Manual
of Child
Psychopathology

Editor

Benjamin B. Wolman
Long Island University

Consulting
Editors

Gerald Caplan, Sol L. Garfield, Norman Garmezy, Wells Goodrich,
Irene M. Josselyn, Lawrence Kohlberg, Carl P. Malmquist, Alan O. Ross

Editorial
Associate

Jean Mundy

Manual of Child Psychopathology

McGraw-Hill Book Company

New York St. Louis San Francisco Düsseldorf Johannesburg
Kuala Lumpur London Mexico Montreal New Delhi
Panama Rio de Janeiro Singapore Sydney Toronto

Manual of Child Psychopathology

Library of Congress Catalog Card Number 78-149722

07-071545-9

1234567890VHVH7987654321

Contents

Contents

Contributors

A. Harvey Baker, Ph.D., Research Psychologist, Educational Testing Services, Princeton, N.J.

Jack I. Bardon, Ph.D., Professor and Chairman, Department of Psychological Foundations, Graduate School of Education, Rutgers University, New Brunswick, N.J.

Morton Beiser, M.D., Associate Professor of Social Psychiatry, Harvard School of Public Health, Boston, Mass.; Assistant Psychiatrist, Massachusetts General Hospital, Boston, Mass.; Senior Psychiatrist, Medfield State Hospital, Harding, Mass.

Virginia D. C. Bennett, Ed.D., Associate Professor, Department of Psychological Foundations, Graduate School of Education; Director, School Psychology Program, Rutgers University, New Brunswick, N.J.

Irving N. Berlin, M.D., Professor of Psychiatry and Pediatrics and Head, Division of Child Psychiatry, Department of Psychiatry, School of Medicine, University of Washington, Seattle, Wash.

Saul L. Brown, M.D., Chief, Department of Child Psychiatry, Cedars-Sinai Medical Center of Los Angeles, Los Angeles, Calif.

Albert Bryt, M.D., Assistant Clinical Professor of Psychiatry, New York University School of Medicine, New York, N.Y.; Training and Supervisory Analyst, William Alanson White Institute, New York, N.Y.

Bradley Bucher, Ph.D., Associate Professor, Department of Psychology, University of Western Ontario, Ontario, Canada

Elaine Caruth, Ph.D., Assistant Clinical Professor of Medical Psychology, UCLA School of Medicine, Senior Clinical Research Psychologist, Reiss-Davis Child Study Center, Los Angeles, Calif.

Jacob Chwast, Ph.D., Director of Mental Health, Consultation Service, The Educational Alliance, New York, N.Y.

Leonard Diller, Ph.D., Chief of Behavioral Science, Institute of Rehabilitation Medicine, New York, N.Y.; Associate Professor of Rehabilitation Medicine, New York University Medical Center, New York, N.Y.

Paul Eiserer, Ph.D., Professor of Psychology and Education, Teachers College, Columbia University, New York, N.Y.

Rudolf Ekstein, Ph.D., Director of the Childhood Psychosis Project at Reiss-Davis Child Study Center, Los Angeles, Calif.; Clinical Professor in Medical Psychology at the University of California at Los Angeles; Senior Faculty Member, Los Angeles Psychoanalytic Society and Institute and Southern California Society and Institute

Stuart M. Finch, M.D., Professor of Psychiatry and Chief of Children's Psychiatric Service, Department of Psychiatry, University of Michigan Medical Center, Ann Arbor, Mich.

Stephen Fleck, M.D., Professor of Psychiatry and Public Health, Yale University, New Haven, Conn.

Seymour Friedman, M.D., Director of Clinical Services, Reiss-Davis Child Study Center, Los Angeles, Calif.; Senior Faculty Member, Los Angeles Psychoanalytic Society and Institute

Marianne Frostig, Ph.D., Founder and Executive Director, Marianne Frostig Center of Educational Therapy; Professor, Mount St. Mary's College and Marianne Frostig Center of Educational Therapy, Los Angeles, Calif.

Jerome D. Goodman, M.D., Director, Pediatric Psychiatry, Bergen Pines Hospital, Paramus, N.J.; Associate in Psychiatry, College of Physicians and Surgeons, Columbia University, New York, N.Y.

Lawrence M. Greenberg, M.D., Associate Professor and Director of Training, Section of Child Psychiatry, Department of Psychiatry, School of Medicine, University of California, Davis, Calif.

H. C. Gunzburg, Ph.D., Consultant Psychologist, Director Psychological Services, Mental Subnormality Hospitals, Birmingham Area, England

William Hahn, Ph.D., Associate Professor of Psychology, University of Denver, Denver, Colo.

Seymour L. Halleck, M.D., Ph.D., Professor of Psychiatry, University of Wisconsin, Madison, Wis.

Christoph M. Heinicke, Ph.D., Director, Research Division, Reiss-Davis Child Study Center, Los Angeles, Calif.

Lewis A. Hurst, M.D., Ph.D., Professor of Psychological Medicine, University of the Witwatersrand, Johannesburg, Republic of South Africa; Chief Psychiatrist, Johannesburg Hospital and Associated Teaching Hospitals

Joseph C. Kaspar, Ph.D., Associate Professor of Pediatrics and Psychiatry, Northwestern University Medical School, Chicago, Ill.

Jane W. Kessler, Ph.D., Director and Professor of Psychology, Mental Development Center, Case Western Reserve University, Cleveland, Ohio

Lawrence Kohlberg, Ph.D., Professor of Educational and Social Psychology, Graduate School of Education, Harvard University, Cambridge, Mass.

Irvin A. Kraft, M.D., Associate Professor, Psychiatry and Pediatrics, Baylor College of Medicine, Houston,

Tex.; Medical Director, Texas Institute of Child Psychiatry, Houston, Tex.

Jean E. LaCrosse, Ph.D., Research Associate, Harvard Graduate School of Education, Cambridge, Mass.

Stanley Lesser, M.D., Chairman, Department of Psychiatry, Jewish Board of Guardians; Associate Clinical Professor, College of Physicians and Surgeons, Columbia University, New York, N.Y.

Samuel Livingston, M.D., Associate Professor of Pediatrics, The Johns Hopkins Hospital School of Medicine; Director and Physician-in-Charge, The Johns Hopkins Hospital Epilepsy Clinic, Baltimore. Md.

Reginald S. Lourie, M.D., Medical Director, Hillcrest Children's Center; Director, Department of Psychiatry, Children's Hospital of D.C.; Professor, Pediatrics (Psychiatry) The George Washington University School of Medicine, Washington, D.C.

John P. McKinney, Ph.D., Professor of Psychology, Michigan State University, East Lansing, Mich.

Carl P. Malmquist, M.D., M.S., Professor, Institute of Child Development, University of Minnesota, Minneapolis, Minn.

Charles Marcantonio, Ph.D., Chief Trainee Development, Division of Trainee Qualification, Office of Citizen Placement, Action, Washington, D.C.

Jerrold M. Milstein, M.D., Ph.D., Assistant Professor, Pediatrics and Neurology (Pediatric Neurology), University of Minnesota Medical School, Minneapolis, Minn.

Jean Mundy, Ph.D., Associate Professor of Psychology, Long Island University, Brooklyn, N.Y., Senior Clinical Psychologist, St. Vincent's Hospital, New York, N.Y.

Edward D. Mysak, Ph.D., Chairman, Department of Speech Pathology and Audiology, Teachers College, Columbia University, New York, N.Y.

Peter Neubauer, M.D., Director, Child Development Center, New York; Associate Clinical Professor, Downstate Medical Center, State University of New York, New York, N.Y.

Russel E. Orpet, Ed.D., Professor of Educational Psychology, California State College, Long Beach, Calif.

Kenneth Purcell, Ph.D., Professor and Chairman, Department of Psychology, University of Denver, Denver, Colo.

A. I. Rabin, Ph.D., Professor of Psychology, Michigan State University, East Lansing, Mich.

David F. Ricks, Ph.D., Professor of Clinical Psychology, Teachers College, Columbia University, New York, N.Y.

Bernard F. Riess, Ph.D., Director of Research, Postgraduate Center for Mental Health, New York, N.Y.

Max Rosenbaum, Ph.D., Editor, *Group Process,* Lecturer, Department of Psychiatry, New York Medical College, New York, N.Y.

Alan O. Ross, Ph.D., Professor of Psychology and Director, Doctoral Program in Clinical Psychology, State University of New York at Stony Brook, N.Y.

Sebastiano Santostefano, Ph.D., Professor of Psychiatry and Psychology, Boston University School of Medicine, Boston, Mass.

Marshall D. Schechter, M.D., Director and Professor, Consultant Professor of Pediatrics, Division of Child Psychiatry, University of Oklahoma School of Medicine, Oklahoma City, Okla.

Jerome L. Schulman, M.D., Professor, Department of Neurology and Psychiatry, Northwestern University Medical School, Chicago, Ill.; Head, Division of Child Psychiatry, The Children's Memorial Hospital, Chicago, Ill.

Daisy K. Shaw, Director M.A. Bureau of Educational and Vocational Guidance, Board of Education of the City of New York, Brooklyn, N.Y.

L. W. Sontag, M.D., Director Emeritus, Fels Research Institute, Yellow Springs, Ohio

John A. Sours, M.D., Assistant Clinical Professor of Psychology, College of Physicians and Surgeons, Columbia University, New York, N.Y.

Richard E. Sternlof, Ph.D., Oklahoma City Psychiatric Clinic, Oklahoma City, Okla.

Kenneth F. Swaiman, M.D., Professor and Director, Pediatric Neurology, University of Minnesota Medical School, Minneapolis, Minn.

Povl W. Toussieng, M.D., Professor of Child Psychiatry, Associate Professor of Pediatrics, University of Oklahoma School of Medicine, Oklahoma City, Okla.

Jonathan Weiss, Ph.D., Associate Professor of Psychology, Yeshiva University, New York, N.Y.; Visiting Associate Professor of Pediatrics, Albert Einstein College of Medicine, New York, N.Y.

Joseph M. Wepman, Ph.D., Professor of Psychology, Surgery, and Education; Director of Speech and Language Clinic and Research Laboratory; Director of Early Education Research Center, University of Chicago, Chicago, Ill.

Benjamin B. Wolman, Ph.D., Professor of Psychology, Long Island University Doctoral Program in Clinical Psychology, Long Island University, Brooklyn, N.Y.; Editor-in-Chief, *International Journal of Group Tension*

Preface

Mental health problems have become the number one national concern. They have grown too big and too complex to be solved in mental hospitals or in offices of private practitioners, and they require the cooperation of several professions and a thorough planning by research.

In their efforts to face this national emergency, responsible professional and community leaders are presumably embarking upon the only feasible road, the road of *preventive action.* Preventive efforts must start at the roots of the problem and attack mental disorders at their onset in childhood.

There has been a growing awareness of the importance of this area, and more thought, planning, and money have lately been put into the training of research workers and practitioners in clinical child psychology, child psychiatry, and related fields.

Yet no adequate effort has been made to put together all the available data in this expanding field of research, study, and practice. There is not a single comprehensive, thorough, and systematic presentation of what is known, what has been done, and what could be done in regard to mental disorders in childhood and adolescence. Training centers and practicing workers badly need a thorough, detailed, authoritative, and up-to-date description and analysis of scientific research and clinical experience in this vital field.

The aim of the *Manual of Child Psychopathology* is to fill this gap.

The *Manual of Child Psychopathology* is prepared as a textbook for doctoral and postdoctoral clinical programs in child psychology for training programs for child psychiatrists, child psychoanalysts, psychiatric social workers, school psychologists, and advanced workers in the fields of counseling and guidance. In addition, the *Manual* is intended to serve as a standard reference book for practitioners in the above-mentioned fields and as a reliable source of information for psychologists, psychiatrists, pediatricians, and other professionals and scholars.

The *Manual* covers the entire field of mental disorders in childhood and adolescence. While uniformity in presentation was neither expected nor advised, the chapters of the *Manual* complement one another so as to give an up-to-date and comprehensive presentation of the field. Each chapter is followed by detailed references.

The *Manual* is divided into nine parts. Part I starts with the description of normal development in childhood and adolescence and proceeds to an analysis of genetic, organic, nongenetic, sociocultural, and intrafamilial factors in the etiology of mental disorders in childhood and adolescence.

The five chapters of Part II describe organic mental disorders, such as brain damage, epilepsies, and disorders caused by metabolic and toxic factors. The chapter on mental deficiencies serves as a transition to the nonorganic disorders.

Part III describes the major neuroses and psychoses of childhood as well as sexual disturbances and antisocial behavior.

Certain specific disorders, such as physical handicap, speech and auditory defects, difficulties in learning, and psychosomatic diseases, are covered in the five chapters of Part IV.

Part V describes in four chapters the diagnostic procedures, especially interviewing, mental tests, and projective techniques, and also diagnosis of learning difficulties.

Treatment methods are described in Parts 6 and 7. The eight chapters of Part VI deal with Freudian and non-Freudian psychoanalytic theory, behavior modification, and nondirective techniques and with group and family therapies and physicochemical methods. Part VII describes special problems.

Part VIII is devoted to research in childhood psychopathology, and its six chapters analyze the contribution of developmental psychology, learning theory, psychoanalysis, Piaget's studies, and organic research. The last chapter dwells on problems of predictability of adult mental health from childhood behavior.

Part IX describes the professions of clinical child psychologists, child psychiatrists, school psychologists, and guidance workers.

I am submitting this *Manual* to colleagues and students with a great deal of anxiety. After several years of preparatory work, of writing and rewriting and editing this huge collective volume, I can appreciate the tremendous amount of work all of us have put into making it as perfect as we could. Unfortunately, we know that it is not perfect, that there are so many issues which are controversial and in so many areas that we have hardly scratched the surface. My co-editors and co-authors have done their best, and I admire their brilliance, goodwill, and cooperation. I could hardly match their excellence, and I must have erred quite often in the use of my editorial pen.

On several occasions I have sought the advice of Alfred L. Baldwin, Gordon F. Derner, Sibylle K. Escalona, Aaron H. Esman, Anna Freud, Florence Halpern, Robert R. Holt, Arthur T. Jersild, Jerome Kagan, Bernard N. Kalinkowitz, Stanley R. Lesser, and Herbert Nechin. Their wise guidance is greatly appreciated.

In the preparation of the manuscript I was assisted by Sandy Gerber, Bernice Gross, and Susan Knapp.

The editors, contributors, consultants, and assistants put me deeply in debt by their kind and cordial cooperation.

Benjamin B. Wolman

part i | Etiologic Factors

1 | Normal Development in Childhood

Peter B. Neubauer

Child development has been the subject of continuing interest particularly since Freud discovered that most of the pathology found in adults has its roots in emotional disorders of early childhood. Freud's genetic approach to the understanding of pathology, through a reconstruction of those early conditions out of which pathology evolves, inevitably led him to undertake an outline of the normal processes of development. Comparatively soon after the publication of his theories, the traditional "commonsense" approach toward children was acknowledged to be inadequate for the explanation of either normal development or the frequency of emotional disorders. It was also recognized that scientific criteria would be required to counteract the tendency of adults to view childhood from the standpoint of the cultural influences of a particular social environment. Then too, increased awareness of the need for early treatment of otherwise irreversible pathological conditions prompted many to concentrate on the study of infants and young children in the search for clarification of normal and pathological development.

To date, most of the research has had to be conducted piecemeal, as part of the work of many disciplines: psychiatry, psychology, biology, education, and so forth. Yet despite the interest in child development, only a very few centers have been established to coordinate the findings contributed by the various scientific fields. The institutional gap is all the more serious when one reflects that this is an area which is especially susceptible to the proliferation of theories. For not only do conceptions of development differ according to the scientific discipline involved, but they also differ according to the different schools of thought within each scientific field.

It is therefore impossible within the compass of a single chapter to formulate a systematic or comprehensive summary of the current state of knowledge. Hence this chapter is confined largely to a formulation which represents a preferred set of propositions frequently embodying concepts of development based on psychoanalytic theory. The material has been divided into two main sections: the first outlines the basic tenets of a developmental psychology, while the second deals with the conception of normality in child development.

FUNDAMENTAL PRINCIPLES OF A DEVELOPMENTAL PSYCHOLOGY

Scope of the Concept

Because child development is often erroneously equated with child psychology, its scope is not always well understood. Whereas the term *child psychology* refers to the totality of a child's psychic experiences—i.e., all the psychic elements contributing to behavior, including external factors—*child development* connotes the unfolding progression through time of the changes which occur in the evolving psychic structure and function as part of the child's normal growth process. The evolvement of psychic structure in a progression of changes results from the continuous interaction of the psychological effects of the biological maturation process and environmental influences.

The developmental psychologist is therefore concerned primarily with understanding the laws that govern the developmental progression and views psychic experiences exclusively within this context. Thus in one sense, child development must be regarded as a specific aspect or focus of child psychology. However, in terms of the comparative scope of the two fields of study, child development is much the broader concept.

The Developmental Process Related to Biological Maturation and Environmental Influences

Whenever a concept comprises several major components, there is always a danger that theorists will give undue prominence to one of them and will formulate an elaborate overall hypothesis which is essentially imbalanced. In the case of child development, many nonpsychologists have tended to overstress the importance of biological maturation or the sociocultural assumptions behind the environmental influences. Those who stressed the latter aspect produced a *tabula rasa* conception of child development, which suggests that the psychic structure is totally unformed at birth and that the child's subsequent personality is shaped primarily by his experience of environmental factors. Conversely, those who stressed the importance of biological maturation proposed a "preformationist" conception of development, which assumes that the basic developmental pattern already exists in a minute anlage at birth; according to this theory the human personality is given and emerges to its full maturity according to a preformed pattern. Not surprisingly, these unbalanced conceptions of development have had serious consequences in terms of practical study. Thus the *tabula rasa* notion excludes by definition genetic factors, innate predispositions within the individual child, and the psychological effects of the maturational process. Similarly, the preformationist conception suggests the view that because the child is simply a small—i.e., preformed—adult, it is not necessary to assist the developmental process by paying attention to his special needs and problems during certain periods of stress.

The emphasis on biological maturation has had another unfortunate consequence—an overconcentration on those aspects of behavior which are manifested in the development of certain performance capacities, e.g., perception and motor skills, which are rooted in the biological processes like neuromuscular maturation. Detailed schedules of biological neurophysiological achievements at given times are then often presented as if they were psychological development schedules. But they do not tell us enough about the psychology of the child. They tell us nothing, for instance, of the impact of the child's newfound capacity to walk on his psychic life—the emotional experiences which accompany the ability to leave the mother and explore new space, the growing sense of control over the body, the emergent self-image, the perception of distance, etc.

If it is true that all psychological processes have an organic substrate and are therefore coordinated with the maturational sequences, then it is no less true that all maturational sequences are accompanied by psychological effects. This is the emphasis which ought to be the concern of developmental psychology. In other words, the student of child development is not interested in describing sequences of biological processes per se but in understanding their effect on developmental sequences, their content and meaning as psychic experiences for the child. Thus the infant's sucking has to be explored from the standpoint of its capacity to release tension connected with feelings of frustration, or as an experience of the gratifying outside world, rather than as an example of muscular development.

It is therefore of prime importance to keep the component parts of the concept of child development in a proper perspective. Biological and environmental factors both *contribute* to the developmental process of the psychic structure, but neither of them is the sole determinant. Since the developmental progression results from the (psychological) interaction of the maturational process and environmental influences, the laws which the developmental psychologist seeks to outline for psychic evolvement must be tested in terms of data on the psychic experiences of both sets of factors.

Development of the Basic Psychic Structure

As will be described below, the theory of development outlined here assumes a progression of changing hierarchies of psychic organization where the various facets of mental structure shift in relationship to one another as they respond to the different requirements of a new biological phase and expanding environmental contact. However, all these facets belong to one or another of the three main elements in the psychic structure—i.e., the id, ego, and superego—which are themselves subject to the development process. Since this tripartite division of mental structure, which forms one of the basic propositions of psychoanalytic theory, is familiar in the field, it is necessary here only to restate the concept in terms of the timetable for its development.

It is assumed that the psychic structure of the fetus consists entirely of the id, or the drives which represent the effects of the biological demands on psychic life. Ego formation does not begin until after the baby is born and is thrust into contact with the outside world. At first the ego exists merely as part of the undifferentiated id-ego matrix; then as the infant becomes steadily more responsive to environmental stimuli with the process of biological maturation, the ego gradually differentiates itself from the id. Thus psychic development during infancy is characterized by the emergence of a rudimentary ego which begins to perform its function of synthesizing and coordinating the internal expression of the drives into an appropriate relationship with the demands imposed by the outside world. Not until between the ages of approximately 4 and 6 years does the superego emerge to direct the child's value relationship with his environment. The function of the superego is to internalize the ethical standards and moral attitudes of family and society by establishing an "ego-ideal" consisting of values that reward and protect the individual. And when the child falls short of achieving this ideal, then it leads to a pathological superego.

Once all three elements of the psychic structure are present, development throughout the rest of childhood is essentially a two-way process of refinement: On the one hand various facets of ego equipment evolve to cope with the changing expressions of the drives in response to new demands of biological maturation, while on the other the superego strives to keep pace by determining the proper value relationship between the new drive expressions and environmental pressures.

Prenatal Development

One of the fundamental propositions of developmental psychology suggests that the pregnant mother's constitutional makeup, eating and sleeping habits, emotional attitudes, and so forth, all may significantly contribute to the particularity of the intrauterine environment to which the fetus responds as a psychic entity. This hypothesis cannot as yet be tested scientifically. At the present time there is no knowledge available about the "psychic life" of the fetus, such as the effect of the various forms of perception on feeling tone or the process of threshold formation in response to stimulus and tension-producing sensations. Nor is (the science of) embryology sufficiently advanced to be able as yet to distinguish those factors contributing to the psychic individuality or predispositions in the neonate which are the result of the effects of the intrauterine environment and of the birth process from factors which are the product of genetic variables. Current statistics indicate that a quarter of a million American children are born each year with abnormalities caused by deviations in prenatal development. But it is not known how many of these abnormalities are due specifically to genetic factors and how many are caused by deviations in the intrauterine environment.

Thus it is impossible today to describe the impact of the pregnant mother's condition either on basic developmental characteristics or on the subsequent emergence of pathology during postnatal life. However, since it is known that the fetus exhibits a degree of responsiveness to various kinds of stimulation, growth-promoting or growth-retarding influences in the intrauterine environment are clearly operative. In particular, knowledge of a given intrauterine environment would throw much light on how the individual fetus is equipped to respond to the all-important event of birth. This event, which many consider to be the first human experience and which may be described in psychological terms as a sudden flooding of stimulation, symbolizes both the traumatic and the growth-promoting effects of the entire development process, just as the baby's first cry is an expression of psychic shock that simultaneously represents a significant biological advance.

In view of the importance of the prenatal period for an assessment of later development, it is to be regretted that current scientific observations of the pregnant mother do not include extensive data on normal variations in the fetal environment, but concentrate almost exclusively on the more severe deviations. Although this may be due in part to the difficulties of scientific investigation in this sphere, it to some extent also reflects a widely held belief that only severe abnormalities in the pregnancy significantly affect fetal development. The developmental psychologist, of course, cannot accept such a restricted view and must await the day when the anticipated breakthrough in observation of fetal life will be achieved, thus opening up an avenue that will meaningfully connect the science of embryology with the study of development.

The Theory of Stages of Psychosexual Development

The psychoanalytic concept of human sexuality takes into account *all* the pleasure-seeking drives that relate to the body. Therefore, sexual pleasure is not confined to genital sensation or to genital activities. By thus extending the concept of sexual pleasure, it was possible to study the sexuality for the entire range of human behavior development from infancy to old age.

As applied to child development, Freud's concept permits a hypothesis of a progression of "libidinal" stages in which psychic organization is built on different constellations of pleasure strivings which are directly linked with the process of biological growth and which exhibit an increasing complexity as the child progresses toward adulthood. Thus, because during infancy pleasure strivings are intensely associated with oral activity, this period has been termed the *oral phase* of psychosexual development. But pleasure-giving activity is associated with the exercise of all bodily functions (functionslust). This is followed by the anal phase, with its pleasure of body function and its controls— weaning, toileting. The next stage, which lasts from approximately 3 to 4 years, is called the *phallic phase* because pleasure strivings are directed largely toward gratifying curiosity about the genital differences between the sexes. Between the ages of 4 and 6½ years, the *Oedipal phase,* the child experiences conflict as he tries to integrate his pleasure activities associated with sex differences within the organization of the family unit. Then comes a period of diminution in sexual strivings, the phase of *latency,* which can last from age 6½ to age 9½. This is followed, between the ages of 9½ and 12, by the biological period of puberty, the phase of *preadolescence,* when psychic experience relates chiefly to the emergence of genital sexuality. Lastly there is the phase of *adolescence* proper, which extends from age 12 to age 18.

In thus referring to specific "stages" or "phases" of development, it is obvious that this theory postulates a certain degree of discontinuity in the process of psychic development. Over the years there have been frequent discussions of the issue of discontinuity versus continuity in the developmental process, and it has now been agreed by most to avoid an either-or position. However, it should be stated that if development were assumed to be a continuous process of unfolding by imperceptible minute steps, then one could not refer meaningfully to separate developmental phases and would have to be content with merely referring to the time periods of biological growth. However, discontinuity is not intended to imply that each phase represents a distinct unit. On the contrary, as will now be described, the entire concept of a developmental phase carries with it the notion of a developmental progression in which each new phase is brought about as the result of the resolution of conflicts during the preceding phase.

The Nature of the Developmental Progression

As has already been implied in the outline of the stages of psychosexual development, the different constellations of pleasure strivings which accompany the process of maturation have to be seen in the context of the total psychic life of the child. These constellations form the focal points of successive conflicts as the competing elements in the psychic structure continually re-form themselves in different organizational hierarchies so as to coordinate the internal expression of new drives with the ever-encroaching demands of the outside world. Thus each phase of development has its characteristic constellations of strivings, which in turn present a characteristic internal organization that challenges or conflicts with the existing structural hierarchy. The resolution of this conflict in the formation of a new organizational hierarchy heralds the start of a new phase of development; then the child is once more subjected to new internal and external demands, and the process of conflict and resolution begins again. And so the process continues throughout the seven successive phases of development until the child finally reaches adulthood and maturity.

Developmental propositions thus often stress the carryover of conflicts from one stage into the next. Sometimes a new stage of development can reactivate a dormant but partially unresolved conflict of an earlier stage. In the transitional periods between the phases, especially, the forward motion of the psychic progression is frequently mixed with regressive tendencies. However, these tendencies can also serve to promote further development, since their fluidity permits new forms of integration.

It is assumed that formation of the basic psychic structure is achieved by the end of the Oedipal phase. Consolidation in each area of psychic life, expansion, and reorganization of old forms are all important aspects of structural development during subsequent phases. But apart from some facets of character formation during late adolescence, the emergence of a new psychic function has not been found to occur after the Oedipal stage.

The Notion of Developmental Crises

It is evident, then, that the concept of the developmental progression embodies several different levels of successive changes, several different ways of regarding the successive changes in psychic structure that take place during the growth process. As we have seen, it can be viewed as the changing expression of the drives, as the evolution of changes in hierarchies of psychic organization, or as the resolution of successive conflicts; depending on one's point of view or study one may emphasize any one of these aspects as the most useful. To enlarge on the aspect of development as the resolution of successive conflicts, the formulation has been suggested that development can most fruitfully be regarded as a series of essential tasks which the child has to master at each phase. Others, however, see the resolution of successive conflicts in terms of a series of developmental crises rather than tasks. The reasoning behind this view is that it helps to remind one that the conflicts are not mere academic categories, but represent a heightening of the struggle within the

psychic life, and that the child may experience them as intense emotional crises. Furthermore, it confirms the basic propositions of development, namely, that conflicts, inhibitions, and symptoms are an integral part of the normal growth process and are not necessarily indications of pathology.

Major/Typical Phasal Characteristics

The following is an outline of the typical characteristics specific to each phase of development. It excludes preadolescence and adolescence, however, since these phases are the subject of another chapter in this volume.

The oral phase (birth to 1½ years). The oral phase of development is characterized by the dominance of oral activity, its pleasure-seeking strivings and its aggressive aims. The appropriate satisfaction or gratification of these needs prepares the way to the next step of development; the various forms of conflict are usually to be found even in this early phase of development. Indeed, some of these conflicts lead to the establishment of early individual character traits which then become integrated into the general personality and achieve a "secondary autonomy." Food fads, overeating, repression of pleasure in eating and a resulting turning away from food, sucking or nail-biting, self-aggrandizement, and depressions connected with the feelings of loss of the object are frequent findings. As character traits they may be expressed as undue dependency on the mother, as restlessness, as optimism anticipating full gratification, as pessimism expecting deprivation, and as various forms of greed and demandingness.

The oral phase is also characterized by object dependency and the emergence of a rudimentary ego equipment. These two aspects of development together lay the foundation for the individual pattern of the later psychic unfolding. The infant is soon able to differentiate between pleasure and pain, between a state of satiation and a state of tension. The rooting activity which follows the demand for satiation and reactions to tension are examples of early reactive forms of behavior or ego-adaptive function and are initiated early. Memory traces, the forerunners of the thought processes that correspond to pleasure-pain reactions, emerge in connection with body function and with the human object to which all infantile experiences are invariably bound. From these processes evolve the mental representation first of the object, then of the outside world, and lastly of the self.

Thus the initial relationship to the human object is the central experience of the oral phase and exercises a decisive influence over subsequent development. Although this relationship is usually subsumed under the general head of *dependency,* it rests on psychic mechanisms such as imitation and identification. The child's needs are object-bound, and so also is the emergence of his fantasy life. Signposts of psychic development are all linked to the human object: the first smile, the ability to differentiate the known object from the stranger (stranger anxiety), and the process of separation, which is linked to the one of individuation. Anticipation of the continuous availability of the mother allows for the development of trust and a causal relationship between internal states and external events. Reality testing, the check between inner feelings of omnipotence and outer reality, becomes more coordinated, and eventually a separation from the mother can be achieved. In this way the appropriateness of emotional and intellectual stimulation, combined with continuity of relationship, can be seen as a basic requirement of normal development. Fear of loss of the object, which in later phases becomes fear of loss of the love of the object, is the primary source of anxiety throughout this phase.

The anal phase (1½ to 3 years). This stage of development is characterized by experiences and pleasure-seeking strivings based on body control, anal activities as they emerge as part of the maturational process, and mother-child interaction. These psychic experiences have their organic substrata in the child's newfound ability to walk, to achieve some degree of neuro-muscular and voluntary sphincter control, and to communicate in speech. Thus it is a period of "training," preceded by weaning, and the child is asked to coordinate his body function according to schedules of time and place and to follow certain explicit rules imposed by the environment.

With the reduction in object dependency come assertive expressions of independence that take the form of age-appropriate negativism, the frequent expression of "no" to outside demands. In this struggle the child usually displays great ambivalence of emotion toward the mother, swinging between extremes of love and hate, of dependence and assertions of independence. There is a heightened pleasure in physical activity, functionslust, as a reflection of the limitless energy available for physical function and practice. The character traits deriving from psychic conflicts likewise express a continuing sense of ambivalence: overorderliness or complete disorderliness, cleanliness or its opposite, rage or meekness as seen in many forms of sadomasochistic tendencies.

The phallic phase (3 to 4½ years). During this phase the child is concerned primarily with the task of differentiating the outside world from himself, and with a clearer awareness of sex differences. It is a phase challenged by curiosity about the genital differences between girls and boys, and between the mother and father as the key representatives of the two sexes. The nature of causal relationships is also tirelessly explored, and the child raises questions about the meaning of each object he encounters. He attempts to understand the details in connection with the whole, and he wants to ask many questions which refer not only to the "what" of experiences but also to the "why" of all his experiences. Equipped with this insatiable curiosity, he can now explore his own body, and just as he may have been anxious in the past over the possible loss of the object, so he may now become anxious over the loss of parts of his body, particularly the genitals.

The Oedipal phase (4½ to 6½ years). This is the stage of development when the child tries to integrate his awareness of sex differences with the organization of the family unit. He now has to find his place as a specific individual in direct conflict with his parents. His dependency on the mother and his longing for her as a sexual object, and the resulting guilt feelings toward the father combined with the anticipation of punishment for his sexual longings, represent the well-known Oedipal conflict. The struggles that take place in this period are manifold and show many variations as the child strives to reconcile his desire for independence with the recognition of the necessity for maintaining the family unit. This is a high order of tasks which never seems to be completely achieved. In order to gain appropriate sex identity, identification with the parent of the same sex is necessary, accompanied by the competition and rivalry with the parent of the opposite sex. Most of the neurotic conflicts in later life stem from this period, which is characterized by the emergence of conscious or unconscious guilt and a specific set of value systems that follows on the emergence of the superego as an independent psychic element.

Latency (6½ to 9½ years). The term *latency* is meant to indicate a reduction of sexual strivings, a reduction in structure formation and conflict constellations.

However, the phase is usually divided into two periods: early latency and later latency. The first period is oriented chiefly toward the resolution of Oedipal conflicts, while the second period is concerned more with rapid expansion of intellectual activity. During the second period, the child is equipped to extend his interest from the family to the outside world. Learning, which in the preceding phases was so strongly bound to imitation, identification, and stimulation within the family, can now proceed to school learning and to learning within the larger community. Causal relationships can be more fully understood as schoolteachers present information about the laws of nature and systems which permit learning to take place on a higher conceptual level. All this does not imply that those conflicts from earlier years have been totally resolved or that structure formation has been completed. Consolidation of superego functions in the context of the values stemming from school peers, and exposure to other families and the community at large is necessary for further superego formation, which in turn permits further repression of the earlier libidinal and aggressive strivings and the sublimation of the drives into the higher forms of function.

Other Psychological Theories of Development

The psychoanalytic theory of development just outlined stresses psychic experience and the formation of psychic structure through a defined progression of specific phases. However, this is only one of several psychological theories in the field. Four of the most influential of these are (1) the theory advanced by Piaget, which stresses development as the acquisition of mental processes; (2) that proposed by Heinz Werner, which embodies an organismic view of development based on orthogenetic aspects; (3) Kurt Lewin's "field theory," which seeks to express the "total situation" contained in the development; and (4) the so-called stimulus-response theory, which views development as the acquisition of different processes of learning (this theory cannot be associated with the work of any single author but has been, so to speak, collectively evolved by a number of like-minded theorists over the years). A brief résumé of each of these theories is given below.

Piaget is one of the most outstanding contributors to the field of developmental psychology. It is difficult to do justice to his theory in a short summary, and one can only hope to stimulate enough interest in the reader so that he will study it for himself.

Because of his biological background, Piaget (1921) has been interested in describing the innate force of equilibrium between those forms of behavior which reflect the changing biological structure. He conceives of mental structure as systems or schemata that include such complex factors as overt motor behavior or thought patterns; cognitive schemata are based on sensorimotor schemata. Assimilation and accommodation are proposed as adaptive processes. Assimilation is the mental activity which reacts to an external situation or stimuli so that the mental structure can start the process of adaptation. Accommodation is the mental activity which actually changes existing schemata in the appropriate manner.

Piaget also proposes concepts which stem from the mathematical concept of the "group." As the child becomes more complex in mental function, it deals with different tendencies which cluster into sets and series.

Resulting systems can be understood by laws of mathematics, corresponding to psychic controls of sets of elements. The relationship of these systems to mental equilibrium and processes of reversibility are carefully stated.

Piaget assumes stages of development. These are both continuous and discontinuous, and the elements of one stage are always integrated into those of the next. This process of unfolding applies to all psychomental areas.

Thus Piaget offers a general theory of development which has a specific reference to the de-

Stage 1—Period of sensorimotor intelligence, birth to 2 years

Period of conceptual intelligence: concrete operation

Stage 2—Preoperational stage, 2 to 7 years

Stage 3—Concrete operation, 7 to 11 years

Stage 4—Stage of formal operation, 11 to 14 years, or period of conceptual intelligence; formal operation

velopment of the child's understanding of concepts of reality—space, time, and causality—and of his capacity to symbolize and use language. Piaget was interested primarily in constructing a genetic epistemology, focused on the cognitive areas of development—that is, perception, memory, and problem solving—and did not include in his work studies of affect, intrapsychic processes, or the relationship of conflicts to pathology.

Heinz Werner's (1930) organismic theory of development stresses inherent mental structures rather than processes of acquiring knowledge. Thus this approach studies development as to its atomistic mechanism. The orthogenetic principle leads him to compare the progression from the thinking of the child to the thinking of the adult with the progression from the thinking in primitive cultures to that of highly advanced industrial societies. Thus Werner states: ". . . development . . . proceeds from a state of relative globality and lack of differentiation to a state of increasing differentiation, articulation and hierarchic integration."

Werner's developmental theory outlines certain qualities based on levels of differentiation, such as syncretic versus discrete, diffuse versus articulated, rigid versus flexible, and labile versus stable function. Like Piaget, Werner is interested in the idea of mental function establishing a progression in its development (and its relationship to adaptation). The atomistic aspects were expressed in a view which explored the role of perception in a short period of time and its relationship to the change from an undifferentiated state to a differentiated quality. This microgenetic approach was tested in many word meanings for the child at different stages of his development.

Kurt Lewin's (1935) field theory is a special strategy in theory formation in that it attempts to prove that the psychological processes in each individual case are "lawful." It searches for the description of the "total situation" in development and for a systematic analysis of causation. Theoretical concepts are exemplified in graphic forms and geometric figures—useful in field theory. This theory shares with others the concept of differentiation in development, but Lewin gives it a quantitative meaning in order to connote an increase in the number of "regions" of a system; these regions became subject to a growing rigidification, that is, a strengthening of their boundaries, as the child proceeds with development.

Development, then, is expressed in the increase in the variety of behavior, in a change of dependency of one form of behavior on other activities in a hierarchical formation of units. Lewin also defines development in terms of the expansion of "life space": "The life space of the child is smaller than that of the adult and the space of free movement increases with growth." Life space is the sum of all the facts that determine a specific form of behavior at a given time. Since only those facts which have relevance to a selected form of behavior are examined, the theory does not assign significance to all present facts, nor does it regard all past facts as being significant.

Psychological environment is thus clearly defined and separated from physical environment. The dynamic aspects of development take on a special importance: Motivation is described as a "need system in a state of hunger," while force and valence are operative as causal factors of action. This dynamic view leads to the formulation of conflict in the field of forces; distance and strength of forces are examined in relationship to valent regions.

Stimulus-response theory embodies the "objective" approach to the study of development. The requirements of testable concepts, rigorous experiment, and operational definitions are overriding considerations. The basic proposition of the theory is that almost all behavior is learned. Genetic-biological factors are not excluded, but the focus is on the "how" of the learning processes. It is assumed that development consists of many different, independent learning processes; each unit of behavior is an "act" of learning, and each is acquired independently. The developmental propositions state that the child learns adult behavior patterns according to the way in which his own behavior is punished or rewarded, reinforced or ignored; these environmental pressures result in the development of values, anxieties, inhibitions, and so forth.

This theory is close to the concept of conditioning and emphasizes instrumental conditioning. Extinction of response, spontaneous recovery, partial reinforcement, and secondary conditioning are integrated with other qualities, such as the generality or specificity of the response to stimuli. The capacity of the organism to respond is related to the drives, activity level, and threshold for response. Habit formation becomes associated with the concept of drive, and reinforcement with drive reduction. In addition to quantitative aspects of drive, the scheduling of reinforcement can achieve an avoidance of extinction.

Since stimulus-response theory also has to include responses that are not overtly manifest or observable, it therefore propounds the notion of mediating responses. Aggression as a response is described in terms of aggression-frustration proportion, consisting of three stages:

1. The stronger the instigation to the frustrated response, the more the frustration is an instigation of aggression.
2. The greater the interference with a frustrated response, the stronger the instigation to aggression.
3. Frustration accumulates.

Stimulus-response theory has also been extended to cover those developmental aspects which deal with the acquisition of various responses within the family "habit hierarchy."

THE PROBLEM OF ASSESSING NORMAL DEVELOPMENT

To assess normal development in a given child or group of children, the psychologist must first elaborate an appropriate conceptual framework for distinguishing individual variations within the developmental process from pathological conditions. This section begins with an examination of different concepts of normality currently employed in the field and then goes on to review some of the inborn, inherent factors contributing to individuality. Lastly, a set of preferred propositions is offered which expresses the view that the developmental process itself constitutes the most appropriate framework for measuring normality.

Some Current Concepts of Normality in Development

Various disciplines have tried to give a specific meaning to the term *normality,* and the resulting interpretations vary greatly with the aim of the inquiry concerned. In the field of child development, several different interpretations are frequently used. For example, normality is often defined as an ideal or hypothetical standard of perfection (and therefore unattainable) against which the actual variations may be measured or appraised. Another important interpretation is that which equates normality with health. However, this use of the term is frequently combined with a third interpretation, which defines normality as a statistical average extrapolated from data on observed developmental rates within a given environment. Thus the term *normal development* is often used to denote both average and healthy development.

Normality defined as an ideal standard of development. Any standard or hypothetical norm for ideal development necessarily reflects specific theoretical assumptions about the nature of the developmental process. In effect, the theorist selects certain factors as the key determinants of the developmental process and uses these as the basis for establishing the criteria of normality. The factors selected vary greatly from author to author. Jahoda (1958) proposes, for instance, six criteria for assessing mental health: attitudes toward oneself, style and degree of growth, integration, independence from social influences, perception of reality, and environmental mastery. Maslow and Middleman refer to self-esteem, spontaneity and emotionality, contact with reality, bodily desires and the ability to gratify them, self-knowledge, integration and consistency, adequate life goals, and so forth. Erikson (1950, pp. 371ff) proposes the criterion balance between basic opposing emotional attitudes, for example, between trust and mistrust, autonomy and doubt, shame and guilt, and initiative and inadequacy. Thomas, Chess, and Birch (1968) suggest that temperament, which they define as the overt behavioral style of the individual child, constitutes one of the basic factors in development. Accordingly, they adduce a concept of normality which relates to the variable of temperament (rather than to the relationship of health and pathology) and propose as their criteria such characteristics as activity level, rhythmicity, approach or withdrawal, adaptability, intensity of reaction, threshold of responsiveness, quality of mood, distractibility, attention span, and persistence.

One of the main purposes of these attempts to construct hypothetical norms of development is, of course, to introduce an element of stability into a field that demonstrably consists largely of imponderables. But the motive itself suggests the limitations of the method, for there is a very real danger that the categories of criteria may be too selective or too arbitrary to bear a meaningful relationship to the process of development as it is actually experienced by the child. Or the categories may be too static to be used as an effective yardstick for measuring normality and pathology in clinical practice. To achieve optimum practical results, the psychologist should seek a concept of normality which adequately expresses the dynamics of the developmental process as a *progression* and yields categories that are sufficiently flexible to accommodate the imponderables which necessarily arise at each successive phase.

Normality defined as health. If normality is equated with health, it becomes difficult to explain why only very few children conform to the expected image of a stable child or follow the sequence of developmental phases without internal and external interferences in the optimum growth. Moreover, the converse proposition, that what is not normal (or not average) is always unhealthy, cannot be consistently maintained. Irregularity in development can sometimes be the result of certain forms of maladaptation to an abnormal environment and as such an expression of health.

An even more serious drawback to the equation of normality with health lies in the difficulty of defining health in positive terms. In fact, since our conception of health has been derived largely from the study of pathology, it is often defined simply as the "absence of pathology." This negative definition clearly has little practical value in assisting the developmental psychologist to bolster the regulatory mechanisms of psychic function that foster healthy development. If the psychologist is to achieve measures of prevention rather than mere elimination of pathology, a far more explicit understanding of the positive factors of health (i.e., normality) is required. The definition of health as the absence of pathology also conflicts with the proposition (outlined under "Fundamental Principles of a Developmental Psychology") that many of the "inhibition symptoms and anxieties" exhibited during childhood are inherent in the developmental process itself. On the basis of this proposition, the problem of defining normality in development becomes essentially one of defining those conflicts and stresses and, at times, symptoms which form an integral part of the developmental progression and of distinguishing them from symptoms that are the result of pathological conditions.

Biological Factors Contributing to Individual Variations in Normal Development

In order to avoid committing errors of judgment, one should bear in mind that there are considerable variations in the process of normal development. One frequently observed type of normal variation is to be found, for example, in differences of overall rate of development.

There are children whose developmental progression unfolds very rapidly; while the normal sequence of successive stages of development is maintained, it seems to be somewhat condensed in time. The other extreme is the slow-motion unfolding, in which every phase lasts longer and the entire sequence appears extended.[1] Such variations are due to inherent factors of individuality that will be discussed below, and they must be distinguished, respectively, from precociously adult behavior caused by overstimulation and from immaturity caused by regression or fixation. Again, many children who have a normal or even superior development in the intellectual sphere may nevertheless display slow affective emotional development. There are also considerable variations in the preferred channels of discharge. For instance, those children who prefer motor to mental activity tend to express their psychic experiences in terms of physical action rather than fantasy of thinking.

Innate predispositions. Most of the basic pre-dispositions—for example, individual variations in the threshold to stimuli, frustration tolerance, motility discharge areas, and perceptual sensitiv-ities—manifest themselves during early infancy. Although some of these individual predispositions may subsequently be modified, many seem to maintain a degree of stability throughout de-velopment. In this way they necessarily con-tribute to higher forms of psychic organization and exercise a significant influence on such important aspects of psychic function as the selectivity of defense mechanisms, anxiety levels, ego strength, and so on. Hence, through a care-ful study of infancy, it is possible to outline a profile characterizing significant facets of the child's individuality and to some extent anticipate the personality trends that will emerge later on during development. Such normal variations in the developmental process are due largely to

---

[1] These variations in the overall time schedule usually encompass large spheres of development. If they are limited to only a few, unevenness in the developmental unfolding may result and create certain areas of conflict specific to the variation.

the effects of certain innate predispositions which are embedded in the individual neuro-physical constitution of the child. These factors represent the "given" aspects of individuality with which the environmental factors interact as the developmental progression unfolds. Ob-viously it is not intended to suggest that all pre-dispositions are normal (i.e., in the common-usage sense of not being unusual or destructive) merely because they are inborn. However, there is a wide range of permissible variation, in regard to both the predispositions themselves and the resulting differences in children's psychic reac-tions to environmental influences. Since it is not always easy to distinguish the effects of normal predispositions from certain kinds of pathological deviations in the developmental process, it seems worthwhile to discuss the subject in some detail.

The effect of the gender variable. The pre-dispositions of the individual child are determined partially by general predispositions that relate to gender. Traditionally, most of the proposi-tions of psychosexual development have put the date for the emergence of significant sex differ-ences at around the third year of life, that is, at the phallic phase. However, there is now enough evidence to suggest that the sex-linked characteristics of psychic organization which emerge during the phallic phase are essentially founded upon, and are a development of, certain gender-related dispositions apparent during in-fancy.

Thus, male neonates display a higher motor-activity level than female neonates, who in their turn show a greater reaction to the removal of a covering blanket and a lower threshold of re-sponse to air stimulation on the abdomen. There is also some indication that girl infants may have a lower threshold to pain. These two categories of sex differences during infancy form the basis of fundamental differences of psychic organization observed throughout the developmental process. For all through their childhood, boys consistently display greater motor activity, and girls a heightened perceptual sensitivity, which significantly affect their respective psychic experiences of pain, pleasure, gratification, and so on. With their higher activity level, boys develop an earlier spatial sense, performing better with form boards and block design. They also tend to express their aggression through physical action and are better equipped to vent their defiance in anger. Girls, on the other hand, tend to use indirect expression of aggression, to repress their anger, and to exhibit the appearance of affect change.

Relating these differences to specific disorders, it is found that enuresis delinquency, behavior disorders, and speech difficulties occur more frequently in boys, whereas girls are more subject to mood disturbances and affective-depressive syndromes. Other early sex-linked characteristics stem from differences in the respective rates of biological maturation. Girls mature much more rapidly in several areas—bone age, speech development, the capacity to verbalize, etc. Hence they usually achieve toilet training earlier than boys, and their earlier facility in verbal communication is usually the chief reason they are so frequently considered to be "precocious."

All these sex-linked biological differences—in motor activity, perception, and maturation rates—find their collective expression in significant differences in the ego equipment, for instance, in mode of object relationships, conflict formulation, body-image development, and symptom clustering. Thus it is clear that such sex-linked differences in the psychic progression constitute an important form of variation within the normal developmental process. Unfortunately, at the present time there are clearer propositions for the development of the boy

(perhaps because his behavior patterns are more overt), and as a result girls are frequently judged by a boy's yardstick of development, which leads to inappropriate comparative judgments—such as that girls are "more precocious" or "more disturbed" than boys—that obscure the understanding of normal development pattern in girls. In order to ensure that sex differences are given full recognition, it would therefore seem worthwhile to evaluate separate pilot schedules delineating gender-linked characteristics for each sex.

Separate schedules would not only facilitate a clearer appreciation of the range of normal variations for both sexes but also make it easier to detect the beginning of pathology in individual children.

The role of genetic variables. The science of genetics seems to be on the verge of significant new discoveries that will either substantiate or drastically alter some of the basic propositions of psychoanalytic developmental theory, and indeed of psychological theory in general. It is already known that certain serious psychic disorders are related to, or caused by, abnormalities in the number and distribution of chromosomes and that disorders can even result from abnormality within a single pair of genes, the small unit of the chromosomes. For example, males displaying the pathological condition referred to as the "Klinefelter syndrome"—abnormal psychosexual behavior in the sexual area, which often includes transvestism—possess additional chromosomes, while many of the males who are jailed for aggressive, antisocial behavior are found to have the rare chromosome combination. Although at present the science of genetics throws more light on the origin of severe psychobehavioral disorders than on normal variations of behavior, it can be expected that further knowledge about the milder genetic deviations will reveal more information on how these factors contribute to the normal predispositions of the child. (Even now it can be assumed that there may exist conditions of "genetic deprivation" or that "genetic susceptibility" may exist even though the child does not exhibit symptoms of genetic abnormality.)

Because the range of possible chromosome variations is so very great, the techniques that are currently being developed to enable scientists to "read" chromosome patterns will have the greatest importance for the study of child development and the promotion of therapeutic psychology. For once these techniques are perfected, it may well become possible to study the interaction of the behavioral effects of different chromosome variations with environmental factors. It is this interaction that determines how the psychic effects of genetic deviations take their final form and the channels through which pathology expresses itself. Thus a study of the interplay between the behavioral effects of known chromosome patterns and given environmental influences suggests the possibility of a therapeutic approach—through appropriate corrective social programs—which could modify or counteract pathological behavior.

The Developmental Progression as a Yardstick of Normality

It has been shown how most of the current concepts of normal development in childhood seem to take inadequate account of the nature of the developmental progression. Now it is proposed that the developmental progression itself be used as the conceptual framework for distinguishing normal variations in behavior from pathological conditions. The formulation of a fixed sequence of explicitly defined developmental phases provides, as it were, a graph or system of reference points for charting the imponderables of the specific manifestations of

individual behavior and psychic experience. On this basis it becomes possible to assert that as long as the child continues to develop, normality —and also health—is maintained.

Thus, one has to measure the difficulties, symptoms, and conflicts of the child in terms of their impact on development and whether they interfere with the psychic progression. Feeding and sleeping problems, hyperactivity, and many other difficulties can therefore be considered within the range of normality as long as the child continues to develop. On the other hand, if these difficulties interrupt the developmental process, they can be said to imply pathology. The significance of certain problems and symptoms cannot be judged without the full evaluation of their influence on development.

Some developmental categories for classifying conflicts and disorders. Nagera (1966) has elaborated a useful set of propositions which express the developmental viewpoint. He defines the concept of developmental interference as "whatever constitutes a disturbance in the typical unfolding of development." As an example of an important cause of such disturbances, he cites cases of environmental interference with certain needs and rights of the child, such as separation of mother and child or the lack of appropriate stimulation. While this type of interference may produce different reactions in different children, the resulting disorders must nevertheless be differentiated from those which are due to later internal conflicts. It is therefore important to study the specific factors that are operative in each case and to relate them to the developmental phase during which the disturbances occur.

Having defined the concept of external interference, Nagera (1966) goes on to distinguish two basic types of conflict: developmental conflicts and neurotic conflicts. Developmental conflicts or conflicts of organization which occur as a result of the effects of environmental demands at a given developmental or maturational level may represent a mixture of different elements of particular internal and external conflicts and may become fully internalized. Since these developmental conflicts are phase-specific, they are usually transitory in nature.

Neurotic conflicts are interstructural conflicts that specifically involve the function of the superego in relation to the other two structural elements (id and ego).

Another conceptual measure for classifying conflicts and disorders in terms of their relationship with the developmental progression is that of reversibility-irreversibility. Conflicts which are seen to interfere with development can be grouped according to whether they have reversible or irreversible effects. To formulate such a category, however, is to assume that the effects of certain disorders can in fact be successfully reversed so that development can be redirected to its proper path and once more proceed in a normal manner. But at the present time psychologists cannot always predict whether the effects of a given disturbance can be reversed successfully. Hence the concept of reversibility is largely a hypothetical one, having a theoretical rather than a practical value. It should also be noted that the reversibility-irreversibility concept bears a close relationship to the psychoanalytic concepts of regression and fixation. Regression is a condition which causes the developmental process to return to an earlier stage, while fixation is a condition which causes a halt in the psychic unfolding. Both these conditions form an integral part of the developmental progression, so that normality of development depends upon a proper balance being maintained between the overall forward drive and the individual regressive tendencies.

A nonconceptual, more empirical approach to the classification of conflicts and disorders is exemplified in a major study of children from infancy to maturity which was conducted by MacFarlane, Allen, and Honzik (1962). They classified the frequency of behavioral problems according to age and sex, and data on each type of problem were arranged to illustrate three propositions: decreasing incidence with age, increasing incidence with age, and the peak age period. This study, which explored the relationship of age to conflict without exploring any of the underlying factors or causes, certainly revealed a high frequency of behavioral problems in a nonclinical group of children. Moreover, some of the findings are very illuminating from a developmental point of view.

The Problem of Reversible Pathology

The foregoing leads us to the importance of the assessment of reversibility. Again, we use this term to refer to reversibility in the sense of the developmental process rather than to changes in adaptation of an individual and his relationship to the outside world. When we find points of interference in development, can they be undone? If so, can development return to its original direction without further sign of the interference? These questions are related to such concepts as regression and fixation—regression referring to the development which gives up its advanced position and returns to an earlier stage, and fixation to an interference with further progression at a given level. It is clear that the assessment of mental health of the psychic conditions is closely connected with the factors of irreversibility or with the balance between progression and regression in the child.

Thus, it is very important to note that the peak period of change is during the preschool years, preadolescence, or both. The tendency toward degrees in frequency is connected with habit formation (e.g., soiling, enuresis, and thumb-sucking) and with social behavior (e.g., destructiveness, temper tantrums, and overactivity). From the age of 3½ to about 6, there is an increase in aggressive behavior, expressed in food fads, irritability, dependency, and so forth. During the latency period no peaks of new problems occur, except for overdependency in girls, and from the age of 10 on, new peaks are reached in certain areas of development. It is furthermore of great significance that the behavioral constellations, problems, and conflict solutions show marked differences in boys and girls, a finding that appears in all studies of the influence of the sex variable in development.

The empirical approach toward the classification of conflicts and disorders was also taken by Thomas et al. (1968) in their longitudinal study of 136 children, which was designed to explore temperament as the basic factor of development. Their concept of temperament and their criteria for judging normality have already been described (see pages 13–14). On the basis of these criteria, their study showed that 42 of the children exhibited clinical behavior disorders and that symptoms in the younger child are primarily abnormalities of overt behavior, reflecting the character of the young organism. Symptoms that developed in functional areas appeared to be the result of standards and values as expressed by parents, teachers, peer groups, and so forth.

The Condition of Deprivation. This is a condition that seems to merit special mention because it is a frequent occurrence among those large segments of the population that are culturally, educationally, and economically disadvantaged. Deprivation here refers to those developmental conditions which are the result of insufficient stimulation and which lead to retarded developmental progression in substantial areas. The deprivation syndrome was first observed in children who had been hospitalized for long periods of time or brought up in orphanages. The findings stressed that many of these pathological syndromes cannot be reversed in later life. Often one finds that the effects of understimulation are mixed with those of overstimulation. While underprivileged children may be understimulated in certain areas, they are frequently overstimulated in others, which results in simultaneous immaturity and precocity and a syndrome of developmental disorganization that is not described under the general syndrome of deprivation. Overstimulation can be due to premature or continuous and overintense exposure to inappropriate experiences—e.g., violent behavior in the family—which are beyond the child's capacity to master.

How can the effects of deprivation be modified? What special modes of intervention should be constructed, and what is the most advantageous period during which to intervene? These are questions that are currently being explored at several levels of social and governmental authority. Today, many programs such as Head Start are attempting to undo some of the effects of deprivation; special educational procedures are being devised to counteract specific forms of deprivation, such as in language development, reading preparedness, and so forth. The general trend, however, is to try to intervene as early as possible, preferably during the first year of life, so as to safeguard development and prevent the occurrence of the syndrome.

Assessing Normality within the Developmental Progression

Although the use of the developmental progression as a yardstick of normality has many advantages, no one would claim that it solves all problems. On the contrary, like any other conceptual framework, it solves certain questions while simultaneously raising new ones. A major problem lies in the difficulty of differentiating transitional disorders from more long-lasting ones and of deciding whether a disorder that lasts for only a short period of time, and only briefly interferes with the developmental process, can usefully be regarded as an abnormality requiring treatment. Then again, in cases where there are severe external pressures stemming from family pathology or abnormal socioenvironmental conditions, it is difficult to determine whether the ongoing resulting disorders continue to be reactive-adaptive in character (and therefore essentially healthy) or have formed part of a fixed developmental deviation.

In a sense, these and other difficulties may be said to reflect an overall difficulty which the psychologist usually experiences in trying to make predictions about development. Escalona and Heider (1959) have found that specific predictions are less successful than the general ones and that the best areas of prediction for children are the life-style of general patterns of behavior and the patterning of interests and values. They also found that prediction based on anticipated environmental factors showed the highest success ratio. Evidently, prediction is more easily achieved with the assessment of the environmental constellation than with the assessment of the child's own developmental process. That is, psychologists can more readily anticipate areas of conflict and pathology on the basis of the pathology of the parents than on the basis of the measure of conflict-free spheres and the normal psychological defenses of the child.

REFERENCES

Beller, K., & Neubauer, P. Sex differences and symptom patterns in early childhood. *Journal of the American Academy of Child Psychiatry*, 1963, **2**, 417–433.

Erikson, E. H. *Childhood and society.* New York: Norton, 1950.

Escalona, S., & Heider, G. *Prediction and outcome: A study in child development.* New York: Basic Books, 1959.

Escalona, S., Leitch, M., et al. Early phases of personality development: A non-normative study of infant behavior. *Monographs of the Society for Research in Child Development,* 1953, **17** (1, Whole No. 54).

Freud, S. *Instincts and their vicissitudes* (1915). London: Hogarth Press, 1958.

Freud, S. *A general introduction to psychoanalysis* (1916). New York: Liveright, 1935.

Freud, S. *The ego and the id* (1923). London: Hogarth Press, 1947.

Inhelder, B., & Piaget, J. *The growth of logical thinking from childhood to adolescence.* New York: Basic Books, 1958.

Inhelder, B., & Piaget, J. *Early growth of logic in the child: Classification and seriation.* New York: Harper & Row, 1964. Pp. 53–55, 107, 144, 238, 241, 262, 263–264, 265, 266, 267, 268, 271–272, 298.

Jahoda, M. *Concepts of mental health.* New York: Basic Books, 1958.

Lewin, K. *A Dynamic theory of personality.* New York: McGraw-Hill, 1935.

Lewin, K. *Principles of topological psychology.* New York: McGraw-Hill, 1936.

Lewin, K. The conceptual representation and measurement of forces. *Contributions to Psychological Theory,* 1938, **1**, 100.

Lewin, K. *Resolving social conflicts.* New York: Harper & Row, 1948.

MacFarlane, J. W., Allen, L., & Honzik, M. P. *A developmental study of the behavior problems of normal children between 21 months and 14 years.* Berkeley: University of California Press, 1962.

Maslow, A. H., & Mittelmann, B. *Principles of abnormal psychology.* New York: Harper, 1941.

Nagera, H. Early childhood disturbances, the infantile neurosis, and the adulthood disturbances: Problems of a developmental psychoanalytical psychology. *The Psychoanalytic Study of the Child,* 1960 (Monog. 2).

Piaget, J. Une forme verbale de la comparaison chez l'enfant. *Archives of Psychology, Genève,* 1921, **18,** 141–172.

Piaget, J. *The origins of intelligence in children.* New York: International Universities Press, 1952.

Piaget, J. *The Construction of reality in the child.* New York: Basic Books, 1954.

Rappaport, D. The structure of psychoanalytic theory. *Psychological Issues,* 1960, **2** (Monog. 6).

Sears, R. R. A theoretical framework for personality and social behavior. *American Psychologist,* 1951, **6,** 476–483.

Spitz, R. A., & Wolf, K. M. The smiling response: A contribution to the ontogenesis of social relations. *Genetic and Psychological Uronographs,* 1946, **34,** 57–125.

Thomas, A., Chess, S., & Birch, H. G. *Temperament and behavior disorders in children.* New York: New York University Press, 1968.

Werner, H. Die Rolle der sprochempfindung im prozess der gestaltung, ausdruckmassig erlebter worter. *Z. Psychol.,* 1930, **10,** 149–156.

Werner, H. *Comparative psychology of mental development.* (Rev. ed.) Chicago: Follet, 1948.

2 Normal Development in Adolescence

Marshall D. Schechter, Povl W. Toussieng, and Richard E. Sternlof[1]

"The cure for adolescence belongs to the passage of time."
Winnicott, 1962, p. 1

HISTORY

G. Stanley Hall is considered the father of the psychology of adolescence. Hall (1916) expanded Darwin's concept of biological "evolution" into a psychological theory of recapitulation. The individual relives the development of the human race from early primitivism, through a period of savagery, to the more recent civilized ways of life, which characterize maturity. He described adolescence as a period of *Sturm und Drang,* full of idealism, commitment to a goal, revolution against the old, expression of personal feelings, passion, and suffering.

Psychoanalytic theory had one fundamental idea in common with Hall. S. Freud (1959) maintained that the individual repeats earlier experiences of mankind in his psychosexual development. He stated the Oedipal complex as a universal phenomenon which marks the onset of the latency phase. Puberty was seen as the time when adult sexuality takes its final shape. All other erogenous zones become subordinated to the genital zone, and there is a shift from primary objects (the parents) to sexual objects outside the family. Erikson (1950), Fromm (1941), Horney (1943), and Sullivan (1953) modified Freud's position, with his emphasis on instincts and biological determinism. They pointed out that social factors can modify development and redirect instinctual impulses.

Rank (1929) broke away from Freud and saw human nature not as repressed and neurotic, but as creative and productive. He criticized Freud's emphasis on the unconscious and returned to the conscious ego as the proper field of psychoanalysis. The core concept in Rank's theory is "will," a positive factor, a force that actively forms the self and modifies the environment. During latency, the will grows stronger and more independent and expands to the point where it turns against any authority not of its own choosing. It is here that the individual "will" encounters a societal "will" represented by parents and expressed in a moral code centuries old.

[1] This work was supported in part by a grant from The Foundations Fund for Research in Psychiatry, New Haven, Connecticut.

In early adolescence, the individual begins to oppose dependency, including both the rule of external environmental factors (parents, teachers, the law, etc.) and the rule of internal cravings. Establishing volitional independence, which society values and requires, becomes an important but difficult developmental task for the adolescent.

E. Jones (1922) indicated, too, that adolescent development is greatly determined by personality factors present during the prelatency phases. Spiegel (1951) reviewed the psychoanalytic contributions to adolescence covering clinical and theoretical as well as treatment aspects of this developmental phase.

A. Freud (1958) explored adolescence more fully and asserted that the factors in the developmental conflicts are:

1. The strength of the id impulse, which is determined by physiological and endocrinological processes during pubescence.
2. The ego's ability to cope with, or yield to, the instinctual forces. This in turn depends on the character training and superego development of the child during latency.
3. The effectiveness and nature of the defense mechanisms at the disposal of the ego. She considered two to be typical: asceticism and intellectualization.

Miss Freud (1958, p. 275) states: "Where adolescence is concerned, it seems easier to describe its pathological manifestations than the normal processes. Nevertheless, there are . . . at least two pronouncements which may prove useful for the concept: (1) that adolescence is by its nature an interruption of peaceful growth, and (2) that the upholding of a steady equilibrium during the adolescent process is in itself normal."

Mead's (1950) book is devoted entirely to the adolescent period. These findings of cultural anthropology are a serious challenge to Hall and Freud in their belief that certain important patterns in development and behavior were universal. Cultural relativism emphasized the importance of social institutions and cultural factors in human development. The Samoan child follows a relatively continuous growth pattern without severe interruptions, interferences, or restrictions. Benedict (1946) discussed three specific aspects of discontinuity in cultural conditioning. Major dichotomies occurring during adolescence in Western society are as follows:

1. Responsible versus nonresponsible status role
2. Dominance versus submission
3. Male versus female roles

Mead agrees with Erikson that the major task facing adolescents today is the search for meaningful identity.

Erikson's (1950) ideas modified Freudian theory in the light of findings from cultural anthropology. The core concept is the acquisition of ego identity. He lists eight basic stages with positive solutions and negative counterparts. He conceived of adolescence as a period in which the youth is confronted with a "physiological revolution" within that threatens his body image and his ego identity. Erikson maintained that the study of identity has become as important as the study of sexuality was in Freud's time.

A *Geisteswissenschaftliche* theory, propounded by Spranger (1928), is influential in Europe. Spranger's "six types of men" is the theoretical frame of reference for Allport's (1937) scale of values. Spranger identifies his theory with (1) developmental psychology and (2) typology. He distinguished three patterns of adolescent development:

1. Rebirth through storm, stress, strain, and crisis, resulting in personality change
2. Slow, continuous growth without basic personality change

3. Growth with conscious, active participation, similar to that proposed by Erikson, in adolescents' need to establish ego unity.

He also distinguished three possible effects:

1. A challenging of all previously unquestioned ideas and relationships—rebellion
2. An increased need for social recognition and interpersonal relationships
3. A need to experiment with different aspects of one's own ego—"Who am I?"

Spranger applied his six types of men to adolescence and put a heavy methodological emphasis on understanding the individual—his values, goals, and total situation.

K. Lewin (1935) was influenced by Freud's psychoanalytic theory but advanced his own widely known field theory. One core concept is that behavior is a function of the person and his environment and that they are both interdependent variables. The sum of these environmental and personal factors in interaction Lewin called the *life space*. Within the life space, objects or goals can have positive or negative valence. This is clearly seen in Lewin's formulation of adolescence, in which the adolescent is viewed as constantly changing his group membership. The adolescent is in a state of "social locomotion," moving into an unstructured social and psychological field. "The individual does not yet have a clear understanding of his social status and obligations, and his behavior reflects this uncertainty" (Muuss, 1962, p. 88). He becomes a "marginal man," standing on the boundary that separates two groups, and experiences a continuous conflict between the various attitudes, values, ideologies, and styles of living. He lacks social anchorage except in his peer group. This conflict results in increased emotional tensions.

Barker (1953) expanded Lewin's theory to show that changes in physiological structure influence behavior. His assumptions are that:

1. Adolescents are in a transitory period.
2. Body dimensions, physique, and endocrinological changes occur at an accelerated speed.
3. The time and speed of these changes vary greatly among individuals.
4. There are great differences within a given individual in the degree of maturity attained by different parts of the body.

An adolescent's behavior will depend on his perception of the situation. Since the adolescent's perceptual structure is unstable, his behavior will be unstable and vacillating. His first realization of the contradictions between the values taught by adults and the failure of adults to live and succeed by their own beliefs presents a new psychological situation that may drastically change his outlook on life. The less stable the situation, the more the individual depends upon small and sometimes unimportant cues. Behavior can be influenced easily, especially by the social group he wishes to belong to. Peer-group conformity is the psychological response to living in an unstable situation. It is an attempt to structure the field.

Gesell's theory of adolescent development (Gesell & Ilg, 1943) is a natural and integral part of his general developmental theory. He saw growth as a process that brings about changes in form and function; it has its "seasons" and "lawful sequences." He considered adolescence the crucial transition period from childhood to adulthood, not necessarily turbulent, erratic, and troublesome. He considered it a ripening process, though not without irregularities.

Davis (1944) defined socialization as the process by which the individual learns and adapts the ways, ideas, beliefs, values, and norms of his particular culture and makes them a part of his personality. He saw development as a process of learning socially acceptable behavior by means of reinforcement and punishment. The anticipated fear of punishment brings about what Davis calls "socialized anxiety." The goals of socialization differ not only from culture to culture, but from social class to social class within a given culture. The culture determines (1) what the goal responses are for a given adolescent and (2) the degree to which the goal responses are available to him. With regard to a great many goals, what is rewarding to a middle-class adolescent may not be so to a lower-class adolescent.

Havighurst's (1951) concept of "developmental tasks" expanded on Davis's ideas. The emphasis shifts from social anxiety to the mastery of developmental tasks in adolescence. An important aspect of this is the sequential nature of these tasks:

1. Accepting one's physique and accepting a masculine or feminine role
2. New relations with age-mates of both sexes
3. Emotional independence of parents and other adults
4. Achieving assurance of economic independence
5. Selecting and preparing for an occupation
6. Developing intellectual skills and concepts necessary for civic competence
7. Desiring and achieving socially responsible behavior
8. Preparing for marriage and family life
9. Building conscious values in harmony with an adequate scientific world picture

Many other authors contributed to the field, and for summaries and excellent bibliographies the reader is referred to Erikson (1950), Hall and Lindzey (1957), Hathaway and Monachesi (1963), Hsu (1961), Jahoda (1959), Muuss (1962), and Offer and Sabshin (1966). Most valuable and productive studies have been reported from a number of longitudinal investigations. A summary of these studies is noted in Kagan (1964).

GENERAL CONSIDERATIONS

We wish to offer the thoughts and conceptualizations of four authors concerning criteria for mental health in "adolescenthood" (Maier, 1965; Toussieng, 1966).

Gardner (1957) feels that the crucial developmental tasks of adolescents are:

1) Modification of their unconscious concepts of parental figures, 2) need for assumption of appropriate standards of morality, 3) identification with biologically determined sex role, and 4) permanent decisions and choices as to educational and vocational future.

Offer and Sabshin (1966) quote Jahoda as saying:

1) Attitudes towards the self; they include the accessibility of the self to consciousness; the correctness of the self-concept; its relation to the sense of identity and the acceptance by the individual of his own self. 2) Growth, development and self-actualization; the extent the individual utilizes his abilities; his orientation toward the future and his investment in living. 3) Integration; the extent to which the psychic forces are balanced; a unifying outlook on life and a resistance to stress. 4) Autonomy; the aim here is to ascertain whether the self-reliant person will be able to decide with relative ease and speed what suits his own needs best. 5) Perception of reality; a relative freedom from need-distortion, and the existence of empathy. 6) Environmental mastery; under this heading is listed: ability to love; adequacy in love, work and play; adequacy in interpersonal relationships; meeting situational requirements; adaption and adjustment; and efficiency in problem solving.

Offer and Sabshin (1966) quote Epstein as saying:

1) The ability to develop love and trust of another human being: to be able to tolerate awareness of negative as well as positive feelings in relation to these loved objects. 2) An inherent sense of autonomy and pride based upon healthy self-esteem. 3) A sense of freedom in the exertion of initiative based upon a satisfactorily developed conscience. 4) An ability and freedom to learn and develop mastery within the limits of the individual's abilities without being forced to hide a sense of inferiority by a too rapid and final retreat to illusory "safe" positions. 5) A sense of ego indentity, in Erikson's terms "the accrued confidence that one's ability to maintain inner sameness and continuity is matched by the sameness and continuity of one's meaning for others." 6) Early signs of an ability to develop interpersonal intimacy as contrasted with a fixed need for excess isolation. 7) The ability to generate what Rado speaks of as "welfare emotions"—happiness, pride, joy and so forth. 8) The capacity to accept and enjoy one's sexual impulses, and the ability to attain healthy gratifications or exert reasonable control without resorting to crippling mechanisms or defeat.

An example of the transition from adolescence to early adulthood was studied by Silber, Coelho, Murphey, Hamburg, Pearlin, and Rosenberg (1961). They noted the tasks required for this movement. Prominent among these were the following: (1) separation from parents, siblings, and close friends; (2) greater autonomy in regard to making important decisions, assuming responsibility for oneself, and regulating one's own behavior; (3) establishing new friendships; (4) pressures (internal and external) toward greater intimacy and adult sexuality; and (5) dealing with new intellectual challenges.

It is our contention, along with Offer and Sabshin (1966) as well as Grinker (1963), that there are indeed psychologically normal, healthy adolescents who meet the above criteria and very adequately accomplish the required tasks. These developments are neither smooth nor easy, internally or externally, but the phasic quality of this evolution (with possible regressions, plateaus, and advancements) seems evident from many sources. It presently appears (this will be detailed below) that there are clear changes in a number of parameters suggesting real differences between ages 9 and 12, 12 and 14, 14 and 17, and 17 and 21. It may appear that we are extending the age groups below and above that which is ordinarily thought of as adolescence proper. Yet, the changes which occur from 9 to 12 clearly presage adolescence in many respects. Psychological forces have been at work long before the onset of the menses or nocturnal emissions or the development of secondary sex characteristics. Also, many adolescents are forced to continue in a dependent position in their families for some time after completing high school because of the demands for specialization in our highly complex modern society.

PSYCHOLOGICAL FACTORS

Blos (1962, pp. 173–174) states:

It might be helpful to define the preconditions which the ego must possess at the onset of adolescence to an appreciable degree in order to develop those qualities and functions that are specifically adolescent and that will bring about those ego transformations which result in the ego of adulthood. The essential ego achievements of the latency period are the following: (1) An increase in cathexis of inner objects (object and self-representations) with resultant automatization of certain ego functions; (2) an increasing resistivity of ego functions to regression (secondary autonomy) with a consequent expansion of the nonconflictual sphere on the ego; (3) the formation of a self-critical ego which increasingly complements the functions of the superego, so that the regulations of self-esteem has reached a degree of independence from the environment; (4) reduction of the expressive use of the whole body and increase in the capacity for verbal expression in isolation from motor activity; (5) mastery of the environment through the learning of skills and the use of secondary process thinking as a means to reduce tension. The reality principle stabilizes the use of postponement and anticipation in the pursuit of pleasure.

Concurrent with these changes are the changes noted in the growth of logical thinking (Inhelder & Piaget, 1958). There is, during the latency and early adolescent phase a distinct shift in thinking from the concrete to the abstract, generalizations about laws of motion, energy, transfer, and conservation, as well as transformation of matter. Shifts also occur in thinking about properties of space and shape. There is a change from simplistic number concepts to generalizations about number systems and transformations in representation of size, position, form, and quantity. There is also a shift in the capacity to deduce items from inferences and the development of a capacity to argue logically. Along with these modifications, there is quite clearly a change in vocabulary and in problem solving. Such changes are reflected in the Rorschach test, as evidenced by an increase in responsivity, and a greater ability to synthesize and organize the inkblots, as well as increased ability to perceive movement in the blots (Beck, 1961). There is some indication that behavior is more likely to be stabilized during the 9-to-12 age period. It is during this period of life that statistically valid comparisons for future achievements are noted with most children (Bayley & Schaefer, 1963; Kagan & Moss, 1962). There is also during this age a much deeper and more long-lasting change in ethnic attitudes which persist into later life (Wilson, 1963) and in regard to the value and impact of religious experience (Elkind & Elkind, 1963).

This early age of preadolescence, 9 to 12, gives evidence of a second step in individuation, the first one having occurred between the ages of 2 and 3 (Blos, 1962; Dennis, 1964). It is during the preadolescent phase that the child is clearly more self-sustaining and self-governing, seeing himself objectively as part of a continuum of past, present, and future (Nixon, 1964). Youths at this age are increasingly distancing themselves from their primary introjects, their parents, and are trying instead to cathect individuals outside the home. This promotes the emergence of adolescent groups, the formation and functions of which are detailed by Sherif and Sherif (1965). Increased independence is evidenced in modes of thinking (Inhelder & Piaget, 1958), as well as in a much greater perception of reality which goes along with a considerably increased mastery over the external environment. Awareness of mind and body prior to the onset of preadolescence depends mainly on the feedback from parents. During this early period of adolescence and then in adolescence proper, there is a considerably increased amount of self-consciousness —an awareness of himself as a functioning, operating, and determining individual. Major self-concepts are determined by the adolescent's peer group as well as by others slightly older than he, who begin increasingly to fit the role of heroes both consciously and unconsciously (Galdston, 1967; Long, 1966).

The preadolescent also begins to observe himself more adequately, and this self-observation expands as he moves into later phases of development. Goldman (1962) suggests that adults may see the adolescent in a more negative light than he sees himself. Medinnus (1965) found that those adolescents who had high scores on a self-regard dimension also perceived their parents as loving. Ostermeier (1967) demonstrated that clothing and appearance are highly valued as having a positive influence on acceptance by peer groups. Carlson (1965) studied sociopersonal orientation as well as self-esteem. Over a six-year period (from age 11 to age 17) girls showed an increase in social orientation, while boys increased in personal orientation. Self-esteem, however, was independent of sex role. Douvan (1960) felt that character development is more rapid in boys than in girls during adolescence. The critical variable for girls, she felt, is their progress in developing interpersonal skills and sensitivities.

Shapiro (1963a, p. 3) states:

> A new capacity for hypothesis formation develops, with the utilization of hypothetico-deductive reasoning and experimental proof. I have postulated that the consistency of this finding in early adolescence justifies an extension of Hartmann's assumptions about autonomous ego development in childhood, to the period of early adolescence, to account for the maturational events of this phase.

New areas of autonomous development can thus be assumed. It is in the remodeling of the psychic structures (Jacobson, 1961) that energies are released for new attachments to new objects and for the development of a feeling of omnipotentiality (Pumpian-Mindlin, 1965). Schechter (1964) suggests that the period of adolescence is one in which there is a destruction of primary introjects with a consequent vigorous drive toward replacement by attachments to new age-appropriate and more satisfactory objects. This is one of the factors which Erikson (1968) thinks is essential in the establishment of an identity and which Blos (1962) suggests as necessary for the consolidation of a sense of self (Bronson, 1959; Hershenson, 1967; Howard, 1960). The superego thus becomes far less archaic and punitive as the preadolescent and early adolescent shifts from primitive imagoes to more realistic and more rational views. Horror movies, which in the past triggered nightmarish dreams, are sought out and enjoyed during this period. Magical and irrational thinking are replaced by a secure hold on the reality principle (Deutsch, 1967).

Shapiro (1963b, pp. 85–86) states:

> These new ego capacities which Jacobson subsumes under secondary autonomy seem related to the new

cognitive capacities delineated by Inhelder and Piaget (1958), and their appearance could be considered a maturational event which is a part of autonomous ego development.

Elkind (1967, pp. 1029–1032) indicates:

> From the strictly cognitive point of view . . . the major task of early adolescence can be regarded as having to do with *the conquest of thought.* Formal operations not only permit the young person to construct all the possibilities in a system and construct contrary-to-fact propositions (Inhelder & Piaget, 1958); they also enable him to conceptualize his own thought, to take his mental constructions as objects and reason about them. . . . Once more, however, this new mental system which frees the young person from the egocentrism of childhood entangles him in a new from of egocentrism characteristic of adolescence.

> Formal operational thought not only enables the adolescent to conceptualize his thought, it also permits him to conceptualize the thought of other people. . . . Accordingly, since he fails to differentiate between what others are thinking about and his own mental preoccupations, he assumes that other people are as obsessed with his behavior and appearance as he is himself. It is this belief that others are preoccupied with his appearance and behavior that constitutes the egocentrism of the adolescent. . . .

> Adolescent egocentrism is thus overcome by a twofold transformation. On the cognitive plane, it is overcome by the gradual differentiation between his own preoccupations and the thoughts of others; while on the plane of affectivity, it is overcome by a gradual integration of the feelings of others with his own emotions.

Two excellent books that deal with information about all phases of adolescence from the viewpoints of nonpsychiatric authors are *The Adolescent through Fiction* (1959) and *The Universal Experience of Adolescence* (1964), both by Norman Kiell. We also would like to call attention to *Selected Problems of Adolescence* (1967), by Helene Deutsch, which indicates problems in terms of group formation as well as some special forms of object relations in both males and females during adolescence.

BIOLOGICAL FACTORS

During the initial phase of our own study of adolescence, it became clear that little had been written on biochemical (especially hormonal) changes that lead up to and are continued during puberty. Certainly little appeared in the literature correlating the biological with the psychological. Hormonal studies were undertaken by Tanner (1963) and Nathanson, Aub, and Towne (1941). It was quite clear that hormonal changes begin in males by age 8 or 9 and that estrogenic substances (or their precursors) can be discovered in females between ages 7 and 8 (Nathanson, et al., 1941; Tanner, 1963). Recently, Kestenberg (1967a,b,c) attempted to draw together information from biochemical and psychological sources and adapted a chart from Talbot, Berman, and MacLachlan (1952) and Wilkins (1965, p. 448). This chart shows a definite shift in hormonal substances in the male and the female with advances in the internal genitalia in the female between ages 7 and 8 and in the external genitalia of the male between ages 10 and 11. There is a suggestion from the work of Bell (1965) that penile and testicular growth perhaps antedates these ages.

It is our observation that one of the peaks of emotional difficulties in females occurs at approximately age 9, correlating with the growth of the bony pelvis and the budding of the nipples. The problem distinguishes itself by the development of what is classically called a *school phobia*. It is suggested that this disorder is one of those which might be seen as being driven by biological forces and perhaps would fall into the diagnostic classification of a normal developmental process. The evidence of estrogenic excretion in girls is noted in ovarian and uterine growth as androgenic

hormones in the male are evidenced by growth of the external genitalia (Jones & Heller, 1966; Livson & McNeill, 1962; Novak, 1966; Riley, 1960; Schonfeld, 1943).

Although in normal, healthy youngsters the capability of making these transitions on a physical as well as a psychological basis is epigenetically determined, it has been the experience of one of us that even in biologically competent organ systems, a definite inhibition in growth may occur without sufficient external stimulation (Schechter, 1964). This experience parallels the work of Blizzard, Powell, Basel, and Raiti (1967) and of Barbero and Shaheen (1967) with infants diagnosed as having failed to thrive because of maternal deprivation.

Early physical maturation has been closely correlated with both psychological and social maturation. M. C. Jones (1957) indicated that early maturers showed signs of occupational stability and ability to make executive decisions, while late maturers evidenced occupational instability. Broverman, Broverman, Klaiber, Palmer, and Vogel (1964) and Broverman (1964) found that early maturers were able to perform simple repetitive tasks well (strong automatizers), in contrast with late maturers, who did the tasks poorly (weak automatizers).

Mussen and Jones (1957) and M. C. Jones (1957) described physically accelerated boys as more independent, self-confident, relaxed, and poised. The slower-growing boys had more negative self-conceptions, felt rejected, and were rebellious. Late-maturing adolescent boys were also described as being more expressive and talkative. M. C. Jones and Mussen (1958) repeated their data collecting with females—slow and accelerated in development—and found essentially the same things as with the males.

Eichhorn and McKee (1958) found that adolescence is characterized by a temporary decrease in intraindividual physiological stability. Douglas and Ross (1964), on longitudinal examinations of 1,700 boys and 1,600 girls tested at ages 8, 11, and 15, found no relationship between social class and the onset of puberty. They did find that children who matured early earned higher intelligence and reading achievement scores, remained in school longer, and were higher in school performance than those who matured late.

Temperament as a constitutional variable has been given little prominence in child development. Thomas et al. (1968, p. 183) state:

> Existing theories emphasize motives and drive states, tactics of adaption, environmental patterns of influence, and primary organic determinants. The central requirement that a concept of temperament makes of such generalizations is that they come increasingly to focus on the individual and on his uniqueness. In other words, it requires that we recognize that the same motive, the same adaptive tactic, or the same structure of objective environment will have different functional meaning in accordance with the temperamental style of the given child. Moreover, in such an individualization of the study of functional mechanisms in behavior, temperament must be considered as an independent determining variable in itself, and not as an *ad hoc* modifier used to fill in the gaps left unexplained by other mechanisms.

Pishkin (1967) suggests a plateauing of information processing between ages 13 and 15 due to interferences from what he terms "puberty noise." Ljung (1965) investigated verbal comprehension in boys and girls between the ages of 9 and 15. He found a growth spurt for girls between 12 and 13 and for boys between 14 and 15. A comparatively slow growth rate seemed characteristic of the period immediately before the spurt, and girls seemed to comprehend better than boys at all the tested ages. Complicating normal growth processes and endocrinological changes are the differences in food intake at different socioeconomic and cultural levels. This may also have an impact on the development of the biological growth spurt and therefore also on psychological development (Remmers, 1962; Riley, 1960).

SOCIOCULTURAL ASPECTS

The works of Benedict (1946), Erikson (1968), and Mead (1950) highlight the importance of mores, attitudes, and cultural settings in the development of the preadolescent and the adolescent. Erikson (1968, p. 94) charts a sequence of developmental tasks and the impingement of psychological and cultural forces. He states: "The diagram formalizes a progression through time of a differentiation of parts. This indicates 1) that each item of the vital personality to be discussed is systematically related to all others, and they all depend on the proper development in the proper sequence of each item; and 2) that each item exists in some form before 'its' decisive and critical time normally arrives" (pp. 93–94).

The importance of socialization and its effects on adolescence are detailed by a number of authors, among whom are Hsu (1961), Mead (1950), and Axelrad (1960–1967). In the prepubertal years, industry and competence as well as increasing autonomy make for a very different child from the one who entered school at age 5. The ability to join peer groups within and without school allows the preadolescent, as well as the early adolescent, the opportunity to be socially accepted and to live by customs and mores which facilitate separation from primary internal objects. School systems show their recognition of these changes from the prepubertal to the pubertal period by creating junior high schools. Generally this introduction into adolescence carries with it a socially approved method whereby group formation is enhanced.

It is during this early adolescent period (12 to 14) that vocational, reality-oriented conceptions take hold, and when adolescents are unable, for whatever reasons, to go through this phase normally and conceptualize themselves with a vocational future, severe depressive states may intervene (Schechter, 1964). Aggression becomes far more channeled along lines that are goal-directed, whether they exist in athletic situations or in the development of omnipotent vocational fantasies. These developments involve both sexes (particularly males); females seem involved primarily with a commitment of femininity and the roles assigned to females in their given society. Differences exist in various socioeconomic and cultural groups. Many in the low socioeconomic groups are unable to see themselves attaining any prestigious vocation. Some of the children may attempt full adult roles during this preadolescent and early adolescent phase. We refer to areas of involvement with work, sexual behavior, interpersonal relationships, and social customs specifically allocated and permitted for adult populations only.

Implications of developmental difference, sexual demands, and conflicts in middle-class adolescents have been reported by Lansky, Crandall, Kagan, and Baker (1961). A recent publication by Brody (1968) describes similar adolescent conflicts among Negroes, Mexican-Americans, Chinese, Japanese, Kiowa-Apache Indians, and Puerto Ricans.

The influence of social structures and some of the effects are detailed in Coleman (1966) and Cole and Hall (1964). It is when the social systems, exemplified by parental authorities or by the Establishment, are unable to accept the development of the mood shifts, the different conceptualizations of problem solving, the change in body image, and the potential threat in competition with the older generation that conflicts between the adult and the adolescent generations begin (Bell, 1965; Duvall, 1965; Friedenberg, 1959). As long as dependency is expressed and parental help is desired by the child, the parent is much more able to tolerate this situation. As soon as evidence of independence begins, the threat to the parent's own autonomy and estab-

lished identity is manifest. It is our impression that separation anxiety is not merely a function of the child leaving his parents, but the reverse also—anxiety in the parents at being able to allow separation and individuation in their teenager.

In previous years, the recognition of the arrival by adolescents into the adult community was occasioned in the United States by religious and puberty rites (Arlow, 1951). These recognitions of the biological and psychological maturation became increasingly meaningless as educational specialization increased the need for a more prolonged adolescence with continued dependency. Previous social acceptance of adulthood at age 13 or 14 by religious puberty rites in the United States no longer holds. The acquisition of the driver's license appears to us far more important in determining arrival at an adult status than any of the religious rites (Coleman, 1966). The adolescent, up to age 15, although biologically mature, is still considered by his own peer society to be a child. This has a distinct effect on systems of thinking and the ability to develop independence, autonomy, and self-esteem.

ADOLESCENCE PROPER

At about the age of 15 many adolescents have completed a major part of the changes caused by puberty and are ready to enter the phase of adolescence proper. They have emerged from the intense self-preoccupation of early adolescence, have gained some distance between themselves and their early love objects, and have begun to attain some mastery over the strong new instinctual pressures. It is important to remember, however, that puberty "normally" can begin in some boys at 15 or 16 and that 17 percent of all males aged 21 studied by Schonfeld (1943) still had not attained full sexual maturation. He studied 1,500 males from birth to age

25. The biological, psychological, and social consequences of the time of onset of puberty and the rate of maturation are considerable. They are too often ignored when "normal" adolescent development is discussed. It is not justified to make late puberty an abnormal occurrence.

We are as yet not able to foretell exactly when puberty will occur and what the rate of growth will be compared with prepubertal body size. Broverman et al. (1964), in restudying the longitudinal growth data on 67 males reported by Stolz and Stolz (1951), found that preadolescent body build contributed more to postadolescent body build than the adolescent growth spurt. However, the earlier the adolescent growth spurt starts, the more growth is likely to take place. Ectomorphy and mesomorphy are no predictors of when physical maturation will take place. In studying a sample of 177 boys drawn from three longitudinal growth studies, Livson and McNeill (1962) divided them into subgroups of contrasting somatotypes and observed the difference in age at reaching 90 percent of mature height. They were not able to confirm earlier reports that mesomorphs mature significantly earlier than ectomorphs, though the trend was in this direction. Yet, 41 percent of extreme mesomorphs matured later than the average ectomorph. They did have findings suggesting that extreme ectomorphs have a very narrow age range of maturation, whereas the mesomorphs have a much wider range.

Fried and Smith (1962) studied the senior-year school health records of 600 girls from well-to-do homes and found that the menarche in most girls leads to decelerated growth. Their growth tends to be less than 4 inches after the menarche. However, in almost 10 percent of the girls there was a growth spurt of more than 4 inches, which could not be predicted from their physical status at the time of the menarche. Fried and Smith stress that the rate of growth is of intense interest to adolescents and that predictions should not be made unless good records of past growth are available and unless a good physical examination is done. X-rays and hormonal assays, as well as knowledge of the past medical history and the adolescent growth history of the parents, can all be of help in making predictions. Growth failure due to illness in childhood may be corrected by a growth spurt of more than 4 inches after the menarche.

Novak (1966), on the basis of his study of eighteen high school athletes and twenty controls, stresses that the desirable weight for athletic adolescents cannot be estimated properly from standard height and weight tables.

The degree to which physical development in adolescents influences personality development was studied by Weatherly (1964). A total of 234 male and 200 female students at the University of Colorado, aged approximately 19, were given the Minnesota Multiphasic Personality Inventory (MMPI) K scale and the Taylor Manifest Anxiety Scale early in the semester. They also rated themselves as to similarity to their mothers, fathers, same-sex best friends, and opposite-sex best friends, along with dimensions of overall personality, intelligence, warmth, orderliness, political views, and religious views. The rate of physical maturation was assessed by responses to a self-rating scale. Approximately 5 weeks later, ninety-six of the boys and ninety-two of the girls were given the Edwards Personal Preference Schedule. On the basis of their own reports, the students were divided into groups of early, average, and late physical maturers, each of which was compared on the personality measures obtained. The results indicated that late physical maturation represents a handicap to the personality development of the boys, while early maturation is no greater asset to personality developments in boys than an average rate of maturation. The effects of late maturation in girls are in the same direction, but are much less profound than in boys. The late-maturing boy, aged 19, is still more inclined to seek attention and affection from others and less inclined to assume the role of dominance and leadership over others. Yet, he is inclined to defy authority and engage in rebellious, unconventional behavior. He experiences more subjective tension and is more ready to indulge in guilt-implying self-abasement than boys who have matured early or at the average time. He also tends to see himself as different from his peers and adults.

Mussen and Jones (1957) found in a Thematic Apperception Test (TAT) follow-up of 17-year-old boys studied earlier that late physical maturation was accompanied by less adaptive social behavior, feelings of inadequacy, negative self-concepts, feelings of rejection and domination, and persistent dependency needs paradoxically coupled with the rebellious quest for autonomy and freedom from restraint. Apparently these difficulties persist into adulthood. In restudying men at an average age of 33, M. C. Jones (1957) found that the late maturers were less capable of conveying a good impression and more inclined to turn to others for help than the early maturers.

These findings contrast with those of H. E. Jones (1949) that at 16, late-maturing girls are more sociable, cheerful, poised, and expressive than early-maturing girls and show more leadership and interest in extracurricular activities. However, in TAT follow-ups of 17-year-old girls, M. C. Jones and Mussen (1958) found the same trend in girls that they had found in boys, though there was less difference between late- and early-maturing girls. Early-maturing girls had more adequate thought processes, a more positive self-image, and a more relaxed, secure view of themselves and their world.

For normal adolescent development in girls a normally functioning central nervous system is important (Hertzig & Birch, 1966). On clinical neurological examination of psychiatrically disturbed adolescent girls, they found neurological dysfunction four to eight times more frequently than in psychiatrically unremarkable populations of children younger in age.

Many normal adolescents tend to worry excessively about serious underlying diseases which will interrupt their progress toward adulthood. They have many minor physical symptoms, usually without objective physical findings (Wessel & LaCamera, 1967). It may be that these complaints are in some way related to attitudes in the families of these adolescents. In analyzing interfamily attitudes of over 200 youths with body-image disturbance, Schonfeld (1966) found that these families exploited the significance of body functions and appearance and that they all overly stressed the importance of "being big" and of "growing up." As a result, the youngsters in these families overvalued the "body beautiful" for security and overreacted to slight deviations in development—sometimes even to features of normal growth. In adolescents with actual body defects, the outcome of psychological development depended more on family and cultural attitudes than on the defects themselves.

Erikson (1959) managed to include all these factors and stressed the struggle in adolescence for an ego identity. This struggle manifests itself at times in an almost morbid preoccupation with how the adolescent appears to others as compared with how he feels he is. He is also very much concerned with how he can connect the roles and skills he cultivated in childhood with the current ideal prototypes. Thus, an understanding of adolescent development in this phase, as well as in late adolescence, must be viewed as an interaction of intrapsychic forces with familial constellations and the social and cultural environment as a whole. In addition, there must be a continuity between the child's experiences in the prepubertal period and in adolescence proper. Erikson, for example, emphasizes the very difficult discontinuity between the more sensual early childhood of some minority groups

(Negroes, Indians, Mexicans, etc.) and the sudden shift in child-rearing attitudes in the parents and teachers away from sensuality at the time of these children's puberty.

Root (1957) concludes from individual case studies that the primary intrapsychic task of adolescence proper is to mourn the infantile attachments which must now be given up to free the way to adult maturity. Also on the basis of psychoanalytic experience, Blos (1962) differentiates adolescence proper from preadolescence by the shift from a merely quantitative drive increase to the emergence of a distinctly new drive quality. The preadolescent regressive position is abandoned, and pregenitality becomes part of *fore*pleasure. In adolescence proper, emotional life becomes wider and richer. The goal of growing up becomes the main focus and orientation. There is a never-ceasing attempt to define the self in answer to the question "Who am I?". Relationships with others move into the spotlight, and active character formation proceeds rapidly, though it will not be completed until postadolescence.

Pumpian-Mindlin (1965), also basing his views on psychoanalytic experience, traces the vicissitudes of infantile omnipotence and stresses that at the start of adolescence proper, infantile omnipotence is transformed into "omnipotentiality." Pumpian-Mindlin (1965, p. 2) defined omnipotentiality as:

> . . . the feeling and conviction on the part of the youth that he can do anything in the world, solve any problem in the world if given the opportunity. And if it is not given, even create it. There is no occupation which is inaccessible, no task which is too much for him . . . nothing is impossible, nothing can be taken for granted. . . . he knows no limits in fantasy and accepts grudgingly any limits in reality. Yet at the same time he finds it difficult to do one thing and follow it through to completion, because to do so would mean to commit himself

to one thing primarily, and this he is not yet prepared to do.

Considerable confusion exists as to exactly what is to be expected intrapsychically in a normal adolescent. Anna Freud (1958) holds the view that adolescence by itself is an interruption of peaceful growth and that the upholding of a steady equilibrium during the adolescent process in itself is abnormal. Disharmony within the psychic structure is to be expected, and defenses become overstressed, overused, or used in isolation, thus creating an external picture of pathological development. However, these defenses must be used in order to regain mental stability, and they remain within the normal range if they are combined with other defenses and used in moderation. Anna Freud considers it important that the adolescent ego experiment while building a viable adult intrapsychic structure. She views the adolescent's inconsistency and unpredictability, his asceticism and sensual sprees, his alternating love and hate for his parents, his excessive independency or dependency, and his alienation or sudden intimacy as such ego-building experimentation. She also includes in this the adolescent's imitation of or identification with others, while searching constantly to find out who he is; his wish to be more idealistic, creative, and unselfish than he will ever be again, while also being self-centered, selfish, and manipulative; as well as his intense suffering and ecstatic happiness. She views these fluctuations as being much healthier than the premature freezing of the personality, which does lead to serenity but is a sign of stunted growth.

Erikson (1968) is much less sweeping in his definition of what is normal in adolescent development, as he sees this development as being partly dependent on how it matches the historical period in which a given adolescent lives. The adolescent who is gifted and well trained in the pursuit of contemporary technological trends does not need to have a stormy adolescence. However, if the adolescent cannot match the historical trends of his time, he is forced into a more "explicitly ideological direction" (Erikson, 1968, p. 130). He may then react with animallike strength to an environment which he sees as depriving him too radically of those forms of expression which he needs to be able to achieve a stable and workable ego identity.

From his intensive study of 101 adolescent outpatients, who were compared with a control group, Masterson (1967) has raised the question as to the exact role of adolescent turmoil in relation to psychiatric illness in adolescence. He berates current psychoanalytic authors who cannot tell during the period of adolescence whether ongoing development is pathological or not, and he insists that healthy adolescent development, at most, produces subclinical levels of anxiety and depression. Masterson explains the discrepancy between his findings and those of others by suggesting that clinical authors on adolescence have been too prone to generalize to all adolescents from one or a few patients. However, Erikson, for example, was associated with several longitudinal studies of normal children while he was formulating his ideas. Even so, the need for further intensive longitudinal studies to settle once and for all the question of adolescent turmoil is more than evident.

After studying intrapsychic aspects of the rebelliousness observed at times in many normal adolescents, Blos (1962) considers it theoretically convincing and clinically demonstrable that the amount of adolescent negativism is inversely proportionate to the degree to which the adolescent has gained mastery over the regressive pull within himself. Such mastery is gained by various defensive and adaptive maneuvers, which prove effective and strengthening to the adolescent's

heterosexual, extrafamilial, nonambivalent object relations. In this way, the adolescent is able to renounce irreversibly the attachments to his parents and his family, which now have resumed incestuous overtones. Special defenses pave the way in this process, particularly those of intellectualization, asceticism, and a turn to inner experience, with an accompanying discovery of beauty and all its possible manifestations. Blos perceives this as a sublimation of the child's love for an idealized parent. Thus, normal adolescence can also be a peak period of intense creativity.

A study of eighty boys and seventy-one girls by Kurtzman (1967) confirms the impression of many authors on adolescence that effective use of creativity in adolescents is evidence of a maturational process which is proceeding well. Creative adolescents tend to be more extroverted and adventurous, and they have a greater tolerance for ambiguity. Creative boys are more self-confident and mature than noncreative boys, while there is no difference as to these two personality characteristics between creative and noncreative girls. Strikingly, creative boys tend to receive greater acceptance from their peer group than noncreative boys, while the more creative girls are less accepted by their classmates than noncreative girls. One of Kurtzman's other interesting findings is that there is a negative relationship between adolescent creativity and a favorable attitude toward school. The implication of this finding is that our current regimented, overly structured junior high and high schools cannot assimilate creative students and therefore inadvertently counteract the effective ongoing psychological maturation in those adolescents. Friedenberg (1959) has offered a chilling picture of the ways in which contemporary high schools try to prevent or abort the maturation process in their students.

Another matter which is causing increasing

concern is the lack of support available for the adolescent maturational process in many contemporary families. Deutsch (1967) feels that this is often due to the fact that many parents are still involved in their own incomplete adolescence. These parents can only be pals on the same level with their children and are unable to provide parental guidance and protection at a very crucial time. Deutsch deplores this, as she feels that attempts to achieve freedom and to protest against authority should first be begun at home and only later taken to the larger field of society. She stresses that in her view, this is especially true for girls and their current so-called sexual freedom.

Indeed, the presence of two effective and mature parents in the home does seem to be crucial for satisfactory psychological maturation in adolescent children. Barclay and Cusumano (1958) studied forty male white and Negro adolescents of an average age of 15.43. Using Wilkins' Rod and Frame test and the Gough Femininity score, they found that adolescent boys who did not have a father in the home were more field-dependent. The Negro boys as a group were more field-dependent than the group of white boys, but the fatherless Negro boys were more field-dependent than the Negro boys who had a father in the home. Strikingly, the boys with a father and those without one did not differ significantly in masculinity scores or in evidence of cross-sex identity. Barclay and Cusumano speculate that boys without fathers come up to the level of their peers with fathers by forming a strong reaction formation to their identification with their mothers' more passive role, an identification which shines through, however, in their greater field dependence.

Grinker (1962, 1963), after intensive study of sixty-five college students, concluded that satisfactory and positive affectionate relationships with both parents contributed to mental health

in his subjects. Parental agreement and cooperation in child raising were important, as were definite and explicit limits and reasonable, consistent punishment.

The presence of a father in the home is equally important for the psychological development of adolescent girls. On the basis of several intensive case studies, Leonard (1966) stresses the importance of the presence of an affectionate but nonseductive father in the home, who will not be seduced by his daughter's fantasies either. If the father is unavailable, girls may either build an idealized father image and seek a love object who is as much like the ideal as possible or begin to place excessive emphasis on being *loved* and thus become unable to give love. Seductive or seducible fathers may prompt extreme defense measures in their daughters, such as intense hate or flight from the home to another (unconsciously similar) love object.

In addition to the inner turmoil and confusion, adolescents today have to try to prepare themselves to live in an adult society which is itself deeply confused as to its values and goals. The world the adolescents enter changes so rapidly that even mature adults have major difficulties in keeping up with them, at least to some degree. Caught in its own dilemmas, society has no understanding of, or sympathy with, adolescent problems and tends to force outdated, rigid patterns of behavior and values on the young (Friedenberg, 1959; Wessel & LaCamera, 1967). Many adolescents are aware of the discrepancy between what they are taught and what is being required of them, on the one hand, and what is actually happening in the world today, on the other. They are therefore caught between their own accurate reality testing and the determined adult demands to accept the picture of the world which is being conjured up in their schools, churches, and homes. Blos (1962, p. 109) has pointed out: "Unreserved submission to social pressures which force the individual to perform in a given way regardless of his corresponding internal capacity to integrate the experience into the continuity of the ego usually produces a state of inner confusion." This confusion is manifested clinically by the adolescent's inability to learn scheduled time, orient himself to the future, adjust to the consequences of his actions, etc.

In many ways, until recent years minority-group adolescents tended to be forced into submission by social pressures. Peck and Galliani (1962) studied 1,217 eighth-grade boys and girls of Anglo-American and Latin-American ethnic backgrounds in three Texas communities. The California Test of Mental Maturity and McGuire's Role Nomination Instrument were used. The results showed that adolescents with great accuracy assess and value intelligence in their peers, even though this intelligence is not reflected in those peers' academic performance. However, Latin American youths win less attention not only from the "Anglos," but from one another as well. They show a deeply passive attitude. Peck and Galliani asked whether this may be due to identification with their parents, to cultural injunction against seeking or gaining social visibility, or to protective withdrawal, or whether the Latin American students secretly accept the cultural tenet of the Anglo-Americans that the Anglos are superior. However, the features observed in these Latin American students might equally well be due to the consequences of submission and to inner confusion, which Blos warns about. In other words, the submission has thwarted further psychological growth.

LATE ADOLESCENCE

Around the age of 17 or 18, with wide variations on both sides, the identity crisis of adolescence proper has been settled sufficiently to allow the adolescent to turn his attention to the role his newly defined self may properly assume in the adult world. As this occurs, he enters the phase of late adolescence, which ends with passage into early adulthood around the age of 21. Deutsch (1967) sees the phase of late adolescence as a "finishing process" (p. 41) in which the adolescent conflicts are being acted out, but in a relatively controlled way. She wonders whether the acting out is possibly also a defensive move to prevent "after-repression of the not-quite-buried forces of adolescence" (p. 41). Pumpian-Mindlin (1965) sees this acting out of inner fantasies as necessary to find out about reality and to make the transition from omni-potentiality to commitment, which Pumpian-Mindlin sees as the main characteristic of young adulthood.

Blos (1962) likewise sees late adolescence, which he calls *postadolescence,* as a phase of consolidation. He enumerates the following characteristics of this period (p. 128): (1) gains in purposeful actions, (2) gains in social integration, (3) gains in predictability, (4) gains in constancy of emotions, (5) gains in stability of self-esteem, (6) greater unification of affective and volitional processes, (7) ability to compromise and delay, and (8) delineation of concerns which really matter in life—not necessarily selfish ones—and which do not tolerate postponement of compromise. Intrapsychically, Blos sees in late adolescence the following characteristics: highly idiosyncratic and stable arrangement of ego functions and interests, an extension of the conflict-free sphere of the ego (secondary autonomy), an irreversible sexual position (identity constancy) with genital primacy, a relatively constant cathexis of object and self-representations, and the stabilization of mental apparatuses which automatically safeguard the integrity of psychic organism (p. 129).

Erikson (1968), speaking of late adolescence as young adulthood, sees this period as the time when young men and women gain the capacity for *intimacy,* which he defines as far more than genital intimacy. For him, true intimacy is the "counterpointing as well as fusing of identities" (p. 135) in friendships, in erotic relationships, or in inspirational groups. True intimacy can be accomplished only by persons who are sure of their identity. Erikson further stresses that the moralism of childhood and the idealism of adolescence proper are replaced in late adolescence by an "ethical sense" which differentiates "competition, the erotic bond and merciless enmity" from each other (p. 136).

Erikson's stress on the achievement of a strong ego identity as a prerequisite for developing an "ethical sense" is not supported by the findings of Heilbrun (1964). Using psychometric measures from sixty-nine male and sixty-three female college students, aged approximately 20, Heilbrun could not demonstrate any relationships between the strength of sexual identification and the consistency between the subjects' social values and their overt social behavior. Heilbrun's other findings, not related to this subject, were that females with a strong female identification were significantly less aggressive than females with a weak identification. Males with a strong male identification tended to be more aggressive than males with a weak identification, but not significantly so. Why the difference is smaller in boys has not yet been satisfactorily determined.

Whittington (1963) has become impressed, in his experiences as a college psychiatrist, with how well Thomas Wolfe has described the late adolescent: the sense of urgency, the restless impatience and joyous grandiosity which collide with the stubborn reality of a drab world, the exhilaration of standing at the entrance to adult life while having major fears about an unpredictable future, and the obsession with using the newly found, supposedly invulnerable and omnipotent self, as well as the black despair

when inevitable defeats and disappointments occur. Time is constantly getting away from the late adolescent, and he fears that it will leave him old before he has even lived. A rich fantasy life promises effortless sexual and other gratifications as well as passionate and tender love relationships. Whittington points out that this pursuit of pleasure, gratification, security, power, respect, and love leaves room in only a few college students for the excitement of learning. The students who do experience this type of exhilaration try to "cram all knowledge into their hungry brains, or sense the thrill of speculation and the ecstasy of a satisfied curiosity" (1963, p. 46).

In view of the intoxication with one's own powers in this period, it is striking to find how much conformity is exhibited in the behavior of many young people in this age group. Silber, Coelho, Murphey, Hamburg, Pearlin, and Rosenberg (1961) studied a small sample of highly competent adolescents from various socioeconomic levels to determine what went into their decision to go to college and their choice of college. In spite of individual differences, by and large the adolescents did not make a conscious decision to go to college. Instead, they acted on the basis of the internalized expectations of their parents, which in turn were strongly reinforced by their schools and their socioeconomic environments. The choice of college, while sometimes limited by financial considerations, nevertheless was by and large left up to the students themselves. However, their need to conform to the expectation to go to college, any college, was reflected in the striking equanimity shown by the students and their parents when the students were rejected by colleges of their choice.

Nixon, like Whittington a college psychiatrist, sees the period of late adolescence as a *cognitive* stage of development, as the adolescent now is capable of perceiving and "knowing" both himself and his setting in an "objective, detached, constructively critical fashion" (1964, pp. 55–56). For these reasons Nixon frowns on counseling late adolescents to stop being so "introspective," "sensitive," "selfish," etc. In studying the impact of college and personality development, Nixon divides college students into three subgroups: (1) the "growers," who have some measure of self-regard, who do experience anxiety but are not injured by it, who question their upbringing at least to some extent, and who protest, but not in a destructively rebellious fashion; (2) the "conformers," who are adored by society but leave college without ever having been touched by their educational experience; and (3) the "rebels," whom colleges feel forced to fight or even expel and on whom colleges therefore have no impact either.

However, because late adolescence is a cognitive stage, Nixon believes there is growth potential in any of these groups. He counsels colleges to recognize the dim beginnings of the students' broadening vision of themselves and their world and to encourage it to expand, though society is notoriously reluctant to allow that vision to grow. Nixon feels that colleges should offer objective and constructive criticism of the social scene and of the students themselves, while showing compassion for the youngsters, supporting them when they temporarily have had too much work, and giving them a firm but kind push forward once they are ready to move again. The students must be respected and recognized as growing young persons, who are sometimes scared, and sometimes overly bold, but always on their own trying to get to know themselves in order to determine their own assets and liabilities.

In view of Nixon's advice, it is interesting to note Nichols' (1964) findings when he studied 796 male and 450 female intelligent high school seniors. Their mothers were studied with the Parental Attitude Research Instrument, while the students were studied through self-ratings, academic performance, and teacher ratings.

Though Nichols warns that many other factors not studied may be involved and may modify his results, his findings nevertheless show a strong trend. There were no significant and mostly low correlations between the mothers' education and the creativity of their children. However, authoritarian child-rearing attitudes on the part of the mothers were negatively related to measures of the creativity and originality of their children, and positively related to the children's academic performance. (These relations were significant at the 0.05 level and were significant only because of the large sample.)

On the other hand, parents can offer a great deal of support to their children even in late adolescence. In discussing the "revolt of youth," Gustin (1961) stresses that parents can help their children to have the courage to face the future and to feel that it is worthwhile. The parents can provide clarity, serenity, and stability for the adolescent as he struggles with his sexual impulses, with the rules of society, and with the mysteries of life.

ADOLESCENT SEXUALITY

Blos (1962) warns of two dangers of adolescence proper: (1) a rush into heterosexuality at the expense of personality differentiation and (2) the massive repression of sexual impulses, which leads to character deformation and deviant emotional development, especially emotional shallowness and sentimentalism (p. 123). He deplores the fact that American adolescents so often are trying to handle their sexual impulses by adopting a group norm either of premature freedom or of denial of sexuality. Deutsch (1967) also observed that overt and successful sexual behavior, even during late adolescence, still does not lead to full genital gratification, with resulting disappointment. She believes that the overt sexual behavior at this age is not related to genital needs nearly as much as it is used to prove masculinity and femininity. Actually, over-emphasis on sexual gratification will lead to impairment of the ability to sublimate and may lead to a *pathological reinforcement* of old object attachments, rather than allowing adolescents to free themselves of them (Deutsch, 1967, pp. 24–25).

Blos (1962) points out that the recent demise of the double standard has not given girls the freedom they had hoped for because the female sexual drive is "far more intimately attached to their ego interests and personality attributes than is the male's" (p. 144). Kirkendall (1961), on the basis of thorough interviews with 200 college-level men (average age—20.2), found that the first experience of intercourse in his sample occurred at the average age of 17.1 (with a range from age 9 to age 26). His data confirm that " . . . the effect of intercourse, in and of itself, on the strengthening or weakening of a relationship is indirect and minimal" (p. 196). Obviously, then, the relationship depends on quite different things. He observed that if sex is to serve a satisfying interpersonal relationship, it must be part of an inherent value system which places stress on the improvement of the interpersonal relationship. The sex impulse must be seen as a positive, life-giving one, which the individual must learn to direct and utilize. It must be open for discussion across age and sex lines and must scrupulously avoid any exploitation and self-centered use of sex. The development of satisfying complementary sex roles in the relationship is stressed (Kirkendall, 1961, p. 252).

Kirkendall's research findings indicate that the negative effects of premarital intercourse per se on later marital adjustment have probably been greatly exaggerated, because previous research efforts ignored personality characteristics and underlying cultural factors in the marital partners. According to his findings, premarital intercourse may damage and disrupt or strengthen the relationship depending on the particular circumstances surrounding the couple at the time. Persons who had been brought up strictly tended to react with more guilt and shame, but it was clear here that severe upbringing was a much more important factor than the sexual experience in itself.

Kinsey, Martin, and Pomeroy (1948) found that close to half of all American males had experienced their first intercourse by age 20, while only 6 percent of females up to age 20 had had sexual intercourse (Kinsey, Gebhard, Martin, & Pomeroy, 1953).[2] After studying 1,873 boys and girls, aged 15 to 19, all over England and Wales, Schofield (1965) found that sexual intercourse had been experienced by 11 percent of boys aged 15 to 17 and by 30 percent of boys aged 17 to 19. The corresponding figures for girls were 6 percent and 16 percent respectively. From his interviews with these young people, Schofield was amazed to discover how ignorant they were about venereal disease, pregnancy, and contraception. Unfortunately, the ones who needed sex education most seemed to be those who were least likely to get it. Schofield also came to the conclusion that the teen-age desire for sexual experiences is created by the adult world, which through movies and the commercial market conveys the idea that sexual satisfaction is all-important. He wryly points out that the only group of teen-agers which "sets out to resist the blandishments of the marketeers are the Beats, and they come in for an extra measure of social hostility" (1965, p. 256).

SUMMARY

At this point, it must be blatantly clear to the reader that the vicissitudes of progress through normal adolescence are considerable. Further, one must not be lulled into thinking that the word *normal* in this case implies any degree of quiescence, calmness, or "averageness." On the contrary, we view normal adolescence as a disruptive, sometimes chaotic and awkward stage of life. Its

---

[2] There is much to indicate that these percentages would be higher today.

very disorderliness defines its normality. It is fascinating to compare the research, clinical pronouncements, and theorizing about adolescence with adolescence itself. The writings on adolescence are considerable, cumbersome, conflicting, varied, optimistic, pessimistic, grandiose, degrading, simplistic, idealistic, and lacking in closure. It is as if the very subject matter itself is reflected in the description of it.

REFERENCES

Allport, G. W. *Personality: A psychological interpretation.* New York: Holt, 1937.

Arlow, J. A. The consecration of the profit. *The Psychoanalytic Quarterly,* 1951, **20,** 375–397.

Barbero, G. J., & Shaheen, E. Environmental failure to thrive: A clinical view. *The Journal of Pediatrics,* 1967, **71,** 639–644.

Barclay, A., & Cusumano, D. R. Father absence, cross-sex identity, and field-dependent behavior in male adolescents. *Child Development,* 1958, **38,** 243–250.

Barker, R. G., Wright, B. A., & Gonick, M. R. Adjustment to physical handicap and illness. *A Survey of the Social Psychology of Physique and Disability,* 1953, No. 55.

Bayley, N., & Schaefer, E. S. Maternal behavior and personality development data from the Berkeley Growth Study. In R. E. Grinder (Ed.), *Studies of adolescence.* New York: Macmillan, 1963.

Beck, S. J., Levitt, E. E., Beck, A. G., & Molish, H. *Rorschach Test I basic processes.* New York: Grune & Stratton, 1961.

Bell, A. The significance of scrotal sac and testicles for the pre-puberty male. *The Psychoanalytic Quarterly,* 1965, **34,** 182–206.

Benedict, R. *Patterns of culture.* New York: Mentor Books, 1946.

Blizzard, R. M., Powell, C. F., Basel, J. A., & Raiti, S. Emotional deprivation and growth retardation stimulating idiopathic hypopituitarism. *The New England Journal of Medicine,* June 8, 1967, 276.

Blos, P. *On adolescence.* New York: Free Press, 1962.

Brody, E. B. *Minority group adolescents in the United States.* Baltimore: Williams and Wilkins, 1968.

Bronson, G. W. Identity diffusion in late adolescents. *Journal of Abnormal and Social Psychology,* 1959, **59,** 414–417.

Broverman, D. M. The automatization cognitive style and physical development in preadolescent males. *Child Development,* 1964, **35**(4), 1343–1358.

Broverman, D. M., Broverman, I. K., Klaiber, E. L., Palmer, R. D., & Vogel, W. Physique and growth in adolescence. *Child Development,* 1964, **35,** 857–870.

Carlson, R. Stability and change in the adolescents' self image. *Child Development,* 1965, **36**(3), 659–666.

Cole, L., & Hall, I. N. *Psychology of adolescence.* New York: Holt, 1964.

Coleman, J. S., & staff. *Equality of educational opportunity.* Washington, D.C.: Department of Health, Education and Welfare, 1966.

Davis, A. Socialization and adolescent personality. *Adolescence: Yearbook of the National Society for the Study of Education,* 1944, **43**(1), 196–216.

Dennis, J. L. *Adolescents: Whose Responsibility?* Presented at the Downtown Lions Club, Oklahoma City, September, 1964.

Deutsch, H. *Selected problems of adolescents.* New York: International Universities Press, 1967.

Douglas, J. W. B., & Ross, J. M. Age of puberty related to educational ability attainment and school leaving age. *Journal of Child Psychology and Psychiatry,* 1964, **5**(3–4), 185–196.

Douvan, E. Sex differences in adolescent character processes. *Merrill-Palmer Quarterly,* 1960, **6,** 203–211.

Eichorn, D. H., & McKee, J. P. Physiological instability during adolescence. *Child Development,* 1958, **29,** 255–268.

Elkind, D. Egocentrism in adolescence. *Child Development,* 1967, **38**(4), 1025–1034.

Elkind, D., & Elkind, S. Varieties of religious experience in young adolescence. In R. R. Grinder (Ed.), *Studies in adolescence.* New York: Macmillan, 1963.

Erikson, E. H. *Childhood and society.* New York: Norton, 1950.

Erikson, E. H. *Identity and the life cycle.* New York: International Universities Press, 1959.

Erikson, E. H. *Identity: Youth and crisis.* New York: Norton, 1968.

Freud, A. *Adolescence.* Vol. 13. *Psychoanalytic study of the child.* New York: International Universities Press, 1958. Pp. 255–278.

Freud, S. *Three essays on the theory of sexuality.* Standard edition. Vol. VII. London: Hogarth Press, 1959.

Fried, R. I., & Smith, E. E. Post menarchael growth patterns. *Journal of Pediatrics,* 1962, **61** (4), 562–565.

Friedenberg, E. J. *The vanishing adolescent.* Boston: Beacon Press, 1959.

Fromm, E. *Escape from freedom.* New York: Rinehart, 1941.

Galdston, R. Adolescence and the function of self-consciousness. *Mental Hygiene,* 1967, **51**(2), 164–168.

Gardner, G. E. Present day society and the adolescent. *American Journal of Orthopsychiatry,* 1957, **27,** 508–517.

Gesell, A., & Ilg, F. L. *Infant and child in the culture of today.* New York: Harper, 1943.

Goldman, S. Profiles of an adolescent. *The Journal of Psychology,* 1962, **54,** 229–240.

Grinker, R. R., Sr. A dynamic study of the "homoclite." *Science and Psychoanalysis.* Vol. 6. New York: Grune & Stratton, 1963.

Grinker, R. R., Sr., Grinker, R. R., Jr., & Timberlake, J. Mentally healthy young males (homoclites). *Archives of General Psychiatry,* 1962, **6,** 405–453.

Gustin, J. C. The revolt of youth. *Psychoanalysis and the Psychoanalytic Review,* 1961, **48,** 78–90.

Hall, G. S. *Adolescence.* New York: Appleton, 1916. 2 vols.

Hall, C. S., & Lindzey, G. *Theories of personality.* New York: Wiley, 1957.

Hathaway, S. R., & Monachesi, E. D. *Adolescent personality and behavior.* Minneapolis: University of Minnesota Press, 1963.

Havighurst, R. J. *Developmental tasks and education.* New York: Longmans, 1951.

Heilbrun, A. B., Jr. Social value, social behavior consistency, parental identification and aggression in late adolescence. *The Journal of Genetic Psychology,* 1964, **104,** 135–146.

Hershenson, D. B. Sense of identity, occupational fit, and enculturation in adolescence. *Journal of Counseling Psychology,* 1967, **14,** 319–324.

Hertzig, M. E., & Birch, H. G. Neurologic organization in psychologically disturbed adolescent girls. *Archives of General Psychiatry,* 1966, **15,** 590–598.

Horney, K. *Neurotic personality of our times.* New York: Norton, 1943.

Howard, L. P. Identity conflicts in adolescent girls. *Smith College Studies in Social Work,* 1960, **31,** 1–21.

Hsu, F. L. K. (Ed.) *Psychological anthropology: Approaches to culture and personality.* Homewood, Ill.: Dorsey Press, 1961.

Inhelder, B., & Piaget, J. *The growth of logical thinking.* London: Routledge, 1958.

Jacobson, E. Adolescent moods and the remodeling of psychic structures in adolescence. Paper presented at the meeting of the New York Psychoanalytic Society and Institute, New York, March, 1961.

Jahoda, M. *Current concepts of positive mental health.* New York: Basic Books, 1959.

Jones, E. *Some problems of adolescence: Papers on psychoanalysis.* London: Baillière, 1922.

Jones, H. E. Adolescence in our society. In *The family in a democratic society.* New York: Columbia University Press, 1949.

Jones, H. W., Jr., & Heller, R. H. Puberty-initiation of and delay of estrogen function. In *Pediatric and Adolescent Gynecology.* Baltimore: Williams & Wilkins, 1966. Pp. 1171–1203.

Jones, M. C. The late careers of boys who were early and late maturing. *Child Development,* 1957, **28,** 113–123.

Jones, M. C., & Mussen, P. H. Self conceptions, motivations and interpersonal attitudes of early and late-maturing girls. *Child Development,* 1958, **29,** 491–501.

Kagan, J. American longitudinal research in psychological development. *Child Development,* 1964, **35,** 1–32.

Kagan, J., & Moss, H. A. *Birth to maturity.* New York: Wiley, 1962.

Kestenberg, J. S. Phases of adolescence: With suggestions for a correlation of psychic and hormonal organizations. Part II. Pre-puberty diffusion and reintegration. *Journal of the American Academy of Child Psychiatry,* 1967, **6**(4), 577–612.

Kiell, N. *The adolescent through fiction.* New York: International Universities Press, 1959.

Kiell, N. *The universal experience of adolescence.* New York: International Universities Press, 1964.

Kinsey, A. C., Martin, C. E., & Pomeroy, W. B. *Sexual behavior in the human male.* Philadelphia: Saunders, 1948.

Kinsey, A. C., Gebhard, P. H., Martin, C. E., & Pomeroy, W. B. *Sexual behavior in the human female.* Philadelphia: Saunders, 1953.

Kirkendall, L. A. *Premarital intercourse and interpersonal relationships.* New York: Julian Press, 1961.

Kurtzman, K. A. A study of school attitudes, peer acceptance, and personality of creative adolescents. *Exceptional children,* 1967, Pp. 157–162.

Lansky, L. M., Crandall, V. J., Kagan, J., & Baker, C. T. Sex differences in aggression and its correlates in middle class adolescents. *Child Development,* 1961, **32,** 45–58.

Leonard, M. R. Fathers and daughters. *International Journal of Psychoanalysis,* 1966, **47,** 325–334.

Lewin, K. *A dynamic theory of personality.* New York: McGraw-Hill, 1935.

Livson, N., & McNeill, D. Physique and maturation rate in male adolescents. *Child Development,* 1962, **33,** 145–152.

Ljung, B. O. The adolescent spurt in mental growth. *Stockholm Studies in Educational Psychology,* 1965, **8,** 350.

Long, R. T. The observing ego and adolescent development. Paper presented at the meeting of the Dallas Neuropsychiatry Society, Dallas, September, 1966.

Maier, H. W. Adolescenthood. *Social Casework,* 1965, **66,** 3–9.

Masterson, J. F., Jr. *The psychiatric dilemma of adolescence.* Boston: Little, Brown, 1967.

Mead, M. *Coming of age in Samoa.* New York: New American Library, 1950.

Medinnus, G. R. Adolescent's self-acceptance and perceptions of their parents. *Journal of Consulting Psychology,* 1965, **29**(2), 150–154.

Muensterberger, W., & Axelrad, S. *The psychoanalytic study of society.* New York: International Universities Press, 1960–1967. 4 vols.

Mussen, P. H., & Jones, M. C. Self conceptions, motivations and interpersonal attitudes of late and early maturing boys. *Child Development,* 1957, **28,** 243–256.

Muuss, R. E. *Theories of adolescence.* New York: Random House, 1962.

Nathanson, I. T., Aub, J. C., & Towne, L. E. Normal excretion of sex hormones in childhood. *Endocrinology,* 1941, **28,** 851–865.

Nichols, R. C. Parental attitudes of mothers of intelligent adolescents and creativity of their children. *Child Development,* 1964, **35,** 1041–1049.

Nixon, R. E. Psychological normality in the years of youth. *Teachers College Record,* 1964, **66** (1), 71–79.

Novak, L. P. Physical activity and body composition of adolescent boys. *The Journal of the American Medical Association,* 1966, **197,** 891–893.

Offer, D., & Sabshin, M. *Normality.* New York: Basic Books, 1966.

Ostermeier, A. L. Adolescent behavior as manifested in clothing. *Child Study Center Bulletin,* 1967, **3** (1), 1–9.

Peck, R. F., & Galliani, C. Intelligence, ethnicity, and social roles in adolescent society. *Sociometry,* 1962, **25** (1), 64–72.

Pishkin, H. Pubertal onset and ego functioning. *Journal of Abnormal Psychology,* 1967, **72** (1), 1–15.

Pumpian-Mindlin, E. Omnipotentiality, youth and commitment. *Journal of the American Academy of Child Psychiatry,* 1965, **4,** 1–18.

Rank, O. *The trauma of birth.* New York: Harcourt, Brace, 1929.

Remmers, H. H. Cross-cultural studies of teenage problems. *Journal of Educational Psychology,* 1962, **53**(6), 254–264.

Riley, G. M. *Gynecologic endocrinology.* New York: Hoeber-Harper, 1960.

Root, N. N. A neurosis in adolescence. *Psychiatric Study of the Child,* 1957, **13,** 320–334.

Schechter, M. D. Adolescent affective states and object relations. *Psychiatry Digest,* 1964, **25** (3), 25–34.

Schofield, M. *The sexual behavior of young people.* London: Longmans, 1965.

Schonfeld, W. A. Primary and secondary sexual characteristics. *American Journal of Diseases of Children,* 1943, **54,** 535–549.

Schonfeld, W. A. Body image disturbances in adolescents. *Archives of General Psychiatry,* 1966, **15**(1), 16–21.

Shapiro, R. L. Action and family interaction in adolescence. Paper presented at the Howard University Conference on Youth and Social Action, Washington, D.C., October, 1963. (a)

Shapiro, R. L. Adolescence and the psychology of the ego. *Psychiatry: Journal for the Study of Interpersonal Processes,* 1963, **26** (1), 77–87. (b)

Sherif, M., & Sherif, C. W. *Problems of youth.* Chicago: Aldine, 1965.

Silber, E., Coelho, G. V., Murphey, E. B., Hamburg, D. A., Pearlin, L. I., & Rosenberg, M. Competent adolescents coping with college decisions. *Archives of General Psychiatry,* 1961, **5,** 517–527.

Spiegel, L. A. A review of contributions to a psychoanalytic theory of adolescence: Individual aspects. *The Psychoanalytic Study of the Child,* 1951, **6,** 375–393.

Spranger, E. *Types of men.* Halle: Neimeyer, 1928.

Stolz, H. R., & Stolz. *Somatic development of adolescent boys.* New York: Macmillan, 1951.

Sullivan, H. S. *The interpersonal theory of psychiatry.* New York: Norton, 1953.

Talbot, N., Berman, R. A., & MacLachlan, E. A. Functional Endocrinology. In *From birth through adolescence.* Cambridge, Mass.: Harvard University Press, 1952.

Tanner, J. M. The course of children's growth. In R. E. Grinder (Ed.), *Studies of adolescence.* New York: Macmillan, 1963.

Thomas, A., Birch, H. G., & Chess, S. *Temperament and behavior disorders in children.* New York: New York University Press, 1968.

Toussieng, P. W. Psychological maturation in adolescenthood. *The Journal of the Oklahoma State Medical Association,* December 1966, 658–664.

Weatherly, D. Self-perceived rate of physical maturation and personality in late adolescence. *Child Development,* 1964, **35,** 1197–1210.

Wessel, M. A., & LaCamera, R. G. The pediatrician and the adolescent. *Clinical Pediatrics,* 1967, **6**(4), 227–233.

Whittington, H. C. *Psychiatry on the college campus.* New York: International Universities Press, 1963.

Wilkins, L. *The diagnosis and treatment of endocrine disorders in childhood and adolescence.* Springfield, Ill.: Charles C Thomas, 1965.

Wilson, C. W. Development of ethnic attitudes in adolescence. *Child Development,* 1963, **34**(1), 247–256.

Winnicott, D. W. Adolescence. *The New Era in Home and School,* 1962, **43,** 1–7.

3 Etiology of Mental Disorders: Genetics

Lewis A. Hurst

This chapter seeks to review and evaluate the genetics of the psychiatric disturbances of childhood and adolescence, of both a primary and a secondary kind. By *primary* we mean those conditions in which the psychological deviation is part and parcel of the clinical condition. Mental subnormality (defect) and the schizophrenic and manic-depressive psychoses are good examples. In contradistinction to this we use the term *secondary* to designate those cases where the psychological disturbance originates indirectly, that is, from the serious problems of adjustment flowing from the inherited disability. The child or adolescent reacting to the handicap resulting from his genetically determined neurological disease, congenital malformation, deafness, blindness, reading difficulties, or stammer may serve to illustrate this second category. The publications on the mental health problems and services of the Department of Medical Genetics of the New York State Psychiatric Institute, Columbia University (Rainer & Altshuler, 1966; Rainer, Altshuler, & Kallmann, 1963; Sank, 1962)

provide a comprehensive overview of the range of psychological adaptive reactions to the problems of early total deafness, hereditary and nonhereditary, in the young and old. The publication by the Superintendent of the California School for the Blind at Berkeley (Lowenfeld, 1956 and 1967) has rendered us a somewhat similar service in the sphere of blindness. Furthermore, everyday experience speaks to us of psychological distress attendant on school failure due to dyslexia, which has, alas, too often escaped detection, and stammering, with the handicap it brings in both social and school life.

To the task of setting forth what is known of the contribution of genetic factors to these ills of childhood and adolescence we now address ourselves.

RELEVANT GENETIC CONCEPTS IN THEIR HISTORICAL SETTING

In order that our information may be precise, as to both our knowledge and our ignorances in this field, let us follow the significance of concepts and terms relevant to our theme in the context of the history of the evolution of scientific genetics. This history divides itself into three stages. The first is the postulation of hypothetical or conceptual hereditary factors by Gregor Mendel on the basis of precise quantitative observations on his hybridization experiments on the garden pea. The second is the identification of the physical basis of inheritance, or discovery of the organic structure, notably the chromosome, in which the hereditary factors, now known as *genes,* are embedded. Thomas Hunt Morgan and his associates at Columbia University are the central figures in this development. The third and current phase, which one may characterize as that of physiological genetics, includes (1) the picture of genes in dynamic, chemical interaction provided by R. Goldschmidt's developmental studies of moths and butterflies; (2) the working out of conceptual models of the chemical mode of gene action by J. B. S. Haldane and others and the discovery of the detailed role of the enzymic processes involved by Beadle, Tatum, and others in their investigations into the inheritance of nutritional requirements of the fungus *Neurospora;* (3) Watson and Crick's great breakthrough as to the structure and replication of DNA, initiating the science of microbiology and the concept of the genetic code and its misprints fundamental to our understanding of genetic disease; and (4) last but not least, the era of precise study of chromosomes and their anomalies resulting from improved cytological techniques culminating in the work of Tjio and Levan on the chromosome number in man and initiating the epoch-making discoveries of Lejeune, Jacobs, Polani, and Penrose and their co-workers in the field of Down's syndrome (Mongolism) and of Ferguson-Smith, Barr, and others concerning human cytogenetics and sex determination, with its ramifications into the areas of intersexuality and allied syndromes, transvestism, and mental retardation (defect).

Fundamentals have not changed since the publication of the companion volume in 1965 (Wolman), and I accordingly refer the reader to a portion of my chapter in that work (Hurst, 1965, pp. 141–151).

CYTOGENETICS OR CHROMOSOMAL GENETICS

Although in this section of the chapter we are dealing with broad principles, the recent discoveries concerning chromosomal anomalies are so plentiful in the field of psychiatry, and furthermore relevant to the period of childhood and youth, that it would be artificial to separate concepts from empirical findings, and our procedure here will be to include the data in the fields of mental defect (subnormality), congenital malformations, and sexual anomalies, not only as illustrations, but as our full coverage of the factual information in these two areas.

Up to 1956 our techniques for the visualization of chromosomes were so imperfect that there were presumed to be forty-eight chromosomes in the human somatic cell. However, improved methods of human tissue culture, of promoting cell division and arresting it at a stage in which the separate chromosomes are most clearly visible, and of making cell preparations under the microscope for well-defined chromosome pictures set the stage for Tjio and Levan's classic paper in 1956, which marked not only the beginning of a new era in cytology but also the point at which cytogenetics became one of the main growing points of human genetics. Tjio and Levan's finding that the human somatic cell has a normal complement of only forty-six chromosomes was soon amply confirmed by other workers using the same refined cytological techniques. A further major advance following rapidly in the wake of the improved methods was the evolution of a standard method of classification, that named the *Denver system,* which finally won international acceptance at a meeting at Denver, Colorado, in 1960. The better visualization of the chromosomes, in the new approach under the influence of colchicine, had made it possible to observe their size, their morphology, and the position of the centromere—the point at which the daughter chromatids are still joined when the division of the chromosome is commonly arrested. An analysis of these features makes possible the recognition of chromosomes individually or at least as belonging to a specified small group. The classification is in descending order of magnitude, number 1 being the largest and number 22 being the smallest of the autosomal chromosomes. Thus number 21 implicated in Down's syndrome (Mongolism) belongs to the shortest group. With regard to the sex chromosomes, we find the female, or X, chromosome in company with the longest autosomes, and the male, or Y, chromosome with the shortest.

AUTOSOMAL ANOMALIES

Down's Syndrome (Mongolism)

The next clearly indicated step in the new chromosomal era was the investigation as to whether anomalies of number and form of human chromosomes are associated with clinical effects. It is significant for child psychiatry that the first autosomal anomaly found to be associated with a clinical syndrome was Down's syndrome (Mongolism), where chromosome 21 was found to be present in triplicate instead of duplicate, the so-called chromosome 21 trisomy, in 1959, three years after the discovery of Tjio and Levan, by the French workers Lejeune, Gautier, and Turpin and the British group consisting of Jacobs, Baikie, Court Brown, and Strong. In this form of Down's syndrome the total chromosome number is forty-seven instead of the normal forty-six. The under-

lying mechanism is nondisjunction during gametogenesis in the female, whereby an ovum with two instead of one number 21 chromosomes originates, which on fertilization results in a trisomy 21. However, a year later Polani and co-workers (1960) and Penrose and co-workers (1961) reported instances of Down's syndrome with the normal total number of forty-six chromosomes and the normal complement of two number 21 chromosomes. One of the forty-six was abnormal in morphology, having apparently arisen from chromosomal fusion or translocation between fractured chromosomes 15 and 21—the translocation type of Mongolism. The larger portions of these broken chromosomes had joined to produce the abnormal chromosome. This type of translocation may involve number 13, 14, or 15 chromosome, as chromosomes of this group are very alike and difficult to distinguish, but for convenience of description the designation chromosome 15 translocation is often adopted. A further abnormality was the absence of one of the pair of number 15 chromosomes. The extra translocated chromosome and the missing number 15 issues in the apparently normal total chromosomal count of forty-six. If we disregard the actual chromosome number, however, and concentrate on the quality of genetic material present, these Down's syndrome cases carry approximately the same amount of chromosomal material in their cells as those trisomic for chromosome 21. Among the mothers and other normal relatives, the same abnormal fused or translocated chromosome is found, but the total chromosome count in their case is only forty-five because of the absence of one member of the twenty-first chromosome pair. Despite the reduction in the total chromosome number, the quantitative balance of chromosomal material is presumed to be correct in their cells. The presence in the normal relatives of translocation Mongols of the same abnormal chromosome indicates a mode of hereditary transmission that results in a very different empirical risk figure as compared with nondisjunction cases, of the utmost importance in genetic counseling; the risk that the mother of a Mongol will have a second affected child approaches 1 in 3 in the case of translocation, while for the more usual case of trisomy it is only 1 to 2 per 1,000.

The role of maternal and paternal age in the origin of Mongolism has been evaluated by Penrose (1961, 1962). In the nondisjunction variety there is, as already explained, failure of separation of chromosomes or of daughter chromatids in cell division, so that one extra chromosome finds its way into a cell. This may occur at different stages, either in the parent at gamete formation or after the zygote destined to become the Mongol has been formed by fusion of the parental germ cells. It is presumed that nondisjunction occurs most often in gametogenesis, and the observed maternal-age effect would implicate the ovum rather than the sperm (Penrose, 1961). Despite this effect, it has been estimated that even at the most advanced maternal age for childbearing, the exceedingly low empirical risk figure already cited is at most quadrupled, giving a figure of, say, 250 to 1 in favor of normality. The highlighting of the later age group of 35 and over by the publicity accorded to the maternal-age factor should not blind us to the fact that this type of Mongolism is common among the offspring of the younger maternal group also. In the translocation group 13 to 15/21 no influence of either maternal or paternal age has been detected, but in the comparatively rare 22/21 translocation an associated late-paternal-age effect has been demonstrated (Penrose, 1962).

Another form of translocation or chromosomal fusion in Down's syndrome is between chromosomes of the group containing chromosomes 21 and 22. Just as in the other translocation type of Mongolism (involving chromosomes in the group 13 to 15 with the twenty-first pair), there

is the normal total cell complement of forty-six chromosomes. One of the group involved, however, is again abnormal in morphology and is abnormally large, so that the Mongol is carrying too much genetic material in the cell. Here, too, in carriers of the fused chromosomes a reduced total chromosome count is found among normal relatives.

Two associations with Down's syndrome and its underlying chromosomal mechanism well worthy of recording here are mosaicism and leukemia. Mosaicism is the phenomenon to which we have made passing allusion, in which a nondisjunctional error occurs at a mitotic division subsequent to fertilization; this could be due either to both members' of one chromosome pair being included in the same daughter cell or to one chromosome's lagging at anaphase and failing to be included in either daughter cell. This would lead to an individual composed of two or more stem lines of cells which may be intermixed in the tissues or separated in different tissues. Clarke, Edwards, and Smallpiece (1961) reported an intelligent child with Mongoloid features who was found to be a trisomy 21/normal mosaic. This type of finding should serve as a caution to the physician and psychologist and bring a ray of hope to parents whose child has Mongoloid features. Leukemia of both the acute and chronic myeloid varieties has been shown by Baikie, Court Brown, Jacobs, & Milne (1954) and de Grouchy and de Nava (1966) to be associated with deletion of material from chromosome 21. The abnormal chromosome resulting, smaller than the smallest normal one, has been named the *Philadelphia chromosome*. As Mongolism results from an anomaly apparently involving the same chromosome, the frequent association of leukemia with Mongolism has become more understandable.

Of a less direct and apparently more fortuitous nature is the coexistence of Mongolism with Klinefelter's syndrome (Ford, Jones, Miller, Mittwoch, Penrose, Kidler, & Shapiro, 1960; Harnden, Miller, & Penrose, 1960), to be discussed later. The karyotype here is trisomy 21 + XXY.

Possible influences of a nongenetic nature in the pathogenesis of Mongolism referred to by Cowie are the physique of the mother associated with the production of a Mongoloid child at a young maternal age (Coppen & Cowie, 1960), which may in turn be dependent upon the endocrinological status of the mother (Rundle, Coppen, & Cowie, 1961). In leaving the theme of Down's syndrome (Mongolism), we should perhaps convey the perspective that although chromosomal anomalies have regularly been discovered in association with it, we are still ignorant of the influences by which they make their effects manifest in so widespread a manner, affecting probably every tissue of the body, and by no means least, mental function. These must, in the last resort, be chemical in nature, and clues of the sort mentioned, relating to the association with leukemia and endocrinological status of the mother, should be followed up.

Congenital Malformations and Mental Subnormality (Defect)

Trisomies of chromosomes in the group 13 to 15 and of chromosomes 17 and 18 are known to produce severe multiple malformations associated with gross mental defect and are usually incompatible with long survival. The former was first described by Patau, Smith, Therman, Inhorn, and Wagner (1960), and the latter by Edwards, Harden, Cameron, Wolff, and Cross (1960). These trisomies are known by the chromosome group numbers because as has been already stated, it is difficult to distinguish between chromosomes 13, 14, and 15 by their size and morphology, and the same is true of chromosomes 17 and 18.

The syndrome associated with trisomy 13–15 consists of multiple deformities including anophthalmia, harelip, cleft palate, polydactyly, cardiac defects, capillary hemangiomata, and a cerebral defect which would no doubt lead to severe mental subnormality if the children lived long enough for it to become fully manifest. They die, however, as a rule in early infancy.

The syndrome associated with trisomy 17–18 includes such features as a peculiar face with low-set ears and a triangular mouth, small chin, cardiac septal defect, many minor physical abnormalities, and spasticity. Again there is evidence of retarded mental development, although these children appear unable to survive infancy.

A syndrome originally described by de Grouchy et al. (1966), involving severe mental retardation, microcephaly, and other gross congenital anomalies, was described more fully by Lejeune, Berger, Lafourcade, and Rethore (1966) at the Third International Congress of Human Genetics and was shown to be associated with partial deletion of the long arm of chromosome 18.

A missing portion of chromosome 5 is responsible for another syndrome comprising multiple congenital anomalies combined with severe mental defect, which was described at the Chicago conference on the basis of the sixty-one cases observed up to April, 1966, by Lejeune and his group. It has been christened with the colorful but not universally appropriate name *cri du chat syndrome,* on the basis of the high-pitched, plaintive cry, resembling the mewing of a cat and resulting from an immature larynx, produced by these infants and originally considered a pathognomonic feature but subsequently found, as the sample increased, to affect fewer than half of the cases. Additional clinical features described by the authors are oligophrenia, somatic hypotrophia, microcephaly, hypertelorism, retrognathism, and dermatoglyphic anomalies, while congenital heart disease is not uncommon. The cytological details of the partial monosomy of chromosome 5 underlying the condition are simple deletion, deletion by translocation, mal-segregation secondary to parental translocation, ring chromosome, and "aneusomie de recombinaison."

ANOMALIES OF THE SEX CHROMOSOMES

The way the sex-chromosome constitution determines sex was shown by Morgan and Bridges in *Drosophila* a half century ago, who described deviations in sex-chromosome constitution in *Drosophila* that have given a clue to abnormalities in man. It will be remembered that the normal human sex-chromosome constitutions are XY in the male and XX in the female. Many clearly defined syndromes associated with the sex chromosomes have been identified. The best known are Klinefelter's and Turner's syndromes and the triplo-X female. In Klinefelter's syndrome the patient is anatomically male with male genitalia, but the sex-chromosome complement is XXY. In Turner's syndrome the patient is anatomically female, but with a deficiency of ovarian tissue and concomitant physical signs, and the sex-chromosome complement is XO (that is, there is only a single X chromosome). In the triplo-X syndrome the patient is also anatomically female, but has the sex-chromosome complement XXX.

Various surveys have shown a higher incidence of sex-chromosome anomalies among the mentally subnormal than in the general population (Ferguson-Smith, 1958; Hamerton, Jagietto, & Kirman 1962; Money & Hirsch, 1963; Prader, Schneider, Züblin, Frances, & Küdi 1958). Thus Money and Hirsch, in a survey of 784 female and 916 male mentally defective patients, picked up three triplo-X and two triplo-X/Y patients. In general, as compared with the autosomal anomalies the mental retardation associated with the sex chromosomes is less severe. A tendency for Klinefelter cases to exhibit schizoid traits as

well as mental subnormality has been claimed by Pasqualini, Vidal, and Bur (1957), and Penrose (1960). Therefore, this is perhaps a good point at which to review the chromosomal studies in schizophrenia relating to the mentally normal and subnormal.

In Money and Hirsch's survey of 1,700 mental defectives, already alluded to, two of the four triplo-X and triplo-XY patients picked up were found to be schizophrenic and had their pedigrees explored as extensively as possible. The authors conclude correctly that schizophrenia, when coexistent with mental deficiency in the triplo-X syndrome, could not be ascribed to the tripling of the X chromosome. For their surmise that ". . . perhaps there is a closer genetic linkage between schizophrenia and mental deficiency than can so far be demonstrated" they provide no shred of evidence.

Tedeschi and Freeman (1962), in a study of sex chromosomes in 248 male schizophrenics, while finding in two cases a count of sex-chromatin cells far above the expected frequency in the normal male (but lower than in the normal female) demonstrated percentagewise, in the series as a whole, that a frequency of positive sex chromatin "not too dissimilar from that found by others in normal and mentally defective males" emerged.

A paper by Raphael and Shaw (1963) describes chromosome studies of ten adult schizophrenics (five men and five women), followed by a more extensive one of 100 male and 100 female cases, and presents in compendious form twenty-seven sex-chromatin surveys (three on newborn infants, eighteen on mental defectives, and six on schizophrenics). The authors conclude that one Klinefelter and one triplo-X syndrome in their series of 210 patients suggest that specific abnormalities of sex chromosomes are more frequent among schizophrenics than in the general population. With regard to the sex-chromatin studies, they comment that while the difference between the mental defectives and the newborn infants is statistically significant, in the case of the schizophrenics, numbers are as yet insufficient to confirm a trend that appears suggestive.

Summarizing one's own impression of these studies, it may be said that to date chromosomal anomalies have been demonstrated in only a very small minority of schizophrenic cases and are probably not above the expectancy figure for the general population.

While cytogenetics opens up promising vistas in the field of schizophrenia, as in so many others, let us temper our enthusiasm with the restraint of Sonneborn, when he says:

> There is still a long way to go. Tomorrow or 10 or 20 years hence there may be breakthroughs, but they cannot at present be foreseen. . . . There are still vast areas of ignorance to be converted into precise knowledge before such human engineering will be possible. For the present and for the foreseeable future, sound application of genetic knowledge to the improvement of man—if it is to be done at all—will necessarily have to be restricted to the slower and less spectacular, but sound methods based on classical genetics.

The role of the contribution of sex-chromosome anomalies to intersexuality and homosexuality merits some consideration. Apart from the physical sexual deficiencies of sex-chromosome origin that we have already encountered in the Klinefelter and Turner syndromes, there are cases of abnormal sex differentiation not uncommonly leading to transvestism even during adolescence. Summarizing the contribution of chromosomal anomalies to these developmental sex abnormalities from Miller, we arrive at the following picture:

1. Congenital agonadism
   a. Ovarian dysgenesis: chromosome complement, XX
   b. Gonadal dysgenesis: chromosome complement, XO or XO/XX
   c. Congenital anorchism: chromosome complement, XY
2. True hermaphroditism
   a. XO/XY mosaicism—bone-marrow culture; XY metaphase cells—skin culture
   b. XXX/XX mosaic or 6-12 trisomy
   c. XXX + small Y fragment
   d. All tissues chromatin positive XX/XXY mosaic. Blood cells: majority, forty-six chromosomes XX; one-seventh of cells, forty-seven chromosomes XXY
   e. XX with forty-six chromosomes

With regard to the much more widespread problem of homosexuality, which may already be the source of grave psychological disturbance in our adolescents, Cowie has correctly pointed out that Lang's theory (1940) that male homosexuals are genotypically female has been overthrown by the failure of new techniques to show a conflict between anatomical and chromosomal sex (Pare, 1956; Pritchard, 1962), as indeed was found to be the case in transvestites (Barr & Hobbs, 1954). However, as Cowie goes on to indicate, this does not by any means exclude a genetic factor in the etiology of homosexuality. Indeed, despite the disproof cited of Lang's specific hypothesis as to the genotypical femininity of male homosexuals, his observation of an increased male/female sex ratio in the sibships of male homosexuals, paralleled in the studies of Darke (1948) and Kallmann (1952), points to a biological component in etiology. Kallmann's twin-family study of a sample of adult male homosexuals in New York, in which the disturbed sex ratio mentioned occurred, presented strong evidence that this biological component is genetically determined. A finding of central importance is that the forty one-egg twin pairs (with Kinsey homosexual ratings of three or more) showed a 100 percent concordance as to homosexuality, although in no single instance had the two members of any twin set indulged in homosexual relations with each other. In the case of vo-egg twins, however, the figures for various insey ratings were very little above the estimates r the general population. On the basis of this rge discrepancy between the concordances of onozygotic and dizygotic twins and the disrbed sex ratio among the siblings, Kallmann as postulated that adult male homosexuality a biologically determined phenomenon on a netic basis, due more specifically to a genetally disarranged balance between male and male maturational tendencies. While this ypothesis is compatible with Freud's psychoynamic picture of homosexuality in terms of rest at the third stage of libidinal orientation, is arrest is seen as genetic and physiogenic ther than, along the lines of psychoanalytic eology, as psychogenic on the basis of earlier sychological conflicts. Nor does Kallmann eny the mechanism of a learned or acquired rm of homosexuality in circumstances where ere is sexual segregation for long periods, in ontrast to the freedom of sexual choice enjoyed y his own sample from the resident population f New York. Finally, he stresses the need for ore extended studies in this area.

Bringing together the autosomal and sexhromosome anomalies, it is important from the oint of view of perspective to attempt an estiate of their incidence. In the Second Report f the World Health Organization Expert Comittee on Human Genetics (1964) we are given is estimate: "The incidence, at birth, of the ore common chromosome abnormalities is bout 1 in 400 among males for Klinefelter's yndrome, 1 in 500 for Down's syndrome, 1 in 00 among females for the XXX syndrome, and in 2,500 among females for Turner's syndrome. f other chromosomal aberrations sufficiently ross to be detected by present techniques are dded, it is reasonable to think that about 1 ercent of all live-born infants have some such armful trait. Moreover, evidence is accumuting that a significant fraction of intrauterine deaths is caused by a variety of chromosomal aberrations." At the Third International Congress of Human Genetics (1966), Curt Stern gave as a global estimate 50 percent of spontaneous abortions are being referable to chromosomal anomalies. One mechanism whereby this can come about is that owing to nondisjunction, the fetus may receive from either sperm or ovum an extra complement of twenty-three chromosomes per cell, which is lethal.

In concluding this section on cytogenetics we should refer to two screening techniques helpful in the search for anomalies of the sex chromosomes which are simpler and quicker than the culturing method applied to chromosomes themselves. Together they are often designated *nuclear sexing procedures.*

The first is the examination of cells, scraped from the buccal mucosa, for chromatin masses. In females with the normal XX sex-chromosome complement, 50 to 70 percent have a clearly staining small intranuclear body close to the nuclear membrane. The basis on which we work is that a cell with n times X chromosomes contains $n - 1$ of these sex-chromatin bodies. Thus a normal XX female would be expected to have $2 - 1 = 1$, and an XXX female $3 - 1 = 2$, of these bodies in a number of her cells. A normal male, by the same token, would be expected to have none of these bodies, as he has only one X chromosome. A male with Klinefelter's syndrome, with an XXY sex-chromosome complement, would be expected to have $2 - 1 = 1$ sexchromatin body in a proportion of his cells. The sex-chromatin bodies and their numerical relationship to X chromosomes were first discovered by Barr and Bertram (1949) in the course of their work on nervous tissue in cats. They are accordingly often called *Barr bodies.*

The second technique is the examination of the nuclei of polymorphs for the presence of club-shaped projections, or "drumsticks," as first reported by Davidson and Smith (1954).

The drumstick phenomenon is not observed in males, while it occurs in approximately 6 out of every 500 females—the basis of a useful blood-smear test.

A final item on the side of methodology worthy of mention is the technique reported by Jacobson (1966) of withdrawal during pregnancy of amniotic fluid, which contains cells sloughed off by the embryo, for karyotyping. This provides a valuable extension to genetic counseling methodology. He cites a case where the recovery of normal fetal cells in this way fortified a woman in her resolve to proceed with her pregnancy, and another where discovery of chromosomal damage in these cells, presumed attributable to excessive exposure to x-rays, led to the therapeutic termination of the pregnancy.

RESEARCH METHODS

Biochemical and cytogenetic methods of research have been reviewed in the foregoing. It remains for us to consider the methods of population genetics.

Methods of Population Genetics

The methods of population genetics include the statistical treatment of material systematically collected from large communities or defined smaller samples for familial patterns of incidence. The collecting of sporadic family data, or pedigree method, is now long outdated. Especially noteworthy studies in population genetics have been carried out in Scandinavia, where geographically circumscribed populations exist in rural areas or on islands. Outstanding recent examples include Böök's genetic-neuropsychiatric study in a northern Swedish population (1953), Øster's study of Mongolism in Denmark (1953), Larsson and Sjögren's genetic-psychiatric study of a large Swedish rural population (1954), and Akesson's investigation of the epidemiology and genetics of mental deficiency in a southern Swedish population (1961). Intermediate between the extensive studies of population genetics and the intensive investigation of a specific condition in a selected and circumscribed sample comes work aimed at extracting more general and varied psychiatric information from a given sample. Cowie's study of the incidence of neurosis in the children of psychotics (1961), entailing statistical analysis of clinical data, illustrates this. It was based on information about the children of hospital patients and was designed to discover whether there is evidence to disprove the hypothesis that there is no increase of neurosis among the children of psychotics.

The intensive study of circumscribed populations selected with respect to one particular condition has contributed greatly to psychiatric genetics. These studies will be dealt with under "Empirical Genetic Studies in Child Psychiatry" in terms of a series of detailed topics such as schizophrenia (including the preadolescent form), dyslexia, epilepsy, and so forth.

For the rationale, design, and statistical methodology for twin, family, and twin-family studies the reader is referred again to my chapter in the companion volume (Hurst, 1965, pp. 152–155).

Behavior Genetics: Its Rationale and Scope

Before examining defined diseases and syndromes, let us consider the range of behavior related to such areas as intelligence, temperament, personality, neuroticism, and anxiety, with regard to the role of a possible genetic component.

This relatively new field of endeavor within human genetics, which has now been raised to the status of a department of its own and has been christened *behavior genetics,* has been comprehensively surveyed in its ideological aspect as well as from the standpoint of its foundation in animal and human experiment by Fuller and Thompson (1960), on whose excellent work I shall draw heavily in my subsequent recital.

At the outset we should adduce salient methodological considerations in this field. With regard to experimental design, heredity as an independent variable can be incorporated in a psychological experiment, as is the case with physiological or experiential factors. The dependent variable can be any form of behavior which interests the investigator. The simplest experiment consists of taking two groups of different heredity, treating them alike in all other respects, and administering a behavior test. The results are compared against the prediction from the null hypothesis, i.e., that the groups differ no more than two independent samples drawn from the same population. If the null hypothesis is not supported, evidence for heritability of the behavior variation has been obtained.

Pathways between genes and behavior. A fundamental ideological problem is that of the pathways between genes and behavior. The ordinary technique of physiological genetics research is to start with a specific, well-developed phenotypic difference and work backward toward genetic sources of variation. The reverse order is more suited to the presentation of general principles. Behavior is the response of an organism to stimulation of external or internal origin. Genes operate at the molecular level of organization, but they are peculiar kinds of molecules, highly individuated carriers of information, whose effects are describable in psychophysiological as well as chemical terms. Enzymes, hormones, and neurones may be regarded as successively complex intermediaries between genes and psychological characters. Instances of the path through enzymes are hyperphagia in the genetically obese mouse, strain differences in audiogenic seizures in mice, superior performance in the Krech hypothesis apparatus by rats with high brain cholinesterase levels, and, in man, phenylketonuria and Williams's genetotropic theory of alcoholism. The

approach to the gene-behavior-character relationship through enzyme studies has the advantage of being close to the gene end of the chain, but this advantage is counterbalanced by distance from behavioral events. One may employ genetic lesions to naturally dissect the nervous system at the metabolic level, but this dissection is not the same as separating natural units of behavior. More must be learned regarding the relationship between biochemical individuality and behavior before the findings of the biochemist can have psychological meaning. In the expanding area of psychochemistry, genetics will have a unique role, for it is only through genes that permanent chemical characteristics can be built into an organism.

Beach (1948) has summarized the potential mechanisms through which hormones might control behavior as follows (quoted by Fuller & Thompson, 1960, pp. 331–332):

> 1. Through effects upon the organism's normal development and maintenance activities. Such effects, exemplified by the multiple deficiencies of the cretin, are relatively nonspecific.
> 2. Through stimulation of structures employed in specific response patterns; for example, the postnatal growth of genital organs is dependent upon hormones, and adult sexual behavior cannot occur until these structures are fully developed.
> 3. Through effects upon peripheral receptors, sensitizing them to particular forms of stimulation— a comparatively little-explored area.
> 4. Through effects on the integrative functions of the central nervous system, investigated by direct injections of hormones into the brain (Fisher, 1956; Harris et al., 1958).

With these generalizations in mind, one should reinforce one's critical attitude by distinguishing between psychophysiological actions of hormones in normal concentrations and psychopharmacological effects of large doses applied in artificial ways, which latter have at most an indirect bearing on the genetics of normal variation. An additional complication in the analysis of the gene-hormone-behavior relationship is that genes might operate upon the source of the hormone, affecting the quality and quantity of the product, or upon the target organs, affecting their response. Furthermore, the endocrine system is physiologically complex, with much interaction between components. None of the four types of mechanism described by Beach, or the two means by which genes might act, are mutually exclusive. The availability of pathways is more than adequate.

Despite the importance of variation in the nervous system as a path along which genes might come to influence behavior, few studies have dealt directly with the problem. Genes which lead to major neurological defects have been found in many species and show a considerable uniformity in their manifestations. One group of these, the lipidoses, is characterized by abnormal lipid deposition in the brain, but these have not yet been related to specific enzymatic processes. A promising area of investigation in this field is the individual variation in the fine structure of the central nervous systems of higher vertebrates and its genetic components and behavioral significance.

Genes and psychological components. One final ideological consideration must engage our attention before we turn to details of the psychological behavior genetics field. It is the general logicostatistical question of the interrelationship of genes and psychological components. The search for anatomical and physiological channels through which genes contribute to variation in behavior has had the limited success just indicated. Physiological and anatomical techniques have the limitation that the measuring devices themselves impair the intactness of the subjects. This has provided a gap, which psy-

chologists have been able to fill by using behavic tests themselves to define psychological con ponents that could have genetic significance The idea is that traits might be found by method such as factor analysis which are biologicall more real than test scores chosen empiricall (Blewett, 1954; Cattell, 1953; Eysenck & Pre 1951; Royce, 1957; Thompson, 1956; Thurstone Thurstone, & Strandskov, 1953).

Although we cannot discuss the whole fiel of factor analysis here, we can perhaps brin home that part of it where we are concerned wit the relationship between multifactor constella tions at various levels, behavioral, physiologica and genetic. In their substantial work entitle *The Meaning and Measurement of Neuroticisr and Anxiety,* Cattell and Scheier (1961) stress th importance of multivariate analysis of a con prehensive array of test-response measuremen in personality assessment. As an extension this theme to various levels and their interrela tionships, the reader is referred to Royce's cor gruent and noncongruent models reproduce in Fuller and Thompson (1960). In his congruer model, using general intelligence as an example he illustrates his concept of the relationship be tween the multiple-factor theory of psycholog and the multiple-factor theory of genetics. Th model is called *congruent* because of the part-fo part correspondence between gene blocks an the three psychological components of genera intelligence selected—space factor, memor factor, and other factors—manifested in th behavioral phenotypes. In contrast to this, th second model is noncongruent, inasmuch as ther is no precise correspondence between genes an traits defined at the physiological and behavior levels. The correlation between the traits and Θ is a function of the contribution of th physiological character ι to each. This characte is in turn controlled by gene D. Both ϕ and ϵ have genetic variances (from genes A, B, C, D

, and F) which are either specific or shared with other traits. The figure also has a portion illustrating chromosomal communality. The covariation between traits Θ and Σ is dependent upon the linkage of genes F and G. The noncongruence in this model implies multiple-factor control of psychological traits and the existence f complex gene interactions in the development f phenotypes. In spite of this complexity, the vidence for lawful genetic effects upon behavior as been amply demonstrated. Further analysis f the gene-character relationship may be possible from experiments in which genotypes are manipulated and phenotypic effects measured.

GENETIC FACTORS IN INTELLIGENCE

We cannot here enter into a critical evaluation of the rival definitions of intelligence or of the dispute as to whether it is made up of a general factor as well as specific components.

Family Studies

The first systematic examination of familial correlation with respect to mental ability was made by Karl Pearson around the turn of the century. Using teachers' rankings based on a seven-point scale of intellectual capacity, he found the correlations between brothers to be .52; between sisters, .51; and between brother and sister, .52. The correlations were in line with those obtained with physical characteristics such as height, hair color, and cephalic index. Cattell and Willson (1938), using a so-called culture-free intelligence test, obtained the figures of .91 for parent-child and .77 for sibling correlations, concluding that parents and children have nine-tenths of their respective levels in common and that four-fifths of the variability in intelligence among families is due to heredity.

As representative of work on special abilities within intelligence, we may take the investigation of Carter (1932) into family resemblance in verbal and numerical abilities. He found that if both parents are superior, they tend to have a high proportion of superior children; if one or both are inferior, this proportion is correspondingly less.

Fuller and Thompson (1960) came to the following conclusions as a result of their survey of these family studies of intelligence:

> In the first place, resemblance in intelligence appears to depend in most populations more on hereditary than environment or experiential factors. Second, degree of resemblance is not different in defferent kinds of populations, such as urban or rural, superior or average, except insofar as these may influence the homogeneity of the sample. If cultural influences on test score are eliminated (Cattell & Willson, 1938), degree of resemblance is increased. Third, there is some evidence to show that resemblances even in school abilities are affected by heredity at least as much as those in general intelligence.

Twin Studies

Twin studies based on intellectual resemblances of dizygotic and monozygotic twins reared together and apart are of the most definitive value. Those of Newman, Freeman, and Holzinger (1937) and of Gardner and Newman (1940), in which intrapair correlations in respect of Binet, Otis, and Stanford achievement tests are recorded, are the best known, but there are four others (Burks, 1942; Gates & Brash, 1941; Saudek, 1934; Stephens & Thompson, 1943). In summary, the evidence on twins reared apart supports the hereditary hypothesis, though there is also little doubt that large differences in environment can affect similarity of monozygotic twins.

A host of studies on special abilities are in line with the broad conclusions in respect of general intelligence. Thus Holzinger (1929), who used among other indices five tests of school ability (word meaning, arithmetic, nature study, history and literature, and spelling), found correlations that ranged from .73 to .87 in monozygotic pairs and from .56 to .73 in dizygotic pairs.

GENETIC FACTORS IN TEMPERAMENT AND PERSONALITY

Genetic work in the wide field of temperament and personality stems from Galton's (1874) pedigree studies. More precise work has been made possible by family correlations and twin resemblances between the results (often including components) of such tests as the Bernreuter, several attitude scales, Maller Character Sketches, Allport Ascendance-Submission, tests of personal tempo (e.g., speed of tapping), the Rorschach (coarctative, introversive, and extroversive), and tests of perceptual and sensory capacities. These investigations may in general be said to support the view that a number of testable dimensions of personality depend on inheritance. However, conclusions such as the nature-nurture ratio are by no means as clear as those in the case of intelligence. Obviously, much remains to be done, particularly in the matter of obtaining a rational and parsimonious description of personality. Experimentation on such points as activity and inactivity and emotionality and nonemotionality in rats offers promise in this direction and has already given rise to precise genetic hypotheses (Brody, 1942, 1950; Hall, 1941).

GENETIC FACTORS IN NEUROTICISM AND ANXIETY

Our next theme is that of genetic factors in neuroticism and anxiety. Eysenck (1956) has by methods of factorial analysis given conclusive evidence that neuroticism and psychoticism are different dimensions of personality. Moreover, Eysenck and Prell (1951) have, on the basis of their study of twenty-five monozygotic and twenty-five dizygotic twin pairs, classified the "neurotic personality factor" as a biological and largely gene-specific entity, estimating the genetic contribution to this neurotic unit predisposition to be 80 percent.

Anxiety, that frequent concomitant of neurosis, is brought together with it (i.e., neurosis) by Cattell and Scheier (1961) for critical statistical scrutiny, and both items are enriched by their treatment. Not only do they confirm Eysenck's finding that neuroticism and psychoticism are separate dimensions, but they also establish the multifactor nature of neurosis on the basis of the method of multivariate analysis. In contrast to neurosis, both trait definition and type definition attach the clinical concept of anxiety to a single second-order factor. The main first-order components in this factor are ergic tension, ego weakness, guilt-proneness, low self-sentiment strength, and protension or suspiciousness, and on these components a valuable clinical test of anxiety has been devised. The general point their analysis has established is that anxiety is part, but not all, of neurosis, which is a broader and more complex concept.

EMPIRICAL GENETIC STUDIES IN CHILD PSYCHIATRY

Genetic studies in psychiatry relevant to infancy, childhood, and adolescence will be reviewed and examined in terms of the following:

1. Psychoneuroses (including enuresis) and personality disorders (including psychopathy and delinquency)
2. Mental subnormality or defect
3. Epilepsy
4. Schizophrenia, childhood schizophrenia, early infantile autism, and manic-depressive psychosis

5. Neurological conditions

6. Developmental (congenital) malformations

7. Severe communication handicaps—deafness, blindness, dyslexia, and stammering (stuttering)

Psychoneuroses and Personality Disorders

Moving now from the general psychological dimension of "neuroticism" (which may also be thought of as at most a predisposition to neurotic reactions) to clinically overt neurosis, we are confronted by Slater's monumental work on psychotic and neurotic illnesses in twins (1959). Here he combined his psychopathic and neurotic twins into one group which comprised eight uniovular twins, forty-three biovular twins, and one pair of doubtful ovularity. Children and adolescents were well represented in the sample.

His results as regards concordance and discordance are summarized in Table 3-1.

Two features of this study are a detailed clinical presentation of all cases and the quotation of actual words and phrases used by informants in characterizing personalities such as the schizoid. Slater (1953, pp. 87–88) summarizes his findings as follows:

(a) Among 8 uniovular pairs in which the propositus suffered from a neurotic or psychopathic state, only 2 pairs were concordant. One of these was a pair of boys with anxiety symptoms, tics and habit spasms, the other was a pair of neurotic wastrels with life-long social and psychiatric abnormality. In neither of these pairs did psychogenic and environmental factors appear to play any significant role.

(b) There were 3 biovular pairs in which, despite marked differences in personality, both twins developed very similar behavior disorders in childhood. In these cases psychogenic precipitation appeared to be highly important.

(c) In the discordant uniovular pairs environmental factors again seemed to be decisive. Thus in one pair it was the twin, who had made an unsatisfactory marriage, who broke down; in another the twin who had to assume greater responsibilities in marriage made a better adjustment. The observation is made that the paths of uniovular twins

TABLE 3-1 PSYCHOTIC AND NEUROTIC ILLNESSES IN TWINS (SLATER, 1953, P. 76)

Diagnosis of Propositus	Uniovular		Binovular	
	Total Number of Propositi	Number with Abnormal Co-twins	Total Number of Propositi	Number with Abnormal Co-twins
Predominantly psychogenic behavior disorders in children	1	1	9	4
Neurotic reactions in adolescents and adults (including psychopaths and defectives)	1		15	2
Psychopathic disturbances in mental defectives			8	1
Other psychopathic states*	6	1	11	1
Total	8	2	43	8

* In this group there was also one pair of doubtful ovularity, twin partner (?) normal.

may diverge only very slightly at first but eventually lead to entirely different circumstances, and the consequences of one false step may lead by a vicious spiral to a progressively lower niveau.

(d) On the whole, neurotic symptoms appear as exaggerations of personality traits detectable at other times. *The form of the symptoms is not so closely related to the form of the stress as it is to the basic personality.*

(e) An examination of the main traits of personality shown by blood-relatives shows rather little tendency towards family resemblance, but the material was not well suited to an investigation on this question.

(f) Psychopathic traits, shown by the abnormal personalities among the relatives of propositi, classified into the four main clinical groups (schizophrenia, affective illness, organic states, and psychopathy and neurosis), are differently distributed. Among relatives of the schizophrenic propositi, paranoid, anergic, eccentric and emotionally cold personality traits are relatively frequent, traits of the depressive and emotional lability and alcoholism relatively infrequent. An excess of personality traits of the depressive and emotionally labile type were relatively common in the relatives of affective propositi, of hysterical and wastrel type among the relatives of psychopathic and neurotic propositi, and of tendencies to elation and depression among relatives of the organic propositi.

(g) There is a striking contrast between the psychoses on the one hand and the psychopathic and neurotic traits on the other. In the latter, uniovular pairs were less frequently concordant, and some of the binovular pairs developed very similar troubles despite big differences in intelligence and personality. The dividing line between adjustment and maladjustment is not so wide as that between sanity and insanity and is more easily overstepped, so that chance, whether favourable or unfavourable, is more important. Once maladjustment has begun, it may contribute to its own continuance. However, personality is of even greater importance in these conditions than in the psychoses.

(h) Finally, from a comparison of uniovular and biovular twins we gain an appreciation of genetical differences between one person and another without which a full understanding of both psychotic and neurotic behavior is impossible and which helps us, moreover, towards that knowledge of fundamental pathology which is the basis of a rational treatment of disease.

Slater's emphasis on grouping neurosis and psychopathy together around the common axis of maladjustment will be noted, in broad contradistinction to the psychoses, which he boldly characterizes as insanity.

Before proceeding to a genetic analysis of the subdivision of the broad neurosis-psychopathy group for which Slater is largely responsible, let us examine a comprehensive study conducted by him and his co-workers (Coppen, Cowie, & Slater, 1965) on a large sample of neurotics and their first-degree relatives, who were assessed on the Maudsley Personality Inventory (MPI) for their neuroticism and extroversion scores.

The patients were derived from a neurosis center (Belmont Hospital). The number accepted for investigation was 266; 939 of their first-degree relatives and spouses were approached, and of them 735 responded and completed an MPI form. Scores of patients and relatives, where necessary, were corrected for age. In the subsequent analysis it was not found necessary to take account of the diagnosis of type of neurosis in the patient.

A raised neuroticism score and a depressed mean extroversion score were found in the patients, as expected, but, contrary to expectation, mean neuroticism scores in different classes of relatives were not found to be raised, and correlation coefficients within classes of relatives were generally low. Omitting spouses, correlation coefficients in ungrouped relationships were only significantly positive in the families of male patients, and in them solely in the relationships between the mother and her children and the patient and his male siblings. These findings were thought to be incapable of explanation along genetic lines. The conclusion was drawn from certain detailed correlation coefficients that there may well be a special affective relationship between the mother and her children in the families of male neurotics that does not obtain in the families of female neurotics.

The negative conclusion as to the role of genetic factors in the neurotic group taken as a whole, arrived at by Slater, has been followed up by him into the subgroups of hysteria and anxiety state. In his Maudsley lecture (1961) he reviews twin data of his own and of Ljungberg (1957) illustrating the heterogeneity of this group and dethroning it from the status of a nosological entity.

Slater's twins, totaling twelve monozygotic (MZ) and twelve dizygotic (DZ) pairs, were collected, as part of a systematized, unselected series of all twins with a neurotic or psychopathic diagnosis, from the inpatient and outpatient material of the Bethlem and Maudsley Hospitals between March 1, 1948, and December 31, 1958, and from Belmont Hospital between November 1, 1950, and June 30, 1953. Number 311 is the diagnostic classification number of the International List of Diseases (1947) indicating "hysterical reaction without mention of anxiety reaction." However, the Belmont diagnoses accepted for inclusion were those of hysteria and anxiety hysteria.

Slater gives us a detailed clinical picture of the cases. The net conclusion is concordance in five MZ and four DZ pairs. The difference is negligible, and we are "driven to the conclusion that specific hereditary factors are not manifesting their presence." Slater then takes the "one further step we can take along genetic lines, and that is an examination of the family history," which takes him to Ljungberg's valuable monograph on hysteria (1957). Ljungberg calculated that the incidences of hysteria in the fathers, brothers, and sons of hysterics were approximately 2 percent, 3 percent, and 5 percent, respectively, against the background of a general population morbidity risk of 0.5 percent. He considered that his findings supported the view that polygenic factors are responsible. Slater's further analysis of the incidence of other psychiatric disorders among the relatives of the propositi in Ljungberg's and his own material issues in the conclusion that *there is no indication that hysteria can claim the autonomy of a genetical syndrome.*

Exploration of environmental factors both in early life and in the adult suggest the importance of reactions to physical factors and illness interacting with particular life situations and intense psychological-stress situations.

In his conclusion Slater raises the question of the justification for regarding hysteria as a syndrome. He indicates here that *the etiology appears to be very various; and the hypothesis of a genetical basis of a specific or indeed important kind has had to be discarded.* In his analysis he stresses the occurrence of the dissociative reaction in psychosis, epilepsy, and focal organic disease and its purely symptomatic status: "If in our patient we find the signs of hysteria and no more, then these are signs that we have not yet looked deeply enough."

In his paper read at the Second International Congress of Human Genetics in Rome, 1961 (pub. 1964). Slater reviews, in addition to the above situation in hysteria, the evidence in respect to the *obsessional neuroses* and *anxiety states* as follows.

> . . . *Of all neurotic syndromes, the evidence relating to genetic predisposition is best in the case of obsessional neuroses* [italics added]. Luxenburger (1930), Lewis (1935), Brown (1942), and Rüdin (1953) have all contributed to this. Luxenburger examined the parents and sibs of 71 obsessionals and found anankastic qualities in 15 percent of fathers, 6 percent of mothers, and 14 percent of sibs. He concluded that the "anakotrope character" was inherited as an entity. Somewhat similar con-

clusions were reached by Lewis. He reported on the familial data on 50 obsessional patients. Of the 100 parents, 37 showed pronounced obsessional traits in one form or another, and of the 206 sibs, 43, or 21 percent, showed mild or severe obsessional traits. In Brown's material, 9 cases of definite obsessional neurosis were found among the parents and sibs of the 3 neurotic groups, 7 among the 96 first-degree relatives of obsessional probands, 2 among the 344 relatives of anxiety neurotics, and none among the 105 relatives of hysterics or the 185 relatives of control cases. Brown differed in his conclusions from other workers, since he did not think his findings supported, as in fact they do, the existence of a specific obsessional predisposition. The most recent report is that of Rüdin. She found that 5 percent of the parents and 2 percent of the sibs of her obsessional probands had had an obsessional illness and that 5 percent of the parents and 3 percent of the sibs had obsessional personalities. Obsessionality in one form or another was found in 8 percent of parents and 5 percent of sibs. The differences between the results obtained by these workers depend in part on the criteria used.

The data relating to anxiety states are very much less in amount. McInnes (1937) examined the relatives of 50 anxiety neurotics and found that 15 of the 100 parents and 28, or 15 percent of the 189 sibs had anxiety neuroses also. There were also small numbers of others suffering from unclassified neurotic states and other psychiatric abnormalities, but anxiety state was the only condition shown in obviously marked excess. Among the relatives of psychiatrically normal control subjects, 4 percent of parents and 5 percent of sibs had anxiety neuroses. Brown found the percent 21 of the parents and 12 percent of the sibs of anxiety neurotics had also had anxiety neuroses, i.e., conditions which at some time had produced some incapacity socially or at work, but such conditions were also found with about half that frequency in the parents and sibs of hysterics and in the sibs of obsessionals. Cohen (1951) worked with Army recruits suffering from "neuro-circulatory asthenia" (NCA), i.e., a form of anxiety neurosis in which the circulatory symptoms predominate. They divided their material into sixty-seven chronic and forty-four acute cases and compared the findings with those obtained from eighteen men convalescent from physical disorders and fifty-four healthy soldiers. It was the group of chronic cases that showed the distinctive findings, 18 percent of the fathers, 55 percent of the mothers, 13 percent of the brothers, and 12 percent of the sisters of these probands suffering also from NCA. Among the relatives of the acute cases the prevalence of NCA was hardly higher than among the relatives of the control groups. The authors considered various possible genetic models for the explanation of their findings, and they thought that a dominant or double-dominant hypothesis fitted the facts best. They add: "In addition, the study of 37 children of 18 NCA parents revealed no evidence of hysteria, depression or obsessional neurosis, although there was a high prevalence of NCA in these children."

Now, if there are specificities in the predisposition to neurosis, then one might expect that in pairs of twins, both of whom develop a neurotic illness, there would be greater qualitative similarity within MZ than within DZ pairs. Shields (1954) has made a number of observations bearing on this point. In his report on thirty-six MZ and twenty-six DZ pairs of normal twin schoolchildren, he shows that 42 out of the total of 124 individuals had a moderately severe degree of psychiatric maladjustment, severe enough to have at some time caused referral to some social agency. The symptoms were of the kind familiar to the child psychiatrist. Analysis of the figures, to distinguish between quantitative and qualitative concordance, showed that MZ twins were only a little more alike than DZ twins in respect of the presence or absence of neurosis or behavior disorder but that they were very much more alike in the type of neurotic symptom or personality trait. *The occurrence or nonoccurrence of neurotic disorder appeared to be determined largely by the environment; the form of the neurosis depended more on the genetic constitution.*

In Shields's study (1962) on MZ twins who had been separated from one another in infancy or early childhood, both similarities and dissimilar-ites in neurotic symptomatology were very striking. Thus at one extreme there was a pair who had both complained at times of globus hystericus and had been submitted to much hospital investigation for physical disorders with negative results, and at the other extreme there was a pair in which only one had been a rebellious child, had made homosexual attachments, and had had three attacks of amnesia, while her twin was normal. In general, illnesses of a hysterical kind showed up in the discordant pairs, while community in respect of anxiety states accounted for several concordant pairs.

In a further study by Slater and his co-workers in the Medical Research Council Genetics Unit, Maudsley Hospital, there were fourteen MZ pairs and five DZ pairs in which both twins had some form of neurotic disorder. In six of the MZ pairs the twins showed close similarity in important respects and very little qualitative difference. There were no such pairs among the DZ twins, who showed wide qualitative differences. Thus we have in the DZ pairs a chronic alcoholic paired with an exhibitionist liable to anxiety states, a chronic hypochondriac paired with a woman who had an anxiety state during a pregnancy, a chronic alcoholic and drug addict paired with an anxious hypochondriac, a chronic obsessional paired with a chronic hysteric, and a suicidally inclined homosexual man whose twin was a truant at school, later became sexually promiscuous and a shoplifter, and had many neurotic complaints, some involving a suggestion of malingering. In the group of twins from the Maudsley Children's Department, whom Slater's team has been following up for a number of years, the same general observation is made: *Concordant MZ pairs are much more alike in their symptomatology than concordant DZ pairs.*

We should not leave the sphere of the subclassification of psychoneurotic syndromes without referring to a yet more specialized syndrome falling within the psychoneurotic-psychophysio-

logical range because of its prevalence in childhood, namely, enuresis.

S. Hallgren's work (1957) is the most substantial in this field and is based on 229 propositi from the psychiatric departments of two children's hospitals and on 173 secondary cases from among their relatives. He argued that nocturnal enuresis is etiologically heterogeneous, there being cases that are genetically determined and others which he terms "nongenetic." Regarding the mode of inheritance in genetic cases Hallgren's results leave us with the alternatives of (1) a single, major, dominant gene whose expression is modified by the environment as well as many genes of small effect and (2) determination of the condition solely by the interaction of polygenes and the environment. On the psychogenic side Hallgren stresses the role of unfavorable environmental factors disturbing the emotional security of the child. A methodological thought relating to the above is the altered conceptual model which we bring to the analysis of the nature-nurture problem in the neuroses; Slater's (1964, pp. 265, 266, 269) formulations of this are best left to him:

> My own interest in the genetical aspects of neurosis and psychopathy dates back to the last war. The circumstances then, in which a great body of men were subjected to physical and psychological stresses of a relatively stereotyped kind, to which they reacted in a variety of ways, were such as to highlight the contribution made by individual differences in personality and predisposition. Statistical investigation of a large case material (Slater, 1943) led to two conclusions.
>
> The first of these in importance was the inverse relationship between the degree of stress undergone and the number of markers indicating abnormality of personality. The more these markers were recorded in an individual case, the less the degree of stress which had been required to produce breakdown. From this the suggestion arose that variation in neurotic predisposition was quantitative in nature, and, on the genetic side, could most plausibly

be attributed to polygenes. However, the close relationship between the type of personality and the type of symptom manifested suggested the existence of qualitative as well as quantitative variation. My brother and I (Slater and Slater, 1944) subsequently formulated the hypothesis more precisely. Clinical observations could be accounted for if the disposition to neurosis was regarded as due to a number of distinct qualities, each of them subject to normal variation. An individual who differed markedly from the mean towards either extreme, in respect to any single such quality, would be more than normally susceptible to stresses of a certain specific kind; and if the stress passed a certain level of intensity he would be likely to break down, and then to show symptoms of specific and related kind. But the majority of men breaking down under stress would, by the laws of chance, be those who showed minor deviations along a number of different lines, rather than those who showed an extreme deviation along one line. They would be liable to break down under a mixture of stresses, and to respond with a variety of symptoms. Variation in the constitutional predisposition to such reactions should correspond to a normal surface in many dimensions.

A hypothesis of essentially the same kind, but much simplified, has been advanced by Eysenck and has been supported by him and his collaborators with a great amount of valuable work. A recent formulation of his theory is given in his *Handbook of Abnormal Psychology* (Eysenck, 1960). The normal surface which Eysenck uses has two dimensions, the polarities being, horizontally, extroversion-introversion and, vertically, neuroticism-normality. With the mental tests employed, persons with anxiety states, obsessionals, and depressives are found on the introverted side of the midline, and psychopaths and hysterics on the extroverted side. On the vertical dimension all these groups cluster fairly close together, but are widely separated from the normals. A multifactorial genetic basis for the neurotic predisposition forms a natural but probably not essential part of Eysenck's theory.

In what follows, I shall endeavor to examine the question of whether we can be satisfied with this theory or whether we should prefer the concept of a pluridimensional field of variation to that of a bidimensional one. The question will be approached from the genetic side. If we find indications of qualitative rather than quantitative differences between groups or if the genetic factors associated with such closely neighboring syndromes as anxiety and obsessionality are found to be different from one another, we shall be inclined to prefer the pluridimensional hypothesis. If no such findings are made, the simpler view should prevail. . . .

Reviewing the evidence, it seems to me that in the field of variation of temperament and personality we have to face much the same situation that we have in the field of variation in intellectual ability. It is a convenience for the psychologist to use the simplest possible hypothesis for the design of mental tests and the calculation of scores. By means of such simple hypotheses a useful part of the total observable variance can be accounted for. In both fields, however, as we refine our studies we find specific traits or constellations of traits of personality which find no place in such simplified models. At this point we have to broaden our working hypothesis.

Turning to twin studies dealing exclusively with childhood maladjustment in the categories of neurosis and of behavior disorder and delinquency, we are indebted to Shields (1954), who has not only described his own work on personality differences and neurotic traits in normal twin schoolchildren but also compiled a table (Table 3-2) summarizing the work of others.

The high concordance as compared with the discordance rate for monozygotic pairs in respect of the categories appearing in the table suggests the operation of hereditary factors. The high concordance rates between same-sex as compared with opposite-sex dizygotic twins, which shows up well in the figures of Rosanoff and his collaborators, especially with respect to juvenile delinquency, is probably an environmental effect. In Shields's own investigation of personality differences and neurotic traits in normal twin schoolchildren, he found closer similarity be-

TABLE 3-2   PERSONALITY AND PSYCHONEUROTIC DISORDERS IN TWIN SCHOOL-CHILDREN (ABSTRACTED FROM SHIELDS, 1954, BY COWIE, 1965)

Condition Studied	Author (Country)	Year	Uniovular Pairs		Same-sex Binovular Pairs		Opposite-sex Biovular Pairs	
			Concordant	Discordant	Concordant	Discordant	Concordant	Discordant
Juvenile delinquency	Rosanoff et al. (U.S.)	1934	39	3	20	5	8	32
Behavior disorder in children	Rosanoff et al. (U.S.)	1934	41	6	26	34	8	21
Institutional reeducation of juveniles with personality abnormality	Kranz (Germany)	1937	7	4	0	3	2	6
Childhood maladjustment	Kent (U.S.)	1949	7	0	4	2	2	1

ween monozygotic twins than between dizygotic twins in respect of personality characteristics. The form taken by neurotic symptoms appeared to be more closely related to hereditary factors than the degree of their severity, where the environment seemed to contribute more. The suggestion was that genes most often influence neurotic behavior through their effect on the physical basis of personality. On this hypothesis, disorders such as juvenile delinquency, less closely related to personality type, are likely to be determined by heredity to a lesser extent than neurotic and psychosomatic disorders.

Gedda has contributed a comprehensive survey, in Italian, of studies of normal schoolchildren (1951) in this field.

In conclusion, one may sum up by stating that these studies support the view that " . . . personality deviation in childhood, whether manifested as juvenile delinquency, non-delinquent behavior disorder or childhood maladjustment is to a considerable extent determined by heredity," to quote Cowie (1965). In neurosis, however, we must distinguish between predisposition, reflected in the dimension of personality "neu-

roticism," which similarly shows a high genetic loading, 80 percent according to Eysenck and Prell (1951), and overt neurosis, where Slater's work has discredited a genetic interpretation. With regard to the predispositional genetic factors in both personality deviation and neurosis, the probability is that we are dealing with a polygenic vulnerability to stress, which may manifest itself, depending upon the environment, at a very early age.

Mental Subnormality

In approaching the area of the inheritance of mental defect, I should like to start by referring to Penrose's Colchester study (1949), lest the brilliant successes scored by chromosomal and biochemical genetic work obscure our perspective as to the relative incidence of these types of abnormality. The Colchester study revealed the fact that some 15 percent of that rather large institutional sample of mental defectives was nongenetic (even albeit congenital) in the sense of being attributable to such factors as cerebral birth conditions (anoxia and hemorrhage) and cerebral infections. This leaves us with a figure

TABLE 3-3 MENTAL RETARDATION AND METABOLIC DISORDER (ADAPTED FROM CROME & STERN, 1967)

Serial No.	Designation, Synonyms, and Variants	Main Clinical Features	Specific Defect	Main Abnormal Substances			Mode of Transmission	Key References in Literature	Remarks
				Urine	Blood	Tissues			
1.	Lipidoses: Gargoylism (Hurler's syndrome, lipochondrodystrophy; Hurler-Pfaunder syndrome)	Usually mental retardation; hepatosplenomegaly; corneal clouding; generalized skeletal and cranial changes; heart changes	Suggested anomalous metabolism of mucopolysaccharides	Excess of chondroitin sulphate B and of heparitin sulphate		Excess of chondroitin sulphate B and of heparitin sulphate; increased brain ganglioside	1. Autosomal recessive 2. Sex-linked (condition tends to be less severe, and there is no corneal clouding)	Maroteau and Lamy (1965); McKusick et al. (1965)	The nervous system shows changes histologically similar to the other lipidoses
2.	Tay-Sachs disease (amaurotic family, idiocy); variants according to age at onset a. Bielschowsky b. Spielmeyer-Vogt c. Batten d. Kufs	Progressive mental deterioration; occasional epilepsy; progressive paralysis; macular and later generalized retinal atrophy with pigmentation	Not known			Neuronal and reticuloendothelial system cells, increase of neuramine acid containing ganglioside	Autosomal recessive	Bogaert (1962); Aronson and Volk (1962); Volk (1964)	
3.	Gaucher's disease	Physical and mental retarda-	Deficiency in B-glyco-			Excess of gluco- or	Autosomal recessive;	Banker, Miller and	There is general-

	Clinical features	Enzyme defect	Biochemistry	Inheritance	References	Notes
—infantile	tion; spleno- and hepatomegaly; hypotonia followed by muscular rigidity; head retraction; cachexia; bulbar palsy	sidase (cerebrosidase)	galactocerebrosides (kerasin)	possibly dominant in some cases	Crocker (1962); Bogaert (1962); Aronson and Volk (1965)	ized involvement of the reticuloendothelial system, and the brain may show changes of lipidosis
4.	Niemann-Pick, disease	Occasional early jaundice; progressive mental deterioration with spleno- and hepatomegaly and widespread involvement of the reticuloendothelial system; sometimes retinal changes as in Tay-Sachs disease	Not known	Increased sphingomeylin in brain and some other tissues	Autosomal recessive	Bogaert (1962); Aronson and Volk (1962, 1965)	Nervous system shows lipidosis as in Tay-Sachs disease; excess of neuraminic acid has been found by Cumings (1962)
5.	Leucodystrophies: Sudanophil; Pelizaeus-Merzbacher; Krabbe's (globoid cell); metachromatic; Alexander; spon-	Clinical picture varies with age at onset; usually progressive mental deterioration, paralysis, and epilepsy	Not known		Often autosomal recessive; often sex-linked in Pelizaeus-Merzbacher type	Poser (1962); Bogaert (1962)	

TABLE 3-3 MENTAL RETARDATION AND METABOLIC DISORDER (ADAPTED FROM CROME & STERN, 1967) *Continued*

Serial No.	Designation, Synonyms, and Variants	Main Clinical Features	Specific Defect	*Main Abnormal Substances*			Mode of Transmission	Key References in Literature	Remarks
				Urine	Blood	Tissues			
	giform diffuse sclerosis; Schilder's disease								
	Aminoacidurias:								
6.	Phenylketonuria	Mental retardation usually present; epilepsy, dilution of pigment; eczema; frequent microcephaly	Lack of hepatic phenylalanine hydroxylase	Excess of phenylpyruvic, phenyllactic, and phenylacetic acids	Excess of phenylalanine; low tryptophan-metabolites, e.g., 5-hydroxytryptamine; low catecholamines		Autosomal recessive	Knox (1966); Lyman (1963); Woolf (1963)	Some improvement on phenylalanine-low diet
7.	Maple syrup urine disease; branched-chain amino-aciduria; leucinosis (late-manifesting	Failure to thrive; vomiting; opisthotonos; severe mental retardation; hypertomicity; maple syrup smell in urine; convulsions	Oxidative co-carboxylation of branched-chain amino acids (probable)	Excess of leucine, isoleucine, and valine; ketoaciduria	Excess of leucine, isoleucine, valine, and alloisoleucine; occasional hypoglycemia		Autosomal recessive	Dancis and Levitz (1966); Scriver (1962); Blattner (1965); Efron (1965)	Smell of the urine is caused perhaps by the alpha-hydroxy acids of branched-chain amino acids

No.	Disorder	Clinical features	Enzymatic defect	Excess (1)	Excess (2)	Excess (3)	Inheritance	Reference	Remarks
8.	Tyrosinosis	Neurological disturbances; evidence of hepatic cirrhosis and renal tubular damage	Deficiency in p-hydroxyphenylpyruvic acid oxidase	Excess of tyrosine, p-hydroxyphenylpyruvic acid	Excess of tyrosine		Not known	Francois et al. (1962); Menkes and Jervis (1961); Halvorsen and Gjessing (1964); Gentz, Jagenburg, and Zetterström (1965); Woolf (1966)	Mental retardation not a constant or typical feature of the disease
9.	Hydroxyprolinemia	Microscopic hematuria; mental retardation	Deficient hydroxyproline oxidase	Excess of hydroxyproline	Excess of hydroxyproline		Autosomal recessive	Efron et al. (1965)	
10.	Hyperprolinemia I	Renal disease; photogenic epilepsy	Deficient proline oxidase	Excess of proline, hydroxyproline, and glycine	Excess of proline		Possibly autosomal recessive	Efron (1965)	
11.	Hyperprolinemia II	Epilepsy; mild mental retardation	Deficient delta-pyrroline-5-carboxylate dehydrogenase	Excess of proline, hydroxyproline, and glycine	Excess of proline		Possibly autosomal recessive	Efron (1965)	
12.	Hyperhistidinemia	Speech defect; mental	Deficient histidase	Excess of histidine	Excess of histidine	Excess of histidine	Possibly autosomal	Ghadimi, Partington,	Urinary ferric

TABLE 3-3 MENTAL RETARDATION AND METABOLIC DISORDER (ADAPTED FROM CROME & STERN, 1967) *Continued*

Serial No.	Designation, Synonyms, and Variants	Main Clinical Features	Specific Defect	*Main Abnormal Substances*			Mode of Transmission	Key References in Literature	Remarks
				Urine	Blood	Tissues			
	(histidinemia)	retardation		and imidazolepyruvic acid		in cerebrospinal fluid	recessive	and Hunter (1961); La Du et al. (1963); Davies and Robinson (1963); Holton, Lewis, and Moore (1964)	chloride reaction may lead to confusion with phenylketonuria
13.	Hyperlysinemia I	Mental deficiency; convulsions; asthenia; anemia	Not known		Excess of lysine		Not known	Ghadimi et al. (1964); Woody (1964)	
14.	Hyperlysinemia II	Mental deficiency	Not known		Excess of lysine and arginine		Not known	Colombo et al. (1964)	
15.	Hyperglycinemia (glycinemia)	Neonatal vomiting; failure to thrive; convulsions; lethargy; mental retardation; neutropenia; thrombocytopenia; osteoporosis	Not known	Glycinuria; ketonuria	Hyperglycinemia; general aminoacidemia; increased globulins ketosis		Not known	Childs, Nyhan, Borden, Bard, and Cooke (1961); Childs and Nyhan (1964); Gerritsen and Waisman (1964),	

No.	Condition	Clinical features	Biochemical defect	Biochemical findings	Genetics	References
16.	Homocystinuria	Mental retardation; epilepsy; increasing spasticity; tremor of iris; mottled and dry skin; hepatomegaly; dislocation of lenses; anemia genu valgum; pes cavus	Not known	Excess of homocystine	Reported in two sisters	Carson and Neill (1962); Carson, Cusworth Deat, and Westall (1963); British Medical Journal, annotation 2 (1963); Menkes (1966)
17.	Hartnup disease	Mental retardation with emotional instability; red, scaly, light-sensitive rash; ataxia, diplopia, and nystagmus (acute stage)	Cellular amino-acid transport disorder in kidney and intestine (possibly)	Aminoaciduria; indoleacetic acid, indoleacetylglutamic acid, and indican	Autosomal recessive	Baron et al. (1956); Watts (1962); Hooft, Laey, Timmermans, and Snoeck (1964); Scriver (1965); Woolf (1966)
18.	Argininosuccinicaciduria	Gradual mental retardation; friability of hair; convulsions; systolic murmur	Deficient argininosuccinase	Excess of argininosuccinic acid; Excess of argininosuccinic acid; Excess of argininosuccinic acid	Possibly recessive	Levin, Mackay, and Oberholzer (1961); Dent (1961); Grosfeld, Mighorst, and Moolhuysen (1964)

TABLE 3-3 MENTAL RETARDATION AND METABOLIC DISORDER (ADAPTED FROM CROME & STERN, 1967) *Continued*

Serial No.	Designation, Synonyms, and Variants	Main Clinical Features	Specific Defect	*Main Abnormal Substances*			Mode of Transmission	Key References in Literature	Remarks
				Urine	Blood	Tissues			
19.	Citrullinuria	Mental retardation in a child at 18 months	Deficient argininosuccinate synthetase	Excess of L-citrulline	Excess of L-citrulline	Excess of L-citrulline in cerebrospinal fluid	Not known	McMurray et al. (1962, 1963)	
20.	Hyperammonemia	Episodic vomiting, lethargy, and stupor; mental retardation with decline of vision; microcephaly	Deficient ornithine-trans-carbamylase	Persistently neutral or alkaline; aminoaciduria	High level of ammonia	High levels of ammonia and glutamine in cerebrospinal fluid	Not known; described in two cousins	Russell, Levin, Oberholzer, and Sinclair (1962)	
21.	Lowe's syndrome (cerebro-oculorenal disease)	Mental retardation; glaucoma; cataracts; osteoporosis; rickets; hypotonia	Not known	Aminoaciduria with occasional glycosuria and proteinuria	Acidosis; azotaemia; alkaline phosphatase may be raised		Thought to be sex-linked	Crome, Duckett, and Franklin (1963); Richards et al. (1965)	
	Other neuro-metabolic diseases:								
22.	Galactosemia	Neonatal jaundice and hepatomegaly, followed by cirrhosis; cataracts;	Lack of galactose-1-phosphate uridyl transferase	Galactosuria; aminoaciduria	Excess galactose-1-phosphate	Excess of galactose-1-phosphate	Autosomal recessive	Holzel (1961); Woolf (1962); Hsia (1965)	Improvement on elimination of lactose from diet

No.	Disease	Clinical features	Biochemical defect	Urine	Blood chemistry		Inheritance	References	Notes
		deafness; mental retardation	activity						
23.	Fructosemia (fructosuria)	Failure to thrive; vomiting; hepatomegaly; transient jaundice; retarded growth; mild mental retardation	Almost total lack of liver aldolase; activity to fructose-1-phosphate and reduced activity to 1:6 diphosphate	Fructosuria; aminoaciduria	Fructosemia after fructose administration; frequent hypoglycemia; low magnesium		Autosomal recessive	Levin et al. (1963); Froesch, Wolf, Baitsch, Prader, and Labhart (1963)	In older children the condition may be symptomless
24.	Generalized glycogenosis (Pompe's disease and glycogen synthetase deficiency disease associated with mental defect)	Failure to thrive; cardiomegaly and later cardiac failure; hepatomegaly; hypotonia and general floppiness; osteoporosis; enlarged tongue; resembles cretinism	Probably lack of a (1-4) glucosidase		Excess of glycogen in blood and leucocytes	Excess glycogen in all tissues.	Autosomal recessive	Hers (1964); Crome, Cumings, and Duckett (1963)	
25.	Nephrogenic diabetes insipidus	Polydipsia; polyuria; dehydration; occasional mental retardation	Renal tubule failure to respond to pitressin	Low specific gravity; polyuria	Hyperelectemic azotamia		Uncertain; mostly sex-linked	Ruess and Rosenthal (1963); Woolf (1966)	
26.	Pseudohypoparathyroidism	Mental retardation; round face; stubby hands; widespread	Not known	Low calcium	Hypocalcemia; hyperphosphatemia		Familial cases; possibly sex-linked	Bartter (1966); Woolf (1966)	Administration of parathyroid extract has

TABLE 3-3 MENTAL RETARDATION AND METABOLIC DISORDER (ADAPTED FROM CROME & STERN, 1967) *Continued*

Serial No.	Designation, Synonyms, and Variants	Main Clinical Features	Main Abnormal Substances			Mode of Transmission	Key References in Literature	Remarks
			Specific Defect	Urine	Blood	Tissues		
		calcification; tetany; epilepsy; fragility of nails; cataracts						no effect
27.	Abetalipoteinemia (Bassen-Kornzweig syndrome)	Steatorrhoea; retinitis plymentosa; acanthocytosis of erythrocytes; cerebellar ataxia and mental retardation	Probably inability to form the betalipo protein molecule		Low serum globulins; absent betalipoprotein; low cholesterol and phospholipids; low vitamin A; no particulate fat; microcytic anemia		Autosomal recessive	Woolf (1965); Forsyth, Lloyd, and Fosbrooke (1965)	
28.	Leigh's encephalomyelopathy (subacute necrotizing encephalomyelopathy)	Failure to thrive, lack of movement, and hypotonia, leading to spasticity, absent reflexes, optic atrophy, nystagmus, and convulsions			High level pyruvates (thiamine-resistant)		Autosomal recessive (possibly atypical dominant)	Richter (1957); Reye (1960)	In one case improvement followed administration of lipoic acid

No.	Condition	Clinical features	Biochemical defect				Inheritance	Reference	Remarks
29.	Nonendemic goitrous familial cretinism	Mental retardation; goiter; signs of hypothyroidism—low basal metabolic rate; course hair and skin; stunted growth							
	Type 1	As above	Failure to bind iodine to tyrosine	Normal	High cholesterol		Autosomal recessive	The Thyroid Gland (1960)	Differentiation of groups greatly assisted by radioactive iodine studies
	Type 2	As above with deafness	Failure to bind iodine to tyrosine				Autosomal recessive		
	Type 3	As in type 1	Inability to couple iodotyrosine to form thyroxine	Increase in mono- and di-iodotyrosine	Increase in mono- and di-iodotyrosine; high cholesterol	Thyroid contains mono- and di-iodotyrosines but no iodothyronines	Possibly dominant	Stanbury (1966)	
	Type 4	As in type 1	Inability to deiodinate mono- and diiodotyrosine due to absence of dehalogenase	Increase in mono- and di-iodotyrosine	Increase in mono- and di-iodotyrosine; high cholesterol		Autosomal recessive	Watts (1962)	

TABLE 3-3 MENTAL RETARDATION AND METABOLIC DISORDER (ADAPTED FROM CROME & STERN, 1967) *Continued*

Serial No.	Designation, Synonyms, and Variants	Main Clinical Features	*Main Abnormal Substances*				Mode of Transmission	Key References in Literature	Remarks
			Specific Defect	Urine	Blood	Tissues			
	Type 5	As in type 1	Not known		Increase of iodinated polypeptides; high cholesterol		Not known		
30.	Undesignated steroid disorder	Mental retardation; lack of secondary sex characters; deaf-mutism; muscular wasting	Not known	Reduced estrogen pregnandiol and total of seventeen neutral ketosteroids			Possibly autosomal recessive	Richards and Rundle (1959)	
31.	Kinky hair disease	Mental and physical retardation; lack of pigmentation in hair; pili torti; trichorrhexis nodosa; epilepsy; microencephaly	Not known	General slight aminoaciduria	Excess of glutamic acid		Consistent with sex-linked transmission	Menkes, Alter, Steigleder, Weakley, and Sung (1962)	Degeneration of cerebral gray matter with secondary changes in white matter; diffuse cerebellar atrophy

of about 85 percent attributable to the genetic factors, whose operation has been abundantly revealed in diverse twin studies, reviewed by Allen and Kallmann (1955). It has been estimated that only about 1 percent is referable to chromosomal anomalies, and 3.5 percent to specific single-factor inheritance, often with a known or partially known chemical basis (see Tables 3-3 and 3-4). This means that the great majority of mental defectives, approximately 80 percent, may be postulated as comprising the tail end of the normal (Gaussian) curve of distribution of intelligence, with a polygenic mechanism of inheritance.

In assessing the genetic counseling implications in connection with a mentally defective child, although biochemical and chromosomal screening should be borne in mind, the matter of obstetrical delivery looms larger than specialized chromosomal and biochemical testing, and even more commonly than that, an unfavorable draw of polygenes from the parental pool. However, in cases of gross mental subnormality, often with recognizable patterns of physical features (e.g., Down's syndrome), chromosomes and specialized biochemistry become of greater concern.

We have already covered the question of chromosomes, and accordingly we now turn our attention to the biochemical genetics of mental subnormality (defect).

Chemical aberrations. Garrod's concept of inborn errors of metabolism, enunciated in 1902, bore fruit in the domain of mental defect in 1934, when Folling drew attention to the association of phenylketones in the urine with mental retardation. To date, 3.5 percent of mental defectives have been shown to possess some presumably etiologically associated biochemical abnormality. They may be broadly divided into errors of carbohydrate, lipid, and protein metabolism, and classification is in terms of blood amino-acid level and chromatographic abnormality.

Phenylketonuria, which may be classified as a single overflow aminoaciduria, has become the paradigm of the chemical mode of action of single gene effects and enzyme blocks.

The complex of biochemical events disclosed in this condition is as follows: Phenylalanine hydroxylase, an enzyme concerned in the conversion of the essential amino acid phenylalanine to tyrosine, is at fault. Consequences of this are the following: (1) There is an accumulation of phenylalanine in the blood and cerebrospinal fluid and an overflow in the urine; (2) phenyl-pyruvic and phenylacetic acids and phenylacetyl-glutamine are therefore in excess and, as the renal threshold is low, are excreted in the urine; and (3) the administration of excess phenylalanine to normals produces a rise in blood tyrosine levels, but none follows in phenylketonurics.

The matter of how directly or completely the mental retardation in this condition is related to failure of conversion of phenylalanine to tyrosine has often been canvassed. Confirmation of the central etiologic role of this mechanism comes from two sources (Hsia, Knox, Quinn, & Paine, 1958; Moncrieff & Wilkinson, 1961), in which it is reported that treatment commenced early (in which dietary phenylalanine was maintained at a bare minimum) gave indications of the prevention of mental retardation.

A test for the detection of carriers in this disease has been evolved, based on the plasma phenylalanine levels 1, 2, and 4 hours after a standard test dose of levophenylalanine had been administered.

The details of the main findings and conclusions in this very active field of research are presented in Table 3-3.

The fact that twelve of these metabolic defects can be treated stresses the importance of screening programs for the newborn.

Grüter (1966, pp. 5–6) has summarized these

TABLE 3-4   GENETICALLY DETERMINED METABOLIC BLOCK AND PATHOLOGICAL CONSEQUENCES IN PHENYLKETONURIA

Block in metabolism of phenylalanine to tyrosine

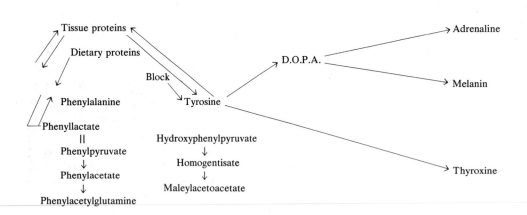

Possible mode of production of mental defect in phenylketonuria (after Knox, 1966)

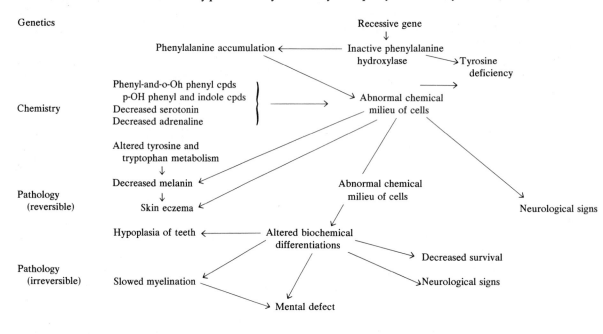

therapeutic endeavors as follows:

> In galactosaemia the patient remains free from symptoms if he is given a diet absolutely free of galactose. Idiopathic hypoglycaemia in early childhood begins in the first two years of life with hypoglycaemic symptoms leading to fainting and convulsions in the morning, and eventually causes irreversible defects of intelligence. Long-term administration of ACTH not only restores the blood-sugar level to normal but also prevents the mental defect. Fructose intolerance results from absence of the enzyme phosphofructaldolase. Physical and mental symptoms can be avoided by a fructose-free diet. Decarboxylation of glutaminic acid to aminobutyric acid is upset in Vitamin B_6 deficiency. Vitamin B_6 can prevent convulsions and death or an irreversible oligophrenia, and maintain the patient in good health. Hormone treatment of familial cretinism may produce good results if started early enough but is at times disappointing. An inadequate renal response to the antidiuretic hormone is the basis of renal diabetes insipidus. If affected children survive the untreated syndrome of dehydration and hypernatraemia they fall victims to a chronic brain syndrome, with progressive mental deficiency as a consequence. An abundant supply of hypoosmolar electrolyte solution is a simple and effective way of overcoming the results of the metabolic error, the children then developing normally.

Glycocoll disease, described in 1961, depends on a primary enzyme defect associated with failure to degrade the amino acid glycocoll and leads to episodes of acetonemia with disturbances of consciousness, leucopenia, and thrombopenia, followed later by convulsive attacks, changes in the EEG, and arrest of development. A possible form of treatment is the use of gamma globulin substitution. Citrullinuria and hyperammonemia, both recently discovered, depend on disturbances in the citric-acid cycle. There are vomiting attacks with disturbance of consciousness and ataxia during the first years of life, followed by gradual and severe impairment of intelligence. A diet poor in protein and administration of alpha-ketoglutaric acid appear to exercise a favorable influence. Maple syrup urine disease, also quite a recent discovery, seems to be due to an enzyme block rendering oxidative decarboxylation of the amino acids leucine, isoleucine, and valine impossible. Toxic symptoms and convulsions give place to a dementia if the children do not succumb in the first months of life. Success has already been obtained by reduction of intake of the amino acids involved to the minimum necessary for life. In the Hartnup syndrome, the condition may be improved by a high-protein diet with addition of nicotinamide and tryptophane. Hepatocerebral degeneration is secondary to a lack of the enzyme-active globulin coeruloplasmin. After years of pathological deposition of copper in various organs, there are sudden discharges of large amounts of copper into the circulation with resultant hemolytic crises and hepatic cirrhosis; similar events have been demonstrated in comparable animal poisonings. Only after some years do the cerebral lesions become manifest through neurological and mental defects. So far, preventive measures have not been undertaken in the subclinical latent stage. In the later stages, an intense mobilization of copper by oral administration of penicillamine has produced impressive improvement in both physical and mental symptoms and signs. By parenteral replacement of coeruloplasmin similar results have been obtained, as well as complete restoration of biochemical changes to normal. Whether this technique can be developed into a practicable therapy of choice will depend on long-term observations on cases in which treatment began during the latent stage. In principle, in all these syndromes, optimum therapy must obviously be by replacement of the missing or incompetent enzyme.

Most extensive experience is in the area of

therapy of phenylketonuria. Independently of each other, Bickel and Armstrong worked out forms of diet low in phenylalanine. One was based on use of casein hydrolysate, and the other on an amino-acid mixture. Several commercial preparations in powder form are now available and can be incorporated in various dishes. In addition, certain natural nutrients may be permitted or even deemed necessary to cover requirements in calories, vitamins, and trace elements. If treatment is begun in the first 6 months, the disease can be completely prevented. A large number of children have been treated regularly up to the age of 8 years and are entirely normal, but we do not yet know how long the diet must be maintained. There is some evidence that after a few years on such diets permanent damage to the brain need no longer be feared, and it is certain that the diet will be superfluous after puberty. Even if it is commenced at a stage when defects are manifest, it may be partially successful during childhood. Bickel, Bosscott and Gerraid (1955) give a comprehensive account of the topic.

Epilepsy

In contrast to the unequivocal findings as to specific unit-factor genetic mechanisms in the major psychoses, schizophrenia and manic-depressive psychosis, to be reviewed later, extensive work in the sphere of epilepsy has not resulted in the same clear-cut conclusions. In fact, the findings of certain substantial studies are in such striking conflict that we are faced with a serious problem as to how they are to be reconciled.

Work stressing the importance of the genetic factor comes from two sources: (1) Conrad's pioneer study of epileptics (1935, 1936) diagnosed as idiopathic, where the expectancy rates were 4.0 percent for siblings, 4.3. percent for two-egg twins, and 86.0 percent for one-egg twins, and (2) the studies of Lennox and the Gibbses

(1944, 1945), employing dysrhythmia in the EEG as the criterion of epilepsy, in which 100 percent concordance was found for one-egg twins and 25 percent concordance for the two-egg variety—the ideal figure for a fully penetrant single dominant gene.

In 1950, in striking contrast to this, came the publication of work by Alström, based on the study of epileptic patients and their families admitted from 1925 to 1940 to a university clinic for neurology in Sweden at the Serefimer Hospital. Salient findings of this study were as follows: In the first place, the expectancy figures for parents (1.3 ± 0.27 percent), for siblings (1.5 ± 0.25 percent), and for children (3.0 ± 0.93 percent) were not significantly higher than those in the general population. Second, families with epilepsy in members other than in the index case were lacking in the majority (i.e., 92 percent) of cases. Third, among the sixteen pairs of twins in this study, two of which were monozygotic, there was not a single case of concordance as to epilepsy. All this notwithstanding, examination of individual pedigrees in Alström's series discloses, according to his own submission, a single-factor genetic mechanism in approximately 1 percent of cases—eleven index cases belonging to eight families in his sample of 897 index cases and their families. This is compatible with the type of genetic mechanism postulated by the Gibbses as being operative throughout their series instead of in only 1 percent. With a view to finding further evidence toward settling the dispute, Hurst, Reef, and Sachs undertook a study at the Meadowlands Clinic (1959 to 1961), where the clinical material held out the special advantage for genetic study of large sibship size (average, 5.8; range, 1 to 16). The study was published in 1961.

The preliminary pilot study produced evidence along the following two lines: (1) the percentage of families showing one or more members exhibiting epilepsy in addition to the index case, for comparison with Alström's low figure cited above, and (2) the types of genetic mechanism exhibited in the pedigrees making up the material. With regard to the first point, there is an incidence of thirteen out of forty-five families, i.e., a figure of 28.3 percent, in contrast to Alström's 8.8 percent—a difference significant at the 0.1 percent level. This comes down very heavily on Conrad's and on Lennox's and the Gibbses' side of the dispute.

Turning to the second point, analyses of the thirteen positive pedigrees (of the forty-six) show that three are suggestive of a penetrant single dominant mechanism and one of irregular dominance, while the remaining nine are equally compatible with recessiveness—or irregular dominance. Therefore, at least a portion of these results is in line with the thesis of single dominance of Lennox and the Gibbses.

Metrakos and Metrakos (1960) and Metrakos (1961) offer a solution which resolves the problem in a most ingenious fashion. On the basis of the EEG of the parents and siblings of 211 probands and 112 controls, he claims that epilepsy of the centrencephalic type may be explained on the basis of a *single dominant gene showing a variable penetrancy with age, such that the penetrance is low at birth, rises rapidly to almost complete penetrance between the ages of 4½ and 16½, and declines gradually to almost zero penetrance after the age of 40½.*

It is of interest to us here that their large sample of 1000 consecutive admissions was made up of the first 1,000 children admitted in 1956 to the Montreal Children's Hospital, as reflected in Table 3-5. The experimental design of the study is unexceptionable.

The prevalence of children with a history of having had at least one convulsion, among 1,000 admissions, was found to be 11.50 ± 1.01 percent. If children who were admitted because of their convulsions are omitted, the prevalence is reduced to 8.76 ± 0.91 percent. The preva-

TABLE 3-5 TOTAL NUMBER OF CHILDREN REPRESENTED BY 1,000 CONSECUTIVE ADMISSIONS (METRAKOS & METRAKOS, 1960)

Number of Times Admitted	Number of Children	Number of Admissions
Once	894	894
Twice	41	82
Three times	3	9
Four times	2	8
Seven times	1	7
Total	941	1,000

lence is reduced still further to 6.55 ± 0.80 percent if children who had convulsions as an associated symptom of their disease are also omitted. The prevalence of individuals with a history of having had at least one convulsion among most of the different orders of near relatives of convulsant patients of a pediatric hospital was significantly higher than that for the near relatives of nonconvulsant patients who were drawn from the same hospital population. When all the near relatives (parents, siblings, aunts and uncles, grandparents, and cousins) are considered together, the prevalence for the convulsant group (3.79 ± 0.45 percent) is 2.9 times and significantly higher ($P = < .001$) than that for the control group (1.3 ± 0.15 percent).

A special problem in this area on which genetic analysis has been brought to bear is the interrelationships between epilepsy and schizophrenia raised by unclear differential diagnostic situations arising clinically. Kallman and Sander (1947), on the basis of their own and of Conrad's studies of the incidence of epilepsy in the family circles of schizophrenics, and of schizophrenia in the family circles of epileptics, have demonstrated that ". . . although there is no evidence of a genetic relationship between the two disorders, it may happen, of course, that some person inherits both predispositions by chance." They go on to endorse Hoch's view, derived from their data, that in most cases showing concurrence of convulsive and schizophrenialike symptoms, ". . . we are dealing with either symptomatic convulsions in true schizophrenics or with a symptomatic schizophrenic syndrome in true epileptics."

Slater and Glithero take up this problem 18 years later (1965, pp. 19–20) as follows:

When we face the crucial problem of the aetiological basis of the psychoses we have described, there are *three main possibilities* to be considered. Either they are to be regarded as *symptomatic schizophrenias of purely epileptic causation;* or they are *independent schizophrenias* which have *appeared in these epileptic subjects coincidentally* as the result of pure chance; or they are forms of schizophrenic illness which have *arisen in individuals predisposed thereto* by the *stresses produced by the epilepsy*. An investigation of the genetical background is capable of producing evidence which would assist in answering this question. If the first hypothesis is correct, the incidence of schizophrenic psychoses in the relatives of our subjects should be no greater than in the general population. If the second hypothesis is correct, the incidence of schizophrenic psychoses in the relatives of schizophrenics is of the usual kind. If the third hypothesis is correct, we would expect an incidence of schizophrenia in the relatives of our patients which would lie somewhere between these two figures.

With this in mind, an investigation of the family history was undertaken along two lines. First, all the hospital records were examined for information about illness or abnormality among first degree relatives. Secondly, one of us (E. G.) contacted the accessible relatives and interviewed them, either at hospital or in their own homes. At these interviews questions were put, not only about the family history, but also about the patient's follow-up history since last admission to hospital, a subject which will be dealt with later. On the family history, relatives were asked for complete data about the patient's parents and sibs, and his children if any, including

age now or at death or when last heard of, illnesses, especially epilepsy or any mental illness, and temperament and personality. Where there was a record of mental illness, data were obtained on the time and the hospital where it had been treated so that further enquiries could be made.

On this basis, we have observed 333.5 risk lifetimes for epilepsy, 286 risk lifetimes for schizophrenia, and 321.5 risk lifetimes for "psychopathic personality." Having found among the relatives eight epileptics two schizophrenics and twelve "psychopathic personalities," we calculate the incidences of these disorders as respectively, 2.4 percent, 0.7 percent and 3.7 percent.

The incidence of schizophrenia among these relatives is approximately what would have been expected from a sample of the general population, and very different from expectation if our subjects had been schizophrenics. Estimates on the expected incidence of schizophrenia in the parents and in the sibs of schizophrenics could hardly be put lower than 4 percent and 8 percent, leading to an expectation of finding 5.32 schizophrenic parents and 12.24 schizophrenic sibs in our material. Our finding of 2 schizophrenics differs from the expected total of 17.56 by a margin which is significant at the 0.001 level.

We conclude accordingly that, for a parent or sib of an epileptic who develops a schizophrenialike psychosis, the risk of epilepsy may well be raised, though our value is subject to a large sampling error; we have found it to be of the same value as has been found by previous investigators for the first-degree relatives of "symptomatic" epileptics.

These findings support the first of the three hypotheses enunciated, that the psychoses which we have investigated are to be regarded as *symptomatic schizophreniform psychoses of purely epileptic causation*—that they are, in fact, *epileptic psychoses* and *not schizophrenic ones from the aetiological standpoint.*

For general perspectives on the comparative biology of convulsive reactions and the range of potential genetic mechanisms underlying them in man, the reader is referred to Kallmann and Sander's (1947) exposition.

TABLE 3-6 TWIN-FAMILY STUDIES (KALLMANN, 1938–1964)

Clinical Condition	Sample Size	Corrected Morbidity Percentages							Postulated Genetic Mechanism
		General Population	Half-sibs	Sibs	DZ Twins	MZ Twins	Parents	Children	
Schizophrenia* (1938) (1946)	13,851† (German); 5,804 (U.S.); twin pairs 953‡	0.9	7.1	*Schizophrenic* 14.2	14.5	86.2 Sep. 77.6 Not Sep. 91.5	9.3	16.4	Single autosomal recessive, 70% penetrant
		2.9	12.5	*Schizoid* 31.5	23.0	20.7	34.8	32.6	
Childhood schizophrenia (1956)	555 twin pairs 52	1.9 hosp. adms.		12.2	17.1	70.6	12.5		As for adult form
Tuberculosis (1943)	2,460 twin pairs 308	1.37	11.9	25.5	25.6	87.3	16.9		Polygenic resistance mechanism
Manic-depressive psychosis (1954)	461 twin pairs 82	0.4	16.7	*Manic-depressive* 23.0	26.3	95.7	23.4		Single autosomal dominant; penetrancy 50% (cycloids included, 90%)
		0.7		*Cycloid* 12.9	30.9	3.7	14.5		
Involutional psychosis (1950)	603 twin pairs 96	1.0	4.5	6.0	6.0	60.9	6.4		Heterozygous carriers of schizophrenic genotype
Senile psychosis (1950)	479 twin pairs 108			6.5	8.0	42.8	3.4		Polygenic plus adaptive personality traits
Adult male homosexuality (1952)	342 twin pairs 85			Sex ratio 1:253	42.3	100.0			Genetically disarranged hormonal sex balance (favoring immature-level libidinal fixation)
Suicide (1949)	N.Y. vital statistics; twin pairs 28	2.0			0.0	5.9			None
Early total deafness (1963)	6,916 twin pairs 37	0.06			35.0	88.0			Autosomal dominant (50% penetrant); 13.4% autosomal recessive 43.3% (at least forty-five genes); sporadic cases 43.3%

*Final figures from United States study, except German figure for schizophrenic children.

†Total number of family members in study.

‡Number of twin pairs in study.

TABLE 3-7   COMPARATIVE TAINT SURVEY IN THE VARIOUS DESCENT GROUPS OF THE PROBAND FAMILIES (ADAPTED FROM KALLMANN, 1938, P. 145)

		Present Study (Estimated According to Abridged Method)		
		Expectation of Schizophrenia		
	Total Number of Adults under Observation		**Clinical Subgroups**	
		Total Material, Percent	**Nuclear Group, Percent**	**Peripheral Group, Percent**
Children	1,000	16.4	20.9	10.4
Grandchildren	543	4.3	5.1	2.9
Great grandchildren	29			
Siblings	2,581	11.5	12.9	8.9
Half sisters and half brothers	101	7.6	7.6	
Nephews and nieces	1,654	3.9	4.7	3.4
Normal average population		0.85		

TABLE 3-8   SCHIZOPHRENIA RATES FOR RELATIVES OF SCHIZOPHRENIC TWIN INDEX CASES (ADAPTED FROM KALLMANN, 1946, P. 313)

		Rates*	
	Number	**Uncorrected**	**Corrected**
Parents	1,191	9.1	9.2
Spouse	254	2.0	2.1
Step-sibs	85	1.4	1.8
Half-sibs	134	4.5	7.0
Full sibs	2,741	10.2	14.3
Two-egg co-twins	517	10.3	14.7
One-egg co-twins	174	69.0	85.8

*Uncorrected—all schizophrenia and all persons over age 15. Corrected—definite schizophrenia and one-half of persons aged 15 to 44 plus all over 44.

Schizophrenia, Childhood Schizophrenia, Early Infantile Autism, and Manic-depressive Psychosis

It may be asked how the so-called functional psychoses, schizophrenia and manic-depressive psychosis, fall within the province of a work on child psychiatry including the period of adolescence. Schizophrenia itself qualifies very substantially, as, by common consent, a sizable proportion of cases of this prevalent psychosis, especially of the hebephrenic and catatonic varieties, occur in the later teens. To this we must add cases falling into the category of childhood or preadolescent schizophrenia and weigh up the genetic position with regard to early infantile autism. Furthermore, the problems of marked introversion and withdrawal, whether in childhood or adolescence, have in their differential diagnosis schizoid and sometimes even schizothymic personality, in the Kretschmerian sense.

There is also widespread agreement that the

TABLE 3-9   VARIATIONS IN SCHIZOPHRENIA RATES OF SIBLINGS AND TWIN PARTNERS ACCORDING TO SEX AND SIMILARITY OR DISSIMILARITY IN ENVIRONMENT (ADAPTED FROM KALLMANN, 1946, P. 316)

	Siblings of Twin Index Cases			Dizygotic Co-twins			Monozygotic Co-twins		
	Male	Female	Total Number	Male	Female	Total Number	Separated	Nonseparated	Total Number
Same sex	15.9	16.3	16.1	17.4	17.7	17.6	77.6	91.5	85.8
Opposite sex	12.5	12.0	12.3	10.5	10.2	10.3			
Total number	14.0	14.5	14.3	14.3	14.9	14.7	77.6	91.5	85.8

occurrence of a full-blown manic-depressive reaction or psychosis before the age of 15 is extremely rare and that from that age throughout the late teens it remains a comparative rarity. However, even apart from the Kleinian dogma that the child during his early development goes through a transitory manic-depressive state, there are specific cases on record during childhood and adolescence by Kasanin (1931); Gareiso, et al. (1940); Beres and Alpert (1940); Sherman (1939); Stürup (1932); Dussik (1934); Baruk and Gévaudien (1937); Cronick (1941); Bender (1937); Yerbury and Newell (1944); Anthony and Scott (1960); and Kanner (1935). A slight impression of incidence may be derived from a study of the last two authors, who found only four manic-depressive cases that had commenced before the age of 16 in 6,000 patients admitted to the Boston Psychopathic Hospital during the 1923 to 1925 period. However, anamnestic data on constitutional depressions, excited episodes, and mood swings in childhood and adolescence are not uncommonly, in the light of full-blown depressions and manic-depressive reactions in later life, susceptible of retrospective interpretation in terms of underlying depressive, hypomanic, and cyclothymic temperament or personality. This lends more weight in numerical terms to the category now under consideration.

Schizophrenia and schizoid personality. Kallmann's German and American studies of schizophrenia may be used in this chapter to illustrate the methodology of the twin-family studies in human genetics. Considerations of space, and the fact that I have dealt with this theme in the companion publication in this series, have led to the decision to present the evidence here in tabular form with minimal exegesis.

In the first of these (Table 3-6), item 1 summarizes the main figures of Kallmann's German (1938) and American (1946) studies best explained by a single recessive genetic mechanism of 70 percent penetrance. Tables 3-7 and 3-8 fill in the details as to disease expectancy in a wider range of blood relationship in respect of the 1938 and 1946 studies. Table 3-9 reflects variations in schizophrenia rates for siblings and twin partners according to sex and similarity or dissimilarity in environment. One feature meriting special comment is the difference in concordance rates for separated and nonseparated monozygotic co-twins of 77.6 percent as compared with 91.5 percent. The difference of 13.9 percent argues that some allowance should be accorded to environmental factors in the precipitation of a schizophrenic psychosis, but its relatively small weight is seen in its true proportions if we contrast this difference with the difference in con-

TABLE 3-10   FREQUENCY OF SCHIZOPHRENIA IN SIBLINGS, PARENTS, AND CHILDREN OF SCHIZOPHRENICS, (ADAPTED FROM KALLMANN, 1938, P. 160)

	Probability of Schizophrenia in Proband Siblings					Probability of Schizophrenia in Children of Schizophrenics	
	Both Parents Non-psychotic, Percent	One Parent Schizo-phrenic or Suspicious of Schizo-phrenia, Percent	Mother Definitely Schizo-phrenic, Father Schizoid or Only Germinally Affected, Percent	One Parent Schizo-phrenic or Suspicious of Schizo-phrenia, the Other Schizoid, Percent	Frequency of Schizo-phrenia in Parents of Schizo-phrenics, Percent	One Parent Schizo-phrenic, the Other Suspicious of Schizo-phrenia, Percent	Both Parents Definitely Schizo-phrenic, Percent
Siblings of Luxen-burger's material of schizophrenic twins	11.4	16.7			16.1		
Siblings of Schulz's and Kahn's schizo-phrenic probands	8.1	11.7					53
Kallmann's material	9.1	14.8	23.9	23.3	10.4	63.4	68.1

cordance rates between monozygotic and dizygotic schizophrenic co-twins of 86.2 percent and 14.5 percent, that is, 71.7 percent, and the essential similarity of the sibling and dizygotic twin figures of 14.2 percent and 14.5 percent, respectively. Table 3-10 reflects the frequency of schizophrenia for various parental combinations in siblings and children of schizophrenics: the findings of Luxenburger (1930), Schulz (1936), Kahn (1923 and Kallmann agree in showing an upward trend with the increased potential genetic loading of the parental combinations. In Tables 3-11 and 3-12 the twin concordance figures of Slater from his British study (1953) and the expectancy figures of Garrone from his Geneva study (1962) are shown to be in close agreement with Kallmann's own. *Particularly impressive is Garrone's well-nigh complete agreement with Kallmann in his formulation of the genetic mechanism involved,* namely, *single recessive autosomal of 67 percent penetrancy.*

Finally, Table 3-13 summarizes schizophrenic twin studies.

Returning to Table 3-10, the reader's attention is directed to the expectancy rates of schizoid

TABLE 3-11   TWIN CONCORDANCE FIGURES (SLATER, 1953)

DZ Twins (41 pairs)	MZ Twins (115 pairs)
14%	76%

personality, the clinical importance of which in the psychiatry of childhood and adolescence has already been stressed. Genetically, the clinical phenomenon may be interpreted in terms of the penetrance of a single imperfectly recessive gene against the background of weak polygenic constitutional modifiers, or the frustrated, partial expression of two recessive schizophrenic genes against the background of strong polygenic constitutional modifiers. A detailed discussion of the role of mesomorphic and ectomorphic constitutional factors and their postulated polygenic substrate in the production of less and more severe degrees of clinical expression of schizophrenia (Kallmann's nuclear and peripheral groups) falls beyond the scope of the present chapter. With regard to schizoid personality itself, however, it is of interest to note from the genetic viewpoint in the monozygotic twin category that the figure takes care of the apparent shortfall from a 100 percent concordance. From a clinical viewpoint, moreover, the considerably higher incidence, as compared with the frank psychosis itself, in several categories of blood relationship indicates the magnitude of the problem of maladjustment, in both individual and sociological terms, referable to this source. Item 3, tuberculosis, item 5, involutional psy-

chosis, and item 9, early total deafness, in Table 3-6, have only oblique reference to the schizophrenic theme—tuberculosis, because of the original belief as to a gene coupling with schizophrenia and the more recent demonstration as to a parallel in constitutional resistance mechanisms; involutional psychosis, because of Kallmann's demonstration of its closer genetic affinity with schizophrenia than with manic-depressive psychosis; and early total deafness, because of the demonstration by Kallmann's team of the primacy of the genetic over the psychogenic isolation-withdrawal factor in the etiology of schizophrenia occurring in this group.

Childhood schizophrenia. The only item that we may single out for detailed description in our present context, however, is item 2 in Table 3-6, namely, childhood schizophrenia, and more particularly Kallmann and Roth's paper on the genetic aspects of preadolescent schizophrenia (1956). One fails to see why Cowie (1965) finds it "not easy to go all the way with Kallmann and Roth in their views" and claims, without stating them, "that there are reasons for regarding both the schizophrenias of adult life and the schizophrenias of childhood, as being each of them heterogeneous groups." It is my belief that

TABLE 3-12 EXPECTANCY FIGURES (GARRONE, 1962)

| General Population | | | | Siblings | | | | | | |
| | | | | | | Parental Combinations | | Offspring of Propositi | Relatives of Propositi | |
Crude	Male	Female	Total	Total	Both Healthy	One Schizophrenic	Double Propositus			Mechanism
1%	1.9%	2.9%	2.4%	14.7 ± 1.3%	13.5 ± 1.3%	28.5 ± 5%	11.9 ± 1.7%	17 ± 4%	7 ± 2%	Single recessive of 67% homozygous penetrance; frequency in Geneva population, 19%

TABLE 3-13 SUMMARY OF TWIN STUDIES OF SCHIZOPHRENIA (AFTER GOTTESMAN & SHIELDS, 1966)

Investigator	Country	Concordance				Sampling				Is Severity Related to Concordance?	Sex with Higher Concordance	Sample Sex Surplus	Hospital vs. Author Diagnosis	Blood and/or Fingerprints in Zyg. Dx.
		MZ Pairs	Per cent	DZ SS Pairs	Per cent	DZ OS Pairs	Per cent	Resident vs. Con-sec. Admit.	Long Stay vs. Short Stay					
Kallmann:														
Preadolescent (1956)	U.S.	15/17	88	8/35*	23	*		R + C	L	?	?	M	A	Yes
Adult (1946)	U.S.	120/174	69	34/296	11	13/221	6	R + C	L	Yes	Neither	F	A	No
Slater (1953)	U.K.													
Resident sample		17/26	65	4/35	11	0/36	0	R	L	Yes	F	F	A	Yes
Consecutive sample		7/11	64	4/25	16	2/18	11	C	L	Yes	Neither	Neither	A	Yes
Essen-Möller (1941)	Sweden	7/11†	64	4/27†	15			C	L	No	Neither	Neither	A	Yes
Rosanoff (1934)	U.S.	25/41	61	7/53	13	3/48	6	R	L + S?	?	F	F	A	Yes
Inouye (1961)	Japan	33/55	60	2/11	18	0/6	0	R + C	L + S	Yes	Neither	F	A	Yes
Luxenburger (1928)	Germany	11/13	58	0/13	0	0/20	0	R + C	L	Yes?	Neither	Neither	A	No
Gottesman & Shields (1966)	U.K.	10/24	42	3/33	9			C	S	Yes	Neither	Neither	H	Yes
Harvald & Hauge (1965)	Denmark	2/7	29	2/31	6	1/28	4	Neither	n.a.	?	?	?	H	Yes
Kringlen (1964)	Norway	2/8	25	2/12	17			R + C	L	No	‡	‡	H	Yes
Tienari (1963)	Finland	0/16	0	0/16	0			Neither	n.a.	No	‡	‡	A	Yes

*DZ pairs not broken down by type and include OS pairs.
†Includes psychoses with schizophreniclike features and Kaij (1960) follow up. On other criteria MZ concordance ranges from 0 percent to 86 percent.
‡Neither Kringlen nor Tienari included female probands.

TABLE 3-14 CONCORDANCE AS TO SCHIZOPHRENIA AND SCHIZOID PERSONALITY (KALLMANN & ROTH, 1956)

	Number of Co-twins	Cases of Schizophrenia		Uncorrected Schizophrenia Rate		Expectancy Rate	
		Under Age 15	Age 15 and Over	Preadolescent Schizophrenia	Total Schizophrenia	Schizophrenia	Schizoid Personality
Present study (preadolescent cases)							
Dizygotic	35	6	2	17.1	22.9	22.9*	25.7†
Monozygotic	17	12	3	70.6	88.2	88.2*	11.8
Previous study (over age 15)							
Dizygotic	517	6	47	1.2	10.3	14.7	23.0
Monozygotic	174	8	112	4.6	69.0	85.8	20.7

* Without further age correction.
†Including five cases "suspected" of schizophrenia.

TABLE 3-15 MENTAL STATUS OF SIBS AND DIZYGOTIC CO-TWINS IN RELATION TO QUALITY OF THE PARENTAL HOME (KALLMANN & ROTH, 1956)

Siblings and Dizygotic Co-twins over Age 4*	Number of Persons, Percent		Adequate Home, Percent			Inadequate Home, Percent		
	Co-twins	Sibs	Good	Fair	Total	Broken	Poor	Total
Schizoid or schizophrenic	16	34	4.0	14.0	18.0	52.0	30.0	82.0
Asocial or retarded	1	16	5.9	5.9	11.8	29.4	58.8	88.2
Normal	18	107	10.4	24.8	35.2	28.0	36.8	64.8
Total	35	157	8.3	20.3	28.6	34.4	36.9	71.4

* Limited to cases with information available about mental status and parental home.

were Cowie to give detailed attention to the studies of Kallmann and others on the genetics of schizophrenia that we have reviewed and to note the parallel of the figures for preadolescent schizophrenia in tables 2, 4, and 6 of their paper (their table 2 appears on page 89 as Table 3-14), she would be driven to seeing more than an analogy between the preadolescent and post-adolescent figures, while honoring the restraint of Kallmann and Roth in their manner of postulating the same mechanism for the two forms.

In passing, the reader's attention is drawn to the figures for schizoid personality appearing in Table 3-14 because of their special clinical importance in child psychiatry, already stressed.

In addition to the genetic twin-family data summarized in Table 3-14, the characteristics of the parental home were studied by Kallmann and Roth. We present the authors' own description of their investigation of this variable, with the relevant table (Table 3-15), and their own summary of the investigation as a whole, so that the reader may judge at firsthand the nature, nuances, and limitations (acknowledged by the authors) of their claim.

Parental home. The last set of variables which may play a part in precipitating an un-usually early onset of a schizophrenic process is related to the quality of the parental home (Table 3-15). In this analysis, we have a somewhat sim-plified and deliberately loaded scheme, com-bining socioeconomic and psychological criteria for classifying the parents' home as well as their personal adjustment. According to this scheme, only those homes have been classified as adequate which (1) appeared good or fair from a socio-economic standpoint; (2) were not "broken" as a result of desertion, divorce, or death of a parent; and (3) were maintained by two well-adjusted parents. The presence of one emotionally dis-turbed or socially inadequate parent was suffi-cient to place the home into the "poor" category, even if there was no economic distress. Since

the entire sample of parental homes includes no unit that has not given rise to an early schizo-phrenic process in at least one child—namely, the index case—a simple correlation between inadequacy of the home and severe childhood disorder developed in this setting can be tested in the present study only in relation to the ad-justive patterns of the sibs and dizygotic co-twins of the index cases. For obvious reasons, the analysis has been limited to family units with adequate information both about the mental status of parents, co-twins, and sibs and about the socioeconomic quality of their home. Un-fortunately, no adequate control data are avail-able on the families and homes of a comparable series of children, of the same age group and social stratification, not distinguished by an early case of schizophrenia in the family. This aspect of the present study has not been completed.

The tabulated data show that of all the homes investigated, 28.6 percent have been broadly classified as adequate, and 71.4 percent as in-adequate. The proportion of adequate homes is reduced to 18.0 percent for the co-twins and sibs diagnosed as schizoid or schizophrenic, and to 11.8 percent for those classified as asocial or mentally retarded. At face value, this part of the analysis indicates a rather close relationship between inadequate home and preadolescent maladjustment in general. In other words, sib-ships characterized by severe maladjustment in more than one child are not likely to come from adequate homes—a finding which is compatible with both genetic and environmental theories.

It is a truism that parents who are unable to establish a stable home or who fail in the up-bringing of well-adjusted children are often un-stable themselves, emotionally as well as socially. However, it is unlikely that the emotional dis-turbance of the parents stems from the inade-quacy of the home, nor can it be said that a poor home is certain to produce early schizophrenia in the children. The inadequacy of the home does not seem to be directly responsible for a preadolescent onset of schizophrenia, any more than an adequate home can be trusted to prevent it in vulnerable children.

This conclusion is supported by the finding that of those co-twins and sibs in the present sample who have been considered normal, only one-third (35.2 percent) have come from adequate homes, and nearly two-thirds (64.8 percent) from inadequate homes. The large proportion of normal sibs from inadequate homes and the more limited series of schizoid and schizophrenic sibs from adequate homes contradict the notion of a simple relationship between a good home and normal behavior or between a poor home and mental disorder. While broadly applicable to the formation of general adjustive patterns, these equations are apparently complicated in early schizophrenia by two factors still unidentified biochemically: (1) a gene-specific vulnerability to stress arising from ordinary environmental circumstances and (2) an apparently nonspecific impairment in the organization of those normal protective functions which bestow on many persons a relatively high degree of resistance to an unfavorable environment.

It seems that children who display schizophrenic personality changes at an early age are distinguished not only by a specific vulnerability factor in the enzymatic range but also by a general constitutional inability, or lowered ability, to control through compensatory activity this basic deficiency in the complex processes of growth and maturation. Why they fail to compensate for this maturational defect is still an unsolved problem. Studies in progress here and elsewhere are aimed at identifying the nature of this constitutional impairment. The investigative data available at this time may be summarized as follows:

1. In comparing the family backgrounds of preadolescent schizophrenia cases (fifty-two twins and fifty singletons under age 15) with those of a comparable adult sample (691 twin index cases), no significant intergroup differences have been found either with respect to twin concordance rates or with respect to the schizophrenia rates for the parents (12.5 percent and 9.2 percent) and sibs (12.2 percent and 14.3 percent) of the index cases. Fathers and mothers contribute equally to the parental schizophrenia rate, while two-egg and one-egg co-twins of schizophrenic index cases differ as much in concordance for preadolescent schizophrenia (17.1 percent and 70.6 percent) as they do with regard to adult schizophrenia (14.7 percent and 85.8 percent). These findings indicate an *early effect in childhood schizophrenia of the same genotype* (gene-specific, deficiency state) *assumed to be responsible for the basic symptoms of adult schizophrenia.* This conclusion is supported by the observation that the psychoses in the co-twins of early schizophrenia cases occur sometimes before and sometimes after adolescence.

2. While the etiologic mechanism underlying the relatively infrequent activation of a schizophrenic psychosis before adolescence has not yet been adequately identified, it would seem to be connected with variable constellations of secondary factors lowering constitutional resistance. There appears to be an increase in the number of early schizophrenia cases among the co-twins and sibs of early index cases, and there is a definite excess of males over females in the preadolescent group. Theories attempting to explain either finding on nonbiological grounds lack substantiation.

3. Because of a dearth of statistically comparable data, it is difficult to appraise the part played by a poor home with disturbed intrafamily relationships in the etiology of childhood schizophrenia as compared with that of adult schizophrenia. It is certain only that there is no simple correlation between inadequacy of the parental home and a preadolescent onset of

schizophrenia and that a late onset of the disease is not always associated with favorable home conditions in childhood. In the present study, 71.4 percent of the homes of all sibs and dizygotic co-twins and 82 percent of the homes of co-twins and sibs diagnosed as schizoid or schizophrenic have been broadly classified as inadequate. In evaluating this finding, it is necessary to bear in mind, however, that of all the normal co-twins and sibs, nearly two-thirds (64.8 percent) have come from an inadequate home identified with the development of schizophrenic phenomena in the index case.

4. Since an adequate home cannot be expected either to preclude an early onset of schizophrenia in especially vulnerable children or to be easily established in the presence of emotionally unstable parents, the need for systematic and intensified research into the genetic aspects of both preadolescent and adult forms of schizophrenia remains a major challenge to our discipline.

Early infantile autism. Having become impressed with the frequency with which twins with autism were being reported, Rimland (1963) attempted to tabulate all cases of probable autism in the literature involving multiple births, as follows:

1. Kallmann, Barrera, and Metzger (1940)—identical twin boys
2. Sherwin (1953)—identical twin boys
3. Bakwin (1954)—identical twin boys
4. Eisenberg and Kanner (1956)—one autistic and one who died too early in infancy to assess whether it was autistic; zygosity undetermined
5. Keeler (1957)—dizygotic, discordant
6. Chapman (1957)—identical twin girls
7. Lehman, Haber, and Lesser (1957)—identical twin boys
8. Keeler (1958)—blind twins (presumed boys)
9. Polan and Spencer (1959)—identical twin boys

10. Bruch (1959)—Negro boys—identical twins
11. Chapman (1960)—two additional sets of identical twins
12. Keeler (1960)—identical twins; sex not stated
13. Ward & Hoddinott (1962)—concordant fraternal twin girls

Rimland, in his use of the term *identical* in an unqualified fashion, implies that identical twins are both monozygotic and concordant.

He comments that the finding of at least eleven sets of monozygotic twins all concordant for infantile autism seems highly significant in terms of the biological etiology of the disease. Of the three dizygotic pairs, one is concordant, another discordant, and the third undetermined.

With regard to family data, Rimland is impressed that the "parents and grandparents of autistic children show a strikingly low incidence of mental illness." Out of 200 parents there was only one case of psychosis (a postpartum depression), and siblings tended to be in good mental health. Both these findings are in marked contrast with the high figures cited in the study of Kallmann and Roth (1956) and with those quoted by Bender in her papers on childhood schizophrenia (1953, 1955, 1956).

Commenting on this, Rimland (1963, p. 75) states: "Writers who attempt to equate autism with schizophrenia find themselves with a discomforting lack of overt schizophrenia in the parents and families of autistic children." He explodes the attempted explanation of this finding on the basis of parents' being merely schizoid or near-psychotic and hence escaping hospitalization and detection.

To sum up, Rimland's argument favors a genetic basis for infantile autism, but argues that schizophrenia is a different clinical entity with a different genetic basis.

Rimland has done us the service of paving the way for a comprehensive twin-family study in the field of infantile autism.

Manic-depressive psychosis. As already indicated, manic-depressive psychosis ranks as very inferior in importance to schizophrenia in the ambit of child and adolescent psychiatry, albeit the underlying personality can make larger claims than the frank manic-depressive psychotic reaction.

Under these circumstances it will suffice here to draw attention briefly to Tables 3-16 and 3-17 and item 4 in Table 3-6.

The Slater and Kallmann's twin studies agree in showing 100 percent concordance for the psychosis in monozygotic twins and approximately 25 percent for dizygotic twins, with the sibling figure very close to it (2 to 3 percent less). For the cycloid personality type in Kretschmer's sense (showing mood swings, greater than the cyclothyme, but not to the degree of frank psychosis), Table 3-16 provides an indication as to the additional percentage in each category where the manic-depressive genotype is present but where full psychotic expression is presumed to be inhibited by polygenic constitutional modifiers. (For details of this constitutional mechanism and associated components of physique, the reader is referred to Kallmann, 1954.) Combining the evidence in Tables 3-16 and 3-17, the mechanism is best explained as being a single autosomal dominant one, of 50 percent penetrancy when disregarding, but of 90 percent penetrancy when including, the cycloid personality types.

Neurological Conditions

I should like to commence this section by indicating general perspectives that have come from the application of genetic principles and insights to neurology. First, the fundamental etiology of a long list of neurological conditions has been established by demonstrating them as being due to single dominant, single recessive, or sex-linked genetic mechanisms. Second, examining the constellation and varying prominence of the signs and symptoms in stated neurological syndromes, in the light of the genetic concepts of *penetrancy* and *expressivity,* makes these more understandable and *diagnosable* and also shows that cases with only a fraction of the total symptomatology are classifiable with the more fully fledged syndromes, the missing features being explicable in terms of deficient penetrancy. And, finally, the now fully recognized fact of the chemical basis of all single-factor genetic mechanisms, such as underlie a long list of neurological disorders, has brought a *reasoned hope of reversibility and cure* in an area hitherto regarded as chronic and without hope.

In summary, there are three main types of genetic mechanisms that may be implicated in neurological disorders—the single dominant, the single recessive, and the sex-linked. Although one of these may be characteristic of a particular neurological disorder, we may find two or all three of these mechanisms in different pedigrees of the same disease, e.g., in Friedreich's ataxia.

The following list gives a picture of the type of mechanisms characteristic of certain of the more common neurological conditions:

1. *Usually single-dominant syndromes.* Marie's heredocerebellar ataxia; status dysrhaphicus (syringomyelia); hereditary essential tremor;

TABLE 3-16 COMPARABLE EXPECTANCY RATES IN MANIC-DEPRESSIVE INDEX SIBSHIPS

| | Siblings | | Co-twins | |
	Half	Full	Dizygotic	Monozygotic
Schulz		14.3–26.1*		
Slater		22.9	24.0	100.0
Kallmann	16.7	22.7	25.5	100.0

*With normal and abnormal parents, respectively.

TABLE 3-17   FREQUENCY OF CYCLOID PERSONALITY TYPES (EMOTIONAL INSTABILITY) IN MANIC-DEPRESSIVE INDEX FAMILY UNITS (HOCH & ZUBIN, 1954, PP. 6–7)

	General Population	Parents	Siblings	Children	*Relatives of Manic-depressive Index Cases* Dizygotic Co-twins	Monozygotic Co-twins
Luxenburger-Schulz et al.	0.8	12.2	18.8	13.4		
Banse-Hoffmann		5.0	2.7	14.4		
Entres-Röll et al.	0.7	1.8		6.1		
Slater				13.4		
Kallmann	0.7	14.5	12.9		30.9	3.7

congenital cataract, glaucoma, and bilateral ptosis; hereditary nerve deafness; paralysis agitans; Thomsen's myotonia congenita; familial periodic paralysis; and some forms of muscular atrophy (Charcot-Marie).

2. *Usually single-recessive syndromes.* Friedreich's ataxia (spinal form); Wilson-Wesfal's pseudosclerosis (progressive lenticular degeneration); microphthalmia; deaf-mutism (hereditary type); most forms of muscular atrophy (Dejerine-Motta) and muscular dystrophy (Duchenne-Erb); and spastic spinal paralysis.

3. *Usually sex-linked syndromes.* Leber's primary optic atrophy; retinitis pigmentosa; hemophilia; and familial eunuchoidism associated with anosmia, color blindness, and mental defect.

It would be out of place to deal comprehensively here with the field of neurological genetics, as our central theme focuses on the handicaps and crippling resulting from these conditions in children and adolescents. For details the reader is referred to the reviews in the 1953 *Proceedings of the Association for Research in Nervous Disease* (the main contributors are Tyler on muscular dystrophies and neurol atrophies, Schut on the

hereditary ataxias, Herndon on the lipidoses, and Goodell et al. on migraine), to Haberlandt and Glanville (1962), and to Hurst (1958, 1961, 1962, & 1964).

Developmental Malformations

The Second Report of the WHO Expert Committee on Human Genetics (1964, p. 11) provides the following general perspective:

Of the variety of conditions known as congenital malformations, for which the mode of inheritance is not yet well understood, some few may perhaps be due to differences in *single chromosomes* or *genes*. Evidence is accumulating, however, that with some others the genetic basis may be *multifactorial*. Maternal health and intra-uterine environment appear to play a considerable part in determining the likelihood of occurrence of these anomalies. There is also some familial concentration, greater than would occur by chance, but seldom sufficient to satisfy the criteria for single gene differences. The frequency of these traits has been estimated to be 1.5% of the live-born, the figure being higher if still births are included. An additional 1% of affected children can be detected at the age of 5 years.

We have already reviewed the known chromosomal instances of developmental malformations with gross physical manifestations and severe mental defect. Reed (1963) has brought together a number of other developmental malformations of which we select central nervous system syndrome, congenital dislocation of the hip, harelip and cleft palate, clubfoot, and congenital heart disease as exemplifying handicaps bringing gross problems of adjustment in their wake, quite apart from the contribution of congenital malformations to infant mortality (10 to 20 percent of all deaths of infants under 1 year of age in Minnesota being due to this, according to Reed).

Central nervous system syndrome. Analyzing the studies of Record and McKeown (1949, 1950) and of Roberts (1962) on anencephaly and hydrocephaly in association with spina bifida, Reed surmises that spina bifida occulta may represent the heterozygous condition, while the homozygous state results in spina bifida aperta and other manifestations of the central nervous syndrome. Edwards (1961) found a few families in which hydrocephalus behaved as a strictly sex-linked trait (one individual family pedigree displaying fifteen affected males). Reed comments that the anomalies shown in these families are not typical of the mass of cases with the central nervous system syndrome and that they indicate the heterogeneity one should expect with common malformations. He assesses the chance of repetition of parents producing a living child with some aspect of the central nervous system syndrome at only 3 percent, but the chance of a miscarriage or still birth at each successive pregnancy as approaching 25 percent. More conceptions are lost because of these central nervous system syndromes than from erythroblastosis.

Congenital dislocation of the hip. Idelberger (1951), in an extensive sample, has found a ratio of 1 boy to 5.4 girls affected. In a small twin sample the concordance rates for monozygotic and dizygotic twins were 42 percent and 2.7 per-

cent, respectively, arguing a substantial genetic factor. Record and Edwards's study (1958) provides evidence that the morbidity risk is 3.6 percent where the patients were boys and 5.2 percent where the patients were girls. Reed (1963, p. 106) summarizes the position as follows:

> The chance of having a second child with dislocation of the hip is about 5 percent at each subsequent pregnancy. Presumably a person with acetabular dysplasia might expect to have 5% of his children affected. If the child is a girl, the chances that she will be affected are about six times as great as those for a boy. If the family history of either member of a married couple gives evidence of dislocated hip, then the girl babies, at least, should be examined radiographically for possible acetabular dysplasia.

Harelip and cleft palate. Metrakos, Metrakos, and Baxter (1958) sifted the twin literature, added ten pairs of their own, and for harelip with or without cleft palate found concordance rates of 42 percent and 5 percent for monozygotic and dizygotic twins, respectively.

The classic paper on cleft lip and palate in man is that of Fogh-Andersen (1943). The empirical risk estimates derived from it are as follows: If one parent is affected and has had an affected child, the risk for each subsequent child is about 16 percent. If neither parent is affected, the risk subsequent to the propositus is about 7 percent. In Reed's experience unions resulting in affected children are typically between one affected and one normal-appearing person. Moreover, Fogh-Andersen found a low percentage of affected children from an affected parent, probably indicating that few of the spouses of the affected persons carried the various recessive genes necessary for the appearance of the trait. Roberts (1962) similarly found only 3.3 percent of affected children in a large series with one affected parent.

The typical counseling problem will concern normal-appearing parents who have had a child with cleft lip and are anxious to learn what their risk is for each future pregnancy. This is of the order of 7 to 10 percent.

Clubfoot. In a small twin sample, Böök (1948) found a 32 percent concordance for monozygotic in contrast to a 3 percent concordance in dizygotic twins. Stewart's study (1951) showed a remarkable difference in relative frequencies of clubfoot, congenital dislocation of the hip, and harelip and cleft palate in the different ethnic groups that make up Hawaii due to different gene frequencies for these three defects. The data indicated that the genetic background for clubfoot is what might be called "subrecessive." A single pair of genes alone is insufficient to produce the abnormality; one or more pairs of other genes are necessary for maximal expression of the character.

Clinically, clubfoot refers to a host of abnormalities of the foot, and it may also be part of another syndrome (e.g., paraplegia). We can nevertheless venture an empirical risk figure on the basis of Böök's study (1948), which included data from three physicians—Fretscher, Isigkert, and Assum (1936). If parents are unaffected and already have a child with congenital clubfoot, the mean risk that the following children will be affected is 3 percent. In Assum's own study (1936), which Reed thinks contains the least statistical bias of the studies of the three physicians mentioned, 8 percent of children born after the propositi had clubfoot. The empirical risk figure may therefore be given as lying between 3 and 8 percent.

Congenital heart disease. McKeown, MacMahon, and Parsons (1953) showed a significant excess of cases of congenital heart disease among the brothers and sisters of the original cases. The risk of only 1.8 percent of a second case in the sibship is helpful in genetic counseling. Anderson (1954) found a risk figure of 1.4 percent for patent ductus arteriosus, which is about five times random expectation, in a fair-sized family study. The four twin pairs included in it were all discordant. Polani and Campbell's study (1960) confirmed the raised incidence of congenital heart disease in the siblings of affected cases.

The role of chromosomal anomalies in cardiac malformations merits further exploration in view of those occurring in Down's syndrome and a study of Böök, Santesson, and Zetterquist (1961), in which an atrial septal defect was found to be associated with an extra chromosome of the 19/20 group.

Communication Handicaps

Communication handicaps in childhood in the areas of hearing, vision, reading, and speech (stuttering or stammering) and the maladjustive psychological repercussions they engender have been adumbrated in the introduction to this chapter. It is now our task to spell out the genetic details in the four clinical areas mentioned.

Deafness. Early total deafness is the variant of special concern to us in the area of child psychopathology and was a central emphasis in the mammoth project for the deaf of the Department of Medical Genetics of the New York State Psychiatric Institute, Columbia University (Rainer & Altshuler, 1966; Rainer, Altshuler, & Kallmann, 1963 Altshuler & Sarlin, 1962) and with many substantial contributions from Sank and Deming. It is not our function here to trace the burgeoning of the statewide investigation of the causes of deafness into the comprehensive mental health services for the deaf, with individual, sexual, marriage, family, education, employment, and hospital aspects, which is reflected in the volume edited by Rainer and Altshuler (1966). Our aim is rather to summarize the genetic aspect (in interrelationship with the individual psychological-psychiatric aspect where they intersect). One of these points of intersection is dealt with by Altshuler and Sarlin (1962). The New York deafness study, as they indicate, comprises a statewide census of deaf schizophrenics, combined with a computation of schizophrenia risk figures for their siblings and parents. Early total deafness was chosen as an additional criterion for the ascertainment of schizophrenic index cases because it imposes unusually stressful and disruptive conditions on childhood development and later life. These stresses include disturbed and distorted communication, developmental imbalances, and marked disorder of parent-child relationships. Here we have an ideal situation for the assessment of the relative roles of a genetic vulnerability factor and nongenetic influences in the molding of life processes in schizophrenia. The net result of the study was that sibship consanguinity to a schizophrenic person results in the expected marked increase in morbidity risk, whether or not there is a perceptual defect in the index case or relative. In other words, *the schizophrenic genetic factor is the significant one, and the severe and varied stresses associated with early total deafness apparently do little to increase the chance of developing clinical symptoms of schizophrenia* (Table 3-18). However, a pathoplastic coloring effect in the schizo-

phrenic symptomatology is observed, for as Altshuler and Rainer (1963) show, an undue prominence of behavior disturbance and, contrary to popular expectation, a tendency to be overly trusting and not suspicious and paranoid characterizes the deaf schizophrenic.

The genetic aspects of early total deafness per se in the New York State census were dealt with by Sank (1962, 1963). The population survey (sampled by mail questionnaire) established that about one-half of the deaf population of New York were *sporadic* cases, appearing to be due to *exogenous causes, complicated modes of inheritance,* or *new genetic mutations.* *Dominant genes* accounted for only 10 percent of all deafness. Professor Howard Levene's analysis revealed an average penetrancy of only 50 percent, as against the nearly complete penetrancy reported for an earlier study of deafness in Northern Ireland (Chung, Robison, & Morton, 1959; Stevenson & Cheeseman, 1956). The remaining cases were *autosomal recessive. High parental cousin-marriage* rates (12 percent) provided strong evidence of the preponderance of a *recessive genetic mechanism* in early total deafness in the population of the state of New

TABLE 3-18   SCHIZOPHRENIC RISK DATA FOR SIBLINGS OF DEAF AND HEARING SCHIZOPHRENICS (ADAPTED FROM RAINER ET. AL., 1963, P. 211)

	Number of Siblings				
	Surviving Age 15	**Definitely Schizophrenic**	**Corrected Frame of Reference**	**Crude Risk, Percent**	**Corrected Risk, Percent**
Of deaf index cases:					
Hearing siblings	303	25	223	8.3	11.2
Deaf siblings*	28	3	19	10.7	15.8
Total	331	28	242	8.5	11.6†
Of hearing index cases (Kallmann, 1946)	2014	184	1288	9.14	14.3

*Includes seven cases with marked hearing loss.
†14.1 percent if probable cases are included.

York. There was further evidence of *many different* recessive genes (upward of forty-five in the gene pool of the population) implicated in this condition.

In summary, we may point to the vast field for clinical psychological study presented by the variable patterns of adjustment in the deaf.

Blindness. The blind offer no less of an opportunity and clinical challenge. The problems of adjustment of the blind are perhaps more widely appreciated and empathized than those of the deaf, and although we have no scientific project comparable with that of the Columbia group for the deaf, which we have barely sampled, the work by Lowenfeld (1956) drives home the human and organizational aspects.

Ophthalmology is particulary rich in genetic research. Waardenburg, Franceschetti, and Klein's two massive tomes (1961–1963) bear eloquent testimony to this fact. We cannot hope to convey the whole riches of this work in the compass of our present chapter, and in lieu of this we supply a brief list of conditions in which the mutation rates as well as the mode of inheritance have been worked out (Table 3-19). Careful scrutiny of the index of this work reveals that there is *not a portion of the eye and its appendages that does not have its genetic diseases, with a total heavy toll of blindness.*

Dyslexia. It is only comparatively recently that the high prevalence of specific dyslexia and the havoc it wreaks on the schoolchild and his educational progress have been recognized. The publication of B. Hallgren's monograph on specific dyslexia (congenital word blindness) (1950) has contributed its mead to the growing enlightenment on the subject. He studied 276 cases, of whom 116 were probands and 160 were secondary cases (sibs and parents of probands). The probands were derived from the Stockholm Child Guidance Clinic and could not be regarded as a random sample of the normal population, as Hallgren was first to point out. The *general-population figure* he estimated as *high as 10 percent* on the basis of a study of consecutive children in a school sample. These data were compatible with a *single autosomal genetic explanation,* and he could find no association with left-handedness or environmental psychological factors such as broken homes. In certain individual cases, however, he could not entirely exclude the contribution of adverse environmental influences to the child's inability to read and write. The *recognition of the single dominant genetic* basis of this widespread disability is a *potential help in recognizing the reason for school failure* in offspring of a parent who can retrospectively be judged as having had a similar handicap in his or her own childhood.

Stuttering. The earlier genetic studies in the field, notably those of Wepman (1935) and West (1943), while providing valuable pointers, fell down on the sides of methods of selection and absence of modern genetic statistical techniques.

Andrews and Harris (1964) have more recently presented us with a sophisticated study. Part of the study conducted by Kay and Garside was a family investigation of two groups, A and B, together referred to as the "clinic cases." Group A consisted of eighty-three children seen in the Speech Therapy Clinic during the period 1950 to 1953—sixty-five boy and eighteen girl probands, with a mean age of 6 years and a range of 2 to 14 years. Group B consisted of fifty-two cases, comprising all the adolescent and adult stutterers under treatment at the clinic during 1963. After a detailed review of possible genetic mechanism, they provide the following conclusions and summary:

1. In both sexes the risk of stuttering among the first-degree relatives of probands was three to four times higher than the risk in the general population.

TABLE 3-19 MUTATION RATES ESTIMATED FOR DISORDERS OF OPHTHALMOLOGICAL INTEREST (WAARDENBURG, FRANCESCHETTI, & KLEIN, 1961, P. 129)

Condition	Mode of Inheritance	Mutation Rate per Million Genes per Generation	Method	Region	Source
Epiloia (tuberous sclerosis)	D	4–8	Direct	England	Gunther and Penrose (1935, 1936)
	D	14	Direct	England	Philip and Sorsby (1949; unpublished, quoted by Haldane, 1949)
		23	Direct	U.S.	Neel and Falls (1951)
		6–7		Southern Germany	Vogel (1957)
Aniridia	D	10	Direct	Denmark	Mollenbach (1947)
Marfan's syndrome	D	4.2–5.8		Northern Ireland	Lynas (1958)
Interocular hypoplasia; hypo-chromatism of iris and hair; deafness	D	3.7	Direct	Netherlands	Waardenburg (1951)
Neurofibromatosis	D	100 130–250 80–100	Direct (indirect)	U.S. (Michigan)	Crowe, Neel, and Schull (1956)
Myotonic dystrophy	D	5		Northern Ireland	Lynas (1957)
Infantile amaurotic idiocy	R	11		Japan	Neel et al. (1949)
Congenital ichthyosis	R	11		Japan	Neel et al. (1949)
General albinism	R	28		Japan	Neel et al. (1949)
Achromatopsia	R	28		Japan	Neel et al. (1949)
Congenital amaurosis (Leber)	R	23		Sweden	Alström and Olsen (1957)
Microphthalmia or anophthalmia with oligophrenia	Gonos. (X and Y) R?	10–20	Direct	Sweden	Sjögren and Larson (1949)
Microphthalmia or anophthalmia without oligophrenia	Gonos. (X and Y) or Autos. D	5 or considerably more	Direct	Sweden	Sjögren and Larson (1949)

Since it is difficult to account for this increase in risk through the operation of nongenetic factors alone, a genetic explanation is preferred for the familial cases. Nonspecific environmental factors, such as low intelligence, social incompetence, or anxiety-proneness among the mothers, may, however, bring to light a latent predisposition to stutter. Among the nonfamilial cases, an unknown proportion may be wholly acquired.

2. The altered sex ratio among stutterers is compatible with sex limitation because of the action of modifying genes. It is pointed out that sex differences (in addition to purely genital ones) exist in children and that girls show relatively greater physiological maturity at all ages. The ease with which speech functions are acquired may be related to this.

3. The sex of the probands affects the risk of stuttering among the relatives. *The highest risk occurs among the male relatives of female stutterers, and the lowest among the female relatives of male stutterers.* An analogy with stature is drawn.

4. Simple monogenic inheritance does not account for the data unless a reduction in rate of manifestation of very marked degree is assumed. This virtually excludes recessive inheritance. *Transmission by a common dominant gene with a multifactorial background appears to be a reasonable hypothesis. Alternatively,* inheritance may be *wholly polygenic.* In either case sex limitation operates. It is impossible to decide between these two alternatives at the present time.

I trust that our survey of four important clinical conditions of childhood and adolescence involving communication handicaps, with their heavy genetic loading, may serve to indicate the *paramount importance of a knowledge of genetic principles to the child clinician in the evaluation of the individual, family, and eventually marriage problems of his young patients.*

CONTROVERSIAL ISSUES

The controversial issues, with which this field bristles, come to focus in schizophrenia, with its rival genetic and nongenetic interpretations. Moreover, they do so in a far richer, more detailed, and more multifaceted fashion than anywhere else. It is for this reason that we take the ideological battlefield of schizophrenia as our paradigm.

At the outset I should like to emphasize that differences of opinion as to the *nature* of the genetic mechanism in schizophrenia are decidedly compatible with substantial agreement as to the *fact* of its existence. Thus protagonists of the single-recessive hypothesis (Kallmann and Garrone), the single-dominance theory of partial expression (Slater and Böök), and two-factor or multiple-factor views (Karlsson, Burch, and Penrose) are foursquare as to the paramount significance of the genetic factor in the etiology of this condition.

It is nonetheless important to recognize that this genetic factor in etiology is eminently compatible with psychological interpretations, psychoanalytic or behavioristic, and with the Chicago and New Haven sociological findings—enriching them with new orienting insights.

The karyotype studies of Money and Hirsch (1963), Raphael and Shaw (1963), and Tedeschi and Freeman (1962) show that in schizophrenia, interpretations of etiology in terms of chromosomes are highly unlikely to oust the explanation on the basis of genes, as has happened, for example, in the case of Down's syndrome (Mongolism). Sonneborn's philosophy, already quoted, applies.

The dominance-recessiveness issue, which at one time presented the facade of a harsh dichotomy, has now assumed a far milder guise, in the light of biochemical advance. Moreover, as Roberts (1959) has explained in evolutionary perspective, a mutant gene diverges from intermediacy to recessiveness or dominance, as generation succeeds generation, according to its advantageousness or the reverse. It is compatible with this position that we find dominant and recessive instances, and these of varying degrees of manifestation, in different cases of the same hereditary pathological condition.

The concept of genetic morphism links up with Roberts's hypothesis. Sir Julian Huxley, Prof. Ernst Mayr, Dr. Humphrey Osmond, and Prof. Abram Hoffer have propounded in *Nature* (1964) that schizophrenia is such a genetic morphism: "All genetic characters which exist in a population at a higher frequency than can be maintained by mutation alone involve morphism; the frequency of a morphic gene is the result of a balance between its selectively favorable and unfavorable properties."

Validity of Genetic Principles and Studies Cited

In view of criticisms of geneticists (e.g., Stern, Harvald and Hauge [see below]) and others (e.g., directly and by implication in the writings of Lidz (1958), Meehl (1962), Pastore (1949), and Rosenthal (1961) and in the work edited by Jackson, [1960]) of certain basic principles and assumptions of human genetics (e.g., the inference that may correctly be drawn from twin studies) and the design of specific studies in the field (e.g., bias, sampling, and diagnosis), it is necessary for us to take stock of these matters now to apprise ourselves of the soundness of the foundation upon which we are raising our theoretical structure.

Twin-study Ideology

Stern (1960) and Harvald and Hauge (1965) see as the main objection to the classical twin method the untenability of equating the environments of identical and nonidentical twins in comparisons between them. Objection is also raised to the partitioning of heredity and environment, and formulas are evolved for characterizing the relative strength of genetic and environmental factors (in interaction). Stern indicates that "These critical considerations are not intended to discredit the importance of twin investigations." They not only show that—as so often happens—a problem initially believed to be simple has turned out complex, but also suggest additional methods of approaching the problem of nature and nurture.

Slater (1953, p. 6), referring to this criticism, states: "It is sometimes assumed that any similarities shown by uniovular twins can be attributed to heredity, any differences to environment, but only the latter half of this assumption can be safely held. From this, however, it does not follow that deductions about the importance of heredity in causing some characteristic cannot be based on the examination of a series of uniovular twins, provided that there is no biased selection and that controls e.g., binovular twins are available." He also makes the point, universally accepted, that ". . . one cannot hope to derive any information from twin studies about the mode of inheritance of a psychiatric abnormality—a pair of uniovular twins are alike not only in respect of any specific gene but also in their entire genetic make-up" (p. 7).

Kallmann has also given minute attention to controversies concerning legitimate inferences from twin studies and has drawn attention to the point make by Darlington that discordance between monozygotic twins is not a measure merely of postnatal or even prenatal environmental effects: it may also have a genetic component through the action of genes sensitive to cytoplasmic asymmetry. Darlington (1964) develops his views on twin-study ideology, which maximizes the genetic weight to be attributed to concordance and minimizes that to be assigned to discordance:

Only one-egg twins which have split early and formed separate membranes should be taken as having nearly identical heredity and pre-natal environments as similar as those of two-egg twins. . . .

Twins are used to establish the contrast between

heredity and environment. And they do so correctly no doubt in ninety percent of cases. But the other ten percent represents, by a strange paradox, the one situation in human life where heredity and environment are not separable, for the process of their origin is external to each but internal to the two. . . .

In general these considerations show that the degree of resemblance found between one-egg twins is a minimum expression of the "influence of heredity," or, more strictly of the force of genetic determination. Where we do find differences in the rate of physical, mental and emotional development in one-egg twins, they are to be ascribed sometimes chiefly to errors in splitting of the egg.

Many who remember the storm of controversy raised by Bronson Price (1950) may see in this a neat turning of the tables.

Family Studies

We have noted that twin studies leave us with no clue as to the *mode* of inheritance. It is to family studies in combination with estimates of the frequency of the character and of cousin marriages in the general population that we turn for this. Slater itemizes estimates of frequency in various classes of relatives of persons suffering from the abnormality and in the children of special crosses of parents who both had the abnormality. Reverting to twin research, he states that it "makes a desirable contribution to all the data that are needed, but it can only supply one part and that not always an essential one."

Twin-family Studies

The case is quite the reverse when family data are incorporated into twin studies, as has been done so effectively by Newman, Kallmann, and Slater. "Kallmann," says Slater (1953), "also has emphasized the importance of combining twin work with family studies and this is the plan that has been followed in the present work." This procedure mutually potentiates the contributions from the twin and family sides of the study and also provides seven sibship categories, with variable degrees of similar genetic endowment for comparison: same-sex monozygotic twins, opposite sex monozygotic twins, same-sex dizygotic twins, opposite-sex dizygotic twins, sibs, half-sibs, and step-sibs.

Bias, Sampling, and Diagnosis

Garb (1964) has collected criticisms under the headings of "bias," "sampling," and "diagnosis" of studies upon which we shall be basing our theoretical deductions.

Bias. Relying partly on Rosenthal, Garb considers that training as or under physicians introduces the possibility of bias in diagnosis, a reductionist frame of mind, and a limited interpretation of findings. Kallmann and Slater are alleged not to have escaped here entirely, despite their efforts to systematize reporting procedures to keep errors and biasing factors low.

Sampling. Pastore's and Rosenthal's criticisms of the sampling procedures of Kallmann's two major studies of schizophrenia show poor acquaintance with the design actually followed by Kallmann, as I have already sought to indicate in my rejoinder to Pastore's (1949) article. It is true that Kallmann did not claim to have obtained a random sample of the general population, but one derived from the hospital population.

Slater, in *Clinical Genetics* (1953, p. 346), gives an objective evaluation covering the point at issue as follows:

Kallmann's contributions of a major kind are two-fold. He made a very extensive family survey (1938) covering the sibs, half-sibs, children and grandchildren, of 1,087 schizophrenic propositi, the study differing in a significant particular from similar studies that had been made before. In earlier studies of the children of schizophrenics, families were almost automatically taken in which there were known to be one or more children. This involved a degree of biased selection of the parents being automatically over-represented whose illness came on late or was so mild that reproduction could still occur after the illness had begun. Kallmann started from a hospital population, without knowledge whether there were children or not. This material contained a fairer selection of the graver forms of psychosis than had been obtained before. His second major contribution has been the collection and examination of a very large series from the New York State mental hospitals. A detailed study of the 794 schizophrenic twin pairs appeared in 1946, when 2,741 sibs as well as parents, consorts and other relatives had been investigated. The material was gathered by a systematic attempt to discover all the twins in a total mental hospital population of some 85,000 persons.

Another criticism under the heading of "sampling" and affecting all five major studies concerns the acceptability of zygosity determinations by the similarity method.

Diagnosis. Rosenthal stresses the point that ideally in studies involving two dichotomous variables, assessment of these should be made by independent investigators. In three of the five major twin studies of schizophrenia assessments were carried out by a single investigator. The edge of this criticism is considerably dulled when we read of the procedure in Kallmann's study as described by Slater (1953, p. 18): "The diagnostic classification was made only after a period of observation of five years or more: it was a common occurrence for patients, who on their first admission to hospital had been diagnosed as manic-depressives, to need, in the light of later developments, re-diagnosis as schizophrenic. Various types of reactive illness were also removed from the manic-depressive group." This thorough study over a prolonged period by a front-rank psychiatrist, who revised diagnoses where necessary in the light of repeated long-term observations, bespeaks the reliability of the diagnostic variable.

Conclusions as to the Validity of Genetic Studies of Schizophrenia

In the light of the above and the broad agreement of morbidity figures for twins, monozygotic and dizygotic, and other categories of first-degree relationship in the major studies, there can be no doubt of the significance of a genetic factor in schizophrenia, even though details as to the precise genetic mechanism are not agreed upon and constitute in large measure the rationale of the present discussion.

What Slater says in concluding his review of twin studies may be extended to family and twin-family studies in psychiatry and is important in providing general and historical perspective in this field (1953, p. 22).

> If therefore we look back over the development of investigations into psychiatric twin material, we see a progressive improvement in technique and range. Such studies have been conducted on a much greater scale in the field of mental disorder than in any other realm of human biology, and in spite of the difficulty of the work much has been learned that otherwise would have been unascertainable. Progress however, has revealed as many new problems as it has supplied partial solutions to old ones; and these must be solved, for one of the most important justifications of work of this kind is that it is a contribution to fundamental theory. We cannot come to any conclusions about the basic pathology of mental illness without taking genetical aspects into account; and the genetics of mental disorder may well in time provide the foundation for a reliable nosology.

GENETIC STUDIES OF SCHIZOPHRENIA
History and Introduction

Of historical interest are the pioneer works of Rüdin (1916), which showed an excessive amount of schizophrenic illness in the sibs of schizophrenics (interpreted by Weinberg [1927] as involving more than one gene); Luxenburger's 1930 systematic twin survey in psychiatry on schizophrenics, which he, however, was inclined to interpret in terms of a recessive autosomal genetic mechanism; and Lenz's (1929) espousal of dominance.

In 1934 Rosanoff, Handy, Plesset, and Brush published their findings on schizophrenic twins. They studied forty-one uniovular, fifty-three same-sex, and forty-eight opposite-sex binovular twin pairs and were impressed by the high concordance for biovular twins (10 percent), contrasting it with Humm's (1932) unreliable figure of 3 percent for sibs. For uniovular twins the concordance is 61 percent. The twin concordance rates agree with those of Slater and Kallmann as to the large discrepancy of monozygotic and dizygotic figures and a ratio of about 6 to 1. A special theory of Rosanoff's is that a large group of cases, predominantly male, seem to occur on a basis of partial "decerebration," mainly of traumatic infective origin, while a psychogenic precipitating factor appeared to him to be more common in women. He also gave attention to prenatal and intranatal factors which may be expected to affect pairs of binovular twins more frequently than pairs of sibs and to an apparently greater general and cerebral vulnerability in the male fetus and infant, which leads to a higher incidence in that sex.

Essen-Möller published his comprehensive Swedish investigations in 1941 and described his twenty-one uniovular pairs in detail. In the schizophrenic pairs included in this number he was impressed with the gross disparities in clinical features. Slater lists these differences under eleven headings. Essen-Möller's study regarding schizophrenia, small as it is, may, in the attention given to clinical detail, be regarded as a forerunner of Slater's own.

Of a special contemporary importance is Slater's (1953) sophisticated twin study (41 uni-

ovular and 115 binovular pairs). Consistent with his own and the generally accepted view that no deduction as to the nature of genetic mechanism can logically be derived from twin studies, he makes no inferences on this point from his own study, which, although it included family as well as twin data, did not do so at a level acceptable to Slater's critical sense for this special purpose.

A point of particular interest is that his concordance rates of 76 percent and 14 percent for uniovular and binovular twins approximated closely those of Kallmann. Among relatives of schizophrenic propositi, schizophrenic females outnumbered schizophrenic males by about 2 to 1. This appears to accord well with observation of Malzberg (1955) from New York State Hospital statistics, analyzed in a novel, significant manner by Burch (1964), as reported further on. As regards type of onset, specific and atypical clinical features, and course of the illness, interesting similarities were observed in related individuals, but not in outcome. A number of curious resemblances in the mode of precipitation were noted, but no figures were obtained which could be statistically tested.

Eiji Inouye (1961) has been influenced by the school of thought differentiating schizophrenia into "reactive" and "process" types and more specifically by Leonhard (1934) in his distinction between "typical" forms of schizophrenia, which take a progressive and malignant course, and "atypical" forms, with a better prognosis. A "blind" investigation that Leonhard, who handled the clinical data, had undertaken with Schulz (1936), who handled the genetics, disclosed incidences of schizophrenia in the parents of propositi of 1 percent and 6 percent, respectively, which suggested to them a preponderance of recessive types in the "typical" and of dominant types in the "atypical" clinical forms of schizophrenia. Inouye, in his study of seventy-two schizophrenic twin pairs, develops his hypothesis that concordant monozygotic twins are those in whom heredity is involved and that discordant pairs are those in whom it is not. With regard to the course of the illness, in the markedly similar concordant group 60 percent showed a chronic progressive type, while 67 percent show a very different course designated as a chronic mild or transient type of schizophrenia.

Inouye's family histories (not based on personal observation) led him to the hypothesis that "the chronic progressive type of schizophrenic is likely to be recessive in most cases, and that the relapsing type is often dominant and genetically more heterogeneous. The chronic mild transient type is often dominant and genetically heterogeneous" (1961, pp. 524–530).

From these studies, important in so many ways, we turn to two authors whose family and twin-family studies fulfill the criteria permitting deductions as to the type of genetic mechanism involved, namely, Kallmann and Garrone.

Kallmann's German and American Studies

The findings of Kallmann's German family study (1938) and American twin-family studies (1946, 1948, 1950,) have been summarized by Slater with admirable clarity, with special relevance to the analyses, from the standpoint of the genetic mechanism involved, to which Kallmann and he himself have separately submitted them.

I have already commented on Slater's introductory background (1953) to Kallmann's studies in connection with the question of sampling. He proceeds to give this useful compendium of percentage expectancy figures:

1. Unrelated: general population, 0.85; stepsibs, 1.8; consorts, 2.1.
2. Relatives: first cousins, 2.6; nephew and nieces, 3.9; grandchildren, 4.3; half-sibs, 7.0–7.6; parents, 9.2–10.3; full sibs, 11.5–14.3; dizygotic co-twins, 12.5; children, 16.4; children of two schizophrenic

twins who had been separated for five years or more, 77.6; monozygotic twins who have not been so separated, 91.5

In Slater's words (1953, p. 346), *"The increasing likelihood of schizophrenia with increasing nearness of blood relationship to a schizophrenic is very striking."*

Slater (1953, p. 18) pays tribute to the general impact that Kallmann's genetic studies of schizophrenia and other psychoses have had on psychiatric ideology:

This evidence of a distinct biological basis for the main psychiatric groupings is important, for it is so often denied. Penrose has maintained (1930) that "it is difficult to believe that common mental disorders are due to single genetical factors. The common reaction types, the effective and the schizophrenic, are not clearly defined entities. To a great extent they are symptomatic diagnoses." Kallmann's work has shown that if strict and careful methods of clinical diagnosis are applied, the main lines of division do correspond with a biological difference. Many of Kallmann's theoretical arguments are based on the familial investigations he made parallel with the twin studies; he is no doubt right in maintaining that the two lines of approach are best combined.

Slater also reflects the emphasis that Kallmann attributes to a constitutional resistance mechanism of genetic modifiers, correlated with the degree of development of the athletic component of physique, and possibly the associated mesodermal defense mechanism (reticuloendothelial system) which affects the manifestation of the *single recessive genetic predisposing mechanism* postulated by Kallmann in such ways as (1) nonappearance of the disease despite the presence of the necessary complement of genes in about 30 percent of cases, attributable to a penetrance of the schizophrenic genotype of about 70 percent; (2) variations in age of onset and severity of progress of the disease in the nuclear and peripheral categories, as well as atypical clinical forms, interpreted in terms of variable expressivity; and (3) the wide prevalence of schizoid personalities on the basis of homozygous schizophrenic genotype of suppressed expression, but also as a result of incomplete suppression of the heterozygous state.

The theme is elaborated by Kallmann (1948), who reports, with three illustrative case histories, that where uniovular twins differ in the severity of a schizophrenic psychosis, the relatively spared twin has larger mesomorphic and endomorphic components as measured by Sheldon's somatotyping technique. The same reflection appears in another article (1948) as well as in his paper read at the Second International Congress of Psychiatry held in Paris in 1950, where he further specified agents which might lower resistance, including physical and emotional strain, pregnancy, acute infections, or a drastic reducing diet.

Finally: "The hypothesis of recessive inheritance in relation to the unitary genotype of schizophrenia is borne out by the taint distribution in schizophrenic index families, showing transmission in the collateral rather than in the direct line of descent, and by an excess of consanguineous marriages among the parents of schizophrenic index cases. In two of our surveys about 5 percent of the index cases originated from consanguineous parental matings" (Kallmann, 1948, p. 257).

Constitutional relationship between schizophrenia and tuberculosis (1938, 1943, 1949, and 1958). Kallmann's earlier work and speculations on the constitutional relationship between schizophrenia and tuberculosis in his German study (1938) were considerably elaborated in conjunction with Reisner (1943), to a degree that won the acclaim of Burks (1938). Detailed studies of the clinical and pathological aspects of pulmonary tuberculosis confirmed that there is a parallel between this disease and schizophrenia, on the side of the second genetic factor of graded *resistance mechanism*. Preliminary evidence was adduced for this residing in the reticuloendothelial system. Rainer (1966) returned to the theme of this physiological basis of the reticuloendothelial system in his review of the contributions of Kallmann to the genetics of schizophrenia. Kallmann sent in an unpublished progress report to the Scottish Rite Committee on Research in Schizophrenia in which he said: "There is a French proverb to the effect that people, as they grow older, tend to return to their first loves. . . ." He went on to say:

Over 30 years ago, while working in pathological laboratories, I became interested in the function of the reticulo-endothelial system as the system which is man's principal organ of defense. At that time we studied in laboratories the regulatory and defensive activities of cell elements in connection with artificially produced fever reactions, first in neurosyphilitics and later in schizophrenics. Ever since, I have had the nagging thought that some systematic work should be done along these lines in order to make it possible to have a connecting link between the psychodynamic and physiodynamic approaches to a pathological state that may be referred to in terms of lack of strength in coping with stress, as well as in those of the organism's inability to maintain a state of adaptiveness in the presence of a non-containable deficit in its biochemistry. Since I have always assumed that genes exert their effects through control of metabolism, although there is a long chain of reactions between the initial gene effects and its observable end products, I never thought of the genetic factor for schizophrenia as something that is static and fixed at birth. Instead we defined it as a specific, complex, and quite dynamic vulnerability factor that leads to adaptive incompetence only when the defense system collapses. Unfortunately, it took many years to obtain whatever statistical data were needed to substantiate the theory that this collapse is more likely to occur in some people than others. With this task accomplished, many fine physicians had an incentive to search for the biological substrate of this presumably gene-specific metabolic deficiency while we finally got a chance to look again into the mysterious activity of reticulo-endothelial cells.

Kallmann went on to describe the function of monocytes, histiocytes, and phagocytes; the importance of studying such cell activity in potential schizophrenics prior to the manifestation of clinical symptoms; and the need to study, therefore, the offspring of two schizophrenic patients and the identical twins of persons with schizophrenic symptoms. Counting cellular elements in blister fluids, he observed tentatively a marked reduction in the total cell count and a rise in the percentage of lymphocytes.

This facet of Kallmann's thought and work relating to the *genetic resistance mechanism* (to both schizophrenia and tuberculosis) has achieved a central importance to the theme of this section and in the linkup with Burch's papers, to be reviewed later on.

Kallmann's formulation of single-locus recessivity in the predisposition to schizophrenia. From the foregoing it is clear that the only meaningful single-locus genetic theory of the etiology of schizophrenia is one that postulates it in relation to *predisposition,* in interplay with a second *resistance mechanism of genetic modifiers,* which Kallmann sees as probably polygenically related to constitution, notably to the development of mesodermal elements, reflected in the somatotype and located in the reticuloendothelial system, which is the body's chief defense mechanism not only in schizophrenia but in pulmonary tuberculosis and other infective illness also.

Kallmann's detailed argument for single-locus recessivity. It is in his monograph on his German study (1938, pp. 40–44, 152–164) that Kallmann develops his argument for the single-locus

recessivity of the genetic mechanism implicated in the predisposition to schizophrenia. The reader is referred to this source for a detailed exposition.

Other Studies by Kallmann

We bring together those relevant to the central argument, even though they may be discussed elsewhere in this chapter.

Involutional psychosis (1950). Involutional psychosis is shown as having affinities with the family circle of schizophrenia rather than with that of manic-depressive psychosis, in Kallman's Paris paper (1950). This accords with clinical features and the prepsychotic personality as reported by Henderson and Batchelor (1962).

Childhood schizophrenia (1956). This study indicates that in preadolescent schizophrenia, we are dealing with the same single recessive genotype as in the adult form, but with exceptionally high penetrance and low resistance of the constitutional modifiers.

Deafness and schizophrenia (1962, 1963). The general effect of these studies is that blood relationship to a schizophrenic rather than the psychological isolation entailed in deafness is of etiological significance in schizophrenia in the deaf.

Slater's Criticisms of Kallmann's Hypothesis

We have already noted the high regard in which Slater holds Kallmann's investigative design and the magnitude of his achievement. However, in his analysis of Kallmann's two major studies he finds "the incidence of schizophrenia in the children of schizophrenics rather more easy to reconcile with the *dominance* hypothesis." Slater is, however, impressed with Kallmann's consanguinity argument. Slater would therefore appear to hold the view that a proportion of cases are referable to a partially penetrant dominant gene and that others involve a partially penetrant recessive mechanism. This would accord with the general evolutionary vista provided by Fraser Roberts in our introduction to this section on controversial issues.

Slater commences his analysis with an expurgated view of Köller's statistical argument against the recessivity hypothesis, involving Dahlberg's formulas regarding the frequency of genes in the homozygotic and heterozygotic form in the population and in various types of matings. It demonstrates that on the recessive view, the expectancy of schizophrenia should be higher among the sibs of schizophrenics than among their children, whereas the reverse is the case. The anomaly cannot be resolved on the basis of assortative mating, for only about 2 percent of consorts are schizophrenic, whereas a much higher figure would be required to save the situation.

Kallmann's finding of a higher incidence of schizophrenia in the children than in the sibs is a "strong indication of dominance. On the dominance hypothesis one would of course expect an equal incidence in children and sibs, but a difference of the extent which actually exists would not be a serious objection to the theory as it may result from a sampling error or be explicable in other ways."

Slater then considers Kallmann's evidence adduced in favor of recessivity that about 5.7 percent of schizophrenics have been found to be the children of consanguineous matings. Using Bell's estimate of the frequency of cousin marriage in England and Wales (as the American figure was unknown to the writer), and assuming that about two-thirds of Kallmann's consanguineous matings were first-cousin marriages, the application of Dahlberg's formula yields a figure which vis-à-vis the incidence of schizophrenia in the general population would imply the involvement of 125 distinct autosomal genes. Although such a figure cannot be discounted on

general grounds, the incidence of schizophrenia found in the children of dual matings rules this totally out of court, as it is much higher than the expectancy rate of the 125-gene hypothesis, which would yield a figure little higher than in the children of one schizophrenic and one normal parent.

In his view of the possible genetic heterogeneity of schizophrenia, Slater includes the schizophreniform reactions with a potentially high environmental component, in addition to the dominant and recessive genetic categories. In his discussion of schizophreniform reactions he cites the claim of Leonhard and Schulz of a preponderance of recessive types in the "typical" and dominant types in the "atypical" clinical group.

The attempt to identify distinct genotypes for the four classical subforms of schizophrenia has failed. Slater has observed from Kallmann's figures "a noteworthy correlation between the form taken by the illness in the propositi and the relative." Furthermore, he found that " . . . the incidence of schizophrenia was more than twice as high in the children of catatonic and hebephrenic propositi than in the children of paranoid and simple cases." Kallmann explicitly recognizes this fact. It finds a ready explanation in the hypothesis that not only the specific genes but the constitutional modifiers determining the malignancy of the schizophrenic process, and hence the clinical forms, are transmitted from parents to children.

Slater concludes: "The matter must be left here, with the important questions still all unanswered, although the available evidence has been far from exhaustively discussed" (Slater, in Sorsby, 1953, p. 349).

Karlsson's Criticisms of Kallmann's Hypothesis

Karlsson draws on Kallmann's data extensively in his analysis of the genetic mechanism involved in schizophrenia. He postulates a basic dominant factor, with a gene frequency of 3 percent, and a predisposing factor, probably recessive, with a gene frequency of 40 percent. He advisedly pits this hypothesis against that of highly penetrant single (70 percent) recessiveness (e.g., Kallmann's) and that of dominance with a 20 percent (heterozygous) penetrance (Slater, Böök). More specifically, he contends that his recessive gene p must have a frequency of 0.40 to account for the risk of one in six in children, taking into account a penetrance of 80 percent. The frequency of his dominant gene S must be 0.3 to explain that almost 1 percent of the population is affected.

Karlsson's failure to recognize the preliminary distortion of human genetic data through the design of collection leads to his impression that only the affected members of schizophrenic families pass on the disorder with a significant frequency—a contention sadly at variance with the evidence that most schizophrenics originate from parents who are both overtly unaffected. His other main objection to Kallmann's recessive hypothesis is that hereditary prognosis in offspring is little affected by the previous reproductive history of the spouse. This proposition, in itself not crucial in discriminating dominant from recessive inheritance, is moreover not borne out in fact in Kallmann's detailed analysis of various parental combinations in his 1938 study, already reviewed in this chapter.

Garrone's Study

If any further confirmation were needed of Kallmann's definitive studies in the field of the genetics of schizophrenia, it would come from Garrone's extensive study of the Geneva population between 1901 and 1950, already referred to. It comprises a census of no fewer than 3,810 cases falling within the stated period and a family study of propositus cases. Salient conclusions are the genetic homogeneity of schizophrenia,

including the matter of clinical subforms and the single recessive mode of inheritance, with a homozygous penetrancy of 67 percent.

The net incidence of schizophrenia in the Geneva population is estimated at 1 percent, the morbidity risk at 2.4 percent, and the prevalence of the schizophrenic gene at 19 percent.

The morbidity distribution closely parallels those of the German and American studies of Kallmann and other workers cited. In particular, its details are in such close agreement with Kallmann's that in the absence of any significant points of disagreement, the reader is referred to Garrone's report (1962) for confirmation and to Tables 3-11 and 3-12.

The Novel Statistical Approach of Burch

Burch, following the application of a new statistical approach to manic-depressive psychosis (1964a), extended it to schizophrenia (1964b) and involutional psychosis (1964c).

The mathematical procedure is based upon age- and sex-specific incidence rates for certain spontaneous, disturbed tolerance, autoimmune diseases conforming to the following general equation:

$$\frac{dN}{dt} = kP_o t^{(r-1)} \exp\left(\frac{-kt^r}{r}\right)$$

where dN/dt is sex-specific incidence minus rate of the disease at age t (age from birth is a good approximation for diseases studied so far) and k is a constant throughout postnatal life. The precise value of k depends upon the details of etiology, but in a special situation, where r specific somatic mutations, at r available sites, must be accumulated in any one of the L cells at risk, in any sequence, $K = r \, (mg)^r$. It is assumed here that m_s is an average rate of somatic mutation (Burch, 1964) applicable to r sites.

In the equation P_o is the fraction of the male or female population at birth that is at risk, through inheritance, with respect to the diseases in question (Burch, 1964a).

Age and sex-specific first admission rates to hospitals in New York State (Malzberg, 1955) are used in conjunction with familial evidence (mainly from Kallmann, 1959) to assess certain aetiological aspects of schizophrenia. It is concluded that this disorder is restricted to a carrier population (about 2.7 per cent at birth of the general male and female population of New York State) that is homozygous for certain alleles (say sa and sb), at two, non-linked autosomal loci (sa and sb). Its phenotypic initiation —in males and females—depends upon the accumulation of two specific random events that are probably autosomal somatic mutations. The average interval, or latent period, between the completion of the second (and final) somatic mutation and first admission to hospital, is about 4 to 5 years longer in females than in males. It is suggested that the somatic mutations may yield (in carriers) a forbidden clone (or clones) of immunologically competent cells, carrying cell-bound auto-antibody. Alternatively, the aetiology of schizophrenia involves disturbances in an unidentified system that shares certain important characteristics with the lymphoid system.

The statistics for age- and sex-specific onset rates for general paresis are contrasted with those for manic-depressive psychosis, schizophrenia, and recognized autoimmune diseases.

Of special interest in the context of our present discussion are the entirely different pictures in manic-depressive psychosis and schizophrenia. In manic-depressive psychosis a common *dominant* allele on the *X chromosome* and a rather rare *dominant autosomal allele* are postulated, and three somatic mutations are probably required, one affecting a gene on the X chromosome and the other two affecting autosomal genes.

In schizophrenia, on the other hand, two separate autosomal *recessive genes* and two autosomal somatic mutations are needed.

On the basis of Burch's evidence on the contrasting positions in manic-depressive psychosis and schizophrenia, could any stronger demonstration on the question of recessivity or dominance of schizophrenia be made.. Or from the intrinsic evidence in schizophrenia, could any stronger confirmation of a single recessive *predisposing factor* interacting with a constitutional *resistance mechanism* residing in the reticuloendothelial system be demanded?

The advance made by Burch's analysis is the demonstration that the resistance mechanism is even more specific than Kallmann had dared to suppose; that is, it is single recessive (like the predisposing mechanism), and not polygenic.

Burch's involutional psychosis paper confirms Kallmann's view that this condition has a schizophrenic component, inasmuch as the specific genetic requirements appear to be a dominant allele at a single X locus and two autosomal recessive alleles, one of which constitutes one of the predisposing genetic factors in schizophrenia.

SYNTHESIS AND CONCLUSIONS: SCHIZOPHRENIC IDEOLOGICAL DISPUTES

In orienting ourselves to our summing up of the situation, it behooves us to remind ourselves of the increasing measure of relativism in the discrimination of dominant from recessive mechanisms in our era of biochemical genetics, molecular biology, and the genetic code. The possibility of the existence of both dominant and recessive mechanisms causing the same conditions was conveyed in evolutionary perspective in our earlier reference to Fraser Roberts. It remains only to direct our attention to the diagram constructed by Kallmann (1962) to picture to ourselves the interaction of biochemical, molecular, subcellular, and cellular mechanisms with threshold factors to produce the individual behavioral phenotype and the family and social expressions thereof. This will give us a more vivid and dynamic picture of the factors controlling the manifestation and expression of genes such as are depicted in Slater's concept of partial dominance, probably involved in certain apparent deviations from the theoretical expectation of monohybrid recessivity in Kallmann's (1938) morbidity distribution, and, indeed, such as may go a long way to cloud the clear recognizability of dominant-recessive genetic mechanisms, all too apparent in these pages. The importance of being able to make this distinction nobody will deny: from the genetic counseling standpoint alone it is extremely important to know whether one or both parents and families are involved in the transmission of the condition and what type of morbidity distribution is to be expected among descendants.

To come, then, to the case for single-factor recessivity of the genetic predisposition to schizophrenia, I should sum it up as follows: First, we have the morbidity distribution in the studies of Kallmann and Garrone, showing transmission in the collateral rather than the direct line of descent. In this connection I would stress Kallmann's plea to regard the effect of figures, such as appear in the tables *as a whole,* recognizing that there may be explanations for deviation from expectation of individual, isolated figures. Difficulties of ascertainment, variability of penetrancy in relation to constitutional modifiers and genetic morphism should be considered in this connection. Second, comes the substantially raised consanguinity in the parental generation. Third, there is the strong confirmation from Burch's new statistical approach of recessivity in schizophrenia in contrast to dominance in manic-depressive psychosis. The details of the genetic mechanism so disclosed are of particular interest because they accord with Kallmann's emphasis on a single-factor *predisposing* genetic mechanism, interacting with a *constitutional, modifying resistance mechanism.* Should this second mechanism turn out to be a single-factor recessive instead of a polygenic one, as Kallmann had supposed on general grounds, it

would have the advantage of definiteness and increased therapeutic manipulability, through exploration of the possible autoimmune factor and further attention to Kallmann's "old love" for the reticuloendothelial system. This raises the fourth point, namely, the heuristic value of the second, modifying mechanism in vindicating the genetic homogeneity of schizophrenia and the notion of a single basic genotype manifesting variously in the four classical subforms as well as in Kallmann's nuclear and peripheral groups. It affords an explanation, moreover, not only of the tendency for the same subgroup to be transmitted to the subsequent generation but also of the different expectancy figures in the co-twins of schizophrenic index cases as compared with those in the offspring of dual mating.

Regarding the two-factor theory of Karlsson and the partial single dominant theory of Slater and Böök, their statistical criticisms of Kallmann's hypothesis are met by Burch's analysis disclosing a single recessive predisposing mechanism and a single recessive resistance or modifying mechanism. He shows that in respect of twin concordance ratios (monozygotic/dizygotic) and the figures for full siblings, half-siblings, step-siblings, marriage partners, and the general population, this hypothesis fits Kallmann's data and "that it is unlikely that any simpler alternative could give better agreement."

It would not, however, appear to answer the vexed question raised by Slater of the relative expectancies in siblings and children. These are probably explained chiefly by difficulties of ascertainment, particularly in respect of the older generation in Kallmann's earlier study (from which these comparative figures are derived), notably in the matter of overlooking affected and tainted parents, referred to in Kallmann's (1938) discussion of Hoffmann's criticism of the hypothesis of recessivity. Differential action of the constitutional modifying mechanisms as between the two categories may also be involved, for there is a conspicuously higher representation of "nuclear" relative to "peripheral" cases in the group of children as compared with that of siblings. Finally, only future research will reveal the extent to which genetic morphism, including the facet of infective and other stressors, and Burch's somatic mutations and autoimmune phenomena (and their relative time sequence) may play a part.

As we come now to the end of this chapter, we are in a better position to indicate a little more precisely similarities between the various genetic theories of schizophrenia adumbrated earlier.

All exponents postulate two genetic factors —Karlsson and Burch in the form of two single genes, and Kallmann and Slater in the form of a single main gene against the background of a mechanism of polygenic modifiers. Kallmann and Burch agree in emphasizing recessive transmission, while Slater and Karlsson are at one in assigning primacy to a dominant mechanism.

Differences between Kallmann and Burch as to whether the second factor is single recessive or polygenic, and between Slater and Karlsson as to whether single dominant and recessive factors are combined in one individual or are separate, may sink into places of relative insignificance in the light of the converging physiological pathways of Kallmann's reticuloendothelial system and Burch's autoimmune disease hypotheses.

PREVENTIVE ACTION

Chemical Reversal of Single Gene Effects

It is the heartening paradox of modern human genetics that rather than the demonstration of the genetic nature of diseases spelling tragedy, resignation, irreversibility, and counsel of despair, it is the focal and growing point of a new and fundamental hope of reversal of the conditions by chemical means, pinpointed by their very genetic nature as being of an identifiable biochemical type of the enzyme-block variety. Indeed, they are in principle and prospect more predictably controllable than diseases of psychogenic causation, as environing psychological influences are for the individual never entirely under control, however careful external supervision may have been. In illustration of this proposition, we have already seen in the single recessive genetic condition phenylketonuria how the pinpointing of its specific single-factor genetic nature followed by the elucidation of the derailed chemistry, consequent upon the genetically determined enzyme block involved, has opened the way to the arrest of the mental subnormality and other clinical abnormalities involved through appropriate chemical reversal by dietetic means. We have also indicated the start that has been made with other forms of mental subnormality, where the genetically induced abnormal train of chemical events is known.

We at the University of the Witwatersrand have initiated a project embodying a similar principle for endogenous depressions as outlined at the Third World Congress of Psychiatry (Hurst, 1961, 1962, 1969). Taking the single dominant genetic nature of the condition with its postulated enzyme block as the fixed point at the one end of our chemical spectrum for investigation and serotonin and noradrenaline at the other, as the two important chemical substances in the human phenotype upon which the actions of two discrete categories of antidepressant drugs (the MAO inhibitors and tricyclic compounds) converge, our aim is to work back through the precursors of serotonin and noradrenaline to the chemistry (enzyme block) of the initiating genetically determined metabolic error. In principle, schizophrenia, with its single-gene basis, and with various leads as to metabolic disturbances (in relation to protein, carbohydrate, adrenaline, electrolyte balance, electron donation, and heme) is also a challenging and most worthy theme for this type of treatment. The importance of a fundamental chemical cure of schizophrenia and the endogenous depressions speaks for itself.

Genetic Counseling

Where the ideal of chemical reversal of the genetically determined psychiatric disorders of childhood has not yet been achieved or is not yet in sight, there is room for consideration of the role of a minimal program of voluntary negative eugenics, through genetic counseling at heredity clinics.

The reader is referred elsewhere (Hurst, 1965) for a discussion of the wider issues of eugenics (positive and negative) and the theoretical and practical contributions of Plato, Galton, and the Oneida Community to the subject and to the organizational aspects of modern heredity clinics, well outlined by Dice (1952) in his Presidential Address to the American Society of Human Genetics. The importance of adequate heredity counseling services and centers for human welfare, health, and happiness cannot be overestimated. It is encouraging, therefore, to note the development of many such centers during the past few decades. In 1956 Hammons listed fifteen such centers in the United States and Canada, one in Denmark, five in England, one in France, one in Germany, two in Holland, one in India, two in Italy, one in Japan, one in Norway, three in Sweden, and one in Switzerland. Two of these are concerned primarily with psychiatric cases. Reed (1963) provides a list of twenty-eight such services, with their addresses, in the United States and Canada; his compendious yet concise volume is recommended for perusal by all those interested in genetic counseling.

We here restrict ourselves to features relating to genetic counseling in conditions relevant to child psychiatry. The stage has been well set in the WHO report already referred to.

Genetic counseling is the most immediate and practical service that genetics can render in medicine and surgery. The proportion of the population which really needs genetic advice is not large, but neither is it negligible. Those who do need genetic advice, however, need it badly, and it is a service to patients which should be available. Experience shows that in some communities, the great majority of inquiries come from couples who have had a deformed or defective child and who want to know what the chances of recurrence may be, should they have another. With recessive defects—and these bulk quite largely at a genetic clinic—the usual finding is a negative family history on both sides; the danger is revealed only by the birth of an affected child. Then with some commoner congenital malformations, the empirical risk of recurrence tends to be rather low. The birth to a relative, even a close one, of a child with, say, spina bifida does not indicate an appreciable risk, but naturally the couples who have had such a child themselves will often be concerned about the risk of repetition. Dominant abnormalities and also sex-linked abnormalities are distinctly rare in comparison, so that queries from people contemplating marriage, or from couples who have not yet had a child, are proportionately not very numerous. It must be mentioned, however, that in some communities, for example, those in which cousin marriage is common, a higher proportion of queries come from those contemplating marriage. With common diseases which have some genetic element in their causation, the increased risk to relatives is usually quite low. Moreover, one or another of these diseases is almost certain to occur in any family history, so that couples may confidently embark upon parenthood. Routine premarital genetic counseling is to be discouraged, except perhaps in some areas with special problems, for example, sickle-cell anemia; it would be very time-consuming and might tend to encourage neurotic tendencies in certain cases.

One general exception must be made, however. This is psychotic illness. Here there are often traditional fears which transcend the fears of ordinary physical illness. A level of risk that might be accepted for, say, diabetes could be considered altogether too large for schizophrenia. Hence, with mental diseases, inquiries will come more often from those not yet married.

The task of giving genetic advice is facilitated by the fact that bad risks are usually associated with simple inheritance. With more complex inheritance, the genetics becomes progressively more obscure, and the empirical chances of recurrence diminish correspondingly. Fortunately, when the genetics is very obscure, it is often known that whatever the type of inheritance may be, the empirical risk is low. Another advantage is that risks tend to cluster around two points, one high and the other considerably lower.

At the worst, and this should not happen often, if the case is really difficult and no reliable estimate of the risk can be made, at least the patient goes away with the knowledge that no one else knows either, and he is then spared the baleful influence of unhelpful comments from friends and relatives and the old wives' tales with which the subject bristles. The majority of inquirers at a genetic clinic can be told that the outlook is good and that the risk of recurrence is small, very small, or perhaps negligible. Only a minority have to be told that the risk is serious. For every couple in the population who have had a second abnormal child but who would have refrained from having more children after the first abnormal child, had they known what the risks really were, there are probably several

couples who have limited their families unnecessarily. In this connection, it must be remembered that in any pregnancy the chance that the child will be born with some severe malformation or will manifest some serious error of development in early life is at least 1 in 40. A special genetic risk not very much greater than this does not, therefore, look very serious to most couples when the facts are explained to them. At present, where, in the field of child psychiatry, genetic counseling is concerned largely with problems relating to mental defect and deformity, we are fortunate in knowing a good deal of the modes of inheritance and of genetic influences operating in different syndromes.

The hard core of genetic counseling is the risk figure of various categories of relatives being affected similarly to the patient. Where the Mendelian mechanism and its penetrancy are known, the risks can be worked out from basic genetic principles, but where this is not so, the empirical risk figures calculated from adequate samples may still provide a firm foundation for providing the guidance required.

If consulted by parents who have had a phenylketonuric child born to them or whose adolescent child has developed schizophrenia, we may picture in our mind's eye the ratios in the hypothetical sibship of four—namely, one having two of the morbid genes, two having one morbid gene each, and one no morbid genes. In these recessive diseases one also bears in mind the emphasis of propagation of the illness along the collateral lines of descent. With single dominant genetic mechanisms such as are involved in epiloia, dyslexia, or manic-depressive psychosis, by contrast, we bear in mind 50 percent of children receiving the gene and 50 percent not receiving it, the inability of the unaffected to transmit the disease as the gene does not remain latent, and the emphasis on transmission in the direct line of descent. The penetrancy figures—for example, 70 percent in schizophrenia and 50 to 60 percent in manic-depressive psychosis—are brought into the calculation. Similarly, in sex-linked recessive diseases, for example, Friedreich's ataxia, the known pattern of the Mendelian mechanism, involving transmission of the defect by a clinically unaffected female to the male, who then manifests it, helps us in our risk calculations in respect of other affected relatives. In arriving at a risk figure, whether from Mendelian considerations or on an empirical basis, we should hold clearly in our mind—and if we feel it necessary to convey the risk figure to the inquirers, we should make it clear to them—that the figure is an expression of average statistical risk which may show marked deviations from average expectation when applied to the small family sample under consideration.

Examples of empirically derived risk figures, where the Mendelian ratios are unknown or are not reasonably certain, are those already cited of 3 percent for central nervous system syndrome, 5 percent for congenital dislocation of the hip, 7 to 10 percent for harelip and cleft palate, 3 to 8 percent for clubfoot, 1.8 percent for congenital heart disease, and 1.4 percent for patent ductus arteriosus.

Epilepsy, despite its known Mendelian genetic mechanism, presents a more complicated problem from the genetic counseling viewpoint than conditions with only empirically derived risk figures because of the complicated penetrancy situation disclosed by Metrakos and Metrakos. Once the possibility that the epilepsy is of a symptomatic nature has been excluded, one approaches the genetic counseling situation in the knowledge that we are dealing with a single dominant genetic mechanism with peculiarities of expression which issues in a net average risk of the condition's manifesting in a disabling form of too low an order to counsel abstention from marriage and propagation on eugenic grounds—although there may be other considerations such as the potential psychological influence on children of a disturbed epileptic parent.

The scope of genetic counseling advice has been extended by the development of techniques for detecting the heterozygote or frustrated homozygote—generally known as *carrier detection.* Neel (1953) lists no fewer than thirty-three conditions in which features indicating carrier status have been studied. Biochemical methods are vital. For example, the clinically unaffected heterozygote for the phenylketonuric gene in his response to a phenylalanine tolerance test is moderately abnormal (Hsia, Drescoll, Troll, & Knox, 1956)—the homozygote is grossly so. This biochemical means of detecting the phenylketonuric heterozygote may be of value to us in genetic counseling. For example, if the sib of a phenylketonuric were contemplating marriage, it could be determined by this test whether he and/or his intended spouse was a carrier and hence a genetic prognosis regarding prospective offspring could be offered. In addition to exploring the biochemical methods of carrier detection, including changes in amino-acid metabolism (McMenemey, 1961; Seakins & Cowie, 1962), in the late-manifesting single dominant condition Huntington's chorea, Folek and Glanville (1962) have devised a sensitive method for recording subclinical hand tremors in an attempt to detect subtle signs of the illness before its overt onset.

Apart from biochemical methods, cytogenetic investigations are contributing new insights in the field of genetic counseling. Discrimination should, however, be exercised as to when requests for the extensive procedures entailed in karyotyping are warranted. Mental defect and congenital malformations are the areas to which these techniques are relevant.

There are, however, as Cowie (1965) points

out, certain circumstances in which the answer to genetic problems may be greatly modified by information from chromosome analysis. For instance, in the case of a young mother, say, under 30, who has borne a Mongol child, chromosome analysis may show that she is a genetically balanced 15/21 translocation carrier. In that case her chances of bearing further Mongols at any age would be likely to be increased. If, on the other hand, her Mongol baby were found to have 21 trisomy and the mother herself and the baby's father had normal karyotypes, we would have no theoretical grounds in cytogenetics for supposing that her chances of bearing further Mongols were greater than those of mothers in the general population. It has been estimated that for mothers who have borne a Mongol under the age of 25 years, the risk of bearing a second Mongol is something like fiftyfold the random risk, whereas there is no increased risk for mothers over 35 (Carter & Evans, 1961). It has been suggested, however, that the increased risk for younger mothers is at least partially explained by instances where one parent or the other has been found to be a translocation carrier.

The WHO report suggests that there are seldom grounds for giving a genetic prognosis for malformations with mental defect worse than that of the 1 in 40 figure for the general population in families with a child affected by a chromosomally determined malformation. Where a translocation mechanism is involved, there is in principle the possibility of a heightened risk, but this aspect has not been sufficiently explored in any syndrome other than Mongolism, where it accounts for only a minority of cases anyway.

In conclusion, I should like to mention some general orientations in genetic counseling:

1. The role of the genetic counselor is advisory: after he has brought all relevant factors to the attention of the inquirer or couple, the final decision as to marriage or procreation is the client's.

2. A clear distinction should be made concerning the conclusion to be drawn from an adverse genetic prognosis, regarding marriage on the one hand and procreation on the other. The decision as to marriage without contemplating having children is a general issue to be left to the couple concerned.

3. The degree of handicap imposed by a genetically determined trait should be weighed up before it is regarded as a contraindication to marriage or to procreation, intrinsically, and the high total prevalence of human genetic defects should also be taken into account. In this context a couple might shy away from a high likelihood of producing a schizophrenic child, while being quite prepared to take the risk of having a child with dyslexia, in respect of whom remedial teaching instituted promptly, where indicated through the valuable genetic warning, will result in an educationally and socially adequate being.

4. In the case of recessive Mendelian mechanisms involved in grave illnesses such as schizophrenia, even when procreation should be discouraged as a counsel of perfection, where this is not accepted, marriage with a spouse likely to be the carrier of the same pathological gene can, in any event, be discouraged.

5. Perhaps most important of all is the matter of the psychological approach of the genetic counselor. To Kallmann (1963) belongs the credit for having repeatedly stressed this point, to the extent of classifying genetic counseling as also being a form of psychotherapy. The good genetic counselor will never lose sight of the fact that the couple seeking his guidance are facing a major crisis, which may involve, for example, a decision to forgo cherished marriage plans. To present a couple with an empirical

risk figure, cold, is in such circumstances, clearly of all things the least desirable.

The portion of the WHO report quoted stresses the tendency of inquirers to overestimate the gloom of the genetic situation and to have been confused and depressed by old wives' tales. This provides the counselor with the happy privilege of disabusing the clients' minds of cruel fallacies, relieving their doubts, and sending them on their way to a happy marriage, which they had begun to feel to be beyond their reach.

Cowie drives home the lesson as follows:

> As our knowledge of genetical mechanisms advances there is perhaps an increasing tendency in genetical counseling to present the gloomy picture of a multitude of unlikely dangers. One should remember that the enquirer is often more anxious than the facts warrant, and usually comes expecting to get pessimistic advice. As a rule those who come to the genetical counseling clinic of their own accord are responsible and conscientious people, of the kind who make excellent parents. It is very sad if, on account of unduly pessimistic advice, they should deprive themselves unnecessarily of children.

Genetic counseling should never be undertaken in a thoughtless or irresponsible manner. Genetic risks should, of course, be explained, but at the same time reassurance should be given wherever possible, and the adviser should do whatever he can to alleviate the guilt borne by so many parents who feel they have almost unwittingly passed on some hereditary condition to their children.

REFERENCES

Åkesson, H. O. *Epidemiology and genetics of mental deficiency in a South Swedish population.* Uppsala: Institute for Medical Genetics, University of Uppsala, 1961.

Allen, G., & Kallmann, F. J. Frequency and types of retardation in twins. *American Journal of Human Genetics,* 1955, **7**(15).

Alström, C. H. A study of epilepsy in its clinical, social and genetic aspects. *Acta Psychiatrica Scandinavica,* 1950 (Suppl. 63).

Altshuler, K. J., & Rainer, J. D. Distribution and diagnosis of patients in New York State mental hospitals. In *Family and mental health problems in a deaf population.* New York State Psychiatric Institute, 1963. Pp. 195–203.

Altshuler, K. J., & Sarlin, B. Deafness in schizophrenia: Interrelation of communication stress, maturation lag and schizophrenia risk. In F. J. Kallmann (Ed.), *Expanding goals of genetics in psychiatry.* New York: Grune & Stratton, 1962. Pp. 60–61.

Anderson, R. C. Causative factors underlying congenital heart malformations.1. Patent ductus arteriosus. *Pediatrics,* 1954, **14,** 143–152.

Andrews, S. G., & Harris, M. (Eds.). *The syndrome of stuttering.* London: Heinemann, 1964.

Anthony, J., & Scott, P. Manic-depressive psychoses in childhood. *Journal of Child Psychology and Psychiatry,* 1960, **1** (1).

Assum, H. W. Untersuchungen über die Erblichkeit des angeborenen Klumpfussleidens. *Zeitschrift fur Orthopsychologie,* 1936, **65,** 1–42.

Baikie, A. G., Court Brown, W. M., Jacobs, P., & Milne, J. G. Chromosome studies in human leukaemia. *Lancet,* 1954, **2,** 425.

Bakwin, H. Early infantile autism *Journal of Pediatrics,* 1954, **45,** 492–497.

Barr, K. L., & Hobbs, G. E. Chromosomal sex in transvestites. *Lancet,* 1954, **1,** 1109.

Barr, M. L., & Bertram, E. G. A morphological

difference between neurones of male and female. *Nature,* 1949, **163,** 676.

Baruk, H., & Gévauden, Y. Periodic psychoses in children; pure forms and forms associated with chorea and with infundibular—hypophyseal syndromes. *Annales Médico-psychologiques,* 1937, **95,** 296–312.

Beach, F. A. A review of physiological and psychological studies of sexual behaviour in mammals. *Physiological Review,* 1948, **27,** 240–307.

Bellak, L. *Manic-depressive psychosis and allied conditions.* New York: Grune & Stratton, 1952.

Bender, L. Behavior problems in the children of psychotic and criminal patients. *Genetic Psychology Monographs,* 1937, **19,** 229–339.

Bender, L. Childhood schizophrenia. *Psychiatric Quarterly,* 1953, **27,** 663–681.

Bender, L. Schizophrenia in childhood: Its recognition, description and treatment. *American Journal of Orthopsychiatry,* 1956, **26,** 499–506.

Bender, L. Twenty years of clinical research on schizophrenic children, with special reference to those under six years of age. In G. Caplan (Ed.), *Emotional problems of early childhood.* New York: Basic Books, 1955. Pp. 503–515.

Beres, D., & Alport, A. Analysis of a prolonged hypomanic episode in a five year old child. *American Journal of Orthopsychiatry,* 1940, **10,** 794–800.

Bickel, H., Boscott, R. J., & Gerrard, J. Observations on the biochemical error in phenylketonuria and its biochemical control. In H. Waelsch (Ed.), *Biochemistry of the developing nervous system.* New York: Academic Press, 1955. Pp. 417–430.

Blewett, D. B. An experimental study of the inheritance of intelligence. *Journal of Mental Science,* 1954, **100,** 922–933.

Böök, J. A. A contribution to the genetics of congenital clubfoot. *Hereditas,* 1948, **34,** 289–300.

Böök, J. A. A genetic and neuropsychiatric investigation of a North Swedish population. *Acta Genetica,* 1953, **4,** 1–100, 133–139, 345–414.

Böök, J. A., Santesson, B., & Zetterquist, P. Association between congenital heart malformation and chromosomal variations. *Acta Pediatrica,* 1961, **50,** 217–227.

Brody, E. G. Genetic basis of spontaneous activity in the albino rat. *Comprehensive Psychological Monographs,* 1942, **17**(5), 1–24.

Brody, E. G. A note on the genetic basis of spontaneous activity in the albino rat. *Psychology,* 1950, **43,** 281–288.

Bruch, H. Studies in schizophrenia. The various developments in the approach to childhood schizophrenia. Psychotherapy with schizophrenics. *Acta Psychiatrica et Neurologica Scandinavica,* 1959, **34** (Suppl. 130).

Burch, P. R. J. Manic-depressive psychosis: Some new aetiological considerations. *British Journal of Psychiatry,* 1964, **110,** 807–817. (a)

Burch, P. R. J. Schizophrenia: Some new aetiological considerations. *British Journal of Psychiatry,* 1964, **110,** 818-824. (b)

Burch, P. R. J. Involutional psychosis: Some new aetiological considerations. *British Journal of Psychiatry,* 1964, **110,** 825–829. (c).

Burks, B. S. A study of identical twins reared apart under different types of family relationship. In Q. McNemar & M. A. Merrill (Eds.), *Studies in personality.* New York: McGraw-Hill, 1942.

Burks, B. S.   Review of twins.   A study of heredity and environment. *Journal of Abnormal and Social Psychology,* 1938, **33,** 128–133.

Carter, C. O., & Evans, K. A., Risk of parents who have had one child with Down's syndrome having another child similarly affected. *Lancet,* 1961, **2,** 785–788.

Cattell, R. B.   Research designs in psychological genetics with special reference to the multiple variance method. *American Journal of Human Genetics,* 1953, **5,** 76–93.

Cattell, R. B., & Scheier, J. H.   *The meaning and measurement of neuroticism and anxiety.* New York: Ronald Press, 1961.

Chapman, A. H.   Early infantile autism in identical twins. *Archives of Neurological Psychiatry,* 1957, **78,** 621–623.

Chapman, A. H.   Early infantile autism: A review. *A.M.A. Journal of Diseases of Children,* 1960, **99,** 783–786.

Chung, C. S., Robison, O. W., & Morton, N. S. A note on deaf mutism. *Annals of Human Genetics,* 1959, **23,** 357.

Clarke, C. M., Edwards, J. E., & Smallpiece, V. 21-trisomy/normal mosaicism in an intelligent child with some mongoloid characters. *Lancet,* 1961, **1,** 1028.

Conrad, K. Erbanlage und Epilepsie. *Zeitschrift gesamte Neurologie und Psychiatrie,* 1935, **153,** 271–326.

Conrad, K. Erbanlage und Epilepsie. *Zeitschrift gesamte Neurologie und Psychiatrie,* 1935, **153,** 254–297, 509–542.

Coppen, A., & Cowie, V.   Maternal health and mongolism. *British Medical Journal,* 1960, **1,** 1843–1847.

Coppen, A., Cowie, V., & Slater, E.   Familial aspects of "neuroticism" and extraversion. *British Journal of Psychiatry,* 1965, **3,** 70–83.

Cowie, V.   The incidence of neurosis in the children of psychotics. *Acta Psychiatrica et Neurologica Scandinavica,* 1961, **37,** 37–87.

Cowie, V.   The genetical aspects of child psychiatry.   In J. G. Howells (Ed.), *Perspectives in child psychiatry.*   Edinburgh: Oliver & Boyd, 1965.   Pp. 38–57.

Crome, L. C., & Stern, J. *Pathology of mental retardation.*   London: Churchill, 1967.   Pp. 198–215.

Cronick, C. H.   A manic-depressive reaction in an eight year old child. *Quarterly Bulletin of the Indiana University Medical Centre,* 1941, **3,** 11–13.

Darke, R. A.   Heredity as an etiological factor in homosexuality. *Journal of Nervous and Mental Disease,* 1948, **107,** 251–268.

Darlington, C. D.   *Genetics and man.*   London: George Allen and Unwin, 1964. P. 230.

Davidson, W. M., & Smith, D. R.   A morphologic difference in the polymorphonuclear neutrophil leucocytes. *British Medical Journal,* 1954, **2,** 6.

Dice, L. R.   Heredity clinics: Their value for public service and research. *American Journal of Human Genetics,* 1953, **4,** 1–13.

Dussik, K.   Manic-depressive psychosis in an 11 year old child. *Psychiatrische Neurologische Wochenschrift,* 1934, **36,** 305.

Edwards, J. H.   The syndrome of sex-linked hydrocephalus. *Archives of Disease in Childhood,* 1961, **36,** 481–493.

Eisenberg, L., & Kanner, L.   Early infantile

autism, 1943-1955. *American Journal of Orthopsychiatry,* 1956, **26**, 556–566.

Essen-Möller, E. Psychiatrische Untersuchungen in einer Serie von Zwillingen. *Acta psychiatrica* (Copenhagen), 1941 (Suppl. 23).

Eysenck, H. J. Neuroticism in twins. *Eugenics Review,* 1951, **43**, 79–82.

Eysenck, H. J. The inheritance of extraversion-introversion. *Acta Psychologica,* 1956, **12**, 95–110.

Eysenck, H. J. Classification of the problem of diagnosis. In H. J. Eysenck, (Ed.), *Handbook of abnormal psychology.* London: Pitman, 1960. Pp. 1–31.

Eysenck, H. J., & Prell, D. B. The inheritance of neuroticism: An experimental study. *Journal of Mental Science,* 1951, **98**, 441–465.

Ferguson-Smith, M. A. Chromatin positive Klinefelter's syndrome (primary micro-orchidism) in a mental deficiency hospital. *Lancet,* 1958, **1**, 928.

Fischer, A. E. Maternal and sexual behavior induced by intracranial chemical stimulation. *Science,* 1956, **124**, 228–229.

Fogh-Andersen, P. Inheritance of harelip and cleft palate. *Opera Copenhagen University,* 1943, **4**, 266.

Folek, A., & Glanville, E. V. Investigation of genetic carriers. In F. J. Kallmann (Ed.), *Expanding goals of genetics in psychiatry.* New York & London: Grune & Stratton, 1962, Pp. 136–148.

Ford, C. E., Jones, K. W., Miller, O. J., Mittwoch, V., Penrose, L. S., Ridler, M., & Shapiro, A. The chromosomes in a patient showing both mongolism and the Klinefelter syndrome. *Lancet,* 1959, **1**, 709.

Fuller, J. L., & Thompson, R. *Behavior genetics.* New York: Wiley, 1960.

Galton, Sir. F. *English men of science: Their nature and nurture.* London: Macmillan, 1874.

Galton, Sir. F. *Memories of my life.* London: Methuen, 1908.

Garb, Judith. *An aetiological investigation of schizophrenia.* Unpublished thesis for the degree of bachelor of arts (Hons), University of the Witwatersrand, Johannesburg, 1964.

Gardner, I. C., & Newmann, H. H. Mental and physical tests of identical twins reared apart. *Journal of Heredity,* 1940, **31**, 119–126.

Gareiso, A., et al. Depressive melancholia syndrome in children. *Archivos Argentinos de Pediatria,* 1940, **11**, 447–468. In Leopold Bellak, *Manic-depressive psychosis and allied conditions.* New York: Grune & Stratton, 1952. P. 32.

Garrone, G. Statistical genetic study of schizophrenia in the Geneva population between 1901 and 1950. *Journal de Génétique Humaine,* 1962, **11**, 89–219.

Gates, N., & Brash, H. An investigation of the physical and mental characteristics of a pair of like twins reared apart from infancy. *Annals of Eugenics,* 1941, **11**, 89–101.

Gedda, L. *Studio dei Gemelli.* Edizione Orizzonte Medico. Roma: Istituto Gregorio Mendel, 1951.

Goodell, H., Lewontin, R., & Wolff, H. G. The familial occurrence of migraine headache: a study of heredity. In Association for research in nervous and mental disease. *Genetics and the inheritance of integrated neurological psychiatric patterns.* (Research Publ. 33). Baltimore: Williams & Wilkins, 1953, Pp. 346–356.

Gottesman, I. I., & Sheilds, J. Schizophrenia in twins: 16 years' consecutive admission to a psychiatric clinic. *British Journal of Psychiatry,* 1966, **112,** 809–818.

Grouchy, J. de, & Nava, C. de. Anomalies chromosomiques dans les leucemies. In *Progrés en Hématologie,* Paris: Flammarion, 1966.

Grouchy, J. de, Bonnette, J., & Salmon, C. H. Délétion du bras court du chromosome 18. *Annales de Génétique,* 1966, **9,** 19.

Grüter, W. Biochemistry and mental retardation. In *Mental Handicap, Documenta Geigy,* Basle, 1966. Pp. 5–6.

Haberlandt, W. B., & Glanville, E. V. Progress in neurological genetics. In F. J. Kallmann (Ed.), *Expanding goals of genetics in psychiatry.* New York, Grune & Stratton, 1962. Pp. 126–135.

Hall C. S. Temperament: A survey of animal studies. *Psychological Bulletin,* 1941, **38,** 909–943.

Hallgren, B. *Specific dyslexia (Congenital word-blindness).* Copenhagen: Munksgaard, 1950.

Hallgren, B. *Enuresis: A clinical and genetic study.* Copenhagen: Munksgaard, 1957.

Hamerton, J. L., Jagietto, J. M., & Kirman, B. H. Sex chromosome abnormalities in a population of mentally defective children. *British Medical Journal,* 1962, **1,** 220–223.

Harnden, D. G. The chromosomes. In L. S. Penrose (Ed.), *Recent advances in human genetics.* London: Churchill, 1961. Pp. 126–135.

Harnden, D. G., Miller, O. J., & Penrose, L. S. The Klinefelter-mongolism type of double aneuploidy. *Annals of Human Genetics,* 1960, **24,** 165.

Harris, G. W., Michael R. P., & Scott, P. P. Neurological site of action of stilbesterol in eliciting sexual behavior. In *Neurological basis of behavior, Ciba Foundation Symposium.* Boston: Little Brown, 1958. Pp. 236–251.

Harvald, B., & Hauge, M. Hereditary factors elucidated by twin studies. In J. V. Neel, M. W. Shaw, K. & W. J. Schull (Eds.), *Genetics and the epidemiology of chronic diseases.* Washington, D.C.: U.S. Department of Health, Education & Welfare, 1965. Pp. 61–76.

Henderson, D., & Batchelor, I. R. C. *Henderson and Gillespie's textbook of psychiatry.* London: Oxford University Press, 1962. Pp. 259–261.

Herndon, C. N. Genetics of the lipidoses. In Association for Research in Nervous and Mental Disease. *Genetics and the inheritance if integrated neurological psychiatric patterns* (Research Publ. 33). Baltimore: Williams & Wilkins, 1954. Pp. 239–258.

Holzinger, K. J. The relative effect of nature and nurture influences on twin differences. *Journal of Educational Psychology,* 1929, **20,** 241–248.

Howells, J. G. (Ed.). *Modern perspectives in child psychiatry.* Edinburgh: Oliver & Boyd, 1963.

Hsia, D. Y., Driscoll, K., Troll, W., & Knox, W. E. Heterozygous carriers of phenylketonuria detected by phenylalanine tolerance tests. *Nature,* 1956, **178,** 1279–1280.

Hsia, D. Y., Knox, W. E., Quinn, K. V., & Paine, R. S. A one-year controlled study of the effect of low-phenylalanine diet on phenylketonuria. *Pediatrics,* 1958, **21,** 178–207.

Humm, D. E. Mental disorders in siblings. *Dissertation,* University of California, 1932.

Hurst, L. A. Application of genetics in psychiatry

and neurology. *South African Journal of Laboratory and Clinical Medicine,* 1958, **4,** 169–205.

Hurst, L. A. Classification of psychotic disorders from a genetic point of view. Vol III. *Proceedings of the Second International Congress of Human Genetics,* Rome, Sept. 6–12, 1961. Pp. 1745–1756.

Hurst, L. A., Reef, H. E., & Sachs, S. B. Neuropsychiatric disorders in the Bantu. I. Convulsive disorders: A pilot study with special reference to genetic factors. *South African Medical Journal,* 1961, **35,** 750–754.

Hurst, L. A. Research implications of converging advances in psychiatric genetics and the pharmacology of psychotropic drugs. In *Proceedings of the Third World Congress of Psychiatry, Montreal, June 4–10, 1961.* Toronto: University of Toronto Press, 1962. Pp. 538–542.

Hurst, L. A. Classification of psychotic disorders from a genetic point of view, *Acta genetical Medical et Gemellologial,* 1961, **11**(3), 320–332.

Hurst, L. A. Research implications of converging advances in psychiatric genetics and the pharmacology of psychotropic drugs. *Medical Proceedings,* 1961, **7,** 417–423.

Hurst, L. A. The current status of psychiatric genetics. *Leech,* 1962, **32,** 5, 120–129.

Hurst, L. A. Trends in psychiatric genetics in South Africa. In F. J. Kallmann (Ed.), *Expanding goals of genetics in psychiatry.* New York: Grune & Stratton, 1962. Pp. 235–243.

Hurst, L. A. Genetics in relation to psychiatry and neurology. *South African Medical Journal,* 1964, **38,** 339–346.

Hurst, L. A. Genetic factors. In B. Wolman (Ed.), *Handbook of clinical psychology.* New York: McGraw-Hill, 1965. Pp. 141–180.

Hurst, L. A. Rival theories of the genetic mechanism in schizophrenia. *Psychological Scene,* 1967, **1,** 9–15.

Hurst, L. A. Research implications of converging advances in psychiatric genetics and the pharmacology of psychotropic drugs. In M. Manosevitz, G. Lindzey, & D. D. Thiessen (Eds.), *Behavioral genetics: Method and research.* New York: Appleton-Century-Crofts, 1969. Pp. 742–749.

Idelberger, K. *Die erbpathologie der sogenannten angeborenen Huftverrenkung.* Munich: Urban & Schwarzenberg, 1951.

Inouye, E. Similarity and dissimilarity of schizophrenia in twins. Vol I. *Proceedings of the Third World Congress Psychiatry, Montreal.* Canada: University of Toronto & McGill Press, 1961. Pp. 524–530.

Jackson, D. A critique of the literature of the genetics of schizophrenia. In D. Jackson (Ed.), *Aetiology of schizophrenia.* New York: Basic Books, 1960. Pp. 27–87.

Jacobs, P. A., Baikie, A. G., Court Brown, W. M., & Strong, J. A. The Somatic chromosomes in mongolism. *Lancet,* 1959, **1,** 710.

Jacobson, C. B. Gestational management in balanced translocation heterozygotes. *Third International Congress of Human Genetics. Chicago, Sept. 5–10, 1966. Abstracts of contributed papers.* Pp. 50–51.

Kahn, E. *Schizoid und Schizophrenia im Erbgang.* Berlin, 1923.

Kaij, L. *Alcoholism in twins.* Stockholm: Almquist & Wiksells, 1960.

Kallmann, F. J. *The genetics of schizophrenia.* Locust Valley, N.Y.: Augustin. 1938.

Kallmann, F. J. Genetic mechanisms in resistance to tuberculosis. *Psychiatric Quarterly,* 1943, **32** (Suppl 17).

Kallmann, F. J. Twin studies on genetic mechanisms in resistance to tuberculosis. *Journal of Heredity,* 1943, **34,** 269.

Kallmann, F. J. The genetics of schizophrenia. An analysis of 691 twin index families. *American Journal of Psychiatry,* 1946, **103,** 309–322.

Kallmann, F. J. Genetics in relation to mental disorders. *Journal of Mental Science,* 1948, **94,** 250–257.

Kallmann, F. J. Genetics of psychoses. *American Journal of Human Genetics,* 1950, **2,** 385–390.

Kallmann, F. J. Genetics of psychoses. *Proceedings of the First International Congress of Psychiatry, Section VI.* Paris: Herman & Cie, 1950.

Kallmann, F. J. Comparative twin study on the genetic aspects of adult male homosexuality. *Journal of Mental Disease,* 1952, **115,** 283–298.

Kallmann, F. J. Genetic principles in manic-depressive psychoses. In P. H. Hoch & J. Zubin (Eds.), *Depression.* New York: Grune & Stratton 1954. Pp. 1–24.

Kallmann, F. J. The genetics of mental illness. In S. Arieti, (Ed.), *American handbook of psychiatry.* New York: McGraw-Hill, 1959.

Kallmann, F. J. Recent cytogenic advances in psychiatry. In *Proceedings of the Third World Congress of Psychiatry, Vol I.* Toronto: University of Toronto Press, 1962.

Kallmann, F. J., Barrera, S. E., & Metzger, H. Association of hereditary ophthalmia with mental deficiency. *American Journal of Mental Deficiency,* 1940, **45,** 25–36.

Kallmann, F. J., de Porte, J., de Porte, E. & Feingold, L. Suicide in twins and only children. *American Journal of Human Genetics,* 1949, **1,** 113.

Kallmann, F. J., & Jarvik, L. F. Twin data on genetic variations in resistance to tuberculosis. In L. Gedda (Ed.), *Genetica della Tubercolosi e dei Tumori.* Rome: Gregorio Mendel, 1958.

Kallmann, F. J., & Rainer, J. D. Psychotherapeutically oriented counselling techniques in the setting of a medical genetics department. *Topical problems in psychotherapy,* 1963, **4,** 101–108.

Kallmann, F. J., & Reisner, D. Twin studies on the significance of genetic factors in tuberculosis. *American Review of Tuberculosis,* 1943, **47,** 549.

Kallmann, F. J., & Roth, B. Genetic aspects of preadolescent schizophrenia. *American Journal of Psychiatry,* 1956, **112,** 599–606.

Kallmann, F. J. & Sander, G. The genetics of epilepsy. In P. H. Hoch & R. P. Knight (Eds.), *Epilepsy.* New York: Grune & Stratton, 1947.

Kanner, L. *Child psychiatry.* Baltimore: C. C. Thomas, 1935. P. 206.

Kasanin, J. The affective psychoses in children. *American Journal of Psychiatry,* 1931, **10,** 897.

Kay, D. W. K., & Garside, R. F. The genetics of stuttering. In S. G. Andrews & M. Harris (Eds.), *The syndrome of stuttering.* London: Heinemann, 1964.

Keeler, W. R. In discussion. *Psychiatric Reports of the American Psychiatric Association,* 1957, **7,** 66–88.

Keeler, W. R. Autistic patterns and defective communication in blind children with retrolental fibroplasia. In P. Hoch & J. Zubin (Eds.), *Psychotherapy of communication.* New York: Grune & Stratton, 1958. Pp. 64–83.

Keeler, W. R. Personal communication, 1960.

Knox, W. E. In Stanbury, J. B., Wyngaarden, J. B., & Fredrickson, D. S. *The metabolic basis of inherited disease.* New York: McGraw-Hill, 1966. P. 258.

Kringlen, E. Schizophrenia in male monozygotic twins. *Acta Psychiatrica* (Copenhagen), 1964 (Suppl. 178).

Lang, T. Genetic determination of homosexuality. *Journal of Nervous and Mental Disease,* 1940, **92,** 55.

Larsson, T., & Sjogren, T. A methodological, psychiatric and statistical study of a large Swedish rural population. *Acta Psychiatrica* (Copenhagen), 1954 (Suppl. 89).

Lehman, E., Haber, J., & Lesser, S. R. The use of reserpine in autistic children. *Journal of Nervous and Mental Disease,* 1957, **125,** 351–356.

Lejeune, J., Turpin, R., & Gautier, M. Le mongolisme: Premier example d'aberration autosomique humaine. *Annales de Génétique,* 1937, **1,** 41.

Lejeune, J., Berger, R., Lafourcade, J., & Rethore, M. O. La deletion partielle long chromosome 18. *Annales de Génétique,* 1966, **9,** 32.

Lennox, W. G., & Gibbs, E. L. The intelligence and the electroencephalograms of normal and epileptic twins. *Transactions of the American Neurological Association,* 1944, **70,** 182–184.

Lennox, W. G., Gibbs, E. L., & Gibbs, F. A. The brain-wave pattern: An hereditary trait. *Journal of Heredity,* 1954, **36,** 233–243.

Lenz, F. *Methoden der menschlichen Erblichkeitsforschung.* Jena, 1929.

Leonhard, K. Atypische endogene Psychosen im Lichte der Familienforschung. *Zeitschrift für gesamte Neurologie und Psychiatrie,* 1934, **149,** 520–562.

Lidz, T. Schizophrenia and the family. *Psychiatry,* 1958, **21**(1), 21.

Ljungberg, L. Hysteria. A clinical, prognostic and genetic study. *Psychiatria et Neurologie Scandinavica* (Copenhagen), 1957 (Suppl. 112), 32.

Lowenfeld, B. *Our blind children.* Springfield Ill.: Charles C Thomas, 1956 & 1967.

Luxenburger, H. Psychiatrische Neurologische Zwillingspathologie. *Zentralblat für gesamte Neurologie und Psychiatrie,* 1930, **56,** 145.

Luxenburger, H. Vorläufiger Bericht über psychiatrische Serienuntersuchungen an Zwillingen. *Zentralblat für gesamte Neurologie und Psychiatrie,* 1928, **116,** 297–326.

Malzberg, B. Age and sex in relation to mental diseases. *Mental Hygiene,* 1955, **39,** 196–224.

McKeown, T., MacMahon, B., & Parsons, C. G. The familial incidence of congenital malformation of the heart. *British Heart Journal,* 1953, **15,** 273–277.

McMenemey, W. H. Immunity mechanisms in neurological disease. *Proceedings of the Royal Society of Medicine,* 1961, **54,** 127–136.

Meehl, P. E. Schizotaxia, schizotypy, schizophrenia. *American Psychologist,* 1962, **17**(12).

Metrakos, J. D., Metrakos, K., & Baxter, H. Clefts of the lip and palate in twins, including a discordant pair whose monozygosity was confirmed by skin transplants. *Plastic and Reconstructive Surgery,* 1958, **22**(2), 109–122.

Metrakos, J. D., & Metrakos, K. Genetics of convulsive disorders. II. Genetic and encephalographic studies in centrephalic epilepsy. *Neurology,* 1961, **11,** 474–483.

Metrakos, J. D. The centrencephalic EEG in epilepsy. *Proceedings of the Second International Conference on Human Genetics,* 1961, 1792–1795.

Metrakos, J. D., & Metrakos, K. Genetics of convulsive disorders. I. Introduction, problems, methods and base lines. *Neurology,* 1960, **10,** 228–240.

Miller, O. J. Developmental sex abnormalities. In L. S. Penrose, *Recent advances in human genetics.* London: Churchill, 1961. Pp. 56–75.

Moncrieff, A., & Wilkinson, R. H. Further experiences in the treatment of phenylketonuria. *British Medical Journal,* 1961, **1,** 763–767.

Money, J., & Hirsch, S. R. Chromosome anomalies, mental deficiency and schizophrenia. *Archives of General Psychiatry,* 1963, **8,** 242–251.

Morgan, T. H., & Bridges, C. B. *Sex-linked inheritance in Drosophila.* Washington D.C.: Carnegie Institute, 1916 (Publication 237).

Nanabhay, R. A study of stuttering in an Indian family with special reference to genetic factors. Unpublished master's thesis, University of the Witwatersrand, Johannesburg, 1967.

Neel, J. V. The detection of the genetic carriers of inherited disease. In A. Sorsby (Ed.), *Clinical genetics.* London: Butterworth, 1953.

Newman, H. H., Freeman, F. N., & Holzinger, K. J. *Twins: A study of heredity and environment.* Chicago: University of Chicago Press, 1937.

O'Gorman, G. Manic-depressive psychoses. In J. G. Howells (Ed.), *Modern perspectives in child psychiatry.* Edinburgh: Oliver & Boyd, 1963. Pp. 485–488.

Osborn, F. Galton and midcentury genetics. *Eugenics Review,* 1956, **48,** 15.

Oster, J. *Mongolism.* Opera ex domo biologiae hereditariae humanae, 32. Copenhagen: Danish Science Press, 1953.

Pare, C. M. B. Homosexuality and chromosomal sex. *Journal of Psychosomatic Research,* 1956, **1,** 247–251.

Pasqualini, R. Q., Vidal, G. & Bur, G. E. Psychopathology of Klinefelter's syndrome: Review of 31 cases. *Lancet,* 1957, **2,** 164–167.

Pastore, N. The genetics of schizophrenia (a special review). *Psychological Bulletin,* 1949, **46,** 285–302.

Patau, K., Smith, D. W., Therman, E., Inhorn, S. L., & Wagner, H. P. Multiple congenital anomaly caused by an extra autosome. *Lancet,* 1960, **1,** 790.

Penrose, L. S. *Biology of mental defect.* London: Sidgwick & Jackson, 1949.

Penrose, L. S. Personal communication, 1960.

Penrose, L. S. Parental age in relation to non-disjunction in man. *Conference on Human Chromosomal Abnormalities,* 1960, as quoted in L. S. Penrose (Ed.), *Recent advances in human genetics.* London: Churchill, 1961. Pp. 35–36.

Polan, C. G., & Spencer, B. L. A check list of symptoms of autism of early life. *West Virginia Medical Journal,* 1959, **55,** 198–204.

Polani, P. E., Briggs, J. H., Ford, C. E., Clarke, C. M., & Berg, J. M. A mongol girl with 46 chromosomes. *Lancet,* 1960, **1,** 721.

Polani, P. E., & Campbell, M. Factors in the causation of persistent ductus arteriosus. *Annales de Génétique,* 1960, **24,** 343–357.

Prader, A., Schneider, J., Zublin, W., Frances, J. M., & Rüdi, K. Die Häufigkeit des echten chromatin-positiven Klinefelter-Syndroms und seine Beziehungen zum Schwachsinn. *Schweizerische Medizinische Wochenschrift,* 1958, **88,** 917–920.

Price, B. Primary biases in twin studies. *American Journal of Human Genetics,* 1950, **2,** 293–352.

Pritchard, M. Homosexuality and genetic sex. *Journal of Mental Science,* 1962, **108,** 616–623.

Rainer, J. D. *The contributions of Franz Joseph Kallmann to the genetics of schizophrenia.* Lecture, The University of Michigan, Department of Psychiatry, May 24, 1966.

Rainer, J. D., & Altshuler, K. Z. *Comprehensive health services for the deaf.* New York: New York State Psychiatric Institute, 1966.

Rainer, J. D., Altshuler, K. Z., & Kallmann, F. J. *Family and mental health problems in a deaf population.* New York: New York State Psychiatric Institute, 1963.

Raphael, T., & Shaw, M. W. Chromosome studies in schizophrenia. *Journal of the American Medical Association,* 1963, **183,** 1022–1028.

Record, R. G., & Edwards, J. H. Environmental influences related to the aetiology of congenital dislocation of the hip. *British Journal of Preventive and Social Medicine,* 1958, **12,** 8–12.

Record, R. G., & McKeown, T. Congenital malformation of the central nervous system. I. *British Journal of Preventive and Social Medicine,* 1949, **3,** 183–219.

Record, R. G., & McKeown, T. Congenital malformation of the central nervous system. II. *British Journal of Preventive and Social Medicine,* 1950, **4,** 26–50. (a)

Record, R. G., & McKeown, T. Congenital malformation of the central nervous system. III. *British Journal of Preventive and Social Medicine,* 1950, **4,** 217–220. (b)

Reed, S. C. *Counseling in medical genetics.* (2nd ed.) Philadelphia: W. B. Saunders Company, 1963.

Rimland, B. *Infantile autism.* London: Methuen, 1963.

Roberts, J. A. F. Methodology in human genetics. San Francisco: Holden-Day, Inc., 1962.

Roberts, J. A. F. *An introduction to medical genetics.* (2nd ed.) London: Oxford University Press, 1959.

Rosenthal, D. Problems of sampling and diagnosis in the major twin studies of schizophrenia. *Psychiatric Research,* 1961, **1,** 116–134.

Rosanoff, A. J., Handy, L. M., Plesset, I. R., & Brush, S. The etiology of so-called schizophrenic psychoses with special reference to their occurrence in twins. *American Journal of Psychiatry,* 1934, **91,** 247–286.

Royce, J. R. Factor theory and genetics. *Educational and Psychological Measurement,* 1957, **17,** 361–376.

Rüdin, E. *Zur Vererbung und Neuenstehung der Dementia Praecox.* Berlin: Springer, 1916.

Rundle, A., Coppen, A., & Cowie, V. Steroid excretion in mothers of mongols. *Lancet,* 1961, **2,** 846–848.

Sank, D. The genetic and adjustive aspects of early total deafness. In F. J. Kallmann (Ed.), *Expanding goals of genetics in psychiatry.* New York: Grune & Stratton, 1962. Pp. 149–165.

Sank, D. *Genetic aspects of early and total deafness in family and mental health problems in a deaf population.* New York: New York State Psychiatric Institute, 1963. Pp. 28–81.

Saudek, R. A British pair of identical twins reared apart. *Character and Personality,* 1934, **3,** 17–39.

Seakins, J. W. T., & Cowie, V. Urinary alanine excretion in a Huntington's chorea family. *Journal of Mental Science,* 1962, **108,** 427–431.

Sherman, L. C. Psychoses in children. *Illinois Mental Journal,* 1939, **75,** 446–450.

Sherwin, A. C. Reactions to music of autistic (schizophrenic) children. *American Journal of Psychiatry,* 1953, **109,** 823–831.

Schulz, B. *Methodik der medizinischen Erbforschung.* Leipzig, 1936.

Schut, J. W. The hereditary ataxias. In Association for research in nervous and mental disease. *Genetics and the inheritance of integrated neurological and psychiatric patterns* (Research Publ. 33). Baltimore: Williams & Wilkins, 1953, 293–324.

Shields, J. *Monozygotic twins brought up apart and brought up together.* London: Oxford University Press, 1962.

Shields, J. Personality differences and neurotic traits in normal twin schoolchildren. *Eugenics Review,* 1954, **45,** 213–246.

Slater, E. Psychotic and neurotic illnesses in twins. *Medical Research Council Special Report Series,* 278, 1953. Pp. 6–7, 75–83, 87–88.

Slater, E. The thirty-fifth Maudsley lecture "Hysteria 311." *Journal of Mental Science,* 1961, **107,** 359–381.

Slater, E. Genetical factors in neurosis. *General Psychiatry,* 1964, **3,** 265–269.

Slater, E. Diagnosis of hysteria. *British Medical Journal,* 1965, **1,** 1395–1399.

Slater, E., & Glithero, E. Schizophrenia-like psychoses of epilepsy. III. Genetic aspects. *International Journal of Psychiatry,* 1965, **1,** 19–20.

Slater, E. Psychiatry. In Arnold Sorsby (Ed.), *Clinical genetics.* Ch. 18. London: Butterworth, 1953. Pp. 332–349.

Sonneborn, G. M. Implications of the new genetics for biology and man. *A.I.B.S. Bulletin,* 1963, **13,** 22–26.

Stephens, F. E., & Thompson, R. B. The care of Millan and George, identical twins reared apart. *Journal of Heredity,* 1943, **34,** 109–114.

Stern, Curt. *Principles of human genetics.* (2nd ed.). San Francisco & London: W. H. Freeman & Company, 1960. Pp. 568–572.

Stevenson, A. C., & Cheeseman, E. A. Hereditary deaf mutism, with particular reference to Northern Ireland. *Annals of Human Genetics,* 1956, **20,** 177.

Stewart, S. F. Clubfoot: its incidence, cause and treatment. *Journal of Bone and Joint Surgery,* 1951, **33 A,** 577–590.

Sturup, G. Manic-depressive psychosis in a 13 year old boy with hyperthymic constitution. *Acta psychiatricia and neurologica,* 1932, **7,** 635–645.

Tedeschi, L. G., & Freeman, H. Sex chromosomes in male schizophrenics. *Arch. gen. Psychiat.,* 1962, **6,** 109–111.

Thompson, W. R. The inheritance of behavior. *Journal of Heredity,* 1956, **47,** 147-148.

Thurstone, T. G., Thurstone, L. L., & Strandskov, H. H. *A psychological study of twins.* Ch. 4. Chapel Hill: University of North Carolina, Psychometric Laboratory, 1953.

Tienari, P. Psychiatric illnesses in identical twins. *Acta psychiatrica* (Copenhagen), 1963 (Suppl. 171).

Tjio, J. H., & Levan, A. The chromosome number of man. *Hereditas,* 1956, **42,** 1.

Tyler, F. H. The inheritance of neuromuscular disease. In association for research in nervous and mental disease. *Genetics and the inheritance of integrated neurological psychiatric patterns* (Research Publ. 33). Baltimore: Williams & Wilkins, 1953. Pp. 283–292.

Waardenburg, A., Franceschetti, A., & Klein, D. *Genetics and ophthalmology.* Assen: Van Gorcum, 1961–1963. 2 Vols.

Ward, T. F., & Hoddinott, B. A. Early infantile autism in fraternal twins. *Journal of the Canadian Psychiatric Association,* 1962, **7,** 191–195.

Weinberg, W. Mathematische Grundlagen der Probandenmethode. *Zeitschrift für Induktive Abstammungs und Verebungslehre,* 1927, **48,** 179–228.

Wepman, G. P. Is stuttering inherited? Proceedings of the American Speech Correction Association, Madison, 1935. As quoted by Bernard C. Meyer, Psychosomatic aspects of stuttering. *Journal of Nervous and Mental Disease,* 1945, **101,** 127–157.

West, R. The pathology of stuttering. *The Nervous Child,* 1943, **2,** 96.

World Health Organization. *Human genetics and public health.* Second Report of the WHO Expert Committee on Human Genetics. Geneva: WHO Technical Report Series, No. 282, 1964.

Yerbury, E. G., & Newell, N. Genetics and environmental factors in psychoses of children. *American Journal of Psychiatry,* 1944, **100,** 599–605.

4 Etiology of Mental Disorders: Prenatal, Natal, and Postnatal Organic Factors

Marshall D. Schechter, Povl W. Toussieng, Richard E. Sternlof, and Ethan A. Pollack

"And surely we are all out of the computation of our age, and every man is some months older than he bethinks him; for we live, move, have a being, and are subject to the actions of the elements, and the malice of diseases, in that other world, the truest microcosm, the womb of our mother." *Sir Thomas Browne, 1642*

Characteristically, Western society has always inferred that life begins at the time of parturition. In 1869 the Catholic Church took a stand against abortion, arguing that the embryo or fetus is a living organism equipped with a "soul" from conception. Any investigation of prenatal influences on later development of personality and even physical capabilities was subsequently discouraged for a long time because it was not possible to draw the full consequences of research findings and totally impossible to take logical action.

In this century increasing attempts at understanding the role of birth defects (of which there are approximately 250,000 in the United States per year) in later behavioral and emotional disorders have created a climate in which many studies of lower animals as well as of humans are being undertaken. This chapter will review pertinent findings in both of these areas.

Certain basic observations can be made:

1. Events during the organism's early development may have a disproportionately greater influence than events of the same type or magnitude occurring later. The effects of early traumatic events are characterized by the extent to which they are generalized, since they often involve a wide variety of tissues, and by their general irreversibility.

2. The proposition that early traumata are important by no means implies that later experiences cannot become equally important. Pasamanick and Knobloch (1962) called this the "continuum of reproductive causality." M. F. A. Montagu (1962, p. 13) defines constitution as follows:

Indeed, there is little that is final about constitution, for constitution is a process rather than an unchanging entity. In brief, it is important to understand at the outset that constitution is not a biological constant, a structure predestined by its genotype, that is to say, the genetic structure or constitution, determined by the number, types and arrangement of genes, to function in a predetermined manner. The manner in which the genotype functions is determined by the interaction of the genotype with the environment in which it undergoes develop-

129

ment. The outcome of this interaction will be expressed as the organism's constitution.

3. Any prenatal, perinatal, or postnatal events which affect sensorimotor development and/or lead to congenital defects can in themselves predispose the child to the development of psychological disorders such as the ones observed in minimal cerebral dysfunction or cerebral dysrhythmias. They may secondarily influence the child's psychological development because the body image has to be built on the basis of a defective body such as in cleft palate, phocomelia, blindness, or deafness. Prenatal and perinatal traumata may also directly impair psychological functioning, e.g., the capacity to understand and integrate environmental stimuli such as in mental retardation and the aphasias. Any of these sequelae are in turn affected by the reactions of important people in the environment (e.g., parents, teachers, physicians) to the child's handicaps and psychological manifestations.

4. Studying the effects of prenatal, perinatal, and postnatal organic conditions and how these factors relate to difficulties in development often necessitates a longitudinal research design. Such research is not easily accomplished, as longitudinal studies are often difficult to carry on. Further, the complexities and the various uncontrollable influences in the life experiences a child undergoes understandably make direct correlations with early organic conditions somewhat obscure and tentative.

PRENATAL INFLUENCES

Masland (1961) outlined and classified three groups of factors which he presumed to be connected with prenatal defects.

The first group he labeled *general factors,* which include social, economic, environmental, and demographic variables. High correlations between maternal age and pregnancy outcome

have been found, with very young women (below age 19) and women over 40 having the least favorable outcome. Paternal age, on the other hand, bears little if any relationship to pregnancy outcome, except for an increased incidence of stillbirths in very young or very old fathers (Yeroshalmy, 1939). In addition, parity beyond four pregnancies carries with it increased risk, especially with young mothers who have had closely spaced pregnancies (Masland, Sarason, & Gladwin, 1958).

Masland notes that the outcome of pregnancy is less favorable in the lower socioeconomic classes than in the higher classes (Brandon, 1957; Burt, 1957; Higgins, 1959). It has also been found that the incidence of prematurity and of certain defects (mental retardation, aphasias, and cerebral palsy) is greatest in the winter months. Wars are also presumed to contribute to difficulties, possibly as a result of altered habits of diet, physical activity, or increased emotional stress (Knobloch & Pasamanick, 1958; Macfarlane, Pennycuik, & Thrift, 1957; Pasamanick & Knobloch, 1958b).

The second group listed by Masland concerns *maternal factors.* Maternal nutrition plays an important role for the developing fetus. Animal research has shown that starvation during critical phases of pregnancy may lead to an unfavorable outcome; however, corresponding evidence from human populations has been difficult to obtain because of confounding environmental variables.

The mother's emotional status is felt to bear some relationship to the outcome of pregnancy. Some authors feel that the emotional state may be related to maternal attitude, while others are of the opinion that it may depend upon preexisting and deep-seated psychosomatic reaction patterns (Cramond, 1954; Scott, Illsley, & Biles, 1956; Scott, Illsley, & Thomson, 1956; Scott & Thomson, 1956a, 1956b).

Too much physical activity by the mother may influence pregnancy outcome, but at present the exact relationship is unclear (Stewart, 1959). There are also suggestions that women of small physique are more subject to prematurity than larger women (Lindsten & Hagert, 1959).

Pregnancy complications such as toxemia and bleeding, as well as long periods of infertility between pregnancies, have adverse effects on pregnancy outcome. The relationship of blood type to erythroblastosis and its subsequent effects have been well substantiated (Nesbitt, 1957). Endocrine dysfunction has been related to pregnancy outcome. In diabetic and prediabetic pregnancy the outcome of the pregnancy may be jeopardized (Dekaban, 1959; Gellis & Hsia, 1959; Wilkerson, 1959).

Maternal immune reactions have been shown to be harmful to the fetus. Maternal antibodies against the fetal thyroid and crystalline lens have produced postnatal disabilities in animals. Anti-brain immunity has been correlated with anencephaly in animals.

The third group of factors Masland outlined he labeled *specific environmental factors*. These include x-rays, toxins, drugs, hormones, and maternal infections. Anoxia and tobacco have been found to be damaging in animals, but their roles in humans have yet to be firmly established.

Masland's outline provides a comprehensive overview of the prenatal factors. We shall elaborate on some of the more important factors in following sections.

MATERNAL FACTORS

M. F. A. Montagu (1962, p. 213) states:

If we could develop means of measuring the significant biological changes in the mother, and thus of those acting upon the conceptus, and relate these to the critical stages of growth and development of the conceptus, it would ultimately be possible to predict something of the behavioral as well as the physical postnatal growth and development of the organism. In any event, it would appear reasonable

to suppose that both personality and behavior in child and adult are to some extent determined by influences operative in the prenatal maternal milieu.

Before getting into this rather complex and unclear area, it is necessary to discuss some of the processes by which substances pass from the maternal organism to the fetal organism and perhaps back again. The so-called placental barrier used to be considered the area of interchange. It was thought that substances could be transported across this semipermeable membrane only if they were of low molecular weight and that they passed through by the simple process of diffusion. In more recent years, it has become clear that the transport routes are far more complex and that a number of different mechanisms are involved. Besides simple diffusion, there is also a carrier system which promotes active transport against a specific concentration gradient. There is also a third process, generally referred to as *leakage*. More complex molecules, such as compounds containing iron, amino acids, and glucose, are probably transported back and forward by these two latter mechanisms. There is now evidence that even intact red blood corpuscles and large protein molecules can cross the placenta. At present this is thought to occur mainly in the direction from the fetus to the mother, but there are observations suggesting that passage in the other direction also occurs. Thus, it can no longer be considered impossible for complex molecules and even foreign substances such as viruses and drugs to pass through the placenta (Cobrinik, Hood, & Chusid, 1959; Gregg, 1941; Hardy, 1965; A. Montagu, 1961; Plummer, 1952; Yamazaki, Wright, & Wright, 1954). It becomes more and more incumbent on us to observe the potential for transmission of maternal hormones and/or catecholamines via the placental barrier, as this potentially may result in long-lasting sensitization and varying other effects on the fetus.

Thompson (1962) states that to illustrate the intimacy of the relationship between mother and fetus, we may cite the following examples: Adrenalectomy of pregnant rats produces compensatory hypertrophy of fetal adrenals (Ingle & Fischer, 1938; Knobil & Briggs, 1955). Since this effect is blocked by maternal hypophysectomy, it seems likely that it depends on the passage of maternal ACTH across the placenta (Knobil & Briggs, 1955). Direct evidence of the function of the pituitary, however, is lacking. The hormones secreted by the placenta include ACTH (Assali & Hameresz, 1954) and corticoid substances (Johnson & Haines, 1952). It may be that these are responsible for the effects on the fetal adrenals. ACTH activity is generally higher in pregnant women. In rats it rises to a peak around the middle of the second week and declines up to parturition when it shows another abrupt rise (Poulton & Reece, 1957). It is quite likely that these hormonal changes underlie the changes in mood and physiology commonly associated with pregnancy in human beings, for example, morning sickness in the early phases, ebullience later on and post-partum depression after the birth of the child.

Thompson (1962) goes on to say that emotional changes and changes in learning and activity level have been reproduced in rats by treating mothers during pregnancy with chemical agents (Thompson & Olian, 1961; Werboff, 1959), alcohol (Vincent, 1958), intense sound (Thompson & Sontag, 1956), anoxia (Meier, Bunch, Nolan & Scheidler, 1960), x-irradiation (Furchtgott & Echols, 1958a, 1958b; Furchtgott, Echols, & Openshaw, 1958; Levinson, 1952), and conditions causing anxiety (Doyle & Yule, 1959; Hockman, 1961; Thompson, 1957, 1960). There seems to be no doubt that both "physical" and "psychological" stress imposed on the mother during pregnancy can affect the behavior of her offspring.

The kinds of change produced are not necessarily adverse. When quantitative behavior traits are studied, deviations from the mean in both directions are found. The direction taken apparently depends heavily on the degree of stress applied to the mother. Vincent (1958) found that rats given small amounts of alcohol produced offspring which were less emotional and more highly motivated and which were better learners than the controls, whereas large dosages had just the opposite effect. The same holds true for the effects of x-irradiation (Furchtgott & Echols, 1958a, 1958b) and epinephrine (Thompson & Olian, 1961) on the activity of the young. That is to say, either less or more active offspring may result (Thompson & Olian, 1961, p. 12).

In view of these studies it is evident that maternal emotions and their physiological concomitants also will influence the fetus during pregnancy and very well may have more long-lasting effects on the child after birth. A thorough discussion of the effects of maternal emotions on fetal development has been contributed by M. F. A. Montagu (1962).

Selye (1950) demonstrated that the female sex organs of rats are highly influenced by systemic stress, which results mainly in ovarian atrophy and suppression of the sexual cycle. Physiologically these changes are related to a decrease in gonadotrophin production from the anterior lobe of the pituitary. As the characteristic response to stress in the human female often includes changes in the ovulatory cycle, a similar mechanism may be operative here as in Selye's rats.

These findings lend credibility and value to the work of Sontag and others from the Fels Institute. Sontag (1944, p. 154) states:

> The fetal behavior pattern as observed in utero may be described in terms of three different types of movement and in variations in heart rate. The amount of sharp kicking movement and slow squirming movement seem to bear some relationship to certain maternal physiological characteristics

usually associated with autonomic function and therefore to what one might call emotional state or psychic constitution.

Maternal emotional state as observed clinically is capable of altering fetal behavior patterns in the direction of much greater amounts of irritative movement as is also severe maternal fatigue.

There appears to be an autonomic component of such irritative behavior which is evident post-natally as gastrointestinal dysfunction and food intolerance.

Hyperactive fetuses store less food as fat than do less active ones.

There is evidence that fetal response patterns of heart rate and movement can be altered by exogenous stimuli.

Later, Sontag (1966) reviewed the work at the Fels Institute on the behavior of the mother-fetus dyad. Measurements of fetal movement and fetal heart rate indicated differences in babies *in utero*. Eight babies whose mothers were profoundly upset at some time during late pregnancy developed into hyperactive, irritable babies. Similarly, the tendency for adults to have a variable heart rate is associated with the variability in the heart-rate records of the same individuals as 8-month fetuses. Thus, tension during pregnancy may have long-lasting, possibly lifelong effects on offspring. The importance of the mother's emotional state not only for the child but also for the occurrence of obstetrical complications such as premature birth has been stressed by Gunter (1963); McDonald, Gynther, and Christakos (1963); and Blau, Slaff, Easton, Welkowitz, Springarn, and Cohen (1963).

Stott (1957, 1961) relates physical and mental handicaps, including a greater frequency of Mongolism, to emotional shocks in early pregnancy. M. F. A. Montagu (1962) notes that a given fetus who, during the period of intense growth of his hypothalamic structures, is exposed to a high level of adrenergic substances, resulting from his mother's psychosomatic response to an external or internal psychic conflict, will adapt to this changed biochemical environment as if it were the normal one. Fetuses who during the same period are exposed to lower levels of adrenergic substances will adapt to those levels. This may lead these organisms to make their adaptive levels permanent after birth. In other words, it is conceivable that certain infants will require a permanently higher or lower production of adrenergic substances regardless of what postnatal environment they live in. This in turn will have an effect on their postnatal tolerance of stress. The exact nature and implications of these relationships are not yet known, but there is now no longer any doubt that these relationships exist.

NUTRITION AND OTHER FACTORS

In the study by Burke, Beal, Kirkwood, and Stuart (1943) all stillborn children and all infants dying during the first few days of life, with one exception, were prematures. Most infants with major congenital defects as well as all the infants considered to be "functionally immature" were born to mothers who had been on diets deficient in a number of substances during their pregnancies. Ninety-four percent of the mothers who were on good to excellent diets during their pregnancies gave birth to babies who were in good to excellent condition at birth. Antonov (1947), reporting on the children born during the siege of Leningrad, found that the stillbirth rate during this period was twice the normal figure and that the rate of prematurity climbed to 41.2 percent of all live births. The neonatal mortality rate was unusually high, 9 percent for those born at term and 30.8 percent for those born prematurely. The average weight of infants born at term during the first half of 1942 was 500 to 600 grams less than the normal. The physiological weight loss normally lasting 3 to 4 days after birth continued for 6 days, and the average weight loss during this period was 9.7 percent of the original weight, considerably above the usual figures. Newborn infants observed by Antonov generally showed lower vitality. The rates of erythema, and of a rare physiological swelling of the mammary glands, were increased. There were some cases of toxic erythema which resulted in subsequent softening of the skull bones. Antonov attributed the unusually high rate of morbidity (32.3 percent) among newborns to their lowered vitality.

Specific dietary deficiencies during pregnancy have been reported in many cultures and geographic areas. The most common example is the one of endemic congenital cretinism, which is related to a deficiency in maternal iodine intake, resulting from iodine-deficient soil.

Billewicz and Thomson (1957) studied 13,322 deliveries in Aberdeen in an attempt to correlate prematurity and perinatal death rates with maternal body height. There was a high correlation between perinatal mortality and prematurity and the height of mothers, suggesting that tall women (above 5 feet, 5 inches) in the lower classes, who lived in an environment where nutritional standards were low, seemed to be at a relatively greater disadvantage than those women with lesser innate growth potential. A higher rate of prematurity and infant mortality occurred among babies of small upper-class women, as compared with those of tall upper-class women. However, small stature in all mothers, whether genetically or nutritionally determined, proved to be a handicap in producing viable babies.

M. F. A. Montagu (1962, p. 89) states:

> In spite of the fact that Negroes may frequently be less well nourished than a random sample of the white population with which they may be compared, Murphy found that the malformation rate was almost twice as high in whites as in Negroes. For individuals born during the same five-year period in Philadelphia, there were 5.7 per 1,000 malformed white babies born as compared with 3.2 per 1,000 malformed Negro babies born. This difference in Negro-white malformation rates holds true for the whole of the United States, and suggests that a genetic factor may be involved, that whites possibly carry more defective genes or perhaps are characterized by more easily disordered cellular processes than Negroes. However, the possibility has to be borne in mind that these differences may reflect nothing more substantial than poorer observation and reporting of Negro cases. Since Negroes are characterized by higher fetal and neonatal death rates, affected individuals would be more frequently removed, and this might also be a factor influencing the reported differences.

M. M. Nelson, Asling, and Evans (1952) report that dietary deficiencies in pregnant rats, created at varying times during the pregnancy, invariably resulted in stillborn litters or multiple congenital deformities. The later the dietary deficiency was introduced during the pregnancy, the milder the ensuing abnormalities were. Kerr, Chamove, Harlow, and Waisman (1968) produced "fetal PKU" by feeding pregnant rhesus monkeys an excess of L-Phenylalanine. There seems to be some evidence that a woman's nutrition prior to pregnancy has an important effect on development of the fetus, as does dietary adequacy during pregnancy (Burke, Stevenson, Worcester, & Stuart, 1949; Ebbs, Tisdall, & Scott, 1941; Pasamanick & Knobloch, 1958b).

The unfortunate consequences of drug intake on fetal development have been well documented (Apgar, 1964; Kline, Blattner, & Lunin, 1964; Shane, 1968; Voorhess, 1967). Massive x-irradiation is also implicated in the development of fetal disorders. Specific hormones in animals have been demonstrated to be damaging, but these have not been shown especially to have a direct effect in human infants. Maternal illness such as syphilis, polio virus, rubella virus, herpes virus, brucellosis, toxoplasmosis, and the Coxsackie virus have all been implicated in the development of congenital malformations with or without mental retardation.

PREMATURITY

W. E. Nelson's (1959) discussion of prematurity illustrates the difficulties in arriving at a clear definition of this concept. Nelson states 1959, p. 306):

> A premature infant is a live-born infant weighing 2,500 grams (5 pounds, 8 ounces) or less at birth. This definition, although in use, is admittedly unsatisfactory, since it includes infants of low birth weight resulting from factors other than prematurity, and excludes those actually premature who would have been of large size if carried to term. The additional qualifications of a crown-heel length of 47 cm. (18½ inches) or less has been little used. The prognosis for survival of premature infants (less than 37 weeks gestation) in any weight group is directly related to gestational age. For example, in one analysis the neonatal mortality rate of a group of 79 infants between 1,000–1,499 grams birth weight was 46%; when the group was divided by recorded gestational age, the infants of less than 30 weeks had a mortality rate of 63%, compared to 21% of those in the same weight range, but with gestational ages of 34 to 37 weeks.

Pieper (1963) reviewed the literature concerning birth weight and viability of premature infants. He notes that of infants who weighed less than 1,000 grams, from 10.40 to 20.50 percent survived. However, among infants whose birth weights were 2,100 to 2,500 grams, 90 percent survived. Pieper cites reports of infants with birth weights as low as 454 grams and 600 grams, but observes that such infants would formerly have been labeled miscarriages (abortions), considered nonviable, and abandoned. Pieper concludes (1963, p. 553): "The limit of viability cannot be stated in figures."

The implications of these various studies are that fetal mortality depends on the amount of damage which has occurred. Many infants who survive with similar birth weights or gestational ages still have suffered definite though nonlethal damage which later may manifest itself in adaptational difficulties (this is discussed in a subsequent section). Developmental deficits of varying extent in those premature infants who survive have been extensively studied (Lubchenco, Horner, Reed, Hix, Metcalf, Cohig, Elliott, & Bourg, 1963). Similar factors of brain damage in prematures were reported by Zitran, Feber, and Cohen (1964).

In studying mental retardation and adaptive functions, Moore (1966) noted that the capacity for adaptive behavior varied significantly with the degree of prematurity. Friedman (1961) reported that nearly one-third of all cases of cerebral palsy were found to have been born prematurely. With regard to psychological processes and the effect of lesions on mental functioning, Luria (1966, p. 50) states:

> In a lesion of a particular area of the cortex, secondary disturbances arise in behavioral processes for which the normal working of the brain is essential, and those forms of psychological activity not including in their structure a factor directly associated with the affected area will remain intact.
>
> For instance, a lesion of the cortex of the left temporal region, which directly causes a disturbance of complex forms of auditory (or, more precisely, audio-speech) analysis and synthesis must lead to a secondary disturbance of the understanding of speech, of writing, and of the verbal notation of objects, all of which are dependent upon the integrity of analysis and synthesis of the phonetic composition of words; whereas processes such as visual

perception of figures, orientation in space or written calculations, the normal course of which is quite independent of the integrity of the auditory analysis the sounds of speech remain intact. On the other hand, a lesion of the occipital (or occipital-parietal) cortex, directly causing a disturbance of visual and visual-spatial analysis and synthesis causes a secondary disturbance of complex mental processes but not including in their structure a factor of spatial analysis and synthesis.

Luria (1966) also suggests that reading and writing disturbances may be different in varying languages. Interference with certain brain tissue in children using one language system rather than another in which the ideographic principle of writing is used instead of the conventional graphic signs might be able to have an opportunity to avoid problems of dyslexia and various forms of aphasia and agnosia, in contrast to those children using "phonematic" (phonetic) speech.

Pasamanick and Knobloch (1961, p. 90) conclude from their ongoing study of infants born to mothers with toxemia, bleeding, and influenza during pregnancy:

> A preliminary scrutiny of the data seems to indicate that prematurity, particularly that precipitated by toxemia of pregnancy or bleeding, is probably involved in the causation of gross and fine brain injury, but that the toxemia and placental difficulties are more likely to create minimal brain damage.

These and other authors also report a highly significant correlation between maternal nutrition and the incidence of prematurity (Braine, Heimer, Wortis, & Freedman, 1966; Drillien, 1957; Masland, 1961; M. F. A. Montagu, 1962; Pasamanick & Knobloch, 1958b, 1961).

The question remains whether it is the prematurity itself or the underlying factors which brought about the premature delivery which must be considered important when one seeks to understand the difficulties many of these children have later in life. A review of the literature indicates considerable divergence within the

thinking on the subject. All we can say at this point is that there are a number of factors which, when they influence both the developing fetus and the maternal organism, may result in premature ejection of the child unequipped for survival on its own within what is at that time of development an essentially hostile environment.

PERINATAL FACTORS

A marked change in the attitude of pediatricians and obstetricians has been taking place concerning the possibilities that adverse perinatal factors may affect the fetus. The direction in which many investigators are going is best illustrated by the example of erythroblastosis fetalis. Erythroblastosis fetalis is a hemolytic disease of the newborn caused by the development of antibodies against Rh-positive fetal red blood. The transfer of the antibodies from the mother's blood into the fetal blood can result in massive hemolysis of the fetal red blood cells. This results in severe jaundice due to the increased amounts of bilirubin and can affect the brain in a condition called *kernicterus,* which is accompanied by severe mental retardation. Exchange transfusions of Rh-positive blood immediately after birth eliminate the antibodies from the mother's blood and prevent the hemolysis and jaundice. In the last few years a new medical speciality, fetology, a middle ground where obstetrics and pediatrics meet, has promoted the development of new techniques which make it possible to counteract adverse influences on the fetus during the pregnancy itself. A technique for intrauterine transfusions had been developed and makes it possible to counteract much earlier any damage which may result from Rh incompatibility between mother and child. This technique is an example of other interventions which may become possible, for example, to prevent spontaneous abortions, miscarriages, stillbirth, and assorted gross birth defects.

Anoxic conditions at birth which can lead to neurological and behavioral disorders may be related to interruptions in fetal blood supply (Courville, 1954; W. E. Nelson, 1959). Placental dysfunction is evidenced often by necrotic placental sections caused, for example, by an abruptio placenta or a placenta praevia.

Besides prematurity, with all its attendent early and late complications, postmaturity has also been identified as a condition which could lead to problems of impaired central nervous system functioning. The etiology of this disorder may not be known until the mechanics of labor are better understood. A number of children born with the postmaturity syndrome also have placental dysfunction which includes clinical signs of cerebral damage due to anoxia and severe respiratory symptoms resulting from aspiration of meconium-containing amniotic fluid (W. E. Nelson, 1959).

One perinatal factor which has assumed increasing importance in our time is related to anesthetic or analgesic drugs administered to the mother during labor and during delivery. Such drugs, which decrease the respiratory capabilities of mother and infant, may result in hypoxia or even anoxia in the fetus. This can in turn lead to permanent death of sensitive brain cells, which may manifest itself later in life through difficulties in cognition and perception (Courville, 1954).

Windle (1966), in a comparative study involving the role of respiratory distress in brain damage in newborn monkeys, found that fetuses at term could withstand about 7 minutes of asphyxia without subsequent neurological symptoms. However, when his monkeys were asphyxiated for 8 minutes or longer, demonstrable, permanent, and structural brain damage occurred. Monkeys resuscitated after 12 to 15 minutes of asphyxia showed at maturity some ability to compensate for their early deficits, although others remained severely crippled throughout life, resembling children with cerebral palsy.

Tucker and Barnaran (1953) found the incidence of anoxia in the newborn to be directly proportional to the degree of trauma suffered by the infant. It seemed to be lowest in natural labor and highest in prolonged labor which was accompanied by the use of forceps. The more difficult the operative procedure was, the higher the incidence and degree of anoxia. They also found that the use of sedation substantially increased the incidence of anoxia. The excessive and forceful use of forceps has also been implicated in the development of later neurological problems by Wile and Davis (1941), who indicate that children delivered with forceps show a general reduction of psychic energy in addition to increased sensitivity and irritability.

While prolonged labor has served as one of the problem areas in the development of brain damage, precipitous delivery, such as in cesarean sections and very short labor, is also known to be the cause of permanent brain dysfunction in a number of children (Nesbitt, 1957). Kenworthy (1927) postulated that children delivered by cesarean section are prone to be less sensitized than children delivered via the vagina. The difficulty in evaluating the results of this study lies in properly weighing the influence of the kind of anesthesia required for a cesarean section as well as that of the blood loss occurring during the procedure. It would be of great interest to repeat this study in a sample of women whose cesarean section was done under hypnosis.

Otto Rank (1929) related the origin of anxiety to the trauma of birth. A number of other authors have supported this notion of birth as being a traumatic experience in itself which predisposes every individual for later anxiety. However, no scientific investigation of this hypothesis has ever been adequately undertaken, and the notion therefore remains speculative.

Birth order can also be a factor in perinatal

difficulties. The birth process in firstborn children is often more difficult than that in subsequent children. Many studies demonstrate the greater frequency of behavior problems in first-born children. Whether these behavior problems are sequelae of possible birth trauma or are related to subsequent experiences remains an open and unanswered question (M. F. A. Montagu, 1962; Nesbitt, 1957).

Questions are being raised at this point about the importance of uterine contractions in determining respiratory behavior as well as in acting as a positive stimulant to central nervous system development. Denenberg (1959) found a suggestion of such a relationship in rats.

Difficulties with delivery can occur with excessive amounts of analgesic medications if they delay uterine contractions. Dystocia (abnormal or difficult labor) can occur because of abnormalities of the expulsive force, e.g., as a result of drugs. Abnormalities of position or presentation or in development of the fetus, such as breech or shoulder presentations, or fetal malformations such as hydrocephalus can lead to dystocia. The presence of abdominal tumors may interfere with normal delivery. A too small pelvis can arrest the process of labor. In this connection it must be remembered that women who have not had medical examinations during the pregnancy and who therefore have not had their pelvises measured may be in arrested labor by the time they finally come to medical attention. If the factor of the narrow birth canal is not thought of at this time, labor is liable to become excessively prolonged, thus increasing the danger of possible brain damage in the children.

Multiple births increase maternal and fetal hazards and in this way relate to an increase in prenatal and perinatal mortality and morbidity (M. F. A. Montagu, 1962; Nesbitt, 1957).

In the last 15 years, hypoglycemia occurring immediately after birth, even in infants of nondiabetic mothers, has attracted increasing attention. The relation between sugar metabolism and cerebral function in the first months of life has not as yet been adequately studied, but it is entirely conceivable that the newborn brain can be damaged in the absence of its main metabolite: glucose. Haworth and Goodin (1960) in reviewing the literature and their own cases, found that in thirty-five children who had been known to have hypoglycemia prior to the age of 6 months, 51 percent had permanent neurological sequelae. In twenty-three children in whom the hypoglycemia occurred after the age of 6 months, only 12 percent showed subsequent brain damage. Apparently, then, hypoglycemia occurring early in life may have dire consequences. The practice of not feeding infants for the first 24 to 28 hours will need to be carefully reevaluated. (For an excellent review of factors involved in hypoglycemia in infancy, see Cornblath & Schwartz, 1966.)

POSTNATAL FACTORS

Postnatal organic factors loom large in the progressive development of the human organism. Various organic processes which occur in the first several weeks of posturine life determine the subsequent destiny of the child throughout his life-span, either by promoting growth and development or by hindering it.

As already discussed, one of the most obvious conditions which affects the well-being of the young infant is his weight at birth. The sequelae of prematurity have been extensively studied by Drillien (1964). Over one thousand mothers who delivered prematurely in two large maternity hospitals took part in a longitudinal study investigating the effect of economic and social factors on development after premature birth. The study revealed that mean developmental quotient scores for singletons and twins fell steadily with decreasing birth weight at all ages from 6 months to 4 years of age. Further, the twins in the study showed consistently lower scores than singletons of like birth weight at all ages. Developmental ability was related to "social grade" (social class) of the mother. "Social-grade" differences increased with age. In average and poor working-class homes, there was little difference in mental ability between those prematures who were 4½ pounds at birth and mature controls; in superior working-class and middle-class homes, children who weighed between 4½ and 5½ pounds at birth were still at a disadvantage at 4 years of age. There seemed to be a marked excess of dull, retarded, and defective children among those who were 4½ pounds or less at birth and more particularly if there were additional adverse factors in the environment, which probably accounts for the lack of differences between the prematures and the mature controls in the lower social grades. Most children who were seen to be dull, retarded, and defective during the preschool period were rather consistently seen in the same manner in later school testings.

Drillien (1964) also examined the preschool and early school behavior of the premature children. He pointed out that the incidence of all types of problems increased when maternal handling was obviously unsatisfactory. Feeding, sleeping, and toilet-training problems and negativism and overdependence predominated when the mother was overanxious, rigid, or indulgent. A small increase in the incidence of problems was found when birth weight was 4½ pounds or less. Using the Bristol Social Adjustment Guide, Drillien made observations on the behavior of children in school at ages 6½ to 7½ years. He found that the proportion of children considered unsettled or maladjusted increased with decreasing birth weight. Further, males showed consistently more adverse behavior than females. Children of all birth weights who were subjected to severe family stress showed an increase in adverse behavior, which was more marked when the birth weight had been 4½

pounds or less. Obstetric complications also added to the behavioral difficulties observed in children in low birth-weight groups. Where there was a history of severe complications of pregnancy and/or delivery, disturbed behavior increased. When premature children were compared with their siblings who were not premature, more disturbances were noticed in the premature group.

Drillien also examined intensively 112 babies whose weight at birth was 3 pounds or less. Defects of vision were found in 37 percent of the children who had passed the age for school entrance. Eight percent of the school-age group had some degree of congenital deficit. Other defects included cerebral diplegia (18 percent) epilepsy (7 percent), and speech defects (8 percent). At 5 years or over, one-third of the 112 subjects were below the 5th percentile for mature controls in weight; nearly one-half were behind in height, and over one-quarter in both weight and height. Sixty-six of the school-age children were given an intelligence test and only 9 percent scored 100 or over. Over one-third of the total were likely to be ineducable in normal schools for reasons of physical or mental defect or both; over one-third were dull children, who could probably be retained in normal schools but would require special educational assistances, and less than one-third were doing classwork appropriate to their age. In terms of behavior, only 30 percent of the school-age children were said to show no disturbance of behavior. Restlessness and hyperactivity were the most commonly reported problems. All in all, three-quarters of the 112 children were found to have some defect and/or mental retardation by the time they reached school age.

Confirmation of Drillien's work is provided by a study by Knobloch, Pasamanick, Harper, and Rider (1959). In this study 500 premature children were compared with 492 full-term infants matched in terms of social and economic circumstances and on a number of other significant variables. The premature infants at 40 weeks of age were ½ to 1 inch shorter and 500 to 1,000 grams lighter than the full term infants. They also had two to three times as many physical defects and 50 percent more illnesses. A significantly greater number of neurological impairments was also found in the premature group.

Braine et al. (1966) examined premature children longitudinally at 4 days, 6 weeks, 7 months, 7½ months, and 13½ months and compared them with a control group of full-term infants who received examinations at 4 days and 13½ months. The examinations included a measure of the strength of the grasp reflex, measures of the amplitude and the normality of the Moro reflex, a measure of gross motor development, and a test of visual following. A standardized mental scale was administered for the last two examinations, and a standardized test for gross motor development was given at the time of the last examination.

The results of this study showed that neonatal complications, hyperbilirubinemia, hypoxia, neonatal weight loss, and neonatal infections all correlated with the birth weight of the infant. Neonatal complications did not seem to be correlated with maternal complications or with socioeconomic ratings. At the time of the final examination at 13½ months of age, the prematures of both sexes scored significantly lower than full-term infants on standardized tests of gross motor development as well as on standardized "mental tests." Male prematures were significantly inferior in their performance on psychological and motor tests when compared with female prematures of the same birth weight at age 13½ months. However, no comparable sex differences were found in the full-term infants. Brain damage was much more frequently present in male when compared with female prematures. With respect to complications, a greater male vulnerability to insult was suggested primarily in relation to toxemia during the pregnancy and hyperbilirubinemia. The males who were affected by their mothers' toxemia during the pregnancy tended to perform as expected on all tests up to the age of 1 year, at which time they began to show gross impairment in motor and psychological functioning. Strikingly, children who suffered from postnatal hypoxia and who lost much weight shortly after birth showed impairment in their cognitive functions almost immediately, including such items as visual following and visual comprehension of objects.

DeHirsch, Jansky, and Langford (1966) found that 8-year-olds who had been born prematurely were below their full-term age-mates in academic achievements. The same observation has been made by Kawi and Pasamanick (1959).

Drillien (1959) and Shirley (1939) observed that prematures as children presented more frequent problems in feeding and possibly also in respiratory, bowel, and bladder functioning. There is the possibility that inadequate cutaneous stimulation may play a role in their greater susceptibility to various disorders of the upper respiratory, gastrointestinal, and genitourinary systems. This possibility has yet to be confirmed by an adequately rigorous research study. Other studies by Kock (1964), Katz and Taylor (1967), and Cutlel, Heimer, Wortis, and Freedman (1965) all point to the deleterious effect of prematurity.

Lubchenco et al. (1963) made the following conclusions from their study of surviving infants whose birth weights were 1,500 grams (3 pounds, 4 ounces) or less. Sixty-eight percent of their sample had central nervous system visual handicaps, with the incidence and severity of handicaps showing an inverse relationship to birth weight. These handicaps included visual defects due primarily to retrolental fibroplasia and brain damage.

Lubchenco et al. (1963, p. 114) also noted that "Growth retardation was severe, social and emotional problems were encountered, and school failures among children with normal intelligence was seen in 30% of the group."

On the basis of their results the authors felt compelled to consider the following points: The high incidence of defects noted among the children in this study causes concern about the twelve children who did not return for the examinations because they were placed in adoptive homes. The adjustment of adoptive parents to unsuspected neurological handicaps must have been difficult and accompanied by feelings uncomplimentary to the adoption agencies. On the basis of findings presented in this review, one would suggest that adoptive parents be fully informed of the possibility of later sequelae of premature birth. Knobloch has shown that one can reasonably be sure of neurological damage by 40 weeks of age. The adverse effects on emotional growth of the child and the difficulty in adoptive-home adjustment when placement is delayed until 10 to 12 months must also be considered.

A number of other organic conditions seem to co-vary at times with low birth weight. Bacola, Behrle, DeSchweinitz, Miller, and Mira (1966a, 1966b) indicate that respiratory disease syndrome is often associated with low birth weight. All the infants in their study considered to be mentally retarded had respiratory disease syndrome in its most severe form. They found an inverse relationship between respiratory disease syndrome, birth weight, and gestational age on the one hand and the incidence of mental retardation on the other.

Idiopathic hypoparathyroidism, while a relatively rare condition, also can result in rather impaired conditions later in life. Kunstadter, Tanman, and Cornblath (1963), who studied this condition in two newborn infants of diabetic mothers, stressed the importance of maintaining normocalcemic levels through adequate vitamin D therapy indefinitely. Failure to control hypoparathyroidism results in convulsive seizures, behavior disorders, mental retardation, and even-

tually nonreversible organic changes. Accordingly in another comparative study Harlow and Griffin (1965) examined the effects of induced biochemical errors in a monkey population. They raised monkeys from birth on a high-L-Phenylalinine diet and found that these animals developed profound mental retardation. They did not recover intellectually after being on this diet for 2 years. Induced phenylktonuria also appears to debase the infant monkey's play pattern. Infants must learn to play early in life in order to develop normal sociosexual lives.

Neonatal hyperbilirubinemia may also result in severe psychological behavioral problems in children. VanCamp (1964) suggests that neonatal hyperbilirubinemia may result in severe neurological involvement. She feels that the effects of this condition may range on a continuum from severe neurological involvement to minor intellectual impairment.

Occasionally an emotionally based condition may have symptoms similar to those seen in organic dysfunction. Powell, Brasel, and Blizzard (1967a) studied thirteen children who had clinical findings suggestive of idiopathic hypopituitarism. Yet the syndrome in each case was thought to be related to a disturbed parent-child relationship. The authors warned that this syndrome is common and must be considered whenever lack of adequate growth is evaluated. Adequate treatment in these cases requires the removal of the child from the home. In a subsequent study (1967b) deficiencies in ACTH and growth hormones were common defects in thirteen short-statured children studied. These children grew at remarkable rates when removed from their emotionally disturbed environments, and the levels of growth hormones returned to normal.

Abnormal light sensitivity in neonates may also contribute to disturbances later in life. Anderson and Rosenblith (1964) studied 700 neonates, four of which showed abnormal sensitivity to light. These four children showed severe disturbances (muscle flaccidity and hypertonicity) in development during the first year of life.

Visual attentiveness in babies is also apparently related to their condition at the time of birth. Lewis, Bartels, Campbell, and Goldberg (1967) found that infants whose Apgar scores were between 7 and 9 were significantly less attentive than infants who rated 10. The difference, in general, held over the first year and appears to indicate that individual differences in attention within the first year of life are in part a function of birth condition.

Stress can have a deleterious effect on the neonate. Klatskin, McGarry, and Steward (1966) studied the developmental test findings of twenty-two infants judged normal at birth and compared them with those of twenty-one potentially stressed infants. At 3 to 4 months of age no differences were found between the two groups. At 6 to 7 months of age the stressed infants were more variable in performance in the adaptive, fine motor, gross motor, and observed language test areas. There was an increased number of failures even at levels below chronological age within the stressed group. The data indicate that it is easier to detect the effects of neonatal stress within the latter half of the first year of life than within the first 6 months. Heider (1966) studied the susceptibility or vulnerability to stress in infants. She found that vulnerability showed an inverse relation to physiological factors such as robust physiques, good energy, and good energy resources. Leonard, Rhymes, and Solnit (1966) relate the effect of stress to failure to thrive in infants. He found that children who fell into this category had often endured considerable stress. The families of these children often were undergoing multiple stress factors. The mothers of these children did not seem able to carry the whole burden for the family without adequate support from their husbands.

Apparently, crying can also have ramifications for later behavior in the child. Karelitz, Fisichelli, Costa, Karelitz, and Rosenfeld (1964) studied the cries of thirty-eight infants aged 4 to 10 days. They measured outburst frequency during the most active 20-second period of crying. The crying scores showed a significant correlation ($+.45$) with Cattell IQ at 15 to 20 months and a nonsignificant trend ($+.32$) with speech ratings at 3 years.

Honzik, Hutchings, and Burnip (1965) compared the performance of 197 full-term babies tested at 8 months of age to determine whether conditions during pregnancy and the perinatal period are related to infants' later development. Assessments made by two pediatricians and a psychologist showed that the mental and motor test scores were significantly related to whether children were classified as definitely suspect, possibly suspect, or not suspect at birth. The definitely suspect group was most clearly differentiated from the other groups (not suspect, possibly suspect, and suspect). As a group, the infants for whom there was most concern at birth about possible neurological involvement were at the age of 8 months most likely to be poorly coordinated, to have short attention spans, to be markedly distractible and hypoactive or hyperactive, and to perform less well on tests of eye-hand coordination and problem solving.

There is some evidence to suggest that infants who are highly prone to develop schizophrenia may be identified in early infancy. Fish, Shapiro, Halpern, and Wile (1965) studied the development of a group of infants at 1 month of age. They were able to classify children as vulnerable to schizophrenia by evaluating them according to the degree of abnormally uneven neurological development, characterized by unusual combinations of retardation and precocity. In their evaluation of sixteen infants they found three who were judged to be "vulnerable to schizophrenia." These children were subsequently evaluated at nine to ten years of age by a psychiatrist and a psychologist who were unaware of their previous classification. This subsequent evaluation characterized all three of the vulnerable children as grossly pathological when compared with other children. Results similar to those obtained in this study were also obtained by Fish and Alpert (1962). While the authors acknowledge that it is difficult to generalize from their small samples, they nevertheless suggest that clinicians should alert themselves to detect such developmental disorders in infants.

Any illness or injury within the first month of life which has a primary or secondary effect on central nervous system functioning can also have long-term behavioral consequences. These include intracranial hemorrhage, trauma, and encephalitis, which are primary destructive forces, and pneumonitis, atelectasis, diaphragmatic hernia, and anemic cardiac decompensation or arrest, which create secondary effects on the central nervous system as a result of lowered oxygen potential (hypoxia). Illnesses which create marked changes in electrolyte balance also might destroy nervous tissues.

Nutritional deficiencies, especially inadequacies in protein intake, have been seen to create innumerable problems during pregnancy. So, too, can severe malnutrition in the first months of life affect total growth patterns, but more specifically it can be the basis of severe to profound mental retardation. It can be assumed that lesser degrees of malnourishment could lead to behavioral and/or learning disorders (avitaminosis, kwashiorkor) (W. E. Nelson, 1959; Protein malnutrition, 1968).

Pneumonia and vomiting combined with inadequate food intake and insufficient external stimulation are part of the total picture in tracheoesophageal fistulas. Following corrective surgery, these children are placed in isolettes with very little handling or stimulation of any sensory input pathways, leading to a state resembling marasmus.

In summing up this chapter, we wish to underline the great number and variety of prenatal, perinatal, and postnatal factors which have been related to neurological, intellectual, emotional, and behavioral disturbances later in life. At the present state of our knowledge we know how to prevent or alleviate many of the factors, while others are still totally beyond our control. More should be done to make sure that what is known is applied in the care of all expectant mothers' and their newborn babies. Prevention is at all times superior to rehabilitation after the damage has already occurred. The research done so far stresses particularly the importance of adequate maternal medical care during the pregnancy and of adequate medical attention to the infant during the first weeks of life.

REFERENCES

Anderson, R. B., & Rosenblith, J. F. Light sensitivity in the neonate: A preliminary report. *Biologia Neonatorum,* 1964, **7**, 83–94.

Antonov, A. N. Children born during the siege of Leningrad in 1942. *The Journal of Pediatrics,* 1947, **30**, 250–259.

Apgar, V. Drugs in pregnancy. *The Journal of the American Medical Association,* 1964, **190**, 840–841.

Assali, H. S., & Hameresz, J. Adrenocorticotropic substances from human placenta. *Endocrinology,* 1954, **55**, 561–567.

Bacola, E., Behrle, F., DeSchweinitz, L., Miller, H. C., & Mira, M. Perinatal and environmental factors in late neurogenic sequelae. *American Journal of Diseases of Children,* 1966, **112**, 359–367.(a)

Bacola, E., Behrle, F., DeSchweinitz, L., Miller,

H., & Mira, M. Perinatal and environmental factors in late neurogenic sequelae. II. Infants having birth weights from 1,500 to 2,500 grams. *American Journal of Diseases of Children,* 1966, **112,** 369–374.(b)

Billewicz, W. Z., & Thomson, A. M. The effect of maternal social class and structure upon the incidence of prematurity. *Proceedings of the Nutrition Society,* 1957, **16,** v.

Blau, A., Slaff, B., Easton, K., Welkowitz, J., Springarn, J., & Cohen, J. The psychogenic etiology of premature births. *Psychosomatic Medicine,* 1963, **25,** 201–211.

Braine, M. D. S., Heimer, C. B., Wortis, H., & Freedman, A. M. Factors associated with impairment of the early development of prematures. *Monographs of the Society for Research in Child Development,* 1966, **31** (4, Whole No. 106).

Brandon, M. W. G. The intellectual and social status of children of mental defectives. *The Journal of Mental Science,* 1957, **103,** 710–724.

Brown, T. *Religio Medici.* (Text established by J. J. Denonian) New York: Cambridge University Press, 1955.

Burke, B. S., Beal, V. A., Kirkwood, S. B., & Stuart, H. C. The influence of nutrition during pregnancy upon the condition of the infant at birth. *The Journal of Nutrition,* 1943, **26,** 569–583.

Burke, B. S., Stevenson, S. S., Worcester, J., & Stuart, H. C. Nutrition studies during pregnancy. Relation of maternal nutrition to conditions of infant at birth: A study of siblings. *The Journal of Nutrition,* 1949, **38,** 453–467.

Burt, C. Inheritance of mental ability. *Eugenics Review,* 1957, **43,** 137–147.

Cobrinik, R. W., Hood, R. T., Jr., & Chusid,

E. Effect of maternal narcotic addition on newborn infants: Review of literature and report on 22 cases. *Pediatrics,* 1959, **24,** 288–304.

Cornblath, M., & Schwartz, R. *Disorders of carbohydrate metabolism in infancy.* Philadelphia: Saunders, 1966.

Courville, C. B. *Cerebral palsy.* Los Angeles: San Lucas, 1954.

Cramond, W. A. Psychological aspects of uterine dysfunction. *The Lancet,* 1954, **267,** 1241–1245.

Cutel, R., Heimer, C., Wortis, H., & Freedman, A. M. The effects of prenatal and neonatal complications on the development of premature children at two and one-half years of age. *The Journal of Genetic Psychology,* 1965, **107,** 261–267.

DeHirsch, K., Jansky, J., & Langford, W. S. Comparisons between prematurely and maturely born children at three age levels. *American Journal of Orthopsychiatry,* 1966, **36,** 616–628.

DeKaban, A. S. The outcome of pregnancy in diabetic women. II. Analysis of clinical abnormalities and pathologic lesions in offspring of diabetic mothers. *The Journal of Pediatrics,* 1959, **55,** 767–778.

Denenberg, V. H. Interactive effects of infantile and adult shock levels upon learning. *Psychological Reports,* 1959, **5,** 357–364.

Doyle, G., & Yule, E. P. Grooming activity and freezing behavior in relation to emotionality in albino rats. *Animal Behavior,* 1959, **7,** 18–22.

Drillien, C. M. The social and economic factors affecting the incidence of premature birth. I. Premature births without complications of pregnancy. *Journal of Obstetrics and Gynaecology of the British Empire,* 1957, **64,** 161–184.

Drillien, C. M. Physical and mental handicaps in the prematurely born. *Journal of Obstetrics and Gynaecology of the British Empire,* 1959, **66,** 721–731.

Drillien, C. M. *The growth and development of the prematurely born infant.* Baltimore: Williams & Wilkins, 1964.

Ebbs, J. H., Tisdall, F. H., & Scott, W. A. The influence of prenatal diet on the mother and child. *The Journal of Nutrition,* 1941, **22,** 515–526.

Fish, B., & Alpert, M. Abnormal states of consciousness and muscle tone in infants born to schizophrenic mothers. *American Journal of Psychiatry,* 1962, **119,** 439–445.

Fish, B., Shapiro, T., Halpern, F., & Wile, R. The prediction of schizophrenia in infancy. III. A ten-year follow-up report of neurological and psychological development. *American Journal of Psychiatry,* 1965, **121,** 768–775.

Friedman, A. M. The effect of hyperbilirubinemia on premature infants. Unpublished report, New York Medical College, 1961.

Furchtgott, E., & Echols, M. Activity and emotionality in pre- and neonatally X-irradiated rats. *Journal of Comparative and Physiological Psychology,* 1958, **51,** 541–545.(a)

Furchtgott, E., & Echols, M. Locomotor co-ordination following pre- and neonatal X-irradiation. *Journal of Comparative and Physiological Psychology,* 1958, **51,** 292–294.(b)

Furchtgott, E., Echols, M., & Openshaw, J. W. Maze learning in pre- and neonatal X-irradiated rats. *Journal of Comparative and Physiological Psychology,* 1958, **51,** 178–180.

Gellis, S. S., & Hsia, D. Y. Y. The infant of the diabetic mother. *A. M. A. Journal of Diseases in Children,* 1959, **97,** 1–41.

Gregg, N. M. Congenital cataract following German measles in the mother. *Transactions of the Ophthalmological Society of Australia (British Medical Association),* 1941, **3,** 35–43.

Gunter, L. M. Psychopathology and stress in the life experience of mothers of premature infants. *American Journal of Obstetrics and Gynecology,* 1963, **86,** 333–340.

Hardy, J. B. Perinatal factors and intelligence. In S. F. Osler & R. E. Cooke (Eds.), *The Biosocial Basis of Mental Retardation.* Baltimore: Johns Hopkins, 1965. Pp. 35–60.

Harlow, H. F., & Griffin, G. Induced mental and social deficits in Rhesus monkeys. In S. F. Osler & R. E. Cooke (Eds.), *The Biosocial Basis of Mental Retardation.* Baltimore: Johns Hopkins, 1965. Pp. 87–106.

Haworth, J., & Goodin, F. Idiopathic spontaneous hypoglycemia in children. *Pediatrics,* 1960, **25,** 748–765.

Heider, G. M. Vulnerability in infants and young children: A pilot study. *Genetic Psychology Monographs,* 1966, **73,** 1–216.

Higgins, J. V. A study of intelligence of the Nam family in Minnesota. *American Journal of Mental Deficiency,* 1959, **64,** 491–504.

Hockman, C. H. Prenatal maternal stress in the rat: Its effects on emotional behavior in the offspring. Paper presented at the meeting of the Eastern Psychological Association, Philadelphia, 1961.

Honzik, M. P., Hutchings, J. J., & Burnip, S. R. Birth record assessments and test performance at eight months. *American Journal of Diseases of Children,* 1965, **109,** 416–426.

Ingle, D. J., & Fisher, G. T. Effect of adrenalectomy during gestation on size of adrenals in newborn rats. *Proceedings of the Society for Experimental Biology,* 1938, **39,** 149–150.

Johnson, R. H., & Haines, W. J. Extraction of adrenal cortex hormonal activity from placental tissue. *Science,* 1952, **116,** 456–457.

Karelitz, S., Fisichelli, V. R., Costa, J., Karelitz, R., & Rosenfeld, L. Relation of crying activity in early infancy to speech and intellectual development at age three years. *Child Development,* 1964, **35,** 769–777.

Katz, C. M., & Taylor, P. M. The incidence of low birthweight in children with severe mental retardation. *American Journal of Diseases of Children,* 1967, **114,** 80–87.

Kawi, A. A., & Pasamanick, B. Prenatal and paranatal factors in the development of childhood reading disorders. *Monographs of the Society for Research in Child Development,* 1959, No. 24.

Kenworthy, M. The pre-natal and early post-natal phenomenon of consciousness. In E. Dummer, (Ed.), *The unconscious.* New York: Knopf, 1927.

Kerr, G. R., Chamove, A. S., Harlow, H. F., & Waisman, H. A. Fetal PKU: The effect of maternal hyperphenylalanmenia during pregnancy in the Rhesus monkey (Mocaca Mulatte). *Pediatrics,* 1968, **42,** 27–36.

Klatskin, E. H., McGarry, M. E., & Steward, M. S. Variability in development test patterns as a sequel of neonatal stress. *Child Development,* 1966, **37,** 819–826.

Kline, A. H., Blattner, R. J., & Lunin, M. Transplacental effect of tetracyclines on teeth. *The Journal of the American Medical Association,* 1964, **188,** 178–180.

Knobil, E., & Briggs, F. N. Fetal-maternal endocrine interrelations: The hypophyseal-adrenal system. *Endocrinology,* 1955, **57,** 147-152.

Knobloch, H., & Pasamanick, B. Seasonal variation in the births of the mentally deficient. *American Journal of Public Health,* 1958, **48,** 1201–1208.

Knobloch, H. B., Pasamanick, B., Harper, P. A., & Rider, E. The effect of prematurity on health and growth. *American Journal of Public Health,* 1959, **49,** 1164–1173.

Kock, H. L. A study of twins born at different levels of maturity. *Child Development,* 1964, **35,** 1265-1282.

Kunstadter, R. H., Oh, W., Tanman, F., & Cornblath, M. Idiopathic hypoparathyroidism in the newborn. *American Journal of Diseases of Children,* 1963, **105,** 499–506.

Leonard, M. F., Rhymes, J. P., & Solnit, A. J. Failure to thrive in infants. *American Journal of Diseases of Children,* 1966, **111,** 600–612.

Levinson, B. Effects of foetal irradiation on learning. *Journal of Comparative and Physiological Psychology,* 1952, **45,** 140–145.

Lewis, M., Bartels, B., Campbell, H., & Goldberg, S. Individual differences in attention: The relation between infants' condition at birth and attention distribution within the first year. *American Journal of Diseases of Children,* 1967, **113,** 461–465.

Lindsten, J., & Hagert, C. G. Congenital malformations in mothers 42 years of age and over. *Nurdisk Medicin,* 1959, **61,** 753–756.

Lubchenco, L. O., Horner, F. A., Reed, L. H., Hix, I. E., Jr., Metcalf, D., Cohig, R., Elliott, H. C. & Bourg, M. Sequelae of premature birth.

American Journal of Diseases of Children, 1963, **106**, 101–115.

Luria, A. R. *Human brain and psychological processes.* New York: Harper & Row, 1966.

Macfarlane, W. V., Pennycuik, P. R., & Thrift, E. Resorption and loss of fetuses in rats living at 35° C. *Journal of Physiology,* 1957, **135**, 451–459.

Masland, R. L. Researches into prenatal factors that lead to neuropsychiatric sequelae in childhood. In G. Caplan (Ed.), *Prevention of mental disorders in children.* New York: Basic Books, 1961, Pp. 52–73.

Masland, R. L., Sarason, S. B., & Gladwin, T. *Mental subnormality: Biological, psychological and cultural factors.* New York: Basic Books, 1958.

McDonald, R. L., Gynther, M. D., & Christakos, A. C. Relations between maternal anxiety and obstetric complications. *Psychosomatic Medicine,* 1963, **25**, 357–363.

Meier, G. W., Bunch, M. E., Nolan, C. T., & Scheidler, C. H. Anoxia, behavioral development and learning ability: A comparative-experimental approach. *Psychological Monographs,* 1960, **74**, No. 1.

Montagu, A. Neonatal and infant immaturity in man. *The Journal of the American Medical Association,* 1961, **178**, 156–157.

Montagu, M. F. A. *Prenatal influences.* Springfield, Ill.: Charles C. Thomas, 1962.

Moore, B. C. Prematurity and adaptive behavior in mental retardates. *Arizona Medicine,* 1966, **23**, 589–591.

Nelson, M. M., Asling, C. W., & Evans, H. M. Production of multiple congenital abnormalities in young by pleroylglutamic acid deficiency during gestation. *The Journal of Nutrition,* 1952, **48**, 61–80.

Nelson, W. E. *Textbook of pediatrics.* (7th ed.) Philadelphia: Saunders, 1959.

Nesbitt, R. E. L., Jr. *Perinatal loss in modern obstetrics.* Philadelphia: Davis, 1957.

Pasamanick, B., & Knobloch, H. The contribution of some organic factors to school retardation in Negro children. *Journal of Negro Education,* 1958, **27**, 4–9. (a)

Pasamanick, B., & Knobloch, H. Seasonal variation in complications of pregnancy. *Obstetrics and Gynecology,* 1958, **12**, 110–112. (b)

Pasamanick, B., & Knobloch, H. Epidemiologic studies on the complications of pregnancy and the birth process. In G. Caplan (Ed.), *Prevention of mental disorders in children.* New York: Basic Books, 1961, Pp. 74–91.

Pasamanick, B., & Knobloch, H. *The epidemiology of reproductive causality.* Paper presented at the Fifth International Congress of Child Psychiatry, Scheveninger, The Netherlands, August, 1962.

Pieper, A. *Cerebral function in infancy and childhood.* New York: Consultants Bureau, 1963.

Plummer, G. W. Anomalies occurring in children exposed in utero to atomic bomb in Hiroshima. *Pediatrics,* 1952, **10**, 687–692.

Poulton, B. R., & Reece, R. P. The activity of the pituitary-adrenal cortex axis during pregnancy and lactation. *Endocrinology,* 1957, **61**, 217–225.

Powell, G. F., Brasel, J. A., & Blizzard, R. M. Emotional deprivation and growth retardation simulating idiopathic hypopituitarism: Clinical evaluation of the syndrome. *The New England Journal of Medicine,* 1967, **276**, 1271–1278. (a)

Powell, G. F., Brasel, M. D., & Blizzard, R. M. Emotional deprivation and growth retardation simulating idiopathic hypopituitarism: Endocrinologic evaluation of the syndrome. *The New England Journal of Medicine,* 1967, **276,** 1279–1283. (b)

Protein Malnutrition may be chief mental growth barrier. *Hospital Tribune,* Oct. 7, 1968.

Rank, O. *The trauma of birth.* New York: Harcourt, Brace, 1929.

Scott, E. M., Illsley, R., & Biles, M. E. A psychological investigation of primigravidae, III. Some aspects of maternal behavior. *Journal of Obstetrics and Gynaecology of the British Empire,* 1956, **63,** 494–501.

Scott, E. M., Illsley, R., & Thomson, A. M. A psychological investigation of primigravidae, II. Maternal social class, age, physique and intelligence. *Journal of Obstetrics and Gynaecology of the British Empire,* 1956, **63,** 338–343.

Scott, E. M., & Thomson, A. M. A psychological investigation of primigravidae. I. Factors and the clinical phenomena of labour. *Journal of Obstetrics and Gynaecology of the British Empire,* 1956, **63,** 331–337. (b)

Scott, E. M., & Thomson, A. M. A psychological investigation of primigravidae, I. Methods. *Journal of Obstetrics and Gynaecology of the British Empire,* 1956, **63,** 331–337. (b)

Selye, H. *The physiology and pathology of exposure to stress.* Montreal: Acten, 1950.

Shane, J. M. Congenital anomalies secondary to maternal drug ingestion. *The Journal of the Oklahoma State Medical Association,* 1968, **61,** 529–532.

Shirley, M. A behavior syndrome characterizing prematurely born children. *Child Development,* 1939, **10,** 115–124.

Sontag, L. W. Differences in modifiability of fetal behavior and physiology. *Psychosomatic Medicine,* 1944, **6,** 151–154.

Sontag, L. W. Implications of fetal behavior and environment for adult personalities. *Annals of the New York Academy of Science,* 1966, **134,** 782–786.

Stewart, A. M. Environmental hazards of pregnancy. *Journal of Obstetrics and Gynaecology of the British Empire,* 1959, **66,** 739–742.

Stott, D. H. Physical and mental handicaps following a disturbed pregnancy. *The Lancet,* 1957, **7,** 1006–1012.

Stott, D. H. Mongolism related in emotional shock in early pregnancy. *Vita Humana,* 1961, **4,** 57–76.

Thompson, W. D. Influence of prenatal maternal anxiety on emotionality in young rats. *Science,* 1957, **125,** 698–699.

Thompson, W. D. Early environmental influences on behavioral development. *American Journal of Orthopsychiatry,* 1960, **30,** 306–314.

Thompson, W. D. The effects of prenatal and early postnatal experience. In S. A. Barnett (Ed.), *Lessons from animal behavior for the clinician.* London: Heinemann, 1962, Pp. 10–17.

Thompson, W. D., & Olian, S. Some effects on offspring behavior of maternal adrenalin injections during pregnancy in three inbred mouse strains. *Psychological Reports,* 1961, **8,** 87–90.

Thompson, W. D., & Sontag, L. W. Behavioral effects in the offspring of rats subjected to audiogenic seizures during the gestation period. *Journal of Comparative and Physiological Psychology,* 1956, **49** 454–456.

Tucker, B. W., & Barnaran, H. B. W. The immediate effects of prolonged labor with forceps delivery, precipitate labor with spontaneous delivery and natural labor with spontaneous delivery on the child. *American Journal of Obstetrics and Gynecology,* 1953, **66,** 540–550.

VanCamp, D. Psychological evaluation of children who had neonatal hyperbilirubinemia. *American Journal of Mental Deficiency,* 1964, **68,** 803–806.

Vincent, N. M. The effects of prenatal alcoholism upon motivation, emotionality and learning in the rat. *American Psychologist,* 1958, **13,** 401.

Voorhess, M. L. Masculinization of the female fetus associated with Norethindrone-Mestranol therapy during pregnancy. *The Journal of Pediatrics,* 1967, **71,** 128–131.

Werboff, J. Developmental effects of prenatal drug administration in the white rat. Paper presented at the third annual meeting of the Midwestern Psychological Association, Chicago, May, 1959.

Wile, I. S., & Davis, R. The relation of birth to behavior. *American Journal of Orthopsychiatry,* 1941, **11,** 320–324.

Wilkerson, H. L. C. Maternal prediabetes and outcome of pregnancy: A preliminary report. *American Journal of Public Health,* 1959, **49,** 1032–1040.

Windle, W. F. Role of respiratory distress in asphyxial brain damage of the newborn. *Cerebral Palsy Journal,* 1966, **27,** 3–6.

Yamazaki, J. N., Wright, S. W., & Wright, P. M. Outcome of pregnancy in women exposed to atomic bomb in Nagasaki. *American Journal of Disturbed Children,* 1954, **87,** 448–463.

Yeroshalmy, J. Age of father and survival of offspring. *Human Biology,* 1939, **2,** 342–356.

Zitran, A., Feber, P., & Cohen, D. Pre- and paranatal factors in mental disorders of children. *The Journal of Nervous and Mental Disease,* 1964, **139,** 357–361.

5 Etiology of Mental Disorders: Sociocultural Aspects

Morton Beiser

The community mental health movement has emerged as a social innovation in response to felt needs within the social system (Seely, 1953). Impetus for the movement was no doubt generated when extraordinarily high rates of psychiatric disorder were found among young men otherwise potentially eligible for military service during the Second World War (Mora, 1959). Caplan has suggested that the continuing widespread interest in mental disorders in the intervening score of years has been motivated partly by the same societal considerations — the need to conserve manpower, especially as it is now required in a period of rapid technological development.

Since the passage of the Mental Health Study Act of 1955 and President Kennedy's message to Congress on February 5, 1963, there has been an increasing assumption of responsibility by government for the general welfare of citizens (Caplan, 1967), and the growth and development of mental health services has been one product of this.

Among the ensuing proliferation of ideologies and approaches, the concept of prevention has assumed increasing prominence. This focuses attention most logically on prevention or treatment of disorders in children. Of this, Caplan (1961, p. 48, quoted in Weinberg, 1967,) has written:

> The focus upon the community rather upon individual children introduces a new viewpoint that transforms some old and rather insignificant side issues into exciting and complicated problems of strategy and tactics in both the research and action fields. For example, as soon as we focus upon the community we can no longer restrict our clinical gaze to those individuals who penetrate the barriers and appear as patients within the walls of our clinics. We must also look outside the walls and we must even go ourselves and work outside the walls. This . . . upsets our previous equilibrium in regard to the deployment of our specialists [sic] resources. We can no longer base our decision on which patients to treat entirely by chance, or upon our therapeutic predictions, or upon the technical interest of the case. Instead we have to develop priorities based also upon community implications of our treatment. From here it is a short step to real-

150

izing the necessity for a careful evaluation of how best to deploy the efforts of our scarce personnel.

This newer and broader focus of effort has highlighted the inadequacies of theory and the relative lack of therapeutic tools which the mental health professions bring to their expanded task. In turn, these inadequacies have limited the mental health worker's sphere of influence, let alone his effectiveness, among groups who seem to be most in need of services (Hollingshead & Redlich, 1958; Myers & Bean 1968; Myers & Schaffer, 1954).

Psychiatric disorder is one of a set of interrelated social problems which must be dealt with at the community level and this calls for revision of theory and practice. This does not mean that we must discard all that we know or have inferred about the nature of psychiatric disorder—in part, the task will be to assemble real knowledge and solid inferences so that creative strategies of intervention can be evolved (Caplan, 1961; Eisenberg & Gruenberg, 1961).

In this chapter we shall attempt to survey systematically what is known and believed about the sociocultural aspects of psychiatric disorder in children.

The survey, while systematic, is not exhaustive. An exhaustive survey will require an adequate theoretical framework, something we do not currently possess.

PSYCHIATRIC DISORDER IN CHILDREN

Research in the behavioral sciences is sometimes characterized as being mainly (1) descriptive or (2) explanatory. In child psychiatry, we suffer from a serious lack of adequate descriptive studies. In part. this is a consequence of not having a generally agreed-upon system of categorization, at least until very recently (Jenkins & Cole, 1964; Rutter, 1963).

The descriptive studies discussed in this chapter are drawn from a variety of diverse sources and employ a variety of different methods. The results described are therefore hardly comparable in any strict sense. However, some common themes are highlighted, which seem to require further study and clarification.

In the interest of clarity, the descriptive studies have been grouped according to whether they deal primarily with groups of children in treatment or with groups in other settings, such as schools.

One can further divide such studies with regard to focus. In this light, we consider studies "general" if they refer to psychiatric disorder as a whole and "specific" if they focus on specific syndromes, like psychosis and mental deficiency. The implications of each approach for research and practice have been discussed elsewhere (Beiser, 1968; A. H. Leighton, 1959).

Without the kind of background such descriptive studies provide, all explanatory or etiologic models must be regarded with reservation. Nevertheless, some extremely convincing reports have appeared. In the main, the focus has tended to be one-sided; the emphasis has tended to be exclusively developmental. While much lip service is paid to the idea of studying the personality in interaction with the current environment, the former has occupied most of our attention. The role of current stresses is frequently considered to be "merely" an activator of deep-seated conflicts in the personality.

While conflicts, defenses, and the various ego functions are of undoubted importance, we have begun to recognize syndromes in which the *balance* of etiologic forces seems to be on the situational side.[1]

---

[1] In adult psychiatry, relatively new diagnostic terms such as *black-patch syndrome* and *war neurosis,* which indicate that the relative balance of the determinants is not in the personality but in the situation, point to recognition of this, in professional circles.

In this chapter, we shall review some of the sociocultural determinants of personality development which have mental health relevance, such as interference with the physiological integrity of the central nervous system, the establishment of human-relatedness, issues of autonomy and control, and the development of skills. We shall also turn our attention to some situations with mental health implications, particularly the school experience.

The general scheme of organization is presented below:

Descriptive Studies: General

1. Groups in treatment settings
2. Groups in community settings:
   a. Studies of school populations
   b. Studies of other community agencies dealing with children
   c. Neighborhood studies

Explanatory Studies

1. Developmental approach:
   a. Interference with the physiological integrity of the central nervous system
   b. Relatedness
   c. Aggression, autonomy, and control
   d. Development of skills
   e. Cognitive map of the social environment
2. Situational approach:
   a. School
   b. Others:
      War
      Disaster
      Migration
      Death and bereavements

"GENERAL" DESCRIPTIVE STUDIES

Descriptive studies give us information about several important questions: (1) What is the extent of psychiatric disorder among children? (2) How is disorder distributed—or, to put the question another way, are there groups of children who seem to be at special risk of developing disorder? It is from such background information that explanatory studies derive their meaning.

Groups in Treatment Settings

Rates and demographic characteristics of patients treated in outpatient clinics (Rosen, Bahn, & Kramer, 1964; Rosen, Bahn, Shellow, & Bower, 1965) have limited utility in studying etiology. This is so because many factors other than psychiatric disorder per se determine clinic attendance (Myers & Schaffer, 1954; Raphael, 1964). So-called treated prevalence figures are often most useful in identifying relationships between psychiatric facilities and the larger social system (Hollingshead & Redlich, 1958; Rosen et al., 1965). They also serve to highlight trends, such as the relationships between various categories of treated disorder and certain demographic variables. The significance of these findings can be studied further by using more representative populations.

As part of a larger study of psychiatric clinic utilization in the United States, Rosen (Rosen et al., 1964) reports some interesting findings regarding children under the age of 18. He presents figures on estimated national and regional rates of terminated cases for all psychiatric clinics for the year ending June 30, 1961. The rate for the group under 18 is 212 per 100,000 children in the general population (using 1960 census data as base line). The rates vary markedly by region from a high of 420 per 100,000 in the Northeast to 140 per 100,000 in the South. This probably reflects differential availability of services and attitudinal differences toward mental health, rather than a "true" picture of crazy Yankees and composed Southerners.

Groups in Other Community Settings

The other studies reported in this section attempt to deal with the problems of underreporting and selection biases inherent in a study of clinic populations alone by broadening the base for observations. Children in the care of general practitioners, children in schools, children who are clients of various community agencies, and children simply living at home —all these have been studied, and the results have been provocative indeed.

How much disorder? Beier, Binder, and Robbins (1961) interviewed a sample of schoolteachers and general practitioners in the state of Indiana and asked them to estimate the number of emotionally disturbed children in their classrooms and in their practices, respectively. The community psychiatric clinics in Indiana produced an estimate of 0.6 percent of the population of children between the ages of 1 and 18 receiving psychiatric services. Teachers estimated 2.1 percent of children as requiring such services, and the general practitioners 4.1 percent.

Hsu's (1966) study is interesting from several points of view. His population consists of most of the children in grades 1 to 6 in schools in Taipei—a total of 8,329 children. "Problem" children were identified by teachers and compared with a 5 percent random sample of the rest of the children in the schools. As a methodological point, he compares the rates of identification of problem children by teachers before and after training by means of a mental health seminar. The percentage so identified leaps from 3.5 to 12 percent.

Several other studies—including those of Cummings (1944); Mensh, Kantor, Domke, Gildea, and Glidewell (1959); and Rutter (1966)—have utilized teachers as case finders. The rates they report are quite similar. Cummings found that 11 of the total of 142 (7.7 percent) of the Leicester schoolchildren ranging in age from 2 to 7 were "seriously disturbed," which was defined as being in need of specialized psychiatric attention. Using a similar criterion, Mensh et al. (1959) identified 8.2 percent of children in thirty third-grade classrooms in St. Louis County as seriously disturbed.

Among a somewhat older group (10- and 11-year-olds) on the Isle of Wight, Rutter established a "minimal" prevalence rate of 6.3 percent, excluding cases of mental subnormality. His finding that 0.7 percent of the study population was actually receiving treatment is remarkably similar to the findings of Beier et al. and Rosen et al. for this age group.

Many studies rely on a symptom checklist, and Lapouse and Monk (1958, 1959) question the validity of this procedure in identifying cases of psychiatric disorder. They interviewed mothers of a systematic sample of 482 children aged 6 to 12, drawn from four different economic quartiles in the city of Buffalo. The mothers were asked about different behaviors in children widely believed to be of pathological import, such as fears and worries, enuresis, and tension phenomena. They found that these "symptoms" were extremely prevalent and, further, that they showed no pattern of interrelationship (such as between enuresis and a large number of fears and worries). In view of the ubiquity of many of these behaviors and because of a failure to demonstrate significant intercorrelations between them, the authors raise serious doubts about the use of such so-called symptoms as indicators of psychiatric disorder, both clinically and for epidemiological purposes. Subsequent methodological studies, however, have demonstrated the utility of the symptom-list method (Sherwin & Schoelly, 1965).

Cummings (1944, 1946) also found such behaviors to be very widespread and reports, moreover, a general tendency for these symptoms to fade out during the 18-month period encompassing her study.

She attaches considerable weight to symptoms which tend to persist and points out that age is an important factor here. Children under 5 show more "spontaneous" improvement, whereas there is a greater tendency toward stabilization of symptoms in children over 5. Since Lapouse and Monk's study is confined to this latter age group, it may be that the symptoms in their sample are more serious than these authors seem to feel.

In addition, Glidewell et al. (1957) found a reliable and positive relationship between the number, frequency, duration, and severity of symptoms reported by a child's mother and the degree of disturbance found on clinical examination. This is in part confirmed by Sherwin et al. (1965). Glidewell used a much more exhaustive list of behaviors than Lapouse and Monk. Further, he did not look for intercorrelations between symptoms, but rather for total symptom scores, a procedure which has shown promise in work with adult populations as well (MacMillan, 1957; Langner, 1962). Rutter (1963) and Mensh et al. (1959) point out that single, *individual* items of behavior formerly thought to be indicative of psychiatric disorder may have no significant association when one considers large groups of children. (One of these items, they suggest, is enuresis.) This does not discount the value of scores on a large group of different symptoms.

Mensh (Mensh et al., 1959) has attempted to distinguish "payoff" items from others—that is, items of behavior in children which, either singly or in combination, will distinguish a group likely to be identified as psychiatrically disturbed on clinical examination. Beginning with a large list of behavioral items, he narrows it to the following, which seem to have discriminatory value: (1) difficulty in interacting with other children, (2) daydreaming, (3) destructiveness, (4) sleep disturbance, (5) overactivity, and (6) nervousness. Of these, item 1 is the most significant of all, and this has been borne out in other studies (Kellam & Schiff, 1967). Most of Mensh's items are not reported in the Lapouse and Monk study.

In addition to teachers' reports and symptom checklists, other instruments to identify maladjusted children have been used, including paper-and-pencil tests by Mangus (1949) and Sewell and Haller (1959) as well as ratings by peers (Mangus, 1949). It is unclear what the relationship of such measures is to psychiatric disorder, but it is abundantly clear that such measures swell the number of children identified as being in need of help.

To summarize, one of our major questions was: What is the extent of psychiatric disorder among children? In answer to this, we have rates going from 0.21 percent of children under 18 to a high of 30 percent of third- and sixth-grade children identified as "maladjusted." The answer clearly depends upon such factors as the population base, the precision of the instruments used, and the scope of the question. The choice of focus is, of course, never purely arbitrary. In planning mental hospital facilities, one might be interested only in the numbers of severely disturbed children in the community, which in turn would probably be a much smaller number than most of the cases reported here. Rutter & Graham (1966), for example, estimate a rate of 2.2 percent for severe disorders, as opposed to 6.3 percent whom they would consider to be definite cases exhibiting psychiatric disturbances. In planning for more comprehensive community services or for certain research questions, the latter figure might be more significant. One might be interested, moreover, in adding cases of mental retardation as well, as some other authors have done. In general, the broader the net and the finer the mesh, the greater will be the number of identified cases.

No matter which figure one chooses, it is clear that the question of psychiatric disorder among children is a significant one. Larger groups of children are affected than can probably ever be serviced by conventional treatment approaches.

Who are the children at special risk? What, then, of the second question? Is it possible to identify high-risk groups and to use such identification as the basis for the search for the cause and, ultimately, for the development of strategies of prevention?

Sex and age trends are of great interest in this regard.

Most studies seem to indicate that boys display more disorder than girls. This is particularly striking in the treated groups, where the ratio of boys to girls is at least 2 to 1 until late adolescence, when girls finally catch up.

One would like to know whether boys really do have more psychiatric disorder or whether this is only an apparent difference. Boys' behavior may be more disturbing to parents and teachers, or adults may expect more from boys than from girls. In either case, boys are more likely to be referred for treatment.

The studies reported so far and summarized in Tables 5-1 and 5-2, as well as others in the literature, indicate that both explanations seem to be operative. Boys do have more troublesome symptoms than girls (Beller & Neubauer, 1963; Bentzen, 1963; Lapouse & Monk, 1958, 1959[2]; Mensh et al., 1959; Rosen et al., 1965), but they also seem to evidence more disorder in general (Cummings, 1944; Hsu, 1966; Mangus, 1949; Rutter & Graham, 1966).

In considering these findings, it is useful to have information about specific breakdowns. The greatest differences between boys and girls

[2] Lapouse and Monks' study also offers indirect confirmation that boys have more problems in general, since they do tend to have more overactivity and more tension phenomena—two of the "payoff" items listed by Mensh et al.

occur in the categories of mental deficiency, personality disorders, and transient situational personality disorders (Rosen et al., 1964).

In late adolescence, girls exhibit an increase in emotional disturbance in general and particularly in psychoneuroses (Matteson, Hawkin, & Seese, 1967; Rosen et al., 1965). One possible explanation is that girls experience more tension at this age, when they move out from the relatively protective environments of home and school and are suddenly confronted with all the cultural ambiguities pertaining to the female role in Western society. Kaffman (1965) observed a remarkably similar pattern for clinic referrals in Israel, for girls both from kibbutzim and from urban centers. He feels, however, that the rise is mainly an apparent one, resulting from the fact that less troublesome symptoms are overlooked in prepubescent girls. In general, his view seems to be contradicted in the English and Chinese literature (Cummings, 1944; Hsu, 1966; Mangus, 1949; Rutter & Grahm, 1966).

We shall consider these and other hypotheses and the evidence for them later in this chapter. For now, we wish to call attention to several other trends which seem apparent from descriptive studies, findings which will also require further elaboration.

Besides sex and age trends, there is a tentative relationship demonstrated between a high prevalence of psychiatric disorder and low socioeconomic status (Hsu, 1966; Lapouse & Monk, 1958, 1959; Sewell & Haller, 1959; Tapia, 1968). The issue here is far from clear. Findings of a positive relationship may be due primarily to the case finders' middle-class biases, thus accounting for overrepresentation of children from the lower socioeconomic classes (Mensh et al., 1959). On the other hand, some investigators have demonstrated a tendency for the bias to operate in the reverse direction, that is, for teachers to overlook significant behavior in

TABLE 5-1   DESCRIPTIVE STUDIES, GENERAL: GROUPS IN TREATMENT

Author	Study Population	Age Range	Instrument	Rates of Disorder, Percent	Summary of Other Important Findings
Rosen et al., 1964	Clinic termination reported by 80% of the 1,589 clinics in the U.S. for year ending June 30, 1961; data used to estimate national and regional termina.ion rates and other features; baseline: 1960	Children less than 18 years of age	Reports by clinics	0.21*	1. Sex: 　a. Termination rates: boy/girl ratio, 2 to 1 2. Age: 　a. Rates lowest for children under 5, and rather steep rise after 5 3. Sex and age: 　a. Rates highest for boys 10 to 14 　b. Rates highest for girls 15 to 17 4. Race: 　a. Non-white—rates lower than average, ages 3 to 11 　b. Higher rates at almost all other ages
Rosen et al., 1965	Clinic termination reported by forty-one states—54,000 of the 104,000 adolescent clinic terminations in the U.S. in 1962	10–19	Reports by clinics	0.62*	1. Sex: 　a. In general, more boys than girls 　b. Presenting complaints by sex: boys, acting-out behavior; girls, listlessness, depression, and "not making it" socially 2. Age: 　a. 14 to 15-year-olds have highest clinic utilization rates 3. Sex and age: 　a. In 10- to 11-year-old age bracket: boy/girl ratio, 2.8 to 1 　b. In 18- to 19-year-old age bracket: boy/girl ratio, 1 to 1

* Secondary calculations by present authors based on data in articles.

lower-class children that they would regard more seriously in middle-class children (Deutsch, 1964; McDermott, 1967; McDermott, Harrison, Schrager, & Wilson, 1965), which would lead to an underestimate of the prevalence of symptoms in the lower-class groups.

It also seems that the types of phenomena considered to be evidences of "psychiatric disorder" will affect the investigation of relationships. If mental deficiency, for example, is included in a study along with other categories of psychiatric disorder, the relationship with social class will no doubt be strengthened accordingly, whereas its exclusion may account in part for the lack of a demonstrated relationship, such as one finds in Rutter and Graham's (1966) study, for example.

Mental deficiency is chosen as an example because it offers such a striking case in point. For mental deficiency of severe degree, the rate of discovery is highest in the 5- to 9-year age group (Gruenberg, 1966; Rosen et al., 1964), and there are *no* marked class differences. On the other hand, moderate and mild deficiency rates reach a maximum at 10 to 14 years, and there is a marked association with race, socioeconomic status, and sex, with boys far outnumbering girls (Gruenberg, 1966; F. McDermott, 1967; Rosen et al., 1964).

The same set of interrelated factors is associated with the likelihood of developing aggressive behavior disorders (J. F. McDermott et al., 1965; Tapia, 1968) and frankly delinquent behavior (Cohen, 1955; W. B. Miller, 1958; Short, 1966).

Race is also somewhat associated with a high prevalence of symptoms (Lapouse & Monk, 1958, 1959; Rosen et al., 1964; Tapia, 1968). Socioeconomic status, rather than race per se, is usually considered the important variable, however (Gruenberg, 1966; Srole, 1962; Tapia, 1968).

The points concerning socioeconomic status and race raise many questions about method-ology, questions which have not been satisfactorily answered.

Mangus (1949) finds that in his rural county, the average level of personality adjustment is higher for rural than for urban children.

Hsu's (1966) and Burt and Howard's (1952) findings point to the importance of considering the school settings, as well as family and neighborhood, in the genesis of disordered behavior.

The findings that differential rates of psychiatric disorder are associated with the age of the child, his sex, and the social environment to which he is exposed in his formative years by virtue of his parents' socioeconomic status and place of residence and the suggestion that there are situations and experiences in society which may cause stress to his personality system (e.g., the school) have acted as guidelines in our selection and reporting of explanatory studies. We have tried to review explanatory studies which seem to relate meaningfully to these findings. Our interpretation of these various explanatory attempts has also been conditioned and oriented by the relationships demonstrated in the descriptive studies.

EXPLANATORY STUDIES

The product of a descriptive study is the demonstration of relationships. Only rarely can one speak about causality. Indeed, when dealing with such complex phenomena as society, culture, and psychiatric disorder, it is difficult to make any definitive statements about cause, given the present state of our knowledge.

We can, however, approach the problem by discussing the process of becoming ill. We may further speak of two major models of process: (1) developmental and (2) functional.

Most psychiatric theory has a strong developmental emphasis. There is a pronounced interest in early experiences, the influence that they exert upon personality structure and function, and the

TABLE 5-2 DESCRIPTIVE STUDIES, GENERAL: GROUPS IN OTHER COMMUNITY SETTINGS

Author	Study Population	Age Range	Instrument	Rates (Estimates) by Source	Summary of Other Important Findings
Beier et al., 1961	Children in the state of Indiana	1–18	Surveys of: 1. Community psychiatric clinics 2. Interviews with teachers 3. Interviews with general practitioners	(Estimates) by Source: 1. 0.6% 2. 2.1% 3. 4.1% *	
Cummings, 1944	239 Leicester school children in: 1. War nurseries 2. Nursery classes 3. Elementary classes	2–7	Interviews with nineteen teachers: 1. Initial contact 2. 6 months 3. After 18 months follow-up; symptom checklist—142 of the 239 children were in the final sample	"Seriously disturbed," 7.7%	1. Sex: a. Boys have more of the "difficult" symptoms, but also more symptoms over all 2. Age: a. General tendency for emotional symptoms to fade out with age b. Significant difference between improvement of children under 5 and those 5 to 7
Sewell and Haller, 1959	1,462 children in a "typically midwestern community characterized by a fairly wide range of social status levels"	4–8	Paper-and-pencil tests	Not reported	3. Social factors: a. Lower-class children seem less well adjusted
Lapouse and Monk, 1958, 1959	Systematic sample of 482 children from four different economic quantities in city of Buffalo	6–12	Structured interviews with mothers' symptom checklist	Not reported	1. Sex: a. More boys than girls are overactive and have "tension" phenomena

Author	Sample	Age	Method	Prevalence	Findings
					b. More girls have a larger number of fears and worries 2. Social class: a. Tendency for children in lower socioeconomic status group to have more fears and worries and more nightmares 3. Race: a. Significantly more Negro children have large number of fears and worries than whites
Burt and Howard, 1952	Schoolchildren in different areas of London	6–14	Referrals by teachers and direct observation by clinicians in classrooms	3–10% "maladjusted"; mental retardation not included here	Relationship between "maladjustment" and social factors: 1. School: a. Presence of uncongenial teacher b. Assignment to classes where work is too difficult 2. Home: a. Lack of affection b. Overstrict discipline c. Presence of stepmother, of foster mother d. Lack of adequate recreational facilities
Hsu, 1966	8,329 children in elementary school in Taipei identified as "problem children" are compared with 5% random sample of the rest of the children	Grades 1–6	Interviews with teachers: 1. Before 2. After training in a mental health seminar	1. 3.5% 2. 12.0%	1. Sex: a. Boy/girl ratio approximately 2 to 1 b. Tendency for boys to have more of all types of problems than girls 2. Age: a. Peak prevalence at fourth-grade level

Author	Study Population	Age Range	Instrument	Rates (Estimates) by Source	Summary of Other Important Findings
					b. Repeating of grades and hence being older than most other children in class seems problematic and stress-inducing
					3. Social factors:
					a. More problem children identified as coming from families of lower socioeconomic status
					b. Association between disorder and a history of school change
Mensh et al., 1959	827 children in third-grade classrooms in St. Louis County	Grade 3	Independent judgment of teachers and trained observers in classrooms compared with mothers' reports of children's symptoms	8.2%*	1. Methodological:
					a. Teachers display middle-class bias in rating maladjustment
					b. Good agreement between ratings by teachers and mental health workers
					c. Relationship between level of adjustment reported in classroom and mothers' reports of symptom patterns
					2. Sex:
					a. Boys more likely to be rated less well adjusted by teachers than girls

Study	Sample	Age	Measures	Prevalence	Findings
					b. No sex difference for frequency of symptom patterns
Mangus, 1949	Third- and sixth-grade children in public schools of an Ohio county: 1. Farm dwellers 2. Nonfarm rural (towns and villages) —573 3. Urban—285	Third and sixth grades	1. California Test of Personality-elementary series 2. Ratings by teachers 3. Rating by students about others in class	17–30%	1. Sex: a. Girls display better personality adjustment b. Girls get on better scholastically 2. Social factors, rural vs. urban: a. Average level of personality adjustment higher for rural than urban
Rutter and Graham, 1966	1. All children resident on the Isle of Wight of the specified ages, with the exception of those who attended private schools 2. All children receiving psychiatric services 3. All children who had come before juvenile court	10- and 11-year-olds	Parent questionnaire; teacher questionnaire; psychiatric examination of screened sample	6.3% "minimal" prevalence rate, excluding mental subnormality (0.7% of children actually receiving treatment)	1. Sex: a. More boys than girls 2. Social factors: a. No association demonstrated between social class and rates of disorder

* Secondary calculations by present authors based on data in articles.

role of unresolved and traumatic early experiences in the genesis of psychiatric disorder. The functional viewpoint (for the most part neglected in psychiatry) stresses the contemporaneous interaction of forces in the development of symptoms. While some psychiatrists still have a tendency to dismiss the role of situations themselves in the production of disorder, a growing body of research in such fields as sensory deprivation, civilian disasters, and other crises attests to a gradual righting of the balance.

This is described as a righting of the balance because we do not mean to imply that the developmental framework should be discarded. Current, real stresses have a significant impact on the personality, but individual differences in perception of the stress and in vulnerability to stress are no doubt dependent upon prior experience. Both viewpoints are necessary—or better, an integration of both viewpoints. In an attempt to be comprehensive as well as clear, we have chosen to divide our discussion of sociocultural influences and explanatory variables into two parts, depending upon whether the variables are conceptually either *mainly* developmental or *mainly* functional.

Developmental	*Functional*
1. Interference with the physiological integrity of the central nervous system	1. Situations: a. School b. Other: War Deaths and bereavements Disaster Migration
2. Relatedness	
3. Aggression, autonomy, and control	
4. Development of skills	
5. Elaboration of a cognitive map of the social environment	

Interference with the Physiological Integrity of the Central Nervous System

Pasamanick (1961) has reported an association between complications of pregnancy and prematurity and (1) cerebral palsy, (2) epilepsy, (3) mental deficiency, (4) behavior disorders, and (5) reading disabilities.

By way of explanation, he advances the very important concept of a "continuum of reproductive causality."

Prematurity and other complications of pregnancy are associated with a high risk of fetal and neonatal death, usually on the basis of injury to the brain. Pasamanick reasons that there must remain a fraction of children who are injured in this way, but who do not die. These children go on to manifest many of the behaviors which we consider psychopathological and which we may mistakenly attribute to early experiences in childhood, such as cultural deprivation, rather than to the more fundamental damage to the central nervous system itself.

Abnormalities of pregnancy are, in turn, associated with certain conditions such as malnutrition, infection, and other forms of stress which are in large part socioeconomically determined. Since poverty is associated with both poor prenatal care and cultural deprivation, the latter may be only an apparent or relatively minor contribution factor in the genesis of psychiatric disorder, at least in many instances. The more basic cause may be minimal and unrecognized brain damage.

A number of studies by Pasamanick's group support this concept.

Many of these were large-scale, retrospective studies of children diagnosed as having various clinical entities. As controls, the next surviving infants of the same race, sex, and socioeconomic status as the case, born in the same hospital to a mother of the same age, were chosen. Significant differences between cases and controls have been found with regard to a history of such anoxia-producing complications of pregnancy as toxemias and maternal bleeding. Such complications are presumably associated with a higher risk of minimal brain damage (Pasamanick, 1961). Newer prospective studies have highlighted the same relationships (Knobloch & Pasamanick, 1966).

Furthermore, an examination of the distribution of complications of pregnancy and birth showed a relationship to socioeconomic status: The incidence of such complications was 5 percent in the highest white economic stratum and 14.6 percent in the lowest white stratum. In the nonwhite lowest stratum, it was 50.6 percent. The complications appear to result from an interaction between inadequate diet, poor prenatal care, poor housing, and gross stress, each of which is associated with pregnancy outcome (Wortis & Freedman, 1968).

These findings are most interesting in view of the tremendously disproportionate contribution of nonwhite children to outpatient clinic admission rosters for mental deficiency (Rosen et al., 1964). They suggest that there may be factors operative in addition to the more popular cultural-deprivation explanation (Pasamanick, 1963).

F. McDermott's (1967) study adds another important dimension. In examining clinic intake records for all children for a 2-year period, he and his co-workers discovered that the diagnosis of chronic brain syndrome was made *less* often in the lowest social-class group than in other groups, in spite of the fact that the historical and clinical data upon which this diagnosis is usually based were equally prevalent in all class groups. Thus, there was a definite bias *against* making this diagnosis in the lowest social classes.

Since most of the referrals came from schools, the authors suggest that the disproportionate rates for such "serious" conditions may be due

in part to teachers' allowing a greater interval of time to elapse between the appearance of disturbance among their socially disadvantaged pupils and the eventual referral for help (a finding of J. F. McDermott et al., 1965, as well). When the children from this group are finally referred, the question of brain damage may be overlooked by the treatment facility.

The authors suggest that both teachers and diagnosticians exhibit a class bias in viewing symptoms. Although the concept of cultural deprivation is extremely important, the teaching profession and the mental health professions may have been "oversold." The result is that they may neglect aberrant behavior, which would be viewed seriously in middle-class children, when it shows up in socially deprived children, particularly in the younger age groups. The tendency is to attribute such behavior to a child's deprived background and hope that he will "grow out of it."

Even if Pasamanick's evidence were not so compelling, and McDermott's so disturbing, the need to improve the quality of prenatal and neonatal care among low-income groups would appear self-evident. This need gains additional perspective when we recognize that it has important implications for the primary prevention of psychiatric disorder in children.

Relatedness

It is commonly recognized that the infant and young child require a consistent and continuous relationship with a mothering figure if satisfactory development is to take place. Interference with such a relationship is followed by difficulties in interpersonal and social interactions which may result in disordered behavior (Bowlby et al., 1966; Elkin, 1960; Erikson, 1963).

Spitz and Wolf (1949), Bowlby et al. (1966), Davis (1947), and others have described the disastrous consequences attendant upon a total lack of mothering or a sudden rupture of the mother-child relationship.

At the level of the social aggregate, it is doubtful that one would find many instances of the kind of almost total affective deprivation with which these studies were concerned. However, Bowlby's later formulations regarding instances of partial deprivation or of inconsistent relationships with parents or parent substitutes have been of great theoretical importance and have influenced many workers in the field.

Rutter (1965), Olenick et al. (1966), and Eisenberg (1968) feel that parental deprivation may be associated with the development of many different types of psychiatric disorder. Wallenstein's work, quoted by Bowlby et al. (1966), substantiates this. The latter surveyed the entire school population of a part of New York City. Children were examined psychologically, and it was demonstrated that those from broken homes had developed less favorably in general than others.

Other workers have been more specific in their formulations and have advanced evidence that parental deprivation tends to be associated with the later development of aggressive and antisocial behavior, rather than neurotic symptoms (Bowlby, 1944; Cummings, 1944; Provence & Lipton, 1962; Wardle, 1961; Wardrop, 1967).

Separation from parents is not inevitably associated with difficulties in interpersonal relationships later in life. Various workers have pointed out that age at separation, quality of the mother-child relationship prior to separation, duration of separation, and constitutional factors all play a role in determining the outcome (Bowlby et al., 1966).

The role of social and cultural factors is, by and large, ignored in the literature. These factors exert an influence in at least two ways: (1) Different social and cultural conditions affect the individual child's *risk* of experiencing depriva-

tion, and (2) if a child is separated from one or both parents, the sociocultural environment will in part determine the *meaning* of this experience.

The risk factor. A set of social conditions, characteristic of what we shall call *sociocultural disintegration,* seems to be regularly associated with an increased risk of experiencing significant separations. (See A. H. Leighton, 1959, for an important discussion of the functioning of a social system.)

Sociocultural disintegration refers to a breakdown in the functioning of a social system and is characterized by material deprivation, lack of a sense of community, a weak and fragmented network of communication, lack of patterns of leadership and followership, and a high frequency of interpersonal hostility.

In discussing poverty, S. M. Miller (1964) describes a subgroup which he calls the "unstable poor," and O. Lewis speaks of a "culture of poverty" (1961, 1966). Both concepts are closely related to sociocultural disintegration. The conditions described are not synonymous with poverty or low socioeconomic class. A different dimension is being dealt with—the functional malaise of a community, with concomitant failures of many aspects of community life, including effective socialization of the young.

The life histories presented in *The Children of Sanchez* (O. Lewis, 1961), for example, have a common and pervasive theme—the evanescence of human relationships. Families reflect the general disorganization of the larger community and are no more successful in stabilizing adult members than they are in socializing children. Parental figures come and go with what must seem bewildering frequency to the young child. The lack of social cohesiveness is further complicated by a great deal of emotional and physical ill health and by the death of parents at relatively young ages.

In the Stirling County reports (Hughes, 1960; A. H. Leighton, 1959; D. C. Leighton et al., 1963), findings from several integrated and disintegrated communities are presented. In the disintegrated communities, 30 percent of the homes were found to be psychologically broken. In two rural integrated communities, one English Protestant and the other French Catholic, the figures were 16 percent psychologically broken and 22 percent physically broken in the former and 5 percent and 11 percent, respectively, in the latter (Beiser, 1965). Rates of illness among adults have consistently been higher in the disintegrated communities.

The meaning of separation. Not all children who experience separation develop symptoms of disordered behavior. One must consider the total sociocultural matrix in which the experience occurs in order to assess the meaning it will have for the individual.

This is demonstrated in a study by Douglas and Blomfield (1958), which consisted of a follow-up investigation of 5,386 live births, constituting a representative sample of all legitimate, single-born children from all parts of Great Britain in the year 1946. Follow-up information was collected by health visitors, school doctors, and school nurses.

They found that 52 percent of the survey children were separated from their mothers at least once during the first six years of their lives; 14 percent were away for at least a month.

There was no suggestion that separation affected children adversely if they remained at home. In this instance, children showed no difference in occurrence of nervous habits, such as nightmares and thumb-sucking, from controls who were never separated. However, children who were separated and away from home showed more nightmares and tension habits. More children who had been sent away from home were attending child-guidance and speech-therapy clinics by age 6 than children in their control groups, although the difference was relatively small.

There was a tendency for types of separation to be associated with social class. Separations in higher-class groups were apt to be instances of parents' going on holiday and leaving children at home with a housekeeper or with relatives. Lower-class separations were apt to be due to stressful events like hospitalization of a parent or of the child himself. Thus the lower-class child experienced the total configuration of the event differently from the way the middle-class child did and it was more likely to be disturbing to him.

Of the 4-year-old survey children, 4.4 percent were living in homes broken by death, divorce, or separation of their parents. Health visitors generally assessed the management and care of the children in these broken homes unfavorably in comparison with that in the unbroken homes.

When the children in broken homes were compared with controls, however, there was no evidence of their being emotionally less stable.

The authors conclude on a cautious note: " . . . since the present report follows them only up to the age of five, this is not regarded as a final conclusion" (Douglas & Blomfield, 1958, p. 149).

Since there is some evidence that emotional instability tends to manifest itself more frequently after age 5 (see Cummings, 1944; Rosen et al., 1964), the authors' point is extremely well taken.

M. Mead (1966) points out the importance of culture, and also of such features of the social system as its complexity, in considering the question of maternal separation.

In complex societies, under certain conditions, child care is assumed by an institution other than the family. It is in institutions that the extreme forms of impersonal care have been observed, although this is not an invariable consequence of institutionalization (Hellman, 1962).

In "primitive" societies, on the other hand:

All the functions served by institutions—care of the orphan, care of the child of a sick mother, care of the handicapped or defective child, care of the illegitimate child—are dealt with in primitive societies either by care of the child within the greater family or neighborhood group on an individual basis which obviates the major trauma-inducing aspect of institutional care—the impersonality of an institution—or drastically, by the elimination of the child by such means as burying the new born child with the dead mother, or exposing immediately or by extinguishing by a process of slow, low level care children who show extreme handicaps. The child who is chosen to live is cared for personally, not impersonally. [M. Mead, 1966, p. 240]

"Multiple mothering" and "multiple fathering," as characteristic patterns in different cultures, have been studied in various ways. Volkart (1957) reports some interesting observations by Spiro among the Ifaluk. Here, social patterning results in a diffusion of intensive relationships among many people, with the result that the process, and presumably also the experience of bereavement, is markedly different from the one commonly observed in Western industrial societies.

Multiple mothering, or at least the availability of mother substitutes, is a feature of Chinese society. Rin (1965) reports that among the Taiwanese, loss of fathers, but not of mothers, is associated with the development of severe emotional disturbance and possibly with the development of schizophrenia in female patients. He suggests that the lack of father substitutes in this culture may in part account for this demonstrated relationship.

By contrast, it has been reported that the death of a father among the Murngin creates few psychological problems for children. All their lives,

children call their paternal uncles "Father," and their relationships with these uncles do not differ very much from their relationships with their biological fathers (Warner, 1937, quoted in Volkart, 1957).

The availability of parental substitutes in general is considerably lessened in complex societies, where there is a tendency toward isolation of the nuclear family (Bossard, 1953; Glasser & Navare, 1965). As a consequence, both generations and both sexes are forced into a more intensive relationship. Child-parent separation becomes a very different thing under these circumstances from what it is among the Ifaluk or the Murngin.

We must not, however, become overly simplistic and equate primitive society with personal care of children, and complex society with familial isolation and hence with catastrophic separations. Many children are separated from their parents for varying periods of time; however, most separations, even those which occur in a complex society, are not traumatic if they are handled with warmth and evidence of concern (Douglas & Blomfield, 1958).

Furthermore, the tendency toward isolation of the nuclear family varies considerably, even between two countries such as England and the United States, apparently so similar in their major social characteristics. There is evidence of greater intergenerational contact throughout the family life cycle in England than in the United States (Townsend, 1963). There is also probably considerable variation according to social class, ethnic derivation, and so forth, within these countries.

Conversely, there is not a simple, one-to-one relationship between the personal and effective care of children and smallness and primitiveness of the society, as Mead seems to imply (1966). This depends upon the level of integration of the system as a whole. Even small societies may cease to function effectively as total systems, and the quality of child care and socialization may deteriorate as a consequence.

By way of example, we have reports concerning an Eskimo village on Saint Lawrence Island:

> At one time, this was a well-integrated community. A disease epidemic, a world war, and dramatic social changes initiated a downward spiral and the bonds of social organization weakened and fragmented. In former days, when there was a true community on Saint Lawrence Island, a child who lost his parents was immediately adopted by another family within the village and blended with the other children of this family. In the latter phases of community disintegration such a child became an "orphan" and was sent to an orphanage on the mainland, far from his birthplace. [Beiser, 1968, p. 93]

Finally, we must turn our attention to difficulties in relatedness which may arise on a basis other than total or partial deprivations at critical ages. Malone (1966, 1967) suggests that slum children are exposed to constant and real threats of physical harm and develop a danger orientation as a consequence. This is characterized by distrustfulness, guardedness, tension, servility to authority figures, a reliance on visual and auditory hyperalertness to orient and protect themselves, and a literalness of imitation, learning, and thinking. Malone attributes this to the disorganized, unpatterned relationships between adults, with the constant threat of violence, which he observed in a small group of skid-row families.

While the generalizability of his findings may prove to be limited, the study does draw attention to an aspect of the social environment which is otherwise overlooked in the literature.

Aggression, Autonomy, and Control

Many investigators have been impressed with the relationship between a child's failure to establish appropriately autonomous patterns of behavior and to channel aggression, and the sub-sequent development of psychopathology (Erikson, 1963; Pavenstadt, 1961; Spitz, 1953).

In the matters of expression of aggression and of self-control, the extrafamilial culture impinges forcibly upon socialization practices. The form in which parents choose to discipline and the issues which they select for disciplinary attention reflect their pattern of sentiments regarding these issues. These sentiments are in turn derived from, and reinforced by, the larger social group to which the family belongs.

This link between parental behavior and cultural patterns has understandably generated a great deal of interest in disciplinary techniques and attitudes in different sociocultural settings (Becker, 1964; Kohn, 1964; Whiting & Child, 1953).

The consequences of discipline for the mental health of children are difficult to assess, and there have been many contradictory findings (Becker, 1964). There is some general agreement, however, that inconsistent discipline may be harmful (Becker, 1964). Minuchin, Montalvo, Guerney, Rosman, and Schumer (1967) studied twelve disorganized lower-class urban families who had produced at least two delinquent children. He offers a fascinating formulation of the process through which difficulties in autonomy are generated by parental inconsistency and of the consequences in terms of behavior disorder, particularly delinquency.

Parents in such families respond unpredictably to a child's behavior; often a disciplinary action is provoked by the parent's own feeling state at the time, rather than by the child's actual actions. Under these patternless conditions, children never have the opportunity to internalize rules of behavior and thus come to rely on adults for guidance in every new situation.

These are often fatherless families, and the mothers feel threatened by excessive demands; they react by disengagement.

Children then turn to their siblings, often to one in particular, who assumes the role of the "parental child." This substitute parent teaches his siblings the lessons, often asocial ones, which he himself has learned on the streets.

The sibling subsystem thus becomes the predominant socializing agent—often directed against the existing authority structure.

Minuchin feels that the antisocial, aggressive activity which ensues is amorphous and ill defined; it is a generalized aggression rather than being object-specific.

Parental inconsistency and the lack of stable identificatory models leave their residue in the personality. There is no feeling of autonomy—what Minuchin calls the child's "focused experience of himself as an agent of change" fails to develop. Thus, the sense of powerlessness among the adult poor (Haggstrom, 1964; Stone, Leighton, & Leighton, 1966) is transmitted to the next generation (Kardiner & Ovesey, 1951).

It should be pointed out that the one-parent family is not synonymous with the disorganized, multiproblem family. However, this structural characteristic is found disproportionately among disadvantaged family units. About 10 percent of the children in the United States are living with only one parent, usually the mother. One-parent families represent one-twelfth of all families with children, but they make up one-quarter of all those classified as poor (Glasser & Navare, 1965).

There is a relationship between social class and delinquent behavior, and also a marked sex trend, with boys far outnumbering girls (Cummings, 1946; Jessor, Graves, Hanson, & Jessor, 1968; Rosen et al., 1964). While biology may account for this difference in part, one cannot neglect the importance of early socialization experiences.

Delinquents often come from broken homes (Bowlby, 1944; Short, 1966; Wardle, 1961; Wardrup, 1967), and broken homes, at least in the United States, are usually fatherless homes. There is some evidence that control of behavior is more affected by the same-sex than by the opposite-sex parent, which would put boys of fatherless families at a disadvantage.

In addition to the father's absence, it is also interesting to note that mothers spend significantly less time interacting with offspring when they are sons than when they are daughters. Also, mothers report exerting more control and regulation over daughters than over sons (Bronfenbrenner, 1961; Jessor et al., 1968). Thus, the mother's lesser effectiveness as an agent from whom to learn self-control is further compounded by an apparent pattern of disengagement. This would lead one to predict what is indeed the case—a preponderance of problematic, asocial behavior among boys.

Development of Skills

In the main, psychodynamic theories relating to the development of psychiatric disorder deal with the conflict-defense system of the personality. The major proposition seems to be that disturbance occurs when the relative balance between impulses and conflict, on the one hand, and defenses, on the other, is upset.

Hartman (1958) called attention to the "autonomous ego functions." He referred to such things as thinking, language, object comprehension, and motor skills, which are dependent upon environmental conditions for their proper unfolding, but which develop relatively independently of conflicts and drives. These are skills which individuals require in order to live in organized societies.

Although there is growing interest in these functions, our theoretical understanding of their role in psychiatric disorder has not progressed much beyond what amounts to a statement of faith on Hartman's part (1958, p. 10): "The concrete study of various disturbances in psychosis and some of the psychophysical interrelations . . . must also take into account the conflict free sphere. None of these problems can be completely resolved in terms of instinctual drives and conflicts."

Much has been made of mental retardation presumably due to cultural deprivation. A few specialized syndromes like reading disability have been traced to failure in the development of autonomous functions like language and abstracting ability (Blank & Bridger, 1967; Siller, 1957) and thence to the social conditions under which the developmental failures occur. However, relatively little has been done to try to incorporate such findings into a broader theory of the causes of what we call "psychiatric disorder." The neglect of this area is puzzling, since it seems quite apparent that a child who develops a broad range of skills has available, by virtue of this, a broad repertoire of problem-solving abilities and insulation against undue stress (Cumming & Cumming, 1963), and this has clearcut implications for treatment and prevention.

How skills develop then becomes an important issue.

One line of investigation has been the failure of socially disadvantaged families to stimulate ego development in children.

Deutsch (1960, 1964, 1967) and his associates have extensively studied schoolchildren from socially deprived backgrounds. They find that many of these children have less language facility, less visual and auditory perceptual ability, and less ability to concentrate than children from middle-class families.

Many authorities feel that these deficiencies are traceable to the marginal social and economic conditions under which these children live (Coleman, 1966; Deutsch, 1967; Hunt, 1961). The child from a disadvantaged family is likely to have been deprived of a substantial portion of the variety of stimuli which he is maturationally

capable of responding to—there are fewer exposures to books and manipulable objects of all types, there is little diversity of home artifacts, and so forth.

In addition to the restriction of variety, Deutsch (1964) postulates that the parts of the stimulus spectrum which are presented in the slum environment tend to have poorer and less systematic sequential ordering and are thereby less useful to the growth and activation of cognitive potential.

In considering findings such as these, conceptual clarity between the child from a poor family and the socially disadvantaged child must be maintained (Riessman, Cohen, & Pearl, 1964). Siller's (1957) research, for example, substantiates the idea of a class difference in conceptual abilities. Careful analysis, however, shows that the effects of poverty are uneven. The statistically significant class differences in conceptual thinking are produced essentially by a subgroup within their low-status population sample, who do very poorly. When this group is removed from the comparison, class differences in conceptual ability disappear. (There is, however, no similar subgroup of very poor performers in the high-status sample.)

Lack of development of skills is usually explained by a deprivation hypothesis. We seem to assume that the lack of stimulation at home is compounded by inadequacies in the ghetto schools, thus resulting in even more apparent intellectual failure. While this is no doubt true, it is an inadequate model in that it assumes that the child is a passive victim of deprivation. In fact, children are not merely passive, and failure to develop skills, at least certain types of skills, may be the result of an active process of renunciation, rather than a purely passive phenomenon.

For instance, Davis (1949, p. 30) reports that, for the slum child, "To study homework seriously is literally a disgrace. Instead of boasting of good marks in school, one conceals them, if he ever receives any."

School achievement, then, is actually something to be feared and concealed, and it further seems as if there is a subcultural force at work to perpetuate the pattern of nonachievement within the Establishment.

In their study of patients from socioculturally disintegrated rural families, Cleveland and Longaker (1957) noted a pattern of self-denigration in certain areas of accomplishment, as well as a generalized tendency to disparage the abilities of others.

They have called this the "disparagement syndrome" and have suggested that it is an interpersonal maneuver with an adaptive component, in that it serves to protect the self from the ridicule of one's fellows.

Malone (1966, 1967) noted that even parents often disparage their children. He observed that skid-row parents frequently tended to derogate their children's efforts to achieve and produce, their expressions of assertion and self-hood, their products, and even their sexual identities. Hughes, Tremblay, Rapoport, and Leighton (1960) report similar observations in a rather different setting.

Besides functioning as a device to protect oneself from the ridicule of others, the disparagement syndrome probably also serves to obviate disappointment, which often seems the inevitable and sole reward for having aspirations, under the difficult conditions in which many people live. As with any neurotic pattern, however, self-protection comes at the price of severe limitations in interpersonal flexibility and failure to recognize and capitalize upon real opportunities when they do appear. Toby (1963, p. 553) summarizes the state of affairs very well: "We assume . . . that the lower-class subculture (uncongenial to social mobility) has its roots in a sour-grapes reaction. This does *not* mean that every lower-class boy yearns for higher socio-economic status at some time or other in his life. Some of them have been socialized into the sour-grapes tradition before having the experience on which they might personally conclude that the grapes are sour."

What literature there is in the area of skills and their development focuses almost exclusively on cognitive abilities like perception, ability to abstract, language facility, and so forth.

Social skills, while less well defined, are probably no less important and have been regrettably neglected. In complex social situations, the recognition of nuances in behavior and the ability to assess another's motivations accurately are important assets. Lack of such discriminatory abilities probably has mental health consequences for children (Griffin & Seeley, 1952; Kellam & Schiff, 1967; Zegans, 1967).

There are provocative leads, but no adequate studies dealing with the failure to develop social skills. Glasser and Navare (1965), for example, posit a relationship between failure to develop social skills and the unique problems of the one-parent family, where adult authority resides in one, rather than in two, individuals. This type of family, as already described, is particularly prominent among low-status, nonwhite groups:

> The diad [*sic*] has unique properties and certainly a uniquely simple power structure. In terms of authority from which the children are more or less excluded by age and social norms, the one-parent family establishes a diadic relationship, between the parent and each child. Society places full responsibility in the parental role; and therefore, the parent becomes the only power figure in the one-parent family. Consequently, the adult in any given situation is either for or against the child. Some experience of playing one adult against the other, as long as it is not carried to extremes, is probably valuable in developing social skills and in developing a view of authority as tolerable and even manipulable within reason, rather than absolute and possibly tyrannical. [Glasser & Navare, 1965, p. 103]

Mattick's (1967) observations of a small group of slum children seem at first to contradict this formulation. In her study, Mattick noted that the children had great skill in outguessing adults by "reading" their facial expressions and by picking up other behavioral nuances, when they spelled potential trouble.

However, Mattick's children, although disadvantaged, apparently did not come primarily from one-parent families. They lived in a densely populated slum with many older people and skid-row alcoholics, whom the children often teased.

It would be of great interest to know what difference the father's presence, and hence the form of the family power structure, makes in the development of social skills. Also, it may be significant that the children in Mattick's study interacted with large groups of adults on the streets, on whom they could test out behavioral limits. Because of the age and infirmity of these adults, the consequences of failing in various maneuvers are presumably not too disastrous, so that social learning of this type may proceed with a minimum of tears. It is also true, of course, that what Mattick is describing is a very limited set of responses to interpersonal behaviors. This ability to read other people is useful within limits, but it is not synonymous with having a broad repertoire of skills which one may call upon in acting on a wider social stage.

Elaboration of Cognitive Map of the Social Environment

Besides interest in the formal aspects of cognition and the possibilities for aberrant development, there has been some attention paid to the *content* of cognitive systems, such as attitudes, beliefs, sentiments, values, and orientations.

Values and orientations are bridging concepts of particular utility in considering sociocultural influences on personality. These variables are important in the study of children as well as in the psychology of adults. Personality development is marked by an emerging self-concept and orientations which involve a child's ideas about himself and about the larger social environment. Furthermore, the child develops a sense of his own relationship to the environment—for example, which roles have been assigned to him and his chance of achieving the things which are valued by his culture—and this sense, this map of the environment and his own locations within it, has important mental health implications (Jessor et al., 1968; G. H. Mead, 1934; Sullivan, 1953).

One of the major orienting axes is one's sex role. Kagan (1964) suggests that the child forms his conception of male and female, upon which his own sex-role identity is based, between the ages of 3 and 7. This is used as a framework for explaining findings such as the one that boys outnumber girls in reading problems from kindergarten through the fourth grade. Kagan's interpretation is that the child perceives school in the early years as a feminine activity and that young boys, who are struggling to master a particular sex role, tend to reject the school on this account.

Ausubel (1958; Ausubel & Ausubel, 1967) also uses an identification model to aid in explaining the well-known preponderance of young boys among clinic referrals. He points out that young girls exhibit less negativism (which is among the major causes of referral) than boys; he feels this is due largely to the fact that they have more readily available to them a same-sex person with whom to identify. Also, girls can obtain more subsidiary primary status than boys can by participating in female household tasks. Weinstein and Giesel (1960) also feel that interaction with the same-sex parent exerts a protective effect. Other studies point to a relationship between adequate sex identity and other mental health measures (Douvan & Adelson, 1966; Mussen, 1961).

As Ausubel implies, the physical presence of the same-sex parent, on a continuing basis, may be a critical factor in developing appropriate sex-role identification. The bulk of research in this area is concerned with the absent father, and there is a strong suggestion that this leads to cross-sex identifications among boys. One reaction to this is defense by means of exaggerated masculine behavior (Burton & Whiting, 1961). One of the most interesting studies in this area concerned 8- and 9-year-old boys in Norwegian sailors' families (Lynn & Sawrey, 1959). The findings indicated that the fathers' absence was linked with less adequate peer adjustment (which, it will be recalled, is a symptom to which Mensh and Glidewell attach considerable weight).

Gordon and Gordon (1958) suggest that moving from a metropolis to a suburb is disturbing to boys, more so than to girls, for the apparent reason that the father must spend much more of his time away from home. Mangus's (1949) finding, considered earlier, that rural schoolchildren show less emotional disturbance than their urban counterparts is intriguing in this respect. Presumably, rural children have more chance of being in contact with their fathers.

Glasser and Navare (1965) point out that poor families tend also to be one-parent families, so that opportunities for adequate role definition are not equally distributed among all sectors of society. In addition to fathers' being absent, mothers in these families are often forced to go out to work and do not have time to care for the home adequately. Thus, there will also be distortion of the female role which involves emotional support and home-centered activities.

The father may be absent from home in other than a purely physical sense. Several authors have pointed to a pattern of paternal disengagement in working-class subcultures in England Dennis, 1956; Young & Willmot, 1957).

Fathers spend their time socializing with their own peer groups, when they are not working, and thus the English "mum" assumes the major role in the socialization process. Children interact with their mothers in a predominantly female society, among female relatives and neighbors.

This creates a difficult situation for the male child—the adult role will call for strict segregation along sexual lines, but he has little opportunity to identify with his father. Socialization then becomes the task of the boy's male peers— the famous "lads"—with, presumably, an increased likelihood of deviant behavior.

Fleck et al. (1959), Lidz et al. (1957), Lidz (1963) and others claim that there is a relationship between the remote father who, even when physically present, does not fill the instrumental leadership role in the family and the development of schizophrenic and homosexual tendencies in children. In the United States, the special difficulty the Negro father has in maintaining his masculine status has often been commented upon. The Negro family, at least the lower-class Negro family, is often characterized by role reversals in the power relationship. The male is further emasculated by the pressure of white society, against which effective retaliation is impossible (Kardner & Ovsey, 1951). Such factors make adequate identification a difficult task.

The perception of his sexual role and the adequacy he feels in filling it are only part of the child's overall sense of self in relationship to his social world. Theorists such as G. H. Mead (1934), Sullivan (1953), and Rogers (1951) have been interested in self-esteem in a global sense, and they attach great importance to deficiencies in self-esteem in the genesis of psychopathology.

More recently, Coopersmith (1967) has shown that boys with low self-esteem interact less in groups, tend to be self-conscious and preoccupied with inner problems, avoid disagreements, are more constricted, and are less creative than boys with medium and high levels of self-esteem.

There has been considerable interest in the

impact of minority-group membership on the development of self-esteem in children (Adams, 1950; Brody, 1963; M. J. Clark, 1939; M. J. Clark & Clark, 1950; Coles, 1967; Dai, 1961; Davis & Dollard, 1940) and in the relationship between self-devaluation and sociocultural deprivation (Deutsch, 1960; Pavenstadt et al., 1967; Stone, 1966). Most of these writings have been polemics —and at best, case studies—designed to expose the injustices of a social system which permits such conditions to exist. It is understandable that we still lack good scientific studies in this area; it is difficult to be scientific when one is outraged. However, Coopersmith's work demonstrates the value of making self-esteem the object of serious study, and it may yet point the way to some desperately needed creative remedial programs.

Such programs will probably call for an extramural extension of effort on the part of clinic personnel, if they are to be truly effective. At present, child-guidance clinics are often the court of last appeal for desperate cases which society does not know how to handle. Rosen et al. (1965), noting the increasing use of the clinic as a referral agency for difficult adolescents by schools and courts, sound a note of caution. They point out that the clinic's role may be becoming more and more an extension of the behavior-controlling institutions of society, such as the police and the courts. The danger is that the emphasis becomes control rather than treatment and rehabilitation: "Though the clinic may relieve the child's disturbance, despondency and anger, his behavior often is in response to the lack of meaningful education or job training opportunities and of a satisfying role in the community, thus requiring society wide action" (Rosen et al., 1965, p. 159).

Situations

The literature dealing with events which may precipitate psychiatric disorder is very scant. There are scattered reports of the impact of war on children (Carey-Trefzer, 1949; Ellis, 1948; Freud & Burlingham, 1944), of immediate reactions to death and bereavements (Alpert, 1964; Arthur & Kemme, 1964; Zeligs, 1967), of the emotional reaction to disasters (Bloch, Silber, & Perry, 1956; Stewart, 1958), and of the effects of migration (Gordon & Gordon, 1958; Sedlis, 1965).

However, there is little evidence of sustained interest in such topics, and they have received nothing close to the amount of attention accorded to developmental issues.

In the main, the "situation" literature indicates that the child's primary group, which usually means the nuclear family, is an important element in his response to stress. If a child is separated from his parents during, or as a result of, a stressful event (Bloch et al., 1956; Ellis, 1948; Freud & Burlingham, 1944), if one of his parents is mentally ill at the time the family is exposed to stress (Bloch et al., 1956; Carey-Trefzer, 1949), or if the intrafamilial dynamics are disturbed (Bloch et al., 1956; Stewart, 1958), the child may respond to stress with disordered behavior.

War, bereavement, disaster, and migration are specialized experiences, by and large, but there is one experience which most children share, at least in most industrialized societies, and which may act as a source of untoward stress. We refer to the experience of going to school.

Criticism of, and dissatisfaction with, the school system is currently widespread. Besides the failures in many areas, its role in the mental health of children has been documented and, to some extent, studied.

Interest has centered, to a large extent, on the lower-class or socially disadvantaged child who enters the school system and on the meaning of this in terms of discontinuities in experience, lack of understanding between such children and middle-class teachers, and lack of social and intellectual readiness for the school experience. Too often this results in the formation of negative attitudes, and possibly in disturbed behavior.

Deutsch, who has studied this process, has this to say:

> The lower class child probably enters school with a nebulous and essentially neutral attitude. His home rarely, if ever, negatively predisposes him toward the school situation, though it might not offer positive motivation and correct interpretation of the school experience. It is in the school situation that the highly charged negative attitudes toward learning evolve, and the responsibility for such large groups of normal children showing great scholastic retardation, the high drop-out rate, and to some extent the delinquency problem, must rest with the failure of the school to promote the proper acculturation of these children. [Deutsch, 1964, p. 186]

Deutsch (1964, 1967) points out that most schools are not equipped to deal with the disadvantaged child or his lack of relevant skills. Furthermore, the child in school is exposed to a material culture, which he may find desirable, but in which he cannot hope to participate. The result is that the intellectual gap between such children and their middle-class peers widens, rather than diminishes, during their school careers (Coleman, 1966; Deutsch, 1964, 1967).

Teachers' attitudes also change during this time. In kindergarten and first grade, teachers often describe lower-class children as "curious," "cute," "affectionate," "warm," and "independently dependent." By the fifth or sixth grade, however, they have become "alienated," "withdrawn," "angry," "passive," "apathetic," or just "troublesome" (Deutsch, 1964). Not only are teachers' middle-class biases apparent to outside observers (Mensh et al., 1959), but there is some evidence that lower-class children are well aware of their teachers' unfavorable attitudes (Davidson & Lang, 1967).

Teachers' use of psychiatric clinics as a referral source increases at about the fifth and sixth grades (F. McDermott, 1967; J. F. McDermott et al., 1965; Rosen et al., 1964). Further, it

appears that the attitudinal change toward the socially disadvantaged child reported by Deutsch is reflected by a higher rate of referral of such children at this age level, whereas younger referrals tend to be disproportionately middle class. Once referred, lower-class children receive more diagnoses of mental deficiency (Rosen et al., 1964) and personality disorder, including borderline psychoses (J. F. McDermott et al., 1965), than other children, and symptoms of overt hostility, impulsivity, affective disturbance, and withdrawal are more marked (J. F. McDermott et al., 1965). McDermott, as already mentioned, suggests that teachers may tend to overlook behaviors in lower-class children which they regard seriously in middle-class children until the child becomes a disruptive factor in class.

While this is an appealing hypothesis, we must also be aware of another possibility—the school may act as a stress which generates certain patterns of disordered behavior (Freud, 1966). The need for further study is self-evident.

In the latter connection, Burt and Howard's (1952) findings are most interesting. They demonstrated a relationship between school conditions and adjustment, particularly (1) an uncongenial teacher and (2) assignment to a class where the work is too difficult. They also point out difficulties which may accrue when the child is promoted or switches schools and is exposed to methods of teaching which are abruptly different. This is particularly apt to be damaging to those who are dull or suffer special disabilities. Burt and Howard do not agree with traditional interpretations of such findings, that is, that school stresses merely serve to unmask previous personality problems or simply reflect problems within the home. In many instances, follow-up demonstrated significant improvement when remedies were directed solely to an alteration of school conditions. Hsu (1966) offers a similar interpretation of the rise of symptoms among fourth-grade children in Taiwan. These studies are interesting in that the school as a stress situation seems to cut across social-class lines and, to an extent, cultural lines.

The school situation offers yet another perspective on the finding that boys exhibit more symptoms and are more frequently referred to psychiatric clinics by teachers than girls. Most teachers in primary grades are women and are more apt to regard boys' behavior as disturbing. Meyer and Thompson (1956) studied teacher-pupil interaction in sixth-grade classrooms over a 1-year period and analyzed behaviors in terms of "approval" and "disapproval" contacts. The finding was that teachers expressed greater approval of girls and greater disapproval of boys. Davidson and Lang (1967, p. 222) suggest:

> More men should be urged to teach at the primary level. Findings . . . suggest the urgency to establish a sexual balance in the teaching staff at the primary grades. Not only is it desirable for boys to have a male model with whom to identify, but conditions may then be created which may assure greater teacher approval for boys and reduce teacher disapproval for behavior which is, to a large extent, culturally instigated.

Chess (1967) points to the possibility of difficulties arising when the child moves actively into functional situations outside the home and encounters severe dissonance between the expectations and demands of the intrafamilial and extrafamilial environments. Although the focus of her study is mainly on temperamental differences as these interact with environmental influences, it is worth noting here since her sample of 139 children included many from the middle class, with highly educated parents. Thus, being raised in a middle-class family does not ensure consonance with predominantly middle-class institutions like the school, although it may increase the likelihood.

The difficulties of the middle-class child in school have been of lesser interest than those of lower-class children, where the problem requiring social intervention is more acute. Chess's study indicates that we must not lose sight of other perspectives, however. At least one author has suggested a theoretical framework for viewing the problems of the middle-class child in school. Green (1946) points out that the transition from life within the family unit to outside is potentially disruptive, a view held by Klein and Lindeman (1961), and Bower (1964). This is made more difficult because of the particular value system of our middle-class Western society, which imposes dual standards on the child—to be obedient in the home, but competitive and achieving in school and with his peer group. Thus the child becomes an instrument of his parents' aspirations: "Everything he accomplishes or fails to accomplish becomes an inevitable part of the family's attempt to maintain or improve its standing in the community" (Green, 1946, p. 40).

These considerations are lent a special poignancy by the fact that the school system should, and could, be an instrument of prevention rather than a generator of psychopathology (Griffin, 1968). Guidelines and findings reported in the literature, however, have received insufficient attention. One can allude to the works of Bower (1964), Ojeman (1958), Schiff and Kellam (1967), and Griffin and Seeley (1952), which offer creative approaches to this problem. Another area which has been studied is the role of the teacher. Eisenberg and Conners (reported in Eisenberg, 1968) were able to demonstrate that improvement in a class of Head Start children could be correlated with measures of the teachers' cognitive, affective, and disciplinary styles. Unfortunately, the characteristics associated with better performance were those incompatible with the rigid, authoritarian attitude suggested by a survey of urban schoolteachers carried out at the same time.

The importance of expectation has not been fully appreciated. Eisenberg (1968), for example, cites a study by Rosenthal and Jacobson (1968) in which children, chosen at random, were identified to their teachers as promising. At the end of the school year, the teachers described these children in more positive terms, and they performed significantly better on achievement tests. Too many schoolteachers, on the other hand, expect little and are not surprised when they get little from disadvantaged children (Roberts, 1967, p. 172).

In an anecdotal fashion, the experience of children from a rural slum in Stirling County as reported by Beiser (1965) points to the possibility of children learning useful social skills within the school framework. The apparent principle underlying success here, however, is too often overlooked. In this case, the gap between the disadvantaged child and his better-off contemporaries was not so wide as to seem insurmountable. For ghetto children in an urban school system, this must seldom be the case.

CONCLUSION

Lip service is often paid to the importance of social and cultural factors in psychiatric disorder, and yet little of any practical or theoretical consequence derives from the ritualistic repetition of formulas such as these.

Another popular ritual is to espouse the need for better theoretical integration of the major behavioral science disciplines; however, the evidence that this is being done is not very encouraging. In spite of our professed infatuation with multidisciplinary approaches, there are few real examples of blissful weddings between the disciplines, productive of theory and findings. One sees instead the parallel evolution of closed theoretical systems explaining many of the same phenomena in an exclusive manner, using biological, psychological, and sociocultural paradigms, to mention those most prominent in the behavioral sciences.

In psychiatry, the sociocultural paradigm has

had nowhere near the impact of the biological and the psychological, particularly in the area of treatment.

It has been repeatedly pointed out, however, that our treatment flounders when we approach those people who are precisely in need of help, and a wholesale revision of theory and treatment practices has been advocated (Myers & Bean, 1968; Riessman et al., 1964).

Such revisions cannot occur without incorporating the sociocultural paradigm. To be more specific, this paradigm should prove useful in conceptualizing the target of our efforts, that is, psychiatric disorders in children. In saying this, we do not mean to revive old arguments in their original form, arguments which now seem excessively naïve, such as, "What is schizophrenic in our culture might be venerated in another." Rather, we wish to call attention to the fact that those inadequacies and maladaptations which we call "psychiatric disorder" cannot be wrenched from a sociocultural context. This is particularly true when the "symptoms" are cast in terms of a deviation from societal norms or expectations, rather than primarily in terms of an internal deficit or as private suffering.

In his survey article dealing with the epidemiology of mental retardation, Gruenberg (1966) highlights the contextual dimension. He points out that the "most important single finding of . . . surveys" is the declining prevalence of retardation with age, after 14, the peak of the so-called schologenic crest. He points out that, in all likelihood, these people "have stopped being retarded in any real sense at all and do not need any special protection, help, or services, in which case one had better change one's concept of what 'real' mental retardation 'really' is" (Gruenberg, 1966, p. 94).

He thus points to the very important possibility that much mental retardation, at least of the borderline type, may well be a cultural artifact.

Cohort studies are obviously needed in this

and other, related fields. Outstanding examples of such studies have been done by Roff (1961) and Robins (1966), both of whom demonstrate the remarkable longevity of antisocial behavior in adults who were diagnosed as delinquent in childhood. One question deserving further study in this regard concerns the influence of being labeled antisocial in childhood and the role of this labeling in the stabilization of symptoms (Scheff, 1967).

The paradigm should also prove useful in terms of progress in theory building and tests of application. Little such progress will take place in the absence of better articulation of the paradigmatic models, such as the sociocultural, with others like the familial and the psychological. We need theoretical models which take into account the mutual interaction of each of these systems before we can evolve treatment strategies or make plans for intervention.

Clearly, sociocultural factors are important in the etiology of psychiatric disorders; however, in children perhaps even more than in adults, one must consider intervening systems between the individual and society at large. Most children function mainly within a familial matrix, which, although subject to sociocultural variation, is a remarkably effective buffer. Early childhood in particular appears to be unusually immune to the pathological sequelae of broad social change: "It is a broad finding from many forms of change that children remain undisturbed provided only that they remain within their family and that their family, in its functioning, does not change" (Murphy, 1961, p. 291).

The younger the child, it seems, the more effective is this protective envelope. Block et al. (1956), for example, found that preschool children were more immune to the effects of a disaster than schoolchildren. If we go back far

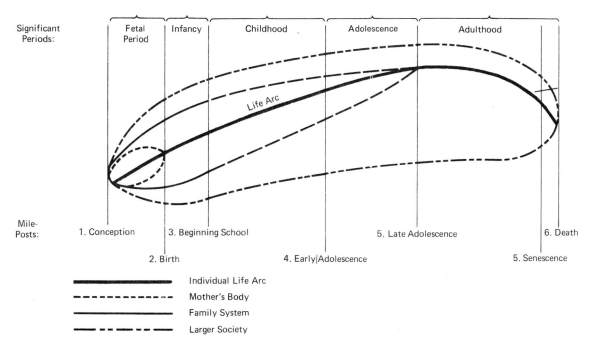

Figure 5-1. Interacting systems in personality development.

enough, to the fetal period, the child is completely protected within his mother's body—all this assuming that the relevant systems, from the physiological one of the mother to the small-group nuclear family, are functioning optimally.

When these systems fail—if the pregnant woman's nutritional intake is inadequate or if the family system is disrupted by death or divorce —there may be pathogenic sequelae. Adequate nutrition and family stability vary with some regularity, as we have seen, with social class and with other important social variables.

Figure 5-1 is a diagram of the various relevant systems in interaction. Obviously, our major concern in this discussion is with events pictured to the left of the milepost: late adolescence.

The individual is pictured as developing in an upward direction to indicate a progressive increase in his facilities and coping abilities, until a peak is reached in late adulthood, with a subsequent decline of abilities.

During a child's development, his loci of interaction evolve and change. In the prenatal period, he is obviously completely within the maternal "envelope." After birth, and as a young child, he interacts mainly with his nuclear family. Note that the line which indicates the boundary of the family system is broken relatively early; this is so because children are exposed directly to the larger society through one of its major institutions—the school—and this happens when they are quite young. As the child continues to develop, the influence of his family of orientation wanes progressively, as he interacts more and more directly with other institutions in the larger society—the school, the adolescent peer group (see Coleman, 1961; Eisenstadt, 1956), and so on.

This model also stresses the idea that smaller systems or subsystems, like the family and the school, must be viewed as being in a constant state of interaction with the larger society.

The model has several implications. For one, we can no longer be content with simplistic or reductionistic explanations of behavior. For example, if we discuss competitiveness as a problem, we can no longer be satisfied with an explanation based solely on instinctual drive (Oedipal strivings) or with one which alludes to experiences purely within the family (e.g., sibling rivalry). We must recognize competitiveness as a culturally determined behavior as well, and we must study the ways in which other major social institutions may foster it, either for good or for ill.

For instance, we offer the following quotation: "[To] succeed in competition with middle-class children in a school taught by middle-class teachers, some communality of experience with their competition seems imperative" (M. H. Roll, quoted in Pavenstadt, 1967, p. 22).

Here is an explicit statement by an educator, not only recognizing competitiveness but also suggesting that we foster it, as an adaptive behavior within our particular society. Here, the lack of competitiveness is seen as a problem, not its presence, as in so much popular theory.

Recognizing the importance of other systems besides the family alerts us to the possibility of major disarticulations occurring between socializing experience at home and in school, for example. This has led at least one author to suggest that parent-teacher societies have mental health implications for children (Wall, 1955), and this has certainly been implicit in programs for disadvantaged children in this country, such as Operation Head Start.

The articulation, or lack of it, between the family and school on the one hand and the opportunity structure and economic system on the other is a complex and difficult one to study and yet is obviously of great importance. The rise in levels of juvenile delinquency, schizophrenia, and neurosis (among girls) in late adolescence is of great interest here and points to the need for studying the interface between these important subsystems.

This chapter, as well as most of the others in this volume, engenders a feeling of optimism about the potentiality for developing effective programs of intervention. We hasten to add that they offer directions, guidelines, and perspectives, rather than definitive answers.

REFERENCES

Adams, W. A. The Negro patient in psychiatric treatment. *American Journal of Orthopsychiatry,* 1950, **20,** 305–310.

Agnew, P. C. Cultural deprivation and mental illness. *Quarterly Bulletin, Northwestern University Medical School,* 1961, **35**(1).

Alpert, J. Death of Kennedy stirs nation's youngsters. *Medical World News,* May 8, 1964, P. 111.

Arthur, B., & Kemme, M. L. Bereavement in childhood. *Journal of Child Psychology and Psychiatry and Allied Disciplines,* 1964, **5,** 37–49.

Ausbel, D. P. *Theory and problems of child development.* New York: Grune & Stratton, 1958.

Ausubel, D., & Ausubel, P. Ego development among segregated Negro children. In J. I. Roberts (Ed.), *School children in the urban slum.* New York: Free Press, 1967. Pp. 231–260.

Becker, W. C. Consequences of different kinds of parental discipline. In M. L. Hoffman & L. W. Hoffman (Eds.), *Review of child development research.* New York: Russell Sage, 1964. Pp. 169–208.

Beier, D. C., Binder, A., & Robbins, C. D. Indiana survey of emotionally disturbed children. Indiana University, Mimeographed Report No. 2, January, 1961.

Beiser, M. Poverty, social disintegration and personality. *Journal of Social Issues,* 1965, **21**(1), 57–78.

Beiser, M. Primary prevention of mental illness: General v. specific. In C. A. Roberts, F. C. R. Chalke, & J. J. Day, (Eds.), *Primary prevention of psychiatric disorders.* Toronto: University of Toronto Press, 1968. Pp. 84–97.

Belkin, M. E., et al. Mental health training program for the child care conference. *American Journal of Public Health,* 1965, **55,** 1046–1056.

Beller, E. K., & Neubauer, P. B. Sex differences and symptom patterns in early childhood. *Journal of the American Academy of Child Psychiatry,* 1963, **2,** 417–433.

Bentzen, F. Sex ratio in learning and behavior disorders. *American Journal of Orthopsychiatry,* 1963, **33,** January, 1963, 92-98.

Bernard, V. W. School desegregation: Some psychiatric implications. *Psychiatry,* 1958, **21,** 149–158.

Blank, M. & Bridger, W. H. Perceptual abilities and conceptual deficiencies in retarded readers. In J. Zubin & G. A. Jervis (Eds.), *Psychopathology of mental development.* New York: Grune & Stratton, 1967. Pp. 401–412.

Blank, M., & Solomon, F. A tutorial language program to develop abstract thinking in socially disadvantaged preschool children. *Child Development,* 1968.

Bloch, D. A., Silber, E., & Perry, S. E. Some factors in the emotional reaction of children to disaster. *American Journal of Psychiatry,* 1956, **113,** 416–422.

Bossard, J. H. S. *Parent and child.* Philadelphia: University of Pennsylvania Press, 1953.

Bower, E. M. The modification, mediation,

and utilization of stress during the school years. *American Journal of Orthopsychiatry,* 1964, **24,** 667–674.

Bowlby, J. Forty-four juvenile thieves: Their characters and home life. *International Journal of Psychoanalysis,* 1944, **25,** 19–53.

Bowlby, J., et al. *Maternal care and mental health.* New York: Schocken Books, 1966.

Brody, E. B. Color and identity conflict in young boys: Observations of Negro mothers and sons in urban Baltimore. I. *Psychiatry,* 1963, **26,** 188–201.

Brody, E. B. Color and identity conflict in young boys. II. *Archives of General Psychiatry,* 1964, **10,** 354–360.

Bronfenbrenner, U. Socialization and social class through time and space. In E. E. Macoby, T. M. Newcomb, & E. L. Hartley, (Eds.), *Readings in social psychology.* New York: Holt, 1958. Pp. 400–424.

Bronfenbrenner, U. Some familial antecedents of responsibility and leadership in adolescents. In L. Petrullo, & B. M. Bass, (Eds.), *Leadership and interpersonal behavior.* New York: Holt, 1961. Pp. 239–271.

Bronfenbrenner, U. Early deprivation in mammals and man. In G. Newton (Ed.), *Early experience and behavior.* Springfield, Ill.: Charles C Thomas, 1966. Pp. 627–764.

Buck, C., & Laughton, K. Family patterns of illness: The effect of psychoneurosis in the parent upon illness in the child. *Actopsychoneurology Scandinavia,* 1959, **34,** 165–175.

Burt, C., & Howard, M. The nature and causes of maladjustment among children of school age. *British Journal of Psychology,* 1952, **5,** 39–59.

Burton, R. V., & Whiting, J. W. M. The absent father and cross-sex identity. *Merrill-Palmer Quarterly,* 1961, **7,** 85–95.

Caplan, G. (Ed.) *Prevention of mental disorders in children.* New York: Basic Books, 1961.

Caplan, G. Community psychiatry: The changing role of the psychiatrist. In S. K. Weinberg (Ed.), *The sociology of mental disorders.* Chicago: Aldine, 1967. Pp. 301–309.

Carey-Trefzer, C. J. The results of a clinical study of war-damaged children who attended the Child Guidance Clinic, the Hospital for Sick Children, Great Ormond Street, London. *The Journal of Mental Science,* 1949, **95,** 535–559.

Casler, L. Maternal deprivation: A critical review of the literature. *Social Research and Child Development,* 1961, **2** (26), 1–64.

Chess, S. Behavior problems revisited: Findings of an anterospective study. *Journal of the American Academy of Child Psychiatry,* 1967, **6,** 321–331.

Chilman, C., & Sussman, M. Poverty in the United States. *Journal of Marriage and the Family,* 1964, **26,** 391–395.

Clark, K. B., & Clark, M. K. The development of consciousness of self and the emergence of racial identification in Negro preschool children. *Journal of Social Psychology,* 1939, **10,** 591–599.

Clark, K. B., & Clark, M. P. Racial identification and preference in Negro children. In T. M. Newcomb & E. L. Hartley (Eds.), *Readings in social psychology.* New York: Holt, 1947. Pp. 169–178.

Clark, M. K., & Clark, M. P. Emotional factors in racial identification and preference in Negro children. *Journal of Negro Education,* 1950, **19,** 341–350.

Clausen, J. A. Family structure, socialization

and personality. In L. W. Hoffman & M. L. Hoffman (Eds.), *Review of child development research.* New York: Russell Sage, 1966. Pp. 1–53.

Cleveland, E. J., & Longaker, W. D. Neurotic patterns in the family. In A. H. Leighton, J. A. Clausen & R. N. Wilson (Eds.), *Explorations in social psychiatry.* New York: Basic Books, 1957. Pp. 167-200.

Cohen, A. K. *Delinquent boys: The culture of the gang.* New York: Free Press, 1955.

Coleman, J. S. *The adolescent society.* New York: Free Press, 1961.

Coleman, J. S. *Equality of educational opportunity.* Washington: U.S. Department of Health, Education, and Welfare, 1966.

Coles, R. Southern children under desegregation. *American Journal of Psychiatry,* 1963, **120,** 332–344.

Coles, R. *Children in crisis.* Boston: Little, Brown, 1967.

Coopersmith, S. *Antecedents of self-esteem.* San Francisco: Freeman, 1967.

Coopersmith, S. Studies in self-esteem. *Scientific American,* 1968, 96-106.

Costello, A. J., et al. Aetiological factors in young schizophrenic men. *British Journal of Psychiatry,* 1968, **114,** 433–441.

Cumming, J. The family and mental disorder: An incomplete essay. *Causes of mental disorder: A review of epidemiological knowledge, 1959.* New York: Milbank Memorial Fund, 1961. Pp. 153–180.

Cumming, J. The inadequacy syndrome. *The Psychiatric Quarterly,* 1963, 1–11.

Cumming, J., & Cumming, E. *Ego and milieu.* New York: Atherton, 1963.

Cummings, J. D. The incidence of emotional symptoms in school children. *British Journal of Educational Psychology,* 1944, **14,** 151–161.

Cummings, J. D. A follow-up study of emotional symptoms in school children. *British Journal of Educational Psychology,* 1946, **16,** 163–177.

Dai, B. Minority group membership and personality development. In J. Masuoka and P. Valien (Eds.), *Race relations: Problems and theories.* Chapel Hill: University of North Carolina Press, 1961. Pp. 181–199.

Davidson, H. H., & Lang, G. Children's perceptions of their teachers' feelings toward them related to self-perception, school achievement and behavior. In J. I. Roberts (Ed.), *School children in the urban slum.* New York: Free Press, 1967. Pp. 215–230.

Davis, A., & Dollard, J. *Children of bondage.* Washington: American Council on Education, 1940.

Davis, A. *Social class influences on learning.* Cambridge: Harvard University Press, 1949.

Davis, K. Mental hygiene and the class structure. *Psychiatry,* 1938, **I,** 55–65.

Davis, K. Final notes on a case of extreme isolation. *American Journal of Sociology,* 1947, **52,** 432–437.

Davis, R. D. Family processes in mental retardation. *American Journal of Psychology,* 1967, **124**(3), 340–350.

Dennis, N., et al. *Coal is our life: An analysis of a Yorkshire mining community.* London: Eyre and Spottiswoode, 1956.

Deutsch, M. P. Minority groups and class status

as related to social and personality factors in scholastic achievement. *Society for Applied Anthropology,* Monograph 2. Ithaca: Cornell University Press, 1960.

Deutsch, M. P. The disadvantaged child and the learning process. In F. Riessman, J. Cohen, and A. Pearl (Eds.), *Mental health of the poor.* New York: Free Press, 1964. Pp. 172-187.

Deutsch, M. P. (Ed.), *The disadvantaged child.* New York: Basic Books, 1967.

Douglas, J. W. B., & Blomfield, J. M. *Children under five.* London: Allen and Unwin, 1958.

Douvan, E., & Adelson, J. *The adolescent experience.* New York: Wiley, 1966.

Eisenberg, L. The psychiatric implications of brain damage in children. *The Psychiatric Quarterly,* 1957, **31,** 72-92.

Eisenberg, L. Child psychiatry: The past quarter century. Address to the Twenty-fifth Anniversary, Department of Psychiatry, McGill University, Montreal, Oct. 3, 1968. (Mimeographed)

Eisenberg, L. & Gruenberg, E. M. The current status of secondary prevention in child psychiatry. *American Journal of Orthopsychiatry,* 1961, **31,** 355-367.

Eisenstadt, S. N. *From generation to generation.* New York: Free Press, 1956.

Elkin, F. *The child and society.* New York: Random House, 1960.

Ellis, R. W. B. Effects of war on child health. *The British Medical Journal,* 1948, **1,** 239-245.

Erikson, E. H. *Childhood and society.* New York: Norton, 1963.

Fairweather, D. V. I., & Ilsley, R. Obstetric and social origins of mentally handicapped children. *British Journal of Preventive & Social Medicine,* 1960, **14,** 149-159.

Fleck, S., et al. The intrafamilial environment of the schizophrenic patient. In J. Masserman (Ed.), *Science and psychoanalysis.* Vol. 2. New York: Grune & Stratton, 1959. Pp. 142-158.

Freud, A., & Burlingham, D. T. *Infants without families.* New York: International Universities Press, 1944.

Freud, A. The relationship between psychoanalysis and pedagogy. In N. Long, W. C. Morse, & R. G. Newman (Eds.), *Conflict in the classroom.* Belmont, Calif.: Wadsworth, 1966.

Fromm, E. Individual and social origins of neurosis. *American Sociological Review,* 1944, **9,** 380-384.

Glasser, P., & Navare, E. Structural problems of the one-parent family. *Journal of Social Issues,* 1965, **21** (1), 98-109.

Glidewell, J. C., et al. Behavior symptoms in children and degree of sickness. *American Journal of Psychiatry,* 1957, **114** (1), 47-53.

Glidewell, J. C., et al. Behavior symptoms in children and adjustment in public school. *Human Organization,* 1959, **18,** 123-130.

Gordon, R. E., & Gordon, K. K. Emotional disorders of children in a rapidly growing suburb. *International Journal of Social Psychiatry,* 1958, **4,** 85-97.

Green, A. The middle class male child and neurosis. *American Sociological Review,* 1946, **11,** 31-41.

Griffin, J. D. Public education and school procedures. In F. C. R. Chalkes & J. J. Day (Eds.), *Primary prevention of psychiatric disorders.* Toronto: University of Toronto Press, 1968. Pp. 149-161.

Griffin, J. D., & Seeley, J. R. Education for mental health: An Experiment. *Journal of Canadian Education,* 1952,

Gruenberg, E. M. Epidemiology of mental retardation. *International Journal of Psychiatry,* 1966, **2,** 78–126.

Haggstrom, W. C. The power of the poor. In F. Riessman, J. Cohen, & A. Pearl (Eds.), *Mental health of the poor.* New York: Free Press, 1964. Pp. 205–226.

Hartman, H. *Ego psychology and the problem of adaptation.* New York: International Universities Press, 1958.

Hellman, I. Hampstead Nursery follow-up studies: Sudden separation and its effect followed over twenty years. *The Psychoanalytic Study of the Child,* 1962, **17,** 159–174.

Hoffman, L. W., & Hoffman, M. L. (Eds.) *Review of child development research.* Vol. 2. New York: Russell Sage, 1966.

Hoffman, M. L., & Hoffman, L. W. (Eds.) *Review of child development research.* Vol. 1. New York: Russell Sage, 1964.

Hoggart, R. *The uses of literacy.* London: Chatto and Windus, 1957.

Hollingshead, A. B., & Redlich, F. C. *Social class and mental illness.* New York: Wiley, 1958.

Hsu, C. C. A study of "Problem Children" reported by teachers. *Japanese Journal of Child Psychiatry,* 1966, 7(2), 91–108.

Hughes, C. C., Tremblay, M. A., Rapoport, R. N., & Leighton, A. H. *People of cove and woodlot.* New York: Basic Books, 1960.

Hunt, J. McV. *Intelligence and experience.* New York: Ronald Press, 1961.

Jenkins, R. L., & Cole, J. O. (Eds.) *Diagnostic classification in child psychiatry.* American Psychiatric Association, Psychiatric Research Report No. 18, October, 1964.

Jessor, R., Graves, T. D., Hanson, R. C., &

Jessor, S. L. *Society, personality and deviant behavior.* New York: Holt, 1968.

Kaffman, M. A comparison of psychopathology: Israeli children from kibbutz and from urban surroundings. *American Journal of Orthopsychiatry,* 1965, **35,** 509–520.

Kagan, J. Acquisition and significance of sex typing and sex role identity. In M. L. Hoffman & L. W. Hoffman (Eds.), *Review of Child Development Research.* New York: Russell Sage, 1964.

Kardiner A., & Ovesey, L. *The mark of oppression.* New York: Norton, 1951.

Kellam, S. G., & Schiff, S. K. Adaptation and mental illness in the first grade classrooms of an urban community. In M. Greenblatt, P. E. Emery, & B. C. Glueck (Eds.), *Poverty and mental health.* • American Psychiatric Association, Psychiatric Research No. 21, 1967. Pp. 79–91.

Klein, D., & Lindeman, E. Preventive intervention in individual and family crisis situations. In G. Caplan (Ed.), *Prevention of mental disorders in children.* New York: Basic Books, 1961. Pp. 283–306.

Knobloch, H., & Pasamanick, B. Prospective studies on the epidemiology of reproductive causality: Methods, findings, and some implications. *Merrill-Palmer Quarterly,* 1966, **12,** 7–26.

Kohn, M. C. Social class and parent-child relationships: An interpretation. In F. Riessman, J. Cohen, & A. Pearl (Eds.), *Mental health of the poor.* New York: Free Press, 1964. Pp. 159–171.

Langner, T. S. A twenty-two item screening score of psychiatric symptoms indicating impairment. *Journal of Health and Human Behavior,* 1962, **3,** 269–276.

Lapouse, R., & Monk, M. A. An epidemiologic study of behavior characteristics in children.

American Journal of Public Health, 1958, **48,** 1134–1144.

Lapouse, R., & Monk, M. A. Fears and worries in a representative sample of children. *American Journal of Orthopsychiatry,* 1959, **29,** 803–818.

Leighton, A. H. *My name is legion.* New York: Basic Books, 1959.

Leighton, D. C., et al. *The character of danger.* New York: Basic Books, 1963.

Lewis, H. *Child rearing among low income families.* Washington: Washington Center for Metropolitan Studies, 1961.

Lewis, O. *The children of Sanchez.* New York: Random House, 1961.

Lewis, O. *La vida.* New York: Random House, 1966.

Lidz, T. *The family and human adaptation.* New York: International Universities Press, 1963.

Lidz, T., et al. The intrafamilial environment of schizophrenic patients. II. Marital schism and marital skew. *American Journal of Psychiatry,* 1957, **114,** 244.

Lynn, D. B., & Sawrey, W. L. The effects of father absence on Norwegian boys and girls. *Journal of Abnormal and Social Psychology,* 1959, **59,** 258–262.

MacMillan, A. M. The health opinion survey: Technique for estimating prevalence of psychoneurotic and related types of disorder in communities. *Psychological Reports,* 1957, 3 (Monog. Suppl. 7), 325–339.

Malone, C. A. Safety first: Comments on the influence of external danger in the lives of children of disorganized families. *American Journal of Orthopsychiatry,* 1966, **36,** 3–12.

Malone, C. A. The psychosocial characteris-tics of children from a developmental view-point. In E. Pavenstadt (Ed.), *The drifters.* Boston: Little, Brown, 1967. Pp. 105–124.

Mangus, A. R. *Mental health of rural children in Ohio.* Ohio Agricultural Experimental Station Research Bulletin 682, March, 1949.

Matteson, A., Hawkin, J. W., & Seese, L. R. Child psychiatric emergencies. *Archives of General Psychology,* 1967, **17,** 584–592.

Mattick, I. Description of the children. In E. Pavenstadt (Ed.), *The drifters.* Boston: Little, Brown, 1967.

McDermott, F. Social class and mental illness in children: The diagnosis of organicity and mental retardation. *Journal of the American Academy of Child Psychiatry,* 1967, **6,** 309–320.

McDermott, J. F., Harrison, S. I., Schrager, J., & Wilson, P. Social class and mental illness in children: Observations of blue-collar families. *American Journal of Orthopsychiatry,* 1965, **35,** 500–508.

Mead, G. H. *Mind, self and society.* Chicago: University of Chicago Press, 1934.

Mead, M. A cultural anthropologist's approach and material deprivation. In A. Bowlby et al., *Maternal care and mental health.* New York: Schocken Books, 1966.

Mensh, I. N., Kantor, M. B., Domke, H. R., Gildea, M. C., & Glidewell, J. C. Children's behavior symptoms and their relationships to school adjustment, sex and social class. *Journal of Social Issues,* 1959, **15,** 8-15.

Meyer, W. S., & Thompson, G. G. Sex differences in the distribution of teacher approval and disapproval among sixth grade children. *Journal of Educational Psychology,* 1956, **47,** 285–396.

Milbank Memorial Fund. *Causes of mental*

disorders: A review of epidemiological knowledge. New York: MMF, 1959.

Miller, S. M. The American lower classes: A typological approval. In F. Riessman, J. Cohen, & A. Pearl (Eds.), Mental health of the poor. New York: Free Press, 1964. Pp. 139–154.

Miller, W. B. Lower class culture as a generating milieu of gang delinquency. Journal of Social Issues, 1958, 14, 5–19.

Minuchin, S., Montalvo, B., Guerney, B., Rosman, B. L., & Schumer, F. Families of the slums. New York: Basic Books, 1967.

Mora, G. Recent American psychiatric developments. In S. Arieti (Ed.), American Handbook of Psychiatry. New York: Basic Books, 1959. Pp. 18–57.

Murphy, H. B. M. Social change and mental health. In Milbank Memorial Fund, Causes of mental disorders: A review of epidemiological knowledge. New York: MMF, 1961. Pp. 280–329.

Mussen, P. H. Some antecedents and consequents of masculine sex-typing in adolescent boys. Psychological Monographs, 1961, 75(2).

Myers, J. K., & Bean, L. L. A decade later. New York: Wiley, 1968.

Myers, J. K., & Schaffer, L. Social stratification and psychiatric practice: A study of an out-patient clinic. American Sociological Review, 1954, 19, 307–310.

Ojeman, R. H. Basic approaches to mental health: The human relations program at the State University of Iowa. Personnel Guidance Journal, 1958, 36, 198–211.

Olenick, M., et al. Early socialization experiences and intrafamilial environment. Archives of General Psychiatry, 1966, 15, 344–353.

Oltman, J. E., & Friedman, S. Parental deprivation in psychiatric conditions. III. In personality disorders and other conditions. Diseases of the Nervous System, 1967, 28, 298–303.

O'Neal, P., & Robins, L. N. The relation of childhood behavior problems to adult psychiatric status: A 30-year follow-up study of 150 subjects. American Journal of Psychiatry, 1958, 115, 385–391.

Palmain, G., et al. Social class and the young offender. British Journal of Psychiatry, 1967, 113, 1073–1082.

Pampian-Mindlin, E. Omnipotentiality, youth and commitment. Journal of the American Academy of Child Psychiatry, 1965.

Pasamanick, B. Epidemiologic studies in the complications of pregnancy and the birth process. In G. Caplan (Ed.), Prevention of mental disorders in children. New York: Basic Books, 1961. Pp. 74–94.

Pasamanick, B. Some misconceptions concerning differences in the racial prevalence of mental disease. American Journal of Orthopsychiatry, 1963, 33, 72-86.

Pavenstadt, E. A study of immature mothers and their children. In G. Caplan (Ed.), Prevention of mental disorders in children. New York: Basic Books, 1961. Pp. 192–217.

Pavenstadt, E. A comparison of the child-rearing environment of upper-lower and very low-lower class families. American Journal of Orthopsychiatry, 1965, 35, 89.

Pavenstadt, E. (Ed.). The drifters. Boston: Little, Brown, 1967.

Pritchard, M., & Graham, P. An investigation of a group of patients who have attended both the child and adult departments of the same psychiatric hospital. *British Journal of Psychiatry,* 1966, **112,** 603–612.

Provence, S., & Lipton, R. *Infants in institutions.* New York: International Universities Press, 1962.

Prugh, D. G., et al. A study of the emotional reactions of children and families to hospitalization and illness. *American Journal of Orthopsychiatry,* 1953, **23,** 70–106.

Raphael, E. E. Community structure and acceptance of psychiatric aid. *American Journal of Sociology,* 1964, **69,** 340–358.

Ried, D. D. Precipitating proximal factors in the occurrence of mental disorders. In Milbank Memorial Fund, *Causes of mental disorders: A review of epidemiological knowledge.* New York: MMF, 1961, **39**(2), 229–258.

Riessman, F. *The culturally deprived child.* New York: Harper, 1962.

Riessman, F., Cohen, J., & Pearl, A. (Eds.). *Mental health of the poor.* New York: Free Press, 1964.

Rin, H. Family study of Chinese schizophrenic patients: Loss of parents, sibling rank, parental attitude, and short-term prognosis. *Transcultural Psychiatric Research,* 1965, **2,** 24–27.

Roberts, J. I. (Ed.) *School children in the urban slum.* New York: Free Press, 1967.

Robins, L. N. *Deviant children grown up.* Baltimore: Williams & Wilkins, 1966.

Roff, M. Childhood social interactions and young adult bad conduct. *Journal of Abnormal and Social Psychology,* 1961, **63,** 333–337.

Rogers, C. R. *Client-centered therapy.* Boston: Houghton Mifflin, 1951.

Rosen, B. M., Bahn, A. K., & Kramer, M. Demographic and diagnostic characteristics of psychiatric clinic outpatients in the U.S.A., 1961. *American Journal of Orthopsychiatry,* 1964, **34,** 445–468.

Rosen, B. M., Bahn, A. K., Shellow, R., & Bower, E. M. Adolescent patients served in outpatient psychiatric clinics. *American Journal of Public Health,* 1965, **55,** 1563–1577.

Rosenthal, R., & Jacobson, L. *Pygmalion in the classroom.* New York: Holt, 1968.

Rutter, M. Some current research issues in American child psychiatry. *Milbank Memorial Fund Quarterly,* 1963, **41,** 339–370.

Rutter, M. Classification and categorization in child psychiatry. *Journal of Child Psychology and Psychiatry,* 1965, **6,** 71–83.

Rutter, M., & Graham, P. Psychiatric disorder in 10 and 11-year-old Children. *Proceedings of the Royal Society of Medicine,* 1966, **59,** 382–387.

Scheff, T. J. *Being mentally ill: A sociological theory.* Chicago: Aldine, 1967.

Schiff, S. K., & Kellam, S. G. A community-wide mental health program of prevention and early treatment in first grade. In M. Greenblatt, P. E. Emery, & B. C. Glueck (Eds.), *Poverty and mental health.* American Psychiatric Association, Psychiatric Research Reports No. 21, 1967. Pp. 92–102.

Schrupp, M., & Gjerde, C. Teacher growth in attitudes toward behavior problems of Children. *Journal of Educational Psychology,* 1953, **44,** 203–214.

Sedlis, E. National history of infantile eczema: Its incidence and cause. *The Journal of Pediatrics,* 1965, **66,** 158–163.

Seeley, J. R. Social values, the mental health

movement, and mental health. *Annals of the American Academy of Political and Social Sciences,* 1953, **286,** 15–24.

Sewell, W. H., & Haller, A. O. Factors in the relationship between social status and the personality adjustment of the child. *American Sociological Review,* 1959, **14,** 511–520.

Sherwin, A. C., & Schoelly, M. Criteria of psychiatric disorder in children. In J. M. Murphy, & A. H. Leighton (Eds.), *Approaches to cross-cultural psychiatry.* Ithaca, N.Y.: Cornell University Press, 1965. Pp. 219–247.

Sherwin, A. C., et al. Determination of psychiatric impairment in children. *The Journal of Nervous and Mental Disease,* 1965, **141,** 333–341.

Short, J. F. Juvenile delinquency: The sociocultural context. In L. W. Hoffman & M. L. Hoffman (Eds.), *Review of child development research.* Vol. 2. New York: Russell Sage, 1966. Pp. 423–468.

Silber, E., Perry, S. E., & Bloch, D. A. Patterns of parent-child interaction in a disaster. *Psychiatry,* 1958, **21,** 159–167.

Siller, J. Socioeconomic status and conceptual thinking. *Journal of Abnormal and Social Psychology,* 1957, **55,** 365–371.

Smelser, N. J., & Smelser, W. T. *Personality and social systems.* New York: Wiley, 1963.

Solomon, H. Civil rights activity and reduction in crime among Negroes. *Archives of General Psychiatry,* 1965, **12,** 227–236.

Spiro, M. *Children of the kibbutz.* Cambridge, Mass.: Harvard University Press, 1958.

Spitz, R. A. Aggression: Its role in the establishment of object relations. In R. M. Lowenstein (Ed.), *Drives, affects, behavior.* New York: International Universities Press, 1953. Pp. 126–133.

Spitz, R. A., & Wolf, K. Autoeroticism. *The Psychoanalytic Study of the Child,* 1949, **3-4,** 85–120.

Srole, L., Langner, T. S., Michael, S. T., Osler, M. K., & Rennie, T. A. *Mental health in the metropolis: The midtown Manhattan study.* Vol. 1. New York: McGraw-Hill, 1962.

Stein, M. R. Sociocultural perspectives on the neighborhood and the families. In E. Pavenstadt et al. (Eds.), *The drifters.* Boston: Little, Brown, 1967. Pp. 299–320.

Stolz, M., et al. *Father relations of war-born children.* Stanford, Calif.: Stanford University Press, 1954.

Stone, I. T., Leighton, D. C., & Leighton, A. H. Poverty and the individual. In L. Fishman (Ed.), *Poverty amid affluence.* New Haven, Conn.: Yale University Press, 1966. Pp. 72–96.

Stouffer, G. A. W. Behavior problems of children as viewed by teachers and mental hygienists. *Mental Hygiene,* 1952, **36,** 271–285.

Sullivan, H. S. *The interpersonal theory of psychiatry.* New York: Norton, 1953.

Tapia, F. Girls with conditions more commonly seen in boys. *Diseases of the Nervous System,* 1968, **29,** 323–326.

Thomas, C. S., & Bergen, B. J. Social psychiatric view of psychological misfunction and role of psychiatry in social change. *Archives of General Psychiatry,* 1965, **12,** 539–544.

Toby, J. Orientation to education as a factor in the school maladjustment of lower-class children. In N. J. Smelser & W. T. Smelser (Eds.), *Personality and social systems.* New York: Wiley, 1963. Pp. 549–558.

Townsend, P. The family of three generations in Britain, the United States and Denmark. Paper presented at the meeting of the International Social Science Seminar in Gerontology, Makkaryd, Sweden, August, 1963.

Volkart, E. H. Bereavement and mental health. In A. H. Leighton, J. A. Clausen, & R. N. Wilson (Eds.), *Explorations in social psychiatry.* New York: Basic Books, 1957. Pp. 281–307.

Wall, W. D. *Education and mental health.* UNESCO, Problems in Education—XI, Holland, 1955.

Wardle, C. J. Two generations of broken homes in the genesis of conduct and behavior disorders in childhood. *British Medical Journal,* 1961, **11,** 349–354.

Wardrop, K. R. H. Delinquent teenage types. *British Journal of Criminology,* 1967, **714,** 371–380.

Warner, W. L. *A black civilization.* New York: Harper, 1937.

Warner, W. L., Havinghurst, R. J., & Loeb, M. B. *Who shall be educated?* New York: Harper, 1944.

Weinberg, S. K. *The sociology of mental disorders.* Chicago: Aldine, 1967.

Weinstein, E. A., & Giesel, P. N. An analysis of sex differences in adjustment. *Child Development,* 1960, **31,** 721.

Whiting, J. W. M., & Child, I. L. *Child training and personality.* New Haven, Conn.: Yale University Press, 1953.

Wickman, E. K. Children's behavior and teachers' attitudes. New York: Commonwealth Fund, 1928.

Wing, J. K. (Ed.) *Early childhood autism: clinical, educational and social aspects.* New York: Pergamon Press, 1966.

Wittenberg, R. M. Personality adjustment through social action. In F. Riessman, J. Cohen, & A. Pearl (Eds.), *Mental health of the poor.* New York: Free Press, 1964. Pp. 378–392.

Wootton, B. A social scientist's approach to maternal deprivation. In J. Bowlby et al., *Maternal care and mental health.* New York: Schocken Books, 1966. Pp. 255–265.

Wortis, H., & Freedman, A. M. The contribution of social environment to the development of premature children. *American Journal of Orthopsychiatry,* 1968, **35,** 57–68.

Yarrow, L. J. Separation from parents during early childhood. In M. L. Hoffman & L. W. Hoffman (Eds.), *Review of child development research.* Vol. 1. New York: Russell Sage, 1964.

Young, M. D., & Willmott, P. *Family and kinship in East London.* Baltimore: Penguin Books, 1957.

Zegans, L. S. An appraisal of etiological contributions and psychiatric theory and research. *American Journal of Psychiatry,* 1967, **124,** 729–739.

Zeligs, R. Children's attitudes towards death. *Mental Hygiene,* 1967, **51,** 393–396.

6 Some Basic Aspects of Family Pathology

Stephen Fleck, M.D.[1]

Throughout history, students of man, particularly those in the helping professions, have concerned themselves with the family. In antiquity, writers and philosophers were preoccupied and fascinated with the subject, and humanity's universal concern with family life and structure is reflected in most religious systems. As the primary transmitter of human experience and institutions across generations, the family, whatever its structure or composition, has also often been the historian's or politician's scapegoat, being held accountable for the cultural, social, or political decline of a group or nation. However, it must be appreciated that the family, although the primary environment for each person, is but one institution in society, and modifications in family styles and characteristics are as likely to arise from within that institution as through forces outside it. Changing

[1] Portions of this chapter have been published in *Comprehensive Psychiatry*, Vol. 7, No. 5 (October) 1966 under the title "An Approach to Family Pathology" and are being reproduced here with the publisher's permission, which is gratefully acknowledged.

cultural mores; political, economic, and climactic conditions; and technological innovations are among the factors that affect family life, and vice versa (Toynbee, 1947).

Family pathology, therefore, cannot be considered something absolute, a *Ding an sich* apart from either external or internal forces, including the individual personality patterns and the emotionally charged interrelationships, none of which are static or unidirectional. The individuals who compose the family undergo evolutionary and nonevolutionary changes, and the adults in it (the parents in the nuclear family) bring to it personalities and behavioral techniques which derive largely from their respective family experiences, which in turn shaped their developing personalities (Lidz, 1963, 1968; Winnicott, 1965).

Even if we knew what a "normal" or "average" family is, it would still have to be defined on different levels of organization, ranging from the cell and chromosomes to the social stratum; from different perspectives and vantage points; and also for different cultures, if not for each socioeconomic class. For instance, Mrs. Marguerite

Oswald, mother of a presumed assassin, twice married and unable to take care of her children much of the time, claimed that hers was just "an average American family" (Stafford, 1965); and an infertile couple, both Ph.D.s in the pursuit of adopting a child, described themselves in the same terms (Fleck, unpublished data).

We cannot deal with family pathology as we can with liver slices, for example. These we establish as normal or abnormal through various chemical and optical observations, but we can also detect cellular abnormalities indirectly by measuring specific functions of the total organ, e.g., certain cellular outputs, without dissecting the organ and without proof of what particular disturbance besets the cells, or which, or how many cells are afflicted. This can be done without complete knowledge of all liver functions or cellular operations.

Similarly, we can distinguish between functional family competence and family disability in those vectors which we have come to understand as essential family tasks. This approach to family pathology seems most appropriate at this time, i.e., to view family abnormalities as failures or deficiencies in essential task accomplishments. It allows for future additions to the list of basic family functions as they may become known and understood, as well as for further refinement and more accurate discernment of those to be considered here.

We shall therefore present first a brief résumé of our current concepts of basic and essential family functions before discussing family pathology as deviations from, or deficiencies in, family functioning. These functions are "normal" in the sense that they are indispensable to the establishment of a family and to the fulfillment of its missions in a given culture. Our considerations will be limited to the nuclear family unless stated otherwise, because it is increasingly the typical family unit in industrialized societies and because our clinical experience as well as most of our relevant concepts pertain to the nuclear

family, the middle-class nuclear family in particular. It should be noted briefly that compared with an extended-family system, the nuclear unit imposes on family life certain disadvantages and special burdens. In the isolated nuclear family the personalities of the parents are more crucial than in the extended family because each parent must function as a model for the child of the same sex. In extended-family systems alternative models and sometimes more wholesome ones than those of the progenitors are readily and continuously available to offspring. Parental role complementarity is most crucial in the isolated nuclear family so that tangible and intangible tasks can be shared, lest a child have to substitute for a parent. Furthermore, industrialization, together with child labor laws, has rendered offspring and grandparents economic liabilities, in contrast to earlier generations, when both were more likely assets, especially on the farm (Parsons, 1964; Parsons & Bales, 1955).

FAMILY TASKS

Before family functions can be outlined as a preliminary to considering pathology, two important and basic divisions that govern family structure and dynamics must be understood. These can be viewed as the two axes of family life. One is the generation boundary which divides the group into parents, who nurture and lead and who direct and teach, and offspring, who are dependent and who follow and learn. This line also divides those members who are sexually active with each other, the parents, from those to whom sexual activity within the family is interdicted. The other division is that between the two sexes, the family being the environment in which sons first learn to be boys and then men and in which daughters learn to become girls and then women. While much identity consolidation, especially with regard to gender security and gender-linked behavior characteristics, is influenced from outside the family, especially by peers in adolescence, the identity anlagen are pre-Oedipal, and basic gender awareness and security derive from constructive resolution of Oedipal issues. Effecting and maintaining these two boundaries is the most important task of family life, a task accomplished more by example and nonverbal cues than explicitly. This paradigm can also be stated as the effective establishment of the incest taboo within the family (Lidz, 1963; Parsons, 1954).

Family functions will be outlined briefly in terms of (1) parental coalition, (2) nurturant tasks, (3) enculturation of the younger generation, (4) emancipation of offspring from the family, and (5) family crises. For the purpose of discussion, these functions are presented as if they were separate, but in actuality they are interrelated and overlap. They parallel in many ways the life cycle, especially the personality development of the child, and much of what is stated here has also been outlined by Erikson (1950, 1964) in his eight stages of development and conceptualized by Parsons (1964) and Parsons and Bales (1955).

The marital coalition may be defined as consisting of those interactional patterns which the spouses develop at first for their mutual needs and satisfaction. Later, in the evolving structure and dynamics of the family, this coalition must serve the age-appropriate needs of the children and still support an area of exclusive relationship and mutuality between parents. One of these parental sectors is sexual activity, interdicted to children in most societies. Mutuality denotes the spouses' interactive patterns on implicit and explicit levels, the sharing of feelings and conveying of respect and appreciation of one spouse to the other as well as to other people. Furthermore, the representation of one spouse by the other to the children and to others is an important item in the parental coalition, especially when one parent has to be absent from the family.

An important function of this coalition in family life is the mutual reinforcement of the spouses' complementary sex-linked roles, so that as parents they represent, respectively, culture-appropriate masculinity and femininity, not only as individuals but also through the other spouse's support and approval. Another facet of the coalition is the conjugal role divisions and reciprocities the spouses establish for themselves, but it should be noted that role allocations in a marriage as well as the decision-making methods vary with different socioeconomic classes (Bott, 1957; Rainwater, 1965). Basically, according to Parsons, fathers are predominantly the instrumentalists in our culture—their activities usually determine the family's social position—whereas mothers are more responsible for the affective and emotional climate in the family (Lidz, 1963; Parsons & Bales, 1955).

The coalition must serve the establishment of triangular relationships when children are born, and these triangles must be flexible, as each additional child at first must be very close to the mother and absorb a great deal of her attention and energy, to which the older family members must adapt. The older child must give up this primary closeness with his mother and learn to tolerate his replacement by a younger sibling. Parental role complementarity is essential to this task. In both psychodynamic and sociodynamic terms, this role complementarity evolved by the parents is an important basis of the group which the family must become. Role allocations affect and involve all family members, and they must change with the age of the family group.

In contrast to synthetic or therapy groups, the family group has built in it biopsychosocial givens and a predetermined evolutionary history with rather distinct age-related tasks and functions. Role flexibility within the family is therefore a necessity and also demonstrates that the needs or welfare of the group sometimes precede individual needs, and vice versa at other times (Bell & Vogel, 1960). Parental role allocations are therefore important demonstrations of how the two sexes divide tasks and attitudes in a particular society. If the parents' behavior in this respect is markedly and consistently deviant from social and class norms, we must entertain the likelihood of abnormal family dynamics and a pathogenic impact on the personality development of the children.

Nurturant family tasks are assigned primarily to the mother, but she can perform these adequately only if supported tangibly and emotionally by a spouse. Even if the husband is absent or dead, the knowledge of his approval of her and of her maternal behavior is important. Nurturant functions encompass more than food and the psychological aspects of feeding. They involve especially the establishment of basic trust (Erikson, 1964). The early nurturance of the child includes helping him learn how to manage and control his body and how to observe, distinguish, and communicate about inner and external experiences, even before he speaks; it also includes providing him with appropriate experiences and learning opportunities. The importance of these nurturant functions very early in the child's life has been appreciated clearly only in recent times. The potential damage to personality development, social adjustment, and educational capacities if these nurturant tasks, besides feeding, are not fulfilled adequately is now a source of much concern and investigation (Bloom, 1964; Bowlby, 1952; Lidz, 1963; Moynihan, 1965).

Weaning is part of nurturance, but more is involved than withdrawing the bottle or breast. The intricate physical closeness with the mother must be loosened and an essentially nonphysical intimacy established with all family members. Weaning involves still more, in that both the process of weaning and its accomplishment are foundation stones in the acquisition of ego boundaries and a sense of separateness (Erikson, 1964).

Mastery of separation can be defined as the child's experiencing the pain of acute loss of supportive closeness to another person and having a good feeling toward, or being dissatisfied with, such a significant person (the parent) without losing faith and trust in the continuity of the relationship and the ultimate restoration of good feeling and a sense of security. Through separation experiences the child learns and grows; he becomes more able to avoid the same impasse and less vulnerable to, and threatened by, subsequent separations or emotional distance from others. This mastery must be facilitated by the opportunity to observe, imitate, and eventually internalize how other family members cope with frustration and "separation anxiety."

It must be obvious from the preceding discussion that any clear line between nurturant and enculturating tasks is arbitrary because these family functions are continuous and overlap, but the passage of the Oedipal phase may be considered the turning from predominantly nurturant issues to enculturating ones. At this point not only should the child have mastered body control together with gender awareness, but he should also have acquired communicative competence and accepted the incest taboo in the sense of feeling comfortable in his deeroticized relationship to each parent. Latency can then begin in the sense of an abeyance of sexual and erotic problems, freeing the child for instrumental learning and increasing his capacity for investment into peer relationships. Family tasks become at this time those of facilitating peer relationships, that is, of allowing the child greater distance from the family circle, as well as teaching him within the family many of the instrumental modes of the culture in shared work and games.

Together with this instrumental teaching, the family helps to inculcate the communicative and social skills and modes of culture, and it defines the sociocultural norms of relationships by example rather than explicitly (Lidz, 1968; Senn & Solnit, 1968). Communicative styles and competence in the family are crucial because significant deviance from the culturally valid patterns will usually create disturbance within the family and will certainly handicap its members in interacting with the surrounding community. Faulty, inadequate, or idiosyncratic intrafamilial communication is, of course, related to other conditions or defects, such as parental psychopathology, or to cultural differences between the family and the community in which they live. Furthermore, language is the basis for conceptual and abstract thinking; therefore, the younger generation's formal education and emotional development depend on instrumentally and relationally valid verbal and nonverbal communication (Lidz, 1963; Whorf, 1956).

Emancipation of offspring from the parental family is an evolutionary task of the nuclear-family system. Emancipation must occur physically and geographically as well as psychologically and socially. To be accomplished successfully, this final separation cannot be abrupt; it must be the culmination of many forms of increasing psychosocial separateness between parents and child. The first step in this evolution was weaning, followed by many partial steps of emancipation and vectorial independence which the family must abet and effect as the child moves through his developmental stages. Among such steps are the first school entrance, camp or other living-away-from-home experiences, dating, job, or college, and the offspring's final achievement of a solid identity and inner self-direction, culminating ideally in marriage and parenthood.

The family tasks in this connection demand mutual tolerance and resilience because adolescents need to experiment with independent behavior and often teeter between their still intense needs for dependence and guidance and their equally intense strivings for independence (Senn & Solnit, 1968). The parental coalition is on trial during the emancipation phases because youths' experimentation with independence often entails much hostility against the older generation, which parents must meet together, and also because they must prepare for and accomplish, living again as a dyad. Emancipation is therefore also the evolutionary dissolution of the family as a group because grandparental functions are limited and not continuous in the nuclear-family system (Bell & Vogel, 1960; Bott, 1957).

From the preventive standpoint these functions and tasks can also be viewed as normal or evolutionary family "crises,." as documented extensively by Lindeman and Caplan (Caplan, 1964). This is a key approach to family pathology and to mental health promotion, and coping with crises is an important standard of family and individual mental health, even though this standard is not measurable in any easy or precise manner at this time (Caplan, 1964).

Moving from the parental dyad to a triad is one of these important crises issues. For instance, do the parents at this time clearly establish a generation boundary, or does one parent remain overly dependent on the other, thereby competing with the child for the spouse's parental nurturance? Equivalent questions arise around the Oedipal phase. For example, does one parent fail to deeroticize his or her relationships to, and behavior with, the child? Has separation been taught and mastered by the family members so that schooling can be begun without undue conflict and hardship? Does parental role complementarity compensate for the needs of an older child when the mother's energy is preempted by a newborn sibling? During the offspring's puberty and adolescence, does the parental coalition present a consistent front against which emancipation experiments can proceed, or does the front give and waver, engulfing the offspring in inconsistency and indecision? Do parents show the capacity to return to dyadic living and face the issues of aging and infirmity together, interdependent but independent for as long as possible? These are some of the crises in which deficiencies in parental personalities and in family functioning can be discerned most readily.

One form of family crisis should be mentioned because its usual absence in present-day family life unavoidably creates an experience deficiency which often handicaps adults; that is, they may live as adults and parents for many years before a death in the immediate family occurs. The absence of shared tragedy and mourning early in life has wrought certain difficulties for families and individuals in facing death and gaining reassurance in the continuity of individual and family life after the loss of a loved one. Stated another way, the work of mourning is best learned as a shared family experience. Paul (Paul & Grosser, 1964) considers unresolved and unshared mourning on the part of a parent a common source of pathological family interaction.

FAMILY-TASK DEFICIENCIES AND FAILURES

This brief compendium of family tasks and functions will permit us now to consider family pathology as deficiencies in family-task performances. Such an approach to family pathology is anchored in present knowledge and data from family studies. While certain characteristics of family pathology have been found to correlate with individual psychopathology in a member, the establishment of reliable and specific correlations between types of family dysfunctions and psychiatric entities is still for the future.

Like family functions, family disturbances must be considered on many levels, and one must be constantly mindful that any one pathogenic "focus" affects the individual members and the family dynamics on more than one level and that these interactive and reactive forces in turn influence the "focus." If so considered,

a concept such as "schizophrenogenic" mother, for instance, becomes untenable. Symbiotic mother-child relationships or incestuous patterns do not exist *in vacuo,* but are part of a family's structure and dynamics. Distinct levels of disturbance or deficiency can be separated, therefore, only at the expense of ignoring other levels of the reactive and interactive forces in the life of the family. However, for the purpose of discussion we shall treat these levels as if they were rather discrete. Besides, a particular defect can be overwhelming and pervasive in the life of a particular family and should alert the physician to watch for familywide disturbances in the way a high fever would direct his thinking about possible causes into the realm of infections.

We shall follow as far as possible our outline for family functions, beginning with intrapersonal problems.

Individual Pathology

Chronic inborn or acquired organic defects or diseases will not be considered here except to the extent that they affect the emotional and psychosocial family climate, but the field of eugenics constitutes, of course, an important sector of family hygiene.

Consideration of deviant parental personalities is germane to our approach to family pathology; this, of course, does not exclude organic defects or illness in a parent. The entire range of neurotic, psychotic, or psychopathic abnormalities is relevant, but the impact of these deviances on family life and family-task performance is not determined solely by the intrapersonal abnormality itself. Schizophrenic mothers can have children whose personality and adjustment may fall within a normal range (Elsaesser, 1952), and psychopathic or alcoholic fathers need not produce offspring with like abnormalities, although these intrapersonal abnormalities leave their mark on the family and on the personalities of its members (Alanen, 1958; Lidz, Fleck, & Cornelison, 1966). Symptoms and behavior can be copied and incorporated by offspring, although we do not know how frequently. It is an impression that neurotic psychopathic traits, especially conversion mechanisms, are transmitted more frequently than psychotic processes (Alanen, 1966; Fleck, unpublished data), but investigations of trait-specific and mechanism-specific intrafamilial transmission are very much needed. Psychopathy is probably the best-documented form of intrafamilial learning of abnormal behavior (Johnson & Szurek, 1952). Young psychopaths often act out overt and covert wishes of parents who themselves may not misbehave grossly. We also noted a high incidence of occupations of the public relations type among the fathers in a small series of young upper-class delinquents (Fleck, unpublished data; Lidz et al., 1966).

Inborn defects in a child, whether inherited or not, have serious implications for the entire family and may distort its structure and dynamics. If the condition is familial and therefore presumably hereditary, family life may become centered around the parents' guilt or shame and other maladaptive mechanisms. A shared defect can dominate family life, as in so-called nests of severely feebleminded individuals. While almost every clinician has encountered such familywide psychological and psychosocial pathology, no systematic investigations of such families seem to have been undertaken.

A pathological phenomenon similar to that created by the presence of a defective child has been pointed out by Green and Solnit (1964), who found that families with a child who recovered despite a fatal prognosis pronounced earlier can suffer from an inability to accept the fact that a mistake in diagnosis had been made or that despite the acute danger, from which recovery was not expected, the child's health and expected life-span did return to normal. Overprotection and infantilization of that child, and even of his siblings, may ensue, and secondary rejection and scapegoating of the child may develop because of his resentment and adverse reactions to this situation (Green & Solnit, 1964). Similar developments have been reported in detail by Caplan (1964) with regard to prematurity or congenital defects; in particular, the prolonged search for whom or what to blame was evidence of familial pathology and inadequate crisis coping.

The most common familial pathology which clinicians encounter incident to handicapped offspring concerns denial of realistic implications of expectable consequences of the condition. We cannot consider or even list the many possibilities and underlying reasons for such a development—among them denial, guilt (whether realistic or unrealistic), and immaturity, evidenced often by confusing the wish for a magic solution with its realizability. A complete discussion of these reactions would require a treatise of all known defense mechanisms on intrapsychic and interactional levels (Ehrenwald, 1963; Senn & Solnit, 1968; Winnicott, 1965).

All too often, iatrogenic contributions to this type of familial pathology occur in the form of confusing or evasive statements that are meant to be soothing, when the physician should educate and help the family toward realistic appraisal and action, even though such a step may be upsetting and painful to all concerned (Fleck, unpublished data).

Parallel considerations of familial pathology are relevant to any chronic illness in the family, especially the problem of dying. The infrequency of acute death and the lack of opportunity for shared mourning have already been stressed, but another element of modern family life concerns the adjustment or maladjustment to dying rather than to death. Most often, death now is not sudden or unexpected, but "occurs" over a long period of time. This imposes on the family the task of adjusting to an inevitable loss through anticipatory mourning, which healthily would result in a gradual emotional disengagement and disinvestment at a pace commensurate with the patient's declining capacity for involvement, without abandoning him. There are many important facets to this process which are not altogether relevant here, but without detailed discussion of them we can state that unrealistic and pathological family processes are commonly observed in the situation of a dying family member similar to those indicated in connection with chronic illness or the presence of defective offspring.

In general, whether a condition is transitory or permanent, congenital, hereditary, or acquired postnatally, and regardless of whether it is located in parent or offspring, the potential for family pathology is increased, but the opportunity for such a family to develop special forms of strength also exists (Caplan, 1964; Rainwater, 1965). The decision to turn over the care of nurturant and enculturating tasks to an extrafamilial agent can be realistic and constructive for the family, or it can constitute abdication of responsibilities, in which case it indicates a serious limitation of the parents' nurturant capacities which could affect all their offspring adversely.

Deviant Parental Coalitions

Parental personality patterns largely determine the character of the parental coalition or lack thereof. Chronic parental disharmony has been found to be a common occurrence among parents of young schizophrenics, especially female patients (Lidz et al., 1966; Wolman, 1965). We have termed the marriages of such parents *schismatic*, resulting in a family in which the children are forced to join one or the other camp of two warring spouses. In a sense the "coalition" is a negative one. One of the major problems for offspring in such a family is that the spouses devalue each other, making it difficult for the child to want to be like either of them

or to appreciate the parent of the opposite sex as the prototype of a desirable love object. This interferes with the development of a clear sexual identity and maturation toward heterosexual orientation. Besides potentially fostering homosexual proclivities in this manner, incestuous problems also may persist because one or both parents engender intimate closeness with one or the other offspring in their war with the devalued spouse. In such a family the child may perceive correctly that one parent values him above his or her spouse. Stated another way, in such situations both axes of the family structure are violated (Fleck, Lidz, Cornelison, Schafer, & Terry, 1959; Lidz et al., 1966).

Overt incest is evidence in itself of gross parental psychopathology as well as of defective family structure. Father-daughter incest is commonest (at least as far as is known, since intersibling incest is much more likely to remain undisclosed, if it is temporary), but both parents are involved in parent-child incest because it is very difficult for one spouse "not to know" of such a relationship within the family. Incest may represent a pattern that serves to maintain a tenuous family equilibrium. For instance, in daughter-father incest, the daughter may fulfill many of the mother's functions, the latter having withdrawn from wifely and parental tasks, often to work outside the home. But the parents maintain in this manner a façade of role competence, and after the "discovery" of incest behavior such families often break up (Weinberg, 1955).

Another form of defective coalition occurs when one or both spouses remain primarily attached to, and involved with, their families of origin, so that parental roles are not really assumed within the nuclear group, and the center for decision making lies outside the primary family. This situation can compound a schismatic marriage, but it also occurs apart from it—for instance, when incompletely emancipated spouses live geographically as a nuclear family but psychologically and emotionally as an extended family. The spouses then abrogate essential parental tasks (Kluckhohn, 1957). This was first described in the families of schizophrenics (Lidz et al., 1966), but occurs in the background of other patients.

Another distortion of the parental coalition has been described as skewed (Lidz et al., 1966). This condition is also rooted in severe psychopathology of at least one spouse, but the other, although usually aware of the severe abnormalities of his or her partner, gives in, appeases, and generally assumes a submissive role to preserve the marriage. Only a very passive person could tolerate such a mode of adjustment, which demands abrogating realistic views in the home while being effectively responsive to reality outside, so that the marital pair can be said to consist of two partners with complementary attitudes or personality patterns, but the ensuing coalition is very lopsided and unsuited to many basic family tasks. This too has been observed in families with schizophrenic offspring (Lidz et al., 1966; Wolman, 1965). In less severe forms such a coupling of psychopathology in two people has been described as a "neurotic marriage"; that is, the spouses' neurotic difficulties are interlocking (Ackerman, 1958; Ehrenwald, 1963).

Coalition deviations and other difficulties can, of course, result in divorce or desertion, which occur significantly more often in the backgrounds of psychopaths and of schizophrenics than in other groups (Lidz et al., 1966). Among schizophrenic patients females are more apt to have been reared in schismatic families, and boys more often in skewed ones, but this does not hold 100 percent.

The most severe form of faulty coalition is of course no coalition, i.e., usually a fatherless family, which is a frequent problem in our poverty population. However, father absenteeism is accompanied by other family distresses and dysfunctions to be discussed further in subsequent sections. Other risks for the one-parent child, especially for an only child, can be overattachment to and overdependence on the parent, and parental overcloseness to the child.

Faulty Nurturance

Nurturance can be defective because the husband either fails to support or actively interferes with the mother's tending to the infant. In other instances, the mother may be ill and cannot nurture adequately or procure an adequate substitute. Some mothers of schizophrenics were found (retrospectively) to have been too anxious and obsessively indecisive to accomplish what they wanted very much, namely, to function as "normal" mothers to their babies (Alanen, 1958; Lidz et al., 1966).

Pathology on the level of parental personality can, of course, have many serious consequences in itself, and because parents with deviant personalities are apt to effect very faulty family patterns, the nurturant dysfunction rarely stands out as a single pathological and pathogenic item. A mother too anxious and obsessive to work out a realistic feeding pattern for her baby or too afraid to bathe him lest he drown is likely to find decisions about the child's play activities and range of distance no easier. The so-called symbiotic mother must be included as another example of deficient nurturance because she cannot wean the child effectively (Alanen, 1958; Winnicott, 1965). Most probably her personality difficulties, unless relieved, will adversely affect her children's development at many stages, and she is not likely to change her overprotective role in the family as its biosocial evolution demands. Similarly, a father jealous of the firstborn child is not likely to change with subsequent offspring, although the sex of the child can make a difference.

Deficient nurturance can occur because parents may quickly acquire more children than they would have opted for had they been able to foresee and predict the limitations on their functioning as parents that would come as a result of the decreasing amount of time, energy, and material resources available to provide for their own needs and ambitions. This excess of nurturant needs over parental resources (Lieberman, 1964; Rossi, 1968) has also been observed in psychosomatic illnesses of parents, and it can be a factor in a child's illness, since the sick child may receive preferential attention in a large family, rendering the sick role an "adaptive" one in the sense that it procures important emotional satisfactions. However, limitations in fulfilling nurturant tasks as defined here are found in smaller families too for the reasons already described in connection with defective coalitions or because of chronic illness of one parent. The battered child is a manifestation of severe parental and family pathology and dysfunction, and has recently been the cause of much concern and legislative action (Fleck, 1964). Battering indicates malfunction of nurturance, but could be listed under any of the deficiency categories.

Nurturance broadly defined as in the first section is often deficient in the lower socioeconomic classes and especially in one-parent families. Feeding itself is usually provided for adequately even by young unmarried mothers (Minuchin et al., 1967; Sarrel, 1967), but there is undernurturance in interacting with the infant as his interest in his world unfolds. There may actually be excessive feeding as such because there is a tendency to perceive all the infant's needs and demands as oral, and weaning itself is therefore delayed and inconsistent (Minuchin et al., 1967). This problem may be aggravated because in many poor families, the oldest child often functions as a substitute mother and may feed the infant conscientiously in a technical sense, but without any maternal or emotional investment or interest in giving the baby any more than minimal care.

Faulty Enculturation

Familial interaction, as stated, depends on the parental personalities and the parental coalition, if any, and children learn through this interaction or fail to learn how to interact with their environment at crucial stages of their development (Lidz, 1968). Manifestations of parental mental ill health are learned by children, if not copied, and there is ample evidence that if the parental interaction is starkly atypical of the culture or subculture surrounding them, the entire family suffers estrangement, and children will be handicapped in their interactions outside the family and can develop intrapersonal conflicts of neurotic or psychotic proportions (Bell & Vogel, 1960; Bott, 1957; Kluckhohn, 1957; Lidz et al., 1966). But culturally deprived parents, especially single parents, are also apt to raise undernurtured children, leading to mental ill health in the form of undereducation, communicative disabilities, and deviant behavior.

It is true that definitions of health, especially of mental health, are impossible in absolute terms, but it is possible to distinguish between "healthier" and "less healthy" in a particular culture and subculture. Rather than seeking definitions that have absolute cross-cultural validity, it must be appreciated that the differences have more to do with values, including health as a cultural value, than with health standards per se. In a society where dentistry is unknown, defective teeth are the "norm," or one might say that, whatever the reasons, the culture gives a low priority to dental health. Similarly, a society without formal educational institutions puts a low value on abstract thought or scientific inquiry, so that relationships are accepted through fixed role ascriptions and expectations instead of through individual aspirations and subtle interpersonal processes. Such value discrepancies also exist within a society, especially in the different socioeconomic classes in Western culture (Rainwater, 1965). It is often said that middle-class standards of health, family health in particular, are not relevant to other classes, especially lower socioeconomic groups, but this argument is specious. Such a formulation may serve to avoid considering effective remedial action with regard to family pathology because of the forbidding complexities of assessment and the well-documented treatment difficulties, aggravated by the usual class differential between therapist and patient or family (Coleman et al., 1957; Minuchin et al., 1967).

Although it is true that studies of lower-class families have tended to be extensive rather than intensive and that middle-class concepts, especially those concerning sources of strength in a family, must be modified, it is also true that the paradigms of family functions as outlined here and the effects of malfunctioning and deficiencies in family dynamics are relevant to a major degree to all classes. If we accept health, optimum education, and individuation within a particular society as valid goals, the family's enculturating effectiveness can, indeed must, be examined and evaluated in these respects. That is, do the family structure and interaction serve these goals, or do they hinder them? For instance, one-parent childhood, especially in the lower socioeconomic classes, is significantly related to school underachievement (Bloom, 1964; Moynihan, 1965). Alanen, who earlier described characteristics of the mothers of schizophrenics (1958), has more recently focused on family process and interaction. Comparison of families with neurotic and schizophrenic offspring, respectively, disclosed some significant differences. In the schizophrenic group he found two types of background: (1) "chaotic" families, which lacked suitable identification figures, contained no consistent relationship patterns, and tended to teach paralogical ideation, and (2) rigid families, which permitted only very stereotyped and limited interactions and in which the patient's personality was usually an extension of that of one of the parents. Neither type occurred among the families of neurotics. Symptomatic behavior was similar in the patient and one parent in 17 percent of schizophrenic and 22 percent of neurotic patients (Alanen, 1966).

Parental expectations of offspring with respect to enculturation may be overly severe, stringent, and even unrealistic. Cohen et al. (1954) found this in the family background of depressed patients, the central issue being family prestige. However, depression also plays a causative role in family malfunction, especially in the form of unresolved mourning. Paul (Paul & Grosser, 1964), on the basis of family studies, and Lindeman and Caplan (Caplan, 1964), on the basis of both clinical and epidemiological observations, stress the preventive value of accomplishing the "work of mourning" and the possible ill effects of "bypassing" the mourning experience after a significant emotional loss or trauma. They consider that the stoic family member, who may gain applause for not being upset in the face of having lost a loved one, is headed for emotional troubles. We have stressed already that learning how to mourn is a family task, although it is more common today for a family to have had no death to mourn before the children reach the ages of their emancipation from their family of origin; yet the evolutionary crises such as separations or sicknesses or accidents do occur, and the family's modes of dealing with these may serve to strengthen or to weaken family functioning and to promote or hinder emotional growth in the individual members. The continuum of successive separations and their mastery by the family as well as by each individual in it can be extended to the issues of loss or death, and if death occurs, separation experiences do serve to some extent as prototypes for shared grief and pain.

The single most important learning instrument is communication, and the family is the major and primary teacher. Verbal communication must fit the nonverbal interaction, and language competence is a *sine qua non* for conceptual and abstract thinking, for reading, and for the cultural ways and styles of perceiving. Again in this respect, lower-class families seem handicapped whether one views their communication as "normal" for the class or as deviant in terms of other values such as the standards for the utility of symbolic and abstract communication characteristic of the educated middle and upper socioeconomic groups. Minuchin and his collaborators pointed out that interaction in their disturbed lower-class families was mostly negatively reactive, i.e., consisted of messages of threat or violence, whether transmitted verbally or physically. Power issues dominate such family scenes, with no demonstration for the contemplative and learning uses of communication. Nor can this pattern of reactive parenting lead to considerations of role-conflict resolution, and role consistency is virtually absent. These psychosocial and communicative handicaps are often compounded by such tangible deficiencies as a child not having his own bed or toys or any space which is clearly and consistently his, which further undermines a sense of self and self-worth. The predominantly reactive interaction also interferes with superego formation because negative and violent reactivity is the model and because reinforcement of appropriate behavior or reaffirmation of welcome feeling states seem virtually absent. Such a family knows and teaches how to make others feel "bad" and how to evoke negative responses but not how to make anybody feel "good," which apparently is somehow thought to be a "normal" state that will come about without any effort on the part of anybody except for feeding on demand as noted earlier. Lastly, there may also be a failure to effect a two-generation structure in that the enculturating tasks may fall upon an older child, a sibling or a peer, an intrafamilial subsystem which is paralleled outside the family in the poverty community by the role of the gang member as a model.

Bateson and Jackson observed and analyzed the frequent contradictory messages in families with a schizophrenic member, a process which they named *double bind* (Bateson et al., 1956). Wynne and Singer (1963) have discovered that analysis of thought and communication styles is more relevant to family pathology than the communicative contents transmitted or educational levels as such. Styles of intrafamilial communication called "amorphous" and "fragmented," respectively, by Wynne and Singer have been found to be related to distinct types of schizophrenic patients, and Lidz et al. (1966) have documented how irrationality is transmitted in families with schizophrenic offspring. Abnormal intrafamilial communication not only is important as a manifestation of family pathology but also holds the best promise to yield to further analysis and classification of family pathology itself and as an indication of thought disorders in individual family members (Lidz et al., 1966; Wild, 1965; Wynne & Singer, 1963).

Emancipation Problems

It has already been stated that the evolution of the nuclear family demands its eventual contraction to the parental dyad after the emancipation of the young from it. Deficient emancipation is usually rooted in earlier defects in family-task accomplishments. Cultural gaps between the generations may also be an important impediment to children's separation from parents and the parental home (Bell & Vogel, 1960; Kluckhohn, 1957). The pathology of incomplete emancipation is probably best known to college mental health services (Keniston, 1965), but in less educated groups is more likely to appear as individual psychopathology after the incompletely emancipated person has undertaken marriage and parenthood (Minuchin et al., 1967; Moynihan; 1965; Rainwater, 1965). As was indicated in the previous section, a pseudo-emancipation occurs often in the lowest socioeconomic groups when a child's care is left to an older sibling or peers outside the family. Obviously a cycle of successive generations with psychopathology and family pathology can occur in this way, and we and others have documentary data for this phenomenon up to four generations (Bloom, 1964; Fleck, unpublished data; Lidz et al., 1966).

COMMENT AND SUMMARY

It is tempting and rewarding, but speculative, to relate specific family problems and constellations to specific psychiatric diagnostic entities. But this is not consistent with our understanding of family dynamics, and our conceptual frameworks of family functions may not be sufficiently succinct and comprehensive to permit this. Equally weighty, however, is the imprecision of psychiatric diagnosis and the lack of specific quantifiable indicators for most diagnostic entities. Further revision and greater precision of diagnostic categories may derive from more acute understanding and delineation of familial and other psychosocial deficiencies and abnormalities. It is clear now that issues and concepts of health are intertwined with sociocultural and educational issues. The family is the original sociocultural milieu as well as the primal teacher for every human being. Crucial to these functions are communication, thinking and conceptual styles, and sociocultural values. These are determinants of character traits as well as aimed-for introjects.

Attention to, and analysis of, these processes as family functions, as exemplified by the work of Wynne and Singer (1963), Kluckhohn and Spiegel (Kluckhohn, 1957), Lidz et al. (1966),

and Wild (1965), seem more promising and fruitful in elucidating psychopathology than attempts to deal with total family constellations or with specific personality features of a parent or child or the particular mode of their pathological relationships. On the other hand, analyzing only the communicational and interactional modes cross-sectionally, as perfected by the Mental Health Research Group in Palo Alto, is too narrow an assessment of family functions and pathology (Jackson & Satir, 1961). Our studies of young schizophrenics demonstrated the multiplicity of family pathology and the fact that most of the families were deviant in most basic family functions (Lidz et al., 1966).

The difficulty of correlating individual and family abnormalities is thus compounded. Besides, some abnormalities, such as deviant communication styles, pervade the entire family and if severe will affect all members, but not necessarily in the same way. While each child lives in the same family, he also lives in a family unique for him. No parent-child triad is identical with another, not even those of twins, as has been demonstrated (Alanen, 1966; Lidz, 1968; Lidz et al., 1966; Winnicott, 1965). It is necessary to understand both the family-wide deviations and the specific distortions of family paradigms in each child's dynamic position and role in the family vis-à-vis his parents and vis-à-vis his siblings.

Research must begin with present knowledge and plausibly derived theories. This points presently toward cross-sectional and historical analysis of family health and strengths and of family pathology. Grasping the entire biopsychosocial complex is difficult, and no one method will suffice, but a concerted and multidisciplinary approach should prove fruitful and rewarding at this time, when total health is becoming an integral part and goal of total human welfare.

Most important, such an approach has preventive and therapeutic relevance because the approach of analyzing family functioning and coping can be accomplished in its entirety only through a therapeutically oriented group process. Certain tests, especially those devised by Wynne and Singer (1963) and Wild (1965), are important, but intrafamilial communication and interaction can be studied best through participant observation incident to a therapeutic effort, or at least—and next best— in a task-oriented session (Ackerman, 1958; Jackson & Satir, 1961; Minuchin et al., 1967).

The approach to family pathology presented here, then, focuses on deficiencies in, and deviations from, salient family functions and tasks. It is not possible at present to establish specific correlation among such defects and clinical psychiatric entities. It may, however, be suggested that from such an approach to family pathology, revisions and reclassification of psychiatric diagnoses could follow. Although for discussion purposes distinctions have been made between intrapersonal, interparental, and family-wide pathological phenomena, it must be stressed that all these are relevant considerations and that each alone is insufficient to understand family process. The most promising approaches to understanding family functioning are the examination of familial communication styles and interaction modes through relevant tests and therapeutically oriented participant observation and the historic evaluation of the validity and effectiveness of the family behavior with regard to basic family tasks and to the crisis-coping competence of the family.

REFERENCES

Ackerman, N. W. *The psychodynamics of family life.* New York: Basic Books, 1958.

Alanen, Y. O. The mothers of schizophrenic patients. *Acta Psychiatrica et Neurologica Scandinavica,* 1958 (Suppl. 124).

Alanen, Y. O. The family in the pathogenesis of schizophrenia and neurotic disorders. *Acta Psychiatrica et Neurologica Scandinavica,* 1966, **24,** Suppl. 189.

Bateson, G. et al. Toward a theory of schizophrenia. *Behavioral Science,* 1956, **1,** 251–264.

Bell, N. W., & Vogel, E. Toward a framework for functional analysis of family behavior. In N. W. Bell & E. Vogel (Eds.), *A modern introduction to the family.* Glencoe, Ill.: Free Press, 1960. P. 691.

Bloom, B. S. *Stability and change in human characteristics.* New York: Wiley, 1964.

Bott, E. *Family and social network.* London: Tavistock, 1957.

Bowlby, J. *Maternal care and mental health.* Geneva: World Health Organization, 1952.

Caplan, G. *Principles of preventive psychiatry.* New York: Basic Books, 1964.

Cohen, M. B., et al. An intensive study of twelve cases of manic-depressive psychosis. *Psychiatry* 1954, **17,** 103–137.

Coleman, J. V., et al. Comparative study of psychiatric clinic and family agency. *Social Casework,* 1957, **38,** 3–8.

Ehrenwald, J. Family diagnosis and mechanisms of psychosocial defense. *Family Process* 1963, **2,** 121–131.

Elsaesser, G. *Die Nachkommen Geistes Kranker Elternpaaren.* Stuttgart: Thieme, 1952.

Erikson, E. *Childhood and society.* New York: Norton, 1950.

Erikson, E. *Insight and responsibility.* New York: Norton, 1964.

Fleck, S., Lidz, T., Cornelison, A., Schafer, S., & Terry, D. The intrafamilial environment of the schizophrenic patient: Incestuous and homosexual problems. In J. Masserman (Ed.), *Individual and familial dynamics.* New York: Grune & Stratton, 1959. P. 218.

Fleck, S. Family welfare, mental health and birth control. *Journal of Family Law,* 1964, **3,** 241–247.

Fleck, S.: Unpublished data.

Green, M., & Solnit, A. J. Reactions to the threatened loss of a child: A vulnerable child syndrome. *Pediatrics,* 1964, **34,** 58–66.

Jackson, D. D., & Satir, V. A review of psychiatric developments in family diagnosis and therapy. In N. W. Ackerman, F. Beatman, & S. Sherman (Eds.), *Exploring the case for family therapy.* New York: Family Association of America, 1961. P. 159.

Johnson, A. M., & Szurek, S. A. The genesis of antisocial acting out in children and adults. *The Psychoanalytic Quarterly,* 1952, **21,** 323–343.

Keniston, K. *The uncommitted.* New York: Harcourt, Brace & World, 1965.

Kluckhohn, F. *Variants in value orientations.* Evanston, Ill.: Row, Peterson, 1957.

Lidz, T. *The family and human adaptation.* New York: International Universities Press, 1963.

Lidz, T. *The person.* New York: Basic Books, 1968.

Lidz, T., Fleck, S., & Cornelison, A. *Schizophrenia and the family.* New York: International Universities Press, 1966.

Lieberman, E. J. Preventive psychiatry and family planning. *Journal of Marriage and the Family,* 1964, **26,** 471.

Minuchin, S., et al. *Families of the slums.* New York: Basic Books, 1967.

Moynihan, D. P. *The Negro family: A case for national action.* Washington: GPO, 1965.

Parsons, T. The incest taboo in relation to social structure and the socialization of the child. *British Journal of Sociology,* 1954, **5,** 101–117.

Parsons, T. *Social structure and personality.* New York: Free Press, 1964.

Parsons, T., & Bales, R. F. *Family, socialization and interaction process.* Glencoe, Ill.: Free Press, 1955.

Paul, N., & Grosser, G. The role of loss and mourning in conjoint family therapy. Paper presented at the First International Congress of Social Psychiatry, London, August, 1964.

Rainwater, L. *Family design.* Chicago: Aldine, 1965.

Rossi, A. S. Transition to parenthood. *Journal of Marriage and Family Living,* 1968, **30,** 26–39.

Sarrel, P. The university hospital and the teen-age unwed mother. *American Journal of Public Health,* 1967, **57,** 1308–1313.

Senn, M. J. E., & Solnit, A. J. *Problems in child behavior and development.* Philadelphia: Lea & Febiger, 1968.

Stafford, J. *An American mother in history.* New York: Farrar, Straus & Giroux, 1965.

Toynbee, A. J. *A study of history.* (Abridgement Vols. I–VI by D. C. Somerwell) New York: Oxford University Press, 1947.

Weinberg, S. K. *Incest behavior.* New York: Citadel Press, 1955.

Whorf, B. *Language, thought, and reality: Selected writings of . . .* (J. Carroll, Ed.) New York: Wiley, 1956.

Wild, C. Disturbed styles of thinking and measuring disordered styles of thinking. *Archives of General Psychiatry,* 1965, **13,** 464–476.

Winnicott, D. W. *The family and individual development.* London: Tavistock, 1965.

Wolman, B. B. Family dynamics and schizophrenia. *Journal of Health and Human Behavior,* 1965, **6,** 147–155.

Wynne, L. C. & Singer, M. T. Thought disorder and family relations of schizophrenics. II. A classification of forms of thinking. *Archives of General Psychiatry,* 1963, **9,** 199–206..

part ii | Organic Disorders

7 Organic Mental Disorders: Brain Damages

Joseph C. Kaspar and Jerome L. Schulman[1]

DIAGNOSTIC STUDIES

Defining the Problem

In order to avoid disagreement as to the meaning of the term *brain damage,* in this chapter we shall begin by defining it. Schulman, Kaspar, and Throne (1965, pp. 4–5) constructed four possible definitions of brain dysfunction:

(1) Patients with psycho-social disturbances. This category includes those disturbances ordinarily classified as "functional" such as adjustment reaction, neurosis and retardation due to cultural deprivation;

(2) Patients at the low end of the normal distribution curve of intelligence. The so-called "familial retardates" comprise the bulk of this group, although it includes some children with mild or isolated delays in neuro-muscular maturation;

(3) Patients with abnormalities of brain development. The significant feature of this category is that the brain does not develop properly due to structural or chemical defects. The brain does

not stop developing at any point, but develops in an abnormal fashion, predicated upon the deficiency involved. Mongolism is a good example;

(4) Patients with a normally formed brain which is subsequently damaged in any fashion. Differentiating this category from Category (3), even in a purely theoretical consideration, poses the most difficult practical problem in this area. The distinction can be made in two ways. One can distinguish on the basis of the time of injury. In most applications, this category implies normalcy in development throughout most of the fetal life, with subsequent damage just before, during, or at various times after birth. Examples include, anoxia at birth, lead poisoning and physical injury to the brain. Unfortunately, this basis of distinction would combine such disparately caused types of injury as phenylketonuria and anoxia. Alternately, one can distinguish on the basis of the etiology of the injury, differentiating according to whether the injury occurred because of some defect of the organism, regardless of the time the defect appeared, or because of the intervention of some external agent.

This chapter will deal with empirical studies of the effects of injury to presumably potentially normal brains on the subsequent function of the

[1] Preparation of this chapter was supported by research grant number NB 06928 from the National Institute of Health, Neurological Diseases and Blindness.

injured child. To the extent that a distinction can be made, we shall be concerned primarily with injuries caused by the intervention of an external agent, occurring just prior to, during, or following the birth process.

Frequently, psychologists have considered the neurological examination to be the definitive criterion for determining the presence or absence of brain injury. Certainly, in those instances in which there is clear neurological evidence of the presence of brain injury or in which the combination of history, physical examination, and electroencephalogram is such that there appears to be compelling evidence of dysfunctioning neural tissue, the task of psychological and other evaluation is that of extending and defining the effects and importance of this injury in the areas of intellectual and social functioning. However, there does exist a question as to whether the diagnosis of brain injury should be made, given negative or equivocal neurological findings. The neurological evaluation can be criticized on two levels. One might consider the first to be a reliability level. Since both the content of the neurological examination and the interpretation of the presence or absence of symptoms vary from clinician to clinician, as is true of any clinical examination, it cannot be assumed that because one competent neurologist has made a particular diagnosis, another equally competent neurologist would also. Obviously, as findings grow more equivocal, one would expect difficulties in reliability to increase.

The second criticism is based upon the fact that the sample of behaviors and functions included in the neurological examination is relatively limited in scope, centering on the assessment of the adequacy of neuromotor functioning. Since there are a large number of areas of functioning which may not be assessed at all in a neurological evaluation, it appears probable that brain injury can exist without being detected during a neurological examination. For example, Clements (Clements & Peters, 1962) has argued

that the neurological examination is sensitive to only 50 percent of brain functioning. It is this logic which has led to the recent concern with concepts such as the minimal brain dysfunction syndrome or the hyperkinetic behavior syndrome. Strauss and Lehtinen (1947, p. 4) state their position as follows: "A brain injured child is a child who before, during, or after birth has received an injury to or suffered an infection of the brain. As a result of such organic impairment, defects of the neuromotor system may be present or absent; however, such a child may show disturbances in perception, thinking and emotional behavior either separately or in combination." Thus, these authors assume that brain dysfunction may occur in a fashion which will not be reflected on the neurological examination. If one does not take the position that psychomotor deficiencies as detected by a neurological evaluation are an inevitable consequence of the presence of brain injury, it is very tempting to substitute another set of symptomatic considerations in their place, leading to the position that some set of symptoms such as the hyperkinetic behavior disorder is perforce indicative of brain injury.

However, if one grants that brain injury can exist without the presence of neurological findings, it seems equally reasonable to grant that it can exist without any specific inevitable consequence. It would also appear reasonable to assume that brain injury can disrupt any form of human activity. Which consequence is obtained in a particular case would depend upon interactions between the age of the patient, the site of the damage, the extent of the damage, the length of time which has transpired since the damage occurred, the source of the damage, whether it is progressive in character or not, and what effects it has on the child's interactions with society, his family, his peers, and the education system.

Thus, in this chapter we shall be discussing the consequences of damage to a normally formed brain, and we shall not presume that such damage will necessarily be detectable on a neurological examination.

Parallel Consequences

While it appears reasonable to assume that any damage to the brain will result in reduced effectiveness of the damaged area, whatever its function, there is also the issue of whether there will be consequences of brain injury which will occur without regard to the nature of the particular area affected. These might be considered supralocal consequences. Strauss and Lehtinen (1947, p. 4) contend that ". . . all brain lesions wherever localized are followed by a similar kind of disordered behavior." This position is not supported by clinical experience or by research evidence. Many children seen clinically with clear-cut evidence of a brain injury such as epilepsy, cerebral palsy, or even removal of a brain tumor do not behave in a hyperkinetic manner. Neither Ernhardt et al. (1963) nor Schulman et al. (1965) found any evidence to support this contention. At present there is little support for the hypothesis that hyperkinesis is a consequence of brain injury and no support for the hypothesis that it is an inevitable consequence.

It is conceivable that consequences of brain injury will be found which occur in addition to the effect to be expected on the basis of the loss of function due to tissue destruction. While to date the argument in this area has been between those who assume that injury would affect only the specific function localized in the specific area destroyed and those who assume that regardless of the site of injury the effect would be identical, it is also possible to assume that there are consequences which are neither universal nor totally specific. Thus, rather than the hypothesis that "hyperkinesis will occur whenever a brain injury has occurred," one might test the hypothesis that "hyperkinesis will occur whenever the injury is such as to produce disorder perceptions."

A second assumption that is frequently made concerning the consequences of brain injury is that all its supposed consequences are related and that brain injury will lead to hyperactivity, distractibility, inconsistency, lability, etc. This type of syndrome can be called *convergent* in the sense that the presence of any symptom greatly increases the probability of the presence of another symptom. In contrast, in a parallel syndrome the presence of any sign or symptom would have no effect on the probability that any other sign would be present. If one assumes that brain injury produces parallel rather than convergent consequences, one would assume that it could lead to hyperactive behavior, neuromotor dysfunction, defects of intelligence, distractibility, and/or pathological electroencephalogram findings, as well as other still undiscovered consequences. Under certain circumstances one would find many of these signs of brain injury concurrently, while under other circumstances only a few would be found, and at times a typical consequence of brain injury would occur without any other evidence that an injury to the brain has occurred. We contend that the consequences of brain injury are parallel and relatively independent, rather than convergent, as described by Strauss and Lehtinen.

The Neurological Examination

One of the difficulties in conceptualizing and understanding the neurological examination derives from the frequent assumption on the part of nonneurologists that this examination is a relatively homogeneous and consistent thing. In fact, however, the content of neurological examinations probably varies considerably among neurologists. An examination will generally include assessments of the intactness of reflex arcs and testing the strength of muscles; the neurologist estimates the quality of both voluntary and involuntary movements. Additionally, a number of visual-motor tasks such as copying geometric figures may be administered, and quality of language may be assessed.

The presence or absence of hyperkinesis is noted. In addition, the electroencephalogram, which will be discussed separately, is frequently used as an index of intactness of cortical functioning. X-rays and certain contrast studies such as the angiogram or air encephalograms are also used in certain circumstances. The air encephalogram involves the substitution of air for spinal fluid in the ventricles or cavities of the brain. Since the air has a different density to x-rays from that of brain tissue or blood, any deviation in size, position, or configuration of these cavities may be indicative of structural changes in the brain. Similarly, in an angiogram, a dye with a different x-ray density from that of brain tissue or blood is injected into the blood vessels in or near the brain, enabling the neurologist to study the distribution of blood supply.

In a neurological examination great weight is always placed upon the patient's history, especially the pattern of symptoms; the mode, sequence, and progression of symptomatic changes provide a context in which the particular current findings are interpreted. Without going into great detail, the point of the discussion is to put forth the notion that the neurological examination should be considered a complex of heterogenous procedures assessing many different levels and types of function. Additionally, there is a good deal of uncertainty as to the reliability and validity of many of the procedures employed. Probably the type of findings relative to a diagnostic determination of developmental delay are among the most difficult to interpret or replicate.

It should be pointed out also that the nature of the distribution generated by any kind of pathological study of a population of subjects is quite different from that of a normal distribution. Given any randomly selected sample of people, one would expect that the large majority would demonstrate no pathological findings on a neurological examination. For the sake of argument let us assume that this would involve 80 percent of the subjects tested. The remaining 20 percent would be divided into three smaller classes. The majority of those remaining would probably fall into a class in which there were equivocal, findings which might or might not be felt to be definitive. This would, let us say, encompass another 15 percent. Of the remaining 5 percent of the subjects, perhaps half would have definitive findings of minor importance, and the other half would have definitive findings related to some major consequence. This type of distribution is obviously not a normal distribution with which psychologists are accustomed to dealing and probably more nearly approaches a Poisson distribution, which applies when the probability of any occurrence is much smaller than the probability of its nonoccurrence. However, those children referred for neurological evaluations are not a random sample of children. Rather, they are children whose functioning is questionable and about whom other findings are equivocal, so that the task of any clinician is to explain the most puzzling 25 or 30 percent of the population. This should be borne in mind when interpreting the studies in this area.

Paine (1962) studied forty-one children who exhibited minimal chronic brain syndrome and found that thirty-one showed definite abnormal neurological signs, while Knobel, Wolman, and Mason (1959), working with forty children exhibiting the same syndrome, concluded that their behavior seemed in no way related to organicity on the basis of developmental history, neurological examinations, psychological tests, or electroencephalograms. Schulman et al. (1965) found no significant correlation between rating of brain damage on a neurological evaluation and any of seven other measures hypothesized to be measures of brain injury. It should be pointed out, however, that this neurological examination was conducted somewhat differently from the traditional one and most notably did not have available a good history on the children.

Anderson (1963) studied thirty hyperkinetic

children between the ages of 8 and 12 with border-line normal or higher intelligence. He found minimal neurological findings, ". . . with the exception of the 'choreiform syndrome,' rostral dominance, right and left confusion, and mild pyramidal tract signs" (p. 970). Electroencephalograms were normal in four of the children. It should be noted that there was no discussion in the paper of whether the various ratings included in this study were done blind or not.

In spite of the minimal nature of his findings, Anderson concluded that ". . . hyperkinetic behavior disorders, with associated learning problems, are organic in origin. The most common element would seem to be that of complication in the prenatal, paranatal or immediate postnatal period" (1963, p. 970). Kennard (1960) found a positive correlation between a diagnosis of organic deficit made through clinical means, such as history, behavioral pattern, and psychological findings, and the presence of eighteen "equivocal" neurological signs. The presence of these signs did not, however, correlate with electroencephalographic findings of abnormality or with reading disabilities. She also found that low intelligence tended to correlate with both the frequency of equivocal signs and organic brain disorders as diagnosed by other means. Thus, the relationship between neurological signs and "minimal brain damage" or "hyper-kinesis" is not at all clear at present.

The Electroencephalogram

In contrast to the neurological examination, which measures the intactness of neuropathways affecting receptors and affectors outside the brain itself, the electroencephalogram is basically a measure of the electrical activity in various portions of the cortex. In those instances in which the wave patterns produced by this measure are not normal, they are graded for the extent to which they are disrupted and dysrhythmic. It should be pointed out that even patients with known seizure disorders may on a particular occasion produce a normal pattern. Similarly, the interpretation of the produced patterns is an extremely complex task, one which requires a great deal of diagnostic skill, which again varies from examiner to examiner.

Psychologists are frequently surprised to discover that neurologists may differ in their opinion concerning the utility of various of their diagnostic instruments, just as psychologists may quarrel about the utility of the Rorschach as a measure of psychopathology. It is clear that false negatives may occur in the electro-encephalogram in which people whose history and behavior clearly indicate a brain injury do not produce abnormal findings. Similarly, in studies of electroencephalograms on subjects with no known neuropsychopathology, a definite incidence of abnormal tracings is generally found. The percentage found may range from 10 to 55 across various studies (E. L. Gibbs, Rich, Fois, & Gibbs, 1960; Miller & Lennoz, 1948; Secunda & Finley, 1942; Solomon, Brown & Deutsche, 1944).

When the electroencephalogram patterns of known pathological groups are studied, it has not generally been found that one can distinguish between patients with psychogenic disorders and those with organic brain diseases. Mueller, Nylander, Larsson, Widen, and Frankenhaeuser (1958) found that the electroencephalogram did not distinguish between a group of 238 patients who had had meningitis and 138 control subjects, nor did the electroencephalogram findings correlate with other clinical or psychometric data. Kennard (1959) found an abnormal electro-encephalogram in 83 percent of subjects with known organic brain disorder. Children with thought disorders and no known organic damage had 40 percent abnormal electroencephalograms, and children with neither organic disorders nor thought disorders had 23 percent abnormal electroencephalograms. It would appear from these studies that an abnormal finding on this instrument can occur without any other evidence of organic difficulties. Silverman and Harris (1954) found that 60 percent of patients who showed no organicity on psychological tests had abnormal electroencephalograms.

In a study of central importance to our conceptualization of the diagnostic study of brain injury, Hanvik, Sherman, Hanson, Anderson, Dressler, and Zarling (1961) found that a medical neurological examination correlated significantly with the psychological examination. However, the neurological examination and the electroencephalogram did not correlate in the study by Schulman et al. (1965) described above; there was a correlation of zero between neurological findings of pathology and electroencephalogram findings of pathology. It should be stressed, however, that this is not a finding which one should be particularly surprised at, given the nature of the events being assessed in each of these examinations.

Another example of the complexity of electroencephalogram interpretation and the lack of agreement among experts in this area is found in Gibbs and Gibbs (1963), who have described their results as indicating that fourteen- and six-per-second spikes "indicate a special form of epilepsy, arising from a part of the brain which is not extremely convulsive, but which is highly susceptible to dysrhythmia." They report the incidence of this finding to be 20 percent of children between 5 and 14; however, the paper is in general a frank attempt to convince the reader of the validity of their observations.

A great deal of work is being done to unite electroencephalography and computer techniques (Burch, Nettleton, Sweeny, & Edwards, 1964; Riehl, 1963; Walter, 1963) in the hope that vastly more detailed analyses of electroencephalogram records will increase the understanding of this technique and its relationship to brain dysfunction. No study could be found in which this technique was applied with children, however.

The data clearly indicate that the neurological examination and the electroencephalogram do not assess the same aspects of neural functioning. The data reported by Schulman et al. (1965) suggested that the neurological examination may correlate better with extensive damage, which is likely to produce low IQ scores, while the electroencephalogram may be sensitive to more specific damage which might differentially affect visual-motor skills or language skills. It also appears reasonable to conclude that neither test is sensitive to all forms of brain injury. Finally, the electroencephalogram has not been shown to be sensitive to brain injury, as opposed to psychosocial disorders or mental retardation.

The Wechsler Intelligence Scale For Children

Before discussing the particularities of this intelligence test, certain findings on the epidemiology of intelligence and retardation should be borne in mind by the clinician. Tarjan (1961) has pointed out that the distribution of intelligence found seems to differ significantly from that which would be predicted on the basis of a normal intelligence curve. The nature of the deviation consists of an excess of children with very low IQs. Tarjan feels that there exists a second distribution of intelligence scores of children with brain damage having a mean of approximately 32. This point is made to introduce the notion that it is not unreasonable to assume that the lower the IQ found in testing a child, the more likely it is that some form of brain damage has occurred. This, of course, is a probabilistic statement which cannot by itself lead to the categorization of a particular child at a particular IQ level as being brain-injured. Beck and Lam (1955) felt that their data suggested that the possibility of organicity increases considerably as the IQ drops below 70 to 80 on the Wechsler Intelligence Scale for Children (WISC). It would appear reasonable, then, to hypothesize that extensive neurological damage will result in a lower IQ.

In general, our discussion of intelligence tests will concern itself primarily with the WISC, which in spite of its age limitations provides a great many data concerning the strengths and weaknesses of any group of children referred for diagnosis. The WISC begins at the age of 5 and continues to 16. However, it seems reasonable that the sample of behavior available for scoring at the lower ages is not sufficient for the clinician to feel comfortable in using it for specific diagnostic interpretations except in a very gross sense. Between the ages of 5 years and 5 years and 3 months, for example, the similarities score of 3 is equal to a scale score of 10. Similarly, an arithmetic score of 3 is equal to a scale score of 10. A block-design score of 4 is equal to a scale score of 10. Since the population with which one is working in attempting to assess brain injury and its consequences generally falls into the lower portion of the IQ scale, one can see that the reliability of the test at these ages with children clinically described as inconsistent and distractible might be limited. The newly developed Wechsler Primary and Preschool Scale of Intelligence, which extends the Wechsler scale downward to an age of 3 years and 10 months, enables the clinician and researcher to deal more effectively with this portion of the population (Wechsler, 1963). However, given the paucity of clinical experience and research investigations with this instrument, great caution should be used in its interpretation.

A number of indices of presumed brain injury are sometimes used in analyzing data gathered on the WISC. The first of these is the difference between the verbal IQ and the performance IQ, which is frequently thought to reflect brain injury. Reitan (1955) and Fitzhugh, Fitzhugh, and Reitan (1962) have demonstrated that adults with left-sided lesions tend to do more poorly on verbal tests than on performance tests, while patients with right-handed lesions in general tend to do better on verbal tests than on perfor-

mance tests. However, these differences are generally found in group means and may not be large enough to be predictive individually. These findings cannot be assumed to relate to the effect of brain injury in children.

Before turning to a study of the research which has been done examining the relationship between verbal IQ and performance IQ in children with known or presumed brain injury and the nature of the distributions of the verbal and performance IQ and full-scale IQ scores, it becomes evident that these two distributions are not identical. For example, if a patient receives a verbal IQ of 50, he needs to achieve a performance-scale score of 21 points or an IQ of 60 to receive a full-scale IQ of 50. Similarly, on the other end of the scale a verbal IQ of 150 and a performance IQ of 150 would yield a full-scale IQ of more than 154. These discrepancies between the three distributions tend to decrease as one proceeds toward an average IQ. Thus, the standardization data themselves as presented in the manual to the WISC do not support the notion that the distributions of the verbal IQ, performance IQ, and full-scale IQ scores are identical. In general, in the lower half of the distribution, if one is to attain a full-scale IQ equal to his verbal IQ, he must attain a performance IQ higher than his verbal IQ. It is not until one attains a verbal IQ of 96 that a performance IQ of 96 will produce a full-scale IQ of 96. In children with above-average IQs the opposite situation obtains. That is, if children's verbal IQs equal their full-scale IQs, their performance IQs will be lower than their verbal IQs. These results do make the assumption that performance and verbal scores on the WISC should be equal and that any deviation from this equality is an indication of some specific pathology more difficult to accept.

In contrast to the Reitan studies quoted above, in which group of subjects with localized lesions were compared, studies of children have generally consisted of an attempt to find a consistent pattern of relationships between verbal and performance IQs in a heterogeneous group of brain-injured children. Hopkins (1964) found the performance IQ significantly higher than the verbal IQ with twenty-two of thirty-three brain-injured children, while Beck and Lam (1955) found that their Ss did significantly better on the verbal than on the performance subtests.

Balthazar (1961) has suggested that there may be a larger number of left-sided brain-damaged cases than of right-sided brain-damaged cases. Reed, Reitan, and Klove (1965) studied children from 10 to 14 years old and concluded that chronic cerebral dysfunction leads to a generalized lowering of intellectual ability. Holroyd and Wright (1965) studied children with differences of 25 or more points between verbal and performance IQs and concluded that a difference of this magnitude is indicative of brain injury when verbal IQ is greater than performance IQ. Thus, the research literature does not support the position that brain injury will have a consistent or constant effect upon the relationship between verbal and performance IQ. The test-retest reliability of the verbal minus performance difference was found to be 0.35 by Schulman et al (1965), who tested thirty-five retarded adolescent boys on two occasions between 3½ and 4 months apart. This finding further underscores the extreme caution with which this measure should be used.

A third technique for using the Wechsler to diagnose brain injury is to attempt to find a particular pattern of subtest scores which is specifically indicative of brain injury. Hopkins (1964) studied thirty-three undifferentiated brain-injured children with a mean age of approximately 8½ years. All IQs were above 80. He found that the arithmetic and coding subscales were involved in eleven significant differences when compared with other subscale scores. In contrast, Spreen and Anderson (1966) found no differences in pattern of subscale scores between brain-damaged and familial retardates.

If we consider that brain injury is a parallel syndrome, as was discussed above, it is difficult to defend the conceptualization that there should be a particular pattern of subscale results which result from brain injury. It would appear to be more reasonable to assume that different forms of brain injury in children would affect the WISC differently. It also cannot be assumed that if brain injury occurs, all other variables such as genetic endowment, family and class background, and family order cease to have an effect upon the child's performance. Rather, it would appear that some attempt to control these variables would be in order, if one is to study consequences of brain injury in children.

It is sometimes assumed that brain injury in children should increase the range of scores across subscales on the WISC. Schulman et al. (1965) found that when the range test was interpreted in this fashion, it correlated negatively with all the other diagnostic indicators of brain injury used in their study except scatter on the Stanford-Binet. These authors reversed the scale so that constricted range was considered pathological. In this form it correlated significantly with IQ, scatter on the Binet, and a poor Draw-A-Person drawing, but not with the neurological examination rating or ratings of the electroencephalogram. They also found the reliability of the range across 3 months to be 0.53. These results suggests that the range is not particularly sensitive to localized brain injury, perhaps because the range across subscales on the WISC is quite large normally. However, it may be that extensive and generalized damage serves to contrict the range of abilities and that this end of the scale may be diagnostic. Further studies of the possibility should be undertaken.

At present the assumption that brain injury can be diagnosed utilizing the WISC has received no empirical support. There do not appear to be any specific patterns of findings which are diagnostic of brain injury, nor is there very much reason to expect that there should be. It would appear that very well-controlled studies of the effect of clearly defined lesions on performance on the WISC must be undertaken if the test is to be of any value in diagnosing the presence of brain injury, as opposed to delineating its consequences.

The Bender Gestalt Test

In assessing the value of the Bender Gestalt Test as a measure of organicity, one should remember that the test consists of a series of cards which are copied by children, producing a series of drawings which are interpreted by clinicians. Schulman et al. (1965) had thirty-five sets of Bender-Gestalt drawings which were produced by retarded adolescents scored by three judges as to the presence or absence of brain injury. Interjudge correlations ranged from .41 to .75. If these results are typical, it would appear reasonable to examine the results of previous studies from the point of view of considering what specific indicators of organicity they are employing. The ultimate of this position is to focus upon a particular system for scoring the test.

Cooper and Barnes (1966) have devised a system to determine the extent to which a given figure deviates from the gestalt presented in a Bender card. This technique has not been used to date with children. Bensberg (1952) found that reversals, repetition of parts, and uses of lines instead of dots significantly differentiated brain-injured from non-brain-injured retardates.

Quast (1958) published a list of ten signs of dysfunction which, when present in any combination of three or more, are suggestive of organic dysfunction. Feldman (1953) employed Pascal and Suttel's scoring system and found that brain-injured children obtained scores more indicative of pathology than did noninjured retardates. Hanvik (1953) found a high correlation between Bender rotation and electroencephalogram abnormalities. However, in an attempt to replicate these findings, Chorost, Spivak, and Levine (1959) found that of those children showing one or more rotation of 30 degrees or more, 69 percent had

abnormal electroencephalograms. The probability of predicting an abnormal electroencephalogram was not particularly improved by using the Bender rotation. Halpin (1955) found no significant differences between fifteen brain-injured and fifteen non-brain-injured carefully matched retardates in the number of rotations. However, she felt that breakdowns of a gestalt did reveal differences between the two groups. Matunas (1961) was unable to distinguish between two groups of seventeen boys between 10 and 15 years of age matched for age and IQ, one group diagnosed as psychotic and the other as having organic brain disease.

Koppitz (1962) has made a study of the effectiveness of the Bender Gestalt Test with children intensively in an attempt to devise a scoring system which would differentiate brain injury in children. "The findings in this study offer support for the claim that the Bender Gestalt Test is a valuable aid in diagnosing BD in children. Both individual scoring items . . . and the total Bender test score . . . proved to have considerable diagnostic value. . . . While very few BD subjects do well on the Bender, not all youngsters who do poorly on this test necessarily suffer from neurological impairment" (Koppitz, 1962, p. 544). Keough (1965) found that the Bender given in kindergarten predicted reading level at third grade, although this finding washed out when intelligence was controlled. Again, good Bender scores were predictive of success, but poor Benders were nonpredictive. Thweath (1963) reported similar results. L. C. Miller, Loewenfeld, Linder, and Turner (1963) reported very high reliabilities for scoring using the Koppitz system.

Wiener (1966) controlled race, sex, social, and maternal variables and verbal IQ and demonstrated a relationship between the Bender and minimal neurological impairment. However, he felt that " . . . socio-economic status, maternal behavior and race were more important contributors to performance on this test" (p. 279). Friedman, Strochak, Gitlin, and Gottsagen (1967) failed to find a relationship between the Koppitz system and medical-neurological diagnosis of brain damage.

Relationships between Bender performance and brain injury tend to occur because a very low percentage of children with difficulties are being found in the group of children who do good Benders for their age. In the data reported by Koppitz (1962), 42 percent of the "bad" Benders were produced by children with no evidence of brain dysfunction. Let us set up the following theoretical distribution of the population: normal, 70 percent; brain-injured, 10 percent; other pathology, 20 percent. If we take as a working example the percentages of good and poor Benders that Koppitz found with 8-year-old subjects, we find that 20 percent of the Benders given by normal subjects were poor and that 93 percent of the Benders given by brain-injured Ss were poor. Let us assume that the percentage of poor Benders among the other pathological groups is the same as that among the normal group, which is clearly not the case, but does serve to underscore the problem. Under these assumptions twenty-seven out of every one hundred Benders scored will be poor, but of these twenty-seven only nine will have been given by brain-damaged subjects, and the psychologist who calls a subject brain-injured on this basis will be wrong 67 percent of the time. These assumptions hold if the sample selected to receive Benders is randomly selected from the general population, which of course it is not. If we assume that 25 percent of the children referred have brain injuries and if we ignore the other diagnostic categories, then thirty-eight out of every one hundred Benders would be poor, and approximately 40 percent would be given by normal subjects. These figures are quoted to point out that one must carefully examine the probability statements quoted in studies in order to understand their clinical meaning.

To summarize, it is meaningless to discuss the Bender-Gestalt Test as an indicator of brain injury or any other form of pathology without carefully specifying what method of interpreting the test is being used. The Koppitz technique has been successful in statistically separating brain-injured children from control groups; however, this has been on the basis that the control groups have produced "good" Benders. Therefore, it cannot be assumed that a "bad" Bender is indicative of brain injury per se.

These results underscore the difficulty involved in devising a measure which will be sensitive to brain injury. It can be assumed until proved otherwise that any test can be affected by a variety of forms of pathology. In order for a test to differentiate clearly among pathological groups, it would seem necessary that there be a sufficient number of different sources of error for pathological groups to react differently to it. In a situation like the Bender, where there are relatively few ways in which a subject can err, the likelihood of this situation obtaining is reduced.

The Draw-A-Person Test

Relatively little recent work has been done concerning the Draw-A-Person Test. Schulman et al. (1965) found that this test correlated significantly with the Bender Gestalt Test and with electroencephalogram ratings of pathology; however, it was found to be very difficult to separate ratings of pathology on this test from intellectual functioning, and the interjudge reliability in this test was found to be unsatisfactory when employed as an index of brain damage.

New Instruments for the Diagnosis of Brain Injury: the Memory-for-Designs Test

A measure which has been devised for the specific assessment of organic consequences of brain injury is the Memory-for-Designs Test (Graham & Kendall, 1960). This test consists of a series of fifteen geometric figures, each of which is seen for a 5-second period, following which the figure is taken away and the patient is instructed to draw it from memory. The drawings are then scored on a four-point scale from zero to three, zero points being given for satisfactory reproductions. If errors are made, but the gestalt is retained, a score of one point is used. If the general configuration is lost, two points are scored. If the design has been rotated or reversed, three points are scored. The scores generated on this test are then compared with a set of standardized norms with the mental age or IQ being taken into account so that there is a method of equating subjects for intellectual functioning.

Graham and Kendall feel that the test "significantly differentiates brain-disordered subjects from those without brain disorder. While there was considerable overlap in the score distributions of these two groups, the overlap is largely due to failure to detect brain disorder rather than to misclassification of normal subjects. That is, with a poor performance, there is a high probability of brain disorder; but a good performance does not indicate an intact brain" (1960, p. 174). They did not find differentiation in the Memory-for-Designs Test results when groups were compared for the location of lesions. The authors feel that the complexity of the act of perceiving, remembering, and copying a figure requires the interaction of so many different skills on the part of the subject that it becomes a supralocal task. Although one might expect parietal functioning to be central in this task, enough other functions are involved in its execution for this expected preeminence not to occur. Unfortunately, the test has not been used to study children with marked mental deficiency, and at the time of publication of the test manual the separate standardization norms for mentally retarded children had not been developed. The test does seem to be sensitive to organic brain injury at least in the direction of having relatively few false positives. It does appear that the Memory-for-Designs Test is one which deserves further

research and study as a tool for the diagnosis of brain injury.

The Illinois Test of Psycholinguistic Abilities

Another test in this area is the Illinois Test of Psycholinguistic Abilities, developed by Kirk and McCarthy (1961) and Kirk, McCarthy and Kirk (1968) at the University of Illinois. The test is based upon a model of communication processes which was developed by Osgood (1953, 1957). It involves two levels of organization: "(a) the representational level which is sufficiently organized to mediate activities requiring the meaning or significance of linguistic symbols, and (b) the integration level which mediates activities of a more *automatic* or habitual nature including the acquisition of linguistic symbol sequences and response change, closure and perceptual speed, and the ability to predict future outcomes from past events" (McCarthy & Kirk, 1963, p. 1).

This test, which has been standardized to be used with children between the ages of 2 and 10, is designed to serve the purpose of helping remediation workers to specify the strengths and weaknesses of a particular child who may be having learning difficulties, whatever the label for these difficulties may be. The test does not, therefore, assess the presence or absence of organicity or retardation per se, but rather attempts to describe the strengths and weaknesses of children. It is divided into nine subscales, six of which assess the representational area. These are separated into three processes and two channels. The channels are auditory-vocal and visual-motor, and the processes are receptive, association, and expressive. In addition, there are four tests which test children's ability to perform automatic, nonsymbolic tasks. The authors present validity studies and subsequent research. One of the conclusions reached is as follows: "It is difficult, indeed, to make an overall judgement about the validity of the ITPA battery and subtest ... generally, the data suggests the concurrent, construct and predictive validities to be adequate, followed by the content and the diagnostic" (McCarthy & Olson, 1964, p. 66).

In spite of its relative newness, a great deal of research has been done to assess the utility and weaknesses of this test, and the authors have demonstrated admirable scientific purpose and restraint in their approach to the test. This test is of great importance to the clinician because it has become a central vehicle in the thinking and training of educators who are developing techniques for remediating difficulties in learning. This being the case, the clinician needs to be familiar with it, since it affords a method of communication between the psychologist and the educator which was not present in the past.

Other Instruments

A number of other new instruments have been developed in the recent past for the purpose of assessing the presence of brain injury; these include the Minnesota Percepto-Diagnostic Test (Fuller & Laird, 1963; Kreitman, 1966; Uyeno, 1963) and the Organic Integrity Test (Tien & Williams, 1965), which measure perceptual motor functioning and color perception, respectively. Elizur (1966) has extended his Elizur's Test for Organicity downward to include children. This test involves figure copying, block-design constructs, and a digit test, and Elizur has stated that a child should be diagnosed as organic only if the results on two of the three scales are in the organic range. Rapin, Tourk, and Costa (1966) described the Purdue Pegboard test as a device for rapid screening of children for more intensive evaluation. Garfield (1964) devised a fascinating test requiring the ability to sustain voluntary motor tasks, defining pathological impersistence as showing impersistence on two or more (of eight) tasks. This finding was present in 3 percent of the normal children and 68 percent of the brain-damaged children, with a screen efficiency of 83 percent. Frostig, Lefever, and Whittlesey (1961) have described a test of perceptual func-

tioning which yields separate scores for five classes of perceptual functioning. All these tests require a great deal of further research and clinical use before their ultimate utility can be assessed, and they are presented here without judgment.

In considering the utility of any diagnostic test, one is confronted with the presence of a number of issues. Basically, however, the issue of the validity of a particular instrument resolves itself to two fairly simple questions: (1) Does this test show a difference in level or quality of performance between a diagnostic group and a control population? (2) Does this test differentiate between children in different diagnostic categories? It is quite difficult at times to answer these questions for any particular instrument or set of instruments. Nevertheless, it is clear at this point that there are no diagnostic procedures, psychological or otherwise, which are or should be considered to be definitive instruments to evaluate the presence or absence of brain injury in a child. Indeed, since the diagnosis of brain damage is usually arrived at inferentially, there may never be any.

The search for test results which are inevitable consequences of brain injury regardless of the site of damage, the age of the child at the time of damage, and the nature of the damaging circumstances is less important than the attempt to comprehend the child, his functional capacities and his strengths. In view of the research just reviewed, it would appear that the diagnosis of brain injury should never be made without confirming medical opinion and that other diagnostic terms such as *perceptual handicap* and *minimal brain dysfunction* should be used with great reluctance. Rather, the psychologist should concern himself with specifying the areas in which a child has difficulties and seeking remediation. Equally important, the psychologist, of all people on the diagnostic team, should be concerned with emotional difficulties which the child is experiencing because of his problems and their consequences.

THE MAIN SYNDROMES

Behavioral Studies

As was discussed above, Strauss and Lehtinen (1947) described a syndrome consisting of a series of behaviors which relate to the child's lack of capacity to inhibit responses from the "old brain." "Remove or diminish the inhibiting effect of the new brain by a disruption of connections or by an impairment of this balancing power and the old brain acts unchecked; excessive emotional reactions and hyperactivity are the result" (Strauss & Lehtinen, 1947, p. 23). Unfortunately, at no point do Strauss and Lehtinen give a precise list of those characteristics of brain-injured children which they feel are definitive. In general, however, the two central aspects of the syndrome are considered to be hyperactivity and distractibility. Emotional lability, inconsistency, and perseveration are also considered parts of the syndrome. When any of these characteristics described above is operationalized in one fashion or another, it has a tendency to dissolve into a group of smaller measures rather than to maintain its intactness. In other words, when one begins assessing distractibility through the creation of a number of measurements of attention, one finds that some of these correlate with one another and that some of them do not. Similarly, when one compares activity readings taken in a situation which requires constraint with activity measures in a relatively free situation, one finds very little correlation between them. All this tends to indicate that even the terms being used to describe the behavior of a brain-damaged child are not as unified as one would suspect from the natures of their use in clinical descriptions. For example, Schulman et al. (1965) found that the structured-task activity measure they developed correlated only .25 with the total-day activity. This correlation is not significant. When these authors examined the relationships among various behavioral indicators purported to relate to the presence of brain injury, they concluded that their data did not support the contention that a brain-damage behavior syndrome existed.

In a study of seventy brain-injured preschool children between the ages of 3 and 5, Ernhardt, et al. concluded that when one examined the rating scales filled out by the parents of brain-injured children ". . . in this heterogenous group of brain-injured children, the parents did not describe their children as showing what has been called the hyperkinetic behavior syndrome, although they did perceive them as having behavior characteristics which might be called undesirable" (1963, p. 27). Further, these authors state: "The present result suggests that the hyperkinetic personality syndrome is not a typical picture, at least in the heterogenous group of brain injured children. Hyperactivity, impulsivity, and distractibility were more common in our brain injured group than in normal children. However, the difference was significant only for Examiner Ratings and not for Parent measures, it was no greater than the impairment in other personality characteristics, and was less than the impairment in the nonpersonality area of functioning" (p. 30).

Thus, neither of these studies supports the contention that the hyperkinetic behavior syndrome is an inevitable, or indeed even likely, consequence of brain injury in children.

The remainder of this discussion will deal with the various aspects of behavior which have been purported to be affected by brain injury in children.

Activity

Cromwell, Baumeister, and Hawkins (1963) describe four methods of measuring activity —direct visual observation, a free-space traversal approach, a kinetometer, and a fidgetometer— and in addition there are rating scales which have been used by a number of investigators. They go on to state that while the amount of work which has been done investigating relationships among activity measures is somewhat limited, that which exists does not support the contention that activity can be viewed as a unified phenomenon. Reliability is also an issue in the measurement of activity. For example, activity measured across a full day correlated between .60 and .71 across three pairs of days in the Schulman et al. (1965) study. As Cromwell points out, the size of the activity reliability coefficient one achieves depends to some extent upon the length of time one measures.

Schulman, Lipkin, Clarinda, and Mitchell (1961) demonstrated that sleeping and waking activity levels are not correlated, using the same instrument, and similar data were cited by Cromwell et al. (1963). The data of Schulman et al. (1965) also indicate that the patterns of correlations generated by measures of activity while performing a structured task and a measure of total-day activity are quite different. It appears that activity level is tied to the instrument with which it is measured and the conditions under which it is measured.

Given the fact that activity level varies so greatly across various instruments and across various states of the organism being assessed, it becomes increasingly difficult to speak of activity as a single dimension and therefore more difficult to define hyperactivity. If the data do not support the contention that certain children are hyperactive at all times and in all places, how can one define hyperactivity? It would appear that the term *hyperactivity* has a large social connotation, in that there is an acceptable activity level for each situation, which is defined by adults, and when a child is designated as hyperactive, it is on the basis of his inability to regulate his level of activity to that which is expected or permitted in the circumstance in which he finds himself. It is, for example, unlikely that a hyperactive child, whether brain-injured or not, would be considered a particular problem because of his activity level on a playground at recess. Clinically, one gets referrals for hyperactivity because children are posing difficulties in structured situations such as the classroom, and it is the structured situation which leads to the designation of certain children as hyperactive.

In spite of the fact that in any given situation people will vary considerably in activity level and that across a number of situations a particular person would probably vary in activity level, it is reasonable to assume that the activity level of a particular person in a particular situation will remain relatively constant across time and to hypothesize a basic tendency in the organism toward a given activity level. If one assumes this to be the case, it becomes possible to further hypothesize a homeostatic control device which attempts to compensate for deviations from the mean optimum activity level that the person is accustomed to. Thus, while people can adjust to wide variations in activity level within relatively short periods of time, it would be hypothesized that variations from the person's optimum level would be followed by a movement toward the mean, so that periods of overactivity would be followed by periods of relative inactivity, and conversely periods of inactivity would be followed by increased activity. Given a situation in which the activity level which is socially acceptable deviates greatly from an individual's own optimum activity level, the issue would be whether the person involved would be capable of adjusting to this deviation. Thus, in children, the relatively constraining school environment would have to be compensated for with a high level of activity outside the school situation, and a wide variety of situational and environmental factors would enter into what would be the socially acceptable activity level at any particular point in time. Again, those children who were not able to adjust their activity level to that which is expected would be designated as hyperactive. However, the same child who does not sit still in the classroom may spend long periods of time quietly watching television.

If one hypothesizes a homeostatic control mechanism for activity, then injury which would directly affect this control mechanism would lead on one extreme to coma and on the other extreme to a kind of classic driven hyperactivity. Laufer and Denhoff (1957), for example, argue that injury to the hypothalamus produces hyperkinesis. On the other hand, either extreme of activity is a relatively rare circumstance, and more frequently the consequence of brain injury would appear to be to render it more difficult for the child to integrate his neuromuscular tendency toward activity with the particular demands of the situation he is in. Schulman et al., (1961) found that a structured activity cluster correlated significantly and negatively with two diagnostic clusters, indicating that more brain-damaged children were less active. One way of dealing with this finding is to conclude that the effect of brain damage on the control mechanism may be one of reducing the child's capacity to adjust his activity level to the demands of the situation, so that he will at times reduce his activity level far below that required, and rather than hyperactivity per se being the probable consequence of brain injury, one might presume that deviations in activity level would be a more general consequence.

Other aspects of activity should also be noted. Kagan (1965; Kagan & Rosman, 1964) has done many studies of cognitive dispositions in childhood, one of which contrasts reflection and impulsivity. He demonstrated, for example, that impulsive children typically have difficulties in reading and pointed out that "... in a recently completed study with first-grade children, poor reproductions of Bender-Gestalt designs were associated with fast response times on MFF (Matching Familiar Figures) and were unrelated to ability to perform perceptual discriminations. These data suggest that poor Bender scores from subjects with reading problems may arise from an impulsive disposition" (Kagan, 1965, p. 627). Kagan's extensive work in this area certainly should be taken into account as an alternative

to the position that impulsive equals hyperactive, which in turn equals brain damage. Nordan (1968) failed to find any relationship between impulsivity and activity level.

Scarr (1966) studied genetic aspects of activity and found a complex function involved in which the number of games a child took part in seemed to be related to his genetic endowment, while the type of game, such as active or sedentary, was not. Presumably, the type of game would be socially determined. Pihl (1967) has discussed the possibility that operant conditioning procedures could be used to reduce activity and provided two case reports in which this technique was employed for this purpose. Certainly the potential value of this technique needs further assessment.

Distractibility

The results of research in the area of the effect of brain injury on attention have produced mixed findings. As has been the case throughout this chapter, many of the inconsistencies in findings may occur as a result of considering both brain injury and distractibility to have unitary, one-dimensional meanings.

Schulman et al. (1965) devised four distinct methods of assessing distractibility and tested children with and without an external distractor. Three of these tests correlated significantly with one another, while the fourth test did not correlate significantly with any of the other distractibility tasks with or without an external distractor. When these tests were analyzed from the point of view of the input and output modalities involved in their solution, neither of these appeared to affect the pattern of correlation as much as the central process characteristics of the task at hand. This leads to the possibility that certain kinds of attentional processes may be affected by brain injury, while others are not, and further that certain kinds of attentional processes may be affected by certain kinds of brain injury and not by others.

These authors found that a cluster of distractibility measures heavily weighted by stimulus-discrimination tasks correlated positively with generalized brain injury and low IQ. Mirsky, Primac, Stevens, and Ajmone-Marsan (1958) found that diffuse brain injury interfered with performance in a continuous performance task, while focal injuries did not.

Stevens, Boydstun, Dykman, Peters, and Sinton (1967) studied a group of minimally brain-damaged children on a series of behavioral tests involving attention, discrimination, motor impersistence, and tone discrimination. They found: "Relative to controls the (26) MBD children were slower to respond, less able to follow verbal instructions, and poorer in tone discrimination and tapping. On the Wechsler Intelligence Scale for Children the MBD's were inferior to normals on the information, arithmetic, digit span and coding subtest. While individually these deficiencies can be quite specific, there was a definite tendency for many of them to be interrelated" (p. 285). Rosvold, Mirsky, Sarason, Bransome, and Beck (1956) found that brain-damaged children did significantly worse than non-brain-damaged children on a revolving-drum problem.

Browning (1967) found that task-irrelevant visual stimuli did not interfere with learning in brain-damaged children and concluded that intelligence may be a more basic variable in distractibility than minimal brain damage. Earlier studies by Milner and Penfield (1955), Schlanger (1958), and Dencker and Lofving (1958) found no relationship between brain injury and distractibility. Cruse (1961) found no general difference between brain-damaged and familial retardates in distractibility. Thus, it would appear that no general relationship between brain injury and distractibility exists, although certain kinds of brain injury may affect certain kinds of attentional processes. In addition, the age of the child and his general IQ level are clearly important intervening variables. And,

as Frank (1964) pointed out, a number of variables other than brain injury can affect attention, and the clinician should be cautious in interpreting distractibility as evidence of brain injury.

Before concluding this section there are two final points to be made concerning distractibility. First, it appears to be highly reliable. Schulman et al. (1965) found that split-half reliability measure correlations ranged from 82 to 98, with six of the reliability estimates being more than 90. Second, distractibility may be responsive to remediation. Martin and Powers (1967) reviewed the literature on attention span and distractibility in retarded and brain-damaged children from an operant conditioning viewpoint and concluded that this technique could improve the capacity of these children to attend.

Affective and Performative Lability

Few studies can be found which investigated the relationship between measures of autonomic lability in children and evidence of brain injury. Similarly, very little work has been done relating variability in performance to brain injury.

Schulman et al. (1965) studied variablity in heart rate and lever-pressing rate, while Ss operated an operant conditioning apparatus on an intermittent reinforcement schedule. After an interval of at least 5 minutes, a loud buzzer was sounded close to the subject. Recording was then continued for a minimum of 7 minutes. The object was to determine the relative variability or lability for each subject before and after the stress. The more variability there was in performance, the more labile the subject was considered. It was found that subjects increased in lability after the stress and that the amount of increase was positively related to the original level of lability. The introduction of the buzzer did not alter the subjects' lever-pressing behavior significantly, nor did it affect the variability in heart rate. Autonomic lability and performative lability were highly related; however, autonomic lability did not relate significantly to either of two clusters of diagnostic measures of brain injury. The performative lability, however, did relate significantly to a diagnostic cluster involving motoric damage, suggesting that inconsistency in lever-pulling rates was another demonstration or consequence of the same form of damage which produced poor Bender drawings, poor Draw-A-Person drawings, electroencephalogram abnormalities, and large performance minus verbal differences.

In a study of great interest, Kagan and Rosman (1964) studied cardiac rate cognitive disposition, and attention and found that "The cardiac data . . . yielded the predicted differences between analytic and nonanalytic children. Analytic boys had lower cardiac rates during the entire experiment, and especially during the four attention episodes. In sum, cardiac rate and respiratory variability differentiated analytic from nonanalytic boys and episodes of attention from contiguous rest periods" (p. 62). These studies suggest the possibility that fluctuations in attention, fluctuations in cardiac rate, and performative lability may reinforce one another and at times produce a situation in which the child spirals out of control.

Summary of Research

In summary, then, the scientific literature to date does not support the contention of a convergent syndrome including hyperactivity, distractibility, performative lability, autonomic lability, and inconsistency as inevitable consequences of brain injury. While there are some possible relationships among various kinds of diagnostic indicators and various kinds of behaviors, these tend to be at best rather modest correlations and have not been sufficiently explored to be accepted as proved. One can only conclude at this time that the existence of a hyperkinetic behavior syndrome has not been demonstrated and that it probably does not exist in the fashion typically assumed. However, the research does suggest that further studies of distractibility, structured task activity, and autonomic lability may provide important clues to the understanding of both brain injury and learning disabilities.

As the reader has almost certainly concluded by this point, it is safe to say that the research evidence in the area of brain injury in children has not produced a body of knowledge which the clinician can utilize in his diagnostic and remediative efforts. Part of the failure in this area can undoubtedly be traced to the sheer difficulty of the task at hand. There appears to be almost no class of events in this area which can be used as indisputable validating criteria, and none of the instruments commonly employed are without difficulties of one kind or another. Under these circumstances the concurrent-validity strategy which underlies most of the work in this area is inappropriate, and a construct-validity approach in which one is attempting to define those processes which contribute to performance in a given area should be adopted. This type of approach can lead to an eventual definition of the aspects of brain functioning which are being measured by current techniques. Further, since large domains of cortical and subcortical behavior are not being sampled by current instrumentation, a construct-validity approach would help to delineate those areas which require further work.

REMEDIATION AND EDUCATION

New Views on Intelligence

One of the frequent consequences for children designated as brain injured is that they are removed from the group of children for whom therapy is available. One of the most exciting and promising current ventures in the field consists of the development of educational therapists who diagnose the child in terms of the functional strengths and weaknesses he shows and who develop specific programs which enable the child to maximize his capacity and to learn as much as is possible.

In addition to the Illinois Test of Psycholinguistic Abilities, mentioned above, a number of other educational and diagnostic approaches have been developed. Bortner (1968) has edited a collection of articles in this area concerning the variety of approaches which have been devised in the recent past to assist children with learning disabilities. Much of the work is at the clinical level; however, it is of value in informing the clinician of the variety of approaches which are being employed. It is obvious that if advances are to be made in the area of work with the brain-injured child, a much higher level of cooperation and communication must be developed between psychological diagnosticians and educators.

In addition to these specific remediational approaches, there is the work of Hunt (1961), who has stressed the value of conceptualizing intelligence as a variety of processes which permit a child or an adult to assess current situations on the basis of the concomitants of the situation itself and on the basis of past data. It is necessary that psychologists begin to think of intelligence as a dynamic process, one which is as complex and exciting as the dynamic psychopathological processes which have for a long time been the center of attention. For too long, intelligence has been considered to be an immutable score generated by an intelligence test, rather than a complex array of functions. The opportunity to study impairment of functioning in children affords one the chance of understanding more clearly many of the processes involved in intellectual functioning, and it is likely that important new conceptions of intelligence, education, and brain functioning will emerge from this direction. Certainly, the growing interest in this area bodes well for the future, both in terms of the child who has difficulties of a nature which leads people to presume that he has brain injury and in terms of the understanding of many of the intellectual and dynamic processes which are involved in human learning which

heretofore have been ignored or subsumed under the all-encompassing rubric of the IQ test.

Psychotherapy and Education

Another unfortunate consequence of the conceptualization of the brain-damage behavior syndrome has been to effectively remove children demonstrating aspects of this "syndrome" from psychotherapeutic efforts. It is simple to consider that if the child is hyperactive because he is "brain-injured," very little can be done to modify his behavior, unless some medical procedure such as drug therapy is available. Children with problems such as these are considered to be appropriate candidates not for psychotherapy, but rather for classification. The child with a chronic learning disability is likely to accumulate secondary emotional problems which can reasonably interfere with the best and most skillful attempts to remediate him. Children of this type frequently feel stupid and inept and find it quite difficult to compete with peers in many academic fields or other interpersonal areas. Withdrawal, feelings of impotence, and immaturity are quite commonly seen. The child may also react to his feelings of deficiency with striking-out behavior and aggression. If these children are placed in an educational setting which will be directed toward their specific learning needs, they may be effectively cut off from peer relationships with other children their age. Frequently they exhibit a combination of passivity and inappropriateness which makes relating to them on a therapeutic level quite difficult. In addition, the therapist is faced with the ongoing problem of the child's continuing difficulties outside his therapeutic relationship. For all these reasons, as well as for some administrative reasons, brain-injured children are frequently not seen as therapy prospects.

Ideally, we should consider the brain-damaged child as a total person who manifests various difficulties in various situations and has integrated certain concepts about himself which tend to exacerbate these difficulties. A diagnostic study which examines the child's emotional situation and his feelings about himself can be of great value to him, his parents, and the educators working with him.

If one can summarize this chapter briefly, the literature indicates that psychological tests are not currently very useful in detecting the presence of brain injury in children. That is, the strategy of attempting to find inevitable supralocal signs of brain injury in children, signs or findings which correlate with all brain injury regardless of the source or diagnostic indication employed, has failed. In view of the variety of ways that brain injury can be manifested, it is unlikely that this approach will ever be successful. If one turns from this, it is possible to conceptualize a second strategy, in which the cognitive and emotional strengths and weaknesses of a child would be described as completely as possible, with brain injury being used as an explanatory variable only when there is strong medical evidence to support the contention that it exists. In other instances the child's difficulties would be labeled without any inference being made as to the source of the problem. While it may someday be possible to distinguish between poor visual-motor performance due to anoxia at birth, poor visual-motor performance due to contra-cue damage, poor visual-motor performance due to experiential deprivation, and poor visual-motor performance resulting from a hysterical response to masturbation guilt, it does not appear that it is possible to do so now, and it is unlikely that the psychologist makes much of a contribution by pretending that it is.

Second, the research literature does not support the contention that the brain-damage behavior syndrome exists as a convergent syndrome, in the sense that the behaviors purported to follow brain injury inevitably do follow it. However, the literature does suggest that distractibility, difficulties in control of activity levels, and possible emotional lability may also be a consequence of some classes of brain injury. Further studies to investigate the relationships among measures of these characteristics, and between measures of these characteristics and various indices of brain injury, are needed to clarify whatever relationships do exist. Finally, it is also necessary that activity level, distractibility, and emotional lability be studied among normal children if studies of children with difficulties are to be properly understood.

REFERENCES

Anderson, W. W. The hyperkinetic child: A neurological appraisal. *Neurology,* 1963, **13,** 968–973.

Balthazar, E. E., & Morrison, D. J. The use of Wechsler intelligence scales as diagnostic indicators of predominant left-right and indeterminate unilateral brain damage. *Journal of Clinical Psychology,* 1961 **17,** 161–165.

Beck, H. S., & Lam, R. L. Use of the WISC in predicting organicity. *Journal of Clinical Psychology,* 1955, **11,** 154–158.

Bensberg, G. J. Performance of brain-injured and familial mental defectives on the Bender-Gestalt Test. *Journal of Consulting Psychology,* 1952, **16,** 61–64.

Bortner, M. *Evaluation and education of children with brain damage.* Springfield, Ill.: Charles C Thomas, 1968.

Browning, R. M. Effect of irrelevant peripheral visual stimuli on discrimination learning in minimally brain-damaged children. *Journal of Consulting Psychology,* 1967, **31,** 371–376.

Burch, N. R., Nettleton, W. J., Jr., Sweeny, J., & Edwards, R. J., Jr. Period analysis of the electroencephalogram on a general-purpose computer. In W. E. Tolles (Ed), *Computers in medicine and biology. Annals of the New York Academy of Science,* 1964, **115,** 827.

Chorost, S. R., Spivak, G., & Levine, M. Bender-Gestalt rotations and EEG abnormalities in children. *Journal of Consulting Psychology,* 1959, **23,** 559.

Clements, S. D., & Peters, J. E. Minimal brain dysfunction in one school age child. *Archives of General Psychiatry,* 1962, **6,** 185–197.

Cooper, J. R., & Barnes, E. J. Technique for measuring reproductions of visual stimuli. II. Adult reproductions of the Bender-Gestalt. *Perceptual and Motor Skills,* 1966, **23,** 1135–1138.

Cromwell, R. L., Baumeister, A., & Hawkins, W. F. Research in activity level. In N. R. Ellis (Ed.), *Handbook of mental deficiency.* New York: McGraw-Hill, 1963. Pp. 632–663.

Cruse, D. B. Effects of distraction upon the performance of brain-injured and familial retarded children. *American Journal of Mental Deficiency,* 1961, **66,** 86–92.

Dencker, S. J., & Lofving, B. Psychometric study of identical twins discordant for closed head injury. *Acta Psychiatrica Scandinavica,* 1958, **33,** Suppl. 122.

Elizur, A. The psychological evaluation of the organic child. *Journal of Projective Techniques and Personality Assessment,* 1965, **29,** 292–299.

Ernhart, C. B., Graham, F. K., Eichman, P. L., Marshall, J. M., & Thurston, D. Brain injury in the preschool child: Some developmental considerations. II. Comparison of brain injured and normal children. *Psychological Monographs: General and Applied,* 1963, **77** (Whole No. 574), 17–33.

Feldman, I. S. Psychological differences among moron and borderline mental defectives as a function of etiology. I. Visual motor functioning. *American Journal of Mental Deficiency,* 1953, **57,** 484–494.

Fitzhugh, L. C., Fitzhugh, K. B., & Reitan, R. M. Sensorimotor deficits of brain-damaged Ss in relation to intellectual level. *Perceptual and Motor Skills,* 1962, **15,** 603–608.

Frank, G. H. The validity of retention of digits as a measure of attention. *Journal of General Psychology,* 1964, **71,** 329–336.

Friedman, J., Strochak, R. D., Gitlin, S., & Gottsagen, M. Koppitz' Bender scoring system and brain injury in children. *Journal of Clinical Psychology,* 1967, **23,** 179–182.

Frostig, M., Lefever, D. W., & Whittlesey, J. R. B. A developmental test of visual perception for evaluating normal and neurological handicapped children. *Perceptual and Motor Skills,* 1961, **12,** 390–391.

Fuller, G. B., & Laird, J. T. The Minnesota Perceptor Diagnostic Test. *Journal of Clinical Psychology,* 1963, **19,** 3–34.

Garfield, J. C. Motor impersistence in normal and brain-damaged children. *Neurology,* 1964, **14,** 623–630.

Gibbs, E. L., Rich, C. L., Fois, A., & Gibbs, F. A. Electroencephalogram study of mentally retarded persons. *American Journal of Mental Deficiency,* 1960, **65,** 236–247.

Gibbs, F. A., & Gibbs, E. L. Fourteen and six per second positive spikes. *Electroencephalography and Clinic Neurophysiology,* 1963, **15,** 553–558.

Graham, F. K., & Kendall, B. S. Memory for Designs Test: Revised general manual. *Perceptual and Motor Skills,* 1960, **11** (Monogr. Suppl. Z–J11), 147–188.

Halpin, V. G. Rotation errors made by brain-injured and familial children on two visual-motor tests. *American Journal of Mental Deficiency,* 1955, **59,** 485–489.

Hanvik, L. J. A note on rotations in the Bender-Gestalt Test as predictors of EEG abnormalities in children. *Journal of Clinical Psychology,* 1953, **9**, 399.

Hanvik, L. J., Sherman, E. N., Hanson, H. B., Anderson, A. S., Dressler, W. H., & Zarling, V. R. Diagnosis of cerebral dysfunction in children. *American Journal of Diseases of Children,* 1961, **101**, 364–375.

Holroyd, J., & Wright, F. Neurological implications of WISC verbal-performance discrepancies in a psychiatric setting. *Journal of Consulting Psychology,* 1965, **29**, 206–212.

Hopkins, K. D. An empirical analysis of the WISC in the diagnosis of organicity in children of normal intelligence. *The Journal of Genetic Psychology,* 1964, **105**, 163–172.

Hunt, B. M. Differential responses of mentally retarded children on the Leiter Scale. *Exceptional Children,* 1961, **28**, 99–102.

Kagan, J. Reflection-impulsivity and reading ability in primary grade children. *Child Development,* 1965, **36**, 609–628.

Kagan, J., & Rosman, B. L. Cardiac and respiratory correlates of attention and an analytic attitude. *Journal of Experimental Child Psychology,* 1964, **1**, 50–63.

Kennard, M. A. The characteristics of thought disturbances as related to electroencephalographic findings in children and adolescents. *American Journal of Psychiatry,* 1959, **115**, 911–921.

Kennard, M. A. Value of equivocal signs in neurologic diagnosis. *Neurology,* 1960, **10**, 753–764.

Keogh, B. K. The Bender-Gestalt as a predictive and diagnostic test of reading performance. *Journal of Consulting Psychology,* 1065, **29**, 83–84.

Kirk, S. A., & McCarthy, J. J. The Illinois Test of Psycholinguistic Abilities: An approach to differential diagnosis. *American Journal of Mental Deficiency,* 1961, **66**, 399–412.

Kirk, S. S., McCarthy, J. J., & Kirk, W. D. *The Illinois Test of Psycholinguistic Abilities.* Revised edition. Urbana: University of Illinois, 1968.

Knobel, M., Wolman, M. B., & Mason, E., Hyperkinesis and organicity in children. *Archives of General Psychiatry,* 1959, **1**, 310–321.

Koppitz, E. M. Diagnosing brain damage in young children with the Bender-Gestalt Test. *Journal of Consulting Psychology,* 1962, **26**, 541–546.

Kreitman, L. A note on the use of the Minnesota Percepto-Diagnostic Test. *Journal of Clinical Psychology,* 1966, **22**, 196.

Laufer, M., & Denhoff, E. Hyperkinetic syndrome in children. *The Journal of Pediatrics,* 1957, **50**, 463–474.

McCarthy, J. J., & Kirk, S. A. *The construction, standardization and statistical characteristics of the Illinois Test of Psycholinguistic Abilities.* Urbana: University of Illinois Press, 1963.

McCarthy, J. J., & Olson, J. L. *Validity studies on the Illinois Test of Psycholinguistic Abilities.* Urbana: University of Illinois Press, 1964.

Martin, G. L., & Powers, R. B. Attention span: An operant conditioning analysis. *Exceptional Children,* 1967, **33**, 565–570.

Matunas, M. D. Test performance of psychotic children with organic brain pathology: A study to determine whether the Bender-Gestalt Test, the Benton Visual Retention Test, the Marble Board Test can detect the presence of organic brain pathology in psychotic children. *Dissertation Abstracts,* 1961, **21**, 1257.

Miller, C. A., & Lennoz, M. A. Electroencephalography in behavior problem children. *The Journal of Pediatrics,* 1948, **33,** 753–760.

Miller, L. C., Loewenfeld, R., Linder, R., & Turner, J. Reliability of Koppitz' scoring system for the Bender-Gestalt. *Journal of Clinical Psychology,* 1963, **19,** 211.

Milner, B., & Penfield, W. The effect of hippocampal lesions on recent memory. *Transactions of the American Neurological Association,* 1955, **80,** 42–48.

Mirsky, A. F., Primac, D. W., Stevens, J. R., & Ajmone-Marsan, C. A comparison of patients with focal and nonfocal epilepsy on a test of attention. *Electroencephalography and Clinical Neurophysiology,* 1958, **10,** 206. (Abstract)

Mueller, R., Nylander, I., Larsson, L., Widen, L., & Frankenhaeuser, M. Sequelae of primary aseptic meningo-encephalitis: A clinical sociomedical electroencephalographic and psychological study. *Acta Psychiatrica Scandinavica,* 1958, **33,** (Suppl. 126).

Nordan, R. *Relation between cognitive style and Rorschach M responses.* Unpublished doctoral dissertation, University of Chicago, 1968.

Osgood, C. E. *Method and theory in experimental psychology.* New York: Oxford University Press, 1953.

Osgood, C. E. A behavioristic analysis of perception and language as cognitive phenomena. In J. Bruner (Ed.), *Contemporary approaches to cognition.* Cambridge, Mass.: Harvard University Press, 1957, Pp. 75–118.

Paine, R. S. Minimal chronic brain syndromes in children. *Developmental Medicine and Child Neurology,* 1962, **4,** 21–27.

Pihl, R. O. Conditioning procedures with hyperactive children. *Neurology,* 1967, **17,** 421–423.

Quast, W. Visual-motor performance in the reproduction of geometric figures as a developmental phenomenon in children. *Dissertation Abstracts,* 1958, **18,** 1111.

Rapin, I., Tourk, L. M., & Costa, L. D. Evaluation of the Purdue Pegboard as a screening test for brain damage. *Developmental Medicine and Child Neurology,* 1966, **8**(1), 45–54.

Reed, H. B. E., Reitan, R. M., & Klove, H. Influence of cerebral lesions on psychological test performances of older children. *Journal of Consulting Psychology,* 1965, **29,** 247–251.

Reitan, R. M. Certain differential effects of left and right cerebral lesions in human adults. *Journal of Comparative and Physiological Psychology,* 1955, **48,** 474–477.

Riehl, J. L. Analog analysis of EEG activity. *Electroencephalography and Clinical Neurophysiology,* 1963, **15,** 1039–1042.

Rosvold, H. E., Mirsky, A. F., Sarason, I., Bransome, E. D., Jr., & Beck, L. H. A continuous performance test of brain damage. *Journal of Consulting Psychology,* 1956, **20,** 343–350.

Scarr, S. Genetic factors in activity motivation. *Child Development,* 1966, **37,** 663–673.

Schlanger, B. B. Results of varying presentations to brain-damaged children of an auditory word discrimination test. *American Journal of Mental Deficiency,* 1958, **63,** 464–468.

Schulman, J. L., Kaspar, J. C., & Throne, F. M. *Brain damage and behavior.* Springfield, Ill.: Charles C Thomas, 1965.

Schulman, J. L., Lipkin, N. P., Clarinda, M., & Mitchell, J. Studies on activity level in children. Paper presented at the meeting of the American Psychiatric Association, Chicago, May, 1961.

Secunda, L., & Finley, K. H. Electrographic

studies on children presenting behavior disorders. *Archives of Neurology and Psychiatry,* 1942, **47,** 1076–1079.

Silverman, A. J., & Harris, V. W. Electroencephalography and psychometric testing in brain damaged patients. *The Journal of Nervous and Mental Disease,* 1954, **120,** 31–34.

Solomon, C. I., Brown, W. T., & Deutsche, M. Electroencephalography in behavior problem children. *American Journal of Psychiatry,* 1944, **101,** 51–61.

Spreen, O., & Anderson, C. W. Sibling relationship and mental deficiency diagnosis as reflected in Wechsler test patterns. *American Journal of Mental Deficiency,* 1966, **71,** 406–410.

Stevens, D. A., Boydstun, J. A., Dykman, R. A., Peters, J. E., & Sinton, D. W. Presumed minimal brain dysfunction in children: Relationship to performance on selected behavioral tests. *Archives of General Psychiatry,* 1967, **16,** 281–285.

Strauss, A. A., & Lehtinen, L. *Psychopathology and education of the brain-injured child.* New York: Grune & Stratton, 1947.

Tarjan, G. Studies of organic etiologic factors, In G. Caplan (Ed.), *Prevention of mental disorders in children.* New York: Basic Books, 1961.

Thweath, R. C. Prediction of school learning disabilities through the use of the Bender-Gestalt Test: A validation study of Koppitz' scoring techniques. *Journal of Clinical Psychology,* 1963, **19,** 216–217.

Tien, H. C., & Williams, M. W. Organic integrity test (OIT) in children. *Archives of General Psychiatry,* 1965, **12,** 159–165.

Uyeno, E. Differentiating psychotics from organics on the Minnesota Perceptor Diagnostic Test. *Journal of Consulting Psychology,* 1963, **27,** 462.

Walter, W. G. Technique-interpretation. In D. Hill & G. Parr (Eds), *Electroencephalography: A symposium on its various aspects.* New York: Macmillan, 1963. P. 65.

Wechsler, D. *Manual for the Wechsler Preschool and Primary Scale of Intelligence.* New York: Psychological Corporation, 1963, 1967.

Wiener, G. The Bender-Gestalt Test as a predictor of minimal neurologic deficit in children eight to ten years of age. *The Journal of Nervous and Mental Disease,* 1966, **143,** 275–280.

8 | Epilepsy in Infancy, Childhood, and Adolescence

Samuel Livingston[1]

The data presented in this chapter are based on studies made of approximately fifteen thousand patients who developed seizures at various ages during childhood. All of them have been followed at The Johns Hopkins Hospital Epilepsy Clinic under my personal supervision. Most of these patients have been observed for years, many for as long as 20 to 33 years.

DIAGNOSIS OF EPILEPSY

A seizure or convulsion is a symptom and may be one of the clinical manifestations of a variety of disorders. Therefore, every person who suffers a seizure should be examined thoroughly for all disorders that are known to be associated with seizures, e.g., intracranial neoplasm and hypoglycemia. Epilepsy should be assigned as a diagnosis in any given case only after all the available diagnostic techniques have failed to elicit a definite cause for the seizures.

[1] The author was assisted in the preparation of this chapter by Irving M. Pruce.

In our clinic, the routine initial work-up on a seizure patient consists of a detailed medical history; general physical and neurological examinations; routine blood-cell counts and blood chemistries, including calcium, phosphorus, and fasting blood-sugar determinations; x-ray films of the skull; a cerebrospinal fluid examination; and an electroencephalographic study.

We perform cerebral examinations such as echoencephalography, brain scanning, pneumoencephalography, and arteriography in those patients who present signs or symptoms of an intracranial neoplasm, cerebral vascular anomaly, or other specific types of cerebral pathology, other than the seizure itself.

The importance of a comprehensive medical history cannot be overemphasized. In most patients, a diagnosis of epilepsy can be made on the basis of the clinical history and the exclusion by physical, neurological, and laboratory examinations of other disorders known to be associated with seizures. Special attention should be directed to the age at onset of the seizures, the occurrence of an aura, and the prodromal features of the symptomatology, since these aspects frequently provide valuable diagnostic clues. For example, true petit mal epilepsy rarely makes its onset during the first 2 years of life or after 15 years of age, and a breath-holding convulsion is almost always preceded by an acute emotional upset and cry.

Electroencephalography should be regarded as a valuable adjunct to, but not as a substitute for, other methods of diagnosing epilepsy, since it does have limitations, particularly in major motor (grand mal) epilepsy. Given, for example, a 5-year-old child who has had recurrent major motor seizures and in whom appropriate diagnostic tests have failed to elicit a cause, a diagnosis of a convulsive disorder of undetermined etiology (epilepsy) must be made, regardless of whether an electroencephalographic examination revealed normal or abnormal findings. On the basis of serial electroencephalograms performed over a period of many years on thousands of our patients who suffered with definite clinical evidence of major motor epilepsy, we would like to emphasize the fact that the incidence of normal electroencephalographic findings in patients with major motor epilepsy is exceedingly high, particularly in young children.

It should be noted that electroencephalographic findings can, in some instances, be pathognomonic, such as the spike-wave discharge of petit mal epilepsy and the hypsarhythmic pattern of myoclonic seizures of infancy (minor motor epilepsy, infantile spasms), and in other instances may be the "key" to the diagnosis, for example:

1. In the case of an individual who presents a history of having experienced an attack which was not completely observed or was poorly described by the historian

2. In those patients who present symptomatology consisting of, for example, recurrent behavioral aberrations and/or bizarre nonconvulsive motor activity in whom the physician is unable on clinical grounds to differentiate between psychomotor epilepsy and an emotional or psychiatric disorder

3. In those patients who suffer with disturbances such as recurrent attacks of abdominal pain, headache, dizziness, or fainting spells in whom the physician is unable on clinical grounds to differentiate between nonconvulsive epileptic equivalent and a functional or emotional disturbance.

The electroencephalogram is exceedingly important in classifying different types of epileptic seizures (see the section entitled "Classification of Epileptic Seizures"), particularly petit mal spells and short psychomotor seizures.

Also, electroencephalography may be of value to the neurosurgeon by assisting him in locating a localized cerebral area exhibiting abnormal electrical discharge.

In some instances, a diagnosis of epilepsy can be made only in retrospect, depending upon the course of the patient's symptoms and the response to specific antiepileptic medication. Obviously, this would apply to those patients in whom the physician is unable at the time of the initial evaluation to make a definite diagnosis on the basis of the clinical history; physical, neurological, and electroencephalographic examinations; and other procedures appropriate for the symptom in question. Some examples of epileptic manifestations which, in our experience, can frequently be diagnosed only in a retrospective manner are dizzy spells, nightmares, laughing spells, night terrors, temper tantrums, somnambulism, recurrent attacks of abdominal pain, recurrent headaches, and behavioral aberrations of various types. On the basis of our experience in the evaluation of hundreds of patients who presented such symptoms, we should like to caution the physician against making a definite diagnosis of epilepsy until he has excluded a psychogenic basis for the patient's symptoms and has also taken into consideration a possible placebo effect of the medications prescribed. Our methods for the differential diagnosis of epileptic manifestations which simulate psychiatric disorders are presented in a recent writing (Livingston & Pauli, 1967).

The problem of whether or not the physician should assign a diagnosis of epilepsy to an individual who suffers a seizure of undetermined etiology remains controversial. In such instances, we assign a diagnosis of epilepsy to those patients in whom the electroencephalographic examination reveals abnormalities such as those seen in overt epilepsy. However, in those patients in whom the electroencephalographic examination reveals normal findings, we make a tentative diagnosis of epilepsy and continue with this diagnosis unless the passage of time proves that the seizure was a manifestation of some other disorder. Details relative to our management of patients who have experienced one seizure of undetermined etiology are presented in previous publications (Livingston, 1960, 1964a) and are briefly discussed later in this chapter under "General Principles of Drug Therapy."

DISORDERS SIMULATING EPILEPSY

Below is a list of a number of disorders which are associated with seizures or spells of various types. The following sections are limited to a

DISORDERS ASSOCIATED WITH SEIZURES OR SPELLS OF VARIOUS TYPES[2]

1. Intracranial infections, e.g., meningitis, encephalitis, cerebral abscess.

2. Intracranial hemorrhage, such as caused by direct injury to the brain (in association with birth or other trauma).

3. Subdural hematoma.

4. Concussion of the brain, e.g., acute trauma to the head.

5. Metabolic disorders, e.g., tetany (hypocalcemia, alkalosis), hypoglycemic states, phenylpyruvic oligophrenia, hypernatremia, pyridoxine dependency.

6. Breath-holding spells.

7. Emotional (functional) disorders, e.g., simple fainting spells, hysterical convulsions.

8. Parasitic brain diseases, e.g., toxoplasmosis, malaria, hydatid cyst, cysticercosis.

9. Narcolepsy and cataplexy.

10. Intracranial neoplastic diseases, e.g., brain tumors.

11. Toxic:
    a. Drugs; e.g., when taken in excess or if sensitivity is present, many of the commonly used drugs such as ACTH, atropine, diphenhydramine hydrochloride (Benadryl), caffeine, cortisone, epinephrine, penicillin, chlorpromazine (Thorazine), and prochlorperazine (Compazine) will cause convulsions.
    b. Acute lead encephalopathy.
    c. Kernicterus.
    d. Immunizations, particularly pertussis (may also be due to fever).
    e. Roseola infantum (may also be due to fever).
    f. Shigella gastroenteritis (may also be due to fever).

[2] Taken in part from Livingston, 1963, p. 15.

12. Cerebral degenerative diseases, e.g., encephalitis periaxialis diffusa of Schilder.

13. Congenital cerebral defects, e.g., tuberous sclerosis, Sturge-Weber syndrome, hydrocephalus.

14. Fever in young children (usually associated with infections such as tonsillitis or otitis media), e.g., simple febrile convulsive disorder.

15. Tetanus.

16. Epilepsy.

discussion of two disturbances encountered in young children which, in our experience, are frequently misdiagnosed as epilepsy: (1) convulsions associated with breath-holding spells and (2) infantile febrile convulsions.

Breath-holding Spells

Holding of the breath during the course of crying is observed frequently in young children. A typical simple breath-holding spell is easily recognized and usually follows a more or less constant pattern. After some event as a result of which the child has become angry or afraid or has injured himself even slightly, he starts crying. As the crying increases in intensity, the child appears to be in a rage, begins holding his breath, and becomes cyanotic around the lips.

The entire episode may terminate in a minute or so. Generally, such spells are of minor significance and should cause little concern either to the parents or to the physician. In other instances, however, the breath-holding spells are of a more violent nature and may be associated with unconsciousness and/or frank convulsive movements. We classify these latter attacks as breath-holding spells of the convulsive type.

Breath-holding spells most often appear during the first 2 years of life, but rarely before 6 months of age. In our group of patients, the average age at onset was 12 months.

The frequency of spells varies considerably. Some of our patients experienced one spell every several months or so, while others had as many as five to ten a day. Generally, breath-holding spells recur infrequently at the beginning of the disorder, but in most cases, the frequency of recurrence gradually increases as the child advances in age. The frequency in our group of patients reached a peak between the ages of 2 and 3 years. These spells usually disappear spontaneously after 5 or 6 years of age.

Breath-holding spells are easily recognized, since the following triad of symptoms is encountered in no other condition:

1. A precipitating factor such as a slight injury or some other minor provocative incident which arouses an acute emotional response (see list below).

2. Violent crying, ending suddenly in respiratory apnea

3. The occurrence of cyanosis, unconsciousness, or convulsions, depending upon the individual child and the duration of the apnea

INCIDENTS OR EMOTIONS WHICH PARENTS CONSIDER TO BE CAUSES OF BREATH-HOLDING SPELLS IN CHILDREN

Bumping his head

Fright

Anger

To get attention

Displeasure with things or people

Hurting himself

Examination by a doctor

Being forced to do something he does not want to do

Having playmates take something he wants

Getting a spanking

Simple breath-holding spells, i.e., those consisting of crying, holding of the breath, and cyanosis, usually do not present major differential diagnostic problems. Breath-holding spells of the convulsive type, however, are frequently erroneously diagnosed as epilepsy and treated accordingly.

The convulsive movements which occur in association with breath-holding spells are basically indistinguishable from those of epilepsy. The duration of a breath-holding convulsive episode is almost always brief, seldom longer than 2 to 3 minutes. An epileptic seizure, on the other hand, may last for a few seconds or continue for several hours or longer.

Some features which assist in differentiation between convulsions associated with breath-holding spells and epileptic convulsions are presented in Table 8-1. Breath-holding convulsions are almost invariably preceded by an

TABLE 8-1 FACTORS WHICH HELP TO DIFFERENTIATE CONVULSIONS ASSOCIATED WITH BREATH-HOLDING SPELLS FROM EPILEPTIC CONVULSIONS

	Convulsions Associated with Breath-holding Spells	*Epileptic Convulsions*
Precipitating factor	Always present	Usually not apparent in young children
Crying	Always present before onset of convulsion	Not usually present
Cyanosis	Always occurs before onset of convulsion	When present, usually occurs after convulsion has been in progress (prolonged convulsion)
Opisthotonos	Usually present	Rarely occurs
EEG	Always normal	Usually abnormal, but may be normal

obvious precipitating factor, whereas in most instances, epileptic seizures occur spontaneously without any apparent preceding disturbing factor. Breath-holding episodes are always preceded by crying and holding of the breath, whereas young children with epilepsy rarely cry before an attack. Cyanosis appears with the crying and precedes the convulsions of breath-holding spells, whereas in epilepsy, cyanosis, if present, usually appears after the onset of the convulsive movements. Opisthotonos almost always occurs in association with breath-holding spells, whereas it rarely occurs with epileptic seizures. The electroencephalogram is normal in patients with breath-holding spells (Low, Gibbs, & Gibbs, 1955; Livingston, 1958), whereas it is abnormal in most patients with epilepsy.

The specific mechanism or mechanisms involved in the production of breath-holding spells have not as yet been definitely established and may vary from patient to patient. Bridge, Livingston, and Tietze (1943) proposed vagotonia as a possible cause (mechanism) of breath-holding spells in some patients. Cerebral anoxia secondary to various factors has been suggested as the most likely cause (mechanism) by Gastaut and Gastaut (1958); Gauk, Langford, and Prichard (1963); and Lombroso and Lerman (1967). A relation between anemia and breath-holding spells was reported by Holowach and Thurston (1963). However, we did not encounter anemia in the hundreds of patients with breath-holding spells observed in our clinic, nor are we cognizant of any other report in the literature describing such a relationship.

Breath-holding spells are, in our experience, essentially innocuous, and the general outlook for children with this disorder is excellent. Follow-up studies made on hundreds of our patients with breath-holding spells over a period of many years revealed an incidence of epilepsy no greater than that which exists in the general population.

Some of our patients with breath-holding episodes manifested behavioral disorders, such as enuresis, head banging, and temper tantrums. In some instances, these latter disturbances appeared during the early years of life concurrent with the breath-holding spells. In others, however, behavioral aberrations did not become apparent until after the breath-holding attacks had disappeared. Kanner (1962) studied a group of children with breath-holding spells and observed similar behavioral disturbances.

We are impressed with the fact that breath-holding spells are observed almost entirely in children with normal intelligence. Only rarely have we encountered a typical breath-holding spell in a brain-damaged child. Long-term follow-up studies made on our group of patients did not present the slightest indication that the apnea and/or convulsions associated with breath-holding spells caused demonstrable evidence of brain damage.

The unconsciousness and convulsions associated with breath-holding episodes are generally brief and require no immediate care. The administration of antiepileptic therapy and/or tranquilizing agents, in our experience, is of no value in preventing the recurrence of these spells.

Treatment consists primarily in parent-child guidance and reassurance. We inform the parents of the harmlessness of the attacks; reassure them that their child does not have epilepsy; advise them that, statistically, the chances of their child's developing epilepsy are no greater than those for the general population; and direct our treatment toward a solution of a parent-child conflict, if such a situation is apparent. Coincident recommendations relative to the psychiatric aspects of treatment have been emphasized by other investigators, notably Hinman and Dickey (1956).

Febrile Convulsions

There is some diversity of opinion regarding the diagnosis, treatment, and prognosis of convulsions which occur in association with an elevation of temperature during early childhood. The findings of most of the investigations relative to this subject, and the recommendations made, are set out by Frantzen, Lennox-Buchthal, and Nygaard (1968); Livingston (1954, p. 79), and Millichap (1968).

We classify febrile convulsions, excluding those which occur with intracranial infections (meningitis, encephalitis, etc.) or with diseases which adversely affect the central nervous system (shigella gastroenteritis, etc.) or other disorders known to be toxic to the brain, into two groups (Table 8-2): simple febrile convulsions and epileptic seizures precipitated by fever.

TABLE 8-2 FACTORS WHICH HELP TO DIFFERENTIATE SIMPLE FEBRILE CONVULSIONS FROM EPILEPTIC CONVULSIONS PRECIPITATED BY FEVER

	Simple Febrile Convulsions	*Epileptic Convulsions Precipitated by Fever*
Age at onset of seizures	Under 6 years	Any age
Duration of seizures	Always very short	Minutes to hours
Character of seizures	Always generalized	Generalized or focal
EEG	Normal	Abnormal in most cases
Relation of seizures to fever	Occurs soon after onset of fever	Any time during febrile episodes
Frequency of seizures	One to four per year	Daily to yearly
Genetic factor	Familial incidence very high	Familial incidence low—same as other forms of epilepsy

We make a diagnosis of a simple febrile convulsive disorder in those children who present the following: generalized seizures of brief duration, seldom lasting longer than several minutes, occurring soon after a rise in temperature; no clinical or laboratory evidence of cerebral infection or intoxication; and a normal electroencephalogram after the patient has been afebrile for at least a week.

A simple febrile convulsive disorder usually makes its initial appearance between 9 and 15 months of age, seldom occurs in infants under 6 months, and rarely, if ever, commences after 5 years of age. Simple febrile convulsions are almost always associated with an extracranial infection such as tonsillitis or otitis media.

Simple febrile convulsions generally appear soon after a sudden rise in temperature, usually within 3 to 6 hours after the onset of the fever. It is very rare for the convulsion to occur later than 12 to 18 hours after the initial appearance of the elevation of temperature.

Our investigations indicate that in children who suffer with simple febrile convulsions, the familial incidence of similar convulsions is exceedingly high. In 1954, we reported that the incidence of a family history of simple febrile convulsions among 201 patients who suffered with similar febrile convulsions was 58 percent (Livingston, 1954). Millichap (1968) reported a familial incidence of febrile convulsions of 30 percent in ninety-five children who themselves suffered from febrile convulsions. Certainly, these figures—58 and 30 percent—are considerably higher than most investigators have reported relative to the familial incidence of epilepsy in patients who suffer with overt epilepsy (nonfebrile convulsions). As stated in a previous publication (Livingston, Bridge, & Kajdi, 1947), we believe that the exceedingly high familial incidence of simple febrile convulsions can be utilized as an additional, supportive criterion in categorizing febrile convulsions and also in prognosticating the outcome in young children who have convulsions in association with an elevation of temperature.

A diagnosis of epilepsy precipitated by fever is strongly indicated by one or more of the following findings: prolonged seizures, focal convulsions of any duration, febrile convulsions in a child over 5 years of age, and electroencephalographic abnormalities such as are seen in overt epilepsy.

Our evaluation and recommendations relative to the prognosis and treatment of the aforementioned two groups of febrile convulsive disorders are based on the results of two independent studies carried out over the past 30 years in the Children's Seizure Clinic of The Johns Hopkins Hospital. The first investigation revealed prognostic data which are presented in a previous writing (Livingston, 1958). Briefly, this investigation consisted of prolonged follow-up studies of 622 children who were seen at our clinic with their first febrile convulsive seizure. None of them presented evidence of specific diseases known to cause convulsions or had a history of any cerebral disorder before this convulsive episode. All of them had been observed for at least 15 years, and many for as long as 22 years at the conclusion of this study. These patients were not treated with regular daily maintenance dosages of anticonvulsant medication on a controlled comparative basis.

Of the 622 patients in this study group, 256 fulfilled, at the time of their initial seizure, our criteria for a diagnosis of a simple febrile convulsive disorder (group A), and 366 our criteria for a diagnosis of epilepsy precipitated by fever (group B).

Of the 256 patients included in group A, only seven (2.9 percent) subsequently developed recurring afebrile seizures (epilepsy). Some of the remaining 249 patients had no recurrence of seizures, but the majority had a recurrence of simple febrile convulsions of varying frequencies (averaging one to four per year) up to 4 or 5 years of age and subsequently no recurrence of seizures of any type at the time this study was terminated.

Of the 366 patients included in group B, 355 (97 percent) subsequently developed various types of epileptic manifestations (seizures unassociated with fever).

Our second investigation was begun approximately nine years ago, and the results will be published at a later date. The material for this study was collected in the following manner. The General Out-Patient Clinic and Emergency Department staffs were instructed to refer to the Special Seizure Unit the first 200 children who were seen in these areas with their first febrile seizure unassociated with evidence of specific cerebral disturbances of any type either before or at the time of the initial seizure. These patients initially received a complete seizure work-up, and were placed consecutively into one of the following four groups. The first group received daily conventional, maintenance dosages of phenobarbital; the second group was given phenobarbital with instructions to administer aspirin at the first sign of fever or infection; the third group was given a placebo; and the fourth group received a placebo with instructions to administer aspirin at the first sign of fever or infection. Placebos were prescribed in this study as an incentive for the parents to return for follow-up visits as well as to determine the effect of no medication in the management of febrile convulsive disorders. The results of the follow-up studies of these patients are now being tabulated, but the data on hand confirm the prognostic findings of our first investigation.

The results of both studies have convinced us that the prognosis of a simple febrile convulsive disorder is excellent, and in addition, the findings of the second study demonstrated that the regular daily administration of conventional prophylactic dosages of phenobarbital is of no value in preventing the recurrence of simple febrile convulsions. The efficacy of intermittent treatment (administration of phenobarbital and/or an antipyretic at the onset of fever) is impossible to evaluate since many children suffering from a simple febrile convulsive disorder do not have a convulsion each time they have a fever. Moreover, this type of therapy often fails because the parent does not realize that the child has a fever until after the occurrence of the convulsion.

We do not prescribe daily prophylactic anticonvulsant medication to children who suffer with simple febrile convulsions, and we strongly disagree with those physicians who advocate the long-term daily administration of antiepileptic agents, particularly diphenylhydantoin sodium (Dilantin), in the treatment of this disorder. It is well known that, in addition to other serious side effects, in many patients this drug causes hyperplasia of the gingivae with concomitant displacement of teeth and, in some, hypertrichosis, which is almost invariably irreversible.

On the basis of the findings of both studies, we would like to emphasize that patients with epileptic seizures precipitated by fever should be treated with daily antiepileptic medication in the same manner as patients who have epileptic seizures unassociated with fever.

We believe that the physician confronted with a child who has experienced his first simple febrile convulsion should advise the parents of the good prognosis. We do not believe, however, that he can be completely dogmatic and inform the parents that there is absolutely no chance of epilepsy developing later in life. We recommend that these patients be observed periodically by the physician. If the patient has a recurrence of seizures other than the kind typical of simple febrile convulsions, if subsequent EEG studies reveal electrical aberrations diagnostic of epilepsy, or if the febrile seizures recur after 6 years of age, the physician should then consider the diagnosis of an epileptic disorder and treat the patient accordingly.

INCIDENCE OF EPILEPSY

Epilepsy is a prevalent disorder. There are no accurate figures available as to the total number of persons afflicted with epilepsy in the United States. This is due primarily to the fact that epilepsy is not a reportable disease in most states.

We conducted a survey (as of December, 1968) of the fifty states and the District of Columbia and learned that epilepsy is reportable to the state health department in the following seven states: California, Connecticut, Delaware, Indiana, Nevada, New Jersey, and Oregon. Attention is directed to the following communication, dated October 4, 1968, and signed by James Chin, M.D., Head, General Epidemiology Section, Bureau of Communicable Diseases, Department of Public Health, State of California: "Epilepsy was a reportable disease in California up to 1966. Since then it is still reportable but has been grouped into those disorders characterized by lapses of consciousness. It is presently not possible to separate out epilepsy as a distinct diagnosis."

Of the many figures relative to the incidence of epilepsy which appear in the literature, the most common is that one in one hundred individuals in the United States suffers with epileptic seizures. However, we believe that the true incidence of epilepsy is higher than this estimate. A survey conducted by Eisner, Pauli, and Livingston (1959) in our clinic indicated that one out of every fifty persons will develop some form of epilepsy during his lifetime. This finding is closely matched in a publication by Miller, Court, Walton, and Knox (1960, pp. 164–165), who reported the incidence of recurrent convulsions in a 5-year study of 845 children to be one in fifty-three.

Over the past years, there has been an increase in the incidence and known number of persons with epilepsy. This can be attributed in great part to the following factors:

1. Because of better obstetric and pediatric care, many infants who, in the past, would have died because of cerebral birth defects and injuries are now survivng, but with varying degrees of residual cerebral pathology which predisposes them to the development of recurrent seizures.

2. Modern medicine is now saving the lives of many victims of disorders, such as meningitis, encephalitis, severe head injuries, and brain tumors. These disorders, however, produce irreversible cerebral changes in some patients which predispose them to developing recurrent seizures.

3. A better understanding of the disorder of epilepsy by the general public has led to a decrease in the stigmata associated with this disease. This has resulted in a greater willingness among epileptics to reveal their condition.

4. The repeal in most communities of restrictive legislation relative to epilepsy has also eliminated some of the barriers which had caused individuals to conceal their illness from public authorities.

5. The increase in the number of known epileptics is due in great measure to the use of the electroencephalograph. With the aid of this diagnostic instrument, the physician has become more aware that disturbances other than the classic convulsive seizure may be manifestations of an epileptic disorder. As examples, one could cite disturbances such as recurrent attacks of dizziness, headache, and abdominal pain and brief periods of impairment of consciousness and syncope, which, in many instances, prior to the advent of electroencephalography, had remained undiagnosed or were considered functional in origin.

AGE AT ONSET OF EPILEPSY

Every individual is subject to a seizure or convulsion at any age from birth to death. All races are equally subject to this disturbance, and there is no true sex incidence.

Epilepsy is primarily a disorder of childhood; approximately 90 percent of all epileptic patients develop their initial symptoms before 20 years of age.

There are two specific times during childhood when epilepsy occurs most frequently: during the first few years of life and at the onset of puberty. The initial appearance of epilepsy during the latter period is observed more often in females than in males.

The high incidence of epilepsy during the first few years of life is thought to be related to cerebral damage occurring either prenatally or at birth. The factors responsible for the relatively high incidence of epilepsy in association with adolescence remain obscure. However, some physicians have postulated that the many complex chemical and physiological changes which take place in the body at this time play some part in the causation of this disorder.

FACTORS WHICH PREDISPOSE SOME INDIVIDUALS TO EPILEPSY

Many hypotheses have been proposed as to the cause of epilepsy. Among these are disturbances which produce defects in the physiological, metabolic, enzymatic, and chemical systems of the brain. Some physicians advocate a genetic basis for the occurrence of epileptic seizures. To our knowledge, however, no evidence has been presented which definitely proves that hereditary factors or any one cerebral abnormality or combination of cerebral abnormalities is unequivocally the cause of epilepsy.

We believe it is fair to state that the etiologic factor or factors in epilepsy have not been precisely established. However, it is known that damage to the brain such as produced by infections (meningitis, encephalitis), cerebral injuries sustained in association with birth or from other causes, and metabolic disorders (hypoglycemia, hypernatremia) predispose some individuals to the development of epilepsy.

It seems obvious that cerebral damage caused by either infection or trauma is not a *sine qua non* in the development of epilepsy since not all individuals with brain damage develop recurrent seizures. Certainly, not all infants who sustain obvious damage to the brain in association with birth develop recurrent convulsions. Also, despite the fact that all children with "cerebral palsy" have brain damage of some type, several investigations, including one of our own, revealed that only about 25 to 30 percent of these children subsequently develop epilepsy. In addition, it is of interest to note that there is a pronounced paucity of seizure disorders among boxers, many of whom are known to have sustained injuries to the brain. The query as to why some individuals with brain damage develop epilepsy and others do not remains unanswered.

It has been postulated by some physicians that individuals who develop recurrent seizures following cerebral injury (due to infection or trauma) were actually "potential epileptics" and that the brain damage increased their "susceptibility" to epilepsy. This assumption is certainly reasonable, but has by no means been definitely proved.

The genetic aspects of the disorder of epilepsy are presented in a subsequent section of this chapter.

PRECIPITATING FACTORS OF EPILEPTIC SEIZURES

It is important that the treatment of an epileptic patient be directed not only to the antiepileptic medication but also to factors which, in some patients, precipitate epileptic seizures. In some instances, a precipitating factor is apparent in association with all the patient's seizures, and in others it is apparent only at certain times. In many patients, however, the physician is unable to elicit a definite precipitating factor. This is particularly true in the very young child.

Emotional disturbances

Emotional disturbances such as excitement, fear, frustration, tension, and anxiety are among the most common, if not the most common, of the precipitating factors of epileptic seizures. This is particularly true in the teen-ager and the younger adult.

The management of the specific emotional disturbance in any given case of epilepsy obviously depends upon the nature and severity of the disturbance. In many instances, the personal physician can minimize or alleviate the emotional aberration by so-called commonsense psychiatric guidance. In other instances it may be advisable to have the patient consult a psychiatrist.

Menstruation

It has long been known that there is a direct relationship between epileptic seizures and menstruation and that some females experience seizures only in association with their menstrual periods. The physiological change or changes which occur during the menstrual cycle and which are responsible for the precipitation of epileptic seizures are not clearly understood and remain a highly controversial subject.

Epileptic seizures may occur or become more frequent at any time during the menstrual cycle; however, the greatest tendency to seizures is observed during the first several days preceding the onset of the menstrual flow. In addition to the fact that the menstrual cycle is associated with an increase in the frequency of seizures in some epileptic patients, it is important to note that many females have their first epileptic seizure between the ages of 11 and 13 years. This is the period of life during which the onset of the menses generally occurs.

Epileptic seizures which occur in association with the menses are frequently difficult to control. Our general plan of treatment for menstrual seizures is to prescribe initially the conventional dosage of antiepileptic medication. If this regimen does not benefit the patient, we continue with the conventional daily dosage and prescribe larger dosages of the same medication starting several days before the expected menstrual period and for about 3 days thereafter. We have also found that in some instances a reduction of fluid intake or the administration of a diuretic such as acetazolamide (Diamox), or both, is helpful.

Sleep

Many patients have their seizures only in association with sleep. Epileptic seizures may occur at any time during the sleep cycle, but they occur most frequently at two specific times: (1) within the first or second hour after falling asleep and (2) 1 to 2 hours before the usual time of awakening.

Drug therapy for patients who suffer with seizures only in association with sleep differs somewhat from that prescribed for patients whose seizures occur during the daytime. We initially prescribe the conventional dosage of the appropriate antiepileptic agent, with the first dose given at lunch, the second dose at supper, and the third dose at bedtime. In the event that this dosage does not control the patient's seizures, (1) we increase the suppertime (second) dosage of the drug to tolerance as indicated for those patients whose seizures occur soon after they fall asleep, (early nocturnal seizures), and (2) we increase the bedtime (third) dosage to tolerance as indicated for those patients who have so-called late nocturnal or early morning seizures.

We have found that the daily administration of a Dexedrine (dextroamphetamine sulfate) Spansule just before going to bed, in addition to the specific antiepileptic agent, is helpful in some instances. This may appear to be paradoxical in view of the fact that the amphetamines are "stimulating drugs." However, the institution of this form of therapy is based on the hypothesis that the occurrence of nocturnal seizures is related to the depth of sleep: The deeper the sleep, the more likely the occurrence of seizures. Therefore, the amphetamines are administered in an endeavor to lessen the depth of sleep. Obviously, their usage should not be continued in those patients who become insomniac.

Environment

A change of environment frequently favorably affects the course of epileptic seizures, particularly in children. We have seen many patients who experienced a decrease in the frequency and even a complete disappearance of seizures upon removal from their homes to other environments such as hospitals, camps, foster homes, and special resident or hospital schools. They continued to do well throughout their stay in this new environment. When these patients returned to their homes, however, the seizures reappeared with the same frequency as before the change of environment.

There are many factors in a patient's environment which may adversely affect the course of his epileptic disorder. The one factor which we believe is by far the most significant is improper management by the family.

Change of environment should be an important consideration for all patients who have not responded to the usual forms of antiepileptic therapy. It has been our experience that this aspect of the treatment of epilepsy has been much neglected. Physicians would do well to heed the advice of Hippocrates, who, in the fifth century B.C., stated that "epilepsy in young persons is most frequently removed by changes of air, of country, and of modes of life."

Fever

The effect of fever in individuals who suffer with epilepsy varies from patient to patient. In some instances, the frequency of seizures is increased, while in others it is lessened, and in still others it remains unchanged. The physician should make every attempt to remove all possible foci of infection in epileptic patients as soon as feasible, particularly in those who have experienced increased frequency or severity of seizures during acute infections.

The treatment and outcome of patients who suffer with epileptic seizures triggered off by fever are essentially the same as in other types of epilepsy.

It is important that the physician differentiate true epileptic seizures triggered by fever from those convulsions occurring in young children in association with an elevation of temperature, which we classify as simple febrile convulsions. Febrile convulsions are discussed in a previous section.

Hyperventilation

As a precipitant of epileptic seizures, hyperventilation is primarily of importance as a means of activation of seizures for diagnostic purposes. This diagnostic procedure, when carried out properly, will precipitate a clinical petit mal spell in practically all patients with this form of epilepsy. Voluntary forced deep breathing rarely, if ever, precipitates other types of seizures.

Many parents have asked us the following question: "Since it is medically known that deep breathing precipitates petit mal seizures, should patients with these spells perform activities which bring about deep breathing, such as running, bicycle riding, and swimming?" We inform the parents that the increased respirations associated with ordinary childhood physical activities are harmless and rarely, if ever, precipitate a petit mal spell.

Miscellaneous Precipitants

Sensory-precipitation epilepsy (also called *reflex epilepsy*) may occur in response to tactile (Calderon-Gonzalez, Hopkins, & McLean, 1966), visual (Keith, Aldrich, Daly, Bickford, & Kennedy, 1952), or startle (Cohen, McAuliffe, & Aird, 1961) stimuli, as well as with more specific situations such as reading (Bickford, Whelan, Klass, & Corbin, 1956), listening to music (Critchley, 1937), or photic stimulation (Livingston & Torres, 1964), including watching television (Livingston, 1952).

It has been our experience, by and large, that sensory-precipitated epileptic seizures are refractory to the standard antiepileptic drugs. Good results in occasional cases with diazepam (Valium) have been reported. However, we have treated many patients with this form of epilepsy with diazepam without benefit.

Patients with so-called photogenic epilepsy can be relieved of their seizures in some instances by wearing specially constructed eyeglasses with Polaroid lenses. It has been our experience, however, that most patients are unwilling to wear such glasses because they are cosmetically unattractive.

Forster (1967, 1968) recently reported improvement in patients with "sensory-evoked seizures" (music, light) by a gradual desensitization to the "stimuli that once evoked" seizures.

Spangler (1943), Dees and Lowenbach (1951), and several other investigators have reported a relationship between allergy and recurrent convulsive seizures. However, a study carried out in our clinic failed to reveal a specific relationship between allergy and epilepsy.

Numerous other conditions and situations are designated by some patients as precipitants of their seizures. Constipation and fatigue are frequently cited, along with many vague situations, such as "with changes of the moon," "on rainy days," "when I eat certain foods," "when it snows," "during certain seasons of the year," and "on weekends." The reader may refer to another publication for a more detailed discussion of the significance of these "factors" in the precipitation of epileptic seizures (Livingston, 1963).

GENERAL CLASSIFICATION OF THE EPILEPSIES

The epilepsies may be classified into two broad groups:

1. Recurrent seizures which develop subsequent to demonstrable evidence of brain damage, such as those which occur in some patients in association with birth, infections of the brain (e.g., meningitis and encephalitis), and cerebral trauma caused by direct injuries to the head, are designated as *secondary* (organic, symptomatic, posttraumatic) epilepsy.

2. When seizures occur in patients in whom the physician is unable to demonstrate specific evidence of cerebral pathology, the disorder is classified as *idiopathic* (cryptogenic, essential, pure, primary, true) epilepsy.

The term *genetic epilepsy* is also assigned by some physicians to this latter group. We do not believe that an etiologic relationship between inheritance and the occurrence of epileptic seizures has been definitely established, and we therefore prefer that this classification not be assigned to all patients who suffer with recurrent seizures of undetermined etiology. The subject of the genetic aspects of epilepsy is discussed in a subsequent section of this chapter.

CLASSIFICATION OF EPILEPTIC SEIZURES

Epileptic seizures are classified by most physicians into specific types by utilizing one or more of the following factors: the clinical manifestations of the attack, the electroencephalographic pattern, and the presumptive anatomic site or origin of the neuronal discharge.

The following classification is a purely pragmatic one, based on direct clinical observations and electroencephalographic studies of thousands of epileptic patients followed for prolonged periods of time in the Epilepsy Clinic of The Johns Hopkins Hospital. It includes only the common types of epileptic seizures encountered in children.

Major Motor (Grand Mal) Seizures

These seizures may be generalized or focal. When generalized, there is always associated impairment of consciousness, either partial or complete. When focal, there is usually no apparent loss of consciousness. The clinical manifestations of a major motor seizure may vary considerably. There are, however, four specific types:

1. Tonic-clonic. This is the most commonly observed type of major motor seizure. It is not necessary to describe this spell, since it is so well known.

2. Tonic. During this seizure the musculature remains in a tonic (boardlike) state throughout the convulsive episode.

3. Clonic. This type begins with rapid jerking movements of the muscles, which continue throughout the acute stages of the attack.

4. Atonic. When the attack is generalized, the patient, if standing, suddenly crumples and falls to the floor in an unconscious state. The musculature remains flaccid throughout the seizure, and there is no apparent clonic or tonic phase. This spell is classified by others as a "drop," "akinetic," or "inhibitory" seizure.

The interseizure electroencephalogram in many patients with major motor epilepsy reveals normal findings, particularly in the very young child; in others, it shows abnormalities such as spikes coming from areas of the brain other than the temporal regions and spike-wave discharges (Figure 8-1) other than the classic spike-wave complex of petit mal and hypsarhythmia. During a clinical seizure, the EEG shows diffuse bursts of multiple spikes which continue throughout the entire period of the active phases of the convul-sion; during the postconvulsive phase, high-voltage slow-wave activity appears in the tracing and continues until the patient completely regains consciousness.

Attention is called to the fact that the term *Jacksonian* is used very loosely in the medical literature, and many patients who suffer with focal major motor seizures of the clonic type are classified as having Jacksonian seizures. A typical Jacksonian seizure is one which initially manifests itself by clonic movements of one part of the body (the hand, for example) which rapidly spread to involve the entire one side of the body. The clonic movements then spread in a similar fashion on the other side of the body and finally terminate in a generalized convulsion of the grand mal type. During the interval that the convulsive movements are spreading over the body, the patient usually maintains consciousness. However, when the seizure becomes generalized, the patient falls into a state of unconsciousness, just as with other types of generalized major motor seizures. It has been our experience that true Jacksonian seizures are rarely encountered in children.

Petit Mal Seizures

Our investigations revealed that "true" petit mal epilepsy is a relatively uncommon type of epileptic disorder (Livingston, Torres, Pauli, & Rider, 1965). Of our total clinic population, only 2.3 percent suffered with this form of epilepsy.

The spells of petit mal epilepsy consist of paroxysmal periodic attacks of altered consciousness, usually lasting from 5 to 30 seconds. During a typical petit mal attack, the patient appears to be staring vacantly into space (staring spell). A characteristic feature of a petit mal spell is the absence of prodromal and postictal phenomena; the attack begins suddenly and terminates abruptly, and the patient is almost always able to continue whatever he had been

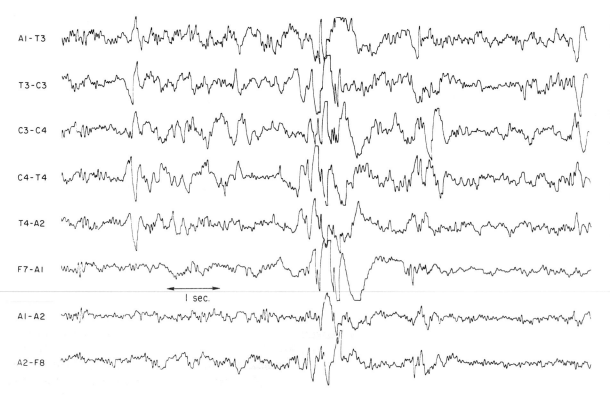

AI-T3

T3-C3

C3-C4

C4-T4

T4-A2

F7-AI

|◄————►| I sec.

AI-A2

A2-F8

Figure 8-1. EEG of a 7-year-old child with generalized major motor (grand mal) epilepsy. This sample of record was obtained during light sleep artificially induced by chloral hydrate. Note the short burst of spike-wave forms. The tracing revealed normal findings during the other three phases of the electroencephalogram (awake, voluntary hyperventilation, and intermittent photic stimulation).

doing before the onset of the spell. Occasionally, however, there are concurrent clinical aberrations such as slight clonic movements of the head or upper extremities, or both. The eyes occasionally "roll back into the head" during these spells. Sometimes there is smacking of the lips, chewing and swallowing movements, and mumbling speech. It is important to note that these latter clinical features are also encountered in many patients with psychomotor (temporal lobe) epilepsy. Occasionally, the patient may sway a little, but rarely falls, and in some instances, particularly in those patients

with prolonged spells, there may be urinary incontinence.

Petit mal epilepsy is primarily a disorder of childhood and seldom continues into adult life. It begins most commonly between 4 and 8 years of age and rarely commences much before 3 or after 15 years of age. Our studies strongly suggest that in some patients petit mal epilepsy disappears spontaneously in association with adolescence.

Petit mal spells recur daily, and some patients may have as many as 50 to 100 or more a day. Although these seizures may appear at any time of the day, many patients experience an increase in the frequency of spells during the first few hours after awakening.

Patients with petit mal epilepsy are prone to develop major seizures, particularly at the time of puberty. However, the occurrence of grand mal convulsions can be prevented in many cases by the administration of a major motor anticonvulsant such as phenobarbital (combined therapy). The subject of combined therapy for the treatment of petit mal epilepsy is presented in a subsequent section of this chapter.

Petit mal epilepsy shows a low prevalence among children with demonstrable evidence of brain damage at the onset of the disorder. It is a relatively benign disturbance and rarely causes pathological cerebral changes regardless of the frequency of the spells, except in those patients who have frequent attacks of petit mal status.

Petit mal spells can be precipitated in essentially all patients by voluntary hyperventilation. In sensitive patients, the spells usually appear after short periods of hyperventilation (1 to 2 minutes), and in other patients, it may be necessary to continue the hyperventilation for as long as 4 to 5 minutes in order to produce a spell.

The electroencephalographic abnormality of petit mal epilepsy is classical and consists of diffuse, bilaterally synchronous spike and wave forms recurring at frequencies of 2½ to 4 per second, but most commonly at a frequency of 3 per second (Figure 8-2).

Myoclonic Seizures

We classify childhood myoclonic epilepsy into two groups:

1. Myoclonic epilepsy of infancy (minor motor epilepsy, infantile spasms, hypsarhythmia). Attacks initially occur during the first year of life, most often between 3 and 6 months of age.

2. Myoclonic epilepsy of older children (Lennox syndrome, petit mal variant, modified hysarhythmia). Attacks commence after 2 years of age, most commonly between 3 and 5 years.

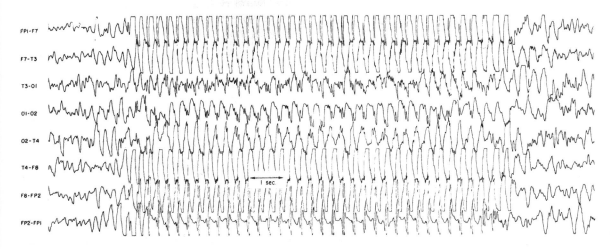

Figure 8-2. EEG of an 8-year-old child with petit mal epilepsy. This section of tracing was obtained during voluntary hyperventilation (2 minutes). Note the diffuse bilaterally synchronous classic three-per-second spike-wave discharge which lasted for approximately 11 seconds. The patient manifested a clinical petit mal spell during this period. The remainder of this patient's tracing revealed normal findings (resting state, sleep, and intermittent photic stimulation).

By and large, the clinical manifestations of myoclonic seizures vary, depending upon the posture of the patient:

1. Recumbent. They consist essentially of sudden flexion or extension of the head with simultaneous extension of the arms and flexion of the thighs on the abdomen. Such attacks in infants are frequently preceded or followed by a short laugh, cry, or giggle. Many patients with myoclonic seizures of this type have been referred to us with a diagnosis of infantile functional colic.

2. Sitting. They generally consist of a sudden jerk of the head, usually forward, with an associated jerk of the arms.

3. Standing. They consist of sudden, forceful contractions of the muscles of the neck and trunk, often followed by a violent fall forward or backward with injury usually to the head. Recurrent injury to the head is a major problem, but can be lessened somewhat by the wearing of protective headgear.

The seizures of myoclonic epilepsy almost always recur daily, and some patients have as many as 100 attacks per day. These spells frequently occur in the early morning hours, soon after awakening. While the duration of the individual seizure is exceedingly brief, usually lasting only a few seconds, myoclonic attacks, particularly in infants, frequently recur in series or clusters lasting 2 to 3 minutes.

As previously defined, we recognize two types of childhood myoclonic epilepsy; however, we question whether these two forms of epilepsy are not essentially the same and believe that the differences in prognosis are related to the age of the patient at the onset of the disorder. Prolonged follow-up studies of 1,300 patients (1,000 with myoclonic epilepsy of infancy and 300 with myoclonic epilepsy of older children) carried out in our clinic revealed that the earlier the onset

of myoclonic seizures, the worse the prognosis, particularly with regard to mental status and motor development.

The most serious hazard of childhood myoclonic epilepsy is not the seizures per se, but the associated mental retardation which is an almost universal finding in patients with this disorder. Livingston, Eisner, and Pauli (1958) reported an incidence of 96 percent mental retardation in a large group of patients with infantile myoclonic seizures. The degree of intellectual deficiency varied from mild to severe, but most patients were severely retarded (both mentally and physically). We have encountered only rare instances of patients with myoclonic epilepsy of infancy who, after prolonged follow-up study, exhibited normal intelligence.

We have not, as yet, completely evaluated the mental status of our 300 patients whose myoclonic seizures commenced later in childhood. However, our current data clearly indicate that most of these children manifest mental retardation, but are by no means as intellectually impaired as those whose myoclonic seizures appeared during infancy.

The electroencephalogram of patients with infantile myoclonic epilepsy almost invariably reveals abnormalities designated as hypsarhythmia (Figure 8-3), which consists of runs of high-voltage isolated spikes or short bursts of multiple spikes followed by high-amplitude slow waves. These abnormalities are diffuse and recur very frequently during the course of the record.

The electroencephalogram of patients with myoclonic epilepsy of older children reveals abnormalities which we classify as modified hypsarhythmia (Figure 8-4), which consists of bursts of irregular spikes and high-voltage slow waves in addition to hypsarhythmia.

It should be noted that many patients with childhood myoclonic epilepsy suffer concomitantly or subsequently with other types of sei-

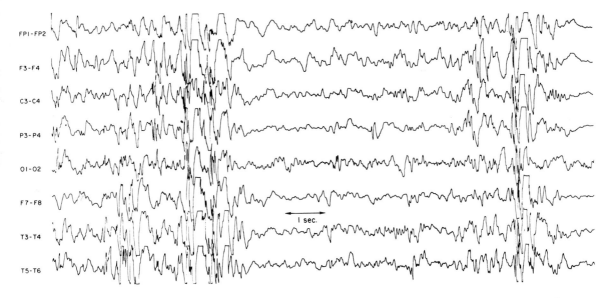

Figure 8-3.   EEG of a 7-month-old child with infantile myoclonic epilepsy (minor motor epilepsy, infantile spasms). Onset of myoclonic seizures was at 4 months of age. Because of patient's age, this EEG study could be carried out only during sleep induced by secobarbital (Seconal). Note the high-voltage diffuse fast spikes, followed by high-amplitude slow waves (hypsarhythmia). These electrical aberrations recurred at least once every 10 seconds during the entire tracing.

zures, particularly grand mal.   Our follow-up studies of a large group of patients revealed that the myoclonic aspects of their seizure disorder disappeared spontaneously in association with adolescence.

The following list presents the disorders considered to be the cause of brain damage in some of our patients with infantile myoclonic epilepsy. *Attention is directed to the fact that we were unable to elicit specific etiologic factors of brain damage in approximately 50 percent of our patients with infantile myoclonic epilepsy and in very few of our patients whose myoclonic epilepsy started later in childhood.*   Similar diagnostic experiences are reported by Jeavons and Bower (1964) in their excellent monograph on infantile spasms.

PRESUMPTIVE PREDISPOSING FACTORS IN SOME PATIENTS WITH INFANTILE MYOCLONIC EPILEPSY

Brain injuries associated with birth

Subdural hematoma (bilateral)

Congenital defects of cerebral development

Infections of the brain (e.g., meningitis, encephalitis)

Trauma not related to birth

Tuberous sclerosis

Toxoplasmosis

Phenylketonuria

Kernicterus

Postpertrussis immunization encephalopathy

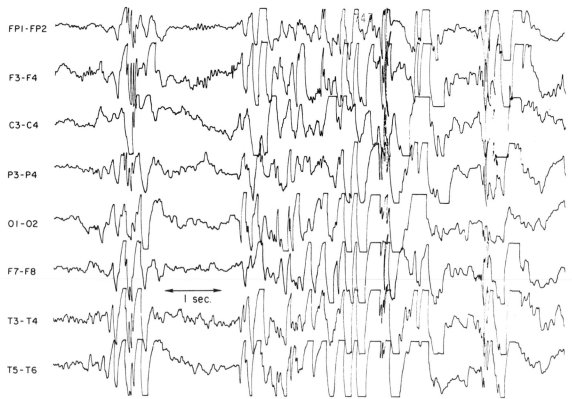

Figure 8-4. EEG of an 8-year-old child with childhood myoclonic epilepsy (Lennox syndrome, petit mal variant). Onset of myoclonic seizures was at 3 years of age. This record was obtained during sleep artificially induced by chloral hydrate. Note the very short bursts of diffuse fast spikes, followed by high-amplitude slow waves and bursts of irregular spikes and high-voltage slow waves lasting about 4½ seconds (modified hypsarhythmia). These electrical abnormalities were present in all leads and occurred during all phases of EEG examination (awake, voluntary hyperventilation, sleep, and intermittent photic stimulation). However, they were greatly accentuated during sleep.

Myoclonic seizures also occur in association with degenerative diseases, e.g., amaurotic familial idiocy of Tay-Sachs (lipidoses) and encephalitis periaxialis diffusa of Schilder, and in disorders such as subacute inclusion body encephalitis of Dawson (subacute sclerosing leucoencephalopathy).

Involuntary jerks of isolated muscles or muscle groups are occasionally observed in the intervals between and also just prior to major attacks in some patients with major motor epilepsy. We classify these spells as "benign" or "simple" myoclonic seizures.

Psychomotor (Temporal Lobe) Seizures

Psychomotor (temporal lobe) epilepsy may occur at any age; in our experience, however, it is encountered most frequently in the older child and adult.

The clinical manifestations of psychomotor

epilepsy vary considerably. In some patients, psychomotor seizures persist for only a moment or so, while in others they may continue for hours. They are most commonly characterized by automatic, stereotyped, bizarre motor movements or a variety of abnormal behavioral performances associated with some clouding of consciousness and at least partial amnesia for the event. Staring episodes with smacking of the lips, chewing movements, and mumbled speech simulating petit mal, and also very brief episodes of purposeless movements of the extremities with picking at the clothing, are common. Disturbances of sleep, such as somnambulism, night terrors, and nightmares, are also sometimes manifestations of psychomotor epilepsy.

In most patients, particularly the older child and adult, the electroencephalogram reveals epileptiform discharges, most commonly in the form of spikes (Figure 8-5), from the anterior temporal areas.

However, in other patients the electroencephalogram shows other types of electrical abnormalities or normal findings.

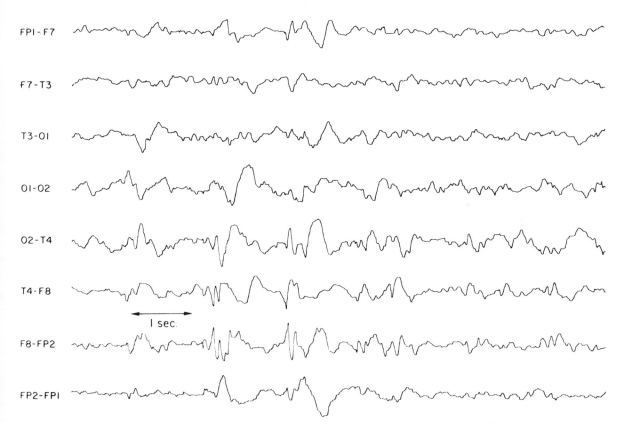

Figure 8-5. EEG of an 11-year-old child with psychomotor (or temporal lobe) epilepsy. This record was obtained during light sleep artificially induced by chloral hydrate. It shows spikes localized to the right anterior temporal area. The spikes were also observed during the awake state, but were more numerous during sleep.

NONCONVULSIVE EPILEPTIC EQUIVALENTS

Disturbances such as recurrent attacks of abdominal pain, headache, dizziness, "fainting," and other symptoms referable to the thalamic and hypothalamic areas of the brain may also be manifestations of an epileptic disorder (Livingston & Escala, 1967; Klinefelter, Greene, Pauli, & Livingston, in press; Lennox, 1960). When we consider these symptoms to be of epileptic origin, we classify them as nonconvulsive epileptic equivalents. These disorders are also designated by a variety of terms, such as *diencephalic epilepsy, autonomic epilepsy, thalamic epilepsy, hypothalamic epilepsy, epileptic equivalent, epileptic variant,* and *nonconvulsive epilepsy.*

We do not make a definite diagnosis of non-convulsive epileptic equivalent unless the electroencephalogram reveals abnormalities such as are seen in patients with overt epilepsy or the symptoms disappear with the administration of antiepileptic drup therapy.

THE FOURTEEN- AND SIX-PER-SECOND POSITIVE SPIKE DISCHARGE (FIGURE 8-6)

In our experience, this electrical discharge is seen in many patients who suffer with all types of clinical epileptic seizures and also in a significant number of persons who are considered "normal," but most commonly in individuals who present symptoms referable to the thalamic and hypothalamic areas of the brain. Many workers in the fields of epilepsy and electroencepha-

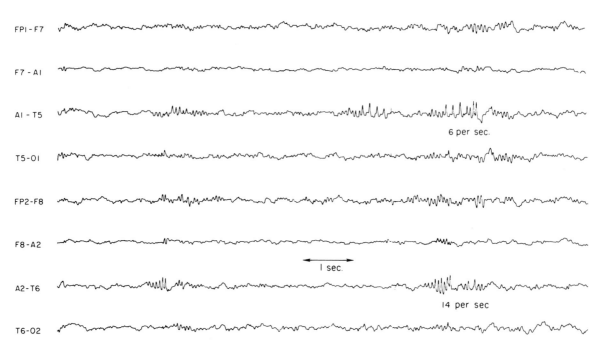

Figure 8-6. EEG of a 12-year-old normal child. No history of epilepsy or related disorders in the family. This record was obtained during light sleep artificially induced by chloral hydrate. Note the six-per-second and fourteen-per-second positive spike discharges.

lography believe that the exact clinical significance of the fourteen- and six-per-second positive spike discharge has not as yet been clearly established. We agree, and in our opinion many more extensive studies with adequate controls have to be carried out before one can definitely state that this electrical discharge is a manifestation of an epileptic disorder. The reader may refer to a previous publication for a detailed discussion of the fourteen- and six-per-second positive spike discharge (Livingston, 1963).

AURAS

An aura, or period of warning, is a disturbance which sometimes precedes an epileptic seizure. Actually, it is an integral part of the attack. Auras may be classified broadly into three groups: (1) sensory, (2) psychic, and (3) motor.

Sensory Auras

These auras may manifest themselves in the following forms: somatosensory, visual, auditory, vertiginous, or olfactory. Of these auras, the somatosensory is the most common in children. A frequent episode is described as "a peculiar sensation which starts in the abdomen (or epigastrium) and then goes up through the chest to the head."

Psychic Auras

Some children exhibit disturbances such as increased irritability or restlessness, fears, anxieties, marked fatigue, mental confusion or dullness, and various types of bizarre behavior for varying intervals before the onset of a frank seizure.

Motor Auras

Some children present muscular twitching or spasms of isolated muscles or muscle groups or a series of generalized myoclonic jerks prior to the onset of a major seizure.

An aura, particularly the sensory aura, is

usually of very short duration, generally lasting less than a minute. However, in some cases, the aura, especially the psychic one, may last for hours. Occasionally, the aura is not followed by the "full-blown" attack and may be the only manifestation of the convulsive episode. This is particularly true in some patients whose seizures have been partially controlled by anticonvulsant therapy.

Many patients, particularly the younger children, who were interrogated about this aspect of their symptomatology, could not give a definite description of such an episode. The following is a list of some of the auras described by our patients:

AURAS DESCRIBED BY SOME EPILEPTIC PATIENTS

A peculiar sensation which starts in the abdomen and then goes up to the chest and then to the head.

I just feel funny all over my body.

I feel different, but just can't describe the sensation.

Abdominal pain or abdominal distress.

Tingling, numbness, or pain in various parts of the body (mostly extremities).

Headaches.

A sensation of movements of the extremities which cannot be seen by the observer.

Spots before the eyes.

Various colors before the eyes.

Impaired vision.

A buzzing sensation.

Sounds of different types of music.

Dizziness or unsteadiness.

Peculiar or disagreeable tastes or odors.

An aura is of particular importance to the neurosurgeon in that it indicates the site of origin of the epileptic discharge. It is also of importance to the patient, since it provides warning of an impending seizure and, if of sufficient duration, enables the patient to protect himself from injury.

The prime value of a classification of any medical disorder, including epilepsy, is that it may serve as a guide to the treatment and prognosis of the disorder in question. Since it is known that the treatment and prognosis vary considerably with the different forms of epilepsy, it is important that one be cognizant of the current classifications of the epilepsies. Therefore, we call attention to the fact that some physicians employ the term *centrencephalic* to classify the clinical spell associated with the classic three-per-second spike and wave discharge. This is the type of spell which we designate as petit mal. Other physicians assign the term *centrencephalic* as a classification for those types of epileptic seizures, regardless of their clinical manifestations, in which spike and wave discharges of any frequency are demonstrated in the electroencephalogram.

Some physicians, particularly electroencephalographers, classify all forms of epilepsy as focal epilepsy in those patients in whom they are able to demonstrate a focal electrical abnormality, regardless of the clinical manifestations of the attack. Many physicians classify psychomotor attacks as focal epilepsy because most patients with this form of epilepsy present electroencephalographic abnormalities, usually spikes, limited to the anterior temporal area of the brain. Other physicians designate clinical generalized major motor epilepsy as focal epilepsy when the electroencephalogram shows unilateral electroencephalographic discharges.

PROLONGED SEIZURE ACTIVITY

A universally accepted definition of *status epilepticus* in the medical literature is lacking, and the interpretation of this term varies from clinic to clinic and from physician to physician. Many authors utilize this designation to refer to a series of recurrent major seizures; others, however, include all types of "prolonged seizure activity" in this classification. Obviously, such nosologic inconsistency has led to pronounced differences of opinion regarding the etiologic, therapeutic, and prognostic aspects of this type of epileptic disturbance.

In our clinic, we employ the term *prolonged seizure activity* to designate epileptic manifestations of long duration, as follows:

Status epilepticus
  Major motor (grand mal) status
  Petit mal status
  Myoclonic status
  Psychomotor status
Prolonged major motor (grand mal) seizure

Major motor grand mal status refers to a state of recurrent major motor seizures between which the patient does not completely regain consciousness. This disorder may continue for 4 or 5 days or even longer.

Petit mal status refers to a state of recurring, almost continuous petit mal spells, during which the patient frequently appears disoriented and confused, but is usually able to walk about and function to the extent that he generally can take medication and nourishment by mouth.

Myoclonic status refers to a state of recurring myoclonic attacks. It is observed in some patients just prior to the onset of a major motor seizure, in patients with myoclonic epilepsy, and most commonly in patients with cerebral degenerative and related diseases.

Generally, *psychomotor status* refers to seizures of relatively short duration; however, we have encountered some patients with psychomotor epilepsy whose attacks persisted for hours. There are also reports of patients who suffered with attacks of amnesia thought to be of epileptic origin that lasted for periods of from several days to as long as 30 days (Gastaut & Vigouroux, 1958).

A prolonged major motor convulsion can occur in association with infections of the brain such as meningitis and encephalitis and also in epilepsy. A *prolonged major motor convulsion* refers to a seizure in which the active stages, generally the clonic aspects, are of long duration. The prolonged clonic features are followed by a postconclusive state of extended duration. The difference between this condition and major motor status epilepticus is that in the former, the patient does not experience a recurrence of the tonic-clonic aspects after termination of the seizure.

Major motor (grand mal) status epilepticus should always be considered a medical emergency. It is difficult to treat, may be lethal, and at times is the cause of irreversible cerebral damage. The reader may refer to a previous writing (Livingston, 1968c) for our methods of treatment of grand mal status and other types of prolonged seizure activity.

TREATMENT OF EPILEPSY

General Principles of Drug Therapy

1. Patient and parental cooperation is important and can be obtained best by understanding the disorder of epilepsy. At the time of the initial visit the physician should explain in simple terms the nature of the disorder of epilepsy to the patient and/or his parents. He should emphasize what the person with epilepsy "can do" and also what he "should not do," e.g., operate a motor vehicle until he has fulfilled the medicolegal requirements of his respective state department of motor vehicles or prepare himself for a vocation or profession which is not suitable for individuals with seizures. The reader may refer to previous writings (Barrow & Fabing, 1966; Livingston,

1963, 1965) for comprehensive discussions relative to these socioeconomic considerations.

Obviously, the ideal goal in every case of epilepsy is to control the seizures completely or at least reduce their frequency to the extent that they do not interfere with the patient's general well-being. The physician should tell the patient and/or his parents that with understanding, cooperation, and proper treatment this desired goal can be attained in the vast majority of individuals afflicted with epilepsy. He should emphasize the importance of taking medication regularly and precisely as prescribed.

In many instances, the physician can lessen the likelihood of a patient's becoming discouraged relative to seizure control by informing him of the fact that it may take a period of time before effective therapy can be determined in any given case. He should tell the patient that antiepileptic medication must be prescribed in a systematic manner: in some patients, the appropriate therapy can be ascertained after a short trial on one drug, and then again in others, it may take a longer time to determine the proper treatment since several drugs may have to be prescribed either individually or in combination before the proper therapeutic regimen is established.

It is of the utmost importance that the physician inform the patient of untoward reactions which may be caused by certain drugs, such as morbilliform rashes or diplopia by diphenylhydantoin sodium (Dilantin) and marked drowsiness by primidone (Mysoline), particularly during the first few weeks of therapy. Of course, the physician definitely should not "frighten" the patient by calling attention to serious disturbances which have occurred on rare occasions in association with the administration of antiepileptic drugs.

2. Regular medical care (routine follow-up visits) is one of the most vital aspects of treatment. During the first year or so of treatment, the physician should see the patient at regular intervals in order to regulate the dosage of his medication, to examine him for untoward drug reactions, and to discuss socioeconomic problems when present. The various untoward reactions to antiepileptic drugs, together with methods for their prevention, detection, and treatment, and the management of pertinent socioeconomic difficulties with which many epileptics are confronted are presented in other writings (Livingston, 1963, 1966a, 1966b, 1968b).

He also should examine the patient for signs or symptoms of a specific cause of the seizure disorder which may have been overlooked or were not present at the time of the initial visit.

It is our general policy to have each patient return in 2 to 3 weeks after the initial administration of a drug, primarily to determine his tolerance to the prescribed dosage. The frequency of the return visits depends on the magnitude of his problems. We see every patient at least once every 6 months during the entire time he is taking anticonvulsant medication; this policy includes those who have been rendered free of seizures.

3. Laboratory examinations should be carried out during the course of therapy with certain drugs. Periodic blood, renal, and liver function tests should be performed on all patients receiving those drugs which are known to have adversely affected the hematopoietic, renal, or hepatic system, such as mephenytoin (Mesantoin), primidone (Mysoline), paramethadione (Paradione), phenacemide (Phenurone), trimethadione (Tridione), and ethosuximide (Zarontin). These examinations should be carried out before the patient is started on such drugs and repeated during the entire course of therapy. In our clinic, we repeat these tests monthly during the first year of therapy and subsequently at 2- to 3-month intervals.

The patient or his parents should be instructed to report promptly any sign or symptom which was not present before the drug was prescribed and should be specifically directed to notify the physician immediately of signs or symptoms indicative of possible damage to the hematopoietic system (e.g., easy bruising, petechiae, ecchymosis, or epistaxis), to the renal system (e.g., hematuria or edema), or to the hepatic system (e.g., jaundice, dark urine, or clay-colored stools).

4. Treatment should be instituted as soon as a diagnosis has been established. Early institution of treatment is important for the following reasons: First, in most cases, the degree of success in the control of seizures bears a direct relation to the duration of the epilepsy—the longer the duration, the less likely it is that a satisfactory result will be obtained; second, it is important to institute measures to prevent a recurrence of seizures, not only because of the seizures themselves, but also because of injuries, brain damage, and emotional disorders which are sometimes associated with the occurrence of seizures.

The problem of whether or not the physician should assign a diagnosis of epilepsy to an individual who suffers a seizure of undetermined etiology and in whom the electroencephalographic examination revealed normal findings remains controversial. We make a tentative diagnosis of epilepsy in such instances and continue with this diagnosis unless the passage of time proves that the seizure was a manifestation of some other disorder. We would like to reemphasize the fact that such patients should be observed very closely for a prolonged period of time for signs or symptoms of a specific cause of the seizure disorder, particularly an intracranial neoplasm.

Our general policy is to prescribe daily medication to patients with one seizure of undetermined cause in essentially the same manner as to those who have experienced recurrent epileptic seizures (Livingston, 1960). We do not utilize this plan of treatment, however, in infants and young children whose first convulsion was of the type which we classify as a simple febrile convulsion. Our plan of therapy for these patients is presented in previous publications (Livingston, 1964a, 1968a).

5. The selection of the drug of first choice for the treatment of any case of epilepsy should be based on the toxicity of the drug and the type of seizure. It is generally agreed that phenobarbital, primidone, and diphenylhydantoin sodium possess significant anticonvulsant properties and are of considerable value in controlling major motor (grand mal) seizures. Our drug of first choice for the treatment of major motor epilepsy is phenobarbital because the toxic reactions associated with its usage are singularly few. When this drug is properly administered, the only major side effects are drowsiness, which is generally dose-related, and hyperactivity simulating the hyperkinetic syndrome, which is not dose-related and is encountered primarily in children. These reactions are not serious, and both are reversible. Diphenylhydantoin sodium is our third choice because the number of adverse reactions which have been observed in association with its usage is considerable (Livingston, 1966a). Some of these side reactions are frequent and disturbing, e.g., gingival hyperplasia; some are irreversible, e.g., hypertrichosis; and others may constitute an actual threat to the patient's life and have, on occasion, terminated fatally, e.g., Stevens-Johnson syndrome, hematopoietic disturbances, and hepatitis with exfoliative dermatitis.

It is true that diphenylhydantoin sodium is currently employed by many physicians as the drug of first choice for grand mal epilepsy (Livingston, 1968d). We would like to direct attention to the fact that in addition to the numerous toxic effects of this drug, there are no reports in the literature of controlled studies which demonstrate that diphenylhydantoin sodium is superior to phenobarbital in the treatment of major motor epilepsy.

In our clinic the use of diphenylhydantoin sodium as the drug of first choice for the control of grand mal seizures is specifically contraindicated in two types of patients for the reasons given below.

Infants. The recognition of diphenylhydantoin intoxication due to overdosage is frequently exceedingly difficult in infants. Ataxia and/or diplopia is the usual initial sign or symptom that the maximal tolerable dosage of this drug has been surpassed. It is obvious that, for example, a 16-month-old child with grand mal epilepsy who is receiving diphenylhydantoin sodium would be unable to describe diplopia to the physician. Also, if this child was just beginning to walk and presented unsteadiness of gait, one might have considerable difficulty in determining whether the unsteadiness was a manifestation of diphenylhydantoin overdosage or was due merely to the fact that the child had not yet mastered the walking technique.

Females, particularly adolescents. It is needless to state that gingival hyperplasia and hypertrichosis of any degree are cosmetically unattractive in any person.

Diphenylhydantoin gingival hyperplasia occurs much more frequently in the younger individual than in the adult. On the basis of observations made in our clinic, we estimate the incidence of this disturbance to be at least 40 percent (Livingston & Livingston, in press), a figure approximating those reported by Babcock (1965) and Panuska, Gorlin, Bearman, and Mitchell (1961).

We have been called upon many times to change the antiepileptic regimen in individuals who had been rendered seizure free with diphenylhydantoin sodium but in whom the drug produced marked gingival hyperplasia. These patients, mostly adolescent females, stated that they would rather have seizures than suffer the embarrassment and emotional distress caused by the "swollen gums." In addition, pronounced hyperplasia frequently causes displacement of the teeth, which is also aesthetically objectionable and necessitates extensive orthodontic and periodontic procedures in many instances.

Hypertrichosis is encountered in approximately 5 percent of patients receiving diphenylhydantoin sodium. When this reaction is marked and occurs on exposed surfaces, it presents a very serious cosmetic problem, particularly in females. It has been our experience that the abnormal growth of hair persists, at least to some degree, in all patients after discontinuance of diphenylhydantoin sodium.

Attention is directed to the fact that some drugs are effective in controlling certain types of epileptic seizures, and, on the other hand, these same drugs often increase the frequency of other types of epileptic seizures. For example, diphenylhydantoin sodium is of value in the control of psychomotor seizures in some patients, but often increases the frequency of petit mal spells. Similarly, trimethadione is an efficacious agent for controlling petit mal attacks, but sometimes precipitates major seizures or increases the frequency of preexisting major motor seizures. Table 8-3 lists the drugs in order of our preference for the treatment of various types of epileptic seizures.

It is generally known that many patients who suffer with pure petit mal epilepsy subsequently develop other types of epileptic seizures, particularly grand mal attacks. On the basis of findings which are presented in a recent publication (Livingston et al., 1965), we recommend the following therapeutic regimen for the treatment of patients with pure petit mal epilepsy.

TABLE 8-3   DRUGS USED FOR CONTROL OF VARIOUS FORMS OF EPILEPSY*

Major Motor (Grand Mal)	Petit Mal	Psychomotor (Temporal Lobe)	Myoclonic	Nonconvulsive Epileptic Equivalent
Phenobarbital	Zarontin	Mysoline	Valium	Same drugs as listed for major motor (grand mal) epilepsy
Mysoline	Tridione	Phenobarbital	ACTH and Corticosteroids (for infants)	
Dilantin	Paradione	Dilantin		
Bromide (for young children)	Celontin	Mebaral		
Mebaral	Milontin	Peganone		
Peganone	Dexedrine			
Gemonil	Diamox	Gemonil		
Diamox (for menstrual seizures)	Atabrine	Mesantoin		
Mesantoin	Phenurone			

* Arranged in order of our preference, based on relative efficacy and toxicity.

Treatment should be started with the conventional dosage of phenobarbital. It is important to note that this drug is prescribed as a prophylactic measure against the development of grand mal seizures and not for the purpose of controlling the petit mal spells. Treatment should be continued with phenobarbital alone for approximately one month, during which time the physician will have the opportunity to determine the patient's tolerance to the prescribed dosage and also to ascertain whether it adversely affects the frequency of the patient's petit mal spells. In the event that the patient does not tolerate this drug satisfactorily, another major motor anticonvulsant such as primidone or mephobarbital (Mebaral) should be prescribed. Since diphenylhydantoin sodium often increases the frequency of petit mal spells, we give this drug as the major motor anticonvulsant only as a last choice.

It has been our experience that petit mal spells are occasionally controlled with phenobarbital, and, obviously, in such instances this drug should be continued as the sole therapeutic agent.

After the patient's tolerance to the major motor anticonvulsant has been determined, a specific anti-petit mal agent should be added to the therapeutic regimen. Our anti-petit mal drugs of choice are ethosuximide and trimethadione, in that order of preference. In the event that the petit mal spells do not respond to these drugs, the physician has no alternative but to prescribe less effective anti-petit mal medications (Table 8-3).

The medication should be continued in full dosage until the patient has been free of clinical petit mal spells for at least 4 years and an electroencephalographic examination performed after this period of freedom from spells does not reveal the classic electroencephalographic discharge of petit mal epilepsy.

We withdraw the anti–petit mal agent gradually over an interval of 6 to 12 months, depending upon the amount of medication the patient had been taking. Since the peak incidence of the development of major convulsions in our group of patients was between 10 and 13 years of age (Livingston et al., 1965), it is important that all patients receive the full dosage of the prophylactic major motor anticonvulsant until they reach 14 years of age. In seizure-free patients, the major motor anticonvulsant should then be withdrawn gradually over the course of the subsequent year.

6. The dosage of anticonvulsant medication varies from patient to patient. The proper dosage of antiepileptic medication for any given patient is that which controls his seizures without producing untoward reactions that interfere with his well-being. Obviously, the ideal goal in the treatment of epilepsy is to attain complete control of seizures. However, the drug dosage necessary for complete control of seizures may, in some patients, produce unpleasant reactions, such as drowsiness, which are more of a handicap to the patient than the seizures themselves. Some patients may be better off leading a normal life between occasional seizures than living seizure-free in a perpetual state of drug-induced drowsiness and confusion. The dosages of the various antiepileptic drugs employed in our clinic are presented in Table 8-4.

In many instances, reactions such as drowsiness can be alleviated somewhat by the daily administration of stimulating drugs, such as dextroamphetamine sulfate (Dexedrine), methamphetamine hydrochloride (Desoxyn), or methylphenidate hydrochloride (Ritalin).

7. Treatment should be started with one drug. Other drugs should be prescribed, if necessary, only after it has been determined that the maximal tolerated dosage of the initial drug failed to produce a satisfactory clinical response. In those patients who suffer with relatively infre-

TABLE 8-4   DOSAGES OF ANTIEPILEPTIC DRUGS*

Drug	Age, Yr.	Starting Dosage		Maximum Dosage	
		Mg	Times/Day	Mg	Times/Day
Bromides	Under 6	320	2	640	3
	Over 6	320	3	1,000	3
Phenobarbital	Under 6	16	3	48	3
	Over 6	32	3	65	3
Mebaral	Under 6	32	3	130	3
	Over 6	65	3	200	3
Gemonil	Under 6	50	3	100	3
	Over 6	100	3	200	3
Mysoline	Under 6	50	3	250	4
	Over 6	125	3	500	3
Dilantin	Under 6	30	3	100	3
	Over 6	100	2	100	4
Mesantoin	Under 6	50	3	200	3
	Over 6	100	3	400	3
Peganone	Under 6	250	3	750	4
	Over 6	500	3	1,000	4
Dexedrine	Under 6	2.5	1	2.5	3
	Over 6	2.5	2	7.5	3
Paradione	Under 6	150	2	300	3
	Over 6	300	2	600	3
Tridione	Under 6	150	2	300	3
	Over 6	300	2	600	3
Milontin	Under 6	250	2	500	3
	Over 6	500	2	1,000	4
Celontin	Under 6	150	3	300	4
	Over 6	300	2	600	4
Zarontin	Under 6	250	2	250	4
	Over 6	250	3	500	4
Diamox	Under 6	125	3	250	3
	Over 6	250	2	250	4
Phenurone	Under 6	250	3	1,000	3
	Over 6	500	3	2,000	3

ACTH and corticosteroids †

Valium ‡

*This table includes only those antiepileptic drugs which are used in our clinic.

quent seizures (monthly or less often), the conventional starting dosage of the appropriate drug should be prescribed initially. The dosage should be increased gradually, if necessary, until a satisfactory control of seizures is attained or until the limit of tolerance for the drug has been reached. In some cases it may be necessary to prescribe a second drug, but this should not be done until after it has been determined that the maximal tolerated dosage of the first drug failed to produce a satisfactory clinical response. If the maximal tolerated dosage of the first drug fails to control the seizures satisfactorily, but does reduce the frequency or severity to some extent, it should be continued at the same dosage, and a second drug should be added to the therapeutic regimen. The dosage of the second drug should be increased as needed to tolerance. However, if the maximal tolerated dosage of the first drug fails to help the patient in any manner, it should be gradually withdrawn simultaneously with the administration of the second drug. If during the process of withdrawal of the first drug and the addition of the second drug a satisfactory combination of dosages of both drugs is found, then the patient should continue with both drugs. Occasionally, it may be necessary to prescribe the maximal tolerated dosage of more than two drugs in order to obtain good control of seizures.

For patients who suffer with relatively frequent (daily or weekly) seizures, the average maximum dosage should be prescribed initially. This dosage should be decreased or increased, if necessary, depending upon the patient's tolerance and the occurrence of the seizures. Other drugs should be added to the therapeutic regimen, if necessary, as previously described.

8. The medication should be taken daily in divided dosages at times of the day which do not interfere with the patient's routine activities, such as with meals, upon returning home from school, and at bedtime. Generally, we recommend that the total daily dose of antiepileptic medication be administered in two to four equal parts throughout the course of the day. However, in the treatment of certain types of epileptic seizures, such as those occurring in association with sleep or the menses, it is frequently of value to administer the medication in a different manner. Our methods for prescribing antiepileptic drugs in such instances are described under "Precipitating Factors of Epileptic Seizures."

Within recent years several investigators have advocated prescribing the total daily dosage of antiepileptic drugs such as phenobarbital and diphenylhydantoin sodium at bedtime. We are not cognizant of controlled studies which have proved that the administration of antiepileptic medication in this manner is superior to, or even as effective as, administration in divided doses throughout the day. Also, Svensmark and Buchthal (1964) have demonstrated that the maintenance of constant serum concentrations of phenobarbital and diphenylhydantoin in children requires the administration of these drugs in divided doses throughout the day.

We can cite two difficulties which we have

---

† The patient should receive a daily intramuscular injection of twenty-five to thirty units of corticotropin (Achar Gel) for a period of 4 to 6 weeks, depending upon seizure response.

If there is no clinical response to six weeks of ACTH therapy, the patient may be given a trial on steroid therapy, administered daily for a period of at least 2 to 3 months. It is important to note that steroid therapy should be discontinued gradually.

‡ In our clinic, we start treatment with Valium in the younger child with 1 mg every 3 hours for five doses daily, and in the older child with 2 mg every 3 hours for five doses daily. The maximum dosage we have employed in the younger child is 25 mg daily, and in the older child, 50 mg daily. Valium in dosages of 2.5 to 10 mg administered intravenously slowly over a period of 1 to 10 minutes is exceedingly effective in controlling prolonged seizure activity [major motor (grand mal) status, myoclonic status, prolonged major motor convulsion] in some patients. This dosage may be repeated in 20 minutes if necessary.

encountered in some of our patients who received the total daily dosage of their medication at bedtime:

a. Some were so drowsy and sleepy that they were unable to perform their routine activities for the greater part of the following morning.

b. Others either forgot or neglected to take their medication at bedtime and experienced a recurrence of seizures the following afternoon or evening. These patients had received no antiepileptic medication for almost 48 hours.

9. The medication should be taken for a prolonged period of time. By and large, it has been our experience that the longer anticonvulsant medication is continued in epileptic patients, the less likely it is that they will experience a recurrence of seizures after therapy has been terminated.

It is our general policy to continue effective and well-tolerated antiepileptic medication in all patients in full dosage for at least 4 years after the time of the last seizure, plus an additional 1 or 2 years, during which time the medication is gradually withdrawn (see principle 10). We do make exceptions, however, to this general plan of duration of therapy, some of which are discussed below.

Shorter periods of therapy. It is needless to state that a drug should be discontinued immediately in patients in whom there is even suggestive evidence that it is causing serious untoward reactions. The physician also should consider withdrawal of medication sooner than the 4-year period (1) in those patients in whom there is an indication that the medication is causing a reaction, regardless of its severity, such as drowsiness, which interferes with the performance of the patient's general duties (scholastic or employment) to his fullest potential and (2) in those patients in whom there is evidence that the taking of the medication per se is causing emotional

difficulties. Many patients, particularly teen-agers, have told us that they "just don't want to be bothered taking medicine every day," that the taking of medication makes them "feel different from their friends," and so forth.

Longer than four year. The onset of puberty, particularly in females, is a time of life when epilepsy frequently makes its initial appearance and also when many controlled epileptics experience a recurrence of seizures. If the 4-year period of freedom from seizures should coincide with the usual age of onset of puberty, the medication should be continued in full dosage throughout the adolescent period.

10. The medication should be discontinued very gradually. A sudden withdrawal of anticonvulsant medication, particularly phenobarbital, is a frequent cause of a recurrence of seizures or grand mal status. Therefore, when the physician decides to withdraw anticonvulsant medication in a patient who has been rendered seizure-free, he should reduce the dosage of the medication very gradually.

The period necessary for complete withdrawal is governed by the severity of the patient's previous seizure state and also by the dosage of the medication which the patient has been taking. In those patients who had suffered with a "mild form of epilepsy" which was controlled by an average dosage of medication, we generally withdraw the medication by a gradual reduction of the dosage over a period of 1 to 2 years. In those patients who had suffered with severe epilepsy and were taking large amounts of medication, we extend the period of withdrawal of medication to 3 or 4 years. It should be noted that we generally withdraw anti-petit mal drugs over a period of 6 to 12 months, as previously described.

If there should be a recurrence of seizures during or subsequent to the period of withdrawal, the patient should be restarted immediately on the same dosage of medication which had previously controlled the seizures, and the physician should consider continuing this medication in full dosage for the rest of the patient's life.

In our clinic we rarely, if ever, utilize information obtained from an EEG examination as a complete indicator of a patient's progress, except in those patients who have petit mal epilepsy. In this latter form of epilepsy, there is a close relationship between normalization of the EEG (absence of the classic bilaterally synchronous spike-wave discharge) and the disappearance of clinical petit mal spells. It has been our experience, however, that many of these patients continue to show other electrical aberrations for many years despite the fact that they have remained free of clinical petit mal spells.

Over the past 25 years or so we have performed yearly EEGs on thousands of epileptic patients, and except for the previously cited relationship of clinical petit mal epilepsy to the classic petit mal electrical discharge, we have not observed a direct relationship between normalization of the EEG and clinical improvement. In many of our patients the EEG became more abnormal even though the patient had fewer or no seizures; in others, the EEG continued to reveal abnormalities in spite of the fact that the patient had remained free of seizures for a period of years. Attention is called to the fact that in many children, the EEG tends to revert to normal during adolescence, regardless of their clinical progress (Livingston, 1962).

Antiepileptic Drugs

Prior to the introduction of diphenylhydantoin sodium by Merritt and Putnam (1938) in 1938, the only antiepileptic drugs of value were bromide and phenobarbital. In the past 25 years, however, a number of new anticonvulsant drugs have been synthesized and successfully employed in the treatment of epileptic seizures. Table 8-3 lists our choice of anticonvulsant drugs for the treatment of various types of epileptic seizures, and Table 8-4 gives the dosages employed at The Johns Hopkins Hospital Epilepsy Clinic. Table 8-5 presents untoward reactions which have been observed in association with the administration of antiepileptic drugs in our clinic and/or reported with sufficient frequency in the literature to incriminate the respective medication as causally related. The interested reader may refer to a previous publication (Livingston, 1966a) for details of these reactions and also for the methods employed in their prevention, detection, and management.

Experimental Drugs

The following drugs are currently being evaluated in our clinic for the control of epileptic seizures:

Tegretol (Carbamazepine)
Conadil; ospolot (Sulthiame)
Co-Ord (Albutoin)

Tegretol (Carbamazepine). This drug is exceedingly effective in the control of psychomotor (temporal lobe) seizures (Livingston, Villamater, Sakata, & Pauli, 1967). The significant side reactions which have been observed with this drug are visual disturbances (diplopia or blurring of vision) and hematopoietic disturbances (aplastic anemia, thrombocytopenia). Several fatal hematopoietic disturbances have occured in association with the administration of Tegretol.

Conadil; ospolot (Sulthiame). This drug has proved to be of value in controlling psychomotor and major motor seizures (Livingston, Villamater, & Sakata, 1967). The major untoward reactions observed in our patients were tachypnea and loss of weight. Paresthesias and a case of renal damage have been reported by other investigators.

TABLE 8-5   UNTOWARD REACTIONS OBSERVED IN ASSOCIATION WITH THE ADMINISTRATION OF ANTIEPILEPTIC DRUGS

Drug	*Reaction*
Barbiturates and related drugs:	
Phenobarbital	Drowsiness; excitability; hyperactivity; impairment of speech (dysarthriclike); malignant lymphoma (?); skin rashes (rare); Stevens-Johnson syndrome (rare)
Mebaral	Similar to phenobarbital, but usually less severe and less frequent
Gemonil	Similar to phenobarbital, but usually less severe and less frequent
Mysoline	Abdominal pain; alopecia; ataxia; diplopia; dizziness; drowsiness; dysarthria; edema of eyelids; headaches; leukopenia; lymphadenopathy (clinically and pathologically simulating malignant lymphomas); malignant lymphoma (?); megaloblastic anemia; nausea; nystagmus; painful gums; personality changes; psychoses; skin rashes (morbilliform); vomiting
Hydantoinates:	
Dilantin	Abdominal pain; agranulocytosis; albuminuria; alopecia; anorexia; aplastic anemia (?); behavioral disturbances; constipation; diplopia; disturbed equilibrium; dizziness; drowsiness; dysarthria; eosinophilia; erythroid aplasia; exfoliative dermatitis; granulocytopenia; headaches; hematoporphyrinuria; hematuria; hepatitis; hyperplasia of gums; hypertrichosis; increases frequency of petit mal spells in some patients; leukopenia; lymphadenopathy (clinically and pathologically simulating malignant lymphomas); macrocytosis; malignant lymphoma; megaloblastic anemia; myocardial damage; nausea; nystagmus; pancytopenia; periarteritis nodosa; pigmentation of the skin; polyarthropathy; psychotic disturbances; pulmonary abnormalities (reported by one physician, but not substantiated by other investigations); purpuric (nonthrombocytopenic) rashes; skin rashes (measleslike and scarlatiniform frequently associated with lymphadenopathy and leukopenia); Stevens-Johnson syndrome; systemic lupus erythematosus; thrombocytopenia; thrombocytopenic purpura; toxic amblyopia; tremors; urticarial rashes; vomiting
Mesantoin	Agranulocytosis; albuminuria (transient); aplastic anemia; ataxia; constipation; diplopia; drowsiness; dysarthria; exfoliative dermatitis; fatal dermatitides; hepatitis; hyperplasia of gums (rare); leukopenia; lymphadenopathy (clinically and pathologically simulating malignant lymphomas); megaloblastic anemia; mental confusion; nausea; nystagmus; pancytopenia; periarteritis nodosa; pigmentation of the skin; polyarthropathy; psychoses; purpuric rashes (associated with thrombocytopenia); skin rashes (measleslike and scarlatiniform); Stevens-Johnson syndrome; systemic lupus erythematosus; thrombocytopenia; vomiting
Peganone	Anorexia; ataxia; depression; diplopia; dizziness; drowsiness; epigastric distress; headaches; lymphadenopathy (clinically and pathologically simulating malignant lymphomas); nausea; nystagmus; skin rashes; vomiting

TABLE 8-5   UNTOWARD REACTIONS OBSERVED IN ASSOCIATION WITH THE ADMINISTRATION OF ANTIEPILEPTIC DRUGS *(Continued)*

Drug	*Reaction*
Succinimides:	
Celontin	Aplastic anemia; ataxia; diaphoresis; diplopia; dizziness; drowsiness; eosinophilia; fever; gastrointestinal disturbances; headaches; hiccups; kidney damage; leukopenia; liver damage; malignant lymphoma (?); monocytosis; personality changes; psychiatric disturbances; skin eruptions
Milontin	Aplastic anemia (?); drowsiness; granulocytopenia; hematuria (microscopic); leukopenia; megaloblastic anemia; nausea; skin eruptions; vomiting
Zarontin	Agranulocytosis; aplastic anemia; dizziness; drowsiness; eosinophilia; gastric distress; headaches; leukopenia; nausea; pancytopenia; psychiatric disturbances; skin rashes; sleep disturbances; systemic lupus erythematosus; thrombocytopenia
Oxazolidinediones:	
Tridione	Abdominal pain; agranulocytosis; albuminuria; alopecia; angioneurotic edema; aplastic anemia; behavioral disturbances; diplopia; drowsiness; eosinophilia; exfoliative dermatitis; headaches; hematuria; hemeralopia (photophobia); hepatitis; hiccups; hypoplastic anemia; increased irritability; leukopenia; lymphadenopathy (clinically and pathologically simulating malignant lymphomas); myasthenia gravislike syndrome; nausea; nephrosis; painful and swollen joints with fever; pancytopenia; personality changes; precipitates initial grand mal seizure or aggrevates preexisting grand mal in some patients; skin rashes (morbilliform and urticarial); Stevens-Johnson syndrome; systemic lupus erythematosus; thrombocytopenia; vertigo; vomiting
Paradione	Marked drowsiness—very frequent; otherwise, similar to Tridione, but usually less severe and less frequent
Phenurone	Adverse change in personality and behavior; deaths from hematopoïetic, genitourinary, and hepatic disturbances

Our experience with Co-Ord at the time of this writing was too limited to allow us to evaluate its efficacy and toxicity adequately.

Miscellaneous Drugs

The following drugs are employed primarily in the treatment of other conditions, but have been found to be quite helpful in some patients with epilepsy: acetazolamide (Diamox), ACTH and corticosteroids, chlordiazepoxide hydrochloride (Librium), dextroamphetamine sulfate (Dexedrine), diazepam (Valium), pyridoxine (Hexa-Betalin, Hexavibex), and quinacrine (Atabrine). Attention is directed to the fact that diazepam (Valium) administered intravenously is exceedingly effective in the control of prolonged seizure activity in some patients. The reader may refer to a previous publication (Livingston, 1966a) for details relative to the dosages and toxicity of these drugs.

THE KETOGENIC DIET REGIMEN

The ketogenic diet was first introduced by Wilder (1921) in 1921 as a treatment for epilepsy. Subsequently, Peterman (1925), Talbot (1930), Wilkins (1937), Bridge (1949), Keith (1963), Dekaban (1966), and others confirmed the beneficial effect of this diet in controlling epileptic seizures. In 1958, we reported excellent seizure control in a large group of patients treated with this regimen and, as of the present, have employed this form of therapy in approximately one thousand patients (Livingston, 1958).

We are, however, impressed with the fact that this type of therapy is not utilized by many physicians who specialize in convulsive disorders. Many of them have expressed the opinion that the ketogenic diet is too rigid a form of therapy, too unpalatable, too difficult to prepare and maintain, much less effective than drug therapy, and generally "not worth all the effort." On the basis of our experience with the ketogenic diet regimen during the past 33 years, we are convinced that these opinions are definitely untrue and unwarranted.

The ketogenic diet is most effective in children between the ages of 2 and 5 years. Favorable results are occasionally obtained in patients between 5 and 8 years of age, but in children older than 8 years, this diet is rarely successful.

There is no absolute relationship between the type of seizure and the likelihood of a satisfactory response to the ketogenic diet. However, we have obtained our best results in the control of myoclonic seizures. In our experience, the ketogenic diet is essentially ineffective in the treatment of petit mal epilepsy.

The feasibility of prescribing the ketogenic diet is governed more by the circumstances within the home than by any other factor. To be effective, this regimen must be rigidly controlled and should not be attempted unless both the patient and his parents are able to cooperate satisfactorily. The parents must be at least moderately intelligent and realize the importance of maintaining the diet and adhering to it steadfastly. Once started, the diet must be followed closely, or its entire beneficial effect is lost. Some children with pronounced dietary likes and dislikes may find it difficult to eat the large amounts of fatty foods contained in the ketogenic diet; therefore, it should not be prescribed if feeding difficulties are anticipated.

The mechanism of action of the ketogenic diet in controlling epileptic seizures is not clearly understood. Most investigators have equated the beneficial results with one or a combination of the physiological effects of acidosis, ketosis, and dehydration. Dekaban (1966) reported that ". . . elevation of various plasma partitioned lipids and of the total lipids appears to parallel the improvement in the control of seizures and is considered to be a good index in predicting the extent of the control of epileptic attacks in children."

It is of interest to note that in addition to its anticonvulsant properties, the ketogenic diet produces a marked tranquilizing effect in some children. Many of our patients were described by their parents before the institution of the ketogenic diet as being "wild as an Indian" and then, after the diet was started, as being "calm as a lamb." In fact, several parents were reluctant to discontinue the diet, in spite of poor seizure control, because their children's restlessness and irritability were so vastly improved while on the ketogenic regimen, as compared to when they were being treated with antiepileptic drugs. Details relative to our method of prescribing and managing the ketogenic diet regimen are presented in a previous publication (Livingston, 1963).

SURGICAL TREATMENT

The primary treatment for a patient suffering with an epileptic disorder is medical, consisting in anticonvulsant therapy, psychotherapy, and social and occupational rehabilitation. It is worth emphasizing that medical treatment should be given an adequate trial in all cases of epilepsy and considered unsuccessful only when all appropriate therapeutic agents have been administered alone and in combination without beneficial results. Surgery should be considered only when these measures have failed. Obviously, if the seizures are symptomatic evidence of a progressive cerebral lesion such as tumor, abscess, or hematoma, surgery is the method of treatment.

Our experience indicates that surgery is not of great value in the treatment of childhood epilepsy. We recommend, however, that surgical investigation be considered in those patients who have not responded to medical therapy and are incapacitated by their seizure disorder. In our clinic, we utilize the following criteria outlined by Walker (1964, p. 1104) for selection of patients for surgical consideration:

1. At least one disabling attack occurs per month despite adequate medication.
2. The focus is clearly defined by electroencephalography at the time of a spontaneous or induced attack.
3. The focus is located where its removal would not further impair functions such as speech and motor power.
4. The patient is not so debilitated that even if the seizures were eliminated, he would still be disabled.

It should be noted that patients with grand mal and/or psychomotor epilepsy are the most likely candidates for surgery; patients with petit mal or myoclonic epilepsy are rarely candidates for surgical intervention.

Surgical excision of an epileptogenic focus does not terminate the treatment. It is only an intermediate stage, and medical therapy must be continued after the operation just as thoroughly as before. Anticonvulsant medication should be started as soon as the patient has regained consciousness and should be continued until the patient has been free of seizures for at least 4 years or even longer.

THE SOCIOECONOMIC ASPECTS OF EPILEPSY

This is a very important phase of the overall management of the epileptic patient and one which is very much neglected. Considerations of space make it impossible to discuss this exceedingly important subject adequately. However, the reader may refer to recent publications for details concerning problems such as education, automobile driving, employment, and marriage (Barrow & Fabing, 1966; Livingston, 1903, 1965, 1966b, 1968b).

HEREDITY AND EPILEPSY

There are those who advocate inheritance as a predominant factor in the pathogenesis of epilepsy on the basis of a higher incidence of electroencephalographic abnormalities in the families of epileptics than in normal control families (Doose, Gerken, & Volzke, 1968; Lennox, Gibbs, & Gibbs, 1940; Metrakos & Metrakos, 1961; Rodin & Gonzalez, 1966). This "speculation" deserves consideration. However, we believe that positive conclusions relative to the inheritability of clinical epilepsy based on electroencephalographic findings must be interpreted with caution for the following reasons:

1. The assumption that electroencephalographic abnormalities are genetically the same as clinical epilepsy, while an attractive hypothesis, has yet to be proved.
2. It is known that a considerable number of

seemingly healthy, "normal" individuals from nonepileptic families present electroencephalographic aberrations. It is also well known that many patients with epilepsy, particularly major motor epilepsy, present normal electroencephalograms.

3. Some types of electrical discharges are considered by one group of electroencephalographers to be indicative of an epileptic disorder, and these same "irregularities" are classified by others as "nonspecific" or nonpathognomonic. The Jack Ruby case is an excellent example of a situation in which electroencephalographers differ in their opinion to electroencephalographic interpretations (Livingston, 1964b).

4. It is known that electrical findings can vary somewhat in the same patient from day to day.

We believe it is fair to state that most authorities in the field of epilepsy today are of the opinion that the inheritability of clinical epilepsy has not been proved. The conclusion we derived from a relatively recent study conducted in our clinic (Eisner et al., 1959) was that we could not prove or disprove hereditary transmission of clinical epilepsy.

We are currently conducting an investigation relative to the incidence of clinical epilepsy in the offspring of the approximately twenty-thousand epileptic patients whom I have studied in our clinic during the preceding 33 years. Since our seizure clinic is somewhat unique in that we care for persons of all ages with epilepsy, we have the singular opportunity to investigate many first-, second-, and third-generation offspring of the proband. On the basis of results on hand, we are not impressed with an incidence of clinical epilepsy in these offspring that is any higher than was demonstrated in our previous study (Eisner et al., 1959) or than that which is quoted for the general population. The results of this study will be reported at a later date.

We base our decision in regard to marriage and children for individuals with epilepsy primarily on the frequency of the patient's seizures and his or her physical and mental ability to raise a family. In addition, there is little evidence for making eugenic recommendations to the parents of an epileptic child. It is generally considered that estimates of risk to siblings of an epileptic patient are not of sufficient magnitude to warrant advising against future pregnancies.

REFERENCES

Babcock, J. R. Incidence of gingival hyperplasia associated with Dilantin therapy. *The Journal of the American Dental Association,* 1965, **71,** 1447.

Barrow, R. L., & Fabing, H. D. *Epilepsy and the law.* New York: Hoeber-Harper, 1966.

Bickford, R. G., Whelan, J. L., Klass, D. W., & Corbin, R. B. Reading epilepsy: Clinical and electroencephalographic studies of a new syndrome. *Transactions of the American Neurological Association,* 1956, 100–102.

Bridge, E. M. *Epilepsy and convulsive disorders in children.* New York: McGraw-Hill, 1949.

Bridge, E. M., Livingston, S., & Tietze, C. Breath-holding spells. *The Journal of Pediatrics,* 1943, **23,** 539.

Calderon-Gonzalez, R., Hopkins, I., & McLean, W. T., Jr. Tap seizures: A form of sensory precipitation epilepsy. *The Journal of the American Medical Association,* 1966, **198,** 107.

Cohen, N. H., McAuliffe, M., & Aird, R. B. "Startle" epilepsy treated with chlordiazepoxide (Librium®). *Diseases of the Nervous System,* 1961, **22,** 20.

Critchley, M. Musicogenic epilepsy. *Brain,* 1937, **60,** 13.

Dees, S. C., & Lowenbach, H.   Allergic epilepsy. *Annals of Allergy,* 1951, **9,** 446.

Dekaban, A. S.   Plasma lipids in epileptic children treated with the high fat diet. *Archives of Neurology,* 1966, **15,** 177.

Doose, H., Gerken, H., & Volzke, E.   Genetics of centrencephalic epilepsy in childhood. *Epilepsia,* 1968, **9,** 107.

Eisner, V., Pauli, L. L., & Livingston, S.   Hereditary aspects of epilepsy. *Bulletin of the John Hopkins Hospital,* 1959, **105,** 245.

Forster, F. M.   Cited in *The National Observer,* Feb. 20, 1967.   P. 10.

Forster, F. M.   Cited in *Medical World News,* July 12, 1968.   P. 18.

Frantzen, E., Lennox-Buchthal, M., & Nygaard, A.   Longitudinal EEG and clinical study of children with febrile convulsions. *Electroencephalography and Clinical Neurophysiology,* 1968, **24,** 197.

Gastaut, H., & Gastaut, Y.   Electroencephalographic and clinical study of anoxic convulsions in children. *Electroencephalography and Clinical Neurophysiology,* 1958, **10,** 607.

Gastaut, H., & Vigouroux, M.   Electro-clinical correlations in 500 cases of psychomotor seizures. In M. Baldwin & P. Bailey (Eds.), *Temporal lobe epilepsy.*   Springfield, Ill.: Charles C Thomas, 1958.   P. 118.

Gauk, E. W., Langford, K., & Prichard, J. S.   Mechanism of seizures associated with breath-holding spells. *The New England Journal of Medicine,* 1963, **268,** 1436.

Hinman, A., & Dickey, L. B.   Breath-holding spells: Review of literature and eleven additional cases. *American Journal of Diseases of Children,* 1956, **91,** 23.

Holowach, J., & Thurston, D. L.   Breath-holding spells and anemia. *The New England Journal of Medicine,* 1963, **268,** 21.

Jeavons, P. M., & Bower, B. D.   Infantile spasms. Clinics in Developmental Medicine No. 15.   London, William Heinemann Medical Books, Ltd., 1964.

Kanner, L.: *Child psychiatry.* (3d ed.)   Springfield, Ill.: Charles C Thomas, 1962.

Keith, H. M.   *Convulsive disorders in children.* Boston: Little, Brown, 1963.

Keith, H. M., Aldrich, R. A., Daly, D., Bickford, R. G., & Kennedy, R. L. J.   A study of light-induced epilepsy in children, *American Journal of Diseases of Children,* 1952, **83,** 408.

Klinefelter, H. F., Greene, C. A., Pauli, L. L., & Livingston, S.   Precordial pain in an epileptic relieved by Dilantin. *Bulletin of the Johns Hopkins Hospital,* in press.

Lennox, W. G.   *Epilepsy and related disorders.* Boston: Little, Brown, 1960.

Lennox, W. G., Gibbs, E. L., & Gibbs, F. A.: Inheritance of cerebral dysrhythmia and epilepsy. *Archives of Neurology and Psychiatry,* 1940, **44,** 1155.

Livingston, S.   Comments on a study of light-induced epilepsy in children. *American Journal of Diseases of Children,* 1952, **83,** 409.

Livingston, S.   *The diagnosis and treatment of convulsive disorders in children.*   Springfield, Ill.: Charles C Thomas, 1954.

Livingston, S.   Breath-holding spells.   In I. Z. Levine (Ed.), *Advances in pediatrics.*   Chicago: Year Book, 1958.   P. 119.

Livingston, S.   Febrile convulsions.   In I. Z. Levine (Ed.), *Advances in pediatrics.*   Chicago: Year Book, 1958.   Pp. 113–119.

Livingston, S. Management of the child with one epileptic seizure. *The Journal of the American Medical Association,* 1960, **174,** 135.

Livingston, S. Valor y limitaciones de la electroencefalografia en el diagnostico, tratamiento y pronostico de la epilepsia en los ninos. El Dia Medico, Edicion Especial, Mayo, 1962, 907–913.

Livingston, S. *Living with epileptic seizures.* Springfield, Ill.: Charles C Thomas, 1963.

Livingston, S. The child who has had one convulsion. *Pediatrics,* 1964, **174,** 1001. (a)

Livingston, S. Epilepsy and murder. *The Journal of the American Medical Association,* 1964, **188,** 172. (b)

Livingston, S. Restrictive measures relative to epilepsy: Comments on the medical aspects. *Archives of Environmental Health,* 1965, **10,** 508.

Livingston, S. *Drug therapy for epilepsy: Anticonvulsant drugs—Usage, metabolism and untoward reactions (prevention, detection and management).* Springfield, Ill.: Charles C Thomas, 1966. (a)

Livingston, S. What the teacher can do for the student with epilepsy. *National Education Association Journal,* 1966, **55,** 24. (b)

Livingston, S. Infantile febrile convulsions. *Developmental Medicine and Child Neurology,* 1968, **10,** 374. (a)

Livingston, S. New freedoms for children with epilepsy. *Parents Magazine,* November, 1968. (b)

Livingston, S. Seizure disorders. In S. S. Gellis & B. M. Kagan (Eds.), *Current pediatric therapy.* Philadelphia: Saunders, 1968. P. 117. (c)

Livingston, S. Treatment of grand mal epilepsy:

Phenobarbital versus diphenylhydantoin sodium. *Clinical Pediatrics,* 1968, **7,** 444. (d)

Livingston, S., Bridge, E. M., & Kajdi, L. Febrile convulsions: A clinical study with special reference to heredity and prognosis. *The Journal of Pediatrics,* 1947, **31,** 509.

Livingston, S., Eisner, V., & Pauli, L. Minor motor epilepsy: Diagnosis, treatment and prognosis. *Pediatrics,* 1958, **21,** 916.

Livingston, S., & Escala, P. Headaches and epilepsy in children. In A. P. Friedman & E. Harmes (Eds.), *Headaches in children.* Springfield, Ill.: Charles C Thomas, 1967. P. 122.

Livingston, S., & Livingston, H. L. Diphenylhydantoin gingival hyperplasia. *American Journal of Diseases of Children,* 1969, **117,** 265.

Livingston, S., & Pauli, L. L. Neurological evaluation in child psychiatry. In A. M. Freedman & H. I. Kaplan (Eds.), *Comprehensive textbook of psychiatry.* Baltimore: Williams & Wilkins, 1967. P. 1338.

Livingston, S., & Torres, I. C. Photic epilepsy: Report of an unusual case and review of the literature. *Clinical Pediatrics,* 1964, **3,** 304.

Livingston, S., Torres, I. C., Pauli, L. L., & Rider, R. V. Petit mal epilepsy: Results of a prolonged follow-up study of 117 patients. *The Journal of the American Medical Association,* 1965, **194,** 227.

Livingston, S., Villamater, C., Sakata, Y., & Pauli, L. L. Use of carbamazepine in epilepsy. *The Journal of the American Medical Association,* 1967, **200,** 204.

Livingston, S., Villamater, C., & Sakata, Y. Ospolot (Sulthiame) in epilepsy. *Diseases of the Nervous System,* 1967, **28,** 259.

Lombroso, C. T., & Lerman, P. Breathholding

spells (cyanotic and pallid infantile syncope). *Pediatrics,* 1967, **39,** 563.

Low, N. L., Gibbs, E. L., & Gibbs, F. A. Electro-encephalographic findings in breath-holding spells. *Pediatrics,* 1955, **15,** 595.

Merritt, H. H., & Putnam, T. J. Sodium diphenyl-hydantoinate in the treatment of convulsive disorders. *The Journal of the American Medical Association,* 1938, **111,** 1068.

Metrakos, K., & Metrakos, J. D. Genetics of convulsive disorders. II. Genetic and electro-encephalographic studies in centrencephalic epilepsy. *Neurology,* 1961, **11,** 474.

Miller, F. J. W., Court, S. D. M., Walton, W. S., & Knox, E. G. *Growing up in Newcastle upon Tyne.* London: Oxford University Press, 1960.

Millichap, J. G. *Febrile convulsions.* New York: Macmillan, 1968.

Panuska, H. J., Gorlin, R. J., Bearman, J. E., & Mitchell, D. F. The effect of anticonvulsant drugs upon the gingiva: A series of analyses of 1048 patients. II. *The Journal of Periodontology,* 1961, **32,** 15.

Peterman, M. G. The ketogenic diet in epilepsy.

The Journal of the American Medical Association, 1925, **84,** 1979.

Rodin, E., & Gonzalez, S. Hereditary components in epileptic patients: Electroencephalogram family studies. *The Journal of the American Medical Association,* 1966, **198,** 221.

Spangler, R. H. Allergic findings in epileptic patients and ancestors. *Annals of Allergy,* 1943, **1,** 91.

Svensmark, O., & Buchthal, F. Diphenylhydantoin and phenobarbital serum levels in children. *American Journal of Diseases of Children,* 1964, **108,** 82.

Talbot, F. B. *Treatment of epilepsy.* New York: Macmillan, 1930.

Walker, A. E. *Surgical treatment of epilepsy: Modern treatment.* New York: Harper & Row, 1964.

Wilder, R. M. The effect of ketonemia on course of epilepsy. *Mayo Clinic Bulletin,* 1921, **2,** 307.

Wilkins, L. Epilepsy in childhood. III. Results with the ketogenic diet. *The Journal of Pediatrics,* 1937, **10,** 341.

9 Organic Disorders Caused by Abnormal Metabolic Conditions

Kenneth F. Swaiman and Jerrold M. Milstein

METABOLIC DISEASES

Metabolic diseases of the immature nervous system can be discussed in terms of these major categories: carbohydrate metabolism, amino-acid–protein metabolism, lipid metabolism, electrolyte metabolism, and endocrine metabolism. The metabolic aspects of these diseases have been reviewed in many articles (Stanbury, Wyngaarden, & Fredrickson, 1966) and books (Holt & Milnar, 1964). The aim of this chapter is to acquaint the reader with diseases in these categories which directly or indirectly cause neurological symptoms and signs.

DISEASES OF CARBOHYDRATE METABOLISM

Carbohydrate, primarily in the form of glucose, is the major energy source of the brain. This circumstance is also true of the newborn period, even though the clinical symptoms of carbohydrate derangement may not be easily recognized. The organ most sensitive to deple-tion of glucose is the brain. The following conditions illustrate the effect of carbohydrate abnormalities on the central nervous system (CNS).

Hypoglycemia

The neurological effects of hypoglycemia were first observed after the discovery of insulin and its clinical use (S. Harris, 1924; Warren, 1926). Later, in the 1930s, hypoglycemia was seen in patients who did not have hyperinsulinism (Shaw & Moriarty, 1924). McQuarrie (1954) first described the syndrome of familial idiopathic hypoglycemia in children. As hypoglycemia became more frequently recognized, it became apparent that the condition could appear sporadically and in the neonatal period (Cornblath & Reisner, 1965; Hartmann & Jaudon, 1937; Pildes, Forbes, O'Connor, & Cornblath, 1967). Although a large number of cases are still regarded as idiopathic, numerous cases embracing many metabolic areas have been reported.

The neurological manifestations of hypoglycemia are closely related to the patient's age. Frequently in the newborn period there are no

270

overt symptoms, particularly in full-term infants. Tremors, cyanosis, seizures, respiratory problems, and eye rolling are the most frequent symptoms of hypoglycemia in the newborn period (Cornblath, Wybregt, Baens, & Klein, 1964). In a series of twenty-four cases, 87.5 percent of infants were below the 10th percentile in weight for gestational age, and the remaining infants were between the 10th and the 25th percentiles. These infants had blood sugars between 0 and 9 mg percent. Cornblath and Reisner (1965) have formulated criteria for diagnosis of neonatal hypoglycemia based on both blood-sugar concentration and patient's age. In infants of low birth weight, blood glucose concentration less than 20 mg percent during the first 48 hours of life is abnormal (Cornblath & Reisner, 1965). After this period a blood glucose value less than 40 to 50 mg percent is abnormal. Symptoms in these children may persist for 4 to 5 weeks. It is not known if hypoglycemia which is unaccompanied by neurological symptoms or signs produces long-range deleterious effects on the brains of these infants.

Hypoglycemia in the newborn period is associated with toxemia of pregnancy, maternal and occasionally paternal diabetes mellitus, prematurity, low birth weight, multiple births, mild hypothermia, cerebral hemorrhage, islet cell adenomas, certain glycogen storage diseases, glycogen synthetase deficiency, galactosemia, fructose intolerance, adrenal hemorrhage, leucine sensitivity, and cerebral gigantism (Cornblath, Joassin, Weisskopf, & Swiatek, 1966; Cornblath & Reisner, 1965; Pildes et al., 1967; Sauls & Ulstrom, 1967).

The infant of the diabetic mother usually has symptoms in the first 4 hours of life, and then again between 24 and 36 hours. Infants of diabetic mothers have increased circulating insulin levels. Intravenous glucose in adequate concentration has been used to treat the hypoglycemic infant of the diabetic mother (Cornblath et al.,

1966). If this therapy fails, then epinephrine can be used. If this therapy too is insufficient, then adrenocorticoids are of benefit.

Low-birth-weight infants, premature infants, and twins appear to have inadequate stores of glycogen to maintain their blood-sugar levels (Cornblath et al., 1964; Cornblath & Schwartz, 1966; Wybregt, Reisner, Patel, Nellhaus, & Cornblath, 1964). Therapy is similar to that employed in the infant of the diabetic mother. Patients with cerebral infection or hemorrhage may have hypoglycemia on the basis of hypothalamic involvement leading to autonomic dysfunction (Ford, 1960). Cerebral infections and hemorrhage are most readily diagnosed by spinal fluid examination, which reveals the presence of pleocytosis or red blood cells. Islet cell adenomas, even though rare in children (Crigler, 1962; Sauls & Ulstrom, 1967), can be diagnosed by determination of serum insulin activity (Floyd, Fajans, Knopf, & Conn, 1964). The adenomas must be surgically removed.

Those patients with glycogen storage disease types I and III and those with glycogen synthetase deficiency are unable to mobilize glucose because of enzymatic blocks in synthesis or degradation of glycogen (Field, 1966). The glycogen synthetase deficiency can be diagnosed from enzymatic analysis of liver and peripheral blood (Field, 1966; Nitowsky & Gronfeld, 1967). The glycogen storage diseases will be discussed in more depth later in this chapter.

The galactosemic patient may present with hypoglycemia after the ingestion of galactose. A detailed discussion of this disease appears later in this chapter.

The hypoglycemia of fructose intolerance is apparent almost immediately after the ingestion of sucrose. Patients with familial fructose intolerance have a deficiency of fructuse-1-phosphate aldolase (Froesch, Wolf, Baitsch, Prader, & Labhart, 1963). This deficiency leads to an inhibition of hepatic release of glucose. Avoidance of fructose-containing foods controls the disease. Adrenal hemorrhage can be reasonably confirmed with tests to determine serum and urine levels of 17-hydroxycorticoids, but can be suspected clinically on the basis of the presence of hypoglycemia with hyponatremia and hypotension. Replacement therapy with adrenocortical hormones and electrolytes is necessary. The child with leucine sensitivity does not have symptoms until the offending agent is ingested. Therefore, symptoms in the first 24 hours of life are highly unusual in this disease. Increased amounts of circulating insulin are present as a result of increased rate of release. Restriction of leucine-containing protein is necessary. Hypoglycemia associated with maple syrup urine disease is thought to occur on the same basis as in leucine sensitivity. Maple syrup urine disease will be discussed later in this chapter.

After the identifiable types of hypoglycemia have been sought, there is still a large group of children who suffer from hypoglycemia and fall into the idiopathic category. Some of these patients suffer from a familial form. They are treated with adrenocorticoids, epinephrine, and partial pancreatectomy. Each form of therapy has been associated with some success, but usually complete remission does not result. A new drug, Diazoxide, has been found to have very little diuretic effect, but has marked hyperglycemic effects (Dollery, 1962). There are some unwanted side effects of the drug such as hirsuitism, but this is of small consequence if the drug is effective in preventing the irreversible cerebral complications of hypoglycemia.

After the newborn period, and before the end of the first year, seizures are almost uniformly present during hypoglycemia. Spells of flaccidity, sweating, and coma are also frequently seen. After the first month of life, but before the end of the first year, any of the above-mentioned etiologies may become manifest, but survey studies indicate that during this period there is a change in the frequency of the various causes of hypoglycemia. In this age period leucine sensitivity becomes the most frequent etiology, and the familial idiopathic type next (Sauls & Ulstrom, 1967). The incidence of mental retardation is around 60 percent in those children who develop hypoglycemia in the first year of life (Haworth & Coodin, 1960; Sauls & Ulstrom, 1967).

The child over 1 year of age frequently may be able to give a more complete assessment of his prodromal symptoms. In addition to the symptoms associated with hypoglycemia in younger children, these patients may also complain of dizziness, light-headedness, and hunger with the onset of the attack. More focal neurological signs have been observed such as ataxia and hemiplegia (Haworth & Coodin, 1960). Of those patients developing hypoglycemia after the first year, only about 10 percent are retarded (Sauls & Ulstrom, 1967). Seizures can later become a permanent feature even though hypoglycemia is no longer present (Plum & Posner, 1966).

After the first year both the leucine sensitivity and the familial hypoglycemia type of difficulties become rare, and a new clinical syndrome becomes more frequent. This syndrome is referred to as *ketotic hypoglycemia* (Colle & Ulstrom, 1964). This syndrome has its highest incidence in children between 18 months and 3 years of age. Symptoms of hypoglycemia occur after a short fast. They can be precipitated by ingestion of a high-fat, low-carbohydrate diet. The laboratory studies reveal consistent ketonuria which precedes the hypoglycemia.

Beginning at about 4 years of age, the relative incidence of islet cell adenomas increases.

Metabolic factors. As was previously mentioned, the CNS manifestations of hypoglycemia are more easily detected than aberrations of other organ systems. While carbon sources, other than glucose, such as other carbohydrates, amino acids, and lipids can be utilized for oxidative decarboxylation and phosphorylation by nervous tissue in the experimental situation, little is known about their utilization *in vivo* in clinical situations. If glucose supply ceased, the glucose needs of the brain would exhaust the glucose content of the brain in 10 to 15 minutes (Geiger, 1958). The respiratory quotient of the brain is close to unity. Thus it appears that carbohydrate is the most readily used material for oxidation. Other carbohydrates such as mannose and fructose can be utilized *in vivo* and prevent symptoms of neuroglycopenia, but cannot reverse the symptoms once they have begun (Dickens & Greville, 1933; Maddock, Hawkins, & Holmes, 1939). Acetoacetate and beta hydroxybutyrate are taken up by cerebral tissue *in vivo* when the animal has been starved to the point of hypoglycemia (Kety, Polis, Nadler, & Schmidt, 1948). Glutamic acid appears to be the only amino acid which has any value in the treatment of hypoglycemia. The amino acid, when injected intravenously, arouses patients who have undergone insulin-induced hypoglycemia (Gomez, Gotham, & Meyer, 1961). Its use has no advantage over the use of glucose.

Pathology. The changes which occur in the brain with hypoglycemia have been studied extensively in autopsy material (Baker, 1939; Blackwood, McMenemey, Meyer, Norman, & Russell, 1963; Etheridge, 1967). Pathologically the changes are most like those seen in anoxia (Courville, 1957). Though there is a significant clinical difference between hypoglycemia affecting those under 1 year of age and hypoglycemia affecting those over a year, there are no pathological studies showing a difference in the manner in which hypoglycemia affects immature brain as compared with mature brain. Courville (1957) surveyed the long-term affects on the brain and found that in those cases in which death occurred within a few hours, there was congestion with some subarachnoid hemorrhage and focal petechiae in the white matter. If the patient survived for several days, there was neuronal loss from the cortex and basal ganglia. Longer survival was characterized by laminar necrosis, mainly of cortical layers III and IV, which progressed to cystic degeneration.

Hyperglycemia

The most common pathological cause of hyperglycemia is diabetes mellitus.

Lack of proper treatment leads to diabetic acidosis after accumulation of keto acids in the tissues and blood. Diabetic acidosis is frequently associated with profound acute neurological findings. The patients are usually obtunded or comatose. The etiology of diabetic coma has not been completely explained. The presence of ketone bodies and organic acids as a result of fatty acid degradation, during a period of decreased availability of intracellular glucose, has experimentally led to coma (Kety et al., 1948). Coma occurs despite maintenance of normal acid-base balance. In disease it is not unusual that multiple factors occurring simultaneously or in rapid sequence account for the ultimate clinical picture. The patient with diabetic coma is often severely dehydrated and may be in shock. Either acidosis or dehydration may lead to coma, no matter what their etiology is. Therapy with fluids, replacement electrolytes, and insulin must be administered immediately.

Cerebral edema was known to be associated with diabetic acidosis as early as 1936 (Dillon, Riggs, & Dyer, 1936) and is often seen in conjunction with fatty liver infiltration in patients who have not received adequate therapy. Recent reports tell of patients who have expired despite adequate therapy (Young & Bradley, 1967). Postmortem examination revealed pronounced cerebral edema. There has been no good explanation of this phenomenon.

Chronic diabetes has been implicated as the

cause of premature vascular changes in the brain and cord (Young & Bradley, 1967), but we are unaware that any cases have been reported in which these changes have caused clinical difficulties in the pediatric population.

Glycogen Storage Diseases

The glycogen storage diseases are a group of diseases characterized by abnormal accumulations of glycogen in various body organs (Field, 1966). The glycogen stored may be of normal or abnormal configuration. Each of the glycogen storage diseases is characterized by specific absence of an enzyme related to carbohydrate metabolism. The enzymatic deficiency is genetically determined. Although almost a dozen diseases of this type have been described, only three forms are of importance to the present discussion concerning the effect of abnormal carbohydrate metabolism on the brain. The glycogen storage diseases are numbered after a system first proposed by Cori (1957).

Glycogen storage disease type I is a disease characterized by the absence of the enzyme glucose-6-phosphatase (Illingworth & Cori, 1952). The absence of this enzyme in the liver results in the accumulation of large amounts of liver glycogen because glycogen cannot be degraded beyond glucose-6-phosphate and subsequently transported into blood in the form of glucose. As a result, hypoglycemia is a frequent problem. Aside from the eventual compromise of hepatic function with its resultant cerebral manifestations, the symptoms of hypoglycemia which have been described above are the prominent cerebral symptoms of this disease. Therapy consisting of numerous small feedings of carbohydrates is moderately successful.

Type III glycogen storage disease is the result of the absence of activity of the debranching enzyme amylo-1,6-glucosidase (Field, 1966). There is a resultant storage of an unusual glycogen with many branched chains primarily in the liver

and kidneys. Because of the difficulty in degradation of the short, outer chains of glycogen, persistant but mild difficulties with hypoglycemia are experienced. The symptoms are not unlike those described above. Treatment is the same as practiced in type I glycogen storage disease.

Type II glycogen storage disease is a disease in which there is a generalized deposition of glycogen in muscle, liver, kidneys, myocardium, and neurons of the brain and spinal cord (Van Creveld, 1934). Hypoglycemia is not present in glycogen storage disease type II. Hers (1963) noted the enzyme defect to be present in lysosomes. He described the absence of the enzyme acid maltase (alpha-1,4-glucosidase) in these patients. The vast majority of these patients are infants who become progressively weak and die before the end of the first year of life due to glycogen deposition in the myocardium.

Recently, patients have been reported with a variety of this disease, which appears to be best called *late infantile acid maltase deficiency,* who have not had cardiac difficulty and at least in one case no concomitant cerebral difficulty (H. L. Smith, Amick, & Sidbury, 1966; Swaiman, Kennedy, & Sauls, 1968).

Enzyme analysis for diagnostic purposes can be performed on peripheral blood cells (Huijing, Van Creveld, & Losekoot, 1963; Nitowsky & Gronfeld, 1967). Pathological changes in the CNS include generalized cellular swelling (Field, 1966) due to the deposition of glycogen. Glycogen appears to be deposited primarily in neurons rather than in glial cells.

No therapy for this condition is known. It is unlikely that successful therapy will be possible until a better understanding of the role of acid maltase in normal carbohydrate metabolism is gained.

Galactosemia

Galactosemia was not recognized as an inborn error of metabolism until 1951 (Gorter, 1951).

In 1956, it was noted for the first time that there was an accumulation of galactose-1-phosphate in erythrocytes in patients with galactosemia (Schwarz, Goldberg, Komrower, & Holzel, 1956). In the same year the enzyme deficiency in galactosemia was described (Isselbacher, Anderson, Kurahashi, & Kalckar, 1956). Following the recognition of the disease entity and the responsible metabolic limitations, it was only a matter of time before dietary therapy was instituted. The incidence of the disorder ranges from 1 per 70,000 to 1 per 18,000 live births (Hansen, Bretthauer, Mayes, & Nordin, 1964).

The patients are normal at birth except for a slightly lower birth weight than their siblings (Hsia & Walker, 1961). Symptoms are not apparent until milk feedings are begun. A frequent early sign is jaundice, which appears between 4 and 10 days and persists longer than would be anticipated with physiological jaundice (Donnell, Bergren, & Ng, 1967). Other symptoms of liver dysfunction include hepatomegaly, edema, and hypoprothrombinemia. Renal involvement with ensuing proteinuria and aminoaciduria is common.

Hypoglycemia occurs in galactosemia, but is usually mild (Donnell, Bergren, & Ng, 1967). The defect purported to be present in galactosemia which leads to hypoglycemia is the inhibition of phosphoglucomutase leading to a decrease in the hepatic output of glucose (Sauls & Ulstrom, 1967). Mild CNS symptoms appear, including lethargy and hypotonia. Following the neurological signs, the patient usually develops the gastrointestinal symptoms of anorexia, vomiting, and diarrhea. Death may occur at this stage of the disease. If the course is less fulminating, the patient will show signs of failure to thrive and will continue to have mild gastrointestinal symptoms. Cataracts appear between 4 and 8 weeks of age (Isselbacher, 1966), and the patient then begins to show evidence of neurological retardation. If untreated, motor and intellectual re-

tardation is moderate to severe and does not have any specific features to differentiate it from other forms of retardation.

In galactosemia there is the presence of a positive reducing material in the urine which is shown not to be glucose by a negative glucose oxidase test. Tests for reducing substance must be repeated because galactosuria may be intermittent, being present only when galactose or lactose has been ingested. A more sensitive indicator is the generalized aminoaciduria which is present when there is only a slight increase of galactose-1-phosphate (Cusworth, Dent, & Flynn, 1955).

The confirmatory laboratory test for galactosemia reveals the absence of galactose-1-phosphate uridyl transferase activity in blood samples (Isselbacher et al., 1956; Kalckar, Anderson, & Isselbacher, 1956). This determination is also helpful in discerning the presence of the heterozygous state in otherwise normal individuals.

The cataracts are a result of accumulation of galactose-1-phosphate (Gitzelmann, Curtius, & Schneller, 1967). Galactose tolerance tests are potentially dangerous and are not used unless no other method of diagnosis is available (Donnell, Bergren, & Ng, 1967).

The pathophysiology of the CNS involvement has not been elucidated. The hypoglycemia associated with the ingestion of galactose is no greater than is seen when secondary to other etiologies and probably does not account for the degree of retardation observed. Galactitol, a reduction product of galactose, has been isolated from urine and tissue from patients (Egan & Wells, 1966) and may be implicated in the pathogenesis of the CNS findings.

Since galactose is not an essential foodstuff, its complete removal from the diet is not followed by complications. The main offending foods are dairy products, but these can easily be avoided with the use of vegetable-product substitutes. Because milk constitutes a large proportion of an infant's diet, it becomes very important to make the diagnosis early in life. With increasing age and body size, the relative amounts of ingested galactose are normally reduced. Therefore, the diet need not be as strict as in the neonatal period. With dietary regulation, all symptoms of the disease can be prevented. If therapy is delayed for a short period, most symptoms including cataracts will regress (Donnell, Bergren, & Ng, 1967). Unfortunately, mental retardation may persist.

DISORDERS OF AMINO-ACID–PROTEIN METABOLISM

No diseases have been described in which there is deficient synthesis of a specific brain protein or in which an abnormal brain protein has been isolated. There is strong experimental evidence that cretinism and certain of the aminoacidurias induce cerebral changes on the basis of interference with brain protein synthesis. The information available at this time permits only a theoretical discussion. Undoubtedly this area of knowledge will greatly expand in coming years, but detailed discussion in this chapter is unwarranted.

Disorders of the brain secondary to aberrations of amino-acid metabolism have been discussed in review publications over the past few years (Efron, 1965a; Efron & Ampola, 1967). The acceleration of interest in research in this area has led to the description of new clinical disease entities each year. One recent review (Efron & Ampola, 1967) implies that the subject will not be capable of treatment by a single review article for much longer. Professional and lay publicity surrounding disorders of amino-acid metabolism has led to great public interest in the detection of, and therapy for, these newly described diseases (Cooper, 1967).

Efron (1965a), in a discussion of the aminoacidurias, divided abnormalities of amino-acid metabolism into two major categories—primary and secondary aminoacidurias. Primary aminoacidurias are those conditions in which there is no known enzymatic or transport defect but in which there is accompanying aminoaciduria. These diseases include severe liver involvement, renal impairment with proximal tubular damage including galactosemia, Wilson's disease, severe burns, and other diseases in which aminoaciduria is present, but unexplained, such as scurvy and rickets. Secondary aminoaciduria and related diseases are not germane to the present discussion.

Primary aminoacidurias can be divided into three categories (Efron, 1965a):

1. Overflow aminoacidurias
2. No-threshold aminoacidurias
3. Renal (transport) aminoacidurias

Overflow aminoacidurias are so named because amino acid appears in the urine as a result of increased plasma concentration of one or more amino acids. The increase in plasma concentration of these amino acids is due to an enzymatic deficiency. The most common overflow aminoacidurias associated with neurological disorders are:

1. Phenylketonuria.
2. Tyrosinosis
3. Maple syrup urine disease
4. Hypervalinemia
5. Isovaleric acidemia
6. Hyperlysinemia
7. Citrullinemia
8. Hydroxprolinemia
9. Hyperprolinemia
10. Histidinemia
11. Oasthouse urine disease
12. Hyper-β-alaninemia
13. Carnosinemia
14. Hypersarcosinemia

No-threshold aminoacidurias are diseases in

which enzymatic deficiencies are present but in which no increase in plasma concentration of these amino acids occurs. Increase in plasma concentration does not occur because the amino acid and its metabolites are readily excreted in the urine as a result of the fact that there are no normal mechanisms for reabsorption of these substances. Substances that fall into this category are frequently intermediates in amino-acid metabolism. Aminoacidurias associated with neurological disorders that fall into this category include:

1. Homocystinuria
2. Argininosuccinic aciduria
3. Cystathioninuria

Renal (transport) aminoacidurias are the result of faulty mechanism of reabsorption of amino acids in the renal tubules. The abnormality lies presumably in the absence of carrier molecules, probably protein, that ordinarily combine with the amino acid in the process of reabsorption. There are accompanying absorption abnormalities of the same amino acids in the gastrointestinal tract. Therefore, in this type of aminoaciduria deficiencies of transport of certain classes of amino acids are found. The common renal aminoacidurias associated with neurological disorders include:

1. Hartnup disease
2. Joseph's syndrome
3. Methionine malabsorption

Unfortunately, certain of the aminoacidurias can be classified under two of these categories because there is both an increase in blood concentration of the affected amino acid and an absence of a renal threshold.

Although mental retardation or cerebral involvement has been noted with most of the aminoacidurias described above, individuals have been reported who suffer from the biochemical abnormality but who do not manifest the expected cerebral consequences of the disease. These asymptomatic individuals have led investigators to attempt to further clarify the mechanism of association of CNS symptoms with the biochemical abnormalities. The specific process by which these diseases compromise cerebral function is not known. Until this type information is available, evaluation and design of therapy for these conditions will remain somewhat arbitrary.

Representative diseases in each category will be discussed.

Overflow Aminoacidurias

Phenylketonuria. Phenylketonuria was the first of this group of amino-acid disorders to be clearly described. The discovery was anticipated by Garrod (1909), when he described expected features of inborn errors of metabolism. In 1934, Følling described a family with phenylpyruvic acid in their urine. Five years later Jervis (1939) noted that the disease was transmitted as an autosomal recessive. Further work by Jervis (1947) demonstrated that there was an enzymatic defect in these patients which resulted in lack of conversion of phenylalanine to tyrosine. The deficient enzyme, phenylalanine hydroxylase, is ordinarily found in the liver.

The usual clinical description of a patient with phenylketonuria depicts a retarded child with blond hair, blue eyes, fair skin, eczema, and microcephaly. These findings were most common in the Northern European populations that were studied early, but it has subsequently been noted that changes in skin and hair pigmentation are not universal. The affected child usually appears normal at birth and may appear so for several months. Study of case history and observation often reveal that evidence of retardation is present in the early months of life and is almost always present by 6 months of age. The usual milestones of motor development are often delayed, and there is commonly a greater delay

TABLE 9-1   OVERFLOW AMINOACIDURIAS ASSOCIATED WITH NEUROLOGICAL DISORDERS

Disease	Amino Acid Increased in Blood	Deficient Enzyme	Clinical Features
Phenylketonuria	Phenylalanine	Phenylalanine hydroxylase	Retardation; seizures; eczema; fair skin; light hair
Tyrosinosis	Tyrosine	Probably p-hydroxyphenyl-pyruvic acid oxidase	Hepatic; renal disease; failure to thrive; mild retardation
Maple syrup urine disease	Leucine; valine	Branched-chain keto acid decarboxylase	Seizures; spasticity; retardation; usually die without therapy
Hypervalinemia (Wada, Tada, Minagawa, Yoshida, Morikawa, & Okamura, 1963)	Valine	Unknown, perhaps valine transaminase	Retardation
Isovaleric acidemia (Tanaka, Budd, Efron, & Isselbacher, 1966)	Leucine	Isovaleric acid dehydro-genase	Sweaty foot smell; mild retardation; episodes of stupor and coma
Hyperlysinemia (Ghadimi, Binnington, & Pecora, 1964)	Lysine	Unknown	Retardation; hypotonia; fine hair
Citrullinemia (McMurray, Rathbun, Mohyuddin, & Koegler, 1963)	Citrulline	Argininosuccinic acid synthetase	Retardation; vomiting; ammonia intoxication
Hydroxyprolinemia (Efron, Bixby, & Pryles, 1965)	Hydroxyproline	Hydroxyproline oxidase	Retardation; hematuria
Hyperprolinemia: Type I (Efron, 1965b)	Proline	Proline oxidase	Retardation; deafness; seizures; renal disease
Type II (Berlow & Efron, 1964)	Proline	Δ^1-pyroline-5-carboxylase dehydrogenase	Retardation; seizures
Histidinemia	Histidine	Histidase	Retardation; speech defects
Oasthouse urine disease (A. J. Smith & Strang, 1958)	Phenylalanine; valine; isoleucine, leucine, methi-onine; tyrosine	Unknown	Retardation; white hair; seizures; body odor (a-hydroxybutyric acid)

TABLE 9-1   OVERFLOW AMINOACIDURIAS ASSOCIATED WITH NEUROLOGICAL DISORDERS *(Continued)*

Disease	Amino Acid Increased in Blood	Deficient Enzyme	Clinical Features
Hyper-β-alaninemia (Scriver, Pueschel, & Davies, 1966)	β-alanine	?β-alanine transaminase	Somnolence; seizures; hypotonia; motor and intellectual retardation
Hypersarcosinemia (Gerritsen & Waisman, 1966b)	Sarcosine	?Sarcosine dehydrogenase	Weakness; motor and intellectual retardation; failure to thrive
Carnosinemia (Perry, Hansen, Tischler, Bunting, & Berry, 1967)	Carnosine	?Carnosinase	Seizures; motor and intellectual retardation

in social and intellectual development. Language acquisition is frequently severely retarded, and many patients do not progress beyond the ability to use single words. Seizures are frequently associated with the disease and have been reported in 26 percent of cases (Paine, 1957). The seizures are usually major motor in type, but on occasion are myoclonic. Accompanying electroencephalographic patterns of hypsarythmia are sometimes seen.

The incidence of phenylketonuria was initially thought to be 4 to 6 per 100,000 (Munro, 1947), but the increase in numbers of newborn infants screened has led to an estimate that 1 per 10,000 infants has phenylketonuria. Cases have been found in every population survey, including the American Indian and Negro (Knox, 1966).

The diagnosis of phenylketonuria is first suspected on the basis of either the finding of an increased phenylalanine concentration in blood or the presence of phenylpyruvic acid in urine. The screening test for increased blood concentration of phenylalanine has been described by Guthrie and Susi (1963) and consists of a bacterial-growth-inhibition test. This test is presently being used in most newborn nurseries in the United States. The presence of phenylpyruvic acid in the urine is detected when the addition of ferric chloride results in a green precipitate. Phenylpyruvic acid frequently is not found in the urine in the first month of life because of the absence of the transaminase which transforms phenylalanine into phenylpyruvic acid. The test is not specific for phenylpyruvic acid and is positive in many other situations. Therefore, both these screening tests must be followed with sophisticated studies designed to demonstrate the inability of the individual to convert phenylalanine to tyrosine. These tests usually include phenylalanine loading and study of plasma concentrations of amino acids (O'Flynn, Tillman, & Hsia, 1967) utilizing automatic ion-exchange chromatography (Spackman, Moore, & Stein, 1958) or fluorometric techniques.

The enzymatic defect has been intensively studied since its description. It has become obvious that a complex system of co-factors is necessary for normal activity of phenylalanine hydroxylase. The actual pathophysiology that leads to compromise of brain function has not been elucidated, although many theories have been proposed. There are a number of individuals who have the metabolic block noted in phenylketonuria but who are not retarded. Many of these individuals, however, suffer from psychiatric illness later in life.

The theories proposed to explain the cerebral difficulties include the accumulation of certain abnormal amines such as phenylethylamine or the relative decrease of certain biogenic amines such as serotonin. Other theories postulate that the high concentration of phenylalanine interferes with protein synthesis. There has been some experimental evidence that protein metabolism in the developing brain can be compromised by high concentrations of phenylalanine (McKean, Boggs, & Peterson, 1968; Neame, 1961; Swaiman, Hosfield, Wolfe, & Lemieux, 1968). Although abnormalities of lipid metabolism have been described, they are not specific for phenylketonuria.

In recent years, low-phenylalanine diets have been employed to treat patients with phenylketonuria. The use of the diet successfully lowers plasma phenylalanine levels. The efficacy of this therapy is still in question. Established and respected investigators are divided in their opinions regarding the status of the presently available therapy. There are those who claim that the diet has not changed the course of the disorder (Bessman, Wapnir, & Due, 1967). Others are convinced of the efficacy of the diet in improving intelligence and feel that the diet has been eminently successful (Bickel, 1967; Koch, Acosta & Fishler, 1967). The diet is not without complications. Most patients do not achieve normal height and weight (Kennedy, Wertelecki, Gates, Sperry, & Cass, 1967). There is also retardation in bone growth. The diet has been associated with hypoglycemia, hypoproteinemia, and megaloblastic anemia. Several deaths have been reported to occur which were likely associated with administration of the diet (Kennedy et al., 1967; Knox, 1966). It is clear that when the diet is employed, it must be monitored by physicians skilled in its use.

In recent years a new problem has been noted.

A number of mothers who have phenylketonuria but who have normal mental abilities have given birth to children who are retarded and who have microcephaly (Mabry, Denniston, & Coldwell, 1966). This phenomenon implies that the increase of blood phenylalanine and its metabolites is detrimental to the fetus.

Certain other aspects of abnormal phenylalanine metabolism may pose problems in the differential diagnosis of phenylketonuria. A number of newborn infants may have delayed maturation of phenylalanine hydroxylase activity and will consequently have abnormally high plasma phenylalanine levels for a few weeks or sometimes longer. After the enzyme activity develops, the patient has no more biochemical difficulties. Other infants may transiently have high concentrations of phenylalanine and other amino acids in the blood because of immature renal function during the first few months of life.

Maple syrup urine disease. Maple syrup urine disease, which was first described by Menkes, Hurst, and Craig (1954), is a disorder of the metabolism of the branched-chain amino acids—leucine, isoleucine, and valine. The enzyme responsible for decarboxylation of the branched-chain keto acids is absent. Since the original description about thirty additional cases have been reported. The disease usually appears within the first week or two of life and is transmitted as an autosomal recessive trait.

In the classical form of the disorder the child is normal at birth, but by the end of the first week of life feeding difficulties appear with emesis and lethargy. About this same time muscular hypertonia and seizures appear. The urine smells like maple syrup.

The children may die within the first few weeks of life and are almost always dead by one year of age if proper diagnosis and treatment are not effected. A few exceptions have been reported. One patient has lived 5 years without any neurological findings and has an IQ between 90 and 100 (Westall, 1967). Dancis and Levitz (1966) report a patient who has survived to 10 years but who is markedly retarded and has severe neurological impairment.

An intermittent form has also been described which has a later age of onset (Dancis, Hutzler, & Rokkones, 1967). The intermittent form of the disease is usually apparent during unrelated illnesses. The patients develop ataxia, irritability, and stupor. During these episodes the maple syrup odor is present in the urine, and investigation at this time will reveal increased concentrations of branched-chain amino acids in blood and urine. The intermittent form of the disease has not been associated with retardation.

The diagnosis is confirmed by the demonstration of elevated blood concentrations of leucine, isoleucine, and valine by amino-acid chromatography. Analysis of the urine reveals the keto acids to be present. The enzymatic defect was first described by Dancis, Hutzler, and Levitz (1963). They were able to demonstrate an absence of leukocyte oxidative decarboxylation of these particular keto acids. They also reported keto-acid decarboxylase activity to be 10 to 20 percent of normal in the intermittent form of the disease (Dancis et al., 1967). The neurological symptoms have been most closely related to elevated blood leucine (Dancis & Levitz, 1966). Hypoglycemia is present in 50 percent of cases (Donnell, Lieberman, Shaw, & Koch, 1967). The mechanism producing the hypoglycemia has not been clearly established. In other instances of hypoglycemia, leucine has been responsible for producing increased insulin secretion, but assays of insulin in these patients have not shown any increase.

Dietary therapy has been used in maple syrup urine disease, and the patients receiving therapy are reportedly doing well. No complications have been noted except for retarded growth. In a few cases the growth was noted to increase when yeast was added to the diet (Snyderman, 1967). The proponents of the diet contend that the IQ attained by the patient is a function of early therapy. Dietary therapy has been used on the intermittent form of the disease only during an acute exacerbation (Dancis et al., 1967).

Histidinemia. Histidinemia was first described by Ghadimi, Partington, and Hunter (1961). They described a family in which two sisters had elevated blood histidine concentration. One of the sisters had delayed speech development. One year later an additional patient was described who was also retarded. Since the original description there have been seventeen reported cases. Fourteen have undergone intelligence testing, and only ten are retarded (Efron & Ampola, 1967). Not all the patients have had speech problems. The clinical picture is not uniform, and there are no pathognomonic clinical features. The only consistent finding is elevated plasma histidine levels. When imadazolepyruvic acid is excreted in the urine, the addition of ferric chloride leads to the appearance of a gray-green color. Oral histidine tolerance tests cause prolonged elevation of plasma histidine (Auerbach, DiGeorge, Baldridge, Tourtellotte, & Brigham, 1962). The deficient enzyme is histidase (Auerbach et al., 1962; La Du, 1966). This enzyme has been found in liver and skin and is necessary for the conversion of histidine to urocanic acid. Only an occasional investigator has employed a low-histidine diet to correct the elevated blood histidine. Waisman (1967) reported that the mother saw no improvement in the child, and the diet was discontinued. No other information is available regarding the other patient who was begun on a low-histidine diet.

Tyrosinosis. This disease was first seen by Medes, Berglund, and Lohmann in 1927 in a patient with the diagnosis of myasthenia gravis. The diagnosis was made after the finding of reducing substance in the patient's urine, which on further

TABLE 9-2   NO-THRESHOLD AMINOACIDURIAS WITH NEUROLOGICAL DISORDERS

	Amino Acid Increased in Blood	*Deficient Enzyme*	*Clinical Features*
Homocystinuria	Homocystine	Cystathionine synthetase	Retardation; seizures; ectopic lenses; thrombotic episodes
Argininosuccinic aciduria (J. D. Allen, Cusworth, Dent, & Wilson, 1958)	Argininosuccinic acid citrulline	Argininosuccinase	Retardation; seizures; fine hair; ammonia intoxication
Cystathioninuria (H. Harris, Penrose, & Thomas, 1959)	Cystathionine	Cystathioninase	Mental retardation; seizures

investigation proved to be p-hydroxphenylpyruvic acid (Medes, 1932), the alpha keto acid of tyrosine. Other patients with myasthenia gravis have not been found to have tyrosinosis. Further investigation has shown that the deficient enzyme is p-hydroxyphenylpyruvic acid oxidase (La Du, 1967).

There may be an acute or chronic clinical course (S. Halvorsen, Pande, Loken, & Gjessing, 1966). In the acute variety the patient presents in the first few months of life with vomiting, diarrhea, enlarging abdomen, and failure to thrive. Examination usually reveals edema, ascites, hepatosplenomegaly, and rickets. The course from the diagnosis to death is usually one of months, but an occasional patient has lived a few years. Death is preceded by coma, probably on the basis of liver involvement.

The chronic type presents with symptoms similar to those which occur in the acute type, but the onset is later in life. These patients present with gastrointestinal symptoms, but in addition have bleeding, growth retardation, and muscular hypotonia. They also have a progressive illness with increasing hepatic failure, and in addition they develop renal tubular dysfunction leading to renal failure. They usually die within the first decade of life. Unlike phenylketonuria, tyrosinosis has not been associated with more than mild to moderate mental retardation.

The presence of p-hydroxyphenylpyruvic acid leads to a positive urinary ferric chloride test. Serum amino-acid chromatography then is necessary for confirmatory data. The serum amino-acid chromatogram usually shows an elevation of both tyrosine and methionine (S. Halvorsen et al., 1966). The methionine elevation is secondary to hepatic involvement. The tubular changes which give rise to proteinuria and generalized aminoaciduria occur late in the course of the disease.

The pathophysiology of tyrosinosis remains to be elucidated. The hepatic and renal involvement are progressive and lead to death.

Therapy has been directed at reduction of blood tyrosine concentration. In this case, therapy requires the reduction of both tyrosine and its immediate precursor, phenylalanine. Problems similar to those seen with the low-phenylalanine diet can be anticipated with a diet low in both phenylalanine and tyrosine. Because there is only a small number of patients with the disorder, they are kept under closer observation, and at present only one major complication has occurred. Scriver, Larochelle, and Silverberg (1967) report one patient who became hypoglycemic on the second day of therapy and died 2 days later. This death may not be related to the diet because severe liver disease may also lead to hypoglycemia. High doses of vitamin D have been used for treatment of the rickets with little success.

No-threshold Aminoacidurias

Homocystinuria. The disorder of homocystinuria was first described in 1962 by Carson and Neill and independently by Gerritsen, Vaughn, and Waisman (1962). The clinical picture includes intellectual defects which range from mild to gross cerebral dysfunction. Other features are ectopic lenses, seizures, sparse hair, occasional spasticity, and thromboembolic phenomena. The latter are frequently the cause of death (Gerritsen & Waisman, 1966a). Many of these patients were previously thought to be suffering from Marfan's syndrome.

The diagnosis is made by means of amino-acid chromatography of urine. The addition of sodium nitroprusside to the urine will result in the formation of a deep red color. Plasma amino-acid analysis will show elevation of both homocystine and methionine. The deficient enzyme responsible for homocystinuria is usually present in liver and brain tissue. The enzyme cystathionine synthetase converts homocystine to cystathionine.

The mechanism by which emboli form in homocystinuria has not been found. There has been speculation that there may be increased platelet stickiness, and changes in platelet adhesiveness have been demonstrated (McDonald, Bray, Field, Love, & Davies, 1964). No beneficial

TABLE 9-3 RENAL AMINOACIDURIAS ASSOCIATED WITH NEUROLOGICAL DISORDERS

	Amino Acid Increased in Urine	Other Biochemical Findings	Clinical Features
Hartnup disease	Proline, glycine; hydroxyproline alanine; asparagine; citrulline; glutamine; histidine, isoleucine; leucine; phenylalanine; serine; threonine; tryptophan; indoxyl sulfate excreted in excess in urine	Associated intestinal absorption difficulties; same amino acids poorly absorbed by intestines	Retardation; pellagralike rash; cerebellar ataxia
Joseph's syndrome (Joseph, Ribierre, Job, & Girault, 1958)	Proline; hydroxyproline; glycine	Unknown	Seizures
Methionine (Hooft, Timmermans, Snoeck, Antener, Oyaert, & van den Herde, 1964)	Perhaps nine, but likely similar to oasthouse urine disease; a-hydroxylbutyric acid in urine and feces	Poor absorption of leucine, isoleucine valine, and methionine; a-hydroxybutyric acid formed in gut by bacterial action from methionine	Retardation; seizures; white hair; abnormal body odor; hyperpnea

changes in platelet adhesiveness occur with dietary therapy.

The age of onset of symptoms in homocystinuria is highly variable, and consequently there is great variation in the ages of patients when dietary therapy is instituted. One patient was diagnosed at birth and was begun on therapy at 9 days of life, when the methionine and homocystine were both elevated (Komrower, 1967). The diet was adequate to keep both the methionine and homocystine in the "normal" range, but cystathionine was not supplemented. The patient was 1 year of age when reported and was developing normally.

Renal Aminoacidurias

Hartnup disease. Hartnup disease is a disease noted in childhood and characterized by a pellagralike rash, transient cerebellar ataxia, renal aminoaciduria, and indicanuria (Baron, Dent, Harris, Hart, & Jepson, 1956).

The rash is present on exposed surfaces, is dry and red, and may become hyperpigmented. The presence of the rash is usually accompanied by the transient symptoms of cerebellar ataxia. Other neurological signs including spasticity, nystagmus, and tremors are sometimes noted. Approximately one-half of the affected individuals are retarded.

The mode of inheritance is not completely understood. In this condition there is transport deficiency of tryptophan and other neutral amino acids both in the epithelium of the gut and in the renal tubules. The urinary amino-acid pattern is highly unusual, and there is a manyfold increase in the urinary concentration of alanine, asparagine, histidine, glutamine, isoleucine, citrulline, leucine, phenylalanine, serine, threonine, and tryptophan (Jepson & Spiro, 1966). The patients also excrete compounds known as *indicans,* of which the primary component is indoxyl sulfate. It appears that indoxyl sulfate excretion is the result of breakdown of tryptophan within the gut,

absorption of the resulting indoles through the intestinal mucosa, further metabolism of the indoles within the liver, and finally excretion of the circulating indoles into the urine through the kidneys. The biochemistry of this disease is not well understood except for the fact there are obviously difficulties in transport mechanisms. The relationship of these mechanisms to the neurological signs and symptoms is unknown.

Therapy with nicotinic acid results in a decrease of excretion of indican, resolution of the skin rash, and cessation of most of the motor neurological abnormalities (K. Halvorsen & Halvorsen, 1963).

There are very few cases of this disease, and little more information is known.

DISEASES ASSOCIATED WITH ABNORMALITIES OF LIPID METABOLISM

Lipids are the major chemical component of the brain. Diseases associated with lipid abnormalities have assumed a new importance in the past decade. Increased interest in this area is directly related to heightened sophistication in techniques of lipid identification and enzymology. Many diseases have been recognized that are associated with accumulation of lipids. It is only recently that enzyme abnormalities in metabolic pathways of lipid synthesis and degradation have been identified.

Sphingolipids

Most diseases of lipid storage accumulation in the brain are the result of abnormal metabolism of sphingolipids. Sphingosine is an eighteen-carbon nitrogen-containing compound that is formed from the condensation of palmitic acid and serine. The combination of sphingosine and a long-chain fatty acid is known as a *ceramide* (Figure 9-1). A ceramide complex is found in most of the sphingolipids of clinical importance. The attachment of

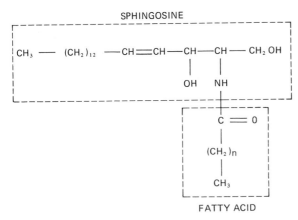

SPHINGOSINE

FATTY ACID

Figure 9-1. A ceramide composed of sphingosine and a fatty acid. Fatty acid chain length is determined by numerical value of n.

Ceramide——Glucose
Ceramide——Galactose

Figure 9-2. Composition of the two important cerebrosides found in brain.

Ceramide——Galactose——Sulfate

Figure 9-3. Composition of a sulfatide. The sulfate is esterified to the third carbon of galactose.

Ceramide-phosphoric acid-choline

Figure 9-4. Composition of a sphingomyelin.

Ceramide——Glucose——Galactose——N——Acetylgalactosamine——Galactose

N-Acetylneuraminic Acid

Figure 9-5. Composition of a ganglioside with a single molecule of N-Acetylneuraminic acid (monosialoganglioside).

galactose or glucose to the ceramide results in the formation of compounds known as *cerebrosides* (Figure 9-2). Cerebrosides are found in excess in the tissues of patients with Gaucher's disease. The esterification of a sulfate group onto the third carbon of galactose of a cerebroside leads to the formation of a compound known as *sulfatide* (Figure 9-3). Accumulation of sulfatide is found in association with sulfatide lipidosis (metachromatic leukodystrophy).

Ceramide complexed with phosphate and choline results in the formation of *sphingomyelin* (Figure 9-4). Accumulation of sphingomyelin is noted in tissues of patients with Niemann-Pick disease.

Ceramide, galactose, glucose, N-acetylgalactosamine, and N-acetylneuraminic acid are joined to form compounds known as *gangliosides* (Figure

9-5). A number of gangliosides have been described on the basis of the type and number of hexoses and molecules of N-acetylneuraminic acid present. An increase of ganglioside concentration in the brain is noted in Tay-Sachs disease.

Cerebromacular Degeneration (Familial Amaurotic Idiocy)

The first of the lipidoses to be described was Tay-Sachs disease. The first case was reported in 1881 by Tay, an ophthalmologist, who described macular changes with a "cherry-red" spot in affected infants. Later Sachs described siblings who had blindness and dementia. The name *amaurotic family idiocy* (Sachs, 1896) was applied to the disorder. About 80 percent of the patients are of Jewish descent (Fredrickson, 1966).

The signs and symptoms of Tay-Sachs disease begin within the first year of life (Schneck & Volk, 1967). Very frequently there are subtle symptoms which, when viewed retrospectively, can be seen to have been present in the first 2 months of life. The most frequent and earliest findings are hyperacusis and the cherry-red macula. Hyperacusis in Tay-Sachs disease becomes progressively more prominent. Very shortly after these symptoms begin, it becomes apparent that the child's head control is poor and that his skeletal muscles are weak and hypotonic. After visual acuity becomes impaired, nystagmus and lack of fixation become prominent. In addition to the hyperacusis, which is accompanied by an abnormal electroencephalographic pattern, there is an associated seizure disorder. The seizures are usually myoclonic and appear before 1 year of age. There is a slow progression of symptomatology with deterioration. After the first year of life the head size is noted to increase above normal limits because of a marked accumulation of gangliosides (Fredrickson & Trams, 1966). Electroretinography is normal in Tay-Sachs disease (Copenhaver & Goodman, 1960). The expected life-span is about 2 years; occasionally a child has survived through age 5. The disease is transmitted in an autosomal recessive pattern of inheritance.

Routine biopsy studies from marrow, liver, and kidney are not helpful in the antemortem diagnosis of Tay-Sachs disease. Rectal biopsy followed by study of the ganglion cells may reveal the presence of storage material.

In the 1940s the chemical pathology was more clearly identified when increased brain gangliosides were noted to be present. In the past 10 years definitive lipid studies have further delineated the chemical pathology. Svennerholm (1963) and Kuhn (Kuhn & Wiegandt, 1963) have described the composition and profile of gangliosides which are normally found in the brain as well as an abnormal ganglioside found in large quantities in Tay-Sachs disease.

The presence of a large amount of this abnormal ganglioside is due to an enzymatic defect in the catabolic pathway. In Tay-Sachs disease the ganglioside that is accumulated lacks a terminal galactose, as compared with the normally present gangliosides. Most likely the terminal galactose has been cleaved from the ganglioside, and the metabolic block involves the enzyme responsible for the subsequent cleavage of neuraminic acid (R. O. Brady, 1966).

The routine laboratory studies in Tay-Sachs patients have not shown any significant abnormalities, with the exception of low serum fructose-1-phosphate aldolase activity (Volk, Aronson, & Saifer, 1964). Heterozygotic individuals also have low fructose-one-phosphate aldolase activity.

Our present state of knowledge is not adequate to explain the pathophysiology of Tay-Sachs disease. Neuronal cell size is increased by the inclusion of ganglioside material. This process is generalized within the brain, causing massive brain enlargement (Fredrickson & Trams, 1966). Neurons in visceral plexuses are also involved (Kamoshita & Landing, 1968). The involved cells show displacement of the nuclei as well as displacement of the Nissal substance. No information is available that details the effects of the ganglioside on neuronal physiology.

Present therapy is supportive only. There is no evidence that benefit accrues from restriction of dietary lipid or carbohydrate, as it does in some of the other metabolic disturbances.

Since the early descriptions of the disorder there have been many case reports of patients with seizures, macular degeneration, and progressive cerebral deterioration. These difficulties occur in older children. There is no cherry-red spot. There is abnormal dark pigmentation of the macular area instead.

The progression of the diseases is much slower than that of Tay-Sachs disease, and the pathology is not the same. These syndromes have a variety of eponyms depending upon the age of onset.

The late infantile form is known as *Jansky-Biel-schowsky disease,* the juvenile form as *Vogt-Spielmeyer disease,* and the adult form as *Kufs disease.* It has not been definitely established that there is a derangement of ganglioside metabolism in these diseases.

Generalized Gangliosidosis

In contrast to Tay-Sachs disease, which clinically appears to affect the CNS only, there is a disease of infants associated with ganglioside accumulation with both cerebral and systemic involvement. The first cases were reported in 1959 (Norman, Urich, Tingey, & Goodbody, 1959). After the initial description many new cases were found, and the disorder is known as both *generalized gangliosidosis* (O'Brien, Stern, Landing, O'Brien, & Donnell, 1965) and *neurovisceral lipidosis* (Landing, Silverman, Craig, Jacoby, Lahey, & Chadwick, 1964).

The ganglioside that is stored in large amounts appears to be of the same structure as a ganglioside normally found in the brain. Patients with generalized gangliosidosis display some clinical manifestations similar to those found in Tay-Sachs disease. In addition to CNS involvement they also have evidence of liver and kidney failure (Landing et al., 1964). They usually expire within the first 2 years of life. Generalized gangliosidosis patients also have some features associated with the mucopolysaccharidoses. Biopsy material from patients with generalized gangliosidosis have revealed foamy histiocytes and x-ray skeletal deformities usually associated with the mucopolysaccharidoses.

Niemann-Pick Disease

A disease with similarities to Tay-Sachs disease was initially described by Niemann in 1914. These cases were later reviewed by Pick (1933), and the common factors were noted. Frequently the patients are of Jewish origin. The earliest symptom in the infantile type is usually failure to thrive with accompanying jaundice and diarrhea (Crocker & Farber, 1958); Schneck & Volk,

1967). Symptoms usually appear by the sixth month of life. Examination usually reveals hepatosplenomegaly and the cherry-red macula. In contrast to Tay-Sachs disease, there are few early abnormal neurological findings. The patients eventually deteriorate, with mental and motor regression accompanied by seizures. There are also electroencephalographic abnormalities, but no specific pattern emerges. The course of the disease is similar to that of Tay-Sachs disease, and only a rare patient lives beyond 2 years. There is no undue enlargement of head size in the second year.

Routine laboratory studies are not diagnostic. Elevated serum lipids have been reported as well as small elevations of transaminase activity. Bone-marrow studies may be diagnostic. Foam cells seen in bone-marrow studies in this disease are called *Niemann-Pick cells.* Liver biopsy reveals parenchymal and reticuloendothelial cells with vacuolated cytoplasm. Light microscopic examination of the brain yields findings nearly indistinguishable from findings in Tay-Sachs disease. The ganglion and glial cells are infiltrated with lipid material. Quantitative studies of liver, spleen, and brain reveal decreased lecithin and increased cholesterol and sphingomyelin (Crocker & Mays, 1961; Fredrickson, 1966).

Sphingomyelin, the abnormally accumulating lipid, is composed of ceramide and phosphorylcholine esterified to it by means of the phosphate moiety.

Decreased activity of the enzyme sphingomyelinase has been found in all organs (R. O. Brady, Gal, Kanfer, & Bradley, 1965) which are involved. The deficiency is also present in the peripheral blood (Kampine, Brady, Kanfer, Feld, & Shapiro, 1966). The enzyme cleaves the phosphorylcholine from sphingomyelin to yield ceramide. Although the enzymatic defect has been described (Roitman & Gatt, 1963), this information has led to no satisfactory explanation of the clinical manifestations.

Review of case reports makes it apparent that

Niemann-Pick disease is not confined to the first year of life. Crocker and Farber (1958) published a series of cases and divided the disease into four types. All have abnormalities in sphingomyelin storage. The first is the classical type, with onset in the first year of life and severe CNS involvement. The patients of the second type are older, have marked visceral involvement, and experience no CNS involvement. The third type begins in late infancy, has not been found in Jewish children, and involves the CNS. Moderate visceral involvement secondary to lipid accumulation also occurs. The fourth type has been described in Nova Scotian Catholics. Symptoms of CNS involvement beginning in early to middle childhood are noted along with mild visceral involvement. The illness runs a chronic course with death occurring between 12 and 20 years.

No specific treatment has been of benefit in Niemann-Pick disease, but liver extracts (Braithwaite & Miller, 1940; Crocker & Farber, 1958), anterior pituitary extracts, and adrenocortical extracts have been used. It is of interest to speculate about the value of infusion of the deficient enzyme or transplantation of a normal spleen or liver. Up to the present time only supportive therapy has been employed.

Gaucher's Disease

The disease described in 1882 by Gaucher has been seen in children under a year of age as well as in adults. The symptom and signs differ in the two types.

The symptoms and signs of infantile Gaucher's disease include hepatosplenomegaly with evidence of cerebral involvement. The CNS abnormalities result in findings of spasticity, opisthotonus, and strabismus. These children die within the first 2 years of life of progressive bulbar involvement, and on microscopic and biochemical examination are noted to have increased storage of cerebroside (Phillippart & Menkes, 1964). Cerebroside is composed of sphingosine and a fatty acid bound to hexose.

The hexose is either glucose or galactose. In the case of Gaucher's disease, the hexose present in the excess cerebroside is glucose in the viscera (Phillippart & Menkes, 1964) and galactose in the brain (Phillippart & Menkes, 1967). The enzyme has been isolated, and its activity can be determined in the involved tissues (R. O. Brady, 1966; R. O. Brady, Kanfer, Bradley, & Shapiro, 1966) as well as in the blood. The enzyme which is deficient in Gaucher's disease cleaves hexose from the sphingosine. The disease is transmitted as an autosomal recessive trait.

The antemortem diagnosis is made by bone-marrow examination, which reveals classical Gaucher cells (Block & Jacobson, 1948). They are foamy and contain vacuoles of cerebroside. Study of liver biopsy material is also abnormal (Volk & Wallace, 1966), demonstrating the accumulation of the cerebroside (Philippart & Menkes, 1964).

The patients also have unexplained elevated serum acid phosphatase activity.

At the present time no adequate therapy is available that will change the course of the disease.

Sulfatide Lipidosis (Metachromatic Leukodystrophy)

One of the later-described sphingolipidoses was called a *leukodystrophy* up until the last 5 years. It was known as *metachromatic leukodystrophy* and is now known as *sulfatide lipidosis* (Moser & Lees, 1966). The term *metachromatic* was applied to this disorder when it was shown that the stored lipid material stained brown when stained with toluidine blue (Austin, 1957). The symptoms of sulfatide lipidosis begin late in comparison with those of most of the previously mentioned lipidoses. The early development of these children is entirely normal until 1 to 1½ years of age. The children then develop gait disturbance which may appear as ataxia or as weakness. Other neurological symptoms may be lacking for another 6 months or more, when bulbar signs become apparent and the weakness progresses to spasticity and severe mental and motor deterioration. The most striking clinical finding at this time is the absence of deep tendon reflexes, ostensibly because of peripheral nerve involvement by abnormal sulfatide deposition. The disease is transmitted as an autosomal recessive trait.

Austin (1959) demonstrated that the biochemical abnormality is the accumulation of sulfatides in both the central and the peripheral nervous system. The deficient enzyme was reported in 1963 to be sulfatase (Austin, Balasubramanian, Pattabiraman, Saraswathi, Basu, & Bachhawat, 1963). The abnormal accumulating molecule is a sulfatide which consists of a cerebroside with a sulfate ester. The deficient enzyme is necessary for cleaving the sulfate ester from the hexose. Arylsulfatase A activity has been found in liver and kidney as well as in the nervous system. Another finding which has been used for diagnosis is the absence of gall-bladder function as assessed with a cholecystogram (Allen, McCusker, & Tourtellotte, 1962). At the present time the diagnosis can be made from urinary studies for the presence of granules or the determination of urinary arylsulfatase A activity.

No therapy has been effective in sulfatide lipidosis, but some attempts have been made to get the enzyme into the nervous system. The enzyme was injected into pig cerebrospinal fluid (Austin, 1967), and days later the cerebrospinal fluid was found to have significant levels of enzyme remaining. Unfortunately, the problem of getting the enzyme into the cell where the deficiency resides remains unsolved.

Some cases reported by Bischel, Austin, and Kemeny (1966) have been called *sulfatide lipidosis variants* because of their excretion of both sulfatide material and mucopolysaccharides. No satisfactory explanation of this phenomenon has been found, and these conditions may represent a bridge between the lipidoses and the mucopolysaccharidoses.

Mucopolysaccharidoses

There are three well-identified diseases associated with abnormal mucopolysaccharide metabolism and two rarer types.

The disease initially described is known as *Hurler's syndrome* and is characterized by short stature; unusual skeletal deformities involving the spine, hands, ribs, and long bones; limitation of movement at the joints; deafness; hepatosplenomegaly; unusual facies; congenital heart disease; mental retardation; and sometimes clouding of the corneas (Leroy & Crocker, 1966). Mucopolysaccharides are excreted in excess in the urine and have been found deposited in an abnormal degree in tissues of these patients. Examination of white blood cells obtained from bone-marrow biopsy reveals the presence of unusual cytoplasmic granules known as *Reilly bodies* (Reilly, 1941). X-rays of the extremities and spine often reveal the typical deformities of tubulation of the metacarpal bones and beaking of the posterior portions of the vertebral bodies. This form of the disease is transmitted in an autosomal recessive pattern.

The patients excrete abnormal amounts of chondroitin sulfate B (CSB) and heparitin sulfate (HS) (Terry & Linker, 1964). There is a preponderance of CSB in their urine.

Another group of patients have been identified as the *Hunter group* (Leroy & Crocker, 1966). These patients have a disease similar to those with Hurler's syndrome, but there are some differences. These children are not as retarded in their motor or intellectual development, although they deteriorate sometime between the second and fourth years. These patients excrete almost equal amounts of CSB and HS. They are all boys because their form of the disease is inherited in a sex-linked recessive manner. Deafness is also commonly observed.

The third disease of this group is known as the *Sanfilippo syndrome* (Leroy & Crocker, 1966). These patients are markedly different from the patients in the first two groups and have none of the skeletal abnormalities of Hurler's and Hunter's syndromes (Terry & Linker, 1964). The clinical pattern of their disease is that of mild early retardation followed by rapid deterioration sometime between the second and fourth years. They do not have the cardiac, skeletal, visceral, or ocular abnormalities seen in the other two syndromes.

These patients excrete HS almost exclusively in their urine and are therefore known as heparitin excreters (Terry & Linker, 1964). Their clinical course is one of relentless neurological deterioration, with death sometime early in the first decade.

Another disease in this group, known as *Scheie's syndrome,* is transmitted as an autosomal recessive trait. The patients have coarse facies, cloudy corneas, limitation of motion at the joints, normal intellect, and cardiac valvular changes which result in aortic regurgitation. CSB is excreted in large amounts in the urine. Another rare disease in this group is known as the *Maroteaux-Lamy syndrome.* It is also transmitted as an autosomal recessive trait, and increased amounts of CSB are found in the urine. The patients are of normal intelligence, but have pronounced corneal clouding and changes in the bones. The latter two diseases have been described in only one or two family groups.

Another mucopolysaccharidosis is known as *Morquio's syndrome.* This disease is transmitted in an autosomal recessive fashion and is characterized by normal intelligence, cloudy corneas, and severe bony changes leading to marked curvature of the spine. The mucopolysaccharide is an unusual material known as *keratosulfate,* which is usually excreted in only trace amounts in normal individuals.

The enzyme deficiency in both Hurler's and Hunter's syndromes is known; beta galactosidase deficiency has been noted in both conditions.

Recently fluid removed by transabdominal anoicentesis was used to obtain fetal cells. *In vitro* culture techniques were followed by study of radioactive sulfate incorporation. The resulting curves revealed an abnormally rapid uptake and accumulation of intracellular mucopolysaccharide. Thus the diagnosis of Hurler's and Hunter's syndromes is possible *in utero.*

These diseases are included in the diseases of abnormal lipid metabolism because there has been noted associated abnormal patterns of brain lipid (Borri, Hooghwinkel, & Edgar, 1966).

DISORDERS OF FLUID AND ELECTROLYTE BALANCE

Disorders of fluid and electrolyte balance may present with CNS manifestations. In general, electrolyte and fluid homeostasis is maintained by CNS controls and peripheral volume receptors (Gilbert & Glaser, 1961).

The osmotic receptors in the hypothalamus respond to electrolyte concentration changes and react by causing the secretion of antidiuretic hormone by the supraoptic and paraventricular nuclei of the hypothalamus. The peripheral volume receptors located in the right atrium and aorta exert their influence through control of adrenal secretion of aldosterone (Logothetis, 1966). There is evidence that aldosterone secretion can also be regulated by the CNS (Gilbert & Glaser, 1961).

Another regulatory center is the thirst center (Leaf, 1962; Logothetis, 1966). This center is postulated to be present in the mid-hypothalamus, on either side of the third ventricle. Injection of hypertonic saline or electrical stimulation of these areas leads to excessive drinking (Andersson, 1953; Andersson & McCann, 1955).

Neurological changes have been described with abnormalities of sodium and water balance, calcium balance, magnesium balance, and acid-base balance (Cooke & Ottenheimer, 1960; Katzman, 1966; Logothetis, 1966; Miller, 1968).

Most common of the above disorders are those

involving the imbalance of sodium and water. Hyponatremia may result from an increase in extracellular fluid volume, a decrease in the concentration of sodium in the extracellular space, or a combination of the two. Extracellular sodium deficiency may result from vomiting, diarrhea, late phases of renal diseases, multiple or large-volume enemas, diuretic therapy, hypoadrenalism (including the adrenogenital syndrome), and burns. An increase in extracellular fluid volume may result from fluid therapy with hypotonic solutions, excessive oral intake of water, and excess secretion of antidiuretic hormones.

The symptoms of hyponatremia are quite similar no matter what the underlying etiology is. In the early phases of hyponatremia the patient may complain of headache and lethargy. Lethargy may progress into coma (Katzman, 1966; Logothetis, 1966). Seizures frequently occur in infants and young children with hyponatremia. Other symptoms and signs have been reported and include ataxia, hypertension, headache, papilledema, and apnea (Cooke & Ottenheimer, 1960). On occasion extremely low levels of serum sodium have been reported with no accompanying neurological deficit. It has been suggested that the presence of symptoms is a function of both the serum sodium concentration and the rapidity of the fall from normal values (Cooke & Ottenheimer, 1960).

The diagnosis of hyponatremia is dependent upon the determination of serum sodium concentration. The severity of the decrease of serum sodium concentration does not shed light on the cause of hyponatremia. Associated laboratory findings or changes in other serum electrolytes can help delineate the underlying disorder. For example, in the presence of excess antidiuretic hormone the urine sodium concentration is increased, while the serum sodium concentration is low. Hypoadrenalism is associated with high serum potassium concentration along with hyponatremia.

Investigations into the pathophysiology of hyponatremia have not been very rewarding. Animals that have been made hyponatremic show increases in brain water (Crawford, Dodge, & Probst, 1958), with minimal changes in brain sodium and decreased brain potassium (Yannet, 1940).

Therapy is dictated by the underlying etiology, but basically it is directed to the addition of deficient sodium or the removal of excess water. In the emergency situation, when the patient is convulsing, infusion of 3 percent sodium chloride can be lifesaving (Miller, 1968). When there is both dehydration and hyponatremia, the patient needs both water and sodium. Many cases of hyponatremia are associated with excess extracellular fluid volume and normal total body sodium. In these instances fluid restriction will suffice unless the symptoms and signs require more vigorous therapy (Cooke & Ottenheimer, 1960; Katzman, 1966). Both intravenous urea and mannitol have been used as diuretics in this situation with success (Katzman, 1966). Recent experience favors the use of mannitol over urea.

Acute hyponatremia may result in death. Serum sodium concentration of less than 100 milliequivalents per liter is reportedly incompatible with life (Leaf, 1962). No good follow-up studies of patients who have suffered from hyponatremia are available.

Numerous clinical and experimental reports have been published describing causes, pathophysiology, and prognosis of hypernatremia (Finberg, 1959; Finberg, Luttrell, & Redd, 1957; Macaulay & Watson, 1967; Morris-Jones, Houston, & Evans, 1967). This syndrome has been studied more than any of the other electrolyte imbalances, and it still carries the poorest prognosis (Macaulay & Watson, 1967).

The signs and symptoms of hypernatremia do not vary with the underlying etiology. Systemic evidence such as hypotension and dehydration may be lacking. Neurological symptoms include lethargy, coma, and hyperirritability to minimal stimuli. Seizures are common and may occur before or after attempted therapy (Cooke & Ottenheimer, 1960). Examination confirms the hyperirritability and also reveals hyperactive deep tendon reflexes, muscular rigidity, and meningismus.

There are two general causes of hypernatremia. The first is an increase in extracellular sodium concentration. This situation is frequently present with accidental administration of excess sodium, oral or parenteral, or the inability of the kidneys to excrete sodium normally. The second cause is a decrease in extracellular volume without change in total body sodium. Associated conditions include excessive water losses from the gastrointestinal tract, excessive renal losses, and diabetes insipidus. Occasionally the abnormal situation is compounded by decreased intake of water. The administration of a hypertonic electrolyte solution to a child with diarrhea is a common antecedent of hypernatremia.

Of all the electrolyte disturbances affecting the CNS, hypernatremia produces the most characteristic pathological findings. Severe hemorrhage involving the cortex, subarachnoid space, and occasionally the subdural space is usually seen (Luttrell, Finberg, & Drawdy, 1959). Cerebrospinal fluid protein is frequently elevated, and this fact has been cited as evidence that there is a breakdown of the blood–cerebrospinal fluid barrier. Thromboses of pial bridging veins have been observed and have been noted to extend into the major dural sinuses. Experimental studies have shown that brain water is reduced about 10 percent (Cooke & Ottenheimer, 1960), while the changes in brain sodium and potassium concentration are negligible. Cerebrospinal fluid pressure is consistently low. When cerebrospinal fluid pressure is maintained experimentally, the hemorrhagic picture described above is not seen (Luttrell et al., 1959). Seizures frequently follow initiation of therapy of hypernatremia, but the mechanism of the onset of seizure activity is unknown (Cooke & Ottenheimer, 1960; Morris-Jones et al., 1967).

The treatment of hypernatremia is dependent on the etiology. In most clinical situations dehydration is paramount, but the water cannot be replaced rapidly because of the possibility of producing cerebral edema and seizures. Consequently, replacement is usually spread over 12 to 24 hours using hypotonic solutions.

Prevention of hypernatremia in patients with diabetes insipidus requires administration of exogenous antidiuretic hormone and the availability of free water. During acute episodes of hypernatremia these patients must also be given antidiuretic hormone and water.

Two recent clinical studies have outlined the prognosis of hypernatremia (Macaulay & Watson, 1967; Morris-Jones et al., 1967). In both studies a high mortality rate was noted with the acute episode. Of the surviving patients, 22 to 37 percent had residual neurological symptoms. These included abnormal electroencephalograms, seizures, intellectual retardation, and spasticity. It is of interest to note that in both surveys, there was an unusually high incidence of preexisting CNS disease.

Hypocalcemia is frequently associated with increased neuromuscular irritability leading to tetany (Katzman, 1966; Miller, 1968). Seizures also occur with hypocalcemia. Hypocalcemia may be present in the newborn child without any known specific etiology, but it has been associated with prematurity and maternal diabetes. Hypocalcemia in the newborn may also be present with seizures rather than with neuromuscular irritability.

Hypoparathyroidism is probably the most common cause of hypocalcemia in older children. These patients may have seizures and lethargy and demonstrate inappropriate affect and behavior. Increased intracranial pressure has also been reported. Calcification in the region of the basal ganglia is sometimes seen in hypoparathyroidism.

Pseudohypoparathyroidism is the result of the failure of the renal tubules to respond to circulating parathyroid hormone. In addition to having hypocalcemia, usually these children are retarded and dwarfed and have wide hands and thumbnails, broad faces, and foreshortened fourth metacarpal bones.

Treatment of hypocalcemia consists primarily of replacement of deficient calcium. In the newborn nursery, hypocalcemia is treated with parenteral calcium. In older children acute hypocalcemia is also treated with parenteral calcium, but chronic hypocalcemia is treated with oral calcium salts and vitamin D. The chronic forms of hypocalcemia are due to parathyroid disorders and to severe chronic renal insufficiency.

Hypercalcemia is a rare disorder in the pediatric population. It usually results from ingestion of excess vitamin D, but on occasion has been seen with parathyroid adenomas and malignancies. An idiopathic form of hypocalcemia has also been described in children. These infants have a peculiar facies, mental retardation, growth failure, hypertension, and muscular weakness (Lightwood, 1952). Associated congenital heart disease is sometimes present.

Hypercalcemia has been observed to cause suppression of CNS activity, ultimately leading to coma. Weakness, hallucinations, and seizures have also been observed during episodes of hypercalcemia (Miller, 1968). The treatment of hypercalcemia is determined by the underlying cause. Phosphate salts have been infused during acute episodes with good results.

Disorders of magnesium metabolism are also very rare. Hypomagnesemia has been reported in the newborn resulting in muscle spasm, tetany, and seizures. More frequently it is seen in older children who have underlying chronic disorders usually including liver failure. The treatment of choice, regardless of the etiology, remains administration of parenteral magnesium.

Hypermagnesemia is much more common among the newborn than in any other population. It usually appears secondary to the treatment of maternal toxemia. The child is frequently somnolent, weak, and areflexic. Hypotension and myoclonus have been observed in older children. Treatment of severe disease in the newborn consists of infusion of calcium salts and occasionally exchange transfusion (J. P. Brady & Williams, 1967).

Disturbances of potassium metabolism are commonly seen in all age groups and are often associated with metabolic disturbances which do not affect primarily CNS function. Potassium metabolism is greatly affected by changes in circulating levels of aldosterone, which acts predominantly on the distal renal tubule to reabsorb sodium at the expense of potassium. Weakness is the most characteristic finding in both conditions (Katzman, 1966; Miller, 1968). The paralysis seen is usually of a flaccid variety. Electrocardiogram changes are frequently seen in these conditions. From the study of clinical material it is apparent that no specific neurological syndrome can be delineated in hyperkalemia or hypokalemia (Katzman, 1966).

The clinical syndromes involving changes in acid-base balance have few specific neurological manifestations. In general, changes in consciousness may be present, and seizures are sometimes noted. Tetany is frequently present in alkalotic conditions. Carbon dioxide retention in respiratory acidosis has been associated with narcosis.

Recently, measurements of cerebrospinal fluid pH have been used as a diagnostic tool in respiratory acidosis (Posner & Plum, 1967). Changes in the level of consciousness were closely related to the changes in the cerebrospinal fluid pH, even though the blood pH had returned to normal. From a therapeutic viewpoint, it was demonstrated that too rapid correction of the systemic pH leads to more profound depression. The etiology of the depression is purported to be due to the depression of respiration, which in turn results in a greater retention of cerebrospinal fluid carbon dioxide.

DISORDERS OF ENDOCRINE METABOLISM

Hypothyroidism

Congenital and acquired hypothyroidism are the two types of hypothyroidism seen in infancy and childhood. Congenital hypothyroidism is also known as *cretinism*. It may be caused by congenital lack of the thyroid gland; the presence of a small, ectopic, and inadequate thyroid gland; errors in the biochemical pathway of thyroid synthesis; and hypothyroidism secondary to drug therapy of a hyperthyroid mother.

Clinical symptomatology is frequently not present in cretins at the time of birth, ostensibly because of the presence of circulating thyroxin from the mother. Over half the children have clinical abnormalities by the first month of life (Lowrey, Aster, Carr, Ramon, Beierwaltes, & Spafford, 1958). In general, the child is lethargic and has thickened facial features involving the lips, eyelids, and tongue. Constipation is usually present, and umbilical hernias are common. The child may also have difficulty with frequent respiratory infections and may eat poorly and fail to gain weight. The cry is often low-pitched and short-lived. Seizures are very rare.

Laboratory studies reveal decreased serum protein-bound iodine and decreased radioactive iodine uptake. The electrocardiogram frequently shows reduced voltage of all complexes. X-ray examination of the bones reveals delayed bone age and failure of epiphysial closure in the long bones. The electroencephalogram is abnormal and is frequently dominated by excessive low-voltage, slow activity (R. Harris, Della Rovere, & Prior, 1965). The electroencephalogram often becomes normal or near normal after replacement thyroid therapy.

Acquired hypothyroidism is much less common in children and may be secondary to goiter formation, ectopic and insufficient thyroid tissue, and ingestion of goitrogens. The symptoms that these children manifest are dependent upon the age at which hypothyroidism is acquired. In general, they become lethargic and placid and do not respond appropriately to their environment. Constipation, loss of appetite, and cold intolerance also appear. The deep tendon reflexes are often hypoactive, and there is delay in relaxation of contraction. Laboratory changes are similar to those seen in congenital hypothyroidism.

On occasion, hypothyroidism presents itself in patients with muscular hypertrophy. These patients do not have true dystrophy, and the hypertrophy and firmness of the muscles resolve with adequate therapy.

Therapy consists of the use of desiccated thyroid. The drug must be begun in small dosages and increased until adequate levels are reached. The drug dosage may be monitored by the regression of clinical symptoms and the maintenance of serum protein-bound iodine within normal limits.

Early therapy of cretinism, before the age of 6 months, allows a fair number of patients to develop intelligent quotients in the low normal range (D. W. Smith, Blizzard, & Wilkins, 1957). These infants do not ordinarily achieve the intelligence levels of their normal siblings, no matter how early and appropriate the therapy.

It is evident from work in recent years that normal thyroid function is necessary for normal development of the CNS. Cretinism is associated with a decrease in the number of neurones and abnormalities in the maturation of the dendritic processes. Other laboratory studies have revealed the dependence of normal protein ‘synthesis in the developing brain upon the presence of thyroxin (Gelber, Campbell, Deibler, & Sokoloff, 1964). It appears that the effect of thyroid hormone on protein synthesis is mediated through mitochondrial metabolism. Recent studies have demonstrated that thyroid hormone also enhances the rate of myelination in the developing brain (Walravens & Chase, 1968).

Hyperthyroidism is unusual in infancy and does not result in any specific neurological deficiency. Other endocrine abnormalities exert their effect on the CNS by means of changes in electrolyte, water, and carbohydrate metabolism and have been discussed earlier in this chapter.

REFERENCES

Allen, J. D., Cusworth, D. C., Dent, C. E., & Wilson, V. K. Disease, probably hereditary, characterized by severe mental deficiency and constant gross abnormality of amino acid metabolism. *The Lancet,* 1958, **1,** 182–187.

Allen, R. J., McCusker, J. J., & Tourtellotte, W. W. Metachromatic leukodystrophy: Clinical, histochemical, and cerebrospinal fluid abnormalities. *Pediatrics,* 1962, **30,** 629–638.

Andersson, B. Effect of injections of hypertonic NaCl solutions into different parts of the hypothalamus of goats. *Acta Physiologica et Neurologica Scandinavica,* 1953, **28,** 188.

Andersson, B., & McCann, S. M. Further study of polydipsia evoked by hypothalamic stimulation in the goat. *Acta Physiologica et Neurologica Scandinavica,* 1955, **33,** 333.

Auerbach, V. H., DiGeorge, A. M., Baldridge, R. C., Tourtellotte, C. D., & Brigham, M. P. Histidinemia. *The Journal of Pediatrics,* 1962, **60,** 487–497.

Austin, J. H. Metachromatic form of diffuse cerebral sclerosis. I. Diagnosis during life by urine sediment examination. *Neurology,* 1957, **7,** 415–426.

Austin, J. H. Metachromatic sulfatides in cerebral white matter and kidney. *Proceedings of the Society for Experimental Biology and Medicine,* 1959, **100,** 361.

Austin, J. H. Some recent findings in leukodystrophies and in gargoylism. In S. M. Aronson & B. W. Volk (Eds.), *Inborn disorders of sphingolipid metabolism.* Oxford: Pergamon Press, 1967.

Austin, J. H., Balasubramanian, A. S., Pattabiraman, T. N., Saraswathi, S., Basu, D. K., & Bachhawat, B. K. A controlled study of enzymic activities in three human disorders of glycolipid metabolism. *Journal of Neurochemistry,* 1963, **10,** 805–816.

Baker, A. B. Cerebral damage in hypoglycemia: Review. *American Journal of Psychiatry,* 1939, **96,** 109–127.

Baron, D. N., Dent, C. E., Harris, N., Hart, E. W., & Jepson, J. B. Hereditary pellagra-like skin rash with temporary cerebellar ataxia, constant renal aminoaciduria and other bizarre biochemical features. *The Lancet,* 1956, **2,** 421–428.

Berlow, S., & Efron, M. L. New cause of hyperprolinemia associated with excretion of Δ^1-pyroline-5-carboxylic acid. *Society of Pediatric Research,* 1964. (Abstract)

Bessman, S. P., Wapnir, R., & Due, D. Amine metabolism in phenylketonuria. In J. A. Anderson & K. F. Swaiman (Eds.), *Phenylketonuria and allied metabolic diseases.* Washington: U.S. Department of Health, Education and Welfare, 1967. Pp. 9–20.

Bickel, H. A critical assessment of the dietary treatment of phenylketonuria: Experiences with 45 cases over the last 6 years. In J. A. Anderson & K. F. Swaiman (Eds.), *Phenylketonuria and allied metabolic diseases.* Washington: U.S. Department of Health, Education, and Welfare, 1967. Pp. 99–115.

Bischel, M., Austin, J., & Kemeny, M. Metachromatic leukodystrophy (MLD). VII. Elevated sulfated acid polysaccharide levels in urine and postmortem tissues. *Archives of Neurology,* 1966, **15,** 13–28.

Blackwood, W., McMenemey, W. H., Meyer, A., Norman, R. M., & Russell, D. S. *Greenfield's neuropathology.* (2nd ed.) Baltimore: Williams & Wilkins, 1963.

Block, M., & Jacobson, L. O. The histogenesis and diagnosis of the osseous type of Gaucher's disease. *Acta Haematologica,* 1948, **1,** 165–177.

Borri, P. F., Hooghwinkel, G. J. M., & Edgar, G. W. F. Brain ganglioside pattern in three forms of amaurotic idiocy and in gargoylism. *Journal of Neurochemistry,* 1966, **13,** 1249–1256.

Brady, J. P., & Williams, H. C. Magnesium intoxication in a premature infant. *Pediatrics,* 1967, **40,** 100–103.

Brady, R. O. The sphingolipidoses. *The New England Journal of Medicine,* 1966, **275,** 312–318.

Brady, R. O., Gal, A. E., Kanfer, J. N., & Bradley, R. M. The metabolism of glucocerebrosides. III. Purification and properties of glucosyl- and galacto-cylceramide-cleaning enzyme from rat intestinal tissue. *The Journal of Biological Chemistry,* 1965, **240,** 3766–3770.

Brady, R. O., Kanfer, J. N., Bradley, R. M., & Shapiro, D. Demonstration of a deficiency of glucocerebroside cleaving enzyme in Gaucher's disease. *The Journal of Clinical Investigation,* 1966, **45,** 1112–1115.

Braithwaite, J. V., & Miller, J. H. D. Hepatosplenomegaly resembling Niemann-Pick's disease: Recovery following liver therapy. *Archives of Disease in Childhood,* 1940, **15,** 61–64.

Carson, N. A. J., & Neill, D. W. Metabolic abnormalities detected in a survey of mentally backward individuals in northern Ireland. *Archives of Disease in Childhood,* 1962, **37,** 505–513.

Colle, E., & Ulstrom, R. A. Ketotic hypoglycemia. *The Journal of Pediatrics,* 1964, **64,** 632–651.

Cooke, R. E., & Ottenheimer, E. J. Clinical and experimental interrelations of sodium and the central nervous system. *Advances in Pediatrics,* 1960, **11,** 81–145.

Cooper, J. D. The role of government and legislation in management of problems in medicine. In J. A. Anderson & K. F. Swaiman (Eds.), *Phenylketonuria and allied metabolic diseases.* Washington: U.S. Department of Health, Education, and Welfare, 1967. Pp. 168–176.

Copenhaver, R. M., & Goodman, G. The electroretinogram in infantile, late infantile and juvenile amaurotic family idiocy. *Archives of Ophthalmology,* 1960, **63,** 559–566.

Cori, G. T. Biochemical aspects of glycogen deposition diseases. *Modern Problems in Pediatrics,* 1957, **3,** 344.

Cornblath, M., Joassin, G., Weisskopf, B., & Swiatek, K. R. Hypoglycemia in the newborn. *Pediatric Clinics of North America,* 1966, **13,** 905–920.

Cornblath, M., & Reisner, S. H. Blood glucose in the neonate and its clinical significance. *The New England Journal of Medicine,* 1965, **273,** 378–381.

Cornblath, M., & Schwartz, R. *Disorders of carbohydrate metabolism in infancy.* Philadelphia: Saunders, 1966.

Cornblath, M., Wybregt, S. H. Baens, G. S., & Klein, R. I. Symptomatic neonatal hypoglycemia. Studies of carbohydrate metabolism in the newborn infant. VIII. *Pediatrics,* 1964, **33,** 388–402.

Courville, C. B. Late cerebral changes incident to severe hypoglycemia (insulin shock). *Archives of Neurology and Psychiatry,* 1957, **78,** 1–14.

Crawford, J. D., Dodge, P. R., & Probst, J. H. Experimental water intoxication. *American Journal of Diseases of Children,* 1958, **96,** 582–583.

Crigler, J. F., Jr. Case records of the Massachusetts General Hospital. *The New England Journal of Medicine,* 1962, **266,** 1269–1275.

Crocker, A. C., & Farber, S. Niemann-Pick disease: A review of 18 patients. *Medicine,* 1958, **37,** 1–95.

Crocker, A. C., & Mays, V. B. Sphingomyelin synthesis in Niemann-Pick disease. *The American Journal of Clinical Nutrition,* 1961, **9,** 63–67.

Cusworth, D. C., Dent, C. E., & Flynn, F. V. The aminoaciduria in galactosemia. *Archives of Disease in Childhood,* 1955, **30,** 150–159.

Dancis, J., Hutzler, J., & Levitz, M. The diagnosis of maple syrup urine disease. *Pediatrics,* 1963, **32,** 234–238.

Dancis, J., Hutzler, J., & Rokkones, T. Intermittent branched-chain ketonuria: Variant of maple-syrup-urine disease. *The New England Journal of Medicine,* 1967, **276,** 84–89.

Dancis, J., & Levitz, M. Maple syrup urine disease. In J. B. Stanbury, J. B. Wyngaarden, & D. S. Fredrickson (Eds.), *The metabolic basis of inherited disease.* (2nd ed.) New York: McGraw-Hill, 1966.

Dickens, F., & Greville, G. D. Metabolism of normal and tumour tissue: Respiration in fructose and in sugar-free media. *Biochemistry,* 1933, **27,** 832–841.

Dillon, E. S., Riggs, H. E., & Dyer, W. W. Cerebral lesions in uncomplicated fatal diabetic acidosis. *The American Journal of the Medical Sciences,* 1936, **192,** 360–365.

Dollery, C. T. Letter to editor: Action of diazoxide. *The British Medical Journal,* 1962, **2,** 337.

Donnell, G. N., Bergren, W. R., & Ng, W. G. Galactosemia. *Biochemical Medicine,* 1967, **1,** 29–53.

Donnell, G. N., Lieberman, E., Shaw, K. N. F., & Koch, R. Hypoglycemia in maple syrup urine disease. *American Journal of Diseases of Children,* 1967, **113,** 60–63.

Efron, M. L. Aminoaciduria. *The New England Journal of Medicine,* 1965, **272,** 1058–1067, 1107–1113. (a)

Efron, M. L. Familial hyperprolinemia: Report of second case, associated with congenital renal malformation, hereditary hematuria and mild mental retardation: Demonstration of enzyme defect. *The New England Journal of Medicine,* 1965, **272,** 1243–1254. (b)

Efron, M. L., & Ampola, M. G. The aminoacidurias. *Pediatric Clinics of North America,* 1967, **14,** 881–903.

Efron, M. L., Bixby, E. M., & Pryles, C. V. Hydroxyprolinemia. II. Rare metabolic disease due to deficiency of enzyme hydroxyproline oxidase. *The New England Journal of Medicine,* 1965, **272,** 1299–1309.

Egan, T. J., & Wells, W. W. Alternate metabolic pathway in galactosemia. *American Journal of Diseases of Children,* 1966, **111,** 400–405.

Etheridge, J. E. Hypoglycemia and the central nervous system. *Pediatric Clinics of North America,* 1967, **14,** 865–880.

Field, R. A. Glycogen deposition diseases. In J. B. Stanbury, J. B. Wyngaarden, & D. S. Fredrickson (Eds.), *The metabolic basis of inherited disease.* (2nd ed.) New York: McGraw-Hill, 1966.

Finberg, L. Pathogenesis of lesions in the nervous system in hypernatremic states. *Journal of Clinical Investigation in Pediatrics,* 1959, **23,** 40.

Finberg, L., Luttrell, C., & Redd, H. Functional, anatomical and biochemical alterations of the brain resulting from experimental hypernatremic dehydration. *A.M.A. Journal of Diseases of Children,* 1957, **94,** 542.

Floyd, J. C., Fajans, S. S., Knopf, R. F., & Conn, J. W. Plasma insulin in organic hyperinsulinsm: Comparative effects of tolbutamide, leucine, and glucose. *Journal of Clinical Endocrinology and Metabolism,* 1964, **24,** 747–760.

Folling, A. Uber ausscheidung von phenylbrenztaubensaure in den harn als stoffwechselanomalie in verbindun mit imbezillitat. *Zeitschrift fuer Physiologische Chemie,* 1934, **277,** 169–176.

Ford, F. R. Diseases of the nervous system in infancy, childhood and adolescence. (4th ed.) Springfield, Ill.: Charles C Thomas, 1960.

Fredrickson, D. S. Cerebroside lipidosis: Gaucher's disease. In J. B. Stanbury, J. B. Wyngaarden, & D. S. Fredrickson (Eds.), *The metabolic basis of inherited disease.* (2nd ed.) New York: McGraw-Hill, 1966.

Fredrickson, D. S., & Trams, E. G. Ganglioside lipidosis: Tay-Sachs disease. In J. B. Stanbury, J. B. Wyngaarden, & D. S. Fredrickson (Eds.), *The metabolic basis of inherited disease.* (2nd ed.) New York: McGraw-Hill, 1966. P. 523.

Froesch, E. R., Wolf, H. P., Baitsch, H., Prader, A., & Labhart, A. Hereditary fructose intolerance: An inborn defect of hepatic fructose-1-phosphate splitting aldolase. *The American Journal of Medicine,* 1963, **34,** 151–167.

Garrod, A. E. *Inborn errors of metabolism.* London: Oxford University Press, 1909.

Gaucher, P. *De l'épithélioma primitif de la rate.* Paris: Thèse de Paris, 1882.

Geiger, A. Correlation of brain metabolism and function by the use of a brain perfusion method *in situ. Physiological Reviews,* 1958, **38,** 1–20.

Gelber, S., Campbell, P., Deibler, G., & Sokoloff, L. Effects of L-thyroxine on amino acid incorporation into protein in mature and immature rat brain. *Journal of Neurochemistry,* 1964, **11,** 221.

Gerritsen, T., Vaughn, J. G., & Waisman, H. A. The identification of homocystine in the urine. *Biochemical and Biophysical Research Communications,* 1962, **9,** 493–496.

Gerritsen, T., & Waisman, H. A. Homocystinuria. In J. B. Stanbury, J. B. Wyngaarden, & D. S. Fredrickson (Eds.), *The metabolic basis of inherited disease.* (2nd ed.) New York: McGraw-Hill, 1966. (a) P. 420.

Gerritsen, T., & Waisman, H. A. Hypersarcosinemia. *The New England Journal of Medicine,* 1966, **275,** 66. (b)

Ghadimi, H., Binnington, V. I., & Pecora, P. Hyperlysinemia associated with mental retardation. *Journal of Pediatrics,* 1964, **65,** 1120.

Ghadimi, H., Partington, M. W., & Hunter, A. A familial disturbance of histidine metabolism. *The New England Journal of Medicine,* 1961, **265,** 221–224.

Gilbert, G. J., & Blaser, G. H. On the nervous

system integration of water and salt metabolism. *Archives of Neurology,* 1961, **5,** 179–196.

Gitzelmann, R., Curtius, H. C., & Schneller, I. Galactitol and galactose-1-phosphate in the lens of a galactosemic infant. *Experimental Eye Research,* 1967, **6,** 1–3.

Gomez, M. R., Gotham, J. E., & Meyer, J. S. Effect of sodium glutamate on leucine-induced hypoglycemia: Clinical and electroencephalographic study. *Pediatrics,* 1961, **28,** 935–942.

Gorter, E. Familial galactosuria: Proceedings of 22nd general meeting of British Paediatric Association. *Archives of Disease in Childhood,* 1951, **26,** 271–272.

Guthrie, R., & Susi, A. A simple phenylalanine method for detecting phenylketonuria in large populations of newborn infants. *Pediatrics,* 1963, **32,** 338–343.

Halvorsen, K., & Halvorsen, S. Hartnup disease. *Pediatrics,* 1963, **31,** 29.

Halvorsen, S., Pande, H., Løken, A. C., & Gjessing, L. G. Tyrosinosis. *Archives of Disease in Childhood,* 1966, **41,** 238–249.

Hansen, R. G., Bretthauer, R. K., Mayes, J., & Nordin, J. H. Estimation of frequency of occurrence of galactosemia in the population. *Proceedings of the Society for Experimental Biology and Medicine,* 1964, **115,** 560–563.

Harris, H., Penrose, L. S., & Thomas, D. H. H. Cystathioninuria. *The American Journal of Human Genetics,* 1959, **23,** 442–453.

Harris, R., Della Rovere, M., & Prior, P. F. Electroencephalographic studies in infants and children with hypothyroidism. *Archives of Disease in Childhood,* 1965, **40,** 612.

Harris, S. Hyperinsulinism and dysinsulinism. *The Journal of the American Medical Association,* 1924, **83,** 729–733.

Hartmann, A. F., & Jaudon, J. C. Hypoglycemia. *The Journal of Pediatrices,* 1937, **11,** 1–36.

Haworth, J. C., & Coodin, F. J. Idiopathic spontaneous hypoglycemia in children: Report of seven cases and review of the literature. *Pediatrics,* 1960, **25,** 748–765.

Hers, H. G. Alpha glucosidase deficiency in generalized glycogen storage disease (Pompe's disease). *The Biochemical Journal,* 1963, **86,** 11–16.

Holt, K. F., & Milnar, J. (Eds.) *Neurometabolic disorders in childhood.* Edinburgh: E. S. Livingstone, 1964.

Hooft, C., Timmermans, J., Snoeck, J., Antener, I., Oyaert, W., & van den Hende, C. L. Methionine malabsorption in a mentally defective child. *The Lancet,* 1964, **2,** 20.

Huijing, F., Van Creveld, S., & Losekoot, G. Diagnosis of generalized glycogen storage disease (Pompe's disease). *The Journal of Pediatrics,* 1963, **63,** 984–987.

Hsia, D. Y-Y., & Walker, F. A. Variability in the clinical manifestations of galactosemia. *The Journal of Pediatrics,* 1961, **59,** 872–881.

Illingworth, B., & Cori, G. T. Structures of glycogens and amylopectins. III. Normal and abnormal human glycogen. *The Journal of Biochemistry,* 1952, **199,** 653.

Isselbacher, K. J. Galactosemia. In J. B. Stanbury, J. B. Wyngaarden, & D. S. Fredrickson (Eds.), *The metabolic basis of inherited disease.* (2nd ed.) New York: McGraw-Hill, 1966. P. 178.

Isselbacher, K. J., Anderson, E. P., Kurahashi, K., & Kalckar, H. M. Congenital galactosemia: A single enzymatic block in galactose metabolism. *Science,* 1956, **123,** 635–636.

Jepson, J. B., & Spiro, M. J. Hartnup disease. In J. B. Stanbury, J. B. Wyngaarden, & D. S.

Fredrickson (Eds.), *The metabolic basis of inherited disease.* (2nd ed.) New York: McGraw-Hill, 1966. Pp. 1283–1299.

Jervis, G. A. The genetics of phenylpyruvic oligophrenia. *The Journal of Mental Science,* 1939, **85,** 719–762.

Jervis, G. A. Studies of phenylpyruvic oligophrenia: The position of the metabolic error. *The Journal of Biological Chemistry,* 1947, **169,** 651–656.

Joseph, R., Ribierre, M., Job, J. C., & Girault, M. Maladie familiale associant des convulsions à début trés précoce, une hyperalbuminoarchie et une hyperaminoacidurie. *Archives Francaises Pediatrie* (Paris), 1958, **15,** 374–387.

Kalckar, H. M., Anderson, E. P., & Isselbacher, K. J. Galactosemia: A congenital defect in a nucleotide transferase. *Biochimica et Biophysica Acta,* 1956, **20,** 262–268.

Kamoshita, S., & Landing, B. H. Distribution of lesions in myenteric plexus and gastrointestinal mucosa in lipidoses and other neurologic disorders of children. *American Journal of Clinical Pathology,* 1968, **49,** 312–318.

Kampine, J. P., Brady, R. O., Kanfer, J. N., Feld, M., & Shapiro, D. Diagnosis of Gaucher's disease and Niemann-Pick disease with small samples of venous blood. *Science,* 1966, **155,** 86–88.

Katzman, R. Effect of electrolyte disturbance on the central nervous system. *Annual Review of Medicine,* 1966, **17,** 197–212.

Kennedy, J. L., Wertelecki, W., Gates, L., Sperry, B. P., & Cass, V. M. The early treatment of phenylketonuria. *American Journal of Diseases of Children,* 1967, **113,** 16–21.

Kety, S. S., Polis, B. C., Nadler, C. S., & Schmidt, C. F. Blood flow and oxygen consumption of human brain in diabetic acidosis and coma. *The Journal of Clinical Investigation,* 1948, **27,** 500–510.

Knox, W. E. Phenylketonuria. In J. B. Stanbury, J. B. Wyngaarden, & D. S. Fredrickson (Eds.), *The metabolic basis of inherited disease.* (2nd ed.) New York: McGraw-Hill, 1966.

Koch, R., Acosta, P., & Fishler, K. Observation of phenylketonuria. In J. A. Anderson & K. F. Swaiman (Eds.), *Phenylketonuria and allied metabolic diseases.* Washington: U.S. Department of Health, Education, and Welfare, 1967. Pp. 116–132.

Komrower, G. M. Dietary treatment of homocystinuria. *American Journal of Diseases of Children,* 1967, **113,** 98–100.

Kuhn, R., & Wiegandt, H. Die Konstitution der Ganglio-N-tetroose und des Gangliosids G_1. *Chemische Berichte,* **96,** 866-880.

La Du, B. N. Histidinemia. In J. B. Stanbury, J. B. Wyngaarden, & D. S. Fredrickson (Eds.), *The metabolic basis of inherited disease.* (2nd ed.) New York: McGraw-Hill, 1966.

La Du, B. N. The enzymatic deficiency in tyrosinemia. *American Journal of Diseases of Children,* 1967, **113,** 54–57.

Landing, B. H., Silverman, F. N., Craig, J. M., Jacoby, M. D., Lahey, M. E., & Chadwick, D. L. Familial neurovisceral lipidosis. *American Journal of Diseases of Children,* 1964, **108,** 503–522.

Leaf, A. The clinical and physiologic significance of the serum sodium concentrations. *The New England Journal of Medicine,* 1962, **267,** 24–30, 77–83.

Leroy, J. G., & Crocker, A. C. Clinical definition of the Hurler-Hunter phenotypes. *American*

Journal of Diseases of Children, 1966, **112,** 518–530.

Lightwood, R. Idiopathic hypercalcemia in infants with failure to thrive. *Archives of Disease in Childhood,* 1952, **27,** 302.

Logothetis, J. Neurologic effects of water and sodium disturbances. *Postgraduate Medicine,* 1966, **40,** 408–417, 621–629.

Lowrey, G. H., Aster, R. H., Carr, E. A., Ramon, G., Beierwaltes, W. H., & Spafford, N. R. Early diagnostic criteria of congenital hypothyroidism. *A.M.A. Journal of Diseases of Children,* 1958, **96,** 131.

Luttrell, C. N., Finberg, L., & Drawdy, L. P. Hemorrhagic encephalopathy induced by hypernatremia. II. Experimental observations on hyperosmolarity in cats. *Archives of Neurology,* 1959, **1,** 153–160.

Mabry, C. C., Denniston, J. C., & Coldwell, J. G. Mental retardation in children of phenylketonuric mothers. *The New England Journal of Medicine,* 1966, **275,** 1331–1336.

Macaulay, D., & Watson, M. Hypernatremia in infants as a cause of brain damage. *Archives of Disease in Childhood,* 1967, **42,** 485–491.

Maddock, S., Hawkins, J. E., & Holmes, E. The inadequacy of substances of the glucose cycle for maintenance of normal cortical potentials during hypoglycemia produced by hepatectomy with abdominal evisceration. *The American Journal of Physiology,* 1939, **125,** 551–565.

McDonald, L., Bray, C., Field, C., Love, F., & Davies, B. Homocystinuria, thrombosis, and the blood platelets. *The Lancet,* 1964, **1,** 745–746.

McKean, C. M., Boggs, D. E., & Peterson, N. A. The influence of high phenylalanine and tyrosine on the concentrations of essential amino acids

in brain. *Journal of Neurochemistry,* 1968, **15,** 235–241.

McMurray, W. C., Rathbun, J. C., Mohyuddin, F., & Koegler, S. J. Citrullinuria. *Pediatrics,* 1963, **32,** 347–357.

McQuarrie, I. Idiopathic spontaneously occurring hypoglycemia in infants: Clinical significance of problems and treatment. *American Journal of Diseases of Children,* 1954, **87,** 399–428.

Medes, G. A new error of tyrosine metabolism: Tyrosinosis. *The Biochemical Journal,* 1932, **26,** 917–940.

Medes, G., Berglund, H., & Lohmann, A. An unknown reducing substance in myasthenia gravis. *Proceedings of the Society for Experimental Biology and Medicine,* 1927, **25,** 210–211.

Menkes, J. H., Hurst, P. L., & Craig, J. M. New syndrome: Progressive familial infantile cerebral dysfunction with unusual urinary substance. *Pediatrics,* 1954, **14,** 462–473.

Miller, R. B. Central nervous system manifestations of fluid and electrolyte disturbances. *The Surgical Clinics of North America,* 1968, **48,** 381–393.

Morris-Jones, P. H., Houston, I. B., & Evans, R. C. Prognosis of the neurological complications of acute hypernatremia. *The Lancet,* 1967, **2,** 1385–1389.

Moser, H. W., & Lees, M. Sulfatide lipidosis: Metachromatic leukodystrophy. In J. B. Stanbury, J. B. Wyngaarden, & D. S. Fredrickson (Eds.), *The metabolic basis of inherited disease.* (2nd ed.) New York: McGraw-Hill, 1966.

Munro, T. A. Phenylketonuria: Data on 47 British families. *Annals of Eugenics,* 1947, **14,** 60–88.

Neame, K. D. Phenylalanine as inhibitor of

transport of amino acids in brain. *Nature*, 1961, **192**, 173–174.

Niemann, A. Ein unberkanntes krankheitsbild. *Jahrbuch kinderh.*, 1914, **79**, 1.

Nitowsky, H. M., & Gronfeld, A. Lysosomal alpha glucosidase in type II glycogenosis: Activity in leukocytes and cell cultures in relation to genotype. *The Journal of Laboratory and Clinical Medicine*, 1967, **69**, 472–484.

Norman, R. M., Urich, H., Tingey, A. H., & Goodbody, R. A. Tay-Sachs disease with visceral involvement and its relationship to Niemann-Pick's disease. *The Journal of Pathology and Bacteriology*, 1959, **78**, 409–421.

O'Brien, J. S., Stern, M. B., Landing, B. H., O'Brien, J. K., & Donnell, G. N. Generalized gangliosidosis. *American Journal of Diseases of Children*, 1965, **109**, 338–346.

O'Flynn, M. E., Tillman, P., & Hsia, D. Y-Y. Hyperphenylalanemia without phenylketonuria. *American Journal of Diseases of Children*, 1967, **113**, 22–27.

Paine, R. S. The variability in manifestations of untreated patients with phenylketonuria. *Pediatrics*, 1957, **20**, 290–302.

Perry, T. L., Hansen, S., Tischler, B., Bunting, R., & Berry, K. Carnosinemia. *The New England Journal of Medicine*, 1967, **277**, 1219.

Philippart, J., & Menkes, J. H. Isolation and characterization of the main splenic glycolipids in Gaucher's disease: Evidence for the site of metabolic block. *Biochemical and Biophysical Research Communications*, 1964, **15**, 551–555.

Philippart, M., & Menkes, J. H. Isolation and characterization of the principal cerebral glycolipids in the infantile and adult forms of Gaucher's disease. In S. M. Aronson & B. W.

Volk (Eds.), *Inborn disorders of sphingolipid metabolism*. Oxford: Pergamon Press, 1967.

Pick, L. Niemann-Pick's disease and other forms of so-called xanthomatosis. *The American Journal of the Medical Sciences*, 1933, **185**, 601–616.

Pildes, R. S., Forbes, A. E., & Cornblath, M. Studies of carbohydrate metabolism in the newborn infant. IX. Blood glucose levels and hypoglycemia in twins. *Pediatrics*, 1967, **40**, 69–77.

Pildes, R., Forbes, A. E., O'Connor, S. M., & Cornblath, M. The incidence of neonatal hypoglycemia: A completed survey. *The Journal of Pediatrics*, 1967, **70**, 76–80.

Plum, F., & Posner, J. B. *The diagnosis of stupor and coma*. Philadelphia: Davis, 1966.

Posner, J. B., & Plum, F. Spinal-fluid pH and neurologic symptoms in systemic acidosis. *The New England Journal of Medicine*, 1967, **277**, 605–613.

Reilly, W. A. The granules in the leucocytes in gargoylism. *American Journal of Diseases of Children*, 1941, **62**, 489–491.

Roitman, A., & Gatt, S. Isolation of phospholipase-C from rat brain. *Israel Journal of Chemistry*, 1963, **1**, 190–191.

Sachs, B. A family form of idiocy, generally fatal, associated with early blindness. *The Journal of Nervous and Mental Disease*, 1896, **23**, 475–479.

Sauls, H. S., & Ulstrom, R. A. Hypoglycemia. In W. C. Kelley (Ed.), *Brennemann's Practice of pediatrics*. Vol. I. Chap. 40. New York: Hoeber-Harper, 1967. P. 1.

Schneck, L., & Volk, B. W. Clinical manifestations of Tay-Sachs disease and Niemann-Pick disease. In S. M. Aronson & B. W. Volk (Eds.), *Inborn disorders of sphingolipid metabolism.* Oxford: Pergamon Press, 1967.

Schwarz, V., Goldberg, L., Komrower, G. M., & Holzel, A. Some disturbances of erythrocyte metabolism in galactosaemia. *Biochemistry,* 1956, **62,** 34–40.

Scriver, C. R., Larochelle, J., & Silverberg, M. Hereditary tyrosinemia and tyrosyluria in a French Canadian geographic isolate. *American Journal of Diseases of Children,* 1967, **113,** 41–46.

Scriver, C. R., Pueschel, S., & Davies, E. Hyper-β-alaninemia, associated with γ-aminoaciduria and γ-aminobutyricaciduria, somnolence and seizures. *The New England Journal of Medicine,* 1966, **274,** 635.

Shaw, E. B., & Moriarty, M. Hypoglycemia and acidosis in fasting children with idiopathic epilepsy. *American Journal of Diseases of Children,* 1924, **28,** 553–567.

Smith, A. J., & Strang, L. B. Inborn error of metabolism with urinary excretion of a-hydroxybutyric acid and phenylpyruvic acid. *Archives of Disease in Childhood,* 1958, **33,** 109–113.

Smith, D. W., Blizzard, R. M., & Wilkins, L. The mental prognosis in hypothyroidism of infancy and childhood. *Pediatrics,* 1957, **19,** 1011.

Smith, H. L., Amick, L. D., & Sidbury, J. B. Type II glycogenosis. *American Journal of Diseases of Children,* 1966, **111,** 475–481.

Snyderman, S. E. The therapy of maple syrup urine disease. *American Journal of Diseases of Children,* 1967, **113,** 68–73.

Spackman, H., Moore, S. D., & Stein, W. H. Chromatography of amino acids in sulfonated polystyrene resins: An improved system. *Analytical Chemistry,* 1958, **30,** 1185–1190.

Stanbury, J. B., & Wyngaarden, D. S. J. B., & Frederickson (Eds.). *The metabolic basis of inherited disease.* New York: McGraw-Hill, 1966.

Svennerholm, L. Chromatographic separation of human brain gangliosides. *Journal of Neurochemistry,* 1963, **10,** 613–623.

Swaiman, K. F., Hosfield, W. B., Wolfe, R. N., & Lemieux, B. Influence of high plasma phenylalanine concentration on incorporation of lysine into protein of developing brain. *Neurology,* 1968, **18,** 300.

Swaiman, K. F., Kennedy, W. B., & Sauls, H. S. Late infantile acid maltase deficiency. *Archives of Neurology,* 1968, **18,** 642.

Tanaka, K., Budd, M. A., Efron, M. L., & Isselbacher, K. J. Isovaleric acidemia: A new genetic defect of leucine metabolism. *Proceedings of the National Academy of Sciences of the United States of America,* 1966, **56,** 236–242.

Terry, K., & Linker, A. Distinction among four forms of Hurler's syndrome. *Society for Experimental Biology and Medicine,* 1964, **115,** 394–402.

van Creveld, S. Investigations on glycogen disease. *Archives of Disease in Childhood,* 1934, **9,** 9–26.

Volk, B. W., Aronson, S. M., & Saifer, A. Fructose-1-phosphate aldolase deficiency in Tay-Sachs. *The American Journal of Medicine,* 1964, **36,** 481–484.

Volk, B. W., & Wallace, B. J. The liver in lipidosis. *The American Journal of Pathology,* 1966, **49,** 203–225.

Wada, Y., Tada, K., Minagawa, A., Yoshida, T., Morikawa, T., & Okamura, T. Idiopathic hypervalinemia. *The Tohoku Journal of Experimental Medicine,* 1963, **81,** 46.

Waisman, H. A. Variations in clinical and laboratory findings in histidinemia. *American Journal of Diseases of Children,* 1967, **113,** 93–94.

Walravens, P. A., & Chase, H. P. Brain lipids and thyroid hormone. Society of Pediatric Research, Program, thirty-eighth annual meeting, 1968. P. 5.

Warren, S. Adenomas of islands of Langerhans. *The American Journal of Pathology,* 1926, **2,** 335–340.

Westall, R. G. Dietary treatment of maple syrup urine disease. *American Journal of Diseases of Children,* 1967, **113,** 58–59.

Wybregt, S. H., Reisner, S. H., Patel, R. K., Nellhaus, G., & Cornblath, M. The incidence of neonatal hypoglycemia in a nursery for premature infants. *The Journal of Pediatrics,* 1964, **64,** 796–802.

Yannet, H. Changes in brain resulting from depletion of extracellular electrolytes. *The American Journal of Physiology,* 1940, **128,** 683–689.

Young, E., & Bradley, R. F. Cerebral edema with irreversible coma in severe diabetic ketoacidosis. *The New England Journal of Medicine,* 1967, **276,** 665–669.

10 Organic Disorders Caused by Infections and Poisoning

Kenneth F. Swaiman

Infectious processes of the nervous system are still of the utmost importance in clinical medicine. The strides that have been made in the diagnosis and therapy of bacterial infections in the past few decades are effective in preserving life, but unfortunately many surviving children are handicapped because the infectious episode has unfavorably altered the growth and development of their nervous system.

Viral infections have become more easily recognized with modern serologic techniques, but only a few can be prevented by immunization, and few if any can be treated specifically after the infection has been established. However, it is the recurring process of the development of reliable diagnostic techniques eventually resulting in practical therapy that leads physicians to an optimistic outlook for the not too far distant future.

Concerning the problem of poisoning, it is difficult to be as optimistic. The modern home is a repository for a myriad of potent chemicals including drugs, insecticides, herbicides, cleaning agents, and hydrocarbons. The diversity of these compounds, their ubiquity, and their potency combine to make recognition and therapy difficult.

Only in recent years have we begun to judge the results of therapy of poisoning on the basis of follow-up physical, neurological, and psychometric examinations. The use of survival alone as a measure of therapeutic efficacy is insufficient and unrealistic.

It is becoming clear that certain children in certain households are more likely than other children to be victims of poisoning, and further studies as well as education of the public may reduce the alarming increase in the incidence of poisonings in children.

VIRAL ENCEPHALITIS

The traditional division of viral encephalitides into those types caused by viruses that attack primarily the central nervous system (CNS) and viral encephalitis occurring secondary to viral infection of other organs is no longer tenable (Johnson & Mims, 1968). It is becoming increasingly clear that the brain is relatively rarely involved in viral infections, which are almost always systemic. It is also becoming apparent that the vast majority of viral encephalitides occur in connection with large-scale epidemics of virus infections in which symptoms of mild aseptic meningitis predominate. There are often accompanying mild symptoms of involvement of other organ systems. The focus of clinical thought is turned on the encephalitic component of the systemic disease because mild aberration in brain function is easily clinically recognized in comparison with mild compromise of hepatic, renal, or pulmonary function. Studies through the years have pointed to the variable route of infection in viral encephalitis. It appears that the hematogenous route is the most common pathway of infection, but it is clear that infection by means of spread to the brain from peripheral nerves and from nasal mucosa is possible and, on occasion, of clinical importance. From the blood the viruses most likely reach the cerebrospinal fluid via the choroid plexus and reach the brain by this route.

Viremia alone is not sufficient to lead to brain infection. Free viruses are cleared from blood in minutes. Both the duration of viremia and the numbers of viruses present are important determinants of cerebral spread from blood. Both of these factors can be enhanced by multiplication of viruses in a protected environment such as that available in white blood cells. Growth in vascular endothelium or lymphatics may provide a similar function. Immunological incompetence in the host for any reason, including immaturity, may allow abnormal production of large numbers of viral particles in infected tissues and blood. Host factors such as age and concurrent infection and viral factors such as size, ability to multiply in white blood cells, and antigenic properties may greatly modify the likelihood of the occurrence of viral encephalitis.

In a chapter of this size it is impossible to cover each type of viral encephalitis that has been rec-

ognized. Rather, representative types of viral encephalitis will be discussed.

Prominent symptoms of viral encephalitis include malaise, headache, fever, lethargy, photophobia, nuchal rigidity, vomiting, seizures, and changes in level of consciousness.

Physical findings are also common to the vast majority of encephalitides, and they include a positive Kernig's sign, nuchal rigidity, signs of increased intracranial pressure, and findings associated with upper motor neuron disease— positive toe signs, ankle clonus, and hyperactive deep tendon reflexes.

In sporadic cases it may be very difficult to quickly establish specific etiology from the presenting clinical symptoms, and in many cases etiology remains unproved despite exhaustive laboratory studies.

Encephalitis associated with viral infection causing distinct systemic signs such as the exanthematous diseases (rubeola, rubella, and varicella) or mumps, Coxsackie, or ECHO virus disease is much easier to diagnose and is common in childhood. Unfortunately, encephalitis caused by these viruses may occur without the recognizable systemic clinical changes.

A number of encephalitic illnesses are thought to be viral, although the viruses have not been isolated, e.g., infectious mononucleosis and acute hemorrhage encephalitis.

The severity of encephalitis varies greatly even during a time of epidemic. It is likely that the vast majority of individuals suffering from a given viral infection during a time of epidemic do not manifest clinical symptomatology readily identified as that of encephalitis. The mechanism by which one individual infected with a given virus develops encephalitis and another individual infected with the same virus develops no symptoms of CNS involvement is unknown and is one of the important problems in the study of infectious disease.

The methods utilized for the definitive diagnosis of viral infection include tissue culture of nasopharyngeal swabbings, cerebrospinal fluid, and stool. Serologic studies including complement-fixation studies are also sensitive and helpful. Minimum study to ascertain etiology of viral encephalitis includes complement-fixation studies for the common viral encephalitides and attempts to culture virus from stool and nasopharynx.

Examination of cerebrospinal fluid is the most valuable routine laboratory study that can be performed. There is often a pleocytosis of mild degree, usually no higher than several hundred cells, and the predominating cell is usually mononuclear. Occasionally early in the disease there may be a predominance of polymorphonuclear cells. Spinal fluid sugar and protein are usually normal. Increased intracranial pressure may be present.

The hemogram usually reveals a normal or lower-than-normal white blood count, oftentimes with a greater percentage of lymphocytes than normal. The sedimentation rate is usually normal or only mildly elevated.

Arthropod-borne Viruses

Eastern equine encephalitis. Eastern and western equine encephalitis are divided on the basis of the geographic location of their initial appearance, east and west of the Appalachian Mountains. Eastern encephalitis was first noted in 1933 (Baker, 1962). Eastern equine encephalitis has occasionally spread west of the Appalachian Mountains. The virus, which appears to be 40 to 50 millimicrons in diameter, infects many animals besides man including domestic pets, birds, and farm animals. The means of transmission is through mosquitoes, both the Ades and the Culex types (Baker, 1962).

Eastern equine encephalitis usually develops rapidly. Initial symptoms include lethargy, vomiting, seizures, and high fever. The patients are seriously ill within a day or two after the onset of the disease (Feemster, 1958). A wide range of symptomatology is possible depending upon the areas of the brain most heavily involved. These difficulties consist of hemiplegia, language disturbances, visual disturbances, including diplopia, and various errors of judgment and memory.

The disease is common in children. In those children who undergo a severe course of the disease, severe residual difficulty is not unusual. Farber and associates (Farber, Hill, Connerly, & Dingle, 1940) reported eight infants and children who suffered from the disease. Five died, and three who recovered were left with severe residual difficulty. Residual symptoms include hemiparesis, intellectual and emotional aberrations, seizures, mental retardation, visual difficulties, and language difficulties.

Pathology of the brain reveals marked congestion and edema. Congestion of the brainstem is often severe. The inflammatory changes are greatest in the brainstem and the basal ganglia but are also usually widespread in the cerebral cortex. Many small arteries are involved and leukocytic reaction of the artery walls with subsequent necrosis is common. Microglia and phagocytes are commonly seen in the areas of neural degeneration (Wesselhoeft, Smith, & Branch, 1938). If the child survives longer, the infiltrations are primarily lymphocytic. Numerous areas of demyelination may be present in those patients who do not succumb to the disease.

Western equine encephalitis. Western equine encephalitis is also transmitted by the Ades and Culex mosquitoes. The mosquitoes bite not only horses but also birds. The horse is a primary intermediate agent in the disease of man. Western equine encephalitis occurs primarily west of the Appalachian Mountains. It does not occur as frequently in children as eastern equine encephalitis. The incubation period is about 2 weeks. It is followed by headache, nausea, and vomiting. The onset of the disease is not as precipitious as in eastern equine encephalitis. Fever develops, and the patient becomes more lethargic. Often the patient complains of vertigo and photophobia. Lethargy may progress to unconsciousness, but more usually the patient has fever and headache and is somewhat obtunded. The usual findings of nuchal rigidity and a positive Kernig's sign are present. Involvement of the cranial nerves and other focal neurological findings are unusual. Seizures are also uncommon although they occur more frequently in children (Finley, 1958).

Finley and his associates reviewed the cases of eighteen children who suffered from an attack of western equine encephalitis in California in the early 1950s (Finley, Fitzgerald, Richter, Riggs, & Shelton, 1967). In this follow-up study, it was clearly demonstrated that the children who had been victimized in the first months of life were much more severely retarded in cerebral development than those who were affected at a later age. Symptoms included temperature elevation, generalized seizures, lethargy, nuchal rigidity, and bulging fontanelle.

Spinal fluid findings included a pleocytosis in which there were equal numbers of lymphocytes and polymorphonuclear cells. The total count ranged from slightly below 100 cells per cubic millimeter to 700 or more cells per cubic millimeter. Protein was frequently elevated, and no change in spinal fluid sugar was usually present.

Follow-up studies with pneumoencephalography revealed usually mild to moderate enlargement of the lateral ventricles. Electroencephalograms were frequently abnormal. The abnormalities were often diffuse, and at times spike- and slow-wave abnormalities were also noted.

Microcephaly was present in twelve of the sixteen children who were affected in the first several months of life. The authors also noted that the children who had sequelae immediately after the acute disease had more severe behavioral and cognitive impairment than children whose sequelae were delayed. The longer the delay in appearance of difficulties, the less severe the clinical abnormalities. Although frequently the children appeared to be regressing, in actuality the problem was one of lack of continuing development. Interpretation of such phenomena must be carefully considered so that mistaken diagnosis of deterioration leading to the necessity of considering the myriad degenerative diseases of childhood can be avoided.

Pathological study of western equine encephalitis reveals the brain to be markedly congested and swollen. The brainstem is greatly involved. The brain is not as severely involved as in eastern equine encephalitis. Neither the arteritis nor the macrophage response is as great. The areas most greatly affected are the basal ganglia and the white matter of the cerebral hemispheres. Small areas of demyelination or necrosis may persist, and on occasion small cysts may appear. Some patients actually have widespread cystic formation within the white matter (Noran & Baker, 1943).

St. Louis encephalitis. St. Louis encephalitis was first noted in the United States in 1933. The disease has appeared several times since then in smaller outbreaks predominantly in the Middle Western United States. The vector is the Culex mosquito, of which several species have been incriminated. Although domestic animals and birds are the usual target of these mosquitoes, man is also among the victims.

St. Louis encephalitis usually strikes abruptly with temperature elevation, headache, and symptoms and signs of meningeal inflammation. The patient becomes more lethargic, somnolent, and confused. Focal neurological findings are rare. Nuchal rigidity is invariably present. Although focal findings are rare early in the disease, if they do appear, they rarely persist.

The patient is usually ill for 2 to 3 weeks, after which improvement occurs, usually rather rapidly. Some difficulties with judgment, emotions, and personality may remain for several months or, on occasion, permanently. Up to one-fifth of the patients with the disease may die. Mortality is much more common in older age groups and is unusual in children.

Residual difficulties are not common in St. Louis encephalitis and Bredeck noted only 5.7 percent of 331 patients to have residuals (Bredeck, Brown, Hempelmann, McFadden, & Spector, 1938). These residuals consisted of seizures and focal weakness. Other patients complain of emotional and nervous symptomatology that are difficult to document.

Vascular changes consisting of lymphocytic infiltration are common, especially in the brainstem, basal ganglia, and cerebral cortex. Mononuclear infiltration of the meninges in the sulci over the convexity of the brain is common. There are also scattered foci of mononuclear infiltration of the brain which may or may not be associated with blood vessels. Neuronal changes are also common (Suzuki & Phillips, 1966).

Japanese encephalitis. Japanese encephalitis has been noted in Japan since 1891. Encephalitis is transmitted by the Culex mosquito. The mosquito usually attacks animals and birds, but man is also an obvious victim.

Japanese encephalitis progresses rather rapidly and runs a tumultuous course which leads to death or almost complete and quick recovery. The temperature may rise alarmingly rapidly and high over the first few days of the disease. Accompanying headaches, confusion, and obtundation are common. Signs of meningeal irritation are common, and nuchal rigidity is present. Paralysis of the limbs is common but usually transient. The disease usually runs its course within several weeks (Huand & Liu, 1940).

Laboratory findings reveal an increase in white cells with the prominent cell type being the polymorphonuclear cell. Although generally Japanese encephalitis leaves no sequelae, there are a few reports of persistent difficulties. These difficulties include paralysis, headaches, judgment and personality changes, and intellectual retardation. Children are especially susceptible to intellectual retardation and severe personality changes (Lewis, Taylor, Sorem, Norcross, & Kindsvatter, 1947).

Pathological findings reveal congestion and mild edema of the brain. Meningeal infiltration along with perivascular infiltration is common. Perivascular infiltration is most common in the gray matter. Polymorphonuclear cells are often seen in the early stages of the disease. Nodules of white cells may be present in the cortex, basal ganglia, and brainstem. These nodules appear to consist primarily of macrophages (Haymaker & Sabin, 1947).

Viruses Spread by Rodents

Lymphocytic choriomeningitis. Lymphocytic choriomeningitis usually develops insidiously with headache, chills and fever, rhinitis, and lethargy. Meningeal irritation followed by seizures and disorientation is common. The patient is ill primarily with changes in sensorium for a period of 10 days, although headache and minor changes in sensorium may persist for a period of 4 weeks.

The disease is rarely fatal and usually is benign. It is transmitted to humans from the secretions of house mice that serve as the reservoir for the virus (Kramer & Som, 1940).

Pathological changes are found primarily in the meninges, in which there is a diffuse, and intense lymphocytic infiltration (Baker, 1947). The meninges are usually thickened, and the contiguity of the subarachnoid space may be compromised in certain areas by resulting fibrosis and adhesion of the meninges with one another. Although the cerebral parenchyma may not be involved, there is frequent perivascular lymphocytic infiltration and occasionally small areas of hemorrhage. Some neuronal swelling and on occasion glial cell reaction may be present (Baker, 1947).

Enteroviruses

Poliomyelitis. Poliomyelitis is caused by three immunologically different types of viruses. Infection type I (Brunhilde), infection type II (Lansing), and infection type III (Leon) do not produce cross-immunity, but infection with a specific type of poliomyelitis virus results in permanent immunity to that type. Paralytic poliomyelitis was seen in frequent epidemics in the summer and early fall in the United States as well as other countries (Weinstein, Shelokov, Seltser & Winchell, 1952). The appearance of both killed-virus and attenuated-live-virus vaccines has greatly reduced the disease incidence. In non-epidemic form the disease most commonly afflicts children, but in an epidemic the average age of the involved population is significantly higher.

The viruses are spread from human to human by secretions of the nose and throat and also by fecal contamination.

Early symptoms include malaise, muscle pains, and stiffness. Headache is often present, and symptoms of upper respiratory infection are prominent in children. As the disease progresses, the patient develops some degree of neck stiffness and frequently a low-grade fever. Tightness of the back and leg muscles then appears. The course of the disease may be relatively fulminating or slowly progressive. The more rapid the progression, the more severe the eventual involvement. The virus attacks primarily the anterior horn cells, resulting in motor weakness that is usually asymmetrical. The most serious threat to life occurs when the lower cranial nerve nuclei are involved along with pronounced involvement of the brainstem reticular formation. The patient becomes markedly weak, and the deep tendon reflexes are unobtainable. Fasciculations may

or may not be present. There is no sensory loss, although later the presence of muscle pain at rest or during stretch is pronounced. If the cranial nerve motor nuclei and the reticular formation are rapidly and progressively involved, stupor and difficulties with respiration and maintenance of blood pressure occur.

The most common difficulty with cranial nerve function is the inability of the patient to swallow, and frequently swallowed material will appear through the nostrils. Difficulties with the autonomic nervous system lead to prominent symptoms of hypertension, perspiration, and occasionally vomiting. Death is much more common in adults than children.

Auld and associates (Auld, Kevy, & Eley, 1960) reported on their experience with 956 cases of poliomyelitis in children in the 1955 Massachusetts epidemic. They noted that 1½ times as many boys as girls were affected. Of the cases, 25.7 percent were nonparalytic, 51.5 percent were spinal, 12.7 percent were bulbar, and 10.0 percent were bulbospinal.

In patients above the age of 1, the sites of predilection appeared to be the same. There was a high incidence of quadriplegia and involvement of the trunk muscles.

In thirty-three cases diffuse encephalitis was noted. Of these thirty-three cases, twenty-four were males and nine were females. Three of these children died. No encephalitis was noted in children below age 5. Four of the encephalitis patients had characteristics of relatively focal cerebral involvement as manifested by seizures, myoclonic jerks, or symptoms of cerebellar involvement.

More boys than girls suffered from bulbar symptomatology than would be expected on the basis of sex incidence alone.

In this series there were forty-nine patients under 1 year of age. The most common involvement was that of the trunk, followed by involvement of the legs and both arms and legs. Bulbar involvement was very rare. The cranial nerves were involved in only two of the forty-nine infant patients. In another series, patients under 1 year had a 90 percent incidence of paralysis, but trunkal paralysis was uncommon (Abramson & Greenberg, 1955).

Most commonly the spinal fluid findings include a pleocytosis with mononuclear cells and normal or slightly increased protein concentration. The spinal fluid glucose is usually normal.

The importance of immunization and prevention cannot be too heavily stressed. Specific treatment of poliomyelitis is not at hand. However, care of bulbar symptomatology with support of respirations and circulation may become necessary. Proper handling of secretions and prevention of pneumonia with early use of tracheostomy techniques may be necessary. The marked flaccidity and weakness of the muscles is soon replaced with spasm and tightness. Passive stretch and heat along with reeducation of the patient's use of affected musculature are very important and may be necessary over a prolonged period of months and years.

ECHO encephalitis. The ECHO viruses produce a large profile of clinical disease. Although there are many serologic types of ECHO viruses, types 4, 6, and 9 have been associated with encephalitis more often than others.

The tendency for any one type of virus to cause a particular clinical picture appears to be the result of virulence of the microorganism and susceptibility of the host. It is impossible to describe a clinical complex that would separate one ECHO type of infection from another. Not only do the symptoms produced by the various ECHO viruses overlap, but there are great areas of overlap with the other enteroviruses — polio and Coxsackie (Sanford & Sulkin, 1959).

Of all the ECHO viruses, ECHO 9 has been as-

sociated most frequently with the large epidemics of infection and encephalitis (Sabin, Krumbiegel, & Wigand, 1958). In the summer of 1956, ECHO 9 viruses were recovered from patients infected during large-scale epidemics in Europe and Canada. During these epidemics ECHO 9 viruses were frequently isolated from the spinal fluid of patients.

A large epidemic of aseptic meningitis in Milwaukee in 1957 is well documented by Sabin and his co-workers (Sabin, Krumbiegel, & Wigand, 1958). They noted a high ratio of male to female patients hospitalized during the epidemic. Almost without exception, the hospitalized adults and children manifested symptoms of aseptic meningitis that in previous years would have been diagnosed as poliomyelitis.

The typical patients suffer from fever up to 103° F for 4 to 6 days with an associated headache. Vomiting is very common in children, and there is frequently abdominal pain. Nonexudative pharyngitis is present in almost all children. Cough and rhinitis are not usually present. Only one-half of the children have a maculopapular rash. Only occasional Kernig and Brudzinski signs are present in children. Spasm of the erector spinae muscles is common. Nuchal rigidity is present in over half of involved children, but does not necessarily parallel the degree of pleocytosis of the spinal fluid. Infants may show more severe symptomatology including chorea, facial weakness, "jerking," and grimacing. Coma, vertigo, and ataxia are sometimes seen. Acute cerebellar ataxia has been reported as the primary symptom in a child with ECHO 9 infection (McAllister, Hummler, & Coriell, 1959).

ECHO 9 viruses can be isolated from the spinal fluid and stools of infants who have only three to five white cells per cubic millimeter in their spinal fluid.

Death is very unusual, and permanent motor sequelae almost nonexistent. Intellectual and personality changes have not been studied in detail for follow-up purposes. On rare occasions mild paresis has occurred with ECHO infection (Magoffin, Lennette, Hollister, & Schmidt, 1961; Wehrle, Lampton, Portnoy, & Mason, 1961).

It is estimated that during the Milwaukeee County epidemic, 40,000 of the 740,000 population were affected and that 85 percent of those infected suffered from clinical difficulties.

Coxsackie encephalitis. Severe Coxsackie encephalitis outside the infant age group is rare, but has been reported (Walker & Togo, 1963). Coxsackie encephalitis is generally a mild affair lasting approximately a week, from the beginning of the prodromal period to the end of the encephalitic phase (McLeod, Beale, McNaughton, & Rhodes, 1956).

The main clinical features include headache, lethargy, vomiting, nuchal rigidity and fever. A mild pleocytosis is present which may be mononuclear or polymorphonuclear.

On occasion mild paresis of facial, abdominal, and back muscles has been reported with Coxsackie virus infection (Magoffin, Lennette, Hollister, & Schmidt, 1961). No residual difficulties of Coxsackie encephalitis have been reported.

Coxsackie virus infection in a newborn can be a calamitous, generalized disease—encephalohepatomyocarditis (Kilbrick & Benirschke, 1958). Coxsackie B viruses are associated with these infections. Infections are probably incurred before birth. A fever occurs during the first few weeks of life and is followed by lethargy, occasionally seizures, and fulminating cardiac difficulty. Pleocytosis of the spinal fluid is present. Death occurs in 80 percent of cases (Kilbrick & Benirschke, 1958). No follow-up is available on the survivors.

Encephalitis Caused by Spread to the Brain from Peripheral Nerve

Rabies encephalitis. Rabies is becoming a rare disease in the Western Hemisphere. The virus is spread from the bite of rabid animals including the dog, skunk, cat, and bat. Rabid animals all manifest the disease within 5 to 7 days after biting their victim. The length of the incubation period in man is related to the area of the bite. Face bites have a shorter incubation than bites incurred in other areas of the body. The incubation period of man is from 30 to 60 days after exposure.

After a bite the disease may be prevented by immunization with the Pasteur, Semple, or avian embryo vaccine. Treatment should be begun within 72 hours. Allergic postvaccinal encephalomyelitis occurs in 1 out of 500 treated patients. Symptoms of allergic encephalomyelitis occur within 5 to 7 days after therapy. Encephalitis appears to be less common in patients treated with the avian vaccine, but there is some question as to its efficacy.

Once the patient shows clinical symptoms of the rabies, death is inevitable. Presenting symptoms include pain, chills and fever, nausea and vomiting, psychiatric difficulties, malaise, dyspnea, headache, paresthesias, vertigo, and dysphagia (Dupont & Carle, 1965). Later the course of the disease is dominated by mental confusion, irritability, hydrophobia, and dysphagia.

Encephalitis Spread by Oropharyngeal Secretions

Herpes simplex encephalitis. Herpes simplex encephalitis in children was first reported in 1941 (Smith, Lennette, & Reames, 1941).

The onset of the illness is frequently heralded by upper respiratory infection, fever, and convulsions (Bellanti, Guin, Grassi, & Olson, 1968). The physician may believe that the seizure is a result of the fever, only to discover later that the child does not awaken but remains unconscious. The seizure pattern is frequently focal (Bellanti, Guin, Grassi, & Olson, 1968).

The temporal lobes are frequently involved, and indeed the involvement may be so concentrated that swelling of the temporal lobe leads to problems associated with an expanding intracranial mass (Pierce, Portnoy, Leeds, Morrison, & Wehrle, 1964).

The electroencephalogram may reflect profound involvement of the temporal lobes (Rawls, Dyck, Klass, Greer, & Herrmann, 1966).

Brain biopsy with resultant finding of the typical intranuclear inclusions seen in neurons and oligodendroglial cells is helpful in early diagnosis (Bellanti, Guin, Grassi, & Olson, 1968; MacCallum, Potter, & Edwards, 1964). Of course, an ultimate diagnosis can be made only by isolation of the virus. The spinal fluid findings are often nonspecific or normal.

Of late, therapy with intravenous administration of 5-iodo-2-deoxyuridine has shown some promise (Bellanti, Guin, Grassi, & Olson, 1968). However, the cellular destruction is so great that arrest of the virus after proper diagnosis may not prove sufficient to allow reasonable remaining brain function.

Encephalitis Associated with Exanthematous Diseases

Rubeola. Rubeola encephalitis will likely become more unusual as prophylactic immunization with attenuated vaccine becomes more common. The incidence of clinically incapacitating encephalitis and rubeola is not specifically known, but is less than 0.5 percent (Tyler, 1957).

The severity of the preceding rubeola infection has little or no bearing on the likelihood of development of clinical encephalitis. Although encephalitis can appear before, during, or several weeks after the appearance of the exanthem, it most commonly appears 4 to 7 days after the rash is present. Thus, it usually appears when the patient's rash is fading and his fever is resolving.

The patient then develops a secondary rise in temperature which is accompanied by headaches, vomiting, signs of meningeal irritation, and lethargy frequently progressing to a comatose state.

On occasion the patient develops seizures as the first symptom of encephalitis and frequently remains comatose after the seizure episode.

A common neurological symptom in almost 25 percent of patients is ataxia (Tyler, 1957). The ataxia is usually mild, but may persist for several weeks to months after all other symptoms of encephalitis have disappeared. The ataxia is usually accompanied by signs of upper motor neuron involvement, and isolated cerebellar ataxia is rarely present. The overall prognosis for ataxia secondary to rubeola encephalitis is good. It is obvious that unrecognized or unsuspected measles encephalitis resulting in cerebellarlike ataxia may pose a difficult diagnostic problem (Griffith, 1921).

The course of the encephalitis is highly variable. Most patients improve markedly after a 3- or 4-day period. Others continue comatose with increased intracranial pressure, status epilepticus, and respiratory failure progressing to death. The mortality rate for measles encephalitis is recorded as 10 percent (Tyler, 1957). It must be borne in mind that a vast majority of cases of measles encephalitis are not hospitalized and that a 10 percent figure is most likely exaggerated. Electroencephalographic studies reveal that over half of the children with rubeola uncomplicated by clinical encephalitis have abnormal electroencephalographic records (Gibbs, Gibbs, Carpenter, & Spies, 1959).

Usually the spinal fluid pressure is increased, and pleocytosis in the form of a mild lymphocytosis is present. Spinal fluid protein is sometimes elevated. Pleocytosis has been found in 46 of 123 cases of uncomplicated measles (Ajala, 1947).

In a study by Ford (1928) there were residual difficulties in 65 percent of the patients. The most common residual was that of ataxia in 30 percent, followed by mental retardation in 12 percent and seizures in 5 percent. Personality changes were also relatively common and caused great problems in formal education.

At times, concomitant myelitis may occur producing a clinical picture of transverse myelitis or disseminated myelitis (Tyler, 1957).

Histological examination reveals perivascular areas of demyelinization, intact axis cylinders, and numerous microglia. The perivascular mononuclear cuffing seen in viral encephalitis is present. There is evidence that the measles virus actually infects brain tissue and causes characteristic intracytoplasmic and intranuclear inclusion bodies to be found (Adams, Baird, & Filloy, 1966).

Varicella. Varicella encephalitis may precede, occur concurrently with, or follow the onset of the eruption (Holliday, 1950). Most commonly, the onset of encephalitis occurs toward the end of the first week of illness (Gibel, Kramer, & Neji, 1960). There is no correlation between the severity of the encephalitis (Krugman & Ward, 1964; Wilson & Ford, 1927). The incidence of varicella encephalitis has been stated to be less than 0.1 percent.

Varicella encephalitis may begin insidiously or may have an explosive concept with sudden onset of seizures, fever, and paralysis. The usual gradual onset is characterized by lethargy, irritability, and ataxia. Many other symptoms have been reported to be present in this disease (Gibel, Kramer, & Neji, 1960). These symptoms include cerebellar difficulties, including titubation and nystagmus; paresis of the legs with accompanying upper motor neuron findings of clonus and positive toe signs; seizures; and bowel and bladder difficulties (Gibel, Kramer, & Neji, 1960). Spinal fluid changes usually include a mild pleocytosis, but there usually are no changes in pressure, protein, glucose, or chloride concentrations (Gibel, Kramer, Neji, 1960).

Persistent focal difficulties are rare. Patients who die usually die within the first week of pneumonia or medullary involvement. In one series 15 percent of patients showed residual difficulties including paresis, ataxia, blindness, retardation,

speech difficulties, and personality changes (Heppleston, Pearce, & Yates, 1959).

The spinal cord has been reported to be occasionally involved, and the presence of myelitis leads to upper motor neuron involvement of the legs and severe bladder and bowel disturbances.

The essential lesion of varicella encephalitis appears to be perivascular demyelinization, but there are also changes in the gray matter in almost all patients (Appelbaum, Rachelson, & Dolgopol, 1953; Heppleston, Pearce, & Yates, 1959). Striking involvement of the dorsal and ventral spinocerebellar tracts may account for some of the cerebellar symptomatology (Appelbaum, Rachelson, & Dolgopol, 1953; Heppleston, Pearce, & Yates, 1959).

Rubella. Rubella is a rare cause of childhood encephalitis. The encephalitis is usually delayed until several days after the rash has appeared. On occasion the rash has completely disappeared before the encephalitis takes place. As might be expected, only severe cases have been reported. For the most part, these symptoms consist of coma and major motor seizures. On occasion the patient will have preceding difficulties with headache, vomiting, and vertigo. The patient may manifest nystagmus and various other difficulties with voluntary eye movements. Upper motor neuron signs may be present, and focal findings such as hemiparesis have been recorded (Steen & Torp, 1956). Death is very rare and usually occurs very early in a fulminating fashion.

Polymorphonuclear cells are found in the spinal fluid. Pressure may be elevated, and there is usually a monocytic pleocytosis. Protein content may be increased, but is usually normal.

Rubella encephalitis is not as great a threat to the CNS in the older child as it is when it is contracted by the fetus (Cooper & Krugman, 1966). Not only is the CNS involved, but numerous other organ systems are involved in prenatal rubella. Common manifestations of rubella involvement include cataracts, deafness, spasticity, microcephaly, mental deficiency, hepatomegaly, congenital heart disease, abnormal dermatoglyphics, and growth retardation (Cooper & Krugman, 1966; Tondury & Smith, 1966).

In a study of brains of nine infants less than 1 year of age who died with the congenital rubella syndrome, Rorke and Spiro (1967) noted gross degenerative changes in leptomeningeal and intrinsic arteries and veins of the cerebral hemispheres. The vascular destruction consisted of areas of focal necrosis localized chiefly in the area of gray nuclei and the deep white matter. In addition these authors noted retardation in myelinization, suggesting gross interference with the normal processes of white-matter maturation. They found no gross developmental malformations and no evidence of inflammation of the nervous tissue.

There is no consensus as to the mechanism by which intrauterine rubella causes CNS embarrassment. The virus is often present in the newborn and excreted for weeks or months after birth (Blattner, 1966). The rubella virus has been isolated from the brain tissue of affected infants (Monif & Sever, 1966). Evidence of gross malformation has been presented only infrequently, and it would appear that the studies of Rorke and Spiro are the most convincing and point to impairment of neural development based on extensive vascular involvement of the meninges and cerebrum.

Encephalitis Associated with Other Systemic Viral Diseases

Mumps encephalitis. Mumps is one of the most frequent causes of viral encephalitis (Christ, 1967; Kilham, 1949). There is no correlation with the severity of the systemic disease, and indeed the patient may have no overt signs of the systemic disease while suffering from a severe episode of mumps encephalitis (Macrae & Campbell, 1949). It is difficult to assess the percentage of patients with mumps who suffer from mumps encephalitis because only the most severe systemic cases are hospitalized and reported. One can hope that with the advent of mumps vaccine (Young, Dickstein, Weibel, Stokes, Buynak, & Hilleman, 1967), there will be many fewer cases of mumps encephalitis. Neurological difficulties usually occur during the latter half of the first week or during the second week after the swelling of the parotid gland appears. On occasion encephalitis or myelitis occurs before parotitis (Silverman, 1949).

The clinical symptoms of mumps include fever, headache, and vomiting. There is often nuchal rigidity. The patient may be lethargic and manifest varying degrees of delirium, stupor, and coma (Aldfelt, 1949). Seizures are very uncommon (Kilham, 1949). Focal symptoms such as hemiplegia, aphasia, and ataxia are frequent. Brainstem symptoms including facial paresis and deafness are also seen. Progressive medullary involvement leads to death. On occasion a myelitis is present, and a peripheral neuritis is rarely present (Silverman, 1949). The patient may suffer difficulties with severe peripheral weakness and sphincter weakness and will manifest the symptoms of both upper and lower motor neuron difficulty.

Changes in the spinal fluid include mononuclear pleocytosis (Brown, Kirkland, & Hein, 1948). The pleocytosis is usually relatively high, in the neighborhood of several hundred cells per cubic millimeter. Occasionally counts as high as 1,000 cells have been noted. There is usually an increase in intracranial pressure and a mild increase in protein.

Mumps encephalitis rarely leads to death. Symptoms usually begin to resolve within 2 weeks after onset. Although residuals are commonly recorded as being rare, the incidence of hearing loss resulting from mumps is obviously much higher than was initially thought. Other residuals are rare but persistent facial weakness, hemiplegia (Block, Hirschil, Turin, & Zaleznak, 1950), and personality changes have been reported. Myelitis is usually followed by permanent residuals in a high percentage of cases.

The usual lesion seen in the brain at postmortem examination is an acute perivascular demyelinization (Donohue, Playfair, & Whitaker, 1955).

Cytomegalic inclusion body disease. Cytomegalic inclusion body disease (CID) is caused by a well-characterized virus (Hanshaw, 1966). Neonatal infection is of primary concern and is the only form to be discussed here.

CID almost always leads to clinical CNS deficit in the neonatal period.

Frequent symptoms and signs include spastic diplegia, microcephaly, seizures, deafness, psychomotor retardation, chorioretinitis, cerebral calcifications, and optic atrophy (Hanshaw, 1966; Medearis, 1964; Weller & Hanshaw, 1962). Hepatosplenomegaly and a petechial rash are frequently present.

Diagnosis can be confirmed by isolation and identification of the pathognomonic cells with their nuclear inclusions in the urinary sediment. The use of concentrating techniques greatly increases the efficiency of the procedure (Blanc & Gaetz, 1962). The virus can also be isolated directly from the urine. Use of the complement-fixation test is valuable in screening suspect neonates because of the near-uniform positive test in affected infants and the 1 percent incidence of positive tests in infants in general (Hanshaw, 1966).

Chronic Viral Encephalitis

Subacute sclerosing encephalitis. Subacute sclerosing encephalitis (SSE) is a disease characterized early by mood, personality, and intellectual regression. Later seizures, frequently of a myoclonic nature, and other adventitious movements appear. Changes in sleep cycle, hallucinations, memory loss, irritability, and hyperactivity may begin to dominate the clinical picture. Increas-

ing stupor, an increase in myoclonic seizure frequency, and extrapyramidal symptoms of rigidity and athetosis become prominent. The child becomes progressively demented. Coma and death follow (Chao, 1962; Foley & Williams, 1953).

The course of the disease usually runs only 2 to 4 months and rarely more than a year. Only 20 percent live longer than a year. Most frequently patients between the ages of 3 and 20 are affected. Spinal fluid findings include normal or increased protein with an increase in gamma globulin. Occasionally a mild pleocytosis is present.

Electroencephalographic findings may include bursts of synchronous high-voltage slow waves followed by periods of relative electrical quiescence (Cobb & Hill, 1950; Petre-Quadens, Sfaello, van Bogaert, & Moya, 1968).

The disease is so named because of the type A inclusion bodies noted in the neuronal and glial cells in the brain (Dawson, 1933).

It is becoming increasingly clear that the inclusion body encephalitis is a result of infection from the rubeola virus or a very closely related organism (Zeman & Kolar, 1968).

Encephalitis of Suspected but Not Proved Viral Origin

Infectious mononucleosis. Infectious mononucleosis has only rarely been described as being associated with encephalitis (Bernstein & Wolff, 1950; Nichols & Athreya, 1962). Only a handful of cases have been reported. Less than 1 percent of cases have neurological difficulty (Gautier-Smith, 1965).

Seizures have been the initial symptomatology in several children. Bonforte (1967) reported a case in a 45-month-old girl who suddenly had a major motor seizure. Temperature was 100.4°F. No symptoms were found except for hyperactive reflexes in the legs. There were a few petechiae scattered over the shoulders. There was no adenopathy.

The liver was palpable 2 centimeters below the

right costal margin, and the spleen 4 centimeters below the left costal margin.

The spinal fluid contained twenty mononuclear cells per cubic millimeter. The morphology of the mononuclear cells suggested the possibility of infectious mononucleosis. Spinal fluid protein and sugar were normal.

Heterophile antibody slide hemagglutination was positive. Serum heterophile antibody studies were positive in a dilution of 1:896 before absorption and 1:488 after absorption with guinea-pig kidney. The child recovered rapidly, and the spinal fluid was normal by the third day.

With rare exceptions the disease is nonfatal and leaves no sequelae.

Encephalitis Secondary to Rickettsial Infection

Rocky Mountain spotted fever. After an incubation period of 3 to 12 days, the onset of Rocky Mountain spotted fever is acute and is accompanied by severe headache, nuchal rigidity, myalgia, high fever, and a typical rash (Woodward, 1959; Woodward & Jackson, 1965). The eruption appears in the fourth day and is maculopapular early. It appears mostly about the ankles, soles, wrists, and palms and is present to a lesser degree about the trunk. Later the rash becomes hemorrhagic. The patient experiences restlessness and insomnia. He may then develop coma or may remain irritable and disoriented for several days. Seizures and athetosis have been reported. Transient deafness is common.

The patient is usually severely ill for less than a week, with rapid recovery. There may be accompanying muscle and soft-tissue tenderness. Less severe cases may be accompanied by signs of aberration in superficial sensory perception including paresthesias and hypesthesias.

The responsible organism, *Rickettsia rickettsi,* is spread by the wood tick *Dermacentor andersoni.* Diagnosis is established by the use of serologic tests and isolation of the organism. Isolation is not a practical method, however.

Rocky Mountain spotted fever is effectively treated with chloramphenicol or tetracyclines (Woodward & Jackson, 1965).

BACTERIAL MENINGITIS

Most cases of bacterial meningitis occur in children below the age of 5. The vast majority of cases of bacterial meningitis in childhood are caused by a handful of types of bacteria. The most common causes of bacterial meningitis are *Diplococcus pneumoniae, Haemophilus influenzae,* and *Neisseria meningitidis* (Swartz & Dodge, 1965). These organisms cause pneumococcal meningitis, influenzal meningitis, and meningococcal meningitis, respectively.

Influenzal meningitis is the most common bacterial meningitis occurring in the pediatric age group (Carpenter & Petersdorf, 1962).

Other less common but not rare types of bacterial meningitis in children include staphylococcal meningitis and streptococcal meningitis.

Although the advent of specific antimicrobial therapy for bacterial meningitis resulted in great expectations for prevention of death and residuals, the expectations have not been completely fulfilled (Alexander, 1952).

Little change in mortality or morbidity rates is now taking place (Haggerty & Ziani, 1963). The death rate is highest in the first year of life and continues to fall to about age 5. Morbidity and mortality rates are higher among boys than girls. The use of declining mortality as an index of successful therapy has great limitations. Children who appear normal at the time of discharge, with no motor difficulties, may subsequently be found to have intellectual retardation, areas of intellectual disability as monitored by psychometric testing, and emotional difficulties. Follow-up studies that do not go through the second year of school may be regarded as incomplete.

In a group of 100 patients, 18 percent demonstrated serious sequelae (Haggerty & Ziani, 1963). Similar findings have been noted in other series

(Desmite, 1955; Kresky, Buchbinder, & Greenberg, 1962; Ross, 1952; Smith, 1954).

Motor difficulties include hemiparesis, spastic diplegia, and occasionally monoplegia. Seizures, mental retardation, emotional disturbances, and deafness are prominent late symptoms. Early difficulties immediately related to the acute infection include subdural effusions, brain abscesses, dural sinus thromboses, and hydrocephalus.

The three types of bacteria that cause the predominant number of cases of bacterial meningitis in childhood are frequent residents of the respiratory tracts of normal adults and children. The vast majority of these individuals do not develop meningitis. Otitis media with subsequent spread of infection through the penetrating veins to the close-by meninges is a common explanation for many cases of meningitis. However, the vast majority of meningitis victims do not have otitis media, and their CNS invasion must take place through hematogenous spread. The intricacies of the bacterial and host factors that modify the likelihood of bacterial meningitis in a given patient are not well understood, and only generalities can be thrust into this crucial gap in our knowledge. Meningococcal meningitis is somewhat different because unlike pneumococcal and influenzal meningitis, it is commonly associated with epidemics.

After the newborn period, symptoms and signs of bacterial meningitis include headache, lethargy, fever, shock, photophobia, vomiting, bulging fontanelle, stiff neck, disorientation, seizures, and coma.

Frequent signs on examination include nuchal rigidity, a positive Kernig sign, and a positive Brudzinski sign.

Symptoms and signs of bacterial meningitis must be followed by diagnostic lumbar puncture to obtain spinal fluid for study. The fluid should be smeared and cultured. Studies should also include cell count, glucose determination, and protein determination. Spinal fluid pressure should be obtained whenever feasible.

These smears should be carefully studied because growth on culture may not occur, although organisms are readily seen on smear. This may likely be the case when the patient has had prior antibiotic therapy (Harter, 1963). The advantage of prompt diagnosis resulting from a positive smear is obvious. Unfortunately, difficulty in identifying bacteria found in smears is sometimes encountered. Although theoretically little difficulty should be experienced in differentiating Gram-positive from Gram-negative organisms, there is a frequent problem. The differentiation of the coccobacillus shape of hemophilus from the diplococcal shape of pneumococcus may be very difficult.

Spinal fluid glucose is usually reduced in bacterial meningitis. The mechanisms are not clear, but are likely related to processes of phagocytosis (Petersdorf & Harter, 1961; Petersdorf, Swarner, & Garcia, 1963), and impairment of glucose transport.

Leukocytes are found in abnormal amounts in almost all cases of bacterial meningitis. Polymorphonuclear cells almost always predominate. The cell counts can range from less than 100 cells per cubic millimeter to 90,000 per cubic millimeter. Counts such as the latter are often associated with rupture of abscesses into the lateral ventricles. High counts may be difficult to assess, and the use of heparinized tubes may be helpful (Haggerty & Ziani, 1963) in keeping the cells from clumping. The cell count drops as treatment progresses, but may remain slightly elevated for weeks after clinical recovery is under way.

Treatment of bacterial meningitis must be undertaken as rapidly as possible following diagnosis. Aspects of specific therapy will be discussed in the appropriate section.

Subdural effusions are a common sequelae of bacterial meningitis, particularly influenzal meningitis (Haggerty & Ziani, 1963). Subdural effusions occur also, however, in meningococcal and pneumococcal meningitis. They are most commonly seen in infants. The reason for this incidence is not entirely clear, but it must always be remembered that the ease of subdural tap through the open fontanelle allows for more ready diagnosis. The fluid almost always appears over the frontoparietal temporal area and rarely can be found in the occipital area alone. The general practice is to attempt to tap the subdural effusions dry over a period of 10 days. No more than 20 to 30 milliliters of fluid should be removed from one side per day. If the effusions have not been cleared within 10 days, then surgical stripping of the membranes should be carried out.

Neonatal Meningitis

Neonatal meningitis occurs in 0.01 percent of full-term infants (Groover, Sutherland, & Landing, 1961). The incidence of meningitis in premature infants is much greater (Groover, Sutherland, & Landing, 1961).

The findings in these infants are frequently subtle and undistinguished early in the course of their disease. Vomiting, anorexia, lethargy, twitchings and tremulousness, an increase in startle response, episodes of cyanosis, jaundice, and irregular respirations may be present.

More specific signs such as bulging fontanelle, nuchal rigidity, seizures, and fever (Berman & Banker, 1966; Haggerty & Ziani, 1958) may or may not be present. Fever may not be present when the child is obviously severely affected.

Subtle indications of the presence of neonatal bacterial meningitis make it necessary for diagnostic lumbar puncture to be performed whenever a newborn is experiencing any of the vague difficulties mentioned above (Berman & Banker, 1966).

Neonatal meningitis is frequently caused by Gram-negative organisms ostensibly acquired from the mother at the time of birth. In a large number of cases maternal perinatal infections are present, and similar organisms are found in infant and mother (Berman & Banker, 1966). Skin infections, including infections of the umbilicus, are the likely source of streptococcal and staphy-

lococcal infections leading to neonatal meningitis (Groover, Sutherland, & Landing, 1961).

The mortality rate in neonatal meningitis is frequently reported as over 60 percent. In a majority of newborn infants with meningitis, death occurs within 4 days from the onset of symptoms (Berman & Banker, 1966). This horrendous record in contradistinction to mortality rates in meningitis of older children is undoubtedly due to late diagnosis and therapy.

The inflammatory changes are frequently seen almost wholly within areas of spinal fluid pathways. There is a paucity of lymphocytes noted in the subacute stage of the meningeal reaction (Berman & Banker, 1966).

Hemophilus Influenzae Meningitis

Hemophilus influenzae meningitis is the most common cause of bacterial meningitis in infancy and childhood. It is associated commonly with otitis media and upper respiratory infections in children. However, Swartz and Dodge (1965) report that in 40 percent of their cases, there was no overt associated infection or evidence of impaired host resistance.

Symptoms are not unique to this type of meningitis and include lethargy, fever, meningeal signs, bulging fontanelle, and seizures.

Almost all strains of Hemophilus influenzae that are associated with meningitis can be serologically typed into type B. Typing is not usually necessary because it has little practical significance in therapy, although it may be necessary to distinguish this organism from another. On Gram smears, the organism in the spinal fluid is shown to be a small Gram-negative pleomorphic coccobacillus. The organism can be cultured on chocolate agar. Hemophilus influenzae meningitis results in a layer of greenish pus over the convexities of the brain if it is not treated properly and promptly. Prompt therapy with ampicillin (Barrett, Eardley, Yow & Leverett, 1966) chloramphevicol can lead to remarkably rapid clinical improvement. In one recent case, ampicillin was noted to fail to eradicate *Hemophilus influenzae* meningitis, and recurrence took place after the drug was discontinued following 14 days of therapy (Young, Haddow, & Klein, 1968). Not uncommonly, a child below the age of 2 who is progressing well after several days of therapy develops anorexia, fever, or seizures. Such a child should be suspected of having developed a subdural effusion, and subdural taps should be performed to determine the presence or absence of subdural effusion. If a subdural effusion is present, repeated tapping over a period of 10 days will often result in a "drying up" of the effusion. If this is not the case or, indeed, if more fluid appears to be accumulating daily, then surgical intervention with removal of the subdural membranes may prove necessary.

The sequelae of *Hemophilus influenzae* meningitis are not unlike those of other bacterial meningitides and include upper motor neuron disease with resultant spasticity, hemiparesis, monoparesis, deafness, intellectual and motor retardation, hydrocephalus secondary to blockage of spinal fluid passage, seizures, and, rarely in the case of *Hemophilus influenzae,* brain abscesses. The mortality rate is less than 5 percent, but the rate of morbidity is still relatively high.

Pneumococcal Meningitis

The child who develops pneumococcal meningitis usually has suffered from a preliminary upper or lower respiratory infection. The pneumococcus is almost constantly present in the respiratory tract of unaffected patients.

The pneumococcus is a Gram-positive diplococcus. It has a thick capsule that can be typed, but as in the case of *Hemophilus influenzae,* this procedure is usually not available or necessary.

Patients with pneumococcal meningitis develop a thick tenacious exudate which layers over the convexity of the brain, with somewhat less predilection for the base of the brain. Pneumococcal meningitis appears to be among the most difficult meningitides to treat successfully, perhaps because of the rather thick layer of purulent material that is rapidly laid down. Although foci of pneumococcal infection in other organs are present, they respond much more rapidly to therapy than the meningitis. Subdural effusions occur in pneumococcal meningitis, but are relatively uncommon.

Therapy with large doses of penicillin, sometimes combined with one of the sulfa drugs, is the therapy of choice. On occasion, chloramphenicol is also added to the regimen.

The usual sequelae of bacterial meningitis are noted most frequently in the presence of pneumococcal meningitis (Desmite, 1955). The relatively greater number of patients with residuals after pneumococcal meningitis may be due to the fact that penicillin does not readily pass the blood–spinal fluid barrier (Dumoff-Stanley, Dowling, & Sweet, 1946; Rosenberg & Sylvester, 1944). For this reason, relatively high dosages of penicillin are employed in treatment of pneumococcal meningitis. Exacerbation of infection after therapy is most frequently encountered in cases of pneumococcal meningitis.

Meningococcal Meningitis

Meningococcal disease is different from the other bacterial meningitides because large-scale epidemics are common. The disease is prevalent throughout the world and is most common in early spring. Males are more heavily affected than females, and almost half the cases occur in children under age 5. Carriers are relatively common in the population even during nonepidemic periods.

The meningococcus is a Gram-negative diplococcus which may be extracellular or intracellular in Gram stain smears. The meningococcus may be present in the respiratory tract and is frequently found in association with septicemia.

The meningococcus elaborates an endotoxin which leads to a petechial rash or frankly purpuric or ecchymotic areas of skin. Mucous membranes may also be involved. The presence of petechial or purpuric lesions in a patient who is acutely ill should immediately suggest the presence of meningococcal septicemia. Hemorrhages and areas of purulent involvement are present throughout the body. There is a purulent involvement of the meninges over the convexity of the brain, primarily posteriorly.

Overwhelming hemorrhage including hemorrhage into the adrenal glands has been termed the *Waterhouse-Friderichsen syndrome,* which usually results in death. It is not clear whether the hemorrhage in the adrenal glands leads to acute adrenal insufficiency or, indeed, whether steroid therapy prevents a fatal outcome. In any event, when this condition is likely to occur, steroid therapy is commonly employed in an attempt to stave off death following acute adrenal failure. It should be pointed out that some patients with meningococcal septicemia do not develop signs of meningitis, possibly because of the intervention of death. On the other hand, some patients who do develop tenderness, joint pains, malaise, and fever are subsequently shown to have meningococcal septicemia and do not develop bacterial meningitis. It is much more common, however, to find the patient to be suffering from the so-called meningitic form, in which there is an accompanying septicemia which does not dominate the clinical picture.

Therapy. Therapy for meningococcal meningitis consists of large doses of penicillin and sulfa drugs. Therapy of meningococcal meningitis if instituted early not infrequently leads to rapid and almost complete recovery of the patient.

Delayed therapy may lead to the chronic form of meningococcal meningitis and resultant sequelae.

Family members and other close contacts should be treated for 2 days with sulfonamides. There is a great likelihood that close contacts are nasopharyngeal carriers (Craig & Bennett, 1959).

Staphylococcal Meningitis

Staphylococcal meningitis is a relatively rare meningitis which usually results from a purulent infection of the skin, ears, or paranasal sinuses. The resultant inflammation and tissue disruption are accompanied by a massive formation of purulent material and often multiple intracerebral and meningeal abscesses.

Staphylococcal meningitis is a serious threat to life, and it is essential that the organism be cultured and sensitivities be determined if proper therapy is to be carried out. Initial therapy with one of the synthetic penicillins and/or ampicillin, followed by specific therapy when the results of sensitivity testing are known, is the best means of therapy known. Drainage of abscesses in primary areas of infection is mandatory.

Aside from abscess formation, the pathology and usual sequelae of staphylococcal meningitis do not differ from those of other purulent meningitides.

Streptococcal Meningitis

Streptococcal meningitis is most commonly found during the first few months of life and is frequently thought to result from a septicemia incurred from a superficial infection about the umbilicus in the newborn. In a manner similar to that noted with staphylococcal meningitis, a focus of infection in the skin, nasopharynx, ears, or other organs is frequently present.

Streptococcal meningitis results in a deposition of a purulent exudate over the convexity of the brain.

Therapy of streptococcal meningitis is basically that of administration of massive amounts of penicillin. Often, other antimicrobial drugs including sulfonamide, chloramphenicol, and tetracycline are employed. Of course, known areas of infection outside the CNS should be drained if possible and properly treated.

The pathology and sequelae of streptococcal meningitis are not greatly different from those of the other purulent meningitides discussed.

Other Purulent Meningitides

There is a large number of other bacterial organisms which from time to time cause bacterial meningitis. These organisms include *Salmonella, Brucella, Listeria,* and others. Specific therapy can be administered only if the organism and its sensitivities are known. No specific sequelae other than those already mentioned occur.

Tuberculous meningitis is a relatively uncommon disease in the United States. It is usually of insidious onset and leads to a basilar meningitis. There is frequently associated pulmonary infection. Antituberculous drugs in large doses are employed in therapy.

OTHER INFECTIOUS PROCESSES

Although viral and bacterial infections are the most common in the CNS, there are others. Infections secondary to protozoans, fungi, parasite worms, and spirochetes also occur. A few of the more common disease processes associated with these organisms are discussed below.

Toxoplasmosis

The protozoan organism *Toxoplasma gondii* causes intrauterine (congenital) and postnatal (acquired) human disease from the period of development to adulthood. *Toxoplasma gondii* is found in many wild and domesticated mammals and birds.

Infection may be mild and inconsequential or severe and devastating (Feldman, 1958).

Most commonly, the CNS of infants is affected by the congenital type of infection. The organism is transmitted via the placenta to the fetus from the mother, who is usually asymptomatic. Subsequent children are usually unaffected. This type of infection can lead to abortion, stillbirth, or premature birth. Symptoms and signs at time of birth include microcephaly, petechiae, thrombocytopenia, hepatomegaly, jaundice, seizures and chorioretinitis (Feldman, 1958; Glasser & Delta, 1965). If the child survives, the brain involvement becomes of paramount importance, and difficulties with seizures and mental retardation are very common. Late sequelae include microcephaly and hydrocephaly.

Granulomata may be seen in all areas of the brain. Cystic changes in the brain hemispheres are well documented. Periventricular calcification is frequently seen on x-ray examination.

The diagnosis can be confirmed by use of the Sabin dye test and subsequent use of the serum complement-fixation test. At postmortem examination the organisms can often be seen in the brain. At times the organisms can be found in the placenta (Glasser & Delta, 1965).

Although a combination of pyrimethamine and sulfonamides has been used with some success in acquired toxoplasmosis, there is no evidence of their efficacy in preventing the CNS damage seen in the congenital disease (Eyles, 1956).

Cryptococcosis (Torulosis)

Fungal infections of the CNS are rare in children.

Cryptococcosis meningitis is frequently associated with leukemia or lymphoma in children (Siewers & Cramblett, 1964). The disease is caused by *Cryptococcus neoformans,* which usually gain entrance through the lungs. Entrance can also be gained through the tonsils and gastrointestinal tract.

The child develops signs and symptoms of meningitis including a positive Kernig's sign, nuchal rigidity, increased intracranial pressure, irritability, somnolence, anorexia, and vomiting. Fever, hepatosplenomegaly, lymphadenopathy, and pneumonitis are usually present (Butler, Alling, Spickard, & Utz, 1964). Routine examination of the spinal fluid usually reveals a mononuclear pleocytosis with a reduction in glucose and an increase in protein concentration. Unless the fluid is studied by means of an India ink preparation, the encapsulated organism will not be seen. Culture on Sabouraud's medium will usually grow the organism. Therapy with Amphotericin B. is the present therapy of choice and is moderately successful (Emanuel, Ching, Lieberman, & Goldin, 1961).

Congenital Syphilis

Congenital syphilis occurs when the fetus is infected with *Treponema pallidum,* a spirochete, after it has crossed the placenta. The disease is becoming more and more rare because of the efficacy of penicillin treatment in afflicted mothers (Nelson & Struve, 1956). Fully a third of infected fetuses are stillborn.

Symptoms and signs in the newborn include rhinitis, skin infections, moist patches around the mouth and arms, and hepatosplenomegaly. Jaundice is common. A third of such infants have abnormal spinal fluid findings (Jeans & Cooke, 1930). Clinical symptoms of meningoencephalitis may be present. The children may experience seizures and paresis during the neonatal period (Dodd, 1964). Retardation and deafness are frequent sequelae.

Laboratory diagnosis may be accomplished by the use of dark-field studies of scrapings from moist patches. Serologic tests at birth may be positive when the mother has had syphilis and the baby is unaffected. A positive, persistent serologic test is significant by six months of age. Babies with clinical signs of disease should be treated immediately (Christ, 1967).

Therapy with large doses of penicillin over 14 to 21 days is the treatment of choice.

TOXINS

It is not the intent of this section to provide the reader with a complete encyclopedia of diagnosis and treatment of acute and chronic poisoning.

Many excellent books and manuals exist which can provide complete information of this type (Arena, 1963; Goodman & Gilman, 1965). It is the intent of this chapter to discuss the CNS effects of certain selected toxins. Toxins that do not frequently involve the CNS will not be discussed. Of necessity, emphasis will be placed on those common toxins which cause acute and short-term chronic changes in brain function. Although the information concerning prevention and treatment of acute episodes of toxicity is highly laudable, information concerning the long-term effects of such toxins would be of considerable help. It is frustrating but understandable that most reports on the subject do not delve into the permanent residuals from acute and chronic toxicity. Such information is needed because often neurologists, psychiatrists, and psychologists are faced with the problem of evaluating the effect of a previously experienced toxic episode on the child's current cerebral function. It must be hastily pointed out that the dissemination of such information may be a noble goal but that, unfortunately, the amount of information available is astoundingly small. Perhaps more will become available in the future.

Prevention is really the keystone to the problem of acute poisoning. Poisoning in children is often looked upon as an accidental and isolated incident. Sobel and Margolis (1965) summarized the feeling of many investigators when they stated: "Our results indicate that the ingestion of poison by a child is not just a chance event but rather is the result of purposeful behavior."

It has been estimated that 25 percent of all childhood poisoning victims have repeat episodes (Wehrle, DeFreest, Penhollow, & Harris, 1961). Repetitive poisoning is associated with hyperactivity, negativism, and other emotional problems. A poor parent-child relationship, marital discord, and a tense family atmosphere are also frequently present (Sobel & Margolis, 1965).

Data also indicate that each year there are 500

childhood deaths from poisoning and 600,000 nonfatal poisonings in the United States (Fleming, 1960). It is also likely that 6 to 9 percent of all children in the United States between the ages of 1 and 4 years poison themselves (Wehrle, Day, Whalen, Fitzgerald, & Harris, 1960).

The following classifications of toxins will be employed in the discussion in this chapter:

1. Drugs
   a. Analgesics
   b. Antihistamines
   c. Anticonvulsants
   d. Autonomic drugs
   e. Corticosteroids and corticotropin
   f. Sedatives
   g. Tranquilizers
2. Agricultural chemicals
   a. Pesticides
3. Household toxins
   a. Organic solvents
   b. Heavy metals
   c. Acids, bases, and oxidizing agents
   d. Gases

Drugs

Analgesics

Salicylates. Acetylsalicylic acid (aspirin) is the most common cause of salicylate intoxication. Oil of wintergreen or methyl salicylate is the next most common offending agent. Salicylates may be introduced by ingestion or through the skin. Accidental salicylate poisoning in children is most common in the 2- to 4-year-old range. Intoxication due to therapeutic overdosage is much more common in the infant age group.

Early symptoms of salicylate poisoning are hyperventilation and vomiting. Initially there is respiratory alkalosis induced by stimulation of respiration through central mechanisms (Krasnoff & Bernstein, 1947; Riley & Worley, 1956). After several hours the respiratory alkalosis is replaced by metabolic acidosis in the form of ketoacidosis.

The onset of metabolic acidosis may be accompanied by lethargy, disorientation, and coma.

The physician is unable to know whether the child is in a state of alkalosis or acidosis without laboratory study of blood pH. Data on carbon dioxide content of the blood are not sufficient to allow this judgment to be made. Therapy in the early stages includes adequate intravenous electrolyte and fluid administration and support of circulation as necessary. After acidosis is present, therapy with sodium bicarbonate is indicated.

Gastric lavage should be carried out whenever salicylate ingestion is encountered. In extreme cases exchange transfusion may be a therapeutic necessity.

Symptoms of chronic toxicity of salicylates include muscle tenderness and spasm, decreased auditory acuity, paresthesias, excitability, delirium, and hallucinations. Toxic levels of salicylates may appear at a blood concentration of 9 mg percent in children. Almost all children show some degree of toxic difficulties if the blood concentration is above 35 mg percent (Riley & Worley, 1956).

Antihistamines. Ingestion of antihistamines which produces toxic blood levels results in CNS stimulation followed by depression. Seizures are common manifestations of cerebral stimulation. On occasion, renal and hepatic difficulties are also noted.

Acute ingestion of large doses of antihistamines usually causes major motor seizures and progressive stupor leading to coma. Chronic toxicity is rarely encountered and usually consists of drowsiness or hematologic abnormalities.

Therapy for acute ingestion includes gastric lavage and supportive efforts. Seizures may be controlled by intravenous barbiturates or paraldehyde or by the use of general anesthetics. Death infrequently occurs, and residual CNS symptoms are rare.

Representative drugs of this group include

brompheniramine (Dimetane), chlorpheniramine (Chlor-trimeton), diphenhydramine (Benadryl), and tripelennamine (Pyribenzamine).

Anticonvulsants. Of the anticonvulsants that cause prominent cerebral symptomatology due to toxicity, phenobarbital will be discussed under sedatives. The other commonly used anticonvulsants that cause cerebral difficulties are diphenylhydantoin and primidone.

Diphenylhydantoin. Diphenylhydantoin was first introduced into medicine in 1938 (Merritt & Putnam, 1938). It is an effective anticonvulsant. Acute intoxication with diphenylhydantoin results in prominent symptoms of ataxia and lethargy progressing to coma. Ataxia is very severe and may lead to the false diagnosis of cerebellar tumor.

Chronic toxicity to the CNS from diphenylhydantoin frequently consists of mild degrees of ataxia, incoordination, and lethargy. Chronic intoxication may involve numerous other organ systems ranging from mild and severe blood disease (Lauriault & Jim, 1966) to skin rashes.

Certain individuals may have a predisposition to diphenylhydantoin toxicity because of an inborn error of metabolism in the pathway of diphenylhydantoin degradation (Kutt, Wolk, Scherman & McDowell, 1964).

Therapy should include gastric lavage and supportive measures if necessary. Permanent changes in cerebellar Purkinje cells have been reported after the chronic administration of large doses of diphenylhydantoin to laboratory animals (Kokenge, Kutt, & McDowell, 1965). Chronic cerebellar changes in man have also been reported (Kokenge, Kutt, & McDowell, 1965).

Primidone. Primidone has become a widely used anticonvulsant in the past 10 years. It is closely related to the barbiturates.

Symptoms of acute toxicity from primidone include ataxia, somnulence, irritability, and coma. Chronic toxicity may lead to incoordination, intellectual deterioration, irritability, and personality change. No long-term residuals have been reported.

Treatment of acute ingestion includes gastric lavage and supportive therapy where necessary. There are no specific antidotes.

Other anticonvulsants. Trimethadione and ethosuximide are anticonvulsants frequently used in therapy of centrencephalic seizures. They are rarely associated with CNS toxicity except for mild lethargy.

Autonomic Drugs

Atropine and related alkaloids. Atropine antagonizes the parasympathetic nervous system by inhibiting acetylcholine effect. Acute toxic symptoms from atropine and related drugs include mydriasis, blurred vision, fever, lethargy, delerium, excitability, confusion, weakness, seizures, and coma. In infants, fever may be in excess of 106° F (Morton, 1939). Chronic toxicity causes the same symptoms.

In cases of acute toxicity, ingestion should be treated with gastric lavage. General measures to control seizures may be necessary. Hyperthermia should be combated with cooling blankets and other cooling measures. Paralysis of smooth muscles may lead to bladder paralysis and urinary retention. Permanent CNS residuals are uncommon.

Representative drugs of this group include atropine, tincture of belladonna, benstropine (Cogentin), cycrimine (Pro-banthine), and trihexyphendyl (Artane).

Epinephrine and related drugs. These so-called sympathomimetic drugs cause stimulation of the sympathetic nervous system with resultant smooth-muscle and glandular changes.

Acute toxicity leads to CNS excitement, irritability, fever, tachycardia, mydriasis, and frequently seizures and ensuing coma. Acute toxicity due to amphetamines may cause auditory and visual hallucinations.

Chronic toxicity may lead to personality disorders, and on occasion addiction may be a problem.

Toxicity should be treated by gastric lavage if large doses have been ingested. A specific anti-sympathomimetic drug is phentolamine hydrochloride. On occasion, chlorpromazine has also been used. Seizures should be controlled by the use of barbiturates or general anesthesia.

Although there are usually no residuals of acute toxicity, chronic ingestion with resultant pyschotic behavior may prove a problem (Norman & Shea, 1945).

This group of drugs is commonly represented by amphetamine (Benzedrine), metaraminol (Aramine), metamphetamine (Desoxyn), and propylhexadrine (Benzedrex).

Physostigmine and related drugs. These drugs are used primarily for the treatment of myasthenia gravis and occasionally for hypotonia of smooth muscle, usually in the urinary bladder. They are parasympathetic in action, and as a result, smooth muscles and glands ordinarily stimulated by the parasympathetic system are involved in intoxication.

Acute toxicity frequently leads to abdominal colic, perspiration, tremors and shaking, bronchospasm, muscle fasciculation, brachycardia with resultant vasovagal collapse, seizures, coma, and death. The picture is usually dominated by respiratory difficulties, colic, and perspiration. Symptoms of chronic toxicity are similar to those found in acute poisoning.

Therapy should include supportive care and the administration of atropine. If there has been no prolonged anoxia or brain ischemia, there are usually no permanent residuals.

Ergot and related drugs. Ergot and related drugs cause contraction of the smooth muscles of the gut, uterus, and arterioles. Acute toxicity may lead to light-headedness, seizures, and coma. Blood-vessel difficulty may cause peripheral numbness and coldness of the fingers and toes.

Chronic cerebral toxicity leads to those difficulties present in acute toxicity except that the circulatory difficulties are more common. Residual difficulties after withdrawal of the offending agent are rare.

Therapy should include gastric lavage for ingestion. Vasodilators should be given intravenously.

Corticosteroids and corticotropin. Corticosteroids and corticotropin therapy result in numerous and protean manifestations of toxicity. In general the CNS is affected because of salt and water retention, induction of hypertension, or body electrolyte changes (Good, Vernier, & Smith, 1957).

Symptoms of acute toxicity range from personality change, including psychosis, to coma. There may or may not be associated hypertension. The patient may have seizures, and although death is uncommon, it may occur.

Chronic abnormalities including electrolyte changes such as hypernatremia and hypokalemia may lead to diffuse weakness, somnulence, convulsions, and coma. Permanent changes are unusual, and withdrawal of the offending drug is usually sufficient therapy. Treatment of electrolyte changes or hypertension in the acutely ill patient may be required until the effects of the offending drug have disappeared.

Sedatives

Barbiturates. Acute toxicity from barbiturates leads to lethargy, mental confusion, and incoordination. Progressive difficulty with coma, hypotension, and respiratory failure may occur. The deep tendon reflexes become progressively depressed. There are electroencephalographic changes consisting of high-voltage fast activity superimposed on moderate-voltage slow waves (Cohn, Savage, & Raines, 1950). Artificial respiration by the use of mechanical respirators is frequently necessary.

Chronic toxicity from barbiturates frequently leads to confusion, incoordination, lethargy, personality changes, and irritability. A number of individuals become addicted to these drugs. Addiction is rare in childhood. Therapy of chronic intoxication should include the slow withdrawal of the drug. Precipitous withdrawal of barbiturates may lead to status epilepticus.

Treatment of apnea secondary to acute barbiturate poisoning with picrotoxin, caffeine, or similar drugs is of little help and may be dangerous (Plum & Swanson, 1957). No good studies of follow-up neurological or psychological evaluation of children with acute toxicity are available. Nonbarbiturate sedatives frequently lead to lethargy, incoordination, and coma. These drugs enjoy relatively little popularity compared with barbiturates.

Tranquilizers

Chlorpromazine and other phenothiazines. The phenothiazines have become very common therapeutic agents over the past decade. They have been used primarily as tranquilizers and antiemetic drugs.

Acute toxicity causes lethargy and in most cases some degree of hypotension. The patient becomes nauseated and ataxic, and later he may develop tremors and occasionally visual difficulties. He may also complain of difficulty with voluntary muscle movement. Coma then follows. Phenothiazines enhance the effect of sedative drugs and may lead to symptoms of acute toxicity in the presence of sedative-drug dosages that usually are not toxic. The phenothiazines may also cause hematologic and hepatic damage.

Acute or chronic toxicity secondary to phenothiazines may result in an unusual clinical picture. The phenothiazines cause a reaction, which is not dose-related, in which symptoms of extrapyramidal involvement appear (Goldsmith, 1959; Shaw, Dermott, Lee, Burbridge, 1959; Swaiman, 1960). There is a profound rigidity of all muscles with arching of the back and opisthotonos in the most severely affected patients. Oculogyric crisis has been reported. The patient may also develop difficulties with seizures and coma.

Therapy consists of removal from drug administration followed by the use of such drugs as Benadryl, atropine, or Cogentin.

Representative drugs of this group include chlorpromazine (Thorazine), prochlorperazine (Compazine), promethazine (Phenergan), and thioridazine (Mellaril).

Phenothiazines are used in children not only for antiemetic purposes but frequently also in high doses to calm hyperactive children. Toxic reactions in these children are unusual and rarely cause residual CNS problems. More often than not, residual problems that occur consist of hepatic and hematologic difficulties.

Reserpine and other rauwolfia preparations. Acute reserpine toxicity leads to lethargy, weakness, salivation, visual blurring, ataxia, headaches, and finally coma. Chronic poisoning leads usually to drowsiness, stuffy nose, and occasionally gastric upset and peptic ulcers.

Reserpine toxicity frequently leads to extrapyramidal symptoms similar to those found in phenothiazine toxicity. Residual CNS dysfunction from reserpine therapy is unusual.

Other tranquilizers. There are many other tranquilizers including meprobamate (Miltown), diazepam (Valium), and chlordiazepoxide (Librium). Chronic overdosage of these drugs leads to weakness, lethargy, vertigo, and finally coma.

Therapy of acute toxicity includes gastric lavage, supportive intravenous therapy, artificial respiration if necessary, and control of seizures if present by judicious use of barbiturates or general anesthetics.

Agricultural Chemicals

Pesticides

Organophosphate poisoning. Organophosphates were first employed as gases during the

First World War. Among them, parathion was not volatile enough or soluble enough in aqueous solution to be employed. This material has been used extensively as an insecticide and serves as the prototype for this group; it is the most frequently employed organophosphate in the world (Durham & Hayes, 1962).

Parathion and its related chemical compounds have become more and more prevalent as a poisoning agent in children.

Organophosphates inhibit acetylcholinesterase, leading to a persistence of the binding of acetylcholine to the receptor sites on the postsynaptic membrane. The continuous stimulation by acetylcholine leads to the symptoms of organophosphate poisoning, which can be divided into two main groups: the muscarinic and the nicotinic effects (Durham & Hayes, 1962).

The muscarinic effects are usually the first noted and consist of nausea, epigastric pain, and excessive perspiration. The method of contact with the toxin determines the early symptomatology. Gastrointestinal difficulties usually appear first if the patient has ingested the toxin, and sweating and muscular fasciculations are frequently seen early when the route of contact has been through the skin. In a similar manner, inhalation of the toxin frequently leads to early respiratory difficulties. Overwhelming exposure by any route results in vomiting, diarrhea, and then the cholinergic symptoms of salivation, lacrimation, perspiration, and dyspnea.

Nicotinic effects appear later and include muscular fasciculations and muscle cramping. Fatigability and weakness are pronounced, and overwhelming exposure leads to marked weakness, including failure of the respiratory muscles.

Not only is the peripheral nervous system involved, but CNS symptoms also arise. Early manifestations include anxiety and restlessness; later confusion, withdrawal, depression, and coma take place.

Most deaths from organophosphate poisoning result from compromise of respiration. Respiration can be hampered by weakness of the respiratory muscles, bronchoconstriction, increased bronchial secretions, and depression of the respiratory centers in the medulla.

Numerous reports of organophosphate poisoning of children are present in the literature. Mackey (1966) reports the poisoning of an 8-week-old girl from parathion spray. The child was successfully treated. The absorption of these compounds through the skin is particularly dangerous to children. The organic solvent utilized in formulating the organophosphate spray is very important in determining the rate of absorption through the skin. Even those children who receive a minimal spray dose which wets their clothes will, after a period of time because of constant exposure, develop symptoms to the chemical.

Diagnosis is made by the determination of cholinesterase activity in the blood or, more specifically, the pseudocholinesterase activity of the red cells. In the case of suspected poisoning, therapy should not be put off until laboratory confirmation is observed. Mild cases of toxicity can be treated with atropine to ward off severe muscarinic effects. Dosages of 1 to 2 milligrams intravenously can be given to small children. If no effect is noted after 8 minutes, intravenous injection of 1 milligram of atropine can be repeated. Atropine administration to anoxic patients potentiates the possibility of cardiac arrythmia, and it is necessary to ensure proper pulmonary exchange before atropine is given. There is some question as to whether atropine has an effect on the CNS symptoms. (Durham & Hayes, 1962). If seizures develop, phenobarbital or a faster-acting barbiturate can be given for seizure control. Under no circumstances should succinylcholine be given because this drug potentiates anticholinesterase drugs.

Specific antidotes to organophosphates have been employed over the past few years. Of those now employed, 2-pyridine aldoxime (2-PAM) appears to be the most efficacious (Durham & Hayes, 1962). Only minimal side effects from this drug have been noted in man. The general group of drugs to which 2-PAM belongs is the oximes. These drugs liberate cyanide *in vitro* or *in vivo,* and those materials which have been on the shelf for some time should be checked periodically for the presence of free cyanide. The oximes have three basic mechanisms of action:

1. Reactivation of inhibited cholinesterase
2. Binding and later inactivation of the organophosphate
3. Inhibition of excess cholinesterase activity

The oximes, including 2-PAM, appear to have little effect on brain cholinesterase levels. Apparently, these compounds do not pass the blood-brain transport system.

Phenothiazines have been reported to potentiate the effect of organophosphates and should not be used in the treatment of organophosphate poisoning (Arterberry, Bonifaci, Nash, & Quinby, 1962). Chronic CNS changes which persist, including changes in personality, judgment, and intellect, have been reported and should be emphasized (Gershon & Shaw, 1961).

Dichloyroidiphenyl trichloroethane (DDT). DDT is one of the most commonly used commercial insecticides in the world. It is also one of the most toxic insecticides. Solutions of DDT in various solvents usually result in a combination that is more toxic than DDT or the solvent alone.

Acute toxicity with DDT leads to irritability, excitability, muscular tremors, weakness, and eventually major motor seizures. Liver changes and renal changes are also common. Fatty changes of the myocardium are common.

Symptoms of chronic exposure to DDT have been unusual, but paresthesias, tremors, and personality changes do occur.

Emergency therapy includes gastric lavage or cleansing of the skin where the contact has been via skin absorption. Anticonvulsant therapy consisting of barbiturates or general anesthetics may be indicated. Patients who have reached the seizure stage are often left with permanent residuals or die. If only muscular tremors are present and the progression of symptomatology goes no further, the prognosis for complete recovery is good.

Household Toxins

Organic solvents

Carbon tetrachloride. Carbon tetrachloride is frequently used as a dry-cleaning agent. It is sometimes employed as an antihelminthic drug. Intoxication may occur by means of ingestion or inhalation. Symptoms are primarily those of liver, kidney, and CNS compromise.

Acute CNS symptoms include lethargy and confusion followed by coma. Extensive liver damage with jaundice and renal damage with anuria may lead to CNS compromise on the basis of the hepatic and renal failure.

Therapy with gastric lavage or emesis is indicated. Close monitoring of the urinary output is also indicated, and therapy for oliguria and anuria may prove necessary.

Chronic poisoning may lead to disabilities with blurred vision, peripheral neuritis, confusion, personality change, and memory loss. Loss of peripheral color vision has been described.

Trichloroethylene. Trichloroethylene is a common industrial solvent that is also found around the house. Inhalation is the usual method of poisoning. Trichloroethylene exposure results in CNS depression initially, leading to light-headed sensations, headache, and hyperactivity followed by coma.

Chronic poisoning may lead to lethargy and personality change. The myocardium may be involved, and cardiac arrhythmias including ventricular fibrillation are not uncommon.

At times liver damage may be the limiting factor in the patient's recovery.

Therapy consists of removing the solvent fumes from the area and giving supportive care.

Ethylene dichloride. Ethylene dichloride is used primarily in industry as a solvent for plastic and rubber adhesives. It is also used, however, by hobbyists and may be present in material ingested or sniffed by children.

The CNS is involved primarily. The liver, kidney, and heart are also involved to some extent. Symptoms of acute poisoning include stupor, progressing to coma along with vomiting and hypertension. Pulmonary edema also occurs.

The patient later may go on to manifest both hepatic and renal difficulty.

Chronic poisoning may lead to similar CNS aberrations. Cerebral difficulties with acute and chronic glue sniffing are thought to stem primarily from toluene and not from ethylene dichloride toxicity.

Methyl alcohol. Methyl alcohol is a common solvent found in industry and around the house. Its ingestion leads to acute acidosis and CNS malfunction ranging from headache and blurring of vision to coma. Vision may remain normal and then after 48 hours begin to fade. Acute symptoms of methyl alcohol toxicity also include mydriasis, dizziness, nausea, and lethargy. Chronic poisoning is usually marked predominantly by visual changes and little CNS abnormality.

Therapy includes gastric lavage and the administration of ethyl alcohol (Roe, 1950) in an attempt to block the degradation of methyl alcohol. The acidosis must be treated with administration of sodium bicarbonate and intravenous fluids. The patient may become hyperexcitable, and therapy with an appropriate sedative may prove necessary.

Ethyl alcohol. Ethyl alcohol is usually found around the home as the main constituent of alcoholic beverages. Serious difficulties, including death, occur in children who have ingested as little as 1.0 milliliter per kilogram of denatured alcohol containing 5 percent methyl alcohol.

Ethyl alcohol leads to CNS symptoms including incoordination, slowing of reaction time, blurred vision progressing to gross incoordination, impairment of judgment, stupor, and coma. Hypoglycemia with attendant seizures has been described in children. Chronic poisoning is not usually a problem in children.

Therapy consists of gastric lavage in acute cases and supportive therapy as necessary.

Ethylene glycol. Ethylene glycol is a frequent component of permanent antifreeze. Metabolism occurs to form oxalic acid, which is a powerful oxidizing agent and can lead to cerebral edema and other changes on the basis of calcium binding. Primary difficulty in the form of renal cortical necrosis and degeneration of the liver also takes place. Calcium oxalate crystals are found in the brain, spinal cord, and kidneys.

In the acute phase of poisoning the patient may be stuporous and comatose and may experience seizures. Anuria may develop rapidly. The patient may also experience pulmonary edema.

Therapy includes gastric lavage and the administration of ethyl alcohol and calcium gluconate.

Chronic poisoning is rarely a problem, but stupor, lethargy, and nystagmus do occur.

Triorthocresyl phosphate. Triorthocresyl phosphate is found in lubricating oil and is employed as a gasoline additive. Ingestion occurs primarily with the inadvertent substitution of lubricating oil for cooking oil. The usual sequelae of ingestion are demyelination of peripheral nerves and to some extent degenerative changes within the spinal cord. Lower motor neuron paralysis, particularly of the distal muscles of the extremities, is common.

Acute poisoning leads to weakness of the distal muscles with foot drop, wristdrop, and loss of deep tendon reflexes. Severe difficulties may include weakness of the ocular, laryngeal, and respiratory muscles.

Chronic poisoning may lead to the above symptoms over a prolonged period of time.

Treatment includes gastric lavage and supportive therapy.

Kerosene. Kerosene exposure usually occurs through ingestion or inhalation. The patient suffers from pulmonary edema, but there is also CNS depression which may lead to coma and seizures.

Chronic exposure to kerosene may lead to peripheral neuritis and personality changes.

Proper acute therapy is not universally agreed upon. The danger of aspiration during gastric lavage with subsequent severe pneumonitis is a real threat. Gastric lavage after insertion of a tracheal catheter and inflation of a cuff has been recommended. Gasoline ingestion causes similar difficulties.

Toluene. Toluene is a common constituent of airplane glue and is thought to be the offending agent in patients who suffer from toxicity secondary to glue sniffing.

Symptoms include light-headedness, euphoria, headache, visual blurring, tremors, and in later stages coma and seizures. Chronic symptoms include personality changes, irritability, and headache.

Acute therapy includes removing the patient from the contaminated atmosphere; in the case of ingestion, gastric lavage should be induced, with care taken to avoid aspiration. Cardiac arrhythmias are common and may be induced with the administration of sympathomimetic drugs.

Naphthalene. Naphthalene is a constituent of mothballs and moth repellent flakes. Although difficulty usually occurs in patients who develop hemolysis because of hereditary deficiency of glucose-6-phosphate dehydrogenase, other patients may develop hyperactivity, coma, and seizures. Renal disease with hematuria and oliguria may be present. Hepatic compromise leading to jaundice may also occur. Inhalation may also lead to headache and confusion.

Therapy includes lavage for ingestion or removal of the patient from the offending atmosphere if exposure is by inhalation. The presence of coma and seizures secondary to the naphthalene exposure usually indicates severe exposure, and death is common.

Heavy metals

Lead poisoning. Acute lead poisoning in childhood, due to ingestion or inhalation, is not unusual. Nausea, vomiting, weakness, and pain in the extremities and abdomen may result. Hemolytic crisis and irreversible renal damage frequently occur.

Chronic lead poisoning is much more common in children than in adults and occurs principally in older homes in slum areas on the East coast of the United States. Lead poisoning is the result of ingestion of old flaked paint. It is now illegal to utilize lead for manufacture of indoor house paint. Children between 1 and 3 years of age make up 85 percent of the cases (Mellins & Jenkins, 1955). A high percentage of children with lead poisoning have pica (Jacobziner & Raybin, 1962).

Lead is absorbed from the gastrointestinal tract in the form of various salt complexes and is deposited and stored primarily in bone but also in many soft tissues. It is deposited in bone in much the same manner as calcium in a phosphate complex. Conditions suitable for calcium deposition are usually suitable for lead deposition, and conditions suitable for mobilization of calcium from bone usually result in mobilization of lead from bone.

The most common neurological manifestation in adult patients with chronic lead poisoning is peripheral neuritis. This neuritis frequently involves important nerves of the arms and legs and classically involves the radial nerve of the forearm, leading to wristdrop. On the other hand, peripheral neuritis is relatively uncommon in childhood. More commonly, chronic lead poisoning in children leads to involvement of the CNS. A large spectrum of cerebral symptomatology is possible from brain involvement secondary to lead poisoning in children, but the most common clinical picture is that of increased intra-cranial pressure with resultant changes in level of consciousness, splitting of the cranial sutures, convulsions, changes in pulse rate, and findings of upper motor neuron impairment including spasticity, clonus, and positive toe signs. The patient may be unconscious or semicomatose. The pathological picture is one of diffuse cerebral edema with marked changes including swelling of neurons. Massive cerebral edema is frequently life-threatening, and emergency therapy is necessary if the patient is not to die from the sequelae of severe increased intracranial pressure. Such therapy includes infusion of hypertonic solutions (i.e., mannitol) and at times craniotomy with removal of portions of the temporal lobe.

Treatment of lead intoxication includes the use of ethylenediamine tetracetic acid (EDTA), which chelates lead and results in excretion of the resulting complex in the urine. Although such therapy effectively lowers blood lead concentration, the problems attendant on mobilization of lead deposited in other tissues, particularly bone, continue to be present. Acidosis must be prevented because of the resulting massive mobilization of lead from bone, leading to marked exacerbation of clinical symptomatology. In the comatose patient, other supportive measures including proper electrolyte therapy and maintenance of a proper airway are necessary.

Concomitant renal symptomatology including albuminuria, hematuria, and glycosuria is benefited by the same therapy.

Diagnosis can be made by determination of urinary excretion of lead over a 24-hour period. Usually, excretion of less than 50 micrograms of lead in a 24-hour period can be considered normal. Excretion of over 80 micrograms per 24 hours is usually indicative of lead toxicity, and excretion of 50 to 80 micrograms of lead in the urine in 24 hours is indicative of increased intake of lead. Urinary coproporphyrins are increased early in lead poisoning, and an increase in their concentration is a reliable and sensitive sign of lead toxicity. Unfortunately, their increase is not always secondary to lead intoxication. Urinary excretion of delta aminolevulinic acid is increased in lead poisoning, but previous techniques of accurate determinations do not lend themselves to screening purposes. There are, however, some new techniques that deserve investigation (Davis & Andelman, 1967).

Study of blood lead levels are not universally available, although normal values between 0.003 and 0.06 microgram per 100 milliliters are known. Blood levels above 0.06 microgram per 100 milliliters are known. Blood levels above 0.06 microgram per 100 milliliters should be suspect.

Effects of therapy can be monitored by determination of urine lead concentration and diminution of urinary coproporphyrin excretion. X-rays of long bones should show diminution in the amount of deposited lead during long-term therapy for lead intoxication. These x-ray findings are frequently not present in children below age 2.

The most important factors in therapy aside from the acute problems of increased intracranial pressure are those relating to prevention. Therapy depends on prolonged excretion of small amounts of lead each day without reexposure. The source of exposure must be determined, and flaked paint must be removed and covered with a safe layer of fresh nontoxic paint. Children should not be allowed to gnaw on old painted surfaces, including those of furniture.

Brain handicaps are commonly found in victims of lead poisoning. Over 39 percent of children in one study had some type of neurological residual (Perlstein & Attala, 1966). Seizures, mental retardation, spasticity, and optic atrophy are commonly found.

Barium. Barium salts are used primarily as pesticides. They are occasionally found in depilatories. Occasionally, soluble barium salts may be present in insoluble barium sulfate used for radiological purposes.

Acute toxicity usually consists of muscle spasms, vomiting, weakness, cardiac irregularities, seizures, and death. Chronic toxicity is very rare.

Therapy includes gastric lavage and the administration of sodium sulfate intravenously. Sulfates should also be given by gastric tube after lavage has been carried out. Atropine may be used for severe gastrointestinal colic. If the patient survives for 20 hours, the prognosis for life is good. Chronic cerebral changes may occur as a result of severe and prolonged episodes of major motor seizures.

Arsenic. Arsenic is found around the house in rat poisons, insecticides, and occasionally in paint and wallpaper. Signs of acute toxicity early after injection are limited mainly to gastrointestinal symptoms of vomiting and watery, bloody diarrhea. In the terminal stages of acute poisoning, seizures and coma are present.

Chronic arsenic ingestion causes peripheral neuritis with dysesthesias and paresthesias. Burning sensations are common. Optic neuritis may be the presenting difficulty. Other symptoms include alopecia, hyperkeratosis of the palms and soles, anemia, nephritis, and chronic gastrointestinal upset (Southly, 1965).

Acute toxicity should be treated with gastric lavage and administration of BAL (dimercaprol).

Chronic toxicity should be treated by removal of arsenic from patient contact and use of BAL.

At autopsy the brain is often congested, and numerous areas of petechiae are present. Both neuronal changes and demyelination may also be present.

Mercury. Mercury in its liquid form is not toxic because it is not absorbed into the gastrointestinal tract. Mercury vapors are toxic. Mercuric salts are found in the house primarily in paints and in calomel (mercurous chloride), a drug of doubtful clinical efficacy. Treatment

with mercurial diuretics can also lead to toxic symptomatology. Mercury acts as the cellular level by binding to sulfhydryl groups.

Acute mercury poisoning leads to gastrointestinal disturbances of vomiting, abdominal colic, and bloody diarrhea. Albuminuria and hematuria are frequent. Death is usually caused by uremia after a period of several days or weeks. Acute toxicity rarely causes prominent CNS symptoms.

Therapy of acute mercury poisoning consists of lavage, supportive measures, and use of BAL (dimercaprol).

Chronic mercury poisoning is accompanied by fatigue, irritability, muscular weakness, and psychotic personality changes. On occasion optic neuritis, peripheral neuritis, ataxia, and seizures may appear.

Chronic intoxication is treated by removal of the mercury from patient contact and the use of Bal (dimercaprol).

Thallium poisoning. Thallium is a toxic heavy metal; it is frequently used to coat grain and peanuts, which makes it susceptible to ingestion by both children and rodents.

Unusual and for the moment unexplained neurological symptoms including myoclonic jerking, dysarthria, and rigidity are frequently noted. Alopecia almost universally results, but does not appear until 3 to 4 weeks after the chemical is ingested (Smith & Doherty, 1964). Early diagnosis can be made by use of a test in which equal amounts of urine, 0.4 percent sodium bismuth in 20 percent nitric acid, and 10 percent sodium iodide are mixed in a test tube. The presence of thallium results in a red precipitate. No precipitate is formed in the absence of thallium. Other heavy metals do not cause false-positive reactions.

Therapy with thiosulfate, EDTA, BAL, and cation-exchange resins has not been highly effective. Studies by Thyresson (1950) demonstrated that cystine and methionine retard alopecia. He also demonstrated that thallium inhibits anaerobic glycosis. Thallium combines with sulfhydryl groups and therefore inhibits enzymes. Cystine and methionine supply excess sulfhydryl groups and in this way probably prevent thallium from reacting with active enzymatic components.

Lund (1956) studied dithizone (di-phenolthiocarbazone) and noted that he could increase thallium excretion by at least 75 percent. This drug theoretically may produce serious side effects. Chamberlain (Chamberlain, Stavinoha, Davis, Kniker, & Panos, 1958) has utilized the drug for therapy in humans and has noted its lack of toxicity and its efficacy in therapy.

Unfortunately, many children who survive chronic thallium ingestion suffer residual cerebral difficulties including intellectual, motor, and personality changes.

Other heavy metals. On rare occasions toxicity from phosphorus, antimony, zinc, copper, silver, gold, and manganese may occur.

Iron poisoning does occur, but CNS symptoms are secondary (Whitten, Gibson, Good, Goodwin, & Brough, 1965).

Acids, bases, and oxidizing agents

Bromates. Bromates are important constituents of home permanent sets, in which they are utilized as neutralizers. Hydrogen bromates are released upon ingestion, and predominant symptoms are those of renal and CNS embarrassment. In acute poisoning the patient begins to vomit violently and experiences colic and diarrhea. Lethargy, coma, and seizures usually follow. Difficulties with anuria are very common and may lead to permanent renal failure and death. Acute therapy consists of gastric lavage or induced emesis. Sodium thiosulfate is frequently given intravenously as an antidote. Renal failure must be treated with customary methods of fluid and electrolyte restriction.

Gases

Carbon monoxide. Carbon monoxide combines with hemoglobin to form a stable bond that precludes the use of bound hemoglobin for oxygen transport. The resultant tissue anoxia leads to the generalized symptomatology. Symptoms of carbon monoxide poisoning range from headache and light-headedness to coma and death. Children may be particularly susceptible to carbon monoxide poisoning on the basis of their increased need for oxygen. An anemic child may suffer disproportionate difficulty.

Therapy includes removal of the patient from the abnormal environment and oxygen administration.

Chronic carbon monoxide exposure may lead to personality change and loss of intellectual ability.

Patients who have been comatose from carbon monoxide poisoning frequently suffer residual extrapyramidal symptoms of rigidity and tremor. Permanent intellectual impairment is also a common consequence.

Neuropathological studies (Schwedenberg, 1959) usually reveal changes in the caudate and putamen, but lesions of the globus pallidus are most common. In severe cases, if the patient survives for several days, the examination of the cerebral cortex may reveal areas of ischemic necrosis and neuronal changes. The Purkinje cells in the cerebellum are frequently severely affected. There have been some reports of the effect of carbon monoxide in the fetus (Hallervorden, 1949). It appears that the lesions in the fetus caused by carbon monoxide poisoning are even more devastating than those in older children.

REFERENCES

Abramson, H., & Greenberg, M. Acute poliomyelitis in infants under one year of age: Epidemiological and clinical features. *Pediatrics,* 1955, **16,** 478–487.

Adams, J. M., Baird, C., & Filloy, L. Inclusion bodies in measles encephalitis. *The Journal of* the *American Medical Association,* 1966, **195,** 290–298.

Alexander, H. E. Advances in the treatment of bacterial meningitis. *Advances in Pediatrics,* 1952, **5,** 13–52.

Appelbaum, E., Rachelson, M. H., & Dolgopol, V. B. Varicella encephalitis. *The American Journal of Medicine,* 1953, **15,** 223–230.

Arena, J. M. *Poisoning.* Springfield, Ill.: Charles C Thomas, 1963.

Arterberry, J. D., Bonifaci, R. W., Nash, E. W., & Quinby, G. B. Potentiation of phosphorus insecticides by phenothiazine derivatives. *The Journal of the American Medical Association,* 1962, **182,** 848–850.

Auld, P. A. M., Kevy, S. V., & Eley, R. C. Poliomyelitis in children. *The New England Journal of Medicine,* 1960, **263,** 1093–1100.

Baker, A. B. Chronic lymphocytic choriomeningitis. *The Journal of Neurophathology and Experimental Neurology,* 1947, **6,** 253–264.

Baker, A. B. Viral encephalitis. In A. B. Baker (Ed.), *Clinical neurology.* New York: Hoeber-Harper, 1962. P. 811.

Barrett, F. F., Eardley, W. A., Yow, M. D., & Leverett, H. A. Ampicillin in the treatment of acute suppurative meningitis. *The Journal of Pediatrics,* 1966, **69,** 343–353.

Bellanti, J. A., Guin, G. H., Grassi, R. M., & Olson, L. C. Herpes simplex encephalitis: Brain biopsy and treatment with 5-iodo-2′-deoxyuridine. *The Journal of Pediatrics,* 1968, **72,** 266–275.

Berman, P. H., & Banker, B. Q. Neonatal meningitis: A clinical and pathological study of 29 cases. *Pediatrics,* 1966, **38,** 6–24.

Bernstein, T. C., & Wolff, H. G. Involvement of the nervous system in infectious mononucleosis. *Annals of Internal Medicine,* 1950, **33,** 1120–1138.

Blanc, W. A., & Gaetz, R. Simplified millipore filter technique for cytologic diagnoses of cytomegalic inclusion disease in examination of urine. *Pediatrics,* 1962, **29,** 61–64.

Blattner, R. J. Congenital rubella, persistent infection of the brain and liver. *The Journal of Pediatrics,* 1966, **68,** 997–999.

Bloch, H., Hirschil, D., Turin, R., & Zaleznak, B. Masked mumps encephalitis complicated by hemiplegia. *American Journal of Diseases of Children,* 1950, **79,** 324–325.

Bonforte, R. J. Convulsion as a presenting sign of infectious mononucleosis. *American Journal of Diseases of Children,* 1967, **114,** 429–432.

Bredeck, J. F., Broun, G. O., Hempelmann, T. C., McFadden, J. F., & Spector, H. I. Follow-up studies of the 1933 St. Louis epidemic of encephalitis. *The Journal of the American Medical Association,* 1938, **111,** 15–17.

Brown, J. W., Kirkland, H. B., & Hein, G. E. Central nervous system involvement (meningoencephalitis and spinal fluid pleocytosis) during mumps. *The American Journal of the Medical Sciences,* 1948, **215,** 434–441.

Butler, W. T., Alling, D. W., Spickard, A., & Utz, J. P. Diagnostic and prognostic value of clinical and laboratory findings in cryptococcal meningitis: A follow-up study of forty patients. *The New England Journal of Medicine,* 1964, **270,** 59–67.

Carpenter, R. R., & Petersdorf, R. G. Clinical spectrum of bacterial meningitis. *The American Journal of Medicine,* 1962, **33,** 262–275.

Chamberlain, P. H., Stavinoha, W. B., Davis, H., Kniker, W. T., & Panos, T. C. Thallium poisoning. *Pediatrics,* 1958, **22,** 1170–1182.

Chao, D. Subacute inclusion body encephalitis. *The Journal of Pediatrics,* 1962, **61,** 501–510.

Christ, N. R.   Acute viral infections of the nervous system. *Proceedings of the Royal Society of Medicine,* 1967, **60,** 24.

Cobb, W., & Hill, D.   Electroencephalogram in subacute progressive encephalitis. *Brain,* 1950, **73,** 392–404.

Cohn, R., Savage, C., & Raines, G. W.   Barbiturate intoxication: A clinical EEG study. *Annals of Internal Medicine,* 1950, **32,** 1049–1065.

Cooper, L. Z., & Krugman, S.   Diagnosis and management, congenital rubella. *Pediatrics,* 1966, **37,** 335–338.

Cragg, J., & Bennett, E. F.   Meningococcal meningitis: A family study. *The Lancet,* 1959, **1,** 248–249.

Davis, J. R., & Andelman, S. L.   Urinary delta aminoevialince and levels in lead poisoning. I. A modified method for the rapid determination of urinary delta-aminolevulinic and using disposable ion-exchange chromatography columns. *Archives of Environmental Health,* 1967, **15,** 53–59.

Dawson, J. R.   Cellular inclusions in cerebral lesions of lethargic encephalitis. *The American Journal of Pathology,* 1933, **9,** 7–15.

Desmite, E. M.   A follow-up study of 110 patients treated for purulent meningitis. *Archives of Disease in Childhood,* 1955, **30,** 415–418.

Dodd, K.   Spirochoetal disease. In W. E. Nelson (Ed.), *Textbook of pediatrics.* Philadelphia: Saunders, 1964. P. 522.

Donohue, W. L., Playfair, F. D., & Whitaker, L.   Mumps encephalitis: Pathology and pathogenesis. *The Journal of Pediatrics,* 1955, **47,** 395–412.

Dumoff-Stanley, E., Dowling, H. F., & Sweet, L. K.   Absorption into and distribution of penicillin in the cerebrospinal fluid. *The Journal of Clinical Investigation,* 1946, **25,** 87–93.

Dupont, J. R., & Earle, K. M.   Human rabies encephalitis. *Neurology,* 1965, **15,** 1023–1034.

Durham, W. F., & Hayes, W. J., Jr.   Organic phosphorus poisoning and its therapy. *Archives of Environmental Health,* 1962, **5,** 21–47.

Emanuel, B., Ching, E., Lieberman, A. D., & Goldin, M.   Crytococcus meningitis in a child successfully treated with Amphotericin B. *The Journal of Pediatrics,* 1961, **59,** 577–591.

Eyles, D. E.   New knowledge of the chemotherapy of toxoplasmosis. *Annals of the New York Academy of Science,* 1956, **64,** 252–267.

Farber, S., Hill, A., Connerly, M. L., & Dingle, J. H.   Encephalitis in infants and children caused by the virus of the Eastern variety of equine encephalitis. *The Journal of the American Medical Association,* 1940, **114,** 1725–1731.

Feemster, R. F.   Eastern equine encephalitis. *Neurology,* 1958, **8,** 882–883.

Feldman, H. A.   Toxoplasmosis. *Pediatrics,* 1958, **22,** 559–574.

Finley, K. H.   Western equine encephalitis: Clinical sequelae. *Neurology,* 1958, **8,** 881–882.

Finley, K. H., Fitzgerald, L. H., Richter, R. W., Riggs, N., & Shelton, J. T.   Western encephalitis and cerebral ontogenesis. *Archives of Neurology,* 1967, **160,** 140–164.

Flemming, A. S.   Accidental poisoning. *U. S. Public Health Reports,* 1960, **75,** 91–92.

Foley, J., & Williams, D.   Inclusion encephalitis and its relation to subacute sclerosing leucoencephalitis. *The Quarterly Journal of Medicine,* 1953, **22,** 157–194.

Ford, F. R.   The nervous complications of measles. *Bulletin of the Johns Hopkins Hospital,* 1928, **43,** 140–184.

Gautier-Smith, P. C. Neurological complications of glandular fever (infectious mononucleosis). II. *Brain,* 1965, **88,** 323–334.

Gershon, S., & Shaw, F. H. Psychiatric sequelae of chronic exposure to organophosphate insecticide. *The Lancet,* 1961, **2,** 1371–1374.

Gibbs, F. A., Gibbs, E. L., Carpenter, P. R., & Spies, H. W. Electroencephalographic abnormality in "uncomplicated" childhood diseases. *The Journal of the American Medical Association,* 1959, **171,** 1050–1055.

Gibel, H., Kramer, B., & Neji, A. F. Encephalitis complicating chickenpox. *American Journal of the Diseases of Children,* 1960, **99,** 669–679.

Glasser, L., & Delta, B. G. Congenital toxoplasmosis with placental infection in monozygotic twins. *Pediatrics,* 1965, **35,** 276–283.

Goldsmith, R. W. Toxicity of phenothiazine compounds. *Pediatrics,* 1959, **23,** 1015–1016.

Good, R. A., Vernier, R. L., & Smith, R. T. Serious untoward reactions to therapy with cortisone and adrenocorticotropin in pediatric practice. *Pediatrics,* 1957, **19,** 95–118.

Goodman, L. S., & Gilman, A. *The pharmacological basis of therapeutics.* (3rd ed.) New York: Macmillan, 1965.

Griffith, J. Acute cerebellar encephalitis. *The American Journal of the Medical Sciences,* 1921, **162,** 781–789.

Groover, R. V., Sutherland, J. M., & Landing, B. H. Purulent meningitis of newborn infants: Eleven-year experience in antibiotic era. *The New England Journal of Medicine,* 1961, **264,** 1115–1121.

Haggerty, R. J., & Ziani, M. Acute bacterial meningitis. *Advances in Pediatrics,* 1963, **13,** 129–181.

Hallervorden, J. Über eine Kohlenoxydvergiftung im Fetalleben mit Entwicklungsstörung der Hirnrinde. *Allgemeine Zeitschrift für Psychiatrie,* 1949, **124,** 289.

Hanshaw, J. B. Congenital and acquired cytomegalovirus infection. *Pediatric Clinics of North America,* 1966, **13,** 279–293.

Harter, D. H. Preliminary antibiotic therapy in bacterial meningitis. *Archives of Neurology,* 1963, **9,** 343–347.

Haymaker, W., & Sabin, A. B. Topographic distribution of lesions in central nervous system in Japanese B encephalitis. *Archives of Neurology and Psychiatry,* 1947, **57,** 673–692.

Heppleston, J. D., Pearce, K. M., & Yates, P. O. Varicella encephalitis. *Archives of Disease in Childhood,* 1959, **34,** 318–321.

Holliday, P. B., Jr. Pre-eruptive neurological complications of the common contagious diseases: Rubella, rubeola, roseola and varicella. *The Journal of Pediatrics,* 1950, **36,** 185–198.

Huand, C. H., & Liu, S. H. Acute epidemic encephalitis of the Japanese type. *The Chinese Medical Journal,* 1940, **58,** 427–439.

Jacobziner, H., & Raybin, H. W. The epidemiology of lead poisoning in children. *Archives of Pediatrics,* 1962, **79,** 72–76.

Jeans, P. C., & Cooke, J. V. (Eds.) Prepubescent syphilis. In *Clinical pediatrics.* Vol. 17. New York: Appleton-Century-Crofts, 1930.

Johnson, R. T., & Mims, C. A. Pathogenesis of viral infection of the nervous system. *The New England Journal of Medicine,* 1968, **278,** 23–30.

Kilbrick, S., & Benirschke, K. Severe generalized disease (encephalohepatomyocarditis) occurring in the newborn period and due to infection with coxsackie virus, group B: Evidence of intrauterine infection with this agent. *Pediatrics,* 1958, **22,** 857–874.

Kilham, L. Mumps meningoencephalitis with and without parotitis. *American Journal of Diseases of Children,* 1949, **78,** 324–333.

Kokenge, R., Kutt, H., & McDowell, F. Neurological sequelae following dilantin overdose in a patient and in experimental animals. *Neurology,* 1965, **15,** 823–829.

Kramer, R., & Som, M. L. Intracranial pathways of infection from diseases of sphenoid and ethmoid sinuses. *Archives of Otolaryngology,* 1940, **32,** 744–770.

Krasnoff, S. O., & Bernstein, M. Acetylsalicylic acid poisoning. *The Journal of the American Medical Association,* 1947, **135,** 712–714.

Kresky, B., Buchbinder, S., & Greenberg, I. M. The incidence of neurologic residual in children after recovery from bacterial meningitis. *Archives of Pediatrics,* 1962, **79,** 63–71.

Krugman, S., & Ward, R. *Infectious diseases of children.* (3rd ed.) St. Louis: C. Mosby, 1964.

Kutt, H., Wolk, M., Scherman, R., & McDowell, F. Insufficient parahydroxylation as a cause of diphenylhydantoin toxicity. *Neurology,* 1964, **14,** 542–548.

Lauriault, C. D., & Jim, R. T. S. Diphenylhydantoin toxicity, lymphadenopathy and low platelet count. *Pediatrics,* 1966, **37,** 341–342.

Lewis, L., Taylor, H. G., Sorem, M. B., Norcross, J. W., & Kindsvatter, V. H. Japanese B encephalitis. *Archives of Neurology and Psychiatry,* 1947, **57,** 430–463.

Lund, A. Effect of various substances on excretion and toxicity of thallium in rats. *Acta Pharmacologica et Toxicologa,* 1956, **12,** 260–268.

MacCallum, F. O., Potter, J. M., & Edwards, D. H. Early diagnosis of Herpes simplex encephalitis by brain biopsy. *The Lancet,* 1964, **2,** 332–334.

Mackey, R. W. Parathion poisoning in a young infant. *American Journal of Diseases of Children,* 1966, **111,** 321–323.

Macrae, J., & Campbell, A. M. G. Neurological complications of mumps. *The British Medical Journal,* 1949, **2,** 259–261.

Magoffin, R. L., Lennette, E. H., Hollister, A. C., & Schmidt, N. J. An etiologic study of clinical paralytic poliomyelitis. *The Journal of the American Medical Association,* 1961, **175,** 269–278.

McAllister, R. M., Hummler, K., & Coriell, L. L. Acute cerebellar ataxia: Report of a case with isolation of type nine ECHO virus from the cerebrospinal fluid. *The New England Journal of Medicine,* 1959, **261,** 1159–1162.

McLeod, D. L., Beale, A. J., McNaughton, G. A., & Rhodes, A. J. Clinical features of aseptic meningitis caused by coxsackie-B virus. *The Lancet,* 1956, **271,** 701–703.

Medearis, D. N., Jr. Observations concerning human cytomegalovirus infection and disease. *Bulletin of the Johns Hopkins Hospital,* 1964, **114,** 181–211.

Mellins, R. B., & Jenkins, C. D. Epidemiological and psychological study of lead poisoning in children. *The Journal of the American Medical Association,* 1955, **158,** 15–20.

Merritt, H. H., & Putnam, T. J. Sodium diphenylhydantoinate in treatment of convulsive disorders. *The Journal of the American Medical Association,* 1938, **11,** 1068–1073.

Monif, G. R. G., & Sever, J. L. Chronic infection of the central nervous system with rubella virus. *Neurology,* 1966, **16,** 111–112.

Morton, H. G. Atropine intoxication. *The Journal of Pediatrics,* 1939, **14,** 755–760.

Nelson, N. A., & Struve, V. R. Prevention of congenital syphilis in pregnancy. *The Journal of the American Medical Association,* 1956, **161,** 869–872.

Nichols, W. W., & Athreya, B. Encephalitis probably due to infectious mononucleosis: Report of 4 cases. *American Journal of Diseases of Children,* 1962, **103,** 72–76.

Noran, H. H., & Baker, A. B. Sequels of equine encephalomyelitis. *Archives of Neurology and Psychiatry,* 1943, **49,** 398–413.

Norman, J., & Shea, J. T. Acute hallucinosis as a complication of addiction to amphetamine sulfate. *The New England Journal of Medicine,* 1945, **233,** 270–271.

Ojala, A. On changes in the cerebrospinal fluid during measles. *Annales Medicinae Internae Fenniae,* 1947, **36,** 321–331.

Oldfelt, V. Sequelae of mumps-meningoencephalitis. *Acta Medica Scandinavica,* 1949, **134,** 405–415.

Perlstein, M. A., & Attala, R. Neurologic sequelae of plumbism in children. *Clinical Pediatrics,* 1966, **5,** 292–298.

Petersdorf, R. G., & Harter, D. H. Fall in cerebrospinal fluid sugar in meningitis. *Archives of Neurology,* 1961, **4,** 21–30.

Petersdorf, R. G., Swarner, D. R., & Garcia, M. Studies on pathogenesis of meningitis. III. Relationship of phagocytosis to fall in cerebrospinal fluid sugar in experimental pneumococcal meningitis. *The Journal of Laboratory and Clinical Medicine,* 1963, **61,** 745–754.

Petre-Quadens, D., Sfaello, Z., Van Bogaert, L., & Moya, G. Sleep study in SSPE (first results). II. *Neurology,* 1968, **18,** 60–75.

Pierce, N., Portnoy, B., Leeds, N., Morrison, R., & Wehrle, R. Encephalitis associated with Herpes simplex infection presenting as a temporal-lobe mass. *Neurology,* 1964, **14,** 708–713.

Plum, F., & Swanson, A. G. Barbiturate poisoning treated by physiological methods. *The Journal of the American Medical Association,* 1957, **163,** 827–835.

Rawls, W. E., Dyck, P. J., Klass, D. W., Greer, H. D., & Herrmann, E. L., Jr. Encephalitis associated with Herpes simplex virus. *Annals of Internal Medicine,* 1966, **64,** 104–115.

Riley, H. D., & Worley, L. Salicylate intoxication. *Pediatrics,* 1956, **18,** 578–593.

Röe, O. The role of alkaline salts and ethyl alcohol in the treatment of methanol poisoning. *Quarterly Journal of Studies on Alcohol,* 1950, **11,** 107–112.

Rorke, L. B., & Spiro, A. J. Cerebral lesions in congenital rubella syndrome. *The Journal of Pediatrics,* 1967, **70,** 243–255.

Rosenberg, D. H., & Sylvester, J. C. Excretion of penicillin in spinal fluid in meningitis. *Science,* 1944, **100,** 132–133.

Ross, A. T. Meningococcic meningitis. *Archives of Neurology and Psychiatry,* 1952, **67,** 89–102.

Sabin, A. B., Krumbiegel, E. R., & Wigand, R. ECHO type nine virus disease. *American Journal of Diseases of Children,* 1958, **96,** 197–219.

Sanford, J. P., & Sulkin, S. E. The clinical spectrum of ECHO-virus infection. *The New England Journal of Medicine,* 1959, **261,** 1113–1122.

Schwedenberg, T. H. Leukoencephalopathy following carbon monoxide asphyxia. *The Journal of Neuropathology and Experimental Neurology,* 1959, **18,** 597–608.

Shaw, E. B., Dermott, R. V., Lee, R., & Burbridge, T. N. Phenothiazine tranquilizers as a cause of severe seizures. *Pediatrics,* 1959, **23,** 485–492.

Siewers, C. M., & Cramblett, H. G. Crytococco-sis (torulosis) in children. *Pediatrics,* 1964, **34,** 393–400.

Silverman, A. C. Mumps complicated by a preceding myelitis. *The New England Journal of Medicine,* 1949, **241,** 262–266.

Smith, D. H., & Doherty, R. A. Thallitoxicosis: Three Massachusetts cases. *Pediatrics,* 1964, **34,** 480–490.

Smith, E. S. Purulent meningitis in infants and children: A review of 409 cases. *The Journal of Pediatrics* 1954, **45,** 425–436.

Smith, M. G., Lennette, E. H., & Reames, H. R. Isolation of the virus of Herpes simplex and the demonstration of intranuclear inclusions in a case of acute encephalitis. *The American Journal of Pathology,* 1941, **17,** 55–67.

Sobel, R., & Margolis, J. A. Repetitive poisoning in children: Psychosocial study. *Pediatrics,* 1965, **35,** 641–651.

Southby, R. Fatal poisoning in children under five years of age. *The Medical Journal of Australia,* 1965, **1,** 533–538.

Steen, E., & Torp, K. H. Encephalitis and thrombocytopenia purpura after rubella. *Archives of Disease in Chldhood,* 1956, **31,** 470–473.

Suzuki, M., & Phillips, C. A. St. Louis encepha-litis: A histological study of the fatal cases from the Houston epidemic in 1964. *Archives of Pathology,* 1966, **81,** 47–54.

Swaiman, K. F. Acute neurologic reaction to promethazine. *The New England Journal of Medicine,* 1960, **263,** 747.

Swartz, M. N., & Dodge, P. R. Bacterial menin-gitis: A review of selected aspects. *The New England Journal of Medicine,* 1965, **272,** 725–731.

Thyresson, N. The influence of dietary factors, experimental brewer's yeast, cystine, and vitamin B in the course of chronic thallium poisoning in the rat. *Acta Dermato-Venereologica,* 1950, **30,** 9–26.

Tondury, G., & Smith, D. W. Fetal rubella pathology. *The Journal of Pediatrics,* 1966, **68,** 867–879.

Tyler, H. R. Neurological complications of rubeola (measles). *Medicine,* 1957, **36,** 147–167.

Walker, S. H., & Togo, Y. Encephalitis due to group B, type 5 coxsackie virus. *American Journal of Diseases of Children,* 1963, **105,** 209–212.

Wehrle, P. F., Day, P. A., Whalen, J. P., Fitz-gerald, J. W., & Harris, V. G. The epidemiology of accidental poisoning in an urban population. II. Prevalence and distribution of poisoning. *American Journal of Public Health,* 1960, **50,** 1925–1933.

Wehrle, P. F., DeFreest, L., Penhollow, J., & Harris, V. G. The epidemiology of accidental poisoning in an urban population. *Pediatrics,* 1961, **27,** 614–620.

Wehrle, P. F., Lampton, A. K., Portnoy, B., & Mason, J. O. Disability associated with ECHO virus infection. *American Journal of Diseases of Children,* 1961, **102,** 500–501.

Weinstein, L., Shelokov, A., Seltser, R., & Winchell, G. D. Comparison of clinical features of poliomyelitis in adults and in children. *The New England Journal of Medicine,* 1952, **246,** 296–302.

Weller, T. H., & Hanshaw, J. B. Virologic and clinical observations on cytomegalic inclusion body disease. *The New England Journal of Medicine,* 1962, **266,** 1233–1244.

Wesselhoeft, C., Smith, E. C., & Branch, C. F. Human encephalitis: Eight fatal cases, with four due to the virus of equine encephalomyelitis. *The Journal of the American Medical Association,* 1938, **111**, 1735–1741.

Whitten, C. F., Gibson, G. W., Good, M. H., Goodwin, J. F., & Brough, A. J. Studies in acute iron poisoning. I. Desferrioxamine in the treatment of acute iron poisoning: Clinical observations, experimental studies. and theoretical considerations. *Pediatrics,* 1965, **36**, 322–335.

Williams, R. D. B. Alterations in glucose transport mechanism in patients with complications of bacterial meningitis. *Pediatrics,* 1964, **34**, 491–502.

Wilson, R. E., & Ford, F. R. The nervous complications of variola, vaccinia and varicella with report of cases. *Bulletin of the Johns Hopkins Hospital,* 1927, **40**, 337–353.

Woodward, T. E. Rickettsial disease in the United States. *The Medical Clinics of North America,* 1959, **43**, 1507–1535.

Woodward, T. E., & Jackson, E. B. Spotted fever rickettsiae. In F. C. Horsfall, Jr., & I. Tamm (Eds.), *Viral and rickettsial infections of man.* (4th ed.) Philadelphia: Lippincott, 1965.

Young, L. M., Haddow, J. E., & Klein, J. O. Relapse following ampicillin treatment of acute Hemophilus influenzae meningitis. *Pediatrics,* 1968, **41**, 516–518.

11 Mental Deficiencies

H. C. Gunzburg

The report of the President's Panel on mental Retardation (1962) states: Mental retardation "afflicts twice as many individuals as blindness, polio, cerebral palsy and rheumatic heart disease, combined." Approximately "5.4 million children and adults in the United States, are afflicted, some severely, most only mildly." "An estimated 126,000 babies born each year will be regarded as mentally retarded at some time in their lives."

Whatever type of definition one adopts and whatever system of classification is applied, mental deficiency represents a formidable problem to society, which has to deal in some way with the social inadequacy that is the most important aspect of this condition. If preventive and curative measures fail to have any effect, people handicapped by lower-than-average mental ability will represent an increasingly heavy burden on the resources of the nation. After a period of pessimism, during which institutionalization of one kind or another was regarded as the only possible method for dealing with the problem, there has been, in recent years, an upsurge of realistic optimism in the belief that much can be done to overcome the consequences of the handicap, and perhaps also to prevent it's occurring at all. This is the result of looking at the problem from new points of view and applying new methods of approach to issues which have so far successfully resisted any real solution.

The following pages attempt to give a survey of the present situation in the field, stressing particularly positive approaches of education and training based on psychological work.

HISTORICAL DEVELOPMENT

Official recognition of the existence of the problem of mental deficiency can be said to have taken place when the first organized provisions for mental defectives were arranged. In 1837 Seguin (1846) founded a center for the training of idiots in Paris, and he developed the treatment methods further after he emigrated, in 1850, to the United States, where his work profoundly affected further developments. England established its first asylum for mental defectives in 1840 and passed an "idiots' act" in 1886; by 1913 some

342

five thousand mentally defective persons were being cared for in these institutions.

The approach to the problem was greatly influenced by the work of the French physician Itard (1962), who had tried to tackle the education and training of a young lad who had been found living wild in the woods and who is now known in literature as the "Wild Boy of Aveyron." Influenced by Itard's ideas of "sense training," Seguin —and later Maria Montessori, Decroly, and Mlle. Descœudres—believed that appropriate teaching would help to socialize the thousands of feebleminded people whose social inefficiency was reflected in crime, illegitimacy, prostitution, alcoholism, and poverty. However, the optimism characterizing the approach of the early workers could not be upheld for long in the face of the poor results of training. In consequence, institutions, which had originally been conceived of as transitional training places, became permanent custodial shelters for people considered incapable of improvement.

This change of emphasis was considerably reinforced by the repercussions of the introduction of intelligence testing and a consideration of the Mendelian laws of heredity. Systematic intelligence testing in the United States before and during the First World War indicated the presence of an unsuspected high number of people with subaverage intelligence. Since it was also shown that a very high proportion of social misfits found in prisons, in workhouses, and on relief obtained low scores on intelligence tests, the conclusion was drawn that low intelligence inevitably causes low social adequacy. This rash and superficial assumption was amplified by many studies, inspired by the eugenics movement, of ne'er-do-well families. Researches into the ancestries of social problem cases, such as the classical studies of the Kallikak family by Goddard (1912) and of the Juke family by Dugdale (1910), seemed to prove, on the basis of data which would be regarded as insufficient nowadays, that subnormal families

show an extremely high incidence of persons of low social competence. Since it was found that the social problem cases, who were characterized by low intelligence, produced particularly large families of low social adequacy, it was easy to calculate mathematically when the proportion of low-ability individuals would be large enough to affect adversely the average level of intellectual functioning and would thus produce a decline in the national intelligence (Goddard, 1914).

These deductions, which subsequent genetic research has proved to be exaggerated and incorrect, led to panic measures, and institutions, which had been turned into custodial shelters, became virtually detention centers to protect the nation from the repercussions of the combination of high fertility and low mental ability. Thus, the "dark ages" of mental deficiency work, lasted until the 1950s, when new legislation in the United States, England, and other nations reflected a growing awareness that the problem of mental deficiency had to be tackled constructively and actively, rather than avoided. The extended pessimistic period of some forty years' duration was characterized by a vicious circle of professional lack of interest in the problem (except in the biological-genetic fields) and the resulting unattractiveness of mental deficiency for most disciplines, such as sociology, psychology, education, and psychiatry.

Some of the lack of progress over many years can undoubtedly be attributed to the term *mental deficiency* itself (or *mental subnormality* or *mental retardation*), which suggests a well-defined category of clean-cut etiology. In fact, we are justified in thinking in terms of a number of mental deficiencies, all resulting in social inadequacy and all characterized by subaverage intelligence, but of various confusing and undefinable etiologies. They require different approaches, different treatments and different specialists, but since the various handicapping conditions which contribute to the social inadequacy cannot be separated and treated by themselves, mental deficiency has nowadays become a meeting place of many disciplines such as biology, biochemistry, education, genetics, neurology, psychology, psychiatry, and sociology. As will be seen in the section on incidence and prevalence of mental deficiency, estimates of the size of the problem vary extremely, and so do the provisions made to meet the requirements. This brings it home that mental deficiency is a disablement relative to the culture of the particular community in which it is found. The acknowledged number of people whose disablements require attention, and whose abilities to adjust to the demands of their communities are impaired, depends by and large on those communities' awareness, resources—financial and otherwise—tolerance and sense of responsibility toward their weaker members. It is not a mere coincidence that the numbers of mentally defective people cared for are highest in the materially most advanced countries.

DIAGNOSIS AND PROGNOSIS

Four main criteria have in the past been accepted as decisive in the diagnosis of mental deficiency, but are no longer considered quite as valid nowadays:

1. Presence of intellectual subnormality
2. Existence of defect during childhood
3. Incurability
4. Need for prolonged social assistance

When considering a child, the first two criteria are diagnostic, based on observation, but the second two criteria are prognostic and often deduced entirely from the first two observations. The difficulties of obtaining valid assessments of intellectual capacity will be discussed later on, but it must be pointed out that there is no generally accepted *dividing-line* IQ which separates normality from subnormality *in the individual case* and that a diagnosis of intellectual subnormality becomes a

matter of judgment in borderline cases. The criterion which requires recognition of the mental deficiency in childhood excludes people who have deteriorated as a result of adult psychosis, but does not differentiate childhood psychosis and autism from mental deficiency. The criterion of "incurability" is quite unacceptable, not only because it reflects a negative and discouraging point of view which affects the development and application of remedial measures, but also because it has been shown untenable in view of intellectual and social changes in people who had once been considered incurable (Baller, 1936; Charles, 1953). This consideration applies also to the last criterion, which depends as much on the complexity of the environment and the tolerance shown as on the mental defective himself.

Nowadays, workers in the field are unwilling to commit themselves to definite prognostic pronouncements except in the cases of the most seriously mentally defective children, and they are content to recognize the condition as a handicap but not necessarily as a permanent disablement of such degree that it cannot be ameliorated. The definition by the American Association on Mental Deficiency is nowadays widely used: "Mental retardation refers to sub-average general intellectual functioning which originates during the developmental period and is associated with impairment in one or more of the following: (1) Maturation, (2) Learning, and (3) Social Adjustment" (Heber, 1959). Here the above-mentioned first two essential criteria are included, but no speculative prognostic forecasts are made regarding the future. The definition refers to the *present* level of intellectual and social functioning and does not exclude the possibility that a person could be accepted as normal at a later stage.

It is also significant for the cautious approach to a problem far more complicated than had been assumed in the past that the etiology of the condition is no longer an integral part of the diagnosis. While in the past authorities regarded as essential the establishment of the "constitutional origin" of the condition (Doll, 1941), the difficulties of ascertaining uncontroversially the causes of a mental defect in the majority of cases thus diagnosed have made it imperative to avoid such a speculative criterion. Mental deficiency is thus recognized in all but the severest cases by the consequences of the condition rather than by a diagnosis based on demonstrable deficiencies in the central nervous system (CNS). While subaverage intelligence is a condition common to all people who are considered mentally defective, people with subaverage intelligence who are socially adequate should not be regarded mentally defective.

CLASSIFICATION

It is important to realize that the decisive criterion for taking action is a social one and that the medical and psychometric evidence provides only one of many possible explanations of why a person is socially inadequate. While it is perfectly true that in a large proportion of cases the biological-genetic factor is so evident that the resultant impairment of adaptive behavior can be directly traced back to inadequate innate resources, a much larger proportion of people labeled "mentally defective" may show only very mild organic factors. It is difficult to think of these factors as being causative of inadequate behavior, even though they may make life difficult. That these factors and measured low intelligence need not affect adequate social functioning is evidenced by the many thousands who never draw our attention.

Difficulties in adapting to the social demands of the environment are usually noticed at three stages of the life career. The most extreme forms of impairment are noticeable at or very soon after birth, such as pronounced physical maldevelopment or very marked deficiencies in physical behavior. Some authorities are quite prepared to diagnose mental deficiency at this very early stage on the basis of inadequate motor development (Gesell & Amatruda, 1947; Illingworth, 1955). Examples of this early diagnosis will be given in the section on etiologic classification.

Less pronounced deficiencies will often be suspected only when the child reaches school age. The increasing educational demands lead to inadequate scholastic progress. An assessment of intellectual ability will disclose the fact of subaverage mental functioning, but care must be taken not to consider a low IQ figure to be a diagnosis of mental deficiency. This will be discussed in the sections on psychometric classification and assessment of intelligence.

While many children progress inadequately at school and their impairment is shown by pronounced learning difficulties, they may somehow succeed in completing their school careers thanks to tolerant teachers and an undemanding environment. For some of them the difficulties arise in the third stage, that of adaptation to occupational demands and social life. Unable to cope with the unprotective environment, they become problem cases and refuse help. If they have not been ascertained previously, the diagnosis of mental deficiency will hinge largely on their proved social inadequacy. This is discussed in the section on social classification.

Etiologic Classification

The most widely accepted etiologic classification method, used by many workers, simply divides mental deficiency into two groups according to clinical etiology. Difficulties, however, arise not only from the near-impossibility of making valid diagnostic decisions in a majority of cases but also from disagreements as to under which of the two major group headings a particular condition should be classified. The indecision is reflected in the many different and confusing names by which reference is made to the two groups.

For practical purposes and to give an overview of the classification method, the terms listed below have been used as if they were nearly equivalent, but it must be realized that many conditions listed by one authority as belonging to one main group are classified by another authority under the other heading.

Primary and secondary causes of mental deficiency. In cases where mental defect is considered to be due to causes *before conception,* the conditions are classified as *primary* by many authorities. In this group are found two very different types of mental deficiency which have apparently little in common. The first type in this group is mental defect due to a major genetic defect caused by rare but specific recessive, dominant, or sex-linked genes. Mendelian laws apply, and the condition of epiloia (discussed below) is a good example of such defects.

Also included in this group are conditions due to aberrant chromosomes, involving autosomes or the sex chromosomes, which lead to certain metabolic disorders. Conditions in this group are generally characterized by profound intellectual subnormality and many pronounced physical stigmata; phenylketonuria, (discussed below) is an example of these defects.

In the second group of mental defects caused by factors obtained before conception are included those in which the influence of specific genes is comparatively small, though a poor genetic endowment in its totality influences adequate mental functioning.

Intellectual impairment is not pronounced, and in the majority of cases there are no very obvious physical deficiencies. This group is numerically the largest and is also known by other names, such as *familial* and *subcultural.* Environmental factors affect functioning to a large extent, and their influence is often considered to be so dominant that the poor genetic endowment is disregarded.

(For example, in the tenth edition of his book on mental deficiency, Tredgold (Tredgold & Soddy, 1963) uses the term *primary* only to refer to subcultural defect, while in previous editions the term referred to both genetic and subcultural defects.)

Secondary causes are considered to be responsible *after conception,* and they operate during the antenatal, intranatal, and postnatal periods. They are mostly of an infectious kind such as the consequences of rubella and syphilis during the fetal period or meningitis and encephalitis during the postnatal period. Most of the cases in this group are characterized by pronounced physical stigmata.

Pathological group. A diagnostic label of pathology is often conveniently attached to conditions which either are genetic in origin or are the result of specific adverse factors obtained during the developmental period before, during, or after birth. This group comprises, therefore, cases of both primary and secondary origin and excludes those "familial" mental defectives in whom no specific damage to the CNS can be shown. (It must, however, also be pointed out that the apparent absence of organic pathology may be due to the inadequacy of the diagnostic tools involved, which may make it impossible to ascertain convincingly the presence of minimal cerebral damage which may be held responsible for the poor mental functioning.)

The members of the pathological group are classified as "idiots" or "imbeciles" depending on the degree of mental functioning, and their IQs do not generally rise above the 50 to 55 mark. This group is contained in the English classification label "severely subnormal" and comprises the moderately, severely, and profoundly retarded mental defectives as they are defined by the American Association on Mental Deficiency (Heber, 1959). However, in both these instances the terms refer to classification according to the degree of adaptive behavior and not to etiology.

The pathological group represents low-ability cases *additional* to the normal variation of mental ability, and their numbers cannot be predicted in any way because they are "biological accidents." The distribution curve of ascertained mental defectives, which follows closely the Gaussian curve, shows an unexpected thickening at the lower end which is brought about by the high number of low-grade mental defectives in excess of what would be expected normally.

In the following section a few examples are given to illustrate the variety of etiology within the pathological group, but for more exhaustive descriptions the relevant textbooks should be consulted (Hilliard & Kirman, 1965; Kanner, 1949; Masland, Sarason, & Gladwin, 1958; Penrose, 1963; Tredgold & Soddy, 1963).

Predominantly genetically determined pathology. Among clinical conditions considered to be the result primarily of harmful genes, probably the most widely known is *epiloia* (tuberous sclerosis). In many cases the condition, which is due to a single gene, is transmitted by a parent, but it may also be due to new gene mutations. Though the condition is not unusual among subnormals, epiloia probably occurs in only 1 in 30,000 people (Penrose, 1963). Summaries of work on epiloia are found in Critchley and Earl (1932); Walsh, Koch, and Brunsting (1938); and Finnlayson (1955). These patients are most easily recognized by a "butterfly" rash on the face consisting of an overgrowth of red- to yellow-colored nodules not larger than small peas. They are associated with neuroglive overgrowth and fibrotic tumors affecting organs such as the kidneys, spleen, lungs, and heart. Patients are usually epileptic and mentally subnormal, but adults with normal intelligence have been reported (Koffman & Hyland, 1959).

If both parents are carriers of a gene responsible for recessive abnormalities, there is an increased risk that the child will inherit the gene in duplicate. Probably the most widely known example of this condition is *phenylketonuria (phenylpyruvic oligophrenia, PKU, Föllings disease),* which is a metabolic disorder (Fölling, 1934) due to a genetic fault. This leads to an absence of enzymes which are necessary for an undisturbed protein metabolism. In consequence, phenylalanine is not converted to tyrosine, and probably the excess phenylalanine leads to intoxication which is associated with mental deficiency. Phenylketonuria cases have attracted attention despite their comparative rarity (approximately 1 percent of the cases of mental deficiency are due to this condition) because treatment seems to hold out hope for final cure. If the condition is spotted by early testing of a baby's urine, it is possible to institute a strict dietary regime (omitting particularly meat, fish, eggs, and bread) which can help to overcome some of the consequences of the condition, particularly lowered intellectual functioning. It is not yet clear how long this treatment has to be continued in order to maintain the improvement resulting from it (Bessman et al., 1967; Fuller, 1967; Woolf, 1970).

Maple syrup urine disease is also caused by the absence of the necessary enzyme and is characterized by a pronounced odor of the urine. It is associated with increasing spastic paralysis (Crome, Dutton, & Ross, 1961). Dietary treatment of children diagnosed early appears to be promising (Ireland, 1964; Westall, 1963).

Hartnup disease is characterized by a pigmentary areola around the nipples and sensitivity, with rough dermatitic areas on body surfaces exposed to light. No treatment has yet been discovered.

Galactosemia is due to incomplete metabolism of galactose and leads to rapid loss of weight and failure to develop. Growth is inhibited, and progressive mental retardation is observed. There may be early death in undiagnosed cases, but the introduction of a lactose-free diet results in an amelioration of the condition, (Segal, Blair, & Topper, 1962).

Hypoglycemia is probably genetically determined and leads to cerebral damage, convulsions, and mental subnormality.

Cerebromacular degeneration (due to degeneration to the retina) is found in *Tay-Sachs disease (amaurotic idiocy)*. Though in this condition the infant appears to be normal up to the third month of development, soon after this he becomes weak in the back and seems to experience difficulties in seeing clearly. Examination reveals a characteristic cherry-red spot in the macula surrounded by a whitish-gray area. It is followed by complete blindness and, in the final stages, by extreme emaciation, which is often associated with muscular rigidity and spasms. It is a fatal disease and is due to a failure to metabolize fat deposited in nerve cells. No treatment has been discovered yet (Aronson & Volk, 1962).

Gargoylism (Hurler's disease) is characterized by a coarse, grotesque face reminiscent of that of a gargoyle; stunted growth; enlarged head; short neck; and thick nose and lips. The majority of patients are severely mentally handicapped, but milder degrees of subnormality have been reported. This disease can be found in those cases in which an autosomal recessive gene occurs but can also be transmitted as a sex-linked recessive affecting only males (Jervis, 1959).

Microcephaly occurs in a small group of mental defectives, probably not more than 5 percent of defective children (Tredgold & Soddy, 1963). They have a marked reduction in cranial circumference (in adults often under 17 inches) *and* characteristic anomalies in shape. Most microcephalics are severely subnormal, but the less handicapped ones may be able to learn to read and write.

Microcephaly is usually due to recessive genes (true microcephaly), but can also be the consequence of various factors in the antenatal and postnatal periods. The Hiroshima disaster caused microcephaly and severe mental deficiency in 63 percent of children at the time unborn.

In cases of *Hydrocephalus* the skull is excessively enlarged the cranial bones are separated, and there is often the general appearance of translucency. The condition is due to an excess of cerebrospinal fluid and is the result of an obstruction to the circulation of the fluid. The obstruction itself may have been caused by birth injury, brain tumors, meningitis, or encephalitis. The patient may not be able to hold his head and must be supported. Early surgical attention may arrest intellectual deterioration. Though the mental functioning of most hydrocephalics is severely impaired, milder cases may function on a mildly subnormal level. Their motor coordination is poor, and some of them have convulsions.

Macrocephaly is shown by some children whose brains grow disportionately to their bodies. They have low intelligence, often have impaired vision, and may have convulsions.

The study of human chromosomal aberrations is of very recent origin, but promises to throw a good deal of light on our understanding of mental defect. It appears that abnormalities in number and morphology are often closely connected with mental deficiency. This new knowledge is illustrated most strikingly in *Mongolism (Down's syndrome)*, which is the commonest single subgroup in mental deficiency. The physical characteristics—flat face, coarse skin, small and slanted eyes, coarse and deeply fissured tongue, short and clumsy hands, wide cleft between the large toe and the other toes, etc.—are very obvious and make a diagnosis comparatively easy. Though most of the Mongols have IQs below 50, it is often overlooked that some Mongols can attain higher intelligence test scores, which permits them to receive the same type of education given to less intellectually impaired mental defectives. Cases of rather literate Mongols have been reported in the literature, and the diagnostic label of Mongolism should not be considered synonymous with severe mental deficiency. Mongols are traditionally considered to have a very placid and "lovable" nature, but research work has shown that, temperamentally, they do not form a homogeneous group, but show the same variations in personality as other human beings.

The incidence of Mongol births (about 1 in every 600 to 700 births) has remained constant, but owing to improved medical care the overall number of Mongols has quadrupled in the last 30 years. Recent research work in cytogenetics has shown the existence of two main groups of Mongols. The "regular Mongol" (three out of four) tends to be born more frequently with advancing maternal age, and he shows a trisomy of chromosome 21 and a karyotype of forty-seven chromosomes. It has been shown that 80 percent of the mothers are aged between 30 and 45 at the time of the birth and that 50 percent of the mothers are past the age of 35 (Goldstein, 1954). The "translocation Mongol" (one out of four) is often born to a young mother and has the normal forty-six chromosomes accompanied by an *abnormal* chromosome constitution. There is a higher risk of repetition in this form of Mongolism (Richards 1970).

Predominantly environmentally determined pathology. Abnormal environmental events occurring before, during, and after birth may cause cerebral damage, the effects of which produce pathological conditions which are as much of a handicap as those resulting from genetic causes.

The agents causing the defect include infection, toxicity, trauma, and endoctrine imbalance. Diagnosis of the etiologic factors is comparatively easy, and in most cases a normal family history can be shown. Infection of the nervous system is said to account for approximately 11 percent of severe subnormality. The infection causes inflammation of the brain or its membranes and severe brain damage.

Syphilitic oligophrenia is transmitted during pregnancy to the fetus. If this infection occurs early, it may lead to miscarriage, but later infection results in certain typical signs of congenital syphilis and diffuse or localized meningovascular lesions. Mental development may be normal, but a proportion of children born with this condition are mentally defective. Thanks to routine serologic tests of pregnant women and subsequent treatment, the occurrence of this type of mental deficiency has been immensely reduced.

Virus infections leading to mental deficiency are *equine encephalitis, mumps,* and particularly maternal *rubella (German measles)* in the early months of pregnancy. The children show many pathological conditions, such as deafness, blindness, heart malformation, and mental deficiency.

Childhood diseases such as chickenpox, whooping cough, scarlet fever, and measles with associated *cerebrospinal meningitis* and *encephalitis* can produce mental deficiency. Personality changes due to encephalitis are often marked. Children so affected are aggressive, destructive, restless, and impulsive, and management of them may be very difficult. The advent of massive antibiotic treatment has reduced the incidence of such patients very considerably.

Among the toxic causes of mental deficiency, lead poisoning has recently attracted much attention. Cheap, mass-produced, brightly colored nursery toys and apparatus, which are licked and gnawed by the young child, have been shown to result in severe mental deficiency, often with accompanying convulsions, if the paint used contains even only small amounts of lead (Moncrieff, Koumidis, Clayton, & Patrick, 1964).

Kernicterus is due to Rh blood-factor incompatibility. This occurs only in a comparatively small proportion of Rh-positive children from Rh-negative mothers, but when it is found, jaundice, anemia, paralysis, and convulsions are typical signs at birth. Later they become mental-defective spastics and show choreoathetosis.

This is probably the most suitable point at which to mention *cerebral palsy (Little's disease),* which, however, shows a wide variety of etiologic factors. It appears that at least 50 percent of cerebral palsy children can be considered mentally defective (Crothers & Paine, 1959; Cruickshank & Rans, 1955).

A great number of abnormal factors are associated with the birth of cerebral palsy children (prematurity, instrumental delivery, jaundice, asphyxia), and it is often argued that lesions due to difficult labor may be a frequent cause of cerebral palsy. From the psychological point of view, it is often extremely difficult but, at the same time, extremely important to ascertain validly the degree of intellectual retardation in cerebral palsy children. On account of the very severe physical handicap and the patient's difficulty in controlling his responses, the standardized and widely accepted methods of assessing intellectual functioning are generally inadequate and give a misleading underassessment of the available intellectual resources. Special techniques have to be applied (Abercrombie, 1964; Illingworth, 1958; Mein, 1967; Woods, 1957).

Cretinism is due to endocrine disturbance. This condition appears as a result of congenital aplasia or of biochemical insufficiency of the thyroid gland, resulting in a low level of excretion. In the sporadic form a goiter is seen, and the endemic condition can be observed in certain mountainous countries with soil poor in iodine content (the Alps, the Rocky Mountains, and the Himalayas). Usually there are no physical signs present at birth, but they appear later, when the infant ceases to develop physically, appears to be apathetic, and is slow in his movements. The skin becomes coarse and dry, anemia oc-

curs, the vocal expression is hoarse, dorsal kyphosis is often present, and infantile genitalia and stunted growth as well as a characteristic puffiness in the face become very pronounced. Though most cretins are profoundly retarded, others, the "cretinoids," can learn simple academic skills and can be usefully occupied.

Thyroid preparations given carefully can help, but these seem to have more effect on the physical development when given in early childhood than on intellectual maturation (Benda, 1946; Collipp et al. 1965).

Another endocrine disturbance affecting the pituitary gland results in the *Froelich syndrome.* There is, however, no constant relationship between a defective gland and mental deficiency. No effective treatment has been devised yet.

Mental deficiency may be caused during birth by birth injuries involving often anoxia and asphyxia. Experts do not agree on the actual incidence of birth injury as a cause of mental deficiency, and estimates range from 1 to 50 percent. While obstetrical injuries could be established retrospectively in some cases, it is nearly impossible to be certain about traumatic conditions. There is now a growing belief that with improvement in delivery techniques, obstetrical hazards would not account for an appreciable number of cases of mental deficiency.

In conclusion, it must be pointed out again that it is in practice very difficult to establish the definite causes of subnormality, even if the particular pathological syndrome has been clearly established. Our inability to understand fully the causative factors in each case has, of course, direct repercussions on prevention and treatment aspects.

Nonpathological group. There is a very pronounced danger that mental defectives who cannot be clearly diagnosed as pathological are automatically classified as belonging to this large group. As a rule of thumb, this group is generally considered to be identical with the group of mental defectives who obtain IQs above 55. However, it would be surprising if there were not pathological conditions with slight brain damage in the higher IQ range, and it is also unacceptable that there should be no mental defectives with IQs below 50 whose limited abilities are the result of normal variations rather than of pathological factors. It is thus more reasonable to look at this classification system as simply suggesting that the lower the IQ the greater the probabilities of pathological involvement, and the higher the IQ, the lesser the likelihood of cerebral and genetic damage. Even though sociocultural and psychological factors appear to be predominant in causing subnormal functioning, minimal cerebral damage and poor genetic endowment could contribute appreciably to the inadequacy.

The group has been variously referred to as consisting of *familial, subcultural,* or *garden-variety* mental defectives. Tredgold (Tredgold & Soddy, 1963) talks of *primary aments,* and Strauss (1955) calls them *endogenous,* reserving the term *exogenous* for the brain-injured mental defective. Kanner (1949) refers to them as displaying *relative feeblemindedness,* and Masland, et al. (1958) proposed the term *mentally retarded* for them to differentiate them from the mentally defective (the pathological group).

This group is made up largely of people described variously as the feebleminded, the borderline morons, and the mildly retarded. The subcultural familial defective appears to be characteristic of the poor social classes, and both heredity and unfavorable environment could be held responsible. In sharp contrast to this, the incidence of brain-damaged children is in no way related to environmental factors, and such children are found in all social strata (Stein & Susser, 1962).

It is difficult, probably impossible, at the present state of knowledge to subdivide this very large group according to some valid system of supposed etiology. Generally there is a preference for singling out various groups on the basis of a characteristic aspect of behavior, such as the psychopaths. However, the diffuse makeup of this large subcultural group, with its multifactorial causation, makes it impossible to present an even superficially useful classification that would bring some sort of order into this heterogenous mass of inadequate human beings, whose common description as "mental defectives" gives a misleading impression of a clinical entity. Even the overall classification contrasting the defective whose development has stopped with the defective who has simply less of everything that matters in this respect is an oversimplification. The inadequate endowment, whether due to genetic or environmental causes, must engender feelings of insecurity and inadequacy, which in turn will undermine the competent handling of meager resources. Thus, a not very favorable situation will be gradually worsened, and the etiology of the social incompetence of the mental defective will be far more complex than is suggested by the classification systems discussed in this section.

Pseudomental deficiencies. Exceptional diagnostic difficulties with possibly very deplorable consequences are presented by a number of conditions which are said to simulate "true mental deficiency," which is characterized by a significant deficit in intellectual development. Children who are diagnosed as mentally defective on the basis of their inadequate behavior and low IQ score could be regarded as "pseudo mentally defective" if their inadequacy is not the result of poor mental endowment. An unhappy constellation of factors, such as auditory or visual handicaps, emotional disturbances, etc., may interfere with the child's emotional and intellectual development to such an extent that a diagnosis of mental defect is only too likely. The inevitable consequence of such a diagnosis is that the child is treated as a mental defective, and no sustained and directed effort is made to overcome the consequences of these handicapping conditions. These children, misdiagnosed and misclassified, therefore are included in the ranks of the genuine mental defectives, when, in fact, an early and correct diagnosis could have initiated remedial measures which would have helped toward increased efficiency in later life. The problem is, of course, not so much mistaken diagnosis as mistaken prognosis (Clarke & Clarke, 1955). The definition of mental deficiency (Heber, 1959) quoted previously relates only to behavior at the time of assessment. It is therefore quite acceptable to classify as mentally defective children who function on that level, irrespective of the etiology of their inadequacy. It is, however, unpardonable and indefensible to make far-reaching prognostic decisions on the basis of one examination which may reflect a temporary dysfunctioning. Repeated reassessments and proper attention to all available evidence should help to spot at an early stage conditions which are not due to mental defect.

This group presents not only diagnostic problems and prognostic dangers but also classification difficulties relating to disposal and remedial action. Wolman (1965) points out three categories of children who are not mentally subnormal, despite low IQs, but who are treated as if they were. The first category contains those whose IQs fall *within the normal curve of distribution.* Though they have low intelligence, this is a normal occurrence, in the same way that there are short and tall people in the normal population. They are largely a social and educational problem, but not a clinical concern.

The second category includes those underprivileged children who obtain low scores on intelligence tests because they have not had average learning opportunities and experiences. Moreover, the tests may not be culture-free, being usually biased toward a middle-class culture.

The third category contains those children whose adequate functioning is affected by psychotic and neurotic conditions.

Adopting this particular viewpoint means that the term *mental deficiency* should be used only when there are accompanying organic disorders, such as described in the preceding section on pathology. A person in the familial, subcultured, endogenous category is not *abnormal* and must therefore not be considered mentally defective.

This viewpoint certainly helps to highlight the different *needs* of mentally handicapped children, and particularly of those whose very low intellectual performance resembles superficially that of the organic group.

The most important examples of conditions which require careful differential diagnosis to establish their etiology are discussed below.

Childhood schizophrenia, autism, and psychosis. These conditions have recently drawn much attention, and efforts are being made to separate children diagnosed under those headings from the "genuine mental defective" because they are said to have normal mental abilities, even though they exhibit the intellectually defective's typical impairment in adaptive behavior. Nine diagnostic pointers to the presence of autism have been suggested, but only the first two are of decisive importance:

1. Extreme and sustained impairment of emotional relationships with people.
2. Low intellectual level, though there are "islets" of normal or near-normal intellectual functioning.
3. Preoccupation with particular objects.
4. Apparent unawareness of a personal identity.
5. Pathological and sustained resistance to environmental changes.
6. Very marked and illogical anxiety.
7. Disturbances in development of speech.
8. Queer mannerisms, rocking postures, etc.

9. Abnormal perceptual difficulties, though no organic abnormality can be established.

This condition is at present very ill understood. It is difficult to decide whether the "schizophrenic picture" presented by this condition is a true psychosis as seen in adults, in view of the fact that criteria applicable to adults cannot legitimately be applied to the growing child, whose development is often rather devious and uneven. Moreover, in a child, the symptoms described above could have a variety of different causes, such as brain damage, and the differential diagnosis is extremely difficult and, at present, unreliable (Wolman, 1970).

Despite the attention which has been given to this condition, there are in fact very few comprehensive studies available (Benda & Melchior, 1959; Bender, 1954, 1960; Kanner, 1957; O'Gorman, 1967; Rimland, 1964); and even less is known about the treatment of this condition, which is probably not surprising, considering that we are still completely ignorant regarding its cause.

It is difficult to estimate the prevalence of psychosis and neurosis in the institutionalized defective, partly because pathological behavior in the severely defective is superficially ascribed to low intelligence. Penrose (1963) estimated that 17 percent of his sample were neurotic and that 6 percent were psychotic. O'Connor and Tizard (1956) suggested that 6 to 12 percent of the feebleminded defectives showed signs of a "severe neurotic handicap" and that 40 percent suffered from an often temporary, but nevertheless disturbing, mild neurotic tendency.

Auditory deficits. The most common type of hearing loss is that of congenital high-frequency deafness, which makes it impossible to perceive sounds such as "s," "sh," and "t." This means not only that the child is unable to perceive properly and therefore misinterprets but also that he is unable to learn to use language adequately. The

concomitant side effects may well be a larger degree of backwardness than necessary and emotional instability. The child will then be diagnosed erroneously as a low-grade mental defective, when, in fact, he may be not only educable but even of normal intelligence.

The few surveys of institutionalized mentally defective children available so far indicate an incidence of deafness ranging from 13 to 49 percent (Kodman, 1963) among mental defectives, compared with some 3 to 10 percent among normal children. Burt (1951), in his studies of British children, showed that among normal schoolchildren, only 1 percent had severe defects of hearing and 4 percent had slight defects but that the figures among children in schools for the mentally retarded were 6 percent and 18 percent, respectively. The auditory pathology represents a particularly defined aspect of the many deficiencies in the sensory apparatus of the mental defective, and absence of remedial action will increase considerably the number of people who will require additional assistance. It is most important that audiometric testing be carried out regularly and that children who have been diagnosed as having hearing defects be given hearing aids, speech therapy, and modified educational curricula.

Visual deficits. Deficiencies in the perceptual processes have been treated with increasing attention in recent years. The figure-background studies, particularly those associated with the names of Werner and Strauss (1941, 1943), have resulted in the development of methods to overcome the deficiencies (e.g., Frostig, 1964). Discrimination processes have been studied, as well as problems of recognition, constancy, and specific optical illusions, and there is now in fact quite a considerable literature on this subject summarized ably by Spivack (1963).

The consesus of these studies is that mental defectives, as a group, are less efficient than people with normal intelligence, but it is by no means clear how much these deficiencies add to the mental defective's difficulties in adjustment, and whether they in fact interfere with it substantially. The decreased efficiency of the perceptual processes will certainly affect learning processes and may give the appearance of inability to learn, when, in fact, there is only a handicap to learning.

Psychometric Classification

Though social inadequacy has generally been recognized as being the decisive criterion in the diagnosis of mental deficiency, the assessment of intellectual subnormality has been regarded as all-important, particularly in childhood. Most authorities agree that pronounced difficulties in adaptive behavior *and* intellectual subnormality must be present for the diagnosis of mental deficiency to be made, but there is no general agreement on how to define intellectual subnormality in exact quantitative terms. This means that a clinical and subjective decision must be made in all cases in which the assessed intelligence level is near the borderline.

The decision regarding the borderline—the IQ figure which separates the "intellectually normal" from the "intellectually subnormal"—is an arbitrary, administrative one and may vary from one test of intelligence to another. Strictly speaking, IQ figures derived from different intelligence tests are not equivalent, and thus the accurate delineation of a "cutoff" score and the subcategories within the range of mental deficiency depend on the test used.

The most widely used tests of intelligence are the Stanford-Binet test and the various Wechsler intelligence scales. Using the statistical concept of standard deviation (SD), the IQ figures of 84 for the Wechsler tests and 83 for the Stanford-Binet test have been accepted as representing the dividing line between intellectual normality and subnormality. This means that 68.26 percent of a given population are regarded as having normal or average intelligence, while the remaining third of the population will be distributed evenly above or below the average IQ range.

The further classification of the intellectually subnormal range is based on statistical conventions.

The *borderline retarded* child obtains an IQ between 70 and 84 on the Wechsler scales and between 68 and 83 on the Stanford-Binet test. At preschool age he will show only a minimal retardation in the sensorimotor areas and will usually be considered normal, but often he will require special education when he reaches school age.

The *mildly retarded* child obtains an IQ between 55 and 69 on the Wechsler scales and between 52 and 67 on the Stanford-Binet test. As a baby he may show a fair amount of motor development and can be managed with moderate supervision. He may be slow in development, but learns to talk and communicate. Special education during the school years will be necessary, but he is capable of elementary attainments in the tool subjects of reading, writing, and arithmetic. The mildly retarded make up a fairly large section of the community, approximately five million in the United States. Approximately twenty-six out of every one thousand children fall into this category.

The *moderately retarded* child obtains an IQ between 40 and 54 on the Wechsler scales and between 36 and 51 on the Stanford-Binet test. As a baby he is frequently unable to profit from training and develops only a few communication skills and poor motor development. When of school age he learns to communicate and can be trained in many self-help skills. He finds tremendous difficulties in acquiring academic skills, and special provisions have to be made for his training. There are probably some 300,000 to 350,000 persons in the United States who fall into this category. It is estimated that three out of every one thousand children born will be moderately retarded.

The *severely retarded* child obtains an IQ between 25 and 39 on the Wechsler scales and between 20 and 35 on the Stanford-Binet test. As a baby he shows severe retardation in all aspects and requires constant nursing care. He can be trained to feed, wash, and dress himself under supervision, but still needs total care even during the school years. He does not really benefit from training for independence.

The *profoundly retarded* child has an IQ below 25 on the Wechsler scales and below 20 on the Stanford-Binet test. Such children need complete nursing care throughout their lives and are unable to feed themselves or to look after their toilet requirements. They are usually unable to walk, or they do so only with help.

The two groups of the severely and profoundly retarded number probably 60,000 to 90,000 persons in the United States, and it is estimated that 1 child out of every 1,000 born belongs to these groups (approximately 4,000 births per year).

The above descriptions of the various groups are necessarily generalizations, and there are many individual exceptions. Many of these are due to the difficulties in obtaining valid IQ assessments and to intellectual changes which occur in the course of maturation and education. It is certainly true that the higher the IQ the less close is the association between intellectual level and social competence, and that it is unwise to predict from one aspect to the other in individual cases.

The literature discussing the advantages and disadvantages of intelligence test figures in mental deficiency has become very large, and it is probably best to accept the IQ figure as an administrative classification label but not to attach too much diagnostic or prognostic importance to it.

(Clarke & Clarke, 1965; Masland et al., 1958; Robinson & Robinson, 1965; Sarason, 1959).

Social Classification

Despite the importance of adaptive behavior for adjustment to the demands made by society, no objective and standardized measures have been developed for classifying levels of social behavior in the same way they have been available for intelligent behavior. This is due mostly to the very different standards set up by society at different times and to the different minimum level of social efficiency required by various sociocultural groups. This means that a person's social competence must be defined simply as relative economic independence and relative absence of support by social agencies such as welfare agencies, and at the same time compliance with the standards of his own socioeconomic group (which may not be very acceptable to the average citizen, but is tolerated by society as a whole).

A classification system similar to the one used for intellectual classification could be applied (Heber, 1959). The evaluation would have to be done in terms of age since the demands of social responsibility will vary with increasing age. At the preschool level, maturational development schedules will be found useful (Bühler & Hetzer, 1935; Catell, 1947; Gesell & Amatruda, 1947; Illingworth, 1960), and later a social-maturity scale such as the Vineland scale (Doll, 1953).

At the adult level, great difficulties arise. Using the definitions of the intellectual classification, the following generalizations can be made. The borderline retarded person is potentially quite capable of social and vocational adequacy, and if he should draw attention to himself by proved social incompetence, an inadequate personality makeup will generally be responsible. The mildly retarded person is able to hold jobs in unskilled and semiskilled occupations. The moderately retarded person can contribute to his self-suppport, but will require mostly sheltered conditions to do so. He is able to look after himself, but needs permanent guidance and supervision. The severely retarded person can never be really independent and needs complete care and supervision, although he can be trained to execute simple remunerative work in a sheltered workshop. The profoundly retarded person has to be nursed and cared for even in adulthood.

Within this broad classification system there are many individual differences, and many mental defectives' social adaptiveness may exceed considerably the level expected on the basis of his IQ classification label or may be well below it. In fact, within each category there will be a range from superior to backward social efficiency, as a result of training, motivation, stimulation, personality makeup, and many other factors, which may improve or retard the utilization of what is essentially a poor endowment. From the diagnostic point of view and for the purpose of remedial therapeutic measures, it will be important not only to state the size of deviation from normality but also to find out the "backward retardate" who deviates markedly and negatively from the standards of his own age and intellectual group. Such standards of social competence for mentally defective children and adults are now available (Gunzburg, 1968), and they permit the comparison of the level of competence of an individual child with that of a large group of others of the same age and with a similar intellectual handicap.

PREVALENCE AND INCIDENCE OF MENTAL DEFICIENCY

An estimate of the number of mental defectives in the community will depend primarily on definitions but also on the validity and reliability of the assessment methods used and, lastly and equally important, on available community resources and willingness to accept the problem. As far as the first point is concerned, the preceding discussion of classification criteria has already shown that much depends on judgment and circumstances. While it is comparatively easy to present uncontroversial figures concerning the incidence of mental deficiency at or shortly after birth, estimates tend to vary when relating to school-age children, and they differ widely in regard to mentally defective adults (Jastak, Macphee, & Whiteman, 1963).

The most pronounced cases of mental deficiency, usually those referred to as "low-grade" or "pathological" mental deficiency of biological-genetic origin, can be diagnosed medically fairly early and with a high degree of certainty. The incidence figure for the preschool age group (below 5) is thought to be about 1.2 per 1,000 (Goodman & Tizard, 1962; Lewis, 1929; Onondaga County Survey, 1955).

The educational demands of school life draw attention to many hitherto scarcely suspect cases of low mental ability, who are unable to benefit by ordinary school education. Estimates of the incidence of mental deficiency among school-age children vary considerably depending on the criteria applied to define the mentally defective child in need of special attention. Kushlick (1968) and Tizard (1964) give prevalence rates of severe subnormality of various age groups. It appears that the incidence rate for severe subnormality rises sharply from 0.5 per 1,000 at ages 0–4 to a maximum of 3.6 at ages 15–19. This rise is due to late notifications and it can be assumed that the figure 3.6 per 1,000 is indicative of the incidence of severe subnormality at birth (Kushlick, 1967). These figures are considerably increased if children with milder forms of mental deficiency are included (IQ 55 +).

It is difficult to estimate the proportion of children in need of extra educational assistance on account of their mental handicap. Varying criteria and estimates are given in different states of the United States. England considers that 1 percent of the schoolchildren require education in special schools but that in addition, 8 to 9 percent need educational help. In France it is estimated that 1.5 percent to 8.6 percent of the school population, depending on age, is educationally subnormal, and the Dutch give a mean rate of 2.6 percent (Wall, Schonell, & Olson, 1962).

While the biological and genetic "accidents" tend to occur without regard to the economic status of the parent, the milder forms of mental deficiency appear to be prevalent in those strata of society which are, economically seen, not successful. Stein and Susser (1962), in their Lancashire surveys, showed that children without brain damage occur predominantly in lower socioeconomic groups, and they regard them as the products of a "subculture" which may account for perhaps 75 percent of the less severely mentally deficient in the school population. Similar findings were reported by others (Onondaga County Survey, 1955; Penrose, 1963).

Once the period of the academic obstacle race has been passed and the mental defective is faced with the practical, and for him better-manageable, problems of occupation and adult life, many become sufficiently competent to disappear from the registers of the authorities. This is reflected in sharply declining prevalence figures for different age groups after age 16 (Lemkau, Tietze, & Cooper, 1942; Lewis, 1929; Onondaga County Survey, 1955). After all, the mental defective's capacity for social adjustment cannot easily be judged at school age. Delayed maturation and the fact that the demands made on adults are different account for the existence of a large proportion of socially now well-adjusted but intellectually subnormal people who were regarded as mentally defective during childhood (Baller, 1936; Baller et al. 1967; Charles, 1953; Kennedy, 1962).

The prevalence rate in the adult population is generally assumed to be the order of about 4 per 1,000. In terms of the population of the United States, this would mean that 5.4 million children and adults have relatively impaired mental resources with which to deal with the demands of the community. Since about 400,000 of these people are so severely defective as to require constant care, there are some 5 million people left who have a handicap which may interfere considerably with their lives but which need not incapacitate them permanently.

ASSESSMENT PROCEDURES

Assessment of Intelligence

Increasing importance is given to the results of intelligence testing, particularly in cases of suspected mild mental deficiency. The IQ is used in practically all assessments as a classification label to indicate the degree of subnormality and is often misused when relied on as the only diagnostic tool to establish mental deficiency. Useful as the IQ measurement is, its shortcomings have to be known to safeguard against placing too much confidence in its implications. These shortcomings are related at one side to weaknesses in test construction and administration and at the other side to the changeability of the human being himself who is being measured. As far as the tests of intelligence themselves are concerned, it should be noted that:

1. Different tests of intelligence often attempt to measure different aspects of intellectual functioning, and the resulting IQs are therefore not equivalent (e.g., IQs obtained from verbal and nonverbal intelligence tests).

2. Most recognized tests of intelligence are in fact batteries of subtests, sampling different aspects of intelligence, and the IQ is a measure of average functioning, which hides the diagnostic significance of extremely high and low achievements in various areas. It has been argued that a

diagnosis of mental deficiency is made impossible if the overall figure of average achievement is taken at its face value without considering the picture presented by the component subtests (Jastak, 1949, 1952).

3. Intelligence tests have been designed primarily to ascertain whether a child has the necessary intellectual endowment to succeed in the ordinary scholastic career. Although there is a high relationship between this type of academic intelligence and the intelligence displayed in other walks of life, intelligence tests are not designed primarily to give a measure of "social intelligence" or a prediction of social adaptability, which is the paramount consideration in mental deficiency.

4. An intelligence test measure is frequently invalidated because it has been obtained without adhering to the standardized administration procedure. Typical incorrect procedures involve testing in a disturbing situation or environment, using an incomplete test, not realizing that a particular test is unsuitable in the situation, and paying no attention to establishing rapport with the subject, to his physical condition, to his misunderstandings, etc.

5. Psychological measurements are not as reliable as physical measurements, such as those obtained by a thermometer. It has, for example, been shown that one in ten children obtaining an average IQ of 100 would on retest obtain an IQ above 112 or below 88 because of errors in measurement (Shapiro, 1951). To attach great significance to minor IQ changes unsupported by other observations is quite unjustifiable because of the unreliability of the test instrument itself, not to mention the "unreliability" of the human being who is being measured.

6. Even after attention has been paid to the point just mentioned, it should be noted that the test, however valid and however reliably and correctly administered, will reflect only functioning *at the time of testing*. If a prediction of future or past functioning is made, it carries the inherent risk of being *an informed guess* rather than a forecast based on scientific laws.

The most important factor, however, which affects the "constancy of the IQ," as it has been termed, is the inconstancy of the human being himself. Maturation and personality aspects interfere quite considerably with the even and consistent mental development which is essential for predicting future status by statistical computations. While prediction can be carried out with considerable success when applied to groups, it has been shown to be often completely unreliable when used in connection with individual children or adults. Some of the significant work carried out in mental deficiency illustrates the following points:

1. There is evidence that different rates of development result in significant changes in intellectual efficiency. It is quite possible that children who obtain a valid low IQ score on one occasion receive a valid and significantly higher IQ score at a later assessment, which is not due to the imperfections of testing as discussed above (Clarke, Clarke & Brown, 1959; Dearborn & Rothney, 1941). IQ changes in the region of fifteen points are not uncommon after a period of several years.

2. Intellectual functioning is affected by environmental factors. It has been shown that adverse factors in upbringing can be responsible for spuriously low intellectual functioning. This has been demonstrated in studies of normal twins, (Newman, Freeman, & Holzinger, 1937), and there is no reason why there would not also be differences due to environmental opportunities in the case of mentally defective children. Studies of children placed in different foster homes suggest that there is a tendency to respond to the influence of the environment in which the child grows up (Freeman, Holzinger, & Mitchell, 1928; Skodak & Skeels, 1949).

3. Special, individualized stimulation may result in remarkable IQ improvements; Skeels and Dye (1939), for example, found that the average IQ of children so stimulated improved by 27.5 points, while children not stimulated lost an average of 26.2 points.

4. Intellectual efficiency as reflected in IQ scores is affected by adverse environmental factors and recovers once those factors are removed (Clarke & Clarke, 1965).

5. There is evidence that intellectual development still continues in adolescence and adulthood and that predictions based on assessments in childhood underestimate later intellectual growth (Bayley, 1955; Bradway & Thompson, 1962; Owens, 1953).

6. An institutional, and therefore probably unstimulating, environment has a deteriorating effect on mental growth compared with that of an ordinary but relatively stimulating home or work environment. This can be shown to apply in the case of children (Lyle, 1959, 1960; McCandless, 1964) and adults (Mundy, 1957).

Summary

Considering the many influences which affect an IQ score and the great confidence put into it by most workers, it cannot be repeated too often that assessments must be given frequently (because mental functioning varies over a period of years), must be carried out with the right instrument to answer particular questions (because different intelligence tests are assessing different aspects of intelligent behavior), and cannot always be interpreted at their face value (because of the presence of many factors which influence the validity of the measure). If these points are kept in mind, then the value of an intelligence test as a means of classifying a person's intellectual functioning (at the time of testing) in relation to the general population cannot be gainsaid. To use it for diagnostic and predictive purposes requires, however, much experience and a thorough knowledge of relevant research work, and thus the interpretation of the test results should be left to the expert.

Assessment of Personality

The insistence with which the mental defective's intellectual behavior has been measured has detracted attention from the fact that behavior cannot exist independently of the person under observation. Yet the demonstrated intellectual inferiority has so overshadowed other issues that one may legitimately wonder whether researchers have become conscious of the fact that they are dealing with a human being who has emotions and feelings. Though there is much accepted evidence that emotional disturbances and maladjustment affect intelligent behavior, learning, and social adjustment, these findings are usually taken into account only when considering the case of a child with average or better-than-average intelligence. If the child has a measured low IQ, his inadequate functioning at school, at home, and in the community is attributed directly and wholly to his intellectual inferiority, and no attention is paid to the influence that emotional disturbance could have on his intellectual functioning or on his efficiency in other directions.

Evidence for the influence of personality disturbance on the even functioning of the mental defective comes mainly from three sources: (1) personality assessments, (2) psychotherapy, and (3) clinical judgments; however, there is much indirect evidence from other sources.

As far as personality assessments are concerned, the literature on this is meager compared with the vast amount of work carried out on the cognitive front. This is probably due partly to the techniques used for this purpose, which prove mostly too difficult for the mentally defective child and adult. Projective tests such as the Rorschach Ink Blot Test and the Thematic Apperception Test (TAT) require some ability to verbalize impressions, and questionnaire techniques demand some degree of self-assessment or judgment of other situations, which is mostly alien to the mental defective.

Jolles (1947), using the Rorschach test on sixty-six children with IQs below 80, found cases of anxiety neurosis, schizoid trends, feelings of inferiority, depression, and compulsions and came to the conclusion that ". . . there is, perhaps, a greater incidence of normals functioning mentally defective than clinicians have believed to be true." At times the evidence of a projective test indicating emotional disturbance can be used to reject a diagnosis of mental deficiency based on a psychometric assessment (Hackbusch & Klopfer, 1946, Ruess, 1958; Sarason, 1945; Sarason & Sarason, 1946; Zubin et al., 1956).

The presence of an undermining personality disturbance is often revealed by the work of the psychotherapist. Because of the difficulties in communication experienced by the mental defective, there has been a delay in introducing psychotherapy in mental deficiency, and methods have had to be adapted to suit the special limitations of the patient. However, there is now a multitude of significant work dealing with the whole range of mental deficiency, except profound retardation, summarized by various authors (Beier, 1964; Bialer, 1968; Cowen, 1963; Gunzburg, 1965b; Masland et al., 1958; Robinson & Robinson, 1965).

Play therapy has been carried out with children, and group therapy with adults. Some individual psychotherapy is psychoanalytically oriented, but most individual work is of a counseling character.

The evidence of the therapeutic value of psychotherapy in mental deficiency is not very convincing, but neither is there unchallenged proof of its effectiveness with people of "normal intelligence." The evidence of the presence of emotional conflict and its destructive effect on the functioning of a person who is mentally ill

equipped to deal with disturbing situations cannot, however, be rejected.

The third source of evidence—clinical experience—tends to remain unrecorded by those who have to deal daily with the difficulties of the mental defective. Comparatively few clinicians have looked at the personalities rather than at diagnostic aspects of their mentally defective patients, but case histories reported by social workers (Adams, 1960) and social investigators (Edgerton, 1967), reflect vividly the personality conflicts experienced by mental defectives, many of which could have been tackled in childhood before they added to the adjustment difficulties of the mentally defective adult. Earl (1961) discussed several personality aspects which, in mental defectives can be held directly responsible for their inadequacy and behavioral difficulties. He points out their characteristic "weakness of drive," perseveration, rigidity, immaturity, instability, and schizoid personality makeup. The mental defective's decreased ability to strive toward a goal, to persist in an effort, and to withstand frustration reduces markedly his ability to make adequate use of his limited mental equipment, which would otherwise be sufficient to survive in today's welfare society.

Instability, which is probably related to disorders in relationship formation (Tredgold & Soddy, 1963), has been singled out by many writers as a very characteristic aspect of the personality makeup which seems to defeat all attempts at permanent adjustment and socialization. This may be caused by failures in relating initially to the mother and the family and leads to inability to orientate socially.

A group labeled by the rather undefined terms *psychopathy* or *sociopathy* tends to be made up of a certain type of high-grade mental defective who represents an unreliable type of individual of defective judgment, liable to impulsive acts which are often both imprudent and inconsiderate, and who is moreover unable to profit by experience. The term is widely misused to cover any type of socially delinquent behavior of repetitive character which could, however, be due to many other causes, such as developmental instability, mental disorder, and sociocultural factors.

How much adverse home conditions affect adequate functioning can be deduced by studies such as those by Clarke and Clarke (1954) and Clarke, Clarke, and Reiman (1958), indicating that mental defectives tend to recoup their efficiency once they are removed from disturbing influences. Longer individual investigations such as those by Baller (1936) and Charles (1953) also suggest that emotional and vocational stability can be achieved at maturation, once the childhood upheavals have been overcome.

The various psychological theories discussed later in this chapter agree generally on the importance of personality factors to the adequate functioning of the mental defective. The literature on this aspect has been ably summarized by Heber (1964).

Assessment of Social Competence and Adjustment

An assumption which has dominated thinking and acting in mental deficiency was the reliance on the value of the IQ for predicting social adjustment. Research had established a high relationship between school intelligence and/or educational achievement and subsequent social status *in groups*. This encouraged the continued use of a familiar and comparatively reliable assessment instrument such as an intelligence scale for predicting the social status of an individual rather than for developing an independent assessment scale of social competence. This explains why even nowadays there are only a few assessment instruments available which could help in the evaluation of the most relevant aspect of the mental defective's behavior, e.g., the Vineland Social Maturity Scale (Doll, 1953), the Progress Assessment Charts of Social Development (Gunzburg, 1963), and the Social Competency Scale (Cain et al., 1963).

The relationship between intellectual status and social competence in mentally deficient individuals is not as close as one would expect because many of the skills required to be socially acceptable, if not competent, are the result of training, experience, and opportunities to learn. By comparing intelligence and social-competence ratings, it has been shown that many mental defectives function considerably better than one would expect on the basis of their mental ages (Gunzburg, 1968), and this has been corroborated through case histories showing the relatively high social and economic status achieved by people of low intellectual efficiency (Baller et al., 1967).

An assessment of social competence is of even less predictive value than an intelligence test score since it reflects largely the impact of circumstances at and up to the time of assessment, even though the mental defective's relatively low mental ability sets a ceiling to social development. The Vineland scale, which is similar to a test of intelligence (Doll, 1953), provides a measure of the deviation from the norms of average social competence of various age groups in the general population. The social age indicates an individual's social maturity compared with his chronological or mental age.

A completely different approach is presented by the PAC technique (Gunzburg, 1963), which draws attention to the uneven functioning in social aspects (Gunzburg, 1968) and evaluates in the Progress Evaluation Index (PEI) whether a mentally retarded child is socially backward, considering his age and limited abilities. The PAC results give a *qualitative* rather than a quantitative assessment of social functioning. The norms of the PEI make it possible to compare the social development of an individual mentally defective child with the average social development of other mentally defective children in the same age group. This technique of comparing a subnormal child with other subnormal children differs from the approach adopted by Doll, who compares the mentally defective child with normal children.

Considering the paramount importance of an assessment of social efficiency, it is disappointing that there are so few useful instruments available which would assist in this task. Techniques which are based on the social achievements of the normal person are of limited value as long as we are ignorant about the *minimum* requirements in social "know-how" required for independent survival in communities of different character.

TREATMENT, EDUCATION, AND TRAINING

As has already been pointed out, the etiology of the mental defective's social inadequacy is of a complex and multifactorial origin, and thus treatment and remedial measures will overlap and can be mutually supportive. It is, however, convenient to discuss some aspects of this work by relating it to the "pathological-nonpathological" dichotomy because it corresponds roughly to the biochemical-medical treatment for one group and to the psychiatric-educational-vocational measures for the other nonpathological group. Even so, biochemical treatment is also used in the nonpathological group in the form of sedatives, and the combined psychiatric, educational, and vocational efforts have recently spilled over into the area of low-grade subnormality.

Preventive Measures

As far as the genetically determined cases of pathology are concerned, the most striking,

even if modest, successes have been achieved in *phenylketonuria*. A special diet low in phenylalanine appears to prevent the development of intellectual subnormality if started early enough in life. However, research has not yet been able to assess how long this special diet has to be continued to establish "permanent normality" (Berman et al., 1961; Fuller, 1967).

There is also now an increasing belief that other metabolic disorders associated with severe mental deficiency (e. g., galactosemia) are likely to be susceptible to biochemical treatment (Penrose, 1963).

The better understanding of genetics and chromosome abnormalities suggests that "genetic family planning" may help to avoid many of the hazards which lead to severe mental defect.

Pathological mental deficiency, caused predominantly by environmental factors before, during, or after pregnancy, might now be on the decrease (Tizard, 1964). For example, a decline of about one-third in the prevalence rate of idiocy and imbecility has been reported for the English county of Middlesex (Goodman & Tizard, 1962). In this group very positive measures can be taken, and the increase of good and active maternal and child health services, improvements in obstetrical practice and in treatment of infections, and the establishment of registers of "children at risk" must lessen the probabilities that children with severe mental defect will be born, and it may well be that in that group, at least, one may confidently hope for a gradual decrease of numbers. On the other hand, improved medical care has resulted in a quadrupling of the prevalence rate of Mongols during the last 30 years (Carter, 1958; Goodman & Tizard, 1962).

There has been a short-lived hope that the administration of certain drugs would improve the intellectual functioning of the mental defective. Glutamic acid was considered potentially able to effect improvement in cognitive functioning, and also *Celastrus paniculata,* but results so far have not been convincing, largely because of inadequate experimental methodology.

Preventive measures are considered applicable mostly to the "pathological" type of mental deficiency, partly because there is some understanding of the etiologic factors involved and partly because the problems are manageable in terms of manpower and resources. Nevertheless, there is a clear recognition that much of the nonpathological, familial, subcultural mental deficiency could be prevented if adequate social planning could be carried out. The President's Panel on Mental Retardation (1962), submitting their Proposed Program for National Action to Combat Mental Retardation, considered that mental defect could be prevented "on a truly significant scale" by improving bad social and economic conditions. It was stated that a broad attack on the fundamental adverse conditions which spawn not only mental retardation but many other health and social problems is necessary to achieve this.

Until effective new social measures have succeeded in eliminating the fertile soil for the development of the subcultural type of mental deficiency, we shall have to learn to live with it and to apply ameliorating measures to specific cases rather than preventive measures to the community.

Ameliorating Measures

Much, if not most, nonmedical work in mental deficiency has been concerned with ameliorating the consequences of subnormal mental functioning. This means, first, the provision of special schools, institutions, and training places which are geared to the mental defective's low speed of learning and limited capacity to acquire knowledge and, second, the organization of shelter and protection for those mental defectives who are unable to survive independently in the community. Opinions as to who requires permanent custodial care and shelter and who could be trained sufficiently to adjust to minimal demands by society can differ widely in individual cases. At present, the initial optimism which characterized the early work in mental deficiency has been revived, largely because it has been seen that even severely subnormal people are capable of performing remunerative work and are thus able to contribute, at times substantially, to their own support. The realization that with proper education and training a mental defective need not be such a liability to his family and community as he was in the past and that an institutional existence is by no means inevitable has encouraged efforts to devise special programs, approaches, and methods to make the mental defective more competent in many aspects of functioning.

These efforts can be conveniently discussed under four headings: environmental manipulation, education and training, occupational training, and social training.

Environmental manipulation. It had been shown by various researchers that unfavorable home circumstances tend to lower mental efficiency, but that, on the other hand, favorable factors in the environment help to raise mental efficiency. This was shown in the case of orphanage children of parents with low mental ability, and it was demonstrated that those children were functioning nearer the level of their adoptive parents than of their real parents. A series of very important researches on this aspect, many of them originating at the University of Iowa (Skeels & Harms, 1948; Skodak, 1939; Skodak & Skeels, 1949), suggested strongly that adverse environmental factors *superimposed* on a poor genetic endowment *result in mental underfunctioning* at first but that the consequence can be remedied to some extent if the child is placed in a more favorable environment. Kirk (1958), in a series of experiments, showed that preschool training of children with IQ scores roughly between 45 and 80 was highly successful in increasing their rate of development, while the twin and sibling controls who did not receive preschool training deteriorated. The significant point in these studies is that early educational remedial action was successful in *accelerating* the role of mental growth and counteracted the effects of psychosocially deprived homes.

The influence of adverse environmental factors may even succeed in making people function on the level of mental defectives *despite* normal intellectual endowment (Davis, 1947; Guertin, 1949, 1950).

The interesting investigation by Tizard (1962), known as the "Brooklands experiment," showed that adequate (normal) stimulation of institutionalized imbecile children resulted in positive changes in social and emotional maturity, affective relationships, and social participation and in a significant increase in intelligence ratings.

The earlier study by Skeels and Dye (1939) showed also very clearly that "normal environments" will help to improve mentally defective children's functioning, while "poor environments" lead to deterioration.

Education and training. Importance is laid on the provision of special education for the severely mentally handicapped. It is, however, clearly recognized that it is futile and even harmful to apply an "academic" educational program which, while simplified and reduced to essentials, is nevertheless based on a syllabus designed for the normal child, with his wide range of adult possibilities. It is becoming gradually accepted practice to emphasize in the "school" for the mentally defective child "social education" which prepares him for his adult life. Several educational programs have been designed for this purpose (Gunzburg, 1965a, 1968; Ingram, 1953; Kirk & Johnson, 1954) which aim at developing the skills of giving satisfaction in employment, managing leisure time, making use of public services, getting on with other people, and managing personal finances. In programs of this kind, the tool subjects of reading, writing, and arithmetic are considered of subordinate value because the mentally handicapped has only a limited ability to understand and to make use of these skills, even though he is capable of mastering them to a fairly high level of competence in a purely mechanical manner. Considerations of this kind lead to the development of educational approaches which are quite distinct from those used in the world of normal education.

Much of the available educational material will not be of use because special requirements regarding content and methods are often disregarded. This applies particularly to content because the aims in this field are different and less ambitious than in normal education, and it will be necessary to develop special teaching aids for the mentally defective child (Gunzburg, 1966). This can be illustrated best by reference to teaching reading. While it is now recognized that even very severely defective children can acquire a very advanced reading skill, comparable to that of normal children of 13 and 14 years of age, this is a useless acquisition if the child is unable to apply this skill owing to his mental limitations. The time spent on teaching a high but useless proficiency in reading could be more usefully spent on the acquisition of social skills. Nevertheless, a certain minimum knowledge of the written word may help the illiterate to orientate himself in the literate world of signs and, notice boards. If the child, and later the adult, is able to recognize certain words or notices and acts accordingly, such knowledge could contribute to his social adequacy. The words of a social sight vocabulary or functional vocabulary, such as "exit," "inquiries," "ladies," "gentlemen," and "no smoking," are obviously of a far more advanced type than the words taught to the normal child at the beginning of this school career, e. g., "house," "apple," "dog," and "cat." Yet there is little virtue in wasting time teaching words which have no particular social significance. If so desired, this social sight vocabulary can provide the basis for learning to read when a certain readiness has been developed (Gunzburg, 1968).

It should also be remembered that many of the teaching aids which are placed in front of the mentally defective child who is supposed to help himself are very ineffective if he is not guided in their use. Using Piaget's theories as a framework for the training of the mentally defective child, Woodward (1963) points out the need to use the various teaching aids in accordance with the developmental stages.

Careful educational programming based on the experimental analysis of behavior and targets to be achieved has attracted much attention recently. The learning process is controlled to the last detail, and the material is presented in small, logical steps. The pupil is informed by reinforcement, rewards, etc., about his success, and if possible, failure is avoided.

Programmed instruction is particularly useful in adjusting to individual learning speeds, but has also been used in behavior-shaping work, for example, to eliminate undesirable behavior such as temper tantrums (Watson, 1967). The widest application of programmed instruction is, however, in connection with teaching machines. Various teaching machines of either the branching or the linear type have been developed and are now commercially available for use in normal education. Specially designed programs have been developed for use with mentally retarded children, particularly for teaching academic skills. The available work with mentally defective children has been fully reviewed by Stolurow (1963), Haskell (1966), Watson (1964), and Malpass (1968). It is difficult to assess the effectiveness of this new method because much of the evidence is marred by poor design, inefficient control of variables, inadequate criteria, etc., but is seems that this method can be utilized in teaching situations with mental defectives and could save, in particular cases, time and energy which the teacher could spend on aspects which require more individual attention.

Though children have been shown to learn from the program, it is not quite clear yet whether there is retention and whether the skills learned in such a manner can be transferred and applied to other situations by a mentally defective person.

The use of teaching machines and a carefully programmed course of instruction which can be carried out without a teacher's constant supervision could be of the utmost value in a field where there is still a scarcity of qualified, trained teachers and a marked need for individual attention. The practical difficulties, and not the least of those is the technical inadequacy of many of the moderately priced machines, are quite formidable, and so are the problems of keeping the children motivated sufficiently to adhere to the programs of the teaching machine. Yet the greatest obstacle to applying this particular form of instruction consistently and economically for prolonged periods is the time required to design individualized programs for the mentally handicapped. Programs which are written for young children of normal intelligence are usually quite inadequate because these children have a faster learning speed, the steps are larger, and, perhaps most important of all, the contents of such programs may not be suitable for the older mentally retarded child and adolescent.

Operant conditioning techniques have been introduced spasmodically in recent years to tackle the problems presented by mentally defective children who had so far not responded to the traditional techniques used. These children have been described as "vegetating" in the wards; rocking and showing stereotyped, manneristic behavior; being uninterested in their surroundings; manipulating pieces of string; sitting and staring; and apparently being quite unable to acquire behavior of an acceptable type.

Operant conditioning appears to be potentially useful in such situations because it requires little or no language understanding and because training and learning are accomplished in a mechanical way. Most work has been carried out in the field of self-help: toileting, dressing, and feeding. A few researchers have investigated the application of this approach to playing activities and general social behavior as well as development of speech and acceptable work habits.

Most programs rely on reinforcement techniques using successive approximation or behavior-shaping procedures, training techniques, etc., but a few researchers have used aversion techniques (Ellis, 1963; Watson, 1967).

Generally speaking, it is very difficult to decide at the present time whether any of the demonstration experiments have in fact established the value of the conditioning principle as such in these particular circumstances. Though there is little doubt that much of the work described has been successful, it seems to demonstrate only that children with this degree of severe mental handicap are capable of acquiring these skills if enough systematic attention is paid to the task of teaching. Whether or not these changes for the better were due to the methodology of operant conditioning cannot be ascertained at present with any certainty, and it may even be argued that operant conditioning was far more successful with the staff than with the children. It is very clear from the accounts that the staff involved were highly motivated, and the same results might have been achieved in the past, without much of the highly sophisticated experimental design, if the staff had applied themselves as systematically and energetically to dealing with the problems as they did in these experiments.

There is at present no evidence as to whether the successes achieved in a comparatively short training period are of a lasting nature. Moreover, the intensiveness of the training and the unavoidable disturbances created by it in the wards' routine suggest that it may well be difficult to use these methods as everyday procedures year after year. It will need a good deal more work, probably of a laboratory character, to establish which elements, principles, and steps in conditioning techniques are of value and can be incorporated in the ward routine. There is, however, no doubt that this is a potentially important and very successful approach to solving the training problems of children who so far have been considered to be untrainable.

Occupational training. Occupational training is usually not introduced before the child has reached adolescence (approximately age 16). Handicrafts (making baskets, rugs, mats, etc.), which are traditional in occupational therapy, are regarded as obsolete and a poor preparation for adult work in an industrial world. Hence there is now an increasing emphasis on introducing industrial work such as assembling, machining, finishing, etc., into training. The aim is not to train a worker who is skilled in one particular trade, but rather to encourage competence in industrial habits and requirements, e. g., timekeeping, fast working, and care of tools and materials.

The success of these training schemes has been impressive, and much of the current literature on the rehabilitation of the mental defective deals with this particular aspect. It has been shown particularly that even the severely retarded imbecile is capable of carrying out industrial processess to an employer's satisfaction. Carefully controlled experimental studies by Tizard, O'Connor, and Clarke (summarized Clarke & Clarke, 1965a) showed that imbeciles can learn many manual skills which help toward contributing to their own support, but certain principles of training have to be carefully adhered to in order to achieve the necessary competence.

The very success of industrial training tends to detract attention from the fact that employment is only one aspect of successful community adjustment. Many of the severely retarded people who obtain an acceptable standard of occupational proficiency can do this only in sheltered conditions. For them, the work training leads to occupation in sheltered workshops organized by various authorities and organizations. Being at work helps them and their families in many ways, but the defective still requires some form of direct custodial care. The literature on this aspect is helpful and encouraging (H. Goldstein, 1964; O'Connor & Tizard, 1956; Stahlecker, 1967; Tizard & O'Connor, 1950a, b).

Social training. The general enthusiasm engendered by the discovery of the mental defective's potential as an industrial worker has tended to underemphasize the fact that he is also a social being who requires social skills when living outside an institution. Training which encourages the acquisition and application of these skills should be initiated at school and must be continued into later life, alongside vocational training. The increased stability, awareness, and maturity of the adolescent mental defective will often make him amenable and receptive to such training only at this later stage, which too often tends to be dominated by vocational training. Social training will be particularly concerned with introducing the mental defective to situations which he might encounter in the community when using public transport, going shopping, asking for a doctor's help, budgeting, etc. These situations have to be discussed, rehearsed, practiced, and analyzed in detail in order to familiarize the defective with ordinary, day-to-day situations and to prevent him from becoming a "stranger in his own country" (Gunzburg, 1960, 1968; Neale & Campbell, 1963).

While there is a hard core of mental defectives who will always require much attention—many of whom belong to the pathological group—a large proportion of the garden-variety or subcultural group disappear from view for long times or altogether. Their social adjustment in later life is probably due to various factors. Delayed maturation may account for a fuller utilization of innate mental potential only later in life. It is also quite possible that the academic work of school life is more stressful than the subsequent demands of adult life, where the mental defective can deal more efficiently with practical situations. Third, the difference between the normal and subnormal in ordinary, everyday functioning becomes less noticeable in time because the slow learner has at last acquired a minimum of social competence.

Studies of the subsequent careers of people who were once classified as mental defectives show a high success rate in continuing adjustment, though such persons will always be highly vulnerable members of society in times of social instability. Studies of social adjustment make interesting reading (Abel & Kinder, 1942; Baller, 1936; Baller et al., 1967; Charles, 1953; Edgerton, 1967; Kennedy, 1948, 1962; Saenger, 1957; Stahlecker, 1967).

PSYCHOLOGICAL THEORY AND MENTAL DEFICIENCY

The following sections will summarize psychological theories as applied to the field of mental deficiency and used to provide a framework for research and working hypotheses, but it must be added that so far, they have had little influence on a general, consistent, approach to treatment and training.

Gestalt and Field Theory

Gestalt psychologists are interested in the effect of present internal and external conditions on the person and his behavior. Perceptual phenomena and their organization and systematic distortions have attracted Gestalt psychologists' persistent interest, and much psychological work in mental deficiency relates to this approach.

The Werner-Strauss school of thought. In a series of experiments and studies of figure-ground perception in the brain-injured (exogenous) Werner, Strauss, and their co-workers observed that brain-injured children tend to be seriously handicapped in the visual, tactual, and auditory fields by background interference, which probably leads to a chaotic and highly disturbing impression of the world around them. On the basis of these findings, special teaching and training approaches were developed (Gallagher, 1960; Strauss & Kephart, 1955; Strauss & Lehtinen, 1947) which aimed at overcoming the excessive distractibility of the brain-injured child by diminishing irrelevant external stimuli and by taking him through a carefully designed program of exercises aimed at teaching him how to tackle perceptual difficulties.

The theory and research have come under heavy criticism regarding both methodology and interpretation, and yet this work has had a far-reaching influence on the teaching and training of mentally defective children in general. Several techniques of assessing perceptual difficulties and of taking remedial action have been developed recently, but little is yet known regarding their effect on successful adaptive behavior in later life (Frostig & Horne, 1964).

The Lewin and Kounin school of thought. Lewin's field theory attempts to explain the familial mental defective in terms of "topological psychology." According to Lewin (1935, 1951) and Kounin (1941), differentiation of the organism's psychic regions increases with age and intelligence. Mental defectives show a noticeable rigidity of the boundaries between the regions, as compared with normal people of the same chronological or mental age. This accounts for the mentally defective person's relative in-

ability to generalize, his perseverative tendencies, his concrete thinking, and his sterotyped, "either-or" inflexible behavior.

Neither Lewin nor Kounin developed this approach further after the initial experiments, but their theories received widespread attention since they seemed to account for much of the clinical picture given by the mental defective. The main attack on the interpretation of the experimental findings came from K. Goldstein (1942), who explained the inadequate behavior of the mental defective in terms of his general theory (1939). According to him, the rigidity observed, and in fact any other perseverative and distractible behavior, is the "catastrophic reaction" to tasks which are beyond a person's capacity and which therefore result in failure. Experience of failure, accouting for much of the mental defective's typical behavior, is also the main theme of Zigler and his associates (Zigler, 1962), who attacked the Lewin-Kounin position. The main point of the argument states that differences between normal people and familial defectives can be explained in terms of motivation. In a series of studies Zigler and his associates (Zigler & Williams, 1963) showed that institutionalized mentally defective children, who usually have a very marked history of deprivation and negative relationships with adults, tend to seek more frequent adult approval than normal children. However, many of these attempts lead to failure, which produces a "higher negative reaction tendency toward adults." If the rigidity, noted by Lewin and Kounin, is typical of the mentally retarded and is inherent in them, it should be present in all mental defectives. However, Green and Zigler (1962), comparing the performance of mentally defective children who were living at home and presumably were not deprived to an extreme extent with that of institutionalized mentally defective children (deprived), found significant differences in performances.

Whether the motivational variable originating

in particular environmental conditions can explain entirely the mental defective's inadequate behavior is doubtful, and yet the weak drive to strive toward a goal or to withstand frustration (Earl, 1961), which in the face of difficult situations leads to typical perseverative behavior, is a common clinical observation, which suggests that Zigler's work may well contribute to preventive action in this field.

The "cortical-satiation" school of thought (Köhler and Wallach). Köhler and Wallach (1944) assume a structural and functional correspondence between experience and the underlying physiological processes. The principle of psychophysical isomorphism suggests that the distribution and structure of a stimulus as perceived by the person correspond to the distribution and structure of its representation in the brain. The representation involves electrical charges and currents which may, if prolonged, fatigue the cortical area "so as to impede further flow of neural processes" (Wolfensberger, 1963).

Perceptual processes, involving reversible figures such as the Necker cube and figural aftereffects, have been used to support this approach. Experimentation suggests that the mentally defective as a group take longer than normal people to induce electrical, chemical, and physical changes in stimulated cortical cells and that it is more difficult for these cells to return to the previous state or to form new or different traces or patterns (Spitz, 1963).

The findings of this experimental work throw new light on the problem of visual perception encountered by the brain-damaged in learning and problem solving, but there is at present no way to apply this work to the actual teaching situation. All findings refer to groups, and there is so much overlapping in the satiation test results of normal and mentally defective subjects that one may well feel that this particular factor does not contribute decisively to the better handling of the problem of mental deficiency.

Hebb's Neurophysiological Theory

It was pointed out at the beginning of this discussion of mental deficiency that practically all accepted definitions of this condition stress the social inadequacy which is associated with intellectual subnormality. Benoit's (1959) definition, based on Hebb's theory of brain function, emphasizes the importance of an impaired CNS. He defines mental deficiency as "a deficit of intellectual function resulting from varied intrapersonal and/or extrapersonal determinants but having as a common proximate cause a diminished efficiency of the nervous system thus entailing a lessened general capacity for growth in perceptual and conceptual integration and consequently in environmental adjustment."

This theory suggests that the impairment is found in the capacity for growth rather than in the ability to learn, which explains why there is a ceiling to learning even if learning at the simple, elementary stages proceeds at the same rate as in normal children.

Hebb suggests that healthy and even development depends on rich perceptual experience, particularly in infancy, and that deprivation of stimuli results in abnormal behavior. Institutionalization at an early stage for whatever reason would lead to an underdevelopment of these basic cell assemblies which are essential for continued learning because the infant is considerably less talked to, played with, fondled, and handled than a baby growing up at home. Living in an impersonal, even if hygienic, institutional environment must therefore interfere with the learning experience, and the child growing up under such conditions will be considerably handicapped in addition to other handicaps such as congenital damage to the CNS. Hebb stresses the effects of damage to the reticular brainstem formation, resulting in difficulties in attention and control. Thus, in such cases the richness of a stimulating environment has to be regulated to channel attention to relevant stimuli and to program learning in easy, slow steps which can be grasped in different perceptual and conceptual experiences (Benoit, 1957; Gallagher, 1960). The neurophysiological approach can provide the basis for a systematic diagnosis and treatment of many educational problems encountered in mental deficiency, such as difficulties in reading.

Rotter's Social-learning Theory

To many workers in the field, the rationale offered by social-learning theory seems to give a better understanding of the inadequate behavior of mentally defective persons. Rotter's theory (1954) emphasizes that behavior depends not only on expectancy regarding the future but just as much on the past experiences of failure and success, punishment and reward. Thus individuals could be categorized as "success-striving" or "failure-avoiding." In the first case, learning will be encouraged by the positive reinforcement of reward. In the second case, learning will be helped by the negative reinforcement of punishment. The difficulty is to conceptualize the success-failure systems and reward-punishment systems which have to be learned. The hedonistic child, attempting to acquire immediate pleasure and to avoid immediate unpleasurable experiences (pain), gradually begins to strive toward less immediate goals which spell success and to avoid situations which mean failure. Success may mean reward, and failure may mean punishment, and yet the older he gets, the more he may realize that he might have to tolerate immediate unpleasantness (punishment) to achieve long-term success and reward.

The ability to regulate behavior on the more mature level, which is not subject to the wish for immediate gratification, is severely diminished in the mental defective. As Rotter's theory suggests, this may be due to many unhelpful experiences in the past, but the end effect is a marked absence of directed drive to overcome difficulties and just as marked a tendency to desire immediate reward and success, noted by many clini-

cians (e.g., Earl, 1961). There is a closer association between emotional maturity and intellectual ability than between emotional maturity and chronological age, but it is quite possible that intellectual functioning in itself is adversely affected by the mentally defective child's unreadiness and unwillingness to expose himself to the intellectual challenge contained in intelligence tests.

The important point in this theory, when applied to the practical work in mental deficiency, is that the effect of promising reinforcing rewards—on which the whole practice of training and education in mental deficiency is based—is greatly weakened by the accumulated experience of the past, which may have produced anticipation or expectance of a kind that contradicts or nullifies the promise of reward. In other words, the mentally handicapped child may not be motivated sufficiently because past frustrations and failures have created an avoidance behavior.

There is now available a series of researches (Cromwell, 1963) which suggest strongly that mental defectives perform in new situations on a level below their ability and that "failure" does not motivate them to extra effort. They show stronger avoidance tendencies than normals, and it is hypothesized that this is due to past experience leading to a generalized expectance of failure (see also Cromwell, 1968; Zigler, 1962).

SPECIAL PROBLEMS

Learning

The emphasis put on the low IQ figure as the *cause* of the mental defective's inadequacy tends to deflect from the fact that the test result reflects impairment in the *learning* process. "Learning" refers to the ability to acquire knowledge and to establish associations between isolated facts and events, to store them in memory, and to reproduce them at will when required. Low intelligence test scores and low learning ability are closely associated but are not identical, and recent research has shown the large number of factors which impair learning as such but which may be independent of innate low intelligence. The whole problem has not yet been adequately discussed or explored, but it has become clear that factors such as motivation, memory, and attention play a decisive part in the final performance we measure in intelligence tests. It may well be that inadequacies in these aspects lead to considerable intellectual underfunctioning and that a mental defective's potential could be much underestimated by accepting his IQ at face value.

The first optimism of Itard (1801) and his co-workers regarding the learning abilities of their subjects soon gave way to the pessimistic outlook of subsequent workers who failed to raise the defective to a normal level. However, recent work has shown that transfer of learning is possible. This is, in fact, extremely important for the future of all education and training because the mental defective's apparent inability to apply to new situations what he has been taught with much effort has bedeviled progress in rehabilitation work.

In particular, research work has shown the following:

1. Though intelligence level is related to efficiency on motor task (i.e., in industrial work), mentally defective people can improve their performance to a greater extent than their IQs would suggest.

2. In simple tasks and with extended practice, their final level of achievement is similar to that of normal people.

3. Even children on the idiot level can learn by discrimination.

4. Transfer of "learning" can take place at low levels of intelligence.

5. It is possible for severely subnormal children to transfer "conceptual strategy" from one task to another which is of a different type but which involves the same strategy.

6. In industrial conditions, the adult imbecile worker can perform as well as a normal worker in certain simple tasks.

These investigations have also shown the decisive influence that various factors have on performance and how misleading experimental conclusions can be if those factors are disregarded. In particular, the following factors have been mentioned in this connection:

1. Incentives. Reports generally indicate that even low-grade imbeciles perform better under incentive conditions.

2. Personality. Individual differences in the ability to learn are, to some extent, associated with personality types.

3. Difficulty of task. Increased learning can take place if difficult tasks are broken down into consistent, simple operations.

4. Verbal reinforcement. Learning is made easier by verbal direction of actions. Evidence for this view is offered by Russian work, but much more work is needed to exploit these interesting concepts.

5. Direction and maintenance of attention have been considered in recent work essential to adequate learning.

6. "Learning sets" can be retained by young imbeciles, but these children have to be taught formally and do not learn spontaneously.

It has been shown in various studies referring to learning reinforcement, delays of reinforcement, schedules of reinforcement, magnitude of rewards, social reinforcement, primary and secondary reinforcement, success versus failure, transfer of training, transposition, and stimulus generalization that by and large, the basic learning processes in mental defectives are not dissimilar from those in normal people. There is, of course, a difference in speed of learning, and also the low ceiling of achievement puts a limit to learning more complex operations. Nevertheless, very often it appears that the low achievement might be due simply to the fact that little is expected and therefore little is achieved.

A factor which needs far more investigation and which is of unknown magnitude is represented by the "institutionalization" of the vast majority of subjects on whom the results are based in these investigations. The effects of prolonged institutionalization and continued deprivation of stimulation and the warm "home," as experienced by the normal child, must have a marked deteriorating effect on mental functioning (as shown, for example, in studies of language development). Many of the reported differences —for example, the different type of reinforcement that is effective with mentally defective children, as compared with normal children of the same mental level—may in themselves be the result of institutionalization rather than mental deficiency. The work on this aspect is reviewed and summarized by Clarke and Clarke (1965b) and Watson and Lawson (1966).

Attention and Remembering

Efficient learning is obviously dependent on the ability to attend to the teaching and to remember over both the short term and the long term. It is widely accepted that mentally defective children and adults have particular problems in this field. Their short attention span, lack of concentration, and excessive distractibility increase their difficulties in discrimination, and thus not only their low intelligence level but also the perhaps very inadequate techniques for learning present serious obstacles to teaching.

Research work suggests that the difficulties in learning are situated mainly in two fields. First, there is limitation in attending to the relevant stimulus dimensions (Zeaman & House, 1963), and second, there is difficulty in selecting the appropriate and correct stimuli from the mass of

stimuli surrounding the mental defective (O'Connor & Hermelin, 1963). Research work also suggests that there is probably not a great difference between normals and subnormals in remembering over both the short term and the long term, once the initial difficulty of registering, perceiving, and selecting the correct cue has been overcome. Many of the traditional techniques of teaching mentally defective children have in many ways anticipated the findings of modern psychological research by realizing that materials have to be presented in a different manner from the one suitable for normal children because relevant cues should be singled out by a combination of attention-attracting factors, such as size, color, and tactile sensations.

Studies of visual discrimination and simple work habits have indicated consistently that the severely subnormal child and adult show a characteristic delay in responding to stimuli before beginning to learn, and this delay may be so long that the investigator, experimenter, trainer, or teacher may be tempted to give up the educational effort because the child does not seem to learn. This delay until the child grasps what is wanted of him will be less frustrating if the teacher takes into account the child's difficulties in singling out the relevant cues. Much of this difficulty is due to inadequate verbal communication between teacher and the child, and it has been shown that the ensuing weaknesses in the encoding and decoding processes are quite considerable.

Communication Deficits

It has been argued that the important mental functions, such as perception, memory, attention, logical thinking, etc., are not inborn properties but are complex processes which are formed in the course of a child's development. If, for one reason or another, the prolonged process of formation is disturbed or interrupted, this disturbance may influence the further mental development of the child to such an extent that he becomes mentally defective. This school of thought (represented by the psychologists Vygotsky, Leontiev, and Luria) suggests that the abnormalities displayed by many mentally defective children can be accounted for by the derangement of normal development owing to an early disease or sometimes an inborn defect which results in a definite missing link which is indispensable for normal development. This missing link or basic disturbance may lead to a number of secondary symptoms and may have widely different consequences, depending on the localization of the lesion and on whether the lesion occurred in early childhood or at a mature age.

From the treatment point of view this approach is extremely important. Instead of accepting the explanation of a general intellectual deficiency which accounts for inadequacy in the absence of established organic or physical impairment, the hypothesis is put forward that ". . . a primary derangement of any particular link may inevitably lead to the disintegration of the whole system" (Luria & Yudovich, 1959). The primary defect may be so slight as to be scarcely detectable and may have no consequences in an adult who can develop compensatory and highly successful techniques to overcome his handicap. On the other hand, the same lesion which, in an adult may be inconsiderable and a purely peripheral defect, may affect learning at the early childhood stage to such an extent that the child's inability to participate normally in the world around may lead to failure, frustration, despair, and total collapse, resulting in functional mental deficiency.

A careful diagnosis to disclose the primary disorder as well as subsequent secondary consequences may well help to develop a perceptive corrective training procedure of practical use (Luria, 1963).

The approach that assumes that adequate mental development has been affected by the presence of a limited, strictly localized defect which has repercussions in general development does not cover all cases of mental deficiency. Besides the extreme cases where an obvious organic pathological defect makes normal development impossible, there are many others, probably the majority of cases, where the handicap is shown by diminished ability to concentrate, by increased impulsiveness, by intractability, by lack of application, by absence of perseverance, etc. These are the children who show sufficient intelligence to be enrolled in a special educational program but who remain social problem cases throughout their adult life.

Any higher nervous activity is characterized by varying degrees of equilibrium between the excitatory and inhibitory processes. Disturbances of the equilibrium lead to pathological behavior, and a person is no longer able to respond adequately to inhibitory signals; thus impulsive, involuntary actions may be frequent. On the other hand, sluggishness may be the result of a predominance of elementary inhibition. The ability to inhibit and to adjust to new conditions (lability) is seriously affected in pathological states. Research workers, particularly Russian psychologists, have shown that the adaptive behavior of a mentally defective patient can be regulated by his use of speech to direct his behavior (Luria, 1963). Use of verbal reinforcement results in improvement in elementary problems, but research has not yet succeeded in applying this method to more complicated problems. Most of the recent Russian work (Leontiev, 1957; Liublinskaja, 1957) stresses the importance of speech for regulating behavior. "Thinking in words," or inner language ability, which is probably of a nature similar to that of Piaget's egocentric speech (1926), represents the individual's ability to manipulate linguistic symbols internally, and therefore a defect in this area could limit the development of the thought processes and, in consequence, intelligence. Published studies suggest a very high relationship between inner language facility and intelligence which may be of a causal nature. The poor expressive linguistic ability of defectives is well known, and many studies of speech skills indicate that factors such as intelligence, etiology, and environmental circumstances influence the ease with which speech is used. Useful summaries of published work covering this aspect are those by Spradlin (1963) McCarthy (1964) and Webb and Kinde (1968).

Concluding Remarks

Mental deficiency has for many years been the Cinderella of the various disciplines which admitted having a stake in the condition. It rapidly became a largely medical concern because of the interest in etiology and because of the humanitarian consideration of keeping "life alive" as long as possible. These views invariably resulted in a "custodial philosophy" and in attempts to provide not only bigger but also better institutions in the sense of making them more "livable" and acceptable. Yet the provision of better custodial facilities for the mentally defective has generally not been able to disguise the fact that few active and imaginative workers in the many disciplines which have a contribution to make have been attracted to a field which seemed barren of the essential rewards of success. While the medical profession and the allied disciplines have soldiered bravely on, nibbling at the problems of etiology with barely any success, other professions have shown a conspicuous lack of enthusiasm in getting down to dealing with the overwhelming problems of what to do once the condition has been established. There is a traditional belief that this is really a dead end for professional endeavor because the mentally handicapped has no place in this competitive world and it is in his own interest to continue his existence in the safe protection of a sheltered environment.

The climate of stagnancy and apathy which is characteristic of the majority of institutions for the mentally defective is not attractive to the worker who looks around for promising and interesting fields of inquiry, although it is his contribution which could improve the situation. This vicious circle can be broken, and this chapter, outlining ideas, researches, and activities which have taken place in this field in recent years, demonstrates the unexplored potential for positive action in this field of work.

Positive actions refer to those measures, whether of a theoretical or a practical kind, which aim at improving the functioning of a person with a handicap, with the ultimate aim of giving him a chance to live *outside* the complete protection offered by the institution. This is more than the largely negative action of accepting the condition and providing a permanent separate community within the large community, irrespective of the size of the handicap.

There is little doubt that emphasis has shifted generally toward a belief that the consequences of mental deficiency can be considerably ameliorated by adequate and early action. There is much disagreement as to the nature of this action and the efficiency of the methods now in use. Yet where progressive thinking and energetic consideration are taking place, the results challenge the prevalent practices of using passive institutionalization as the only realistic means of disposing of the problem complex.

There is no dissident voice regarding the desirability of *early* action in childhood. There is, however, much evidence that the early diagnosis of mental deficiency is generally equivalent to a sentence of eternal damnation because professional people, unaware of the new developments summarized in this chapter, give advice based on discarded notions. Worse, because of the lack of belief that something positive can be done, little active, consistent, and persistent action is taken, and in consequence, the mentally defective child will fail to progress and is likely to deteriorate. Being handled with kindness and tolerance, but without belief in his abilities and the possibility of genuine progress, his obvious stagnation seems to support the apparent correctness of the widespread prejudice that a mental defective can function on only a primitive level in a sheltered community.

Research results available now, originating from a multidisciplinary approach which has superseded the one-sided medical-genetic-biological angle, have opened up promising and exciting vistas. Which of them will result in decisive steps forward is by no means clear yet, but it is certainly essential to rid ourselves of oversimplified and misleading notions of mental deficiency to clear the way for progress.

This short survey of the mental deficiencies and recent work in this field can give only glimpses of what promises to become more interesting and more rewarding, the more interest and effort are devoted to it. There are now many new comprehensive works available which deal with the problems on a wide front and in novel ways, and interested readers should consult them for elaboration of what has been said here or for information which has been omitted in this chapter. The number and quality of these works indicate the wide scope of the work and the increased importance given to questions of adequate diagnosis and remedial work.

REFERENCES

Abel, T. M., & Kinder, E. F. *The subnormal adolescent girl.* New York: Columbia University Press, 1942.

Abercrombie, M. L. J. *Perceptual and visuomotor disorders in cerebral palsy.* London: Heinemann, 1964.

Adams, M. *The mentally subnormal: The social casework approach.* London: Heinemann, 1960.

Aronson, S. M., & Volk, B. W. *Cerebral sphingolipidoses.* New York: Academic Press, 1962.

Baller, W. R. A study of the present social status of a group of adults who, when they were in elementary schools, were classified as mentally deficient. *Genetic Psychological Monographs,* 1936, **18,** 165–244.

Baller, W. R., Charles, D. C. & Miller, E. L. Mid life attainments of the mentally retarded. *Genetic Psychological Monographs* 1967, **75,** 235–329.

Bayley, N. On the growth of intelligence. *American Psychologist,* 1955, **10,** 805–818.

Beier, D. C. Behavioral disturbances. In H. A. Stevens & R. Heber (Eds.), *Mental retardation.* Chicago: University of Chicago Press, 1964.

Benda, C. E. *Mongolism and cretinism.* New York: Grune & Stratton, 1946.

Benda, C. E., & Melchior, J. C. Childhood schizophrenia, childhood autism and Heller's disease. *International Record of Medicine,* 1959, **172,** 137–154.

Bender, L. Symposium in juvenile schizophrenia. In *Neurology and psychiatry in childhood.* Association for Research in Nervous and Mental Diseases, Baltimore: Williams & Wilkins, 1954.

Bender, L. Diagnostic and therapeutic aspects of childhood schizophrenia. In P. W. Bowman and H. V. Mautner (Eds.) Mental retardation: *Proceedings of the First International Medical Conference.* New York: Grune & Stratton, 1960. Pp. 453–468.

Benoit, E. P. Relevance of Hebb's theory of the organization of behavior to educational research on the mentally retarded. *American Journal of Mental Deficiency,* 1957, **61,** 497–507.

Benoit, E. P. Toward a new definition of mental retardation. *American Journal of Mental Deficiency,* 1959, **63,** 559–564.

Berman, P. W., Graham, F. K., Eichman, P. L., & Waisman, H. A. Psychologic and neurologic status of diet treated phenylketonuric children and their siblings. *Pediatrics*, 1961, **28**, 924.

Bessman, S. P., due Logue, D., & Wapnir, R. A. Phenylketonuria: Certainty versus uncertainty. *Proceedings of the First Congress International Association Scientific Study of Mental Deficiency*, 1967, 182–193.

Bialer I. Psychotherapy and other adjustment techniques with the mentally retarded. In A. A. Baumeister (Ed.) *Mental retardation.* London: University of London Press, 1968. Pp. 138–180.

Bradway, U. P., & Thompson, C. W. Intelligence at adulthood: A twenty-five year follow up. *Journal of Educational Psychology*, 1962, **53**, 1–14.

Bühler, C., & Hetzer, H. *Testing children's development from birth to school age.* New York: Rinehart, 1935.

Burt, C. *The backward child.* (3rd ed.) London: University of London Press, 1951.

Cain, L. F., Levine, S., & Elzey, F. F. *Cain-Levine Social Competency Scale.* Palo Alto, Calif., Consulting Psychological Press, 1963.

Carter, C. O. A life table for Mongols with the causes of death. *Journal of Mental Deficiency Research*, 1958, **2**, 64–74.

Catell, P. *The measurement of intelligence of infants and young children.* New York: Psychological Corporation, 1947.

Charles, D. C. Ability and accomplishment of persons earlier judged mentally deficient. *Genetic Psychological Monographs*, 1953, **47**, 3–71.

Clarke, A. D. B., & Clarke, A. M. Cognitive changes in the feebleminded. *British Journal of Psychology*, 1954, **45**, 173–179.

Clarke, A. D. B., & Clarke, A. M. Pseudo-feeblemindedness: Some implications. *American Journal of Mental Deficiency*, 1955, **59**, 507–509.

Clarke, A. D. B., Clarke, A. M., & Reiman, S. Cognitive and social changes in the feebleminded: Three further studies. *British Journal of Psychology*, 1958, **49**, 144–157.

Clarke, A. D. B., Clarke, A. M., & Brown, R. I. Regression to the mean: A confused concept. *British Journal of Psychology*, 1959, **51**, 105–117.

Clarke, A. D. B., & Clarke, A. M. The abilities and trainability of imbeciles. In A. M. Clarke & A. D. B. Clarke (Eds.), *Mental deficiency: The changing outlook.* London: Methuen, 1965. Pp. 356–384. (a)

Clarke, A. M. & Clarke, A. D. B. (Eds.) *Mental deficiency: The changing outlook.* London: Methuen, 1965. (b)

Collipp, P. J., Kaplan, S. A., Kogut, M. D., Tasem, W., Plachti, F., Schlamm, V., Boyle, D. C., Ling, S. M., & Koch, R. Mental retardation in congenital hypothyroidism. *American Journal of Mental Deficiency*, 1965, **70**, 3.

Cowen, E. L., & Trippe, M. J. Psychotherapy and play techniques with the exceptional child and youth. In W. M. Cruickshank (Ed.), *Psychology of exceptional children and youth.* Englewood Cliffs, N.J.: Prentice-Hall, 1963.

Critchley, H., & Earl, C. J. C. Tuberose sclerosis and allied conditions. *Brain*, 1932, **55**, 311–346.

Crome, L., Dutton, G., & Ross, C. F. Maple syrup urine disease. *The Journal of Pathology and Bacteriology*, 1961, **81**, 379.

Cromwell, R. L. A social learning approach to mental retardation. In N. R. Ellis, (Ed.), *Hand-*

book of mental deficiency. New York: McGraw-Hill, 1963.

Cromwell, R. L. Personality Evaluation. In A. A. Baumeister (Ed.) Mental retardation. London: University of London Press, 1968. Pp. 66–85.

Crothers, G., & Paine, R. S. The natural history of cerebral palsy. Cambridge, Mass.: Harvard University Press, 1959.

Cruickshank, W. M., & Rans, G. M. Cerebral palsy: Its individual and community problems. Syracuse, N.Y.: Syracuse University Press, 1955.

Davis, K. Final note on a case of extreme isolation. American Journal of Sociology, 1947, 52, 432–437.

Dearborn, W. F., & Rothney, J. W. M. Predicting the child's development. Cambridge, Mass.: Science and Art Publishers, 1941.

Doll, E. A. The essentials of an inclusive concept of mental deficiency. Proceedings of the American Association on Mental Deficiency, 1941, 46, 214–219.

Doll, E. A. The measurement of social competence: A manual for the Vineland Social Maturity Scale. Washington: Educational Test Bureau, 1953.

Dugdale, R. L. The Jukes. New York: Putnam, 1910.

Earl, C. J. C. Subnormal personalities: Their clinical investigation and assessment. London: Baillière, 1961.

Edgerton, R. B. The cloak of competence. Berkeley: University of California Press, 1967.

Ellis, N. R. Toilet training the severely defective patient, and S-R reinforcement analysis. American Journal of Mental Deficiency, 1963, 68, 98–103.

Finlayson, A. Tuberous sclerosis. American Journal of Mental Deficiency, 1955, 59, 617–628.

Fölling, A. Uber ausscheidung von phenylbrenztraubensaure in den harn. Hoppe-Seylers Zeitschrift fuer Physiologische Chemie, 1934, 227, 169–176.

Freeman, F. N., Holzinger, K. J., & Mitchell, B. C. The influence of environment on the intelligence, school achievement and conduct of foster children. Yearbook of the National Society for the Study of Education, 1928, 27, 103–217.

Frostig, M., & Horne, D. The Frostig program for the development of visual perception. Chicago: Follett, 1964.

Fuller, R. Treated phenylketo muria: Analysis of psychological results. Proceedings of the First Congress Int. Ass. Scientific Study of Mental Deficiency, 1967, 305–313.

Gallagher, J. J. The tutoring of brain-injured mentally retarded children. Springfield, Ill.: Charles C Thomas, 1960.

Gesell, A., & Amatruda, C. S. Developmental diagnosis, normal and abnormal child development. New York: Harper, 1947.

Goddard, H. H. The Kallikak family. New York: Macmillan, 1912.

Goddard, H. H. Feeblemindedness: Its causes and consequences. New York: Macmillan, 1914.

Goldstein, H. Social and occupational adjustment. In H. A. Stevens & R. Heber (Eds.), Mental retardation. Chicago: University of Chicago Press, 1964.

Goldstein, K. The organism. New York: American Book, 1939.

Goldstein, K. Concerning rigidity. *Character and Personality*, 1942, **11**, 209–226.

Goldstein, S. A study of mongolism and non-mongoloid mental retardation in children. *Archives of Pediatrics*, 1954, **71**, 11–28.

Goodman, N., & Tizard, J. Prevalence of imbecility and idiocy among children. *British Medical Journal*, 1962, **1**, 216–219.

Green, C., & Zigler, E. F. Social deprivation and the performance of retarded and normal children on a satiation type task. *Child Development*, 1962, **33**, 499–508.

Guertin, W. H. Mental growth in pseudo-feeblemindedness. *Journal of Clinical Psychology*, 1949, **5**, 414–418.

Guertin, W. H. Differential characteristics of the pseudo-feebleminded. *American Journal of Mental Deficiency*, 1950, **54**, 394–398.

Gunzburg, H. C. *Social rehabilitation of the subnormal.* London: Baillière, 1960.

Gunzburg, H. C. *Progress assessment charts of social development (P-A-C).* London: National Association of Mental Health, 1963.

Gunzburg, H. C. Educational problems in mental deficiency. In A. M. Clarke & A. D. B. Clarke (Eds.), *Mental deficiency: The changing outlook.* London: Methuen, 1965. Pp. 328–355.(a)

Gunzburg, H. C. Psychotherapy with the feebleminded. In A. M. Clarke & A. D. B. Clarke (Eds.), *Mental deficiency: The changing outlook.* London: Methuen, 1965. Pp. 417–446.(b)

Gunzburg, H. C. Teaching aids for the subnormal. In H. C. Gunzburg (Ed.), The application of research to the education and training of the severely subnormal child. *Journal of Mental Subnormality,* 1966 (Monogr. Suppl.). Pp. 61–68.

Gunzburg, H. C. *Social competence and mental handicap.* London: Baillière; Baltimore: Williams & Wilkins, 1968.

Hackbusch, F., & Klopfer, B. The contribution of projective techniques to the understanding and treatment of children psychometrically diagnosed as feebleminded. *American Journal of Mental Deficiency*, 1946, **51**, 15–34.

Haskell, S. H. Programmed instruction and the mentally retarded. In H. C. Gunzburg (Ed.), The application of research to the education and training of the severely subnormal child. *Journal of Mental Subnormality,* 1966 (Monogr. Suppl.). Pp. 15–24.

Heber, R. A manual on terminology and classification in mental retardation. *American Journal of Mental Deficiency* 1959 (Monogr. Suppl.).

Heber, R. Personality. In H. A. Stevens & R. Heber (Eds.), *Mental retardation.* Chicago: University of Chicago Press, 1964.

Hilliard, L. T., & Kirman, B. H. *Mental deficiency.* London: Churchill, 1965.

Holzel, A. In *Neurometabolic disorders in childhood.* London: Livingstone, 1963.

Illingworth, R. S. Mental retardation in the infant and preschool child. *British Medical Journal*, 1955, **2**, 1–7.

Illingworth, R. S. *Recent advances in cerebral palsy.* London: Churchill, 1958.

Illingworth, R. S. *The development of the infant and young child, normal and abnormal.* London: Livingstone, 1960.

Ingram, C. P. *Education of the slow-learning child.* New York: Ronald Press, 1953.

Ireland, J. T. *Biochemical approaches to mental handicap in children.* London: Livingstone, 1964.

Itard, J. M. G. *The Wild Boy of Aveyron* (1801).

(Transl., 2nd ed.) New York: Appleton Century Crofts, 1962.

Jastak, J. A rigorous criterion of feeblemindedness. *Journal of Abnormal and Social Psychology,* 1949, **44,** 367–378.

Jastak, J. Psychological tests, intelligence and feeblemindedness. *Journal of Clinical Psychology,* 1952, **8,** 107–112.

Jastak, J. E., Macphee, H. M., & Whiteman, M. *Mental retardation: Its nature and incidence.* University of Delaware Press, 1963.

Jervis, G. A. The mental deficiencies. In S. Arieti (Ed.), *American handbook of psychiatry.* New York: Basic Books, 1959.

Jolles, I. The diagnostic implications of Rorschach's test in case studies of mental defectives. *Genetic Psychological Monographs,* 1947, **36,** 89–197.

Kanner, L. *A miniature textbook of mental deficiency.* New York: Child Care Publications, 1949.

Kanner, L. *Child psychiatry* (3rd ed.) Springfield, Ill.: Charles C Thomas, 1957.

Kennedy, R. J. R. *The social adjustment of morons in a Connecticut city.* Hartford, Conn.: State Office Building, 1948.

Kennedy, R. J. R. *A Connecticut community revisited: A study of the social adjustment of a group of mentally deficient adults in 1948 and 1960.* U.S. Office of Vocational Rehabilitation, 1962.

Kirk, S. A. *Early education of the mentally retarded.* Urbana: University of Illinois Press, 1958.

Kirk, S. A., & Johnson, G. O. *Educating the retarded child.* London: Harrap, 1954.

Kodman, F. Sensory processes and mental deficiency. In N. R. Ellis (Ed.), *Handbook of mental deficiency.* New York: McGraw-Hill, 1963.

Kodman, F., et al. The incidence of hearing loss in mentally retarded children. *American Journal of Mental Deficiency,* 1958, **63,** 460–463.

Koffman, O., & Hyland, H. H. Tuberous sclerosis in adults with normal intelligence. *Archives of Neurology and Psychiatry,* 1959, **81,** 43–48.

Köhler, W., & Wallach, H. Figural after-effects: An investigation of visual processes. *Proceedings of the American Philosophical Society,* 1944, **88,** 269–357.

Kounin, J. S. Experimental studies of rigidity. *Character and Personality,* 1941, **9,** 251–282.

Kushlick, A. A comprehensive service for the mentally subnormal. In H. Freeman & J. Farndale (Eds.), *New aspects of the mental health services.* London: Pergamon Press, 1967.

Kushlick, A. Social problems of mental subnormality. In E. Miller, *Foundations of child psychiatry,* London: Pergamon Press, 1968. Pp. 369–411.

Lemkau, P., Tietze, C., & Cooper, M. Mental hygiene problems in an urban district. *Mental Hygiene,* 1942, **26,** 275–288.

Leontiev, A. N. The nature and formation of human psychic properties and processes. In B. Simon (Ed.), *Psychology in the Soviet Union.* London: Routledge, 1957.

Lewin, K. *A dynamic theory of personality.* New York: McGraw-Hill, 1935.

Lewin, K. *Field theory in social science: Selected theoretical papers.* New York: Harper & Row, 1951.

Lewis, E. O. *Report on an investigation into the*

incidence of mental deficiency in six areas: 1925–27. London: H. M. Stationery Office, 1929.

Liublinskaja, A. A. The role of language in the development of a child's perceptual ability. In B. Simon (Ed.), *Psychology in the Soviet Union.* London: Routledge, 1957.

Luria, A. R. (Ed.) *The mentally retarded child.* London: Pergamon Press, 1963.

Luria, A. R., & Yudovich, F. I. *Speech and the development of mental processes in the child.* London: Staples Press, 1959.

Lyle, J. G. The effect of institution environment upon the verbal development of imbecile children. I. *Journal of Mental Deficiency Research,* 1959, **3,** 122–128.

Lyle, J. G. The effect of institution environment upon the verbal development of imbecile children. II. *Journal of Mental Deficiency Research,* 1960, **4,** 1–13.(a)

Lyle, J. G. The effect of institution environment upon the verbal development of imbecile children. III. *Journal of Mental Deficiency Research,* 1960, **4,** 14–22.(b)

McCandless, B. R. Factors to environmental relation of intellectual functioning. In H. A. Stevens & R. Heber (Eds.), *Mental retardation.* Chicago: University of Chicago Press, 1964.

McCarthy, J. J. Research on the linguistic problems of the mentally retarded. *Mental Retardation Abstracts,* 1964, **1,** 3–27.

Malpass, L. F. Programmed instruction for retarded children. In A. A. Baumeister (Ed.), *Mental retardation.* London: University of London Press, 1968. Pp. 212–238.

Masland, R. L., Sarason, S. B., & Gladwin, T. *Mental subnormality.* New York: Basic Books, 1958.

Mein, R. Changes in intelligence test scores in cerebral palsied patients under treatment. *Proceedings of the First Congress of the International Association for the Scientific Study of Mental Deficiency,* 1967, 429–433.

Moncrieff, A. A., Koumidis, O. P., Clayton, B. E., Patrick, A. D., Renwick, A. G. C., & Roberts, G. E. Lead poisoning in children. *Archives of Disease in Childhood,* 1964, **39,** 1–13.

Mundy, L. Environmental influence on intellectual function as measured by intelligence tests. *British Journal of Medical Psychology,* 1957, **30,** 194–201.

Neale, M. D., & Campbell, W. J. *Education for the intellectually limited child and adolescent.* Sydney: Ian Novak, 1963.

Newman, H. H., Freeman, F. N., & Holzinger, K. J. *Twins: A study of heredity and environment.* Chicago: University of Chicago Press, 1937.

O'Connor, N., & Hermelin, B. *Speech and thought in severe subnormality.* London: Pergamon Press, 1963.

O'Connor, N., & Tizard, J. *The social problem of mental deficiency.* London: Pergamon, 1956.

O'Gorman, G. *The nature of childhood autism.* London: Butterworth, 1967.

Onondaga County Survey: *A special census of suspected referred mental retardation,* Community Mental Health Res., New York State Department of Mental Hygiene Report, 1955.

Owens, W. A. Age and mental abilities: A longitudinal study. *Genetic Psychological Monographs,* 1953, **48,** 3–54.

Penrose, L. S. *The biology of mental defect.* London: Sidgwick & Jackson, 1963.

Piaget, J. *The language and thought of the child.* New York: Harcourt, Brace, 1926.

President's Panel on Mental Retardation, *A proposed Program for National Action to Combat Mental Retardation*. Washington: Superintendent of Documents. U.S. Government Printing Office, 1962.

Richards, B. W. (Ed.) *Mental subnormality: Modern trends in research*. London: Pitman.

Rimland, B. *Infantile autism*. New York: Meredith Press, 1964.

Robinson, H. B., & Robinson, N. M. *The mentally retarded child: A psychological approach*. New York: McGraw-Hill, 1965.

Rotter, J. B. *Social learning and clinical psychology*. Englewood Cliffs, N.J.: Prentice-Hall, 1954.

Ruess, A. L. Some cultural and personality aspects of mental retardation. *American Journal of Mental Deficiency*, 1958, **63**, 50–59.

Saenger, G. *The adjustment of severely retarded adults in the community*. Albany, N.Y.: Interdepartmental Health Resources Board, 1957.

Sarason, S. B. Projective techniques in mental deficiency. *Character and Personality* 1945, **13**, 237–245.

Sarason, S. B. *Psychological problems in mental deficiency*. (3rd ed.) New York: Harper, 1959.

Sarason, S. B., & Sarason, E. K. The discriminatory value of a test pattern in the high-grade familial defective. *Journal of Clinical Psychology*, 1946, **2**, 38–49.

Segal, S., Blair, A., & Topper, Y. J. Oxidation of carbon-14 labelled galactose by subjects with congenital galactosaemia. *Science*, 1962, **136**, 150.

Seguin, E. *Traitement moral, hygiène et éducation des idiots et des autres enfants arrières*. Paris: Balliere, 1846.

Shapiro, M. B. An experimental approach to diagnostic testing. *The Journal of Mental Science*, 1951, **97**, 748–764.

Skeels, H. M., & Dye, H. B. A study of the effects of differential stimulation on mentally retarded children. *Proceedings of the American Association of Mental Deficiency*, 1939, **44**, 114–136.

Skeels, H. M., & Harms, I. Children with inferior social histories: Their mental development in adoptive homes. *Journal of Genetic Psychology*, 1948, **72**, 283–294.

Skodak, M. Children in foster homes. *University of Iowa Studies in Child Welfare*, 1939, **16**, 1–156.

Skodak, M., & Skeels, H. M. A final follow-up of one hundred adopted children. *Journal of Genetic Psychology*, 1949, **75**, 85–125.

Spitz, H. H. Field theory in mental deficiency. In N. R. Ellis (Ed.), *Handbook of mental deficiency*. New York: McGraw-Hill, 1963.

Spivack, G. Perceptual processes. In N. R. Ellis (Ed.), *Handbook of mental deficiency*. New York: McGraw-Hill, 1963.

Spradlin, J. Language and communication of mental defectives. In N. R. Ellis (Ed.), *Handbook of mental deficiency*, New York: McGraw Hill, 1963.

Stahlecker, L. V. *Occupational information for the mentally retarded*. Springfield, Ill.: Charles C Thomas, 1967.

Stein, Z., & Susser, M. Mental retardation: A 'cultural' syndrome. *Proceedings of the London Conference on the Scientific Study of Mental Deficiency*, 1962, **1**, 174–178.

Stevens, H. A., & Heber, R. *Mental retardation*. Chicago: University of Chicago Press, 1964.

Stolurow, C. M. Programmed instruction for the

mentally retarded. *Review of Educational Research*, 1963, **33**, 126–136.

Strauss, A. A., & Kephart, N. C. *Psychopathology and education of the brain injured child.* New York: Grune & Stratton, 1955.

Strauss, A. A., & Lehtinen, L. E. *Psychopathology and education of the brain injured child.* New York: Grune & Stratton, 1947.

Tizard, J. The residential care of mentally handicapped children. *Proceedings of the London Conference on the Scientific Study of Mental Deficiency,* 1962, **2**, 659–666.

Tizard, J. *Community services for the mentally handicapped.* London: Oxford University Press, 1964.

Tizard, J., & O'Connor, N. The employability of high-grade mental defectives. I. *American Journal of Mental Deficiency*, 1950, **54**, 563–576. (a)

Tizard, J., & O'Connor, N. The employability of high-grade mental defectives. II. *American Journal of Mental Deficiency*, 1950, **55**, 144–157. (b)

Tredgold, R. F., & Soddy, K. *Tredgold's textbook of mental deficiency*. London: Bailliere, 1963.

Wall, W. D., Schonell, F. J., & Olson, W. C. *Failure in school.* Hamburg: UNESCO, 1962.

Walsh, M. N., Koch, F. L. P., & Brunsting, B. A. The syndrome of tuberous sclerosis, retinal tumours and adenoma sebaceum. *Proceedings of the Mayo Clinic*, 1938, **13**, 155–160.

Watson, L. S. Programmed instruction with the retarded. *Mental Retardation Abstracts* 1964, **1**, 28–30.

Watson, L. S. Application of operant conditioning techniques to institutionalised severely and profoundly retarded children. *Mental Retardation Abstracts* 1967, **4**, 1–18.

Watson, L. S., & Lawson, R. Instrumental learning in mental retardates. *Mental Retardation Abstracts* 1966, **3**, 1–20.

Webb, C. E., & Kinde, S., Speech, language and hearing of the mentally retarded. In A. A. Baumeister, *Mental retardation.* London: University of London Press, 1968. Pp. 86–119.

Werner, H., & Strauss, A. A. Pathology of figure background relation in the child. *Journal of Abnormal and Social Psychology,* 1941, **36**, 58–67.

Werner, H., & Strauss, A. A. Impairment in thought processes of brain-injured children. *American Journal of Mental Deficiency,* 1943, **47**, 281–295.

Wolfensberger, W. Conceptual satiation: An attempt to verify a construct. *American Journal of Mental Deficiency*, 1963, **68**, 73–79.

Wolman, B. B., & Heiser, K. F. Mental deficiencies. In B. B. Wolman (Ed.) *Handbook of Clinical Psychology.* New York: McGraw-Hill, 1965.

Wolman, B. B. *Children without childhood.* New York: Grune & Stratten, 1970.

Woods, G. E. *Cerebral palsy in childhood.* Bristol: Wright, 1957.

Woodward, M. The application of Piaget's theory to research in mental deficiency. In N. R. Ellis (Ed.), *Handbook of mental deficiency.* New York: McGraw-Hill, 1963.

Zeaman, D., & House, B. J. The role of attention in retardate discrimination learning. In N. R. Ellis (Ed.), *Handbook of mental deficiency.* New York: McGraw-Hill, 1963.

Zigler, E. Rigidity in the feebleminded. In E. P. Trapp & P. Himmelstein (Eds.), *Readings on the exceptional child*. New York: Appleton-Century-Crofts, 1962.

Zigler, E., & Williams, J. Institutionalization and the effectiveness of social reinforcement.

Journal of Abnormal and Social Psychology, 1963, **66**, 197–205.

Zubin, J., Eron, L. D., & Sultan, F., Current status of the Rorschach test. I. A psychometric evaluation of the Rorschach experiment. *American Journal of Orthopsychiatry*, 1956, **26**, 773–791.

part iii | **Sociogenic Disorders**

12 | Neurosis in Childhood

Jane W. Kessler

DEFINITION OF NEUROSIS

Neurosis, an abbreviation of *psychoneurosis,* is a broad, inclusive term which is often used synonymously with *emotional disturbance,* mainly to differentiate certain behavior deviations from psychoses, which are more pervasive and profound in their effect, and from behavior disorders, which are presumed to be organic in origin. Clinicians with a psychoanalytically-oriented background use the term *neurosis* only to refer to a special form of emotional disturbance where there is an internalized, partially unconscious conflict, as opposed to those disorders which result from a conflict between the child and his environment or those which are a direct reaction to environmental conditions. However, many other clinicians, particularly those who take a learning-theory position, seriously question the validity of such a distinction and use the term for any behavior disorder which is neither psychotic nor organic. In view of the current controversy between the so-called disease model and the learning model, we shall try to avoid an a priori commitment and shall

first discuss the problems of neurosis in its more general, operational usage.

There is agreement that neurosis can take many forms, and this chapter is concerned with those emotional problems which are included in the diagnostic categories of phobias, hysteria, and obsessive-compulsive neurosis. These categories have two things in common which justify grouping them together. First, in all three states, the child is aware of feeling anxious. The specific symptom may be used to ward off this feeling—for instance, giving in to a compulsion or avoiding a phobic object may reduce anxiety—but it is rarely successful in the total elimination of anxiety. So we deal here with children who know what it means to feel anxious. The second common factor is that the child suffers more than the people in his environment, in contrast to those behavior disorders which involve antisocial acting out. As long ago as 1931, Ackerson distinguished between those disorders which result primarily in suffering for the child, "personality problems," and those which create suffering for others, "conduct problems." More recently, sophisticated efforts at classification have employed factorial approaches and have reached the identical conclusion, even sometimes to the words selected. Peterson identified two factors: "The first implied a tendency to express impulses against society and was labelled 'conduct' problem. The second contained a variety of elements suggesting low self-esteem, social withdrawal, and dysphoric mood. It was called 'personality' problem" (1961, p. 208). Achenbach factor-analyzed the symptoms from the case histories of 300 male and 300 female child psychiatric patients between the ages of 4 and 16 years and identified a bipolar first principal factor given the label of *internalizing* versus *externalizing*. The author states: "The label is not intended to carry dynamic implications. It means only that the symptoms at the externalizing end describe conflict with the environment, while those at the other end describe problems within the self" (1966, p. 10). Somatic complaints and obsessive factors (including obsessions, compulsions, and phobias) were two of the eight rotated factors identified, and it was found that all subjects classified by these two factors had already been classified by the internalizing end of the first principal factor, so Achenbach suggested that these factors represented subtypes within the one principal category. It is interesting to note the clear-cut sex difference reported in his study. When the subjects were classified according to the first factor, there were nearly twice as many externalizing boys as internalizing boys (128 to 68, respectively), whereas for girls, the reverse was true, with 63 externalizers and 143 internalizers. Comparing this finding with the usual sex ratio of 3 boys to 1 girl referred to clinics because of behavior disorders strongly suggests that adult persons (who, after all, are responsible for getting help for children) are far more concerned about the externalizers than about the internalizers. It also tells us that the problems with which this chapter deals are more characteristic of girls than of boys, which confirms the author's impression from clinical experience.

Factor-analytic studies such as those cited above give an empirical basis for grouping phobias, hysteria, and obsessive-compulsive neurosis together. Although such studies attempt to be operational and atheoretical, the investigators must perforce draw their material from clinical settings, where this terminology and categorization are traditional, which may influence the kind of clinical data available for factor analysis. However, investigators of many theoretical persuasions concur in differentiating behavior disorders along the dimension of the inward or outward effect of the symptom. Children with phobic, hysterical, obsessional, and compulsive symptoms share a tendency toward what is variously called *internalization, intropunitiveness, introversion* (in the sense the term is used by Eysenck), or *intrapsychic conflict*. This conclusion says nothing about the acquisition or maintenance of the neurosis, but says only that neurotic symptoms involve special inhibitions or demands which are imposed primarily on the self rather than acted out against others. This attribute, common to all neuroses, provides a consensual basis for a major differentiation within the broad category of emotional disturbance.

THEORIES OF NEUROSIS

Pursuing the topic of neurosis beyond the aforementioned generalizations leads into the current great debate as to the usefulness of the so-called medical or disease model and the learning model for explaining maladaptive behavior. Albee has been one of the most articulate spokesmen for the view that neurotic individuals are not "sick" and should be called something other than "patients" (1966b). He feels that psychiatrists, psychoanalysts, psychologists, and others who use the traditional terms regarding "mental illness" are making the assumption that behavioral problems are the result of a biological defect (1966a). He would propose instead that maladaptive behavior be understood in terms of past learning according to the same psychological principles used to explain "normal," or adaptive, behavior. *Behavior therapy* is a term coined by Eysenck (1959) to denote a system of psychotherapy which systematically applies learning theory to the problem of changing overt behavior patterns. One form or another of behavior therapy has been tried with almost every kind of psychopathology seen in children or adults with reported rates of cure generally higher than those reported for psychotherapy (Wolpe, 1965). Reading the popular as well as the professional literature gives one the impressing of a tug-of-war in which the learning theorists are depicted as pulling ahead, and the "traditional," psychoanalytically oriented clinicians are depicted as pulling backward (Hunt, 1967). Unfortunately, many workers feel that they must choose sides and have felt it necessary to sell or defend their position by simplifying their opponents' beliefs or by exaggerating their differences. At the present time, it is not at all in style to attempt reconciliation in the fashion of Shoben (1949) or Dollard and Miller (1950), who translated psychoanalytic concepts into the terminology of Hullian learning theory. Ullman and Krasner point out that these translations did not change the basic premises as to the importance of undoing repression and reconstructing the original cause of the neurotic symptom (1965). The present-day behavior therapists are seeking a revolution in our views about neurotic behavior whereby we would forget the issues of cause and the notion of an "unconscious" and look at the neurosis as "bad habits" to be extinguished by a systematic program. This is not an entirely new stand, but at the time of the first appearance of what would now be called "behavior therapy" (Watson & Rayner, 1920), there was no opposing Establishment. In the current struggle, professional identity is one issue, as the psychologists lay claim to the basic tenets of behavior therapy, but there are also strong medical proponents such as Wolpe. Whenever a comparison is made between psychoanalytic and learning-theory views, one should keep the following points in mind: (1) There is significant diversity of opinion within the two major camps; (2) some of the differences can be reduced to semantics; (3) some of the differences can be interpreted in terms of what is considered central versus peripheral; (4) some of the differences can be understood in terms of what is considered exceptional versus usual; (5) some of the differences exist more in theory than in practice; and (6) there is major irreconcilable disagreement on at least one point, namely, the role of internal factors in the acquisition and maintenance of neurotic symptoms.

Historical Development of the Psychoanalytic Theory of Neurosis

The essential ingredients of the psychoanalytic theory of neurosis have changed little since Freud's original exposition at the beginning of this century. One of his first contentions was that neurotic behavior is similar in kind to normal behavior, which was the major reason for his great interest in the psychology of dreams and the psychopathology of everyday life, such as forgetfulness, slips of the tongue, etc. The importance of Freud's study of dream psychology is twofold. First, dreams provide access to the unconscious mind and are thus useful in psychotherapy. Second, the interpretation of dreams, using dream symbols and the associations of the dreamer, is helpful in understanding the development of neurotic symptoms. Briefly, Freud enumerated three sources of dreams: (1) physical sensations impinging upon the sleeper, (2) the day's residue (i.e., memories and thoughts left over from the day's events), and (3) instinctual wishes. Such wishes become relatively stronger during sleep, when the vigilance of the ego is less and the potential for regression is greater. Even in sleep, however, the ego maintains some guard and reacts with anxiety if forbidden wishes are crudely expressed. If the anxiety is sufficiently great, the sleeper wakes up apprehensive and, in any case, discontinues the dream. It is assumed that the sleeper is motivated to preserve sleep and that, as long as possible, he defends himself against waking by disguising forbidden wishes, usually in such a way that the dream seems completely illogical. Neurotic symptoms, like dreams, are a compromise formation between a repressed element and the defenses of the ego. They also have an unconscious meaning which has been successfully disguised, at least to the patient, although the forbidden wish may be obvious to the onlooker. In his preface to the first edition of *The Interpretation of Dreams,* which appeared in 1900, Freud stated:

> The dream is the first member of a class of abnormal psychical phenomena of which further members, such as hysterical phobias, obsessions and delusions are bound for practical reasons to be a matter of concern to physicians. As will be seen in the sequel, dreams can make no such claim to practical importance; but their theoretical value as a paradigm is on the other hand proportionately greater. Anyone who has failed to explain the original of dream-images can scarcely hope to understand phobias, obsessions or delusions or to bring a therapeutic influence to bear on them. [1953, p. xxiii][1]

The premise of continuity has remained unchanged. Brenner remarked that the "phenomena of human mental functioning and behavior range from the normal to the pathological in much the same way as the spectrum of an incandescent solid ranges from red to violet, with no sharp line separating one color from the next" (1955, p. 197).

A second contention, somewhat related to the

[1] In this chapter, the dates given for works by Freud are the dates of publication of the *Standard Edition,* not the original dates of publication, which appear in the References.

first, is Freud's belief that there is a universal application of determinism to mental life and that it should be possible in theory to discover the psychological determinants of the smallest detail of the processes of the mind. No one would disagree that anything which occurs in the mind has some relationship to past events, but there would, of course, be disagreement as to the nature and importance of this relationship.

In understanding the relationship between present behavior and past events, Freud employs the concept of the unconscious mind in a way that learning theorists do not. In *On the History of the Psychoanalytic Movement,* he declares that "The theory of repression is the cornerstone on which the whole structure of psychoanalysis rests" (1957b). The starting point of psychoanalytic theory was clinical observations of adult patients who suffered such florid somatic symptoms as partial anesthesias, paralyses, epileptiform states, amnesias, etc., symptoms which legitimately brought them to the attention of the neurologists of that day. Initially, Freud related the onset of such symptoms to real-life experiences, although he realized that the long-lasting reaction was disproportionate to the actual event and suggested that the connection was often a "symbolic relation between the precipitating cause and the pathological phenomenon, a relation such as healthy people form in dreams" (1955d, p. 5). In his early writings, Freud was greatly occupied with the question of why the same event is experienced as traumatic by one person and dismissed by another, still a very important question. To understand the significance of a reality occurrence to an adult, he felt that one must go back to prior experiences in childhood which rendered him susceptible to trauma. The effects of such idiosyncratic trauma persist because of repression of affects (occasioned in part by the association with prior childhood experience), a hypothesis which he substantiated by observations of treatment results: "Each individual hysterical symptom immediately and permanently disappeared when we had succeeded in bringing clearly to light the memory of the event by which it was provoked and in arousing its accompanying affect, and when the patient had described that event in the greatest possible detail and had put the affect into words" (1955d, p. 6). He suggested that even though the original cause was no longer operative, the results lingered on, and he proposed that "hysterics suffer mainly from reminiscences," but he stressed that recall without abreaction was of little therapeutic value. These ideas regarding the acquisition of neurosis are somewhat similar to classical conditioning, where a stimulus evokes a response because of its similarity to a previous stimulus, and the treatment bears some resemblance to the desensitization procedures employed by present-day behavior therapists. There is, of course, a major difference in the role assigned to repression and the importance of verbalization in discharging the repressed affect.

Later on, Freud was to pay less attention to reality events and more attention to inner events, that is, fantasies and affects aroused as much by drives as by external circumstances, and here is where learning theory and psychoanalysis completely part company. In his expository lectures at Clark University, Freud asserted that the origin of neuroses was predominantly of a sexual nature: "The imperishable, repressed wishful impulses of childhood have alone provided the power for the construction of symptoms, and without them, the reaction to later traumas would have taken a normal course. But these powerful wishful impulses of childhood may without exception be described as sexual" (1957a, p. 41). This was the period when he was concerned with establishing the fact of infantile sexuality, its "polymorphous perverse nature," and the complications of the Oedipal complex. There would seem to be little doubt that sexual feelings, particularly when they are attached to homosexual or incestuous objects or when they are associated with oral or anal activities, evoke guilt and anxiety, repression, and subsequent symptom formation; however, it has been argued that Freud assigned too much importance to sexuality on the basis of the specific Victorian culture with which he was familiar. Much later, Freud modified his theory of drives to include aggression as the second basic drive: "In all that follows I adopt the standpoint therefore that the inclination to aggression is an original, self-subsisting instinctual disposition in man, and I return to my view that it constitutes the greatest impediment to civilization" (1961, p. 122). Clinical observations, as well as everyday experience, certainly bear out the impression that the manifestations of aggressive feelings cause a great deal of conflict between people and, subsequently, within a person.

A discussion of this dualistic theory of basic drives would lead far afield because ultimate validation will depend on biological rather than psychological theories. It is important to consider briefly to what extent Freud offered an "organic" explanation for neurosis. In a general, abstract way, he attempted to do so. His earlier training as a neurologist led him to resist the acceptance of psychological explanations as ultimate, and he sought a physical basis to explain *all* mental phenomena. He was particularly attracted to concepts of energy and thought in terms of a closed system. This accounts for the importance of the discharge of affects—so that the energy attached to the memory of the event can be released. Along this line, he offered the general "principle of constancy": "The mental apparatus endeavours to keep the quantity of excitation present in it as low as possible or at least to keep it constant" (1955b, p. 9). The energy concepts, or what are known as the "economic" aspects of psychoanalysis, are the most controversial and speculative of Freud's original contributions, and most clinicians have tended to slide over these concepts, finding them irrelevant to clinical practice. The important point is, however, that Freud was attempting to use the same biological principles for normal and abnormal behavior alike, and he did not think of neurosis as a disease. "Neuroses, unlike infectious diseases, for instance, have no specific determinates. It would be idle to seek in them for a pathogenic factor" (1964, p. 183).

Present use of psychoanalytically oriented concepts of neurosis as applied to children. The term *neurosis* appears in most present-day diagnostic nomenclatures. Definitions are not given in terms of the result or nature of the symptoms (as in the factor-analytic approach), but rather in terms of the source of the symptoms. The concept of internalization is the key point in one definition: "When the behavioral difficulties in a reactive behavior disorder have become fixated patterns which the child brings even to favorable circumstances, the term 'neurotic' is appropriately used" (Chess, 1959, p. 89). She distinguishes three types—neurotic behavior disorders, neurotic character disorders, and neurosis—on the basis of the degree of fixation and severity of the disorder. A more restricted definition is proposed by the Committee on Child Psychiatry of the Group for the Advancement of Psychiatry (GAP): "This category [psychoneurotic disorders] is reserved for those disorders based on unconscious conflicts over the handling of sexual and aggressive impulses which, though removed from awareness by the mechanism of repression, remain active and unresolved. Such neurotic conflicts are ordinarily derived from earlier conscious conflicts between the child and significant persons in his environment such as parents and siblings" (1966, p. 229). The report describes seven subdivisions based on the nature of presenting symptoms: anxiety type, phobic type, conversion type, obsessive-compulsive type,

depressive type, and the ubiquitous "other." In the GAP report, the general category of psychoneurotic disorders is differentiated from the other major categories of healthy responses, reactive disorders, developmental deviations, personality disorders, psychotic disorders, psychophysiological disorders, brain syndromes, mental retardation, and "other." As the fourth item in this list, psychoneurosis ranks as relatively healthy, compared with the disorders which follow it. In the sense the term *psychoneurosis* is used here, this diagnosis implies a level of social and intellectual maturity rarely reached before the age of 6 or 7 years. At this point, the conscience is an internalized part of the personality, so that the child suffers guilt and anxiety, which are no longer based on fear of external detection and punishment. From the intellectual side, the child is far more logical and seeks internal consistency for his various ideas and wishes. Although this kind of maturity has many good and desirable benefits for both the child and the parent, at the same time it renders the child vulnerable to internalized conflicts for which there is no easy escape.

Although problems of diagnostic nomenclature plague workers who deal with adults, the task of diagnostic labeling is far more difficult in the case of children. As a source of information, the child is notably unreliable. He changes unpredictably, depending on circumstances and on his feeling about the interviewer. Since the child seldom comes to an appointment on his own, it takes skill, or luck, to elicit significant psychological material, and the results vary with the experience and personality of the examiner. The diagnostician must rely heavily on secondhand information provided by parents, teachers, and pediatricians, all of which is subject to certain distortions. This is one reason why many have moved toward "family diagnosis," in which one hopes to make a direct observation of family relationships and problem behavior (Scherz, 1964).

Even more important, however, is the fact that the child is an immature organism. One cannot be sure about adults, but one can be sure that a child will grow and change. Diagnosis becomes, in part, an answer to the question: How much will the child grow out of this in the natural course of events? Most, if not all, problem behavior in childhood occurs normally at certain ages and is considered abnormal when the child is too old for its expected continuance. Also, one sees relatively rapid changes in child behavior because the child is still responsive to external circumstances. Many times parents backtrack on their own teaching spontaneously. For instance, if a child seems excessively kindly or sympathetic, his parents will try to reassure him about feeling or acting agressively under appropriate circumstances. Such action may stop a symptom in the process of "becoming." Even after a particular symptom-producing conflict is internalized, the child will need the support and encouragement of his parents in the change process.

Another corollary of the immaturity of the child is that neurosis rarely appears in the classical forms observed in adult individuals. Child analysts have been particularly aware of this phenomenon. Anna Freud remarked: "In children, symptoms occur just as often in isolation, or are coupled with other symptoms and personality traits of a different nature and unrelated origin. Even well-defined obsessional symptoms such as bedtime ceremonials or counting compulsions are found in children with otherwise uncontrolled, restless, impulsive, i.e., hysterical personalities; or hysterical conversions, phobic trends, psychosomatic symptoms are found in character settings which are obsessional" (1965, p. 151). Discussing the loose relationship between child problems and later adult disorders, Nagera commented: "What is observable in the large majority of cases [child] are not finished products in terms of character or neurosis but rather less well-defined, much more diffuse

neurotic and character organizations. There is a feeling of fluidity, or lack of definition, or processes potentially capable of developing in several directions, the final line not yet having been decided upon" (1966, p. 58).

In the face of so much fluidity and change, many have questioned the usefulness or validity of diagnostic classifications for children (Rexford, 1966). Hersch (1968) contrasted the contemporary intake procedures of two community clinics, operating under the same auspices (state of Massachusetts), one of which supports an extended and sophisticated diagnostic process, while the other curtails the process as much as possible. At present, diagnostic labels as such have little communicative value except in small circles of workers well acquainted with one another. However, the diagnostic process should not have labeling as its prime purpose, but rather a comprehensive description of behavior. This should be sufficiently broad-based and operationalized so that anyone can make use of any case-history record, but in current practice it is difficult to compare data from different sources.

The rapidly changing nature of children raises two other questions of practical concern which should be mentioned briefly: (1) How are children selected for referral? (2) How are children selected for treatment? As to the first question, many writers have complained that ". . . many things thought by some (psychiatrists) to be signs of serious abnormality are not so" (Valentine, 1956) and that ". . . symptoms figuring among the 'traits' found in the histories of 'problem children' are apt to be given too prominent a place, far out of proportion to their role as everyday problems or near-problems of the everyday child" (Kanner, 1960). Lapouse and Monk studied representative samples of school-age children using interviews of mothers and children and found that a great many so-called psychiatric problems were reported in these apparently normal samples (1959). Shepherd, Oppenheim, and

Mitchell (1966) carried out a similar survey in England. They questioned the parents and teachers of 6,920 schoolchildren, covering every tenth child between the ages of 5 and 15 attending guidance clinics with a partner of similar age, sex, and behavior from the "normal" school group. They concluded that the clinic children were *not* any more severely disturbed than the matched children, that 65 percent of the clinic group and 61 percent of the matched children had improved at the time of a 2-year follow-up, and that the only real difference between the two groups was in their mothers, with the clinic mothers seeing themselves as more "nervous." Such reports have led some to conclude that by concerning ourselves with those individuals who "happen" to appear in child-guidance clinics, we are offering the most treatment time to those who need it least (Lapouse, 1965). The whole question of "who is sick" and therefore of "whom to treat" has been a major issue in what Hersch (1968) has called the "discontent explosion in mental health" in the child-guidance field.

In this author's opinion, the survey findings of so much "abnormal" behavior in "normal" samples is not surprising and simply confirm the fact of a continuum from adaptive to maladaptive behavior, an idea which is often stated but rarely believed. It is particularly important to note that those symptoms which are considered in this chapter to be in the category of "psychoneurosis" are especially likely to appear in normal or unidentified populations. It is entirely possible for people to "get by" almost indefinitely with mild or moderate degrees of psychoneurosis for the very reason that it affects the individual more than those around him.

Probably the selection for treatment is more troublesome than the selection for referral since the latter could consist of a simple process of screening, whereas treatment is much more of a commitment for everyone concerned. Certain descriptive criteria are usually applied to test the need for treatment: (1) frequency of occurrence of symptom, (2) number of symptoms, (3) degree of social disadvantage, (4) the child's discomfort, and (5) intractability of behavior (Kessler, 1966). Intractability is implied, in part, in the criterion of frequency. It is conceivable that a child persists in behavior which is abnormal for his age simply because no one has suggested that he change. In neurosis, however, ordinary efforts to discourage the symptomatic behavior have proved futile. Another descriptive criterion is general personality appraisal in terms of the child's ability to get along with a variety of people and in a variety of situations. Anna Freud suggests that one should take a longitudinal look at the child's development rather than evaluate only the degree of impairment of current functioning:

> There is only one factor in childhood the impairment of which can be considered of sufficient importance in this respect (that is, indicating need for psychoanalysis), namely, the child's capacity to move forward in progressive steps until maturation, development in all areas of the personality, and adaptation to the social community have been completed. Mental upsets can be taken as a matter of course so long as those vital processes are left intact. They have to be taken seriously as soon as development itself is affected, whether slowed up, reversed, or brought to a standstill altogether. [1965, p. 123]

At a special psychoanalytic meeting devoted to problems of infantile neurosis, Hartmann commented that when Freud first approached this problem, neurosis was frequently taken to be naughtiness, but that he, Hartmann, observed a subsequent swing to the opposite extreme, where ". . . every naughtiness, actually every behavior of the child that does not conform to the textbook model, every developmental step that is not according to plan, is considered as neurotic" (Hartmann & Kris, 1954, p. 33). Many other psychoanalysts could be quoted to the same point, namely, that no symptom or bothersome behavior per se indicates a neurosis. The cardinal feature is the internalization of conflict within different structures of the personality (that is, the structures of id, ego, and superego). In discussing the role of external and internal factors, Anna Freud remarked that external events are distorted in the translation into internal experience and that once the external and internal pathogenic factors are intertwined, ". . . pathology becomes ingrained in the structure of the personality and is removed only by therapeutic measures which effect the structure" (1965, p. 51). Learning theorists strongly oppose such a distinction, which asserts that alterations in external reality are ineffective after a certain point, and have proposed instead that environmental manipulation continues to modify behavior, regardless of how ingrained it has become or what internal purposes it might serve.

Learning Theory and Neurosis

Early learning theorists were concerned with normal behavior and relied mainly on carefully controlled animal experiments for their data. Although Pavlov received the Nobel Prize in medicine in 1904, there is no mention of his work on conditioning experiments in Freud's writings because there was no apparent connection between the salivary reflex of dogs in Russia and the hysterical paralyses of neurotic women in Vienna. The general principles of classical conditioning, sometimes known as *respondent learning,* are generally familiar and acceptable. Classical conditioning consists essentially in the modification of a naturally occurring reflex pattern through substitution of a neutral or conditioned stimulus for the natural or unconditioned stimulus so that the former elicits the same response as the latter. Like Freud, Pavlov was concerned with relating behavior to the operations of the nervous system, which was in the scientific *Zeitgeist* of the times, but behaviorist psychologists soon discarded this particular goal. In the words of Wolman, "Hull, for example, did to Pavlov what

Horney did to Freud; Horney continued psychoanalysis without libido; Hull continued conditioning without the nervous system" (1960, p. 62).

In 1920, Watson demonstrated that fears in children could be established by classical conditioning. His subject was Albert, aged 11 months, who was first shown to be totally unafraid of furry animals such as a rabbit or a white rat. His natural reaction to a loud noise, however, was one of fear, and after a 7-day period during which a steel bar was struck with a heavy hammer at the moment Albert reached for the white rat, he came to react to the animal in the same fearful way. Watson then tested Albert with a rabbit, a dog, a fur coat, and cotton wool and found that the fear reaction had generalized to all furry objects and, further, that the reaction persisted for at least a month without repetition of the unconditioned stimulus (1920). This work was followed by studies of deconditioning children's fears by bringing the feared object into association with a pleasant stimulus (Jones, 1924). There was then a hiatus of some thirty years before these ideas were again picked up and used in the treatment of phobias. In the animal laboratory, Pavlov described another experimental neurosis evolved from classical conditioning principles, namely, the confusion and distress resulting when the animal cannot discriminate stimuli associated with pleasant and unpleasant events (1927), a situation somewhat analogous to the double-bind hypothesis of schizophrenia in which the person receives conflicting signals (Schuham, 1967).

The second kind of conditioning, now called *operant conditioning, Skinnerian conditioning,* or *instrumental learning,* involves voluntary behavior more than responses referable to the autonomic central nervous system (CNS), and the stimulus is less important than the response in the S-R formula. The central thesis here is that the choice of behavior is determined by the consequences or reinforcement which followed the same act on previous occasions. This was first stated by Thorndike, who called it the *law of effect:*

> Of several responses made to the same situation, those which are accompanied or closely followed by satisfaction to the animal will, other things being equal, be more firmly connected with the situation, so that when it recurs, they will be more likely to recur; those which are accompanied by or closely followed by discomfort to the animal will, other things being equal, have their connection with the situation weakened so that, when it recurs, they will be less likely to occur. The greater the satisfaction or discomfort, the greater the strengthening or weakening of the bond. [Thorndike, 1911]

Hull followed the same principle, although he used the term *need reduction* and felt that conditioning was dependent on need reduction, in opposition to some other learning theorists, such as Guthrie, who asserted that association by contiguity in time was the most important principle of conditioning (1935). The best-known contemporary exponent of operant conditioning is Skinner, who rephrased the law of effect as follows: "Instead of saying that a man behaves because of the consequences which are to follow his behavior, we simply say that he behaves because of the consequences which have followed similar behavior of the past. This is, of course, the Law of Effect, or operant conditioning" (1938, p. 87). This slight switch in verb tenses implies that man does not voluntarily choose a behavior because of what he expects but that he involuntarily repeats behavior which was successful in the past. All kinds of disturbed behavior can be evoked when the same response has been associated with pleasant *and* unpleasant consequences. After learning a response to obtain food, Masserman's cats displayed a great variety of reactions when the same response was paired with shock (1943). Here the confusion is not in the discrimination between stimuli but, rather, is due to the animal's inability to predict the results of his behavior.

Both psychoanalysts and learning theorists tend to minimize the idea of "free will" in man, although the former see man as the victim of his instinctual drives and past memories encapsulated in his unconscious, and the latter see him as the victim of past external events. A notable exception to this rule is Mowrer. Although he uses the language of learning theory, he takes a unique position with reference to free will and responsibility: "It is our thesis that in psychopathology the primary, basic *cause* is deliberate, choice-mediated behavior of a socially disapproved, reprehensible nature which results in emotional disturbance and insecurity because the individual is objectively guilty, socially vulnerable, and, if caught, subject to criticism or punishment" (1965, p. 243). It seems paradoxical that Mowrer contends that other behavior therapists, Wolpe, for instance, retain a basically Freudian theory, whereas Mowrer's formulation neatly fits the analytic concept of intrapsychic conflict between the ego and the superego—taking out the role of the unconscious. This is but another instance of the problem of categorization of theories; they do not fit into neat pigeonholes, and it is necessary to go beyond the general classification of a theory, take it apart, and inspect the component parts.

There are two premises basic to learning theory which deserve close inspection when we seek to use them in understanding the development of maladaptive behavior. The first is stimulus generalization, which, in learning-theory terms, means that there is a range of environmental events which are likely to produce a learned response. It is agreed that the more similar these stimuli are to those of the learning situation (whether in classical or respondent learning), the greater is the chance that the conditioned behavior will occur. The question is: What stimuli will be perceived as essentially similar, and why? Albert generalized from the white rat to all furry objects, and this is relatively simple, but why did he not generalize to all white objects or all moving objects? The range of generalizability varies from individual to individual, and this requires explanation. The second premise, even more troublesome, is the nature of reinforcement. The law of effect follows the psychoanalytic pleasure principle, "that the course of those events [mental] is invariably set in motion by an unpleasurable tension, and that it takes a direction such that its final outcome coincides with a lowering of that tension—that is, with an avoidance of unpleasure or a production of pleasure" (S. Freud, 1955b, p. 7). The key issues here are: What constitutes pleasure? What constitutes pain? Werry and Wollersheim touch briefly on this problem: "The efficacy of a given reinforcer depends on several factors such as the need state of the individual (food is unlikely to be effective if the subject has just satiated himself) and, in the human, a degree of idiosyncrasy stemming from the complex uniqueness of individual experience and our capacity for symbolism" (1967, p. 349). In their critique of learning theory, Breger and McGaugh comment that the concept of reinforcement is of only explanatory usefulness when it is specified in some delimited fashion. Otherwise, we arrive at "a state of affairs where any observed change in behavior is said to occur because of reinforcement, when, in fact, the change in behavior is itself the only indicator of what the reinforcement has been" (1965, p. 346).

Some very important contributions to the theory of reinforcement (and motivation) have been made by Bandura and his co-workers in their studies of identification, which they describe as "learning which apparently takes place in the absence of an induced set or intent to learn the specific behaviors or activities in question" (Bandura & Huston, 1961). Berger (1961) suggested the term *vicarious reinforcement* to account for the fact that under some circumstances, an individual may observe another person behaving, observe reinforcements being delivered to the other person in such a way that they seem contingent upon particular responses, and thereby have his own response tendencies altered in a congruent manner. This has led to a number of child studies investigating the social contexts in which vicarious reinforcement is effective. It is interesting to note one of these studies, which indicated that implicit reinforcement is most likely to be effective when the observer and the model are engaged in some sort of competitive task or when they perceive the amount of available reinforcement to be a discrete quantity, so that when one is praised, the other is correspondingly deprived (Sechrest, 1963). This is the situation which normally obtains for the young child, accounting for some of his intense jealousies and possessiveness as well as his susceptibility to vicarious reinforcement. Here one gets a hint of the importance of the nature of the perceiving organism exposed to certain stimuli and reinforcements in the S-R formula. Another such hint is provided in a clinical report of Peterson and London (1965) describing the combined use of verbal and behavioral measures in the treatment of a toilet-training problem in a 3½-year-old boy. These authors point out that understanding, acquired through verbal instructions and explanations, facilitates normal learning processes and is no less effective in the correction of maladaptive behavior. Without doing violation to either theory, this would seem to offer an avenue of legitimate rapprochement between traditional, psychoanalytically oriented techniques of psychotherapy and those of behavior therapy.

Learning theory and diagnosis. As one would expect, behavior therapists, by and large, have been little concerned with problems of diagnosis or classification of behavior disorders. Many behavior therapists agree with Eysenck's pronouncement that the presenting symptom is itself the neurosis, which obviates any need to search for specific causes (1959). When the traditional categories of phobia, hysteria, and obsessive-compulsive neurosis are used, it is only to provide a surface description of the deviant behavior. An example of symptom diagnosis is provided in the case of the *brat syndrome;* this term is used by Bernal, Duryee, Pruett, and Burns (1968) to describe the child who often engages in tantrums, assaultiveness, threats, and other aversive behavior. The authors describe the behavior-modification program of training the mother to set limits and enforce control, but it is interesting to note that before starting this, some major changes were made in the marital situation, with subsequent clarification for the boy. From the standpoint of diagnosis, the authors were content to assume that the aggressive behavior was the direct result of parental mishandling and tacitly suggest that this would be true in all such cases.

Pick (1961) is one of the behavior therapists who proposed a system of classifying children's problems in learning-theory terms by subdividing his "learning-psychological" diagnostic category into those disturbances attributable to (1) lack of learning, (2) inappropriate learning, and (3) learning of conflict. *Lack of learning* is another way of saying *lack of training* and refers to parental deficiencies in child rearing. *Inappropriate learning* refers to deficiencies in the models which parents provide for indentification. *Learning of conflict* is regarded as a special case of inappropriate learning in which anxiety or guilt is attached to behavior instrumental to need reduction. A simple example of this is furnished by the toddler who learns to climb on a chair to reach the cookies. His behavior is instrumental to his getting the cookies, which is need-reducing since he is presumably hungry and wants to eat them. But if the child is forbidden to eat the cookies, he learns a conflict. His disobedience gets him the cookies, but it also creates the danger of parental disapproval. This simple formulation is easy to follow because the conflict is between im-

mediate gratification and the possibility of disapproval, and both are real. The formulation becomes much more complicated when a series of displacements have occurred and when the troublesome conflicts are compounded of fantasy as well as reality.

Kanfer and Saslow proposed a guide to functional analysis of behavior which was written with adults in mind but which applies equally well, if not better, to children (1965). The outline is proposed as a guide for setting specific treatment goals and for determining the motivational controls which are at the disposal of the clinician. There are seven sections. The first is *analysis of the problem situation,* in which the individual's major complaints are categorized into classes of behavioral excesses and deficits with descriptions of frequency, intensity, duration, and stimulus-arousing conditions. The second is *clarification of the problem situation,* with consideration given to the people and circumstances which tend to maintain the problem behavior. The third is *motivational analysis,* in which the hierarchy of particular persons, events, and objects which serve as reinforcers is established. The other four sections are *developmental analysis, analysis of self-control, analysis of social relations,* and *analysis of the social, cultural, and physical environment.* This behavior analysis is no less complex, time-consuming, or elusive than the developmental profile proposed by Anna Freud (1965). However, the behavior therapist is interested in the details of present and past events so that he can understand what specific behavior has been learned, and under what circumstances, in order to change environmental conditions to permit new learning. Kanfer and Saslow make the important point that a diagnostic evaluation is never complete until the end of treatment. Only in retrospect can one ascertain with some degree of accuracy the factors which were crucial in maintaining the problem.

PHOBIAS IN CHILDHOOD

Definition of a Phobia

A *phobia* can be defined as an irrational and severe anxiety which is aroused in specific situations or by specific objects. There are two elements in this definition which require close examination: the irrationality of the fear and the intensity of the anxiety reaction. Many authors have proposed that anxiety be distinguished from fear on the basis that anxiety is a response to a subjective danger and fear is a response to an objective danger (Jersild, 1968). However, there is no difference in the psychological experience. It feels the same; the same somatic mechanisms are activated; and, further, it is often difficult to distinguish a real danger from an imagined one. For example, if a young child is afraid that a dog will bite him, his fear has a real basis if the dog is vicious and an imagined basis if the dog is friendly. If a child is afraid that a bridge will fall down as he passes over it and if the bridge is flimsy and rickety, his fear has a real basis. But it has an imaginary basis if the bridge is sturdy. In almost every instance, anxiety about external danger is at least compounded by the child's imagination, and the younger the child, the more difficult it is to evaluate the "objectivity" of his fears. Conversely, fears which take on phobic dimensions can be rationalized in some measure by objective considerations. Fears about traveling are justified when one considers the number of automobile and airplane accidents, but most of us dismiss such fears on the basis of probabilities and take the trip nevertheless.

Fears and phobias can be distinguished to some extent on the basis of the severity of the anxiety. In phobias, the reaction has the nature of an overwhelming panic which renders the child practically helpless. Also, phobias often contain a kind of obsessional quality, so that the person always has it in mind. Describing a patient who had a doll phobia, which does not sound too serious, Rangell remarked: "When one chooses an object for a phobia, he in a sense becomes married to the object. In order to avoid it, his eyes seek it out. He finds it in obscure places, he sees it with his peripheral vision" (1952, p. 43). It is the secondary avoidance behavior which is so handicapping in phobias of specific objects or animals.

It is very difficult to get a good idea of the real incidence of phobias in childhood because casual surveys do not differentiate between reported phobias and true phobias. A school-age child may express a dislike for dogs and be uneasy if one is nearby; this is a reported fear. If the child is preoccupied with the possibility of encountering a dog and is in a constant state of anticipatory anxiety, he may not want to walk to school, visit friends, or leave the house at all, to avoid the possibility of seeing or hearing a dog. This is a phobia. The hallmark of a phobia is the child's preoccupation with the object or situation he fears.

Developmental Aspects

Since there is little distinction between fears and phobias in very young children in the objectivity-subjectivity dimension, it is pertinent to examine briefly the empirical data on age trends in respect to fears. There are many typical fears which appear only when a child reaches a certain developmental level. For example, the fear of strangers which usually appears between the ages of 5 and 10 months is the by-product of the perceptual discrimination, memory, and emotional preferences of the age. Similarly, the separation anxiety of the 2-year-old involves some ability to anticipate what is going to happen in the near future and the way he is going to feel when his mother leaves him. In his review of this topic, Jersild (1968) points out that a child who is precocious or advanced in his development may be afraid of things which do not disturb other children. In an experimental laboratory study (Holmes, 1935), there was a positive correlation between intelligence and number of fears which declined with age (from .53 at age 2 years to .10 at age 5 years). There is also a characteristic change in the kind of fears, progressing from concrete objects to imaginary, unlikely objects or possibilities. One could say that a child learns to be afraid.

Although the young child has an excellent memory for things which he has perceived, it is easy to forget how much he misunderstands. On the basis of the egocentrism normal for the pre-school child, he assumes that everyone and everything shares the identical experiences with him and at the same moment, "essentially a phenomenon of undifferentiation, i.e., confusion of his own point of view with that of others or of the activity of things and persons with his own activity" (Piaget, 1951 p. 74). According to this view, objects and animals are alive and endowed with all the feelings and intentions of human beings like himself (animism). For instance, a little girl of 2 years who had a great fear of vacuum cleaners visited her grandmother and immediately asked where the vacuum cleaner was. Her grandmother, seeking to reassure her, replied, "The vacuum cleaner is in the closet taking a nap." After a moment's silent reflection, the child began to cry in terror. The fanciful explanation had not allayed her fears because anything which can sleep can also wake up, anything which can wake up can walk around, and anything which can walk around can be very loving or very angry and scary. The limitations in concepts of size, time, and distance also render the young child susceptible to fears which have no basis in external reality. For example, it is common for a toddler to develop a morbid fascination with plumbing drains, vacuum cleaners, and objects which make things disappear. There is nothing

which tells the toddler that he is too big to disappear in a like fashion. When people disappear, he cannot understand where they go or for how long. Also, we have to appreciate the concreteness of his thinking and the literal interpretation given to words with no judgment to temper what he sees and hears according to probabilities or logical impossibilities. When he hears his mother complain that "ants eat everything up," he imagines that he could be consumed as well as sugar. The special effects on television programs and commercials cannot but further convince him that anything imaginable is possible. Finally, the young child vastly overrates the power of his own words and thoughts. Since his first words usually resulted in something happening in reality, it takes a long time for him to understand that this magic occurred through the medium of communication with another person. To him, words and thoughts, which are poorly distinguished, have all kinds of powers to affect reality, whether there is anyone around to hear them or not. This accounts, in part, for the child's fear of his own aggression, i.e., that his bad wishes can very well come true. As later discussion will show, the same kind of primitive thinking is often involved in the formation of a neurotic phobia at later ages.

As children grow older, there is a decline in overt expression of fear, partly because imaginary fears do not elicit the same kind of visible, immediate reaction as that evoked by specific objects and partly because of the general tendency to suppress emotional reactions. In a survey of supposedly normal school-age children, Lapouse and Monk found that mothers frequently reported a child as having fewer fears and worries than the child himself reported (1959). As mentioned before, anxiety feelings bother the child much more than those around him and therefore are likely to go unnoted.

In dealing with young children, the reciprocal relationships between cognitive and emotional developments are relatively clear. Fears become increasingly ideational, linked with experiences which provide the material for imagined possibilities loosely generalized to all sorts of stimulus cues. Many times a young child's so-called phobic fear can be relieved by simple educational means to correct his misunderstandings. Other fears disappear spontaneously with the reassurance of greater experience. With much less attention to cognitive factors, psychoanalysts have spoken of phobias normal for certain ages, particularly around 4 to 5 years of age. Although these may have all the diagnostic criteria for a true phobia, they are usually transitory. Anna Freud speaks of such difficulties as "ubiquitous, inevitable, and, in fact, part of life itself." At this age, they are understood as a reflection of the Oedipus complex, which is "the prototype of an upsetting love affair, complete with hopes, expectations, jealousies, rivalries, and inevitable frustrations" (A. Freud, 1968, p. 39). The spontaneous resolution occurs then, not as a result of reassurance or intellectual understanding, but rather as the result of the child's moving away from the emotional entanglements with his family.

Acquisition of Phobias

In deference to the behavior therapists, we shall use the term *phobia* in the general sense of persistent, severe, and unreasonable fears rather than restrict it only to those special fears which psychoanalysts label *neurotic symptoms*. The preceding discussion indicated some causes of fears rooted in (1) growing awareness of potential dangers and (2) misunderstanding of what can happen and why. In the discussion to follow, the emphasis is on the origin of fears which persist beyond the expected time. Also, we shall use illustrations of animal phobias because of their frequency and relative simplicity. A high incidence of fear of animals in the age range from about 3 to 8 years has been found in a number of studies (Jersild, 1968); generally, such fears decrease in middle childhood. When the fears persist into adulthood, people manage to circumvent the anxiety by simple avoidance. Although dogs are the common feared animal, a large proportion of animals dreaded by children are creatures they will never encounter in the flesh, such as lions and wolves.

Proceeding from the simplest explanation to the most complicated, some fear is engendered by parental warnings to thoughtless toddlers to "be careful." Told that a dog can bite or that a cat can scratch, the toddler has no way of knowing when or why and may be overcautious. The explanation on the next level is simple conditioning; that is, the child is frightened by an animal biting, knocking him over, or whatever, or he sees this happen to another child and avoids all animals, as the burned child dreads the fire. To appreciate the anxiety of the young child confronted with even a well-intentioned but boisterous dog, one must take account of his small physical size and consequent feeling of helplessness. The case of little Albert involved a modification of direct conditioning in that the animal was innocent but associated with an unconditioned, fear-evoking stimulus. This does not happen frequently in real life, but it does illustrate the principle of generalization. It must be noted that Albert was only 11 months old and therefore could have no concept of the lack of any realistic causal relationships between the noise and the animal. An older child would not be so easily conditioned in just this way.

A third source is the child's imagination (or misunderstanding, if you will) regarding the potential danger of an animal. Occasionally a young child is quite comfortable with large, familiar animals but deathly afraid of tiny insects, which at first seems illogical. It is usually the biting of these insects which is overestimated, coupled with the fact that tiny animals appear and disappear very suddenly. For some children, the fragility of such animals causes a further complication. The squashing of a fly, mosquito, or crawling ant gives him a sense of power, but at the same time it seems possible, or likely, that someone in the animal world will seek revenge. The young child has no feeling that he can "get away with murder."

 Proceeding to the next level of complexity, or indirectness, <u>many fears arise from identification with someone else who is patently afraid.</u> Bandura (1967) illustrated this in reverse, that is, in the process of eliminating a fear. Nursery school children who were afraid of dogs were assigned to one of four groups. Children in the first session participated in eight brief sessions in which they watched a child without fear interact more and more closely with a dog in the setting of a "party," designed to make them generally comfortable. The children in the second group saw the same modeling but in a neutral context. The children in the third group saw the dog in a party setting, and the children in the fourth group joined the party without exposure to dog or child model. Experimental testing for avoidance behavior showed that most of the children who had received the modeling treatment had lost their fear of dogs. Again, there is probably a developmental factor to take into account in that the nursery school child is more prone to take over the attitudes and behavior of others than the school-age child.

The most complex acquisition of a phobia involves psychological defenses against internal impulses, as illustrated by the horse phobia of 5-year-old Hans reported by Freud (1955a). In his discussion of this phobia, Freud tied it in with concurrent nightmares, fantasies, and behavior of the child to show that Hans was in a state of intensified sexual excitement (with nightly masturbation) and also that he was concerned about the missing penis of the woman, interpreting the anatomic sex difference as a possible consequence of masturbation. Hans was afraid not only of horses biting him but also of carts, furniture vans, buses, horses that started moving, horses that looked big and heavy, and horses that drove quickly. He was afraid of horses falling down and soon included in his phobia everything that seemed likely to facilitate their falling down. After considerable talking (the analysis was carried out by the parents with the guidance of Freud), Hans recalled that just before the outbreak of the phobia he saw a horse fall down and kick about with its feet. He was terrified and thought the horse was dead, and from that time on he thought that all horses would fall down. This soon led to the expression of the wish that his father might fall down in the same way and be dead. The fact that his father had played "horsey" with Hans and allowed him to ride him like a horse helped in this identification. Freud pointed out a number of life events which stimulated Hans's jealousy of his father, for example, the fact that when his father was away, Hans slept with his mother. "Hans had learnt from experience how well-off he could be in his father's absence and it was only justifiable that he should wish to get rid of him." Further, as was common then, the stork was used to explain a baby sister's birth, a story which Hans easily recognized as a gross evasion. There were further elaborations involving Hans's confusion about impregnation and identifying birth as an anal process. "But this father, whom he could not help hating as a rival, was the same father whom he had always loved and was bound to go on loving, who had been his model, had been his first playmate, and had looked after him from his earliest infancy: and this it was that gave rise to the first conflict" (1955a, p. 134). This conflict forced the first step in defense, namely, repression of his death wishes. The second step was projection, a fear that something would do to him what he in fact wished to do himself, and the third step was displacement to an object outside the house, namely, the horse, which served as a father surrogate.

This synopsis does not do justice to the very full development in the case history, with a wealth of material spontaneously provided by the boy. In his final statements, Freud commented on the impression that such material would make on an uninitiated reader. At that point (1909), Freud was not so sure of the universality of the Oedipal complex and suggested that perhaps such early sexual feelings are correlated with intellectual precocity. He also commented on child-rearing philosophy: "It seems to me that we concentrate too much upon symptoms and concern ourselves too little with their causes. In bringing up children we aim only at being left in peace and having no difficulties, in short, at training up a model child, and we pay very little attention to whether such a course of development is for the child's good as well" (1955a, p. 143). It was no doubt remarks of this nature which were taken as a recommendation that instincts should be indulged and not suppressed. However, it is interesting in reading the case to see how much sexual seduction was practiced unwittingly because the possibility of exciting a small child was unthinkable 60 years ago. Basically, this triad of repression of a forbidden or conflicting wish, projection, and displacement still forms the base of the psychodynamic explanation of neurotic phobias of any particular form.

The care with which Freud teased out all the ramifications of Hans's dread of horses illustrates diagnosis as well as treatment. In the psychodynamic view, it is not enough simply to state that a child has been afraid of a particular object for some period of time; one would like to know precisely what characteristics of the object are feared, what are the surrounding circumstances which make the object safe or unsafe, what prior associations with the object existed for the child, and what event preceded the outbreak of the phobia. In psychoanalytic theory, such an external event is not regarded as the true cause (as it might be in learning theory), but it is important in illuminating the nature of the repressed conflict. Assuming that the phobia mirrors the repressed impulse by projection, the choice of object may give some hint as to its nature. For instance, lions and tigers are favorite choices for 5- and 6-year-olds because they so well represent wild, ferocious feelings which can get out of control. Robbers may represent the wish to steal something from someone. It is not hard to detect the repressed wish of a 10-year-old girl who was afraid to go to sleep for fear that a cobra would crawl into the bedroom of her New Jersey suburban home! In situational phobias, the circumstances may give the same clues. Using the example of a travel phobia, the disturbing factor may be the physical sensation of motion, the close contact with strange people, the fear of not returning, the possibility of accidents caused by wild drivers, and so on. One 9-year-old girl felt safe with women drivers, but only for short trips. On long trips, even with women drivers, she was afraid that they might be attacked by highway robbers. Another girl would travel only with some member of her family. She could not take school trips with her class because she foresaw that terrible catastrophes would befall them, but she was quite happy to stay behind and imagine them perishing. The fantasies of these two girls suggest that the first was struggling mainly with sexual wishes, and the second primarily with aggressive feelings. Sometimes the phobia represents more the expectation of punishment than the wish itself. A child who feels chronically bad considers himself deserving of punishment and anticipates it in various forms. He deserves to be sick, hurt, or even killed by the improbable dangers in his environment; he expects to fail an examination, he is sure no one likes him, and so on. Reassurance and actual experiences to the contrary do not change his expectations.

The fact that it usually takes time to get all the details about a phobia shows the continuing process of repression. As the child remembers how it all began, he also begins to remember what he was thinking at the moment of its occurrence. It is not expected that the specific psychodynamics of a phobia are known before starting psychotherapy, but these are the kinds of possibilities that the therapist would be considering.

Ancillary Causative Factors

All theories of neurosis tend to ignore the vexing question as to why one person develops symptoms and another does not under apparently the same environmental circumstances. It is, of course, true that no two people can have identical experiences throughout their life, but that seems to many like an evasion of the question. The founders of both learning theory and psychoanalysis postulated constitutional or inborn differences as important determinants of behavior, normal or abnormal. Pavlov suggested that there were constitutional differences in the nervous system (1941). According to Kalish, "Three types of nervous systems were identified: the strong in which inhibitory processes are considerably weaker than the excitatory; the weak, in which both processes are insufficient, especially the inhibitory; and the balanced, where inhibitory and excitatory processes begin at the same level. . . . While neurosis is produced by an individual's specific contact with life, the type of nervous system is exceedingly important in determining not only whether neurosis will occur but also what the specific form of the neurosis will be" (1965, p. 1246). Freud also placed considerable weight on heredity: "We divide the pathogenic determinants concerned

in the neuroses into those which a person brings along with him into his life, and those which life brings to him—the constitutional and the accidental—by whose combined operation alone the pathogenic determinant is, as a rule, established" (1958, p. 317).

The best-known contemporary exponent of the importance of constitutional factors is Stella Chess. She speaks of "temperament as an organismic contributor to the course of behavioral development" and defines temperament as "a phenomenologic term used to describe the characteristic tempo, rhythmicity, adaptability, energy expenditure, mood, and focus of attention of a child, independently of the content of any specific behavior" (Thomas, Chess, & Birch, 1968, p. 4). Although she feels that it is not immutable, it represents a "given" in understanding a child's susceptibility to his environment. Starting at the time of birth, Chess and her colleagues followed 136 children for a period of 12 years. Their families were upper middle class, predominantly Jewish (78 percent), residing in the New York City area. Forty-two of the children developed behavioral disturbances, as determined by the presence of symptoms and a psychiatric evaluation, although only one was officially diagnosed as a "neurotic behavior disorder." (The great majority were diagnosed as reactive behavior disorders.) In comparison with the rest of the sample, these children were different in temperament well before the development of symptoms, although there was overlap between the groups. The conclusion is carefully stated: "Therefore, to understand the etiology of behavior disorders it is insufficient to refer to temperamental organization alone. Such organization clearly modifies the degree or risk, but does not directly convert risk to reality" (Thomas, Chess, & Birch, 1968, p. 70). The longer a person works with children, the less content he is with any simplistic explanation of behavior disorders. For practical reasons, he may elect to work on a single aspect of a problem, but the principle of multiple causation should not be forgotten.

Once a phobia has been acquired, there are usually factors which serve to maintain it. This reinforcement can be real or apparent agreement with the child that his anxiety is justified. The parents may be so terrified of the child's anxiety attack that they assist him in avoidance, which gives him the impression that he is quite justified. Or they may even share the phobia to a lesser degree, so that their attempts at reassurance ring hollow. Another kind of reinforcement is in the secondary gains from the symptom. Freud points out that Hans's phobia was an obstacle to his going into the street and thus served as a means of allowing him to stay at home with his beloved mother. In this way, his affection for his mother triumphantly achieved its aim, albeit in a disguised, innocuous form, so that: "The true character of a neurotic disorder is exhibited in this twofold result." There is no doubt that any phobic child obtains extra attention and enjoys a perverted sense of power as the parents try helplessly to deal with the tyrannies of his symptom. The reinforcement provided by such secondary gains must be minimized in a treatment program dictated by either psychodynamic or learning-theory principles. In behavior therapy, this is extinction due to nonreinforcement and is accomplished by "withholding reward" (Werry & Wollersheim, 1967) or "omission training" (Kalish, 1965). This technique alone is rarely sufficient; it is a first step.

Principles of Treatment

Behavior therapy. Behavior therapy started in 1924 with the reports of Mary Cover Jones on the elimination of children's fears. Her method was to combine eating with the appearance of the feared object. The object was placed far enough away so that the child continued to eat and then was brought closer and closer until the child was able to ignore its presence (1924a). These were young children described as eating in high chairs. In the case of 3-year-old Peter, who had a fear of white rats, rabbits, fur, cotton, wool, and other such stimuli, she added the "modeling" technique. Peter was placed in a play group with three fearless children, and the rabbit was brought into the room for short periods each day (1924b). These experiments were a deliberate effort to follow the pattern of Watson and Rayner (1920) and to show that fears could be created and extinguished by the same conditioning processes. After this abortive beginning, behavior therapy went into a latency period, partly because of the ascendancy of psychoanalysis and partly because of the psychologists' inclination to keep their science "pure" in the laboratory.

In the recent renaissance period, behavior therapy has been reported with individuals of all ages and kinds of problems. Basically, behavior therapy techniques involve variations or combinations of two basic themes: changing the stimulus conditions which arouse the maladaptive response and changing the response by modifying the reinforcement. If the stimulus is specific and known, as in the case of phobias, the former approach is preferred. When the maladaptive behavior is diffuse and aroused by a great variety of nonspecific stimuli, as in the case of psychosis, delinquency, or the "brat syndrome," the response is attacked directly through some combination of reward, omission, and punishment reinforcement schedules. In the present context, it is more appropriate to discuss the first model, which is derived from classical conditioning principles, specifically those of reciprocal inhibition. The method of "systematic desensitization" has been carefully detailed by Wolpe (Wolpe & Lazarus, 1966), and in its present form consists of three steps. By the person's own report, an *anxiety hierarchy* is established in which the phobic themes are identified and then is subdivided into a list of specific stimuli, graduated according to the degree of anxiety aroused. Wolpe comments that this is not easy to do because the first report may not be an accurate report of the true source of fear. In the process of establishing this anxiety hierarchy, the professional person must go through a careful exploration of the reported phobia, not unlike the initial procedures of the psychoanalyst. In discussing some snags and pitfalls of desensitization therapy, Wolpe mentions the failure to identify the "true source" of the phobia because the generalization, or displacement, is so highly symbolized as to be unrecognizable. In his opinion, these are the unusual cases, but may be "what led Freud to the presumption that all phobias have a hidden 'real' source" (Wolpe & Lazarus, 1966, p. 93).

The second step, which is unique to behavior therapy, is the *training in relaxation* of the deep muscles. This may be accompanied by drug therapy or light hypnosis, but it is necessary by some means to establish a definite relaxation response as a physiological state incompatible with anxiety, which then acts to inhibit the anxiety response. The third step is to instruct the patient to imagine himself in anxiety-generating situations, starting with the least frightening in the hierarchy, and this imagery is alternated with deliberate relaxation. There are some other features which are referred to in a peripheral way, such as "other interviews in which a desensitization session does not occur" and "assertive training," which "covers a range of methods of promoting change of behavior in the patient's life situation" (Wolpe & Lazarus, 1966, p. 38).

Bentler reports the treatment, using reciprocal inhibition therapy (1962), of an 11-month-old child with a fear of water. His basic rule was that Margaret should be exposed to only small amounts of anxiety, and attraction toward toys and body contact with the mother were used to elicit responses which were presumed to be incompatible with anxiety. By being gradually reintroduced to the bathtub, the scene of the original trauma of falling, Margaret overcame her fear in a month's time. It is important to point out the very young age of this child; one would not expect a fear in an 11-month-old to have much ideational content. The procedures followed were certainly thoughtful and appropriate to her age. It should be pointed out that many infants have a transient fear of water, or the bathtub, and sensitive parents are likely to follow much the same procedures. It would be the unusual mother who would (1) force a screaming child back into the bathtub or (2) spare the child any kind of further exposure to water. The phobias of school-age children are admittedly much more complicated, and a further account of desensitization procedures will be given later in the discussion of school phobias.

Rachman (1967) recently reviewed the experimental investigations of systematic desensitization and concluded that the alternation of confrontation (in imagery) and relaxation is essential for best results. From his review, he concludes that response to treatment is not related to suggestibility; that relaxation or hypnosis, with or without interpretive therapy, does not reduce the phobia; that desensitization without relaxation is less effective; and that the establishment of a therapeutic relationship does not in itself reduce the phobia. He states that the learning process involved is conditioned inhibition rather than simple extinction and that it is in no way dependent on insight as to cause, for either the therapist or the patient. The fact that the treatment works in the majority of cases, without subsequent relapses or symptom substitution, he takes as further confirmation that underlying causes are unimportant. This is the essence of the position of the behavior therapists.

Psychoanalytic therapy. The essence of psychoanalytic treatment is treatment of the underlying cause rather than the overt symptom. There are many who do not choose psychoanalysis as the specific form of treatment but who use similar principles in group therapy, family therapy, or other types of psychotherapy. However, not every childhood fear should be considered a phobia. Lippman contrasts neurotic anxiety with "objective fears which can be troublesome and very disturbing to the child" and suggests that a "discussion of the reasons for their reality fears may help them to accept the fears and later to overcome them." He goes on to suggest that a fearful child may be "unconditioned by games that are pleasant or rewards that give him pleasure" (1967, pp. 83–84). The guidelines for differential diagnosis are not well spelled out in the literature, but the children with neurotic phobias tend to have multiple, persistent, and overwhelming fears which have supposedly resisted ordinary educational efforts of reassurance and encouragement. In addition, there are usually character traits of exaggerated dependency and avoidance defenses for any kind of difficult or unpleasant situation.

Given the diagnosis of neurotic phobia, psychodynamically oriented therapists assert that suppression of the symptom without modification of the underlying cause will lead to symptom substitution. The validity of this contention has caused great debate in the literature (Bookbinder, 1962; Holland, 1967; Speigel, 1967; Yates, 1958b, 1962). The theory of symptom substitution rests on the assumption of a "closed-energy" personality system, with the symptom serving as a mechanism for the expression of an internal conflict of drives. The empirical evidence comes in part from case histories and also from follow-up studies of hypnotic "cures" (Bookbinder, 1962; Holland, 1967). It was the failure to achieve lasting results with hypnosis or suggestion which

originally led Freud to the technique of psychoanalysis, where the patient remains wholly conscious and an active participant. In his review of the controversy, Cahoon (1968) points out the communication problem between the dynamic therapists and the behavior therapists, who reject the concept of symptom altogether. Continuing difficulties to the behavior therapist mean that " . . . the contingent stimuli that previously maintained the maladaptive behavior may come to support other maladjustive behavior" (1968, p. 153), and the behavior therapists are in agreement that removal of symptoms must be followed by retraining of new behavior. The cause and cure, however, remain in the environment. There is no easy resolution to this argument because both sides tend to see what they expect. One important point should be kept in mind when evaluating follow-up reports: The notion of symptom substitution does not imply that one phobia will be replaced by another; it is more likely to take quite a different form. For example, some children with chronic learning inhibitions have a history of a brief school phobia which has been handled by the parents by rigid enforcement that "you must go to school," without any consideration for the child's feelings. Isolated cases of this sort do not prove that all children cured of school phobias will have learning problems, or vice versa, but they do illustrate the principle that the new symptoms may look entirely different from the old.

The principal means of dynamic therapy are (1) child-therapist relationship, (2) work with the mother, (3) spontaneous play with conversation, (4) release and acceptance of feelings, and (5) interpretation. For the sake of simplicity, we shall draw illustrations from the analytic reports of phobias in preschool children. An excellent description of the total treatment of a 3-year-old girl with stammering and an insect phobia is given by Kolansky (1960). This treatment, which extended over a 40-day period with thirty-six sessions, was carried out with the mother present, which is not unusual in the case of young children. Kolansky felt that being present helped the mother to understand and change her educational ways at home and also that "Many of the interpretations made to Ann were immediately reinforced by the mother, making Ann's acceptance of these more immediate." It is obvious that it is very difficult for a child to be getting different messages from therapist and parents; this can only exacerbate any loyalty conflict the child may have in his feelings of allegiance to one or the other. Although the therapist tries to establish a positive relationship in which the child can trust him completely with his "secrets," he does not want to replace the mother in the child's affections or leave the mother feeling out in the cold. In the long run, it is the parents who will have the greatest influence on the child, and they must be able not only to support the treatment but also to continue when it is finished.

Play has been used in various ways in child therapy (Woltmann, 1952). In analytic therapy, the child's spontaneous play is used as a way of gaining an understanding of his conflicts and feelings, a natural substitute for the technique of free association in the adult person. Some analysts, of the Kleinian school, feel that all play can be interpreted in the light of the unconscious; others, who follow Anna Freud's thinking, are more cautious in interpretation and watch for repetitions or unusual themes. However, with preschool children it is in the context of play that release of feelings and interpretations take place. Again, there are differences between the dynamic therapists as to how much verbal explanation must take place. For example, in Levy's "release therapy," it is sufficient to abreact the original traumatic events and to express the inhibited instinctual wishes with the approval of the therapist but without comment. Kolansky

points out that in psychoanalysis, there is a systematic analysis and interpretation of the symptom picture. For instance, when Ann was playing the "bee game," Kolansky suggested that perhaps she had wanted a bee to bite her younger sister, or that perhaps even she had wanted to bite her. Since the death of this sister had been explained as the result of a "bad bug" (infectious disease), Kolansky later connected these ideas for Ann and then reassured her that she would not die, not even if a "bug" bit or stung her. Working with a 2-year-old child with many animal phobias, Sperling noted that Linda was very frightened when a piece of a paper doll was accidentally cut off. Then she proceeded to tear the doll up saying, "Nothing happens, we can even cut it up, nothing happens. It is only a paper doll" (Sperling, 1952, p. 119). Later, she connected this with the child's experience of a tonsillectomy and her observation of the sex difference.

The analytic case reports are unanimous in showing a conflict over aggression, specifically in the fear of biting or soiling (representing a defiant act against the mother's expressed wishes), and in analysis the projected fear is traced back to the source in the child and then followed by the reassurance that he is still a "good" child, that he is still loved, that retaliation is not forthcoming, and that nothing terrible will happen. Something similar to this interpretation occurs in the analysis of phobias in children of any age. It "works" to change behavior because "Exposure of the unconscious death wishes results in a devaluation of the magical qualities attached to unconscious thought processes" (Sperling, 1967). Contrasted with this psychoanalytic explanation, Rachman and Costello reinterpreted the psychoanalytic cases according to the principle of desensitization (1961).

It is interesting that almost all the early child phobias reported in the analytic literature have involved little girls (Bornstein, 1935; Kolansky, 1960; Schnurmann, 1949; Sperling, 1952); and that another theme has been the missing genital, which the little girls often thought had been bitten off, taken away as punishment, or in some way destroyed by their own doing. It is true that girls are more likely than boys to develop phobias and other inner-directed neuroses, whereas boys are more likely to identify with the aggressor and express their conflicts by acting out, perhaps because the expression of fear is more allowable for girls. Boys, much more than girls, may show obvious counterphobic mechanisms where they are irresistibly drawn to the objects they fear most, trying to master their fears by denying their existence. The denial is betrayed in the fact that they may actually endanger themselves despite repeated warnings.

Results of treatment with phobias, by any method, are generally good and relatively rapid, so there is no way of validating theory by comparing efficacy of treatment. As indicated, treatment methods in practice tend to be contaminated by a mixture of explanation, desensitization, uncovering the repressed or "forgotten," and acceptance of feelings (the assertive training in Wolpe's program, for example). It is hard to determine the critical factor. In the author's view, one should keep an open mind to all possibilities. Particularly with young children, one should start with the most parsimonious explanation and the simplest procedures, including (1) education as to reality, (2) gradual desensitization, (3) elimination of secondary gains, and (4) presentation of adult and child models who are *not* afraid. However, one should be prepared for more complex possibilities. If the anxiety is not lessening within a matter of weeks, one should consider the complications introduced by the defense mechanisms of repression, projection, and displacement of aggressive wishes and/or sexual anxieties and start the unraveling process leading to eventual insight. Unfortunately, those who are skilled in behavior therapy tend to limit themselves to these tools, and con-

versely, the psychoanalysts tend to look at all expressed fears as if they had the complexity of a neurotic symptom.

School Phobia

Without question, the phobia of greatest concern (and one unique to childhood) is school phobia. Because of compulsory school attendance laws, it invariably comes to the attention of the authorities, who must distinguish phobia from truancy. In the former case, the child refuses to go to school and remains at home with the parents' knowledge, if not their consent. Truant children, on the other hand, show no inclination to remain at home, and their whereabouts are unknown to their parents. As Davidson expressed the idea, "While the truant runs away from school, the school phobic runs back to mother" (1961). Whatever superficial similarity there may be in sharing the problem of refusal to attend school is completely overshadowed by major differences in related characteristics, home backgrounds, school history, and personality dynamics between the two groups (Hersov, 1960a, 1960b).

Reviewing the literature for characteristics of children with school phobia indicates no sex difference. In fact, the data given in nine reports indicate an even number (106) of girls and boys (Coolidge, Willer, Tessman, & Waldfogel, 1960; Davidson, 1961; Eisenberg, 1958; Hersov, 1960b; Klein, 1945; Suttenfield, 1954; Talbot, 1957; Van Houten, 1947–1948; Waldfogel, Coolidge, & Hahn, 1957). School phobia may occur at any age and seems to have little to do with the "newness" of the school itself; for instance, it is much more common in the first grade than in kindergarten. The onset of phobia may be related to changing expectations in the school situation, however, but it is hard to validate this hypothesis from the data in general surveys. The epidemiology of school phobia has not been investigated systematically, but it seems to be a phenomenon of higher socioeconomic levels (Hersov, 1960b). Milman suggests that perhaps when school phobia occurs in underprivileged groups, it is labeled "truancy" and handled in an authoritarian rather than in a sympathetic manner (1966), but there are probably other social and cultural influences which operate before the child demonstrates the first sign of refusing to go to school. It would be interesting to know the incidence of school phobia in the homes of working mothers, for instance, where the secondary gains would be minimal. Interestingly, children with school phobia tend to be bright (which may go along with the social and cultural factor) and generally are doing well in their schoolwork. This is most clearly demonstrated in Hersov's comparison of fifty truant, fifty phobic, and fifty control children, where only four of the phobic, as compared with thirty-one of the truant and eighteen of the control group, had a "poor standard of school work" (1960). It is one of the paradoxes in the psychopathology of childhood that youngsters with school phobia who are "successful" in school by objective standards are frightened away, whereas other children who are having learning problems continue to attend with apparent enjoyment. It provides a clue that the source of the phobia is in the perceived rather than the actual reality of school.

Most children have expressed some reluctance to go to school either directly in words or by alleged aches and pains. Usually, their desire to be with their friends, and the parents' firm insistence, overcomes their resistance. In the case of a school phobia, the reluctance is transformed into an acute anxiety reaction which makes the parents uncertain and starts a vicious circle within the child, who then becomes afraid of the anxiety symptoms per se. Once the phobia is there, it cannot be ignored. Lippman gives a graphic portrayal of what happens:

> The next morning when it was time for Anne to leave for school, her parents became anxious. Her father was annoyed by what he termed "nonsense";

there was nothing to fear. Anne admitted as much. He had to go to work and he became angry as Anne started to cry and he insisted that she put on her wraps and come along with him to school. When the mother acted as though she felt he was doing the wrong thing, he became more annoyed; the mother's behavior increased his doubts about what he was doing. Realizing that this was no time to change his mind, however, since that would only confuse Anne more, he got into the car with her. Anne cried all the way to school, saying she knew she could not make it. Her father assured her that she would get along well as soon as she was at her desk with all her friends around her. Anne and her father walked up the school steps, but as they approached the entrance, Anne grew pale and vomited. [1956, p. 86]

In the specific instance of school phobia, there has been a great deal said about the causative role of the parents. Davidson treats school phobia as a manifestation of family disturbance and describes the mothers as ambivalent and so afraid of their aggression, which they often show in outbursts of exasperation, that they cannot support the child with any degree of firmness and tend to be inconsistent in their handling. Coolidge et al. also attribute the overprotectiveness of the mothers to their ambivalence (1962). Davidson describes the mother as immature and dependent on the maternal grandmother, tending to repeat the relationship with the child that she has with her own mother. Although she may profess to be encouraging the child to return to school, she unconsciously acts in the opposite direction (1961). A. M. Johnson shares this view, considering school phobia a specific form of separation anxiety, a fear of separation shared equally by mother and child, with the mother's problem antedating the problem in the child (Johnson, Falstein, Szurek, & Svendsen, 1941). Eisenberg described the behavioral cues by which mother and child communicate their anxiety about separation to each other (1958), and Estes, Haylett, and Johnson (1956) talk about the complementary neurosis of the mother (1956).

These writers stress the fact that children with school phobia are generally dependent and immature well before the outbreak of the phobia, confirming Andrews's hypothesis that phobic individuals tend to avoid *any* activity which involves independent, self-assertive handling of difficult situations (1966). The learning of the phobia as well as the development of the dependent character are explained in a social-learning context, with the mother as both the model and the reinforcer. These conclusions are particularly interesting because none of the writers cited would consider himself or herself a behavior therapist.

In this author's opinion, the responsibility of the mother is nowhere near as clear-cut as it might seem at first glance. First, the same kind of psychopathology has been observed in mothers of children with very different problems (e.g., psychosis or psychosomatic diseases). Second, school phobia does not run in families, so the affected child must have a special susceptibility. Third, we have no way of knowing how many other mothers have the same problems since our information is gathered *after* the children's symptoms are reported. In reading case histories, it is hard to tell which came first, the child's distress or the mother's overprotectiveness. However, whatever the origin of the phobia in the child, an immature mother will have a more difficult time in coping with the child's anxiety and so may unintentionally prolong it.

Sperling makes a useful distinction between what she calls an "induced school phobia," where "we are dealing with a more insidious traumatization of the child due to the pathological parent-child relationship," and the "traumatic or common type of acute school phobia" (1967). She would treat the parent in the first case and the phobic child in the second. If a precipitating event can be identified, it speeds up the treatment process. The event is seen as the cause only because of its symbolic meaning. "The traumatic event is usually one that represents a danger to the child's ability to control reality; that is, a danger of loss of control over a situation or object (usually the mother). In the final analysis, this extreme need for control reveals itself as a wish for control over life and death, and the fear of the phobic patient (child or adult) is a fear of death" (Sperling, 1967, p. 378). Behavior therapists also have identified the fear of death as basic. Lazarus commented that a child of 9 years "was in fact not afraid to go to school, but was afraid that her mother might die before she returned home from school" (1960, p. 117), and Garvey and Hegrenes found that their case "had an intense fear of losing his mother, illustrated by his fantasies about the various kinds of harms that could happen to her and by his fantasies about what would happen to the family if his mother were to leave" (1966, p. 149). In a similar vein (although from a different background), Coolidge et al. state that "The central concern in the child is the fear of abandonment by the parents. The child fears that some danger from the outside world will befall the parents, particularly the mother, and that thus abandoned, he will either die of lack of care or because of lack of protection be a victim of violence from the outside world" (1962, p. 330). Davidson found a high incidence of deaths or threatened deaths, in the form of severe illness, preceding the onset of school phobia in her thirty cases (1961). Here we see remarkable agreement among workers of differing theoretical persuasions concerning the nature of the fantasies of the child with school phobia. The extent to which the child's conviction that his worst fears will come true can be justified by external events would be more debatable.

Notwithstanding this clinical documentation, again in the author's opinion, it would be a mistake to label all school phobias as separation anxiety revolving around the fear of permanent loss. There are some children with school phobia who are quite comfortable about their parents' leaving them at home or who are comfortable about leaving home for some place other than school. There are fear-arousing features of school beyond the single fact of separation from parents. There are some children who fear the teacher, greatly exaggerating her punitive attributes. There are others who fear their classmates and anticipate ridicule or bullying, again out of proportion to the facts. There are still others who have an unreasonable fear of failure. Although aggression, in its imagined consequences, is paramount in school phobias, there may be guilt over sexual feelings with expectation of punishment. The case of Mary Ann, whose treatment was reported in some detail by the author (Kessler, 1966), contained many sexual fantasies as well as overt sexual behavior, about which she was tremendously anxious and guilty. This girl verbalized her wish to replace her mother in her father's affection and her jealousy of grown-up women, which had been displaced to her teacher. After this displacement, she was able to tolerate separation from her mother except in school. She was particularly content if her mother left her home with her father. Although aggression was involved, it was stimulated by her sexual wishes. One would suspect that the dynamics for girls might be quite different from those for boys; perhaps boys with school phobias are more generally immature and dependent, with less sexual involvement.

The treatment reports contain the variety one would expect, although most of them report success in fairly short order and are unanimous in recommending that the child return to school at the earliest moment, at any level of school participation that he can tolerate. This gradual return to school is systematically programmed in behavior therapy with varied application of classical and operant conditioning methods. Garvey and Hegrenes give the most straightforward account of the small steps by which 10-year-old Jimmy was "desensitized" to school. The therapist and Jimmy began by coming to school early in the

morning when no one else was present. Jimmy was told to report any uncomfortable feelings, and when he said he was feeling afraid, the therapist immediately indicated that it was time to return to the car and generously praised Jimmy for what he had accomplished. After a period of 20 days, he returned to school completely. The authors explained the success on the basis of counterconditioning, or reciprocal inhibition. "Since Jimmy and the therapist had a good relationship, the presence of the therapist may be considered as a relatively strong stimulus evoking a positive affective response in the patient," and this inhibited the anxiety response connected with school. They point out that ". . . a cue weak in evoking anxiety is paired with a cue strong in evoking a positive response, and the stronger anxiety-evoking cues are approached gradually"; otherwise, the fear response becomes attached to the therapist. Although they emphasize the classical conditioning procedures, they also used operant conditioning by giving generous praise for whatever approaches he made, and they were accepting of his feelings, allowing him to control the pace of his treatment (Garvey & Hegrenes, 1966).

In Jimmy's case, there is no indication of work with the parents, but others have involved the parents in reinforcement procedures. Patterson (1965) describes the treatment of 7-year-old Karl, in which desensitization was started by doll play structured in the office to reproduce the situation of going to school. Reinforcement consisted of both praise and candy, which were given whenever Karl reported that the boy doll was not afraid, in marked contrast to the method of Garvey and Hegrenes, who permitted the child to express his anxiety. After twenty-three 15-minute sessions, four times a week, Karl returned to school. Patterson concluded that ". . . one of the crucial variables involved in this procedure is the reinforcement contingencies being used by social agents other than the experimenter" and felt that ". . . the highly structured interviews with the parents are of particular importance in insuring generalization of conditioning effects from the laboratory to the home." In his opinion, the difficulties of the parents were not due to their emotional problems but rather to a lack of awareness as to what it was in the child that they were reinforcing. Like Garvey and Hegrenes, he feels that the therapist must make it a point to become associated with a wide range of pleasant stimuli before attempting any behavior manipulation; hence the initial use of candy reinforcers (Patterson, 1965). Lazarus and Abramovitz (1965) offer another modification of these basic procedures by establishing "emotive imagery" for the anxiety-inhibiting response. They point out that relaxation training or feeding in the presence of the anxiety-evoking stimulus is not always feasible and instead encourage the child to imagine happy situations or heroic figures. At the same time, the child is allowed to indicate feelings of anxiety, which results in removal of the anxiety-producing stimulus. Lazarus, Davison, and Polefka (1965) describe this treatment with 9-year-old Paul. The application of numerous techniques in the consulting room was abandoned because "It was obvious that his verbal reports were aimed at eliciting approval rather than describing his true feelings," and they started going to school in fact. In the company of the therapist, "Paul's feelings of anxiety were reduced by means of coaxing, encouragement, relaxation and the use of emotive imagery, i.e. the deliberate picturing of subjectively pleasant images such as Christmas and a visit to Disneyland, while relating them to the school situation." For the parents, "A long list of do's and don'ts was drawn up and discussed"; for instance, the mother was instructed not to allow him in the house during school hours. A mild tranquilizer was also prescribed. In the latter stages, when anxiety was less but avoidant behavior continued, operant conditioning was used by giving him tokens and

rewards contingent upon his entering school and remaining there alone. The authors comment that the presence of the therapist (although several were involved) seemed to have as much reward value as the comic books and tokens. This treatment extended over 4½ months and required the therapist to make a lot of on-the-spot judgments. For instance, when Paul left the classroom to seek out the therapist (who was sitting in the library) because he was scared, the therapist had to decide whether to reassure him or urge him to return. The critical factor in determining the appropriate procedure was the degree of anxiety as judged by the therapist (Lazarus et al., 1965).

Review of these cases shows that the therapist needs considerable sensitivity to judge the child's anxiety and win his confidence. Also, it is apparent that there must be active cooperation on the part of the parents and the school staff, although the reports vary in the details. The reports of behavior therapy are similar in that there is no attempt to probe further as to why the child is afraid, and the goal is to get rid of the anxiety by brief exposures, by distraction (emotive imagery), by rewarding verbal statements of denial, or by pairing the frightening situation with a nonfrightening one such as the presence of the therapist. One might ask whether a real change results or merely suppression of affect. Behavior therapists say that the proof is in the overt behavior change of the child: If he does not act on his fear, then he does not have it.

Review of "psychodynamic" treatment reports of school phobics reveals a diversity in philosophy and techniques equaling that found in the behavior therapy literature. For a number of years, the staff at Judge Baker Guidance Center in Boston conducted a clinical investigation into the causes and treatment of school phobia. They reported a close relationship between prompt therapeutic intervention and remission of symptom; twenty out of twenty-one children treated during the same semester in which the symptom appeared returned to school within 3 months (Waldfogel, Tessman, & Hahn, 1959). In view of this experience, they undertook a project of early intervention at the first signs of an incipient school phobia. A total of thirty-six children with symptoms of school phobia were referred to the Judge Baker field unit during its 2 years of operation in the Newton public school system. Sixteen of these were treated successfully in the school with ten or fewer half-hour interviews. Four others were referred to the clinic for treatment, five recovered spontaneously, and eleven were not treated because of staff time or refusal by the parents. The authors make a special point of the advantages of treating in the school, where ". . . the therapist can offer direct support to the child in the feared situation," which sounds very much like "reciprocal inhibition" by another name. In explaining their treatment philosophy, reference is made to the concept of the "corrective emotional experience" advanced some years ago by Alexander and French (1946). Although Alexander and French were psychoanalysts, their final statements emphasize the role of learning in neurosis:

> The main therapeutic result of our work is the conclusion that, in order to be relieved of his neurotic ways of feeling and acting, the patient must undergo new emotional experiences suited to undo the morbid effects of the emotional experiences of his earlier life. Other therapeutic factors, such as intellectual insight, abreaction, recollection of the past, etc., are all subordinated to this central therapeutic principle. Re-experiencing the old, unsettled conflict but with a new ending is the secret of every penetrating therapeutic result. Only the actual experience of a new solution in the transference situation or in everyday life gives the patient the conviction that a new solution is possible and induces him to give up the old neurotic patterns." [p. 338]

In their case reports, Waldfogel, Tessman, and Hahn did more than encourage the mother and child to master the anxiety by keeping the child in school. They considered the phobic reaction as a crisis situation which made internal conflicts more accessible to brief psychotherapy. In the case of Sue, aged 5½, fourteen interviews elicited a good deal of material about her fears for her mother and her fantasies about her mother's pending operation for ear trouble. Clarification was made by the mother as to the real facts, and the therapist relieved Sue's guilt about her hostile wishes.

Sperling makes a distinction between "induced school phobia," where there is a long-standing symbiotic relationship between mother and child, and "acute school phobia," which starts suddenly after some traumatic event (1967). She reports success after relatively brief psychotherapy in cases of acute phobia (1961), such as that of 7-year-old Peter, who had been out of school for 3 weeks following a sudden panic while listening to the teacher play the piano in assembly. He associated the music with the funeral of a neighbor who had committed suicide while her child was in school. "For the purpose of bringing him back to school, it was sufficient to make him aware of his fear that this could happen to his mother and to link it with the unconscious wish by remarking casually that boys sometimes when they are angry have such wishes and are afraid that they might come true. His phobia cleared up immediately" (Sperling, 1967, p. 379). The dynamics here are the same as in the case of Sue, fear for the mother's welfare because of unexpressed hostile wishes. As mentioned before, with these dynamics, separation rather than school is feared; in other school phobias, the psychodynamics involve a more complex network of displacements and projections on to some feature of the school.

In trying to compare the validity of different treatment philosophies, the crucial question is not so much whether the psychodynamic explanations are correct, but whether it is necessary to "detoxify" unconscious wishes in order to (1) cure the phobia and (2) prevent later neurotic difficulties. Davison makes the astute observation that ". . . from evidence regarding efficacy in changing behavior, one cannot claim to have demonstrated that the problem evolved in an analogous fashion" (1968, p. 98). The converse may also be true. Although phobia may well start by touching off an unconscious wish (which was obviously latent before the phobia), it may not be necessary for the child to recognize the wish in order to regain his former equilibrium. All the treatment approaches agree on the importance of the child's continued exposure to school, however brief, and are also unanimous in opposing coercive measures. They all capitalize on the child-therapist relationship and, with few exceptions, encourage the child's expression of feelings and fantasies. The rate of recovery seems to be related more to promptness of intervention than to kind of treatment, so therapists still have the option of choosing for themselves what they consider the most important factor in success.

HYSTERIA

History and Incidence

In contrast to childhood phobias, about which so much has been written, there is very little on the topic of hysteria in childhood. In the classification of psychopathological disorders proposed by the Group for the Advancement of Psychiatry Committee on Child Psychiatry (1966), hysteria is not listed as a separate entity. There is a diagnostic classification of "hysterical personality disorder" for children, mostly girls, "who show tendencies toward overdramatic, flamboyant, overlabile, overaffective, oversuggestible, coy, or seductive behavior. They often appear to be overly dependent upon their environment for the establishment of their own independent identities and may exhibit a pseudosocial poise or veneer" (pp. 240–241). The same classification system lists two types of psychoneurosis which cover the Protean forms of hysterical symptoms. In *psychoneurosis, conversion type,* the symptoms are mainly somatic and can mimic those of almost any organic disease. *Psychoneurosis, disassociative type,* includes such florid alterations in conscious awareness as amnesia and split personalities as well as minor alterations such as sleepwalking or motor tics of which the person is not aware. For reasons indicated earlier in this chapter, people working with children, regardless of their theoretical background, prefer to use diagnostic terms which are descriptive of the current problem behavior rather than medical labels which imply a relatively fixed condition.

Although the literature on hysteria in childhood is scant, there are volumes on adult hysteria. Since 2000 B.C., hysteria has interested physicians faced with the problems of differentiating between the "real" and the "imagined" or between the "organic" and the "functional." Freud followed an ancient heritage in ascribing the cause to frustrated sexual needs. The word itself was coined by Hippocrates. It comes from the Greek word *hysteron,* meaning "uterus," since it was originally applied to a convulsive condition said to occur in widows and spinsters, presumably because of migration of the uterus. Veith (1965) quotes an English physician, Robert Carter, who in 1853 described three main factors in the etiology of hysteria: "the temperament of the individual, the event or situations which trigger the initial attack, and the degree to which the affected person is compelled to conceal or repress the exciting causes. 'Sexual passion' . . . is far the most frequent and important of all immediate etiological agents." It remained for Freud to illustrate how complicated and conflictful "sexual passion" could be in all its polymorphous forms.

All discussions contain some reference to the remarkable suggestibility of persons with hysterical symptoms. Hysterical personalities seem to "pick up" symptoms through social contact without remembering their model. Freud has pointed out that "Identification is a highly important factor in the mechanism of hysterical symptoms.

It enables patients to express in their symptoms not only their own experiences but those of a large number of other people; it enables them, as it were, to suffer on behalf of a whole crowd of people and to act all the parts in a play single-handed" (1953, p. 149). He goes on later to say that hysterics identify most readily with people who are involved in their sexual life, real or fantasied. With or without the sexual component, there is no argument about the suggestibility of hysterical characters. It is perhaps most clear in the dissociative reactions. In these states, one part of the mind, in an effort to blot out a conflicting wish, represses another part in which free expression of the forbidden impulse is permitted. Sometimes the wish is so transparent to the onlooker that the person's conscious innocence can hardly be believed. This kind of hysterical state is similar to the condition which exists in hypnosis. The hypnotist artificially, and temporarily, produces hysteria. In the execution of a posthypnotic suggestion, the source of the suggestion is repressed; the person has no conscious volition or awareness of why he is performing the acts. Not everyone is susceptible to this kind of suggestion; subjects who are easily hypnotized usually have hysterical personalities.

It has been suggested by some that hysteria is disappearing from the contemporary scene. There is no doubt that the symptoms, which are bound to reflect contemporary culture, have changed and perhaps are not recognized as easily as the major paralyses and anesthesias of Charcot's day. Discussing the incidence of hysteria in childhood, Proctor (1967) points out that hysteria is seen more often in medical settings, where the cases are often treated medically, symptom relief is obtained, and the patient is discharged without further study. In addition to failure in recognition, other explanations have been offered in terms of social and cultural factors. Waelder suggested that a shift in symptoms could be understood in terms of changes in philosophy of child rearing. In Victorian times, management of children was strict, with a general policy of suppression. In the event of psychological difficulties, repression was the only recourse available to the child. When indulgence and permissiveness became the fashion, the characteristic defense mechanisms of children so reared changed to avoidance, acting out, and pleasure seeking rather than repression and inhibition, which provided the substratum of classical neuroses (Waelder, 1960). Society's attitude toward sexuality has softened, so that the demands for repression are less. "The present cultural climate, particularly in adolescence, leads not so much to repression of the id but of the superego. The main problem for the analyst is the fact that this development has not led to an improvement in the mental health of the generation which has grown up in this altered climate but rather to a change in pathology" (Lowenfeld, 1968, p. 103).

The most extensive reports on hysteria in childhood have been provided by Proctor (1958, 1967). In his sample of 191 consecutively diagnosed cases in the child psychiatric unit of the Department of Psychiatry, University of North Carolina School of Medicine, 13 percent were diagnosed as conversion hysteria or dissociative hysteric reactions. "Our cases are often of a dramatic nature and, from perusal of the literature, it seems they are more often florid than commonly seen in other areas of the country; for example, tic-like pelvic thrusts associated with a request for circumcision in a 10-year-old Negro boy; paraplegia in an 11-year-old Negro female" (1958, p. 397). His figures indicated that the diagnosis is at least as common with boys as with girls, that hysterical children tend to be older than the other patients in child psychiatry, and that relatively more Negroes than whites are so diagnosed.

The fact that hysterics tend to be older than the others coming to a child psychiatry clinic does not mean that younger children do not have hysterical symptoms. Far from it—the preschool child is more likely than the older child to use his body to express his feelings. Some of these transitory symptoms are direct, physiological manifestations of anxiety, and some are indirectly derived by association with some idea or event. Preschool children identify readily with others; if a nursery school or kindergarten child is seriously hurt, it is common to see others faint, vomit, etc. At first this might seem to be genuine sympathy for the injured one, but closer inspection shows that the other children are neither helpful nor solicitous, but act as if they themselves had been injured and are in need of attention. The identification is basically egoistic and reflects the precarious state of self-identity. In the indirectly derived somatic symptoms, one sees examples of concrete thinking, where a "bad" arm or leg is punished for aggressive or destructive behavior. Many temporary aberrations appear in connection with eating and defecation, both of which are extremely important to the young child and filled with mystery. However, at younger ages no one would consider a special label for such symptoms. We expect the preschool child to be suggestible, labile in his emotional reactions, more likely to express feelings somatically than in words, and more concrete in his concepts about body functions. The young child is a "normal hysteric"; it is amazing to see how much this psychology continues to operate in hysterical individuals, who often appear so mature and sophisticated on the surface. Intimate experience with the thought processes of the child between 1 and 3 years of age is very helpful in making sense out of hysteria.

To help explain the high incidence he found in North Carolina, Proctor described the "Bible Belt" culture, with its vivid depiction of punishment and awesome magic. He suggested that extreme inconsistency between action and word is the breeding ground for hysterical reactions. The child's sexual feelings and Oedipal wishes are activated by the parents' unconscious stimulation, while at the same time sexuality is despised and linked with horrible punishments. The child, caught in the middle, can neither express nor forget his sexual feelings, so they emerge as a hysterical symptom which discharges some of the tension without arousing anxiety since they are disguised. Proctor, like Waelder, thus relates the patient's culture to his choice of symptom.

Somatic Symptoms

Somatic symptoms with major psychological causes can be subdivided into three categories: (1) temporary physical changes related to acute emotional states, (2) somatic reactions expressing an inner conflict in symbolic form, and (3) tissue changes and organic disease resulting in part from long-standing emotional problems. In the first category, we have all the somatic symptoms associated with acute anxiety—faintness, palpitations, vomiting, loss of bladder or bowel control, and so on. These are usually aroused very suddenly and are accompanied by a subjective feeling of anxiety. In the third category belongs the whole host of psychosomatic diseases. Hysterical conversion symptoms belong in the second category and are usually distinguished by their chronicity and the fact that they are *not* accompanied by anxiety. In fact, the person may seem quite comfortable with his symptom, the so-called "belle indifference" of the hysteric. Examples which may appear in childhood are inability to swallow or strange abdominal complaints. One 11-year-old girl was very much preoccupied with a feeling of pulsation in her stomach. In treatment, it developed that she thought that this must be a baby, although she had the intellectual knowledge about sexual intercourse and "knew" it was impossible. Sometimes the inability to swallow is limited to certain types of foods which betray the meaning of the symptoms, for example, eggs or seed-containing foods (fear of, or wish for, impregnation) frankfurters (fear of, or wish for, fellatio or oral sadism), and so on. There may be disturbances in sensation, for instance, a tickly, crawling feeling or numbness. Occasionally, there is a real loss of function of arms or legs, or it is even possible for a stiff neck to represent a turning away from something. Disturbances in vision usually take more subtle forms than outright blindness, for instance, double vision, blurred vision, tubular vision, or seeing things characteristically larger (macropsia) or smaller (micropsia) than they are. Even after degenerative brain disease or space-occupying lesions are ruled out, these disturbances in visual perception are hard to diagnose as definitely "functional." Usually one depends on evaluation of the total personality, the person's spontaneous explanations, and what use he may make of the symptoms. The list of possible somatic conversion symptoms is endless because any organ or function of the body can be drawn into a psychological conflict requiring defensive inhibition of some aspect. Obviously, these symptoms challenge the skill of the medical profession first and may be dismissed lightly when no organic basis is found. It is also quite possible for the patient to dismiss them as well on the basis of his characteristic suggestibility, but hysterics have a way of coming back with something new.

A rather special problem exists with the convulsive disorders, which may present a bewildering combination of organic and hysterical features. The few detailed clinical reports of convulsive activity and the sequence of events leading to it have been contributed by Gottschalk (1953, 1955, 1956). He feels that the grand mal attack has no symbolic significance, although it can at times be precipitated by emotional conflict. However, he suggests that "In less generalized forms of epileptic discharge, such as psychomotor epilepsy and related automatisms or in certain manifestations of petit mal epilepsy and especially in 'psychic equivalent seizures,' it is likely that epileptic manifestation may symbolize in microcosmic forms some aspects of the subject's old

and recent emotional conflicts" (1956, p. 379). He gives the treatment report of a 10-year-old boy with various kinds of "spells," one form of which turned out to be a hysterical conversion phenomenon. The symptom complex (staring and hand shaking) condensed and symbolized both the peeping which the boy had earlier engaged in, when he tried to discover what his parents were doing in *his* bedroom, and his guilty fear of his love for his mother and his resentment of his father. Immediately before and during one of these particular spells, he could report thoughts and feelings that were highly unacceptable to him. Gottschalk pointed out that other boys with similar conflicts and psychological mechanisms do not have seizures. Both the hysterical character disorder and the paroxysmal cerebral dysfunction were necessary to produce the clinical syndrome.

Despite the diagnostician's eagerness to separate organic factors from functional ones, nowhere is their interdependence more clear than in the hysterical conversion symptoms. Not everyone can somatize his psychological conflicts; it requires compliance from the body, a predisposition which must have been laid down before birth or very early in life, possibly as the result of the kind of maternal care and concern provided in infancy. On the other hand, many "honest-to-goodness" organic symptoms acquire a hysterical overlay or persist for psychological purposes after the organic cause has passed.

Tics

Disturbances in motility can take the form of either inhibition (paralysis or difficulty in the use of motor functions for walking or writing) or excessive, involuntary movements. The latter, however, are much more common and deserving of more attention. In this context, we are concerned only with stereotyped, discrete motor patterns which have become chronic automatisms for the child. Tic responses are closely related to general fidgetiness and motor restlessness. The line between what is "normal" and what constitutes "hyperactive" (suggestive of minimal cerebral dysfunction) is very fuzzy and depends a good deal on the adult's tolerance level. Describing normal preadolescent behavior, Redl comments that "... the most striking thing about them is their extreme physical restlessness. They can hardly stand still, running is more natural to them than walking, the word 'sitting' is a euphemism if applied to what they do with a table and a chair. ... Funny gestures and antics seem to turn up overnight with little or no reason—such things as facial tics, odd gestures and jerky movements, long-outgrown speech disorders and the like" (1966, p. 398). In the Lapouse and Monk study of reported problems in 482 unselected children of elementary school age, 57 percent of the boys and 42 percent of the girls were described by their mothers as "overactive" (1959, 1968). In MacFarlane's (1954) investigation of behavior problems in normal children between 21 months and 14 years of age, the mothers reported the peak of overactivity for boys at ages 4 (44 percent) and 5 (46 percent) and for girls also at ages 4 and 5 (35 percent).

Tics usually involve the musculature of the face, neck, and head, as in blinking the eye, wrinkling the nose, stretching or twisting the mouth, rolling the tongue around outside the mouth, clearing the throat, yawning, shrugging the shoulders, or some combination of these. In diagnosis, a tic must first be differentiated from neurological conditions (e.g., postencephalitis or infectious chorea). Transitory tics, for instance, eye blinking, are extremely common in childhood and are best ignored. In the same Lapouse and Monk study cited above, 12 percent of the schoolchildren were reported as having "unusual movements, twitching or jerking [tics]," but the epidemiologic significance of the figure is limited by the fact that there is no indication given of the persistence or frequency of the move-

ments. In the MacFarlane study, "tics and mannerisms" reached their peak with the girls at 6 years (10 percent) and with the boys at 7 years (11 percent). One-quarter of her sample demonstrated "tics and mannerisms" at some age during the 12-year period of observations. Rarely is treatment instituted only for a tic symptom unless it is remarkably complicated and conspicuous. A child with a tic which has persisted for months usually has other demonstrable psychological problems as well.

When we look for explanations and approaches to treatment, we find the usual difference of opinion as to whether the symptom is a simple learned response which is self-perpetuating or whether it is an outward expression of inner conflict. In learning theory, tics are considered "symptoms which developed originally as conditioned avoidance responses, became reinforced through satisfying temporary needs and thereafter existed as learned responses separated from the original circumstances which first occasioned them" (Rafi, 1965, p. 264). One of the classic treatment reports is that of Yates, who used the method of "negative practice" suggested by Dunlap many years before (1932). The method involves voluntary repetition of the tic as fast as possible in brief periods of time interspersed with brief rest periods. In the original case (a 25-year-old woman), the frequency of voluntary tic movements declined, and there was a corresponding decline in the involuntary tics as well (Yates, 1958a). In a later report on two adult patients, Rafi found that one responded with this method and that one required a different approach modeled on classical conditioning lines (1965).

Walton described the behavior therapy of an 11-year-old boy who had had facial tics since the age of 5. At about 10 years of age, these tics generalized to major jerking movements of the arms and legs, accompanied by explosive speech utterances such as "Fool, fool, fool." Walton diagnosed the situation as follows: "The patient was an over-privileged child who wished to claim, and was used to claiming, all the parents' attention, but of late the mother had attempted to discipline him. This constituted a threat to his over-indulged self, which produced anxiety, resentment, and considerable tension. The tics could be regarded as tension-reducing phenomena" (1961, p. 149). The boy was treated in a hospital with a total of thirty-six daily sessions lasting from 15 to 30 minutes. During these sessions, he was "forced to practice voluntary evocation of his tics." Considerable relief was attained, and a year later he showed only a minor facial tic.

The explanation of how this works utilizes some of the most complicated concepts in learning theory, derived from Hull and modified by Eysenck and others. It is postulated that the constant, rapid repetition of a single act builds up a reactive inhibition on a neurophysiological base. When this reactive inhibition, which might be called "satiation," reaches a critical point, the person is forced to rest, or "not do" the act. Then, this new habit of "not doing is associated with drive reduction because it releases 'I$_r$.'" The new habit becomes self-perpetuating since a new and different drive has been established around it. It is a fascinating theory which lends itself to all kinds of experimentation, but there are many underlying assumptions. It may be that "negative practice" works because the subject is sincerely desirous of stopping the tic and finds deliberate production of it distasteful. Another way of looking at the cure may be that deliberate practice changes the involuntary character of the tic. The subject is made thoroughly conscious of what he is doing and when; it is thereby reduced to a motor behavior which he can elect to do or not to do.

In the psychodynamic approach, the therapist also wants to make the subject fully conscious of his tic, not only as a motor movement, but also in terms of what external and internal events (i.e., feelings) elicit it and what its symbolic significance might be. Many times the tic contains a clue to the underlying conflict. Some facial grimaces, for instance, look suspiciously as if the person is aggressively making a face at somebody. The head shaker could be saying "No, no" to an unconscious wish. Wrinkling of the nose seems to say, "Something doesn't smell good around here." Blinking the eye suggests an attempt to blot out something which was seen. Usually the onset is so insidious that it provides no help in understanding the tic. Sometimes it is clear that the tic serves an unconscious aggressive purpose because it is so disturbing to everyone in the child's presence. Kessler reported on a 7-year-old girl who had a loud throat-clearing tic which the mother had explained, for months, as the result of a postnasal drip. This noise was very bothersome to everyone at home and at school, and it disappeared when it was steadfastly ignored. The little girl had many other problems, however, which did not yield to such simple measures (1966, p. 444).

Proctor gives a good example of psychodynamic treatment of a 14-year-old boy, John, who developed an acute anxiety state about losing his mind which was associated with a horizontal head-nodding tic and nocturnal enuresis. The symptoms started very suddenly about 3 days before treatment, and after six visits (spread over 2 weeks) he had rapid symptom relief. He then was continued on a twice-a-week basis for the next year so that the therapist could get a better understanding of what the symptoms represented. Only the observations related to the tic will be quoted, but it is important to note that Proctor was concerned with the total symptom complex, which he diagnosed as hysteria.

John had an eye-blinking tic that lasted approximately a year when he was about 5, and he had been cured of enuresis with an alarm device at age 8. These symptoms had appeared immediately prior to and following his father's departure to a mental hospital. He was then symptom-free until the adolescent outbreak. The night before, he was baby-sitting for a 5-year-old boy whom he observed to masturbate in the bathroom. Although John handled the young boy kindly, the observation triggered off memories of himself at that age. As a result of the work done during treatment, Proctor concluded:

> The horizontal head-nodding tic was closely related to the eye-blinking tic in that it was a conversion symptom condensing the impulse to look (turning the head toward) and the prohibition against the impulse (turning the head away). The head shaking itself was an important element in this symptom and was a condensation of father's habit of shaking his head when saying "no" (the superego prohibition), and his own habit of shaking his penis as a child (masturbation and the associated fantasies—the impulse-wish system). Thus, the head-shaking aspect of the symptom was an upper displacement of the impulse to masturbate and a compromise with the prohibition, expressing both the impulse and defense against the impulse. [1967, pp. 130, 131]

Proctor describes John's course of therapy, after the first immediate symptom relief, as dramatic and sometimes agonizing, revolving around the content of early memories and dreams. Obviously a great deal of work was done regarding the psychosis of his father—how this explained his erratic behavior toward John and its irrelevance as far as his own sanity was concerned. The good therapy outcome should be understood as resulting not from the intellectual formulation of the psychodynamics of his tic but rather from the reconstruction and abreaction of that entire period of his life and from his transference relationship with the therapist, who served as a "sane" father model at a time when John most needed one.

Disassociative Reactions

There is no single disassociative reaction which occurs with any great frequency in childhood. It is rare for preadolescents to be sufficiently aware of themselves to report any kind of disassociation or depersonalization. Once in a while a school-age child will complain that he does not know what he is doing, that he is an automaton, or that everything seems unreal, but his remarks are likely to be met with skepticism by his parents and teachers, who suspect that he is finding an excuse for some misdemeanor. It is conceivable that some of the poor memory manifested by children with learning disorders has a hysterical base, a partial amnesia, but it is usually so embedded in the total learning problem that it cannot be isolated as a separate symptom. Of the more obvious disassociative reactions, sleepwalking would perhaps be the most innocuous example and hallucinations the most serious.

In contrast to adult pathology, psychotic children rarely have hallucinations, and children who have hallucinations are usually hysterical (Bender & Lipkowitz, 1940; Despert, 1948; Weiner, 1961). Brenner (1951) and Esman (1962) presented clinical reports of seven children from 2 to 7 years of whom only one was diagnosed as psychotic. All the hallucinations were visual, and what the children "saw," in many instances, were scenes in which a phobia appeared to come true—a biting rat or dog, a butterfly, or crawling bugs, roaches, or snakes. It is quite possible that hallucinatory experiences in preschool children are more common than we know, since such an experience would be brushed aside by both parent and child if it were not accompanied by intense anxiety. In the cases described in the literature, the experiences were recurrent and very frightening, indicating that more than a simple confusion between reality and "make-believe" was involved. Weiner explained the hallucinatory experiences as "attempts to deal with internal emotional stimuli by translating them into concrete perceptual material that will allow the child to utilize his previously learned stimulus-response patterns (1961, p. 550). This is similar to the psychodynamic mechanisms involved in a phobia, namely, repression, displacement, and projection in order to put distance between the self and the source of conflict. The hallucination goes one step further in projection and concretization.

It has been suggested that some children may be constitutionally endowed with a more vivid fantasy life and that some such constitutional difference may explain the greater incidence of hallucinations in Negro than in Caucasian children. Although Esman made the same observation regarding incidence, he thought it more probable that ". . . many Negro children, due to well-defined socio-cultural influences, suffer from significant deviations in ego development, particularly in the area of reality testing and impulse control, so that the pathways to direct discharge and loss of differentiation are more open to them" (1962, p. 340). His five cases corroborate Proctor's thesis that excessive stimulation combined with punitive moralism provides fertile ground for the development of a hysterical symptom. Specifically, Esman suggests that repeated *visual* exposure to sexual scenes and adult genital organs (in families where sexual attitudes alternate between extreme laxity and extreme Puritanism) is characteristic of children suffering from visual hallucinations.

Brenner describes a case of childhood hallucinosis which appeared suddenly in a little girl of 3½ years. On going to bed, she was terrified by bugs that she imagined were crawling all over her, on the bedclothes, and on the walls. These vivid night terrors lasted about a week and then tapered off in the next 6 months, leaving her, however, with a marked insect phobia. In this example, we see how close dreams, phobias, and hallucinations can come. In Brenner's case, the acute outbreak of anxiety was related to her wish to have a baby and confusion which had resulted from her older sister's explanation to her about insemination. She rejected the facts regarding the role of the father and substituted free-flying bugs for semen. One might well ask why the wish to have a baby still should occasion so much conflict after imaginative modification of the process, but it is made understandable by other details in the case report.

Kessler reports a case which is a little different in that the hysterical hallucination was auditory rather than visual (1966). At the age of 14 years, this girl had decided to give up masturbation for the sake of her health, and shortly after this resolve she heard the "warning signal" for the first time. Her first association was to a recurrent dream she had had as a younger child. In the dream, a rocket was about to take off, and the hallucinatory signal was like a whistle to warn bystanders of the takeoff. The whistle was also like the "wolf" whistle of boys attracted to a girl, a whistle she would have liked to hear. When everything was very quiet, her mind wandered to romantic fantasies about herself and boys. The warning whistle stopped the fantasies. Thus, the hallucination expressed both the wish to be sexually attractive and a warning about the dangers of sexuality. It was midway between the normal person's voice of conscience and the malignant voices of schizophrenia. In the case of this girl, no one would have raised the question of psychosis in view of her general outgoing (albeit hysterical) personality.

A word should be said about the special vulnerabilities of adolescents. The onset of puberty often occasions a rash of hysterical symptoms, which is not surprising in light of our earlier formulation of hysteria. Sexual feelings are intense, but with the taboos of society and the habits the child has already acquired in his own short life, some repression is almost a necessity. Other characteristics of hysterical personalities, such as the suggestibility, ease of identification, craving for attention, and emotional lability, are also typical of many adolescents. At this age, feelings of depersonalization and unreality are not uncommon and reflect the adolescent's concern for identity. Very bizarre symptoms may appear and still be in the range of neurosis. In a study of the

Rorschach records of 300 supposedly normal adolescent girls, Frank et al. (1953) commented on the number whose records could have been interpreted as psychotic *if* they had been the reactions of adult subjects (1953). More license is allowed in applying diagnostic criteria to adolescents; it is much better to err on the conservative side and adopt a wait-and-see attitude. Premature diagnosis may lead to unnecessary hospitalization, thereby confirming an adolescent's greatest fear—that of losing his mind.

OBSESSIVE-COMPULSIVE NEUROSIS

Diagnosis

There are very few published reports on the specific topic of obsessive-compulsive disorders in childhood. It is not clear whether such disorders are really so infrequent or whether they are not properly identified. Despert suggested that the very severe obsessive-compulsive neuroses are often mistakenly diagnosed as childhood schizophrenia (1955). On the other hand, the milder forms look like simple fears or habit disturbances. Obsessional ideas often start with a phobia, but when avoidance of the external object does not suffice to reduce anxiety, the person becomes obsessed with the idea of it. It is like a continuous self-torture in which the person has to think about the very thing which is most frightening or upsetting to him. In general, there seem to be two types of obsessional preoccupations: those which are precautionary, for instance, ideas about safeguarding health and about cleanliness, and those which are repugnant, for instance, obsessive fantasies about hurting someone, sexual perversions, or doing something "dirty" and shocking. Usually compulsions have been preceded by obsessions; the person can no longer control his anxiety by selected thoughts, but has to do something in addition. Again, compulsive acts seem to fall into two major categories: those which serve as restrictions, prohibitions, or precautions (such as wiping doorknobs free of germs or repeated checking of locks and gas jets) and those which symbolize penances, atonements, and punishments (such as ritualistic counting). Ordinary everyday activities such as eating, dressing, washing, etc., may be elaborated into highly complicated rituals, sometimes caricaturing parental demands for care and cleanliness. In its very early stages, such behavior may seem laudable, and it takes the parents a long while to realize that the child has lost control and is compelled to repeat the hand washing, the bed making, or whatever it may be.

There are obsessional states which are more subtle and diffuse and even more difficult to recognize. For instance, the obsessional child who broods, constantly checks himself and others, and cannot make up his mind may very well look like an irresponsible dawdler to his impatient parents. In making the diagnosis of obsessive-compulsive neurosis in adulthood, there are subjective statements which help greatly. The adult person complains about his own inability to control certain thoughts or actions which he himself views as ridiculous. There is much more self-awareness in obsessive-compulsive states as compared with hysteria, for instance. The person performing a tic does not know he is doing it, whereas the person with a compulsion to clear his throat a specified number of times is miserably aware of what he is doing. The person with a phobia sees the source of his anxiety as outside himself, whereas the person with an obsession knows that it is his own imagination which is giving him trouble. Curiously, children rarely complain about their own psychology—their moods, feelings, unwanted thoughts, or undesired impulses—so that their diagnoses are usually made on the basis of overt manifestations alone.

There are normal variants of compulsive behavior, with peaks around the age of 2 years, at 7 to 8 years, and in early adolescence. The 2-year-old tends to be very upset with any change in his physical surroundings or daily routines and clings tenaciously to established habits. Custom becomes law, and any departure from the usual routines is regarded with suspicion and alarm. Part of the rigidity of this age is the 2-year-old's attempt to control his environment in his search for autonomy, and part of it reflects his magical thinking. He assumes that if a certain sequence of events (around bedtime, for instance) preceded a "happy ending" (waking up safe and sound), the whole sequence is necessary to ensure the same fortunate result. He applies this *post hoc, ergo propter hoc* reasoning to all situations and makes no discriminations between chance circumstances and essential causes. The adult compulsive person may use exactly the same kind of reasoning, but recognizes it as superstitious. There is still another common feature of 2-year-old behavior which relates to obsessive-compulsive personalities, and that is the overconcern shown in relation to cleanliness. At this age, it is easy to see how the child is trying to fight off the devil of temptation by setting up extraordinary barriers, not only with respect to his newly acquired toilet control, but also with respect to any and all demands for "goodness." His wishes are still very close to the surface, and it is a real battle within himself as to which side to take. A 2-year-old with a crayon in hand may stand for a long time staring at a wallpapered surface, saying "No, no" but unable to tear himself away. In a microcosmic form, this is not unlike the person who is obsessed with the possibility of his doing some terrible thing, saying a dirty word, for instance. He tries to control the impulse by constant thinking about the prohibition, but then finds that the defense of intellectualization has become uncontrollable.

Around the age of 7 or 8 years, a variety of compulsive rituals are often observed in children who seem generally happy and well adjusted. These may be related to the superstrictness of the child's conscience. At this age, the child is going off on his own for the first time, he is faced with many temptations, and he is beginning to realize how much he could do and escape detection, so he is very much dependent on the dictates of his conscience for self-control. Benjamin Spock used the example of stepping over sidewalk cracks with the accompanying rhyme "Step on a crack, break your grandmother's back" to show how a compulsion can be related to unconscious aggression (1957). In her discussion of play in relation to libidinal phases, Peller points out that one feature of school-age games is the strictness of the rules, which are regarded as absolute by the players. "Their meticulous observance gives independence from external superego figures" (Peller, 1954, p. 191). "The plot is codified, and the roles, too, are frozen and conventional. Rules, ceremonies, rituals, are essential elements of all games" (p. 192). As the child approaches 9 or 10 years, there is more flexibility in the observance of rules and a diminution of ritual behavior. The child has learned to live more comfortably with his conscience. The differentiation between normality and pathology in school-age children is not difficult. The common compulsions are like games which the child enjoys playing by himself or with others, and he has no feeling of inner coercion. In the pathological form, the compulsion is unique to the child, and he derives no pleasure or social benefits from it. Obsessional manifestations which occur as part of the child's effort to control his behavior through thought and deliberate action appear normally as part of the forward thrust of development. It is only when these defenses escalate, or when the child continues to use them to control external reality events according to the magical thinking of the very young child, that one considers the diagnosis of "obsessional neurosis" (Sandler & Joffe, 1965).

The adolescent, aroused by heightened sexual drives, has another set of temptations to ward off. In her classical description of the internal struggles of the adolescent, Anna Freud discussed two defenses which are particularly marked in this age period, namely, asceticism and intellectuality (1946). Asceticism represents a total repudiation of all forms of instinctual gratification in which the adolescent may actually injure his health in his self-imposed restrictions in matters of eating, for instance. This may also take more circumscribed forms in which the adolescent sets himself specific tasks of willpower, perhaps the renunciation of some pleasure or the assumption of some extra burden. This behavior looks very compulsive, although the adolescent rarely complains. These rituals are usually private, with no gamelike quality, but the adolescent sees them as "his choice" and therefore does not bring them to anyone's attention as a problem. In psychotherapy, it often appears that the adolescent's reason for setting himself these unnecessary hurdles to strengthen his willpower can be traced back to his guilt over failure to resist masturbation. In learning theory, such behavior is interpreted in terms of "overdoing" that which has been generally recommended as "good."

The intellectuality of adolescents, as manifested by their love of discussion, the alacrity with which they seize the most difficult problems to "solve," and their sharp criticism of all that has gone before, may take on an obsessional coloration. Action is divorced from intellectualization, and they may get so entangled in their own thought processes that they are unable to fulfill everyday responsibilities at home or at school. Although this is a little different from asceticism, the essential purpose is the same, namely, to control instinctual feelings. Usually these problems are time-limited; as the adolescent becomes accustomed to his new feelings and finds some satisfactory outlets, the defenses fade. On the other hand, adult obsessional-compulsive neurotics often date their difficulties from this period, so in the exceptional case, it can become a way of life. It is probably most important that those

working with adolescents recognize these mechanisms and take care *not* to reinforce them with praise and admiration.

A word should be said about the term *compulsion* as applied to addicts or fetishists. Some people include any kind of repetitious behavior which the person cannot control under the umbrella of "compulsion." In this presentation, we are distinguishing between out-of-control behavior which yields to temptation (however perverse) and out-of-control behavior which represents a defense against temptation. Glue sniffers, drug users, and so on, give themselves some pleasure even if it goes against their conscience, and the same can be said about transvestites, fetishists, exhibitionists, and so on. To include all that kind of behavior with the defense compulsions, which bring no pleasure except anxiety reduction, would give us no logical basis for categorization since almost any behavior disorder could be called "compulsive" in the ordinary dictionary sense.

Differentiation of obsessive-compulsive neuroses from other behavior disorders is not always easy. As mentioned before, obsessive thoughts or compulsive acts may be so bizarre and intense that they resemble the delusional ideas of schizophrenic patients. However, it is rare for the childhood forms to be so severe. Differentiation from hysteria is made not only on the basis of symptoms, and the person's attitude toward same, but also on the basis of accompanying personality characteristics. The obsessive does not have the outgoing, labile, suggestible personality of the hysteric; on the contrary, he tends to be introspective, depressive, and resistant to change (making therapy very difficult).

Below the surface, there are characteristic differences in the defense mechanisms employed in the two major neuroses, although both involve repression and displacement. Often, the displacement in compulsion neurosis is onto a small detail which is magnified out of all proportion to its real significance. By total concentration on the substitute, the obsessive-compulsive attempts to reduce the anxiety and guilt which the "real" wish would arouse. The two neuroses differ in that the obsessive-compulsive neurotic makes less use of projection and conversion and more use of reaction formation, undoing, and isolation. Reaction formation was described as common in the preschool child whose excessive virtue reveals the strength of latent wishes. The obsessive-compulsive is likely to set impossible standards for himself and others and may suffer great guilt from his too strict conscience. The obsessional neurotic behaves as if he were divided into both the bad child and the stern parent. He does a bad thing, or thinks a bad thought, and then metes out his own punishment. "Undoing" mechanisms are magical devices for appeasing, serving penance, or warding off imagined danger. Repetition, often taking the form of undoing, is described by Fenichel:

> The idea is that for the purpose of undoing, an activity has to be repeated with a different intention. What was once done with an instinctual intention must be repeated with a super-ego attitude. The warded-off instinct, however, tends to enter the repetition and has to be repeated. Usually, the number of necessary repetitions quickly increases. "Favorite numbers," the choice of which may have a separate unconscious meaning, are set up, and determine the number of necessary repetitions; eventually, the repetitions may be replaced by counting. [1945, p. 288].

The mechanism of isolation is very prominent in common compulsions about touching and not touching. The patient tries to put things into tight categories (e.g., dirty or clean, nice or not nice, feminine or masculine). The slightest suggestion of contact contaminates the object or thoughts belonging to the desired category. Zetzel proposes that the obsessive-compulsive thinks in terms of inexorable either-or categories as a result of a failure to integrate emotions which are initially experienced as mutually exclusive, such

as love and hate (1966). One of the developmental tasks is to learn to tolerate ambivalence and to fuse contradictory emotions so that there is some constancy which cannot be destroyed by a momentary anger. The obsessive-compulsive in some of his defenses tries to reestablish the simplistic state of affairs obtaining for the very young child.

Explanations

There is very little epidemiological information available about obsessive-compulsive neuroses, in children or adults. One reason for this is the relatively low incidence. Judd reviewed the records of 405 children under 12 years of age who had been evaluated at the psychiatric services at the University of California, Los Angeles, and found thirty-four children who had obsessive-compulsive symptoms, but in only five cases were these symptoms the most prominent evidence of psychopathology in the total clinical picture (1965). He reported that the same incidence was found in the adult case load (1.2 percent). It is often said that this neurosis is more common in people of above-average intelligence, and this was confirmed by the five cases in this survey. However, it is not restricted to this population. The author was acquainted with a mildly retarded adolescent boy (measured IQ in the 70s) who spontaneously asked his teacher for help with classical compulsions—repeated hand washing, checking and rechecking, and indecisiveness to the point of physical immobility at times. As usual, this behavior had had an insidious onset some years earlier, when his parents first noted that he required an inordinate amount of time for his newspaper route because he had to place and re-place the newspapers in a "just-so" position. This youth was considered a model by his teachers and parents. He was conscientious, considerate, polite, neat, and clean, characteristics which they thought would go a long way to compensate for his mental retardation. No discussion or recognition had been given to his sexual feelings, nor was he given any indication as to what he might anticipate in the way of dating or marriage. He was tremendously preoccupied with fantasies about girls which he was totally unable to verbalize or to find outlets for in social relationships. The crucial factor does not seem to be IQ as such, but whether the child has achieved an internalized conscience.

Explanations for the origin of obsessive-compulsive symptoms vary in the expected way according to theoretical orientation. In the psychoanalytic view, it is the instinctual content of the anal-sadistic phase which is warded off by means of the obsessional symptomatology (A. Freud, 1966). Reconstructions made in the course of psychoanalytic treatment lead back to trauma and confusion in the 2- to 4-year age period; in his analysis of the "wolf man," Freud expressed disbelief that the fantasies regarding anal functions could have been the thoughts of a child of 4½ and suggested that the patient referred back to the remote past the thoughts which had arisen later in his life (1955c). However, there is ample material from direct analysis of young children to show that they are indeed capable of the most complicated, albeit erroneous, associations and connections between oral, anal, genital, and aggressive activities. Ramzy's (1966) report of a 3½-year-old boy who was treated for severe constipation showed clearly how far a child's mind can go in linking up anal functions with various forms of fears and terrors of injury, destructiveness, retaliation, abandonment, and loss. The giving or withholding of bowel movements is inextricably tied in with the loving and hating aspects of the ambivalent relationship to the mother; it gets entangled with body image and fear of permanent damage, and cleanliness becomes the symbol for "goodness." Although the hysteric is usually conflicted about expression of his sexual feelings, the obsessive-compulsive is even more so because sex is tied in with anality and is viewed as dirty

and disgusting. The aggression also has a more regressed character in that it reflects the sadistic wishes for destruction and hurting which are common in the 2-year-olds (Wolman, 1970).

The learning theorists have not agreed on an explanation of obsessive-compulsive behavior (Metzner, 1963; Meyer, 1966; Taylor, 1963). Metzner draws some analogies between animal experiments and obsessional behavior and interprets the latter as traumatic avoidance responses. The avoidance response is first learned in some traumatic anxiety-provoking situation, and then it reappears as a response to any anxiety-provoking situation, with anxiety being the stimulus cue. Both Metzner and Meyer talk about inner sources of anxiety such as frequently recurring impulses or ideas which are not under the patient's voluntary control. Meyer points out that the same stimulus may be both an "approach incentive" and also an "anxiety-evoking conditioned stimulus" and that a compulsion may both satisfy an approach response and also reduce learned anxiety. In a different language this is equivalent to the psychoanalytic view that a neurotic symptom is a compromise and persists because it gives partial discharge to an impulse (approach incentive) in a form so disguised that it does not arouse the anxiety which would be aroused by conscious recognition of the wish.

Published reports of behavior therapy of obsessive-compulsive symptoms thus far concern only the treatment of adults, and degree of success has been more limited than with other behavior disorders. Walton and Mather (1963) discuss the treatment in two phases: reciprocal inhibition for the conditioned autonomic drive (CAD)—for instance, the anxiety associated with aggressive wishes—and retraining of the motor reaction to the CAD. Meyer took a slightly different approach to the desensitization of the anxiety state which prompts the obsessive-compulsive reactions. He introduced the concept of expectancies and suggested that if the patient's fearful expectations could be disproved, new expectancies would evolve which would in turn mediate new behavior. His technique was to force obsessional persons to remain in feared situations without permitting them to carry out their ritualistic defenses. This treatment requires, of course, total control of the environment. In his report of two cases, the outcome was favorable in reducing the overt symptoms, although the character inhibitions remained. If we think of this approach applied to children, it is always helpful to be able to prove in fact that their worst fears are groundless, but often it is difficult to do this by any external action. The feared expectation may be an event in the unspecified future or a change in someone's feeling for them, and it is hard to convince them otherwise.

The pathology of the obsessive-compulsive individual invariably reflects a disorder of conscience functions with exaggerated guilt, either consciously recognized or projected in the form of expected punishments. All Judd's cases were described as possessing a rigid, absolute, adult-like moral code, more rigorously active than one would expect. He describes a 7-year-old boy who "tells of how naughty he feels all the time and in spite of many people saying he isn't, he is unable to feel any differently. He told his mother that although she considered him to be a nice boy, he was really quite naughty" (1965, p. 139). If this overstrict conscience is to be understood in terms of past learning, we must consider closely the reality nature of the negative experiences which so traumatized the child. It may seem paradoxical that severe physical punishment does not produce this effect on the individual; the parents of the obsessive-compulsive person are usually strict, mildly compulsive, idealistic, devoted parents who relied on moral disapproval for punishment. Many times they are themselves perplexed by the child's harsh conscience and are far more tolerant of misbehavior than one would expect. The child's conscience, in terms of both the standards

he sets for himself and the strength of guilt which he feels, is more than a carbon copy of that of his parents. In obsessive-compulsive neuroses, it is clear that the guilt is aggression turned against the self, and one gets a feeling of the tremendous amount of aggression which would otherwise be directed toward the outside. A vicious circle is then set in operation because such a person is so miserable that he cannot help but be angry at the world, which makes him so anxious that he must keep himself even more closely in check. In understanding the development of an obsessive-compulsive neurosis, one has to consider not only the past history of direct punishment (disapproval) of manifest behavior but also the covert transmission of attitudes which would block the expression of aggressive or sexual feelings. To understand any neurosis, but particularly this one, one must be very sophisticated in the devious ways of communication between people, in terms of both the messages sent out and the distortions introduced by the perception of the receiver. There is not a one-to-one correspondence between what the parents intend to say and what the child hears.

The writer's bias toward psychoanalytic explanations for neurotic problems has undoubtedly become clear by this point. This implies that one looks at the symptomatic behavior as a defense against some feeling which is struggling for expression. Treatment then is designed to elicit the feeling and identify the dangers with which it is associated in the mind of the person. Past learning experience is extremely helpful in understanding the choice of defenses and the reasons why the feeling has been deemed so dangerous. It is hoped that with full insight, the unrealistic anxieties can be removed and the child can find ways to express his feelings which are acceptable to himself and to others. Behavior therapy directed at changing the overt behavior may be more efficacious in some instances and may suffice to get the child back into the mainstream of development. However, the possibilities for generalization to new situations are limited, so that it has little instructive value for the child. In behavior therapy, the child does not acquire new coping mechanisms which he can elect to use when faced with difficult situations of a different nature. Werry and Wollersheim (1967) make the excellent point that behavior therapy should not be viewed as supplanting traditional therapies and suggest that it be the treatment of choice (1) when there are discrete symptoms; (2) where the patient or his parents are symptom- rather than insight-oriented; (3) where, because of clinical conditions or mental age, the patient is not amenable to conflict-insight-verbalization approaches; and (4) where child therapists are scarce. Combined insight and behavior therapy approaches are still rare, but to this author, it seems logical to work both from the outside in and from the inside out. One would suspect that in a true neurosis, some insight would be necessary, but if the symptoms disappear before this is achieved, one should keep a weather eye on the child's continuing development and keep the door open to return. Certainly one would hope that at least the child therapist has some insight into the cause of the neurotic behavior so that the environment can be modified to support maximum emotional development in the future.

REFERENCES

Achenbach, T. M. The classification of children's psychiatric symptoms: A factor analytic study. *Psychological Monographs,* 1966, **80,** 1–37.

Ackerson, L. *Children's behavior problems.* Chicago: University of Chicago Press, 1931.

Albee, G. W. The dark at the top of the agenda. *Clinical Psychologist,* 1966, **1,** 7–9. (a)

Albee, G. W. Give us a place to stand and we will move the earth. *Mental health manpower needs in psychology: Proceedings of a conference.* Lexington: University of Kentucky Press, 1966. (b)

Alexander, F., & French, T. M. *Psychoanalytic therapy.* New York: Ronald Press, 1946.

Andrews, J. D. W. Psychotherapy of phobias. *Psychological Bulletin,* 1966, **66,** 455–480.

Bandura, A. Behavioral psychotherapy. *Scientific American,* 1967, **216,** 78–89.

Bandura, A., & Huston, A. C. Identification as a process of incidental learning. *Journal of Abnormal and Social Psychology,* 1961, **63,** 311–318.

Bandura, A., & Walters, R. H. *Social learning and personality development.* New York: Holt, 1963.

Bender, L., & Lipkowitz, H. Hallucinations in children. *American Journal of Orthopsychiatry,* 1940, **X,** 471–509.

Bentler, P. M. An infant's phobia treated with reciprocal inhibition therapy. *Journal of Child Psychology and Psychiatry,* 1962, **3,** 185–189.

Berger, S. M. Incidental learning through vicarious reinforcement. *Psychological Reports,* 1961, **9,** 477–491.

Bernal, M. E., Duryee, J. S., Pruett, H. L., & Burns, B. J. Behavior modification and the brat syndrome. *Journal of Consulting and Clinical Psychology,* 1968, **32,** 447–456.

Bookbinder, L. J. Simple conditioning vs. the dynamic approach to symptoms and symptom substitution: A reply to Yates. *Psychological Reports,* 1962, **10,** 71–77.

Bornstein, B. Phobia in a two-and-a-half year old child. *The Psychoanalytic Quarterly,* 1935, **4,** 93–119.

Breger, L., & McGaugh, J. L. Critique and re-formulation of "learning-theory" approaches to psychotherapy and neurosis. *Psychological Bulletin,* 1965, **63,** 338–359.

Brenner, C. A case of childhood hallucinosis. In *Psychoanalytic study of the child.* Vol. VI. New York: International Universities Press, 1951. Pp. 235–244.

Brenner, C. *An elementary textbook of psychoanalysis.* New York: International Universities Press, 1955.

Cahoon, D. D. Symptom substitution and the behavior therapies: A reappraisal. *Psychological Bulletin,* 1968, **69,** 149–157.

Chess, S. *An introduction to child psychiatry.* New York: Grune & Stratton, 1959.

Coolidge, J. C., Tessman, E., Waldfogel, S., & Willer, M. L. Patterns of aggression in school phobia. In *Psychoanalytic study of the child.* Vol. XVII. New York: International Universities Press, 1962. Pp. 319–334.

Coolidge, J. C., Willer, M. L., Tessman, E., & Waldfogel, S. School phobia in adolescence: A manifestation of severe character disturbance. *American Journal of Orthopsychiatry,* 1960, **30,** 599–608.

Davidson, S. School phobia as a manifestation of family disturbance: Its structure and treatment. *Journal of Child Psychology and Psychiatry,* 1961, **1,** 270–288.

Davison, G. C. Systematic desensitization as a counterconditioning process. *Journal of Abnormal and Social Psychology,* 1968, **73,** 91–100.

Despert, L. Delusional and hallucinatory experiences in children. *American Journal of Psychiatry,* 1948, **104,** 528F–537F.

Despert, L. Differential diagnosis between obsessive-compulsive neurosis and schizophrenia in children. In P. H. Hoch & J. Zubin (Eds.), *Psychopathology of childhood.* New York: Grune & Stratton, 1955. Pp. 240–284.

Dollard, J., & Miller, N. E. *Personality and psychotherapy: An analysis in terms of learning, thinking, and culture.* New York: McGraw-Hill, 1950.

Dunlap, K. *Habits: Their making and unmaking.* New York: Liveright, 1932.

Eisenberg, L. School phobia: A study of communication of anxiety. *American Journal of Psychiatry,* 1958, **114,** 712–718.

Esman, A. Visual hallucinosis in young children. In *Psychoanalytic study of the child.* Vol. XVII. New York: International Universities Press, 1962. Pp. 334–344.

Estes, H. R., Haylett, C. H., & Johnson, A. M. Separation anxiety. *American Journal of Psychotherapy,* 1956, **10,** 682–695.

Eysenck, H. J. Learning theory and behavior therapy. *The Journal of Mental Science,* 1959, **105,** 61–75.

Eysenck, H. J., & Rachman, S. *The causes and cures of neurosis: An introduction to modern behavior therapy based on learning theory and the principle of conditioning.* San Diego, Calif.: Knapp, 1965.

Fenichel, O. *The psychoanalytic theory of neurosis.* New York: Norton, 1945.

Frank, L. K., et al. Personality development in adolescent girls. *Monographs of the Society for Research in Child Development,* 1953, **16.**

Freud, A. *Ego and mechanisms of defense.* New York: International Universities Press, 1946.

Freud, A. *Normality and pathology in childhood.* New York: International Universities Press, 1965.

Freud, A. Obsessional neurosis: A summary of Congress view. *International Journal of Psychoanalysis,* 1966, **47,** 116–123.

Freud, A. Indications and contraindications for child analysis. In *Psychoanalytic study of the child.* Vol. XXIII. New York: International Universities Press, 1968. Pp. 37–47.

Freud, S. *The interpretation of dreams* (1900). Standard Edition. Vols. IV-V. London: Hogarth Press, 1953.

Freud, S. *Analysis of a phobia in a five-year-old boy* (1909). Standard Edition. Vol. X. London: Hogarth Press, 1955. (a)

Freud, S. *Beyond the pleasure principle* (1920). Standard Edition. Vol. XVIII. London: Hogarth Press, 1955. (b)

Freud, S. *From the history of an infantile neurosis* (1918). Standard Edition. Vol. XVII. London: Hogarth Press, 1955. (c)

Freud, S. *On the psychical mechanism of hysterical phenomena: Preliminary communication* (1893). Standard Edition. Vol. II. London: Hogarth Press, 1955. (d)

Freud, S. *Five lectures on psychoanalysis* (1910). Standard Edition. Vol. XI. London: Hogarth Press, 1957. (a)

Freud, S. *On the history of the psychoanalytic movement* (1914). Standard Edition. Vol. XIV. London: Hogarth Press, 1957. (b)

Freud, S. *The disposition to obsessional neurosis* (1913. Standard Edition. Vol. XII. London: Hogarth Press, 1958.

Freud, S. *Civilization and its discontents* (1930). Standard Edition. Vol. XXI. London: Hogarth Press, 1961.

Freud, S. *Outline of psychoanalysis* (1940). Standard Edition. Vol. XXIII. London: Hogarth Press, 1964.

Garvey, W. P., & Hegrenes, J. R. Desensitization techniques in the treatment of school phobia. *American Journal of Orthopsychiatry,* 1966, **36,** 147–152.

Gelfand, D. M., & Hartmann, D. P. Behavior therapy with children: A review and evaluation of research methodology. *Psychological Bulletin,* 1968, **69,** 204–216.

Gottschalk, L. A. Effects of intensive psychotherapy on epileptic children. *Archives of Neurology and Psychiatry,* 1953, **70,** 361–368.

Gottschalk, L. A. Psychologic conflict and electroencephalographic patterns. *Archives of Neurology and Psychiatry,* 1955, **73,** 656–663.

Gottschalk. L. A. The relationship of psychologic state and epileptic activity. In *Psychoanalytic study of the child.* Vol. XI. New York: International Universities Press, 1956. Pp. 352–381.

Group for the Advancement of Psychiatry. *Psychopathological disorders in childhood: Theoretical considerations and a proposed classification.* Vol. VI. New York: GAP, 1966.

Guthrie, E. R. *The psychology of learning.* New York: Harper, 1935.

Hartmann, H., & Kris, E. Problems of infantile neurosis: A discussion. In *Psychoanalytic study of the child.* Vol. IX. New York: International Universities Press, 1954. Pp. 16–75.

Hersch, C. The discontent explosion in mental health. *American Psychologist,* 1968, **23,** 497–507.

Hersov, L. A. Persistent non-attendance at school. *Journal of Child Psychology and Psychiatry,* 1960, **1,** 130–137. (a)

Hersov, L. A. Refusal to go to school. *Journal of Child Psychology and Psychiatry,* 1960, **1,** 137–146. (b)

Holland, B. C. Discussion. Appended to H. Spiegel, Is symptom removal dangerous? *American Journal of Psychiatry,* 1967, **10,** 1282–1283.

Holmes, F. B. An experimental study of the fears of young children. In A. T. Jersild & F. B. Holmes (Eds.), Children's fears. *Child Development Monographs,* 1935, **20,** 167–296.

Hunt, M. M. A neurosis is "just" a bad habit. *The New York Times Magazine,* June 4, 1967. Pp. 38–48.

Jersild, A. T. *Child psychology.* (6th ed.) Englewood Cliffs, N.J.: Prentice-Hall, 1968.

Johnson, A. M., Falstein, E. I., Szurek, S. A., & Svendsen, M. School phobia. *American Journal of Orthopsychiatry,* 1941, **11,** 702–711.

Jones, M. C. The elimination of children's fears. *Journal of Experimental Psychology,* 1924, **7,** 382–390.

Jones, M. C. A laboratory study of fear: The case of Peter. *Pedagogical Seminar,* 1924, **31,** 308–315.

Judd, L. L. Obsessive compulsive neurosis in children. *Archives of General Psychiatry,* 1965, **12,** 136–144.

Kalish, H. J. Behavior therapy. In B. B. Wolman (Ed.), *Handbook of clinical psychology.* New York: McGraw-Hill, 1965. Pp. 1230–1253.

Kanfer, F. H. & Saslow, G. Behavioral analysis. *Archives of General Psychiatry,* 1965, **12,** 529–539.

Kanner, L. Do behavioral symptoms always indicate psychopathology? *Journal of Child Psychology and Psychiatry,* 1960, **1,** 17–25.

Kessler, J. W. *Psychopathology of childhood.* Englewood Cliffs, N.J.: Prentice-Hall, 1966.

Klein, E. The reluctance to go to school. In *Psychoanalytic study of the child.* Vol. I. New

York: International Universities Press, 1945. Pp. 265–281.

Kolansky, H. Treatment of a three-year-old girl's severe infantile neurosis. In *Psychoanalytic study of the child.* Vol. XV. New York: International Universities Press, 1960. Pp. 261–286.

Lapouse, R. Who is sick? *American Journal of Orthopsychiatry,* 1965, **35,** 138–143.

Lapouse, R., & Monk, M. A. Fears and worries in a representative sample of children. *American Journal of Orthopsychiatry,* 1959, **29,** 803–818.

Lapouse, R., & Monk, M. A. An epidemiologic study of behavior characteristics in children (1958). In H. Quay (Ed.), *Children's behavior disorders.* Princeton, N.J.: Van Nostrand, 1968. Pp. 3–21.

Lazarus, A. A. The elimination of children's phobias by deconditioning. In H. J. Eysenck (Ed.), *Behavior therapy and the neuroses.* New York: Pergamon Press, 1960. Pp. 114–122.

Lazarus, A. A., & Abramovitz, A. The use of "emotive imagery" in the treatment of children's phobias. In L. P. Ullman & L. Krasner (Eds.), *Case studies in behavior modification.* New York: Holt, 1965. Pp. 300–304.

Lazarus, A. A., Davison, G. C., & Polefka, D. A. Classical and operant factors in the treatment of a school phobia. *Journal of Abnormal Psychology,* 1965, **70,** 225–230.

Levy, D. Trends in therapy. III. Release therapy. *American Journal of Orthopsychiatry,* 1939, **9,** 317–376.

Lippman, H. S. *Treatment of the child in emotional conflict.* New York: McGraw-Hill, 1956.

Lippman, H. S. The phobic child and other related anxiety states. In M. Hammer & A. M. Kaplan (Eds.), *The practice of psychotherapy with children.* Homewood, Ill.: Dorsey Press, 1967. Pp. 73–95.

Lowenfeld, H. Book review of *Hysteria: The history of a disease,* by Ilza Veith. *International Journal of Psychoanalysis,* 1968, **49,** 101–103.

MacFarlane, J. W., Allen, L., & Honzik, M. P. *A developmental study of the behavior problems of normal children.* Berkeley: University of California Press, 1954.

Masserman, J. H. *Behavior and neurosis.* Chicago: University of Chicago Press, 1943.

Metzner, R. Some experimental analogues of obsession. *Behavior Research and Therapy,* 1963, **1,** 231–236.

Meyer, V. Modifications of expectations in cases with obsessional rituals. *Behavior Research and Therapy,* 1966, **4,** 273–280.

Milman, D. H. School phobia: Clinical experience. *New York State Journal of Medicine,* 1966, **66,** 1887–1891.

Mowrer, O. H. Learning theory and behavior therapy. In B. B. Wolman (Ed.), *Handbook of clinical psychology.* New York: McGraw-Hill, 1965. Pp. 242–276.

Nagera, H. *Early childhood disturbances, the infantile neurosis, and the adulthood disturbances.* New York: International Universities Press, 1966.

Patterson, G. R. A learning theory approach to the treatment of the school phobic child. In L. P. Ullman & L. Krasner (Eds.), *Case studies in behavior modification.* New York: Holt, 1965. Pp. 279–284.

Pavlov, I. P. *Conditioned reflexes.* (Trans. by G. V. Anrep). London: Oxford University Press, 1927.

Pavlov, I. P. *Lectures on conditioned reflexes.* New York: International Universities Press, 1941.

Peller, L. Libidinal phases, ego development and plan. In *Psychoanalytic study of the child.* Vol. IX. New York: International Universities Press, 1954. Pp. 178–199.

Peterson, D. R. Behavior problems of middle childhood. *Journal of Consulting Psychology,* 1961, **25,** 205–209.

Peterson, D. R., & London, P. A role for cognition in the behavioral treatment of a child's eliminative disturbance. In L. P. Ullman & L. Krasner (Eds.), *Case studies in behavior modification.* New York: Holt, 1965. Pp. 289–295.

Piaget, J. *Play, dreams, and imitation in childhood* (1945). (Trans. by C. Gattegno & F. M. Hodgson). New York: Norton, 1951.

Pick, T. Behavior theory and child guidance. *Journal of Child Psychology and Psychiatry,* 1961, **2,** 136–147.

Proctor, J. T. Hysteria in childhood. *American Journal of Orthopsychiatry,* 1958, **28,** 394–407.

Proctor, J. T. The treatment of hysteria in childhood. In M. Hammer & A. M. Kaplan (Eds.), *The practice of psychotherapy with children.* Homewood, Ill.: Dorsey Press, 1967. Pp. 121–151.

Rachman, S. Systematic desensitization. *Psychological Bulletin,* 1967, **67,** 93–104.

Rachman, S., & Costello, C. G. The aetiology and treatment of children's phobias: A review. *American Journal of Psychiatry,* 1961, **118,** 97–106.

Rafi, A. A. Learning theory and treatment of tics. In L. P. Ullman & L. Krasner (Eds.), *Case studies in behavior modification.* New York: Holt, 1965. Pp. 263–268.

Ramzy, I. Factors and features of early compulsive formation. *International Journal of Psychoanalysis,* 1966, **47,** 169–177.

Rangell, L. The analysis of a doll phobia. *International Journal of Psychoanalysis,* 1952, **33,** 43–54.

Redl, F. Pre-adolescents: What makes them tick? In F. Redl (Ed.), *When we deal with children.* New York: Free Press, 1966. Pp. 395–409.

Rexford, E. N. Discussion of Dr. Solnit's paper, Who deserves child psychiatry? A study in priorities. *Journal of Child Psychiatry,* 1966, **5,** 24–34.

Sandler, J., & Joffe, W. G. Notes on obsessional manifestations in children. In *The psychoanalytic study of the child.* Vol. XX. New York: International Universities Press, 1965. Pp. 394–425.

Scherz, F. H. Exploring the use of family interviews in diagnosis. *Social Casework,* 1964, **45,** 209–216.

Schnurmann, A. Observation of a phobia. In *Psychoanalytic study of the child.* Vols. III–IV. New York: International Universities Press, 1949. Pp. 253–271.

Schuham, A. J. The double-bind hypothesis a decade later. *Psychological Bulletin,* 1967, **68,** 409–416.

Sechrest, L. Implicit reinforcement of responses. *Journal of Educational Psychology,* 1963, **54,** 197–201.

Shepherd, M., Oppenheim, A. N., & Mitchell, S. Child behavior disorders and the child guidance clinic: An epidemiological study. *Journal of Child Psychology and Psychiatry,* 1966, **7,** 39–52.

Shoben, E. J., Jr. Psychotherapy as a problem in learning theory. *Psychological Bulletin,* 1949, **46,** 366–392.

Skinner, B. F. *The behavior of organisms.* New York: Appleton-Century-Crofts, 1938.

Sperling, M. Animal phobias in a two-year-old child. In *Psychoanalytic study of the child.* Vol. VII. New York: International Universities Press, 1952. Pp. 115–126.

Sperling, M. Analytic first aid to school phobias. *The Psychoanalytic Quarterly,* 1961, **30,** 504–518.

Sperling, M. School phobias: Classification, dynamics, and treatment. *Psychoanalytic study of the child.* Vol. XXII. New York: International Universities Press, 1967. Pp. 375–402.

Spiegel, H. Is symptom removal dangerous? *American Journal of Psychiatry,* 1967, **10,** 1279–1282.

Spock, B. *Baby and child care.* New York: Pocket Books, 1957.

Suttenfield, V. School phobia: A study of five cases. *American Journal of Orthopsychiatry,* 1954, **24,** 368–381.

Talbot, M. Panic in school phobia. *American Journal of Orthopsychiatry,* 1957, **27,** 286–295.

Taylor, J. G. Behavioral interpretation of obsessive-compulsive neurosis. *Behavior Research and Therapy,* 1963, **1,** 237–244.

Thomas, A., Chess, S., & Birch, H. G. *Temperament and behavior disorders in children.* New York: New York University Press, 1968.

Thorndike, E. L. *Animal intelligence: Experimental studies.* New York: Macmillan, 1911.

Ullman, L. P., & Krasner, L. *Case studies in behavior modification.* New York: Holt, 1965.

Valentine, C. W. *The normal child.* Baltimore: Penguin, 1956.

Van Houten, J. Mother and child relationships in 12 cases of school phobia. *Smith College Studies in Social Work,* 1947–1948, **18,** 161–180.

Veith, I. *Hysteria: The history of a disease.* Chicago: University of Chicago Press, 1965.

Waelder, R. *Basic theory of psychoanalysis.* New York: International Universities Press, 1960.

Waldfogel, S., Coolidge, J. S., & Hahn, P. The development, meaning and management of school phobia. *American Journal of Orthopsychiatry,* 1957, **27,** 754–781.

Waldfogel, S., Tessman, E., & Hahn, P. B. A program for early intervention in school phobia. *American Journal of Orthopsychiatry,* 1959, **29,** 324–333.

Walton, D. Experimental psychology and the treatment of a ticqueur. *Journal of Child Psychology and Psychiatry,* 1961, **2,** 148–155.

Walton, D., & Mather, M. D. The application of learning principles to the treatment of obsessive-compulsive states in the acute and chronic phases of illness. *Behavior Research and Therapy,* 1963, **1,** 163–174.

Watson, J. B., & Rayner, R. Conditioned emotional reactions. *Journal of Experimental Psychology,* 1920, **3,** 1–14.

Weiner, M. F. Hallucinations in children. *Archives of General Psychiatry,* 1961, **5,** 544–553.

Werry, J. S., & Wollersheim, J. P. Behavior therapy with children. *Journal of Child Psychiatry,* 1967, **6,** 346–370.

Wolman, B. B. *Contemporary theories and systems in psychology.* New York: Harper and Row, 1960.

Wolman, B. B. (Ed.) *Handbook of clinical psychology.* New York: McGraw-Hill, 1965.

Wolman, B. B. *Children without childhood.* New York: Grune & Stratton, 1970.

Wolpe, J. *Psychotherapy by reciprocal inhibition.* Stanford, Calif.: Stanford University Press, 1958.

Wolpe, J. The comparative clinical status of conditioning therapies and psychoanalysis. In J. Wolpe, A. Salter, & L. J. Reyna (Eds.), *The conditioning therapies.* New York: Holt, 1964. Pp. 5–20.

Wolpe, J., & Lazarus, A. A. *Behavior therapy techniques.* Oxford: Pergamon Press, 1966.

Woltmann, A. G. Play and related techniques. In D. Bower & L. E. Abt (Eds.), *Progress in clinical psychology.* New York: Grune & Stratton, 1952. Pp. 278–287.

Yates, A. J. The application of learning theory to the treatment of tics. *Journal of Abnormal and Social Psychology,* 1958, **56,** 175–182. (a)

Yates, A. J. Symptoms and symptom substitution. *Psychological Review,* 1958, **65,** 371–374. (b)

Yates, A. J. A comment on Bookbinder's critique of Symptoms and symptom substitution. *Psychological Reports,* 1962, **11,** 102.

Zetzel, E. R. 1965: Additional "Notes upon a case of obsessional neurosis": Freud, 1909. *International Journal of Psychoanalysis,* 1966, **47,** 123–130.

13 | Sociopathic Behavior in Children

Jacob Chwast

The term *sociopathy* has had its antecedents through the years. Prichard (1835) described those suffering from what he called "moral insanity"; Koch (1891) then suggested the expression "psychopathic inferiority"; Kahn (1931) described the dynamics of the "neurotic character"; and Henderson (1939) wrote about "psychopathic states." It was Partridge (1930) who introduced the designation *sociopath* to diagnostic terminology. Essentially, today, the terms *psychopathy* and *sociopathy* are interchangeable, although the latter is preferred generally because it does not carry the connotation of constitutional irreversibility.

DEFINITION

In the official listing (American Psychiatric Association, 1952), sociopathic personality disturbance is seen as consisting of four types of personality disorders: (1) antisocial reaction, (2) dissocial reaction, (3) sexual deviation, and (4) alcoholism and drug addiction. By almost universal consensus, the first type of disorder listed is considered characteristic of the true sociopath,

i.e., sociopathic personality disturbance and antisocial reaction. Such persons are described as

> . . . chronically antisocial individuals who are always in trouble, profiting neither from experience nor punishment, and maintaining no real loyalties to any person, group or code. They are frequently callous and hedonistic showing marked emotional immaturity with lack of sense of responsibility, lack of judgment, and an ability to rationalize their behavior so that it appears warranted, reasonable and justified. [1952, p. 38]

The diagnosis of dissocial reaction, on the other hand, is applied to individuals

> . . . who manifest disregard for the usual social codes, and often come in conflict with them, as the result of having lived all their lives in an abnormal moral environment. They may be capable of strong loyalties. These individuals typically do not show significant personality deviations other than those implied by adherence to the order or code of their own predatory, criminal, or other social group. [1952, p. 38]

Cleckley (1959) prefers to refer to the "sociopathic personality disturbance and antisocial reaction" as the psychopath. The diagnostic criteria he uses in distinguishing the core of psychopathy are the following: unexplained failure, undisturbed technical intelligence, absence of neurotic anxiety, persistent and inadequately motivated antisocial behavior, irresponsibility, peculiar inability to distinguish between truth and falsehood, inability to accept blame, failure to learn by experience, incapacity for love, inappropriate or fantastic reactions to alcohol, lack of insight, shallow and impersonal response to sexual life, suicide rarely carried out, and a persistent pattern of self-defeat.

Schmideberg (1961) considers psychopathy to be basically a failure in socialization, but not necessarily of a criminal nature: "The psychopath is unable to tolerate delay or frustration, has little sense of responsibility, lacks self-control and is anti-socially oriented. He tries to use the other person because of his fear of being used by him" (p. 734). She further depicts the psychopath as excessively narcissistic with underlying grandiosity. He is unable to tolerate anxiety because it would expose his human vulnerability, and he has a blunted conscience rather than none at all. The psychopath, Schmideberg continues, is one who immunizes himself to anxiety and guilt. While he denies his emotions to some extent, he is nonetheless "unhappy, frustrated and lonely." He manifests disturbed thinking and reality relations but not of psychotic proportions, and he spends "an inordinate amount of time creating complications, troubles and excuses" (p. 734).

Wolman (1966) designates the sociopathic or psychopathic personality as a *hyperinstrumental character neurosis*. He sees the hyperinstrumental as always wanting something for nothing. These individuals "show no consideration for fellow men, not even for their own parents, marital partners, or children; they act convinced that the world owes them a living, but they don't owe anything to anyone in return" (p. 53). The hyperinstrumental treats life like a bank that can be robbed or an oil field that can be exploited. Such individuals love no one but themselves. They are selfish, brutal, and exploitative, and they display sentimentality only for themselves. The hyperinstrumental feels sorry for himself, but has no mercy for another. He never blames himself, but always projects it onto somebody else. He views himself as weak but friendly and as hemmed in by enemies who are unfair and selfish.

"Hyperinstrumentals," Wolman goes on, "are dishonest, and disloyal. Yet they believe in their own innocence. They believe the world is hostile and they are resentful whenever others refuse to serve them" (1966, p. 53). The hyperinstrumental is overly sensitive to his own suffering, but he shows no empathy or concern for another person. Lacking moral restraints or compassion, he may or may not become criminal, depending upon whether he anticipates retaliation. This kind of sociopathic symptom formation offers the individual both primary and secondary gains. First, it offsets feelings of weakness and helplessness, and second, it helps in wresting privileges from those about him.

Wolman (1966, p. 53) describes the personality structure of the hyperinstrumental or psychopath as follows:

> His libido is self-hypercathected; he has never outgrown the primary narcissism of an infant and is in love with himself. He has no true object love for others; whatever object-relations he has, they are on an exploitative, primitive-instrumental, oral-cannibalistic level. He uses people and is inclined to destroy them for his own use. His friends are to be used and not helped; those who resent being used must be "liquidated," as enemies.

The hyperinstrumental views others as enemies who are bound to devour him unless he devours them first. He regards himself as weak, friendly, poor, and innocent. Although he feels sorry for himself, the hyperinstrumental cannot feel sorry for those he victimizes.

In essence, the hyperinstrumental possesses no moral principles or ethical standards and feels no human obligations. He operates only on the basis of his needs, with a superego that is virtually non-existent. "His ego may be weak or strong, but always siding with the id" (Wolman, 1966, p. 54).

Rosen and Gregory (1965), after reviewing the literature, summarized the characteristics of the typical antisocial sociopath. They see him (anti-social sociopaths are predominantly males, they believe) as having had his first psychiatric contact in adolescence or as a young adult. Sociopaths are concentrated in the lower socioeconomic classes. The sociopath manifests an uninhibited acting out of impulses and is unable to postpone rewards. His superego is defective or absent, with minimal or no guilt manifested because of serious antisocial activities. The sociopath is amoral, unreliable, and irresponsible. He may be addicted to drugs or alcohol, and he may express hostilities directly and violently unless such expression would interfere with immediate goals. The sociopath is indifferent to the opinions of others, except when such opinions frustrate his immediate needs. Confident and carefree, without long-range plans, the sociopath uses his superficial charm and plausibility to manipulate others. Incapable of true affection, his sexual behavior tends to be uninhibited and promiscuous. Among sociopaths, EEG abnormalities are frequent, and one finds a tendency toward a mesomorphic body build. Frequently, sociopathy has been found in the parents and siblings of sociopaths. Rosen and Gregory also note that one finds "Parental deprivation, discord, deceit, lack of supervision, occasionally overindulgence. Association with delinquent peers or siblings. Truancy, job instability and nomadism. . . . Record of conflict with police or military authorities" (1965, p. 353).

Even more succinctly, McCord and McCord (1956) present the profile of the psychopath as asocial, driven by primitive desires, highly impulsive, aggressive, feeling little guilt, and having a warped capacity for love.

ETIOLOGY

The etiology of psychopathy is accounted for variously by the many students of this disorder. The debate ranges from purely genetic factors as initially proposed by Koch (1891) to views such as proposed by Guttmacher (1953), who sees it as the "result of affect starvation during the first year of life." Karpman (1941) takes the position that two forms of psychopathy are discernible; the first is *idiopathic,* or *primary, psychopathy,* also called *anethopathy,* and the second is *symptomatic,* or *secondary, psychopathy,* which is of psychogenic origin.

Meerloo (1962), in reviewing the concept of psychopathy, considers psychopathy an innate deviation which is in a state of constant flux and will probably vanish when more is learned of "the personality and the specific genes that are related to impaired adjustment" (p. 651).

McCord and McCord (1956) also review psychopathy along causal lines as revealed in the literature, and they cite those such as Kraepelin (1915) and Rosanoff, Handy, and Plesset (1941) who support the hereditary approach; those who consider the neurological approach, such as Henderson (1939) and Thompson (1953); and those who are concerned with environmental factors including family influences, such as Partridge (1928), Field (1940), Szurek (1942), Lindner (1944a), Friedlander (1947), Bender (1947), Bowlby (1952), Levy (1937), Newell (1934), Wolberg (1944), Wolman (1971), and Symonds (1939). McCord and McCord conclude that there are two causes for psychopathy: "First, severe rejection, by itself. Second, mild rejection in combination with damage to the brain area (probably the hypothalamus) which normally inhibits behavior (1956, p. 69).

They are also aware of the need to take into account social and cultural forces in the predisposition toward psychopathy.

Although the dissocial sociopath is perceived

as much less disorganized and uncontrolled, Rosen and Gregory (1965) make the point that since in so many cases a combination of antisocial and dissocial traits occurs, ". . . the two reaction types should be considered the extremes of a continuum with the majority of sociopaths distributed somewhere in the middle" (p. 358).

THE CHILD

In his work in Vienna, Aichhorn (1935) observed two types of delinquent children. The first type he described is the child whose dissocial behavior is manifested symptomatically as an expression of an underlying neurotic difficulty. The second, basically sociopathic, is the child who exhibits dissocial behavior without neurosis. Such children received no affection when young and often have been treated severely and brutally.

Whereas Anna Freud (1949) clings to a purely psychosexual intrapsychic orientation, other psychoanalysts such as Szurek (1942, 1949), Johnson (1949), and Eissler (1949) see the child as carrying out the parents' unconscious impulses.

Eissler views the child as also being punished for doing this. Hence, both the unconscious hostile wishes of the parents toward the child and the demands of the superego are simultaneously satisfied. Johnson (1949) considers that antisocial acting out stems from unconscious parental initiation and fostering that is due to poorly integrated forbidden impulses in the parents. These impulses and the permission for their enactment are usually unconsciously communicated to the child.

Bender (1947) has observed that the psychopathic child is similar to the adult psychopath in his impulsivity, asociality, aggressiveness, lack of guilt, and poor ability to form relationships. Lippman (1959) confirms this observation in recalling that it is not unusual to find delinquents in child-guidance clinics whose behavior is similar to that described for adult psychopaths. Such

children have usually had inadequate relationships with one or both parents and frequently manifest an intense dislike for the parent to whom disciplinary action has been entrusted. They have also usually been truants from school, have been aggressive toward teachers, have had difficulties with the law early, and have drifted into predatory associations and gangs. Also observed among these children were frequent feeding problems, prolonged enuresis, and homosexual tendencies and activities.

Spitz (1950) finds little anxiety clinically among children who later become psychopathic. He describes the lack of inclination and application to any task demanding continued effort, and also motor hyperactivity such as rocking. Greenacre (1945) adds that such children have little tolerance for pain. Most important, they display an inability to appreciate time factors and to learn from experience. Lowrey (1951) contends that psychopathic reactions are multiple, repetitive, and overdetermined. These reactions are also inadequate, rather damaging to the self, and not modified by experience. Furthermore, such reactions are not adapted to social integration, for although conscious guilt and anxiety may be present, these are projected outward rather than inward toward the self. He concludes that although these reactions are not present in children, they are nascent very early.

After reviewing the evidence concerning organic factors as connected with psychopathy among children, Karpman (1959) concludes that ". . . psychopathic development for the most part indicated a clear-cut psychogenetic relationship with inadequate opportunity in the first years for the establishment of a meaningful primary mother relationship or cathexis" (pp. 143–144). He further declares that, in most instances, there is revealed "the absence of accepting parents, who under normal circumstances provide the child with the capacity or wish to become socialized" (p. 144).

The lack of parental response, especially maternal, is also emphasized by Berkowitz and Rothman (1960) and by Levy (1943, 1951). The latter is most impressed by the relationship between later psychopathy and primary affect hunger. In consequence of maternal attitudes, Levy traces two types of psychopaths. First, he speaks of the *deprived* psychopath. This individual is unable to adjust to life because he has not been able to form a close, personal relationship with anyone in infancy. As a consequence, emotional deficit develops within him, and he is ostensibly unaffected by the need to be loved. The superego thus emerges as weak in such a child, and the capacity to develop standards is defective because of an inability to identify with anyone. Second, Levy describes the *indulged* psychopath. Because his mother could never deny him anything as a child, his aggressiveness has been allowed to develop freely, and he therefore has become immune to punishment. In addition, the superego in the indulged psychopath is weak because the identification with the indulgent, loving mother has been so strong. Similar etiologic findings have been reported by Wolman (1971).

Lippman (1951) observes that children who have been rejected from the outset may become psychopathic. Such children have been unwanted or rejected by neurotic, sadistic, and ambivalent parents. As a result, ego formation is pathological and leads to extreme narcissism and instinct-driven behavior. Lippman maintains: "It is the narcissism, resulting from rejection, which accounts for the inability of the child to form an object relation to his mother in the first year of life, to his father and siblings later, and to those in the external world with whom he comes in contact" (p. 226). The child has failed to become socialized because he has had little to gain thereby. The usual rewards of affection from his parents have not been forthcoming because they have been unable to provide them.

Commenting upon the effect of early separation from the mother in shaping the personality of the psychopath, Spitz (1950) holds that the mother's unpredictable and rapidly changing personality makes the establishment of object relations impossible in the first year of life. This encourages narcissism and impairs identification. Spitz also notices that specific emotional factors are related to specific maternal personalities. In one case, identification with the mother is impossible because of contradictory, inconsistent, and rapidly fluctuating affective reactions. In another, it is possible that the child may encounter several rapidly changing mother substitutes. Under such circumstances, the varying and contradictory personalities of these substitutes make them just as unpredictable insofar as the child is concerned.

Michaels (1955) considers psychopathy to be representative of sexualization of antisocial behavior, while Banay (1948) links social deviation to an excessive emotional tie, usually to the mother, and an unresolved Oedipal complex. Chwast (1963), on the other hand, notes the relevance of Sullivan's concept of the "malevolent transformation" to antisocial, sociopathic forms of behavior.

Sullivan (1953) and Mullahy (1948) believe that a chronically hostile mother will induce an intense and chronic anxiety in her child. She does not provide him with tenderness, the lack of which will drastically affect his well-being and happiness as he grows older. As the child becomes more and more aware of the significant people about him, he learns to manifest behavior which will help him gain approval and escape punishment and disapproval. The experiencing of tenderness, approval, and good feelings leads to a perception of the self as "good-me," whereas disapproval and anxiety lead to a perception of the self as "bad-me." The earliest years thus have a profound effect on the course of future development. Perforce the attitudes, codes, and behavior of the child's parents or surrogates are uncritically accepted. The child will acquire a respecting and loving attitude toward himself if the significant people in his life have been respecting and loving toward him: "If they are derogatory and hateful, then he will acquire a derogatory and hateful attitude toward himself. Throughout life, save perhaps for the intervention of extraordinary circumstances and allowing for some modification through later experience, he will carry the attitudes towards himself he learned early in life around with him just as surely as he will carry his own skin" (Mullahy, 1948, p. 298).

When certain impulses cannot be openly expressed because they might stimulate retaliation and disapproval, the child may integrate them and then release them in a camouflaged way, which circumvents the appearance of anxiety. Since sublimation in this manner cannot always be achieved, the child may regress. Another possibility, however, is that the child might undergo a malevolent transformation of personality in seeking tenderness from his parents. The awareness of a need for tenderness, in consequence, becomes connected with rebuff, and "bad-me" is manifested when the child feels this need. Additionally, since feelings of disapproval and resultant anxiety accompany "bad-me," the child begins to experience anxiety whenever a need for tenderness occurs. Furthermore, the child may temporarily conceal his anxiety with anger, by preparing himself to counterattack his parents with his own hostility as they evoke anxiety within him by their hostility. Feeling unceasingly endangered, the child refuses to risk experiencing the anxiety that becomes attached to any expression of tenderness.

Sullivan (1953, p. 214) continues that the child learns that it is

... highly disadvantageous to show any need for tender cooperation from authoritative figures about him in which case he shows something else: and that something else is the basic malevolent attitude, the attitude that one really lives among enemies. . . .

And on that basis . . . later in life . . . the juvenile makes it practically impossible for anyone to feel tenderly towards him or to treat him kindly; he beats them to it, so to speak, by the display of his attitude.

From this it would seem that the malevolent transformation could lead to antisocial activity as the child is confronted by the "derogatory and hateful" attitudes of his parents. Among serious delinquents, many of whom were psychopathic, Redl and Wineman (1951) have noticed both the conscious and unconscious rejection by the parents. Bowlby (1944), Clothier (1944), Kanner (1944), Wolberg (1944), and Wolman (1971) have also observed this rejection among psychopathic children.

Evidently, severely traumatized children such as these aggressive delinquents cannot allow themselves to bear the pain that comes with expecting tenderness from others or expressing it toward others.

Bloch (1954) develops Sullivan's point of view further. He contends that the delinquent deals with his anxiety by manipulating others so that they will respond in a manner similar to that of his parents. The delinquent thus elicits from others rejection and punishment. Such treatment serves the added function of preventing the emergence of dependency needs, with their potential for unbearable anxiety. Because feelings of dependency are too difficult to handle and closeness can cause panic, the delinquent feels safer in remaining hostile.

Chwast (1958, 1963) reports the results of a study in which predelinquent boys were compared with nonpredelinquent boys in the perception of parental attitudes at two levels of awareness. He concludes that the predelinquent boys showed discrepancies in their perceptions, which indicates that the malevolent transformation is a process extending in time and not limited to the childhood and juvenile period. Thus in the case of the predelinquent the process is at an intermediate state which may still be heading toward its eventual resolution. In consequence, the chronically hostile mother can create anxiety in the child which may, in turn, be converted into hostility by the latter as he "beats the adult to it." The disastrous consequences of the malevolent transformation may be ushered in thereby as repeated small conversions of parental hostility into child hostility occur. Carried far enough, psychopathy might ensue as the end product.

TREATMENT

Treatment approaches to sociopathy have run the gamut of known techniques.

Physical methods have included the use of dilantin (Silverman, 1944), benzedrine (Shovron, 1947), and amphetamine (Hill, 1947). More drastic procedures have also been utilized, such as shock treatment (Darling, 1945; Green, Silverman, & Geil, 1944) and lobotomy (Banay & Davidoff, 1942).

Although psychoanalysis and psychotherapy have usually been reported to have failed with the sociopath (Lippman, 1949; Szurek, 1949; Whitaker, 1946), Friedlander (1947) and Lindner (1944b) have been quite encouraged, and Schmideberg (1949) is even more optimistic.

Chwast (1965, 1966) reports on the methods used in treating offenders, old and young and largely sociopathic, as observed in the clinic of the Association for the Psychiatric Treatment of Offenders (APTO). He contends that it is essential to utilize controlling and uncovering techniques in their treatment. Specifically, he highlights the creation of a viable treatment structure, the maintenance of rapport, realistic goal setting, the handling of crises, concrete assistance, uncovering and supporting maneuvers, the evocation of appropriate guilt and anxiety, ways of deflating and challenging, the encouragement of normalization, the therapist's flexibility, multiple relational supports, the building on positive strengths, and cooperative work with other agencies.

Aichhorn's (1935) early success with milieu therapy has been tried subsequently in several different settings. Redl and Wineman (1952) believed that the approach was effective despite the fact that their institution did not survive for lack of financial support. Powdermaker, Levis, and Touraine (1937) did not report success with this method at the Hawthorne Cedar-Knolls School, although good results were obtained at Wiltwyck. In connection with the latter institution, McCord and McCord (1956), as a result of intensive study, aver that ". . . milieu therapy improves the child psychopath in many ways" (p. 162).

The conclusions of McCord and McCord (1956) with regard to the effects of treatment—i.e., that forced institutional conformity does not usually improve the child psychopath; that narcotherapy may bring temporary relief or, conversely, aggravate the condition; that psychotherapy can be useful to some extent; and that milieu therapy has affected changes among some psychopaths—still seem valid.

In sum, if one considers all that has been written and said about sociopathy in children up until the present, the conclusion is inescapable that we are faced with many serious gaps in our knowledge. Open questions still persist in regard to the nature of sociopathy, its expression, and the underlying mechanisms, apart from the more pressing issues of the prevention, control, and treatment of this pathological personality formation.

REFERENCES

Aichhorn, A. *Wayward youth.* New York: Viking Press, 1935.

Alexander, F. The neurotic character. *International *Journal of Psychoanalysis,* 1930, **2,** 292–311.

American Psychiatric Association, Mental Hospital Service. *Diagnostic and statistical manual.* Washington: American Psychological Association, 1952.

Banay, R. S. *Youth in despair.* New York: Coward-McCann, 1948.

Banay, R. S., & Davidoff, L. Apparent recovery of a sex psychopath after lobotomy. *Journal of Criminal Psychopathology,* 1942, **4,** 59–66.

Bender, L. Psychopathic behavior disorders in children. In R. M. Lindner & R. V. Seliger (Eds.), *Handbook of correctional psychology.* New York: Philosophical Library, 1947. Pp. 360–377.

Berkowitz, P., & Rothman, E. *The disturbed child.* New York: New York University Press, 1960.

Bloch, D. A. Some concepts in the treatment of delinquency. *Children,* 1954, **1,** 49–55.

Bowlby, J. Forty-four juvenile thieves: Their character and home life. *International Journal of Psychoanalysis,* 1944, **25,** 19–53, 107–127.

Bowlby, J. *Maternal care and mental health.* Geneva: World Health Organization, 1952.

Chwast, J. Perceived parental attitudes and pre-delinquency. *Journal of Criminal Law, Criminology and Police Science,* 1958, **49,** 116–126.

Chwast, J. The malevolent transformation. *Journal of Criminal Law, Criminology and Police Science,* 1963, **54,** 42–47.

Chwast J. Control: The key to offender treatment. *American Journal of Psychotherapy,* 1965, **14,** 116–125.

Chwast J. Principles and techniques of offender therapy. In J. H. Masserman (Ed.), *Current*

psychiatric therapies. Vol. 6. New York: Grune & Stratton, 1966. Pp. 136–144.

Cleckley, H. M. Psychopathic states. In S. Arieti (Ed.), *American handbook of psychiatry.* Vol. 1. New York: Basic Books, 1959. Pp. 567–588.

Clothier, F. The treatment of the rejected child. *Nervous Child,* 1944, **3,** 89–110.

Darling, H. F. Shock treatment in psychopathic personality. *The Journal of Nervous and Mental Disease,* 1945, **101,** 247–250.

Eissler, R. S. Scapegoats of society. In K. R. Eissler (Ed.), *Searchlights on delinquency.* New York: International Universities Press, 1949. Pp. 288–305.

Field, M. Maternal attitudes found in 25 cases of children with primary behavior disorder. *American Journal of Orthopsychiatry,* 1940, **10,** 293–311.

Freud, A. Certain types and stages of social maladjustment. In K. R. Eissler (Ed.), *Searchlights on delinquency.* New York: International Universities Press, 1949. Pp. 193–204.

Friedlander, K. *The psycho-analytical approach to juvenile delinquency.* London: Kegan Paul, Trench, Trubner, 1947.

Green, E., Silverman E., & Geil, G. Petit-mal electro-shock therapy of criminal psychopaths. *Journal of Criminal Psychopathology,* 1944, **5,** 667–695.

Greenacre, P. Conscience in the psychopath, *American Journal of Orthopsychiatry,* 1945, **15,** 495–509.

Guttmacher, M. Diagnosis and etiology of psychopathic personalities as perceived in our time. In P. Hoch & J. Zubin (Eds.), *Current problems in psychiatric diagnosis.* New York: Grune & Stratton, 1953. Pp. 139–156.

Henderson, D. K. *Psychopathic states.* New York: Norton, 1939.

Hill, D. Amphetamine in psychopathic states. *British Journal of Addiction,* 1947, **44,** 50–54.

Johnson, A. Sanctions for superego lacunae. In K. R. Eissler (Ed.), *Searchlights on delinquency.* New York: International Universities Press, 1949. Pp. 225–245.

Kahn, E. *Psychopathic personalities.* New Haven, Conn.: Yale University Press, 1931.

Kallmann, F. *The genetics of schizophrenia.* Locust Valley, N.Y.: Augustin, 1939.

Kanner, L. The role of the school in the treatment of the rejected child. *Nervous Child,* 1944, **3,** 228–248.

Karpman, B. On the need for separating psychopathy into 2 distinct clinical types: symptomatic and idiopathic. *Journal of Criminal Psychopathology,* 1941, **3,** 112–137.

Karpman, B. The psychopathic delinquent child. *American Journal of Orthopsychiatry,* 1950, **20,** 260–265.

Karpman, B. Psychopathic behavior in infants and children: A critical survey of existing concepts. *American Journal of Orthopsychiatry,* 1951, **21,** 223–224.

Karpmen, B. (Ed.). *Symposia on child and juvenile delinquency.* Washington: Psychodynamics Monograph Series, 1959.

Koch, J. L. A. *Die psychopathischen Minderwertigkeiten.* Ravensburg: Maier, 1891.

Kraepelin, E. *Psychiatrie.* Leipzig: Barth, 1915.

Levy, D. M. Primary affect hunger. *American Journal of Psychiatry,* 1937, **94,** 643–652.

Levy, D. M. *Maternal overprotection.* New York: Columbia University Press, 1943.

Levy, D. M. The deprived and indulged forms

of psychopathic personality. *American Journal of Orthopsychiatry,* 1951, **21,** 250–254.

Lindner, R. M. A formulation of the psychopathic personality. *Psychiatry,* 1944, **7,** 59–63. (a)

Lindner, R. M. *Rebel without a cause.* New York: Grune & Stratton, 1944. (b)

Lippman, H. S. Difficulties encountered in the psychiatric treatment of chronic juvenile delinquents. In K. R. Eissler (Ed.), *Searchlights on delinquency.* New York: International Universities Press, 1949. Pp. 156–164.

Lippman, H. S. Psychopathic reactions in children. *American Journal of Orthopsychiatry,* 1951, **21,** 227–231.

Lippman, H. S. The "psychopathic personality" in childhood. In B. Karpman (Ed.), *Symposia on child and juvenile delinquency.* Washington: Psychodynamic Monograph Series, 1959. Pp. 4–8.

Lowrey, L. G. The development of psychopathic reactions. *American Journal of Orthopsychiatry,* 1951, **21,** 242–249.

McCord, W., & McCord, E. *Psychopathy and delinquency.* New York: Grune & Stratton, 1956.

Meerloo, J. A. M. The concept of psychopathy. *American Journal of Psychotherapy,* 1962, **16,** 645–654.

Michaels, J. J. *Disorders of character.* Springfield, Ill.: Charles C Thomas, 1955.

Mullahy, P. *Oedipus myth and complex.* New York: Hermitage, 1948.

Newell, H. W. Psychodynamics of maternal rejection. *American Journal of Orthopsychiatry,* 1934, **4,** 387–401.

Partridge, G. E. A study of 50 cases of psychopathic personality. *American Journal of Psychiatry*, 1928, **7**, 953–973.

Partridge, G. E. Current conceptions of psychopathic personality. *American Journal of Psychiatry*, 1930, **10**, 53–99.

Powdermaker, F., Levis, H. T., & Touraine, G. Psychopathology and treatment of delinquent girls. *American Journal of Orthopsychiatry*, 1937, **7**, 58–71.

Prichard, J. C. *Treatise on insanity.* London: Gilbert & Piper, 1835.

Redl, F., & Wineman, D. *Children who hate.* Glencoe, Ill.: Free Press, 1951.

Redl, F., & Wineman, D. *Controls from within.* Glencoe, Ill.: Free Press, 1952.

Rosanoff, A. J., Handy, L. M., & Plesset, I. R. *The etiology of child behavior difficulties, juvenile delinquency and adult criminality with special reference to their occurrence in twins. Psychiatric Monographs,* **1.** California Department of Institutions, 1941.

Rosen, E., & Gregory, I. *Abnormal psychology.* Philadelphia: Saunders, 1965.

Schmideberg, M. The analytic treatment of major criminals: Therapeutic results and technical problems. In K. R. Eissler (Ed.), *Searchlights on delinquency.* New York: International Universities Press, 1949. Pp. 174–189.

Schmideberg, M. Psychotherapy of the criminal psychopath. *Archives of Criminal Psychodynamics,* 1961, **4**, 724–735.

Sheldon, W. H. *Varieties of delinquent youth.* New York: Harper, 1949.

Shovron, J. J. Benzadrine in psychopathy and behavior disorders. *British Journal of Addiction*, 1947, **44**, 58–63.

Silverman, D. E.E.G. and treatment of criminal psychopaths. *Journal of Criminal Psychopathology,* 1944, **5**, 439–466.

Spitz, R. A. Possible infantile precursors of psychopathy. *American Journal of Orthopsychiatry,* 1950, **20**, 240–248.

Sullivan, H. S. *The interpersonal theory of psychiatry.* New York: Norton, 1953.

Symonds, P. M. *The psychology of parent-child relations.* New York: Appleton-Century, 1939.

Szurek, S. A. Notes on the genesis of psychopathic personality trends. *Psychiatry,* 1942, **5**, 1–6.

Szurek, S. A. Some impressions from clinical experience with delinquents. In K. R. Eissler (Ed.), *Searchlights on delinquency.* New York: International Universities Press, 1949. Pp. 115–127.

Thompson, G. N. *The psychopathic delinquent and criminal.* Springfield, Ill.: Charles C Thomas, 1953.

Thompson, G. N. Psychopathy. *Archives of Criminal Psychodynamics,* 1961, **4**, 736–747.

Whitaker, C. A. Ormsby Village: An experiment with forced psychotherapy in the rehabilitation of the delinquent adolescent. *Psychiatry,* 1946, **9**, 239–250.

Wolberg, L. R. The character structure of the rejected child. *Nervous Child,* 1944, **3**, 74–88.

Wolman, B. Classification of mental disorders. *Psychotherapy and Psychosomatics,* 1966, **14**, 50–65.

Wolman, B. B. *Call no man normal.* New York: International Universities Press, 1969.

14 | Schizophrenia in Childhood

Benjamin B. Wolman[1]

HISTORICAL REMARKS

In 1672, Willis, a British brain anatomist had described children who "passed into obtuseness and hebetude during adolescence." Esquirol (1772–1840) believed that this "acquired idiocy" developed as a result of masturbation, head injury, etc.

The first attempt to actually study disturbed or abnormal children was made in the late 1700s by Itard when he undertook the study of the "Wild Boy of Aveyron," who was found at the age of 12 living in the woods and who was considered to be a feral child.

Morel, in 1857, introduced the name *démence précoce* and emphasized the disease characteristics of arrest in mental development and "degeneration" that inevitably led to a state of dementia. In 1863, Kahlbaum described mental deterioration in adolescence, calling it *paraphrenia hebetica*; 11 years later he described a case of catatonia. He believed that catatonia was

a brain disease leading to disturbances in motility. The states of melancholia, mania, stupor, and confusion follow, and finally dementia takes place. In 1871, Kahlbaum's disciple and friend, Hecker, described hebephrenia in detail as a progressive disease of adolescence that starts with depressive moods, leads into a stage of wild excitement, and ends in a progressive mental decline. Both Kahlbaum, in 1890, and Hecker, in 1877, also published monographs in which they described a juvenile form of mental illness—hebephrenia.

In 1893, Kraepelin introduced a systematic classification of mental disorders. He distinguished two major psychoses—the manic-depressive psychosis and dementia praecox. Later, in 1896, Kraepelin elaborated his system, distinguishing three types of dementia praecox: (1) catatonia (Kahlbaum), (2) hebephrenia (Hecker), and (3) vesania typica (Kahlbaum), which is characterized by delusions of persecution and auditory hallucinations and which was later called the *paranoid* type of dementia praecox. Still later Kraepelin added the simple type of dementia

[1] Assisted in the preparation of this chapter by Susan Knapp, doctoral candidate in clinical psychology.

446

praecox to his system. While these types of dementia praecox usually occur in later adolescence and adulthood, Kraepelin, in his earlier writings (1883), indicated that similar types of pathology could be found in early childhood.

As a result of Kraepelin's influence, several childhood types of dementias were described in the early 1900s, and de Santis gave these the label *dementia praecocissima*.

E. Bleuler (1950),[2] who published in 1911 the now classic monograph entitled *Dementia Praecox or the Group of Schizophrenias,* accepted Kraepelin's idea of the nosological entity of this disorder and maintained that forms of it or similar to it can be found in childhood. Bleuler, however, was opposed to Kraepelin's emphasis on intellectual decline. He regarded emotional and associative disturbances as the essential features of schizophrenia, emphasizing the disturbance of affectivity expressed by indifference, on the one hand, and uncontrolled affects, on the other.

Bleuler, also, shifted the emphasis from dementia, the eventual outcome of the process, to the morbid process itself. He introduced the concept of autism, which is characterized by withdrawal from reality into a private world of one's own thoughts and emotions unrelated to those of other individuals. With this concept Bleuler created the impetus for future studies that emphasized social relations as determinants of schizophrenia, as opposed to Kraepelin's emphasis on metabolic disturbances.

Bleuler stressed that the outstanding features of the illness are the loosening of the associative function and the disruption in the continuity of personality. Accordingly, *schizophrenia* seemed to be a proper name for this split (schism) in the patient's mind (phrenos).

---

[2] The dates given in parentheses are the dates of publication of the works cited in the References, not necessarily the original dates of publication.

In 1896, in his first paper on schizophrenia, Sigmund Freud described a paranoid type of schizophrenia and the mechanism of projection. He stated that he believed early childhood experiences, especially those of a sexual nature, are represented in the delusions. The resulting guilt feelings and self-criticism are projected on the environment and experienced by the schizophrenic as ideas of reference and auditory hallucinations.

In 1907, Abraham, one of Freud's disciples, discussed the etiologic importance of early sexual traumata:

> Experiences of sexual nature whether they have the true value of a trauma, or produce a less severe impression upon infantile sexuality, are not the causes of illness, but merely determine its symptoms. They are not the cause of delusions and hallucinations; they merely give them their particular content; they are not responsible for the appearance of stereotyped words and postures; they merely determine the form which such manifestations take in an individual case. [1955, p. 58]

Freud believed that the conflict around the negative Oedipus complex and homosexuality leads to a paranoid delusional system. In schizophrenia the libido regresses from object love to autoeroticism, and at the same time it struggles to regain contact with the objects in restitution symptoms. Thus, according to Freud, loss of object and efforts for restitution are the content of the schizophrenic disorder.

In further studies (1914 and 1915) Freud explained the narcissistic regression in schizophrenia and the nature of its mental processes. The primary processes of displacement and condensation, which usually take place in dreams, occur in schizophrenics during the waking state. The libido withdraws from objects, but the retention of cathexis "of the verbal idea is not part of the act of repression (the withdrawal phase of the illness) but represents the first attempt at recovery or cure which so conspicuously dominates the clinical picture of schizophrenia" (Freud, 1925–1950, Vol. 4, p. 98).

A clear presentation of Freud's ideas on schizophrenia was given by Fenichel, who wrote:

> The infant starts out in a state of "primary narcissism" in which the systems of the mental apparatus are not yet differentiated from each other, and in which no objects exist as yet. The differentiation of the ego coincides with the discovery of objects. An ego exists in so far as it is differentiated from objects that are not ego. The schizophrenic has regressed to narcissism; the schizophrenic has lost his objects; the schizophrenic has parted with reality; the schizophrenic's ego has broken down. In schizophrenia, the collapse of reality testing, the fundamental function of the ego, and the symptoms of "disintegration of the ego" which amounts to a severe disruption of the continuity of the personality, likewise can be interpreted as a return to the time when the ego was not yet established or had just begun to be established. [1945, pp. 414–416]

Thus Freud proposes that schizophrenia has its roots in early childhood.

INCIDENCE

Mahler (1955) believes that there is a widespread reluctance to describe a child as a psychotic. Therefore, many euphemistic terms are used, among them *pseudopsychotic, prepsychotic,* and *incipient* and *borderline psychotic,* to describe children who show a clear evidence of psychotic behavior. Once, however, the term *childhood schizophrenia* was introduced as a diagnostic category, more and more children have been diagnosed as suffering from this disorder.

Milt (1963) reports that there are approximately four thousand psychotic children in state hospitals and approximately twenty-five hundred in residential treatment and day-care centers, while about three thousand schizophrenic children are seen in outpatient clinics. Milt further states that there are tens of thousands of children suffering from childhood schizo-

phrenia and that some estimates run as high as half a million.

SOCIOCULTURAL VARIABLES

Hollingshead and Redlich (1958) found in their Yale study that severity of mental disorder was inversely related to socioeconomic class. The prevalence rate of schizophrenia in the lowest class was eight times higher than that in the highest class. Also, Hare (1955) found a positive correlation between schizophrenia and low socioeconomic status in England. Goldhamer (Goldhamer & Marshall, 1949), however, questioned the reliability of the Hollingshead and Redlich study because of their small number of cases.

Stein (1957), in her study of mental disorders in London, found a higher incidence of schizophrenia in two boroughs. While there was a lower rate of schizophrenia in the more wealthy borough, a higher rate was found in the lowest economic class of each borough.

Morris (1959) remarked that although the incidence of schizophrenia is highest in the lowest socioeconomic class, the fathers of schizophrenics represent all socioeconomic classes. The low socioeconomic status of schizophrenics may therefore not be a cause but rather a result of schizophrenia. Kanner's study (1948b) is a case in point. Kanner found that most parents of schizophrenic children belong to the middle and upper social classes. It seems that schizophrenics treated in private practice belong to the middle and upper social classes, while schizophrenics in public hospitals belong mostly to the lower socioeconomic classes (Wolman, 1957, 1961, 1970). Schizophrenia is therefore not a class privilege. Families of wealthy schizophrenics, as a rule, seek help from private practitioners, while schizophrenics from low-income classes are most frequently committed to mental institutions.

Studies of the relationship between schizophrenia in adults and social mobility and urbanization (Faris & Dunham, 1939) suggest that there is some connection between these factors. R. Freedman's findings (1950) of the relationship between high mobility and high hospital admission rates of schizophrenics did not support Faris's and Dunham's hypothesis.

In a review of the pertinent literature, Lemkau and Crocetti concluded that " . . . there is a great deal of evidence justifying the speculation that there is an etiological relationship between schizophrenia and urbanization. However, the nature of the relationship or even its unchallenged existence has not yet been completely demonstrated" (1958, p. 73).

Von Brauchitsch and Kirk (1967) found that schizophrenia is more frequently discovered in children from the upper socioeconomic classes, while it is least frequent among children from broken homes, hard-core multiproblem families, and families in which the parents show overt mental illness. Furthermore, the prognosis of schizophrenia in the upper classes is less favorable and the disorder most closely resembles adult forms of psychoses, while children in the lower classes seem to lapse in and out of schizophrenic behavior. Von Brauchitsch and Kirk state: "It is possible that certain characteristic features of the disease (i.e. autistic and symbiotic symptoms and poor prognosis) are related to parental attitudes and ultimately to social group pressure rather than to the disease proper." (1967, p. 400)

Migration is believed to be highly correlated with schizophrenia. Malzberg and Lee (1956) found that psychosis rates among migrants are twice as high as those among nonmigrants, but it was not clearly evident that rates of schizophrenia are especially high. Yet studies by Odegaard (1932, 1945) and Wolman (1946, 1949) point to the conclusion that problems due to *acculturation* related to migration (but not migration as such) create emotional conflict. In most cases migration affects the socioeconomic status of fathers.

People migrate because they have not been successful in their homeland and expect a radical improvement in the new country. Unfortunately, migration often brings serious disappointments, or at least for awhile. Children go to school, learn the new language, and may adjust quickly. Parents, and especially breadwinners, may find their skills inadequate, their earning capacity limited, and their foreign customs and language subject to ridicule. Migratory groups have a difficult time adjusting to their new homes, and fathers of families find it hardest. They remain "greenhorns" for a long time, and their adjustment hardships invoke lack of respect from the members of their own families. My research cited above (Wolman, 1946, 1949) has pointed to this particular decline in paternal authority in migratory families as a significant factor in producing childhood schizophrenia.

ETIOLOGY

Genetics

Many research workers believe that schizophrenia is an inherited disorder. One of the strongest proponents of the inheritance theory of schizophrenia is Kallmann (1938, 1946, 1948, 1953), who found that children with one schizophrenic parent have a 16.4 percent probability of becoming schizophrenic, while children with two schizophrenic parents have a 69.1 percent probability. Furthermore, a comparison of fraternal and identical twins showed that where one fraternal twin has developed schizophrenia, there is a 16.4 percent probability that the other twin will also become schizophrenic, while identical twins have an 86.2 percent chance of both becoming schizophrenic. In a study of 691 twins, Kallmann demonstrated that dizygotic twins have shown concordance with schizophrenia in 14.7 percent of the cases, as compared with 77.6 to 81.5 percent in monozygotic twins. This higher percentage of 81.5 percent refers to twins who have been together for five years prior to their breakdown. Therefore, Kallmann concludes that ". . . inheritance of schizophrenia follows a biological genetic pattern" (1946, p. 318).

Kallmann, however, does not overlook environmental factors, for he states that schizophrenia is "the result of intricate interaction of varying genetic and environmental influences."

A tabular summary of Kallmann's studies (1962) of expectancy of schizophrenia shows:

One-egg twins	86.2%
Two-egg twins	14.5%
Siblings	14.2%
Half-siblings	7.1%
General population	0.85%

Altshuler (1957) confirms Kallmann's findings, stressing the fact that the expectancy rates for relatives of schizophrenics are much higher than those for the general population. And Vorster (1960) found a 17 percent incidence of schizophrenia among two-egg twins, as compared with a 70 percent incidence among one-egg twins.

The findings of Kallmann, Altshuler, and Vorster show a higher correlation between schizophrenia and consanguinity. Kallmann further hypothesized that inheritance of schizophrenia is probably due to a recessive gene.

Böök (1960) and Slater (1953, 1958) strongly criticized Kallmann's hypothesis of recessive heredity. They point out that since the corrected risk figures for schizophrenia "do not differ to a significant degree between parents, siblings, and children with one or no affected parent" (Böök, 1960, p. 29), the hypothesis becomes untenable. Furthermore, Gregory (1960) notes that the incidence of schizophrenia among various kinds of relatives follows neither a simple dominant nor a simple recessive pattern.

Böök hypothesizes that schizophrenia could be caused by gene differences expressed in homozygotes in a recessive fashion and occasionally in heterozygotes in a dominant fashion. The

basis for this hypothesis is the concept of "reduced penetrance," i.e., that the presence of a genetic factor does not necessarily affect the individual carrying it. Böök admits (1960, p. 31) that the applicability of the concept of penetrance to humans has been questioned, and yet Garrone (1962) applied the penetrance hypothesis to a study of the population of schizophrenics in Geneva and his findings show that schizophrenia is inherited according to a simple recessive mode with 67 percent of homozygous penetrance.

Bender (1956) also favors a genetic theory of schizophrenia. She proposes that schizophrenia is a process of dysmaturation and an arrestment of development at the embryonic level which is determined by genetic factors. The schizophrenic child is born with a kind of "*primitive plasticity.*" The entire neurological system of the child shows evidence of an organic lag in development. The infant's sleep, respiration, blood circulation, muscular tone, and metabolic processes are disturbed. The trauma caused by birth activates certain defense mechanisms which develop into the typical behavior patterns of schizophrenia; thus schizophrenia can be seen as a sort of encephalopathy.

Many workers seem to support Bender's hypothesis. Fish (1959) reported that a child diagnosed as schizophrenic at the age of 5 may have shown neurological and physiological disturbances as early as 1 month of age. Goldfarb (1961), however, found no significant differences in physical appearance between normal and schizophrenic children. And Eisenberg (1957) questioned the anatomical evidence of Bender's theory of encephalopathy. On the other hand, Bergman and Escalona (1949) reported unusual sensitivity in infants who were later diagnosed as psychotic. Their information, however, is based on parental observation, and there is no evidence demonstrating whether these sensitivities are inherited or acquired.

Roth (1957) states that " . . . no simple genetic

hypothesis accords with all the facts." Rosenthal, who is in favor of a genetic interpretation of schizophrenia, still admits that the question of what is actually inherited will remain unclear "until the specific metabolic error can be located or the specific patterns of influence defined or established" (1960).

D. D. Jackson (1960) examined the literature pertaining to genetics in schizophrenia and found that schizophrenia does not seem to follow the rules of dominant heredity. Furthermore, if schizophrenia were a product of recessive heredity, as Kallmann maintains, the rate of expectancy for monozygotic twins and for children of two schizophrenic parents would be 100 percent. Yet Kallmann's rates are substantially lower, and therefore the hypothesis of recessive heredity is also invalid (D. D. Jackson, 1960, p. 46). On the basis of these figures it would seem that since schizophrenia follows neither a dominant nor a recessive pattern, it cannot be considered to be an inherited disorder.

Yet heredity in schizophrenia is far from being a closed issue, and intensive research on the genetics of schizophrenia is being conducted at the present time in several scientific centers in different parts of the world.

Physique

The etiology of schizophrenia has often been thought to be related to bodily structure. In 1921 Kretschmer published his popular work *Körperbau und Charakter (Physique and Character),* in which he introduced a new version of the ancient Hippocratic theory of the relationship between bodily structure and personality type and applied it to mental disorders. The Hippocratic theory of the four bodily fluids has influenced the thinking of several generations. Galen, for example, in the second century, modified the four Hippocratic fluids, or "humors," introducing a theory of nine temperaments which result from combinations of the basic fluid.

While in modern times, Esquirol ascribed monomanic states and attributed what is now called "schizophrenia" to the *lymphatic* type. Lypomanic states, on the other hand, correspond to what is now called "affect" (or "manic-depressive") psychosis, and were attributed to the sanguine temperament.

The body-temperament tradition is still very much a part of European psychology and psychopathology. Kretschmer distinguished three physical types: the leptosomatic (asthenic), the athletic, and the pyknic. Kretschmer found that the three physical types were applicable to the general population and correlated with normal personality traits. Normal individuals with leptosomatic or athletic bodily structure were classified as normal schizothymics. If these individuals were to deteriorate mentally and become mental patients, their disorder would be schizophrenia.

Kretschmer's studies were, for a while, quite influential, for not only does he imply a normality-abnormality continuum, but he also relates mental disorders to tangible physical characteristics.

Sheldon (1940) and Lindegarde (1953) modified Kretschmer's theories, and there has been a great deal of theorizing about schizophrenia based on the constitutional theories of these three men. Yet empirical research has given little if any support to these theories. M. Bleuler (1955), Rees (1957), and others failed to find a definite relationship between schizophrenia and somatic types, while other workers (Bellak & Holt, 1948) tried unsuccessfully to relate certain schizophrenic syndromes to bodily types. Reviewing this literature, Rees (1957) wrote: "The proportion of individuals with the pyknic type of body-build was similar in the schizophrenic and normal group." Furthermore, research workers found a "considerable overlapping in the distribution of physical types between the manic depressive and the schizophrenic group" (Rees, 1957, pp. 8-9). Rees did not reject Kretschmer's ideas; yet he clearly states; "Modern methods of analyzing and classifying variations in body-build have indicated the existence of a continuous variation rather than the existence of physical types as discrete and independent entities" (1957, pp. 8–9).

Biochemical and Related Factors

Many research workers relate schizophrenia to biochemical factors, which may or may not have a clear genetic explanation. Baruk (1949) proposed that schizophrenia is caused by "cerebral anemia." It has been demonstrated that one can artificially impair cerebral blood circulation by injecting mescaline, adrenaline, and other toxic elements, with the resulting reactions being very similar to the symptoms of catatonic schizophrenia, especially with regard to inhibition of voluntary process. Yet Kety et al. (1948) demonstrated that the overall blood circulation in schizophrenics is normal.

Sackler, Sackler, La Burt, Tui, and Sackler (1952) related childhood schizophrenia to neuroendocrine factors. They found a high incidence of thyroid dysfunctions in mothers and frequent endocrine disorders, and they suggested that an adrenocortical excess is related to the etiology and pathogenesis of schizophrenia. Among the children in their study, the onset had occurred before the age of 4, and in thirteen out of nineteen children it had occurred before the age of 2.

Several researchers (see H. Freeman's review of the literature, 1958) have related schizophrenia to an alleged increase in cerebrospinal protein level. Katzenelbogen (1953) did not find evidence of a higher cerebrospinal protein level in schizophrenics, as compared with normals, and Davidson (1960) and Hyden (1961) did not find any evidence with regard to the role of RNA and protein in the etiology of schizophrenia. Other research workers, among them Gjessing (1938), Hoskins (1946), Hoagland (1952), Reiss (1954), and others, believe hormonal disbalance to be the cause of schizophrenia. Yet these workers have not been able to agree as to whether it is thyroid or adrenaline or any other endocrine disorder that acts as the cause. M. Bleuler (1954), H. Freeman (1958), and others stated, however, that at that time, there was no established connection between schizophrenia and endocrine factors. Hendrickson believes that schizophrenia is "an organic abnormality of the nervous system, really a complex and subtle type of neurological disorder" (1952, p. 10). Yet even the most detailed research in brain activity (Davidson, 1960; Hyden, 1961) has not reached the point where one could conclusively state that schizophrenic behavior *is* caused by a smaller amount of RNA in the ganglion cells, as compared with that found in normal individuals.

As previously mentioned, Bender believes that organic determinants are the cause of schizophrenia. She states that ". . . childhood schizophrenia involves a maturational lag at the embryonic level . . . characterized by a primitive plasticity in all areas from which subsequent behavior results" (1956, p. 499). Similar views have been expressed by A. M. Freedman (1954).

Kety expressed serious doubts as to whether "a generalized defect in energy metabolism . . . could be responsible for highly specialized features of schizophrenia" (1960), and Böök (1960, p. 32) found that the data on toxicity were very controversial. Richter (1957), on the basis of his own work and that of others, including Fisher, De Jong, Hoagland, and Munkvael, concluded that no evidence had been found indicating the presence of free aminos or any specific toxic compounds or abnormal metabolites in the blood of schizophrenics.

Heath (1960) proposed that ". . . schizophrenia is a disease characterized by alterations in the metabolic pathways for the breakdown of certain endogenously occurring compounds" (p. 146). The presence of taraxein in the bloodstream causes formation of a toxic compound that alters the activities of certain parts of the brain and results in schizophrenic behavior. Kety reported (1960) that injection of taraxein caused symptoms resembling schizophrenia, but there is no evidence that taraxein causes schizophrenia. Furthermore, there is no evidence supporting the amino-acid metabolism hypothesis. "The chromatographic search for supportive evidence is interesting and valuable," wrote Kety, but ". . . the preliminary indications of differences that are characteristic of even a segment of the disease rather than artifactual or incidental has not yet been obtained" (1960, p. 127). For instance, the presence of phenolic acids in the urine of schizophrenics has been, according to the study of Mann and Lambrosse, "better correlated with the ingestion of this beverage [coffee] than with schizophrenia" (Kety, 1960, p. 127). Kline (1958) pointed out that the alleged link between biochemical aberrations and psychosis is often a product of the peculiar food intake of institutionalized patients.

Research studying the possibility of biological determinants of schizophrenia goes on, however. For example, Wooley's hypothesis (1958) with regard to the role played by the serotonin enzyme has been tested in the so-called model psychosis. Yet studies reported by Kety (1960), Szara (1958), and others failed to find significant differences between normal controls and schizophrenics.

Reviews of research by H. Freeman (1958), Overholser and Werkman (1958), Werkman (1959), and Kety (1960) did not disclose any clearly determined causal relationships between organic factors and schizophrenia.

More recent studies seem to focus on neurological determinants of schizophrenia, pointing to the interaction between these determinants and disturbed relationships between parents and children who are diagnosed as schizophrenics.

As early as 1949, Bergman and Escalona stated that children who show uneven development and who eventually manifest psychotic disorganization are characterized from a very early age by extreme sensitivity to various types of stimuli.

They propose that in these children, there is a defect in the organic or neurophysiological barrier against these stimuli and that the aberrant behavior of such children is an attempt to protect themselves against overpowering stimuli.

Pasamanick and Knobloch (1963), after a study of the literature regarding early feeding problems and the eventual development of schizophrenia, report that it may be erroneous to correlate these problems with maternal rejection, as many writers have. They state that one of the most prominent causes of difficulty in nursing are brain injuries in the child. Therefore, they suggest that a child with some sort of mild physical abnormality will exhibit behavior, such as refusal to suckle, which in turn may cause the mother to become anxious and even rejecting. The child's disability and the reaction to it on the part of the mother may eventually result in childhood schizophrenia or autism. Therefore, Pasamanick and Knobloch state that it would be "advisable, at this time, to reconsider both the etiology and diagnosis of much of 'childhood schizophrenia' or 'infantile autism,' and possibly assign these cases to relevant chronic organic brain syndromes" (1963, p. 76).

As a result of a study of prenatal and perinatal factors in childhood schizophrenia, Taft and Goldfarb reported that ". . . symptoms of childhood psychosis are expressions of adaptation to a diversity of elements, and that, in addition, brain damage can in itself be a primary causative agent for the ego deficits of some children in the constellation of children designated by the label of childhood schizophrenic" (1964, p. 32). In their study they found that a number of children diagnosed as schizophrenic had been traumatized and neurologically impaired in the course of the reproductive process. Taft and Goldfarb further add: "The cerebral dysfunction restricts the child's adaptive competence; the direct expressions of cerebral dysfunction stimulate responses from his parents; and these parental responses in turn, become stimuli which reinforce behavior

in the child which we term 'schizophrenic'"
(p. 42).

Gittelman and Birch (1967) made a similar
study, and their findings support those of Taft
and Goldfarb. Yet they feel that their data point
to a theory proposing a continuum of psychogen-
icity interrelated with organismic factors. They
state that psychotic children possess primary
disorders of the sensory and response systems
which predispose them to abnormal patternings
of organism-environmental interactions and
which affect the totality of perceptual, cognitive,
and interpersonal experiences which are vital to
psychological growth.

Ornitz and Ritvo (1968) believe that there is
a single, psychological process which is common
to early infantile autism, certain cases of childhood schizophrenia, the atypical child, symbiotic
psychosis, and children with unusual sensitivities.
While the symptoms of all these disorders include
disturbances of perception, mobility, relatedness,
language, and developmental rate, Ornitz and
Ritvo state that perceptual disturbance is fundamental to the disorders and is evidenced by a very
early failure to distinguish between self and the
environment and the inability to imitate and to
modulate sensory input. These writers propose
that schizophrenic children are unable to maintain perceptual constancy because of "an underlying failure of homeostatic regulation within
the central nervous system so that environmental
stimulations are either not adequately modulated
or are unevenly amplified" (Ornitz & Ritvo, 1968,
p. 88). Furthermore, the child's various symptoms are not merely due to this "pathophysiology"
but are often the result of the child's attempt to
adjust to the pathophysiology.

Psychosomatics

With regard to biochemical defects, the question is one of causal order. Is schizophrenia a
result of biochemical defects, or does it cause
them? The somatopsychological theories stress

somatic factors, but, as Richter points out, "It is
always difficult to distinguish between cause and
effect" (1957, p. 68).

Several workers (Arieti, 1955; Wolman, 1967)
point to the possibility of a reverse causal order
and view schizophrenia as a psychosomatic
or, rather, a sociopsychosomatic disorder.

Chitty (1955), Krech et al. (1960), Hyden (1961),
and many others have found that social interaction can produce lasting biochemical changes.
Krech concluded his study of cholinesterase
activity by saying: "We have now shown that
cerebral CHE activity . . . can in turn be modified by behavioral and environmental circumstances."

Hoskins (1946), Shattock (1950), Doust (1952),
and others observed several pathological phenomena in schizophrenics, including cyanosis,
or bluing, of feet and hands caused by venous
stasis and other defects in their vasomotor system
such as a decrease in the volume of flow of blood
and a tendency to vasoconstriction. Yet Kety
et al. (1948) could not detect significant differences between the oxygen consumption and the
flow of blood in the brains of schizophrenics
and normal controls. There was no evidence
of cerebral anoxemia, and yet the disturbances
in the circulatory system of schizophrenics are
a well-established fact.

Therefore, a *psychosomatic* interpretation
of these phenomena seems to be justified. Arieti
states that vasoconstriction in schizophrenics
is a compensatory mechanism which prevents
dissipation of body heat, while the bizzare postures of catatonics activate antigravity vasocon-
strictor mechanisms. "Without these mechanisms, edema due to blood stasis would be very
frequent" (Arieti, 1955, p. 395).

Many physiological peculiarities have been
observed in schizophrenics, such as little reactivity to stimuli, reduced sensitivity to pain,
strong inclination to skin diseases, frequent colds
and increased sensitivity to cold, sharpening of

olfactory sensitivity, and lowered body temperature (Arieti, 1955; E. Bleuler, 1950; Buck, Caescallen, & Hobbs, 1950; Wolman, 1957, 1966b, 1967; and others).

These symptoms can be interpreted in light of the experimental studies of interoceptive conditioning (see Bykov, 1957; Ivanov-Smolensky, 1954; Pavlov, 1941). These studies show that the magnitude of general metabolism can be changed by conditioning through word signals. For example, in Shatenstein's experiment as reported by Bykov (1957, p. 179), a man who remained lying quietly on a couch showed a definite increase in metabolic rate when it was suggested to him that he had just finished an exerting, hard physical effort. Thus neuropathological changes can be interpreted as a result rather than a cause of schizophrenia, and Wolman (1967) maintains that schizophrenia is a sociopsychosomatic disorder.

Psychogenic factors

In 1896 Freud related schizophrenia to an early repression of libido, but then in 1907 he shifted the emphasis from sexual traumata to more general concepts of libido development. In that same year Abraham (1955) elaborated on this point of view by saying: "Experiences of a sexual nature, whether they have the true value of a trauma or produce a less severe impression upon infantile sexuality, are not causes of illness, but merely determine its symptoms."

In 1908 Abraham hypothesized that schizophrenia is caused by a regression of libido from object relationship into the autoerotic stage. According to the Freud-Abraham timetable, mental disorders are a product of fixation and/or regression, while more severe disorders are a product of earlier fixations.

"The psychosexual characteristic of dementia praecox is the return of the patient to autoeroticism, and the symptoms of this illness are a form of autoerotic activity," wrote Abraham in 1908.

"The autoeroticism is a source not only of delusions of persecution but of megalomania" (Abraham, 1955, pp. 74-75). "The psychosexual constitution of dementia praecox is based, therefore, on an inhibition in development." It is "an abnormal fixation to an erotogenic zone—a typical autoerotic phenomenon" (p. 77). In dementia praecox " . . . a person who has never passed out of the primary stage of his psychosexual development is thrown back more and more into the autoerotic stage as the disease progresses" (p. 78).

Freud (in 1911 and 1912) accepted Abraham's ideas regarding the pathogenesis of schizophrenia and viewed schizophrenia as a struggle between the regression of libido and its withdrawal from object relations and its efforts to recapture or restitute the object relations. Later in this chapter the theoretical explanations of schizophrenia given by Freud and other psychoanalysts will be discussed.

Freud's theorizing left several questions open in regard to the etiology of schizophrenia. His ideas include the biologically determined developmental stages and socioculturally determined human interactions. Assuming that all human beings go through the Freudian stages, the way in which they go through them depends upon interactional patterns. Whether a child will pass safety through an oral or anal stage or remain fixated or regress eventually depends on the amount and quality of the satisfaction and frustration he experiences in the *interaction* with his close environment. For, according to Freud, "Owing to the general tendency to variation in biological processes it must necessarily happen that not all these preparatory phases will be passed through and completely outgrown with the same degree of success; some parts of the function will be permanently arrested." The development can be "disturbed and altered by current impressions from without" (1949a, pp. 297ff.).

Sullivan studied these impressions from without. He noted peculiarities in the personalities of parents of schizophrenics and related the origins of schizophrenia to a state of panic disastrous to the patient's self-esteem (1931). Thus Sullivan perceived parent-child relationships which prevent the establishment of the "self-system," and especially panic states producing dissociation (the "not-me" feeling), as causes of schizophrenia (1947, 1953).

Sullivan's theory of interpersonal relations stimulated many workers to study the peculiar parent-child relationships. Whether these relationships caused schizophrenia as interpreted by a Freudian hypothesis of withdrawal of libido, by Sullivanian dissociation, or by any other theory, the nature of these relationships became a major topic in research in schizophrenia.

Interactional Determinants

Studies of the incidence of schizophrenia do not clearly indicate that schizophrenia is related to any peculiar century or type of civilization (see R. Linton, 1956). And the hypothesis that certain intrafamilial interactional patterns produce schizophrenia lacks final evidence.

A study of the research seems to indicate that parents of schizophrenics are not necessarily schizophrenic themselves, nor do they form a clear-cut pathological group. Kanner (1948a), Kanner and Eisenberg (1955), Despert (1951), Rank (1955), Nuffield (1954), Rosen (1953), and others found the parents of schizophrenics, and especially the mothers, to be highly disturbed, narcissistic, cold, etc. Some writers have used the term *schizogenic mother,* but there has been no agreement in regard to the personality traits that make a mother schizogenic.

Furthermore, research workers failed to find any definite pathology in the parents of schizophrenics. Alanen (1958) found 10 percent of the parents of schizophrenics to be disturbed and slightly over 5 percent to be schizophrenic. While I have found (Wolman, 1961, 1967) that

about 40 percent of fathers and 30 percent of mothers of schizophrenics display a great variety of pathological conditions, it is impossible to state that schizophrenia in offsprings is caused by any peculiar mental type of parents.

The current trend of research has been directed at the study of the intrafamilial interaction.

Kanner and Eisenberg, in a follow-up study of 105 cases, wrote the following about both parents: "The majority of parents . . . were cold, detached, humorless perfectionists" (1955, p. 228). Arieti found that among the parents of schizophrenics there is a predominance of a "domineering, nagging and hostile mother, who gives the child no chance to assert himself, [who] is married to a dependent, weak man, too weak to help the child" (1955, p. 52).

Research workers at the James Jackson Putnam Center called their little patients children with "atypical development" (Putnam, 1955; Rank, 1949, 1955; and others). They believe that the most important etiologic factors were related to "profound disturbance" in the early parent-child relationship and to traumatic events, especially separation from parents (Rank, 1955, p. 493). Rank points to a "fragmented ego" that is "the result of the infant's unsuccessful struggle to obtain vital satisfaction from his parents" (1955, p. 493). This "paralyzed ego" retreats into a world of fantasy and "coexists" with the development of certain functions. This leads to disparity in the intellectual development of schizophrenic children.

Bateson, Jackson, Haley, and Weakland (1956) studied peculiar patterns of self-contradictory mother-child communications, called the *double bind* (1956). Hill described the parents of schizophrenics as follows: "These mothers were ill. They needed their sons and daughters to give them a reason for existence. These mothers are devastatingly, possessively all-loving of their child who is to be schizophrenic. The father was often aggressive, but this belligerence was that of a very unwilling agent of his wife" (1955, pp. 106–107).

Lidz and associates (Lidz et al., 1957; Lidz et al., 1958; Lidz & Fleck, 1960) found lack of mutual understanding and cooperation between the parents of schizophrenics:

> We realized soon, that the intrapsychic disturbances of the mothers were not nearly as relevant to what happened to one or more children in the family (especially to the child who became schizophrenic), as was the fact that these women were paired with husbands who would either acquiesce to the many irrational and bizarre notions of how the family should be run or who would constantly battle with and undermine an already anxious and insecure mother. [Fleck, 1960, p. 335]

Similar findings have been reported by Wolman (1957, 1961, 1966b), Lu (1961, 1962), and many others.

Apparently the etiology of schizophrenia "requires . . . the failure of the father to assume his masculine controlling function. . . . To produce schizophrenia it appears necessary for the mother to assume the father's role" (Whitaker, 1958, p. 108). "The parents follow a pattern very much like divorced parents who share their children. The mother, the overadequate one in relation to the inadequate child, is in charge of the child. . . . The father is then in the functioning position of a substitute mother" (Bowen, 1960, p. 363).

Szurek (1956) found that in all instances in which a child was diagnosed to be schizophrenic, both parents were found to have suffered severe intrapsychic conflicts prior to the development of the child's disorder. Szurek states that the psychotic child's disorder represents his identification with, and rebellion against, each of the parents' disorders, while the healthy aspects of the child seem to be correlated with his integrative experiences with his parents. Furthermore, the child's symptoms are often a caricature of what he sees in his parents.

With regard to infantile autism, Bettelheim (1967) states that the precipitating factor "is the parent's wish that his child should not exist" (p. 125). Accordingly, autism represents a defense on the part of the infant, erected to protect himself against an environment which he perceives to be totally annihilating. Because he is not wanted by the parent, the child is not heard, and his cries become more and more impotent. Finally, the child feels that there is no response and no love and that he is powerless and forsaken. The mother, in turn, by failing to respond to the infant "may force him to exist only or mainly as an extension of herself, as a passive object of her care" (Bettelheim, 1967, p. 28). The infant responds to his mother's denial of his being by slowly withdrawing from her and the environment. He feels that since his environment is insensitive to his reactions, he has no power to influence it in any way. Thus, in a desperate attempt to survive, the child is forced into a state of hopelessness and despair.

Family Structure

All these studies indicate peculiarities in intrafamilial relationships, and while the reported data may differ in detail, all show an almost uniform pattern of interaction. Therefore, a sociopsychological theory has been proposed which could link all the data into a coherent system (Wolman, 1957, 1958b, 1965, 1966b, 1970).

According to this theory, three types of social relationships, depending upon the objectives of the participants, have been distinguished. Whenever an individual enters into a relationship with the objective of receiving, the relationship is of the *instrumental* type, for the partner or partners are used for the satisfaction of the individual's needs. The infant-mother relationship is the prototype of instrumentalism. The infant is weak, while the mother is strong; the infant must receive, but he cannot give. Whenever an individual enters into a relationship with the objective of satisfying his own needs and also the needs of others, the relationship is a *mutual* one. Friendship and marriage represent mutualism. Sexual intercourse is probably the prototype of mutualism. Whenever an individual's objective is to satisfy the needs of others, the relationship is *vectorial*. Parenthood is the prototype of vectorialism; parents give love and support and protect their children.

Normal adults are capable of interacting in all three ways. In business they are instrumental; in friendship and marriage, mutual; and in parenthood and in their ideals, vectorial.

In normal families, children perceive their parents as strong and friendly adults who relate to each other in a giving and receiving (that is, *mutual*) fashion and who have a *vectorial* attitude toward the children, irrespective of what these children may be or do. Parental love must be unconditional; the smaller and weaker the child, the more vectorial the parental attitude. This protecting (vectorial) attitude of the parents enables the totally dependent (instrumental) infant to move toward higher, more complex levels of interindividual relations. At the anal stage of development, the child may graciously accept toilet training, with its demands to give something away. Throughout his development the growing child "generalizes" this give-and-take or mutual-acceptance attitude and learns reciprocity in his relations with his peers. This social development, which is brought about by both maturation and learning processes, enables the child to grow to the point at which he is able to adopt a protective (vectorial) attitude toward his own children.

Schizogenic families. Detailed case studies and interviews have demonstrated that it is not the "weak father" and "strong mother" that produce schizophrenia. Were this true, *all* siblings of a schizophrenic would also be schizophrenic, and empirical evidence shows that they are not. Furthermore, domineering mothers and submissive fathers often produce manic-depressives. It seems that *the main cause of schizophrenia is frustrated instrumentalism in the interparental relationship* (Wolman, 1957, 1961, 1964, 1966b). A woman who has been frustrated in her attempt to make a father out of her husband eventually grows to hate him and seeks the child's love and support instead. A father who is disappointed because his wife does not act like his mother may try to compete with or seduce his own child.

This morbid intrafamilial relationship does not fall into the usual descriptive categories of rejection, overprotection, overindulgence, etc. The schizogenic family relationship represents a *reversal of social positions* which creates in the child, who eventually becomes schizophrenic, a confusion regarding social roles of age, sex, and family position.

The mother confuses the child by presenting herself as the tyrant who controls the entire family. She adopts a protective-hostile manner, telling the child that he is weak, sick, stupid, or ugly and that she must protect and care for him. Yet at the same time she presents herself as a self-sacrificing, suffering, almost dying person.

This tyrant-martyr ambivalence with constant accusation of ingratitude and incessant demands for appreciation is, as far as the content of communication goes, a "double bind" (Bateson et al., 1956). But the issues at stake are more than a matter of communication.

These mothers cannot tolerate in the child any independence, any growth, or any successes which they themselves do not bring about. They are possessive, they control the child's life, and they demand from him an unlimited amount of love, gratitude, and self-sacrifice for the self-sacrificing tyrant-martyr mother (see Davis, 1961; Foudraine, 1961; Lu, 1961, 1962; Weakland, 1960; Wolman, 1961, 1965b, 1966b; Wynne et al., 1958; and many others).

The normal reaction to this kind of emotional extortion is hate, but the preschizophrenic child is not able to express his hate toward those who are hurting him. For at the same time that the mother is destroying the child, she is constantly professing that she loves him. She makes him hate himself for feeling hostile toward his self-sacrificing protector. He becomes frightened and confused and forces himself to deny his true hostile feelings. As Federn (1952) states it, the frightened child is forced to hypercathect his love objects at the expense of self-cathexis.

The future schizophrenic starts his life like any other child, helpless and dependent on aid from the outside. Yet he soon realizes that his parents are weak and dependent, and he lives under a constant threat of losing them. All schizophrenics, as Sullivan observed (1953), are panic-stricken. The child worries about his parents and takes on a premature and much too costly protective, *hypervectorial* attitude toward them, for in order to survive, he must protect his protectors (Wolman, 1957, 1958a, 1959, 1961, 1962, 1965, 1966b, 1970).

No woman could, however, destroy her child without the active or tacit assistance of her husband, and all fathers of schizophrenics participate in producing schizophrenia in their children.

Often it is the father who triggers the tragic involvement with his child. He, too, expects the child to give him what he cannot get from his wife. He tends to become seductive toward children of both sexes, causing confusion with regard to age and sexual identification. Some fathers fight against their own wives and children, and many schizophrenic families live in fear of the angry father.

Manic-depressive patients wish to be sick or dying in order to elicit their mother's love. They perceive their mother as a strong, hostile person whose sympathy and favors can be won only by weakness or illness. Schizophrenics and other hypervectorial types, on the other hand, cannot expect anything in sickness. They will be blamed for getting sick and burdening their martyred mother.

Schizophrenics' fantasies take a grandiose direction. They wish to be God, Creator, Messiah, Savior; they want to become superfathers and supermothers. They often dream of how they will destroy the entire world and put an end to their misery. They dream about power, while manic-depressives dream about weakness. When they hallucinate, they hallucinate a super-parental power (Fenichel, 1945; Wolman, 1966b).

THEORETICAL INTERPRETATIONS

Psychoanalytic Theories

The primary question to be asked with regard to disturbed, disorganized, or abnormal behavior is: What is its cause? Causation is not an observable fact; what is observable is merely a temporal sequence of events. Yet the causal principle is an exceedingly useful and methodologically necessary postulate which helps in relating events in a coherent and intelligible manner (see Wolman, 1960a, pp. 523ff.). All theories dealing with psychopathology endeavor to relate observable phenomena to the underlying causes and deal with the explanation of past causes and prediction of future results.

Kraepelin believed that schizophrenia is an incurable process of deterioration. In 1898, in a paper entitled "The Diagnosis and Prognosis of *Dementia Praecox*" (later called *schizophrenia* by E. Bleuler) he visualized an endogenous, deteriorating, and incurable disease of organic origin. Kraepelin first related the disease to brain pathology, but later favored a metabolic explanation and maintained that catatonic symptoms may end in the death of the patient (1919).

E. Bleuler accepted, in 1911, the organic theory of schizophrenia, but refuted Kraepelin's ideas of deterioration, incurability, and lack of affect. Bleuler reported several cases of recovery in schizophrenia, with and without specific treatment. He felt that the core of schizophrenia consists of dereistic and autistic thinking, disturbances in associations, emotional ambivalence, and withdrawal from reality into a world of fantasy (1950).

Bleuler's theory was influenced by the Freud-Abraham studies, which were mentioned previously. Freud assumed that the fixation point of schizophrenia lies in the transition from the autoerotic stage toward the beginning of object relations. He stated that schizophrenia is a "narcissistic neurosis" in that the patient is unable to develop object relations. The origins of the ego are related to the "differentiations from objects that are not ego." Schizophrenia is a regression to narcissism, i.e., loss of objects, loss of contact with reality, and breakdown of the ego. As a result, schizophrenics are incapable of transference (see Fenichel, 1945, pp. 415ff.).

During the period from 1911 to 1914, Freud stressed the inner struggle that takes place in schizophrenia. On the one hand, schizophrenia is a process of regression and withdrawal of libido from objects, but on the other hand, it is at the same time a restitutive struggle to regain object relations. This effort of recathexis of objects with libido, wrote Freud in 1915, "represents the first of the attempts at recovery or cure which so conspicuously dominate the clinical picture of schizophrenia" (1925–1950, Vol. 4, p. 136).

Freud related delusions of persecution to repressed homosexual impulses. In the famous Schreber case (1911) the patient tried to ward off homosexual urges by reaction formation and by projecting his hate onto his love object. Schizophrenic ideas of reference and "influencing machine" have been interpreted by Tausk (1933) as projection; at the pre-ego and pre-object-relations stage there is no clear dividing line between the organism and the outer world. Thus the schizophrenic may perceive his own sensations as if they were coming from without.

In the later development of psychoanalytic thinking, Abraham (1955) in 1916 and Nunberg (1948) in 1921 related schizophrenia to the oral stage, in which introjection is the only possible object relationship. At this stage there are no definite boundaries between the organism and the outer world; therefore, incorporation and projection take place easily. In 1924, Abraham concluded that introjection may also be anal (see Abraham, 1955). At the same time Freud introduced the concept of a tripartite personality structure composed of id, ego, and superego, and he characterized psychoses as the ego's loss of contact with reality and surrender to the id.

Later Developments

Orthodox Freudians such as Fenichel, Federn, Hartmann, Katan, Roheim, and others elaborated, with some deviations, on the Freud-Abraham interpretation of schizophrenia. Hartmann (1955) hypothesized that the schizophrenic ego is unable to "neutralize" aggressive energy, while Katan (1954) stressed the importance of homosexual conflict. Roheim (1955) proposed that oral trauma, such as loss of the mother, is the essence of schizophrenia and that the illness represents a regression to the infantile fantasy of the internalized mother.

In his successful treatment of schizophrenics, Federn discovered that they do develop transference. He pointed out that schizophrenia is not a withdrawal of object cathexis but a hypercathexis of objects. The patient's ego has not lost its love object—it has lost the cathexis. The ego of the schizophrenic is impoverished, inadequately cathected, and unable to test reality (1952).

Federn also introduced the concept of "ego boundaries," a sort of center of perception of the "ego feeling." This feeling distinguished "everything that belongs to the ego" from everything else. In schizophrenics the poorly cathected ego boundary breaks down; consequently, there is no correct perception of reality.

Klein and her school represent an independent point of view which deviates sharply from that of Freud. Klein (1946) rejected the concept of primary narcissism, proposing that there are very early object relationships. The earliest objects, the breast and later the penis, are perceived as good or bad. Early projection and introjection of the bad breast typifies the "paranoid position," ascribed by Klein to infants in their third year of life. Under the pressure of threats of dissolution, the ego may fall apart. Klein writes that this "falling of the ego to pieces" underlies the "states of disintegration in schizophrenics." The infant identifies the object with hated parts of himself, and this hateful introjection and projection is, according to Klein, the essence of schizophrenia.

Another British psychoanalyst, Rosenfeld (1953), accepted some of Klein's ideas regarding early introjection. He believed that schizophrenics are afraid that they might destroy their love objects by introjection and that therefore they withdraw from objects. Rosenfeld stressed the preponderance of aggressive impulses in schizophrenics and their fear of these impulses.

Non-Freudian Psychoanalytic Views

Non-Freudian analysts have also devoted considerable attention to schizophrenics.

In 1906, Jung disagreed with Kraepelin's interpretation of schizophrenia and stressed emotional overinvolvement which leaves little energy for facing real problems. Jung wrote:

> The separation of the schizophrenic patient from reality, the loss of interest in objective happenings, [all this] is not difficult to explain when we consider that he persistently stands under the ban of an invincible complex. . . . He dreams with open eyes and psychologically no longer adapts himself to his surroundings. [1936, p. 89]

The schizophrenic complex, Jung believed, is rooted in the collective unconscious. The unconscious archaic, atavistic material may be the essence of schizophrenia.

Sullivan traced the origin of schizophrenia to *disastrous interpersonal relations* between the schizophrenic and his parents and/or other significant adults. The severe anxieties experienced in childhood lead to parataxic distortions, which as described by Sullivan resemble autistic thinking as Bleuler describes it, and to dissociation, which is analogous to Freud's repression. Thus schizophrenia, according to Sullivan, is basically a "regressive preponderance" associated with a profound loss of self-esteem, panic states, and regression to the uncanny, weird, prototaxic mode.

Sullivan's idea of "regressive preponderance" and Von Domarus's (1944) principle of "paleological thinking" have been further developed by Arieti. Arieti (1955) feels that schizophrenia is a regression "because less advanced levels of mental integration are used." Furthermore, this regression is teleological because ". . . the regression seems to have a purpose, namely to avoid anxiety by bringing about the wanted results" (1955, p. 192).

At this point, it should be noted that Freudians and non-Freudians alike stress regression, aggression, unconscious processes, and loss of contact with reality.

Kretschmer's Theory

As previously stated, Kraepelin believed in an organic, chemogenic, or endocrinogenic origin of schizophrenia, and several workers have supported the organic interpretation.

Kretschmer (1925) developed a systematic theory of schizophrenia, associating it with asthenic (leptosomic), athletic, and often dysplastic bodily structures. Kretschmer's theory, in addition to its constitutional ideas, presented all mental disorders, including schizophrenia, on a continuum starting with normal schizothymics. Accordingly, any individual of the above-mentioned bodily structures could be a normal introvert with some tendency to abstraction and fantasy life. Should the normal schizothymic individual deteriorate and become psychotic, his psychosis must be schizophrenic.

"Model Psychosis"

Experiments with mescaline and LSD 25 have aroused considerable interest and a great deal of speculation concerning the nature of schizophrenia. The symptoms which have been produced in these experiments resemble those of schizophrenia; the volunteering subjects experienced disturbance in thought processes, severe states of anxiety, general confusion, and delusions (see Baruk, 1949; Linton & Langs, 1962; Savage & Cholden, 1956).

The fact that mescaline and lysergic acid produce symptoms resembling those of schizophrenia cannot serve as evidence that schizophrenia is a chemogenic disorder. For example, baldness can be produced by electric current, and yet this is not the way men usually get bald. Furthermore, symptoms produced by mescaline and lysergic acid are not specific; nonschizophrenics may display some of these symptoms, and schizophrenia may occur without most of them. Criticism has been raised also in regard to the use of volunteers and the validity of the results in general (see Esecover, Malitz, & Wilkens, 1961; Wolman, 1962; and others).

Pavlov's Theory

Pavlov (1928, 1941) suggested a neurophysiological theory of schizophrenia. He hypothesized that schizophrenia is a protective reaction of weak cortical centers. Schizophrenics are easily excitable and overreact to strong stimuli. When overstimulated, they may burst out in a raging fury. Thus schizophrenia is interpreted as a general *protective inhibition* of the cortex to protect overstimulation of nerve cells. In catatonia the protective inhibition spreads to subcortical and autonomic nerve centers. Outbursts of violence have been interpreted by Pavlov as a lack of control of the weak cortex over subcortical centers.

Extensive research has been conducted in the Soviet Union along the lines of Pavlov's theory. Several empirical studies offer support to Pavlov's general ideas in regard to the role of the cortex, but this does not prove or disprove Pavlov's interpretation of schizophrenia.

Learning Theory

There have been some efforts to interpret schizophrenia in terms of Hull's learning theory. Mednick (1958) proposes that acute schizophrenics are in a state of "heightened drive" which tends to increase the strength of responses. Accordingly, a high-drive group should display faster conditioning than a low-drive group. The studies by Taylor and Spence (1954) and Spence and Taylor (1953) have discovered faster eyeblink conditioning in schizophrenics than in normals.

Garmezy (1952) and Mednick (1957), in experiments of generalization of pitch and of space dimensions, respectively, found higher generalizations in schizophrenics than in normals. However, contrary to Hull's theory, Dunn (1954) found that normal controls generalize better than schizophrenics do with social materials.

According to Hull's theory, organisms in high drive turn to irrelevant and incorrect responses. The fact that schizophrenics perform poorly on complex tests (Hunt & Coffer, 1944; Mednick, 1957) has been explained by Mednick in a Hullian fashion as follows: "The schizophrenic performance has been retarded by irrelevant, incorrect response."

Multiple-factor Theories

A multiple-factor theory of schizophrenia was proposed by Bellak, who doubts whether there is one principal cause for schizophrenia. He compares schizophrenia to "fever" as diagnosed in early studies of medicine. Schizophrenia can be produced by LSD 25, by perceptual isolation, and by several other physiochemical or psychological factors. "Schizophrenia lies at the low end of the continuum of ego strength," wrote Bellak (1958, p. 53). "Schizophrenia was designated as a syndrome characterized by a final common path of disturbances of the ego, with a primary etiology of chemogenic, histogenic, genogenic, or psychogenic nature and combinations thereof, different in each individual case, but probably identifiable as clusters in subgroups" (pp. 61–62).

A comparative developmental theory of schizophrenia based on Werner's work has been introduced by Goldman. Goldman views schizophrenia as a "regression," meaning "the structural re-emergence of developmentally lower levels of functioning as the more advanced and more recently developed levels are disorganized" (1962). Thus emotions become uncontrolled, aggressive and impulsive feelings are fused, and the emotional experience of an acute schizophrenic becomes similar to that of a young child, labile and unpredictable. There is a regression in perception, and attention is shifting. Schizophrenics perform poorly on complex tests, and their total behavior is indicative of low-level performance.

Adolf Meyer (see Lief, 1948) stressed the gradual deterioration in mental life. Schizophrenia may start as a series of "trivial and harmless subterfuges" such as decline in interest in the outside world, gradual withdrawal into fantasy life, and moodiness that may eventually lead into a schizophrenic reaction.

Existential psychology has interpreted schizophrenia chiefly as a "hypotonia of consciousness." The schizophrenic's sense of reality has been affected. He experiences himself "as so limited in his full humanity that he no longer can feel himself as really 'existent'" (Frankl, 1955).

Structural-deficiency Theory

Des Lauries (1962, 1967) describes schizophrenia in terms of *structural deficiency*. The schizophrenic child is unable to relate to others because he is unable to experience himself as differentiated from others. He cannot define the boundaries of his own identity, and therefore he is unable to experience others as separate from himself. Yet this deficiency is also dynamic and functional because as a result of this ego deficit, instinctual strivings have no adequate and satisfactory instrument of expression or gratification (Des Lauries, 1967, p. 195). The schizophrenic child is suffering from a lack of sufficient narcissistic cathexis of his body boundaries, which makes it impossible for him to develop the necessary psychological structures vital to his experience of reality and his individual position in reality. Des Lauries states that the schizophrenic child, despite the hypotheses of many writers, has not withdrawn from reality in order to live in a private world. On the contrary, the schizophrenic child is unable to experience reality as it exists for others. Moreover, the schizophrenic child's seemingly bizarre behavior is a desperate attempt on his part to establish the boundaries of his identity. He is not avoiding contact with reality; he is unable to experience reality because of his deficiencies in ego structure (1962).

Sociopsychosomatic Theory

An effort has been made to bring together all the relevant factual data and to present schizophrenia in a sociopsychosomatic continuum. This continuum is, however, a reversal of Pavlov's somatopsychological continuum, the starting point being the overt behavior (Wolman, 1966b, 1970).

The psychological frame of reference of this theory is a modified Freudian personality model, somewhat influenced by Sullivan's interpersonal theory.

The study of manifest social relations has been conducted experimentally in the framework of the *power and acceptance* theory. Power has been defined as the ability to satisfy needs;

acceptance, as the willingness to do so. Furthermore, a distinction has been made between the instrumental (take), mutual (give-and-take), and vectorial (give) types of interaction (Wolman, 1958b, 1960b).

In schizogenic families the parent-versus-parent relationship is hostile-instrumental. The mother-versus-child relationship is pseudovectorial, actually exploitative-instrumental, while the father-versus-child relationship is frankly instrumental in that he is either seductive or competitive. The child is thus forced to worry about his parents instead of their worrying about him. In this reversal of social roles the child becomes the "protector of his protectors."

This noxious social relationship represents, in a modified Freudian framework, a disbalance of interindividual cathexes. The child who is normally a "taker" (instrumental) is forced prematurely into a precocious giving (hypervectorial) relationship; hence, *vectoriasis praecox,* the proposed new name for schizophrenia (Wolman, 1966b). This abundant, premature object cathexis inevitably leads to an inadequate self-cathexis. Whatever exists, exists in some quantity; an abundant object cathexis of libido adversely affects self-cathexis of libido (see Federn, 1952), and hence the lowered vitality and general decline in behavior proficiency.

All living organisms struggle for survival, and the preschizophrenic's struggle involves sacrificing himself, as it were, to protect those who are supposed to protect him. When, however, he reaches an exceedingly low level of libido self-cathexis, destrudo (the hostile impulse) takes over. A wounded animal either flees in mortal fear or attacks everyone in terror. Paranoid and catatonic hostility resembles the rage of a wounded animal.

Thus schizophrenia can be interpreted as a process of *downward adjustment in an irrational struggle for survival.* In the "hebephrenic" type there is less fight and more regression: the "simple" type represents resignation and surrender.

Schizophrenia starts in childhood as a paradoxical action of an organism that abandons its own protection to protect those who should protect it. It is a severe disbalance of libido and destrudo cathexes; in its milder, latent stages it represents a struggle of the individual against his own hostile impulses and his fear that they may break through. In psychoanalytic terms, the superego is overgrown, demanding, and dictatorial, and the ego struggles to prevent the outburst of id impulses. As long as the struggle goes on, it is a neurotic, character neurotic, or latent psychotic stage. When the ego fails and the unconscious impulses and primary processes disrupt the conscious control, it is a manifest psychosis. In some cases the destroyed personality structure lies in shambles in a dementive state.

Obviously these profound psychological changes must affect the function of the central and autonomous nervous systems and usually they affect endocrine and other organic processes too. Somatic symptoms in schizophrenia are therefore interpreted as psychosomatic ones. These symptoms could be interpreted as a result of an inadequate libido self-cathexis; the hypocathected organs are affected first (Wolman, 1967).

Symptomatology

Adults suffering from schizophrenia are characterized by a variety of symptoms including signs of mental deterioration or impaired intellectual functioning, unusual access to the unconscious, frequent and prolonged periods of depression and periods of elation when they hallucinate power and omnipotence, extreme self-neglect, sexual disturbances, withdrawal from interpersonal relationships, and feelings of depersonalization.

Many of these symptoms are also characteristic of childhood schizophrenia. Rank (1949, 1955), Putnam (1955), and others stated that the outstanding symptoms of their little patients are "withdrawal from people, retreat into a world of fantasy, mutism or the use of language for autistic purposes, bizarre posturing, seemingly meaningless stereotyped gestures, impassivity or violent outbursts of anxiety and rage, identification with inanimate objects or animals, and excessively inhibited or excessively uninhibited expression of impulses" (Rank, 1955, pp. 491–492).

Kanner (1943, 1948b; Kanner & Eisenberg, 1955), in his writings about children suffering from early infantile autism, describes the overt behavior of these children as dehumanized, mechanical, lacking in vitality and spontaneity, rigid, and lifeless.

Hinsie and Campbell (1960), in their *Psychiatric Dictionary,* define childhood schizophrenia as a "clinical entity occurring in childhood usually after the age of one and before the age of 11, characterized by disturbance in the ability to make affective contact with the environment and by autistic thinking."

Schizophrenia in Childhood and Adulthood

Some research workers believe that childhood schizophrenia is not exactly the same clinical entity as schizophrenia in adulthood. Bradley (1947) pointed to withdrawal from reality, escape into the world of fantasy, lack of social contacts, and improper emotional response as the outstanding symptoms of childhood schizophrenia. In addition, he noticed a decline in physical activity and exceeding sensitivity to criticism. Speech disturbances, fear of death, and world-destruction fantasies were observed by Despert (1955).

Maturational Lag

Bender, as previously stated, regards childhood schizophrenia as a "maturational lag at the embryonic level characterized by a primitive plasticity." She describes vasovegetative disorders which include excessive flushing and perspiration; cold extremities; unpredictable reaction to physical illness; occasional high temperatures; disturbances in eating, sleeping,

and bowel and bladder control; disturbances in menstruation; awkwardness; fear of climbing stairs, of swinging, of riding a bicycle, and of engaging in new motor activities; and, in some of these children, a tendency to whirl and rotate. The emotional disturbances include anxiety and apathy and states of panic and bewilderment. Socially, these children are rather attractive and empathetic, and they try to lean on, and even incorporate, the other person, be he a parent or a therapist. Their perceptions are bizarre, with the primary and secondary processes mixed together. If there is speech, it is frequently disturbed, and there is a tendency to use the third person instead of "I." These children are also preoccupied with problems of their own identity, of body, and of bodily functions.

On the basis of her extensive studies, Bender (1956) suggested dividing childhood schizophrenia into three types: the autistic, or pseudo-defective; the pseudoneurotic; and the pseudo-psychopathic with paranoid ideas. Bender goes on to define childhood schizophrenia

> . . . as a maturational lag at the embryonic level in all the areas which integrate biological and psychological behavior; an embryonic primitivity or plasticity which characterizes the pattern of behavior disturbance in all areas of personality functioning. It is determined before birth and heredity factors appear to be important. It may be birth itself, especially a traumatic birth. Anxiety is the organismic response to this disturbance which tends to call forth symptom formation of a pseudo-defective, pseudo-neurotic, or pseudo-psychopathic type. [1955, pp. 512–513]

There is no doubt that Bender's empirical data evidence certain somatic disorders in childhood schizophrenia. However, the lack of adequate proof of inherited and prenatal, intrauterine etiologic factors would lead one to believe that somatic symptoms are a *product* of psychological changes which are precipitated by social causes. The occurrence of gastrointestinal and respiratory dysfunctions, allergies, and metabolic irregularities offers support to the sociopsychosomatic theory of schizophrenia. There is no evidence whatsoever that the infant's disturbed sleep, crying, screaming, and refusal to take food in the first months of life are inborn or inherited. Those research workers

> . . . who have taken part in well-baby clinics or in studies of personality development from birth on, are keenly aware of the daily, almost hourly shifts in a young infant's behavior, as manifested in tension or relaxation, in response to or coincident with tensions or relaxation in the mother. We have all seen newborn babies, who ate and slept quite peacefully in the hospital, go through periods of extreme upset at home. [Putnam, 1955, p. 521]

Adaptive Aberrations

Goldfarb (1963), in his study of schizophrenic children, notes three important phenomena which are characteristic of schizophrenic children: (1) defective self-awareness, (2) perceptual aberrations, and (3) marked anxiety states. He says that schizophrenic children fail to perceive the stability and structural continuity of the total environment, an ability which is essential to the attainment of clear and stable self-awareness (1963, p. 55). "The schizophrenic child's deficient self-awareness is most dramatically demonstrated in his impaired consciousness of his body in terms of its anatomy and its physiology"; he is unable to feel his body, and he suffers from difficulties related to normal physiological functioning (1963, p. 49). With regard to perceptual aberrations, the child has extreme difficulties in dealing with normal stimulation from the outside world (1963, p. 52).

Goldfarb states: "The schizophrenic child merely seems to be equipped with a narrower repertoire of responses than is the normal child (1964, p. 621). The "schizophrenic child's adaptive aberrations are seen as highly individualized accommodations to the very special requirements of his psychosocial environment" (1964, p. 621). Goldfarb says that children diagnosed as schizophrenic show the following

symptoms: impaired relationships, disturbances in personal identity, resistance to change, marked anxiety, perceptual difficulties, communicative defects, bizarre mobility, unusual preoccupations, and at all times severe intellectual retardation (1964, p. 621). In his study of the schizophrenic child, Goldfarb chooses to focus on the reciprocating influence of the child and his environment, for, as he says, ". . . schizophrenic children suffer defects in orientative and manipulative functions that are normally the foundation of self-regulation behavior" (1964, p. 625). Furthermore, Goldfarb says that schizophrenic children experience severe panic and anger because they are unable to recognize the permanence, the wholeness, and the predictability of self and nonself (1964, p. 625).

Alderton, in a review of the literature on childhood schizophrenia, states that the symptoms of a schizophrenic child may be described as:

> 1. Lack of firm self-identity, disturbed body image and lack of clear ego boundaries. This may be directly apparent or may be determined by the use of projective methods of drawings. These difficulties constitute the core problem and are essential to the diagnosis.
> 2. Dereistic feelings, thinking, and behavior.
> 3. The simultaneous presence of impaired and precocious psychological functioning.
> 4. A loss of normal interests or regressive ones.
> 5. Language disturbances in content or in rhythm, intonation, pitch, stress or volume.
> 6. Deficient social relationships with impaired capacity to empathize and a tendency toward withdrawal. Certainty about individual identity and what lies outside and inside the ego is essential for normal relationships. [1966, p. 283]

THE MAIN SYNDROMES

Reactive versus Process

Some research workers, describing schizophrenia in adults, distinguish between *process* schizophrenia, which is characterized by a gradual decline of activity, dullness, autism, ideas of reference, and thought disturbances, and *reactive* schizophrenia, which is characterized by oscillations between excitement and stuporous depression and by periods of almost normal functioning alternating with states of confusion. Yet workers such as Arieti (1955), Becker (1956), Wolman (1957, 1965, 1966b), and others did not find clear indications for a reactive versus a process distinction. Phillips (1953), Garmezy and Rodnick (1959), and others have seemed to believe that such a distinction has some prognostic value; however, the premorbid history of each patient is determined to a great extent by his environment.

The schizophrenic personality is exceedingly labile and easily influenced by interaction with other individuals. A schizophrenic is not always schizophrenic; the fact is that even the so-called chronic schizophrenics respond to human warmth and kindness and show surprising improvement (see T. Freeman, Cameron, & McGhie, 1958; Rosen, 1953; Schwing, 1954; Wolman, 1966b).

Symptom Formation

Wolman (1958a, 1964, 1966b) proposes a division of symptoms of schizophrenia in terms of ego strength. The *ego-protective* symptoms indicate the struggle of the ego to retain control over the unconscious impulses. All defense mechanisms and varieties of neurotic symptoms belong to this category. The preschizophrenic has been called "pseudoneurotic" by Hoch and Polatin (1949); most probably he is, however, a latent schizophrenic (Wolman, 1958a, 1958c). The main ego-protective symptom of this hypervectorial or preschizophrenic neurotic is the overmobilization of the ego, reflected in his constricted, introverted, high-strung, tense personality. The preschizophrenic neurotic is overconscientious, moralistic, and dogmatic. He often develops phobias, obsessive-compulsive behavior, and partial withdrawal from social contacts. All these ego-protective symptoms may postpone or even prevent psychotic breakdown.

Whether the ego-protective symptoms will prevent the onset of manifest psychosis depends on a variety of benign and noxious factors (see Arieti, 1955; Bychowski, 1952; Hill, 1955). When these symptoms fail, a series of *ego-deficiency* symptoms starts, indicating an insidious or sudden collapse of the ego. Loss of contact with reality, paranoid delusions, hallucinations, inability to control unconscious impulses, violence, stupor, and depersonalization, as well as motor and speech disturbances, are among the ego-deficiency symptoms. No schizophrenic has lost contact with reality completely and irreversibly. The therapeutic work of Federn (1952), Fromm-Reichmann (1950, 1952, 1959), Rosen (1953), Arieti (1955), Schwing (1954), Sechehaye (1956), Eissler (1947, 1952), Sullivan (1947, 1953), Wolman (1957, 1966b), and scores of others indicates that even severely deteriorated schizophrenics are accessible and responsive to treatment. Whether this "treatment" is a planned therapeutic interaction or a result of an unplanned but exceedingly helpful interaction with a friend is an open question. There is, however, no doubt that schizophrenics in remission develop *ego-compensation* symptoms, as if going back from psychosis toward normality. How far back they can go is still a controversial issue (see Arieti, 1955; Brody & Redlich, 1952; Dawson, Stone, & Dellis, 1961; English, Hanupe, Bacon, & Settlage, 1961; Knight, 1953; Riemer, 1950; Rifkin, 1957; Scher & Davis, 1960; Wolman, 1959, 1965, 1966b).

One can present schizophrenia and related disorders in a continuum using sociopsychological determinants as the uniting factor. According to the previously mentioned sociopsychosomatic theory (Wolman, 1966b, 1967), schizophrenia, in the broad sense of the word, starts with peculiar disbalance of libido cathexes. Precocious object hypercathexis and resulting self-hypocathexis—or, in terms of overt social behavior, a precocious hypervectorialism—is the core of hypervectorial disorders.

The Five Levels

One may distinguish five *levels* of mental disorders: neurosis, character neurosis, latent psychosis, manifest psychosis, and the dementive level. In hypervectorial or schizo-type disorders the neurotic step includes phobic, neurasthenic, and obsessive-compulsive patterns. The schizoid character neurosis corresponds to what is usually called the *schizoid personality*. The next step in schizophrenic deterioration is latent schizophrenia, in which the ego is still in control but is on the verge of breakdown. Next comes manifest schizophrenia, called *vectoriasis praecox*. The last level, the dementive level, is the end of the decline and a complete collapse of personality structure. All five levels represent an ever-growing disbalance of cathexes of sexual and hostile impulses. The decline of the controlling force of the ego is the most significant determinant of each level. As long as the ego exercises control, it is neurosis. When the ego comes to terms with the symptoms, it is character neurosis. When the ego is on the verge of collapse, it is latent psychosis. When the ego fails, it is manifest psychosis, or a full-blown schizophrenia in one of its four syndromes (paranoid, catatonic, hebephrenic, and simple). A complete diliapidation of the ego and behavior on the id level are typical of the severely deteriorated, dementive stage (Wolman, 1966b).

The Diagnostic and Statistical Manual

The *Diagnostic and Statistical Manual of Mental Disorder* (American Psychiatric Association, 1968) describes nine types of schizophrenic reactions:

1. The simple type, which is "characterized chiefly by reduction in external attachments and interests and by impoverishment of human relations [and] adjustment on a lower psychobiological level of functioning, usually accompanied by apathy and indifference [and] an increase of the severity of symptoms over long periods, usually with apparent mental deterioration. . . ."

2. The hebephrenic type, which is "characterized by shallow, inappropriate affect, unpredictable giggling, silly behavior and mannerisms, delusions, often of a somatic nature, hallucinations, and regressive behavior."

3. The catatonic type, which is "characterized by conspicuous motor behavior, exhibiting either marked generalized inhibition (stupor, mutism, negativism, and waxy flexibility) or excessive motor activity and excitement. The individual may regress to a state of vegetation."

4. The paranoid type, which is "characterized by autistic, unrealistic thinking, with mental content composed chiefly of delusions of persecution, and/or of grandeur, ideas of reference, and often hallucinations. It is often characterized by unpredictable behavior, with a fairly constant attitude of hostility and aggression."

5. The acute undifferentiated type, which "includes cases exhibiting a wide variety of schizophrenic symptomatology, such as confusion of thinking and turmoil of emotion, manifested by perplexity, ideas of reference, fear and dream states, and dissociative phenomena."

6. The chronic undifferentiated type, which is characterized by "a mixed symptomatology, and when the reaction cannot be classified in any of the more clearly defined types, it will be placed in this group."

7. The schizo-affective type, which includes "those cases showing significant admixtures of schizophrenic and affective reactions."

8. The childhood type, which characterizes "those schizophrenic reactions occurring before puberty. The clinical picture may differ from schizophrenic reactions occurring in other age periods because of the immaturity and plasticity of the patient at the time of onset of the reaction. Psychotic reactions in children, manifesting primarily autism, will be classified here."

9. The residual type, which characterizes "those patients who, after a definite psychotic, schizophrenic reaction, have improved sufficiently to be able to get along in the community,

but who continue to show recognizable residual disturbance of thinking, affectivity, and/or behavior."

Four Syndromes Related to Childhood Schizophrenia

According to the sociopsychosomatic theory of schizophrenia (Wolman, 1966b, 1967), four syndromes can be distinguished. The first syndrome corresponds roughly to what has usually been described as *paranoid schizophrenia* and is characterized by the ego's losing contact with reality and leaving it to the superego. In the second syndrome, the *catatonic,* the superego takes over control also of the motor apparatus. In the *hebephrenic* syndrome the ego yields to the id; the superego is defeated, and the id takes over. In the *simple deterioration* syndrome there is a process of losing life itself. Alderton (1966), in a review of the literature on childhood schizophrenia, describes the following syndromes:

1. Early infantile autism, which is characterized by extreme self-isolation, independence, insensitivity, a desire to preserve the various objects in the environment in an unchanged state, a ritualistic involvement with objects, distorted speech patterns, and repetitive movements.

2. Symbiotic infantile psychosis, which usually occurs in children aged 2½ to 4 and which is characterized by an inability on the part of the child to separate himself from his mother. Maturation and progressive social demands often result in a psychotic breakdown. The child frantically attempts to define the outer world as different from himself and tries to introject or fuse with adults. This syndrome can lead to secondary autism.

3. Pseudoneurotic schizophrenia, which is characterized by neurotic symptoms which are extremely intense and which cannot be explained in terms of the current life situation.

4. Pseudopsychopathic schizophrenia, which is characterized by the use of delinquency as an attempt to deal with the illness.

Comparing Schizophrenia in Childhood and Adulthood

A retrospective search into the life histories of adult schizophrenics shows that these adults manifested various degrees of severity of schizophrenia in childhood. The main difference between infantile and adult schizophrenia is due to developmental factors. Adult schizophrenics improve or deteriorate. Infant schizophrenics are also subject to growth and maturation processes that complicate the disease.

All schizophrenia-type symptoms represent a downward adjustment for survival, and a hurt child may react in many ways. Thus there are several schizophrenia-type behavioral patterns in childhood, depending on the age of the child, his sex, the severity of the damage, his level of development, specific family influences, etc. One important distinction should, however, be made: *Schizophrenia in adulthood is a failure of the impoverished ego.* The ego lost most of its resources in object cathexis, was hard pressed ("overdemanded") by the superego to overcontrol its id, failed in that, and finally has become unable to control the id and has ceased to be the steering wheel of the organism. Schizophrenia in infancy, *vectoriasis praecocissima,* on the other hand, is a *mental catastrophy that took place even before the ego had the opportunity to grow and to assert control over the id.*

The symptomatology of schizophrenia in adults has been examined in order of increasing severity, ending in the dementive level. The symptomatology of infantile schizophrenia should be presented in a *reverse* order, starting with the most severe syndromes. With regard to adult schizophrenics, the personality structure is *regressed;* in childhood schizophrenia, *growth was prevented.*

Four Syndromes of Childhood Schizophrenia

The first and most severe level, *pseudoamentive schizophrenia,* corresponds roughly to dementive schizophrenia in adults, the last and most severe level of regression. The second and slightly less severe level is *autistic schizophrenia* in children, which corresponds to simple deterioration and hebephrenia in adults. The third level in order of decreasing severity is *symbiotic schizophrenia* in children, more or less corresponding to catatonia in adulthood. The fourth level, the belligerent *aretic schizophrenia* in childhood, corresponds to adult paranoid schizophrenia.

The proposed types of infantile schizophrenia correspond, to some extent, to the five stages and manners in which the hypervectorial disorder was produced. Pseudoamentive childhood schizophrenia is formed on a preverbal, pre-ego formation level. The other types are formed slightly later, but all of them probably originate in the first 2 years of life.

The pseudoamentive syndrome. The disturbance in the pseudoamentive schizophrenic child begins as early as in the oral stage. The child apparently senses or empathizes with the mother's demanding attitude and the father's selfishness. Refusal to suckle, vomiting, and sleep disturbances are among the earliest symptoms which suggest that these children are too frightened to grow. Fear of eating, inability to chew food, avoidance of new foods (especially solids), lack of assertiveness, and lack of initiative have been observed by several workers (Bettelheim, 1950; Ribble, 1938; Wolman, 1970; and many others).

In these most severe cases of infantile schizophrenia development was stopped before it had the chance to start. Practically everything has been affected: motor coordination, metabolism, sleep and waking states, food intake, speech, and mental development. Sometimes the process looks congenital, but in all the cases which I have studied (since 1932) the child was born normal, but the family pattern was schizogenic. Furthermore, whenever the mothers of these children received guidance or therapy, the child improved.

". . . new born babies, who ate and slept quite peacefully in the hospital, go through periods of upset at home, and subsequently reassert their potential for easy normal behavior if and when it became possible for mother to modify her attitude favorably," observed Putnam (1955, p. 521).

The nature of the symptoms depends primarily on the nature of the offense. Some children are exposed to the schizogenic family pattern from the day they are born or the day they come home from the maternity hospital. From that day on they sense or empathize or are somehow made to feel that the mother does not want them because *she herself wants to be taken care of.*

The schizophrenic child is not, however, a "rejected" child. The schizogenic mother does take care of her child, but she does it in a hostile and pseudovectorial manner, yelling, crying, screaming, beating, and forcing food down the child's throat "for his own well-being." Often she delivers a tirade to the infant in the crib: "Why can't you sleep? See how tired I am. You are the worst child ever born!"

The severity of the initial offense and of subsequent ones is an important, if not the most important, factor. Most ambulatory or hospitalized adult patients have had some years of close to normal or at least neurotic life, but infantile pseudoamentive schizophrenics were never normal or neurotic, for there was no opportunity for developing ego-protective, neurotic symptoms. Infantile schizophrenia, or vectoriasis praecocissima, usually starts in the first year of the infant's life. Sometimes it is so severe as to affect practically everything: emotions, mobility, overall personality structure, intellectual functions, metabolism, physical growth, etc.

The main symptoms of these pseudoamentive infants resemble those found in severe mental deficiency. These pseudoidiotic children are frequently institutionalized as mental defectives. Richards (1951) found twenty-two cases of schizophrenic children in an institution for mental defectives. One of my first patients was diagnosed as a severe imbecile, whereas he was really a pseudoamentive schizophrenic who responded partially to treatment.

The autistic syndrome. E. Bleuler (1911; English translation, 1950), in his analysis of autistic thought, stated that autistic thinking occurs in healthy adults "when the emotions obtain too great a significance." Autistic thinking is detached from reality, for in autistic thinking the material comes from the individual himself, appearing in the form of daydreams, fantasies, delusions, and hallucinations. Arieti (1955) believes that autistic thinking is not a pathological form of logic but an archaic form described by Levy-Bruhl, who studied primitive cultures. Autistic thinking and language can be seen as a regression in that both are "motivated only or predominantly by an inner or intra personal need of the individual" (Arieti, 1955). Piaget maintained that autistic thought is the first stage of development of intelligence in the normal child. It tends not to establish truths but to satisfy desires. It remains incommunicable by language and is expressed in images and symbols such as myths.

In pathological manifestations of autistic thought a complete detachment from reality takes place, " a peculiar alteration of the relation between the patient's inner life and the external world, [wherein] the inner life assumes pathological predominance" (Despert, 1958).

No child is born autistic (Rimland, 1964). Autism is a part of the schizophrenic downward adjustment. It is a withdrawal made in an attempt to avoid further damage (Nagelberg, Spotnitz, & Feldman, 1953). The autistic child is a child who has given up growth, desire, initiative, emotions, and social contacts in order to survive. Moreover, when it is impossible to survive on a human level, the organism may try to survive on a subhuman level (Bettelheim, 1956).

The pseudoamentive child is a child whose overall maturation process was prevented and inhibited by hostile parental instrumentalism in the first months of life. The autistic child is one whose ego was badly damaged before it had the opportunity to protect the system. Autism represents a regression of the infantile ego into the id. An autistic child's libido was robbed and was forced to turn inward, and yet some initial development took place, and the child's overt behavior is one step ahead of that of the pseudoamentive schizophrenic.

The most characteristic symptom of children manifesting early infantile autism is their inability to relate to other people. Many do not speak, and those who do rarely actually communicate with their words. In children who do talk there is an echolalia type of reproduction and an absence of spontaneous sentence formation. Other characteristics include apathy, withdrawal from social contacts, obsessive insistence on routine and sameness, fear of change, and use of the third person when the child is talking about himself (Kanner, 1948b).

In a follow-up study of forty-two autistic children, Kanner and Eisenberg (1955) found that around the age of 14, most of these children had retained their early characteristics but had lost some symptoms such as echolalia and pronunciational reversals. Of the nineteen nonspeaking children, eighteen remained in a state of complete isolation and were hardly distinguishable from mentally defective children. Children who have not learned to talk by 4 years of age are prognostically bad cases. In Kanner's follow-up study, eighteen out of the nineteen nonspeaking children showed no improvement whatsoever.

The twenty-three children who used language represented a more encouraging picture in the follow-up study. Of these children, thirteen had been able to function at home and in the community, although they remained schizoids and maintained a tenuous contact with reality.

Autistic children *apparently* fail to respond to

human affection, and yet their avoidance of human contact is neither complete nor absolute. These children may not be able to endure the looks of others or to look straight into the eyes of another, but they may accept close physical contact, which seems to increase their feeling of identity.

Mutism in autistic children was interpreted by L. Jackson (1950) as an effort to be immobile, to feign death. Feigning death is one of the primitive mechanisms for escaping a terrifying threat. The reader is reminded of our interpretation of the catatonic stupor and mutism. Several catatonics in remission or recovery have explained their mutism as a protective device: "If I keep my mouth shut, I could not say anything wrong. If I refrain from doing anything I will not get into trouble."

Autistic children frequently display preferences for olfactory contact with the environment. One can see these children smelling and sniffing things and touching objects with their noses. Goldfarb (1956) noticed their preference for using "contact receptors" such as smell, touch, and taste and their avoidance of "distant receptors" such as sight and hearing. This regression to lower sensory contacts seems to fall in line with the overall trend of adjustment for survival on a lower level of functioning.

Mahler distinguished two types of infantile psychosis: *autistic* and *symbiotic*. In the first type, the mother never seems to have been perceived emotionally by the infant, and the primary representation of outer reality, the mother as a person, as a separate entity, does not seem to be cathected. The mother remains a part of object, seemingly devoid of specific cathexis and not distinguished from inanimate objects (1952, p. 289). "The instinctual forces, both libido and aggression, exist in an unneutralized form, due to the absence of the synthetic function of the ego. There is an inherent lack of contact with the human environment" (1952, p. 289).

Early infantile autism develops when the infant

. . . devoid of emotional ties to the person of the mother is unable to cope with external stimuli and inner excitations, which threaten from both sides his very existence as an entity. Autism is, therefore, the mechanism by which such patients try to shut out, to hallucinate away (negative hallucination) the potential sources of sensory perception, particularly those which demand affective response. The most striking feature is their spectacular struggle against any demand of human (social) contact which might interfere with their hallucinatory delusional need to command a static, greatly constricted segment of their inanimate environment in which they behave like omnipotent magicians. . . . These patients experience outer reality as an intolerable source of irritation, without specific or further qualifications. [Mahler, 1952, p. 297]

Mahler believes that the autistic disorder is probably "the basic defense attitude of these infants for whom the beacon of emotional orientation in the outer world—the mother as primary love object—is non-existent" (1952, p. 297).

The early signs of the autistic syndrome have been described as a lack of "anticipatory posture" in the infant prior to being picked up. Instead of smiling in the rather spontaneous way that the normal child does at the sight of a parent, the autistic infant shows nothing but a vacuous, distant stare (Eveloff, 1960).

Behavior problems are often unnoticed in the first or even the second year of life. A common parental comment is that "It just seemed as if he wanted to be left alone." Some parents feel for quite awhile that they have a very well-behaved but quiet baby. Pediatric examinations reveal only occasional and unrelated physical abnormalities that can be easily explained as psychosomatic and interoceptive conditioning (Wolman, 1966b).

The autistic child's passion for *sameness* can

be recognized in his awareness of slight changes in the environment which might go unnoticed by most people. Yet any change in the environment can easily throw the autistic child into a rage or panic. Therefore, most of his activities are aimed at the preservation of sameness in a rigid, restricted set of rituals. People as well as objects must remain unchanged. A visible scar or wart evokes instant comment and yet no sympathy or solicitude is offered.

The general attitude of the autistic child toward people is put concisely in Eveloff's (1960) statement: "Except when they choose to make contact to get something, humans seem to exist for them only as meddlesome intruders or agents of frustrations."

Pronovost (1961) noticed that the autistic child's comprehension of spoken language greatly exceeds his use of it. It is difficult to elicit speech from an autistic child, though in most cases he understands what he is told. He can discriminate environmental sounds and voices of adults, recognize names of people, and distinguish objects and actions, but there is much less comprehension of abstract or complex language.

A severe perceptual defect is brought about by the difficulty in differentiating figure from ground and part from whole. The autistic child recognizes voices but not faces, pictures but not people. He does not distinguish himself from the outer world and may even attack his own arms and legs without feeling the injury, and he is therefore extremely accident-prone. The poor differentiation of self from others explains the observed reversal of pronouns.

Everyday routines appear as complicated processes to the autistic child. Upon waking, he conveys the feeling that something is happening to his body rather than to the world around him. He shows an active locking out of the environment by covering up his eyes and ears. He may keep his eyes closed, though awake, even when being dressed and toileted. The autistic child does not reveal any apparent interest in his clothing, "nor did being clothed become incorporated into [his] mode of living" (Maier & Campbell, 1957).

A normal infant craves milk and love. Yet when in his first encounter with his mother love is not given because the mother is also instrumental and stronger than the infant, he may also be forced to give up his contacts with the outer world altogether (Wolman, 1970).

The symbiotic syndrome. The neonate has no ego. His entire mental apparatus consists of the id, "a cauldron of seething excitement":

> Within the id, the organic *instincts* operate, which are themselves composed of fusions of two primal forces (Eros and destructiveness). . . . The one and only endeavor of these instincts is toward satisfaction. But an immediate and irresponsible satisfaction of instinct, such as the id demands, would in most instances lead to perilous conflicts with the external world and to extinction. . . . The other agency of the mind . . . the ego . . . was developed out of the cortical layer of the id. . . . Its constructive function consists in interposing between the demand made by an instinct and the action that satisfies it, an intellectual activity which . . . endeavors by means of experimental actions to calculate the consequences of the proposed line of contact . . . just as the id is exclusively motivated to obtain pleasure, so the ego is governed by considerations of safety. The ego has set itself the task of self-preservation which the id appears to neglect. . . . In its efforts to preserve itself in an environment of overwhelming mechanical forces, the ego is threatened by dangers that come in the first instance from external reality, but not from them alone. Its own id is a source of similar dangers . . . an excessive "stimulus" from the external world. [Freud, 1949a, pp. 108–111]

The weak, immature, "archaic ego of the first phase of childhood becomes a storage of self-cathectical libido" (Freud, 1949a, pp. 213–214).

Sometimes the weak and immature ego of the first phase of childhood is permanently damaged by the strain put on it in the effort to ward off the dangers that are peculiar to that period of life. Children are protected against the dangers threatening them from the external world by the care of their parents; they pay for this security by a fear of losing their parents' love, which would deliver them over, helpless to the dangers of the external world" (Freud, 1949a, p. 112).

This is precisely what happens in childhood schizophrenics. When the newborn is not offered protection and is exposed to violent scenes, verbal and nonverbal, his ego may not emerge from the id, may not become a libido-cathected, separate entity. This is probably the situation in the pseudoamentive schizophrenic.

When in the first months some protection is offered to the infant accompanied with great stress and instrumental demands, his weak, just-emerging ego may regress. It is no longer primary narcissism, for his infantile ego has already rushed to cathect his mother. In a self-protective move, the ego shuns contacts with anybody and anything. This is the autistic withdrawal and regression of the infantile ego.

Some schizogenic mothers are rejecting-protective, and some are symbiotic-parasitic. Children of the latter group of mothers receive more support than children of rejecting-protective parents. Their mothers are somehow more willing to give them affection; they are not so harsh, though they are no less dictatorial. They are, indeed, unable to give. *But when they perceive the child as part of themselves, giving away becomes giving to oneself* (Hill, 1955).

These are the mothers of symbiotic schizophrenic children. They protect the child and "invade" his personality. *Many of the adult manifest catatonic schizophrenics were symbiotic as infants.* Their mothers conquered them in childhood as one conquers a foreign territory and claimed absolute possession. They sub-

jugated the child to their own emotional needs and prevented his normal growth. Yet their attitude is less destructive than that of the rejecting-protective mothers of the pseudoamentive and autistic children.

In terms of personality dynamics, a symbiotic childhood schizophrenia is caused by a *premature, precocious formation of an overdemanding, dictatorial, primitive superego.* The child identifies with the mother by introjection of her image and renounces his own identity, ceasing to be a separate individual.

Maintaining this symbiotic, subservient pattern of living, in which the child renounces his independence, his strivings and ambitions, and even his pain and pleasure, seems to be the only way of securing his mother's love and protecting her and, resultingly, his own life. The schizophrenic paradox of giving up everything to protect those who are supposed to be protectors is the leading motive in the symbiotic schizophrenic.

Mahler (1952, 1955) states that during the first 12 or 18 months, the infant is "almost completely a vegetative being, symbiotically dependent on the mother" (Mahler & Gosliner, 1955, p. 195). Normally, however, if the first 12 to 18 "symbiotic" months have been adequately satisfying for the infant, he undergoes 18 to 36 months of separation individuation.

The mechanisms of the symbiotic psychosis are "introjective-protective" ones, said Mahler, that aim at a "restoration of the symbiotic parasitic delusions of oneness with the mother and thus are diametric opposites of the function of autism . . . clinical symptoms manifest themselves between the ages of two and a half to five, with a peak of onset in the fourth year of life. These infants' reality ties depend mainly upon the delusional fusion with the mother (unlike those of the autistic who had no reality ties to begin with)" (1952, pp. 247–248).

Mahler believes that symbiotic psychotic

children are constitutionally vulnerable: "The very existence of the constitutional ego defect in the child helps create the vicious circle . . . by stimulating the mother to react to the child in an overanxious way" (1955, p. 201).

I see, however, no reason to postulate "constitutional defects." It seems methodologically preferable to assume that the id is the constitutional part of personality and that both ego and superego develop in interaction with the environment through conditioning and cathexis. The etiology of the symbiotic syndrome is adequately interpreted by the social interaction in the family. Some little patients in the Sonia Shankman Orthogenic School (Bettleheim, 1950), in comparing their counselors with their parents, stated that parents love, but counselors "becare." To these children love is a demanding attitude, while becare is a giving, vectorial attitude. The schizophrenic child learns that strings are always attached to parental love.

Hill (1955, p. 109) writes: " . . . these mothers are devastatingly, possessively, all loving of their child who is to become schizophrenic . . . the condition for their love is one which the schizophrenic child cannot meet. If he does, to a degree, meet it, in so doing, he sacrifices his realization of a personality of his own, independent of hers."

Mothers of symbiotic children are anxiously possessive, affectionately overprotective, and jealously preventing of normal contacts between the child and the outer world.

This maternal symbiotic attitude forces the formation of the superego prior to an adequate formation of the ego. Normally, part of the ego develops into a superego in the Oedipal conflict. In these children, the superego starts at the anal or perhaps even the oral stage. The precociously formed superego takes over and distorts reality testing; although the child may have good mental abilities and use them properly in certain areas, he is anxious to give the "right answer," i.e.,

the answer that pleases his mother. The therapist once asked a preschool child: "Do you like these blue booklets?" The child's reply was, "Mommy says that blue is a nice color."

The precocious formation of superego leads to hallucinated feelings of omniscience and omnipotence with world saving and world destruction as frequent themes. For the schizophrenic, who has lost his grip on reality, imagines himself as being capable of taking care of or destroying his parents.

In the symbiotic syndrome the child's identification with his mother prevents further growth, other identifications, and independent thought or action. He avoids other children and cannot relate to them; all his thoughts and feelings go out to his mother.

With this overidentification, separation must represent a terrible threat. The moods of a symbiotic child resemble those of the adult catatonic. The child has no initiative of his own, no interest, no ambitions to be fulfilled. He repeats what his mother says; he tries to read her mind and to be the way he feels she wants him to be. He follows her wherever she goes. He showers her with questions to make sure that his thoughts follow hers, and above all he cannot share her with anyone else, for his security depends on a religious adherence to her, to fixed rules, and to definite schedules. The slightest deviation from routine and the mildest frustration throw the child into a state of panic and unleash the catatonic type of "terror" hostility.

The aretic syndrome. The term *aretic* (belligerent) is derived from the name of the Greek god of war Ares and applies to schizophrenic children who display unusual aggressiveness and unprovoked cruelty. A 5-year-old boy was brought to my office after he almost strangled a playmate. His previous experiences included biting his 2-year-old sister and hitting another child with a heavy stick. Aretic children have bitten, scratched, torn hair, and badly hurt other children or themselves. Boatman and Szurek (1960), in their comprehensive study of childhood schizophrenics, reported a girl who hit the head of another child against a concrete wall and a 4-year-old girl who deliberately slammed the door on her own finger.

When a child is persistently rejected but is still able to protect himself, most likely he will develop hyperinstrumental pathology with both distinct secondary gain symptoms (Wolman, 1971).

A schizophrenic child is not a rejected child. Schizogenic mothers take care of their children and are very proud of being ideal, self-sacrificing, overprotective mothers. They are, however, unwilling parents; their alleged self-sacrificing, vectorial attitude is a cover for selfish instrumentalism, and their communication conveys their ambivalent feelings.

An aretic schizophrenic is a child who receives sufficient affection to enable some ego growth, but not enough to overcome his resentment against the instrumental, robbing mother. The child would like to please his mother, to protect her when she claims he makes her sick. He would like to be her quiet, nice little child. He enjoys bits of the high-priced parental approval. He may even have some sort of development of superego and identification with one of his parents. Yet he is unable to accept the complete surrender of his own personality. His ego is not strong enough to accept frustration and control of his destructive impulses, nor can he believe that his mother is always good and kind no matter what she does. He carries the image of the bad mother who cares but hurts, and this feeling makes him and everyone else bad (Sullivan, 1947, 1953).

Aretic children are symbiotic but rebellious. They cling to their parents and yet attack them. They resent being left alone even for awhile, and yet they do not seem to enjoy proximity either. A 4-year-old girl went into tantrums whenever her mother left her home with the baby-sitter. Yet when the mother returned, the child screamed, hit, and clawed at her. Boatman and Szurek (1960, p. 395) described some of these children in the following manner:

> Even the child who clings to his parents usually does so in a possessively demanding and often physically hurtful way, showing little relaxation or enjoyment in contact with them. However indifferent or hurtful he is, particularly with his mother, he is clearly "dependent" upon her and experiences panic or separation from her. We have seen somatic malfunction as an indirect manifestation of this struggle and panic, e.g., anorexia or bulimia, constipation or diarrhea, asthma and exema.

The dependent-independent syndrome plays a most significant role in aretic childhood schizophrenia. The child rebels against being engulfed by his mother. He not only attacks her when in despair, as a symbiotic child would do, but also uses abusive language frequently and consciously and physical force in order to see what will happen. The child, such as Tommy, a 5½-year-old aretic schizophrenic, seems to enjoy performing malicious, destructive, hurtful deeds, in almost a testing fashion, as if he were trying to see whether he is really the bad, dangerous person or the killer that his mother describes him to be.

Moreover, in the case of Tommy, punishment did not seem to have much restraining influence. It rather increased his *paranoid* projections and introjections. When beaten, he was reassured that he was an evil person and that the world was full of malice. The little boy fantasized and talked about killing, burning, and torturing. Occasionally, he acted out his fantasies. Thus it seems that *anal-sadistic* impulses play an outstanding role in the development of the aretic syndrome, analogously to the role they play in paranoid schizophrenia in adults (Wolman, 1966b, 1970).

Anal conflicts are of significance in the development of all types of schizophrenia. At the time of toilet training, the child learns "to postpone or to renounce a direct instinctual gratification out of consideration for the environment . . . but simultaneously the hitherto 'omnipotent' adult becomes dependent, to a certain extent, on the will of the child" (Fenichel, 1945).

At the time when anal conflicts arise, some parents become exceedingly involved with the child. The child's resistance reawakens their own anxieties and makes them unhappy, angry, or both. The child is aware of how dependent his parents are upon him. Thus he may experience elimination as a great self-sacrifice; he gives up the pleasure of retention in order to please the demanding mother. He renounces the cathexis of something which is in his body and overcathects an external object, the mother. Obviously, a similar process may also take place in normal cases, but in schizophrenic children, toilet training is always severe and too successful. The schizophrenic child surrenders pleasure to duty and develops compulsory cleanliness as a reaction formation to his desire to rebel and be dirty.

As a result of the anal conflict, the child may develop *anal fears* and *phobias.* He may fear that something wrong will happen to his parents, should he fail them in terms of cleanliness. Anal fears and phobias play a significant role in the personality structure of all schizophrenics. Psychoanalytic theory explains the nature of these fears as follows: "As a retaliation for anal-sadistic tendencies, fears develop for what one wished to perpetuate anally on others, will now happen to oneself. Fears of physical injury of an anal nature develop, like the fear of some violent ripping out of feces or of body contents" (Fenichel, 1945, p. 68). In many cases, mothers of schizophrenic children have actually forcefully "ripped feces" out of the child's body by an application of enemas (Fleck et al., 1959). The overanxious toilet training is perceived by

the child as a part of the mother's overall robbing attitude. The mother takes away from the child his libido, his possessions, even the contents of his body. This seems to be the origin of ideas of reference.

The aretic child is more active than an autistic or symbiotic one, and his ego has attained a higher level of organization. Yet neither his ego nor his superego is capable of exercising rational control. He has not had the opportunity to rationalize, to displace, or to develop other defense mechanisms. Either there is a complete subservience to the mother or the impulses go wild. It is either superego or id, with the ego crushed in between.

Bender (1959) observed pseudopsychopathic symptoms in schizophrenic children. Many of them steal, lie, assault people, and destroy property. Many of them are "children who hate" (Redl & Wineman, 1960).

There is, however, a profound difference between aggressive psychopaths and aretic schizophrenics. Psychopaths attack for gains. They are hyperinstrumental and steal money to use it; they attack other children to force submission and to take away toys or money. They are delinquents who fight for gain and never attack anyone who can retaliate.

A schizophrenic aggressor, on the other hand, is a child who has failed to control his hostility toward his parents. He is tortured by guilt feelings whenever he attacks others and wishes to be restrained. Yet he is often carried away and unable to control his impulses. His thefts are often senseless; he attacks people who are stronger than himself; he assaults foe and friend alike; and he exposes himself to terrible retaliation. His hostile, destructive acts may be acts of compulsion with paranoid hallucination.

The aretic child fights against "bad people" because he was told (and felt it was true) that he was the "bad boy." He projects self-accusations against others and, with a typical infantile psychotic lack of self-restraint, attacks everyone.

The Neurotic Level

Not all individuals exposed to schizogenic parents become full schizophrenics. Some arrest at a neurotic level.

Despert compared (1955) four cases of obsessive-compulsive neurosis with two cases of childhood psychosis. Despert noticed a break with reality and an impairment of abstract thinking in schizophrenics and a strong guilt reaction in obsessive-compulsives. He interpreted the preoccupation with death as self-punishment. Bakwin (1953) based differential diagnosis on the child's early life history. Disturbances in sleep, vomiting, refusal to take solid food, diarrhea, respiratory diseases, and speech disorders were signs of psychosis.

In neurosis, the main ego function, reality testing, shows little if any damage, whereas in schizophrenia it is badly shattered. The essence of the infantile hypervectorial neurosis is the desperate struggle of the child to please and protect his protectors.

The overdemanding attitude of the mother fosters a too early formation of the superego. The hypervectorial neurotic child surrendered to the demanding mother without surrendering his ego; a surrender of the ego would mean psychosis. The hypervectorial neurotic child develops phobias, compulsions, and other ego-protective symptoms, and his precocious superego dominates his personality.

This overgrowth of the superego is one of the most important aspects of personality deformation in all schizophrenic disorders. Wexler (1952) aptly states that " . . . a primitive, archaic, and devastatingly punitive superego plays an important role, along with urgent instinctual demands, in producing schizophrenic disorganization (p. 185). Also, Hartmann (1955) believes that the *overgrowth of superego* is undoubtedly

an important feature in the formation of schizophrenia.

A typical sympton is *a perplexing fear of and preoccupation with death.* Some children ask questions about the future of the earth, mankind, rivers, or stars; they worry about the age of their parents and fear physical exertion. These children dread change in the daily life routine; moving to another city or even neighborhood is a frightening experience to them.

It seems that the child's insistence on sameness (Kanner, 1943, 1948b, 1949; Wolman, 1970) is an expression of that fear. As long as life continues in an unchanged fashion, the child feels that he has everything under his control; change represents a threat to the continuation of life.

The diversity in symptoms of the hypervectorial neurotic child depends on his life history and the peculiar interaction patterns within his family.

Schizophrenia in Later Childhood and Adolescence

Without planned therapeutic or unplanned compensatory interaction, the psychotic child may get worse as he grows up. Often a friendly relative, neighbor, or teacher may offer the child a supportive relationship which will make possible the compensatory development of his ego.

Some of these children represent the gloomy clinical picture of pseudoamentive, autistic, or symbiotic schizophrenia. In some the disease appears to become milder as they grow up, and yet even while they are of school age, they still have difficulties and exhibit behavioral symptoms of their disorder.

SCHIZOPHRENIA IN SCHOOL-AGE CHILDREN

All hypervectorial (schizophrenia-type) school-age disorders can be divided into three groups: manifest psychosis, latent psychosis, and neurosis.

Manifest Childhood Schizophrenia

Boatman and Szurek (1960, p. 394) define psychosis by saying: "We consider a child to be psychotic when his disorder is so great that almost all affective expression is distorted and when, in addition, his capacity to experience real satisfaction and to learn at his age level is seriously interfered with."

Intellectual and academic performance. The intellectual performance of schizophrenic children varies from deep mental deficiency to superb intellectual achievement; in some cases there is both. Measures of intelligence of schizophrenic children are not always valid or reliable. Since the level of performance of schizophrenic children depends on their mood and their rapport with the examiner, the results cannot be taken as a measure of their intelligence (Des Lauries & Halpern, 1947; Margolies-Mehr, 1952–1953; Wolman, 1966b, 1970).

Schizophrenic children frequently display peculiar cognitive functions and an astonishing memory, a result of their easy access to their unconscious. The schizophrenic child tends to force his energy on only those facets of learning which have personal meaning to him. Moreover, schizophrenics have access to many experiences that normal individuals usually forget because of repression or extinction.

School life. The learning situation represents a great challenge to the schizophrenic child. Learning always involves trial and error, and the schizophrenic child is afraid of both. His self-esteem is already very low, and his daydreams about great achievements increase the gulf between his desire to be strong and the reality of his being weak. The child, constricted by his desire to be perfect, makes no effort at all rather than risk failure. Yet the majority of schizophrenic children should and can attend regular schools and make satisfactory scholastic progress. Their problems lie usually in the realm of inter-individual relations with teachers and other children rather than in academic achievement.

The schizophrenic child often relates better to adults than to other children, and thus he may easily form an attachment to his teacher. If she responds, he learns eagerly and may even accept the school, gain self-confidence, and relate better to his peers. Yet in the present school situation, the schizophrenic child rarely gets the attention he needs. Often the teacher becomes one more hostile adult who drives the child deeper into his psychotic reaction.

The schizophrenic child is afraid of other children because he feels different and feels that he has no one to protect him. Thus, even when the children are friendly to him, the schizophrenic child can hardly accept this friendship. Schizophrenic children are suspicious and afraid of being used, and they fear and project their own hate. Most of them are so overinvolved with their parents that they have little object libido left for normal relationships with other children.

When the schizophrenic child does make a friend, he tends to become overattached to him and makes excessive demands. A schizophrenic child tends to be exceedingly jealous and irrational in his demands. Thus, despite his profound desire to have friends and to be nice to them, he soon finds himself isolated, rejected, sneered at, and humiliated.

Home environment. The symptoms of childhood schizophrenia are plastic, changeable, and fluctuating, depending on the child's interaction with his home environment. Unfortunately, the schizophrenic child is exposed to a most unstable and unfriendly environment, with frequent verbal or physical clashes between the parents. Violence on the part of the parents forces the child to worry more and more about them, to fear death more, and to become more and more psychotic (Wolman, 1965, 1966b, 1970).

Similar findings have been reported by several workers:

> Those children who are mute or who talk about themselves in the third person are often children whose parents talk about them in their presence as if they were not there. . . . It is a frequent occurrence for a parent to answer for a child when the child is spoken to. . . . Many parents behave toward the child as if he were stupid. . . . Threats about her (i.e. mother's) wish never to return again may also appear, only to be followed by renewed efforts to get the child to say he loves her. . . . Some parents urge a child to dress or feed himself, [only] to take over once he starts, presumably because he is so slow or clumsy. . . . Lack of discussion between parents is very frequent. . . . Angry projections, even if unverbalized, are frequent between the parents and toward the child. [Each parent has experienced] intensified unconscious needs for exclusive, all-loving, undemanding, tender care and understanding from the spouse. [Boatman & Szurek, 1960, pp. 414–416]

Some mothers treat the child as if he were an inanimate object and their sole property. Resultingly, many psychotic children do not have any notion of personal property. Possession is a concept which is gradually acquired by the child. It starts with the anal stage, this stage thus being important in the formation of schizophrenia. Yet here the mother takes the feces out forcefully, just as she takes the toys she gave to the child, as if they belonged to her and not to him. Thus the idea of personal ownership does not become a reality for the child.

Acting out. A schizophrenic child knows what is right and what is wrong. Moreover, he fears doing wrong, but his ego fails in the exercise of self-control. For example, when defenses fail, the schizophrenic child is most likely to act out his confused sexual impulses. Schizophrenics, as a result of the peculiar confusion of sex and age roles in their family, are frequently confused in regard to their own sex identification. More-

over, they do not have much opportunity for development of rational inhibitions and sublimations. Frequently, they act in an uninhibited, polymorphously perverted manner.

Acting out of destructive impulses takes on several forms in childhood schizophrenia. When a schizophrenic child acts negativistically, defying his parents and destroying objects, he is often testing to see the limits of his parents' love.

When hostility turns inward, he mutilates himself by pulling his hair, scratching his face, or banging his head. Often he provokes a fight to be beaten up and to prove to himself that he is bad and that the world is hostile and retaliatory. When the inner pressures become unbearable, he projects his hostility in a paranoid fashion.

Sometimes he acts out in order to see just how destructive he can be. Is he really a dangerous person, the only cause of his parents' sickness and misfortunes?

At other times, however, the child's behavior is not due to testing. A slight provocation may throw him into a state of uncontrollable aggressiveness, such as vicious self-assaultiveness, head banging, face slapping, tongue biting, and face scratching. And when interfered with, this behavior leads to attacks on others.

In childhood schizophrenia, there is an easy transition from secondary to primary processes. Normal children may experience fears and have a rich fantasy life, but they are always able to distinguish between true and "pretended" experience. The schizophrenic child, however, easily loses the distinction, especially when in fear or in a rage.

All children have fears, but the more protection they receive, the more easily they overcome their fears. The schizophrenic child is one who has not felt protected. The fear of death, which is a major preoccupation of the schizophrenic child, is experienced as a panic of ceasing to be oneself. The feeling of "not-me," of not being oneself, represents a loss of identity, a sign of the decline of the ego, and these feelings of depersonalization are, in latent schizophrenics, signs of the oncoming breakdown (Bychowski, 1952; Federn, 1952; Sullivan, 1947; Wolman, 1966b).

Latent Childhood Schizophrenia

Latent schizophrenia develops in children when the superego is strong enough to prevent the victory of the id over the ego. The ego, subservient to the superego, is capable of testing reality and exercises a tenuous control, but it is unable to prevent occasional vehement outbursts of emotions.

The latent schizophrenic's anxiety causes him to adhere to rigid, inflexible rules. He becomes more compulsive than the obsessive-compulsive neurotic. To be orderly, punctilious, neat, and clean is, to him, literally a matter of life and death.

One of the outstanding features of latent schizophrenia in childhood is the fluctuation between the neurotic, ego-protective and the psychotic, ego-deficiency symptoms (Ekstein & Wallerstein, 1956; Wolman, 1966b). His behavior varies from normal to bizarre. He tries to be perfect, and his failures terrify him.

Sometimes he makes the strange compromise of the character neurotic who loves someone and finds in his great love justification for his hatred and cruelty toward anyone else.

Sometimes a desperate struggle goes on between the hostile impulses and the controlling apparatus. This desperate struggle characterizes latent schizophrenia.

Latent schizophrenic children are torn by the dependence-independence conflict. To grow means to be independent, but to be independent means to use one's own judgment, to care less for the mother, to neglect her. Thus growth causes guilt feelings, and dependence-independence becomes a major conflict.

Geleerd (1960, p. 158) describes latent schizophrenic children, often referred to as being in the "borderline state." These children show lack of tolerance for frustration, emotional immaturity, uneven mental development, uncontrollable id impulses, and lack of social adaptation.

Geleerd (1946) describes prepsychotic children, saying that they

> ... display a far lesser degree of control over their aggressive actions than do other children of the same age. Also they show a lack of control over their anal and sexual impulses. ... In most of their activities they tend to present an uncontrollable impulsive behavior. Their temper tantrums differ from those of the normal or neurotic child and their aggressiveness is dangerous both to themselves and to the environment. The child is out of control with reality and believes himself to be persecuted [and] becomes more paranoid where treated with firmness. He considers it proof of his paranoid ideas. ...

Similar observations were reported by Ekstein and Wallerstein (1956) on several borderline cases of childhood schizophrenia. Under the mildest stress the child's ego defenses fall apart, and he plunges into world-destructive or even oral-cannibalistic fantasies.

Sometimes these children burst out in laughter when they act destructively, as if experiencing triumph and a great feeling of power, and their omnipotent fantasies come close to the pattern of delusion.

Parents are frequently the targets of the child's outbursts of destrudo, and the more the parents quarrel between themselves, the more they stimulate the child's destrudo. He desperately needs the security of strong, loving parents and panics when he sees that they are weak (Wolman, 1970).

Hypervectorial childhood neurosis. The hypervectorial neurotic child is a child whose ego has remained relatively intact, despite the instrumentalism of his parents. Their instrumentalism has forced him to adopt a hypervectorial attitude that may eventually lead to schizophrenia. The impoverished, neurotic ego develops a series of ego-protective symptoms, such as self-sacrifice, conformity, renunciation of pleasures, and a too early development of a distorted reality principle.

Under the threat of losing his hypercathected love object—the mother—the child introjects her image as early as the anal stage. This leads to a precocious formation of a despotic, rigid, over-demanding superego.

In hypervectorial childhood neurosis, the main symptoms reflect repression of hostile impulses. Such children are anxious and often hypo-chondriacal, and may have phobias and compul-sions. As a result of the struggle of the ego against both the id and the superego, the child is constantly tense and anxious. However, no matter how hard he tries, he can never satisfy the demands of his nagging mother.

Character neurosis. Sometimes these neurotic mechanisms may not suffice, and a powerful *character armor* develops. Obsessive-compulsive children easily accept authority and are, as a rule, compliant and conforming. Many of them are model students in the lower grades, where con-formity with the teacher's demands is rewarded.

The child feels that absolute conformity, strict routine, and rigidity are the best protection against his doing something wrong.

One of the main reasons for forming compul-sive action patterns is the *fear of losing self-con-trol.* Many children worry that they may lose control of their bowels or will be tempted to mas-turbate, or perhaps that they will get indigestion and vomit. All these have been perceived by the mother as an intentional defiance of her orders, and the child is terrified that he will accidentally incur her wrath.

Any kind of change is a threat and challenge to the child's aspiration for mastery over himself

and his environment. The child's displaced fears turn into a series of taboos, restrictions, rituals, and compulsive acts, including *délire de toucher,* a compulsion of touching, agoraphobia, and claustrophobia.

Obsessive-compulsive neurosis is the first step in the downward adjustment in hypervectorial disorders (Wolman, 1957, 1966b). The same dynamic factors act in obsessive-compulsives as in a full schizophrenic, in both childhood and adulthood (Fenichel, 1945). In all hypervectorial disorders there is the object-hypercathected attitude toward parents, the fear of one's own hos-tile impulses, and an overgrown superego.

The differential diagnosis between manifest childhood schizophrenia and obsessive-compul-sive childhood neurosis represents a serious prob-lem. Despert (1951, 1952, 1955) stressed the fact that a neurotic child is aware of the irrationality of his experiences and fantasy distortion. In the psychotic child there is a break with reality and impairment of intellectual functions. Weil (1953) found obsessive-compulsive symptoms. Sleep disturbances, hypochondriacal complaints, etc., are found in both neurosis and psychosis. The severity of symptoms offers the clue for differen-tial diagnosis. A combination of several symp-toms, such as fears, obsessions, and anxieties, is indicative of psychosis.

There are, as a rule, fewer fluctuations in neurosis than in manifest psychosis. The mani-festly schizophrenic child acts sometimes like a neurotic and is sometimes almost normal. The neurotic child, however, does not act like a psy-chotic. Ekstein and Wallerstein (1956) pointed to the stronger ego of the neurotic child, which protects primary processes. Some workers have not noticed the continuum of all hypervectorial disorders, while my observations point to this continuum (Wolman, 1959, 1966b). The obses-sive-compulsive symptoms in childhood are ego-protective; when they fail, ego-deficiency or psy-chotic symptoms appear. Neurosis and psychosis in childhood and adulthood are not opposites; they are distinct levels of the same disorder, distinguished by the fighting or failing ego, respectively.

As long as the child is aware of the irrationality of his obsessive thoughts and compulsive acts, he is a neurotic, no matter how strange his thoughts and acts are. As long as he knows that his fantasies are fantasies and more or less controls his impulses, he is not yet psychotic.

SCHIZOPHRENIA IN ADOLESCENCE

The onset of schizophrenia has frequently been associated with adolescence. Undoubtedly, adolescence is a time of great emotional changes and personality formation. Several workers believe this to be a period of trial and challenge to one's mental apparatus; yet even the most stormy adolescence of a normal youngster has little, if anything, in common with that of a mild schizophrenic.

Schizophrenia does not start at adolescence. Some cases are "overstayed" cases of childhood schizophrenia. Some are cases of childhood schizophrenia that improved for awhile and, under the impact of biological growth and the social-role readjustment faced by all adolescents, slowly or rapidly regressed into manifest psychosis (Beres, 1956). Thus, there is fairly good reason to believe that adolescence may activate latent conflicts and aggravate the already existing hypervectorial disorder.

The aggravation of symptoms and personality deterioration may be caused by both biological and social factors. The growth of the organism, with its metabolic and endocrine changes, has a disturbing impact on all adolescents and represents a challenge to the shaky personality structure of the hypervectorial neurotic or latent psychotic.

The other challenge comes from the environment. Adolescents face serious problems of adjustment to their future sex roles and occupations, and to adult society.

The identification is closely related to the forming of the superego in adolescence.

Abnormal adolescents go through considerable difficulties before they find their way in absorbing the cultural values of their society, reshaping their superegos, and forming their own philosophy and set of values. These difficulties can be insurmountable for neurotic and latent psychotic individuals. The increased pressures of their infantile, maternal, dictatorial superegos may come to a point where any activity is believed to be wrong. A complete rigidity and tense passivity may lead into a catatonic stupor at this age.

During the elementary school years, characterized by socially regulated patterns of behavior, and during the biopsychologically not so stormy latency period, the neurotic ego-protective mechanisms keep the ego going without major setbacks. But when the human body grows and changes rapidly and the adolescent faces new social roles and expectations, the existing safety valves may prove inadequate, and a flood may start. This is probably the reason for the frequent onset of manifest schizophrenia in adolescence in individuals who were hypervectorial neurotics or latent psychotics in childhood.

DIAGNOSTIC METHODS

Interactional Influences

Halpern (1965) has done extensive work concerning diagnosis of childhood disorders. She states: ". . . any evaluation of a child's adjustment, of the adequacy of his functioning, whether or not he is suffering from a 'disorder,' must take into account the fact that he is still a developing organism that has not yet reached complete physical, mental, or emotional status" (p. 621). Therefore, diagnosis at any age must be based on the knowledge of the normal child's responses and behavior patterns at any age. At each age level the child, because of the development of his ego, shows different ways of coping with anxiety and responding to new situations. Moreover, the tester must note that there are certain aspects which must be considered when testing the child. First, the child is totally dependent on his environment, and both physical and psychological separation come only gradually. The tester must be fully aware of the nature of the child's environment. The tester must also be aware of the fact that the child does not come for testing with an awareness of his needs, but is brought by others. Therefore, it is necessary for the tester to establish a good rapport with the child in order to ensure his cooperation.

The major emphasis in testing is an attempt to measure the strength of the child's ego in terms of his ability to function in a variety of areas. The tester is interested in only a clinical classification of the child.

Early Predictions

Diagnosis of schizophrenia can be made as early as infancy. For example, on the basis of Bender's theory of schizophrenia, Fish (1957, 1959, 1960) studied a small number of infants and designated those who showed a tendency toward schizophrenia. Later studies, which included extensive psychological testing, substantiated her predictions. Fish states that her conclusions were based on the manifestation of hypersensitivity on the part of these infants in response to certain forms of stimuli, erratic developmental patterns, and a combination of marked retardation in some areas and precocious functioning in others.

Escalona and Heider (1959) found that one of the best predictions of schizophrenia is based on the infant's early response to space. They found that schizophrenic children often show severe difficulty with regard to spatial orientation and become confused and get lost more easily than

normal children. Moreover, this weakness is seen on tests involving spatial relations, such as the object-assembly test on the Wechsler Intelligence Scale for Children and the Bender Gestalt test.

Intelligence Tests

With older children suffering from schizophrenia, a variety of test signs can be indicators of the disorder. In intelligence testing the schizophrenic child often shows an erratic scatter in terms of ability. On the Stanford-Binet he may be a base age 2 years below his chronological age and yet continue to pass tests at levels as great as 7 or 8 years beyond his chronological age, while on the WAIS such a child may show as much as a twelve-point range between his highest and lowest scores. Even more typical of the schizophrenic child is the unevenness of his functioning on any one subtest, for he often fails very easy items and yet passes more difficult ones. There is often very little correlation between the difficulty of the test items and his performance. Moreover, in the testing situation he shows erratic attentional effort and often volunteers fragmented and somewhat bizarre observations on his environment (Wolman, 1970).

The Rorschach Test

On the Rorschach, the schizophrenic child manifests his feelings of being overwhelmed by stimuli by giving highly disorganized responses. His thinking shows primary process activity, lack of reality testing, and confusion. "The child simply uses the test stimulus as a springboard for his own highly idiosyncratic associations and makes no effort to bring these in line with more usual concepts" (Halpern, 1965, p. 629). On some occasions, the schizophrenic child displays a strange combination of both excessive concreteness and inadequate organizing and integrative abilities. Other schizophrenic children will attempt to make sense out of their confused inner world by using a variety of common neurotic defenses such as withdrawal, denial, repression, blocking, and projection. Thus the results of the testing will show many neurotic features, and yet there will be certain responses which could not come from either a neurotic or a brain-damaged child.

Thematic Tests

The schizophrenic child's response to the CAT or TAT will be similar to his response to the Rorschach. For while he may be stimulus-bound when he begins his response to a particular card, he will often show more and more bizarre thinking as he proceeds, and by the end of the story he has lost almost all contact with the card itself.

The schizophrenic child's entire behavior within the diagnostic setting will reflect his underlying pathology. The autistic child may or may not respond to the situation, depending on whatever internal activity is going on at that moment. The symbiotic child, on the other hand, will react with terror and refuse to be separated from his mother.

Interviews

The interview with the schizophrenic child differs from that with other children in that the schizophrenic child responds to all aspects of the interview in a highly subjective manner. He often ignores the questions, and even the presence of the interviewer, and will continue to discuss only what interests him. His conversation is often characterized by expressions of excessive hostility, references to excretory and sexual activity, and bizarre comments about the everyday events in his life.

Thus observations and interviews alone often are enough to establish whether or not a child is schizophrenic. Yet testing can be helpful to determine more specific information about a particular child. For example, intelligence testing can show to what extent the child's illness interferes with his intellectual functioning and learning ability and in which areas he is advanced or retarded for his age. Personality testing, on the other hand, shows how the child perceives both himself and his world, the way in which he copes with the forces in his environment, and the adequacy or inadequacy of his defenses.

REFERENCES

Abraham, K. *Selected papers on psychoanalysis.* New York: Basic Books, 1955.

Alanen, Y. O. The mothers of schizophrenic patients. *Acta Psychiatrica et Neurologica Scandinavica,* 1958, **33** (Suppl. 724).

Alderton, H. R. A review of schizophrenia in childhood. *Canadian Psychiatric Association Journal,* 1966, **11,** 276–285.

Altshuler, K. Z. Genetic elements in schizophrenia. *Eugenics Quarterly,* 1957, **4,** 92–98.

American Psychiatric Association. *Diagnostic and statistical manual of mental disorders.* Washington: APA, 1968.

Arieti, S. Autistic thought. *Journal of Nervous and Mental Disorder,* 1950, **111,** 288–302.

Arieti, S. *Interpretation of schizophrenia.* New York: Brunner, 1955.

Bakwin, H. The early development of children with schizophrenia. *The Journal of Pediatrics,* 1953, **43,** 217–219.

Baruk, H. Experimental catatonia and the problem of will and personality. *Journal of Nervous and Mental Disorder,* 1949, **110,** 218–235.

Bateson, G., Jackson, D. D., Haley, J., & Weakland, J. Toward a theory of schizophrenia. *Behavior Science,* 1956, **1,** 251–264.

Becker, W. A genetic approach to the interpretation and evaluation of the process reactive distinction in schizophrenia. *Journal of Abnormal and Social Psychology,* 1956, **53,** 229–236.

Bellak, L. (Ed.) *Schizophrenia: A review of the syndrome.* New York: Logos, 1958.

Bellak, L., & Holt, R. R. Somatotypes in relation to dementia praecox. *American Journal of Psychiatry,* 1948, **104,** 713–724.

Bender, L. Childhood schizophrenia. *American Journal of Orthopsychiatry,* 1947, **27,** 68–79.

Bender, L. Childhood schizophrenia. *The Psychiatric Quarterly,* 1953, **27,** 663–681. (a)

Bender, L. *Child psychiatric techniques.* Springfield, Ill.: Charles C Thomas, 1953. (b)

Bender, L. *A dynamic psychopathology of childhood.* Springfield, Ill.: Charles C Thomas, 1954.

Bender, L. Twenty years of clinical research on schizophrenic children. In I. G. Caplan (Ed.), *Emotional problems of early childhood.* New York: Basic Books, 1955. Pp. 503–518.

Bender, L. Schizophrenia in childhood: Its recognition, description, and treatment. *American Journal of Orthopsychiatry,* 1956, **26,** 499–506.

Bender, L. The concept of pseudopsychopathic schizophrenia in adolescence. *American Journal of Orthopsychiatry,* 1959, **29,** 491–512.

Bender, L., & Faretra, G. Organic therapy in pediatric psychiatry. *Diseases of the Nervous System,* 1961, **22** (Monogr. Suppl.).

Bender, L., Faretra, G., & Cobrinik, L. LSD and UML treatment of hospitalized disturbed children. *Recent Advances in Biological Psychiatry,* 1963, **5,** 84.

Bender, L., Goldschmidt, L., & Sankau, D. S. Treatment of autistic schizophrenic children with LSD25 and UML419. *Recent Advances in Biological Psychiatry,* 1962, **4,** 170.

Bender, L., & Gurevitz, S. Results of psychotherapy with young schizophrenic children. *American Journal of Orthopsychiatry,* 1955, **25,** 162–170.

Bender, L., & Woltman, A. Play and psychotherapy. *Nervous Child,* 1962, **1,** 17–39.

Beres, D. Ego deviation and the concept of schizophrenia. In *The psychoanalytic study of the child.* Vol. 11, New York: International Universities Press, 1956. Pp. 164–235.

Bergman, P., & Escalona, S. K. Unusual sensitivities in very young children. In *The psychoanalytic study of the child.* Vols. 3–4. New York: International Universities Press, 1949. Pp. 3–4.

Bettelheim, B. *Love is not enough.* Glencoe, Ill.: Free Press, 1950.

Bettelheim, B. *Truants from life.* Glencoe, Ill.: Free Press, 1955.

Bettelheim, B. Schizophrenia as a reaction to extreme situations. *American Journal of Orthopsychiatry,* 1956, **26,** 507–518.

Bettelheim, B. Childhood schizophrenia symposium 1955, #3. *American Journal of Orthopsychiatry,* 1964, **3,** 488–497.

Bettelheim, B. *Infantile autism and the birth of self.* New York: Free Press, 1967.

Betz, B. J. A study of tactics for resolving the autistic barrier in the psychotherapy of the schizophrenic personality. *American Journal of Psychiatry,* 1947, **107,** 267–273.

Blake, P., & Moss, T. The development of socialization skills in an electively mute child. *Behavior Research and Therapy,* 1967, **5,** 349–356.

Bleuler, E. *Dementia praecox or the group of schizophrenias.* New York: International Universities Press, 1950.

Bleuler, M. *Endokrinologische Psychiatrie.* Stuttgart: Thieme, 1954.

Bleuler, M. Research and changes in concepts in the study of schizophrenia. *Bulletin of the Isaac Ray Medical Library,* 1955, **3.**

Boatman, J. J., & Szurek, S. A clinical study of childhood schizophrenia. In D. D. Jackson (Ed.), *The etiology of schizophrenia.* New York: Basic Books, 1960. Pp. 389–440.

Böök, J. A. Genetic aspects of schizophrenic psychoses. In D. D. Jackson (Ed.), *The etiology of schizophrenia.* New York: Basic Books, 1960. Pp. 23–36.

Bowen, M. A family concept in schizophrenia. In D. D. Jackson (Ed.), *The etiology of schizophrennia.* New York: Basic Books, 1960. Pp. 346–372.

Bradley, C. Early evidence of psychoses in children with special references to schizophrenia. *The Journal of Pediatrics,* 1947, **30,** 529–540.

Brody, E. B., & Redlich, F. C. (Eds.) *Psychotherapy with schizophrenics: A symposium.* New York: International Universities Press, 1952.

Buck, C. W., Carscallen, H. B., & Hobbs, G. E. Temperature regulation in schizophrenia. *A.M.A. Archives of Neurology and Psychiatry,* 1950, **64,** 828–842.

Bychowski, G. *Psychotherapy of psychosis.* New York: Grune & Stratton, 1952.

Bykov, K. *The cerebral cortex and the inner organs.* New York: Chemical Publishers, 1957.

Chitty, D. Adverse effects of population density upon the viability of later generations. In J. B. Cragg and N. W. Pirie (Eds.), *The numbers of men and animals.* London: Oliver & Boyd, 1955.

Davidson, G. A social learning therapy program with an autistic child. *Behavior Research and Therapy,* 1964, **2,** 149–159.

Davidson, J. N. *The biochemistry of the nucleic acids.* New York: Wiley, 1960.

Davis, D. R. The family triangle in schizophrenia. *British Journal of Medical Psychology,* 1961, **34,** 53–63.

Dawson, J. G., Stone, H. K., & Dellis, N. T. (Eds.),

Psychotherapy with schizophrenics. Baton Rouge: Louisiana State University Press, 1961.

Des Lauries, A. *The experience of reality in childhood schizophrenia.* New York: International Universities Press, 1962.

Des Lauries, A. The schizophrenic child. *Archives of General Psychiatry,* 1967, **16,** 194–201.

Des Lauries, A., & Halpern, F. Psychological tests in childhood schizophrenics. *American Journal of Orthopsychiatry,* 1947, **17,** 57–67.

Despert, J. L. Some considerations relating to the genesis of autistic behavior in children. *American Journal of Orthopsychiatry,* 1951, **21,** 335–350.

Despert, J. L. Diagnostic criteria of schizophrenia in children. *American Journal of Psychotherapy,* 1952, **6,** 148–163.

Despert, J. L. Differential diagnosis between obsessive-compulsive neurosis and schizophrenia in children. In P. Hoch & J. Zubin (Eds.), *Psychopathology of childhood.* New York: Grune & Stratton, 1955. Pp. 240–253.

Despert, L., & Sherwin, A. Further examination of diagnostic criteria in schizophrenic illness and psychosis of infancy and early childhood. *American Journal of Psychiatry,* 1958, **114,** 784.

Doust, J. W. Spectroscopic and photoelectric oximetry in schizophrenia and other psychiatric states. *The Journal of Mental Science,* 1952, **93,** 143–160.

Dunn, W. L. Visual discrimination of schizophrenic subjects as a function of stimulus meaning. *Journal of Personality,* 1954, **23,** 48–64.

Eisenberg, L. The fathers of autistic children. *American Journal of Orthopsychiatry,* 1957, **27,** 715–724.

Eissler, K. R. Dementia praecox therapy: Psychiatric ward management of the acute schizophrenic patient. *Journal of Nervous and Mental Disorders,* 1947, **105,** 397–402.

Eissler, K. R. Remarks on the psychoanalysis of schizophrenia. In E. B. Brody & F. C. Redlich (Eds.), *Psychotherapy with schizophrenics: A symposium.* New York: International Universities Press, 1952.

Ekstein, R. *Children of time and space, of action and impulse.* New York: Appleton-Century-Crofts, 1966.

Ekstein, R., & Wallerstein, J. Observations on the psychology of borderline and psychotic children. In *The psychoanalytic study of the child.* Vol. 9. New York: International Universities Press, 1956.

English, O. S., Hanupe, W. W., Bacon, C. L., & Settlage, C. F. *Direct analysis and schizophrenia.* New York: Grune & Stratton, 1961.

Escalona, S., & Heider, G. *Prediction and outcome.* New York: Basic Books, 1959.

Esecover, H., Malitz, S., & Wilkens, B. Clinical profiles of paid normal subjects volunteering for hallucinogen drug studies. *American Journal of Psychiatry,* 1961, **117,** 910–915.

Eveloff, H. H. The autistic child. *Archives of General Psychiatry,* 1960, **3,** 66–81.

Faris, R. E. L., & Dunham, H. W. *Mental disorders in urban areas.* Chicago: University of Chicago Press, 1939.

Federn, P. *Ego psychology and the psychoses.* New York: Basic Books, 1952.

Fenichel, O. *The psychoanalytic theory of neurosis.* New York: Norton, 1945.

Fish, B. The detection of schizophrenia in infancy. *The Journal of Nervous and Mental Disease,* 1957, **125,** 1–24.

Fish, B. Longitudinal observations of biological deviations in a schizophrenic infant. *American Journal of Psychiatry,* 1959, **116,** 25–31.

Fish, B. Involvement of the central nervous system in infants with schizophrenia. *Archives of Neurology,* 1960, **2,** 115–121.

Fleck, S. Family dynamics and the origin of schizophrenia. *Psychosomatic Medicine,* 1960, **22,** 333–344.

Fleck, S., Lidz, T., Cornelison, A., Schafer, S., & Terry, D. The intrafamilial environment of the schizophrenic patient. In J. H. Masserman (Ed.), *Individual and family dynamics.* New York: Grune & Stratton, 1959.

Foudraine, J. Schizophrenia and the family: A survey of the literature 1956–1960 on the etiology of schizophrenia. *Acta Psychotherapeutica,* 1961, **9,** 82–110.

Frankl, V. E. *The doctor and the soul.* New York: Knopf, 1955.

Freedman, A. M. Maturation and its relation to the dynamics of childhood schizophrenia. *American Journal of Orthopsychiatry,* 1954, **24,** 487–491.

Freedman, A. M. Treatment of autistic schizophrenic children with marsilid. *Journal of Clinical and Experimental Psychopathology,* 1958, **19,** 138 (Suppl. 1).

Freedman, A. M. Day hospitals for severely disturbed schizophrenic children. *American Journal of Psychiatry,* 1959, **115,** 893–899.

Freedman, R. *Recent migration to Chicago.* Chicago: University of Chicago Press, 1950.

Freeman, H. Physiological studies. In L. Bellak (Ed.), *Schizophrenia: A review of the syndrome.* New York: Logos, 1958. Pp. 174–215.

Freeman, T., Cameron, J. L., & McGhie, A.

Chronic schizophrenia. New York: International Universities Press, 1958.

Freud, S. *Collected papers.* London: Hogarth Press and the Institute of Psychoanalysis, 1925–1950. 5 vols.

Freud, S. *The ego and the id.* London: Hogarth Press, 1927.

Freud, S. *A general introduction to psychoanalysis.* New York: Perma Giants, 1949. (a).

Freud. S. *An outline of psychoanalysis.* New York: Norton, 1949. (b)

Fromm-Reichmann, F. *Principles of intensive psychotherapy.* Chicago: University of Chicago Press, 1950.

Fromm-Reichmann, F. Some aspects of psychoanalytic psychotherapy with schizophrenics. In E. B. Brody & F. C. Redlich (Eds.), *Psychotherapy with schizophrenics: A symposium.* New York: International Universities Press, 1952.

Fromm-Reichmann, F. *Psychoanalysis and psychotherapy.* Chicago: University of Chicago Press, 1959.

Garmezy, N. Stimulus differentiation by schizophrenic and normal subjects under conditions of reward and punishment. *Journal of Personality,* 1952, **20,** 253–276.

Garmezy, N., & Rodnick, E. H. Premorbid adjustment and performance in schizophrenia. *The Journal of Nervous and Mental Disease,* 1959, **129,** 450–466.

Garrone, G. Statistical genetic study of schizophrenia in the Geneva population between 1901–1950. *Journal of Genetic Psychology,* 1962, 89–219.

Geleerd, E. R. A contribution to the problem of psychoses in childhood. In *The psychoanalytic study of the child.* Vol. 2. New York: International Universities Press, 1946. Pp. 271–291.

Geleerd, E. R. Borderline states in childhood and adolescence. In J. Weinreb (Ed.), *Recent developments in psychoanalytic child therapy.* New York: International Universities Press, 1960. Pp. 154–171.

Ginott, G., & Harms, E. Mental disorders in childhood. In B. B. Wolman (Ed.), *Handbook of clinical psychology.* New York: McGraw-Hill, 1965. Pp. 1094–1118.

Gittelman, M., & Birch, J. G. Childhood schizophrenia: Intellect, neurologic status, perinatal risk, prognosis and family pathology. *Archives of General Psychiatry,* 1967, **17,** 16–25.

Gjessing, R. Distribution of somatic function in catatonia with a periodic course and their compensation. *The Journal of Mental Science,* 1938, **84,** 608.

Goldfarb, W. Receptor preferences in schizophrenia. *A.M.A. Archives of Neurology and Psychiatry,* 1956, **76,** 643–653.

Goldfarb, W. *Childhood schizophrenia.* Cambridge, Mass.: Harvard University Press, 1961.

Goldfarb, W. Self awareness in schizophrenic children. *Archives of General Psychiatry,* 1963, **8,** 47–60.

Goldfarb, W. An investigation of childhood schizophrenia. *Archives of General Psychiatry,* 1964, **11,** 620–634.

Goldhamer, H., & Marshall, A. W. *Psychosis and civilization.* New York: Basic Books, 1949.

Goldman, A. E. A comparative-developmental approach to schizophrenia. *Psychological Bulletin,* 1962, **59,** 57–69.

Gregory, I. Genetic factors in schizophrenia. *American Journal of Psychiatry,* 1960, **116,** 961–972.

Hall, K. R., & Crookes, T. G. Studies in learning impairment. I. Schizophrenic and organic patients. *The Journal of Mental Science,* 1951, **97,** 725–737.

Halpern, F. Diagnostic methods in childhood disorders. In B. B. Wolman (Ed.), *Handbook of clinical psychology.* New York: McGraw-Hill, 1965. Pp. 381–408.

Hare, E. H. Mental illness and social class in Bristol. *British Journal of Social Medicine,* 1955, **9,** 191–195.

Hartmann, H. Notes on the theory of sublimation. In *The psychoanalytic study of the child.* Vol. 10. New York: International Universities Press, 1955. Pp. 9–29.

Heath, R. G. A biochemical hypothesis on the etiology of schizophrenia. In D. D. Jackson (Ed.), *The etiology of schizophrenia.* New York: Basic Books, 1960. Pp. 146–158.

Hendrickson, W. J. Etiology in childhood schizophrenia: An evolution of current views. *Nervous Child,* 1952, **10,** 9–18.

Hill, L. B. *Psychotherapeutic intervention in schizophrenia.* Chicago: University of Chicago Press, 1955.

Hinsie, L. E., & Campbell, R. J. *Psychiatric dictionary.* (3rd ed.) New York: Oxford University Press, 1960.

Hirsch, E. A. Interpretive flexibility as a condition set by schizophrenic children—in psychotherapy. *American Journal of Orthopsychiatry,* 1961, **30,** 397–404.

Hoagland, H. Metabolic and physiologic disturbances in the psychoses. In S. S. Cobb (Ed.), *The biology of mental health and disease.* New York: Hoeber-Harper, 1952.

Hoch, P. H. Drugs and psychotherapy. *American Journal of Psychiatry,* 1959, **116.**

Hoch, P. H., & Pennes, H. H. Electric convulsive treatment and its modification. In L. Bellak (Ed.), *Schizophrenia: A review of a syndrome.* New York: Logos, 1958. Pp. 428–455. (a)

Hoch, P. H., & Pennes, H. H. Insulin shock treatment. In L. Bellak (Ed.), *Schizophrenia: A review of a syndrome.* New York: Logos, 1958. Pp. 397–422. (b)

Hoch, P. H., & Polatin, P. Pseudoneurotic forms of schizophrenia. *The Psychiatric Quarterly,* 1949, **23,** 248.

Hollingshead, A. B., & Redlich, F. *Social class and mental illness.* New York: Wiley, 1958.

Hoskins, R. G. *The biology of schizophrenia.* New York: Norton, 1946.

Hunt, M. V., & Coffer, C. N. Psychological deficit. In M. V. Hunt (Ed.), *Personality and the behavior disorders.* New York: Ronald Press, 1944. Pp. 971–1032.

Hyden, H. Satellite cells in the nervous system. *Scientific American,* 1961, **205,** 62–70.

Ivanov-Smolensky, A. G. *Essays on the pathophysiology of higher nervous activity.* Moscow: Foreign Language Publishers, 1954.

Jackson, D. D. (Ed.) *The etiology of schizophrenia.* New York: Basic Books, 1960.

Jackson, L. Non-speaking children. *British Journal of Psychology,* 1950, **23,** 87–100.

Jung, C. G. *The psychology of dementia praecox.* New York: Journal of Nervous and Mental Disorders Publishing Co., 1936.

Kalinowsky, L. B. Convulsive shock treatment. In S. Arieti (Ed.), *American handbook of psychiatry.* New York: Basic Books, 1959. Pp. 1499–1520.

Kallmann, F. J. *The genetics of schizophrenia.* Locust Valley, N.Y. Augustin, 1938.

Kallmann, F. J.   Genetic theory of schizophrenia: Analysis of 691 twin index families. *American Journal of Psychiatry,* 1946, **103,** 309–322.

Kallmann, F. J.   Genetics in relation to mental disorders. *The Journal of Mental Science,* 1948, **94,** 250.

Kallmann, F. J.   *Heredity in health and mental disorders.*   New York: Norton, 1953.

Kallmann, F. J. (Ed.).   *Expanding goals of genetics in psychiatry.*   New York: Grune & Stratton, 1962.

Kanner, L.   Autistic disturbances of affective contact. *Nervous Child,* 1943, **2,** 217–250.

Kanner, L.   *Child psychiatry.*   Springfield, Ill.: Charles C Thomas, 1948.   (a)

Kanner, L.   Early Infantile autism. *American Journal of Orthopsychiatry,* 1948, **19,** 416–426.   (b)

Kanner, L., & Eisenberg, L.   Notes on the follow-up studies of autistic children.   In P. H. Hoch & J. Zubin (Eds.), *Psychopathology of childhood.* New York: Grune & Stratton, 1955.   Pp. 227–234.

Katan, M.   The importance of the nonpsychotic part of the personality in schizophrenia. *International Journal of Psychoanalysis,* 1954, **35,** 119.

Katzenelbogen, S., & Fang, A. D.   Narcosynthesis effects. *Diseases of the Nervous System,* 1953, **14,** 85–88.

Kety, S. S.   Recent biochemical theories of schizophrenia.   In D. D. Jackson (Ed.), *The etiology of schizophrenia.*   New York: Basic Books, 1960.   Pp. 120–145.

Kety, S. S., et al.   Cerebral blood flow and metabolism in schizophrenia: Effects of barbiturate semi-narcosis, insulin coma. *American Journal of Psychiatry,* 1948, **104,** 765–770.

Klein, M.   *Contributions to psychoanalysis.* London: Hogarth Press, 1946.

Knight, R. P.   Management and psychotherapy of the borderline schizophrenic patient. *Bulletin of the Menninger Clinic,* 1953, **17,** 139.

Kraepelin, E.   *Dementia praecox and paraphrenia.*   Chicago: Chicago Medical Book, 1919.

Krech, D., et al.   Interhemispheric effects of cortical lesions on brain biochemistry. *Science,* 1960, **132,** 352–353.

Kretschmer, E.   *Physique and character.*   London: Kegan Paul, Trench, Trubner & Co., 1925.

Lehman, E., Haher, J., & Lesser, S. R.   The use of reserpine in autistic children. *Journal of Nervous and Mental Disorders,* 1957, **125,** 351–356.

Lemkau, P. V., & Crocetti, G. M.   Vital statistics of schizophrenia.   In L. Bellak (Ed.), *Schizophrenia: A review of the syndrome.*   New York: Logos, 1958.   Pp. 64–81.

Lidz, T., & Fleck, S.   Schizophrenia, human integration, and the role of the family.   In D. D. Jackson (Ed.), *The etiology of schizophrenia.* New York: Basic Books, 1960.   Pp. 323–345.

Lidz, T., et al.   The intrafamilial environment of schizophrenic patients. II. Marital schism and marital skew. *American Journal of Psychiatry,* 1957, **114,** 241–248.

Lidz, T., et al.   The intrafamilial environment of schizophrenic patients. IV. Parental personalities and family interaction. *American Journal of Orthopsychiatry,* 1958, **28,** 764–776.

Lief, A.   *The commonsense psychiatry of Dr. Adolf Meyer.*   New York: McGraw-Hill, 1948.

Lindegarde, B.   *Variations in human body build.* Copenhagen: Munksgaard, 1953.

Linton, H. B., & Langs, R. J.   Subjective reactions to lysergic acid and diethylamide (LSD-25). *Archives of General Psychiatry,* 1962, **6,** 352–368.

Linton, R. *Culture and mental disorders.* Springfield, Ill.: Charles C Thomas, 1956.

Lovaas, O. I., Freitag, G., Gold, V., & Kassorla, I. C. Experimental studies in childhood schizophrenia: Analysis of self-destructive behavior. *Journal of Experimental Child Psychology,* 1965, **2,** 67–84.

Lovaas, O. I., Freitag, G., Nelson, K., & Whalen, C. The establishment of imitation and its use for the development of complex behavior in schizophrenic children. *Behavior Research and Therapy,* 1967, **5,** 171–181.

Lovaas, O. I., Schaeffe, B., & Simmons, J. Q. Building social behavior in autistic children by use of electric shock. *Journal of Experimental Research in Personality,* 1965, **1,** 99–109.

Lu, Y. C. Mother-child role relations in schizophrenia. *Psychiatry,* 1961, **24,** 133–142.

Lu, Y. C. Contradictory parental expectations in schizophrenia. *Archives of General Psychiatry,* 1962, **6,** 219–234.

Mahler, M. S. On child psychosis and schizophrenia: Autistic and symbiotic infantile psychoses. In *The psychoanalytic study of the child.* Vol. 7. New York: International Universities Press, 1952. Pp. 286–305.

Mahler, M. S. Childhood schizophrenia: Round table, 1953 discussion. *American Journal of Orthopsychiatry,* 1954, **24,** 523.

Mahler, M. S. Discussion of chaps. 13–16. In P. Hoch et al. (Eds.), *Psychopathology of childhood.* New York: Grune & Stratton, 1955. Pp. 285–289.

Mahler, M. S. Autism and symbiosis: Two extreme disturbances of identity. *International Journal of Psychoanalysis,* 1958, **39,** 77.

Mahler, M. S., & Gosliner, B. J. On symbiotic child psychosis: Genetic, dynamic and restitutive aspects. In *The psychoanalytic study of the child.* Vol. 10. New York: International Universities Press, 1955. Pp. 195–212.

Maier, H. W., & Campbell, S. Childhood psychosis. III. Routines: A pilot study of three selected routines and their impact upon the child in residential treatment. *American Journal of Orthopsychiatry,* 1957, **27,** 701–709.

Malzberg, B., & Lee, E. S. *Migration and mental disease.* New York: Social Science Research Council, 1956.

Margolies-Mehr, H. Application of tests to schizophrenia in children. *Nervous Child,* 1952–1953, **10,** 63–93.

Mayer-Gross, W., Slater, E. J., & Roth, M. *Clinical psychiatry.* Baltimore: Williams & Wilkins, 1955.

Mednick, S. A. Generalization as a function of manifest anxiety and adaptation to psychological experiments. *Journal of Consulting Psychology,* 1957, **21,** 491–494.

Meyer, M., & Ekstein, R. The psychotic pursuit of reality. *American Journal of Orthopsychiatry,* 1967, **37,** 359–400.

Milt, H. Serious mental illness in children. *Public Affairs,* 1963, No. 352.

Morris, J. N. Health and social class. *Lancet,* 7, 1959, 303–305.

Nagelberg, L., Spotnitz, H., & Feldman, Y. An attempt at healthy insulation in the withdrawn child. *American Journal of Orthopsychiatry,* 1953, **13,** 238–252.

Nuffield, E. J. A. The schizogenic mother. *The Medical Journal of Australia,* 1954, **2,** 283–286.

Nunberg, H. *Practice and theory in psychoanalysis.* New York: Journal of Nervous and Mental Disorders Publishing Co., 1948.

Ødegaard, O. Emigration and insanity. *Acta Psychiatrica et Neurologica,* 1932, **4.**

Ødegaard, O. The distribution of mental diseases in Norway. *Acta Psychiatrica et Neurologica,* 1945, **20,** 247–284.

Ornitz, E. M., & Ritvo, E. R. Perceptual inconsistency in early infantile autism: The syndrome of early infant autism and its variants including certain cases of childhood schizophrenia. *Archives of General Psychiatry,* 1968, **18,** 76–98.

Overholser, W., & Werkman, S. L. Etiology, pathogenesis and pathology. In L. Bellak (Ed.), *Schizophrenia: A review of the syndrome.* New York: Logos, 1958. Pp. 82–106.

Pasamanick, B., & Knobloch, H. Early feeding and birth difficulties in childhood schizophrenia: An exploration note. *Journal of Psychology,* 1963, **56,** 73–77.

Pavlov, I. P. *Lectures on conditioned reflexes.* New York: Liveright, 1928.

Pavlov, I. P. *Conditioned reflexes and psychiatry.* New York: International Publishers, 1941.

Peck, H., Rabinovitch, R., & Cramer, J. A treatment program for parents of schizophrenic children. *American Journal of Orthopsychiatry,* 1949, **19,** 592–598.

Phillips, L. Case history data and progress in schizophrenia. *Journal of Nervous and Mental Disorders,* 1953, **117,** 515–535.

Pronovost, P. Speech behavior and language comprehension of autistic children. *Journal of Chronic Diseases,* 1961, **13,** 228–233.

Putnam, M. C. Some observations on psychosis in early childhood. In G. Caplan (Ed.), *Emotional problems of early childhood.* New York: Basic Books, 1955. Pp. 519–524.

Rank, B. Adaptations of the psychoanalytic technique for the treatment of young children with atypical development. *American Journal of Orthopsychiatry,* 1949, **19,** 130–139.

Rank, B. Intensive study of preschool children who show marked personality deviations or "atypical development" and their parents. In G. Caplan (Ed.), *Emotional problems of early childhood.* New York: Basic Books, 1955. Pp. 491–502.

Redl, F., & Wineman, D. *Children who hate.* (2nd ed.) New York: Free Press, 1960.

Rees, L. Physical characteristics of the schizophrenic patient. In D. Richter (Ed.), *Schizophrenia: Somatic aspects.* New York: Macmillan, 1957. Pp. 1–14.

Reiss, M. Correlations between changes in mental states and thyroid activity after different forms of treatment. *The Journal of Mental Science,* 1954, **100,** 687–703.

Ribble, M. A., Redl, F., & Wineman, D. Clinical studies of instinctive reactions in newborn babies. *American Journal of Psychiatry,* 1938, **15,** 149–160.

Richards, B. W. Childhood schizophrenics and mental deficiency. *The Journal of Mental Science,* 1951, **97,** 290–372.

Richter, D. (Ed.). *Schizophrenia: Somatic aspects.* New York: Macmillan, 1957.

Riemer, M. D. Mental status of schizophrenics hospitalized for over 25 years into their senium. *The Psychiatric Quarterly,* 1950, **24,** 309.

Rifkin, A. H. *Schizophrenia in psychoanalytic office practice.* New York: Grune & Stratton, 1957.

Rimland, B. *Infantile autism.* New York: Appleton-Century-Crofts, 1964.

Roheim, G. *Magic and schizophrenia.* New York: International Universities Press, 1955.

Rosen, J. N. *Direct analysis.* New York: Grune & Stratton, 1953.

Rosenfeld, H. Considerations regarding the psychoanalytic approach to acute and chronic schizophrenia. *International Journal of Psychoanalysis,* 1953, **35,** 135.

Rosenthal, D. Confusion of identity and the frequency of schizophrenia in twins. *Archives of General Psychiatry,* 1960, **3,** 297–304.

Roth, M. Interaction of genetic and environmental factors in the causation of schizophrenia. In D. Richter (Ed.), *Schizophrenia: Somatic aspects.* New York: Macmillan, 1957. Pp. 15–31.

Sackler, M. D., Sackler, R. R., La Burt, H. A., Tui, C., & Sackler, A. M. A psychobiologic viewpoint of schizophrenia in childhood. *Nervous Child,* 1952, **10,** 43–59.

Savage, C., & Cholden, L. Schizophrenia and model psychoses. *Journal of Clinical and Experimental Psychopathology,* 1956, **17,** 405–413.

Scher, S. C., & Davis, H. A. *The out-patient treatment of schizophrenia.* New York: Grune & Stratton, 1960.

Schwing, G. *A way to the soul of the mentally ill.* New York: International Universities Press, 1954.

Sechehaye, M. A. New psychotherapy in schizophrenia. (Trans. by G. Ruben-Rabson). New York: Grune & Stratton, 1956.

Shattock, M. F. The somatic manifestations of schizophrenia: A clinical study of their significance. *The Journal of Mental Science,* 1950, **96,** 32.

Sheldon, W. H. *The varieties of human physique.* New York: Harper, 1940.

Slater, E. *Psychotic and neurotic illnesses in twins.* Medical Research Council, Special Report No. 278. London: H. M. Stationery Office, 1953.

Slater, E. The monogenic theory of schizophrenia. *Acta Genetica,* 1958, **8,** 50–56.

Spence, V. W., & Taylor, J. A. The relation of conditioned response strength to anxiety in normal, neurotic, and psychotic subjects. *Journal of Experimental Psychology,* 1953, **45,** 265–272.

Stein, L. Social class gradient in schizophrenia. *British Journal of Preventive and Social Medicine,* 1957, **11,** 181–195.

Sullivan, H. S. Sociopsychiatric research: Its implications for the schizophrenia problem and for mental hygiene. *American Journal of Psychiatry,* 1931, **10,** 77–91.

Sullivan, H. S. *Conceptions of modern psychiatry.* Washington: W. A. White, 1947.

Sullivan, H. S. *The interpersonal theory of psychiatry.* New York: Norton, 1953.

Szara, S. The comparison of the psychotic effect of tryptamine derivatives with the effects of mescaline and LSD-25 in self-experiments. In S. Garattini & V. Ghetti (Eds.), *Psychotrophic drugs.* London: Cleaver-Hume Press, 1958.

Szurek, S. A. Psychotic episodes and psychotic maldevelopment. *American Journal of Orthopsychiatry,* 1956, **26,** 519–543.

Taft, L. T., & Goldfarb, W. Prenatal and perinatal factors in childhood schizophrenia. *Developmental Medicine and Child Neurology,* 1964, **6,** 32–43.

Tausk, V. On the origin of the influencing machine in schizophrenia. *The Psychoanalytic Quarterly,* 1933, **2,** 263.

Taylor, J. A., & Spence, K. W. Conditioning

level in the behavior disorders. *Journal of Abnormal and Social Psychology,* 1954, **49,** 497–503.

Von Brauschitsch, H. K., & Kirk, W. E. Childhood schizophrenia and social class. *American Journal of Orthopsychiatry,* 1967, **37,** 400.

Von Domarus, E. The specific laws of logic in schizophrenia. In J. S. Kasanin (Ed.), *Language and thought in schizophrenia.* Berkeley: University of California Press, 1944.

Vorster, D. An investigation into the part played by organic factors in childhood schizophrenia. *The Journal of Mental Science,* 1960, **106,** 494–522.

Weakland, J. H. The double-bind hypothesis of schizophrenia and three party interaction. In D. D. Jackson (Ed.), *The etiology of schizophrenia.* New York: Basic Books, 1960. Pp. 373–388.

Weil, A. Clinical data and dynamic considerations in certain cases of childhood schizophrenia. *American Journal of Orthopsychiatry,* 1953, **23,** 518–529.

Werkman, S. L. Present trends in schizophrenic research. *American Journal of Orthopsychiatry,* 1959, **29,** 473–480.

Wexler, C. A. The structural problem in schizophrenia. In M. Brody & F. C. Redlich (Eds.), *Psychotherapy with schizophrenics.* New York: International Universities Press, 1952. Pp. 179–201.

Whitaker, C. A. (Ed.) *Psychotherapy of chronic schizophrenic patients.* Boston: Little, Brown, 1958.

Wolman, B. B. Juvenile delinquents in Palestine (Hebrew). *Hachinuch Quarterly,* 1946, **17,** 50–79.

Wolman, B. B. Intellectual development in adolescence. *Hachinuch Quarterly,* 1948, **19,** 131–148.

Wolman, B. B. Disturbances in acculturation. *American Journal of Psychotherapy,* 1949, **3,** 601–615.

Wolman, B. B. Social relations as a function of power and acceptance. Paper presented at the annual convention of the American Sociological Society, Boston, Mass., 1955.

Wolman, B. B. Leadership and group dynamics. *Journal of Social Psychology,* 1956, **43,** 11–25.

Wolman, B. B. Explorations in latent schizophrenia. *American Journal of Psychotherapy,* 1957, **11,** 560–588.

Wolman, B. B. The deterioration of the ego in schizophrenia. Paper presented at the meeting of the Eastern Psychological Association, 1958. (a)

Wolman, B. B. Instrumental, mutual acceptance, and vectorial groups. *Acta Sociologica,* 1958, **3,** 19–29. (b)

Wolman, B. B. Libido and destrudo in pseudoneurotic symptoms in schizophrenia. Paper presented at the meeting of the American Psychological Association, 1958. (c)

Wolman, B. B. Continuum hypothesis in neurosis and psychosis and the classification of the mental disorder. Paper presented at the meeting of the Eastern Psychological Association, 1959.

Wolman, B. B. *Contemporary theories and systems in psychology.* New York: Harper, 1960. (a)

Wolman, B. B. Impact of failure on group cohesiveness. *Journal of Social Psychology,* 1960, **51,** 409–418. (b)

Wolman, B. B. The fathers of schizophrenic patients. *Acta Psychotherapeutica,* 1961, **9,** 193–210.

Wolman, B. B. Research in etiology of schizophrenia. Paper presented at the meeting of the Eastern Psychological Association, 1962.

Wolman, B. B. Non-participant observation on a closed ward. *Acta Psychotherapeutica,* 1964, **12,** 61–71.

Wolman, B. B. Family dynamics and schizophrenia. *Journal of Health and Human Behavior,* 1965, **6,** 147–155.

Wolman, B. B. Classification of mental disorders. *Acta Psychotherapeutica,* 1966, **14,** 50–65. (a)

Wolman B. B. *Vectoriasis praecox or the group of schizophrenias.* Springfield, Ill.: Charles C Thomas, 1966. (b)

Wolman, B. B. The socio-psycho-somatic theory of schizophrenia. *Psychotherapy and Psychosomatics,* 1967, **15,** 373–387.

Wolman, B. B. *Children without childhood: A study in childhood schizophrenia.* New York: Grune & Stratton, 1970.

Wolman, B. B. *Call no man normal.* New York: International Universities Press, 1971.

Wooley, D. W. Serotonin in mental disorders. *Research Publication of the Association of Nervous and Mental Disorders,* 1958, **36,** 381–400.

Wynne, L. C., et al. Pseudo-mutuality in the family relations in schizophrenics. *Psychiatry,* 1958, **21,** 205–220.

15 | Depressive Phenomena in Children

Carl P. Malmquist

The occurrence of painful feeling states associated with sadness is probably the most prevalent form of suffering experienced by children as well as adults. Such experiences also have the potential for subsequent developmental and psychopathological consequences. The term *depression* itself has a variety of meanings. Three main usages employed refer to an affective state, a syndrome, and a nosological entity which some would consider an "illness." Sad *affective states* may be elicited in response to persons, situations, or objects, in contrast to the more enduring and sad *moods,* which lend a particular coloring to the personality or ego state of the individual child (Jacobson, 1957). Clinical investigations in the past few decades have extended the spectrum of depressive phenomena back to infancy. The goal has been to delineate varying manifestations of how depressive affect is dealt with by children at different developmental stages as well as the clinical consequences of this state. Many workers remain skeptical of a "disease entity" of depression in childhood comparable to the adult diagnoses, at least before the preadolescent period. At the other extreme, almost all clinicians who work with children seem agreed that children experience mood disturbances. Between these extremes, most clinicians hold to a complex of manifestations in children which are referred to as *accompaniments* or *equivalents* of depression. It is parsimonious to view children as manifesting various signs and symptoms of mood lability in response to environmental or internalized alterations which will be labeled as *depressive phenomena.* A variety of problems are encompassed under this rubric, such as depressive reactions in children, the origins of depressive proneness, grief in children, object loss as related to depressive states, suicidal impulses, and psychodynamic patterns within the child and family as related to depressions. There are also biological correlates in terms of genetic and biochemical predispositions as well as in terms of individual drive endowments of the child which predispose toward depression.

INFANTILE DEPRESSIVE PHENOMENA

Discussions of "infantile depressions" are frequently blended within the context of maternal deprivation. Many of these reports are based retrospectively on data of patients who have various types of emotional disorders later in life, although in recent years there have been attempts to extend the deprivation hypothesis directly to anterospective follow-up studies of such children. Many of the early papers dealt with children of different ages in nurseries, foster homes, hospitals, and institutions, where a repeated observation was made of a disruption in the capacity to form consistent and tender human attachments. Efforts to treat these children were made in the context of attempting to extend psychoanalytic hypotheses to the earliest childhood periods via direct work with children. This began in the 1920s and 1930s, and a few examples will illustrate this early beginning. Levy (1937) reported on an 8-year-old girl who had been in a succession of foster homes and was finally adopted but who continued to manifest an incapacity to form attachments, coupled with a lack of emotional responsiveness and "hunger" for affect. Goldfarb (1943) studied thirty children, aged 34 to 35 months, and concluded that fifteen of the children brought up in institutions had lower IQs by twenty-eight points than those raised in foster homes since the age of 4 months. Children placed in the Hampstead nursery during the bombing of London were studied by Burlingham and Freud (1943), who noted that maternal deprivation has less serious repercussions as the child grows older but who felt that the younger the child is when the deprivation occurs, the more serious the effects will be. It should be noted that the matter has still not been settled, by either observational research or psychoanalytic reconstruction, of whether the earlier an affective disturbance takes place, the greater damage it necessarily does to emotional development, although clinical impressions favor this hypothesis. It may be a matter of the younger organism's being more vulnerable in some respects but also having a greater adaptive capacity, such as being able to accept substitute objects.

Spitz (1946) elaborated on the syndrome of *anaclitic depression*. Pediatricians had long been aware of such a condition and had referred to it as *marasmus,* classifying it as a form of wasting disease. Separation from a maternal object after the period of specific recognition at about 6 months was held to lead to a grief reaction. It is now realized that various types of perceptual and attachment behavior to objects occur long before 6 months. Infants in such situations were described as sad, weepy, and apathetic, with immobile faces and a distant expression; they reacted slowly to stimuli, their movements were slow, their appetite and sleep patterns were poor, and they had a distaste for locomotion. Spitz believed these to be phenomena of an anaclitic depression since the infants appeared so similar to adults who were depressed. These infants had been having a satisfactory relationship with the maternal object up to that time. After 3 months of such separation, a full restoration appeared to be rare. Similar symptoms and signs were observed in children who had been institutionalized in infancy and permanently separated from their mothers and who had not had adequate stimulation and fondling. This had more serious overtones since both mental and physical development lagged and repeated infections were common, as well as cachexia and sometimes death. This clinical picture was described as *hospitalism* because of its frequent association with children in hospitals or institutions. The infant with a gastric fistula described by Engel and Reichsman (1956) was similar. She showed a "depression-withdrawal reaction" in the presence of a stranger, with descriptive features of inactivity, hypotonia, sad facial expression, decreased gastric secretion, and finally sleep.

Subsequent studies have attempted to expand and critically evaluate this earlier work. Criticism has centered on methodological considerations and questions as to the adequacy of the organic evaluation processes in this syndrome. It is thus striking that infants with nutritional deficiencies may appear indistinguishable in some cases from those subject to prolonged institutionalization, as indeed the term *marasmus* indicates. Even more striking is the similarity of these studies to separation studies with nonhuman primates, who show distress similar to the anaclitic depression in human infants (Kaufman & Rosenblum, 1967).

This led to the 1952 monograph *Maternal Care and Mental Health,* which reviews previous studies and presents new formulations. "Prolonged breaks during the first three years of life have a characteristic impression on the child's personality. Clinically, such children appear emotionally withdrawn and isolated" (Bowlby, 1952, p. 32). Subsequent clinical appraisal has cast doubt upon the conclusion of such a personality development universally occurring from such early experiences. Why it is not universal is not definitely known, but it may be related to individual susceptibility or to fortuitous factors, such as certain children having the opportunity to develop different types of object ties. This work also stressed a literal physical separation in early childhood as the "deprivation" which needed amending.

Depressive phenomena may be associated with deprivation situations. However, what must be questioned about all the work on deprivation is the lack of a necessary connection between depressive phenomena in childhood and depressive illness in later life. That they do lead to present suffering, and probably long-range character changes, cannot be doubted. Yet the *sine qua non* of a clinical depression cannot be solely unhappiness and descriptive features, such as sad faces, since an affective state of depression oc-

curs all along a continuum of normal reactivity and probably in all types of psychopathology. A distinction must be noted between a painful affective state experienced by the ego, with the associated defenses mobilized against this pain, and a depressive condition that may eventually result.

There are other related criticisms of the work of the maternal-deprivation theorists. One is the multiplicity of possible outcomes, such as psychosis, neurosis, or delinquency, which have all been attributed to deprivation. It can be asked whether the deprivation concept has any relevance to the emergence of depressions or depressive vulnerability in childhood or later adolescence and adulthood. Even though the details concerning the specific mechanism that causes some children to be fortunate enough to be excluded from later consequences are not known, the hypothesis may yet be viable. A theoretical criticism pertains to the heavy emphasis in maternal-deprivation formulations on the view that later behaviors, such as depressions, are rigidly proscribed in the earliest months of a child's life. Without appraising deterministic philosophical arguments, there appears to be a tacit assumption that certain early mother-child relationships will inevitably lead to certain personality manifestations, even though we might not know beforehand the exact outcome. Hope still resides in the deterministic position that if we knew all the variables, such as a chance relationship with someone in an institution, we could predict with certainty the depressive, psychopathic, or whatever outcome might be expected to result from maternal deprivation. Such a degree of specificity has not been established. The concept is weighted in the direction of placing an overemphasis on early infantile experiences' leading to an unalterable outcome, without taking cognizance of other significant variables in the child's life, such as the role of the father and siblings. Wooton (1959) has pointed out that subsequent broader sociocultural influences in a child's life are also not sufficiently accounted for, such as school associations, vocation, and marriage, and that the seeming irreversibility may not actually be strictly true.

EARLY WORK

Many workers have contributed to attempts at understanding the nature of depressive phenomena. Not all their work can be considered; rather, only that which is pertinent to childhood depressions will be discussed. Early psychodynamic formulations usually considered childhood only to the extent of the "trauma" which had left the child vulnerable as an adult to depressive illness, and these were viewed primarily as retrospective curiosities. Concepts such as orality, introjection, turning against the self, narcissistic injury, loss of object, anal-sadism, and ambivalence were proposed as relevant for later depressions. Abraham's 1911 paper emphasized that the patient's repression of aggression leads to depression, which is analogous to the "actual neuroses" postulate that repressed sexuality leads to anxiety (Abraham, 1966a). Elaboration of the psychosexual stages led to reconstructive efforts to account for periods of fixation and subsequent regression. Freud (1957)[1] had stressed the importance of introjective processes, with their attendant ambivalence, but also the regression to the anal-sadistic, as well as successively to the oral cannibalistic, stage. Regressions could be precipitated by the loss of a love object. Abraham (1966b) subsequently expanded this by the double introjection, where the original love object is introjected as part of the ego-ideal and conscience as well as the introject being the target for a hostile attack. Developmentally, the child treats the object to

[1] The dates given in parentheses are the dates of publication of the works cited in the References, not necessarily the original dates of publication.

which he becomes attached as something over which he exercises ownership similar to his ownership of the contents (feces) of his body. Loss of such an object is unconsciously equivalent to expulsion of a stool. A cognitive connection is made by children between losing-destroying and retaining-controlling. The unfolding of depressive-prone development in a child would then show an emphasis on control and orderliness much like that of an obsessional. In fact, the compensated depressive would have a compulsive character structure.

Abraham also listed five developmental factors which, if they all occur, will predispose children to later depressions. The first is a constitutional element, not viewed as a direct genetic inheritance, but rather as a predisposed tendency to oral eroticism. This was seen as an excessive demand by some children for gratification via the mouth and body surfaces from various oral activities and from warm contact with the mother's own body. If the demands are powerful or are strongly frustrated, a regressive readiness is present and is manifested by a constant clamor for gratification. Much subsequent work has led to formulations stressing the genesis of moral masochism as part of the structure of a depressive character. The fixation on frustrated early oral and skin erotic needs is viewed as the basic substratum of depression. Patterns of distorted affectional relations leave a vital need for being loved and forming tender attachments ungratified. This leads to behaviors and attitudes which seek gratifications vicariously and pervertedly by frustration, and nonlove, from the person whose love is needed. Through demanding and incorporating oral activities and the need for bodily contact, the child absorbs—and later unconsciously seeks—displeasure, sadness, and suffering instead of being loved, and he assimilates these feelings into his personality. As development progresses, highly sophisticated and unconscious mechanisms operate to lead the child not only to seek approval and acceptance from individuals who do not and cannot meet these requests but also to unwittingly involve himself in dependent relations with others who may inflict pain. Self-pity is an accompaniment to suffering since such purification leads to a feeling that love has been earned and that if it is not forthcoming, one may justifiably be self-righteous. The defect is that a chronic state of feeling one has never received his "due" is present, which has narcissistic ramifications.

A second factor proposed by Abraham is the contribution of oral eroticism based on the antecedent of oral fixation. The consequence is an increase in demands for oral indulgence or low frustration if they are not met. Another predisposing influence is a severe injury to infantile narcissism as a result of repeated childhood disappointments which are caused by those toward whom the child is most affectionate and which leave a psychic "wound." Early examples of such influences are the birth of a sibling, repeated humiliations, and a realization that the child is not a favorite or that the parents are actually not genuinely fond of him. The effect of these disappointments is that the child feels deserted and repetitively seeks to gain the love of a person of the opposite sex. A fourth cumulative factor holds that the first major disappointment occurs prior to the resolution of Oedipal strivings. The importance of this lies in the child's making a move toward "object love" which is then rebuffed as a reinforcing later disappointment. Toward the end of the phallic phase, the object has acquired distinct recognition as a separate object toward whom a mixture of strivings is directed. Cognitions revolve about this new object mixed with sensual and tender feelings. Prior to this a mixture of love and hate predominated, and the strivings were mainly of the "partial" instincts variety, which focus on part of the object, or erogenous zones, in contrast to a wish to possess the entire object. A

fusion of tender with oral-sadistic strivings allows a fusion of sensuality and aggression. Yet the disappointment occurs in transit when "oral-sadistic instincts are still in force," and consequently the mother is blamed for the disappointment rather than a rivalrous father. This is believed to be the basis for observations that depressive characters continue a highly ambivalent relationship with maternal figures throughout their life. This first disappointment is the "primal parathymia," whose occurrence is necessary but not sufficient for later depressions. Finally, the repetition of the primary disappointment in some form later in life is the precipitant that elicits a depressive reaction with an accompanying upsurge of hate and other mechanisms of self-directed aggression; the abandoned or abandoning object cannot psychologically be dismissed without psychological processes' first disposing of the internalized object. It is thus not merely a matter of choosing to forget or give up the object, since the object is part of the self. The object representation has become part of the self-representation in such a way that states of contentment depend on the harmonious relationship to the internalized object.

Subsequent work continued to focus on intrapsychic alignments, but the role of the developing superego was introduced. Weiss (1932) felt that the processes of introjection and identification were equivalent to an object being destroyed. When children put themselves in the place of another, the latter may be eliminated and then subsequently re-created as part of the superego structure, which thus inherits magical powers to destroy. The future melancholic becomes dependent for his narcissistic satisfaction on the libido which the superego chooses to give the ego. At the same time, Rado (1928) was elaborating this in terms of the precarious balance of self-esteem in the depressive due to the overwhelming dependence of self-esteem maintenance on the approval of others. Subsequent depressions in the latency period are often triggered by minor disappointments and associated with the primitive rage of the infant from hunger or satiation from sucking ("alimentary orgasm"). The paradigm of self-esteem based on the "feeding" by others leads to a dependency on external narcissistic supplies. A series of intrapsychic maneuvers develops with respect to expiatory efforts of the ego toward the superego. Since part of the anger and rage is directed against the internalized representatives of past and present objects, guilt develops with reparative efforts to atone. "Splitting of the incorporated object" permits anger to be directed against the object or received from it. These self-regulatory mechanisms cannot operate effectively until the child experiences guilt for transgressions in thought, word, or deed, at which point he has acquired a depressive character. Maneuvers are then observed, such as interpersonal ingratiation and cautiousness with aggression, which are efforts of the ego toward the superego to reinstate a loving and beloved superego in place of a predominantly primitive one (Schafer, 1960). Gero (1936) later felt that the perpetuation of infantile demands for approval and affection was associated with conflicts which had occurred during the Oedipal period which led to anxieties, aggression, and suffering and which prevented the later fulfillment of object relations based on adult tenderness without prominent ambivalence.

These ideas led some to give a predominantly characterological interpretation to the emerging depressive-prone child. This was early noted in the "individual psychology" of Alfred Adler and his followers, who focused on the exploitative behavior of the child: "The discouraged child who finds that he can tyrannize best by tears will be a cry-baby, and a direct line of development leads from the cry-baby to the adult depressed patient" (Adler, 1967). Early infantile passive-aggressive activities such as pouty, whiny behavior or feeding disturbances were viewed

as forerunners of the way the child will exact tribute from others. The childhood prototype of the potential suicide is saying in essence, "It serves my mother right if I break my leg." Similarly, the prototype of the manic-depressive is the child who begins everything with great enthusiasm, only to give it up with crying and protest behavior just as quickly if brilliant success is not forthcoming. Such a child then alternates between pessimistic ruminations about not having performed well, having no friends, etc., mingled with a feeling of superiority. This framework has been expanded to view the depressive as a hostilely manipulative child who has to outcompete others and who resents personal demands since he feels others are trying to manipulate him. Consequently, such a child is unwilling to provide gratifications for others unless he is receiving himself. If he is not receiving, he seeks to inflict punishment or retaliation on others. The guilt proneness is viewed not as part of a mature conscience but either as part of manipulating others by inducing guilt or as part of reality-based guilt for having attempted to make others unhappy. These traits are laid to childhood socialization experiences where the needs of the child for sincere solicitous care were unfulfilled. Manipulative efforts toward peers and authorities are repeating patterns for dealing with extractive and manipulative parental figures. "He has been deprived, and he feels gypped and is angrily determined to get what is rightfully his. . . . In this defiant, stubborn, angry, begrudging battle of something-for-nothing, he loses the enjoyments of adolescence, of young adulthood, and of later adulthood" (Bonime, 1966). What can be said about these astute documentations? Such character traits can be seen to emerge in children and acquire perfection, and yet other aspects of the depressive process seem underemphasized. This emphasis would make proneness to depressive mood states in children almost equivalent to a character disorder rather than a mixture. Also, the family background as described may lead to many types of pathology. There is thus a need for more developmental and longitudinal data. There is also the question of such explanations' being confined to empirical observations. Constructs with a higher degree of explanatory power for the origins and ramifications of depressions are lacking.

OBJECT-RELATION ASPECTS OF DEPRESSION

No discussion of childhood depressions is complete without a consideration of Melanie Klein's theories. Again, only those aspects of Kleinian theory of child development will be used which are relevant to childhood depressions. In many ways hers is the epitomy of the intrapsychic model, although actually denying an early narcissistic phase preceding the development of object relations. Rather, she held that from the beginning of extrauterine life, introjective-projective processes are being transacted. Most striking is the telescoping of psychological processes into the first year, which are usually viewed as spread out and occurring throughout childhood. The "depressive position" is believed to develop in association with the loss accompanying weaning between 3 and 12 months. This is viewed as a normal and unavoidable developmental situation and not an illness. It parallels the child's ability to throw things away, which is taken as an indication that losses can be mastered. The depressive position succeeds an earlier "paranoid position," from which it is genetically derived. Superego development is also posited during the first year, but it is associated with experiences related to destructive possessiveness toward a parent rather than incestuous wishes (Klein, 1964). The "depressive position" develops in moving from a "part" to a "whole" object relation. In the predepressive position there are only part-object relations, such as to the breast. During the depressive position the mother is perceived as a whole object, which permits ambivalence and also anxiety about the loss of the loved object. The infant then experiences a guilty anxiety, with a need to preserve the good object, which leads to efforts at magical repair. Reparative work is an effort to make amends or undo sadistic attacks on introjected objects, as well as from actual situations where the excited infant achieves instinctual gratification, such as during breast feeding. The object which is "attacked" is the same one which provides security. If reparative activities are unsuccessful, there is a despair and fear that the good object will disappear. This is characteristic of the depressive position as well as of any future clinical depressions. The infantile depressive position is related to the possibility of later depressions in that those children for whom the loved object is not securely present in the ego have a lack of assurance of the mother's love and remain predisposed to return to the depressive position with the concomitant affects associated with a depressed state. Anxiety over the loss of loved objects is believed to be the most painful affect in human development and is the motive behind reparative efforts to regain the lost object. Anxiety over the status of internalized objects leaves the depression-prone child and later adult always subject to fears of abandonment and loss, in contrast to the security of one whose internalized objects are accepted as bestowing love and security. "It seems that after a time the individual can build up memories of experiences felt to be good, so that the experience of the mother holding the situation becomes part of the self, becomes assimilated into the ego. In this way the actual mother gradually becomes less and less necessary" (Winnicott, 1958). Thus, despite such theorizing, which is not empirically based but consists of retrospective reifications based on work with older children and adults, Klein's work is still based on the mother-child relationship, which will permit or not permit the child to overcome fears of persecutory objects, ambivalence, and anxiety over losses.

Implicit in much of this discussion is the entire topic of object relations and their relationship to depressions. Although not all theorists would agree that some type of literal or symbolic object loss is absolutely necessary for a depression, few would deny that the periods of infancy and early childhood are sensitive periods for both "objects" and "losses"; this is particularly so when the terms encompass not only internalized aspects but also interpersonal relations with animate and inanimate things, as well as abstractions when the cognitive capacity of the child evolves so as to make him capable of relations with institutions and values. Hence, a few general comments prefatory to a discussion of John Bowlby's work on childhood grief and mourning are in order. Current theories on the development of object relations seem to vary between two extremes (Gewirtz, 1961). One holds that need satisfaction is basic and that developing awareness of an "object" is merely incidental to this process. This theory of *secondary drives* holds that in the process of satisfying his physiological needs, the infant gains accompanying learning about the source of the gratifications. Social needs are then viewed as acquired, and the object is seen as a means to the end of need satisfaction. The opposite viewpoint is represented by those who believe the infant has a built-in need for an object in its own right and independent of strict need reduction, such as in eating. This theory is referred to as that of *primary object clinging*. Many attempts have been made to combine the two major viewpoints by various theorists. There are certain ethological implications inherent in the latter theory of the genesis of object relations. "Priming" mechanisms may operate in the

infant and be connected to intrinsic central nervous system regulation. The subsequent presence of "releasing" stimuli evokes behavior patterns toward a presented object. The motivational or directional pattern would be initially internal in origin, and the external object would serve as a trigger. Five "instinctual response systems" have been considered in this category for humans: sucking, clinging, following, crying, and smiling (Bowlby, 1958). The importance of each of these response systems to the mother-child tie is due partly to their survival value. The infant is believed to develop an attachment to the maternal figure, independent of biological satisfactions in the strict sense, because of a psychological attachment that these built-in mechanisms promote. This combined biological-psychological attachment and its vicissitudes form the matrix from which a predisposition to depression can emerge since they are related to being able to give and receive supplies which are related to narcissistic aspirations. Argument centers about the extent to which learning may affect the development of attachment and its consequences.

Bowlby has discussed grief and mourning in infancy when responses mediating attachment behavior are activated and the maternal figure continues to be unavailable (1958, 1960, 1961a, 1961b, 1963). This work is important not only for raising the issue of the nature of childhood bereavement but also for hypotheses regarding the pathogenic potential of mourning processes and the reaction to losses when they take a pathological turn. Removal of young children from their mothers initiates three successive psychological phases, according to Bowlby: protest, despair, and detachment. These each have an accompanying parallel response of separation anxiety, grief and mourning, and defense, although they all operate as part of a unitary process. An earliest phase of *numbness* has recently been added before protest behavior.

Mourning refers to a psychological process set in motion by loss of a loved object, while *grief* is a parallel subjective state in such a loss. *Depression* is the affective state when mourning is occurring, as distinguished from the clinical syndrome of melancholia. One of Bowlby's postulates is that the loss of a mother figure between 6 months and 3 to 4 years has a high degree of pathogenic potential for subsequent personality development because of the occurrence of mourning processes. He also believes that Kleinian theory has exaggerated the importance of weaning and that the major trauma is the loss of a maternal object or the mother's love in early childhood.

The initial phase of protesting behavior manifests itself in crying, motoric restlessness, and angry efforts to regain the lost object by means of these demands for its return. This phase is believed to sow the seeds for later psychopathology. Subsequent disorganization with painful despair leads, it is hoped, to a reorganization in connection with relinquishing the image of the lost object as helped by the presence of new objects. Anger is believed essential for efforts to recover the lost object, since yearning is mixed with repeated disappointments in not recovering the lost object. Grief is then associated with an irretrievable loss, while separation anxiety is a response to a situation where hope that the loss is retrievable still exists.

Persistance of efforts to regain a lost object may lead to four main variants of pathological response:

1. A persistent and unconscious yearning to recover the lost object, which can appear as an "absence of grief" without an overt protest.

2. An intense anger and reproach against the self and other objects in which the goal seems to be a reunion. There is a displacement of reproaches to what appear to be inappropriate objects, or "mourning at a distance" may occur

sometime later. When angry reproaches are directed against the self, guilt is present. Guilt may be generated via reality-based realizations that the person played a role in the loss or that he had wished for the object to be destroyed; reproaches once aimed at the object may be turned against the self—which was Freud's initial model. The pathology of displacement is due to the prolongation of anger without direct expression. The chronicity in turn leads affectionate components to wane.

3. An absorption in caring for others who are bereaved, which succors others instead of grieving oneself. This employs a mechanism of projective identification with vicarious mourning. These are the seeds for children who may be dogged by ill fortune and compulsive pitying of others or who are perhaps led into the "helping" professions vocationally.

4. A denial of the permanency of object loss, which operates on a conscious level and hence necessitates a split in the ego. It is believed that acute losses have a greater tendency to result in such denial and that children are particularly prone to react to losses in such a manner. This predisposes them to retain the object without going through the psychological processes of mourning. Losses predispose the child to character changes, but are also believed to leave the child in a state of readiness for evoking similar reactions to any subsequent type of developmental, psychological, or environmental loss. This would operate in much the same way that a sensitized allergic child remains susceptible to the allergen whenever he is exposed, although certain preventive efforts may be made to protect him from exposures, too heavy dosages, etc.

Theoretical controversy has arisen over Bowlby's theories. He holds that no qualitative difference exists between children and adults in the mourning processes since descriptively their behavior is similar. This has been challenged as a confusion of observational data with a theoretical explanation. Various models of mental functioning, such as the structural, are believed to have been ignored by Bowlby in his explanation. It is felt erroneous to ignore differences between the toddler and the adult in such areas as the formation of object relations since there are differences in their perceptual processes which would alter mourning processes. The criticism is, then, that Bowlby has not considered the differences in successive developmental stages and how they affect psychological processes of responding to object loss (Freud, 1960). It would be agreed that young children grieve, but whether they mourn would remain debatable, since mourning presupposes more elaborate psychological structures. Bereavement reactions of young children would be viewed as governed primarily by the pleasure-pain principle rather than by psychological processes which accompany more elaborate mental development. A further question has been raised as to whether there may not be a lack of developmental readiness to mourn prior even to adolescence:

> Until he has undergone what we may call the trial mourning of adolescence, he is unable to mourn. Once he has lived through the painful, protracted decathecting of the first love objects, he can repeat the process when circumstances of external loss require a similar renunciation. When such loss occurs, we may picture the individual who has been initiated into mourning through adolescence confronting himself with the preconscious question: "Can I bear to give up someone I love so much?" The answer follows: "Yes, I can bear it—I have been through it once before." Before the trial mourning of adolescence has been undergone, a child making the same tentative beginning of reality testing in regard to a major object loss is threatened with the prospect of overwhelming panic and retreats into defensive denial in the way we have observed. [Wolfenstein, 1966, pp. 116–117]

There is a further criticism that Bowlby has ignored the distinction between biology and psychology in that psychology does not deal with drive activity per se, such as attachments, but with their mental representations. The concept of narcissism is cited as an example; Bowlby describes narcissistic infants as withdrawn, whereas the concept does not have reference to observed behavior, but is rather a metapsychological concept referring to an early phase of libido distribution. Thus the height of attachment behavior may correspond with the height of infantile narcissism.

The concept of loss has subsequently been extended to include all varieties of subtle and less obvious disruptions and distortions in the parent-child relationship. These have the possibility of being as devastating in their effects as gross maternal deprivation or separation. Thus it may not be simply separation from parents that is crucial, or even a "loss," unless the concept is so broadened that it loses its meaning, with everything contributing to depressive-proneness being called a "loss." What is crucial, rather, is the adequacy and subtleties of the emotional supplies given to a child and the nature of their mutual involvement (Prugh & Harlow, 1962). A child may thus have meaning to a parent primarily from being required to respond to or fulfill parental wishes or goals. The child is then not perceived as autonomous with his own needs and wishes. Instead of family life then serving the process of socialization, the child is caught in a bind of guilt-inducement processes if he resists or if he complies and functions as an extension of the parental wishes. This situation "fudges" object boundaries and leads the child to overresponsiveness to others and their wishes. In contrast to schizophrenic withdrawal, it leads the child to be hyperaware of his surroundings and the affect of others, with the use of denial being difficult. The development of the child who will be plagued by depressive problems is characterized by difficulty in denying his perceptions. When extended, it is seen as a hypercritical belittling of the self, in contrast to projective devices of accusing the world of hating him. Another situation is that of the child who has little specific meaning to his parents because their preoccupations with their own conflicts hinder their capacity to give adequately to him; giving may be performed in a legal or moral obligatory sense, with an absence of tender affect. Thus a parent with narcissistic conflicts may be precluded from giving in a meaningful way to a child. The amount of giving that is available for a child may be depleted by current environmental crises which are not resolved, such as the death of a loved one, miscarriages, overwhelming family responsibilities, or depression on the part of the parents.

Object loss is then a concept much broader than the original concept of a literal loss or separation. Effects on the child may occur which will make him depression-prone, even though the parent is physically present and, further, is without gross signs of disturbances. Anna Freud has noted that depressed moods of the mother during the first 2 years after birth create in the child a tendency to depression, although it may not be manifest until many years later. What happens is such that infants achieve their sense of unity and harmony with the depressed mother not by means of their developmental achievements but by producing the mother's mood in themselves (A. Freud, 1965). Those children who have an "as-if" existence, in which they are perceived as necessary only for whatever needs the parent wishes to validate, are reacted to much like a negative hallucination. This type of existence leaves the child in a constant perplexity as to whether *his* needs will be met or whether he will be abandoned (Brodey, 1965). Serious and chronic preoccupations in the parents similarly leave little room for their spontaneous curiosity and interaction with the child in his world.

Empirical work tells us that not all children

who will have "narcissistic vulnerability" have lost an external object, nor will all who have not remain free of the vulnerability. The missing variable is the intrapsychic processes relating to loss processes. Such processes are partially attendant upon developmental lines striving for object constancy via attempts at separation and individuation. Beginning differentiation then gives rise to a period of greater psychomotor activity from 10 to 18 months in which the mood is believed to be one of infantile elation. Actively leaving and returning with a maternal readiness for the infant's separation and return are steps toward acquiring an internal object constancy. "Giving up" the fusion with an object, along with its supposed magical powers, is a concomitant process (Mahler, 1961). Depressive moods are believed to be generated by relinquishment of the child's belief in his omnipotence, a feeling that the parents are withholding power from him, and uncertainty as to parental availability when needed. Such moods may manifest themselves by separation and grief reactions "marked by temper tantrums, continual attempts to woo or coerce the mother, and then giving up in despair for awhile; or it may be revealed in impotent resignation and surrender (in some cases with marked masochistic coloring). On the other hand, discontentment and anger may persist after a shorter period of grief and sadness" (Mahler, 1966). The natural history of these early mood states in the pre-Oedipal child is interesting since they may continue or give way to a premature earnestness which shows up as an "unchildlike" concern possibly indicating precocious superego formation. Failure to attain object constancy with respect to mood disturbances reveals itself in signs of separation difficulties, ambivalence, precocious overidentification, pseudo self-sufficiency, and a flattened affective capacity. Multiple other developmental processes are also simultaneously contributing.

Other psychological processes may have

serious implications in terms of implanting a depressive nucleus in a child. The self-concept evolves via others' evaluation. By repetitive introjections of self-depreciatory attitudes, feelings of unworthiness become internalized and become part of the child's self-concept. Angry, rejecting behavior which increases interpersonal distance and isolation from family members puts the child into a nuclear conflict. Since he is by necessity dependent on his parents, he is in no position to understand or appraise the situation. Most typically, the mother herself, for example, does not comprehend, nor is she aware of the innumerable ways her reaction to the child is manifested. One 4-year old, caught between the mutually rejecting behavior of both parents, who were locked in marital conflict, had ceased talking except for the stereotyped repetition of the phrase, "I'm a nuttin'." A 12-year-old described himself in solemn tones and with a sad countenance as a "lifetime prick." Such is the forerunner of what will be seen in the adult depressions as self-depreciatory components which may reach delusional proportions. It is an elaboration of a distorted childhood concept that the child is intrinsically undesirable or dis-appointing. Objectively, despair or detachment may reign, while subjectively the child feels pain-fully alone or abandoned. A 10-year-old girl with feelings of not being as "valuable" as her two younger siblings thus recalled with tears a Christmas episode when all the gifts were brought in except hers; after all the presents had been opened, her father noticed her sitting silently and attempted to "joke," as though the forgetting had been planned to amuse all the family. When the gift was brought in, it was a huge dollhouse which the maintenance man had been asked to build. It was received with a feeling of added disappoint-ment, since the girl had never played with dolls. In the ensuing year, it continued to sit unused and conspicuous in her room.

Only two components of the complicated superego functioning relevant to depressive phenomena in children will be noted. The first is that others' feelings and reactions are "taken in" and form the basis for a self-concept. External criticizing and hateful objects then irrevocably become the child's for use throughout life. Self-esteem has become wedded not only to what others think and feel about him but also to their self-perpetuating internal representations. The more destructive the early model, the less able the older child or adolescent will be to stand apart objectively and feelingly and question whether the early model of himself has necessarily been accurate. This is often seen in therapy, when the child surprisingly realizes that the appraisal by the therapist does not correspond with what he has long felt others thought of him and what he thinks of himself. This is a step toward resolution of the depressive core, with its chronic guilt and shame reactions, so that self-esteem may be restored, although there is the possibility of parental termination of therapy if such changes in a child are not in correspon-dence with changes in the way they wish to perceive the child. The second relevant compo-nent of superego functioning is the emergence of conscience, which takes place parallel to an emer-gence of self-concept. As noted earlier, precur-sors of the superego are functioning from early childhood. Introjections and projections appear to be continuously in operation, with the result that the child's picture of the prohibiting and threatening parents is an exaggerated one (Jones, 1966). More particularly, the punitive aspects of the superego may "hypertrophy" when the external danger is magnified. This is due to the internalized object's being less tolerant than the parents themselves may be, since actual parents are not completely intolerant. There are limits to parental anger, while this is not necessarily true of a superego. Also, there is no appeal to external objectivity from an internalized criticizer; hence, a possible explanation for the excessively severe superego which develops in the depression-prone child. Integrally related to this are the unattainable ideals, with subsequent failure and self-condemnation. This leads to the early tendencies toward "hero worship" that such children have, which persist in a lifelong quest for the hero-ideal, as well as attempts to escape from overcritical parents and introjects by seeking out substitutes. Such children eventually find therapy a beneficial experience since the therapist can give acceptance without requiring the child to be good, clean, or compliant and without having to teach him anything. This permits the child to share with the therapist in discovering and resolving his conflicts.

From the above theoretical material, some direct clinical applications are possible. The groundwork is laid for understanding varieties of pathological self-esteem regulation (Reich, 1960). Excessively strict and uncompromising standards give the child a feeling of helplessness and hopelessness, which are viewed as the hallmarks of depressive states. Parental isolation and aloofness, far from making the child autonomous, seem to produce exaggerated dependency needs for tender affectivity, which has never been adequately received and for which the child "hungers."

Character traits noted begin to emerge during the widening process of socialization. The child may be noted to be extremely sensitive and easily rejected. Demanding, clinging, or "sucking" behavior evolves with a constant seeking of approval. If there are talents, such as athletic or intellectual ones, ways may be found for temporary approval, but it is never too successful since the approval must always be sought externally and the need is insatiable. It is often perplexing for some clinicians to see a perfectionistic child resorting to periodic antisocial behavior, particularly in adolescence. Yet if the usual compulsive covering is considered as part of a depressive nucleus, the defensive aspects become more obvious. Perfectionism as a reaction formation against angry feelings may be realized in the picture of a conforming, ingratiating child, but the threat of suffering from the breakthrough of depressive affect may mobilize a more vigorous type of defense. The earlier and unresolved defect in self-esteem is manifested by an ever-present seeking for, and demanding of, attention and admiration from others, which appear unquenchable. If frustrated in their demands, they may aggressively seek ways to coerce compliments and praise, which further alienates others. Their angry responses and ambivalence toward others are further demaging since these conflict with their own wish to be good and loving and increase their disappointment. The aggressivity seems related to warded-off painful longings of the child which tend to emerge if the "feeding" of praise and reward is not forthcoming. This description refers to the narcissistic character formation as the special vulnerability which is present in the depression-prone child. Such a child may try all manner of maladaptive devices to ward off depressive feelings which threaten. Depressive equivalents may be in the form of somatic symptoms, antisocial behavior of varying types and degrees, or oral taking-in activities such as using drugs or alcohol in adolescence. When these fail, the depressive symptoms emerge more forcefully since the vulnerability to the rejections and indifferences which permeate maturational stresses will be present.

The question of the origin of the narcissistic character has been prevalent throughout much of this discussion in light of clinical and theoretical work viewing it as one of the crucial variables in the dispositional state in depressions. One hypothesis ties this in with the devalued self-image seen in children with some form of early deprivation, neglect, or loss. Repeated rebuffs or losses reaffirm to the child that a significant object does not value him and that consequently he is worthless and should be discarded (Rochlin, 1965).

These transactional processes occur during infancy and early childhood and hence may be a present reality as well as giving rise to the potentiality for unconscious loss within a regressive context, as in adult depressions. Since object relations at this stage are primarily on a narcissistic basis, impairment in obtaining gratification from external objects results in a heightening of narcissism, which in some children may manifest itself as a deficit in reality testing. This is in accord with the principle that an increase in narcissism occurs as the importance of real objects diminishes. Yet this substitute gratification in itself is unsatisfactory to children and leads to "restitutive" attempts to restore an object. These appear to be some of the earliest processes in the development of the child who will later be prone to depressive tendencies.

In the young child, "losses" may be met not only by an increase in narcissism but also by a greater flexibility owing to their seeking and accepting substitute objects. Pathogenic possibilities as described by Bowlby were noted earlier. When the structural division of mental activity has been achieved, with superego processes, self-esteem becomes the great regulator of mood. Loss of self-esteem then becomes the consequent response to a loss, but also to frustrations in attaining idealized goals and images of the self. Loss of self-esteem as a response to loss is not thought to appear until the structural division of mental activity has been accomplished. At that stage object constancy has also been attained, so that mourning as a process of detachment from an inner image can occur. "Depression is the psychology of disappointment, not frustration. Psychoanalytic work with young children who have experienced object loss, in fact or fantasy, to separation, deprivation, or in whom adequate object relationship has failed to develop, has shown that the clinical picture is ruled by the infantile vicissitudes of aggression" (Rochlin, 1961). Only when the object itself is valued does

object loss lead to self-devaluation. At that time, the aggression may be retroflexed and witnessed in masochistic phenomena as part of a depressive picture. It has been pointed out that when an object becomes important, the child becomes concerned with the question, "Who will love me when I am left?" and the answer, "No one may want you" (Rochlin, 1961). When one has no worth, one is not claimed but is rather abandoned. Such reactions appear to be operating in many children in the latency and adolescent periods; these children can critically, and with a razor humor, deride themselves in their usually compensated obsessional states.

Accompanying these cognitive distortions in self-appraisal are individual variations in moodiness which emerge as prominent personality characteristics. Somatic manifestations appear to be the template for similar symptoms in later depressions, such as motor restlessness, sleep upsets, and gastrointestinal problems, which correspond to the heightened narcissism seen in hypochrondriasis. Accompanying these cognitive and somatic reactions are individual variations in moodiness which can be seen as prominent personality characteristics. Jacobon (1957) notes three main characteristics in children's moods, in contrast with those of adults: (1) Affective manifestations are more intense because of insufficient ego-superego control, (2) they are of briefer duration and change rapidly because of the instability of children's object relations and their greater readiness to accept substitute objects and gratifications, and (3) their affective range is more limited as a result of the lack of ego differentiation. When a propensity toward pathological mood disturbance is developing, there is actually less variety and spontaneity of moods, although a more exaggerated quality is present such as in persistent forlornness and sadness.

Family configurations offer another vantage point for the study of depressive children. Some of these theories have a kinship with the earlier Adlerian formulations. There is a keen sensitivity in the family members to the norms of the wider group to which they aspire to belong but from which they feel alien. Not only is the child used as a vehicle for the family to gain entrance into this wider group, such as by his accomplishments, but also his acceptance within the family is conditional upon his succeeding in a chosen enterprise. Further, there is a high price put on conformity to an austere parental figure who is displeased by nonconformity. Here is the origin of the duty-bound, self-conscious child who will be the compulsive "organization man," afraid of not being accepted. Affection must be earned, and if it is not forthcoming, it is because the child has not performed adequately to merit it.

Being selected as a favorite child further gives rise to the "Joseph theme" syndrome, which takes its name from the Biblical story in which the child is unconsciously fearful of arousing envy and jealousy in others (Arieti, 1959). To counteract these fears, children commonly use two defensive techniques: a pattern of chronically underselling themselves and altruistic behavior of constantly feeling they have to help or give to others. Being competitive with, and envious of, others who are successful, they quickly sense siblings and peers who feel this way toward them. Also, there is some indication that the fathers in such families may be relatively unsuccessful by the family standards, and yet have emotional warmth, so that the dethroned parent is the one to whom the child is most attached. A host of symptomatic disturbances may be associated with this configuration which are not specifically connected with depressions, such as learning disorders and patterns of chronic underachievement in whatever is attempted. This would be the equivalent of "success phobias" in adults. The unconscious goal is to have others like one at whatever personal cost, and yet at the same time the child has been selected to compete aggressively and

carry the family banner. Success may lead not only to envy but also to actual abandonment by others. Not only does aggression have a primary "instinctual" basis in this formulation, but it is also secondarily engendered by the competitive learning situation; this learning situation provokes envy and counteraggression from peers, which reinforces an anticipated rejection for self-assertive activities. The interpersonal school tends to view the development of such mood disturbances not as being associated with genuine guilt, but rather as representing the use of guilt maneuvers to exploit others. In contrast to this, intrapsychic theorists feel that an essential component in transient depressions as well as in depressive illnesses would be a sense of guilt associated with the aggression. "Nor does the guilt stem directly from the helplessness, the narcissistic injury, or the object loss, but from the unconscious fantasies evoked by the experience, whether related to preoedipal or oedipal conflicts" (Beres, 1966).

The following outline is a tentative classification of the various types of depressive phenomena encountered in childhood. It combines several criteria, such as descriptive features, age, and etiology. There is not an elaboration of psychodynamic models, which are discussed below. Some of these patterns may at different ages also be viewed as primarily a different entity, such as anorexia nervosa, but they are included here from the prominence of depressive affect.

CHILDHOOD DEPRESSIVE PHENOMENA: TENTATIVE CLASSIFICATION

I. Associated with organic disease states
   A. Part of the organic disease process
      1. Leukemia
      2. Degenerative diseases
      3. Infectious diseases—juvenile paresis
      4. Metabolic diseases, such as pituitary disease, juvenile diabetes, thyroid disease, etc.
      5. Nutritional or vitamin deficiencies

B. Secondary (reactive) to a physical disease
process

II. Deprivation syndromes—the reality-based reactions to an impoverished or nonrewarding environment
A. Anaclitic depressions
B. "Affectionless" character types

III. Syndromes associated with difficulties in individuation
A. Problems of separation individuation, such as symbiotic psychotic reactions
B. Depressive aspects of school phobias
C. Developmental anlage of moral masochism

IV. Latency types
A. Associated with object loss
B. Failure to meet unattainable ideals or standards
C. "Depressive equivalents" (depression without depressive affect)
1. Somatization (hypochondriacal patterns)
2. Hyperactivity
3. Acting out
4. Delayed depressive reactions: mourning at a distance, overidealization processes, postponing response, and denial patterns
5. Anorexia nervosa–obesity syndromes
D. Manic-depressive states
E. "Affectless" character types (generalized anhedonia)
F. Retroflexed anger and rage

V. Adolescent types
A. Mood lability as a developmental reaction
B. Reactive to a current loss
C. Unresolved mourning from current losses
D. Earlier losses ("traumata") which are now dealt with by the ego
E. Schizophrenias with prominent affective components
F. Continuation of earlier types (I to IV)

LATENCY DEPRESSIVE PHENOMENA

In the current rash of preoccupation with depressive manifestations in infancy, adoles-cence, and adulthood, depressive phenomena in the latency age group are often ignored. The occurrence of such phenomena in this group is more frequent than is usually realized. Conceptual clarity is often lacking with formulations about latency-age children who manifest depressive feelings with respect to losses, physical illness, or unmet dependency needs (Bierman, Silverstein, & Finesinger, 1958). The same type of theoretical confusion which permeates the "depression question" with younger children still operates in this age group. Although the more complex model of mental functioning which has evolved opens the possibility for depressive symptoms and syndromes and their equivalents, some continue to question whether the concepts of depression can appropriately be applied to childhood at all (Rie, 1966). Conceptual confusion may be due to the "latent" manifestations of depressions in this age group, in which there is often an absence of overt symptomatology customarily associated with depressions, such as crying, overt self-condemnation, guilt, etc. Parents' needs to deny that their children are sad and unhappy also mask the true incidence. Also, at adolescence the more florid picture of mood disturbances, increased aggressive activity, resurgence of pregenital activities, and heterosexual activity may be associated with depressive reactions and suicidal ideation and tend to conceal earlier and less dramatic depressive phenomena.

Both clinical and developmental studies have confirmed that latency is not the quiescent period it was once considered to be. Mechanisms for handling sexual and aggressive impulses can in reality never be a quiescent affair. Coupled with this is the recent emergence of a perfected inner control system relative to the first few years of life. The existence of "actual" clinical depressions in the latency period is not debatable among theorists, as it is with respect to infantile depressive phenomena. Thus, the argument as to whether a young child governed mainly by pleasure and pain can be regarded as suffering from a depression, beyond an immediate grief reaction, if he has not elaborated a superego structure, has been superseded by the time the child reaches latency. In fact, superego functions seem particularly prone to disturbance in view of their recent structuralization. It is not unusual to observe latency-age children placing demands on themselves which are more severe than those of their parents. This may be explained in terms of the immaturity of their superego or a projection of aggression onto the internalized object by the child, which is then used against his own ego to ensure that no transgression will occur since he is now "on his own."

Sandler (1965) has extracted data recorded in the Hampstead index in terms of the depressive reactions of children to a wide range of internal and external precipitating circumstances. These have been utilized here to construct a list of the characteristics of depressed children, in conjunction with cases which the author has also reviewed and treated:

1. A physiognomy which records a sad, depressed, or unhappy-looking child. It is not that the child complains of unhappiness, or even that he is aware of it; rather, he presents a psycho-motor behavioral picture which conveys sadness.

2. There is withdrawal and inhibition with little interest in any activities. It is a listlessness which may give an impression of boredom or physical illness and often leads an observer to a conclusion that the child must be physically ill.

3. Physical or vegetative signs may be present, such as physical pain, insomnia, and sleeping or eating disturbances—the "depressive equivalents."

4. A quality of discontent is prominent. An initial impression is that the child is dissatisfied and experiences little pleasure, and in time the clinician gets the added impression that somehow others—even the examiner, who has barely met the child—are responsible for his state.

5. A sense of feeling rejected or unloved is present, with a readiness to turn away from disappointing objects.

6. Reports of observations of low frustration tolerance, coupled with self-punitive behavior when goals cannot be attained.

7. Although the child conveys a sense of needing or wanting comfort, it is then accepted as his due, or he remains dissatisfied and discontent, although he is often in ignorance as to why.

8. Reversal of affect, where the child may clown and deal with underlying depressive feelings by foolish or provocative behavior to detract from assets or achievements.

9. Provocative behavior which stirs angry responses in others and leads others to utilize the child as a focus for their own disappointments. Such scapegoating exhibits the child's suffering, which leads to descriptions of him as a "born masochist."

10. Tendencies to passivity or having needs met by expecting others to anticipate them.

11. Sensitivity and high standards, with a readiness to condemn himself for failures.

12. Obsessive-compulsive bahavior in connection with other types of regressive, magical activities.

What is the phenomenological or pathological experience of depression-prone children? They are likely to be sensitive and easily hurt because of their problems in the narcissistic realm. This does not imply a degree of narcissism that is not object-directed, but rather implies that object ties seem labile and easily threatened. This lends such children a quality of inner hesitancy, which may appear as a fear of committing themselves in school, at play, or in peer relationships. It is as though they are never sure whether objects are reliable and will remain steadfast. Consequently, the clinician often senses a cautious seeking for object ties both in the course of therapy and in the daily lives of these children. They very much wish to relate and attempt to do so, and yet they are fearful of abandonment. In contrast to the schizoid child, who prefers his withdrawal, the depressed child hungers for a relationship. With depressed children, it is rather that their object ties are perpetually and endlessly in doubt. One can note the connection in this regard to the simultaneous presence of obsessional personality characteristics. Although the child may seem externally forlorn and sad, he is usually unaware of the reasons for his altered mood or of why he periodically reacts this way.

Qualities of nostalgia and self-pity emerge at age 3 to 4 in most children. The children may then verbalize their feelings directly to a parent who has temporarily left about how the parent was missed. Sensitive observers may note mild depressive affect when a parent, pet, or friend is absent for more than a short period. There may be displays of narcissistic mortification which amuse an adult. Thus, a 4-year-old may refuse to participate in an activity which he enjoys a great deal when something is denied him or he is reprimanded. A miscarried attempt to hurt the frustrating and controlling object by not cooperating in some activity he knows also pleases the other party may ensue. This permits further self-pity to emerge for the self-imposed deprivation. Families which utilize these mutual behavior patterns are basically pursuing retaliatory aims, which also permits the child to indulge his wounds in this manner. Many types of personality attributes in the parent or other important people in the child's life affect this ongoing internalization process. A predominance of unresolved conflicts centering around aggression, masochism, guilt over aggression or success, and patterns of expiation then develops.

Historically, a frequently seen pattern is that of the intermittently depressed parent or adult who is present from the child's early years into the latency period. An emotional tone of sadness and loneliness attendant upon introjecting the "bad" with the "good" results. The sad feeling tone seems to leave a particular imprint on each psychosexual and psychosocial stage which the child passes through. It is thus not only an oral pessimism and oral hunger for an object, but also a sadness upon giving up any attachment or possession and a heightened ambivalence. Similarly, the disappointment coming in the Oedipal period may fall on a sensitized child who has already accumulated interpersonal and intrapsychic vulnerabilities.

Children with clinical depressions thus vary in their symptomatology from pathetic, long-suffering, individuals to those with other symptoms which may not overtly impress an observer as manifestations of a depressive process. They frequently have been seen by physicians for problems of weight loss, declining academic performance, or somatic complaints for which no explainable organic pathology has been demonstrated. The most frequent somatic symptoms are headaches, dizziness, abdominal pain, nausea, and difficulty in sleeping. These are equivalents of "masked depressions" in adults. Indeed, in two successive series of 100 children investigated for recurrent abdominal pain ("little belly-achers"), only 8 percent of children in the first series and 6 percent of children in the second were found to have an organically explainable etiology (Apley, 1959). Not only abdominal complaints but also anorexia, pruritus, and migraine headaches have been viewed as depressive equivalents in children (Sperling, 1959). Severe encopresis has also been considered a depressive equivalent in children in which there is much less concealment of the aggression. Reports may indicate that the child is a "loner" and does not enjoy play activities with other children. In some there is a quality of profound pessimism, alternating with teasing and sadistic behavior, as a response to their feelings of loneliness and of being unwanted and unacceptable to other children and adults. This may appear as taking pleasure in seeing others commit errors or get injured, which seems incongruous with other aspects of their socially conforming behavior when with adults, such as schoolteachers. In some of these children an acute shift in behavior may indicate a depression. Thus, a previously alert child who shows signs of withdrawal and apathy, inability to study, and lack of interest may reveal a depression. Similarly, previously outgoing and carefree children may grow quiet and preoccupied, or conforming children with obsessional tendencies may show more mood variations with breakthroughs of "delinquent" behavior. A superior student whose achievement is reflective of high aspirations and ideals will more likely react with depressive manifestations if the rewards for his hard work are not forthcoming or if he overachieved when younger. Unmitigatingly high standards and reactivity proneness when such ideals cannot be maintained make them vulnerable. These strivings are often in association with perfectionistic standards and an overdeveloped superego. Obsessional activities in the depressed child may represent efforts to compensate for the feelings of helplessness present in the depression by a resort to magical maneuvers. Jarvis (1965) noted an association between loneliness and compulsivity in children in which the compulsions served as a defense against sadness and loss. These feelings were evoked in response to a pattern of "withdrawn mothering" in which the physical needs were adequately met but in which the mother was emotionally absent and hence unable to gratify some of the basic psychological needs of the child.

Hyperactive and restless behavior may be present in the depressed child, which often seems paradoxical. This may be an equivalent of the hypomanic behavior seen in adult patients in an attempt to ward off depressive feelings, although it may all too frequently be passed off as a symptom of "brain damage" in children. In some cases rebellious behavior may be a reflection of maladaptive mechanisms in the child. The child then repeats a situation of provocative and parental rejecting behavior within and without the family. He may behave in a hyperactive or antisocial manner, which brings parental condemnation and allows the parent to focus on this behavior, while the long-standing underlying mutual hostility is bypassed. There has been an increasing amount of clinical work confirming the view the certain forms of antisocial behavior or acting out in children are a response to a depressive core. In his original monograph, Bowlby (1952) suggested that there is a specific connection between prolonged deprivation in the early years and the development of a personality capable of only shallow relationships with others, poor impulse control, and an "affectionless, psychopathic character." The association of this same deprivation with a disposition toward subsequent depression in the child has been noted, and also criticized on the basis of its explaining too much. It has also been questioned on the grounds that the effects of this type of deprivation are not equivalent to a depressive personality structure.

Problems of object relations which later lead to some form of antisocial behavior need not necessarily be a reflection of a depressive nucleus since ambivalence may not be present. There may rather be a predominance of unmitigated hate toward an object and its introject (Berman, 1959). Concentration is then laid on the lack of symptom formation in a strict sense, and a defective conscience is ascribed to the absence of love for a maternal object and a related lack of guilt for this behavior. Others focus on the depressive nucleus which is present in later impulse-ridden character behavior. The concept of early object loss as a trauma which is experienced by the child as a state of painful discomfort is felt to set a depressive framework. The antisocial behavior is further related to the anxiety of object loss (separation) in which attacking or taking from the environment expresses feelings of anger and rage about a loss. By mechanisms of acting out, denial, and isolation, children attempt to ward off their feelings, while therapy, which sets limits, will necessitate their having to deal with their underlying depression. The emerging depression will often appear in the form of somatic complaints. Forms of unconscious self-destructive behavior may be present as a response to the strong hate for oneself. This may be manifested in provocative behavior toward other children and teachers, as a means of seeking punishment, or in a pattern of repetitive self-injury during play. Aggressive behavior itself may be used to avoid depressive feelings, especially when the child's adequacy is directly threatened, when he cannot deny his cravings for affection, or when past feelings of worthlessness are recalled (Burks & Harrison, 1962). Kaufman has written extensively on this problem (1955; Kaufman et al., 1963). Not only may acting out and delinquent patterns represent an attempt at coping with a depressive nucleus or a defense against experiencing depressive feelings, but also questions arise about the nature of distortions in ego development and about the extent to which they are actually reversible. There is the fundamental question as to when a "depressive character" becomes relatively fixed irrespective of the reversibility of certain overt depressive symptoms.

Acting-out behavior obviously has various psychodynamic and personal meanings for a child. In the context of depressions, it is viewed as a defense against experiencing the psychological pain and anxiety associated with a depressed state. Theoretical opinions vary as to the extent and prominence of acting-out behavior in association with childhood depressions. There are those who believe it is present in a primary fashion in a majority of cases; others view depressive affect as a secondary phenomenon subsequent to acting

out if it is associated with different diagnostic categories, such as the impulse-ridden character, antisocial development, or a schizophrenic process. The problem is a conceptual one in part since the primary theorists would view depressive affect as crucial to whatever overt diagnostic features are present. In the case of such children, a history of their preschool years may be obtained showing a prominence of hyperactive, rebellious, and aggressive behavior. When the child is seen in the latency period, a progressive pattern of hatred and destructive behavior in fantasy, play, and overt behavior is present. Object relations are on a primarily narcissistic basis, with striking ambivalence. Beneath the externals of an aggressive attack, the acting-out depressed child reveals a denigrated self-concept. The child and parent may both be mutually identifying with the "bad" part of each other, which reinforces a feeling of worthlessness. Repetitive play themes or fantasies may relate to destroying bad things, followed by magically reconstituting them.

The formulations of Benedek (1956) regarding the "depressive constellation" are relevant to the elaboration of depressive states. In those situations where the oral demands and frustrations of the infant reactivate similar conflicts in the mother, the transactions between them will be based on an ambivalent core. Child and mother then interact on a projective and introjective bipolar basis of aggression in an attempt to escape from the feeling of being a "bad child" and a "bad mother." The mother is also ambivalently identified with her own critical mother, who is condemnatory of the child, as well as with her own child, who is on the receiving end since the child is a burden and provocateur. The hypothesis is that certain parents have had childhood experiences which heighten their "ambivalent core." A pattern of mutually reinforcing hostility is set in motion and gains momentum. The child feels estranged and angry, which is superimposed on the parent's disappointment. The parent then feels justified in condemning the angry, sullen child, who in time develops feelings of deep shame, which lead to increasing distance. Repetitive acting out may then ensue, with the depressive nucleus being deeply buried.

A fairly frequently seen type of patient was a 9-year-old boy whom the school authorities felt could no longer be tolerated in class. Although of average size, he would constantly provoke fights without regard to the sex of the person whom he was attacking. An active type of behavior had been present since infancy, and the black eyes and disturbing classroom behavior did not lead to a school suspension until stealing commenced.

Various professional contacts had begun at age 2, when a series of pediatricians had been consulted for his restlessness. Although neurological examination, EEG, and skull films were all negative, he had been diagnosed as either "brain-damaged" or a "developmental problem." He had entered school with these labels, although most of the school authorities has little idea of whether this was the explanation or excuse for his behavior. Psychological testing revealed a WISC of 127 and no organic deficits on brain-damage batteries. Several medications, from amphetamines to tranquilizers and antidepressants, had not produced any alteration of his unpredictable behavior.

An armor of distrust and his provocative behavior were his main approaches to others. Observationally, he appeared restless and fidgety. His attitude toward most people was characterized by the height of contempt and disrespect. His fourth-grade teacher was unwilling to tolerate the boy coming to her desk for the express purpose of passing flatus, as teachers in earlier grades had. His mother was oblivious to this behavior, and when it was brought up, she stated that she had long ago trained herself to ignore it as part of the brain problem over which her boy had no control.

Several thought trends would be condensed by this boy, with an assumption that others should

know what he was attempting to communicate. If they honestly told him they did not understand, he reacted with anger and as though they were deceiving him. Angry outbursts occurred both verbally and physically. This provoked rejection, which he then interpreted as others' turning away from him.

Denial of a request for a nickel by his mother in the waiting room one day, on the basis of his having overdrawn the next two weeks' allowance, led to a temper tantrum like that of a 3-year-old, during which he lay on the floor and kicked.

Without elaboration in detail about the family and personal psychodynamics, as therapy progressed, many of the features of a depressed and bitter child became evident. After much testing and maneuvering, self-depreciatory material emerged with tears. The process of testing and retesting, in and out of therapy, may go on for a prolonged period. As therapy progressed, somatic concerns coupled with anxiety also became prominent as the acting out decreased. The point is that such behavior may be the overt manifestation of a depressed child, although no one, least of all the patient, will present with the chief complaint of "feeling depressed."

ADOLESCENT DEPRESSIVE PHENOMENA

Mood fluctuation is often regarded as an inherent part of adolescence. The mood swings seem to reflect the loosening of identification ties with the parents so that other "objects" may take their place. This loss necessarily involves grief work. Periodic regressions to attempt refusions and identifications with more primitive narcissistic objects also take place (Geleerd, 1961). Adolescent depressions cannot be viewed as having one standardized explanatory model; they involve many types of conflicts and dynamic mechanisms:

An adolescent's unhappiness may express his grief about childhood objects and pursuits that he must relinquish; his sadness may be tinged with painful longings because he can neither go back to them nor yet reach new levels of achievement, of personal investments and pleasures. He may be depressed because he cannot gain the love of a girl he woos, or because he has failed in his work or in other personal conquests and feels physically and personally inadequate, intellectually and mentally inferior. But at other times his depression may be caused by guilt conflicts, either from sexual sources or because of his disproportionate, severe hostility. His depressive moods may be then devoid of regressive features, and then again involve a retreat to homosexual or sadomasochistic positions, or even a hostile and deeply narcissistic withdrawal from the world. [Jacobson, 1961]

Early adolescence may be a time when struggles with problems of self-esteem, values, and guilt, as related to the self-image and body image, come closest to producing a personality adjustment that may appear to be psychotic. If depressive features become prominent, it may be difficult to distinguish the depressive affect from that seen in clinically depressed adults on initial consultation. Yet, over a period of time the fluctuating state of the mood lability as an adolescent phenomenon helps to distinguish it from a clinical depression. Most adolescents go through such phases and emerge with an ego capable of curbing demands for impulse gratification and without the need to resort to defenses based on ascetic "otherworldly" demands prompted by a severe superego. In contrast, an emerging schizophrenic process in adolescence does not appear to involve a persistent need to seek out new objects; rather, the schizophrenic seeks to maintain a progressive state of schizoid withdrawal or shows signs of ego diffusion and fragmentation.

Depressed adolescents present with a mixed symptomatology, discussed below, which can be present in transient form. One of the most typical features is that there are periods of alternation between apathy and indifference and overactive garrulousness. This need not be viewed as a manifestation of an adolescent form of manic-depressive disease, as some have held (Harms, 1952). There are no reports of manic reactions in the same form in adolescents as in adults, presumably because the adolescent's ego functions are not usually capable of such a degree of defensive specificity. Cyclothymia must be differentiated from the mood lability that is present developmentally in most adolescents. This requires evaluation of the general aspects of personality functioning and past performance. A second typical feature is that unresolved dependency conflicts related to depressive reactions now become more prominent. Frequently, a conscious recognition of the need to become emancipated exists contemporaneously with an increasing sense of despair over the ability to emancipate oneself. Somatization, hypochondriac concerns, or actual psychophysiological disease may begin during these crises. A picture of increasing anger and rage may take the form of hostile attacks on parents, family, or external authority, but without the capacity to identify whatever the difficulties may be. In some cases actual physical violence may occur as well as verbal sarcasm and attack. In others there is a pattern of forays of impulsive acting out with subsequent returning home. Despite such forays, which may involve periodic episodes of absenting, the past and home may be nostalgically reminisced about when the adolescent is absent, with past difficulties repressed or ignored. This is similar to the "homesickness" of the latency-age child when he is separated from his home; the depressed adolescent has often suffered this homesickness earlier. During extended adolescent absences from home, fantasies are indulged in about the old home, where all one's needs and wishes were somehow met.

A deeply unhappy 17-year-old boy was referred for therapy. Since the age of 13 he had become aware of a "wall" which had grown up between him and his father, with whom he had previously had a close relationship. His mother had always seemed more involved with his older sisters, and he had now been upset by his father's anger when he had begun to spend more time going to downtown areas with boys. Although he had always striven to meet his father's perfectionistic demands, he now felt sad and pessimistic about meeting his father's goals for him. Accompanying this change was a feeling of emptiness, since he had previously felt a sense of his father's presence with him whenever he needed him, and this was now gone. At 15 the beginning of several unsuccessful attempts at separation commenced which took the form of brief absences from home. By 17 years some of his departures had taken him to various parts of the country, from which he always returned on his own because of a feeling that he had inexplicably "wronged Dad." The father then offered the patient a "partnership" in his local business which also involved the boy's marrying a girl he had dated for several years and "had the deepest respect for." Once the wedding date was set, a period of indiscriminate sexual activity began which had not previously occurred. Two weeks after the wedding he drove his wife back to her parents' home and sobbingly moved back with his parents. Back home he alternated between his absenting periods and his returns home in an attempt to reinstate the old relationship with his father or "at least make him happy." At the time of referral there was a sense of deep despair with suicidal ideation. His attempts to leave were then taking the form of distant trips followed by great anxiety and a return home, from which he might leave again within days. He intellectually recognized his difficulty in emancipating himself, but had no idea as to why he was in the predicament he was, although his inability to do anything beyond leaving and returning gave him a feeling of "not wishing to continue to live if there is no way out."

Superego activity with adolescent depressions takes several forms. There may be a great sensi-tivity and proneness to overreact to any criticism. Peer relations may manifest a conservative conformity, while relations with adults show prominent ambivalence which fluctuates between angry outbursts and subsequent undoing. The depressed adolescent has a chronic feeling of being unable to satisfy himself in terms of ideals, ambitions, or self-concept. He is dissatisfied with having to deal with an impulse life as well as dissatisfied that satisfactory gratification may not be obtained, and he then experiences qualms and hesitancies when he does obtain gratification. There is a self-disappointment manifested in despair and guilt which lowers self-esteem. Rebelliousness against the environment, and the superego, as well as demands for impulse gratification, leaves the ego in a state of impoverishment with a predominant affect of guilt. Reenactment of earlier competitive relationships, often again with disappointing results, similarly contributes to a feeling of inadequacy.

Acting out can be expected to some extent in most depressed adolescents. This mode of handling their rage against the external world and the internalized representatives is manifested by attacking one and seeking an escape from the other. The acting out may function as a defense against the affects of despair and helplessness, but it may also have two additional meanings in a depressed adolescent: It may be a maladaptive effort to consolidate an identity, and it may also be a coercive effort to extract security from the environment. Various sexualized and aggressivized acts, such as promiscuity, cheating, theft, and acts of physical aggression and violence, may be used to serve these ends. Such precarious devices for dealing with feelings in a person subject to self-reproaches also raise serious possibilities for suicidal ideation and occasionally genuine attempts. Most frequently this is manifested in "chance-taking" phallic exhibitionistic behavior in the form of joy rides, drag racing, Russian roulette, attempts to drink themselves "under the table," or exploits with various types of drugs; these may masochistically provoke punitive measures by adults or social institutions or eventuate in "accidental" suicides.

An insatiable need for affection at any price may be a maneuver in adolescents for dealing with their depression. This is in part a need to capture what they feel never existed, the lack of which now raises a threat to their well-being; hence, the compulsive aspect in their affection seeking. All relationships with males and females may hold out the hope of becoming the tender and trusting relationship that is repetitively sought; frequently the result is another disappointment and disillusionment.

Confusion in identification is associated with an impaired self-image and groping for an idealized adult figure who can solve their predicament. When feeling depressed, new object relations are not developed, but there may rather be an indulgence in what life could be like "if only" or in what it will be like in the future. If reality demands are too prominent and these fantasies are interfered with, a profound sense of hopelessness may ensue. Such groping for the idealized adult may persist into adulthood as a perpetual quest for the "hero," with disappointments and searches for new heros. The hero may take an institutional form, such as an omniscient church, which will last to the consummation of the world and never betray or abandon one. Such idealized institutions may also combine maternal and paternal qualities.

Confusion in identity may lead to what Erikson (1955) has called a syndrome of "acute identity diffusion." This is precipitated by a need for commitment to physical intimacy (sexual and otherwise), choices about vocation, competitive strivings, and psychosocial definition. The clinical manifestations are indecisiveness, a feeling of inner estrangement and loss of continuity, a renewed struggle with archaic introjects, an inability to work or concentrate, and the choice of a negative identity. The latter is based on a scornful and snobbish hostility toward the roles offered as desirable in a community. It takes a personal form of a perverse identity based on what is most undesirable or dangerous. It has been further postulated that the depressed adolescent carries his defective identification models through successive developmental stages: "The inadequacy of early love objects, of a permissive ego-ideal and later the superego, are responsible for disturbed identity formation in the adolescent" (Lorand, 1967).

Heightened self-condemnatory patterns may denote a clinically depressed adolescent. Many of their activities are disparaged as having a materialistic or ulterior motive and as therefore being unworthy. These experiential components have had earlier developmental precursors, such as the utterances of the 4- to 6-year-old who repetitively tells himself "I'm stupid" for minor transgressions and whose self-condemnations are not modified by reassurance. This type of self-depreciatory component is not merely an affective factor where the child states "I hate myself for being so stupid," for a cognitive distortion is present accompanying the feeling. A viable question concerns whether the cognitive disturbance is actually an antecedent to the subsequent affective component of hating oneself; that is, is the essence of the predisposition toward depressive states actually due to the primacy of a cognitive aberration with a mood disturbance secondarily induced? It would appear that such dispositions develop very early, whatever the predisposing factors may be—genetic mechanisms, early losses, or reinforcement of self-derogatory cognitive appraisals. The dispositional tendency to misinterpret subsequent experiences then inheres and generalizes. The misinterpretation is not one of being attacked by external forces but rather the ascription of any failures or misfortunes in oneself or others to a personal shortcoming for which he somehow feels culpable. Such a child then interprets himself as responsible not only for his own failings but also for others' miseries. The burdens of the world are then his. It is from this type of cognitive disturbance that the potentiality for delusional thought content emerges, which is present in the psychotically depressed.

RETROSPECTIVE STUDIES

Most clinicians have the impression that children who are prone to depressive phenomena, as well as adults, have sustained a significant object loss of some type in childhood. This has given rise to a host of retrospective studies with depressed or mentally ill adults in an attempt to determine whether such losses occurred in an earlier period of their life and whether there is statistical significance, compared with a control group. These empirical studies are worthy and interesting, but will not be reviewed in this chapter. Rather, they are noted only for the following points of summary:

1. Empirical studies which are based on retrospective object losses have dealt with adult patients, and there is the pervasive problem of reconstructing for large numbers of patients' details of their developmental period—even apart from deliberate falsification.
2. Patients used in investigations often represent extremely skewed samples, such as those in institutions. Hence, it remains difficult to offer generalizations about the effects of object loss on a general population who may have had no contact with mental hospitals or clinicians.
3. Difficulties in obtaining a valid control group for comparison purposes are apparent from the perspective of any number of variables, such as socioeconomic factors, family constellations and dynamics, and genetic backgrounds, as well as the usual sex and age factors.
4. The prevalence of "object loss" for individuals may not necessarily correspond with one of the categories used in empirical inquiries. Thus, it could be maintained that an object loss occurring in fantasy could have the same potency as one occurring externally, besides the occurrence of idiosyncratic experiences, which have significance for some children. This would involve all manner of "losses" that would be difficult to detect, especially when investigated years later and when the research is restricted to overt response categories, such as death, divorce, etc. Nor must a loss have a precise correspondence with a selected category specified in a given retrospective investigation. It must also not be forgotten that few clinicians, of whatever theoretical persuasion, would be willing to say that all depressions in childhood or later adulthood must have originated in a loss in childhood and that depressions are inconceivable without such a predisposing loss. The stress may be put more upon discrepancies between self-appraisal and actual attainments, so that object loss per se is not a sufficient measure to encompass the variety of depressive responses.

PSYCHODYNAMIC MODELS

How early internalized representations of objects later function within the psychological economy is subject to different interpretations. One hypothesis distinguishes two primary affects of unpleasure: anxiety and depression-withdrawal (Engel, 1962). These unpleasurable affects are experienced and reacted to by the ego. When a danger situation threatens, such as a loss or an insult to narcissistic integrity, a series of psychological and biological responses are initiated to seek relief from the unpleasurable state. If the anxiety signal does not operate successfully to restore esteem or the lost object, depression-withdrawal may be utilized defensively to conserve emotional and physical resources. This is an attempt at self-isolation from an environment which is depriving and not providing the hoped-for emotional supplies. This extends the original concept of depression as an acute response to object loss, while anxiety is viewed as a response to a danger which threatens or accompanies a loss or some other realization which is experienced by the ego as a painful loss of well-being.

The creation of the "good" object as one which alleviates pain and the "bad" object as one which produces or maintains suffering operates externally and by internalization. Not only are external objects felt to be good or bad, but also how one feels about oneself is elaborated as the child matures. Concepts of a "good me" and a "bad me" develop within the dependency context. The basis for self-depreciatory cognitions accompanying depressive affect in childhood is established. The child cognizes and emotes "goodness" when he experiences approval and self-acceptance, and "badness" when there is a converse disapproval or lack of self-acceptance. Since parental appraisals are accepted uncritically by the child, feelings of hate and contempt toward him become internalized and the basis for a derogatory and hateful self-concept. These are accentuated when some type of failure or limitation becomes manifest, especially when the failure is with respect to some narcissistic aspirations. The very quest for dependency needs to be met with tenderness may come to be viewed as "bad" and evidence of worthlessness. Various types of character structures may be elaborated in attempts to deal with these painful and persistent feelings. One extreme is the "malevolent transformation," in which dependency needs have been repressed since their expression has led to anxiety and depression as a result of their unacceptability. The external façade is then that of an angry, defensive child who is poised to strike out against a hateful external world (Sullivan, 1953), or the child uses various maneuvers for hanging onto others, such as ingratiating or seductive behavior, to secure dependency or esteem, which may be observed routinely in

many children, described earlier, who present with mixtures of depression.

Depressions in children involve all varieties of distorted interpersonal relationships in their genesis with a regressive pull toward early object attachments in their clinical manifestations. When the ego is no longer functioning effectively to ward off overt depressive affect by defenses against disturbed narcissism, various degrees of withdrawal may be noted. There is not only a general inhibition of activity, but also an impairment in ego functions in both intrapsychic and interpersonal dimensions. In addition, vegetative signs such as physical wasting or sleep disturbances may be viewed as part of the depressive complex to taper the impact of external stimuli as well as a reflection of "giving up." Some believe that in the preadolescent age group, a depression with primary vegetative signs is more prevalent than the morbid guilt and turning-inward pattern of aggression that Freud and Abraham proposed.

There are several alternative psychodynamic models which give a different perspective on what should be given explanatory primacy to account for depression proneness in children. The models have evolved from the following theoretical constructions, which also illustrate changing emphases from empirical observations and clinical work:

1. Loss of an object leads to a depressive response with retroflexed rage and aggression directed against the self and the introjected object; this has an accompanying regression in object relations, drive discharge, and control mechanisms, which lead to the end stage of impaired self-esteem (feelings of worthlessness, helplessness, etc.).

2. Subsequent modifications lead to a shift wherein the child loses a significant object in reality or fantasy. This leads to impaired self-esteem, which leads to a depressive response.

This is a shift perhaps as important as Freud's revision in anxiety theory, where instead of repression leading to anxiety, the converse was proposed; so with this shift in the ontogenesis of depression proneness, where instead of depression leading to an impairment in self-esteem, the converse is proposed, with depression then the end result.

3. The ego is now placed at the center of development for later depressive symptomatology. Bibring (1953) conceptualized depression as an affective state of the ego, which views itself as helpless and powerless to accomplish anything.

4. A further extension may then be proposed: Cognition of inability to achieve a goal or ideal state (actual, fantasized, symbolic, or idealized), or the affect accompanying a loss, threatens the child's narcissistic well-being. This leads to a painful ego state, which may lead to despair, inhibition, and lowered self-esteem—which are the accompaniments of a depressive response.

The psychological pain experienced by the ego, whatever its cause and extent, may be viewed as reflecting a discrepancy between an actual state of the self and an ideal, wished-for state. Although clinically, states of object loss are dealt with, what is lost in object loss is ultimately viewed as a state of the self for which the object is the vehicle (Joffe & Sandler, 1965). For young children the pain may initially be related to biological gratifications whose absence threatens existence itself. This would be related to earlier work on oral deprivation, but is now extended and generalized to the level of psychological loss of self-esteem in response to anything interpreted or felt as a failure, be it environmental or in response to internalized goals or values. The passivity or "giving up" may then correspond to the ultimate of despair or helplessness. Also to be accounted for are biological and developmental variations in the capacity to tolerate object losses, or individual differences in the capacity to tol-

erate discrepancies between ideals and achievement (Zetzel, 1965).

Of crucial significance to this capacity is the development of the ego function related to the acceptance of reality. Part of this would then be the ability to accept helplessness in the face of overwhelming odds or when a situation realistically demands limit setting on goals for accomplishment. Variations in superego development are also relevant in this regard. It is in this context that experiencing and dealing with depressive affect are necessary elements in development. For those children who may be biologically predisposed in temperament and drive endowment and who in addition sustain either an excessive indulgence or an excessive deprivation, or both, coupled with highly ambivalent object relations, the acceptance of reality is most difficult. The superego may reinforce these tendencies in three ways: (1) by holding up ideals which are largely unattainable, (2) by punitively reacting when self-evaluative processes reflect that the ideals are not met, and (3) by condemning hostile acts or feelings in the ego subsequent to a failure or loss. Narcissistic ideals require an inflated or grandiose self-image, and hence the connection with infantile development, with its narcissistic participation with the maternal object before individuation and object constancy are attained. This is why the acceptance of reality is so difficult and the persistence of unattainable ideals so tenacious, with all the accompanying frustration, personal pain, and interpersonal jealousy. The egos of such children develop with a greater degree of "depressive readiness" than those of children with fewer of the predisposing factors noted.

Two of the most painful, unpleasurable affects experienced by the growing child are guilt and shame. For this reason, they are believed by many to play a significant role in regulating self-esteem, in controlling impulses, and in laying the basis for different types of depressive phenomena.

The development of *guilt* is believed related to the fear of punishment or retaliation, while *shame* has its origins in the threat of abandonment because of failure to meet introjected parental standards. It is further held that guilt is related to a conflict between the ego and the superego, while shame reveals conflicts between the ego and the ego-ideal (Piers & Singer, 1953). The guilt reaction develops in the mutual interplay between the child and his parents where a transgression of a parental rule has occurred. The displeasure of the parent is communicated to the child, which leads to a sense of distance or personal estrangement from the parent. Such feelings are believed to be present at a very young age and to be sufficiently uncomfortable so that the child wants to do something about them. The child becomes cognizant that there are steps that will relieve such painful feelings in the form of atonement or "taking one's punishment" which will lead to the restoration of the tender relationship with the parent and the resumption of having dependency needs met (Rado, 1956).

Shaming occurs in a different context. Although the transgressing behavior or failure may be identical, the technique of handling it will vary widely from that which induces guilt. In the same situation, the emotional distance from the parents is not only maintained but also increased over time. The interpersonal context is that in which the child feels isolated and alone, with a sense of personal humiliation and degradation for his behavior, which is viewed as bad since it emanates from him. The large number of emotional factors in the parent-child relationship which give rise to this damaged self-concept have a connection with the ego state of the depressed child. There is also the absence of a means for atonement, which means that the depressive core is maintained and not resolved. Character manifestations of increased defiance and difficulty with impulse control are seen since the rewards of affection and dependency gratification for

control are absent. It would thus be hypothesized that there is a loss of support or emotional deprivation whose manifestations will vary, depending on whether the developing control system has been guilt-based or shame-based (Barry, 1962). Self-esteem regulated by shame has much less possibility of altering the unattainable ideals in view of the lack of resolving the painful ego state in the context of supporting and forgiving parental objects.

The sense of loneliness and isolation, so often seen in the seriously depressed child, appears to be related to the inherent feeling of worthlessness that accompanies shaming; it is associated with the tacit assumption that *you* as a person are unworthy and that inasmuch as you can really never alter your basic self, you will remain essentially despicable. The closeness which would permit dependency needs to be met is thus impossible; this mobilizes much anger and resentment. When the superego has structuralized, the formulation is, "If you are to be accepted (loved), you must regard yourself as an inferior, depreciated object." This is seen in repetitive patterns of behavior where worthy accomplishments are continuously underrated or depreciated. A 13-year-old with natural athletic ability and straight "A" marks repetitiously described himself to his therapist with the utmost gravity as "stupid." A 10-year-old, who was the butt for much of his obsessional father's hate, had always been referred to as "retarded" by all members of the family; although he tested 115 on the WISC, he continued a lonely pathway of clowning.

The child may seek to be maintained as a shamed one. This permits him to have an illusory sense of power over a masochistically oriented parent who can point to the child as the one responsible for causing so much suffering. This reaction appears to be noted in children with a "martyred" parent who believe that somehow they have caused the parent's unhappiness and dissatisfaction. A divorced mother with a 4-year-old girl brought her child to a child psychiatrist after several visits to pediatricians in an attempt to establish why there were alterations in the child between unruly, defiant behavior and withdrawn behavior. The mother interpreted this behavior as personally intended by the daughter to hurt her, which was dynamically accurate in part; however, all the mother's difficulties in her past and present life were assigned to the child. A 14-year-old girl began to prostitute herself while in the depths of a depressed state manifested by preoccupations that she had long been responsible for much of the misery and depression her mother had endured since the time of her birth. An awareness that her mother's unhappiness would actually continue, despite the girl's presence or absence, produced an intolerable situation from which she could not escape, with the result that she resorted to the most depreciatory act she could think of in adolescence.

Depression may function as an attempt to avoid shame by shaming and to avoid the "shameful feelings" of aggression by self-inflicted suffering. Self-reproach may be viewed as a disturbed attempt to maintain, or create, a relationship between the child and parent at a primitive, narcissistic level, where the self and object are fused (Leveton, 1962). Such theories utilizing guilt, shame, loneliness, and self-mortification have been portrayed in many novels and works of a semiautobiographical nature about adolescence, illustrating the acme of depressed feelings at this period of "cutting the cord." Some have discussed this in association with the period of identity crises noted earlier. It may also be viewed in terms of unresolved wishes and nostalgia for a reunion which never in fact existed but is retrospectively distorted. This is similar to the mourning process involved in losing any desired object. In these cases, there is the addition of a fantasied state or relationship which is then mourned even though it never existed. With younger children the anger at the lack of a tender relationship which would not be characterized by shame or abandonment evokes direct aggression against people or toys. It may in time also show a displaced reaction formation where toys are collected rather than used since using things is too close to destroying them; they are also identified with these objects and hence do not wish to "lose" them. Such children may then not only exhibit a pattern of "getting lost" themselves, for which they blame others, but also reenact this with their possessions by becoming chronic losers:

> They forget and mislay their money, their caps and articles of clothing wherever they are. We feel tempted to say that not only are their possessions strewn around, but they actually run away from the children. What we discover in their analyses first is an inability to cathect the inanimate, owing to the general damage done to their capacity for involvement with objects; next, that they direct to their possessions the whole hostility aroused by the frustrations and disappointments imposed on them by their parents. It is only behind these fairly obvious causes that a further, even more far-reaching motive comes into view: by being chronic losers, they live out a double identification, passively with the lost objects which symbolize themselves, actively with the parents whom they experience to be as neglectful, indifferent, and unconcerned toward them as they themselves are toward their possessions. [Freud, 1967]

It is noted in the compulsive pattern of absenting from home, followed by calling on the phone or returning. This pattern has been observed in some cases over years and has been observed perpetuated into the third and fourth decades of life.

Suicidal Problems

Suicide as a phenomenon associated with depressive manifestations in children and adolescents cannot be casually ignored. Although not every child who seriously makes a suicidal effort will or should be given a diagnosis of depression, the prominence of depressive affect is usually conspicuous, and it is for this reason that it is discussed here. Two approaches have emerged in studying this problem: the epidemiologic and the psychodynamic. The former approach deals with the incidence of suicide at various age levels, sex differences, techniques employed (pills, weapons, etc.), and the frequency ratio of "successful" to "unsuccessful" attempts. The psychodynamic approach seeks to utilize material such as that presented earlier in this chapter to render explanations as to why a particular child in a given family and social matrix resorts to suicidal activities on occasion. Epidemiologic studies reveal suicide in the 15- to 19-year age group, as well as in the group from 20 to 24, to be the fourth leading cause of death in the United States after accidents, neoplasms, and homicide, with about six hundred deaths reported as occurring annually in each of these categories (U.S. Bureau of the Census, 1963). Three of these four categories are related to some type of dyscontrol in the realm of aggression. In addition, over one hundred suicides per year are now being reported for children between the ages of 10 and 15, and about 10 per year for children under the age of 10. This appears to parallel a progressive upswing in the hospitalization of children for mental illness in the preadolescent and adolescent age brackets. Inaccurate reporting plagues incidence studies of suicide among children, as it does among adult populations. True incidence is estimated as being underreported by a factor of at least five to twenty times the recorded rate. In New York City there are fifty known attempts for every successful suicide among persons under 20 years of age, and 3 percent of successful suicides are under 20 (Schrut, 1964).

Bergstrand and Otto (1962) reported on 1,727 Swedish children (351 males and 1,376 females)

under 21 years who were seen in 465 different hospitals in connection with suicide attempts over a 5-year period. There was a pattern of progressive frequency with age, but also a great majority of them (83 percent) came from lower-income groups; this would raise a question of a biased selection, overreporting from certain social classes, or social factors' playing a significant role as a predisposing factor. There is thus a correlation between social class and family disorganization, alcoholism, parental separation, or emotionally disturbed parents—all of which could contribute to a suicidal predisposition. In 87 percent of the cases drug ingestion was the chosen method. Although the admissions were greater among girls, the boys employed more violent methods and more often repeated the attempts. Precipitating factors were listed as "love problems" (30 percent) and "family problems" (25 percent). These figures correspond with those of American studies indicating a correlation between suicide attempts, family disorganization, and delinquency (American Journal of Psychiatry, 1962). The same sample has been analyzed from different perspectives. Thus, 42 of the 1,727 cases were under 14 years of age, and these revealed a more even sex distribution, with home and parental problems predominant (Otto, 1966). Attempts to delineate a presuicidal syndrome which would predict the "high-risk" suicidal child have not led to a set of reliable indices (Otto, 1964). The most frequent personality change was noted in 581 of the patients who were retrospectively investigated for the 3 months preceding the suicide attempt; it was found that depressive symptomatology, anguish, anxiety, sleep disturbances, and psychosomatic disturbances were most prevalent. This corresponds to other clinical reports such as those of Bakwin and Bakwin (1960), who stressed signs of depression in children as a suicidal danger signal, and Jacobinzer (1965), who warned that sudden personality changes should be viewed as a sign of difficulty in the control of aggressive impulses. Detection is difficult, not only because of the diverse picture of depressions in children, but also because of the constant emphasis on suicide attempts in children as being impulsive acts without prior suicidal preoccupation (Despert, 1952). Methodologically, the problem is extremely difficult owing to the requirement of being able to predict which particular subset of a group will commit an act, when a group may share similar characteristics and the act is one that is a rare occurrence.

Early in the century some concern was expressed about the increasing suicide rate among young people, although then, as now, there was reference to the conflicting statistical evidence. It is startling to find Stekel commenting in 1910 that: "Suicide is triggered off more easily in children. Their tendency to be emotional, together with a characteristic overvaluation of emotions, means that in similar circumstances, children are more likely to translate the idea of suicide into action. The occasions for suicide are often ridiculously trivial. Their very triviality seems to me evidence that we must seek stronger forces behind the triggering impulse" (Stekel, 1967). Contemporary explanations which do not proceed beyond stressing this impulsive quality in childhood suicides have not progressed beyond this early formulation. Stekel believed that the "stronger forces" to which he alluded referred to a motivational need for punishment for forbidden fantasies. Hence, "No one kills himself who has never wanted to kill another, or at least wished the death of another."

The cognitive correlates of death in children were subsequently felt to be important since it seemed presumptuous to assume that children who killed themselves at different stages of development would be assigning the same content to their act. This would hold apart from any motivational formulations. Chadwick (1929) thus attempted a correlation between the fear of death

and various clinical phenomena utilizing the structural theory. Schilder and Wechsler (1934) ascribed various meanings to death in children, such as escape from an unbearable situation, a maneuver to force others to give more love than they had received in life, an equivalent for an idealized sexual union, a narcissistic perfection which would give an eternal significance, and gratification of masochistic wishes. Until the last few years only two subsequent psychological studies had been carried out dealing with the cognitive components of the child and death. S. Anthony (1940) demonstrated that school-age children have many thoughts about death which are detectable in their fantasies and play as well as in their reactions to separations, losses, and grief. Nagy (1948) delineated three stages of child development for ideas of death: ages 3 to 5 years, when death as a process with finality is denied; ages 6 to 9, when death is personified but not yet conceptualized as a universal; and the last stage, when death is perceived as the dissolution of bodily life (Nagy, 1948). The point would seem indisputable that adequate developmental concepts regarding death are necessary for a sufficient psychodynamic explanation of why children at different cognitive and chronological ages may attempt suicide. Surprisingly, only recently has interest been renewed (Grollman, 1967; Maurer, 1964).

Psychodynamic patterns leading to self-destructive behavior in children can be quite variable and are related to the earlier formulations presented with respect to helplessness and despair (Gould, 1965). Self-destructive impulses may be expressed by many unconscious and deceptive acts which are as "masked" to the child as to the adult. Acting-out behavior may thus not only have a defensive function but also serve to elicit punishment from others. In the extreme case, this may lead to suicide. A depressed 14-year-old with average intelligence and a long record of unsuccessful efforts at car theft was noted on a careful history always to have driven the stolen automobile in the same neighborhood from which it was stolen or to have driven it past parked police cars. His last apprehension came when he drove such a stolen car into the parking lot of a drive-in hamburger stand and parked directly opposite a squad car. Repetitive or increasing "accidents" may be the expression of self-destructive impulses. An example would be a depressed 9-year-old who had repetitively injured himself by cuts, letting himself get hit by baseballs, and finally getting hit by a car, which were all dramatic changes that had become prominent within a few months' time. During the course of therapy, he revealed that a few months earlier he had been playing with a rival male cousin who lived with them and whom he greatly envied because of his abilities and the erotic attention his mother paid to him; while "playing," he had pushed this cousin in a baby buggy behind a garbage truck, which had subsequently reversed and killed him. Shortly thereafter the "accidents" began occurring. Some accidents in children may thus represent suicidal equivalents. In this case the self-injurious behavior began subsequent to what actually amounted to killing a rival.

Early childhood precursors of self-injurious behavior patterns also exist. What are referred to as "accidental" poisonings would be rife with etiologic possibilities from their great prevalence. Rather than resting content with explanations ascribing these deaths to the "carelessness" of someone, a more intensive psychological autopsy might reveal contributory predisposing patterns. In the infant and parental object where pleasurable cooperation is lacking, the infant may well experience an ego deficit in learning certain danger signals:

> Thus, a two-year-old child whose ego development has lagged in establishing a capacity for unpleasure created by id demands that are dangerous is more likely to stumble to a fracture, injest aspirin or a toxic household agent in a life-threatening way, or walk into a swimming pool where only ordinary precautions have been taken. The reasons for this developmental lag in a physically normal child are most likely to be found in the pattern of the early experiences with the mother, i.e. in the area of object relationships. [Solnit, 1965]

These patterns may persist as the child ages, with many contributory factors, such as an exhaustive or conflicted maternal figure, family conflicts, or wishes of the parent to be rid of the child—all of which impair the capacity of the child to identify and learn safety measures. Such patterns begin to manifest themselves in qualities of recklessness or a lack of concern for danger. A 13-year-old boy who alternated between moody withdrawal and being the leader of a peer group in acting out expressed little concern when he drove a speedboat into an anchored rowboat in which several people were sitting. On inquiry one finds that in such cases, it is as though there has been a failure to cognitively register a danger signal. Persistence in handling conflicts by action rather than fantasy contributes to the tendency for accidents to recur (Frankl, 1965).

Acts of self-punishment or self-mutilation may represent an attempt to expiate profound guilt feelings, which can be conscious or deeply repressed. Self-humiliating behavior consisting of being taken advantage of repeatedly can be part of the self-abasement in an overall shaming process. Some of these children appear to be seeking ways to propitiate and thus avoid punishment, while others seem to be seeking a way out of yielding to forbidden desires. Suicidal fantasies in depressed children at times have a quality of returning to an "oceanic state," where, through wish fulfillment, all one's dependency needs are gratified. This is a restitutive effort to recapture what in fact may never have been—a beatific union with a maternal object. It may also represent an angry act and escape from an insoluable predicament, as illustrated earlier in the case of the 17-year-old boy who had an ambivalent relationship with his father. Variations of the re-union fantasy seem to be a constantly recurring theme with children who have had a lifelong pattern of living in boarding homes or foster homes or of moving from one relative to another, interspersed with occasional institutional placements. The parallel theme of social isolation is also contributory (Jacobs & Teicher, 1966).

Deep-seated feelings of loneliness and emptiness may be apparent in these children, and these form the nucleus for a suicidal disposition later in life. However, it should be noted that among twenty-two children who attempted suicide, most of whom had overtly deprived backgrounds, none killed themselves in the ensuing 14 years (Bender & Schilder, 1964). Rather, they appeared to turn to antisocial or delinquent behavior or to acquiesce in an intolerable situation with emotional and intellectual flattening. Since deprivation has such variable meaning, it would be quite important in longitudinal studies to differentiate the specific type of deprivation present. A feeling of desolation and abandonment may be shared by many of these children. This may eventually lead to an act which is overdetermined, where some children act with a conscious content of altruistically sparing their parents the burden of continuing to have them around. In some cases there is an extended element of taking siblings along with them into paradise, which results in the performance of a homicide-suicide. This is movingly portrayed in Thomas Hardy's novel *Jude the Obscure,* published in 1895. Another literary masterpiece, *The Counterfeiters,* by André Gide, portrays a 13-year-old schoolboy who has been subjected to an early paternal death and maternal overstimulation, followed by a series of subsequent disappointments in his close attachments. This eventually leads to his selection by schoolmates for a suicide, which the boy permits in an ambivalent and collusive act (Sterba, 1951).

An intensification of lonely and abandoned feelings in the depression-prone child may occur during holiday seasons, such as Christmas and Thanksgiving, when most children are experiencing some of their happiest moments. An older child may be engulfed in nostalgia for earlier holidays which leads to a suicide attempt; such feelings are analogous to the "anniversary reactions" seen in adults. The overt fantasy of being reunited with a deceased parent may then be acted upon. This reunion with a parent the child has never known or seen, owing to death or desertion, also occurs, in which the child impulsively decides to "join" the parent.

In one case a 16-year-old illegitimate girl living with foster parents was called by her biological mother and was informed that her biological father, whom she had never seen, had recently died. For the remainder of the day a mixture of feelings of disappointment, nostalgia, and anger preoccupied her. There was a recurrent thought, "Now I will never be able to see him." A lifelong wish to meet her father someday would now be impossible. A day later these ruminations were still present when the patient was staring out of a window of the foster home. She felt a sense of loss, but she also felt helpless ever to remedy the situation. Within minutes she had impulsively set fire to a parked car without any thought of whose car it was, and during therapy she verbalized her need at the moment to destroy something. In the turmoil of thoughts of suicide she had set the fire. Many factors coalesced to produce this act, and it also served many functions, such as indiscriminate aggressive discharge, self-injury, obtaining help, and punishing her mother, the agency that had placed her, and her irretrievably departed father.

The actual fantasy need not be of death in a physical sense, but rather of being restored "in heaven" with the absent one, or a denial mechanism can function regarding the actual reality of death (Kubie, 1964). A young adolescent girl whose mother had died when she was an infant lived 3 miles from the cemetery in which her mother was buried, but had never visited it since "this would mean Mother really might be dead." She was brought to the hospital after taking a full bottle of aspirin and quietly going to bed. The bottle was found replaced on the shelf by a relative who returned home from work with a headache. Adolescents who have had a parent die by suicide seem particularly prone when depressed to recapitulate the same mode of dying. A 14-year-old boy whose father had died in a hunting "accident" while leaving a suicidal note carefully rigged up an apparatus with the same shotgun to pull the trigger at a distance of a few yards; it succeeded in shattering his hip and thigh. This appears to operate in a manner similar to the internalization of parental moods noted earlier. Self-injurious fantasies, and at times acts, may be related to feelings of rage which become mobilized with the feeling of a need for vengeance toward a loved person toward whom there is also much ambivalence. There may be an accompanying concealed fantasy of enjoying the suffering that their death has caused loved ones. Some of these children and adolescents may be depressed and have a fragmented ego, with indulgence in narcissistic fantasies of being present at their funeral or in a coffin surrounded by grieving relatives.

Descriptive diagnoses vary widely in such cases when a suicide is attempted by a child or adolescent. Some tend toward the viewpoint that many are schizophrenic, especially when the act may be a response to a hallucinatory command or a preoccupation with attaining an oceanic reunion (Balser & Masterson, 1959). Others are more impressed with the characterologic features, such as the excessive reactivity to minor stress and acting-out behaviors, such as truancy, promiscuity, absenting, and overt family disharmony (Toolan, 1962). The earlier reference to Adler's emphasis on emerging manipulative qualities in the depressive child would be relevant here. The self-injurious behavior is viewed as a retaliatory, or anxiety-provoking, act in the child directed toward love objects. A more subtle psychodynamic hypothesis has been advanced that the family dynamics in such cases involve mutual filicidal-matricidal wishes between the child and parent. The child may react to the wish that he destroy himself in some manner, or he may defend himself against this by a displacement of homicidal or matricidal impulses (Liebermann, 1953). All manner of sado-masochistic maneuvers are evident as derivatives of these impulses. Even in these cases the theme of retaliatory abandonment of a rejecting world is evident in the form of, "Since you left me, I will leave you" (Ackerly, 1967). The previously internalized anger is projected so that escape from what is viewed as an annihilatory world is effected by a suicidal act. Contributory to this is the observation that adolescent boys who are actively suicidal have mothers with suicidal preoccupations. To ensure that no loss will occur, the boys identify with their mothers' depressed suicidal state (Margolin & Teicher, 1968).

In deeply unhappy children with physical or congenital defects, fantasies of being reborn and starting over occur, which may provide the motivational background for actual attempts at self-destruction. Children with fatal illnesses do not appear to become as depressed and suicidal as adults in similar circumstances, perhaps because of their greater use of denial. Another problem occurs with perversions and wishes to change sex which are related to suicidal acts. Transvestite children have been known to kill themselves as a result of binding themselves with ropes and chains around their neck and limbs (Schechter, 1957). The relationship between effeminacy and suicidal tendencies in male children is in need of clarification. A confusing depressive phenomenon is related to the achievement of sudden success which the child feels too unworthy to receive. This may be seen in gradations, from the child who has outstanding athletic ability but who "holds back" to prevent himself from becoming a star, which produces an affective tension state, to the 16-year-old who is number one in his high school class with a scholarship to a leading college but who takes a bottle of barbiturates and leaves a note reading, "Lay not up for yourselves treasures upon earth." Freud talked of such individuals as those "wrecked by success," and they are currently discussed in the adult literature as having "success phobias." Many of these same determinants operate in certain depressive and suicidal children.

BIOLOGICAL FACTORS

Two main lines of biological approach to the etiologic bases for clinical depressions exist: the genetic and the biochemical. These may ultimately be regarded as sequentially related aspects when their interrelationships become unraveled. Some initial caveats are in order. Almost the entire expanding literature on these two approaches has been based on work with adults. This is partially a reflection of the lag in clinical thinking up until quite recently, as well as in basic observations, on the nature of depressive phenomena in childhood, which are necessary before any investigations can delineate biological correlates. In the absence of a test which could rule out false positives and indicate with a high degree of probability a given clinical entity, such as the inferences from a serologic test, investigation must initially proceed by establishing a clinically reliable grouping of behavioral aspects into syndromes which can then be investigated for biological factors. As indicated earlier, we are only now at this latter point, and several theoretical arguments as to the nature, or even delineation, of clinical depressive phenomena in childhood are still raging.

Besides the fact that the biological work has been restricted to adults, there has also been the intrinsic problem of a "disease" which is basically either self-limiting or cyclical in nature even in its most extreme states, providing the patient survives an acute state by not committing suicide as an adult or "wasting away" as a child. There are also the problems posed in the evaluation of any treatment measures; such evaluations lead to formulations which may be relevant only to the particular stage of evolution or devolution of the cycle the patient is at; the same type of thinking applies to developmental differences in the manifestations of depressions, such as those with a chronic type of depressive character versus a cyclothymic type. An additional limitation to the adult investigations is their restriction to certain psychoses, such as manic-depressive illness, involutional melancholia, or schizo-affective schizophrenia. These are conditions obviously not manifesting themselves in childhood, with the exceptional clinical report of a case of manic-depressive illness in a child. Milder types of depressions of the neurotic variety are customarily viewed as reactive or exogenous in nature by this approach, and the more malignant types are considered endogenous. The controversy as to whether the dichotomy "exogenous-endogenous" has any validity also continues unabated. That psychotic depressions may not manifest themselves until some period of adulthood is not a criticism of efforts to delineate the possibility of genetic loading or chemical alterations. It does illustrate that milder types of depressions are less susceptible to these modes of investigation, and conclusions applicable to children at this point can be discussed only hypothetically within a context of surmise.

With these limitations in mind, a brief summary of the types of investigations and lines of research being pursued will be given which may have future relevance for children exhibiting depressive phenomena. Genetic work proceeds on the basis of some type of genetic combination providing the necessary predisposing element for depression proneness to develop, which may lead to depressive reactions or illness. The genetic predisposition may be viewed as a tertiary dispositional state which permits the emergence of a capacity to become depressed. Under the necessary eliciting circumstances, internal or external, the depressive potential unfolds, which is the secondary dispositional state. Such depression proneness then endures as a potentiality, and when a depressive picture is present, a primary dispositional state has become manifest. The question is: What is the empirical evidence in support of the theory that a genetic factor leads to a tertiary disposition toward depression? Early work tended to look for a clearly delineated factor, and the major gene hypothesis was frankly proposed by Slater in 1936 as a single autosomal dominant gene with reduced penetrance which would have about one-third of carriers affected (Slater, 1936). Stenstedt's later work with manic-depressives stressed the same factors with variable expressivity (1952). An estimate of the "heritability" can be obtained by comparing the concordance rates of dizygotic and monozygotic twins for affective disorder. Data from combining various twin studies reveal that 68 percent of monozygotic pairs are so concordant, whereas only 23 percent of same-sex dizygotic pairs are (Price, 1968a).

Theories other than the major gene hypothesis employ some variation of a polygenically determined continuum as the predisposing factor for depression proneness. This may involve several alleles at one locus, or several loci, as well as multiple polygenic systems which could operate independently and not necessarily by summation (Price, 1968b). In such a system one gene might be an inhibitor, while another was "phasic" for a particular depressive trait. Another group proposes a cyclothymic model, which would not suffice by itself for manic-depressive episodes since these are posited to require an additional specific factor (Leonhard, Korff, & Schalz, 1962). This theory polarizes manic-depressive reactions into bipolar and monopolar types related to the

cyclicity or its absence as part of the depressive process. Dispositional tendencies would also be related to a theory which proposes that manic-depressive disease, like many others, may have a quasicontinuous variation; if a disease pattern is relatively frequent, there may be a certain threshold barrier to symptom manifestations which, at a certain point of extension, appears as an all-or-none phenomenon, such as many of the metabolic diseases. There might thus be partial or mild degrees of cyclothymic manifestations without manic-depressive illness (Edwards, 1960). The apparently greater tendency of females toward affective illness was early given consideration as being related to a sex-linked gene, but this hypothesis was abandoned when it was realized that fathers should then transmit this tendency primarily to their daughters, which in fact they do not. This hypothesis would raise questions related to the greater propensity toward depressions of boys with more feminine attributes, whatever their source.

More elaborate statistical theories have been propounded more recently to render the genetic hypothesis viable. There has been a hypothesis of two dominant genes, one sex-linked and one autosomal, which lead to a somatic mutation (Burch, 1964). The variability in depressive manifestations is more conducive to a theory which does not view depression proneness as a simple dichotomy between the "haves" and "have-nots," but rather adopts the quasicontinuous model, which permits accompanying quantitative variations. This would also be more compatible with biochemical possibilities.

An initial confrontation with biochemical and neurophysiological explanations of depressions leads to some immediate hesitancies. Not only is the old problem of differentiating between a symptom, a syndrome, and a nosological entity still operating to confuse any research conclusions, but also many of the studies do not appear to differentiate the subjects beyond noting that they are a depressed group. Many other research limitations are also present, such as the lack of controls and the inherent problem of investigating a problem which has a cyclical structure such that the "disease" is often self-limiting, even apart from waggish comments that this may be so as a result of suicide. Differentiating primary and secondary biochemical alterations would also be important, although confirmatory knowledge of either would be an accomplishment. Patients investigated have not always been screened for drugs they may have been taking, as well as for some concurrent medical illness, either of which could produce chemical changes. These specific contaminating effects must be noted, as well as the usual complications in any study, such as placebo effects from drugs and the halo effect of the investigator as part of environmental alterations. It must be noted that almost all biochemical work has been confined to adult patients. This is partially due to the rarity with which depressive disorders are even considered by clinicians dealing with children; a 1952 study dealing with 1,000 emotionally disturbed children did not contain a single affective diagnosis of a child under the age of 13 (Barton-Hall, 1952). The scarcity also reflects the milieu on which debate focuses, such as the issue of whether manic-depressive psychosis exists in children or not (J. Anthony, 1960). Probably most compelling in terms of the lack of basic biochemical hypotheses is the clinical confusion due to lack of delineating, until quite recently, such basics as the descriptive features of what a depressed child even looks like. Such delineation is a prerequisite to proposing any psychodynamic constructs, let alone carrying out any meaningful chemical or physiological investigations. Hence, the comments offered here are with these current limitations on the status of our knowledge of childhood depressive phenomena acknowledged.

The biological aspects of depression cover a wide range of possibilities. A few of the main alterations which have been investigated will be noted. The stimulus for this work seems to have been the early medical model of disease in which a condition is reversed to status quo ante, with the symptom then disappearing. Therefore, elimination or arrest of the causative agent, such as the spirochete for the accompanying mood disturbances in general paresis, is the treatment model. There is a subtle distinction that one must be alert to in all such extended formulations from these original hypotheses: That an organic treatment may alleviate a psychological manifestation is not necessarily an argument that the etiology is organic, nor is the converse so—that a psychological treatment argues against an organic etiology. Replacement therapy for a deficiency was a variation of the medical model which had some direct implications for depressive phenomena. Pellagra has a depressive effect as a prominent symptomatic component of its "dementia," and this was one of the first diseases to yield to a metabolic model of treatment. Administration of nicotinic acid leads to an alleviation of most of the symptoms, including the mental ones (Jolliffe & Wortis, 1941). Similar findings were made with respect to the depressive symptoms associated with thiamine deficiency, as well as part of the syndrome associated with pantothenic acid deficiency (Bean, Hodges, & Daum, 1955).

Recent theorizing has taken three related routes: those of the monoamines, the electrolytes, and the endocrines. These will be summarized with reference to the lines of supporting evidence. The monoamine theory of depression posits a basic deficiency of monoamines, such as catecholamines or 5-hydroxytryptophan. Empirical evidence from the use of reserpine for hypertension leading to a significant incidence of depression is cited since reserpine depletes the brain of Its amine stores (Snyder, 1967). Supporting work has dealt with the effects of monoamine oxidase inhibitor drugs to alleviate depressed states. There have been attempts to specify which of the amines seems to be most involved, with suggestions that serotonin or tryptamine is the prime amine. At present it cannot be stated that brain amines are involved when a clinical depression is present, but there is suggestive evidence that the catecholamines and indole-amines need to be investigated (Schildkraut & Kety, 1967).

Theories proposing electrolyte disturbances as a cause or accompaniment of depressions extend back to the early years of the twentieth century. The fluctuating nature of manic-depressive states was suggestive that a lack of electrolytes or water balance was contributory. There is the problem with such theories, as with theories concerning amine metabolism, that alterations in brain metabolism may not be correlated with measurements performed on the blood or urine. There have been attempts to study the distribution of electrolytes, such as potassium and sodium, between the cells and the extracellular fluid via radioactive isotopes. Such studies indicate an increase in intracellular sodium during depressed states and a lowering of intracellular potassium. What effect on the central nervous system these alterations have is not known beyond the alterations in evoked potentials which would be an accompaniment related to a neuroexcitatory theory of depression. It is also interesting that in manic states, the intracellular sodium also increases and even more so than in depressions (Coppen, 1967)—hence, subsequent work using lithium salts as a therapeutic gambit in mania, since they are the only ion capable of being transported across cell membranes by the sodium transport mechanism. Lithium appears to affect adversely the permeability of the cell membrane to sodium. Those who see clinical improvement when utilizing lithium point to this as further evidence for the electrolyte abnormality theory of depressions. Of course, it still leaves unanswered the basic question as to what promotes such disturbances originally as well as any relationship

to amine metabolism that might be present (Schou, 1968). There is also the old question of whether such alterations are secondary to psychogenic mood states.

Endocrinological theories of depression date back to the hypothesis that involutional depressions are associated with a hormonal alteration as well as depressed states in the premenstrual woman. Constitutional theories proposed the pyknic habitus as predisposing toward cyclothymia. In addition, clinicians have long been aware of depression as being an initial or prodromal sign of certain physical diseases which could accompany metabolic or endocrine changes. Such diseases as Cushing's syndrome, carcinoma of the lung or pancreas, and thyroid disease are believed to have depression as a primary finding, rather than being secondarily induced by knowledge of the disease. Similarly, depression is viewed as one of the most frequent symptoms in diabetes, in which the patients seem to be reacting to something beyond the disease picture (Eiduson, Geller, Yuwiler, & Eiduson, 1964). Endocrine work related to depressions has dealt primarily with thyroid hormone and cortisol and its derivatives. There have been two limitations on this research: the general response of the adrenal cortex to any stress, so that implicating corticosteroids as causal in depressions is very precarious, and technical difficulties which have impaired the investigation of other hormones. This leaves many psychoendocrine factors yet to be evaluated, such as anterior and posterior pituitary functioning, androgens, estrogens, aldosterone, etc. (Fawcett & Bunney, 1967). The variety of inquiries into the possible biological bases for depression appear to have a "shotgun" approach at present, wherein a hope resides that one of the shots will somehow connect and validate a hypothesis. These include such studies as blood types, anti-gammaglobulin activity in the serum, calcium metabolism, and altered sleep patterns and EEG responses in the depressed.

What does all this biological work have to do with depressive phenomena in childhood? It can only illustrate the diversity of investigatory approaches currently being utilized with depressions, which will need appraisal with children when diagnostic and psychodynamic thinking become better clarified. It is also evident how little is really known about what is probably one of the most ancient emotional disturbances of man, which is mentioned in the Bible as well as in the writings of Hippocrates, who prescribed mandrake as a cure for depressions. As for childhood depressive phenomena, we are at the beginning of our knowledge.

REFERENCES

Abraham, K. Notes on the psycho-analytical investigation and treatment of manic-depressive insanity and allied conditions (1911). In B. D. Lewin (Ed.), *On character and libido development.* New York: Norton, 1966. Pp. 15–34. (a)

Abraham, K. A short study of the development of the libido, viewed in the light of mental disorders (1924). In B. D. Lewin (Ed.), *On character and libido development.* New York: Norton, 1966. Pp. 67–150. (b)

Ackerly, W. C. Latency age children who threaten or attempt to kill themselves. *Journal of the American Academy of Child Psychiatry,* 1967, **6,** 242–261.

Adler, K. A. Adler's individual psychology. In B. B. Wolman (Ed.), *Psychoanalytic techniques.* New York: Basic Books, 1967. Pp. 299–337.

American Journal of Psychiatry, 1962, **119,** 119–228.

Anthony, J., & Scott, P. Manic-depressive psychosis in childhood. *Journal of Child Psychology and Psychiatry,* 1960, **1,** 55–72.

Anthony, S. *The child's discovery of death: A study of child psychology.* New York: Harcourt, Brace, 1940.

Apley, J. *The child with abdominal pain.* Springfield, Ill.: Charles C Thomas, 1959.

Arieti, S. Manic-depressive psychosis. In S. Arieti (Ed.), *American handbook of psychiatry.* Vol. I. New York: Basic Books, 1959. Pp. 419–454.

Bakwin, H., & Bakwin, R. M. *Clinical management of the behavior disorders in children.* Philadelphia: Saunders, 1960.

Balser, B., & Masterson, J. F. Suicide in adolescents. *American Journal of Psychiatry,* 1959, **116,** 400–405.

Barry, M. Depression, shame, loneliness and the psychiatrist's position. *American Journal of Psychotherapy,* 1962, **16,** 580–599.

Barton-Hall, M. Our present knowledge about manic-depressive states in childhood. *Nervous Child,* 1952, **9,** 319–325.

Bean, W. B., Hodges, R. E., & Daum, K. Pantothenic acid deficiency induced in human subjects. *The Journal of Clinical Investigation,* 1955, **34,** 1073–1084.

Bender, L., & Schilder, P. Suicidal preoccupations. In L. Bender (Ed.), *Contributions to developmental neuropsychiatry.* New York: International Universities Press, 1964. Pp. 301–326.

Benedek, T. Towards the biology of the depressive constellation. *Journal of the American Psychoanalytic Association,* 1956, **4,** 389–427.

Beres, D. Superego and depression. In R. Lowenstein, L. Newman, M. Schur, & A. Solnit (Eds.), *Psychoanalysis: A general psychology.* New York: International Universities Press, 1966. Pp. 479–498.

Bergstrand, C. G., & Otto, U. Suicidal attempts in adolescence and childhood. *Acta Paediatrica Scandinavica* 1962, **51,** 17–26.

Berliner, B. Psychodynamics of the depressive character. *Psychoanalytic Forum,* 1966, **1,** 244–264.

Berman, S. Antisocial character disorder: Its etiology and relationship to delinquency. *American Journal of Orthopsychiatry,* 1959, **29,** 612–621.

Bibring. E. The mechanism of depression. In P. Greenacre (Ed.), *Affective disorders.* New York: International Universities Press, 1953. Pp. 13–48.

Bierman, J. S., Silverstein, P. B., & Finesinger, J. E. A depression in a six-year-old boy with acute poliomyelitis. In *The psychoanalytic study of the child.* Vol. 13. New York: International Universities Press, 1958. Pp. 430–450.

Bonime, W. The psychodynamics of neurotic depression. In S. Arieti (Ed.), *American handbook of psychiatry.* Vol. III. New York: Basic Books, 1966. Pp. 239–255.

Bowlby, J. *Maternal care and mental health.* (2nd ed.) Geneva: World Health Organization, 1952.

Bowlby, J. The nature of the child's tie to the mother. *International Journal of Psychoanalysis,* 1958, **39,** 350–373.

Bowlby, J. Grief and mourning in infancy and early childhood. In *The psychoanalytic study of the child.* Vol. 15. New York: International Universities Press, 1960. Pp. 9–52.

Bowlby, J. Childhood mourning and its implication for psychiatry. *American Journal of Psychiatry,* 1961, **118,** 481–498. (a)

Bowlby, J. Processes of mourning. *International Journal of Psychoanalysis,* 1961, **42,** 317–340. (b)

Bowlby, J. Pathological mourning and childhood mourning. *Journal of the American Psychoanalytic Association,* 1963, **11,** 500–541.

Bowlby, J. Separation anxiety. *International Journal of Psychoanalysis,* 1960, **41,** 89–113.

Brodey, W. M. On the dynamics of narcissism. I. Externalization and early ego development. In *The psychoanalytic study of the child.* Vol. 20. New York: International Universities Press, 1965. Pp. 165–193.

Burch, E. Manic depressive psychosis: Some new aetiological considerations. *British Journal of Psychiatry,* 1964, **110,** 808–817.

Burks, H. L., & Harrison, S. I. Aggressive behavior as a means of avoiding depression. *American Journal of Orthopsychiatry,* 1962, **32,** 416–422.

Burlingham, D., & Freud, A. *Infants without families.* London: G. Allen, 1943.

Chadwick, M. Notes upon the fear of death. *International Journal of Psychoanalysis,* 1929, **10,** 321–334.

Cohen, M. B., et al. An intensive study of twelve cases of manic-depressive psychosis. *Psychiatry,* 1954, **17,** 103–137.

Coppen, A. The biochemistry of affective disorders. *British Journal of Psychiatry,* 1967, **113,** 1237–1264.

Despert, J. L. Suicide and depression in children. *Nervous Child,* 1952, **9,** 378–389.

Edwards, J. H. The simulation of mendelism. *Acta Genetica et Statistica Medica,* 1960, **10,** 63–70.

Eiduson, S., Geller, E., Yuwiler, A., & Eiduson, B. T. *Biochemistry and behavior.* Princeton, N.J.: Van Nostrand, 1964.

Engel, G. Anxiety and depression withdrawal: The primary affects of unpleasure. *International Journal of Psychoanalysis,* 1962, **43,** 89–97.

Engel, G., & Reichsman, F. Spontaneous and experimentally induced depressions in an infant with a gastric fistula. *Journal of the American Psychoanalytic Association,* 1956, **4,** 428–456.

Erikson, E. H. The syndrome of identity diffusion in adolescents and young adults. In J. M. Tanner & B. Inhelder (Eds.), *Discussions on child development.* Vol. III. New York: International Universities Press, 1955. Pp. 133–154.

Fawcett, J., & Bunney, W. E., Jr. Pituitary adrenal function and depression. *Archives of General Psychiatry,* 1967, **16,** 517–535.

Frankl, L. Susceptibility to accidents: A developmental study. *British Journal of Medical Psychology,* 1965, **38,** 289–297.

Freud, A. Discussion of Dr. Bowlby's paper. In *The psychoanalytic study of the child.* Vol. 15. New York: International Universities Press, 1960. Pp. 53–62.

Freud, A. *Normality and pathology in childhood.* New York: International Universities Press, 1965.

Freud, A. About losing and being lost. In *The psychoanalytic study of the child.* Vol. 22. New York: International Universities Press, 1967. Pp. 9–19.

Freud, S. Mourning and melancholia (1917). Standard Edition. Vol. 14. London: Hogarth Press, 1957.

Geleerd, E. R. Some aspects of ego vicissitudes in adolescence. *Journal of the American Psychoanalytic Association,* 1961, **9,** 394–405.

Gero, G. The construction of depression. *International Journal of Psychoanalysis,* 1936, **17,** 423–461.

Gewirtz, J. L. A learning analysis of the effects of normal stimulation, privation and deprivation on the acquisition of social motivation and attachment. In B. M. Foss (Ed.), *Determinants of infant behavior.* London: Methuen, 1961. Pp. 213–303.

Goldfarb, W. Infant rearing and problem behavior. *American Journal of Orthopsychiatry,* 1943, **13,** 249–265.

Gould, R. E. Suicide problems in children and adolescents. *American Journal of Psychotherapy,* 1965, **19,** 228–246.

Grollman, E. A. *Explaining death to children.* Boston: Beacon Press, 1967.

Harms, E. Differential pattern of manic-depressive disease in childhood. *Nervous Child,* 1952, **9,** 319–325.

Jacobs, J., & Teicher, J. D. "Broken homes" viewed as a process: An important aspect in the progressive social isolation of adolescent suicide attempters. *International Journal of Social Psychiatry,* 1966, **13,** 139–149.

Jacobson, E. On normal and pathological moods. In *The psychoanalytic study of the child.* Vol. 12. New York: International Universities Press, 1957. Pp. 73–113.

Jacobson, E. Adolescent moods and the remodeling of psychic structures in adolescence. In *The psychoanalytic study of the child.* Vol. 16. New York: International Universities Press, 1961. Pp. 164–183.

Jacobziner, H. Attempted suicides in adolescence. *The Journal of the American Medical Association,* 1965, **191,** 7–11.

Jarvis, V. Loneliness and compulsion. *Journal of the American Psychoanalytic Association,* 1965, **13,** 122–158.

Joffe, W. G., & Sandler, J. Notes on pain, depression, and individuation. In *The psychoanalytic study of the child.* Vol. 20. New York: International Universities Press, 1965. Pp. 394–424.

Jolliffe, N., & Wortis, H. Encephalopathia Alcoholia. *American Journal of Psychiatry,* 1941, **98**, 340–346.

Jones, E. The genesis of the superego (1947). In *Papers on psychoanalysis.* Boston: Beacon Press, 1966. Pp. 145–152.

Kaufman, I. Three basic sources for pre-delinquent character. *Nervous Child,* 1955, **11**, 12–15.

Kaufman, I., et al. Delineation of two diagnostic groups among juvenile delinquents: The schizophrenic and the impulse-ridden character disorder. *Journal of the American Academy of Child Psychiatry,* 1963, **2**, 292–318.

Kaufman, I. C., & Rosenblum, L. A. The reaction to separation in infant monkeys: Anaclitic depression and conservation-withdrawal. *Psychosomatic Medicine,* 1967, **29**, 648–675.

Klein, M. *Contributions to psycho-analysis: 1921–1945.* New York: McGraw-Hill, 1964.

Kubie, L. S. Multiple determinants of suicidal efforts. *The Journal of Nervous and Mental Disease,* 1964, **138**, 3–8.

Leonhard, K., Korff, I., & Schalz, H. Die temperamente in den familien der monopolaren und bipolaren phasischen. *Psychiatrie et Neurologie,* 1962, **143**, 416–434.

Leveton, A. F. Reproach: The art of shamesmanship. *British Journal of Medical Psychology,* 1962, **35**, 101–111.

Levy, D. Primary affect hunger. *American Journal of Psychiatry,* 1937, **94**, 643–652.

Liebermann, L. P. Three cases of attempted suicide in children. *British Journal of Medical Psychology,* 1953, **26**, 110–114.

Lorand, S. Adolescent depression. *International Journal of Psychoanalysis,* 1962, **48**, 54.

Mahler, M. S. On sadness and grief in infancy and childhood. In *The psychoanalytic study of the child.* Vol. 16. New York: International Universities Press, 1961. Pp. 332–354.

Mahler, M. S. Notes on the development of basic moods. In R. Lowenstein, L. Newman, M. Schur, & A. Solnit (Eds.), *Psychoanalysis: A general psychology.* New York: International Universities Press, 1966. Pp. 152–168.

Margolin, N. L., & Teicher, J. D. Thirteen adolescent male suicide attempts: Dynamic considerations. *Journal of the American Academy of Child Psychiatry,* 1968, **7**, 296–315.

Maurer, A. Adolescent attitudes toward death. *Journal of Genetic Psychology,* 1964, **105**, 75–90.

Nagy, M. The child's theories concerning death. *Journal of Genetic Psychology,* 1948, **73**, 3–27.

Otto, U. Changes in the behavior of children and adolescents preceding suicidal attempts. *Acta Psychiatrica Scandinavica,* 1964, **40**, 386–400.

Otto, U. Suicidal attempts made by children. *Acta Paediatnica Scandinavica,* 1966, **55**, 64–72.

Piers, G., & Singer, M. B. *Shame and guilt: A psychiatric and cultural study.* Springfield, Ill.: Charles C Thomas, 1953.

Price, J. S. Genetics of the affective illnesses. *Hospital Medicine,* 1968, **4**, 1172–1179. (a)

Price, J. S. Neurotic and endogenous depression: A phylogenetic view. *British Journal of Psychiatry,* 1968, **114**, 119–120. (b)

Prugh, D. G., & Harlow, R. G. Masked deprivation in infants and children. In *Deprivation of maternal care.* Geneva: World Health Organization, 1962. Pp. 9–29.

Rado, S.   The problem of melancholia.   *International Journal of Psychoanalysis,* 1928, **9,** 420–438.

Rado, S.   Emergency behavior with an introduction to the dynamics of conscience.   In *Psychoanalysis and behavior.*   New York: Grune & Stratton, 1956.   Pp. 214–239.

Reich, A.   Pathologic forms of self-esteem regulation.   In *The psychoanalytic study of the child.* Vol. 15.   New York: International Universities Press, 1960.   Pp. 215–232.

Rie, H. E.   Depression in childhood: A survey of some pertinent contributions.   *Journal of the American Academy of Child Psychiatry,* 1966, **5,** 653–685.

Rochlin, G.   The dread of abandonment.   In *The psychoanalytic study of the child.*   Vol. 16. New York: International Universities Press, 1961. Pp. 451–470.

Rochlin, G.   Loss and restitution.   In *Griefs and its discontents.*   Boston: Little, Brown, 1965. Pp. 121–164.

Sandler, J., & Joffe, W. G.   Notes on childhood depression.   *International Journal of Psychoanalysis,* 1965, **46,** 88–96.

Schafer, R.   The loving and beloved superego in Freud's structural theory.   In *The psychoanalytic study of the child.*   Vol. 15. New York: International Universities Press, 1960.   Pp. 163–188.

Schechter, M. D.   The recognition and treatment of suicide in children.   In E. S. Shneidman & N. L. Farberow (Eds.), *Clues to suicide.*   New York: McGraw-Hill, 1957.   Pp. 131–142.

Schilder, P., & Wechsler, D.   The attitudes of children toward death.   *Journal of Genetic Psychology,* 1934, **45,** 406–451.

Schildkraut, J. J., & Kety, S. S.   Biogenic amines and emotion.   *Science,* 1967, **156,** 21–30.

Schou, M.   Lithium in psychiatric therapy and prophylaxis.   *Journal of Psychiatric Research,* 1968, **6,** 67–95.

Schrut, A.   Suicidal adolescents and children. *The Journal of the American Medical Association,* 1964, **188,** 1102–1107.

Slater, E. T. O.   The inheritance of manic-depressive insanity and its relation to mental defect. *The Journal of Mental Science,* 1936, **82,** 626–634.

Snyder, S. H.   New developments in brain chemistry.   *American Journal of Orthopsychiatry,* 1967, **37,** 864–879.

Solnit, A. J.   A tribute to Heinz Hartmann.   *The Psychiatric Quarterly,* 1965, **33,** 475–484.

Sperling, M.   Equivalents of depression in children.   *Journal of the Hillside Hospital,* 1959, **8,** 138–148.

Spitz, R.   Anaclitic depression.   In *The psychoanalytic study of the child.*   Vol. 2.   New York: International Universities Press, 1946.   Pp. 113–117.

Stenstedt, A.   A study in manic-depressive psychosis.   *Acta Psychiatrica et Neurologica Scandinavica,* 1952 (Suppl. 79).

Sterba, E.   The schoolboy suicide in André Gide's novel "The Counterfeiters."   *American Imago,* 1951, **8,** 307–320.

Sullivan, H. S.   *The interpersonal theory of psychiatry.*   New York: Norton, 1953.

Toolan, J. M.   Depression in children and adolescents.   *American Journal of Orthopsychiatry,* 1962, **32,** 404–415.

U.S. Bureau of the Census, 1963.

Weiss, E.   Regression and projection in the superego.   *International Journal of Psychoanalysis,* 1932, **13,** 449–478.

Winnicott, D. W. The depressive position in normal emotional development (1954). In *Collected Papers*. New York: Basic Books, 1958. Pp. 262–277.

Wolfenstein, M. How is mourning possible? In *The psychoanalytic study of the child*. Vol. 21. New York: International Universities Press, 1966. Pp. 93–126.

Wooton, B. *Social science and social pathology.* London: G. Allen, 1959.

Zetzel, E. Depression and incapacity to bear it. In M. Schur (Ed.), *Drives, affects, behavior.* Vol. 2. New York: International Universities Press, 1965. Pp. 243-276.

16 | Delinquency

Seymour L. Halleck

In a rapidly changing and sometimes tumultuous world, more and more adolescents are willing to break the law. According to FBI statistics, the number of juveniles arrested each year since 1952 has increased more rapidly than the number of older persons arrested. In 1963, the largest group of persons arrested for all crimes was made up of sixteen-year-olds. Seventeen-year-olds constituted the second largest group of offenders. Fifteen- and eighteen-year-olds, who had almost equal arrest rates, were third (Cohen & Short, 1966).

The problem of juvenile delinquency has become so intimately related to political and social conflicts within our society that there is reason to question whether the community's interests are served by considering this phenomenon in psychopathological terms. One way of looking at a great deal of delinquency is to consider it as an attempt to relieve oppression or as a kind of social activism or dissent. In violating the law, the delinquent is often directly or indirectly clamoring for change within his family unit or within his society. In the last few years, the boundaries between social dissent and crime have become increasingly unclear. Youth who protest the war and oppression of minority groups must often break the law to make their point. On the other hand, much of what appears to be selfish crime, such as rioting and looting, is also having an increasing influence in bringing about social change. Lawless rioting of youth in our cities has probably had more influence in helping the poor and the Negro than most lawful pleas or demands for change.

Within such a social context the behavioral scientist must move carefully in making analogies between delinquency and psychopathology. There are probably some elements of psychopathology involved in every delinquent act, but often these are not the major determinants. The approach of the behavioral scientist who identifies himself with the healing arts must be a limited one. If he becomes too enamoured of the disease model of delinquency, he merely takes society "off the hook," by providing it with an excuse for ignoring its own imperfections and weaknesses. He becomes an agent of the Establish-

541

ment, a person who does little more than provide a rationalization to those who wish to preserve the status quo.

DEFINITIONS OF DELINQUENCY

Delinquency can be defined either in legalistic or in behavioral terms. A child can be adjudicated delinquent if he violates a criminal statute by committing an act which would have been defined as a crime if it were committed by an adult. But a child can also be adjudicated delinquent for committing acts for which adults would not be legally accountable. Our current juvenile court system allows for commitment of youth for such vaguely defined behaviors as immoral or indecent conduct, incorrigibility, or promiscuity. It should be apparent that legalistic definitions of delinquency are often based on value judgments which are not held consistently by all elements in our society. A behavior considered delinquent in girls might not be considered delinquent in boys. Similar discriminations occur with regard to ethnic groupings and social class. Legalistic definitions therefore present us with an eccentric picture of the total delinquency problem (Eissler, 1948; Sellin, 1938).

Behavioral definitions would include as delinquent all those youth who have antisocial attitudes and who commit antisocial acts for which they could have been adjudicated delinquent if they had been apprehended and prosecuted. Obviously, many more individuals commit delinquent acts than are adjudicated delinquents. The problem with behavioral definitions is that they are too broad, and they fail to define a population which can be studied (Tappan, 1947).

Most behavioral scientists agree that it is impossible to derive a comprehensive or logical definition of delinquency. For the purposes of this discussion, delinquency will be considered in terms of the behaviors that will bring a child to the attention of those clinicians and those social agencies which are involved in disciplining, rehabilitating, or treating offenders. Such attention is called for when a child repeatedly engages in acts which either are illegal or offend the morality of the greater community and which are defined as a problem by the child himself, by his parents, or by the community.

SOME DATA ON DELINQUENCY

Whatever definition one invokes, it is impossible to determine the true extent of delinquency in this country. There is very little we know for sure. We do know that approximately 2 percent of all children aged 10 to 17 were involved in court cases each year after 1954. We also know that the trend is toward youth's representing the largest group of offenders for most types of crime. Most observers feel that juvenile crime is increasing, but even this assumption has been questioned (Cohen & Short, 1966).

There has been a change in the ratio of boys to girls appearing before juvenile courts. In recent years this ratio has dropped to about 5 to 1. Around the turn of the century it was closer to 50 or 60 to 1. Delinquency rates among Negroes are especially high. Rates among Puerto Ricans, Mexicans, and American Indians are also higher than would be expected on the basis of their representation in the total population. In general, ethnic groups who are plagued by poverty and discrimination are likely to have higher delinquency rates. Such findings, however, must be interpreted carefully. Minority groups may have a high propensity for antisocial behavior, but it is also true that society is exceptionally quick to define such groups as delinquent.

Delinquency rates are highest in urban areas and lowest in rural areas. In large cities delinquency is more of a lower-class phenomenon. As the size of the community becomes smaller, the rates of delinquency among the various social classes become more similar. Any data dealing with social class must of course be interpreted in the light of our knowledge that lower-class youth are far more likely than upper-class youth to be adjudicated delinquent, even when the behaviors of both groups are similar.

THEORIES OF DELINQUENCY

In no other field in the behavioral sciences is there as much theoretical confusion as there is in the area of delinquency and crime. Because delinquency is such an arbitrarily defined concept to begin with, many have questioned whether it is even worth searching for a theory of delinquency. The difficulties of formulating an inclusive theory to explain such variant behaviors as murder, looting, incorrigibility, stealing, and sodomy should be readily apparent.

In recent years there has been some trend toward restricting theoretical formulations to specific types of crime. Gibbons (1965), for example, has described nine specific categories of juvenile delinquency, each of which he views as having a different etiology. Johnson (1959) has followed the lead of many other psychiatrists in attempting to make a relatively sharp differentiation between the individual delinquent, whose problems are psychological, and the sociological delinquent, whose problems are generated by the inequities and conflicts within the greater society. Halleck (1967b) has attempted to restrict psychiatric theorizing to that form of crime or delinquency which can be labeled *unreasonable*.

Even when the category of delinquency to be considered is rigidly defined, there is still much controversy as to how the theorist should go about his task. Traditionally, there has been a deplorable tendency among biologists, psychiatrists, and sociologists to search for a single cause of crime. Such efforts have never been successful. The multiple-factor approach developed by Healy (1944) and Burt (1915) and preferred by most clinicians is an effort to understand delinquency causation in terms of the wide variety of stresses to which the delinquent is exposed. While this approach is more realistic than global theorizing, it has been widely criticized by sociologists (Cohen, 1951; Vold, 1958). A theory of crime should be able to describe the complex processes by which various factors exert a delinquent influence. Unfortunately, in the hands of many behavioral scientists the multiple-factor approach has been conceptualized as a static, multilinear model in which factors are seen as distinct variables whose relative influence can be precisely weighed or measured. The multiple-factor approach is, indeed, of little theoretical value unless some effort is made to define the interrelatedness of factors and to describe the manner in which each factor exerts its influence.

While all-inclusive theories of antisociality are still occasionally invoked, most sophisticated theoreticians in the field of delinquency appreciate the need for integrated field or process models. To understand a given delinquent act, one must examine both personality variables and situational variables. A psychiatrist cannot explain delinquency as the result of one or more personality traits since among individuals with quite similar traits, some will be delinquent and others will not. The sociologist cannot explain delinquency in terms of factors in the immediate environment since people exposed to similar situations often behave differently.

We are in need of a conceptual framework which will integrate biological, psychological, and social data. Such a framework can be derived from that sociopsychological methodology which is based on the assumption that human behavior is an adaptation to stress. Different varieties of behavior can be classified as adaptations. The factors that generate the behaviors are stresses. To understand the behavior of a delinquent youth, it is necessary to understand the kinds of stress he experienced in early childhood as well as the kinds of stress he experiences in his immediate existence. But, while it is stress that moves man to act, the direction of his action is determined by social conditions. It is therefore also necessary to describe those conditions which favor socially acceptable adaptations and those which favor alienated or delinquent adaptations.

As our technological skills have increased, the number of natural stresses which threaten man has gradually diminished. While biological stress is still an important factor in shaping behavior, the major problems of our era are man-made. Moden man experiences the most severe stresses when he feels that he is arbitrarily controlled, deprived, or abused. Such stresses can be categorized under the heading of *oppression*. Usually, oppression implies neglect, selfishness, or malevolence on the part of others. The stress of oppression may be a direct product of social injustice, or it might be experienced as a more personal force which emanates from interactions with one's family and immediate neighbors. Unfortunately, human beings, because of conflicting learning experiences, frustration, and deprivation, also come to devise means of inflicting pain upon themselves. Most of us, at times, perceive more oppression in the world than actually exists, and we have learned to make life miserable for ourselves even when it seems that living conditions are optimum. Those who regularly and incorrectly perceive the world as more oppressive than it actually is are in a sense predisposed to maladaptive responses, and one such response is delinquency.

Oppression is also experienced when one senses that the world created by his fellowman has failed to provide enough joy, enough gratification, or enough meaning to make life worthwhile. Stress here is at least in part impersonal. The structures created by man may assume an autonomy of their own, and they then have the power to suppress and frustrate. Technology and progress, for example, are not products of malevolence, but they often generate oppressions in our life which are intolerable.

When a person experiences himself as oppressed (whether or not he is accurate in his perceptions), he must respond or adapt. For the purpose of clarity it is possible to define certain consistent patterns of behavior or adaptational styles which occur with some regularity. Perhaps the commonest response to most varieties of stress is tolerance or conformity. Most of us can tolerate minor stresses without feeling the need to change the conditions which created them. But people are also capable of conforming under extreme conditions of oppression by altering something about themselves—their physiology, their attitudes, or their expectations. Conformity is especially favored by those individuals who can believe in a better future during life or who have faith in a divinity who guarantees a new life after death. The "Uncle Tom" or "Good Negro" is an example of an individual who uses the conforming adaptation. Tolerance or conformity is favored in a society which is homogeneous, which honors its historical values, which has strong religious beliefs, and which has faith in its future.

A more aggressive but still socially approved response to oppression is legal activism. An oppressed Negro may elect to better his lot by using legally sanctioned channels to protest and change those things which are troubling him. The early leaders of the NAACP and the Urban League, for example, were men who elected the legal-activism adaptation. Socially approved activism is favored in a society in which communication between those in power and those who are seeking power is at a high level and in which channels for social change are readily available to all individuals.

Under certain conditions an oppressed individual may despair of tolerating a situation or of changing it through legal means. He then has two alternatives. He can withdraw from the society, or he can attack it by illegal means. Both are actually alienated responses. In either adaptational style the individual comes to feel estranged from the social processes which the greater community endorses. He rejects the values of his community, and if he was raised in that community he also rejects the values of his own past.

The withdrawn individual responds to oppression by trying to detach himself from the forces which created it. He develops his own subculture and his own way of life, which are maintained at the expense of the derision of the mass of society. In a sense he is struggling with the rest of society, but it is a struggle in which he seeks power through passivity. Often his life is dominated by nihilism, fantasy, and drugs. Withdrawal is a more likely adaptation in a society which does not have good communication between the masses and the leaders and which is highly tolerant of peculiarity and inactivity.

The adaptation of illegal activism is a last recourse available to those who cannot conform to what is distasteful to them in their society, who despair of changing it by legal means, and who are also unwilling or unable to withdraw. It is an aggressive form of alienation which takes the form of insurrection, civil disobedience, or delinquency. These behaviors all have some elements in common. They are all generated by a sense of oppression. They also produce a sufficient reaction on the part of the rest of society to lead to a certain degree of social change. Illegal activism is likely to occur in a society in which there is poor communication between the oppressed and the oppressors and which is limited in its capacity to control those who violate its laws.

The above is a grossly oversimplified description of the nature and variety of adaptational alternatives. None of the adaptations described is wholly characteristic of any one individual at a given time. They are dominant forms of behavior or life-styles which vary with changes in circumstances. In a given period of time certain individuals may utilize several adaptations to deal with an oppressive situation.

Because man is basically a social animal, he tends to elect conventional adaptations such as conformity or legal activism unless oppression is great. The selection of a particular adaptation is also determined by the availability of that adaptation within that social structure at a given moment. If the society, for example, is unable to control delinquency through its law-enforcement apparatus, antisocial behavior will increase. A decrease in the availability of any adaptation will force individuals to seek other adaptations. If, for example, legal activism is not possible, people must either conform or adopt an alienated stance.[1]

In this conceptual framework, the delinquent act must be viewed as a response to the perception of massive oppression coupled with a perception that no other adaptation is available. Phenomenologically, the individual who experiences this condition perceives himself to be helpless. The criminal act can then be viewed as an effort to deal with the perception of helplessness by attempting to attack and thereby alter an oppressive environment. Even if the criminal act fails to change the environment in a manner that meets the delinquent's needs, it still provides him with some attenuation of the feeling of helplessness insofar as the act itself provides a certain degree of freedom and hope for change. Undoubtedly, some individuals are predisposed to criminality by virtue of childhood experiences which make them perceive more oppression and helplessness than actually exists. Other delinquent acts are more directly related to a sense of oppression and helplessness created by the immediate environment.

[1] The above model is essentially similar to that presented in Halleck's *Psychiatry and the Dilemmas of Crime* (1967b). The model is expanded in Halleck's "Process of Student Unrest" (in press).

Delinquent acts can also be viewed as having a communicative purpose. The delinquent is trying to say something through his behavior. Sometimes his illegal behavior is an effort to communicate with his society or his family. In other instances the type of communication is more private. Often the delinquent act must be viewed as an unreasonable or unconscious communication toward introjects or as an effort to resolve conflicts which were generated during early life.

Conceptual frameworks such as the above make it possible to derive explanations of delinquency which account for both personal and social factors. Much of the new work in psychology and sociology is based on integrated approaches. There is still some tendency, however, to retreat to the ways of the past, and members of the disciplines that work with the delinquent will often propose single-factor or global theories, which are supposed to explain every variety of delinquency. From an adaptive or integrative standpoint, however, each of these theories is better considered as describing only a single factor or stress which favors the adaptations of illegal activism. Some of the stresses described in these theories exert their influence in a manner which predisposes the individual to later delinquency. Other stresses emanate from the immediate environment and have a more direct influence. For purposes of clarity and convenience, theories of delinquency will be examined in terms of their conventional categories: the biological, the psychological, and the sociological. The reader must understand, however, that delinquency cannot be understood in terms of linear models. No biological or psychological stress can be understood outside its social context. Nor can one understand the meaning of a social stress unless he is aware of the psychological makeup of the man who is experiencing it.

Biological Theories

Biological theories of crime assume a hereditary basis in physical deficiencies or malfunctions which predispose some individuals toward delinquent action. While no biological factor has ever been proved to be a major cause of delinquency, the exact importance of biological stresses or factors is at this moment unknown. Few criminologists of either a psychological or a sociological orientation believe that they are crucial factors in delinquency. From a historical standpoint, however, it will be worthwhile to review briefly the kinds of biological theories that have been put forth as total explanations of criminality.

In 1876 the Italian psychiatrist Cesare Lombroso first presented the doctrine that criminals and delinquents have not advanced as far along the evolutional scale as normal men. They are "atavistic throwbacks," individuals whose skulls and brains, in Lombroso's opinion, are more similar to those of prehistoric or primitive man than to those of modern man. Because the future delinquent is afflicted with primitive instincts, he has no choice but to lead a predatory life similar to his ancestors'. He is a "born criminal" endowed with a "criminal brain" (Lombroso, 1911).

Although Lombroso's theory has been convincingly refuted, the conviction that inborn constitutional traits produce criminal behaviors has continued to receive periodic reinforcement through new studies. In our own era, Hooton (1939) and Sheldon (1949) have presented anthropological and anatomical data which suggest that the delinquent is physically different from the normal person. The only finding of these two researchers which has not been thoroughly refuted is Sheldon's discovery of a high degree of mesomorphism in delinquent boys. The correlation between mesomorphism and delinquency, which has also been described by Glueck and Glueck (1956), does not, however, mean that a physical factor is the cause of delinquency. As will be noted later, the association of these two variables can be explained in other ways.

If constitutional defects are the cause of delinquency, such defects are most likely to be transmitted through hereditary processes. Efforts to demonstrate a hereditary factor in crime, however, have been notably unsuccessful (McLearn, 1964). Most of the important research in this area has involved twin studies which look for rates of concordance in criminal behavior in one-egg and two-egg twins. Although it does appear that twins with a similar heredity are more likely to be similar with regard to criminal behaviors, the data are not strong enough to rule out the relevance of environmental factors involved in rearing one-egg twins (Montagu, 1951). At this moment no evidence of a hereditary factor that is present in delinquents but absent in non-delinquents is available. Even if such evidence were found, constitutional or hereditary theories would still be of limited usefulness unless they could also explain how bodily defects influence behavior. It must also be noted that researchers who have supported biological theories usually fail to appreciate the arbitrary nature of delinquency. In some ways it makes little sense to suppose a common genetic cause of such widely variant forms of delinquency as check forgery and sodomy.

In the early part of this century, most American psychiatrists and psychologists believed that feeblemindedness or mental deficiency was a major cause of delinquency (Anderson, 1919). It was not until psychological tests were standardized with Army recruits during the First World War and not until other inadequacies in test administration were discovered that the doctrine of the feebleminded delinquent began to decline. Today most behavioral scientists find little evidence to support the hypothesis that crime is caused by defective intelligence. Some delinquents, particularly those who are institutionalized with Army recruits during the First World of mental deficiency than is found in a nondelinquent population, but this finding can also be explained in terms of the general social ineffectiveness of the intellectually limited person.

At various times during the history of research into delinquent behavior, a number of observers have been convinced that they have found endocrinological or neurological defects present in delinquents that are not present in nondelinquents (Berman, 1932; Hill & Watterson, 1952; Thompson, 1953). A careful review of each of these findings, including the alleged presence of electroencephalographic abnormalities in the delinquent, has failed to show any consistent differences between delinquents and nondelinquents. One interesting speculation about crime causation which has not as yet been disproved is that of Eysenck (1964), who suggested that the criminal has an innate predisposition to form "weak and fleeting" conditioned responses. Eysenck acknowledges the complex social and psychological nature of delinquency, but believes the basic problem may be an inherited defect in conditioning ability. More recent studies of the chromosome structures of highly aggressive men also suggest some linkage between innate neurological characteristics and aggression (Polani, 1967). It must be noted, however, that aggressiveness is not synonymous with delinquency and that delinquency may often be characteristic of nonaggressive persons.

Most modern scientists believe that heredity operates by setting upper limits or potentialities, which are then brought out or expressed only in certain environments. The environment is not capable of influencing change beyond those limits. In approaching a subject such as delinquency, behavioral scientists today are concerned with the manner in which environmental and hereditary influences collaborate or interact so as to lead to antisocial behavior. If a child is born in the slums of a large city in the United States and if he is a Negro, the color of his skin may be a factor favoring criminality. A muscular or mesomorphic boy from the same environment may find that his innate physical endowment provides him with better equipment for criminal activity than his pyknic counterpart. In different environments, however, neither a dark-skinned nor a muscular habitus would necessarily encourage criminal delinquency. Biological factors will therefore play a role in determining delinquent adaptations, but they are not sufficient causes of delinquency.

Psychological Theories

For the most part, psychological theories of delinquency focus upon those learning experiences and conflicts of early life which predispose the child to view the world as an oppressive place. In such a world he must sometimes behave in a delinquent manner if he is to survive. The crucial learning experiences which favor delinquency are believed to take place within the family. Schools and other community agencies are viewed as resources which might be enlisted to prevent delinquency, but they are not usually viewed as the critical settings in which delinquency is generated.

There has been much speculation as to the influence of separation from the mother at an early age as an important factor in the genesis of delinquency and other personality disturbances. At one time a number of researchers claimed a direct relationship between maternal separation in early life and later development of delinquent personality traits (Bowlby, 1951). Subsequent research has not confirmed this claim. At this point students of the problem believe that maternal separation has an unfavorable impact upon the adaptive capacity of the organism, but they are unwilling to make more specific statements as to the type of personality traits which may develop as a response to such separation (Yarrow, 1964).

There is more general agreement among behavioral scientists that prolonged neglect and an absence of a significant mothering person in a child's early life may have a profoundly unfavorable effect upon his future adjustment. The child who is rejected by maternal figures yearns for closeness, but begins to associate this yearning with feelings of helplessness and anticipated rejection. Several observers have noted that delinquents suffer from chronic depression. This is especially true of those who had inadequate mothering during the early years of life. They tend to equate closeness with helplessness and begin to experience deep discomfort whenever interpersonal relationships become more intimate. "Dependency anxiety," or a tendency to react aggressively whenever one is placed in a situation which threatens to remind him of his dependency or to make him more dependent, is a striking characteristic of many delinquents (Bandura & Walters, 1958).

Parental hostility or violence toward young children has also been invoked as a predisposing factor toward delinquency. Some researchers believe that expression of hostility toward the child is not a sufficient cause for delinquency but that when hostile attitudes are combined with lax modes of discipline, delinquency is quite likely to result. According to these studies, an unloved child who is raised strictly might develop a form of mental illness, but an unloved child who is raised with few restrictions would have a tendency to learn to act out antisocial impulses (Becker, 1964). Direct parental violence may also play a role in creating delinquent tendencies. We now know that brutality toward children is not uncommon. It seems likely that violence does beget violence, and we know that some of the most aggressive delinquents with whom society must deal were exposed to extremely brutal conditions in their own homes.

Inconsistency in the kind of discipline imposed by parents has long been felt to be a primary cause of delinquency. There is remarkable agreement among both clinicians and researchers as to the importance of this factor (Bandura & Walters, 1959; Glueck & Glueck, 1956; McCord, McCord, & Zola, 1959). The issue of inconsistency actually encompasses many more factors than discipline. There can be inconsistency between attitudes, between behaviors, and between attitudes and behaviors. Sometimes verbal communications are themselves inconsistent in that they present "double messages" to which the child cannot possibly respond in a satisfactory manner. Paradoxical communication or communication which puts the child into a "double bind" is sometimes invoked as an important etiologic factor in creating severe emotional disturbance and juvenile delinquency (Bateson, Jackson, Haley, & Wealkand, 1955).

Overprotectiveness or overcontrol of children is not generally seen as a factor in creating delinquent tendencies. In fact, parental overcontrol is usually thought of as a factor which predisposes the child to passive or neurotic personality traits. There is one complicated form of overcontrol, however, which is directed toward satisfying the needs of the entire family unit and which may predispose certain individuals to delinquency. Some families have a distinct tendency to "scapegoat" one particular child. One of the members of the family is identified as the "bad child" and is regularly put into a position in which other members of the family anticipate and unconsciously support his delinquent activities (Haley, 1963).

Personality disorders. Much of psychiatric and particularly psychoanalytical theorizing in the area of delinquency deals with the origin of personality traits which define a type of character structure which predisposes one to delinquency. Aichorn (1935) was the first to develop the concept of "latent delinquency." The personality traits of the latent delinquent include a tendency to seek immediate gratification (impulsivity), a tendency to consider satisfaction of instincts more important than gratification from objects (poor relationships with other people), and a subordination of regard for right and wrong to instinctual gratification (lack of guilt). According to Aichorn, the latent delinquent is a child who will easily succumb to overt delinquency when he encounters stressful situations in adolescence.

Bowlby described the "affectionless" character who cannot make friends, who is inaccessible, who lacks emotional response, and who takes part in pointless lying and deceiving. According to Bowlby (1951), such character traits develop as a response to maternal deprivation. Freidlander (1945) ascribes the characteristics of Aichorn's latent delinquent to defects in the development of the ego and superego. She believes that the child, because of insufficient exposure to maternal love, withdraws interest from objects and stays fixated at a developmental level which is concerned primarily with gratification of needs. This basic defect is carried through the various phases of psychosexual development, so that the child fails to develop an independent superego, that is, a superego which is not dependent upon external control and reinforcement. Where there is no internal system which automatically evaluates an act as right or wrong, control of impulses in the delinquency-prone child is governed by the chances of being discovered and punished.

Lampl-DeGroot (1949) views the basic defect in the character structure of the delinquent as residing in only one portion of the superego, the ego-ideal. That part of the superego which contains the parent's internalized standards is believed to be defective. The child seems unable to say to himself, "I want to be like my parents and to have their ideals." Johnson and Szurek (1952) have described delinquents who can be thought of as having specific defects in the structure of their superegos. Such children conform in most ways, but seem to be driven toward one specific type of antisocial conduct. It is believed that the parents of such children have subtly encouraged them to engage in specific forms of misconduct which vicariously gratify the parent's own need. A timid father may raise a son who is a bully, or a sexually frustrated mother may indirectly encourage her daughter to be promiscuous. The inadequacies of conscience formation in such individuals are referred to as *superego lacunae*.

The personality disturbance referred to in the literature as the *psychopathic* or *sociopathic* personality has received considerable attention in the literature on adult criminology. There has been considerable reluctance, however, to apply terms such as *psychopathic* or *sociopathic* to an adolescent. Few clinicians are willing to concede that a person still in the formative stage of development should be considered to have such a fixed personality disorder. It is also true that the concept of psychopathy itself is an extremely confused one. Some writers consider psychopathy a distinct entity, an emotional disorder or syndrome which is characterized by antisociality, aggressivity, impulsivity, lack of guilt, and inability to form lasting bonds of affection with other human beings (McCord & McCord, 1956). Other writers think of psychopathy as more similar to other forms of psychoneurosis and describe it as a type of neurotic character structure which can be understood quite clearly in psychoanalytic terms (Alexander, 1930). In the recent literature there is an increasing trend toward viewing psychopathy as more of a tendency or reaction pattern than a syndrome (Halleck, 1966). There is also a much clearer understanding that psychopathy is in no sense synonymous with delinquency or criminality and that, in fact, the person with psychopathic tendencies may adapt quite well in modern society.

Limitations of psychological theories. The weakness of psychological explanations which attempt to describe how one develops behavioral patterns which predispose toward delinquency is that they do not fully consider the adaptive value of much delinquent behavior. Psychoanalytic theory which deals with the expression or control of antisocial impulses also tends to over-simplify the problem. Much psychoanalytic theorizing is concerned with motivation. Consideration of motivational aspects of personality cannot by itself provide a comprehensive understanding of the problem of delinquency. Clinicians, more than most other men, appreciate that antisocial tendencies are universal. The fact that one understands the motivations behind an act does not mean that he can explain it, since for every person who violates a law, there are many others who have similar antisocial inclinations but do not express them.

If it is assumed that deviancy from social standards is generally bad, then there is a tendency to consider all deviant behavior as a defect, and, indeed, psychoanalytic theory often seems to be directed toward discovering a defect in the superego, a defect that allows for a direct expression of antisocial impulses. This is a linear form of thinking which does not consider the complex processes involved in the actual expression of antisocial tendencies.

Some delinquent acts require a great deal of control. Even if we consider those crimes which seem to be a clear expression of antisocial impulses, it is not possible to describe a linear relationship between such expressions and an ego or superego defect. Rather, the alleged personality defect must be examined within the total situation. Consider the example of a child who has been brain-damaged. Such a child would be described as having a damaged ego. If he then behaved in an antisocial manner, his behavior might be explained as being directly related to a defect in control mechanisms. This assumption would be too simplistic. Actually what would be happening would be a general shift in equilibrium between the child and his environment. With his damaged brain cells, the child would be exposed to many new social stresses and would experience some lack of capacity to find useful adaptations. Delinquency might then occur with greater frequency because in his new state of ego impairment, the child would find himself in a world in which antisocial behavior might be the best adaptation available. This is quite a different kind of causality from that implied in the usual thinking about delinquency as a breakdown in control mechanisms.

Psychological theories are also limited by their inability to explain why two individuals with similar predispositions often behave differently. The clinician sees many individuals who have been heavily exposed to the kinds of stresses described earlier but who never become delinquent. He also sees many delinquents who were not exposed to such stresses. The inability to explain adaptational or symptom choice is, of course, one of the grave deficiencies of all psychological theory. It is no less a weakness in the area of delinquency.

Stress During Adolescence

Psychological stress is related to delinquency in more ways than are included under the concept of predisposition. Stress which is present during the adolescent years may also provide an impetus toward delinquency. The adolescent occupies a peculiar role in modern American society. Often he possesses all the physical attributes of the adult, and yet in many ways he is treated like a child, someone who is not entitled to the responsibilities and privileges given to adults. The discrepancy between his physical development and his social status constitutes a formidable stress in itself.

Physical strength by itself is a factor militating toward delinquency. The preadolescent may experience criminal impulses, but he does not have the biological equipment with which to act upon them. The adolescent has sufficient physical strength to transform antisocial wishes into antisocial conduct. Other physical changes occurring during adolescence such as sexual maturation, rapid changes in body appearance, changes in energy levels, and changes in eating and sleeping habits constitute new stresses to which the adolescent must adapt. Sometimes eccentric rates of maturation play a role in delinquency. The physically precocious girl may be an easy sexual target for more mature men or boys. And the boy whose physical development proceeds rapidly is likely to be invited to participate in antisocial pursuits before he is equipped to evaluate the consequences of these activities.

The adolescent is also concerned with finding his identity, in terms of both his capacity to be productive or creative and his capacity to relate to other individuals as potential sexual partners. If during these crucial years he is confronted with a family situation which is exploitative or depriving, or if he must live in social circumstances that sap the strength and dignity of him and his family, he develops certain conflicts which favor a delinquent adaptation (Blos, 1962).

In our society many disturbed families are prone to use the male child to fulfill social roles which properly belong to the father. Such situations arise when the father is physically absent, is emotionally distant, or fails to provide an adequate model for his son. The adolescent is then pushed closer to his mother, and because he is uncertain as to what his proper relation with her should be, he may come to experience an insidious discomfort with any masculine role. Often in such situations the mother tries to use the son to provide the intimacy and social closeness which should have been provided by her husband. The adolescent then becomes uncertain as to his sexual identity. He is liable to become deeply preoccupied with fears of being considered a "sissy" or effeminate. If he also perceives his own latent homosexual tendencies, he is even more threatened.

In our culture young men tend to defend themselves against fears of homosexuality or of feminization by displaying strength or aggressivity. A significant proportion of male juvenile delinquency can be described as "masculine proving behavior." It is characterized by actions which involve tests of courage and risk taking. In this regard it is interesting to note that the Negro culture in America, which for various reasons is dominated by strong mothers and weak fathers, is characterized by exceptionally high rates of delinquency. The social dislocations engendered by poverty and discrimination produce additional psychological stresses which fall most harshly upon those who are already deprived (Kardiner & Ovesey, 1951).

Adolescence is a time during which youth must begin to resolve dependency conflicts. An adolescent must learn to free himself from over-reliance upon his family, and he must find a certain degree of autonomy. Often this process is thwarted by the selfish needs of his parents. Some parents are overprotective. Others are too quick to push the child out of the home. Either type of parental reaction may, under certain circumstances, make the child excessively concerned with his identity and status. Sometimes the adolescent feels he has no choice other than to react violently against his parents and adult society. He may prematurely disavow all dependency feelings. Or he may view explosive rebelliousness as the only behavior through which he can find a reasonable degree of freedom. Either reaction leads to behaviors which are likely to be defined as delinquent.

Adolescence is also a time when one begins to discover the deviousness, the inconsistencies, and the inadequacies of the adult world. The adolescent learns to perceive the double bind, and at this phase in his development he has some ability to break out of it. He is particularly sensitive to the issue of "phoniness." It may be that much of the rebelliousness of the adolescent is related to his discovery of fact and truth. Some delinquency may well represent an angry reaction to his disillusionment with the hypocrisy and the double standards of the adult world.

Finally, adolescence is also a time when man's tendency to form clubs, cliques, and other associations of peers reaches its peak. Many adolescent groups are organized around participation in antisocial activity. The gang is a particularly appropriate instrument for temporarily solving the problems of the oppressed adolescent.

A basic need provided by the gang is protection from other violent youth and sometimes from the police or other adults. The gang also offers friendship and an opportunity to find new identifications. It may be an outlet for aggressive energies or a social structure which allows many uncertain adolescents to prove their masculinity and worthwhileness. It is also true that the gang may, in itself, stimulate delinquency. Sometimes the gang becomes an autonomous force whose behavior is not predictable through an understanding of its individual members. A group of rebellious youngsters can be stimulated to perform more antisocial acts when together than any individual member would dare to perform alone (Geis, 1965).

During adolescence, youth are enormously influenced by peers. One of the traditional functions of gangs or peer groups has been to gradually acquaint the youngsters with certain ritualistic activities characteristic of the adult world which might at the same time be defined as delinquency if performed by those under the legal age of maturity. In past years, adolescent drinking was a major problem which worried our society. It was frowned upon by many in the adult world, but by and large drinking in moderation was tolerated, particularly among middle- and upper-class adolescents.

Because of changes in the overall direction of our society, which will be described later, there is a new and far more difficult problem today related to the adolescent's use of drugs. Marijuana, LSD, and other drugs are widely used on our university campuses, but they are also becoming quite prevalent in our high schools. The simple act of using or possessing these drugs is a serious offense for either an adult or a child. Selling illegal drugs, which is not an uncommon activity among high school students, is an extremely serious offense. A large proportion of adolescents do not believe that drugs are harmful, and they appreciate that they can gain status by using them. Adolescence then becomes an especially hazardous time since peer groups put much pressure upon many youths to indulge in a behavior which is clearly illegal. There are certain by-products of using marijuana and other illegal drugs which may make youth more susceptible to other forms of delinquency. The young person perceives that for the most part the drugs are not nearly as harmful to his well-being as he has been told by adult members of the community. He also knows that the chances of being apprehended for using drugs are extremely remote. He then begins to question the validity of other laws and to wonder whether they are based on as little substance as those which govern the control of marijuana and other drugs. There is also some danger that he will feel increasingly alienated from society. Once a youngster has broken a major law, he is less likely to be too conscience-ridden when he breaks other laws.

Similar considerations apply to the sexual conduct of adolescents. While the revolution in sexual behavior has not as yet caught up with the revolution in sexual attitudes, we can anticipate that more and more adolescents will be participating in a wider variety of sexual activity. The gang or peer group will support these activities. Yet most of these activities are still defined as illegal, and they place the adolescent in jeopardy of being adjudicated delinquent.

Sociological Theories

Sociological theories of delinquency are of two varieties. Some focus upon the process by which delinquency is learned in various social contexts. These theories are quite consistent with adaptational and other psychological models of behavior. Other sociological theories focus upon specific social stresses—upon those disruptions, inequities, and oppressions which exist within all societies and which exert a pernicious influence upon the behavior of the individual.

Sutherland's theory of differential association is a classical view of delinquency as a learned process (Sutherland & Cressey, 1960). Those sociologists who hold to this view see the future delinquent as a person who has been exposed to an excess of learning experiences favorable to a violation of law over learning experiences unfavorable to a violation of law. In recent years some sociologists have included under Sutherland's "definitions favorable to the violation of the law" defensive personality patterns which are used to rationalize and justify the criminal act even before it is committed (Sykes & Matza, 1956). Other sociologists have suggested that susceptibility to learning delinquent behavior is related to the individual's self-concept and identifications (Glaser, 1956). In expanding upon the basic theory of differential association, such sociologists are utilizing concepts which are quite familiar to psychologists and psychiatrists.

Other sociological theorists are concerned with the powerful impact of learned social roles upon delinquent behavior. A simplified definition of role is that it is a pattern or sequence of learned actions and attitudes which a person takes in an interaction situation. Some roles may be chosen by the individual, while others may be forced upon him by social situations. Once a role is learned, it takes on a certain power and autonomy of its own. The person who is put into a social role such as that of a delinquent gang member may experience himself as having had little alternative but to commit antisocial acts (Korn & McKorkle, 1959). Role therapists of course recognize that social climates which support delinquent rules are created by inequities and oppression within the greater society.

Those sociological theories which view delinquency as a product of conflict and disorganizations within a given culture seem richer and more diversified than the more general theories which view delinquency as learned behavior. Sellin (1938) has proposed that delinquency thrives when an individual is placed under social pressures which direct him to respond to norms or values that are at variance with those of the general culture. Such culture conflict arises through clashes or inconsistencies in the values of divergent social groups. Merton argues that success goals in the United States are not coordinated with available means to obtain such goals. He states: "The cultural demands made upon persons in this situation are incompatible. On the one hand they are asked to orient their conduct toward the prospect of accumulating wealth and on the other hand they are largely denied effective opportunities to do so institutionally" (1938). Merton believes that these inconsistencies produce anomie and social deviancy. Cloward and Ohlin (1960), expanding upon Merton's theory, argue that in the absence of legitimate means for obtaining success and wealth, the direction of delinquency will also be dependent on the kinds of illegitimate means which society can provide for obtaining similar goals. Cohen (1955) argues that the nonutilitarian malicious and negativistic actions of the juvenile delinquent arise as a frustrating response to his perception of middle-class values. Being unable to obtain the rewards of middle-class life, the delinquent develops a subculture whose values become a perversion or mockery of middle-class values.

Ecological theories of delinquency which developed in the 1920s have gained a new respectability in the past decade. Reasoning that the means by which humans compete for space and economic advantages must influence the direction of behavioral patterns, Burgess (1926) postulated that if one demarcated specific zones in a city radiating outward from the center, each

zone would be characterized by different stages of competitive adjustment and by different rates of crime. He postulated that delinquency would be highest in "interstitial zones," areas in the throes of change from residential dwellings to business activities, and that delinquency would be less prevalent as one moved away from the center of the city. With a few exceptions these findings have been consistently replicated (Shaw, Zorbaugh, McKay & Cottrece, 1929). In the present decade it seems apparent that the inner cores of our cities are populated by those who are exposed to unusually severe oppressive stress in the form of poverty and discrimination. In such settings opportunities to gain status through legitimate means are limited. Families with broken homes are common. A sense of alienation from the physical comforts and pleasures of middle-class life is a part of every child's upbringing. In view of such conditions, it should not be surprising that delinquency is so largely a matter of urban living.

Classical sociological theory has been limited and rendered somewhat sterile by its neglect of unconscious motivations and processes. Just as psychological theories have failed to account for a selective criminality of individuals with similar personality traits, so have sociological theories been unable to account for the selective criminality of individuals exposed to similar situations. In fairness, however, it should be noted that sociologists have been more ready than clinicians to comprehend the deficiencies of single-factor theorizing and are showing a new appreciation of the relevance of psychological variables.

Social Stress in the 1960s and 1970s
Granted the relevance of classical psychological and sociological theories of delinquency, they do not account for the widespread impression, if not the fact, that there has been more unrest among youth in this decade than our world has seen for some time. A discussion of the

issue of delinquency in modern American society would be incomplete without some emphasis upon that general oppressive stress which is characteristic of our modern technological world. In the rapidly changing world created by technology, everyone is a little restless, but the stresses seem to fall hardest upon youth. The young are naturally fearful of a future that does not promise a certain degree of stability. If they are to accept a conforming adaptation, they must have some hope of a better life, but they are now faced with a future that holds the threat of a distinctly unpleasant life.

Every child growing up in the United States has reason to wonder whether his life will end prematurely in nuclear holocaust, slow starvation, or respiratory failure caused by lack of proper air. At one time only cranks or religious fanatics worried about the end of the world. Today, knowledgeable scientists cooly talk about such possibilities, and when they speculate as to the gruesome consequences of overpopulation and pollution, few of their colleagues stand up to refute them. This is a severe oppressive stress whose impact upon the psyche of our youth is rarely acknowledged. While it is unlikely that young people can seriously contemplate the end of the world, they are so deluged with fearful facts regarding overpopulation and pollution that they do begin to fear for their future.

In a situation in which future gratifications seem remote, there is a natural tendency of man to search for gratifications in the present. Much of the demandingness of youth throughout the world may well be a result of their sensing the possibility of there being no world. One must take whatever he is going to get right now. The quality of searching for gratifications in the present used to be considered a maladaptive-lifestyle characteristic of those who are more or less psychopathic. Today, life in the present has certain adaptive advantages. At the same time, however, living in the present produces a demand

for immediate experience and gratification, which makes youth less likely to develop the patience and hope that go with a law-abiding existence. This tendency is illustrated by a popular quip of the late 1960s: "If you're sailing on the S.S. 'Titanic,' you might as well go first class."

Even if we reject the horrendous possibility of man's total annihilation, youth have reason to fear that overpopulation and pollution will lead to a world in which the gratifications provided by privacy and beauty will gradually disappear. Youth should be a time for optimism, but it is hard to find a young person today who is very hopeful for the world's future. Those who currently live in poverty see no way of getting out. Those who are more privileged recognize that underdeveloped and overpopulated racial groups and nations will not sit back and starve quietly while more fortunate people are allowed to enjoy wealth and peace. Our cities have always had their share of poverty. Yet those of us who have lived in cities in the 1960s have come to appreciate how much more oppressive, callous, and impersonal they become as they grow larger. Living in an overpopulated, dirty world is a severe stress, and when youth correctly foresee that things are more likely to get worse than better, they are justifiably restless.

Overpopulation and pollution are by-products of progress—progress in medicine and progress in technology. There are also more subtle stresses upon youth related to the process of technological growth itself. Technological progress has become so rapid and the rate of progress has increased so rapidly that we now live in a world in which nobody can predict the everyday conditions of life in 20, 10, or even 5 years. As a young person attempts to prepare himself for the future, he has no guidelines as to which psychological qualities will be adaptive. This too militates toward a life in the present. Those who work with youth have noticed that they are not nearly as impressed as the older generation with the relevance of such values as patience, hard work, and responsibility. Such values have meaning only when the rate of change of the conditions of everyday life has a certain stability or predictability (Kenniston, 1960).

As old values have been losing their influence, our society has been unable to develop a stable set of new values to replace them. It is very difficult for adults to try to tell children what is right and wrong. In today's world every value is debatable, whether it be chastity, marriage, fidelity, patriotism, success, or filial loyalty. Our youth drift in a climate of meaninglessness, a world in which an occasional antisocial act is not too likely to elicit guilt, remorse, or even self-questioning.

Our modern society also dramatizes the difference between the haves and the have-nots. The pleasures and conveniences associated with material comforts are so great that the deprivation of such comforts is maddening to those who do not have them. The media make the harsh realities of oppression known to everyone. A poor Negro youth knows how his affluent neighbors live because he can watch much of their behavior on television. The media also have a more general effect upon the entire population. It is very difficult to keep anything hidden from our youngsters. Youth learn the harsh realities of life at an earlier and earlier age. The media make it ridiculously easy to expose the hypocrisies of elders. Television, in particular, cruelly exposes the weaknesses of those who would serve as models or leaders. Few young people have any heroes these days. In such a social climate conformity is unlikely, but rebelliousness is favored.

As our society advances and changes with incredible rapidity, there is a new need for flexibility in our political, social, and ethical institutions. Yet as these institutions have grown and solidified, they have become less, rather than more, susceptible to change. This may be related in part to man's selfishness. No adult wants to change those things which he has had a part in creating because he fears that such change will adversely reflect upon the meaningfulness of his earlier works and beliefs. On the other hand, much of the inertia of our institutions is purely a product of their size. There are so many conflicting pressure and interest groups in our society that it is extremely difficult to develop the kind of communication and efficient assignation of power that will lead to useful social change. Youth are becoming increasingly skeptical of trying to bring about social change by working through conventional channels. In their disillusionment with the Establishment, they are ever more willing to break laws to express their grievances.

Some have argued that if we would end all military commitments and do away with racial discrimination our society could again gain a certain degree of stability. Certainly such changes would reduce the level of oppression experienced by large groups of youth in our society and might for a time be reflected in lower rates of delinquency. It should be noted, however, that youthful unrest and delinquency are worldwide phenomena which are characteristic of all societies today, including those which are peaceful and unfamiliar with racial prejudice. The psychological consequences of technological progress at this moment seem to be overwhelming to the youth of many nations. It is unlikely that we shall know much peace until we can find means of slowing the rate of technological change or until we can find better means of adapting to such change.

A Note on Female Delinquency

For the most part when young girls break the law, they do not victimize anyone but themselves. The two commonest forms of female delinquency, sexual promiscuity and running away from home, may offend society's sense of propriety, but they are in no sense dangerous to other individuals or to other persons' possessions. While there are some indications that stealing and fighting among girls may be increasing, female delinquency remains largely a self-destructive adaptation. The primary reason for labeling girls delinquent is that they tend to offend the community's values.

Unfortunately, it is also true that a girl is rarely adjudicated delinquent unless she comes from a lower-class family. Middle- or upper-class girls are practically never seen in training schools. Yet it is obvious that promiscuity, shoplifting, and drug usage are not confined to the lower classes. Quite often the lower-class girl is viewed as delinquent because her family is in conflict and is unable to bear the twin burdens of their child's troublesome behavior and poverty. Sometimes the main motivation for putting a troublesome child out of the way is an economic one. If she sexually tempts her father or embarrasses or threatens her mother, she creates levels of family tension which her parents are unwilling to tolerate.

Many girls who regularly participate in rule-breaking behavior demonstrate a collection of character traits which constitute what psychiatrists refer to as the *hysterical personality.* Such girls are often seductive, flirtatious, and promiscuous. They tend to dramatize their plight in a histrionic manner. They are prone to periods of deep depression and anxiety which follow one another with rapidity. Such individuals have a certain degree of flexibility in that their "radar" is exquisitely tuned to the environment. Above all, such girls are illness-prone and extremely dependent (Chodoff & Lyons, 1958).

The girl who develops hysterical personality traits has despaired of obtaining gratification in life through direct, honest means, usually because she has been deprived and exploited in her relationships with her parents. Often she has been rejected by her mother and has turned to her father for gratification of oral needs. Too often the father-daughter relationship becomes eroticized and may be characterized by overt sexual interaction. During adolescence such girls will run away when they are threatened by erotic feelings toward paternal figures, and in their search for nurturance and comfort from others they tend to be sexually promiscuous.

The hysterical delinquent girl learns to deal with what she perceives as a basically oppressive world by attempting to control others through her passivity. She is skilled in using "helpless" roles to manipulate others. She has also learned to move through life as though she were not responsible for any of her actions. Such traits are particularly conducive to those socially deviant behaviors associated with the feminine role which our society chooses to define as delinquent (Halleck, 1967a).

TREATMENT OF THE JUVENILE DELINQUENT

There are three different varieties of activity which allow the mental health clinician to make a contribution to the treatment of delinquents. In recent years there has been significant expansion of opportunities for clinicians to involve themselves in programs for the prevention of delinquency. There has also been an increasing tendency for juvenile courts to seek the advice of experts in human behavior when determining the disposition of their clients. Finally, the clinician has always been accepted whenever he has been willing to lend his services to the institutional or outpatient treatment of the individual delinquent.

Prevention

The expansion of community mental health resources makes it possible for more and more clinicians to collaborate with agencies that are working to prevent delinquency. In stable middle-class communities the clinician is able to assist the treatment process by offering increased understanding of behavior to those who have the primary responsibility for dealing with the child. He is also able to assist in the process of finding cases of youth who appear likely to have future antisocial difficulty. Often he can, in a very few sessions, help resolve the problems of individual delinquents by working directly with the disturbed boy, with his family, or with his social worker.

Community mental health in an impoverished, overcrowded neighborhood is a somewhat different matter. The clinician must work not only with disturbed individuals and families but also within a social milieu which is basically oppressive. Here the prevention of delinquency must begin with the society making an effort to change those oppressive conditions which create delinquency. The clinician who involves himself in such communities must invariably become something of a social activist, a person who is constantly trying to change those political and social conditions which oppress minorities and the poor. Much is accomplished by setting up programs which provide jobs and educative skills, programs such as the Job Corps, the Teachers Corps, and Head Start, which are efforts to compensate for the retardation that takes place when one grows up in poverty. The administration of such programs does not require exceptional skills in the behavioral sciences. Those clinicians who involve themselves in these programs either rely on their own administrative skills or help other administrators by offering consultative services.

It should be clear that the crucial forces which affect delinquency rates are outside the sphere of influence of the clinician. In this regard it is interesting to speculate as to the future effects of the new black militancy. Under some circumstances black militancy seems to reduce rates of delinquency. Here there is a question of whether the militancy itself will become defined as delinquency. If it does not, it will quite likely lead to a kind of purpose, a pride in race, and a new sense of identity which will stabilize the black community.

Juvenile courts. The system of correctional justice for juveniles has been based largely upon a medical model of treatment. When the first juvenile court in the United States was established in Cook County, Illinois, in 1899, its aim was to offer adolescent offenders individualized justice and treatment, rather than impartial justice and punishment (Davidoff & Joestel, 1951). Today all juvenile courts are at least in principle committed to the same aims. The child who is adjudicated delinquent is not a criminal. He retains status, and his disposition is determined is much the same way as that of a person who is legally defined as mentally ill.

The principles under which the courts operate are in theory benevolent, but in practice the juvenile courts often perpetrate certain injustices. An obvious problem is that the suspected delinquent is not afforded due process. He can be arrested and institutionalized without any proof that he committed a crime. The recent Galt decision allows him to be assisted by an attorney, but he is still in jeopardy of being committed to an institution for activities which are not defined as crimes when they are carried out by adults. This is especially true in the case of girls.

Some have argued that the current juvenile court system puts the adolescent in a situation in which he is discriminated against by the rest of society (Ketcham, 1961; Tappan, 1949). Some even consider this kind of oppression to be an important cause of delinquency (Matza, 1964). Certainly too many children are institutionalized simply to serve the needs of inadequate parents or to placate an enraged community rather than to serve the needs of the child. These practices are especially discriminatory against members of the lower socioeconomic classes.

The medical model of treatment of juvenile delinquency is justifiable if the child is actually provided with the kind of treatment he needs. This is unlikely to happen in the majority of our juvenile institutions. Many of them are no less cruel or barbaric than adult prisons. The problem is compounded by indeterminate commitment laws which allow the court to keep the child institutionalized until he reaches the age of 21. An especially frightening aspect of juvenile court systems is that a child confined to a juvenile institution can be transferred to an adult institution even if he has never committed a criminal act. When a child becomes a serious disciplinary problem in the training school and particularly as juvenile institutions become overcrowded, he is in jeopardy of being transferred to an adult prison.

In practice, the courts commit too many children to institutions who simply do not have to be there. Most of those who are committed could be adequately treated in the community if the proper agencies were alerted and if the proper resources were available. It is likely that for most delinquents who are committed to training institutions, the harmful experiences they encounter will exceed their beneficial experiences. It is in this area that the mental health clinician can be extremely useful to the courts. He can demonstrate the relative harmlessness of so many delinquent acts and can recommend the many simple and inexpensive social and psychological treatments which can be carried on in the community and which will in all likelihood produce better results, and certainly far less expensive results, than institutionalization. He can also offer direct therapeutic services to those who come before the court and in so doing provide

the judge with an immediate option other than institutionalization.

Psychotherapy

While the majority of training schools do not provide adequate social, educational, or psychological treatment, there are some notable exceptions. Programs of treatment have been developed which have been based upon psychoanalytic group interactional and upon behavioral models. The Boys Industrial School in Topeka is an outstanding example of an institution which has been able to provide psychotherapy for most of its clients and which has introduced principles of mental hygiene into the daily living situation. Sociologists, using the technique of guided group interaction, have in a number of institutions reported that combining a work program with constant group attention to the maladaptive nature of the individual boy's delinquency produces excellent results. A few institutions have been experimenting with systems of carefully measured reward and punishment based on the new techniques of behavior therapy. The use of aversive conditioning techniques on involuntary clients certainly raises certain ethical questions. Programs based on rewarding acceptable behavior are more immune to this criticism. Those who have been using operant techniques with delinquents seem enthusiastic about their results, although they have thus far not comprehensively reported them in the literature.

Beginning with Aichorn, psychoanalysts and other therapists have demonstrated the value of psychotherapy for delinquents. Individual or group psychotherapy with delinquents is an effective treatment when available. The problem is that the availability of such treatments is restricted almost entirely to the middle and upper classes.

Psychotherapy with delinquents is primarily an educative process in which the young person learns to discriminate between oppression which is imposed upon him by others and oppression which he brings upon himself. The delinquent is encouraged to continue to react to, and defend himself against, real oppressions in his life. At the same time he learns to understand and control his maladaptive responses to internal conflicts which cause him to see more oppression than actually exists. Psychotherapy with adolescents is unlikely to be effective unless the therapist is rigidly honest with his client. The therapist must define his purposes, must clarify his dual responsibilities to his client and his community, and must recognize the appropriateness of many of the delinquent's aggressive responses. The therapist must also be prepared to be a "real person" in his interactions with the delinquent. This means that he must be willing to communicate his values and even his prejudices whenever they are relevant to the delinquent's situation

In the past few years therapists have been learning that much can be accomplished through family therapy, that is by conducting interviews with two or more members of the family at the same time. Family therapy clarifies the nature of oppression and conflict within the family unit. It is a technique which allows the therapist to suggest small modifications in the power structure of the family which will have large and favorable effects upon the family member who is defined as the patient. As family members learn to stop hurting one another and to start helping one another, the possibility that any member of the family unit will engage in highly maladaptive behavior decreases. While family therapy with delinquents has not yet been utilized on a large scale, our experiences with nondelinquent families and our theoretical knowledge of delinquency suggest that it may eventually become the most important therapeutic resource for dealing with antisocial behavior.

REFERENCES

Aichorn, A. *Wayward youth.* New York: Viking Press, 1935.

Alexander, F. The neurotic character. *International Journal of Psychoanalysis,* 1930, **11,** 292–311.

Anderson, V. V. Mental disease and delinquency. *Mental Hygiene,* 1919, **3,** 177–198.

Bandura, A., & Walters, R. H. Dependency conflicts in aggressive delinquents. *Journal of Social Issues,* 1958, **14,** 52–65.

Bandura, A., & Walters, R. H. *Adolescent aggression.* New York: Ronald Press, 1959.

Bateson, J., Jackson, D., Haley, J., & Weakland, J. Toward a theory of schizophrenia. *Behavioral Sciences,* 1955, **1,** 251–264.

Becker, W. C. Consequences of different kinds of parental discipline. In M. L. Hoffman & L. N. W. Hoffman (Eds.), *Review of child development research.* Vol. 1. New York: Russell Sage, 1964.

Berman, L. Crime and the endocrine gland. *American Journal of Psychiatry,* 1932, **12,** 215–235.

Blos, P. *On adolescence: A psychoanalytical interpretation.* New York: Free Press, 1962.

Bowlby, J. *Maternal care and mental health.* World Health Organization, Monogr. Series, No. 2, 1951.

Burgess, E. W. The natural area as the unit for social work in the large city. *Proceedings of the National Conference of Social Work,* 1926.

Burt, C. *The young delinquent.* London: University of London Press, 1944.

Chodoff, P., & Lyons, H. Hysteria: The hysterical personality and hysterical conversion. *American Journal of Psychiatry,* 1958, **114,** 734–740.

Cloward, R. A., & Ohlin, L. E. Illegitimate mean and delinquent sub cultures. *Delinquency and opportunity.* Glencoe, Ill.: Free Press, 1960. Pp. 145–152.

Cohen, A. Juvenile delinquency and the social structure. Doctoral Dissertation, Harvard University, 1951.

Cohen, A. K. *Delinquent boys.* New York: Free Press, 1955.

Cohen, A. K., & Short, J. F. Juvenile delinquency. In R. K. Merton & R. A. Nisbet (Eds.), *Contemporary social problems.* (2nd ed.) New York: Harcourt, Brace, 1966. Pp. 84–136.

Davidoff, E., & Joestel, E. S. *The child guidance approach to juvenile delinquency.* New York: Child Care Publication, 1951.

Eissler, F. (Ed.). *Searchlights on delinquency.* New York: International Universities Press, 1948.

Eysenck, H. J. *Crime and personality.* Boston: Houghton Mifflin, 1964.

Friedlander, K. Formation of the anti-social character. In *The psychoanalytic study of the child.* Vol. 1. New York: International Universities Press, 1945. Pp. 189–204.

Geis, G. *Juvenile gangs.* Washington: Presidents' Committee on Juvenile Delinquency and Youth Crime, 1965.

Gibbons, D. *Changing the law breaker.* Englewood Cliffs, N. J.: Prentice-Hall, 1965.

Glaser, D. Criminality theories and behavioral images. *American Journal of Sociology,* 1956, **61,** 433–445.

Glueck, S., & Glueck, E. *Physique and delinquency.* New York: Harper, 1956.

Haley, J. *Strategies of psychotherapy.* New York: Grune & Stratton, 1963.

Halleck, S. L. Psychopathy, freedom and crime. *Bulletin of the Menninger Clinic,* 1966, **30,** 127–140.

Halleck, S. L. The hysterical personality. *Archives of General Psychiatry,* 1967, **16,** 730–737. (a)

Halleck, S. L. *Psychiatry and the dilemmas of crime.* New York: Hoeber-Harper, 1967. (b)

Halleck, S. L. The process of student unrest. *Proceedings of the New York Academy of Medicine.* (In press.)

Healy, W. *The individual delinquent.* Boston: Little, Brown, 1915.

Hill, D., & Watterson, D. Electroencephalographic studies of psychopathic personalities. *Journal of Neurology and Psychiatry,* 1952, **5,** 47.

Hooton, E. A. *Crime and the man.* Cambridge, Mass.: Harvard University Press, 1939.

Johnson, A. M. Juvenile delinquency. In S. Arieti (Ed.), *American handbook of psychiatry.* Vol. 1. New York: Basic Books, 1959. Pp. 840–856.

Johnson, A., & Szurek, S. A. The genesis of anti-social acting out in children and adults. *The Psychoanalytic Quarterly,* 1952, **21,** 323–343.

Kardiner, A., & Ovesey, L. *The mark of oppression: Psychosocial study of the American Negro.* New York: Norton, 1951.

Kenniston, D. *The uncommitted.* New York: Harcourt, Brace, 1960.

Ketcham, W. The unfulfilled promise of the

juvenile court. *Crime and Delinquency*, 1961, **7**, 97–130.

Korn, R. W., & McKorkle, L. W. *Criminology and penalogy.* New York: Holt, 1959.

Lampl-DeGroot, J. Neurotics, delinquents and ideal formation. In F. Eissler (Ed.), *Searchlights on delinquency.* New York: International Universities Press, 1949. Pp. 248–258.

Lombroso, C. *Crime: Its causes and remedies.* (Trans. by H. P. Horton). Boston: Little, Brown, 1911.

Matza, D. *Delinquency and drift.* New York: Wiley, 1964.

McCord, N., & McCord, J. *Psychopathy and delinquency.* New York: Grune & Stratton, 1956.

McCord, N., McCord J., & Zola, I. K. *Origins of crime.* New York: Columbia University Press, 1959.

McLearn, G. E. *Genetics and behavioral development.* In M. L. Hoffman & L. N. W. Hoffman (Eds.), *Review of child development research.* New York: Russell Sage, 1964. Pp. 433–481.

Merton, R. Social structure and anomie. *American Sociological Review*, 1938, **3**, 672–682.

Montagu, A. The biologist looks at crime. *Annals of the American Academy of Political and Social Science*, 1951, **217**, 55.

Polani, P. E. Occurrence and effect of human chromosome abnormalities. In R. Platt & A. S. Parkes (Eds.), *Society symposium: Social and genetic influences on life and death.* New York: Plenum Press, 1967.

Sellin, T. Culture conflict and crime. *Social Science Research Council Bulletin 41,* 1938.

Shaw, C. R., Zorbaugh, G. H., McKay, H. D., & Cottrece, L. S. *Delinquency areas.* Chicago: University of Chicago Press, 1929.

Sheldon, W. H. *Varieties of delinquent youth.* New York: Harper, 1949.

Sutherland, E., & Cressey, D. *Principles of criminology.* (6th ed.) Philadelphia: Lippincott, 1960.

Sykes, G. M., & Matza, D. Techniques of neutralization: A theory of delinquency. *American Sociological Review,* 1956, **21**, 744–746.

Tappan, P. W. Who is the criminal? *American Sociological Review,* 1947, **12**, 96–182.

Tappan, P. W. *Juvenile delinquency.* New York: McGraw-Hill, 1949.

Thompson, G. N. *The psychopathic delinquent and criminal.* Springfield, Ill.: Charles C Thomas, 1953.

Vold, G. *Theoretical criminology.* New York: Oxford University Press, 1958.

Yarrow, L. J. Separation from parents in early childhood. In M. L. Hoffman & L. N. W. Hoffman (Eds.), *Child development research.* Vol. 1. New York: Russell Sage, 1964. Pp. 89–137.

17 | Phallic-Oedipal Development: Deviations and Psychopathology of Sexual Behavior in Children[1]

John A. Sours

In any discussion of psychosexual deviations and psychopathology, it is important to consider normal patterns of development during the phallic-Oedipal stage as well as the developmental sequences and variations that antedate this stage, make it possible, and lead to disturbances during the phallic-Oedipal years and throughout development into adulthood.

The *phallic-Oedipal phase* of development—also called the *nursery school years,* the *preschool years,* and the *stage of initiative versus guilt* (Maier, 1965; Mussen, 1965)—takes place between 3 and 5 years of age. There are, however, variations from child to child in its chronology. Some aspects of developmental issues during this phase may be seen any time from 3 to 7 years. Its features are usually clear-cut and distinguishable by the time the child is 5 years old. Personality traits are, in many respects, well established, though subject to modification and emendation during latency and adolescent de-

velopment. The component parts of the phallic-Oedipal phase (A. Freud, 1965; S. Freud, 1955a, 1955b, 1961a, 1961b)[2] include the phenomena of infantile sexuality (Frank, 1949; Spitz, 1965), discovery of sex differences, sexual curiosity, erotic-genital exploration, sexual play, and attachment to the contrasexual parent with expectation of loss of love, injury, and retaliation from the isosexual parent (Chodoff, 1967). Castration anxiety is the pivotal force in the Oedipal situation.

During the course of the phallic-Oedipal period the child strives to increase his capacities in many areas. He comes alive with energy and initiative. Erikson refers to the *phallic-intrusive* mode of development: "being on the make," "making," and pleasure in the conquest (Baldwin, 1967; Maier, 1965; Mead, 1958). This behavior is more marked in boys, but has its counterpart in girls in terms of reaching out, "catching," and

[1] The study on which this chapter is based was supported in part by N.I.M.H. Career Teacher Grant 1T1 MH-10066-01.

[2] In the references to the works of Freud in this chapter, the dates in parentheses are the dates of publication of the *Standard Edition,* not the original dates of publication, which appear in the References.

being more attractive and endearing in both the human and the nonhuman worlds. For the girl, the mother becomes the anticipatory rival.

The child is now able to conceptualize his place in his family and his relationship to other people in general. He assumes a social role in his group, and his sex role becomes more clearly defined. He receives indications, starting at about the age of 3 to 4 years, that he is no longer a small child, but on the other hand he quickly realizes that he is hardly an adult. He repeatedly suffers defeat and humiliation in his competitions and transactions with his family, nursery school teachers, and peer group. His aspirations are inevitably frustrated. He fumbles his way through his fears and failures and tries to remain hopeful.

He asks many questions about the relationship of his parents. He becomes curious about genital differences and reproduction. He is now more apt to ask his mother whether he can marry her. Whatever he tries now reinforces his sense of inferiority, anxiety, and guilt. He is smaller than adults. He is not as strong. He is unable to run as fast. He cannot throw a ball as well as his father. He wants to drive his father's car and run his father's power mower and snowblower. His sense of failure reinforces his feeling of smallness and his overawareness of genital underdevelopment. His phallic-Oedipal struggle meets with defeat, which is much like his experience in toilet training, when he attempted to assert his power and autonomy. It is a hopeless fantasized situation which leads to guilt and resignation. The joys of his giant fantasies turn to the horrors of his monster dreams.

EGO DEVELOPMENT DURING THE PHALLIC-OEDIPAL PERIOD

In order to reach the phallic phase of psychosexual development and then to resolve the Oedipal conflict, a considerable degree of maturation (Barton, 1966) and learning (Flavell, 1963; Laurendeau & Pinard, 1962) is required, as well as experience in socialization both within the family and in peer groups (Mussen, 1965). Between the ages of 3 and 5, the average boy grows about 5 inches and gains almost 10 pounds. The average girl is slightly shorter and lighter. Growth is very rapid during the preschool years; by the fifth year, 75 percent of the weight increase is due to muscular development. The most rapid organ development through the phallic period is that of the central nervous system. By the time the child is 5 years old, 90 percent of the nervous system has developed (Mussen, 1965). Myelination has been completed in the higher brain centers. Although genital organs are morphologically immature at this time, the neural system controlling erotic excitement and orgasm is intact, but the threshold for stimulation remains comparatively high until sexual hormones are secreted in puberty and the threshold for erotic stimuli is lowered (Beach, 1965; MacLean, 1962).

Psychomotor development by the age of 4 years permits smoother movements, better running, and standing broad jumps. There is less totality in body movements. Yet the child is still awkward in overhand throwing. At 5 years of age the child has a better sense of balance but is still unable to hop, skip, and jump smoothly. Fine digital movements are better executed. He is now able to pick up pellets smoothly, draw straight strokes, and copy squares and triangles. Consequently, he has many adult motor patterns which allow him to use tools and more complicated toys with some skill. Now able to throw a ball more smoothly, the child can better engage in sports, which can put the boy in more direct competitive contact with his father. With his new motor skills he tries to play the roles of engineer, truck driver, athlete, and other model figures who seem to have power in their environments.

Language development has progressed from the basic phonemes to the simple sounds or morphemes which are developed at the age of 3. Morphological rules which are necessary for the construction of words and syntactical rules are learned to some extent by the age of 5 years. Thus, the 5-year-old child can organize subject, predicate, and adjectives into sentences with a good choice of vocabulary. Through the use of words the child is able to decrease fantasy time and ludic play, establish connections between thoughts and words, and make increasing strides toward closer object relations. He uses language to describe, classify, and better comprehend phenomena he encounters every day.

At age 3 his use of words is undifferentiated and syncretic. Words stand for objects and events as well as actions and fantasies. For a 3-year-old a dog is in the class of all animals with four feet. A child syncretically thinks of words such as "eat" as meaning food and being fed, as well as the process of eating. At age 5, however, words are differentiated in meanings to apply to specific objects and events. Classes of objects and things in common are now possible.

In his communications the child is egocentric up to age 4 to 5. He is unable to put himself in the place of others. As he passes through the phallic-Oedipal period, his object relations and transactions become sociocentric. His speech becomes more socially oriented. Fantastic and symbolic play is less employed as the child moves during the latency years into sociocentric communications with his peer group. The child now has less need for fantasies and imaginary companions. There is less need for dramatizations of different roles.

As a child develops in the phallic-Oedipal period, his perceptual capacities increase (Baldwin, 1967; Falkner, 1966; Hoffman & Hoffman, 1964, 1966; Kidd & Rivoire, 1966). A preschool child can better differentiate stimuli in his environment. Stimuli become more distinct when specific language labels can be applied to them. By the age of 5 years, the child can label the compo-

nent parts of stimuli. He is now able to attend to both the whole and the part. A 5-year-old, however, has difficulty in detecting differences between shapes and mirror images. Only with increasing age can the child regard spatial organization of objects as relevant dimensions. This is due in part to his learning the labels "right" and "left" as well as "up" and "down."

It is difficult in the intellectual development of the child to separate perception and language from cognition. The child's intellectual ability is dependent upon the acquisition of language, increasing memory capacity, the differentiation of perceptual experiences, and the learning of rules of mathematics and logic and their application (Decarie, 1965; Kidd & Rivoire, 1966; Laurendeau & Pinard, 1962). From age 2 to age 4, according to Piaget, the child begins to form a representational world (Flavell, 1963). During the preconceptual phase of intelligence, the child develops a symbolic representation of the world. He acquires labels for the things that he now perceives. From age 4 to age 7, he is better able to articulate simple representations. He now can construct more complicated images and more elaborate concepts. Nevertheless, his understanding of concepts is still based on the perceptual aspects of the stimulus. For instance, at 4 years his concept of quality is dependent upon the perceptual aspect of the stimuli. Beads in a tall, cylindrical jar are thought to be greater in quantity than the same number held in a short, squat jar. From age 5 to age 7, however, the child begins to understand that the amount of the beads remains constant regardless of changes in the shape of the containers. Thus, the phallic-Oedipal child adds thought to his perception and is better able to comprehend his world. This is what Piaget means when he says that the phallic child develops the capacities of reversibility and conservation.

The child's relationship with his peers changes as he enters the phallic-Oedipal stage. Up until age 3, his peers are relatively unimportant to him. Reciprocal play is minimal. His contacts with children stylistically reflect his learning experience at home. In the nursery school situation, however, the child finds that many of his responses which his parents rewarded prove unacceptable elsewhere and, in fact, that they result in punishment, shame, or rejection. This awareness brings about changes in his social behavior as he moves into the preschool years. The child goes from solitary to parallel play, then to cooperative play, and finally to reciprocal play. His play activity is important not only for the discharge of energy but also for the practice of new skills and the opportunity to try new roles and modes of behavior.

Thus, the phallic-Oedipal phase of development is both a psychosocial and a psychosexual period with considerable developmental overlap. In order to complete this phase of the development and the resolution of the Oedipal situation in his family, a child must reach a considerably higher level of maturation, both cognitive and perceptual, as well as learning and socialization within the family. Psychosocially, the child's main emphasis is on the realization of goals, many of which can be gratified only in play and fantasy. Genital arousal and pleasure are obtainable only through fantasy, masturbation, and sexual exploration.

A male-female gender polarity is apparent even at the phallic-Oedipal phase. The child often feels guilt over his initiative when he approaches people or seeks goals which belong to others or when he approaches them in a way reserved for others. This is an important aspect of the Oedipal situation. The boy wants to take over his mother; the girl wants to be like the mother in order to take over the father. The boy does in his fantasies what his father can do in everyday life. And this provides a fertile soil for guilt feelings which can undercut the child's sense of initiative. His guilt is much greater than the

shame and doubt he experienced at the anal-muscular stage of development. Ideally, the child has enough initiative left after his multiple disappointments and guilt feelings so that he can still optimistically enter first grade and commence his stage of industry.

Each child has a unique Oedipal experience determined by his earlier intrapsychic years, the external and internal events of the phallic period, his interactions with his parents, his instinctual drives, and the extent of his ego development. Death, illness, the birth of a new sibling, and sexual seduction are further influences on phallic-Oedipal development.

MALE PHALLIC PSYCHOSEXUAL DEVELOPMENT

The boy early in his phallic stage becomes aware of anatomical gender differences (Casuso, 1957). His recognition of the male genitalia helps him in his identification with his father, brothers, and male peers. It enables the boy to feel that he can do what his father does and gives him an increased awareness of his father's relationship with his mother, particularly what he thinks his father does with his mother. The boy wants to exhibit his phallus to his mother. He may ask her to go to the bathroom with him, or he may openly exhibit himself at bedtime or bathtime. His fantasy of the penis is one in which it is used as a penetrating instrument. It is seen also as an instrument of pleasure—at first as part of pleasurable body areas and later as a special pleasure structure of the body, which he has discovered through masturbation, exhibition, and sex play.

The boy sees himself as a little man; his father is his adult rival. His mother is the object of his pleasures, around whom he weaves a not too innocent "romance." He may become very protective of his mother, imitating his father in this respect, or he may mock or openly attack his father.

Another alternative for him is to play games involving the father's role. He may make up stories and fantasies about larger rivals whom he easily overcomes, like "Jack and the Beanstalk." The father's size, dominance, and strength, however, make his competition pointless. The father is a threatening figure, and the threat he represents takes the form of castration anxiety, which ushers in a new developmental aspect. The threat may exist solely in the child's fantasies and have no relationship to the intimidation. The conflict around castration eventually leads to a repudiation of his Oedipal wishes through suppression, repression, and a shift in defense organization. Evidence for this developmental sequence is found in children's play and fantasies, fairy tales, anthropological studies of totemic animals, dreams, children's graphic productions, and psychoanalytic reconstructive data.

The boy may be stirred to a jealous rage against his mother because of her rejection of his wishes for exclusive possession of her. This can either reinforce or give rise to his wish to kill her and to be loved by the father in her place. The negative Oedipal complex can also lead to fears of injury and castration which also must be repressed. Fears of retaliation by an omnipotent parent, conflicts over love and admiration and longing and dependency, and fears of parental disapproval and punishment for wanting to destroy a younger sibling can occur. Both negative and positive wishes in the Oedipal period arouse castration anxiety.

The readiness of the boy to respond to this situation with fear of castration has a number of possible determinants. The erogenous phallus is an object of attention, pleasure, and fantasy. The boy's concern with uncontrollable phallic tumescence gives rise to fears that his fantasies may be exposed to his parents. His discovery of the female external genitalia leads him to conclude that the girl has lost a penis. Direct and indirect threats of punishment from either the father or the mother reinforce this fantasy. In addition, his earlier experiences of losing the breast in weaning and in losing feces in defecation are pre-Oedipal experiences antecedent to body loss and castration anxiety. Castration anxiety can be manifested by overt concern with the body, excessive fear of injury, phobias, and nightmares. The boy must resolve his Oedipal conflict by renouncing his wishes or by holding them in check through superego controls, available defense mechanisms, and other ego techniques for resolution of conflict.

FEMALE PHALLIC PSYCHOSEXUAL DEVELOPMENT

The girl's psychosexual development is much more complicated and less well understood than the boy's (Benedek, 1963). Her desire to play the man does not flounder on castration fear. The girl is psychosexually much like the boy, starting out with the mother as the main libidinal object (Kestenberg, 1956). Her earliest erotic fantasies also involve the mother as object. At ages 2 and 3 the little girl begins showing a preference for the father. Much like the boy, the girl begins to masturbate. The clitoris becomes the main erogenous zone. It is here that a gender difference in psychosexual development is thought to occur. Later in her development, particularly during adolescence, the girl was thought to make a switch from the clitoris to the vagina as the primary erogenous zone. Research in female sexuality, however, has disproved this theory (Chodoff, 1967). The second decisive gender difference occurs when the little girl must shift her libidinal strivings from her first object, the mother, to the father in order to achieve adult heterosexual status. This theoretical construct, unlike the previous one, still is correct; it is readily seen in mid-adolescent girls as well as in girls during the phallic stage. Turning from the mother to the father may be abrupt or quite gradual. The shift can also involve a great deal of antagonism and hostility toward the mother. Frequently, the girl registers many complaints about her mother. The shift occurs at the time the little girl notices anatomical differences between herself and a male child. Her first impulse is to repudiate the sexual difference. She may later attempt a masculine identification. The fantasy of having been deprived of the penis by the mother furthers her antagonism toward the mother and increases her fear of the latter's retaliation. The wish for the penis facilitates interest in the father and brothers. Penis envy, evidenced by shame, inferiority, jealousy, and rage, is quite common. The girl shows a passive wish for the father's penis. She turns to the father as her principal love object. Sooner or later rebuffed by the father, she is forced to renounce and repent her Oedipal wishes. Castration analogues for the girl are jealousy and a sense of mortification as well as a fear of genital injury, which is partly a consequence of the wish to be penetrated and impregnated by the father.

Between the ages of 2 and 4 years, children of both sexes derive an increasing sense of pleasure from genital stimulation, particularly masturbation. The boy discovers his penis, and the girl is quickly made aware of her deficiency. The phallic child displays marked body curiosity. He explores his body, checking every orifice. There is a marked increase in body narcissism, manifested not only by a preoccupation with body functions but also by the child's dread of injury. The slightest injury is regarded by the child as worthy of a band-aid. The discovery of sexual differences suggests to the boy that the little girl has lost her penis (Casuso, 1957; Jones, 1933). He is then frightened that he too may suffer the same fate. He may resort to ego-defensive maneuvers and feel that everybody is built like himself. He may try to convince himself that the little girl has a penis which is hidden inside her vulva, or he may believe that the girl's penis will grow back someday. He may openly exhibit himself. He may play games in which he hides his penis between his legs and allows it to pop forth. He may displace to other parts of his body his concern over castration. He may deprecate girls. His anxiety may lead to increased masturbation, which is done as a way of reassuring himself that his penis is still intact, or he may threaten others with castration. The little girl, on the other hand, may deny the fact that she has no penis. She may feel that the mother took it away from her. She may repress her awareness of anatomical differences until she reaches adolescence. A child's view of parents' external genitalia can intensify castration fears. The boy feels inferior to his father. The little girl is frightened of her father's penis. A boy may think that his mother's penis is inside her pubic hair. Visual or auditory awareness of parental intercourse is exciting, stimulating, or frightening to the child. Because of muscular activity, sounds of breathing, and vocal noises the child may view parental intercourse as an act of aggression. A child's awareness of a mother's pregnancy is another source of information during this stage of development. The pregnancy can be seen as a result of ingestion through the mouth, and the birth as a result of and expulsion from the anus.

Only a few systematic observations of childhood sexual behavior have been made (Kinsey, 1948; Ramsey, 1943; Reevy, 1961). Childhood sexual responsiveness, defined in terms of stimulation of one's own or another's genitals for pleasure, denoting a response to genital stimulation analogous by adult standards to manifest sexual excitement, is verifiable by clinical and anthropological data. Ford and Beach (1951) found that preadolescent children, by the age of 6 to 8 years, openly masturbate. Malinowski, in his studies in Melanesia, made observations of societies in which childhood sexuality is openly permitted and expressed. Furthermore, children in Melanesian, African, and Indian tribes actively participate in sexual intercourse several years before the onset of puberty. They receive active instruction from the older members of the society. Prepubertal children have the capacity to respond sexually before the onset of pubescence. Ramsey and Kinsey demonstrated by surveys that exhibitionism, homosexual play, masturbatory behavior, and attempted intercourse are readily observable at the age of 6 and increase in frequency through middle childhood and adolescence. Furthermore, observations, including those of Kinsey, strongly suggest that even infants are capable of orgasmic responses. Kinsey suggested that about one-third of boys are capable of orgasm within the first year. The number rises to about 80 percent before the coming of puberty.

PRE-OEDIPAL SEXUAL IDENTIFICATION AND LOVE OBJECTS

Both the male and the female child have initially an undifferentiated primary identification with the mother (Blauvelt & McKenna, 1961; Bowlby et al., 1956; Brenner, 1957; Kagan, 1965; Koff, 1961; Lampl-DeGroot, 1946; Sperling, 1963; Spitz, 1955, 1964, 1965; Yarrow, 1964). Later the child internalizes parts of both parents (Koff, 1961). At around 2½ or 3 years, the girl imitates the mother and carries on a flirtation with the father. At this stage most of her investment is with the mother, and in this sense the little girl is experiencing her negative Oedipal complex. With separation, individuation, and autonomy, the little girl proceeds into the positive Oedipal complex, in which she reaches out much more affirmatively toward the father. She aggressively devalues the mother. For the girl, the negative Oedipus complex involves transfer of her aggression to the father; she attaches her libidinal drives to the Oedipal mother. For the male at age 2 to 3½, the identification shifts from the mother to the father. The boy, in his negative Oedipal feelings, remains aggressively attached to the

mother and regards her as engulfing, overprotecting, and often ungiving. If he can resolve these feelings, he will then switch in his allegiances to the mother and transfer his aggression to the father. The mother is now valued, and the father is seen as a competitor.

If his development cannot proceed in this phase-specific way, his feminine attachment to his father will intensify. He remains aggressively attached to the mother, with whom he identifies. The boy then is in a passive stage in which he subordinates his active wishes for his mother. In later development, if no Oedipal resolution is made, a separation of tenderness from sexuality occurs. In the Madonna-prostitute complex, the Madonna is the Oedipal woman, and the prostitute is the pre-Oedipal deprecated female. In the negative Oedipus complex, there are two possibilities. The boy may have sexual wishes toward the father in which he wants to put himself in the father's place and play a passive role. The boy may also want to supplant the mother and be loved by the father.

In early ego-identification the child proceeds from his primary identification to a bisexual identification with both parents, with increasing contrasexual intensification of castration fear. Eventually, Oedipal resolution takes place. In the process of identification the child internalizes the parental values and attitudes. An internalized image is created in which the ego takes over characteristics of the parental image. The ego-identification leads to prohibiting and facilitating superego functions. In the Oedipal resolution, the superego becomes independent of the ego and goes on during latency to modify its form and function.

THE OEDIPUS COMPLEX

The Oedipus complex is seen as a triadic developmental family phenomenon involving the child's sexual strivings which brings him face to face with erotic feelings toward the parent of the opposite sex. The desire for affection and stimulation from the contrasexual parent forces the child into a competitive relationship with the isosexual parent. For the boy this results in a fear of castration. This triad is the Oedipus complex; it is an apprenticeship for heterosexuality and a necessary developmental stage for male and female psychosexual identity. The boy's Oedipus complex develops out of the phase of phallic sexuality. Under the influence of castration anxiety, he is forced to abandon his Oedipal feelings at about the age of 5 or 6 years (Parsons, 1954; Slater, 1959). According to Freud, castration anxiety terminates the Oedipus complex in boys. In girls, however, there is no castration anxiety in the same sense. A little girl may envy the boy's penis and see his masculinity as an advantage which he enjoys with the mother (Brown, 1958). She may attempt to resolve her Oedipus complex by emulating the father. Under these circumstances, she may pass through a period of masculine identification, often referred to as the latency and early adolescence stage of "tomboyism." The girl's Oedipus complex begins with the discovery of genital differences, but it is not resolved until puberty or adulthood. No castration threat can make the little girl give up her father. Her relationship with the father develops slowly into adolescence until a shift back to the mother occurs.

The developmental factors that lead to the Oedipus complex and its resolution involve the child's long obligatory dependency on his parents (Fenichel, 1945) and his need to be loved by and to love his parents—his first love objects. The biologically determined sexual development before physiological sexual maturity and incestuous and parenticidal impulses become increasingly strong during this period of development. Oedipal development for the boy springs from phallic sexuality. He abandons his Oedipal wishes under the influence of castration anxiety, thereby re-

pressing and sublimating his incestuous wishes and further identifying with his father. Castration anxiety therefore terminates the Oedipus complex for the boy. The little girl, however, must shift from the first object, the mother, to the father. This occurs when she notices genital anatomical differences. She feels antagonistic and hostile toward her mother. Her first impulse is to repudiate the genital difference by attempting a masculine identification with the father. She entertains the fantasy of the penis having been taken away by the mother. This engenders antagonism toward her mother and fear of her mother. Her wish for a penis leads to increasing interest in her father and her brothers. Because of guilt she may give up masturbation for awhile, or her wish for possession of her father's penis may become stronger. Rage and despair increase the little girl's rivalrous relationship with the mother. She turns to her father as her principal love object. She is later rebuffed by her father, so that she must now renunciate and repress the Oedipal wishes. In passing through the tomboy stage, she gains some elements of a masculine identification with the father. The shift back to the mother occurs later in adolescence. Its timing and degree depend on a number of factors.

Neo-Freudian Formulations of the Oedipus Complex

The neo-Freudians take issue with Freud's postulations, particularly infantile sexuality. Adler viewed the Oedipal child as a pampered child (Mullahy, 1948). He felt that the normal attitude of the phallic child is that of equal interest in the father and the mother. He acknowledged the possibility of a boy's overstimulation by the mother, but he saw sexual pleasure as incidental to the quest for power over the mother. Thus for Adler, the Oedipus complex was simply one of many forms of child pampering. The child eventually becomes the victim of his fantasies toward the mother.

Jung, on the other hand, viewed the Oedipus complex as involving issues of independence and autonomy (Mullahy, 1948). If there is no freedom for the child, the Oedipus complex can lead to a conflict. He introduced the term *Electra complex* to denote a girl's conflict between the fantasized infantile-erotic relationship with the father and her will to power. Failure to achieve moral autonomy and the need to return to the relative security of the father are key factors in the Electra complex.

Rank saw the Oedipus complex as the origin and destiny of man (Mullahy, 1948). He believed that the average person never really overcomes his birth trauma. From the primal horde followed the primal family, the group family, and eventually matriarchal society. He viewed the Oedipus complex as a saga, a sociological phenomenon, a compromise between the wish to have no children and the necessity to renounce one's own immortality in favor of children. He saw the Oedipus complex as a reaction to coercion by the human species, which prescribes marriage and fatherhood as forces against the individual's will.

Horney regarded the child's fixation to parents as not biological (Mullahy, 1948). She saw the family relationship as a force in molding the matrix of character formation. A conflict lies between dependency on the parents and hostile impulses toward them, giving rise to anxiety and the need to cling to the parents for love and security. She doubted whether sexual yearnings toward parents are as strong as Freud thought.

Fromm regarded the Oedipus complex as a rebellion of the son against patriarchal authority (Mullahy, 1948). He agreed with Freud that there are sexual strivings in children, that the tie to the contrasexual parent is often not severed, and that the father-son conflict is characteristic of patriarchal society. He questioned whether the Oedipus complex is the result of sexual rivalry. And Fromm doubted the universality of the Oedipus complex. He alluded to cultures in which there is no rivalry and no patriarchal authority. He also questioned whether the tie to the mother is primarily sexual. He believed that the fixation to the mother is caused by maternal dominance.

Harry Stack Sullivan postulated that the feeling of familiarity toward the child on the part of the isosexual parent leads to an authoritarian attitude which produces resentment and hostility in the child (Mullahy, 1948). A parent treats the child of the opposite sex with more consideration because of a sense of the child's strangeness. A parent feels justified in dictating to a child who seems to be like himself. The feelings of strangeness deprive the parent of motives for control of the child's life. Consequently, he treats the child more carefully. The freedom from pressure results in the child's feeling greater affection for the contrasexual parent and being more attracted to him.

Another formulation of the Oedipus complex is provided by the adaptational view, which rejects bisexuality and constitutional factors, as well as the role of phylogenetic memories from the "primal horde." This view was most strongly espoused by Rado (1956), who formulated an ontogenesis of family relations. He asserted that the parents furnish the child with conditions that foster the development of omnipotence. These feelings the child delegates to the parents during the anal-muscular phase of development. A rewarding relationship between the child and the parents generates tender affects and parental idealization. Thus the child's object choice is "learned" and is not a reflection of inborn instinctual drives and their vicissitudes. The child's first sexual pleasure is from autoerotic manipulations. A subsequent shift to other objects comes only after the child has established an affectionate tie to the mother. He learns that he must share the mother with the father and siblings. This initially intensifies his need for exclusive possession of the mother as a dependency object. Thus both boys and girls in the family are interested in the mother primarily as the libidinal object. In this sense, there is no essential difference in sexual development between the sexes. The striking gender difference is in the attitude of the little girl toward her genital equipment. She attributes cultural privileges of greater masculine freedom in play and assertiveness to the fact that the boy possesses a penis. This is the root of the girl's penis envy, a repressed wish to castrate the boy as a means of resolving her dependency needs.

According to the adaptational view (Kardiner, Karush, & Ovesey, 1959), the boy clings to the mother. Consequently, he meets with overt disapproval from both parents. This leads to the incest taboo (Parsons, 1954). The child's response to parental intimidation is hostility to the father, which must be repressed because of the fear of castration. The child must further protect himself by repressing libidinal desires for the mother. As the mother becomes more inaccessible, he retreats autoerotically to his own genitals and indulges in sexual play with other children. If these activities are not blocked, the Oedipus complex is resolved initially by substitution of himself and later by substitution of nonincestuous objects for his mother. If there is parental interference, sexual intimidation and inhibition are apt to occur. Since our society is still moderately sexually inhibited, the likelihood of intimidation is still quite high. As a consequence, all sexual gratification for the child must be given up. Thus the child falls back on the mother again as his sexual object since the inhibition of his independent executive action forces him to return to earlier dependency attachments. The Oedipus complex is thus perpetuated from one generation to another. Heterosexual objects are identified by the boy with his forbidden mother, which heightens his castration anxiety.

In the adaptational view—and this is true also for the classical view of the Oedipus complex— the sexual development of the girl is more complicated and not so well understood. The first sex-

ual object for the girl is her mother. She then turns to her father, not because of sexual differences, but because of subtle persuasion by both the mother and the father. The mother discourages the daughter's sexual interest in herself. She shifts the little girl's attention to the father through the multiple examples of her own behavior to the father. Thus she helps the girl identify with her. The father offers no objection. Through his own playful seduction of his daughter he facilitates her identification with the mother. The shift of the daughter to the father is reinforced by the social institutions of our culture which emphasize attachment to a man as the highest goal for a woman. A contradiction soon arises for the girl if the parents become alarmed at the dramatic shift they have encouraged. Alarm arises because of sexual overtones in the heightened relationship between father and daughter. This leads to sexual intimidation of the girl in much the same manner that this occurred for the boy. The little girl has become aware of genital differences. She unconsciously attributes her lack of a penis to castration by the mother because of her Oedipal strivings toward the father.

In this formulation castration anxiety for boys and girls appears after parental intimidation; it does not follow discovery of genital differences. The sexual development of the girl then proceeds in the same manner as that of the boy. The adaptational view takes issue with Freud's contention that castration anxiety terminates the Oedipus complex in boys but initiates it in girls. In the adaptational view, the relationship of castration anxiety is the same for both sexes. It sets in motion the repression of the Oedipus complex. Sexual inhibition in the woman is enhanced by social institutions regarding the role of the female. The woman must present herself as chaste, virtuous, and uninterested in sex. This facilitates the repression of her sexuality. Contrapuntal cultural attitudes toward men and women reinforce the latter's penis envy. Intercourse is seen frequently as an instrument in the battle for dominance-submission. The woman often feels vulnerable to injury by the man, which she handles by a reparative fantasy of taking away the man's penis. She fears retaliation by the man. Penetration by the penis arouses repressed Oedipal strivings and associated guilty feelings of punishment by the mother, thus adding another increment of retaliatory fear. The result for the woman is withdrawal and flight from men and denial of sexual yearnings for them.

The Resolution of the Oedipus Complex

In the resolution of the Oedipus complex, changes in the aims and object of biological drives occur. There is progressive modification of the relationships with past objects like parents and siblings (Tennes & Lampl, 1965). Anaclitic and erotic aspects of objects are dissociated. Development of new object relations free of the incest taboo takes place (Minuchin, 1965). Further sexual differentiation occurs. The child enters the phase of latency, which phenomenologically commences with the shedding of the first deciduous teeth and is dynamically associated with the resolution of the "family romance" and the diminution in the child's narcissistic preoccupation with his body, its functions, and its orifices (Sours, 1966). Latency extends to the prepubertal growth spurt of adolescence. During this time further sexual identification and ego differentiation proceed (Kagan, 1964). Peer interactions are more frequent as the child spends less time with his family. When he enters school, he starts to develop academic skills. In his relationship with other authoritarian figures, as well as in his relationship with peers, there is a strengthening of superego and ego-ideals. In the first half of latency (ages 6 to 8 years) repression and regression are phasically seen. The ego and drives undergo temporary regressions to pregenitality with reaction formations of shame, disgust, and guilt.

The superego during this time is quite strict. In many ways it functions as a "foreign body"

leading to heightened reaction formations. Ambivalence is augmented, particularly toward the isosexual parent. A "second edition" of masturbation occurs. No longer does the child masturbate openly, as he did in nursery school. Now autoerotic activity is pursued with much more discretion. In addition, masturbatory equivalents arise including nail-biting, scratching, and head banging, some of which have large sadomasochistic components. Between the ages of 8 and 10, the ego is better equipped cognitively to deal with the environment. Sublimation is more frequently used, and cognitive functions have matured. These factors allow for better environmental and intrapsychic discrimination and control. The superego is less strict toward the end of the latency years, partly because of increased self-awareness and discrimination. In addition, the child's delegated omnipotence is now taken back from the parents by him.

Since Alpert's phenomenological research on latency sexuality, there have been increasing numbers of reports indicating that sexuality is not quiescent during this stage of development (Sours, 1966). While it is true that the child does not openly masturbate and acts as if he were ignorant of his parents' sexuality, he nevertheless has sexual strivings and sexual fantasies. Sexuality in the latency period is later suppressed and repressed. Repression is most prominent in terms of the child's awareness of parental intercourse. Latency suppression of sexuality is fostered by our culture in the service of education and cognitive development (Sours, 1966).

Longitudinal Aspects of the Oedipus Complex

Although the Oedipus complex occurs in the phallic stages of development and involves isosexual rivalry and contrasexual stimulation and attraction, this triadic transaction is not limited to the phallic-Oedipal period of development. In early adolescence there is a resurgence of many aspects of the Oedipus complex. And in adulthood, often prior to a son's marriage, there is a reappearance of Oedipal feelings on the part of the father vis-á-vis his future daughter-in-law. This, of course, can also occur for the mother in her feelings toward her newly found son-in-law. Later in life, grandparents may experience a return of their rivalrous feelings toward a son-in-law or daughter-in-law after the birth of grandchildren. And in senescence, if aging takes its toll on cognitive ability and the capacity for instinctual delay, a man can give vent to long-repressed Oedipal urges through molestation of young girls.

Unsatisfactory Resolutions of the Oedipus Complex

The reasons for unsuccessful resolutions of the Oedipus complex are multifactorial. Some are particularly common. If the child has no sustaining relationship with his two parents, he is apt to suffer multiple deprivations leading to failure in relating to adult objects (Blauvelt & McKenna, 1961). Impairment in psychosexual development and sexual identity can occur (Bowlby et al., 1956; Brenner, 1957). Fragile control of sexual and aggressive impulses with little pleasure capacity can result (Katin, 1960). Harlow's studies have demonstrated in the subhuman primate that female infants who are deprived of their mothers grow up to be inadequate mothers. Males who have experienced the same sort of mother-child relationship have difficulty in expressing aggression and sexuality. If either extreme frustration or extreme overindulgence at the preschool level has occurred, Oedipal involvement may be impeded. If the parent of the opposite sex is removed at the beginning of the child's phallic development and remains absent, the child's contrasexual object relations can remain strained. He may become overattached to the parent of the same sex, leading in some cases to a homosexual object choice. Other objects such as siblings, relatives, and friends,

however, offer other identification models. The outcome also depends on whether the parent views the child as a symbolic substitute for the lost spouse. The opposite-sex parent can behave in an unduly seductive way toward the child. This can lead to extreme stimulation of the child, with intensification of the unresolved Oedipal situation (Kaplan, 1960). Death, illness, injury, or desertion of the parent of the same sex during the Oedipal period can lead to sexual conflicts because these events coincide with unconscious or thinly disguised wishes of the child. Because of increased magical thinking, whereby a wish or fantasy is viewed as tantamount to an act, illness or death of a parent is seen by the child as the result of his aggressive wish or fantasy.

Normal heterosexual development is contingent on many things. Clinical and developmental studies point to several factors in the family matrix. First, the isosexual parent should be non-punitive and strong enough to be a model for identification. Second, the contrasexual parent must not be punishing, emotionally unpredictable, or seductive, in order that the child can place full confidence in members of the opposite sex. Third, parents must show no indications of rejection of the child's genetic sex; gender role behavior must not be obfuscated by the parents in terms of their teaching cross-sex role responses. Fourth, the child must identify with the parents' acceptance of marriage in terms of the desirability and eventuality of his own marriage.

Harsh and punitive attitudes on the part of the father make it more difficult for Oedipal resolution. For instance, a boy may give up all women and assume a passive, compliant attitude toward his father. He may aspire to be the main object in the life of a young woman and see his mother as her rival. This can lead to exaggerated character traits of passivity, compliance, ingratiation, and timidity. On the other hand, the boy can overly identify with the father and develop very aggressive pseudomasculine traits. The girl can assume a masochistic attitude toward the father and regard the penis as a sadistic weapon to be passively accepted by the woman. In this situation, frigidity is common. If the mother is aggressive and a relatively masculine person and if the father is passive and feminine in character, the boy must deal with his aggressive, punitive mother. His inadequately masculine father cannot help him and is not a satisfactory identification model. The boy may follow in the father's footsteps in a passive-feminine masochistic way.

The girl may feel that she was deprived by the mother during pre-Oedipal development. She may believe that her feminine attitude has been depreciated by the mother. She can adopt a passive attitude toward the mother, maintain the mother as an object, depreciate the father as a weak and withholding man, and enter into homosexual relationships. Or she may assume a maternally protective attitude toward the father, establishing strong bonds with him which she is never able to really relinquish. Older siblings of the opposite sex often provide a substitute for the parents, and Oedipal problems may therefore be displaced to these siblings. An only child may suffer in competitive ability since he took part without siblings in the "family romance." When siblings are much younger, older children may fantasize a mother role toward them.

BEHAVIORAL SCIENCE RESEARCH AND INFANTILE SEXUALITY

In the course of theoretical development Freud postulated a number of factors which he thought essential to infantile sexuality (A. Freud, 1965; S. Freud, 1955a, 1955b, 1961a, 1961b). First of all, he suggested that there is a prepubertal sexuality commencing in infancy. Psychosexual development, he felt, leads to specific characterological constellations. Affective residua of childhood experiences frequently lead to neurosis, "a negative of a perversion." He regarded

the Oedipal constellation as having a biological foundation. He encouraged the study of unconscious fantasies and memories. He advanced the concept of biological bisexuality and, in addition, postulated the clitoral-vaginal transfer theory. He also postulated that an infantile amnesia is part of the repression following resolution of the Oedipus complex, and he presented in a number of papers a Lysencko-type anthropology. Central to Freud's theories of infantile sexuality is his theoretical construct of libido theory.

Psychoanalytic theorists after Freud have considered the existence of infantile sexuality to be proved on the basis of (1) direct observation of children, (2) sexual foreplay, (3) adult sexual perversions, (4) psychosis, (5) results of regression, (6) public opinion, and (7) psychoanalytic reconstruction of infantile sexual life (Brenner, 1957; Waelder, 1960).

Although a number of analytic theorists consider the propositions of infantile sexuality "to have been amply proved," Clara Thompson was among the first neo-Freudians to challenge Freud's mechanistic-biological hydrodynamic theory of infantile sexuality. She emphasized the importance of environmental factors. Fromm-Reichman regarded Freudian psychosexuality as pathological family interaction.

Many facets of infantile sexuality warrant further investigation. Advances in the behavioral sciences can contribute in some instances to our knowledge of childhood sexuality. With the marked emphasis on methodology and electronic instrumentation for the study of infancy, the phallic-Oedipal period and infantile sexual behavior have been relatively neglected in research. Children's fantasies, dreams, wishes, and other mental events have hardly been investigated at all. Castration fears, primal-scene experiences, penis envy, birth fantasies, and Oedipal masturbatory fantasies are phallic phenomena that warrant research. The nature of infantile amnesia is poorly understood, partly because of our ignorance about memory mechanisms in general. Evidence regarding the patterns and developmental nuances of the female Oedipus complex and its resolution is fragmentary (Barton & Ware, 1966; Benedek, 1959, 1963; Kestenberg, 1956).

Chodoff has suggested, as did Rado (1956), that Freud's concept of constitutional bisexuality is without scientific basis. Embryologic research has demonstrated that initially, every embryo is female. When the genetic determinance is male, energy reaches levels high enough to change the female embryo into a male embryo. In anatomical sexual differentiation of the embryo, each embryo starts with gonads and internal accessory structures *(anlagen)* for both male and female sexual development. What follows for both sexes is that one set of genital structures regresses and the other set proliferates and differentiates. The external genitalia structures are also differentiated from the same external anlagen. For example, from the genital tubercle come both the penis and the clitoris. A hormonal organizing substance, stimulated by the gonads and produced by the hypothalamus, regulates differentiation. There is a critical period for genital-duct differentiation of the gonads. In male differentiation the changes are brought about by increasing titers of androgen.

Many of the postulates of infantile sexuality are not easily tested by empirical methods. Controlled research in this area is extremely difficult. Young children cannot easily report experiences. Play techniques are useful as modes of expression, but translation from play to language is necessary, with considerable room for distortion (Levy, 1940). Direct observations of children do not offer incontestable or necessarily relevant confirmatory evidence for psychoanalytic constructs. Neurophysiological speculations attempting to relate orality and sexuality by way of contiguous neural limbic pathways do not at this time supply a physiological support to psychoanalytic concepts (Beach, 1965; Ford & Beach,

1951; MacLean, 1962). The association of thumb-sucking with masturbation has been questioned by Wolff, who views rhythmic infant activities as motor discharges rather than autoerotic movement (Chodoff, 1967). The connection between oral and infantile pleasures and adult foreplay, as well as regressive sexuality and perversions, is analogical in form and not necessarily continuous in dynamics or in ego functioning (Barton & Ware, 1966). And the relevance of sleep penile erections to infantile sexuality is put into some doubt by the fact that penile erections occur mainly during periods of rapid eye movement and may be merely manifestations of altered metabolic states.

Hampson and Money have studied the variables of sex differentiation (Money, Hampson, & Hampson, 1957). Genetic sex, hormonal sex, gonadal sex, and the morphology of both internal and external reproductive organs are the important variables in sex determination. Their studies of pseudohermaphrodites have demonstrated that a psychosexual differentiation takes place as an active process of editing and assimilating experiences that are gender-specific and reinforced by the individual's genital appearance. The gender role of assignment and early gender learning are the most critical factors in psychosexual differentiation (Birdwhistell, 1964; Brown, 1958). Money has concluded from clinical studies of intersex patients that the sex of assignment must be made clear by the eighteenth month in order to avoid future psychosexual deviation. Early learning, often called *imprinting,* takes place before and at the toddler stage. Gender role is then well established. The acquisition of gender role and sexual identity is similar to that of language in that there is a critical period operative for both. Hormones which bring about early sexual maturation apparently do not have any definite determining influence on the direction of psychosexual development or any effect on perceptual, memory, and dream imagery.

The role of cognitive development in sex-role behavior is important. A child cognitively organizes his social world along sex-role dimensions. This patterning is based on the child's concepts of physical things; he cognitively organizes the social-role concept in terms of universal physical dimensions. The organization of role perception and role learnings depends on his concepts of his body and his world. The schemata that cement events together include his concepts of the body, the physical and social world, and general categories of relationships, including substantiality, causality, space, time, quantity, logical identity, and inclusion. The child develops an unchangeable sexual identity which has its analogues in his concepts of the invariable identity of physical objects. From the patterning arises a self-categorization as boy or girl which is a basic organizer of sex-role attitudes. These basic self-categorizations influence basic gender values. Masculine-feminine values arise from the child's need to see things as either consistent or inconsistent with the self. Once masculine-feminine values have been acquired, a child identifies with isosexual figures. In other words, the wish to be masculine results in the desire to imitate a masculine model, which in turn intensifies an emotional attachment to the object. Kohlberg (1966) suspects that parental attitudes regarding sex roles may be more negative than positive in terms of the development of appropriate sex-role attitudes. Parental sex-role anxiety may be a strong inhibitor of the cognitive organization necessary for sex-role behaviors.

There are no recent developmental studies of memory in children (Schachtel, 1959; Whitty & Zangwill, 1966). Such studies are requisite to an understanding of infantile amnesia. Massive repression at 5 to 6 years of age with resolution of the Oedipus complex is a countercathexis which impedes release of memory traces into consciousness (S. Freud, 1955a, 1955b). Childhood memory, however, is most likely an immaturely developing ego function. Memory depends not only on previous experience and storage of information but also on an ability to reason. A child classifies experience differently from the way an adult does. In all likelihood, changes in cognitive ego style in the Oedipal phase facilitate repression and allow for amnesia.

Fear of incest is central to the classical formulation of the Oedipus complex (Mullahy, 1948; Parsons, 1954; Slater, 1959). Family studies of incest have been made, but few developmental studies of children involved in incest are reported (Raphing, Carpenter, & Davis, 1967; Weinberg, 1965). The frequency of incest between mother and son, siblings, and father and daughter is poorly understood from both a statistical and a clinical standpoint. Incest has been best studied in father-daughter units where the family functions ineffectively and where the pursuit of socially approved goals and conformity with socially defined values are held in high regard. In such a relationship, the girl has a pregenital dependency need on the father. Her contact with the father may reflect her defense against the sexual inadequacy of both parents. Incest may also express revenge by the daughter against the mother. Incestuous behavior can also be a way of fending off separation anxiety. In addition, incestuous behavior is a mechanism whereby the father can maintain a facade of role competence. The sexual role of the daughter undergoes role reversal of mother and daughter.

Stoller's research has corroborated much of Money's earlier work (Stoller, 1964a, 1964b, 1965a, 1965b). Stoller has pointed out that gender identity depends in the beginning upon sex assignment and that it is set by the age of $2\frac{1}{2}$ to 3 years. Gender identity arises from experiential rather than constitutional factors and occurs before the resolution of the Oedipus complex. He views this process as leading to core gender identity. He believes that biological forces silently augment the formation of identity. Therefore, gender identity is not the result of fixation by conflict but rather the effect of imprinting at a critical period upon a passively developing identity. Thus, castration anxiety, penis envy, etc., change only the quality of gender identity.

The clitoral-vaginal transfer theory has been challenged by a number of investigators. Genetic sex at fertilization is later changed during the first 6 weeks by a number of forces. At first the embryo is female but has a bipotentiality and eventually a unipotentiality as the testicular inductance substance forms and leads to the production of androgen between the seventh and twelfth weeks. In the male, the "exaggerated clitoris" becomes a penis. From the crura and bulb emerge the male external genitalia. Masters and Johnson have suggested that female sexual drive is based on clitoral eroticism (Chodoff, 1967). They believe that it is impossible to separate the vaginal from the clitoral orgasm. No such thing as a vaginal orgasm exists; it is an orgasm of the circumvaginal venous chambers. During the luteal phase there is increasing pelvic congestion with transudation and an increase in sexual desire. Psychosexual excitation leads to an increase in the vasocongestive reaction.

Thus, it is apparent that Freud's theories of infantile sexuality encompass many phenomena and postulates at various levels of conceptualization. Fears of bodily injury, preoccupation with bodily functions and integrity, masturbation, response to primal-scene experience, and transactions of the child vis-à-vis isosexual and contrasexual parents are phenomenological. Child therapists encounter these phenomena daily in their work. They are observable facts available to child developmentalists for possible validation. At another level of observation are dreams, fantasies, and memories of phallic and latency children. The child must report this material by either verbal or nonverbal means. Research methodology in this area is problematic. At still another level of conceptualization are postulates

relating to the libido theory. These postulates are transcendental. Empirical data are not relevant to economic postulates and do not allow for testable hypotheses about behavior. Nevertheless, there are many important areas of ego psychology which can be empirically evaluated. Research in the development of memory, cognitive style shifts from the phallic to the latency period, perceptual gender differences in terms of erotic arousability, and the role of olfaction (Bieber, 1959; Kalogerakis, 1963) in psychosexual development may yield information relevant to phallic-Oedipal development.

PSYCHOSEXUAL DEVIATIONS AND PSYCHOPATHOLOGY

The correlations and continuities between child and adult perversions are not clear. Longitudinal and follow-up studies need to be done. The phenomenology of both child and adult perversions is also unclear. The phenomenology of both child and adult perversions can be identical. Nevertheless, metapsychologically the age difference becomes a crucial factor. For adults, perversion implies that genital primacy has not been reached, established, or maintained. Consequently, prepubertal children, by definition, cannot be properly called perverts. A child has a polymorphously perverse tendency which can result in expression of components of infantile sexuality, out of phase chronologically or quantitatively. These deviations from the norms of development are related to the strength of drive components, vicissitudes of environmental factors, ego balance, and defensive organization.

Homosexuality

Until recent years, homosexuality has been viewed as a result of constitutional blockage and fixation in the flow of libido. Freud regarded homosexuality as a fixation, as an erogenous interest in one's own genitals during the autoerotic period. Over the years he viewed homosexuality as the result of castration anxiety with Oedipal frustration leading to regression from object love to a narcissistic identification. The individual behaves toward an object as he wishes his mother had behaved toward him. Freud suggested anal and homosexual fixation as important factors. He also postulated the dynamics of returning in favor of somebody else, a competitive rivalry held in check by its transformation into homosexual love. Freud therefore viewed homosexuality as a result of blockage leading to fixation. He did not see homosexuality as a symptom of neurosis and a defense against castration anxiety by phobic avoidance of the female genitalia.

It was Clara Thompson who suggested that homosexuality is an expression of a neurotic process. In doing this, she encouraged a therapeutic approach to the problem. Homosexuality was viewed as a symptom of a neurosis.

Bieber, Gaylin, Ovesey, and Westwood have added to the formulation of homosexuality qua neurosis (Bieber, 1962; Marmor, 1965; Ovesey & Gaylin, 1965). Nevertheless, the concept of constitutional bisexuality is still espoused in classical psychoanalytic circles. "This innate bisexuality is intensified in the preoedipal period by identification with both male and female parents and remains the constitutional basis for any homosexual inclination which arises later" (A. Freud, 1965). Anna Freud adds that ". . . what determines the direction of development are not the major infantile events and constellations in themselves, but a multitude of accompanying circumstances . . . [which] include external and internal, qualitative and quantitative factors (1965).

Various trends in development have been implicated in the etiology of homosexuality: (1) narcissism and the need to choose a sexual partner in the image of oneself; (2) constitutional bisexuality; (3) excessive love of, and dependence on, the mother or father or marked hostility toward one parent; (4) traumatic visual exposure to the female genitalia; (5) oral and anal fixations; (6) envy of the mother's body; and (7) sibling rivalry turned into love of a brother as a sexual object (A. Freud, 1965). These components are part of every boy's development. Whether they become pathogenic depends on a number of circumstances, both quantitative and qualitative, too numerous to enable prediction of homosexuality in childhood. For example, intense castration anxiety can encourage boys to avoid girls and push them toward homosexuality; on the other hand, castration anxiety can push boys out of the negative Oedipus complex into heterosexuality. Anaclitic object attachment, excessive narcissism, investment of pleasure at the anus, passivity during anal development, excessive penile stimulation, and persistence of the negative Oedipus complex enhance the possibility of homosexuality. On the other hand, the positive Oedipus complex, reaction formations against passive-feminine wishes, anality, and a high endowment of aggressive drive can augur well for heterosexuality. In addition, adequacy of parental models, parental psychopathology, and vicissitudes of family life are also determinants of psychosexual development.

Homosexuality cannot be diagnosed during latency. Diagnosis is possible only after puberty, if the homosexual object love represents the adolescent's ideal self and is the exclusively preferred love object (A. Freud, 1965). In latency the object choice among contemporaries is based on identification and not object love. Nevertheless, in latency as well as in late phallic development, one can encounter boys who inordinately manifest homosexual wishes as well as effeminate behavior. In latency, their sexual activities and curiosities are much more erotically tinged and neurotically colored. This is particularly true of those boys who do not complete the negative Oedipus complex and remain in a passive-oral position with feminine wishes to male objects.

Markedly effeminate behavior is seen in boys with narcissistic identifications. They are in adhesive ties with a mother who is possessive, indulgent, overgratifying, and overstimulating. These boys are usually adept at role playing and play acting. They are highly artistic and are often exhibitionistic with adults. The prognosis for a boy with excessive preadolescent homosexual behavior and effeminacy is dependent on a number of factors. Ego strength, positive masculine identification, relative absence of anxiety in peer groups, and the capacity for heterosexual stimulation are some positive signs for heterosexual development.

A paradigm for male homosexuality is love for the woman with phobic avoidance of her genitalia. It is not merely or always flight from a feared and hostile castrating woman. The male is both feared and hated. The father is not supportive, constructive, or loving with the son; he does not protect the boy from the mother. The mother is seen as seductive, overly close, possessive, dominant, overprotective, emasculating, and preferring the son to the husband. In the Oedipal situation, the son is easily stimulated. Often he has been excessively stimulated by the mother. He worries about displeasing the mother, often acts as her adviser and confidant, and frequently disrespects the father. The father is frequently aloof from the son. He tends to minimize his achievements and remains detached and hostile. He is not admired by his wife. The boy cannot identify with his father. If the father is absent because of divorce, military service, or death, his image is mostly negative and is negatively reinforced by the mother. The son views sex from a disinterested standpoint, often responding with the reaction formation of disgust, fear, and aversion in regard to the female genitalia. The dynamic constellation of dependency and power is a prominent reparative maneuver which attempts to undo castration and equate the penis with the breast. If these dynamics exist

without erotic stimulation and the use of sex in male transactions, the man is viewed as a pseudo-homosexual. Those homosexuals for whom there is active erotic involvement display frank disturbances of ego functions: poor peer-group relationships, minimization of competition, tendency toward isolation, and, in general, inhibition of assertive and aggressive behavior. This overall model of homosexuality, however, ignores the individuality of the boy: qualitative and quantitative factors such as the degree of castration anxiety, fixation to aggressive-sadistic or passive-oral wishes (and, respectively, the push to either the positive or the negative Oedipus complex), the extent of phallic strivings, and, in general, his push to complete development.

A paradigm for the female homosexual is more difficult to conceptualize in that the female Oedipal resolution is less well understood and various forms of female homosexuality are not as easily discriminated as those of the male. It is apparent that the most common female homosexual pattern is related developmentally to an active chronic struggle between the mother and the daughter. The hostility between them belies their anaclitic relationship. The mother is usually overbearing, dominant, intolerant, and anti-heterosexual. The daughter frequently desires children, wishes to be a mother, and may even have exposure to heterosexual experiences. Nevertheless, she views men as detached, uninterested, withdrawn, unassertive, and exploitative of women. The daughter remains in hostile rebellion to the mother. Indifference is most marked. The daughter's separation anxiety about the mother is often crippling. In her peer-group relations the daughter is hostile to isosexual peers, is frequently extremely competitive, and usually appears as a "tomboy." The daughter adopts homosexuality as a defense against the Oedipus complex and against maternal hostility. The female homosexual can be highly masculine, the so-called bull-dyke, whose psychosexual identification is defensively masculine to an extreme and whose aggressive needs and competitive capacity are very striking. As with males, the more ego-syntonic the homosexuality, the greater the compulsive drive, the more severe the defiant exhibitionism, and the less the heterosexual arousal capacity, the worse the prognosis for treatment is.

Fetishism

For the adult and for the child, there is no particular metapsychological identity when it comes to fetishism. A child's fetish is "merely a stage in a process which may or may not lead to adult fetishism" (Sperling, 1963). The only similarity is the cathexis of narcissistic or object libido with a body part or article of clothing. For adults the part object is symbolized by a fetish which is equivalent to the imaginary penis of the phallic mother, to which the adult is tied for sexual gratification. For the child, the fetish can have a number of symbolic meanings and can be related to a number of purposes (Dickes, 1963). For instance, for a child a fetish can be substituted for the mother's body or breast; it can be a transitional object. The child may need a fetish for falling asleep, for separating from the mother, and for withdrawing interest from the object world to himself. In normal development, a fetishistic object need have no serious pathological implication. The preschool child's use of a transitional object at bedtime is an ordinary pattern. Later the fetish can represent the ambivalent object or the imaginary penis. In late adolescence and early adulthood, particularly during the college years, it is not unusual for a girl to have stuffed animals which psychologically serve as fetishes. It is only when the fetishistic object is erotically exciting that it should be considered to imply a serious disorder meriting treatment.

Transvestism

Children's interest in adult clothes and in the game of "dressing up" is ubiquitous and healthy; games provide opportunities for role playing within parental identifications. Any articles of clothing or objects belonging to parents are used as gender and status symbols, often with disregard for gender appropriateness. For phallic girls "transvestism" is part of tomboyism: imitation and identification with boys as a defense against penis envy and castration damage and guilt over masturbation. It is not pathological unless the girl absolutely refuses to wear feminine dress or uses the transvestism as a means of sexual excitation. For the boy, cross-dressing is a serious symptom after the age of 3 years. Dynamically, his transvestism can be a denial of phallic masculinity and a means of ensuring a tie to the mother, regaining the lost maternal object, or bidding for the mother's love (Charatin & Calef, 1965). Invariably, the boy's mother has encouraged his feminine wishes by actively letting him know she prefers girls. She can be subtly collusive with the boy by giving in to his wishes for feminine clothes or by ignoring the whole situation.

For both the female and the male, transvestic symptoms can be explained in terms of a "fixation to a level to which part of an object is accepted as a substitute for the whole and on which, accordingly, easy displacements are made from the (male or the female) body to the clothes which cover it" (A. Freud, 1965).

In the classical formulation of transvestism, the symptom is seen as both a defense and an expression of bisexuality. Anna Freud refers to "quantitative alterations in his (or her) libido economy." Neo-Freudian formulations, on the other hand, stress identificatory learning and defense organization as the focus for transvestism. By identifying with the rejecting mother, the boy hopes to retain her. He maintains a sadomasochistic relationship with her which defends him from Oedipal guilt, and in terms of early pre-Oedipal needs, he plays the role of mother to fulfill his own oral needs and avoids the risk of incorporation (Segal, 1965).

In children, cross-dressing for girls is phase-determined for penis envy; for boys it is phase-determined for anal-passive femininity, the negative Oedipus complex, and regressions to these phases of development. As long as the behavior is a defense against anxiety and not a mode for masturbatory activities, fantasies, and sexual excitement, cross-dressing is not truly a perversion, although the probability of adult transvestism is increased. Its occurrence in adulthood can be in the absence of homosexuality and schizophrenia, although the likelihood of both is increased in the presence of narcissism. Likewise, fetishistic and transsexual behavior can accompany transvestism (Benjamin, 1965).

Transsexualism

The transsexual is usually aware of having felt at an early age (between 2 and 4 years) a sense of contrasexual core gender identity. The development of cross-dressing and feminine mimicry in prephallic boys represents not merely rejection of the male gender role but also an early conviction of contrasexual core gender identity (Pauly, 1965; Stoller, 1965a). More so than the transvestite, the transsexual as a child is noteworthy for his capacity for role playing, his hyperaestheticism, and his heightened artistic ability. Money (1965), Benjamin (1965), and Stoller (1965a, 1965b) have noted the existence of transsexuality without concomitant homosexuality and ego disintegration. Transsexuals, however, are usually characterologically deviant. Because of their rejection of the masculine gender role, they shun sports and isosexual peer activities. Peer teasing and humiliation force them into withdrawal and isolation, which is secondarily disruptive to their development. The sex frequency of transsexualism is from 1:8 to 1:3, with a preponderance of males (Benjamin, 1965). There are many more male transsexuals, just as there are many more male homosexuals and transvestites.

The reasons are not in the least clear. Benjamin (1965) has discussed biological, psychological, and etiologic speculations. Stoller has pointed to certain transsexuals as exceptions to his postulate that gender identity depends primarily on sex assignment. He has described one group of male transsexuals with an infancy history of excessive tactile contact with the mother. Another group was "propelled inexorably by biological forces so that from infancy on they behaved as if they were members of the opposite sex" (Stoller, 1964a, 1964b, 1965a, 1965b).

Sadomasochism

Sadism and masochism are pairs of opposites in the child (Brenner, 1959). They express the active and passive aspects of partial instinctual drives in psychosexual development. At first sadism is present as oral sadism, and it then passes through anal and phallic transformation by way of sublimation and reaction formations, adding to characterological development. In 1920 Freud identified masochism as complementary to sadism: masochism becomes sadism turned against the self. The sadist in perversions gets a genital discharge and releases an aggressive discharge against the object he wants to humiliate. The partner is usually a masochist, but the partner may also be coerced, as in rape and murder. The punishment produces genital stimulation in the masochistic pervert. Usually the masochistic pervert is also a moral masochist who seeks defeat under conditions unconsciously provoked. The masochistic behavior which leads to punishment is attained through identification with the aggressor and provocation of the aggressor. Through unconscious identification with his sadistic partner, the masochist can gratify his own sadistic needs and return to a sense of infantile omnipotence.

In Freud's earlier writings, masochism was seen as derived from sadism. Freud initially denied a primary masochism. He later postulated its existence in terms of the death instinct, with refusion and diffusion representing movement of both erotic and aggressive drives. In *The Ego and the Id,* instinctual activity aiming at unpleasure is postulated. The fixation is viewed as an infantile misidentification and a distortion of the female role. Masochism is also viewed as a defense against castration. Beating fantasies represent an anal-sadistic regression of Oedipal strivings that is due to the influence of the superego and the need for punishment. Three forms of masochism are (1) erogenous masochism, in which pleasure versus pain is the principal issue; (2) moral masochism, in which a sense of guilt is prominent with a wish to be beaten by the father, expressed in terms of guilt riddance; and (3) feminine masochism, which is manifested by fantasies arising through an identification with a humiliated woman.

Bieber's (1953) adaptational view of masochism presents it as a choice of lesser evils and a defense against castration. He does not view it as instinctual. A fear of success often goes hand in hand with masochism. Its mechanisms include a pathological dependency secondary to neurotic inhibition of function. It may also serve as a technique for getting attention and love. Its purpose may also be circumvented—to cover up unacceptable ideas. Masochism is a facade to cover up hostile responses. It may also operate through repetition compulsion as a way of surmounting and maintaining a painful traumatic event in the past. Rado has described masochism as a defense against original oral-frustration pains. Defiant rage leads to pain dependency. Pain becomes a stimulus for pleasure (Rado, 1956).

Self-mutilation and injury of psychotic children characterize a complicated variant of masochism. Studies of self-destructive young children, often with ego deviations, have suggested multiple etiologic factors. It can be postulated that rocking, an adaptive and initially unlearned response, leads to increased sensory input with gradual delineation of ego boundaries. In early infancy, there is no conflict, and there is no fantasy. Through rocking, the infant in a random way bangs his head and finds the pain pleasurable. This activity increases the sensory input; through conditioning he may persist in head banging. This behavior continues through the toddler and preschool stages, when fantasy life is greater and when reinforcement of head banging by the parents occurs. The parents may respond only when the child bangs his head. The response is often hostile and critical. It is also common for such patients to have been subjected to parental physical attacks, which, because of family deprivations, are experienced as pleasurable and as a necessary mode for obtaining attention and affection. At this stage of development, operant conditioning occurs in the parental transactions with the child. Fantasy life is much more vivid. The child is now capable of substituting the self for an object as a target of his aggression. Operating with psychotic defenses of introjection and projection, the child is apt to turn to himself in order to subordinate pain to pleasure.

Predicting the outcome of perverse behavior in children is difficult. How can we be certain that genitality will assume primacy? Only at puberty can one make any sort of prediction. The force of regressive pulls, the strength of genital drives, the desire and push to complete development, and the opportunity for genital gratification are certainly important factors for assessment and prognosis.

REFERENCES

Baldwin, A. L. *Theories of child development.* New York: Wiley, 1967.

Barton, D., & Ware, T. D. Incongruities in the

development of the sexual system. *A.M.A. Archives of General Psychiatry,* 1966, **14,** 614–623.

Beach, F. A. (Ed.). *Sex and behavior.* New York: Wiley, 1965.

Benedek, T. Parenthood as a developmental phase. *Journal of the American Psychoanalytic Association,* 1959, **7,** 389–417.

Benedek, T. An investigation of the sexual cycle in women. *A.M.A. Archives of General Psychiatry,* 1963, **8,** 311–322.

Benjamin, H. *The transsexual phenomenon.* New York: Wiley, 1965.

Bieber, I. The meaning of masochism. *American Journal of Psychotherapy,* 1953, **7,** 433–448.

Bieber, I. Olfaction in sexual development and adult sexual organization. *American Journal of Psychotherapy,* 1959, **13,** 351–359.

Bieber, I., et al. *Homosexuality.* New York: Basic Books, 1962.

Birdwhistell, R. L. *The tertiary sexual characteristics of man.* Montreal: AAAS, 1964.

Blauvelt, H., & McKenna, J. Mother-neonate interaction: Capacity of the human newborn for orientation. In B. M. Foss (Ed.), *Determinants of infant behavior.* New York: Wiley, 1961. Pp. 38–49.

Bowlby, J., et al. The effects of mother-child separation: A follow-up study. *British Journal of Medical Psychology,* 1956, **29,** 211–247.

Brenner, C. *An elementary textbook of psychoanalysis.* New York: Doubleday, 1957.

Brenner, C. The masochistic character. *Journal of the American Psychoanalytic Association,* 1959, **7,** 197–226.

Brown, D. G. Sex-role development in a chang-ing culture. *Psychological Bulletin,* 1958, **55,** 232–242.

Casuso, G. Anxiety related to the discovery of the penis. In *The psychoanalytic study of the child.* Vol. 12. New York: International Universities Press, 1957. Pp. 169–174.

Charatin, F. B., & Calef, H. A case of transvestism in a six-year-old boy. *Journal of the Hillside Hospital,* 1965, **14,** 160–177.

Chodoff, P. A critique of Freud's theory of infantile sexuality. *International Journal of Psychiatry,* 1967, **4,** 35–48.

Decarie, T. G. *Intelligence and affectivity in early childhood.* New York: International Universities Press, 1965.

Dickes, R. Fetishistic behavior: A contribution to its complex development and significance. *Journal of the American Psychoanalytic Association,* 1963, **11,** 203–330.

Falkner, F. (Ed.). *Human development.* Philadelphia: Saunders, 1966.

Fenichel, O. *The psychoanalytic theory of neurosis.* New York: Norton, 1945.

Flavell, J. H. *The developmental psychology of Jean Piaget.* Princeton, N.J.: Van Nostrand, 1963.

Ford, C. S., & Beach, F. W. *Patterns of sexual behavior.* New York: Ace Books, 1951.

Frank, R. L. Childhood sexuality. In P. Hoch & J. Zubin (Eds.), *Psychosexual development.* New York: Grune & Stratton, 1949. Pp. 143–158.

Freud, A. *Normality and pathology in childhood.* New York: International Universities Press, 1965.

Freud, S. *Analysis of a phobia in a five year*

old boy (1909). Standard edition. Vol. 10. London: Hogarth Press, 1955. Pp. 3–148. (a)

Freud, S. *The sexual life of human beings* (1917). Standard edition. Vol. 10. London: Hogarth Press, 1955. Pp. 3–148. (b)

Freud, S. *Dissolution of the oedipus complex* (1924). Standard edition. Vol. 19. London: Hogarth Press, 1961. Pp. 173–179. (a)

Freud, S. *Some physical consequences of the anatomical distinction between the sexes* (1925). Standard edition. Vol. 19. London: Hogarth Press, 1961. Pp. 243–260. (b)

Gifford, S. Repetition compulsion. *Journal of the American Psychoanalytic Association,* 1964, **12,** 632–649.

Green, A. H. Self-mutilation in schizophrenic children. *Archives of General Psychiatry,* 1967, **17,** 234–244.

Hendrick, I. *Facts and theories of psychoanalysis.* New York: Knopf, 1958.

Hertz, J., et al. Transvestitism. *Acta Psychiatrica Scandinavica,* 1961, **37,** 283–294.

Hoffman, M. L., & Hoffman, L. N. W. (Eds.), *Review of child development research.* Vol. 1. New York: Russell Sage, 1964.

Jones, E. The phallic phase. *International Journal of Psychoanalysis,* 1933, **14,** 1–33.

Kagan, J. Acquisition and significance of sex typing and sex role identity. In L. W. Hoffman & M. L. Hoffman (Eds.), *Review of child development research.* Vol. 1. New York: Russell Sage, 1964. Pp. 137–168.

Kagan, J. The concept of identification. In P. H. Mussen, J. J. Conger, & J. Kagan (Eds.), *Readings in child development and personality.* New York: Harper, 1965. Pp. 212–224.

Kalogerakis, M. G. The role of olfaction in sexual development. *Psychosomatic Medicine,* 1963, **25,** 420–432.

Kaplan, B., & Wapner, S. (Eds.). *Perspectives in psychological theory.* New York: International Universities Press, 1960.

Kardiner, A., Karush, A., and Ovesey, L. A methodological study of Freudian theory. *The Journal of Nervous and Mental Disease,* 1959, **129,** 11–19, 133–143, 207–221, 341–356.

Katin, A. Distortions of phallic phase. In *The psychoanalytic study of the child.* Vol. 15. New York: International Universities Press, 1960. Pp. 208–214.

Kestenberg, J. S. Vicissitudes of female sexuality. *Journal of the American Psychoanalytic Association,* 1956, **4,** 453–477.

Kidd, A. H., & Rivoire, J. L. (Eds.). *Perceptual development in children.* New York: International Universities Press, 1966.

Kinsey, A. C., et al. *Sexual behavior in the human male.* Philadelphia: Saunders, 1948.

Kinsey, A. C., et al. *Sexual behavior in the human female.* Philadelphia: Saunders, 1953.

Koff, R. H. A definition of identification: A review of the literature. *International Journal of Psychoanalysis,* 1961, **42,** 362.

Kohlberg, L. A cognitive-developmental analysis of children's sex-role conceptions and attitudes. In E. Maccoby (Ed.), *Development of sex differences.* Stanford, Calif.: Stanford University Press, 1966. Pp. 82–172.

Lampl-DeGroot, J. The pre-oedipal phase in the development of the male child. In *The psychoanalytic study of the child.* Vol. 2. New York: International Universities Press, 1946. Pp. 75–83.

Laurendeau, M., & Pinard, A. *Causal thinking of the child.* New York: International Universities Press, 1962.

Levy, D. Studies of reaction to genital differences. *American Journal of Orthopsychiatry,* 1940, **10,** 755–762.

MacLean, T. D. New findings relevant to the evolution of psychosexual functions of the brain. *The Journal of Nervous and Mental Disease,* 1962, **135,** 289–301.

Maier, H. W. *Three theories of child development.* New York: Harper, 1965.

Marmor, J. (Ed.). *Sexual inversion.* New York: Basic Books, 1965.

Mead, M. The childhood genesis of sex differences in behavior. In J. M. Tanner and B. Inhelder (Eds.), *Discussions on child development.* Vol. III. New York: International Universities Press, 1958. Pp. 13–90.

Minuchin, D. Sex-role concept and sex typing in children as a function of school and home environments. *Child Development,* 1965, **36,** 1033–1048.

Money, J. Psychosexual differentiation. In J. Money (Ed.), *Sex research.* New York: Holt, 1965. Pp. 3–23.

Money, J., Hampson, J. G., & Hampson, J. L. Imprinting and the establishment of gender role. *A.M.A. Archives of Neurology and Psychiatry,* 1957, **77,** 333–336.

Mullahy, P. *Oedipus: Myth and complex.* New York: Hermitage Press, 1948.

Mussen, P. H., Conger, J. J., & Kagan, J. *Child development and personality.* New York: Harper, 1965.

Ovesey, L., & Gaylin, W. Psychotherapy of male homosexuality. *American Journal of Psychotherapy,* 1965, **19,** 382–396.

Parsons, T. The incest taboo in relation to social structure and the socialization of the child. *British Journal of Sociology,* 1954, **5,** 101–117.

Pauly, I. B. Male psychosexual inversion: Transsexualism. *A.M.A. Archives of General Psychiatry,* 1965, **13,** 172–181.

Rado, S. An adaptational view of sexual behavior. In *Psychoanalysis of behavior.* Vol. I. New York: Grune & Stratton, 1956. Pp. 201–203.

Ramsey, G. V. The sexual development of boys. *American Journal of Psychology,* 1943, **56,** 217–233.

Rangell, L. The role of the parent in the oedipus complex. *Bulletin of the Menninger Clinic,* 1965, **19,** 9–16.

Raphing, D. L., Carpenter, B. L., & Davis, A. Incest: A genealogical study. *A.M.A. Archives of General Psychiatry,* 1967, **16,** 505–512.

Reevy, W. R. Child sexuality. In A. Ellis & A. Abarbanel (Eds.), *The encyclopedia of sexual behavior.* Vol. I. New York: Hawthorn Books, 1961. Pp. 258–267.

Salzman, L. Psychology of the female. *A.M.A. Archives of General Psychiatry,* 1967, **17,** 195–204.

Schachtel, E. G. *Metamorphosis.* New York: Basic Books, 1959.

Segal, M. M. Transvestitism as an impulse and as a defense. *International Journal of Psychoanalysis,* 1965, **46,** 209–217.

Slater, M. K. Etiological factors in the origin of incest. *American Anthropologist,* 1959, **61,** 1042–1047.

Sours, J. A. Growth and emotional development

of the child. *Postgraduate Medicine,* 1966, **40,** 515–522.

Sperling, M. Fetishism in children. *The Psychoanalytic Quarterly,* 1963, **32,** 374–392.

Spitz, R. A. A note on the extrapolation of ethological findings. *International Journal of Psychoanalysis,* 1955, **36,** 162–165.

Spitz, R. A. The derailment of dialogue. *Journal of the American Psychoanalytic Association,* 1964, **12,** 752–775.

Spitz, R. A. *The first year of life.* New York: International Universities Press, 1965.

Stoller, R. J. A contribution to the study of gender identity. *International Journal of Psychoanalysis,* 1964, **45,** 220–226. (a)

Stoller, R. J. The hermaphroditic identity of hermaphrodites. *The Journal of Nervous and Mental Disease,* 1964, **139,** 453–457. (b)

Stoller, R. J. Passing and the continuum of gender identity. In J. Marmor (Ed.), *Sexual inversion.* New York: Basic Books, 1965. Pp. 190–210. (a)

Stoller, R. J. The sense of maleness. *The Psychoanalytic Quarterly,* 1965, **34,** 207–218. (b)

Tennes, R. H., & Lampl, E. E. Stranger and separation anxiety in infancy. *The Journal of Nervous and Mental Disease,* 1965, **139,** 247–254.

Velikovsky, I. *Oedipus and acklination.* London: Sidgwick & Jackson, 1960.

Waelder, R. *Basic theory of psychoanalysis.* New York: International Universities Press, 1960.

Weinberg, S. *Incest behavior.* New York: Citadel Press, 1965.

Whitty, C. W. M., & Zangwill, O. L. *Amnesia.* London: Butterworth, 1966.

Yarrow, L. J. Separation from parents during early childhood. In M. L. Hoffman & L. N. W. Hoffman (Eds.), *Review of child development research.* Vol. I. New York: Russell Sage, 1964.

part iv | **Other Disorders**

18 | Psychological Aspects of Physically Handicapped Children

Leonard Diller

Of the 28 million handicapped and ill in the United States, it is estimated that approximately 6 million are under 21 years of age. There are, generally, six major types of handicapping conditions: (1) mental retardation and emotional disturbances, (2) orthopedic, (3) blind and partially blind, (4) deaf and partially deaf, (5) cardiac, (6) tuberculosis and respiratory. We will be concerned with all these groups except for the mentally retarded and the emotionally disturbed. The orthopedic group, which will be our largest concern at this time, includes cerebral palsy, spina bifida, amputees, paraplegics, and muscular dystrophy. These conditions have in common two major characteristics. One is that the disability is visible to all, and the second is that there are impairments in movements. It has been estimated that 1 out of every 200 births in this country will produce brain damage, resulting in neuromuscular disability. Interest in the handicapped child is highly related to, and reflective of, the triumphs and failures in scientific technology, as well as the delivery of services in our industrial society. With the introduction of the Salk vaccine, for example, a major category of handicapping conditions—poliomyelitis—has been eliminated. However, with the recent popularity of drugs, the well-known effects of thalidomide compounds, which were ingested during pregnancy, have aroused widespread public interest in congenital limb deformities and brain damage in the newborn. From other quarters come more reports of the increased evidence of handicapping conditions associated with poverty and technological lag (Gruenberg, 1964; Knoblock & Passamanick, 1959). Some have even suggested that hunger is the largest source of potential handicapping conditions in the world.

In this chapter, we will briefly describe some of the major physically handicapping conditions, including their definitions, incidence, etiology, and medical management. We will then point up some of the social, educational, and psychological considerations which are pertinent to the understanding of individuals and institutions that are associated with these conditions. Finally, we will discuss the psychological diagnosis and treatment of these conditions.

VARIETIES OF PHYSICAL HANDICAPS

Before describing the varieties of physically handicapping conditions, we must note several critical points. First, a handicap is not a disease or illness. It is a condition or state of disability, which may be the result of disease, illness, or trauma. The handicapped person is not sick. Second, the term *handicap,* as we are using it, refers to a condition which prevents an individual from performing competently or being accepted by other people. The adolescent girl with acne, the boy who is too short or fat, and the child with facial disfigurement may consider themselves handicapped. In some instances, other people also consider them handicapped. In a sense, any person who is deviant or imagines himself deviant may be handicapped in one way or another. Many of the psychological problems of so-called normal people have their analogues in the problems of the people whom we will be discussing. The psychological problems of the disabled may be merely a magnification of the problems of nonhandicapped people. Indeed, some students of the problem argue that the situation of the handicapped person serves as a useful experiment in nature for the study of fundamental social processes. Roger Barker (1963), on the basis of his observations of the limitations of opportunities for social interaction in handicapped children, developed a methodology for studying the ecology of nonhandicapped people in their settings. In this chapter, we will be concerned with handicaps which are primarily manifested in atypical physical conditions which impair functional competence in movement or language. While psychological characteristics associated with atypical physique—e.g., dwarfism, obesity—may have much in common with neuromuscular impairment, they will not be our primary concern.

Third, handicapping conditions, which we will describe, seldom result in a limited or circumscribed area of difficulties. They tend rather to be the central point of a whole network of interrelated problems, each of which pulls others along. For example, the child who cannot walk may experience a frustration in being limited in his movements, but he also may be exposed to fewer social contacts; he may have to be bussed to a school outside of his neighborhood, so that his parents may have to move. He may need special clothing, and he may pose a problem with regard to his recreational needs since he cannot be admitted to a normal summer camp. To describe the alterations in this child's life, or to compare him with a nondisabled child on one or two sets of parameters, for example, intelligence tests or personality tests, may yield a grotesque distortion of the most salient parts of his life. For even if there are no differences manifested on the test, the question of whether the child's personality or life-style is different from that of normal children, or the question of whether his personality is affected by his disability, may remain unanswerable.

Fourth, although a handicap is not an illness and is relatively static compared with illness, the individual who is handicapped is not static. It, therefore, makes a difference whether the disability is congenital or acquired, the age at which the disability is acquired, and the length of time since the onset of the disability. There are very few studies which consider the parameters associated with time in life and disability. Those studies which exist have been more concerned with the area of aging than with childhood, or they have been concerned with the effects of brain damage on performance on mental tests (Belmont & Birch, 1960; Hebb, 1949). There is even a paucity of information about how children at different ages experience what a handicap is. Is a 3-year-old child with a congenital amputation of his leg aware that he differs from other people?

At what age does he become aware of his difference? There are very few hard answers to this kind of simple question.

CEREBRAL PALSY

Definition

Cerebral palsy is a "condition characterized by paralysis, weakness, incoordination or any other aberration of motor function due to the pathology of the motor control center of the brain" (Perlstein, 1952). However, cerebral palsy is more than a "motor problem." Despite this definition, the motor system must be seen as only one of the sources of dysfunction. Indeed, it might be more appropriate to consider cerebral palsy as an aggregate of handicaps with neuromuscular, sensory, mental, and emotional disturbances. In general, cerebral palsy may be divided into a number of subtypes, with the following frequencies of occurrence: spastic (45 percent), athetoid (23 percent), rigidity (11 percent), ataxic (11 percent), and other or mixed (7 percent). The subtypes are divided on the basis of the nature of the motor disturbance (Cruickshank, 1966). These types differ in terms of the neurological source of the disturbance, as well as in some of the sequelae which are pertinent. For example, the incidence of mental retardation is greater for spastic children. The occurrence of deafness and speech involvement is greater for athetoid children (Hopkins, Bice, & Colton, 1954).

Severity of disability is generally characterized by the number of limbs affected. Impairment of one limb is referred to as *monoplegia*. Impairment of one-half of the body along the vertical (right-left axis) is known as *hemiplegia*. Impairment of three limbs, which is rare, is known as *triplegia*. Impairment of all four limbs is called *quadriplegia*. Where the paralysis (plegia) is incomplete, it is referred to as *paresis* (weakness). As a general rule, the more severe the disability,

the greater the degree of brain damage and the greater the degree of other defects, including mental retardation.

While opinion as to the incidence of mental retardation among the cerebral-palsied children has fluctuated, it is currently thought that approximately 50 percent are borderline and below in intelligence (Cruickshank, 1966). It is of interest to note that when the great boom in rehabilitation of cerebral palsy started in this country immediately after World War II, it was thought that the cerebral-palsied were typically of average intelligence but had suffered from lack of opportunity and lack of adequate rehabilitation treatment. Current students of the problem are not so optimistic (Cruickshank, 1966). This recognition is accompanied by a shift in attitudes from concern with the motor disturbance as the primary problem to a concern with the less visible aspects of the problem, which may be more handicapping than the visible disability.

The concern with the possible sources of difficulty can be appreciated by noting that approximately 60 percent of individuals with cerebral palsy have a variety of difficulties in the visual area. These difficulties range all the way from severe blindness to minor disturbance in visual acuity, visual versatility, and visual capacity to disturbances in squinting and color vision (Donlon, 1966).

Field defects (Tizard, Paine, & Crothers, 1954) and muscle imbalance (Guibor, 1955) range all the way from 35 to 70 percent, depending on the sample studied. Similarly, auditory defects reveal a variety of subproblems (Nober, 1966) which might impair hearing. Disturbances in sensation have also been noted by many students of the problem (Hohman, Baker, & Reed, 1958; Tizard, Paine, & Crothers, 1954; Wilson & Wilson, 1967). Evaluation of these disturbances is extremely difficult. Consider the fact that in order to obtain a reliable response, one must have a cooperative subject who is able to either talk, move, or indicate. Consider, also, the fact that one must have the subject's attention. Finally, many of the tests of acuity are intertwined with mental functions. For example, a child with limited intelligence may fail to read a visual chart for many reasons. It is, therefore, very difficult to tell what the source of failure is when a child does not perform.

Incidence and Etiology

There are approximately 600,000 individuals with cerebral palsy in this country (Allen, 1962; McCavitt, Diller, & Orgel, 1966). It is estimated that over one-third of these individuals are under 21 years of age. It is also estimated that for each 100,000 births per year, there are 7 children with cerebral palsy. There have been many studies on the etiology of cerebral palsy, and indeed, there have been attempts to induce experimental cerebral palsy in animals (Windle, 1962). The major sources which have been implicated and their incidence are as follows: birth injury, including anoxia and hemorrhage (55 percent); congenital cerebral defect (23 percent); postnatal injury to the head (5 percent) and encephalitis meningitis (4 percent); and other causes (13 percent). Prematurity and anoxia have been implicated as the major conditions which result in multiply handicapped children.

Medical Treatment

Medical treatment of the child with cerebral palsy is complex. The technical treatment may involve specialties ranging from pediatrics, orthopedics, psychiatry, neurosurgery, and orthopedic surgery. Nonmedical professionals may include psychologists, social workers, physical therapists, occupational therapists, recreational therapists, speech therapists, audiologists, speech educators, and vocational counselors. Despite the recent wide publicity afforded to specific approaches (Doman et al., 1960), there have been no spectacular breakthroughs in this field.

Furthermore, since several modalities are affected simultaneously and many different treatment procedures have to be conducted at the same time, it is difficult to test for the efficacy of any single treatment procedure. The evaluation of physical therapy, occupational therapy, and speech therapy remains in an even more primitive state than the evaluation of psychotherapy. In general, the goals of treatment are to make the individual as competent as possible in his functional activities, to give him the appearance of being normal, to provide him with education which is realistic, and to prepare him for vocational self-sufficiency. Psychological adjustment is generally regarded as a by-product of these activities. With regard to the attainment of functional competence, the field of rehabilitation medicine has developed a number of scales, called Activities of Daily Living Scales, which consist of the most common daily activities which are needed to carry out self-care. These include dressing activities, feeding, and ambulation (Brown, 1960). These items are similar to those found in the well-known Vineland Social Maturity Scale (Doll, 1953) and the Gesell scales, which pertain to the motor aspects of independence. They are perhaps the most critical instruments developed in the field of rehabilitation since they are often used as criteria for admission and discharge from rehabilitation programs. It is important to note that the scales emphasize functional motor skills, rather than motor skills per se. For example, the child is taught to feed himself and to walk. The acquisition of these skills touches on diverse fields relating to neurophysiology, engineering psychology, developmental psychology, and the psychology of learning. While there are studies on the relationship of walking to intelligence and age (Perlstein & Hood, 1957), there has been little study of how a cerebral palsy child learns to walk. There has been even less study of how much the cerebral palsy child actually does walk. The technical scaling of activities of daily living presents an important problem, which has not as yet been treated with psychometric sophistication (Diller, 1966). Because the scales are so highly functional, items have content validity, in contrast to achievement or intelligence tests, in which the items have statistical or construct validity. If a child can button a garment, it seems reasonable to think he is more independent. But if a person knows how far it is from New York to Chicago, an item on the intelligence scale, it is not so apparent that he is more intelligent than an individual who cannot answer this particular question. Many of the observations with regard to speech are similar to those made with regard to physical therapy. The problem of language development, its measurement and its treatment in the child with cerebral palsy, has received only scattered attention (Lencione, 1966). Denhoff and Holden (1951) have developed a table for expectancies of motor and language maturation in children with cerebral palsy. For example, in comparing their findings, based on a study of 100 children with cerebral palsy, with normative data provided by Gesell, they point up such factors as: The typical normal infant reaches for objects at 3 to 5 months, while the child with cerebral palsy reaches for objects at 14 months. The typical normal child crawls at 7 to 8 months, while the cerebral palsy child crawls at 26 months. The typical normal child uses single words at 9 to 10 months, while the cerebral palsy child uses single words at 27 months.

This type of normative profile can be a very useful tool to the pediatrician and the psychologist. It can provide him with a frame of reference for what he might expect in the development of these children. It might be noted that there has been very little work which utilizes some of the more current notions derived from psycholinguistics (Lenenberg, 1966) with regard to the language development of the child with cerebral palsy.

SPINA BIFIDA

Definition

Spina bifida is a birth defect which involves a developmental failure of the bilateral dorsal laminae of the vertebrae to fuse in the midline and develop a single dorsal spinal process. If the developmental failure is not accompanied by spinal-cord or nerve-root abnormality and if it is covered by normal skin, it is not visible externally and is referred to as *spina bifida occulta*. This defect is very common. The incidence is reported to range from 2 to 54 percent in adults (Karlin, 1935) and from 58 to 82 percent in children (Fawcett, 1959). The higher incidence figures in children suggest that fusion of the spine occurs with growth and development in later childhood. Spina bifida occulta is generally without clinical signs or symptoms, although some (Gillespie, 1946) believe that it predisposes to back instability.

The children with whom we are concerned have a spina bifida which is associated with a defective formation of the spinal cord. The defective cord and the meninges are visible on the back, and the skin attaches to the protruding mass, so that there appears to be a lump protruding from the spinal column. This malformation is generally accompanied by muscle weakness, skin sensitivity below the defective part of the spinal cord, poor innervation of the bowel and bladder, and various degrees of hydrocephalus.

Spina bifida manifesta is known technically as *myelomeningocele* and is the most frequent type associated with deviant normal development. There are various subclassifications of the type of defect associated with spina bifida manifesta (Swinyard, 1966).

Incidence and Etiology

In the past, spina bifida was considered a medical curiosity because of the low survival rate. However, in the more recent present, with increasing hopefulness, more accurate data are being gathered. In England and Wales, where epidemiological problems have been studied in more sophisticated ways, it has been reported that spina bifida occurs in 2 to 3 cases per 1,000 live births (Swinyard, 1966). In New York City in 1959, the estimate was 8 cases per 1,000 live births. Spina bifida occurs more often in females than in males. It also appears to be more severe in females than in males. It is of interest to note that spina bifida (like clubfoot) has a low incidence in nonwhite populations.

Although the etiological factors which cause human spina bifida remain unknown, there is little doubt that the causative factors are profoundly influenced by the genetic constitution of the individual concerned. Studies associating spina bifida with epidemics, maternal health, seasonal variation, and environmental factors are suggestive but inconclusive.

Medical Treatment

The care of the child with spina bifida and its associated difficulties probably requires more continuous study and delicate juxtaposition of therapies than does any other handicapping condition. This study is not well known to the medical profession (in addition to ignorance on the part of psychologists, educators, and laymen).

Since the spina bifida is often accompanied by hydrocephalus, neurosurgical intervention, which might be useful in arresting the enlarged head size, may be necessary. This requires continued alertness on the part of the parents and the physician, especially during the first year of life. If the neurosurgical procedure is carried out, continued observation is required afterward because of the danger of malfunctioning of a shunt, which is placed in the skull. The shunting procedure, which is one of the modern developments of neurosurgery, may be considered to be a great lifesaver in children who otherwise would

have been doomed to death a few years ago. As the child grows older, the parents will become aware of the difficulty in bladder and bowel incontinence. Extra procedures for the care of bowel and bladder have to be taught to the parents. This involves dietary intake, as well as a regularized schedule of voiding. With increasing maturation, neuromuscular problems then come to the fore. Difficulties in walking, requiring bracing, and dangers of muscle imbalance, leading to curvatures in posture, have to be considered. These obvious disabilities may obscure the presence of more subtle ones, including problems in sensation and perception (Badell-Ribera, Swinyard, Greenspan, & Deaver, 1964). Because of the fact that the spina bifida group had, until modern surgical and rehabilitation techniques, been considered hopeless, not as much is known about their behavioral and neurological impairments as in the case of the cerebral palsy group, who have been well studied for almost a century.

The child with spina bifida may require continued rehospitalization for neurological and urological reasons. In addition, a program of habilitation in which the child may be taught ambulation, self-care, toilet habits, and a variety of motor skills has to be considered. Since these skills differ at different age levels, repeated hospitalization is required. It has been estimated, for example, that the child with spina bifida loses an average of two months of school per year.

Since so little is known about this child and since he appears to be so verbally facile, he will often confuse the teacher, who may expect more of him than he is capable of producing. Consequently, the child may be subjected to school pressures to perform beyond his level of ability.

Some of the problems, particularly in the personality and cognitive domains, do not emerge until later in life—in contrast, for example, with the cerebral palsy child, whose personality style and temperament are clear from early childhood.

There is some evidence that while children with spina bifida, particularly those with hydrocephalus, may be very attractive socially as young children, this attractive quality turns to withdrawal and depression in adolescence (Diller, Paddock, Badell-Ribera, & Swinyard, 1966). The child then is a puzzle both to his family and to the professionals who come into contact with him.

It has been noted that the speech of the child with spina bifida appears to be hyperaccelerated in development. The verbal output is similar in some respects to that of a hyperactive child with minimal brain damage, who moves a lot without purpose. This chatterbox quality, which may serve to obscure fundamental problems in thinking, perception, and action, has been referred to as the *cocktail party personality.*

AMPUTATIONS

Definition

With the increase of congenital malformations associated with brain injuries (Apgar & Stickle, 1968), there has been an increase in interest in children with amputations. Practically all children who have limb deformations or amputations incur these deformations at birth. However, amputations sometimes occur as a result of trauma after birth or surgery to correct a congenital malformation. While malformations or amputations could occur in all four extremities, the majority affect only one limb, and these are known as *unilateral* amputations. The site of amputation is fundamental; that is, if it is the hand, it is critical whether it is above or below the elbow, and if it is the leg, it is critical whether it is above or below the knee. With regard to the fitting of a prosthetic device or to the attainment of functional activities, amputees are generally, therefore, identified in terms of which and how many limbs are missing, as well as the locus of amputation. In general, as the number of joints

lost—that is, ankle, knee, hip, or wrist, elbow, shoulder—increases, the extent of functional potential decreases. Amputees can be described as *unilateral* (one arm or leg affected), *bilateral* (two arms or two legs affected), *double* (one leg and one arm affected), or *multiple* (more than two extremities affected).

While amputations, per se, need not affect central nervous system (CNS) function, in congenitally malformed or amputated children, CNS disorder is not unusual. In one study (Siller, 1968), it was found that 18 percent of the children showed associated impairments which could be indicative of CNS dysfunction. It has also been stated (Fishman, 1962) that there are twice as many amputations of the upper extremities as of the lower extremities. This is in contrast with adults who undergo amputations of limbs. Adults show a ratio of 3½ as many lower-extremity amputations as upper-extremity amputations.

Incidence and Etiology

Figures on the incidence of congenital amputations vary. Most authorities agree that amputations occur much more often in adulthood than in childhood. Some have estimated that 75 percent of amputations take place in adulthood, particularly among the elderly (Fishman, 1962). Fishman estimates there are 25,000 juvenile amputees in this country. The causes of congenital malformation or amputation are complex.

Medical Treatment

Perhaps the most important aspect of the medical management of the child with an amputation is the management of parental attitude. The physician who is forced to inform the mother that she has given birth to a monster is put in a terribly difficult situation. A number of parents report that the doctor "appeared angry with me." Others report that the doctor "did not inform me and didn't let me see the child. I only found out through the nurses." The feelings of guilt and disgust on the part of the mother and the father may often color their relationship and their attitudes toward the child for years to come.

From the technical medical standpoint, one of the major tasks in the management is the introduction and fitting of an appropriate prosthesis. The prosthesis must be changed with age and must be introduced under carefully controlled circumstances. There is often a dilemma in the timing of the prosthesis. If one introduces it too early, the child will not use it. If one introduces it too late, the child will have to unlearn a set of skills which have served to substitute for the missing extremity.

Where amputation occurs following surgery, the trauma and care following surgery must be carefully monitored. There also must be continued alertness for the occurrence of clinical problems of contractures (shortening of muscle), skin irritations, scar tissue, etc. In general, there are prosthetic teams which include, in addition to the physician, a prosthetist, occupational therapist, and physical therapist.

A fascinating problem, which has been associated with amputation, has been the phenomenon of phantom limbs. Phantom limbs may be viewed as a type of illusion in which the individual perceives that his missing part still exists in one way or another. For example, the person may feel that the amputated leg may still itch and reach down to scratch it. He may feel he can wiggle his fingers or toes or flex his wrist or ankle, despite the fact that the limb is missing. A patient may step on a phantom foot and fall. The observations on phantom limbs have served as an important background for a modern approach to the understanding of the body image, following the reasoning of Henry Head, who argued that phantom limbs suggest that all perception which enters the body is recorded on a scheme, which is built up through experience. It is of interest to note that phantom limbs generally do not occur in congenitally handicapped children. The incidence of phantom limbs tends to increase with age, so that if a child is 8 years old when

he has an amputation, it is highly likely that he will experience a phantom. If he is 2 years of age when he undergoes amputation, it is unlikely he will experience a phantom. Simmel (1967) has presented data on the incidence of phantom phenomena in childhood amputees.

One of the major problems as the child grows older is the fact that he becomes aware that his appearance differs from that of normal children. This becomes most critical at the time of adolescence. If a prosthesis is to be introduced, it often takes a great deal of preparation, particularly during the adolescent years.

MUSCULAR DYSTROPHY

Definition

Progressive muscular dystrophy is primarily a progressive degeneration of striated musculature of the body. There are, generally, five types of muscular dystrophy—the classification being dependent upon appearance of muscles, the group of muscles primarily involved, age of onset, or changes in muscle tone and reactivity. The natural histories of these types vary somewhat, and the incidence and prognosis of these types vary somewhat, so that the differential diagnosis is very important (Rusk, 1964).

Progressive muscular atrophies are neurological diseases in which failure of development or progressive degeneration of lower motor neuron cell bodies results in atrophy of the nerves and paralysis of the muscles. In both groups of disease entities, the primary problem is a progressive loss of muscular control. While there has been a traditional attitude of fatalism which accompanies these diagnoses, this fatalism does not apply to some of the subtypes, and indeed, a rehabilitation program may be quite useful. This program emphasizes different degrees of self-care activity, which are consonant with the degree of muscle impairment. Physical therapy is useful for maintaining muscle power.

Incidence and Etiology

Fortunately, the incidence of this disease is less than is generally believed, although from a prognostic standpoint it is one of the most serious problems. There is some controversy over the prevalence and incidence of the disease. Some considerations in this regard and a bibliography may be found in Rusk (1964).

Although it is generally agreed that the disease is hereditary in basis, the mechanism of the defective gene which produces the disease is unknown. Most investigators believe it to be a biochemical defect (Rusk, 1964).

Medical Treatment

In both muscular dystrophy and muscular atrophy, the primary problem is a progressive loss of muscular control, eventually involving the entire muscular system. The child gradually becomes weaker and weaker until the point of death. Respiratory disease may be the precipitating cause of death. The signs and symptoms of muscular dystrophy are often first manifested in early childhood when the parent notices that the child has difficulty climbing stairs. In response to the weakness, the child develops compensation, so that movements proceed in a side-to-side sway or waddle. Medical treatment usually consists of a rehabilitation program oriented around muscle strengthening or exercise to support and maintain the child's ability to take care of himself and to prevent physical deformities. Careful monitoring of his physical status is necessary. In addition to the rehabilitation program, there is some experimental work utilizing drug therapy on the theory that the disease is due to a metabolic deficiency which might be replaced by proper medication.

The progressive nature of the disease and its possible tragic consequences cause profound emotional difficulty for both the patient and the family, as well as for the staff who come into contact with the child. Truitt (1954), Austin (1954), and Wexler (1951) have described some of the psychological problems which exist in this situation.

BLINDNESS

Definition

The National Association for the Prevention of Blindness defines the blind child as one who "has central visual acuity of 20/200 or less in the better eye with correcting glasses, or central visual acuity of more than 20/200 if there is a field defect in which the peripheral field has contracted, so that the widest diameter of visual field extends an angular distance of no more than 20 degrees." In practice, 20/200 may be considered to be blind; 20/70 to 20/200 may be considered to be partially blind.

Incidence and Etiology

It is thought (Apgar & Stickle, 1968) that there are today 500,000 who were born blind or with serious loss of vision in this country. A survey of the school population of the United States in 1954 indicated that 0.2 out of every 1,000 children are blind and 2 out of every 1,000 children are partially blind. The causes of blindness are as follows: (1) infectious diseases, (2) trauma, (3) poisoning, (4) neoplasms, (5) prenatal difficulties, (6) etiology not specified. More than half of the causes are prenatal in origin.

Medical Treatment

While we will reserve discussion of the psychological problems and the difficulties in assessment of blind children, it can be stated, in general, that blind children are of normal intelligence (Pinter et al., 1941). Blind children begin to talk later than seeing children since they must learn to imitate movements of speech which they have never seen. This delay is often aggravated by the fact that parents may be uninformed of the necessity of therapy for speech problems or that the child may be raised in an environment which is unstimulating. Speech difficulties are common. Once speech is learned, however, blind children indulge in it more than seeing children, asking a great many questions about objects and environment. Blind children tend to favor proper names.

Although blind children can learn as well as normal children, they are unable to take advantage of imitation, a process which greatly facilitates learning to walk and take care of oneself. There is, therefore, a lag in the development of skills which are pertinent to the activities of daily living. The blind child also lacks the stimulation which the seeing child constantly receives through vision. Objects must, therefore, be brought to his attention, and the auditory and tactile modalities must be reinforced. Blind children, for example, should be told when a person is entering the room. The individual who moves should talk in order that the child can follow his movement. Because of the absence of visual cues, fear may be a great factor in deterring walking. Blind children, for example, rarely creep. Sounds may be used to reinforce walking. The objects that a child bumps into should be carefully placed and removed so that he will get to know obstacles and avoid them. Running, at first, should be discouraged since falls are frightening. Reaching out with the hand as a protection should be discouraged since this is an unpleasant mannerism.

Learning to behave without undue mannerisms presents a major problem in rearing a blind child. The isolation of the child can impose as great a handicap as the actual physical disability. Children should be encouraged to travel and become familiar with the community. This could be facilitated by careful supervision, planning, and adequate verbal cues which describe for the child what to expect (Carroll, 1961).

The blind child also should be taught neatness and orderliness, since he does not have visual cues to check on his appearance.

The educational problems of the child who is blind are complex. Two guiding principles have been enunciated. First, the child should be given a knowledge of the realities of the world in which we live through the application of special methods in his teaching. Second, he should be given confidence to deal with these realities. And, third, he should be given a feeling that he is recognized and accepted as an individual in his own right.

Among the special methods of education for the blind are Braille reading and writing, typewriting from the fourth grade on, talking books to compensate for the slowness of Braille, diagram drawings and the use of forms in geometry, and special maps for teaching geography. Modeling is a useful creative activity, as are drama and music. The learning of a musical instrument is particularly difficult, for the musician must read Braille with his fingers. Since he cannot use his fingers at the same time to play the instrument, he must rely on memory in practicing as well as in performing. Handicrafts, physical education, and hiking are important parts of the program. Among the special methods which have received recognition are (1) individualization, (2) concreteness of instruction, (3) unified instruction, (4) additional stimulation, (5) self-activity.

It has been estimated that over 80 percent of all blind children receiving special education are attending residential schools, most of which are state-supported. These schools should attempt to develop programs which integrate their children with seeing children in the community. The question of whether the child should be sent to a residential school or kept in the home to attend a special program in the public school system has long been debated by experts in this field (Lowenfeld, 1952). The trend in the country is toward the loosening of institutional and residential approaches.

DEAFNESS

Definition

Deafness is an impairment of hearing so that verbal communication with other people is impaired. People whose hearing is defective but functional, with or without a hearing aid, are referred to as *partially deaf*. The partially deaf may be able to acquire language through normal channels, although more slowly than normal children. The profound disability of deafness is both insidious and obvious, for language is both the key to our culture and an important key to mental development.

Incidence and Etiology

It has been estimated that there are 3 million children with some kind of auditory defects in this country. It is further estimated that 0.1 percent of the school population in the United States are deaf and 1.5 percent are hard of hearing. Approximately 60 percent of hearing difficulties in children are due to congenital reasons. The remaining 40 percent are due to acquired reasons. One of the greatest sources of acquired hearing impairment is meningitis. The defects in hearing associated with meningitis are particularly severe. That is, the incidence of total deafness is greater following meningitis than it is following scarlet fever or measles. Congenital deafness usually affects several members of the same family. This is often encouraged by the fact that deaf individuals intermarry.

Medical Treatment

Levine (1962) has outlined the considerations entering into medical management. Testing for auditory acuity is a particularly difficult problem in the case of infants or the mentally retarded. Deafness is generally not detected until after the age in which language is expected to develop. A careful developmental history is important. For example, at 6 months of age, a hearing child may move his eyes in the direction of sound, trying to locate it; a deaf child will not.

Gesell and Amatruda (1952) present a list of signs which are useful in the developmental evaluation of deafness. Techniques utilizing operant conditioning have been developed to detect deafness. Since language is impaired in deaf people, it is not surprising that the intelligence tests of the deaf reveal that they lag behind normal people. Nevertheless, there is a great deal of individual difference within the group as a whole. Experts in the field disagree on two major issues: (1) whether the child should be taught sign language primarily or lip reading, (2) how much a language impairment actually does affect thinking (Furth, 1966). As can be expected, reading is extremely difficult for the deaf child. The development of good reading habits should be encouraged. Books of high vocal level and high interest are useful. Written language and grammar also affect the reading of the deaf. The typical deaf child is two to three years below his expected achievement level by the time he is 12 years of age.

Where the deaf child is not impaired in his motor movements, he is free to explore his environment. He should be encouraged in diverse interests and occupations. He should be encouraged to participate in family conversations and discussions; otherwise, he may acquire the habit of not listening or watching and may have difficulty learning to lip-read. The isolation, both social and cultural, which accompanies deafness may pose greater constraints on the personality than the more obvious problems associated with the child who is visibly crippled. Most deaf children can be taught to talk. The parents must be very observant, beginning with the infant's early babbling and cooing. Whatever small remnants of hearing exist may be found to be useful. Most authorities who have dealt with the deaf (Bakwin & Bakwin, 1963) encourage all who come into contact with deaf children to talk a great deal. Talking is often helpful if it is close to the child's ear and accompanied by visual or tactile demonstration. The head should be kept still so as not to distract the child from the difficult task of watching lips and mouth. The face should be kept at a level with the child's.

Whole sentences are important, for the child learns to fill in. Good pronunciation is useful. Since the child can see, imitation is useful, and methods of matching and teaching are therefore encouraged. In general, a hearing aid is useful if the hearing loss in the better ear is more than 30 decibels in the speech range. Hearing aids differ in type and must, therefore, be carefully prescribed. Fitting of hearing aids and training in their use are to be recommended. Children as young as 2 and 3 years of age have used them. The newer hearing aids are small, compact, efficient, and attractive.

CARDIAC PROBLEMS

Definition

Heart disease in children falls into three general categories: (1) There is the infectious group, of which rheumatic fever is the largest and most important. (2) There are children with congenital heart disease. This group is a small but important number, since a large percentage of them are curable by surgery. (3) There is a large group of so-called potential or possible cases, who have no heart disease but whose diagnosis is based on a vague history resembling rheumatic fever or on the incidental presence of an innocuous or meaningless murmur.

Rheumatic fever is a disease in which inflammation of many tissues of the body occurs simultaneously, and the symptoms are due to localization of this inflammation. It may occur in joints, skin, brain, or the heart. Consequently, it has varied manifestations. It may occur in a mild form, with vague symptoms, or in a severe form. In the heart, rheumatic fever may heal with scarring and thus produce permanent heart disease. The valves may not close sufficiently, or they may not open sufficiently. In the mild case, with adequate treatment, there may be total disappearance of the symptoms and the inflammation. The child, indeed, may never give evidence

of heart disease and can be returned to normal activity following appropriate rest. If there is valve damage, competitive sports may be eliminated but normal life resumed. If the damage is severe, a special school may be required. Although no heart damage may occur in the first attack, the diagnosis is very important since forestalling further attacks can be instituted with appropriate medication.

The second group, children with congenital heart disease, generally show abnormality of the heart and/or its blood vessels at birth. This abnormality interferes with the passage of blood. Since 1938, modern techniques of surgery can often correct or partially correct this defect, and adequate diagnosis is again useful in prevention. It should be pointed out that the consequences of cardiac defect range from none to severe, so that limitations of the disability vary widely.

The third group, which is perhaps the largest in number, is very important because there is often suspicion of disease, with an attending anxiety in both the parent and the child. Rheumatic fever is often difficult to diagnose even by experienced observers. Functional heart murmurs are not at all uncommon in children. Children with heart disease had received little attention until the past two decades.

Incidence and Etiology

A survey of children in the New York City school system indicates that approximately 1 percent may be considered cardiac children with known disease. Approximately half of these suffer from consequences of rheumatic fever, and the other half suffer from congenital defect (Wrightstone, 1961).

More recent studies have indicated that cardiac nondisease may be more disabling than cardiac disease. There is also evidence to indicate how children with congenital heart defects often respond to stress.

Personality difficulties have been studied by

a number of investigators (Josselyn et al., 1955; Kir-Stimon, 1962). Finally, children with cardiac conditions have been shown to have a lag in reading and arithmetic (Wrightstone, 1961).

Medical Treatment

The specific treatment varies with the type of cardiac disease. In the case of rheumatic fever, the child may have to be observed periodically after the acute disease has passed. This is also true in the case of the child with congenital heart disease. However, in the former instance, the cardiologist is interested primarily in prophylactic treatment against the recurrence of the rheumatic state. In a recent study of a large sample of children (Wrightstone, 1961), it was found that by far the greatest problems were misdiagnosis in more than one-half of the sample and an over-restriction of activity in 83 percent of the cases. Since restrictions in activity can be lifted, depending on the condition of the child, it is important that medical follow-up be rigorously adhered to.

SOCIAL FACTORS IN DISABILITY

While a disability comes to our attention because of an impairment in biological functioning, social factors enter in both overt and covert ways. It is clear, for example, that a physical handicap in one set of circumstances may be disabling whereas in another set of circumstances it is not. There are very few studies on cross-cultural attitudes toward the disabled. Whiting and Child (1953), working with the data in the Yale cross-cultural files, have demonstrated the interrelationships of religious beliefs, perceived cause of disability, and child rearing. These interrelationships, which have been demonstrated for primitive cultures, may exist in our society, but they may be obscured by factors, such as universal education, which tend to flatten differences in belief systems. Differences in our society may,

therefore, be less pronounced. Hanks and Hanks (1948) have argued that the physically handicapped in nonoccidental societies are treated in accordance with the level of production in the society, so that the more primitive the level of production, the more the handicapped individual is denigrated or devalued. This hypothesis is similar to the kind McClelland and his associates (1953) have put forward with regard to achievement drive, in which it has been suggested that the need for achievement in different societies is correlated with the level of economic productivity. Indeed, attitudes toward a handicapped child may be related to achievement drive. Many of the methods of McClelland's group, e.g., the analysis of children's stories, novels, or drawings, would lend themselves as useful devices for testing the hypothesis.

In viewing attitudes toward the disabled in current Western civilized countries, one finds little hard data on the effects of different cultures on attitudes toward the disabled. One of the few studies in this area (Sanua, 1967) has shown that cerebral-palsied individuals in different European countries regard themselves and their disabilities differently. Indeed, in some societies, particularly in the northern parts of Europe, the disabled receive much more opportunity for participating in normal society. Taylor and Taylor (1960) have analyzed the approaches to special education in different European countries, basing their information on the legislative history of these countries and the current status of handicapped children. It is difficult to demonstrate coherence between countries in accordance with any single hypothesis. However, it is easy to demonstrate the lack of adequate facilities in the education of children in different countries.

In addition to cross-cultural differences, there have been a number of investigations showing the effects of social class with regard to handicapping conditions. Farber (1959) has demonstrated that the mentally retarded boy has a much greater disruptive effect in lower-class families than does a mentally retarded girl, whereas this is not the case for middle-class families. Lower-class mothers think in terms of the practical problems the child poses in terms of their role, e.g., arrangements for baby-sitting, caring functions, transportation, etc. The middle-class mother thinks typically in terms of "Why did this happen?" It has also been suggested, in the case of the mentally retarded, that a child who is born early in the marriage, that is, to a young couple, tends to affect the progress of the father's occupational development, so that there is less mobility on an occupational ladder (Farber & Jenne, 1963). A similar effect does not take place if a child is born once the occupational ladder has been set. Similar patterns are highly likely among the cerebral-palsied and other congenitally damaged groups.

Social class factors enter in other ways. For example, in this country the pattern of care of handicapped children has been strongly influenced by the roles of parent groups, which are usually organized to promote services for their handicapped children (Katz, 1961). These parent groups stem from the middle-class segment of our population. It has been demonstrated, for example, that a great deal of money was invested in the cure and prevention of poliomyelitis, even though the incidence of poliomyelitis is much lower than that of other disabling conditions. This has been largely due to the fact that poliomyelitis had a much higher incidence in middle-class groups than did other disabling conditions. Heber et al. (1968) have argued that mild mental retardation is often cultural in origin and, therefore, occurs in a disproportionate amount in lower-class groups. By way of contrast, severe mental retardation, that is, IQs below 50, is probably organic in origin and may be culturally induced only indirectly, that is, insofar as lower socioeconomic factors heighten the conditions for difficult pregnancies and deliveries. Although there are strands of evidence for the differences in social class affecting the incidence and perceived cause of disability and the parental roles (Farber, 1959; Farber & Jenne, 1963; Kelman, 1964), by far the greatest impact in social class is probably in the area of delivery of services.

Religious differences also enter with regard to the physically handicapped. It is clear that many people perceive the handicap as "God's will." However, the meaning of religious belief and attitude toward disability is less clear. A number of studies (Boles, 1956; Zuk, 1959) present data to suggest that Catholic mothers are more accepting of a handicapped child than are Protestant and Jewish mothers. Zborowski (1952) and Sanua (1960) have demonstrated similar patterns of differences in the case of response to pain and amputation. Manjos (1966) was able to find similar differences among cerebral-palsied individuals with different religious beliefs. McCavitt, Diller, and Orgel (1966) were able to confirm these differences in studying attitudes toward disability in cerebral-palsied individuals, as well as in their parents. There appears to be evidence from a variety of quarters that expectancies with regard to the disabled are influenced by cultural, social class, and religious differences. The effects of these differences on response to treatment and management of the disabled have not yet been articulated. For example, why do some religious beliefs facilitate acceptance while others do not?

Cultural influences in attitudes toward the disabled have also been investigated from another standpoint. Davis (1961, 1963), Gofman (1963), and Becker (1963) have argued that the disabled represent a deviant group. An individual's response to a disabled person, therefore, is indicative of how he responds to someone who deviates from himself (Cowan, 1960). Richardson (1963) has called attention to the fact that individuals may often be overly polite to a handicapped person because they do not know how to respond to him. He cites the instance of the person who was with a disabled individual, listening to a long story even though he was in a hurry to get away. The individual felt too uncomfortable to excuse himself and terminate the situation, so that he remained in it, partially listening, partially patronizing, and partially thinking about how he could extricate himself. These brief interpersonal encounters, therefore, serve to elicit a variety of defense mechanisms manifested in distancing techniques or ways of reducing tension, e.g., denial, avoidance, circuitous conversations, overbluntness, or humor. Davis (1963) interviewed a number of articulate handicapped people who were able to speak of these situations. Richardson has argued that if it is indeed the case that the handicapped person is receiving different kinds of responses in interpersonal encounters, then he is being subjected to abnormal feedbacks. For example, the young child may be continuously overpatronized, overindulged, or overavoided, and he is not informed of the appropriateness of his reactions as other children are. The distortion of interpersonal feedback may lead to inadequate development of skills in fulfilling the variety of roles an individual must perform in interpersonal encounters (Kelley, 1967). This hypothesis, which has not yet been experimentally tested, would account for an immaturity which has been noted among congenitally handicapped children by a number of observers. For example, the job placement rate among individuals with cerebral palsy has been alleged by earlier investigators to be related to the degree of physical handicap. However, Glick (1953) and McCavitt, Diller, and Orgel (1966) have pointed out that vocational placements among the cerebral palsy group, even in individuals with mild handicaps, are below expected levels.

There have been a number of other pertinent studies in attitudes toward the disabled. Yuker, Block, and Campbell (1960) and Siller (1963, 1968) have been devising objective scales of attitudes toward disabled people. The basic hypothesis put forward by Yuker, Block, and Campbell (1960) and Cowan (1960) is that individuals who reject handicapped people also reject other minority-group members, including the aged, and score in the authoritarian direction on the F scale. Siller (1963) and Whiteman and Lukoff (1964) have attempted to break down the components of attitudes toward the handicapped and have argued that the handicapped may be viewed in terms of more than a single dimension of accepting or rejecting. Siller has proposed, for example, that there may be different dimensions for different kinds of handicapping conditions. Nash (1962) and Granofsky (1959) have used Thematic Apperception Test (TAT) type pictures to investigate attitudes toward handicapped individuals with similar results. Richardson (1963) and Richardson et al. (1963) have used a picture-preference technique in which it has been demonstrated that there is a rank order of preference for different kinds of physical deviations, for example, obesity versus wheelchair versus amputation. Richardson found a correlation between the attitudes of parents as reflected on this scale and the attitudes of their children. He therefore proposed that attitudes toward the handicapped present an excellent example of the transmission-of-values system, which can be studied in the pure form since it is outside the domain of most value-conflict areas in our society. Other approaches to the problem have been to study the effects of a handicapped person on the responses of other people in social situations. This could be done in the laboratory situation, for example, where a handicapped person acts as a stooge or confederate in a conformity situation (Kleck, 1966) or where a handicapped person might actually enter a restaurant or apply for housing (Hastorf et al., 1964) to study the effects on both bystanders and participants. All studies demonstrate prejudiced attitudes toward the handicapped. The prejudiced attitudes of society toward the handicapped have an obvious influence on the handicapped person's attitude toward himself. Just as normal individuals will avoid looking at an amputee in the aniesekonic lens technique, so will an amputee avoid looking at the picture of an amputee. Lipp et al. (1968) have demonstrated that the avoidance of a recognition of a handicap which may be found on tachistoscopic presentation is related to other features of denial, including locus of control, i.e., whether the person was himself responsible or whether an outside force is responsible. Farina, Sherman, and Allen (1968) found that the stigma of physical handicap did not arouse uniform and unambiguous responses. On the contrary, contempt and sympathy often occurred in the same person.

The importance of the vantage point of the perceiver is illustrated in the study of Barker, Schoggin, Schoggin, and Barker (1952), who interviewed all the teachers and physicians and a good sampling of laymen in a county in Kansas, asking them to list whomever they knew as disabled. The investigators found different degrees of reporting by each. It was further found that specialized training was not a critical facet. Barker (1963) has developed a theory of behavior settings and methods of measuring behavioral occurrences as they unfold in the environment.

Studies using sociometric approaches to the handicapped (Force, 1956) found that physically handicapped children were chosen significantly less often as companions, both as playmates and as workmates. This study was conducted in an integrated school setting. Holden (1962) and Holmes (1966), using sociometric approaches of integrated groups in camps or recreational programs, found similar underpopularity of handicapped children. In an unpublished study (Diller, 1966) of a group of cerebral-palsied individuals, where an attempt was made to see what the basis of choice is within a group of handicapped

people, there was some evidence that less handicapped people were chosen more often than the more severely handicapped. However, this evidence was secondary to another major finding. When an attempt was made to match the individual chosen with the chooser, in terms of similarity or difference on the following dimensions: high IQ versus low IQ, wheelchair-bound versus ambulatory, speech impaired versus speech normal, age, Jewish versus Catholic, male versus female, there were only two major dimensions which indicated affinity between chooser and chosen. The primary factor was the same sex. That is, even though the population averaged 20 years of age, there were very few cross-sex choices. This tends to support the notion of sexual immaturity in this group. This finding was repeated when the study was conducted for a second year. A second finding which is of some interest is that at the beginning of the program individuals also chose on the basis of similar religion, i.e., Jewish individuals chose Jewish people and Catholics chose Catholics. When the study was repeated a year later, after the individuals knew each other, the dimension of religious affinity was dissipated but the sex dimension was maintained.

There are very few studies on the courting, dating, and marriage patterns of children who are handicapped. Although there are reports that some handicapped groups, e.g., the deaf (Kelley, 1967), tend to intermarry, there are no hard data on this area. Skipper, Fink, and Hallenbeck (1968) have discussed adjustment problems in husband-wife relationships.

Although early students of the problem have commented that the physically handicapped person poses an interesting experimental test of the Freudian theory of psychosexual development, there has been very little creative work or even tests of this model. Block (1954), using the Blacky Pictures Test, which had been designed specifically to tap the Freudian theory of psychosexual development, found little evidence that a group of individuals with cerebral palsy differ from a normal group. However, clinical experience suggests that it is difficult to generalize about the sexual adjustment of the handicapped.

Diller (1970) found that the figure drawings of handicapped children, measures which might reflect psychosexual development, did not point to a particular difficulty associated with a particular handicapping condition; rather, they reflected the general organismic level of personal adjustment. The earlier positive findings of Bender (1948) on the Draw-A-Person Test, which suggested that a figure drawing might reveal the individual's body image, or the disability itself, might be explained by the fact that Bender's group were seen in a psychiatric setting and were severely disturbed mentally. It therefore might be argued that the Draw-A-Person Test represents a combination of attitudes affected by the disability and the levels of defense of personality. Where the defenses are down, the attitude toward the disability will be reflected. In another study, it has been shown that children with congenital amputations demonstrate an increased use of mechanisms of avoidance on figure drawings when administered in adolescence.

EDUCATIONAL PROBLEMS

The education of the handicapped child poses a special problem for both parents and community. The problem may be viewed on two levels; one is cognitive, and the second is personality. From a cognitive standpoint, the handicapping condition, as in the case of cerebral palsy, will often directly impair the child's ability to learn, so that special methods of diagnosis and education might be called for. The past decade has seen an explosion of technologies for the evaluation of learning problems in brain-injured and handicapped children, as well as suggested solutions. There are new journals, e.g. *Journal of Learning Disabilities, Journal of Special Educa-*

tion, Journal of Child Psychology, Journal of School Psychology, as well as a revamping of classical journals, e.g., *Exceptional Children.*

Procedures for education range all the way from piling a group of cerebral palsy children into confined spaces so that they brush up against each other and, consequently, develop an awareness of their body image and create more intimate contact with other people (Jones & Sisk, 1967) to the use of "prosthetic environments" (Lindsley, 1964). There is no hard-and-fast evidence at this stage of our knowledge of the superiority of any single method. At a second level, the problems of education pertain to the personality of the handicapped child. Here, the whole issue of the child's being different enters. Is it better to send a child to an integrated school or to a special school? Would handicapped children benefit from having handicapped instructors? Opinions on these questions have not been subject to vigorous testing, so that a school which has designed a program for handicapped children or a parent who is considering the education of his handicapped child must fall back on his own experiences and judgments.

The problems, which have been the traditional concerns of psychologists, have been compounded by ecological considerations and practical difficulties, which have not been considered by psychologists. For example, the problem of transportation is critical when you consider the fact that a handicapped child may spend an hour and a half going to school on a school bus, in each direction, and that this time is nearly equivalent to the amount of time spent in school. The bus driver, in fact, may spend more time with the child than the teacher does. He may have to settle arguments, deal with children who are late, and contend with indifferent parents and with hyperactive children. The school itself poses many architectural problems. How large should the class be? How many children should there be to a teacher? The curriculum also poses a problem. What should the subject matter be? Should it be the same as for nondisabled children? If it is the same, how can one take into account the social isolation once the handicapped child goes home from school? How can one take into account the fact that if he is wheelchair-bound, then his opportunities in the vocational world may be limited, and how can one prepare the child for this? At what age should vocational counseling begin? Can one devise an index of a child's "vocational maturity" which could be used as a measure of his readiness?

The education of a handicapped child is further complicated by the fact that handicapped children generally are dispersed throughout the community, so that there is usually not enough of a population concentration of handicapped children to foster a neighborhood-school concept.

There are only rudimentary beginnings of efforts on the part of psychologists to bring their tools to bear on these problems. Barker (1963) and his students have begun to study some of the parameters of behavior settings. It is clear that the problems, which are now coming into major focus in the eyes of the parents and the institutions that care for the handicapped and the professionals who work with the handicapped, will play an important role in the management of the child. Since it is often asserted that institutions impose their own kinds of pathology —indeed, the use of intelligence test requirements in education is really a tool to help an institution sort its children—the psychologist working with the handicapped must become increasingly sophisticated in terms of the subtleties which different institutionalized restrictions impose.

PSYCHOLOGICAL EVALUATION

Psychological assessment is used for several purposes: (1) when there is a complaint with regard to a behavioral disturbance, a learning difficulty, or a developmental lag; (2) when there is a need on the part of the institutions which are concerned with the management of the child to define who the child is and certain critical parameters. The latter assessment will occur in school settings, rehabilitation settings, and vocational programs. In this type of setting, the issue is generally twofold; one is to define the child on a set of parameters, and the second is to determine how this definition fits the definition of what the institution has to offer. While diagnosis from the standpoint of the needs of an individual and assessment from the standpoint of the institutional setting are often congruent, sometimes they are not. Let us consider, for example, the role of norms in the case of the child with cerebral palsy. We may find that the mental development of the average child with cerebral palsy who enters a rehabilitation program is below that of 90 percent of the normal population. From one standpoint in planning a program, this is highly important. However, the question arises of what the goals of a program for such a child should consist of. Here, the comparison with external norms may be quite irrelevant. If we ask how we can optimize a child's potential, we would have to rephrase our consideration of norms, and we would be much more accurate if we spoke of norms which were specific to a setting and a subtype of the population.

In considering the evaluation of the child with a physical handicap, four factors must be dealt with:

1. Sensory limitations. For example, poor hearing may diminish responses to verbal tasks.

2. Motor limitations. Paralysis or motor weakness may inhibit or delay the patient's manual response.

3. Speech handicaps, which may curtail his responses to verbal questions.

While most clinicians will suspend time limits to supplement the judgment based on the test standards, there are no normative studies on what the effects of extended time limits are. In adult brain damage (Costa & Vaughan, 1962), it has been demonstrated that increasing time limits facilitates performance in individuals with damage to the major hemisphere on a block design task but does not affect the performance of individuals with damage to the minor cerebral hemisphere. Briggs (1963), in a study of patients with poliomyelitis, has demonstrated that the motor handicap on manipulative tasks, such as object assembly, is not critical.

4. Cultural impoverishment. Many disabled children do not have the advantage of normal environmental stimuli. For example, a study of children with muscular dystrophy who have become homebound indicates that their verbal intelligence is below average (Morrow & Cohen, 1954). Congenitally disabled cerebral-palsied persons show less creative and imaginative records than those with acquired disability, even when they are matched for intelligence (Richards & Letterman, 1956). The lag in auditory discrimination skills has been related to a lag in reading and verbal intelligence in children without any known physical handicaps.

All these considerations point to the absence of appropriate norms for handicapped children. The standards used to measure the performance of an individual are compiled generally from samplings of performances of physically abled persons who suffer from none of the preceding limitations.

INTELLECTUAL EVALUATION

The evaluation of intelligence in children stems historically from the tradition of Alfred Binet and Henri Simon, a physician and an educator, who attempted to devise a scientific way of separating slow learners from other children in the school system of Paris at the turn of the century. The model which they proposed, and which was accepted with a great deal of success, involved the accumulation of a variety of tasks which could be graded in order of difficulty, in accordance with age-generated norms. The tasks presented to the child yielded specific and objective information, which could be easily recorded and compared with the performances of other children. This model is still the major one utilized in the assessment of handicapped children. There are several developments, however, within the model.

1. Included are attempts to devise tests which would not penalize handicapped children, for example, the Columbia Mental Maturity Scale, the Peabody Picture Vocabulary Test, the Benton Multiple Choice Visual Retention Test. These tests increase the samplings of behavior that the clinician may legitimately tap. However, the findings derived from these measures must be interpreted cautiously, for they tend to sample only a narrow range of the child's ability.

2. Within the traditional psychometric approach, there are many studies devoted to the examination of the scatter of an individual's ability. It has been observed for over half a century that children and adults with difficulties tend to show uneven mental functioning. This observation, stemming from the early work of Witmer (1911) and Wells (1927) down through the modern era of mental testing (Rapaport, Gill, & Schafer, 1964–1965), has received widespread attention from clinicians. Although the hypothesis and findings generated by scatter approaches have failed to produce a consistent body of replicable findings which can be used in differential diagnosis, interest in this approach persists to the present day. In part, this stems from the fact that clinical observations of deviance exist and that perhaps the psychometric investigations do not do justice to these clinical observations. It also stems from the fact that

there appears to be an underlying, implicit model of mental functioning. Mental functions may be viewed as being composed of a composite of abilities which act in concert in normally developing children. In individuals with behavioral and learning problems, these abilities become dissociated. This is the underlying thought of the students of mental development (Guilford, 1967). The topography of the structure-of-intellect which has been proposed in the statistical approaches to intelligence is similar in some respects to the organization of a chemist's table of elements, and the search for patterns of scatter would appear to be similar to the search for the chemist's pattern of elements to explain deviant compounds. Indeed, Guilford (1967) has posited a table with 120 elements, of which approximately 80 are known. Recent interest in tying together clinical observations with the approach of the factor analyst, who may provide a tool which permits statistical analysis along these lines, may be found in the works of Belmont and Birch (1966); Jastak (1949); and Jastak, McPhie, and Whiteman (1963). These works are pertinent to the psychometric approach to brain damage.

3. There have been attempts to develop a miniapproach to mental development, that is, the isolation of segments of mental development for specific purposes. For example, the Illinois Test of Psycholinguistic Abilities is an attempt to devise a battery of tests to yield a profile of communication ability. The Frostig Test of Visual Motor Development (Frostig et al., 1961) is an attempt to devise a test sensitive to the development of perceptual disturbances. Both of these approaches are attempts to develop an assessment technique which can be used to diagnose children with learning problems. They represent only two of a score of similar endeavors. These tasks have been used for differential diagnosis in children with physical handicaps.

4. A fourth approach has been that of developing a specialized tool which would minimize the sensory motor and cultural lag of the handicapped child. Haeussermann (1958) has developed a set of materials which are easier to grasp and to see and more capable of eliciting responses in impaired children. The findings from this instrument, in contrast with previous approaches, are not designed to yield scores which can be compared with those obtained from normative groups. On the contrary, both the materials and the approach are designed to capitalize on the child as an individual.

5. A fifth approach, which has gained more currency in European psychology than it has in America, is not only to examine the child's successes and failures but also to attempt to revise the test conditions to facilitate success. Luria (1961), utilizing Vygotsky's notion of zone of potential development, has argued that these additional samples of behavior can yield useful insights into mental functioning. For example, a cerebral palsy child can pass a block design task if it is presented as a multiple-choice recognition problem but not if he has to perform it in the regular way (Bortner & Birch, 1960).

PERCEPTUAL EVALUATION

Psychologists working with children with cerebral palsy and spina bifida and with other types of brain-injured children are frequently asked to evaluate the effects of perceptual difficulties on learning. However, perceptual assessment in its current state is highly primitive. We lack, for example, a basic taxonomy of the subtypes of perceptual disturbances (Teuber, 1959), nor do we have an adequate theory or rationale to explain task failure in the case of a child who fails to copy a figure correctly (Birch, 1964). Furthermore, it is often impossible to tease out the relationships between performance on complex tasks, e.g., drawing, and primary sensory disturbances (Diller & Birch, 1964). While there have been widespread attempts to devise perceptual batteries which can be used for both diagnosis and treatment (Frostig et al., 1961), the approach must be used with caution since there is still considerable controversy in this area (Cruickshank, 1967).

Perceptual evaluation has been utilized clinically in a number of different ways. It is most often used to determine whether or not a child is brain-damaged or to determine whether or not a disability is associated with brain damage. This point of view has been widely associated with the work of Lauretta Bender and the Bender Visual Motor Gestalt Test. The drawing tasks, particularly the Bender, have been widely adopted in the United States as part of clinical procedures. Although there has been evidence for the efficacy of using this approach with children, there is a danger that the disturbance on the task is automatically equated with the presence of brain damage, so that other disciplines, e.g., neurologists and psychiatrists, tend to look upon the Bender-Gestalt and similar tests as confirming the presence of CNS disorders in the absence of other kinds of neurological signs. This stems, in part, from the tradition laid down by Strauss, Werner, and Lehtinen, who argued that many children with behavioral disturbances are, in truth, victims of brain damage which is too subtle to be detected in classical neurological examinations, so that the disturbance of the CNS may be manifested perhaps in a disturbance in perception, even though sensation is intact. As a result of the confirmation of these findings by other investigators, perceptual evaluation is now regarded as one of the best measures of *soft signs of organicity*. Disturbances in perception may generally be associated with hyperactivity, short attention span, and difficulties in learning.

While this formulation has been useful in sensitizing clinical observers to different ways of looking at the etiology of a problem, it has also created difficulties. For example, it is possible to be brain-damaged without showing signs of perceptual disturbance. If a child shows a perceptual disturbance, it might also be possible that this disturbance is related to difficulty in vision or to emotional problems. Children may show perceptual disturbances for many reasons, including those which have very little to do with the presence of brain damage. Finally, there is the danger that the psychologist will be content to label a child as having perceptual disturbances, equating this notion with the presence of brain damage and refusing to think further about either the nature of the disturbance or the nature of the brain damage. In short, it has tended to obscure thinking as much as facilitate it. If the brain-damaged child cannot draw a diamond, why is he not able to draw it? Is it that he does not see it, or that he cannot translate what he sees into action? Under what conditions can he succeed in drawing the diamond?

An additional problem with the perceptual-evaluation approach in working with brain-injured children is that it has been basically agenetic. It is puzzling that although Werner and Bender, two of the pioneer workers with brain-injured children, were both keen students of developmental psychology, they never viewed brain-injured children from a longitudinal standpoint. Interest in the longitudinal approach to visual motor perception in both normal children (White, Castle, & Held, 1964) and brain-injured handicapped children (Belmont & Birch, 1966; Birch & Lefford, 1964; Kahn & Birch, 1968) has only been recent.

PERSONALITY EVALUATION

The major method of assessment of personality of handicapped children has been the use of standard projective techniques or the modification of techniques to obviate the difficulties imposed by the handicap. With regard to the use of projective techniques, there appears to be little evidence that a specific disability is associated with a specific personality. Since there is a fairly large literature in this area, we will consider some of the approaches in terms of the specific disabilities which we have outlined above.

Cerebral Palsy

Rorschach studies of individuals with cerebral palsy (Kimmel, 1959; Richards & Hooper, 1956; Sarason & Sarason, 1947) seem to indicate an impairment in fantasy and a sparseness in the inner life of individuals with cerebral palsy. These findings are supported by the study of Holden (1959), using the Children's Apperception Test (CAT), in which cerebral palsy children gave more literal descriptions to the cards than did normal children. However, in both the Rorschach and the CAT studies, it is difficult to assess what these differences are due to. Wenar (1954) found, for example, in a study of thirty adolescents with motor handicaps, that there appeared to be no differences when compared with nonhandicapped adolescents, so that the findings in the case of the cerebral palsy child may be a function not of the motor handicap but of the presence of brain damage or social deprivation. Other studies, utilizing level-of-aspiration approaches (Wenar, 1953), found that cerebral palsy individuals tended to differ in level of aspiration with the unfolding of the task, so that the goal setting of the handicapped children started out the same as that of the normal children but tended to diverge over time.

There have been a number of attempts to modify standard projective tests for use with cerebral-palsied as well as other motor-handicapped individuals. Gruenbaum, Quatere, Carruth, and Cruickshank (1953), Broida, Izard, and Cruickshank (1950), and Wenar (1956) have introduced modifications into standard projective tests. These might include changing the figures on TAT cards, or modifying the stimuli on the World Test so that they could be handled by the handicapped. A word of caution should be entered with regard to standard projective personality tests and inventories. Item analysis indicates that items which may be considered neurotic if responded to by normal people would obviously lead to wrong conclusions if interpreted in the same way for the handicapped; e.g., consider the following item: "I have never been paralyzed or had any unusual weakness in muscles."

Spina Bifida

There are almost no formal studies of the personality development of children with spina bifida. Unpublished findings suggest the following: (1) standard projective tests are useful for evaluating the child with spina bifida; (2) children with more severe motor handicaps tend to have more impairment in judgment of reality on the Rorschach test and more immature fantasies. The data suggest that a salient part of the dynamics of the adjustment of the disability group is a function of the lack of integration of verbal and nonverbal skills.

Often the child who can solve a problem cannot explain his solution, and the child who can explain the solution cannot solve the problem. This lack of integration is not found, for example, in a control group of children with congenital amputations. The disability itself touches on many areas of psychic adjustment which do not produce a single kind of reaction. The most profound area is the absence of bowel and bladder control, which is common to this disorder. The lack of bowel control does not create a unique characterological imprint. In most instances, it merely serves as a vehicle for the child's low self-esteem. While the TAT has been used with children with spina bifida, the analysis has been primarily in terms of psycholinguistic interpretations rather than dynamics. But even here, findings are of interest, for they indicate an irrelevancy in the thought processes of the child with spina bifida, particularly if it is associated with hydrocephalus. This irrelevancy may be one of the correlates of the poor integration of verbal and nonverbal skills.

The figure drawings of children with spina bifida present an interesting tool for study. The drawings are immature and take the form of mechanical, stick figures or empty, doll-like figures. The presentation of a distorted or paralyzed limb is seldom present. The defense system of the child with spina bifida appears to be organized around a very crude and primitive denial. For example, while an amputee child will not draw a figure with a missing limb, he may draw a person with his hands behind his back, a girl standing in a swimming pool with water up to her hips, or someone holding a book so that the fingers do not have to show. The spina bifida child does not use these mechanisms for disguising the disability; rather, there appears to be a total lack of recognition of the disability on the figure drawings.

Amputees

Individuals with amputations have no handicap which prevents them from performing on psychological tests. There are very few formal studies of the personalities of children with amputations. Siller (1968) argues that the amputee child shows the gamut of responses to his disability. However, there is no unique profile. The projective technique which has attracted the greatest attention with amputees is the Draw-A-Person Test. Although the findings on the Draw-A-Person Test appear to be ambiguous with regard to personality (Swensen, 1968), there is an absence of longitudinal data in this field. For example, in a recent study it has been suggested that the figure drawings of adolescents with amputations tend to show signs of adjustment difficulties. These difficulties are manifested by the use of denial and by withdrawal mechanisms.

Muscular Dystrophy

Clinical studies suggest that children with muscular dystrophy generally do not manifest any major emotional disorders. These children have not developed any dominant or prevailing modes of defense (Sherwin & McCully, 1961). Nevertheless, these children have been shown to rely heavily on fantasy (McCully, 1961). There is some suggestion that increased fantasy is related to impaired motility. However, this finding is not unequivocal. While it is generally alleged that in nonhandicapped people increased fantasy is related to an inhibition of movement, this hypothesis, which has become central in current ego psychology, has obvious implications for an individual who cannot move. However, the findings here are unclear. Morrow and Cohen (1954) have demonstrated the effect of environmental influences in the impoverishment of children with muscular dystrophy who are homebound and socially isolated as a result of their disability.

Blindness

With regard to blind children, there has been more work on developing special personality tests to bypass the impairment which the disability offers than in the case of other disabilities. Lebo and Harrigan (1957) have developed verbal TAT with the blind. David (1969) has described an Auditory Apperception Test, which consists of individuals listening to different sounds, human and mechanical, and then responding. Brieland (1950) used a sentence-completion test with 250 blind children. The blanks consisted of either large print or Braille. Dean (1957) used a Rotter Incomplete Sentences Blank. In general, most of these studies do not demonstrate any differences between blind children and others. However, this is unclear, for one of the few projective tests designed to meet the needs of the blind is the Sargent Insight Test (Sargent, 1956). This instrument reveals that blind individuals appear less adjusted than nondisabled persons.

With regard to objective tests, there are a number of studies using personality inventories. Greenberg and Jordan (1957) have used the Bernreuter and California F Scale, while the Minnesota Multiphasic Personality Inventory (MMPI) has been used by a number of people

(Bonk, 1955, Cross, 1947; Potter, 1947). In general, the MMPI seems the most practical method. A combination of the Rotter sentence-completion tasks, the Sargent Insight Test, and the MMPI would provide the best methods of assessing personality.

Deafness

With regard to the deaf, the problems posed by the handicapped are particularly profound in trying to assess personality. With the exception of the Vineland Social Maturity Scale and teacher ratings, there appears to be little work with non-projective tests for the deaf.

The Rorschach has been used with the deaf; however, it is important to have an examiner who is trained in sign language administer the test. Those techniques which are most useful might be the Rosenzweig Picture-Frustration Test (Kahn, 1957) and the Draw-A-Person Test. In general, there are very few definitive studies on the personality of the deaf.

In reviewing the actual work done with personality assessment of the handicapped individual, it is clear, then, that adequate evaluation of personality can be obtained for most disabled people using standardized clinical assessment procedures or adaptations. It is also clear that it is difficult to associate specific personality traits with specific disabilities. The clinician is usually called upon to assess personality to answer specific problems. We have found it useful to organize data, which are derived from projective tests, according to the following outline:

1. Current problems actually facing the child
2. The child's perception of these current problems
3. The child's style of adaptation to the world
   a. Anxiety level
   b. Ego strength, i.e., inner resources to cope with problems
   c. Defenses
4. Pertinent psychological conflicts
   a. Self-acceptance
   b. Dependency needs
   c. Body image
   d. Attitude toward disability
   e. Reaction to authority
   f. Frustration tolerance
   g. Sex role
5. Genetic sources of tensions and defenses
   a. Sources of strength of identification
   b. Level of aspiration
   c. Ability to plan
   d. Ability to relate to workers
6. Recommendations

In general, the effects of the disability and the setting must be taken in their appropriate context. Tuttman (1955) found that the adjustment of children with poliomyelitis was more a function of parental attitudes than of the disability. For example, children of parents who were punitive, rigid, and authoritarian tended to be more constricted and anxious than children with less punitive parents. They failed to accept their disabilities and either denied them or used them as an excuse for not adjusting to their peers. Severity of handicap had no relationship to adjustment.

PSYCHOLOGICAL PRINCIPLES IN THE MANAGEMENT OF HANDICAPPED CHILDREN

While most psychologists think of management in terms of strategies of approach in psychotherapy, it is important to take a broader view of management, for often psychotherapy may not be feasible because of limitations of transportation and time and other considerations both of a realistic and of a psychodynamic nature. The management of the child should take into account not only the functioning of the child but the functioning of the setting in which he is being seen. It may be useful, therefore, to consider a number of points—first, the levels of direct psychotherapeutic contact; second, the notions of support.

With regard to the levels of psychotherapeutic contact, it is important to distinguish the following: In some instances, direct psychotherapy is not feasible despite the existence of profound psychopathology. Contact with the child may be largely for diagnostic rather than therapeutic purposes. This occurs when the child is not responsive to the psychotherapist's approach because of communication difficulties, negativism, or contrary expectancies. In this particular kind of situation, the psychologist might be more helpful, not via direct intervention, but through acting as a consultant for those people working with the child.

A second level of intervention can take place where the psychologist has brief, superficial contact with the child and/or his parents. These contacts may be frequent and extend over a period of time, or they may be on one or two occasions. The psychologist in this case may function best by operating largely within the reality framework of the setting and taking his cues from the child. Doll play, for example, may be encouraged as part of the therapy, but the interpretations are made, not with the view toward uncovering significant dynamic aspects of the relationships, but rather with the aim of facilitating the therapeutic sessions. Often, this might be the level at which one can relate to the child.

At a third level of intervention, one can often engage in meaningful, psychotherapeutic encounters, either by direct verbal confrontations or by play experiences with children. At this level, one can make interpretations and deal with dynamics, and one can deal with confrontation of the child with the intent of his own behavior. Freud (1952) has described modifications of classical psychoanalytic procedures which have been applied to handicapped children. Watson and Johnson (1956) have described a similar modification of psychotherapy with a child hospitalized for surgical procedures.

Fourth, in conjunction with each of the other levels, or perhaps by itself, an important part of psychotherapy with the handicapped child might be supportive therapy. This is based on the development of a relationship in which the therapist is seen as being basically a helpful, parentlike figure. This approach is most often useful in residential or institutional settings that children with physical handicaps attend, not for reasons of personal maladjustment, but because of the need for developing skills or for medical treatment.

While levels of intervention are not mutually exclusive and while they do not necessarily apply to children in the same way at all times, we have found them helpful as a framework for defining an important structural aspect of psychotherapeutic goals with children. We have also found that there need be no correlation between the severity of personal adjustment, per se, and the type of therapeutic approach used. Indeed, it is probable that the children who are best adjusted benefit from confrontation types or interpretive types of therapy. An important therapeutic role for the psychologist in management of the child is to act as a kind of conscience for the staff. That is, there is often a tendency to wish to promulgate shortcut, quick treatment procedures by individuals in different disciplines who get overly involved with treating the disability rather than the child. The psychologist can play a role in dampening extreme expressions of this attitude.

The psychologist can play another subtle role in management. Rehabilitation programs and education programs, in general, are more oriented toward developing styles of behavior which suit a person for work. For example, there are continuing emphases on achievements, progress, and mastery. While this is to be encouraged, it may run into the problem of overlooking the child's needs for intimacy and affection. Part of the psychologist's role, then, is to help create this kind of atmosphere.

There have been a number of approaches to management which are based on learning-theory principles. Myerson (1963), for example, has demonstrated a film in which operant conditioning has been used to help a cerebral palsy child learn to walk. Goodkin (1966) has also shown how operant conditioning can be used to improve language productivity. Most of the studies in operant conditioning have been applied to the development of skills. There has been an expansion of this interest to influencing attitudes as well as skills. Fordyce (1962) has used operant conditioning to treat complaints of pain. In general, rehabilitation workers in other disciplines who are concerned with skills—for example, speech therapists and physical and occupational therapists—have been very eager to promulgate operant-conditioning procedures for hard-core cases in rehabiliation. There are a number of problems, however, aside from the philosophical implications in behavior-shaping approaches, which should be called to the attention of students in this field:

1. Operant conditioning requires an environment in which there is almost total effective control.

2. In considering operant conditioning, there is always a problem of what behavior should be shaped. How does one define this, and why? For example, in a perceptual motor task, the problems may be at the afferent level, so that whatever feedback there is is offered not after the child performs but concurrent with performance (Freedman, 1968; Smith & Smith, 1960).

3. Psychological problems seldom exist in isolation, so that it is often difficult to treat one problem apart from others.

4. In working with brain-damaged children, there is a particular problem of carry-over; that is, the child may be conditioned, for example, to sit still in one setting or to ambulate in one setting but not carry over when the setting is changed. In problems of the CNS, immaturity becomes more manifest in the course of carrying over than in the original condition itself.

REFERENCES

Allen, R. M. Cerebral palsy. In J. F. Garrett and E. S. Levine (Eds.), *Psychological practices of the physically disabled.* New York: Columbia University Press, 1962. Pp. 159–196.

Apgar, V., & Stickle, G. Birth defects: Their significance as a public health problem. *Journal of the American Medical Association,* 1968, **204,** 408–415.

Austin, E. Participation of the family and patient in a program of rehabilitation. *Proceedings of Third Annual Conference, Muscular Dystrophy Association of America.* New York, 1954, 116–118.

Babcock, H. An experiment in the measurement of mental deterioration. *Archives of Psychology,* 1930, **117** (whole).

Badell-Ribera, A., Swinyard, C. A., Greenspan, L., & Deaver, G. Spinal bifida with meningomyelocele: Evaluation of rehabilitation potential. *Archives of Physical Medicine and Rehabilitation,* 1964, **45,** 443–453.

Bakwin, H., & Bakwin, R. M. *Clinical management of behavior disorders in children.* Philadelphia: Saunders, 1963.

Barker, L. S., Schoggen, M., Schoggen, P., & Barker, R. G. The frequency of physical disability in children: A comparison of three sources of information. *Child Development,* 1952, **23,** 215–226.

Barker, R. *The stream of behavior.* New York: McGraw-Hill, 1963.

Barrett, M. L., Hunt, V. V., & Jones, M. H. Behavioral growth of cerebral palsied children from group experience in a confined space. *Developmental Medicine and Child Neurology,* 1967, **9,** 50–58.

Becker, H. *Outsiders.* New York: Free Press, 1963.

Belmont, L., & Birch, H. G. The relation of time of life to behavioral consequence in brain damage. I. The performance of brain-injured adults on the marble board test. *The Journal of Nervous and Mental Disease,* 1960, **131,** 91–97.

Belmont, L., & Birch, H. G. The intellectual profile of retarded readers. *Perceptual and Motor Skills,* 1966, **22,** 787–866 (Monograph Suppl. 6-V22).

Bender, L., & Silver, A. Body image problems of the brain damaged child. *Journal of Social Issues,* 1948, **4**(4) 84–89.

Birch, H. G. *Brain damage in children.* Baltimore: Williams & Wilkins, 1964.

Birch, H. G., & Lefford, A. Two strategies for studying perception in brain damaged children. In H. G. Birch (Ed.), *Brain damage in children.* Baltimore: Williams & Wilkins, 1964.

Block, W. E. Personality of the brain injured child. *Exceptional Children,* 1954, **21,** 91–100.

Boles, G. Personality factors in mothers of cerebral palsy children. *Genetic Psychology Monographs,* 1956, **59,** 159–218.

Bonk, E. Counseling implications of the MMPI for blind people in selected occupations. *Dissertation Abstracts,* 1955, **15,** 2095.

Bortner, M., & Birch, H. G. Perception and perceptual-motor dissociation in cerebral palsied children. *The Journal of Nervous and Mental Disease,* 1960, **130,** 49–53.

Brieland, D. Personality problems of the blind and visually handicapped as revealed by a projective technique. *American Psychologist,* 1950, **5,** 340.

Briggs, P. F. Validity of the Porteus Maze Test completed with the non-dominant hand. *Journal of Clinical Psychology,* 1963, **29,** 427–429.

Broida, D., Izard, C., & Cruickshank, W. Thematic apperception reactions of crippled children. *Journal of Clinical Psychology,* 1950, **6,** 243–248.

Brown, M. E. The patient's motion ability: Evaluation methods, trends and principle. *Rehabilitation Literature,* 1960, **21,** 46–58, 78–90.

Carroll, T. M. *Blindness.* Boston: Little, Brown, 1961.

Costa, L., & Vaughan, H. G. Performance of patients with lateralized cerebral lesions. I. Verbal and perceptual tests. *The Journal of Nervous and Mental Disease,* 1962, **134,** 162–168.

Cowan, E. L., Underberg, R. P., Verrillo, R. T., & Benham, F. G. *Adjustment to visual disability in adolescence.* New York: American Foundation of the Blind, 1960.

Cross, O. Braille edition of the Minnesota Multiphasic Personality Inventory for use with the blind. *Journal of Applied Psychology,* 1947, **31,** 189–198.

Cruickshank, W. *Cerebral palsy: Its individual and community problems.* Syracuse, N.Y.: Syracuse University Press, 1966.

Cruickshank, W. *Teaching the brain-injured child.* Syracuse, N.Y.: Syracuse University Press, 1967.

David, A. Ego functions in disturbed and normal children, aspiration, inhibition time estimation and delayed gratification. *Journal of Consulting Psychology,* 1969, **33,** 61–71.

Davis, F. Deviance disavowal: The management of strained interaction by the visibly handicapped. *Social Problems,* 1961, **9**(2), 120–132.

Davis, F. *Passage through crisis.* Indianapolis: Bobbs-Merrill, 1963.

Dean, S. Adjustment testing and personality factors of the blind. *Journal of Consulting Psychology,* 1957, **21,** 171–177.

Denhoff, E., & Holden, R. H. Significance in delayed development of diagnosis of cerebral palsy. *Journal of Pediatrics,* 1951, **38,** 452–456.

Diller, L. Attitudes towards the disabled: An extension to clinical research. Paper read at the American Personal Guidance Association, Washington, 1966.

Diller, L. Current status of behavioral approaches to the improvement of motor and sensory capacities in the vocational rehabilitation of hemiplegics. In A. L. Benton (Ed.), *Behavioral changes in cerebrovascular disease.* New York: Harper and Row, 1970. Pp. 81–105.

Diller, L., & Birch, H. G. Psychological evaluation of children with cerebral damage. In H. G. Birch (Ed.), *The brain damaged child.* Baltimore: Williams & Wilkins, 1964.

Diller, L., Paddock, N., Badell-Ribera, A., & Swinyard, C. A. Verbal behavior in children with spina bifida. In C. A. Swinyard (Ed.), *Comprehensive care of children with spina bifida manifested.* Cited in *Rehabilitation Monographs,* 1966, **31.**

Doll, E. *Measurement of social competence: A manual for the Vineland Social Maturity Scale.* Minneapolis: Educational Test Bureau, 1953.

Doman, R. J., Spits, E. B., Zucman, E., Delcato, C. H., & Doman, G. Children with severe brain injuries: Neurological organization in terms of mobility. *Journal of the American Medical Association,* 1960, **174,** 257–262.

Donlon, E. T. Implications of visual disorders for cerebral palsy. In W. Cruickshank (Ed.),

Cerebral palsy: Its individual and community problems. Syracuse, N.Y.: Syracuse University Press, 1966.

Farber, B. Effects of a severely mentally retarded child on family integration. *Child Development,* 1959, **24**(2).

Farber, B., & Jenne, W. C. Interaction with retarded siblings and life goals of children. *Marriage and Family Living,* 1963, **25,** 96–98.

Farina, A., Sherman, M., & Allen, J. G. Role of physical abnormalities in interpersonal perception and behavior. *Journal of Abnormal Psychology,* 1968, **73,** 590–593.

Fawcett, J. Some indilogical aspects of congenital anomalus of the spine in childhood and infancy. *Proceedings of the Royal Society of Medicine,* 1959, **50,** 321–333.

Fishman, S. Amputation. In J. F. Garrett and E. S. Levine (Eds.), *Psychological practices with the physically disabled.* New York: Columbia University Press, 1962. Pp. 1–50.

Force, D. G., Jr. Social status of physically handicapped children. *Exceptional Children,* 1956, **23,** 104–107, 132–133.

Fordyce, W. F. The behavioral modification of pain in rehabilitation. *Proceedings of the First Interdisciplinary Conference on Rehabilitation,* Chicago, 1962.

Freedman, S. *The neuropsychology of spatially oriented behavior.* Homewood, Ill.: Dorsey Press, 1968.

Freud, A. The role of bodily illness in the mental life of children. In *The psychoanalytic study of the child.* Vol. 7. New York: International Universities Press, 1952. Pp. 69–81.

Frostig, M., LeFever, D. W., & Whittlesey, J. R. B. A developmental test of visual perception evaluating normal and neurologically handicapped children. *Perceptual and Motor Skills,* 1961, **12,** 383–394.

Furth, H. G. *Thinking without language: Psychological implications of deafness.* New York: Free Press. 1966.

Gesell, A., & Amatruda, C. B. *Developmental diagnosis.* New York: Hoeber-Harper, 1952.

Gillespie, H. W. Radiological diagnosis of lumba intervertebral disc lesions. Report on 160 cases. *British Journal of Radiology,* 1946, **19,** 420–428.

Glick, S. J. *Vocational, educational, and recreational needs of the cerebral palsied adult.* New York: United Cerebral Palsy of New York City, 1953.

Gofman, E. *Stigma.* Englewood Cliffs, N.J.: Prentice-Hall, 1963.

Goodkin, R. Case studies in behavior research in rehabilitation. *Perceptual and Motor Skills,* 1966, **23,** 171–182.

Granofsky, J. Attitudes of the non-handicapped to the handicapped. Unpublished doctoral dissertation, Yeshiva University, 1959.

Greenberg, H., & Jordan, S. Differential effects of total blindness and partial sight on several personality traits. *Exceptional Children,* 1957, **24,** 123–124.

Gruenbaum, M., Quatere, T., Carruth, B., & Cruickshank, W. Evaluation of a modification of the Thematic Apperception Test for use with physically handicapped children. *Journal of Clinical Psychology,* 1953, **9,** 40–44.

Gruenberg, E. Some epidemiological aspects of congenital brain damage. In H. G. Birch (Ed.), *Brain damage in children.* Baltimore: Williams & Wilkins, 1964.

Guibor, G. P. Cerebral palsy: A practical routine for discerning occula motor deficits in cerebral palsy children. *Journal of Pediatrics,* 1955, **47,** 333–339.

Guilford, J. P. *The nature of human intelligence.* New York: McGraw-Hill, 1967.

Haeussermann, E. *Developmental potential of preschool children.* New York: Grune & Stratton, 1958.

Hanks, J. R., & Hanks, L. M., Jr. The physically handicapped in certain non-occidental societies. *Journal of Social Issues,* 1948, **4**(4), 95–101.

Hastorf, A. H., Jones, E. E., Kelley, H. H., Thibaut, J. W., & Usdane, W. Some problems from social psychology research in the handicapped. *Rehabilitation Research.* American Psychological Association, 1964.

Hebb, D. O. *The organization of behavior.* New York: Wiley, 1949.

Heber, R., Dever, R., & Conry, J. The influences of environmental and genetic variables on intellectual development. In H. Prehm, L. A. Hamerlynck, & J. E. Crosson (Eds.), *Behavioral research in mental retardation.* Monograph No. 1. Eugene, Ore.: Research and Training Center in Mental Retardation, 1968.

Hohman, L., Baker, L., & Reed, R. Sensory disturbances in children with infantile hemiplegia, triplegia, and quadriplegia. *American Journal of Physical Medicine,* 1958, **37,** 1–6.

Holden, R. H. The Child's Apperception Test with cerebral palsied and normal children. *Child Development,* 1956, **27,** 5–8.

Holden, R. H. Motivation, adjustment and anxiety of cerebral palsy children. *Exceptional Children,* 1959, **24,** 313–317.

Holden, R. H. Changes in body image of physically handicapped children due to summer camp experience. *Merrill-Palmer Quarterly of Behavior and Development,* 1962, **8**(1).

Holmes, D. The use of structured observational schema in evaluating the impact of integrated social experiences upon orthopedically handicapped children. Paper presented at the meeting of the American Psychological Association, Washington, D.C., 1966.

Hopkins, T. W., Bice, H. V., & Colton, K. C. *Evaluation of the cerebral palsied child.* Washington: Council for Exceptional Children, 1954.

Jastak, J. F. Problems of psychometric scatter analysis. *Psychological Bulletin,* 1949, **46**, 177–197.

Jastak, J. F., McPhie, H. M., & Whiteman, M. *Mental retardation: Its nature and incidence.* Newark, Del.: University of Delaware Press, 1963.

Jones, R. L., Gottfield, N. W., & Owens, A. The social distance of the exceptional: A study at the high school level. *Exceptional Children,* 1966, **32**, 555–556.

Jones, R. L., & Sisk, D. A. Early perceptions of orthopedic disability. Paper presented at the meeting of the American Psychological Association, Washington, D.C., 1967.

Josselyn, I. M., Simon, A. J., & Eells, E. Anxiety in children convalescing from rheumatic fever. *American Journal of Orthopsychiatry,* 1955, **25**, 109–119.

Kahn, D. Responses of hard of hearing and normal children to frustration. *Exceptional Children,* 1957, **24**, 155–159.

Kahn, D., & Birch, H. G. Development of auditory-visual integration and reading achievement. *Perceptual and Motor Skills,* 1968, **27**, 459–468.

Karlin, I. W. Incidence of spina bifida occulta in relation to age. *American Journal of Diseases of Children,* 1935, **49**, 125–134.

Katz, A. H. *Parents of the handicapped: Self-organized parents and relative groups for treatment of ill and handicapped children.* Springfield, Ill.: Charles C Thomas, 1961.

Kelley, H. H. Attribution theory in social psychology. In D. Levine (Ed.), *Symposium on motivation.* Lincoln, Neb.: University of Nebraska Press, 1967.

Kelman, H. R. The effect of a brain-damaged child on the family. In H. G. Birch (Ed.), *Brain damage in children.* Baltimore: Williams & Wilkins, 1964.

Kimmel, J. A comparison of children with congenital and acquired orthopedic handicaps on certain personality characteristics. *Dissertation Abstracts,* 1959, **19**, 3023–3024.

Kir-Stimon, W. Rehabilitation counseling with cardiac children. *Personnel and Guidance Journal,* 1962, **32**, 89–95.

Kleck, R. Emotional arousal in interactions with stigmatized persons. *Psychological Reports,* 1966, **19**, 1226.

Kleck, R., Hastorf, A. H., & Ono, H. The effects of physical deviance upon face to face interaction. *Human Relations,* 1966, **19**, 425–430.

Knobloch, H., and Passamanick, B. The syndrome of minimal cerebral damage in infancy. *Journal of the American Medical Association,* 1959, **70**, 1384–1387.

Kogan, K. L. Standardization of the Childrens Picture Information Test. *Journal of Clinical Psychology,* 1959, **16**, 405–411.

Lebo, D., and Harrigan, M. Visual and verbal presentation of TAT stimuli. *Journal of Consulting Psychology,* 1957, **21**, 339–341.

Lencione, R. M. Speech and language problems in cerebral palsy. In W. Cruickshank (Ed.), *Cerebral palsy: Its individual and community problems.* Syracuse, N.Y.: Syracuse University Press, 1966.

Lenenberg, E. *The biological foundations of language.* New York: Wiley, 1966.

Levine, E. S. Auditory disability. In J. F. Garrett and E. S. Levine (Eds.), *Psychological practices with the physically disabled.* New York: Columbia University Press, 1962.

Lindsley, O. R. Geriatric behavioral prosthetics. In O. R. Lindsley (Ed.), *New thoughts on old age.* New York: Springer, 1964. Pp. 41–60.

Lipp, L., Kolstoe, R., James, W., & Randall, H. Denial of disability and internal control of reinforcement. *Journal of Consulting and Clinical Psychology,* 1968, **32,** 72–75.

Lowenfeld, B. The child who is blind. *Exceptional Children,* 1952, **19,** 96–102.

Luria, A. R. An objective approach to the study of the abnormal child. *American Journal of Orthopsychiatry,* 1961, **31,** 1–17.

Manjos, T. A study of attitudes of cerebral palsy individuals of different religious persuasion. Unpublished doctoral dissertation, New York University, 1966.

McCavitt, M. E., Diller, L., & Orgel, M. *A demonstration and research project to study methods for facilitating the adaptation of adults with cerebral palsy to personal, social and vocational instrumental roles.* Washington: Vocational Rehabilitation Administration, 1966.

McClelland, D. C., Atkinson, J. W., Clark, R. A., & Lowell, E. L. *The achievement motive.* New York: Appleton-Century-Crofts, 1953.

McCully, R. Human movement in the Rorschach material in a group of pre-adolescent boys suffering from progressive muscle loss. *Journal of Projective Techniques,* 1961, **25,** 205–211.

Morrow, R. S., & Cohen, J. The psycho-social factors in muscular dystrophy. *Journal of Child Psychiatry,* 1954, 3, No. 1.

Myerson, L. Somatopsychology of physical disability. In W. Cruickshank (Ed.), *Exceptional children and youth.* Englewood Cliffs, N.J.: Prentice-Hall, 1963.

Nash, M. A study of attitudes of a group of non-handicapped people towards the orthopedically handicapped. Unpublished doctoral dissertation, New York School of Social Education, Columbia University, 1962.

Nober, E. H. Hearing problems associated with cerebral palsy. In W. Cruickshank (Ed.), *Cerebral palsy: Its individual and community problems.* Syracuse, N.Y.: Syracuse University Press, 1966.

Perlstein, M. A. Infantile cerebral palsy classification and clinical correlations. *Journal of the American Medical Association,* 1952, **149,** 32–34.

Perlstein, M. A., & Hood, P. N. Infantile spastic hemiplegia: Intelligence and age of walking and talking. *American Journal of Mental Deficiency,* 1957, **61,** 534–542.

Pinter, R., Eiserson, J., & Stanton, M. *The psychology of the physically handicapped.* New York: Appleton-Century-Crofts, 1941.

Potter, G. S. A method for using the Minnesota Multiphasic Personality Inventory with the blind. In W. Donahue and D. Dabelstein (Eds.), *Psychological diagnosis and counseling with the adult blind.* New York: American Foundation for the Blind, 1947.

Rapaport, D., Gill, M., & Schafer, R. *Diagnostic psychological testing.* Vols. 1 and 2. Chicago: Year Book, 1964–1965.

Richards, T. W., & Hooper, S. Brain injury at birth (cerebral palsy), perceptual response during childhood and adolescence. *The Journal of Nervous and Mental Disease,* 1956, **123,** 117–124.

Richards, T. W., & Letterman, R. A study of action in fantasy of the physically handicapped. *Journal of Clinical Psychology,* 1956, **2,** 188–189.

Richardson, S. A. Some social psychological consequences of handicapping. *Pediatrics,* 1963, **32,** 291–293.

Richardson, S. A., Goodman, N., Hastorf, A., & Dombush, S. Variant reactions of physical disabilities. *American Sociological Review,* 1963, **28,** 429–435.

Rusk, H. A. *Rehabilitation medicine: A text book on physical medicine and rehabilitation.* St. Louis: Mosby, 1964.

Sanua, V. Sociocultural factors to stressful life situations. The behavior of aged amputees as an example. *Journal of Health and Human Behavior,* 1960, **1,** 17–25.

Sanua, V. A cross-cultural study of children with cerebral palsy. Prospective report submitted to Vocational Rehabilitation Administration, 1967.

Sarason, S., & Sarason, E. K. The discriminatory value of a test pattern with cerebral palsied defective children. *Journal of Clinical Psychology,* 1947, **3,** 127–130.

Sargent, H. Insight Test prognosis in successful and unsuccessful rehabilitation of the blind. *Journal of Projective Techniques,* 1956, **20,** 429–441.

Sherwin, A. C., & McCully, R. S. Reactions to a crippling, progressive, and fatal illness (muscular dystrophy) observed in boys of various ages (10–14). *Journal of Chronic Diseases,* 1961, **13,** 59–68.

Siller, J. Reaction to physical disability. *Rehabilitation Counseling Bulletin,* 1963, **7,** 12–16.

Siller, J. Psychological concomitants of amputation in children. Paper presented at the meeting of the American Psychological Association, Washington, D.C., 1968.

Simmel, M. L. The body percept in physical medicine and rehabilitation. *Journal of Health and Social Behavior,* 1967, **8**(1), 25–32.

Skipper, J. K., Fink, S. L., & Hallenbeck, P. N. Physical disability among married women. *Journal of Rehabilitation,* 1968, **34,** 137–139.

Smith, K. U., & Smith, M. F. *Cybernetic principles of learning and educational design.* New York: Holt, 1960.

Swensen, C. F. Empirical evaluation of human figure drawings. *Psychological Bulletin,* 1968, **70,** 20–44.

Swinyard, C. A. Comprehensive care of the child with spina bifida. *Rehabilitation Monographs,* 1966, **31** (whole).

Taylor, W. W., & Taylor, I. W. *Special education of physically handicapped children.* New York: International Society for Welfare of Crippled, 1960.

Teuber, H. L. Perception. In J. Field (Ed.), *Handbook of physiology.* Vol. 3. Washington: American Physiological Association, 1959.

Tizard, J. P., Paine, R. S., & Crothers, B. Disturbances of sensation in children with hemiplegia. *Journal of the American Medical Association,* 1954, **155,** 628–632.

Truitt, C. J. Personal and social adjustment of children with muscular dystrophy. *Proceedings of the Third Medical Conference of the Muscular Dystrophy Association of America.* New York, 1954, 124-128.

Tuttman, S. Parental attitudes and adjustment of handicapped children. Unpublished doctoral dissertation, New York University, 1955.

Watson, E. J., & Johnson, A. M. Psychotherapy in facial disfigurement. *Proceedings of the Staff Meeting of the Mayo Clinic.* 1956, **31,** 537–544.

Wells, F. L. *Mental tests in clinical practice.* Tarrytown-on-Hudson, N.Y.: World, 1927.

Wenar, C. The effects of a motor handicap on personality. I. The effects of level of aspiration. *Child Development,* 1953, **24,** 123–130.

Wenar, C. The effects of a motor handicap on personality. II. The effect on interpretative ability. *Child Development,* 1954, **25,** 287–295.

Wenar, C. The effects of a motor handicap on personality. III. The effects on certain fantasies and adjustive techniques. *Child Development,* 1956, **27,** 9–15.

Wexler, M. Mental hygiene and the muscular dystrophy patient. *Proceedings of the First Medical Conference of the Muscular Dystrophy Association of America.* New York, 1951, 58–67.

White, B. L., Castle, P., & Held, R. Observations on the development of visually directed reaching. *Child Development,* 1964, **351,** 349–364.

Whiteman, M., and Lukoff, I. *Public attitudes towards blindness.* New York: American Foundation for the Blind, 1964.

Whiting, J. W. M., & Child, I. L. *Child training and personality.* New Haven, Conn.: Yale University Press, 1953.

Wilson, B. C., & Wilson, J. J. Sensory and perceptual functions in the cerebral palsied. I. Presence thresholds and two point discrimination. *The Journal of Nervous and Mental Disease,* 1967, **145,** 53–60.

Windle, W. F. Neuroanatomy in relation to experimental neurology. In J. D. French (Ed.), *Frontiers in brain research.* New York: Columbia University Press, 1962.

Witmer, L. *The special class for backward children.* Philadelphia: Psychological Clinic Press, 1911.

Wrightstone, J. W. *Adolescents with cardiac limitations.* New York: Bureau of Educational Research, Board of Education, 1961.

Yuker, H. E., Block, J. R., & Campbell, W. J. *A scale to measure attitudes toward disabled persons.* Albertson, N.Y.: Human Resources Foundation, Division of Abilities, 1960.

Zborowski, M. Cultural components in response to pain. *Journal of Social Issues,* 1952, **8,** 16–3

Zuk, G. H. Artistic distortions in parents of retarded children. *Journal of Consulting Psychology,* 1959, **23,** 171–176.

19 | Child Speech Pathology

Edward D. Mysak

The purpose of this chapter is to present modern developments in theories, research, and clinical practice in child speech pathology. Before beginning the central discussion of the chapter, a brief statement on the history and purposes of American speech pathology and audiology should prove useful to the many health specialists who may refer to this manual.

A BRIEF PERSPECTIVE ON AMERICAN SPEECH PATHOLOGY AND AUDIOLOGY

The history of the science and profession of speech pathology and audiology in the United States is relatively short compared with that of many other health-related fields. For example, the first doctoral degree was granted in 1922, and the national association, the American Speech and Hearing Association (ASHA), was incorporated in 1925 (under the name of the American Academy of Speech Correction). The field has grown rapidly; some of the milestones of this growth include (1) the beginning of publication of the *Journal of Speech and Hearing Disorders*

(1936), the *Journal of Speech and Hearing Research* (1958), and the *DSH* (deafness, speech, and hearing) *Abstracts* (1960); and (2) the establishment in 1959 of the American Boards of Examiners in Speech Pathology and Audiology, which include an education and training board and a professional services board.

As of 1970, there were about 13,000 members listed in the *Directory of Members of the American Speech and Hearing Association.* The directory contains a geographical list of members and also identifies those members who hold the Certificate of Clinical Competence in Speech Pathology or Audiology. ASHA also publishes a listing of graduate training programs and of available speech and hearing services in the United States; these publications are entitled *A Guide to Graduate Education in Speech Pathology and Audiology* and *A Guide to Clinical Services in Speech Pathology and Audiology,* respectively, and can be obtained by writing to the national office.[1]

[1] American Speech and Hearing Association, 9030 Old Georgetown Road, Washington, D.C., 20014.

The field is defined as follows in the ASHA bylaws:

> The purposes of this organization shall be to encourage basic scientific study of the processes of individual human communication, with special reference to speech, hearing, and language, promote investigation of disorders of human communication, and foster improvement of clinical procedures with such disorders; to stimulate exchange of information among persons and organizations thus engaged; and to disseminate such information.

It has been found frequently that many specialists are either uninformed or misinformed about the nature, scope, and development of American speech pathology and audiology. Some of the reasons for this situation may be related to the relatively recent emergence of the field as a serious health profession, the tendency toward microspecialization in the health fields, the relative lack of cooperative training programs in the health sciences, and the tendency for members of older, established health fields to perceive developing ones from old or inaccurately conceived standpoints.

As indicated, the purpose of this chapter is to present modern developments in theories, research, and clinical practice in that portion of the field of speech pathology and audiology which may be designated as child speech pathology. Specifically, the chapter will be concerned with the development and disorders of spoken communication of children from about 1 year through the age of puberty. The chapter is divided into two parts. The first is devoted to disorders which are relatively simple and speech-system specific, such as disorders of spoken language, the articulation of such language, its phonation, and its rhythm. The second is devoted to speech-system complexes associated with severe hearing disorders, cleft palate, and various neurodevelopmental and psychodevelopmental conditions.

SPEECH-DISORDER SIMPLEXES

Childhood speech disorders which appear to be simple and relatively confined to the speech system may be described as *speech-disorder simplexes*. For example, some children may appear equal in all respects except that they begin to speak later than expected or do not articulate some of the speech sounds well, or their voices or speech rhythms are atypical. In any regular school, upwards of 5 percent of the population may fall into this category of children with speech disorders. Each discussion of a speech simplex will include developmental information, descriptions of forms of the disorder, and diagnostic and therapy considerations.

SPOKEN LANGUAGE AND ITS ARTICULATION

Because of the close relationship between a child's development of spoken symbols and the sounds of which they are composed, it was decided to discuss these two aspects of speech communication under one heading.

Speech Articulation

Carrell (1968, p.1) recently stated, "Disorders of articulation are the most frequent and potentially handicapping of all speech disorders." Black (1964, p. 7) reported that in the Illinois public schools in 1962–1963, 82 percent of the speech case load was comprised of articulatory problems. Powers (1957, p. 711) summarizes her examination of major survey reports with the comment, ". . . it is safe to say that functional articulation defectives represent between 75 to 80 percent of all speech defectives in the school population."

The following comments by Milisen (1957, pp. 252–253) should also prove informative:

> In the first grade, from 15 to 20 percent of the children are likely to be described as having defec-

tive articulation. There is a marked decrease . . . in the percentages through the first three or four grades, after which the decline is likely to become small or nonexistent. . . . Apparently, articulation is likely to improve until the age of 9 or 10; but after that age, for the most part, misarticulated sounds remain defective unless therapy is provided.

Developmental patterns. Speech sounds emerge during at least two stages: the audiovocal, or prespeech, stage and the audioverbal, or true speech, stage (Mysak, 1966a, chap. 3). The audiovocal stage includes a reflexive vocalization period (approximately the first 4 to 6 weeks), a babbling period (up to about 6 months), a lalling period (up to about 9 months), and an echolalia period (up to about 12 months). During these first 12 months or so, the child theoretically utters forms of all the sounds he will need to utter during the true-speech stage. About three periods also appear discernible in the audioverbal stage, which extends from the period of the acquisition of about twenty words by about 18 months to the period of adultlike symbolic intercommunication by 7 or 8 years. Speech sound development is taking place throughout this 7- or 8-year period; however, only the developmental trends observed during the verbal period will be presented here.

The earliest age levels at which 75 percent of children tested by Templin (1957) correctly articulated certain consonant sounds are as follows: 3.0 years: *M, N, NG, P, F, H, W;* 3.5 years: *Y;* 4.0 years: *B, D, K, G, R;* 4.5 years: *S, SH, CH;* 6.0 years: *T, L, V, TH;* 7.0 years: *TH* (voiced), *Z, ZH, J.* An earlier study by Davis (1938) reported findings on the earliest age levels at which 100 percent of the children she tested correctly articulated the following consonants: 3.5 years: *M, P, B, W, H;* 4.5 years: *N, T, D, NG, K, G, Y;* 5.5 years: *F, V, S, Z;* 6.5 years: *SH, ZH, L, TH, TH* (voiced); and 8.0 years: *R, WH, S, Z.* The reason for listing *S* and *Z* twice, according to Davis, is that after these sounds appear in words at about 4 or 5 years, they frequently become

distorted because of loss of upper deciduous incisors but are usually automatically corrected with the appearance of permanent anterior dentition at about 8 years of age.

As with other developmental schedules, individual differences exist from child to child. The articulatory schedules presented, however, should at least provide specialists with a general idea of when certain speech sounds are expected to develop and, perhaps more importantly, should remind them that sounds do develop as a function of time and that many appear in developmental forms before they reach full maturity.

Disorder patterns. Since the nomenclature in speech pathology is still not well established, descriptive rather than etiologic terms will be used as often as possible to identify various articulatory problems. The discussion of disorder patterns is divided into two parts: the first is on articulatory immaturity patterns, or those reflecting late, slow, or incomplete development; and the second is on articulatory dysmaturity patterns, or those reflecting disturbed development.

Articulatory immaturity cases are those in which speech sound patterns typical of a younger child persist well past normal time limits and where they may remain incomplete unless there is therapeutic intervention. Ingram and Barn (1961) include such problems under the heading of specific developmental speech disorders which, according to them, may involve articulation only or language development and articulation. They state, "Children suffering from these conditions show unexpectedly slow development of intelligible speech, though in other respects their development is usually normal and their health is good. . . ." and "Specific developmental speech disorders are the commonest cause of abnormal speech in the general child population. . . ." Powers (1957, p. 718) describes articulatory immaturity in this way: ". . . the pattern of speech sound production which research has shown to be typical of normal speech development in the first several years of life is reflected at later age levels. . . ."

Carrell (1968, pp. 15–22), in discussing articulatory immaturity, points out that the problem can range from mild involvement to completely unintelligible speech. Some of the most frequently involved sound substitutions, according to Carrell, are *W* for *R, TH* for *S, TH* (voiced) for *Z, F* for *TH, V* for *TH* (voiced), *T* for *K, D* for *G, W* or *Y* for *L,* and *SH* for *CH.*

Articulatory dysmaturation cases present speech sound patterns which reflect interference with normal maturational processes by certain identifiable factors. Such factors include mild hearing loss (i.e., the kind which does not interfere with the child's ability to learn language) (Carrell, 1968, p. 22); developmental articulatory dyspraxia (Morley, 1965, p. 175); possible disturbances in articulatory system proprioceptive and tactile feedback (Carrell, 1968, p. 9); problems in auditory discrimination and span for speech sounds (Powers, 1957, pp. 740–746); anomalies of the mouth, lip, tongue, and dental occlusion (Bloomer, 1957, pp. 632–644); isolated dysarthria (Morley, 1965, pp. 178–184); oroneuromotor dysmaturation (Mysak, 1968b, pp. 91–92); and relatively specific neurologic involvement and combinations of involvement of lips, tongue, soft palate, and laryngeal and pharyngeal muscles due to congenital suprabulbar paresis, meningitis, poliomyelitis, and the Mobius syndrome (Worster-Drought, 1968).

Diagnosis and therapy. The diagnostic responsibility of the speech pathologist in these cases is first, to determine whether the articulatory patterns presented by the client may in fact be within normal limits. It is not infrequent for mothers or friends of the family to hear developmental varieties of *S, R, L,* for example, and perceive them as defective rather than as developmental forms.

If, however, the diagnostician believes that there is a problem of some kind, he should then consider whether the symptoms are of the immaturity or of the dysmaturity variety. He should also determine whether it is a relatively speech-specific problem or one symptom of a complex. On the basis of a thorough and complete analysis of a particular case of articulatory immaturity or dysmaturity, the speech pathologist may recommend either prior orthodontic work followed by a speech-symptom unlearning and relearning therapy program or a basic speech sound stimulation program. For discussions of various approaches to articulation therapy, the reader is referred to Carrell (1968, chap. 7), Powers (1957, chap. 24), Van Riper (1963, chap. 10), and Mysak (1966a, chap. 6).

Spoken Language

After the first year of life, speech sounds develop together with the comprehension and formulation of speech symbols. Hence, we should expect various relationships to exist between the developmental and disorder patterns of speech symbols and their manner of production. However, there are exceptions to such expected relationships.

Powers (1957, p. 718) identifies at least two forms of speech immaturity: infantile perseveration and delayed speech. She comments that when the child's problem is basically with speech sounds, it may be referred to as *infantile perseveration.* However, if, in addition to speech sound lapses, the onset of speech is late and various oral language deficiencies are present, the condition may be referred to as *delayed speech.* On the other hand, Carrell (1968, p. 10) reports that there are children with certain types of intellectual deficits in which speech sounds may be normally produced even though there is a "severe limitation of verbal capacity."

Developmental patterns. For an excellent chapter on the development of speech in the human race and on speech development in children, the reader is referred to Simon (1957, chap. 1). There are numerous other chapters on speech development in the speech pathology literature. Some more familiar ones include Berry and Eisenson (1956, chap. 3, "The Normal Development of Speech"), Van Riper (1963, chap. 4, "Speech Development"), and West (1968, chap. 2, "The Normal vs. the Abnormal"). More recent ones include Winitz (1966, chap. 3, "The Development of Speech and Language in the Normal Child") and Mysak (1966a, chap. 3, "Speech Development"). Developmental patterns in spoken communication will be limited here to a discussion of the age at which first words and two- or three-word sentences develop in children.

Darley and Winitz (1961) examined the results of fifteen studies of the age of appearance of the first word in twenty-six groups of children. They state: "From the results of these studies it appears that the average child begins to say his first word by approximately one year. Delay of appearance of first word beyond 18 months may indicate a serious physical, mental, or hearing involvement."

Statements by various authorities in speech pathology on the emergence of the first spoken word follow: "Somewhere between twelve and 18 months of age, the 'average child' really begins to talk" (Berry and Eisenson, 1956, p. 21); ". . . most commonly occurring between 12 and 18 months but which may include the 9 to 24 months span . . . speech is learned most efficiently and thoroughly" (Simon, 1957, p. 27); "Girls begin to speak about the fourteenth month after birth and boys about the fifteenth month" (West, 1968, pp. 53–54); "From about 18 months to two years, a child usually acquires between 10 and 20 words" (Wood, 1964, p. 10); and ". . . first words . . . appear between 10 and 14 months of age" (Brown, 1967, p. 331). Finally, in a sample of 114 children, Morley (1965, p. 34) reported that the average age for the first use of words was 12 months but that the range extended from 8 to 30 months. It is apparent that there is a range of months during which authorities expect

first words to appear in normal children. In general, however, it may be said that the first word is expected by about 1 year of age.

Van Riper (1963, p. 108), in discussing the onset of speaking in phrases and sentences, states that "any child who is not using at least a few understandable two-word phrases or sentences by the age of thirty months should be referred to a physician or speech therapist immediately." Morley (1965, p. 27) reported that in her study, "The average age at which these children first used word sequences was 18 months, and the age range was from 10 to 44 months." The average infant, according to Brown (1967, p. 332), should be using combinations of words and simple sentences by 21 to 24 months. Worster-Drought (1968) states that "most normal children can produce short sentences by the age of two years." However, he reports that "there are some exceptions when otherwise normal children are later in acquiring normal speech, even up to the end of their third year. Sometimes such a late development of speech is a family characteristic." He also believes that if a child does not speak by 3 years, "some defect in the speech mechanism is usually present." In general, then, it is expected that the average child should be using at least simple, two-word utterances by about 30 to 36 months of age.

Spoken-language immaturity. The discussion of immaturity of spoken language is limited here to those instances in which all other aspects of the child's development appear generally within the normal range. A possible background for such immaturity is specific developmental language retardation, where speech sounds and spoken language develop more slowly than expected but where all other aspects of development may be roughly within normal limits, except possibly for a family predisposition toward delayed and slow language learning.

Such types of specific developmental language

retardation have been described by Ingram and Barn (1961) and by Berry and Eisenson (1956, p. 89). Related to this concept of specific language immaturity is Bloodstein's (1958, pp. 23–24) finding that among 108 children between 2 and 6 years of age examined by him because of stuttering, one-third were described by their parents as "late talkers," as persisting in the use of "baby talk," or as "difficult to understand" prior to the onset of stuttering. Except for these speech symptoms, the children were relatively free of other clinical manifestations.

Diagnosis and therapy. Many questions must be considered by the speech pathologist when he is confronted with a case of possible specific language retardation. First, is the language behavior physiological or pathological? If it is outside of normal limits, is it actually a case of specific developmental language immaturity, or is it secondary to mental retardation, serious hearing loss, brain dysfunction, emotional disturbance, or some combination of these factors?

Formulating appropriate habilitation plans is also complex. For example, is this a case of language retardation which will resolve itself as a function of time alone? Or if intervention is considered appropriate, is parental counseling on how to facilitate speech development sufficient? Or should there be professional intervention in the form of enrollment in a nursery school or kindergarten and/or actual speech therapy? For discussions of various approaches to language habilitation, the reader is referred to Berry and Eisenson (1956, chap. 7); Van Riper (1963, chap. 6); Wood (1964, chap. 4); and Mysak (1966a, chap. 4).

PHONATORY BEHAVIOR

Voice is the carrier tone of spoken communication. It also serves as a signal system during the preverbal stage since parents often report that they can distinguish various meanings in their infants' wails and cries (Perkins, 1957, p. 848). Disorders of voicing are not too common among children; however, it has been estimated that 1 to 2 percent of schoolchildren do present clinical voice problems (Curtis, 1967, p. 200).

Developmental Patterns

This writer (Mysak, 1966b, pp. 150–155) recently described vocal evolution and involution of the male and female voice. The discussion was based on my findings with respect to middle-aged and older males and the incorporation of these findings with those of numerous investigators of male and female voices at various developmental stages. This discussion will be limited to the evolutional stages for the speaking fundamental frequency of boys and girls through the postpubertal period. Fundamental frequency of boys' voices at various developmental stages (measured in cycles per second) are as follows: 7 years: 294 cps; 8 years: 297 cps; 10 years: 269.7 cps; 14 years: 241.5 cps; and 18 years: 137.1 cps. For girls, they are: 7 years: 273.2 cps; 8 years: 286.5 cps; 11 years: 258.0 cps; 13 years (premenarcheal): 251.7 cps; 13 years (postmenarcheal); 237.7 cps; and 15 years: 229.5 cps. The developmental trends for males and females for speaking fundamental frequency is one of a progressive lowering of pitch level from 7 years until after puberty. As would be expected, the amount of lowering is much greater for males. Most of this difference can be attributed to the much greater growth and development of the larynx among boys during the pubertal period.

Metraux (1950), who studied various aspects of the speech development of 207 children at 18, 24, 30, 36, 42, 48, and 54 months, also described certain voice changes during this period. Some prominent features of voice change were as follows: 18 months: not well controlled and tends to become high-pitched and strained; 24 months: better pitch control, pitch lower, still some straining, and squeaking is common; 30

months: voice continues to show wide pitch variability, under stress voice may change quickly from a low-pitched tone to a high, thin, nasalized squeak; 36 months: usually well controlled and in general shows an even, normal loudness, begins to use whispered voice to gain attention; 42 months: normal speaking tone characterized by high, full-volumed yell, whispered voice still used but readily changes to a yell if responses to requests are slow; 48 months: voice somewhat subdued, many children (especially boys) persist in use of loud voice, inflections tend to be marked; and 54 months: voice becomes well modulated, girls' voices may become imitative of their mothers.

Developmental trends discernible in Metraux's observations are the tendency for the child to experiment with pitch, loudness, and quality dimensions of voice and the progression toward increased control and monitoring of voice, no doubt in keeping with environmental models and rewards.

Disorder Patterns

In the ensuing discussion, *vocal immaturity* will refer to conditions which may *retard* the maturation and function of the laryngeal structures and *vocal dysmaturity* will refer to various conditions which may directly *interfere* with the development and function of the laryngeal structures.

Vocal immaturity. One reason for a postpubertal adolescent to continue to speak with the voice of a child would be the dysfunctioning of the sex glands to the point of inhibiting laryngeal growth and development. There are cases of prepubertal or pubertal hoarse-husky voices which appear related to the advent of maturity rather than to some immaturity disorder. Van Riper and Irwin (1958, pp. 169–170) indicate that school speech clinicians frequently have children aged 10 to 12 years referred to them because of complaints of hoarse or husky voices. However, these vocal

differences often disappear after puberty. It is acknowledged that various investigators view huskiness and hoarseness as characteristic of the prepubertal or pubertal period and as heralds of approaching voice change.

Vocal dysmaturity. There are numerous conditions which may directly disturb vocal behavior through the pubertal period. Schwartz (1961) has reported on the infantile voice involvement of *congenital laryngeal stridor*. Possible causes offered include immaturity of the larynx, abnormally shaped larynx, and excessive rehearsal of the laryngeal closing reflex during aquatic fetal life. Complete or partial loss of the larynx in childhood due to cancer or trauma (rare), allergies, asthmatic conditions, and physical weakness have also been cited as contributors to childhood voice problems. Van Riper and Irwin (1958, pp. 185–203) discuss various specific laryngeal pathologies which may affect voicing; among them is *vocal nodules*. Most authorities agree that vocal nodules are the result of abuse of the voice. Since children frequently shout and yell excessively, it is not uncommon to find "screamer's nodes" and hoarseness in childhood (Brodnitz, 1959, p. 61; Wilson, 1961). Greene (1957b, p. 69) indicates that such children often suffer from chronic hoarseness and that it is common between the ages of 5 and 10 years.

Contact ulcers, also commonly the result of misuse and abuse of the cords, "only rarely . . . appear in children" (Van Riper & Irwin, 1958, p. 193). *Neurogenic involvement of the larynx* is also a rare occurrence in children (Worster-Drought, 1968), except in cases of cerebral palsy. Hoarseness due to *inflammation of the cords* because of colds is common in children. *Laryngeal webs*, often congenital but also possibly due to diphtheria, is a relatively uncommon condition.

Hypernasality, a rather common voice disorder, may be found in children for various reasons. One obvious reason is a congenital cleft palate. Transient hypernasality (about 4 to 6 weeks in duration) may follow an adenotonsillectomy (Greene, 1957a). Various differences in the anatomy and physiology of the velopharyngeal closure mechanism may also account for a certain number of cases of childhood hypernasality. Hypernasality is also often found as a sequela to bulbar poliomyelitis or diphtheria (Worster-Drought, 1968).

Diagnosis and therapy. The first action taken by a speech pathologist upon receiving a referral of childhood voice disorder is to make sure a laryngological examination has been performed. Following medical clearance, he must decide whether or not the presenting phonatory pattern is a reflection of a developmental phase. If not, he must determine whether there are possible ongoing socioemotional backgrounds for the problem. Consultation with psychology-psychiatry is important here. Regardless of the background of the vocal misuse, he must also determine whether the misuse may eventually result in an abuse of laryngeal tissue, possibly resulting in nodes, polyps, or ulcers.

With respect to therapy, decisions have to be made as to whether the vocal symptoms are amenable to medical, otolaryngological, or psychologic-psychiatric procedures alone or in various combinations; or whether voice symptom therapy needs to be provided because the misuse has led to tissue change once and, regardless of the medical, surgical, or psychological attention, will very likely again result in tissue change because of the habituation of an inefficient and injurious phonatory pattern. The pathologist must also decide whether voice symptom therapy should be provided simultaneously with psychotherapy and/or parental counseling because the child's phonatory patterns are of the nature which may eventually cause pathologic tissue change. For information on voice symptom unlearning

and relearning therapy procedures which may be employed by the speech pathologist, the reader is referred to Murphy (1964, chap. 8), Curtis (1967, pp. 212–228), Perkins (1957, pp. 857–874), Van Riper and Irwin (1958, chap. 9), and Mysak (1966a, chap. 5).

SPEECH FLUENCY

Stuttering is familiar to most adults and rather easily "diagnosed" by laymen. The incidence of the disorder among schoolchildren is approximately 0.7 to 1 percent, and the sex ratio is from 3:1 to 10:1 in favor of boys. Because of its audible and visible symptomatology and its social implications and because of the progressive increase in self-awareness of and sensitivity toward the symptoms by the child who stutters, it is perhaps one of the most painful childhood speech disorders.

Developmental Nonfluency

Speech fluency, like other aspects of speech production, develops as a function of time, and adultlike fluency patterns may not be observed until the latter part of the first decade of life. Not as much is known about developmental fluency patterns as would be desirable from a clinical standpoint. Data that are available follow.

Johnson (1957, pp. 901–902), in summarizing the results of various studies of children's fluency, states:

> In general, these investigators have found that repetitions of sounds or syllables, whole words, and phrases or combinations of two or more words are relatively common in the speech of children from two through five years of age. . . . The range is from less than 10 to approximately 100 instances of repetition per 1000 running words, and the mean is approximately 45 instances per 1000 words.

Johnson also points out that these repetitions are tension-free, that the children do not appear to be "emotional" or "conscious" of them, and that the speech gradually becomes more fluent as a function of time (i.e., they may be considered to be normal developmental nonfluencies). Worster-Drought (1968) refers to these nonfluencies as *physiological stammering* and as *purely transient phenomena.*

In Metraux's (1950) study of children's speech between 18 and 54 months, the following observations were made with reference to what can be termed developmental nonfluency patterns: (1) 18 months: repetition of syllables or words more frequently than not; (2) 24 months: use of "uh" and "uh, uh" before many responses and compulsive repetition of word or phrase; (3) 30 months: compulsive repetition of phrase even more marked and an increase in such repetition now caused by inter- rather than intracommunication factors (*developmental stuttering* evidenced for the first time at this age—i.e., repetition of syllable or first word often progressing to a tonic block which can be easily broken); (4) 36 months: return to easy repetition without compulsive character, use of "uh" or "um" as starter for speech, infrequent tonic block on initial syllables; (5) 42 months: frequent repetitions, developmental stuttering is again prominent, speech blocking may be accompanied by grimacing, cocking of the head, and so on; (6) 48 months: reduction in repetitions (however, repetitions and blocking episodes may continue in those children who previously manifested "developmental stuttering"); and (7) 54 months: use of "um" or "uh" at beginning of phrase, infrequent appearance of repetitions, except for those children who showed earlier tendency toward speech blocking.

Finally, Wingate (1962) summarizes a review of the literature of the speech characteristics of young children by stating that children show considerable individual variation in the type, amount, and frequency of fluency irregularities but that certain kinds of irregularities, that is, predominantly syllable repetitions and prolongations, are found more frequently in children later identified as stutterers.

Developmental patterns that emerge from this discussion of childhood fluency, at least up to 5 years or so, include:

1. Nonfluencies of various kinds appear physiologic in children's speech.

2. There is a progressive reduction in these nonfluencies as a function of time.

3. Amount and frequency of nonfluency appear related to internal factors first (e.g., searching for a certain word or phrase) and then to external factors (e.g., attempting to gain or fearing to lose a listener's attention).

4. A small number of children appear to manifest certain types of nonfluencies (immaturity characteristics) which later appear more like disfluencies (dysmaturity characteristics).

Forms of Stuttering

The growing interest in studying developmental fluency patterns should continue to make important contributions to stuttering theory. Another important development has been the slow shift from the age-old physiogenic-versus-psychogenic battle over the cause of stuttering to the increased recognition that various forms of the disorder known as stuttering may exist.

In summing up his discussion of the origins of stuttering, Van Riper (1963, p. 327) states, " . . . stuttering has many origins, many sources . . . the original causes are not nearly so important as the maintaining causes, once stuttering has started." West's (1968, chap. 5) most recent discussion of stuttering identifies at least three probable causes: (1) atavistic heredity, (2) brain injury, and (3) hysteroid disfluencies. In short, there is growing acceptance that the overt symptoms identified as stuttering behavior may, like the symptom of fever, have numerous sources or combinations of sources.

This author (Mysak, 1960) has hypothesized

about the existence of at least four categories of stuttering behavior. Only three will be discussed here since the fourth, the psychogenic category, will be reviewed in a later section of the chapter.

Neurogenic forms. It has been stated that fluency may be affected if there is periodic uncontrolled release of electrical potential in areas of the brain which subserve speech formulation or which innervate articulatory musculature. For additional information in this area, the reader is referred to West's (1958, pp. 178–179) comments about speech epilepsy.

Sensorimotor forms. Fluency may also be affected if there is a physiological delay in the return of various sensory dimensions of the speech signal back to the speaker. For comments on the effects of delayed auditory and proprioceptive feedback on speech production, the reader is referred to Mysak (1966a, pp. 91–92) and Dinnerstein and Lowenthal (1966).

Evaluational forms. Speech fluency may also be affected if significant others regularly overmonitor and are critical of a child's developmental nonfluencies and if the child eventually introjects this tendency, overmonitors, and becomes hypercritical of his own nonfluencies, thus disturbing the automaticity of speech (Johnson, 1957, chap. 28).

Common childhood stuttering. Finally, for purposes of this section of the chapter, it is important to define forms of stuttering which can be designated as *common childhood stuttering*. The basis of a good portion of this definition is from Johnson (1957, chap. 28).

The onset of common childhood stuttering is between 2 and 4 years, with a peak at 3 years; however, occasionally onset is associated with entrance into school. At the time of onset, stuttering almost always takes the form of *developmental repetitive nonfluencies* or, in some cases, *developmental repetitive disfluencies*

which are produced relatively without self-awareness or tension. It occurs most often in the presence of significant adults who have begun to listen to "how" rather than "what" is being said and who in some way indicate disapproval of the nonfluencies or disfluencies. It occurs in children who are relatively free of any significant neurological or psychological symptomatology (although many have positive family histories of stuttering), and it occurs in children whose parents are essentially normal except perhaps for their overconcern about their child's speaking ability. Finally, the diagnosis of stuttering in these cases is almost always made first by a layman.

If the onset of stuttering is at a different age, if it occurs in a different type of child, if its character is different, and so on, a diagnosis other than common childhood stuttering should be considered.

Formation and Transformation of Symptoms in Common Childhood Stuttering

Regardless of whether the child first exhibits developmental nonfluencies or disfluencies, if they are basically articulatory repetitions and prolongations, if they are relatively free of increased articulatory muscle tension, and if the child is generally unaware and unconcerned about them, the child is still not exhibiting the full speech symptom complex usually identified as stuttering. This statement has important theoretical as well as practical implications.

However, if significant others (or through them, the child; or for some, the child himself) respond to the child's speech automaticity or basal fluency level in a punitive fashion, symptom formation which may eventually be interpreted as stuttering may begin ("Johnson effect"). In other words, the child may eventually react in childish "forceful" ways to his developmental nonfluencies or actual disfluencies by attempting to reduce their number and/or frequency at a time when he is neurophysiologically unable to. This may result in heightened articulatory muscle tone and consequently, his simple repetitions may become episodes of articulatory hyperclonicity. Similarly, his attempts at reducing syllable prolongation time may cause his simple prolongations to become episodes of articulatory hypertonicity. And now "true" stuttering symptoms become observable. Further symptom formation takes place in time. For example, the abnormal increase in articulatory muscle tone usually irradiates to muscles of the face, head, neck, and so on; also, the child may begin to use "arm swings," "leg swings," "thoracic sways," and so on, as "blockbusters" and distraction devices. In addition to the acquisition of these overt articulatory and extraneous movement parakineses, the child may develop an array of covert symptoms such as sound and word fears, fears of certain speaking situations, use of verbal "starters" and circumlocutions and synonyms for "hard" words, and also the conscious avoidance of speaking situations.

In short, then, the overt and covert symptoms commonly regarded as stuttering may be viewed as childish reactive symptoms or as learned behavior in response to imagined or to actual deficits in one's basal speech-fluency level.

Stuttering symptomatology also undergoes various transformations. A rather thorough discussion of these changes in stuttering symptomatology as a function of time has been presented by Bloodstein (1960a, 1960b, 1961). Bloodstein described four stages of stuttering:

1. The preschool stage: episodic repetitions at the beginnings of sentences and on minor parts of speech. The child shows little evidence of concern.

2. The early elementary-school stage: chronic blocks on major parts of speech. The child considers himself a stutterer but still shows little or no concern.

3. The junior high and high school stage: stut-

tering chiefly in response to specific situations. There are the appearance of sound and word fears and the use of word substitutions and circumlocutions, but essentially no avoidance of speaking situations and little or no evidence of embarrassment.

4. The high school and older stage: strong anticipation of stuttering, feared sounds, words, and situations, the frequent use of word substitutions and circumlocutions, and embarrassment and avoidance of speaking situations.

Bloodstein cautions by stating that the stages are variable and are typical rather than universal and that the changes are continuous and gradual.

Diagnosis and Therapy

In suspected cases of childhood stuttering, the speech pathologist must first determine whether the problem is in the "ear of the parent" (or other significant adults), so to speak, or is actually in the "mouth of the child"—that is, is it a case of developmental nonfluency? Or is there an actual increase in the amount and frequency of articulatory repetitions and prolongations—that is, is it a case of developmental disfluency? In either case, we do not as yet have childhood stuttering unless the child also manifests some of the reactive symptoms previously described. However, in the case of suspected developmental disfluency, further studies should be made, for example, by pediatrics, neurology, and psychiatry-psychology, in order to help determine whether the disfluency is secondary to environmental speech pressures or, more seriously, secondary to some form of neurological and/or psychological distress.

If the diagnosis points to some form of secondary disfluency, speech therapy may wait until causal therapy is provided to counteract the primary disorder, or speech therapy may be recommended simultaneously with some other therapy in the hopes of preventing or retarding the development of reactive speech symptoms.

On the other hand, if the diagnosis is developmental nonfluency, therapy may take the form of a series of counseling sessions with the parents on speech-fluency hygiene. Also, if it is a case of developmental disfluency which appears relatively speech-system specific, that is, without remarkable physiological or psychological findings, therapy may take the form of parental speech counseling alone or counseling done simultaneously with fluency facilitation work for the child. If the child is older and reactive symptoms or "true" stuttering symptomatology is manifested and if the case is still viewed as relatively speech-specific, various kinds of speech symptom approaches to therapy are available to the clinician. For examples of speech therapy for stuttering, the reader is referred to the following authors: Van Riper (1963, chap. 12), Eisenson (Ed.) (1958, chaps, by Bloodstein, Eisenson, Sheehan, Van Riper, & West), Mysak (1966a, chap. 7), and Luper and Mulder (1964). For recent discussions on the application of learning theory to stuttering therapy, the reader is referred to books by Gregory (Ed.) (1968) and Brutten and Shoemaker (1967).

This concludes the first division of the chapter, devoted to speech-disorder simplexes, that is, disorders based specifically on problems of the speech system that present relatively simple symptom patterns.

SPEECH-DISORDER COMPLEXES

This division of the chapter is concerned with speech-disorder complexes associated with congenital cleft palate and congenital severe hypacusis, as well as those associated with more generalized childhood conditions such as cerebral palsy, mental retardation, and childhood psychoses. It is here that the speech pathologist frequently encounters the "rare," "exotic," and "unclassifiable" disorders of speech communication. Such cases are more likely to confront the speech pathologist in the hospital setting, and diagnosis and treatment are usually a team effort.

Each discussion of a speech complex will include descriptions of forms of the complex and diagnostic and therapy considerations.

Because absence or severe limitation of speech comprehension and formulation in a child is so obvious and so handicapping in our "talking society," children whose speech-communication disorders may be secondary to mental retardation or some form of childhood psychosis are often referred to a hospital speech and hearing service first. Therefore, the service often provides a screening function as well as a place to confirm the presence of suspected primary or secondary speech and hearing conditions. A good service will include a doctoral-level speech pathologist and audiologist and a social worker. Also, all referred children should be examined by a pediatrician and otolaryngologist. The services of a neurologist, a psychiatrist, and a psychologist should also be available. This kind of team examination allows for the thorough evaluation of a child's speech, hearing, and language functions, as well as of his intellectual, socioemotional, and visual and motor functioning. When a child has received such a work-up, diagnostic impressions and recommendations are usually made at a team conference.

From such team evaluations may emerge the impression that the case is primarily a speech and hearing complex and should receive speech and hearing therapy—as, for example, in certain cases of childhood language dysmaturation, anacusis, or stuttering—or that the child is primarily retarded or emotionally disturbed and appropriate referrals should be made. In many of the latter cases, interim and/or supplementary speech and hearing therapy may also be offered. As might be expected, such a service often becomes involved with problems of placement at schools or classes for the retarded, brain-damaged, and emotionally disturbed. The experienced social worker is indispensable in offering assistance at these times. Opportunity for parental counseling is also frequently provided.

The discussion of speech-disorder complexes is presented under the following headings: congenital and infantile anacuses, cleft palate speech syndromes, neurodevelopmental speech syndromes (including mental retardation, cerebral palsy, and minimal brain dysfunction), and psychodevelopmental speech problems. Since all the areas mentioned have voluminous literature associated with them, the present discussions are based on recent references and on those which are more specifically concerned with speech and hearing processes.

CONGENITAL AND INFANTILE ANACUSES

Congenital and infantile anacuses refers here to those hearing losses, from whatever cause, which are severe enough to retard or prevent the development of spoken language unless there is professional intervention. Di Carlo (1964, p. 43), in his review of definitions of childhood deafness, states, "There now seems to be a general agreement that a hearing loss of 80 db or more in the speech range, if present prior to the acquisition of language and speech, should be accepted as a satisfactory definition of deafness."

Etiological Factors

Morley (1965, pp. 98–99) reported on 110 children with hearing loss sufficient to cause language retardation. Eighty-four of the problems were considered to be congenital, while twenty-four children had illnesses in infancy which might have caused the problem. For the greater number of the congenital cases, the cause was unclear; however, in one case maternal rubella was suffered during pregnancy and in another the child was kernicteric soon after birth. In the history of the twenty-four suspected cases of acquired hearing loss, the following diseases were found: meningitis, severe measles, severe whooping cough, pneumonia, and mumps. These findings reflect the overall conclusion reached by

Di Carlo (1964, p. 44) in his review of research into the etiology of deafness, namely, that it has multiple origins. Kendall (1966, p. 216), in his extensive review of the literature on auditory problems in children, comments, ". . . most retrospective studies have been unable to assign a definite or fairly certain etiology to more than about fifty percent of the child population with severe hearing impairment. . . ."

Speech and Language Functioning

The speech complex of the severely hypacustic or anacustic child includes not only the inability to hear, and hence the inability to learn to comprehend spoken language, but also the inability to learn to produce speech symbols and the sounds of which they are formed. The complex is further complicated because of the importance of intraverbalizing and interverbalizing behavior to emotional, social, and intellectual development.

Of the 110 severely hypacustic children discussed by Morley (1965, p. 102), 29 did not say any words and 28 of the remaining 81 children spoke their first words by 4 years. Di Carlo (1964, pp. 94–95) states, "Unless the deaf child has had intensive early instruction, he probably has less than twenty-five words at the age of five years." He states further (1964, p. 99) that evaluation of the speech of the deaf reveals severe delay and restriction in "vocalization from birth, the time at which single words appear, the use of single sentences, the proficiency of articulation of speech sounds, the general length of the speech responses in communication, the amount of speech output, and the vocabulary usage."

Diagnosis and Habilitation

There has been increasing emphasis on detection of hearing loss in infancy and on more accurate diagnoses of the type and severity of the loss. Both of these factors have important implications for habilitation. Kendall (1966, chap. 10), in his extensive review of the literature, presents data on types of childhood auditory disorders, including hypacusis, anacusis, dysacusis, combined dysacusis and hypacusis, and functional problems. He also discusses various ways of assessing auditory behavior. These include knowledge of developmental stages of auditory behavior in infants up to 9 months of age, the use of reflex testing for auditory screening of neonates up to 10 days, and the use of various auditory tests developed for use with children up to 6 years of age, including play audiometry, speech audiometry, and various electrophysiological approaches to hearing measurement. Another good review of auditory diagnostic procedures for children has been presented by Di Carlo (1964, pp. 48–63).

The first goal of the speech pathologist and/or audiologist and his health colleagues with respect to congenital or infantile hypacusis or anacusis is the earliest possible identification of the disorder. Next, an attempt must be made to differentiate a relatively isolated involvement of the peripheral hearing mechanism from various kinds of deviant auditory behavior which may accompany brain dysfunction, severe emotional disorder, mental retardation, or combinations of these disorders. Myklebust (1954) presents data which he states serves to differentiate among children with peripheral deafness, aphasia, psychic deafness, and mental deficiency.

When language retardation is secondary to a primary severe hearing loss and when there may also be secondary problems in intellectual, social, and emotional development, the habilitation process is necessarily long and complex. For example, early use of hearing aids (even during infancy) and special auditory training and speech stimulation carried out by the speech and hearing clinician and by parents are recommended. Di Carlo (1964, p. 106) indicates that there is a growing conviction among educators of the deaf that an early program of training leads to more satisfactory speech development, and he states that many schools and clinics are now providing this early instruction to both deaf children and parents. Ongoing evaluation of the child's progress in language development, as well as of his intellectual, social, and emotional development, must also be made in order to make early decisions about whether the child should be placed in a regular school, in a special class in a regular school, or in a special school for the deaf.

Finally, Di Carlo (1964, p. 116) states, "Teaching speech to the deaf requires consummate skill, infinite patience, time, and a devotion to the oral method. . . . It appears desirable that the deaf should have an opportunity to acquire an education which is conducive to the development of oral communication."

CLEFT PALATE SPEECH SYNDROMES

Areas of concern in congenital cleft palate are numerous. Much has recently been written in the areas of classification, incidence, embryology, etiology, anatomy and physiology, and evaluation and management (including surgical, orthodontic, prosthetic, otological, dental, psychological, and speech and hearing) of congenital cleft lip and palate. The discussion here will focus on what is considered the most important sequela of cleft palate, that is, the common disturbance of the child's speech communication. Two good books on the topic are by Morley (1966) and Spriestersbach and Sherman (Eds.) (1968).

Background Data

Congenital clefts of the palate and lip have occurred in man for a long time. Symptoms of such clefts have been found among the remains of some early inhabitants of Egypt, and a repair of a cleft lip was reported in the first century. Today the incidence of congenital clefts of the palate and/or lip has been estimated to be 1 in 750 to 800 live births. The immediate cause of such clefts is a failure in embryogenesis; specifically, a failure in the complete development, by about the first 8 to 10 weeks, of one or more of the five embryonic processes of the face.

Clefts of the lip and palate can range from a bifid uvula, or a lip pit, to a combination of complete cleft of the soft and hard palates and complete bilateral clefts of the lip. Etiology of such conditions has been divided into genetic and environmental categories. Family histories have been reported in 27 percent of isolated cleft lip cases, in 19 percent of isolated cleft palate cases, and in 41 percent of combination cleft lip and palate cases. Possible environmental causes that have been reported include maternal radiation, thyroid deficiency, basal metabolism irregularity, dietary deficiencies, infection, and stress; parental age and number and recency of color fusions in the maternal ancestry have also been cited as possible causal factors. It is not unusual for children with cleft lip and palate to exhibit multianomalies (about 20 to 25 percent) since the heart, limbs, and skeleton are also developing during the fifth to the tenth weeks of embryonal life.

Some comments made by Goodstein (1968, pp. 220–222) in the recapitulation of his chapter "Psychosocial Aspects of Cleft Palate" are also appropriate here:

1. There is no evidence that, in general, parents of children with cleft palate are poorly adjusted to any substantial degree.

2. There is minimal evidence that children with cleft palate are in general somewhat retarded physically and socially.

3. There is substantial agreement that, as a group, children with cleft palate suffer a moderate degree of intellectual impairment.

4. There is little, if any, evidence that children with cleft lip and palate are in general psychologically disturbed or emotionally maladjusted.

Speech and Hearing

About 40 percent of these children may exhibit hearing problems. Upper-respiratory-system infection and eustachian tube anomalies are the causes usually cited for these problems. Factors that may contribute to the speech syn-

drome include taut upper lip, missing or supernumerary teeth, various malocclusions, alveolar ridge and dental arch anomalies, oronasal fistula, palatal vault anomalies, short soft palates or palates with inadequate rates of diadochokinesis (postsurgery), and flattened nasal ala. Intellectual and socioemotional deficits may also serve as compounding factors.

The author (Mysak, 1961) presented a review of the commonly encountered voice and speech sound deficits in individuals with cleft palates. In any one case, the child may manifest language immaturity (Moll, 1968, p. 110), phonatory-resonatory irregularities due to oronasal and velopharyngeal structural anomalies, and articulatory dysmaturity associated with chronic hearing problems and with lip, alveolar ridge, dental-occlusal, and palatal vault anomalies.

Diagnosis and Therapy

Evaluation and management of children with cleft lip and palate are best done through cleft palate teams. Such teams are usually composed of a pediatrician, plastic surgeon, otolaryngologist, orthodontist, prosthodontist, dentist, social worker, psychologist, and speech pathologist. A listing of cleft palate teams by state may be found in the membership directory of the American Cleft Palate Association.

If a child with a cleft lip and/or palate appears at a team conference within a few weeks of his birth, the role of the speech pathologist is basically one of providing speech counseling for the parents. In this regard, the writer (Mysak, 1961; 1966b, p. 172) has described techniques which might encourage the development, during the first months of life, of more normal oropneumodynamics for voice and speech sound production. This counseling, plus periodic demonstrations of techniques and follow-up, could be described as preventive speech therapy designed to ensure maximum development of speech processes during the first 12 months of life.

As time goes on, the speech pathologist will

urge that palatal closure take place as early as possible, hopefully before 9 months. Such early closure may allow the infant to create intraoral breath pressure and oralized speech airstreams during at least part of the prespeech period of vocal activity, which is important to later speech development. If for one reason or another palatal surgery is planned at a year or beyond, the speech pathologist should request an interim speech appliance or oral prosthesis. Early and ongoing monitoring of the child's auditory behavior is also done since these children are vulnerable to conductive hearing losses. The speech pathologist also evaluates and reports to the team on the possible speech repercussions of anomalous dental and occlusal situations. Further, he must be alert to all the factors which, in addition to their negative effects on voice and speech production, may also retard the development of spoken language. This includes reduced or inappropriate speech stimulation due to frequent hospitalization and/or negative parental attitudes.

Finally, with the cooperation of the entire team, including the parents, every effort is made by the speech pathologist to provide the type and amount of speech and hearing services needed, especially during the first 4 or 5 years of life, so as to ensure the development of the highest level of speech communication of which each child is capable.

NEURODEVELOPMENTAL SPEECH SYNDROMES

The discussion of neurodevelopmental speech syndromes includes descriptions of speech and hearing disorders associated with childhood conditions popularly referred to as mental retardation, cerebral palsy, and minimal brain dysfunction. Two of the reasons for grouping these complex problems are (1) a child from any one of these groups frequently has dysfunctions common to all three; and (2) in each case, the clinician should collect data on medical problems, on motor behavior, on vision, on intellectual and socioemotional functioning, and most importantly from the standpoint of the present chapter, on speech, hearing, and language abilities.

Mental Retardation and Speech

Since there is a vast literature concerned with the field of mental retardation in general and a substantial amount specifically concerned with the speech and hearing of such children, only the more salient data in each of these areas are presented here.

Background information. Retardates are those who are relatively generally, rather than specifically, involved with respect to motor, perceptual-conceptual, socioemotional, and speech and language developments. Wood (1964, p. 36) defined mental retardation as "a reduced ability to learn adequately from any experience within his environment, whereas children with aphasia, hearing loss, or emotional disturbance are able to learn from certain types of experience, depending upon their individual problems." Etiologies for the various brain dysfunctions in mental retardation include chromosomal abnormalities, central nervous system (CNS) impairment, familial tendencies, or various combinations of these factors.

With respect to relationships between speech and mental retardation, Matthews (1957, p. 532) states, "In our own clinical experience, mental retardation has been one of the most frequently encountered factors associated with language and speech retardation." Similarly, Morley (1965, p. 76) states that when hearing is normal, retarded mental development is the most common cause of speech retardation.

Speech and language. In defining the nontrainable child, many authorities include the criterion that the child is nonverbal or capable of learning only a few monosyllabic words. Brown (1967,

p. 335) states, "In general, the degree of speech retardation parallels the degree of mental deficiency." In Darley and Winitz' (1961) review of research on the time of appearance of the first word among the mentally retarded, they report a range of approximately 30 to 60 months. They conclude, "Intelligence is apparently an important factor in the age of appearance of the first word." Myklebust (1954, chap. IX), in his discussion of mental deficiency and speech acquisition, indicates that those children classified as idiots usually do not acquire speech, while those classified as imbeciles may begin to use words at approximately 3 years of age and those classified as morons may begin to use words at approximately 18 to 24 months of age. An interesting clinical observation on the first use of words by retardates has been made by Brown (1967, p. 337). He reports that some retarded children may develop a few words at a nearly normal time which are used for a few days or even several months, only to disappear and not return. He indicates that with such a history, "one may be almost certain that the child is seriously retarded mentally."

Matthews (1957, chap. 17) offers the following conclusions based on a review of the literature of the speech and hearing of the mentally retarded:

1. On the average, the mentally retarded child acquires language considerably later than the normal child.

2. When speech does emerge, the incidence of disorders is considerably higher than in the general population.

3. There is no evidence that the disorders differ in kind from those disorders of nonretarded children.

4. There appears to be a relationship between intellectual level and degree of speech involvement.

5. The incidence of hearing loss is considerably higher than in a nonretarded population.

Of 280 children referred with delayed development of speech, Morley (1965, chap. 7) indicated that 71 cases were associated with general mental retardation. The intelligence quotient was ascertained in 32 of the 71 cases; the average IQ was 60, with a range of 37 to 87. The mean age for the first use of words was 3 years, and the mean age for the first use of phrases was 4 years. Morley also reported the following findings on the speech of eighty-two hospital patients with severe mental retardation: (1) the outstanding feature was the absence or poverty of speech rather than defective articulation; (2) the onset of speech was severely delayed, and when it developed it was extremely limited; and (3) speech comprehension was better than expression. The statement by Berry and Eisenson (1956, p. 9) that "Lack of intelligence is much more likely to be the direct cause of linguistic inadequacy than of speech defect" supports Morley's findings.

Diagnosis and therapy. When confronted with a child with speech involvement possibly associated with mental retardation, the clinician must estimate whether the deficit is merely one part of the child's retardation in overall abilities or whether parts of the speech disorder may be attributed to hearing loss, emotional disturbance, specific types of CNS impairment, glandular dysfunction, institutionalization, and so on. It should be clear that for the speech pathologist to arrive at a good analysis of the child's speech and language profile, he requires examination data from other specialists, for example, the pediatrician, psychiatrist, psychologist, and audiologist.

If the child's speech problem appears to be secondary to mental retardation, the speech pathologist needs to consider how speech habilitation procedures might fit into the total management plan. For example: Is the retardation so severe and the learning potential so limited that speech therapy is not indicated except, perhaps, in the form of some suggestions to the parents if the child is still at home? Or is the degree of retardation sufficient to require special-school placement and, until this placement is effected, interim speech therapy and home suggestions? If a child has been placed but there is no speech service available at the school and the child shows potential for speech progress, supplementary speech therapy plus school and home speech-stimulation suggestions should be offered. There are also times when the speech pathologist determines that speech progress is in keeping with overall development and hence special speech therapy may not be indicated. There are also cases in which the child may manifest interesting amounts of unactualized potential in speech and language functioning and hence becomes a candidate for speech therapy.

With reference to speech therapy for the retarded, Brown (1967, p. 335) comments, "Of course it is possible to improve the speech of a mentally retarded child by intensive training, and it is also possible to improve his intelligence scores somewhat." Matthews's (1957, chap. 7) review of the literature also concludes that speech therapy with mentally retarded children can be beneficial. Rigrodsky and Steer (1961) reported on their study with mentally retarded children designed to compare an experimental articulation-therapy technique based upon Mowrer's autistic language-development theory with a traditional stimulus method. At the conclusion of speech training, the upper intellectual group (IQ scores ranging from 45 to 79) achieved better scores than the lower intellectual group (IQ scores ranging from 12 to 44) on certain articulation tests. No significant differences were found between the two groups receiving the speech therapy when compared with each other or with the control groups. However, observation revealed that "the children in the experimental program appeared to become more spontaneously verbal and more favorably inclined to the therapy sessions than were the children receiving the traditional therapy programs."

Cerebral Palsy and Speech

As is well known by specialists working with children classified as cerebral-palsied, the term is quite general and usually refers to a wide range of chronic childhood brain syndromes with observable sensorimotor deficits. In this group of children may also be found those with major intellectual, hearing, and emotional problems. For rather inclusive discussions of the multifaceted problems found in cerebral palsy—for example, neuromuscular, orthopedic, seizure disorder, visual-perceptual, social, emotional, intellectual, educational, and vocational problems, as well as problems in speech, hearing, and language—the reader is referred to texts by Cardwell (1956) and Cruickshank (1966). For texts which are more specifically concerned with the speech and hearing concomitants, the reader is referred to texts by McDonald and Chance (1964), Mecham et al. (1966), and Mysak (1968b).

Background information. The condition now known as cerebral palsy appears to date back to earliest recorded time. Some carvings on ancient Egyptian monuments reflect individuals with this problem. Descriptions suggestive of the problem are found in ancient Hebrew and Greek scriptures and in the New Testament. The first clinical description was offered by Dr. Little, an English physician, in 1843. Incidence figures today range from 1 to 6 in every 1,000 births. Etiological factors include heredity and various environmental problems, of which the major ones are prematurity, anoxia, malformations, birth trauma, kernicterus, and multiple pregnancies. Frequently recognized types of cerebral palsy include spasticity, athetosis, rigidity, ataxia, tremor, atonia, and mixed.

This discussion will be confined to the frequently encountered problems among those with childhood cerebral palsy in the development of speech, hearing, and language.

Speech and hearing. This discussion of cerebral palsy speech disorders and its habilitation is based on the extensive review of the literature made by the author in preparation for his writing of two chapters on the topic for the new *Handbook of Speech Pathology and Audiology* (1971).

The incidence of speech-communication problems among the cerebral-palsied is high. Numerous reports give figures which range from 70 to 86 percent. There does not appear to be a particular speech syndrome characteristic of the cerebral-palsied. A high proportion of the cases are mixed, and the speech communication of the cerebral-palsied may range from a complete absence of communication to little if any differences from the normal.

Excluding the frequent complications of major problems of mental retardation and emotional disorder, cerebral palsy speech syndromes may take the form of various combinations and degrees of the following involvements: infantile breathing patterns plus paralytic breathing symptoms; symptoms of auditory immaturity and otopathology, speech-sound immaturity, and various forms of dysarthria; symptoms of infantile laryngeal functioning and of laryngeal paralysis; symptoms of speech-rhythm immaturity as well as of pathology of speech-rhythm mechanisms; and symptoms of oral-language immaturity as well as of pathology. In short, cerebral palsy speech syndromes take many forms and have multiple backgrounds, and the speech pathologist must examine for every possible type and combination of speech pathology.

Diagnosis and therapy. With respect to the speech diagnosis, the clinician must determine whether major hearing, intellectual, and emotional problems are present. He must decide whether the presenting problem is a relatively specific dysarthria or some complex of auditory, articulatory, phonatory, rhythm, and linguistic symptoms. Further, he should determine how much of each of the symptoms reflects immaturity secondary to the brain lesion and how much

is due to primary paralysis directly associated with the brain involvement.

Because of the complexity of many of the speech syndromes presented by the cerebral-palsied child, wide-spectrum treatment approaches to speech habilitation is usually recommended in the hopes of ensuring that each child will actualize his maximum potential for speech communication.

This means that the speech clinician should start his work as soon as possible after the child is identified, even if this be very soon after birth. He should develop preventive speech-therapy procedures for the preverbal period designed to minimize possible secondary problems; causal speech-therapy procedures for the speech age designed to ameliorate those factors which appear to be directly responsible for certain speech symptoms (e.g., stimulating tongue-tip elevation if this appears to be a problem); speech symptom procedures designed to ensure that the child use all the speech sounds and symbols he is capable of at any one time in his therapy program; and speech compensatory techniques designed to help the child develop compensatory sounds when certain sounds are impossible for him to make or, when necessary, to help him use, for example, a language or conversation board to supplement or to replace his efforts at speech communication.

Minimal Brain Dysfunction and Language Disorder

Minimal brain dysfunction in childhood is the last topic under the heading of neurodevelopmental speech syndromes. Such children are classified in different ways by different specialists. *CNS-impaired, cerebral dysfunction, minimal brain damage, minimal chronic brain syndromes, brain-injured, perceptually handicapped, and cerebrally handicapped* are some of the terms used. These are the children who may not manifest observable neuromotor problems and in whom the diagnosis of childhood neurological disorder may be based entirely on behavioral manifestations. These are also the children who may show varying degrees and combinations of sensory, perceptual, integrative, motor, and behavioral symptoms—and, importantly from the standpoint of this section of the chapter, symptoms of language dysmaturation.

Speech and hearing. It is among the children who usually fit the category of minimal brain dysfunction that developmental or acquired childhood aphasia or oligophasia may be found. In a recent chapter on disorders of oral communication among such children (Mysak, 1968a, chap. 1), the following kinds of possible speech and hearing symptoms in various combinations and degrees were reported: (1) auditory: possible acuity loss as well as problems with span, discrimination, figure ground, and sequencing; (2) articulatory: subtle or frank neurological deficits of the tongue and velum and slow and disturbed development of speech sounds; and (3) linguistic: retardation or lack of speech formulation, problems in speech comprehension, unusual differences between speech comprehension and formulation abilities, compensatory use of speechreading and gesture to assist speech comprehension, use of the agrammatisms, omission of functional or small words in speech, problems in organizing sentences and sequences of sentences, lack of or inconsistent meaning associated with verbalization, atypical verbal associations during reading or speaking, word-finding problems, use of circumlocutionary speech, echolalia, and verbal perseveration.

Worster-Drought (1968) identifies two types of aphasia in children: receptive aphasia and executive aphasia. In auditory receptive aphasia, the otherwise intelligent child finds it difficult to comprehend spoken language and consequently also suffers secondary expressive problems. In executive or expressive aphasia, the child may comprehend well but is very slow or unable to express himself in spoken language; however, he usually compensates for his verbal problem with gesture and mime.

Worster-Drought believes that receptive aphasia in childhood is best termed congenital or developmental auditory aphasia. The diagnostic profile of such a child shows limited or absent speech comprehension, limited and frequently unintelligible speech expression, average nonverbal IQ, and a normal or near normal audiogram. Most of these children spontaneously acquire some sounds and words and may gradually acquire a language of their own, that is, an idioglossia understood only by those close to them (he believes congenital auditory imperception is the basis of true idioglossia); in addition, such speech is invariably telegrammatic and characterized by omissions of syllables and word endings. Also, because of their comprehension limitations, these children may echo questions directed at them and request the frequent repetition of new words (reflection of their defective auditory word memory). Some of these children attempt to speechread but do not do so consistently unless taught. Worster-Drought recognizes three grades of congenital auditory imperception: (1) pure word deafness only; (2) word or language deafness with additional inability to distinguish between cruder sounds; (3) the previous deficits plus some actual peripheral hearing loss, including those children who are impervious not only to spoken language but to any ordinary sound (the only evidence of hearing is via cortical audiometry). The most likely cause of the problem is "a biological variation of the nature of an aplasia or agenesis affecting both sides of the brain in the temporal lobe cortex and including the auditory word area" (p. 435).

In developmental executive aphasia, speech comprehension may be adequate but speech formulation is considerably delayed and, upon its appearance, is characterized by single words usually associated with gesture; the further development of speech is marked by dysarticulation. Both kinds of aphasia may be found in acquired cases associated with head injury, brain abscess or tumor, encephalitis, and epilepsy.

The following points are made by Myklebust (1954, chap. 7) in his discussion of childhood aphasia: Aphasia is a relatively specific disorder of symbolic functioning and reflects itself in various degrees of inability to comprehend speech (predominantly receptive aphasia), to speak (predominantly expressive aphasia), or to use language for thought (central aphasia), irrespective of whether it is congenital or acquired. Children who exhibit predominantly expressive aphasia comprehend speech well but rarely engage in vocal activities such as jargon or imitative speech. Those who have less disability may exhibit intermittent ability to use words, phrases, or sentences. Children who exhibit predominantly receptive aphasia can hear speech but cannot comprehend it. They may begin to ignore speech as well as other sounds or to intermittently and unexpectedly comprehend a word. They also experience secondary speaking problems. Those who have mixed aphasia are difficult to differentiate from those with predominantly receptive problems. In short, receptive and expressive aphasias are impairments of interverbalization, while central aphasia is an impairment of intraverbalization. For other discussions of childhood aphasia, the reader is referred to Morley (1965, chap. 9) and Wood (1964, chap. 2).

Finally, Eisenson (1968) offers some impressions of childhood aphasia based on his recent years of experience with nonverbal children. He indicates that relatively few children he has seen "qualify" as truly aphasic, and he states, "With rare exception, developmentally aphasic children are essentially those who have auditory perceptual involvements." He states further

that unless "there is clear evidence to suspect an underlying dysarthria or oral apraxia, expressive manifestations in the child may be considered just another aspect of auditory aphasia."

There is still substantial disagreement among speech pathologists about the existence of true congenital aphasia, and there is disagreement about its forms and etiologies among those who do agree about its existence.

Diagnosis and therapy. Irrespective of the beliefs of the speech pathologist, he is often asked to diagnose relatively specific language disorders in children suspected of suffering from minimal brain dysfunction. His first task with such referrals is to determine whether the child's language development is in fact outside of normal limits. Then he must determine whether the language symptoms can be explained on the basis of serious hearing loss, mental retardation, emotional disturbance, or combinations of these. Here he will need data from pediatrics, neurology, psychiatry, psychology, and otolaryngology. Ultimately, he will need to collect the kind of speech and hearing data which will allow him to test the hypothesis that the language disturbance is on the basis of relatively specific involvement of central neural mechanisms subserving language function. The length of time that a child suffers from a relatively primary language disturbance is also critical to, and may complicate, diagnosis and habilitation, since a primary language disturbance can be expected to produce repercussions in social, emotional, and intellectual development.

Habilitation of children with minimal brain dysfunction and relatively specific language disorder is complex. Language therapy in the form of home activities as well as professional therapy should be offered as soon as possible. Depending on the progress made in developing speech communication, special schooling and other therapies may eventually be required. For a discussion of language therapy for children, the reader is referred to Wood (1964, chap. 4).

PSYCHODEVELOPMENTAL SPEECH PROBLEMS

This last section of the chapter is divided into two parts: the first concerns those childhood socioemotional problems which may disturb the voicing, articulation, and rhythm aspects of spoken symbols; the second has to do with those childhood socioemotional problems which may disturb the comprehension and formulation of spoken symbols. The causes of such problems may range from meager stimulation or inappropriate reward for speech communication to childhood neuroses and psychoses.

Van Riper (1963, pp. 2–11) has discussed the roles of speech in thinking, in intercommunication, in emotional expression, in social control, and in the identification of self. His discussion is supportive of the important and reciprocal relationships that obtain among intellectual, socioemotional, and speech developments. Hence, primary socioemotional problems which may affect speech development may give rise to a vicious spiral of childhood dysmaturation, and conversely, primary speech problems which may affect socioemotional development may also give rise to a vicious spiral of childhood dysmaturation. Early identification and analysis for possible primary and secondary factors in a childhood behavioral disorder which includes speech symptoms are therefore important.

SPEECH-PRODUCTION SYMPTOMS OF PSYCHODEVELOPMENTAL ORIGIN

Environmental conditions which may affect the development of the voice, articulation, or rhythm dimensions of speech may or may not seriously affect the child's emotional and social developments. However, each case requires careful study if the "vicious spiraling" previously referred to is to be avoided.

Articulatory Symptoms

Symptoms of articulatory dysmaturity may stem from factors such as foreign accent and nonstandard speech-sound models, reduction in the amount of speech stimulation (Carrell, 1968, pp. 34–38), and hospitalization during the speech-sound learning period. Regression in articulatory development is sometimes seen when certain children desire or need the amount and kind of attention a younger sib may be receiving. These regression patterns may be surprisingly similar to those of the younger sib. West (1958, p. 50) has stated that speech develops earliest and best in a child whose environment provides rich speech experiences (with both children and adults), a real need for and pleasure to be derived from speaking, and daily rewards for steady improvement in speech.

Phonatory Symptoms

Disorders of human vocalization can originate for various socioemotional reasons and at different periods in a child's life. For example, early negative conditioning of an infant's vocalization has been seen as one possible contributor to disturbance in vocal development, and Brodnitz (1959, p. 49) states, "Many of the deviations from normal vocal behavior that we find in the adult can be traced to the mutational change during puberty."

Negative conditioning of the infantile voice. Perkins (1957, pp. 848–849) hypothesized about early negative conditioning of an infant's vocalization. For example, if an infant is deprived of experiencing early contented vocalization because of being in a state of continual discomfort (stemming, for example, from colic, parental rejection, or "crying it out"), his patterns of tense vocalization may tend to be reinforced. There are no data on just how such early reinforcement of tense vocal patterns may affect later vocal maturation. Along these lines, Murphy (1964, p. 31), in discussing the genesis of abnormal voice in children, states, "Throughout the vocal learning process, the voice acquired by the child depends upon how he imitates or identifies with important adults in his environment." He believes normal vocal development depends upon approval and success in earlier phases of communication, that is, satisfactions derived from vocal play and imitation.

Postmutational voice disorders. Brodnitz (1959, pp. 50–51) describes three types of postmutational voice disorders in males which he ascribes to psychological influences.

The mutational falsetto is a relatively rare condition, in which a male with normal vocal cords speaks in a high, squeaky voice and often with a pitch that is higher than a child's voice. *Incomplete mutation* describes a voice which began to descend during mutation but which leveled off before reaching the full depth of the adult male pitch. These conditions are interpreted by Brodnitz as resulting from a rejection at puberty of the maturity and responsibility of adulthood or from a refusal to accept vocal masculinity because of a rejection of the father. In their review of the literature, Van Riper and Irwin (1958, p. 229) find the following additional reasons for rejection of the mature voice: (1) because it requires more breath and effort, (2) as a response to ridicule of the changing voice ("physiologic puberphonia"), and (3) as a means of avoiding stuttering.

The mutational basso is the third type of postmutational voice disorder. It is characterized by the use of an abnormally deep voice, which, according to Brodnitz, represents an attempt to express vocally a maturity that is premature or not genuine.

Mutational voice disturbances in females have been observed less frequently. True mutational falsetto in a female is rather rare, but an upwardly displaced pitch level is more common (Brodnitz, 1959, p. 52). Abnormally deep female voices are sometimes encountered and may be reflective of a male identification.

Phonation and personality types. Murphy (1964, p. 31) reported his survey of the literature on personality and voice descriptions—a type concept which he believes is not too useful. The following possible relationships were found: weak voice and weak, submissive, shy personalities; loud voice and vital, aggressive, dominant personalities; thin, high voice and stingy, indecisive personalities; monotonous voice and a lack of imagination; breathy voice and fearful, passionate personalities. Other personality-voice relationships reported include harsh voices and aggressive, antagonistic, competitive, and hypertense individuals (Van Riper & Irwin, 1958, p. 233); and harsh quality with high pitch and chronic feelings of anxiety and insecurity (Curtis, 1967, p. 208). To the extent that such relationships may be justifiable in any one case, it could be considered a basis for vocal dysmaturation.

Hysterical aphonia. Hysterical aphonia is rare in children. Such sudden loss of voice may be precipitated by extreme fright or disappointment. Berry and Eisenson (1956, p. 232) report that the condition occurs more frequently in girls and may appear as early as puberty (or sometimes even earlier). They believe that deeply seated emotional problems are the "true etiological agents" of hysterical aphonia.

In conclusion, it should be noted that rather simple explanations for voice differences may also exist, such as poor speech models (Curtis, 1967, p. 208) and faulty vocal learning (Murphy, 1964, pp. 33–34).

Fluency Symptoms

As indicated, there has for some time been substantial controversy over the cause and treatment of stuttering. In its simplest form, the controversy has existed among investigators who could be identified as "organicists," "environmentalists," and "interactionists." Throughout the long history of stuttering research, conclusive data have not been found to support any one position over the others. An interesting development has been the move by many clinicians to a multicausal approach to the problem, a move that is so often necessary and productive when clinicians deal with human disorders and diseases.

That psychogenic forms of stuttering exist would be difficult to deny. The "to speak or not to speak" conflict, and hence the frequent compromise of incomplete speaking or stuttering, may arise because (1) the speaker fears that he may automatically process thoughts into words which are socially unacceptable (Travis, 1957, chap. 29), and (2) the child's attempts at speaking are accompanied by feelings of guilt or hostility (Sheehan, 1958, pp. 123–166). Other current theories worthy of consideration are Glauber's (1958, p. 78) theory that stuttering is a symptom of a pregenital conversion neurosis and Berry and Eisenson's (1956, p. 270) theory that stuttering is a psychological perseverative manifestation. Worster-Drought (1968) reports that "purely hysterical stammer is uncommon in children." When it appears, it is more frequent in girls and usually appears at about the time of puberty or later.

SPEECH-CONTENT SYMPTOMS OF PSYCHODEVELOPMENTAL ORIGIN

Those conditions which affect socioemotional development to the point where they prevent or interfere with the development of spoken language will be the concern of this final section of the chapter. With respect to childhood emotional problems, for example, a neurosis may affect the way in which speech symbols are produced and a psychosis may affect whether or not such symbols are acquired. However, as indicated below, not all cases of environmentally induced language dysmaturation are based on serious emotional disturbance.

Insufficient and/or Inappropriate Stimulation and Rewards

Numerous authorities have offered various environmentally based reasons for language retardation in childhood (e.g., Berry & Eisenson, 1956, pp. 88–116; Brown, 1967, pp. 340–352; Van Riper, 1963, pp. 112–113; Wood, 1964, p. 14). Some of the categories of reasons are *insufficient stimulation* because of absence of one or both parents (social isolation) or because of "quiet" parents ("silent" environment); *reduced motivation* because parents or sibs anticipate the child's needs and desires; *inappropriate rewards* for "baby talk"; *inadequate rewards* for the child's actual progress in language development; and *inappropriate stimulation* due to exposure to excessive verbal discipline and "angry talk' or to poor language models or to models using more than one language poorly. Other background factors cited are shock, accident, parental rejection, birth of a younger sibling, negativism, and hospitalization.

Childhood Psychoses and Speech

Recently, De Hirsch (1967) attempted to differentiate between "primary, specific communicative disorders—sometimes called 'aphasic'—and those communicative difficulties which are secondary to psychopathology. . . ." She indicated that such differentiation "is rarely, if ever, straightforward." Points made in her review of the literature should help identify some of the speech and hearing characteristics of the psychotic child.

In terms of *auditory comprehension* of speech, both schizophrenic and aphasoid children present limitations—aphasoids, because of their symbolic deficits, and schizophrenics, because their experiences "are so fragmented that they cannot integrate meaningful information into an already existing framework." The *auditory memory span* of aphasoids is extremely short in contrast to that of schizophrenics, whose memory for meaningless material may be excellent (e.g., they may reproduce long TV commercials or unexpectedly and spontaneously produce words and sentences of a highly complex structure). Also, schizophrenics may occasionally experience *auditory hallucinations*.

In terms of speech, the psychotic child may be characterized by at least three features (de Hirsch, 1967). First is the frequent total *absence of "communicative intent."* That is, language for the schizophrenic "is not an instrument of interpersonal behavior." This is reflected in their reduced and sometimes inappropriate gestures (in contrast to gestures used by many aphasoids) and their frequently severely limited verbal output. Further, the echolalic speech of the schizophrenic is "mechanical, high-pitched, birdlike" in quality, in comparison to the more normal pitch and inflection of the aphasoid. Second, there is a *loss of the symbolic status of words*. For example, words are treated as things instead of symbols for things. Words may become "heavily emotionally invested, played with, juggled. . . ." Third, schizophrenic language is subject to *"primary process distortion"*; that is, the language is tied to early instinctual processes. For example, some verbal symbols may be invested with "highly personalized meanings" and may symbolize fears of aggression and retaliation.

Shervanian (1967), in his review of the literature on speech, thought, and communication disorders in childhood psychoses, presents the following general information: (1) Speech and language disturbances are key symptoms of childhood psychoses. (2) Childhood psychoses are not a single disease entity; the major subtypes include the nuclear schizophrenic child, early infantile autism, the symbiotic psychotic child, the very young, severely disturbed child with unusual sensitivities, and schizophrenic adjustment to neurological dysfunction.

In terms of auditory impairment, Shervanian reports a range from hypersensitivity to a simulation of anacusis. With respect to speech, he states:

1. There is no single entity which could be "called typical of the communication process of psychotic children"; however, there is much "to suggest the possibility of a number of syndromes of psychotic speech, thought, and communication" with variations influenced by numerous variables.

2. There may be severe language retardation from the very beginning, or normally developing speech may cease or regress.

3. "There may be a cessation of speech for communicative purposes." Other peculiarities reported include silence, except for animal sounds; long periods of silence interspersed with the utterance of complete sentences and the display of numerous voice, articulation, and rhythm defects by the speaking child; the possession of a large and complex vocabulary, which the child does not combine into usable sentences; and, finally, the production of echolalia, delayed echolalia, neologisms, logorrhea, and verbal perseveration.

For recent discussions of speech and language evaluation and language symptom therapy for psychotic children, the reader is referred to articles by Rubin et al. (1967) and Ruttenberg and Wolf (1967).

Diagnosis and Therapy

One of the first concerns of the speech pathologist when he suspects a psychodevelopmental basis for presenting speech symptoms in a child is the matter of level of involvement. Is it due to insufficient or inappropriate speech stimulation? Or is it one symptom of a complex associated with some form of serious childhood emotional disorder? The speech pathologist needs psychiatric-psychological data before a final speech diagnosis can be made. If, in fact, the disorder is of emotional origin, the speech pathologist must consider the possible role of speech therapy in the total habilitation program. Sometimes the use of language symptom therapy will be considered before, during, or after psychotherapy. When such symptom therapy is offered, the close collaboration of the psychotherapist is required.

CONCLUDING COMMENTS

Child speech pathology is a large and complex clinical area. Diagnostic expertise requires training to the doctoral level in addition to years of clinical experience. It is no longer possible for any one speech pathologist to be equally competent in diagnosis in all aspects of this complex area. Also, the speech pathologist must function well in the team diagnostic approach.

As with other developmental areas, the speech clinician deals with developing organisms and hence with symptoms which vary in form and importance as a function of time. Also, because of the importance of speech communication to perceptual, conceptual, and socioemotional developments, the primacy of speech problems is not always easy to establish; conversely, when primary speech disorders are present for certain lengths of time, relatively specific speech disorders rapidly develop into childhood complexes. Further, it is more often the case that serious speech problems in childhood have multiple origins. It is also important to adequate diagnosis and habilitation for the speech pathologist to analyze speech disorders with respect to im-

maturity versus dysmaturity aspects and to examine for individual symptom complexes.

Finally, the child speech pathologist must be prepared to enter into combination therapy approaches and to develop individualized, preventive, causal, symptom, and compensatory speech therapy programs.

REFERENCES

Berry, M. F., & Eisenson, J. *Speech disorders: Principles and practices of therapy.* New York: Appleton-Century-Crofts, 1956.

Black, M. E. *Speech correction in the schools.* Englewood Cliffs, N.J., Prentice-Hall, 1964.

Bloodstein, O. Stuttering as an anticipatory struggle reaction. In J. Eisenson (Ed.), *Stuttering: A symposium.* New York: Harper, 1958.

Bloodstein, O. The development of stuttering. I. Changes in nine basic features. *Journal of Speech and Hearing Disorders,* 1960, **25,** 219–237. (a)

Bloodstein, O. The development of stuttering. II. Developmental phases. *Journal of Speech and Hearing Disorders,* 1960, **25,** 366–376. (b)

Bloodstein, O. The development of stuttering. III. Theoretical and clinical implications. *Journal of Speech and Hearing Disorders,* 1961, **26,** 67–82.

Bloomer, H. H. Speech defects associated with dental abnormalities and malocclusions. In L. E. Travis (Ed.), *Handbook of speech pathology.* New York: Appleton-Century-Crofts, 1957.

Brodnitz, F. S. *Vocal rehabilitation.* Rochester, Minn.: Whiting Press, Inc., 1959.

Brown, S. F. Retarded speech development. In W. Johnson and D. Moeller (Eds.), *Speech handicapped school children.* New York: Harper & Row, 1967.

Brutten, E. J., & Shoemaker, D. J. *The modification of stuttering.* Englewood Cliffs, N.J.: Prentice-Hall, 1967.

Cardwell, V. E. *Cerebral palsy.* New York: Association for the Aid of Crippled Children, 1956.

Carrell, J. A. *Disorders of articulation.* Englewood Cliffs, N.J.: Prentice-Hall, 1968.

Cruickshank, W. M. (Ed.). *Cerebral palsy.* Syracuse, N.Y.: Syracuse University Press, 1966.

Curtis, J. F. Disorders of voice. In W. Johnson and D. Moeller (Eds.), *Speech handicapped school children.* New York: Harper & Row, 1967.

Darley, F. L., & Winitz, H. Age of first word: Review of research. *Journal of Speech and Hearing Disorders*, 1961, **26**, 272-290.

Davis, I. P. The speech aspects of reading readiness. *17th Yearbook of the department of elemantary school principals,* National Education Association, 1938, **17**, 282–289.

De Hirsch, K. Differential diagnosis between aphasic and schizophrenic language in children. *Journal of Speech and Hearing Disorders,* 1967, **32**, 3–10.

Di Carlo, L. M. *The deaf.* Englewood Cliffs, N.J.: Prentice-Hall, 1964.

Dinnerstein, A. J., & Lowenthal, M. Anxiety, perceptual latency and behavioral disability. *Journal of Nervous and Mental Diseases*, 1966, **142**, 562–567.

Eisenson, J. (Ed.). *Stuttering: A symposium.* New York: Harper, 1958.

Eisenson, J. Developmental aphasia: A specula-tive view with therapeutic implications. *Journal of Speech and Hearing Disorders*, 1968, **33**, 3–13.

Glauber, P. I. The psychoanalysis of stuttering. In J. Eisenson (Ed.), *Stuttering: A symposium.* New York: Harper, 1958.

Goodstein, L. D. Psychosocial aspects of cleft palate. In D. C. Spriestersbach and D. Sherman (Eds.), *Cleft palate and communication.* New York: Academic Press, 1968.

Greene, M. C. L. Speech of children before and after removal of tonsils and adenoids. *Journal of Speech and Hearing Disorders,* 1957, **22,** 361–370. (a)

Greene, M. C. L. *The voice and its disorders.* London: Pitman Medical Publishing, 1957. (b)

Gregory, H. H. (Ed.). *Learning theory and stuttering therapy.* Evanston, Ill.: Northwestern University Press, 1968.

Ingram, T. T. S., & Barn, J. A description and classification of common speech disorders associated with cerebral palsy. *Cerebral Palsy Bulletin,* 1961, **3**, 57–69.

Johnson, W. Perceptual and evaluational factors in stuttering. In L. E. Travis (Ed.), *Handbook of speech pathology.* New York: Appleton-Century-Crofts, 1957.

Johnson, W., Darley, F. L., & Spriestersbach, D. C. *Diagnostic methods in speech pathology.* New York: Harper & Row, 1963.

Kendall, D. C. Auditory problems in children. In R. W. Rieber & R. S. Brubaker (Eds.), *Speech pathology: An international study of the science.* Amsterdam: North-Holland Publishing, 1966.

Luper, H. L., & Mulder, R. L. *Stuttering: Therapy for children.* Englewood Cliffs, N.J.: Prentice-Hall, 1964.

Matthews, J. Speech problems of the mentally retarded. In L. E. Travis (Ed.), *Handbook of speech pathology*. New York: Appleton-Century-Crofts, 1957.

McDonald, E. T., & Chance, B. *Cerebral palsy*. Englewood Cliffs, N.J.: Prentice-Hall, 1964.

Mecham, M. J., Berko, M. J., Berko, F. G., & Palmer, M. F. *Communication training in childhood brain damage*. Springfield, Ill.: Charles C Thomas, 1966.

Metraux, R. W. Speech profiles of the preschool child 18 to 54 months. *Journal of Speech and Hearing Disorders*, 1950, **15**, 37–53.

Milisen, R. The incidence of speech disorders. In L. E. Travis (Ed.), *Handbook of speech pathology*. New York: Appleton-Century-Crofts, 1957.

Moll, K. L. Speech characteristics of individuals with cleft lip and palate. In D. C. Spriestersbach and D. Sherman (Eds.), *Cleft palate and communication*. New York: Academic Press, 1968.

Morley, M. E. *The development and disorders of speech in childhood*. Baltimore: Williams & Wilkins, 1965.

Morley, M. E. *Cleft palate and speech*. Baltimore: Williams & Wilkins, 1966.

Murphy, A. T. *Functional voice disorders*. Englewood Cliffs, N.J.: Prentice-Hall, 1964.

Myklebust, H. *Auditory disorders in children: A manual for differential diagnosis*. New York: Grune & Stratton, 1954.

Mysak, E. D. Servo theory and stuttering. *Journal of Speech and Hearing Disorders*, 1960, **25**, 188–195.

Mysak, E. D. Pneumodynamics as a factor in cleft palate speech. *Plastic and Reconstructive Surgery*, 1961, **28**, 588–591.

Mysak. E. D. *Speech pathology and feedback theory*. Springfield, Ill.: Charles C Thomas, 1966. (a)

Mysak, E. D. Phonatory and resonatory problems. In R. W. Rieber and R. S. Brubaker (Eds.), *Speech pathology: An international study of the science*. Amsterdam: North-Holland Publishing, 1966. (b)

Mysak, E. D. Disorders of oral communication. In M. Bortner (Ed.), *Evaluation and education of children with brain damage*. Springfield, Ill.: Charles C Thomas, 1968. (a)

Mysak, E. D. *Neuroevolutional approach to cerebral palsy and speech*. New York: Teachers College, Columbia University, 1968. (b)

Mysak, E. D. Cerebral palsy speech syndromes. Cerebral palsy speech habilitation. In L. E. Travis (Ed.), *Handbook of speech pathology and audiology*. New York: Appleton-Century-Crofts, 1971.

Perkins, W. H. The challenge of functional disorders of voice. In L. E. Travis (Ed.), *Handbook of speech pathology*. New York: Appleton-Century-Crofts, 1957.

Powers, M. H. Functional disorders of articulation—Symptomatology and etiology. In L. E. Travis (Ed.), *Handbook of speech pathology*. New York: Appleton-Century-Crofts, 1957.

Rigrodsky, S., & Steer, M. D. Mowrer's theory applied to speech habilitation of the mentally retarded. *Journal of Speech and Hearing Disorders*, 1961, **26**, 237–243.

Rubin, H., Bar, A., & Dwyer, J. H. An experimental speech and language program for psychotic children. *Journal of Speech and Hearing Disorders*, 1967, **32**, 242–248.

Ruttenberg, B. A., & Wolf, E. G. Evaluating the communication of the autistic child. *Journal of Speech and Hearing Disorders,* 1967, **32,** 314–324.

Schwartz, A. B. Congenital laryngeal stridor— Speculations regarding its origin. *Pediatrics,* 1961, **27**, 477–479.

Sheehan, J. Conflict theory of stuttering. In J. Eisenson (Ed.), *Stuttering: A symposium.* New York: Harper, 1958.

Shervanian, C. C. Speech, thought, and communication disorders in childhood psychoses: Theoretical implications. *Journal of Speech and Hearing Disorders,* 1967, **32**, 303–314.

Simon, C. T. The development of speech. In L. E. Travis (Ed.), *Handbook of speech pathology.* New York: Appleton-Century-Crofts, 1957.

Spriestersbach, D. C., & Sherman, D. (Eds.) *Cleft palate and communication.* New York: Academic Press, 1968.

Templin, Mildred C. Certain language skills in children. *Institute of Child Welfare Monograph Series.* University of Minnesota Press, Minneapolis, 1957, No. 26.

Travis, L. E. The unspeakable feelings of people with special reference to stuttering. In L. E. Travis (Ed.), *Handbook of speech pathology.* New York: Appleton-Century-Crofts, 1957.

Van Riper, C. *Speech correction.* Englewood Cliffs, N.J.: Prentice-Hall, 1963.

Van Riper, C., & Irwin, J. V. *Voice and articulation.* Englewood Cliffs, N.J.: Prentice-Hall, 1958.

West, R. An agnostic's speculations about stuttering. In J. Eisenson (Ed.), *Stuttering: A symposium.* New York: Harper, 1958.

West, R., & Ansberry, M. *The rehabilitation of speech.* New York: Harper & Row, 1968.

Wilson, D. K. Children with vocal nodules. *Journal of Speech and Hearing Disorders,* 1961, **26**, 19–26.

Wingate, M. E. Evaluation and stuttering. Part I. Speech characteristics of young children. *Journal of Speech and Hearing Disorders,* 1962, **27**, 106–115.

Winitz, H. The development of speech and language in the normal child. In R. W. Rieber and R. S. Brubaker (Eds.), *Speech pathology: An international study of the science.* Amsterdam: North-Holland Publishing, 1966.

Wood, N. E. *Delayed speech and language development.* Englewood Cliffs, N.J.: Prentice-Hall, 1964.

Worster-Drought, C. Speech disorders in children. *Developmental Medicine and Child Neurology,* 1968, **10**, 427–440.

20 | Auditory Imperception: A Perceptual-Conceptual Developmental Construct[1]

Joseph M. Wepman

INTRODUCTION

While certain knowledge of the neurophysiological substrata underlying cognitive and adaptive behavior, including the language acts of speech and reading, is as yet unknown, the maturation and development of these higher mental processes are behaviorally evident. The present paper explores certain underlying assumptions concerning the early stages of learning in children relating to the acquisition of language. Many of the aspects to be discussed have been demonstrated empirically or are either clinically observable or logical parallels of what is known.

It is a basic tenet of the present concept that children go through a series of critical stages in the development of the skills and aptitudes required for speech and reading. The nervous system is thought to follow an innate pattern of maturation marked by critical stages of readi-

ness for the development of function, which always proceeds from the simple to the complex. These critical stages, or states of readiness for the next step in the learning process, are demonstrably discrete and distinguishable one from the other. They come into being in a given order or sequence, each dependent for their full development upon the adequacy attained by the development of the preceding stage.

Each modality or input pathway is seen as having its own developmental sequence; however, the modalities are not seen as being necessarily interrelated in their developmental patterns, i.e., speed of development in auditory processing of signals has been found to have little if any relationship to either speed or slowness of development of the ability to process visual or tactual signals (Morency, 1967).

The modality distinction separating auditory from parallel visual and tactual/kinesthetic development can be seen to play a particular although far from exclusive role in the acquisition of speech, in the increased accuracy of articulation with age, and in the ability as well

[1] This study was partially supported by the Department of Health, Education, and Welfare, Office of Education, Project No. 7-0461.

653

as the inability of certain children to learn to read.

Perhaps the most telling effect of the differential development of the input modalities is to be found in Charcot's principle of learning typology (Freud, 1953). Charcot held that each person has a propensity for learning along one modality or another; he is either "audile," "visile," or "tactile" in learning. Stated differently, some people learn best by ear, some by eye, and some by touch. While little, if any, empirical evidence for this viewpoint has been forthcoming, the generalization seems easily observable.

A second major tenet of the position expressed here, one held by many child psychologists (Flavell, 1963; Osgood, 1963) and described at some length previously by the present writer (Wepman, 1962, 1964) is that there exists a hierarchy of learning, beginning with reflex behavior evident at birth and proceeding through a recognition/imitation level to the highest level of comprehension/intentful behavior in keeping with the known dedifferentiation that occurs in the central nervous system (CNS). For clarity of exposition, these are called the "reflex," "perceptual," and "conceptual" levels, although it is difficult at times to establish hard-and-fast borders for them.

Figure 20-1 presents a schematic model which accommodates both the modality differential and the hierarchy of learning. Auditory perception and imperception will be discussed in terms of this model.

AUDITORY PERCEPTION[2]

The focus of the present paper is on the processing of auditory signals at the prelinguistic,

[2] Much of what will be said here relating specifically to auditory perception and imperception seems equally true of visual and tactual perception and imperception. The total concept of perceptual-conceptual modality-oriented learning appears to function through parallel, but not directly intersecting, vectors.

nonmeaningful, perceptual level and on the motor acts which are consequent to them. It is at this level that the child gains his knowledge of the sounds of the verbal community in which he lives, the melodic patterns of speech that go to form his own intonational patterns, and the integration between his aural reception and parallel signals gained from other modalities. It is this integration and synthesis of multichanneled reception that permit the child to form the imitative and echoic speech that characterizes his earliest stage of learning to speak. Later, it is the adaptation of this alphabet of sounds that he uses for his expression of meaningful speech at the higher conceptual level. It is evident from this formulation that perceptual, phonemic learning must precede conceptualized expression; otherwise, the latter would be (as it so often is in the very early phases of children's attempted speech) quite unintelligible to the listener.

Halle (1967) points out in his recent discussion of the modern study of speech sounds that "speech events or utterances are thought to be sequences of discrete entities, the speech sounds . . .," a viewpoint that is held by a majority of phoneticians. While he goes on to say quite correctly that speech consists not of the enunciation of a series of discrete units but rather of the combination of units into syllabic groups, yet the discrete sound remains the basic and fundamental subject of study.

Perception, considered here as a CNS capacity, has its initial roots in acuity; i.e., an organism cannot perceive what it does not receive. Auditory acuity, or the ability to transform an airborne wave form which impinges on the receptor mechanism of the ear into a neural impulse which traverses the nervous system, goes through a developmental process of its own. Beginning with the relatively gross capacity to react to sound, the ear differentiates into an instrument capable of transforming fine distinctions in the wave form which correspond to the phonemes of the language. While no absolute order of acquisi-

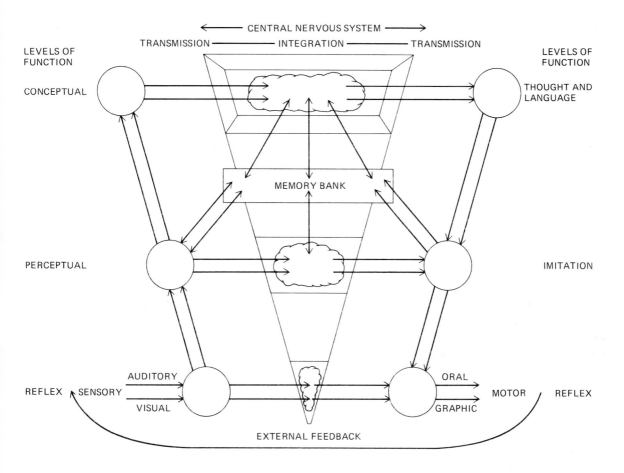

Figure 20-1. An operational diagram of the levels of function in the central nervous system.

tion of this acuity ability for transmitting individual acoustic patterns has been established, there seems to be comparative agreement that the vowel sounds, which are the lowest in the speech sound spectrum, can be transmitted early and the higher-pitched consonants somewhat later, as the organ of Corti comes to its full maturation. Without becoming involved in a lengthy and necessarily technical discussion of modern concepts of auditory-acuity function, it is believed that children who have the capacity to hear sounds no more than 20 decibels below the base line of audition can be said to have "normal" hearing (Hollien & Thompson, 1967).

In those children whose hearing curve indicates an inability to hear sounds at the 20-decibel level, any consideration of perceptual ability as it is discussed later would need to be interpreted in the light of a hearing handicap. Our discussion of perception will be limited for the most part, then, to the children whose acuity is normal, i.e., in whom the ear is capable of and does transform and transmit the sounds adequately and correctly.

The critical stages, or readiness levels, of maturation that must be reached by the child and that have been identified are (1) auditory discrimination, or the ability to distinguish between sounds; (2) auditory memory for discrete units, or auditory phoneme span; and (3) auditory memory for sequential units. While these are seen as independent readiness stages, each of which must develop before the next step can be undertaken, their interdependence is probably greater than their independence. Thus, the ability to discriminate between sounds seems to have its own rate of development, differing in different children, just as auditory memory has its own developmental rate. Memory for discrete sound units can only be as good as the discrimination ability permits. Similarly, recall of sequential units is dependent upon both discrimination of the sounds heard and memory for discrete units.

Following the development of a reasonable degree of adequacy in discrimination and memory, the capacity to relate the units processed along the auditory modality to similar units developed in parallel along other modalities (what has been called "intermodal transfer" or "integration") goes through its own series of developmental characteristics. It is only as this ability to synthesize the perceptual modalities comes to complete development that the child can be said to be ready to (1) articulate the sounds of the language with accuracy, (2) read the orthographic symbols and obtain full meaning from them, (3) spell using the orthographic symbols in combination with the phonemic ones, and (4) develop a vocabulary based upon the speech of the community. It also should be pointed out at least parenthetically that as the child progresses through the developmental stages, while his speech, reading, spelling, or other verbal forms are being used, his feedback system, both internal (kinesthetic and tactual) and external (aural and visual), continuously provides stimulation, which assists in further perceptual development.

Studies have shown that the development of the perceptual factors follows a recognizable pattern. Each of the aspects tested to this point shows a tapering off in the normal population sometime within the eighth year of life. That is not to say or even imply that all children develop these capacities over the 8-year span, but rather that some children, about 25 percent of them, continue to show a progressive improvement through that age range. Quite naturally, some children (those that Charcot would have called "audile") seem to have a relatively complete development of the different facets of perception along the auditory modality as early as the second year of life. They show it by the early development of articulate, intelligible speech and sensitivity to sound and sound patterning. They are inclined to listen to instructions rather than follow the speaker with their eyes. When offered training in a second language, they acquire both comprehension of it and the ability to speak it at an early age. Since cognitive ability means, in part, adaptiveness, they easily learn to attend by ear.

On the other hand, the visile child, who may not be so rapid in the development of his auditory abilities, learns to speak more slowly, using his auditory abilities only as they come to some higher degree of efficiency and adequacy with time. Such children do poorly at learning a second language (at least to speak it) and pay more attention to what they see than to what they hear.

The tactile child, to complete the picture, may be slow in both visualization and auditorization and yet, because of his rapid development of motoric skills, keeps pace with his peers through touch and motion learning.

In any of these children (audile, visile, and tactile), it is evident that intelligence—the generalized ability to integrate and formulate conceptually—must be at least adequate. The child whose basic intellectual ability is high will adapt to the singleness of his learning typology with greatest ease. The child, however, whose intellectual ability is low will rarely adapt easily but must be led to such adaptation through training.

Fortunately, the great majority of children can learn by almost any pathway. They are broadly stimulated, and they select the learning typology best suited to their innate ability to learn.

It is important to determine the learning modality of choice for each child, but it is vital to do so for the child who shows a specific lag in modality development. Since auditory perception is so important for the first stages of learning to speak and therefore for the first stages of interpersonal communication, recognition of a lag in this modality is of greatest importance.

Competency in auditory discrimination among all the perceptual factors has been most widely studied (Deutsch, 1964; Weiner, 1967; Wepman, 1960). It is defined as the ability to differentiate among the auditory signals representing the sounds of spoken language. This decoding process permits the child to hear the difference between such words as /cat/ and phonetically similar words such as /cap/, /cad/, /cab/. In this example, the difference lies in a single phone, the final stop /t/ being recognized as different from the final /p/, /d/, and /b/. Auditory discrimination can be said to be fully developed when all or most of the sounds of the language can be contrasted and differentiated from each other. One needs only to listen to the occasional error in pronunciation or the occasional error in adult recognition of such differences to realize the task faced by the child in his early, formative years.

Relatively recently, linguists have identified a series of "distinctive features" for each sound (Halle, 1964). Such features, which permit recognition of difference by contrast, are almost certainly never heard by children—yet below the level of awareness, the distinctive features provide the basis for auditory discrimination. While other phoneticians (Peterson & Shoup, 1966) prefer a different basis for making the distinction from that of "distinctive features," relying on acoustic differentials or physiologically based

phonetic analysis, the results in terms of the child are relatively the same. He must in some way distinguish among the sounds of the language. Auditory perception has this basic competency to develop—as it does so, the other perceptual factors become useful. Without or until discrimination develops, the other factors are limited in the role they can play in speech and language production.

Auditory memory for discrete units, auditory memory and recall for sequential ordering, and intermodal transfer of auditory and other perceptual factors are believed to follow a developmental pattern of their own. Some evidence for this has been forthcoming, especially in the area of auditory memory (Beebe, 1944; Blakenship, 1938; Munn, 1954); however, standardized tests to assess the changes with age are not as far developed as those in the area of auditory discrimination.

Auditory perception, then, is held to be a series of relatively discrete competencies which, following the maturation of the nervous system to the point where they can begin to develop, show a progression of ability through early childhood. It is during this period of time that the child needs to develop his speech, his reading, and his other academic language achievements. Of greatest importance is the fact that the developmental period seems to continue through the eighth year of life, at least. A failure to recognize this fact by society, parents, and educators alike may underlie a significant proportion of the early school failures that have commanded so much attention recently.

AUDITORY IMPERCEPTION

Developmental Imperception

Within the population of children who may be said to suffer from auditory imperception, undoubtedly the largest number are those who, for no pathological reason but rather for relatively simple developmental reasons, lag behind their peers in the rate of development of competency in auditory perception. Properly stated, such children can be said to be competent for their age but at the nether end of the develop-

tile children with a proclivity in another modality, which would agree with Charcot's principle of differential learning typology. They may, due to genetic factors, have a lag in this specific modality, or they may come from homes where no premium is placed on accuracy of auditory perception (or on the critical attitude toward anything). For whatever reason, they are often looked upon as being behavior problems, delayed in general development, or even mentally retarded.

The imperception frequently lasts in such children until, in the normal course of events, the auditory processes demonstrate their development. This occurs in almost all children by the age of 9. The problem for these children lies in the expectation of significant others in their environment—parents who expect their children to speak early and with accuracy frequently pose a problem even in the preschool years; teachers in the kindergarten or early elementary grades who think of accuracy of speech as a reflection of intelligence also pose problems, as do peers, who tend to embarrass and deride children whose speech accuracy is less than perfect.

The earliest direct effect of auditory imperception on behavior is the inadequate role it plays in guiding the articulatory efforts of the child. Poor discrimination shows in speech by substitution articulatory patterns; poor discrete auditory memory shows in the tendency of the child to drop final sounds or elide sounds in multisyllabic words; and poor auditory sequencing shows itself by the reversal of sounds and syllables as words are spoken.

The next most evident effect is seen as the child begins to read. Here the auditory imper-

ception blocks the phonic/orthographic match, which is so vital for reading acquisition.

A commonly observed effect in school achievement is difficulty with spelling, since so often this is taught as an auditory-verbal or auditory-graphic skill. When auditory imperception is grossly inadequate, spelling, whether out loud or in writing, is very likely to be defective.

Some children, fortunately few in number, never develop adequate auditory perceptual ability yet show no pathology to account for their lack of development. When they are of superior intellectual ability, their capacity to adapt their learning through the other modalities presents little or no problem to them, especially after the earliest phases of learning. This is best illustrated by a boy who had mastered the compensatory adaptation necessary to learn to speak with accuracy with the aid of a speech therapist, to learn to read from solely visual cues, and to learn to spell with a series of mnemonic devices. As he entered high school, he began to experience difficulty with algebra since most of the initial instruction was given orally. It took considerable ingenuity on the part of both the boy and his teacher to devise visually oriented cues to algebraic formulations, and this was only possible, it was believed, because the boy had the basic intellectual capacity to adapt with relative ease.

Another child, who had similarly mastered the art of adapted learning (needed because of an apparent permanent auditory imperception), had only temporary setbacks in school until he reached the point of graduation from his state university. One of the requirements for graduation was the ability to use French conversationally. This he found to be literally impossible for him. He could read French without difficulty, but mastering the enunciation of the language was more difficult than it had been for him to learn to speak English with accuracy. All his articulatory inaccuracy in his native tongue had not been completely resolved through his first 13 years of life. The learning of conversational French would probably have taken as long, if not longer. It was only by intervention with the school authorities that he was permitted to graduate without the requirement being fulfilled.

These two brief examples are admittedly selected from a host of others who were not so fortunate. Skillful adaptive compensatory modality learning requires intelligence, motivation, and recognition by others of the task to be performed. With only average intelligence the chance of successful adaptation is reduced, and when the intellectual level is below normal, the chance is almost nil.

Pathological auditory imperception, as differentiated from the developmental variety, may result from any agenesis or trauma that affects the transmission of sounds at the perceptual level. As indicated earlier, the neurophysiological substrata underlying cognitive functioning of any kind are as yet unknown. Specific localization of neural trauma producing perceptual handicaps cannot, therefore, be isolated. However, there is little question as one studies learning behavior of brain-injured children that specific imperceptions do exist. Children with known birth defects may show no acuity loss yet acquire speech and language as though they were deaf or deafened. Such children frequently show behavior in the presence of sound that indicates a marked sensitivity to sound—as though their systems had received the sound but were incapable of handling it at any level. Some authorities have considered children of this nature as aphasic, or unable to develop language usage because of a neural insult affecting the maturation of their CNS. It is thought by the writer that they are just as likely to be children suffering from a specific modality defect—auditory imperception —and properly classified as suffering from auditory agnosia. For the child involved, this is not a semantic labeling difference but a real one. If he is indeed aphasic, then his difficulty is thought to be in the integrative process of verbal comprehension, formulation, and use; whereas if he is an agnosic child, the other modalities of sensory input should be available to him and the integrative processes of conceptualization should be unaffected. At least, consideration of this possibility should be given to every child who appears to be delayed in the development of speech and language.

The telling difference between children who are merely delayed in the development of their auditory perceptual skills and children who are pathologically delayed lies in the overall consistency of the problem in the latter group. While the developmentally delayed children show progressive changes with age, the others do not. In the developmentally delayed, each of the auditory perceptual aspects seems to show an interrelated but somewhat independent developmental progression. In the organically impaired child, all aspects of the perceptual mechanism seem similarly affected. Finally, in the developmentally delayed child, training seems to have some direct effect, according to recent studies (Seidler, 1967; Zedler, 1956). No such results have been reported, however, for the neurologically impaired child.

SUMMATION

Auditory imperception is presented against a background of a perceptual-conceptual model of learning. In this operational schema for the neural processing of stimuli, the prelinguistic perceptual level is seen as providing the basis for conceptual formulation and use of language. Auditory perceptual learning provides the establishment and organization of the phonemic alphabet and, in conjunction with the visually acquired orthographic alphabet, the basis for reading and spelling and other language acts. Auditory imperception is seen as any developmental lag, agenesis, or trauma which obviates, distorts, or delays the acquisition of the critical stages of readiness for aural learning—such as discrimination, retention, and recall of discrete phonemic units and sequential ordering of these units—as well as the development of the capacity to interrelate auditory events with parallel-learned visual and tactual perceptualized units.

While the most direct or immediate effect of auditory imperception is seen in the oral production of speech, it has a similarly telling effect on learning to read and to spell.

The significance of auditory imperception in the initial stages of learning is seen by the number of children entering school who are not yet ready for conceptual training and should have attention paid to the prelinguistic aspects, which are the building blocks necessary for operational development.

Developmental auditory imperception is seen as affecting close to 25 percent of all children—a not insignificant number. Pathological auditory imperception affects fewer children but is even more devastating in its effect on learning. The argument is made for considering children from the viewpoint of their predilection for one learning modality over another as one approach to the equalization of educational opportunity.

REFERENCES

Beebe, H. H. Auditory memory span for meaningless syllables. *Journal of Speech Disorders,* 1944, **9,** 273–276.

Blakenship, A. A. Memory span: A review of the literature. *Psychological Bulletin,* 1938, **35,** 1–25.

Deutsch, C. Auditory discrimination and learning. *Merrill-Palmer Quarterly of Behavior and Development,* 1964, **10,** 277–296.

Flavell, J. H. *The developmental psychology of Jean Piaget.* Princeton, N.J.: Van Nostrand, 1963.

Freud, S. *On aphasia.* New York: International Universities Press, 1953.

Halle, M. On the basis of phonology. In J. A. Fodor & J. A. Katz (Eds.), *The structure of language.* Englewood Cliffs, N.J.: Prentice-Hall, 1964.

Halle, M. On the modern study of speech sounds. *International Social Science Journal,* 1967, **19** (1).

Hollien, H., and Thompson, C. L. A group screening test of hearing. *Journal of Auditory Research,* 1967, **7,** 85–92.

Morency, A. Modality approach to reading problems. *Proceedings of the 12th Annual Convention of the International Reading Association,* Seattle, 1967.

Munn, N. L. Learning in children—memory. In L. Carmichael (Ed.), *Manual of child psychology.* New York: Wiley, 1954. Pp. 407–430.

Osgood, C. E. On understanding and creating sentences. *American Psychologist,* 1963, **18,** 735–751.

Peterson, G. E., and Shoup, J. A physiological theory of phonetics. *Journal of Speech and Hearing Research,* 1966, **9,** 5–67.

Seidler, A. Paper presented at the American Speech and Hearing Association Convention, Chicago, 1967.

Weiner, P. S. Auditory discrimination and articulation. *Journal of Speech and Hearing Disorders,* 1967, **32,** 19–28.

Wepman, J. M. Auditory discrimination, speech and reading. *Elementary School Journal,* 1960, **60,** 325–333.

Wepman, J. M. Dyslexia: Its relationship to language acquisition and concept formation. In J. Money (Ed.), *Reading disability.* Baltimore: Johns Hopkins, 1962.

Wepman, J. M. The perceptual basis for learning. In H. A. Robinson (Ed.), *Meeting individual differences* (Suppl. Education Monogr. 94). Chicago: University of Chicago Press, 1964.

Zedler, E. Effect of phonic training on speech sound discrimination and spelling performance. *Journal of Speech and Hearing Disorders,* 1956, **21,** 245–250.

21 | Learning Disturbance in Childhood[1]

Christoph M. Heinicke

INTRODUCTION AND DEFINITION

The interest in understanding the causes of learning disabilities in the child, as well as bringing about alleviation of these difficulties, has increased greatly in the last ten years. There is a journal specifically devoted to this topic, *Learning Disabilities,* and several comprehensive volumes have appeared in the last few years: Hellmuth (1965, 1966, 1968); Frierson and Barke (1967); and Johnson and Myklebust (1967). This recent acceleration of interest as part of a generally greater emphasis on new programs in education must be added to the long-standing research on learning difficulties associated with several different disciplines—education, psychiatry, psychology, neurology, to mention only a few.

Despite this great acceleration in interest,

there is so far little consensus on either a classification of the different types of learning disturbance or the etiology associated with such different types. It is the purpose of this chapter to summarize what is known about these disturbances and to integrate this knowledge in a way that will enhance progress in their diagnostic classification, in the understanding of their etiology, and in their treatment.

The number of approaches potentially relevant to such an integrated summary is very large. Furthermore, the individual experience of different professionals in handling learning disturbances varies greatly. Unfortunately, this very experience has often been described in such a way as to limit its impact to those who share the views of the author in the first place. This review has therefore concentrated on those approaches which not only reflect extensive experience but also have aroused considerable professional interest and have been defined by relevant research findings. Further, in the interest of objectivity, this writer has confined his

[1] The preparation of this chapter was made possible through the generous financial support of the W. T. Grant Foundation, New York. We are particularly indebted to all those authors who took the trouble to send us their writings and to Mrs. Claire Bernstein, who assisted us in all phases of the work.

interpretative remarks to the "Discussion" and "Concluding Remarks" sections.

Learning disturbances are here defined somewhat loosely as those deviations in the learning processes which are associated with an educationally significant discrepancy between apparent intellectual capacity and actual performance on academic tasks. While learning disturbances can occur in all areas of development, this chapter focuses on those developmental tasks which are relevant to and defined by the school environment. The nature of the literature and interest is such that within this area most of the focus has been on the discrepancy between apparent capacity and actual performance in reading. This chapter therefore deals with certain general issues around learning disturbances, but specifically applies mostly to reading disturbances.

Using the above definition as a point of departure, three major questions will be posed and discussed:

1. What methods have been used to diagnose and further specify the specific nature of the learning disturbance? ("The Diagnosis of the Learning Disturbance")

2. What common characteristics do children with learning disturbances have, and what are the implications of these characteristics for the etiology of the learning disturbance? ("An Outline of the Four Etiological Hypotheses"; "Characteristics of the Children Reading below Their Potential")

3. What treatment programs have been used to alleviate the learning disturbance, and to what extent have these programs resulted in permanent gains? ("Programs to Enhance the Development of the Child Reading below His Potential")

The manner in which each of these questions is answered will be very much determined by the individual's point of view. Most workers would no doubt acknowledge the unity of mind and body and that the complete understanding of a learning disturbance must include the continuing longitudinal interaction of organism, psyche, and environment. In actual practice, authors tend to conceptualize explanations of the learning disturbance either in terms of deficiencies in the biological characteristics of the child or in terms of those psychological characteristics which are the product of his experiences and particularly his family experiences. This, in turn, will influence their diagnostic and treatment approach.

At the risk of oversimplification and recognizing that the various etiological hypotheses are not necessarily contradictory, we have focused on four of them:

1. Learning disturbance as a function of maturational lag

2. Learning disturbance as a function of a constitutionally determined pattern of disturbed neurological organization

3. Learning disturbance as a function of minimal brain dysfunction

4. Learning disturbance as a function of intrapsychic and external psychological conflict

These hypotheses are not to be seen as any kind of classification, but rather as a reflection of those etiological concepts that have received the greatest attention. One might well have included, among other things, those direct deficits and subsequent disturbances which result from socio-cultural-educational deprivation. Our focus on individual psychopathology, as well as limitations of space, suggested exclusion of this particular area.

The essence of the above hypotheses will be formulated as part of a summary of those characteristics which are hypothesized as being associated with the occurrence of learning disturbances. We turn first, however, to a discussion of diagnostic techniques.

THE DIAGNOSIS OF THE LEARNING DISTURBANCE

As has already been stated, the nature of the approach to learning disturbances will govern not only the treatment of the child but also the strategy and methods of diagnosis. Often less explicit are the criteria which select the population of learning disturbances to be diagnosed and how these, in turn, influence the types of diagnostic tools that are likely to be appropriate. The method of choosing a population may be to ask a teacher to pick out those children "who are not doing well in class." Or the design of a study may call for a sample of learning-disturbance children who speak English, have rated IQs within 1 standard deviation above and below 100, present no significant sensory defects, and show no evidence of psychopathology. The first group of children will require a very wide screening device, whereas diagnosis of the second group is not likely to concentrate on issues of intrapsychic and external psychological conflict.

Whatever the group chosen, the trend in diagnosis of the learning disturbances has been to specify through the use of a battery of tests the child's areas of strength and weakness. The concepts of profile or pattern are frequently employed. Although the general intelligence and academic achievement tests still play an important role, extensive testing of the child's perceptual-motor and linguistic functioning is now emphasized. Below we cite some of the different diagnostic batteries that have been employed.

Diagnosing Maturational Lag

Beginning with an interest in the type of maturational hypothesis discussed particularly by Bender (1958), De Hirsch et al. (1966) have developed for predictive purposes a battery of thirty-seven tests of perceptual-motor and linguistic development. Specifically, measures of patterning of behavior, motility, gross and fine motor skills, laterality, body image, visual and auditory per-

ceptual patterning, reading readiness, and style (ego strength and work attitude) were included. To assess the predictive power of these tests, the same children were given the following tests at the end of the second grade: a writing test (four dictated sentences), the Gates Advanced Primary Reading Test, the Gray Oral Reading Test, and the spelling subtest of the Metropolitan Achievement Test. Rank-order correlations were computed between each of the kindergarten tests and the child's reading, spelling, and writing performance as assessed at the end of the second grade.

The choice of the above battery of kindergarten tests not only reflects extensive clinical experience with the problem of inadequate academic progress but readily yields a profile of the child's functioning. Certain omissions, probably in part reflecting the author's primary interest in maturation, should also be noted. Data on the parental background are limited, and only two variables, ego strength and work attitude, can be related to considerations of psychological conflict. Emphasis on maturation and neurological integration would lead one to expect the inclusion of data from the physical and neurological examination of the children. Though reported elsewhere, it is not included in the predictive battery. Consideration of the effects of premature birth on later learning disturbance is included, however.

Diagnosing Patterns of Disturbed Neurologic Organization

As illustrated by the diagnostic approach of Rabinovitch et al. (1954), Rabinovitch (1968), Cohn (1964), and Critchley (1968), diagnosis of the primary reading retardation or developmental dyslexia relies heavily on the techniques of the neurologist. As given in some detail by Rabinovitch et al. (1954), other techniques have supplemented these assessments: (1) psychometric evaluation, (2) achievement testing, (3) psychiatric evaluation, and (4) response to specific remedial reading therapy. The diagnostic techniques of this team of clinicians are noteworthy both because a determined effort is made to integrate a variety of findings and because the results of therapeutic efforts are used to confirm or correct the diagnostic impressions.

Diagnosing Minimal Brain Dysfunction

Interest in the differential diagnosis of minimal brain dysfunction is likely to lead to the type of diagnostic battery used by Cruickshank et al. (1961). The psychological assessments included several intelligence tests, detailed assessments of academic achievement, the Bender Visual Motor Gestalt Test, the Vineland Social Maturity Scale, the Ammons Full Range Picture Vocabulary Test, the Marble Board Test, the Tactual Motor Test, the Syracuse Visual Figure Background Test, and the Rorschach. A pediatric and developmental history was taken, including detailed information gathered on the prenatal, natal, and postnatal events. Each child was examined physically and neurologically. EEGs were done, and speech and hearing were also evaluated. Some interview data were available on the parents, and each child was also seen by a psychiatrist.

This is clearly one of the most thorough assessment efforts, and it accurately reflects the extensive and detailed diagnostic efforts of the workers interested in minimal brain dysfunction. Considerations of family and intrapsychic dynamics were by no means ignored but, in fact, played a minimal role in the data collection and analysis. Extensive psychiatric interview data on the child were presented but not related to the rest of the data analysis. Even the neurological data (with the exception of the EEG) could not be incorporated into the findings. These comments demonstrate once more the immense difficulty of developing a diagnostic team that can both collect and integrate a variety of data.

Another major difficulty of this type of attempt to assess cerebral damage has been discussed by Reitan and Heineman (1968). They point out that it is often assumed that a certain type of brain damage has a certain effect in impairing performance. Not only are such 1-to-1 relations unlikely, but the particular deficit in performance may be not at all associated with brain damage. Nevertheless, Reitan accepts that certain specific behavioral impairments, highly differential performance on a given test, and lateralized differences may well be areas to explore in the development of a neuropsychological battery. The basic procedure is to develop a series of tests that differentiate normal children from those who have definitive cerebral damage. Various tests of the Halstead Battery and a series of tests of sensory-perceptual disturbances have been adapted for children (Reed, Reitan, & Klove, 1965; Reed, 1968; Reitan, 1964). This battery can then be applied to patients where the question of cerebral damage is in doubt. This allows one to determine the number of tests on which the results fall into the range characteristic of the performance of brain-damaged as opposed to normal children.

Diagnosing Intrapsychic and External Psychological Conflict

The diagnostic profile outlined by Anna Freud (1965) facilitates the integration of a variety of data by providing a theoretical frame of reference for the assessment of development and by insisting that each piece of data be interpreted in context. No simple 1-to-1 relationships between behavior and underlying determinants are posited. All aspects of the personality (the organic, the psychic, the environmental, etc.) are taken into account in assessing the child's drive, ego, and superego development and in describing the regressions, the fixations, and the nature of the conflicts.

As part of a study of the child psychotherapy of learning disturbances Heinicke (1965a, 1965b, 1969) has used the profile to organize a variety of test and interview data. The material of these profiles in turn served as a basis for making forty-six different ratings on the children. These ratings could then be further organized in terms of four major factors: the level of ego integration, the degree of ego flexibility, the extent of the child's peer relations, and the extent of his move toward self-reliance. The derivation of these factors in turn makes case comparison and the diagnostic grouping of children possible. Included in the ego-integration factor are ratings of the capacity to sublimate, the effectiveness of the defense organization, the extent of academic ambition, the ability to persist in a task, the absence of denial or avoidance of the academic problem, and so forth.

The very strength of providing a theoretical base for the meaningful integration of a variety of data may for some also be a detriment, in that factual data and theory are too intertwined. As one solution to this problem, Heinicke's (1969) work illustrates how a meaningful diagnostic abstraction can be derived in clinical profile terms and can then guide the analysis of test scores derived independently of these abstractions.

Diagnosing Language Capabilities

Among the tests developed to provide a specific picture of the child's strengths and weaknesses in the psycholinguistic area, those designed by Kirk and McCarthy (1961) are probably the most frequently used. Based on the theoretical models of Osgood (1957), the Illinois Test of Psycholinguistic Abilities includes nine subtests designed to differentiate defects in (1) the three processes of communication (decoding, association, and encoding), (2) the levels of language organization (representational versus automatic-sequential), and/or (3) the channels of language input and output (auditory, visual, vocal, and motor). Tests 1 to 6 deal with the representational or meaning level of organization. Tests 1 and 2 tap the decoding (interpretation) process;

Test 1 deals with auditory decoding, and Test 2 with visual decoding. Tests 3 and 4 emphasize testing of the association processes; either auditory-vocal (Test 3) or visual-motor (Test 4) channels are used. Tests 5 and 6 assess vocal and motor encoding (expression of intentions). Tests 7 to 9 deal with the less complex, more automatic processes. Defects at this level interfere with sequential imitation and the ability to retain sequences of visual and/or auditory stimuli. The tests assess the following: auditory-vocal automatic abilities (a grammar test), auditory-vocal sequential abilities (a digit-repetition test), and visual-motor sequential abilities (a visual sequential memory test).

Use of the test battery results in a psycholinguistic profile of the assets and deficits of the child and can thus serve as a specific guide to the remedial work. Research involving the use of the test has recently been reviewed by Bateman (1965).

Another diagnostic language test, the Parson Language Sample (PLS) (Spradlin, 1963) is systematically derived from the learning theory developed by Skinner. The emphasis is on the delineation of observable vocal and nonvocal responses so that the conditions controlling these responses can also be defined. Seven subtests were developed, and these reflect Skinner's major classes of language behavior: tact (naming response), echoic (verbal repetition response), comprehension (response showing comprehension), intraverbal gesture (gestural exchange), and mand (demand response). The first three subtests assess vocal responses; the next three, nonvocal responses; and the seventh, both vocal and nonvocal responses. With the exception of the Mand Test, the reliability achieved for the subtests is high. Of the remaining six, only the Gestural Intraverbal Test does not correlate with the others. As Spradlin (1963) suggests, the predictive value of the PLS is not added to by retaining each of the five subtests. Of particular interest is the fact that the total PLS vocal score correlates to the extent of .74 with the Verbal Scale of the Wechsler Intelligence Scale for Children (WISC) and with independently derived ratings of the child's speech. By contrast, the nonvocal items do not correlate with either the Performance Scale of the WISC or independent ratings of nonvocal behavior.

The possibility of a behavioral and more exact definition of the child's language behavior, as well as of its relation to the operant-conditioning mode of behavior change, makes the PLS of particular interest. Difficulties in establishing the reliability of the Mand Test may reflect certain more pervasive limitations of this diagnostic instrument. The Mand Test requires that the examiner present a discriminative stimulus that will motivate the child to ask for something. Apparently there are times when the child does not show an interest in anything. In order to assess what stimuli will elicit a verbal request, it may well be necessary to explore on a more individual basis the meaning and motivational value of the stimulus. It would seem that the procedure does not call for such exploration. That is, the very precision that allows for accurate definitions of language behavior may not make it possible to explore certain areas of that behavior.

AN OUTLINE OF THE FOUR ETIOLOGICAL HYPOTHESES

Examination of the literature on the characteristics of children with learning disturbances tends to support a conclusion reached about many other symptom pictures. There is no one profile of associated behaviors. Only as one narrows one's definition of the group of children being studied is one likely to find a pattern of common characteristics and to be able to make inferences about the underlying etiology. This does not remove the necessity of examining a given aspect of behavior in the context of individual functioning, but it does serve as a guide to such assessment.

Patterns of Characteristics Relevant to the Maturational-lag Hypothesis

Bender's writings (1958) best state the hypothesis that learning disturbances and, specifically, reading disabilities must be understood as part of more pervasive indications of maturational lag. A variety of areas are examined to assess the nature of the lags: (1) the development of the child's perceptual motor experiences as measured by the well-known Bender Visual Motor Gestalt Test; (2) the development of the most specific of these perceptual motor gestalten, namely, the body image (Schilder); (3) the development of patterned postural reflexes; and (4) the development of the ego as outlined by psychoanalytic theory. The individual child's progress is then judged against these recognized maturational patterns. A maturational lag is posited when there is a slow differentiation in these patterns. The hypothesis does not imply a structural defect, deficiency, or loss. The concept of plasticity as used by embryologists is central, implying as it does the yet unformed but capable of being formed. With this postulate of differential rates of "forming" in mind, Bender hypothesizes that those parts of the neopallium which serve the human functions of unilateral dominance, handedness, eyedness, auditory and visual recognition of symbols, and spoken and written language show a wider range of maturation age than do other parts associated with other patterns.

More specifically, Bender (1958) defines the following characteristics as indicative of the existence of maturational lags:

1. A slow maturation of language skills and, specifically, the inability to read

2. A slow maturation in neurological patterning, as revealed in:

    a. The developmental history of motor

skills, motility awkwardness, and hyper-kinesis, and

b. "Soft" neurological signs

3. An uneven pattern of intellectual development, as revealed by:

a. Repeat testing, or

b. Intertest variability

4. Poor establishment of cortical dominance in one form or another

5. Right-left confusion or lack of orientation in relation to:

a. Body

b. Time

c. Space

6. Immaturity in personality development

Not listed as specific criteria but certainly emphasized by Bender (1958) and elaborated most recently by De Hirsch et al. (1966) are:

7. Retention of primitive experiences in perceptual-motor patterning, as evidenced in:

a. Body imagery of human-figure drawing

b. Figure-ground organization

c. Bender Visual Motor Gestalt Test

8. Difficulties in auditory perceptual patterning and, according to Schilder, the integration of sound and written words

9. A tendency to uncontrolled obstructiveness in the form of compulsiveness, rigidity, and correctness

10. A tendency to forget both the disability and the learning process that attempts to correct it.

Patterns of Characteristics Relevant to the Hypothesis of a Constitutionally Determined Disturbance in the Neurological Organization

A second major hypothesis stresses that the learning disability reflects a disturbed pattern of neurological organization. As Rabinovitch et al. (1954) have stressed, the disturbance is primary in the sense of representing a constitutionally de-termined neurological defect rather than being caused by definitive postnatal or later insults to the nervous system.

Needless to say, definite brain damage can well be responsible both for a disturbed pattern of neurological organization and for difficulties in tasks necessary for learning (Reed, Reitan, & Klove, 1965). Mention of this area was made in the context of the discussion of minimal brain damage.

While questions of disturbed neurological patterns are also linked to a consideration of maturational lag, the emphasis on a primary defect in the structure as present at birth differs from a stress on the integration and differentiation of maturational patterns.

Rabinovitch et al. (1954) and Rabinovitch (1968) have defined some of the characteristics from which they inferred developmental dyslexia. Not only was the reading retardation of these children greater than among the other diagnostic groups, but the dysfunction was qualitatively different. Despite their obvious intelligence, their efforts at reproducing a sentence led to incomprehensible results. The authors noted that many of these children could not even recognize letters, suffered from letter reversals, showed no ability for word attack, and had difficulty in maintaining left-right direction.

Rabinovitch (1968) stresses that both the visual and the auditory techniques required for reading, and particularly the ability to master sight vocabulary, are impaired in the primary reading retardation. Not that perceptual discrimination per se is a problem, but the letter forms cannot be translated into meaningful wholes. Results of the administration of the WISC and particularly the large discrepancy between a low verbal IQ and a relatively higher performance IQ are cited to demonstrate the dyslexic's difficulty with abstract thinking.

More specifically, within the general concept-symbolization deficiency, these authors stress the dyslexic's difficulty with orientational concepts. Deficiencies in dealing with time tend to be the most severe. To explore this further, Rabinovitch and his colleagues have developed the Hawthorn Center Concept-Symbolization Test.

Their experience with these children also points to language deficits other than the reading itself. Imprecise articulation, difficulty in specific name finding, and immature syntax occurred frequently.

Rabinovitch et al. (1954) indicate that there was no evidence of abnormality in the routine neurological examination of these children, but that abnormalities were found in the expanded neurological assessment. These included non-specific awkwardness and clumsiness in motor function; such sensory defects as delay in appreciation of the simultaneous stimulation of the face and hand, right-left confusions but no clear findings on laterality, confusion of similar-sounding words but no inability to name objects, the inability to write spontaneously but only slight interference with copying, and the inability to spell aloud.

Patterns of Characteristics Relevant to the Minimal Brain Dysfunction Hypothesis

A third major hypothesis concerning the etiology of learning disturbances focuses on the concept of minimal brain dysfunction. The writings of many authors provide the background for this thinking, but it was particularly the work of Strauss and Lehtinen that accelerated interest in what was initially referred to as minimal brain damage.

Both the volume of writing and the controversy regarding the minimal brain dysfunction hypothesis have been extensive. A recent effort to clarify the problem of terminology and identification has therefore been most helpful (Clements, 1966). First of all, this project succinctly defined the two opposing views in the controversy concerning the plausibility of the hypothesis of minimal brain dysfunction. The two extreme views are summarized as follows:

1. The purist point of view is that "minimal brain dysfunction" is in most instances an unproven presumptive diagnosis. Therefore, the concept can have little meaning and acceptance until such time as our knowledge is greatly increased and our diagnostic skills remarkably refined. Brain dysfunction can only be inferred until physiologic, bio-chemical, or structural alterations of the brain are demonstrated.

2. The pragmatic case might be presented in the following manner: With our limited validated knowledge concerning relationships between brain and behavior, we must accept certain categories of deviant behavior, developmental dyscrasias, learning disabilities, and visual-motor perceptual irregularities as valid indices of brain dysfunctioning. They represent neurologic signs of a most meaningful kind, and reflect disorganized central nervous system functioning at the highest level. To consider learning and behavior as distinct and separate from other neurologic functions echoes a limited concept of the nervous system and of its various levels of influence and integration. . . .

[Thus] the term "minimal brain dysfunction syndrome" refers . . . to children of near average, average, or above average general intelligence with certain learning or behavioral disabilities ranging from mild to severe, which are associated with deviations of function of the central nervous system. These deviations may manifest themselves by various combinations of impairment in perception, conceptualization, language, memory, and control of attention, impulse or motor function. [Clements, 1966, pp. 6–7 and 9]

These aberrations may be due to genetic variations, biochemical irregularities, perinatal brain insults, or other illnesses or injuries sustained during the years which are critical for the development and maturation of the central nervous system (CNS). Even early sensory deprivation can result in CNS alterations which may be permanent.

Following review of more than a hundred publications, Clements (1966) derived an extensive list of ninety-seven symptoms and signs that have been posited to indicate minimal brain dysfunction. Of these, ten have been cited most frequently:

1. Hyperactivity
2. Perceptual-motor impairments
3. Emotional lability
4. General coordination deficits
5. Disorders of attention (short attention span, distractibility, perseveration)
6. Impulsivity
7. Disorders of memory and thinking
8. Specific learning disabilities
   - a. Reading   c. Writing
   - b. Arithmetic   d. Spelling
9. Disorders of speech and hearing
10. Equivocal neurologic signs and electroencephalographic irregularities

The authors stress the individual-profile approach to each child. That is, they stress that no two children are going to evidence the same syndrome with identical signs. Yet they suggest that the abstraction of certain general syndromes such as "hyperkinesis" or "hypokinesis" may well be possible.

Examination of the characteristics hypothesized to be associated with minimal brain dysfunction reveals that they are not unlike those posited by Bender (1958) for maturational lag. The indices emphasized and the way in which they are conceptualized do stress the underlying difference between a model of dysfunction and one stressing the slow differentiation of patterns. Bender makes explicit that her hypothesis does not imply a structural defect or loss.

Patterns of Characteristics Relevant to the Psychological Conflict Hypothesis

A fourth major hypothesis emphasizes the role of intrapsychic and external psychological conflict in the etiology of learning disturbances. Just as the maturational lag and minimal brain dysfunction hypotheses have stimulated the search for syndromes, so the positing of the importance of psychological conflict has led to efforts to isolate typical intrapsychic conflict patterns and typical forms of family interaction associated with the development of the learning disturbance in the child. But while this effort has persisted, no definitive statement as to typical conflict or familial patterns is available. Rather, Blanchard's (1946) conclusion is still implicitly or explicitly assumed: "There is no single situation of personality maladjustment which can be isolated to explain the development of reading disability."

A useful framework for evaluating a particular learning disturbance is Anna Freud's diagnostic profile (Freud, 1965). The nature of this assessment method has already been discussed. Certain further points are particularly relevant to the discussion of the etiology of learning disturbance. Similar to certain considerations of uneven differentiation derived from the maturational-lag hypothesis is Anna Freud's statement that pathology is likely to result where development proceeds at different speeds in different areas of the personality. The importance of organic or early developmental deficiencies is also recognized in the fifth diagnostic category of those listed below. In categorizing a particular disturbance, the clinician considers the following:

1. that, in spite of current manifest behavior disturbances, the personality growth of the child is essentially healthy and falls within the wide range of "variations of normality";

2. that existent pathological formations (symptoms) are of a transitory nature and can be classed as by-products of developmental strain;

3. that there is permanent drive regression to previously established fixation points which leads to conflicts of a neurotic type and gives rise to infantile neuroses and character disorders;

4. that there is drive regression as above plus simultaneous ego and superego regressions which lead to infantilisms, borderline, delinquent, or psychotic disturbances;

5. that there are primary deficiencies of an organic nature or early deprivations which distort development and structuralization and produce retarded, defective, and nontypical personalities;

6. that there are destructive processes at work (of organic, toxic, or psychic, known or unknown origin) which have affected, or are on the point of affecting, a disruption of mental growth. [A. Freud, 1965, p. 147]

Within this framework, and keeping in mind that the search for single or even typical conflict situations contradicts the spirit of the framework, it is nevertheless useful to ask if certain intrapsychic emphases or family relationship patterns are more frequently associated with children suffering from learning disturbances than with those having other or no disturbances.

Among the foci of intrapsychic conflict associated with learning disturbances, those involving the scoptophilic impulses (the wish to see) have been consistently stressed since S. Freud's (1949) paper on hysterical blindness. Given the exorbitant demands of the sexual "lust of the eye," he concluded that this calls forth "some retaliatory measure from the side of the ego-instincts, so that the ideas which represent the content of its strivings are subjected to repression and withheld from consciousness." Abraham (1913) specifically applied Freud's ideas to the problem of reading. Later, S. Freud (1959) was to place this example of inhibition of function into the context of a larger discussion of inhibition, symptoms, and the restriction brought about by the impoverishment of the ego. The writings of Strachey (1930), Fenichel (1937), and Jarvis (1958) further emphasize the relation between the psychological meaning of the act and content of vision and disturbances of the learning process. Thus, Jarvis stresses that the active looking needed for reading (the word attack) may be associated with identification and fantasies involving aggression. By contrast, passive television viewing of even frightening content is thoroughly enjoyed.

Several authors have suggested that in many instances of learning disturbance the child's inhibition of curiosity may have to be maintained in order not to embarrass the parent. Hellman (1954) points out that the mother may even "confess" one secret in order to hide another. This seriously impairs the child's ability to distinguish between reality and fantasy and tends in general to equate active curiosity about mother's secrets with the possible loss of a very intimate relationship. Sperry et al. (1958) stress that as part of a family tendency to deny and distort reality, feelings associated with particular secret family events are also suppressed. The child must accommodate to this pressure and thus inhibits his curiosity.

Implied in the above is the inadequate differentiation of aggression and assertiveness, with its implications in boys for the development of an age-appropriate identification with the masculine role. Clearly, these problems are again not specific or exclusive to learning disturbances. Moreover, many different developmental patterns will be associated with the adequate or inadequate Oedipal resolution and the child's identification with the active and passive roles of parental intercourse.

Sperry et al. (1958) again approach the problem of aggressiveness and competition from the point of view of the family interaction. The children suffer from a learning disability because they are most eligible for the role of the unsuccessful one in the family. They present themselves as unaggressive, compliant, and in need of help. Through their helplessness, their dependent needs are gratified. The child's tendency toward renunciation is further linked by these authors to a general family tendency to approve self-sacrifice and decry aggressive competition. Buttressing this renunciation, in turn, is a general family denial of aggression.

Buxbaum's (1964) findings concerning the nature of learning disabilities are also very relevant to issues of the boy's adequate masculine identification. She distinguishes the all-pervasive learning disturbance and the success neurosis. In the latter the inadequate resolution of Oedipal conflicts plays a primary role. In the cases cited, the boys were so intimidated by their fathers that they were unable to function in areas which the fathers maintained as their prerogative, for example, the use of money or tools. They resolved their Oedipal conflicts by not exercising their ego functions, which they considered aggressive and competitive, and instead became passively aggressive. Contrary to the findings of Sperry et al. (1958), the fathers studied by Buxbaum were not failures but tended to be potent in reality.

Still another focus of the discussion of the psychological determinants of learning disturbance is on the vicissitudes of anal and oral sadism. As Blanchard (1946) pointed out, one of these vicissitudes places the learning disturbance in the role of a neurotic symptom. That is, the symptom represents a compromise between the wish to gratify an impulse and the need to refuse gratification or even to deny that such an impulse exists. "Failure in reading may represent a hidden antagonism to adults expressed in passive resistance rather than in openly rebellious behavior, and thus may also conceal repressed attitudes" (Blanchard, 1946).

While again stressing the fact that unresolved oral sadism potentially plays a role in all disturbances, various authors have stressed its particular importance in discussing what Buxbaum (1964) has termed the *all-pervasive learning disturbance*. This oral sadism, as well as intense longing for the mother, is seen in the context of a partially symbiotic relationship (Buxbaum, 1964; Hellman, 1954; Rubenstein et al., 1959). The mother and child maintain the child's feeling that he cannot function alone in certain areas. When alone, the child is anxious, but when with her, he feels omnipotent. When the child cannot do something, he becomes furious. Both mother and child are tied up in a relationship in which each expects and demands miracles from the other. All these factors are likely to interfere seriously with the child's independent learning.

The above discussion reflects the intrapsychic and external conflict components that various psychotherapists have considered to be important in understanding and treating the child with a learning disturbance. Again it must be stressed that the actual combination of factors will vary greatly from case to case and that, therefore, no combination of determinants can be thought of as typical for the learning disturbance. The careful delineation of subgroups within the overall heading of learning disturbance may, of course, make it possible to say that for a specific subgroup certain types of intrapsychic and external conflicts are more frequently found than in other subgroups.

CHARACTERISTICS OF THE CHILDREN READING BELOW THEIR POTENTIAL

In summarizing the evidence describing the general characteristics of children reading below their potential, a set of subheadings was developed which are relevant to the theoretical hypotheses stated and reflect what evidence is indeed available. Careful note should be made of the fact that the general issues of the learning disturbance are now specifically focused on the reading disturbance.

The most frequent approach to the problem of isolating the characteristics of the disturbed reading learner has been to define two or more groups of children in terms of differing progress in their reading and then to contrast them in terms of other dimensions. It is important here to differentiate those studies which contrast selected clinic samples with normally progressing readers and those that begin with a fairly large population and, on the basis of extensive testing, differentiate out a number of subgroups. Greater control is likely to be introduced if the contrast groups are drawn from the same population.

Another way of defining the characteristics of the slowly as opposed to the rapidly progressing reader is to assess the child in terms of a wide variety of characteristics, say at kindergarten, and then to see which of these characteristics are significantly associated with reading performance in the first and second grades.

Both forms of evidence, current correlates and predictive correlates, will be used in evaluating the hypotheses stated in the following sections. Where the definition of the original criterion groups was hard to specify and where the data were not analyzed systematically, less weight was given to a particular study.

Performance on the Wechsler Intelligence Scale for Children

Hypothesis 1—Children who perform below expectation in reading also have lower scores on the Full Scale, Verbal Scale, and Performance Scale of the WISC.

Most relevant to this hypothesis is the study by Belmont and Birch (1966). Groups of retarded and normal readers were defined on the basis of test scores available in a large public school population of 9- and 10-year-old Scottish children. Retarded readers were classified as such if they fell at or below the tenth percentile. The resulting 173 children were matched with members of the remaining group on the basis of birth date, sex, and school class. From these two groups, a sample of 150 retarded and 50 normal readers was chosen randomly. Comparison of the two groups on the Full Scale, the Verbal Scale, and the Performance Scale of the WISC showed that the mean score for the normal readers was significantly higher. This finding is supported by the studies of Altus (1956), Barratt and Baumgarten (1957), and Coleman and Rasof (1963). Another study (Shimota, 1964), based on seventy-four 14-year-old institutionalized emotionally disturbed or delinquent children, found no difference on the Full Scale, Verbal Scale, or Performance Scale.

Because of the great care taken by Belmont and Birch (1966) in defining the retarded and normal reader and because differences in total IQ scores are likely to emerge more clearly when working with extreme groups in a large population, this reviewer is inclined to give most weight to their study and to conclude that the above hypothesis is given considerable support.

Hypothesis 2—Children who perform below expectation in reading also have relatively higher performance as opposed to verbal scores on the WISC.

Belmont and Birch (1966) found that 60 percent of their retarded readers had higher performance than verbal IQs, while 60 percent of the normal comparison group had higher verbal than performance IQs. This difference was maintained even when the differences in Full Scale score were controlled for statistically. A review of thirteen other studies as summarized by Belmont and Birch also supports the above hypothesis.

Further support for this hypothesis, as well as an indication of the possible need to define certain small subgroups, comes from the study of children showing discrepancies of 20 points or more in verbal and performance scores (Kinsbourne & Warrington, 1966). Children who had a much higher performance than verbal score consistently had difficulty in expressive and receptive language functions but, interestingly, passed tests of finger differentiation and order and showed no selective impairment of arithmetical or constructional abilities. The opposite is true for the children with the higher verbal score. As for many of these findings, it may well be very important to consider the possible different meanings of such IQ discrepancies at the different ages.

Hypothesis 3—Children who perform below expectation in reading also tend to perform more poorly on *each* of the Verbal Scales and, relatively speaking, to perform *more adequately* on the Performance Scales of the WISC. Specifically, they score lower on Information, Arithmetic, Vocabulary, and Digit Span and tend to score higher on Picture Arrangement, Block Design, and Object Assembly.

Despite considerable variation in the samples contrasted, the above WISC profile of intellectual functioning does tend to characterize the child who is performing below expectation in reading. For the Similarities, Comprehension, and Coding Scales, the findings are contradictory. Listed below are those scales which have consistently been found to differentiate the slow and normal school-aged readers in the middle IQ ranges.

Readers below their potential in reading score *lower* on:

Information—Altus (1956); Barratt and Baumgarten (1957); Belmont and Birch (1966); Burks and Bruce (1955); Coleman and Rasof (1963); Dockrell (1960); Kallos, Grabow, and Guarino (1961); Neville (1961); Robeck (1960, 1962, 1963); Sheldon and Garton (1959).

Arithmetic—Altus (1956); Barratt and Baumgarten (1957); Belmont and Birch (1966); Burks and Bruce (1955); Coleman and Rasof (1963); Dockrell (1960); Dudek and Lester (1968); Graham (1952); Hirst (1960); Kallos, Grabow, and Guarino (1961); Neville (1961); Paterra (1963); Robeck (1960, 1962, 1963); Sawyer (1965); Sheldon and Garton (1959).

Vocabulary—Barratt and Baumgarten (1957); Belmont and Birch (1966); Coleman and Rasof (1963); Dockrell (1960); Graham (1952); Paterra (1963); Rabinovitch (1962); Rabinovitch et al. (1954); Sawyer (1965).

Digit Span—Coleman and Rasof (1963); Dudek and Lester (1968); Hirst (1960); Neville (1961); Robeck (1960, 1962, 1963); Shimota (1964).

Readers below their potential in reading score *higher* on:

Picture Arrangement—Barratt and Baumgarten (1957); Burks and Bruce (1955); Hirst (1960); Neville (1961); Shimota (1964).

Block Design—Barratt and Baumgarten (1957); Burks and Bruce (1955); Coleman and Rasof (1963); Graham (1952); Kallos, Grabow, and Guarino (1961).

Object Assembly—Barratt and Baumgarten (1957); Belmont and Birch (1966); Graham (1952); Sawyer (1965); Shimota (1964).

In further evaluating these results, particular weight was given to the research of Belmont and Birch (1966), Coleman and Rasof (1963), and Sawyer (1965). All these studies controlled for differences in full-scale IQ. The directions of the differences are those indicated by the hypothesis. The first two reported that the subtests Information, Arithmetic, Vocabulary, and Object Assembly most strikingly discriminated the child developing normally as opposed to the one reading below his potential. Using both an eleven- and a seven-variable Discriminant Functions data analysis, Sawyer (1965) found that for her total sample the subtests Arithmetic, Vocabulary, and Object Assembly were particularly useful in distinguishing between the mildly and severely disabled readers. Information does not emerge in the analysis, and this author also reports some interesting age differences.

The importance of age as a factor determining which subtest best differentiates good and poor readers is underlined by research reported by Reed (1968). Arithmetic, Vocabulary, Information, and Similarities are among the best differentiators at age 10, but Picture Arrangement, Information, Similarities, and Block Design best separate the readers at age 6. While there is thus considerable overlap in the subtests which differentiate the two groups, the inability to perceive and express visuospatial relations as reflected in the lower scores on Picture Arrangement and Block Design is more characteristic of the 6-year-old having difficulty in learning to read. It is most likely, therefore, that the hypothesis under discussion applies best to the child who is about 10 years old.

Hypothesis 4—Children who perform below expectation in reading are particularly characterized by the slow development of their vocabulary.

The evidence showing the differential performance of slow and normal readers on the vocabulary scale of the WISC has already been cited. In a study attempting to predict reading performance at the end of second grade from tests administered in kindergarten, De Hirsch et al. (1966) found that the number of words used by the child in telling the story of the Three Bears was indeed predictive. In emphasizing the importance of vocabulary as indicative of the generally poorer verbal performance of the slow reader, Belmont and Birch (1966) report that the retarded reader can define fewer of even the simplest words, uses more descriptive as opposed to categorical definitions, and in general knows fewer words than the normal reader.

Perceptual Functioning in the Child Reading below His Potential

A great number of studies have stressed that normal and retarded readers also differ in the efficiency of their perceptual functioning. In examining these results, it is of interest to ask whether any differences found can be accounted for in terms of differences in IQ. That a particular perceptual function correlates with the IQ does not, of course, mean it is unimportant in either reading or the general intellectual functioning. Following the model used by Sterritt et al. (1967), the question instead becomes whether variation in the perceptual function can account for variation in reading achievement not already accounted for by the IQ.

Hypothesis 5—Children who develop below their potential in reading also have particular difficulty with auditory-visual integration and with the perception of the auditory stimuli per se.

Beginning with an emphasis on the importance of the integration of various intersensory experiences, Birch and Belmont (1964) reasoned that the integration of auditory and visual stimuli might be of particular importance in reading. Specifically, they expected that children having difficulty in reading would also have difficulty recognizing the visual pattern equivalent for dot patterns that had been tapped out with a pencil.

In their initial study, based on the sample of 9- and 10-year-old Scottish children previously mentioned, they did find that a child whose reading scores fell into the lowest 10 percentile also performed less well than the control group on the auditory-visual (A-V) integration test (Birch & Belmont, 1964). A correlation of .38 between the A-V test and IQ was also reported.

In a second study, this association was *not* replicated for the third and fourth grades (Birch & Belmont, 1965). That is, these grades would be roughly equivalent in age to the ages in the first study. Significant associations between the A-V test and reading performance were found, however, for the first and second grades. Also, the IQ and the A-V test scores were significantly associated from grades 1 to 5.

Since the children taking the A-V test saw as well as heard the taps made by the pencil, Sterritt and Rudnick (1966a) reasoned that both auditory and visual stimuli were involved and should be studied independently. Using both earphones and blinker lights, they developed separate A (auditory) and V (visual) tests modeled on the original A-V test of Belmont and Birch. These tasks do, of course, still involve identifying the correct corresponding pattern on a piece of paper. Using regression equations, they found that at the fourth-grade level, mental age accounted for 55 percent and the A (auditory) test for an additional 23 percent of the variance. For the third grade, mental age accounted for 32 percent, the V (visual) test for 14 percent, and the A (auditory) test for 11 percent of the variance (Rudnick, Sterritt, & Flax, 1967). Both studies demonstrated that Belmont and Birch's A-V test made no significant contribution independent of mental age.

From an extensive review of studies of the relation between auditory discrimination skills and reading, Dykstra (1966) concluded that a significant though low association had been found in most of them. Only the research based on unselected populations gave inconsistent results. The results of his own carefully executed study are consistent with those reported by Sterritt and Rudnick (1966a) — certain auditory discrimination measures given before the first grade make a significant but small contribution beyond IQ to the prediction of reading at the end of first grade.

The above results can be interpreted as indicating that perception of auditory pattern per se is more difficult for the retarded reader and/or that the ability to transpose from the auditory to the visual modality is interfered with. Studies by Raab, Deutsch, and Friedman (1960) and Katz and Deutsch (1963) indicate that slow as opposed to normal readers do have greater difficulty shifting from one mode to another. Thus, Katz and Deutsch (1963) found that the poor as opposed to good readers reacted more slowly when the mode of presentation was changed. Thus, a visual presentation, rather than being followed by another visual stimulus, was followed by an auditory presentation. The rapid attentional shifts between modalities required for this task may well be of importance in reading. Performance on this task was not significantly associated with IQ.

That the perception of the auditory pattern per se is more difficult for the slow reader is also supported. Katz and Deutsch (1964) found that auditory as opposed to visual presentation was more difficult for all children but that for the retarded as opposed to normal reader, the discrepancy between their auditory and visual test performances was particularly striking. Of particular interest is the fact that the poor readers gave a greater proportion of incorrect and idiosyncratic verbal responses. Thus, "spoon" might be given for "cup." More of these idiosyncratic responses occurred during the auditory as compared with the visual presentation.

In further research, Katz (1967) has demonstrated that the familiarity of the stimulus material clearly influences the response to the item, whether presented in a visual or an auditory form. But holding familiarity constant, more errors were again made in relation to the auditory as opposed to the visual presentation.

In summary, the above evidence indicates that children who develop below their potential in reading have particular difficulties in establishing the equivalence of auditory and visual stimulations, cannot shift as easily from an auditory to a visual mode of presentation, and have difficulty in discriminating the auditory pattern per se.

Hypothesis 6 — Children who develop below their potential in reading also have difficulties at the automatic sequencing-integrative level.

The formulation of this hypothesis has been influenced in particular by research involving the Illinois Test of Psycholinguistic Abilities (ITPA). Research summarized by Bateman (1965) had shown that children with learning difficulties were particularly characterized by difficulties at the rote or automatic-sequential level, as opposed to the comprehension or representational level of language usage. Ragland (1964) and Kass (1962) found that disabled readers actually did well in the Visual Decoding subtest designed to measure ability to interpret meaningful visual stimuli.

Findings reported by McLeod (1967) further support this hypothesis discussion. Data from all twelve subtests of the WISC, the nine subtests of the ITPA, and four other tests were available on twenty-three second-grade children with reading difficulties and their matched controls. The other tests included Wepman's Auditory Discrimination Test, the Northwestern University Auditory Test No. 4, the auditory reproduction of words in context, and the written reproduction of tachistoscopically presented letter sequences. Answers to a questionnaire which has been found to discriminate significantly between children with reading disabilities and controls (the Dyslexia Schedule) were also available.

Factor analysis of the twenty-nine variables resulted in five factors, four of which correlated highly with reading ability. The first of these factors, entitled *sequencing-integrative,* had a heavy loading on all three ITPA tests at the automatic-sequential level, the WISC Digit Span, the two tests involving the written reproduction of printed letter sequences, and the ITPA Auditory-Vocal Association Test. There was also a substantial loading on the WISC Picture Arrangement and on the McLeod Dyslexia Schedule. McLeod (1967) stresses the fact that both auditory and visual tests are represented in the factor but that it does not load on tests involving semantic mediation such as the WISC verbal subtests. That is, the significant defects are at the automatic-sequential level and not the representational level.

The second of the factors that contributed particularly significantly to differences in the development of reading was entitled *auditory language input capacity.* It was primarily defined by the four tests involving the reproduction or discrimination of auditorily presented words and also had loadings on the ITPA Auditory Decoding and the Dyslexia Schedule.

The other two factors that contributed significantly to the prediction of reading disability were named *encoding* and *planning factors.* The ITPA subtests tapping the representational level as well as four verbal WISC subtests (Vocabulary, Similarities, Comprehension, and Information) load on this factor. The loading of Arithmetic and Comprehension in the planning factor also suggests the importance of semantic mediation.

That the first of the above four factors is the best predictor of the child's membership in the reading-disability group does lend support to the hypothesis under discussion. Since the other factors relating to problems of auditory input and semantic mediation are, however, also significant, further support is given to hypotheses previously discussed in this chapter.

In using a factorial design to determine what sources of variance are important, it may well be important as to whether one is using a normal population, a clinical population, or a combination of the two. McLeod (1967) employed a combination of normal and clinical populations.

Hypothesis 7—Children who develop below their potential in reading also have visual perceptual difficulties.

Noting that many of the children who were referred to her for learning difficulties also showed disturbances in visual perception, Frostig and her colleagues (Frostig et al., 1964) have developed and standardized their Developmental Test of Visual Perception in order to understand better this aspect of the child's total disturbance.

Following the model of IQ testing, a perceptual quotient is derived from summarizing the scores of five subtests: (1) A test of *eye-hand coordination;* (2) a test of *figure-ground perception;* (3) a test of *form constancy* involving, for example, recognizing the same letter represented in different sizes; (4) a test of perception of *position in space* as reflected in mirror writing; and (5) a test of difficulties in analyzing *spatial relationships* as reflected in a tendency to reverse the order of letters in a word. It should be noted that the first of these is a test of visual-motor skills and the rest are tests of visual discrimination.

A variety of studies do suggest a significant

association between total performance on this visual perceptual test and other areas of functioning. For example, of the kindergarten children with perceptual quotients of 90 or less, 70 percent fell below the midpoint on the Reading Achievement Test (Frostig et al., 1964).

Olson (1966) found that the total, as opposed to the subtests, of the Frostig showed the highest association with measures of reading. For example, the Reading Vocabulary Test of the California Achievement Test correlated with the total Frostig score to the extent of .44 and .41 for the second and third grades, respectively. Correlations with the specific subtests were lower.

Using the Children's Perceptual Achievement Forms, Di Meo (1967) also found that the total visual discrimination score as opposed to its specific components showed the highest association with a test of word recognition in a kindergarten population. The correlation was .53.

Given these findings on the importance of the summary as opposed to specific measures of visual discrimination, and given the previous finding by Sterritt and Rudnick (1966a) showing that the purely visual integration tests accounted for very little or none of the variation in reading ability not accounted for by IQ, the question arises as to how these summary indices of visual discrimination relate to IQ. Olson (1966) did find a correlation of .66 between the total Frostig score and the California Short-Form Test of Mental Maturity. The total visual discrimination score developed by Di Meo (1967) was not correlated with IQ scores. Further research is needed, therefore, to determine what contribution beyond IQ these total visual discrimination test scores or the subtests make in predicting reading development. At this point, one can conclude that the child reading below his potential also performs less well on general measures of visual discrimination.

Visual Motor Skills in the Child Reading below His Potential

The child's ability to copy or repeat a standard stimulus pattern has been tested in a variety of ways and has often been related to his performance in word recognition and reading comprehension. Most frequently, though, the standard pattern has been presented visually and the child is asked to copy it on a blank piece of paper; of these tests, the Bender Gestalt is the best known. Facets of these skills, and particularly the ability to integrate auditory and visually presented patterns, have already been discussed. The specific hypothesis suggested by review of the literature relating visual-motor skills and reading is discussed below.

Hypothesis 8—Children who develop below their potential in reading also have particular difficulty copying a visually presented standard pattern.

In one of the earliest systematic studies reported, Potter (1949) tested a group of first-graders at the beginning of the year on a number of visual discrimination and visual-motor tests. In the visual discrimination test, the stimulus (a shape and two-letter, three-letter, and four-letter words) was exposed briefly and a subsequent matching to the standard was made in a multiple-choice situation. The total perceptual discrimination score derived from these tests correlated .47 with reading as assessed at the end of first grade. When controlled for IQ, the coefficient dropped to .35. Of the various subtests, the ability to avoid mirror errors on two-letter words and the matching of shapes showed the highest correlation with reading; in each instance, the coefficient was .47. There was little evidence, though, that the skills involved in these tests were significantly more important than those in the other subtests. This evidence is again supportive of hypothesis 7.

The test of matching shapes was also used to

ask the child not only to *recognize* the match but actually to *reproduce* the shape from memory. Visual-motor skills were thus involved. For these first-graders, this test did *not* predict reading ability at the end of the year. It may well be that asking the child to draw from memory rather than having the standard in front of him, as in the Bender Gestalt, makes an important difference.

Goins (1958) administered fourteen perceptual tests to 120 first-graders and found that pattern copying (.519), reversals (.491), and combined perceptual scores (.495) correlated most highly with reading achievement.

That the copying of a visually present standard stimulus is associated with reading performance is further supported by the research of Barrett (1965), Koppitz and her colleagues, and De Hirsch et al. (1966). Barrett (1965) used a multiple regression analysis to relate performance on visual discrimination tasks at the beginning of first grade to reading performance at the end of the year. Reading letters and numbers made by far the strongest contribution to the equation, and the test of pattern copying previously used by Goins (1958) was second in importance. Barrett emphasizes that while the multiple correlation coefficients derived from these and other tests were statistically significant, other factors not tapped by the battery must be included to achieve adequate prediction of reading performance.

In a series of studies, Koppitz (1958), Koppitz, Sullivan, Blyth, and Shelton (1959), and Koppitz, Mardis, and Stephens (1961) report associations ranging in the .60s between the Bender Gestalt administered at the beginning of first grade and achievement on the Metropolitan Achievement Test at the end of first grade. These coefficients are enhanced if the results of the Figure Drawing Test are included in a multiple battery. It was also found (Koppitz, 1958) that, especially during grades 1 and 2, performance on the Bender and IQ tests is highly interrelated.

More recently, De Hirsch et al. (1966) have reported that among the thirty-seven kindergarten tests given, the Bender Gestalt was one of the better predictors of reading achievement at the end of the second grade; the coefficient was .44. Since a multiple regression analysis was not included, it is difficult to assess from this study whether or not the prediction of reading was enhanced by inclusion of this test.

In summary, the above evidence does indicate that children who are reading below their potential also tend to have difficulty with visual-motor tasks.

Laterality and Right-Left Discrimination

Since Orton (1937) first hypothesized a possible connection between atypical laterality and backwardness in reading, much controversy has been generated regarding this point. As part of the most frequently quoted discussion of this hypothesis, Zangwill (1962) doubts the value of studies which merely compare the incidences of a typical laterality in matched groups of backward and normal readers. It may be more useful to ask whether certain forms of reading backwardness exist in which anomalies of laterality are especially prominent. How do these differ from instances of reading backwardness in which there are no anomalies of laterality? We will return to these points after presenting the research that is available. Four hypotheses will serve to organize the findings on the role of cortical dominance in reading disability.

Hypothesis 9—Children who develop below their potential in reading will more frequently show signs of weak, mixed, or inconsistent lateral preferences.

O. L. Zangwill stated the hypothesis in this form in 1962. He cites studies by Orton (1937), Macmeeken (1939), Galifret-Granjon and Ajuriaguerra (1951), Harris (1957), Ingram and Reid (1956), and Ingram (1959, 1960) in support of this hypothesis. But as Zangwill also indicates, there are many reading-disability patients in whom laterality is well established and there is no family history of mixed-dominance sinistrality.

Review of studies investigating the relation of lateral preferences and reading disability tends, in general, to suggest that there is no relationship. Of the studies that did find a relationship, that reported by Harris (1957) has been quoted most often. Moreover, his carefully worked out Test of Lateral Dominance (1947) has frequently been used by subsequent investigators. Harris (1957) found that at both age 7 and age 9, children with reading disability, as opposed to an unselected school population, are more frequently characterized by mixed hand dominance on a total index derived from five subtests. Consideration of only one of these five subtests, namely, Hand Preference, suggests greater mixed hand preference among the reading-disability cases at 7 years, but this is not true at 9. At the latter age, mixed hand preference within the usage of one hand is actually slightly greater in the control group. More important, many children had a strong right-handed preference on most tasks but a strong left-handed preference on certain other tasks. If one takes this switching of hands on different tests as an index of mixed dominance, then, of course, a total score based on all the tests is going to suggest mixed dominance. The work of Douglass (1965) throws doubt, however, on the use by Harris of mixed but consistent eye-hand usage as an index of poor lateralization. He had shown that mixed but clear right-left preferences are actually associated with the development of a clear sense of spatial direction. Further questions are raised by other research.

Using Harris's test of dominance, Balow (1965) attempted to replicate the above findings but found that there was no combination of hand dominance and eye dominance, hand-eye dominance and knowledge of right and left, or strength of dominance and knowledge of right and left that was significantly associated with three different tests of reading achievement in first grade. Two factors could account for the fact that Harris's and Balow's results differ. Balow randomly chose his subjects from thirteen first-grade classrooms; subgroups within this large population were defined in terms of test results. Harris compared an unselected normal group with clinic cases of extreme reading disability. Perhaps even more important, Balow carefully matched all his subgroups on IQ, whereas in Harris's study this was an uncontrolled factor.

Two other studies drawing on normal populations are particularly noteworthy. The sample and definition of reading retardation used by Belmont and Birch (1966) to study the intellectual characteristics of the slow reader have already been described (see page 673). Measures of eye and hand preference, and thus hand-eye dominance, were also available on these children but did not differentiate the normal and retarded readers. Similarly, results on tests of hand preference administered to the kindergarten child showed no relation to reading achievement at the end of second grade (De Hirsch et al., 1966).

Since the studies of Harris (1957) and Belmont and Birch (1963) make it clear that in the normal population, hand dominance is not predominantly established until about the eleventh year of life, it is important to examine studies involving older age groups. The effect on reading of weak or mixed laterality may be more pronounced at this time. But even in studies sampling ages with a mean of 11 years or more, Silver and Hagin (1960) and Coleman and Deutsch (1964) found no relation between eyedness, handedness, and footedness on the one hand and degree of reading disability on the other hand. Other studies reported more recently similarly find no relation between the extent of laterality and reading disability (Chakrabarti & Barker, 1966). It is concluded, therefore, that the hypothesis under discussion has not received sufficient support in its present form. We stress present form because it may well be, as Zangwill (1962) has suggested, that within the larger group of children with reading disabilities, those who also show weak or mixed lateral preferences differ in important ways from those slow readers who are fully dextral.

Hypothesis 10—Children who develop below their potential in reading will more frequently show a discrepancy between the cerebral dominance indicated by the extended arm and the dominance indicated by the hand used for writing.

In view of the questions as to whether handedness is a true indication of cerebral dominance, Silver and Hagin (1960), following Schilder, used the discrepancy between the dominance indicated by the hand on the extension-of-arms test and the hand used in writing as a sign of mixed dominance. If the person wrote left-handed but raised his right hand higher on the extension test, mixed dominance would be indicated. Among the thirty reading-disability cases studied by Silver and Hagin, 74 percent showed such a discrepancy while none of the controls showed such mixed dominance. In most instances, there was a left-hand elevation and the concomitant use of the right hand. In subsequent reports, including a follow-up of the children when they were 20 years old, further information was noted. The significant difference between the reading-disability group and the control group noted in childhood was again found. In the first follow-up report, the percentage of cases showing a discrepancy on the elevation test was no different for a developmental versus an organic subgroup of the reading-disability children. In a further report using a subsample of the follow-up study, the developmental group did show a significantly higher discrepancy score on the elevation test: 89 percent versus 50 percent.

This raises certain questions about the stability of the findings and also makes one ask why children with established organic defects would show fewer indications of mixed dominance, but this is, of course, possible. Unfortunately, this finding has not been replicated. Since IQs of the children in the reading-disability and control groups were not equivalent, this matching should certainly be a part of the replication. Despite the above reservations, this research, including the very useful follow-up, remains the best piece of evidence supporting the hypothesis of a connection between reading disability and mixed cerebral dominance.

Hypothesis 11—Children who develop below their potential in reading will at age 6 show more errors of finger localization on the left as opposed to the right hand and at age 10 show more errors on the right as opposed to the left hand.

Previous work on finger agnosia (Benton, 1959; Kinsbourne & Warrington, 1966) suggested to Reed (1967) that finger-localization errors might well be related to achievement in reading. Starting with the general observation that unilateral finger agnosia in adults with known brain damage is associated with a lesion in the contralateral cerebral hemisphere, he specifically suggests that finger-localization errors which occur primarily on the right hand are often found among adult patients who have a loss in language skills and in reading. Similarly, finger-localization errors which occur primarily on the left hand are often found among adult patients who have a disturbance in the appreciation of spatial relations. The further steps in the author's reasoning were that predominantly right-handed finger-localization errors in children may be associated with difficulty in actual *reading comprehension* and that the presence of predominantly left-handed finger-localization errors may be associated with difficulty in *learning to read.* That is, it is assumed that impairment in spatial relations is likely to be of importance at the younger age, when the child is acquiring the reading skill. Using the above assumptions, Reed then stated the hypothesis as given above.

Analysis of the results lends support to the second part of the hypothesis, namely, that children who develop below their potential in reading at 10 tend to make more errors of finger localization on the right as opposed to the left hand. The hypothesis for the 6-year-old group was not supported.

Noting that these children were not brain-damaged, Reed discusses his finding in terms of individual variations. Just as there may be individual variations in the energy available, so there may be differences in cerebral integrity which affect both finger localization and reading comprehension.

Need for replication of this study derives not only from the fact that the general hypothesis was not given support at the 6-year level but also from questions about the adequacy of the tests of finger localization and differentiation (Kinsbourne & Warrington, 1966). Pending further study, the hypothesis is of particular interest in the conceptualization of individual differences and their relation to contralateral cerebral control.

Hypothesis 12 — Children who develop below their potential in reading will more frequently show errors in right-left discrimination.

Many questions must be raised at the outset concerning relevance of errors in right-left discrimination to problems of laterality. Such difficulties in orientation are very likely influenced not alone by maturation but by many other factors (Douglass, 1965).

As part of their previously cited research, Belmont and Birch (1965) developed an extensive battery of tests to assess the 9-year-old child's awareness of right and left on his own body and his conceptions of right and left in relation to self,

to others, and to the environment. In all instances, failure to discriminate right and left was related to reading achievement.

Since Benton and Kemble (1960) had also found such relationships but had indicated that they could be accounted for more parsimoniously in terms of general verbal and IQ differences, Belmont and Birch related indices of right-left awareness to the IQ measures. A significant relation to the performance but not the verbal IQ measures was found.

Harris (1957) also reported that the retarded 7-year-old reader showed greater right-left confusion but that this relation no longer held at the 9-year-old level. Similarly, Silver and Hagin (1960) found that 92 percent of their reading-disability group had defects in right-left discrimination while no instances were observed in their control group. In both of these studies, IQ was not controlled. Where such control was part of the design, the relation between reading disability and right-left discrimination was no longer significant (Balow, 1963). The study by Coleman and Deutsch (1964) is clearly the most relevant to this issue. They found that their normal group of readers did differ from the retarded readers on the Benton Right-Left Discrimination Test. However, these differences were no longer significant when the associated differential intellectual levels were controlled through analysis of covariance. It remains for future, more precise research to determine if difficulties in right-left discrimination beyond variations in IQ can make prediction of reading disability more accurate.

Review of the above findings reveals that there is, in general, little support for the hypothesized relation between inadequate cerebral dominance and reading disability. The studies of Silver and Hagin are the outstanding exception to this conclusion and therefore need to be replicated by other investigators. Noting the controversy existing in this area, Silver and Hagin (1967) pointed to the importance of finding an adequate index of cerebral dominance. As has been emphasized in this review, they still feel that Schilder's arm-extension test is the best available.

Disturbance in the Pattern of Neurological Organization

Hypothesis 13—Reading disability is likely to be one of several clinical indices of neurological dysfunction.

The well-known study of Rabinovitch et al. (1954) was among the first to demonstrate the difference between children with obvious indications of neurological dysfunction—the so-called primary reading disturbances in which brain dysfunction is clearly indicated by a number of clinical indices—and children with secondary reading disability, in which the disturbance is part of a larger pattern of poorly resolved internal and external conflicts.

Cohn (1961) contrasted a group of 7- to 10-year-olds considered by the school authorities to show "specific" reading and writing difficulties with a control group on a great variety of indices derived from four areas of neurological study: (1) language, (2) somatic receiving and expressive systems, (3) personal spatial organization, and (4) social adaptation. Each element was rated from 1 to 4, with 4 indicating maximum deficit. The following indices were particularly sensitive in differentiating the specific reading disability from a normal control: writing, reading, right-left orientation, ability to resolve paired tactile stimuli, time disorientation, inability to synthesize simple action pictures, abnormal deep tendon reflexes, Babinski sign, coordination, mechanical speech, and abnormalities in the EEG. In interpreting these findings, Cohn stressed that the reading difficulties were not isolated phenomena dependent on specific lesion but were the result of generalized brain dysfunction.

The manner of choosing the reading-disability groups in both the Rabinovitch and the Cohn studies may well be of importance in determining what proportion of reading-disturbance cases show generalized brain dysfunction. The impression is that these children did represent extreme instances of difficulty. It is also noteworthy that neither study included statistical analysis of the group differences on the neurological indices. Despite these reservations, the hypothesis under discussion does receive considerable support from these two pieces of thoughtful research.

Both investigators make explicit that the difference in neurological dysfunction is not due primarily either to specific brain lesions or to maturational lags. Instead, they stress the endogenous or biological and constitutional source of these differences. Critchley (1968) is very explicit about this point and cites two kinds of supportive evidence. Hallgren (1950) found a greater frequency of severe reading retardation in certain families. The explanation that this higher frequency could be a function of the common poor-family environment rather than genetic transmission is not likely to account for another finding cited by Critchley: For twelve monozygotic twins with dyslexia, 100 percent concordance was reported; for the dizygotic series in which one twin had dyslexia, only 33 percent concordance was observed.

Minimal Brain Dysfunction

The above evidence supports the observation that there is little disagreement in the literature about the importance of the potential link between learning disturbances and brain dysfunction, as studied both neurologically and behaviorally. By contrast, assumptions concerning the link between minimal neurological signs, the assumed minimal brain damage, and reading disability are considerably more controversial. Cohn (1964) has persuasively argued against equating minimal brain damage and minimal neurological signs. He suggests, first, that what is minimal in one context may not be minimal in another context. Second, the relation of known brain damage and its clinical signs is too little known to make ready interpretations of these signs. Third, it must be recognized that the neurological findings are heavily dependent on the philosophy of the neurologist and the tests used.

Hypothesis 14—Children who develop below their potential in reading will more frequently show signs of minimal brain dysfunction.

Although it is reasonable to assume that brain dysfunction and its effects on behavior are not an either/or matter, as already indicated, the task of demonstrating the brain-behavior relationship becomes difficult when conventionally accepted evidence of cerebral dysfunction is unavailable. Reitan's approach to this problem has already been cited. He and his colleagues have developed a test battery which clearly distinguishes children with cerebral lesions from their normal controls (Reed, Reitan, & Klove, 1965). This battery can then be used to aid in the diagnosis of children suspected of having brain lesions (Reed, 1963). Needless to say, the continued use of more conventional neurological techniques is not thereby eliminated. Moreover, as Reitan and his colleagues stress, the results of the application of the battery which includes the WISC are not that easy to interpret. Application of their tests shows again that children with reading difficulties evidence a wide variety of other disabilities. Inference of specific effects is therefore likely to be more difficult (Reed, 1968; Reitan, 1964). Their findings also suggest that measures of language and visual-motor ability tend to be the best differentiators of advanced and retarded readers (Reed, 1968); Reitan, 1964. For example, Reed found that of the tests selected from the Reitan battery, the subtests of the WISC were the best differentiators of good and poor readers. Since the WISC result is likely to be influenced by many factors, cerebral lesion can be assumed in only certain cases. Reitan and his colleagues have therefore taken great care to make such inferences only in the context of a profile of assessments.

A second approach to the problem of investigating minimal brain dysfunction has been to study the frequency of suggestive indications of neurological abnormality (the so-called soft signs) in groups of children reading below their potential and to compare them with matched controls. Cohn (1961) included in his research a group of normal controls not evidencing reading problems, the group of children previously described (see above) as evidencing generalized brain dysfunction, and a second control, or contrast, group who showed varying intensities of difficulty with reading but who were retained in the normal schoolrooms. This latter group of reading disturbances was neurologically indistinguishable from the normal controls. Cohn stresses in his comments on this study that those indications of neurological abnormality that normal controls did show were found among the so-called soft signs.

Other studies also fail to give convincing clues as to how to establish the presence of minimal brain dysfunction. Stevens et al. (1967) compared twenty-six children assigned to the category of minimal brain dysfunction (MBD) with a matched control group. They found that MBD children tap more slowly, make more errors of an impulsive type, have longer response latencies, make more errors as a function of the complexity of instructions, and are poorer in tone discrimination.

Since, however, it is not clear how the children were assigned to the MBD category in the first place, this study does little to provide support for the hypothesis under discussion. The results obtained could easily be a function of interacting factors other than the presumed minimal brain dysfunction. For example, would the results have been obtained had the full IQ of the two groups been matched? Since eight of the twenty-six MBD children had lost their parents before the age of 5 and this was in no case true in the control group, this factor might also be of some importance in accounting for the behavioral differences.

Starting with the need to find a psychological test battery that would make the referral of the underachieving child for a medical neurological examination more efficient, Zedler (1968) has demonstrated impressive correlations between behavioral items derived from the administration of the WISC and sixty-one variables making up a Medical Examination Index. The correlation coefficient is .65; $P < .01$. While this is clearly a very useful finding, two major questions arise in the context of the discussion of the present hypothesis. It would be important to know the frequency with which the signs making up the Medical Examination Index are found in an adequately achieving population and in one not as extreme in its underachievement as the one studied by Zedler.

But even if one could establish a differential frequency of these medical examination signs in different populations, their interpretation as indicating minimal brain damage needs further study. To correlate the Medical Examination Index with global ratings made by the panel of physicians on these patients would give a valuable indication of reliability but would not clarify the issue. As Zedler points out, the frequency of occurrence of disorder in such items of the neurological section of the Medical Examination Index as gait and station, stride and strength of legs, and coordination tends to provide face validity for the assumption of underlying minimal brain damage. They could, however, also be cited as evidence of constitutionally determined defects in the neurological integration. More convincing proof of the inference of brain damage is therefore more likely to come from the investigative approach adopted by Reitan.

While the relation between behavioral indications and the presumed minimal brain dysfunction, therefore, needs further clarification and demonstration, the above negative evidence does not, of course, mean that in individual instances the construct of minimal brain dysfunction is not likely to be very useful. If, however, the inference is made from behavioral ratings rather than known neurological indices, then the concept of individual differences may initially be more applicable than that of minimal brain damage. These differences, in turn, may be influenced by a great variety of interacting factors. Thus, Rubin and Braun (1968) found that a group of maladjusted children, as defined by the teacher, not only differed from a control group but was made up of at least two major subgroups: those who showed much cognitive motor dysfunction and those who did not. Even though the extensive battery of tests used is highly relevant to the list of symptoms assumed to be indicative of minimal brain damage, it does not follow (nor do the authors so conclude) that those maladjusted children showing this cognitive-motor dysfunction suffer from minimal brain damage while those maladjusted children who do not show their disturbance in this way are free of brain dysfunction. Rather, we would prefer initially to conceptualize these as individual differences in expressing maladjustment. These differences could, in turn, be a function of certain or (more likely) several factors: constitutional variation; early insults to the CNS, including minimal brain damage; developmental lags; psychological conflicts; inadequate stimulation; poor educational experiences; and so forth.

The Personality and Environmental Situation of the Child Reading below His Potential

Ever since Freud's 1910 paper on the psychogenic visual disturbances (S. Freud, 1949), there has been extensive interest in the association between the nature of intrapsychic conflict, its resolution as reflected in certain types of personality configurations, and the associated disruption or strengthening of certain functions, such as perception, attention, reading. More recently, increased attention has also been given to those environmental conditions, and particularly the nature of the family-child and teacher-child interaction, which impede or favor the child's academic progress. The major proportion of the individual papers—Hellman (1954), Sperry (1958), Jarvis (1958), Buxbaum (1964)—and the systematic reviews—Blanchard (1946), Pearson (1952)—have relied on the analysis of clinical cases. A valid picture of the essential internal and external conflict determinants of a reading disability is indeed likely to be reached through the extensive study associated with the treatment of the child. At the same time it must be recognized that generalizing from one or a few cases must be done with great care.

Review of the conclusions of the various clinical papers suggests the following two general hypotheses:

1. The learning disturbance of the child is frequently associated with and primarily determined by inadequate resolution of internal and external conflicts.
2. There is no specific type of internal and external conflict or specific resolution of conflict that characterizes the child with a learning disturbance.

Given these hypotheses, what additional and more systematic evidence can be found to support them?

Hypothesis 15—Children who develop below their potential in reading are also characterized by less adequate resolution of internal and external conflicts.

Anna Freud's profile reflects well the assumption that inadequate progressive development, including such a function as reading, can be the resultant of many different internal and external conflict configurations and resolutions. Great care is taken to examine all the facets of the child's unique functioning, but comparison with other children of this age is also implicit and explicit. In an effort to facilitate such case comparison, Heinicke (1969) has developed a series of forty-five ratings derived from the profile. Profiles were written on a sample of

7- to 10-year-old boys at the beginning, at the end, and after the end of their treatment. As discussed previously, four clusters which characterized the variation of the functioning of these children at *each* of the assessment points were derived. The first of these clusters, named the *level of ego integration*, included the following ratings: the level of ego integration, the capacity to sublimate, the absence of primary-process breakthrough, the effectiveness of the defensive organization, the capacity to tolerate anxiety, the level of self-esteem as a function of the child's achievement, the ability to assert himself, the extent of academic ambition, the ability to persist in a task. The terms "intactness" and "unity of functioning," as well as "effective adaptation," are suggested. A certain level of adequate resolution is also implicit.

The second cluster was named the *extent of ego flexibility* and included the following ratings: the capacity to express a variety of affects, the extent to which a variety rather than a few defenses are available to the child, the nondefensive use of humor, and a minimum repression of aggressive derivatives. This cluster, then, suggests that in addition to adequate integration of areas of functioning, the child's ability to respond in a variety of ways is important. The absence of extensive repression of aggression in particular suggests the more adequate resolution of intrapsychic and external psychological conflicts.

The two other factors were the capacity for forming peer relationships and the extent of self-reliance. These were, relatively speaking, of lesser importance since the first factor accounted for approximately 54 percent and the second about 15 percent of the variance.

Given the importance of the ego-integration cluster in describing the variations in the personality configurations, then the fact that scores based on this cluster correlated at the beginning of treatment with the rate of achievement in reading, arithmetic, and spelling and negatively with a rating of the extent to which the child's family environment impeded his potential for development does tend to support the hypothesis under discussion. That is, variations in the nature of the resolution of intrapsychic and external conflicts are related to variations in the rate of academic achievement.

The ego-integration scores were also related significantly to the Stanford-Binet IQ. This raises the question of whether variations in IQ may in part be related to the nature of conflict resolution. Previous findings by Sontag, Baker, and Nelson (1958) and Bayley and Schaefer (1964) tend to support the possibility of such an association. It also suggests that a multiple regression equation involving measures of ego integration, ego flexibility, and IQ should be developed.

A series of studies by Shaw (1968) and his colleagues using well-thought-out measures of underachievement have consistently demonstrated that the underachiever as opposed to the adequate achiever experiences a more negative self-concept and more hostility toward the social environment. These findings are consistent with findings on self-esteem and resolution of aggression cited by Heinicke (1969). They do not, however, demonstrate that these difficulties as opposed to other personality-linked disturbances are specific to the underachiever.

A number of short-term longitudinal studies provide evidence that personality variables are related to reading achievement in samples not chosen to represent extremes of underachievement. Thus, Kagan (1965) has developed a series of measures of reflection-impulsivity in order to predict reading performance at the end of first grade. To what extent can the child reflect over alternative solution possibilities in contrast to making an impulsive selection of a solution? This dimension appears very similar to attributes included in the ego-integration cluster. Using as a measure of reflection the length of response time to a visual-recall test (MFF), Kagan found that the longer the response time at the beginning of first grade, the fewer the reading errors

at the end of first grade. This relation remained significant ($r = .28$) even when the influence of verbal skills derived from the WISC were partialled out. The multiple correlation using word errors as the criterion and verbal skills and length of response time as separate predictors was .51 for boys and .59 for girls. The advantage of such a predictive study for assessing the effect of personality or other variables on reading is that the secondary effects of failure in reading on the nature of conflict resolution are initially eliminated. Two other predictive studies stress the usefulness of such general personality variables as ego integration and flexibility in predicting reading performance.

Ames and Walker (1964) studied the association between the nature of the Rorschach responses in kindergarten and the performance on the reading sections of the Stanford Achievement Test at the end of the fifth grade. The good readers tended to have a lower W percentage, a high D percentage, a lower F percentage, and a greater number of FM responses. These results persisted when IQ was controlled for, and a tendency for the good readers to have shown more color responses at the kindergarten level also emerged. The correlation of a prognostic Rorschach score and reading was .53. Kindergarten IQ related to reading to the extent of .57, and the multiple R between the two predictors and reading was .73.

Ames and Walker interpret these and other results as indicating that the greater use of color and movement by the better reading groups, concomitant with their lower F percentage, evidently reflects their greater emotional maturity, a more differentiated experiencing, and greater openness to stimulation. The reviewer would suggest that these authors are dealing with attributes very similar to ego integration and flexibility.

De Hirsch et al. (1966) have also studied the association between test response at the kindergarten level and reading achievement at the end of second grade. While many tests were employed and, in fact, associated with later reading, two predictors—ego strength and work attitude—are clearly similar to the various ratings included in the ego-integration cluster.

The above evidence therefore supports the hypothesis that certain general personality characteristics here summarized in part in relation to the concepts of ego integration and ego flexibility are associated with variations in reading performance. While the study of Heinicke (1969) in particular showed the link of these general characteristics to variations in the nature of internal conflict resolution, it does not follow that this alone would account for variations in something like the child's ego integration. Clearly, though, the nature of the child's intrapsychic conflict resolution will have to be at least considered in any explanation of reading failure and its remediation.

Similar arguments apply to the role of external psychological conflicts. We have already noted that general measures of a negative psychologically significant environmental impact did relate to variations in ego integration and academic achievement at the point of referral (Heinicke, 1969). Brodie and Winterbottom (1967) have also shown that 7- to 10-year-old boys referred for a learning disturbance had experienced a greater number of specific traumas and had lived in a more traumatic milieu. It should be noted that these indices are global and summary in nature.

Many different types of family interaction have been described as potentially associated with learning disturbance or underachievement. A particularly close (symbiotic) mother-child relationship (Buxbaum, 1964; Hellman, 1954) has been found in certain cases. Others have suggested that the father plays an inadequate role (Grunebaum et al., 1962; Morrow & Wilson, 1961; Sperry et al., 1958). By differentiating the children with the all-pervasive learning disturbance

from those whose inability to learn is tied to a success neurosis, Buxbaum (1964) found that the first group were characterized by a partial symbiotic tie to the mother but that this was less true for the success-neurosis group. Given the unresolved Oedipal conflicts of this latter group, it is not surprising that some of the fathers were potent in reality and not as self-devaluating as suggested by Grunebaum et al. (1962).

Another etiological hypothesis focuses less on the mother-child or father-child relationship than on the whole family organization from which the learning disturbance of a given child emerges as resultant in order to maintain a certain equilibrium (Miller & Westman, 1964; Sperry et al., 1958). The child responds to the family demands to be the unsuccessful one—to be the nonlearner.

While the above clinical studies, involving as they do a considerable number of cases, do support the hypothesis that the nature of the family relationships is of importance as a determinant of the child's learning disturbance, more systematic research is needed to determine what specific types of environmental circumstances, if any, are of importance in which type of learning disturbance.

Studies of the sources of variation in academic achievement among nonclinical populations do suggest the importance of certain family variables, but even here much of the evidence is contradictory. Many studies stress the importance of an adequate level of parental warmth and involvement as a prerequisite to adequate development and learning (Heinicke, 1953; Skeels, 1966; Yarrow, 1964). The importance of adequate parental verbal stimulation and assistance has also been stressed by many studies: Bing (1963), Hess (1965), Milner (1951). Children of superior intellectual ability, achievement motivation, and actual achievement tend also to come from homes where intellectual achievement is stressed. Wolf (1964), using data obtained from mother interviews of fifth-grade students, found that the children's IQ was predicted to the extent of .69 by the following scales: the parents' intellectual expectations for the child, the amount of information that the mother had about the child's intellectual development, the opportunities for enlarging the child's vocabulary, the extent to which the parents created situations for learning in the home, and the extent of assistance given in learning situations related to school and nonschool activities. Dave (1963) derived an Index of Educational Environment from the scales developed by Wolf; it was associated with an Educational Achievement Score (composed of such areas as word knowledge, spelling, reading, and arithmetic computation) to the extent of .80. While these associations are impressive, it should be noted that general and summary types of scores are again being employed.

As Freeberg and Payne (1967) point out in their recent review of the literature, there is less consensus on the specific role in learning of the acceptant-democratic-indulgent versus the authoritarian-restrictive atmosphere. The same applies to the question of the extent and timing of training for self-reliance as a factor in learning.

Hypothesis 16—Children who develop below their potential in reading evidence a specific type of internal and external conflict configuration and mode of resolving that conflict.

Evidence reported in relation to the previous hypothesis has already suggested that there is little consistent evidence that any one type of internal or external conflict is associated with a child's tendency to develop below his potential in reading. The search for such a configuration has nevertheless been consistently pursued. Research involving the grouping and comparison of several children will be briefly reviewed below.

One area of focus has been on those factors which interfere with the child's active exercise curiosity. Intrapsychic conflict as related to the meaning of active looking and finding out has been stressed by many authors and was discussed in our review of the four etiological hypotheses above. Few systematic studies are available. Walters et al. (1961) showed that advanced as opposed to retarded readers take less time to find a nude male doll with a penis. As the authors themselves indicate, the reluctance to open a box and look at a nude doll does not necessarily indicate a fear of looking. The quickness of the advanced readers could again be a function of their intelligence. More intensive and extensive studies will have to be done in order to be able to make more specific statements about the role of conflicts around curiosity in accounting for the child's difficulty in reading.

The environmental contribution to the child's difficulties in "knowing" has also been stressed (Brodie & Winterbottom, 1967; Hellman, 1954; Sperry et al., 1958). For various reasons, secrets have had to be maintained in the family, or one secret has been confessed to hide an even more painful one. Not only is the exercise of curiosity impeded, but the picture of reality tends to be distorted. Brodie and Winterbottom (1967) found that mothers of children with learning problems were more secretive than the mothers of a matched control group. As the authors indicate, however, this secretiveness may not be specific to a learning disturbance. Mothers of children showing other types of psychological disturbance may also be more secretive than a nondisturbed family. The fact that a condition is not specific to a reading disturbance does not, of course, make it unimportant.

Survey of the clinical literature suggests many other internal and external factors. Dudek and Lester (1968) offer the following hypothesis: The personality of the underachiever will be expected to show a pattern of passive resistance to authority, marked by a "facade of compliance and passivity." Study of a group of 13- to 17-year-old underachievers revealed that by comparison with the normal achiever, these adolescents had great difficulty dealing with their aggression. They coped mainly through passive resistance, withdrawal into fantasy, or both. Particularly striking was the marked inhibition of the expression of oral and oral-aggressive content. They more frequently saw their fathers as inadequate, and their responses reflected difficulties with their mothers. Their predominant response was a "good-child facade."

While this study again points to the importance of psychological conflict in understanding the learning disturbance, clearly not all children with learning disturbance fit into the good-child facade. Nor can one usefully talk of an "under-achievement syndrome" if the factors isolated apply equally frequently to other types of symptomatology.

Still other specific conflict constellations have been suggested as of particular significance in boys. Frequently related to the inadequate exercise of curiosity and problems around activity-passivity is the difficulty in identifying with an assertive masculine role (Buxbaum, 1964). This is, in turn, of course dependent on many other factors, and there are again no studies to indicate that the adequate assumption of masculine identification is specific to learning or more crucial in learning than in other disturbances.

We conclude, therefore, that while the above and many other aspects of external and intrapsychic conflict are likely to be of great importance in individual cases, the evidence available at this point does not support the hypothesis that there is one or even a limited number of specific external or internal conflict configurations or modes of resolving them that characterize the slow reader.

PROGRAMS TO ENHANCE THE DEVELOPMENT OF THE CHILD READING BELOW HIS POTENTIAL

A great variety of programs have been designed to facilitate the development of the slow reader. Although excellent case studies are available, this review is confined to the consideration of systematic studies of change. The various studies are best organized in terms of the orientation and theory that guided their development: (1) training to overcome maturational lag, (2) training to compensate for minimal brain dysfunction, (3) training to develop perceptual skills, (4) remedial education, (5) application of behavioral modification techniques, and (6) psychotherapeutic techniques.

Review of this research underlines the great difficulty of changing the development of the slow reader. Where gains are made during the period of the program, they are often not retained once the help is removed. As far as this reviewer is aware, only the extensive procedure of child psychoanalysis goes some way in ensuring continued progressive development after the period of treatment.

Training to Overcome a Maturational Lag

Implicit in the maturational-lag hypothesis is that certain aspects of the problem will be resolved in the course of time. Training procedures have also been reported to facilitate this process (Bender, 1958). A more systematic study attempting to remedy areas of deficit was carried out, but apparently not too successfully (Silver & Hagin, 1967). A further study concentrating on the development of skills in which the child has already shown some facility is now in progress (Silver & Hagin, 1967).

The Doman-Delacato theory of neurological organization is quite specific in delineating the ontogenetic developmental progressions through which the child must proceed to attain the higher levels of neural functioning. If a lower level is incomplete, all succeeding higher levels are affected. Emphasis is placed on both psychomotor and cognitive development. As in the formulations of Bender, the attainment of adequate cerebral dominance is seen as very important. To facilitate this, as well as to resolve deficiencies at lower levels of neural organization, various forms of creeping and crawling, other forms of physical exercise, certain sleeping positions, and procedures for enhancing lateralization have been recommended. It is hypothesized that insofar as these programs are successful, various cognitive deficits, including difficulties of reading, will be eliminated.

Glass (1966) has raised serious doubts about the studies cited by Delacato to support his hypothesis. Two systematic studies of the impact of programs outlined by Delacato have been reported by other investigators (Kershner, 1968; Robbins, 1967). Exercises involving creeping and crawling, other physical activities, and procedures encouraging lateralization were sequentially structured according to the neurological stages of development. Robbins did not find the postulated relationship between neurological organization (as measured by creeping and laterality) and reading achievement. Nor did the addition of the Delacato program to the ongoing curriculum of the retarded readers enhance their reading development. Kershner (1968) found that the special training given to an experimental as opposed to a control group did bring about differential gains in creeping and crawling and in the scores on the Peabody Picture Vocabulary Test (PPVT). However, the control group showed as much motor-proficiency improvement as those experiencing the special training. As the author points out, the difference in PPVT scores could well be a function of the facts that the groups differed on the pretest scores and that the teacher of the experimental group was more effective and enthusiastic in areas directly affecting the PPVT.

Since no follow-up studies are included as part of either of the two studies and since, in general, the results tend to be negative, there is so far little support for the hypothesis that specific activities based on the Doman-Delacato theory of neural organization are likely to benefit the retarded reader.

Training to Compensate for Minimal Brain Dysfunction

Among the studies that have evaluated teaching programs designed for children who are hyperactive and behaving as if minimal brain dysfunction were present, that by Cruickshank et al. (1961) has rightly been cited very frequently. In a carefully designed study including a control and an experimental group, a detailed effort was made to apply to these hyperactive children techniques that had been effective with children clearly diagnosed as brain-injured. The environmental stimulation was reduced; for example, each student had his own cubicle. The educational sequence was carefully structured so that the child experienced success before going to the next area. Efforts were also made to increase the tactual and visual value of the material. Coordination of eyes and hands in situations such as the Bender Visual Motor Gestalt Test, discrimination of sounds, writing skills, arithmetic, and reading were covered in great detail.

Extensive pretesting and posttesting revealed no significant differences on either the IQ or achievement testing. The experimental as opposed to the control group did, by the end of the program, show significant gains on certain of the items of the Bender Visual Motor Gestalt Test, the Syracuse Visual Figure Background Test, and the Vineland Social Maturity Scale. But, as the authors themselves summarize, after the program had been terminated for a year, the experimental children no longer did significantly better than the control group on a single scoring category.

Important to note in relation to the minimal brain dysfunction hypothesis is that differences between the obviously and less obviously brain-injured were not associated with differential development.

Very similar results were obtained by Gallagher and Kirk (1960) in a carefully designed study of the tutoring of brain-injured mentally retarded children. So long as the tutoring was in effect, there were gains not only in perceptual abilities but also on the verbal IQ and achievement tests. In contrast to the Cruickshank study, greater emphasis was placed on the personal relationship to the teacher. This is likely to be of particular importance in an institutional setting and may well be related to the gains on the Vineland Social Maturity Scale and the children's increased ability to pay attention. But most important, not only were there serious decrements after the tutoring had been withdrawn but a follow-up of the experimental group when they had been without the special stimulation for two years revealed that all gains had essentially been lost.

Training to Develop Perceptual Skills

Starting with the observation that the development of reading skills is in part dependent on visual and auditory skills, various authors have reasoned that training in these perceptual skills will enhance the reading of the slow developer.

This hypothesis is central to the work of Frostig and her colleagues. Although they reported some preliminary results on the effectiveness of their program in perceptual skills, systematic work in this area is limited. Rosen (1966) found that a Frostig program for the development of visual perception did improve the first-graders' response to the Frostig test but did not improve their reading. In terms of one subtest, Grasp of Significant Ideas, the control actually did better. This was attributed to the fact that during the time when the experimental group was receiving perceptual training, the control was given time in reading instruction. The fact that there is no follow-up study should again be noted.

Given their extensive research on the role of both auditory and visual perceptual factors in the development of reading, it is not surprising that the research group headed by Martin Deutsch would also assess the effect of training in auditory skills on the child's development of reading.

Working with deprived children of third-grade level and carefully controlling for the initial level of the IQ and the reading and auditory skills, Feldmann, Schmidt, and Deutsch (1968) found that the auditory training had no significant effects. What they did find was that the students of certain tutors performed significantly better on four of the reading tests. The authors cite earlier studies by Duggins (1956) and Murphy (1943), who did find a relation between auditory perceptual training and reading improvement in first graders. Given the inclusion of two follow-up assessments in the Feldmann, Schmidt, and Deutsch (1968) study and given a generally excellent methodology, this reviewer is at present inclined to give greatest weight to their work. One would also anticipate that perceptual training as part of a broad intensive remedial effort might well be effective. Preliminary results reported by McConnell (1968) support such an anticipation.

Remedial Education

A great number of different studies have shown that remedial education leads to a definite gain in the rate of reading improvement (Balow, 1965; Bliesmer, 1962; Bond & Fay, 1950; Davids & Andrews, 1964; Lovell, Byrne, & Richardson, 1963; Lovell, Johnson, & Platts, 1962; Mouly & Grant, 1956). In general, wherever follow-up assessments were made, it became clear that once the remedial work is withdrawn, the students tend to return to the rate of improvement seen before the period of special help. Balow (1965) could show that where at least some help was continued, the rates of improvement did not decline as much. Moreover, the fact that the remedial help had brought the children to a higher absolute level of reading is very important. But as Balow (1965) stresses, even the intensive two hours a day of involvement in remedial help is not likely to change the reading disability to the point where the child can continue to develop at an acceptable rate once the help is withdrawn. Similarly, Smith (1962) has demonstrated that a general language-development program designed for the mentally retarded made a significant impact on their psycholinguistic abilities but that this advantage was not sustained during the period after treatment (Mueller & Smith, 1964).

Application of Behavior-modification Techniques

Although the various learning theories and the modification efforts based on them are clearly relevant to the difficulties of the slow learner, systematic research based on the principles of operant conditioning are so far the most productive. In one such study, designed by Staats et al. (1967) and carried out by high school seniors and adult volunteers, slow readers in the seventh and eighth grades were reinforced in a variety of ways in relation to their learning of a sequence of material developed from Science Research Associates. A total of 40 hours of training was involved. On a test of vocabulary drawn from that material, the group which experienced this program of reinforcement did significantly better than a comparable control group. There were, however, no significant differences on the more general tests of reading, such as the Iowa Test of Basic Skills. Nor were there any indications that the children developed the type of reading skill that would allow them to decipher new words. Since there is also no evidence as to the children's progress in reading after the reinforcement procedures were terminated, questions concerning the generalization and permanence of these results remain unanswered.

In a more extensive program covering a period of a year, Wolf et al. (1968) conducted a special class, which met for 2½ hours after school as well as on Saturday and during the summer. Every phase of the child's environment likely to be relevant to his academic learning was manipulated through a great variety of ingenious reinforcers. For example, the instructors were given a bonus of $10 if their student showed an improvement over his previous six-weeks report. The authors refer to this as a remedial program. This is clearly a correct description since a wide variety of factors, including the relationships to the adults, were no doubt of importance.

By comparison with a control group, the children showed significant gains on both their report cards and the total battery of the Stanford Achievement Test. The latter result contrasts with those by Staats et al. in that this remedial program led to changes which were generalized to achievement tests.

Yet the question of the generalization of the results must be raised. As part of their study, the authors demonstrated that the reading rate in individual students was highly dependent on the reinforcement system used. This, in turn, suggests that when the reinforcement system is withdrawn at the end of the program, the student will return to slower reading rates. A follow-up assessment after the remedial program has ceased is therefore highly desirable.

Psychotherapeutic Techniques

Although many case presentations illustrate the changes brought about in a reading disability by psychotherapeutic techniques, very few systematic studies are available. Heinicke (1965a, 1965b, 1969) studied the differential development of two matched groups experiencing psychoanalytic psychotherapy either one or four times a week. The Anna Freud developmental profile, clinical ratings of this profile material, and test results were used as measures of outcome. The most general finding was that the children experiencing the more intensive treatment evidenced a higher level of ego integration, greater ego flexibility, and in general, a better adaptation following the end of treatment. The rate of improvement in reading as measured by achievement tests reflects this general finding. While the children seen more frequently made little progress during the first year of treatment, their reading accelerated greatly toward the end and particularly in the two years following the termination of treatment. Most important for this review is the fact that the children seen once a week did increase the rate of their improvement in reading during the first year but showed a striking drop in that rate in the year following treatment. This result is very similar to those obtained for the effects of remedial education. Although considerable gains were made in both forms of help during the period it was available, when this terminated, the child showed a serious drop in the rate of improvement.

While the above findings may well be restricted to the population actually studied, namely, school-aged boys in whom the reading disability was associated with poorly resolved psychological conflict, they are noteworthy because they indicate one form of treatment which does ensure a continuing high level of development after termination. This is not to underestimate the value of other techniques in bringing about immediate and often critical changes.

Where specific learning deficits are present as a by-product, for example, of central nervous dysfunction, ingenious methods of training must be tailored to the child and may have to be continued for long periods of time. It is, of course, also often necessary to combine various forms of help either at the same time or in a time sequence.

DISCUSSION

The primary conclusion emerging from this review is that no single factor or even set of factors can account for the heterogenous group of children included in the category of learning or reading disturbances. Insofar as the concept of specific learning disability implies one specific etiology, it is likely to be misleading. Some

systematic evidence was available in support of each of the four etiological hypotheses discussed. In certain groups of cases, the reading disturbance could be related to inadequate maturation; in others, to indications of brain dysfunction; and in still others, to the inadequate resolution of internal and external conflicts.

Our review also suggests that further efforts to derive support for these hypotheses should (1) derive a classification based on assessments of the child and family that tap all aspects of functioning and (2) attempt to isolate longitudinally those factors which predict the later development of learning disturbance.

In regard to the assessment of the child that is already disturbed, much lip service has been given to multiple assessments but few, if any, investigators or clinicians have in fact achieved this goal. It ought to be possible to combine the techniques suggested by Reitan, those developed by De Hirsch, those used to test in a variety of perceptual-cognitive areas, and those necessary to derive the kind of data needed to construct the Anna Freud diagnostic profile. The above review chapter could be seen as supplying promising suggestions as to which variables and assessments to include.

While for certain questions the application of such multiple assessments to unselected school populations may be most appropriate (Birch & Belmont, 1965), review of the literature suggests the need to define carefully the population to be studied. What criteria have been used to define the learning disturbance? Many studies have failed to specify the level of IQ performance. Other population characteristics only implicitly discussed in this chapter must be considered. A preponderance of boys among learning-disturbance children points to the importance of the sex distribution in the sample. Many interrelationships among variables vary as a function of sex (De Hirsch et al., 1966). The age of children is clearly important. Some of the evidence differentiating between the 6-year-old children who are trying to *learn* to read and the 10-year-old children whose task is to enhance their *performance* has been reported in this chapter. There is considerable evidence to indicate that the sociocultural and associated school opportunities have an important effect on determining the percentage of children reading below their potential (Eisenberg, 1966). For purposes of deriving a classification of different kinds of learning disturbance, it may also initially be important to consider and possibly control for gross variables such as clear-cut evidence of malnutrition, chronic illness, and obvious sensory or motor defects.

While it is possible that there are almost as many types of learning disturbance as there are children who suffer from one, some meaningful grouping ought to result from such multiple cross-sectional assessments. The validity of such a classification would then have to be tested further both by relating it to etiological factors and by studying the response of the various types of children to various forms of treatment.

Even if the above steps are taken and some fairly clear results emerge, the naming and arranging of the various types or clusters will not be easy. Review of the existing studies does indicate that the concepts of integration and flexibility of functioning should be considered in future classification efforts. Heinicke (1965a, 1969) used these concepts in organizing the profile data derived from the psychological assessment of the reading-disability child. Although the correlation of ego-integration scores with verbal IQ suggests the possible importance of semantic mediation factors in achieving integration, many other factors are obviously involved. The items in the ego-integration cluster indicate that inadequate resolution of psychological conflict and motivational factors are likely to affect this integration and, thus, IQ. That types of integration independent of the representational level

may have to be considered is suggested by the research done with the Illinois Test of Psycholinguistic Abilities. The sequencing-*integrative* factor isolated by McLeod (1967) stresses certain automatic-sequential integrative processes that are independent of functions measured by the verbal IQ. Birch and Belmont (1964) stress the importance in reading of adequate auditory-visual *integration*. Further work by Sterritt and Rudnick (1966a) emphasized that it is particularly the integration of pure auditory stimuli and visual-spatial representations of those stimuli that are likely to be difficult for the slow readers. Further research is needed to assess the specific role of visual perceptual and motor-coordination factors in the integration and flexibility of the child's functioning.

The concepts of integration and flexibility do also lend themselves to a discussion of the role of brain dysfunction or maturational lag in the child's reading disability. Cohn (1961) thinks in terms of the biological integrity of the child, and Rabinovitch (1968) discusses the quality of the neurological integration. Either deficits or insults are likely to interfere with integration and/or flexibility. The concept of inadequate integration is certainly implicit in Bender's (1958) discussion of the differential rates at which various patterns mature. It is very possible, then, that the dimensions of integration and flexibility in functioning can serve as a useful starting point for the classification of profiles of learning disturbance. Also implied by the emphasis on these concepts is the conclusion that a chronic reading disability tends to reflect disturbance which pervades many aspects of the child's personality. That is, the disturbance is not too often confined to one area of functioning.

Review of the various efforts to enhance the progressive development of the slow reader once more underlines the pervasive nature of these disturbances. It would seem, first of all, that considerable changes can be brought about in a year's time if the program is sufficiently intensive and broad in scope. Results obtained by Cruickshank et al. (1961) with a program of structured and sequenced teaching, by Wolf et al. (1968) with operant conditioning, by Balow (1965) with remedial education, by McConnell (1968) with an intensive sensory-perceptual language-training program, and by Heinicke (1965a, 1969) with once-a-week psychotherapeutic treatment of child and family are all impressive and well documented. Common to these various programs is the availability of help from an interested adult. As is clear from the follow-up evidence, when that person is no longer available, then the children tend to either lose all gain or revert to their previous rate of improvement. The question thus becomes one of determining those additional factors that bring about the type of change that is ultimately independent of the immediate presence of the helping person.

It may well be that some of the intensive programs now being developed can bring about changes which will ensure the continued and more adequate progress of the child. Heinicke (1965a, 1969) has demonstrated that child psychoanalysis is one such program. How far these findings can be generalized, however, remains to be seen.

Given the difficulty of reversing the disturbance once failure and further inadequate adaptation have been compounded, many investigators and clinicians have increasingly turned to the longitudinal study of normal populations in order both to trace the development of learning disturbances and to treat them at an early date. The general association between early signs of difficulty and later difficulty in school has already been well documented (Cohen, 1963; Kagan & Moss, 1962; Thomas, Chess & Birch, 1968; Westman et al., 1966). Needed now is the more specific longitudinal delineation of the different types of learning disturbance and what combination of variables accurately anticipates which of the children are going to have difficulty in a given environment. To facilitate this task, the variables that have been found to be predictive are summarized below. Included here are studies which made assessments of the child at the very beginning of first grade or before and which used as criteria various measures of reading achievement available on the child at the end of first grade or later.

Of the variables assessed during the first three years of life, only low birth weight and certain indices of possible neurological abnormality have come to the attention of this reviewer. In a review by Wiener (1962), a number of studies are cited showing a relation between premature birth and later reading difficulties. For example, Kawi and Pasamanick (1959) found that low infant birth weight and such childbearing experiences as toxemias of pregnancy and bleeding during pregnancy are associated to a slight extent ($P < .05$) with reading difficulties in the middle school years. Kawi and Pasamanick themselves recognize that using only those hospital records that were complete may have had an unknown biasing effect on the selection of the reading-disability and control groups.

Studies by De Hirsch et al. (1966) and Wiener et al. (1968) have also found a slight but significant relation between premature birth and reading difficulties in the early grades. Less consistent are the findings correlating variations in birth weight with the degree of later reading difficulties.

The most important fact to notice about the period soon after birth until entrance into kindergarten is the scarcity of studies relating child behavior to later reading achievement. As part of the extensive Fels longitudinal study, Kagan and Moss (1962) report that the child's involvement in task mastery (achievement behavior) at age 3 to 6 predicts this same achievement behavior from 6 to 10 years and his intellectual achievement from 10 to 14 years. IQ as assessed at 6 is also associated to the above two measures. It is further of interest to note that the ratings of intellectual achievement at ages 10 to 14 correlated .76 with the degree of protection shown by the mothers of boys during the first three years. This encouragement of dependency in the early years, followed in ages 3 to 10 by the encouragement and acceleration of mastery behavior, was most likely to lead to involvement in intellectual achievement.

As part of their study relating variables gathered in nursery school to later school adjustment, Westman et al. (1966) also found that of various indices anticipating the later adaptation, one relating to the family, namely, deviance in the family structure, correlated most strongly with later academic achievement. Deviance included consideration of such factors as parental death, divorce, adoption, remarriage, and a working mother.

Quite a number of studies have demonstrated a relationship between the child's behavior in kindergarten and reading performance from grades 1 to 5. The research of De Hirsch et al. (1966) specifies further the types of variables within this broad association that are likely to predict reading performance. Nineteen of thirty-seven kindergarten tests used correlated significantly with a reading achievement score in second grade. Many of these kindergarten tests demanded skills directly related to reading, for example, the ability to recognize and reproduce the words "boy" and "train." The Bender Visual Motor Gestalt Test was also an outstanding predictor. Only two personality tests were included, ratings of ego strength and work attitude, but each was predictive of later reading.

Two longitudinal studies have related personality dimensions as assessed in kindergarten to reading performance in the fifth grade. Ames and Walker (1964) found a significant association between a Rorschach prognosis score and later reading. A high Rorschach prognostic score in

this case indicated greater emotional maturity, more differentiated experiencing, and greater openness to stimulation. Attwell, Orpet, and Meyers (1967) reported the following kindergarten test behavior variables as relating to fifth-grade reading: the ability to concentrate on the test task, the effort displayed, the interest shown in the task, the self-confidence approaching the task, and the manual dexterity shown.

If the prediction from kindergarten tests has been one area of concentration, many studies have also focused on the interval from beginning first grade to the end of first grade. Kagan (1965) suggests that a certain amount of delay in a visual discrimination task is associated with reading scores at the end of first grade. Similarly, performance on auditory (Dykstra, 1966) and visual (Potter, 1949) discrimination tasks is slightly related to reading at the end of first grade. Tests demanding visual-motor as opposed to perceptual discriminatory skills are, in general, better predictors (Barrett, 1965; Koppitz, Mardis, & Stephens, 1961).

Examination of the above studies warrants few general conclusions. Clearly, a multitude of predictive variables need to be considered. It would seem, however, that the young child's ability to engage and persist in a task deserves much further study. The child's involvement in task mastery (Kagan & Moss, 1962), work attitude De Hirsch et al., 1966), the ability to concentrate on the test task, and the interest shown in the task (Attwell et al., 1967) all relate to this variable. It will be recalled that the ability to persist in a task was also a significant member of the ego-integration cluster (Heinicke, 1969).

CONCLUDING REMARKS

The overwhelming impression emerging from this review of the work of many investigators is that the very same degree and quality of reading disability and the very same form of behavior, such as hyperactivity or discrepancy in verbal versus performance IQ, not only are understood in very different ways but may indeed be linked to very different correlates and antecedents. Given this situation, many workers have abandoned the pursuit of issues of etiology and have concentrated on finding more efficient ways of helping the child.

Others, including this reviewer, feel that the issue of the etiology and classification of learning disturbances must be investigated not only for scientific but also for very practical reasons. There are many articles in the literature decrying the exclusive and tenacious use of psychotherapy with children who show clear evidence of neurological as well as personality dysfunction. More recently, other voices have been raised against the too ready diagnosis of minimal brain dysfunction and perceptual handicaps (Rabinovitch, 1968). Clearly, if the etiological predispositions of the clinician, whether explicit or not, prevent a child from getting the total kind of help he needs, then tragic consequences can easily emerge.

REFERENCES

Abraham, K. *Selected papers on psycho-analysis.* London: Hogarth, 1913, 1949.

Altus, G. A WISC profile for retarded readers. *Journal of Consulting Psychology,* 1956, **20,** 155–160.

Ames, L. B., & Walker, R. N. Prediction of later reading ability from kindergarten Rorschach and I.Q. scores. *Journal of Educational Psychology,* 1964, **55,** 309–313.

Attwell, A. A., Orpet, R. E., & Meyers, E. C. Kindergarten behavior ratings as a predictor of academic achievement. *Journal of School Psychology,* 1967, **6,** 43–46.

Balow, B. The long-term effect of remedial reading instruction. *The Reading Teacher,* 1965, **18,** 581–586.

Balow, I. H. Lateral dominance characteristics and reading achievement in the first grade. *The Journal of Psychology,* 1963, **55,** 323–328.

Barratt, E. S., & Baumgarten, D. L. The relationship of the WISC and Stanford Binet to school achievement. *Journal of Consulting Psychology,* 1957, **21,** 144. (Abstract)

Barrett, T. C. Visual discrimination tasks as predictors of first grade achievement. *The Reading Teacher,* 1965, **18,** 276–282.

Bateman, B. *The Illinois Test of Psycholinguistic Abilities in current research: Summaries of studies.* Urbana: University of Illinois Press, 1965.

Bayley, N., & Schaefer, E. Correlations of maternal and child behaviors with the development of mental abilities: Data from the Berkeley Growth Study. *Monographs of the Society for Research in Child Development,* 1964, 29, No. 6 (Whole No. 97).

Belmont, L., & Birch, H. G. Lateral dominance and right-left awareness in normal children. *Child Development,* 1963, **34,** 257–270.

Belmont, L., & Birch, H. G. Lateral dominance, lateral awareness, and reading disability. *Child Development,* 1965, **36,** 57–71.

Belmont, L., & Birch, H. G. The intellectual profile of retarded readers. *Perceptual and Motor Skills,* 1966, **22,** 787–816.

Bender, L. Problems in conceptualization and communication in children with developmental alexia. In P. M. Hoch & J. Zubin, *Psychopathology of communication.* New York: Grune & Stratton, 1958.

Benton, A. L. *Right-left discrimination and*

finger localization. New York: Hoeber-Harper, 1959.

Benton, A. L., & Kemble, J. D. Right-left orientation and reading disability. *Psychiatria et Neurologia,* 1960, **139,** 49–60.

Bing, E. Effect of child rearing practices on development of differential cognitive abilities. *Child Development,* 1963, **34,** 631–648.

Birch, H. G., & Belmont, L. Auditory-visual integration in normal and retarded readers. *American Journal of Orthopsychiatry,* 1964, **34,** 852–861.

Birch, H. G., & Belmont, L. Auditory-visual integration, intelligence and reading ability in school children. *Perceptual and Motor Skills,* 1965, **20,** 295–305.

Blanchard, P. Psychoanalytic contributions to the problems of reading disabilities. *Psychoanalytic Study of the Child,* 1946, **2,** 163–185.

Bliesmer, E. T. Evaluating progress in remedial reading programs. *The Reading Teacher,* 1962, **15,** 344–350.

Bond, G. L., & Fay, L. C. A report of the University of Minnesota Reading Clinic. *Journal of Educational Research,* 1950, **43,** 385–390.

Brodie, R. D., & Winterbottom, M. R. Failure in elementary school boys as a function of traumata, secrecy and derogation. *Child Development,* 1967, **38,** 701–711.

Burks, H. F., & Bruce, P. The characteristics of poor and good readers as disclosed by the Wechsler Intelligence Scale for Children. *Journal of Educational Psychology,* 1955, **46,** 488–493.

Buxbaum, E. The parents' role in the etiology of learning disabilities. *Psychoanalytic Study of the Child,* 1964, **19,** 421–447.

Chakrabarti, J., & Barker, G. Lateral dominance and reading ability. *Perceptual and Motor Skills,* 1966, **22,** 881–882.

Clements, S. D. Minimal brain dysfunction in children. *NINDB Monograph* No. 3, U.S. Department of Health, Education, and Welfare, 1966.

Cohen, T. B. Prediction of underachievement in kindergarten children. *Archives of General Psychiatry,* 1963, **9,** 444–450.

Cohn, R. Delayed acquisition of reading and writing abilities in children. A neurological study. *Archives of Neurology,* 1961, **4,** 49–60.

Cohn, R. The neurological study of children with learning disabilities. *Exceptional Children,* 1964, **31,** 179–185.

Coleman, J. C., & Rasof, B. Intellectual factors in learning disorders. *Perceptual and Motor Skills,* 1963, **16,** 139–152.

Coleman, R. I., & Deutsch, C. P. Lateral dominance and right-left discrimination: A comparison of normal and retarded readers. *Perceptual and Motor Skills,* 1964, **19,** 43–50.

Critchley, M. Isolation of the specific dyslexic. In A. Keeney and V. Keeney (Eds.), *Dyslexia.* St. Louis: Mosby, 1968. Pp. 17–20.

Cruickshank, W. M., et al. *A teaching method for brain-injured and hyperactive children: A demonstration-pilot study.* Syracuse, N.Y.: Syracuse University Press, 1961.

Dave, R. H. The identification and measurement of educational process variables that are related to educational achievement. Unpublished doctoral dissertation, University of Chicago, 1963.

Davids, A., & Andrews, J. Changes in academic attainment and personality characteristics following a special educational program for underachieving secondary school boys. *Psychology in the Schools,* 1964, **1,** 388–391.

De Hirsch, K., et al. *Predicting reading failure: A preliminary study of reading, writing and spelling disabilities in preschool children.* New York: Harper & Row, 1966.

Di Meo, K. *Visual motor skills: Response characteristics and pre-reading behavior.* Winter Haven, Fla.: Winter Haven Lions Research Foundation, 1967.

Dockrell, W. B. The use of Wechsler Intelligence Scale for Children in the diagnosis of retarded readers. *Alberta Journal of Educational Research,* 1960, **6,** 86–91.

Douglass, M. P. Laterality and knowledge of directions. *The Elementary School Journal,* 1965, **66,** 69–74.

Dudek, S. Z., & Lester, E. P. The good child facade in chronic underachievers. *American Journal of Orthopsychiatry,* 1968, **38,** 153–160.

Duggins, L. Experimental studies in auditory perception in beginning reading. *Bulletin of Southeastern Louisiana College,* 1956, **12,** 12–18.

Dykstra, R. Auditory discrimination abilities and beginning reading achievement. *Reading Research Quarterly,* 1966, **1,** 5–34.

Eisenberg, L. The epidemiology of reading retardation and a program for preventive intervention. In J. Money (Ed.), *The disabled reader.* Baltimore: Johns Hopkins, 1966. Pp. 3–19.

Feldmann, S. C., Schmidt, D. E., & Deutsch, C. P. Effect of auditory training on reading skills of retarded readers. *Perceptual and Motor Skills,* 1968, **26,** 467–480.

Fenichel, O. The scoptophilic instinct and identification. *International Journal of Psychoanalysis,* 1937, **18,** 24.

Freeberg, N. E., & Payne, D. T. Parental influence on cognitive development in early childhood: A review. *Child Development,* 1967, **38,** 67–87.

Freeman, R. D. Special education and the electroencephalogram. Marriage of convenience. *Journal of Special Education,* 1967, **2,** 61–71.

Freud, A. *Normality and pathology in childhood.* New York: International Universities Press, 1965.

Freud, S. *Psychogenic visual disturbance according to psychoanalytic conceptions* (1910). Standard edition. Vol. 11. London: Hogarth, 1949.

Freud, S. *Inhibitions, symptoms, and anxiety* (1926). Standard edition. Vol. 20. London: Hogarth, 1959.

Frierson, E. C., & Barke, W. B. *Educating children with learning disabilities: Selected readings.* New York: Appleton-Century-Crofts, 1967.

Frostig, M., et al. The Marianne Frostig Developmental Test of Visual Perception, 1963 standardization. *Perceptual and Motor Skills,* 1964, **19,** 463–499.

Galifret-Granjon, N., & Ajuriaguerra, J. de. Trouble de l'apprentisage de la lecture et dominance laterale. *Encephale,* 1951, **3,** 385–398.

Gallagher, J. J., & Kirk, S. *The tutoring of brain-injured mentally retarded children.* Springfield, Ill.: Charles C Thomas, 1960.

Glass, G. V. A critique of experiments on the role of neurological organization in reading performance. *ERIC Document Reproduction Service,* 1966, ED 013 523.

Goins, J. T. Visual perceptual abilities and early reading processes. *Supplementary Educational Monographs,* 1958, 1–108.

Graham, E. E. Wechsler-Bellevue and WISC

scattergrams of unsuccessful readers. *Journal of Consulting Psychology,* 1952, **16,** 268–271.

Grunebaum, M. G., Hurwitz, I., Prentice, N. M., & Sperry, B. M. Fathers of sons with primary neurotic learning inhibitions. *American Journal of Orthopsychiatry,* 1962, **32,** 462–472.

Hallgren, B. Specific dyslexia ("congenital word-blindness"). A clinical and genetic study. *Acta Psychiatrica et Neurologica Scandinavica,* 1950, Suppl. 65.

Harris, A. J. *Harris tests of lateral dominance.* New York: Psychological Corporation, 1947, 1956.

Harris, A. J. Lateral dominance, directional confusion, and reading disability. *Journal of Psychology,* 1957, **44,** 283–294.

Heinicke, C. M. Some antecedents and correlates of guilt fear in young boys. Unpublished doctoral dissertation, Harvard University, 1953.

Heinicke, C. M. Frequency of psychotherapeutic session as a factor affecting the child's developmental status. *Psychoanalytic Study of the Child,* 1965, **22,** 42–98. (a)

Heinicke, C. M. Notes on the strategy of a child psychotherapy project. *Reiss-Davis Clinic Bulletin,* 1965, **2,** 80–86. (b)

Heinicke, C. M. Frequency of psychotherapeutic session as a factor affecting outcome. Analysis of clinical ratings and test results. *Journal of Abnormal Psychology,* 1969, **74,** 553–560.

Hellman, I. Some observations on mothers of children with intellectual inhibitions. *Psychoanalytic Study of the Child,* 1954, **9,** 259–273.

Hellmuth, J. (Ed.). *Learning disorders.* Vols. 1, 2, and 3. Seattle: Special Child Publications, 1965, 1966, 1968.

Hess, R. D. Effects of maternal interaction on cognitions of pre-school children in several social strata. Paper presented at the meeting of the American Psychological Association, Chicago, September, 1965.

Hirst, L. S. The usefulness of a two-way analysis of WISC sub-tests in the diagnosis of remedial reading problems. *Journal of Experimental Education,* 1960, **29,** 153–160.

Ingram, T. T. S. Specific developmental disorders of speech in childhood. *Brain,* 1959, **82,** 450–467.

Ingram, T. T. S. Paediatric aspects of specific developmental dysphasia, dyslexia and dysgraphia. *Cerebral Palsy Bulletin,* 1960, **2,** 254–277.

Ingram, T. T. S., & Reid, J. F. Developmental aphasia observed in a department of child psychiatry. *Archives of Disease in Childhood,* 1956, **31,** 161–172.

Jarvis, V. The visual problem in reading disability. *Psychoanalytic Study of the Child,* 1958, **13,** 451–470.

Johnson, D. J., & Myklebust, H. R. *Learning disabilities.* New York: Grune & Stratton, 1967.

Kagan, J. Reflection-impulsivity and reading ability in primary grade children. *Child Development,* 1965, **36,** 609–628.

Kagan, J., & Moss, H. A. *Birth to maturity.* New York: Wiley, 1962.

Kallos, G. L., Grabow, J. M., & Guarino, E. A. The WISC profile of disabled readers. *Personality and Guidance Journal,* 1961, **39,** 476–478.

Kass, C. E. Some psychological correlates of severe reading disability. Unpublished doctoral dissertation, University of Illinois, 1962.

Katz, P. A. Verbal discrimination performance of disadvantaged children: Stimulus and subject variables. *Child Development*, 1967, **38**, 233–242.

Katz, P. A., & Deutsch, M. Relation of auditory-visual shifting to reading achievement. *Perceptual and Motor Skills,* 1963, **17**, 327–332.

Katz, P. A., & Deutsch, M. Modality of stimulus presentation in serial learning for retarded and normal readers. *Perceptual and Motor Skills,* 1964, **19**, 627–633.

Kawi, A. A., & Pasamanick, B. Prenatal and paranatal factors in the development of childhood reading disorders. *Monographs of the Society for Research in Child Development,* 1959, **24**, 4.

Kershner, J. R. Doman-Delacato's theory of neurological organization applied with retarded children. *Exceptional Children,* 1968, **34**, 441–450.

Kinsbourne, M., & Warrington, E. K. The developmental Gerstmann syndrome. In J. Money (Ed.), *The disabled reader.* Baltimore: Johns Hopkins, 1966. Pp. 59–71.

Kirk, S. A., & McCarthy, J. J. The Illinois Test of Psycholinguistic Abilities. An approach to differential diagnosis. *American Journal of Mental Deficiency,* 1961, **66**, 399–412.

Koppitz, E. The Bender Gestalt test and learning disturbances in young children. *Journal of Clinical Psychology,* 1958, **14**, 292–295.

Koppitz, E. M., Mardis, V., & Stephens, T. A note on screening school beginners with the Bender Gestalt test. *Journal of Educational Psychology,* 1961, **52**, 80–81.

Koppitz, E. M., Sullivan, J., Blyth, D. D., & Shelton, J. Prediction of first grade school achievement with the Bender Gestalt test and human figure drawings. *Journal of Clinical Psychology,* 1959, **15**, 164–168.

Lindemann, E. B., Rosenblith, J. F., Allinsmith, W., Budd, L. M., & Shapiro, S. Predicting school adjustment before entry. *Journal of School Psychology,* 1967, **6**, 24–42.

Lovell, K., Byrne, C., & Richardson, B. A further study of the educational progress of children who had received remedial instruction. *British Journal of Educational Psychology,* 1963, **33**, 3–9.

Lovell, K., Johnson, L. R., & Platts, D. A summary of a study of the reading ages of children who had been given remedial teaching. *British Journal of Educational Psychology,* 1962, **32**, 66–71.

Macmeeken, A. M. *Ocular dominance in relation to developmental aphasia.* London: University of London Press, 1939.

McConnell, F. Sensory-perceptual language training to prevent school learning disabilities in culturally deprived preschool children. *Office of Education Progress Report,* February, 1968.

McGlannan, F. K. Familial characteristics of genetic dyslexia. Preliminary report from a pilot study. *Journal of Learning Disabilities,* 1968, **1**, 185–191.

McLeod, J. Some perceptual factors related to childhood dyslexia. *Slow Learning Child,* 1967, **14**, 5–12.

Miller, D. R., & Westman, J. C. Reading disability as a condition of family stability. *Family Process,* 1964, **3**, 66–76.

Milner, E. A study of the relationship between reading readiness in grade one school children and patterns of parent-child interaction. *Child Development,* 1951, **22**, 95–112.

Morrow, W., & Wilson, R. Family relations of bright high-achieving and underachieving high school boys. *Child Development,* 1961, **32,** 501–510.

Mouly, G. J., & Grant V. A study of growth to be expected of retarded readers. *Journal of Educational Research,* 1956, **49,** 461–465.

Mueller, M., & Smith, J. O. The stability of language age modifications over time. *American Journal of Mental Deficiency,* 1964, **68,** 537–539.

Murphy, H. A. Evaluation of specific training in auditory and visual discrimination on beginning reading. Unpublished doctoral dissertation, Boston University, 1943.

Neville, D. A comparison of the WISC patterns of male retarded and nonretarded readers. *Journal of Educational Research,* 1961, **54,** 195–197.

Olson, A. V. Relation of achievement test scores and specific reading abilities to the Frostig Developmental Test of Visual Perception. *Perceptual and Motor Skills,* 1966, **22,** 179–184. (a)

Olson, A. V. School achievement, reading ability, and specific visual perception skills in the third grade. *The Reading Teacher,* 1966, **19,** 490–492. (b)

Orton, S. T. *Reading, writing and speech problems in children.* New York: Norton, 1937.

Osgood, C. E. *Contemporary approaches to cognition: A behavioristic analysis.* Cambridge, Mass.: Harvard University Press, 1957.

Paterra, M. E. A study of thirty-three WISC scattergrams of retarded readers. *Elementary English,* 1963, **40,** 394–405.

Pearson, G. H. J. A survey of learning difficulties in children. *Psychoanalytic Study of the Child,* 1952, **7,** 322–386.

Potter, M. C. Perception of symbol orientation and early reading success. *Contributions to Education,* No. 939. New York: Teachers College, Columbia University, 1949.

Raab, S., Deutsch, M., & Friedman, A. Perceptual shifting and set in normal school children of different reading achievement levels. *Perceptual and Motor Skills,* 1960, **10,** 187–192.

Rabinovitch, R. D. Dyselxia. Psychiatric considerations. In J. Money (Ed.), *Reading disability. Progress and research needs in dyselxia.* Baltimore: Johns Hopkins, 1962. Pp. 73–79.

Rabinovitch, R. D. Reading problems in children. Definitions and classifications. In A. Keeney and V. Keeney (Eds.), *Dyslexia.* St. Louis: Mosby, 1968. Pp. 1–10.

Rabinovitch, R. D., et al. A research approach to reading retardation. *Research Publication of Association of Nervous and Mental Disease,* 1954, **34,** 363–387.

Ragland, G. G. The performance of educable mentally handicapped students of differing reading ability on the IPTA. Unpublished doctoral dissertation, University of Virginia, 1964.

Reed, H. B. C. Some relationships between neurological dysfunction and behavioral deficits in children. Paper presented at the Conference on Children with Minimal Brain Impairment, University of Illinois, Urbana, 1963.

Reed, H. B. C., Reitan, R. M., & Klove, H. Influence of cerebral lesions on psychological test performances of older children. *Journal of Consulting Psychology,* 1965, **29,** 247–251.

Reed, J. C. Lateralized finger agnosia and reading achievement at ages 6 and 10. *Child Development,* 1967, **38,** 213–220.

Reed, J. C. The ability deficits of good and poor readers. *Journal of Learning Disabilities,* 1968, **1,** 134–139.

Reitan, R. M. Relationships between neurological and psychological variables and their implications for reading instruction. In H. A. Robinson (Ed.), *Meeting individual differences in reading.* Chicago: University of Chicago Press, 1964. Pp. 100–110.

Reitan, R. M., & Heineman, C. E. Interactions of neurological deficits and emotional disturbances in children with learning disorders: Methods for differential assessment. In J. Hellmuth (Ed.), *Learning disorders.* Vol. 3. Seattle: Special Child Publications, 1968. Pp. 95–135.

Robbins, M. P. Test of the Doman-Delacato rationale with retarded readers. *Journal of the American Medical Association,* 1967, **202,** 389–393.

Robeck, M. C. Subtest patterning of problem readers on WISC. *California Journal of Educational Research,* 1960, **11,** 110–115.

Robeck, M. C. Intellectual strengths and weaknesses shown by reading clinic subjects on the WISC. *Journal of Developmental Reading,* 1962, **5,** 120–129.

Robeck, M. C. Readers who lacked word analysis skills: A group diagnosis. *Journal of Educational Research,* 1963, **56,** 432–434.

Rosen, C. L. An experimental study of visual perceptual training and reading achievement in first grade. *Perceptual and Motor Skills,* 1966, **22,** 979–986.

Rubenstein, B. O., et al. Learning problems. 2. Learning impotence: A suggested diagnostic category. *American Journal of Orthopsychiatry,* 1959, **29,** 315–323.

Rubin, E. Z., & Braun, J. S. Behavioral and learning disabilities associated with cognitive-motor dysfunction. *Perceptual and Motor Skills,* 1968, **26,** 171–180.

Rudnick, M., Sterritt, G. M., & Flax, M. Auditory and visual rhythm perception and reading ability. *Child Development,* 1967, **38,** 581.

Sawyer, R. I. Does the Wechsler Intelligence Scale for Children discriminate between mildly disabled and severely disabled readers? *The Elementary School Journal,* 1965, **66,** 97–103.

Shaw, M. C. Underachievement: Useful construct or misleading illusion. *Psychology in the Schools,* 1968, **5,** 41–46.

Sheldon, M. S., & Garton, J. A note on "A WISC profile for retarded readers." *Alberta Journal of Educational Research,* 1959, **5,** 264–267.

Shimota, H. E. Reading skills in emotionally disturbed institutionalized adolescents. *Journal of Educational Research,* 1964, **58,** 106–111.

Silver, A. A., & Hagin, R. Specific reading disability: Delineation of the syndrome and relationship to cerebral dominance. *Comprehensive Psychiatry,* 1960, **1,** 126–134.

Silver, A. A., & Hagin, R. A. Specific reading disability: An approach to diagnosis and treatment. *Journal of Special Education,* 1967, **1,** 109–118.

Silver, A. A., Hagin, R. A., & Hersh, M. F. Reading disability: Teaching through stimulation of deficit perceptual areas. *American Journal of Orthopsychiatry,* 1967, **37,** 744–752.

Skeels, H. M. Adult status of children with contrasting early life experiences. A follow-up study. *Monographs of the Society of Research in Child Development,* 1966, **31** (3, Whole No. 105).

Smith, J. O. Effects of a group language development program upon the psycholinguistic abilities of educable mental retardates. *Peabody College Special Education Research Monograph Series,* 1962, No. 1.

Sontag, L., Baker, C., & Nelson, V. Mental

growth and personality development. A longitudinal study. *Monographs of the Society for Research in Child Development,* 1958, **23** (2, Whole No. 68).

Sperry, B., et al. Renunciation and denial in learning difficulties. *American Journal of Orthopsychiatry,* 1958, **28,** 98–111.

Spradlin, J. E. Assessment of speech and language of retarded children: The Parsons Language Sample. *Journal of Hearing and Speech Disorders,* 1963 (Monogr. Suppl. 10).

Staats, A. W., et al. Cognitive behavior modification: "Motivated learning" reading treatment with subprofessional therapy-technicians. *Behavior Research and Therapy,* 1967, **5,** 283–299.

Sterritt, G. M., & Rudnick, M. Auditory and visual rhythm perception in relation to reading ability in fourth grade boys. *Perceptual and Motor Skills,* 1966, **22,** 859–964. (a)

Sterritt, G. M., & Rudnick, M. Reply to Birch and Belmont. *Perceptual and Motor Skills,* 1966, **23,** 662. (b)

Sterritt, G. M., Rudnick, M., & Martin, V. E. Research design problems. Paper presented at the meeting of the Society for Research in Child Development, New York, 1967.

Stevens, D. A., Boydstun, J. A., Dykman, R. A., Peters, J. E., & Sinton, D.W. Presumed minimal brain dysfunction in children. Relationship to performance on selected behavioral tests. *Archives of General Psychiatry,* 1967, 281–285.

Strachey, J. Some unconscious factors in reading. *International Journal of Psychoanalysis,* 1930, **11,** 322–331.

Sylvester, E., & Kunst, M. S. Psychodynamic aspects of the reading problem. *American Journal of Orthopsychiatry,* 1943, **13,** 69–76.

Thomas, A., Chess, S., & Birch, H. *Temperament and behavior disorders in children.* New York: New York University Press, 1968.

Walters, R. H., et al. A study of reading disability. *Journal of Consulting Psychology,* 1961, **25,** 277–283.

Westman, J., et al. Relationships between nursery school behavior and later adjustment. Paper presented at the meeting of the American Orthopsychiatric Association, San Francisco, 1966.

Wiener, G. Psychologic correlates of premature birth: A review. *The Journal of Nervous and Mental Disease,* 1962, **134,** 129–144.

Wiener, G., Rider, R. V., Oppel, W. C., & Harper, P. A. Correlates of low birth weight. Psychological status of eight to ten years of age. *Pediatric Research,* 1968, **2,** 110–118.

Wolf, M. M., Giles, D. K., & Hall, V. R. Experiments with token reinforcement in a remedial class room. *Behavior Research and Therapy,* 1968, **6,** 51–64.

Wolf, R. M. The identification and measurement of environmental process variables related to intelligence. Unpublished doctoral dissertation, University of Chicago, 1964.

Yarrow, L. J. Separation from parents during early childhood. In M. L. Hoffman & L. W. Hoffman (Eds.), *Review of child development research.* Vol. 1. New York: Russell Sage Foundation, 1964.

Zangwill, O. L. Dyslexia in relation to cerebral dominance. In J. Money (Ed.), *Reading disability.* Baltimore: Johns Hopkins, 1962.

Zedler, E. Y. Screening underachieving pupils for risk of neurological impairment. In J. Hellmuth (Ed.), *Learning disorders.* Vol. 3. Seattle: Special Child Publications, 1968. Pp. 251–274.

22 | Certain Psychosomatic Disorders[1]

Kenneth Purcell, Jonathan Weiss,
and William Hahn

Any chapter whose title includes the word *psychosomatic* ought at least to indicate the posture of its authors on the definition of the problem. An excellent paper by Graham (1967) proposes that *psychological* and *physical* refer to different ways of talking about the *same* event and not to different events. Thus, *mental* and *physical* are regarded as names of different languages, not of different events. Choice of language is governed by convenience, suitability, precision, and personal preference. Quoting Graham (1967, p. 59), ". . . psychosomatic or psychophysiologic research is the effort to write the dictionary between the two languages." This point of view suggests that all illness and all normal functioning are "psychosomatic."

There are many implications of the choice of definitions. The observer's view of the term *psychosomatic* may have important practical implications both for his research and for his clinical practice. One connecting link here is the common use of the terms *functional* and *organic*. Often the *mind* is not believed capable of producing structural or organic changes (how can a thought produce a hole in the duodenum?), although it is held that *mental* influences can produce functional disorders. These assumptions frequently lead to the conclusion that functional disorders are not physical, despite the fact that one can easily provide a physical language description of something as traditionally functional as anxiety.

This line of reasoning may also be associated with serious distortion in the evaluation of symptom severity. A frequently acted-on belief appears to be that a somatic symptom induced by psychological provocation cannot really be serious—certainly not as serious as the same symptom induced by physical provocation. For example, the belief that emotionally triggered asthma is "fake asthma" has been found not only among relatives of the patient but also, on occasion, among physicians. The latter situation once led to a patient in the early stages of status asthmat-

[1] Preparation of this chapter was supported in part by U.S. Public Health Service research grants HD 01060 and HD 01529 to the senior author.

icus (severe, continuous asthma resistant to treatment) being referred for psychotherapy with the physician feeling that "it can't really be serious since everybody knows this patient's asthma is all psychic."

Thus, labeling a disorder *psychological* can bias the observer (clinician or researcher) against making a vigorous attempt at a physical language description of the somatic processes underlying functional symptoms. This, in turn, may blind one to effective therapeutic procedures which are associated with "physical" descriptions and concepts. Similarly, applying the label *physical* to a disorder makes unlikely any serious effort to determine psychological or emotional factors in the etiology or maintenance of the syndrome. In brief, either a purely physical or a purely psychological approach violates the psychosomatic concept.

THE CHILD AND PSYCHOSOMATIC DISORDER

In general, investigations of psychosomatic disorders have dealt with adults. Yet the literature on the biological effects of varying early experience is impressive. Perhaps most dramatic has been the observation that institutionalized infants receiving apparently adequate physical care but little stimulation frequently become extremely apathetic, develop severe symptoms of wasting, and die (Spitz, 1945). While aspects of Spitz's methodology have been justifiably criticized (Pinneau, 1955), he nevertheless correctly drew attention to social stimulation as a variable affecting the biological well-being of a young organism. Previously this syndrome had been described solely in the language of physical causation.

The more extensive and systematic data from research with animals clearly point to the profound biological consequences of differential early experience. For example, Krech, Rosenzweig, and Bennett (1966) have found that exposing rats to complex experiences increases cortical weight and certain aspects of cerebral chemistry activities as compared with brains of littermates kept under colony conditions or isolated. Ader and his colleagues (Ader, 1965; Ader & Friedman, 1965a, 1965b) have reported that rats handled in the first twenty-one days of life showed decreased susceptibility to gastric lesions induced by immobilization and to the growth of transplanted tumors than did control groups. Levine and Mullins (1966) have emphasized that most effects of differential rearing conditions on young organisms are mediated via hormonal pathways. Levine (1967), for example, has reported data showing the relevance of the adrenocortical response in determining the effects of handling.

Thus, there is little doubt that psychologically defined stimulation in young organisms may be associated with significant physiologically and biochemically defined changes. Moreover, these early experiences play a part in psychophysiological reactions in later life. Therefore, one cannot stress too much the need for understanding events in the life of the developing child simultaneously in the languages of psychology, physiology, endocrinology, etc.

PSYCHOSOMATIC MODELS

It is the purpose of this section to outline, briefly and for background only, the major conceptual approaches that have been generated to account for psychosomatic disorders. The problems to which these models are directed are: (1) Person specificity—who is likely to develop a psychosomatic symptom and why? (2) Organ specificity—what factors determine the "target" organ? (3) Mediating mechanisms—how are psychological experiences translated into physiological symptoms? The mechanisms problem as it is raised in relation to a psychosomatic disorder may be interpreted in at least two different ways. The more traditional questions involving mechanisms are: What are the pathways between the site at which relevant stimuli impinge and the end organs at which symptoms are manifested? What are the specific end-organ responses, e.g., spasm, hypersecretion, giving rise to the symptom? A second type of question is: Are symptoms the peripheral manifestation of a unitary, organismic response to relevant stimuli, or does that organismic response merely lay the groundwork for the action of other factors, such as bacterial invasion, that are responsible for the appearance of symptoms? Thus, Karush and Daniels (1953) point to the possibility that the same chemical and neurophysiological defects leading to disintegrative psychological responses may produce disintegrative behavior of the peripheral organ.

There have been a number of theoretical models proposed over the past several decades. The majority of these grew out of experience with clinical material and are formulations couched in clinical language. Two are more closely bound to the laboratory, tend to involve animal experimentation, and are couched in learning-theory terms.

Freud's early thinking held that psychosomatic symptoms are essentially conversion reactions and represent symbolic expressions of repressed feelings and thoughts. Many current theorists reject these views. Later, Dunbar (1943) attempted to correlate personality profiles and types of psychosomatic disorder. She believed that some common agent exercises control over both voluntary behavior patterns and the behavior of the vegetative system and that it therefore made sense to seek correlations between these. Alexander (1950), in turn, suggested the core concept of conflict or emotional specificity. For example, the formation of ulcers was hypothesized to be associated with unresolved dependency conflicts. Organ choice, as in this example involving the gastrointestinal tract and dependency wishes, was thought to be related to the

nature of the conflict. Alexander also included biological predisposition as a significant factor in organ choice. Another type of specificity explanation has attempted to link crucial early-life situations to later disorder, e.g., toilet-training problems leading to constipation and diarrhea (Halliday, 1948). In a 1955 review of specificity investigations, Hamilton (1955, p. 205) concluded that "in spite of the repeated claims made that there exists a specific type of personality for each particular psychosomatic disorder, in fact, the descriptions of the different types are monotonously alike."

In recent years, Graham and his colleagues (Graham & Graham, 1961; Graham, Kabler, & Graham, 1962; Graham, Lundy, Benjamin, Kabler, Lewis, Kunish, & Graham, 1962; Graham & Kunish, 1965) have proposed a sophisticated offshoot of the specificity concept which involves a learned covariation between an attitude and a physiological response. On the basis of both interview and experimental studies, these investigators concluded that a given attitude is associated with a given psychosomatic disorder and with a physiological response consistent with that psychosomatic disorder. For example, the attitude of feeling in danger and on guard was found, as predicted, to be more applicable to hypertensive patients than to nonhypertensive patients. Moreover, healthy subjects were given, on separate days, two attitude suggestions under hypnosis. One was associated with hypertension (that he had to be on guard against assault) and the other with hives (feelings of being unfairly treated and not able to think of anything to do about it). Diastolic blood pressure rose significantly more during the hypertension suggestion than during the hives suggestion, with the reverse being true of skin temperature.

One of the broadest and most productive viewpoints has been that of Wolff (1950), who thought in terms of life stress eliciting a biological reaction pattern to which the individual is genetically predisposed. Many of the studies emanating from investigators identified with this viewpoint stress the careful, detailed, and quantitative exploration of the individual case, a much needed element in psychosomatic research (Holmes, Treuting, & Wolff, 1950; Stevenson, 1950; Wolf & Wolff, 1943).

We shall devote somewhat more space to learning theories of psychosomatic symptoms, as these may be less familiar to the reader. Some of the innate responses elicited by an emotion, such as fear, are physiologically defined and may produce a variety of psychosomatic symptoms (e.g., cardiac, respiratory, gastrointestinal). Most investigators and clinicians working in the field of psychosomatic disorders are aware of the mechanism of classical conditioning of glandular and visceral responses. Gantt (1944) conducted a renowned experiment demonstrating the classical conditioning of persistent and abnormal visceral responses. Working with a dog, Nick, Gantt produced an experimental neurosis by putting the animal in a situation requiring difficult or impossible discriminations between stimuli. Throughout Nick's laboratory life, a marked tachycardia was noted whenever he was brought into the experimental environment or exposed to any specific stimuli connected with his environment, such as a metronome. Changes in gastrointestinal, respiratory, and genital-urinary system function were also noted in association with conditioned stimuli. Gantt observed that the existence of the pathological state (the experimental neurosis) greatly enhanced the ease with which these conditioned responses were formed, caused their prolonged persistence without further exposure to the unconditioned stimulus, and substantially increased their stability and intensity as compared with conditioned responses developed in nonpathological animals.

Graham and Graham (1961) also discuss the question of how disease can occur as a learned response without prior occurrence as an unlearned response. They suggest that physiological activities of the same type as in disease, but of less intensity or duration, can become associated through learning with stimuli previously ineffective in provoking them. It is then possible for these physiological responses to be evoked with sufficient intensity and duration to be labeled *disease*. The conditions under which this might occur include increases in drive (perhaps analogous to Gantt's experimental neurosis) and presentation of a complex stimulus whose individual components have been separately conditioned to the response. Still another possibility for acquiring disease as a learned response without the need of its occurring as an unlearned response involves mediated learning. By way of a mediating response such as a word or image, a variety of stimuli could become associated with the relevant physiological activity without the need for the unconditioned stimulus to occur.

As suggested already, the traditional view has been that psychosomatic symptoms, mediated by the autonomic nervous system, are subject only to classical conditioning. By contrast, Miller and his associates (DiCara & Miller, 1968; Miller & Banuazizi, 1968; Miller & Carmona, 1967) have produced an impressive series of studies showing that visceral or glandular responses such as heart rate, rate of intestinal contraction, and salivation are subject to instrumental learning. The heart-rate study (Miller & DiCara, 1967) will illustrate the general paradigm: Two groups of rats started with initial heart rates of about 400 beats per minute. The individual animal's heart rate, as is true of other biologic functions, shows a degree of spontaneous fluctuation, i.e., slight increases or decreases. By first rewarding small changes in the desired direction and then setting the criteria at progressively more difficult levels, Miller was able to shape rats to learn larger changes, averaging 20 percent, in heart-rate increases or decreases. Follow-up tests (Miller, 1969) showed—and this is most impressive and important in terms of its clinical implications — that instrumentally learned changes in heart rate can be retrained for at least a three-month period without further practice. Further studies have shown that such responses as blood pressure and rate of urine formation in the kidney can be modified by immediate reward (Miller, 1969).

The clinical significance of these findings lies in the fact that instrumental learning is so much more flexible than classical learning. Reinforcement of changes in visceral responses is not limited to unconditioned stimuli which elicit as an unconditioned response the specific change to be learned. Instead, any one of a variety of rewards and punishments, including what are commonly described as secondary gains, that may produce learning of skeletal responses may also modify visceral responses involved in psychosomatic symptoms. Miller (1966) offers the example of two children who are extremely frightened by school examinations and who display a variety of psychosomatic symptoms. If the mother of one child is concerned about pallor and fainting, she will reward the occurrence of those cardiovascular-based symptoms by keeping her child away from school on the day of an examination. Conversely, if the second child is ignored when he shows fainting symptoms but is rewarded by escape from school when he shows gastrointestinal symptoms, then he should learn to produce the latter type of symptom.

We have chosen to organize the remainder of this chapter around three psychosomatic disorders, partly to explore the research approaches taken with different symptoms and partly to examine specific hypotheses that have been developed to explain specific disorders, as contrasted to the more general theoretical statements reviewed above. Asthma is the most common disorder in children which is associated with the label *psychosomatic* and, for this reason, will be explored in the greatest depth.

ASTHMA

Historically, bronchial asthma has traversed the path from being viewed first as a symptom of central nervous system (CNS) origin, then as a fundamentally immunological disorder, and now as a symptom whose interpretation depends on the particular professional spectacles through which one is peering. Most clinical allergists contend that asthma is caused primarily, if not exclusively, by sensitization to allergic elements in the patient's environment. Professionals in the mental health fields assert that psychological conflicts serve as the triggering agent and/or basic cause of asthma in many patients. Pediatricians and internists seem to fall somewhere in between, although usually closer to the allergist group. Infection is recognized by all as a frequently relevant factor. Often the medically oriented practitioner will note the aggravating effects of emotional stress on asthma while exempting emotional processes from any significant etiological role. The attitudes of each discipline are at least partially rooted in clinical reality in that a number of factors are relevant to the symptom of asthma, with the significance of each factor varying from one patient to the next and even from one appearance of the symptom to the next in the same patient.

Description

Asthma is a symptom complex characterized by an increased responsiveness of the trachea, major bronchi, and peripheral bronchioles to various stimuli and manifested by extensive narrowing of the airways, which causes impairment of air exchange, primarily in expiration, and wheezing. A narrowing of the airway may be due to edema of the walls, increased mucus secretion, spasm of the bronchial muscles, or collapse of the posterior walls of the trachea and bronchi during certain types of forced expiration. The significance of these factors may vary from patient to patient and from attack to attack in the same patient. Similarly, the nature of the stimulation triggering these physiological processes may vary from patient to patient and attack to attack.

Hereditary factors. Incidence of asthma in the families of asthmatic patients appears to be relatively high when compared with a similar group of nonasthmatic patients (Criep, 1962; Ratner & Silberman, 1953; Schwartz, 1952). However, it is also possible to find substantial numbers of asthmatics with essentially negative family histories. After surveying their own experience, Ratner and Silberman (1953, p. 374) comment, "It seems to us, from the data of Schwartz, that what may be inherited is not the capacity to become sensitized (immunologically), but a respiratory tract which may react with the production of asthma or rhinitis due to a multiplicity of stimuli, one of which may be the antigen-antibody mechanism." This hypothesis of organ vulnerability is similar to what is postulated for patients who may develop cardiovascular or gastrointestinal symptoms.

Incidence. The incidence of asthma in the population has been observed to be between 2.5 and 5 percent, depending upon the method of estimate. A survey by the Public Health Service in 1957–1958 suggested that nearly 4,500,000 persons in this country were suffering from asthma at that time. About 60 percent of the population of asthmatics was below the age of 17. Asthma occurs in boys twice as often as among girls, although the sex ratio evens out during the adult years. There are no well-documented explanations for this sex difference. Although asthma is relatively uncommon in infancy (Smyth, 1962), it has been diagnosed during the first few months of life and has been reported to start as late as the seventh decade.

Symptom course. On the one hand, there is reason to be moderately optimistic about the future

of a large percentage of asthmatic patients who first exhibit the symptom in childhood. Rackeman & Edwards (1952) reviewed 449 patients who were first seen before 13 years of age and reevaluated twenty years later. Of the entire group, 71 percent had done extremely well, with improvement generally beginning sometime during or soon after adolescence. On the other hand, it is well to remember that asthma can be a life-threatening symptom. A report by Mustacchi, Lucia, and Jassy (1962) indicates that the fatality rate for this condition averages 1.5 deaths per 1,000 asthmatic persons per year. Moreover, Gottlieb (1964) reports that each year since 1949, from 4,000 to nearly 7,000 deaths in the United States were certified as primarily due to asthma. He notes (p. 276), "Asthma was noted on death certificates in 1960 about one-half as often as pulmonary tuberculosis, about one-third as often as malignant neoplasms of the lung, eight times as often as meningococcal infections, and 13 times as often as accidents to occupants of commercial aircraft."

Some indication of the socially disabling nature of this symptom is contained in the data of the U.S. National Health Survey, which indicate that in 1963 an average of about 64 million days were lost to industry, schools, and other "necessary activities" because of asthma and hay fever. Asthma was estimated to be responsible for nearly one-fourth of the days reported lost from school because of chronic illness conditions in children (Schiffer & Hunt, 1963).

In general, unfavorable prognosis is associated with the older patient, a disease of long duration, the presence of organic disease in the respiratory or circulatory organs, frequent and lengthy attacks, incomplete recovery between attacks, chronic cough, and failure to detect a clear "triggering stimulus."

Assessing the symptom. Asthma is a highly unstable symptom which requires careful evaluation in order to obtain a reasonably accurate assessment of frequency and severity. Some patients have long free periods between attacks. Other patients are chronically short of breath and begin wheezing very quickly in response to a whole array of stimuli, e.g., exertion, dust, laughing hard.

An accurate estimate of the frequency and severity of the symptom is important for several reasons, one of which is to assist in gauging the impact of the symptom on the psychological well-being of the patient and his family. The inability to breathe is a frightening experience. Patients who have experienced severe episodes of asthma may be prone to panic reactions even during mild to moderate attacks. These panic states sometimes accentuate the respiratory difficulty.

By way of contrast, teen-age boys or men who need to present a strong masculine image may underplay the severity of their symptoms. Such individuals frequently delay taking medication or take reduced amounts in the effort to convince themselves that they are "normal." As might be expected, this type of defensive denial sometimes leads to serious and incapacitating asthmatic episodes.

Chai, Purcell, Brady, and Falliers (1968), in a study assessing the effects of experimental separation from the family on asthma in children, report a series of intercorrelations among the following measures of asthma: (1) expiratory peak flow rate taken four times daily (the peak flow rate is perhaps the simplest of all the measures of airflow which the pulmonary physiologist can obtain); (2) a physician's clinical examination scaling the severity of asthma at a given moment and done once daily; (3) daily history of a child's asthma, as reported by his mother; (4) amount of medication administered to a child, as reported by his mother.

The highest average correlation was between the history of severity of asthma and the amount of medication given (.60). This was not unexpected since each of these two measures describes an entire twenty-four-hour period as perceived by the same person—in this case, a child's mother. The other measures are momentary—the clinical examination describes the state of a child's symptom during a 1-minute period out of 24 hours, and the average peak flow represents lung function during four 1-minute periods of the day. The substantial variability of the peak-flow measures obtained within the same day dramatically illustrates the intermittent character of the asthmatic symptom. This variability exists after conditions of testing and degree of subject cooperation are well standardized.

Of interest is the fact that the correlation between history of asthma and amount of medication for individual subjects ranged from a low of .25 to a high of .74. The amount of medication taken by a child was, in a number of instances, determined by many factors, e.g., fluctuating anxiety and symptom denial, other than simple symptom severity. Sometimes a parent adhered to a fixed quantity of medication regardless of symptom variability.

The Role of Psychological Variables
Can asthma be induced by psychological stimulation?

Asthma induced by emotional provocation. Promising results have been obtained by investigators employing emotional-provocation techniques. Several studies have included direct clinical observation, often with some objective measurement, of an induced asthmatic attack. Stein (1962) noted that enclosing a patient in a whole-body plethysmograph represented a severe emotional stress, which in some patients precipitated an asthmatic attack. Dekker and Groen (1956) used the technique of selecting emotional stimuli from a patient's case history and then applying psychological provocation tests. Of twelve patients, three showed minor respiratory symptoms and three exhibited frank asthmatic attacks. These investigators noted that high intensity of emotion in itself was not sufficient to produce an attack of asthma. Instead, they suggested that the emotional setting must not only have a certain intensity but also be of a more or less specific quality. Owen (1964), using another form of stimulus specificity, has shown that asthmatic children, contrasted to control subjects, showed (1) increased variability and amplitude of respiration and (2) more abnormal patterns of respiration when listening to their own mother's voice than when listening to the voice of an unknown female adult. Asthmatic wheezing, however, was not demonstrated.

Stevenson (1950) obtained respiratory tracings during an interview with a patient with bronchial asthma. He noted that the occurrence of wheezing coincided with increased secretion of bronchial mucus associated with feelings of resentment and anxiety provoked during the discussion of stressful situations. In another study of twenty-two patients (fifteen asthmatic and seven with anxiety states), Stevenson and Ripley (1952) found that respiratory patterns varied closely with emotional state during an interview. Increased rate or depth, or both, were found with anxiety and sometimes during anger; irregularity of respiration was frequently noted with anger and occurred during weeping. In three asthmatic patients, wheezing occurred which was related to both emotional changes and changes in the pneumograph pattern.

Treuting and Ripley (1948) found that in five patients it was possible to induce asthma by a stress interview without exposure to pollen. In another investigation of hay fever sufferers (Holmes, Treuting, & Wolff, 1950), the investigators demonstrated that a discussion of significant personal conflicts was capable of inducing nasal hyperemia, swelling, hypersecretion, and obstruction. It was noted that the nasal and bronchial mucosa are parts of a continuous membrane which is almost physiologically identical.

A rather different type of mechanism has been described by Faulkner (1941), who observed changes in the size of the bronchial lumen associated with emotional changes. While bronchoscoping one patient, he noticed that the recall of unpleasant incidents evoking resentment was accompanied by bronchial narrowing; in another, depressing thoughts caused the bronchial wall to lose tone, become flabby, and collapse.

Masuda, Notske, and Holmes (1966) studied biochemical variables in relation to asthma. Of seventeen patients interviewed so as to permit a reliving of emotions around their individual asthmatic attacks, seven showed an increase in asthmatic symptoms during the interview. The reactors were differentiated from the nonreactors by their lower excretion levels of metadrenaline in the interview, reflecting a nonresponsive adrenal medulla. Consistent with this was the major finding that during an asthmatic attack, whether naturally occurring or induced, there was an increase in the normetadrenaline/metadrenaline ratio, indicating a disproportionate increase in sympathetic nervous activity. Noting also that the asthmatic had lower daily levels of metadrenaline than seen in other groups of subjects, the investigators suggest that the adrenal medulla functions at a lower level in asthmatics and fails to respond in stimulus situations tending to evoke attacks of asthma.

A series of studies by Dudley and his colleagues (Dudley, Holmes, Martin, & Ripley, 1964; Dudley, Martin, & Holmes, 1964; Dudley, Masuda, Martin, & Holmes, 1965) are of interest because they focus on the experimental induction of various affect states and associated changes in the pulmonary ventilation of normal subjects as well as some suffering from pulmonary tuberculosis or obstructive-airways disease. Respiratory changes (various measures of gas exchange such as ventilation, carbon dioxide production, oxygen uptake, alveolar ventilation) occurring during anger or anxiety were similar to those occurring during real or suggested exercise, and changes during depression were similar to those occurring during real or suggested sleep. Some of the patients with a history of asthma developed attacks of asthma in response to hypnotic suggestion of adverse life situations (Dudley, Martin, & Holmes, 1964).

Two studies have been aimed at evaluating a summation-of-stimuli hypothesis, i.e., that diverse stimuli such as emotional arousal and pollen may effectively combine to produce symptoms, whereas a given quantity of either type of stimulation is insufficient for symptom production. Holmes et al. (1950), in their study of nasal reactions, found that when ragweed-sensitive subjects who had been exposed to a ragweed pollen room and had reacted only mildly were led to discuss conflictual, anxiety-arousing material, their hay fever symptoms became markedly exacerbated. As a result of observing nasal function following a brief unilateral stellate ganglion block, it was concluded that parasympathetic neural impulses to the nose appeared to be the cause of the nasal hyperfunctioning accompanying the patient's reaction to a conflict situation. Treuting and Ripley (1948) were able to induce attacks of asthma in a pollen room during interviews covering a stressful topic, whereas pollen alone did not produce symptoms.

Luparello, McFadden, Lyons, and Blocker (1968) have induced significant increases in airway resistance among asthmatic Ss by suggesting that they were being exposed to pollen when, in fact, they were exposed only to nebulized saline solution. A number of these Ss reportedly developed clinically observable asthma attacks. These investigators indicate that the peripheral mechanism by which suggestion influences airway resistance is the vagal efferent stimulating smooth-muscle constriction in the bronchi and/or bronchioles. They demonstrated that atropine blocks the effect of suggestion on airway reactivity.

"Conditioned" asthma. In 1941, French and Alexander (1941) felt that the available evidence permitted them to conclude that there was ample support for the statement that asthma attacks may be precipitated by a conditioned reflex mechanism. The famous example given by Mac-Kenzie in 1886 of a woman who was supposedly allergic to roses and who developed asthma when an artificial rose was held before her has been cited many times in the literature. The "hoarse, labored breathing" of Nick, the experimentally "neurotic" dog (Gantt, 1944), has also been frequently cited in support of the psychogenic production of asthma. In our judgment, however, "conditioned" asthma has yet to be demonstrated under controlled conditions in either human beings or animals.

For example, references have often been made to the results of Liddell (1951), who produced experimental neuroses in sheep, as well as to the results of Gantt (1944). In both, impressive evidence is presented of altered respiration accompanying the neurotic behavior in the sheep and in the dog. A number of writers have pointed to these data as evidence that asthma can be produced experimentally by psychological manipulation. However, examination of the monograph by Gantt discloses a clear statement that Nick was examined for asthma and that there was no evidence of the sounds of asthma despite the fact that respiration was clearly affected. Liddell, on the other hand, did not report any clinical examination for asthma. One of the early and widely cited reports is that of Ottenberg, Stein, Lewis, and Hamilton (1958), who appeared to show successful classical conditioning of asthma in the guinea pig. The criterion for conditioned asthma was an observer's visual judgment about the animal's heavy, labored respiration and use of accessory muscles. Attempts to replicate these observations with the use of objective recordings of the respiratory pattern have not been successful. Stein (1962) has noted that all that was definitely established in the original study was that a marked respiratory disturbance occurred, perhaps associated with anxiety. Airway obstruction with the prolonged expiration characteristic of asthma was not demonstrated.

Herxheimer (1951) studied the response of human asthmatic subjects to inhalational challenge tests, i.e., having subjects breathe a substance to which they were sensitive. Part of Herxheimer's procedure was to have the subject blow hard into a spirometer, a device for measuring pulmonary function, prior to being exposed to the challenging substance. Herxheimer noted that in some subjects asthma appeared to develop after the subject had blown hard a few times but *before* they were exposed to the antigen. A number of psychologically oriented investigators have referred to this as evidence of conditioning. It is, however, a known fact that all that is necessary to trigger asthma in some asthmatics is to have them blow hard several times. This respiratory stimulation is often accompanied by coughing and/or wheezing.

In the late 1950s, Dekker, Pelser, and Groen (1957) published an article reporting the successful classical conditioning of asthma in two subjects. These were two patients out of approximately a hundred for whom conditioning was attempted. In a personal communication dated October, 1961, Dekker reported that he was unable to replicate even these results.

Knapp (1963), who has conducted a careful and elaborate series of experiments on conditioned asthma in human beings, summarizes his impressions as follows: "Our negative results would lead me at this moment to feel confident that conditioning, conceived in the most simple, mechanical model, cannot account for attacks of asthma in the human, but that 'learning,' particularly with the right kind of emotional concomi-

tants, may well be important in certain individuals."

In sum, it appears accurate to state that with either animals or human beings, the successful conditioning of asthma remains to be demonstrated, even in the opinion of those investigators whose original positive reports on conditioning are cited frequently.

Mechanisms for the operation of psychological variables. Intensive review of clinical experience and clinical research studies leads to the overriding impression that the kinds of behavioral antecedents most immediately relevant to asthma are emotional or affect states rather than personality types or patterns of interpersonal relationship. There are at least four major mediating mechanisms through which emotional states may influence asthma. First, autonomic activity associated with emotional arousal can initiate the airway obstruction characteristic of an asthmatic attack by stimulating mucus secretion, vascular engorgement, or bronchial constriction. For example, it is known that vagal stimulation produces rapid bronchospasm and secretion. Second, emotional states are often associated with certain respiratory behaviors, e.g., crying, laughing, coughing, hyperventilation, which can lead to airway narrowing by reflex mechanisms. In these cases, a vagal reflex arc may be activated by the stimulation of subepithelial cough receptors (Simonsson, Jacobs, & Nadel, 1967). The autonomic discharge and the respiratory mechanisms mediating the effects of emotions are by no means mutually exclusive. Hyperventilation, for example, may occur in association with certain emotional states and patterns of autonomic arousal. Or autonomic activity may initiate mucus secretion, provoking a cough followed by reflex bronchoconstriction. Third, emotions have been shown to influence significantly endogenous adrenal steroid output (Hamburg, 1962; Handlon, Wadeson, Fishman, Sacher,

Hamburg, & Mason, 1962), which may, in turn, alter the course of asthma. Reinberg, Chata, and Sidi (1963), for example, report data suggesting some correspondence between the occurrence of nocturnal asthma attacks and the nightly periodic decrease in adrenocortical activity. Fourth, the physiological responses of mucus-secretion bronchospasm or vascular engorgement may, through learning, be increased in intensity and duration to the point of inducing significant airway obstruction. Finally, it is possible, but not yet demonstrated, that CNS processes may influence the immunological phenomena (antigen-antibody reactions), producing tissue change associated with narrowing of the airways.

Other reviews of mechanisms and other issues discussed in this section may be found in recent articles by Freeman, Feingold, Schlesinger, and Gorman (1964), Lipton, Steinschneider, and Richmond (1966), and Purcell (1965).

Is there a personality constellation specific to asthmatics?

Nuclear conflict or personality traits. Out of a large body of literature, mainly descriptive and nonexperimental case studies, have come suggestions regarding a common personality profile descriptive of asthmatic patients or a specific type of nuclear conflict, for example, unresolved dependency on the mother, as especially applicable to asthmatics. Many authors have implied that these characteristics bear a causal relationship to the development of the asthmatic symptom; others have noted that they appear secondary, resulting from the symptom and its effects on the patient and his family. Asthmatics, particularly children, have been described as anxious, dependent, conforming, insecure, lacking in self-confidence, and hypersensitive. Our own view is that a careful examination of the literature does not suggest that any specific personality constellation, nuclear conflict, or form of interpersonal

relationship is uniformly and etiologically associated with asthma. This assertion, which does not deny the observation that asthmatics and their families often manifest more behavioral disturbance than do normal subjects, is based on several lines of evidence.

First, Neuhaus (1958) found that both asthmatic and cardiac patients (children) were significantly more maladjusted (anxious, insecure, and dependent) than a normal control group but did not differ from each other. He concluded that chronic illness may be the variable most relevant to the production of behavioral maladjustment in asthmatics rather than some process associated specifically with asthma.

A suggestion that unresolved dependency conflicts are central in the development of asthma is contained in the influential writings of French and Alexander (1941), who further hypothesize that asthma may often be viewed as a suppressed cry, with the stated implication that asthmatic children cry less than nonasthmatics, particularly around critical periods of separation conflict. To our knowledge, there is no systematic survey of crying behavior to support this assertion. Nevertheless, clinicians have sometimes noted a tendency for crying to be distorted in a silent, awkward way in certain of their patients. Purcell (1963) has suggested an alternative interpretation of this observation. He notes that a number of patients report that crying, like laughing and coughing, can trigger attacks of asthma and, further, that these patients sometimes deliberately seek to avoid crying and laughing hard so as not to provoke asthma. Thus, the occasionally observed inability to cry or the silent, suppressed manner of crying may reflect a learned attempt to avoid initiating the uncomfortable experience of an asthmatic attack.

Second, evidence supporting the contention that asthma is a heterogeneous symptom has been mounting. Clinicians have long noted the wide variety of stimuli, e.g., allergic, infective, emotional, and mechanical, capable of triggering asthma and have attempted to classify patients in terms of precipitant stimuli. The underlying assumption has been that success in categorizing the types of *stimuli* which initiate the physiological sequence leading to the clinical symptom of asthma should lead to more effective, individualized treatment. Many investigators have recognized that multiplicity of precipitating stimuli, e.g., dust, infections, hyperventilation, is the rule and have been concerned with efforts to define the relative predominance of these factors and their reciprocal interactions for the individual case.

Differential response to institutionalization. Within this framework, Purcell and his collaborators (Purcell, 1963; Purcell, Bernstein, & Bukantz, 1961; Purcell & Metz, 1962; Purcell, Turnbull, & Bernstein, 1962) have separated subgroups on the basis of whether or not spontaneous remission of symptoms occurred within a short time after admission to the Children's Asthma Research Institute and Hospital. Certain psychological differences between groups, particularly between rapidly remitting groups (those who remain virtually symptom-free and require no medication during the 18 to 24 months of residency) and steroid-dependent groups (those requiring continuous maintenance doses of corticosteroid drugs), have been found. For example, in response to a structured-interview technique, rapidly remitting children report significantly more often than do steroid-dependent children that emotions such as anger, anxiety, and depression trigger asthma. Furthermore, the results of a questionnaire device to assess parental childrearing attitudes have indicated that both mothers and fathers of rapidly remitting children show authoritarian and punitive attitudes to a greater degree than the parents of steroid-dependent children.

The present hypothesis of these investigators suggests that among rapidly remitting children, in contrast to steroid-dependent children, the symptom of asthma may be more intimately associated with neurotic conflict and affective reactions. The asthmatic symptom of steroid-dependent children, on the other hand, is viewed as a response more regularly linked to the influences of allergic and infectious factors. The differences between these groups are regarded as relative rather than absolute.

The above remarks make it clear that a large segment of the population of severely asthmatic children become essentially asymptomatic without any medication when they leave their homes in all parts of the country and enter CARIH in Denver. The vast majority of the remainder of the population show substantial, although not as dramatic, improvement. Other residential centers for asthmatic children report similar experiences, as do pediatricians who hospitalize asthmatic children for a brief time. Thus, there is clear evidence that removal from the family home and placement in an institutional setting often have a profoundly ameliorative effect on asthma in children.

However, removal from the family home represents a change in the total physical as well as psychological environment of the child. The evidence implicating physical environmental factors in the perpetuation of asthma in certain patients is quite clear. Therefore, it becomes of central importance to find a way of drastically altering the significant psychological environment without modifying the physical environment.

Differential response to experimental family separation. One approach to this problem has been to measure the effects on asthma of separating a child from his family while maintaining an essentially constant physical environment. Purcell and his collaborators (1969) studied chronically asthmatic children on a daily basis during periods in which they lived with their own families and during a period in which they had no contact with their families but were cared for in their own homes by a substitute mother. A total of twenty-five children were evaluated. On the basis of the selection instrument—a detailed, structured interview for assessing parental and child perceptions of the precipitants of asthma attacks—it was predicted that thirteen of these children would respond positively to the experimental separation while twelve would show no improvement in asthma. For the thirteen predicted positives, all measures of asthma, including expiratory peak flow rates, amount of medication required, daily history of asthma, and daily clinical examination, indicated significant improvement occurring during the period of family separation for the group as a whole. For the group of twelve predicted nonresponders, only the daily history suggested improvement during separation. None of the other measures showed any difference between the separation and nonseparation periods.

Personality characteristics and allergic potential. Finally, Block, Jennings, Harvey, and Simpson (1964) carried out a careful study illustrating another method of subdividing asthmatic patients. These investigators developed an Allergic Potential Scale (APS) for evaluating a patient's predisposition to allergic reaction. The APS is based on such items as family history of allergy, skin-test reactions, eosinophil count, and ease with which a particular clinical symptom may be diagnosed as related to specific allergens. Using a thematic analysis of projective tests, these investigators concluded that the low-APS group (less disposed to allergy but not significantly different from the high-APS group on severity of asthma) were more pessimistic and conforming and had lower frustration tolerance. Mothers and fathers independently described these children more often as nervous, jealous, rebellious,

and clinging than did high-APS parents. The results of observations of mother-child interaction, quantified by an adjective Q-sort technique, indicated that low-APS mothers were more intrusive, angry, rejecting, depriving, etc. Scores on the Parental Attitude Research Instrument (PARI) substantiated this evidence of undesirable maternal attitudes. Personality assessment of the mothers using the Minnesota Multiphasic Personality Inventory (MMPI), the Thematic Apperception Test (TAT), and Rorschach suggested that low-APS mothers were more fearful, anxious, and self-defeating, with more evidence of psychopathology. Interviews and observations of mother-father interaction indicated that the low-APS group of parents showed more ambivalent, destructive, and pathological relationships than the high-APS group.

A recent paper by Jacobs, Anderson, Eisman, Muller, and Friedman (1967) questions the inverse relationship between allergic potential and psychopathology found by Block et al. among two groups of asthmatic children matched for symptom severity. Jacobs et al. found a very low, nonsignificant positive correlation between an index of biological predisposition (eosinophil reaction to histamine injection) and an index of psychological disturbance. They also failed to find psychological differences between allergic Ss scoring high and low on the biological index. There are many differences between the two studies, at least two of which may be critical. First, Jacobs' allergic group of twenty-nine college-student subjects consisted of thirteen with symptoms of asthma and sixteen with seasonal hay fever symptoms. Second, no data are provided on symptom severity within the allergic group. Thus, when this group was divided into a high and low biological reaction group (in order to compare them on the psychological dimension) there was no indication of how well equated these two biological reaction groups were on either symptom type or symptom severity. The authors' suggestion that biological and psychological variables are best conceived of as independent factors (neither positively nor negatively correlated) is not necessarily inconsistent with the views of Block et al. (1964). Jacobs et al. measured the correlation between these two variables within individuals without regard for symptom severity, the resultant of these two and other factors. It is possible for this correlation to be zero and, at the same time, for an inverse biological-psychological relationship to emerge between groups were symptom severity held equal in two large, well-matched groups differing only in biological reactivity. A valuable contribution of the Jacobs study was the addition of a normal comparison group, with the finding that an index combining both biological and psychological measures discriminated best between allergic and normal groups.

At the least, the results obtained from subgroup studies point to the heterogeneity of the asthmatic population. They also suggest the importance of discriminating among asthmatics so as not to obscure relationships that may exist only for a portion of the population. By inference, the data offer some assistance in making a more informed judgment about whether or not to include some form of psychotherapeutic intervention as a part of the treatment program for a particular asthmatic.

Tools and cues for assessing the relevant variables. The usefulness of conventional psychodiagnostic tests in evaluating the role of emotional factors in asthma is questionable because it is not now possible to specify with any precision the relevant test cues. Instead, as we shall try to show, the creation of specialized research instruments for evaluating the functional relationships between various classes of stimuli and the asthmatic response is a more promising approach. The tools and cues found useful are those which have successfully, albeit imperfectly, discrimi-

nated among asthmatic subgroups. There are four classes of information involved: (1) the patient's or, in the case of a child, his parents' perception of events related to the onset of asthma attacks; (2) the nature of the symptom response to separation from significant figures; (3) patient and parental personality characteristics; (4) biological characteristics of the patient. Only a brief account of these classes of information will be offered since a more complete description may be found in a chapter on asthma oriented more toward the clinician (Purcell & Weiss, 1970).

Perception of events related to the onset of asthma attacks. This information is obtained from the structured interview that successfully distinguished rapid remitters from steroid-dependent children (Purcell, 1963) and predicted responders and nonresponders rather successfully in the experimental separation study (Purcell et al., 1969). The objective is to secure a rank-order listing of the various stimuli which the interviewee has observed capable of triggering asthma attacks.

Response to separation. An effort is made to determine whether significant changes in the life situation have sometimes relieved asthma. Most often these changes have to do with separation from significant persons such as parents or siblings. One must always keep in mind that frequently separation from significant persons is accompanied by a change in the physical environment, which itself may be associated with alterations in asthmatic symptoms. When fairly unambiguous data are available on this point, e.g., a patient repeatedly improving during separation with any accompanying changes in the physical environment appearing insignificant, these data deserve to be heavily weighted in evaluating the role of psychological variables.

Patient and/or parental personality characteristics. The personality characteristics and attitudes said to be more typical of (1) low-APS children and their parents (Block et al., 1964), (2) low-skin-reactive adult female patients (Feingold, Gorman, Sinder, & Schlesinger, 1962), and (3) parents of rapidly remitting children (Purcell et al., 1961; Purcell & Metz, 1962) have already been noted. While substantial evidence of a disturbed-personality constellation is a cue to the operation of psychological influences on the production and maintenance of asthmatic symptoms, it is, in our opinion, a relatively weak one. For one thing, the evidence is more ambiguous on this point than on the others. Dekker, Barendregt, and de Vries (1961), for example, failed to find differences in neuroticism between a group of adult female asthmatics showing "manifest allergy" and those showing "no manifest allergy" based on skin reactivity and inhalation tests. Similarly, Purcell, Turnbull, and Bernstein (1962), using a large battery of tests, found no difference in overall psychopathology between a group of rapidly remitting children and a group of steroid-dependent children.

Biological characteristics. Biological data are only of indirect interest to the researcher interested in assessing psychologically relevant variables. Yet the information may be useful in matching groups for certain experiments. The strength of constitutional disposition toward allergy varies directly with the degree of positive finding in the following items (Block et al., 1964): (1) family history of allergy, (2) total number of allergies in patient, (3) ease of diagnosis of specific allergens, (4) skin-test reactivity, (5) blood eosinophil percentage.

Finally, a careful scrutiny of the correlation between infection and the occurrence of asthma is useful. Infection plays a major role in precipitating asthma frequently and severely in some patients, and where this is the case, psychological intervention is likely to be less effective.

A cautionary note in all this is the fact that asthma is almost always a multiply triggered symptom. In the individual case, asthma precipitated by physically defined stimuli almost invariably coexists with asthma precipitated by psychologically defined stimuli. Therefore, a seemingly high score on biological characteristics does not preclude the significance of emotional stimuli, with the reverse being true as well. As noted earlier, these determinants of asthma are independent of each other.

Treatment Techniques

It is probably safe to say that, at one time or another, almost every variety of psychotherapeutic technique has been applied in the treatment of bronchial asthma, including psychoanalysis (Fenichel, 1945), group psychotherapy (Groen & Pelser, 1960; Miller & Baruch, 1956; Sclare & Crockett, 1957), environmental manipulation (Long, Lamont, Whipple, Bandler, Blom, Burgin, & Jessner, 1958; Mullins, 1960; Purcell et al., 1969), hypnosis (Edwards, 1960; Fry, 1957; Maher-Loughnan, MacDonald, Mason, & Fry, 1962; Smith & Burns, 1960; White, 1961), behavior therapy (Cooper, 1964; Moore, 1965; Wolpe, 1958), and tranquilizers (Baum, Schotz, Gumpel, & Osgood, 1957; Eisenberg, 1957; Friedman, 1963; McGovern, Haywood, Thomas, & Fernandez, 1963; Thomas, 1962; Tuft, 1959). With the single exception of electroconvulsive therapy, claims of success have been filed in all instances. It is unfortunately true, however, that these claims have often been based upon studies that have failed to meet one or another of the criteria of adequate treatment studies, namely: (1) unbiased subject-selection procedures, (2) adequate therapist samples, (3) standardized treatment methods, (4) matched control groups not treated by the experimental method, (5) acceptable criteria for evaluation of treatment effects, (6) sufficiently long follow-up to rule out normal variability of the symptom, and (7) large enough samples for statistical evaluation.

There are several mechanisms whereby a technique may produce symptom change, including: (1) modification of some basic physiological function, e.g., alteration in adrenocortical hormone output or autonomic reactivity; (2) reduction of the range of effective triggering stimuli, e.g., removing the child from a tense family situation, treating the family to reduce tensions, or treating the child in order to alter his anxiety level; (3) modification of the patient's attitude toward his symptom, with resulting reduction of what might be considered "secondary symptoms," e.g., training the child to relax rather than panic at the onset of an attack. The first two approaches might be considered "curative" or "preventive" in the sense that the goal is to eliminate or reduce attacks, and the third might be seen as having the reduction of the severity of symptoms as its primary goal. On the basis of current knowledge, it would appear that each technique, regardless of its primary aim, may result in any one or more of these changes. The reader interested in a more thorough review of treatment procedures may consult Purcell and Weiss (1970).

Summary

Asthma is conceptualized as a symptom arising from an overreactivity of the respiratory apparatus (probably on a hereditary basis) to a multiplicity of stimuli, e.g., infectious, allergic, psychological. The prime psychological stimuli are affective states associated with major endocrine and autonomic system alterations as well as with certain respiratory behaviors, e.g., crying and hyperventilation, all of which may lead to the clinical symptom of asthma. However, it is clear that the simple presence of emotional disturbance is not sufficient evidence of its etiological relevance since disturbance often results from stresses imposed by the symptom.

Laboratory studies on the experimental induction of asthma and associated respiratory change probably constitute the best available evidence for the role of psychological factors in asthma. The investigation of experimental family separation extends these findings into the naturalistic setting and provides information on the functional significance of psychological variables for the course of asthma in different children.

Suggested mechanisms for the operation of psychological variables include excessive vagal activity, reflex bronchial constriction associated with various respiratory behaviors, alterations in adrenal steroid output, and modification of physiological responses, e.g., bronchospasm and mucus secretion, through learning.

ULCERATIVE COLITIS

It is, perhaps, reversing the order of things to initiate this section with a conclusion, namely, that ulcerative colitis is an enigmatic disease and that "its etiology remains obscure, and its treatment unscientific" (Lepore, 1965). There is little one can point to by way of a coherent, factually based formulation of the role of emotional factors in this disease process. Certain striking similarities exist between the literature on asthma and that on ulcerative colitis. Like asthma, ulcerative colitis has been regarded as an allergic, an infectious, or a psychological disorder. Like asthma, ulcerative colitis has been linked to a broad variety of nosological categories—most notably, obsessive-compulsive character traits, exaggerated dependence, psychosexual immaturity, depression, inhibited aggression, and inadequate personality. Like asthma, ulcerative colitis has been attributed to a faulty mother-child relationship, and like asthmatics, ulcerative colitis patients have been said to suffer from marked separation anxiety. To what can this similarity be attributed? Two possibilities exist. On the one hand, the similarities may indicate the existence of a "psychosomatic complex" basic to both conditions but differing in manifestation because of different genetic predispositions or because of the "shaping" of different behavior patterns by essentially similar mothers whose major difference may be in orientation toward one organ system rather than another. On the other hand, the very pervasiveness of the similarity, taken together with the absence of a convincing demonstration of the fruitfulness of the methods and concepts employed, suggests that what is being reflected is merely the application of preconceived theoretical and methodological systems derived from research on very different phenomena. As Feldman, Cantor, Soll, and Bachrach (1967) have pointed out, psychiatric and nonpsychiatric investigators studying the same patients have often had very different things to say about them. Similarly, Engel (1954) has noted that the persistent attempts in some psychoanalytic theories of ulcerative colitis to attach central significance to the symbolism of diarrhea ignore the probability that bleeding is the primary symptom, followed only later by diarrhea. It is possible that recent advances in asthma research may serve as useful guidelines for research on ulcerative colitis.

Description of the Disorder

Ulcerative colitis is defined as a chronic, inflammatory disorder of the colon and/or rectum, with stools containing blood and/or pus. The medical diagnosis is fairly simple and can be very reliably established on the basis of clinical, radiological, and proctological signs.

Both the basic causes and the onset of the disease remain uncertain, although Engel (1954), as mentioned above, stresses bleeding as the primary symptom. Age of onset of ulcerative colitis varies widely from early childhood to late adulthood. According to Engel (1954), it is questionable whether the kind of tissue reaction typical of the disease has its counterpart in infancy. In any event, the majority of cases occur prior to the fourth decade. While sex distribution has not been firmly established, estimates range from a slight edge in favor of males to a 1:2 ratio in favor of females (Askevold, 1964).

The course of ulcerative colitis, as is the case in asthma, is variable, with periods of exacerbation alternating with periods of relative remission. The basis for this pattern has not been established, although some effort has been made to link it to psychological factors such as separation from home (Langford, 1964) and alternation with emotional symptoms (Daniels, 1940; Wittkower, 1938). Neither of these has been clearly demonstrated. Information obtained from the U.S. Public Health Service indicates the mortality rate to be 0.5 per 100,000 people. Approximately 10 percent of patients now die of the disease.

Emergence of Ulcerative Colitis as a Psychosomatic Disorder

The first paper to discuss ulcerative colitis as a psychosomatic condition appeared in 1930. Murray (1930) studied twelve patients and concluded, first, that a relationship existed between the onset of the disease and the occurrence of a traumatic emotional experience, most commonly around marriage, and second, that a generally infantile and inadequate adjustment characterized his patients.

Wittkower (1938) and Cullinan (1938) followed up and supported Murray's initial findings. Wittkower, for example, found that out of the forty cases he studied, twenty-eight showed clear-cut patterns of onset associated with a particular traumatic event. He expressed the belief that more psychopathology existed in his sample than "would have been expected" in a similar nonulcerative colitis sample. To further bolster the psychosomatic hypothesis, Wittkower, and later Daniels (1940), noted an alternation of "mental" and ulcerative colitis symptoms. All investigators were impressed by the general immaturity and dependency of the patients.

These observations established the initial basis for considering ulcerative colitis as a psychosomatic condition. It is clear, in light of subsequent developments, that the early papers were at best only suggestive and at worst misleading. In a number of ways they were methodologically naïve, and their conclusions were grossly over-generalized.

The investigation of ulcerative colitis in children began with Sperling (1946), and some 14 years later, Prugh (1951) remarked that Sperling's writings still stood as the only thorough discussion of the disease in children. Briefly, it was Sperling's position, on the basis of extensive psychoanalytic investigation of two cases, that ulcerative colitis is a disease of childhood traceable to specific mother-child relationships. In subsequent papers (1964, 1967), Sperling has reaffirmed her position and has stated that even ulcerative colitis which first appears in adulthood nevertheless originates in childhood and remains clinically latent until its later emergence.

Despite the generally high regard for Sperling's work, the bulk of attention has continued to focus on adult patients. The importance of studying the early course of the disease has apparently not been much appreciated, even though Engel (1954) has clearly pointed out that the picture seen in the later course of the disease is complicated by secondary physical factors, e.g., response to infection once the tissue damage has taken place, or by secondary psychological effects, e.g., the adjustment to ulcerative colitis as a stressor. In all, there have been no more than about a dozen psychological investigations of ulcerative colitis in children.

Studies of Children with Ulcerative Colitis

There are several main questions around which the studies reviewed here may be conveniently grouped: (1) Are there specific experiences related to the onset of ulcerative colitis? If so, what are they? (2) Is there a specific personality profile characteristic of the child with ulcerative colitis? (3) Is there a specific interaction pattern characteristic of the family of the patient? (4) What is the role of psychological factors in determining the course of the disease? (5) What are the mechanisms involved in the disease?

Specific factors related to onset. The early observations of Murray (1930) and Wittkower (1938), reporting an apparent relationship between the disease onset and the occurrence of traumatic emotional events, have been paralleled in research with children by Prugh (1951), who related the onset of the disease in twelve out of sixteen cases to such "firsts" as going away to school, being severely punished by the father, or having sex play with another child. Earlier, Sperling (1946) implicated the threat of separation from the mother or mother substitute in a setting of mutual dependence or "toilet symbiosis" established during the first three years of life. Although the relationship between the occurrence of a trauma and the onset of the disease has been noted by a number of investigators, no specificity or uniformity of those events has been found (Finch & Hess, 1962). Thus, it is not possible to conclude with any certainty that such factors as mutually dependent mother-child relationships are either (1) specific to ulcerative colitis or (2) etiological rather than the result of an illness-fostered interaction.

There is one premorbid factor noted by a number of investigators that is of some interest. Sperling (1946), Prugh (1951), Engel (1954), and Langford (1964) have all commented upon preoccupation with bowel functions on the part of the parents of ulcerative colitis patients prior to the onset of the disease. While no investigators have taken up the origins of these preoccupations, the observation is strikingly similar to the observation on asthmatics that that illness was, in a number of instances, preceded by the exposure of the patient to a significant experience involving respiratory distress (e.g., Knapp & Nemetz, 1957). The suggestion is that conditions which foster specific anxieties or specific learned associations may be capable of triggering or perpetuating the disease process. Thus, Prugh (1951) has reported a case in which attacks of ulcerative colitis were triggered by the patient seeing another child soiling his pants, and Engel (1954) has, conversely, described the case of a woman whose symptoms remitted when she was given to believe that a vagotomy which would help her condition had been performed. In the case of asthma, one of the authors (Weiss) is currently investigating the effects of induced awareness and apprehension of asthma on respiration. Similar experimental work on ulcerative colitis might be revealing of the role of specific anxieties in that disease.

The personality of children with ulcerative colitis. With minor variations, nearly all studies on this question have concluded that the child with ulcerative colitis is rigid, dependent, distrustful, unable to express hostility, depressed, inhibited, and generally immature both intrapsychically and interpersonally (Alexander, 1965; Finch & Hess, 1962; Josselyn, Littner, & Spurlock, 1966; Langford, 1964; Prugh, 1951). These studies, however, have almost uniformly suffered from methodological and conceptual shortcomings. None, for example, has employed a comparison group of any kind. It is, therefore, not possible to conclude how much of what was observed is specific to ulcerative colitis and how much is simply illness-related. In addition, use has often been made of psychodiagnostic tests, interviews, and some direct observations, either in therapy sessions or on hospital wards, with little or no attention to their reliabilities or to the potential bias of observers who are aware of the patient's diagnosis.

Conceptually, it has not often been kept in mind that demonstrating similar personality characteristics among patients does not necessarily imply any etiological (as opposed to reactive) significance of those characteristics. In the one study in which this consideration was raised explicitly (Finch & Hess, 1962), it was concluded that while ulcerative colitis patients shared similar personality profiles, no characteristics could be discovered to have any etiological role.

Finally, no attention at all has been given to the

possibility that, as has been shown to be true for asthmatics, there may be subgroups of ulcerative colitis patients for whom emotional factors are more important than they are for others. The attempt to discover universal traits has distracted investigators from studies of how variations in personality traits may relate to symptom variables. Such studies are strongly to be recommended.

The family of the child with ulcerative colitis. A major problem with the work on family relationships in ulcerative colitis is that, with the exception of the analysts, investigators have made little effort to determine which aspects of familial interactions are relevant to the disease process under investigation. For example, there has been some agreement that the mothers of ulcerative colitis children are domineering, manipulative, and often seen by their children as martyrs (Arthur, 1963). Fathers are described as passive, ineffectual, dissatisfied men (Jackson & Yalom, 1966), and the family as a unit is said to be rigid, inhibited, and "restrictive" (Jackson & Yalom, 1966). Nevertheless, it has not been shown that these observations are specific to the families of ulcerative colitis patients, that they precede the appearance of the disease, or how they relate specifically to the disease process. Surely it must be true that certain interaction patterns are more relevant to the disease than are others. For example, the observation that mothers of ulcerative colitis children are preoccupied with cleanliness and bowel functions would appear to be potentially more relevant than the observation that father-son relationships are generally cool and father-daughter relationships deep and seductive (Finch & Hess, 1962). However, we shall not know with certainty until more careful attention has been paid to the issue. In this respect, the analytic investigators (e.g., Prugh, 1951; Sperling, 1946) have maintained a sharper focus than have some of the others.

In addition to this conceptual difficulty, studies

of the families of ulcerative colitis patients suffer from the same methodological shortcomings already mentioned elsewhere. Jackson and Yalom (1966), for example, have alone indicated the necessity and the intention to compare their findings on ulcerative colitis families with those on other, nonulcerative colitis chronic-illness groups. These authors are also to be credited for using direct observational techniques rather than relying upon clinical interviews or psychological tests, as have others (e.g., Alexander, 1965; Arthur, 1963; Prugh, 1951).

In summary, then, it may be said that while a general pattern appears to have been observed in the families of ulcerative colitis children, we do not yet know if or how this pattern contributes specifically to the disease. Such techniques as Purcell's (Purcell et al., 1969) experimental family separation might be useful in determining to what extent, and in which cases, the familial context contributes to the symptom picture. In addition, the use of direct observations rather than case histories or diagnostic testing is much to be desired. Finally, the need for adequate controls cannot be overemphasized.

The effects of psychological factors on the course of ulcerative colitis. Prugh (1951) reports an inverse relationship between premorbid adjustment and rapidity of development of the disease, with more adequately adjusted patients showing slower development. A similar relationship has been reported between assessed adjustment and prognosis (Langford, 1964). Thus, in twenty-four cases who came from severely disturbed environments, 75 percent died or required surgical intervention, while in twelve cases who came from relatively good homes, 66 percent improved and 33 percent died or required surgery.

Evidence with regard to the precipitant effect of emotional factors derives from two types of studies. First, tissue reactions have been observed directly under varying experimentally induced stress conditions. Grace, Wolf, and Wolff (1951), for example, observed that induced fear and dejection were associated with hypofunction of the bowel while anger, resentment, and hostility were associated with hyperfunction. Second, a number of naturalistic observations have suggested that severity varies at least in part with emotional upset. Prugh's (1951) description of the case in which sight of another child soiling induced an attack and Engel's (1954) case of remission following a placebo operation have already been cited. Langford (1964) noted remission of symptoms in forty-five cases within four to six weeks following hospitalization regardless of whether or not the patient was on medication. Parental visits to the hospital were said to produce short-lived symptom recurrences. The histories of these patients revealed that other separations, e.g., going to camp, had in a number of instances produced similar good results and that return home had resulted in relapse. Pasnau (1964) reports a single case of an 8-year-old girl in which decreased maternal visits to the hospital, encouragement of independence, and decreased emphasis on bowel functions had at least temporarily beneficial effects.

One of the criteria offered by Feldman et al. (1967) for "true" psychosomatic disease is the efficacy of psychotherapy in reducing symptom severity. Only two studies assessed the effects of psychotherapy on ulcerative colitis in children. Prugh (1951) reported on eight cases seen in therapy for between 4 weeks and 10 months. Recognizing that his observations were few, he nevertheless reported a trend toward an inverse relationship between degree of aggressive expression in the therapy hour and symptom severity. Weinstock (1961), on the other hand, questioned the effectiveness of intrusive, short-term therapy because, in his experience, about the same proportion (50 percent) of treated patients eventually required surgery as did nontreated patients.

Mechanisms. Karush and Daniels (1953) have hypothesized that the psychological (i.e., cerebral and subcortical) and the peripheral characteristics of ulcerative colitis comprise two aspects of the same chemical and neurophysiological process. Portis (1949), on the other hand, has suggested that the final tissue response in ulcerative colitis is the result of bacteria invading the colon damaged by excessive parasympathetic stimulation. The autonomic nervous system has been suggested as a mediator on the basis of such findings as that parasympathomimetic drugs (e.g., methacholine) can induce temporary diarrhea in man (Kern & Almy, 1952). Moreover, it will be recalled that Grace, Wolf, and Wolff (1951) observed the effects of affect states on spasm, edema, and secretion of the colonic mucosa. Which of these end-organ responses, however, is necessary or sufficient remains unknown.

Summary

Without going into the merits or shortcomings of individual studies, there is sufficient evidence to support the view that psychological factors contribute to the variability of the ulcerative colitis process. However, much remains to be done by way of identifying (1) what these factors are, (2) the patients for whom they are especially significant, and (3) the mediating mechanisms whereby they produce their results.

PEPTIC ULCER

Incidence

There is general agreement that the reported incidence of childhood ulcer is increasing. Several surveys indicate that this increase is due to improved diagnostic aids, such as the use of radiological equipment, rather than to a real increase in incidence. When careful diagnostic procedures are used routinely, approximately 10 percent of the children observed are found to have peptic ulcers. This compares with rates as low as 0.1 percent when data from autopsy only are used (Tudor, 1967). It seems reasonable to accept the higher figure as the more accurate one, not only because it is obtained when improved techniques are used but also because many adult ulcer patients report an early age of onset of ulcer symptomatology which was not correctly diagnosed during childhood.

Children who develop peptic ulcers are likely to have a positive family history of ulcer. According to one report, most patients seen had at least one parent suffering from ulcers (Prouty, 1962), and according to another report, a 30 percent incidence of positive family history for ulcer is found (Tudor, 1967). Children who have ulcers are likely to grow into adults who have ulcers, although exact figures on the persistence rate are difficult to obtain due to diagnostic problems, surgical intervention, and other complications. A study of 109 patients at the Mayo Clinic showed that there is a 50 percent chance that a duodenal ulcer in childhood will persist or recur in adolescence or adulthood if medical treatment alone is administered (Barber, Lynn, & Dushane, 1964).

According to the authoritative figures of the Quain and Ramstad Clinic, peptic ulcers occur with a fairly even distribution over the age range of birth to 16 years, with duodenal ulcers seventeen times as frequent as gastric ulcers and with a slightly greater incidence of ulcers in male than in female children—a ratio of 1.6 to 1 (Tudor, 1967).

Classification systems have been proposed which are based on differentiation by either age or severity of ulceration (Bird, Limper, & Mayer, 1941; Tudor, 1967). For the most part, this article will not deal with different classifications of childhood ulcer. It should be mentioned, however, that ulcers occur with relatively high frequency in neonates, due possibly to wide fluctuations in gastric acid during this period. Elevated levels of total acid are obtained during the first forty hours after birth, a greatly suppressed level for the next seven to ten days, and normalization at adult levels by the third week of life (Miller,

1941). The possibility that psychogenic factors play a role in these wide fluctuations during the first few days of life has not been investigated.

Gastric Physiology

A brief description of the physiological processes involved in the production of peptic ulcers may facilitate understanding of subsequent material. Peptic ulcer results when a portion of the mucous membrane of the stomach or duodenum is destroyed by the action of the acid gastric juice. The normal digestive process consists of a number of interacting neural and hormonal factors.

At birth, all the glandular elements of the adult gastrointestinal mucosa are present. The body and base of the stomach contain parietal and chief cells secreting hydrochloric acid and pepsin. In the newborn child, the first stimulus for gastric secretion is the chewing and swallowing of food; conditioning soon occurs, and the sight, odor, or taste of food can then initiate the "cephalic" or "psychic" stage of digestion, and gastric secretion is set in motion. When food reaches the antrum of the stomach, the second, or gastric, phase begins and secretion of the hormone gastrin occurs. Gastrin itself, released into the bloodstream, causes further acid secretion. The release of pepsin and gastrin are controlled by vagal stimulation as well as pH levels and mechanical distension of the antrum of the stomach.

Peptic ulcers can result from various processes which increase or prolong gastric acid secretions beyond the levels necessary for digestion or from a breakdown of normal resistance levels of the gastrointestinal mucosa. For example, when a fistula was inserted in the esophagus of dogs which then received "sham" feeding, a high incidence of ulcers resulted, presumably from the acid secretion provoked by the "cephalic" phase of digestion (Kirstner & Palmer, 1952). When storage capacity for food was surgically reduced, dogs were forced to eat small amounts of food for

many hours. Under these conditions, acid secretion in the excised but normally innervated stomach was greatly increased and led to development of gastric ulcers in 100 percent of the dogs studied. If the antrum was excised, the stimulating effects of gastrin were abolished, but prolonged effects of the neural or cephalic stage were still sufficient to produce ulcers in 45 percent of the subjects. By contrast, only one of twenty-one dogs developed lesions under these conditions following bilateral vagotomy (Sauvage, Schmitz, Storer, Kanar, Smith, & Harkins, 1953). It has also been shown that pharmacological methods of blocking vagal impulses block development of ulcers in experimental animals (Alexander & Merendino, 1952). At the same time, however, presence of food in the antrum can be prolonged by pyloric stenosis or by decreased gastric motility. Thus, if one attempts to reduce acid secretion by vagotomy, the ensuing decrease in motility may lead to prolonged gastrin secretion through the continued presence of food in the antrum of the stomach. It is this delicate balance among chemical, mechanical, neural, and humoral processes which is responsible for obtaining optimal and efficient levels of gastric juices. There is abundant evidence that these functions can be severely disrupted by psychological as well as physiological stimuli.

Experimental Results with Animals

Among the earliest attempts to induce ulcers by manipulation of the psychological environment are the studies by Sawrey and colleagues (Sawrey, Conger, & Turrell, 1956; Sawrey & Weisz, 1956). For 47 out of every 48 hours, rats were forced to cross an electrically charged grid in order to obtain food and water; for the last hour, they were allowed free access to the food and water. This treatment continued for 30 days, and a control group was subjected to a 47-hour deprivation schedule for the same amount of time. With high shock levels, 76 percent of the experimental animals developed gastric ulcers, whereas none of the control animals had ulcers. Evidently, ulceration was associated with the conflict arising from the fact that the experimental animals could sense the food and water but not obtain it without experiencing pain. However, in this study the painful experience itself, resulting from contact with the charged grid, cannot be ruled out as a possible cause of the ulcers. In other studies establishing a similar conflict situation, a significant level of ulceration was again obtained, and it was also shown that rats separated from their mothers at 15 days of age were significantly more susceptible to ulcers than controls weaned at 21 days—an effect that was not due to nutritional differences (Ader, 1962; Ader, Tatum, & Beels, 1960). It has since been shown that a wide variety of conditions, including housing, handling, complexity of environment, early levels of sensory stimulation, and propensity for activity, can have significant effects on rate of ulceration in rats (Ader, 1964; Sines, 1965; Stern, Winokur, Eisenstein, Taylor, & Sly, 1960; Weininger, 1956). Many of these studies can be criticized, however, on the grounds that the relevant stimuli contain important physical elements as well as psychological differences. For example, studies of housing, handling, and activity all involve potentially important thermoregulatory changes, which may have direct effects on efficiency of the digestive process through effects on hormonal secretion rates or gastric motility. It is also appropriate to question whether the psychological processes of rats are comparable to the complex emotions thought to be ulcerogenic for humans. For answers to these questions, one can examine research findings with higher infrahuman species, in which a fairly high level of experimental control is still available.

Psychogenic ulcers have been produced in monkeys in a manner which largely avoids the criticism of differential physical experience. Experimental subjects were required to press a bar every 20 seconds for a period of 6 hours in order to avoid being shocked. Yoked control monkeys were subjected to exactly the same experience, including equal frequency and intensity of shock, but did not have the option of pressing a button to avoid shock. Under these conditions, two experimental monkeys developed ulcers while their controls did not (Porter, Brady, Conrad, Mason, Galambos, & Rioch, 1958). In subsequent work similarly executed, four pairs of monkeys were run under the avoidance conditions for six hours, with six-hour rest periods intervening. The experimental animal of the first pair of monkeys died after 23 days of the experiment. The experimental animals of the third and fourth pairs also expired after 25 and 9 days, respectively, and the second-pair experimental animal was sacrificed after 48 days, having entered a moribund condition.

> In all instances, gross and microscopic analysis revealed extensive gastrointestinal lesions with ulceration as a prominent feature of the pathology of the experimental animals. However, none of the control animals . . . showed any indications of such gastrointestinal complications. [Brady, 1962, p. 369.]

In continuing investigations, a gastric cannula was inserted so that measures of the gastric secretions could be obtained during various phases of the experiment. It was found that there was a marked suppression of gastric acid during the actual avoidance conditioning trials while dramatic elevations above base-line measures occurred during the rest periods. In a similar fashion, pepsinogen remained below base-line level for most of a continuous 72-hour stress period but rose to several times basal levels in the poststress period and remained elevated for several days (Mason, Brady, Polish, Bauer, Robinson, Rose, & Taylor, 1961).

Psychogenic Aspects of Peptic Ulcer in Children and Adults

Four general types of studies which are relevant to psychogenic aspects of ulcer appear in the literature: (1) individual case-history reports, (2) definition of personality types associated with ulcers, (3) studies of gastric secretion rates in groups of subjects experiencing a common stress situation, and (4) studies of the effects of various emotional states on gastric activity in an individual.

In each of the studies to be discussed below, it is well to remember that in both child and adult one is usually dealing with some kind of biological predisposition toward ulceration. In addition to the high incidence of ulcers in the family history of ulcer patients (Muggia & Spiro, 1959; Prouty, 1962; Tudor, 1967), a study by Weiner, Thaler, Reiser, and Mirsky (1957) offers evidence that high resting levels of gastric acid are present in those individuals who later develop ulcers. Serum pepsinogen levels were obtained on thousands of army inductees, and after eight to sixteen weeks of basic training, 15 percent of the hypersecretors had developed duodenal ulcers whereas none of the hyposecretors had ulcers. Mirsky (1953) was able to identify elevated serum pepsinogen levels in infants, some of whom presented levels comparable to those of adults suffering from active duodenal ulcers.

Individual case-history reports provide a useful source of data for the psychogenic aspects of ulcer but do not permit the synthesis of general formulations from the data obtained. One of the earliest attempts to relate a psychological variable to childhood ulcer is contained in the report of Goldsberry (1951). According to this report, the patient had experienced recurring abdominal pain since age 3. Following a panic reaction to a fireworks display at age 5, he became constantly ill, and x-ray examination showed a definite ulcer crater. The author describes the child as having "a sense of inferiority and insecurity" and being in a "mental and emotional no-man's land" and suggests that these factors, plus the fear inspired by the fireworks display, were psychogenic clues which aided in the diagnosis of peptic ulcer. At the same time, it is observed that the father had a chronic duodenal ulcer and the mother frequent gastric symptoms and that the child lived in a very atypical environment, in which there were no other children and four adults shared in his supervision. From the data available, there is no way of ascertaining whether the panic reaction actually led to a flare-up of the ulcer condition or whether this was only a natural worsening of the condition, which had been present for two years. The timing of events is most uncertain, as the author merely states, "After this incident the child was constantly ill." One cannot tell if the interval is hours, days, or weeks or how being "constantly ill" after this time differs from the experience of recurrent abdominal pain before this event. The personality traits of inferiority and insecurity could easily be a result of the unusual interpersonal environment and/or the fact that he was ill and "undersized," rather than a cause of the ulcer condition. Another study, by Millar (1965), presented five cases of peptic ulcer in children, noted these patients' reluctance to attend school, and concluded that the parents' failure to set limits for the children and conflict over mother-child separation were related to the ulcer syndrome. It seems equally possible that the children wished to stay home near mother because mother could give medicine to alleviate stomach pains and that, as appears to be true with asthmatics, their reluctance to attend school might have been related to the embarrassment and discomfort associated with becoming ill in class. These studies illustrate the limitations of the case-history technique, principally the presentation of temporally ordered or concomitant events without the demonstration of functional links between these events.

In a few studies, acid secretion rates have been evaluated as a function of a common stress applied to a group of individuals. It has been shown that anticipating the demands of an examination or the anticipation of an operation produces increased amounts of gastric acid in subjects (Dragstedt, Oberhelman, & Smith 1951; Mahl, 1953). Such studies have not, however, been designed for the analysis of the individual case. It seems highly unlikely, for example, that an event such as an examination arouses the same intensity or quality of emotional reaction in diverse individuals, and when group means are presented, it is always possible that a small percentage of hyperreactors are responsible for the elevated levels of gastric secretion. In experiments with groups of individuals in which no consistent group trends are found, the results may be attributable to the fact that while individuals show consistent reaction patterns to a given stimulus, one person may show an increase in gastric secretion to the same stimulus that provokes a decrease in another individual. Wittkower (1935), for example, found increased secretion in some subjects and decreased secretion in others even when the individuals seemed to be exhibiting similar affect states.

A rare, but very useful, opportunity for the study of gastric activity and psychological states is presented by the subject with a gastric defect or fistula in whom the effects of a psychological stimulus on gastric function can be immediately and directly evaluated. An exceptionally careful and detailed study of this kind was conducted by Wolf and Wolff (1943), and 25 years later, it remains both a milestone and a prototype for studies of emotions and gastric function. The authors had the opportunity to study a subject ("Tom") who, at the age of 9, had the anterior portion of his stomach surgically exteriorized due to esophageal stricture. He had learned to feed himself through the opening and lived a relatively normal life. At age 57 he agreed to cooperate with the authors in detailed and lengthy studies of gastric function. After their subject was well adapted to investigative procedures, the authors categorized various affect states, such as fear, tension, hostility, and resentment, and studied the effects of these states on various measures of gastric function. They were aided in this evaluation (1) by an intimate knowledge of the subject and therefore some knowledge of what situations would

produce certain emotional reactions and (2) by the fact that the subject worked within the hospital, where information about important environmental situations and stresses was available to the investigators. Thus, the situation provided the unusual advantages of allowing the authors to explore "real-life" stresses rather than artificially induced ones and to obtain concomitant measures of gastric functions.

With the experience of sudden fright or a depressive mood, a marked gastric hypofunction was observed, including pallor and blanching of the exposed mucosa and inhibited gastric secretion. On some occasions this reaction was intense enough to inhibit the increase of vascularity and secretion that normally followed the introduction of beef broth into the abdominal defect. Aggressive feelings of resentment and hostility, on the other hand, were regularly associated with levels of gastric secretion and motility as much as three times normal. In addition to the effects of acute stress situations, it was observed that periods of several weeks of sustained emotional tension were related to increased reddening of the mucosa and increased parietal cell hydrochloric acid output for the same period. When the subject was involved in one of these periods of emotional turmoil, he ate little, due to lack of appetite, and even sleeping did not result in any reduction of the gastric hyperfunction.

An opportunity to study a young child under similar circumstances arose when 15-month-old Monica was admitted to Strong Memorial Hospital, Rochester, New York, on October 12, 1953. Monica was born with congenital atresia of the esophagus, and a gastric fistula was inserted three days after birth to allow her to obtain adequate nutrition until corrective surgery could be performed (Engel, Reichsman, & Segal, 1956). Monica lived on the ward from age 15 to 22 months, during which time detailed analysis of behavioral and affect states were obtained, together with frequent measures of gastric hydrochloric acid secretion rates. The results of this study are remarkable for two reasons: (1) the highly significant differences in acid secretion rates associated with different affect states and (2) the similarity between these findings and those in the study of "Tom." Gastric secretion was lowest during depression—significantly lower than rates for all other affects. Rage was associated with significantly higher levels of secretion than in all other affects. Behavioral categorizations in this study were evaluated by two observers, neither of whom had any knowledge of the results of concomitantly obtained gastric samples.

Summary

The studies using animals as experimental subjects show rather convincingly that various conflict situations can produce increased gastric acid secretion and gastroduodenal ulceration. Experiments with primates demonstrate that experimentally induced ulcers are a result of the psychological and emotional components of the stressful situation and are not due to the experience of pain or to physical aspects of the stress complex. No work has come to our attention which deals with manipulation of behavioral events in an attempt to influence healing rates of established ulcers in experimental animals. Study of behavioral methods of healing induced ulcers might yield results of both theoretical and practical value.

In reviewing the studies of adults and children, it is an easier task to describe approaches which have not yielded substantial findings than to present a convincing case for approaches which are fruitful. The kind of investigation which most successfully deals with specifiable functional relationships is that which has taken advantage of prolonged contact with an individual whose gastric system is exposed to frequent and direct observation. The classic study of the patient "Tom" provides very convincing data for the supposition that emotional states, both acute psychological

reactions and long-term mood changes, profoundly influence gastric functioning. Failure to demonstrate functional relationships between personality traits and ulcers, the considerable overlap in traits assigned to various psychosomatic disorders, and the disappearance of trait differences when appropriate control groups are used suggest that some of the more widely explored "psychogenic" aspects of peptic ulcer are more likely to be psychological derivatives of chronic illness.

CONCLUSIONS

Psychosomatic disorders frequently involve multiple possible etiologies. Since this chapter is psychologically oriented, those etiologies most appropriately described in biological terms have been relatively neglected. The psychosomatic researcher cannot, however, afford to omit from his thinking either these other possible pathways to the symptom or the relevant process descriptions in physical language.

Some form of constitutional predisposition to particular psychosomatic disorders is a pervasive concept. For example, recent investigations (Bridger & Reiser, 1959; Lipton, Steinschneider, & Richmond, 1961) strongly suggest that individual differences in cardiac rate and reactivity show the effect of genetic and/or constitutional factors. Longitudinal depth studies of certain high-risk infant or fetal populations and family members are most desirable. Such an approach would be relatively efficient in disorders of early onset, such as asthma and eczema. Using the design suggested by Mednick (1967) in his study of schizophrenia, one might select two high-risk children, perhaps from within the same predisposed family, as well as one from a nonpredisposed family. With the relatively high yield of patients in allergically predisposed families, the chances of obtaining one patient and two controls would be good.

The obvious reason for studies oriented toward

investigation of the emergence of disorder is that otherwise one cannot ever be sure of the time relationships between adjustment problems and illness. A recent report by Lebovits et al. (1967) on prospective and retrospective psychological studies of coronary heart disease illustrates this. These investigators found *affirmative* answers to two very important questions concerned with potential sources of error in retrospective studies. The questions are: (1) Do survivors of the illness differ, on behavior and personality variables, from persons who die before they can be included in a retrospective study? (2) Is occurrence of the illness associated with systematic changes in these variables among survivors?

In our judgment, a focus on the life events immediately preceding the onset of a disorder is more valuable than a description of the personality constellations of family members. To the extent that learning processes are implicated in the development of psychosomatic disorder, the conditions of the psychological environment in which the symptom originated and is maintained are of utmost importance. Contingencies of reinforcement associated with the symptom deserve special attention.

As already emphasized, the complexity of psychosomatic disorders is indicated by the likelihood of multiple causes, which, in turn, points to the need for careful specification of subpopulations. Still another complication is that life experiences, whether naturally occurring or experimentally imposed, often have meanings unique to the individual. The recent work by Thomas, Birch, Chess, Hertzig, and Korn (1963), for example, suggests that each child has an individual pattern of primary behavioral reactivity, identifiable in early infancy and persisting in later periods of life. Such a finding strongly implies that different infants or young children will probably not respond in the same fashion to a given environmental influence. It also reinforces the importance of intensive studies of the individual and his particular psychological surroundings while conducting group investigations.

In sharp contrast to the above suggestions for exploring the psychosocial origin of a disorder, perhaps with an eye toward prevention, it appears highly desirable to experiment with some newly created and relatively simple therapeutic possibilities. The opportunities opened up by the demonstration that visceral responses are subject to instrumental learning depend relatively little upon extensive knowledge of the individual patient. For example, by recording blood pressure in a hypertensive patient and rewarding first small and then larger drops in blood pressure, it may be possible to change undesirable visceral responses to more desirable ones. While it is likely that the conditions of learning in humans will not be quite so simple, the results obtained by Miller suggest that it would be highly worthwhile to give this method a thorough clinical trial.

Little has been said of conventional psychotherapeutic techniques, primarily because there is no indication of specificity of approach for particular disorders. Even the behavior-modification technique of desensitization has, when used, focused more on the anxiety presumed to underlie the symptom than on the symptom itself. Milieu changes, such as those brought about by hospitalization or sometimes by other forms of separation from families, clearly can produce beneficial results in some children with asthma or ulcerative colitis. However, the diagnosis of ulcerative colitis or asthma does not necessarily call for psychological treatment. As repeatedly stressed, detailed evaluation of the individual patient is required for an educated guess as to the relevant mechanisms.

REFERENCES

Ader, R. Social factors affecting emotionality and resistance to disease in animals. III. Early weaning and susceptibility to gastric ulcers in the rat. A control for nutritional factors. *Journal of Comparative and Physiological Psychology,* 1962, **55,** 600–602.

Ader, R. Gastric erosions in the rat: Effects of immobilization at different points in the activity cycle. *Science,* 1964, **145,** 406–407.

Ader, R. Effects of early experience and differential housing on behavior and susceptibility to gastric erosion in the rat. *Journal of Comparative and Physiological Psychology,* 1965, **60,** 233–238.

Ader, R., & Friedman, S. B. Differential early experience and susceptibility to transplanted tumor in the rat. *Journal of Comparative and Physiological Psychology,* 1965, **59,** 361–364. (a)

Ader, R., & Friedman, S. B. Social factors affecting emotionality and resistance to disease in animals. V. Early separation from the mother and response to transplanted tumor in the rat. *Psychosomatic Medicine,* 1965, **27,** 119–122. (b)

Ader, R., Tatum, T., & Beels, C. C. Social factors affecting emotionality and resistance to disease in animals. I. Age of separation from the mother and susceptibility to gastric ulcers in the rat. *Journal of Comparative and Physiological Psychology,* 1960, **53,** 446–454.

Alexander, F. *Psychosomatic medicine. Its principles and applications.* New York: Norton, 1950.

Alexander, J. W., & Merendino, K. A. A study of the mechanisms involved in the protection against ulcer formation afforded by vagotomy in the shay-preparation rat. *Surgery,* 1952, **31,** 859–869.

Alexander, T. An objective study of psychological factors in ulcerative colitis in children. *Applied Therapy,* 1965, **7,** 837–839.

Arthur, B. Role perception of children with ulcerative colitis. *Archives of General Psychiatry,* 1963, **8,** 536–545.

Askevold, F. Studies in ulcerative colitis. *Journal of Psychosomatic Research,* 1964, **8,** 89–100.

Barber, K. W., Jr., Lynn, H. B., & Dushane, J. W. Surgical treatment of complicated duodenal ulcer in childhood. *Postgraduate Medicine,* 1964, **35,** 175–179.

Baum, G. L., Schotz, S. A., Gumpel, R. C., & Osgood, C. The role of chlorpromazine in the treatment of bronchial asthma and chronic pulmonary emphysema. *Diseases of the Chest,* 1957, **32,** 574–575.

Bird, C. E., Limper, M. A., & Mayer, J. M. Surgery in peptic ulceration of stomach and duodenum in infants and children. *Annals of Surgery,* 1941, **114,** 526–542.

Block, J., Jennings, P. H., Harvey, E., & Simpson, E. Interaction between allergic potential and psychopathology in childhood asthma. *Psychosomatic Medicine,* 1964, **26,** 307–320.

Brady, J. V. Psychophysiology of emotional behavior. In A. J. Bachrach (Ed.), *Experimental foundations of clinical psychology,* New York: Basic Books, 1962.

Bridger, W. H., & Reiser, M. F. Psychophysiologic studies of the neonate: An approach toward the methodological and theoretical problems involved. *Psychosomatic Medicine,* 1959, **21,** 265–276.

Chai, H., Purcell, K., Brady, K., & Falliers, C. J. Therapeutic and investigational evaluation of asthmatic children. *Journal of Allergy,* 1968, **41,** 23–36.

Cooper, A. J. A case of bronchial asthma treated

by behavior therapy. *Behavior Research and Therapy,* 1964, **1,** 351–356.

Criep, L. H. *Clinical immunology and allergy.* New York: Grune & Stratton, 1962.

Cullinan, E. R. Ulcerative colitis: Clinical aspects. *British Medical Journal,* 1938, **2,** 1351–1355.

Daniels, G. E. Treatment of a case of ulcerative colitis associated with hysterical depression. *Psychosomatic Medicine,* 1940, **2,** 276–285.

Dekker, E., & Groen, J. Reproducible psychogenic attacks of asthma. *Journal of Psychosomatic Research,* 1956, **1,** 58–67.

Dekker, E., Pelser, H. E., & Groen, J. Conditioning as a cause of asthmatic attacks. *Journal of Psychosomatic Research,* 1957, **2,** 97–108.

Dekker, E., Barendregt, J. T., & DeVries, K. Allergy and neurosis in asthma. In A. Jeres & H. Freyburger (Eds.), *Advances in psychosomatic medicine.* New York: Brunner, 1961. Pp. 235–240.

DiCara, L. V., and Miller, N. E. Changes in heart rate instrumentally learned by curarized rats as avoidance responses. *Journal of Comparative and Physiological Psychology,* 1968, **65,** 8–12.

Dragstedt, L. R., Oberhelman, H. A., & Smith, C. A. Experimental hyperfunction of the gastric antrum with ulcer formation. *Annals of Surgery,* 1951, **134,** 332–345.

Dudley, D. L., Holmes, T. H., Martin, C. J., & Ripley, M. S. Changes in respiration associated with hypnotically induced emotion, pain, and exercise. *Psychosomatic Medicine,* 1964, **24,** 46–57.

Dudley, D. L., Martin, C. J., & Holmes, T. H. Psychophysiologic studies of pulmonary venti-

lation. *Psychosomatic Medicine,* 1964, **26** (6), 645–660.

Dudley, D. L., Masuda, M., Martin, C. J., & Holmes, T. H. Psychophysiological studies of experimentally induced action oriented behavior. *Journal of Psychosomatic Research,* 1965, **9,** 209–221.

Dunbar, F. *Psychosomatic diagnosis.* New York: Hoeber-Harper, 1943.

Edwards, G. E. Hypnotic treatment of asthma: Real and illusory results. *British Medical Journal,* 1960, **5197,** 492–497.

Eisenberg, B. C. Role of tranquilizing drugs in allergy. *Journal of the American Medical Association,* 1957, **163,** 934–937.

Engel, G. L. Studies of ulcerative colitis. II. The nature of the somatic processes and the adequacy of psychosomatic hypotheses. *American Journal of Medicine,* 1954, **16,** 416–433.

Engel, G. L., Reichsman, R., & Segal, H. L. A study of an infant with a gastric fistula. I. Behavior and the rate of total hydrochloric acid secretion. *Psychosomatic Medicine,* 1956, **18,** 374–398.

Faulkner, W. B. Influence of suggestion on the size of the bronchial lumen. *Northwestern Medicine,* 1941, **40,** 367–368.

Feingold, B. F., Gorman, F. J., Sinder, M. T., & Schlesinger, K. Psychological studies of allergic women. *Psychosomatic Medicine,* 1962, **24,** 195–202.

Feldman, F., Cantor, D., Soll, S., & Bachrach, W. Psychiatric study of a consecutive series of 34 patients with ulcerative colitis. *British Medical Journal,* 1967, **3,** 14–17.

Fenichel, O. *The psychoanalytic theory of neurosis.* New York: Norton, 1945.

Finch, S. M., & Hess, J. H. Ulcerative colitis in children. *American Journal of Psychiatry,* 1962, **118,** 819–826.

Freeman, E. H., Feingold, B. F., Schlesinger, K., & Gorman, F. J. Psychological variables in allergic disorders: A review. *Psychosomatic Medicine,* 1964, **26,** 543–575.

French, T. M., & Alexander, F. Psychogenic factors in bronchial asthma. *Psychosomatic Medicine Monographs,* 1941, **4,** No. 1.

Friedman, H. T. Librium-theophylline-ephedrine compound in bronchial asthma. *Annals of Allergy,* 1963, **21,** 163–167.

Fry, A. The scope for hypnosis in general practice. *British Medical Journal,* 1957, **11,** 1323–1328.

Gantt, W. H. *Experimental basis of neurotic behavior.* New York: Harper, 1944.

Goldsberry, J. J. Gastric ulcer in the preschool child: Report of a case. *New England Journal of Medicine,* 1951, **245,** 844–847.

Gottlieb, P. M. Changing mortality in bronchial asthma. *Journal of the American Medical Association,* 1964, **187,** 276–280.

Grace, W. J., Wolf, S., & Wolff, H. G. *The human colon.* New York: Hoeber-Harper, 1951.

Graham, D. T. Health, disease, and the mind-body problem: Linguistic parallelism. *Psychosomatic Medicine,* 1967, **24,** 52–71.

Graham, D. T., & Graham, K. F. Specific relations of attitude to physiological change. Progress Report for U.S. Public Health Service Research Grant M-2011, 1961.

Graham, D. T., Kabler, J. D., & Graham, F. K. Physiological response to the suggestion of attitudes specific for hives and hypertension. *Psychosomatic Medicine,* 1962, **24,** 159–169.

Graham, D. T., Lundy, R. M., Benjamin, L. S., Kabler, J. D., Lewis, W. C., Kunish, N. O., & Graham, F. K. Specific attitudes in initial interviews with patients having different "psychosomatic" diseases. *Psychosomatic Medicine,* 1962, **24,** 257–266.

Graham, F. K., & Kunish, N. O. Physiological responses of unhypnotized subjects to attitude suggestions. *Psychosomatic Medicine,* 1965, **27,** 317–329.

Groen, J. J., & Pelser, H. E. Experiences with, and results of, group psychotherapy in patients with bronchial asthma. *Journal of Psychosomatic Research,* 1960, **4,** 191–205.

Halliday, J. L. *Psychosocial medicine.* New York: Norton, 1948.

Hamburg, D. A. Plasma and corticosteroid plasma levels in naturally occurring psychological stresses. In S. Korey (Ed.), *Ultrastructure and metabolism of the nervous system.* Baltimore: Williams & Wilkins, 1962.

Hamilton, M. *Psychosomatics.* New York: Wiley, 1955.

Handlon, J. H., Wadeson, R. W., Fishman, J. R., Sacher, E. J., Hamburg, D. A., & Mason, J. W. Psychological factors lowering plasma 17-hydroxicorticosteroid concentration. *Psychosomatic Medicine,* 1962, **24,** 535–541.

Herxheimer, H. G. Induced asthma in man. *Lancet,* 1951, **1,** 1337–1341.

Holmes, T. H., Goodell, S., Wolf, S., & Wolff, H. G. *The nose.* Springfield, Ill: Charles C Thomas, 1950.

Holmes, T. H., Treuting, T., & Wolff, H. Life situations, emotions and nasal disease. In H. G. Wolff (Ed.), *Life stress and bodily disease. Proceedings of the Association for Research in*

Nervous and Mental Diseases. Baltimore: Waverly Press, 1950.

Jackson, D. D., & Yalom, I. Family research on the problem of ulcerative colitis. *Archives of General Psychiatry,* 1966, **15**, 410–418.

Jacobs, M. A., Anderson, S., Eisman, H. D., Muller, J. J., & Friedman, S. Interaction of psychologic and biologic predisposing factors in allergic disorders. *Psychosomatic Medicine,* 1967, **24**, 572–585.

Josselyn, I. M., Littner, N., & Spurlock, J. Psychologic aspect of ulcerative colitis in children. *Journal of the American Medical Woman's Association,* 1966, **21**, 303–306.

Karush, A., & Daniels, G. The psychoanalysis of two cases of ulcerative colitis. *Psychosomatic Medicine,* 1953, **15**, 140–167.

Kern, F., & Almy, T. P. The effects of acetylcholine and methacholine upon the human colon. *Journal of Clinical Investigation,* 1952, **31**, 555–560.

Kirstner, J. B., & Palmer, W. L. The problem of peptic ulcer. *American Journal of Medicine,* 1952, **13**, 615–639.

Knapp, P. H. Personal communication, 1963.

Knapp, P. H., & Nemetz, S. J. Personality variations in bronchial asthma. *Psychosomatic Medicine,* 1957, **19**, 443–465.

Krech, D., Rosenzweig, M. R., & Bennett, E. L. Environmental impoverishment, social isolation, and changes in brain chemistry and anatomy. *Physiology and Behavior,* 1966, **1**, 99–104.

Langford, W. S. The psychological aspects of ulcerative colitis. *Clinical Proceedings of the Children's Hospital,* Washington, 1964, **30**, 89–97.

Lebovits, B. Z., Shekelle, R. B., Ostfeld, A. M., & Oglesby, P. Prospective and retrospective psychological studies of coronary heart disease. *Psychosomatic Medicine,* 1967, **29**, 265–272.

Lepore, M. J. The importance of emotional disturbance in chronic ulcerative colitis. *Journal of the American Medical Association,* 1965, **191**, 819–824.

Levine, S. Maternal and environmental influences on the adrenocortical response to stress in weaning rats. *Science,* 1967, **156**, 258–260.

Levine, S., & Mullins, R. F., Jr. Hormonal influences on brain organization in infant rats. *Science,* 1966, **152**, 1585–1591.

Liddell, H. The influence of experimental neuroses on respiratory function. In H. Abramson (Ed.), *Somatic and psychiatric treatment of asthma.* Baltimore: Williams & Wilkins, 1951.

Lipton, E. L., Steinschneider, A., & Richmond, J. B. Autonomic function in the neonate. IV. Individual differences in cardiac reactivity. *Psychosomatic Medicine,* 1961, **23**, 472–484.

Lipton, E. L., Steinschneider, A., & Richmond, J. B. Psychophysiologic disorders in children. In L. W. Hoffman & M. L. Hoffman (Eds.), *Review of child development research.* Vol. 2. New York: Russell Sage Foundation, 1966.

Long, R. T., Lamont, J. H., Whipple, B., Bandler, L., Blom, G. E., Burgin, L., & Jessner, L. A psychosomatic study of allergic and emotional factors in children with asthma. *American Journal of Psychiatry,* 1958, **114**, 890–899.

Luparello, T., McFadden, E. R., Jr., Lyons, H. A., & Blocker, E. The influence of suggestion on airway reactivity. Paper presented at meeting of the American Psychosomatic Society, Boston, 1968.

Maher-Loughnan, G. P., MacDonald, N., Mason, A. A., & Fry, L. Controlled trial of hypnosis in the symptomatic treatment of asthma. *British Medical Journal,* 1962, **11**, 371–376.

Mahl, G. F. Physiological changes during chronic fear. *Annals of the New York Academy of Science,* 1953, **56,** 240–252.

Mason, J. W., Brady, J. V., Polish, E., Bauer, J., Robinson, J., Rose, R., & Taylor, E. Patterns of corticosteroid and pepsinogen change related to emotional stress in the monkey. *Science,* 1961, **133,** 1596–1598.

Masuda, M., Notske, R. N., & Holmes, T. H. Catecholamine excretion and asthmatic behavior. *Journal of Psychosomatic Research,* 1966, **10,** 255–262.

McGovern, J. P., Haywood, T. J., Thomas, O. C., & Fernandez, A. A. Studies with a benzo-diazepine derivative in various allergic diseases. *Psychosomatics,* 1963, **4,** 203–206.

Mednick, S. A. The children of schizophrenics: Serious difficulties in current research methodologies which suggest the use of the "high-risk group" method. In J. Romano (Ed.), *The origins of schizophrenia.* Amsterdam: Excepta Medica Foundation, 1967. Pp. 179–199.

Millar, T. P. Peptic ulcers in children. *Canadian Psychiatric Association Journal,* 1965, **10,** 43–50.

Miller, H., & Baruch, D. Allergies. In S. R. Slavson (Ed.), *The field of group psychotherapy.* New York: International Universities Press, 1956.

Miller, N. E. Experiments relevant to learning theory and psychopathology. *Proceedings of the 18th International Congress of Psychology,* Moscow, 1966.

Miller, N. E. Psychosomatic effects of specific types of training. *Annals of the New York Academy of Sciences,* 1969, **159,** 1025–1039.

Miller, N. E., & Banuazizi, A. Instrumental learning by curarized rats of a specific visceral response, intestinal or cardiac. *Journal of Comparative and Physiological Psychology,* 1968, **65,** 1–7.

Miller, N. E., & Carmona, A. Modification of a visceral response, salivation in thirsty dogs, by instrumental training with water reward. *Journal of Comparative and Physiological Psychology,* 1967, **63,** 1–6.

Miller, N. E., & DiCara, L. V. Instrumental learning of heart-rate changes in curarized rats: Shaping, and specificity to discriminative stimulus. *Journal of Comparative and Physiological Psychology,* 1967, **63,** 12–19.

Miller, R. A. Observations on the gastric acidity during the first month of life. *Archives of the Diseases of Childhood,* 1941, **16,** 22–30.

Mirsky, I. A. Psychoanalysis and the biological sciences. In F. Alexander and H. Ross (Eds.), *20 years of psychoanalysis.* New York: Norton, 1953.

Moore, N. Behavior therapy in bronchial asthma: A controlled study. *Journal of Psychosomatic Research,* 1965, **9,** 257–276.

Muggia, A., & Spiro, H. M. Childhood peptic ulcer. *Gastroenterology,* 1959, **37,** 715–724.

Mullins, A. Asthmatic children take the waters. *Lancet,* 1960, **21,** 440–441.

Murray, C. D. Psychogenic factors in etiology of ulcerative colitis and bloody diarrhea. *American Journal of Medical Science,* 1930, **180,** 239–248.

Mustacchi, P., Lucia, S. P., & Jassy, L. Bronchial asthma: Patterns of morbidity and mortality in United States. *California Medicine,* 1962, **96,** 196–200.

Neuhaus, E. C. Personality study of asthmatic and cardiac children. *Psychosomatic Medicine,* 1958, **3,** 181–186.

Ottenberg, P., Stein, M., Lewis, J., & Hamilton, C.

Learned asthma in the guinea pig. *Psychosomatic Medicine,* 1958, **20,** 395–400.

Owen, F. W. Patterns of respiratory disturbance in asthmatic children evoked by the stimulus of the mother's voice. *Acta Psychotherapeutica et Psychosomatica,* 1964, **2,** 228–241.

Pasnau, R. Therapy of ulcerative colitis in children: A combined pediatric-psychiatric-surgical approach. *Psychosomatics,* 1964, **5,** 137–143.

Pinneau, S. R. The infantile disorders of hospitalism and anaclitic depression. *Psychological Bulletin,* 1955, **52,** 429–452.

Porter, R. W., Brady, J. V., Conrad, D. G., Mason, J. W., Galambos, R., & Rioch, D. Some experimental observations on gastrointestinal lesions in behaviorally conditioned monkeys. *Psychosomatic Medicine,* 1958, **20,** 379–394.

Portis, S. A. Idiopathic ulcerative colitis: Newer concepts concerning its cause and management. *Journal of the American Medical Association,* 1949, **139,** 208–214.

Prouty, M. "Red alert" for duodenal ulcer in children. *Wisconsin Medical Journal,* 1962, **61,** 387–390.

Prugh, D. G. The influence of emotional factors on the clinical course of ulcerative colitis in children. *Gastroenterology,* 1951, **18,** 339–354.

Purcell, K. Distinctions between subgroups of asthmatic children: Children's perceptions of events associated with asthma. *Pediatrics,* 1963, **31,** 486–494.

Purcell, K. Critical appraisal of psychosomatic studies of asthma. *New York State Journal of Medicine,* 1965, **65,** 2107–2109.

Purcell, K., Bernstein, L, & Bukantz, S. C. A preliminary comparison of rapidly remitting and persistently "steroid dependent" asthmatic children. *Psychosomatic Medicine,* 1961, **23,** 305–310.

Purcell, K., Brady, K., Chai, H., Maser, J., Molk, K., Gordon, N., & Means, J. The effect on asthma in children of experimental separation from the family. *Psychosomatic Medicine,* 1969, **31,** 144–164.

Purcell, K., & Metz, J. R. Distinctions between subgroups of asthmatic children: Some parent attitude variables related to age of onset of asthma. *Journal of Psychosomatic Research,* 1962, **6,** 251–258.

Purcell, K., Turnbull, J. W., & Bernstein, L. Distinctions between subgroups of asthmatic children: Psychological test and behavior rating comparisons. *Journal of Psychosomatic Research,* 1962, **6,** 283–291.

Purcell, K., & Weiss, J. Asthma. In C. G. Costello (Ed.), *Symptoms of psychopathology.* New York: Wiley, 1970. Pp. 597–623.

Rackeman, F. H., & Edwards, M. D. Medical progress: Asthma in children: Follow-up study of 688 patients after 20 years. *New England Journal of Medicine,* 1952, **246,** 815–858.

Ratner, B., & Silberman, A. E. Critical analysis of the hereditary concept of allergy. *Journal of Allergy,* 1953, **24,** 371–378.

Reinberg, A., Chata, D., & Sidi, E. Nocturnal asthma attacks and their relationship to the circadian adrenal cycle. *Journal of Allergy,* 1963, **34,** 323–330.

Rosenzweig, M. R. Environmental complexity, cerebral change, and behavior. *American Psychologist,* 1966, **21,** 321–332.

Rosenzweig, M. R., Krech, D., Bennett, E. L., & Diamond, M. C. Effects of environmental complexity and training on brain chemistry and anatomy: A replication and extension. *Journal of Comparative and Physiological Psychology,* 1962, **55,** 429–437.

Sauvage, L. R., Schmitz, E. J., Storer, E. H., Kanar, E. A., Smith, F. R., & Harkins, H. N. The relation between the physiologic stimulatory mechanisms of gastric secretion and the incidence of peptic ulceration. *Surgical Gynecology and Obstetrics,* 1953, **96,** 127–142.

Sawrey, W. L., Conger, J. J., & Turrell, E. S. An experimental investigation of the role of psychological factors in the production of gastric ulcers in rats. *Journal of Comparative and Physiological Psychology,* 1956, **49,** 457–461.

Sawrey, W. L., & Weisz, J. D. An experimental method of producing gastric ulcers. *Journal of Comparative and Physiological Psychology,* 1956, **49,** 269–270.

Schiffer, C. G., & Hunt, E. P. *Illness among children.* Children's Bureau, U.S. Department of Health and Welfare, 1963.

Schwartz, M. Heredity in bronchial asthma: A clinical and genetic study of 191 asthma probands. *Acta Allergologica,* 1952, **5** (Suppl. 2), 1–288.

Sclare, A. B., & Crockett, J. A. Group psychotherapy in bronchial asthma. *Journal of Psychosomatic Research,* 1957, **2,** 157–171.

Simonsson, B. G., Jacobs, F. M., & Nadel, J. A. Role of autonomic nervous system and the cough reflex in the increased responsiveness of airways in patients with obstructive airway disease. *The Journal of Clinical Investigation,* 1967, **46,** 1812–1818.

Sines, J. O. Pre-stress sensory input as a non-pharmacologic method for controlling restraint-ulcer susceptibility. *Journal of Psychosomatic Research,* 1965, **8,** 399–403.

Smith, J. M., & Burns, C. L. C. The treatment of asthmatic children by hypnotic suggestion. *British Journal of Diseases of the Chest,* 1960, **54,** 78–81.

Smyth, F. S. Allergy. In E. L. Holt, R. McIntosh, & H. L. Barnett (Eds.), *Pediatrics.* (13th ed.) New York: Appleton-Century-Crofts, 1962.

Sperling, M. Psychoanalytic study of ulcerative colitis in children. *The Psychoanalytic Quarterly,* 1946, **15,** 302–329.

Sperling, M. A case of ophidiophilia: A clinical contribution to snake symbolism, and a supplement to "Psychoanalytic study of ulcerative colitis in children." *International Journal of Psychoanalysis,* 1964, **45,** 227–236.

Sperling, M. Transference neurosis in patients with psychosomatic disorders. *The Psychoanalytic Quarterly,* 1967, **36,** 342–355.

Spitz, R. A. Hospitalism: An inquiry into the genesis of psychiatric conditions in early childhood. *Psychoanalytic Study of the Child,* 1945, **1,** 53–74.

Stein, M. Etiology and mechanisms in the development of asthma. In J. H. Nodine & J. H. Moyer (Eds.), *Psychosomatic Medicine.* Philadelphia: Lea & Febiger, 1962.

Stern, J. A., Winokur, G., Eisenstein, A., Taylor, R., & Sly, M. The effect of group vs. individual housing on behavior and physiological response to stress in the male albino rat. *Journal of Psychosomatic Research,* 1960, **4,** 185–190.

Stevenson, I. Variations in the secretion of bronchial mucus during periods of life stress. In H. G. Wolff (Ed.), *Life stress and bodily disease. Proceedings of the Association for Research in Nervous and Mental Diseases.* Baltimore: Waverly Press, 1950.

Stevenson, I., & Ripley, H. S. Variations in respiration and in respiratory symptoms during changes in emotion. *Psychosomatic Medicine,* 1952, **14,** 476–490.

Thomas, A., Birch, H. G., Chess, S., Hertzig, M., & Korn, S. *Behavioral individuality in early childhood.* New York: New York University Press, 1963.

Thomas, J. W. Resprium in the treatment of bronchial asthma and respiratory allergy. *Annals of Allergy,* 1962, **20,** 789–793.

Treuting, T. F., & Ripley, H. S. Life situations, emotions and bronchial asthma. *Journal of Nervous and Mental Diseases,* 1948, **108,** 380–396.

Tudor, R. R. Peptic ulcerations in childhood. *Pediatric Clinics of North America,* 1967, **14,** 109–139.

Tuft, H. S. Prochlorperazine as an aid in the treatment of bronchial asthma. *Annals of Allergy,* 1959, **17,** 224–229.

Weiner, H., Thaler, M., Reiser, M. F., & Mirsky, I. A. Etiology of duodenal ulcer. I. Relation of specific psychological characteristics to rate of gastric secretion (serum pepsinogen). *Psychosomatic Medicine,* 1957, **19,** 1–10.

Weininger, O. The effects of early experiences on behavior and growth characteristics. *Journal of Comparative and Physiological Psychology,* 1956, **49,** 1–9.

Weinstock, H. I. Hospital psychotherapy in severe ulcerative colitis. *Archives of General Psychiatry,* 1961, **4,** 509–512.

Weiss, J. H. Mood states associated with asthma in children. *Journal of Psychosomatic Research,* 1966, **10,** 267–273.

White, H. C. Hypnosis in bronchial asthma. *Journal of Psychosomatic Research,* 1961, **5,** 272–279.

Wittkower, E. Studies on the influence of emotions on the functions of the organs. *Journal of Mental Science,* 1935, **81,** 533–682.

Wittkower, E. Ulcerative colitis: Personality studies. *British Medical Journal,* 1938, **2,** 1356–1360.

Wolf, S., & Wolff, H. G. *Human gastric function.* New York: Oxford, 1943.

Wolpe, J. *Psychotherapy by reciprocal inhibition.* Stanford, Calif.: Stanford University Press, 1958.

Wolff, H. G. (Ed.). *Life stress and bodily disease. Proceedings of the Association for Research in Nervous and Mental Diseases.* Baltimore: Waverly Press, 1950.

part v | **Diagnostic Methods**

23 | The Psychiatric Interview

Jerome D. Goodman

A technique for interviewing children must grow from the examiner's love and care about young people as total personalities. Children are neither miniature representatives of adults nor wooden marionettes. They have the capacity for feeling anguish and suffering, which, were it not by fortune of their abilities for repression and rapid restitution, would mar them more than daily. They are rarely at a loss for long in an interviewing situation and can often cope amazingly well if the examiner makes active efforts to enter their domain. There are certain basics in approaching children which are common to the interviewing techniques of all examiners, regardless of their theoretical orientation. These basics, to be outlined later, include a way of talking and relating with children. For the purposes of exposition, the age range pertinent to this discussion encompasses children from ages 3 to 10. There is a triad of parameters which, more than others, guide the interviewer toward a meaningful diagnostic contact with children. These parameters include the child's age, sex, and relative ego strength. A mind's-eye expectation of

usual thinking and behavior, given as a point of departure the age and sex of the child, serves as a guideline from which all observations are brought into focus by extrapolation. A thorough grounding in principles of child development, with observational experience with normal children of various age groups and in diverse settings, is essential to the cultivation of this mind's-eye frame of reference. The child psychiatrist becomes aware of the expected gap that must be traversed between children of different ages and himself. Slowly he collects a built-in, almost kinesthetic sense of what is necessary on his part to bridge that gap. The more altered the child, the more remote from expectation, and thus the more stimulated are the psychiatrist's enteroceptors calling for increased active effort in producing a working relationship with that child.

The psychiatric examination of children is one part of a larger diagnostic process. Traditional child-guidance work had its wellsprings in the interdisciplinary team approach, with the diagnostic process in child psychiatry a resultant of three parts. In the conventional model used in

743

clinic settings, the mother (and less often the father) is interviewed for the developmental and social history, her estimate of the child's current functioning, and a description of the usual relationships in the home. This body of "data" is often unreliable. Wenar (1963) has described the overall picture of reliability of mothers' histories. He found that the information that is most accurately recalled includes details of motor development and weight gain. Much less accurate are details given by the mother about interpersonal relations and child-rearing practices. Wenar concludes that the heart of reconstructive studies —and, by extension, diagnostic inferences—is based on the least valid data, which often can mislead more than inform. The social-developmental history becomes more acceptable as a clinical interview and is equally valuable in that function as in its information-gathering role. For the child-focused diagnostic process, the social-developmental history may present many seeming paradoxes. A child may be reported to have attained motor milestones easily but to have become clumsy and motorically backward suddenly and without apparent cause. Or perhaps a child who presented with grace and excellent motoric coordination was reported as a stumbling and awkward younger child. Other children of easy-going manner were reported to have been terrors at home; and so on, through endless poor fits of social-developmental report and clinical impression. Parents always filter and distort in varying degrees. But there are more instances than the clinician is comfortable in acknowledging in which the child's psychopathogenesis just does not conform to our usual models. Often the paradoxical situation (including many more examples than given above—object relations, anxiety levels, sexual identity, etc.) presents and requires further search for other sources of information outside of traditional methodology. At times, a home visit for diagnostic interviewing in child psychiatry is indicated. Freeman (1967) finds its

use best suited for "very young and immature children; highly anxious, disturbed and unmanageable children; those who are not verbal in office settings, but are reported to talk at home; those who have had multiple medical and surgical experiences, or who have had, or may have, a combination of handicaps requiring careful differential diagnosis." Home movies, if available, are an excellent source of data. Allen and Goodman (1966) described their role in validating the developmental history, in providing information about the child's reactions to environment, parents, siblings, and friends. They also are often frozen documents of child-rearing technique. When they are viewed with parents, the feelings of the parents are instantly mirrored as they participate again in the emotional experience. In certain instances, the clinician may become the unobserved observer, seeing longitudinally a child in his natural environment.

Attitudes, expectations, and bias of the parent form a halo which illuminates the information about the child. All experienced workers in the child-guidance field are sensitive to nuances of thought and feeling emanating from parents in their reportorial productions. It is common for the child psychiatrist to be familiar with the material gathered from the parent(s)—either directly or by briefing—before seeing the child. There are variations on the theme, however. It is not at all uncommon in some clinics, and especially in private practice, for the psychiatrist to incorporate a part of this history taking into the examination of the child. There is an advantage accrued from watching the attendant child-parent interaction while part of the anamnestic material is being gathered. There is a distinct disadvantage to this practice as employed in the diagnostic study of children who are age 5 or over. Generally, the psychiatric examination of school-age children is best conducted without the continual presence of a parent. Interviewing families together is a complex and difficult procedure which provides a wealth of clinical material but tends to obscure the focus. If whole-family interviews are contemplated, they are often employed to greater value following the individual interview with the child. The very separation of the child from the parent is the first bit of information to be gathered in the interview. If the mother of younger children is interviewed in the presence of the child, it is valuable to have her separated from the child and remain in a waiting room at some distance from the office when the child is being interviewed.

Psychological testing is the other traditional part of the diagnostic process. In addition to the common function of psychometric and projective test materials, as well as testing perceptual-motor function, the psychological testing period becomes another chance for clinical examination. The psychologist records his observational findings but, unlike the psychiatrist, will usually confine his interaction to a more narrow range. This range is often defined more by limited activity than by limited acceptance. In child-guidance clinics, the psychologist team member reports not only the test results but his clinical impression as well. The usual temporal sequence of the diagnostic process, particularly in clinic settings, is (1) social and developmental history, (2) psychiatric interview, and (3) psychological testing. Some child psychiatrists routinely read psychological test protocols prior to interviewing children. This practice is to be discouraged.

A historical review of the approach to the psychiatric examination of children will emphasize the very recent and rapid development in sophistication of approach, largely the function of a latter-day recognition of normative developmental patterns for children. Until the nineteenth century, with rare exception, the affliction of children suffering either mental retardation or emotional disturbance was attributed to extracorporeal forces, usually demonic or divine. Children were not spared from witch-hunts, but

curiously, imbeciles were often held in high regard and were studied for supposed cryptic supermentation. The astronomer Brahe kept an idiot in his laboratory and listened at length to the senseless mutterings aspiring to gain some special knowledge. Most of the early psychological observations of children sprang from an interest in the thinking of retarded or organically impaired children. Benjamin Rush wrote in 1812 that the rarity of madness prior to puberty could be attributed to the instability of the minds of children; they were thought to be too unstable for mental impressions to produce more than transient effects. Esquirol, on the other hand, described several cases of mental illness in children between the ages of 8 and 11. He drew a very sharp distinction between what he termed *dementia* and *idiocy,* considering the latter to define a congenital defect. This distinction was important prognostically. "Recovery," Esquirol wrote, "is possible from dementia, its symptoms can be suppressed." The use of diary recording of child development was very much in keeping with the observational approach of the nineteenth-century scientists, including Darwin's *Biographical Sketch of an Infant.* It has recently regained favor in such longitudinal studies as those of Chess, Thomas, and Birch. Kerlin, writing in 1879, thought juvenile insanity to be linked to hereditary predisposition. Diagnostic evaluation, for him, consisted of comparing the patient's reactions with ordinary standards of childhood. Insanity, he wrote, manifested itself in excitation of an intense state in the presence of normal speech, sight, and hearing. He found insane children to be suspicious, violent in their likes and dislikes, and morally unsound. He contrasted such children to idiots and imbeciles, who were found to be truthful and kind. Kerlin, much as Esquirol, categorized children with profound disturbances into either a demented-insane group or a retarded-imbecilic group. In 1887, Emminghaus, in *Psychic Disturbances of Childhood,* treated the problems of children as distinct and different, even incommensurable with those of adults. His work was largely ignored, for childhood disorders were still amalgamated at that time with those of adults. Adolph Meyer, advocating a holistic observational diagnostic process with children, urged abandonment of mere questioning, citing often erroneous information derived from this method. In 1895, he wrote: "If you wish to find peculiar symptoms in the child, you can always produce them by simply arousing the intense desire for mimicry and the suggestability of the child." The entire climate surrounding the problems of children, their clinical disorders, their rights as individuals, and their particular needs as patients changed rapidly around the turn of the century. As in other areas of medicine, social reform preceded and galvanized clinical expertise. The history of the approach to interviewing children since 1900 is inseparable from the history of modern child psychology and child psychiatry, with the major ingredients arrayed around the development of psychometry, psychoanalytic theory, play therapy, and the child-guidance group.

MODELS FOR INTERVIEWING

Many partial models for examining children psychiatrically have been published, most of them of relatively recent vintage. One of the trendsetters in the field, whose studies brought to light many of the accepted modalities now incorporated into play therapy, was David Levy. Levy (1924) described a psychiatric examination of children which included a physical examination. He found that children were readily willing to talk about their physical attributes and were remarkably perceptive about small cosmetic defects, which would have escaped undetected had they not been encouraged to verbalize in a gaming relationship.

Another early guide was that of Nolan D. C.

Lewis (1934). In his outlines for psychiatric examinations, Lewis included a chapter devoted to the examination of children. In his mental examination, Lewis listed (1) general attitude, conduct, and appearance; (2) stream of mental activity; (3) emotional reactions; and (4) mental attitude (spontaneous accounts of problems and life history, attitude toward home and members of the family, attitude toward school and playmates, and attitude toward self). Lewis understood the special nature of child psychopathology and found the examination of children not to be a matter of determining the presence of thought disorders and pathological variations in mood. He wrote that the mental examination aimed to secure an understanding of the child's feelings and attitudes toward life experiences.

There were many landmarks, including the first textbook devoted to child psychiatry, written by Leo Kanner (1935). In the first edition of this textbook, a chapter is devoted to the psychiatric examination proper. An abbreviated mental-status examination is included but was deleted in subsequent editions. A chapter by Paul L. Schroeder in *Child Guidance Procedures* (1937) is quite specific about interviewing procedures and is, for its day, a rare exercise in straightforward exposition of the problem. Sampling from that work, one learns that in the total effort to understand the causes of a child's behavior, the special contribution of the psychiatrist was the discovery and elucidation of the child's inner motives as they were revealed by his behavior in a relatively well-controlled setting. The child in this way was encouraged to give his own account of his attitudes, motives, conflicts, and other inner states. The authors noted that the psychiatrist was afforded an opportunity to observe a child's manner, blocking, tensions, responsiveness, and many other things besides the content of his speech, all of which furnished clues to ideas and emotions. In contrast to later work in family interviews, this account stressed that except in very rare instances, the psychiatrist interviewed only one person at a time. The value of the interview is claimed to depend to a considerable extent upon placing a child in a very simple situation. A third person in the room, stated the authors, complicated the situation to a quite undeterminable degree.

There have been a number of models proposed since the late 1940s concerning highlights of the child psychiatric examination in contradistinction to usual adult models. There has been continuing refinement of these models and a more recent emphasis on the tempering of the diagnostic process to fit the prevailing behavior of the child—to wit, the diagnostic interview of an autistic child proceeds in quite a different manner from the interview of an adjustment-reaction child.

Axline (1947) established a guide of basic principles applicable to nondirective therapy with children which reflects the influence of Carl Rogers. These principles, which can serve as guides to the interviewing circumstances as well as therapy proper, stress the importance of acceptance of the child exactly as he presents himself. The interviewer is urged to express warmth and friendliness with permissive overtones. The child's actions and thoughts are not directed, and only those limitations that are essential are imposed. Structuring for Axline is accomplished through the medium of relationship rather than given through verbal direction. In a similar vein, Moustakas (1959) has discussed the values of limit setting and structuring in early phases of therapy. The limitations of time, of the use of play materials, and of motion within the playroom are all built into the establishment of a relationship. Moustakas emphasizes the unique nature of every child and urges the therapist to present himself as unique to each different child. The inherent experience of growth evolving from the encounter of two individuals within the framework of existentialism pervades this approach to child-therapist interaction.

Ackerman (1953) proposed a guide for evaluation of personality functioning of a child which was inclusive of most of the material gathered in total diagnostic process. He emphasized the adaptational and interactive features of the child's behavior in his environmental context. Those parts of the guide which had particular reference to the psychiatric interview proper included (1) general appearance and behavior, (2) reality adaptation, (3) interpersonal relations, (4) quality of affects, (5) anxiety reactions, (6) patterns of control, (7) defense patterns, and (8) central conflicts. Under patterns of control, Ackerman further listed (1) general capacity for control of emotion, (2) degree of impulsiveness, (3) capacity for pleasure experience, (4) capacity for displeasure experience, and others. Ackerman noted:

> Since the personality organization of a child is continuously changing, dominant behavior reactions are prone to shift in accordance with the integrational pattern and character of the interaction of the environment which prevails at a given time. The younger the child and the less formed its personality, the more difficult it is to discriminate between normal reactions to stress and pathological anxiety responses.

The Group for the Advancement of Psychiatry (1957) Report No. 38 was one of the most explicit and comprehensive forays into the field and remains a landmark. Yarrow (1960) has emphasized the need for effective techniques in interviewing children. Although his discussion is oriented toward research aspects of the interview, he included much methodology which was clinically applicable.

Thomas, Chess, Birch, Hertzig, and Korn (1963) have been gathering continuing information since the 1950s about the individual behavioral style of children, starting in infancy and following into latency and beyond. The nine categories of reactivity that this group uses in their assessments are (1) activity level, (2) rhythmicity, (3) approach or withdrawal, (4) adaptability, (5) intensity of reaction, (6) threshold of responsiveness, (7) quality of mood, (8) distractability, and (9) attention span and persistence. Most of these categories can be incorporated into a psychiatric examination and provide basal values for follow-up interviews. The authors have noted that in many children the consistency of expression of temperament in repeated assessments has been striking. When behavioral disturbance occured in the group of children followed from infancy, it resulted, stated this group, from the interaction of a child with a given pattern of temperament and specific features of his developmental environment, notably the temperament of the mother. Thus, they concluded, the accuracy of differential diagnosis depends upon an assessment of characteristics for *both* the mother and the child. If the psychiatrist has not gathered the social history, he must then—at least—gather some impressions about the mother at some time during the diagnostic process. In partial response to critics who found this approach superficial and descriptive rather than dynamic, the following argument has been used by these authors:

> The typologic and the reactive development positions may be viewed as complementary rather than antagonistic. If one considers the aspects of functioning with which each has been concerned, it becomes clear that typology has focused its interest in problems of temperament, whereas reactive theories have dealt with adaptive organizations of the personality. It is of interest that, when confronted with temperamental questions, reactive theory, as illustrated by Freud, tends to fall back upon constitutionalism and inborn difference in energy level. Conversely, typologies use reactive conceptualizations in order to account for motive and adaptation.

Bransford (1965) has devised a form based on clinical inferences which attempts to standardize, via ratings, seven dimensions of children's behavior. These dimensions are (1) central nervous system (CNS) deficit or dysfunction (neurological examination and behavioral observation

and others), (2) neurotic component (factors relating to the expression of or defense against excessive anxiety or fear), (3) psychotic component (distorted or bizarre perceptions, associations, or behavioral responses), (4) sociopathic component (factors relating to egocentral, manipulative, or retaliative behavior), (5) intellectual functioning, (6) milieu (impression of factors relating to intrafamilial, intrapersonal, and community relationships), and (7) estimated functioning level (combined evaluation and recommendations for therapeutic intervention). Bransford commented on several problems which confront the student of clinical ratings of behavior in children. These problems include the rapid change of the child over time, the variability of the child in changing contexts (settings), and the bias of the rater or clinician. Not the least of the difficulties in devising rating scales had to do with the complexity of behavior, which could only be sampled rather than encompassed in a scale. (A psychiatric examination is hardly a finalized document, and the clinician is well advised to consider his assessment as a biopsy of a protean organism rather than a cross-sectional representation.)

A diagnostic profile in Anna Freud's *Normality and Pathology of Childhood* (1965) includes a comprehensive delving into developmental and social history as well as psychiatric evaluation. Those parts of the profile which are most pertinent to the psychiatric examination proper include (1) *description of the child* (personal appearance, moods, and manner), (2) *assessment of some general characteristics* (frustration tolerance, sublimation potential, attitude toward anxiety, progressive developmental forces versus regressive tendencies), (3) *ego and superego development* (intactness or deficit of ego apparatus, defense organization—whether the defenses are gauged adequate, balanced, effective, or employed specifically against individual drives and whether defense activity interferes with ego achievement), (4) *genetic assessment* (fantasy activity, manifest behavior, symptomatology), and (5) *conflicts* (external, internal, and internalized). Anna Freud stated in this work that descriptive methodology in diagnosis ("direct scrutiny of the surface of the mind") could penetrate structure, functioning, and content of personality. She deplored, however, thinking in descriptive terms, which she called "disastrous when taken as a starting point for analytic inferences." Reconciling the seeming paradox in the above, Anna Freud found it useful to describe the appearance and behavior of a child (surface phenomena) at a given point in time but tended to translate the phenomenological data into psychoanalytic terms. In other words, the totality of the diagnostic process became the starting point for analytic inferences rather than the sample descriptive features of the clinical interview.

In creating a typology of children's psychiatric disorders, which was applied to an evaluation of treatment, Fish and Shapiro (1965) described guides for assessment, which they incorporated into a short series of psychiatric interviews. The subheadings for these guides to evaluation included (1) relation to examiner, (2) relations to peers, (3) relation to environment (within the interview), (4) speech, (5) affect, (6) motility, (7) adaptive function. Fish and Shapiro found that children arranged themselves into four prototypic groups, which they labeled types 1 to 4, when these seven subheadings of behavioral function were used as an evaluating guide. They further stated that their observations of function at different levels did not necessarily point toward etiology but did indicate the depth to which a disorder affected the substratum underlying behavior. The authors have continued their studies, and later, Fish et al. (1968) stated that their categories described a nosology on the basis of functional impairment. Their schemata are relevant for longitudinal studies as well as comparative studies of diverse etiologies.

McDonald (1965) conducted a review and discussion of the literature of child psychiatry with reference to the psychiatric evaluation proper.

She included those few brief descriptive reviews of methodology found in textbooks, mentioned several references which were related to fragments of the diagnostic process, and noted the all too frequent references which merged evaluation with treatment. McDonald, like other workers in the field (Goodman & Sours, 1967), was hard pressed to find more than scant references to the diagnostic interview of children until the 1960s. She commented that her search of the literature found that the clinical diagnostic evaluation of children had been either ignored, presented in the briefest of surveys as a descriptive rather than a dynamic procedure, or abdicated by psychiatrists to other disciplines.

Goodman and Sours (1967) addressed themselves to technical aspects of the child psychiatric interview. They described special techniques for talking with and playing with children, including a neurological examination cast entirely within the framework of play. These authors combined a phenomenological and a dynamic approach and stressed the importance of comprehensive observational detail gathered while tempering their interaction according to the progress of the interview. In the mental-status examination proper, the following headings were described: (1) size and general appearance, (2) motility, (3) coordination, (4) speech, (5) intellectual function, (6) modes of thinking and perception, (7) emotional reactions, (8) manner of relating, (9) fantasies and dreams, and (10) character of play. With regard to play, the authors stated that the characteristics of play confirm the content of play. They found that play content offered more genetic hypotheses while play characteristics offered more dynamic hypotheses. They described an evocative role of the psychiatrist with the child and presented their material as a conceptual guide rather than a formalized outline of approach.

In *A Handbook of Child Psychoanalysis*, edited by Pearson (1968), the authors consider the examination of the child in the expectation of possible candidacy for analysis. They note that the child also evaluates the examiner, looking over the setting and the person of the analyst. They comment that the new circumstance of diagnostic encounter should be reasonably comfortable and inviting for the child. If play is incorporated into the diagnostic interview, the authors caution the analyst not to provide the child with a playmate but rather to show interest, participate if invited, and focus his efforts on learning about the child rather than becoming engrossed in the play activity. They do not advocate telling the child about confidentiality unless the child asks about it. Commenting that an evaluation is incomplete if a child leaves the office or refuses to return, the authors suggest that it is at times necessary to extend participation in the initial relationship to a greater degree than usual in order to accomplish diagnostic goals. Discussion about the advisability of various play materials and the physical composition of the office is also included.

Beller (1962) and Werkman (1965) have written about certain technical aspects of the diagnostic interview. Simmons (1969) has outlined many features of a psychiatric examination of children. He places that examination within the context of the total diagnostic process. Simmons urges the use of the mental status of a child as a documental reference. Summing up the historical aspects of the child psychiatric interview, one must conclude that its development has been recent and accelerating—neither of which conditions permits more than limited historical perspective.

The feelings of parents about their disturbed children have been relatively more constant through history. Although in former times parents may have ascribed their child's ailment to fate or deity, they did not escape the anguish of their lot. Lately, and largely as the product of popularized information distributed through mass media, parents have felt more keenly a sense of failure and active participation in the psychopathology of their children. It is an implied ad-

mission of failure for parents to seek professional help, and they must receive active support about their feelings of guilt and apprehension. Those who work with children are rarely callous to the plight of parents who come to them for assistance. All parents must be briefed prior to the child's interview. They have usually made contact with one of the members of the interdisciplinary team prior to the start of the diagnostic process and can be given a few simple instructions at that time or when the social history is taken. The child should be prepared by the parent. The parents should tell the child that they are concerned about certain aspects of his behavior, that the child will be taken to a special kind of doctor who talks to children about their worries and problems, that the doctor sees other children with similar difficulties, and that the doctor will know a little about the child's particular difficulties and will be able to help the child if he can tell the doctor more about them. It is best to minimize the lag between the time of informing the child of the impending visit and its actuality.

SPECIAL FEATURES IN INTERVIEWING CHILDREN

Children are sent by parents, often at the instigation of schools, referring physicians, courts, or other agencies, to see the psychiatrist. They are, if anything, negatively motivated toward the visit. Children rarely suffer as acutely from their emotional symptoms as they do from even minor physical ones. Anna Freud (1965) has remarked that we have to become accustomed to the paradoxical situation that the correspondence between psychopathology and suffering, normality and equanimity, as it exists in adults is reversed in children. She found that the most seriously disturbed children were completely oblivious of illness. Contrasted to what is expected in adults, compliant and resigned children often arouse clinical suspicions as to abnormal processes at work within them. To counteract the prevailing set of absent or negative motivations in children, the child psychiatrist approaches the young patient with special techniques and surroundings. Helen Beiser (1962) considered that most child psychiatrists over a period of time unconsciously sort and compare various observations and slowly reach conclusions as to what influences behavior in various directions. At the same time, she wrote, they probably develop a technique which, if not formalized in the strict sense, at least becomes a fairly stable pattern for them. This developed technique—a customary way of approaching children with built-in expectations for the child's responses according to age, sex, and ego strength and with an ongoing appraisal of those aspects of appearance, behavior, and verbal material which range outside of empirical expectations—constitutes the very core of the diagnostic method during the psychiatric interview.

There are few rules, no absolutes, but many guidelines about the physical setting of an office where diagnostic interviews with children are conducted. The interviewing area should be designed so that it is separated from the waiting room by another room or corridor. The distance traversed by the child in separating from the parent is often the setting for important diagnostic information in child-parent interaction. Some children look back to wave or receive other support from parents. Some children are nonchalant and unconcerned, even eager to come along with the strange doctor. Some of the physical attributes of the child (gait, resemblance to parent, alacrity of response) and his manner of relating—whether trusting and friendly or shy and wary—are first impressions along the way to the office. From the GAP Report of 1957 we learn that an examination of the child really begins in the waiting room, where the psychiatrist meets and briefly welcomes the child and his parents, utilizing this opportunity to note the interaction of parents and child and their anticipatory attitudes about the coming session. Thus he can observe the child's physical appearance and note any striking resemblances or lack of them to the parents. In addition, the psychiatrist becomes particularly attuned to the counterpoint in the child versus his parents with respect to temperament. Especially in those disorders in which the child is noted as ebullient in contrast to placid parents (or vice versa) does such disparity in temperament often have cueing value for symptomatology and predictive value for choice of treatment modality.

The examiner then enters the waiting room with all the receptivity he can muster. The initial encounter is often the most informative moment in the entire diagnostic process, rivaled only by the farewell. Some children, especially preschool-age children, will not separate easily from their mothers. If the interviewer attempts to force them, to coerce separation, he is usually courting a battle (often with mother an unwitting adversary). Some coaxing, perhaps a deliberately disarming approach, can help. But if the child will not separate easily, the mother should be invited along. In these instances, the examiner wishes to evaluate the mother's role via her prompting, verbal and nonverbal. If the mother does come along and if the child is engageable—and does, in fact, settle down in the office—some attempt should be made to have the mother withdraw. Perhaps as many as half of those children who have been so chaperoned initially will tolerate the separation. Nothing is lost in the attempt, and much can be gained diagnostically about the outcome. For those children who do separate initially—and they are the majority—the psychiatrist does well to avoid uncalled-for reassurances. It is not necessary to reassure the child, without his asking, that mother will wait for him. Shaw (1966) discusses "Rules of the Diagnostic Interview," which he finds useful but not necessarily of universal application. One of these pertains to the clinician's appearance.

Shaw finds no positive value, and much of negative value, in the wearing of a white coat. But perhaps of greater importance, Shaw advises that the child not be deceived about the fact that he is seeing a psychiatrist and the reasons for the interview. He also urges the clinician not to whisper or attempt to communicate with an accompanying adult (parent or social worker) in the child's presence. As a corollary, he urges the doctor to actively greet the child as the person of maximum importance rather than the accompanying chaperone.

The child should not be interviewed in a veritable toy shop. A large number of elaborate toys allows the child to take flight into play and cheerfully avoid talking about himself. The simpler the play materials, the more information they can provide. The toy box or shelf should contain the following unstructured playthings: clay, crayons and paper, children's scissors, wooden blocks, pipe cleaners, balloons, and paper clips. A few play originals are chosen largely because they can create scenarios and also demonstrate the child's ability to coordinate and manipulate objects. A doll or two, vehicles (especially trains or trucks that can be linked together), plastic soldiers or a family set, magnets, and a pack of cards are most of what is needed. Small rubber balls, pickup sticks, or jacks can be included, and they often provide significant information about neurological functioning. A blackboard, freestanding or on a wall, is very helpful. The most important design feature of the office is the incorporation of those pieces of furniture and the arrangement of space so that the child's-eye view and scale of perception prevails. There should be enough free space to allow the child to move about but not so much as to appear cavernous. The room should be well lighted, and drapes or shades on the windows are best kept open. There should be a small table with low wooden chairs, at least one of which is sturdy enough to hold the examiner. Play material should be placed close

to the floor. If windows are hung high on the wall, the placement of a chair near one of them will allow the child a view of the outside. Running water and a lavatory should adjoin the play area; it will often become the center of the child's activities. A ticking clock can serve as an aid in the structuring of the interview. Children often ask how long they will be seen, and the presence of a clock—even though their time sense is tremendously expanded in comparison with an adult's—can be used to show them just how long the interview will last. There are several other optional items that can be incorporated into the interviewing area, including a mirror, paintings (but not nursery primitives), and a child's clothing rack. The fewer breakable objects, the better. Almost all examiners see adults and adolescents as well as children in their offices. Practicality dictates that the office contain furniture and equipment other than the above. Dictating machines, telephones, and other mechanical devices are diverting distractions for children and can be kept relatively remote. The physical composition of the office is a constant within which the psychiatrist observes the child. It is less important than his expertise in relating to children, but it is one component which can be relatively controlled and which offers information about the child's natural responses. For a résumé, GAP Report No. 38 (1957), *The Diagnostic Process in Child Psychiatry,* formulated by the Committee on Child Psychiatry, states:

> It is desirable that the interviewing room be set up to provide the child with a reasonable balance of freedom and protection and to offer simple play materials appropriate to his age, affording both creative and aggressive expression. Physical examining rooms or luxurious adult offices rarely afford an appropriate setting for a psychiatric session with a young child.

What are some of the examiner's responsibilities toward the child during the interview? As an adult, he cannot permit the child total free rein for aggressive activities. Whatever the ego strength of the child, it is destructive of his reality testing to allow him to smash, shout, or run completely at will. Neither should the psychiatrist expect the child to dutifully sit in place and give an orderly or well-behaved account of himself. The child psychiatrist approaches a young patient in a more active, friendly, and supportive manner than he would older patients. He seeks to enter the child's world, but he carefully avoids doting or patronizing attitudes and allows the child to initiate approach-avoidance behavior. Millar (1968) has written about the roles of limit setting in the psychological maturation processes of the child. He underscores the need to supply children with guidelines serving to help them sustain ego growth from their earlier position of omnipotence, egocentricity, and limited capacity for delay. The interviewer, like the parent, has a responsibility to provide a positive and, to some extent, gratifying experience for the child. He must also disapprove, however, of behavior which is out of bounds and destructive. Such behavior most often cries out for control and guidance. If the child displays aggressive outbursts, it is not necessary to allow these to run their full course during an interview. It is also informative to note the child's response to firm yet understanding disapproval. For the diagnostic interview, as in child rearing, Millar has stated that appropriate controls can be achieved by maintaining expectations at the maturity level of the child and reinforcing them at that level.

TALKING WITH CHILDREN

Talking with children in an attempt to gain information is a practiced art. The early studies of Piaget (1928, 1932) are replete with just those areas of limitation by age of a child's conceptual processes which disallow adults egress into their world via adult models. Shaw (1966) has written of the use of humor in parlance with children.

In his text, he finds that clues in diagnosis can progress from the response of the child to an initially humorous approach. He finds that a joke now and then helps to set a tone for the interview and deplores the clinician who is unable to relax in his dignity. He states that a child cannot tolerate a situation well which is stiff and formal. On the other hand, many children are prepared to work hard even in the initial interview. Particularly 7- to 10-year-old children expect often to accomplish something and, at times, feel the same uneasiness with merriment and levity that other children feel with formality and restraint. The initial use of humor is usually advisable, but its continuation—as with other approaches of the clinician—requires feedback.

Note that the progression of a child's thinking pattern from egocentric to socialized thought must always temper clinical inferences about "thought disorders" in children. There is often a fallacious and loose assumption in the mind of the examiners that paleologic (Arieti, 1955) is roughly equivalent to a young child's thought processes. Arieti feels that autistic thought occurs at a very early age in children when they use paleological thinking. He is inclined to view the occurrence of autistic thought as a propensity rather than a necessity. The propensity is automatically overcome if the child relates well and becomes socially integrated. The primary-process thinking of Freud (1960), though present in plentitude in children, is inhibited and overlaid by secondary-process thought relatively early. In addition, this primitive thinking, which Freud postulated, is relatively unavailable to the child and is usually repressed readily. Although this thinking can be heard distinctly at times in adult psychotic patients, it is not a passkey to children's thought, even in psychotic children. Tessman and Kaufman (1967) have used the primary process in the treatment of schizophrenic children. They make note of the concretisms, condensations, symbolisms, timelessness, and primitive logic that is experienced as reality by the schizophrenic child. They believe that the child's retention of this thinking is overdetermined and maintained by a parent-child interaction in which there is often a symbiotic tie and in which the child's "craziness" is fostered. In therapy, the clinician's stance tends toward understanding the child's need to use this thinking rather than toward direct interpretations and communications through its medium. If the examiner, well intentioned, attempts to capture the child's imagination and interest by commenting in a replica of primary process, the child will more likely than not ignore him or indicate that the examiner is "crazy." Such parlance constitutes one of the empirical violations of interviewing children. One does not try baby talk or crazy talk or any other variety of primitive talking in order to reach a child diagnostically. What, then, are some of the ways of talking with children which are empirically effective and productive?

First, the examiner is well advised to speak slowly and in simple rather than compound sentences. Children forget the central point of sentences which run on with dependent clauses. As an illustration, compare the following: "When you get up in the morning on school days, are you able to get dressed yourself or does your mother have to help you with the buttons?" versus "Can you dress yourself?" "All the time?" "How about buttons?" "Does your mother help?"

Second, repeated questioning turns the interview into an inquisition—yet there are many things the examiner wants to know. Questions can be disguised and muted by asking them rhetorically, directing them toward a hypothetical third person, and conveying them through thinking aloud. Questions can also be implied through the use of hyperbole and distortion for dramatic effect. Using the example above, the series of questions and answers can become:

> "I'm wondering if you dress yourself."
> "Yeah."

> "Well, that's something! Most 5-year-old children *can't* dress themselves."
> "I do."
> "I bet you don't do it *all* by yourself. Not *all* the time."
> "Well, sometimes . . ."
> "Even buttons?!!"
> "My Mommy buttons me . . . but I can do some . . . you wanta see?"

Third, the use of the subjunctive is an open invitation for the child to participate. Many phrases, including "Suppose you were . . ." and "What if you . . . ?" and "Let's pretend that. . . ," are very effective toward bridging the adult-child gap. There is a gaming quality about the subjunctive which allows the child to let down his guard, "almost as though it didn't count." Many children are sensitive to failure and try mightily to avoid making mistakes. They want approval and fear censure. The "let's pretend" way of talking circumvents the demands of a classroom model or the authoritarian adult figure. Other children seize the initiative offered them in the subjunctive mode and give vent to elaborate stories and tall tales. It is usually easier, however, to guide them back from an invitation to fantasy than it is to ask for fantasies and dreams as a segmental part of the interview alone. Liberal usage of this subjunctive mode, particularly with younger children, sets a tone in the interview which prepares the way for some probing in depth.

Fourth, the examiner should modulate his or her voice and speak quietly, yet audibly. Loud voices, especially *basso profundo,* frighten children. Many youngsters respond warmly to song, and singing or humming during otherwise silent activities can be helpful. Whistling or humming is a signal, usually, that all is going well. If the examiner finds humming, singing, or whistling out of character for him, then it is better to talk or remain silent. Children are usually quick to detect dissimulation, and the most natural approach on the part of the examiner bids for trust.

Fifth, there is often the temptation on the part of an adult to alter grammar and vocabulary to approximate the child's. Many interviewers have learned in talking with adults of foreign birth that a phrase in their mother tongue can go far in establishing rapport. Not so with children. A deliberate infantilization of speech rarely accomplishes much more than signaling regression in a child.

Sixth, the interviewer should space his questions and have them proceed from the innocuous to the searching. All examiners want to ask the child about his understanding of what has brought him to the office. This question can be reserved, in most instances, for the terminal part of the interview; at times it is not apt. Other subject matter that can be held in abeyance, to be asked later—if at all—includes questions about fears, symptoms, and worries. The interviewer's combined intuitive guesses and reasoned approach can allow him to recognize those children who have a need to talk about their symptoms. These children, usually in the later latency group, are best served if they can ventilate at some length. Denying such children free expression of their concern, either by monopolizing the options of subject material or by drawing them away from talking into play, can raise the level of their anxiety.

Seventh, the psychiatrist should ask questions in such a manner that the answer is not implied. Almost all children have encountered many adults whose questions are in reality veiled commands. The psychiatrist is also in danger of misleading himself if he puts his own words into the child's productions. With older children who are in serious difficulty and who are particularly attuned to their recent behavioral problems, a disarming preliminary can often arouse suspicion about an unpleasant task or discussion to follow. For them, if the clinician so senses, it is better to come to the point rapidly. They cannot give easily of themselves while waiting for the sword to fall.

Eighth, the interviewer should attempt to strike a balance between questioning and commenting versus allowing the child to talk spontaneously. Some children will play and chatter on, if so permitted, throughout the interview. Others will dutifully answer and offer little on their own if the interview is structured in that manner. Ideally, the child psychiatrist starts off as a friendly and supportive interviewer, allows (and actively sponsors) the child to capture the initiative during the middle part of the interview, and gathers the more searching information toward the end, especially if a relationship has caught on. Children are rarely suitable historians and should not be expected to present lengthy anamnestic responses to any probings about their problems. It is the temperament and personality of the child which guide, and the psychiatrist adapts his interviewing techniques to fit the child's behavior and verbalization. Checklists and formalized sets of questions do not capture the experience of an interview with the child.

NARROWING THE RANGE OF DIAGNOSTIC POSSIBILITIES

The clinician is relatively nondirective during the early part of the interview and samples rather than probes. Midway in the interview he takes his hunches drawn from myriad sources (appearance and behavior, the presenting symptomatology—in brief, a mental-status examination) and applies them. Every interview poses different requirements. Those children who appear to have perceptual-motor impairment will perforce be investigated in a much different manner than those who present with well-integrated parlance about conflicts and fears. Once the gist of the child's problem has been surmised, the pathway toward appropriate and more special investigating procedures is established. The interview is thus divided into thirds, for which only the first third is in any way standardized. In the first third, the child is encouraged, supported, and allowed fairly random choice. His activity is limited only by those considerations which are dictated by the psychiatrist's role as a responsible adult. At the end of the first third of the interview, the clinician will have clicked off major categories in his mind and assigned the child as representational of a gross diagnostic category. The first third, then, is basically observation and typologic. The interviewer, as an analogy, walks along a corridor looking into rooms on either side and gathers a notion at the end of this walk as to whether he has passed by familiar and animated areas or barren and disordered places. He has used his clinical senses in a scanning manner. At the end of the first third of the interview, or thereabouts, the clinician will have sorted the child in his thinking into perhaps one of the following categories: (1) normal, developmental lag, or situational reaction; (2) neurotic traits, habit or conduct disturbance, or psychoneurosis; (3) mild organic impairment, psychophysiological reaction, or mild mental retardation; (4) psychotic reaction, toxic disturbance, major organic impairment, or profound mental retardation. The precision of labels is not so important as the ability to narrow down the scope of possibilities.

The second third of the interview is a pursuit of the differential assortment. It combines descriptive and psychodynamic methodology. If a child looks fairly healthy and well integrated (remembering the social-developmental history and chief complaint), is there a disparity in parental report and clinical impression? Perhaps the child will change with a measure of challenge and stress; or maybe the "immaturity" is more a function of experiential deprivation than of regression. If the child has appeared anxious, worried, and fearful, is there pervasive disturbance or sector impairment? Does the child regard his disturbance as ego-alien and intrusive, or is he relatively unconcerned about it?

If the child has initially seemed dull, is there overall intellectual deficit or circumscribed areas of perceptual-motor impairment? If he appears clumsy and poorly coordinated, does his performance vary according to his level of comfort during the interview? If the child has appeared bizarre, is his thinking also disjunct and his way of relating distant? Is his strange appearance a passive deficit in communicating ability or an active attempt to avoid contact? The second third of the interview is more active than the first, as the clinician moves toward the child, testing hypotheses.

The last third of the interview is the most artful and demanding part. Having tentatively formed a clinical impression, the psychiatrist will attempt to implement this clinical judgment by moving still closer to the child and interrelating with him. If the child is seen as organically compromised, perhaps the psychiatrist will conduct a neurological play examination. If the child is seen as psychotic, the psychiatrist will identify those islands of relatively intact ego functioning and will try to relate through them, perhaps in play, perhaps through the child's projected or expressed fantasies. If the child is found to be neurotic, the psychiatrist will gauge those coping mechanisms which are brought into the foreground through interaction, play, and general pursuit through indirect means of unconscious material. If the child is seen as relatively healthy, perhaps the parent can join the last part of the interview and the interaction of child and parent can be further explored. The last third of the interview looks more to strength than weaknesses. It capitalizes on the accrual of goodwill founded on an educative and nonthreatening relationship developed earlier in the interview. It also comes closer to learning about the child's conception of the primary problem, his self-estimate, and his desire for help. It varies with each child. The child psychiatrist may conduct himself in a more standardized manner in the opening moments, but the close of the interview is in every sense therapeutic and thus a function of the child, the clinician, and the way they get along together.

The first third of the interview attempts to answer the question: What does the child look like? The second third seeks the answers to the questions: What kind of trouble is this? and How serious is the disturbance? The last third seeks the answers to the question, What can we do about it? and investigates those strengths that the child brings with him that will provide the framework for prognostic considerations and choice of treatment modality. The approaches to the interview of the child discussed next (whether they are phenomenological, analytic, or transactional) are points of emphasis rather than totalities and are readily melded together in a compatible whole. The child's blend and uniqueness of personality dictate methodology, not the examiner's theoretical preferences. There is some question as to whether children develop a transference reaction. They probably do transfer somewhat their expectations, but they probably do not develop the transference neurosis. The psychiatrist, especially in the diagnostic interview, should approximate the parent as to the child's conception of their role. It is rarely appropriate in an initial interview for the examiner to interpret out of hand or comment sagaciously about play activity to the child, relating this activity to unconscious processes. Borrowing from Winnicot (1963), we learn that parents who interpret the unconscious to their children are in for a bad time. A psychiatrist who thinks he has the child well pegged should bridle his enthusiasm and not blurt out his discoveries. The child can rarely use this information and can be put off for future therapy.

DIFFERENTIAL DIAGNOSIS

Prior to a consideration of the more common differentials, some attention should be directed to common artifacts of interviewing and the mistakes that can ensue from these artifacts. Engaging a child inappropriately for either age or sex will produce artifacts. In those parts of the interview when the psychiatrist is most active, his approach is determined not only by his individual temperament and the instrumentation of his accustomed manner but also by the age and sex of the child. He would not, for example, shake hands vigorously with a latency girl or speak in timid tones with a 3- or 4-year-old boy. He will expect more histrionic display and need for attention from a 6-year-old girl—and will respond in some measure to same—than he would expect from an 8-year-old boy. He will tend to approach the child with a greeting and demeanor fitting to age and sex and will also adapt to the flash intuition that proceeds from the first appraisal of the child. No singular approach is universally applicable. The "How are 'ya, buddy?" jovial and masculine greeting could conceivably signal the start of a rapid-moving and productive interview with the appropriate boy; conversely, it could be a nearly irreversible and threatening barrier for all that follows with the inappropriately selected child.

Too few girls are seen in child-guidance clinics and in private practice. If the events of the third decade of life, when women are often seen in some form of therapy, have long antecedents, it is apparent that casefinding with young girls has lagged behind other developments in the field. Very often the problems of young girls are actively disguised and protected by well-intentioned parents. Yet even more commonplace are those young girls who appear reserved and industrious, just the model of "little ladies"—their presenting symptomatology, in fact. Our diagnostic skills with young girls need to be refined to recognize early problems that masquerade as "feminine" reticence.

Children are affected by the slightest of physical disturbances and reflect physical discomfort in behavior. The child with a full bladder wiggles. The child with an infection appears disinterested. The child who is tired is often irritable.

The child with a fever is somnolent. The child who is hungry may appear whining and dependent. It is of maximum importance to inquire after these possibilities if some of this behavior is manifest. Much of it can be corrected or at least ameliorated in the office. And with regard to regressive behavior that proceeds after more mature activities, the length of time for reconstitution and the quanta of input necessary from the examiner are important diagnostically.

It is artifactual to spring surprises on children. It is productive of artifacts to talk about the "forbiddens" during the initial interview. But by far and away the leading source of artifacts issues from the personal involvement of the psychiatrist. If the examiner is tired or bored or negatively disposed toward the child, his attitude will communicate and may be returned in kind. Children are great for mimicry and will accommodate themselves to a situation either favorably or adversely.

Those differential diagnoses which plague, challenge, and exhaust the child psychiatrist are arranged between childhood psychosis, mental retardation, and organicity. The treatment of these conditions varies so drastically that their assortment is crucial. Probably fewer essential retardates are placed in the other categories than is the case with the other two conditions. Generally, it is all too frequent that social values creep into diagnostic considerations. It is socially more acceptable to be "minimally brain damaged" than psychotic—and it is more acceptable socially to be psychotic as a child than retarded.

GAP Report No. 66 (1967), *Mild Mental Retardation,* lists the presence of at least two characteristics that are required for an empirical definition of mental retardation: impaired intelligence and impaired adaptation. The report goes on to classify the mildly retarded children into two groups, A and B. Group A is drawn from those children who come from larger families of lower socioeconomic status, often broken homes, with other factors of educational and emotional deprivation. Group A children have less in the way of organic factors. Group B are from smaller, intact, higher-socioeconomic-status families with more resources in education and medical care. These children are found to have organic factors more frequently. The Group B child, smaller perhaps in number, is well known to physicians, unlike Group A children. The child psychiatrist is frequently called upon to examine and treat these children, whose parents have frequently overstimulated them and demanded more of them than they could deliver without pathological emotional response. The report also emphasizes early symptoms of mildly retarded preschool-age children: immaturity, passivity, repetitiousness of behavior with inflexibility, scant social play, "self-centeredness that leads to social isolation." Often it is the psychiatrist who is in private practice who sees Group B children and the clinic psychiatrist via school, agency, or court referral who diagnoses and treats Group A children. Also, Group B children are often diagnosed with greater frequency as "brain-injured." The above influences, largely societal, must be avoided unless a diagnostic classification evolves based upon social class and privileged treatment.

In data presented from psychiatric evaluation in children diagnosed as psychotic, McDermott et al. (1967) found no significant difference in the incidence of psychoses among five social-class groups. They found, however, that the expression of the psychotic illness correlated with the social class. Autism and withdrawal were found in high representation in the professional executive group, and both disturbances occurred significantly more in both professional executive and skilled working-class groups. This study also considers the pragmatic significance of labeling children either "psychotic" or "mentally retarded" (at times, psychotic children are deliberately misdiagnosed as retarded for the purpose of gaining special education and placement).

The majority of psychiatric examinations can be accomplished in one interview. The indications for repeated interviews include problems in differential diagnosis, disruptive conditions (child physically ill, very negativistic, or aggressive), and most cases which present with hyperactivity. Disorders of motility, one of the most common presenting symptoms, especially for boys, often requires the dimension of a clinical trial with medication as part of the diagnostic process. Freedman (1958) pointed out that psycho-pharmaco therapy was more popular and widespread in child psychiatry before its recent vogue in adult psychiatry precisely because hyperactivity was such a frequent presenting symptom in children and also because of the reluctance on the part of the psychiatrist to resort to other, more drastic therapies available in the treatment of adults. There is diagnostic value in a clinical trial of one versus another of several classes of medication available. In general—and closely correlated with sex, age, and weight—there are different inferences to be made concerning whether the child responds to sedating versus ataractic versus stimulating compounds. It is often the case that hyperactivity which responds well to amphetamines but not to phenothiazine or antihistamine is more indicative of cerebral dysfunction (brain damage or developmental lag) than the hyperactivity of a functional disorder. Conversely, that form of hyperactivity which can yield to and absorb relatively large dosages of ataractic agents (phenothiazine) yet become exacerbated by amphetamines points toward a more primary functional disturbance and tends to rule out organicity. There are many exceptions to this empirical observation. Barbiturates are usually contraindicated in the treatment of hyperactivity of children. Many authors noted that hyperactivity may be part of a cerebral dysrhythmia and advocate the use of anticonvulsant compounds. However, some studies indicate that anticonvulsant agents are of little or negative value unless the child is seizure prone.

The psychiatrist should always maintain a high index of clinical suspicion about cryptic progressive cerebral pathology. It need hardly be emphasized that the earlier signs of a space-taking lesion or degenerative disease have behavioral manifestations. Weighing the risk of missing psychodynamic material against the calamity of overlooking treatable early organicity, psychiatrists should not be so concerned with an image as a superbenign (nonphysical) doctor that they avoid certain physical and neurological examination procedures within the psychodiagnostic process.

The differential between organicity and psychotic reactions, particularly childhood schizophrenia, is especially difficult. Eaton and Menolascino (1967), in a five-year follow-up study of psychotic children, were impressed by the number of children designated as "chronic brain syndrome with psychoses" who showed increase in the neurological symptoms during the first five-year follow-up. Some of these children had progression from initial questionable or minor signs of damage to definite major findings (electroencephalogram changes, seizures, or onset of neurological signs). In their group of cases of chronic brain syndrome with psychosis, a quite high percentage had initial handicaps in the realm of speech.

In describing autistic children, Ruttenberg and Wolf (1967) found that the eight most significant areas to focus upon are relationship, communication, vocalization, sound and speech reception, interest in mastery, social skills, perceptual and conceptual abilities, and psychosexual development. Certainly speech and, in broader terms, communication are a critical determinant in differential diagnosis. Brown et al. (1967) have found that the length of responses which a child produces when shown pictures or toys is a useful index of a child's developmental status in language. Roughly, the child responds with the same number of words or one more than his age. They also point out that children through age 5 normally repeat as many as 49 of every 1,000 running words in conversation—hardly pathological stuttering.

One of the better clues toward the schizophrenic child is his greater drive for antigravity play. These children—often walled off from human contact—will suffer contact with adults if it is in the context of antigravity activity. Metzger (1968), reflecting Bender's work, noted the preoccupation in schizophrenic children with whirling and spinning objects as well as a tendency to accompany such activity in their bodies.

Bender (1963) has described the wide disparity between boys and girls for particular syndromes. Four or five boys to every girl, for example, are found to be schizophrenic, especially in the latency group, and a ratio of 2 boys to 1 girl is found in all emotional disturbances. Bender also describes statistically the number of boys exceeding girls in all types of growth and developmental disorders, especially those found in association with mental retardation.

Differential diagnosis is arduous and often tentative. All known methods which point toward definitiveness should have been exhausted in particularly difficult cases. Such methods include chromosomal studies, various chemical laboratory determinations, electroencephalograms, and other neurological procedures. It is important for the child psychiatrist to become the coordinator, guiding the family through offices and laboratories in the quest for information. Often the therapeutic trial, whether psychopharmacological or psychotherapeutic, is the last recourse and hindsight settles the matter at a later date. It is one of the primary goals of the field to relegate such cases to rarities rather than to common occurrences.

CASE EXAMPLE

The following case was chosen as illustrative of the abundance of data and richness of interaction which is commonplace in the interviewing of children. It also illustrates a growing circumstance, namely, the fresh interview of a child who has been in therapy previously. Every interview of diagnostic importance must start from scratch. Even though many details may be forthcoming from prior sources, the child must be approached for the first time as if it were his first interview. Indeed, because of the maximum importance of transactional data, a diagnostic interview is always a matter of primacy.

Clinical Synopsis

Larry was adopted at age 6 weeks through an agency. He was an only child. He was reported to have been a full-term infant, weighing 9 pounds 2 ounces at birth. Motor milestones were said to have been within normal limits. There were no unusual childhood illnesses, hospitalization, or separations from parents. He was weaned easily at 18 months and was fully trained for bowels at 2 years. He was bladder-trained at age 3 years. He was described as an active infant who rarely napped after the second year. He had never given up the practice of entering the parental bedroom in the early hours of the morning, taking his place next to his mother in bed. He started in kindergarten at age 5 and continued in parochial school, where he learned fundamentals easily. Although his school adjustment was never a problem, he had few friends and tended to prefer solitary play. His few friends were one to three years senior to him, as a rule. He rarely fought in school or in play but preferred contact sports. His father, a civil engineer, devoted much time to him, encouraging manual skills and athletics as well as various outdoor hobbies. His mother, a nervous and sensitive woman, tended to magnify any physical ailment of Larry's and was quick to take her son to various physicians for minor problems.

He first came to psychiatric attention at age 8, referred by a pediatrician for hyperactivity and outbursts of violent temper, apparently confined to his home and occurring most frequently in the late afternoon. These symptoms started in the second grade, shortly after Larry had been told by his mother that he had been adopted. They were grafted onto the previous history of pervasive hyperactivity and occasional flares of temper.

Psychotherapy with the first psychiatrist began on a twice-a-week basis shortly after Larry's eighth birthday, with the focus in therapy directed toward a playing out of anger and resentment thought to stem from the knowledge of his adoption. After six months of therapy, Larry's aggressive outbursts at home still continued unabated, and his mother complained of bruised shins attendant to her son's kicking fits. The psychiatrist curtailed some of the discussions and play and attempted to seal over Larry's hostile impulses through supportive interpretations. As therapy progressed, Larry started to tear apart the playroom to a point requiring physical restraint from the psychiatrist to avert further damage. He was placed on a number of medications, including an amphetamine and numerous phenothiazines, all to no avail. When his dosage of chlorpromazine had been raised to 100 mg. t.i.d. and the display of temper remained unchecked, the family sought another psychiatric opinion. His mother had been titrating the dosage of phenothiazines, unknown to the first psychiatrist, and had lowered them when her son complained of fatigue or somnolence. She had also raised the dosage whenever the outbursts of temper flared.

Larry was brought to the office by his parents for the first interview. He was 9 years and 5 months old. He had been without medication for ten days. His mental status on initial interview was as follows:

Mental Status

Size and general appearance. His large size was striking. He was powerfully built and looked to be older than 9 years of age. He wore a school blazer with a tie. His face was mobile, with fleeting expressions which changed rapidly and which might have been fixed into grimacing if they were played in slow motion. He had a sallow complexion. There were some marks of old lacerations and bruises. His hair was pale blond with patchy thinning over the right temple. His fingernails were dirty and long. His carriage and poise were erect and hypermasculine. He was chewing gum, which he cracked loudly.

Motility. He was nearly always in motion. He paced around the office, frequently gesturing in broad strokes. He climbed on a radiator to gain a better view from a window. When sitting, his hands were usually moving. There were no tic-like movements. There were a few moments of relative bradykinesia, especially while he seemed to be musing, looking out of a window. His muscles were taut, and there was little evidence of relaxation at any time. He could respond to a game of "playing possum" and could hold a pose. His breathing was deep and at times noisy, especially when sighing.

Coordination. His gross coordination appeared excellent. He walked in a self-assured manner. In finer movements, his fingers seemed to race ahead of his intent—as, for example, in making a paper airplane, when he folded the paper more hurriedly than aerodynamic trial would permit, requiring a second plane, which was hardly improved. He drew and wrote easily and well, with rapid strokes and little hesitation. His sample of three of four of the Bender Gestalt figures was accurate. His laterality was dominant and uncrossed on the right. He could not, however, stand on his right leg alone and wavered in the Romberg. There was no evidence of weakness in his right leg, and he seemed to be angry with himself about this discovered "infirmity," repeating the trial several times.

Speech. He had a deep, loud, and at times raucous voice. There seemed to be problems in modulation, though there was no hint of pubertal change. The voice had a raspy, hoarse quality, but there was some variation in inflection and tempo. At times his phrases came in rushes, but there was no evidence of stammering or stuttering. His grammer was precise, and he used many action-oriented verbs. He used slang freely and expressed no neologisms or other bizarre verbiage. He tended to use a "grown-up" vocabulary. There was a lack of feeling associated with most of the words that he spoke, which, coupled with the lack of modulation in volume, gave his verbal production a belligerent cast.

Intelligence. His vocabulary was advanced and filled with technical terms from scientific fields. His fund of information about medical matters reflected his frequent exposure to doctors. He was resourceful and alert and used his intelligence aggressively. He did well with arithmetic calculations. He read with no difficulty, offering to read from a medical text. He was acutely aware of the passage of time, wanting to know how much longer the interview would last. He was interested in the examiner's opinion of his intelligence and guessed that he was "pretty smart."

Emotional reactions. His affect tended to be flat, and there was little constancy between his facial expressions and the feeling tenor of his verbal productions. Although he had an expressive face, it was not a communicative one. At most times he was anxious and tense, and he appeared to overreact to small stimuli such as noises from outside of the room. The only

spontaneous clue to possible dysphoric feelings came in sighing. When asked about feeling sad, he quickly changed the subject. There were no temper outbursts. He talked about his temper as though it were a foreign body, commenting about it passively. There was no contrition or evidence of shame.

Manner of relating. From the moment of his entry into the office, he attempted to take charge and master an unfamiliar situation. He related in a bragging and bluffing manner and seemed anxious to impress the psychiatrist with his strengths and talents. He performed an elementary card trick with some difficulty and looked for approval. He was always aware of the psychiatrist's presence and took pains to establish a superficial familiarity. He often anticipated questions with, "You'll probably ask me about . . .," but he did not hesitate to provide answers to his own posed queries. He acknowledged the need for help, perhaps too much so, commenting that he was a "diagnostic problem . . . you probably won't know how to treat me, just like the other doctor." He could accept controls and direction best if they were spelled out in advance, so that he had foreknowledge to prepare him for most eventualities. He was well versed in bargaining to advantage. Above all, he sought not to be surprised or alarmed.

Thinking trend. He used the words "strong," "big," "tough," and "brave" repeatedly. He had much concern about his body and his physical prowess. He deprecated authority figures and tried to disarm the psychiatrist by calling him "just another doctor." He was acutely aware of his adopted status and was concerned about his place in the family. "They picked me out, and they will have to get me cured." He knew that his mother was biologically childless and thought his parents were "lucky" to have him. There was restriction of spontaneous thought involving school or peers. He ruminated about how long it would take him to grow up and assume "command" of the household. He spoke ambitiously of careers in either the police force or the military. There was a hint of fatalism in his resignation about his continuing problem with temper. Much of his mental energies were directed toward bolstering his prestige and improving his worth. He tended to project blame onto responsible adults and, though admitting that there was much that might be changed about himself, distanced himself from primary obligation for that change. He denied all fears categorically except for a past fear of monsters, which he claimed that he had "overcome."

Fantasy life. His fantasy life seemed meager compared with the force of his manner of relating and his creative intelligence. His earliest memory was of riding a pony. He told two dreams after some urging. He could elaborate on neither of them. The first dream was of winning a race and getting a trophy. The second was a recent one of falling out of a tree (he once had broken his arm) which he had climbed to pick fruit. He denied daydreams but said he often wondered how long it would take for him to "grow into a man."

Character of play. He sought to demonstrate strength and agility through various physical feats. He proved that he could lift the psychiatrist by having the psychiatrist place full weight on his shoulders as he pushed upright from a leaning-forward position. He had practiced this game with his father. He asked for puzzles, tests, challenges, guessing games—whatever could assure himself by convincing the psychiatrist of his abilities. His span of attention for this proving type of play was prolonged, and he seemed not to tire in its repetition. He sought various avenues of demonstrating mastery, offering to operate a typewriter, a telephone, the venetian blinds. His play was not solitary or removed. In a last effort at demonstrating

mastery, he proposed an arm-wrestling match. After he lost in this match, he proposed a return match "after I grow some more."

Follow-up

Larry was seen ten times over a period of four months, and then contact was lost, as the family moved away. A more formal neurological examination found him again unable to balance on his right foot. No pathological reflexes or localizing signs were found. An activated electroencephalogram was reported as within normal limits. After the electroencephalogram, the patient was placed on dilantin—100 mg. b.i.d. His office visits were exercises in control, with little psychodynamic exploration. His idea of temper as an isolated foreign body was supported. He became more comfortable with the idea of a larger person being stronger than he. "It would be silly if I could beat you," he said. His parents were counseled about the need to restrict him from the bedroom and about the desirability of providing more adequate disciplinary measures. Whether it was the brief therapy or the dilantin, the boy managed to have less severe temper outbursts and did not mention his adoptive status again. His parents, who were on the verge of hospitalizing him, attributed his improvement to the new-found medicine.

This case illustrates the two most imposing difficulties in a diagnostic interview with a child—a problem in differential refining of diagnosis and the problem of remembering normal developmental patterns and comparing the child with age-expected behavior. Here was a boy who, on a psychodynamic level, was a 4-year-old (bluffing, counterphobic, actively aggressive, and full of body references). He had the equipment of a much older boy in size and intellect. So much of his personality was distributed over different age levels—part precocious, part regressed, less at age level. There were neurotic slants. There were organic factors. There were also characterological problems. Since every diagnostic interview is a preparation for possible therapy, those clues which guided the therapy with this youngster had to do with his excellent response to limit setting. Had he not responded to limits in the office, more profound ego problems would have been entertained in diagnosis. Above all, the examiner remembered always that Larry was but a child and that his brash behavior was a plea for control.

CONCLUSION

In summary, the history of child psychodiagnostics is short but the momentum of recent new knowledge is impressive. The average examiner is much more sophisticated in his approach toward children and minimizes the artifacts that were commonplace thirty or forty years ago. As newer modalities of therapy open up, the interviewer takes on new dimensions as a more critical appraiser of differential diagnostic entities. He realizes increasingly that there are allowable deviations which expand with his knowledge of normal behavioral patterns. He has been trained and continues to work in a multidisciplinary field, utilizing psychological testing and social developmental histories as integral parts of the diagnostic procedure. He individualizes his approach to the child but maintains a core of usual approach against which he gauges the child's responses. As Hirschberg (1966) has written:

> Interviewing children requires not only specialized knowledge of children, but also specialized knowledge of the particular language and modes of every age group. As a result, the child psychiatrist brings to any setting a specialized interviewing skill and a specialized awareness of the use that individuals make of themselves in both the interviewing and the therapy of children.

We have come a long way from the pronouncements of Rush and the first distinctions of Esquirol. All the more headlong, then, is the hurry into the discoveries of the future.

REFERENCES

Ackerman, N. W. Psychiatric disorders in children—Diagnosis and etiology in our time. In P. H. Hoch & J. Zubin (Eds.), *Current problems in psychiatric diagnosis.* New York: Grune & Stratton, 1953. Pp. 205–230.

Allen, T., & Goodman, J. Home movies in child psychodiagnostics. *AMA Archives of General Psychiatry*, 1966, **15**, 649–653.

Arieti, S. *Interpretation of schizophrenia.* New York: Brunner, 1955.

Axline, V. *Play therapy.* Boston: Houghton Mifflin, 1947.

Beiser, R. Psychiatric diagnostic interviews with children. *Journal of the American Academy of Child Psychiatry*, 1962, **1**(4), 652–670.

Beller, E. K. *Clinical process.* New York: Free Press, 1962.

Bender, L. Genetic data in evaluation and management of behavior disorders in children. *Diseases of the Nervous System,* 1960, **21**(57), 318–342.

Bender, L. Mental illness in childhood and heredity. *Eugenics Quarterly,* 1963, **10**(1), 21–36.

Bransford, P. W. Experimental demonstration of the difficulties in the development of a classification for children's behavior disorders. Doctoral dissertation, University of Michigan. Ann Arbor, Mich.: University Microfilms, 1965.

Brown, J. R., Darley, F. L., & Gomez, M. R. Disorders of communication. In J. G. Millichap

(Ed.), *Symposium on pediatric neurology, Pediatric clinics of North America*. Philadephia: Saunders, 1967.

Chess, S. The role of temperament in the child's development. *Acta Paedopsychiatrica*, 1967, **34**, 91–103.

Copel, L. *Psychodiagnostic study of children and adolescents*. Springfield, Ill.: Charles C Thomas, 1967.

Eaton, L., & Menolascino, F. J. Psychotic reactions of childhood—A follow-up study. *American Journal of Orthopsychiatry*, 1967, **37**(3), 521–529.

Fish, B., & Shapiro, T. A typology of children's psychiatric disorders—Application to a controlled evaluation of treatment. *Journal of the American Academy of Child Psychiatry*, 1965, **4**(1), 32–52.

Fish, B., Shapiro, T., Campbell, M., & Wile, R. A classification of schizophrenic children under five years. *American Journal of Psychiatry*, 1968, **124**(10), 109–117.

Freedman, A. Drug therapy in behavior disorders. In H. Bakwin (Ed.), *Symposium on behavior disorders, Pediatric clinics of North America*. Philadelphia: Saunders, 1958.

Freeman, D. The home visit in child psychiatry. *Journal of the American Academy of Child Psychiatry*, 1967, **6**(2), 276–293.

Freud, A. *Normality and pathology in childhood*. New York: International Universities Press, 1965.

Freud, S. *The interpretation of dreams*. New York: Basic Books, 1960.

Goodman, J., & Sours, J. *The child mental status examination*. New York: Basic Books, 1967.

Group for the Advancement of Psychiatry. The diagnostic process in child psychiatry. *GAP Report*, 1957, No. 38.

Group for the Advancement of Psychiatry. Mild mental retardation: A growing challenge to the physician, *GAP Report*, 1967, No. 66.

Hirschberg, J. C. Basic functions of a child psychiatrist in any setting. *Journal of the American Academy of Child Psychiatry*, 1966, **5**(2), 360–366.

Kanner, L. *Child psychiatry*. Springfield, Ill.: Charles C Thomas, 1935.

Kerlin, I. N. Juvenile insanity. *Transactions of the Medical Society of Pennsylvania*, 1879, **12**, 611–620.

Krug, O., et al. (Eds.). *Career training in child psychiatry*. Report of the Conference on Training in Child Psychiatry, American Psychiatric Association, 1964.

Levy, D. M. The physiologic and psychiatric examination. *American Journal of Psychiatry*, 1924, **11**, 669–673.

Lewis, N. D. C. *Outlines for psychiatric examinations*. Utica, N.Y.: State Hospitals Press, 1934.

McDermott, J. F., Harrison, S. I., Schrager, J., Lindy, J., & Killins, E. Social class and mental illness in children: The question of childhood psychosis. *American Journal of Orthopsychiatry*, 1967, **37**(3), 548–557.

McDermott, J. F., Harrison, S. I., Schrager, J., Wilson, P., Killins, E., Lindy, J., & Waggoner, R. W., Jr. Social class and mental illness in children: The diagnosis of organicity and mental retardation. *Journal of the American Academy of Child Psychiatry*, 1967, **6**, 309–320.

McDonald, M. The psychiatric evaluation of children. *Journal of the American Academy of Child Psychiatry*, 1965, **4**, 569–612.

Metzger, L. Early recognition of emotional difficulties. *New York State Journal of Medicine,* 1968, **68**(5), 638–642.

Millar, T. T. Limit setting and psychological maturation. *Archives of General Psychiatry,* 1968, **18**, 214–221.

Moustakas, C. E. *Psychotherapy with children.* New York: Harper, 1959.

Paul, L. The psychiatric interview. In Staff of Institute for Juvenile Research, *Child guidance procedures, The century psychology series.* New York: Appleton-Century, 1937.

Pearson, G. H. J. (Ed.). *A handbook of child psychoanalysis.* New York: Basic Books, 1968.

Piaget, J. *Judgment and reasoning in the child* (1924). New York: Harcourt, Brace, 1928.

Piaget, J. *The language and thought of the child* (1923). (2nd ed.) London: Routledge, 1932.

Rubenstein, E. Childhood mental disease in America. *American Journal of Orthopsychiatry,* 1948, **18**, 314–321.

Rush, B. *Medical inquiries and observations upon the diseases of the mind.* Philadelphia: Kimber and Richardson, 1812. Pp. 56–57.

Ruttenberg, B., & Wolf, E. Evaluating the communication of the autistic child. *Journal of Speech and Hearing Disorders,* 1967, **22**(4), 314–324.

Shaw, C. R. *The psychiatric disorders of childhood.* New York: Appleton-Century-Crofts, 1966.

Simmons, J. E. *Psychiatric examination of children.* New York: Lea and Febiger, 1969.

Tessman, L. H., & Kaufman, I. Treatment techniques, the primary process, and ego development in schizophrenic children. *Journal of the American Academy of Child Psychiatry,* 1967, **6**(1), 98–115.

Thomas, A., Chess, S., Birch, H., Hertzig, M., & Korn, S. *Behavioral individuality in early childhood.* New York: New York University Press, 1963.

Walk, A. The pre-history of child psychiatry. *British Journal of Psychiatry,* 1964, **110,** 754–767.

Wenar, C. The reliability of developmental histories. *Psychosomatic Medicine,* 1963, **25**(6), 505–509.

Werkman, S. L. The psychiatric diagnostic interview with children. *American Journal of Orthopsychiatry,* 1965, **35**, 764–771.

Winnicot, D. W. Dependence in infant care, in child care, and in the psychoanalytic setting. *International Journal of Psychoanalysis,* 1963, **44**, 339–344.

Yarrow, L. J. Interviewing children. In P. H. Mussen (Ed.), *Handbook of research methods in child development.* New York: Wiley, 1960.

24 | Intelligence Tests and Childhood Psychopathology

A. I. Rabin and John P. McKinney

Standardized intelligence tests were originally devised for practical purposes—for classification and diagnosis. They were not devised with a specific definition or theory of intelligence in mind. The definition of intelligence was, perhaps, implicit in the particular operations demanded by the tests. Efforts to make the concept of intelligence more explicit have not met with great success or with general consensus. Throughout the decades of use of tests by applied psychologists, there has been a reciprocal relationship between the instrument and theory. Refinement of tests and cumulative experience with them have contributed to the attempts at sharpening the definition of the construct. On the other hand, greater sophistication and discrimination in definition and theory have stimulated more effective and useful test designs.

Moreover, the utilization of intelligence tests in the assessment of a great variety of deviations and disorders has given psychologists some important data regarding the relationship between intellectual deficit and psychopathological processes. We have learned something about the effects of various organic conditions upon intellectual functioning and cognitive processes; we have also had the opportunity to assess the influence of sundry antecedent circumstances in the life of individuals upon their efforts to deal with the reality about them and to adjust effectively to it.

Standardized methods, used widely, provide a common base for comparison of data from various sources and an opportunity to test the generality of conclusions obtained via their use. The following pages present a survey, albeit incomplete, of the history and current status of intelligence tests, in the process of increasing our knowledge and understanding of childhood psychopathology and its diagnosis.

EVALUATION OF THE CONCEPT OF INTELLIGENCE

Definitions of Intelligence

Intelligence is undoubtedly as elusive a concept as any that psychology has attempted to define. Definitions vary widely, depending on the assumptions one makes concerning the nature of ability. Learning theorists have tended to emphasize the transferability of solutions from task to task or learning sets (Thorndike, 1903), while psychometrically oriented psychologists have emphasized the commonality among the tasks themselves and among approaches to solution (Kelley, 1928; Spearman, 1927). Some psychologists have defined intelligence as primarily innate ability (Galton, 1870; Garrett, 1961–1962; Woodworth, 1910), and others have stressed the formative importance of the environment (Hunt, 1961; Liverant, 1960). Operational approaches have stressed the importance of the measuring instrument (Spiker & McCandless, 1954); neurophysiological definitions have included the plasticity of the human central nervous system (Hebb, 1949). Wesman (1968), in a recent address, indicates that with so much inconsistency among definitions of the concept it is not surprising that psychologists and educators are not agreed on the best methods of its measurement. On the other hand, the continuous attempt to come to grips with the notion of intelligence and its measurement attests to the central importance that psychologists have ascribed to that concept in the understanding of human behavior. Indeed, as has been suggested elsewhere (McKinney, 1962), perhaps we have expected too much of a unitary dimension of intelligence while overlooking the importance of a multidimensional approach to the understanding of human ability.

What the various definitions do have in common, if little else, is the underlying notion of ability, i.e., competence to perform a task. Almost everyone will agree that individuals differ with respect to their ability to perform almost any task. Few people, however, will agree on the basis for those individual differences, on their invariance with respect to age, growth, past experience, and cultural setting, or on their invariance across tasks. It is within the context of these disagreements that psychologists and educators have attempted to resolve several troublesome issues concerning the topic of ability. Many of these issues can be expressed as distinctions between (1) the effect of heredity and the effect of environment on human ability, (2) intelligence as an entity and intelligence as a logical construct, (3) ability and achievement, (4) general ability and specific abilities, (5) cognitive factors and personality factors in intelligence.

Current Criticisms of the Concept

The major difficulty with such distinctions is that they have usually been stated as dichotomies, as mutually exclusive. The either-or proposition is a poor substitute for a scientifically sound set of alternatives. This is best demonstrated, perhaps, by Anastasi's (1958b) discussion of the heredity-environment issue, in which she outlines the history of the scientific thinking about the influence of nature and nurture on intelligence. Anastasi asserts that psychologists have traditionally asked the wrong questions concerning the genesis of psychological traits, i.e., they have asked either (1) whether the trait was a product of heredity *or* environment or (2) how much variability among people could be attributed on each trait to heredity or environment. While the latter at least assumes that both factors are operative, it still asks for a trait-specific formula for predicting the separate extent of the effect of heredity and environment on behavior. However, a third alternative, suggested by Anastasi, is the question of how environment and heredity interact with one another in the production of intelligent behavior. Rather than considering the contribution of each factor separately, as if each were independent of the other, Anastasi suggests an examination of the lawful interaction between them, i.e., their effect on one another with respect to intelligence.

Aside from the approach she takes to the

heredity-environment issue, a second change is also implicit in Anastasi's paper when compared with several earlier writers. She is writing about "the operation of heredity and environment in the etiology of *behavior*" (Anastasi, 1958, p. 197; italics added). By reminding oneself that the response measure is always an observable behavior which is an expression of, but not identical to, the construct itself, one avoids the temptation to reify a psychological construct such as intelligence. This caution was expressed a few years earlier by Cronbach and Meehl (1955) in an analysis of test validity. It is essential to avoid granting the term *intelligence* the status of an entity if one is going to examine its scientific value. One author (Liverant, 1960) felt that the construct was in need of careful reexamination:

> The importance of the concept of intelligence in understanding and predicting human behavior appears so obvious that the value of this term in a science of behavior has seldom been questioned by psychologists. . . . By leaving open the possibility that the concept may be unnecessary, and even an obstacle, in explaining behavior, perhaps we can arrive at a better solution to the problems now subsumed under the rubric of intelligence. [Liverant, 1960, p. 101]

A more recent statement by Wesman (1968) continues to provide a similar caution:

> We have all too often behaved as though intelligence is a physical substance, like a house or an egg crate composed of rooms or cells; we might better remember that it is no more to be reified than attributes like beauty, speed, or honesty. There are objects which are classifiable as beautiful; there are performances which may be characterized as speedy; there are behaviors which display honesty. Each of these is measurable, with greater or lesser objectivity. Because they can be measured, however, does not mean they are substances. We may agree with E. L. Thorndike that if something exists it can be measured; we need not accept the converse notion that if we can measure something it has existence as a substance. [Wesman, 1968, p. 267]

In addition to the heredity-environment issue, there are other dichotomies which tend to plague the mental-testing movement. One is the distinction between ability (of which intelligence is accepted as the most general case) and achievement. Classically, *ability* has been the term used to designate potential, or capacity for future learning and performance, while the term *achievement* has been reserved to mean past accomplishment. With studies of the effects of early experience on later performance, sensory deprivation, etc., it has become clear that this distinction is no longer practically valid. Implied in this distinction is the notion that physiological states are inherited and are responsible for ability while experiential differences are the basis for achievement within the limits of one's genetically determined capacity. Hebb's (1949) theory suggests that changes in the central nervous system are themselves the result of experience and, further, that certain experiences are required for the development of cell assemblies and phase sequences which are the basis for further learning. In that sense, learned patterns (achievement) also provide the potential (ability) for further learning. The old dichotomy becomes less meaningful. This should be familiar ground to those involved in mental testing, since IQ tests themselves often contain items of information and verbal skill which are based on experience and sensorimotor tasks on which performance would certainly be improved with practice.

Assuming that the distinction between ability and achievement is not a clear-cut and maximally useful distinction, one is still left with the question of the generality of the construct of ability. Toward the end of the nineteenth century, Francis Galton discovered a mathematical way to express the degree of correspondence between two variables. Karl Pearson later developed the formula further and emphasized its application in the social sciences. It was Spearman (1904) who, on the correlation analyses of Galton and Pearson, based his Theorem of Intellective Unity and its corollary, the Hierarchy of Specific Intelligences. He found high correlation co-efficients between various sensory capacities and intellectual capacities, the latter defined by peer and teacher ratings. This led him to believe that a certain proportion of the variance in any intellectual task could be explained by a factor of "general intelligence." To the extent that behavior did not contribute to this g factor, he found it necessary to postulate a corollary notion of specific intelligences: ". . . all branches of intellectual activity have in common one fundamental function (or group of functions), whereas the remaining or specific elements of activity seem in every case to be wholly different from that in all others" (Spearman, 1904, p. 284). There are other commonalities, however, among a group of tasks, but not among all, which are not included in Spearman's two-factor theory. Apparently, however, he was not unaware of their existence (Anastasi, 1958a) but felt that they were relatively unimportant.

The current view of intelligence, however, and of trait organization in general includes a large number of relatively broad factors. The work of Kelley (1928) and particularly of Thurstone (1948) not only introduced the idea of group factors of intellective ability but began to question the importance of a general factor. Kelley believed that the general factor could be explained by the heterogeneity of the subjects being tested and by the heavy loading of verbal items on the instruments used (Anastasi, 1958a). Since Kelley's day, there have been a number of other psychologists who have opted to discredit the importance of general intelligence. Such things as situational specificity and cultural milieu have made it clear that the amount of variance which can be attributed to a g factor has limited predictive usefulness.

In the whole discussion of general versus specific intelligence and the importance of group factors, another issue emerges, namely, that of the relation of personality factors to intellectual ability. While the group factors first proposed by Thurstone (1938) can truly be considered "mental abilities," the more recent classification given by Guilford (1959) includes groups of intellectual abilities which would appear to border on being personality traits as well; he lists five major groups: cognition, memory, convergent thinking, divergent thinking, and evaluation. It becomes a moot point, then, to what extent one can speak of intellectual ability without becoming involved with so-called noncognitive factors. We will return to this issue later in discussing the history of the testing movement. Wechsler, for example, in developing his intelligence test for adults, insisted that general intelligence could not be isolated from the personality as a whole (Wechsler, 1950).

ATTEMPTS TO MEASURE INTELLIGENCE

Early Mental-testing Movement

The formulation of a theory of intellectual development during the past 70 years has gone hand in hand with attempts to create diagnostic instruments for the evaluation of intellectual ability. One of the earliest such attempts, as is well known, is represented by the work of Binet shortly after the turn of the century. Thus, as scientific constructs go, the notion of intelligence as a measurable variable has a relatively short history. It may be instructive to take a brief look at the historical development of the construct in terms of attempts at measurement, if only to become aware that many of the current criticisms of the construct of intelligence have been the recurring dissatisfactions of people involved in the work of differential diagnosis.

As early as 1905, long before operational definitions as such became the vogue in psychology, Binet and Simon (1961) complained, "What is lacking is a precise basis for differential diagnosis." Their complaint was twofold: first, investigators were not universally agreed on what they meant by the term *intelligence* and secondly, what measurements were made lacked precision. Not only did physicians differ with respect to what behaviors they considered to be characteristic of subnormality, but they also tended to be highly subjective in their assessment and description of the behaviors.

More than simply a vague enumeration of symptoms, Binet longed for the quantitative expression of a limited and generally accepted set of behaviors to define intelligence. Simultaneously with Binet's concern with the plight of the subnormal, Spearman (1904) was working out the mathematical justification for his Theorem of Intellective Unity and its corollary, the Hierarchy of Specific Intelligences. By calling that variance which was common to all in a group of tests *intelligence*, Spearman was paving the way for a half century of psychologists and teachers who would use and abuse his notions of a general intelligence and too often forget his very important corollary of specific abilities.

A good many of the problems which center around the notion of intelligence today have their origins back in the days of Binet and Spearman. For example, the differentiation between achievement and ability is made explicit in a remark of Binet's to the effect that, "It is understood that we here separate natural intelligence and instruction" (Jenkins & Paterson, 1961, p. 93). In attempting to measure this "natural intelligence," Binet claimed to have "succeeded in completely disregarding the acquired information of the subject." One wonders what Binet would have answered to the modern-day objection that perception itself is a learned phenomenon. It is curious, however, that the major proponent of the view, D. O. Hebb, whose research has shown perhaps more than any other the effects of early experience on later behavior, still maintains a

distinction, not unlike Binet's, between two sorts of intelligence. In *The Organization of Behavior* (1949), Hebb distinguishes between intelligence A, which he calls "an *innate potential,* the capacity for development, a fully innate property that amounts to the possession of a good brain and a good neural metabolism," and intelligence B, "the functioning of a brain in which development has gone on, determining an average level of *performance or comprehension* by the partly grown or mature person." Hebb's intelligence A sounds like Binet's concept of natural intelligence, while Hebb's intelligence B compares with Binet's ideas of the effect of instruction on performance. But we are getting ahead of ourselves in the historical development of the idea of intelligence.

By returning to Spearman, the father of correlational psychology, we get some notion of the excitement that was occurring about the turn of the century around the general area of intellectual ability. Faculty psychology, an offshoot of scholastic philosophy, was being rejected as an explanation for differential abilities. Spearman presented his position with the following statement of intentions:

> The present article, therefore, advocates a "Correlational Psychology," for the purpose of positively determining all psychical tendencies, and in particular those which connect together the so-called "mental tests" with psychical activities of greater generality and interest. . . .
>
> For finding out the classes and limits of these individual functions, modern psychology seems to have mainly contented itself with borrowing statements from the discredited "faculties" of the older school, and then correcting and expanding such data by inward illumination. [Spearman, 1904, p. 205]

Thorndike's *law of effect* (1903) and the empirically specific and testable hypotheses concerned with transfer of training were invoked to account for the fact that persons well trained on one task would more easily perform a related task. The "relatedness" of the tasks was spelled out in Thorndike's notion of *identical elements*. The more elements two tasks had in common, the greater was the likelihood that proficiency in one task would facilitate the learning of the second. The extent to which two tasks had elements in common was not restricted to substance but included procedures as well. This overlap or commonality of elements is not unlike Spearman's more quantitatively precise notion of a *g* factor defined by the correlation between tasks. Intelligence for Thorndike was the ability to transfer behavior acquired in one setting to novel situations.

Increased Flexibility in Viewing IQ and Mental Age

Several changes have occurred over the years in the conceptualization of intelligence since the time of Binet. In large measure these were the consequence of research done in the 1930s which indicated that intelligence could change as a result of experience. The work of Sherman and Key (1932) with deprived children in the Hollows area of Virginia and the studies by Wheeler (1942) and Skeels and Fillmore (1937) on children from underprivileged homes indicated the intellectually debilitating effect of such an environment. In addition, it was shown that the school also contributed to changes in a child's intelligence quotient (Worbois, 1942). On the positive side, Skeels et al. (1938) demonstrated the enhancing effect of an enriching nursery school experience. More recently, with retarded children, Rheingold and Bayley (1959) and McKinney and Keele (1963) have shown the positive effects of modification of the social environment by increasing maternal care.

In other words, the modifiability of intelligence has been demonstrated by the changes that occur both as a result of an impoverished environment and by enriching the environment. Hunt (1961), who has reviewed the research related to this topic, concludes that the belief in a fixed intelligence and the belief in predetermined development are outmoded. As mentioned earlier, we have come to think of intelligence as a construct rather than as an entity and, in addition, as a highly plastic construct.

Some Commonly Employed Scales

In the present section an attempt will be made to deal with the findings obtained with several of the more common tests employed in the assessment of intelligence in children. There are many more tests for children than will be mentioned in the present context. We shall merely sample a few, point up some salient characteristics based on data reported, and suggest closer perusal of the details concerning scoring, administration, etc., to the interested reader.

The use of infant and preschool intelligence tests has been recently reviewed by Stott and Ball (1965). In their review of the tests in current use, they included both those used with normal children and those used in the diagnosis of childhood disorders. In talking about infant mental testing, it is important to keep in mind a point made by Rabin (1967, p. 430) that the "levels of capacities sampled by infant scales and tests of mental development vary markedly during the first few years of life." Indeed, such different skills are being tapped at this early age, compared with what one calls intelligence in later childhood or adulthood, that the predictive validity of these tests, as we shall see later, is extremely low. The poor predictability of infant and preschool scales was also stressed by Bayley (1955), but reports by Knobloch and Pasamanick (1967) make this conclusion far from unanimous.

According to Stott and Ball (1965), the Stanford-Binet is by far the most frequently used scale at the preschool level (90 percent of their sample). "The next most widely used tests, in order of frequency were, Goodenough's Draw-a-Man, the WISC, the Gesell Schedules, the Cattell Infant Scale, Ammons Picture-Vocabulary, and the Merrill-Palmer Scale" (Stott & Ball,

1965, p. 136). Since the authors of that monograph have given an excellent description of each of these instruments, there is no need to describe them in detail here. It should be recalled, however, that these scales at the lower age levels heavily emphasize those components of intelligence dealing with perceptual and motor skills. This is necessary since these are the aspects of the child's intellectual development which are a major part of his behavior repertoire at that stage. On the other hand, the predictive validity of these measures is thereby weakened, since the tests given at the later ages are mainly measures of cognitive skills.

The two most popular intelligence tests for school-age children in the clinical setting are, of course, the Wechsler Intelligence Scale for Children (WISC) and the Stanford-Binet, the most recent edition of which is Form L-M (Terman & Merrill, 1960). These have a long and illustrious history (Rabin, 1965). The two tests differ structurally; the former is a point scale, consisting of eleven relatively homogeneous subtests, whereas the latter is an age-level scale. Furthermore, as has been mentioned, the Stanford-Binet is designed to cover the preschool years (excluding infancy), whereas the WISC is actually a "downward extension" of the Wechsler Adult Intelligence Scale (WAIS) and does not extend below the 5-year level. In an early summary review of the WISC, Rabin (1959, p. 561) states:

> For the present it may be stated that although . . . the WISC measures the same thing as the Wechsler Bellevue and the Stanford Binet, its sensitivity and discrimination at the lower end of the range (5–6 years) and at the higher end (14–15 years) are inferior to those of the time-honored instruments. Serious difficulties in diagnosis of mental deficiency and discrimination within that category are noted.

A more recent study (Beldoch, 1963) points out the possible invalidity of WISC IQs obtained at age 5 with gifted children. The report concludes with a recommendation for "a revision of the extrapolated norms" and raises the question as to the diagnostic usefulness of the WISC with 5-year-olds. This and similar studies have pointed up the need for a further "downward extension" of Wechsler's tests. The recently published Wechsler Preschool and Primary Scale of Intelligence (Wechsler, 1967) was designed to fill that need. On the other hand, when WISC and WAIS data on 16-year-olds are compared (Rose & Morlege, 1964), it is concluded that the transition from one test to another does not introduce any serious errors in determining the IQ. Littell (1960) is rather critical of the composition of the WISC, mostly on theoretical rather than empirical grounds.

The Goodenough Draw-A-Man Test, more recently revised by Harris (1963), is one of the most popular brief methods in the assessment of intellectual maturity in school-age and preschool populations. Correlations between the Goodenough and other standard measures seem to vary—depending on the nature of the subject groups. For a normal group of 10-year-olds with an average WISC IQ of 102, the correlations with the Full, Verbal, and Performance Scales are in the .70s (Dunn, 1967). The correlations between the Goodenough and the Stanford-Binet with a Head Start population (ages 4 to 6 years) of average intelligence range only between .43 and .46— considerably lower than those obtained by either Goodenough or Harris (Oliver & Barclay, 1967).

A more recently devised technique which is applied to special populations is the Peabody Picture Vocabulary Test (PPVT) (Dunn, 1959). There seems to be some controversy regarding the usefulness and validity of this method for the assessment of intellectual functioning. On the one hand, Burnett (1965), who compared the PPVT with the Binet and Wechsler with a group of "educable retardates," found the PPVT a useful screening device, although the IQs obtained with it were significantly higher than those achieved on the other tests. The PPVT correlated moderately with the WISC ($r = .63$) when employed with a group of emotionally disturbed children (Himelstein & Herndon, 1962). Another study with educable mental defectives (Kimbrell, 1960) indicates rather modest correlations with the WISC Full and Verbal Scales and an insignificant correlation with the Performance Scale. In contrast to the .40 correlation between the WISC MAs and grade placement, the correlation between PPVT and grade placement is a rather low $r = .11$. The author concludes that "when overall academic achievement scores among educable mental defectives are taken as the criterion, PPVT scores appear to be poorly validated."

Another test on which some recent research data are available is the Columbia Mental Maturity Scale (CMMS). The scale does not require the use of language, nor does performance require manual dexterity to any extent. It correlates highly with the IQs of the Stanford-Binet (Form L), although the MAs and IQs obtained by means of the CMMS tend to be somewhat higher. The test instructions are somewhat difficult for the younger preschool population (Hirschenfang, 1961).

GENERAL TRENDS IN INTELLECTUAL FUNCTIONING AND PERSONALITY

Longitudinal Studies and the Problems of Prediction

In an earlier section we discussed the construct validity of intelligence. It is appropriate here to consider the validity of the measures themselves, namely, their empirical validity. The sort of empirical validity of importance to the clinical tester is predictive validity. That is, to what extent will scores on an intelligence test correlate with measures of intelligence given at a later date? The correlation, obviously, will not be perfect, partly because of the unreliability of the instrument. But there is another reason. There is so-called "real" change in IQ, which can be mea-

sured and which has been associated with a number of factors. An interesting issue with respect to test-retest reliability comes up at this point. Should intelligence tests be so well behaved with respect to reliability that they are insensitive to these real changes? The tests which we have discussed are generally sensitive to these changes, which are a function of a number of factors to be discussed later.

In general, it has been found (Anderson, 1939; Honzik et al., 1948), first, that the correlation between two intelligence tests, given some time apart, is related to the time of the first testing and the length of time between the testings; that is, the earlier the first test is given, the less satisfactory it is as an adequate predictor of future IQ. Moreover, a test is a better predictor of intelligence in the near future than of intelligence in the distant future. The correlation between the two measures falls off considerably as the time between the two tests increases. It is evident, then, that infant intelligence scales lack this predictive validity. One reason for this has already been cited, namely, that the infant tests are measuring different skills than later intelligence tests. While childhood and adult intelligence tests are heavily loaded with verbal items, the infant measures are limited to the child's rather restricted behavioral repertoire, which consists largely of perceptual and motor behaviors. Also, the infant's intelligence is developing much more rapidly than the older child's or the adult's, so that from day to day he may shift dramatically with respect to a normative group of his age-mates because of sudden development of new skills.

One of the early and impressive longitudinal studies in developmental psychology was the Berkeley Growth Study (Jones & Bayley, 1941). Among other aims, this research was designed to study developmental changes in intellectual ability. In a number of research papers which have resulted from the study, various aspects of the organization of mental ability and the changes in this organization over time have been reported. Bayley (1933) reported evidence which was later corroborated by the observations of Honzik (1938), Anderson (1939), and Honzik, Mac-Farlane, and Allen (1948) to the effect that infant measures of intelligence are not highly predictive of later intelligence.

In a later paper, Bayley (1940a) cited some of the correlates of growth in mental ability, particularly emotional and attitudinal variables. Two later studies have been reported which deal with maternal behaviors and child development (Bayley & Schaefer, 1964; Schaefer & Bayley, 1963). The latter is concerned with the correlation between maternal behaviors and the development of mental abilities. Using mental test scores covering the years from birth to age 18, the authors correlated the results with maternal and child behaviors gathered in observations and interviews during those years. In general, the environmental influence in the case of maternal behaviors has a more lasting correlation with the mental ability of the boys. Boys with hostile mothers score lower on intelligence tests than boys with loving mothers. While the same is true for girls during the first three years, this influence is not observed in the later years.

By the time the children of the California Growth Study were 8 years old, Bayley (1940b) reported that only one-fifth of them had retained any degree of stability in intelligence scores from their first testing as infants. Some fascinating results have emerged from the long-term study of individual children in the California Growth Study (Bayley, 1955). By plotting their intelligence test scores at each age in terms of the 16-year standard deviations from the mean scores on the Wechsler-Bellevue and the Stanford-Binet, Bayley was able to construct individual growth curves for her subjects which covered the years from infancy until age 25. A number of observations can be made from examination of these individual curves. Bayley observed the striking way in which each child followed his own almost idiosyncratic timetable of mental growth. Each child seemed to reach his own plateaus, his own rapid upswings, his own slow decelerations in his own unique pattern. While the curves begin from a common origin and initially diverge only slightly, they quickly, after 5 or 6 years, diverge and establish their own individual patterns. As Bayley notes, however, there is a good deal of consistency in these patterns after 5 or 6 years. Children who forge ahead at that time tend to remain superior, and those who lag behind tend, in the main, not to catch up. "There is some shifting of position, but the changes are gradual over rather long periods of time" (Bayley, 1955, p. 814).

Another well-known longitudinal study, conducted at the Fels Research Institute, has also focused on the mental development of normal children (Kagan et al., 1958; Sontag et al., 1958). The Sontag et al. study dealt with the personality correlates of IQ changes. One hundred and forty Fels children were selected; they had received intelligence tests from infancy through 10 years. Changes in IQ between ages 4½ and 6 and between ages 6 and 10 were correlated with data from personality rating scales. Changes during the preschool years were associated with ratings on independence, and changes during the primary school years were associated with ratings on independence, aggressiveness, self-initiation, problem solving, anticipation, competitiveness, and scholastic competition. In other words, just as IQ itself had been shown to be related to certain so-called nonintellective factors, Sontag and his associates demonstrated that improvement in IQ was associated with a distinct pattern of personality variables.

Two questions come to mind in reading these studies. The main emphasis in the Berkeley Growth Study and the Fels study has been on normal growth and development. What of the child who is intellectually subnormal? Under what conditions might changes in intelligence occur, that is, a dramatic shifting in position? It has been observed (Rabin, 1967) that longitudinal studies of the intellectually subnormal are practically nonexistent. One follow-up study (Skeels, 1966) has been reported which, after a lapse of 21 years, followed up the entire group of twenty-five children who had been studied as institutionalized babies in their infancy. Thirteen of the children had been judged mentally retarded in infancy, while the contrast group of twelve children had IQ scores which were higher, most of them in the low normal and average range.

Dramatic shifts in intelligence, however, followed an early experimental treatment. The children in the experimental group, having been transferred to an improved environment for from 6 to 52 months, showed marked improvement in their mental ability. The contrast group, who did not get such treatment, showed a corresponding decline. The change in each group was so marked that their mental status was reversed, so that the mean IQ for the experimental group was 91.8 while that for the contrast group was 60.5. The main result of the 20-year follow-up of these subjects was that these differences in mental ability had persisted into their adulthood. The close social interaction with an interested adult during those early years had made enough of a difference that the experimental subjects were living relatively normal lives. They had completed high school for the most part, and some had even gone on to college (one completed some graduate work!). Now in adulthood, they were all self-supporting and were living well-adjusted lives. The contrast group, by comparison, were relatively uneducated (median of less than the third grade) and were either unemployed or had jobs of low status and income. While most of the experimental group were married and had normal, healthy children, only two of the contrast group had married. The one child which resulted from one of those marriages was mentally retarded.

The exciting conclusion from this study is that appropriate intervention in the early life of a child can make a dramatic difference in his adult welfare. While the effects of early environment on intelligence had already been demonstrated (Skeels, 1940; Skeels & Fillmore, 1937), as had been the enhancing effects of improving the environment (Skeels & Dye, 1939; Skodak, 1939), the important contribution of the follow-up was in demonstrating the long-term effects of such changes.

There are other reasons, however, for the lack of predictive efficiency of intelligence tests given early. Some of the social correlates of IQ changes have already been discussed. Children from impoverished backgrounds are more likely to lose IQ points over the years than children from enriched backgrounds. The effect of the milieu will be greater during the earlier years, as the major skills, particularly language, are developing. On the positive side, it has been shown (Kagan et al., 1958) that marked increases in IQ over a number of years during childhood are related to certain personality characteristics. Children whose IQ showed a significant increase between the ages of 6 and 10 showed a higher need for achievement, a higher display of intellectual curiosity, and less passivity on Thematic Apperception Test (TAT) themes than did children whose IQs decreased during those years. In other words, it would be difficult, if not impossible, to separate intellectual ability from those motivational characteristics which appear to be a major contributor to the child's intellectual development. This was the thrust of a paper by Wechsler (1950), in which he states:

> To realize that general intelligence is the function of the personality as a whole and is determined by emotion and cognitive factors is also just a beginning. We need to know what non-intellective

factors are relevant and to what degree. This is the task which lies immediately before us. [Wechsler, 1950, p. 83]

Kagan and his associates have discovered some of those nonintellective factors as mentioned above, such as intellectual curiosity and need for achievement. They have suggested that a number of others might fruitfully be investigated, notably, parental encouragement for academic achievement. If the early social milieu of the child is as important to intellectual growth as it appears, one of the crucial factors is undoubtedly the attitudes of adult models toward intellectual performance. The recent development of Head Start programs may be successful not only because of the content of instruction during those early years but also because of the formation of attitudes toward academic success.

Recently, Crandall, Katkovsky, and Crandall (1965) have developed an instrument to measure children's beliefs with respect to the control of reinforcement in academic situations. The scale is designed to tap the dimension of internal versus external locus of control, which has been described by Rotter (1966) and also by Lefcourt (1966). The Crandall et al. technique involves pairs of statements, one of which the child is asked to identify as more descriptive of him. In each pair, one statement describes a belief in external control of reinforcement and the other describes a belief in internal control. For example: "If a teacher passes you to the next grade, would it probably be: a) because she liked you or b) because of the work you did?" (Crandall et al., 1965, p. 95). In a more recent study, Katkovsky, Crandall, and Good (1967) have found that children's beliefs in their own internal control of reinforcement in academic situations is highly influenced by parental behavior: "The relations which stand out most strongly in the two studies are between children's beliefs in internal control of reinforcements and the degree

to which their parents are protective, nurturant, approving, and nonrejecting" (p. 774). Finally, it has been found (McGhee & Crandall, 1968) that belief in internal control of reinforcement is positively related to academic achievement. It would appear that this is another personality dimension which is extremely important as an antecedent to intellectual performance.

CHILDREN'S INTELLIGENCE TESTS AND THEIR USE IN ASSESSMENT

Intelligence tests were originally devised as predictive instruments for the purposes of classification of school populations. The concern of the early workers in the field of intelligence testing was with the degrees of educability of their subjects within the confines of the conventional school system. The intelligence tests were employed as predictors. Those pupils who scored within the average range or better were retained in the several conventional school programs. Those who were somewhat retarded on the basis of the test data obtained either were retained in the grades below their chronological ages or were permitted to progress at their own rate of speed under special provisions made available in the school systems. There were still others who were decreed to be entirely unsuitable for the usual school programs because of their limited intellectual capacities. Moreover, their presence in the ordinary classroom was felt to have a deleterious effect upon the more capable students because the presence of such retarded persons was expected to siphon off the energies and attention of the teacher disproportionately. Such retarded individuals were considered "feebleminded" or "mentally defective." Often, the removal from school of the more severely retarded was followed by their institutionalization in special "homes" or "training schools," where allegedly they were to be given appropriate training and instruction in order to maximize their opportunities for extrainstitutional adjustment upon maturity. Actually, in most instances such dynamic programs were not followed, and those institutionalized remained there for many years — often for life. In many instances the diagnosis of mental deficiency was based solely on intelligence test findings, and in most of these instances a *single* test administration served as a basis for such determination.

Intelligence tests thus emerged as instruments offering primary criteria for the diagnosis of mental deficiency and were the bases upon which serious courses of action have been undertaken. This trend was a regression to some extent, since prior to the invention of intelligence tests, multiple criteria were employed in the determination of mental deficiency. To be sure, the criteria were imprecise, not numerical, and not scientific, but they were based on fairly long periods of observation of the individual in the community. With the advent of intelligence tests, especially during the earliest period following their introduction into the world of education and psychology, in many instances a single criterion, the IQ, was substituted and employed as the sole diagnostic indicator of mental deficiency.

Some of the underlying assumptions in such uses of the IQ belonged to the early era. Among these assumptions were the notions regarding the stability of the IQ and its unalterability throughout one's life: that the IQ is a result of hereditary factors, i.e. that you are "born with a certain IQ," and that the magical number of 70, or 3 standard deviations below the mean, marks the dividing line between mental defect and relative mental normality.

Recent decades have witnessed the development of a more balanced and sober view of the "almighty" IQ. Research produced in the 1940s and subsequently, discussed earlier in this chapter, has shown that the IQ is an unstable index and that it is vulnerable to environmental circum-

stances. Its universal stability and predictability have been cast into doubt. The notion has developed that intelligence tests are measures of *current functioning* of the individual; that changed circumstances, especially in the lives of children, may markedly alter the test results; and that chances for more accurate and stable determination of a person's standing relative to the general population (IQ) are considerably enhanced when a test (or tests) is repeated two or three times over a fairly sizable span of time and a high degree of consistency in the results is achieved.

In view of the above, the arbitrary dividing line of an IQ of 70 as an index of mental deficiency was, by and large, abandoned long ago. There is recognition that there is nothing magical about 3 standard deviations or about the number 70. These are statistical concepts which are related highly, but not perfectly, to behavioral criteria concerned with the individual's adjustment to his society and with his development of a high degree of independence within it. Some people with low IQs are helpless in their environment and are socially ineffective, while others are able to achieve adequate social status. Thus, greater attention to a number of social criteria, *including* the IQ, has become the more reasonable procedure in the diagnosis of mental deficiency.

Mental deficiency (or retardation or feeble-mindedness) is, therefore, diagnosed by a number of biographical and social criteria. First, it is not a disease but a condition or a state. Second, it exists from birth or early childhood; it is not something acquired later in life. Third, it persists into maturity; it is not a transitory state. Fourth, the educational and social incompetence of the person is affected; he is unable to meet the environmental demands placed upon members of society. Fifth, this incompetence and inadequacy are due primarily to incomplete intellectual development. It is in the determination of this last criterion that the intelligence tests become of value. However, the several remaining criteria, especially the one concerning social incompetence, must be taken into account before a diagnosis of deficiency or retardation is made with any degree of confidence (Sarason, 1959).

It appears, from a number of studies, that the prediction of social incompetence in adulthood on the basis of intelligence tests given to children is not always valid (e.g., Charles, 1953; Muench, 1944). Intelligence test findings in childhood, especially if close to the borderline level (IQ of 70+), are not always predictive of social incompetence in adulthood. Moreover, marked changes in the IQ itself often take place as a result of a variety of circumstances (Rabin, 1965, 1967). However, the changes appear to be minimal in clear cases of exogenous (nonfamilial) mental retardation and in those who achieve extremely low IQs at the initial testing. Children who are diagnosed as "educable" mentally retarded (IQs of 50 and above) have thus more of a chance of rising above the level of mental retardation than those considered as only "trainable" (usually IQs in the 30s) when diagnosed early in life. Generally, as indicated above, the data from the test are used as a guideline and as an index of current functioning, without excessive implications or commitments for the future.

Psychologists are not interested solely in the single minimal index of the IQ that is obtained with standard intelligence tests. They are also concerned with the breakdown of the total performance, with the successes and failures, the pattern and "scatter" represented by the several components that constitute the conventional intelligence scales. The question they wish to answer is: Are all the abilities which make up the global "general intelligence" equally affected by this or that personality disturbance, neurological defect, or congenital malfunctioning of an endogenous (familial) or exogenous nature?

Mental retardation in general is said by Wechsler (1958) to be characterized by relatively limited intratest as well as intertest variability. According to him the retarded, especially the adult retarded, achieve "consistently low scores on arithmetic, Digit Span and Digit Symbol, and relatively good scores on Comprehension and Object Assembly." Although a number of investigators obtained consistency with Wechsler's pattern, Mueller's review (1964) of Alpers' data with 713 mentally retarded children notes that Comprehension, Similarities, Picture Completion, and Object Assembly were relatively high, "while Arithmetic, Vocabulary, Picture Arrangement and Coding were consistently low." Thus, as we remarked previously (Rabin, 1967), "This pattern is rather broad; it contains Wechsler's pattern, is consonant with it, but goes beyond it."

Factor analysis of the WISC, especially of results on a normal sample, yields, as might be expected from the design of the test, a verbal and a performance factor (Cropley, 1964). However, Baumeister and Bartlett (1961–1962) identified a "short-memory" factor, in addition to the conventional two factors, in the mentally retarded. Arithmetic, Picture Arrangement, Coding, and Digit Span loaded on this factor.

Familial Subnormality and Brain Injury

There is little agreement among investigators regarding differences in patterning of intellectual function in the endogenous and exogenous retarded (Miller, 1960–1961). Gallagher (1957) found no important differences between carefully matched groups of brain-injured and non-brain-injured mentally retarded on successes and failures on the items of the Stanford-Binet test. On the other hand, Fisher (1960–1961) reports WAIS data on 508 subnormal persons of a wide age range which indicate a higher verbal than performance IQ in those diagnostic groups "due to central nervous system infection and other organic nervous diseases." It is difficult, however, to separate the factor of organicity from a number of other variables which were not controlled in this study. A later review of WISC data with retardates (Baumeister, 1964–1965) reports higher scores on the Performance Scale on the part of "cultural familial, undifferentiated retardates" and no clear confirmation of a typical organic pattern. Baumeister reports that brain-damaged retardates tend to perform more evenly across the Verbal and Performance Scales of the WISC.

The comparison of organics and familial retardates by means of the Stanford-Binet Form L-M (Rohrs & Haworth, 1962) yields a higher mean score and greater scatter in the organics. However, only one item of the test (VII-2, Memory for Stories: The Wet Fall) differentiated between the two groups, with a greater proportion of organics passing this item.

A review of scatter on the WISC and WAIS led Baumeister to conclude that the search for scatter patterns beyond the Verbal-Performance Scales discrepancy "appears futile." The status of conclusiveness of intratest variability, especially with children, is even more shaky than that with adults (Rabin, 1965). We may conclude that the familial mentally subnormal tend to perform better on the Performance Scale than on the verbal items of the WISC. This pattern is not true with organics, with whom the trend of discrepancy is in the opposite direction. The inapplicability of findings on adult patients and the fact that there are many kinds of "organicity" have been justifiably pointed out by Hopkins (1964), who studied groups of children of normal intelligence.

Children with Learning Disorders

A fairly extensive report on "intellectual factors in learning disorders" was presented by Coleman and Rasof (1963). They compared 126 "underachievers" and 20 "overachievers" with an age range of 7.5 to 16 years on the WISC.

Their results indicate that underachievers score significantly lower on WISC subtests which demand "sustained concentration and memory," while they do well on the subtests which, according to factor analytic studies, are "loaded with perceptual organization and informal learning." Overachievers showed a lower score on the Performance Scale and a high amount of scatter on the WISC subtests.

An unpublished report on "educationally handicapped" pupils who were compared with their siblings and with successful students (Owen, 1967) concludes with the following generalizations:

Educationally handicapped pupils were superior to the controls in selected performance areas as measured by the WISC.

Educationally handicapped pupils were significantly impaired in arithmetic reasoning, general information, memory for digit span, and the visual-motor task of coding as measured by the WISC.

There is some similarity between the "underachievers" and the "educationally handicapped" of these two studies. The WISC subtests which are closely related to school performance are rather low. Moreover, in general, we may note a similarity between this average, or better, group and the familial mentally retarded discussed in the previous section. Both are relatively superior on the WISC Performance Scale and, of course, inferior on the Verbal Scale.

The Effects of Affects

That measures of anxiety show consistently negative correlations with indices of intellectual functioning has been demonstrated in a number of studies (Hafner & Kaplan, 1959; Sarason et al., 1960; Sarason, Hill, & Zimbardo, 1964). It seems that IQ is also a factor in the degree of anxiety, for Feldhusen and Klausmeier (1962) found higher levels of anxiety in their low (56 to 81) IQ (WISC) group as compared with the high (120 to 146) and average (90 to 110) IQ groups.

There seems to be some inconsistency between

the results discussed above and the data obtained with emotionally disturbed children. One study (Granick, 1955), for example, reports no differences on the Stanford-Binet between twenty-seven children with "mild personality disturbance" and a matched sample of nondisturbed controls. The Cornell-Coxe Scale, however, yielded significant differences between the groups, especially on the Block Design and Memory for Design items. Particular distortion was noted in the configurations of the latter item. However, the author concludes that these group differences cannot be viewed as signs of maladjustment or as practical aids in individual diagnosis.

Even less encouraging is Wolf's (1965) report on "nonpsychotic, nonorganic and nonretarded emotionally disturbed children from lower and lower middle class families." These children, diagnosed as neurotic or with personality disorder, "did not differ significantly from their 'normal' control siblings on standardized intellectual measures at either the kindergarten, second grade or fourth grade level" (p. 906). The Lee-Clark test was used with the kindergarten children, and the Kuhlmann with those in grade school.

The overall impression gained from data concerning the relationship between emotional disturbance and measurable intelligence in children is that of ambiguity. Despite the consistently negative relationship between intelligence and anxiety, (mildly) emotionally disturbed children do not differ from matched controls or siblings. Perhaps when gross indices such as IQs are employed, no marked differences may be noted. The diagnostic clues should be sought in minute aspects of individual idiosyncratic performance on specific items. There are some hints in other directions, but we do not as yet have specific information that might serve as objective indices. The acumen of the particular clinician must therefore be relied upon.

An interesting study of changes in intellectual functioning of emotionally disturbed children who were hospitalized was reported by Hiler and Nesvig (1961). A group of twenty children (mean age: 13.6 years) was tested on admission and retested 2 to 3 months and 12 to 24 months later. Results of the retest following the longer period of hospitalization are probably uninfluenced by practice effects and are of special interest. Improvement in verbal IQ, full-scale IQ, and digit span as well as in oral reading tests "was significantly related to clinical improvement." The authors further state that "most hospitalized children have problems which cause them to be retarded in verbal skills; as they improve their verbal IQ rises." It is further concluded by the authors that the performance rather than the verbal IQ may be a better estimate of the intellectual potential of emotionally disturbed children.

It is doubtful that much can be generalized from the data of this limited sample of emotionally disturbed children. This appears to be a special group with histories of acting out and school failures. "Many of the children in this hospital were transferred to it from correctional schools or sent to the hospital as an alternative to correctional school." Thus, the data reported are probably most relevant in connection with a later section that deals with intellectual functioning in delinquency.

Schizophrenia

A discussion of emotional factors in intellectual and cognitive functioning would be incomplete without a consideration of what might be called the most incapacitating mental disturbance—schizophrenia. The concept of "childhood schizophrenia" is perhaps even less clearly defined and agreed upon than Bleuler's original term. Nevertheless, children do get diagnosed as schizophrenic and exhibit many of the symptoms of adult schizophrenia in addition to those unique during the developmental period.

That lower levels of intellectual functioning

are frequent concomitants of severe psychosis, such as schizophrenia, has often been observed and reported. It is not clear, however, whether lower levels of mental functioning are a part of the predisposition to schizophrenia or that these often observed findings are a *function* of the disordered process itself. The available literature offers some support in both directions (Rabin & Winder, 1969).

On the one hand, such studies as the one by Rapaport and Webb (1950), who compared the IQs of schizophrenics with their premorbid IQs, report an average deficit of 33.7 points. On the other hand, Griffith et al. (1962) and Fitzherbert (1955) not only fail to note any deficit but, to the contrary, report a rise in the IQs of schizophrenics when compared with their premorbid test achievement. The deficit is obviously easier to explain, whether on the basis of withdrawal, poor cooperation and motivation in the testing situation, or confusion. However, *improvement* in IQ following the onset of psychosis directs attention to the need for detailed investigation of the period of time which intervened between test and retest and possible constraints on performance prior to official onset.

Evidence concerning the originally low level of intelligence in schizophrenics, even in the premorbid state, is fairly consistent. The work of Mason (1956) and of Lane and Albee (1965), who compared the intellectual levels of children who later became schizophrenic with those of their siblings who did not, shows consistently and significantly lower IQs in the former. Developmentally, although not defective intellectually, the potential schizophrenic is below the level of his peers and siblings. These data are consistent with the "scapegoat" hypothesis concerning the schizophrenic in his family.

A survey of studies on childhood schizophrenia between 1937 and 1965 (Pollack, 1967) indicates "remarkable agreement" that "at least one-third of the children scored below 80. . . . When compared with the nonschizophrenic patient controls, all studies reported the 'schizophrenic patients' significantly inferior" (p. 469). This condition of childhood schizophrenics seems to be less easily reversible than it may appear to be in older schizophrenics. One study (Schachter et al., 1962) indicates that retarded rather than schizophrenic children show some gain in IQ following a year of psychotherapy. Generally, according to a British survey (Rutter, 1964), "Abnormality of intelligence does not seem to be a factor of major importance in child psychiatric disorders but is worthy of attention for other reasons."

Delinquency

A significant discrepancy between the Verbal and Performance Scales on Wechsler's adult tests in favor of the latter in delinquents and young sociopaths has often been noted. Wechsler (1958) notes that in addition to the higher Performance Scale, the "adolescent sociopath" does particularly well on Picture Arrangement and Object Assembly and rather poorly on Information and Arithmetic. The discrepancy between the scales is well supported by data on 500 delinquents obtained by the Gluecks and cited by Wechsler. Whether these patterns carry over to the WISC is not particularly clear. Moreover, a review of some other studies concerned with this issue (Guertin et al., 1962) presents a good many data that are not altogether consistent with the aforementioned pattern. It has been pointed out that this discrepancy in favor of the Performance Scale holds *if* the delinquents are also poor readers. This is not surprising, for we have noted a similar performance pattern in underachievers and in educationally handicapped children who apparently were not sociopaths. Perhaps many delinquents and sociopaths are recruited from a population with this type of cognitive style, which, incidentally, includes the familial mentally retarded. Thus, the discrepancy in favor of the Performance Scale is hardly a discriminating and specific characteristic of a particular diagnostic group. It obviously has limited use as a differential diagnostic pattern.

Intelligence Tests in the Diagnostic Endeavor

In the foregoing pages we noted certain trends and patterns of intellectual functioning in subjects of several diagnostic categories. We have concentrated on global IQs and scatter indices, or patterns, which cannot serve as sole bases for differential diagnostic statements. The IQ and the intratest pattern—the relationship between the achievement levels on the several subtests—give us a hint and narrow down the choice of syndrome but do not point specifically and conclusively to any diagnostic category. This is, actually, not a great limitation, for "labeling" is not an important or major objective of the clinical enterprise. Diagnosis goes beyond this circumscribed undertaking.

In an earlier discussion of the "Diagnostic Use of Intelligence Tests" (Rabin, 1965), four levels of analysis of test data were proposed. These levels are:

I. Numerical indices of intellectual functioning
II. Indices of interest variability
III. Intratest scatter
IV. Qualitative analysis of responses

Levels I and II have been discussed, to some extent, in the previous sections. Under level I, the reference is primarily to the IQ and/or MA, which are the major numerical and quantitative indices in intelligence testing. Essentially, these indices give us some information regarding the standing of a particular person—subject, client, or patient—relative to a representative sample of the general population or relative to the "unselected" sample which represents the standardization population for that particular intelligence test. We obtain a global impression

with respect to relative retardation, advancement, or normality in the intellectual sphere. This level is unconcerned with the so-called nonintellective factors obtainable by means of intelligence tests. If the examiner stops at this level of application, the use of intelligence tests is rather circumscribed and unqualified and does not differ much from the way they were employed some 40 or 50 years ago.

The second level of analysis and interpretation, that of scatter of subtests, still remains on the formal and quantitative level. Discrepancies between verbal and performance IQs on the WISC, deviations of various subtests from the vocabulary level, etc., are indications of diagnostic trends, based primarily on empirical data with various diagnostic groupings. These scatter patterns are rather shaky in the diagnosis of adults but even less reliable in the case of children whose functioning styles and patterns are not yet crystallized and in whom much variability may be expected as a function of the developmental process. Nevertheless, on a descriptive level, patterns and profiles of individuals, considered as patterns of *current* intellectual developmental status, produce useful material for the clinician. Even with infants, the descriptive profile based on locomotor, personal-social, hearing and speech, hand and eye coordination, and performance factors (Griffiths, 1954) are very informative and useful in viewing the current developmental picture of the child. The use of individual subtests of batteries in the descriptive diagnosis of the brain-damaged (Taylor, 1959) is another example.

Level III involves a further penetration into the test material, for the concern is with "intratest" scatter—the failures and successes on individual items which are not consistent with their arrangement according to order of difficulty. This intra-subtest variability is, probably, even greater in children than intertest variability, and for the reasons we mentioned above.

The "order of difficulty" within tests is based on statistical data with a large sample of children. Such data mask individual differences and unique styles of performance, which may be dependent on the special experiences to which a particular child has been exposed. Nevertheless, the failure on easy items, on the information subtest, in the case of an otherwise bright youngster who passes many of the more difficult items may be interpreted in a way similar to that of adults, as possible use of repression as a major defensive mode. The "forgetting" of certain easy items may be due to the valence they have assumed as a consequence of association with painful and anxiety-arousing content which has irradiated to a variety of related topics.

The foregoing levels of the diagnostic operation involve the utilization of tests as psychometric instruments, whether the large and global indices are employed or the ratios and indices of parts of the tests, as in levels II and III. In all of these, responses to tests and test items are defined in terms of success and failure, with the content of the responses themselves being irrelevant. Level IV, however, deals with the content analysis of the responses per se, without the consideration of their formal correctness or incorrectness. At this level of analysis and interpretation, what the respondent says, and especially the errors that he makes, are grist for the interpreter's mill (Blatt & Allison, 1968). The clinician regards the content of the responses as material from a "personal document" or data from a "projective technique." Deviations in response, as compared with the standard answer, are said to represent the uniqueness of the respondent and to yield something especially characteristic of him. Thus, the material of the intelligence test is employed not only as a measure of an isolated function or set of functions subsumed under the term *intelligence,* but also as a means for a broader personality assessment and diagnosis, whether deviant or within the normal range.

At this level, "interpretation depends, to a considerable extent, upon the experience (private norms?), dynamics, and theoretical orientation and sophistication of the examiner-interpreter. The kinds of inferences he is going to make about the personality examined strongly depend upon the conceptualization of personality (intervening) variables and dynamics" (Rabin, 1965).

One notable example of the influence of theoretical predilection is the schema, proposed by Fromm (1960), for the analysis and interpretation of responses to infant and intelligence scales. From a psychoanalytic vantage point, she suggests a number of personality variables, sorted into such categories as id-ego, ego development, ego-ideal, and superego, which might be elicited from the behavior of the subject, client, or patient in the testing situation. This is a more formal type of analysis and interpretation than is customarily involved in the operations of the clinician. It has the virtue, however, of providing a more systematic framework for analysis and possible quantification of data.

In concluding the present section, it may be well to reiterate the statement made by Terman and Merrill in their last manual (1960 p. 13):

> The skillful and experienced clinician may make meaningful, even if unquantified, observations on the qualitative aspects of a subject's performance, his methods of work, his approach to problems, and many other clinically significant areas of his behavior in the standard situation presented by the test. Many important personality characteristics are and may be observed in the course of testing. . . . *And, of course, the problem of the validity of the clinician is as pertinent to the effectiveness of testing as the validity of the tests.*

SUMMARY

In the preceding pages we attempted to present a statement concerning the nature of intelligence tests and their relation to psychopathology of childhood. We have surveyed briefly the history of intelligence tests and have dealt with some of the definitional and theoretical difficulties involved. We have also reviewed some of the recent findings with various infant and intelligence scales, their predictive validity and changes in the course of human development, from infancy to maturity. The effects of various chronic and long-term conditions upon intellectual functioning as reflected in standardized measures of intelligence were considered, and the resulting deficits were related to psychopathology of childhood and to deviation in the developmental process. Finally, the application of intelligence tests in the diagnostic endeavor was described, following a brief review of recent empirical findings with intelligence tests with several nosological groupings of childhood disorders.

REFERENCES

Anastasi, A. *Differential psychology.* New York: Macmillan, 1958. (a)

Anastasi, A. Heredity, environment, and the question "How?" *Psychological Review,* 1958, **65,** 197–208. (b)

Anderson, J. E. The limitations of infant and preschool tests in the measurement of intelligence. *Journal of Psychology,* 1939, **8,** 351–379.

Baumeister, A. A. Use of the WISC with mental retardates: A review. *American Journal of Mental Deficiency,* 1964–1965, **69,** 183–194.

Baumeister, A. A., & Bartlett, C. J. A comparison of the factor structure of normals and retardates on the WISC. *American Journal of Mental Deficiency,* 1961–1962, **66,** 641–646.

Bayley, N. Mental growth during the first three years. *Genetic Psychology Monographs,* 1933, **14,** 92.

Bayley, N. Factors influencing the growth of intelligence in young children. In G. M. Whipple (Ed.), *The thirty-ninth yearbook.* National Society for the Study of Education. Part II. Intelligence: Its nature and nurture. Bloomington, Ill.: Public School Publishing Co., 1940. Pp. 49–79. (a)

Bayley, N. Mental growth in young children. In G. M. Whipple (Ed.), *The thirty-ninth yearbook.* National Society for the Study of Education. Part II. Intelligence: Its nature and nuture. Bloomington, Ill.: Public School Publishing Co., 1940. Pp. 11–47. (b)

Bayley, N. On the growth of intelligence. *American Psychologist,* 1955, **10,** 805–818.

Bayley, N., & Schaefer, E. S. Correlations of maternal and child behaviors with the development of mental abilities: Data from the Berkeley Growth Study. *Monographs of the Society for Research in Child Development,* 1964, **29,** No. 6.

Beldoch, M. Application of the norms of the Wechsler Intelligence Scale for Children to five-year-olds. *Journal of Consulting Psychology,* 1963, **27,** 263–264.

Binet, A., & Simon, T. The development of intelligence in children. In J. J. Jenkins & D. G. Paterson (Eds.), *Studies in individual differences.* New York: Appleton-Century-Crofts, 1961. Pp. 81–111.

Blatt, S. I., & Allison, J. The intelligence test in personality assessment. In A. I. Rabin (Ed.), *Projective techniques in personality assessment.* New York: Springer, 1968.

Boring, E. G. The use of operational definitions in science. *Psychological Review,* 1945, **52,** 243–245.

Burnett, A. Comparison of the PPVT, Wechsler-Bellevue, and Stanford-Binet on educable retardates. *American Journal of Mental Deficiency,* 1965, **69,** 712–715.

Charles, D. C. Ability and accomplishment in persons earlier judged mentally deficient. *Genetic Psychology Monographs,* 1953, **47,** 3–71.

Coleman, J. C., & Rasof, B. Intellectual factors in learning disorders. *Perceptual and Motor Skills,* 1963, **16,** 139–152.

Crandall, V. C., Katkovsky, W., & Crandall, V. J. Children's beliefs in their own control of reinforcements in intellectual-academic achievement situations. *Child Development,* 1965, **36,** 91–109.

Cronbach, L. J., & Meehl, P. E. Construct validity in psychological tests. *Psychological Bulletin,* 1955, **52,** 281–302.

Cropley, A. J. Differentiation of abilities, socioeconomic status, and the WISC. *Journal of Consulting Psychology,* 1964, **28,** 512–517.

Dunn, J. A. Note on the relation of Harris Draw-A-Woman to WISC IQ's. *Perceptual and Motor Skills,* 1967, **24,** 316.

Dunn, L. M. *Peabody Picture Vocabulary Test Manual.* Nashville, Tenn.: American Guidance Services, 1959.

Feldhusen, J. F., & Klausmeier, H. J. Anxiety, intelligence, and achievement in children of low, average, and high intelligence. *Child Development,* 1962, **33,** 403–409.

Fisher, G. M. Differences in WAIS and performance IQ's in various diagnostic groups of mental retardates. *American Journal of Mental Deficiency,* 1960–1961, **65,** 256–260.

Fitzherbert, J. Increase in intelligence quotient at onset of schizophrenia: Three adolescent cases. *British Journal of Medical Psychology,* 1955, **28,** 191–193.

Fromm, E. Projective aspects of intelligence testing. In A. I. Rabin and M. R. Haworth (Eds.),

Projective techniques with children. New York: Grune & Stratton, 1960.

Gallagher, J. J. A comparison of brain injured and non-brain injured mentally retarded children on several psychological variables. *Monographs of the Society for Research in Child Development,* 1957, **22,** No. 2.

Galton, F. *Hereditary genius: An inquiry into its laws and consequences.* New York: Appleton, 1870.

Garrett, H. The equalitarian dogmatism. *Perspectives in Biology and Medicine,* 1961–1962, **4,** 480–484.

Granick, S. Intellectual performance as related to emotional instability in children. *Journal of Abnormal and Social Psychology,* 1955, **51,** 653–656.

Griffith, R. M., Estes, W., & Zerof, S. A. Intellectual impairment in schizophrenia. *Journal of Consulting Psychology,* 1962, **26,** 336–339.

Griffiths, R. *The abilities of babies.* New York: McGraw-Hill, 1954.

Guertin, W. H., Rabin, A. I., Frank, G. H., & Ladd, C. E. Research with the Wechsler Intelligence Scales for Adults: 1955–1960. *Psychological Bulletin,* 1962, **59,** 1–26.

Guilford, J. P. Three faces of intellect. *American Psychologist,* 1959, **14,** 469–479.

Hafner, A. J., & Kaplan, A. Children's manifest anxiety and intelligence. *Child Development,* 1959, **30,** 269–271.

Harris, D. B. *Children's drawings as measures of intellectual maturity.* New York: Harcourt, Brace & World, 1963.

Hebb, D. O. *The organization of behavior.* New York: Wiley, 1949.

Hiler, W. E., & Nesvig, D. Changes in intellectual functions of children in a psychiatric hospital. *Journal of Consulting Psychology,* 1961, **25,** 288–293.

Himelstein, P., & Herndon, J. S. Comparison of WISC and PPVT with emotionally disturbed children. *Journal of Clinical Psychology,* 1962, **18,** 82.

Hirschenfang, S. Further studies on the Columbia Mental Maturity Scale (CMMS) and revised Stanford-Binet. *Journal of Clinical Psychology,* 1961, **17,** 171.

Honzik, M. P. The constancy of mental test performance during the preschool period. *Journal of Genetic Psychology,* 1938, **52,** 285–302.

Honzik, M. P., MacFarlane, J. W., & Allen, L. The stability of mental test performance between two and eighteen years. *Journal of Experimental Education,* 1948, **17,** 309–324.

Hopkins, K. D. An empirical analysis of the efficacy of the WISC in the diagnosis of organicity in children of normal intelligence. *Journal of Genetic Psychology,* 1964, **105,** 163–172.

Hunt, J. McV. *Intelligence and experience.* New York: Ronald Press, 1961.

Jenkins, J. J., & Paterson, D. G. *Studies in individual differences.* New York: Appleton-Century-Crofts, 1961.

Jones, H. E., & Bayley, N. The Berkeley Growth Study. *Child Development,* 1941, **12,** 167–173.

Kagan, J., Sontag, L. W., Baker, C. T., & Nelson, V. L. Personality and I.Q. change. *Journal of Abnormal and Social Psychology,* 1958, **45,** 261–266.

Katkovsky, W., Crandall, V. C., & Good, S. Parental antecedents of children's beliefs in internal-external control of reinforcements in intellectual achievement situations. *Child Development,* 1967, **38,** 765–776.

Kelley, T. L. *Crossroads in the mind of man: A study of differentiable mental abilities.* Stanford, Calif.: Stanford University Press, 1928.

Kimbrell, D. L. Comparison of Peabody, WISC, and Academic Achievement scores among educable mental defectives. *Psychological Reports,* 1960, **7,** 502.

Knobloch, H., & Pasamanick, B. Prediction from assessment of neuromotor and intellectual status in infancy. In J. Zubin and G. A. Jervis (Eds.), *Psychopathology of mental development.* New York: Grune & Stratton, 1967.

Lane, E. A., & Albee, G. W. Childhood intellectual differences between schizophrenic adults and their siblings. *American Journal of Orthopsychiatry,* 1965, **35,** 747–753.

Lefcourt, H. M. Internal vs. external control of reinforcement: A review. *Psychological Bulletin,* 1966, **65,** 206–220.

Levine, M. Psychological testing of children. In W. Hoffman and M. L. Hoffman (Eds.), *Review of child development research.* Vol. 2. New York: Russell Sage Foundation, 1966.

Littell, W. M. The Wechsler Intelligence Scale for Children. *Psychological Bulletin,* 1960, **57,** 132–156.

Liverant, S. Intelligence: A concept in need of re-examination. *Journal of Consulting Psychology,* 1960, **24,** 101–110.

Mason, C. F. Pre-illness intelligence of mental hospital patients. *Journal of Consulting Psychology,* 1956, **20,** 297–300.

McGhee, P. E., & Crandall, V. C. Beliefs in internal-external control of reinforcements and academic performance. *Child Development,* 1968, **39,** 91–102.

McKinney, J. P. A multidimensional study of the behavior of severely retarded boys. *Child Development,* 1962, **33,** 923–938.

McKinney, J. P., & Keele, T. Effects of increased mothering on the behavior of severely retarded boys. *American Journal of Mental Deficiency,* 1963, **67,** 556–562.

Miller, M. B. Psychometric and clinical studies in mental deficiency, 1954–1959: A selective review and critique. *American Journal of Mental Deficiency,* 1960–1961, **65,** 182–193.

Mueller, M. W. Mental testing in mental retardation: A review of recent research. *Training School Bulletin,* 1964, **60,** 152–168.

Muench, G. A. A follow-up of mental defectives after 18 years. *Journal of Abnormal and Social Psychology,* 1944, **39,** 407–418.

Oliver, K., & Barclay, A. Stanford-Binet and Goodenough-Harris test performances of Head-Start children. *Psychological Reports,* 1967, **20,** 1175–1179.

Owen, F. W. The study of hearing disorders in childhood. Paper presented at the San Francisco Psychoanalytic Institute fall symposium, 1967.

Pollack, M. Mental subnormality and "childhood schizophrenia." In J. Zubin & G. A. Jervis (Eds.), *Psychopathology of mental development.* New York: Grune & Stratton, 1967.

Rabin, A. I. Wechsler Intelligence Scale for Children. In O. K. Buros (Ed.), *The fifth mental measurements yearbook.* Highland Park, N.J.: Gryphon Press, 1959.

Rabin, A. I. Diagnostic use of intelligence tests. In B. Wolman (Ed.), *Handbook of clinical psychology.* New York: McGraw-Hill, 1965.

Rabin, A. I. Assessment of abnormalities in intellectual development. In J. Zubin & G. A. Jervis (Eds.), *Psychopathology of mental development.* New York: Grune & Stratton, 1967.

Rabin, A. I., & Winder, C. L. Psychological studies of schizophrenia. In L. Bellak & L. Loeb (Eds.), *The schizophrenic syndrome.* New York: Grune & Stratton, 1969.

Rapaport, S. R., & Webb, W. B. An attempt to study intellectual deterioration by premorbid and psychotic testing. *Journal of Consulting Psychology,* 1950, **14,** 95–98.

Rheingold, H. L., & Bayley, N. The later effects of an experimental modification of mothering. *Child Development,* 1959, **30,** 363–372.

Rohrs, F. W., & Haworth, M. R. The 1960 Stanford-Binet, WISC, and the Goodenough tests with mentally retarded children. *American Journal of Mental Deficiency,* 1962, **66,** 853–859.

Rose, R. L., & Morlege, J. Comparison of the WISC and WAIS at chronological age sixteen. *Journal of Consulting Psychology,* 1964, **31,** 331–332.

Rotter, J. B. Generalized expectancies for internal vs. external control of reinforcement. *Psychological Monograph,* 1966, **80,** No. 1.

Rutter, M. Intelligence and childhood psychiatric disorder. *British Journal of the Society of Clinical Psychologists,* 1964, **3,** 120–129.

Sarason, S. B. *Psychological problems in mental deficiency.* New York: Harper, 1959.

Sarason, S. B., Davidson, K. S., Lighthall, F. F., Waite, R. R., & Ruebush, B. K. *Anxiety in elementary school children.* New York: Wiley, 1960.

Sarason, S. B., Hill, K. J., & Zimbardo, P. G. A longitudinal study of the relation of test anxiety to performance on intelligence and achievement tests. *Monographs of the Society for Research in Child Development,* 1964, **29,** No. 7.

Schachter, F. F., Meyer, L. R., & Loomis, E. A. Childhood schizophrenia and mental retardation: Differential diagnosis before and after one year of psychotherapy. *American Journal of Orthopsychiatry,* 1962, **32,** 584–594.

Schaefer, E. S., & Bayley, N. Maternal behavior, child behavior, and their intercorrelations from infancy through adolescence. *Monographs of the Society for Research in Child Development,* 1963, **28,** No. 3.

Sherman, M., & Key, C. B. The intelligence of isolated mountain children. *Child Development,* 1932, **3,** 279–290.

Skeels, H. M. Some Iowa studies of the mental growth of children in relation to differentials of the environment: A summary. *The thirty-ninth yearbook.* National Society for the Study of Education. Bloomington, Ill.: Public School Publishing Co., 1940. Pp. 281–308.

Skeels, H. M. Adult status of children with contrasting early life experiences. *Monographs of the Society for Research in Child Development,* 1966, **31,** No. 3.

Skeels, H. M., & Dye, H. B. A study of the effects of differential stimulation on mentally retarded children. *Proceedings and Addresses of the American Association of Mental Deficiency,* 1939, **44,** 114–116.

Skeels, H. M., & Fillmore, E. A. The mental development of children from under-privileged homes. *Journal of Genetic Psychology,* 1937, **50,** 427–439.

Skeels, H. M., Updegraff, R., Wellman, B. L., & Williams, H. M. A study of environmental stimulation: An orphanage preschool project. *University of Iowa Studies in Child Welfare,* 1938, **15,** No. 4.

Skodak, M. Children in foster homes: A study of mental development. *University of Iowa Studies in Child Welfare,* 1939, **16,** No. 1.

Sontag, L. W., Baker, C. T., & Nelson, V. L. Mental growth and personality development: A longitudinal study. *Monographs of the Society for Research in Child Development,* 1958, **23,** No. 2.

Spearman, C. "General intelligence" objectively determined and measured. *American Journal of Psychology,* 1904, **15,** 201–292.

Spearman, C. *The abilities of man.* London: Macmillan, 1927.

Spiker, C. C., & McCandless, B. R. The concept of intelligence and the philosophy of science. *Psychological Review,* 1954, **61,** 255–266.

Stott, L. H., & Ball, S. Infant and preschool mental tests. *Monographs of the Society for Research in Child Development,* 1965, **30,** No. 3.

Taylor, E. M. *Psychological appraisal of children with cerebral defect.* Cambridge, Mass.: Harvard University Press, 1959.

Terman, L. M., & Merrill, M. A. *Stanford-Binet Intelligence Scale.* Boston: Houghton Mifflin, 1960.

Thorndike, E. L. *Educational psychology.* New York: Lemcke and Buechner, 1903.

Thurstone, L. L. Primary mental abilities. *Psychometric Monograph,* 1938, No. 1.

Thurstone, L. L. Psychological implications of factor analysis. *American Psychologist,* 1948, **3,** 402–408.

Wechsler, D. *Wechsler Intelligence Scale for Children.* New York: Psychological Corporation, 1949.

Wechsler, D. Cognitive, conative, and non-intellective intelligence. *American Psychologist,* 1950, **5,** 78–83.

Wechsler, D. *The measurement and appraisal of adult intelligence.* (4th ed.) Baltimore: Williams & Wilkins, 1958.

Wechsler, D. *Manual for the Wechsler Preschool and Primary Scale of Intelligence.* New York: Psychological Corporation, 1967.

Wesman. A. G.   Intelligent testing.   *American Psychologist,* 1968, **23,** 267–274.

Wheeler, L. R.   A comparative study of the intelligence of East Tennessee mountain children. *Journal of Educational Psychology,* 1942, **33,** 321–334.

Wolf, M. G.   Effects of emotional disturbance in childhood intelligence.   *American Journal of Orthopsychiatry,* 1965, **35,** 906–908.

Woodworth, R. S.   Racial differences in mental traits.   *Science,* 1910, **31,** 171–186.

Worbois, G. M.   Changes in Stanford-Binet IQ for rural consolidated and rural one-room school children.   *Journal of Experimental Education,* 1942, **11,** 210–214.

25 The Use of Projective Techniques with Children

Jean Mundy

The purpose of this chapter is to present the current methodological use of projective techniques. These projective methods are insufficient in themselves, but like all other specialized techniques, they represent a necessary component in a clinical assessment program aimed at understanding the whole child. The personality of the child is a complex entity and therefore cannot be assessed by any one instrument. The major types of instruments in use today are designed to systematically measure the inner life of the child by minute examination of his verbal and motor responses to ambiguous stimuli.

Some projective techniques deal primarily with the verbal productions of the child, others with graphic or motor responses. While these three modes of functioning are usually positively correlated, to ensure against error all three modes must be examined in each child. In this paper, the projective techniques are grouped according to these three modes.

The author wishes to thank Dr. Carole Bare, Miss Susan Knapp, and Miss Gail Geddis

The following tests will be discussed: the Rorschach; thematic apperception, word-association, and sentence-completion techniques; tests eliciting verbal responses; the various drawing and construction techniques which require the child to build or make something or to play with toys or other materials; and other tests which elicit motor responses.

RATIONALE UNDERLYING THE PROJECTIVE METHODS

If we are to understand children and their deepest feelings of satisfaction, disappointments, longings, bewilderment, and confusion, we need methods which will make this private inner world directly accessible. Unfortunately, verbal communication between children and adults is frequently not direct. Children are usually unable to express their feelings in words. Moreover, many important psychological processes, such as perception and structuring of the life space, cannot be expressed well in words, no matter how strong is the need to communicate.

Projective techniques have been designed to supplement verbal communication channels. They minimize face-to-face, question-answer interchange and maximize subject-to-task interaction. While the child is absorbed in performing the task, minute observations are made, which are later subjected to detailed analysis.

Not all tasks are well suited for such analysis. To yield the most revealing behavior samples, the task must meet certain criteria. The assignment must be relatively novel to the child so that he cannot imitate other people's responses. The situation has to be interesting and nonthreatening, and it must allow for a wide range of individual differences in responses. The greatest possible amount of freedom is given to the child in order that his uniqueness can be manifested, and yet enough limitations are imposed so that his responses can be interpreted in terms of those of other children.

In using a projective technique, the examiner provides a standard ambiguous task for the child, giving him minimal instruction. In performing the test, the child projects something of his own inner world and reveals his habitual mode of structuring perceptions and organizing his life space.

Ambiguous material is used because it serves to determine the individual nature of the child as opposed to his cultural assimilations. If a child is asked to answer a question and all he has to do is recall a specific answer which he has been taught, the result indicates only how well he has learned specific material. If he echoes the teacher's words, saying, for example, "Two plus two is four" or that a picture of an apple is called "apple," he indicates his degree of socialization. If two children call the picture of an apple by that name, we erroneously assume that both children are thinking, feeling, and perceiving identically at that moment, but the experience may be quite different for each, depending on their respective past experience with apples. However, if a child calls an inkblot "apple" and another child calls the same part of the blot "ball," the interesting question is raised: What made each child see it that way? The principle of psychic determinism precludes the answers from being due to chance. In attempting to understand the child's response to the inkblot, we must explore the stimulus itself, i.e., the inkblot, and the immediate environment, i.e., the effect of the adult examiner, and the child's feelings, his past experiences, his physiology, etc. In so exploring, we gain a tremendous amount of information about the subject's inner world. Substituting an ambiguous reality for an obvious reality forces the child and the clinician to explore the child's unique personal world.

Another reason for using ambiguous material is that the ambiguity serves as a catalyst. Some children become creative; others panic. The adult leaves the child to his own devices in coping with an unknown situation, unlike the usual child-adult interaction. Therefore, the child's individual mode of acting in a stress situation can be observed. The projective test record is a documented account of how a particular child reacts when faced with an ambiguous reality.

CURRENT APPLICATION OF PROJECTIVE TECHNIQUES

The analysis of the child's habitual mode of approach to problems can give guidelines for effective treatment programs. Projective test records supplement information gained from the case history and thus aid the clinician in selecting the most beneficial therapy method. There are at least four possibilities which may result from this combination: (1) symptoms may appear in behavior but not in the psychological protocol, (2) symptoms may appear in both strata, (3) symptoms may appear in neither overt nor covert records, (4) symptoms may be seen in the psychological test even though they are not manifested in behavior.

When these discrepancies appear, diagnosticians are puzzled, and some choose to ignore the results of either the case histories or the test battery. Actually, the contradiction lies not in the approach to the patient but in the patient himself. When Machover (1949) was challenged about the validity of projective techniques, she replied, "They are as valid as the patients are." Some people, after all, are wearing shoes that do not fit their feet, and some live out a public role which does not fit with their inner life.

Differences or contradictions must not be glossed over or "solved" by ignoring some aspects of the patient's behavior but should be used in selecting treatment procedures. For example, if the child appears well adjusted on the surface but underlying pathology is revealed by the test, the therapist must either support the present defenses or, using proper safeguards, carefully bring the pathology to the surface and work the problems through with the child. Quite often, pathology appears in the test material before it appears on the surface, and thus anticipated overt problems could be prevented. On the other hand, a child's projective records may indicate many underlying strengths which are hidden by shyness or antisocial behavior. The diagnosis based on overt symptoms may be confirmed by the child's reaction to projective materials, which may indicate a different therapeutic approach than in the overt-covert discrepancy situation.

A second method which is useful in mapping out a therapeutic approach to the child involves the following: Some parts of these personality tests require the examiner to be direct and forceful with the child, while other parts require letting the child have his own way. The examiner can then note how the child reacts in these two situations and communicate his observations to the therapist, enabling the therapist to predict what will happen if he encourages fantasy or introduces structure.

Since children often relate better to some adults than to others, personality tests can be used to help in choosing the most effective therapist for a given child. The test can point out whether the child needs a firm paternal surrogate or a warm, accepting parental figure, etc.

Moreover, if the projective tests are administered properly, the testing situation may become a therapeutic experience for the child. A different kind of communication channel is opened between the child and the adult, for the projective procedure can supplement or even replace verbal communication. The child who cannot express himself well in words or who needs a buffer between himself and the adult will find the projective methods a means of filling in this void. The child gains a comfortable distance from the adult by concentrating on the materials at hand rather than answering the questions directly. And since some materials allow more psychological distance than others, the adult can adjust the intensity of contact by judicious use of materials and can introduce materials which require more personal interaction whenever the child is ready for it.

The examiner can also use the projective materials as a means of communication and can talk to the child in the same way a puppeteer talks through a puppet. Feelings and attitudes which are not clear to the child can thus be expressed by him and brought into the conscious realm.

LIMITATIONS OF PROJECTIVE TECHNIQUES

Halpern (in Wolman, 1965) points out that the testing of children is essentially different from the testing of adults because the examiner cannot assume that the child is motivated to do his best in the testing situation. Moreover, the child is usually brought to the session by the adults in his environment, rather than coming because he wants to or feels that he should be tested. Quite often, the child has no understanding of why he should perform for a strange adult. Finally, the child's attention span must be taken into consideration, for the willingness to begin or end a project according to a time clock is a learned cultural value that not all children accept.

Difficulties of Administration

The limitations of projective techniques begin with the difficulty of administering the test properly. The child is easily influenced by adults in general, and he is even more suggestible when faced with ambiguity. The training and personality of the examiner are crucial factors in projective testing. The examiner may consciously or unconsciously influence the child instead of allowing him true freedom of expression. An adult may be shocked by what the child says and unwittingly reveal his disapproval. The examiner may, therefore, by gestures and facial expressions encourage the child to produce certain kinds of responses and to eliminate others. An examiner who is afraid that the test will reveal pathology, for example, may seriously inhibit the child or score the test in a highly subjective rather than a detached manner. The examiner may impose his own personality, anxieties, and premature conclusions into the situation and fail to recognize that his own projections are being scored rather than those of the child.

It is difficult to train examiners to be able to keep rapport and degree of influence constant. The examiner must attempt to elicit maximum cooperation from each child. Furthermore, the length of time spent on the test is influenced by immediate environmental factors, which are generally difficult to control. To simplify the work of recording significant behavior during the testing situation, the examiner must be carefully trained.

Only the child's behavior need be recorded; the examiner's behavior is predetermined by the standard test procedure. However, in interpreting the test, it is essential that even minor deviations from the standard procedure on the part of the examiner be registered and their effect taken into consideration. It is almost pointless to compare test results of one examiner with the results of another examiner if the examiners are not equally well trained or if they use a different approach.

Difficulties of Scoring

Errors may be introduced into the test by the scoring procedure. The personality test measures global factors, yet the scoring must be made on the basis of discrete items. Much of the meaning of the test is lost if scores are taken out of context, for by taking scores out of context one loses sight of the child's manner of reasoning. The manner of performing that is the process of test performance may be sometimes more important than the final answer. For example, the response "Cars stop at red lights" would appear rational, but the author is reminded of a child who based this conclusion on the premise that the red light sent out powerful waves of energy which forced the cars to stop. Scoring this response as correct in this instance fails to reveal the child's bizarre thinking process.

Difficulties of Interpretation

Because these tests measure inner life, it is difficult to find a comparable measure of inner life with which to make comparisons. Since inner life and overt behavior do not always correspond, overt or external criteria do not suffice. Furthermore, it is not sufficient to match test results to judges' ratings if the reliability of these ratings cannot be established.

Although it is essential to use ambiguous materials to elicit projections, using such items has some disadvantages. Because of the wide range of possible responses, it is difficult to know what an individual response means. The technical procedure used to overcome this problem is the development of norms. By standardizing the stimuli and the procedure, it is possible to collect comparable records of hundreds of children. The scoring and tabulating of the scores from these records have generated frequency response tables and responses found to be typical of a certain age and occurring only rarely at another, thus providing indicators of normal development.

A further consideration is that some responses are found in one diagnostic group and not in others; thus their presence indicates a particular syndrome. In a word, the individual response becomes meaningful in comparison with the record of other children. And we can readily determine if a child is developing atypically.

Difficulties of Predicting

The use of projective techniques for prediction of the child's actual behavior has frequently been misunderstood, for in most instances the test records cannot predict the future within a satisfactory level of probability. Projective techniques can merely outline the subject's inner life at the present time. Yet if it could be established clinically what kinds of needs, what kind of impulse control, etc., lead to a certain type of behavior, the projective methods could help in prediction of behavior.

SUMMARY

Because of the inherent problems in administration, scoring, and interpretation and predicting, there has been a great deal of misunderstanding concerning the projective methods. Those who use statistics designed to test correct answers reject the projective tests as inconclusive. Those who mistakenly assume that the tests must predict future behavior directly have rejected the tests because the predictions were found to be in error. But in spite of these problems, interest in these tests has increased rather than diminished. Clinicians continue to supplement idiographic methods of personality analysis with nomothetic methods. Methods are used because they fulfill a function. The refinements of the technique and why it works frequently are not fully understood until after several decades of use.

There are over a hundred different projective methods in use today (Buros, 1959, 1965). Over seven thousand references are available for just one of these tests (Kiell, 1965). Journals such as the *Journal of Projective Techniques and Personality Assessment* have been entirely devoted to projective techniques. In this chapter we shall classify these materials into two major categories and shall include information which is useful to the practicing clinician. The first category includes those techniques which are primarily directed to record verbal responses, and the second, those which elicit motor responses. Verbal and motor behaviors are the two principal modes of interaction with others, but it is rare to find a child equally competent in both modes, and so it is necessary to allow each child to express himself in these two media.

Projective techniques can be used to describe the inner world of children and as an aid to diagnosis and therapy. The rationale of projective techniques has been stated as follows: By providing the child with an ambiguous task to perform, we highlight his unique way of coping with reality. However, his uniqueness compounds the problem of making comparisons of his behavior with that of other children. By standardizing as many variables as possible, by a choice of stimuli, administration, and scoring, we attempt to make the child's responses comparable without destroying their uniqueness. The child is an integrated entity, but for practical reasons we divide his personality into components, such as intelligence, attitudes, self-concept, and motor behavior, and design specific tests for these specific areas. Each of the tests presented here describes a part of the whole. It remains for the experienced clinician to reconstruct the composite picture. A major symptom can be isolated and then put in proper perspective by understanding the personality background in which it exists. To date, we can guarantee reliability and validity only by restricting our measures to small units of behavior. As we attempt to measure larger units of behavior, we are unable to secure reliability and validity. In the attempt to predict future behavior, we lose even more accuracy. The task remains for present and future scientists to assess the total personality and its pathology without sacrificing objectivity. The projective techniques illustrated here are a step toward these goals.

PROJECTIVE TECHNIQUES REQUIRING VERBAL RESPONSES

The Rorschach Inkblot Method

Description. The child is asked to tell what he sees in the ten Rorschach (1942) inkblots. Verbatim records and response times are kept, as well as detailed notes of the child's expressive movements. An "Inquiry" is then made about each of the responses given. At times a third step is taken, "Testing the Limits," during which the child is prompted to give certain responses.

Rationale. The Rorschach instrument helps the examiner analyze the child's perceptual functioning and his habitual mode of testing reality. The child's process of interpreting the inkblots is basically the same as his process of comprehension in everyday visual perception (Murphy, 1956). The record indicates the child's degree of control, his ability to integrate and organize, and his emotional reactions to his perceptions (Halpern, 1953). The child's responses from the age of 2 throughout childhood reflect his growing awareness and acceptance of reality, his development of a self-concept, his maturing emotional life, and the mechanisms he develops for dealing with his problems. Acceleration or retardation in any of these areas of personality can be easily detected when the child's reactions are compared with those of his peers.

Scoring. There is no one accepted approach to Rorschach scoring. The most commonly ac-cepted interpretational scorings are those designed by (1) Rorschach and Oberholzer (Rorschach, 1942) and Beck et al. (1961), who are empirical, experimental and statistical; (2) Klopfer and Kelley (1942), who are phenomenalists; (3) Hertz (1951), who bases her nomothetic interpretations on firm statistical footing; (4) Piotrowski (1957), who is unique and imaginative and who believes in insight but is also comfortable with programming IBM machines to generate typed reports (1964); and (5) Schafer (1954), who represents the psychoanalytic school. The Rorschach continues to be a complex instrument open to new interpretations.

The validity and reliability of the Rorschach continue to be an open question. It is not a test, in the strict sense of the word, but a technique which represents an extension of the interview. (No projective technique is a test, and the word *test* is used here only because of its convenience.)

There are more than twenty scoring factors to be considered in a Rorschach analysis. For a complete analysis of the attempts at validation of these scores, the reader is referred to Wolman's *Handbook of Clinical Psychology* (1965). To avoid repetition, only two Rorschach scores will be considered here as brief examples, and Halpern's (1953) use of the Rorschach in determining school readiness will be considered.

Form scores. Awareness of reality is reflected by the form scores. If the child gives responses which actually correspond with the shape of the blot, he is aware of reality. By the time the child is 4½ or 5 years of age, he should no longer give the same response to differently shaped blots, and more of his percepts should be a better match for the shape of the blots. The percentage of such good form matches rises from a low of 20 to 40 percent at age 2 to close to 60 percent by age 4 or 5. By 6 years of age, the percentage of good form responses is about 80 percent. Thus, while the reactions of the 6-year-old tend to be somewhat crude and lacking the richness that older children possess, there is no longer any appreciable tendency to disregard reality. Some departures from good form represent a momentary failure of judgment, a tendency to be overambitious and daring, whereas frequent misperceptions give evidence of a more serious disturbance.

Human percepts. A second commonly used measure is the quantity and quality of human shapes reported by the subject. Perceiving human figures on the Rorschach indicates ego strength, and, therefore, a child of 6 or 7 who does not give a single human-form response on the Rorschach is manifesting some disturbance in his development. The child's perception of himself can be seen by examining his animal, humanlike, and human forms. For example, the child who gives such interpretations as "crawling worms" and whose only human response is that of "a giant" is probably a child who feels small and inadequate in the face of an overpowering and frightening adult world. By the time the child is about 10 years old, these immature concepts should have been replaced by human forms of more orthodox shape. Further examples are presented in Table 25-1, but for a more complete understanding, the reader is urged to select his particular interest from the 3,000 references available.

School readiness. A special caution must be noted when using Rorschach methods with very young children. It is advisable to have two or three records from a toddler over a period of several months to a year, so that minor fluctuations are not viewed as manifestations of pathology. However, if the examiners are experienced and proceed cautiously, Rorschach records of preschoolers can be used to ascertain school readiness.

The child's reaction to the Rorschach situation is analogous to his reaction to new school experiences. When given the Rorschach, the child is placed in a new and surprising situation in which he is required to make a continuous effort and to keep his uninterrupted attention on a series of ten plates at one sitting. The child's reaction to the first plate indicates his reaction to novelty, and throughout the test he is taken through many emotional reactions by the changing pattern of stimuli.

The second Rorschach plate has some red color combined with black forms. The red coloring provokes an excited or shocked reaction. The third plate has some familiar elements with regard to the other cards because it also is black and red, and, therefore, the reaction reveals the child's mode of perceiving a semifamiliar situation. Plate IV is the blackest one, and as such it often creates a feeling of unpleasant surprise in the child. His associations to fear and his ways of handling unpleasant situations and unpleasant emotions are the keynotes here. Plate V is clearly defined and also black, but lacks the shock value of Plate IV. On Plate V, the child has a chance to recover from unpleasantness and strangeness if he has the necessary inner resources, and the examiner is given an indication of tolerance level. Plate VI is difficult to interpret as a unit, for it has several distinct units. Moreover, it has some sexual implications due to its phalliclike form. Plate VII is light, vague, and open, and to many children it is a delight, but some are made uneasy by it. However, the child's response to this plate tells the examiner about the child's need for freedom as opposed to limitations. Plate VIII is the first full-color plate. This requires that the child again adjust to a new situation—some children need time to forget that the black color is no longer there; some feel great excitement because there is so much color. Plate IX is also in full color, but it is less distinct. By comparing his responses to the two full-color plates with those to the previous two black-and-white cards, the examiner can note whether the child gives healthier responses when he is emotionally stimulated than when he is not so stimulated. Whether emotional experiences are traumatic or stimulating to his growth can also be judged by his reaction to these and other

TABLE 25-1   DEVIATIONS IN RORSCHACH PATTERNS*

Category†	Attitude	Self-concept	Emotions	Coping Mechanisms	Rorschach Scoring
Inhibited	Fear of failure	Weak	Barren, depressed	Severe inhibition; conforms	Good W; average F+%; tame animals predominate over wild animals
Neurotic	Overly sensitive	Small, helpless, or hiding "badness"	Fearful of rebellious impulses	Denial, projection, repression, blocking, sublimating	Low F+%†; in some, early appearance of FC, high F+, high P, and little else
Antisocial	Ignoring and defying of reality	Egocentric, unstable, primitive, "lone wolf"	Impoverished, no empathy, shallow affect	Gives way to impulses	Poor Ws; low F+%‡; many CF or C, or no Cs with many Fs and few FMs; sees wild animals
Passive-aggressive	Passive on surface; covert aggression	Vacillates between seeing self as good and then as bad	Resentful, hostile	Compliance	Both passive and aggressive content; high F%, sporadic CFs with M
Schizophrenic	Poor reality testing; withdrawal	No stable or meaningful self-concept	Morbid, brutal, impulsive, anxious, nightmarish	Preoccupations with aspects of objects, time, and space	All categories either higher or lower than expected norms; denies his responses; bizarre responses; variations in form level; no H, or high Hd; M−, or M with CF, CF−, C
Prepuberty	Uncertain, introversive (girls more so than boys)	Reevaluates self	Fluctuates	Repression	High F%, low sum C, F+% drops but responses not bizarre; shading and texture noted for first time

* Adapted from Halpern (1953).

† Many children resist such dichotomies; this is a suggested frame of reference.

‡ The low F+% of the neurotic is due to a poor attempt to resolve his percepts with his needs, while the low F+% of the acting-out child is due to carelessness and indifference.

colored plates. Plate X is a colored picture book to most children. They find familiar forms of animals with great ease and enjoy the variety of forms. Other children are too shaken by previous experiences to enjoy this inkblot and give up or react in a defensive way. By analyzing the sequence of reactions and responses that the child has gone through in taking the test, we can estimate what his reaction will be to the school situation (Halpern, 1953).

Variations of the Rorschach

1. Holtzman et al. (1961) have attempted to eliminate some of the scoring problems of the Rorschach by designing two sets of forty-five inkblots and requiring only one response to each card. This helps scoring procedure but may result in some loss of the subject's individuality.

2. The Behn-Rorschach (Behn, 1956) is designed to be a parallel set to the original Rorschach. It is useful for research or with subjects who are already overly familiar with the Rorschach set.

3. Group administration of the Rorschach is possible, and a multiple-choice form for screening purposes has been devised (Harrower-Erickson, 1941, 1943).

Thematic Apperception Methods

Rationale. The second most widely used verbal method is thematic apperception (Sundberg, 1961). Henry's (1947) bibliography contains almost a thousand titles on its use. A discussion of the problem of norms can be found in Rosenzweig (1949). Theoretically, the Rorschach reveals the child's perceptual processes of testing reality while the thematic methods tap cognition and characteristic problem-solving reactions in interpersonal relationships (Moriarty, 1968).

The stories told in response to the pictures are directly related to the child's attitudes, viewpoints, role relationships, conflicts with people, and dispositions toward others. The strength of basic drives is indicated by the frequency of their occurrence within the story. For example, a child may be shown ten different pictures but tell eight stories involving a hero who runs away from aggressive authority figures. The plot indicates what the child anticipates as a result of his behavior. Identification with the hero is usually conspicuous and describes the child's self-concept or the ideal self-concept. By questioning aspects of the child's story, the examiner can further explore his preoccupations, troubles, daydreams, coping devices, and adaptive functioning.

Description of the thematic materials. Essentially, a series of pictures are presented and leading questions are asked to prompt clinically rich stories. There are many sets of pictures available, and it is left to the discretion of the examiner to choose stimuli which will elicit material in the area of immediate concern. Some subjects are aided in identifying with the characters portrayed when the pictures are clearly similar in age, sex, and culture to the subject. For others, vague, nonspecific materials aid projection. Some very young children are more comfortable with pictures of humanlike animals. These and other variations of the Thematic Apperception Test (TAT) are outlined below.

1. The Children's Apperception Test—CAT (Haworth, 1966). The CAT is the most widely used set of animal pictures for children ages 3 to 10 (Bellak, 1954). It is a series of pictures of anthropomorphic animals. For example, one card portrays adult monkeys sitting on a sofa drinking from teacups while an adult monkey in the foreground is talking to a baby monkey.

The CAT pictorial situations enable the examiner to probe for fears in play situations, interpersonal problems in the classroom, fantasies about being an adult, competitiveness with others, illness, bathroom problems, sexual fears, etc.

2. The Make-A-Picture-Story Test—MAPS (Shneidman, 1947). The examiner may allow the subject to change the stimulus in the MAPS. The test materials consist of twenty-two pictorial

backgrounds (e.g., a living room, bedroom, bathroom, schoolroom, cave, and a blank card), which are held upright in a wooden frame. The cast of characters consists of sixty-seven cutout figures—men and women of various ethnic backgrounds, some nudes, children, legendary characters, silhouettes, and figures with blank faces. The child chooses some cutouts, inserts them into wooden bases, and arranges them in front of the chosen background. The child (ages 3½ to 16) then tells a story in the same manner as in the TAT. The test requires forty-five to ninety minutes.

The MAPS protocol can be subjected to elaborate formal scoring schemes (Shneidman, 1947). In clinical practice, however, the protocol is most often interpreted in a holistic and impressionistic manner. It yields the same type of psychological insights as the TAT, the major difference being that the examiner allows the child to select the test materials.

3. The Picture-Frustration Test (Rosenzweig, 1953). The children's form of this test (ages 4 to 13) is an extremely useful device for sampling reactions to frustration and for determining whether the child's aggression is directed inwardly or externally. The pictures are highly structured scenes of interpersonal frustration events, such as, for example, the destruction of a treasured object. The scoring system is relatively objective.

4. The Hand Test (Wagner & Medvedeff, 1963). This test is a projective technique in which the child (ages 6 and over) is shown a series of nine drawings of a hand in various ambiguous poses and is asked what the hand might be doing. The last card is blank and requires the subject to imagine a hand and describe what it is doing. The scoring is similar to that of Rorschach and TAT and provides measures of affection, dependence, aggression, tension, etc.

5. The Paired Hands Test of Friendliness (Zucker & Jordan, 1969). Reasoning that two hands would allow for a finer measure of interaction, Zucker presents slides of a black and a white hand in various positions. He simplifies group administration and scoring by providing the child with a multiple-choice answer sheet and secures meaningful data about the child's social relatedness.

6. The Blacky Pictures Test (Blum, 1949). Blum's cartoons of a dog family are used by clinicians of the psychoanalytic persuasion (Granick & Scheflen, 1958). The questions are patterned after the analytic approach, and the subject's answers are fitted into that framework. For example, questions focus on sexual activity, sibling rivalry, and castration fears.

7. Test of Family Attitudes (Jackson, 1950). When the examiner wishes to explain the attitude of the child toward his parents and siblings, he may use this test, which consists of seven pictures portraying situations between children and adults.

8. The Family Relations Indicator (Howells & Lickorish, 1963). Similar to the Test of Family Attitudes is the Family Relations Indicator, which has less structured pictures of child and father, child and mother, child alone, child and baby, siblings together, and parents alone and with children.

9. The Picture World Test (Buhler & Manson, 1955). This test differs from the standard format of related tests in that the subjects (ages 6 and over) write their own stories and can add additional figures and objects from a list of thirty-six. The scenes are interestingly drawn and are unambiguous and reality-oriented. The subject is instructed to "make up a world as it is or as you would like it to be." This is essentially a picture version of the World Test, which will be discussed later.

10. The Picture Impressions Test (Libo, 1957). This form is specifically designed to study the patient's expectations regarding the therapist and is suitable for adolescents and adults. The four pictures have drawings of a person in a short white laboratory coat, and as in the other variations, specific questions are asked.

11. The Auditory Apperception Test (Stone,

1950). This projective is similar to the TAT but with auditory rather than visual stimuli. The test materials consist of ten sets of three sound situations. There is no rationale for using auditory stimuli with normally sighted subjects, but the instrument would be useful with visually handicapped subjects (ages 9 and over).

12. The Michigan Picture Test—MPT (Hartwell, Hutt, Andrew, & Walton, 1951). The MPT focuses on school difficulties. Two of the pictures—the father and daughter and the girl alone in a classroom—deserve particular attention because they are not matched in the Murray TAT set. The pictures are dated, however, and may not be appealing to contemporary children.

13. The Object Relations Technique (Phillipson, 1955). Phillipson's two sets of four pictures of one-person, two-person, three-person, and group relationships are more ambiguous than the TAT pictures and are in color. He proposes that color intensifies the threat element and encourages emotional involvement. The second series pictures kitchen, bedroom, outside, and a public place.

14. The Symonds (1949) twenty pictures were designed for administration to adolescents (grades 7 to 12). The test pictures parallel the TAT scenes but contain more youthful figures. The pictures are depressive in tone and repetitious, and therefore they are not favored over the Murray (1943b) TAT.

15. The Adult-Child Interaction Test (Alexander, 1955). The distinctive feature of this eight-card TAT-type instrument is the system developed for categorizing various features of the stories on a recording blank. The scores are grouped according to (1) the occurrence and organization of a series of defined story elements—the behaviorial continuum; (2) the stimulus elements used—symbolization; and (3) the positive and negative feelings and actions—the emotional perception.

16. The Thompson (1949) modification of the TAT is for blacks (ages 4 and over). It parallels the TAT using black characters and ethnically appropriate backgrounds. This form might also be used with white subjects to tap social attitudes toward blacks.

17. The South African Picture Analysis Test—SAPAT (Nel & Pelser, 1960). This test is the only TAT-type set which purports to measure the child's relationship to God as well as to man. The stories are interpreted by the authors in an existential framework, yet not without the influence of American empiricists. The pictures were picked after surveying children to ascertain their preferences. This set presents both human and humanlike animals as characters.

18. Rock-a-bye Baby (Haworth, 1962). A film is now available as a substitute for the static TAT pictures. Rock-a-bye Baby is a 35-minute 16-mm. sound film for the investigation of sibling rivalry, self-concept, jealousy, aggression to parents, guilt, anxiety, and obsessive trends. It is suitable for groups of nine to sixteen children aged 5 to 10.

19. The Pickford Projective Pictures (Pickford, 1963). The Pickford set has 120 ambiguous line drawings of people in a variety of situations, and it is recommended for therapeutic interaction with children from ages 5 to 15. The manual points out that the pictures can serve as a cathartic experience for the child as well as help in understanding the child's dynamics. In addition to being designed as an aid to therapy, it is unique in that so many of the pictures are attractive. This set partially fills the gap between the TAT and the CAT. The examiner does not need to prod the child since children generally find it more desirable to tell a large number of short stories rather than a few drawn-out ones. The recurrent themes reflect some of the child's preoccupations and worries. The interpretation guidelines in the manual are not restricted to a single theory, although they are analytically inclined.

20. The IES Test (Dombrose & Slobin, 1958). This test is designed to measure impulses, ego, and superego in children ages 10 and over. The

subtests are the Arrow-Dot Test, the Photo-Analysis Test, a questionnaire about the motives of pictured characters, the Picture Story Completion Test, and the Picture Title Test. It is based on an explicit psychoanalytic framework. It is well designed and easily administered and scored, and it captures the interest of the subjects, but few norms are available for children.

Picture-arrangement tests. Tests of this sort have certain advantages in that the subject is allowed to arrange a set of pictures into a sequence rather than respond to discrete scenes. For not only will the subject construct a personally relevant sequence, but three or four pictures in a row automatically lead to a story which has a beginning, a middle, and an end. The arrangement of the pictures has more stimulus pull than verbal directions. Sequential stories shed light on the subject's long-term solutions of conflict situations, and furthermore, notations of the arrangement can be objectively scored separately from the story content. Examples are (1) the WISC Picture Arrangement Test (Wechsler, 1949); (2) the Van Lennep Four-Picture Test (Van Lennep, 1951), which allows the subject to write his own stories after he has arranged the colored plates; (3) the Tomkins-Horn Picture Arrangement Test (PAT) (Tomkins & Miner, 1959), which provides twenty-five sets of three pictures, mainly in industrial settings. IBM scoring is available.

Supplementary questions for TAT techniques. In addition to the usual series of probes, i.e., "How did it turn out?" "What is he thinking and feeling?" "What led up to this scene?", one may ask, "What would be different in the story if that were a man rather than a woman?" "Where did you get the ideas for your stories?" "What is the one thing that could *not* be happening in this picture?" And finally, after the cards have been replaced, memory can be investigated by asking the subject to recall as many of the pictures as he can in as much detail as possible.

Interpreting the TAT. After having administered the appropriate thematic materials and made whatever variations on the theme are necessary for the immediate situation, the examiner must consider scoring. The TAT has no succinct scoring system available,* but using even an imperfect system of scoring develops the examiner's sensitivity to the subject's form and content. With the TAT this sensitization process is more important than the numerical scores. "Any research in objects of organized complexity, such as we humans are, must, after the nomothetic parameters have been set up, take the next step, to idiography" (Beck, in Buros [Ed.], 1959, p. 274).

Murray's (1943) system of interpretation lists five elements of TAT content which can be examined in each story: the hero, the needs of the hero, the environmental forces, the theme, and the outcome. Rapaport (1946) recommends that one attend to the emotional tone of the narrative and also to the figures, their strivings, and the obstacles that confront them.

A basic rule in the interpretation of TAT content is that the interpersonal scenes described cannot be taken at face value to indicate actual relationships, past or present. While it is possible that the content reflects real life, other possibilities are equally likely. The relationships may be wished for, feared, defensively presented to cover significant issues, pointed to a polar opposite, or based on perceptions of others. TAT stories can be composites of these possibilities and reflect several facets simultaneously (Allison, Blatt, & Zimet, 1968; Mundy, 1971a, b).

Word-association Techniques

While the thematic techniques allow the examiner to measure logical thinking, they inhibit spontaneity. The word-association techniques are an attempt to overcome this difficulty. Sup-

---

* A recent exception is the scoring sheet proposed by Exner (1971).

posedly, by asking for a one-word answer rather than full sentences, one allows for more spontaneity. It is also assumed that spontaneity is further enhanced by encouraging the child to react quickly. In the word-association method, a series of words rather than a set of pictures is presented to the child, with the directions, "Say the first word that comes into your mind when I say a word." The first series of experimentally chosen words was Kent and Rosanoff's (1910). The list contained emotionally tinged as well as neutral words. The differences in reaction time between the emotion-provoking words and the neutral words are interpreted as well as the actual content of the responses. Delays in response words can be further used as a basis for interview by asking the child what prompted his associations. Furthermore, the associations themselves often provide provocative clues to an astute clinical psychologist. A measure of interest in the technique may be found in the fact that up-to-date lists of popular responses are published periodically (Jenkins & Russell, 1960; Palermo, 1963; Tresselt & Mayzner, 1964).

However, it appears that the given association is as much a function of the stimulus and contemporary linguistics as of intrapsychic factors, and thus it would seem that these techniques are of limited value in a clinic setting.

Semantic Differential

The Semantic Differential (Osgood, Suci, & Tannenbaum, 1957) merits consideration because it both has a simple structure and is the only instrument available which has sound statistical structure. The otherwise ubiquitous note which follows every experimental analysis of projective techniques, "no significant data on reliability and validity," cannot be made of Osgood's research. One would think that in a field in which reliability and validity are continually sought, the Semantic Differential would be the most popular technique, and it is indeed strange that it is almost universally ignored.

Perhaps the Semantic Differential is not used routinely because it provides the clinician with no record of the subject's mode of arriving at his judgments but offers his final judgments only. Such judgments are very useful but do not lead to generalizations about the patient's personality. Knowing that the acrobat moved from trapeze to platform is not as interesting as seeing *how* he did so.

Administration is short and simple and interesting to the subjects. It can be administered individually or in groups, although the lower age limit is not specified. A mimeographed form is provided as follows:

(Concept to be related)

rough __:__:__:__:__:__:__smooth
fair __:__:__:__:__:__:__ unfair
active __:__:__:__:__:__:__ passive, etc.

Basically, the directions are, "If you feel that the concept at the top of the page is very closely related to one end of the scale, you should place your check mark there." Any concept can be selected by the experimenter, e.g., mother, family, self, ideal. The resulting semantic spaces can be defined statistically. Three-dimensional models of the particular subject's definitions can be constructed. For instance, *white rosebuds–gentleness–sleep* may be associatively similar in a subject's mind but at a psychological distance from *quicksand–death–fate.*

The Semantic Differential can be used to answer a wide range of questions, such as: Is the subject's meaning of *father* significantly different from that of *mother?* Is the definition of *me* different at the end of therapy from what it was at the beginning? Do other people have a different concept of the patient than the patient does? Is the patient's meaning of *independence* the same as the therapist's meaning?

The Q-Sort

Stephenson (1953) also provides a technique for evaluation of subjective meanings. Here the testee sorts descriptive sentences along a seven-point rating scale. Although administration time is rather lengthy, the data can be factor-analyzed and understood in statistical terms.

Sentence-completion Techniques: Rationale

A technique which combines the word-association method and the greater freedom of the thematic approach is the sentence-completion form. Printed forms containing from 25 to 100 incomplete sentence stems are given to the child with the directions, "Someone started to write a sentence but didn't finish. Will you please write the rest of the sentence?" The form can be group-administered, or the child can dictate his responses. Some blanks request the subject to respond as quickly as he can, as in the word-association technique, so that speed will limit defensive maneuvers. Other forms encourage the subject to "work at his usual speed," to provide a sample of typical behavior.

Changing the content of the stems allows for investigation of specific facets of personality. Hanfmann and Getzels (1953) found that first-person stems, i.e., "I wish my father . . . ," tend to encourage responses more related to conscious and manifest aspects of the person, whereas the third person, i.e., "One should. . . ," reveals less overt material.

Sentence-completion methods were designed for adults, but Sanford (1943) extended their use for children in the third to the eighth grades. The Payne Sentence Completion Blank (Rohde, 1957) is for children in the upper grades and high school, whereas Rotter and Rafferty's (1953) children's form is directed toward measurement of personal adjustment in grades 9 to 12. The Holsopple and Miale (1954) adult form is in the process of being adapted for children. The Forer (1950) Structured Sentence Completion Test (ages 10 to 18) is excellent for investigation of interpersonal relationships, wishes, causes of aggression, anxiety, failure, guilt, inferiority feelings, responsibility, and school life.

The Curtis Completion Form (Watson, 1955), for ages 11 and over, is unusual in that the scoring method provided is partially objective, making possible the derivation of a cumulative point score which serves as the primary basis for personality inferences. This contrasts with the most common methods of clinical inference. Factors scored include antagonism, suspicion, jealousy, self-pity, insecurity, social inadequacy, environmental deprivation, and severe conflict. The authors include scores for graphic style, i.e., erasures, crossed-out content, and punctuation. Consideration of form as well as content always enriches projective interpretation.

Interpreting sentence-completion forms. As in the word-association method, variations in performance from one item to the next are highly significant. Breaks in logical structure are interpreted in the context in which they occurred. Original and popular items are noted in comparison with samples provided in the test manuals. Most sentence items can be taken both literally and symbolically. For example, the sentence stem "When fire starts . . ." may be taken as referring to a real fire. The responses, "Put it out," "Call the fire department," "Watch it burn," and "Get out" suggest independent action, appeal to authority, passive-aggressiveness, and avoidance behavior, respectively. But symbolically the stem can be seen as referring to one's emotional life. In the latter case, the responses suggest a squelching of impulses, a desire for outer rather than inner controls, a dissociative stance, and hysteria. These are not to be taken as valid interpretations but rather as an exercise in forming hypotheses about the patient which need to be checked out by other sentence stems, other techniques, observation, and interview.

Incomplete-story Techniques—Insight Test

The Insight Test combines the advantages of the sentence-completion methods with the thematic approach. Sargent (1944) originated this test. A series of cartoonlike pictures are presented, and a story is begun for the child. The child is asked to add the ending. For example, "A boy came home from school and found his dog had run away. What did he do? How did he feel?" Other stories deal with the child's mode of problem solving in relation to his parents, other adults, children, school failure, loss of a loved one, illness, and concepts of distance and time. A separate form is available for boys and girls (Engel, 1958).

Scoring procedures help analyze expressions of affect, defenses against affect, and thought processes which are indicative of maladjustment. As with other projective techniques, the more the examiner encourages free expression on the part of the subject, the more difficult he makes his own task of test interpretation. However, even the inexperienced clinician can profit from thematic investigation, for he has a written record which can be studied at leisure and interviewing time can be saved by pinpointing significant areas.

PROJECTIVE TECHNIQUES ELICITING MOTOR BEHAVIOR

A child manifests his personality to the astute observer by expressive movements as well as through verbal behavior. Collecting drawings and observing play are the two main approaches to obtaining samples of motor behavior. Drawing has the advantage over play techniques because of ease of administration and collecting records. Play is probably just as significant, but as recording devices are much more complex, the technique has not been as popular.

Drawings as Projective Technique: Current Usage

Drawings highlight the distinction between projective testing of personality and nonprojective testing. In projective analysis, the content of the subject's productions is considered separately from the form and a record is made of the processes the subject goes through to arrive

at a finished product. Theoretically, content is the subject's reaction to day-to-day stimulation, whereas the formal elements of verbal and motor behavior are a kind of personal equation that remains with the individual during his lifetime. Not only is the *modus operandi* relatively permanent, but its pervasive influence affects every area of the person's life space.

In order to illustrate the current uses of drawings as an aid to the investigation of personality, three of the most popular instruments—the Bender Gestalt, the Draw-A-Person, and the optional-content drawings—will be considered with their variants. These three tests are usually combined into a battery of tests for one individual. An excellent example of a complete series of tests is "The Case of Gregor" (Bell, 1949). Such a series separates formal processes from content and the permanent from the temporary. The Bender Visual Motor Gestalt Test method keeps the content in the drawings standard (all subjects copy the same nine designs) and so accentuates the subject's individuality in formal aspects (line quality, size, erasures, etc.). The DAP and variations restrict the content to relatively narrow limits (man, woman, boy, girl, baby, house, tree), while the optional-drawing methods, in which the subject chooses what to draw, allow for wide variation in content. Finally, the drawing-completion methods are designed to restrict the formal elements by requiring the subject to begin with printed graphic elements of a known stimulus pull (Sisley, 1971).

The Bender Visual Motor Gestalt—B-G. The original test, consisting of the nine Wertheimer designs and the instruction to "copy these," has been in use since 1938 (Bender) with children ages 4 and over. The many modern modifications consist primarily of alterations in administration procedure, such as asking for a second set of drawings from memory, and new scoring systems, such as those of Koppitz (1964), Clawson (1959), Hutt (1969), and Pascal and Suttell (1951), although they have retained all the original test materials. However, Fuller and Laird (1963), in an attempt to make the instrument more sensitive to organic pathology, have selected two of the designs for presentation in three different spatial orientations. The incidence of rotations is carefully noted as a possible symptom of brain damage. The authors state that the test is suitable for children ages 8 to 15 and manifests emotional as well as neurological disturbances.

It is difficult to ascertain which scoring system is the most popular, but Koppitz (1964) has many followers. She demonstrated that deviations from the model designs were conspicuous and indicative of the child's visual-motor coordination even after age norms were taken into account. Coordination correlates with intelligence (also see Chapter 26 in this manual), school achievement, and emotional disturbances. Koppitz found in her study of 1,000 children that the B-G drawings of the emotionally disturbed children differed from those of the normal children in the following ways: confused arrangement, wavy lines for figures 1 and 2, dashes drawn instead of circles, progressive increase in size of certain figures, fine lines, reinforced lines, false starts, expansion or constriction of figures. Of course, these test signs are not sufficient in themselves and cannot be used out of their context.

The Myokinetic Psychodiagnosis — MKP. Another example of controlled content is the MKP. Mira (1940) did not provide models but requested the children (ages 10 and over) to draw a few straight and curved lines, some with their eyes closed and with the nonpreferred hand. Two sessions, a week apart, were conducted. The manual describes seventy-nine measurements of the finished product. This, like the B-G, is useful with nonverbal children, and it allows for more individuality than the B-G. Mira's work is one more bit of evidence that motor activities express personality.

The Draw-A-Person Technique and variations. Although all drawings reflect the artist's personality, they are not all equally interpretable. To make interpretations possible, the conditions under which the drawing was done must be known and objective evaluation norms must be available. Ideally, the drawing should be done in the presence of a trained observer and at his request, so that expressive movements and interpersonal behavior can be recorded.

Norms have limited use unless standard testing procedures have been adhered to. The standard procedure was established by Machover (1949). Basically, a human figure is drawn in pencil on typing paper. A second figure, of the opposite sex, is then drawn. Time and sequence are noted, and a series of questions about the drawing are asked. Machover (in Rabin & Haworth, [Eds.], 1960) provides a list of thirty-three items; for example: "How old is the subject drawn?" "What is he/she doing?" "Will he/she marry?" "How old will he/she be when he does marry?" Many psychometrists use questions of their own, such as, "What does he need most?" The technique can readily be combined with the thematic approach by saying, "Tell me a story about your drawing."

The principle of changing the test format to reveal different aspects of personality was discussed with reference to verbal techniques and can be applied to drawings. The format of the House-Tree-Person drawings was originally suggested by Buck (1948). It is still widespread, though few have retained his half-size sheets and many now request that all three drawings be executed on a single sheet to indicate interrelatedness.

The Draw-A-House is followed by questions of social interaction. The Draw-A-Tree may be interpreted as a kind of self-portrait of the subject's body image (Buck, 1949). Requests for Draw-An-Animal, theoretically at least, allow for an expression of attitude toward one's own primitive impulses. Draw-A-Family focuses on feelings about the immediate family life. Craddick (1963) points out the usefulness of the Draw-A-Self-Portrait. Gorman and Mundy (Gorman, 1969) studied drawings of Draw-A-Brain and other body parts as an aid to understanding body image.

In addition to these modifications, there are others. The Draw-a-Person-In-the-Rain attempts to evaluate the body image under conditions of environmental stress, as represented by the rain. As Hammer (1958) points out, this drawing frequently provides useful information when compared with the child's drawing of a person under standard conditions. Catalano (1971) questions the degree to which the rain truly symbolizes a stressful condition for most children and compares figure drawings "in the rain" with drawings "in a storm." Catalano finds that both graphic and thematic differences are obtained in figure drawings under storm and rain instructions, suggesting that the storm symbolizes a more stressful condition.

Caligor (1957) and Hammer (1958) have modified both the content and the medium. Caligor requires his subjects (ages 7 and over) to redraw the human figure eight times, drawing each successive portrait while viewing only the immediately preceding drawing. Hammer follows suit but introduces color by providing the subject with a box of crayons. It is believed that adding the color dimension leads to more primitive and emotional content, while the crayons prevent the subject from making corrections in his drawing. According to Hammer, the redrawing approach allows reaction formation to be manifested and allows for the exaggeration of personally significant elements in the drawing. Caligor provides a complex scoring system.

There are almost as many variations as there are clinicians. There is no one definitive reference work but rather a large mosaic of tiny bits. Lyons' (1955) study of "The Scar on the H-T-P Tree" is an example of the contemporary research approach.

The Visual Apperception Test—VAT. The VAT (Khan, 1960) has twelve plates consisting of lines randomly drawn under controlled conditions. The subject is told to color in whatever object or pattern he sees in the doodles and title the finished drawing. Choice of colors, content, and titles is interpreted for subjects ages 12 and over. This appears to be a way to help the subject draw his own TAT-type picture and add his own emotional coloring.

Interpretation of figure drawings. The figure drawings are used to assess general personality traits, to supplement diagnosis, and as an aid to therapy. Brief examples of each application follow.

Description of personality. To interpret the drawing as a personality test, one must work on the principle that the drawing is a self-portrait. The child may draw a combination of real, ideal, or imagined characteristics of himself and others. The examiner, however, must be well aware of developmental norms in motor development before making assessments about self-concept. Machover (in Rabin & Haworth [Eds.], 1960) studied the drawings of over one thousand New York school children and drew a composite portrait for each age. For example, the 8-year-old boy does not continue to draw passive body forms, but in contrast to the 7-year-old, he expresses his dissatisfaction with his own weakness by much labeling, balloon talking, and strident humor, with which he announces his declaration of rights. There is still reliance upon symbols of stature such as hats and heavy heels, but his male drawings have more active postures and broader shoulders than when he was 7. The 8-year-old's attitude toward girls is seen in his drawings of females. The female figure is drawn larger than the male, is given the more assertive stance, is indicated as the older of the set more often, and is drawn first more at this age than at any other. He is now less amiable toward the female and more frequently gives her angry expressions to replace the contrived pleasantness given her at ages 6 and 7.

Diagnosis. It is obvious that brain-injured children vary greatly from one another, and there is no one personality common to them all. Hence, it stands to reason that brain-injured children do not all draw the same way. Nevertheless, many signs are present in the drawings of damaged children which do not frequently appear in the drawings of noninjured children. The presence of such signs could be the basis for a referral to the appropriate diagnostician, such as a neurologist. For example, the following signs occur more frequently, but not exclusively, in the drawings of brain-injured boys (Koppitz, 1968): gross asymmetry of limbs, figure slanting by 15 degrees or more, omission of bodies in subjects older than 6, omission of the neck (in subjects older than 10), tiny figures less than 2 inches in height, hands cut off. It is important to note that these signs denote immaturity, poor integrative capacity, impulsivity, and instability, as well as poor self-concept, feelings of inadequacy, and helplessness. It is more accurate to see the drawing not as a sign of brain injury as such but as personality attributes of the brain-injured child. Even the brain-injured child has hopes, fears, attitudes, etc., which are revealed in the drawing. Personality tests supplement the diagnosis of brain injury by assessing how the damage is affecting the child's total personality.

Therapy. The human-figure drawings done by the child may be useful in assessing the progress of treatment. The drawings are an indication of the child's self-concept and of his attitude toward others, and these, in turn, are central to the child's emotional adjustment. Successive drawings done by a single child, taken over a long period of time, would reveal any change or lack of change in the child's attitude toward himself and others (Koppitz, 1968).

The act of drawing human figures and other content is in itself therapeutic for most subjects.

The act of drawing helps the artist cope with the period of crisis and inner turmoil. Completing a drawing may be a catharsis for emotions which have no other mode of expression. Naumburg (1947) states that normal children need to draw in order to develop a well-balanced ego. The release of the unconscious into imaginative and spontaneous art productions is of vital importance. The act of drawing can be therapeutic if it is done in a setting planned by the therapist which fosters the transference relationship. Drawing is an integrative rather than a disintegrative process because the various components of personality, intellect, affect, and motor skills must be used simultaneously to complete the drawing. Furthermore, a child who is not responsive to direct questions will usually feel free to talk about his drawing and even tell elaborate stories about its content. Youngsters may continue to make drawings until they are comfortable enough with the therapist to use direct verbal communication. Upsetting events which are too painful to talk about are commonly drawn in symbolic form by disturbed children. They do not want their drawings interpreted. The therapist must accept the finished drawing and preserve it. The child may later want reassurance that the drawing has been saved. However, if the material drawn is really too threatening, the child will mutilate the drawing himself. One therapist (Flora Hogman) reported that her 7-year-old patient, who had a schizophrenic mother, drew a picture in each session which was a symbol of her mother, then slowly and carefully tore it into many pieces, and then reassembled it with scotch tape. The turning point in her treatment was dramatically illustrated when the child performed this ritual for the umpteenth time and then no longer needed to repair her drawing. According to Dr. Hogman, the patient diminished the anxiety associated with her powers of destruction by her experience with the drawings. Instead of being the victim of her fears, she became their master. As a general rule, the series of drawings has a therapeutic effect when each drawing is closer in manifest content to the disturbing event. It seems as though the traumatic event no longer has any power to harm the child after the child can picture the event as it occurred to him. It is as though the process of drawing lifts a burden from the child and gives him some control over disturbing elements in his life.

Optional-content drawings

Controlled Projection for Children. The Ravens test is in its second edition (Ravens, 1951). The child is asked to "draw anything that comes into your head" and simultaneously relate a story about an imaginary child. The framework of the story is provided by the psychologist; the details, by the child in response to eleven questions about preferences, fears, fantasies, feelings, and parents. This is offered as a global test of social attitudes, habits, and personal relationships for children ages 6 to 12. The manual provides test records and case histories. This instrument could be classified as one of the TAT modifications as well as a drawing method, for both the story and the drawing are interpretable.

Drawing-completion forms. There are several drawing-completion techniques in the literature, but the popularity of each is not known. The Symbol Elaboration Test (Krout, 1950) provides eleven stimulus patterns to be elaborated by drawing. It is designed for children ages 6 and over. The Franck Drawing Completion Test (Franck & Rosen, 1949) is particularly geared for the assessment of masculinity-femininity in children ages 6 and over. The Horn-Hellersberg (Hellersberg, 1945, 1949, 1950) form has the advantage of a published list of popular responses for grade school children (Ames & Hellersberg, 1949).

The Wartegg form will be discussed here as a typical example. It is not necessarily the most widely used, but the test forms and a manual are readily available. The Wartegg form has eight 2-inch boxes, each containing a small stim-

ulus line or dots or geometric detail. The child (ages 5 and over) is told, "Someone started to draw but didn't finish; would you please finish the drawing?" Titles and a judgment of "best liked" and "least liked" are recorded, as well as the usual observations of behavior (Kinget, 1952).

The rationale for the drawing-completion technique is unlike that for the previous drawing test, in which specific content is asked but the form the drawing takes is left up to the child. The drawing-completion technique allows the child to choose what to draw, but the form the finished product takes is restricted by the test blank. The stimuli on the printed form are bits of reality. How the child interacts with reality is ascertained by noting how he uses the given stimulus. For example, if the finished drawing is unrelated to the stimulus, the clinician would formulate the hypothesis that the child is ignoring reality. On the other hand, the drawing may reflect a distortion of the stimulus or show affinity for it by capitalizing on the stimulus characteristics. The child's creativity level is demonstrated by the way he works the stimulus detail into a meaningful whole, and his degree of motor control can be judged by his ability to meet the restrictions imposed by the printed matter. Furthermore, the content provides the clinician with interesting material concerning what is on the child's mind at the moment. The value judgments are indicated by the chosen likes and dislikes. Thus, the test is offered as a means of analyzing certain structural and functional aspects of the child's personality.

The eight stimuli on the Wartegg blank were chosen because they represent different Gestalt qualities. The qualities are as follows:

Qualities of the Drawing Completion Stimuli

1. Small, light, round, unimposing except for central location
2. Lively, mobile, loose, fluttering, flowing, organic, dynamic

3. Rigid, order, austere, regular progression, gradual development, methodical construction
4. Heavy, solid, massive, angular, static, concrete, inorganic, inert
5. Conflict, oppositional forces, construction, or mechanical
6. Matter-of-fact, sober, dull, or mundane
7. Delicateness, round and supple, complex fine structures, awkward location
8. Roundness and flexibility, restfulness, fluency, organic, and vastness

The Gestalt properties of the stimuli have psychological analogues. While the Gestalt qualities have been partially assessed by experimentation, the psychological properties are idiographic. The stimuli can be classified by subjects as masculine or feminine, happy or sad, natural or manmade. The second stimulus, for example, appears to be more akin to pleasant emotional states than the fourth. If a child is unable to draw a picture with stimulus 2, the examiner may probe for affective disturbances. These hypotheses are helpful in that they suggest areas to explore. Samples and interpretations are given by Kinget (in Hammer, 1958), and it can be seen that her insights are far more provocative than her scoring system.

In the samples of normal children, one sees more appropriate use of the stimuli, elaborated figures, better motor control, and harmony between drawings and titles. Relationships between the drawings and the titles are examined as indications of the child's ability to communicate. If his titles are not clear but the pictures are, it is assumed that verbal modes of communication are more difficult for him than graphic.

The intelligence of a child is appropriately measured by standard intelligence tests. However, drawing tests can indicate the level of aspiration the child sets for himself.

The manifest content is also taken as a sample of the child's mood. Drawing guns and bombs is indicative of more aggressive feelings than drawing flowers, for example.

In addition to the consideration of content, formal execution of the drawing is noted. Particularly striking in this field is the emergent agreement on the significance of various aspects of formal analysis—e.g., area used, whether expansive or compressed; smooth and flowing as against angular lines; intensity of pressure; vertical and horizontal lines; choice of color (Stone, in Harrower, 1950). For example, heavy slash lines indicate impulsive, aggressive drives, while light, sketchy lines suggest a greater degree of self-control.

Developmental stages of optional-content drawings. Ames and Hellersberg (1949) have summarized the developmental stages in children's drawings based on the Horn-Hellersberg Drawing Completion Test.

Developmental Stages of Drawing

Age

THREE Scribbles, then names his product; may achieve closed figures.

FOUR Traces; some enclosures with embellishing lines.

FIVE Many closed figures; embellishing; naming of the figure; stays within frames.

SIX Drawing simple objects, well within the frame of the picture, is now common. The child names the completed drawing rather than planning ahead what to draw.

SEVEN A marked change; tracings and simple closures with additions no longer occur. Some children draw elaborate closed figures, others make small figures with additions, a few draw unified scenes planned in advance. Perseveration of forms is typical, e.g., many wheels, windows, and scallops.

EIGHT Elaboration of one big, single form. Many children plan in advance, name, and draw several small objects or, more likely, one unified scene. Abstract ideas appear for the first time. A shift from whole human beings to heads and faces only. Guns, bombs, explosions are drawn more frequently at this age than at any other.

NINE Another marked change occurs; the most

characteristic drawing is now a unified scene or a large elaborate form. This is the age for designs and abstractions.

TEN   Unified scenes are common, decided upon well in advance and drawn neatly.

Constructive Response Test

If one gives a preschool child some version of Guilford's (1967) Universal Uses Test (a test of creativity for older children, which requires the child to say all the ways he can think of to use common objects), he will show no inspiration; but if one gives him the object to manipulate, he will use it in diverse and unexpected ways.

The way in which a subject manipulates objects is also projective. There is no single standardized play technique which the majority of psychologists use. However, the Mosaic Test and the T-A 3-DPT are relatively popular and will serve to illustrate the use of constructive techniques.

Description of the Mosaic Test. The material of the test consists of a collection of small flat pieces of plastic in red, yellow, blue, green, black, and white. Each color is available in five different shapes—circles, triangles, squares, etc. A tray containing the 456 pieces is placed before the child, together with a tray table. The tray table has a raised edge; the inside dimensions are 10 by 12 inches. The child (ages 2 and over) is requested to make something on the tray using as many pieces as he likes (Lowenfeld, 1939). The method of procedure, as well as the finished product, is analyzed in terms of choices of pieces and colors and the finished design (Rioch, 1954).

Contributions of the Mosaic Test. Like the other projectives considered here, the test requires choice and organization of ambiguous forms. Unlike the previous examples, it does not rely on the child's verbal responses. It is a measure of global personality traits, and while it can be used with any child, it is indispensable with the nonverbal child and with the child who is reluc-

tant to draw pictures. As in other projective methods, the formal aspect of the process by which the child goes about performing the task is analyzed separately from the content of the finished work. For example, signs of disorganization of personality are the following: low output, breaking up of the field into unrelated small parts, exclusion from the field of anything but identical parts, and a poor or incomplete Gestalt.

Verbal-Motor Constructive Tests

The Twitchell-Allen Three-dimensional Personality Test—T-A 3-DPT. The T-A 3-DPT materials consist of a set of twenty-eight ceramic figures, which are laid out in a predetermined order in front of the child. The test designer has resolved the technical problem of allowing freedom of expression but recording a considerable mass of data. Each child tells three stories and names each piece. Two of the stories are told in response to pieces he selects and arranges, and, for easier comparison with other children, one story is in response to three standard pieces selected and arranged by the examiner. The pieces were designed by Twitchell-Allen (1947) and are relatively culture-free; they are not bound to one fashion of dress but are of free form and in a neutral color. The examiner records both verbal associations and stories and expressive motor behavior, such as gestures, facial expressions, and movements.

This is one of the most complex personality tests, for it combines the verbal-association and the thematic-apperception methods and provides a record of the child's motor behavior. One recommended analysis of the resulting data shows the relationships of the T-A 3-DPT to Rorschach-type devices. In the Naming Test, the subject's responses are categorized as to content, determinants (movement, color, form, texture, and size), form quality (F+ and F−), and originals. A second approach uses the psychodrama technique, that is, listing the critical areas (sexual, relationship to authority, competence, struggle between independence and dependence) and understanding the person in terms of his dynamics. A third approach is the analysis of verbal form and content (such as in the TAT) and takes into account the number of words, parts of speech, number of different persons included in the stories, etc. This latter technique is ideal for comparing before-and-after changes in openness of personality and goal orientation (Allen et al., 1958). Lastly, a type of play-interview analysis is suggested by Shoben (Buros [Ed.], 1953).

The test was designed to reveal both content and structure of the child's inner world, that is, to present mood and basic attitude. This test has been used in connection with the Children's International Summer Villages, and it has been found that children project into their stories their attitude toward home, degree of dependency on significant people (Fein, 1960), self-concept, sexuality, natural elements, etc. (Allen et al., 1958, vol. 5). It is also one of the few standardized projective techniques for use with the visually handicapped person (Twitchell-Allen, 1958).

Family Relations Test: An objective technique for exploring emotional attitudes in children. The test materials consist of twenty cardboard figures representing people of various ages. The child (ages 3 to 15) picks out his "family" and selects statements applicable to their description. Attitudes of love-hate, dependence, indulgence, etc., are manifested in scorable form (Anthony & Bene, 1957). This test is more objective than other projective techniques because the range of possible responses is limited.

Play Techniques

Other constructive methods, such as play techniques, allow the subject much greater choice of media and objects to use, but resultingly, these techniques cannot be easily requested by standard principles of administration, recording, scoring, and interpretation. The usefulness of these techniques, like psychodrama, depends largely on the skill of the clinician. Generally, the child acts out his inner world by using objects or people to play roles. Either the child or the adult selects the actors and plot, either ahead of time or spontaneously. The most relevant material is the very process of acting out these roles; thus no formal scoring is commonly available. Play techniques have been found useful for both diagnosis and therapy (Mussen, 1960). Examples can be found in the miniature life toys method (Murphy, 1956) and the World Test (Bolgar & Fischer, 1947; Lowenfeld, 1939) and in the Driscoll Playkit (Driscoll, 1952).

The Lynns' Structured Doll Play Test (Lynn & Lynn, 1959) for children ages 2 to 11 uses cardboard figures and objects and four background cards. As children readily project their feelings and fantasies onto dolls, the format is reasonable, but children find cardboard cutouts less attractive than three-dimensional dolls. The data produced survey, in a single interview, common conflicts, the parts played by mother and father in the child's mental schema, as well as attitudes about school and doctors' visits. In nearly every scene, the child is forced to make a choice between objects or people; this method is useful in discovering the child's identifications. It is basically a cross between the MAPS (Shneidman, 1947), the Duss-Despert Fables (Duss, 1940), and the Miniature Situation Test of Santostefano (1962).

The child's favorite instruction, "Now you can play," has no doubt been given to children since antiquity. The first organized approach to study children's play is found in *Floor Games* by H. G. Wells (1911). Psychotherapists—notably, Lowenfeld (1938), Buhler and Kelly (1941), Klein (1932), Erikson (1940), and Murphy (1956)—have contributed to the understanding of the psychodynamics of play. Buhler (1951) standardized the materials and scoring and noted the number of elements used, the presence of aggression, distortions, disarrangements, rigid arrangements, symbolic arrangements, etc. An empty, sparse, unpopulated world, for example, may indicate retardation and various kinds of emotional disturbance.

The Kahn (1957) Test of Symbol Arrangement can be administered and interpreted in a more orderly way than free play. Children from age 6 on find it easy to arrange the set of sixteen small plastic objects, such as dogs, hearts, stars, and butterflies. Although the manual is carefully prepared, the basic diagnostic criteria are based on psychiatric evaluation of adults.

It is difficult to assess the child's personality from his play, and it is even more difficult to train psychologists in this technique. Buhler's (1938) observation that manual skill (freehand scissors cutting of circle, heart, and star) is related to adjustment level in children but not related to age, sex, or intelligence can be demonstrated to psychologists by the Five Task Test. Although the test is not popular in the field today, it deserves mention at least as a training device.

The Lowenfeld Kaleidoblocks (ages 2.5 and over) (Ames & Learned, 1954) consists of painted pieces of wood; the child is asked both to construct whatever he pleases and to build standard forms. It allows for the study of spontaneous behavior and imaginative ability. The blocks are geometric shapes; there are no animate forms. The instrument aids the clinician in assessing the developmental level of mathematical understanding.

Projective Questions

After the testing experience, most children are more open to direct interviewing. The following questions are useful as a supplement to the interview when formal projective techniques are required:

What animal would you like to be? Why?
What animal would you least like to be? Why?
If you had three wishes, what would you wish?

When you look in the mirror, what do you see?
If you could change one thing about yourself, what would you change?
If you could change one thing about your family, what would you change?
What name would you like to have as a nickname? Why?
If you won a million dollars, what would you do?

These questions have not been investigated systematically, with the exception of the animal questions (Freed, 1965). Generally, such questions aid in the establishment of rapport with the child and provide further interview material.

A final word

Rorschach's invaluable observation that the form of behavior can be studied independently of content is the keystone of projective techniques. The multiplicity of devices currently used for separating form from content (content-free inkblots, standard-content pictures, and analyzing graphic form) have been reviewed. To use these techniques, one must go beyond the data gathered and, in so doing, violate scientific principles. However, we must continue to use projective techniques because they provide us with an example of personality processes by giving us an indication not only of what the child sees but of how he sees.

REFERENCES

Allen, D. T., Scheusele, T., & Schurian, W. Before-and-after measure at a C.I.S. village of openness of personality and goal orientation. *Research Remarks,* 1958, 5(1), 2–3.

Allison, J., Blatt, S. J., & Zimet, C. N. *The interpretation of psychological tests.* New York: Harper & Row, 1968.

Ames, L. B., & Hellersberg, E. The Horn-Hellersberg test: Responses of three to eleven-year-old children. *Rorschach Research Exchange and Journal of Projective Techniques,* 1949, **13,** 415–432.

Ames, L. B., & Learned, J. Developmental trends in child Kaleidoblock responses. *Journal of Genetic Psychology,* 1954, **84,** 237–270.

Anthony, E. J., & Bene, E. A technique for the objective assessment of the child's family relationships. *Journal of Mental Science,* 1957, **103,** 541–545.

Beck, S. J., Beck, A., & Molish, H. B. Rorschach's test. I. Basic processes. (3rd ed.) New York: Grune: & Stratton, 1961.

Behn, G. *Behn Rorschach Test.* New York: Grune & Stratton, 1956.

Bell, J. E. The case of Gregor: Psychological test data. *Rorschach Research Exchange and Journal of Projective Techniques,* 1949, **13**(2), 155–205.

Bellak, L. *The Thematic Apperception Test and the Children's Apperception Test in clinical use.* New York: Grune & Stratton, 1954.

Bender, L. *A Visual Motor Gestalt Test and its clinical use.* New York: The American Orthopsychiatric Association, 1938.

Blum, G. S. A study of the psychoanalytic theory of psychosexual development. *Genetic Psychology Monograph,* 1949.

Bolgar, H., & Fischer, L. K. Personality projection in the World Test. *American Journal of Orthopsychiatry,* 1947, **17,** 117–128.

Buck, J. N. The H-T-P technique: A qualitative and quantitative scoring manual. I. *Journal of Clinical Psychology,* 1948, **4,** 319–396.

Buck, J. N. The H-T-P technique: A quantitative and qualitative scoring manual. *Clinical Psychology Monograph,* 1949, No. 5.

Buhler, C. The Ball and Field Test as a help in the diagnosis of emotional difficulties. *Character and Personality,* 1938, **6,** 257–273.

Buhler, C. The World Test: A projective technique. *Journal of Child Psychiatry,* 1951, **2,** 4–23.

Buhler, C., & Kelly, G. *The World Test: A measurement of emotional disturbances.* New York: Psychological Corporation, 1941.

Buhler, C., & Manson, M. P. *The Picture World Test.* Beverly Hills, Calif.: Western Psychological Services, 1955.

Buros, O. K. (Ed.). *The fourth mental measurements yearbook.* Highland Park, N.J.: Gryphon Press, 1953.

Buros, O. K. (Ed.). *The fifth mental measurements yearbook.* Highland Park, N.J.: Gryphon Press, 1959.

Buros, O. K. (Ed.). *The sixth mental measurements yearbook.* Highland Park, N.J.: Gryphon Press, 1965.

Caligor, L. *A new approach to figure drawing: Based upon an interrelated series of drawings.* Springfield, Ill.: Charles C Thomas, 1957.

Catalano, F. K. A comparison of figure drawings under standard conditions with instructions to draw-a-person in-the-rain and draw-a-person in-a-storm. (Paper in preparation, 1971.)

Clawson, A. The Bender Visual Motor Gestalt Test as an index of emotional disturbance in children. *Journal of Projective Techniques,* 1959, **23,** 198–206.

Craddick, R. A. The self image in the Draw A Person test and self portrait drawings. *Journal of Projective Techniques and Personality Assessment,* 1963, **27**(3), 288–291.

Dombrose, L. A., & Slobin, M. S. The IES Test.

Psychological test specialists. *Journal of Perceptual and Motor Skills,* 1958, **8,** 347–389.

Driscoll, G. P. *The Driscoll Playkit.* New York: Psychological Corporation, 1952.

Duss, L. La methode des fables en psychoanalyse. *Archives de Psychology,* Geneva, 1940, **28,** 1–51.

Engel, M. The development and applications of the Children's Insight Test. *Journal of Projective Techniques,* 1958, **22**(1), 13–25.

Erikson, E. H. Studies in the interpretation of play. Clinical observations of play disruption in young children. *Genetic Psychology Monograph,* 1940, **22,** 557–671.

Exner, J. E., Jr. *Thematic Apperception Test* (work sheet). Unpublished mimeograph, 1971.

Fein, L. G. *The three-dimensional personality test: Reliability, validity and clinical implications.* New York: International Universities Press, 1960.

Fine, R. A scoring scheme and manual for the TAT and other verbal projective techniques. *Journal of Projective Techniques,* 1955, **19,** 306–316.

Forer, B. R. A structured sentence completion test. *Journal of Projective Techniques,* 1950, **14,** 15–30.

Franck, K., & Rosen, E. A projective test of masculinity-femininity. *Journal of Consulting Psychology,* 1949, **13,** 247–256.

Freed, E. X. Normative data on a self-administered projective question for children. *Journal of Projective Techniques and Personality Assessment,* 1965, **29**(1), 3–6.

Fuller, G. B., & Laird, J. T. The Minnesota Perceptodiagnostic Test. *Journal of Clinical Psychology,* 1963, **19,** 3–34.

Gorman, W. *Body image and the image of the brain.* St. Louis: Warren H. Green, 1969.

Granick, S., & Scheflen, N. A. Approaches to reliability of projective tests with special references to the Blacky Pictures Test. *Journal of Consulting Psychology,* 1958, **22,** 137–141.

Guilford, J. P. *The nature of human intelligence.* New York: McGraw-Hill, 1967.

Halpern, F. A. *Clinical approach to children's Rorschachs.* New York: Grune & Stratton, 1953.

Hammer, E. F. *The clinical application of projective drawings.* Springfield, Ill.: Charles C Thomas, 1958.

Hanfmann, E., & Getzels, J. W. Studies of the sentence completion test. *Journal of Projective Techniques,* 1953, **17,** 280–294.

Harris, D. B. *Children's drawings as measures of intellectual maturity: A revision and extension of the Goodenough Draw-A-Man Test.* New York: Harcourt, Brace & World, 1964.

Harrower, M. R. *Recent advances in diagnostic psychological testing.* Springfield, Ill.: Charles C Thomas, 1950.

Harrower-Erickson, M. R. Directions for administration of the group test. *Rorschach Research Exchange,* 1941, **5,** 331–341.

Harrower-Erickson, M. R. A multiple choice test for screening purposes. *Psychosomatic Medicine,* 1943, **5,** 331–341.

Hartwell, S. W., Hutt, M. L., Andrew, G., & Walton, R. E. The Michigan Picture Test. Diagnostic and therapeutic possibilities of a new projective test for children. *American Journal of Orthopsychiatry,* 1951, **21,** 124–137.

Haworth, M. R. Responses of children to a group projective film and to the Rorschach, CAT, Despert Fables and DAP. *Journal of Projective Techniques,* 1962, **26,** 47–60.

Haworth, M. R. *The CAT: Facts about fantasy.* New York: Grune & Stratton, 1966.

Hellersberg, E. F. The Horn-Hellersberg test and adjustment to reality. *American Journal of Orthopsychiatry,* 1945, **15,** 690–710.

Hellersberg, E. F. Horn-Hellersberg test: The case of Gregor: Interpretation of test data. Symposium presented at American Psychological Association meeting, Denver. *Rorschach Research Exchange and Journal of Projective Techniques,* 1949, **13,** 461–463.

Hellersberg, E. F. *The individual's relation to reality in our culture: An experimental approach by means of the Horn-Hellersberg test.* Springfield, Ill.: Charles C Thomas, 1950.

Hellersberg, E. F. The Horn-Hellersberg test. *Monographs of the Society for Research in Child Development,* 1953, **16**(53), 138–170, 214–316.

Henry, W. E. The thematic apperception technique in the study of culture-personality relations. *Genetic Psychology Monograph,* 1947, **35,** 3–135.

Hertz, M. R. *Frequency tables to be used in scoring the Rorschach Inkblot Test.* (3rd ed.) Cleveland: Western Reserve Medical School, 1951.

Holsopple, J., & Miale, F. *Sentence completion: A projective method for the study of personality.* Springfield, Ill.: Charles C Thomas, 1954.

Holtzman, W. H., Thorpe, J. S., Swartz, J. D., & Herron, E. W. *Inkblot perception and personality: Holtzman inkblot technique.* Austin: University of Texas Press, 1961.

Howells, J. G., & Lickorish, J. R. The family relations indicator: A projective technique for investigating intra-family relationships designed for use with emotionally disturbed children. *British*

Journal of Educational Psychology, 1963, **33,** 286–296.

Hutt, M. L. *The Hutt adaptation of the Bender-Gestalt test.* New York: Grune & Stratton, 1969.

Jackson, L. Emotional attitudes towards the family of normal, neurotic and delinquent children. *British Journal of Psychology,* 1950, **41,** 35–51.

Jenkins, J. J., & Russell, W. A. Systematic changes in word association norms: 1910–1952. *Journal of Abnormal and Social Psychology,* 1960, **60,** 293–304.

Kahn, T. C. Kahn Test of Symbol Arrangement: Clinical manual. *Perceptual and Motor Skills,* 1957, **7,** 97–168.

Kent, G., & Rosanoff, J. A study in association in insanity. *American Journal of Insanity,* 1910, **67,** 37–96.

Khan, R. Z. *Visual Apperception Test.* Mound, Minn.: Midwest Psychological Services, 1960.

Kiell, N. *Psychiatry and psychology in the visual arts and aesthetics.* Madison: University of Wisconsin Press, 1965.

Kinget, G. M. *The drawing completion test.* New York: Grune & Stratton, 1952.

Klein, M. *The psychoanalysis of children.* London: Hogarth, 1932.

Klopfer, B., & Kelley, D. M. *The Rorschach technique.* Tarrytown-on-Hudson, N.Y.: World, 1942.

Koppitz, E. M. *The Bender Gestalt test for young children.* New York: Grune & Stratton, 1964.

Koppitz, E. M. *Psychological evaluation of children's human figure drawings.* New York: Grune & Stratton, 1968.

Krout, J. Symbol Elaboration Test (S.E.T.): The reliability and validity of a new projective technique. *Psychological Monograph,* 1950, **64,** 1–67.

Libo, L. M. The projective expression of patient-therapist attraction. *Journal of Clinical Psychology,* 1957, **13,** 33–36.

Lowenfeld, M. The theory and use of play in the psychotherapy of childhood. *Journal of Mental Science,* 1938, **84,** 1057–1058.

Lowenfeld, M. The world pictures of children. *British Journal of Medical Psychology,* 1939, **18,** 65–101.

Lynn, D. B., & Lynn, R. The Structured Doll Play Test as a projective technique for use with children. *Journal of Projective Techniques,* 1959, **23,** 335–344.

Lyons, J. The scar on the H-T-P Tree. *Journal of Clinical Psychology,* 1955, **11,** 267–270.

Machover, K. *Personality projection in the drawing of the human figure.* Springfield, Ill.: Charles C Thomas, 1949.

Mira, E. Myokinetic psychodiagnosis: A new technique for exploring the conative trends of personality. *Proceedings of the Royal Society of Medicine,* 1940, **33,** 173–194.

Molish, H. B. Can a science emerge from Rorschach's test: Book review. *Contemporary Psychology,* 1958, **3,** 189–192.

Moriarty, A. E. Normal preschoolers' reactions to the CAT: Some implications for later development. *Journal of Projective Techniques and Personality Assessment,* 1968, **32,** 413–419.

Mundy, J. Content analysis: TAT card 12BG— the rowboat as a symbol for female body image and sexual activity. *Psychological Reports,* 1971, **28,** 219–222. (a)

Mundy, J. An addition to Hartmann's basic TAT set. *Journal of Personality Assessment,* 1971 (in press.) (b)

Murphy, L. B. *Personality in young children.* New York: Basic Books, 1956. 2 vols.

Murray, H. A. *Explorations in personality.* New York: Oxford, 1943. (a)

Murray, H. A. *Thematic Apperception Test.* Boston: Harvard, 1943. (b)

Mussen, P. H. (Ed.). *Handbook of research methods in child development.* New York: Wiley, 1960.

Napoli, J. A finger painting record form. *Journal of Psychology,* 1948, **26,** 31–43.

Naumburg, M. Studies of the "free" art expression of behavior problem children and adolescents as a means of diagnosis and therapy. *Nervous and Mental Diseases Monographs,* 1947, No. 71.

Nel, B. F., & Pelser, A. J. K. *The South African Picture Analysis Test.* Johannesburg: Swets and Zeitlinger, 1960.

Osgood, C. E., Suci, G. J., & Tannenbaum, P. H. *The measurement of meaning.* Urbana: University of Illinois Press, 1957.

Palermo, D. S. Word associations and children's verbal behavior. In L. P. Lipsitt & C. C. Spiker (Eds.), *Advances in child development and behavior.* Vol. I. New York: Academic Press, 1963. Pp. 31–68.

Pascal, G. R., & Suttell, B. J. *The Bender-Gestalt test: Its quantification and validity for adults.* New York: Grune & Stratton, 1951.

Phillipson, H. *The object relations technique.* London: Tavistock Publications, 1955.

Pickford, R. W. *Pickford projective pictures.* London: Tavistock Publications, 1963.

Piotrowski, Z. A. *Perceptanalysis.* New York: Macmillan, 1957.

Piotrowski, Z. A. Digital-computer interpretation of inkblot test data. *Psychiatric Quarterly,* 1964, **38**(1), 1–26.

Rabin, A. L. & Haworth, M. R. (Eds.). *Projective techniques with children.* New York: Grune & Stratton, 1960.

Rapaport, D. The Thematic Apperception Test. In D. Rapaport, *Diagnostic psychological testing: The theory, statistical evaluation, and diagnostic application of a battery of tests.* Vol. 2. Chicago: Year Book, 1946. Pp. 395–459.

Rapaport, D., Gill, M., & Schafer, R. *The word association test in diagnostic psychological testing.* Chicago: Year Book, 1946.

Ravens, J. *Controlled projection for children.* New York: Psychological Corporation, 1951.

Rioch, M. J. The Mosaic Test as a diagnostic instrument and as a technique for illustrating intellectual disorganization. *Journal of Projective Techniques,* 1954, **18**, 89–94.

Rohde, A. R. Explorations in personality by the sentence completion method. *Journal of Applied Psychology,* 1946, **30**, 169–181.

Rohde, A. R. *The sentence completion method: Its diagnostic and clinical application to mental disorders.* New York: Ronald, 1957.

Rorschach, H. *Psychodiagnostics: A diagnostic test based on perception.* (4th ed.) New York: Grune & Stratton, 1942.

Rosenzweig, S. Apperceptive norms for the Thematic Apperception Test. I. The problems of norms in projective methods. *Journal of Personality,* 1949, **17**, 475–482.

Rosenzweig, S. Rosenzweig Picture-Frustration Study. In A. Weider (Ed.), *Contributions toward medical psychology: Theory and psychodiagnostic methods.* Vol. 2. New York: Ronald, 1953.

Rotter, J. B., & Rafferty, J. E. Rotter Incomplete Sentences Blank. In A. Weider (Ed.), *Contributions toward medical psychology: Theory and psychodiagnostic methods.* Vol. 2. New York: Ronald, 1953.

Sanford, R. N. Personality patterns in school children. In R. G. Barker, J. S. Kounin, & H. F. Wright, *Child behavior and development.* New York: McGraw-Hill, 1943.

Santostefano, S. Miniature situation tests and a way of interviewing children. *Merrill-Palmer Quarterly,* 1962, **8**, 261–269.

Sargent, H. D. An experimental application of projective principles to a paper and pencil personality test. *Psychological Monographs,* 1944, **57**, No. 5.

Schafer, R. *Psychoanalytic interpretation in Rorschach testing: Theory and application.* Austen Riggs Foundation Monograph Series, No. 3. New York: Grune & Stratton, 1954.

Sears, R. P. Influence of methodological factors on doll play performance. *Child Development,* 1947, **18**, 190–197.

Shneidman, E. S. The Make-A-Picture Story (MAPS) projective personality test: A preliminary report. *Journal of Consulting Psychology,* 1947, **11,** 315–325.

Sisley, E. L. *Measuring the meaning of stimuli used in a drawing-completion test.* Ph.D. dissertation. New York: Long Island University, 1971.

Sluyter, G. V. The Kinget Drawing-Completion Test: Reliability and validity approaches. Unpublished master's thesis, University of Oklahoma, 1964.

Stephenson, W. *The study of behavior: Tech-*

nique and its methodology. Chicago: University of Chicago Press, 1953.

Stone, D. R. A recorded Auditory Apperception Test as a new projective technique. *Journal of Psychology,* 1950, **29,** 349–353.

Sundberg, N. D. The practice of psychological testing in the clinical services in the United States. *American Psychologist,* 1961, **16,** 79–83.

Symonds, P. M. *Adolescent fantasy: An investigation of the picture-story method of personality study.* New York: Columbia University Press, 1949.

Syngg, D. The need for a phenomenological system of psychology. *Psychological Review,* 1941, **48,** 404–424.

Tendler, A. D. A preliminary report on a test for emotional insight. *Journal of Applied Psychology,* 1930, **14,** 122–136.

Thompson, C. E. The Thompson modification of the Thematic Apperception Test. *Rorschach Research Exchange and Journal of Projective Techniques,* 1949, **13,** 469–478.

Tomkins, S. S., & Miner, J. B. *PAT interpretation: Scope and technique.* New York: Springer, 1959.

Tresselt, M. E., & Mayzner, M. S. The Kent-Rosanoff Word Association: Word association norms as a function of age. *Psychonomic Science,* 1964, **1,** 65–66.

Twitchell-Allen, D. A three-dimensional apperception test: A new projective technique. *American Psychologist,* 1947, **2.**

Twitchell-Allen, D. *Revised guide for recording and administration of the Twitchell-Allen Three Dimensional Personality Test.* Chicago: Stoelting, 1958. (Currently available only from the author at the University of Cincinnati.)

Van Lennep, D. J. The Four-Picture Test. In H. H. Anderson & G. L. Anderson, *An introduction to projective techniques.* Englewood Cliffs, N.J.,: Prentice-Hall, 1951. Pp. 149–180.

Wagner, E. E., & Medvedeff, E. Differentiation of aggressive behavior of institutionalized schizophrenics with the Hand Test. *Journal of Projective Techniques,* 1963, **27,** 111–113.

Watson, W. S. The validity of the Curtis Completion Form as a predictor of college student personality deviates. *Yearbook of National Council Measurements,* 1955, **12,** 82–85.

Weaver, W. Science and complexity. *American Scientist,* 1948, **36,** 536–544.

Wechsler, D. *Wechsler Intelligence Scale for Children.* New York: Psychological Corporation, 1949.

Wells, H. G. *Floor games.* London: F. Palmer, 1911.

Wolff, W. *Expressive Movement Chart: Evaluation of emotional trends in pre-school children.* New York: Grune & Stratton, 1948.

Wolman, B. B. (Ed.). *Handbook of clinical psychology.* New York: McGraw-Hill, 1965.

Zucker, K. B., & Jordan, D. C. The Paired Hands Test: A technique for measuring friendliness. *Journal of Projective Techniques,* 1969, in press.

26 | Cognitive Theories and Diagnostic Procedures for Children with Learning Difficulties[1,2]

Marianne Frostig and Russel E. Orpet

In the past, psychological tests were used primarily as predictive and classifying instruments rather than as diagnostic tools. However, a trend is currently emerging of aiming to assess the psychological functions which are basic to the adjustment and learning of children so as to obtain a more efficient basis for a planned educational, prescriptive, or other interventive program.

The purpose of this chapter is to consider the theoretical foundations of the diagnostic procedures that have been found beneficial in working with children with learning difficulties and also to scrutinize the instruments themselves. The usual process in the evolvement of test instruments is that theoretical foundations are laid by scholars in child psychology, linguistics, epistemology, etc., and test construction follows later. Without the theoretical foundations, the development of many tests would not have been possible.

[1] Supported in part by National Institute of Child Health and Human Development research grant HD 02368-01.

[2] Appreciation is expressed to Phyllis Maslow and Donna Joseph for their many suggestions throughout the preparation of this chapter.

The three positions presented below were selected because, in the opinion of the authors, either (1) they have exerted a major influence on the development of currently used diagnostic procedures or (2) they are considered likely to exert a major influence upon the development of future diagnostic procedures.

The specific tests or other diagnostic procedures selected for discussion do not represent a comprehensive study of all available diagnostic tools. An attempt was made to select diagnostic procedures which have been found particularly appropriate for use with children having learning difficulties and which have not been discussed in previous chapters of this volume.

THEORETICAL FOUNDATIONS

The three areas of study and research which are the subject of this discussion have either given rise to a large number of testing devices or are presently exerting an influence on the development of diagnostic procedures. The first is the concept of multivariate cognitive functions;

the second, the study of cognitive development; and the third, the study of behavioral deviations, especially of perceptual disturbances in adults and children with brain injury.

The most influential and representative of the first approach is Guilford, who has developed a theoretical model of the structure-of-intellect. The second approach is exemplified by Piaget, who painstakingly explores children's development. The third approach was heralded by the work of members of the Gestalt school, especially that of Kurt Goldstein. All three approaches focus on cognition, but while Guilford and his colleagues follow the psychometric tradition, Piaget, like many other students of child behavior, is interested in a developmental or genetic approach. Kurt Goldstein, Strauss, Cruickshank, and a host of others have been mainly concerned with the study of pathological changes, especially in perception and overt behavior. Neither Guilford nor Piaget have been primarily interested in testing devices, whereas the scholars working with brain-damaged adults and children have attempted to devise diagnostic instruments. But because both Piaget and Guilford have given impetus to so many studies which have resulted in evaluative procedures and are currently exerting an influence on the development of diagnostic tools, a short discussion of their basic theoretical positions is included.

Multivariate Cognitive Theories

Guilford's theoretical model. Guilford's theoretical model has led to many factor analytic studies of psychological abilities and has been instrumental in bringing to the attention of many psychologists and educators the fact that the total scores of an intelligence test are a much less helpful guide for setting up educational and treatment procedures than an analysis of the child's profile of abilities.

For example, the structure-of-intellect model (Figure 26-1) directs the educator's attention to

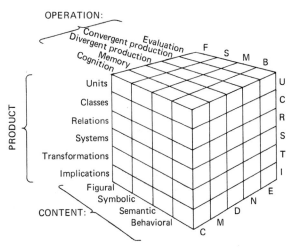

Figure 26-1. Guilford's Structure-of-Intellect Model (Guilford, 1967).

dimensions of mental abilities which are often neglected and is a helpful guide to selecting methods for remedying weaknesses in the child's performance. Educators will find that in any particular child the ability to comprehend, the ability to remember, and the ability to produce a variety of possible solutions or to find the right answer to a question or to evaluate critically may all be at different levels of development. They will also find that some children may be able to remember a figural content but be unable to understand or remember symbols, and some may be able to comprehend units while others of their age level are already thinking in terms of classes, relations, systems, and so on.

Thus Guilford has fertilized the field of diagnosis and treatment of children with learning difficulties. In spite of certain shortcomings, Guilford's model promises to grow in influence. Tests using his schema of the structure-of-intellect are currently being developed, and educational methods based on this model are being tried out (Meeker, 1968). Well-known and widely used tests such as the Wechsler Intelligence Scale for Children (WISC), the Binet, and the Illinois

Test of Psycholinguistic Abilities (ITPA) have been analyzed according to Guilford's model (Meeker, 1968; Meyers, 1968).

Guilford's structure-of-intellect has not been accepted without criticism. Wesman (1968) points out:

> When expounding upon the theory of factor analysis, experts almost invariably agree that factors are merely descriptive categories; they are not functional entities. But when engaged in interpreting the factors which have emerged from their studies, some analysts apparently succumb to the mystic charm of rotating axes and perceived entities which, they have told us, do not exist. . . . Though the authors of such creations have sometimes demonstrated in other writings that they well understand the difference between the reality of descriptive categories and the illusion of underlying entities, some of their disciples and many of their readers seem less clear in their perception.

Another criticism of Guilford is that there has been no neurological support for Guilford's system of factors; however, the use of a multiple-abilities measurement has been a fruitful approach for the assessment of the diverse facets of organic brain damage (Haynes & Sells, 1963). In addition, the theory does not help to explain global or temperamental characteristics which color all of a person's behavior—such as alertness, energy level, or persistence, which strongly influence all cognitive functions. In pathological states, characteristics are seen which are often described as global characteristics; i.e., where there is brain dysfunction all the abilities of the child seem to be affected, and he is likely to be generally disorganized, poorly motivated, and unpredictable. These global characteristics are not taken into account in Guilford's model. A satisfactory theory taking all these facets into account is not yet available.

Illustrative of the strong support of Guilford's approach are the following comments by Bayley (1955):

> I see no reason why we should continue to think of intelligence as an integrated (or simple) entity or capacity which grows throughout childhood by steady accretions. . . . Intelligence appears to me, rather, to be a dynamic succession of developing functions with the more advanced and complex functions in the hierarchy depending upon the prior maturing of earlier simpler ones. . . . If intelligence is a complex of separately timed, developing functions then to understand its nature we must try to analyze it into its component parts.

Similar conclusions were reached by Stott and Ball (1965), who stated:

> The recent research has provided a better understanding of the nature of intelligence, its determinants, and the nature of its developmental change, thus furnishing a sounder basis for new scale construction. The users of presently available tests generally feel the need for improved testing devices and techniques. Our analyses of scale content have demonstrated a great lack of consistency among and within the scales now in wide use, in terms of factor content and meaning, thus pointing up the need for more consistent and adequate test scales. Any attempt to develop a new intelligence scale, if it is to be an improvement over what is now available, must first and foremost be guided by, and be consistent with, the best conceived and most solidly based theory of the nature of mentality. Research has made it quite clear, that the human being, even at very early ages, possesses not just one single general ability factor, but a number of abilities. It should not be assumed without proof, however, that the same repertoire of mental abilities would be found at all levels of development.

For a detailed and comprehensive discussion of Guilford's theory, the reader is referred to Guilford (1967); a briefer and less technical discussion is provided in a more recent paper (Guilford, 1968).

Osgood's psycholinguistic theory. The development of one of the most significant psychological test batteries to appear in several decades (the

ITPA, which will be discussed in the section on diagnostic procedures) owes its existence to Osgood's (1954) psychological theory of the communication process. According to Osgood's theoretical model (see Figure 26-2), the three major dimensions of the communication process are (1) channels of communication, (2) levels of organization, and (3) processes.

Channels of communication. Communication consists of various combinations of stimulus input and response output. The three major channels of sensory input are auditory, visual, and tactual. The major modes of output are vocal and motor. Therefore, the channels of communication include auditory-vocal, auditory-motor, visual-vocal, visual-motor, tactual-vocal, and tactual-motor combinations.

Levels of organization. Osgood hypothesizes three distinguishable levels of organization: (1) the representational level, which mediates activities requiring the meaning of linguistic symbols; (2) the integration level, which mediates activities of a more habitual or automatic nature; and (3) the projection level, which deals with innate physiological processes.

Processes. Processes involve the acquisition and use of skills required for normal language usage. The three major kinds of processes to be considered are (1) decoding, or the ability to obtain meaning from either auditory or visual linguistic stimuli; (2) encoding, which is the ability to express a communication in words or gestures; and (3) association, which represents the sum total of skills that have been developed which are required to manipulate linquistic symbols.

Developmental Point of View

The development of the child's psychological functions occurs in a predictable sequence. The developmental point of view has been emphasized by Piaget (1926, 1952), Werner (1957), Bühler (1935, 1939), and others. The ideas of Piaget are of particular significance.

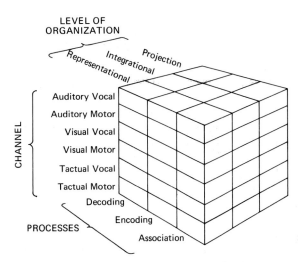

Figure 26-2. Osgood's Psycholinguistic Model (Osgood, 1954).

Piaget, Bühler, and other genetic psychologists maintain that the nature of cognition changes in a predictable and orderly sequence through various stages of intellectual development. Piaget states that the fundamental ingredients of intellectual functioning are the processes of assimilation and accommodation. *Assimilation* refers to the cognitive encounter with an environmental object which involves some kind of cognitive structuring of that object in accord with the nature of the organism's existing intellectual organization. *Accommodation* is a process of adapting the internal intellectual organization to the various requirements and conflicts posed by the environment.

The child's intellectual development proceeds by the assimilation of new information, which results in modification of some existing cognitive structure. His possession of the modified cognitive structure results in altered behavior toward the environment. The two processes of assimilation and accommodation, together called "equilibration," operate throughout life.

Another fundamental concept is Piaget's notion of "schema." A schema is:

... a flexible mental structure, the primary unit of mental organization. . . . The organism experiences and reacts to the environment always in terms of an existing organization. All experiences of a particular kind are molded into the already present schema, and in turn alter it according to the reality conditions. Hence, experiences are not recorded as isolated stimulus-response connections, or engrams impressed on a passive brain field, but are integrated into a constantly changing structure. [Tuddenham, 1966]

Schemas occur at all ages of development, including infancy. They are mobile and grow through assimilation and accommodation.

According to Piaget, the four major periods of the child's intellectual development are sensorimotor intelligence, preoperational thought, concrete-logical operations, and formal thinking operations.

Sensorimotor intelligence. The maximum development of sensorimotor intelligence continues from birth to about 2 years of age. During the sensorimotor period, the infant changes from a primarily reflexive organism responding in an undifferentiated way to his environment to a relatively coherent organization of sensorimotor behavior. Piaget attributes great importance to this first period of human development and has devoted more detailed analysis to the first 2 years of life than to any subsequent period. He divides the sensorimotor period into six successive stages, but space does not permit discussion of these.

Preoperational thought. During the preoperational period of early childhood, from 2 to about 6½ or 7 years of age, the individual makes his first relatively organized but crude attempts to cope with the new world of symbols. In general, children at the preoperational period of development are characterized by egocentric thinking, inability to manipulate abstract symbols, and inability to deal with more than one characteristic of an object at a time. They are not able to con-

ceive of the perceptual world in terms of impersonal, abstract, reality-oriented concepts (Piaget, 1954).

Concrete-logical operations. During the period of concrete-logical operations, from about 7 to 11 years of age, the child first begins to seem logical, rational, and well-organized in his adaptations. He appears to have a fairly well-organized conceptual framework, which he utilizes in his perceptual world. One of the most important components of the transition from preoperational to concrete operational thought is the acquisition of various conservations, that is, the cognition that certain properties remain invariant or are conserved in the face of certain transformations.

Formal thinking operations. During this period, from about 11 to 15 years of age, the individual is able to perform truly logical and abstract thinking and conceptualization. He is able to use hypothetical deductive procedures of logical thought (Inhelder & Piaget, 1958). For a more complete discussion of Piaget's developmental psychology, the reader is referred to Flavell (1963).

Piaget tests. The developmental psychology of Piaget suggests an approach to the psychological assessment of children different from the typical psychometric-quantitative approach. Piaget's approach to diagnosis stresses a qualitative and genetic analysis, which attempts to understand how the child arrived at his answer rather than only determine whether his response was correct or incorrect.

If it is true that cognitive development proceeds through a series of invariant stages, then it should be possible to develop assessment procedures that would determine the child's level of conceptual development.

A number of investigators are attempting to develop test materials based on Piaget's experiments. Inhelder and Vinh-Bang at the University of Geneva are standardizing and norming about thirty Piaget tasks for children 4 to 12 years of age. According to Inhelder (1968, p. 308), "such an ensemble of tests constitutes a diagnostic instrument in the form of a genetic scale which reveals both the hierarchical and the synchronic operations." Preliminary description of selected tests from the Inhelder and Vinh-Bang battery, which is currently being developed, is provided by Inhelder (1968, pp. 308–320). A similar project has been carried out at the University of Montreal by Laurendeau and Pinard (1963). In the United States, Tuddenham (1968) is standardizing and norming selected Piaget tests. In the opinion of the authors, the further development and refinement of Piaget-type tests would add a significant dimension to the diagnostic study of a child.

Developmental test batteries. There are a number of other theorists with a developmental point of view who have constructed developmental scales chosen for assessing the level of behavior development of the child. The developmental scales chosen for brief discussion are examples of preschool or infant batteries. The distinction between these batteries and those based on Piaget is that the former derive from normative procedures based on empirical observation, in contrast to Piaget's clinical-observational methods devised to substantiate his epistemological theories.

Gesell Developmental Schedules. The Gesell Developmental Schedules (Gesell & Amatruda, 1947) have been used primarily by pediatricians and neurologists and consist of a detailed observational schedule of a young child's (1 month to 6 years) developmental status. The four major areas assessed by the schedules are (1) motor development, (2) adaptive behavior, (3) language behavior, and (4) personal-social behavior. Data for the schedules are obtained by direct observation of the child's responses to standardized situations and are supplemented by information provided by the mother. Detailed verbal descrip-

tions of the behavior typical of different age levels are provided. Knobloch and Pasamanick (1960) found that with adequate training, there was substantial agreement ($r = .95$) between examiners.

Bayley Infant Scales of Development. Another carefully standardized developmental test is the one by Bayley (1968), which is a revision and restandardization of the California First-Year Mental Scale. This scale is applicable for infants from birth to 15 months. The items include postural and motor development, perception, attention to objects and to people, vocalization, manipulation of objects, understanding simple language, naming objects, and solving simple form boards. The norms are based on a carefully selected sample at each age level. Extensive longitudinal data on other groups of infants are provided to supplement the normative data.

Psychological Evaluation of Brain Injury

The attempt to isolate and describe abilities, illustrated by Guilford's structure-of-intellect, and the findings of research in child development, highlighted by Piaget's work, are two fields of importance for the development of evaluative procedures. A third area of research influential in pointing up disabilities has been the psychological evaluation of cerebral functioning of brain-damaged patients. The scientist who pioneered research in the area of the behavioral effects of brain damage was Kurt Goldstein (1923, 1927). On the basis of his observations of World War I soldiers who had been brain-damaged, Goldstein formulated his theory concerning the behavioral changes associated with cerebral trauma. The major symptom that Goldstein and his associates observed in brain-damaged adults was their relative inability to function abstractly.

The inability to assume an "abstract attitude" manifests itself by difficulty in (1) abstracting common properties from objects, (2) grasping the essential quality of a given whole, (3) breaking up a whole into its parts, or (4) shifting from one aspect of a situation to another.

Goldstein and Scheerer (1941) devised a test battery to detect impairment in abstract behavior. The battery was developed for adults and consisted of five subtests: (1) Color-Form Sorting, (2) Color Sorting, (3) Object Sorting, (4) Stick Test, and (5) Cube Test.

Two studies concerning the use of the Goldstein-Scheerer test with children have been published. Heald and Marzolf (1953) investigated the utility of the Stick Test and the Color-Form Sorting Test as a means of measuring the child's abstract-thinking ability. Their normative study of 138 children between the ages of 6 and 10 years indicated that the majority of school-age children are capable of abstract behavior as measured by the above two Goldstein and Scheerer tests. The percentages of correct responses to the Stick Test were: at age 6, 90 percent; at 7, 94 percent; at 8, 98 percent; at 9, 99 percent; and at 10, 100 percent. The percentage at each age level who were capable of shifting the method of sorting color-form blocks was: at age 6, 71 percent; at 7, 89 percent; at 8, 92 percent; at 9, 93 percent; and at 10, 100 percent.

Heald and Marzolf concluded:

(1) the majority of elementary school children are capable of abstract behavior insofar as such behavior is measured by the tests used; (2) there are no sex differences in the performance on these tests; (3) there is improvement in test response associated with age; and (4) tentative norms for use in evaluating results with supposedly brain-injured children of these ages are provided which, in terms of standard errors, are reasonably reliable.

Halpin and Patterson (1954) used three of the Goldstein-Scheerer tests—the Cube Test, the Color Sorting, and the Stick Test—with matched groups of brain-injured and non-brain-injured children. The purpose of their research was to discover whether or not significant differences between the two groups could be demonstrated. Analysis of the data indicated that there were no significant differences between the two groups on Color Sorting and the Cube Test; however, there was a very significant difference between the two groups on the Stick Test. They concluded that the Stick Test would be a useful adjunctive instrument for analyzing perceptual-motor disturbances in children. They also found that rotations and breakdowns of Gestalt on the figures in the Stick Test are more prevalent in brain-injured children than in non-brain-injured children.

Following Goldstein's work with adults, Alfred A. Strauss and his associates (Strauss & Kephart, 1955; Strauss & Lehtinen, 1947; Werner & Strauss, 1941, 1943) investigated the behavioral characteristics of brain-injured children. They described the distinctive perceptual, cognitive, and personality characteristics of the brain-damaged child. The differential diagnosis of cerebral dysfunction is compounded by the knowledge that many of the functions that are disrupted by neurological difficulties are also impaired by emotional factors, such as anxiety.

In contrast to the "pure science" approach of Guilford and Piaget, Goldstein, Strauss, and their associates were interested in applying their clinical observations to diagnosis and treatment, and especially to the education and remediation of brain-damaged adults and children. Their work had led to the development of a number of diagnostic tools and to the development of special educational approaches for brain-injured children.

DIAGNOSTIC PROCEDURES

Children with learning and behavioral difficulties usually show developmental lags in one or more of the following six areas of psychological functions: sensorimotor abilities, language, perception, higher cognitive processes, emotional development, and social adjustment. A thorough diagnostic evaluation of a child should pinpoint the nature and degree of specific disabilities and strengths in each of these developmental areas.

A comprehensive diagnostic study of a child's physical and psychological characteristics depends upon an appropriate battery of psychological tests supplemented by observation of the child, a physical examination and evaluation of vision and hearing, interviews with the child and parents, and information gathered from other sources. From this should emerge a picture of the child's developmental status in the six areas of psychological functions as well as insight into the child's past and present life situation. This information is required before appropriate recommendations can be made concerning the child's educational program and medical-psychological needs. For a more complete discussion of the six aspects of development, the reader is referred to a paper by Frostig (1968).

Since previous chapters of this volume were concerned with higher thought processes and social-emotional dimensions, the authors are concentrating their discussion on the psychological functions of sensorimotor, perceptual, and linguistic domains.

Appraisal of Sensorimotor Functions

A considerable amount of emphasis has recently been placed upon the importance of sensorimotor functions to child development and learning. Piaget, in particular, has stressed the importance of sensorimotor activity as the basic building block of the child's total development (Piaget, 1952). Several motor-development scales have been constructed to measure the motor abilities of children.

Lincoln-Oseretsky Motor Development Scale. The most frequently used sensorimotor diagnostic test battery at the present time is probably the Lincoln—Oseretsky Motor Development Scale (Sloan, 1955). The original Oseretsky was first published in Russia in 1923. The test was pub-

lished in English in 1946, and the Lincoln adaptation was first published in 1948 and was revised in 1955. Sloan's revision of the test reduced the number of items from the original eighty-five to thirty-six. The deleted items were eliminated on the basis of unreliability and of possible injury to the subject being tested. This test appears to have high reliability and good discrimination between 6 and 14 years of age. The Lincoln-Oseretsky test has proved useful in research and in evaluating the motor development of children in special programs. The major limitation of the test is that it requires approximately one hour to administer. In addition, the test appears to be a measure of general motor ability rather than a differential evaluation of psychomotor abilities (Thams, 1955).

California Infant Scale for Motor Development. Another early test battery of motor development is the California Infant Scale for Motor Development (Bayley, 1935), which was constructed for use with infants from birth to 3 years of age. The subtests of the battery were adapted from previously developed motor tests, such as the Oseretsky. The scale consists of seventy-six items; sample items are as follows:

3.5 months—Sits with support.
6.2 months—Sits alone thirty seconds or more.
9.3 months—Able to pick up a pellet with thumb and forefinger.
13.0 months—Walks alone two or three steps without support.
16.9 months—Walks backward several steps.
20.3 months—Walks upstairs with help.
24.3 months—Walks upstairs alone.
28.0 months—Jumps off floor with both feet.
32.1 months—Jumps from chair.
35.5 months—Walks upstairs, alternating forward foot.
39.7 months—Able to jump at least 36 centimeters.

50.0 months—Walks downstairs, alternating forward foot. (This is the last item in the test.)

Purdue Perceptual-Motor Survey. The Purdue Perceptual-Motor Survey (Roach & Kephart, 1966) attempts to "assess qualitatively the perceptual-motor abilities of children in the early grades." The survey consists of twenty-two scorable items divided into eleven subtests: (1) walking board (dynamic balance), (2) jumping, (3) identification of body parts, (4) imitation of movement, (5) obstacle course, (6) Kraus-Weber muscular strength tests, (7) angels in the snow (bilateral and cross-lateral body movement), (8) chalkboard (ability to match motor performance with visual control), (9) rhythmic writing, (10) ocular control, (11) visual achievement forms (perceptual-motor). Normative data are provided on 200 children, 50 at each grade level (grades 1 to 4). The correlation between the perceptual-motor survey and the teaching ratings of overall academic performance was .65. A comparison of test-retest scores on a group of thirty children indicated a reliability coefficient of .95.

Movigenic Movement Scale. An experimental approach, the "movigenic curriculum" for children with learning disabilities, which stresses the sensorimotor aspect of development has been developed by Barsch (1965); however, the Movigenic Movement Scale is still in the early stages of development. Consequently, normative data and reliability and validity data are not presently available. In Barsch's approach, the children are observed individually or in groups performing activities in the following twelve dimensions: (1) dynamic balance, (2) spatial awareness, (3) muscular strength, (4) body awareness, (5) visual dynamics, (6) auditory dynamics, (7) kinesthesia, (8) tactuality, (9) bilaterality, (10) flexibility, (11) rhythm, (12) motor planning. Preliminary data concerning this scale indicate that it is a potentially valuable clinical instrument; however, further development and research are needed.

Appraisal of Language Abilities

The assessment of language abilities and research concerning language has been greatly facilitated by the relatively recent development of diagnostic language tests. Of particular interest is the ITPA (Kirk & McCarthy, 1961; Kirk, McCarthy, & Kirk, 1968).

Frostig Sensory-Motor and Movement Skills Checklist

The "Frostig Checklist" (Orpet and Heustis, 1971, in press) was developed for the primary purpose of assisting classroom teachers, school psychologists, and other professional school personnel to observe and evaluate selected aspects of the child's motor development. The checklist is intended for use in conjunction with the *Frostig Move-Grow-Learn* program (Frostig, 1969) and *Movement Education: Theory and Practice* (Frostig, 1970).

Seven broad areas of sensory-motor and movement skills (attributes of movement) have been identified: (1) coordination, (2) agility, (3) strength, (4) flexibility, (5) speed, (6) balance, and (7) endurance. The checklist is not a standardized psychometric instrument in which developmental norms are provided at each age level. It is based upon the examiner's observations of the child in classroom and playground activities. Suggestions for teaching the seven "attributes of movement" are provided by Frostig (1969 and 1970).

Illinois Test of Psycholinguistic Abilities. The ITPA attempts to assess differential language abilities that are considered important to communication and learning disorders. The theoretical framework for this test was Osgood's (1957a, 1957b) communication theory, which was previously discussed in this chapter. The early work on the development of the test was done by Sievers (1955), and the experimental edition of the ITPA, consisting of nine subtests, was published six years later (Kirk & McCarthy, 1961). As of this writing, approximately seventy-five research articles have been published concerning the experimental ITPA. Four monographs that summarize selected studies on the test have also been published (Bateman, 1965, 1968; McCarthy & Olson, 1964; Sievers et al., 1963).

The revised edition of the ITPA (Kirk, McCarthy, & Kirk, 1968), assesses the same abilities as the original ITPA (Kirk & McCarthy, 1961) but includes several changes. (1) Three additional subtests were added—Visual Closure, Auditory Closure, and Sound Blending. (2) The norms were extended, and scale scores with a mean of 36 and a standard deviation of 6 are now provided for ages 2 to 10 years. (3) The names of several subtests were changed because of modifications in terminology; e.g., *reception* was substituted for *decoding, expression* for *encoding, organized process* for *association,* and *sequential memory* for *sequencing.* In the discussion of the revised subtests, the experimental-edition terms are included parenthetically following the revised-edition title.

The revised ITPA consists of twelve subtests, which attempt to assess the child's communication skills in (1) three processes of communication (decoding or reception, encoding or expression, and organized process), (2) two levels of language organization (representational and automatic), (3) two channels of language input (auditory and visual), and (4) two channels of language output (verbal expression and manual expression). The subtests are as follows:

1. *Auditory Reception* (Auditory Decoding) is a test of the child's ability to understand spoken words.

2. *Visual Reception* (Visual Decoding) measures the child's ability to comprehend or gain meaning from visual stimuli.

3. *Auditory-Vocal Association* assesses the child's ability to manipulate linguistic symbols in a meaningful way through the use of verbal analogies.

4. *Visual-Motor Association* is a test of the child's ability to relate, organize, and manipulate visual symbols in a meaningful way. The subject selects which of four pictures is associated with a stimulus picture. He must comprehend the relationship by pairing objects that are used together or that serve a similar purpose. At the upper levels, visual-analogy items are used.

5. *Verbal Expression* (Vocal Encoding) attempts to measure the child's ability to express ideas with spoken words.

6. *Manual Expression* (Motor Encoding) is a test of the child's ability to express ideas through movement. He is required to demonstrate by gestures how various objects are used.

7. *Grammatic Closure* (Auditory-Vocal Automatic) assesses the child's ability to produce the correct patterns of standard American language, primarily involving syntax and grammatical inflections.

8. *Auditory Sequential Memory* (Auditory-Vocal Sequencing) is a test of immediate auditory memory that is assessed by a digit-repetition test presented at the rate of two digits per second.

9. *Visual Sequential Memory* (Visual-Motor Sequencing) is a visual memory test in which the subject is required to reproduce sequences of nonmeaningful visually presented figures from memory.

10. *Visual Closure* measures the child's ability to identify a common object from an incomplete visual presentation in which the objects are seen in varying degrees of concealment.

11. *Auditory Closure,* Supplementary Test 1, assesses the child's ability to fill in the missing parts which were deleted in the auditory presentation and to produce a complete word.

12. *Sound Blending,* Supplementary Test 2, is a test in which the child has to synthesize the separate parts of the word spoken by the examiner and produce an integrated whole word.

The following studies of the ITPA are all concerned with the experimental edition since the revised edition has not been published at the time of this writing.

Validity studies. Validity studies that have been done with the ITPA are, in general, supportive of the concurrent, construct, and predictive validity for the battery. However, the following cautions to test users are made by McCarthy and Olson (1964): (1) The data suggest that the encoding subtests, especially the Auditory-Vocal Automatic subtest, may deviate from the definition in the examiner's manual. It is important when a diagnosis or prescription for remediation is based on the results of these subtests that other evaluation procedures be used to confirm performance on them. Of the three encoding subtests, Vocal Encoding appears to be the most valid. (2) In the diagnosis of children with linguistic defects, such as dyslexia, it is recommended that auxiliary tests accompany the use of the ITPA. Concerning this point, Kass (1966) concluded that the ITPA subtests that appear to be most related to reading are three subtests at the integrational level (Grammatic Closure, Auditory Sequential Memory, and Visual Sequential Memory) and also Auditory-Vocal Association at the representational level. Specific tests recommended by Kass to supplement the ITPA are Visual Automatic-Visual Closure (Kass, 1962, 1966), Sound Blending (Monroe, 1932), Mazes (Wechsler, 1949), Memory-for-Designs (Graham & Kendall, 1960), and Perceptual Speed (Thurstone & Thurstone, 1954). In other words, Kass recommends supplementing the nine subtests of the experimental ITPA with five additional measures. It should be noted that the revised ITPA includes a Visual Closure Test and a Sound Blending Test.

Factor-analytic studies of the ITPA. Meyers (1968), after reviewing and synthesizing sixteen different factor analytic studies employing the ITPA, concluded that the test appears to tap some half-dozen separate abilities. While it taps more than one general ability, it certainly does not measure one separate component per subtest. To determine what it does measure, Meyers drew upon Guilford's model. On the basis of Meyers' synthesis, the following factors from Guilford's structure-of-intellect appear to be represented in the ITPA: (1) cognitive-convergent semantics (Auditory-Vocal Association and Auditory-Vocal Automatic), (2) convergent semantic relations (Visual Decoding and Motor Encoding), (3) cognitive semantic relations (Visual-Motor Association and Visual-Motor Sequencing), (4) visual memory for figural system (Visual-Motor Sequencing), (5) convergent semantics (Auditory Decoding), (6) memory for symbolic systems (Auditory-Vocal Sequencing and Visual-Motor Sequencing), and (7) divergent semantics (Vocal Encoding).

According to Bateman (1968), "One of the greatest contributions of the ITPA is that it has provided a frame of reference which makes it easier to know which behavior to observe, facilitates the observation, and provides guidelines for planning the modification of those behaviors through remediation."

The empirical findings from the many studies done on the experimental ITPA have helped the test developers to modify and improve the instrument. The revised edition, which should be available by the time this chapter is published, should be a valuable diagnostic tool for psychologists and educators working with children with learning disabilities.

Parsons Language Sample. Spradlin (1960) designed an instrument for sampling language behavior, the Parsons Language Sample (PLS), which was based primarily on Skinner's (1957) theoretical system of language behavior. The two subsections of the PLS are vocal and nonvocal. The vocal subsection consists of three subtests: (1) Tact Subtest, which requires the subject to name a series of objects and pictures; (2) Echoic Subtest, which requires the subject to repeat a series of words, phrases, or sentences of varying degrees of complexity; and (3) Intra-Verbal Subtest, in which the subject is required to answer questions, e.g., "What do we do when we are hungry?" and "In what way are an egg and a seed alike?" The nonvocal subsection consists of three subtests: (1) Echoic Gesture Subtest, in which the subject is required to imitate a series of motor acts first demonstrated by the examiner; (2) Comprehension Subtest, in which the examiner asks the child to follow simple directions; and (3) Intra-Verbal Gesture Subtest, in which the subject responds to questions by either a vocal or a gestural response. Only the gestural responses are scored. Examples of items are "Where is your ear?" and "What do you do with a handkerchief?"

The PLS was administered to 275 ambulatory institutionalized 8- to 15-year-old mental retardates at Parsons State Hospital and Training Center. Odd-even reliability for the subtests ranged from .85 to .96. The correlations between the subtests of the PLS indicate that similar abilities are tapped by most of the subtests with the exception of the Intra-Verbal Gesture Subtest, which is sampling a different ability.

The ITPA and the PLS are both experimental instruments that are based on a theoretical model. The development of assessment procedures that are based on a sound theoretical foundation represents, in the opinion of the authors, an important trend in diagnostic procedures. Of the two instruments, the ITPA appears to be a more promising diagnostic tool for children with learning difficulties.

Appraisal of Perceptual Abilities

For the purpose of this discussion, perception is defined as the discrimination and meaningful interpretation of stimuli impinging upon the senses. It is a process occurring in the brain, not within the sense receptors. In other words, perception involves the extraction of information from sensory stimuli. Three sensory modalities are of particular significance for formal learning tasks such as reading: visual, auditory, and haptic (tactile-kinesthetic). One or more of the perceptual channels of children with learning difficulties is frequently impaired.

Visual-perception tests. A major characteristic of brain-damaged adults suffering from disturbances of "abstract attitude" observed by Goldstein was disability in visual perception. Later it was found that disturbances in visual perception were among the symptoms that occurred most frequently in children who, on the basis of a neurological examination, were diagnosed as brain-damaged. The appraisal of perceptual abilities has therefore been attempted by workers engaged in the diagnosis and treatment of children and adults with cerebral dysfunction as well as by factor analytic studies in unselected populations (Thurstone, 1944). The interest that was focused upon perceptual dysfunctions, rather than on perceptual functions, led to the development of the first perceptual tests that were used in clinical settings to evaluate perceptual functions.

The following visual-perceptual tests will be discussed: Bender Visual Motor Gestalt Test (Bender, 1938), Developmental Test of Visual-Motor Integration (VMI) (Beery & Buktenica, 1967), Frostig Developmental Test of Visual Perception (Frostig et al., 1964), Benton Visual Retention Test (Benton, 1955), and Memory-for-Designs Test (Graham & Kendall, 1960).

Bender Visual Motor Gestalt Test. The Bender Gestalt is probably the most frequently administered perceptual-motor test (Sundberg, 1961). The test utilizes nine cards, each containing a geometric figure, which the subject copies. The designs were selected by Bender from a longer series used by Wertheimer (1923) in his early research on visual perception. Although the Bender has been administered to children for many years, its usefulness has been greatly facilitated by the development of an objective scoring system (Koppitz, 1964) for 5- to 11-year-old children.

Relatively high scorer reliability coefficients ranging from .88 to .96 are reported; however, retest reliability over a four-month interval was found to range between .55 and .66. Evidence of validity is indicated by significant relationships between the Bender and achievement in reading and arithmetic and by group differences between total scores on the Bender of brain-injured and normal children.

In addition to the Bender Gestalt being useful as an indication of visual perceptual-motor development and for detecting possible cerebral dysfunction, Koppitz also provides a set of eleven "emotional indicators," six of which have been found to show statistically significant group differences between children who were emotionally disturbed and a control group.

Developmental Test of Visual-Motor Integration. The VMI (Beery & Buktenica, 1967) is a recently developed form-copying test in which norms are provided for age groups of 3 to 14 years. The VMI appears to have good reliability even at the younger age levels, which is probably due to the larger number of items and more gradual increase in difficulty between items. This test also lends itself readily to group administration and can be easily administered as a screening test.

Frostig Developmental Test of Visual Perception. The Frostig test (Frostig et al., 1964) was designed to measure five operationally defined perceptual functions: (1) visual-motor coordination—the ability to coordinate vision with movements of the body or parts of the body; (2) figure-ground perception—the ability to attend to one aspect of the visual field while perceiving it in relation to the rest of the field; (3) perceptual constancy, which refers to the fact that an object is perceived as possessing invariant properties such as shape, position, and size in spite of the variability of the sensory impression; (4) perception of position in space—the perception of

an object in relation to the observer; (5) perception of spatial relationships, which denotes the ability to perceive the position of two or more objects in relation to each other.

The Frostig test is the only presently available perceptual test that provides a profile of perceptual abilities. It attempts to diagnose the specific areas of deficiency that the child has rather than merely providing a total score of perceptual development. Silverstein (1965) analyzed the Frostig test to determine the variance components of its five subtests. He found:

> On the average, the proportion of the total variance accounted for by the specificity of the subtests was approximately equal to that accounted for by their communality. This finding lends some support to the premise that a number of relatively distinct areas of perception can be delineated. . . . And that it may be of value to direct perceptual training toward the specific functions disturbed in each case.

The test-retest reliability of the perceptual quotient is reported as .80; the test-retest reliability coefficients for the subtest scale scores range from .42 (figure-ground) to .80 (form constancy).

Austin (Buros, 1965), after reviewing the test, concluded:

> The Frostig test appears to be a significant one. It has proved useful as a screening tool with groups of nursery school, kindergarten, and first-grade children, primarily because it permits identification of those children who need special perceptual training in five important areas of visual perception. It should also be valuable as a clinical tool with children beyond first grade.

Benton Visual Retention Test. The Benton (1955) test consists of ten geometric designs; each design is exposed for 10 seconds, and the child is told to draw what was on the card after it is removed. The test requires visual perception, immediate memory, and psychomotor reproduction of the design. The Benton was developed for use with children 8 years of age and older;

therefore, it has limited diagnostic usefulness with a clinical population of children because of the difficulty of the tasks. The Benton has been found to be useful in detecting severe brain damage in older children.

Memory-for-Designs Test. The Memory-for-Designs Test (Graham & Kendall, 1960) is intended for subjects 8½ years old and older. It consists of fifteen geometric designs, which the child is required to draw from memory after he has looked at the design for five seconds. The test is similar to the Benton. Test-retest reliabilities are reported as ranging from .72 to .90. Studies of the validity of the test in predicting organicity indicate that it is a valuable tool in the diagnosis of severely brain-damaged cases (Korman & Blumberg, 1963) but that it is of limited usefulness in identifying the child with mild neurological impairments (Kerekjarto, 1962).

Evaluation of auditory perception. Buktenica (1966) investigated the relationship between auditory and visual perception in reading and spelling achievement in first grade. A battery of tests which included two tests of auditory perception and one of visual perception was administered to 342 first-grade children. Buktenica found that visual perception correlated .50 with first-grade achievement and the two auditory-perception tests correlated .46 and .51 whereas the IQ test correlated .47. It was also found that visual perception and auditory perception were relatively independent of each other; the multiple correlation between reading and the auditory and visual-perception tests was .61. The relationship between auditory-discrimination abilities and reading achievement has also been found by Dykstra (1966) and Wepman (1960).

Wepman Test of Auditory Discrimination. The Wepman (1958) test is an individually administered instrument that requires five to ten minutes to administer and attempts to determine whether or not auditory-discrimination deficits are present. The subject is required to determine whether two words pronounced by the examiner are alike or different. The test-retest reliability of this instrument is reported as .91.

Peabody Picture Vocabulary Test (PPVT). The PPVT (Dunn, 1959) is a decoding or receptive vocabulary test in which the child is required to understand the words spoken by the examiner and to select which of four pictures is most like the word pronounced. In addition to requiring "auditory perception," the PPVT also appears to be a measure of "cognition of semantic units" in Guilford's structure-of-intellect model. The test is untimed and takes about ten minutes to administer. Norms are provided for ages 2 to 18 years. Alternate-form reliability coefficients for different age levels ranged from .67 to .84.

Evaluation of haptic perception. The evaluation of haptic (tactile-kinesthetic) perception has long been included in the diagnostic evaluation by neurologists in that difficulties in haptic perception are considered indicative of organicity (Alpers, 1945). The typical method of evaluation is to have the subject identify an object placed in his hand without the aid of vision.

Relatively little basic research concerning haptic perception has appeared in the literature. Only scattered studies (Ayres, 1965; Birch & Lefford, 1963; Buckner, 1964; Pick, Pick, & Thomas, 1966; Vaught, 1968) have been published. Benton and Schultz (1949) designed a haptic-perception test with norms for 3- to 6-year-old children. Prior to the administration of the test, the subject was asked to name the objects. If he could name them correctly, the test objects were removed from sight and he was asked to identify the objects by feeling them with one hand.

Mills (1955) developed a standardized procedure for determining which of four learning approaches is most effective for presenting new words to a child. The four approaches are (1) visual, (2) auditory or phonetic, (3) kinesthetic or tracing, and (4) a combination of the visual, auditory, and kinesthetic. The procedure followed is: (1) forty words are selected that the child was not able to read; (2) the words are arranged into four sets of ten words each; (3) fifteen minutes are spent teaching the first set of words using a visual approach; (4) an immediate recall test and delayed recall test are administered on the words taught. On subsequent days, a similar procedure is followed with the auditory, kinesthetic (Fernald, 1943), and combination approach.

Cross-modal integration. In addition to having difficulties in visual, auditory, or haptic perception, children with learning disabilities have frequently been found to have difficulties in the ability to integrate two or more perceptual abilities. Birch (Money, 1962) found children with learning disabilities to have problems in visual-tactual and visual-kinesthetic coordination. Kass (1966) also found that children with reading disabilities tended to have difficulty in integrating perceptual modalities. Similar observations have also been made at the Frostig Center.

Piaget's explanation of cross-modal integration is that a representative schema is built up that serves as a common referent for two or more modalities. In Piaget's words, "The whole trend of events appears to suggest that the power to imagine the shapes visually, when they are perceived through the sense of touch alone, is an expression of the sensorimotor schema involved in their percention" (Piaget & Inhelder, 1956).

In the above paragraph, Piaget points out that perception itself is an integrative act. Already during the preschool years, the child learns to master the task of perceiving something visually by integrating the visual image with previous experiences with the same object. These experiences include memories of touch, sound, taste, etc. The child looks at a piece of metal and remembers that it feels cold and smooth, and the coldness and the smoothness of the metal become just as much a part of the image gained through visual perception as its color or its shape. For the purpose of exploring a child's perceptual ability, it is important that the examiner be aware of the fact that perceptual deficits may occur because the child has difficulties perceiving the characteristic of an object through the sense modality to which it is exposed. For example, the child may not be able to recognize a square visually while it is shown to him but may be able to recognize it by touch, or the child may have difficulties in the recognition of an object because of a deficit in cross-modal integration (imagery). He may look at the square and see it as a square but be unable to recognize its tactile qualities, for example, to perceive that it is made of either a rough or a smooth material. In testing perceptual functions, the examiner must always know whether or not he is requesting a response which requires cross-modal integration.

A test which measures perception only in the sense modality through which the child perceives the object will probably be less predictive because perception is usually multimodal; however, the single-channel perceptual test will indicate whether or not the child has difficulties in that aspect of perception. A test which requires the child to integrate cross-modal perceptions or to integrate perceptual and motor tasks may be more predictive of school achievement, such as in reading or writing.

On the basis of both theoretical and research evidence, it appears that a complete diagnostic evaluation of the perceptual abilities of children with learning difficulties should include single-channel perception, cross-modal perception, and perceptual-motor tasks. Such an evaluation is necessary for an estimate of the child's present perceptual functions and for the purpose of determining which abilities are intact and which are in need of remediation.

USE OF TEST BATTERIES

Learning is the main task of the child, learning which occurs in and out of school. Any disturbance in the child's development seems to be reflected in his diminished ability to acquire new skills, knowledge, and adaptive behavior and to progress in his schoolwork.

The most important purpose of the tests discussed in this chapter is to diagnose disabilities and thus to make remediation possible, especially remediation of those disabilities which handicap the child in his school learning. To serve this purpose, a single test does not suffice. It is necessary to tap the whole gamut of psychological functions. Even though the teacher bases her program primarily on the results of those tests which evaluate cognitive abilities, the emotional, social, perceptual, and language functions also have to be explored if the underlying causes and accompanying symptoms of learning difficulties are to be fully understood.

The school program itself may be based upon a careful assessment of each child's strengths and weaknesses in each of six developmental areas: sensorimotor, perceptual, language, higher thought processes, social, and emotional. These findings, which are quantified whenever possible, can be used as the basis for remedial programs that are specifically adapted to each child's needs.

Assessment in the six areas is attempted on the basis of test results, observations, and interview data. In addition to the diagnostic evaluation being a basis for the child's educational program, decisions regarding classroom management, child-teacher relationships, and auxiliary services for the child and his family (medical-psychological casework) may also be based on these findings.

At the Frostig Center, four tests have been found to be especially helpful and are invariably included in the battery. They are the ITPA, the Wepman Test of Auditory Discrimination, the Frostig Developmental Test of Visual Perception, and the WISC. These tests provide an assessment of language functions, auditory perception, visual perception, and higher cognitive functions and involve three of the six developmental areas listed above.

The ITPA and the WISC are broad-gauge instruments which evaluate a wide range of abilities. The WISC tests mainly higher cognitive functions but also includes perceptual abilities and language functions. The ITPA is even broader in scope. It focuses on language but takes into account a very wide range of abilities, such as visual-perceptual memory, auditory memory, ability to think logically, and ability to form concepts.

The advantage of broad-gauge tests lies in the panoramic view of the child that they provide. Their disadvantage is that they provide less detailed data in any single area on which to base remedial strategy. The Frostig and Wepman tests, on the other hand, are narrow-gauge tests, designed to evaluate the specific abilities of visual perception and auditory discrimination of speech sounds, respectively. They have the advantage of specificity but the limitation of evaluating only a narrow range of the child's functioning.

In order to make the most effective use of both broad- and narrow-gauge tests, it is necessary to use a battery of tests, because no single test covers the wide span of developmental functions. Such a test battery may include instruments which overlap in function. This overlap should not be regarded as a disadvantage since the low reliability of many of the individual subtests makes it desirable that the examiner look at single scores within the context of the entire battery. He should further observe the child and check discrepancies of findings of the subtests designed to evaluate similar areas of functioning.

Discrepancies between test results and observed behavior may be fruitfully studied. For example, a child who functioned poorly on digit span may not evidence deficits in auditory memory functions in his behavior. Another child with above average scores on all WISC subtests may have great difficulty with geometry. Careful analysis may show that the child cannot master a task in which the manipulation of spatial relationships is combined with the use of symbols.

Another reason for discrepancies between behavior and test results may be the child's ability to successfully perform the task through the utilization of abilities other than the ones hypothesized. For example, a great amount of research shows clearly that perceptual abilities are necessary for reading; nevertheless, there are children who are able to read with a minimum of perceptual functioning. Often we do not know exactly what other abilities are used in these cases. To give a clinical example, Eskga was able to do arithmetical calculations fairly quickly, although her test results indicated extreme deficiencies in memory for digits and arithmetic fundamentals. Observations and interviews revealed that this youngster was able to substitute for her inability to remember number facts by extremely rapid and imperceptible movements of her toes as she counted.

The tests used at the Frostig Center, in addition to the four mentioned above, are chosen according to individual requirements. But these four tests, together with an evaluation of psychomotor functions and of school achievement, are given to all children of the appropriate ability level and form the basis for remedial programming.

How may teachers utilize the results of this or a similar battery? Test results can be used to determine the best teaching approach for a single child or for a group. A somewhat different approach is required in programming a single child than is used in developing a training program for a whole class.

In the latter case, the teacher uses a chart, such as that shown in Figure 26-3, which refers to a group of seven children. By listing each child's performance in all areas evaluated, the teacher can see at a glance the difficulties which occur most frequently in the group and can plan the program accordingly. The arrows indicate the areas on which she would concentrate.

Two of the children, Verje and Gomgr, have perceptual difficulties not shared by the others. As this is the case, they will receive perceptual training while the other children are working on other tasks. Cowro and Kayje need to share this training also, but for a shorter period. Cowro and Gomgr also need training in auditory perception.

The teacher needs to consider each subtest score and provide appropriate training (special training programs have been developed at the Center, based on the tests for visual perception and language functions). But as valuable forms of ability training need to integrate several underlying skills, the teacher of a group can also, without fear of wasting time, employ exercises which focus primarily on areas in which an individual child is not deficient. Such activities will be of value to the child, not only by training other particular skills which are requisite to the activity in which he may be weak but also by helping him integrate and associate his various abilities. Later evaluation may suggest that a child requires more individualized work in one or more areas.

The following are examples of the use of test results for the training of an individual child. Pretest results are shown as well as later test results, to indicate the change in psychological functions that were assessed.

Varcl (Figure 26-4) was referred to the Center because of difficulties in writing and spelling and because of poor performance in physical education. He was assigned to an individual teacher for tutoring. The program was devised for all his relatively low areas, with special emphasis upon visual-motor sequencing and motor encoding. It was probably his disability in visual-motor sequencing which had contributed both to his

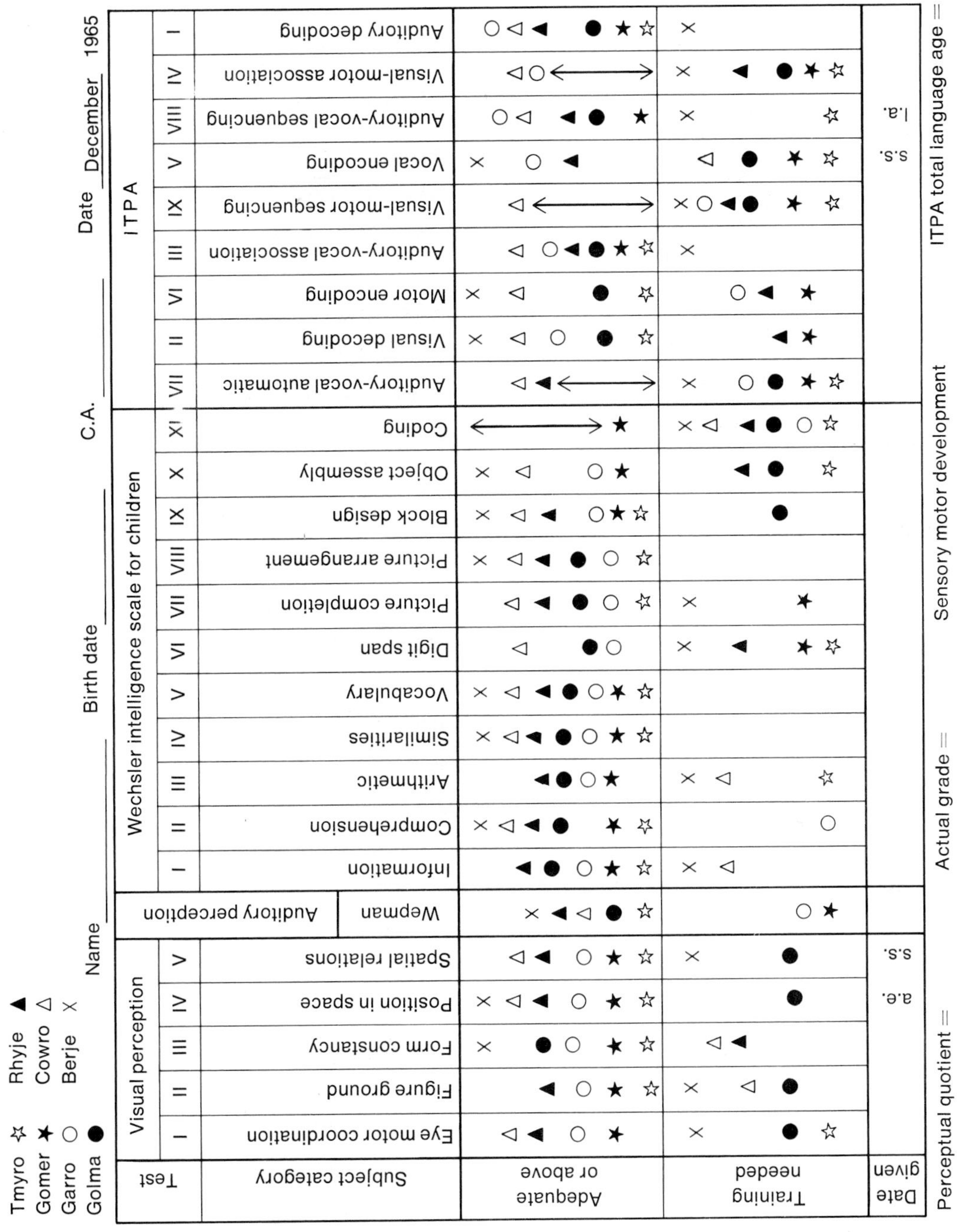

Figure 26-3. Basic test results.

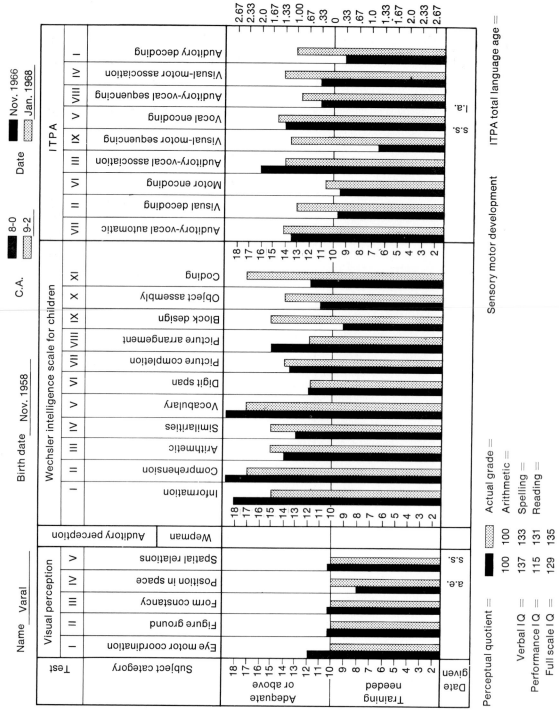

Figure 26-4. Basic test results.

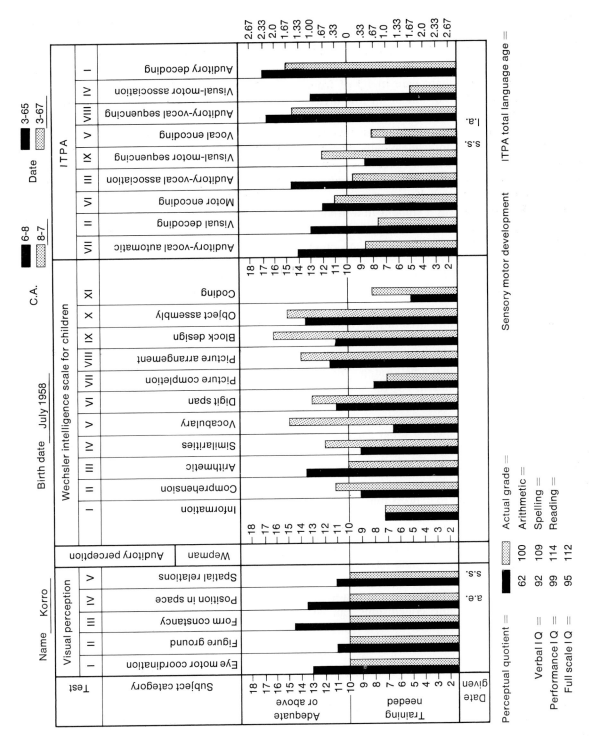

Figure 26-5.   Basic test results.

839

clumsy movements and to his difficulties in writing and spelling.

Retesting showed a slight gain in IQ of from 129 to 135, with a leveling out of all low areas, so that his profile is currently a very even one. At the present time he is progressing satisfactorily without special help in an academically demanding private school. A physical education teacher reports improvement, although physical education was not taught remedially.

Korro (Figure 26-5) was a student in a private, highly competitive school, where the academic requirements were great. He came to the Center for tutoring, which had to be concentrated in the academic area because he was threatened with failure.

Korro tested above average in visual perception and in the performance area of the WISC on intake at the Center, and his scores have continued at this level. His very slight auditory-perceptual deficit has been ameliorated. But in spite of a gain of 17 points in IQ, the low areas on his test profile have stayed the same: information, picture completion, and coding. Only his vocabulary score has shown a great change, as language was extensively developed in his program. The poor score on visual-motor association on the ITPA may be an artifact because Korro is rather reluctant to express himself freely in a tense situation and easily feels threatened; this is probably reflected in his vocal-encoding scores also. Of the two ITPA subtests which were formerly somewhat low, one has remained low, and a few other additional low points can now be discerned, but ITPA scores are not so highly reliable that definite conclusions can be drawn from these scores alone.

This case illustrates that if the teacher needs to concentrate on academic work and neglect ability training, the discrepancy between scores on tests of developmental functions may even increase. Academic work may strengthen the child's existing strong points without ameliorating his deficits.

The same results occur in some children when individual differences are not taken into account. Teacher F used intensive training focusing on visual-perceptual functions for all children in his group. Those children with high performance scores on the WISC were given the same program as those children with low WISC performance scores. Retesting indicated that all children increased their performance scores; however, the children who had low performance scores initially showed a much more even profile after training.

An attempt has been made to illustrate how the use of a test battery can be helpful in a diagnostic-prescriptive educational program. Testing, which is only part of a complete diagnostic evaluation, will be of optimum value if the results of an appropriate battery of tests are taken into account in the planning of the child's curriculum.

REFERENCES

Alpers, B. J. *Clinical neurology.* Philadelphia: Davis, 1945.

Ayres, A. J. Patterns of perceptual-motor dysfunction in children: A factor analytic study. *Perceptual and Motor Skills,* 1965, **20,** 335–368.

Barsch, R. *A movigenic curriculum.* Madison, Wis.: State Department of Public Instruction, 1965.

Bateman, B. *The Illinois Test of Psycholinguistic Abilities in current research.* Urbana: University of Illinois Press, 1965.

Bateman, B. *Interpretation of the 1961 Illinois Test of Psycholinguistic Abilities.* Seattle: Special Child Development, 1968.

Bayley, N. The development of motor abilities during the first three years. *Monographs of the Society for Research in Child Development,* 1935, **1.**

Bayley, N. On the growth of intelligence. *American Psychologist,* 1955, **10,** 805–818.

Bayley, N. *Bayley Infant Scales of Development.* New York: Psychological Corporation, 1968.

Beery, K. E., & Buktenica, N. A. *Developmental Test of Visual-Motor Integration.* Chicago: Follett, 1967.

Bender, L. A visual motor Gestalt test and its clinical use. *The American Orthopsychiatric Association Research Monograph,* 1938, **3.**

Benton, A. L. *Benton Visual Retention Test.* (Rev. ed.) New York: Psychological Corporation, 1955.

Benton, A. L., & Schultz, L. M. Observations on tactual form perception in preschool children. *Journal of Clinical Psychology,* 1949, **5** (4), 359–364.

Birch, H. G., & Lefford, A. Intersensory development in children. *Monographs of the Society for Research in Child Development,* 1963, **28**(5).

Buckner, L. J. The relationship of tactual-visual reciprocity to the intelligence and achievement of fourth-grade children. Unpublished doctoral dissertation, University of Colorado, 1964.

Bühler, C., et al. *The child and his family.* New York: Harper, 1939.

Buktenica, N. A. Relative contributions of auditory and visual perception to first-grade language learning. Unpublished doctoral dissertation, University of Chicago, 1966.

Buros, O. K. (Ed.) *The sixth mental measurements yearbook.* Highland Park, N.J.: Gryphon Press, 1965.

Dunn, L. M. *Peabody Picture Vocabulary Test manual.* Nashville, Tenn.: American Guidance Service, 1959.

Dykstra, R. Auditory discrimination abilities and beginning reading achievement. *Reading Research Quarterly,* 1966, **1**(3), 5–34.

Fernald, G. M. *Remedial techniques in basic school subjects.* New York: McGraw-Hill, 1943.

Flavell, J. H. *The developmental psychology of Jean Piaget.* Princeton, N.J.: Van Nostrand, 1963.

Frostig, M. Education for children with learning disabilities. In H. Myklebust (Ed.), *Progress in learning disorders.* Syracuse, N.Y.: Syracuse University Press, 1967.

Frostig, M., Lefever, W., & Whittlesey, J. *Developmental Test of Visual Perception.* Palo Alto, Calif.: Consulting Psychologists Press, 1964.

Gesell, A., & Amatruda, C. A. *Developmental diagnosis.* New York: Hoeber-Harper, 1947.

Goldstein, K. Die Funktionen des Stirnhirns und ihre Bedeutung für die Diagnose der Stirnhirnerkrankungen. *Medizinische Klinik,* 1923, **28** and **29.**

Goldstein, K. Die Lokalisation in der Grosshirnrinde. *Handb. Norm. Pathol. Physiologie.* Berlin: J. Springer, 1927.

Goldstein, K., & Scheerer, M. Abstract and concrete behavior: An experimental study with special tests. *Psychological Monographs,* 1941, 239.

Graham, F. K., & Kendall, B. S. *Memory-for-Designs Test.* Psychological Test Specialist, 1960.

Guilford, J. P. *The nature of human intelligence.* New York: McGraw-Hill, 1967.

Guilford, J. P. Intelligence has three facets. *Science,* 1968, **160,** 615–620.

Halpin, V., & Patterson, R. M. The performance of brain-injured children on the Goldstein-Scheerer tests. *American Journal of Mental Deficiency,* 1954, **59,** 91–99.

Haynes, J. R., & Sells, S. B. Assessment of organic brain damage by psychological tests. *Psychological Bulletin,* 1963, **60,** 316–325.

Heald, J. E., & Marzolf, S. S. Abstract behavior in elementary school children as measured by the Goldstein-Scheerer Stick Test and the Weigl-Goldstein-Scheerer Color-Form Sorting Test. *Journal of Clinical Psychology,* 1953, **9**, 59–62.

Inhelder, B., & Piaget, J. *The growth of logical thinking from childhood to adolescence.* New York: Basic Books, 1958.

Kass, C. Some psychological correlates of severe reading disability. Unpublished doctoral dissertation, University of Illinois, 1962.

Kass, C. Psycholinguistic disabilities of children with reading problems. *Exceptional Children,* 1966, **32**(8), 533–539.

Kerekjarto, M. B. Untersuchung über die Diskrimierungskraft dreier Tests zur Erfassung zerebraler Schäden. In G. Lienert (Ed.), *Bericht über den 23 Kongress der Deutschen Gesellschaft fur Psychologie.* Göttingen: Hogrefe, 1962.

Kirk, S., & McCarthy, J. *Illinois Test of Psycholinguistic Abilities.* Urbana: University of Illinois Press, 1961.

Kirk, S., McCarthy, J., & Kirk, W. *Illinois Test of Psycholinguistic Abilities.* (Rev. ed.) Urbana: University of Illinois Press, 1968.

Knobloch, H., & Pasamanick, B. An evaluation of the consistency and predictive value of the forty week Gesell developmental schedule. *Psychiatric Research Reports,* 1960, **13**, 10–41.

Koppitz, E. M. *The Bender-Gestalt test for young children.* New York: Grune & Stratton, 1964.

Korman, M., & Blumberg, S. Comparative efficiency of some tests of cerebral damage. *Journal of Consulting Psychology,* 1963, **27**, 303–309.

Laurendeau, M., & Pinard, A. *Causal thinking in the child; A genetic and experimental approach.* New York: International Universities Press, 1963.

McCarthy, J. J., & Olson, J. L. *Validity studies on the Illinois Test of Psycholinguistic Abilities.* Urbana, Ill.: Authors, 1964.

Meeker, M. Differential syndromes of giftedness: A four-year follow-up. *Journal of Special Education,* 1968, in press.

Meyers, C. E. What the ITPA measures: A synthesis of factor analytic studies. American Association of Mental Deficiency Annual Convention, 1968.

Mills, R. E. *Learning methods test.* Fort Lauderdale, Fla.: Mill Center, 1955.

Money, S. (Ed.) *Reading disability: Progress in research needs in dyslexia.* Baltimore: Johns Hopkins, 1962.

Monroe, M. *Children who cannot read.* Chicago: University of Chicago Press, 1932.

Osgood, Charles E. A behavioristic analysis. In *Contemporary approaches to cognition.* Cambridge, Mass.: Harvard University Press, 1957. (a)

Osgood, Charles E. Motivational dynamics of language behavior. In *Nebraska symposium on motivation.* Lincoln, Neb.: University of Nebraska Press, 1957. (b)

Piaget, J. *The language and thought of the child.* New York: Harcourt, Brace, 1926.

Piaget, J. *The origins of intelligence in children.* New York: International Universities Press, 1952.

Piaget, J. *The construction of reality in the child.* New York: Basic Books, 1954.

Piaget, J., & Inhelder, B. *The child's conception of space.* New York: Humanities Press, 1956.

Pick, A. D., Pick, H. L., & Thomas, M. L. Cross-modal transfer and improvement of form discrimination. *Journal of Experimental Child Psychology,* 1966, **3**, 279–288.

Roach, E. G., & Kephart, N. C. *The Purdue Per-ceptual-Motor Survey.* Columbus, Ohio: Charles E. Merrill Books, 1966.

Sievers, D. Development and standardization of a test of psycholinguistic growth in preschool children. Unpublished doctoral dissertation, University of Illinois, 1955.

Sievers, D., McCarthy, J. J., Olson, J. L., Bate-man, B. D., & Kass, C. E. *Selected studies on the Illinois Test of Psycholinguistic Abilities.* Ur-bana, Ill.: Authors, 1963.

Silverstein, A. B. Variance components in the Developmental Test of Visual Perception. *Per-ceptual and Motor Skills,* 1965, **20,** 973–976.

Skinner, B. F. *Verbal behavior.* New York: Appleton-Century-Crofts, 1957.

Sloan, W. *Lincoln-Oseretsky Motor Develop-ment Scale.* Chicago: C. H. Stoelting, 1955.

Spradlin, J. E. Assessment of language skills among mentally retarded children. *Parson's Research Project Working Paper,* 1960, No. 29.

Stott, L. H., & Ball, R. S. Infant and preschool mental tests: Review and evaluation. *Mono-graphs of the Society for Research in Child Devel-opment,* 1965, **30** (3) (Ser. No. 101).

Strauss, A. A., & Kephart, N. C. *Psychopathol-ogy and education of the brain-injured child.* Vol. 2. New York: Grune & Stratton, 1955.

Strauss, A. A., & Lehtinen, L. E. *Psychopathol-ogy and education of the brain-injured child.* Vol. 1. New York: Grune & Stratton, 1947.

Sundberg, N. D. The practice of psychological testing in clinical services in the United States. *American Psychologist,* 1961, **16,** 79–83.

Thams, P. F. A factor analysis of the Lincoln-Oseretsky Motor Development Scale. Unpub-lished doctoral dissertation, University of Mich-igan, 1955.

Thurstone, L. L. A factor analysis study of per-ception. *Psychometric Monograph,* 1944, **4.**

Thurstone, L. L., & Thurstone, T. G. *SRA pri-mary mental abilities, for ages five to seven.* Chi-cago: Science Research Associates, 1954.

Tuddenham, R. D. Jean Piaget and the world of the child. *American Psychologist,* 1966, **21,** 207–217.

Vaught, G. M. Form discrimination is a function of sex, procedure, and tactual mode. *Psycho-nomic Science,* 1968, **10**(4), No. 151–152.

Wechsler, D. *Wechsler Intelligence Scale for Children.* New York: Psychological Corpora-tion, 1949.

Wepman, J. *Wepman Test of Auditory Discrimi-nation.* Chicago: Language Research Associates, 1958.

Wepman, J. Auditory discrimination, speech, and reading. *Elementary School Journal,* 1960, **60,** 325–333.

Werner, H. *Comparative psychology of mental development.* New York: International Uni-versities Press, 1957.

Werner, H., & Strauss, A. A. Pathology of figure-background relation in the child. *Journal of Ab-normal and Social Psychology,* 1941, **36,** 236–248.

Werner, H., & Strauss, A. A. Impairment in thought processes of brain-injured children. *American Journal of Mental Deficiency,* 1943, **47,** 291–295.

Wertheimer, W. Studies in the theory of Gestalt psychology. *Psychological Forsch,* 1923, **4.**

Wesman, A. G. Intelligent testing. *American Psychologist,* 1968, **23**(4), 267–274.

part vi | Overview of Treatment Methods

27 Psychoanalysis with Children

Stanley R. Lesser

LITTLE HANS

The basic techniques of child analysis were formulated by Anna Freud in 1926 (English publication, 1946) and by Melanie Klein in 1932 (English publication, 1949). Some twenty years earlier, in 1909, Sigmund Freud (1955) had published the *Analysis of a Phobia in a Five Year Old Boy* (commonly known as the "case of Little Hans"). Freud supervised the boy's father in analysis of his son. This landmark case confirmed the reality of childhood sexuality, the psychic conflicts, and their direct relationship to the neurotic symptomatology, which had been derived until then only from adult analysis. The case of Little Hans further indicated that the hidden and unconscious fantasies and emotions of the child could be exposed and interpreted; moreover, through the child's understanding of the roots of his fantasies (insight), the phobic symtomatology could be dissolved. Nevertheless, Freud believed that only a father could be vested with the authority necessary for the positive transference of a child. Freud believed that the father's intimate knowledge of the child's history and habits was essential for the treatment of the child.

Although formal psychoanalysis of children was relegated to the future, from the earliest days of psychoanalysis, observation of their own children was carried on by psychoanalysts and those influenced by their teachings, among them some educators. The unconscious and not yet conscious motivations and feelings, less disguised in the child than in the adult, were noted and used to augment, to support, or to revise psychoanalytic theory and technique. This cross-fertilization between adult and child studies has enriched both and continues to the present day.

One may recall that Freud revised his hypothesis that adult seduction of children was a major etiological factor in neurosis when he discovered the low incidence of actual child seduction and the frequency of seduction fantasies in children. Again, overt wish-fulfillment dreams in his own children (S. Freud, 1950b) supported the theory of the latent wish content in the more obscure adult dreams.

847

A second source of information about the emotional development of the child came through the attempts to prevent neuroses and enhance mental health through changes in child-rearing practices and in the education of children. This concentrated attention on the child's productions—drawings, diaries, etc.—contributed to the understanding of the relationship between the development of the normal child, his inner experiences, and the relationship to pathological deviation. Other important contributions, such as the learning of the child's language, his preferred mode of communication, and the toys and other materials through which he is able to express himself, later became major tools in child analysis. Ferenczi's (1950, 1955) "active therapy," his experiments in forcing fantasies in adult patients resistant to free association, opened the possibility of approaching children neither able nor willing to free-associate. More specifically, when Ferenczi urged a young patient to fantasize, the patient, unable to verbalize, asked if he could draw and play.

MELANIE KLEIN

Melanie Klein (1949) began to analyze children, using their play with small toys as raw material coequal, in her opinion, with the free associations of the adult. Subsequently, she was able to demonstrate that the child's behavior, his feelings and ideas about her, reflected patterns and conflicts formerly lived through with the parents. Hence her conviction that children were able to develop transference manifestations subject to interpretation and understanding in much the same manner as adult analysands. She assumed that play could be directly interpreted by symbolic translation—such as an elongated object representing the penis; rotund objects, breasts; and cars running into each other, the primal scene.

Concomitantly, she found manifestations of introjection of the parental objects and of guilt in very young children. These manifestations induced her to assume the presence of an internalized superego by the end of the first year of life; this was a major revision of classical Freudian theory, which postulates the internalization of the superego as cotemporal with the inauguration of the latency period, at the age of 5 to 7 years. Oedipal fears, the "pound of flesh" demanded by the primitive internalized conscience, and the intense retaliatory fears for the infant's own destructive impulses are, according to her views, part and parcel of every infant's experience. All libidinal stages are thus telescoped temporally into the oral stage.

Melanie Klein and her followers, the so-called English School, then extended their theoretical constructs to include the ubiquitous development of psychoticlike conflicts in the first year of life, the paranoid and depressive positions. Life, according to this view, starts with conflict, anxiety (persecutory anxiety), and guilt (depressive guilt). Further development of the infant entails an uphill battle of building defenses against these affects (manic defenses) and relating to good objects in an attempt to neutralize the inner bad objects. Two psychic positions are postulated: the paranoid-schizoid (destructive rage and greed toward the mother—retaliatory murder) and the depressive (love-hate ambivalence toward the object—self-punishment to preserve the loved object). The Kleinian orientation, although extremely valuable in focusing attention on the importance of earliest mother-child interactions and in describing the earliest roots of superego formation, has not been widely accepted in the United States but remains the dominant orientation for many English child analysts.

Despite the rejection of Kleinian theory, much of Melanie Klein's technique has been incorporated in our present practice of child analysis, especially in the analysis of the prelatency child. The nondirective play with small toys, water, graphics, etc., and the noninterference with the development of the transference manifestations are common currency among all child analysts.

ANNA FREUD

Anna Freud has been the major figure in the development of child analysis and of psychoanalytic child psychology from her Vienna lectures in 1926 until today. Three books of hers—*The Psychoanalytic Treatment of Children* (1946a), *Ego and Mechanisms of Defense* (1946b), *Normality and Pathology in Childhood* (1965)—constitute the bible for child analysts. She has always stressed the differences between child analysis and the analysis of adults, differences inherent in the immature psyche of the child and in his life situation.

To Anna Freud, the child patient differs in his motivation for analysis, in his incapacity to free-associate, and in his difficulty in forming a transference neurosis. Most adult patients seek analysis because they are troubled by their anxiety or depressive mood, their thoughts, and/or their behavior. The child, with his tendency to externalize and to act when painful feelings or thoughts intrude, does not for the most part recognize his distress as coming from his own affects and actions but rather sees in his stress a fault of his environment. Thus, the psychoneurotic adult is a distress to himself, whereas the psychoneurotic child distresses his environment. Second, as Anna Freud has noted (1946a), the child's dependency on his parents and their desire to alleviate his suffering cushion him against the full extent of his anxiety. This cushioning by the parents is a generally desirable state of affairs in the emotional development of the child, though not conducive to the child's readiness to undergo analysis. The mother sits with her child when he is tense falling asleep; she works with him should he be inhibited in learning and accompanies him should he have a street phobia. One might remember the difficulty of analyzing a phobic adult patient should he obtain a collaborator to mask his phobia. Often the child is brought for treatment at the point where the parent no longer has the capacity for or loses the desire to offer protection and secondary gain to the child. A child's symptoms on entrance to school, while at camp, on following the illness of the mother may be a recrudescence of long-smoldering conflicts which now have lost their "tranquilizer."

The decision for child psychoanalysis rather than for one of the "crisis intervention" therapeutic techniques makes it essential to differentiate those symptoms emerging from their suppression through the "cotton batting" from those directly related to change in environmental circumstances (reactive disorders). Here a broad diagnostic evaluation of object relationships, predominant defenses, and adaptational techniques—in the past as well as the present—will usually settle the issue.

The Hempstead Child Guidance Institute, under Anna Freud's general direction, has formulated a developmental profile (Nagera, 1963) which has proved helpful in this as in many other regards. At times, nonetheless, it is necessary to work out the immediate crisis before one can be certain of the underlying situation.

THE OBJECTIVES

I was consulted about Lotte, a 7-year-old girl, who had developed asthmalike breathing difficulties and a fear of leaving her mother. She had been reared from birth by her grandmother and had several months previously come to live with her newly remarried mother. Her distress was so severe that it was difficult to tell whether it was due entirely to the change in mother figures or whether old conflicts were the primary source. (Further history from the grandparents confirmed the impression that she had been a tense and emotionally labile child, who, supposedly because of her night fears, had slept on a cot next to her grandparents.) Lotte's adamant refusal to leave her mother necessitated the use of symbolic appearance and disappearance games (e.g., hide-and-seek, blindman's buff), which rapidly allowed her to part from her mother. At this point, Lotte was able to shift her frozen attention from her mother and become interested in her relationship with her analyst. Gradually, with the lessening of the (traumatic) anxiety and with her renewed curiosity about people and events of the present, she developed an awareness that, despite her own desire to please herself and her parents, tension and conflicts prevented her from enjoyment. At this juncture Lotte was able to utilize a formal psychoanalysis.[1]

The adaptation of adult analytic techniques to the child patient is favored by some aspects of the child's psychological situation and is hampered by others. The naïveté and openness of the child, as well as his greater tolerance toward divergent impulses and affects, allow him to express his fantasies and emotions more openly and with less secondary elaboration.

A 7-year-old boy opened his analysis by expressing his fear of looking at an illustration in which a dog was killing a rabbit. He proceeded to describe his horror when his own dog was killed, and shortly thereafter he began to play with toy animals, alternately playing the parts of murderer and victim. The child's fantasies have an analytic role in elucidating unconscious materials, as do dreams for the adult. These fantasies are communicated mainly through play with toys, dramatic role play, and graphics— drawing, painting, modeling. The child's attitudes and feelings toward the analyst are the other major mode of fantasy communication. Sometimes there will be an accompanying verbal commentary, explanation, or elaboration; at other times, the communication will be completely nonverbal and the analyst must be able to translate this "talk in action."

[1] All case histories have been taken from the author's personal records.

Of prime necessity in child analytical techniques, therefore, is the development of a milieu consistent with the child's maturation, development, and individual psychological equilibrium, in which the child can spontaneously express his fantasies and their concomitant affects. The aim is to allow the form and the content to come from within (projection and externalization) rather than be structured and directed by the analyst. Toys and other materials should be small, able to be adapted for many roles and purposes, familiar to the child, and within his cognitive and manipulative skills. Typical materials should include a small doll family, small cars and animals, blocks, crayons, finger paints, plasticine. Exotic or unfamiliar toys produce "novelty shock"; overdifficult materials induce a "task demand situation"; board games and cards promote stereotypy; large cars, bicycles, etc., call for action without observation. Materials such as these may, in fact, obscure the analytic purpose and psychological communication. Special materials may be required in any one case because of ego weakness, rigid defensive systems, idiosyncratic traumas, etc., or they may be introduced for a special purpose in a specific phase of the analysis. For the most part, however, they muddy rather than clarify the child's own psychic structures and processes.

These pragmatic details serve to illustrate the relation of the methods to the goals of child analysis. The major goal is to free the developmental process which has been retarded, inhibited, or deviated by the present derivatives of past emotional traumata and/or fixations (A. Freud, 1945, 1965). The technique of child analysis involves mutual investigation of the child's emotional life by the child and the analyst, especially of those parts of his emotional life of which he is unaware (unconscious) or only dimly aware. Fantasy, emotions, and behavior are the important pathways of expression of unconscious conflicts, attitudes, impulses, and motivations.

These fantasies and emotions, properly integrated with other ego functions, serve as alternative satisfactions, as signals evoking internal and external responses, and as coping methods for mastering the real world.

INTERPRETATION

The Kleinians equate fantasy play with the free associations obtained in the analysis of the adult and interpret the fantasy play and behavior directly; i.e., they translate the symbolic content of the fantasy into its original impulse. The so-called Vienna School, led by Anna Freud, emphasizes the progressive interpretation of emotion rather than the interpretation of the defenses and, finally, the interpretation of underlying conflict and impulses (Bornstein, 1945, 1949, 1951, 1953). The Vienna School criticizes the direct symbolic interpretations on several grounds. The Kleinian one-to-one relationship between the symbol and the deepest conflict seems overly simplistic, and the Kleinians seem to ignore the complex defensive systems that have overlaid the original anxiety (Glover, 1945).

> Toby, 3 years old, entered analysis because of screaming tantrums at the slightest frustration and severe anxiety over separation from her mother. In the course of her analysis she modeled clay "oranges." That these symbolized her mother's breasts became clear when she began to go to nursery school with real oranges in her sweater ("like Mommy's"). Presently she played out and related the fantasy: "I'll eat the oranges; I'll be as big as the clouds; I'll eat you [the analyst]." Following this, she excitedly jumped around the room, fell down, and played dead.

A Kleinian might directly interpret her desire to incorporate the feeding organs, her grandiosity in possessing these valuable and dangerous (frustrating and retaliatory) objects. Her death fantasy would then symbolize her fear of the wish to extract from her mother and a need for punishment to expiate this guilty fear. Instead, a series of prior interpretations were considered necessary: her anger at the analyst for separating her from her mother (displaced and projected from her rage at her mother); her feeling that the analyst could never satisfactorily feed-love her (again a displacement from the mother—this time in the transference); her trying to feel good inside by being Mommy (a formulation for Toby of the process and a motivation for imitative identification); her need to be a giant because of the fear of the analyst's overwhelming size (mechanisms of compensation, identification with the aggressor, and reversal of roles); and finally death as punishment for greed and rage (retaliatory principle and the beginning of a primitive conscience formation). Thus the fantasy and its attendant behavior were used for clarification and interpretation of object relationships, defense mechanisms, and transference distortions. It of course served to connect the unconscious conflicts to her present productions.

The working through of the child's defenses and other ego maneuvers allows insight not only into the unconscious conflicts but also into the ways in which he has dealt with the conflict. No longer do the fearful thoughts, the panicky feelings, and the "bad" behavior seem "the way of the world," inexplicable and arbitrary. Internal stress and external press can, at least in part, be separated, and their interconnections are then capable of being understood.

Secondary-process thinking, involving cause-and-effect relationships and the time trajectory—separation of past and present and anticipation of the future—begins to replace primary-process thinking, in which time relationships are telescoped and emotional correspondence connects objects and events.

> A vignette from 3-year-old Toby's analysis: Toby in her second year of analysis utters a mock scream each time she enters the playroom. "How come the

scream?" "So Mommy will know where I am." "She'd forget?" "No! I used to scream a lot; now I scream so I won't be sad when I have to leave you." Reason and time are beginning to bring order to Toby's emotional relationships.

Most child analysts draw their theoretical and technical principles from three sources:

1. *The developmental continuum,* as formulated by Anna Freud (1945). Progressive development along an inherently preprogrammed trajectory emerging in an "average expected" environment (Hartman) has become the major assessment and treatment focus (A. Freud, 1945, 1962).

Nightmares occurring in a 4-year-old child might be, developmentally, an expected phase during this phallic-Oedipal period. They would, in themselves, not indicate the need for therapeutic intervention. On the other hand, less strident events (or nonevents), such as a 4-year-old's lack of spontaneous fantasy and play, might indicate excessive fear of libidinal and aggressive drives and, even more importantly, the truncation of a crucial ego function. Such ego arrests do not allow the proper resolution of the phase conflicts and their attendant anxieties which permits forward development to the next era (Erikson, 1950). Moreover, the inhibition of spontaneous play prevents learning, with its attendant strengthening of the ego. Hence the inhibition or stereotypy of fantasy and play is a prime indication for child analysis.

The developmental concept stresses the normal sequential ordering of the expected internal and external psychic events in the child and allows these events to be juxtaposed to the more usual deviations and those excessive deviations, which we then see as pathology. It thus is inclusive of both the normal and the abnormal and, more importantly, allows us to assess clinically the abnormal in relation to the normal.

Anna Freud (1965) has delineated the usual

developmental course in the different segments of the child's unfolding personality. She has labeled these "developmental lines"—e.g., from dependency to emotional self-reliance and adult object relationships, from egocentricity to companionship, from body to toy, and from play to work. These developmental lines, "when assembled, convey a convincing picture of an individual child's personal achievements or, on the other hand, of his failures in personality development" (A. Freud, 1963).

2. *The concept of the independent roots and autonomous though interrelated (with the id) development of the ego* has stemmed from the discoveries of child analysis and, in turn, has influenced its principles and practices (Hartman, 1939; Hoffer, 1952, Kris, 1950.

3. *The epigenic concept* of Eric Erikson (1950, 1959) further amplifies the developmental concept in positing the necessary achievement of developmental "tasks" in adequate age sequences. Should these "tasks" not be fulfilled, deleterious attitudes and postures to the external and internal world ensue. "Trust," "autonomy," "initiative," "work," and "identity" are some of these developmental tasks. Erikson's constructs include the intermeshing of human and cultural forces with the maturational unfolding, uniting the biological and the social.

TRANSFERENCE

No area of child analysis is more open to question and controversy than transference. The difference between Anna Freud's views in 1926 and her more recent (1965) revision emphasizes the problem. Miss Freud originally (1946a) held that the continued presence of, and the child's continued dependency upon, the parents prevented and made unnecessary for the child a displacement of the affects, fantasies, and desires from the parents to the analyst. Hence the formation of a transference neurosis, in which the conflicts and their symptomatic expression are withdrawn from figures in the extra-analytic world and focused on the analyst, would not occur spontaneously in a child analysis. This opinion was revised, though not wholly countermanded, by A. Freud (1965):

> Taught by experience, by the elimination of the introductory phase (except in selected cases), and by the deliberate use of defense analysis as an introduction, I have modified my former opinion that transference in childhood is restricted to single "transference reactions" and does not develop to the complete status of a "transference neurosis." Nevertheless, I am still unconvinced that what is called transference neurosis in children equals the adult variety in every respect.

The acceptance of transference capacity in the child is reflected by the increasing emphasis on transference and transference interpretation as a major technical tool for the exercising of therapeutic leverage, as it is in adult psychoanalysis. The repetition of past attitudes, conflicts, and emotions with an object (the analyst) about whom, from a rational perspective, there would be relatively little reason for such reactivity to be induced sets up a gap between the logical and the emotional, between fantasy and reality, between primary (wish-fulfillment) and secondary (adaptive) process, and between the present and the past. This gap can then be narrowed through observation, formulation, interpretation, and reconstruction, whether by the analyst or by the child's self-observing ego, allowing alternate (nonneurotic) solutions to internal conflicts.

The roots of the transference are embedded in the life history of the child during his development. He simultaneously forms a more or less realistic picture of his parents and a distorted picture based on his own wishes, needs, fantasies, and emotions. Both the more factual representation and the more fantasied one remain psychically active for the child as internal representations (Fairbairn, 1952; Sandler, 1962). As the child grows older, these internal representations reciprocally influence his later perception of his parents and in varying degrees are modified by new experiences with his parents. The developmental level that has been achieved, as well as the particular course of any one child's experiences with his parents, will determine his capacity to separate old relational experiences from fresh ones and will determine the mode by which he will integrate his past human experiences with his new ones. Blind fusion of his parents with the analyst and, conversely, absolute differentiation both serve as resistances to transference and to the therapeutic use of transference interpretations. We are familiar with the child who views the analyst only as a beneficial protective figure (the partial introject of the "good mother") and with the child who treats the analyst as though any relationship with him will mean the loss of his parent (a fixation on the so-called "stranger anxiety" and the symbiotic developmental phase) (Mahler, 1958, 1968). Any "absolutism" does not allow the distance needed for the expression of transference feelings and fantasies. In the "good mother" transference, any negative thoughts or feelings would threaten the return of the split-off "bad mother"; and in the "dangerous stranger" transference, any positive expression threatens disintegration of the poorly integrated internal representation of the mother. In children with early ego fixation or during times, in or outside the analysis, when strong affects or primitive fantasies force ego regression, the child's expression of his feeling toward the analyst may be limited or absent. Transference interpretations will be unattended or reacted to with hostility. Hence an original strong, positive attachment to the mother, with the internalized image of the whole mother, is a prerequisite for a workable analytic transference. Put another way, the child must be able to trust that strong feelings toward an object will not result in destructive retaliation by the object or in loss of past object representation in the self (Erikson, 1959).

> Evan, a 7-year-old boy, was given to destructive rages (Lesser, in press). This rage concealed panic whenever he felt there was any obstacle to his return to his mother. School was unbearable. "The school gates," as he later expressed it, "were the prison bars, and the classrooms were a desolate empty desert." Suffering from a constitutional exacerbation of the oral drive, Evan was unable to be orally satiated as an infant. (He had sucked the skin off both thumbs by 1 week of age and had chewed through the bars of his crib when he was 6 months old.) He regarded his mother as a food bank that had at all times to be at hand—either in sight or, at least, with the path to her fully mapped out. A long introductory phase to his analysis was necessary, during which time his mother always carried food for him. This concretization of the feeding source was then carried over by the analyst, who gradually was able to place the food in a cupboard, where Evan could obtain it upon demand. The "analytic" situation at this time allowed Evan a relationship with the analyst while the symbolized mother was secure and accessible in the cupboard. Later, more abstract mother symbols sufficed, e.g., a map of his house or a gum wrapper. Once Evan had achieved greater certainty in his maternal relationship, he was able to use the analyst as a transference object, projecting earlier relationships with his parents. Not only did he transfer his early attitudes toward his parents, but as his developmental inhibitions were released, the more mature relationships which developed were, in turn, reflected in the transference.

It is necessary here to note that in children with gross early fixations, in pre-Oedipal children, and at times of rapid developmental transition (for instance, in early puberty), the transference is complicated by the projection onto the analyst not only of past relationships but of developing new relational modes. Thus Evan, originally fixated on an oral and one-to-one relationship, as his development processes were released in analysis, entered a belated (age 9 years) triangular Oedipal rivalry with his father; and when he had resolved the Oedipal rivalry and repressed the sexual fantasies toward his mother, he began to treat the analyst as a rival. Evan, during his Oedipal rivalry, had refused to speak his father's native language. He attacked his father for his foreignness, contrasting his own Americanism with his father's European ways, and by the time he entered his latency, he had "forgotten" his father's language. A year later, when the repetition of the paternal rivalry with the analyst was interpreted, he suddenly "remembered" his father's language and could again speak it fluently.

Selma Fraiberg (1951, 1966) hypothesized that those affects and fantasies that have undergone full repression can have their reexpression limited to the transference situation whereas those which have not been fully repressed will often be expressed around the original parental objects.

Repression becomes the predominant defense mechanism as the child enters latency. It is the major mechanism in hysterical symptoms and character neuroses and, often, the barrier to phallic and Oedipal conflicts so prevalent in the analysis of the school-age child. Children whose main conflicts are phallic-Oedipal, who have entered latency and whose principal defense mechanism is repression, and who diagnostically show hysterical characteristics are the best candidates for child psychoanalysis. They can be treated with minimal environmental intervention and with an "open-field" analytic situation. They are capable of forming, at least at times and at least partially, a transference neurosis.

However, it would be mistaken to assume that most material brought into the analysis, even by those who are most analyzable children, is necessarily related to the analyst or, if so related, follows the characteristics of a transference neurosis. In the pre-Oedipal child almost ubiquitously, in those school-age children who have not as yet arrived at the surcease of latency, and in all children during regression induced by severe emotional stress, the analyst may directly be the target of a transference reaction. In all these instances, there is a carry-over into the analysis of displaced responses to present-day figures rather than of those repressed in the past.

> A 4-year-old boy would not or could not speak directly to his father, who had several months previously left the home. When the analyst suggested that he might be sad because his father no longer lived with him, the youngster began to berate the analyst: "You're bad; you're a bad man. I am going to kick you." The anger was a defense against the breaking down of the denial that his father was really gone. When the analyst so interpreted, the child retorted, "You're bad like my father. All husbands are bad." Here he was indicating the displacement of the rage from the father to the analyst. The next time his father visited him, he told the father to get out. He did not want him.

Later in the analysis this child insisted that the analyst become his father. The insistence on the analyst becoming a parental replacement is common in children who have lost a parent. In this case, it served other functions, namely, as a murderous attack on the real father and as a defense against his Oedipal rivalry with the analyst, as well as a boy's developmental need of a father.

The analyst is depicted in a social role compatible with the child's knowledge of social reality. This may be the analyst's own or *another social role,* e.g., doctor, teacher, counselor, nursemaid. The role into which the analyst has been cast, as well as that which the analyst may have formulated with the child, e.g., "problem doctor," serves as a background screen upon which the transference phenomena are projected. In the youngest children, this "reality" aspect of the relationship is very hazy for the child and represents the earliest maternal functions—as

the protector of the ego against overly strong stimuli and internal excitements (Winnicott, 1958).

The analyst may serve as an *externalized representative of the child's sugerego and/or id.* In the toddler, in the immature child, or in a borderline psychotic, the analyst can represent various ego faculties. Almost all children view the analyst as an authority and usually have at least a lurking notion that they are brought to him for punishment for their real or fantasied misdeeds. At times, especially with pre-Oedipal children, the sugerego and id aspects of the therapist are not delineated. These children see the analyst at once as a seducer and as an entrapper. Some children try to use the analyst as an ally against the restrictions and controls of their parents. The parents here often serve as a projective screen for the child's own overrestrictive superego. Other children use the parents to defend themselves against the drive temptations that arise during an analysis. These preobsessional or obsessional analysands may be paralyzed without direct permission from their parents to deal with themselves, with the analyst, or with their environment.

COUNTERTRANSFERENCE

Countertransference behavior colors all child analysis. The analyst's ability to realize (through self-analysis or supervision) the irrational aspects of his conduct, their source within himself, and their connection with the child's material is a keystone of a successful analysis.

Countertransference difficulties can be considered in three categories:

1. General reactions to children (essentially a countertransference reaction rather than countertransference itself)
2. Displaced reactions from the analyst's current life
3. Unresolved unconscious problems of the

analyst, often touched off by his child patient or the patient's family

Adults are often made uneasy by the impulsive behavior and labile emotionality of the child. The fear of the unanticipated may provoke the analyst to overreact, with overstructuring and overcontrol. The child's impulsivity may evoke in the analyst an unconscious desire for the child to act out the analyst's own inhibited impulses. The forms are myriad. One of the most common is the provocation of the child to show rage to his parents, which is a result of unresolved hostility in the therapist against his own parents.

Other countertransference reactions include the inability to endure anxiety or depression in a child based on reaction formation against rivalry with a sibling, identifications with a depressive parent, rage at parental separation.

THE ROLE OF THE PARENTS

The child's partially developed ego must be complemented by that of his parents. Most child analysts find it necessary to relate to one or both parents in the course of their child's analysis. Obviously, the practical arrangements, fees, and time can be settled only between adults; but more importantly, the parents usually make the original decision to seek aid and supply the force to continue the analysis should there be resistance during its initial phases. Also, it is essential to prepare the child for analysis and the parents for the management of the emotional eruptions that commonly occur during the course of the child's analysis.

The parents are, in most cases, the richest and most organized source of information for developmental data, the history of the symptomatology, the familial interrelationships, and the present adaptation and functioning of the child. Many analysts, although there is much variation, form a strong working relationship with the par-

ents by including them in their assessment of the child and in the general directions and goals of the analysis. During the early phases of the analysis, they are seen weekly or biweekly for information about the significant events in the child's life. It is uncommon for a child younger than 10 or 11 to relate systematically his extra-analytic emotional life. Without this knowledge, it is difficult to integrate the fantasy material produced in the analytic situation with the emotional interaction which may have elicited it. For example, the information garnered from the parents may be compared with the day residue in the interpretation of a dream.

Later in the analysis, the child learns to trust the analyst and to report more fully. Also, the analyst learns the characteristic affective reaction patterns and can more easily discern the source of a veering trend, an unexpected mood, or an abrupt transference shift. Hence contact with the parents, in this phase of the analysis, is less essential and is in many cases gradually attenuated and then terminated.

There are other, less tangible advantages in the analyst's relation to the parents. Some parents, usually the mothers, react as though they had lost their child to the analyst and feel empty and deserted. This separation reaction is compounded by their feelings of guilt about rearing a troubled child. Those parental affects are communicated to the child, who then reacts with guilt about his parents' suffering and attacks himself and/or projectively the analyst. Not infrequently this elicits overt antagonism or indifference by the child in the analytic relationship. Should this depressive reaction be severe, the parent must herself seek treatment with a therapist different from that of her child.

Simultaneous analysis of a mother and child, although sometimes efficacious and extremely important in the understanding of child-mother relationship (Burlingham, 1954), can create a disruptive home environment and delay both analyses. It is better for the parents to be in guidance therapy or a psychoanalytically oriented psychotherapy. If psychoanalysis for one or both parents is necessary, it is better to phase either the child's or the parents' analysis until the turmoil of the initial stages of the first analysis has subsided.

Other neurotic parental responses toward the child's analysis may create obstacles. The child's relationship with the analyst may arouse old conflicts in the parents with their own parents. Envy of the child's "favored" position can result in a mother's attempt to "invade" the analysis, e.g., demanding more time for herself or rationalizing the missing of the child's appointments or, defensively, withdrawing herself from the child. These regressive oral conflicts are sometimes accompanied by anal conflicts, such as control and manipulative maneuvers, as well as by rigidity in the face of the child's freer and more spontaneous emotionality and behavior.

Analytic motivation in children is rarely present at the induction of an analysis. The parents must exercise the initial pressure. Rather, the patient's capacity to become interested in the analytic exploration and his capacity to tolerate the discomforts (frustration tolerance) and obstacles of the analysis substitute for the testing of motivation in the adult. The child cannot conceive of the idea of disease and cure (neither the concept nor the causality involved). At best he hopes for relief from his fears by an adult in whom his parents have vested some of their now reduced omnipotence. He often taps his narcissism and becomes emotionally fascinated by the exploration of himself and intellectually interested in connections between seemingly isolated phenomena which he is able to discover. These secondary motivations emerging in the course of the analysis become part of the "alliance with the healthy part of the ego," the "therapeutic alliance" (Sterba, 1934, 1940) which helps overcome the resistances and defenses. Pride in himself

as a feeler of feelings enhances his ego strength and its tolerance even for unacceptable affects. "I am capable of hating my father." The hero is born, and rather than setting out to kill the father-dragon, his efforts are utilized to fight against the inner representation of the dangerous father. (Sandler, 1960, 1962; Fairbairn, 1952). Now he can bring out his past jealousies, his competitivenesses, his desires for his father.

Another important motivating force that develops in the course of the analysis, although originating from the earliest relations between the child and his mother, is the attachment to the analyst as an understander and a resonator of his inner feelings. Developmentally, the infant has no knowledge of what he needs to satisfy his hunger feelings and his other discomforts. The mother's "reading" of his feelings produces food or whatever she hopes will satisfy his needs. Later, her communication, verbal or nonverbal, of her understanding of his desires and emotions allows delay of their discharge. If this has taken place, it is one evidence of the shift from the need-gratifying object to object constancy (A. Freud, 1965). Certain feelings cannot and should not be "read" (empathized with) by the parents. The child's joy in immersing himself in his feces and his sexual feelings for his mother cannot enjoy this parental empathy, as they are repressed in the parents themselves. Should the parent consistently, as happens in analytically sophisticated households, intellectually formulate these feelings, it focuses attention on the child's inner life, fixates rather than solves the conflicts inherent in such affects, supports the pleasure principle over the reality principle, and fixates the child to his parents. The analyst is desirous, in contradistinction to the parents, of exploring the inner life, and this "emotional feeding" serves both as fuel and as an entrée into the underlying defenses and conflicts (Bornstein, 1949).

The child's motivation, in the sense of his desire for treatment, is not nearly as important as his capacity to delay discharge, accept affects as part of himself, and continue to relate to the analyst despite strong conflicts. Should these be sufficiently developed, the motivations for treatment blend with the analytic process itself.

CHILD PSYCHOANALYTIC SITUATION

The child usually sees the analytic situation as punishment for his guilty impulses and feels guilty for causing anxiety in his parents. He is faced at frequent (four to five times per week) intervals by a stranger about whose expectations he is unfamiliar. Yet, unless there is a psychotic detachment, the child will draw on his earlier parental experiences to form a relationship. The relational polarity may be positive or negative, submissive or aggressive, frank or hidden. These attitudes become the basis of the unconscious, "irrational" facet of the therapeutic alliance.

The child's preparation for the analysis and the work of its earliest phase represent what might be called the "rational" facet of the therapeutic alliance. Proper preparation can clarify for the child a communality of interest and purpose between the child and the analyst. A contract is entered, under which the child will permit observation of his play, his words, his dreams and daydreams in order to find the source of his worries, of his unhappy feelings, of his feeling bad about himself. The analyst, on his part, contracts (covertly) to accompany the child in this search and be present for the child when fearful and dangerous impulses and thoughts emerge. The major objective in this initial phase is to create some distance and perspective between the conscious ego and the neurotic symptomatology and/or behavior. It is, in this sense, a reworking of the original ego defense mechanisms which unconsciously attempted to create a distance and a modulation of the original drives. Here one tries to convey to the child that the bothersome feelings and actions are at once part of him and yet able to be viewed (as the "me") with some detachment (by the "I").

Piaget (Wolff, 1960) has observed that children below the age of 6 or 7 years do not have the cognitive development to be able to describe an object from different vantage points. They cannot, imaginatively, reposition themselves. Psychoanalysis has taught us that the id and ego are not fully differentiated until about the same age, i.e., with the onset of the latency period, and that more complete neutralization of language itself, which permits words to be readily shifted from one level of abstract feelings and thoughts to another, begins in preadolescence and is completed by early adolescence. Therefore, the stage of development, as well as the personality and pathology, will determine not only the analytic technique employed but also the level of the "rational" therapeutic alliance.

In the prelatency child the therapeutic alliance and the transference proper are formed simultaneously. The major technique here is the formulation of suppressed, displaced, or reversed affects (Bornstein, 1949). The use of the child's name—"Peter has a Mommy gone feeling," "Peter is saying that he gets mad (feels like hitting) when sister touches his toys"—begins to create a third being partly related to Peter's feelings, actions, and play and partly related to Peter's and the analyst's observations of Peter's affects and impulses. Observing oneself then gradually becomes incorporated into the child's own ego functioning. The reciprocal process of relating the child's pretense and dramatic play to the child's own fantasy and the underlying drives can then proceed; the child's demonstrations and observations intertwine with the analyst's interpretations.

Mark, a 3-year-old, entered analysis because of compulsive excoriation of his skin. His constricted emotionality was evident from the set, frozen expression on his face. He began his analysis by a listless play with the doll family. No trend was obvious in the play except that the baby doll was frequently dropped and run over. Once this "accident" occurred, Mark would look bewildered and stop the play. "Mark did not like the new baby to be in the family." Mark caressed the baby. "It feels cuddly and good when someone pats Mark's skin." Mark looked at his arm and said, "My skin is no good; it's all scratched up. Paul [his 2-year-old brother] scratches it." "Mark gets very mad inside at Paul." Mark put his head next to the analyst.

For the next several sessions, Mark alternately vented his rage at the brother doll and pretended to scratch his own skin. Mark had become more animated and regaled the analyst with stories of Paul's malefactions, Paul's spankings, Paul's crying. By the thirtieth session, the analyst was able to formulate Mark's sadness whenever his mother turned her attention from himself to Paul. Mark answered: "Not sadness; hungriness."

LATE CHILDHOOD AND ADOLESCENCE

Latency children have gained the cognitive capacity to view themselves as others see them and can have achieved a psychic development with the internalization of the superego and the ego-ideal, potentially capable of self-observation and self-critique. The principles and precepts of child analysis were originally formulated with children of this age group, 7 to 11 years of age. This group constitutes the majority of patients treated by the methods of child analysis.

Children of this age who have developed a psychoneurosis not only suffer anxiety but also feel bad about their symptoms, and their symptoms make them feel bad, that is, lower their self-esteem. The narcissistic injury stems in part from the guilt of the pathogenic conflict and also from the threat to the ego integration and synthesis as well as to the observation of difference from their coevals. The polarities of operational and observing ego; of the good and bad parts of the self; of affects, thoughts, and actions within

awareness and control and those beyond volition; of causal chains of events and disruption in the linkages; of the pleasures and anxieties of fantasy differentiated from the satisfactions and fears of reality are all, at least potentially, within the mental grasp of the latency child. The symptoms and aberrant character traits are, or during the course of the analysis become, *ego-dystonic,* and the search for their causation and alleviation form the nexus of the therapeutic alliance between the child and his analyst. Play becomes more purposeful—less a part of the child and more his instrument. Words and understanding gradually replace dramatization and action as the child gains insight into unconscious affect fantasies and drives.

In preadolescence, the psychoanalytic situation is different from that with the latency child. Spoken language for the most part replaces dramatic play. The age-appropriate tendency for assertiveness and aggressiveness in reality (Deutsch, 1944) serves as an additional resistance to the production of fantasy and other inner thoughts and sentiments. The dependency component is frequently resisted. Should it not be, the analyst is commonly related to as a model, displaced from the parent. Under these circumstances, the negative aspects of the transference remain hidden, transference dissolution is difficult, and the analysis is abruptly terminated by the patient with the onset of pubescence. However, despite these difficulties, it is important to accomplish as much analytic work as possible because of the obstacles to analysis in the early adolescent. It is often necessary to introduce technical modifications; constructive projects, literature, playwriting, etc., congruent with the child's special interests and aptitudes may constitute the early core of the analysis around which both the relationship is developed and the fantasies can be elicited.

Child analysis, like its adult counterpart, may be described as a special technique for the treatment of psychoneuroses and some personality and behavior disorders. Its influence, however, extends into almost all other clinical and scientific areas dealing with the psychology of childhood and the development of the child. Child analysis is the base from which the most widely practiced child psychotherapies are derived. In all therapies, transference manifestations must be understood and utilized and countertransference difficulties minimized. Facets of the analytic method are emphasized and/or restricted in specialized therapeutic techniques: release therapy—catharsis and mastery (Levy, 1939); guidance—formulation and intellectual understanding; corrective object relations—identification (A. Alpert, 1959); corrective emotional experience—regressive and progressive development (Alexander, 1946).

CHILD OBSERVATION

Child analysis and direct child observation (A. Freud, 1951; E. Kris, 1950) reciprocally influence each other in the study of the development and maturation of the child. Child observation permits the study of the developmental origins in the first two to three years of life, a most crucial era from which child analysis is excluded. Counterwise, child analysis is able to penetrate the inner life of the child—the sentience, the feelings, the fantasies, and the hidden motivations which accompany and affect the external stimuli and his outer behavior. Observation is the inspective arm; psychoanalysis, the introspective.

The application of knowledge garnered from psychoanalysis to enhance the development of the normal child and to ameliorate his psychic discomforts is both complex and controversial. We have learned that some conflicts are inherent in maturation, and attempts to encourage the child to avoid rather than resolve these conflicts often backfire. Delayed ego development, with poor tension and frustration tolerance, may be

the price paid for the relief of neurotic anxiety. Nevertheless, a knowledge of psychoanalytic principles and findings is an essential in the armamentarium for those professionals who accept the responsibility of planning for the education and emotional welfare of children. The discoveries of child analysis have opened avenues beyond psychological treatment to the awareness of the vicissitudes of the normally developing child.

REFERENCES

Abbate, G. M. (Reporter) Panel on child analysis: Different developmental stages. *Journal of the American Psychoanalytic Association,* 1964, **12,** 135–150.

Alexander, F., et al. *Psychoanalytic therapy.* New York: Ronald, 1946.

Alpert, A. *Reversibility of pathological fixations.* Vol. 14. *The psychoanalytic study of the child.* New York: International Universities Press, 1959.

Balint, M. Sandor Ferenczi's technical experiments. In B. B. Wolman (Ed.), *Psychoanalytic techniques.* New York: Basic Books, 1967.

Becker, T. E. (Reporter) Panel on latency. *Journal of the American Psychoanalytic Association,* 1965, **13,** 584–590.

Bornstein, B. *Clinical notes on child analysis.* Vol. 1. *The psychoanalytic study of the child.* New York: International Universities Press, 1945.

Bornstein, B. *The analysis of a phobic child.* Vols. 3–4. *The psychoanalytic study of the child.* New York: International Universities Press, 1949.

Bornstein, B. *On latency.* Vol. 7. *The psychoanalytic study of the child.* New York: International Universities Press, 1951.

Bornstein, B. *Fragments of analysis of an obses-*

sional child. Vol. 8. *The psychoanalytic study of the child.* New York: International Universities Press, 1953.

Bowlby, W. Maternal care and mental health. *World Health Organization Monograph, Geneva,* 1951, No. 2.

Bowlby, W. The nature of the child's tie to his mother. *International Journal of Psychoanalysis,* 1958, **39,** 350–373.

Burlingham, D. Simultaneous analysis of mother and child. In M. Haworth (Ed.), *Child psychotherapy.* New York: Basic Books, 1954.

Burlingham, D. Child analyst and the mother. In M. Haworth (Ed.), *Child psychotherapy.* New York: Basic Books, 1964.

Deutsch, H. The psychology of women. Vol. 1. New York: Grune & Stratton, 1944.

Ekstein, K., & Friedman, S. W. The foundation of acting out, play action and play acting in the psychoanalytic process. *Journal of the American Psychoanalytic Association,* 1957, **5,** 581–629.

Ekstein, K., & Wallenstein, R. S. *The teaching and learning of psychotherapy.* New York: Basic Books, 1958.

Erikson, E. H. *Childhood and society.* New York: Norton, 1950.

Erikson, E. H. Identity in the life cycle. In G. S. Klein (Ed.), *Psychological issues.* No. 1. New York: International Universities Press, 1959.

Fairbairn, W. R. D. *Psychoanalytic studies of personality.* London: Tavistock, 1952.

Ferenczi, S. On forced fantasies. (1924) In *Further contributions to the theory and techniques of psychoanalysis.* New York: Basic Books, 1950.

Ferenczi, S. Child analysis in the analysis of adults. (1931) In *Further contributions to problems and methods of psychoanalysis.* New York: Basic Books, 1955.

Fraiberg, S. *Clinical notes on the nature of transference in child analysis.* Vol. 6. *The psychoanalytic study of the child.* New York: International Universities Press, 1951.

Fraiberg, S. Technical aspects of the analysis of a child. *Journal of the American Psychoanalytic Association,* 1962, **10,** 338–367.

Fraiberg, S. *Further considerations of the role of transference and latency.* Vol. 21. *The psychoanalytic study of the child.* New York: International Universities Press, 1966.

Fraiberg, S. Problems of transference in child analysis. *Journal of the American Psychoanalytic Association,* 1966, **14,** 528–537.

Fraiberg, S. *Further considerations of the role of transference in latency.* Vol. 21. *The psychoanalytic study of the child.* New York: International Universities Press, 1966.

Freud, A. *Indications for child analysis.* Vol. 1. *The psychoanalytic study of the child.* New York: International Universities Press, 1945.

Freud, A. *The psychoanalytic treatment of children.* (1926) New York: International Universities Press, 1946. (a)

Freud, A. *Ego and mechanisms of defense.* (1936) New York: International Universities Press, 1946. (b)

Freud, A. *Observations on child development.* Vol. 6. *The psychoanalytic study of the child.* New York: International Universities Press, 1951.

Freud, A. *Some remarks on infant development.* Vol. 8. *The psychoanalytic study of the child.* New York: International Universities Press, 1953.

Freud, A. *Psychoanalysis and education.* Vol. 9. *The psychoanalytic study of the child.* New York: International Universities Press, 1954.

Freud, A. *Assessment of childhood disturbances.* Vol. 17. *The psychoanalytic study of the child.* New York: International Universities Press, 1962.

Freud, A. *The concept of developmental lines.* Vol. 8. *The psychoanalytic study of the child.* New York: International Universities Press, 1963.

Freud, A. *Normality and pathology in childhood: Assessments of development.* New York: International Universities Press, 1965.

Freud, S. *Dynamics of transference.* (1912) Vol. 2. *Collected Papers.* London: Hogarth, 1948.

Freud, S. *Analysis terminable and interminable.* (1937) Vol. 5. *Collected Papers.* London: Hogarth, 1950. (a)

Freud, S. *The interpretation of dreams.* (1901) Vol. 5. *Collected Papers.* London: Hogarth, 1950. (b)

Freud, S. *Inhibitions, symptoms and anxiety.* (1926) Vol. 20. (Standard ed.) London: Hogarth, 1951.

Freud, S. *Analysis of a phobia in a five-year-old boy* (1909). Vol. 10. (Standard ed.) London: Hogarth, 1955. (a)

Freud, S. *From the history of an infantile neurosis.* (1918) Vol. 17. (Standard ed.) London: Hogarth, 1955. (b)

Freud, S. *The ego and the id.* (1923) Vol. 19. (Standard ed.) London: Hogarth, 1961.

Geleerd, E. R. *The psychoanalysis of a psychotic child.* Vol. 2. *The psychoanalytic study of the child.* New York: International Universities Press, 1946.

Geleerd, E. R. (Ed.) *The child analyst at work.* New York: International Universities Press, 1967.

Glover, E. *Examination of the Kleinian systems of child analysis.* Vol. 1. *The psychoanalytic study of the child.* New York: International Universities Press, 1945.

Goldfarb, W. Variations in adolescent adjustment of institutionally reared children. *American Journal of Orthopsychiatry*, 1947, **17**.

Hartman, H. *Psychoanalysis and developmental psychology.* Vol. 5. *The psychoanalytic study of the child.* New York: International Universities Press, 1950.

Hartman, H. *Mutual influences in development of ego and id.* Vol. 8. *The psychoanalytic study of the child.* New York: International Universities Press, 1952.

Hartman, H. *Ego psychology and the problems of adaptation.* (1939) New York: International Universities Press, 1958.

Hartman, H., & Kris, E. *The genetic approach in psychoanalysis.* Vol. 1. *The psychoanalytic study of the child.* New York: International Universities Press, 1945.

Hoffer, W. *Mouth, hand and ego integration.* Vols. 3–4. *The psychoanalytic study of the child.* New York: International Universities Press, 1949.

Hoffer, W. *Mutual influences in development of ego and id: Earlier stages.* Vol. 7. *The psychoanalytic study of the child.* New York: International Universities Press, 1952.

Klein, M. *The psychoanalysis of children.* (1932) London: Hogarth, 1949.

Klein, M. On the development of mental functioning. *International Journal of Psychoanalysis,* 1958, **39**, 84–90.

Klein, M. *Narrative of a child's analysis.* London: Hogarth, 1961.

Klein, M., Heiman, P., Isaacs, S., & Riviere, J. *Developments in psychoanalysis.* London: Hogarth, 1952.

Kris, E. *Notes on development.* Vol. 5 *The psychoanalytic study of the child.* New York: International Universities Press, 1950.

Lesser, S. *Derivatives of a constitutional deviation,* in press.

Levy, D. M. Release therapy. *American Journal of Orthopsychiatry,* 1939, **9.**

Mahler, M. Autism and symbiosis. *International Journal of Psychoanalysis,* 1958, **39,** 77–83.

Mahler, M. *On human symbiosis and the vicissitudes of individuation.* New York: International Universities Press, 1968.

Nagera, H. *The developmental profile: Notes on some practical considerations regarding its use.* Vol. 18. *The psychoanalytic study of the child.* New York: International Universities Press, 1963.

Nagera, H. *Early childhood disturbances.* Monograph 2. *The psychoanalytic study of the child.* New York: International Universities Press, 1966.

Pearson, G. H. J. *A handbook of child psychoanalysis.* New York: Basic Books, 1968.

Peller, L. *Libidinal phases, ego development and play.* Vol. 9. *The psychoanalytic study of the child.* New York: International Universities Press, 1954.

Piaget, J. *The origins of intelligence in children.* (1936) New York: International Universities Press, 1952.

Piaget, J. *The construction of reality in the child.* (1937) New York: Basic Books, 1954.

Provence, S., & Lipton, R. C. *Infants in institutions.* New York: International Universities Press, 1962.

Reich, W. *Character analysis.* (1933) New York: Orgone Press, 1949.

Sandler, J. *On the concept of superego.* Vol. 15. *The psychoanalytic study of the child.* New York: International Universities Press, 1960.

Sandler, J., & Rosenblatt, B. *The concept of the representational world.* Vol. 17. *The psychoanalytic study of the child.* New York: International Universities Press, 1962.

Segal, H. Melanie Klein's technique. In B. B. Wolman (Ed.), *Psychoanalytic techniques.* New York: Basic Books, 1967.

Spitz, R. A. *Hospitalism.* Vol. 2. *The psychoanalytic study of the child.* New York: International Universities Press, 1945.

Spitz, R. A. Countertransference. *Journal of the American Psychoanalytic Association,* 1956, **4,** 256–265.

Sterba, R. The fate of the ego in analytic therapy. *International Journal of Psychoanalysis,* 1934, **5.**

Sterba, R. The dynamics of the dissolution of the transference resistance. (1929) *Psychiatric Quarterly,* 1940, **9.**

Sylvester, E. *Discussion of techniques used to prepare young children for analysis.* Vol. 7. *The psychoanalytic study of the child.* New York: International Universities Press, 1952.

Van Dam, H. (Reporter) Problems of transference in child analysis. *Journal of the American Psychoanalytic Association,* 1966, **14,** 528.- 537.

Weiss, S., et al. Technique of child analysis: The problems of the opening phase. *Journal of the American Academy of Child Psychiatry,* 1968, **7** (4).

Winnicott, D. W. Transitional objects and transitional phenomena. *International Journal of Psychoanalysis,* 1953, **34.**

Winnicott, D. W. *Collected papers.* New York: Basic Books, 1958.

Wolff, P. H. Developmental psychologies of Jean Piaget and psychoanalysis. In G. S. Klein (Ed.), *Psychological issues.* No. 5. New York: International Universities Press, 1960.

Zetzel, E. R. Current concepts of transference. *International Journal of Psychoanalysis,* 1956, **37.**

28 Non-Freudian Methods of Psychoanalysis with Children and Adolescents

Albert Bryt

FRAMEWORK AND SCOPE

Sine Qua Non *of Psychoanalysis*

In 1914, Sigmund Freud (1957b) quite properly claimed that psychoanalysis was his "creation" and that therefore no one could "know better than I do what psychoanalysis is" (p. 7). Hence, the psychoanalytic methods discussed in this presentation not only should be relevant to the treatment of children and adolescents but also should satisfy two preconditions held essential to the use of this quasi-protected term. They should postulate unconscious mental activity "peculiar to psychoanalysis" (*ibid.*, p. 16) and acknowledge "two striking and unexpected facts of observation" *(ibid.),* namely, transference and resistance. Differences in other aspects of theory would still satisfy his criteria for: "Any line of investigation which recognizes these two facts and takes them as the starting point of its work has a right to call itself psychoanalysis, even though it arrives at results other than my own" *(ibid.)* In so establishing the framework for this essay, it is not with the expectation of stilling all controversy. This may not be possible except through the strictest adherence to what may appear as a dogma.[1]

NON-FREUDIAN PSYCHOANALYSIS

The authors whose views are included do not subscribe to Freud's formulation of infantile sexuality. Nor do they hold that neurotic conflicts are solely expressive of the vicissitudes in the child's psychosexual development. Hence, the term *non-Freudian* here is meant to refer to psychodynamic theories other than the libido theory.

However, it is less the uniform disagreement with Freud's postulates which prompts the present grouping. It is less the absence of the pursuit of the regressive transference neurosis (Thompson, 1950, p. 234) as the cornerstone of the

---

[1] The following quote from a recent book review may serve as an illustrative documentation: "David Rapaport, like his main source of inspiration, Heinz Hartmann, has undermined many of Freud's original conceptions. The future of psychoanalysis depends, in my opinion, on Freud's conceptions being first of all preserved, and then built upon." [Zelmanowitz, 1968, p. 299.]

analysis. Rather, these non-Freudian theories recognize a variety of etiological factors in the genesis of the neurotic personality. They value the importance of the present, the here and now, including the analytic situation as a real situation. They pay attention to the patient-doctor relationship, not limited to the analysis of the transference (Jung, 1933, p. 49). They agree on the "basic direction forward of the organism" (Sullivan, 1947, p. 48), the tendency of the personality toward mental health. They are also alert to the neurotogenic property of anxiety (Horney, 1937, p. 101) and to the consequent neglect of personal potentials for the sake of protective cultural uniformity (Schachtel, 1959, p. 185).

The stress on "outer" threats to self-fulfilling personality development may be found as one unifying element. Another is the preponderance of interest in feeling and experiencing, in emotional action and interaction of the patient and his environment, not omitting the reality of the analytic situation. The need for authenticity of the analyst's human reactions is but a third distinguishing and unifying feature.

Thus an ensemble of theories can be recognized, each of which leads to a therapeutic technique which is likely to provide a climate favorable for a corrective emotional and therapeutic experience for a child who suffers from his inability to rely on others and to predict their reactions realistically.

Non-Freudian theories on childhood development, akin to Freud's theories, are based on inferences and on interpolations.

PSYCHOANALYSIS WITH CHILDREN AND ADOLESCENTS

Psychoanalytic treatment of children and adolescents may be traced to the 1920s with Hug-Hellmuth, Bernheim, and Aichhorn, all followers of Freud's theories. Non-Freudian modes of child and adolescent analysis were introduced at about the same time by Alfred Adler and the creation, under his impetus, of child-guidance clinics in Vienna. Carl Jung also applied his theories to the analysis of patients in these age groups. Frances Wickes, one of the early adherents of analytical psychology, devoted her work more exclusively to them.

The broader application of non-Freudian theories to the analysis of children and adolescents, however, is a more recent phenomenon. It came with the New York split in American psychoanalysis in the 1940s, the establishment of psychoanalytic training institutes outside of the American Psychoanalytic Association, and the eventual organization of the American Academy of Psychoanalysis in 1956 (Millet, 1966).

Publications, more so in child than in adolescent analysis, over the last fifteen years, cannot always be sorted with comfortable certainty as to the authors' fundamental theoretical positions, Freudian or other. It is as though a cross-fertilization of ideas, back and forth, had taken place, during which "trademark" identifications, mostly linguistic in nature, became lost.

At present one need not be a Jungian or follow Horney's or Fromm's thinking in order to accept the working hypothesis that the manifestations of a child's neurotic difficulties interfere with his creative self-realization. Freudian analysts show concern with interpersonal conflicts without indicating whether they have been inspired by Sullivan. Sullivanians use the terms *transference* and *ego* instead of *parataxic distortions* and *self* and may have lost the precise meaning of the concepts out of their own vocabulary.

No longer is individuation credited to the Jungian framework, nor sibling rivalry or inferiority feelings to that of Adler. Separation anxiety has ceased to be identified with Rank's thesis of the birth trauma, and the adaptational viewpoint may be espoused by many who omit to consider Rado as the originator of this particular approach. Basic anxiety has become a byword of psychoanalysis, though Horney is not always identified with the concept. The conceptualization of adolescence into early, mid, and late adolescence, following Sullivan's observations, has been quite generally adopted.

There is other evidence bearing testimony to the readiness for modification—or "deviationist tendency," as some might call it—of practice, if not of theory, by child analysts. Anna Freud's (1948) classical contribution is a case in point, particularly if viewed retrospectively, at the time of its first publication in 1937. More recently a number of publications in the psychoanalytic study of the child might almost have come from the pens of non-Freudians were it not for some characteristic phraseology (Beres, 1958; Olden, 1958; Spiegel, 1967).

Thus, a variety of reasons concur in dictating not to attempt a presentation of distinct current practices of the different non-Freudian "schools" of psychoanalytic thought. Therefore, in this essay, contributions from several of the more important non-Freudian viewpoints will be discussed with a view to their relevance to the psychoanalysis of children and adolescents.

The elaboration of analytic techniques with adolescents, though having its beginnings contemporaneously with child analysis, was longer in the making and encountered more formidable obstacles. Adler's work with this age group was limited. Jung had stressed primarily the importance of the age of adolescence for the first experience of neurotic difficulties, thus implying the possibility of treatment.

But there was also the impression, until Sullivan made his important contributions, that adolescence was but a transient phase of revival of infantile conflicts. It had been noted, furthermore, that adolescent patients could not be counted upon to develop a transference neurosis or to obey the fundamental rule of psychoanalysis, both held to be conditions *sine qua non* for effective therapy.

This viewpoint, which may still be shared by some, judged adolescents to be unsuitable for analysis lest one succeed in a first phase of treatment "of making the delinquent analyzable, that is to say neurotic" (Eissler, 1958, p. 231). Thus, then, the analyst must fulfill a dual role: the more difficult one of transforming the patient's character difficulties into a psychoneurotic conflict and, only then, the one of applying analytic treatment proper (Society for Adolescent Psychiatry, 1959).

DEPARTURE FROM CLASSICAL CONCEPTS

It is remarkable that in the face of so much, and so well-engrained, pessimism, modifications in analytic technique appropriate to the treatment of adolescents were eventually established. It seems impossible to trace whence the impetus came. But is is fair to assume that the ferment within psychoanalysis itself lent it strength. The separation between Freud and his earliest followers, Adler and Jung, needs to be mentioned here. Also, the revolutionary suggestions for reforms in technique advanced, and then toned down, by Ferenczi (1952b) but carried forward by Rank (1945) belong here. Lastly, the determined innovations advanced by Wilhelm Reich (1949) undoubtedly had their impact.

It is also fair to assume that without a parochial stubbornness, almost pathognomonic of psychoanalysis, these changes might have been more generally adopted much earlier. But here were Freud's early associates, and others as well, whose main concern for some time seems to have been to disassociate themselves from him. Much effort must have been spent to tease out differences, to refute established theories, and to justify a new name, maybe only for the sake of personal pride, thereby making the consideration, let alone the adoption, of new theories and practices a question of loyalty.

THE NON-FREUDIANS

Adler found it necessary to call his system *individual psychology*; Jung, to christen his *analytical psychology*. Both made telling contributions. In so doing, they found themselves partly forced to taint them, but in part, they seem to have delighted in tainting them. This may seem less true for Rank, yet in creating his *will therapy*, he took a long step away from the Freudian schemata and, by the same stroke, aimed at demolishing Adler and Jung as well. This in no way diminishes the importance of his contribution, adopted since then by many, which draws attention to the fundamental trauma of the physical separation at birth of the infant from the mother.

Psychoanalysis, in the course of its development and as a result of the recognition of the impact of social and cultural forces on personality formation, had moved away substantially from the biological orientation which had been so prominent in Freud's earliest writings. This may have been one reason which prompted Rado to emphasize the interplay of the physiological and the psychological forces in determining human behavior. His body of theory stresses biological forces more than any of the other theories do. Whether this necessitated a new name, *adaptational psychodynamics*, is a question which need not be answered here.

None of the authors have failed to present cogent justifications for rejecting the label *psychoanalysis*. No more, in any event, than the psychoanalytic movement failed to advance plausible reasons for rejecting these contributions as not being germane to the existing body of theories. Possibly on these grounds, but more especially because of his empirical and operational orientation, Sullivan found it in order to redefine the field as the *study of interpersonal relations*. In so doing, he meant, first of all, to lay the foundations for a scientific validation of psychological hypotheses.

A distinction may be in order between those authors who departed early from the Freudian fold and the others who made their contributions within the last three decades (though Rado and Sullivan fit neither with one group nor the other). Those who departed earlier—Adler, Jung, and also Rank—seem to have carried out a rebellious move; they are, and they wanted to be, deviationists. Therefore, they needed a new name. This view is also Glover's (1945). The more recently elaborated differences with Freud's theories—those of Fromm, Horney, and Schachtel—appear more like modifications, built on Freud's postulates, consistent with Guntrip's (1961) and Thompson's (1950) views.

In any event, what have been called *splinter groups* in the United States have also formed abroad. From among the authors who seem to have been most intent on disassociating themselves not only from the theory but from the name as well, Schultz-Hencke, mentioned by Horney (1937) and given a place of importance by Wyss (1966), stands out. His ideas are similar to those advanced by Fromm, Horney, and Sullivan. Schultz-Hencke pleads for a recognition of the flexibility of adaptation inherent in the human being. This view, quite important in child and in adolescent analysis, is in diametrical opposition to Freud's. Wyss quotes him as saying (p. 291): "And man is a creature who is quite happy to abandon one form of gratification, which has been rendered loathsome to him, and turn to another, which at that particular time contains no menace." This is a unique position in psychoanalysis, which deserves further exploration in order to determine what accounts for the interference with this readiness. In the theoretical frameworks of other authors, substitutions are said to impair satisfaction, at least partially. In any event, Schultz-Hencke would belong among the non-Freudian analysts grouped in this study by virtue of the importance he gives to "expressive tendencies," self-expression and self-realization.

The challenge to and the rejection of some original formulations of Freudian psychoanalysis have not led all innovators to either minimize their differences or repudiate the name.

Fromm, Horney, Schachtel, and Thompson may be counted among the outstanding analysts who, building on the original framework, have made significant contributions relevant to child and adolescent analysis.

Though these authors had no other choice, ethically, but to separate themselves from the analytic establishment, they continued to credit Freud as the originator in the field. They also suggested the modifications of his contributions in the name of psychoanalysis, almost unperturbed by the ostracism from their erstwhile colleagues.

Horney was probably the most outspoken and certainly among the most militant critics of traditional psychoanalysis. Her holistic theory belongs in the context of this inquiry (Kelman, 1949; Rubins, 1967).

Fromm's (1964) appreciation of the mother-child relationship for the transmission of cultural values (pp. 201–342) is essential for an understanding of character formation. The work with adolescent patients is particularly apt to benefit from it. It is remarkable, though, that Fromm in his own writings barely mentions adolescence and seemingly fails to recognize the very important changes and solidifications of character structure occurring at that time.

This is different with Thompson (1964). Sharing Horney's views, she took a fresh and fairly exhaustive look at feminine psychology, especially as it crystallizes during adolescence (pp. 298–320). The care with which she considered the limits of knowledge available to her is remarkable. The absence of sweeping general-izations and her attempts at extrapolating known variables lend a refreshing quality to her communications.

Schachtel's (1959) comprehensive presentation of a theory on affects (pp. 19–77) touches on a topic long neglected in non-Freudian psychoanalysis. In combination with his observations on "attention and memory" (pp. 251–322), he adds substantial information useful in work with children and adolescents. Moreover, he presents a framework which finds useful application in programs for the promotion of positive mental health (Bryt, 1971).

OTHER INNOVATORS

Before undertaking a more detailed review of non-Freudian methods, let us look briefly at some dimensions of the topic which will not be covered.

Where do Melanie Klein's theories find their place? She and her followers seem to think of themselves as Freudians. But are they? They espouse the libido theory and Freud's theory of the development, structure, and dynamics of the personality, and they subscribe to Freud's theory of drive and affects (Klein, 1950). But they also have been rejected by some prominent Freudians (Glover, 1945) on the grounds that they "have reduced to complete confusion the basic Freudian concepts . . ." (p. 116). They concern themselves with the nature of "object relations" and with the interpersonal experiences which are influenced by and in turn influence the "internal world he (the child) is building up" (Klein, 1955, p. 21). A similarity to Adler's and to Sullivan's formulations can be recognized. Should they therefore be placed within the interpersonal school of psychoanalysis?

Melanie Klein and her students also emphasize inborn tendencies and the role of instincts in the determination of childhood actions and reactions, postulating the existence of a well-established and actively functioning ego and superego within the first year of life. This, in fact, separates them from the Freudians, as it does from the non-Freudians. So it seems to make sense for them to remain Kleinians.

How should one classify Erik Homburger Erikson? Is he a non-Freudian? He holds (Erikson, 1950) that Freud's libido theory tries to explain human behavior in terms of automatic responses to mythical libidinal drives. He also cautions that "we must become sensitive to the danger of forcing living persons into the role of marionettes of a mythical Eros . . ." (p. 60). (Horney has taken a similar position.) He speaks of childhood development as having to conform to roles imposed by the culture, though those may be inimical to mental health. (Jung and Fromm have taken a similar position.) He also clearly differs with Freud's hedonistic viewpoint.

Erikson describes adolescence as an age where personal identity evolves definitively. (So does Sullivan.) He also sees the adolescent as having to arrive at a definition of self, not just in terms of yesterday but in terms of a new, emancipating differentiation. (This is a position close to Sullivan's and to Jung's.)

Or is Erikson a Freudian? One cannot miss recognizing his pointed efforts to reconcile his presentation with the basic tenets of Freud's libido theory (Erikson, 1959, p. 101).

Similar problems arise with regard to some authors from the so-called English School — Fairbairn, Guntrip, and Winnicott, to name but those whose writing on childhood could be examined.

Some brief references may illustrate the point. Fairbairn (1954) seems to present certain Jungian insights in the Freudian framework from a position which resembles that of Melanie Klein. His terminology is Freudian. Yet he has "come to adopt underlying scientific principles which differ from his (Freud's). It is the accompaniment of

the similarity of method by a difference of underlying principle that accounts for the fact that my views simultaneously correspond and diverge from his" (p. 149). He praises Melanie Klein's views as an advance in the development of psychoanalysis. He adopts her views on the paranoid and schizoid positions, but he objects to her acceptance of Freud's hedonistic viewpoint.

His original contribution stems from his major concern with object relations. Thus he speaks of a "breast phase" rather than of an "oral phase" in the infant's development. Therapeutic implications are clearly contained in his view on the separate effects of the maternal love for the child and the acceptance of the child's love by the mother (*ibid.*, p.163).

While not parallel, Winnicott's (1965) and Guntrip's (1961) views would lend themselves to comparable appraisals. Both, even more so than Fairbairn, are concerned with the study of psychodynamic theories, with "a practical aim in view, namely its ultimate bearing on the problem of psychotherapy" (Guntrip, 1961, p. 34). Winnicott also offers some interesting observations on the importance to the child of the mother-father relationship.

It is obvious, therefore, that the choice of authors to be included here must be arbitrary, guided by the purpose of presenting non-Freudian methods of psychoanalysis, not to offer an analysis of the departures from original Freudian theories and their technical applications.

THEORIES AND CLINICAL PRACTICE

An earlier observation bears repeating in this context, albeit with a slightly different focus. In child and in adolescent analysis, there seems to be only little reliable correspondence between clinical practice and the practitioner's commitment to one fundamental theory. The clear-cut development of distinctly individualized schools of practice seems to have spared child and adolescent analysis—except, possibly, for the Kleinians.

SELF-REALIZATION, A UNIFYING PRINCIPLE

A therapeutic technique seems to have evolved, eclectic almost, drawing on several theoretical conceptualizations. The guiding principle seems to be to arrive at a technical approach appropriate to the situation presented and conducive to the correction of neurotic warp and to the unfolding of the child's potentials for self-realization.

Certain therapeutic practices seem to be shared by most analysts: for instance, play therapy with children, following Melanie Klein's refinements of Hug-Hellmuth's technique (Klein, 1955); or the more active interaction of analyst and adolescent patient, in line with Ferenczi's *active therapy* (Ferenczi, 1952a, 1952b) and corresponding to Sullivan's conceptual model of the "participant observer" (Sullivan, 1954, pp. 103–104); or yet the "collaborative investigation" by the two participants (Bryt, 1966, p. 80) in the treatment.

Writings in child and adolescent analysis are replete with theoretical abstractions. Accounts of actual therapeutic transactions between analyst and patient are rare. This contributes to the fact that the views presented here are largely based on personal impressions, as gleaned from the literature and from conversations with colleagues.

Research in child development, and in child psychiatry in general, longitudinal studies now covering more than twenty years, and some carefully designed experiments have recently been reported in the *Review of Child Development Research* (1964). These concern themselves with the testing and reevaluation of a number of important and fundamental theories in child psy-

choanalysis. The data presented shed some light on the natural history of human psychological development and operations. Allowances must be made for the fact that neither the findings nor their interpretations can be free from bias. Nonetheless, there does not seem to be any evidence for an attempt to have preconceptions confirmed. The overall impression, therefore, is that no theory of child development seems accurate in most of its essential aspects. On the other hand, it would appear that as many essential aspects of a given theory have been verified as have not. There seems enough evidence, though, to support the thesis that the interaction of the organism and its environment is of prime importance, within certain limits, irrespective of organic, biological endowment.

Such findings support the impression that no one theoretical framework guarantees better therapeutic results than another. In a given analytic situation, the therapeutic technique used may appear closer to one theoretical conceptualization than to another. But the same analyst in a different situation may use a technical approach more congenial with another theory. In either instance, he may have applied primary theoretical convictions different from his own. This seems to be more often the case in the analysis of adolescents than in work with children.

THE CONCEPTS OF TRANSFERENCE AND RESISTANCE

Nonetheless, significant differences in conceptualization do exist and may affect treatment. An examination of the concepts of resistance and transference may serve as an illustration.

Resistance implies attack and defense. Depending on what is attacked and what defended against, the action may seem welcome or undesirable. An important concept in the Freudian framework, the phenomenon of resistance has received close attention in non-Freudian psychoanalysis as well.

Seen in the light of Levy's (1956) comments on infantile negativism, resistance becomes a "protective and self-propelling function that enables the child to overcome infantile dependency" (p. 126). Without it, the neurotic child feels endangered and is left with only one alternative, namely, his submission and subserviance to the analyst's powerful authority. Thus a situation might find itself repeated that is similar to the one in which the child may be expected to have found himself with his mother. Given these circumstances, the resistance may deserve support as a cementing factor for the maintenance of the child's personal integrity and for purposes of encouraging him toward self-assertive, productive development. Contrariwise, to interpret it as antagonistic, would-be-defeating behavior would, in fact, amount to joining the camp of his oppressors and enemies. The eventual success of the analysis may hinge on the position taken by the analyst.

In a general way, assuming just one of two extreme positions, the respect for the child's resistance may permit the fruitful continuation of the analysis, whereas the view that it is but an illegitimate defense may spell the unrewarding end of therapy.

The dynamics of the behavior of the adolescent who tarries, verbally or otherwise, in the face of the analyst's interest and urging may be compared with those of the 2- or 3-year-old who stops all play activity at the analyst's approach or in response to his helpful hints (Levy, 1956).

It is probable that there would be no disagreement among analysts of differing persuasions that resistance operates as an obstruction in the analysis. But the effective and dynamic meaning given to it depends on the theoretical vantage point whence it is evaluated.

In the Adlerian system (Adler, 1917), the neurotic power struggle would be highlighted, with the purposeful attempt at overcoming feelings of inferiority by controlling the analyst, as all other persons in authority, by depreciating him and "enjoying his [the child's] hidden superiority" (p. 337) over him, the analyst. This need is said to arise in "accordance with his life plan toward his family" (p. 336). It is the child's fear to turn to the "useful" side of life which frequently causes him to put up his resistance. To overcome this fear, the patient should not be forced into activity, but rather he should be guided "very gently towards his easiest approach to usefulness" (Adler, 1964a, p. 73). However, when it is clearly a case of "exaggeration of self-importance," a confrontation is in order; "one would inculcate in her [the child] the conviction that the only person who brags is one who believes he is inadequate himself" (Adler, 1930, p. 7).

Certain similarities to Freud's formulations on resistance can be recognized in Adler's presentation. However, the differences are more striking. The fact that he places consciousness in the center of the personality, as does Jung, albeit to a lesser extent, is only one aspect. The emphasis on the hostile antagonistic components is like an exaggeration of Freud's position.

Adler's formulations on resistance are unique. Those to be found in, or inferred from, the writings of the other authors are much closer to Freud's view, except broader than his in that the implication of instinctual urges, to the exclusion of all others, is absent.

For Jung specifically, though, transference and resistance both appear as irrelevant considerations prior to adolescence, the time of "psychic birth" (Jung, 1933, p. 99). However, in the analytic treatment of adolescents, both transference and resistance come into play. Resistance is likely to be manifest in two areas of inquiry: that which concerns the conflict between conscious and unconscious personality trends, that is, the domain of the "persona," and which includes constructive and desirable personality aspects and, more especially, that which touches on the shadowy presentations of the personality. However, as the patient recognizes that "even what is worthless or inferior" (p. 35) belongs to him and that if he has substance he is bound to cast a shadow, resistance presumably vanishes.

Both Horney (1939) and Sullivan (1954) agree that resistance is a form of protection against the coming into awareness of "repressed feelings or thoughts" (Horney, 1939, p. 34). Sullivan adds the further observation that "anxiety may be regarded as 'resistance'" (Sullivan, 1954, p. 219). Therefore, any concept that carries with it the anticipation that it will unfavorably influence the therapist's "esteem of the patient will rouse anxiety" *(ibid.)*.

The patient's difficulties in cooperating in analysis are indicative of his neurotic needs to protect his subjective values, to ward off self-hate and self-contempt, and to avoid recognition of unfulfilled "shoulds," the very basis of the neurosis.

Fromm (1941) and Schachtel (1959), on the other hand, would be more likely to stress the child's fears of unknown dangers, inherent in the freedom for self-expression. Hence, resistance can be viewed as an indication of the child's craving for that which is harmful to his own growth so as to avoid the threatening loneliness of being mature. The absence of maternal love, presumably, has contributed to that fear and to the wish to remain within the secure confines of *embeddedness* (Schachtel's term). Schachtel would also stress the existence of anxiety aroused by the neurotically expected exploitative intentions of the analyst. Both would agree with Sullivan and Horney that the fear of disapproval, culturally determined and therefore variable in varying settings, in the last analysis accounts for the difficulties in engaging in collaborative efforts with the analyst.

This stance corresponds essentially to that taken by Rank when he states that man is fighting not the outside world but his inner world, "taken in from the outside by means of identification" (Rank, 1945, p. 211).

Rado subsumes a biological emergency reaction which enters into effect in the face of transferentially anticipated frustration from the analyst. Resistance is thus a misdirected emergency reaction, in lieu of aggression against the frustrator.

The common element in these various perspectives, with reservations as to Adler's formulations, is the stress on the self-preserving and protective if not outrightly constructive aspects of resistance. The therapeutic implication derived therefrom indicates a twofold aim. First, respect is required for the patient's reaction; then, the transferential, hence presently inappropriate, purpose must be clarified. The interpretation of resistance is in terms of the dynamics and of its nefarious aspects against the self, rather than against the analyst or for the protection of some unspeakable pleasure seeking.

ANXIETY FUNDAMENTAL TO NON-FREUDIAN FORMULATION

Thus the views on resistance and on transference occupy one differentiating position with bearing on the analytic situation. The concepts of anxiety and of unconscious mental functioning occupy another and also merit inquiry in the present context.

Anxiety is considered a causative factor of neurosis rather than a symptomatic expression thereof. The differences among the several authors are to be found in what they consider the basic cause for anxiety. The stipulation of the underlying conflictual constellation differs. However, there is general agreement that the conflict is brought about by culturally determined factors. There is agreement also that the neurosis involves the total personality rather than only those areas of functioning which are related to an unresolved conflict. Adler called this the person's *life-style.* Jung gave the name *personality type* to the same phenomenon. Horney's *neurotic personality* and Fromm's *neurotic character* refer to the total involvement of the person in the neurotic adjustment. This is true, also, for Sullivan's concept of *self-dynamism,* as it is for Rado's *neurotic adaptation.*

Horney (1937) conceived of the cause of what she called *basic anxiety* as the absence of warmth in the child's environment, which causes feelings of insecurity, and the absence of motherly love, which causes feelings of hostility. As a result, the child develops "an insidiously increasing, all pervading feeling of being lonely and helpless in a hostile world" (p. 89). Feelings of anxiety, as a result of loneliness, and feelings of hostility, as a result of helplessness, concur to produce the neurotic constellation. This basic conflict between two mutually exclusive strivings, the wish for love and the hostile desires, necessitates the neurotic system of defenses, which is expressed in the neurotic personality. However, the defenses themselves may be in conflict and give rise to secondary anxiety as a result of their interference with interpersonal adjustment, mostly because of personal withdrawal or because of projection of personal hostility.

As can be seen from this example, the dynamics are formulated similarly to Freud's description. But where Freud sees the effect of an innate instinct in the genesis of the hostility, Horney sees it as a consequence of interpersonal frustration, privation, and disapproval.

This general view is also expressed by Fromm (1947, 1955) and by Sullivan (1947, 1953). Fromm (1955) sees the basic conflict as between the wish to feel secure and the inability to tolerate insecurity without "panic and undue fear" (p. 196). In Fromm's view, a fictitious sense of security can be achieved by way of alienation from the self, alienation fostered by parental attitudes and the restrictions imposed by other significant

people in the child's life. This interferes with free development and the free expression of his assets. As a result, the child experiences himself as a thing—"an investment, to be manipulated by himself and by others, he is lacking in a sense of self. This lack of self creates deep anxiety" (p. 204). Thus the child may have to betray his best potentialities in order to avoid disapproval. Then any opportunity for the expression of potential assets may give rise to secondary anxiety.

Thompson (1950) has indicated that there "has been much exchange of opinion and free discussion among these three" (p. 122) referring to Horney, Fromm, and Sullivan and to the fact that their theories on anxiety complement each other.

However, a significant difference seems to exist between Fromm and Sullivan, since the latter (1953), in contrast to Fromm, sees the basic conflict arise as a consequence of the fact that security cannot be pursued without undue anxiety. The child seeks satisfaction in order to find himself in what Sullivan called a "state of euphoria." However, when the pursuit of satisfaction threatens disapproval from the mother, feelings of insecurity are induced. This translates itself in a sudden shift "from a condition of moderate euphoria to one of severe anxiety" (p. 160). Therefore, as early as infancy, a "self-system" is elaborated which "can be said to rest on the irrational character of culture or, more specifically, society" (p. 168), whence mother's disapproval is motivated. Thereafter, opportunities for satisfaction may arouse secondary anxiety.

Schachtel's (1959) view on the basic conflict, the resulting anxiety, and the consequent neurotic defenses bears great similarities to those of Sullivan and of Fromm. Yet, while Fromm (1941) thinks that "what we can observe as the kernel of every neurosis, as well as of normal development, is the struggle for freedom and independence" (p. 178), Schachtel presents a different definition of the human conflict. It means "above all, that within the world into which he [the child] is born he can remain tied to the past, to the ways of family, peer group, community, trying to fit in and thus to retain the security of embeddedness, or he can try to be born more fully, to emerge from such embeddedness and to become capable of interest in and love for the larger and richer world in which he lives" (Schachtel, 1959, p. 14). The unaided tendency of the child is not to venture beyond these secure circumstances. He needs encouragement to leave the comfort of embeddedness and to develop an allocentric orientation. Without this encouragement, which is given through maternal love and warmth, the child leaves unused his "capacity to become interested in the totality of any object and not merely in the immediately need satisfying aspects of need related objects" (*ibid.,* p. 221). In turn, the child then does not enjoy the potential richness of his world because he tends to maintain his tie to the mother. Anxiety results, presumably from an uncanny sense of self-betrayal.

Rank (1952) also was of the opinion that the child's failure to fulfill his potentials is related to anxiety. However, he stipulated very different dynamics. The trauma of the physical separation from the mother at birth creates a sense of anxiety in the newborn. This situation is the prototype for any subsequent moves toward growth and independence, which always entail separation. The opposition of these two forces— one the desire to regain the former safety of intrauterine existence, the other the desire to mature —and the anxiety accompanying it is the basic neurotic constellation.

Rank is alone among the non-Freudians, as grouped in this essay, to postulate a purely intrapersonal genesis of the original conflict. But, as far as later conditions of life are concerned, these always proceed from an interpersonal situation and interpersonal separation. Under those circumstances, there is a reenactment of the original dilemma. This applies also to the conditions prevailing in the analysis, more especially at termination.

DIFFERING PERSPECTIVES ON UNCONSCIOUS MENTAL CONTENT

All that has been said about resistance and transference and about neurotic manifestations and defensive operations implies a persistence of character traits, of a set of nearly automatic, patterned reactions in response to external stimuli (Reich, 1949). The child is unaware of these reactions and, more particularly, of their purposiveness, even when he becomes conscious of their consequences, as he sometimes does. Certain of these operations might escape notice by direct observation as well, were it not for the inferences which suggest themselves by more or less abrupt changes in behavior or speech or by seemingly unwarranted delays in the child's reactions in his interplay with another person (Sullivan, 1953, p. 176), as for example in the analytic situation.

Those and related phenomena are explained by assuming unconscious psychological operations of mental functioning predicated on unconscious mental content.

In non-Freudian psychoanalysis, unconscious mental content is said to be derived from personal experiences, as is conscious content, except that these experiences, occurring under the strain of accompanying anxiety or the threat thereof, cause a repression of the experience. However, personal experience is considered irrelevant in Jung's (1933) formulation of a *collective unconscious,* which contains "all the patterns of life and behavior inherited" (p. 185) by the individual from his ancestors.

There is general agreement that the unconscious components of the self may be most desirable personality traits. In fact, their repression may have been the cause for neurotic adjustment, as when outside interference blocks strivings for self-realization. Unconscious mental activity is also believed to have problem-solving potentials and to serve this function especially in dreaming.

It is recognized that behavior is often in the pursuit of unconscious goals. But the question of whether it is of therapeutic advantage to interpret the unconscious meaning of overt behavior is not answered uniformly. Nor is there a consensus about the relevance of the identification of specific unconscious mental content, its derivation from past personal experience, and its purpose in present pursuits.

Most writers assume a basic conflict common to all neuroses. Rank's view in this respect has been spelled out above. Adler (1963) and Horney (1939; Boigon, 1965) recognize an historic origin of the difficulties. They agree with Rank that neurotic behavior accrues from efforts at overcoming the basic neurotic conflict. They also think that defensive operations are directed at present life situations. Therefore, it may be more important to identify these aspects than their specific historical antecedents.

Adler incriminates strivings for power in response to feelings of inferiority and of helplessness. The specific ways, the personal style of life (Adler, 1931, p. 200) through which the wish for power manifests itself depend on the individual experiences which have produced the best results in this direction. It is striving for power for the sake of power.

Adler (1964a) believes that by 4 or 5 years of age, "the full development of the ego, and the complete fixation of its attitudes to life" (1963, p. 3) is established. This brings with it certain observable "automatised attitudes" (1964a, p. 7), which express the unconscious constellation.

ADLER AND JUNG: CONSCIOUS AND UNCONSCIOUS COMPLEMENTARY ELEMENTS

Adler distinguishes between conscious and unconscious, not as "separate and conflicting entities, but (as) complementary and cooperating parts of one and the same reality" (1964a, p. 29). Under favorable circumstances, both enter into the formation of the creative self. Inherited endowment and opportunities and impressions from the environment work in combination. The creative power of the individual, presumably a given, can be recognized as the child's ability to utilize all potentials constructively. Unfavorable circumstances imposed by external conditions may interfere with his creative powers. This makes him feel inferior. He then turns all his efforts toward achieving power and superiority. Thus, in terms of Adler's "psychology of use" (p. 204), the child's relationship to the outside world is governed by the concurrence of conscious and unconscious potentials or by its absence.

For purposes of treatment, this orientation, with consciousness and social orientation at the center of the personality, translates itself in the conviction that the child has to recognize that he exerts efforts in pursuing the "useless" side of life. Provided that he *really* recognizes this, he will correct his error. Adler (1963), subsuming a human given, thinks that "really to recognize the error and then not to modify it runs counter to human nature" (p. 3).

The differences between Adler's position and that of Jung are not always clear. They both stress the importance of the conscious recognition of the neurotic way of life. Exchange *unconscious* for *collective unconscious*, and the neurotogenic disharmony in Jung's system is formulated. Yet there are differences. There are Jung's (1933) detailed schemas on the organization of the collective unconscious and his personality types. There is his view that consciousness and neurotic problems are the warp and the woof of the same fabric, by virtue of the fact that "there are no problems without consciousness" (p. 98). There is the conviction that coherent consciousness of self begins coincidentally with puberty and that, consequently, the disharmony between self-awareness and the foundations of one's personality in the collective unconscious cannot be experienced before then.

Jung's observation may have been influenced by the then prevailing view of what was called the *latency period*. Certainly the clinical evidence, even that presented by Wickes (1938, pp. 67ff.), who set out to support his theories, bears witness to the existence of neurotic, that is, self-experienced, problems in childhood.

Jung fails to specify which unconscious element he considers common to all neuroses except, in a general way, the conflict between personality elements rooted in the collective unconscious and those not so rooted. It seems quite true, as Glover (1950) has endeavored to show, with what appears undue and unending acrimony, that Jung's theory of mental mechanisms (a term abhorred by Sullivan) bears no resemblance to Freud's. It "*substitutes for Freudian repression the concept of voluntary suppression*" (p. 78), among other steps in the direction of making it an "*all-inclusive conscious psychology*" *(ibid.).*

However, as Jung (1933) has pointed out, "psychic happenings have an objective side. In large measure they are withdrawn from our conscious control, [and] we are dependent to a startling degree upon the proper functioning of the unconscious psyche" (pp. 182–183).

From this it follows that one of the analytic tasks consists in exploring the collective unconscious. When working with a prepuberty child, this is done in order to discover the nature of the unrealized personality potentials and to facilitate their expression (Wickes, 1927) without interpreting them. With the adolescent, where the conflict is said to be in awareness, the interpretation of what is repressed, not only the facilitation of its expression, contributes to the ultimate strength of the personality by establishing the foundations for self-realization.

There is fairly general agreement among non-Freudian analysts that the child's early experiences, especially with the mother, have a telling effect on personality formation, that is, on the sum total of individual characteristic action patterns. These are predicated on unconscious mental content, formulated in accordance with the respective author's system of thought, and on the belief of their relative fixity after childhood.

SULLIVAN'S POSITION

Sullivan (1953) is an exception to this rule. He postulates not only ongoing developmental maturation beyond childhood but also the not exceptional possibility for spontaneous changes for the better as a result of the ongoing maturation.

The notion that developments other than the sexual may effect psychological adjustment in adolescence has been advanced by Jung (1933) also, especially the "feeling of inferiority which springs from an unbearable sensitivity" (p. 101). But Jung, like most other non-Freudian analysts, does not offer a precise and detailed schema for the understanding of adolescence; Sullivan does.

Sullivan's contribution, anticipating more recent research findings (Douvan & Gold, 1966), is sufficiently significant to warrant a somewhat more detailed review. He thinks, as does Thompson (1964), that sexual maturation not only is a significant milestone in the course of normal development but also may have considerable salutary effect on neurotic adjustment. He writes: "In fact, if one overlooks his experience with loneliness, he may well think that lust is the most powerful dynamism in interpersonal relations" (Sullivan, 1953, p. 266).

He agrees with all those of the non-Freudian authors who have expressed themselves on the matter that negative attitudes toward sexual considerations, including feelings toward one's own genitalia, are culturally and socially and experientially determined rather than instinctually. (Jung, 1954, p. 18).

Sullivan's presentation of developmental progression in adolescence actually needs to be traced to the end of childhood, the juvenile era (Sullivan, 1953, pp. 127ff.), to the significant steps in the direction of becoming social. Here one can notice for the first time, what remains true thereafter, that "as one passes over one of these more-or-less determinable thresholds of a developmental era, everything that has gone before becomes reasonably open to influence" (p. 227). Thus the unfortunate effects of earlier experiences can be spontaneously corrected by virtue of the flexibility inherent in what one might call a *threshold situation*. This spontaneous possibility also points to therapeutic possibilities and priorities at these times.

The possible correction of earlier interpersonal difficulties accounts for the fact that the formation of chumships, except in fairly extreme cases, proceeds without too much trouble. Also, as a further consequence in the ensuing, relatively brief phase of preadolescence, "one finds oneself more and more able to talk about things which one has learned during the juvenile era not to talk about" *(ibid.)*.

Of special importance are "the experience of social subordination" and "the experience of social accommodation," neither of them imposed from the outside, which help the preadolescent to "compare his parents with other parents, with teachers, and so on" (p. 131) and to free himself from the previously imposed belief in the parental infallibility. This has something to do with the observable rebelliousness, especially against parental authority (Gesell, 1956, pp. 69ff., 90ff.), which Horney might have called a liberation from the "tyranny of the shoulds."

Sullivan (1953) points out that as a consequence of this acquired relative freedom, together with a fair degree of needed stability-in-time of the preadolescent's social milieu and "any good fortune" (p. 243), an adequate orientation toward living will be the eventual outcome.

The next developmental step is contingent upon the thus accomplished sense of personal freedom. The prior liberation from anachronistic shackles is indispensable to being able to involve oneself in an intimate way and to "care for the welfare of another person," a phrase used by Sullivan (1953) to describe "psychiatrically defined *love*" (p. 245).

The fruitful development of the chumship during preadolescence has brought with it a real sensitivity for what matters to another person. This enables the person to go beyond the familiar dynamisms of minimizing anxiety, i.e., aiming at shoring up feelings of security and self-esteem, or of gaining a state of euphoria, i.e., aiming at achieving emotional satisfaction.

Assuming that all has gone well, the next developmental task could be successfully accomplished, namely, the simultaneous integration of the lust dynamism and of the need for intimacy, were it not for "the cultural influences which are borne in upon each person [and which] include very little which prepares members of different sexes for a fully human, simple, personal relationship together" (p. 264).

Sullivan is mindful of the fact that lustful pursuits, particularly adolescent and premarital ones, are handicapped in our society. Therefore, the "collision between one's lust and one's security" (p. 266) is almost inevitable. Although the specific consequences of this conflict are different for each of the two sexes, both are caught in a double bind between the wish for sexual satisfaction and the threat to one's self-esteem and hence to the feelings of security.

A seemingly safe, do-nothing stance in fact offers no solution to the boy but is made feasible through the continuation of autoerotic activity in combination with the appropriate fantasies. More frequently, "a very bold approach in the pursuit of the genital object" (p. 269) is the reaction. This necessitates a prior distinction between those girls with whom there is a likelihood of success with this approach and those with whom there is not—the "prostitute" and the "good girl." Now, "since the bad girls are unworthy and not really people in the sense that good girls are" (*ibid.*), the solution also is only a partial one and is likely to leave a damaged self-esteem. So, despite all the possible corrections of earlier warp, the new difficulties make "*a fully human or mature repertory of interpersonal relations*" (p. 297) almost impossible.

The general suggestions in Sullivan's theory of maturational phenomena, other than sexual, that are characteristic of adolescence are confirmed by the reports of Engle and her collaborators (1967), the findings of Inhelder and Piaget (1958), and the accounts by Douvan and Gold (1966), albeit these findings, while confirming Sullivan's hypotheses, also go far beyond them.

However, Sullivan's (1953) rule of thumb remains valid. He says: "When difficulties in the sex life are presented by a patient as his reasons for needing psychiatric help . . . such problems show . . . what ails their living with people" (p. 295), namely, difficulties in achieving an intimate relationship and problems with their self-esteem.

This brings Sullivan to the comment that "the mark which . . . separates early adolescence from late adolescence is not a biological maturation, but an achievement" *(ibid.)*. In a social organization, he muses, geared to meet the needs and strivings of adolescents—primarily genital, it would seem—such a division would appear unwarranted and artificial. The extension of adolescent problems into young adult years therefore must be looked upon as a cultural phenomenon.

The analytic task, as derived from Sullivan's theories, is the clarification of the conflict between the strivings for satisfaction and those for security and the identification of the personal antecedents which made such a conflict unavoidable.

The main body of Sullivan's theories applies to both boys and girls. He has called attention to the differences in interpersonal experience when he saw them, though he has mostly not concerned himself with gender differences. In fact, these seem fairly irrelevant to his system, which was not meant to present a definitive theory of human psychology. In this respect his approach is almost epistemological. It may be this, and mostly the fact that he underplayed the importance of sexuality, which accounts for Guntrip's (1961) judgment that Sullivan could "barely be called an analyst but rather as one who at most has taken suggestions from psychoanalysis and pursued his own independent psychiatric way" (p. 174).

THOMPSON'S CONTRIBUTIONS TO AN UNDERSTANDING OF FEMALE PSYCHOLOGY

Thompson's (1964) papers on the evolution of womanhood and femininity present a viewpoint which is akin to Horney's. The data presented are indispensable to arriving at a complete picture of the psychosexual vicissitudes in adolescence in our culture. She points out that "in girls the actual physiological demands are usually less overt than in boys" (p. 298); but also the prohibitions are stronger, and there is the challenge of sex as a commodity and of sexual activity for social approval. This makes it difficult for the girl to take advantage of the possibility, acquired in preadolescence, to "care in an unselfish way about the happiness of another person" (p. 299).

The emancipation from parental domination also is more difficult for girls. The girl often is confronted with the "tightening of the vested interests each parent has in the child" (p. 301). Thus it may come to be that the daughter of an attractive competitive mother will play down her own feminine charm. On the other hand, the girl whose father is suspicious of any interest she may show in boys may become sexually promiscuous by incorporating into her own self-image the father's expectations of her. Thompson sees a third possibility, in which the father-daughter attachment is "so great that she does not become interested in any other man" (p. 311).

Thompson finds that adolescent girls' daydreams are more predominantly erotic than those of adolescent boys. She also noticed that girls have a more pronounced tendency to replace reality with daydreams and that this is more frequently associated with severe psychopathology. It must be concluded that Thompson believed in sexual maturation as the only dominant issue in adolescence.

For purposes of analysis, the problem of the shift of the girl's interest from the clitoris to the vagina (p. 320) and of a comparable shift, psychologically speaking, directing her interest to the adult feminine goal, that of motherhood, is kept in the foreground.

Thompson agrees with Fromm and Sullivan in seeing cultural factors as the principal constituents of the basic neurotic conflict. Little weight is given to biological and innate tendencies, other than sexual, when they become manifest in adolescence and conflict with social requirements.

FROMM'S EMPHASIS ON HUMAN POTENTIALITIES

Adler's view of the "givens" with which the child embarks on the process of socialization and is guided toward constructive achievement has been presented. Similarly, in Fromm's (1941) writings a "tendency to grow, to develop and to realize his potentials" (pp. 287–288) is assumed to exist in the child. This tendency presumably has been developed "in the course of history" (p. 288). But Fromm goes beyond this general assumption in setting forth that the child's state of powerlessness gives rise to a sense of justice and truth, which may now be regarded as being part of the "potentialities common to man as such" (p. 289).

Fromm, like Sullivan, assumes that the child's healthy development will proceed unless interfered with. Thus he believes that the human potentialities as such, together with the needed "system of orientation and devotion" (p. 49), can be counted on as the "more powerful sources of energy in man" *(ibid.)*.

His theory is based, as is Jung's, on the assumption that despite psychological qualities and potentials, human nature is essentially "historically conditioned," that humans are social beings, and that the basic direction, therefore, is toward accommodation with others. Because man is not self-sufficient, his social needs and individual frustrations, arising in the course of the individual's historical experiences, may lead him to neurotic adjustments and other self-defeating psychological reactions.

Fromm's explicit concern is with the chronologically mature member of Western society. His thesis, however, rests on the principle that "the childhood shews the man, as morning shews the day" [Milton (1671), 1938, line 220]. He thinks, as does Horney, that the child's need for motherly love must be fulfilled lest dire psychological consequences result. The analyst working with the child, therefore, will enhance his effectiveness by being aware of the fact that "the child's tie to the mother, and the child's fear of the mother are two elements which are rooted in the child's unconscious experience" (Fromm, 1964, pp. 105–106).

Thus it is obvious that Fromm attaches less importance to a facilitating environment than does Winnicott, for example. He concerns himself more with its devastating influences. Social experiences in Western society are found to be overwhelmingly detrimental to the unfolding of constructive personality traits (Fromm, 1947). At first sight, a similarity to the positions of Freud and Sullivan can be recognized. Yet Fromm differs from Freud in seeing the fundamental basis of character not in "various types of libido organization but in specific kinds of a person's relatedness to the world" (Fromm, 1947, p. 58). He differs from Sullivan mainly by assigning more importance to the effects of constitutional and unconscious forces (Fromm, 1964).

However, Fromm's concept of character is reminiscent of Sullivan's concept of self-dynamism and of Adler's formulation of life style, namely, as the relatively permanent form in which "human energy is canalized in the process of assimilation and socialization" (Fromm, 1947, p. 59).

It has been said that Jung's and Adler's positions as analysts are mostly not defensible because they both underplayed the importance of personal unconscious forces. A similar objection has not been raised about Rank. This may be due partially to the fact that he lost much of his earlier influence as an analyst. His work is reviewed here mainly because of the wide application of Rankian principles to psychotherapy with children. He (1947) contended that "Freud's theory has lifted it [the unconscious] to the most powerful factor in psychic life," not as a consequence of psychological experience but because of a "moral necessity," namely, to "find an acceptable substitute for the concept of God" (p. 28). He felt, by and large, as did Horney, that the emphasis on the past and on the unconscious and on instinctual drives favored denial of the present dilemma and therefore interfered with true understanding (p. 41).

Fromm has recorded the differences between his own theories and those of Sullivan (Fromm, 1941, 1947), and he has drawn attention also to the existing similarities.

The basis of Sullivan's theories can be found in his concern with the development of the "dissociated" part of the self, Sullivan's term for what others called "unconscious," and in his interest in and recognition of the importance to personality of social forces.

Alone among non-Freudians, Sullivan has offered a comprehensive theory of child and adolescent development (1947, 1953). He posits that repression is a consequence of the "collision" of a need for satisfaction "with anxiety at the behest of the social censor, of the acculturating person" (1953, p. 194). From this theory of repression, explaining dissociation from awareness, Sullivan also formulated the concept of "sublimatory processes" (1947). Here, similar to Freud's proposition, Sullivan suggests that these processes permit the sacrifice of the overt pursuit for satisfaction, since satisfaction, at least partial, can still be found through covert operations. These "forbidden activities," whatever their nature, are said to be still faithfully expressed in actual performances in early childhood but become suppressed in later childhood and especially in adolescence. Sullivan held that sexual satisfaction—"lustful activity," as he called it—cannot be sublimated (1953, p. 195) or suppressed. This may lead to neurotic conflicts, but as a consequence of interpersonal difficulties which make intimacy impossible (1953).

Schachtel (1959) fills a void that has been left relatively untouched by non-Freudian analysts, though Sullivan (1947) concerned himself with the topic to some extent. This is the issue of childhood amnesia and of other instances of not remembering.

Schachtel (1959) takes specific exception to the theory that childhood memories are repressed because of their libidinal content. Instead, he holds that *"the categories or schemata of adult memory are not suitable receptacles for early childhood experiences and therefore not fit to preserve these experiences and enable their recall"* (p. 284). In line with Inhelder and Piaget's (1958) findings on the shift in the mode of thinking from causal to hypothetico-deductive in adolescence, Schachtel's hypothesis would seem to be applicable to adolescence, in which difficulties in recall of childhood memories are a common occurrence. Reich had found that forgotten experiences could be recovered when the individual was freed of his muscular rigidity. Schachtel (1959, p. 315), building on this, concluded that repressed or forgotten material was liable to recovery through "memory of the body" rather than through involuntary memory in the conscious. Schachtel holds that the psychoanalytic method of free associations is a useful road to these repressed memories provided that the patient can successfully relax from the purposeful, useful pursuit of some thought or activity. Since this is mostly not the case because of neurotic difficulties, Schachtel agrees with Alexander that the recovery of memories "is not the cause, but the result of therapeutic progress" (p. 316).

Schachtel's basic argument is that repression is unrelated to libidinal drives, but he considers that childhood amnesia "covers those aspects and experiences of the early personality which are incompatible with the culture" (p. 320).

A corollary to his thesis on childhood amnesia is to be found in his presentation of "focal attention and the emergence of reality" (pp. 251–278). The concept of focal attention as opposed to global attention is essential, in Schachtel's thinking, to an understanding of repression. Focal attention is "the tool, the distinctively human equipment, by means of which the capacity for object interest can be realized" (p. 268). Focal attention is responsible for the fact that focal acts, i.e., several approaches from different angles, are possible. Focal attention, on the other hand, is incompatible with severe anxiety. Therefore, "the development of focal attention and the emergence of the object world presupposes relative freedom from basic need tension" (p. 274). It follows that when there is tension, and consequently anxiety, focal attention is jeopardized, events and occurrences are dissociated, and repression takes place.

A very similar thesis is advanced by Sullivan

(1947, 1953). According to Sullivan, it is in the juvenile era that the control of focal awareness becomes especially pronounced. Two related phenomena can be observed. *Selective inattention* is one of them. This is "nondiscriminating" behavior, that is, behavior that is consciously not noticed because its recognition would cause anxiety. Such behavior can be brought into awareness retrospectively by an observer, such as the analyst, by way of retracing the context.

The other phenomenon is behavior which is totally dissociated. This is the result no longer of the anticipation of anxiety but of its actual occurrence, when behavior[2] and attitudes are completely unacceptable to the image one wishes to preserve of oneself. Such behavior and the fact that it has been dissociated can only be inferred from careful contextual observation (Sullivan, 1947, p. 70).

DREAMS, REVERIES, AND FANTASIES: INTEGRATIVE DIVERSIONS OF NONCOGNITIVE MENTAL FUNCTIONING

In the preceding pages, unconscious mental function has been considered mainly from the point of view of its relevance to neurotic disturbances. Therefore, "normal" aspects of unawareness have not received the attention they deserve. However, the point needs to be made that in non-Freudian theory unconscious determinants of behavior are not thought of as limited to defensive purposes or as characteristic of neurosis. This applies of course also to views on dreams, which will presently be discussed.

For a long time, speculations about and speculative investigations of dreaming, particularly during sleep but also including daydreams, reveries, and fantasies, were the only sources of

---

[2] The term *behavior*, as used by Sullivan, does not refer only to external relations to others. It bespeaks a general tone of actions, concerns, moral attitudes, judgments, and reactions.

information concerning dream processes. This is reflected in many of the current dream theories.

More recently, the scientific investigation of dreaming and of dream processes during sleep has provided the basis for certain reformulations of earlier theories (Berger, 1963; Hall, 1959; Hall & Domhoff, 1963; Offenkrantz & Rechtschaffen, 1963; Verdone, 1965; Witken & Lewis, 1967; Wolpert & Trosman, 1958). The maintenance of sleep, a function of dreams to which many psychoanalytic authors subscribe, seems at best only of minor psychological significance. Also, dream content has been found to be subject to experimental modifications. This may warrant a reexamination of conceptions regarding its symbolic meaning.

The observation of REM sleep in infancy (De Martino, 1959) may be a further indication that dreaming during sleep does not always portend a relationship to intrapsychic conflict, as older, and particularly Freud's, theories assumed.

Modern investigators of dream processes have not paid as much attention to the symbolic significance of dream content as was the case in the earlier days of psychoanalysis. Experimental verification of dream theory usually confirmed the respective investigator's hypothesis, despite remarkable differences among theories (Adelson, 1963). Some of these findings might be of interest here. However, this transcends the scope of the present essay.

Non-Freudian psychoanalytic theories, generally, have recognized the significance of dreams. With some authors, such as Jung (1933), Jung, Von Franz, Henderson, Jacobi, and Jaffee (1964), and Fromm (1951), dreams and their meaning and interpretation take a central position in psychoanalytic work. They are an exquisite means for discovering the unconscious. With others, such as Adler (1927), Horney (1939), and Sullivan (1953), the understanding of dreams and their interpretation in the traditional mode are but an incidental complement to the patient's analysis.

Rank's position is unique and all the more interesting because of his earlier (1900) collaboration on dream theory with Freud (1953). As far as Rank is concerned, the real importance of dreams, and their essence, is that they convey in the transference the reestablishment of the biological tie to the mother (Rank, 1945). He does not share the view, advanced by Fromm particularly, that the dreamer means to convey something to the analyst. He maintains that dreams have "an auto-therapeutic effect . . . especially in the end phase of treatment" (p. 18) but that they are otherwise irrelevant for analysis, the focus of which "should be present oriented" (p. 34) and not concerned with the recovery of past memories.

MANIFEST DREAM CONTENT

The importance attached to the manifest dream content, characteristic of Jung's approach, is an innovation in non-Freudian dream analysis. So is the insistence on the problem-solving function of dreaming, be it during sleep or during the wakeful state. In their attempts to delineate their own views, the dissenters from Freud's theories have also reexamined representations and symbolizations in manifest dream content.

It is fair to say that the recognition of the importance of the manifest dream content can now also be found in other writings. The work of French and Fromm (1964) needs to be mentioned, and that of Erikson (1954, 1964), who was impressed by the connection between the manifest dream content and the style of dream representation as a reflection of the dreamer's basic orientation. Here then, as elsewhere (as was mentioned), Erikson's position hardly differs from that of the non-Freudian analyst. Indeed his views seem very close to what Jung (1933) wrote and to what can be found in Fromm's work (1951).

Perhaps, and it is to be hoped, this indicates a narrowing of the gap between differing psychoanalytic schools and theories, in spite of the misgivings at such a prospect voiced by Glover (1950).

Jung's mysticism (Mahoney, 1966) can express itself ideally in dream interpretation. But he has also pointed out the practical significance of dreams (Jung, 1933) as a "direct expression of the unconscious" (p. 1). Dreams give a "true picture of the subjective state, while the conscious mind denies that this state exists" (p. 5). Stripped of the artifacts of consciousness, dreams need not be deciphered as to their deceptive value. Indeed they are apt to give a glimpse of the dreamer's true strivings if the interpreter does not "pare down the meaning of a dream to fit some narrow doctrine" (p. 11). He should "establish the context with minute care" (p. 12), and without prejudice, in order to read the dream clearly.

In varying degrees this orientation can be found expressed throughout the writings of non-Freudians. Thus Schachtel (1959), undoubtedly impressed by the problem-solving potential of dreams, described them as "widening the scope of human life" (p. 308) while providing an access road to unconscious memories.

Adler (1930, pp. 109–111) suggested that the power drive, that ubiquitous force behind the neurotic style of life, is expressed unhampered in dreams. He was struck by the fact that this "false guiding ideal" (1966, p. 166) came to be superimposed upon the constructive aspects of the individual, almost masking the wish for self-realization, the "forward to the goal" (Adler, 1964b, p. 359) tendency. By way of these tendencies, dreams are a preparation for the mastery of actual difficulties in living, a "rehearsal for life" (Adler, 1932), and they can be seen as the "expression of the creative faculty of the soul" (Adler, 1946).

Fromm's (1951) extensive use of dreams is predicated on the belief that the dreamer while asleep can look at his inner self because he is "free, freer than when awake" (p. 27) and on the conviction that the patient's report of his dreams, and his relevant associations as well, can be relied upon to permit a "look at the hidden occurrences" (p. 167) in his soul. The analysis of the manifest content gives insight into the dreamer's general character trends and refers to the "qualities of hidden desires and fears but not to their quantities" (*ibid.*). Insight into the magnitude and significance of trends, however, can be gained only through a "quantitative" dream analysis, for which the dreamer's associations, among other background data, are needed (p. 168).

Assessing the manifest dream also, Tauber (1963) held that dreams were expressive of the individual's ways of organizing his life experiences. This view corresponds to Adler's ideas on life style and to similar ideas expressed by others. But Tauber points out that one represents oneself in dreams "in a symbology which is usually strikingly different from that which exists in waking life," thereby offering the possibility in the analysis of transcending the logic of wakefulness.

Critical concern with manifest dream content is also to be found in Boidon (1962) and in Ullman (1958), as it is in other writings. Tauber and Green (1959), using an approach consistent with Sullivan's interpersonal theories, have elaborated on and correlated emotional content with manifest dream content and with transference-countertransference aspects.

Differing with Sullivan (see p. 885), they hold "that it is not man's hostility and man's guilt that are the most obstructive dynamism" (p. 65) but his fear of knowing himself. Agreeing with Fromm and Horney in this respect, they also recognize that the fear of loving and of being loved is a potential resistance to dream analysis, as to analysis generally.

However, Tauber and Green (1959) find also that dream analysis makes revealing oneself easier because the dream experience "is shared by somebody and is not discussed in the logical terms of syntactical relationships" (p. 73). Resistance is lowered because the "peculiar quality of separation and togetherness" does not appear in its inherent contradiction. Clarification of symbolizing activity as a creative endeavor is therefore possible. The implicit symbolic meaning of dreams, neglected because of "the unwarranted assumption of gratification" (p. 151), thereby gains unsuspected importance.

Sullivan's thesis on dreams belongs in the broader content of his developmental theories. He agreed in many ways with Freud on the significance and the purpose of night dreams (1947, pp. 34–35; 1953, pp. 329-343; 1956, pp. 19–20). Though, at variance with Freud, Sullivan (1962) insisted that "primitive thinking in more normal sleep solves many problems, and, in the remembered dream, brings up for assistance many an unresolved problem with which we now feel able to deal" (p. 20). He also believed that sexual strivings are not subject to sublimation and that hostile wishes and anger are particularly unacceptable in our culture. Therefore these are more likely to find their way into dreams. Thereby, tension is relieved and the individual can achieve what Sullivan called a *state of euphoria*, a condition antithetical to anxiety. His views are shared by Balint (1952), who pointed out that the child through fantasies and dreams may be able to lessen the dread of losing parental love.

Sullivan did not advise the exploration of dreams over the investigation of daydreams and reveries. He thought (1956) that there is never a "total absence of the self-system as a functional entity" (p. 20), so that parataxic distortions are likely to intrude in sleep as well. Therefore, when important tensions are associated with the satisfaction of a need, the effectiveness of night dreams for lessening anxiety in the course of symbolic operations is no greater than that of daytime reveries.

Daydreams, as "constructive reveries" (Sul-livan, 1947, p. 97) are attractive also, as White (1966) proposed, because of the ease with which solutions are reached "much more satisfactorily than we could hope to work out in real life" (White, 1966, p. 249). Therefore, he says, "great accomplishments before they are actually brought to pass exist in fantasy only," where "our ambitions find their first expression" *(ibid.)*.

Sullivan (1953) ascribed an integrating function to daydreams (pp. 21ff.). In childhood in particular, almost wholly undisguised reveries serve a socializing purpose. With advancing age they lose some of this original usefulness. They grow more symbolized, as do night dreams, until in the juvenile period they disappear from awareness and henceforth are manifest fully symbolized and in covert operations only.

In the analysis with children, there may be direct transposition from the manifest dream to its actual meaning. In work with adolescents, dreams as symbolic and as sublimated representations have to be reckoned with. However, Sullivan (1953) recommends that primary attention be paid to the feelings in the course of dreaming as preserved in recall and to the feelings experienced by the patient in relating dreams (p. 321). He thought that content is not reported reliably, anyway, except in hysterical conditions and that therefore excessive attention to it is of little practical value. Moreover, he noted that the recall of dream content recedes as waking time elapses, an observation which Schachtel (1959) confirmed.

Both Sullivan and Schachtel have tried to explain "resistance" to the recall of dreams on psychodynamic grounds. According to Sullivan (1956), if "as a result of someone else's attempt at interpretation . . . these dreams come to interfere with the self-system's suave function of keeping the dissociated tendency out of awareness, then the person will cease to recall any dreams whatsoever" (p. 180). Schachtel (1959) agrees with this formulation of "resistance to and repression of a specific dream thought" (p. 308), but he adds that the "transschematic quality . . . of dreams . . . makes it difficult or impossible for the memory schemata to preserve and recall voluntarily" *(ibid.)* details of their occurrence. The resistance appears therefore directed against "the whole quality and language of the dream" (p. 306). The fact that the individual while asleep is not bound by the rules of logic and reason is antithetical to waking life, at least once childhood is passed.

Certain research findings as reported by De Martino (1959) lend support to this thesis. De Martino noted that dream content was affected by both the child's immediate and his general environment, including the socioeconomic conditions of his milieu. More intelligent children, according to his findings, recalled dreams more frequently than others. This may reflect greater creative aspects of dreaming itself. De Martino commented also on the fact that children's reactions to their dreams depended on their age. So did the content of their dreams. Children up to 5 years of age did not seem able to discriminate between reality and dreaming. Contrariwise, by 7 all children recognized dreams as unreal.

The findings suggest the possibility of gauging developmental maturation by the child's reactions to his dreams and also that of assessing transient regression from achieved maturation under the impact of severe anxiety or organic insult—as, for example, serious physical illness.

Several broad facts seem to stand out from this cursory survey. Dreams can be seen "as part of a general spectrum of thought processes participating in the development of mental activities from infancy through childhood into adulthood" (Green, Ullman, & Tauber, 1968, p. 162). Dream productions are subject to modifications from extrapersonal as well as intrapersonal sources. Therefore, it may be expected that patients' dreams will be in tune with their analyst's pet theories (*ibid.,* p. 175). Disagreements and significant variables about the meaning of dreams are related to conceptualizations of unconscious mental content. Freud's (1909) dictum appears valid that "the interpretation of dreams is in fact the royal road to the knowledge of the unconscious" (1957, p. 33).

FUNDAMENTALS OF NON-FREUDIAN METHODS OF PSYCHOANALYSIS

External Threats Leading to Neurotic Adaptation

Non-Freudian methods of psychoanalysis are predicated on a conception of neurosis as a reaction to external threats. Neither the threat nor the reaction to it is consciously perceived for what it is. Here is an area where unique contributions have been made by Schachtel (1959) and by Sullivan (1953) through their clarifications of developmental characteristics in infancy. The observations on speech development suggest new directions of worthwhile psychoanalytic inquiry, as do Sullivan's on the issue of sleep (Sullivan, 1962, p. 153).

Sullivan (1956) observed that the infant empathically senses the mother's anxiety. The physiological distress and the physiological reaction thus engendered are the prototype for all subsequent anxiety reactions. Because anxiety becomes associated with a sense of disapproval, the child's self-concept is damaged whenever anxiety occurs. Situations in which his wishes and pursuits would have earned him disapproval in the past remain potential threats.

A defensive system, therefore, becomes established to signal impending anxiety or, when it is too late for that, to deal with the present situation either through the use of dissociation from awareness in severe instances or through the use of selective inattention under more benign circumstances.

By far the more effective way to cope with all

possible anxiety is to remain unaware of unacceptable wants and to deny them. Thus in infancy a "self-system" comes into existence with "good-me," "bad me," and "not me" personifications (Sullivan, 1953, pp. 161–163). "Good me" conforms with mother's expectations and holds the promise of reward. "Bad me" likewise meets maternal attitudes, but those which condemn, therefore creating anxiety. "Not me," finally, also is a conformist adaptation, but under the gradual impact of intense anxiety which has prevented the organization of personal experiences into clearly recognizable cause-and-effect situations.

These slants in personality representation may cause the child to disregard what really matters to him, beyond the avoidance of anxiety, and to lower his self-esteem (pp. 233–234). The child's behavior in the analysis can give clues to his distorted self-concept once the characteristics of his parataxic integration with the analyst have been recognized. The present purpose and the historical antecedents can be derived from this.

THE ANALYST AS "PARTICIPANT OBSERVER"

The extent of the distortion in self-perception and the consequent distortions in the perception of others are therefore a measure of the child's anxiety and of the severity of impairment of interpersonal relationships and, hence, of psychopathology (Searles, 1967). Anxiety also interferes with learning about oneself or about others. The analysis, therefore, in order to be effective must provide not only a setting free of threats but one which will permit the patient to anticipate some benefit for himself (Sullivan, 1954, p.7). He can do so only after "a valid relationship has come into being" (p. 142). Such a relationship, it is hoped, will at all times satisfy the criteria of the analyst as "participant observer" (pp. 19–25).

Two aspects of non-Freudian analysis bear restatement because of their importance in treatment and treatment goals.

One is the fact that neurosis, or its maintenance, is seen as a reaction to threats, actual or imagined, to the individual in the present. These threats interfere with self-expression in the individual's present life situation although, more often, they result from earlier frustrations.

It has already been said that the child's striving for power, which Adler incriminated as central to every neurotic manifestation, is compensatory for feelings of inferiority, which his experiences usually have confirmed. This urge for power must be handled cautiously in order not to increase the child's feelings of powerlessness, where in the past these may have been experienced as actual threats to the survival of the organism. Therefore, the child needs to develop "a plus factor of safety" (Adler, 1946, p. 24), an overcompensation which must be preserved for a time at least.

It is important in the analysis to recognize and to help the child recognize that the overcompensation established as "a false guiding ideal" (Adler, 1966) now interferes with other productive efforts, since all the energies go into ensuring control over others.

Often the wish to gain control is acted out by the child through helplessness and negativism. Frequently, also, parents respond to this by wanting to be "helpful"; they are eager to do things for the child. Adler cautions against this reaction, feeling that it only increases the neurotic tendency toward omnipotence (Adler, 1963).

PRESENT PURPOSIVENESS OF NEUROTIC INTERACTION

A further fact in non-Freudian theory is the recognition of the importance of the present and *the present purposiveness of the neurosis.*

The person is seen in constant interaction with his environment. The child's potentials and the use of his abilities in a positive or negative way unfold in response to the opportunities offered and the restrictions imposed by the environment. Hostility and aggression in particular are seen as related to external conditions rather than as a consequence of inborn qualities or drives.

Thompson (1950) has pointed out that strivings for power and greater mastery or even the pursuit of curiosity may appear as destructive aggression. This is likely to be the case when the child's legitimate aspirations are actively suppressed. When he is prevented from asserting his rights in a cooperative atmosphere, he fails to achieve a sense of mastery over his environment, needed for continued growth and eventual emancipation (Ovesey, 1966). Therefore, aggressive behavior and negativism appear or persist.

Levy (1955), as has been indicated earlier, looked upon oppositionalism in much the same way. Rado (1956a) also saw such behavior as situation-appropriate, though not constructive, self-assertion. Rank (1947) suggested that negativism was but an "autonomous organizing force in the individual which does not represent any particular biological impulse or social drive but constitutes the creative expression of the total personality and distinguishes one individual from another" (p. 212). The counterwill, therefore, though neurotic, may be seen as the best possible reaction under the given circumstances.

Similar views are reflected by Parsons (1949), who sees "structured patterns of aggression in childhood . . . rooted in normal reactions to strain and frustrations in human relations . . . when the individual is particularly vulnerable" (p. 272). He lists among the sources of aggression "the withdrawal of love to which the child has become accustomed," the expectation "to do things which one is unable to achieve," and the sense of unfairness which derives from unjust punishment *(ibid.)*.

Thus modern sociological thinking, as Fromm-Reichmann (1949) pointed out, is in agreement with Sullivan's concept of "a person's adjustment to reality in terms of adaptation to interpersonal relationships" (p. 125). This adjustment does not appear to have been established once and for all in early childhood, as Adler saw it. Rather, there seems to be an inherent flexibility in line with Pepitone's (1950) theory of *facilitative distortion*, which seeks to achieve "a better state of affairs" for the subject (p. 71).

AUTONOMOUS STRIVING FOR GROWTH

Non-Freudian analysts foresee normal progression of growth and development unless there is interference by the child's environment. Horney (1950) is one of the authors who postulates an inherent, positive, autonomous striving for growth, change, and self-realization. She suggests that growth requires a balance in orientation of the child's "direction toward," expressive of his dependency needs, his "direction away from," implying a need for separation and for independence, and his "direction against," indicative of a natural aggressive tendency against external efforts at molding him.

Circumstances may affect this balance. Absence of maternal love endangers it and may destroy it. This is when basic anxiety arises (Boigon, 1965; Horney, 1950), leading to ultimate neurotic adjustment. Then one or the other of these basic directions becomes dominant (Allen, 1963; Horney, 1945) because the child sees himself as "being isolated and helpless in a potentially hostile world" (Horney, 1945, p. 41). Accepting his powerlessness and the privation of motherly love, he tries to win the affection of others. In a situation in which the direction "toward" gains priority, he tries to lean on others in spite of his fears. "Only in this way can he feel safe with them. If there are dissenting parties in the family, he will attach himself to the most powerful person or group. By complying with them, he gains a feeling of belonging and support which makes him feel less weak and less isolated" (p. 42).

He may still try to secure mother's love by seeking to fulfill the ideal image of himself, a replica of what he unconsciously believes mother wants him to be. He may thus totally neglect his optimal possibilities. Sullivan, as has been said earlier, assumed a similar sequence of events.

Horney (1945) recognized that this wish to secure the mother's love and the expectation of not succeeding are carried into the analysis and work as an obstacle. Under such conditions, major efforts are directed at warding off self-hate, self-contempt, and a sense of failure at having fulfilled all of mother's "shoulds."

Because the imbalance in direction manifests itself in the here and now, Horney attached no particular importance to detailed historical antecedents. She felt that the balance must be established or reestablished in the present (Allen, 1963), that "by working through the consequences [of the imbalance] the patient's anxiety is so much lessened . . . that he can dispense with the neurotic trends" (Horney, 1939, p. 282). Hence she advocated investigating primarily the consequences of these trends and recommended that "the analyst should deliberately conduct the analysis" (p. 286) in order to help "the individual to become discriminately friendly toward others instead of indiscriminately hostile" (p. 282).

Incidentally, some of Horney's followers have felt that her stress on the present and the future resulted in an undue neglect of personal antecedents. Without disagreeing with her emphasis on the loveless mother-child relationship, they see advantages to the recovery of personal antecedents, especially in the treatment of adolescents (Rubins, 1967).

THE HERE AND NOW OF THE ANALYTIC SITUATION AS REALITY

The here and now of the analytic situation, and particularly the nature and the quality of the relationship to the analyst, have commanded increased attention from non-Freudian analysts (Alexander, 1961, pp. 310, 313–314; Enelow & Adler, 1965; Fromm-Reichmann, 1950, pp. 7–31; Tauber, 1954; Tauber & Green, 1959, pp. 113–126; Thompson, 1964, pp. 168–178).

The aim of the analysis is believed to be not the healing of an illness but the treatment of a disturbance. Therefore, the analyst must respect "the patient's own courage and use it as much as possible" (Reid, 1967, pp. 145–146). He must refrain from giving false explanations, as he must avoid insisting that the child accept the true ones (Wickes, 1927). The analyst must take care not to become a partner to the "suppression of the mind's development" (Jung, 1954, p. 34). By respecting the child's rights, he will help him to achieve a sense of fullness of life through being faithful "to the law of one's own being" (ibid., p. 179).

The analyst can assist in the struggle against the imposition of "self-betrayal" and the sacrifice of the wish for self-realization and for freedom (Fromm, 1941, pp. 257–258). As the emerging person is thus supported (Horney, 1950), the ominous unknown (Fromm, 1947), implicit in progressive development, can be faced with more confidence.

Then the neurotic resistance to abandon the familiar, and mostly comfortable, setting of his neurosis, manifest in the analysis as in other aspects of life, may be overcome. Being enabled to become productively true to himself, loneliness and isolation may loom less threateningly. He may be able to dispense with the protective, incestuous attachment to the mother (Fromm, 1964). He may be eager to exchange the safety of his childhood embeddedness for the zestful experience of independent creativity (Schachtel, 1959). He may consider giving up clinging "to the sources of pleasure" (Rank, 1952, p. 18) and confront the anxiety of separation.

There is thus fairly general agreement on the

analyst's role in the analysis. From among the various factors contributing to his usefulness, several are of special importance: the analyst's interest in and ability to learn the child's language rather than trying to impose his own (Rank, 1945; Sullivan, 1954); and, also, his endeavor to remain humanly attuned to the patient, to provide an atmosphere of warm acceptance (Braatoy, 1954; Raush & Bordin, 1957), of personal commitment to the analysis (Sullivan, 1954; Will, 1964), and of significant emotional contact (Auerbach, 1963). The growing trust, then, in the reliability of the analyst and in his noncoercive attitudes encourages the child to venture again into relationships of intimacy. Once he need not fear any longer a repetition of parental tyrannization (Kovar, 1966), he can move on toward individuation and independence, the ultimate developmental accomplishments.

THE NEED TO BELONG, A CRUCIAL PHENOMENON

Finally, but not least, the view must be recorded that nonneurotic development is the unfolding without clogs, not the control, of innate potentials, that it is "a positive process not just an avoidance phenomenon" (Rank, 1952, p. 9).

Adler (1963, p. x) placed great stress on the feeling of isolation and loneliness that results from a lack of identification with the community and communal goals.

Isolation from others and feelings of loneliness, or the fear thereof, are seen as the cause for neurotic adaptation by other non-Freudians as well (Fromm, 1941, 1947; Horney, 1937; Rank, 1952; Schachtel, 1959). Their views differ from Adler's in that the social order and the cultural values of society are held to impose isolation unless the child is willing to forego self-realization. Neurosis, then, is an attempt at compromise and at solution of the dilemma. Since

mental health is jeopardized in isolation from others, neurosis therefore is still an expression of the tendency of personality toward the state "that we call mental health or interpersonal adjustive success" (Sullivan, 1947, p. 48). This does not imply that there is no withdrawal from interpersonal contact in the neurosis. There is, but under duress. Indeed, the child's adjustive efforts, his dynamisms, are still directed toward the achievement of an interpersonal sense of security. It is to this end that he is "willing" to exchange satisfaction and euphoria for apathetic disinterest and withdrawal from others (Sullivan, 1953). Thus curtailing his exposure, he hopes to be able to avert rejection in his now restricted world.

GENITAL MATURATION SEEN IN A NEW LIGHT

The willingness to forego satisfaction for the sake of security undergoes a dramatic change with the advent of puberty and the beginning of adolescence (Sullivan, 1953). This change can be traced to the overwhelming strength of the "lust dynamism," which brings it on a par with the thus far unique concern with self-esteem, personal worth, and in general, feelings of security (Sullivan, 1953, p. 266).

Douvan and Gold (1966) have pointed out that "the early emphasis of psychoanalysis on the instincts and their vicissitudes led to a view of adolescence as primarily, if not entirely, a recapitulation of earlier Oedipal conflict and resolution" (pp. 469–470).

At some variance with this emphasis, non-Freudian theories have advanced the notion of the unprecedented importance of the maturation of the sexual genital ability and have made all other developments contingent on it. However, in addition, Jung and Sullivan, primarily, drew attention to other developmental facets of this age period.

FURTHER MATURATIONAL DYNAMICS IN ADOLESCENCE

Jung (1933) was the first to indicate that "the conscious distinction of the ego from the parents, takes place in the normal course of things at the age of puberty with the eruption of sexual life" (pp. 98–99). One could argue that in actual fact the 3-year-old child seems to have a distinct "I" awareness, but it is "fashioned in large part by parental attitudes toward him" (Swift, 1964, p. 277). There is other evidence indicating that the conscious awareness of the self as a person, psychologically speaking, is coincidental with adolescence. It is in adolescence that the ability matures to look at oneself critically, to take stock, to compare oneself with others, to be objective about oneself and about others, to "manipulate ideas in themselves" rather than merely as objects, as had been the case earlier (Bryt, 1966, 1968; Inhelder & Piaget, 1958; Schachtel, 1959; Sullivan, 1953).

Thus Jung's contention is supported that at puberty the child begins to free himself from "the spell of the family," trying to separate himself as much as possible from them, yet inwardly is tied "the more firmly to the parental image. The frequent and often very deep depressions of puberty emanate from this" (Jung, 1910, pp. 246–247).

Jung also proposed that: "A person is only half understood when one knows how everything in him came about. . . . Life is not made up of yesterday only. . . . Life has also a tomorrow" (Jung, 1920, p. 390). Rank and Horney subscribed to this. Fromm (1964) agrees that the fundamental basis of incestuous desire is the thought or impulse of becoming a child again (Jung, 1927, p. 44) and that the child may at the same time like and fear his mother.

Sullivan's (1947, 1953) seminal contribution to a deeper understanding of adolescence has been touched on. His thinking, namely, that the lust dynamism is not liable to sublimation and always expresses itself directly, approaches Jung's view that with the eruption of sexual life, bodily needs assert themselves "without stint or measure" (Jung, 1933, p. 99).

Sullivan (1947) stressed the ability for intimacy as a prerequisite for rewarding sexual relationships. He defined love as the ability to give equal significance to one's own needs and to "the satisfaction and the security which are being experienced by someone else, some particular other person" (p. 20). The ability to do so depends on whether one has been able to achieve a critical objectification of oneself. It is paralyzed if one's basic attitude toward others is hostile, as when the child has developed a "malevolent attitude" in response to having had his needs for tenderness severely frustrated and to having been treated so as to have experienced "anxiety or even in some cases pain" (Sullivan, 1953, p. 214).

Such children develop an unremitting suspiciousness lest they be caught in the "trap" of tenderness and affection from others. Therefore, they are extremely recalcitrant candidates for analytic treatment.

The mother-child relationship and the mother's role have received increasing attention in non-Freudian thought. Horney (1939) and Thompson (1964) have traced the foundations of "feminine psychology" to this relationship. The issues of masochism in women and of penis envy have been dealt with extensively by these two authors. Obviously, so basic an orientation should deserve more extensive coverage than the mere mention of it, especially since it is of extraordinary therapeutic importance. However, in this context it must suffice to indicate that the positions of both Horney and Thompson agree with that expressed by Fromm (1941) and Sullivan (1947), that specific cultural conditions, transmitted through the child-mother relationship, bring about specific qualities, abilities, and aspirations in both girls and boys.

Gender identification and self-concept, modeling influences, and style setting are not viewed, however, as being exclusively, or even mostly, in the domain of the mother. Forrest (1967) and Deutscher (1968), among others, have highlighted the role of the father in relation to the developmental progress of the boy and the girl (Forrest, 1966).

Consistent with non-Freudian theories on adolescents are reports from the field of sociology. Thus Bealer and Willits' (1961) judgment that the popular image of "rebellious youth" is an inaccurate interpretation of the "individual resistance to specific authority patterns" supports the contention of the determining influence of the milieu on individual adjustment.

This general view may also be gathered from Freedman's (1963) *Longitudinal Study of College Women,* which illuminates commonly disregarded therapeutic possibilities in showing the constructive resourcefulness of adolescents and the fact that traumatizing experiences may first occur in adolescence. Similar observations can be found in a paper by Spiegel (1966), who suggests, too, that the father-daughter relationship contributes to the woman's self-image.

SUMMARY

Non-Freudian analysts have attempted to distinguish between those aspects of child and adolescent development which seem to be genotypical phenomena and those which appear clearly phenotypical. The consensus at this reading seems to be that constructive tendencies for growth, development, and self-realization are inherent in human nature and can be counted on to make their effects felt in the analytic situation. There is agreement also on the special importance of sexual, genital urges and their effects on interpersonal relationships beginning with adolescence. All authors also attach impor-

tance to the conditions prevailing during the childhood years and their lasting effect on personality patterns.

However, the notion that any patterning in personality could arise outside of the influences of a facilitating or inhibiting environment is rejected (Ackerman, 1957). There would be agreement, rather, with Linton (1945) that the basic personality type is characteristic of the society in which it is observed and that "changing conditions in the life of a society may result in changes in the technique of child care with a corresponding modification, over time, in the society's basic personality type" (p. ix).

A comparable notion, it would seem, from the Freudian position has been expressed by Friend (1952) with regard to the "culture conflict" between therapist and child, where "lack of appreciation of details of different cultures tends to prevent the dynamic understanding of actual interplay. . . . What is needed by the child therapist is the capacity for inner freedom, so that alien customs are not transposed into fixed images" (p. 227).

Other followers of Freudian tenets, not the least of whom is Erikson, have been impressed with the interdependence of cultural influences and personality dynamics.

Such developments give added weight to a related warning by Sullivan, to which Spiegel (1966, p. 117) has referred, "about taking over fact and theory about the male psyche and applying them to the female without starting with fresh, uncluttered observations."

Psychoanalysis with children and adolescents may also have to recognize with Allport (1955) that "people are busy leading their lives into the future whereas psychology for the most part, is busy tracing them into the past" (p. 51). Far too often, children are seen as reactors only, rather than as actors "with purposiveness, goal directedness, unity, self-consistency and uniqueness" (Ansbacher, 1967). Too frequently, perhaps, therapy pursues the ravels of the child's avoidance operations when it might be more fruitful to ask with Kraus (1967) "what goal the person is afraid of failing to reach."

Bergson has placed emphasis upon the opposing duality of reproduction and individuation. Non-Freudian analysts have shown that in freeing themselves from what is outdated in Freud, they did not have to forswear him completely. It is as Erikson has said (1964), that "much depends on the interplay of generations in which human strength can be revitalized or human weakness perseverated into the second and third generation" (pp. 119–120). Analysis can well afford, without dishonor to its "creator," to take into account new insights gained from extensive experience.

The contemporary child analyst, therefore, can in good faith make "attempts to reduce anxiety with deliberate speed" (Ginott, 1968, p. 292) and evaluate analytic interpretations not by their accuracy but by the patient's responses to them (Spotnitz, 1968, p. 109). Bloch's formulation (1968) accurately depicts the non-Freudian position: "The nuclear problem," she says, "is the parent-child relationship" (p. 203). The central issue in analysis, therefore, is the relationship between analyst and patient.

It is not unlikely that under the impetus of child and adolescent analysis there will develop in the not-too-distant future a true field of study of human psychology and human relations and a discipline for the treatment of emotional disturbances. Then, with considerations of power and of loyalty to doctrine out of the way, there may be room for dissent and for divergence of opinion. Recent developments in ego-psychology and in psychology of object relations have brought traditional psychoanalysis so much closer to non-Freudian theory that this hope appears more than chimerical.

REFERENCES

Ackerman, N. W. A changing conception of personality. *American Journal of Psychoanalysis,* 1957, **17,** 78–86.

Adelson, E. T. Facts and theories of the psychology of dreams. In E. T. Adelson (Ed.), *Dreams in contemporary psychoanalysis.* New York: Society of Medical Psychoanalysts, 1963. Pp. 1–33.

Adler, A. *The neurotic constitution.* (Tr. by B. Glueck & J. F. Lind.) New York: Moffat, Yard, 1917.

Adler, A. *The practice and theory of individual psychology.* New York: Harcourt, Brace, 1927.

Adler, A. *The neurotic condition.* New York: Dodd, Mead, 1930.

Adler, A. *What life should mean to you.* (Ed. by Alan Porter.) Boston: Little, Brown, 1931.

Adler, A. The fundamental views of individual psychology. *International Journal of Individual Psychology,* 1935, **1,** 5–8.

Adler, A. *Practice and theory of individual psychology.* New York: Harper, 1936.

Adler, A. *Understanding human nature.* (Tr. by W. B. Wolfe.) New York: Greenberg, 1946.

Adler, A. *The problem child.* New York: Capricorn Books, 1963.

Adler, A. *Problems of neuroses.* (Ed. by P. Mairet.) New York: Harper & Row, 1964. (a)

Adler, A. *The individual psychology of Alfred Adler.* (Ed. by H. L. Ansbacher & R. R. Ansbacher.) New York: Harper & Row, 1964. (b)

Adler, A. The psychology of power. (1929) *Journal of Individual Psychology,* 1966, **22,** 166–172.

Alexander, F. *The scope of psychoanalysis.* New York: Basic Books, 1961.

Allen, F. *Positive aspects of child psychiatry.* New York: Norton, 1963.

Allport, G. W. *Becoming.* New Haven, Conn.: Yale University Press, 1955.

Ansbacher, H. L. Life style: A historical and systematic review. *Journal of Individual Psychology,* 1967, **23**, 191–212.

Auerbach, A. H. An application of Strupp's method of content analysis to psychotherapy. *Psychiatry: Journal for the Study of Interpersonal Processes,* 1963, **26**, 137–148.

Balint, M. On love and hate. In *Primary love and psychoanalytic technique.* London: Hogarth, 1952. (As quoted by D. L. Takeo. Some thoughts on helplessness and the desire to be loved. *Psychiatry, Journal for the Study of Interpersonal Processes,* 1963, **26,** 266–277.)

Bealer, R. C., & Willits, F. K. Rural youth. A case study in the rebelliousness of adolescents. *The Annals of the American Academy of Political and Social Sciences,* 1961, **338**, 63–69.

Beres, D. *Vicissitudes of superego functions and superego precursors in childhood.* Vol. 13. *The psychoanalytic study of the child.* New York: International Universities Press, 1958. Pp. 324–351.

Berger, R. J. Experimental modifications of dream content by meaningful verbal stimuli. *British Journal of Psychiatry,* 1963, **109**, 722–740.

Bloch, D. The use of interpretation in the psychoanalysis of children. In E. F. Hammer (Ed.), *Use of interpretation in treatment.* New York: Grune & Stratton, 1968.

Boidon, W. *The clinical use of dreams.* New York: Basic Books, 1962.

Boigon, H. W. Horney's concept of basic anxiety. *American Journal of Psychoanalysis,* 1965, **25**, 142–157.

Bonime, W. *The clinical use of dreams.* New York: Basic Books, 1962.

Braatoy, T. *Fundamentals of psychoanalytic technique.* New York: Wiley, 1954.

Bryt, A. Modifications of psychoanalysis in the treatment of adolescents. In J. H. Masserman (Ed.), *Science and Psychoanalysis.* Vol. IX. New York: Grune & Stratton, 1966. Pp. 80–90.

Bryt, A. Discussion of a paper, "Reactionary and rebel, siblings under the skin?" by S. B. Cohen. In J. H. Masserman (Ed.), *Science and Psychoanalysis.* Vol. XII. New York: Grune & Stratton, 1968. Pp. 52–55.

Bryt, A. Application of theory to prevention. Presented at the 25th Anniversary Celebration of the William Alanson White Institute, October, 1968. New York: Basic Books, 1971.

De Martino, M. F. *Dreams and personality dynamics.* Springfield, Ill.: Charles C Thomas, 1959.

Deutscher, M. Adult work and developmental models. *American Journal of Orthopsychiatry,* 1968, **38**, 882–892.

Douvan, E., & Gold, M. Modal patterns in American adolescence. In L. W. Hoffman & M. L. Hoffman (Eds.), *Review of child development research.* Vol. 2. New York: Russell Sage Foundation, 1966. Pp. 469–528.

Eissler, K. R. Notes on the problem of techniques in the psychoanalytic treatment of adolescents. In *The psychoanalytic study of the child.* Vol. 13. New York: International Universities Press, 1958. Pp. 223–254.

Enelow, A. J., & Adler, L. M. The "here and now" as the focus of psychotherapy. In J. H.

Masserman (Ed.), *Science and psychoanalysis.* Vol. VIII. New York: Grune & Stratton, 1965.

Engel, M., Marsden, G., & Woodaman, S. Children who work and the concept of work style. *Psychiatry, Journal for the Study of Interpersonal Processes,* 1967, **30,** 392–404.

Erikson, E. H. *Childhood and society.* New York: Norton, 1950.

Erikson, E. H. The dream specimen in psychoanalysis. *Journal of the American Psychoanalytic Association,* 1954, **2,** 5–55.

Erikson, E. H. The problem of ego identity. In G. S. Klein (Ed.), *Psychological issues.* New York: International Universities Press, 1959. Pp. 101–171.

Erikson, E. H. *Insight and responsibility.* New York: Norton, 1964.

Fairbairn, W. R. D. *An object relation theory of personality.* New York: Basic Books, 1954.

Ferenczi, S. On the technique of psychoanalysis. (1919) In *The selected papers of Sandor Ferenczi. Theory and technique of psychoanalysis.* New York: Basic Books, 1952. Pp. 177–189. (a)

Ferenczi, S. The further development of an active therapy in psychoanalysis. (1920) In *The selected papers of Sandor Ferenczi. Theory and technique of psychoanalysis.* New York: Basic Books, 1952. Pp. 198–217. (b)

Forrest, T. Paternal roots of female character development. *Contemporary Psychoanalysis,* 1966, **3,** 21–38.

Forrest, T. The paternal roots of male character development. *The Psychoanalytic Review,* 1967, **54,** 278–295.

French, T., & Fromm, E. *Dream interpretation.* New York: Basic Books, 1964.

Freud, A. *The ego and the mechanisms of defense.* (1937) (Tr. by C. Bains.) London: Hogarth, 1948.

Freud, S. The interpretation of dreams. (1900) In *The complete psychological works.* Vols. IV–V. London: Hogarth, 1953.

Freud, S. Five lectures on psychoanalysis. (1909) In *The complete psychological works.* Vol. II. London: Hogarth, 1957. (a)

Freud, S. On the history of the psychoanalytic movement. (1914) In *The complete psychological works.* Vol. XIV. London: Hogarth, 1957. Pp. 7–66. (b)

Friedman, M. B. Some theoretical and practical implications of a longitudinal study of college women. *Psychiatry, Journal for the Study of Interpersonal Processes,* 1963, **26,** 176–187.

Friend, M. R. An evaluation from the psychiatric point of view. In O. Pollak et al., *Social science and psychotherapy for children.* New York: Russell Sage Foundation, 1952. Pp. 221–231.

Fromm, E. *Escape from freedom.* New York: Farrar & Rinehart, 1941.

Fromm, E. *Man for himself.* New York and Toronto: Rinehart, 1947.

Fromm, E. *The forgotten language.* New York: Rinehart, 1951.

Fromm, E. *The sane society.* New York: Rinehart, 1955.

Fromm, E. *The heart of man.* New York: Harper & Row, 1964.

Fromm-Reichmann, F. Recent advances in psychoanalytic psychotherapy. In P. Mullahy (Ed.), *A study of interpersonal relations.* New York: Hermitage, 1949. Pp. 122–129.

Fromm-Reichmann, F. *Principles of intensive*

psychotherapy. Chicago: University of Chicago Press, 1950.

Gesell, A., Ilg, F. L., & Ornes, L. B. *Youth, the years from ten to sixteen.* New York: Harper, 1956.

Ginott, H. G. Interpretation and child therapy. In E. F. Hammer (Ed.), *Use of interpretation in treatment.* New York: Grune & Stratton, 1968.

Glover, E. *Examination of the Klein system of child psychology.* Vol. 1. *The psychoanalytic study of the child.* New York: International Universities Press, 1945. Pp. 75–118.

Glover, E. *Freud or Jung.* New York: Norton, 1950.

Green, M. R., Ullman, M., & Tauber, E. S. Dreaming and modern dream theory. In J. Marmor (Ed.), *Modern psychoanalysis.* New York: Basic Books, 1968. Pp. 146–186.

Guntrip, H. *Personality structure and human interaction.* London: Hogarth, 1961.

Hall, C. S. *The meaning of dreams.* New York: Dell, 1959.

Hall, C. S., & Domhoff, B. A ubiquitous sex difference in dreams. *Journal of Abnormal and Social Psychology*, 1963, **66**, 278–280.

Hoffman, M. L., & Hoffman, L. W. (Eds.) *Review of child development research.* (2 vols.) New York: Russell Sage Foundation, 1964.

Horney, K. *The neurotic personality of our time.* New York: Norton, 1937.

Horney, K. *New ways in psychoanalysis.* New York: Norton, 1939.

Horney, K. *Our inner conflicts.* New York: Norton, 1945.

Horney, K. *Neurosis and human growth.* New York: Norton, 1950.

Inhelder, B., & Piaget, J. *The growth of logical thinking.* (Tr. by A. Parsons & S. Milgram.) New York: Basic Books, 1958.

Jacobi, J. *The psychology of Jung.* (Tr. by K. W. Bash.) New Haven, Conn.: Yale University Press, 1945.

Jung, K. G. The association method. (Tr. by A. A. Brill.) *The American Journal of Psychology*, 1910, **21**.

Jung, K. G. *Collected papers on analytic psychology.* (2nd ed.) (Tr. by E. Long.) London: Baillière, 1920.

Jung, K. G. *The psychology of the unconscious.* (Tr. by B. M. Hinkle.) New York: Dodd, Mead, 1927.

Jung, K. G. *Modern man in search of a soul.* (Tr. by W. S. Dell & C. F. Baynes.) New York: Harcourt, Brace, first published 1933.

Jung, K. G. *The development of personality.* (Tr. by R. F. C. Hull.) Vol. 17. New York: Pantheon, 1954.

Jung, K. G., Von Franz, M., Henderson, J., Jacobi, J., & Jaffe, A. *Man and his symbols.* New York: Doubleday, 1964.

Kelman, N. Child analysis and Horney theory. *The American Journal of Psychoanalysis*, 1949, **9**, 38–47.

Klein, M. *The psychoanalysis of children.* London: Hogarth, 1950.

Klein, M. The psychoanalytic play technique. In M. Klein, P. Heimann, & R. E. M. Kryle (Eds.), *New directions in psychoanalysis.* New York: Basic Books, 1955. Pp. 3–22.

Kovar, L. A reconsideration of paranoia. *Psychiatry,* 1966, **29,** 289–305.

Kraus, H. H. Anxiety: The dread of a future event. *Journal of Individual Psychology*, 1967, **23**, 88–93.

Levy, D. M. Developmental psychoanalytic aspects of oppositional bahavior. In Sandor Rado & George E. Daniels (Eds.), *Changing concepts of psychoanalytic medicine.* New York: Grune & Stratton, 1956. Pp. 114–134.

Linton, R. *Foreword to the psychological frontiers of society.* A. Kardiner, R. Linton, C. Du Bois, & J. West. New York: Columbia University Press, 1945. Pp. v–xiii.

Mahoney, M. F. *The meaning in dreams and dreaming. The Jungian viewpoint.* New York: Citadel, 1966.

Millet, J. A. P. Psychoanalysis in the United States. In F. Alexander, S. Eisenstein, & M. Grotjahn (Eds.), *Psychoanalytic pioneers.* New York: Basic Books, 1966. Pp. 546–596.

Milton, J. Paradise regained. (1671) In H. C. Beeching (Ed.), *The poetical work.* Book IV. London: Oxford University Press, 1938.

Mullahy, P. A theory of interpersonal relations and the evolution of personality. In *Conceptions of modern psychiatry.* Washington, D.C.: William Alanson White Foundation, 1947. (Reprinted from *Psychiatry, Journal of the Biology and Pathology of Interpersonal Relations,* **3**(1) and **8**(2).

Offenkrantz, W., & Rechtschaffen, A. Clinical studies of sequential dreams. *Archives of General Psychiatry*, 1963, **8**, 497–508.

Olden, C. Notes on the development of empathy. Vol. 13. *The psychoanalytic study of the child.*

New York: International Universities Press, 1958. Pp. 505–518.

Ovesey, L. The phobic reaction. In S. Goldman & D. Shapiro (Eds.), *Developments in psychoanalysis at Columbia University.* New York: Hafner, 1966.

Parsons, T. Certain primary sources and patterns of aggression in the social structure of the Western world. In P. Mullahy (Ed.), *A study of interpersonal relations.* New York: Hermitage, 1949. Pp. 223–296.

Pepitone, A. Motivational effects in social perception. *Human Relations,* 1950, **3**, 57–76.

Rado, S. Adaptational developments in psychoanalytic theory. In S. Rado & G. E. Daniels (Eds.), *Changing concepts of psychoanalytic medicine.* New York: Grune & Stratton, 1956. (a)

Rado, S. *Psychoanalysis of behavior.* Vol. 2. New York: Grune & Stratton, 1956. (b)

Rank, O. *Will therapy, truth and reality.* New York: Knopf, 1945.

Rank, O. *The trauma of birth.* New York: Brunner, 1952.

Raush, H. L., & Bordin, E. S. Warmth in personality development and in psychotherapy. *Psychiatry,* 1957, **20,** 351–364.

Reich, W. (1933) *Character analysis.* (3rd ed.) (Tr. by T. P. Wolfe.) New York: Orgone Institute Press, 1949.

Reid, A. M. Discussion. In R. W. Gibson (Ed.), *Crosscurrents in psychiatry and psychoanalysis.* Philadelphia: Lippincott, 1967. Pp. 145–146.

Rosenblatt, B. A severe neurosis in an adolescent boy. Vol. 18. *The psychoanalytic study of the*

the child. New York: International Universities Press, 1963. Pp. 561–602.

Rubins, J. L. Changing concepts of the growth process. *The American Journal of Psychoanalysis,* 1967, **27,** 3–13.

Schachtel, E. G. *Metamorphosis.* New York: Basic Books, 1959.

Searles, H. The schizophrenic individual's experience of his world. *Psychiatry,* 1967, **30,** 119–131.

Society for Adolescent Psychiatry. Goals of treatment of adolescents. P. Bloss, R. Evans, S. Green, & W. Hulse (panelists); A. Bryt (moderator). Unpublished panel discussion, Oct. 14, 1959.

Spiegel, N. T. An infantile fetish and its persistence into young womanhood. Vol. 22. *The psychoanalytic study of the child.* New York: International Universities Press, 1967. Pp. 403–425.

Spiegel, R. The role of father-daughter relationship in depressive women. In J. Masserman (Ed.), *Science and psychoanalysis.* Vol. X. New York: Grune & Stratton, 1966. Pp. 105–119.

Spotnitz, H. The maturational interpretation. In E. F. Hammer (Ed.), *Use of interpretation in treatment.* New York: Grune & Stratton, 1968.

Sullivan, H. S. *Conceptions of modern psychiatry.* Washington, D.C.: William Alanson White Foundation, 1947. (Reprinted from *Psychiatry, Journal of the Biology and Pathology of Interpersonal Relations,* **3**(1), and **8**(2).

Sullivan, H. S. *The interpersonal theory of psychiatry.* (Ed. by S. Perry & M. L. Gawell.) New York: Norton, 1953.

Sullivan, H. S. *The psychiatric interview.* (Ed.

by H. S. Perry & M. L. Gawell.) New York: Norton, 1954.

Sullivan, H. S. *Clinical studies in psychiatry.* (Ed. by H. S. Perry, M. L. Gawell, & M. Gibbon.) New York: Norton, 1956.

Sullivan, H. S. *Schizophrenia as a human process.* New York: Norton, 1962.

Swift, J. W. Effects of early group experience. The nursery school and day nursery. In M. L. Hoffman & L. W. Hoffman (Eds.), *Review of child development research.* Vol. I. New York: Russell Sage Foundation, 1964. Pp. 249–288.

Tauber, E. S. Exploring the psychotherapeutic use of counter transference data. *Psychiatry,* 1954, **17,** 332–336.

Tauber, E. S. The dream in the therapeutic process from the therapist's standpoint. In E. Adelson (Ed.), *Dreams in contemporary psychoanalysis.* New York: Society of Medical Psychoanalysts, 1963.

Tauber, E. S., & Green, M. R. *Prelogical experience.* New York: Basic Books, 1959.

Thompson, C. M. *Psychoanalysis: Evolution and development.* New York: Hermitage, 1950.

Thompson, C. M. The role of the analyst's personality in therapy. In M. R. Green (Ed.), *Interpersonal psychoanalysis. The collected papers of Clara M. Thompson.* New York: Basic Books, 1964.

Ullman, M. The dream process. *American Journal of Psychotherapy,* 1958, **12,** 671–690.

Verdone, P. P. Variable related to the temporal reference of manifest dream content. *Perceptual and Motor Skills,* 1965, **20,** 1253–1268.

White, W. A. Higher levels of mental integration. In C. M. Child, K. Koffka, J. F. Anderson,

J. B. Watson, E. Sapir, W. I. Thomas, M. E. Kenworthy, F. L. Wells, & W. A. White, *The unconscious; A symposium.* Essay Index Reprint series. Freeport, N.Y.: Books for Libraries Press, 1966. Pp. 242–260.

Wickes, F. A. *The inner world of childhood.* New York: Appleton-Century-Crofts, 1927.

Wickes, F. A. *The inner world of man.* New York and Toronto: Farrar, Straus and Rinehart, 1938.

Will, O., Jr. Schizophrenia and the psychotherapeutic field. *Contemporary Psychoanalysis,* 1964, **1,** 1–29.

Winnicott, D. W. *The maturational processes and the facilitating environment.* New York: International Universities Press, 1965.

Witkin, H. A., & Lewis, H. R. (Eds.) *Experimental studies of dreaming.* New York: Random House, 1967.

Wolpert, E. A., & Trosman, H. Studies in psychobiology of dreams. *Archives of Neurology and Psychiatry,* 1958, **79,** 603–606.

Wyss, D. *Depth psychology.* (Tr. by A. Onn.) New York: Norton: 1966.

Zelmanowitz, F. Review of the collected papers of David Rapaport, edited by M. M. Gill, New York, Basic Books, 1967. *Psychiatry, Journal for the Study of Interpersonal Processes,* 1968, **31,** 292–299.

29 | Behavior Therapy

Alan O. Ross

HISTORY

Behavior therapy rests on the premise that psychological disorders represent learned behavior, so that principles of learning can be applied to the modification of these disorders. The last two decades have seen a number of attempts to relate the principles embodied in theories of learning to the process of psychotherapy. Shoben (1949), Mowrer (1950), and Dollard and Miller (1950) were among the first to make systematic attempts at translating psychoanalytic constructs into learning-theory terms, but these writers did not succeed in deriving a new and distinct treatment approach from learning principles. It was not until Skinner (1953), Eysenck (1957), Wolpe (1958), and Bandura (1961) suggested that laboratory-derived and tested methods could be applied to the modification of psychological disorders that behavior therapy, as we know it today, came into its own. From the point of view of the history of science and ideas, it is interesting to note that the prototype of the application of learning principles

to the alleviation of a child's psychological problem dates back to 1924, the year when Mary Cover Jones published the case of Peter, whose generalized fear of furry objects she had treated by applying the principles of classical conditioning. A few years later, Krasnogorski (1925), Ivanov-Smolenski (1927), and Gesell (1938) pointed to the relevance of Pavlovian conditioning to the treatment of psychological disorders; but it seems that the time for this obvious idea had not yet come, for although, in the intervening years, Mowrer and Mowrer (1938) described the treatment of enuretics by conditioning techniques, it was not until Wolpe (1958) "rediscovered" the work of Jones some 30 years later that behavioral approaches to treatment began to find wider acceptance.

Though the prototype of behavior therapy was the treatment of a 3-year-old, early application was almost exclusively with adult cases. When Ross (1964) discussed the application of learning theory to therapy with children, the literature contained reports on but six children thus treated (Boardman, 1962; Lazarus, 1960; White, 1959;

900

Williams, 1959). Not until operant approaches were brought to bear on work with institutionalized children (Ferster, 1961; Ferster & DeMyer, 1962) did behavior therapy become more widely applied in the treatment of children.

THEORETICAL BACKGROUND

The behavior therapist applies principles of learning in the treatment of psychological disorders. These can be roughly classified into two major groupings: deficient behavior and maladaptive behavior. In the case of the former, the child has failed to learn adaptive responses and the therapeutic task is to teach him these responses. In the case of the latter, the child makes responses under inappropriate circumstances and he must be taught to modify these responses so as to make his behavior more adaptive to the demands of his environment. In either case, treatment involves learning, unlearning, and relearning; this corrective action has come to be referred to as *behavior therapy*.

Whether the problem behavior is deficient or maladaptive, the behavior therapist operates on the assumption that it can be modified by studying the *current* conditions under which this behavior occurs and planning remedial action on the basis of the information thus obtained. While the learning orientation logically includes the implicit acceptance of past events as contributing to the development of the child's present difficulty, the behavior therapist considers a detailed knowledge of the child's history unnecessary to arriving at his treatment plans. The historical antecedents of a current problem are thus deemphasized. Instead, behavior therapy demands a detailed and intensive assessment of the current conditions under which the behavior in question takes place or fails to take place, for behavior therapy consists of the modification of these conditions or of the client's reactions to these conditions.

The principles of learning which behavior therapists bring to bear on the analysis and modification of maladaptive behavior suggest that two basic kinds of conditioning affect the establishment and elimination of responses: respondent conditioning and operant conditioning. Space does not permit a detailed, technical presentation of these learning principles. A brief summary must suffice, but anyone wishing to apply these principles in clinical work should first acquire the relevant theoretical background.

Respondent Conditioning

At times called *Pavlovian* or *classical* conditioning, this kind of learning involves the modification of a response that the organism is innately capable of making by substituting a conditioned stimulus for the natural, or unconditioned, stimulus. A well-known example is the case of little Albert (Watson & Rayner, 1920), who was conditioned to make a fear response to the stimulus of a white rat by having the rat repeatedly paired with a loud noise, a stimulus that elicits fear, apparently innately. Prior to this conditioning, the rat had been an object of curiosity to the child, who was thus shown to have learned to fear the animal. It is a distinctive aspect of respondent conditioning that an innate response is *elicited* by a stimulus which *precedes* it and that the organism is *passively responding* to potent environmental events or external stimuli. The responses in question usually involve the autonomic nervous system, and respondent conditioning is probably always involved when emotional responses come to be attached to previously neutral stimuli.

A number of phenomena that have been intensively studied in the psychological laboratory are of particular relevance to the behavior therapist. These are stimulus generalization, extinction, conditioned inhibition, and differential inhibition. Wolpe (1958) and others who treat maladaptive emotional reactions by what they variously call *counterconditioning* or *reciprocal inhibition* produce a decrement of a conditioned response by eliciting an incompatible response to the same conditioned stimulus.

Operant Conditioning

In respondent conditioning, the environment elicits a response from a relatively passive organism. The situation is essentially reversed in the case of operant conditioning. Here the organism actively emits a response to which the environment reacts; in other words, the response is instrumental in bringing about an environmental event. The importance of this sequence lies in the fact that it is the *consequence* of the response that serves to change the probability of that response's recurrence under similar conditions at a later time. The conditions (stimuli) under which the organism has encountered certain consequences to its response will come to control this response, in the sense that the response will occur with greater probability when these conditions pertain than when they do not, but the conditions do not elicit the response, as does the conditioned stimulus in the case of respondent conditioning. Operant behavior is a function of its consequences, and when such behavior is to be modified, the contingencies under which these consequences occur must be changed.

In technical terminology, the sequence of operant conditioning is the presence of a discriminative stimulus, the emission of an operant response, and the presentation of a reinforcing stimulus, which is usually followed by a consummatory response. The discriminative stimulus thus represents a signal that indicates the likelihood of the appearance of the reinforcing stimulus once the response has been emitted. As a signal, it may or may not have an effect on the organism, depending on its then current state, which is a function of such "setting events" as deprivation or satiation for the particular reinforcer.

Since the operant response cannot be reinforced until it has been emitted, the response must be one that is already in the organism's repertoire. Where this is not the case, someone in the environment—parent, teacher, or therapist—must select a similar, already established response and, by selectively reinforcing successive approximations of the desired response, "shape" the necessary behavior.

As in respondent conditioning, the stimulus in operant conditioning exhibits the phenomenon of stimulus generalization. That is, not only the original discriminative stimulus but a range of similar stimuli come to be capable of controlling the response. The more similar these stimuli are to the original, the greater will be the probability that the learned response will occur. On the other hand, a learned response that is repeatedly emitted in the absence of reinforcing consequences will gradually occur with decreasing probability, a process that is labeled *extinction* in both operant and respondent conditioning.

Inasmuch as the operant response is a function of its consequences, an examination of possible consequences is essential if one is to attempt the modification of the response. Consequences can fall in one of three classes: positive, negative, or neutral. Positive consequences will strengthen the response in the sense that they will increase the likelihood of its recurrence under similar circumstances; negative consequences will reduce the likelihood of the response, i.e., they will weaken it; and neutral consequences, being those that have no reinforcing effect, will result in extinction. There are two conditions that can represent positive consequences and two that can represent negative consequences. The presentation of a satisfying stimulation (reward) and the termination or avoidance of noxious stimulation (negative reinforcement) both represent positive consequences, whereas the presentation of noxious stimulation (punishment) and the removal of satisfying stimulation (time out from positive reinforcement) both represent negative consequences.

It will be apparent that when either positive or negative stimulation is to be withdrawn, the relevant stimulation must already be present. Similarly, positive reinforcement depends for its effectiveness on the setting condition of deprivation. This makes the delivery of noxious stimulation the only manipulation that can be presented without preparation and regardless of the condition of the organism, yet despite its ready availability, punishment is complex both in its effect and in its current theoretical status in learning research.

Among the effects of punishment appears to be a physiological arousal state that can become conditioned to the stimuli present when punishment is delivered. While these stimuli may be relevant to the particular behavior being punished, so that this behavior will come to be avoided or suppressed by incompatible responses, the stimuli may also be relevant to the person delivering the noxious stimulation, so that this person will come to elicit fear and hence avoidance or escape responses.

In addition to these emotional and interpersonal aspects of punishment, there is the consideration that it does not actually eliminate the punished behavior but that it simply leads to a suppression of the behavior due to the arousal of incompatible emotional responses and their consequences. Punished behavior will remain suppressed only so long as the conditioned aversive stimuli are present; once these are absent, the punished behavior will reappear, particularly where it carries its own natural reinforcer, as in the case of taking cookies out of the cookie jar. For this reason, it is important that punishment, when used in treatment or child rearing, be paired with positive reinforcement of desirable responses that are incompatible with the responses to be weakened.

A phenomenon which permits a wide range of stimuli to serve as reinforcers is that variously called *conditioned, secondary,* or *acquired* reinforcement. A previously neutral event that repeatedly precedes a reinforcing stimulus takes on reinforcing properties in its own right. This makes it possible to reinforce a child's responses not only with such primary reinforcers as food but also with such secondary reinforcers as approval, praise, tokens, or grades on report cards. Premack (1959) has pointed out that a response with a high probability of occurrence can be used to reinforce a response of lower probability. In the case of children, this means that play can be used to reinforce work, shouting can reinforce being quiet, etc. The principle of secondary reinforcement also holds in the case of punishment. Thus, when verbal reprimands, frowns, or threats have been paired with the administration of more direct, physical punishment or the removal of positive stimulation, the more symbolic, social stimuli can acquire punishing properties in their own right.

Implications for Treatment

As this cursory summary of theoretical principles suggests, a variety of specific treatment approaches are available to the therapist wishing to modify the maladaptive behavior of a child. These approaches can be used alone or in combination, depending on the specific needs of the particular case. When a given child's problem takes the form of a behavioral deficit, the responses missing from his repertoire can be established. When the problem is maladaptive or excess behavior, the responses in question can be modified or replaced by more adaptive behavior. In either case, treatment involves learning (conditioning), and whether the respondent or the operant paradigm is to guide treatment will largely depend on whether the responses in question are skeletal-motor-muscular (voluntary) or vascular-visceral-autonomic (involuntary) in nature. Behavior therapists generally assume that the operant paradigm is best suited for the modification of responses in the skeletal-motor realm while the respondent paradigm should be followed when fear, anxiety, or related autonomic responses are the focus of treatment. This distinction follows the logic of a two-factor theory of learning (Mowrer, 1951), but recent research (e.g., DiCara & Miller, 1968) has demonstrated that visceral responses mediated by the autonomic nervous system can be modified through operant conditioning, suggesting that assigning operant conditioning to the motor realm and respondent conditioning to the autonomic realm may be a gross oversimplification.

Regardless of the adequacy of current theoretical assumptions, the therapeutic operations presently in use can be discussed in terms of the two basic paradigms. When the respondent conditioning paradigm guides the treatment approach, the therapist will have to present stimuli to the child that are intended to elicit fear-incompatible responses so that these can be paired with the stimuli to which the child had been responding with fear. In such a situation, the child is essentially a passive participant in therapy; he is the responder, the therapist the initiator. Despite the child's passivity, it would be wrong to conclude that the therapist manipulates an unwilling or unwitting "victim," for unlike the animal in the classical conditioning experiment, the child is not in a restraining harness. He is quite able not to attend to the stimuli presented to him or not to remain in the room, or he can emit responses that are incompatible with those the therapist is trying to elicit. These circumstances make respondent conditioning treatment best suited to situations where children are

motivated for getting help with a problem they recognize as troubling them. Cooperation in treatment is essential, and since this is more likely to be found with less severely impaired children in nonresidential clinic settings, it is from there that most reports of the use of treatment based on the respondent paradigm have emanated.

Where the operant conditioning paradigm guides the treatment approach, the child is a very active participant because he engages in an operation—does something to the environment. The therapist arranges the environment in such a way as to ensure that the child's operant responses occur under particular conditions and are followed by planned consequences. This contingency management requires that the therapist have some control over the stimulus and reinforcement conditions that the child will encounter, and the level of possible control will largely determine the effectiveness with which treatment can be conducted. Inasmuch as a therapist's opportunity for such control is greatest in an institutional setting, where, with the help of institutional personnel, he can influence the delivery of primary and secondary reinforcements, most reports of treatment using operant methods have come from such settings. In order to conduct this form of treatment in nonresidential settings, the therapist needs to obtain the close cooperation of the child's parents or teachers since these are in a better position to manage reinforcement contingencies than the therapist, who has only occasional contact with the child.

For purposes of presentation, the foregoing had to imply that it is always possible to state with certainty whether a given therapeutic approach is respondent or operant in nature. In reality, of course, all treatment, like any complex human learning, entails both operant and respondent aspects. When a given response constellation is being learned, it is rarely possible to identify the exact principles involved, at least not at the present state of knowledge about learning.

An example of the interrelationship of operant and respondent factors in complex behavior can be taken from the realm of deficient control over eliminative functions and its treatment. By the time a child who has not learned age-appropriate toilet behavior comes to treatment, he is likely to have acquired, as a result of punishment experiences in connection with toilet training, at least some conditioned anxiety to stimuli associated with wetting or soiling. While treatment can be planned in terms of the operant paradigm such that appropriate toilet behavior receives positive reinforcement (e.g., Neale, 1963), respondent factors will also play a role because each time an appropriate toilet response is made, anxiety that had become associated with soiling is being avoided. As frequency of soiling decreases, the anxiety associated with it will also decrease in frequency, and the training sequence must therefore be viewed as involving more than simple operant conditioning, as Hundziak, Maurer, and Watson (1965) have suggested. This is especially the case when aversive stimuli and negative reinforcement are introduced in connection with the training procedure, as in the work of Giles and Wolf (1966), who also suggested that their approach was purely operant.

Not only is it unlikely that any complex learning can ever be said to be purely operant or purely respondent, but specific cases may indeed be best treated if the therapist explicitly plans a combination of operant and respondent approaches, as was the case in the work with a 9-year-old school-phobic boy, reported by Lazarus, Davison, and Polefka (1965). Assessment of this boy's problem revealed not only that his school-phobic behavior involved an intense fear of the school situation itself but that avoiding school was also being maintained by attention and other secondary reinforcers delivered by parents, siblings, and therapists. It was therefore decided to treat the high level of anxiety by respondent (counterconditioning) techniques in the early phases of treatment and then to introduce operant strategies by making positive reinforcements contingent on school attendance. In order to ensure treatment effectiveness, the different techniques had to be carefully chosen and properly timed, with the anxiety level at each stage of treatment carefully assessed.

Lazarus, Davison, and Polefka (1965) stress the risk involved in the inappropriate use of the operant model by pointing out that under conditions of high anxiety, premature exposure to the feared school situation would probably lead to heightened sensitivity and further escape and avoidance responses, reinforced by anxiety reduction. Conversely, treatment can also be impeded by the inappropriate use of the respondent model because attempts to induce relaxation and give reassurance may provide positive reinforcement, strengthening dependent, school-avoiding behavior.

The rudiments of the basic principles of behavior therapy are relatively easy to grasp, making it appear simple and easy to apply. This apparent simplicity should not lead anyone to believe that behavior therapy can be planned and directed by untrained or poorly trained individuals. The treatment is not without its risks. Mary Cover Jones (1924) recognized this long ago when she wrote in her pioneering paper on Peter:

> This method obviously requires delicate handling. Two response systems are being dealt with: food leading to a positive reaction, and fear-object leading to a negative reaction. The desired conditioning should result in transforming the fear-object into a source of positive response (substitute stimulus). But a careless manipulator could readily produce the reverse result, attaching a fear reaction to the sight of food. [P. 388]

TREATMENT PROCEDURES

As stated earlier, the treatment of psychological disorders can be grouped into two major classifications, the treatment of deficient behavior and the treatment of maladaptive behavior. The following discussion will be organized along the lines of this somewhat arbitrary classification—arbitrary because any individual child will usually manifest both types of disorder. Even where a behavior deficit is clearly present, as in the case of enuresis, it is difficult to decide whether the child lacks the response of sphincter control or whether he maladaptively makes the wetting response under inappropriate stimulus conditions (bed instead of toilet).

The Treatment of Deficient Behavior

One of the most common behavior deficits is insufficient or absent sphincter control over bowel or bladder elimination. Enuresis, in particular, has been treated by conditioning methods for many years (Mowrer & Mowrer, 1938). The basic bell-and-pad approach has the child sleep on a pad which is wired in such a way that a single drop of urine will close a circuit and activate a bell or buzzer that continues to sound until it is manually turned off, either by the child or by an adult attendant.

Werry (1966) reviewed twenty studies reporting on the treatment of enuresis by conditioning techniques and concluded that this approach is generally effective, and a comparative study by DeLeon and Mandell (1966) found conditioning techniques superior to traditional psychotherapeutic methods. While the conditioning approach to the treatment of enuresis has thus been found to work, the question of the mode in which it works has not yet been satisfactorily answered. Lovibond (1963) raised the issue of whether this form of treatment represents an instance of classical conditioning, in which the response of sphincter contraction is learned to

the stimulus of bladder distension, or whether it should be viewed as avoidance learning, in which case the contraction would be the response that avoids the loud and sleep-disrupting noise. An experiment (Lovibond, 1964) designed to compare these alternative explanations favored the avoidance-conditioning formulation, but a high relapse rate was noted regardless of the conditioning method used.

The relapse rate in the treatment of enuresis may be viewed as a reflection of the fact that in this case, as in similar cases of the treatment of behavior deficits, one is not simply establishing a response that was previously absent from the child's repertoire but is introducing into the repertoire a response that is antagonistic to one already established. An enuretic child is not simply one who lacks appropriate sphincter control; he is one who makes a micturition response to the stimulus of bladder distension. The therapeutic task must thus be viewed as establishing a complex series of behaviors that includes sustained sphincter contraction and micturition under the appropriate stimulus conditions of the toilet. One must thus strengthen an adaptive response pattern while simultaneously weakening its maladaptive reciprocal, and this would seem to involve a combination of classical, avoidance, and operant factors, the latter coming into play in relation to the secondary reinforcements the child receives for not wetting his bed. If these secondary reinforcements are not, at least intermittently, forthcoming, the staying-dry behavior may well undergo extinction, so that the innate competing response once again becomes prepotent, thus resulting in a relapse. For this reason it is important to reinforce dry nights either by such social reinforcement as praise or such self-reinforcement as pride of accomplishment. This can be helped if, as Lovibond (1964) suggests, the child is an active partner in the treatment plan, helping with the necessary record keeping and receiving praise for his progress.

Since relapse is not found in all children treated for enuresis by conditioning methods, it is possible that those for whom relapse is recorded represent a different population of enuretics. Children who are enuretic can be divided into two groups: one composed of those who have never been dry at night and the other containing those who had once learned to sleep through the night without wetting but who regressed to the innate response in later years. In the first group, treatment would consist of teaching a new response, not previously available. In the second group, where one is dealing with children for whom an adaptive response has undergone extinction, a previously learned response must be relearned. It would stand to reason that the two groups should differ not only in acquisition rate but also in the resistance to extinction of the response pattern being established in the course of treatment.

Some support for the above speculation comes from a study by Novick (1966), who treated twenty-two chronic and twenty-three regressed enuretics by a symptom-focused form of supportive therapy followed, for those who failed to improve (80 percent), by a conditioning technique using a wetting-alarm apparatus. With this combination of treatments, all but four of the subjects reached the cure criterion of fourteen consecutive dry nights. Novick reports that the regressed enuretics, that is, those who had acquired enuresis after an initial period of dryness, reached the cure criterion sooner and with more rapid decrease in the wetting. This would suggest that those who merely had to reestablish a previously learned response relearned more quickly than those who had to acquire an entirely new response. On the other hand, the regressed cases were also more likely to display relapse or new problems than the chronic group, as revealed by follow-up interviews extending over a period of one year. It may well be that the relapsed cases reported in other studies are also primarily

those for whom enuresis represents a regression. There may be at least two explanations for this phenomenon. The first is that the regressed children reach an acceptable level of dryness sooner than the chronic, thus receiving fewer reinforced training trials, with concomitant instability of the adaptive response. Further—and often quickly successful—courses of treatment would thus increase the number of training trials and more firmly establish the desired response. Indeed, DeLeon and Mandell (1966) report this to be the case. The second (and related) explanation of the relapse phenomenon would seem to lie in the reinforcement contingencies that operate in the regressed child's environment. These may be such that the response of wetting or other maladaptive behavior is strengthened while the adaptive responses involved in staying dry are weakened. This would explain why these children not only regressed originally but relapsed after apparently successful treatment. Therapists would thus do well to work not only with the child but also with the parents, who manage the crucial contingencies.

While Novick's (1966) report that many of his subjects developed new symptoms is difficult to evaluate in the absence of a no-treatment control group and irrelevant to the question of symptom substitution in behavior therapy because he confounded supportive and conditioning treatments, a study by Baker (1967) addressed itself directly to this question. Baker treated ten enuretic children with a conditioning device and compared treatment outcome with equal numbers of children in a no-treatment, waiting-list control and in a group that received a control treatment which duplicated all aspects of the conditioning treatment except the conditioning procedure itself. The conditioning group showed significantly more improvement than either control group, and with most of the children in the wake-up group eventually shifted to conditioning, the overall cure rate was 74 percent, another 15 percent showing very marked improvement. Four of the cured subjects relapsed during a six-month follow-up, but when two of these underwent a second course of treatment, they became dry again. In order to investigate the questions of symptom substitution and generalization of improvement, an investigator who did not know to which group a given child had been assigned obtained measures of the child's adjustment from the parents and teachers of the children and from the children themselves. These data revealed no symptom substitution, but the cured children showed improvements in areas such as peer relations, school behavior, and general adjustment even though none of these had been directly treated. There was no instance of a worsening of the child's general adjustment.

The bell-and-pad method, which is derived from the respondent conditioning paradigm, is the most frequently used but not the only form of behavior therapy for enuretic children. Several studies report training methods that are explicitly based on the operant model. Hundziak, Maurer, and Watson (1965) made candy, paired with light and tone stimuli, contingent on elimination in the commode. Eight mentally retarded boys between the ages of 7 and 14 with IQs ranging from 8 to 33 underwent such training. They showed a significant increase in appropriate toilet use compared with a group of boys who were trained by conventional techniques. The training had been conducted in a special cottage, but once the appropriate responses had been established, they generalized to the boys' original living unit. Similar success was reported by Giles and Wolf (1966), who toilet-trained five severely retarded males through the application of operant conditioning methods.

The work of Giles and Wolf (1966) serves to underscore the importance of finding and using a suitable reinforcer for each child. What is reinforcing for one child may be aversive for the next, and only careful assessment can ensure reinforcer effectiveness. One boy in the Giles and Wolf group refused candy but accepted baby food; others considered a ride in a wheelchair, taking a shower, or returning to bed worthwhile rewards. These authors also found that training could be improved by combining positive reinforcement of the desired response with the delivery of aversive stimuli following the changeworthy inappropriate behavior. When exhaustive use of positive reinforcement had failed to produce results, they introduced punishment consisting of physical restraint. Since this restraint could be removed when appropriate toilet behavior was emitted, it came to serve as a negative reinforcer in addition to its aversive function. This combination of operant techniques resulted in all subjects consistently using the toilet.

A combination of positive and negative reinforcement was also used by Gelber and Meyer (1965), who treated a 14-year-old with an IQ of 117 whose chronic encopresis and smearing were reported to be his only problem behaviors. After hospitalizing the boy in order to gain contingency control, the therapists made time off the ward the reinforcer for appropriate toilet behavior. By introducing an aversive condition (being confined to a hospital ward) which was terminated following a desired response, negative reinforcement was possible, while punishment for undesirable response could be introduced by limiting time off the ward and restricting the privilege of walking around the hospital grounds.

While lack of age-appropriate sphincter control is a social handicap, a deficit more crucial to social adaptation is the absence of or gross deficiency in language, such as is frequently encountered in autistic children. This highly complex behavior can be analyzed in operant terms. Accordingly, a word or words emitted by the child are reinforced by the social environment. This paradigm has served as the basis for therapeutic techniques in which reinforcements are made contingent on the production of sounds or words, and by this method therapists have succeeded in establishing speech in nonverbal or echolalic children. Because a response must occur before it can be reinforced, the child must actively participate in the treatment. The therapist can do little to elicit a word, and when a child is completely nonverbal, speech must be shaped by using any available vocalization and reinforcing successive approximations of language. In some instances (Risley & Wolf, 1967), the child's echolalic behavior can be used as a starting point, while in others (Hewett, 1965), training in social imitation must precede speech training.

Like many children with as gross a disorder as absence of speech, Peter, the 4½-year-old boy treated by Hewett (1965), manifested other deviant behaviors that interfered with attempts to develop language. His high distractibility and low attention span made it necessary to train him in a specially constructed booth that not only reduced extraneous stimuli but also permitted the introduction of isolation and darkness contingent upon inappropriate responses. Appropriate responses were reinforced with candy and light, but these artificial reinforcers were soon supplemented by the natural reinforcers dispensed by the social environment when a child engages in acceptable and nonaversive behavior. Peter had acquired a 32-word vocabulary after six months of speech training, and after a further eight months, his speaking vocabulary had grown to 150 words, the beginnings of spoken language. During the latter part of training, generalization to the natural environment was stressed, the boy's parents participating in the program. It is significant that Peter's change in behavior altered the reactions of others toward him. The nursing staff came to seek him out for verbal interaction, giving him cues for imitation and insisting on speech before granting requests. Generalization of appropriate speech from the therapy setting to the child's own environment can be enhanced if the therapist sees to it that speech is reinforced

under a variety of conditions. Risley and Wolf (1967) have suggested that the child be trained to respond appropriately to a variety of individuals and in a variety of settings, including his own home or the family car.

Social reinforcement. The reinforcement value of such social stimuli as praise and approval represents the learning of a generalized reinforcer. Children with severe psychological disorders have frequently failed to acquire this secondary reinforcer, so that therapists wishing to strengthen desirable behaviors must resort to the use of such primary reinforcers as food in the initial stages of treatment. This obviously limits the situations in which learning can take place to those where food can be readily dispensed and requires that the child be in a state of relative deprivation in order for food to be an effective reinforcer. For these reasons, an early therapeutic task with such severely disturbed children is the establishment of generalized social reinforcers which can be delivered at any time and are readily available in the child's environment. Ferster (1967) has pointed to the distinction between arbitrary and natural reinforcers. A natural reinforcer is one that the child's environment delivers in spontaneous reaction to his behavior, and when this behavior is adaptive, these natural reinforcers will maintain the behavior in a variety of situations. Once social reinforcers have acquired effectiveness, they will serve to maintain behavior even after the artificial reinforcers used initially have been withdrawn. Patterson et al. (1965) have advanced the hypothesis "that the importance of any change in behavior lies in the effect which it produces upon the reactions of the social culture," and it is this reaction which serves to maintain adaptive behavior.

The thesis has been advanced (Ferster, 1961) that autistic children fail to be responsive to generalized social reinforcers because of the erratic reinforcement schedules used by their parents. It is assumed that the child has not been rewarded consistently with primary reinforcements to endow stimuli such as adult attention and praise with reinforcing properties. The therapist will thus have to address himself to increasing social-reinforcer effectiveness, and this would be true whether the basic deficit is as Ferster postulates or follows the formulation advanced by Rimland (1964), according to whom the autistic child is unable to associate primary reinforcements with accompanying social stimuli because of a central nervous system dysfunction.

Lovaas, Freitag, Kinder, et al. (1966) focused on the establishment of social reinforcers in their work with two 4-year-old identical twins, who were described as schizophrenic with marked autistic features. Following the classical conditioning paradigm, they paired the delivery of food with the social stimulus "good," but despite several hundred trials, this word did not acquire secondary reinforcement properties; the child's behavior did not change when it was accompanied by the word "good." The child did not seem to attend to the social stimulus, and the authors suggest that a basic problem of autistic children is this failure to attend to social stimuli. If this is the case, the therapeutic task becomes one of teaching the child to attend to the stimulus, as a first step in developing its generalized reinforcement properties. In the study cited, Lovaas et al. (1966), having found the classical paradigm ineffective, shifted to the operant model and successfully established a discriminative social stimulus for the primary reinforcer. The child thus learned that the presence of the social stimulus signaled the availability of food. This training required the child to attend to the social stimulus, and once this discrimination had been established, it was possible to use the social stimulus alone to maintain a simple operant response. Using intermittent reinforcement, it was possible to show that the social stimulus retained its acquired reinforcement property over an extended

period of time, so long as it continued to be discriminative for food.

This significant study not only lends strong support to the speculation that the basic problem of autistic children lies in their deficient attending behavior; it also suggests that any treatment that fails to take this into account is unlikely to succeed since a child must attend to a conditioned stimulus if learning is to occur. Failure to attend represents deficient orienting behavior, and such a deficit may well be related to a neurophysiological dysfunction. Davison (1965) has stated that such an organic hypothesis regarding the basic defect in infantile autism leads to a pessimistic prognosis. This is not so. A constitutional deficiency challenges the therapist to find a method for teaching the child despite his handicap; it does not make his task impossible. This is borne out by a number of successful attempts to treat autistic children with operant techniques (Davison, 1964, 1965; Wetzel, Baker, Roney, & Martin, 1966; Wolf, Risley, Johnston, Harris, & Allen, 1967; Wolf, Risley, & Mees, 1964).

Disruptive behavior. Some behavior will disrupt the acquisition of adaptive responses because it is incompatible with learning or with the response that is to be acquired. A child who attends to stimuli other than those presented by the therapist (distractibility) or who makes repetitive and excess responses (hyperactivity) engages in behavior that must be brought under control before treatment can progress. In this instance, it is somewhat difficult to decide whether one is establishing missing behavior (e.g., sitting still) or reducing surplus behavior (fidgeting), since the one is the reciprocal of the other. The paradox is illustrated in studies reported by Patterson, Jones, Whittier, and Wright (1965) and by Patterson (1965), in which treatment of hyperactive children led to a decrease of such nonattending behaviors as arm and leg movements, shuffling of chair, looking out of window, fiddling, talking to self, and wiggling of feet. The treatment method called for the delivery of candy contingent on the "nonoccurrence of nonattending behavior," a method known as *differential reinforcement of other behavior (DRO)*. The formulation involving the double negative is dictated by the need to focus on observable behavior. It is possible to keep an objective, reliable record of such behaviors as fingering a box of crayons; it is not possible to observe "paying attention" in any direct manner. For this reason, treatment focused on the absence of the observable behavior, with reinforcement made contingent on the nonoccurrence of the defined event.

Risley and Wolf (1967) were able to eliminate disruptive behavior by using *time-out from positive reinforcement (TO)*. Working on the development of speech in echolalic children, these experimenters found distractibility and hyperactivity to interfere with the training process. They were able to bring mildly disruptive behavior under control by simply looking away until the child once again sat quietly in his chair. More severe forms of disruptive behaviors were dealt with by having the therapist leave the room for a set period. The room was reentered only when the child had not engaged in the disruptive behavior for a short length of time. The therapist's coming back into the room thus served as a negative reinforcer for desired behavior since being alone was an aversive condition for the child, a condition that was being terminated contingent on the behavior to be reinforced.

Instructions and contingency announcements. In the treatment of children with whom verbal communication is possible, the therapist can tell the child the conditions under which he will encounter reinforcement of his behavior. This was done in the Patterson studies previously cited, in which not only the hyperactive child but his entire class were told that the aim of the procedure was to help him sit still so that he could study better. The class was told that when the boy sat still, he would earn candy for himself and the rest of the children in the room. This reduced the amount of distraction offered by the classmates and, in one case (Patterson, 1965), led to clapping and cheering at the end of a trial—social reinforcement delivered by the peer group.

Spelling out contingencies would seem to be an obvious procedure when working with a child in therapy, but to the psychologist with a background in laboratory conditioning techniques, it represents an unusual procedure, since in laboratory work with humans, instructions of this kind would confound the experiment, making it impossible to ascertain whether a newly established response is a function of the independent variable or the result of the subject's compliance with the experimenter's stated intentions. As long as it is necessary to test the effectiveness of a specific therapeutic procedure, a verbal statement of the contingencies announced to the client would indeed confound the experiment, but where a therapeutic program has advanced beyond the experimental stage, anything that enhances the treatment process, including verbal instructions, ought to be used by the therapist.

It was around this point that Doubros and Daniels (1966) took issue with Patterson's approach of announcing the contingencies to the child and his classmates. They felt that this introduces uncontrolled social reinforcement and awareness, factors they attempted to control in their own work on the reduction of hyperactivity in six mentally retarded boys. As a result of this controlled experiment, it is now possible to state that differential reinforcement of other behavior (DRO) is an effective method for reducing hyperactivity and increasing constructive play. On the other hand, Doubros and Daniels carried out their work in a playroom where each child was treated by himself, so that it is not known whether the responses they learned there generalized to other surroundings.

Deficient academic and social skills. School-age children who are nonreaders manifest a behavioral deficit that calls for the establishment of missing responses. Operant techniques have been applied in a number of studies dealing with such cases. To consider learning to read as operant discrimination learning, it is necessary to view the learning task as one in which the child emits the correct verbal response while looking at the written stimulus, the response being followed by some form of reinforcement. It is not necessary to make any assumptions about the nature of covert cognitive processes in order to plan a training program along these lines. Thus, Staats and Butterfield (1965) applied operant principles to the treatment of a 14-year-old boy with a long history of school failures and delinquencies. He was reading at second-grade level when treatment began. Following forty hours of training, he not only read at the 4.3 grade level but also passed all his courses for the first time and his misbehavior in school had completely dropped out. This case not only demonstrates that improvement generalizes to areas not specifically designated as treatment targets, but it also illustrates how extrinsic reinforcers (money) can be gradually withdrawn as reading itself becomes reinforcing and other sources of reinforcement come into play and maintain the newly established behavior.

When reading is defined as making the correct verbal response to a particular written stimulus, it can be readily monitored. This, however, is not the case in silent reading, in which only subsequent changes in performance permit one to infer that reading has taken place. The boy in the Staats and Butterfield (1965) study had been reinforced for silent reading, and as these authors point out, there was the danger of reinforcing the behavior of just looking at a printed page when no actual reading was going on. A double contingency was introduced in an attempt to guard against this possibility. Several levels of reinforcers (tokens representing different amounts of money) were used, so that for looking at a page, a low-value reinforcer was presented while higher-value reinforcers were made contingent on correctly answering questions about the content of the reading material. Unfortunately, the design still does not permit an unequivocal answer to the question of whether the boy was attending to the printed words instead of merely staring at them, because the questions he had to answer were based on the story used for silent reading which had previously been the material for oral reading. This makes it barely conceivable that he had learned the answers to the questions during the readily monitored oral phase, after which he did no more than sit and look at the story when he presumably engaged in silent reading.

A flexible use of reinforcement schedules in the course of training is illustrated in a study by Hewett, Mayhew, and Rabb (1967), who taught basic reading skills to mentally retarded, neurologically impaired, emotionally disturbed, and autistic children. During the first three lessons, reinforcement was on a continuous basis, with one unit of reinforcement for each correct response. After this, each child had to make five correct responses before receiving one unit of reinforcement (a 1:5 fixed ratio schedule). Reinforcements were such tangibles as candy or money at this point, but in addition, the experimenters began to phase in a token reward in the form of marks on a card, given on a 1:1 ratio schedule. The tangible reinforcers were later placed on a 1:10 schedule, and ultimately, 200 check marks were needed before they could be exchanged for one tangible reinforcer and a 1:200 schedule with a delay until the end of the session was thus in operation.

Deficient social skills and complex social

behaviors have also been treated by the application of operant principles. Thus, Lovaas et al. (1967) and Metz (1965) established imitative behavior in schizophrenic children for whom the ability to imitate an adult was a necessary first step toward the later acquisition of such socially adaptive behavior as playing games, taking care of personal hygiene, and engaging in appropriate sex-role behavior. Metz (1965) found that imitation generalized to tasks for which specific imitation training had not been given.

What is probably the most ambitious attempt yet in applying operant techniques to the establishment of socially adaptive behavior is the well-controlled study by Schwitzgebel (1967). He recruited forty-eight male adolescent delinquents from city streets and gave differential reinforcement to positive statements and constructive behavior, such as prompt arrival at work, that would make the youths more employable. Reinforcements took the form of verbal praise and small gifts, which were delivered on a variable-ratio schedule while the subject talked into a tape recorder. This procedure resulted in a significant increase in the number of positive statements and an improvement in punctuality of arrival for those subjects who had been specifically reinforced for these behaviors. A series of interviews within an operant conditioning framework thus led to dependable and prompt attendance and similar prosocial behaviors in a group that had been notoriously unresponsive to nearly all other forms of treatment. Schwitzgebel appropriately asks why this knowledge is not put to use in treatment programs across the country.

The Treatment of Maladaptive Behavior

In the treatment of behavior deficits discussed above, the goal is to teach the missing response and the technique involves the use of positive reinforcement. Where maladaptive behavior is to be modified, a variety of techniques are available, and these can be used either singly or in combination. The therapist can strengthen behavior that is incompatible with the maladaptive responses (counterconditioning); he can bring about extinction of the maladaptive responses by changing the reinforcement contingencies; he can introduce aversive consequences (punishment) for the maladaptive responses and thus bring about the suppression of the behavior in question; or he can modify the target behavior by eliminating or greatly increasing the stimuli that precede it (stimulus deprivation or satiation). The choice of the particular technique or techniques to be used will depend not only on the nature of the target behavior and the stimuli which maintain it but also on the conditions under which the child manifests that behavior. Careful assessment is therefore of prime importance.

Fears. Avoidance responses maintained by fear reduction are frequently maladaptive and call for modification or elimination. One behavior in this category is what is usually labeled *school phobia,* a refusal to attend school that may entail either fear of school or fear of leaving the home. Only the former is, strictly speaking, a school phobia. Behavior as complex as refusal to attend school has components of both a respondent and an operant nature, for while the avoidance response may originally have served a fear-reducing function, it is likely that it is later being maintained and complicated by the reinforcements available in the home to a child who is not going to school. Many school-phobia cases thus become difficult to treat once the behavior has a long reinforcement history. This consideration led Kennedy (1965) to develop a rapid treatment procedure for children with sudden school phobia of recent onset. His procedure has six essential components: (1) good communication with referral sources, so that children can be referred on the second or third day after onset of the phobia; (2) a deemphasis of somatic complaints, with (3) decisive insistence on school attendance, including the use of force where necessary; (4) a structured, success-focused interview with the parents, stressing the need for a matter-of-fact approach to the problem and the importance of complimenting the child for his going to school and staying there, no matter how brief or stormy that attendance; (5) a brief interview with the child, held after school hours, in which the importance of going on in the face of fear and the transitory nature of a phobia are stressed; (6) an informal telephone follow-up. Using this approach over a period of eight years, Kennedy treated a total of fifty carefully selected cases, all of whom responded with complete remission. Follow-up failed to reveal evidence for the emergence of other problems, and the children continued to attend school.

Garvey and Hegrenes (1966) report the treatment of a school-phobia case by a modified form of desensitization. The therapist and the child approached the school together in a series of steps graded from the least anxiety-evoking situation (sitting in a car in front of the school) to the most anxiety-evoking condition (being in the classroom with the teacher and other students present). The authors view this approach as similar to that used by Wolpe (1958) and formulate it in terms of the respondent conditioning paradigm. This, as Lazarus, Davison, and Polefka (1965) have pointed out, overlooks the fact that both respondent and operant factors are at work. Clearly, the therapist's implicit and explicit approval of approach responses reinforces and strengthens such responses and thus contributes to the treatment.

Conditioning methods were used in the treatment of children's fears as early as 1924, when Mary Cover Jones reported her pioneering study with Peter. She reduced this child's fear by gradually strengthening a fear-incompatible response, a method that has since come to be known as *counterconditioning,* or therapy by reciprocal inhibition. Relaxation is the fear-incompatible

response most frequently used in work with adults (Wolpe, 1958), but this is rarely applied in work with children, possibly because training in deep muscle relaxation is difficult with young subjects. For this reason, Lazarus and Abramovitz (1965) explored the use of "emotive imagery," an approach that is based on the assumption that it is possible to inhibit anxiety by the induction of child-appropriate imagery with positive emotional content. Images that presumably serve an anxiety-inhibiting function are those that arouse such feelings as self-assertion, pride, affection, mirth, or fearlessness. The child is instructed to imagine a situation associated with such a feeling, and once such imagery is induced, the therapist presents anxiety-eliciting images, carefully graded from mildly to highly anxiety-arousing. On each step of this previously established anxiety hierarchy, the pleasant imagery is paired with anxiety-arousing stimuli, and when treatment is successful, the child should be able to make his fear-incompatible emotional response when the previously anxiety-arousing situation is presented in imagery and, presumably, when it is encountered in real life.

Lazarus and Abramovitz (1965) report success with the method of emotive imagery, but since no systematic research on this approach has been published, there remain many untested assumptions. It is, for example, unknown whether the positive imagery is accompanied by a physiological state that is incompatible with fear, as the notion of reciprocal inhibition would suggest, nor is it known whether verbally presented imagery stimuli do indeed result in a conditioned-stimulus pairing, as would be demanded by the respondent conditioning model that is supposed to be applicable. "Emotive imagery" has interesting implications, but its assumptions remain untested and its claim to efficacy is based on only a few clinical reports.

A variation of desensitization therapy was used in a case reported by Straughan (1964). An 8-year-old girl was referred by her mother because the child "was not as happy as she should be." Vaguely worded, general complaints of this nature can usually be broken down into more discrete maladaptive response classes, and this case was no exception. Further investigation revealed that the child was inhibiting much age-appropriate spontaneous emotional expression in the presence of her mother. Treatment was therefore directed at desensitizing the child to her mother, who had come to be an anxiety-eliciting stimulus. The method used was to have the child in the playroom and to introduce the mother into the girl's presence while she was happily and enthusiastically engaged in play. After five play sessions, the child had indeed learned to be relaxed in the mother's presence and the mother, in turn, was able to learn to interact with the child in a natural and spontaneous manner.

The usual treatment of avoidance behavior involves gradual exposure of the subject to the feared stimulus, but it is also possible to reduce fear by having the subject observe another child who is making approach responses to the fear-arousing object. A report by Bandura, Grusec, and Menlove (1967) showed that after having observed a peer model fearlessly make progressively stronger approach responses toward a dog, children who had displayed fearful and avoidant behavior toward dogs showed stable and generalized reduction in such behavior. While vicarious extinction is possible, the mechanisms involved in such extinction are not fully understood. Cognitive factors may play a role, but inasmuch as verbal reassurance about the harmlessness of a feared object did not serve to reduce fear in a control group, it would appear that the vicarious elimination of conditioned emotionality mediates the reduction of avoidance behavior.

Maladaptive operant responses. Where maladaptive behavior is maintained by its consequences, removing or changing these consequences should modify the behavior. In many instances, the reinforcing consequence of maladaptive behavior is the attention this behavior calls to itself by its demand characteristics. It has been repeatedly demonstrated that the selective use of adults' attention can modify problem behaviors of nursery school children, including regressed crawling (Harris et al., 1965), isolate behavior (Allen et al., 1965), excessive crying and whining (Hart et al., 1965), and deficient motor skills (Johnston et al., 1966). In each of these studies, adult attention was withheld from the target behavior and given to behavior that was incompatible with it. To test the efficacy of this manipulation, the contingencies were experimentally reversed; a resulting recurrence of the maladaptive behavior demonstrated that adult attention was indeed the independent variable responsible for the behavior modification. Following this experimental reversal (see below), the therapeutic contingencies were obviously reinstated, so that the end result of the intervention was adaptive behavior on the part of the child. This design makes it possible to evaluate the effectiveness of a given reinforcer by using each subject as his own control, thus permitting research in clinical situations where control groups are difficult to obtain because of the low incidence of a particular problem behavior.

The reinforcement principles applied in the relatively simple case of nursery school behavior have also been applied in cases of complex multiple problem behaviors (Patterson & Brodsky, 1966), in the treatment of stuttering (Browning, 1967; Rickard & Mundy, 1965), and in such difficult situations as the case of an autistic child (Wolf, Risley, & Mees, 1964) and of a child whose excessive scratching had resulted in large sores and scabs (Allen & Harris, 1966). Where complex behavior or behavior patterns must be modified, a combination of treatment methods may be required and the manipulation of only one reinforcement contingency may not be sufficient to bring about the desired change.

The case of Dicky, reported by Wolf, Risley,

and Mees (1964) and Wolf et al. (1967), serves to illustrate the use of a combination of techniques, including the manipulation of a variety of contingencies in conditioning and extinction procedures and the introduction of a form of aversive control in order to reduce the frequency of grossly maladaptive behavior. Dicky was 3½ years old and had been diagnosed as a case of childhood schizophrenia. He engaged in such self-destructive behaviors as head banging, hair pulling, face slapping, and scratching. He lacked adaptive social and verbal repertoires, refused to sleep alone, and did not eat in an age-appropriate fashion. His case became critical because he was in danger of losing his eyesight. Due to cataracts in both eyes, he had to have surgical removal of the lenses, and since he refused to wear glasses, permanent retinal damage was very likely.

The therapists first attacked the boy's refusal to wear his eyeglasses and his throwing of his eyeglasses because that seemed the most serious, immediate problem. Glasses-wearing was gradually established by reinforcing it with food and later on with opportunities to take walks, go on rides, or play. Because the child's glasses-throwing behavior was incompatible with glasses-wearing, a mild form of punishment was made contingent on glasses-throwing. Following each glasses-throw, Dicky was put in his room for ten minutes, a form of time out from positive reinforcement (TO) if one views being in the company of others as a positively reinforcing condition. The same TO method was used to eliminate tantrums, self-slapping, and the pinching of teachers and other children in the nursery school. The effectiveness of this technique was demonstrated by experimental reversal (Wolf, Risley, & Mees, 1964). Glasses-throwing had taken place at the rate of approximately two times per day before treatment was initiated. Within five days of instituting the TO procedure, the rate of this behavior had decreased to zero, but when Dicky was no longer put in his room for throwing the glasses, thus reversing

the contingencies, the rate of glasses-throwing returned to its original high level after about three weeks. When Dicky was once again put in his room whenever this behavior occurred, it quickly decreased in frequency and virtually disappeared within six days.

Reversal is an applied behavior analysis that permits one to evaluate the reliability of a treatment procedure (Baer, Wolf, & Risley, 1968). The first step in this analysis is to measure the behavior in question and to examine the measure over time until its stability is established. The particular contingency is then introduced, and the behavior continues to be measured in order to ascertain whether the experimental variable produces a behavioral change. If such a change occurs, the contingency is altered or discontinued, and if the behavioral change does indeed depend on it, this change should be lost or diminished (hence, "reversal"). Following this, the experimental variable is once again applied to see whether the behavior change can be reinstated. If it can, the contingency in question continues to be used inasmuch as it has been shown to be a reliable treatment method. If further tests of reliability are desired, reversal can be repeated, although many treatment settings may make it undesirable to bring back the maladaptive behavior in order to demonstrate that it can be modified by manipulating known contingencies.

Reversal can be carried out only if the target behavior is carefully and objectively measured, but the need for such measurement goes beyond the requirements of behavior analysis, for without it, treatment becomes unsystematic and the outcome impossible to define. This is illustrated in further work with Dicky, as reported by Wolf, Risley, Johnston, Harris, and Allen (1967). After some of his more bizarre behavior had been modified during hospitalization, Dicky was enrolled in a nursery school, where he emitted a high rate of pinching teachers and other children. At first, an attempt was made to put this behavior on an extinction schedule by ignoring it, but when this failed to change the pinching rate, Dicky was sent to a specially set-aside small room whenever pinching occurred. After the first use of this time-out contingency, the rate of pinching decreased drastically, only four more instances of it being recorded over the next seventy-four class sessions. Prior to the introduction of the TO procedure, a teacher had attempted to modify the pinching by reinforcing patting, which was seen as an incompatible response. Patting behavior stabilized at a moderate rate within a few sessions when Dicky was encouraged and praised for emitting this response. At this point, the teachers reported that they were succeeding in replacing pinching by patting. However, the observer's record, on which instances of both patting and pinching had been entered for every ten-second interval, clearly showed that, contrary to the teachers' impression, the pinching rate had not decreased and that it did not decline until the TO procedure was instituted some thirteen sessions later. Without the quantitative observer record, the teachers would have been under the mistaken impression that the development of a substitute response had been responsible for the decrease in the undesirable behavior. Inasmuch as Dicky's parents were to be instructed in the use of behavior-modification techniques so that they could supplement the treatment at home, such an erroneous conclusion might have contributed to treatment failure and disappointment. With the variety of approaches used in Dicky's case over a period of three years, the boy was eventually able to attend a special education class in public school, where he made a good adjustment and learned to read at the primary level.

Punishment

Reinforcement theory holds that responses that are consistently and immediately followed by an aversive condition (pain) should become suppressed. The self-injurious behavior of such grossly disordered children as Dicky thus represents an apparent paradox because such responses as self-hitting are maintained despite their negative consequences. Some have assumed that the child has a "need" to hurt himself, that he "enjoys" the self-inflicted punishment. If this explanation were correct, then any treatment that involved the introduction of negative consequences contingent on self-injurious behavior should serve to further strengthen such behavior. Yet reports by Wolf, Risley, and Mees (1964), Risley (1968), Lovaas et al. (1965), and Tate and Baroff (1966) vitiate the "masochism" explanation inasmuch as these investigators were able to reduce the incidence of self-injurious behavior by the introduction of aversive consequences (punishment) to such behavior.

The contingencies surrounding self-injurious behavior were analyzed by Lovaas, Freitag, Gold, and Kassorla (1965), who concluded that such behavior is maintained not by the "pleasure" the child gets out of hurting himself but by the social reinforcement entailed in the attention such behavior almost invariably calls to itself. These investigators showed that self-injurious behavior decreases when it is ignored but increases when it is followed by such solicitous, "interpretive" comments as, "I don't think you are bad." While effective, the extinction process involved in ignoring self-injurious behavior is often too slow, and the risk of permanent physical harm frequently demands that the behavior be modified at a more rapid rate. In addition, behavior tends to increase in frequency, intensity, or duration when an extinction schedule is first introduced and before the rate gradually declines. For these reasons, Risley (1968) and Tate and Baroff (1966), as well as Lovaas and his co-workers (1965), stress the rapid response suppression possible when electric shock is made contingent on self-injurious responses, particularly when this approach is combined with the positive reinforcement of incompatible, adaptive behavior.

Physical punishment should be used only when the behavior in question must be quickly suppressed because delay would endanger the child or make the learning of adaptive responses impossible. In most cases, the negative consequences involved in time out from positive reinforcement, such as social isolation or deprivation of privileges, appear sufficiently potent to weaken undesirable responses. Even such ordinarily intractable behavior as the antisocial acts of institutionalized adolescent delinquents can be modified by the use of a fifteen-minute period of isolation when it is introduced immediately and consistently as a consequence of every instance of specified undesirable behaviors (Burchard & Tyler, 1965; Tyler & Brown, 1967). Since stealing carries its own inherent reinforcement, it would seem to be particularly difficult to treat, but Wetzel (1966) succeeded in eliminating the stealing behavior of an institutionalized boy by using a time-out procedure. In order to have something that could be withdrawn contingent on the boy's stealing, it was necessary to create a condition of positive reinforcement, in this case the privilege of visiting with the institution cook, but once these visits had acquired positive reinforcement value, the loss of this privilege became a potent aversive condition.

There appears to be a paradox in the fact that such relatively mild punishment as having to spend 15 minutes in an empty room can effectively modify behavior of delinquents for whom far more severe punishments have usually been ineffective. Burchard and Tyler (1965), for example, succeeded in reducing the antisocial behavior of a 13-year-old institutionalized delinquent boy through the use of isolation combined with positive reinforcement for clearly defined periods that he did not have to spend in isolation. Yet this same boy had spent a total of 200 days in an individual isolation room during the year prior to the onset of the reported study, and during that time his behavior had become increasingly unmanageable. The prime difference between the systematic and the unsystematic use of punishment would seem to explain this apparent paradox. In the systematic application of operant principles, negative consequences to unacceptable behavior are *immediately* and *consistently* introduced whenever unacceptable behavior occurs. When punishment is used unsystematically, unacceptable behavior usually has to reach a given magnitude before the adults in the environment intervene, and even then punishment is usually introduced as a last resort. A great many interpersonal events take place between the incipient onset of the unacceptable behavior and the eventual introduction of the negative consequences, and these events tend to serve a reinforcing and not a suppressing function.

Burchard and Tyler (1965) describe the temporal sequence of staff behavior to the disruptive behavior of one boy as follows: When Donny first begins to "act up," staff members try to ignore this behavior for as long as possible. During this time, peer approval and attention tend to reinforce the behavior. As the behavior continues and increases in magnitude, attendants turn to attempts at supportive persuasion to desist. When this (reinforcement) is unsuccessful, the staff becomes frustrated, angry and ambivalent, and only at that point is punishment finally introduced. But that is not all. Staff members now feel guilty, and this reaction manifests itself in sympathy and visits to the child in the isolation room. With the contingencies structured in this fashion, it is not surprising that Donny's unacceptable behavior increased over time, for staff and peer attention occurred immediately after the response and punishment was delayed and ambivalent. The time-out program instituted by Burchard and Tyler, on the other hand, had Donny immediately and perfunctorily placed in his isolation room as soon as he displayed any unacceptable behavior. The staff was instructed to approach this intervention in a matter-of-fact way and at the onset of the target behavior, that is, before they themselves had become emotionally aroused by the behavior. It was stressed that isolation had to be on an all-or-none basis and that it should never be used as a threat. It is very likely that the systematic nature of punishment when used in the operant frame of reference is the principal factor in its efficiency. In everyday child rearing, punishment tends to be used in the unsystematic, last-resort fashion described by Burchard and Tyler, and this probably explains why it is rarely an effective technique for the suppression of undesirable behavior.

Treatment by Nonprofessionals

Because the operant techniques can be described in relatively simple terms and their application taught in a short time, treatment using these techniques can be carried out by nonprofessional people working under the direction of a professional person who has expert knowledge of the theoretical basis and works out the details of the treatment program. It has thus been possible to involve ward attendants, nursery school teachers, and parents in treatment programs. Wahler, Winkel, Peterson, and Morrison (1965), O'Leary, O'Leary, and Becker (1967), Hawkins et al. (1966), and Zeilberger, Sampen, and Sloane (1968) have all reported the successful use of mothers as behavior therapists for their own children. If behavior is to be modified, the modification must take place when and where the behavior manifests itself. This is rarely the therapist's consulting room, and as a consequence, behavior therapists working with children frequently find themselves working through the adults who are in a position to be present when the target behavior takes place and who have control over the contingencies of reinforcement. In the case of children in schools or institutions, these adults are teachers, nurses, and attendants.

In the case of children living at home, the parents become the logical contingency managers and, hence, therapists.

In order to engage a parent as the child's actual therapist, it is necessary to train him or her in the essential techniques, including objective recording, and in some instances, in the ability to discriminate the incipient stages of the objectionable behavior. This was done by Hawkins et al. (1966) in having a mother treat her 4-year-old boy, who had been extremely difficult to manage and control. He would kick objects and people, tear at his clothing, hit himself, and generally require almost constant attention. At first the mother found it difficult to recognize the incipient stages of the target behavior and to be consistent in her response to it. She was therefore taught by the professional therapist, who entered the home for this purpose, when to use praise, attention, affectionate physical contact, verbal commands, and isolation. This mother quickly learned both the necessary discrimination and the appropriate reactions and was able to carry the treatment to successful conclusion.

THE EFFECTIVENESS OF BEHAVIOR THERAPY

Several well-controlled studies (Lang, Lazovik, & Reynolds, 1965; Paul, 1966, 1967; Paul & Shannon, 1966) have demonstrated the effectiveness of behavior therapy with adults, but most of the experimental support for the behavioral approach to the treatment of psychological disorders in children rests on studies using the "reversal" design, where each subject serves as his own control (e.g., Hart et al., 1965; Hawkins et al., 1966; Wolf & Risley, 1967). This design permits a demonstration of the reliability of a given procedure, but it does not answer the question of whether this procedure is more effective than a traditional psychotherapeutic approach. With the exception of some studies dealing with the treatment of enuresis (Baker, 1967; DeLeon & Mandell, 1966; Lovibond, 1964), which showed the superiority of conditioning techniques over traditional psychotherapy, the only systematic comparison of behavior therapy with psychotherapy and a no-treatment control was conducted by James Humphery (cited by Eysenck, 1967).

Humphery used seventy-one children referred to child-guidance clinics for a variety of disorders, excluding those with brain damage and psychosis, and divided these into three groups. A control group of thirty-four children was evaluated at the beginning and again at the conclusion of the study, receiving no treatment of any kind in between. The remaining children were divided into two groups; one received behavior therapy (desensitization), while the other was given traditional psychotherapy. Evaluation of all children was on a five-point scale of severity of disorder, "cure" being defined as a rise of two or more points on this instrument. Clinicians who did not know to which group a given child had been assigned conducted the evaluations.

Treatment for each case was terminated when the therapist and a consulting psychiatrist decided that maximum benefit had been obtained. By this criterion of termination, the children who had been in psychotherapy received twenty-one sessions, spread over 31 weeks, while those in behavior therapy received nine sessions, spread over 18 weeks. On the basis of the criterion measure, 75 percent of the children in behavior therapy were rated as cured at the termination of treatment, compared with 35 percent of those who had been in psychotherapy. Follow-up, 10 months later, revealed that 85 percent of those who had received behavior therapy were now rated as cured while only 29 percent of those who had received psychotherapy were still considered cured. Of the no-treatment control group, 18 percent were found to be cured when they were reevaluated at follow-up.

Several flaws detract from the validity of the conclusions of this unpublished study. A five-point rating scale of severity of difficulty would seem a relatively insensitive instrument with which to detect changes in a child's behavior, and the unusually brief time devoted to psychotherapy raises the question of whether that treatment was represented in its most typical form. Furthermore, a bias in sampling had resulted in the assignment of more seriously disturbed children to the behavior-therapy group than to the psychotherapy group. The behavior-therapy group thus had a higher severity rating at the beginning of treatment, so that a ceiling effect made it less likely for them to achieve the two-point rise that defined cure. All told, a definitive experimental comparison of behavior therapy and psychotherapy with children, using a typical child-guidance population with heterogeneous problems, remains to be conducted.

While it is thus possible to maintain a controversy as to the superiority of traditional forms of treatment over behavior therapy, this may well be a moot question. Available studies do attest to the effectiveness of behavior therapy in the kind of cases with which it has been used. There is also no question but that behavior therapists reach their defined treatment goal more quickly than psychotherapists reach their criterion for terminating a case. Even if behavior therapy were no more effective than psychotherapy, it is certainly more efficient, in terms both of time and of professional effort. The important research question now to be asked is what kinds of problems are best treated by which kind of therapy, by what therapists, and under what conditions. It is unlikely that behavior therapy as it is practiced today is the panacea for every conceivable psychological disorder. In all probability, other aspects of psychology, in addition to the conditioning and social learning models, will eventually be brought to bear on clinical problems; developmental phenomena, cognitive processes, modeling, and group dynamics would seem to contain a wealth of knowledge awaiting clinical application.

REFERENCES

Allen, K. E., & Harris, F. R. Elimination of a child's excessive scratching by training the mother in reinforcement procedures. *Behaviour Research and Therapy,* 1966, **4**, 79–84.

Allen, K. E., Hart, B. M., Buell, J. S., Harris, F. R., & Wolf, M. M. Effects of social reinforcement on isolate behavior of a nursery school child. In L. P. Ullmann & L. Krasner (Eds.), *Case studies in behavior modification.* New York: Holt, 1965. Pp. 307–312.

Baer, D. M., Wolf, M. M., & Risley, T. R. Some current dimensions of applied behavior analysis. *Journal of Applied Behavior Analysis,* 1968, **1**, 91–97.

Baker, B. L. Symptom treatment and symptom substitution in enuresis. Paper presented at the First Annual Meeting of the Association for Advancement of the Behavioral Therapies, Washington, 1967.

Bandura, A. Psychotherapy as a learning process. *Psychological Bulletin,* 1961, **58**, 143–159.

Bandura, A., Grusec, J. E., & Menlove, F. L. Vicarious extinction of avoidance behavior. *Journal of Personality and Social Psychology,* 1967, **5**, 16–23.

Boardman, W. K. Rusty: A brief behavior disorder. *Journal of Consulting Psychology,* 1962, **26**, 293–297.

Browning, R. M. Behavior therapy for stuttering in a schizophrenic child. *Behaviour Research and Therapy*, 1967, **5**, 27–35.

Burchard, J., & Tyler, V., Jr. The modification of delinquent behaviour through operant conditioning. *Behaviour Research and Therapy*, 1965, **2**, 245–250.

Davison, G. C. A social learning therapy programme with an autistic child. *Behaviour Research and Therapy,* 1964, **2**, 149–159.

Davison, G. C. An intensive long-term social-learning treatment program with an accurately diagnosed autistic child. *Proceedings of the 73rd Annual Convention of the American Psychological Association,* 1965.

DeLeon, G., & Mandell, W. A comparison of conditioning and psychotherapy in the treatment of functional enuresis. *Journal of Clinical Psychology,* 1966, **22**, 326–330.

DiCara, L. V. & Miller, N. E. Instrumental learning of vasomotor responses by rats: Learning to respond differentially in the two ears. *Science,* 1968, **159**, 1485–1486.

Dollard, J., & Miller, N. E. *Personality and psychotherapy.* New York: McGraw-Hill, 1950.

Doubros, S. G., & Daniels, G. J. An experimental approach to the reduction of overactive behavior. *Behaviour Research and Therapy*, 1966, **4**, 251–258.

Eysenck, H. J. New ways in psychotherapy. *Psychology Today,* 1967, **1**, 39–47.

Eysenck, H. J. *The dynamics of anxiety and hysteria.* New York: Praeger, 1957.

Ferster, C. B. Positive reinforcement and behavioral deficits of autistic children. *Child Development,* 1961, **32**, 437–456.

Ferster, C. B. Arbitrary and natural reinforcement. *Psychological Record*, 1967, **17**, 341–347.

Ferster, C. B., & DeMyer, M. K. A method for the experimental analysis of the behavior of autistic children. *American Journal of Orthopsychiatry,* 1962, **32**, 89–98.

Garvey, W. P., & Hegrenes, J. R. Desensitization techniques in the treatment of school phobia. *American Journal of Orthopsychiatry*, 1966, **36**, 147–152.

Gelber, H., & Meyer, V. Behaviour therapy and encopresis: The complexities involved in treatment. *Behaviour Research and Therapy*, 1965, **2**, 227–231.

Gesell, A. The conditioned reflex and the psychiatry of infancy. *American Journal of Orthopsychiatry,* 1938, **8**, 19–29.

Giles, D. K., & Wolf, M. M. Toilet training institutionalized severe retardates: An application of operant behavior modification techniques. *American Journal of Mental Deficiency*, 1966, **70**, 766–780.

Harris, F. R., Johnston, M. K., Kelley, C. S., & Wolf, M. M. Effects of positive social reinforcement on regressed crawling of a nursery school child. In L. P. Ullmann & L. Krasner (Eds.), *Case studies in behavior modification.* New York: Holt, 1965. Pp. 313–319.

Hart, B. M., Allen K. E., Buell, J. S., Harris, F. R., & Wolf, M. M. Effects of social reinforcement on operant crying. In L. P. Ullmann & L. Krasner (Eds.), *Case studies in behavior modification.* New York: Holt, 1965. Pp. 320–325.

Hawkins, R. P., Peterson, R. F., Schweid, E., and Bijou, S. W. Behavior therapy in the home: Amelioration of problem parent-child relations with the parent in a therapeutic role. *Journal of Experimental Child Psychology*, 1966, **4**, 99–107.

Hewett, F. M. Teaching speech to an autistic child through operant conditioning. *American Journal of Orthopsychiatry*, 1965, **35**, 927–936.

Hewett, F. M., Mayhew, D., & Rabb, E. An experimental reading program for neurologically impaired, mentally retarded, and severely emotionally disturbed children. *American Journal of Orthopsychiatry*, 1967, **37**, 35–48.

Hundziak, M., Maurer, R. A., & Watson, L. S., Jr. Operant conditioning in toilet training of severely mentally retarded boys. *American Journal of Mental Deficiency*, 1965, **70**, 120-124.

Ivanov-Smolenski, A. G. Neurotic behavior and teaching of conditioned reflexes. *American Journal of Psychiatry*, 1927, **7**, 483–488.

Johnston, M. K., Kelley, C. S., Harris, F. R., & Wolf, M. M. An application of reinforcement principles to development of motor skills of a young child. *Child Development*, 1966, **37**, 379–387.

Jones, M. C. A laboratory study of fear: The case of Peter. *Journal of Genetic Psychology*, 1924, **31**, 308–315.

Kennedy, W. A. School phobia: Rapid treatment of fifty cases. *Journal of Abnormal Psychology*, 1965, **70**, 285–289.

Krasnogorski, N. I. The conditioned reflex and children's neuroses. *American Journal of Diseases of Children*, 1925, **30**, 753–768.

Lang, P. J., Lazovik, A. D., & Reynolds, D. J. Desensitization, suggestibility, and pseudotherapy. *Journal of Abnormal Psychology*, 1965, **70**, 395–402.

Lazarus, A. The elimination of children's phobias by deconditioning. In H. J. Eysenck (Ed.), *Behaviour therapy and the neuroses.* New York: Pergamon, 1960.

Lazarus, A. A., & Abramovitz, A. The use of "emotive imagery" in the treatment of children's phobias. In L. P. Ullman & L. Krasner (Eds.), *Case studies in behavior modification.* New York: Holt, 1965. Pp. 300–304.

Lazarus, A. A., Davison, G. C., & Polefka, D. A. Classical and operant factors in the treatment of a school phobia. *Journal of Abnormal Psychology*, 1965, **70**, 225–229.

Lovaas, O. I., Freitag, G., Gold, V. J., & Kassorla, I. C. Experimental studies in childhood schizophrenia: Analysis of self-destructive behavior. *Journal of Experimental Child Psychology*, 1965, **2**, 67–84.

Lovaas, O. I., Freitag, G., Kinder, M. I., Rubenstein, B. D., Schaeffer, B., & Simmons, J. W. Establishment of social reinforcers in two schizophrenic children on the basis of food. *Journal of Experimental Child Psychology*, 1966, **4**, 109–125.

Lovaas, O. I., Freitag, L., Nelson, K., & Whalen, C. The establishment of imitation and its use for the development of complex behavior in schizophrenic children. *Behaviour Research and Therapy*, 1967, **5**, 171–181.

Lovibond, S. H., Intermittent reinforcement in behavior therapy. *Behaviour Research and Therapy*, 1963, **1**, 127–132.

Lovibond, S. H. *Conditioning and enuresis.* New York: Pergamon, 1964.

Metz, J. R. Conditioning generalized imitation in autistic children. *Journal of Experimental Child Psychology*, 1965, **2**, 389–399.

Mowrer, O. H. *Learning theory and personality dynamics.* New York: Ronald, 1950.

Mowrer, O. H. Two-factor learning theory: Summary and comment. *Psychological Review*, 1951, **58**, 350–354.

Mowrer, O. H., & Mowrer, W. M. Enuresis—A method for its study and treatment. *American Journal of Orthopsychiatry*, 1938, **8**, 436–459.

Neale, D. H. Behaviour therapy and encopresis in children. *Behaviour Research and Therapy*, 1963, **1**, 139–149.

Novick, J. Symptomatic treatment of acquired and persistent enuresis. *Journal of Abnormal Psychology*, 1966, **71**, 363–368.

O'Leary, K. D., O'Leary, S., & Becker, W. C. Modification of a deviant sibling interaction in the home. *Behaviour Research and Therapy*, 1967, **5**, 113–120.

Patterson, G. R. An application of conditioning techniques to the control of a hyperactive child. In L. P. Ullmann & L. Krasner (Eds.), *Case studies in behavior modification.* New York: Holt, 1965. Pp. 370–375.

Patterson, G. R., & Brodsky, G. A behavior modification programme for a child with multiple problem behaviors. *Journal of Child Psychology and Psychiatry*, 1966, **7**, 277–295.

Patterson, G. R., Jones, R., Whittier, J., & Wright, M. A. A behaviour modification technique for the hyperactive child. *Behaviour Research and Therapy*, 1965, **2**, 217–226.

Paul, G. L. *Insight vs. desensitization in psychotherapy.* Stanford, Calif.: Stanford University Press, 1966.

Paul, G. L. Insight versus desensitization in psychotherapy two years after termination. *Journal of Consulting Psychology,* 1967, **31**, 333–348.

Paul, G. L., & Shannon, D. T. Treatment of anxiety through systematic desensitization in therapy groups. *Journal of Abnormal Psychology,* 1966, **71,** 124–135.

Premack, D. Toward empirical behavior laws. I. Positive reinforcement. *Psychological Review*, 1959, **66**, 219–233.

Rickard, H. C., & Mundy, M. B. Direct manipulation of stuttering behavior: An experimental-clinical approach. In L. P. Ullmann & L. Krasner (Eds.), *Case studies in behavior modification.* New York: Holt, 1965. Pp. 268–274.

Rimland, B. *Infantile autism; The syndrome and its implications for a neural theory of behavior.* New York: Appleton-Century-Crofts, 1964.

Risley, T. R. The effects and side effects of punishing the autistic behaviors of a deviant child. *Journal of Applied Behavior Analysis,* 1968, **1**, 21–34.

Risley, T., & Wolf, M. Establishing functional speech in echolalic children. *Behaviour Research and Therapy*, 1967, **5**, 73–88.

Ross, A. O. Learning theory and therapy with children. *Psychotherapy: Theory, Research and Practice*, 1964, **1**, 102–108.

Schwitzgebel, R. L. Short-term operant conditioning of adolescent offenders on socially relevant variables. *Journal of Abnormal Psychology*, 1967, **72**, 134–142.

Shoben, E. J. Psychotherapy as a problem in learning theory. *Psychological Bulletin*, 1949, **46**, 366–392.

Skinner, B. F. *Science and human behavior.* New York: Free Press, 1953.

Staats, A. W., & Butterfield, W. H. Treatment of nonreading in a culturally deprived juvenile delinquent: An application of reinforcement principles. *Child Development*, 1965, **36**, 925–942.

Straughan, J. H. Treatment with child and mother in the playroom. *Behaviour Research and Therapy*, 1964, **2**, 37–41.

Tate, B. G., & Baroff, G. S. Aversive control of self-injurious behavior in a psychotic boy. *Behaviour Research and Therapy,* 1966, **4**, 281–287.

Tyler, V. O., Jr., & Brown, G. D. The use of swift, brief isolation as a group control device for institutionalized delinquents. *Behaviour Research and Therapy*, 1967, **5**, 1–9.

Wahler, R. G., Winkel, G. H., Peterson, R. F., & Morrison, D. C. Mothers as behavior therapists for their own children. *Behaviour Research and Therapy,* 1965, **3**, 113–124.

Watson, J. B., & Rayner, R. Conditioned emotional reactions. *Journal of Experimental Psychology,* 1920, **3**, 1–14.

Werry, J. S. The conditioning treatment of enuresis. *American Journal of Psychiatry*, 1966, **123**, 226–229.

Wetzel, R. Use of behavioral techniques in a case of compulsive stealing. *Journal of Consulting Psychology*, 1966, **30**, 367–374.

Wetzel, R. J., Baker, J., Roney, M., & Martin, M. Outpatient treatment of autistic behavior. *Behaviour Research and Therapy*, 1966, **4**, 169–177.

White, J. G. The use of learning theory in the psychological treatment of children. *Journal of Clinical Psychology*, 1959, **15**, 227–229.

Williams, C. D. The elimination of tantrum behavior by extinction procedures. *Journal of Abnormal and Social Psychology*, 1959, **59**, 269.

Wolf, M., & Risley, T. Analysis and modification of deviant child behavior. Paper presented at American Psychological Association meeting, Washington, D.C., 1967.

Wolf, M., Risley, T., Johnston, M., Harris, F., & Allen, E. Application of operant conditioning procedures to the behavior problems of an autistic child: A follow-up and extension. *Behaviour Research and Therapy*, 1967, **5**, 103–111.

Wolf, M., Risley, T., & Mees, H. Application of operant conditioning procedures to the behaviour problems of an autistic child. *Behaviour Research and Therapy*, 1964, **1**, 305–312.

Wolpe, J. *Psychotherapy by reciprocal inhibition.* Stanford, Calif.: Stanford University Press, 1958.

Zeilberger, J., Sampen, S. E., & Sloane, H. N., Jr. Modification of a child's problem behaviors in the home with the mother as therapist. *Journal of Applied Behavior Analysis*, 1968, **1**, 47–53.

30 Nondirective Treatment Methods

Charles Marcantonio

What is the essence of human life? What is its aim, and in what way can we help to attain that aim during our ephemeral lives? Our answers to these questions are bound to be influenced by factors such as our own experience or our cultural setting. Most of all, they are influenced by our courage to face these issues and realize that our truth may become another's folly. What is humbly offered as tentative opinion may be reified into an established school of thought. Let me present some trends that received impetus from the philosophy of nondirective therapy (Axline, 1947b; Rogers, 1942, 1951). Also, related trends will be explored (Allen, 1942; Moustakas, 1959; Taft, 1933). From this exploration, emergent values will be discussed and an attitude toward man's view of himself will be conveyed.

BASIC PRINCIPLES OF NONDIRECTIVE PLAY THERAPY

Axline (1947b), acknowledging the profound influence of the work of Rogers (1942) on her thinking, presented what she considered to be the eight basic principles of nondirective play therapy. They are as follows:

1. The therapist must develop a warm, friendly relationship with the child, in which good rapport is established as soon as possible.
2. The therapist accepts the child exactly as he is.
3. The therapist establishes a feeling of permissiveness in the relationship so that the child feels free to express his feelings completely.
4. The therapist is alert to recognizing the feelings the child is expressing and reflects those feelings back to him in such a manner that he gains insight into his behavior.
5. The therapist maintains a deep respect for the child's ability to solve his own problems if given an opportunity to do so. The responsibility to make choices and to institute change is the child's.
6. The therapist does not attempt to direct the child's actions or conversation in any manner. The child leads the way; the therapist follows.
7. The therapist does not attempt to hurry the therapy along. It is a gradual process and is recognized as such by the therapist.

8. The therapist establishes only those limitations that are necessary to anchor the therapy to the world of reality and make the child aware of his responsibility in the relationship.

Underlying this approach to play therapy is the notion of an actualizing tendency in the individual. Axline (1947b) stated:

> This force may be characterized as a drive toward independence, maturity, and self direction. It goes on relentlessly to achieve consummation, but it needs good "growing ground" to develop a well balanced structure. . . . The individual needs the permissiveness to be himself, the complete acceptance of himself—by himself, as well as by others—and the right to be an individual entitled to the dignity that is the birthright of every human being in order to achieve a direct satisfaction of this growth impulse.

Students of play therapy were taught, as were those of other orientations, that play is the child's most revealing self-expression. Given the opportunity, the child would play out his conflicts. The therapist could structure the play situation and guide the child's play or interpret his actions. But to be consistent with the nondirective approach, the therapist had to leave the responsibility and direction for play with the child. Note that these are beliefs of the nondirective therapist, not hard-core empirical facts. It was felt that the individual had within himself the capacity to solve his own problems.

Needless to say, the therapist is not a passive participant in the therapeutic process. As Rogers (1951) and Axline (1947b) repeatedly pointed out, it is the therapist's belief in the client as well as the atmosphere he creates that is essential to successful therapy. The counselor achieves his therapeutic results by developing empathic understanding and the capacity to accurately reflect or clarify the emotional expressions of the client. For some illustrations of the process of nondirective play therapy, see Axline (1947b, 1964) and Dorfman (1951).

RESEARCH

The early research on nondirective therapy attempted to elucidate the process of therapy as well as offer support for the efficacy of this approach. Landisberg and Snyder (1946) reported on play therapy done with four children between the ages of 5 and 6—hardly an adequate sample. Three therapists were involved. They found that the child's expression of feeling increased during the therapeutic process. This reflected the emphasis on the expression of feeling in therapy. Among their major conclusions was that in the four play-therapy cases studied, no statements were found which could be classified as insight. It was proposed that the amount of insight achieved in play therapy is related to age and intellectual maturity. They suggested that "for the younger child, the value of such therapy may be cathartic." Axline (1950) reported a similar finding after getting follow-up descriptions of the play-therapy process as reported by the children involved. She found that the children tended to ascribe more insight and self-awareness to therapy than they revealed during the therapy. It is possible that the children achieved a greater synthesis of their emotional learning and their intellectual understanding after the therapeutic relationship ended. The self-actualization and awareness continued outside the context of the therapy situation.

In order for play therapy to be effective, it is necessary to provide suitable play equipment. Age and maturity are factors that should be considered in the selection of equipment. Lebo (1956) found that play-therapy toys used for 4- to 10-year-olds inhibited the expressiveness of 12-year-olds. Consequently, nondirective play therapy did not seem appropriate for these children. It was strongly urged that "future research on twelve year olds and older might contrast verbalizations made in a playroom containing special toys for those ages with a straight face-to-face counseling situation in a room without toys." Toys suggested for use were the following: hand puppets, science materials, construction sets, electric train equipment, painting materials, models, more difficult creative equipment. As any therapist who has used a playroom will know, an inadequate collection of toys for any age group could drive the child from the playroom and seriously hamper the therapeutic efforts.

Nondirective play therapy has found interesting uses. For example, several studies were undertaken with children who had reading difficulties. Studies by Axline (1947a) and Bills (1950) found that as a result of play therapy, significant changes in reading ability occurred. Personality changes occurred with as few as six individual and three group sessions. Bills (1950) realized the limitation of his study and stated:

> The change which occurs in the child as a result of a non-directive play therapy experience is a change in self-concept. More adequate measures of self-concept must be devised in order to test the hypothesis that the change in reading ability of some retarded readers following a non-directive play therapy experience is related to the change in the child's self-concept. Experimentation is also needed to determine how the therapy experience enables the child to change and what techniques are most valuable in facilitating this change.

The kind of experimentation called for at that time necessitated a theory of personality development and change that was not present in the nondirective movement. Other research conducted during this period is summarized and evaluated by Dorfman (1951). Dorfman called for more follow-up studies of a large number of cases at regular intervals. She also called for further investigation of the assessment of personal adjustment before and after therapy (Dorfman, 1958). Another question that still awaits evaluation is how effective this kind of therapy is in ameliorating psychotic symptoms in children.

Lebo (1958) criticized the theory developed to explain the results of nondirective play therapy. He thought the emphasis was placed too much on process studies. Consequently, the concept of aggression or a theory of personality change with advancing age was lacking from the formulations of the therapy process. He stated:

> The empirical progress made in psychoanalysis and learning theory has been anticipated by the construction of adequate theory. Further development in nondirective play therapy would seem to require suitable theory. Without such a theoretical framework nondirective play therapy may be in danger of becoming enmeshed in the "regularity" of its process, until, like introspection, it becomes process bound and unproductive.

Though Rogers (1959) has since refined and made more inclusive his theories of personality development and therapy, they have not as yet directly influenced research in the area of nondirective play therapy.

RELATIONSHIP THERAPY

Closely related to nondirective therapy was the development of relationship therapy, which was espoused by Allen (1942) and Moustakas (1953, 1959). Taft (1933), influenced by Rank (1936), did exploratory work on the process and procedure of relationship therapy with children. Moustakas (1959) made a distinction between relationship therapy, psychoanalytic therapy, and client-centered therapy. He wrote:

> In relationship therapy, the relationship is both means and end. The relationship is the significant growth experience. In psychoanalytic approaches, the relationship is the means through which other goals are achieved. Client centered therapy, a significant approach in its own right, comes close to relationship therapy, but here the focus is not on the relationship itself but on the therapist and child as separate individuals with the therapist making reflections and clarifications, conveying empathic

understanding and having unconditional regard for the client.

This approach is clearly different from psychoanalytic therapy in that the therapist does not see predetermined sexual symbolism in the child's play. The focus is on the child's experiencing of himself. Empathy and the capacity to see each play situation as a unique, living experience that can free the child to share himself and to be himself are required of the therapist. The therapist's primary emphasis is on being there, interacting with the child by observing, listening, and making statements of recognition (Moustakas & Schalock, 1955). Central to Moustakas' thinking is the concept of the self. Self-alienation seems to characterize the disturbed child. Moustakas (1959) reported:

[The] disturbed child has been impaired in his growth of self. Somewhere along the line, he began to doubt his own powers of self development. His faith in himself and his self-reliance have been shattered. He does not trust himself and he does not trust others. He is unable to utilize his potentiality to grow with experience. . . . The disturbed child has lost touch with his real self. He no longer knows who he is or what he can do. It is this loss of self which is his basic suffering.

The therapeutic process was found to involve five basic phases (Moustakas 1955a, 1955b, 1959). First, the child's emotional expressions are diffuse and pervasive. Negative emotions are expressed with high frequency and intensity. In the second phase, the child generally fluctuates between generalized anxiety and generalized hostility. During the next phase, the hostility and fears are more focused and more directly expressed. The fourth phase is characterized by ambivalence—the revealing of both positive and negative attitudes. In the final phase, the feelings become separated and clear.

The therapeutic relationship helps the child to achieve a sense of personal worth. In a cli-

mate of understanding and acceptance, the child is freed from the damaging effects of his hostility and anxiety and recovers himself as a unique individual. The child becomes free to venture into new experiences and relationships. Allen (1942) stated:

Each move the therapist makes that helps the child to be a participant in his own change is one that helps that child to assume responsibility for a self which he can accept as uniquely his, and which is the very core of his living.

The journey toward the realization of the potentialities of being human begins. Miyamoto (1960) reported similarities between relationship therapy and Zen in play therapy.

In his recent book, Moustakas (1966a) comments further on the nature of relationship therapy, or what is currently called *experiential* or *existential* child therapy. He wrote that the experiential therapist

does not adhere to vested schools, although in practice he reflects his background and his affiliation. But this reflection is incorporated as one dimension of the self. He, the therapist, stands out on his own firm ground, not in terms of concepts and theory; but he stands out, exists, present to his own self as a whole, integrated being, present to his own resources as they emerge and unfold in his experiences with the child. He is committed to spontaneous, flowing, human processes and potentialities that are engendered and sparked in the communion of a significant relationship.

The therapists do not follow custom or technique but "only the guiding spirit of the integrated self and the direction of their own senses." Two important concepts developed in his introduction to the book and explored at greater length in an earlier article (Moustakas, 1962) are confrontation and encounter. A confrontation arises when there is a conflict between the therapist and the child that creates a crisis in the relationship. This could happen when a therapy limit is being tested by the child. (See Bixler, 1949; Dorfman, 1951; Moustakas, 1959; and Wells, 1967, for discussion of limits in therapy.) Here the therapist is required to remain firm, with both he and the child remaining together until the feelings are resolved. They may terminate the confrontation still at odds on the issue but not at odds with each other. The child must be free to trust his own senses and maintain his own individuality. Moustakas (1966b) defines the confrontation as

> a way to an authentic life between persons, but each person must maintain a living awareness of his feelings and must be honest enough and courageous enough to let the initial breach heal through the silent, sacred, covenant of love, and strong enough to maintain the human sense whatever else may be cancelled out in the issue or dispute.

The encounter is an experience in which the therapist and the child meet in harmony and communion. It is an experience of depth and relatedness. Such a moment is a creative experience in which the child, no matter how disturbed, reveals himself openly and directly and the therapist enters into this reality with receptiveness and openness. A beautiful example of an encounter is expressed by Alexander (1966). He described the experience of therapy with a child as something that occurred spontaneously in such a way that

> each ceased to be a thing apart and the two of us, the room, the hour, became an organic whole. We did not pause to analyze the other, to estimate the other's motivation, to dissect the other's feelings. We responded to each other naturally in a thinking, feeling, dynamic flow.

Alexander raises the question that is at the heart of relationship therapy: "Could not just the deep dialogue of expressive movements and sharing release in itself a powerful therapeutic growth experience?" Wells (1967) stated that Rank and students of Rank would feel a kinship to the experiential therapist. Both believe that growth eventuates from the therapeutic relationship and not from a particular technique or treatment plan based on the diagnosis of an illness. The child needs a human helper who is patient, caring, and firm. Increasingly, therapists are sensing that, as Seeman (1966) stated, "The therapist had to be involved in a real relationship rather than a role relationship. This real relationship came about when the therapist communicated his real self to the client."

Seeman (1966) reported that the current phase of nondirective or client-centered therapy is characterized by the study of therapist variables. Concepts such as genuineness (Rogers, 1961), expressivity (Gendlin, 1967), and spontaneity (Butler, 1958) are being explored as crucial qualities of the therapist. A related trend is the development of paraprofessionals as psychotherapists. One reason this has come about is that we realize that we do not have the required number of professionals to meet the needs of the community. Another reason is that the usual professional training and degrees may not be prerequisites to engage in successful psychotherapy. Guerney (1964), following the philosophy and procedures developed by Rogers, Axline, and Moustakas, has trained parents as play therapists. The approach is called *filial therapy*. Parents were trained to conduct play therapy with their own children. After the training, the parents were given corrective feedback in group meetings with a psychotherapist. The preliminary research showed that the parents and children responded very well, with a large number of parents reporting great improvement in their children. Fuchs (1957) reported an earlier illustration of the efficacy of play therapy in the home. She wrote of her experience as a play therapist with her own child. Stover and Guerney (1967) found that mothers could be trained to make more reflective statements and less directive statements in their play sessions. Thus they could successfully pattern their interaction after the role behavior of client-centered therapists. Stover and Guerney reported that future studies will aim at studying the process of filial therapy and what effect filial therapy will have on the child's emotional adjustment as well as on the overall relationship between the parent and the child. Future research should also keep up with current theoretical conceptions and should consider such important therapist variables as congruence, empathy, and expressivity and their effects on the outcome of play therapy. Studies could also be devised to investigate the interaction of these qualities in the therapist and the child.

A VALUE ORIENTATION

Questions dealing with the goals of therapy or the essence of human life are questions of values. It is generally agreed today that a therapist cannot avoid value judgments, whether implicit or explicit, in the course of his therapeutic work (Ford & Urban, 1965). An important notion developed by Rogers (1964) is that of the organismic valuing process. This valuing process is within the individual. It is characterized by flexibility, change, and openness to new experiences. New experiences are weighed and selected depending on whether or not they tend to actualize the organism. When circumstances make the individual distrust his own felt experiencing, then he begins to introject values from his environment. He learns to adopt values in order to obtain approval and favor with others. When not based on his own experiencing, the individual's values become fixed and rigid. The process of psychotherapy, by helping the individual to become in tone with his own experiences, relocates the valuing process back in the individual and away from introjected values. When the valuing process is located in the individual, he has the capacity to make choices and determine which experiences will enhance his

growth. Also, he develops a sense of responsibility for being true to himself (Moustakas, 1966b). By trusting himself, the individual takes charge of himself and becomes responsible for his actions. After the individual is able to confirm himself, he is able to confirm the other. A sense of mutuality develops. The individual realizes that a mutual dependence is established with the other, in which both can value each other's freedom and sense of identity. Ideally, this feeling emerges in play therapy. The conditions of therapy described by Rogers (1951) and Moustakas (1959, 1966a) facilitate this valuing process. Rogers (1964) stated:

> The process is complex, the choices often very perplexing and difficult, and there is no guarantee that the choice which is made will in fact prove to be self-actualizing. But because whatever evidence exists is available to the individual and because he is open to his experiencing, errors are correctable. If a chosen course of action is not self-enhancing this will be sensed and he can make an adjustment or revision.

The notion of the actualizing tendency is critical for accepting the notion of the organismic valuing process and how it functions.

Note that the above description does not make individuality the central value. Self-acceptance and affirmation are important, but so are mutuality and responsibility. Buber (Buber & Rogers, 1960) makes the distinction between individuals and persons. An individual is a human being with a certain uniqueness. Buber stated:

> I have a lot of examples of man having become very very individual, very distinct of others, very developed in their such-and-such-ness without being at all what I would like to call a man. . . . But a person, I would say, is an individual living really with the world. And with the world, I don't mean *in* the world. But just in *real contact,* in real reciprocity with the world in all the points in which the world can meet man. I don't say only with man,

because sometimes we meet the world in other shapes than in that of man. But this is what I would call a person and if I may say expressly yes and no to certain phenomena, I'm against individuals and *for* persons.

A NOTE ON THE USE OF SCIENCE AND THEORY

Science involves an attempt to generalize. This could involve formulating general laws from a single case or studying a large sample from a population of subjects. By using scientific methods, our results are potentially replicable and able to meet the standard of interpersonal validation. Tentative assumptions can become "facts" and achieve an "existence" beyond that of an individual person. General statements do not have to hide the unique. For example, in our therapeutic work we may have a person speak of a relationship with a loved one and begin to cry. Many tears fall, and a tense, constricted individual becomes unburdened and relaxed. The release of emotion seems to have a freeing effect. Now this person's tears, his story, cannot be replicated. He is unique. The moments with him can be experienced with empathy, joy, pain, or whatever emotions are aroused in you. But the experience cannot be repeated in the same way. However, this does not mean that we cannot generalize from this experience. Later we may reflect on what happened and relate it to similar experiences we have had in other relationships. The concept of emotional catharsis may come to mind. This concept helps us to relate isolated, unique experiences and provides us with therapeutic guidelines. The theory and laws developed around this concept give us further guidelines. The efforts of other scientists working within the same theoretical framework increase our chances of understanding, controlling, and predicting human behavior. Thus we can respect the uniqueness of a single case as well as generalize from it.

If we remain open to our therapeutic experience, we can have a productive interaction of each new experience and our theoretical point of view. We make use of our past while remaining open to the present. A danger arises when we "reify" our theory and, in effect, make it a closed system. We become identified with our theory and become a Freudian, Rogerian, Jungian, or whatever may be the current vogue. We begin to meet our clients in terms of our theory. The new individual becomes defined or classified in terms of our system, and a deadening interpersonal process emerges. Instead of creatively experiencing this individual's uniqueness, we try to reproduce an effect. We tie ourselves in a theoretical knot and play our role. A relationship with limitless possibilities becomes theory-bound. The use we make of theory cannot be detached from the use we make of ourselves in a therapy relationship. In effect, I am suggesting that whatever our theoretical orientation, we should approach each client as unique. In this early stage of our science, each client is more likely to increase the horizons of our theoretical framework than support our favorite hypothesis about human behavior.

REFERENCES

Alexander, E. D. An hour's journey with Cindy. *Psychotherapy: Theory, Research, and Practice,* 1966, **3,** 88–90.

Allen, F. H. *Psychotherapy with children.* New York: Norton, 1942.

Axline, V. M. Nondirective therapy for poor readers. *Journal of Consulting Psychology,* 1947, **11,** 61–69. (a)

Axline, V. M. *Play therapy.* Boston: Houghton Mifflin, 1947. (b)

Axline, V. M. Play therapy experiences as described by child participants. *Journal of Consulting Psychology,* 1950, **14,** 53–63.

Axline, V. M. *Dibs: In search of self.* New York: Ballantine Books, 1964.

Bills, R. E. Nondirective play therapy with retarded readers. *Journal of Consulting Psychology,* 1950, **14,** 140–149.

Bixler, R. H. Limits are therapy. *Journal of Consulting Psychology,* 1949, **13,** 1–11.

Buber, M., & Rogers, C. Dialogue between Martin Buber and Carl Rogers. *Psychologia,* 1960, **3,** 208–221.

Butler, J. M. Client-centered counseling and psychotherapy. In D. Brower & L. E. Abt (Eds.), *Progress in clinical psychology.* Vol. III. New York: Grune & Stratton, 1958.

Dorfman, E. Play therapy. In C. R. Rogers (Ed.), *Client-centered therapy.* Boston: Houghton Mifflin, 1951.

Dorfman, E. Personality outcomes of client-centered child therapy. *Psychological Monographs,* 1958, **72,** 1–22.

Ford, D. H., & Urban, H. B. *Systems of psychotherapy: A comparative study.* New York: Wiley, 1965.

Fuchs, N. R. Play therapy at home. *The Merrill-Palmer Quarterly,* 1957, **3,** 89–95.

Gendlin, E. T. Subverbal communication and therapist expressivity: Trends in client-centered therapy with schizophrenics. In C. R. Rogers & B. Stevens (Eds.), *Person to person: The problem of being human.* California: Real People Press, 1967.

Guerney, B. G., Jr. Filial therapy: Description and rationale. *Journal of Consulting Psychology,* 1964, **28,** 304–310.

Landisberg, S., & Snyder, W. U. Non-directive play therapy. *Journal of Clinical Psychology,* 1946, **2,** 203–213.

Lebo, D. Age and suitability for non-directive play therapy. *Journal of Genetic Psychology,* 1956, **89,** 231–238.

Lebo, D. A theoretical framework for nondirective play therapy: Concepts from psychoanalysis and learning theory. *Journal of Consulting Psychology,* 1958, **22,** 275–280.

Miyamoto, M. Zen in play therapy. *Psychologia,* 1960, **3,** 197–207.

Moustakas, C. E. *Children in play therapy.* New York: McGraw-Hill, 1953.

Moustakas, C. E. Emotional adjustment and the play therapy process. *Journal of Genetic Psychology,* 1955, **86,** 79–99. (a)

Moustakas, C. E. The frequency and intensity of negative attitudes expressed in play therapy: A comparison of well-adjusted and disturbed young children. *Journal of Genetic Psychology,* 1955, **86,** 309–325. (b)

Moustakas, C. E. *Psychotherapy with children: The living relationship.* New York: Harper & Row, 1959.

Moustakas, C. E. Confrontation and encounter. *Journal of Existential Psychiatry,* 1962, **2,** 263–290.

Moustakas, C. E. (Ed.), *Existential child therapy.* New York: Basic Books, 1966. (a)

Moustakas, C. E. *The authentic teacher.* Cambridge, Mass.: Howard Doyle, 1966. (b)

Moustakas, C. E., & Schalock, H. D. An analysis of therapist-child interaction in play therapy. *Child Development,* 1955, **26,** 143–157.

Rank, O. *Truth and reality and will therapy.* New York: Knopf, 1936.

Rogers, C. R. *Counseling and psychotherapy.* Boston: Houghton Mifflin, 1942.

Rogers, C. R. *Client-centered therapy.* Boston: Houghton Mifflin, 1951.

Rogers, C. R. A theory of therapy, personality, and interpersonal relations, as developed in the client-centered framework. In S. Koch (Ed.), *Psychology: A study of science.* Vol. II. *General systematic formulations, learning, and special processes.* New York: McGraw-Hill, 1959.

Rogers, C. R. *On becoming a person.* Boston: Houghton Mifflin, 1961.

Rogers, C. R. Toward a modern approach to values: The valuing process in the mature person. *Journal of Abnormal and Social Psychology,* 1964, **68,** 160–167.

Seeman, J. Perspectives in client-centered therapy. In B. B. Wolman (Ed.), *Handbook of clinical psychology.* New York: McGraw-Hill, 1966.

Stover, L., & Guerney, B. G., Jr. The efficacy of training procedures for mothers in filial therapy. *Psychotherapy: Theory, Research, and Practice,* 1967, **4,** 110–115.

Taft, J. *The dynamics of therapy in a controlled relationship.* New York: Macmillan, 1933.

Wells, R. G. The vein of iron—An essay in review of *Existential child therapy,* Clark Moustakas (Ed.). *Journal of the Otto Rank Association,* 1967, **2,** 81–92.

31 | Group Psychotherapy for Children

Max Rosenbaum and
Irvin A. Kraft

The theory conceptualized in group psychotherapy of children proposes to support the patient's ego growth while he learns to master the chaotic emotions within himself and achieve an adequate interaction with the external world. The family-like setting provides the background for corrective emotional experiences by the maintenance of a maximum of constancy and gratification and a minimum of frustration (Block, 1961; Scheidlinger, 1960). Patients in the group are aided in resolving their differences in a constructive fashion by the therapist, who guides (reacts) with "directness, protective restraint, and verbal clarification" (Scheidlinger, 1960).

The concept of group psychotherapy for children began to emerge when Witmer recognized the importance of a child's emotional adaptation to the school situation. In 1896, he established at the University of Pennsylvania the first psychoeducational clinic for emotionally disturbed children.

A therapeutic classroom differs from group psychotherapy, however, by its goal of education of the intellect. The teacher primarily concen-

trates on bolstering the child's ego by exploring conscious manifestations of his unconscious patterns rather than by utilizing the classroom group in a directed way to promote emotional health. Undoubtedly, therapeutic use of peer group occurs, but it is not group psychotherapy as defined here.

In 1934, Slavson (1947) began activity group therapy with latency-age children. For the first time, children were placed in a deliberately designed situation in which certain actions of the leader were predicated according to a theory of personality and behavior. This contrived group differed from other groups of children, such as a scout troup or swimming team, by its purpose as well as by the special restrictions enforced.

Instead of direct interpretation, controlled group play in a permissive environment afforded patients the opportunity to act out conflicts and emotions. Control resulted when specific limits and ground rules were declared. Slavson believed that relative control of impulsivity could be learned in the group psychotherapy setting. Recognizing that individuation of approach is

935

essential in both group and individual psychotherapy, he noted that children communicate predominantly through motor activity. For a child, play activities issue from inner fantasies that seek expression and resolution. With a child's insight limited, action is his language; the therapist discerns meaning in behavior. Regardless of the approach used in therapy for an individual child, Slavson stressed that feelings of helplessness and dependency characteristic in most children must be recognized as well as the often extreme reaction to criticism, discipline, and punishment from adults.

The goal of group psychotherapy—the education and control of the emotions—is accomplished by various techniques designed to provide an aura of acceptance rather than rejection of feelings and of specific types of behavior. The therapist, as leader of the group, attempts to provide situations which encourage behavior that reveals information from which the emotional content can be extracted and translated intellectually. For example, after a child experiences an outburst of anger in a psychotherapy group, the therapist translates, "Anger is a difficult emotion to control." The child feels better. He gains experiential insight by the verbalization of the feeling and by realizing that retribution does not follow the admission of one's true feelings. Experiential insight may come through interaction with other group members, identification, rationalization, denial, catharsis, or identification with the aggressor. Defense mechanisms tend to be enacted and utilized within the psychotherapy group in an environment of impunity and safety.

Response to treatment can be measured in terms of each child's verbal or nonverbal behavior, activity level, and interrelationships with other children in the group as well as with the leader. Patients bring selected segments of their outside life to the treatment group, and learnings in the group are transmitted through behavior to their outside life. But the child's behavior in treatment is not the same as in his outside life.

Client-centered psychotherapy, Adlerian concepts, and classical psychoanalytic principles dominate the practice of group psychotherapy for children. The literature describes commonalities of assumptions in the work performed by a therapist, regardless of his orientation in theory. These commonalities include the existence of unconscious thinking, psychic determinism, infantile sexuality, the Oedipal conflict, and a topological construct of mind. Overriding these factors, however, awareness of developmental vectors and forces always strongly influences the therapist's ultimate therapeutic patterns.

The child's ego is different from that of the adult in that it is still in the process of evolving. The balance between primitive impulses and restraint has not been established. Slavson (1964) reported, "Whether impulses or restraining forces predominate, each person has worked out a relation between the two, which is the foundation of his character. This is not the situation with the young child."

Under such conditions of ego turmoil, methods and techniques used in adult psychotherapy cannot be applied to children without significant alterations and changes. The child needs freedom to act out feelings and to speak his mind, but the therapist clarifies the limits. In general, the motor acting out of small children in the group is accepted, since the adult therapist can intervene at any time. The therapist uses his theoretical information and his guided or supervised experiences to evolve an individualized treatment style which enables him to work well and comfortably with his patients. His choice of a framework of several conceptual schemes may coincide with recent trends of increasing ambivalence regarding the value of psychoanalytic theory. Enthusiasm for attempting techniques such as operant conditioning or behavior therapy is increasing. Caution dictates that ready simplification of approaches to treatment of children leads to many blind alleys.

As an example, the few studies in print seem to support the hypothesis of parental rejection as primary in children's problems in living, but this rejection is also related to the type of disturbance. Some children in treatment see parents as excessively psychologically controlling; others wish for greater parental control. The great variety of parental descriptions that may emerge complicates group treatment of children. Goldin (1969) summarizes the literature on parental behavior as reported by children. His review should prove helpful to those who wish to form children's groups.

GROUP FORMATION IN CHILDHOOD

Most naturalistic observations of our culture's childhood behavior indicate a trend toward group formation in the latency period, especially in its later years (Block, 1966; Boulanger, 1965; Coolidge & Grunebaum, 1964). In the field of psychoanalysis, Buxbaum (1945) introduces an intriguing formulation regarding group formation. She believes that two peak periods of group formation occur in the lives of children. The first is in the 5- to 7-year age period; the second occurs during adolescence. Posing the question of the needs for which the child seeks and finds satisfaction in the group more than in any other social setting, she suggests that the childhood period of group formation occurs during the phallic phase, when the child is forced to give up his physical dependence on his mother. The child's close relationship with his mother undergoes severance gradually as he achieves independence in motility, expression, and body care. He no longer needs his mother for survival. His relationship to her changes from an anaclitic one to one of an object libidinal character. Rejection of his sexual wishes for her leaves him frustrated and drives him into transferring his feelings for her to other people. In the group, the young child finds support for his newfound physical independence from the mother. Feeling deserted, ousted from a protective atmosphere upon which he used to rely, he finds a welcome shelter in the group experience. The fear of separation from mother and home is overcome by transferring allegiance to the group leader. Transference becomes an essential and causative factor in childhood and adolescent group formation, serving as a principal motivating force in group formation and a principal cohesive force among group members.

Social scientists have attempted to understand childhood group processes from another viewpoint. Muzafer Sherif and Hadley Cantril (1947) proposed a sophisticated theory with a dynamic conception of the individual and his relationship to society which elaborates on the work of Cooley (1902, 1909, 1918). While dynamic and effective, Cooley's work was somewhat mystical. Although his work often is overlooked by group therapists, he stated that social process and control, basic to all group dynamics, are based on the intimate, face-to-face interactions which form the hallmark of the primary group. Cooley stated that the primary group has a psychological structure represented by close identification or intimacy. Later, George Herbert Mead (1934) defined the self process, but his formulations were incomplete because they were cognitive. Sherif (1948) borrowed the term *reference group* from social psychologist Herbert Hyman (1942) to designate the influence of the group upon the values and attitudes of the individual. While it developed that Sherif was referring to a different phenomenon than that which Hyman had described, both were interested in how groups affect people, according to each individual's distinctive relationship to the group (Turner, 1966). Sherif's major concern was how the individual acquires the attitudes and values of a group.

Sociologists until that time had concentrated on the group's reaction to the individual (Thibaut & Kelley, 1959).

Since group formation occurs as a natural phenomenon in childhood development, the age and developmental stage of the child have influenced the growth of group psychotherapy techniques more than perhaps any other factor. Therapists group children by age and often by the nature of their presenting difficulties (Anthony, 1965; Kraft, 1967; Sobel & Geller, 1964). Children are grouped into five categories: preschool and early school age, late latency (ages 9 to 11), pubertal (ages 12 and 13), early adolescence (ages 13 and 14), and middle through late adolescence (14 to 17). The most useful periods of group therapy are the second and fifth. This chapter concerns the first two or three categories. Just as developmental patterns lead to age divisions of group members, the settings in which therapists operate influence their procedures.

TREATMENT SETTINGS

Group psychotherapy of children occurs almost anywhere disturbed children are involved in some type of therapeutic procedure. The diagnostic category may or may not be important for the composition of the group, for authors vary in their experiences and their recommendations. Group therapy may occur in a state hospital (Sobel & Geller, 1964). Different forms of group therapy, such as puppetry, have been used in hospital wards. Hospitals not specifically oriented to psychiatric disturbances, such as a hospital for asthmatic children, also include group therapy as part of their total regimen of medical care of the child.

In residential treatment settings, group psychotherapy is used, especially in small units, depending on the treatment philosophy of the director. In larger units, the manpower prob-

lems tend to make the increased use of group methods a necessity. Another, more common site for group therapy is the day hospital. Psychoeducational settings lend themselves effectively to various kinds of group therapy.

Probably the most frequent setting for group therapy is the outpatient clinic. Through the years, group psychotherapy of children, independent of or concomitant with treatment of the parents, has been used even in the most orthodox child-guidance center (Boulanger, 1965; Ganter & Yeakel, 1965; Novick, 1965; Slavson, 1964; Smolen & Lifton, 1966). A fifth setting in which group therapy is being used more often is the public school (Frey & Kolodny, 1966). Beard et al. (1958) describe involvement of children in unusual settings, such as an adult prison.

COMPOSITION OF THE THERAPY GROUP

The child's developmental age and the therapist's setting strongly influence the selection of children for group psychotherapy. The group therapist, whether beginner or expert, must look at his patient population and decide what types of children to include in his therapeutic program. The diagnostic categories convey the entire spectrum of nomenclature. Work has been done with psychotic children by Sobel and Geller (1964) and Speers and Lansing (1964). Reports describe group psychotherapy with severe psychoneurosis, personality trait disorders, behavior disorders, retardation, school failures, school phobias, and delinquency.

A therapist involved in any therapeutic program decides what type of child he is going to treat on the basis of his own interests and by considering the availability of children for the specific procedure.

Examples of these various categories may help the less experienced group psychotherapist.

Frey and Kolodny (1966) demonstrate social-group treatment methods in their care of the alienated child in a school environment. Their subjects had failed to find ways of relating to the school without excessive fear or anger. Boulanger (1965) excludes from his analytic psychodrama "children who are hyperactive, physically or intellectually defective, delinquent or predelinquent, prepsychotic, psychotic. . . ." He includes children with psychoneurotic character structure from birth, symptom formation, and inhibition. Sobel and Geller (1964) suggest that in their therapy in a hospital setting, the level of functional and behavioral integration of the child was the important factor. "Ability to get along in a structured setting was actually necessary for participation. . . ." Coolidge and Grunebaum (1964) demonstrated the effects of group psychotherapy in conjunction with other inabilities on a child with severe school-phobia symptomatology. Ginott (1961) suggests, "A therapeutic group must consist of children with dissimilar syndromes so that each child will have the opportunity to associate with personalities different from and complementary to his own." Speers and Lansing (1964) described their program with preschool psychotic children.

An intriguing sequence of techniques for kindergarten and latency children was described by Anthony (1965). He termed these the *small-table* and *small-room* methods:

> The circle, which constitutes the top of the table, is divided into five sectors, each of which is separated from the other by a low, removable wall. Between the walls lies the place or "territory" of the individual member. The walls end at the center of the table at a trough containing water. This is, therefore, common to all the members of the group. Each territory is equipped with a set of playthings, and each set has its own special color, making it distinguishable from other sets. The transactional processes in this nursery group are carried out on both the concrete and verbal level. On the concrete level, the children may scale the miniature walls with ladders or tunnel under them. They may borrow or lend their toy equipment, helping to construct their own themes or the themes of others.

He described the work with latency children in equally interesting fashion:

> With this method, a contract was made with the group whereby an activity period of their own choosing followed a period of talking. As I became more and more experienced with groups of this kind, I gradually shortened the activity period, until now I have done away with it altogether, in favor of a group session in which activity occurs spontaneously, and is then generally interpreted in terms of defense. The group is treated in an analytic way, and the role of the therapist is strongly interpretative. The one cardinal rule is that all interpretations are, from the very beginning, directed towards the group, however personally directed the comments of the individual members may be. The group is allowed to develop classically, without a program and without an occupation, and is confronted with its own tensions and silences.

Gender has not played a major role, except that the frequency of children being brought to attention ranges from three or four boys to one girl. Thus, by availability, boys are more frequently seen in group psychotherapy in the childhood age group as compared with the middle to late adolescent groups. There are reports of mixed groupings, but both the source of supply and proclivity by the leaders have led primarily to the use of separate gender groups.

Composition may be seen more as a function of the therapeutic outlook and concepts of the therapist, the setting, and the availability of patients than as the result of a particular theoretical position. Some investigators in state hospitals have found that even with a large number of children available (Sobel & Geller, 1964), the group membership is selected by the criteria of accessibility to insight and the character of the group. Therapists tend to group their children by their availability, such as including psychotic children in a group but excluding a delinquent or mildly disturbed child. This was true in the work done in the East Bay area, except there they found that they could use a "provocateur," or healthier child, with a group of psychotic children in a constructive way.

The composition of groups, therefore, can be of almost any kind if the therapist is flexible enough in his outlook. It seems that the degree of ego strength would be a major factor in forming a group as well as the degree of hyperactivity and the amount of disturbance created by impulse-ridden children. This hyperkinesis, which is thought to be a function of ego strength in the extreme, would be too disruptive to a group of late-latency children, who are involved primarily in school-performance problems.

Intellectual Quotient

The intellectual level of a child often is predictive of his functioning in a therapy group for children, depending upon the age and IQs of the other children. Therapists generally believe that children with average intelligence or above-average levels can function adequately in a group. The major problem rests with children who either are extremely brilliant or have IQ levels below 85. It is difficult for children with lower IQ levels to function adequately in a group because they do not understand what is going on and are often the butt of jokes injected by the brighter group members. It is cruel in most cases to expect a group of bright children to accommodate to the slow pace and often grossly immature development of a retardate, in spite of the fact that emotionally disturbed children often show significant immaturity. But the kind of imma-

turity shown by most disturbed children of normal intelligence differs from the emotional levels and slow development of disturbed retardates. Most investigators prefer to place retardates in groups which are homogenous with reference to intellectual quotient.

Sternlicht (1965) strongly supports group therapy for children who are mentally retarded, taking issue with the assumption that insight is necessary for successful personality change. Neham (1951) views group therapy with children who are mentally retarded as mainly ego-supportive, and Stevenson and Knights (1962) see their group therapy as social reinforcement. Cowen (1962) stresses group play techniques in his work with the "exceptional" child. In general, therapists working with mentally defective patients stress the importance of careful screening for membership balance, even as they maintain it should be done with nondefectives.

Family Structure

A child's previous or present family structure influences his performance and production within a group, but his orientation to his peers tends to be paramount in importance. Since no attempt is made to replicate life in the therapy group, except in groups with two therapists of opposite sex, the family structure is not too important. The child is more involved with his peer relationships than he is in a direct way with his family, expecially in the mid- to late-latency group and the preadolescent group. Thus, the group tends to be ego-supportive and helps the child reorient himself to his family and his peer group through his group work with his peers. This is the purpose for which the group is designed. Thus, the child may discuss his parents and may react to the therapist as if he were a parent, but his interaction in the group is determined predominantly by his peer-oriented discernment. He may treat his peers as if they were siblings, which would reflect the viewpoints in the family structure about children.

Other criteria for selection suggest that children who show a common social hunger, the need to be like their peers and to be accepted by them, should be included. Usually the therapist excludes the child who has never realized a primary relationship, as with his mother, since individual psychotherapy could help the child more. For his preschool groups, Ginott (1961) rejects children with murderous attitudes toward siblings, sociopathic children, children with perverse sexual experiences, habitual thieves, and extremely aggressive children. The children he usually selects are effeminate boys, shy and withdrawn children, and children with phobic reactions and primary behavior disorders. For groups composed of latency-age children, therapists tend to exclude incorrigible or psychopathic children, homicidal children, and overt sexually deviant children. The severely threatened, ritualistic, socially peculiar children who cannot establish effective communications at any useful level with the group members fail to do well in these groups.

PSYCHOTHERAPY TECHNIQUES

The techniques of group psychotherapy of children vary according to the propensities of the therapist, the facilities available to him, and the age of the patients involved. A survey of the literature indicates that many variations occur within the limits of nonexploitation of the patient. A sense of balance must be provided by the therapist. There is a delicate balance between that which is ethical and that which is not acceptable as appropriate technique.

In a field where few guidelines exist and little work has been done compared with the volume of work done with adults, it seems dangerous to let people go on their own. But what standards do we have to go by? Perhaps the best safeguard is the professional competency and integrity of the therapist himself. The setting in which he works, usually an institution, may act as a safeguard in protection for the children. Few articles have been published describing the private-practice patterns used by solo practitioners in their treatment of children. Most of the literature cites work in institutional settings, perhaps because group therapy for children requires a physical plant to accommodate children with different emotional conditions.

We still face the question of the lack of standardization of techniques. Certain characteristics of techniques are generic, however. Children are grouped with some commonality. Children who have syndromes that seem incompatible with those of the other children are excluded, as pointed out by Boulanger (1965) in his article on analytic psychodrama of children.

Other basic techniques include those imitative of individual interviews, activity interviews, group psychotherapy with an analytic framework (Kraft, 1967) to activity group therapy, which is the most commonly fostered sponsored group therapy technique (Scheidlinger, 1960). Most group psychotherapy of children, up to the adolescent group, includes some involvement of play. In interview-type group psychotherapy, the boys and girls need some type of play period or feeding situation at the end of the session.

Many therapists agree that the general pattern of talking does not relieve enough of the tensions, so that at the end or at some point of the therapy, kinesics or active play becomes necessary. In our culture, at most levels of involvement, food is also considered part of social intercourse. Since groups at play often involve a snack or other type of feeding at some point, this is often found as part of a group therapy procedure with children. Eating can be a very useful psychological adjunct for the therapist. As Slavson (1964) pointed out, "Some group therapists who placate their patients by various means, rationalize it as playing out the 'good parent role'." Feeding the patients fulfills the needs of the therapist. Children eating together participate in social interaction in a situation which is present in school life (eating lunch at school) and in homelife. We assume that many families tend to aggregate around the transmittal of food from the parents to the children.

Dream Interpretation

Few reports on the use of dreams in group therapy of children appear in the literature. Certainly in the younger age group, dreams may be reported spontaneously, but they usually are not elicited or interpreted by the therapist in a direct way. Dreams can help, however, by being used as a focus for discussion of all the group members by simply having the child who narrates the dream seek comments from the other group members on similar dreams that they have had. "What do you think Johnny might be saying by his night thinking?" as dreams are often termed. In one case, we found that we could use both dreams and responses to Rorschach cards in the same way. The children tended to have fantasies and comment on each other's productions in their forty-five minutes or so of interview group therapy in a late-latency group. This might be hard to do with children of preschool level or of the Oedipal period.

Free Association

Free association is used in the sense of translating play. This certainly would occur in children who play together under the aegis of the therapist. The use of free association and other devices to obtain unconscious mate-rial is not clearly defined in the literature. The assumption is made that unconscious material is pertinent and involved in the treatment process, although it is not necessarily pointed out to the children. Usually the techniques involve ego-oriented interpretations, providing the opportunity for expression of strong, basic emotions. "It's all right to let your angry feelings out, so long as you know what to do with them," or "When parents do something like that, children may feel sad."

Time Factors in Therapy

Frequency of group meetings may vary from daily to once a week. The frequency of meetings is determined to a great extent by the time flexibility of therapists and the availability of patients, which depends upon the setting, transportation, and other variables. Few studies exist that show comparisons between matched groups with multifrequency meetings versus meetings once a week or less frequently. In actuality, the therapist who is going to work with children considers the frequency primarily on the basis of the mechanisms and involvements of his setting rather than by any theoretical consideration of what would seem to be the best number of times to meet. This same question remains unsettled in adult group therapy and in individual psychotherapy.

The duration of a session varies also. In most of the prescriptions for group psychotherapy of children, the duration of a session is partly a function of the mechanics and proclivities of the therapist and partly determined by the availability of the children and other factors. Once again, no scientific study has compared the various possible time intervals in a controlled way. The amount of time per session usually is determined by the child's concentration span and the type of group psychotherapy involved. With psychotic children, such as those reported by

Speers and Lansing (1968), a session might continue ·for hours. Smolen and Lifton (1966) reported on brief sessions.

The question of the length of therapy is answered in view of the situation. In group psychotherapy to prepare children for individual or residential treament, Ganter, Yeakel, and Polansky (1965) used it for three years with positive results. Duration of treatment is a function of the continued availability of the child, the parents' commitment to bring the child to the setting if it is nonresidential, and other factors. Since group psychotherapy usually is not considered the only treatment for children, depending upon the diagnostic category, other factors may determine discharge and treatment rather than the group psychotherapy itself. Some groups are set up on a time-limited basis. Burdon and Neely (1966) used a short-term group-therapy approach in their work with boys aged 7 to 12 who showed repeated school failure. The therapy, limited to from three to five months, with involvement of child, mother, and father in mandatory group therapy, was held once a week for 90 minutes. The families studied were Caucasian and culturally homogeneous, mostly "blue-collar" and office workers. The entire treatment program with intact family structure was organized around the concept of family responsibility and involvement.

Instrumentation in Psychotherapy

Instrumentation in the life sciences and in psychotherapy is increasing. Schwitzgebel (1968) reviewed about fifty electromechanical devices used for psychotherapeutic purposes. In time, we will apply these techniques to groups of children. Skinner (1938, 1953) emphasized the function of contingent consequences in shaping and maintaining behavior. A logical outgrowth was the designing of an apparatus for more precise environmental control and response measure-

ment. Simple mechanical devices have been devised for prompting the behavior of preverbal children (Biddleston, 1953). Quarti and Renaud (1962) invented an apparatus for the treatment of chronic constipation. Thus, technology finally is moving into psychotherapy and, more specifically, behavior therapy.

The implications for treating children in groups become clearer as therapists speak of ignoring the person (intrapsychically speaking) and altering the relevant environment via mechanical means. Schwitzgebel (1968) suggests:

> An unhappy mother might be taught to love her incontinent child in order to modify his behavior, but the mutual frustration might be avoided by the use of a toilet-training device which functions somewhat independently of the mother's knowledge or mood. The improvement of psychotherapeutic endeavors can likely be hastened by the invention of better social mouse traps.

Behavioral Techniques

The need for shortcuts, as well as public pressure on psychotherapists to produce results, will lead to increasing instrumentation and a behavioral mechanistic approach to child therapy. After all, children rarely have friends at the bar of justice. The unhappy adult's complaints bring children to the attention of therapists. It is reasonable to assume that psychotherapists who practice in the decade ahead will be heavily pressured by a culture which insists on teaching children to conform. Intensive psychotherapy is increasingly challenged as new "gimmicks" are brought to the field of psychotherapy. It is unfortunate that behavior therapists are unaware of much psychoanalytic experience. For example, long before behavior therapists used the technique, Eissler (1949), who was psychoanalytically trained, gave money at times to juvenile delinquents in treatment. He was aware of the dangers in such an approach. Currently, therapists who use the technique seem less aware.

Desensitization techniques, originally used by Wolpe (1958) and Lazarus (1961) and later by Paul and Shannon (1966) in work with college students aged 19 to 24, lend themselves readily to work with children. For years, experienced clinicians have used behavioral techniques selectively. Toussieng and Schechter (1967) use group therapy for children until introspection becomes more tolerable; then they use individual psychotherapy. Using group therapy selectively, they note that schizoid children with fears of social contact do poorly in groups until they have gained more social confidence in individual psychotherapy, at which time group therapy is helpful in developing better social skills. In residential treatment settings, the child is provided with an environment which can accept his assaults without retaliation. Here the child often joins a group and interacts and then may withdraw while he works through some areas without pressure. Clement and Milne (1967) used playtherapy groups with eleven third-grade boys. They applied a behavioral model with children who were referred by their teachers because of shy, withdrawn behavior. They used operant conditioning techniques, including brass tokens which could be used to buy other tokens, trinkets, and candy. Again, they were apparently unaware of the early work done by pioneers in child therapy who used reward mechanisms. While their study is well designed and makes a contribution to research in child therapy, their results are not significant.

Stimulated by the work of Paul and Shannon (1966), Kondas (1967) in Czechoslovakia worked with groups of twenty-three children using group desensitization as a method for reducing stage fright. His results were generally positive, but his goals were limited. Among behavior therapists, Clement and Milne (1967) may be considered the strongest exponents of operant conditioning. Often, behavior therapists use simple reinforcement techniques, such as letting the child talk into a tape recorder. Schwitzgebel and Kolb (1964) describe this in detail in their work with adolescent delinquents. Occasionally, investigators in allied fields become enthusiastic about working with groups of children and adolescents. They may or may not have positive results, but there is rarely a theoretical rationale behind the work. An example of this is in the report of Laeder and Francis (1968), in which they provided group therapy for stutterers in junior-senior high school in a rural setting. They noted the isolation of students in rural settings and praised the idea of workshops in rural settings.

Psychodrama has been used for children of all ages. Boulanger (1965) reports on a most fascinating use of this form of therapy in a technique he terms *group analytic psychodrama*. He suggests, "Psychodrama offers the unique possibility of meeting the therapeutic needs of the latency child by using action for a symbolic dramatization of his conflicts." He uses a plot which is enacted by the patients and co-therapists.

Personality of Therapist

No studies on the personality patterns of therapists are known or have been reported. A few reports delineate the role of the gender of the therapists. Some people assume that if there is female and male, the children react as if the therapists were creating duplications of the mother-father initial role relationships to the children. The gender of the therapist often is immaterial except in working with delinquent or incorrigible boys who have tremendous acting-out problems. It would be difficult for most women to handle these situations without the help of some forceful agent, presumably the male therapist or co-therapist.

FAMILY THERAPY

Family therapy in its multiple variations includes children in a group-therapy situation.

Environmental factors determine frequency, numbers in the group, and the format used. Wilmer, Marks, and Pogue (1966) began an experiment in group therapy at San Quentin Prison in 1964. They included thirteen inmates in group treatment with their wives and their thirty-five children, aged 2 to 17 years, who met monthly at the prison. The children's group was largely oriented around game playing and was devoted to helping the children work through feelings about fantasy fathers who ostensibly had deserted them.

The rationale was based on the work of Anna Freud and her associate, Burlingham, in their study (1944) of fatherless children in England during World War II. They noticed the children's intense and persistent attachment to a fantasy father. In the case of the fantasy father, the child replaced the long lost or missing father with an omnipotent father, endowed with all the desired elements of the benign parent. Or the child went to the opposite extreme and imagined the father as hating, rejecting, and cruel.

Wilmer and his colleagues met with the entire family for 30 to 40 minutes and then divided the participants into three groups: husbands and wives, children under 9 years of age, and children over 9 years of age. While Wilmer's sample may be considered atypical, his findings may be relevant for therapy with disordered family settings, such as hard-core poverty settings. He found that initial separation of the participants, with the children meeting in a group separate from the parents, reinforced the children's separation anxiety as well as the parents' suspicion about what the youngsters were saying about the mothers and fathers. Finally, the families met together, and then at the children's request the children met alone. A female psychiatric nurse and a male correctional officer led the children's group.

Much rewarding work remains to be done in correlating family therapy, parents' groups, and children's groups. Most therapists agree that concomitant therapy with the parents is helpful. Some therapists believe that parental psychotherapy, such as a mothers' group, will be sufficient and more than adjunctive to remedying the problems with preschool through latency-age children. Multiple impact therapy can serve as both a diagnostic instrument and an intake device in family therapy. In these circumstances, one often sees clearly how the child patient can serve as the emotional radar of the family (Ganter & Yeakel, 1965; Macgregor, 1964; Speers & Lansing, 1964).

CONCLUSIONS

For group therapy of children, the decade ahead should reflect the moves toward a mechanistic approach to psychotherapy. The literature reveals a paucity of clear thinking concerning therapy of children. We may anticipate more contributions from social psychologists and academic contributors, which should be welcomed by struggling clinicians. Rosenbaum (1965, 1969) has called attention to the confusion exhibited by clinicians as they plunge ahead without studying the ethical and philosophical issues involved in psychotherapy. The current emphasis on immediate consumption and instant gratification, the antithesis of the much-vaunted Puritan ethic, which stressed the saving of money, the postponement of desires, and the pursuit of long-range goals, is bound to be reflected in treatment goals in work with children. It is critical that issues be studied by clinicians, who often enter community settings, particularly hard-core poverty areas, with minimal awareness of the social structure that is being disturbed (Heacock, 1966).

Another intriguing aspect is the extremely broad extension of group therapy into social areas. A significant aid to clinicians is the work of Makarenko (1936), a Soviet educator, who was hostile to psychological concepts and believed they were of little help to him. A brief summary of his work is germane. After the Bolshevik Revolution and World War I, the Russians were faced with the problem of 7 million war orphans, called "wild boys," roaming the countryside in packs. Makarenko set himself to the task of reclaiming these children. He became disillusioned in attempting to find help in the work of educators preceding him and became so bitter that he developed a profound antagonism toward any educational procedure which stressed psychology. His hero was Maxim Gorki, and he founded a colony for youngsters named the Gorki Colony. His aim was to develop a consciousness of the primacy of the group participatory leadership rather than supervisory leadership. He finally developed the concept of the collective, a concept found in the Israeli *kibbutzim*. When we consider that he worked with children from shattered family groups, in which there was destruction of traditional values, his work shows relevance for today's workers in community mental health. While the reader may disagree with the uses made of his concepts in the Soviet culture, his experiences and conclusions are important (Makarenko, 1936, 1953, 1954, 1955). To Soviet parents, he is what Spock is to American parents.

What can practicing clinicians look forward to in the decade ahead as they contemplate group therapy with children? The trend is toward a pragmatic view. However, theoretical positions overlap. Clinicians find their way to heaven only to find that someone else has been there before them, but the newcomer did not know about the previous voyage. Greater commonalities among the findings of different schools emerge more consistently than the advocates care to recognize.

In a specific review of the psychotherapy of phobias, a term used with roughly the same meaning by psychotherapists of many orientations—behavior therapists, psychoanalysts, school-phobia workers, and logotherapists— Andrews (1966) found that the psychotherapists were consistent in recognizing the underlying problem with school phobias. All the different schools noted the subtle collusion of work among family members, including the child, to prevent loss and separation. Thus, Fenichel (1945) noted that a common factor in all phobias is the regression to childhood, and this represents the psychoanalytic view. In describing a patient, Lazarus (1964), a devoted exponent of behavior therapy, states, "Overprotective and anxious parents provided abundant opportunity for the acquisition of neurotic habits (phobias)." A major disagreement among practitioners is exemplified by Haley (1963) and Fry (1962), who consider symptoms as tactics in human relationships, and by the behavior therapists who reject the idea that there is any purposive element in neurotic symptoms (Wolpe, 1958).

There are many indications for the use of group psychotherapy as a treatment modality. Some indications can be described as situational, when the therapist works in a reformatory setting in which group psychotherapy seems to have reached the adolescents better than individual treatment. Economics indicate therapy groups, since more patients can be reached simultaneously. Perhaps more appropriate would be the necessity to use a treatment procedure that will best help the child for a given age, developmental stage, and type of problem. In the younger age group, the child's social hunger and his potential need for peer acceptance help determine his suitability for group therapy. Criteria for unsuitability are controversial.

The results of group psychotherapy with children are difficult to evaluate. Favorable results were reported in one study of nondirective play therapy and another of delinquents in which control groups were used. Evaluating the results of group psychotherapy of children proves as difficult as assessing individual psychotherapy of children. Since few studies have been controlled for time as well as for other factors, including follow-up evaluations (Novick, 1965), one can say that group therapy does not supplant or replace individual therapy. It is a tool that the therapist might become familiar with by using it under supervision. In crowded child psychiatric clinics, for example, various group techniques help relieve pressures at intake, diagnosis, and treatment levels. Impressionistically, certain results can be indicated. Group psychotherapy helps children feel unconditionally accepted by the therapist and the groups members.

Failures can be seen as part of each child's development. Complexes of feelings and ideation gain expression. Feelings of guilt, anxiety, inferiority, and insecurity find relief. Group psychotherapy of children is still young and undeveloped in its full potential for study and treatment.

REFERENCES

Aichorn, A. *Wayward youth.* New York: Viking, 1935.

Andrews, J. D. W. Psychotherapy of phobias. *Psychological Bulletin,* 1966, **66,** 455–480.

Anker, J. M., & Walsh, R. P. Group psychotherapy: A special activity program and group structure in the treatment of chronic schizophrenics. *Journel of Consulting Psychology,* 1961, **25,** 475–481.

Anthony, E. J. Age and syndrome in group psychotherapy. *Group Psychotherapy Today,* 1965.

Astrachan, M. Group psychotherapy with mentally retarded female adolescents and adults. *American Journal of Mental Deficiency,* 1955, **60,** 152–156.

Beard, J. H., Goertzel, V., & Pearce, A. J. The effectiveness of activity group therapy with chronically regressed adult schizophrenics. *International Journal of Psychoanalysis,* 1958, **8,** 123–136.

Berschling, C., & Homann, J. A proposal for the establishment of a group psychotherapy program for adolescents. *Psychiatric Communications,* 1966, **8**(1), 17–36.

Biddleston, R. J. Time and activity clock device. Patent No. 2,629. *United States Patent Gazette,* 1953, 186.

Block, S. L. Multi-leadership as a teaching and therapeutic tool in group psychotherapy. *Comprehensive Psychiatry,* 1961, **2**(4), 211–218.

Block, Stanley L. Some notes on transference in group psychotherapy. *Comprehensive Psychiatry,* 1966, **7**(1), 31–38.

Boulanger, J. B. Group psychoanalytic therapy in child psychiatry. *Canadian Psychiatric Association Journal,* 1961, **6**(5), 272–275.

Boulanger, J. B. Group analytic psychodrama in child psychiatry. *Canadian Psychiatric Association Journal,* 1965, **10,** 427–431.

Burdon, Arthur P., & Neely, James H. Chronic school failure in boys: A short-term group therapy and education approach. *American Journal of Psychiatry,* 1966, **122**(11), 1211–1219.

Buxbaum, E. Transference and group formation in children and adolescents. *The psychoanalytic study of the child.* Vol. 1. New York: International Universities Press, 1945. Pp. 351–365.

Buxbaum, E. *Your child makes sense.* New York: International Universities Press, 1949.

Case, M. E. The forgotten ones: An exploratory project in the use of group activities for the therapy of deteriorated psychotic patients. *Smith College Studies in Social Work,* 1951, **21,** 199–231.

Clement, P. W., & Milne, D. C. Group play therapy and tangible reinforcers used to modify the behavior of eight year old boys. *Behaviour Research and Therapy,* 1967, **5**, 301–312.

Cooley, C. *Human nature and the social order.* New York: Scribner, 1902.

Cooley, C. *Social organization.* New York: Scribner, 1909.

Cooley, C. *Social process.* New York: Scribner, 1918.

Coolidge, J. C., & Grunebaum, M. G. Individual and group therapy of a latency age child. *International Journal of Group Psychotherapy,* 1964, **14**, 84–96.

Cowen, E. L. Psychotherapy and play techniques with the exceptional child and youth. In W. M. Cruickshank (Ed.), *Psychology of exceptional children and youth.* Englewood Cliffs, N.J.: Prentice-Hall, 1962.

Durkin, H. E. *The group in depth.* New York: International Universities Press, 1965.

Eissler, K. (Ed.) *Searchlights on delinquency.* New York: International Universities Press, 1949.

Epstein, N. Activity group therapy. *International Journal of Group Psychotherapy,* 1960, **10**, 180–194.

Fenichel, O. *Psychoanalytic theory of neurosis.* New York: Norton, 1945.

Freud, A., & Burlingham, D. T. *Infants without families.* New York: International Universities Press, 1944.

Frey, L. A., & Kolodny, R. L. Group treatment for the alienated child in the school. *International Journal of Group Psychotherapy,* 1966, **16**, 321–337.

Fry, W. F. The marital context of an anxiety syndrome. *Family Process,* 1962, **1**, 245–252.

Ganter, G., Yeakel, M., & Polansky, N. A. Intermediary group treatment of inaccessible children. *American Journal of Orthopsychiatry,* 1965, **35**, 739–746.

Ginott, H. *Group psychotherapy with children.* New York: McGraw-Hill, 1961.

Goldin, P. C. A review of children's reports of parent behaviors. *Psychological Bulletin,* 1969, **71**, 222–236.

Gratton, L., & Rizzo, A. E. Group therapy with young psychotic children. *International Journal of Group Psychotherapy,* 1969, **19**(1), 63–71.

Haley, J. *Strategies of psychotherapy.* New York: Grune & Stratton, 1963.

Heacock, D. R. Modifications of the standard techniques for out-patient group psychotherapy with delinquent boys. *Journal of the National Medical Association,* 1966, **58**(1), 44–47.

Heinicke, C. M., & Goldman, A. Research on psychotherapy with children: A review and suggestions for further study. *American Journal of Orthopsychiatry,* 1960, **30**, 483–494.

Hyman, H. The psychology of status. *Archives of Psychology,* 1942, 269.

Kondas, O. Reduction of examination anxiety and "stage fright" by group desensitization and relaxation. *Behaviour Research and Therapy,* 1967, **5**, 275–281.

Kraft, Irvin A. Group therapy. In A. M. Freedman & H. I. Kaplan (Eds.), *Comprehensive textbook of psychiatry.* Baltimore: Williams & Wilkins, 1967. Pp. 1463–1468.

Laeder, R., & Francis, W. C. Stuttering workshops: Group therapy in a rural high school setting. *Journal of Speech and Hearing Disorders,* 1968, **33**, 38–41.

Lazarus, A. A. Behavior therapy with identical twins. *Behaviour Research and Therapy,* 1964, **2**, 313–320.

Lazarus, A. A. Group therapy of phobic disorders by systematic desensitization. *Journal of Abnormal and Social Psychology,* 1961, **63**, 504–510.

Macgregor, R. *Multiple impact therapy with families.* New York: McGraw-Hill, 1964.

Makarenko, A. S. *The road to life.* (Tr. by Stephen Garry.) Vol. 1. London: Stanley Nott, 1936.

Makarenko, A. S. *Learning to live.* Moscow: Foreign Languages Publishing House, 1953.

Makarenko, A. S. *A book for parents.* Moscow: Foreign Languages Publishing House, 1954.

Makarenko, A. S. *The road of life: An epic of education.* Moscow: Foreign Languages Publishing House, 1955.

Matis, Edward E. Psychotherapeutic tools for parents. *Journal of Speech and Hearing Disorders,* 1961, **26**, 164–170.

Mead, G. H. *Mind, self and society.* Chicago: University of Chicago Press, 1934.

Moe, M. Group psychotherapy with parents of psychotic and neurotic children. *Acta Psychotherapeutica et Psychosomatica,* 1960, **8**, 134 and 146.

Mullan, H., & Rosenbaum, M. *Group psychotherapy.* New York: Free Press, 1962.

Neham, Sara. Psychotherapy in relation to mental deficiency. *American Journal of Mental Deficiency,* 1951, **55**, 557–572.

Novick, Jack I. Comparison between short-term group and individual psychotherapy in effecting change in nondesirable behavior in children. *International Journal of Group Psychotherapy,* 1965, **15**, 366–373.

Paul, G. L., & Shannon, D. T. Treatment of anxiety through systematic desensitization in therapy groups. *Journal of Abnormal Psychology,* 1966, **71**(2), 124–135.

Quarti, C., & Renaud, J. A new treatment of constipation by conditioning: A preliminary report. *La Clinique,* 1962, **57**, 577–583.

Rosenbaum, M. Group psychotherapy. In B. B. Wolman (Ed.), *Handbook of clinical psychology.* New York: McGraw-Hill, 1965.

Rosenbaum, M. Current controversies in psychoanalytic group psychotherapy and what they mask. In L. Eron & R. Callahan (Eds.), *The relation of theory to practice in psychotherapy.* Chicago: Aldine, 1969.

Sager, C. J. Combined individual and group psychoanalysis, symposium, 1959: 2. Concurrent individual and group analytic psychotherapy. *American Journal of Orthopsychiatry,* 1960, **30**, 225–241.

Scheidlinger, S. Experimental group treatment of severely deprived latency-aged children. *American Journal of Orthopsychiatry,* 1960, **30**, 356–368.

Schwartz, Martin. Analytic group psychotherapy. *International Journal of Group Psychotherapy,* 1960, **10**, 195–212.

Schwitzgebel, R. L. Survey of electromechanical devices for behavior modification. *Psychological Bulletin,* 1968, **70**, 444–459.

Schwitzgebel, R., & Kolb, D. A. Inducing behavior change in adolescent delinquents. *Be-*

haviour Research and Therapy, 1964, **1,** 297–304.

Sherif, M. *An outline of social psychology.* New York: Harper, 1948.

Sherif, M. Superordinate goals in the reduction of intergroup conflict. *American Journal of Sociology,* 1958, **63,** 349–358.

Sherif, M., & Cantril, H. *The psychology of ego-involvements.* New York: Wiley, 1947.

Sherif, M., Harvey, O. J., White, B. J., Hood, W. R., & Sherif, C. W. *Intergroup conflict and cooperation: The robbers cave experiment.* Norman, Okla.: Institute of Group Relations, 1961.

Sherif, M., & Sherif, C. W. *Groups in harmony and tension.* New York: Harper, 1953.

Skinner, B. F. *The behavior of organisms.* New York: Appleton-Century-Crofts, 1938.

Skinner, B. F. *Science and human behavior.* New York: Macmillan, 1953.

Slavson, S. R. (Ed.) *The practice of group therapy.* New York: International Universities Press, 1947.

Slavson, S. R. (Ed.) *The fields of group psychotherapy.* New York: International Universities Press, 1956.

Slavson, S. R. The scope and aims of the evaluation study. *International Journal of Group Psychotherapy,* 1960, **10,** 176–179.

Slavson, S. R. *A textbook in analytic group psychotherapy.* New York: International Universities Press, 1964.

Slavson, S. R. Para-analytic group psychotherapy: A treatment of choice for adolescents. *Pathways in Child Guidance,* 1964, **6,** 1–15.

Smolen, E. M., & Lifton, Norman. A special treatment program for schizophrenic children

in a child guidance clinic. *American Journal of Orthopsychiatry,* 1966, **36,** 7736–742.

Sobel, D., & Geller, J. J. A type of group psychotherapy in the children's unit of a mental hospital. *Psychiatric Quarterly,* 1964, **38,** 262–270.

Speers, R. W., & Lansing, C. Group psychotherapy with preschool psychotic children and collateral group therapy of their parents: A preliminary report of the first two years. *American Journal of Orthopsychiatry,* 1964, **34,** 659–666.

Speers, R. W., & Lansing C. Some genetic-dynamic considerations in childhood symbiotic psychosis. *Journal of the American Academy of Child Psychiatry,* 1968, **7,** 329–349.

Sternlicht, M. Psychotherapeutic techniques useful with the mentally retarded: A review and critique. *Psychiatric Quarterly,* 1965, **39,** 84–90.

Stevenson, H. W., & Knights, R. M. Social reinforcement with normal and retarded children as a function of pretraining. *American Journal of Mental Deficiency,* 1962, **66,** 866–871.

Thibaut, J., & Kelley, H. *The social psychology of groups.* New York: Wiley, 1959.

Toussieng, P. W., & Schechter, M. D. Treatment of emotional problems in childhood. *Journal of Oklahoma State Medical Association,* 1967, 198–205.

Turner, R. H. The contributions of Muzafer Sherif to sociology. Read at the American Psychological Association meeting, Sept. 4, 1966.

Wilmer, H. A., Marks, I., & Pogue, E. Group treatment of prisoners and their families. *Mental hygiene,* 1966, **50**(3), 380–389.

Wolpe, J. *Psychotherapy by reciprocal inhibition.* Stanford, Calif.: Stanford University Press, 1958.

32 | Group Therapy with Adolescents

Max Rosenbaum

This chapter will be devoted to both the theoretical and the clinical problems involved in the treatment of adolescents. The definition of adolescence itself in any discussion of psychotherapy creates some problems. Technically adolescence may be considered the second decade of life. Therefore, in an age span ranging from age 10 to age 20, we are considering a variety of theoretical concepts as well as techniques.

ADOLESCENCE DEFINED

This chapter was written in the spring of 1968, and any observer of the upheaval to be found in secondary schools and universities as well as the sense of discontent to be found among those who are age 17 to 20 may well question the very definition of the word *adolescent*. The word itself is derived from the Latin verb *adolescere*, which means to grow up. Theoretically adolescence terminates at the age of majority, generally age 21. In fact, we deal with a twilight zone when defining early adolescence as well as later adolescence. Of course, this confuses therapeutic

practice. Now that the United States Congress has passed a law which gives the right to vote to those who are 18 years of age or older, we may have to redefine what is the age of majority and what is maturity. For this writer, adolescence is best described as the period between childhood and adulthood, the no-man's-land where patterns of childhood are no longer applicable and where patterns of adulthood are yet to be arrived at. Physiologically an additional problem erupts since in this decade children arrive at maturity several years earlier than their parents did. This is especially so with girls, who demonstrate a marked growth spurt when contrasted with their mothers. This complicates the study of adolescence if we use concepts that are outdated.

THE FAMILY DEFINED

In a discussion of adolescence it is profitable to define first the family background within which adolescents must live and react. First, then, let us define what constitutes a family. Presum-

951

ably a family comprises an aggregate of persons related to one another by blood or marriage. It does *not* include all persons so related. Sometimes it includes persons who are treated as if they were so related but who are people who were adopted by certain kinship practices. Beyond this, two separate lines of conceptual development are possible and necessary. The first would add to the definition of the family the note of common residence and would consider as members of the same family unit those persons who live in the same dwelling and share the daily round of life by participating in one "domestic economy," eating meals together, and so forth. This is the *family of residence.* There is a second line of development, which recognizes the fact that relationships among kin may be strong and highly significant even though the relatives do not share the same residence and, indeed, may live at a considerable distance from one another. This is the *family of interaction,* which ranges from those who have frequent face-to-face interaction to those who interact through letters or telephone calls. If one were interested in sources of influence on an individual's behavior, his family might well be delimited to include relatives with whom he has no current interaction but who constitute a significant reference group for the individual as a consequence of early socialization. (There is also the treatment of extended kin, but we will not deal with this area.)

ADOLESCENT ROLE PLAYING

As this author perceives adolescents, they are constantly trying out new roles. In the process of detaching themselves from their parents, there is a profound sense of loss and isolation, which accounts very often for the adolescent's frantic turning to the outside world in search of sensory stimulation. To the outside world this appears to be aimless activity. It is possible in our current culture that adolescent behavior may appear even more frantic than ever before because bar-

riers have been removed and the historically noted suppressive forces that have been used to help the young people maintain control are fast disappearing. This is especially noted on college campuses and creates tremendous anxiety for both faculty and students. We are, then, in a complex situation, in which we should be helping the adolescents to master their drives but in which, on the other hand, we find that the adolescents are surrounded with suggestions of things they are not ready for. To repeat, the adolescent often feels quite exposed and vulnerable, in a no-man's-land where he is quite unwilling to be seen as a child and yet not ready to move toward adulthood. In addition, in a culture which is often confused and in which, for example, fathers may dance like teen-agers and mothers may dress like little girls, the adolescent in the struggle for identity loses the model for adult behavior. We find, then, a picture in which the adolescent is looking to the adult for a model and in which the adult, due to his own problems of alienation and confusion, appears to be identifying with the adolescent.

In the school setting, further problems ensue. As long as the teacher can function as a benign influence, all is seemingly well. However, the adolescent challenges and provokes. This results in a countertransference response from the teacher, who is supposed to serve as the adult model. The countertransference response stimulates a good deal of aggression within the teacher, and the teacher is unwilling to accept this hostility coming from himself. At this point both the adolescent's aggression and the teacher's reaction are denied, with resultant chaos. The adolescent is told to "cool it," but the steam must go somewhere.

THEORETICAL MODELS

The Psychological Model

This author has found the most helpful theoretical model in the study of adolescence to be the psychoanalytic model. A note of caution is indicated. Freud (1905) warned that direct observation of children is easily misunderstood without knowledge of the child's motivation. Therefore, research on adolescence must be seen against the background of this warning. The period of ages 11 to 13 may be identified as preadolescence. Deutsch (1944) identified preadolescence with the functions of responsiveness to and mastery of social reality. According to Deutsch, the child's drive for growth and independence is most manifest and consciously valued at preadolescence. The "process of adjustment to reality grows more and more active and reaches its apex at the end of the latency period, in prepuberty . . . it is a phase when sexual instincts are at their weakest and the development of the ego most intense" (pp. 2–4).

Harry Stack Sullivan (1953), a representative of the cultural school of psychoanalytic inquiry, noted: "The great remedial effect of preadolescence occurs because of the real society which emerges among the pre-adolescents so that the world is reflected in the pre-adolescent microcosm. . . . This is an educative, provocative and useful experience in social assessment."

Both of the theorists we have cited, one from the more traditional psychoanalytic point of view and the other from the cultural point of view, have stressed the fact that the adaptive theme of preadolescence is not a transitory response to current inner tensions (as it might have been in earlier years or will be again in puberty) but is a conflict-free widening of the child's awareness of reality and a permanent legacy for his psychological health in adulthood.

The Sociological Model

Sociologists describe the transition from childhood to adolescence somewhat differently. Cohen (1964) contrasts two societal types. The first is described as stressing sociological independence: ". . . the individual's sense of responsibility is to his own nuclear family rather than to his community or to his kinsmen outside his nuclear family." The second type is characterized as valuing sociological interdependence: an individual's sense of responsibility (and identity) lies "as much with his community of kinsmen (his descent group) outside his nuclear family as it does with his nuclear family." Therefore, sociological *independence* is established by individual liability. Sociological *interdependence* is established by joint liability.

Applicability of the models. Some (Maccoby, 1966) have questioned the psychoanalytic model as applied to adolescence, noting that Freud's views on sex and his theoretical formulations seemed more compatible with the psychology of the male than with that of the female. Further, studies of college students have resulted in much questioning of basic psychoanalytic concepts. Freedman (1967) asserts that late adolescence is the time of high readiness for change. He contrasts his findings with the psychoanalytic truism that the direction of development is basically fixed by the age of 6 with the thesis that growth levels off and stabilizes by early adolescence, and with the widely shared view that little personality change can occur in young adults. Freedman questions other widely held truisms: that late adolescence is a time for emotional upheaval, marked primarily by an identity crisis; that sexual impulses are really sources of conflict and motivation; that sexual license is on the increase. However, his evidence appears limited.

Sanford (1967) asks the question: If it is so that human development is not as fixed and predetermined as psychological dogma has long held, what promotes growth and openness to change? He postulates two conditions: (1) readiness for change; (2) challenges sufficiently strong to distrust adaptation but not intense enough to provoke unconscious defensive reactions. He states that colleges have failed to meet the challenge of older adolescents because they have narrowed their conception of the educational mission.

They have replaced the historic humanist and generalist tradition with competitive and specialized interests.

The questions are crucial. The cognitive-orientation researchers (with a bow toward Geneva and Piaget) and those with a social-learning orientation (with a bow to Palo Alto) ask how the child develops a sex-role identity. Kohlberg (Maccoby, 1966) cites evidence on boys from father-absent families to emphasize the point that early identification need not be crucial to the development of a basic sex-role concept. He places sex-role development into a broader social context, emphasizing the role of extra-familial models and experiences as well as the influence of later experiences in the child's developmental progress.

With what appears to be a ferment among researchers, there is good reason for clinicians to question accepted truisms of clinical practice. In a study using another longitudinal sample, Macfarlane (1938) and, later, Livson and Peskin (1967) found ratings of behavior made during preadolescent and early adolescent periods (ages 11, 12, and 13) to be more predictive of adult mental health than were data from the early childhood or the later adolescent years. The authors suggested, as one possible explanation, that the preadolescent and early adolescent period is most "trustworthy" in the sense that behavior is more direct and, hence, more reliably assessed at this time. Recently Besdine (1968) has questioned the lack of attention given by practicing psychoanalysts to the importance of the mother. He notes the increasing dominance of the mother in the family structure. Since his views are those of a traditional psychoanalyst, they are worth noting.

As for the treatment of adolescents in group psychotherapy, there have been many presentations of clinical experience. These will be discussed in some detail. However, there is a noticeable failure to sustain a theoretical model in the presentation of clinical experience. As for clinical practice, when one considers that in the entire field of group psychotherapy, publications in the relatively brief period of 1956 to 1964 have exceeded the previous 50-year period, it is unusual that in this same period of 1956 to 1964 there has been a relative paucity of articles on treatment of adolescents with the technique of group psychotherapy. For example, in 1956 five articles are to be found in the literature on group psychotherapy concerning the treatment of adolescents. By 1960 ten articles for that yearly period had been published. Between 1960 and 1964 there was no significant increase. Thus, in 1961 nine articles are to be found. In 1963 ten articles are to be found. In 1964 twelve articles are to be found. In 1965, ten articles; in 1966, eleven articles; in 1967, four articles. When one compares this output of publications, it becomes a matter of concern as to what sort of progress is being made in the treatment of adolescents in the field of group psychotherapy. This is especially so when one considers that Corsini located 1,747 items in the entire field of group psychotherapy in the period of 1906 to 1955.

Clinicians' Theoretical Models

Before we survey some of the work that has been done, let us again note the possible theoretical contributions made by clinicians. Lampl-De Groot (1960) has described in detail the therapist's difficulties in working with adolescents. Anna Freud (1958) observed that the adolescent lacks interest in the past as well as in the psychoanalyst who is treating him. His concern is solely with the present. Selma Fraiberg (1955) commented on the difficulties a female therapist has in treating early adolescents, particularly girls. She, as well as other therapists, prefers groups composed of adolescents of the same sex. Another group of therapists has not found this to be so. For example, Nathan Ackerman (1955) states that the mixed group is the more realistic. The use of a male therapist seems to reduce some of the early resistance. This appears to create a less threatening situation. It apparently removes male adolescents from mother and mother substitutes and provides a male figure with whom they can identify and about whom they can have fantasies.

The same theoretical construct would appear to apply for a group of girls who are in treatment with a female therapist, but Ackerman (1955) has questioned the premise. However, in treatment of adolescents the group psychotherapist must use a flexible approach. At any moment he may have to shift from interpretive to supportive work. The therapist will have to set limits. He will have to set controls, and he will often have to intervene actively and use the environmental situation whenever possible. This is where the factor of environmental manipulation in treatment of adolescents becomes quite important. Ultimately, according to Rosenbaum (1965), the therapist's skill with adolescents and not the sex of the therapist determines the effectiveness of treatment.

Group procedures are an effective treatment modality for the adolescent since many of the problems of the adolescent age group center around individual and group peer relationships. In very deprived socioeconomic areas, as well as in situations in which there are broken homes, peer relationships have often failed to establish healthy values and positive group goals. In this respect, then, the group experience has provided a therapeutic learning medium as well as a corrective experience and can often serve as an entry into other group experiences, such as community groups and adolescent recreations. It is advisable also that one parent or both parents receive some type of counseling during the period that the adolescent is being treated. This would seem to minimize both conscious and unconscious interference by the parents with the adolescent's treatment. Ostensibly, we have just noted technique,

but again this is related to a theoretical consideration of the goals of treatment. The adolescent feels forced by his superego to change and comply with new demands. He is asked to relinquish old attachments and form new ones. The ego is in revolt against these demands. Unable to express aggression, it is overwhelmed by feelings of helplessness, and there is often a desire to regress to an earlier and less conflict-ridden state of development. The *goal* in treating adolescents should center on the expansion of the ego. This is achieved by concentrating on the distortions of the ego as well as identification difficulties. The analyst may come to represent a transient ego-ideal for the adolescent and encourage a positive change. The life history of many adolescents in therapy indicates the absence of a loving, permissive, and approving mother. To work toward the initial therapeutic alliance with the adolescent, the therapist must concentrate on building a relationship. The therapist may give the adolescent direct support as well as help him cope with his daily conflicts and current problems in life. From this alliance a positive transference may be established. The therapeutic alliance cannot be formed if the adolescent does not want to work with the therapist, and the group is an extra bridge in the therapist's endeavor.

What has been noted is the "ideal" situation. For example, the majority of mental-hospital programs for children and adolescents are makeshift and "stopgap" programs. Although younger patients have needs that are different from those of adults, the programs for children and adolescents can fit quite readily into administrative structures that have been designed for adults. Some institutions have resolved problems of treating the adolescent by setting up a school unit geared toward the "most-well" adolescent rather than the "most ill." The school generally has a standard curriculum and a staff that can be educative and therapeutic. A school concept appears to be logical because it is close to the environment that the adolescent would find outside of a hospital setting. What is of interest to all therapists is that the reports from those mental hospitals that have set up schools indicate that firm and consistent controls are basic to a successful program of treatment for adolescents. The disturbed adolescent appears to be able to adapt to even arbitrary limits but finds it impossible to adapt to or modify his behavior when limits keep changing.

Some observers of adolescent treatment units have encountered the same problems as with adult units. They note that some staff members attempt to work through "rescue fantasies." They offer "love, understanding, and acceptance" without setting limits. The adolescent will often test these offers of the therapist until he receives the expected reaction—rejection—which has been the customary experience and is the one he knows how to live with. Rosenbaum (1965, 1966), in his writings, has stressed the importance of authenticity in psychotherapy. It seems that no one is better at spotting artificiality than an adolescent, and treatment often founders on this point. The adults who overreact to music enjoyed by the adolescent, to hair styles that seem absurd, and to food fads that seem just short of bizarre are unable to accept deviations from adult value judgments. Therapists are often locked into this pattern of rigidity. The introduction of an adolescent treatment unit in the mental-hospital setting may result in resentments since the unit is geared for innovations in program and requires particularly high-grade staff. Everything in the adolescent unit appears to be some form of group psychotherapy, from the school to formal psychotherapy, with its reliance on peer relationships as an important avenue toward effecting change.

Meeks (1967) has observed adolescent group leaders in two contrasting socioeconomic classes and has successfully used nonprofessional volunteers as leaders. He has emphasized the importance of setting limits with adolescents and has noted that this is the area in which group leaders experienced the greatest conflict, particularly because of the adolescent's tendency to question authority.

Beckett (1965), in discussing treatment of adolescents in a hospital using techniques of group therapy, is concerned about how to make adolescents behave themselves in a hospital. Missing in this description is an appreciation of young people and of their genuine role conflicts in contemporary society. The problems of adolescents are defined mainly in intrapsychic terms and only somewhat in intrafamilial terms.

Recently Reckless (1968) has summarized his work with adolescents in a variety of settings by stating that group therapy is the most effective treatment. He considers certain requirements to be essential. These include intelligence, motivation, willingness to cooperate with the therapist, the capacity for insight and awareness of the aberrant nature of the behavior, and finally, the reversibility of the disorder. His conclusions are based in 1968 on his work with pseudosociopathic neurotic girls.

Apparently Reckless looks for more resources in his adolescent pseudosociopathic girls than other therapists are willing to count upon. Bartlett (1932), the great British psychologist, stated: "When human beings are confronted with experiences which are not comprehensible to them in terms of previous experiences, they are driven to find meaning—sometimes any meaning—and the more awesome the experience the more quickly they will evolve some rational construction." This would seem particularly so with the adolescent, and his rational construction appears completely irrational to the adult. Studies of adolescents in a mental hospital have confirmed the need for compassionate yet strong leadership (Hartmann et al., 1968).

Carter (1968), in his work with adolescent

foster children, in which he offered group counseling, stressed the leader's use of himself as he attempted to use the group method as a helping process and to establish himself as an acceptable helping person. He noted that group work with adolescent foster children offered no shortcut. If often created the need for more services as the leader offered more insights. It is interesting to note that his clients wanted group leaders to talk to the caseworkers involved with them, and confidentiality was quite secondary to help in the more immediate sense.

Practically all the therapists who obtained good results using group techniques with adolescents believed in the procedure. This seems to be a truism of any therapy approach, namely, that the therapist believes in his technique. Slavson (1965), in a 6-year study of delinquent boys, using a selected and small sample, offered an ego-oriented psychoanalytic psychotherapeutic approach and claims good results. Maddox and McCall (1964), in studying drinking among teenagers, used a sociological interpretation and frame of reference and ended up rather optimistically, stating: "Drinking as it is described here appears to be an improvised rite of passage between adolescence and adulthood." This conclusion seems rather overoptimistic and appears to ignore many problems. Lest the reader confuse psychotherapy with faith healing, we stress the importance of an approach, any approach, which the therapist designs and attempts to follow, hopefully with some degree of flexibility.

Slivkin and Bernstein (1968) obtained good results with retarded adolescents. However, their group psychotherapy was goal-directed in nature. The boys in the group ranged from age 15 to age 19. The group leader set up a system of rotation of leadership among the group members. The thought that the therapist felt they might have leadership qualities and could accept a responsible role came as a totally unexpected surprise to the group members. This led to

improved functioning on their part. In terms of technique, the therapist related to the group of retarded adolescent boys in precisely the same way in which he had previously related to schizophrenic patients in group therapy—he was always direct and honest. He attempted deeper dynamic exploration in this group, although it is described as goal-directed psychotherapy.

There are different parameters involved. Child therapy groups would not reach for the deeper dynamics explored for in adolescent groups. Activity groups, supportive groups, and anxiety-suppressive groups are all directed toward limiting disruptive feelings and avoid clarification and interpretation at other than a superficial level. The therapist must always decide what level he aims for.

Niles, Stout, et al., (1966) have been encouraged in their work with retarded adolescents. They worked with adolescents who were mentally retarded due to organic defects and treated them with a combination of individual and group analysis plus social-activity group therapy along with the simultaneous analytic treatment of one parent. Interpretations were limited to the simplest language understandable to the patient, initially given on a very concrete level and only gradually extended into more abstract meanings. This approach has produced a significant rise in the patient's IQs and improvement in their social functioning, their ability to learn, and their capacity to work, including those patients who were considered unemployable before therapy.

Finger (1957, 1966), in her work with unmarried adolescent mothers and their parents, and Kaufmann and Deutsch (1965, 1967) changed many of the "rules" that others may have proposed for group treatment of adolescents. Kaufmann and Deutsch found pregnant adolescent girls to be largely angry, deprived, and immature. They did not use a male therapist. They chose a warm, flexible therapist who would refrain from imposing her middle-class values and standards and who would be capable of feeding these girls both symbolically and realistically. The therapist, a widow, turned out to be warm and maternal. This confirms the experience of Rosenbaum (1965), who served as a consultant to programs in the "hard-core inner-city" slum areas, where all types of modified group-therapy programs were used.

The primary effort was made to provide oral gratification for markedly emotionally deprived adolescents. Essentially, an effort was made to provide parent substitutes who would not desert the adolescent. Later, adult group leaders were provided after whom the adolescents might model themselves and, it was hoped, thus find an ego-ideal.

Roemele and Grunebaum (1967) worked toward "helping the helpers." They offered group therapy for six adolescent black girls who were employed as teachers in a remedial after-school program. Rosenbaum (1966) has noted that the more we enlist nonprofessionals in offering services to the community, the more we will have to provide therapy for the "helpers," lest their impact be destructive as well as constructive.

In a world that appears so fragmented to adults, it is easy to imagine the torment of the adolescent. Added to the self-destructiveness of a culture, we have the anxieties of the changing adolescent. The age of puberty seems to be a crucial period as far as the development of active self-destructive drives are concerned. Childhood suicides, according to Zilboorg (1937), appear more to be impulsive acts. His theoretical position is that in puberty ". . . the task of the ego is to assert itself as quickly as possible by means of asserting the instinctual drives with which it must make or is inclined to make an unconditional alliance." Kestenbaum (1959) and Bakwin (1957) have surveyed the field of suicide in adolescence. It is to be noted that the death rate among adolescents has fallen, owing principally

to control of infectious diseases. However, suicide has emerged as one of the leading causes of death in teen-agers. Fortunately, as of this writing, the trend in suicide is downward, especially among girls.

Faigel (1966) noted that suicide reaches a peak incidence between the ages of 15 and 19, when it is the third most common cause of death. He comments, "the iminodibenzyl antidepressants are useful in treating a depressed child, but only psychotherapy for the child and his family group can cure him." Shneidman (1966), a leading investigator of suicides, states that "any suicidal gesture—attempted or threatened—should be seen as an important psychologic and psychiatric crisis and as a 'cry for help' which should not be ignored . . . the therapy for the self-destructive adolescent is to cater to his wants and to help him fulfill his emotional life."

After surveying the work in the field, it is relevant to note that Shaw and Schelkun (1965), who evaluated studies done by different investigators, concluded that in many cases the dynamics may never be understood but the child can get better anyway. They note: "As one investigator has emphasized, in most of child psychiatry the therapist operates not by helping the child work through his conflicts, but rather by helping him to live with them." In would seem that adolescents may be of great help to one another when they share their feelings of despair in a group setting. As in adult group psychotherapy, it is reassuring to find that you are not alone (Mullan & Rosenbaum, 1962). This author has noted the manifest suicidal efforts, but much narcotic addiction, experiments with LSD, and automobile accidents are part of the suicidal effort.

BEHAVIOR THERAPY

Up to this point much of what has been discussed has been within the psychoanalytic framework. Currently there has been a tremendous interest in behavior therapy. Traditional psycho-therapeutic approaches are usually based upon "closed-energy" personality systems, within which the symptom may be conceived of as a mechanism for the expression of psychic conflicts. In contrast to this view, behavior therapists consider symptoms as behavior that can best be accounted for by reference to variables known to control learning in general. Compared with adults, children and adolescents have become an increasingly popular client population for behavior therapists. Among the reasons which may account for the surge of enthusiasm is the brevity of treatment, as compared with more traditional techniques. In addition, the child's environment can be controlled with ease, as compared with that of the adult. For most behavioral therapists, manipulation of the environment is essential in order to eliminate undesirable patterns of behavior. It is easier to do this with a child or adolescent in a school or home situation, where there is dependence upon adults. In this manner the parents, teachers, or school may be instructed as to how to cope with the adolescent or child. This is also reassuring to the parent who likes to be absolved of any responsibility. The direct suggestions that behavior therapists give to parents are generally accepted with enthusiasm, as contrasted with the traditional therapist's advice to be giving and accepting. Also, when treating adults, one rarely finds people who can control the adult in treatment, as contrasted with parents, who can direct or guide adolescents or children.

The term *behavior therapy*, as used by this writer, refers to techniques derived from theories of learning and aimed at the direct modification of problem behavior. This does *not* include techniques that are aimed at effecting more general and less specific personality changes. Behavior therapists assume that social responses, whether they be desirable or deviant, are learned, and their treatment techniques are based on laboratory-tested learning procedures, including operant conditioning and classical conditioning. Behavior therapy generally is aimed at well-defined symptoms such as phobia or bed-wetting.

Gelfand and Hartman (1968) have reviewed behavior therapy for subjects between infancy and 18 years of age. They appear generally positive about its effectiveness. They note that therapists have used positive reinforcement in a classroom setting to control hyperactivity in 9- and 10-year-old boys diagnosed as brain-damaged. This is the kind of immediate result which appeals to many educators.

Recently Sarason (1968) presented a report using behavior-therapy approaches to juvenile delinquency. An early activity of the project was the development of the project's research assistants' skills in role playing and working with groups. He used leaders as models, guided group discussions, and used closed-circuit TV for feedback. His models were primarily middle-class psychologists in training. His project failed in the use of peer models. He found that those who had worked through delinquency had negative attitudes toward delinquent boys. Essentially, this project does not appear to be different from any project in which the concept of ego-ideal is used, whether it be called behavior therapy or psychoanalytic therapy.

Paul (1968) conducted a two-year follow-up of systematic desensitization in therapy groups. His subjects were forty male college undergraduates, ages 19 to 24. He stated that his combined group desensitization procedure required an average of less than two hours of therapist time per client; the short-term, time-limited approach not only was effective but was efficient as well. It is interesting to note that the therapists in this project did attach importance to the establishment of a personally involved relationship.

Schwitzgebel (1967) described two matched groups of adolescent male delinquents who were informally recruited from street corners. They were differentially treated during the course of twenty tape-recorded interviews on four classes of operants: hostile statements, positive statements, prompt arrival at work, and general employability. He reported positive results. None of the concepts which value peer relationships, insight, etc., was employed at all. In an earlier study, Schwitzgebel and Kolb (1964) gathered forty juvenile delinquents and offered them part-time jobs talking into a tape recorder about anything they wished. A simple reinforcement procedure was used, and attendance at work became dependable and prompt within twenty-five meetings. A three-year follow-up of the first twenty employees showed a significant reduction in the frequency and severity of crime as compared with a matched-pair control group. The delinquents were gathered from street corners and pool halls. Both authors cite Alexander and French, the psychoanalysts, to the effect that no insight, no emotional discharge, no recollection can be as reassuring as success in the actual life situation in which the individual has previously failed.

Adolescents have been described as being difficult to get into treatment because they tend not to cooperate, tend to miss appointments, and are seldom punctual. Psychoanalysts suggest that the rapidly changing emotional patterns of the adolescent leave little energy to be invested in the analyst. According to many behavior therapists, these characteristics may not be descriptive of the age but may instead be artifacts of the treatment procedure. Therefore, the approach that is borrowed from B. F. Skinner (1953) is strictly applied to changing specific behavior patterns. As noted earlier, this may please adults who have to live with adolescents through their "impossible years," but does this really get through to any deeper levels for the tormented adolescent? This author would still orient the practitioner to an approach which values insight and the use of the peer relationship.

Every cultural setting, whether rural or urban, would appear to benefit from this approach.

Laeder and Francis (1968) recently described stuttering workshops that they have conducted for seven years. Schools with an average enrollment of 300 were scattered over three sparsely populated counties. Students were from socially, culturally, and financially adequate agricultural families in Michigan. Workshops which were composed of from eleven to as many as twenty-seven students (in more recent ones) achieved successful results. These workshops were all-day and were held twice each year. The important influence appeared to be the peer relationship and the leader.

SUMMARY

As of this writing, the field is wide open for imaginative practitioners to apply the techniques of the group in work with adolescents. But the leader must be defined in his goals, flexible in his technique, and able to shift rapidly. Finally, he must be authentic. Ross and Anderson (1968) in a study pointed up the overlooked obvious. They worked with two therapists. Their reasoning was that, since the group was composed of blind clients who were so deprived, they would use two therapists so that the group would continue even during times of illness or vacation of a therapist. They point out that many people of the lower socioeconomic class have never had a pattern of regularity or regular attendance in any life venture. Here, two therapists established the pattern. Their results were successful. Perhaps this is what adolescents finally hope to find: adults who are willing to get off the treadmill of life and listen to them—at least for awhile.

Many mental hospitals have noted a sharp rise in the influx adolescents and young adults. Over the last decade the admission of patients aged 15 to 25 has changed from 1 in 10 to 1 patient in 2. A decade ago the patient in the 15- to 25-year-old group was essentially passive and withdrawn. Today, we find this age group to be composed of angry and rebellious individuals who challenge the established social institutions. They often form groups to gain courage from one another. It would appear that group psychotherapy musters all the positive forces to be found in the formation of an angry group and uses this energy in a meaningful way.

REFERENCES*

Ackerman, N. Group psychotherapy with a mixed group of adolescents. *International Journal of Group Psychotherapy*, 1955, **5**, 249–260.

Bakwin, H. Suicide in children and adolescents. *Journal of Pediatrics*, 1957, **50**, 749–769.

Bartlett, F. C. *Remembering.* London: Cambridge, 1932.

Beckett, P. G. S. *Adolescents out of step: Their treatment in a psychiatric hospital.* Detroit: Wayne State University Press, 1965.

Besdine, M. Jocasta and Oedipus: Another look. *Pathways in Child Guidance*, Board of Education, New York, 1968, **10**, 1–8.

Carter, W. W. Group counseling for adolescent foster children. *Children*, 1968, **15**, 22–27.

Cohen, Y. *The transition from childhood to adolescence.* Chicago: Aldine, 1964.

Deutsch, H. *Psychology of women.* Vol. 1. New York: Grune & Stratton, 1944.

Faigel, H. C. Suicide among young persons. *Clinical Pediatrics,* 1966, **5,** 187–190.

*For the interested reader, in addition to the references cited in this chapter, which are listed here, the author has listed all references from 1956 to 1967 which apply to group therapy with adolescents. These are included as "Additional References," following the "References" section.

Finger, S. Group therapy with unmarried mothers. Paper presented at National Conference of Jewish Communal Service, Atlantic City, N.J., May 24, 1957.

Finger, S. The therapeutic use of groups of the interplay created by concurrent groups of adolescent unmarried mothers and their parents. Paper presented at the 23rd Annual Conference of the AGPA, Philadelphia, Jan. 26, 1966.

Fraiberg, S. Some considerations in the introduction to therapy in puberty. Vol. 10. *The psychoanalytic study of the child.* New York: International Universities Press, 1955. Pp. 264–286.

Freedman, M. B. *The college experience.* San Francisco: Jossey-Bass, 1967.

Freud, A. Adolescence. Vol. 13. *The psychoanalytic study of the child.* New York: International Universities Press, 1958. Pp. 255–278.

Freud, S. *Three essays on the theory of sexuality.* Vienna: International Psychoanalytic Library, 1905.

Gelfand, D. M., & Hartmann, D. P. Behavior therapy with children. *Psychological Bulletin*, 1968, **69**, 204–215.

Hartman, E., Glaser, B. A., Greenblatt, M., Solomon, M. H., & Levinson, D. J. *Adolescents in a mental hospital.* New York: Grune & Stratton, 1968.

Kaufmann, P. N., & Deutsch, A. L. Group therapy for adolescents and their parents: An out-patient clinic of a general hospital in a low socio-economic area. *Journal of Psychoanalysis in Groups*, 1965, **1**, 59–63.

Kestenbaum, R. Time and death in adolescence. In H. Feifel (Ed.), *The meaning of death.* New York: McGraw-Hill, 1959. Pp. 99–113.

Laeder, R., & Francis, W. C. Stuttering workshops: Group therapy in a rural high school setting. *Journal of Speech and Hearing Disorders*, 1968, **33**, 38–41.

Lampl-De Groot, J. On adolescence. Vol. 15. *The psychoanalytic study of the child.* New York: International Universities Press, 1960. Pp. 95–103.

Livson, N., & Peskin, H. The prediction of adult psychological health in a longitudinal study. *Journal of Abnormal Psychology*, 1967, **72**, 509–518.

Maccoby, E. E. (Ed.) *The development of sex differences.* Stanford, Calif.: Stanford, 1966.

Macfarlane, J. W. Studies in child guidance. I. Methodology of data collection and organization. *Monographs of the Society for Research in Child Development*, 1938, **3**, No. 6.

Maddox, G. L., & McCall, B. C. *Drinking among teen agers: A sociological interpretation of alcohol use by high school students.* New Brunswick, N.J.: Rutgers Center of Alcohol Studies, 1964.

Meeks, J. E. Some observations on adolescents: Group leaders in two contrasting socioeconomic classes. *International Journal of Social Psychiatry,* 1967, **13,** 379–386.

Mullan, H., & Rosenbaum, M. *Group Psychotherapy.* New York: Free Press, 1962.

Niles, G., Stout, W., et al. A modified psychoanalytic treatment program for mentally retarded adolescents. Horney Clinic report to the American Psychiatric Association, January, 1966.

Paul, G. L. Two year follow-up of systematic desensitization in therapy groups. *Journal of Abnormal Psychology*, 1968, **73**, 119–130.

Reckless, J. B. Pseudosociopathic neurotic behavioral disturbances in adolescent girls. *North Carolina Medical Journal*, 1968, **29**, 1–12.

Roemele, V., & Grunebaum, H. Helping the helpers. *International Journal of Group Psychotherapy*, 1967, **17**, 343–356.

Rosenbaum, M. *Group psychotherapy and psychodrama.* In B. B. Wolman (Ed.), *Handbook of clinical psychology.* New York: McGraw-Hill, 1965. Pp. 1254–1274.

Rosenbaum, M. Some comments on the use of untrained therapists. *Journal of Consulting Psychology*, 1966, **30**, 292–294.

Ross, E. K., & Anderson, J. R. Psychotherapy with the least expected: Modified group therapy with blind clients. *Rehabilitation Literature*, 1968, **39**, 73–76.

Sanford, N. *Where colleges fail: A study of the student as a person.* San Francisco: Jossey-Bass, 1967.

Sarason, I. G. Verbal learning, modeling and juvenile delinquency. *American psychologist*, 1968, **23**, 254–266.

Schwitzgebel, R. L. Short-term operant conditioning of adolescent offenders on socially relevant variables. *Journal of Abnormal Psychology,* 1967, **72**, 134–142.

Schwitzgebel, R., & Kolb, D. A. Inducing behavior change in adolescent delinquents. *Behaviour Research and Therapy*, 1964, **1**, 297–304.

Shaw, C. R., & Schelkun, R. F. Suicidal behavior in children. *Psychiatry,* 1965, **28,** 157–168.

Shneidman, E. S. Suicide among adolescents. *California School Health*, 1966, **2**, No. 3, 1–4.

Skinner, B. F. *Science and human behavior.* New York: Macmillan, 1953.

Slavson, S. R. *Reclaiming the delinquent: New tools for group treatment.* New York: Free Press, 1965.

Slivkin, S. E., & Bernstein, N. R. Goal directed group psychotherapy for retarded adolescents. *American Journal of Psychotherapy*, 1968, **22**, 34–45.

Sullivan, H. S. *The interpersonal theory of psychiatry.* New York: Norton, 1953.

Zilboorg, G. Considerations on suicide, with particular reference to that of the young. *American Journal of Orthopsychiatry*, 1937, **7**, 15–31.

ADDITIONAL REFERENCES (1956–1967)

Abrahams, D. Y. Observations on transference in a group of teen age delinquents. *International Journal of Group Psychotherapy*, 1956, **6**, 286–290.

Becker, B. J., Gusrae, R., & Berger, E. Adolescent group psychotherapy: A community mental health program. *International Journal of Group Psychotherapy*, 1956, **6**, 300–316.

Cohen, A. A. Use of group process in an institution. *Social Work*, 1956, **1**, 57–61.

Fried, E. Ego emancipation of adolescents through group psychotherapy. *International Journal of Group Psychotherapy*, 1956, **6**, 358–373.

Stubblebine, J. M., & Roadruck, R. D. Treatment program for mentally deficient adolescents. *American Journal of Mental Deficiency*, 1956, **60**, 552–556.

Baumler, F. Multidimensional treatment of stuttering of children and adolescents in speech therapy groups. *Zeitschrift für Psychotherapie und medizinische Psychologie,* 1957, **7**, 99–104.

Boenheim, C. Group psychotherapy with adolescents. *International Journal of Group Psychotherapy*, 1957, **7**, 338–345.

Brown, P. M. A comparative study of three therapy techniques used to effect behavioral and social status changes in a group of institutionalized delinquent negro boys. Doctoral dissertation, New York University, 1957.

Daniels, M. The influence of the sex of the therapist and of the co-therapist technique in group psychotherapy with boys: An investigation of the effectiveness of group psychotherapy with eighth grade, behavior problem boys, comparing results achieved by a male therapist, by a female therapist and by the two therapists in combination. Doctoral dissertation, New York University, 1957.

Miller, D. H. The treatment of adolescents in an adult hospital by a preliminary report. *Bulletin of the Menninger Clinic*, 1957, **21**, 189–198.

Schneer, H. I., Gottesfeld, H., & Sales, A. Group therapy as an aid with delinquent pubescents in a special public school. *Psychiatric Quarterly Supplements*, 1957, **31**, 246–260.

Schulman, I. Modifications in group psychotherapy with anti-social adolescents. *International Journal of Group Psychotherapy*, 1957, **7**, 310–317.

Eliasoph, E. A group therapy-psychodrama program at Berkshire Industrial Farm. *Group Psychotherapy*, 1958, **11**, 57–62.

Kaldeck, R. Group psychotherapy with mental defective adolescents and adults. *International Journal of Group Psychotherapy*, 1958, **8**, 185–192.

Kassoff, A. L. Advantages of multiple therapists in a group of severely acting-out adolescent boys. *International Journal of Group Psychotherapy*, 1958, **8**, 70–75.

Lebovici, S. Group therapy in France, 1958. *International Journal of Group Psychotherapy*, 1958, **8**, 471–472.

Masterson, J. F., Jr. Psychotherapy of the

adolescents: A comparison with psychotherapy of the adult. *Journal of Nervous and Mental Diseases*, 1958, **127**, 511–517.

Staples, E. J. The influence of the sex of the therapist and of the co-therapist technique in group psychotherapy with girls: An investigation of the effectiveness of group psychotherapy with eighth grade behavioral problem girls, comparing results achieved by a male therapist, by a female therapist, and by the therapists in combination. Doctoral dissertation, New York University, 1958.

Straight, B., & Werkman, S. L. Control problems in group therapy with aggressive adolescent boys in a mental hospital. *American Journal of Psychiatry*, 1958, **114**, 998–1001.

Bloch, G. Remarks on psychotherapeutic activities in Israel. *International Journal of Group Psychotherapy*, 1959, **9**, 303–307.

Franklin, G. H. Group Psychotherapy with delinquent boys in a training school setting. *International Journal of Group Psychotherapy*, 1959, **9**, 213–218.

Gadpaille, W. J. Observations on the sequence of resistances in groups of adolescent delinquents. *International Journal of Group Psychotherapy*, 1959, **9**, 275–286.

Harris, L. M., & Sievers, D. J. A study to measure changes in behavior of aggressive mentally retarded adolescent girls in a permissive classroom. *American Journal of Mental Deficiency*, 1959, **63**, 975–980.

Levitt, M., & Rubenstein, B. O. Acting out in adolescence: A study in communication. *American Journal of Orthopsychiatry*, 1959, **29**, 622–632.

Powles, W. E. Psychosexual maturity in a therapy group of disturbed adolescents. *International Journal of Group Psychotherapy*, 1959, **9**, 429–441.

Peltz, W. L., & Goldberg, M. A dynamic factor in group work with post-adolescents and its effects on the role of the leader. *Mental Hygiene*, 1959, **43**, 71–75.

Schulman, I. Transference, resistance and communication problems in adolescent psychotherapy groups. *International Journal of Group Psychotherapy*, 1959, **9**, 496–503.

Stranaham, M., & Schwartzmann, C. An experiment in reaching social adolescents through group therapy. *Annals of the American Academy of Political and Social Sciences*, 1959, **322**, 117–125.

Alder, J., Berman, I. R., & Slavson, S. Multiple leadership in group treatment of delinquent adolescents. *International Journal of Group Psychotherapy*, 1960, **10**, 213–226.

Barnwell, J. E. Group treatment of older adolescent boys in a family agency. *Social Casework*, 1960, **41**, 247–253.

Baxter, W. M. Fragments of a psychodramatic experience within a religious setting. *Group Psychotherapy*, 1960, **13**, 40–46.

Engle, M. Shifting levels of communication in treatment of adolescent character disorders. *Archives of General Psychiatry*, 1960, **2**, 104–109.

Epstein, N. Recent observations on group psychotherapy with adolescent delinquent boys in residential treatment: Activity group therapy. *International Journal of Psychotherapy*, 1960, **10**, 180–194.

Friedman, A. Some notes on psychotherapy with a group of adolescents. *Acta Psychotherapeutica et Psychosomatica*, 1960, **8**, 147–155.

Jacks, I. A study of accessibility to group therapy of a group of incarcerated adolescent offenders. *Doctoral dissertation*, New York University, 1960.

Kraft, I. A. The nature of sociodynamics and psychodynamics in a therapy group of adolescents. *International Journal of Group Psychotherapy,* 1960, **10,** 313–320.

Phelan, J. F., Jr. Recent observations on group psychotherapy with adolescent delinquent boys in residential treatment: Introduction. *International Journal of Group Psychotherapy,* 1960, **10,** 174–179.

Schwartz, M. Recent observations on group psychotherapy with adolescent delinquent boys in residential treatment: Analytic group psychotherapy. *International Journal of Group Psychotherapy,* 1960, **10,** 195–212.

Slavson, S. R. Recent observations on group psychotherapy with adolescent delinquent boys in residential treatment: The scope and aims of the evaluation study. *International Journal of Group Psychotherapy,* 1960, **10,** 176–179.

Cohn, I. H., & Hulse, W. C. The use of a group psychotherapy program for adolescents as a training unit in child psychiatry. *American Journal of Orthopsychiatry,* 1961, **31,** 521–535.

Feder, S. M. Limited goals in short-term group psychotherapy with institutionalized adolescent delinquent boys. *Doctoral dissertation,* Columbia University, 1961.

Goldenberg de Antin, L. R. Rational group psychotherapy as a form of treatment for adolescents. *Acta Neuropsiquiatrica,* Argentina, 1961, **7,** 204–206.

Hirsch, R. Group therapy with parents of adolescent drug addicts. *Psychiatric Quarterly,* 1961, **35,** 702–710.

Kraft, I. A. Some special considerations in adolescent group psychotherapy. *International Journal of Group Psychotherapy,* 1961, **11,** 196–203.

Lebovici, S. Psychodrama as applied to adolescents. *Journal of Child Psychology and Psychiatry,* 1961, **1,** 298–305.

Odenwald, R. P. Outline of group psychotherapy for juvenile delinquents and criminal offenders. *Group Psychotherapy,* 1961, **14,** 50–53.

Parrish, M. M. Group techniques with teenage emotionally disturbed girls. *Group Psychotherapy,* 1961, **14,** 20–25.

Stockey, M. R. A comparison of the effectiveness of group counseling, individual counseling and employment among adolescent boys with adjustment problems. Doctoral dissertation, University of Michigan, 1961.

Epstein, N. & Slavson, S. R. "Breakthrough" in group therapy of hardened delinquent adolescent boys. *International Journal of Group Psychotherapy,* 1962, **12,** 199–210.

Feder, B. Limited goals in short-term group psychotherapy with institutionalized delinquent adolescent boys. *International Journal of Group Psychotherapy,* 1962, **12,** 503–507.

Garland, J. A., Kolodny, R. L., & Waldfogel, S. Social group work as adjunctive treatment for the emotionally disturbed adolescent: The experience of a specialized group work department. *American Journal of Orthopsychiatry,* 1962, **32,** 691–706.

Goolishian, H. Family treatment approaches. II. Brief psychotherapy program for disturbed adolescents. *American Journal of Orthopsychiatry,* 1962, **32,** 142–148.

Hals, H. Experiment with youth groups in a "somatic" hospital. *Nordisk Psykiatisk Tidskrift,* 1962, **16,** 366–375.

Head, W. A. Sociodrama and group discussion with institutionalized delinquent adolescents. *Mental Hygiene,* 1962, **46,** 127–135.

Heigel, F. A prognostically decisive character trait in a neglected youth. *Praxis Kinderpsycholie Kinderpsychiatrie,* 1962, **11,** 197–201.

Hersko, M. Group psychotherapy with delinquent adolescent girls. *American Journal of Orthopsychiatry,* 1962, **32,** 169–175.

Karmiol, E. Some observations on concomitant individual and group treatment of adolescents. *International Journal of Group Psychotherapy,* 1962, **12,** 374–375.

Krevelon, A. V. Group psychological aspects in the treatment of neurotic youngsters. *Zeitschrift für Psychotherapie und Medizinische Psychiatrie,* 1962, **12,** 186–194.

Krevelon, D. A. On the problem of therapeutic pairing in neurotic youngsters. *Acta Psychotherapeutica et Psychosomatica,* 1962, **10,** 233–245.

Rosenberg, A. Difficulties and possibilities in social therapy and psychotherapy of mentally disturbed delinquents. *Nederlands Tijdschrift voor Geneeskunde,* 1962, **106,** 1746–1747.

Slavson, S. R. Patterns of acting out of a transference neurosis by an adolescent boy. *International Journal of Group Psychotherapy,* 1962, **12,** 211–224.

Wassell, B. Parent-adolescent group therapy. *Journal of Psychoanalysis in Groups,* 1962, **1,** 94.

Annesley, P. T. Group psychotherapy in an adolescent psychiatric unit. *International Journal of Social Psychiatry,* 1963, **9,** 283–291.

Becker, B. J., Gusroe, R., & MacNicol, E. A clinical study of a group psychotherapy program for adolescents. *Psychiatric Quarterly,* 1963, **37,** 685–703.

Brandzel, R. Role playing as a training device in preparing multiple handicapped youth for employment. *Group Psychotherapy,* 1963, **16,** 16–21.

Corrothers, M. L. Sexual themes in an adolescent girls' group. *International Journal of Group Psychotherapy,* 1963, **13,** 43–51.

Elliot, M. A. Group therapy in dealing with juvenile and adult offenders. *Federal Probation,* 1963, **27,** 48–54.

MacLennan, B. W., & Rosen, B. Female therapists in activity group psychotherapy with boys in latency. *International Journal of Group Psychotherapy,* 1963, **13,** 34–42.

McCarthy, K. Experience with supportive group therapy with the adolescent children of psychiatric patients. *Journal of Fort Logan Mental Health Center,* 1963, **1** (1), 37–42.

Perl, W. R. Use of fantasy for a breakthrough in psychotherapy groups of hard-to-reach delinquent boys. *International Journal of Group Psychotherapy,* 1963, **13,** 27–33.

Rybak, W. S. Disguised group therapy: An approach to the treatment of hospitalized teen-aged patients. *Psychiatric Quarterly Supplement,* 1963, **37,** 44–55.

Biermann, W. Group therapy in children and adolescents with behavior disorders and their parents. *Praxis Kinderpsychologie,* 1964, **13,** 40–47.

Burdon, A. P., & Keely, J. H. Emotionally disturbed boys failing in school: Treatment in an outpatient clinic school. *Southern Medical Journal,* 1964, **57,** 829–835.

Craft, M., Stephenson, G., & Granger, C. A

controlled trial of authoritarian and self-governing regimes with adolescent psychopaths. *American Journal of Orthopsychiatry,* 1964, **34,** 543–554.

Elsassen, E. Contribution to the role of the cotherapist in analytic group therapy of adolescents with special reference to fundamental differences between psychoanalytic, individual and group psychotherapy. *Praxis Kinderpsychologie,* 1964, **13,** 47–51.

Fine, R. H., & Dawson, J. C. A therapy program for the mildly retarded adolescent. *American Journal of Mental Deficiency,* 1964, **69,** 23–30.

Godenne, G. D. Outpatient adolescent group psychotherapy. I. Review of the literature of use of co-therapists, psychodrama and parent group therapy. *American Journal of Psychotherapy,* 1964, **18,** 584–593.

Jacks, I. Accessibility to group psychotherapy among adolescent offenders in a correctional institution. *American Journal of Orthopsychiatry,* 1963, **33,** 567–568.

McDavid, J. W. Immediate effects of group therapy upon response to social reinforcement among juvenile delinquents. *Journal of Consulting Psychology,* 1964, **28,** 409–412.

Reiner, E. R., & Quist, C. C. Using psychotherapy groups to observe and supervise personnel relationships with adolescent offenders. *Psychiatric Studies and Projects,* 1964, **2,** No. 4.

Richmond, A. H., & Schechter, S. A spontaneous request for treatment by a group of adolescents. *International Journal of Group Psychotherapy,* 1964, **14,** 97–106.

Saddock, B., & Gould, R. E. A preliminary report on short-term group psychotherapy on an acute adolescent male service. *International Journal of Group Psychotherapy,* 1964, **14,** 465–473.

Silver, A. W. A therapeutic discussion group in a detention home for adolescents awaiting hospital commitment. *International Journal of Group Psychotherapy,* 1964, **14,** 502–503.

Sternlicht, M. Establishing an initial relationship in group psychotherapy with delinquent retarded male adolescents. *American Journal of Mental Deficiency,* 1964, **69,** 39–41.

Wolk, R. L., & Reid, R. A study of group psychotherapy results with youthful offenders in detention. *Group Psychotherapy,* 1964, **17,** 56–60.

Brandes, N. S. Understanding the adolescent in group psychotherapy. *Clinical Psychiatry,* 1965, **4** (4), 203–209.

Cohn, I. H. Intrapsychic changes in an adolescent girl during group psychotherapy. *Topical Problems of Psychotherapy,* 1965, **5,** 176–188.

Duffy, J. H., & Kraft, I. A. Group therapy of early adolescents: An evaluation of one year of group therapy with a mixed group of early adolescents. *American Journal of Orthopsychiatry,* 1965, **35** (2).

Evans, J. Inpatient analytic group therapy of neurotic and delinquent adolescents: Some specific problems associated with these groups. *Acta Psychotherapeutica et Psychosomatica,* 1965, **13**(4), 265–270.

Finger, S. Concurrent group therapy with adolescent unmarried mothers and their parents. *Confinia Psychiatrica,* 1965, **8**(1), 21–26.

Godenne, G. D. Outpatient adolescent group psychotherapy. II. Use of co-therapists, psychodrama, and parent group therapy. *American Journal of Psychotherapy,* 1965, **19,**(1), 40–53.

Harrington, R. C., & Stinson, S. R. Poor academic performance in bright adolescent boys: A study in group psychotherapy. *American Journal of Orthopsychiatry,* 1965, **35**(2), 345–346.

Heacock, D. R. Group approaches with adolescents: Modifications of standard techniques for outpatient group psychotherapy with delinquent boys. *American Journal of Orthopsychiatry,* 1965, **35**(2), 371.

Siegel, M. Group psychotherapy with gifted underachieving college students. *Community Mental Health Journal,* 1965, **1**(2), 188–194.

Slavson, S. R. Para-analytic group psychotherapy: A treatment of choice for adolescents. *Acta Psychotherapeutica et Psychosomatica,* 1965, **13**(5), 321–331.

Zeise, W. J., & Elsaesser, E. Individual observations during psychoanalytic group therapy with adolescents. *Acta Psychotherapeutica et Psychosomatica,* 1965, **13**(4), 314–320.

Berschling, C., & Homann, J. A proposal for the establishment of a group psychotherapy program for adolescents. *Psychiatric Communication,* 1966, **8**(1), 17–36.

Burden, A. P., & Neely, I. H. Chronic school failure in boys: A short-term group therapy and educational approach. *American Journal of Psychiatry,* 1966, **122**(11), 1211–1219.

Caplan, L. M. Identification: A complicating factor in the inpatient treatment of adolescent girls. *American Journal of Orthopsychiatry,* 1966, **36**(4), 720–724.

Evans, J. Analytic group therapy with delinquents. *Adolescence,* 1966, **1**(2), 180–196.

Heacock, D. R. Modifications of the standard techniques for outpatient group psychotherapy with delinquent boys. *Journal of the National Medical Association,* 1966, **58**(1), 41–47.

Knorr, N. J., Clower, C. G., & Schmidt, R. W. Mixed adult and adolescent group therapy. *American Journal of Psychotherapy,* 1966, **20** (2), 323–331.

Marcilio, M. P. Adolescent mixed group psychotherapy. *Excerpta Medica, International Congress,* Ser. No. 117, 290–291. (World Congress of Psychiatry, Madrid, September 1966. Abstract.)

Teicher, J. D. Group psychotherapy with adolescents. *California Medicine,* 1966, **105**(1), 18–21.

Traux, C. B., Wargo, D. G., Carkhuff, R. R., Kodman, F., & Moles, E. A. Changes in self-concepts during group psychotherapy as a function of alternate sessions and vicarious therapy pretraining in institutionalized mental patients and juvenile delinquents. *Journal of Consulting Psychology,* 1966, **30**(4), 309–314.

Traux, C. B., Wargo, D. G. & Silber, L. D. Effects of group psychotherapy with high accurate empathy and nonpossessive warmth upon female institutionalized delinquents. *Journal of Abnormal Psychology,* 1966, **71**(4), 267–274.

Kaufman, P. N., & Deutsch, A. L. Group therapy for pregnant unwed adolescents in the prenatal clinic of a general hospital. *International Journal of Group Psychotherapy,* 1967, **17**, 309–320.

Miezio, S. Group therapy with mentally retarded adolescents in institutional settings. *International Journal of Group Psychotherapy,* 1967, **17**, 321–327.

Roemele, V., & Grunebaum, H. Helping the helpers. *International Journal of Group Psychotherapy,* 1967, **17**, 343–356.

Spruiell, V. Countertransference and an adolescent group crisis. *International Journal of Group Psychotherapy,* 1967, **17**, 298–308.

33 | Family Group Therapy

Saul L. Brown

OVERVIEW

The use of family therapy for psychological disturbances of childhood rests upon the realization that a child's disturbance usually fulfills dynamic functions for the family system. It may simultaneously satisfy intrapsychic needs in one or both parents. The clinical literature which supports these views is extensive and derives from work in child-guidance clinics over the last three decades, from experiences in family service agencies, from parallel or coordinated psychoanalysis of parents and their children, and from the growing body of developmental studies of children. Added to all this are the dramatic examples from family therapy itself which show how parents' and child's problems interrelate.

Field Theory

The view that a child's disturbance flows out of interpersonal dynamics operating within the family system and that his disturbance fulfills a dynamic function for that system is based upon a field-theory perspective, which emphasizes reciprocal interaction rather than linear cause and effect. It is important to recognize this in order to avoid the simplistic view that parents cause their children's problems. The most influential presentation of field theory has been by Kurt Lewin (1954). There are many published elaborations of this viewpoint as it relates to clinical practice. Reports 12 and 38 of the Group for the Advancement of Psychiatry (1950, 1957) provide clear presentations. Side by side with field theory as a basis for family therapy lie two other major theoretical perspectives. These are psychoanalytic theory and systems theory.

Psychoanalytic Theory

From psychoanalysis of both adults and children, it becomes amply clear how children are frequently the representations for their parents of past relationships and of still unresolved conflicts around aggression or sexuality or past object loss. Ongoing fantasy systems within the parents become expressed or externalized through the children. Anxiety and guilt within the parents deriving from old conflicts or deprivations or traumata are reexperienced in the current family transactions. Boszormenyi-Nagy (1965) has subsumed some of this in his references to "acting-out within the family." There are many clinical papers in the psychoanalytic literature that illustrate the ways in which parental, usually maternal, fantasies are activated in the interaction with infants and young children. Specific to this theme has been the work of Therese Benedek (1959), Rank, Putnam, and Rochlin (1948), Sperling (1955, 1958, 1959), Johnson and Szurek (1952), Rexford and Van Amerongen (1957), and various others.

Systems Theory

Viewing the family unit as a biosocial subsystem within a larger cultural-social system helps define the actual complexity of family life and again avoids an overly simplistic conception of family therapy. The coordination of outside social systems with role designations and role functions within the family has been effectively demonstrated by Talcott Parsons and Robert Bales (1955). More recently, concepts from general systems theory have also found applicability to families. The designation of transactional subsystems within families and the focusing upon intrafamilial communication mechanisms as the vehicles for such subsystem transactions have opened a way to newer comprehension of intrafamilial function. Some of this was anticipated in the work of Ruesch and Bateson (1951) in their reliance upon cybernetic theory as a basis for describing human socialization. John Spiegel (1956) has also developed the theme of systems within families. The work of Von Bertalanffy (1956), apropos of general systems theory, has been quite directly applied to clinical work with families by various family therapists, such as E. J. Carroll (1966, 1967), H. P. Laquer (1968), and A. Curry (1966). Car-

roll, in his effort to characterize process in the family system, uses terms such as *feedback, self-correction, directional pathways, storage of information, internal organization of segments of the subsystem* and *hierarchal levels of system.* Using the concept of *steady state* in the family system, he has attempted to observe how variables such as *affect* produce change in that state.

Laquer, referring to the interaction of multiple families, uses terms such as *breaking the familial code, amplification and modulation of signals, overload, delay in feedback loop,* and *inflexibility.*

Running through the systems concepts about family, whether organized in terms of role function or communication or systems processes, is the recurring observation of how tenaciously certain family systems resist change and how communication mechanisms are used to maintain a steady state even when it is severely pathogenic for individual members.

CLINICAL REALITY

Because family therapy for the psychological dysfunctions of childhood has found only recent acceptance in child psychiatric centers, some specific justifications for its use are in order. This requires a brief retracing of what this author would like to designate *clinical reality.*

Clinical reality has its beginning when a child's psychological dysfunction discomfits the parents enough so that they feel the need for outside help. What happens then depends upon a variety of factors. Some of the factors that shape the emerging clinical reality are:

1. The degree of organization or disorganization of the family

2. The parental sophistication about psychological problems and their readiness to turn to a mental-health resource for help

3. The actual availability of appropriate mental-health resources

4. The pressures—both encouraging and discouraging—arising from school or social group or from within the extended family re the use of such services

5. The definitiveness and persistence of the child's dysfunction

6. The emotional pain engendered in the parents by his problems

7. The degree of consensus between the parents that professional help is needed

These determine not only whether the parents seek clinical help but also what kind of help they expect. What the parents expect to gain from a clinical resource affects the subsequent flow of clinical events and therefore needs early and repeated clarification.

Factors more specific to the inner life of the family also shape the clinical reality. These are:

1. The level of ego development of each of the family members. This refers, in the case of the parents, to whether strong regressive tendencies or fixations at early childhood levels are dominant in their ego functions, or whether there are split-off or dissociated ego dynamisms of a relatively infantile or immature nature which show up behaviorally.

2. The major ego defenses and the psychodynamics of the patient and of each family member—especially the parents.

3. The presence of obtrusive psychopathology in any of the family—e.g., recurring depressions, thinking disorders, alcoholism, chronic or recurring psychotic states, impulse disorders, or chronic sociopathic behavior.

4. The existence of major somatic disorders of a chronic or recurring type in any of the family members.

5. The current status of the marriage and the dynamics of the marital dyad.

6. The nature of the family communication systems, the modes of affect expression, the role designations and behavior, the family myths, the family secrets, the family image of itself, etc.

7. Traumatic events that have affected the family in the recent or remote past.

8. Recent or ongoing crises.

The preceding series reflects the existential complexity that may underlie any clinical problem. It demands a departure from traditional psychiatric diagnostic phraseology based upon a medical model since this can only be an oversimplification and therefore misleading. Clinical reality is multifactorial. Although most well-trained clinicians are in some fashion cognizant of the many factors reviewed above, their diagnostic-clinical *procedure* may or may not make contact with them. It is in this complex context that the use of family diagnosis and therapy must be understood.

Every clinical resource, whether private or public, eventually sets some limit to the range of factors it is inclined to work with both in diagnosis and in therapy. This evolves out of the peculiar history of a given clinical setting, the theoretical frame of reference that is dominant there, the training backgrounds of the professionals working in it, its socioeconomic surroundings, and the nature of the social pressures playing upon it. A modern mental-health center, for example, expects to relate to a very broad range of these factors. The same might be true for a family service center.

Clinical interviewing of whole families brings the clinical resource into direct contact with the multiple factors that constitute the clinical reality of the child with dysfunction. Through family interviews, indicated channels for psychotherapeutic action can be defined. It may turn out that such channels are not available in that particular clinical setting. Should this be the case, meeting with the whole family helps to clarify limitations and opens the door to joint planning in accordance with what might be realistically available.

Resistance to Change

It has been this author's thesis (Brown, 1966) that a central challenge for psychotherapeutic intervention, whether with children or adults, is to comprehend the ways in which resistance to change operates in the life of a family. Psychotherapy, if it seeks to induce change, succeeds or fails according to the way the many factors constituting the clinical reality of a given family either facilitate or resist such change. Basic to this is the realization that psychological dysfunction often reflects a family's difficulty in accommodating to or encompassing the inevitable changes that arise out of the unfolding of the life cycle and out of the stresses of daily life. The clinician needs therefore to define the nature of the resistance to change and how it works in a given family system and in the individual members both prior to therapy and during the course of therapy. An initial and continuing appraisal of all the factors mentioned above has to be made in order to understand and respond to the resistances to change which on the one hand may have precipitated a dysfunction and on the other hand serve to impede clinical effort. Direct interview contact with the entire family group, rather than extensive collection of historical data, provides a pragmatic mechanism for this.

Resistance to *therapeutic* change per se may in some instances be more deeply centered in the socioeconomic or ethnocultural range of factors than in the psychodynamic ones. It may lie in some instances in the functional disorganization of the family. It may be anchored to a major physical illness in one member. In another family it may be a function of ignorance or naïveté about psychological-emotional phenomena. On the other hand, the mere absence of psychological sophistication resulting from socioeconomic deprivation may not necessarily block responsiveness to psychotherapeutically induced change. The rigidity of the resistance to change cannot be judged a priori or according to theory. It needs to be felt out through actual clinical engagement with the family group. The barriers to therapeutic responsiveness soon enough become evident in this way, but also the resources within the family that will support developmental and therapeutic change become evident through this experience.

In regard to pathological phenomena, it is *perpetuation* rather than original causation that dominates the clinical concern.

The Clinical Resource Also Shapes Clinical Reality

In addition to the factors listed earlier, including the ways in which resistance to change operates in a family group, the interests and attitudes of the clinicians themselves also shape the clinical reality of the child with psychological dysfunction.

If, for example, through the medium of an initial family interview the therapist discerns undercurrents of disagreement between the parents about their child's problem and he actively probes this difference in the presence of the whole family, he immediately shapes a different clinical reality from one in which a more traditional diagnostic and history-taking interview is held with the parents. In the latter case the therapist, even if he discerns that the parents are in conflict, can use such an observation in only a limited way because of the unwritten contract that underlies that interviewing system. He may tell the parents that they need to look into their problems, and he may suggest a resource for this. He may even urge them to do this before they bring their child to a therapist. But this is still a quite different experience from one in which underlying conflicts are actively underlined with the whole family group participating. In such an approach a new family process becomes set into motion which may have far-reaching implications for all the members, sometimes in a relatively short time.

In the kind of initial family interview just defined, the therapist's comments may awaken each member of the family to new perceptions of each other. If handled appropriately, this may loosen pathological repression because expression of feelings is encouraged. Also, the child's role as "the patient" becomes defined now in the context of a total family problem, and the participation of other family members in his problem becomes open to review. The parents have an opportunity to reevaluate the meaning of the child's dysfunction for them. This need not always be an elaborate verbal process within the interview itself. A new self-orientation on the child's part and a more empathic attitude toward him by his siblings may evolve from this, and the siblings may become now more self-observing. The institution of psychotherapy for one child in the family now has a different coloration than if the parental or other intrafamilial conflicts had never been openly shared. The working through of all this in subsequent family group sessions may reduce resistance to later one-to-one psychotherapy, if and when this is indicated in each member's case.

Reviewing Clinical Reality with the Family

Other aspects of clinical reality mentioned earlier are met through the use of initial family interviews. Situational factors can be brought into the foreground of the family's awareness and jointly assessed. Environmental pressures playing upon the family can be talked about. The family's view of the school or of local authorities or of their economic or social circumstances can be shared in a constructive fashion. The inner life of the family related to recurring psychotic states or to chronic illness in one of the members or to various acting-out character disorders can also be talked about; shame, guilt, resentments, and even certain family secrets can be faced. All this shapes the way in which the therapy will

evolve for the designated patient, and it engages all family members on a new level of mutual responsibility. If out of the subsequent process of therapy—whether individual or family—new problems emerge in family members other than the designated patient, a family group understanding of this phenomenon becomes more immediately possible.

In summary, clinical family interviewing has evolved out of the empirical realization that the many factors making up clinical reality have needed to be met in more flexible ways than the traditional clinical system has allowed for. Having evolved, family diagnosis and interviewing now tend to actively reshape what has been traditionally considered to be clinical reality.

HISTORICAL BACKGROUND

Pioneers

Psychotherapy with whole family groups has a relatively short history. This is in spite of the fact that many clinicians have long recognized that family influences are operative in psychological disturbance and in spite also of the long-existing awareness in child psychiatry of how psychopathology in children is affected by family experience. Precise dating of the origin of a technique is rarely possible. Jay Haley (1962), in a provocatively humorous review, caricatures the "furtive" admissions to each other by a few therapists in the late 1940s that they had made attempts with this type of therapy. An article by Rudolf Dreikurs (1951) of Chicago describes some of his experience in interviewing families with all children present. Ackerman and Sobel's paper (1950) pointed directly to the use of family interviews in relation to young children.

The flow of clinical reports and of theoretical formulations began to be augmented in the mid-1950s and the early 1960s when a variety of papers by those now considered the "pioneers" in family therapy appeared. Most prominent among these early contributors are Nathan Ackerman of New York; Donald Jackson, John Weakland, Jay Haley, and Virginia Satir, all originally working in Palo Alto, California; Theodore Lidz and Stephen Fleck at Yale University; Lyman Wynne, Murray Bowen, and Warren Brodey, all associated at one time at the National Institute of Mental Health in Maryland; Robert MacGregor at the University of Texas Medical School; Ivan Boszormenyi-Nagy, James Framo, and Alfred Friedman, all working in Philadelphia; and John Elderkin Bell, whose report of a series of interviews with a Scottish family was published as a U.S. Public Health Service monograph in 1961. The work of each of these is based upon extensive clinical experience, some of it having its roots in psychoanalytic theory. Several had been trained and had worked as psychoanalysts. Curiously, there is a glaring absence of trained child psychiatrists in the pioneer group.

Many of the early clinical reports were related to manifestly disturbed families with schizophrenic individuals in them. This may have provided an initial coloration to family therapy, with a resulting emphasis upon major failures of communication and a deemphasis of intrapsychic dynamics. Various clinical studies were addressed to defining the ways in which intrafamilial homeostasis and equilibrium were maintained or disrupted. Apropos of this, communication mechanisms and problems of role definition and complementarity were in the center of focus (Ackerman, 1960; Bateson, Jackson, Haley, & Weakland, 1956; Bowen, Dysinger, & Basamania, 1957; Epstein & Westley, 1959; Jackson, 1959; Spiegel, 1957; Wynne, Ryckoff, Day, & Hirsch, 1958). This is not to suggest that the various contributors just noted ignored intrapsychic mechanisms. Indeed the work of Lidz, Cornelison, Fleck, and Terry (1957a) emphasizes the constant interplay of intrafamilial dynamics and individual dynamics, as does Ackerman's basic contribution (1958). It is evident in the literature,

however, that some of the leading clinicians in family therapy have tended to an increasing impatience with the use of psychodynamic interpretations based upon psychoanalytic understanding of intrapsychic function. This is epitomized in letters which Andrew Ferber and C. Christian Beels exchanged with Jay Haley, published in *Family Process* (March, 1967). The exchange of letters was a result of Jay Haley's depreciatory review of the book *Intensive Family Therapy*, edited by Ivan Boszormenyi-Nagy and James Framo (1965), which appeared in *Family Process* in 1966. In their criticism of Haley's review, Ferber and Beels state:

1. Repetitively patterned and mutually distressful ("sick") behavior among family members is in large part the result of past experience between them.

2. That experience is preserved and is dynamically active in the individual minds of the family members, and some especially important parts of it are unconscious.

3. The experiences are of a sort which hinder separation and individuation of family members. In particular, with parental figures strong fantasied relationships are maintained which interfere with realistic appraisal of the self and others.

4. These core aspects of the members' personalities are very difficult to change, and what change is possible takes time.

The contributors to the book share a background of study, and in many cases, a practice of psychoanalysis. Some of them have chosen to move to the study and treatment of the family without ignoring their experience in psychoanalysis.

In response, Haley states:

There is no question that Dr. Nagy and Dr. Framo are serious participants in the family field.

If both Dr. Nagy and Dr. Framo had not shown wisdom and experience in their other writings, this reviewer would not have reacted so sharply to their presentation of a method of treating the family of the schizophrenic.

They claim they brought together a collection of

authors who "operate in a psychoanalytic manner" when these authors do not, whatever else they might have in common. They use such terms as "deep" and "intensive" which are part of the gamesmanship of psychoanalysis to sell a method when one cannot offer outcome results.

The authors also, it seems to me, become almost incoherent in their attempt to describe the behavior of several family members in a language and with a theory specifically designed to describe only a single person.

As they gained experience, most family therapists abandoned this method [psychoanalytic interpretation of unconscious dynamics] with this type of family because it was not producing results as good as spontaneous remission. Perhaps more important, some therapists began to notice that it can be pointlessly painful to the family. Whatever the merits of interpreting unconscious dynamics to individuals in privacy, when this is done in the conjoint situation it is a different matter.

As I travel around the country, I find the only family therapists who use this approach are either new to the field or they are more experienced but work in the large urban centers where psychoanalysis and interminable treatment, has great prestige.

Although the above quotations are somewhat out of context, they reveal some central issues. Haley goes on in his letter to review the theme which is at the core of his theoretical and clinical work. It is the one of bringing about significant change in a total system. He observes that introducing change in a system foments antagonisms and loyalties, which then lead to new ways of thinking. This is applicable to professional-theoretical systems and to families.

The above quotations not only illustrate some of the interpersonal ferment in the field of family therapy but also define significant problems. Does the language and conceptual system of individual psychodynamic psychotherapy obstruct the effective use of family therapy? Are the insights gained from a half century of pain-

staking psychoanalytic work with thousands of patients irrelevant in relation to altering pathological intrafamilial dynamics? Does the effort to introduce "depth insight" truly hamper productive therapeutic flow in family interviews? Is there one kind of family therapy for families with schizophrenic members and another kind for families with lesser disturbance? Is family therapy related to problems of young children significantly different from that with older patients and/or schizophrenic patients?

This writer has found it possible to work in what he believes to be an enlightened eclectic fashion, which requires a continuous flexibility of clinical choice and intervention based upon a combination of psychoanalytic and group transactional understanding. Haley would probably view this as reflecting an inability to break out of a constrictive loyalty to psychoanalysis unrelated to realistic clinical process. Be that as it may, much of what follows in this chapter is cast within a frame of reference that combines rather than dichotomizes. Additional comments about the clinical origin of family therapy follow.

CLINICAL ORIGINS

Group Therapy

It is of interest to note some of the sources of technique in family therapy. A major one is in psychodynamically based group therapy, which emerged as a major clinical procedure in the 1940s. Fundamental to group therapy is a therapist-set in which no group member is the "primary" patient. Even for psychoanalytically oriented groups, major content of each group session tends toward interaction and here-and-now exchanges, with genetic data tending to become deemphasized as the group develops stability and interpersonal ease. Each of these, the therapist-set and the focus upon here-and-now transactions, characterizes much of family-therapy technique. It appears that experience with group therapy provides a comfortable transition for therapists into the work with families. Handlon and Parloff (1962) emphasize that the two modalities differ in that the permissive tone of group therapy is not practical in family therapy, where in fact the family has assigned the patient role to one of its members and the therapist has the task of altering this preexisting family view. Also they note that the family group begins therapy with shared mythology and distortions, which became a major target for the therapist's clarification. It has been the current writer's observation also that because of the qualitatively different nature and function of mutual dependency in families as contrasted with standard therapy groups, the ultimate purpose of the interpersonal communications is quite different. The ultimate objective in family therapy is to create or retrieve a relatively stable equilibrium for day-to-day living together. In standard group therapy the ultimate objective is toward increased self-awareness for each patient. Stability of the therapy group per se is important as a vehicle for each patient's individual progress, but it is not an end in itself since the group members have no day-to-day dependency upon one another. The very structure of a family group, with its intergenerational hierarchy of parents and children also creates a different set of expectations of the therapeutic process than does a standard group, in which authority and decision making are no greater for one patient than for another. Withal, Parloff's comment (1961) that the influence of group therapy has provided "the greatest single advance in the interpersonal relationship treatment technique" summarizes the ultimate importance of group therapy for family therapy. Grotjahn (1960) describes very effectively his own sense of floating attention and his readiness to identify with each family member in turn during a family interview. This is basic to and perhaps even arises from clinical experience in standard group therapy.

Psychoanalytic Psychotherapy

Some of the issues apropos of the influence of psychoanalysis on family therapy have been reviewed earlier in this chapter. The overt techniques of these two modalities are manifestly divergent from each other. The training of the psychoanalytic psychotherapist is one which leads to a calculated remoteness on the therapist's part, a suppression of his own overt emotional reactions, a "passive" or waiting attitude, and an overall pattern of behavior which leaves the patient knowing as little as possible about the therapist—all in order that the patient's projections upon the professional person of the therapist become maximized and subject to subsequent analytic clarification. It is well known that in spite of this traditional and seemingly highly refined model, the actual behavior of psychoanalytic therapists with their patients varies widely. Psychoanalysts have at times reiterated that they do not function without affect. Greenson (1967) makes it clear, speaking from a more or less traditional psychoanalytic position, that a "working alliance" must first be forged between patient and analyst before the analytic work can take place. Psychoanalytic therapy invites strong affective expressions related to here-and-now events, such as the therapist's vacations, late arrival, personal habits, office decor. These are not rejected as "unreal," but the analyst connects these to other levels of emotion in the patient. The emphasis is often upon process rather than content, and this antedates the same emphasis in family-therapy relationships. Understanding "displacement" and "projection" is essential to family therapy.

The analytic therapist's training is toward sensitivity to nuances of feeling and oscillations of affect and toward awareness of the subtle mechanisms through which anger or guilt or anxiety is masked. Communicative techniques must be learned which are flexible enough to effectively get through a particular patient's defenses as they are *currently* operating. Again, this is all clinical foundation for what is done in family therapy.

From psychoanalysis has come the tradition of intensive self-evaluation of the psychotherapist's own motivational system. Personal psychoanalytic experience provides a therapist with knowledge of his own latent countertransference reactions. A constant internal scanning of the therapist's countertransference reactions is crucial in family therapy.

The continuing preoccupation of the psychoanalytic therapist is with his patient's unconscious resistance. Resistance to the subjective awareness and tolerance of anxiety or hostility or sexual impulses or regressive tendencies or guilt feelings results in the elaboration of complex ego mechanisms of defense. Analytic therapeutic technique is designed to help the patient recognize his conflicts about various impulses and the ways in which he organizes defenses against the emotions which relate to them. The "working-through" process of psychoanalytic therapy is aimed at a constant review with the patient of the ways in which he organizes his defensive resistance to experiencing or tolerating uncomfortable or unwelcome emotion. A major aim in family therapy is the sharing and toleration of ambivalent feelings. Reduction of resistance is therefore a problem common to both modalities.

Psychoanalytic technique is often considered to focus totally on genetic origins of behavior. But psychoanalysts do not always agree on the importance of genetic reconstruction for the achievement of self-awareness and for the reduction of exaggerated or unnecessary defenses. Franz Alexander, one of the most influential of psychoanalytic teachers in the United States during the 1930s and 1940s, evolved the concept of the *corrective emotional experience* as being of central significance for therapeutic change (1961), and he was inclined to view the patient's formal understanding of his genetic

past as of lesser significance. Timely use of genetic data in order to clarify an issue and to deepen understanding is again common to both modalities and is subject to selective use in both.

All this is presented out of the current writer's concern that a tendency, prevalent in many academic and clinical centers, to stereotype and caricature the psychoanalytic therapeutic process may cut off the development of family therapy from a crucial source of depth. Ackerman's article (1962a) is of importance relative to this general theme. Donald Jackson and Virginia Satir in a review article (1961) observe that psychoanalysis has acted both in a positive and in a negative sense to expedite the family movement, and they particularly note that the concept of family diagnosis and therapy owes much of its current position to psychoanalysis. They go on, however, to point out their view of the limitations of psychoanalytic conceptual terminology for family therapy. They place major emphasis upon the "monadic" focus of psychoanalytic therapy and upon its reliance upon transference phenomena for its therapeutic leverage. Ackerman (1967) has expanded more recently on his views of the limitations of psychoanalytic technique. He cites the artificiality of the situation in which there is a relatively anonymous therapist and questions whether the working through of distortions relative to this "as-if" interpersonal relationship provides enough grist for "action" in the patient's real life. "Since life is movement and there can be no living without action, in effect the psychoanalyst is in the position of trying to stem the tide of life. Insofar as such an effort is inherently unreal, it complicates and burdens the therapeutic exertion toward achieving a higher level of adaptation." He refers to his concept of *acting in* (in contrast to acting out) developed in an earlier paper, "Transference and Countertransference" (1959), as a theoretical base for this. It is in the family group session that constructive "acting in" occurs, which obviates the need for the acting out that is associated with transference and other kinds of resistance in individual psychoanalytic therapy. Ackerman implies that the acting in that occurs in family group meetings hastens the clarification of distortions, which in psychoanalytic therapy await the slow evolution of a transference regression and then a prolonged working-through process with the therapist and then with persons in the patient's current life.

Indeed the slowness of change that characterizes the psychoanalytic process does induce a therapist orientation which in some instances seems to reinforce a disengagement from dealing with current life problems. On the other hand, the results of family therapy suggest that therapist patience is a virtue for that modality too and that the great resistance to change which characterizes many families does not necessarily yield to energetic therapist interventions. Patience and "timing" derive from psychoanalysis.

Finally, a word about the importance of fantasy in psychoanalytic therapy and in family therapy: The literature of family therapy includes references to such phenomena as family myths (Ferreira, 1966), family secrets (Framo, 1965), and congruence of images (Hess & Handel, 1967). Although discovery of these phenomena in family life cannot be laid to psychoanalytic therapy alone, the recognition of them as complex shared fantasy systems is certainly at least in part derived from long-standing psychoanalytic knowledge about the coping and defensive functions of fantasy.

Marriage Therapy

Still another important clinical origin for family group therapy has been the field of marital counseling. Publications in that field predate the subsequent flow of articles about conjoint treatment of marital pairs that have accompanied those about family therapy. Skidmore and Garrett (1955) reported their work with three cases in which joint interviews with married or engaged couples were utilized. In "Simultaneous Psychotherapy with Marital Partners," an article published in 1956, Thomas describes work with eight cases. Geist and Gerber (1960) describe their use of joint interviews of husband and wife together in a family service agency in Cincinnati. A growing number of clinical reports have paralleled the work in family therapy. Some of the contributions have been by Brody (1961), Carroll, Cambor, Leopold, Miller, and Reis (1963), Gehrke and Moxom (1962), Haley (1963a), Lehrman (1963), Watson (1963), and Satir (1965). These are just a sampling of articles. Satir notes that it was Don Jackson who introduced the term *conjoint therapy* in relation to work with marital pairs.

Child Psychiatry

Although there is an absence of child psychiatrists in the pioneer group of family therapists, it is this writer's belief that child psychiatry and particularly child guidance have had importance for the development of family therapy. Nathan Ackerman, who has influenced family therapy as much as any single contributor, was for years a consultant to family service agencies in New York City, where the child-guidance procedure was usual. His early interest in family diagnosis and his subsequent interest in family therapy arose in some major degree from that experience and from his contact with the problems of child psychiatry. Certain individuals in child psychiatry have made particularly significant clarifications through their research and teaching of the way in which psychopathology is organized in the parent-child interaction and of how its reduction is dependent upon effective therapeutic work with parents.

The publications of Helen Witmer (1946) and Gordon Hamilton (1947) in social work; Melitta Sperling (1955, 1958), Irene Josselyn (1953), Ritvo and Solnit (1958), Rexford and Van Amerongen (1957), and Stanislaus Szurek (1959) in child psychiatry; and Frederick Allen (1942) in child guidance are a few examples. Innumerable others might be mentioned. Moreover, Frederick Allen's emphasis upon the here-and-now separation-individuation process in therapeutic sessions with children provides another relevant basis for the therapeutic transactions with children in family interviews.

Although there have been occasional allusions in the classical child psychiatry literature to a parent's participation in the play-therapy room, none has demonstrated the involvement of the parents on an active transactional level. Some of these include Schwarz (1950), some references in Moustakas (1953), and more recently, Kolansky (1960). There may be others which this writer has not come upon.

THEORY

Categories

Theorizing about family therapy converges around the concept that the family is a biosocial system with deeply entrenched transactional patterns, or "subsystems," which function so as to preserve equilibrium. These can be understood through a variety of conceptual formulations. There are in the literature a number of broad reviews of the theoretical basis of family therapy. Fundamental to all is *The Psychodynamics of Family Life*, by Nathan Ackerman (1958). A valuable critical review is by W. W. Meissner in *Family Process* (1964). Meissner organizes the early contributions of various workers in the field under four subheadings: *personality development, communication and homeostasis*, and *family mechanisms*.

Developmental perspective. The work of Lidz and Fleck reflects a primary interest in the issues of personality development. They are concerned (1960) with the vicissitudes of early object and subsequent intrafamilial relationships as they affect the identification process. Using a developmental frame of reference, Lidz et al. (1957a, 1957b) have described the evolution of intrafamilial "schisms" in certain very disturbed families. In such families there is a chronic failure over many years to achieve appropriate complementarity of roles in the marriage. The result is a distortion of sex-linked role relationships and in some cases a chronic competition for the children's loyalty, with a failure of intrafamilial and parental unity. Accordingly, where "schism" prevails, the mother tends to be severely devalued by the father. The female child allies with father, suffers a faulty identification with her mother, and is unable to work through a viable sex-role identity. In the "skewed" family, one parent, often the mother, is overwhelming and engulfing. A precarious family equilibrium may be achieved but with the penalty that a son in such a situation fails to achieve well-defined autonomous masculine identity. In either case, the real issue underlying these pathological relationships is the desperate need by everyone to avoid anxiety. Individuation is experienced as total separation and loss. "Masking" is also referred to by Lidz et al. (1958) as characteristic of some families, in which significant realities in the family life are obscured and become a covert element in the intrafamilial communication system. Again, while this serves to preserve everyone in the family from the felt anxiety that more realistic perception might precipitate, it cripples the natural process of identification and individuation that should occur in each child.

Personality development also engages the interest of Nathan Ackerman and of Lyman Wynne. In their theorizing, emphasis is placed upon complementarity of role function and upon the failures of genuine complementarity. Ackerman emphasizes the role conflicts in a family that arise from the developmental process of separation and individuation. Wynne coined the word *pseudomutuality* to demonstrate how in some families interpersonal relationships fail to develop to the level of genuine individual identity and autonomy. There is an absence of vibrant, empathic growth inducing interest in each other even while family members remain painfully bound together (Ackerman, 1958).

Murray Bowen's interest in the difficulties of differentiation from the "undifferentiated family ego mass," which he sees to be prevalent for individuals in families with schizophrenic members, also represents the personality-development orientation in family therapy. Bowen (1961) has emphasized the intergenerational carry-over of the failure to achieve individuation. Again, underlying all this is the issue of profound separation anxiety in each person.

Communication and homeostasis. Within the framework of communication and homeostasis, Bateson, Jackson, Haley, and Weakland's (1956) development of the concept of the double-bind communication in schizophrenic families is a derivative of work with whole families. An accurate grasp of this concept is important. There are five components: (1) interaction or communication between two or more persons, i.e., a dyad; (2) repeated experience sufficient to make the double-bind structure a habitual expectation; (3) a primary negative injunction at one level of communication involving a threat of punishment (arousal of anxiety); (4) a secondary injunction conflicting with the first at another level of communication and similarly reinforced with the threat of punishment; and (5) a tertiary injunction prohibiting escape from the field of interaction. The idea of *levels of communication* is crucial in this. Bowen has demonstrated something similar in showing how a demand placed upon a child in some families that he be mature is in conflict with a deep expectation that he must remain a child. Bateson's views are related to schizophrenic processes. Bowen's are possibly more general.

Within the communication-and-homeostasis frame of reference lies the same group's elaborations upon homeostatic mechanisms as a basic conceptual model for viewing the family system. Implicit in this is the concept that a family can be viewed as a system with many interacting components which are constantly readapting to each other so that a relative homeostasis is maintained. Subsystems of communication can function so as to disrupt equilibrium and homeostasis, or they may preserve an uneasy equilibrium. Communication may be geared to avoid or block individuation of family members, with attendant danger of separation and anxiety. Resistance to change characterizes such families, and communication subsystems serve that purpose.

Role theory. This viewpoint converges with the concept of equilibrium-disequilibrium in role relations used by Spiegel and elaborated upon in clinical theory by Ackerman (1956). In their writing, communication patterns per se are not emphasized so much as are the role functions which resist change or which perpetuate pathology. Ackerman characterizes *complementarity* of roles as "specific patterns of family role relationships that provide satisfaction, avenues of solutions of conflict, support for a needed self-image, and buttressing of crucial forms of defenses against anxiety." He points out major sources of disequilibrium in role relations deriving from differences in cultural value orientations and social role expectations, as well as from intrapsychic defensive organization. He sees therapy as directed to reestablishing patterns of complementarity in such a way that new equilibrium will occur with a relief of anxiety and a reduction of pressure upon a given child. Wynne's concept of pseudomutuality in schizophrenic families illustrates the way in which role complementarity may be maintained at the expense of vibrant individuation and identity formation.

Family dynamisms and mechanisms. In the context of family mechanisms as they become discernible in family interviews is Warren Brodey's (1959) concept of "externalization." He shows how an individual in the family selectively perceives another's behavior in such a way as to validate his own prior projections onto that partner. In certain pathological relationships, the partner complies with that expectation of him—i.e., he introjects the other's expectation of him. A rigid reciprocal system operates between them. There is a locking in a pathological ties. Apropos of this, Murray Bowen clarifies that a mother may project her sense of helplessness onto her child, who, sensing this expectation of itself, introjects this identity and develops role behavior which validates the mother's assumption. The mother then continues to relate to the child as helpless. A self-perpetuating system evolves which resists reality influence. Father for his own reasons supports this (Bowen, 1961). The system perpetuating this may be described in role-theory terms, in communication terms, and in psychodynamic phraseology.

The cumulative clinical experience in family therapy has revealed a variety of family mechanisms and phenomena other than those already alluded to in the preceding pages. Also, it provokes new research. "Family games and rules" (described by Haley in 1963), "family secrets" (described by Wynne), "family myths" (described by Ferreira), "family coalitions and alliances," and "family defensiveness" are all examples. A "family projection process," perhaps the most crucial of all insofar as individual psychodynamics converge with transactional events, has been alluded to by Bowen and Brodey in earlier references.

Titchener and co-workers (1960) refer to family "patterns" and "styles" in reference to repetitive sequences of action and to the organization of basic defenses, coping mechanisms, values, etc.

Decision making has been studied in families by Ferreira (1963). "Unanimous decisions," "majority decisions," "dictatorial decisions," and "chaotic decisions" have been differentiated. Also, *rejection* and the modes by which it is experienced in families have been studied by Ferreira (1964). These provide provocative possibility for understanding how certain aspects of intrafamilial phenomena become systemized as pathology. Decision making has also been studied by Ravich, Deutsch, and Brown (1966). They note in thirty-eight couples the following as characteristic of their decision making in an experimental game situation: "sharing," 24 percent; "dominating and submitting," 13 percent; "inconsistent," 26 percent; "intensely competitive," 7 percent; and "dysjunctive" (i.e., asymmetrical and individualistic), 10 percent. A follow-up of this, apropos of effects on children, was made at the American Orthopsychiatric Association meeting in 1966. Between married partners and between parents and children, the timing, the multiple emotions, and the subtle communications that operate around decision making have enormous significance for the way in which the family system functions.

Familial mechanisms in relation to *object loss* and *mourning* have been intensively studied through the medium of family therapy, principally by Norman Paul and George Grosser (1964, 1965). In a presentation of his views at the Pennsylvania Hospital Award lecture in 1966, Paul unified some of his observations under the title, "The Use of Empathy in the Resolution of Grief." He notes the powerful nonverbal element in empathy and defines it as "an interpersonal phenomenon in which the empathizer recognizes that he shares kindred feelings with the object." This, he notes, presupposes the existence of the other person as a separate individual entitled to his own feelings, ideas, and emotional history. "The empathizer makes no judgments about what the other should feel . . . ." Paul also develops the theme of "affective empathy" as his major focus of interest. Moving on from this, he reviews some of the issues pertinent to object loss and grief. He reviews theories relative to mourning that derive from individual psychoanalytic therapy, and he draws upon the work of Freud, Abraham, Klein, Deutsch, Lindemann, Parkes, and others to substantiate these apropos of family experience. He observes that in many families, especially those exhibiting rigid resistance to developmental change, there is a history in the previous generation of maladaptive response to death of loved persons, with a resulting "fixity of symbiotic relationships in the family."

> Although the original loss or losses may have occurred as much as fifty years ago, the response to them exercises a lingering influence on the present. Such losses were usually suffered by one or the other parent, often before the current family unit came into existence. This response to loss appears to generate and be generated by a relative paucity of empathy and the related lack of respect for individuality in the family system. Affects and attitudes toward the deceased remain essentially unchanged, and the family's inability to cope with the original loss, produces a family style which is variably unresponsive to a wide range of changes including losses and disappointments. This unresponsiveness is expressed in an attempt to deny the passage of time which often takes the form of unwittingly keeping one family member in an inappropriate dependent position.

As one works with seriously disturbed family groups, it becomes evident how communication subsystems function so as to fortify the phenomenon of emotional isolation and the relative absence of empathy that Paul describes. Pathogenic patterns in families may also reflect similar origins. How heuristic his concept is for the myriad forms of family pathology that are observable remains to be seen. Application of Paul's views to therapy will be referred to later.

Family language and structure in the *low-socioeconomic groups* have been studied intensively by Salvador Minuchin and co-workers,

(1967). Their work has focused upon communication patterns, role function, and personality development, but other items have become highlighted along with these. *Failure of focal attention* apropos of "listening" is graphically illustrated in a group of families of delinquent boys treated at the Wiltwyck School in New York. Failure to carry a conversational theme through to completion once any interruption occurs was also noted. Disruptive shifts to new themes, alternating with total disengagement from conversation, was characteristic. Exploration and clarification of meaning often failed to occur. Derogation of each other with phrases such as "You are an idiot" tended to replace a working-through of differences in views.

"Noise," or "sound power," was also noted as providing a main source of influence and dominance in interpersonal exchanges. Clarifications or explanations were rare. Together with mounting noise, there was, in the family meetings, a peculiar disruptive motility, in which children would unpredictably change chairs, grab objects from each other, etc.

Affect exchanges were seen to alternate in an all-or-nothing pattern, much as did other elements of transaction. Individuals oscillated between extreme involvement and seemingly total disengagement. The two main affects expressed were related to aggression and affection, expressed through nurturance. Through various verbal and nonverbal mechanisms, threats of violence or retaliation were made, as well as diffuse and confusing references to giving or withholding nurturance (affection). Gradations of affects in terms of empathy, tenderness, concern, subjective uneasiness, or guilt were rare.

> In our observations, this response of the parent is seldom clearly related to the nature of the child's action. There are no guiding cues for future behavior implied in the parents' move. The child's

encounter with this frequent abruptness seems to him to be capricious and incomprehensible. He appears to be somewhat helpless in a "suddenness world" which cannot be modified by his own actions.

These global experiences give the children few chances to estimate themselves and their behavior accurately, and handicaps their contact with, and knowledge of, their feelings.

Their impulsive expressions of aggression become, functionally, not too different from their impulsive nurturance demands. They seem to have the purpose not of opening the gap between self and others, but of closing or repairing it. Any signs of incipient separation apparently triggers off the so-called "acting out" behavior in order to avoid the threat of having to cope with interpersonal gaps.

Minuchin suggests that the "negativistic" or "rebellious" components of delinquent behavior may be as much an effort *against* self-differentiation as toward it since, in the families he has observed, differentiation is experienced as dangerous and the mechanisms for it are deficient. Implications of Minuchin's work for therapy will be discussed later in this chapter.

Cognitive styles and patterns have also come under scrutiny in the context of intrafamilial communication and as elements in family mechanisms. Leaders in this area of study have been Lyman Wynne and Margaret Thaler Singer (1963, 1966). Their report of 250 families, of which 75 contained normal offspring, 60 contained neurotic offspring, 25 borderline and 90 contained schizophrenic offspring, is of long-term significance. In addition to observations of transactional phenomena, the Rorschach, Thematic Apperception Test (TAT), Object Sorting Tests, Proverbs, etc., were given to all parents. Excerpts from psychotherapy sessions were studied. The parental style of communication and relating and their forms of affect expression could all be discerned as predictive of particular forms of thinking style, types of affect expression, and severity of ego impairment in their offspring.

Major headings under which their reactions to experimental tests were grouped are (1) *disruptive behavior,* in which parents ask extraneous questions, get off on tangential speeches, play with words; (2) *negativistic commentary,* in which peculiar but indirect depreciation is expressed; (3) *closure problems,* in which the parents embed responses with contradictions within speeches, so that one is not sure what has happened to the response; (4) *peculiar forms of verbalization,* which include odd grammatical constructions, mispronunciations, slips of the tongue, and violations of conventional usage and logic, such as "This seems like along inside of a human's outer shape or something."

The observations summarized above introduce new levels of understanding of cognitive and perceptual mechanisms operating within family systems. They represent an intersection of the individual perceptual and cognitive experiences of various family members with affective exchange and subsystems of communication. Their role in the precipitation or perpetuation of developmental failures in children are suggestive, even if they are not as yet substantiated as "causative." Implications for family therapy will be raised later.

The phenomenon of *"focal symbiosis"* has been of interest to the current writer. The phrase is used by Phyllis Greenacre (1959). In studies of families with nursery-school-age children who manifest personality disturbances, a peculiar bond between one of the parents and the troubled child can often be observed. The symbiosis is "focal" in the sense that a particular set of ego functions are involved. In some cases, this may occur around bodily exchanges—skin or anal or oral. In other cases, it occurs around intellectual function. Inordinate parental investment in certain of the child's ego functions becomes evident. In some cases, the motor skills of the child are the vehicle for the symbiosis; in yet others, it is the fantasy elaborations verbalized by the child which keep parent and child in a tight bond. Other areas of ego function remain outside of the pathological bond. For each participant a combination of mutual regression and mutual fixation is acted out. The effects upon the family life are complex, and the persistence of such focal symbiotic involvements may be very stubborn (Brown, 1966).

A comprehensive review and critique of various theoretical perspectives in family therapy are presented by Gerald Handel (1967). In his chapter entitled "Psychological Study of Whole Families," Handel emphasizes particularly Bell and Vogel's (1960) idea of "scapegoating" in families. Vogel and Bell have shown how the scapegoating of a child places him in a role which involves inconsistent expectations. Such a child and his parents are closely bound in a way which serves to mask any conflict between the parents. Proceeding from the fear of facing conflict between them, negative feelings are discharged through one of the children, who evolves a behavioral pattern which meshes with the scapegoating needs of the parents. In this situation the parents see themselves as victims of the child's difficult behavior, and the subsystem becomes self-perpetuating.

Handel's (1967) restatement of formulations offered by Hess and himself in 1959 apropos of family function are of interest. Their view has been that the primary issue in family life is one of working out "separateness" and "connectedness." Another central notion is that "behavior in a family may be viewed as the family's effort to attain a satisfactory congruence of images through the exchange of suitable testimony." They note that each family member's image of every other member and of himself is compounded of realistic and idealized components in various proportions. Cultural values, role expectations, and residues of experiences in each parent's respective family of origin all play into

this. A conception of others in the family is gradually developed, which then shapes one's action in relation to the other. "The image is one definition of the other as an object for one's own action or potential action." This borders upon the psychoanalytic view that archaic superego attitudes are projected upon each other in family relationships.

The congruence-of-images concept is of importance in the technique of family therapy, in which much of the therapeutic work involves airing and correcting these images. More recently, Westman et al. (1966) working in a child psychiatric clinical framework, has approached this using the terminology *inner identities, external identities,* and *subidentities* to designate action factors in family transactions. Hess and Handel, in the volume just referred to, also make much of the issue of "the family theme" as a unifying element in determining family behavior. It is often useful in the course of family interviews to help a family define a sense of its own unifying theme—i.e., to gain a view of itself in terms of goals, shared values, historical roots, etc. This is especially so when parents have not been able to consolidate this for themselves.

Handel and Hess elaborate on the issue of the "family's boundaries." The ways in which life-space is defined and experiences are filtered lead to a shared sense of boundaries. This is important for defining a historical-ethnic-social and economic understanding of a family. Its usefulness for clinical intervention is perhaps more as a guide for the therapist than as an explicit theme in the therapy.

Family typology is yet another outgrowth of family therapy. Various categorizations of families have occurred, but no classification scheme appears to have become a central one. Significantly, process rather than classification appears to be in the center of interest. Lidz's designation of "skewed" and "schismatic" families has already been alluded to. Families characterized by "pseudomutuality" and "pseudohostility" are described by Wynne and co-workers.

In a valuable annotated bibliography of articles on psychiatry and the family, edited by Haley and Glick and published by *Family Process* in 1965, the following types of families are designated, reflecting published papers:

Families with schizophrenia
Families with a retarded child
Families of a child with a school problem
Families with an adolescent problem child
Families with a delinquent
Families with neoneurosis
Families with psychosomatic disorder

Warren Brodey, in Ackerman et al. (1967), states: "Each family has its own kind of psychological movement, growth, and change signature . . . . We are constantly changing within a pattern that retains consistency enough so that other people can continue to recognize us." He offers a typology that is illustrative of his emphasis upon the issue of change. He designates the *static family,* the *responsive family,* and the *neutral family.* In the static family, a static equilibrium is maintained, and "if one tries to start something in this family by intervention, one will perhaps find that the family members can be budged just a little bit, but very soon they will return to where they were before, repeating, oscillating within the old structure."

Among the "responsive families," Brodey observes, the members seem to make changes quickly, although they may soon return to their earlier position; others, in response to great therapist pressure, seem to go through change but stop once the pressure is reduced. Brodey concludes, "the therapist must recognize that change is dependent, not on what he says, but on the fact that he has managed to ease the family out of its rut, a process in which he engages without worrying about the point to which the family will move. Essentially, one is engaged in producing change without necessarily directing it."

In regard to the "neutral family," Brodey observes that such families do not establish their own equilibrium but instead reflect what the therapist introduced.

What is important in Brodey's typology is the effort to encompass family systems as they relate to change rather than as they exist in a more temporal and structural-descriptive sense. His categories do not do much more than emphasize such an orientation, and in fact, they reflect some pessimism which may not be shared by most family therapists.

In the same volume, Boszormenyi-Nagy attempts to classify families in a way that reflects feelings they engender in him. He refers to *slippery families* and to *tough families.* In slippery families, members are poorly differentiated. "Their actions and their ways of referring to themselves always imply a we." Whenever the therapist thinks he has pinned them down on an issue, they "somehow slip away . . . . Yet these jelly-like people are quite intelligent when it comes to building up a defensive strategy against therapy."

In tough families, there may be much overt emotionality and conflict. Yet all this turns out to be a mask for basic failures of individuality. The rigid surface behaviors and roles cover up underlying confusion of individuation. "The 'good' members need and stimulate the 'bad' actions of the others; they live through each other vicariously."

Ackerman, in the same volume, concludes that the typing of families must respond to at least three levels of evaluation: "1) The family members' own self evaluations, images and diagnoses of life; 2) The therapist's way of experiencing that family with himself as an intervening agent; and 3) The way the community—either the extended family, the larger community, or both—has experienced and diagnosed the family."

Growing out of his work with families, which has been described by MacGregor et al. (1964), MacGregor has suggested four family types:

1. Schizophrenic—those presenting infantile functioning in an adolescent
2. Autocrats—those presenting childish functioning in an adolescent
3. Intimidated youth—those presenting juvenile functioning in an adolescent
4. Rebels—those presenting preadolescent functioning in an adolescent

MacGregor's typology is limited to using the behavior of adolescents in the family as an index of family maturity. This is a deceivingly simple formulation based on very complex conceptions of intrafamilial function. Implicit is a developmental orientation in which psychiatric illness is viewed as an arrest in the development of a family unit and a failure to adapt to maturational change in its offspring. "Family members interact in ways that require each to go on repetitively performing his function or role in the system." MacGregor sees this function as becoming a stalemate for developmental growth of certain individuals when it is reflective of the whole unit's failure to meet change. Thus an infantile adolescent is the result of a schizophrenic family group, an adolescent who functions "childishly" reflects an autocratic family group, etc. MacGregor's views, when one tries to extend them as a classification scheme, become somewhat difficult to apply since he notes that a family (presumably the parents) may function as one type in relation to one of the children and as another type in relation to a sibling. There tends to be a shifting of family function relative to the kinds of immaturity noted. Withal, he very well shows how in severely dysfunctional families, a relatively closed system is maintained which blocks

growth and individuation for each child in ways that follow fairly well-defined patterns.

A satisfying classification seems not yet at hand. Descriptive characterizations of families are everyday language among family therapists. These include such terms as *sick* families, *chaotic* families, *multiple-problem* families, *psychosomatic* families, *obsessional-compulsive* families, *regressive* families, *hostile* families, *timid* families, *cold* families, *warm* families, *depressed* families, *hypomanic* families, *sensitive* families, *violent* families, families with a sense of destiny, families with purpose, stable families, stable-unstable families, likable families, and difficult families. In Friedman et al. (1965), several family therapies are described, with euphemistic names offered for each. They are *The Island Family* (Jungreis & Speck), *The Rituell Family* (Jungreis & Speck), *The Oracle Family* (Boszormenyi-Nagy & Spivack), and *The Ichabod Family* (Sonne & Lincoln).

Therapists and Theories

Discussion of theory in this chapter has revolved about communication, resistance to change, homeostatic mechanisms, role function and complementarity of roles, and the various intrafamilial transactional dynamisms which reflect each of the above and which simultaneously represent "intrapsychic" functions for each family member.

Formulations about how theory and technique relate to each other are inevitably subject to the bias of the clinical reporter. These are issues that have often stirred acrimonious exchanges between psychotherapists. The relatively recent use of tape recordings of psychotherapy interviews and the even more recent use of one-way viewing windows and of audiovisual tapes have helped to clarify the relationship between theory and technique by making the therapeutic process observable and thereby subject to consensual review. Even so, questions of personal style and individual therapist need remain open variables.

Through clinical writings and demonstrated interviews, certain unifications of theoretical emphasis with technique have been presented by well-known family therapists. What appears to be common for all is an active effort to grapple with the resistance to change that is so pervasive in even "unstable" families. All family therapists agree that family therapy requires a considerable degree of therapist energy. This finds its theoretical expression in the conception of the family as an energy system which seeks to maintain a steady state and which requires the introduction of outside (therapist) energy to disrupt subsystems which maintain that steady, even if pathological, state.

A few characterizations. Nathan Ackerman, Donald Jackson, Jay Haley, Virginia Satir, John E. Bell, Carl Whitaker, Salvador Minuchin, Norman Paul, and a few others have emerged as prototype family therapists in the field, perhaps because of their ability to write about what they do with a combination of flair, integrity, and infectiousness. There are a growing number of descriptions of technique in the family-therapy literature which suggest how various clinicians work. Some of these are in the volumes edited by Alfred Friedman et al. (1965), Boszormenyi-Nagy and Framo (1965), Minuchin et al. (1967), and Ackerman, Beatman, and Sherman (1967), and in the *Casebook on Family Diagnosis and Treatment,* published by the Family Service Association of America (1965). Those therapists mentioned above have reproduced enough direct samples of interviews in films and transcriptions so that they provide templates for discussion of theory and technique. In *Techniques of Family Therapy,* edited by Jay Haley and Lynn Hoffman (1967), are transcriptions of single-session family interviews done, respec-

tively, by Fulweiler, Satir, Jackson, Whitaker, and Pittman, Flomenhaft, and De Young. Reproduced with these are running commentaries involving each of these therapists in turn and the editors (Haley & Hoffman), in which the therapists' actions in the therapy sessions are reviewed. In reading these transcriptions, one gains a vivid picture of the multidimensional process of family interviewing. The questions put to the therapists by the editors, and their answers, help define their theoretical frame of reference, although the intention of the book is not one of explicating theory.

Satir. Satir's interview technique moves quickly into inviting openness to affect. She uses questions such as "Who's hurting?" or "Where does the pain come from?" She is committed to the issue of helping each person experience "individuation," and she therefore makes sure each is drawn into the discussion at appropriate times. She repeatedly refers issues and observations back to the family as a group, with the idea that this forces them to become conscious of themselves as a "system." She draws out implicit family "rules." One example is in relation to silence in the family and what the unstated rules are relative to it. Over and over she rephrases or forces definitions in such a way as to make the family members stand outside of and become more perceiving of the meaning behind their "communications." She shares personal affect at times in order to teach the safety of this and to block denial and isolation. Satir seems to make very little use of role terminology in discussing her technique. She does gather a "family chronology" over several interviews, and she also forces implicit and unstated fantasies to the surface by overstating or exaggerating. The family interview as Satir does it is lively, and her presence is very much evident. She perceives herself as being an authoritative "administrator" in the meetings but does not see herself as running them. At times she introduces a change of roles by asking family members to act like someone else in the family.

Jackson. Like Satir, Jackson shows great care in involving each person in the family and defining a commitment to the mutual effort. He does this through patient, often provocative, questions but not through pedantic statements. Also as with Satir, Jackson works toward removing the stereotyped image the family members have of the designated patient and turns their attention from the patient to the family process and feelings. He notes that "even in family therapy I don't think you can focus on more than one person at a time." He demonstrates his ability to press each person to take seriously what someone else is saying and to attend to feelings. He disregards content in favor of responding to shifts in commentary or attention, which he conceives of in terms of maintaining or disrupting homeostasis. He does the same with nonverbal communication. At times he makes what appear to be educative comments to the family, but he views these as forcing them to pay attention to meaning behind their communications. He does not view his comments as providing the family members with "insight." At times he openly identifies with or seems to take the side of one member or another, as if to explain that person's position. At times he provokes one or the other to overt interaction with each other. One senses in Jackson's technique a finely drawn skill in manipulating family members into active interaction while his affective self remains somewhat more elusive than does Satir's. In his discussion of his technique he is surprisingly avoidant of the kind of theorizing that occurs in his papers.

Whitaker. Whitaker demonstrates a tendency to fairly quick confrontation of the family members with the contradictions in their behavior and their verbalized statements. He makes a demand of them to actively stand by or look into what they have said. In spite of the suggestion of toughness and sharply defined directness that comes through in his interviews, Whitaker evidences great flexibility and a readiness to back off if the resistance is too great. He states: "I see all therapy as expansion therapy, as leading fundamentally toward growth. The patient is up to the same thing I'm up to." This reveals that he feels very much a participant in a give-and-take experience. He quotes himself in one instance as stating to a family, "You're not desperate enough. You're not disturbed enough to really have a go at this thing." He views anxiety as "the motor that makes therapy move." Again, as with Satir and Jackson, he forces the issue of family responsibility in the endeavor and works so as to move them out of a passive inertia and a stereotyping of the named patient. Whitaker's commentary about his actions is relatively free of theorizing.

John E. Bell. Bell reviewed his family-therapy meetings with a Scotch family in a monograph published in 1961. This is a classic presentation of technique and process. Bell characterizes the phasic sequence of the series of meetings as "first conference," then "child-centered phase," "parent-child interaction," "father-mother interaction," "sibling interaction," and "termination phase."

In the *child-centered* phase, the therapist sets himself to building a relationship with the children. This phase may continue for several meetings. Bell as therapist offers support to the children's requests for changes in parental rules and action. He tends to ignore parental criticisms of the child. In the phase of *parent-child* interaction, Bell notes that the therapist needs still to be careful that the parents' angry complaints about the child do not disturb the child's sense of security in the sessions. It is his task to balance this. Intrafamilial interaction is difficult to maintain. Parents and children may resist this by slipping into talking *about* rather than *to* each other.

The phase of *father-mother interaction* brings problems of decision for the therapist related to protecting the parents' role as parents while at the same time encouraging open exploration of their conflicts. *Sibling interaction* occurs throughout the sessions.

Jay Haley. Haley has emphasized the view that family members enter into a struggle for control with the therapist (1963b). The therapist is put upon to devise stratagems—often on the spur of the moment within a given session—which will sidestep or deflate or "pull the rug out from under" the family's efforts to wrest authoritative control from him. Haley argues that the family comes to a therapist with the assumption that he is an authority. Mild-mannered egalitarian behavior on the therapist's part does not change the fact that he will be responded to as an authority. The family members will seek to undo his effectiveness out of their need to establish or retain a homeostatic state. Disequilibrium induced by the therapist is not easily tolerated because it is accompanied by profound anxiety. Family members may at times demonstrate pseudocompliance with the therapist, or even pseudohostility, may defer and demur, may try to envelop him in warmth or friendliness, etc. But each of these must be responded to by the therapist in such a way that the family turns back onto itself and is forced into genuine and appropriate communication with him and with one another. Clearly, this will often require difficult affective explosions, and the therapist needs to be able to ride these out long enough so that when his clarifying comments are made, there is an openness to them. The therapist's empathy and his tolerance of dysjunctive feeling provide a lasting demonstration to the family members that their exaggerated defenses against affect may be unnecessary.

Gerald Zuk. Zuk has reiterated a series of principles of procedure for family therapists which tend to be an extension of Haley's view

that the family struggles to keep control out of its resistance to disruption of homeostasis (1967). Zuk uses the somewhat unfortunate phrase the *go-between* to describe what he considers to be the necessary actions of a family therapist. Zuk defines the family-therapy technique as one which attempts to shift the balance of pathogenic relating among the family members so that new forms of relating become possible. He emphasizes that the requisite energy for shifting a fixed pattern of relationship is generated through the open conflict between family members.

In his go-between role, the therapist actively probes issues as they arise, defines conflicts, and encourages them. In doing this, he at times takes one person's side, then another's. He offers his support, or he becomes translator or apologist from time to time. Reactions to this may be in the form of pseudocompliance or pseudohostility or of such mechanisms as making him out a judge or throwing decisions to him —all of which are unwittingly aimed at distracting the therapist from upsetting the family equilibrium.

The therapist needs constantly to assign his own priorities to the conflicts he will catalyze or energize. He is therefore constantly restructuring the situation and, in terms of Zuk's *go-between* concept, "holding the purse" until a conflict becomes clarified.

His determination to understand and to hear someone out provides a new experience for many families. Zuk's view is that "families change in order to forestall the therapist's expected demands for much greater change or in order to foil his other attempts to control the relationship."

The quality of contest and battle implied in Zuk's statement may be an overemphasis, but family therapy is not a modality for a passive therapist orientation. It is indeed a procedure that requires constant alertness and a willingness to doggedly pursue, to confront, and to provoke,

but always out of empathic concern for the ultimate sensitivity that lies behind each person's
defenses.

THE PRACTICE OF FAMILY THERAPY

The Broader Compass

While family therapy viewed in the narrower
sense can simply be one of a variety of therapeutic modalities, used in an imaginative and
flexible fashion it reorganizes the framework within which psychotherapy is practiced. It can become the encompassing basis for diagnosis and
consultation as well as an integrative system of
clinical management. In his pioneer volume,
The Psychodynamics of Family Life (1958), Nathan Ackerman points out that in the course of
psychotherapy involving the whole family, a
variety of other interventions may be indicated:

> Thus a pattern of procedure evolves that is a
> flexible combination of individual psychotherapy
> and group psychotherapy, involving salient family
> pairs or threesomes or the entire family group. The
> planning of sessions with individuals and sessions
> with two or more family members must be discrimi-
> natingly timed in accordance with indications that
> derive from the active and flexible implementation
> of the principles of family diagnosis. From one
> stage of therapy to the next, as the balance of rec-
> iprocity in family role relations shifts and the focus
> of pathogenic disturbance moves from one part
> of the family to another, the therapist must be ready
> to institute corresponding shifts of the level of thera-
> peutic intervention into the family disturbance.

Diagnosis

The earlier references in this chapter to the
ways in which family therapy connects with clinical reality have relevance for diagnosis. Communication systems in the family, modes of affect
control and expression, collusive or symbiotic
or sadomasochistic pairings, schisms, masking,
pseudomutuality in a family, displacement, projection and externalization, confusion of role
functions, mutual regressions, scapegoating,

infantilization, guilt provocation, and innumerable other transactional phenomena all are grist
for the diagnostic family interview.

When the designated patient is a young child,
the diagnostic procedure must clarify the status
and nature of the child's dysfunction at the same
time that it assesses how the dysfunction reflects
aspects of the family system apropos of the child.
An estimation needs to be made of whether his
dysfunction represents defects in maturational
capacity, failure or lag in developmental progression, internalized (neurotic) conflict, or response to situational or parental or familial stress.
Each of these may be overlapping in some degree.
Anna Freud (1965) has provided a valuable outline of diagnostic criteria in her concept of *developmental guidelines.* Much of this kind of
evaluation can be accomplished in family interviews.

Ego functions. Defensive and coping processes
are evident from moment to moment during the
family exchanges. Language and other cognitive
functions can be assessed in a general way.
Modes of expressing and controlling affect are
observable. Motoric and perceptual skills can
often be noted. The level of fantasy organization and expression can be determined. Mental
mechanisms such as denial, projection, and intellectualization can be recognized during the
family interaction. The nature of the child's
identification with either parent, his level of
anxiety and hostility, and his tolerance for self-
perception can all be estimated. Much of this
occurs in the context of the verbal and nonverbal
transactions but also, in many cases, through
the unstructured use of play materials during the
session. The nature and quality of object relations are the essence of a family interview. Fluctuations of attitudes toward primary objects
(parents) can be seen *in situ.*

Drives. During the course of an interview, children often move to or away from one or the other
of the parents, press or rub against them, sit on

laps, touch body parts, posture, involve themselves in symbolic play with toys that runs parallel to and often directly reflects the ongoing discussion. The interviewer who is knowledgeable about the meaning behind such fleeting items of behavior in children can draw conclusions about the nature and level of the child's sexual and aggressive drives. It is not unusual to see a 4- or 5-year-old boy point a rubber-tipped dart gun at his father in the midst of a family discussion or to see a child of that age attempt to fondle mother's breasts or turn rear end up in a provocative fashion. Masturbatory excitation is often seen in the midst of some discussions. Regressive demands by the children for physical gratification often occur during an interview, and insight into what has been referred to earlier as "focal symbiosis" becomes possible since parental participation in the regression is observable.

Superego. Deals and bargaining between siblings or between the children and the parents often occur in an interview. Self-punitive gestures or remarks also reveal superego functions. Provocative acts that are sure to invite retaliation give evidence of distorted or overactive superego function, as do sudden bits of depressiveness. The ways in which parental sanctions and demands are transmitted are perhaps the most obvious content of family interviews, as is the "testing" behavior of children.

Ultimate objectives. Diagnostic evaluation is of practical use only to the degree that it leads to a clarification of what familial changes need to occur and what is necessary to bring them about. Understanding the way in which a family system may be perpetuating a developmental lag or a neurotic conflict leads to the introduction of measures that will neutralize this. When, for example, a serious marital conflict is found to be present, this may constitute a resistance to change which will require resolution before a child's dysfunction can be relieved. Often, however, a full resolution of the parental conflict

may not be practicable. However, the airing of it in the relative safety of the family diagnostic interviews objectifies the source of the anxiety that the child is experiencing. Great relief can occur if, as the parental conflict grows, the child is helped by the therapist to acknowledge what he feels about it. At these times his symptoms can be seen to improve. In the course of all this, it becomes possible to determine whether the parents are able to isolate their conflicts with each other from their interactions with the child. This is rarely an absolute possibility. If the parents can free the child from their problems with each other, the diagnostic process turns to estimating the child's ability to disengage himself from his involvement with them. The degree of developmental failure and/or of internalization of conflict that has occurred within him is observable in this way. If the latter is great, individual therapy is indicated. Again, absolute estimations are rarely possible. Diagnosis in family therapy, as in other therapy, is a process, not an event. Included in the process may be a variety of interventions—meeting with family pairs, with individuals, etc. Through all this, appropriate action evolves. Mordecai Kaffman, in a study of the uses of short-term family therapy (1963), concluded that decision about the appropriateness of family therapy as a treatment modality for a given family could be made only through an initial use of diagnostic family interviews. In the course of such interviews, the responsiveness of a family to this modality could be estimated. Other treatment alternatives were seen to be indicated in thirty-one out of seventy-five families studied.

An example from a first diagnostic interview follows:

> The participants were Mark, age 4, Betsy, 6, and both parents. Mark was "the patient" because of his persistent refusal to use the toilet. His parents were inclined to see this as willful since he showed no overt anxiety and seemed simply to turn his back

on their cajoling and urging and even their punishment. In the beginning of the session he removed himself to intense play with a train set while discussion went on between the therapist and his parents. (This very significant masculine interest was noted by the therapist but not commented upon.) Efforts to draw Mark into the discussion were met with quiet disconnection. His sister by contrast was much more outgoing and enthusiastic, similar to mother. Father was competent but retiring. Discussion eventually turned to specific issue of Mark's refusal to make bowel movements in the toilet. When therapist asked him if he disliked the "b.m. coming out," he quite directly said he did. When asked if he felt it to be "scary," he again agreed. Mother appeared pained. She commented on the pointlessness of her punishments if his whole problem was fear.

The therapist asked Mark if he had some idea about where babies came from. Mark firmly said he would have a baby when he gets big. Discussion ensued over whether boys or men can have babies and Betsy energetically assured Mark this was impossible. Mother said this whole subject had been gone into at home several months ago and she was dismayed to hear that Mark had not really accepted what he had been told. Therapist asked Mark where babies came out. Mark became uneasy and Betsy was more than happy to tell him they came from vaginas and that he did not have one. He listened carefully but insisted he did have one.

Therapist suggested some sculpting with Play-Doh and Betsy immediately made a figure with a penis and declared to Mark that was what he had. He vaguely disagreed and insisted he could some day have a baby. Therapist expressed open surprise that Mark would doubt he had a penis. Mother then commented that Betsy had at various times made it clear to Mark that she thought it was better to have babies than a penis.

Throughout all of this father, significantly, made no comment. He quickly agreed that Mark seemed to have a confusion of belief but he offered no elaboration of his feeling about this. The relative role reversal in the parents manifested by mother's dynamic vivacity and father's distance could be seen to be general determinants for Mark's wavering

gender identity. His sister's aggressive expression of penis envy was succeeding in overpowering Mark.

Most impressive about this family system was the mildness of the males and the retreating, withholding behavior of the father. Mark's developmental lag (feces retention) had become entangled with fantasies about the vulnerability of his penis and confusion about the relative merits of vaginas and penes. The specific source for this was his sister's castrative communication to him, which appeared to arise out of her frustration over her father's remoteness from her (and her mother). Mark's gender identity was wavering seriously, and his vivacious mother had become a fantasied castrative threat against whom he was defending himself with omnipotent fecal control, identifying in this way with his father. A focal symbiosis between Mark and his mother had evolved around anal function. In this regressive involvement, the mother's enormous frustration and helplessness with her husband were being masked. Her anger and perhaps her erotic needs and her guilt were all being absorbed through her involvement with Mark's symptom, which in turn kept her bound to him. Father acted out passive aggressive behavior toward her through his tacit acceptance of Mark's anal symptoms, which he knew made his wife angry and helpless. The latent and barely contained disequilibrium in the marriage was being compensated for in Mark's dysfunction. Had mother been inclined to continue her focal symbiotic involvement with Mark and to ignore her marital frustration, she would not have sought clinical help. Instead, her need to free herself from the ungratifying relationship with her husband brought her to the clinical situation, but her focus was on Mark. The diagnostic family sessions made it clear that Mark first needed buttressing of his phallic development. This occurred in a few individual sessions with him, and his mother soon reported more appropriate aggressive responses to his sister and other children. His fecal retention continued, however. It soon became clear that the major resistance to change in this family lay in the severe marital failure, which now became manifest. Overt arguments between the parents increased, and separation became a possibility. Out of this came the fact that father had indeed moved out twice in the past year, and Mark's symptom could now be understood in that context also.

If it becomes apparent that an extended series of family interviews promises to be of value, family therapy in the somewhat narrower sense of the term is begun. However, even a series of family interviews may be subject to flexible alternations with other procedures as resistances to change come to the fore. Some resistances may seem to be better met through individual or conjoint-pair sessions or through some device other than the whole family meeting. Parallel assignment of one or another family member to a standard group therapy may seem desirable. In some cases individual therapy with the child who came as "the patient" seems to be needed in addition to regular or sporadic family meetings.

Because the family meeting allows for assessment and reassessment of current need as it continually unfolds, it appears to this writer to offer the most encompassing framework for clinical management.

Audiovisual Taping

An important innovation in technique has been the use of audiovisual (A-V) tapes. Paul (1966) has described the effects of selective use of A-V tapes in activating repressed grief reaction. Perlmutter et al. (1967) have made use of selective playback of A-V tapes both for diagnosis and for therapy with families. They use it to demonstrate to a family how some of their communication patterns operate. Parents are required in this way to acknowledge the impact of nonverbal as well as verbal exchanges between them and their children. Therapists also have an opportunity to see how their own interventions affect communication in the family system. The authors observe that the playback often leads family members from an initial perceiving of their own actions to a more active effort to modify behavior.

Ian Alger, in a presentation of his use of A-V playback to a meeting of the Southern California Group Psychotherapy Association in 1967, demonstrated its use as a means for very active confrontation of rigidly defended family members who seem impervious to usual verbal commentary.

A-V technique promises a great deal, but it also stresses a clinical process because of the time necessary for planning and review. Also, it requires the presence of at least one technician so that the clinician's energies are not dissipated. It does sharpen the focus upon the family subsystems and how they operate.

SOME USES OF FAMILY THERAPY

The uses and applications of family therapy have become so varied that the following can do no more than provide a sampling. The categories used are simply for convenience of presentation.

Facilitating Development

From the *developmental* frame of reference, interviews with whole families offer a means for reducing resistances or barriers to the normal developmental progress of young children in the family. In the sessions parental anxieties are revealed, roles and identities are defined, and better parenting techniques evolve. The natural phases of ego development, including the emergence and encouragement of autonomy in its many facets as well as language and cognitive process, all require appropriate parental reinforcement. Failures of parenting arising out of marital conflict, disturbance in one or both parents, maturational lags in the child, or whatever may be understood and reduced in the course of a series of family meetings.

For young parents, participation in a few sessions in which a therapist points out the meaning behind their child's actions or verbalizations may lead to a long-term deepening of their understanding. With some parents, the mere demonstration of how to help their 3-year-old to focus attention or to stay with a task to completion in spite of his anxiety can be an enlightening experience. Clarifying with the parents their ambivalence about their child's aggressive behavior or his sexual curiosity may lead them to a deep reorganization of their feelings on several levels.

Failures of urinary or bowel training, excessive separation anxiety, timidity, failure to develop effective speech, phobic reactions, sleep disturbance, hyperactivity, aggressiveness, and severe sibling jealousy are all indications of a failure of even ego development. In more frankly pathological situations, severe parental ambivalence about a child or either covert or manifest interparental conflict may need to be dealt with. The presenting problems in the child and between the child and the parents may need to be met through a mixture of educative demonstration and interpretive commentary. A young child's behavioral response to interparental tensions is extremely rapid and can be pointed out as it occurs. This helps the parents disengage the child from the problems they are experiencing with each other. Where psychopathology in the parents is not rigidly organized around the child and when the symbiotic involvements are not overly intense and regressive, a few family interviews may bring clear-cut results. In many instances, however, the family meetings may be extended over many months, and in work that this writer has been associated with, they have been extended to two or three years.

The Department of Child Psychiatry at Cedars-Sinai Medical Center in Los Angeles has two therapeutic nursery schools associated with it. This has led staff to much involvement with family therapy in relation to the very young child. Reports of this work have been made by Augenbraun, Tasem, and Brown (1965), Augenbraun and Tasem (1966), and Brown (1966). Williams (1967a) discusses work in this same department oriented to brief educative family meetings which are aimed toward both a direct aid to the family and a consultative aid to the referring source.

Safer (1965) provides a clear outline or procedure and possibilities with young families.

Crisis

A collection of papers edited by Howard J. Parad includes several contributions related to families and crisis. Selection No. 4, "A Framework for Studying Families in Crisis," by Parad and Caplan, provides insight into the dimensions of a family crisis, the defenses employed by the family members, and the therapeutic challenge inherent in this. In this illustration a mother required extended hospitalization for pulmonary tuberculosis, which eventually led to meningitis and a near death. The authors analyze such intrafamilial factors as the family life style, the family values, the patterning of roles, the network of communication, and the problem-solving mechanisms and relate these to the situational stress. A profile of the crisis itself is drawn in terms of the time duration of the illness, the emotional tax placed upon each family member, the threat to long-term goals of the family, and the mobilization of intrapsychic problems in family members.

In this family, denial mechanisms took the form of humor used to depreciate tender feelings and of scapegoating aimed toward one of the siblings. A gradual evolution of more open acknowledgement of painful feelings by all family members is well described.

Unfortunately, examples of the verbal commentary made by the therapy-research personnel with the family are not given. But the ways in which family-therapy sessions can be of help in a major situational crisis become quite clear.

In another paper in this same volume, Lydia Rapoport describes work with eleven families, each in crisis around the event of a premature birth. The therapy included a variety of situational casework efforts on behalf of each of the families, in addition to family interviews per se. Again, technique of interviewing is omitted, but the case material suggests that in various instances all family members in the household were helped to work through the ambivalent feelings precipitated by the birth of a premature infant. These connected with the complications of hospitalization, the guilt residing in the parents over the event itself, and the interpersonal problems evolving from this. A crucial aspect of the clinical work was the encouragement of a modified mourning process. This example illustrates how complex certain familial crises can be and how the reverberations in each family member need to be met in order to forestall a chain of subsequent pathogenic reactions. Family interviews that allow each member to ventilate feelings and that also help clarify cognitive confusion about the event itself reduce the possibility for distortions of behavior that may derive from the situation. Intrafamilial acting out of guilt and anxiety in the form of provocations, displacements, isolation of feeling, projection, and scapegoating are thereby reduced. Working out of these in the family sessions is what is essential. A mere didactic or educational commentary is not enough.

Donald Langsley et al. (1968) provide a significant contribution to this whole subject. The focus of this extensive report is upon the clinical management of a series of seventy-five cases of acute psychosis through outpatient family therapy over a six-month period. This is balanced against the treatment of seventy-five cases in a six-month psychiatric hospitalization. The results show clearly that although outpatient family therapy in such instances may not be dramatically superior to carefully provided inpatient treatment, it is at least equally successful, and it is much less expensive. The designated patient in each of these instances was not a child. It is important to note, however, that an acute psychosis in one family member, especially a parent, has enormous circular impact upon the children. The use of family therapy at the time of such a crisis may provide the children with a crucial emotional experience. This has even greater significance if the psychotic person continues to live in the home, but it has applicability to the crises that occur when a family member treated by hospitalization returns home.

The concept of crisis in a family is elastic. Family therapy defined in this context might be equally well defined in some other context, such as family reaction to a retarded child, to a major illness in the family, to death, to separation and divorce, to adolescent turmoil. Approaches to each of these and many other possibilities have been described in the family-therapy literature. (See the References at the end of this chapter.) As noted earlier, Paul and Grosser have made significant contributions to understanding how failure in a family to work through grief and mourning in reaction to death may have long-term consequences. Paul (1966) has used selective playback of taped family interviews to activate a long-buried grief reaction in one of the members, with a resulting reduction of emotional isolation in the family. Jensen and Wallace (1967) note how recent object loss through death leads to a shift in role expectations for the family members. Thus not only is sharing of the grief experience itself of importance in such a family crisis intervention, but along with it there needs to be a working through of the changed family balance and the new role functions. Paul's emphasis upon empathy referred to earlier in this chapter is a crucial one in such a process. Each family member needs help to understand the others' experience.

Consultation and Demonstration

The family interview provides a medium for consultation within an ongoing clinical process. Augenbraun, Reid, and Friedman (1967) have described this in relation to pediatric practice. In several cases, a series of three family meetings held in response to the pediatrician's request led to the resolution of symptoms in a young child. The pediatrician was not present in these interviews.

Family interviews observed together by the whole staff of a clinic serve to weld the professional group together around common objectives. The subsequent discussion by the staff of their joint observation leads to a useful sharing of countertransference attitudes toward certain difficult families and to a more realistic definition of clinic responsibility and limitations in such cases.

Interviewing of family groups in the presence of other professionals who are rendering service to the children in the family can be very productive. In one section of the Department of Child Psychiatry at Cedars-Sinai Medical Center, this has become a major activity in relation to pre-school children with disturbances. Project Head Start personnel or standard nursery school teachers, pediatricians, and others are invited to be present at such interviews. Mutual planning evolves out of them. This can also be done with physicians in relation to illnesses and with teachers in special educational settings (Minuchin et al., 1967; Brown, 1968). Various professionals, such as probation workers, public health nurses, and outside caseworkers, can also be involved in joint family interviews for the sake of clarifying objectives and problems.

Brief Therapy

In general, the duration of family therapy as it is described in most outpatient settings tends to be relatively brief. Kaffman's paper "Short Term Family Therapy," published in 1963, provides a definitive description of treatment organized through a series of ten sessions. Based upon initial family interviews, twenty-nine out of a group of seventy families seemed suitable for the planned series of ten family meetings. Symptoms of the children of these twenty-nine cases included phobic reactions, chronic night fears, separation anxiety, hyperaggressiveness, and long-lasting enuresis and encopresis. In twenty of the twenty-nine cases, the symptoms were of long duration. The results were that in ten of the cases a total symptomatic improvement occurred, in none were symptoms aggravated, and in three-fourths there was a definitive improvement. The families were told from the beginning that there would be a limit of ten meetings. The participants in these meetings varied from week to week, according to therapist decision. The length of each session was not rigidly limited to one hour. It is important to note that of the seventy families interviewed, only twenty-nine seemed suitable for the brief family treatment. This is pointed out in order to neutralize any impression that family therapy is the procedure of choice in most cases. Kaffman emphasizes, however, that selection of cases suitable for such a procedure cannot be made a priori but needs to be made on the basis of initial diagnostic family interviews. These provide a more reliable indicator than does a formal history or a diagnosis.

A report by Markenson, Emerson, Barry, and Nolan at the American Orthopsychiatric Association meeting in 1966 described a high success rate in reducing symptoms in fifty families that they treated. In these instances, the families were seen for three or four sessions, beginning within one month of application. Sessions were spaced two, four, and six weeks apart. The child's symptoms were found to be better in 63 percent of the families in the 6-month follow-ups.

The school reports showed a 55 percent improvement.

Safer (1966) has reported on "short-term therapy" with twenty-nine children showing behavior disorders. Most of these were low-socioeconomic "multiproblem" families. A great deal of active focusing was done with these families in relation to chores, discipline, locus of authority, etc. Trial changes in family actions were suggested. When parent behavior began to change, new problems were seen to emerge requiring conjoint marital sessions, encouragement of extrafamilial activities, etc. Of the twenty-nine families, eleven discontinued after one or two sessions. With the remaining eighteen, the average number of meetings was eight. In follow-up 4 to 16 months after termination, twelve of the twenty-nine showed successful outcomes. Five showed no change, and six showed some improvement. Three showed partial improvement, and three were unrelated.

Adolescence

A growing number of reports describe work with behavioral disorders of adolescence. Robert Counts (1967) emphasizes that the precarious equilibrium of the adolescent and the peculiar form in which his conflicts emerge revive old parental conflicts, which now become masked in the family through scapegoating or through unwitting provocation of the adolescent. The very behavior that is characteristic of adolescence invites this from parents. Also, the sexuality of the adolescent provokes reactions in the parents. Some of this is amenable to clarification and modification through family meetings.

Donner and Gamson (1968) report their efforts with randomly selected teenagers in a community psychiatry clinic. In their contact with families, they note a characteristic initial stage of sullenness on the part of the adolescents and open anger in the parents. An evolution occurs in the course of several sessions, during which

there may be frank and even violent confrontations. A stage of warmth supersedes. The authors note the great importance of keeping the fathers involved in the sessions.

A brief but intensive therapy program with adolescents was described by Goolishian (1962). This same program was more elaborately reported by MacGregor et al. (1964). The clinical work was done at the University of Texas, Galveston. A 2- to 3-day intensive process was provided in which the whole family was asked to participate. Meetings with various segments of the family were flexibly interlaced in such a way as to introduce an intensive process of exchange and to maximize those transactions which might lead to an alteration of the family system. A therapy team, rather than a single therapist or a pair of therapists, participated in each case.

Involvement of parents in the treatment of hospitalized adolescents has been described by Rinsley and Hall in 1962. The complexity of inpatient treatment is seen to require appropriate working through of the family and staff interactions so as to avoid the confusions that so commonly arise around inpatient treatment of adolescents.

The current writer has participated in a variety of family efforts with families of adolescents and has consulted in several clinical centers in the southern California area that now make use of family therapy. Generalizations about procedure and result are extremely difficult since procedure varies, as does socioeconomic background and the kinds of dysfunctions dealt with. As noted in the first section of this chapter, the expectations a family brings to the therapy situation are of major significance. Upper-middle-class families with much psychological sophistication enter into such interviews with eagerness and often with fairly immediate success when the problem is one of general adjustment, role transition, separation-individuation, etc. The adolescents in such families are often open to the experience, although very shortly they evolve to a desire for therapy away from their parents. Where the adolescent has become a "scapegoat," however, and the parents are in a strong collusion, family sessions move very slowly. Indeed, as the parents become faced with their own covert anxiety, their resistance often leads them to discontinue the process. In some cases the scapegoated adolescent can be seen to almost determinedly resume his provocative behavior, as if to protect the parents from their anxiety. On the other side of the scapegoat coin, one finds a self-sacrificing lamb.

In the less pathogenic situations the opportunity the adolescent finds in telling feelings to his parents without danger of immediate suppression offers relief to him. Also, understanding of the parental dilemmas leads to toleration of frustration and limitations. With delinquent adolescents, on the other hand, movement is slow and requires a fairly extended initial phase during which trust of the therapist needs to be welded. The very explosiveness of the situation makes this difficult.

The sheer power of a narcissistic, infantile adolescent to aggravate and stir up his family places the family therapy in some jeopardy. Relative degrees of success are not uncommon, however. In the writer's observation, a few months of family therapy need to be followed by many months of additional help for the adolescent alone and for the parents. Not infrequently, one or another sibling reveals depression or anxiety and requires help.

The Low-socioeconomic Population

The use of family interviews and therapy in *lower-socioeconomic groups* has been reported in various publications. The most comprehensive of these is the recent volume *Families of the Slums: An Exploration of Their Structure and Treatment* (1967). Minuchin and his colleagues demonstrate the use of family interviews as a means for opening up and refining perception and communication of feelings and for helping family members to perceive and to attend to a variety of perceptual and cognitive experiences have been of great significance for those who work with this population group. Some of their techniques find applicability to other kinds of families as well. Minuchin and his colleagues have attempted to work with families through active manipulation of the structure of the therapy sessions (Minuchin, Auerswald, King, & Rabinowitz, 1964). They separate segments of the family, often the parents, and bring them to an observation room, leaving the children to interact alone. Parents' reactions to how the children interact are then responded to by the therapist who is with the parents. Also, specific tasks oriented toward the development of focal attention may be introduced. In the families they have worked with, members need to experience listening to each other and need opportunities to formulate and fully verbalize a reaction or an observation. Techniques for doing this require an educational orientation in which very limited goals may be set from one session to the next.

The phases described are:

    I. Induction and entry into the family system
   II. Therapeutic work with the family system
  III. Disengagement and solidifying of the family's autonomy

Phase I required occasions on which the therapists made themselves available to the family in concrete active ways, such as carrying out personal services for them. The authors state: "There were times when we incurred the family's anger, but we were willing to back up our value systems against their delinquent ones. We taught, intervened, showed affection. We were committed to the family's well-being."

Others working with this population group have emphasized the value of home visits. R. A.

Levine (1964) provides a valuable review of this. Charles Hersh (1968) reports on his work with multiproblem families and refers to the use of home visits and the importance of focusing upon concrete issues.

Sager, Masters, Ronall, and Norman (1968) describe their work during 1966 and 1967 in a psychiatric walk-in clinic in a low-socioeconomic area. They define *engagement* as occurring when the patient and his family came for at least six sessions. Of 157 patients seen for screening, 50 percent were asked to participate in family sessions. Seventy-five percent of these did so and became "engaged."

Home Visits

The use of home visits in family therapy has been described by various clinicians. R. V. Speck (1964) designated fourteen reasons for going into the home setting. Much of his work has been with schizophrenic patients. He has described very well how the movement in the household during family sessions has its own major communicative power. Also, the importance of pets in sessions at home has been described.

R. Fisch (1964) has described his home visits as a part of private practice. Egan and Robison (1966) have given a detailed description of their use of home visits.

Psychosomatic Problems

Not much has been reported of family therapy around psychosomatic problems, even though these would appear to invite such an intervention. Complexity of arranging this and the well-known resistance those with psychosomatic disorders show to psychological approaches may be factors. The dangers of precipitating somatic symptoms tend to limit the effort. Titchener, Riskin, and Emerson (1960) reported their work in a case of ulcerative colitis. The current writer's experience has been with one case of a 14-year-old girl with recurrent regional ileitis and a school phobia. In the family meetings, an intense focal symbiotic tie between father and daughter became revealed. This had been masked for many years by the more manifest dependency manipulations by the daughter of her mother occurring around the somatic illness. Family sessions and ancillary group therapy for mother helped her to disengage from her ambivalent overprotection of her daughter. Daughter's symptoms became even more severe, however, and father and daughter's deep alliance then became evident. This brought resistance to further therapeutic intervention.

Tips and Lynch (1963) report on their use of family meetings. In their provocative paper, they review the great importance of involving a whole family in interviews relative to the possibility of genetic disorders occurring in the offspring. Tips and Lynch are not family therapists, but their grasp of its applicability in medicine is impressive.

Learning Disorders

Robert Friedman described "A Structured Family Interview in the Assessment of School Learning Disorders" at the American Orthopsychiatric Association meeting in 1968. In a single session he looks for "operational resultants" rather than for underlying psychodynamics. He has been able to discern fairly specific factors which appear to perpetuate the learning block. In fifty-three such interviews, oriented toward the learning problem per se, he observed double-bind messages, encouragement or permission to fail, inadequate parent models apropos of learning, confused communications in response to achievement, disagreement between parents, and overexpectations of the child. In formulating these, possibilities for specific action with the family apropos of the learning problem became possible. His experience suggests that with some families such issues may be dealt with quite directly. With others, a variety of educational and clinical interventions may be needed. These may include individual therapy for the child, extended family therapy, and tutorial work. The family interview provides an opportunity for defining what needs to follow.

Messer (1964) has described the use of family therapy in a school-phobic child. This is a detailed description of a two-year therapy.

Minuchin's description of specific educational approaches with families of low-socioeconomic children has been noted. Miller and Westman (1964) have described several families in which the existence of a long-term and major learning disorder in an adolescent has served profound dynamic purposes for the family. Their cases illustrate the great potential for decompensation in one of the parents when a learning disorder in the child begins to improve. This suggests the importance of family therapy along with any specific approach to a chronic learning disorder.

Character Disorders

A report by Cutter and Hallowitz (1962) describes family interviews in relation to fifty-six children with such diagnoses. Behavioral descriptions include generalized immaturity; egocentricity; weak ego controls manifested by stealing, fire setting, sex play, and destructiveness; poor superego function; enuresis; hypochandriasis; and poor school social adjustment. Most of the children were between ages 12 and 16, and 80 percent were boys. All had shown symptoms for at least two years. Sixty-six percent were from skilled, white-collar, or professional families. Family therapy was flexible. In some cases, the process was brief; in others, it covered many months. Intercurrent crises during the course of therapy were common. Direct interventions were often required with court, school, or police. Improved familial communication became the guide for the therapists. In some instances characterological changes in

individuals and reorganization of the marital dynamics occurred, but these were not the major therapeutic objective. Sixty percent showed "good progress," and 15 percent "none."

Multiple Family Therapy

Laquer, LaBurt, and Marong (1964) have described their method for bringing families together in therapy groups. Laquer and LaBurt (1964) have shown the ways in which family groups can be meaningfully involved with ward activities in a hospital.

Davies et al. (1966) have described meetings with several families in the context of a psychiatric day center.

Landes and Winter (1966) describe the evolution of a program in a residential treatment center in which visiting families were brought into therapeutic interaction with each other on scheduled visiting days. The authors use the term "communal family therapy" to describe the flexible but very active program built around family weekend visits to the ranch where the center is located.

REFERENCES

Ackerman, N. W. The unity of the family. *Archives of Pediatrics,* 1938, **55,** 51–62.

Ackerman, N. W. *The psychodynamics of family life.* New York: Basic Books, 1958.

Ackerman, N. W. Family focussed therapy of schizophrenia. In S. C. Scher & H. R. Davis (Eds.), *The outpatient treatment of schizophrenia.* New York: Grune & Stratton, 1960. Pp. 156–173.

Ackerman, N. W. Family psychotherapy and psychoanalysis: The implications of a difference. *Family Process,* 1962, **1,** 30–43. (a)

Ackerman, N. W. Adolescent problems. A symptom of family disorder. *Family Process,* 1962, **1,** 202–213. (b)

Ackerman, N. W. *Treating the troubled family.* New York: Basic Books, 1966.

Ackerman, N. W., Beatman, F., & Sherman, S. *Exploring the base for family therapy.* New York: Family Service Association of America, 1961.

Ackerman, N. W., Beatman, F., & Sherman, S. (Eds.) *Expanding theory and practice in family therapy.* New York: Family Service Association of America, 1967.

Ackerman, N. W., & Behrens, M. L. The family group and family therapy: The practical application of family diagnosis. In J. H. Masserman & J. L. Moreno (Eds.), *Progress in psychotherapy.* Vol. 3. New York: Grune & Stratton, 1959.

Ackerman, N. W., & Sobel, R. Family diagnosis: An approach to the preschool child. *American Journal of Orthopsychiatry,* 1950, **20,** 744–753.

Alexander, F. Unexplored areas in psychoanalytic theory and practice. In *The scope of psychoanalysis.* New York: Basic Books, 1961. Part II.

Alexander, I. E. Marriage and family living. *Family Therapy,* 1963, **25,** 146–154.

Allen, F. *Psychotherapy with children.* New York: Norton, 1942.

Augenbraun, B., & Tasem, M. Differential techniques in family interviewing with both parents and preschool child. *Journal of the American Academy of Child Psychiatry,* 1966, **5**(4), 721–730.

Augenbraun, B., Tasem, M., & Brown, S. L. Family group interviewing with the preschool child and both parents. *Journal of the American Academy of Child Psychiatry,* 1965, **4**(2), 330–340.

Bateson, G., Jackson, D. D., Haley, J., & Weakland, J. Toward a theory of schizophrenia. *Behavioral Science,* 1956, **1,** 251–264.

Bell, J. E. Family group therapy. *Public Health Monograph,* U. S. Department of Health, Education and Welfare, No. 64, 1961.

Bell, J. E. Recent advances in family group therapy. *Journal of Child Psychology and Psychiatry,* 1962, **3,** 1–15.

Bell, N. W., & Vogel, E. F. (Eds.), *A modern introduction to the family.* Glencoe, Ill.: Free Press, 1960.

Belmont, L. P., & Jasnow, A. The utilization of co-therapists and of group therapy techniques in a family oriented approach to a disturbed child. *International Journal of Group Psychotherapy,* 1961, **11,** 319–328.

Benedek, T. Parenthood as a developmental phase: A contribution to the libido theory. *Journal of the American Psychoanalytic Association,* 1959, **7,** 389–417.

Boszormenyi-Nagy, I. Intensive family therapy as process. In I. Boszormenyi-Nagy and J. L. Framo (Eds.), *Intensive family therapy: Theoretical and practical aspects.* New York: Harper & Row, 1965.

Boszormenyi-Nagy, I., & Framo, J. L. (Eds.) *Intensive family therapy: Theoretical and practical aspects.* New York: Harper & Row, 1965.

Bowen, M. Family psychotherapy. *American Journal of Orthopsychiatry,* 1961, **31,** 40–60.

Bowen, M. The use of family theory in clinical practice. *Comprehensive Psychiatry,* 1967, **7,** 345–374.

Bowen, M., Dysinger, R. H., & Basamania, B. The role of the father in families with a schizophrenic patient. *American Journal of Psychiatry,* 1957, **115,** 117–120.

Brodey, W. M. Some family operations and schizophrenia: A study of five hospitalized families each with a schizophrenic member. *Ar-*

chives of General Psychiatry, 1959, **1,** (4), 379–402.

Brodey, W. M. *Changing the family.* New York: Clarkson Potter, 1968.

Brody, S. Simultaneous psychotherapy of married couples. In J. Masserman (Ed.), *Current psychiatric therapies.* New York: Grune & Stratton, 1961. Pp. 139–144.

Brown, S. L. Clinical impressions of the impact of family group interviewing on child and adolescent psychiatric practice. *Journal of the American Academy of Child Psychiatry,* 1964, **3,** (4), 688–696.

Brown, S. L. Family therapy viewed in terms of resistance to change. In I. M. Cohen (Ed.), *Psychiatric Research Reports of the American Psychiatric Association,* 1966, No. 20.

Brown, S. L. Coordinating professional efforts for children with school problems. *Children,* 1968, **15,** (6), 214–218.

Carek, D. J., & Watson, A. S. Treatment of a family involved in fratricide. *Archives of General Psychiatry,* 1964, **11,** (5), 533–542.

Carroll, E. J. Treatment of the family as a unit. *Pennsylvania Medical Journal,* 1960, **63,** (11), 56–62.

Carroll, E. J. General systems theory and psychotherapy. *Current Psychiatric Therapies,* 1966, **6,** 8–12.

Carroll, E., Cambor, C., Leopold, J., Miller, M., & Reis, W. Psychotherapy of marital couples. *Family Process,* 1963, **3,** 25–33.

Casebook on family diagnosis and treatment. New York: Family Service Association of America, 1965.

Caudill, W. F., Redlich, C., Gilmore, H., & Brody, E. Social structure and interaction processes on a psychiatric ward. *American Journal of Orthopsychiatry,* 1952, **22,** (2), 314–334.

Charny, E. J. Context of analysis of family interactions. Paper presented at the American Orthopsychiatric Association meeting, Washington, D.C., March, 1967.

Charny, I. W. Integrated individual and family psychotherapy. *Family Process,* 1966, **5,** (2), 179–198.

Clower, C. G., & Brody, L. Conjoint family therapy in outpatient practice. *American Journal of Psychotherapy,* 1964, **18,** 670–677.

Cohen, I. M. (Ed.) *Family structure, dynamics and therapy. Psychiatric Research Reports of the American Psychiatric Association,* 1966, No. 20.

Coolidge, J. Asthma in mother and child as a special form of communication. *American Journal of Orthopsychiatry,* 1956, **26,** 165–178.

Counts, R. Family crisis and the impulsive adolescent. *Archives of General Psychiatry,* 1967, **17,** 1–7.

Coyle, G. L. Concepts relevant to helping the family as a group. *Social Casework,* 1962, **43,** (7), 347–354.

Cutter, A. V., & Hallowitz, S. Diagnosis and treatment of the family unit with respect to the character disordered youngster. *Journal of the Academy of Child Psychiatry,* 1962, **1,** (4), 605–618.

Curry, A. E. The family therapy situation as a system. *Family Process,* 1966, 5(2), 131–141.

Davies, J., Ellenson, G., & Young, R. Therapy with a group of families in a psychiatric day center. *American Journal of Orthopsychiatry,* 1966, **36,** (1), 134–135.

Donner, J., & Gamson, A. Multifamily, time-limited outpatient groups. *Psychiatry,* 1968, **31**(2).

Drechsler, R. J., & Shapiro, M. I. A procedure for direct observation of family interaction in a child guidance clinic. *Psychiatry,* 1961, **24,** (2), 163–170.

Dreikurs, R. Family group therapy in the Chicago Community Child Guidance Center. *Mental Hygiene,* 1951, **35,** (2), 291–301.

Egan, M., & Robison, O. Home treatment of severely disturbed children and families. *American Journal of Orthopsychiatry,* 1966, **36,** (4), 730–735.

Epstein, N. B., & Westley, W. A. Patterns of intrafamilial communication. In D. E. Cameron & M. Greenblatt (Eds.), *Psychiatric Research Reports,* 1959, **11,** 1–12.

Ferreira, A. Decision making in normal and pathologic families. *Archives of Genetic Psychiatry,* 1963, **8,** 68–73.

Ferreira, A. Interpersonal reception among family members. *American Journal of Orthopsychiatry,* 1964, **34,** 64–70.

Ferreira, A. Family myths. In I. M. Cohen (Ed.), *Family structure, dynamics and therapy. Psychiatric Research Reports of the American Psychiatric Association,* 1966, No. 20, 85–90.

Ferreira, A., & Winter, W. D. Stability of interactional variables in family decision-making. *Archives of General Psychiatry,* 1966, **14,** (4), 352–355.

Ferreira, A., & Winter, W. D. Decision-making in normal and abnormal two child families. *Family Process,* 1968, **7,** 17–36.

Fisch, R. Home visits in a private psychiatric practice. *Family Process,* 1964, **3,** 114–126.

Fox, R. The effect of psychotherapy in the spouse. *Family Process,* 1968, **7,** (1).

Freud, A. *Normality and pathology in child-hood.* New York: International Universities Press, 1965.

Friedman, A. S., Boszormenyi-Nagy I., Jungreis, J. E., Lincoln, G., Mitchell, H. E., Sonne, J. C., Speck, R. V., & Spivack, G. *Psychotherapy for the whole family.* New York: Spring Publishers, 1965.

Friedman, R. A structured family interview in the assessment of school learning disorders. Paper presented at the 45th annual meeting of the American Orthopsychiatric Association, Chicago, March, 1968.

Friend, M. R. The historical development of family diagnosis. Proceedings of the conference on family diagnosis, Chicago, 1960. *Social Science Review,* 34 (1), 2–16.

Flugel, J. C. *The psychoanalytic study of the family.* London: Hogarth, 1921.

Gehrke, S., & Moxom, J. Diagnostic classifications and treatment techniques in marriage counseling. *Family Process,* 1962, **1,** 253–264.

Geist, J., & Gerber, N. Joint interviewing: A treatment technique with marital partners. *Social Casework,* 1960, **41,** 76–83.

Goldberg, F., Lesser, S., & Schulman, R. A conceptual approach and guide to formulating goals in child guidance treatment. *American Journal of Orthopsychiatry,* 1966, **36,** 125–133.

Gomberg, M. R. Family diagnosis: Trends in theory and practice. *Social Casework,* 1958, **39,** (2–3), 73–83.

Goolishian, H. A brief psychotherapy program for disturbed adolescents. *American Journal of Orthopsychiatry,* 1962, **32,** 142–148.

Greenacre, P. On focal symbiosis. In L. Jessner & E. Pavenstedt (Eds.), *Dynamic psychopathol-*

ogy in childhood. New York: Grune & Stratton, 1959.

Greenberg, I. M., Glick, I., Match, S., & Riback, S. Family therapy: Indications and rational. *Archives of General Psychiatry,* 1964, **10,** (1), 7–24.

Greenson, R. *The technique and practice of psychoanalysis.* Vol. 1. New York: International Universities Press, 1967.

Grotjahn, M. *Psychoanalysis and family neurosis.* New York: Norton, 1960.

Group for the Advancement of Psychiatry. *Basic concepts in child psychiatry. Report No.* 12, 1950.

Group for the Advancement of Psychiatry. *The diagnostic process in child psychiatry.* Report No. 38, 1957.

Grunebaum, M. G. A study of learning problems of children: Casework implications. *Social Casework,* 1961, **42** (9),

1

Haley, J. Whither family therapy. *Family Process,* 1962, **1,** 69–100.

Haley, J. Marriage therapy. *Archives of General Psychiatry,* 1963, **8,** 213–234.(a)

Haley, J. *Strategies of psychotherapy.* New York: Grune & Stratton, 1963.(b)

Haley, J., & Hoffman, L. (Eds.) *Techniques of family therapy.* New York: Basic Books, 1967.

Hallowitz, D., & Stulberg, B. The vicious cycle in parent-child relationship breakdown. *Social Casework,* 1959, **40,** 268–275.

Hamilton, G. *Psychotherapy in child guidance.* New York: Columbia, 1947.

Handel, G. (Ed.) *The psychosocial interior of the family: A source-book for the study of whole families.* Chicago: Aldine, 1967.

Handlon, V. H., & Parloff, M. B. The treatment of patient and family as a group: Is it group psychotherapy? *International Journal of Group Psychotherapy,* 1962, **12,** 132–141.

Hess, R. D., & Handel, G. The family as a psychosocial organization. In G. Handel (Ed.), *Psychosocial interior of the family.* Chicago: Aldine, 1967.

Hersch, C. Child guidance service to the poor. *Journal of the American Academy of Child Psychiatry,* 1968, **7** (2), 223–229.

Howells, J. G. Extra interview therapy in family psychiatry. *Public Health,* 1963, **77** (6), 368–372.

Hubbard, R., & Adams, C. Factors affecting success of child guidance clinic treatment. *American Journal of Orthopsychiatry,* 1936, **6,** 81–102.

Jackson, D. D. Family interaction, family homeostasis, and some implications for conjoint family psychotherapy. In J. Masserman (Ed.), *Science and psychoanalysis.* Vol. 2. New York: Grune & Stratton, 1959.

Jackson, D. D., & Satir, V. A review of psychiatric development in family diagnosis and therapy. In N. Ackerman, F. Beatman, & S. Sheim, (Eds.), *Exploring the base for family therapy.* New York: Family Service Association of America, 1961.

Jensen, G., & Wallace, J. G. Family mourning process. *Family Process,* 1967, **6** (1), 56–65.

Johnson, A. M., & Szurek, S. A. The genesis of antisocial acting out in children and adults. *Psychoanalytic Quarterly,* 1952, **21,** 323–343.

Josselyn, I. M. The family as a psychological unit. *Social Casework,* 1953, **34,** 336–343.

Kaffman, M. Short-term family therapy. *Family Process,* 1963, **2** (2), 216–234.

Kemph, J., Harrison, S., & Finch, S. Promoting the development of ego functions in the middle phase of treatment of psychotic children. *Journal of the Academy of Child Psychiatry,* 1965, **4** (3).

Kerdman, L., & Cooper, B. An experimental approach to treatment of an adolescent delinquent girl: Family therapy and the use of two therapists in court referred service. Paper presented at the 43rd meeting of the American Orthopsychiatric Association, New York, April, 1966.

Kolansky, H. Treatment of a three-year old girl's severe infantile neurosis: Stammering and insect phobia. Vol. 15. *The psychoanalytic study of the child.* New York: International Universities Press, 1960. Pp. 261–285.

Kwiatkowska, H. Family art therapy. *Family Process,* 1967, **6**(1), 37–55.

Landes, J., & Winter, W. A new strategy for treating disintegrating families. *Family Process,* 1966, **5** (1), 1–17.

Langsley, D., Pittman, F., Mochatka, P., & Flomenhaft, K. Family crisis therapy: Results and implications. *Family Process,* 1968, **7** (2), 145–158.

Laquer, H. General systems theory and multiple family therapy. In J. Masserman (Ed.), *Current psychiatric therapies,* New York: Grune & Stratton, 1968.

Laquer, H., & LaBurt, H. Family organization in a modern state hospital ward. *Mental Hygiene,* 1964, **48,** 544–551.

Laquer, H., LaBurt, H., & Marong, E. Multiple family therapy. In J. Masserman (Ed.), *Current psychiatric therapies.* New York: Grune & Stratton, 1964. Pp. 150–164.

Lehrman, N. S. The joint interview: An aid to psychotherapy and family stability. *American Journal of Psychotherapy,* 1963, **17,** 83–94.

Lennard, H., Beaulieu, M., & Embrey, N. Interaction in families with a schizophrenic child. *Archives of General Psychiatry,* 1965, **12** (2), 166–183.

Levine, R. A. Treatment in the home: An experiment with low income, multiproblem families. In F. Riessman, J. Cohen, & A. Pearl (Eds.), *Mental health of the poor: New treatment approach for low income people.* New York: Free Press, 1964. Pp. 329–335.

Lewin, K. Behavior and development as a function of the total situation. In L. Carmichael (Ed.), *Manual of child psychology.* New York: Wiley, 1954. Chap. 15.

Lidz, T., Cornelison, A., Fleck, S., & Terry, D. Intrafamilial environment of the schizophrenic patient. I: The father. *Psychiatry,* 1957, **20,** 329–342. (a)

Lidz, T., Cornelison, A., Fleck, S., & Terry, D. Intrafamilial environment of schizophrenic patients. II: Marital schism and marital skew. *American Journal of Psychiatry,* 1957, **114,** 241–248. (b)

Lidz, T., Ginelison, A., Carlson, D. T., & Fleck, S. Intrafamilial environment of the schizophrenic patient: The transmission of irrationality. *Archives of Neurology and Psychiatry,* 1958, **79** (3), 305–316.

Lidz, T., & Fleck, S. Schizophrenic human integration and the role of the family. In D. D. Jackson (Ed.), *Etiology of schizophrenia.* New York: Basic Books, 1960. Pp. 323–345.

MacGregor, R., Ritchie, A., Serrano, A., Schuster, F., McDonald, E., & Goolishian, H. *Multiple impact therapy with families.* New York: McGraw-Hill, 1964.

Markenson, D., Emerson, R., Barry, R., & Nolan, R. A follow-up investigation of family group consultation as a primary child guidance clinic service. Reported at the 43rd meeting of the American Orthopsychiatric Association, Washington, D.C., April, 1966.

Meissner, W. W. Thinking about the family: Psychiatric aspects. *Family Process*, 1964, **3**, 1–40.

Menzies, M., Bedlek, S., & McRae, O. An intensive approach to brief family diagnosis in a child guidance clinic. *Canadian Psychiatric Association Journal*, 1961 **6**, (5), 295–298.

Messer, A. Family treatment of a school phobic child. *Archives of General Psychiatry*, 1964, **11** (5), 548–555.

Midelfort, C. F. *The family in psychotherapy*. New York: McGraw-Hill, 1957.

Miller, D. R., & Westman, J. C. Reading disability as a condition of family stability. *Family Process*, 1964, **3**, 66–75.

Miller, D. R., & Westman, J. C. Family teamwork and psychotherapy. *Family Process*, 1966, **5**, 49–59.

Minuchin, S. Family structure, family language, and the puzzled therapist. *American Journal of Orthopsychiatry*, 1964, **34**, 347–358.

Minuchin, S. Conflict resolution in family therapy. *Psychiatry*, 1965, **28**, 278–286.

Minuchin, S. Psychoanalytic therapies and the low socio-economic population. In J. Marmor (Ed.), *Modern psychoanalysis*. New York: Basic Books, 1968.

Minuchin, S., Auerswald, E., King, C., & Rabinowitz, C. The study and treatment of families who produce multiple acting out boys. *American Journal of Orthopsychiatry*, 1964, **34**, 125–133.

Minuchin, S., Montalvo, B., Guerney, B., Rosman, B., & Schumer, F. (Eds.) *Families of the slums: An exploration of their structure and treatment*. New York: Basic Books, 1967.

Mitchell, C. B. The use of family sessions in the diagnosis and treatment of disturbance in children. *Social Casework*, 1960, **41** (6), 283–290.

Mittleman, B. Complementary neurotic reactions in intimate relationships. *Psychoanalytic Quarterly*, 1944, **13**, 479–491.

Moustakas, C. E. *Children in play therapy*. New York: McGraw-Hill, 1953. Pp. 101–203.

Oberndorf, C. P. Folie a deux. *International Journal of Psychoanalysis*, 1934, **15**, 14–24.

O'Shea, J. A six year experience with non-traditional methods in a child clinic setting. *Orthopsychiatry*, 1967, **37** (1), 56–63.

Parloff, M. B. The family in psychotherapy. *Archives of General Psychiatry*, 1961, **4**, 445–451.

Parsons, T., & Bales, R. F. *Family, socialization and interaction process*. Chicago: Free Press, 1955.

Paul, N. L. Effects of playback on family members of their own previously recorded conjoint therapy material. In I. M. Cohen (Ed.), *Family structure, dynamics and therapy*. *Psychiatric Research Reports of the American Psychiatric Association*, 1966, No. 20, 175–187.

Paul, N. L. The use of empathy in the resolution of grief. *Perspectives in biology and medicine*, 1967, **11** (1), 153–169.

Paul, N. L., & Grosser, G. H. Family resistance to change in schizophrenic patients. *Family Process*, 1964, **3**, 377–401.

Paul, N. L., & Grosser, G. H. Operational mourning and its role in conjoint family therapy. *Community Mental Health Journal,* 1965, **1,** 339–345.

Perlmutter, M. S., Loeb, D., Gumpert, G., Ohara, F., & Smith-Higbie, I. O. Family diagnosis and therapy using video tape playback. *American Journal of Orthopsychiatry,* 1967, **37**(5), 900–906.

Rank, B., Putnam, C., & Rochlin, G. The significance of emotional climate in early feeding difficulties. *Psychosomatic Medicine,* 1957, **10,** 279–283.

Ravick, Deutsch, & Brown. An experimental study of marital discord and decision making. In I. M. Cohen (Ed.), *Family structure, dynamics, and therapy. Psychiatric Reports of the American Psychiatric Association.* No. 20, 1966.

Rexford, E., & Van Amerongen, S. The influence of unsolved maternal oral conflicts upon impulsive acting out in young children. *American Journal of Orthopsychiatry,* 1957, **27,** 75-87.

Richmond, A., & Langa, A. Some observations concerning the role of children in the disruption of family homeostasis. *Orthopsychiatry,* 1963, **32**(4), 757–759.

Ritvo, S., & Solnit, A. Influence of the early mother-child interaction on identification processes. Vol. 13. *The psychoanalytic study of the child.* New York: International Universities Press, 1958.

Ruesch, J., & Bateson, G. *Communication, the social matrix of psychiatry.* New York: Norton, 1951.

Safer, D. J. Conjoint play therapy for the young child and his parent. *Archives of General Psychiatry,* 1965, **13**(4), 320–326.

Safer, D. J. Family therapy for children with behavior disorders. *Family Process,* 1967, **5,** 243–255.

Sager, C. J. The development of marriage ther-

apy: An historical review. *American Journal of Orthopsychiatry,* 1966, **36,** 458–468.

Sager, C. J., Masters, Y., Ronall, R., & Norman, W. Selection and engagement of patients in family therapy. *American Journal of Orthopsychiatry,* 1968, **38**(4), 715–723.

Satir, V. *Conjoint family therapy.* Palo Alto, Calif.: Science and Behavior Books, 1964.

Satir, V. Conjoint marital therapy. In B. Greene (Ed.), *The psychotherapies of mental disharmony.* New York: Free Press, 1965.

Schopler, E., Fox, R., & Cochrane, C. Teaching family dynamics to medical students. *American Journal of Orthopsychiatry,* 1967, **37**(5), 906–912.

Schwarz, H. Mother in the consulting room. Vol. 5. *The psychoanalytic study of the child.* New York: International Universities Press, 1950. Pp. 343–357.

Serrano, A. C., & Wilson, N. Family therapy in the treatment of the brain damaged child. *Diseases of the Nervous System,* 1963, **24,** 732–735.

Shellow, R. S., Brown, B. S., & Osberg, J. W. Family group therapy in retrospect: Four years and sixty families. *Family Process,* 1963, **2**(1), 52–67.

Sherman, M. H., Ackerman, N., Sherman, S. W., & Mitchell, C. Non verbal cries and reenactment of conflict in family therapy. *Family Process,* 1965, **4,** 133–162.

Singer, M. T., & Wynne, L. Differentiating characteristics of the parents of childhood schizophrenics, childhood neurotics, and yount adult schizophrenics. *American Journal of Psychiatry,* 1963, **120,** 234–243.

Skidmore, R. A., & Garrett, H. V. The joint

interview in marriage counseling. *Marriage and Family Life,* 1955, **17**(4), 349–354.

Speck, R. V. The home setting for family treatment. *International Journal of Social Psychiatry,* 1964, special ed. 2, 47–53.

Sperling, M. A study of deviate sexual behavior in children by the method of simultaneous analysis of mother and child. In L. Jessner & E. Pavenstadt (Eds.), *Dynamic psychopathology in childhood.* New York: Grune and Stratton, 1959. Pp. 221–242.

Sperling, M. Etiology and treatment of sleep disturbances in children. *Psychoanalytic Quarterly,* 1955, **24,** 358–368.

Sperling, M. Pavor nocturnis. *Journal of the American Psychological Association,* 1958, **6,** 79–94.

Spiegel, J. The resolution of role conflict within families. In N. W. Bell & E. F. Vogel (Eds.), *A modern introduction to the family.* Glencoe, Ill.: Free Press, 1960. Pp. 375–377.

Spiegel, J. P. The resolution of role conflict within the family. *Psychiatry,* 1957, **20,** 1–16.

Spiegel, J. P., & Bell, N. The family of the psychiatric patient. Vol. I. *American handbook of psychiatry.* New York: Basic Books, 1959.

Staver, N. The child's learning difficulty as related to the emotional problem of the mother. *American Journal of Orthopsychiatry,* 1953, **23,** 131–141.

Straughan, J. Treatment with mother and child in playroom. *Behavior Research and Therapy,* 1964, **2,** 37–41.

Szurek, S. Playfulness, creativity, and schisis. *American Journal of Orthopsychiatry,* 1959, **29** (4).

Szurek, S., & Berlin, I. Elements of psychothera-

peutics with the schizophrenic child and his parents. *Psychiatry,* 1956, **19,** 1–9.

Thorman, G. Family therapy: Help for troubled families. *New York Public Affairs Pamphlet,* February, 1964, No. 356.

Tips, R., & Lynch, H. The impact of genetic counseling upon the family milieu. *Journal of the American Medical Association,* 1963, **184,** 183–186.

Titchener, J. L., Riskin, J., & Emerson, R. The family in psychosomatic process. *Psychosomatic Medicine,* 1960, **22**(2), 127–142.

Watzlawick, P. A structured family interview. *Family Process,* 1965, **5**(2), 256–260.

Von Bertalanffy, L. General systems theory. *General Systems,* 1956, **1**(1).

Von Bertalanffy, L. General system theory and psychiatry. In S. Arieti (Ed.), *American handbook of psychiatry.* New York: Basic Books, 1966.

Watson, A. The conjoint psychotherapy of marriage partners. *American Journal of Orthopsychiatry,* 1963, **33,** 912–922.

Weakland, J. H. The "double-bind" hypothesis of schizophrenia and three-party interaction. In D. D. Jackson (Ed.), *The etiology of schizophrenia.* New York: Basic Books, 1960, Pp. 373–388.

J. Westman, D. Miller, & B. Arthur. Psychiatric symptoms and family dynamics as illustrated by the retarded reader. In I. M. Cohen (Ed.), *Family structure, dynamics and therapy. Psychiatric Reports of the American.* Psychiatric Association, 1966, No. 20, 115–120.

Whitaker, C. A., Felder, R., & Warkentin, J. Countertransference in the family treatment of schizophrenia. In I. Boszormenyi-Nagy & J. Framo (Eds.), *Intensive family therapy: Theoretical and practical aspects.* New York: Harper & Row, 1965.

Williams, F. S. Community treatment services and prevention: What are the issues? Paper presented at the American Orthopsychiatric Association meeting, Washington, 1967. (a)

Williams, F. S. Family therapy: A critical assessment. *American Journal of Orthopsychiatry,* 1967, **37**(5), 912–920. (b)

Witmer, H. *Psychiatric interviews with children.* New York: Commonwealth Fund, 1946.

Witmer, H., et al. Outcome of treatment in child guidance clinic. *Smith College Study Social Work,* 1933, **3**, 339–399.

Wynne, L. C., Ryckoff, I. M., Day, J., & Hirsch, S. I. Pseudo-mutuality in the family relations of schizophrenics. *Psychiatry,* 1958, **21**, 205–220.

Wynne, L. C., & Singer, M. T. Communication styles in parents of normals, neurotics, and schizophrenics: Some findings using a new Rorschach scoring manual. In I. M. Cohen (Ed.), *Family structure, dynamics and therapy. Psychiatric Reports of the American Psychiatric Association,* 1966, No. 20, 25–38.

Zuk, C. H. The go-between process in family therapy. *Family Process,* 1967, **5**, 162–178.

34 | Physiochemical Treatment Methods[1]

*Lawrence M. Greenberg
and Reginald S. Lourie*

In the past many types of physical therapy have been used in the treatment of disturbed and psychotic children. Of these, only psychopharmacology continues to play an important part in contemporary therapeutics. Electricity and such chemical agents as metrazol and insulin were used to induce convulsions in the treatment of psychotic children up through the 1950s (Bakwin & Bakwin, 1960), but since the advent of the tranquilizers, shock treatments are rarely employed. Sleep therapy and psychosurgery, techniques that have been utilized occasionally in the treatment of adults, have not been used with children. Physical measures such as restraints and confinements are no longer part of the treatment of children. A broad definition of the term "physicotherapy" may include recreational and occupational therapy. While these therapies are most useful, particularly with hospitalized or severely disabled children, they will not be reviewed in this chapter. This chapter is an at-

tempt to assess the current status of clinical child pharmacotherapy and related research.

The psychoactive properties of medications have often been discovered empirically. For example, the antidepressants were developed after it was observed that a chemically related drug used in treatment of tuberculosis had mood-elevating effects. Similarly, the use of diphenylhydramine as an antihistamine with children led to the serendipitous discovery that this drug has anxiety-relieving and sedative properties. Astute clinicians and researchers found a wide range of situations in which such drugs were helpful, and modifications of the formula were devised which made a broader range of minor tranquilizers available.

In psychiatric work with children, there has always been a need for relaxants, sleep enhancers, "knockout" medications, stimulants, and tonics. Twenty to thirty years ago, chloral hydrate, the bromides, alcohol, paraldehyde, and the barbiturates were often prescribed in the treatment of pyloric stenosis, colic, sleep disturbances, severe panic and anxiety states, psychotic storms, and

[1] This work was supported in part by U. S. Public Health Service Grant MH 15134 from the National Institute of Mental Health.

1010

so on. Since development of many new psycho-pharmacological agents began in the early 1950s, the usefulness of many of the older medications is often underestimated.

Nor are the new drugs being used to best effect. Recent unpublished surveys conducted in the metropolitan Washington, D.C., area indicate that clinicians tend to be remarkably conservative in prescribing medications for children with emotional problems. Clinicians of different specialties in medicine appear to prefer and prescribe different pharmacological agents. For example, pediatricians tend to favor use of the minor tranquilizers in the treatment of hyperactivity, while child psychiatrists prescribe stimulants.

Regardless of preferences, however, it appears that few clinicians prescribe medications for long enough periods or in sufficiently large doses to obtain the desired clinical effects, even in chronic conditions. This conservatism may be due in part to the paucity of reliable information about the correct dosages and effects of the various drugs and in part to fear of encouraging the misuse of drugs. We live in a drug-oriented society, in which alcohol, sedatives, and tranquilizers are readily available and widely used. Many young people are carrying this "drug-age" approach to life one step further by using "mind expanders," or psychotomimetic drugs such as LSD and marijuana, in many uncontrolled experimental ways. This indiscriminate use of drugs is, of course, often destructive, but it should not be allowed to confuse assessments of the controlled use of medication as a valuable tool in reducing handicapping symptoms of disturbed or psychotic children and in enhancing their emotional adjustment and subsequent performance. Review of the literature emphasizes the importance of selecting the most appropriate medication for each condition and prescribing adequately, thorough pharmacotherapy once the selection has been made.

Psychopharmacology should be viewed as only one part of a comprehensive therapeutic program designed to deal with external and internalized stresses. In hyperactivity, for example, medication can improve the child's functioning, but the complete treatment program may need to involve psychotherapy to improve self-esteem, counseling to enable the parents to reinforce the child's efforts to improve his functioning, and special education to overcome related learning handicaps.

Similarly, pharmacotherapy should not be the only treatment offered when anxiety-determined symptoms or behavior are present. With children as with adults, the most important therapeutic function of psychoactive medications is to help the organic components of the ego become better organized so that a steadier, higher level of functioning is maintained. This, in turn, makes the patient more accessible to other therapeutic interventions which can help him reorganize his defenses and deal more effectively with stress and anxiety, whether these arise from external or internal conflicts. When the stresses are external, other facets of the treatment may need to focus primarily on improving the child's environment. When the problems are internalized, the psychopharmacological agent may help the child respond to psychotherapy directed toward resolving his conflicted thoughts, wishes, urges, and fears.

The importance of pharmacotherapy in psychiatric treatment has been well documented in the literature dealing with adult patients (Efron, 1968). Pediatric psychopharmacology is a newer field, and the research is less extensive and less well controlled than studies of drug effects in adults. In part this may be because research and therapy with children are more complex than work with adults; many additional variables must be considered. For example, because the central nervous system (CNS) of the child and adolescent is still developing, the clinician and investigator may encounter a wide range of individual variations in responses to drug therapy. This is equally true for drugs which act on the CNS itself and for those affecting neural mechanisms of functioning. The fundamental factors underlying anxiety responses and their control can be clarified by studying the effects of drugs at the cellular level in the developing organism. A number of exciting and promising investigations of the influence of drugs on the developing nervous system are being conducted (see Woodbury, 1968), but definitive information is not yet available.

The major focus of research in the psychopharmacotherapy of children is on the effect of drugs on behavior. However, behavioral findings in research will be valid only if specific physiological and psychological factors are considered and controlled. Because these factors interrelate in so many ways, it is often difficult to identify particular ones as sources of variation. A drug, for example, may be known to produce, almost universally, a specific physiological reaction, yet its effects on behavior may vary widely because of the influence of variables relating to the drug itself, to the reactions of individual patients, to the attitudes of parents and other authority figures, to the expectations and interpretations of the investigative team, and to socioeconomic factors.

Additional variables, such as the institutional setting in which the investigation is to be conducted, must also be considered in selecting the research design. Differences in administrative structure, types of personnel, and types of patients receiving care can affect the results of the study.

In certain types of studies, valid findings can be obtained only by use of a group of normal patients as a control group. However, normal controls are not usually used in pharmacotherapy research because the hypothesis being tested usually centers specifically on the effects of a given drug on aberrant behavior. A placebo group is customarily used, however, to help the investigator distinguish between the effects of the drug and the effects of such nonspecific factors as the increased attention the child patient receives while under treatment. In evaluating study findings, distinctions between open, blind, and double-blind research designs need to be clearly identified, since the findings of one type of study cannot be generalized to cover studies of other types.

Of the many complex problems in research design, the selection of the dependent variable—the target behavior or trait around which the investigation is to center—and the techniques for assessing this behavior are the most critical. It is difficult to measure most behaviors and traits objectively, and it is still more difficult to determine which behavioral changes are directly related to the effects of the drug. Although valuable, clinical judgments are not, by themselves, adequate measures of change. Nor are familiar clinical tests and experimental tasks such as the Stanford-Binet Intelligence Scale, the Wechsler Intelligence Scale for Children, and the Bender Gestalt test completely reliable as objective measures of behavior. In studies of the therapeutic effects of drugs, findings based on the use of such tests have been inconclusive with both adults and children. Although behavioral changes are apparent in children who receive drugs, review of the pharmacotherapy literature indicates that it has proved difficult to relate these changes to performance on the standard psychodiagnostic tests. A number of investigators have been attempting to develop tasks and measures which may prove more sensitive to drug-behavior interaction.

It is manifestly impossible to control all possible variables in a study. Thus, to give his study maximum validity, the researcher must be selective; he must limit the range of his study to realistic parameters within which certain major variables can be controlled.

The Psychopharmacology Research Center of Children's Hospital, Washington, D.C., has begun a three-year study of the effects of various medications on the behavior of hyperactive children. Using a double-blind research design, investigators administer various performance and learning tasks to five groups of study subjects before and after a course of treatment. Each group, consisting of eighty male children ages 6 to 10, receives a different type of medication. The types of medication being used are a major tranquilizer, chlorpromazine; a minor tranquilizer, hydroxyzine; a stimulant, dextroamphetamine; an anticonvulsant, dyphenylhydantoin; and a placebo. The study will be completed in 1971.

Within the limitations of one brief chapter, it is impossible to review the findings of all the many contradictory and inconsistent studies of child pharmacotherapy over the past thirty years. The remainder of this chapter will therefore center on reports of the clinical aspects of pharmacotherapy of children, including the specific drugs, their actions, indications for therapy, dosages, and complications.

PHARMACOTHERAPY OF CHILDREN: CLINICAL ASPECTS

In the following section, the pharmacotherapeutic agents currently most used with child patients are classified by overall use into six principal categories: hypnotics and sedatives, major tranquilizers, minor tranquilizers, psychostimulants, anticonvulsants, and psychotomimetics. Some of the drugs have been known and used for centuries; others have been in use for less than a decade. Much remains to be learned about the exact mechanisms by which they produce

their effects and about their long-range implications.

Some of the categories include many drugs in current use, of which only one or two reference medications are reviewed as representative of their group in terms of history, pharmacological action, therapeutic uses, and complications. "Recommendations for Pharmacotherapy" summarizes the recommended drugs and dosages for the more commonly encountered psychiatric symptoms in children.

RECOMMENDATIONS FOR PHARMACOTHERAPY

I. Acute anxiety or fear
  A. Diphenylmethane derivatives
    1. Diphenylhydramine (Benadryl) (1–5 mg/pound/day)
    2. Hydroxyzine (Atarax) (1–5 mg/pound/day)
  B. Phenothiazines (particularly if severe or a teen-ager)
    1. Chlorpromazine (Thorazine) (2–8 mg/pound/day)
    2. Thioridazine (Mellaril) (2–8 mg/pound/day)
    3. Perphenazine (Trilafon) (0.01–0.1 mg/pound/day)
    4. Prochlorpriazine (Compazine) (0.025–0.3 mg/pound/day)
    5. Trifluoperazine (Stelazine) (0.0025–0.2 mg/pound/day)
  C. Barbiturates
    1. Phenobarbital (Luminal) (1–3 mg/pound/day)
    2. Pentobarbital (Nembutal) (1–3 mg/pound/day)
II. Hyperactivity, impulsivity, hyperdistractibility, low attention span, and aggressivity
  A. Stimulants
    1. Amphetamines—dextroamphetamine

(Dexedrine) (10–30 mg/day): amphe-
tamine (Benzedrine) (20–60 mg/day)
2. Methylphenidate (Ritalin) (20–80
mg/day)
B. Diphenylmethane derivatives
C. Diphenylhydantoin (Dilantin) (1.5–4.5
mg/pound/day)
D. Phenothiazines
III. Psychosis (including transient psychoticlike
states)
A. Phenothiazines
B. Diphenylmethane derivatives
IV. Acute sleep disturbance
A. Chloral hydrate (5–15 mg/pound/night;
not to exceed 1 g/dose)
B. Diphenylmethane
C. Barbiturates
V. Depression (adolescent)
A. Tricyclics
1. Imipramine (Tofranil) (100–250 mg/
day)
2. Amitriptyline (Elavil) (100–250 mg/
day)
3. Nortriptyline (Aventyl) (100–250 mg/
day)
VI. Enuresis
A. Imipramine (Tofranil) (25–50 mg/day)
B. Amphetamines

Hypnotics and Sedatives

The use of medication to promote sedation
and sleep dates back many centuries to the discovery of alcohol, opium, and belladonna. In
the mid-1800s, bromide, chloral derivatives, and
paraldehyde were major additions to the list of
soporific agents. Chloral hydrate (one of the
chloral derivatives) and paraldehyde have continued to be used in the short-term treatment of
childhood disorders. However, since the early
1900s barbiturates have been the most popular
of the hypnotic and sedative drugs. At first they
were prescribed somewhat indiscriminately as a
chemical replacement for mechanical restraints.

Experience with their use has indicated a need
for greater caution, yet the barbiturate group
remains one of the more important and frequently
used pharmacological means of supporting the
psychotherapeutic process.

The basic chemical structure of the barbiturate family can be modified to produce such
well-known and useful drugs as phenobarbital
(Luminal), methobarbital (Mebaral), amobarbital
(Amytal), pentobarbital (Nembutal), secobarbital (Seconal), and thiopental (Pentothal). Each
of these compounds has specific clinical properties determined by its particular chemical composition. The clinician can choose the most appropriate one on the bases of the desired mode of
administration (oral, intramuscular, or intravenous); the rapidity of onset, peaking, and
duration of effectiveness; potency; and specific
effects (Sharpless, 1965).

The barbiturates are cellular depressants
which cause progressive inhibition of body functions with increasing increments of medication.
Paradoxically, however, they occasionally induce excitation in children and aged adults, and
research is needed to clarify the underlying mechanisms. The CNS is particularly sensitive to the
barbiturates, even when they are administered in
relatively low concentration, and barbiturates
appear to affect all levels of the CNS without a
particular receptor site. However, the role of
the reticular activating system, which mediates
both excitatory and inhibitory functions, has
been the focus of considerable speculation and
investigation because of its very sensitive responses to depressants (Killam, 1962).

It may be that the apparently paradoxical
results of barbiturate-induced wakefulness and
agitation in some patients, instead of the anticipated progressive sedation, are due to this juxtaposition of two opposing functions in the same
neural system. The subcortical network may
serve an excitatory function; the cortical areas,
an inhibitory function. Perhaps, in some cases,

the barbiturates depress the cortex, thereby releasing the alerting or exciting systems of the subcortical impulses. This could result in the excitation observed in some patients. Why the barbiturates should affect some patients this way and induce sedation by affecting the excitatory systems of the subcortical areas in others is not understood, and possible explanations of the phenomenon remain in the realm of speculation at present. It may be that the excitation is simply a manifestation of the organism's attempt to combat the action of the drug and maintain the normal level of alertness.

Barbituates are used therapeutically:

1. In low dosages, as a sedative to promote relaxation and decrease excitability in the acutely tense, anxious child
2. As a hypnotic to facilitate sleep in the acutely anxious child
3. As an anticonvulsant
4. Very rarely, as a diagnostic and therapeutic aid in narcotherapy with adolescents

Contrary to what one might expect, barbiturates are not generally successful in the treatment of hyperactivity in children. In fact, investigators have found that they tend to make this symptom worse rather than better (Laufer & Denhoff, 1957). Exceptions have, however, been reported (Burket, 1955; Carter, 1966).

In spite of their proven value in the treatment of some conditions, barbiturates should be used with caution and only as one aspect of an integrated therapeutic program. Even as an adjunctive therapeutic measure, they should be used only in the treatment of psychological conditions characterized by acute anxiety. Long-term treatment with barbiturates, except as an anticonvulsant, may mask other significant symptoms and precipitate a variety of undesirable complications. The most important of these are the effects of the drugs on many organs of the body, the development of a tolerance to the drug which requires progressively larger dosages, and the development of addiction.

As a cellular depressant, barbiturates affect many organs besides the CNS. In large dosages, excessively rapid intravenous administration, and idiopathic hypersensitivity reactions, barbiturates may seriously depress respiratory, cardiovascular, gastrointestinal, kidney, and liver functioning and cause death. Because of these effects, barbiturates are not given to agitated accident patients who are suspected of having sustained a head injury which may adversely affect the cardiovascular and respiratory centers. In long-term barbiturate treatment, the potential for complications greatly increases. Barbiturates depress consciousness, cognitive functions, and learning ability. Although these effects are often not of serious magnitude, toxicity can also occur. Toxic manifestations include a "hangover," a condition resembling alcoholic inebriation with excitement and delirium, a chronic brain syndrome, or even coma.

Tolerance to barbiturates is a particularly insidious complication because it can occur without warning side effects. Because of increased metabolism and cellular adaption, the patient's body requires increasing amounts of the drug. Yet the lethal dosage level remains the same and may be reached with no intimation of danger.

Addiction occurs when the patient becomes physiologically dependent on the drug and manifests a variety of symptoms known as the *abstinence syndrome* when the medication is withdrawn. One particularly dangerous symptom of addiction which may be encountered upon withdrawal, even with the use of relatively low levels of barbiturates, is *status epilepticus.*

A further hazard in the use of the barbiturates with depressed adolescents is that the drugs are not infrequently used in suicide attempts. It is beyond the scope of this chapter to review the contributing sociological, psychological, and somatic factors of the treatment of acute or chronic poisoning, but the dangers must be kept clearly in mind.

The Major Tranquilizers

The major tranquilizers include the rauwolfias and the phenothiazines. The use of the former stretches back over many centuries, but refinement of clinical application of these two groups of drugs did not take place until the early 1950s.

The rauwolfias. In the Asian countries, extracts of the rauwolfia plant have been used for hundreds of years in the treatment of the psychoses. While reports of their effectiveness as an antipsychotic and antihypertensive agent date back to 1931 (Sen & Bose), it was not until 1954, when Kline published the results of his work with a purified rauwolfia alkaloid extract, reserpine (Serpasil), that these compounds began to receive psychiatric attention in the United States. At the same time that reserpine and the other rauwolfia compounds appeared, the phenothiazines were also being introduced. The rauwolfias were soon eclipsed by the more spectacular results and fewer complications of these other tranquilizers and are therefore infrequently used at the present time.

Reserpine produces a generally depressant effect. Although the mechanism of action is not understood, the drug is known to decrease the tissue catecholamines (norepinephrine) and 5-hydroxytryptamine in the CNS. However these altered amine levels have not been adequately studied to delineate their relationship to behavioral changes.

Reserpine has been used in the treatment of psychotic, hyperaggressive, and hyperactive children. Early uncontrolled studies indicated promising results, but later work has demonstrated that reserpine is less effective than chlorpromazine (Adamson, Nellis, Rurge, Cleland, & Killian, 1958; Beley, Foncin, & Leyrie, 1956) and may show no greater effect than the use of placebos (Freedman, Effron, & Bender, 1955; Kirk & Bauer, 1956). Although some clinicians continue to use reserpine with some success, its primary current use is in treatment of children who have not responded to or have shown a toxic reaction to the phenothiazines. To obtain an adequate clinical response, reserpine levels must be increased slowly and maintained for at least a month.

Initially reserpine causes considerable sleepiness but is usually tolerated well after several days. However, this hypnotic effect may hinder learning processes, particularly in the retarded, hyperactive children for whom it is most often prescribed. Nasal congestion is an annoying but not serious problem. The drug induces some increase in heart rate, decrease in blood pressure, and excessive salivation. In high dosages, it may cause parkinsonian symptoms, but these respond rapidly to appropriate concomitant medication. Reserpine can also induce profound depression and severe hypotension.

The phenothiazines. Although the phenothiazines were discovered decades before, their potent sedative and antihistamine properties were first used with clinical success in the 1930s. However, it was not until 1952 that Deley, Deniker, and Harl reported the antipsychotic properties of a phenothiazine derivative, chlorpromazine, which was also used in anesthesia and in the treatment of nausea and vomiting. Since that time, many new clinically useful phenothiazines have been synthesized and evaluated. However, since there is no clear evidence that any of the more recent derivatives are substantially superior (Cole, Goldberg, & Davis, 1966), chlorpromazine continues to be the reference drug for the phenothiazines and the one most frequently prescribed.

The basic phenothiazine nucleus is altered by chemical additions to produce three groups of psychiatrically important derivatives. These are the aliphatic group, which includes chlorpromazine; the piperizine group, which includes such compounds as perphenazine, prochlorperazine, and trifluoperazine; and the piperidine group, represented by thioridazine. The groups differ in potency and side effects, so the clinician needs to select the compound which will best meet the treatment needs of each patient.

As with other psychoactive medications, the mechanism of action of the phenothiazines is not fully understood. They act as depressants in the hypothalamic, limbic, extrapyramidal, and reticular areas and exert direct, but apparently insignificant, cortical influences. Hawke and McGreat (1964) speculated that the phenothiazines may increase the filtering activity of the reticular formation, which would, in turn, decrease the number of extraneous stimuli going to higher centers; but further study of this possibility is needed. The phenothiazines are generally classified as antihistamines. They appear to exert their tranquilizing effect by blocking norepinephrine and enhancing serotonin in the CNS.

Therapeutically, the phenothiazines have been shown to be effective in a variety of etiologically different conditions, including psychoses of childhood, chronic brain syndromes, minimal brain dysfunction, and constitutional hyperactivity. They are useful in sedating the acutely agitated child; reducing motor activity of the hyperactive or hyperaggressive child; reducing impulsiveness, excitability, hyperdistractibility, and anxiety; and exerting an overall calming effect. Tranquilization resulting from the medication is frequently associated with reduction of hallucinations, delusions, faulty ideas of reference, and disorientation. Thought processes become better organized, and social participation and self-care improve. These results have been well documented in both adults and children (Ayd, 1957; Freed & Peifer, 1956a; Freedman, Effron, & Bender, 1955; Garfield et al., 1962; Goldberg, Klerman, & Cole, 1965; Harman &

Winn, 1966; Hunt, Frank, & Krush, 1956; Hunter & Stephenson, 1963; Johnston & Martin, 1957; Lapolla, 1967; Miksztal, 1956; National Institute of Mental Health, 1964; Tarjan et al., 1957). It is generally accepted that the phenothiazines are the most important pharmacotherapeutic agents now available for psychotic and severely agitated children. They are particularly effective when integrated with sound psychotherapeutic techniques. Irwin (1968), among others, has suggested that some of the observed effects, such as reduction of hallucinations and disorientation, may not be the result of any specific antipsychotic action of the drug but may represent, rather, effects secondary to the general calming effect and the reduction of hyperexcitability to stimuli. Clinical observations tend to support this notion, since reduction in hallucinations and so on often occurs several weeks after improvement in the level of activity.

Phenothiazine treatment also appears to be effective in some acute, severe neurotic and tension states, but it is less effective in chronic anxiety states and personality disorders than psychotherapeutic management.

While attempts have been made to delineate symptom specificity for the various phenothiazine compounds (Fish, 1960; Overall et al., 1963), no conclusive findings have been reported to indicate preferential use of one drug or another. Gwynne et al. (1962) reported that the piperizine group was somewhat more effective than the other groups in the treatment of withdrawn, apathetic schizophrenic patients, but this finding has not been replicated by other investigators (National Institute of Mental Health, 1964).

Hypnotic effects of the various phenothiazine compounds vary, but this does not seem to be an important factor in their antipsychotic properties. Initially, chlorpromazine has a potent sleep-inducing effect, but compensatory tolerance usually develops within several days. However, the rebound insomnia and hyperalertness frequently observed when the medication is terminated (Greenberg & Roth, 1966) suggest that some sedation persists in attenuated form throughout the duration of use of the medication.

Clinically, chlorpromazine does not appear to significantly reduce alertness, arousal time, or cognitive functioning in general. Dosages vary considerably in relation to the age, size, and weight of the child and the severity of the symptoms. Dosages range from 30 to 150 mg per day for children and higher for adolescents. As with all medications, it is advisable to begin conservatively. The daily dosage is divided into two or three separate doses spaced throughout the day. To obtain a rapid onset of symptom control, intramuscular preparations can be used. These are best administered in a monitored environment such as a hospital. Long-term or sustained-release forms of medication are sometimes used, but without any particular benefit. Chlorpromazine is relatively slow in building up to full chemical effectiveness and should be continued for at least 3 or 4 weeks to ensure optimal results. In addition, the clinician may find it necessary to adjust the dosage upward if the initial dosage is ineffective.

Although numerous studies of the relapse rate following termination of phenothiazine therapy with adult chronic schizophrenic patients have been done (Diamond & Marks, 1960; Good, Sterling, & Holtzman, 1958; Greenberg & Roth, 1966; Rothstein, Zeltzerman, & White, 1962), little is known about the relapse rate of child patients. Optimal duration of medication for psychotic children has not been established. It is known that the therapeutic activity of the phenothiazines is of unusually long duration, and traces of the drug have been shown to be present in the body for up to 12 months after termination. Most clinicians appear to agree that medication can be gradually reduced and terminated within a few months after successful results have been obtained with acutely ill children. However, no such consensus exists in regard to the treatment of chronically psychotic children, and current practice varies greatly. In view of the absence of reports of such complications as tolerance and addiction, the evidence supporting maintenance of medication over a period of years with adults suggests a similar policy with chronically ill child patients.

However, one must question the advisability of prolonged use of extremely potent drugs, with their intrinsically high risk of complications, in treatment of protracted but less severe symptoms such as hyperactivity. When hyperactivity is associated with brain impairment, phenothiazines may exacerbate the pathological activity. In such cases, it is therefore preferable to employ equally effective but less dangerous medications described elsewhere.

Because the phenothiazines can produce a number of serious complications as well as various minor ones, their use necessitates routine monitoring of the vulnerable organ systems. As noted above, the drowsiness and lethargy which occur when the medication is first begun usually subside within a few days. Occasionally, however, the dosage must be reduced to eliminate these symptoms.

However, toxic reactions sometimes occur which seem to be independent of the dosage level. This indicates hypersensitivity to the drug and is an indication for discontinuing its use. Since these potent depressants can heighten the effects of other nervous-system depressants, such as alcohol and barbiturates, the use of such drugs must be restricted for patients receiving the phenothiazines.

Sudden decreases in blood pressure when the patient sits up or stands up may be encountered during the early days of treatment. Treated symptomatically, this reaction usually disappears within a few days. If it does not, a reduction or change in medication may be indicated.

Jaundice is an infrequent complication in

patients receiving phenothiazine treatment, especially children. However, the clinician should be alert to the possibility. Even though permanent liver damage is exceedingly rare, most authorities recommend that the use of the drug be terminated if jaundice should appear.

The clinician must also watch the patient closely and rely on frequent laboratory examinations to rule out the possibility of dramatic bone-marrow depressions. These occur infrequently, but when they do, they can result in serious or fatal decreases of white and/or red blood cells. If bone-marrow depression occurs, further treatment with phenothiazines is contraindicated.

Skin reactions are relatively common in patients receiving phenothiazines, especially on exposure to sunlight. These are reversible with withdrawal of the drug or protection from sunlight. However, abnormal deposits of pigments in many organs have been reported, particularly in females on high dosages for long periods of time (DeLong, 1968). To date, this phenomenon has not been reported in children, but the possibility speaks for close observation.

Convulsions have sometimes been observed as a complication of phenothiazine treatment in children with both known and latent convulsive disorders (Adamson et al., 1958; Tarjan et al., 1957). Since concomitant anticonvulsive management can be instituted or increased, occurrence of convulsions is not necessarily a contraindication for use of this medication unless other serious complications occur simultaneously.

Although extrapyramidal complications were first reported to be infrequent in children receiving the phenothiazines (Fish, 1960b), more recent reports indicate such complications in up to one-third of the children treated with certain phenothiazines (Ayd, 1961; Gupta & Lovejoy, 1967; Shaw et al., 1963). The aliphatic group, including chlorpromazine, and the piperidine group, including thioridazine, are of about equal potency, but the latter is associated with fewer extrapyramidal effects. The piperizine group, which includes the higher-potency phenothiazines, produces fewer cardiovascular and hypnotic complications but more extrapyramidal effects than the aliphatic group.

The extrapyramidal reactions may appear with suddenness, but they may also be intermittent and hard to diagnose. They include parkinsonian symptoms such as muscular rigidity, immobile facies, resting tremor, and salivation; akathisias or motor restlessness; and the dystonias, involuntary motor movements with muscular rigidity. When such symptoms occur, reduction of the dosage or concomitant treatment with antiparkinsonian medication, such as trihexyphenidyl (Artane), biperiden (Akineton), or diphenylhydramine (Benadryl), is usually successful. Rarely, these complications may be permanent, particularly in cases with prior neurological impairment (Dabbous & Bergman, 1966). Thus extreme caution in the use of these valuable drugs must be maintained.

The Minor Tranquilizers

The minor tranquilizers include the diphenylmethane compounds, the benzodiazepine compounds, and meprobamate. Some of these non-neuroleptic agents are chemically related to the aliphatic group of the phenothiazines. Although the use of some of them goes back to the mid-1940s, surprisingly little controlled research has been done to substantiate early clinical impressions. It is therefore difficult to assess their efficacy in the treatment of childhood disorders.

These drugs are prescribed primarily for such clinical conditions as anxiety, phobic states, insomnia, irritability, and hyperactivity. Occasional success has been reported in the treatment of psychotic children, especially those with acute reactive conditions. The drugs are most effective when used in combination with other therapeutic measures such as psychotherapy and parental counseling.

Since motor impairment, dependency, and addiction may result from large dosages of these drugs, they must be used in moderation. When administered at the desirable levels, the minor tranquilizers are less effective in reducing activity and excitability levels than the phenothiazines. However, they do seem to promote socialization and, perhaps secondarily, reduce passive avoidance behaviors associated with anxiety and phobic symptoms.

For a variety of reasons, including the wide publicity these drugs have received and the tendency of conservative clinicians to avoid more potent and dangerous drugs, the minor tranquilizers appear to be overvalued and overprescribed at the present time. A series of well-controlled studies with adults and children is needed to clarify the effectiveness of these drugs.

The diphenylmethane compounds. The diphenylmethane compounds consist of diphenylhydramine (Benadryl) and hydroxyzine (Atarax, Vistaril). Diphenylhydramine was discovered and reported in 1946 by Loew, MacMillan, and Katser as a potent treatment for allergies, motion sickness, and parkinsonism. By 1953, its clinical use in the treatment of behavior problems in children was well established (Effron & Freedman, 1953).

Diphenylhydramine acts as a depressant on the CNS. The mechanism of action is not clear, but there is some suggestion that the antagonism of histamine and acetylcholine may be responsible. The drug also has some CNS-stimulating action, but this is not frequently observed clinically.

Effron and Freedman (1953), Fish (1960b), Freedman (1958), and Freedman, Effron, and Bender (1955) all reported favorable results in the use of diphenylhydramine in treating behavior disorders with high anxiety levels. The medication has been reported to be highly effective in treating anxious normoactive and hyperactive children and children broadly diagnosed as schizophrenic. However, much further research is needed to substantiate the clinical impressions reported in these studies.

Following oral administration, the onset of effect is between fifteen and thirty minutes, with peaking at one hour and a duration of three to six hours. Dosage range is from 1.0 to 5.0 mg per pound per day or from 30 to 150 mg per day. A clinical impression that the drug's usefulness in behavior disorders falls rapidly after age 10 has been frequently quoted (Fish, 1960b).

Although toxic reactions and other complications are reported to be very rare, diphenylhydramine can cause considerable sedation, dizziness, and incoordination. Even less commonly, symptoms of excessive CNS stimulation such as insomnia, nervousness, and tremors, gastric upset with anorexia, and dryness of the mouth have been reported, as have various cardiovascular, urinary, and bone-marrow reactions.

Although hydroxyzine, the other diphenylmethane compound, is a somewhat popular medication among pediatricians, its usefulness has not been adequately substantiated. Many clinical reports (Dongan, 1962; Freedman, 1958; Litchfield, 1960) indicate its effectiveness as an agent to reduce hyperactivity and mild-to-moderate levels of anxiety, but the few controlled studies (Craft, 1957; Segal & Tansley, 1957) are not very persuasive. In general, dosage levels and complications are similar to those of diphenylhydramine.

The benzodiazepine compounds. The benzodiazepine compounds, which include chlordizepoxide (Librium) and diazepam (Valium), have been the subject of many clinical reports but few controlled investigations. It is therefore difficult to make definitive statements about them at the present time.

Both of these drugs appear to act by suppressing excitation within the reticular activating area. Their sedative action appears to be intermediate between that of the barbiturates and that of phenothiazines. Both drugs also seem to block convulsive activity elicited by drugs or electricity and to promote muscular relaxation via the CNS.

Clinically, their use is advocated primarily in states of mild to moderate anxiety and/or hyperactivity (D'Amato, 1962; DiFrancesco, 1963; Kraft, Ardali, Duffy, Hart, & Pearce, 1965; Krakowski, 1963; Sylvester, 1963), but evidence for their effectiveness is inconclusive (LaVeck & Buckley, 1961).

Dosage range has not been well established, and the clinician is advised, as with all psychoactive medication, to begin with small doses and increase until therapeutic effects are obtained or the advisable limit is reached. Peak drug effect is reached by eight hours, and some effectiveness is maintained for several days following administration.

Complications are seldom encountered but may include skin rash, weight gain, CNS depression with resulting lethargy, or CNS stimulation with resulting gait disturbances and irritability or euphoria. There are reports of withdrawal symptoms in adults similar to those seen with the barbiturates, but dependence and habituation have not, to date, been described in children.

Meprobamate. Although meprobamate (Miltown, Equanil) has been widely used in the treatment of anxiety states and behavior disorders (Freedman, 1958; Kugelmass, 1956; Litchfield, 1957), the few controlled studies which have been done (Craft, 1958; Cytryn, Gilbert & Eisenberg, 1960; Heaton-Ward & Jancor, 1958; Laties & Weiss, 1958) fail to substantiate the clinical impressions of the earlier studies. Because of the absence of conclusive data, dosage range and recommendations for prescribing meprobamate for children cannot be made firmly at this time.

Psychostimulants

Psychostimulants include the amphetamines, methylphenidate, and the antidepressants. These drugs are most effective when combined with psychotherapy and parental counseling, and their independent use should not constitute the entire treatment plan. If parents are, for example, given adequate counseling in the management of hyperactive behavior, a relatively short period of regular medication will frequently suffice to bring the symptom under control. After that, periodic doses on "bad days" may be sufficient to maintain the general level of improvement. Although psychotherapy without medication has been successful in a significant number of cases, the addition of medication can sometimes hasten the child's favorable response to psychotherapy.

The amphetamines. The amphetamines have been used since the early 1930s to treat adults with narcolepsy, obesity, and certain toxic conditions of the CNS. Lourie first demonstrated empirically that thyroid extract can be used to control certain behavioral disorders in children, even those who do not have thyroid disease. The effectiveness of other stimulants in controlling behavioral disturbances was then investigated. These investigations were described by Lourie in 1964. The amphetamines were known to be useful as antidepressants in treatment of adolescents and adults, but Bradley's report (1937) of their successful use in treating behavioral disturbances of children stimulated their wider use to control such symptoms as hyperactivity, hyperaggressivity, hyperdistractibility, and learning disorders.

Three forms of amphetamines are available: dextroamphetamine (Dexedrine), the levorotary form, and the racemic form (Benzedrine). A related compound, metamphetamine (Desoxyn), is prescribed infrequently because of its cardiovascular effects when given in high dosages. Of the two forms in common use, dextroamphetamine is the most frequently prescribed because of its greater potency as a CNS stimulant and its fewer cardiovascular effects. It is therefore also most frequently used as the index drug in reviews of amphetamine use in the pharmacotherapy of children.

The amphetamines are among the most potent of the sympathomimetic drugs as CNS stimulators. They cause the release of norepinephrine from adrenergic neural storage sites and, perhaps more importantly, act directly on the effector cells, thereby facilitating neural transmission. Acting in the cortical and reticular activating areas, they increase alertness, responsiveness to stimuli, concentration, motor activity, pulse, and blood pressure. They decrease fatigue and sleepiness, and they suppress appetite not related to exercise.

It seems paradoxical that CNS stimulants such as the amphetamines are sometimes effective in calming or slowing down hyperactive children, and the exact reasons for this effect are not understood. It is assumed that the hyperactive child may be overactive because of a low threshold to stimuli at some levels of the nervous system. Although it remains to be demonstrated whether the amphetamines raise this abnormal threshold or enhance the child's ability to focus his attention, much of the striking clinical improvement noted with amphetamine therapy seems to be due to the improved span and level of attention. It is, of course, generally accepted that both emotional factors and neurological impairments can produce motor and cognitive hyperactivity, but it is beyond the scope of this review to examine their precise roles in producing the symptoms of disorders variously diagnosed as hyperkinetic child syndrome, minimal brain dysfunction, constitutional hyperactivity syndrome, and brain damage. For this information, the reader is referred to Bakwin (1967), Laufer and Denhoff (1957), Lourie (1963), Paine (1963), and Sainz (1966).

The amphetamines are prescribed for children who are hyperactive, hyperaggressive, emotionally labile, and hyperdistractible with short attention spans (Conners, Eisenberg, & Barcai,

1967; Ginn & Hohman, 1953; Levy, 1966; Lindsley & Henry, 1942). Presence of these symptoms is often established by the history obtained from the child's parents and teachers and (less so) through observation in the clinician's office. Reports place the incidence of significant improvement with amphetamine treatment at anywhere from 50 to 100 percent. This lack of consistency in reported results, the need to delineate clinical differences shown in different types of hyperactivity, and the effort to distinguish organic from nonorganic hyperactivity on the basis of the response to drug therapy have stimulated many studies.

Dextroamphetamine is usually administered at breakfast and lunchtime. If sustained-release capsules are prescribed, they are given in the morning only, to patients for whom low dosages are adequate. Occasionally a child will show a tendency to become hyperactive in the afternoon or early evening, and the time of administration is adjusted accordingly. The clinical effect of dextroamphetamine is often apparent within 30 minutes of oral administration. Peak effect is reached at two to three hours.

Although it is important to begin dextroamphetamine treatment with small dosages, physicians tend to be too conservative in prescribing medication and frequently discontinue treatment before an adequate dosage level has been reached or before it has been maintained long enough to produce the desired effects. Since hyperactivity tends to be a chronic condition, short-term treatment is not apt to be effective, although exceptions have been reported (McDermott, 1965).

Amphetamine dosage is usually begun at 2.5 to 5 mg and increased gradually until adequate clinical results are obtained or complications necessitate reduction or termination of use. Raising the dosage level too rapidly can cause unfavorable reactions. A child who failed the initial clinical trial of medication may later react favorably to the same drug if the dosage is increased more slowly and his optimal level is not exceeded. While smaller dosages may be successful, up to 20 mg per day may be required for an 8-year-old and up to 30 mg per day for a 10- to 12-year-old to secure adequate clinical results. As the child's symptoms become better controlled, periodic attempts should be made to decrease the dosage level.

In order to avoid overdosage and complications, some clinicians routinely reduce or withhold medication during weekends and school holidays. With many children, this can be done without significant aggravation of symptoms.

Some children again become hyperactive as they build up tolerance to the drug. Occasionally this can be controlled by alternating every few days between low dosage levels and the previously effective level to allow the child's tolerance to the drug to decrease. If this is not effective, it may be necessary to discontinue the dextroamphetamine and prescribe a different amphetamine or some other stimulant. It is not unusual to have to try out several different drugs with one patient before an adequate clinical response is achieved, and failure with one should not be assumed to mean that response to all drugs will be poor.

Since the danger of addiction to amphetamines in adults and adolescents has been demonstrated and since hyperactivity often diminishes spontaneously after puberty, medication with amphetamines is not usually continued after puberty. Addiction has not been encountered in children.

During the first few days of treatment with amphetamines, children frequently show bothersome side effects, such as sleeplessness, appetite depression, elevated blood pressure, and mild exacerbation of hyperactivity. These symptoms usually cease within a week. If they continue beyond this time, the dosage may need reduction. If the child is receiving only a low dosage (2.5 mg) and significant aggravation of his symptoms persists, medication should be terminated.

Toxic effects such as dizziness, irritability, restlessness, and tremors have been reported in some children. Except for the very rare child with an idiosyncratic hypersensitivity to the drug (Ney, 1967), more serious toxic symptoms such as confusion, delirium, panic, psychosis, cardiac arrhythmia, and hypertension have not occurred in children receiving proper dosages.

Methylphenidate. Like the amphetamines, methylphenidate (Ritalin) is a CNS stimulant frequently prescribed for the treatment of hyperactive children (Conners, Eisenberg, & Sharpe, 1964; Knobel, Wolman, & Mason, 1959; Sainz, 1966). The literature on clinical experience with methylphenidate appears to indicate that this drug has about the same level of effectiveness as the amphetamines in treatment of hyperactivity. However, few comparative studies of the two drugs have been done, so the clinician must for the present choose between them on the basis of personal experience and preference.

Methylphenidate is usually administered in morning and noon dosages, but modification of this schedule may be necessary to meet the needs of the individual patient. Initial dosage is 5 mg, and dosage can be increased gradually until levels of approximately 40 mg per day for an 8-year-old and 80 mg per day for a 10-year-old are reached.

Complications of treatment appear to be similar to those encountered with the amphetamines, although there have been some reports that methylphenidate suppresses appetite less than the amphetamines.

The antidepressants. The antidepressant drugs currently in use are divided into three groups: the amphetaminelike compounds, the monoamine oxidase inhibitors, and the tricyclic compounds. The amphetaminelike compounds have already been described. The monoamine oxidase inhibitors include tranylcypromine (Parnate), phenelzine (Nardil), and nialamide (Niamid). This group of drugs is infrequently prescribed because they have not been clearly demonstrated to be of value in childhood depressions or psychoses (Connell, 1965; Davies, 1961; Frommer, 1967; Heaton-Ward, 1962).

The third group, the tricyclic compounds, consists of iminodibenzyls with imipramine (Tofranil) and the dibenzocycloheptenes, which include amitriptyline (Elavil) and nortriptylene (Aventyl). Of these, imipramine is the most frequently prescribed for both depressions and enuresis in children. It will therefore be used as the reference drug for this review.

Because of their chemical relationship to the phenothiazines, the tricyclic compounds were first tested as antihistaminics and then later as antipsychotic agents. While they did not prove particularly successful in either of these uses, their antidepressant actions were delineated in the clinical trials and observations (Kuhn, 1958). In 1960, MacLean reported beneficial effects of imipramine with enuretic children.

Considerable work has been done to delineate the mechanisms of action of the tricyclic compounds, but no definitive conclusions can yet be stated. In general, they appear to act by altering cellular permeability, thereby decreasing the storage or degradation of norepinephrine. These drugs do not inhibit monoamine oxidase.

Imipramine and related drugs have been shown to have therapeutic effect in the treatment of depression in adults (Klerman & Cole, 1965). Some favorable work with adolescents has been reported (Lucas, Lockett, & Grimm, 1965), but this has not been systematically investigated. While depressive symptoms occur in both childhood and adolescence, it is generally accepted that depression in childhood is a reactive condition secondary to separation anxiety or is the result of an impaired physical condition. Adolescent depressions, on the other hand, are similar to the adult illness, and antidepressants are sometimes useful adjuncts to psychotherapy. Dosages for adolescents are generally begun at 25 mg three times per day and are increased every few days

until the dosage reaches 100 to 250 mg per day. Clinical effectiveness is frequently not observed for one to three weeks after treatment is initiated.

The tricyclic compounds have been used in treatment of childhood autism and behavior disturbances, but the results are too inconclusive for such use to be routinely recommended at this time (Bender & Faretra, 1961; Carter, 1966; Kraft, 1966; Kurtis, 1966; Rapoport, 1965).

In addition to MacLean's 1960 report on reduction of enuresis with use of imipramine, a number of other studies have demonstrated significant results in both children and adolescents with this symptom (Alderton, 1965, 1967; Poussaint & Ditman, 1965; Smith & Gonzalez, 1967). While the relative effectiveness of the tricyclic compounds and the amphetamines has not been compared, there seems to be general acceptance of the usefulness of imipramine in the treatment of enuresis in patients with relatively superficial anxieties expressed through uncomplicated bladder instability. The mechanism of effect is not clearly understood, but it is known that imipramine causes smooth-muscle relaxation and may reduce the irritability of bladders. For children with more severe, multidetermined enuresis, other therapeutic endeavors may be necessary. Treatment of enuresis is generally accomplished with 20 to 50 mg of imipramine given in the evening.

Although serious complications have occurred in use of the antidepressants with adult patients, side effects in children are usually mild and tolerable. Irritability, anorexia, sweating, dry mouth, constipation, postural hypotension, and tremor are sometimes noted early in treatment, but they tend to be minor and to improve in time or with a reduction in dosage. In adults, convulsions and liver, bone-marrow, allergic, and hypersensitivity reactions have been reported, but they are rare and not noted in children. Because additive clinical effects and severe complications may result, the tricyclic compounds are not prescribed for at least one week following use of monoamine oxidase inhibitors.

Anticonvulsants

Among the anticonvulsants, diphenylhydantoin (Dilantin) is the most commonly used in childhood behavior disorders. This compound was the product of deliberate attempts to synthesize a new agent which would be of specific therapeutic value because of its chemical relationship to the barbiturates. Merritt and Putnam reported their original findings in 1938, and the drug has been widely used as an anticonvulsant since that time. In addition, soon after its discovery, its value in the treatment of behavior disorders in children and adults was observed empirically. Subsequent studies have shown this drug to be useful in the treatment of a surprisingly large number of apparently unrelated clinical conditions, including neuralgias, migraine, neuromuscular disorders, and a variety of cardiac abnormalities. In this chapter, however, only its use in the treatment of behavioral disorders of children will be reviewed.

Unlike the barbiturates, to which it is chemically related, diphenylhydantoin is not a general CNS depressant and does not produce hypnotic effects. Rather than decreasing the cellular threshold against electrical and chemical excitation, this drug appears to act by decreasing the spread and amplification of the response to the stimulus. In so doing, it exerts a stabilizing effect, which reduces potentiation of cellular excitation. It is thus a much more specific therapeutic agent for psychomotor excitation than, for example, the barbiturates.

It appears that diphenylhydantoin is often efficacious in the treatment of children with diagnosable convulsive disorders associated with behavior problems (Itil, Rezzo, & Shapiro, 1967; Walker & Kirkpatrick, 1947). However, results reported in the treatment of behavior disorders in which hyperactivity is a predominant symptom are highly variable. Most of the clinical studies to date (Brown & Solomon, 1942; Gross & Wilson, 1964; Lindsley & Henry, 1942; Walker & Kirkpatrick, 1947) have been done with children who have had known or strongly suspected neurological impairment, usually in association with an abnormal electroencephalogram. Results do not seem particularly promising in cases with minimal or questionable neurological impairment. More definitive controlled studies are needed before reliable assessments can be made of the effectiveness of this drug.

With nonpsychotic children manifesting hyperactivity, impulsivity, distractibility, and hyperaggressivity with significant anxiety, the recommended dosage is from 1.5 mg per pound, or about 30 mg, for preschoolers to 4.5 mg per pound, or about 100 mg, for older children given two to three times per day. With convulsive patients, the dosage is not uncommonly increased to the point of toxicity and then reduced. However, hyperactive children without frank organic impairment seem to respond to dosages well below the toxic level, so it is advisable to begin medication conservatively with low dosages and increase the medication gradually until the desired effect is obtained. Diphenylhydantoin takes several days to reach peak clinical effectiveness. Its effects persist for a relatively long but unspecified period of time.

Diphenylhydantoin is a relatively safe drug. It may produce mild toxic complications, but these usually subside if the level of medication is reduced slightly. When medication reaches toxic levels, a number of CNS symptoms can be observed, such as unsteady gait, nervousness, tremors, drowsiness, fatigue, and headache. Serious toxic complications such as idiosyncratic bone-marrow depressions, hepatitis, and jaundice occur very rarely. Skin rashes are a fairly common complication and necessitate temporary cessation of the medication. Hyperplasia of the gums is also rather common but is not usually serious enough to warrant termination of treatment. Gastric upsets can be controlled by administering the drug at mealtime.

The Psychotomimetics

The psychotomimetic drugs include mescaline, psylocybine, and lysergic acid diethylamide (LSD). LSD has been used in the treatment of childhood autism and in the psychotherapy of adolescents, but results have not been encouraging. Since these drugs are not part of the clinician's armamentarium, they will not be discussed in detail here. The interested reader is referred to Jarik (1965, pp. 204–208) and Efron (1968, pp. 1185–1275).

In a field as fluid as the pharmacotherapy of children, it is difficult to make definitive statements about future use of drugs. Despite the incompleteness and inconsistency of findings at the present time, enough concrete guidelines have been developed to help clinicians select appropriate therapies. In addition, findings of recent studies suggest many potentially productive channels for further research.

REFERENCES

Adamson, W. C., Nellis, B. P., Rurge, G., Cleland, C., & Killian, E. Use of tranquilizers for mentally deficient patients. *American Journal of the Diseases of Children,* 1958, **96,** 159–164.

Alderton, H. R. Imipramine in the treatment of nocturnal enuresis of childhood. *Canadian Psychiatric Association Journal,* 1965, **10** (2), 141–151.

Alderton, H. R. Imipramine in childhood nocturnal enuresis: Relationship of time of administration to effect. *Canadian Psychiatric Association Journal,* 1967, **12** (2), 197–203.

Ayd, F. J., Jr. Emotional problems in children: The uses of drugs in therapeutic management. *California Medicine,* 1957, **87,** 75–80.

Ayd, F. J., Jr. Phenothiazine tranquilizers: Eight years of development. *Medical Clinics of North America,* 1961, **45** (4), 1027–1040.

Bakwin, H. Developmental hyperactivity. *Acta Paediatrica Scandinavica,* 1967, **172,** 25–29.

Bakwin, H., & Bakwin, R. M. *Clinical management of the behavior disorders in children.* Philadelphia: Saunders, 1960.

Beley, A., Foncin, J. F., & Leyrie, J. Quelques inconvenients des doses élevêrs de réserpine chez le jeune arriéré turbulent; Indications posologiques. *Encephale,* 1956, **45,** 802–810.

Bender, L., & Faretra, G. Organic therapy in pediatric psychiatry. *Diseases of the Nervous System,* 1961, **22** (Suppl. 4), 110–111.

Bradley, C. The behavior of children receiving Benzedrine. *American Journal of Psychiatry,* 1937, **94,** 577–585.

Brown, W. T., & Solomon, C. I. Delinquency and the electroencephalograph. *American Journal of Psychiatry,* 1942, **98,** 499–503.

Burket, L. C. New method of sedation in hyperkinetic children. *American Journal of Medical Science,* 1955, **229,** 22–24.

Carter, C. H. Nortriptyline HCL as a tranquilizer for disturbed mentally retarded patients: A controlled study. *American Journal of Medical Science,* 1966, **251,** 465–467.

Cole, N. O., Goldberg, S. C., & Davis, J. M. Drugs in the treatment of psychosis: Controlled studies. In P. Solomon (Ed.), *Psychiatric drugs.* New York: Grune & Stratton, 1966. Pp. 153–180.

Connell, P. H. Suicidal attempts in childhood and adolescence. In J. G. Howells (Ed.), *Modern perspectives in child psychiatry.* London: Oliver & Boyd, 1965. Pp. 403–427.

Conners, C. K., Eisenberg, L., & Barcai, A. Effect of dextroamphetamine on children. *Archives of General Psychiatry,* 1967, **17,** 478–485.

Conners, C. K., Eisenberg, L., & Sharpe, L. Effects of methylphenidate (Ritalin) on paired-associate learning and Porteus Maze performance, in emotionally disturbed children. *Journal of Consulting Psychology,* 1964, **28,** 14–22.

Craft, M. Tranquilizers in mental deficiency: Hydroxyzine. *Journal of Mental Science,* 1957, **103,** 855–857.

Craft, M. Tranquilizers in mental deficiency: Meprobamate. *Journal of Mental Deficiency Research,* 1958, **2,** 17.

Cytryn, L., Gilbert, A., & Eisenberg, L. The effectiveness of tranquilizing drugs plus supportive psychotherapy in treating behavior disorders of children: A double-blind study of eighty patients. *American Journal of Orthopsychiatry,* 1960, **30,** 113–128.

Dabbous, I. A., & Bergman, A. B. Neurological damage associated with phenothiazines. *American Journal of Disabled Children,* 1966, **111,** 291–296.

D'Amato, G. Chlordiazepoxide in management of school phobia. *Diseases of the Nervous System,* 1962, **23,** 292–295.

Davies, T. S. A monoamine oxidase inhibitor (Niamid) in the treatment of the mentally subnormal. *Journal of Mental Science,* 1961, **107,** 115–118.

Deley, J., Deniker, P., & Harl, J. M. Utilisation en therapeutique psychiatrique d'une phenothiazine d'action centrale élective (4560RP). *Annals Medico-Psychologiques* (Paris), 1952, **110,** 112–117.

DeLong, S. L. Ocular reactions to psychopharmacologic drugs. In D. H. Efron (Ed.), *Psychopharmacology: A review of progress, 1957-1967.* Washington,: Public Health Service Publication No. 1836, 1968. Pp. 515–580.

Diamond, L. S., & Marks, J. B. Discontinuance of tranquilizers among chronic schizophrenic patients receiving maintenance dosage. *Journal of Nervous and Mental Disorders,* 1960, **131,** 247–251.

DiFrancesco, A. Diazepam, a new tranquilizer. *American Journal of Psychiatry,* 1963, **119,** 989–990.

Dongan, H. T. Hydroxyzine syrup (Atarax) in the management of pediatric behavior problems. *Medical Times,* 1962, **90,** 551–554.

Effron, A. S., & Freedman, A. M. The treatment of behavior disorders in children with Benadryl. *Journal of Pediatrics,* 1953, **42,** 261–266.

Efron, D. H. (Ed.) *Psychopharmacology: A review of progress, 1957-1967.* Washington: Public Health Service Publication No. 1836, 1968.

Fish, B. Drug therapy in child psychiatry: Psychological aspects. *Comparative Psychiatry,* 1960, **1,** 55–61. (a)

Fish, B. Drug therapy in child psychiatry: Pharmacological aspects. *Comparative Psychiatry,* 1960, **1,** 212–227. (b)

Freed, H., & Peifer, C. Treatment of hyperkinetic emotionally disturbed children with prolonged administration of chlorpromazine. *American Journal of Psychiatry,* 1956, **113,** 22–26. (a)

Freed, H., & Peifer, C. Some considerations on the use of chlorpromazine in a child psychiatry clinic. *Journal of Clinical Experimental Psychopathology and Quarterly Review of Psychiatric Neurology,* 1956, **17,** 164–169. (b)

Freedman, A. M. Drug therapy in behavior disorders. *Pediatric Clinics of North America,* 1958, **5,** 573–584.

Freedman, A. M., Effron, A. S., & Bender, L. Pharmacotherapy in children with psychiatric illness. *Journal of Nervous and Mental Disorders*, 1955, **122**, 479–486.

Frommer, E. A. Treatment of childhood depression with anti-depressant drugs. *British Medical Journal*, 1967, **1**, 729–732.

Garfield, S. L., Helper, M. M., Wilcott, R. C., & Muffley, R. Effects of chlorpromazine on behavior in emotionally disturbed children. *Journal of Nervous and Mental Disorders*, 1962, **135**, 147–154.

Ginn, S. A., & Hohman, L. B. The use of dextroamphetamine in severe behavior problems of children. *Southern Medical Journal*, 1953, **46**, 1124–1130.

Goldberg, S. C., Klerman, G. L., & Cole, J. O. Changes in schizophrenic psychopathology and word behavior as a function of phenothiazine treatment. *British Journal of Psychiatry*, 1965, **111**, 120–125.

Good, W. W., Sterling, M., & Holtzman, W. H. Termination of chlorpromazine with schizophrenic patients. *American Journal of Psychiatry*, 1958, **115**, 443–448.

Greenberg, L. M., & Roth, S. Differential effects of abrupt versus gradual withdrawal of chlorpromazine in hospitalized chronic schizophrenic patients. *American Journal of Psychiatry*, 1966, **123** (2), 221–226.

Gross, M. D., & Wilson, W. C. Behavior disorders of children with cerebral dysrhythmia. *Archives of General Psychiatry*, 1964, **11**, 610–619.

Gupta, J. M., & Lovejoy, F. H. Acute phenothiazine toxicity in childhood: Five year survey. *Pediatrics*, 1967, **39**, 771–774.

Gwynne, P. H., Hundziak, M., Kautschitsch, J., Lefton, M., & Pasamanick, B. Efficacy of tri-fluoperazine on withdrawal in chronic schizophrenia. *Journal of Nervous and Mental Disorders*, 1962, **134**, 451–455.

Harman, C., & Winn, D. Clinical experience with chlorprotrixene in disturbed children—A comparative study. *International Journal of Neuropsychiatry*, 1966, **2**, 72–77.

Hawke, W. A., & McGreat, I. A. Tranquilizers. *Clinical Pediatrics*, 1964, **3**, 192–196.

Heaton-Ward, W. A., & Jancor, J. A controlled clinical trial of meprobamate in the management of difficult and destructive female mental defectives. *Journal of Mental Science*, 1958, **104**, 454–456.

Hunt, B. R., Frank, T., & Krush, T. P. Chlorpromazine in the treatment of severe emotional disorders of children. *AMA Journal of Diseases of Children*, 1956, **91**, 268–277.

Hunter, H., & Stephenson, G. M. Chlorpromazine and trifluoperazine in the treatment of behavioral abnormalities in the severely subnormal child. *British Journal of Psychiatry*, 1963, **109**, 411–417.

Irwin, S. A rational framework for the development, evaluation, and use of psychoactive drugs. *American Journal of Psychiatry*, 1968, **624** (Suppl.), 1–19.

Itil, T. M., Rezzo, A. E., & Shapiro, D. M. Study of behavior and EEG correlation during treatment of disturbed children. *Diseases of the Nervous System*, 1967, **28**, 731–736.

Jarik, M. E. Drugs used in the treatment of psychiatric disorders. In L. S. Goodman & A. Gilman (Eds.), *The pharmacological basis of therapeutics*. New York: Macmillan, 1965. Pp. 159–214.

Johnston, A. H., & Martin, C. H. The clinical use of reserpine and chlorpromazine in the care of the mentally deficient. *American Journal of Mental Deficiency*, 1957, **62**, 292–294.

Killam, E. K. Drug action on the brain stem reticular formation. *Pharmacology Review*, 1962, **14**, 175–224.

Kirk, D. L., & Bauer, A. M. Effects of reserpine on emotionally maladjusted high grade retardates. *American Journal of Mental Deficiency*, 1956, **60**, 776–780.

Klerman, G. L., & Cole, J. O. Clinical pharmacology of imipramine and related antidepressant compounds. *Pharmacological Reviews*, 1965, **17**, 101–141.

Knobel, M., Wolman, M. B., & Mason, E. Hyperkinesis and organicity in children. *AMA Archives of General Psychiatry*, 1959, **1**, 310–321.

Kraft, I. A. Use of amitriptyline in childhood behavioral disturbances. *International Journal of Neuropsychiatry*, 1966, **2**, 611–614.

Kraft, I. A., Ardali, C., Duffy, J. H., Hart, J. T., & Pearce, P. A clinical study of chlordiazepoxide used in psychiatric disorders of children. *International Journal of Neuropsychiatry*, 1965, **1**, 433–437.

Krakowski, A. J. Chlordiazepoxide in treatment of children with emotional disturbances. *New York State Journal of Medicine*, 1963, **63**, 3388–3392.

Kugelmass, I. N. Psychochemotherapy of mental deficiency in children. *International Records of Medicine*, 1956, **169**, 323–338.

Kuhn, R. The treatment of depressive states with B22355 (imipramine hydrocloride). *American Journal of Psychiatry*, 1958, **115**, 459–464.

Kurtis, L. B. Clinical study of the response to nortriptyline on austic children. *International Journal of Neuropsychiatry*, 1966, **2**, 298–301.

Lapolla, A. A double-blind evaluation of chlorpromazine versus a combination of perphenazine and amitriptyline. *International Journal of Neuropsychiatry*, 1967, **3**, 403–405.

Laties, V. G., & Weiss, B. A critical review of the efficacy of meprobamate (Miltown, Equanil) in the treatment of anxiety. *The Journal of Chronic Diseases*, 1958, **7**, 500–519.

Laufer, M. W., & Denhoff, E. Hyperkinetic syndrome in children. *Journal of Pediatrics*, 1957, **50**, 463–474.

La Veck, G. D., & Buckley, P. The use of psychopharmacologic agents in retarded children with behavior problems. *Journal of Chronic Diseases*, 1961, **13**, 174–183.

Levy, S. The hyperkinetic child — A forgotten entity. Its diagnosis and treatment. *International Journal of Neuropsychiatry*, 1966, **2**, 330–336.

Lindsley, D. B., & Henry, C. E. The effect of drugs on behavior and the electroencephalograms of children with behavior disorders. *Psychosomatic Medicine*, 1942, **4**, 140–149.

Litchfield, H. R. Clinical evaluation of meprobamate in disturbed and pre-psychotic children. *Annals of the New York Academy of Science*, 1957, **67**, 828–831.

Litchfield, H. R. Clinical pediatric experience with anataractic agent in less severe emotional states. *New York State Journal of Medicine*, 1960, **60**, 518–523.

Lourie, R. S. The contributions of child psychiatry to the pathogenesis of hyperactivity in children. *Clinical Proceedings at Children's Hospital (Washington, D.C.)*, 1963, **19**, 247–251.

Lourie, R. S. Psychoactive drugs in pediatrics. *Pediatrics*, 1964, **34**, 691–693.

Lowe, E. R., MacMillan, R., & Katser, M. E.

The antihistamine properties of benadryl, beta-bimethythaminoethyl benzhydryether hydrochloride. *Journal of Pharmacology and Experimental Therapeutics,* 1946, **86,** 229–238.

Lucas, A. R., Lockett, H. J., & Grimm, F. Amitriptyline in childhood depressions. *Diseases of the Nervous System,* 1965, **26,** 105–108.

MacLean, R. E. G. Imipramine hydrochloride (Tofranil) and enuresis. *American Journal of Psychiatry,* 1960, **117,** 551–556.

McDermott, J. F. A specific placebo effect encountered in the use of Dexedrine in a hyperactive child. *American Journal of Psychiatry,* 1965, **121,** 923–924.

Merritt, H. H., & Putnam, T. J. A new series of anticonvulsant drugs tested by experiments on animals. *Archives of Neurology and Psychiatry,* 1938, **39,** 1003–1015.

Miksztal, M. W. Chlorpromazine (Thorazine) and reserpine in residential treatment of neuro-psychiatric disorders in children. *Journal of Nervous and Mental Disorders,* 1956, **123,** 477–479.

National Institute of Mental Health, Psychopharmacology Service Center Collaborative Study Group. Phenothiazine treatment in acute schizophrenia. *Archives of General Psychiatry,* 1964, **10,** 246–261.

Ney, P. G. Psychosis in a child associated with amphetamine administration. *Canadian Medical Association Journal,* 1967, **97,** 1026–1029.

Overall, J. E., Hollister, L. E., Honigfeld, G., Kimbell, I. H., Jr., Meyer, F., Bennett, J. L., & Caffey, E., Jr. Comparison of acetophenazine with perphenazine in schizophrenics: Demonstration of differential effects based on computer-derived diagnostic models. *Clinical Pharmacological Therapy,* 1963, **4,** 200–208.

Paine, R. S. The contributions of neurology to the pathogenesis of hyperactivity in children. *Clinical Proceedings of Children's Hospital (Washington, D.C.),* 1963, **19,** 235–246.

Poussaint, A. F., & Ditman, K. S. A controlled study of imipramine (Tofranil) in the treatment of childhood enuresis. *Journal of Pediatrics,* 1965, **67,** 283–290.

Rapoport, J. Childhood behavior and learning problems treated with imipramine. *International Journal of Neuropsychiatry,* 1965, **1,** 635–642.

Rothstein, C., Zeltzerman, I., & White, H. R. Discontinuance of maintenance dosages of ataractic drugs on a psychiatric continued treatment ward. *Journal of Nervous and Mental Disorders,* 1962, **134,** 555–560.

Sainz, A. Hyperkinetic disease of children: Diagnosis and therapy. *Diseases of the Nervous System,* 1966, **27,** 46–50.

Segal, L. J., & Tansley, A. E. A clinical trial with hydroxyzine (Atarax) on a group of maladjusted educationally subnormal children. *Journal of Mental Science,* 1957, **103,** 677–681.

Sen, G., & Bose, K. C. *Rauwolfia serpentina,* a new Indian drug for insanity and high blood pressure. *Indian Medical World,* 1931, 194–201.

Sharpless, S. K. Hypnotics and sedatives. I. The barbiturates. In L. S. Goodman & A. Gilman (Eds.), *The pharmacological basis of therapeutics.* New York: Macmillan, 1965. Pp. 105–128.

Shaw, C. R., Lockett, H. J., Lucas, A. R., Lamontagne, C. H., & Grimm, R. Tranquilizer drugs in the treatment of emotionally disturbed children. *Journal of the American Academy of Child Psychiatry,* 1963, **2,** 725–742.

Smith, E. H., & Gonzalez, R. Nortriptyline hydrochloride in the treatment of enuresis in mentally retarded boys. *American Journal of Mental Deficiency,* 1967, **71,** 825–827.

Sylvester, R. E. A controlled cross-over trial of chlordiazepoxide (Librium) in mental deficiency. *Proceedings of 2nd International Congress on Mental Retardation,* 1963, **2,** 137–146.

Tarjan, G., Lowery, V. E., & Wright, S. W. Use of chlorpromazine in 278 mentally deficient patients. *AMA Journal of Diseases of Children,* 1957, **94,** 294–300.

Walker, C. F., & Kirkpatrick, B. B. Dilantin treatment for behavior problem children with abnormal electroencephalograms. *American Journal of Psychiatry,* 1947, **103,** 484–492.

Woodbury, D. M. Effects of drugs on various parameters of the developing nervous system. In G. M. McKhann, S. J. Yaffe & G. S. Sharon (Eds.), *Drugs and poisons in relation to the developing nervous system.* Washington: Public Health Service Publication No. 1791, 1968. Pp. 227–243.

part vii | # Specific Treatment Methods

35 The Psychoanalytic Treatment of Childhood Schizophrenia

*Rudolf Ekstein, Seymour Friedman,
and Elaine Caruth*

HISTORICAL REMARKS

The history of mankind's struggle to master the phenomenon of childhood schizophrenia in its totality reminds us of the fable of the blind men and the elephant. Each sightless individual, powerless to identify the whole animal in its total form, can experience only the fragmented part of it available to his limited and hence limiting perceptual apparatus. He then turns this part perception into a quasi-whole identity.

Similarly, scientists seeking to explore the mystery of this inadequately understood human experience of childhood schizophrenia appear to single out those aspects that have meaning to them in terms of their own inner experience and knowledge, that is, in terms of their own limited and hence limiting psychic apparatus, itself determined and influenced by the prevailing scientific *Zeitgeist* as well as by the special and acquired powers of insight available to a few forerunners within this particular area of scientific investigation. Rather than blind, we might perhaps characterize such investigators as victims of a kind of professional scotoma arising out of their particular ideological orientation.

Historically, psychosis was first understood in terms either of deviltry or witchcraft or of supernatural or mystical forces and, as a result, was either demonized or deified. Only gradually was the approach to psychosis modified under the aegis of naturalistic, biological, and psychological principles, becoming broadly identified with somatic pathology and, more specifically, with disorders of the central and autonomic nervous systems, as well as with endocrine and metabolic disturbances. Specific psychological viewpoints were subsequently differentiated within an overall medical, as opposed to theological or moralistic, approach to the understanding of mental illness.

Nevertheless, many specific viewpoints still can find meaningful only certain fragmented aspects of the total disease. Thus, it has come to be regarded variously as the outcome of and a disease of cortical cell degeneration, reticular or autonomic nervous system dysfunction, or disordered adrenalin metabolism. Others have

1035

suggested as determining factors a rejecting or overcontrolling mother; a brutalizing or weak father; unfeeling, mechanical parents; or victimization by symbiotic fusion with a cannibalizing, parasitizing mother. Other viewpoints of psychosis have emphasized the eruption of instincts and the dominance of id over ego, the fragmentation of ego, the weakening or loss of synthesizing and integrating functions of the ego, the helpless state of a psychic apparatus that has lost the nourishing and cementing internal object, etc. Still other viewpoints emphasize ego defect, thought disorder, primary-process functioning over rational secondary processes, disturbances of affect and emotions, and so forth. Each of these viewpoints, undoubtedly correctly perceived, is at the same time only that aspect of the total unity that can be taken in by the particular viewer, who can find only what he is capable of perceiving.

However, epoch-making events in the history of scientific investigation did provide a key of infinite potential leverage that helped toward the resolution of this dilemma inherent in the understanding and treatment of childhood schizophrenia. Although subsequently described by Freud as "the three major narcissistic blows delivered by science to mankind," they nevertheless opened the road to increasingly broader horizons leading to even greater restoration of man's self-esteem, arising out of increasing knowledge of himself and his environment. These events were (1) the Copernican explanation of a heliocentric universe, which replaced the Ptolemaic egocentric view of the earth as the center of the universe, remindful of the infant's omnipotent fantasies; (2) Darwin's theory of evolution, which discounted both theological and prevailing anthropological concepts of man as a product of divine creation uniquely different from unreasoning animals; and (3) Freud's discovery of the unconscious and his formulation of the topographic

model of personality, which challenged man's faith in his rational uniqueness and forced him to consider himself as not only biologically but also psychologically akin to animals, driven similarly by instinctive and nonrational forces. These three great advances in the history of science were essentially changes in viewpoint, which stimulated the observation of new data as well as of new relationships between existing data, leading toward a more unified view of mankind and the world.

In similar fashion, the introduction of the tripartite model of the personality, resulting in a more unified view of psychopathology, in which normality, neurosis, and psychosis were no longer regarded as essentially different and separate (Freud, 1961c) and in which the variety of part aspects of this complex disease could be integrated and synthesized into a total disease condition manifesting itself in a variety of ways, led to what might be considered as a fourth narcissistic blow to mankind on the part of science, which again opened the road to the increase of self-esteem derived from increasing mastery.

Current views of the psychopathology of childhood schizophrenia can best be understood in relationship to historical contributions to the study of schizophrenia in general. One of the early major contributors to the work of diagnosis and classification of the symptomatology of schizophrenia was Kraepelin, who emphasized the process aspects of all diseases, including schizophrenia, in which he felt the prognosis was dementia. Additional major contributions stemmed from Bleuler, who was particularly concerned with the thought and affect disorders in schizophrenia, even though he remained within the nineteenth-century conceptualization of psychosis as equivalent to insanity and dementia. It was only with the twentieth-century extensions of ego psychology that we developed an understanding that the thought disorder implies rather that such patients operate under an order which we do not as yet comprehend (Meyer & Ekstein, 1970).

Freud's major contributions to the study of psychosis (1961a, 1961b) were derived from the tripartite model of the personality and emphasized the loss of reality testing and the loss of capacity for normal object relations in schizophrenia.

CONCERNING THE CAUSE OF THE CURE

If we examine the different emphases of these theoretical approaches, we can see that what appear manifestly as different etiological views of the illness are also reflections of latent views concerning the "cause of the cure" (Ekstein & Friedman, 1968) and involve a hidden commitment to a specific treatment philosophy and technique. In these approaches to treatment we can see how a limited and limiting theoretical bias, or even a valid, reliable bias, with respect to a part of the treatment process has been equated with the whole process and is thereby limited in its perception and knowledge of how to resolve the illness. Thus, a variety of treatment techniques emphasizing merely part aspects of the total treatment process, such as contact and communication, become, as the result of a constricted and constricting emphasis, merely ill-founded and ill-effective overgeneralizations, again repeating the fallacy of the part being taken for and misrepresenting the whole.

Elaboration of treatment techniques should be based upon the capacity to integrate and conceptualize our ever-developing knowledge of the psychic structure of the patient and the formulation of models of personality which integrate the greatest number of these features.

Freud's topographic model of the personality was presented in 1900 in *The Interpretation of Dreams* (Freud, 1953) and is derived from the hypothetical assumption of a mythical, ideal analytic patient, who is stable and whose psychic organization provides the necessary and sufficient structure for the therapeutic process. This model, originating from the classical conception of analysis, has to be adapted to the unique problems of schizophrenia (as well as of child therapy) by integrating it with the tripartite model.

When treatment techniques were based largely on the concept of psychosis derived from the topographic model, the illness was considered a breakthrough of unconscious forces, conceived of as a wild jungle in which neither structure, logic, time sequence, nor evidence of reality testing could be found (a kind of primitive Pandora's box). Accordingly treatment, dictated by social pressures and needs, could consist only of sealing over the seething caldron and driving back the dangerous destructive forces. Clinical maneuvers designed to "put the lid" on these forces are, in our current psychoanalytic framework, considered not as treatment but as a kind of manipulation leading to so-called reconstitution—which, in fact, is an untreated, covered-up disease process. Paradoxically, the consideration of schizophrenia as an "organismic reaction resulting from evolutionary problems and having its onset in the maturational embryonic period" (Bender, 1967) also led to similar manipulative substitutes for psychotherapeutic processes.[1]

The tripartite model of personality portrays the psychic organization in terms of id, ego, and superego structures which are best described in terms of their functions and processes or, as

[1] We have suggested elsewhere in reviewing her work (Ekstein & Friedman, 1968) that Bender and her coworkers' skill and strength could best be used if new insights into the nature of schizophrenia were to be found through studies of the treatment process. We would suggest again that we emphasize the search for techniques for changes, rather than causes of cure—the more popular preoccupation of many workers in the field.

Beres (1965) has suggested, as a functional model of the personality with emphasis on purpose, function, development, and processes. The dynamic relationship between the psychic organizations makes obsolete the Pandora's box metaphor and rather stresses the conflict between impulse and defense, between wish and reality-testing capacity, between impulsivity and delay functions. Such a model permits the recognition of the quasi-adaptive resolution of a conflict represented in symptom formation. It also recognizes that conflict can take place on any level of the psychic organization, which is perceived as a hierarchy of structures and in which there are functional relationships between the different aspects of these personality structures. We suggest here that we combine these two models and conceive of the tripartite model as operating in depth, as it were. Thus, various levels of consciousness may perhaps best be construed as different layers of psychic organization forming a hierarchy developing out of an undifferentiated archaic phase, in which can be found latent dispositions that will later develop into the organizers of more complex structure within the personality. Such an integrated model allows for a more refined and subtle description of the specific ego deviation suffered by psychotic children and thus allows for refinement of treatment techniques to deal with such clinical problems as need for distance devices (Ekstein & Caruth, 1967; Ekstein & Meyer, 1961), need for metaphoric communication (Cain & Maupin, 1961; Caruth & Ekstein, 1966), and need for psychotic acting out (Ekstein & Caruth, 1966), as well as the resulting and unique countertransference problems (Caruth & Ekstein, 1964; Ekstein & Caruth, 1965a; Ekstein, Wallerstein, & Mandelbaum, 1959).

Knight (1953) has amplified this model in order to differentiate further between neurotic and psychotic ego organization through the metaphor of the island separated from the mainland by the intervening sea of primary process. With the neurotic patient, this symptomatology is like the outer island separated from the main continent of adaptive functioning. With the psychotic patient, however, the small amount of adaptive functioning is the outer island isolated from the main continent of psychotic structure. Treatment—the causeway between the island and the continent—can easily be inundated by a breakthrough of primary-process functions and structures in the case of psychotic patients. With such patients, all that is predictable is that fluctuations within the personality structure may occur rapidly in seemingly unpredictable fashion. In treating such patients, we must understand that we are faced with the problem that they are able to maintain the object only so long as the object is present (Ekstein & Friedman, 1967). This may result in their capacity to retain the memory of the spoken voice only so long as the sound waves are present. As the waves die out, the voices recede into an unstable and unreliable memory. The power of interpretation with such patients is limited by this unreliability or lack of object constancy. The voice of the therapist may appear powerful at first, but it does not persist and will die out with his absence. The initial impact cannot be sustained, and little permanent, reliable effect can be assumed from the original powerful impact.

To supplement Knight's model of islands of fragmented ego functioning for the borderline and psychotic patient, we might add the model of the Möebius strip (Caruth, 1968) to further describe the psychic organization of the psychotic patient with respect to the lack of clear-cut differentiation between inside and outside, between conscious and unconscious, between self and object, between fantasy and reality. Such understanding helps to develop more specific techniques for dealing with the problems of how to contact, communicate with, and influence such patients (Ekstein & Caruth, 1967). This is in contrast to Reich's metaphor of an onion to be peeled as a rough description of the necessary working through of systematic layers of impulse and defense in order to get to the underlying conflict. Derived from a topographic model of the personality and applicable for normal and neurotic psychic organization, it is not applicable in the case of borderline and schizophrenic patients, in whom there is no stable personality organization but rather one that is fluctuating, unpredictable, and unreliable.

BASIC MODELS OF ANALYTIC TREATMENT

In addition to a basic model of personality organization, the development of a rational treatment philosophy is aided by the use of a related model of the treatment process. Fifteen years ago the senior author (Ekstein, 1956) described a basic model of the analytic process with adults based upon the then current view that interpretive intervention emanated from outside the treatment process. (See Figure 35-1.) This model therefore did not include the impact of the

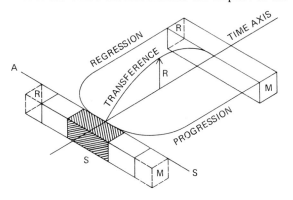

R = Repressed aspects of ego
S = Symptomatology
M = Unavailable—either repressed or undeveloped—functions
    of mature ego
Line AS = Analytic situation

Figure 35-1. Basic model of the analytic process.

process on the analyst and its function in the treatment process. Today we recognize that treatment necessarily involves an interaction of patient and therapist, even though the essential process is an intrapsychic one and the interaction a very unique one. We do not consider psychotherapy exclusively as either an interpersonal process, an interactional process, or a communication process. However, we now recognize that in order to understand the intrapsychic process in psychotherapeutic change, it is also necessary to understand the impact upon it of extrapsychic processes during the period of change.

In our present revised model (see Figure 35-2) of the analytic treatment process, the basic observational data consist, as in the earlier model, of the free associative process, which is the primary activity on the part of the patient. However, we have now included the interpretive process as the primary activity on the part of the analyst. The process of communication between the patient and therapist is set up under conditions which, unlike a social relationship, dictate a different set of rules with a different focus and function for each, even though they both share the same long-range purpose: intrapsychic change in the patient and restoration of autonomous psychic functioning on an age-appropriate level. In psychoanalytic treatment the therapeutic contract defines the activities of the analyst as well as the patient. Basic rules govern both. For the patient, the basic task is to attempt to "talk" freely (be it in the language of words, actions, play, or even silence), and for the therapist the basic task is to attempt to listen freely. Thus, the free associations of the patient are met by the freely suspended attention of the therapist, which must encompass such elements as transference, adaptive and defensive mechanisms, regressive behavior, and unconscious communication, which he will interpret to the patient. The doctor thus has a dual function in which there are elements paralleling the regressive and progres-

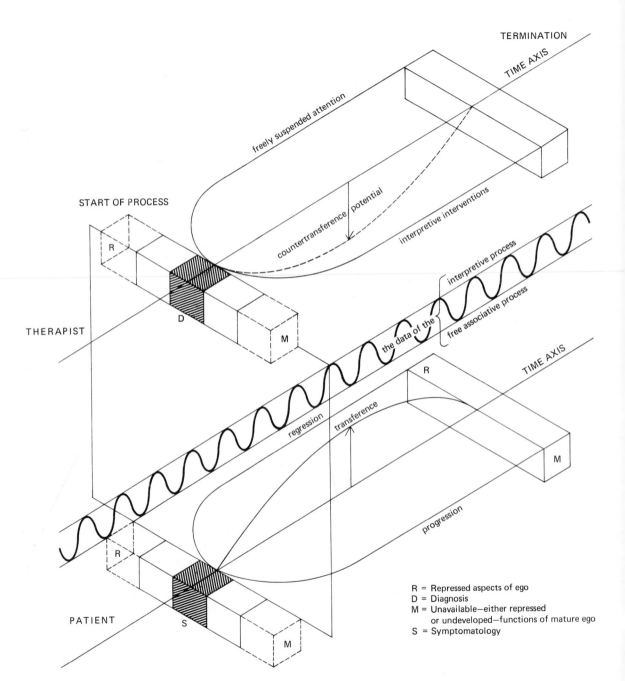

Figure 35-2. Revised model of the analytic process.

sive elements of the therapeutic process in the patient. In this model we see that the transference development of the patient is matched by a countertransference potential of the therapist. The countertransference potential must be kept within the service of the treatment and be an identification to help the patient, rather than an overidentification to act out with him, often employing the fine line between controlled empathy and the loss of analytic equidistance.

For this updated model of treatment, therefore, the basic observational data are the productions of both the patient and the doctor. The free associations of the patient are met by the freely suspended attention and interpretive interventions of the doctor. In many ways it would appear that the rules for the patient and the doctor are like mirror images. They are very similar in that neither can act as in ordinary social situations, and the rules define all behavior within the analytic framework. The patient must reveal his needs rather than demand gratification of them from the therapist. The therapist must accept his needs rather than repress them and must utilize them in the service of understanding instead of letting them deteriorate into countertransference reactions.

However, in dealing with children, especially psychotic children, it is almost impossible to maintain this classical analytic framework, at least with regard to the external conditions. The child does not free-associate in words; the child does not understand the rules of our game, as it were. It may well be necessary to see how this basic model of classical analytic treatment requires modification in order to encompass treatment of children, both neurotic and psychotic. It may be necessary in the future to further elaborate the model for such special cases, requiring a structure which can be maintained despite the breakthrough of inundating forces before they have been absorbed through interpretations or parameters.

Specific approaches to the treatment of childhood schizophrenia must understand pathology in relationship to the totality of psychic growth and development. We have seen how schizophrenia is a global human phenomenon, affecting all areas and facets of human life and personality—biological, psychological, and social. To comprehend the nature and meaning of childhood schizophrenia is to appreciate the total organization of the psychotic personality as a molar state of human functioning, even though, paradoxically, schizophrenia is a state of functioning characterized by fragmentation, disorganization, and disassociation, so that part features dominate the whole.

We deal with an illness which is derived from disturbances in the beginning phases of development, before there was an individual wholeness—the period prior to and including the early mother-child unit, which is characterized by a prolonged state of helplessness and dependency of the infant upon the mother. It is a relationship in which the mother is not an object and the baby is not a self; rather self and object either do not exist or else are fused in a symbiotic arrangement which permits little or no differentiation between self and object, between "I" and "not I," between inner and outer reality. Any delay in immediate gratification of impulse is compensated for by the hallucinated wish fulfillment via which the baby also seeks to restore the union and communion with the mother and thus reestablish the oneness of their fused beings. Only if this early symbiosis between mother and child is a nonpathogenic one can the infant develop the subsequent capacity for individuation and separation. This capacity for individuation and separation is achieved only as there is a beginning constancy of self and object representation. There now emerges a capacity for delay functions, permitting the integration and synthesizing of drive organizations, initially organized around the object as a kind of external steering device to help negotiate between the impulse and the demands of reality. As the individual develops a greater degree of individuation and a more differentiated image of himself as a separate person, he simultaneously develops the capacity to perceive the people around him as separate objects with whom he is able to have a variety of relationships, which change in nature as his psychological development proceeds. Normally, this progression in object relationships moves from the early autistic and symbiotic positions to one in which the child begins to take in the object through the mechanisms of imitation, incorporation, and introjection, leading ultimately to the capacity to achieve mature and stable identifications.

Language serves to facilitate the developing object relations as they proceed from fusion to separation, to introjection, and to identification. Language, according to Buhler's Organon model, begins as a means of expression and appeal but subsequently acquires the functions of representation and communication, proceeding from echolalia, through delayed echolalia, to descriptive and symbolic speech (Ekstein, 1964).

With the schizophrenic child,[2] however, we see a failure to achieve this progression from the earliest mother-child fusion to normal object relatedness. There develops, rather, a prolonged and distorted version of the normal symbiotic relationship, expressed instead as an ambivalent, pathological struggle between the autistic and symbiotic positions and the process of individuation. As the infant struggles unsuccessfully to establish some separation as a defence against the loss of identity which is experienced in the ambivalent, negative symbiosis, he can only retreat to an autistic withdrawal, in what Mahler described as the psychotic analogue of the nor-

mal child's negativism. As such children mature, their psychological development does not proceed normally due to this basic flaw, which subsequently permeates the total psychic organization and often results in a variety of symptomological manifestations, many on a behavioral level, to which, unfortunately, many so-called psychotherapeutic techniques are exclusively addressed—such as the work of the behavior therapists, as exemplified by Lovaas (1965a, 1965b, 1966a, 1966b)—rather than understanding the symptomatology as secondary to the primary thought disorder, to which may be referred many of the features found in childhood schizophrenia.

NATURE OF THE PRIMARY THOUGHT DISORDER

The primary thought disorder—actually not a disorder, but rather an order according to rules different from those governing the thinking of the nonpsychotic—is characterized by the prolonged presence of the pleasure-principle—dominated, primary-process functioning of the primitive, archaic mental organization. This is in contrast to the growth of secondary-process functioning, dominated by the reality principle, which increasingly characterizes the maturing, healthy child and which leads to the capacity for delay and postponement of immediate gratification and the subsequent capacity to obtain gratification in reality from love and work relationships and commitments.

Schizophrenic children live in a world in which they cannot differentiate inner from outer reality; a world in which impulse reigns and the only way to control the impulse may be to identify with it and deny or fail to perceive the existence of the object and the need for delay; a world in which perception and conceptualization may be fused and confused; a world in which the instinctual organization dominates and rules and in which there can only be rule of the part over the whole

---

[2] Pollock (1964) suggests that pathogenic symbiotic ties may be seen in all psychopathological states, and he describes in detail symbiotic neuroses.

and representation of the part for the whole. Theirs is a world characterized by a need for ceaseless instinctual discharge, a world which knows not of delay nor has knowledge about or trust in the future. In such a world the object is experienced only as the aim of the drive. These children are unable to maintain a relationship with the real world other than through the empty, sterile, imitative devices available to them, in which there is no real contact with the object (Ekstein, 1964). They populate their inner world with introjects—fragmented remnants of earlier primitively perceived objects and self-representations—or else with deanimated objects (Ekstein & Friedman, 1967), in a return to the earliest autistic retreat from all contact. These introjects, often monsterlike distortions of early parental images, are projected onto the people around them, who are frequently seen as paranoid, delusional objects that, at the same time, function as precursors of an archaic superego and as an aid in organizing, strengthening, and sustaining the total psychic functioning (Ekstein & Caruth, 1965b). These children, still dominated by primary-process functioning, have not developed the capacity for higher-level, autonomous ego function with which to control, integrate, and synthesize the basic drive organization. One is often confronted with the helpless, impulse-ridden, seemingly meaningless behavior characteristic of many such children. In the process of establishing control over the primitive, archaic, instinctually dominated process, they develop the paranoid objects—the monsters and creatures—in order to ward off the primitive impulses, even as the very means of warding them off are derived out of primitive and archaic defenses. These children are limited in their ability to differentiate the thought from the act, and hence they are not capable of ideational reflection; they tend instead to think via action (Ekstein & Friedman, 1957) and to act out, as a substitute for thinking out, their feelings (Ekstein & Caruth, 1966).

When such children do show indications of higher-level ego functioning, it is often of an unstable, fragmented nature. There are islands of advanced functioning (Knight, 1953), which may suddenly be inundated by regressive floods of archaic material and by sudden shifts in the level of ego organization available to them (Ekstein & Wallerstein, 1954). Thus, fluctuating ego states, sudden massive regressions, and isolated advanced capacities or skills may all characterize different children within this complex disease process (Ekstein & Wallerstein, 1956).

The major dilemma for the psychotherapeutic commitment and task in dealing with these children is the characteristic fragmentation, disintegration, pseudo-whole-parts dichotomy, primary-process nature of the archaic, primitive functioning, which has never become subordinated to advanced ego control and which provides the dominant character of the psychotic personality. Furthermore, treatment is complicated by the fact that the psychotic child experiences that his existence and survival can be maintained only through his autistic, delusional, omnipotent control over any part of his world, including the therapist (Ekstein, Friedman, Caruth, & Cooper, 1968). In his need for complete autistic control, the schizophrenic child must create a narcissistic sameness, a world that comes within his orbit, producing an impregnable, unassailable symbiosis with the nurturing object environment to maintain his delusional autonomy. Such children must turn the therapeutic object and environment into an image of themselves (Caruth & Ekstein, 1964; Ekstein & Caruth, 1965b) to make of the outside what they feel within, in an attempt to render the outside as impotent and ineffectual as their own underlying inward feeling, against which they defend by means of the delusional omnipotence. Unlike the neurotic child, who struggles to feel loved, the schizophrenic child struggles to *feel*, to be, to survive. Change is experienced as a threat to the very survival of the self, which can exist only so long as there is immediate gratification of instinctual drives by part objects, which must mirror the psychosis of the patient and hence can only feed the psychosis—in the process, starving the potential for normal living.

THE TASKS OF THE THERAPIST

The basic tool of change is, as in all analytic therapy, the relationship with the therapist, that is, the transference by which are exposed the motivations, fears, and conflicts that drive these children away from mastery of the external world into delusional gratifications which reinforce their retreat to an autistic, inner world. To treat, there must be this contact, and this becomes the crucial beginning problem: how to bridge the chasm between the patient's inner world and that of the therapist (Ekstein, 1963). The therapist retaining one foot, as it were, in his own secondary-process world so as not to join fully in the symbiosis sought for by the patient. At the same time, he must be capable of entering it sufficiently to allow for the restoration in the transference of the patient's feelings of communion and fusion, even as he introduces the speck of reality around which there can be the further growth and psychic development that, it is to be hoped, will proceed along healthier lines.

When the therapist is permitted into the inner world of the patient and is successful in restoring contact, he is paradoxically faced with a double bind: if the symbiosis is totally restored, this, too, will terrify the patient and cause him to retreat. Optimal contact can be restored under those conditions in which the therapist conveys his understanding of the patient's language and, at the same time, avoids the terrifying aspect of the double bind by skillfully remaining in a position in which he does not enter the symbiosis too completely. The therapist must then compromise between his language and that of the patient; he accepts both and rules out neither. In so doing, he must also accept the patient's varying needs for distance from the therapist, from the conflict, and from his own feelings. This can often be achieved through an acceptance of the metaphor of the patient's level of communication (Caruth & Ekstein, 1966; Ekstein, 1965).

The technical interventions are basically interpretive, yet adjusted to the specific communion and communication difficulties of the schizophrenic child. These interventions must make use of psychotic transference manifestations, which frequently require the maintenance of therapeutic alliances via "cooperation" with psychotic structures, delusional systems, and the like (Ekstein, 1955), in the service of restoring the continuity between various aspects of the psychic organization that have heretofore been unavailable because of paralyzing struggles between forces of impulse and forces of delay and adaptation. We have moved to a concept of treatment that does not aim at suppression of the psychosis but whose goal is restoration of the continuity of functioning between the primitive and advanced psychic organizations, as well as the development and establishment of stable structure within the personality organization which will permit predictable and self-controlled choices at whatever level of psychic organization is available at any given moment. Our goals are not to compensate for ego impairment that prevents outer solutions and resolutions but to seek, rather, to restore ultimately the capacity for functioning and the development of structure which will enable the patient's own learning and mastery of reality to develop. We seek to help him give up the retreat to the inner world, where he can attempt to restore only delusionally and by giving up reality testing the early mother-child union, in which self and object were fused in a symbiotic arrangement.

These concepts can be graphically illustrated

in clinical data of a schizophrenic adolescent girl who, at the time of her diagnostic evaluation, fended off an open psychosis by regressing to the fantasies of the latency period, through which inadequate psychic maneuvers she protected herself from panic and terrifying fantasies. In analytic treatment this patient repeatedly demonstrated that she could function on a marginal level within the limits of what we would describe as the secondary process only until the pressure of primary-process material overwhelmed the capacity of the ego to control the flood of archaic material, leading to regression, to archaic and primitive levels of psychic functioning, and to a reliance upon her psychic invention of the *Creature, a delusional introject* and precursor of the archaic superego, *"who" served to organize, strengthen, and sustain her psychic functioning.* This Creature became her delusional, terrifying, yet protective object, which helped her to maintain some level of integration as she continued to deal with the archaic material that flooded her. We could follow the appearance of the Creature at those times when the patient needed to strengthen her determination to talk "nice" and thus avoid the influx of primary-process material. *The struggle not to communicate the "not nice" material interfered with the process of communication and led to paralysis.* A progressive breakdown in her ego organization was accompanied by a breakdown in the level of superego structure. For, as the flood of disruptive material became more primitive and archaic, it was necessary to counter this with more primitive and archaic defense means. Low-grade defenses were used to ward off low-grade primitive impulse derivatives. The Creature, in order to avoid danger, created a virtual paralysis of advanced ego organization, which in the end resulted in regression to the very archaic primary-process level from which the danger originally emanated.

Since she did not have available normal thinking as a form of trial action and delay, she used as a substitute delay mechanism the introduction of the Creature in order to ward off impulsivity and acting out. However, lacking reality testing and realistic discrimination, this form of primitive control device, even though it served to ward off impulsivity and self-destructive action, also indiscriminately warded off all action at any level and led to the paralysis and unavailability of higher ego functions.

Despite the regressive aspects of the Creature (who is generally experienced by both patient and therapist as an enemy, a paranoid delusion, and an external persecutor), this primitive precursor of the superego has the primary adaptive function of serving to avoid a complete breakthrough of the primary process, of instinct, and of archaic functioning. It also functions to ward off the temptation of outside dangers. Thus, although the Creature derives its energy from the id, its function is to wall off the id lest it overwhelm the ego. Paradoxically, the Creature is derived from the same material that it serves to counteract, having a similar origin but having been differentiated into a different person.

As the therapeutic hour of this psychotic girl continued, archaic primary-process material overran the primitive police power of the Creature and inundated the ego's secondary-process functioning. It is at this point that the therapist would feel helpless to understand or to apply his therapeutic skills if he were to insist that the treatment process be the same for a psychotic as for the normal or neurotic child. The failure to modify the model of treatment under these circumstances places the therapist in the situation of meeting the patient with his own psychosis, as it were. The resultant failure in therapeutic effectiveness would further arouse anxiety and terror in both therapist and patient and would lead to a breakdown in the treatment process.

An understanding of the function of the Creature, as well as of its relationship to the function of the therapist, must become an integral part of the therapeutic model. Observation and analysis of the patient led to the insight that the Creature appeared when the doctor was absent. When analyzing the various vicissitudes and functions of the Creature, we can observe that it serves as a projected paranoid delusional defense against the archaic process and thus is a measure of the intrapsychic process and that it describes a particular functional relationship to the doctor, a tension system between patient and doctor, and therefore is a measure of the interpersonal process. The Creature functions as a helper, as an agent to delay and to ward off the psychotic process, and as a tempter who brings about that very same aspect of the psychotic process against which it also helps to defend.

The Creature, therefore, is a primitive psychological device that works both for the delay function of the ego and for impulse discharge of the id. Its adaptive power and value make it a necessary adjunct to the therapeutic process and lead to the importance of the therapeutic philosophy of establishing an alliance with the monster (Ekstein & Caruth, 1965b), the therapeutic work of committing the Creature, like the therapist, to work in the service of the patient's recovery. In her desperate attempt to stem the flood of the archaic material which emerged as the hour proceeded, and in her attempt to comply with the injunction of the Creature not to talk, express, or let loose harmful primary-process thoughts and impulses, this patient was often led to communicate in what appeared to be a harmless device of talking about borrowed fantasies from the movies. These fantasies, even though they were introduced by external stimuli, were related to her inner world, thus providing the patient with a means of communication by which she could both escape from her own inner world and, at the same time, relate the content of her inner world to the therapist. She could thus dis-

avow her connection with her own inner world, complying with the injunction of the Creature to suppress the "not nice" thoughts and escaping its threatened punishment. At the same time she acquiesced to the imagined requirement of the therapist that she talk about the inner world. While maintaining an equidistance between inner and outer worlds, between id, demands of superego, and the remote and still unaccepted ego-therapist, the patient resolved for the moment the conflict that would otherwise inevitably paralyze her functioning. She maintained her position via the invention of the Creature in much the same way that the neurotic conflict is often temporarily resolved through symptom formation.

Inevitably there was a breakdown of this facade, and more primitive aspects of her ego organization began to appear. Fluctuations in ego states are characteristic of such patients, who undergo shifts from higher levels of functioning to more primitive ones. Primitive autistic experiences of death and the struggle to remain alive, the desperate need for the helper to appear, and at the same time the certain belief that such a helper could not be trusted and could not save her emerged into open relief.

The eruption of the archaic primary process created in this patient the feeling of having lost her mind, of being dead but half-alive. The impending thought disorder was manifested by concretistic language and primitive archaic symbolism by which she began to communicate psychotic fantasies of total isolation in an objectless world where no one would accept her or believe her language. She was reduced to the terror of the underlying psychotic fantasy that, alone and isolated, she was but a living corpse. The therapist understands and accepts this experience, which he interprets as a consequence of the lack of autonomous ego functioning, a true living death (Ekstein, 1966b).

We have used the preceding clinical illustration in an attempt to show how our philosophy of treatment, based upon our conceptualization of the psychic structure of the psychotic patient's personality, has enabled us to borrow Freud's uncanny gift of turning obstacles to treatment and insight into instruments of advance and to advocate an alliance with the very monsters and devils which both the patient and society would enjoin us to banish. Our understanding of the positive adaptive function of delusional systems in the life-and-death struggle of such children has thus led to techniques for helping establish ego dominance over id forces rather than to an attempt to exorcise a very essential part of the patient's psychic structure. Understanding of the fragmented, islandlike nature of ego functioning in such patients has led to interpretive innovations (Caruth & Ekstein, 1966) which permit the restoration of continuity within the personality— a restoration which could not have been achieved by conventional therapeutic techniques that were not adapted to the available psychic structure of the patient (King, 1964; King & Ekstein, 1967). The catastrophic discontinuities experienced by these patients have led us to experimentation with new models and to the establishment of a persistent commitment to the exploration of new treatment techniques.

FURTHER ANALYTIC CONTRIBUTIONS

We are not alone in this commitment to constant exploration and examination of our philosophy and technique. Mahler's extensive clinical and research contributions (Mahler, 1958, 1965; Mahler & Elkisch, 1958; Mahler & Furer, 1960) and those of her collaborators, such as Elkisch (Elkisch & Mahler, 1959) and Furer (1964), to psychoanalytic therapy of childhood psychosis, as well as her training of a number of valuable contributors to the field, center around a variety of germinal notions which have become commonly accepted as the basis for clinical thinking. The continued study of the autistic and symbiotic condition, which she initially defined and identified, has led to insights which consider autism not as a static position but as the indication of an arrested process. She speaks of autism as the negativism of the symbiotic child's struggle. Thus she gives us insight into the peculiar nature of psychotic transferences which allows the evolvement of appropriate techniques to unfreeze autistic positions, that is, animate deanimated states or humanize machines which "influence" the mind of the patient. Her current studies of normal phases of autism and symbiosis during the first two years of life and of normal and pathological mothering arrangements also offer opening wedges toward reaching the seemingly inaccessible patient whose disorder stems from such early periods.

Kaufman and his collaborators (1957, 1960, 1962, 1963) have contributed a variety of publications through the years, culminating in recommendations to create subdivisions in the classification of schizophrenic children and their parents along a scale of decreasing severity of overt disturbance, permitting a better estimate of potential ego growth and reality orientation as well as the utilization of techniques directly related to the specificity of these subdivisions, presently described in five steps from minimal ego development to pseudoneurotic schizophrenia. He and his co-workers believe that such considerations permit more manageable research undertakings and more specificity of treatment techniques.

Thomas (1966), of the Hampstead Child-Therapy Clinic, has attempted to utilize the Anna Freud profile with four "atypical," or borderline, children who had been considered amenable to a modified form of analytic therapy. She and her collaborators found the profile helpful in highlighting the children's chaotic development and reaction to treatment, but they felt it was necessary to modify the profile in order for it to differentiate more clearly among children suffering from different types and degrees of severe disturbance.

Bettelheim's pioneer work in the residential analytic treatment of the autistic and schizophrenic child (1959, 1965, 1967) takes cognizance of the fact that the seriously disturbed child cannot fit himself into his existing environment and that the environment, rather, must fit into the child's needs, even though the ultimate goal of treatment is to help the child slowly change so that he can live in the everyday world. Assuming that such children have the capacity to distinguish the good from the bad environment, Bettelheim advocates accepting the child where and as he is, "going with him" with the expectation that as the child sees and experiences the loving creations provided for him, he will become capable of change. He emphasizes the child's need for experimentation with and discovery of caring and pleasure in his basic functions, even and especially those of his bodily products, in a new atmosphere in which the adult's empathy and emotional involvement in ministering to his functions will replace the earlier experience of pathological mothering. His insightful and compassionate accounts of these very sick children are rooted primarily, however, in generic terms of treatment environment, with relatively little concern (conveyed, at least, in his published writings) about formal analytic therapy (Ekstein, 1968). His primary concern, derived from his philosophy that the cause of the illness is the emotional rejection of the child by his parents, is with the affective deprivation resulting from the mechanical, deanimated way in which the parents relate to the child. He believes this must be counteracted by a kind of rebirth experience in a better and more human way than had been originally experienced so that the child may experience his own feelings and thereby become

human rather than be a mechanical puppet.

Other analytic workers have attempted to deal with these problems on an outpatient basis. Alpert and Pfeiffer (1964) describe the application of Alpert's "corrective object relations" technique for children with severe maternal deprivation (1959) in their history. The goals of the technique are in three phases: first, to establish a dependent relationship on the therapist; second, to move into a so-called regressive phase of an anaclitic, incorporative level of relating, in which the child becomes maximally educable through this incorporation and identification with the therapist; and finally, to achieve restitution and corrective manipulation by the therapist.

Weiland and Rudnik (1961), however, suggest that the fearful child who defends against involvement with human beings because he sees them as dangerous can benefit from such techniques only if they offer a therapeutically corrective life experience. These authors suggest that progress beyond a pseudo-object type of relationship is seldom obtained by psychotherapy, and they propose modifications in the basic analytic orientation to therapy with such children.

Kemph, in a number of publications (1964a, 1964b, 1965, 1966) has also dealt with the treatment of such severely disturbed children and has described a process of three phases in therapy, two of which might be considered precursors of the stage at which the child is actually available for more conventional psychotherapeutic techniques. Kemph describes these phases as (1) breaking through the autistic barrier to establish contact, (2) developing ego functions, and (3) dealing with intrapsychic and interpersonal conflict by providing uncovering therapy. He goes on in other publications to distinguish between treatment techniques for the autistic, the symbiotic, and the borderline psychotic child. The major task with the autistic child is breaking through the autistic barrier by making contact with and establishing communication with and through those parts of the organism that will receive incoming stimuli and will respond. At the vegetative level, this can be accomplished by giving food. Occasionally the child responds with minimal ego functioning. The aim is to establish contact with the child and to get him to become more aware of the therapist by increasing physical contact and primitive precursors to play associated with minimal frustrations. As awareness increases, the child becomes symbiotic with the therapist. With the symbiotic child, the therapist initially strives to become a part of the symboisis with the child, adopts the mother's system of cues and signals which bind and interrelate the mother-child symbiosis, and gradually replaces and substitutes for the mother as the need-satisfying and gratifying part object. After the symbiosis is established, he gradually frustrates the child's efforts to remain fused with the therapist, forcing separation and individuation in the therapeutic process, which provides an overall permissive, accepting environment. Communication with the child involves both verbal and nonverbal processes, varying with the child's particular deficits in ego functioning.

The problem of communication with the psychotic child has occupied many workers in this field, and Rice and Klein (1964) have suggested that the schizophrenic child's behavior can best be understood by its emotional impact upon others, with the therapist needing to become aware not only of the countertransference but also of the relevance of his primitive feelings to the child's struggle and missing affects.

Griffith and Ritvo (1967) have described the therapeutic difficulty arising out of the inability to establish a communicative bridge of secondary-based verbal communication with the echolalic child. Parker (1962) follows in her book the course of analytically oriented psychotherapy with a schizophrenic youth whose need to both communicate and conceal and to maintain distance by means of metaphoric communication and whose difficulty in establishing trust in both the therapist and himself led to a plasticity of approach in maintaining a meaningful relationship, the primary condition of his treatment. Stewart et al. (1965) describe the special problems of communication and transference as they are manifested in bold relief in work with a blind schizophrenic child.

Des Lauriers (1962, 1967) has also attempted to describe therapeutic techniques in childhood schizophrenia derived from the theoretical explanation of the disease within the framework of psychoanalytic ego psychology. He views schizophrenia as a structural deficiency involving the severe diminution of narcissistic cathexis of bodily boundaries, resulting in a lack of differentiation of self from nonself and the consequent loss of reality contact. He believes that the therapist should forcibly intrude his presence in order to direct the patient's attention to his own bodily self, establish body boundaries, draw attention to the patient's feelings and experiences as being his own, and provide space and time orientation. However, in his insistence that the therapist should represent reality and not permit delusional or autistic behavior to occur, one is reminded of those workers who ignore the developments of ego psychology and advocate repressing the psychosis. In surprisingly similar fashion, Des Lauriers emphasizes what the schizophrenic mode of behavior represents and reflects, and while recognizing the symptomatic behavior of the schizophrenic child as an expression of a central ego deficiency, paralleling an inadequate development of the experience of bodily limits that separate the child from the mother, he believes that for a rational therapeutic strategy the etiology must be ignored for the focus on what the condition is. The inability to experience himself as a separated and differentiated individual and the experiencing of himself as the subject of whatever happens to him arise out of his experiencing his body as being invaded and transgressed by the mother's sensory and stimulating intrusion in his life. It is this type of intrusion which Des Lauriers suggests must become the model for treatment and must define the specific therapeutic attitude.

Problems of countertransference in childhood schizophrenia have been described with respect to both the conflict that can be created between various members of the hospital team during treatment of a psychotic symbiotic child (Ekstein, Friedman, Caruth, & Cooper, 1968) and the phenomenological aspects of certain countertransference experiences (Caruth & Ekstein, 1964) and their consequent expressions in the therapeutic interaction (Ekstein & Caruth, 1965a). Christ (1964) has described the specific problems of sexual countertransference with a psychotic child which emerged in the course of eighteen months of treatment of a nearly mute 14-year-old schizophrenic girl. In a discussion of the literature and a presentation of his treatment process, he points out how the patient's progress was delayed by his lack of awareness of the countertransference. Identification and clarification of his own defense mechanisms led to change in the patient's behavior.

Concerned with this same problem, Szurek and Berlin (1956) have suggested that the therapist, who in their setting is usually a student, be engaged in a supervision experience consisting essentially of his own treatment. They advocate this in a milieu in which the therapist's contact with the child is comparatively short and not intensive, although based upon analytic principles. They report that under such conditions approximately 10 percent of the cases improve and that success is usually achieved when treatment is started at an early age and when there is adequate ego strength available.

Prall and Dealy (1965) have dealt in detail with the powerful unconscious countertransference attitudes that are likely to occur in the treatment of psychotic children, which become evident in the training and supervision of the therapist. They feel that these attitudes must be dealt with in the supervision, although they would differentiate supervision from personal treatment or analysis of the therapist student. They describe such common reactions as rescue fantasies and expectations for rapid improvement, which lead to discouragement and pessimism; overidentification with the regressive behavior, aggression, or particular defense mechanisms; difficulty in handling primary-process id expressions, aggression, or polymorphous perverse sexuality; discomfort for the therapist from the extensive bodily contact; inability to tolerate the necessary symbioticlike relationship, which may turn into a subsequent difficulty in giving it up when necessary to foster the separation-individuation process in the child; and, finally, the excessive, reverberating kind of anxiety which may be provoked in the therapist by the massive anxiety of the patient.

Rosenfeld and Sprince (1965) also are concerned with some of the countertransference issues and their relevance to techniques of psychotherapy with borderline children. They concern themselves primarily with the initial stages of treatment, which they acknowledge can extend over years and which are aimed at making the child more analyzable; by this they mean that the internalized conflict can become the center of the treatment, which, as Fordham (1966) emphasizes, can be of an interpretive nature even in childhood autism. They discuss how each child's level of ego and object relations is at a different stage of development and how there is frequently a need for ego-supportive techniques in order to make meaningful contact and follow the child into his psychic world—which, however, leads to such problems as that of becoming relatively active in this therapy. They concern themselves particularly with the influence on the treatment of the children's fragmentary ego, their proneness to acute anxiety, and their low level of object relations.

Sperling (1963) deals specifically with the problems of developing criteria for evaluating the treatment potential of schizophrenic children. She describes some criteria based upon her own work with treatment or supervision of treatment of schizophrenic children for whom an unfavorable prognosis had been predicted, and she suggests that on the basis of her successful experiences, a reevaluation of some of the criteria heretofore used for treatability should be attempted. She suggests that diagnostic interviews should be in a form of trial treatment, focusing on the child's accessibility to therapy rather than upon diagnosis. She points out that for the autistic schizophrenic child, prognosis on the basis of the usual criteria would be considered most unfavorable, more so than with the symbiotic child, yet in actual clinical work this has not always been the case. She describes a number of cases illustrating the necessity for varying the approach to the evaluation according to the situation but, in all cases, utilizing all the data that can possibly be obtained, such as medical and psychological reports, hospital records, opinions of other doctors, detailed developmental, social, and school history, as well as a number of diagnostic interviews. She emphasizes the role of the parents in the total evaluation of the treatment potential and the final prognosis of the schizophrenic child. She suggests that if a reliable relationship with even one of the parents can be established, a schizophrenic child can be treated successfully even in difficult situations.

The need to abandon rigidly prescribed techniques in the diagnosis and treatment of schizophrenic children has also been dealt with by Hirsch (1960), who has emphasized the necessity for flexibility of interpretation in work with schizophrenic children and, as a matter of fact, "as a condition set by" these children, who need to make use of the therapist as "an auxiliary ego"

who makes his own capacities available to the child, thereby enabling the child to function on a higher level. Hirsch refers to the work of Rank, who, like others described above (Alpert, Kemph), has suggested that therapy with a schizophrenic child be carried on in three phases: The first of these is "a restitutional phase," in which the therapeutic effort is to make up to the child for the frustrations of the past. The second phase is one of "ego strengthening," the purpose of which is to help the child make the necessary steps toward socialization, toward the ability to postpone immediate gratification, and toward developing relationships with people. The third stage involves helping the child to differentiate himself from the therapist. Hirsch proposes that the first two stages can frequently be carried on concurrently and that the very process of ego strengthening actually leads to the process of gratification. He suggests that the therapist allow himself to be used symbolically as an auxiliary ego in order to enhance the child's capacity to function in a more organized, modulated, delaying fashion. He describes his work with a Southard schoolchild (previously treated and described in the literature by Ekstein and Friedman) in order to illustrate the child's use of distance devices as a way of regulating and controlling the therapeutic interventions as well as their impact.

Spotnitz (1961, 1962), in a remark not specifically concerning children, speaks of the patient's "need for insulation" rather than a specific need for distance and postulates that self-hatred is the nuclear problem to be worked with in treating the schizophrenic patient. He suggests that the primary reason for the schizophrenic's withdrawal from people is to prevent himself from acting as his impulses tell him to act, thus "unconsciously sacrificing his ego to preserve his object."

Speaking from a specifically Kleinian frame of reference, Souza (1960) suggests that annihilation of the object which accompanies the annihilation of parts of the self is a psychotic type of object relationship. Using Melanie Klein's techniques, he describes the play-therapy analysis of a 2-year, 10-month-old schizophrenic child, which purports to demonstrate how the annihilation of the perception of the object and of the object relationship, as well as the annihilation of verbal communication and capacity for integration, was "related to the ego's integration and capacity for feeling responsible for the object's condition and facing the unbearable guilt connected with the depressive position."

In addition to a number of descriptions of individual instances of psychotherapy with schizophrenic and autistic children (Dolto-Marette, 1958; Ford et al., 1960; Hafilena, 1957; Lefort, 1956; Nichtern et al., 1966; Seidman, 1961), there has been an annotated bibliography on childhood schizophrenia compiled by Tilton (1966), which covers the years from 1955 to 1964, thus overlapping slightly with the comprehensive bibliography of Ekstein, Bryant, and Friedman (1958) covering all the literature through 1956. Wolman (1968, in press) includes a chapter on psychotherapy which has a review of different philosophies of psychotherapeutics with schizophrenic children, including that of analytic orientation. And finally, of course, the senior author has recently published *Children of Time and Space, of Action and Impulse* (Ekstein, 1966a), which offers a vivid, detailed description of all phases of intensive therapy with very sick children, many of whom were considered untreatable (Lippman, 1967).

SUMMARY

In summary, we would like to suggest that the history of the psychoanalytic treatment of childhood schizophrenia represents a culmination and synthesis of the extreme swings in attitude toward the treatment of the severely ill—from the early attempts to control, dominate, overpower, and restrain these patients through chains, torture, exorcism, and snake pits; to efforts of those like Pinel, who struck off the chains; to the other extremes of those like Szaz, who would close the hospitals and completely deny the very existence of the illness and hence really eliminate its treatment. Psychoanalysis recognizes that neither destructive hate nor helpless love is enough. Psychoanalytic treatment of the schizophrenic child has developed out of a scientific understanding of the psychic organization of the total personality rather than out of a moralistic or humanistic value system that concerns itself only with symptoms, the part representation of the patient. Although the severity of the illness of these children and the resulting distortions in personality organization and function that arise out of this illness have led inevitably to the introduction of additional parameters (Morgan, 1964; Sechehaye, 1960; Weiland & Rudnik, 1961) to supplement the basic analytic model of treatment, a total integrated treatment program for such children can be organized around the dominant psychoanalytic ethic that we are dealing with a human being whose basic integrity and identity must be respected even as his illness is recognized and treated. Understanding and restoration of choice must remain the primary technique and goal and must not be sacrificed to the expediency of manipulative techniques which aim at control and conformity. There will always be those who speak of the social problems attendant upon the treatment approach that requires such intensive and extensive commitments; and we can only maintain that a commitment to treatment permits of no compromise with any demands except those of the illness.

REFERENCES

Alpert, A. Reversibility of pathological fixations associated with maternal deprivation in infancy.

Vol. 14. *The psychoanalytic study of the child.* New York: International Universities Press, 1959. Pp. 169–185.

Alpert, A., & Pfeiffer, E. Treatment of an autistic child: Introduction and theoretical discussion. *Journal of the American Academy of Child Psychiatry,* 1964, **3,** 591–616.

Bender, L. Childhood schizophrenia: A review. *Journal of the Hillside Hospital,* 1967, **16,** 10-22.

Beres, D. Structure and function in psychoanalysis. *International Journal of Psychoanalysis,* 1965, **46,** 53–63.

Bettelheim, B. Joey: A "mechanical boy." *Scientific American,* 1959, **200,** 116–127.

Bettelheim, B. The orthogenic school. *University of Chicago Magazine,* 1965, **57,** 2–9.

Bettelheim, B. *The empty fortress: Infantile autism and the birth of the self.* New York: Free Press, 1967.

Cain, A. C., & Maupin, B. Interpretation within the metaphor. *Bulletin of the Menninger Clinic,* 1961, **25,** 307–311.

Caruth, E. The onion and the Moebius strip: Rational and irrational models for the secondary and primary process. *Psychoanalytic Review,* 1968, **55** (3), 416.

Caruth, E., & Ekstein, R. Certain phenomenological aspects of the countertransference in the treatment of schizophrenic children. *Reiss-Davis Clinic Bulletin,* 1964, **1,** 80–88.

Caruth, E., & Ekstein, R. Interpretation within the metaphor: Further considerations. *Journal of the American Academy of Child Psychiatry,* 1966, **5,** 35–45.

Christ, A. E. Sexual countertransference problems with a psychotic child. *Journal of the Ameri-can Academy of Child Psychiatry,* 1964, **3,** 298–316.

Des Lauriers, A. M. *The experience of reality in childhood schizophrenia.* New York: International Universities Press, 1962.

Des Lauriers, A. M. The schizophrenic child. *Archives of General Psychiatry,* 1967, **16,** 194–201.

Dolto-Marette, F. (Psychoanalytic therapy with the aid of the "flower doll.") *Praxis Kinderpsychologie Kinderpsychiatrie,* 1958, **7,** 93–99.

Ekstein, R. Vicissitudes of the "internal image" in the recovery of a borderline schizophrenic adolescent. *Bulletin of the Menninger Clinic,* 1955, **19,** 86–92.

Ekstein, R. Psychoanalytic techniques. In D. Brower & L. E. Abt (Eds.), *Progress in clinical psychology.* Vol. II. New York: Grune & Stratton, 1956.

Ekstein, R. The opening gambit in psychotherapeutic work with severely disturbed adolescents. *American Journal of Orthopsychiatry,* 1963, **33,** 862–871.

Ekstein, R. On the acquisition of speech in the autistic child. *Reiss-Davis Clinic Bulletin,* 1964, **1,** 63–79.

Ekstein, R. Puppet play of a psychotic adolescent girl in the psychotherapeutic process. Vol. 20. *The psychoanalytic study of the child.* New York: International Press, 1965. Pp. 441–480.

Ekstein, R. *Children of time and space, of action and impulse: Clinical studies on the psychoanalytic treatment of severely disturbed children and adolescents.* New York: Appleton Century Crofts, 1966. (a)

Ekstein, R. The Orpheus and Eurydice theme in psychotherapy. *Bulletin of the Menninger Clinic,* 1966, **30,** 207–224. (b)

Ekstein, R. Book review: Bettelheim, B., *The empty fortress. Psychoanalytic Quarterly,* 1968, **37**, 296.

Ekstein, R., Bryant, K., & Friedman, S. Childhood schizophrenia and allied conditions. In L. Bellak (Ed.), *Schizophrenia: A review of the syndrome.* New York: Logos Press, 1958. Pp. 555–693.

Ekstein, R., & Caruth, E. To sleep but not to dream: On the use of electrical tape recording in clinical research. *Reiss-Davis Clinic Bulletin,* 1965, **2**, 87–92. (a)

Ekstein, R., & Caruth, E. The working alliance with the monster. *Bulletin of the Menninger Clinic,* 1965, **29**, 189–197. (b)

Ekstein, R., & Caruth, E. Psychotic acting out: Royal road or primrose path. In R. Ekstein, *Children of time and space, of action and impulse.* New York: Appleton Century Crofts, 1966. Pp. 298–308.

Ekstein, R., & Caruth, E. Distancing and distance devices in childhood schizophrenia and borderline states: Revised concepts and new directions in research. *Psychological Reports,* 1967, **20**, 109–110.

Ekstein, R., & Friedman, S. W. The function of acting out, play action and play acting in the psychotherapeutic process. *Journal of the American Psychoanalytic Association,* 1957, **5**, 581–629.

Ekstein, R., & Friedman, S. W. On the meaning of play in childhood psychosis. In L. Jessner & E. Pavenstedt (Eds.), *Dynamic psychopathology of childhood.* New York: Grune & Stratton, 1959. Pp. 269–292.

Ekstein, R., & Friedman, S. W. Object constancy and psychotic reconstruction. Vol. 22. *The psychoanalytic study of the child.* New York: International Universities Press, 1967. Pp. 357–374.

Ekstein, R., & Friedman, S. W. Cause of the illness or cause of the cure? *International Journal of Psychiatry,* 1968, **5**, 224–229.

Ekstein, R., Friedman, S., Caruth, E., & Cooper, B. The intra-relatedness of childhood schizophrenia: Therapeutic implications for a working alliance with environmental support systems. *The Reiss-Davis Clinical Bulletin,* 1969, **6** (2), 111.

Ekstein, R., & Meyer, M. Distancing devices in childhood schizophrenia and allied conditions. *Psychological Reports,* 1961, **9**, 145–146.

Ekstein, R., & Wallerstein, J. Observations on the psychology of borderline and psychotic children. Vol. 9. *The psychoanalytic study of the child.* New York: International Universities Press, 1954. Pp. 344–369.

Ekstein, R., & Wallerstein, J. Observations on the psychotherapy of borderline and psychotic children. Vol. 11. *The psychoanalytic study of the child.* New York: International Universities Press, 1956. Pp. 303–311.

Ekstein, R., Wallerstein, J., & Mandelbaum, A. Countertransference in the residential treatment of children. Vol. 14. *The psychoanalytic study of the child.* New York: International Universities Press, 1959. Pp. 186–218.

Elkisch, P., & Mahler, M. S. On infantile precursors of the "influencing machine" (Tausk). Vol. 14. *The psychoanalytic study of the child.* New York: International Universities Press, 1959. Pp. 219–235.

Ford, E. S., Robles, C., & Harlow, R. G. Psychotherapy with child psychotics. *American Journal of Psychotherapy,* 1960, **14**, 705-718.

Fordham, M. Notes on the psychotherapy of infantile autism. *British Journal of Medical Psychology,* 1966, **39**, 299–312.

Freud, S. *The interpretation of dreams.* (1900) Vol. IV. (Standard ed.) London: Hogarth, 1953.

Freud, S. *The ego and the id* (1923). Vol. XIX. (Standard ed.) London: Hogarth, 1961. (a)

Freud, S. The loss of reality in neurosis and psychosis (1924). Vol. XIX. (Standard ed.) London: Hogarth, 1961. (b)

Freud, S. Neuroses and psychoses (1924). Vol. XIX. (Standard ed.) London: Hogarth, 1961. (c)

Furer, M. The development of a preschool symbiotic psychotic boy. Vol. 19. *The psychoanalytic study of the child.* New York: International Universities Press, 1964. Pp. 448–469.

Griffith, R., & Ritvo, E. Echolalia: Concerning the dynamics of the syndrome. *Journal of the American Academy Child Psychiatry,* 1967, **6,** 184–193.

Hafilena, F. P. A case of child psychosis. *Journal of the Philippine Medical Association,* 1957, **33,** 473–480.

Hirsch, E. A. Interpretive flexibility as a condition set by schizophrenic children in psychotherapy. *American Journal of Orthopsychiatry,* 1960, **30,** 397–404.

Kaufman, I. Relationship between therapy of children and superego development. *Journal of the American Psychoanalytic Association,* 1960, **8,** 130–140.

Kaufman, I., et al. Childhood psychosis. 1. Childhood schizophrenia: Treatment of children and parents. *American Journal of Orthopsychiatry,* 1957, **27,** 683–690.

Kaufman, I., et al. Success and failure in the treatment of childhood schizophrenia. *American Journal of Psychiatry,* 1962, **118,** 909–1015.

Kaufman, I., et al. Adaptation of treatment techniques to a new classification of schizophrenic children. *Journal of the American Academy of Child Psychiatry,* 1963, **2,** 460–483.

Kemph, J. P. Communicating with the psychotic child. *International Psychiatry Clinics,* 1964, **1,** 53–72. (a)

Kemph, J. P. The treatment of psychotic children. *Current Psychiatric Therapy,* 1964, **4,** 74–78. (b)

Kemph, J. P. Psychotic children treated in a child guidance clinic. *Diseases of the Nervous System,* 1966, **27,** 317–320.

Kemph, J. P., et al. Promoting the development of ego functions in the middle phase of treatment of psychotic children. *Journal of the American Academy of Child Psychiatry,* 1965, **4,** 401–412.

King, P. Theoretical considerations of psychotherapy with a schizophrenic child. *Journal of the American Academy of Child Psychiatry,* 1964, **3,** 638–649.

King, P., & Ekstein, R. The search for ego controls: Progression of play activity in psychotherapy with a schizophrenic child. *Psychoanalytic Review,* 1967, **54,** 639–648.

Knight, R. Borderline states. *Bulletin of the Menninger Clinic,* 1953, **17,** 1–12.

Lefort, R. L'enfant au loup. (The child with the wolf.) *Psychoanalyse,* 1956, **2,** 145–164.

Lippman, H. Book review: Ekstein, R., *Children of time and space, of action and impulse. American Journal of Psychiatry,* 1967, **123,** 1043–1044.

Lovaas, O. I., et al. Building social behavior in autistic children by use of electric shock. *Journal of Experimental Research in Personality,* 1965, **1,** 99–109. (a)

Lovaas, O. I., et al. Experimental studies in childhood schizophrenia: Analysis of self-destructive behavior. *Journal of Experimental Child Psychology,* 1965, **2,** 67–84. (b)

Lovaas, O. I., et al. Acquisition of imitative

speech by schizophrenic children. *Science,* 1966, **151,** 705–707. (a)

Lovaas, O. I., et al. Establishment of social re-inforcers in two schizophrenic children on the basis of food. *Journal of Experimental Child Psychology,* 1966, **4,** 109–125. (b)

Mahler, M. Autism and symbiosis, two extreme disturbances of identity. *International Journal of Psychoanalysis,* 1958, **39,** 77–83.

Mahler, M. On early infantile psychosis. The symbiotic and autistic syndromes. *Journal of the American Academy of Child Psychiatry,* 1965, **4,** 554–568.

Mahler, M., & Elkisch, P. Some observations on the disturbances of the ego in a case of in-fantile psychosis. Vol. 8. *The psychoanalytic study of the child.* New York: International Universities Press, 1958. Pp. 252–261.

Mahler, M., & Furer, M. Observations on re-search regarding the "symbiotic syndrome" of infantile psychosis. *Psychoanalytic Quarterly,* 1960, **29,** 317–327.

Meyer, M., & Ekstein, R. The psychotic pursuit of reality. *Journal of Contemporary Psycho-therapy,* 1970, **3** (1), 3–12.

Morgan, P. Application of "symbolic realiza-tion" to the removal of hallucinations in child-hood schizophrenia. *American Journal of Psy-chotherapy,* 1964, **18,** 59–65.

Nichtern, S., et al. Disturbance in introjection and projection in a schizophrenic adolescent girl: A case report. *Journal of the Hillside Hospi-tal,* 1966, **15,** 211–238.

Parker, B. *My language is me.* New York: Basic Books, 1962.

Pollock, G. On symbiosis and symbiotic neuro-sis. *International Journal of Psychoanalysis,* 1964, **45,** 1–30.

Prall, R., & Dealy, M. Countertransference in therapy of childhood psychosis. *Journal of the Hillside Hospital,* 1965, **14,** 69–82.

Rice, G., & Klein, A. Getting the message from a schizophrenic child. *Psychiatry,* 1964, **27,** 163–169.

Rosenfeld, S. K., & Sprince, M. Some thoughts on the technical handling of borderline children. Vol. 20. *The psychoanalytic study of the child.* New York: International Universities Press, 1965. Pp. 495–517.

Sechehaye, M. Techniques de gratifications en psychotherapie analytique. II. Indications et contre-indications. *Evolution Psychiatric,* 1960, **25,** 559–582.

Seidman, F. Outpatient treatment of a seriously disturbed child in a child guidance center. *Journal of Clinical Psychology,* 1961, **17,** 220–225.

Souza, D. Annihilation and reconstruction of object relationship in a schizophrenic girl. *Inter-national Journal of Psychoanalysis,* 1960, **41,** 554–558.

Sperling, M. Some criteria on the evaluation of the treatment potential of schizophrenic chil-dren. *Journal of the American Academy of Child Psychiatry,* 1963, **2,** 593–604.

Spotnitz, H. The narcissistic defense in schizo-phrenia. *Psychoanalysis,* 1961–1962, **48,** 24–42.

Spotnitz, H. The need for insulation in the schizophrenic personality. *Psychoanalysis and Psychoanalytic Review,* 1962, **49,** 3–25.

Stewart, R., et al. The psychotherapy of a blind schizophrenic child. *Journal of the American Academy of Child Psychiatry,* 1965, **4,** 123–132.

Szurek, S., & Berlin, I. Elements of psycho-therapeutics with the schizophrenic child and his parents. *Psychiatry,* 1956, **19,** 1–9.

Thomas, R. (in collaboration with R. Edgcumbe, H. Kennedy, M. Kawenoka, & L. Weitzner) Comments on some aspects of self and object representation in a group of psychotic children. Vol. 21. *The psychoanalytic study of the child.* New York: International Universities Press, 1966. Pp. 527–580.

Tilton, J., et al. *Annotated bibliography on childhood schizophrenia (1955–1964).* New York: Grune & Stratton, 1966.

Weiland, I., & Rudnik, R. Considerations of the development and treatment of autistic childhood psychosis. Vol. 16. *The psychoanalytic study of the child.* New York: International Universities Press, 1961. Pp. 549–563.

Wolman, B. *Children without childhood: A study of childhood schizophrenia.* New York: Grune & Stratton, 1970.

36 | Helping Children in School

Jack I. Bardon
and Virginia D. C. Bennett

One of the few incontestable facts about childhood in the United States is that children attend school. For better or for worse, somewhere between the ages of 4 and 6, virtually every child capable of learning at all is sent to school, including the vast majority of those described as emotionally and socially maladjusted. Current estimates are that about 4 million children are in need of some kind of assistance because of emotional difficulties and that anywhere from a half million to a million of these children are so disturbed that they require immediate intervention (Gorman, 1968). The Center for Studies of Mental Health of Children and Youth of the National Institute of Mental Health in a report to Congress in 1967 noted that there were about 25,000 children in mental institutions in 1965 and that approximately 300,000 children are seen in outpatient psychiatric clinics each year, with only one of every three children receiving services beyond routine diagnostic interviews (Gorman, 1968). It should be clear from these estimates that most children needing attention for psychological disorders are not receiving

inpatient or outpatient help—and that they are in schools.

As Donahue (1967) has pointed out, schools can and should adapt to the needs of emotionally disturbed children. The school system in America is the only social institution in our culture in a position to deal systematically with the problems of the emotionally disturbed child. Schools have staffs of professional people who are oriented, to some extent at least, to the developmental problems of children. And there is a widely held belief in this country that separating the severely disturbed child from his normal environment is not desirable for most of these children.

When considering helping children with psychological disorders in the school setting, it is important to keep in mind that the school is a social institution different from others in important respects. The grouping of children by ages, teacher-pupil-administrator relationships, school rules and regulations, and community values influence the social climate of the school in unique ways (Bardon, 1968; Coleman, 1961). White and Charry (1966) remind us that the importance of the term *school* in school disorder cannot be overemphasized; school disorder is school defined.

This chapter attempts to bring together opinion and data specifically related to helping emotionally disturbed children in the school setting. It is necessarily "second-order," dealing largely with modifications of theories and methods developed in the behavioral and medical sciences. Whenever possible, the special contribution of the school is emphasized. The material reviewed deliberately avoids topics which are likely to be comprehensively handled in other chapters.

HISTORY

The schools have long been concerned with those pupils who are markedly different from the majority of children: children who seem unable to learn, who resist learning, or who behave in ways the school finds difficult to manage. As early as 1871, the schools of New Haven, Connecticut, isolated children labeled *contumacious aggressors* in a special class (Cutts, 1955). The mental-health professions, particularly psychology, have their roots in concern for the problems of children in the schools. Witmer's clinic, established at the University of Pennsylvania in 1894, is usually credited as the first clinic in the United States. Witmer's concern was for children who were having trouble in school. His clinic was a psychoeducational clinic, and his training program at the University of Pennsylvania was directed to produce a "psychological expert, who should find his career in connection with the school system" (Cutts, 1955, p. 18).

Three years after Witmer's clinic was started, the Chicago Board of Education established a Department of Child Study, whose function was to carry out physical measurements of school pupils, scientific study of educational problems, examination of individual problem children, and instruction of teachers on psychoeducational matters (Magary, 1969).

The development of psychological testing, usually considered a fundamental aspect of all psychology, also had its roots in concern for children in the school. Binet's famous and durable instrument was devised to estimate children's learning potential for the purpose of school placement or, in Binet's day, school exclusion. Goddard in 1908 and Terman in 1916, the promulgators of the use of Binet's scales in the United States, were both concerned with the use of the tests in educational settings.

A concurrent development in the late nineteenth and early twentieth centuries which affected school approaches to helping emotionally disturbed children was the establishment of child-guidance clinics. Clifford Beers's famous diatribe against "insane asylums" spearheaded the formation of the National Mental Hygiene Society in 1909. The gradual acceptance of a mental-hygiene point of view led to modifications of two early clinic models, Witmer's psychoeducational clinic and Healy's Chicago Juvenile Psychopathic Institute. The first modern agency to call itself a child-guidance clinic was started in St. Louis in 1922. In 1924 the first child-guidance clinic under the direction of a board of education was established in Minneapolis, and schools in major cities began to establish similar clinics within their school systems.

This welding together of the two approaches— the one from nineteenth-century psychology and the other from early twentieth-century psychiatry—had rather expectable results. Help for children in the schools was originally focused on primary concern for children's learning problems, with a shift to concern for the "whole child" and for children's emotional problems.

After World War II, the medical-model child-guidance clinic grew rapidly in numbers and services, and help to children in schools became strongly flavored by professionals trained in the psychoanalytic tradition. Psychological testing remained the major technique in the battery of the psychologist working in the schools, but testing became a source for clinical interpretation as well as for the determination of mental ability, especially with the development of the Wechsler tests (1949).

Since World War II, then, the schools have become increasingly involved in attempting to offer help to pupils judged disturbed or maladjusted. Stimulated by political action of enlightened parents of retarded children pressing for special school provisions for their children, major changes in school programming have taken place. Some state legislatures and Congress responded to this pressure, and as federal and state monies became available to help schools make provision for children with various handicaps (Balow, 1966a), states in increasing numbers began to pass legislation for special services and special classes for, at first, the physically handicapped and the mentally retarded and, more recently, the emotionally and socially maladjusted pupil.

A parallel development of the late 1950s and 1960s has been within the professional field itself. Mental-health professionals have recognized the need for involvement in effecting social change, with schools becoming a logical setting in which psychiatrists, psychologists, sociologists, and social workers might apply their knowledge (Bardon & Bennett, 1967; Yale Conference on Learning, 1966). The professional field itself has been reevaluating its approaches to the problems of children in the schools (Balow, 1966a). The strong clinical orientation of the post-World War II decades produced a rash of literature dedicated to alerting both school and special-services personnel to the need to understand children's emotional needs, with emphasis on permissiveness in the classroom, lowered academic expectations, and recognition of individual differences (e.g., D'Evelyn, 1957; Hymes,

1947, 1949; Joint Committee on Health Problems in Education, 1956). Although this point of view is still widely supported, and concern for the individual child with his unique problems has not been negated, the awesome problems of whole groups of children and the problems of society itself have presented the schools with the burden of attempting to change what is evil in society while maintaining its position as the perpetuator of the society which supports it. Mental-health professionals, responding to the needs of society as expressed in the schools, have turned to other models for helping children in the schools. There has been a resurgence of interest in the application of learning theory to the solution of the problems of schoolchildren (Balow, 1966a).

The realization that the number of professionals available to help individual children in the schools falls far short of need has resulted in the development of professionals to be consultants to the schools (Caplan, 1961; Newman, 1967). These consultants work primarily with teachers, administrators, teacher aides, and other school personnel. The recent formation of the Division of Community Psychology of the American Psychological Association underscores professional recognition of the need for a different kind of approach to the problems of our social institutions.

DEFINITION OF MALADJUSTMENT IN THE SCHOOLS

Two major factors influence the definition of maladjustment in schools: the developmental condition of the child and the fact that he is being judged in the school by school personnel for reasons having to do with the aims and goals of the school. Cummings (1962), in considering the "developmental stage contingency principle" in clinical practice with children, noted that the meaning to be inferred from any given behavioral sample is relative to certain developmental conditions—the child's chronological age, the developmental sequence characteristic of that behavior function or system, and the child's personal history of progress through his developmental sequence. Unless these conditions are considered, children may appear simply as "psychotic dwarfs with good prognoses" (p. 3). Schools are organized so that consideration of chronological age and developmental sequence is built into the system. Schools are less well equipped to deal with the child's personal history of developmental progress, although attention to individual differences is an important part of current public school philosophy, if not practice.

A major distinction can be made between emotional disturbance as viewed by mental-health professionals in clinics and hospitals and emotional disturbance as viewed by school personnel. While the clinical view is reasonably specific and based most often on intrapsychic phenomena coupled with manifest symptomatology, the school view is based on a variety of behaviors which are related to performance and conduct in the school setting as interpreted and assigned values by those judging (Beilin, 1959). The classic study by Wickman (1928), despite its serious methodological flaws (Beilin, 1959; White & Harris, 1961), points out what has been mentioned in other studies as well: teachers tend to be concerned with problem behavior related to morality, disobedience, and failure to learn, whereas clinicians tend to place stronger emphasis on withdrawal symptoms and repressive and recessive characteristics in children (Hunter, 1957; Ritholz, 1959; Thompson, 1940). Perhaps the important point is neither the efficacy of these studies nor their merit but that they point up the differences in frames of reference between clinicians and school personnel about problem behavior. Further complications in defining maladjustment in the school setting are seen in

the results of a study by Mutimer and Rosemier (1967). They used the Wickman instrument of fifty behaviors to secure ratings from children in grades 7 to 12 and from their teachers as to the seriousness of the behaviors. Based on results from 400 children and 40 teachers in a northern Illinois community, disagreement was observed between boys and girls, among grades, and between students and teachers. Teachers rated the behaviors of masturbation, enuresis, profanity, and restlessness as being less serious than did students and tended to rate disobedience, obscene notes and talk, nervousness, and unhappiness as being more serious than did students. School-maladjustment problem behavior, therefore, may depend in some measure on who in the school is making the judgment.

Still another difficulty with using clinical definitions of emotional disturbance in the school is the tendency of school personnel to attach meanings to the definitions used, often with negative results. Combs and Harper (1967), for instance, studied the effects of clinical labels on the attitudes of experienced and inexperienced educators toward four categories of exceptional children. While the effects on attitudes were not consistent for different labels, descriptions of children labeled psychopathic and schizophrenic were rated more negatively than were unlabeled descriptions of the same children.

In order to deal with the problem of frame of reference, attempts have been made to develop school-related definitions of maladjustment and, at the same time, to objectify them so that common meanings might be discerned. White and Charry (1966) use the term *school disorder* when describing that subpopulation in the school which has a variety of judged maladjustments in school culture. The term includes "learning difficulties, social difficulties, emotional disturbances, and deviant or antisocial behavior, or any combination of these" (p. 1). In their investigation of the relationship between school disorder and a number of related factors, children referred to school psychologists were operationally defined as those having school disorder. Within the broad limits implied by this term, it is probably true that many children referred to the present-day school psychologist do have serious problems. If the term is interpreted as a very broad, composite title to identify children seen by others as having problems, it is probably useful. But it must be remembered that it only differentiates those children identified from others not identified. The definition is in no way inclusive, tied as it is to the functioning of a specialist in the school rather than to behaviors per se which can be reliably identified.

Hewett (1968) seeks to avoid using the term *emotional disturbance* because it has little pragmatic value in the classroom. For him, the term implies a medical orientation, which leads to a search for underlying causal factors and avoids consideration of the child's educational problems. He admits, however, that the term *emotionally disturbed* will continue to be used because of its widespread acceptance. Hewett prefers to consider the emotionally disturbed child as a socialization failure. "Underlying all of the specialization terms and complex diagnostic labels used to describe him is the implication that his behavior, for whatever reason, is maladaptive according to the expectations of the society in which he lives" (p. 1). Thus, at each age level, there are certain behaviors, capabilities, knowledges, beliefs, and customs which must be acquired if successful adaptation is to take place. *Maladaptive behavior* is Hewett's preferred term. Maladaptive behavior interferes with learning, and it can be modified in the classroom by teachers' using resources unique to the school.

Perhaps the most widely used term related specifically to school maladjustment is *emotionally handicapped,* as defined by Bower (1960). Bower chose *handicap* in preference to *distur-*

bance as having a more lasting and persistent quality, having less of the rigid connotation of a disease, and being more illustrative of the degree and nature of emotional problems. His definition is based on five characteristics, which are visible to teachers and are judged as related to emotionally handicapped children when they occur to a marked extent and over a period of time, although Bower does not say how marked an extent or what the time period might be.

1. An inability to learn which cannot be explained by intellectual, sensory or health factors.
2. An inability to build or maintain satisfactory interpersonal relationships with peers and teachers.
3. Inappropriate types of behavior or feelings under normal conditions.
4. A general, pervasive mood of unhappiness or depression.
5. A tendency to develop physical symptoms, pains, or fears associated with personal or school problems. (Bower, 1960, p. 8).

Bower's definition and his description of its five subareas have received widespread publicity and have been produced in essentially the same form in journals, book chapters, and books of readings since 1960.

The use of educationally oriented definitions of maladjustment poses a dilemma. As White and Harris (1961) have pointed out:

Whatever definition we use, . . . we find ourselves making judgments about behavior which are unavoidable but dangerous. If we insist upon tying our horse to the educational hitching post, we will automatically call emotionally maladjusted a large number of pupils who are making a poor school adjustment but who, in the eyes of many sociologists at least, are making an appropriate adjustment to their own cultural group. And if we don't use adjustment in school as a measure, what can we use? [P. 146]

It is self-evident that the definition of emotional disturbance or maladjustment in the school is influenced by a variety of factors which may or may not directly relate to maladjustment per se. Kitano (1962) suggests that diagnosis of problem children is apparently made on the basis of evidence other than that supplied by the behavior in the specific situation. He recommends that any definition of "problem child" should be based on an analysis of the total situation of the child, including the various demands or expectations placed on him. Burt and Howard (1952), in a factorial study of English children in school, found four conditions which discriminated between a control group and 273 maladjusted children: uncongenial teacher and difficult work, disorganized and neglectful home, general educational backwardness, and emotional instability. Bower (1967), in a comprehensive review of factors related to the prediction of school adjustment, finds evidence that IQ, achievement in school subjects, age-grade relationships, socioeconomic status (SES), and truancy are related to the prediction of school adjustment.

The relationships among school maladjustment, IQ, and SES are exceedingly complex. Previous reviews of the literature indicate not only that SES and IQ are related to school maladjustment but that SES and intelligence test scores are also positively related and that school adjustment, as previously mentioned, is in part based on difficulty with school learning, or school achievement (Morse & Dyer, 1963; White & Harris, 1961). Some clarification is offered by White and Charry (1966) in their study of the relationships among school disorder, IQ, and SES, although their criterion for school disorder is based solely on 2,866 referrals to school psychologists in Westchester County, New York. They find that school disorder, as they define it, is related more highly to low IQ than to low SES. Further, when they divide school disorder into two groups, the educationally disturbed versus the emotionally disturbed, they find that these are two different groups with respect to IQ, SES, and achievement, with the emotionally

disturbed group having higher scores on all three. Based on the general finding that there is a negative relationship between social class and adult mental illness, White and Charry conclude that the educationally disturbed are more likely to become mentally ill as adults than those considered to be emotionally disturbed as children, with educational failure as the critical component.

INCIDENCE OF SCHOOL MALADJUSTMENT

The estimates of numbers of schoolchildren who evidence psychopathology obviously vary with the definition used. In fact, the word *psychopathology* rarely appears in the literature dealing with school pupils. Other terms have become more commonly used and apparently are more acceptable—such as the previously noted conceptions of behavior disorder and emotional handicap. Professionals working in an educational setting prefer school-related terminology when pupils deviate moderately from normal behavior; the terms *emotionally disturbed* and *seriously emotionally disturbed* have become the nomenclature for pupils whose problems clinicians might label *psychosis* or *indicative of extreme psychopathology.*

It should be pointed out that the incidence of pupils with emotional handicaps in the school population is not necessarily a prediction or forerunner of later overt mental disorder. White and Harris (1961) reviewed the literature through 1958 and concluded that there were no definitive studies which indicate what proportion of maladjusted school pupils later become delinquents, psychotics, neurotics, or untreated and unlabeled maladjusted adults. On the other hand, there are a few retrospective studies indicating that adults judged to be poorly adjusted were identified as maladaptive when school pupils (Bower, Shellhamer, & Daily, 1960; O'Neal & Robbins, 1958). Glavin and Quay's recent review (1969) of research investigating the persistence of emotional disturbance led them to conclude that the majority of disturbed children improve without intervention. The studies reviewed referred to children who remained in regular classes in the public schools; studies investigating severely disturbed (psychotic) children suggest a much poorer prognosis.

White and Harris (1961) surveyed studies conducted between 1928 and 1958 to determine the incidence of emotional maladjustment in the school population. Problems of definition as well as variation in sampling techniques led White and Harris to conclude that the incidence of mild maladjustment in the schools is impossible to estimate; the incidence of serious maladjustment seems to fall within a range of 4 to 7 percent of the school population. Other estimates of incidence have been provided by Pate (1963), who suggests that 0.5 percent of the school-age population represent pupils in need of intensive special education. Abrahamson (1955) and Bower (1961) agree that approximately 10 percent of schoolchildren need some help for emotional problems. Glavin (1968) surveyed children in Tennessee and found that 12.9 percent could be considered emotionally disturbed. In a Minnesota school district, Stennett (1966) found 22 percent either moderately or seriously emotionally handicapped. Morse (1967) reports that teachers judged 8 percent of junior high school students severely maladjusted. Hewett (1968) contends that if a broader definition of the problem were employed, the incidence of emotional disturbance or maladaptive behavior which a teacher would be concerned with would far exceed the 10 percent figure. Regardless of the specific figure used to determine incidence, it is perfectly apparent that the number of American schoolchildren in need of professional help runs into the millions and that every schoolteacher is likely to have to cope with two or three extremely troublesome children in the classroom.

IDENTIFICATION OF MALADJUSTED CHILDREN IN SCHOOL

A wide variety of techniques and approaches has been used in an effort to identify school pupils with problems of adjustment. Interestingly enough, despite the plethora of studies dealing with complicated, difficult, and expensive procedures to identify maladjusted children, the result of all these studies may be summed in a very simple statement: Ask the teacher.

Past research has widely used teachers' judgments as a criterion measure for studies of maladjustment, and more recent studies have continued the practice and have, in general, found teachers' identification of problem children to be relatively valid and reliable. Sixth-grade teachers accurately predicted which boys would become delinquent and which would not (Scarpitti, 1964); Glidewell, Domke, and Kantor (1963) found high agreements (70 percent) between teacher and parent identifications. Other studies involving teacher identification are Bower (1961); Seeman (1963); Glidewell, Domke and Kantor (1963); Vane and Eisen (1962); Maes (1966); Westman, Rice, and Bermann (1967); and Pimm and McClure (1967).

Most studies on identification, including those using teachers as identifiers, use a variety of techniques: rating scales, inventories, personality tests, adjustment scales, sociometric techniques, school records, achievement tests, intelligence tests, recorded observations, and spontaneous reports (White & Harris, 1961). Identification of the emotionally handicapped by the use of multiple techniques is probably best exemplified by the instruments and process developed by Bower, Tashnovian, and Larson (Lambert & Bower, 1961), in which teacher, peer, and self-ratings are utilized. Cowen and Zax (1968) combined psychological evaluation, social work interviews with mothers of pupils, classroom observation, and reports by teachers. Teachers' and mothers' reports of symptoms for screening behavior disorders were used by Glidewell, Domke, and Kantor (1963). Woody (1969) suggests that a variety of school personnel contribute their expertise in order to make the identification process a meaningful beginning step toward remediation. Friedman (1968), also with remediation in mind as the ultimate goal of identification, has discussed the value of a structured family interview in order to assess school learning disorders. Sociometric devices together with teachers' ratings were found by Barclay (1966) to be effective in identifying children who need help. Werry and Quay (1968) have described a technique consisting of direct frequency counts of observed behaviors as a useful means of identification, with the added value that the technique can be used by a relatively unskilled observer.

Glavin and Quay (1969), reviewing screening and predictive measures of school behavior disorders, conclude that although the widespread use of teacher judgment in screening for disturbed children is generally justifiable, teacher estimations alone are not as valid an index of disturbance as are teacher judgments in combination with other criteria. Bower (1967), in his review of identification procedures, offers evidence that teacher ratings, self-descriptive data, and peer ratings when combined give the clearest, most comprehensive, and economical picture of the adjustment status of schoolchildren. Teacher ratings are better predictors of emotional handicaps expressed in overt behavior; self-descriptive data are more effective evaluators of feelings, attitudes, and inner tension. Next to teacher judgment, peer perception seems the most valid and reliable indicator of pupil and personality development (Zax, Cowen, Izzo, & Trost, 1964). Other factors found to be related to the prediction of school adjustment are delinquency, visual-perception disorders (Balow, 1966a), and as mentioned earlier, IQ, achievement in school

subjects, SES, truancy, and age-grade relationship (Bower, 1967).

The numbers of school pupils identified as emotionally handicapped make it obvious that identification per se has little value unless it can provide information that can lead to intervention and/or remediation within the educational framework. Teacher ratings are perhaps not only reasonably valid and reliable but also extremely important for future educational planning. It is, after all, the teacher who first observes the maladaptive behavior in school and who must deal with the school disorder. It is also the teacher who is most likely to be able to implement the kinds of ameliorative techniques available for use in the classroom. Identification procedures in schools are most useful if rooted in observations of behavior that are relevant to the classroom and other aspects of the educational setting.

MANAGEMENT AND EDUCATION OF EMOTIONAL DISTURBANCE IN THE CLASSROOM

The emotionally disturbed child presents the school with a potential conflict of goals. His behavior is such that the school must be concerned with control of his behavior and with his emotional stability. But the school is an educational agency, charged with teaching skills and passing on knowledge. Reconciliation of the conflict between these goals appears possible. Bower (1966) expresses a current view that "the instruction of emotionally disturbed children is moving rapidly toward conceptualizations and programs which are based on the *educational* needs of children, rather than on their physiological, neurological, or psychodynamic disabilities" (p. 131). Rhodes (1967), Hobbs (1966), and Kelly (1968) strongly suggest that an ecological approach to the education of emotionally disturbed children is needed, in which a reciprocal relationship is acknowledged between the child, his school environment, and the larger environment in which both function. Hobbs (1966) has outlined twelve concepts which are related to an ecological view of the process of reeducation of emotionally disturbed children: (1) life is to be lived now; (2) time is an ally; (3) trust is essential; (4) competence makes a difference; (5) symptoms can and should be controlled; (6) cognitive control can be taught; (7) feelings should be nurtured; (8) the group is important to children; (9) ceremony and ritual give order, stability, and confidence; (10) the body is the armature of the self; (11) communities are important; (12) a child should know joy. Hewett (1968) also believes that all emotionally disturbed children are ready to learn *something* and that despite their deviant behavior, the goal for the school is to get them ready for school while they are actually in school. The complexity of the task of educating deviant children in schools is presented by Hollister and Goldston (1962) in their exposition of the kinds of psychoeducational processes relevant to the education of emotionally disturbed children in special classes: administrative processes, screening and diagnosis, planning, placement and continuous assessment, classroom relationship, classroom-motivation developmental processes, perceptual-retraining process, behavior management, behavior reeducation, academic education, rehabilitation to the regular classroom, clinician-education liaison, and school-home liaison. If anything, the complexity is increased when the emotionally disturbed child is considered as part of the regular classroom.

Teaching

With an emphasis on helping the emotionally disturbed child in the classroom, whether it be a regular or a special class, the ability of the teacher to teach and manage the child becomes of paramount importance. Stark and Betzen

(1958) describe with compassion the difficulties encountered by teachers when confronted with difficult-to-manage children. A teacher's reactions to a child's learning and behavior difficulties may involve excessive fear and anger, with the result that he neglects or punishes the child (Sarason, Levine, Goldenberg, Cherlin, & Bennett, 1966). These authors go on to cite other ways in which teachers may—and do—react to emotionally disturbed children, using such descriptive words as *insulting, threatening, harried, distraught, retaliating, vindictiveness*. In a detailed survey of public school classes for children designated as emotionally and socially handicapped, based on a mail survey of 117 program and site visits to seventy-four classrooms, Morse, Cutler, and Fink (1964) concluded that teachers of these special classes tend to have had little or no special preparation for dealing with such pupils. It is likely that regular classroom teachers will have had even less special training.

Yet qualifications and competencies *have* been suggested for teachers who work with emotionally disturbed children (Balow, 1966b; Berkowitz & Rothman, 1960; Hewett, 1966; Mackie, Kvareceus, & Williams, 1957). Hewett (1966), attempting to develop a concise and parsimonious list of teacher characteristics, presented a hierarchy of importance (from most basic to highest level) which emphasizes that the teacher of the emotionally handicapped child should be objective, flexible, structured, resourceful, a social reinforcer, a curriculum expert, and an intellectual model. These characteristics appear suitable for any teacher, anywhere, at any level.

Classroom Organization

When the school is faced with the education of emotionally disturbed children, it organizes itself on the basis of at least two variables: the number of children who are disturbed and the degree of the disturbance. To the extent possible, schools may try to match children with teachers or group children with similar difficulties, although the Morse, Cutler, and Fink survey (1964) suggests that most programs bear little explicit relationship to the specific pathologies of the children involved. LaBenne (1967) has proposed that consideration be given to a system of classification of psychoeducational disturbances based on a modification of a system developed at the University of Michigan in 1964. In a comprehensive study of a large city school for the emotionally disturbed, LaBenne identified three major diagnostic categories: neurotic externalizing pupils, primitive neglected pupils, and affectionless personality pupils. For each of these categories, LaBenne proposes differing psychoeducational treatment. He suggests that the neurotic externalizing pupil be educated based on knowledge relating anxiety to learning, that primitive neglected pupils might best be handled by approaches which emphasize self-concept development, and that affectionless personality pupils might best be approached through methods of control which emphasize reinforcers, both negative and positive. Based on a number of empirical research studies, Quay (1963) has developed two major syndromes: the acting-out syndrome (the "conduct problem") and the withdrawn syndrome (the "personality problem"). His recommendations for educational approaches are similar to LaBenne's for neurotic externalizing and affectionless personality pupils. The problem of mixing emotionally disturbed children with others, particularly with brain-damaged children, has been a subject of some controversy. A particularly sharp division of opinion is seen in a debate between Mesinger and Bower (1965), in which Mesinger contends that these groups are different and need differing educational programs. Bower claims that groups ought to be made up of a wide variety of children able to function within each other's limits and that our current classifications do not contain

the distinctions necessary for educational decisions. The question of placement in regular or special classes is also a highly controversial one. Research on special-class placement of the retarded tends, at this time, to point to the deficiencies of special-class placement as compared with pupil placement in regular classes (Dunn, 1968). However, the one study located which compares emotionally disturbed children in regular and special classes indicates that emotionally disturbed children in the regular class achieved less well on the Wide Range Achievement Test and the Behavior Rating Scale than did similar children in special classes. Further, the emotionally disturbed children in the regular classes were less well accepted than the normal children in those classes (Vacc, 1968). The study is limited to only sixteen special-class children, and results must be accepted cautiously.

Still another way in which schools have attempted to organize themselves to deal with emotionally disturbed children is through what Hewett (1967) calls *educational engineering,* in which the classroom itself, as well as instructions and procedures, is planned for certain educational experiences. Hay (1967) has also described room planning for managing and teaching emotionally disturbed children.

Within recent years, mounting support for structured approaches to the education and management of disturbed children in the schools has been presented in the literature. Haring and Phillips (1962) and Whelan and Haring (1966) compared a structured classroom approach, a permissive classroom approach, and a control approach (regular classroom) for academic achievement and behavior. Their findings provide research evidence for the efficacy of the structured approach. Interest in behavior-modification techniques, to be discussed later, undoubtedly has contributed to support for a structured approach to handling emotional disturbance in the schools. But other studies may be cited which indicate that structure versus nonstructure may be too simple a dichotomy. Grimes and Allinsmith (1961) found that selected pupil personality characteristics interacted with teaching methods to affect achievement at the primary grade level, with anxious children in unstructured settings showing the most difficulty with achievement. Quay (1968), from the findings of a series of studies, proposes an educationally relevant taxonomy based on the learning characteristics and the peculiar demands these might make on the instructional process. He has developed a conceptual framework of forty-one cells, each of which represents the point of interaction of a function and modality with a parameter of learning. For Quay, "structure versus nonstructure" would be insufficient to describe educational needs of children with behavior disorders.

Educational literature has been surfeited for years with articles, pamphlets, and exhortations concerning principles teachers should follow in helping children to develop emotionally in the regular school classroom. Included in this literature has been reference to discipline and classroom management problems. More recently, attention has been given to working with (managing) the more seriously disturbed child in school. Generally, the advice given is similar to that given for nondisturbed children, with special cautions to be sensitive to the special needs of the severely disturbed. For instance, Tift (1968) recommends that teachers develop sensitivity to disturbed children (and thereby be more tolerant) by seeing the motion picture *David and Lisa,* visiting an accredited school for emotionally disturbed children, and reading a book which deals with emotionally disturbed children in the classroom!

Johnson and Rubin (1964), in discussing a school follow-up study of children discharged from a psychiatric hospital, recommend that schools adjust school schedules and classroom atmosphere. They are, however, pessimistic about the prognosis for adequate adjustment in school, after discharge from a psychiatric ward, for those children whose illness includes an organic or a psychotic component.

Perhaps the most succinct summary of methods for handling behavior in the classroom is based on Redl's four alternatives: permitting, tolerating, interfering, and preventive planning (Long & Newman, 1965). Redl emphasizes that no one of these alternatives is better than any other; the task is to find the correct combination of techniques for each child.

A number of texts have been published to aid teachers' understanding of maladjusted children, whether the children are in special classes or regular classes. Among them are texts which emphasize structured approaches to teaching and managing emotionally disturbed children (Haring & Phillips, 1962; Hewett, 1968; Woody, 1969). Still other texts tend to be more traditional or eclectic in point of view (Blackham, 1967; Grossman, 1965; Long, Morse, & Newman, 1965; Thomas, 1967).

Descriptions of programs and approaches to handling emotionally disturbed children in special and regular classrooms may be found in the literature (Haan, 1957; Leaverton, 1965; Linton, 1969; Miller, 1964; Moller, 1964; Smith, 1967). These descriptions are broad gauge and describe program procedures, administrative problems, and subjective estimates of program results.

Specific Educational Approaches

In addition to establishing special classes for the emotionally disturbed in the schools, schools have sought ways to individualize programs within the regular classroom and to restructure portions of the school day to accommodate emotionally disturbed children. In planning special events and interventions in the classroom, it is useful to use Bower's (1966) conceptualization of five levels of ego ineffectiveness: level I, children with minor or transient learning or behavior disorders; level II, children with initial and persistent learning and behavior problems; level III, children with recurrent and fixed problems; level IV, children with marked and severe problems; level V, highly disturbed malfunctioning.

It is not likely that many level V children will be found in the regular classroom. Most will be in a 24-hour residential program in a private or public facility, in a special class in the schools, or in a home-tutoring program in which the school furnishes a teacher to work with the child in his home.

Level IV children are usually accommodated in special day schools (Hay, 1967) or in special classes in regular schools (Morse, Cutler, & Fink, 1964). One variation of the concept of placement within the regular class was attempted in California (Bower, 1961). In this approach, small classes were organized consisting of a majority of well-adjusted children but including two or three emotionally disturbed children. The rationale for this program was based on the potential influence of a stable peer group and the teacher's ability to use most of the class as instructional allies.

Level III children often have lost interest—or never established interest—in learning skills and have failed to develop competence in basic academic areas. For these children, attendance at school includes the constant frustration of having to deal with materials and relationships which point up incompetence. Remedial efforts, either in the classroom or presented by special remedial personnel, have been found to be effective as compared with other educational and therapeutic approaches. Bower (1961) reported a two-year study involving 1,200 children which attempted to answer the following question: "Are emotionally handicapped children significantly affected by each of the special programs (used in the study) as shown by a comparison of school be-

havior after one and two years with that of a similar group of emotionally handicapped children who have not been in special programs?" (p. 27) Of the eleven approaches used—most of them involving forms of special classes or therapeutic intervention—learning-disability grouping or remedial education for those with academic deficits proved to be one of the four most useful approaches in producing changes in IQ, academic achievement, peer rating, and teacher rating. The other approaches receiving positive ratings according to Bower's criteria for determining total ratings were (1) special classes at the elementary level, (2) special classes at the secondary level, and (3) adolescent group counseling (Bower, 1961).

Bower (1966) reports on a program called "systematic suspension" used by schools when the usual methods of handling children (rewards, penalties, social pressure, curriculum adjustment) have failed to work.

> The main thrust of the "systematic suspension" is to make the teacher and the school "passive" observers and place the burden of change on the child. This is done by informing the child that the school has given up all attempts to control him. If he breaks a rule, he must go home. The teacher as administrator of this rule will present him with a green slip of paper as a "go home" signal. His parents who have, of course, been consulted in this matter are asked not to scold or punish him when he arrives. In some cases the child may be sent home ten or twenty consecutive days. He may, however, return the next day for a fresh start. [P. 139]

According to Bower, teachers are positively affected by this approach, as it helps to reduce interpersonal friction and gives the teacher a way out. It is hoped that the approach will minimize friction to the extent that the teacher may be able to find "instructional pathways for herself and the . . . child."

Level II and level I programs fall within the

range of preventive programs and screening programs, handled elsewhere in this and other chapters of this manual.

Morse (1964) described a number of classroom interventions which can be used in special and regular classes. In his view, these interventions cannot be labeled as *educational* or *therapeutic* or *management* since therapeutic education encompasses all three. Rejecting the efficacy of one-to-one teaching in the classroom, Morse proposes consideration of group-organized curricula using the project method; the use of integrated several-level teaching units specifically incorporating multisensory activities; parallel but discrete learning sequences which are individualized for different pupils; group discussion about academic affairs, used to "reduce the emotional change attached to academic work"; and interventions designed to control anxiety, such as avoiding tension-producing curricula or conditions, developing neutral approaches which do not arouse negative reactions, and doing nothing at all in reaction to a child's behavior. Other interventions include the intensification of reward for proper responses and the use of what Morse calls *captivating gadgeteering*. By this he means the use of a variety of machines and devices which divest the educational experience of the need to oppose the people controlling it. A very important set of interventions are those planned after diagnosis of individual learning inadequacies, i.e., an attempt to match remediation with problem. Peters (1965) has called this process *prescriptive teaching* and has discussed it at length.

Behavior-modification Approaches in the Classroom

Perhaps the most thorough educational system for using a behavior-modification strategy in the classroom is that of Hewett (1968). Based on a hierarchical developmental sequence of educational goals (attention, response, order, exploratory, social, mastery, achievement), Hewett has developed a system of tasks, rewards, and environmental structures at each developmental level. Certainly the use of rewards and punishments is not new to the educational scene, nor is the idea of teaching with consideration for developmental sequence. But as Hewett (1968) and Whelan and Haring (1966) point out, what *is* new is *systematic* application of what is known about the principles of behavioral control and developmental tasks.

Most of the literature concerned with behavior-modification applications to the classroom is concerned either with special-education classes (see O'Leary & Becker, 1967; Quay, Werry, McQueen, & Sprague, 1966; Whelan & Haring, 1966) or with concentrated attention on one child in the classroom by teachers assisted by teacher aides or outside consultants (see Carlson, Arnold, Becker, & Madsen, 1968; Dyer, 1968). Although mention is made of the possibility of using operant techniques in the regular classroom, little detailed information appears to be available. Valett (1966) has described in very simple terms procedures which can be adapted by teachers in regular classes.

A concern expressed in a number of sources is that behavior-modification techniques will be viewed as a panacea because of their common-sense approach and their relationship to what teachers tend to do anyway, but in a sporadic fashion. Porter (1962) warns that human behavior is so complex and teaching so subtle that "dealing with them must involve complicated techniques." Whelan and Haring (1966) suggest that "skeptical, cautious acceptance and application of behavioral modification techniques are certainly indicated." They go on to say that while data from laboratory studies and with small groups of children demonstrate a high degree of reliability, they have not been validated to any extent in regular and special classroom situations.

MANAGEMENT OF EMOTIONALLY HANDICAPPED CHILDREN BY USE OF SPECIAL SERVICES

Most writers agree that every school system should have available mental-health professionals as part of its staff so that teachers can receive supportive counseling and special help in dealing with problem children (Board of Education of the City of New York, 1962). A few, however, propose that special services should exist outside the administrative unit of the school—mental-health units with which lines of communication should be kept open (Krugman, 1958). What is the most effective use of special-services personnel remains a cloudy issue. Positive change in the behavior of children as the result of intervention by special-services personnel is difficult to measure, especially when the intervention takes such diffuse forms as the use of special-services personnel to the teacher (information giving, recommendations for specific classroom techniques, supportive counseling, in-service training), to parents (information and advice giving, counseling), to administrators (suggestions for curriculum and school policy modifications), and to pupils (counseling, therapy, tutoring, group activities). The issue of the effectiveness of special-services personnel is further confounded because the kinds of specialists in any school system vary widely, both in type of specialty and in level of training within the specific specialty.

Fortunately or unfortunately, lack of definitive evidence as to their effectiveness does not prevent mental-health professionals and paraprofessionals from joining the ranks of the school staff in ever-increasing numbers (Bardon, 1968). Nor does lack of definitive evidence prevent energetic and prolific writers from offering an infinite variety of ways and means in which emotionally handicapped children in the schools may be helped by mental-health professionals. Balow (1966a),

reviewing the literature, makes it clear that despite the flurry of activity in the study of maladjustment affecting children in school, the vast majority of publications in the area have been subjective descriptions and clinical case studies. Glavin and Quay (1969), in a later review, cryptically comment that no substantive research has been reported on "therapeutic educational provisions."

Special-services personnel may consist of any one or any combination of (among the professionals) the following specialists: school psychologist, clinical psychologist, social psychologist, psychiatrist, school physician, psychiatric social worker, school social worker, guidance counselor, elementary counselor, child development specialist, learning disability specialist, school nurse, home-school counselor, remedial-reading teacher, curriculum supervisor, director or coordinator of pupil personnel services, coordinator of pupil personnel or special services.

One of the major questions to be answered is: Who (among special-services personnel) can be most helpful where? Ross (1962) castigates clinical psychologists for making little progress in coming to a better understanding of children's school problems and suggests distinguishing among different categories of learning difficulties in order to determine whether the particular child needs special education, tutoring, therapeutic education, therapy, or a combination of these various interventions. Obviously, the specialist used will vary according to the categorization. "Who helps where?" becomes further confused when guidance counselors, psychologists, social workers, and psychiatrists all "counsel;" when psychologists, social workers, and psychiatrists "assess" and offer "therapy;" when child development specialists, elementary counselors, learning disability specialists, and psychologists all "test" (Bardon & Bennett, 1966).

For the purposes of this chapter, it is helpful to distinguish the mental-health professional from the psychologically oriented educational professional and to exclude the voluminous literature devoted to help for troubled children from the various school counselors and remedial specialists—except as these people become part of the school mental-health team concept. In many states in rapidly growing numbers (Bardon, 1968), the psychologist has become the primary special-service person to whom the school looks for help. If the psychologist is a member of the staff, he is usually a school psychologist; if he consults on a part-time basis, he may be a school, clinical, or social psychologist. A number of books have been devoted to how a psychologist should function in the school situation (Eiserer, 1963; Gottsegen & Gottsegen, 1960, 1963; Hirst, 1963; Magary, 1969; Valett, 1963; White & Harris, 1961), and two professional journals are devoted to the subject *(Psychology in the Schools, Journal of School Psychology).* A few generalities may be made regarding the kind of help the psychologist offers disturbed children in the schools: The psychologist offers diagnosis (assessment), remedial techniques (classroom management or direct counseling/therapy), parent counseling, teacher counseling and in-service education, and consultation with other special-services personnel and other community agencies. In many states it is the psychologist who must certify for placement in any special class, whether the class is for the retarded, the neurologically impaired, or the emotionally and socially maladjusted.

Special-services Personnel as Consultants

When the availability of special-services personnel extends beyond a single, lonely psychologist, the use of consultants as a team is a common recommendation. Newman (1967), for example, reports on the use of a psychiatric social worker, remedial teacher, therapeutic teacher, and two psychologists as consultants available for continuous and regular consultation to children, teachers, and administrators. A problem child

was typically the focus of the consultation, and Newman contends that "new pathways of behavior" (on the part of the pupils) and "new understandings" (on the part of school personnel) "made possible desired changes of a lasting nature" (p. 4). Knoblock and Garcea (1965) report on two clinical psychologists together with a psychiatric social worker serving as consultants to a school system which had a large number of disturbed children referred for special-class placement. The school system, however, had inadequate facilities for such placement. These consultants visited regular classrooms (of which the disturbed children were members) and met with teachers regularly for discussion groups. The authors professed belief that their experiment was successful.

Another proponent of the "team" approach is Woody (1969), who recommends formal in-service training for teachers, as well as "coffee cup seminars."

Bower (1967) discusses mental-health consultation to the schools in Caplan's (1961, 1964) terminology: an interview process between the consultant (usually a psychiatrist, psychologist, or psychiatric social worker) and a consultee (teacher). Bower suggests that such a consultant is likely *not* to be a regular member of the school staff.

Morse (1967) worked with teachers to enable them to conduct "life-space interviewing" with pupils with problems. Life-space interviewing involves the use of a professional specialist who spends considerable time helping the teacher to listen to the child and learn the child's point of view. "Other steps follow, such as exploring the depth of the issue, inquiring as to the generality of a particular problem in other situations, and going on to discuss what might be done in such a situation. The teacher explores the child's recognition of the need for change and particular coping mechanisms that might be taught to him. There is always an attempt to close an interview with some minor alteration so that behavior can be more acceptable in the future" (p. 285). Another Morse (1965) suggestion is the "crisis teacher," who serves as "an immediate resource for the teacher when there is significant deterioration in the classroom group learning process. Help must be available without stigma or recrimination. . . . A new hand is required, but of a special type. Not only must the new person help the school at large, but he must provide immediate succor to the pupil as well . . . [the pupil] needs help with two things—his school work and the feelings which distort his efforts at the moment" (p. 252). Morse describes the crisis teacher as one who knows curriculum, who is steeped in remedial teaching techniques, and who is skilled in life-space interviewing. Morse suggests that the crisis teacher operate from the base of a small classroom with a pleasant anteroom and with books and materials of all sorts at hand. It is essential that the crisis teacher, in order to be effective, receive support from the entire staff. This way of handling deviant children in the school might be referred to as an "in-and-out" policy; disturbed children participate "in" the regular classroom but, at times of stress, are "out" of the regular classroom, often on an episodic rather than a regular basis.

School administration, school social work, psychology, and psychiatry offered consultation to a project reported by Connor and Muldoon (1967). Disturbed teen-agers considered too openly aggressive or withdrawn to be maintained in the public schools or "too motivated" or "too impulsive" to be offered regular agency services were placed in a "Resource Program" within the facilities of a local high school. The plan is similar to that of Morse (1965) in that a special "resource programmer" was available for counseling with these teen-agers, who were then accepted into the public school system. The program is presented as exploratory; no definitive evaluation is suggested.

Gordon (1967) described the use of school psychologists as leaders of teacher groups. These groups assemble each week, and each teacher collects data on a single child in his class. As the data accumulate, the teachers learn to structure them in a variety of ways to probe their meaning. The involvement in sharing understanding about children seems to result in enhancement of teacher self-understanding. The psychologist who is involved also learns in the process; his role is to open up a way of experiencing that will develop each member's inner resources.

Andronico and Guerney (1967) suggest an approach to schoolchildren with problems through the specific technique of "filial therapy." Filial therapy (Guerney, 1964) is a method of teaching parents to relate empathically to their emotionally disturbed children at home for prescribed periods of time. The parents learn methods of interacting with their children modeled after nondirective play-therapy techniques and are taught to use these principles at home when they conduct special play sessions with their children. Andronico and Guerney (1967) suggest that the school psychologist or other trained special-services team members work with parents and conduct filial therapy within the school setting, similar to the way it is conducted in a clinical setting. Expected results are that both school and parents are enabled to help children modify their behaviors, with parents a vital part of the child's treatment. Parents are in constant contact with the school and are more likely to accept discussions with school personnel. Filial-therapy principles are also being used by special-services personnel in working with teachers (Vieland, 1968); teachers learn the nondirective play techniques of filial therapy and engage children in play sessions conducted in the school. As this project has increased in scope, the supervisory time of the specialist has decreased, enabling the specialist to work with many more groups of teachers. These teachers are being taught specific techniques for enhancing the child's self-concept and are increasing their own understanding of situations from a child's viewpoint. The technique of clarifying children's feelings while at the same time firmly enforcing certain limits on behavior is another important technique practiced and learned. Teachers, like parents, may become more favorably disposed to discuss freely with professional specialists their problems with children in the classroom, feel more directly involved with the problem children they encounter, and have fewer feelings of frustration and helplessness.

North (1968) reminds special-services personnel that needed help for children with school problems is often bypassed because teachers fail to alert parents to such problems. He suggests that school psychologists, in particular, develop in-service training with teachers, utilizing role-playing techniques, in order to help teachers motivate parents to seek professional services when needed.

School phobia, a particular manifestation of school disorder, has received the attention of special-services personnel. There is agreement that school phobia may indeed be a manifestation of serious emotional disturbance in the pupil but that there are various categories of school phobia—some purely situational and temporary and not necessarily reflective of deep pathology (Coolidge, 1957; Leventhal & Sills, 1964). The consensus of the studies is that the various special-services personnel (particularly psychiatrist, psychiatric social worker, and psychologist) should consult intensively with child, parents, and teacher to effect attendance in school immediately (Coolidge, Brodie, & Feeney, 1964; Cooper, 1966; Leavitt, 1964; Leventhal & Sills, 1964). Learning-theory principles have also been applied in school-phobic cases (Garvey & Hegrenes, 1966; Lazarus, Davidson, & Polefka, 1965).

In contrast to the subjective nature of the consultant approaches discussed above, psychologists (particularly, but not exclusively) have been offering help to disturbed children in the structured form of behavior-modification therapy. The recent surge of interest in the application of learning theory to the problems of schoolchildren may partially be due to its straightforward nature—help to disturbed children can be specifically programmed, and changes in pupil behavior are frequently dramatic and measurable. Balow (1966a) has reviewed comprehensively the considerable literature dealing with behavior modification in the schools, and more recently Glavin and Quay (1969) warn that the results of the suggested classroom paradigms are still in the preliminary stages. Typical examples of the use of special-services personnel to implement behavior modification with disturbed schoolchildren are the models of Hewett (1968), McNamara (1969), and Woody (1969). A model training (or retraining) program for psychologists working in the schools and based on the learning-theory approach was found by Barclay (1968) to be effective, both in changing the behavior of the psychologists and in changing the behavior of pupils in the schools in which the psychologists were functioning.

Paraprofessionals

The incidence figures for the prevalence of disturbed children in the schools, together with the recognition that the schools represent a captured social system to which professionals have access, have led professionals to recognize the need to extend their services beyond direct consultation with school personnel. Growing in popularity is the use of paraprofessionals—people who are assigned (or volunteer) to work directly with disturbed children in the schools, usually on a one-to-one basis.

Donahue and Nichtern (1965) mobilized a New York State community in an effort to provide for seriously disturbed children within the framework of the public schools. Their approach emphasized low public cost as well as extended services to emotionally disturbed children. They enlisted the services of volunteers, "teacher-moms," women who worked with emotionally disturbed children on a one-to-one basis. The function of the teacher-moms was primarily instruction, but the professional team of educators, psychologists, and psychiatrists worked with the "moms" to help them establish meaningful relationships with the children. The authors offer their model as a demonstration of the methods and results of a program that can be practically pursued and economically structured in any school district.

Another use of paraprofessionals is exemplified by college students working with disturbed schoolchildren (Cowen, Zax, & Laird, 1966). The purpose of this program was to provide a meaningful relationship and beneficial experience for emotionally disturbed children by pairing them with enthusiastic college student volunteers. Each volunteer met with his assigned child immediately following the regular school day for a period of about 70 minutes. Small groups (five to seven in number) of the volunteers were under the direct supervision of an advanced clinical psychology graduate student— the latter under the supervision of the clinical psychologist directing the program. At the end of each afternoon's activity in the school, the volunteer group and the graduate student leader held a discussion session. This program was evaluated, despite the admitted design problems, and provides some preliminary information: The original idealistic attitudes of the volunteers toned down as a result of participation in the program, and a significantly more favorable set of attitudes developed toward the disturbed children themselves. There were also some understandings derived about the nature of volunteer-child interactions and some preliminary estimates

as to why certain interactions were preferred, why some interactions had limited frequency, and why some interactions changed over time.

Campbell (1967) described a program in which children in the primary grades of a public school system who were having learning and behavior difficulties were seen for therapeutically oriented tutoring by college students training to become teachers. The program was developed and supervised by a clinical psychology professor and a school psychologist and was designed within the framework of a course in which students could learn some of the techniques and approaches involved in understanding, relating to, and educating children with problems of emotional adjustment. The course consisted of (1) lectures and readings on child development and (2) a supervised practicum. In the practicum each student teacher saw a child twice a week for supervised individual tutoring sessions at the child's school during the course of the regular school day. The technique of therapeutic tutoring is described as differing from therapy in that the emphasis is on the reality situation but with selected therapeutic techniques, such as accepting, reflecting, and clarifying negative feelings yet imposing essential limits in a firm and accepting manner. According to Campbell, the schools see the program as bridging an important gap between the busy classroom teacher and the professionals; the college hopes that its graduates will become more sensitive and knowledgeable teachers.

The writings cited above are merely samples of the approaches suggested. In general, there is a tendency to attempt to maximize use of special-services personnel by having the specialists serve as consultants, trainers, and/or supervisors of others working in the schools with disturbed children. On the other hand, it is generally believed that problem children in the public schools are benefited by individual attention and educational therapy and that it is desirable to attempt to maintain these children in the regular class-room, with support for the teacher supplied from other special-services personnel.

PSYCHOTHERAPY IN THE SCHOOLS

Most studies dealing with psychotherapy with children discuss therapy in a clinical setting and emphasize ways of understanding the psycho-dynamics of the developmental period and how the dynamics of development affect the inter-action of patient and therapist (Peters & Watten-berg, 1966). The studies focusing on the inter-action of a mental-health professional and a school pupil usually label this interaction *counsel-ing*. There are several reasons why the word *therapy* is infrequently found in literature deal-ing with the schools:

1. Of all the social institutions, the schools are most vulnerable to public scrutiny and public criticism, and the use of the medical terminology is likely to lead the public to conclude that the schools are offering treatment of illness, a func-tion that should be reserved for the medical pro-fession.

2. Educators themselves see therapy as a function of the clinic or private practitioner, not the school.

3. Professionals working in the schools see therapy—especially individual therapy—as a time-consuming process limited to a few children, thus interfering with a more appropriate role for the professional, that of consultant mental-health specialist with prime concern for preventive rather than curative measures.

4. The research offers conflicting evidence as to the effectiveness of therapy, in or out of the school setting (Lewis, 1965).

Professionals have long engaged in philo-sophical discussions (especially at the graduate school level) about definitions of and distinc-tions between counseling and psychotherapy.

As no single definition of either will satisfy the practitioners of each, it seems wise to accept Smith's (1967) suggestion that for the purposes of discussion the terms be used interchangeably. Smith further warns that from a practical stand-point, the terms *counseling* and *reeducation* are more appropriately used to describe profes-sional activities in the school setting, reserving the word *therapy* for the activities of the psy-chiatrist and clinical psychologist in the clinic or in private practice.

In order to keep this chapter within reason-able limits, and in an effort not to overlap the focus of other chapters, discussion will be limited to those techniques used in schools which have as their goal the behavior change (or modifica-tion of behavior) in those children judged dis-turbed or maladjusted—exclusive of those tech-niques used by teachers, remedial specialists, and psychologically oriented educators (guid-ance counselors, child-development specialists).

When therapy is offered in the schools it may take the form of (1) individual therapy, (2) group therapy (counseling groups, activity groups), (3) play therapy (individual or group). Another way of looking at therapy in the schools is long-term versus short-term, with short-term therapy more prevalent (Losen, 1962; Smith, 1967). Still another approach is that of the "ayes" versus the "nays." A number of mental-health pro-fessionals state unequivocally that psychotherapy (usually with the connotation of deep, psycho-analytically oriented therapy) has no place in the schools (Losen, 1962; Patterson, 1966; Ross, 1962; Smith, 1967; Woody, 1969). The severely dis-turbed child whose problems are deeply rooted in family relationships is more appropriately referred to an agency or practitioner outside the school, with referral seen as one of the key func-tions of the school personnel. Another reason for questioning the appropriateness of individual therapy in the schools is the suggestion that many school mental-health personnel may not be adequately trained to render such services (Henriquez, 1964; Losen, 1962; Ross, 1962; Smith, 1967). When a case is made for individual psychotherapy in the schools, it is usually on the basis of the existence of a cliniclike service available to a school system (Henriquez, 1964; Jackson & Bernauer, 1968) or of individual therapists working with children who have school problems (Baruch, 1965; Freud, 1965).

The growing popularity of group techniques has had its counterpart in the schools. Balow (1966a) reviews a number of studies in which group techniques have been used in the schools, and Peters and Wattenberg (1966) have reviewed work with adolescents. These reviewers state that despite the difficulties in conducting research on psychotherapeutic and counseling approaches, positive gains have been reported in some studies in academic achievement, personality, and overt behavior. Other studies, however, present equivocal results or evidence of "spontaneous remission" in control groups (Balow 1966a; Peters & Wattenberg, 1966). Typical of group-counseling research are lack of theoretical frames of reference, failure to state duration and intensity of the experience, and paucity of interpretations of counseling-behavioral interaction (Eells, 1962; Johnson, 1964; Koeppe & Rothney, 1963; Moore & Popham, 1960; Watson, 1961).

Group counseling may take different forms, ranging from courses in personal adjustment or human relations, which are used to "promote discussion" (Bower, 1960), through role-playing techniques in which spontaneous dramatization of group ideas (sociodrama) or of personal ideas (psychodrama) are used as forms of psychotherapy (Smith, 1967), to activity therapy, client-centered techniques, loosely defined *group therapy*, and sensitivity training. There are few reports on group therapy in the school setting; and there is certainly no evidence that it is more effective than other therapeutic activities in the schools (Jackson & Bernauer, 1968; Smith, 1967). Complications are (1) variations in level of training of group therapists and/or leaders and (2) members of school groups having social contact with each other outside the group, interfering with confidentiality.

Play therapy is suggested for elementary (primary grades) schoolchildren, who are less likely than other children to be able to express their feelings verbally. No research has been located on the efficacy of play therapy in the schools, and it remains primarily a suggested technique (Smith, 1967).

Psychotherapy in the schools, especially in the form of group therapy/counseling, has received considerable attention in the literature, in that many descriptive and hortative articles have appeared. However, the dearth of definitive research leads reviewers of the research to comment that there is "a trend away from the traditional procedure of treating the individual child to the more comprehensive application of behavior modification principles to the entire classroom" (Glavin & Quay, 1969, p. 95). It should be reiterated that the ease of adapting behavior-modification procedures based on learning theory to research design may have contributed to this conclusion. Although there is a trend away from focus on therapy with the individual child, there is still considerable indication that therapeutic models other than those based on learning theory are extensively practiced in the schools.

ISSUES AND TRENDS

An issue frequently raised (Smith, 1967) is whether or not the schools should assume the responsibility of trying to help the child with serious psychopathology. The representative literature (Bower, 1966; Gottsegen & Gottsegen, 1960; Smith, 1967; Valett, 1963; White & Harris, 1961) indicates general agreement that there are some children who are so severely disturbed that they cannot be contained either in regular or in special classes in the schools. The role of the mental-health professional in the school is seen, in these cases, as one of helping parents to understand the nature of the problem and of assisting with appropriate placement and/or referral outside the school. Such children may be placed on "home instruction"; the school provides a visiting teacher who tutors the child a few hours each day in the child's home. There has also been a growing tendency, primarily as the result of parent pressure groups, for schools to assume part of the financial burden for a child's placement in a treatment center. On the other hand, institutions are crowded and frequently have waiting lists; private treatment centers are prohibitively expensive for most parents, even with partial help from the school system; and child-guidance clinics have waiting lists. Consequently parents exert more and more pressure upon the schools to make some provision for these children within the school itself. In addition, there is some support for the notion that deviant children, if tolerable, are helped to learn appropriate behavior in the structure of a classroom. In fact, Kanner and Eisenberg's (1955) discussions of autistic children suggest that probably the best placement for such children may be in a classroom of normal children.

The point of view cited in other sections of this chapter, i.e., that a structured, orderly environment combined with the establishment of firm behavioral limits by an authority figure is helpful to the child with problems, adds weight to the school's responsibility to provide for these children. An unanswered question is: How tolerable is tolerable? Are there not limits to the kinds of behavior that a classroom teacher may be expected to handle? It is obvious that individual teachers vary widely in their ability to tolerate extremely deviant children. These children can be sorely trying and can interfere with the teacher's ability to teach other children. On the other hand, there is occasionally indication that the troubled child may be merely troublesome. The teacher's lack of preparation and of certain kinds of knowledge and techniques for dealing with such children may make her unable to tolerate a child who might otherwise be contained in class. Teacher training of yesterday produced teachers with strong notions of discipline; deviant behavior was not tolerated, and classroom discipline was strong—and frequently effective. Teacher training today includes enough psychology to alert teachers to the possibility that they may inadvertently traumatize a child, with the result that many of today's teachers are fearful of imposing firm limits and, under the rubrics of "permissiveness" and "understanding the individual child," fail to exert appropriate classroom controls.

Along with the recommendations for a structured environment is the emphasis on educational therapy (Bower & Hollister, 1967; Hewett, 1968; Lewis, 1967; Smith, 1967). The point of view is probably best expressed by Bower (1967). The goals of the school are seen as educational, and the behavioral sciences in education attempt to assist schools in reaching such goals for all children. Educational success is a necessary ingredient for adult functioning, and effective education results in behavior modification and optimum growth and development. Bower (1967) contends that a major aim of education is to help children become more effective information processors and mediators, implying a cognitive-affection transaction. Education becomes the vehicle for the child's development of coping skills and appropriate ego processes. It is further assumed that the development of coping skills for educational processes is related to the development of coping skills—appropriate defense mechanisms—for taking one's place in adult society. Supporting this idea are the many studies reviewed by Balow (1966a) and by Glavin and Quay (1969) clearly showing the high negative relationship between school achievement and judgments of emotional disturbance among schoolchildren. The positive relationship between school achievement and success in society has long been known. In other words, if the school can help the disturbed child to master academic skills, the school has helped the child in his ego development and has helped him attain coping skills that will help him function in society.

Another important issue has to do with the realization by both educators and behavioral scientists that the quality of the help offered children in the schools cannot be isolated from the setting in which it is offered. The words *therapy, treatment,* and *remediation,* take on a meaning in the schools that is different from the usual clinical connotation. There has been a shift from emphasis on analyzing and basing treatment upon a study of the child's personality to an emphasis on analysis of and remediation for the child from a learning point of view (Bardon, 1968). The child's affective state is not ignored (Bower, 1967) but is considered in the context of the child's interaction with the school (Bardon, 1968; Hobbs, 1968; Hunt, 1968; Kelly, 1968). The mental-health professional who attempts to help children in the school without recognizing that the school is an influential social institution in society with its own unique *modus operandi* is likened to an industrial psychologist who attempts to deal with personnel problems in an industry without having an understanding of that industry's goals and ways of operation. Still another issue is raised when the disturbed child is considered as he interacts with the school as a social system. The upheavals in our current society are reflected in the schools. The schools are under attack for *not* performing their task of educating all children; a drastic change in the current educational methods—perhaps even educational goals—is being called for. The previous discussion of the need to develop coping

skills raises the question: Coping for what? Does learning to function in our society mean learning to function in terms of our present-day, middle-class definitions of successful functioning? Is the achievement motivation that is deemed so important for children in our current educational processes an invalid concept?

Educators and mental-health professionals tend to share a common value judgment about behavior, school performance, and occupational aspiration. Kluckhohn, in her dramatic presentation of the educational implications of her work with a large sample of high school boys in diverse areas of the Eastern seaboard, says, "Many of the problems in disturbed families as well as in the disturbed personalities of children in such families are in some large part traceable to value orientation conflicts" (p. 313) and that "the task [for educators] is that of providing a milieu of understanding so that dominantly oriented *students* in a school do not heavily penalize their variantly oriented fellow students" (p. 313).

Perhaps these cogent issues are best expressed by Bower and Hollister (1967) when they ask: First, what is the nature of the various cognitive-affective ego skills that need to be developed in all schoolchildren, including the deviant? Second, what is needed to change in our social and humanizing institutions (of which the school is primary) to make these institutions more effective ego developers? "What are the kinds of . . . experiences that help to potentiate and/or create mental strengths and how do schools . . . develop programs to do this?" (p. 530)

These authors see education as mankind's most effective tool for building human beings; they affirm the development of a technology for strengthening or repairing cognitive-affective functions of children:

> The long years of the mental health sciences' long and significant contributions to educational methodology and goals are coming to full cycle.

Now education is beginning to give back to mental health scientists new tools to fulfill our fondest dreams—the creation of the mentally healthy, actualized, effective, and competent person. Together the mental health and educational professions will continue to search for new and better ways of enhancing each other's work and of realizing our goals for a healthier, better educated society. [Bower & Hollister, 1967, p. 531.]

REFERENCES

Abrahamson, D. Status of mental hygiene and child guidance facilities in the public school in the United States. *Journal of Pediatrics*, 1955, **46,** 107–118.

Anastasi, A. *Psychological testing.* New York: Macmillan, 1957.

Andronico, M. P., & Guerney, B., Jr. The potential application of filial therapy to the school situation. *Journal of School Psychology,* 1967, **6,** 2–7.

Balow, B. The emotionally and socially handicapped. *Review of Educational Research*, 1966, **36,** 120–133. (a)

Balow, B. A program of preparation for teachers of disturbed children. *Exceptional Children,* 1966, **32,** 455–460. (b)

Barclay, J. R. Rationale and technique for effecting behavior change in the elementary school. *Personnel and Guidance Journal,* 1966, **44,** 1067–1076.

Barclay, J. R. *Changing the behavior of school psychologists: A training rationale and method.* Hayward, Calif: California State College, 1968.

Bardon, J. I. School psychology and school psychologists: An approach to an old problem. *American Psychologist,* 1968, **23,** 187–194.

Bardon, J. I., & Bennett, V. D. C. The perception of the role of the school psychologist as related to teaching experience and educational background. *Journal of School Psychology,* 1966, **4,** 52–58.

Bardon, J. I., & Bennett, V. D. C. Preparation for professional psychology: An example from a school psychology training program. *American Psychologist,* 1967, **22,** 652–656.

Baruch, D. One little boy. In N. J. Long, W. C. Morse, & R. G. Newman (Eds.), *Conflict in the classroom.* Belmont, Calif: Wadsworth, 1965. Pp. 164–177.

Beilin, H. Teachers' and clinicians' attitudes toward the behavior problems of children: A reappraisal. *Child Development,* 1959, **30,** 9–25.

Berkowitz, P. H., & Rothman, E. P. *The disturbed child: Recognition and psychoeducational therapy in the classroom.* New York: New York University Press, 1960.

Blackham, G. J. *The deviant child in the classroom.* Belmont, Calif: Wadsworth, 1967.

Blom, G. E., Rudnick, M., & Searles, J. Some principles and practices in the psychoeducational treatment of emotionally disturbed children. *Psychology in the Schools,* 1966, **3,** 30–38.

Board of Education of the City of New York. *The emotionally disturbed child: A bibliography.* New York: 1962.

Bower, E. M. *Early identification of emotionally handicapped children in school.* Springfield, Ill.: Charles C Thomas, 1960.

Bower, E. M. *The education of emotionally handicapped children.* Sacramento: California State Department of Education, 1961.

Bower, E. M. Psychoeducational approaches to the education of emotionally handicapped children. *Review of Educational Research,* 1962, **32,** 450–453.

Bower, E. M.   A conceptual framework for the development of programs for emotionally disturbed children.   In E. Landy & A. M. Kroll (Eds.), *Guidance in American education. III: Needs and influencing forces.*   Cambridge, Mass.: Harvard University Press, 1966.   Pp. 131–144.

Bower, E. M.   The school psychologists's role in the identification and adjustment of socio-emotionally handicapped children.   In J. F. Magary (Ed.), *School psychological services in theory and practice: A handbook.*   Englewood Cliffs, N.J.:   Prentice-Hall, 1967.

Bower, E. M., & Hollister, W. G. (Eds.)   *Behavioral science frontiers in education.*   New York: Wiley, 1967.

Bower, E., Shellhamer, T., & Daily, J.   School characteristics of male adolescents who later became schizophrenics.   *American Journal of Orthopsychiatry,* 1960, **30,** 712–729.

Burt, C., & Howard, M.   The nature and causes of maladjustment among children of school age.   *British Journal of Psychology,* 1952, **5,** 39–59.

Campbell, E. H.   Consultation and supervision of student teachers in a program of therapeutic tutoring.   *Journal of School Psychology,* 1967, **6,** 7–13.

Caplan, G. (Ed.)   *Prevention of mental disorders in children.*   New York: Basic Books, 1961.

Caplan, G.   *Principles of preventive psychiatry.*   New York: Basic Books, 1964.

Carlson, C. S., Arnold, C. R., Becker, W. C., & Madsen, C. H.   The elimination of tantrum behavior of a child in an elementary classroom.   *Behavioral Research and Therapy,* 1968, **6,** 117–119.

Coleman, J. S.   Social climates in high schools.   *Cooperative Research Monographs.*   Washing-ton, D.C.: Office of Education, U.S. Department of Health, Education & Welfare, 1961, No. 4.

Combs, R. H., & Harper, J. L.   Effects of labels on attitudes of educators toward handicapped children.   *Exceptional Children,* 1967, **33,** 399–403.

Connor, E. M., & Muldoon, J. F.   Resource programming for emotionally disturbed children.   *Exceptional Children,* 1967, **34,** 261–265.

Coolidge, J. C., Brodie, R. D., & Feeney, B.   A ten-year follow up study of sixty-six school phobic children.   *American Journal of Orthopsychiatry,* 1964, **34,** 675–684.

Coolidge, J. C., Hahn, P. B., & Peck, A. L.   School phobia: Neurotic crisis—A way of life.   *American Journal of Orthopsychiatry,* 1957, **27,** 296–306.

Cooper, M. G.   School refusal.   *Educational Research,* 1966, **8,** 115–127.

Cowen, E. L., & Zax, M.   Early detection and prevention of emotional disorder: Conceptualizations and programming.   In J. W. Carter (Ed.), *Research contributions from psychology to community mental health.*   New York: Behavioral Publications, 1968.

Cowen, E. L., Zax, M., & Laird, J. D.   A college student volunteer program in the elementary school setting.   *Community Mental Health Journal,* 1966, **2,** 319–328.

Cummings, S. T.   Psychotic dwarfs with good prognosis.   Paper presented at the meeting of the American Psychological Association, St. Louis, September, 1962.

Cutts, N. (Ed.)   *School psychologists at mid-century.*   Washington: American Psychological Association, 1955.

Deutsch, A., & Fishman, H. (Eds.)   *The ency-*

clopedia of mental health. New York: Frank-lin Watts, 1963.

D'Evelyn, K. *Meeting children's emotional needs.* Englewood Cliffs, N.J.: Prentice-Hall, 1957.

Donahue, G. T. A school district program for schizophrenic, organic, and seriously disturbed children. In E. L. Cowen, E. A. Gardner, & M. Zax (Eds.), *Emergent approaches to mental health problems.* New York: Appleton Century Crofts, 1967. Pp. 369–386.

Donahue, G. T., & Nichtern, S. *Teaching the troubled child.* New York: Free Press, 1965.

Dunn, L. M. Special education for the mildly retarded—Is much of it justifiable? *Exceptional Children,* 1968, **35,** 5–22.

Dyer, V. An example: Reinforcement principles in a classroom for emotionally disturbed children. *Exceptional Chldren,* 1968, **34,** 597–599.

Eells, K. Voluntary versus compulsory counseling with regard to college entrance plans. *Personnel and Guidance Journal,* 1962, **41,** 234–239.

Eiserer, P. E. *The school psychologist.* Washington, D.C.: The Center for Applied Research in Education, 1963.

Felix, R. H. *Mental illness—Progress and prospects.* New York: Columbia, 1967.

Freud, A. The relation between psychoanalysis and pedagogy. In N. J. Long, W. C. Morse, & R. G. Newman (Eds.), *Conflict in the classroom.* Belmont, Calif: Wadsworth, 1965. Pp. 159–163.

Friedman, R. A structured family interview in the assessment of school learning disorders. Paper presented at the 45th annual meeting of the American Orthopsychiatric Association, Chicago, March, 1968.

Garvey, W. P., & Hegrenes, J. R. Desensitization techniques in the treatment of school phobia. *American Journal of Orthopsychiatry,* 1966, **36,** 147–152.

Glavin, J. P. "Spontaneous" improvement in emotionally disturbed children. *Dissertation Abstracts,* 1968, **28,** No. 9, 3505A.

Glavin, J., & Quay, H. C. Behavior disorders. *Review of Educational Research,* 1969, **39,** 83–102.

Glidewell, J. C., Domke, H. R., & Kantor, M. B. Screening in schools for behavior disorders: Use of mothers' report of symptoms. *Journal of Educational Research,* 1963, **56,** 508–515.

Gordon, J. W. The psychologist as a consultant in an in-service program of child and youth study. *Journal of School Psychology,* 1967, **6,** 18–21.

Gorman, M. A national program for emotionally disturbed children. Paper presented at the 20th Anniversary Meeting, Dade County Children's Psychiatric Center, Miami, January, 1968.

Gottsegen, M. G., & Gottsegen, G. B. (Eds.) *Professional school psychology.* Vol. I. New York: Grune & Stratton, 1960.

Gottsegen, M. G., & Gottsegen, G. B. (Eds.) *Professional school psychology.* Vol. II. New York: Grune & Stratton, 1963.

Grimes, J. W., & Allinsmith, W. Compulsivity, anxiety, and school achievement. *Merrill-Palmer Quarterly,* 1961, **7,** 247–271.

Grossman, H. *Teaching the emotionally disturbed: A casebook.* New York: Holt, 1965.

Guerney, B., Jr. Filial therapy: Description

and rationale. *Journal of Consulting Psychology,* 1964, **28,** 304–310.

Haan, N. When the mentally ill child returns to school. *Elementary School Journal,* 1957, **57,** 379–385.

Haring, N. G., & Phillips, E. L. *Educating emotionally disturbed children.* New York: McGraw-Hill, 1962.

Hay, L. The education of emotionally disturbed children: A new school channel for helping the troubled child. *American Journal of Orthopsychiatry,* 1953, **23,** 676–683.

Hay, L., & Cohen, S. Perspectives for a classroom for disturbed children. *Exceptional Children,* 1967, **34,** 577–580.

Henriquez, V. S. The case for psychotherapy in the schools. *Pathways in Child Guidance,* Bureau of Child Guidance, Board of Education of the City of New York, 1964, **6,** 3–8.

Hewett, F. M. A hierarchy of competencies for teachers of emotionally handicapped children. *Exceptional Children,* 1966, **33,** 7–11.

Hewett, F. M. Educational engineering with emotionally disturbed children. *Exceptional Children,* 1967, **33,** 459–467.

Hewett, F. M. *The emotionally disturbed child in the classroom.* Boston: Allyn and Bacon, 1968.

Hirst, W. E. *Know your school psychologist.* New York: Grune & Stratton, 1963.

Hobbs, N. Helping disturbed children: Psychological and ecological strategies. *American Psychologist,* 1966, **21,** 1105-1115.

Hobbs, N. Reeducation, reality, and community responsibility. In J. W. Carter, Jr. (Ed.), *Research contributions from psychology to community mental health.* New York: Behavioral Publications, 1968. Pp. 7–18.

Hollister, W. G., & Goldston, S. E. Psychoeducational processes in classes for emotionally handicapped children. *Exceptional Children,* 1962, **28,** 351–356.

Hunt, J. McV. Toward the prevention of incompetence. In J. W. Carter, Jr. (Ed.), *Research contributions from psychology to community mental health.* New York: Behavioral Publications, 1968. Pp. 19–45.

Hunter, E. C. Changes in teachers' attitudes toward children's behavior over the last thirty years. *Mental Hygiene,* 1957, **41,** 3–11.

Hymes. J. L., Jr. *A pound of prevention.* New York: Teachers Service Committee on the Emotional Needs of Children, 1947.

Hymes, J. L., Jr. *Teacher listen: The children speak.* New York: New York Committee on Mental Health, 1949.

Jackson, J. H., & Bernauer, M. (Eds.) *The school psychologist as a therapist.* Milwaukee: Milwaukee Public Schools, 1968.

Johnson, J. L., & Rubin, E. Z. A school follow-up study of children discharged from a psychiatric hospital. *Exceptional Children,* 1964, **31,** 19–24.

Johnson, L. E. Personality changes in emotionally disturbed students during counseling. *Dissertation Abstracts,* 1964, **24,** 2985–2986.

Joint Committee on Health Problems in Education. *Mental hygiene in the classroom.* Chicago: American Medical Association, 1956.

Kanner, L., & Eisenberg, L. Notes on the follow-up studies of autistic children. In P. Hoch & J. Zubin (Eds.), *Psychopathology of childhood.*

New York: Grune & Stratton, 1955. Pp. 227–239.

Kelly, J. G. Toward an ecological conception of preventive interventions. In J. W. Carter, Jr. (Ed.), *Research contributions from psychology to community mental health.* New York: Behavioral Publications, 1968. Pp. 76–100.

Kitano, H. H. Adjustment of problem and non-problem children to specific situations: A study in role theory. *Child Development,* 1962, **33,** 229–233.

Knoblock, P., & Garcea, R. A. Toward a broader concept of the role of the special class for emotionally disturbed children. *Exceptional Children,* 1965, **31,** 329–335.

Koeppe, R., & Rothney, J. W. M. Evaluation of first steps in the counseling of superior students. *Personnel and Guidance Journal,* 1963, **42,** 35–39.

Krugman, M. (Ed.) *Orthopsychiatry and the schools.* New York: American Orthopsychiatric Association, 1958.

La Benne, W. D. Differential diagnosis and psychoeducational treatment for the emotionally disturbed. *Psychology in the Schools,* 1967, **4,** 366–370.

Lambert, N., & Bower, E. M. *Technical report on in-school screening of emotionally handicapped children.* Princeton, N.J.: Educational Testing Service, 1961.

Lazarus, A. A., Davidson, G. C., & Polefka, D. A. Classical and operant factors in the treatment of school phobia. *Journal of Abnormal Psychology,* 1965, **70,** 225–229.

Leaverton, L. Can the home school provide adequate help for the emotionally disturbed child? *Psychology in the Schools,* 1965, **2,** 269–272.

Leavitt, A. C. Treatment of an adolescent with school phobia. *American Journal of Orthopsychiatry,* 1964, **34,** 334–335.

Leventhal, T., & Sills, M. Self-image in school phobia. *American Journal of Orthopsychiatry,* 1964, **34,** 685–695.

Lewis, W. W. Continuity and intervention in emotional disturbance: A review. *Exceptional Children,* 1965, **31,** 465–475.

Lewis, W. W. Project Re-Ed: Educational intervention in discordant child rearing systems. In E. L. Cowan, E. A. Gardner, & M. Zax (Eds.), *Emergent approaches to mental health problems.* New York: Appleton Century Crofts, 1967. Pp. 352–368.

Linton, T. E. The European educateur program for disturbed children. *American Journal of Orthopsychiatry,* 1969, **39,** 125–133.

Long, N. J., Morse, W. C., & Newman, R. G. (Eds.) *Conflict in the classroom: The education of emotionally disturbed children.* Belmont, Calif: Wadsworth, 1965.

Long, N. J., & Newman, R. G. Managing surface behavior of children in school. In N. J. Long, W. C. Morse, & R. G. Newman (Eds.), *Conflict in the classroom.* Belmont, Calif: Wadsworth, 1965. Pp. 352–362.

Losen, S. M. The role of the psychologist as consultant to the teaching staff and to administrators. In H. O'Shea (Chm.), *Shall school psychologists conduct psychotherapy?* Symposium presented at the American Psychological Association, St. Louis, 1962.

Mackie, R. P., Kovaraceus, W. C., & Williams, H. M. *Teachers of children who are socially and emotionally maladjusted.* Washington, D.C.: U.S. Office of Education, 1957.

Maes, W. R. The identification of emotionally

disturbed elementary school children. *Exceptional Children,* 1966, **32,** 607–609.

Magary, J. F. *School psychological services in theory and practice.* Englewood Cliffs, N.J.: Prentice-Hall, 1969.

McNamara, J. R. Behavior therapy in the classroom: A case report. *Journal of School Psychology,* 1969, **7,** 48–51.

Mesinger, J. F., & Bower, E. M. Emotionally disturbed and brain damaged children—should we mix them? *Exceptional Children,* 1965, **32,** 237–240.

Miller, N. L. A motivational reading program for disturbed children. *Exceptional Children,* 1964, **31,** 91–92.

Moller, H. The treatment of childhood schizophrenia in a public school system. *Psychology in the Schools,* 1964, **1,** 297–304.

Moore, M. R., & Popham, W. J. Effects of two interview techniques on academic achievement. *Journal of Counseling Psychology,* 1960, **7,** 176–179.

Morse, W. C. Intervention techniques for the classroom teacher of the emotionally disturbed. In P. Knoblock (Ed.), *Educational programming for emotionally disturbed children: The decade ahead.* Syracuse, N.Y.: Syracuse University Press, 1964. Pp. 29–41.

Morse, W. C. The crisis teacher. In N. J. Long, W. C. Morse, & R. G. Newman (Eds.), *Conflict in the classroom.* Belmont, Calif: Wadsworth, 1965. Pp. 251–254.

Morse, W. C. Enhancing the classroom teacher's mental health function. In E. L. Cowen, E. A. Gardner, & M. Zax (Eds.), *Emergent approaches to mental health problems.* New York: Appleton Century Crofts, 1967. Pp. 271–289.

Morse, W. C., Cutler, R. L., & Fink, A. H. *Public school classes for the emotionally handicapped: A research analysis.* Washington: Council for Exceptional Children, NEA, 1964.

Morse, W. C., & Dyer, C. O. The emotionally and socially handicapped. *Review of Educational Research,* 1963, **33,** 109–125.

Mutimer, D. D., & Rosemier, R. A. Behavior problems of children as viewed by teachers and the children themselves. *Journal of Consulting Psychology,* 1967, **31,** 583–587.

Newman, R. G. *Psychological consultation in the schools.* New York: Basic Books, 1967.

North, G. E. Behavior reporting to parents: A forgotten approach to behavior problems. *Journal of School Psychology,* 1968, **6,** 117–122.

O'Leary, K. D., & Becker, W. C. Behavior modification of an adjustment class: A token reinforcement program. *Exceptional Children,* 1967, **33,** 637–642.

O'Neal, P., & Robbins, L. N. The relation of childhood behavior problems to adult psychiatric status: A 30 year follow-up study of 150 subjects. *American Journal of Psychiatry,* 1958, **114,** 361–369.

Pate, J. Emotionally disturbed and socially maladjusted children. In L. Dunn (Ed.), *Exceptional children in the schools.* New York: Holt, 1963. Pp. 239–283.

Patterson, C. H. Psychotherapy in the school. *Journal of School Psychology,* 1966, **4,** 15–29.

Peter, L. J. *Prescriptive teaching.* New York: McGraw-Hill, 1965.

Peters, M., & Wattenberg, W. W. Adolescence: Behavior disorders and guidance. *Review of Educational Research,* 1966, **36,** 474–484.

Pimm, J. B., & McClure, G. A screening device for early detection of emotional disturbance in a public school setting. *Exceptional Children,* 1967, **34,** 647–648.

Porter, D. What does learning theory contribute to the classroom? *Audio-visual Instruction,* 1962, **7,** 14–15.

Quay, H. C. Some basic considerations in the education of emotionally disturbed children. *Exceptional Children,* 1963, **30,** 27–31.

Quay, H. C. The facets of educational exceptionality: A conceptual framework for assessment, grouping, and instruction. *Exceptional Children,* 1968, **35,** 25–32.

Quay, H. C., Werry, J. S., McQueen, M., & Sprague, R. L. Remediation of the conduct problem child in the special class setting. *Exceptional Children,* 1966, **33,** 509–515.

Reger, R. *School psychology.* Springfield, Ill.: Charles C Thomas, 1965.

Reger, R. A program for children with learning or behavioral problems. *Psychology in the Schools,* 1967, **4,** 317–324.

Rhodes, W. R. The disturbing child: A problem of ecological management. *Exceptional Children,* 1967, **33,** 449–455.

Ritholz, S. *Children's behavior.* New York: Bookman Associates, 1959.

Ross, A. O. The school psychologist's role seen from the child guidance clinic. In H. O'Shea (Chm.), *Shall school psychologists conduct psychotherapy?* Symposium presented at the American Psychological Association, St. Louis, 1962.

Sarason, S. B., Levine, M., Goldenberg, I. I., Cherlin, D. L., & Bennett, E. M. *Psychology in community settings: Clinical, educational, vocational, social aspects.* New York: Wiley, 1966.

Scarpitti, F. R. Can teachers predict delinquen-

cy? *Elementary School Journal,* 1964, **65,** 130–136.

Seeman, J. Teacher judgments of high and low adjustment. *Journal of Educational Research,* 1963, **57,** 213–216.

Smith, D. C. Counseling and psychotherapy in the school setting. In J. F. Magary (Ed.), *School psychological services in theory and practice.* Englewood Cliffs, N.J.: Prentice-Hall, 1967. Pp. 142–170.

Smith, S. A. An educational program for emotionally disturbed children. *Psychology in the Schools,* 1967, **4,** 280–283.

Stark, W., & Betzen, F. The integration of the emotionally disturbed child in the normal school setting. In M. Krugman (Ed.), *Orthopsychiatry and the school.* New York: American Orthopsychiatric Association, 1958. Pp. 82–95.

Stennett, R. G. Emotional handicap in the elementary years: Phase or disease? *American Journal of Orthopsychiatry,* 1966, **36,** 444–449.

Thomas, R. M. *Aiding the maladjusted pupil: A guide for teachers.* New York: McKay, 1967.

Thompson, C. E. The attitudes of various groups toward behavior problems of children. *Journal of Abnormal and Social Psychology,* 1940, **35,** 120–125.

Tift, K. F. The disturbed child in the classroom. *NEA Journal,* 1968, **57,** 12–14.

Vacc, N. A. A study of emotionally disturbed children in regular and special classes. *Exceptional Children,* 1968, **35,** 197–206.

Valett, R. E. *The practice of school psychology: Professional problems.* New York: Wiley, 1963.

Valett, R. E. A social reinforcement technique for the classroom management of behavior disorders. *Exceptional Children,* 1966, **33,** 185–189.

Vane, J. R., & Eisen, V. W. The Goodenough Draw-A-Man Test and signs of maladjustment in kindergarten children. *Journal of Clinical Psychology,* 1962, **18,** 276–279.

Vieland, C. Teacher education programs: Princeton regional schools. Princeton. N.J.: 1968.

Watson, G. H. Evaluation of counseling with college students. *Journal of Counseling Psychology,* 1961, **8,** 99–104.

Werry, J. S., & Quay, H. C. A method of observing classroom behavior of emotionally disturbed children. *Exceptional Children,* 1968, **34,** 461–470.

Westman, J. C., Rice, D. L., & Bermann, E. Nursery school behavior and later school adjustment. *American Journal of Orthopsychiatry,* 1967, **37,** 725–731.

Whelan, R. J., & Haring, N. G. Modification and maintenance of behavior through systematic application of consequences. *Exceptional Children,* 1966, **33,** 281–289.

White, M. A., & Charry, J. (Eds.) *School disorder, intelligence, and social class.* New York: Teachers College, 1966.

White M. A., & Harris, M. W. *The school psychologist.* New York: Harper & Row, 1961.

Wickman, E. K. *Children's behavior and teachers' attitudes.* New York: Commonwealth Fund, 1928.

Wolman, B. B. (Ed.) *Handbook of clinical psychology.* New York: McGraw-Hill, 1965.

Woody, R. H. *Behavioral problem children in the schools.* New York: Appleton Century Crofts, 1969.

Yale conference on learning. Muncie, Ind.: NDEA National Institute for Advanced Study, 1966.

Zax, M., Cowen, E. L., Izzo, L. D., & Trost, M. A. Identifying emotional disturbance in the school setting. *American Journal of Orthopsychiatry,* 1964, **34,** 447–454.

37 Prevention of Mental and Emotional Disorders of Childhood

Irving N. Berlin

Prevention has been classified roughly into three categories: primary, secondary, and tertiary (Caplan & Grunebaum, 1967). Primary prevention is reserved for those methods which anticipate disease or disorder before it has become manifest in any way. Although the ideal of all prevention models in mental health, it is the most difficult to both conceptualize and utilize. Primary prevention requires the use of two public-health methods—massive research and widespread interventions—to determine the cause-and-effect relationship in disorders with multi-variant factors which need to be isolated and controlled. To be effective, it usually requires changes which include large population groups. There are, however, a number of primary preventive efforts in mental disorders of children which can and have been effective.

Secondary prevention essentially requires early diagnosis, case finding, and intervention so that a disease or disorder may be rapidly brought under control and therefore have only minor impact on the sick individual. Most large-scale preventive efforts in mental disorder are of this nature (Eisenberg & Gruenberg, 1961).

When we discuss tertiary prevention, we are in our most familiar territory. Until recently we have been primarily engaged in those endeavors which reduce disability and most quickly return the individual to some degree of functioning in his normal environment.

Our discussion will include all three preventive methods. However, we must keep in mind that in prevention of mental disorder in children we are dealing with the entire family in relation to the child. Thus, our efforts with the child, and often with the parents, usually also have important preventive implications for the child's parents and siblings.

PRIMARY PREVENTION

At what point does an infant or young child have a disorder which requires intervention and which can be delineated as such (Caplan & Grunebaum, 1967). It may be termed *primary prevention* when one finds that a nursing mother seems to have little feeling for her child and is indifferent to its complaints, bodily position, and other physiological needs (Call, 1963; Rutter, Birch, Thomas, & Chess, 1964; Sayegh & Dennis, 1963). Sometimes mother and child do not seem to get along—for example, a torporous, sleepy baby who will not suck with any vigor from the breasts of his very vital, eager mother; mother then reacts with acute disappointment, hurt, and later anger because she is being cheated of the nursing experience. We have seen a few instances in which a rather shy, withdrawn, and energyless young mother responded to her lusty baby's vigorous sucking at her breasts with ill-concealed horror and aversion. Help for the troubled mother in these instances may be primary prevention for the infant if no symptoms of disturbance have yet been noted in the child (Thomas, Chess, & Birch, 1963). However, it may be early intervention and secondary prevention in the emotional disorder of the mother. Investigation usually reveals that mother reacts to the infant in a particular way because of a variety of factors which occur singly or (usually) in combination. Examples are unconscious expectations of self and child, marital problems, and often emotional conflicts about mothering. If these feelings of hurt, disappointment, and ensuing anger are not dealt with promptly, mother-child alienation occurs, producing not only a disturbed child but also a disturbed mother and perhaps a ripple effect on other family members (Ainsworth, 1962; Bibring, Dwyer, Huntington, & Valenstein, 1961; Blodgett, 1963; Bowlby, 1951, 1969).

In this context the parents (especially the mother of a malformed, mentally retarded, or otherwise physically handicapped child) require prompt professional help. The fact that they live through the initial shock, seem to regain equilibrium, and talk little about the problem is no sign that they have in any way integrated or worked through the trauma so that it will not seriously affect their future lives. The many parents who go from one physician or diagnostic and treatment center to another, never satisfied with the diagnosis and recommendations, indicate the need for early preventive efforts and help with problems precipitated by the birth of a defective child. Experience indicates that attention to the deep hurt, help in verbalizing guilt feelings and self-blame, and repeated open discussion about the fear that something in them is defective begin to help parents feel less conflictual about the situation. They are then better able to consider a course of action for their child and themselves. When, as is usual, such help is not forthcoming early, the guilt, anxiety, anger, and normal death wishes toward the defective child are unrelieved. The need to blame someone else for their painful, unrelieved, conflicted, and troubled state of being then becomes fixed. Subsequently, both the estrangement between the parents and the problems in raising the child are much more difficult to resolve. Here primary prevention focuses on the mental health of the defective child. These efforts may also have primary preventive effects on other children in the home and on the parents (Ambrosino, 1960; Berlin, 1966).

Prenatal and Postpartum Maternal Depression

Several investigators have shown that maternal depression during pregnancy is highly predictive for both postpartum maternal depression and early mother-child alienation, with potentially serious aftermath for child, parents, and siblings (Bibring et. al., 1961). These studies have also indicated that prenatal maternal depression can be readily identified and successfully treated not only by individual psychotherapy but especially by group therapeutic methods involving both parents. The results appear excellent (Call, 1963).

Another important area of primary prevention results from the studies of children at risk. It has become clear from numerous investigations that both prematurity and low birth weight due to maternal malnutrition during pregnancy are predictive for developmental, psychological, and learning problems in later life. Recent efforts to overcome the poor prognosis due to prematurity for normal maturation and functioning in childhood, adolescence, and adult life have led to a variety of investigations (Caplan & Grunebaum, 1967; Cravioto et al., 1966; deHirsch, Jansky, & Langford, 1966; Leonard, Rhymes, & Solnit, 1966; Patton & Gardner, 1963; Winick, 1968). Efforts to stimulate the central nervous system and to reduce the isolation of the premature infant, using appropriate stimuli, have been reported. Handling of the premature baby by his parents while hospitalized is still rare because of the need to keep the tiny infant in an isolette with regulated temperature, oxygen, etc. Some of these investigations give promise of effective intervention methods (Birns, 1965; Blank, 1964; Greenberg, 1965).

The effect of maternal malnutrition on the infant is a pervasive result of poverty. Social legislation and funds are required to prevent maternal malnutrition because these mothers give birth to malnourished infants, with possible brain damage occurring before birth.

Postpartum Depression and Mother-Child Alienation

For unwed or economically deprived mothers, therapeutic efforts must be coupled to action-oriented programs which vigorously alter the anticipated serious socioeconomic and family problems often related to such depression. Identification of postpartum depression and signs of early mother-child alienation are important primary prevention measures. When specially trained, the obstetrical nurse is often the first

to detect this. When prompt help to mother is provided, both mother and child may avoid the serious consequences. The treatment of the mother, of course, depends on the diagnostic assessment of causes. Several studies indicate that young mothers who have not yet lived very fully in married life and have little mothering and child-care experience to draw on may be greatly helped by casework in the hospital. Assistance can also be provided for some weeks or months after the mother leaves the hospital by homemakers who support the mother in learning the mothering role and techniques. Mothers who have had little nurturance in their own infancy and early childhood require some models of nurturance in order to care for their own children. They also need the continued concern of someone until they are able to begin to receive pleasure from the care of and interaction with the infant. Work with both mothers and fathers during the early weeks of their infant's life have been effective in many instances (Bowlby, 1969; Caplan & Grunebaum, 1967; Keller, 1963; Lidz, 1961; Robertson, 1962).

Perhaps the most important areas of primary prevention are in the work of pediatricians in private practice and in well-baby and well-child clinics. Alert pediatricians and general practitioners who notice estrangement of mother and child in the office (e.g., mother not able to cuddle child; a child who fusses, kicks, and squirms so he cannot be held by mother but relaxes in the nurse's arms) need to look upon such behavior as data to be recorded and followed up. Mother's complaints about such problems as feeding and sleeping difficulties, constant irritability, head rolling and banging, reversal of sleep patterns, and incessant crying, as well as comments about the "good" baby who sleeps all the time and requires little stimulation, must be seriously considered as data to be followed closely. Most physicians react quickly to nutritional problems or failure to gain weight and grow and will begin to investigate these. However, frequently they are not so alert to possible psychological causes for retarded development (Braun, 1965; Call & Liverman, 1963; Caplan & Grunebaum, 1967; Levy, 1959; Townsend, 1964).

Identification of Organic Problems as Primary Prevention

The kindergarten and primary school years may provide the first opportunity that trained and experienced observers have to assess a child. Studies of Bower (1960) and others have shown that schoolteachers' observations are usually accurate and sensitive indications of early childhood disturbance. The mildly organically impaired child, when faced with a variety of learning tasks in school which his peers are able to master, begins to reveal areas of minor impairment. Thus, perceptual disturbances, sensory-motor difficulties, etc., come to light fairly early. However, they may not be evaluated or attended to if neither teacher nor physician defines, as early and explicitly as possible, the disorder present (Birch, 1964).

Discrimination between emotional disturbance and mild organic impairment is more easily made in the first and second grades than later because learning patterns may still be examined before frustration, disappointment, failure, and hyperactivity become a circular and fixed set of responses. There is then time for special and often precise remedial efforts to be made so that the child may be selectively protected by gearing his work and its presentation, via appropriate sensory and motor modalities, to his learning capacity.

A vital corollary is the effort to help reduce the expectations of parents and child so they are consonant with actual capacity. There is, then, a consequent reduction of serious emotional trauma for both child and parents, as well as reduced tension in the home. Often school people, physicians, and mental-health consultants to schools do not consider sufficiently the circular emotional disturbances (a kind of reverberating and accelerating circuit of tensions) that result from not clarifying issues of impairment early. This continues despite the fact that most of us know that parental disappointment and high expectations of the child lead to his high self-expectations, hurt, and anxiety. These, in turn, lead to anger and increased turmoil as his best efforts do not satisfy his parents and are not as good as those of his age-mates. Such circular expectation leads to reduced effectiveness in learning, with aggravation of the parent-child and child-teacher relationships. If not altered quickly, the child acquires a defensive set necessary for his psychological homeostasis, resulting in truculence, aggressiveness, indifferent withdrawal, unpredictable and angry outbursts which are self-perpetuated, and sometimes even suicide. In contrast, if these youngsters do have the opportunity to learn without pressure and if methods and materials geared to minimizing their deficit through their particular sensory-motor modalities are used, behavior problems are usually greatly minimized and the children tend to adapt, learn in school at their own rate, and accomplish a good deal. In fact, there is evidence that some of these children may in time come very close to family expectations in their capacities to learn.

SECONDARY PREVENTION

Developmental Framework for Prevention

When developmental sequences are markedly delayed during infancy and the first few years of life, beginning emotional illness may be indicated. Thus, when a child's sitting, crawling, standing, walking, or talking is seriously retarded, there is cause for a closer look. Parents' anxieties about their child's failure to reach certain developmental landmarks as soon as a friend's or relative's child need to be attended to carefully. This may indicate not only competitiveness and keeping up with the neighbors but also a realistic anxiety about their child, stemming from a disturbed parent-child relationship or poor parent-child compatibility, which the parents indicate in this way.

The effort of the physician to spend time with the mother talking about the infant and how it has affected the parents' lives and relationships often begins to bring out disappointments and unrealized expectations of satisfactions and pleasure in the new baby. Many mothers whose children have problems are so inexperienced and uncertain that only repeated help and instruction in dealing with specific problems relieves their tension. Thus, it becomes clear that reassurance alone, a "Don't worry; everything is going to be okay," is of no help to concerned mothers. Serious attention to anxiety about a feeding problem sometimes reveals that it is due to an inadequate amount of handling of the baby. Interest in the mother's problem, followed by a suggestion that she carry out some clearly demonstrated holding of and playing with the infant at prescribed times, may not only alter the baby's feeding problems, but it may help the mother to begin to experience some pleasure with the baby (Call, 1963; Levy, 1959).

Often the public-health nurse's visits, evident interest in the mother's other problems and troubles, encouragement and demonstration of handling and playing with the baby, and follow-up visits in which mother's efforts are supported and praised have been decisive factors in helping her to provide mothering experiences necessary to the child's development. Thus, demonstration and instruction enable many young mothers who, for various reasons, are estranged from their babies to begin to enjoy them and to

be more nurturant. Psychologists who have been trained in child development are now more frequently employed in well-child clinics, and their observations may provide stimuli for investigation and intervention.

Preschool Precursors of Emotional Disorder

Early manifestations of later troubles become evident in the preschool years, and a variety of neurotic disorders and psychophysiological disturbances may be seen. In psychophysiological disorders, environmental stress, interpersonal conflicts, and genetic predisposition all need to be kept clearly in mind as requiring evaluation to determine relevant intervention. Speech abnormalities such as stuttering or loss of speech may become warning signals, as may excessive seclusiveness, withdrawal, or unbridled aggression. Signs of neurological handicap and retardation become more discrete as large and small muscle coordination and organization of speech provide clear landmarks for developmental evaluation. The preventive aspects of such evaluation and early intervention are enormous (Bower, 1964; Brody, 1961; Cary, 1967; Furman, 1957).

Outside of home, the psychosocially deprived child's aberrant behavior becomes most evident in preschool programs. Preventive aspects of preschool interventions through development of relationships, engagement in many kinds of sensory-motor stimuli, and development of a variety of skills have been frequently described (Deutsch, 1965; Pasamanick, Knoblock, & Lillienfield, 1956). Nursery schools provide an opportunity to see the child in a comparative setting, and the teacher is often the first to call attention to marked isolation, speech disturbances, irreducible hyperactivity, hyperaggressiveness, and inability to focus attention on pleasurable activities for any length of time. Children require help when their behavior in a new setting does not alter with familiarity and when there is no change in isolation, fear of attending school, withdrawal, assaultiveness, destructive behavior, or general fearfulness.

Prevention in Psychophysiological Problems

The so-called psychosomatic problems of children may involve both serious emotional problems and physiological problems. Although discussed in detail elsewhere in this volume, I would like to mention some secondary-prevention aspects since primary prevention of eczema, asthma, allergy, ulcers, ulcerative colitis, etc., are particularly difficult, and early intervention cannot occur until these disorders are identified and diagnosed (Berlin, Boatman, Sheimo, & Szurek, 1951; Bruch, 1947; Sperling, 1951).

Secondary prevention depends on prompt recognition of the mixed physiological and psychological factors in each disorder and on an effort to work with all aspects. The psychological elements are usually related to ongoing family conflicts and internalized conflicts from the child's past experiences. Psychotherapeutic work with parents is also essential to the reduction or elimination of the disability. This is especially true if the disease is identified early and efforts with the parents can be supportive of their parenting role rather than critical of them for the contributions their problems have made to the child's disorder. In several instances of infantile eczema the young mothers felt very angry because their babies required so much attention, which the mothers also very badly needed. We enlisted the help of a team consisting of a social worker, public-health nurse, and nurse's aide. They were able to provide mother, father, and infant with a wide variety of help so that, unlike previous experiences, the eczema did not become chronic and recurrent.

Once the disease process in the tissues has

taken hold and both the inter- and intrapersonal conflicts have become circular and self-perpetuating, tertiary prevention requires much more heroic measures in both physiological and psychological treatment and is often not very successful.

The Disadvantaged Child

Prevention through early intervention into the problems of the disadvantaged child has been frequently discussed. It may be sufficient to stress that signs of childhood psychosis, brain damage with hyperactivity, evidence of slow motor and speech development, and many learning difficulties with evidence of gross mental retardation may all disappear when psychosocially deprived youngsters are provided required personal attention, sensory-motor stimulation via a wide variety of learning materials, and activities in a fairly structured setting of sufficient duration. This is especially true if disadvantaged mothers are included in the program. As mothers are stimulated through observing activities of their child and other children, they bring new vitality into their homes. The relation of nutritional deprivation to the total picture of emotional, physical, and intellectual retardation has also been shown to be important (Leighton et al., 1963; Pasamanick et al., 1956).

Secondary Prevention in Neurotic Disorders

Prevention of neurotic adaptations and character disorders occurs only when beginning symptoms are identified and intervention with the child, family, and school occurs rapidly. While phobic symptoms, especially school phobia, are most readily recognized, socially shy or lonely behavior, exclusive preoccupation with schoolwork or fantasies, lack of friends, and extensive daydreaming with reduced capacity to learn may all be indicative of beginning neurotic disorder or more serious emotional difficulties. In a similar vein, enuresis, encopresis, nightmares, sleepwalking, excessive eating, or excessive dependency may be complained of by parents to their physician and may also indicate beginning neurotic disturbances.

Perhaps the most pervasive character disorder seen in children is heralded by school underachievement (Bower, 1960; Zax & Cowen, 1967). While etiological factors may vary, they all reflect a severe degree of parent-child and sometimes teacher-child disturbance. When investigated, learning problems are often indicative of a host of negativistic attitudes toward others, such as tantrums and teasing, which result in reduced self-esteem and self-defeating behavior in every situation. Repeatedly, the parents evidence similar feelings, have little love or nurturance to give, and require nurturance for themselves (Newman, 1961).

Paradoxically, the too good child (exemplary student, mother's pride and joy who is never in trouble, a leader in his class, self-sacrificing in many situations—in fact, a model child) may also be indicating incipient character disorder, especially those children who derive little fun or pleasure from activities. Such exemplary children sometimes become violent toward their parents or self-destructive and suicidal. In adolescence many are unable to form close and intimate relationships; their rebellion and striving for independence are turned inward, and they may become obsessive or schizoid (Burks & Harrison, 1962).

Many child-guidance clinics which work closely with schools are able to effect an alliance to work therapeutically with child and parents. The teacher and counselor use the learning situation to help the child feel more competent and effective, both through mastery of academic work and through social interaction. The conscious use of a teacher or counselor, seen frequently as a model and ego-ideal, may be very effective in helping a child and preventing further disturbance or deterioration. Some of us have had the opportunity to observe group workers in schools working with nonlearners, disaffected and defiant teen-agers, and lonely, withdrawn youngsters. It has been our impression that such group work is particularly effective when the worker is honest and straightforward and can use his human feelings as a springboard for the tentative sharing of the students' own fears and troubles with one another and with the worker.

Prevention of Antisocial Behavior by Early Identification

Several investigations have revealed the high predictive relationship between aggressive, hostile, acting-out behavior in primary grades and antisocial delinquent behavior in adolescents (Balser, Wacker, Gratwick, Mumford, Clinton, & Balser, 1965; Bower, 1960; Glueck & Glueck, 1959). When aggressive behavior is a result of the child's immaturity and the school's inability to find curriculum and activities to engage him, diagnostic evaluation and remediation may lead to primary prevention. When the aggressive behavior is symptomatic of sociocultural or family problems and the inability of society and the school to cope with them, efforts on the part of the school to modify its techniques of reaching these children and helping them learn may be significant preventive efforts. In other instances, the aggressive-destructive behavior may be the result of severe internalized conflicts resulting from continuing and destructive pathological relationships in the family. The teacher's early recognition of a pupil's emotional problems is of increasing importance for necessary early intervention to prevent further disability as measured in impaired learning and interpersonal relations.

Secondary Prevention in Retardation

We have learned that we can best help parents of retarded youngsters by involving them in activities tangibly helpful to their child's learning, socialization, and fuller development. Thus, we have encouraged parents to observe our teacher, occupational therapist, educational psychologist, or other professional person persist in presentation of material or in helping the child learn to carry out a task until he succeeds. Parents thus learn how long it takes for the child to learn in this setting, what kind of persistence is required, and also that there is no special magic and they, too, can learn to be helpful to the child.

Parents need very early to understand the importance of discipline to the child's and their own living. As parents observe professional workers with the child in various activities, they usually note first that their youngster is more cooperative here than at home. They then notice the kind but very firm attitude of the workers which helps the child settle down and begin to learn. Parents need repeated help to recognize the importance of firmness and discipline in helping the child acquire adaptive behavior so important to socialization and learning. Hostile, destructive, and even assaultive behavior may develop without firmness and early efforts to help him adapt. The child's handicap and the frustrations it imposes must be reduced by clear, consistent, and persistent messages from the parents that help him find conflict-free adaptive and social behavior. These early efforts at firmness and establishment of discipline often make the difference between a child's being able to live at home as a useful and nondisruptive member of the family and his needing to be institutionalized because of uncontrollable and impulsive behavior. Here, indeed, is an area of early prevention crucial to the life of the child and to the homeostasis of the entire family (Berlin, 1966; Philips, 1966).

Intervention with Parents

Suicide in children has been attributed to failure in school, lack of friends or peer relationships, isolation, and a sense that no one is really concerned with the depressed, despondent child. Often the teacher may be the first to note the signs and is thus in a position to alert mental-health personnel and parents. Perhaps the greatest problem after teacher identification of a severe psychological problem in a child is finding a way to obtain parental cooperation and acceptance of the need for help. Since in most instances this also implies help for parents, the obstacles are greatly increased.

Efforts to deal with the problem of helping parents accept their child's disturbance have led to the development of several methods. These efforts have been most effective when the principal discusses the findings and their implications with the parents in the teacher's presence. When available, a school psychologist or social worker has been brought into the process as a mediator of information. The central issue is finding a way to discuss the child's emotional problems without blaming the parents. We found that data gathered from teachers and the school nurse could be pieced together to form a picture of the child's functioning in the school setting. The major areas of difficulty could then be delineated, along with steps to be taken to deal with them, without blaming the parents. In many instances parents felt less blamed and were more cooperative when school people could put into words their understanding of the parents' problems in living with the child and could demonstrate their awareness of the intercurrent external pressures and circumstances which affected the parents' lives.

We also found helpful a firm but respectful attitude which outlined the kinds of troubles the youngster had had and predicted clearly what troubles he might encounter in learning, relating to people, holding a job, and becoming a responsible and effective adult if he did not receive treatment. One principal helped a reluctant and hostile father seek psychiatric care for his young schizoid-obsessive son by stating clearly that he was determined to keep bringing up this child's need for help as long as necessary until the father understood and felt able to do something about it. In another instance, very angry and disturbed parents felt less blamed and could better accept the child's need for treatment and the need for their participation when the social worker pointed out that the history indicated that the disturbance began at a time when mother became severely depressed and father was away for long periods on a new job.

In preventive efforts related to instances of psychosocial deprivation, the parents also are seriously socioculturally disadvantaged. Parental cooperation can be elicited by the mental-health professional and physician only when they prove their interest and concern to the parents and demonstrate their usefulness to the family in practical ways. Only then can engagement occur so that discussion and efforts at resolution of the emotional problems of child and parents can begin. In several instances repeated home visits were necessary to convince a mother of the social worker's concern with her well-being. Helping the mother with budgets, arranging transportation for clinic visits, etc., were all steps which were preliminary to and a vital part of working with the mother around her child's psychoticlike behavior and her own serious chronic depression.

It has been of interest to find that psychotherapeutic efforts with parents of very young emotionally disturbed children are often better carried out in groups than in individual sessions (Ambrosino, 1960). Parents become aware of common problems and of one another as people with troubled children, which often makes it easier for them to consider their own troubles. In addition, the group situation helps them feel less sensitive to suggestions about considering alternative ways of dealing with the child or handling certain routine living situations. Discussions and suggestions seem to be felt less as individual criticism when the group discusses how certain problems can be handled by each parent in his own setting. For example, in a group of parents of neurologically handicapped and emotionally disturbed children, the common problem of handling tantrums and aggressive outbursts was discussed. This led to a comment from the teacher that she found it best to sit with the child and let him have his tantrum, remaining close to prevent self-injury with restraint. One angry father said he'd be damned if he'd sit by and just watch his kid scream, kick, and yell; if he spanked him hard enough, he usually stopped. Other parents related their experiences that spanking did not seem to help and expressed the feeling that other ways needed to be found. The father finally reluctantly agreed to try staying at his child's side through a tantrum, but it was clear he actually did not intend to follow through. With encouragement, the parents discussed how their efforts worked out in handling this problem, and as others reported a reduction in frequency and intensity of tantrums, he was encouraged to persist. Finally, with mother's support, he described with some pleasure that the tantrums had decreased. He also related that as he sat through a tantrum with his 5-year-old son, keeping a hand on his arm, he began to recognize how frightened the boy was; he had never noted this aspect of the boy's tantrums before.

Similarly, with young parents of retarded children the group setting made it possible to discuss some very troublesome areas and possible alternative ways of handling these critical situations. As the discussions became more spontaneous and the parents grew more at ease in talking about sensitive areas, they reported that living with their retarded children was becoming easier. Especially helpful were those interchanges which brought to the surface parents' unrealized strong, angry, hateful, and guilty feelings toward the children. It then became easier to help parents expect of their children what in reality they could accomplish. Thus, some of these children began to function on a level closer to their actual capacities.

CRISIS INTERVENTION AS PRIMARY OR SECONDARY INTERVENTION

Caplan (1960), Klein and Lindemann (1961), and Parad (1966) have very nicely described how intervention during such family crises as premature birth, severe illness of a parent or child, and adolescent turmoil may help a family mobilize its resources and become more effective in dealing with problems, rather than falling apart and producing major mental-health problems for all family members. Other workers have described how the death of a parent or impending death of a child (overwhelming crises in most families) may have reduced impact if mental-health workers are available to facilitate communication in the family and between family members and caregivers.

It has also been our experience that family crises resulting from antisocial behavior of a child, out-of-wedlock pregnancy, or psychotic breakdown of a parent or child have potential for increasing or decreasing the integrative capacities of families. Thus, if help is available to the family on a consistent basis, serious aggravation of psychological problems in other family members may be avoided. Task-oriented help in coping with problems of living and relating may strengthen family members' capacities to cope with a wide variety of problems in living — capacities which seem to be maintained after the crisis is over.

Family crises as reflected in the schoolchild, especially in elementary school, are especially important opportunities for prevention of disability. The teacher who notes sudden onset of depression, isolation, withdrawal, or hyperactive, distractible, and sometimes aggressive behavior needs to make inquiry about changes in the family picture. Thus, death of a parent or close relative, divorce, loss of a job of a parent, birth of a sibling, or serious illness in the family may seriously disrupt a child's equilibrium and lead to unusual behavior or aggravation of previous behavior patterns. The child who feels suddenly isolated, alone, and without external resources or anchor will often respond to the inquiry, concern, and attention of a teacher, counselor, principal, etc., with a return of the feeling that someone cares. He needs a clear sense that someone is available for him to turn to, even in terms of helping him make plans for his immediate future.

In one instance a 12-year-old girl who suddenly began to lash out with fists and feet toward classmates revealed to her sympathetic teacher her mother's emergent hospitalization for cancer. Her concern was that if her mother died, her father might abandon her and her three younger siblings. She revealed great fear and anger at her unstable father. She also felt helpless and panicky because there was no one to look to for aid. The teacher immediately arranged a conference with the girl, principal, and school social worker, who were able to discuss with her in detail some contingency plans which they would be ready to help her with at a moment's notice; both teacher and social worker gave her their home phone numbers should she need help outside of the classroom. Her previous low-average work began to improve and continued even after her mother's return home several weeks later.

One person potentially most effective in early prevention of mental disorder is the school attendance worker. His role in working with children and families is not sufficiently understood and utilized in instances of crisis such as school phobia, early antisocial and delinquent behavior, recurrent psychosomatic illnesses that are exploited by the child or parents, and early chronic truancy—all signs of potentially serious emotional disorder. It has been difficult to help mental-health consultants in schools recognize the potential effectiveness of the attendance worker. This is made possible by collaboration, especially when he is afforded sufficient understanding of the case and some idea of what interventions and ego-supportive techniques might be helpful to child and parents. The consultant also needs to be available to the attendance worker around crises, and under these circumstances the worker can perform an effective job in secondary prevention.

In one instance the attendance worker's consistent, repeated efforts to bring to the parents' attention the minor delinquencies of their 11-year-old son forced the boy and his parents, who had regarded these as boyish pranks, to focus seriously on the problem. In conferences held with them, the effects of the parents' drinking, marital discord, and inconsistent attitudes about many aspects of the boy's behavior came out. As a result of these discussions and the attendance worker's continued visits to the home with each truancy, the family sought help at the child-guidance clinic, with marked shift in the boy's behavior. He was no longer the "bad" one in the family since all the intrafamilial problems were now being considered.

Hospitalization of Children: An Opportunity for Primary and Secondary Prevention

Spitz (1945); Bowlby (1951); Mason (1965); Prugh, Staub, Sands, Kirschbaum, and Lenihan (1953) and many others have shown that separation of the young child from the mother by hospitalization for a variety of medical and surgical problems may produce more or less lasting trauma for the child. Despite many publications which document such trauma, few hospitals have changed their policies to permit parents to be with the child during the hospital experience.

For the relatively normal young child, such separation may result in lasting fear of separation; the child who has already experienced some neurotic problems with mother or father may be more seriously traumatized. He may view the separation as abandonment and punishment for his hostile, angry feelings toward the parent with whom he is in conflict. For the child in the midst of an Oedipal struggle, hospitalization may be seen as punishment for his desire to supplant the parent of the same sex and may lead to prolonged depression. Trauma around hospitalization, and especially around major surgery, may be greatly reduced by planning which allows the child to be comforted by his parents during hospitalization. Straightforward information and explanations, rather than evasion by medical staff, and continued personal contact, encouragement, and support by the same staff are important preventive measures, especially during periods of acute pain and discomfort.

Adolescent Crises

Preadolescent and adolescent crises need to be mentioned because of their prevalence and importance in secondary prevention. Areas of early intervention that need consideration are related primarily to sudden shifts in behavior, which may portend serious psychiatric illness. This is especially true of early signs of schizophrenic break in adolescents who have previously been excellent students or active in church or scout activities but then withdraw, begin to fail in school, and become asocial and intensely preoccupied with religion, politics, science, etc. Intervention when such signs are noted may prevent the acute break with reality and prolonged hospitalization. Similarly, a sudden increase in aggressive, hostile behavior, especially assaultiveness, in a youngster previously not antisocial or overtly aggressive may portend an incipient psychotic break with possible murderous consequences as the adolescent is flooded with sexual feelings and anxieties about his identity. The youngster with antisocial behavior associated with adolescent turmoil should be brought to the attention of physician or mental-health personnel (Abend et al., 1968; Balser et al., 1965; Barger, 1964).

Out-of-wedlock pregnancy can sometimes be avoided if one is alert to shifts in behavior patterns. According to recent studies (Guttmacher, 1967), teachers, parents, and especially physicians must take special pains to be aware of depression, reduction of outside interests, and reduced association with former girl friends. They must also be aware of increased avoidance of authority figures rather than the usual adolescent pattern of confrontation and rebellion directed against parents and teachers. Physicians need to be alert to changes in customary peer relations and increased self-absorption, with many somatic complaints which often speak for the adolescent's hunger and increased need for someone's concern and close attention. When these needs are not met, they are often sought after with the unwed's partner.

One special note concerns those girls who have been singularly unattractive, with few social opportunities until adolescence. At this time developing secondary sexual characteristics suddenly make them attractive to boys and easy targets for sexual acting out. Teachers are often the first to note these changes—shifts in peer relationships, sudden acute excitements and reduced interest in all schoolwork, and association with boys in the antisocial element in the school. Their early alerting of parents and school counselors may lead to consultation with the family physician and efforts to deal with these problems in a variety of ways. In one school system, girls' groups at the junior high school level have been very effective in reducing pregnancy rates for this high-risk population.

TERTIARY PREVENTION

Tertiary prevention has been briefly mentioned in each discussion of secondary prevention for cases in which early identification and intervention does not occur. To ameliorate the disorder and restore some degree of equilibrium in children with neuroses, character disorders, and psychosomatic or psychotic disorders, an all-out effort is required. Psychotherapy with child and parents, protective and selective environment, special school arrangements, and active intervention in home management of the child may be in order.

Perhaps most difficult for those engaged in psychotherapeutic work with children is the awareness that such youngsters may need either continuous or intermittent help throughout their lives. We are reluctant to recognize that marginal adjustments with continued psychotherapeutic support are far better than hospitalization. However, we need to take into account the effect of such a child on siblings and family. We also need to be alert to the exacerbation of illness brought on by crises of maturation, family illness, and death and to expect and allow for the kind of involvement over many years which is required of the therapist or institution. To some degree educational institutions, sheltered workshops, and community efforts have made tertiary prevention more possible and effective.

Tertiary Prevention of Psychoses of Childhood

There is little question, from the work of Spitz (1945); Bowlby (1951); Brown, Monck, Carstairs, and Wing (1962); Bettelheim (1967); Harlow and Zimmermann (1959); and others;

that maternal deprivation through absence of the mother, because of her severe depression or alienation, produces infants and children who by their behavior can be characterized as withdrawn, autistic, or psychotic. It is equally clear, from recent investigations of the battered child and severe child neglect, that such traumatic experiences may produce severely disturbed and psychotic children, sometimes of an assaultive, hyperactive type. Early identification and concern with assessment of the degree of disturbance in each child are essential.

The preventive aspects are indicated by studies which reveal that intensive casework with parents of the abused child usually results in their being able to keep the child and to work out those problems which previously led to the expression of hostile feelings toward their child. Follow-up studies are too recent to permit validation of the impression that such casework services enhance the parenting process and reverse the child's previously poor relationship with his parents.

The degree to which nurturance in a therapeutic setting will reverse psychosis for severely emotionally deprived young children is still being examined. Data which evaluate both degree and duration of such severe deprivation, as well as data on prognostic implications of studies on critical developmental periods during which such deprivation occurs, are now being gathered and assessed. Certainly tertiary prevention, that is, reduction of the most severe disability with some return to school and capacity to live without too much difficulty at home, has been achieved in only relatively few of these children to date (Syurek, 1956).

Tertiary Prevention in Antisocial Delinquent Behavior

The current evidence of the relationship between poverty and antisocial delinquent crimes, as judged by arrests and convictions, is striking.

It is also clear that at other socioeconomic levels delinquent and antisocial behavior is frequent and disturbing but does not lead to arrest and conviction. There is some discussion that the act of apprehension and conviction may indeed be critical in the labeling process and in producing recurrent delinquency (Deutscher, 1967; Hobbs & Osman, 1967).

The literature also shows that treatment of delinquents after arrest and conviction, both in institutions and on parole or probation, is extremely difficult (Berlin, 1966; Sarason, 1966; Schwitzgebel, 1965, 1967; Shah, 1966). Efforts at using psychodynamic individual and group approaches have been most frequent. Intervening in gang behavior and use of identification and modeling techniques, as well as behavior-modification techniques, have recently been investigated. Each of these approaches has its adherents and claims of effectiveness. To date no very effective method of tertiary prevention for acting-out delinquent behavior has been proved, though an admixture of techniques reported by several authors seems promising.

Prevention and School Mental-health Consultation

School is a major resource not only for early identification of mental-health problems but also for early intervention. Secondary prevention thus requires not only sensitive awareness by teachers of the child's difficulties, as manifested in school, but also use of a school-parent and mental-health team approach to intervention. It is clear that there will never be enough mental-health professionals to work with disturbed children and that educational approaches may, for many children, be the most effective intervention. This has been indicated by Project Re-Ed and other efforts to enhance competence of the child and to help him feel more effective as a person, as suggested by Lewis (1967) and White (1965).

In addition, teachers who are attuned to developmental crises may be available to students who have learning and behavior problems in the lower grades. However, on moving into junior high school, the parent surrogate is lost as the student moves from class to class. The onset of pubescence and efforts at achieving independence and one's own identity may produce crises. Consultation from mental-health professionals can often reduce the decompensation and increased learning disabilities noted in many children. Their effort to help parents at such times to be attuned to the child's needs may provide key support to a child during a critical period.

Helping teachers understand the therapeutic effects of mastering schoolwork and thus feeling more competent and in control of self is a very significant part of the consultant's role. The mutual efforts of teacher and consultant to assess where and how to help a child to function more effectively and to continually assess these efforts in light of the child's emotional needs help the educator to use teaching and learning more therapeutically.

Both educator and consultant use their professional skills to evaluate the child's capacity for learning as related to growth and development, to assess the emotional needs of the child in light of his family history and previous behavior in school, and to work out a plan to help the child function more effectively in the classroom. Thus the student is helped to reduce his malfunctioning and nonlearning behavior with prevention of increased maladaptive and self-destructive behavior (Berlin, 1967; Caplan, 1961).

SUMMARY AND CONCLUSIONS

Primary prevention of disorders in childhood depends on anticipation of problems in the prenatal and postnatal period and on evaluation of parents' earliest complaints to their physician, followed by suitable interventive methods.

Secondary prevention requires early identi-fication of disturbance in all age groups, often by school personnel, sometimes as a result of parents' concerns, which are expressed to any one of the helping professions. Treatment for child and parents and modification of the learning environment may all be indicated.

Tertiary prevention depends on very active therapeutic efforts after the disorder has been established. Such efforts usually include not only the child or adolescent but also significant parental figures, as well as consultative help to the schools.

The hope for more effective primary and secondary prevention may depend on the use of public-health models which involve large population groups, extensive screening efforts, and perhaps modification of social structure — for example, to provide better nutrition for pregnant mothers and their infants. Earlier efforts at sensory stimulation and development of relationships with deprived children through widespread preschool and day-care programs are also required. In addition, educational and supportive efforts for parents who have had little experience with children and have themselves been emotionally deprived are essential. The application of psychodynamic principles to public-health measures must be worked out to make primary and secondary prevention effective.

REFERENCES*

Primary Prevention

Ainsworth, M. D. The effects of maternal deprivation: A review of findings and controversy in the context of research strategy. *World Health Organization Public Health Papers,* 1962, **14,** 97–165.

Almy, M. New views on intellectual develop-

*References are divided into three sections. Since each section provides a general overview, the student should consult the entire bibliographs to find a particular text reference.

ment in early childhood education. In *Intellectual development: Another look.* Washington: Washington Association for Supervisors and Curriculum Development, 1964.

Ambrosino, S. A project in group education with parents of retarded children. In *Casework papers.* New York: Family Service Association of America, 1960. Pp. 95–104.

Bayley, N., & Schaefer, E. S. Maternal behavior, child behavior, and their intercorrelations from infancy through adolescence. *Monographs of the Society for Research in Child Development,* 1963, **28**(3).

Becker, D., & Margolin, F. How surviving parents handled their young children's adaptation to the crisis of loss. *American Journal of Orthopsychiatry,* 1967, **37**(4), 753–757.

Berlin, I. N. Consultation and special education. In I. Philips (Ed.), *Prevention and treatment of mental retardation.* New York: Basic Books, 1966. Pp. 270–293.

Bibring, G. L., Dwyer, T. F., Huntington, D. S., & Valenstein, A. F. A study of the psychological processes in pregnancy and of the earliest mother-child relationship. I. Some propositions and comments. In R. S. Eissler et al. (Eds.), *The psychoanalytic study of the child.* Vol. 16. New York: International Universities Press, 1961. Pp. 9–24.

Birch, H. G. The problem of "brain damage" in children. In H. G. Birch (Ed.), *Brain damage in children: The biological and social aspects.* Baltimore: Williams & Wilkins, 1964.

Birns, B. Individual differences in human neonates' responses to stimulation. *Child Development,* 1965, **36**, 249–265.

Blank, M. Some maternal influences on infants' rate of sensorimotor development. *Journal of Child Psychology,* 1964, **3**, 668–687.

Blodgett, F. M. Growth retardation related to maternal deprivation. In A. J. Solnit & S. A. Provence (Eds.), *Modern perspectives in child development.* New York: International Universities Press, 1963.

Bower, E. M. *Early identification of emotionally handicapped children in school.* Springfield, Ill.: Charles C Thomas, 1960.

Bowlby, J. Maternal care and mental health. *World Health Organization Bulletins, Monograph No. 2,* 1951, **3**(3), 357–533.

Bowlby, J. *Attachment and loss.* Vol. 1. *Attachment.* New York: Basic Books, 1969.

Braun, S. The well baby clinic: Its prospects for building ego strength. *American Journal of Public Health,* 1965, **55**(12), 1889–1898.

Brim, O. G., Jr. *Education for child rearing.* New York: Russell Sage Foundation, 1959.

Bullard, D. M., Jr., Glaser, H. H., Heagarty, M. C., & Pivchik, E. Failure to thrive in the "neglected" child. *American Journal of Orthopsychiatry,* 1967, **37**(4), 680–690.

Call, J. D. Prevention of autism in a young infant in a well-child conference. *Journal of the American Academy of Child Psychiatry,* 1963, **2**(3), 451–459.

Call, J. D., & Liverman, L. Opportunity for preventive mental health practice in a well-child conference. *Proceedings of a workshop on the public health social worker and the pre-school child.* New Orleans: Tulane University, March 4–8, 1963. Pp. 50–84.

Caplan, G., & Grunebaum, H. Perspectives on primary prevention. *Archives of General Psychiatry,* 1967, **17**(3), 331–346.

Carbonara, N. T. *Techniques for observing normal child behavior.* Pittsburgh: University of Pittsurgh Press, 1961.

Castello, D.   Importance of the mother-child relationship in hospitalized premature infants. *Minerva Pediatrics,* 1966, **18,** 331–336.

Cravioto, J., DeLicarie, E. R., & Birth, H. G. Nutrition, growth, and neuro-integrative development: An experimental and ecologic study. Supplement to *Pediatrics,* 1966, **38** (2, part II).

De Hirsch, K., Jansky, J., & Langford, W. S. Comparisons between prematurely and maturely born children at three age levels. *American Journal of Orthopsychiatry,* 1966, **36**(4), 616–628.

Escalona, S., & Leitch, M.   *Early phases of personality development: A non-normative study of infant behavior.*   Evanston, Ill.: Child Development Publications, 1953.

Greenberg, N. H.   Developmental effects of stimulation during early infancy: Some conceptual and methodological considerations. *Annals of the New York Academy of Sciences,* 1965, **118** (art. 21), 831–859.

Korner, A. F., & Grobstein, R.   Visual alertness as related to soothing in neonates: Implications for maternal stimulation and early deprivation.   *Child Development,* 1966, **37,** 867–876.

Kvaraceus, W. C.   Forecasting delinquency: A three-year experiment. *Exceptional Children,* 1961, **27,** 429–435.

Leonard, M. F., Rhymes, J. P., & Solnit, A. J. Failure to thrive in infants. *American Journal of Diseases of Children,* 1966, **111**(6), 600–612.

Levy, D. M.   *The demonstration clinic: For the psychological study and treatment of mother and child in medical practice.*   Springfield, Ill.: Charles C Thomas, 1959.

Lewis, W. W.   Project Re-Ed: Educational intervention in discordant child rearing systems. In E. L. Cowen, E. A. Gardner, & M. Zax (Eds.), *Emergent approaches to mental health problems.* New York: Appleton Century Crofts, 1967.   Pp. 352–368.

Lindemann, E.   Symptomatology and management of acute grief.   *American Journal of Psychiatry,* 1944, **101**(2), 141–148.

Moore, T.   Difficulties of the ordinary child in adjusting to primary school. *Journal of Child Psychology and Psychiatry and Allied Disciplines,* 1966, **7**(1), 17–38.

Morgan, M. I., & Ojemann, R. H.   The effect of a learning program designed to assist youth in an understanding of behavior and its development. *Child Development,* 1942, **13**(3), 181–194.

Ojemann, R. H.   Investigations on the effects of teaching an understanding and appreciation of behavior dynamics.   In G. Caplan (Ed.), *Prevention of mental disorders in children.* New York: Basic Books, 1961. Pp. 378–397.

Oppe, T.   Emotional aspects of prematurity. *Cerebral Palsy Bulletin,* 1960, **2,** 233–237.

Patton, R. G., & Gardner, L. I.   *Growth failure in maternal deprivation.*   Springfield, Ill.: Charles C Thomas, 1963.

Robertson, J.   Mothering as an influence on early development: A study of well-baby clinic record.   In R. S. Eissler et al. (Eds.), *The psychoanalytic study of the child.*   Vol. 17. New York: International Universities Press, 1962. Pp. 245–264.

Sayegh, Y., & Dennis W.   The effect of supplementary experiences upon the behavioral development of infants in institutions. *Child Development,* 1963, **36,** 81–90.

Schwartz, L. H., Snider, J., & Schwartz, J. E. Psychiatric case report of nutritional battering with implications for community agencies.

Community Mental Health Journal, 1967, **3**(2), 163–169.

Scrimshaw, N. S. Infant malnutrition and adult learning. *Saturday Review of Literature,* March 16, 1968, 64–67.

Siegel, E., Dillehay, R., & Fitzgerald, C. J. Role changes within the child: Health conference. *American Journal of Public Health,* 1965, **55**(6), 832–841.

Silber, E., Coelho, G., Murphey, E., Hamburg, D., Pearlin, L., & Rosenberg, M. Competent adolescents coping with college dscisions. *Archives of General Psychiatry,* 1961, **5**(6), 517–527.

Silber, E., Hamburg, D., Coelho, G., Murphey, E., Rosenberg, M., & Pearlin, L. Adaptive behavior in competent adolescents coping with the anticipation of college. *Archives of General Psychiatry,* 1961, **5**(4), 354–365.

Stennett, R. G. Emotional handicap in the elementary years: Phase or disease? *American Journal of Orthopsychiatry,* 1966, **36**(3), 444–449.

Steward, A. H., Weiland, I. H., Leider, A. R., Mangham, C. A., Holmes, T. H., & Ripley, H. S. Excessive infant crying (colic) in relation to parent behavior. *American Journal of Psychiatry,* 1954, **110**(9), 687.

Thomas, A., Chess, S., & Birch, H. C. *Behavioral individuality in early childhood.* New York: New York University Press, 1963.

Toby, J. An evaluation of early identification and intensive treatment programs for pre-delinquents. *Social Problems,* 1965, **13**, 160–175.

Townsend, E. H. The social worker in pediatric practice: An experiment. *American Journal of Diseases of Children,* 1964, **107**(1), 77–83.

White, R. W. Ego reality in psychoanalytic theory. *Psychological Issues,* 1963, **3**(3), (Mono. No. 2).

Winick, M. Changes in nucleic acid and protein content of the human brain during growth. *Pediatric Research,* 1968.

Wohl, M. D., & Goodhart, R. S. (Eds.) *Modern nutrition in health and disease.* Philadelphia: Lea & Febiger, 1960.

Zax, M., & Cowen, E. L. Early identification and prevention of emotional disturbance in a public school. In E. L. Cowen, E. A. Gardner, & M. Zax (Eds.), *Emergent approaches to mental health problems.* New York: Appleton Century Crofts, 1967. Pp. 331–351.

Zimiles, H. Preventive aspects of school experience. In E. L. Cowen, E. A. Gardner, & M. Zax (Eds.), *Emergent approaches to mental health problems.* New York: Appleton Century Crofts, 1967. Pp. 239–251.

Secondary Prevention

Abend, S. M., Kachalsky, H., & Greenberg, H. R. Reactions of adolescents to short-term hospitalization. *American Journal of Psychiatry,* 1968, **124**(7), 949–954.

Arsenian, J. Situational factors contributing to mental illness in the United States: A theoretical summary. *Mental Hygine,* 1961, **45**(2), 194–206.

Augenbraun, B., Reid, H. L. & Friedman, D. B. Brief intervention as a preventive force in disorders of early childhood. *American Journal of Orthopsychiatry,* 1967, **37**(4), 697–702.

Balser, B. H., Wacker, E., Gratwick, M., Mumford, R. S., Clinton, W., & Balser, P. Predicting mental disturbance in early adolescence. *American Journal of Psychiatry,* 1965, **121** (Suppl. xi–xix).

Barger, B. The University of Florida mental health program. In *Higher education and mental health.* Gainesville: University of Florida, 1964.

Berlin, I. N., Boatman, M. J., Sheimo, S. L., & Szurek, S. A. Adolescent alternation of anorexia and obesity. *American Journal of Orthopsychiatry,* 1951, **21**(2), 387–419.

Biber, B., et al. *The psychological impact of school experience.* New York: Bank Street College of Education, 1962.

Bolman, W. M., & Westmen, J. C. Prevention of mental disorder: An overview of current programs. *American Journal of Psychiatry,* 1967, **123**(9), 1058–1068.

Bower, E. M. The modification, mediation and utilization of stress during the school years. *American Journal of Orthopsychiatry,* 1964, **34**(4), 667–674.

Brody, S. Preventive intervention in current problems of early childhood. In G. Caplan (Ed.), *Prevention of mental disorders in children.* New York: Basic Books, 1961. Pp. 168–191.

Bruch, H. Psychological aspects of obesity. *Psychiatry,* 1947, **10**(4), 373–381.

Burks, H. L., & Harrison, S. I. Aggressive behavior as a means of avoiding depression. *American Journal of Orthopsychiatry,* 1962, **32**(3), 416–422.

Caplan, G. (Ed.) *Prevention of mental disorders in children.* New York: Basic Books, 1961.

Cary, A. C., & Reveal, M. T. Prevention and detection of emotional disturbances in preschool children. *American Journal of Orthopsychiatry,* 1967, **37**(4), 719–724.

Cornely, P. B., & Bigman, S. K. Some considerations in changing health attitudes. *Children,* 1963, **10**(1), 23–28.

Crow, M. Preventive intervention through par-
ent group education. *Social Casework,* 1967, **67**(3), 161–165.

Deutsch, M. The role of social class in language development and cognition. *American Journal of Orthopsychiatry,* 1965, **35,** 78–88.

Eisenberg, L. If not now, when? *American Journal of Orthopsychiatry,* 1962, **32**(5), 781–791. (a)

Eisenberg, L. The sins of the fathers: Urban decay and social pathology. *American Journal of Orthopsychiatry,* 1962, **32**(1), 5–17. (b)

Eisenberg, L., & Gruenberg, E. M. The current status of secondary prevention in child psychiatry. *American Journal of Orthopsychiatry,* 1961, **31**(2), 355–367.

Engel, G. L. Is grief a disease? *Psychosomatic Medicine,* 1961, **23**(1), 18–22.

Faberow, N. L., & Schneidman, E. S. *The cry for help.* New York: McGraw-Hill, 1961.

Freeman, H. E., & Sherwood, C. C. Research in large-scale intervention programs. *Journal of Social Issues,* 1965, **21**(1), 11–28.

Freud, A. *Normality and pathology in childhood.* New York: International Universities Press, 1965.

Fried, M. Effects of social change on mental health. *American Journal of Orthopsychiatry,* 1964, **34**(1), 3–28.

Furman, E. Treatment of under-fives by way of parents. In R. S. Eissler et al. (Eds.), *The psychoanalytic study of the child.* Vol. 12. New York: International Universities Press, 1957. Pp. 250–263.

Glass, A. J. Observations upon the epidemiology of mental illness in troops during warfare. In *Walter Reed Army Institute of Research: Symposium on preventive and social psychiatry.* Washington: U. S. Government Printing Office, 1958. Pp. 185–198.

Glueck, S., & Glueck, E. *Predicting delinquency and crime.* Cambridge, Mass.: Harvard University Press, 1959.

Guttmacher, A. F. Unwanted pregnancy: A challenge to mental health. *Mental Hygiene,* 1967, **51**(4), 512–516.

Hess, R. D., & Shipman, V. C. Early experience and the socialization of cognitive modes in children. *Child Research,* 1965, **36**(4), 869–886.

Hyman, E., et al. *Application of methods of evaluation.* Berkeley: University of California Press, 1965.

John, V. P. The intellectual development of slum children: Some preliminary findings. *American Journal of Orthopsychiatry,* 1963, **33**(5), 813–822.

Kagan, J., Moss, H. A., & Sigel, I. E. Psychological significance of styles of conceptualization. In J. C. Wright & J. Kagan (Eds.), *Basic cognitive processes in children. Monographs of the Society for Research in Child Development,* 1963, **28**(2, Ser. No. 86), 73–112.

Keller, S. The social world of the urban slum child: Some early findings. *American Journal of Orthopsychiatry,* 1963, **33**(5), 823–831.

Kenyon, F. E. Hypochondriasis: A survey of some historical, clinical, and social aspects. *British Journal of Medical Psychology,* 1965, **38**(2), 117–133.

Kiessler, F. Is this psychiatry? In S. E. Goldston (Ed.), *Concepts of community psychiatry: A framework for training.* Washington: Public Health Service Publication No. 1319, 1965. Pp. 147-157.

Kubzansky, P. E. The effects of reduced environmental stimulation on human behavior: A review. In A. D. Biderman & H. Zimmer (Eds.), *The manipulation of human behavior.* New York: Wiley, 1961. Pp. 51–95.

Leighton, D., Harding, J. S., Macklin, D. B., Macmillan, A. M., & Leighton, A. H. *The character of danger.* New York: Basic Books, 1963.

Lidz, T. The marital relationship, family structure, and personality development. Vol. 3. *Proceedings of the Third World Congress of Psychiatry.* Montreal: University of Toronto Press, 1961. Pp. 117–120.

Mechanic, D. The concept of illness behavior. *Journal of Chronic Diseases,* 1962, **15**, 189–194.

Newman, R. G. Conveying essential messages to the emotionally disturbed child at school. *Exceptional Children,* 1961, **28**(4), 199–204.

Pasamanick, B., Knoblock, H., & Lillienfeld, A. M. Socioeconomic status and some precursors of neuropsychiatric disorder. *American Journal of Orthopsychiatry,* 1956, **26**(3), 594–601.

Pearl, A., & Riessman, F. *New careers for the poor.* New York: Free Press, 1965.

Peck, H. B., Kaplan, S. R., & Roman, M. Prevention, treatment, and social action: A strategy of intervention in a disadvantaged urban area. *American Journal of Orthopsychiatry,* 1966, **36**(1), 57–69.

Philips, I. (Ed.) *Prevention and treatment of mental retardation.* New York: Basic Books, 1966.

Provence, S. A., & Lipton, R. C. *Infants in institutions.* New York: International Universities Press, 1962.

Rahe, R. H., Meyer, M., Smith, M., Kjaer, G., & Holmes, T. H. Social stress and illness onset.

Journal of Psychosomatic Research, 1964, **8**(1), 35–44.

Rutter, M., Birch, H. G., Thomas, A., & Chess, S. Temperamental characteristics in infancy and the later development of behavioral disorders. *British Journal of Psychiatry,* 1964, **110**(468), 651–661.

Scott, J. P. Critical periods in behavioral development. *Science,* 1962, **138**(3544), 949–955.

Skeels, H. M. Adult status of children with contrasting early life experiences: A follow-up study. In H. M. Skeels (Ed.), *Adult status of children with contrasting early life experiences. Monographs of the Society for Research in Child Development,* 1966, **31**(3, Ser. No. 105).

Sperling, M. Mucous colitis associated with phobias. *Psychoanalytic Quarterly,* 1950, **19**(3), 318–326.

Sperling, M. The neurotic child and his mother: A psychoanalytic study. *American Journal of Orthopsychiatry,* 1951, **21**(2), 351–362.

Srole, L., Langer, T. S., Michael, S. T., Opler, M. K., & Rennie, T. A. Vol. I. *Mental health in the metropolis: The Midtown Manhattan study,* New York: McGraw-Hill, 1962.

Tasem, M., Augenbraun, B., & Brown, S. L. Family group interviewing with the preschool child and both parents. *Journal of the American Academy of Child Psychiatry,* 1965, **4**(2), 330–340.

Wender, P. H., Pedersen, F. A., & Waldrop, M. F. A longitudinal study of early social behavior and cognitive development. *American Journal of Orthopsychiatry,* 1967, **37**(4), 691–696.

Westman, J. C., Rice, D. L., & Bermann, E. Nursery school behavior and later school adjustment. *American Journal of Orthopsychiatry,* 1967, **37**(4), 725–731.

White, R. W. Motivation reconsidered: The concept of competence. *The Psychological Review,* 1959, **66**(5), 297–333.

Wiener, G., Rider, R. V., Oppel, W. C., Fischer, L. K., & Harper, P. A. Correlates of low birth weight: Psychological status at six to seven years of age. *Pediatrics,* 1965, **35**(3), 434–444.

Crisis Intervention, Hospitalization, Tertiary Prevention, and Consultation

Berlin, I. N. Mental health consultation with a juvenile probation department. In I. N. Berlin & S. A. Szurek (Eds.), *Learning and its disorders.* Palo Alto, Calif.: Science & Behavior Books, 1966. Pp. 158–166.

Berlin, I. N. Preventive aspects of mental health consultation to schools. *Mental Hygiene,* 1967, **51**(1), 34–40

Bettelheim, B. *The empty fortress.* New York: Free Press, 1967.

Brown, G. W., Monck, E. M., Carstairs, G. M., & Wing, J. K. Influence of family life on the course of schizophrenic illness. *British Journal of Preventive and Social Medicine,* 1962, **16**(2), 55–68.

Cadden, V. Crisis in the family. In G. Caplan (Ed.), *Principles of preventive psychiatry.* New York: Basic Books, 1964. Pp. 288–296.

Caplan, G. Patterns of parental response to the crisis of premature birth. *Psychiatry,* 1960, **23**(4), 365–374.

Caplan, G. *An approach to community mental health.* New York: Grune & Stratton, 1961.

Caplan, G., Mason, E. A., & Kaplan, D. M.

Four studies of crisis in parents of prematures. *Community Mental Health Journal,* 1965, **1**(2), 149–161.

Coleman, R. W., & Provence, S. Environmental retardation (hospitalism) in infants living in families. *Pediatrics,* 1957, **19**(2), 285–292.

Deutscher, I. The social causes of social problems: From suicide to delinquency. In H. E. Mizruchi (Ed.), *The substance of sociology.* New York: Appleton-Century-Crofts, 1967.

Green, M., & Solnit, A. Reactions to the threatened loss of a child: A vulnerable child syndrome. *Pediatrics,* 1964, **34**(1), 58.

Harlow, H. F., & Zimmermann, R. R. Affectional responses in infant monkeys. *Science,* 1959, **130**(3373), 421–432.

Hobbs, D. B., & Osman, M. P. From prison to the community. *Crime and Delinquency,* 1967, **13**, 317–322.

Klein, D. C., & Lindemann, E. Preventive intervention in individual and family crisis situations. In G. Caplan (Ed.), *Prevention of mental disorders in children.* New York: Basic Books, 1961. Pp. 283–306.

Mason, E. A. The hospitalized child—His emotional needs. *New England Journal of Medicine,* 1965, **272**(8), 406–414.

Mechanic, D. Therapeutic intervention: Issues in the care of the mentally ill. *American Journal of Orthopsychiatry,* 1967, **37**(4), 703–718.

Milowe, I. D., & Lourie, R. S. The child's role in the battered child syndrome. *Journal of Pediatrics,* 1964, **65**(6, Part 2), 1079. (Abstract).

Parad, H. J. (Ed.) *Crisis intervention: Selected readings.* New York: Family Service Association of America, 1965.

Parad, H. J. The use of time-limited crisis intervention in community mental health programming. *Social Service Review,* 1966, **40**, 275–282.

Prugh, D. G., & Harlow, R. G. "Masked deprivation" in infants and young children. In *Deprivation of medical care: A reassessment of its effects. World Health Organization Public Health Papers,* 1962, **14**, 9–29.

Prugh, D. G., Staub, E. M., Sands, H. H., Kirschbaum, R. M., & Lenihan, E. A. A study of the emotional reactions of children and families to hospitalization and illness. *American Journal of Orthopsychiatry,* 1953, **23**(1), 70–106.

Rapoport, L. Working with families in crisis: An exploration in preventive intervention. *Social Work,* 1962, 7(3), 48–57.

Sarason, I. G. The human reinforcer in verbal behavior research. In L. Krasner & L. P. Ullmann (Eds.), *Current research in behavior modification and its clinical implications.* New York: Holt, 1966. Pp. 231–243.

Schwitzgebel, R. *Streetcorner research.* Cambridge, Mass.: Harvard University Press, 1965.

Schwitzgebel, R. Short-term operant conditioning of adolescent offenders on socially relevant variables. *Journal of Abnormal Psychology,* 1967, **72**, 134–142.

Shah, S. A. Treatment of offenders: Some behavioral concepts, principles, and approaches. *Federal Probation,* 1966, **30**, 29–38.

Spitz, R. A. Hospitalism: An inquiry into the genesis of psychiatric conditions in early childhood. In O. Fenichel et al. (Eds.), *The psychoanalytic study of the child.* Vol. 1. New York: International Universities Press, 1945. Pp. 53–74.

Syurek, S. A. Psychotic episodes and psychotic maldevelopment. *American Journal of Orthopsychiatry,* 1956, **26**, 519–543.

Waldfogel, S., & Gardner, G. E. Intervention in crises as a method of primary prevention. In G. Caplan (Ed.), *Prevention of mental disorders in children.* New York: Basic Books, 1961. Pp. 307–322.

Weissman, A., & Hackett, T. P. Psychosis after eye surgery: Establishment of a specific doctor-patient relation in the prevention and treatment of "black patch delirium." *New England Journal of Medicine,* 1958, **258**(26), 1284.

White, R. W. The experience of efficacy in schizophrenia. *Psychiatry,* 1965, **28**(3), 199–211.

Zetzel, E. R. Depression and incapacity to bear it. In M. Schur (Ed.), *Drives, affects, behavior.* Vol. 2. New York: International Universities Press, 1965.

part viii | # Research in Childhood Psychopathology

38 The Contribution of Developmental Psychology

Sebastiano Santostefano
and A. Harvey Baker

In spite of its early beginnings and active history, the field of developmental psychology has begun, only recently, to be integrated with the fields of general and abnormal psychology (Baldwin, 1960; Dennis, 1949; Harris, 1957). Generating much interest in the early 1900s within the mainstream of psychology, developmental psychology gradually moved in another direction, focusing on physical-growth studies. It was not until the 1940s that the entire posture changed. Very likely because of the influence of Freud's writings, the field turned to studying the effects of child-rearing practices on the psychological development of children and the relations between childhood experiences and adult personality. With this shift in emphasis, developmental psychology reentered the fields of general psychology and psychopathology.

This relatively recent return presents three major implications and complications for any survey of research contributions made by developmental psychology to the field of child psychopathology. First, the literature is only beginning to reflect the return of developmental psychology—revealing, for the most part, its segregated status. On the one hand, writings concerned with psychopathology in children (e.g., Jessner & Pavenstedt, 1959; Kessler, 1966) frequently employ a primarily psychodynamic, descriptive approach and do not emphasize developmental propositions in their treatment of the subject matter.[1] On the other hand, empirical studies concerned primarily with psychological developmental, while employing systematized research designs and methods, typically do not take some form of psychopathology as the subject of study. Rather, such studies explore motivational and socializing variables that have held the interest of child-development researchers for the past twenty years, e.g., aggression (Bandura & Walters, 1963), achievement (Crandall, 1963), dependency (Hartup, 1963), and parental discipline (Becker, 1964).

[1] Exceptions do exist in several texts (e.g., Ausubel, 1952; Engel, 1962), which, however, are not primarily reports of empirical research but conceptual discussions of personality development and psychopathology.

The second complication concerns the fact that the concept of "development" as used in the general psychological literature is a protean one (Kaplan, 1959; Nagel, 1957; Zigler, 1963), with development variously taken to refer to growth, achievement of a new response, attainment of an ideal end state, change occurring over time, or any study employing children, especially if of different ages.

Thirdly, no single, generally accepted theory of psychological development exists at this time. Rather, several schools of development have been stimulating a rapidly growing number of studies, each emphasizing particular questions and classes of behavior and offering various concepts to account for observations made. Among these schools are social-learning theory; psychoanalysis; the cognitive-developmental theories of Jean Piaget, Heinz Werner, and Jerome Bruner; the field theory of Kurt Lewin; the sociological theory of Talcott Parsons and Robert Bales; and the biological-systems theory of Ludwig von Bertalanffy.

Because of this state of affairs, the present writers found it necessary to delimit clearly the areas of developmental research which would be surveyed. To accomplish this we decided to construct a single conceptual scaffold which would not only sharply define the research territory to be covered but also assist us in giving some organization to the numerous and widely varying published investigations concerning development and psychopathology in children.

Which planks, of the many offered by developmental theories in vogue, should go into the scaffold that will guide our survey? The framework we selected derives primarily from three of the schools noted above, namely, the developmental theory of psychoanalysis represented by recent writings in ego psychology (e.g., Hartmann, 1958; Rapaport, 1960; Rapaport & Gil, 1959), the cognitive-developmental theory

of Piaget (e.g., Flavell, 1963), and the organismic-developmental theory of Werner (Werner, 1957; Werner & Kaplan, 1963). The framework we chose is very much in accord with systems theory (von Bertalanffy, 1966), with Thorne's (1967) recently presented conceptualization of "integrative psychology," and with Lewin's developmental position (Baldwin, 1967).[2]

There are two justifications for this choice, beyond the writers' obvious preference for these particular schools and the fact that contributions of learning theory are considered elsewhere in this volume. First, the three schools selected share several basic features: each assumes that "development" is not a phenomenon as such but a set of assumptions defining a point of view from which any behavior can be observed and conceptualized; each was formulated initially within a biological orientation, resulting in a numer of similar propositions; and each conceptualizes normal development as an ideal course of evolving processes and psychopathology as deviations from this course.[3]

Second, the common features of these three schools constitute a framework that is consistent with recommendations made by Baldwin (1967), which he formulated after critically evaluating six major developmental positions, and with those of Harris (1957). In the opinions of Baldwin and Harris, a general theory of development should conceive of organisms as active systems maintaining some degree of integrity, stability, or self-regulation; should view change as

[2] Research contributions of psychoanalytic, cognitive, and biological theories are considered elsewhere in this volume; this report limits itself to research which focuses particularly on the developmental aspects of these positions.

[3] While deviation from some ideal course was most emphasized by Freud, also considered by Werner, and more or less ignored by Piaget, current investigators using the latter two positions show growing interest in psychopathology (e.g., Feffer, 1959, 1967; Goldschmid, 1968; Strauss, 1967; Wapner, 1964).

a transition toward complexity of organization, involving multilevel functioning and organized wholes; should allow for intrinsic development as well as change due to external stimulation; should account for the acquisition of new behaviors (i.e., the occurrence of a response for the first time); and should include as content for study overt behavioral acts, thoughts, feelings, fantasies, drives, inhibiting acts, and peremptory as well as voluntary behaviors.

Since the broader developmental propositions suggested by the theories of Piaget, Werner, and psychoanalytic ego psychology are not available in the usual research report, we have elected to outline them here primarily to aid the reader in locating each study and issue discussed within a particular context of development and in part to inform him of the limits we set in our literature survey.

We acknowledge that the outline presented emphasizes certain features common to each theory and ignores other aspects that are inconsistent. Systematic, comparative discussions of the critical similarities and differences represented by these theories are available (e.g., Baldwin, 1967; Decarie, 1965; Kaplan, 1959; Rapaport, 1960; Wolff, 1960), as well as provocative theoretical critiques of issues presented by developmental psychology (Spiker, 1966; Zigler, 1963).

In taking liberty to interpret and combine aspects of the three positions, we must of course assume responsibility for the end result. Our selection, however, was certainly not arbitrary, nor totally due to personal preference, but was guided by the suggestions of Baldwin and Harris noted above and by the goal of constructing a framework for this review broad enough to guide our search for, and organization of, a wide range of studies involving various pathological groups and numerous aspects of behavior.

Lastly, since the fundamental position regarding development shared by Piaget, Werner,

and Freud is oriented to constructs stemming from biology, the term *biodevelopmental* will be used throughout the remainder of this paper to distinguish the view of development under consideration here from others reported in the literature.

SOME MAJOR ASSUMPTIONS AND PROPOSITIONS OF THE BIODEVELOPMENTAL FRAMEWORK

The biodevelopmental framework includes several basic assumptions which, in turn, lead to a number of propositions. Each of these should be viewed as interrelated while at the same time emphasizing a particular consideration. Alone or in combination, they have guided investigators in formulating various questions for study.

Psychological Givens

Man does not experience and react to stimulation passively. Rather, he brings into play, from birth, innately given behavioral and structural organs and modes of functioning, such as motoric rhythm patterns and sensory thresholds, by which he actively approaches, avoids, shapes, and organizes stimulation confronting him and by which he acts upon the environment in order to effect a change in the person-object relation. A connection is guaranteed between these innately given structures and functions, on the one hand, and stimulation on the other, so that throughout the life-span, certain types of experiences, objects, or persons represent inherent nutriment for them.

Directiveness of Behavior

The behaviors of an individual represent inherently directed activities that serve him in realizing goals. In meeting the basic tasks of human development, he directs and regulates responses at a pace which ensures harmony, coordination, and mutuality between his evolving psychological equipment and the changing demands and stimulations of the environment. Thus he maintains his integrity in the face of highly variable internal and external conditions and ensures that his interactions with the environment result in nutrition-providing experiences.

The tendency to maintain an integrated existence in the midst of changing stimulations is related to the tendency of the individual to develop toward a relatively mature state under the widest range of conditions. Whenever development occurs, it proceeds from a state of relative globality and lack of differentiation to a state of increasing differentiation, articulation, and hierarchic integration.

Structural Changes, Emerging Systems, and Epigenesis

Throughout the life-span, these differentiating psychological structures and functions undergo transformation, both continuously and discontinuously, as a function of two interdependent factors: (1) intrinsically developing (maturating) organismic factors and (2) experience and learning. New behaviors derive from earlier ones (e.g., delayed action from impulsive action), while others show elements that did not exist before and are discontinuous with the past (e.g., fantasy representations of an act versus physical performance of the act).

Holism

The properties and meaning of any unit of behavior (a percept, act, fantasy, or social interact) are in large measure determined by the context of which it is a part. Thus two manifestly similar responses could represent different meanings if they are embedded in different contexts (e.g., aggressive acts by a 5-year-old boy and a 25-year-old man) and two materially different responses could represent the same meaning if embedded in similar contexts (e.g.,

a 5-year-old injures the family's newly acquired pet kitten, and he breaks his baby brother's rattle).

Given these basic assumptions, several additional propositions can be identified which specify further the concept of development and facilitate its application to psychopathology.

Multiple Levels and Mobility of Functions

The assumption of an inherent course of change, from global-diffuse to differentiated-integrated, leads to the proposition that each of the individual's various behaviors (e.g., perceptual, motor, emotional) can be ordered along continua, with global levels of organization defining developmental immaturity and the more differentiated and integrated levels defining developmental maturity.

Differentiated and integrated forms of behavior emerge from more diffuse and global ones. The early forms of functioning are not replaced during this process but become subordinated by and hierarchically integrated with higher forms. Although subordinated, earlier forms remain potentially active, so that at each point in development they codetermine all subsequent structures and functions.

This latent potential of subordinated functions relates to the concept of mobility (regression-progression). At any point in his life-span, the individual does not operate only at a single level but has available a range of operations, each representing different levels of the hierarchy. The genetically immature individual is characterized by a narrow hierarchy of levels and is relatively unable to shift from one to another in response to changes in stimulation, opportunities, and limitations, whereas the mature individual is characterized by a broad and mobile hierarchy of levels, each easily activated to optimize growth and development.

Multiple Modes and Goals and Stages of Development

The construct of differentiation when applied to two interdependent areas, self-world relations and modes of functioning, leads to the proposal that development is represented by an ideal sequence. The immature individual is viewed as fused with his world; gradually he becomes differentiated, constructing a complex and delineated self-world relation. Similarly his modes of behaving (e.g., intellectual activity, drive expressions) are viewed early in development as simply organized. Gradually they become differentiated into numerous instrumentalities, each related to specific goals.

Taken together, these simultaneously occurring processes define a progressive sequence: an immature individual functions with a few globally organized modes that require physical contact with the environment for their operating. At a more mature level of development, the individual functions with many highly differentiated and organized modes capable of operating in contact with, or in the absence of, the related environmental object (for example, the stages from sensory-motor to perceptual to conceptual modes of intellectual functioning and the stages from action expressions of drives to expressions in thought and symbolic behaviors).

The progression from one stage or point in a sequence to the next higher one, therefore, results in multiple means by which the individual can achieve a goal (the child can imagine his baby brother being frightened by a monster, or he can frighten his baby brother) and in multiple goals which can be served by a single mean (the child when frustrated by mother can fantasy retaliating against her, and when lonely in her absence he can fantasy receiving affection from her). The availability of multiple means and alternative ends frees the individual from the demands of the immediate situation, enabling him to express behavior in more delayed, planned, indirect, organized, age-appropriate terms and to search for detours which acknowledge both opportunities and limitations of the environment but still permit successful adaptation.

The developmental status, primitive versus advanced, of a stage or of a level of functioning is assessed not in terms of its time of occurrence but in terms of the organizational characteristics revealed by the behavior or stage, the range of levels available to the individual—whether as a consequence of his current developmental history or as a consequence of situational factors influencing his psychological state—and environmental circumstances and expectations. Thus the diffuse fantasy of a 5-year-old is not primitive in terms of ideal development of fantasy organizations, whereas the diffuse fantasy of a psychotic adult is.

Motivating Forces and Regulating Structures[4]

From birth, "long-range" and "short-range" motivating forces that are goal-directed and require particular qualities, types, and degrees of stimulation activate the individual's innately given motoric, perceptual, and cognitive apparatuses. Long-range forces correspond to needs or instinctual drives and arise from psychophysiological imbalances, inherently coordinated and directed to certain classes of objects in the environment which alone can reestablish psychophysiological balance.

Experience and intrinsically maturing modes of functioning, in interaction, not only play a role in shaping and modifying the behavioral expressions of long-range forces but also give rise to regulating structures. Experience teaches the individual to utilize substitute goal objects and alternative means, whenever the sought-

---

[4] This section borrows from Wolff's (1960) formulation and from Rapaport (1960).

for objects or preferred means of expression are restricted or prohibited by environmental circumstances.

Maturing modes make available new instruments for expression. For example, with the emergence of fantasy and representational thought, the child can now express a long-range motive in a mentally constructed scene of events rather than in action. In this way, regulating mechanisms develop which block, delay, modify, or redirect long-range forces so as to coordinate their expression with changes in available goal objects.

The short-range motivating forces include the "need to function" and ego-motivational states such as "interest" and "curiosity." They arise when organizations of the individual's perceptual and cognitive apparatus undergo change from the assimilation of a new experience. Change in organization of mental structures represents a state of disequilibrium which defines a condition of "nutriment hunger," a need for a particular quality or degree of informational stimulation. These short-term forces have inherent coordination not to external objects but rather to various organizations of information.

The Adaptive Process[5]

The adaptive process involves reciprocal relating between an individual and his environment (e.g., parent, family), with each of these systems attempting to influence the other to achieve a mutually agreed-upon degree of coordination.

The individual phases in and presents to the environment an evolving series of average and expectable behavioral organizations (e.g., perception, cognition, and affectivity) that more or less match environmental expectations,

opportunities, and limitations. The environment, in turn, presents the individual with a continuous, evolving series of average, expectable organizations of stimulation; i.e., the stimulation more or less fits the sensing and responding equipment of the individual. These stimulations, moreover, activate the psychological structures already available to the individual and are suited (preadapted) to handle the confrontation.

However, the environment is never perfectly matched with the individual's psychological equipment and continually changes its opportunities and expectations. In adapting to these environmental fluctuations, therefore, the individual shifts from a more recently acquired level of responding to earlier levels, or he evolves newly differentiated modes (e.g., thought in place of action).

Although this adaptive process occurs continuously, there are periods within the life-span when particular behavioral systems are ready to deal with and assimilate a particular class of stimulation. If the critical experience is not made available, the behavioral system assumes a deviant line of growth.

The environment determines, in part, which behaviors are adaptive. What is average and expectable stimulation in one context may represent an atypical stimulus in another, so that an adaptive response on the part of the individual in one situation could represent developmental failure in another.

THE BIODEVELOPMENTAL FRAMEWORK AND PSYCHOPATHOLOGY

It can be seen that applying the biodevelopmental framework to the study of psychopathology and its development leads to particular questions and interests while excluding others.

In most general terms, whether studying a patient's perceptual activity, problem-solving behavior, conceptual thinking, fantasy life,

---

[5] This discussion is stimulated especially by, and borrows from the writings of, Hartmann (1958) and the works of Sander (1962, 1964).

feelings, or overt actions, the framework would require that methods be devised, subjects be selected, and questions raised which consider the role of psychological givens and of long- and short-range motivating forces, which assess responses in terms of the total context and the hierarchical status of the behavioral mode under study and the goals associated with it, and which take into account the individual and his environment as systems each accommodating to and influencing the other.

For example: Does the infant show evidence of variations in sensory thresholds (e.g., hypersensitivity) which relate to the subsequent formation of ego characteristics (marked avoidance or passivity in the face of information) that signify significant deviation from the ideal sequence of development (i.e., active, sensory-motor explorations of the environment)? Does the adolescent patient show a degree of differentiation of some mode (e.g., Rorschach percepts are vaguely defined and poorly organized) or of some goal (e.g., winning a game is fused with and experienced as equal to destroying the person defeated) that is associated in ideal development with normal individuals functioning at earlier, more immature stages of development (4-year-olds)? Can the latency-aged patient flexibly shift his mode of responding among the levels which ideal development conceptualizes as available to him (e.g., from action expressions of aggression to language or symbolic ones), in keeping with changes in environmental expectations and limitations (e.g., from ghetto neighborhood or playground to classroom)?

SURVEY OF INVESTIGATIONS RELEVANT TO THE BIODEVELOPMENTAL FRAMEWORK

With the biodevelopmental point of view outlined before us, we now turn to the task of surveying studies of child psychopathology conducted within this framework. Our main goal is to present a sampling of studies (not an exhaustive review) that illustrates the potential value of the biodevelopmental framework for guiding efforts to describe, conceptualize, and understand the development of a variety of deviant and psychopathological behaviors in children.

Accordingly, we have selected studies that meet two or more of the following criteria: (1) some deviant form of behavior in children was the main concern of the study; (2) the questions raised, the methods or subjects employed, or the organization given the observations made direct use of one or several biodevelopmental propositions; (3) the study represents an effective illustration of the heuristic value of the propositions and/or has received considerable attention in the literature; (4) systematic methods were employed, and the observations were statistically treated.

Since the biodevelopmental framework proposes that the same processes and principles of organization can be used to conceptualize development from infancy to old age and encourages comparisons between children and adults in order to study these organizing principles, selected instances of studies of normal children and psychopathological and normal adults are included whenever these serve to highlight the issue under consideration. Moreover, because recent reviews are available (Hoffman & Hoffman, 1964; Mussen, 1960; Stevenson et al., 1963) of research conducted with variables that have occupied the interest of child-development researchers over the past two decades (e.g., parental discipline, peer relations, infant care, the effects of separation), only relevant evaluative statements from these sources that bear directly upon the biodevelopmental framework are included here. The majority of studies reported in this review have not been dealt with thus far in the usual review sources.

Our examination of the literature suggested four main lines of investigation, each dealing with questions and hypotheses derived from one of the propositions outlined earlier. These are reviewed in turn below: (1) innate givens, (2) differentiation-integration and levels of organization, (3) multiple modes and stages of development, (4) the adaptive process.

Following the literature review, a concluding section considers implications of the biodevelopmental research reported to date.

Psychological Innate Givens

The proposition of psychological givens views the individual as employing from birth a unique organization of psychobiological functions (e.g., sensory thresholds, activity rhythms) to select, ward off, and organize surrounding stimuli and to direct responses that influence or yield to this stimulation. Innate givens are seen as playing a critical role in the evolution of various psychological structures and functions (e.g., drive level, coping mechanisms) and accordingly in the formation of deviant behavior.

The proposition of innate givens has been of interest especially to clinically oriented investigators in accounting for various carefully detailed observations of infants and children. After studying some 200 newborn infants, Fries and Woolf (1953) proposed the construct of "congenital activity type." Five such activity types are suggested, ranging from very active to very quiet, to account for the amount, tempo, rhythm, and intensity of body movements which are observed fromthe first months of life and which are organized as unique, stable patterns. These activity patterns are held to influence parental attitudes and modes of relating (e.g., a hyperactive infant upsets and stresses his compulsive, controlled mother) and to become critically implicated in the ways in which the infant first tests and masters reality (e.g., the needs of the hypoactive child are waited on and anticipated). Fries and Woolf related these observed innate activity types to the develop-

ment of defense mechanisms and psychopathology—suggesting, for example, that the very quiet activity type is associated later in childhood with marked withdrawal and schizoid traits.

Along the same line, Mittelmann (1954), stimulated by longitudinal observations of children and adults, conceptualized motility as an "urge or drive" and as showing a unique pattern of expression which can be observed as implicated in many other functions of the growing child (e.g., mastery and testing of the environment, control of impulses, expressions of emotion, and sense of self-evaluation). Mittelmann further details how inappropriately coordinated responses by the parent to the child's motor activity leads to the formation of psychopathology. He suggests, for example, that sustained restrictions of motility, especially during the second year of life, when motility is a dominant urge, results later in childhood in severe anxiety reactions and compensatory overactivity.

Bergman and Escalona (1949) reported a study of the role played by the infant's "unusual sensitivities" to stimulation (i.e., easily stressed, or stimulated to enjoyment, by variations in sensory impressions that make little or no difference to the average child). Five children who subsequently developed child psychosis showed during the first year of life atypical sensitivity to, for example, light, human voice, cold air, and certain odors. Ordering their observations in terms of reactions to stimulus intensity (e.g., a whisper produces a startle, or a loud blast produces no reaction) and to stimulus quality (e.g., fascination with red, upset by texture of wool) and employing Freud's concept of "stimulus barrier" (i.e., an innately given ego function employing perceptual apparatus as protection against stimuli). Bergman and Escalona noted that their data suggest that these children start life either with a "thin stimulus barrier" (overexcitable child) or a "thick stimulus barrier" (underexcitable child). Moreover, they propose that both conditions, in the absence of appropriately timed and modulated stimuli by caretakers, result in the infant's evolving premature ego functions to handle his incoordination with available stimuli. These premature ego functions break down under new and more complex stress later in development, resulting in psychotic functioning. An illustration is the child who loses his language capacity during psychosis after a premature development of this function.

Relevant to this work by Bergman and Escalona, Brazelton (1962) used the concept of stimulus barrier to account for his observation that some newborns show the ability to fend off seemingly unwanted stimulation, and Alpert, Neubauer, and Weil (1956) discussed in detail unusual variations in drive endowment observed in neonates.

The studies by Chess and her associates (e.g., 1963, 1967) can be viewed as systematically pursuing the role of psychological givens in the development of psychopathology suggested by these several reports concerning patterns of sensitivity, motility, and drive endowment observed in the first years of life. To organize detailed and extensive longitudinal descriptions of children from the age of 2 or 3 months on, these workers introduced the construct of "temperament," defined as an inborn behavioral style, identifiable early in life, persisting through childhood, and involving, for example, activity level, mood, rhythmicity, approach, withdrawal, adaptability, intensity of reaction, and sensory thresholds. These longitudinal observations, including systematic psychiatric evaluations, of a large group of children have enabled Chess to study "temperamental styles" operating in children who subsequently develop emotional symptoms. For example, in one analysis of the data, the premorbid temperamental styles of children who, on follow-up, presented symptoms classified as "active" were compared with those of children who presented "passive" symptoms, as well as with those of children who were symptom-free. From the third month of life to the onset of the psychiatric disturbance, the children with active symptoms showed a higher degree of irregularity, nonadaptability, intensity of reaction, and negative mood.

Recent studies comparing body type, motivation, and temperament also illustrate interest in the role of constitutional givens in the development of psychopathology. Cortes and Gatti (1965), assessing body types and temperament in adolescent boys and girls, found that endomorphs rated themselves as "kind, relaxed, warm," mesomorphs as "confident, energetic, enterprising," and ectomorphs as "detached, tense, and shy"—findings which are in accord with those obtained by Davidson and his associates (1957) with 7-year-old children. In another study, Cortes and Gatti (1967) reported a relation between achievement motivation and body type with delinquents and nondelinquents. In considering their several findings, these workers proposed that body build may predispose an individual to certain temperamental traits, influencing his earliest reactions to and experiences with stimulation.[7]

Noting a need for explicating the relations between congenital factors and behavior, Waldrop, Pederson, and Bell (1968) related mild congenital anomalies (e.g., fold of upper eyelid, high steepled palate) with preschool behavior, both revealed by children who had been observed from birth and whose delivery was judged as occurring free from complications. They found, for example, that a primitive behavioral quality (e.g., inability to delay gratification,

---

[7] The reader may be interested in contrasting this proposal with that of Kagan (1966), who suggests that body build plays a role in cognitive impulsivity versus delay in terms of the social reactions the child's body build elicits.

diffuse play, spilling and throwing) was associated with the presence of these physical defects. As a result, they bring attention to the role played by physical organization and anomalies in the uniqueness of an individual's behavioral responses. Along the same line, observing multiple somatic and neurological defects in emotionally disturbed children, Stott (1968) proposed that genetic factors are major determinants of individual differences in behavioral disorders.

In contrast to the interest shown in the concept of psychological givens by the more "clinically oriented" investigators, experimentalists in American psychology have not taken to the notion (Freedman, 1964), probably because it is discordant with the prevailing view, held during recent decades, of the child shaped by socializing forces. However, recent writings suggest that a shift is taking place in this regard. For example, as a result of a careful and extensive review of animal and human studies, Bell (1968) recently proposed that the unidirectional interpretation of the direction of effects, offered by studies of socialization, cannot effectively account for the various findings reported. He contended that evidence supports congenital factors as significant contributors to the uniqueness of child behaviors (e.g., sensory-motor, assertive, person-oriented), which in turn influence the behavior of parents.

Similarly, in his review of studies of the effects of separation from parents during early childhood, Yarrow (1965) points out that congenital factors such as sensory thresholds and temperament levels should be considered in assessing an infant's reactions to, and the effects of, separation from a caretaker.

Freedman, Loring, and Martin (1967), reviewing studies of twins, longitudinal observations, emotional responses in infancy, and cultural differences in child rearing, and reminding us of the long-standing biological basis of psychoanalytic theory, cogently and provocatively argue for the inclusion of constitutional-bio-logical factors in personality study. Moreover, they present a creative, biologically based model of personality development conceptualized as a series of evolving structures and adaptations. The sentiment they express with the quote "One hundred years without Darwinism is enough!" seems to be shared by a growing number of investigators interested in the role of psychological givens in development and psychopathology.

Differentiation-Integration and Levels of Organization

The largest number of studies systematically conducted within the biodevelopmental framework has been stimulated by the proposition that development defines a transition from global and diffuse to differentiated and hierarchically integrated levels of psychological organization (see Werner, 1957). This principle has led workers to search for and compare formal similarities and differences in the *organization* of some behavioral response elicited from pathological groups, on the one hand, and younger normal children, on the other. Similarity between responses of a patient and a younger normal child is taken to signify, in the former, developmental immaturity and the disease process. This approach has been employed as an analytical tool to classify patient populations, to study enduring individual differences in cognitive functioning in psychopathological groups (cognitive styles and controls, future-time perspective, body image), and to aid in conceptualizing and understanding psychiatric symptoms or patient populations. This section reviews studies illustrating each of these applications.

Developmental classifications of patient populations. One line of investigation saw its roots at Clark University about fifteen years ago when Friedman devised a rating scale to assess the level of differentiation-integration (and therefore the level of presumed perceptual maturity) revealed by Rorschach responses. The response "a pile of rocks" to card I is rated as global-undifferentiated and taken as an index of a genetically immature perceptual organization; while, to the same card, "two kids dancing around a pole" suggests a high degree of organization and integration of discrete areas of the blot and, accordingly, maturity.

Hemmendinger (1960) has discussed Friedman's Rorschach genetic-scoring system and studies, presenting convincing evidence that the more seriously impaired clinical groups (e.g., hebephrenics, brain-damaged) and younger normals show a preponderance of genetically lower responses while the less severely impaired (e.g., paranoids) and older normals show a preponderance of mature responses.

The success of this initial work has stimulated and influenced other applications. Becker (1959) introduced the Rorschach genetic-scoring system and the concept of levels of organization into the study of the process-reactive distinction applied to schizophrenics. Questioning the heuristic and clinical value of attempts to account for the two types in terms of organic versus psychological etiologies, Becker suggested it may be useful to consider them as defining a continuum reflecting the level of organization reached by a given personality in its growth toward maturity. The process syndrome suggests a lack of personality differentiation (e.g., narrow interests, dependent behaviors), and the reactive syndrome, a higher level of differentiation (e.g., varied interests). To test this proposal, Becker used the Rorschach genetic-scoring system and found that reactive schizophrenics produced more differentiated responses than process schizophrenics, whose performance was characterized by percepts which were similar in organization and structures to those of young children, a relation observed by others (e.g., Judson & Katahn, 1964; Zimet & Fine, 1959).

This same approach has shown that mothers of schizophrenic children produce more immature percepts to the Rorschach than mothers of normals (Winder & Kantor, 1958), and Goldman (1962) has compared various research findings obtained with schizophrenics and children to illustrate the developmental immaturity of the former.

Van De Castle (1965) recently reported a "perceptual maturity scale" more easily administered and objectively scored than the Rorschach genetic scale (the patient indicates his preference for designs presented) but equally effective in distinguishing normal children and adults, delinquents and schizophrenics.

Workers interested in comparisons between the psychological performance of pathological groups and children should consider the caution (e.g., Bibace & Gruen, 1968; Buss & Lang, 1965) that while formal similarities between the perceptual organizations of adult psychopathological groups and normal children can be identified, there are also qualitative differences. Consideration of such differences is critical in understanding the totality of functioning, be it normal or pathological.

The importance of maintaining an holistic position is illustrated by the findings of Smith and Phillips (1959). Administering the Rorschach and Vineland Social Maturity Scale to normal children, they found that with 11- and 12-year-olds, the higher the social maturity, the less the number of developmentally immature responses on the Rorschach; with 13- to 15-year-olds, a slight tendency was observed toward an inverse relation; and with 16- to 18-year-olds, social maturity was associated both with a greater number of a particular type of developmentally primitive Rorschach response (e.g., contaminations, confabulations) and with a greater number reflecting perceptual integration. Thus in late adolescence primitive thought expressed in integrated forms is associated with social adequacy, pointing to the importance of taking into account as much of the total psychological context as possible and suggesting a caution against using, alone, the similarity observed between the perceptual organizations of children and those of older pathological groups.

The concept of differentiation and levels of organization has also been applied by Phillips and his associates in a series of studies concerning the relations between symptom complexes and social-adaptive adequacy. To search for a theoretical basis for conventional psychiatric categories, Phillips and Rabinovitch (1958) systematically examined presenting symptoms of large numbers of hospitalized patients and identified three categories: (1) avoidance of others (e.g., withdraws, feels suspicious, hallucinates); (2) self-indulgence and turning against others (e.g., threatens assault, emotional outbursts, irresponsible behavior); (3) self-depreciation and turning against the self (e.g., suicidal ideas, depression, compulsions). By introducing developmental theory, they conceptualized the social role orientations of these symptom categories in terms of the differentiation principle: the avoidance-of-others category represents a genetically early period, in which the boundaries between the self and the world are relatively diffuse; the self-indulgence category represents a subsequent period of self-centeredness, in which separation of self and world has occurred but with little recognition of the rights of others; and the self-depreciation category represents the most advanced developmental level, in which self identity is maintained and social standards are internalized, as revealed in self-punitive symptoms.

The value of this classification was subsequently illustrated in a series of studies by Zigler and Phillips (e.g., 1960, 1961, 1962). As a result of relating the developmental levels represented by symptoms to biographical categories reflecting social adequacy (e.g., work history, heterosexuality, education) and to types of illness, they were able to offer several interpretations and propositions concerning psycho-

pathology which, although deriving from the study of adult patients, suggest considerable general heuristic value. For example: (1) Symptom processes are differentially related to the adaptive adequacy of the individual and his role orientation in society. (2) Manifest symptoms, and congruent levels of adaptive adequacy, reflect the level of psychological development an individual has achieved and define a developmental continuum of stages applicable to all psychopathology.

A comparison of this attempt to construct a developmentally conceptualized classification with that of Patterson (1964) may be helpful in evaluating the value of the differentiation principle as a guide to conceptualizing symptoms and behavior. Criticizing conventional psychiatric classifications of children's disorders as inadequate, Patterson devised a checklist, based on children's presenting problems, to guide his observations at psychiatric clinics when children first meet the psychologist for an appointment. Observations recorded include "no smile when greated," "unkempt," "cries during interview," "likes to read," "puts finger in mouth." No conceptual rationale is offered for the inclusion of these behaviors rather than others or for the five pathological groups defined by a factor analysis of the observations made, i.e., hyperactive, withdrawn, immature, aggressive, and anxious. When relating the findings of Phillips and his associates (discussed earlier) to Patterson's, a developmental continuum is suggested to the present writers which ranges from withdrawn-immature child symptoms, signifying a low genetic status, to hyperactive-aggressive and to anxious, as developmentally more advanced, respectively. Whether ordering symptoms and behaviors in this way facilitates the study of treatment of choice, prognosis, or adaptive adequacy of children must wait, of course, for evidence. Some evidence, however, is already available in typologies for child disorders recently reported which make use of the concept of levels of differentiation (Borowitz & Hirsch, 1968; Fish & Shapiro, 1965).

Cognitive styles and controls. The principle of differentiation-integration and of levels of organization has been widely applied in a now large, and still rapidly growing, body of systematic research concerned with the concept of cognitive controls or cognitive styles.[8]

The concept of cognitive style or control arose from a body of work which has been designated in the literature by the general heading of "personality and perception." This designation served to crystallize a change in emphasis in the study of perception from "formal aspects" (i.e., the nature of the stimuli giving rise to the perceptual experience) to "functional aspects" (i.e., the ways in which cognitive behaviors serve the adjustment of the organism to changing environments). The bulk of this work in recent years has been reported by (Witkin, Dyk, Faterson, Goodenough, & Karp, 1962), Klein (e.g., 1958), and Kagan (e.g., Kagan et al., 1963) and their associates and followers. Although concerned primarily with the relations between cognition and personality, some empirical work with the concept of cognitive style has focused on psychopathology. Illustrations of only the latter studies are summarized here.

Over more than two decades of research, using the now well-known body-adjustment, rod-and-frame, and embedded-figures tests, Witkin observed that the style of an individual's perceptual activity, as assessed by these procedures, extended across many psychological domains, e.g., intellectual functioning, body and

self evaluations, problem solving, and defenses. As a result, he found it necessary recently to reconceptualize the cognitive style (i.e., field dependence-independence) he initially employed to account for these observed consistencies and to propose a broader cognitive style (a continuum of levels of cognitive organization from global to articulated), the definition of which relies directly upon the principle of differentiation-integration (Witkin, 1965, p. 319).

In a recent review of studies applying this concept to problems of psychopathology and their treatment, Witkin (1965) noted that evidence indicates pathology tends to occur at both extremes of the differentiation continuum and that individuals located at either of the extremes show very different forms of pathology when they break down. For example, a global, undifferentiated cognitive style, as measured by Witkin's three tests, is associated in children with severe identity problems, asthma, poor impulse control, and ineffective coping, whereas the pathology observed when more differentiated personalities break down includes rigid controls, emotional withdrawal, excessive intellectualizing, and restricted interpersonal relations (Dyk & Witkin, 1965). Along a similar vein, Voth (Voth, 1962; Voth & Maynam, 1963) has developed the interesting concept of "ego-close–ego-distant," which suggests some relation to Witkin's global-differentiated style, and he has reported findings which also indicate that extreme ego positions are associated with psychopathology.

The work of Klein and his associates (e.g., Gardner, Holzman, Klein, Linton, & Spence, 1959; Klein, 1958) has given more emphasis to the relations between cognitive controls and motivation and to the role cognition serves an individual as he attempts to adapt to changing environments. These investigators define cognitive controls as mechanisms in the conflict-free sphere of ego activity which govern

---

[8] Critical methodological differences distinguish studies employing the concept of cognitive controls from those employing cognitive styles. These issues, however, are outside the main concern of this paper. The reader is referred to Wallach (1962) and Santostefano (1969). For the purpose of this review, the terms "cognitive controls" and "cognitive styles" are used interchangeably.

the amount and organization of information that becomes available to an individual perceiver attempting to achieve adaptation and which evolve in part as a function of life experiences and personality development. Explicit in this framework is the notion that there are several such ego controls or mechanisms (in contrast to the single principle proposed by Witkin), each dealing with particular informational requirements. In numerous studies using adult normals and psychopathological groups, the unique processes of several cognitive controls have been delineated, e.g., leveling-sharpening, field articulation, equivalence range, and constricted-flexible.

Santostefano (Santostefano, 1964, 1969; Santostefano & Paley, 1964; Santostefano, Rutledge, & Randall, 1965) has investigated the development of several of these cognitive controls in children and their functioning in clinical and normal groups (e.g., orphaned, retarded, brain-damaged, poor readers, and children of different age groups). One of the suggestions of this work that is of direct relevance to the principle of differentiation, is that each cognitive control can be represented as a continuum from global to differentiated cognitive functioning. In one study, for example, older institutionalized orphaned children attending public schools processed contradictory information (i.e., field articulation control) at a level of organization resembling that of younger, non-orphaned children, and in another study, retardates were characterized by a primitive level of attention deployment. This work further suggests that taken together, these several cognitive controls also represent a progression from diffuse to more differentiated and complexly organized information-processing ego strategies. The cognitive control which dominates in the processing of information is a function of the developmental level represented by the individual. Thus early in development (or in individuals assuming genetically primitive

levels of functioning), the cognitive control of focal attention (actively directing attention and scanning broad segments of the field) characterizes the individual's processing of information; at higher levels, field articulation (withholding attention from irrelevant information and focusing on relevant information), leveling and sharpening (articulating ongoing changes in information), and equivalence range (constructing commonalities, or conceptual links, among objects) operate respectively, each integrating the process of the next lower level.

The proposition of differentiated levels of cognitive organization has guided Shapiro's (1965) creative formulation of "neurotic styles." He proposes that the innately given psychobiological equipment of the newborn (e.g., sensory threshold, activity level) represents an "initial organizing configuration" which, from birth, actively organizes internal tensions and external stimuli and thereby contributes to the evolution of styles of experiencing, emoting, acting, thinking, and perceiving. Shapiro artfully describes psychopathological forms of these styles observed in adult patients. It is tempting to speculate that the temperament styles studied by Chess (see above) may be the forerunners of neurotic styles in adult life as defined by Shapiro.

Future-time perspective. The view of cognition as defining a series of developmental levels has recently stimulated a number of studies concerning the concept of future-time perspective. The organization an individual imposes on his perspective of time is seen as related to his developmental status and also to the formation of functions concerned with delaying gratification, controlling impulses, and anticipating alternative routes toward goals.

In an extensive study, Farnham-Diggory (1966) compared psychotic, brain-damaged, and normal children in terms of perspective of time, postponement of gratification, and future self.

To assess time perspective, the child was asked, for example, to pretend that he was looking ahead into the future and to locate on a printed line where "two weeks ahead would be," "one day," "five years," etc. Both psychotic and brain-damaged children showed they experienced the near present (e.g., three hours, one day) as longer and the more distant future (e.g., five years) as shorter. In another aspect of the study, the children were given a choice of taking a small candy bar immediately or a larger one "next week." Here brain-damaged and normals waited, while fifteen of the twenty-four psychotic children chose the immediate gratification. Moreover, these fifteen showed a severely impaired (shortened) future-time perspective when compared with all other groups, and they tended to experience time as passing slowly. To assess the experience of future self, the children were asked, e.g., "What do you expect to do tomorrow?" "Next week?" etc. In reply, the nonnormals made more reference to proximal places (e.g., home) and to a few, childlike activities (e.g., play); this was interpreted as a less differentiated sense of the future.

The significance of this study is elaborated if related to two others concerned with the phenomenon of time perspective in normal and deviant development. Lessing (1968) correlated measures of future-time perspective in a large number of normal 10- to 16-year-olds with various personality and demographic variables. Whenever a significant relationship was found, extended and differentiated future-time perspective was always associated with more favorable psychosocial attributes (e.g., intelligence, academic success, good adjustment); moreover, with an increase in age, unrealistic, childish fantasies concerning the distant future decreased.

Klineberg (1967), using propositions from psychoanalysis and Piaget, postulated that in childhood, the greater the sense of frustration and unhappiness, the more likely it is that images of the distant future will be used to project wish-fulfilling fantasies, but that in adolescence, when society requires future-oriented planning and ego-identity consolidation, maladjustment is associated with a more restricted future outlook. Asking emotionally disturbed boys and normals (10 to 16 years), for example, to list events which might happen to them in the course of their lives and to specify their probable age at each event, Klineberg found that the emotionally disturbed 10- to 12-year-olds showed an extended future-time perspective elaborated with wish-fulfilling fantasies, whereas the disturbed 13- to 16-year-olds showed a more restricted outlook on the future. These results are supported by Stein, Sarbin, and Kulik's (1968) work with institutionalized delinquent boys.

Taken together, the results of these several studies suggest that normal children show a progressively increasing and more differentiated concern with distant events, that severely disturbed children (e.g., psychotics) show an immature, undifferentiated, present-oriented perspective of the future, and that the less disturbed children (e.g., neurotics) show phase-specific relations with exaggerated extensions characterizing future-time perspective in childhood and exaggerated restrictions characterizing future-time perspective in adolescence.

Body-world differentiation: The barrier score. Over a long series of studies, Fisher and Cleveland (1958) and Fisher and Fisher (1959) have formulated a framework and a set of procedures to study various dimensions of body image and body reactivity. Of these, the "barrier score," a measure of body-image boundaries, has received increasing attention in studies of child psychopathology. The barrier score is obtained from an evaluation of Rorschach responses and has been interpreted as signifying the degree to which the individual represents, and experiences, the boundaries of his body as definite and delineated from his environment or as inarticulate and fused with his environment. A count is made of the number of Rorschach responses which describe containing, decorative, or protective qualities to the bounding peripheries, e.g., "knight in armor," "animal with striped fur." The higher the barrier score, the greater the definiteness of body-image boundaries. This Rorschach index has been shown, for example, to increase from psychotics to neurotics to normals and has been studied in normal development.

In a recent study (Fisher, 1966), a group of elementary school children, referred because of a variety of behavioral problems reflecting extreme lack of control (e.g., jumping in and out of seats, hitting other children, darting around the room), showed significantly lower barrier scores than did controls. In another study (Megargee, 1965), juvenile delinquents confined for incorrigibility and assault showed significantly lower barrier scores than did nondelinquents, and with the former group, the scores correlated inversely with ratings of aggressive behavior by resident counselors. These findings, taken as a whole, provide evidence for a relationship between the degree of body-world differentiation, as expressed in cognitive organization, and the developmental status of behavioral regulating systems, especially those concerning the monitoring and delaying of aggression.

Symptoms and clinical populations. Workers with primary interest in clinical populations or symptoms have also introduced the principle of differentiation into their work in order to organize observations and increase their understanding of the phenomenon in question.

Noting the high incidence of enuresis in persistent delinquents, Michaels (1955, 1964) and his co-workers found in a series of studies that not only did enuresis occur more often in combination with other symptoms (e.g., temper tantrums, nail-biting) than in isolation but also these various symptoms were found more often when enuresis was present than when it was absent, raising the question of a unique deviant organization possibly underlying these several behaviors.

To explore this possibility, Michaels interrelated observations of delinquents concerning various domains (e.g., medical-physical, mood, EEG tracings) and findings from relevant published studies (e.g., naval disciplinary cases and young adult prisoners showed a significantly high incidence of enuresis beyond the age of 5 years). On the basis of his analyses, he concluded that enuretic delinquents show a unique psychological organization which suggests ill-balanced integration across several levels— biological, neurological, and psychological (e.g., low sensitivity to stimuli yet greater diffuseness of responses, paucity of fantasy life). He also offered that this ill-balanced organization underlies the lack of appropriate control mechanisms over impulsivity, which results in various forms of symptomatic behavior in childhood (including, in particular, enuresis) and in young adulthood (asocial behavior). For Michaels, the delinquent's inability to control his bladder as a child relates to the same psychological organization that underlies his urgency as an adolescent to discharge tension explosively.

Guyette (1965) introduced the differentiation principle to shed further light on the problem-solving effectiveness of mental retardates. She successfully devised a test procedure to distinguish retardates whose cognitive organization was characterized primarily by the process of differentiation without integration (stimuli were articulated into parts but not combined) from those whose cognitive organization was characterized by both processes (differentiation and integration). The former group was conceptualized as representing a lower level of development, since younger normal children also showed the dominance of the single process. Guyette then demonstrated that the retardates who only articulated information also performed at a lower developmental level with various tasks (e.g., spatial localization, concept formation), suggesting the possibility that relevant diagnostic and educational procedures could be devised to assist retardates characterized by the more immature level.

Use of the differentiation concept is also illustrated by Shore, Massino, and Mack (1965) to aid in evaluating the effectiveness of a therapeutic program for delinquents, by Mack (1965) to analyze nightmares of children of different ages, and by Webster (1963) in studying and conceptualizing the emotional development of retarded children.

Multiple Modes and Stages of Development

The proposition that in ontogenesis differentiating behavioral modalities define an ideal sequence of stages, each distinguished by a unique organization of the mode in question, has stimulated studies concerning sensory, psychosexual, and psychosocial stages and the modalities of action and thought.

Sensory stages. Schopler (1966) investigated Schachtel's proposition that modes of perceiving, by which the individual objectifies his environment and shapes his experiences, define an ontogenetic hierarchy ranging from the dominance of "autocentric" modes (i.e., olfactory, gustatory, tactile) to the dominance of "allocentric" ones (i.e., auditory, visual, the former resulting in global, inarticulate experiences early in development and the latter resulting in detailed and objectified ones. Asking whether schizophrenic and brain-damaged children (5 to 10 years old) would show developmentally earlier stages of receptor preferences versus controls, Schopler administered cleverly devised tests which forced a choice between the visual and tactual modes (e.g., the child could either look at colored slides of animals and scenery or place his hand on a vibrating box). He observed the time each subject remained engaged with the mode selected and found that schizophrenics preferred the tactual mode and normals preferred the visual, with retardates falling between. O'Connor and Hermelin (1965) have also studied sensory dominance in autistic and retarded children, and the consequences of the dominance of a genetically early mode (tactile) for training retardates has been discussed (Hill, McCullum, & Scheau, 1967).

Psychosexual stages. Although using normal subjects, two studies of psychosexual stages proposed by psychoanalytic theory should be noted because the ingenious methods and systematic analyses employed could be of value in planning studies of disturbed children. Rosenwald and his associates (1966) asked adolescents to feel a cutout which was immersed in water, in one condition, and in crankcase oil and flour ("fecal material") in another and to match it with one of several shapes displayed. Differences in performance (speed and success) were viewed as reflecting the adequacy with which the subject managed anal conflicts and prevented associated anxiety from interfering with intellectual activity. Subjects were also administered questionnaires assessing anal character traits (e.g., "I am a punctual person") and anal anxiety (e.g., "I get very upset when I waste time"). Rosenwald found that subjects who performed poorly in the oil condition (versus the water condition) reported higher anal anxiety and that those who matched quickly and accurately in both conditions reported the presence of anal traits but low anal anxiety.

Rosenwald interpreted these findings as supporting several psychoanalytic propositions concerning fixation at the anal stage.

Using a large group of normal children (5 to 16 years) in an extensive study of the concepts of castration anxiety and Oedipal conflict, Friedman (1952), in one aspect of his study, administered incomplete fables. For example, on hearing a story about a dog "with a beautiful large tail he admired and enjoyed wagging," the child was asked to describe what happened. The age differences observed in story completion (e.g., "the tail was cut off") were interpreted by Friedman as supporting predictions of higher castration anxiety during the Oedipal and prepubertal stages versus latency.

Action, fantasy, and language modes. Santostefano (1970) has proposed that action, fantasy, and language represent alternative modes for expressing the same drive and that the dominance of the action mode defines a primitive stage of development, while fantasy and language define higher genetic stages. To assess developmentally drive expressions in the action mode, the child performs three acts (e.g., breaking a light bulb, hammering a nail, and carefully cutting paper), selecting first the act he prefers doing most. With the fantasy mode, the child selects a story (told by the examiner with reference to ambiguous pictures) that best accounts for "what you imagine is going on" (e.g., "Does this show a car crashing or men chopping down a tree?"). And to assess drive expression in the language mode, the child is presented with a stimulus word (e.g.,"knife") and is asked to speak aloud free associations in the form of single words. These associations are then assigned a genetic rank ranging from primitive expressions (e.g., "kill") to regulated ones (e.g., "peel"). In one of the studies reported, for example, a group of fourth- and sixth-grade children representing adjustment problems showed that action expressions of aggression were dominant, as did normal first-graders, whereas normal sixth-graders showed fantasy as the dominant mode.

Related approaches to the notion of stages concerned with various drive expressions or modalities can be found in the studies by Gourevitch and Feffer (1962) with normal children and adults and by Phillips and Zigler (1964) and Hill and Zigler (1964) with normal adolescents and adult patients. The former study was based upon Maslow's concept of a motivational hierarchy. Concrete, directly engaged goal objects characterize early stages of development, and more abstract, delayed, and distant goals represent later stages. The latter study proposed a two-modality hierarchy, action and thought, with action representing unmodulated, physical responses to external stimuli and thought representing indirect, symbolic or verbal behaviors, which characterize maturity.

Shore and Massimo (1967) reported a study involving treated antisocial delinquents and nontreated controls. The treated group showed a decrease in overt hostility and, on pre- and post-TAT (Thematic Apperception Test) evaluations, a significant increase in the number of words used—but only in response to one of the behavioral areas assessed by the stimulus cards, i.e., control of aggression. These findings were interpreted as supporting the proposition that verbal modes, in substituting for action, play a role in the evolution of control over overt aggression.

One aspect of the extensive and in-depth study by Prugh and his associates (1953) of the emotional reactions of children to hospitalization suggests that the developmental status of the action, fantasy, and language modes which characterize a child's functioning at the time of hospitalization not only gives a unique shape to his behavioral and emotional expressions but also relates to the success with which he masters the stresses inherent in hospitalization. Prugh observed that the younger children (2 to 5 years) in mastering anxiety showed more action expressions, revealing more primitivity and disintegration at various levels (e.g., explosive acting out of aggression, thumb-sucking); that the middle age group (6 to 9 years) showed these behaviors to a much lesser degree and showed a higher incidence of play, typically involving vigorous aggression and concerning anxieties about mutilation and punishment; and that the older children (10 to 12 years) used play to a greater degree along with verbalizing hostility and fears.

Psychosocial stages. Empirical evidence for Erikson's (1959) eight ego stages (each defining a crisis which the maturing ego masters before moving to the next phase) has been reported by Boyd (1964). Using normal children and adults, he systematically rated interview protocols and responses to specially designed TAT-like pictures. Younger children, for example, revealed more concern with initiative and guilt (the third stage), while adolescents showed concern regarding identity and role diffusion (the eighth stage). A number of other investigations using normal adolescents and various assessments of personal adjustment have focused in particular on the stage of ego identity (e.g., Block, 1961; Gruen, 1960; Marcia, 1966, 1967).

In a promising formulation relating an elaboration of Piaget's concept of egocentrism and Erikson's stages, Elkind (1967a, 1967b) recently proposed the concepts of "imaginary audience" (the adolescent believes that others are as admiring or critical of him as he is of himself) and of "personal fable" (the adolescent experiences his beliefs and feelings as unique), which he has found useful in the psychotherapeutic treatment of adolescents.

The concept of developmental lines, recently proposed by Anna Freud (1965), conceptualizes normal and deviant development in terms of coordinated sets of stages (e.g., from irresponsibility to responsibility, from egocentricity to companionship). This formulation has received some empirical support from Wolman (1967), who found evidence with a large sample of normal children and adults (5 to 22 years) for the hypothesized progression of stages concerning object relations. With an increase in age, there is a shift from experiencing persons as oriented to oneself to experiencing persons as independent of oneself.

The Process of Adaptation

In considering the process of adaptation, the biodevelopmental point of view proposes that the individual and environment yield to and influence each other in a continuous, more or less coordinated process of give and take. The individual actively copes with, assimilates, and accommodates to, but also influences, stimulation directed from the environment. The environment defines expectations, sets limits, and provides stimulation for the individual while also coordinating its activity with his needs and changing competence. A number of studies have been conducted explicity employing this view of adaptation as a guide. These are grouped for convenience in this review in terms of the particular element of the adaptive process emphasized: (1) styles of adaptation suggested by the coping efforts of children, (2) the reciprocal influences exerted by the individual and environment on each other, and (3) temporary changes that occur within the organizations of the adapting individual as he coordinates himself with brief changes in environmental circumstances, and (4) critical periods.

Styles of adaptation. Studies of styles of adaptation have focused on the enduring behavioral patterns children show when managing various environmental stresses. The content of these patterns usually involves a complex configuration of various modes and qualities of behavior, such as assertive, delayed, and avoidance behaviors; passivity; expressions of joy, sadness, fear; verbalizations; and mechanisms of defense.

On the basis of extensive research over the past two decades, Lois Murphy (1962) has evolved the concept of "coping styles" to organize numerous richly detailed, longitudinal observations made of essentially normal children dealing with various stresses, demands, new opportunities, and social situations (e.g., psychiatric, pediatric, and psychological examinations; trips to the zoo; parties; and automobile rides to and from the clinic).

For Murphy, coping styles refer both to the steps by means of which a child comes to terms with stresses and makes use of opportunities and to the unique organization suggested by various modes and modalities employed by the child in these adaptive efforts. For example, to ward off the mounting stress represented by a continuous stream of psychological test demands, one child reverses roles and asks if he can have a turn at asking a question of the examiner, another escapes cognitively in interrupting the testing to talk about an incident that occurred at school, and a third escapes physically by walking around the room restlessly. Murphy also documented progressive shifts in the coping styles employed by the same child over time. For example, at 2 years of age, one child was terrified by thunder and passing jet planes; at 3 years, she was able to seek out her older sister and accept comfort. Later the child reported to her parents that her younger brother was afraid of thunder, and she reassured the brother. "It's just noise, and it won't hurt you." This sequence suggested to Murphy an evolving series of coping resources from overt expression of fearful affect and helplessness to seeking comfort actively and then to internalizing the image of the supportive person while projecting fear onto the younger brother.

Other workers, some influenced directly by Murphy's methods and concepts, have described coping styles employed by different clinical groups in the face of various stresses: by retardates, to deal with separation from mother (Kessler, Ablon, & Smith, 1968); by hemophilic children (Mattson & Gross, 1966) and by parents of children with leukemia (Chodoff, Friedman, & Hamburg, 1964), to deal with the psychological stress of a fatal illness; by adolescents, to deal with the stressful transition from high school to college (Coelho, Hamburg & Murphey, 1963); and by parents, to deal with delinquency in their children (Hurwitz & Kaplan, 1962).

The variable of future-time perspective, discussed earlier, has also been proposed as a coping mechanism. Smart (1968) found that, as compared with social drinkers, alcoholics show incoherent and shortened perspective of future time (characteristic of young children). He proposed that a shortened time perspective represents a coping mechanism developed by the habitual drinker to manage the several negative consequences the future holds in store as a result of the alcoholism (e.g., loss of job). Similarly, observing shorter time orientation in institutionalized delinquents, Stein and his colleagues (1968) suggested that the cognitive activity concerned with organizing a longer perspective of future time may serve as a coping mechanism operating to bind tension, delay impulses, and anticipate more appropriate plans for the future.

Reciprocal influences of individual and environment. In the past few years, interest in the role of cultural deprivation in the formation of child pathology has increased sharply. Deutsch's (1965) work serves as one example of an approach to this problem area appreciably influenced by the biodevelopmental point of view. Questioning the value of studies which relate social class to a single variable in order to understand the environment's influence on development, Deutsch included in his method subjects representing various levels of developmental maturity (children of different age levels), a microanalysis of the environment (e.g., family structure, communication patterns, economic circumstances, child-rearing practices), and a microanalysis, developmentally conceptualized, of the language mode (e.g., measures of language were employed representing a hierarchy of complexity ranging from labeling, through relating, to categorizing). Deutsch's goal was to identify patterns of environmental influences that relate to patterns of cognitive and linguistic behaviors at various developmental stages. One of his observations, the "cumulative-deficits phenomenon," appears promising in increasing our understanding of environmental influences in the development of deviant behavior. Although the economically disadvantaged first-graders showed a significant language deficit, this difference became more marked in successive grades. Deutsch concluded that the persistent influences of the disadvantaged environment result in a cumulative slow-up in the intrinsic development of the child's language mode. Not only is the older child expected by the school to employ higher levels of language, such as categorizing and relating, but the lower level of language, concerned with labeling, must be used in more complex and differentiated ways. Thus, with each passing year, the child's language functioning becomes more poorly matched with the changing requirements of the school environment toward increasing complexity.

This study points to the proposition emphasized by Hartmann (1958) that society plays a role in defining what is pathological or developmentally mature. The children Deutsch observed showed a language deficit in terms

of environmental expectations located outside the geography of their immediate family. Would these same children show that they are meeting quite adequately the language standards defined within their family setting?

The extensive study reported by Hertzig and her associates (1968) relates directly to this question in showing that behaviors of lower-class children, frequently interpreted by school personnel as reflecting disinterest and lack of curiosity, may be quite adaptive and adequate in the child's home culture. Hertzig compared behaviors and verbalizations produced in response to each item of the Stanford-Binet by 3-year-old children of Puerto Rican, Spanish-speaking, working-class families with those of 3-year-olds from professional families. Significant aspects of the method included: (1) both groups had been followed longitudinally from 3 months of age and had shown no notable deviations in developmental milestones; (2) a bilingual psychologist administered the test to the Puerto Rican children in the child's most competent language.

Observations were organized according to whether the child responded initially with "work behavior" (he engaged the item administered) or "nonwork behavior" (the item administered was avoided by some means) and whether the work and nonwork responses were verbal (e.g., "Yours [tower of blocks built by the examiner] is smaller than mine"; "I don't like to do it") or nonverbal (e.g., the child works at the item with no comments; the child plays with a truck instead of stringing beads as asked).

Although the IQs obtained were comparable for the two groups, marked stylistic differences were observed. For example, middle-class children tended to use verbalizations in both work and nonwork responses, while Puerto Rican children used gestures and silent unresponsiveness. Middle-class children made work responses with equal frequency when confronted with either verbal or performance test demands, whereas Puerto Rican children made work responses more frequently to the latter.

Hertzig also pointed out that while these stylistic differences were observed in response to specific test demands, the Puerto Rican children engaged the examiner in frequent verbal exchanges before, during, and after the testing. Taking these observations together, she concluded that the Puerto Rican children have language capacity but differ from middle-class children in not using language as a response to demands for cognitive performance.

Because the samples and method employed ruled out, as possible explanations of the deficit observed, variables typically offered by other workers (e.g., broken home, poor mothering, IQ differences, language barrier), Hertzig and her associates formulated an alternative hypothesis based upon detailed observations of the family lives of their subjects. They hypothesized that the style of the Puerto Rican child, while adequately fitting the affective-language style of his home, is not adapted to the requirements of the usual school situation (verbal behavior in response to work demands) and, therefore, could lead to inferior school performance. On the other hand, the style of the middle-class child, adaptive at home, is also consonant with school expectations.

The therapeutic techniques of Minuchin and his associates (e.g., 1964, 1967) to rehabilitate the verbal and affective communicating styles of lower-class multiproblem families and their children relate both to Deutsch's observation of a cumulative language deficit and to Hertzig's of a nonverbal style, in suggesting ways of helping children from lower social cultures to develop adaptive capacities that suit requirements of environments outside the home.

Maternal separation and institutional care, as environmental influences in the formation of child psychopathology, have also recieved considerable attention by investigators. Since excellent reviews of this work are available (Ainsworth, 1962; Yarrow, 1961), one recent study (Provence & Lipton, 1962) will be sketched here primarily because the observations were organized and interpreted in terms of biodevelopmental principles concerning the fit constructed by the organism and the environment.

Over a two-year period, Provence and Lipton compared seventy-five institutionalized infants with a group reared in family settings by means of naturalistic observations, developmental tests, and interview of parents and institution attendants, with follow-up evaluations after the infant left the institution.

Observations reported of the feeding situation provide illustrations of the consequences associated with the environment's failing to coordinate itself with the infant's developmental changes. In contrast to home-reared babies, the institution infants were not encouraged to be active at feeding time, and although maturationally ready at various points for a larger world and a more complicated interchange with the environment, they were presented with narrowly constricted stimulation, poorly suiting their maturating equipment. This incoordination between caretaker's level and timing of stimulation and the infant's changing psychological organization was associated with the observation that as early as 6 or 7 months of age, the institutional infant showed a high degree of passivity and a low degree of exploration and curiosity (e.g., toys were not grasped and actively manipulated, as observed with family-reared children), in spite of the fact that their earliest grasping behaviors were observed to be normal.

Research conducted over the past 40 years concerning parent-child interactions as influences in the development of psychopathology has been reviewed recently by Frank (1965). Organizing his survey in terms of major psycho-pathologies considered and methods of data collection employed, he concluded that no factors in the family and parent-child interaction of various psychopathological groups could be identified as unique to them. In attempting to explain this failure on the part of research, Frank pointed out that studies tend not to take into account the totality and complexity of the behavior selected for study (i.e., the holistic approach), that traditional methods employed (questionnaire, interview, direct observation, history) present significant limitations (e.g., parent-child relations change over time; life conditions are poorly recalled), that traditional diagnostic categories may not provide the appropriate grouping to which some life experience is related, and that in spite of Freud's interest in constitutional factors in the development of psychopathology, researchers have not concerned themselves with this factor, tending instead to emphasize the role of experience proposed by psychoanalysis.

Although some have disagreed with aspects of Frank's conclusions (Zuckerman, 1966) or have responded with a methodological examination of research approaches to family etiology (Fontana, 1966), the weaknesses in past research which he outlines serve to raise the issue: Would biodevelopmental principles concerning adaptation help clarify further the role of early family experiences in the formation of psychopathology?

Weinstock's (1967) recent study concerned with early life experience and the development of defenses and coping mechanisms suggests an affirmative reply. Applying an holistic approach (e.g., ratings, home visits, and office interviews were used to assess a wide spectrum of situational variables, coping and defensive behaviors) and alert to the reciprocal, changing influences individual and environment exert on each other (e.g., changes in interaction variables were assessed longitudinally from the subject's infancy to adulthood), Weinstock was able to identify complex life-experience–defense configurations. For example, the use of isolation as a defense was found related to a shift from a warm, friendly mother-son relation in infancy to a strained, tense mother-son relation in adolescence, accompanied by rejection of the son by the father. Moreover, Weinstock observed that if an adolescent is exposed to considerable family conflict after a reasonable childhood, the defenses and coping mechanisms he organizes to handle the conflict equip him to deal much better during adulthood with external and internal conflicts of his own.

Similarly emphasizing that child and family influence each other, a number of recent studies have focused on the role of communication in the formation of pathology in children (e.g., Lennard, Baulieu, & Embrey, 1965; Stabenau, Tupin, Werner, & Collin, 1965). In this area of investigation, Singer and Wynne's framework (see Singer & Wynne, 1966, for a bibliography of this work) is prototypic, and their numerous findings are receiving increased attention. They propose that personality development is affected from birth on, to a large extent, by the infant's capacity to engage and become oriented to the caretaker and by the caretaker's ability to engage the infant's attention and orient him to those aspects of speech, perception, and thinking that will be important in his expectable life experiences. If this sharing of attentional processes by parent and child is poorly coordinated, the first ego organizations are impaired, resulting subsequently in psychopathology. In testing their framework, Singer and Wynne (1963) have been remarkably successful, for example, in distinguishing, blind, test protocols of the parents of schizophrenic, neurotic withdrawn, and neurotic aggressive children. The protocols were examined with well-formulated rating systems evaluating the degree of differentiation and organization suggested by the percept, thought processes, and verbalizations elicited by Rorschach stimuli. The work of Dyk and Witkin (1965) in showing, with normal subjects, a relation between the degree of differentiation characterizing the cognitive organizations of the mother and those of the child lends support to and extends the significance of the findings of Singer and Wynne.

The concept of mother and child mutually influencing each other has been studied most directly by Sander (1962, 1964). A multidisciplinary team collected detailed observations, including a regular schedule during the first three years of the infant's life, consisting of well-baby clinic visits, developmental testing, play interviews, and home visits. To guide observations and to organize data collected in terms of specifying the role mother-infant interactions play in personality formation, Sander has creatively formulated a model which proposes that mother and child participate continuously in an evolving series of mutual adaptations. In this series, nine stages are identified, each concerning a particular developmental issue around which mother and child "negotiate a fit"; i.e., mother accommodates to, yields to, and resists the child's more differentiated and integrated functioning, and the child accommodates to, yields to, and resists the mother's changing responses and expectations.

To illustrate, three of the issues and their proposed timetables supported by Sander's data are:

1. One to three months: the first issue of initial regulation. To what degree, in the interaction between mother and child, will the cues of the infant be met by a specific and appropriate response on the part of the mother?

2. Seven to nine months: the issue of initiative. To what extent will the initiative of the infant be successful in establishing social contacts

with mother, especially in the form of a reciprocal interchange with her?

3. Fourteen to twenty months: the fifth issue of self-assertion. With the advent of locomotion, to what extent does the child establish and determine his own behavior, often in the face of maternal opposition, and in what areas?

For Sander, these several issues specify the interactive process by which the give-and-take between mother and child results in early ego structures in the child from which emerge developmentally higher, more complex structures and functions concerned with reciprocation, regulation, adaptation, and information processing.

Changes in level of functioning in adaptation. In contrast to the focus on more enduring interactions coordinated and negotiated by individual and environment, the studies discussed in this section emphasize that aspect of adaptation concerned with the individual's intrinsic capacity to shift, more or less briefly, from one level of organization to another within a mode or from one mode of functioning to another in order to coordinate himself adaptively with a relatively brief change in the environment. Labeled variously by the major biodevelopmental theories (*fixedness-mobility*, Werner, 1957; *regression in the service of the ego,* Kris, 1952; *perceptual activity,* Flavell, 1963), this proposition essentially concerns studying the conditions under which the individual shifts from some level of functioning to one more primitive or advanced.

Although this concept has stimulated some research among workers studying normal cognitive functioning (e.g., Haronian & Sugarman, 1967), it has not been *formally* investigated to any great extent by those interested in psychopathology, who nonetheless have given it considerable theoretical and clinical attention.

To explore the concept of regression in the service of the ego, Wild (1965) administered word-association and object-sort tests to professional art students, schoolteachers, and adult psychotics (in good contact) in a precondition and in two experimental conditions. In one condition, the subject was read a character sketch of a conventional, "regulated" person, and in the other condition, a sketch of an "unregulated" person who has fanciful thoughts was presented; the subject was asked to respond to the tests as if he were the person described.   Analyses showed that with both tests, art students produced more original and pathological responses following the "unregulated" instructions and more adaptively original responses following the "regulated" instructions, findings interpreted as a greater capacity to shift in the service of the ego on the part of art students.

Workers employing concepts of cognitive style and controls (see above discussion) in the study of psychopathology have also concerned themselves with mobility of levels of functioning.

Kraidman (1958) found support for the hypothesis that stress would have a regressive effect on the conceptual mode of functioning (because it is the most advanced ontogenetically) versus the perceptual mode in the performance of a group of heart-surgery patients.   Their responses to word-meaning and object-sort tests shifted prior to surgery to a lower level of organization than that of a control group of adults, resembling the response level of a group of children.

Guthrie (1967) has studied mobility in both regressive and progressive directions as adaptive in terms of particular environmental changes. The conceptual model he employed to predict direction of change (developed by Santostefano, 1969) proposes that in "average" and "expectable" environments the individual employs a level of cognitive control that represents his characteristic way of organizing information.   However, if he deals with an environment that is not average and

expectable, he shifts the level of cognitive style employed toward a more global or differentiated level, whichever results in a more adaptive fit with the information presented and fosters coping.

In one part of his study, Guthrie administered a test of leveling-sharpening (articulating ongoing changes in information) (1) to novice parachutists in their homes 2 weeks before they were scheduled to perform a jump and a second time at the airport 1 hour before they boarded a plane and (2) to a control group of novice jumpers at home and at the airport before and after a 2-week period when no jump was scheduled.   The experimental group showed a significant shift before jumping toward increased sharpening.   In a second part of the study, adult patients were assessed with a leveling-sharpening procedure a few hours prior to surgery and compared with hospitalized nonsurgical controls, the results indicating that the former organized ongoing information diffusely and globally, so that changes went unnoticed (i.e., more leveling of information). Taken together, the findings with the parachutists were interpreted as supporting the hypothesis that under the stress of jumping, it is more adaptive to articulate changes in information since these changes are to be used for survival, whereas under the stress of imminent surgery, it is more adaptive to insulate oneself from subtle changes in information since the situation forces passivity and the information cannot be used.

The results of the two studies, although not testing directly shifts in cognitive organization, are of interest in showing that a characteristic cognitive style which is found to be adaptive in one environmental context can be quite maladaptive in another.

Wolitzky (1967) assessed whether smokers were characterized by the constricted cognitive control (intrusive peripheral information is more readily observed) or the flexible cognitive control (such information is ignored).   The latter is interpreted as more mature cognitive functioning. Relating these styles with the subjects' responses to published information linking smoking with cancer, Wolitzky found that the constricted-control smokers acknowledged the established link (and showed in the preceding year a tendency to cut down their smoking), whereas the flexible-control smokers denied the possibility.

Fisher (1967) found that women with high barrier scores obtained from Rorschach protocols (interpreted to represent independence and definite body boundaries—see discussion above) delayed longer in seeking medical attention after first discovering symptoms suggesting the possibility of their having cancer.

In both of these studies, the more developmentally advanced index of cognitive organization was associated with a maladaptive approach to available information. Witkin (1965) and Silverman (1964) have noted that individuals at either extreme of a cognitive style tend to show less of a capacity to shift to another level. Whether Wolitzky's subjects represent extremes in flexible control and Fisher's extremes in body definiteness and whether these subjects are thus unable to shift and acknowledge or act upon intrusive information even when survival is at stake are interesting questions that must await study.

Some attempts have been reported to modify, with systematic treatment procedures, styles judged as inflexible and ill-suited for optimal adaptation. Santostefano and Stayton (1967), noting that retarded children do not look actively at information and scan only narrow segments (i.e., exhibit a deficiently operating style of focal attention), reasoned that a change to a higher level (active and extensive scanning) should result in their registering more information and therefore in improving their efficiency with various tasks. Accordingly, a specially devised program was administered by

mothers of retardates at home for a period of four months on a daily basis. The trained retardates, versus matched controls, showed a significant improvement in handling various tasks.

Similarly, Blank and Solomon (1968), proposing that programs for the disadvantaged child should rehabilitate specific cognitive deficits, devised and administered a program to a group of preschoolers intended to raise the developmental status of the "abstract attitude." Compared with matched controls, the trained children showed significant gains in intelligence measures.

Critical periods. In the concept of critical periods, the biodevelopmental framework brings together propositions concerning adaptation and short- and long-range forces. This concept proposes that at various periods or stages in the process of differentiation, behavioral organizations require, and are ready to deal with and assimilate, particular classes of stimulation. If the experience and stimulation, viewed as representing critical nutriment for the behavioral organization in question and necessary for its further growth, are not made available by the active efforts of the individual or the environment, the behavioral system assumes a deviant line of development. While related to the concept of stages of development, the concept of critical periods emphasizes the extent to which stimulation introduced by the environment is timed appropriately in terms of the individual's developmental status and needs.

While this concept has been extensively investigated in research with animals (e.g., Hess, 1959; Scott, 1962; Sluckin, 1965), recent studies with humans conducted within, or of interest to, the biodevelopmental framework have introduced the critical-periods concept primarily to account for various observations already made. A few studies are noted here as illustrations. Stunkard and Burt (1964), comparing children obese both in childhood and in adolescence with children obese either in childhood or in adolescence, concluded that disturbances in body image associated with obesity originate during a relatively short period of time in early adolescence when derogatory communications by peers and parents are incorporated by the obese child.

Reviewing numerous studies of the effects of separation from parents during early childhood, Yarrow (1965) proposed that the data can be interpreted within the framework of critical periods. Numerous findings point to the period of time between 6 months and 2 years of age, when, if separated from parents, the infant is observed subsequently to develop more serious personality disturbances. Along the same line, Menlove (1965), finding a higher incidence of various aggressive symptoms (e.g., fire setting, temper tantrums, sadism, impulsivity) in adopted children, stressed the need to study the optimum time for adoption and placement in new foster homes in terms of the critical-period concept.

Similarly, attention is brought to critical periods by Marks and Gelder (1966) in a study of ages of onset of phobias, by Davis (1967) in a study of the families of mentally retarded children, by Becker (1964) in his review of studies of the effects of parental restrictions on child development, and by Weinstock (1967) in his investigation of the role of family conflict in the development of ego defenses and coping mechanisms. It may be of interest to note that Watson (1965) made central use of the critical-periods hypothesis in organizing his text of child development, and accordingly he brings attention to many and various observations concerning the critical timing of stimulation.

CONCLUSIONS AND IMPLICATIONS

The studies considered in this review indicate that biodevelopmental propositions have been used to guide the investigation of (1) unusual sensitivity to stimulation, activity patterns, and physical anomalies observed in infants; (2) similarities and differences in the organization of perceptual-cognitive behavior of emotionally disturbed individuals and normal children of younger ages; (3) distortions of time perspective and body boundaries in neurotic, psychotic, and brain-damaged children; (4) childhood symptoms and pathological populations viewed as representing different levels of development; (5) deviations in functioning (e.g., drive expressions, sensory preferences) from an ideal developmental sequence defined by the dominance of particular modes and modalities; (6) coping strategies employed by children in various stressful and stimulating situations; (7) enduring conditions in the child and/or environment that disrupt the coordinated give-and-take between them, leading to deviant development; and (8) relatively brief regressive or progressive shifts in the individual's psychological organization, viewed as representing attempts to maintain an adjustment in the face of changing environments.

What overall conclusion can we draw concerning the contribution which these studies have made to our understanding and treatment of child psychopathology? If we examine these findings from the vantage point of the clinician working daily with complex emotional disturbances presented by children and their families, we would conclude that the contribution of biodevelopmental research considered here is indeed a meager one. Certainly the recent body of research inspired by this framework is a long way from being in the position of offering the practitioner a relatively complete and systematic body of knowledge concerning the conceptual understanding and effective treatment of particular psychological disorders in children.

Although short on systematic information which could be applied in practice, in our eyes these studies as a group suggest that there is considerable value in viewing processes of normal and pathological development, in clinical practice and research, from the perspective of the assumptions and propositions outlined at the start of this review. Our overall conclusion, therefore, is that the contribution of the biodevelopmental position and the research it has stimulated are not represented primarily in the content of its findings to date but in the heuristic perspective it offers as a theoretical and methodological guide, assisting clinicians and researchers alike as each makes his way through the thickets of diagnosing and treating psychopathology.

In order to give some support to this conclusion, let us briefly consider what help the biodevelopmental framework offers to practitioners and researchers in handling inconsistencies and controverises contained in two areas concerned with the development of psychopathology: one of these, of possible major interest to clinicians, is located within the specialty of psychopathology and concerns the relation between childhood symptoms and adult pathology; and the other, of possible major interest to investigators, concerns the effects of mass media on aggression in children.

As many clinicians may have noted, a number of recent follow-up studies relating childhood symptoms or histories to adult outcome have reported discouraging results in observing little or no relationship. For example, Roff and his colleagues (1966) examined the child-clinic and military records of 10,000 males and noted that with some cases, the adult outcome (adequacy of adjustment to military service; psychiatric diagnosis) was predictable on the basis of the behavior observed in childhood (especially if noted during adolescence) but that with others, the connection was difficult or impossible to make. Similarly, Robins (1966) interviewed a large number of adult patients, representing

various diagnoses, who had been seen thirty years earlier in child-guidance clinics and observed that for the majority of the categories, the behaviors involved showed little correspondence to the types of symptom behaviors these individuals manifested as children. In a related study, Renaud and Estess (1961) found evidence in the histories of symptom-free adults of events considered traditionally to result in adult psychopathology and noted that, among other possibilities, such findings may challenge theories which link the development of emotional illness to early experience.

The biodevelopmental framework helps with this problem in first pointing out that these follow-up studies, in searching for some degree of isomorphism between child and adult behaviors, are asking inappropriate questions of their data according to several developmental propositions concerned with the relation between early and later forms of behavior. That is, the biodevelopmental framework assumes that with development, a unit of behavior undergoes transformation and reorganization so that early forms are subordinated and integrated into later, more complex emerging forms; therefore, one would not expect the content of an adult symptom to resemble its counterpart in childhood. Moreover, it is also assumed that a unit of behavior is determined and defined by the context of which it is a part; therefore, two materially different symptoms could represent the same meaning if embedded in the same behavioral organization—such as, for example, one concerning aggression and its control.

Investigators following children longitudinally from the vantage point of these assumptions (e.g., Chess, Thomas, & Birch, 1967; Escalona & Hieder, 1959; Murphy, 1962) have emphasized recently that while alterations of behavior from infancy throughout childhood can be noted and while no single behavior remains the same over time, the underlying continuity of the child's behavioral styles and patterns of adaptation is observable. Moreover, it was by means of these propositions as guides that Michaels (1964) was able to gather relevant data and to meaningfully conceptualize a relationship between two dramatically different behaviors (i.e., enuresis in early childhood and explosive delinquent behavior during adolescence) and that Gomberg (1968) was able to relate poorly controlled, overt aggression observed in latency with alcoholism in adulthood.

The biodevelopmental framework, therefore, is of potential help to workers interested in this problem area by offering propositions that caution us, in collecting and interpreting our data, to look not for isomorphism between child and adult behaviors but for the common organizational features the behaviors suggest that allow us to formulate a theoretically meaningful and clinically useful connection between them.

In addition to suggesting propositions to guide the relating of two materially different behaviors, the biodevelopmental framework also offers concepts that can be of use in conceptualizing the process which could account for the emergence of symptomatic behaviors in an adult that appear radically different from his childhood symptoms. Let us illustrate by examining briefly one of the clinical cases (the case of Daniel) reported in rich detail by Roff et al. (1966, pp. 13-24) in the study noted above. We acknowledge that in discussing this case we select and consider only a few of the details provided in the original report to illustrate our point.

Daniel, we learn, was brought to the clinic at age 5 because he was unusually resistant, fought and struggled with mother, and could not mingle easily with peers. At the age of 21, he was rejected from military service with the diagnosis of schizoid personality. How could we understand that this boy, reported by mother and observed by the psychiatrist as hyperactive,

destructive, provocative, and defiant, was given a diagnosis 16 years later which presumed an emotionally cold, flat, and socially guarded young adult? To approach this question, the biodevelopmental framework would first take special note of the fact that at the age of 5 years, ego-personality structures concerned with participating emotionally and reciprocating with others (especially mother) and with the regulation of aggression and independence were already assuming a deviant course of development. Moreover, between 5 and 21 years, these structures became severely modified from expressing opposition and destructiveness to expressing emotional withdrawal and coldness. Since Daniel's child and adult symptomatic behaviors both involved structures concerned with regulation of aggression and independence and reciprocating interpersonally, the biodevelopmental framework would require (borrowing a leaf from Sander, 1962—see discussion of this work in the section on the adaptive process) that we ask questions about particular aspects of Daniel's interaction with his mother during the second and third years of his life, interactions that are taken to define the developmental stage during which the child is presumed to first test out and establish, in numerous negotiations with his mother, his independence, assertiveness, and style of emotional responsivity. Specifically, we would ask: When Daniel showed greater and more complex locomotion and aggressivity during his second and third years, to what extent and by what means did mother protect him from excessive stimulation? To what extent did Daniel establish and determine his behavior in the face of mother's limit setting? To what extent did mother extend her interacting to include speech and symbolic play as she attempted to deal and negotiate with his aggression and independence in arriving at a mutually defined set of opportunities and limits?

Roff's excellent case description provides

us with samples of behaviors required by these propositions and considerations. When Daniel was 20 months of age, mother, a tense, dominant person, located a large number of adult relatives in a room to surprise Daniel on Christmas morning. When he toddled in to see the tree and his gifts, he became very frightened, cried, and would not touch his gifts, and thereafter he always reacted "strangely" to any surprise event. As Daniel showed more curiosity and independence, mother increased her restrictions and controls: She trained him not to touch any of her belongings. Later, when she found him playing with matches, she ran a lighted match through his fingers. When he pulled the dog's tail, mother pulled Daniel's hair. When he kicked the door, mother kicked him. When he began running out into the street, she arranged to have a truck pass near him.

If these data are organized in terms of the considerations noted above, we would conclude that mother failed to protect Daniel from stimulation which he was not equipped to handle and that, as he became more mobile and attempted to negotiate the issue of establishing independence and expressing aggression, mother severely limited and restricted his assertiveness with primitive (and very likely traumatizing) behaviors. Moreover, she failed to handle the task expected of her in ideal development, that of gradually including and coordinating in her responses to his aggression and independence more advanced modes such as speech and play.

By the age of 5, then, mother and Daniel had failed to negotiate successfully a pattern of aggressivity and independence appropriate for Daniel's style of functioning, an issue which should have been settled in its basic components by this age. When seen at the clinic, each was still struggling with this issue, as suggested by Daniel's employing inappropriately primitive and destructive means for expressing his aggression and independence (e.g., in the clinic, he provocatively threatened to damage many objects and was almost successful in destroying the psychiatrist's desk blotter) and as evidenced by mother's coming to the clinic because her primitive, restricting behaviors were not curbing Daniel to her requirements.

Roff's report does not go beyond Daniel's fifth year, except to state the outcome that he was rejected for military service at the age of 21 with a diagnosis of schizoid personality. However, the clinician could conjecture that mother negotiated with Daniel throughout his childhood with the same severe restrictions (this seems likely since she discontinued her clinic visits after the third session because, the social worker felt, mother could not be in "full command" of the clinic situation) and that gradually, before the age of 21, Daniel gave up the struggle, arriving at a negotiated settlement with mother (and subsequently with his extended environment) in which he assumed an emotionally withdrawn, guarded, and severely regulated mode of functioning. To explore this formulation, the concept of negotiation would direct the clinician to focus on the continued give-and-take between Daniel and his mother concerned specifically with his expressions of independence and aggression. Such data, coupled with those obtained during the critical period when Daniel was 2 and 3 years old, would aid the clinician in studying the process that antecedes the formation and modification of ego structures concerned with emotional reciprocation and regulation of aggression and that are unique to the adult schizoid personality.

The second major area which we have selected to exemplify the heuristic value of the biodevelopmental model involves inconsistencies revealed by research concerned with the effects of violence portrayed in mass media on the aggressive behavior of children. Recent reviews of work in this area (Bandura & Walters, 1963;

Maccoby, 1964) show that a number of studies conclude, on the basis of their findings, that viewing violence portrayed in a film offers an individual the opportunity to discharge aggression vicariously (i.e., the cathartic effect) since less aggression is observed in subjects following exposure to some film and that other studies conclude that filmed violence arouses aggression since an increase in aggressive behavior is observed.

Various explanations for this inconsistency have been offered, for example, that change in aggressive behavior relates to the degree to which the anger is aroused prior to viewing the film and/or the extent to which the victim of aggression in the film is associated by the viewer with his own frustrations. While these have led to new research approaches (Berkowitz & Rawlings, 1963), they have far from settled the controversy (e.g., one study, in which the anger of children was aroused before they were exposed to a film of violence, observed an increase in aggression).

In approaching this problem area, the bio-developmental framework would add two inter-related suggestions, based upon the proposition of stages of development, which should be of help in planning further studies to clarify the controversy: first, investigators should take into account the developmental stage, represented by the subjects employed, with respect to the dominance of action, fantasy, and language modes; and second, investigators should note systematically whether tests of action, fantasy, or language are employed to assess expressions of aggression following exposure to film.

Let us examine these suggestions briefly. The empirical work discussed earlier concerning multiple modes and stages of development suggests that the action mode dominates the young child's experiencing and expressing of drives and that fantasy and language, as fully developed modes, emerge only later, subordinating and integrating action. This would suggest that if young children are used as subjects, one would expect that exposing them to crime and fights portrayed in films would result (assuming their aggressive feelings are stimulated) in increased aggression because the fantasy mode is not sufficiently developed in them to permit the displacing or redirecting of the aroused aggression in representational and symbolic terms. From the biodevelopmental point of view, then, an appropriately organized and developed fantasy mode would be a necessary precondition for the cathartic effect.

Some support for this suggestion is provided by the observation that with studies reviewed by Maccoby, those employing children report an increase in aggressive activity following exposure to film, while those using adults and adolescents report a decrease. More direct support comes from two recent studies. Pytkowitz, Wagner, and Sarason (1967), in one aspect of their investigation, determined by questionnaire the extent to which their subjects (college students) fantasied in everyday living. The subjects were then exposed to a laboratory-induced insult condition (designed to arouse aggression), after which they were allowed to sit quietly and let their minds roam freely. Pre- and postassessments of aggression showed that the fantasy experience resulted in a significantly greater cathartic effect for the high daydreamers versus those who did not use fantasy characteristically.

Along the same line, Santostefano and Marshall (1967) divided college students into an action-oriented group and a fantasy group (the first chose to stick a pin into a pincushion, and the second to look at a picture of a bullfight, when presented as a forced-choice situation). Half of each group was exposed to a film of violence, and the other half to a condition requiring them to act aggressively on objects (e.g., breaking light bulbs). Measures of fantasy and action expressions of aggression obtained before and after the two conditions suggested that aggression in the action-oriented subjects was catharted in the action condition but aroused by the film, whereas aggression in the fantasy-oriented subjects was catharted in the film condition, but aroused in the action condition. These results suggested to the investigators that concordance and discordance between the preferred mode of expressing aggression, on the one hand, and the type of aggressive experiences permitted the subjects with the methods employed, on the other, are critical in predicting whether fantasy experiences will arouse or dissipate aggression.

This study leads us to the issue concerning the selection of methods to assess aggression following exposure to a film. An examination of the studies reviewed by Maccoby and by Bandura and Walters indicates that investigators have, for example, asked subjects to tell stories to TAT cards, to check adjectives, and to wander freely in a room filled with toys and have noted the number of aggressive pushes directed toward peers in a free situation. From the viewpoint of the biodevelopmental framework, each of these measures relates to a different mode (action, fantasy, or language). Individuals are presumed to differ in the extent to which they have reached developmentally, and made dominant use of, one or another of these levels. Thus the effects of mass media on aggressive behavior and on the development of aggressive controls in children could be obscured unless the subjects and methods are selected with a systematic rationale that takes into account the several developmental issues considered here.

In introducing biodevelopmental considerations into the problem areas concerned with the relation between child and adult symptoms and with the effects of mass media, we have attempted to illustrate to the practitioner and researcher the value of viewing normal and pathological development from this particular perspective. Other illustrative examples are represented in a number of ongoing areas of investigation which, in introducing aspects of the biodevelopmental framework, are suggesting exciting inroads into old problems: e.g., Kohlberg's (1966) provocative and creative formulation linking psychosexual identity to cognitive development; Gutmann's (1965) stimulating proposal that quite different primary-secondary process structures are adaptive for the male versus the female; Freedman's (Freedman, Loring, & Martin, 1967) integration of evolutionary biology and personality development; Harvey and Schroder's (Harvey, Hunt, & Schroder, 1961; Schroder, Driver, & Streufere, 1967) systematic detailing of information-processing modes serving the individual in adaption; studies of moral development in children and adolescents (e.g., Kohlberg, 1964; Turiel, 1966); Kaplan's (1959) superb analysis of pathology in language; and Arieti's (1965) formulation of cognitive psychiatry.

We agree with Cummings (1967) and Korner (1962) that a regrettable lag exists between the methods and concepts used in conventional practice with children, on the one hand, and the rich propositions of developmental psychology and the methods stimulated by them in recent research, on the other. On the basis of our examination of the literature of the latter field, we could add, however, that a growing number of researchers and clinicians are approaching the study and treatment of child psychopathology through the developmental theories of psychoanalytic ego psychology. Werner and Piaget are now on the threshold of discovering provocative theoretical insights and innovations in practice while at the same time furthering the integration of development, as a way of inquiring about problems, with the puzzles presented by emotionally disturbed children.

REFERENCES

Ainsworth, M. *Reversible and irreversible effects of maternal deprivation on intellectual develop-*

ment. New York: Child Welfare League of America, 1962. Pp. 42–52.

Alpert, A., Neubauer, P. B., & Weil, A. P. Unusual variations in drive endowment. Vol. 11. *The psychoanalytic study of the child.* New York: International Universities Press, 1956. Pp. 125–153.

Ariteti, S. Conceptual and cognitive psychiatry. *American Journal of Psychiatry,* 1965, **122,** 236–367.

Ausubel, D. P. *Ego development and the personality disorders: A developmental approach to psychopathology.* New York: Grune & Stratton, 1952.

Baldwin, A. L. The study of child behavior. In P. Mussen (Ed.), *Handbook of research methods in child development.* New York: Wiley, 1960. Pp. 3–35.

Baldwin, A. L. *Theories of child development.* New York: Wiley, 1967.

Bandura, A., & Walters, R. H. Aggression. In H. W. Stevenson, J. Kagan, & C. Spiker (Eds.), *Child psychology: The sixty-second yearbook of the National Society for the Study of Education.* Chicago: University of Chicago Press, 1963. Pp. 364–415.

Becker, W. C. The process-reactive distinction: A key to the problem of schizophrenia. *Journal of Nervous and Mental Disorders,* 1959, **129,** 442–449.

Becker, W. C. Consequences of different kinds of parental discipline. In M. L. Hoffman & L. W. Hoffman (Eds.), *Review of child development and research.* New York: Russell Sage Foundation, 1964. Pp. 169–208.

Bell, R. Q. A reinterpretation of the direction of effects in studies of socialization. *Psychological Review,* 1968, **75,** 81–95.

Bergman, P., & Escalona, S. K. Unusual sensitivities in very young children. Vols. 3–4. *The psychoanalytic study of the child.* New York: International Universities Press, 1949. Pp. 333–352.

Berkowitz, L., & Rawlings, E. Effects of filmed violence on inhibitions against subsequent aggression. *Journal of Abnormal and Social Psychology,* 1963, **66,** 405–412.

Bibace, R., & Gruen, G. A comparative developmental analysis of cognitive processes in populations representing various sequences of development. Unpublished manuscript, Clark University, 1968.

Blank, M., & Solomon, F. A tutorial language program to develop abstract thinking in socially disadvantaged preschool children. *Child Development,* 1968, **39,** 379–389.

Block, J. Ego identity, role variability, and adjustment. *Journal of Consulting Psychology,* 1961, **25,** 392–397.

Borowitz, G. H., & Hirsch, J. G. A developmental typology of disadvantaged four year olds. *American Journal of Orthopsychiatry,* 1968, **38,** 213–214. (Abstract)

Boyd, R. D. Analysis of ego-stage development of school-age children. *Journal of Experimental Education,* 1964, **32,** 249–253.

Brazelton, T. B. Observations of the neonate. *Journal of the American Academy of Child Psychiatry,* 1962, **1,** 38–58.

Buss, A. H., & Lang, P. J. Psychological deficit in schizophrenia. I. Affect, reinforcement, and concept attainment. *Journal of Abnormal Psychology,* 1965, **70,** 2–24.

Chess, A., Rutter, M., Thomas, A., & Birch, H. G. Interaction of temperament and the environment in the production of behavioral disturbances in children. *American Journal of Psychiatry,* 1963, **120,** 142–147.

Chess, S., Thomas, A., & Birch, H. G. Behavior problems revisited: Findings of an anterospective study. *Journal of the American Academy of Child Psychiatry,* 1967, **6,** 321–331.

Chodoff, P., Friedman, S. B., & Hamburg, D. A. Stress, defenses and coping behavior: Observations in parents of children with malignant disease. *American Journal of Psychiatry,* 1964, **120,** 743–749.

Coelho, G. V., Hamburg, D. A., & Murphey, E. B. Coping strategies in a new learning environment. *Archives of General Psychiatry,* 1963, **9,** 433–443.

Cortes, J. B., & Gatti, F. M. Physique and self-description of temperament. *Journal of Consulting Psychology,* 1965, **29,** 432–439.

Cortes, J. B., & Gatti, F. M. Physique and motivation. *Journal of Consulting Psychology,* 1967, **30,** 408–414.

Crandall, V. J. Achievement. In H. W. Stevenson, J. Kagan, & C. Spiker (Eds.), *Child psychology: The sixty-second yearbook of the National Society for the Study of Education.* Chicago: University of Chicago Press, 1963. Pp. 416–459.

Cummings, S. T. Psychotic dwarfs with good prognoses or what? Developmental contingencies in clinical child psychology. *Psychological Reports,* 1967, **20,** 451–456.

Davidson, M., McGinnis, R., & Parnell, R. Distribution of personality traits in seven year old children: A combined psychological, psychiatric, and somatotype study. *British Journal of Educational Psychology,* 1957, **27,** 48–61.

Davis, D. R. Family processes in mental retardation. *American Journal of Psychiatry,* 1967, **124,** 340–351.

Decarie, T. G. *Intelligence and affectivity in early childhood: An experimental study of Jean Piaget's object concept and object relation.* New York: International Universities Press, 1965.

Dennis, W. Historical beginnings of child psychology. *Psychological Bulletin,* 1949, **46,** 224–235.

Deutsch, M. The role of social class in language development and cognition. *American Journal of Orthopsychiatry,* 1965, **35,** 78–88.

Dyk, R. B., & Witkin, H. A. Family experiences related to the development of differentiation in children. *Child Development,* 1965, **36,** 21–55.

Elkind, D. Egocentrism in adolescents. *Child Development,* 1967, **38,** 1023–1034. (a)

Elkind, D. Middle class delinquency. *Mental Hygiene,* 1967, **51,** 80–84. (b)

Engel, G. L. *Psychological development in health and disease.* Philadelphia: Saunders, 1962.

Erikson, E. H. Identity and the life cycle. *Psychological Issues,* 1959, **1**(1), 1–165.

Escalona, S., & Hieder, G. M. *Prediction and outcome: A study in child development.* New York: Basic Books, 1959.

Farnham-Diggory, S. Self, future and time: A developmental study of the concepts of psychotic, brain-damaged and normal children. *Monographs of the Society for Research in Child Development,* 1966, **31**(1, Whole No. 103).

Feffer, M. H. The cognitive implications of role taking behavior. *Journal of Personality,* 1959, **27,** 152–168.

Feffer, M. H. Symptom expression as a form of primitive decentering. *Psychological Review,* 1967, **74,** 16–28.

Fish, B., & Shapiro, T. A typology of children's psychiatric disorders. *Journal of the American Academy of Child Psychiatry,* 1965, **4,** 32–52.

Fisher, R. L. Failure of the conceptual styles test to discriminate normal and highly impulsive children. *Journal of Abnormal Psychology,* 1966, **71,** 429–431.

Fisher, S. Motivation for patient delay. *Archives of General Psychiatry,* 1967, **16,** 676–678.

Fisher, S., & Cleveland, S. E. *Body image and personality.* Princeton, N. J.: Van Nostrand, 1958.

Fisher, S., & Fisher, R. A developmental analysis of some body image and body reactivity dimensions. *Child Development,* 1959, **30,** 389–402.

Flavell, J. H. *The development psychology of Jean Piaget.* Princeton, N. J.: Van Nostrand, 1963.

Fontana, A. F. Familial etiology of schizophrenia: Is a scientific methodology possible? *Psychological Bulletin,* 1966, **66,** 214–227.

Frank, G. H. The role of the family in the development of psychopathology. *Psychological Bulletin,* 1965, **64,** 191–205.

Freedman, D. G. Smiling in blind infants and the issue of innate vs. acquired. *Journal of Child Psychology and Psychiatry,* 1964, **5,** 171–184.

Freedman, D. G., Loring, C. B., & Martin, R. M. Emotional behavior and personality development. In Y. Brackbill (Ed.), *Infancy and early childhood: A handbook and guide to human development.* New York: Free Press, 1967. Pp. 429–502.

Freud, A. *Normality and pathology in childhood: Assessments of development.* New York: International Universities Press, 1965.

Friedman, S. M. An empirical study of the castration and Oedipus complexes. *Genetic Psychology Monographs,* 1952, **46,** 61–130.

Fries, M. E., & Woolf, P. J. Some hypotheses on the role of the congenital activity type in

personality development. Vol. 8. *The Psycho-analytic study of the child.* New York: International Universities Press, 1953. Pp. 48–52.

Gardner, R. W., Holzman, P. S., Klein, G. S., Linton, H. B., & Spence, D. P. Cognitive control: A study of individual consistencies in cognitive behavior. *Psychological Issues,* 1959, **1**(4), 1–185.

Goldman, A. E. A comparative-developmental approach to schizophrenia. *Psychological Bulletin,* 1962, **59,** 57–69.

Goldschmid, M. L. The relation of conservation to emotional and environmental aspects of development. *Child Development,* 1968, **39**, 579–589.

Gomberg, E. S. Etiology of alcoholism. *Journal of Consulting and Clinical Psychology,* 1968, **32,** 18–20.

Gourevitch, V., & Feffer, M. H. A study of motivational development. *Journal of Genetic Psychology,* 1962, **100,** 361–375.

Gruen, W. Rejection of false information about oneself as an indication of ego identity. *Journal of Consulting Psychology,* 1960, **24,** 231–233.

Guthrie, G. D. Changes in cognitive functioning under stress: A study of plasticity in cognitive controls. Unpublished doctoral dissertation, Clark University, 1967.

Gutmann, D. L. Women and the conception of ego strength. *Merrill-Palmer Quarterly of Behavior and Development,* 1965, **11,** 229–240.

Guyette, A. M. A developmental analysis of cognitive functioning in mental retardates. Unpublished doctoral dissertation, Clark University, 1965.

Haronian, F., & Sugarman, A. Fixed and mobile field independence: Review of studies relevant to Werner's dimension. *Psychological Reports,* 1967, **21,** 41–57.

Harris, D. B. Problems in formulating a scientific concept of development. In D. B. Harris (Ed.), *The concept of development: An issue in the study of human behavior.* Minneapolis: University of Minnesota Press, 1957. Pp. 3–14.

Hartmann, H. *Ego psychology and the problem of adaptation.* New York: International Universities Press, 1958.

Hartup, W. W. Dependence and independence. In H. W. Stevenson, J. Kagan, & C. Spiker (Eds.), *Child psychology: The sixty-second yearbook of the National Society for the Study of Education.* Chicago: University of Chicago Press, 1963. Pp. 333–363.

Harvey, O. J., Hunt, D. E., & Schroder, H. M. *Conceptual systems and personality organization.* New York: Wiley, 1961.

Hemmendinger, L. Developmental theory and Rorschach method. In M. A. Rickers-Ovsiankina (Ed.), *Rorschach psychology.* New York: Wiley, 1960. Pp. 58–79.

Hertzig, M. E., Birch, H. G., Thomas, A., & Mendez, O. A. Class and ethnic differences in the responsiveness of preschool children to cognitive demands. *Monographs of the Society for Research in Child Development,* 1968, **33** (1, Whole No. 117).

Hess, E. H. Imprinting. *Science,* 1959, **130,** 133–141.

Hill, K. T., & Zigler, E. The action-thought dimension and performance in an action versus thought conflict situation. *Journal of Personality,* 1964, **32,** 666–681.

Hill, S. D., McCullum, A. H., & Scheau, A. G. Relation of training and motor activity to development of right-left directionality in mentally retarded children: Exploratory study. *Perceptual and Motor Skills,* 1967, **24,** 363–366.

Hoffman, M. L., & Hoffman, L. W. (Eds.) *Review of child development research.* Vols. 1–2. New York: Russell Sage Foundation, 1964.

Hurwitz, J. I., & Kaplan, D. Parental coping patterns and delinquency. *Journal of Offender Therapy,* 1962, **6,** 2–4.

Jessner, L., & Pavenstedt, E. (Eds.) *Dynamic psychopathology in childhood.* New York: Grune & Stratton, 1959.

Judson, A. J., & Katahn, M. Levels of personality organization and production of associative sequences in process-reactive schizophrenia. *Journal of Consulting Psychology,* 1964, **28,** 208–213.

Kagan, J. Body build and conceptual impulsivity in children. *Journal of Personality,* 1966, **34,** 118–128.

Kagan, J., Moss, H. A., & Sigel, I. E. Psychological significance of styles of conceptualization. *Monographs of the Society for Research in Child Development,* 1963, **28**(2, Whole No. 86).

Kaplan, B. The study of language in psychiatry: The comparative developmental approach and its application to symbolization and language in psychopathology. In S. Arieti (Ed.), *American handbook of psychiatry.* Vol. 3. New York: Basic Books, 1959. Pp. 659–688.

Kessler, J. W. *Psychopathology of childhood.* Englewood Cliffs, N.J.: Prentice-Hall, 1966.

Kessler, J. W., Ablon, G., & Smith, E. C. Separation reactions in young, mildly retarded and brain damaged children. *American Journal of Orthopsychiatry,* 1968, **38,** 216–217. (Abstract)

Klein, G. S. Cognitive control and motivation. In G. Lindzey (Ed.), *Assessment of human motives.* New York: Rinehart, 1958. Pp. 87–118.

Klineberg, S. L. Changes in outlook on the future between childhood and adolescence. *Journal of Personality and Social Psychology,* 1967, **7,** 185–193.

Kohlberg, L. Development of moral character and moral ideology. In M. L. Hoffman & L. W. Hoffman (Eds.), *Review of child development and research.* New York: Russell Sage Foundation, 1964. Pp. 383–431.

Kohlberg, L. A cognitive-developmental analysis of children's sex-role concepts and attitudes. In E. E. Maccoby (Ed.), *The development of sex differences.* Stanford, Calif.: Stanford University Press, 1966. Pp. 82–173.

Korner, A. S. Developmental-diagnostic dimensions as seen through psychological testing. *Journal of Projective Techniques,* 1962, **26,** 201–211.

Kraidman, E. Developmental analysis of conceptual and perceptual functioning under stress and non-stress conditions. Unpublished doctoral dissertation, Clark University, 1958.

Kris, E. *Psychoanalysis explorations in art.* New York: International Universities Press, 1952.

Lennard, H. L., Baulieu, N. R., & Embrey, N. G. Interaction in families with a schizophrenic child. *Archives of General Psychiatry,* 1965, **12,** 166–183.

Lessing, E. E. Demographic, developmental and personality correlates of length of future time perspective (STP). *Journal of Personalities,* 1968, **36,** 183–201.

Maccoby, E. E. Effects of the mass media. In M. L. Hoffman & L. W. Hoffman (Eds.), *Review of child development and research.* New York: Russell Sage Foundation, 1964. Pp. 323–348.

Mack, J. E. Nightmares, conflict and ego development in childhood. *International Journal of Psychoanalysis,* 1965, **46,** 403–428.

Marcia, J. E. Development and validation of ego identity status. *Journal of Personality and Social Psychology,* 1966, **3,** 551–559.

Marcia, J. E. Ego identity status: Relationship to change in self-esteem, "general maladjustment," and authoritarianism. *Journal of Personality,* 1967, **35,** 118–133.

Marks, I. M., & Gelder, M. G. Different ages of onset in varieties of phobia. *American Journal of Psychiatry,* 1966, **123,** 218–221.

Mattson, A., & Gross, S. Adaptation and defensive behavior in young hemophiliacs and their parents. *American Journal of Psychiatry,* 1966, **122,** 1349–1356.

Megargee, E. I. Relations between barrier scores and aggressive behavior. *Journal of Abnormal Psychology,* 1965, **70,** 307–311.

Menlove, F. L. Aggressive symptoms in emotionally disturbed adopted children. *Child Development,* 1965, **36,** 519–532.

Michaels, J. J. *Disorders of character.* Springfield, Ill.: Charles C Thomas, 1955.

Michaels, J. J. The need for a theory of delinquency. *Archives of General Psychiatry,* 1964, **10,** 182–186.

Minuchin, S., Auerswald, E., King, C. H., & Rabinowitz, C. The study and treatment of families that produce multiple acting out in boys. *American Journal of Orthopsychiatry,* 1964, **34,** 125–133.

Minuchin, S., Chamberlain, P., & Graubard, P. A project to teach learning skills to disturbed, delinquent children. *American Journal of Orthopsychiatry,* 1967, **36,** 558–567.

Minuchin, S., & Montalvo, B. Techniques for working with disorganized low socioeconomic families. *American Journal of Orthopsychiatry,* 1967, **37,** 880–887.

Mittelmann, B. Motility in infants, children, and adults: Patterning and psychodynamics. Vol. 9. *The psychoanalytic study of the child.* New York: International Universities Press, 1954. Pp. 142–177.

Murphy, L. *The widening world of childhood.* New York: Basic Books, 1962.

Mussen, P. *Handbook of research methods in child development.* New York: Wiley, 1960.

Nagel, E. Determinism and development. In D. B. Harris (Ed.), *The concept of development: An issue in the study of human behavior.* Minneapolis: University of Minnesota Press, 1957. Pp. 15–24.

O'Connor, N., & Hermelin, B. Sensory dominance. *Archives of General Psychiatry,* 1965, **12,** 99–103.

Patterson, G. R. An empirical approach to the classification of disturbed children. *Journal of Clinical Psychology,* 1964, **20,** 326–337.

Phillips, L., & Rabinovitch, F. M. Social role and patterns of symptomatic behaviors. *Journal of Abnormal and Social Psychology,* 1958, **57,** 181–186.

Phillips, L., & Zigler, E. Role orientation, the action-thought parameter, and outcome of psychiatric disorder. *Journal of Abnormal and Social Psychology,* 1964, **68,** 381–389.

Provence, S., & Lipton, R. C. *Infants in institutions.* New York: International Universities Press, 1962.

Prugh, D. G., Staub, E. M., Sands, H. H., Kirschbaum, R., & Lenihan, E. A study of the emotional reactions of children and families to hospitalization and illness. *American Journal of Orthopsychiatry,* 1953, **23,** 41–79.

Pytkowitz, A. R., Wagner, N. N., & Sarason, I. G. An experimental study of the reduction of hostility through fantasy. *Journal of Personality and Social Psychology,* 1967, **5,** 295–305.

Rapaport, D. Psychoanalysis as a developmental psychology. In B. Kaplan & S. Wapner (Eds.), *Perspectives in psychological theory.* New York:

International Universities Press, 1960. Pp. 209–255.

Rapaport, D., & Gil, M. The points of view and assumptions of metapsychology. *International Journal of Psychoanalysis,* 1959, **40,** 1–10.

Renaud, H., & Estess, F. Life history interviews with 100 normal American males: "Pathogenicity" of childhood. *American Journal of Orthopsychiatry,* 1961, **31,** 786–802.

Robins, L. N. *Deviant children grown up: A sociological and psychiatric study of sociopathic personality.* Baltimore: Williams & Wilkins, 1966.

Roff, M., Mink, W., & Hinrichs, G. *Developmental abnormal psychology: A casebook.* New York: Holt, 1966.

Rosenwald, G. C., Mendelsohn, G. A., Fontana, A., & Portz, A. T. An action test of hypotheses concerning the anal personality. *Journal of Abnormal Psychology,* 1966, **71,** 304–309.

Sander, L. W. Issues in early mother-child interaction. *Journal of the American Academy of Child Psychiatry,* 1962, **1,** 141–166.

Sander, L. W. Adaptive relationships in early mother-child interaction. *Journal of the American Academy of Child Psychiatry,* 1964, **3,** 231–264.

Santostefano, S. Cognitive controls and exceptional states in children. *Journal of Clinical Psychology,* 1964, **20,** 213–218.

Santostefano, S. Cognitive controls versus cognitive styles: An approach to diagnosing and treating cognitive disabilities in children. *Seminars in Psychiatry,* 1969, **1,** 291–317.

Santostefano, S. The assessment of motives in children. *Psychological Reports,* 1970, **26,** 639–649.

Santostefano, S., & Marshall, B. The effects of action and fantasy aggressive experience in terms of the developmental status of modes for expressing motives. Unpublished manuscript, Boston University, 1967.

Santostefano, S., & Paley, E. Development of cognitive controls in children. *Child Development,* 1964, **35,** 939–949.

Santostefano, S., Rutledge, L., & Randall, D. Cognitive styles and reading disability. *Psychology in the Schools,* 1965, **2,** 57–62.

Santostefano, S., & Stayton, S. Training the preschool retarded child in focusing attention: A program for parents. *American Journal of Orthopsychiatry,* 1967, **37,** 732–743.

Schopler, E. Visual versus tactual receptor preference in normal and schizophrenic children. *Journal of Abnormal Psychology,* 1966, **71,** 108–114.

Schroder, H. M., Driver, M. J., & Streufere, S. *Human information processing: Individuals and groups functioning in complex social situations.* New York: Holt, 1967.

Scott, J. P. Critical periods in behavioral development. *Science,* 1962, **138,** 949–958.

Shapiro, D. *Neurotic styles.* New York: Basic Books, 1965.

Shore, M. F., & Massimo, J. L. Verbalization, stimulus relevance, and personality change. *Journal of Consulting Psychology,* 1967, **31,** 423–424.

Shore, M. F., Massimo, J. L., & Mack, R. Changes in the perception of interpersonal relationships in successfully treated adolescent delinquent boys. *Journal of Consulting Psychology,* 1965, **29,** 213–217.

Silverman, J. Scanning-control mechanisms and "cognitive filtering" in paranoid and nonparanoid schizophrenia. *Journal of Consulting Psychology,* 1964, **28,** 385–393.

Singer, M. T., & Wynne, L. C. Differentiating characteristics of childhood schizophrenics, childhood neurotics, and young adult schizophrenics. *American Journal of Psychiatry,* 1963, **26,** 234–243.

Singer, M. T., & Wynne, L. C. Principles for scoring communication defects and deviances in parents of schizophrenics: Rorschach and TAT scoring manuals. *Psychiatry,* 1966, **29,** 260–288.

Sluckin, W. *Imprinting and early learning.* Chicago: Aldine, 1965.

Smart, R. G. Future time perspectives in alcoholics and social drinkers. *Journal of Abnormal Psychology,* 1968, **73,** 81–83.

Smith, L. C., & Phillips, L. Social effectiveness and developmental levels in adolescents. *Journal of Personality,* 1959, **27,** 239–249.

Spiker, C. C. The concept of development: Relevant and irrelevant issues. *Monographs of the Society for Research in Child Development,* 1966, **31**(5, Whole No. 107), 40–51.

Stabenau, J. R., Tupin, J., Werner, M., & Collin, W. A comparative study of families of schizophrenics, delinquents, and normals. *Psychiatry,* 1965, **28,** 45–59.

Stein, K. B., Sarbin, T. R., & Kulik, J. A. Future time perspective: Its relation to the socialization process and the delinquent role. *Journal of Consulting and Clinical Psychology,* 1968, **32,** 257–264.

Stevenson, H. W., Kagan, J. N., & Spiker, C. (Eds.) *Child psychology: The sixty-second yearbook of the National Society for the Study of Education.* Chicago: University of Chicago Press, 1963.

Stott, D. H. *Studies of troublesome children.* New York: Humanities Press, 1968.

Strauss, J. The clarification of schizophrenic concreteness by Piaget's tests. *Psychiatry,* 1967, **30,** 294–301.

Stunkard, A., & Burt, V. Obesity and the body image. II. Age at onset of disturbances in the body image. *American Journal of Psychiatry,* 1964, **124,** 1443–1447.

Thorne, F. The structure of integrative psychology. *Journal of Clinical Psychology,* 1967, **23,** 3–11.

Turiel, E. An experimental test of developmental stages in the child's moral judgements. *Journal of Personality and Social Psychology,* 1966, **3,** 611–618.

Van De Castle, R. L. Development and validation of a perceptual maturity scale using figure preferences. *Journal of Consulting Psychology,* 1965, **29,** 314–319.

von Bertalanffy, L. General system theory and psychiatry. In S. Arieti (Ed.), *American handbook of psychiatry.* Vol. 3. New York: Basic Books, 1966. Pp. 705–721.

Voth, H. M. Ego autonomy, autokinesis and recovery from psychosis. *Archives of General Psychiatry,* 1962, **6,** 288–293.

Voth, H. M., & Mayman, N. A dimension of personality organization. *Archives of General Psychiatry,* 1963, **8,** 366–380.

Waldrop, M. F., Pederson, F. A., & Bell, R. Q. Minor physical anomalies and behavior in preschool children. *Child Development,* 1968, **39,** 391–400.

Wallach, M. A. Commentary: Active-analytical vs. passive-global cognitive functioning. In S. Messick & J. Ross (Eds.), *Measurement in personality and cognition.* New York: Wiley, 1962. Pp. 199–218.

Wapner, S. Some aspects of a research program based on an organismic-developmental approach to cognition: Experiments and theory. *Journal of the Academy of Child Psychiatry,* 1964, **3,** 193–230.

Watson, R. I. *Psychology of the child.* (2nd ed.) New York: Wiley, 1965.

Webster, T. G. Problems of emotional development in young retarded children. *American Journal of Psychiatry,* 1963, **120,** 38–43.

Weinstock, A. R. Family environment and the development of defense and coping mechanisms. *Journal of Personality and Social Psychology,* 1967, **5,** 67–75.

Werner, H. The concept of development from a comparative and organismic point of view. In D. B. Harris (Ed.), *The concept of development: An issue in the study of human behavior.* Minneapolis: University of Minnesota Press, 1957. Pp. 125–148.

Werner, H., & Kaplan, B. *Symbol formation: An organismic-developmental approach to language and the expression of thought.* New York: Wiley, 1963.

Wild, C. Creativity and adaptive regression. *Journal of Personality and Social Psychology,* 1965, **2,** 161–169.

Winder, C. O., & Kantor, R. E. Rorschach maturity scores of the mothers of schizophrenics. *Journal of Consulting Psychology,* 1958, **22,** 438–440.

Witkin, H. A. Psychological differentiation and forms of pathology. *Journal of Abnormal Psychology,* 1965, **70,** 317–336.

Witkin, H. A., Dyk, R. B., Faterson, H. F., Goodenough, D. R., & Karp, S. A. *Psychological differentiation.* New York: Wiley, 1962.

Wolff, P. H. The developmental psychologies of Jean Piaget and psychoanalysis. *Psychological Issues,* 1960, **2**(1, Whole No. 5).

Wolitzky, D. L. Cognitive control and cognitive dissonance. *Journal of Abnormal and Social Psychology,* 1967, **5,** 486–490.

Wolman, R. N. A developmental study of the perception of people. *Genetic Psychology Monograph,* 1967, **76,** 96–140.

Yarrow, L. J. Maternal deprivation: Toward an empirical and conceptual reevaluation. *Psychological Bulletin,* 1961, **58,** 459–490.

Yarrow, L. J. Separation from parents during early childhood. In M. L. Hoffman & L. W. Hoffman (Eds.) *Review of child development and research.* New York: Russell Sage Foundation, 1965. Pp. 89–136.

Zigler, E. Metatheoretical issues in developmental psychology. In M. H. Marx (Ed.), *The-ories in contemporary psychology.* New York: Macmillan, 1963. Pp. 341–369.

Zigler, E., & Phillips, L. Social effectiveness and symptomatic behaviors. *Journal of Abnormal and Social Psychology,* 1960, **61,** 231–238.

Zigler, E., & Phillips, L. Social competence and outcome in psychiatric disorders. *Journal of Abnormal and Social Psychology,* 1961, **63,** 264–271.

Zigler, E., & Phillips, L. Social competence and the process-reactive distinction in psychopathology. *Journal of Abnormal and Social Psychology,* 1962, **65,** 215–222.

Zimet, C. N., & Fine, H. J. Perceptual differentiation and two dimensions of schizophrenia. *Journal of Nervous and Mental Disease,* 1959, **129,** 435–441.

Zuckerman, M. Save the pieces: A note on "Role of the family in the development of psychopathology." *Psychological Bulletin,* 1966, **66,** 78–80.

39 | Learning Theory

Bradley D. Bucher

Research in human and animal learning has made numerous contributions to current concepts of pathological behavior. The major viewpoints have been those of Pavlov, Hull, and Skinner, who are also the major current influences in American learning. Dollard and Miller (1950) used Hullian theory to attempt to unify the therapy and theory of dynamic psychology with results emerging from learning laboratories. They retained the usual dynamic clinical viewpoint and tried to redefine its concepts in the terminology of learning. Theirs was the first major attempt in this direction. Later formulations have been generally more restricted in scope and have not always taken dynamic psychology as the basis for observation and discussion. Ferster (1961), for example, recently presented an analysis of child autism in learning terms, without assuming the predominant significance of those behaviors that have been stressed by traditional clinicians or the validity of the concepts used to explain them. He was interested in behavior that could be produced and measured using operant research methods. These behaviors may not seem

of especial importance from the dynamic point of view. Bijou (1966) presented a similar analysis of the behavior of the mentally retarded. Specific analyses have been presented for such delimited problems as enuresis, hyperactivity, and almost any of the pathological behaviors to be discussed here.

To reduce the material for this review to manageable proportions, emphasis will be given to research studies that have used change in pathological behavior as the focus of interest. Only a portion of the learning research into pathological processes has been primarily concerned with changing the observed behaviors. In this chapter the methods and successes of this work will be surveyed. After some preliminary comments, work on creation of "experimental neurosis" in animals will be examined, as the first major attempt to demonstrate the relevance of learning for development of pathological behaviors and to find learning conditions for animals that might produce analogues of human neurotic behavior. A similar body of experimental work with humans is, of course, not available for review. Then research efforts to modify pathological behaviors will be discussed. This latter portion will concentrate on the sizable body of recent work with disturbed children and will not include similar research with adults and animals.

Emphasis on learning in the study of pathological behavior implies emphasis on environmental events, as factors shaping and maintaining behavior, and consequently on the search for methods of manipulating the environment to produce behavior changes. Of course, it is generally recognized that behavior is responsive to changing circumstances, but this recognition does not imply an emphasis on learning unless it is also accepted that environmental manipulation can actually lead to generalized and lasting changes in behavior. Many clinicians have not agreed to this latter proposition. Indeed, much of our adaptability to circumstances does not involve new learning but merely reflects discriminated learning previously acquired. If nothing more than this were achieved in attempts to control human behavior in the laboratory, little generalization outside could be expected. Useful learning involves lasting change in behavior in the presence of given stimuli, as a result of specific experiences with such stimuli. The behavior of a child with a book is an example. Gross behavior differences can be produced by teaching a child to read, since this skill involves the child in a quite different relation to the book than casually looking at the pictures or ripping out the pages. In a sense, the environment reacts on the child in a new way. A similar attitude can be taken toward pathological behavior, as representing unusual and maladaptive relations to the environment. These relations can be influenced directly by controlled learning experiences to bring about behavior changes which then alter the environment and which, in favorable circumstances, the environment will then maintain —much as our hypothetical child's new relation to books is maintained by the (presumably)

greater satisfaction to be gotten from reading. Social behavior is also an excellent example of this point.

Anyone familiar with both the learning and clinical approaches to behavior will recognize the discrepancy between the remarks above and the typical clinical emphasis on the emotional accompaniments of behavior disorders. Learning theories have not ignored emotion, as the mass of research involving the concept of anxiety illustrates. However, in devising means to change behavior, it generally has seemed preferable to work at the level of responses that are directly observable. Anxiety is a concept or construct rather than a class of behaviors, and changes in such conceptual dimensions must always be determined by inference, from changes in more clear-cut behavior classes.

In the application of learning theory to human behavior, much use is made of results of experimentation with animals. Use of animals permits more control and more variety in environmental manipulations and thus facilitates investigation. However, the more complex forms of human behavior, such as speech, cannot be studied directly in animals. Therefore, learning models contain fewer of the complex mediational concepts that have been proposed by psychologists studying human behavior, and learning theorists have preferred models positing a more direct relation between stimuli and behavior.

Concepts such as "awareness," "voluntary behavior," and "expectation" are not usually included in the terminology described here, except as terms available for brief inexact description, even though they may often seem quite appropriate. The avoidance of these concepts makes the application of operant terminology seem artificial, mechanical, and incomplete to many psychologists. Children in conditioning experiments, for example, often verbalize the experimental contingencies (correctly or incorrectly) and sometimes appear to be reacting more in accord with their verbalizations than with the actual contingencies. Sometimes these children, mistaken at a verbal level about experimental circumstances, may appear very contrary or stupid in their reactions, and typical animal behavior may appear more appropriate and uniform. Such data indicate that humans are different from animals, although there is not conclusive evidence that the differences are qualitative, in the sense that radically new concepts are necessary to describe human behavior.

To demonstrate that animal research and concepts derived therefrom can be useful for understanding human behavior, then, data are required that show that operations that produce reliable changes in animal behavior can be carried across for application to humans. Results cannot be transferred directly. Humans exist in quite different environments. Concepts such as reinforcement, discriminative stimulus, and fear can be transferred from animal to human events, but the specific stimuli and operations of animal learning cannot. Instead, empirical demonstration must be given that the same functional relationships hold across operations in the different environments. If the important functional relations do not transfer, it cannot be asserted confidently that variables comparable to those that operate in animal research also control the human behavior being studied. Consequently, research to manipulate human behavior directly has special value for learning models; and the importance of animal learning for human psychopathology can be shown most clearly by demonstrations of animal-human similarities in response to similar controlled environmental manipulations—the emphasis of this review.

Thus, the approach judged most useful here is to attempt to apply to humans the concepts developed in work with animals, adding to them or modifying them, with reluctance, when the data require. The use of this approach implies, of course, some degree of prophecy fulfillment, since phenomena are likely to be chosen for study partly on the basis of observed regularity and conformity to the customary experimental procedures with animals. In this, the learning analyst does not differ from his colleagues in other fields of science, and the judgment of the value of the model must depend finally on its achieved scope.

EXPERIMENTAL ESTABLISHMENT OF PATHOLOGICAL BEHAVIOR

A major example of an attempt to find pathological behavior in animals analogous to that of humans is the research in experimental neurosis. In this work, the cross-species translation is made from observations on humans to research with animals, rather than in the other direction. Broadhurst (1961) has given an excellent review of this work. He borrowed a definition of neurosis from Hebb (1947): "Neurosis is in practice an undesirable emotional condition which is generalized and persistent; it occurs in a minority of the population and has no origin in a gross neural lesion." Broadhurst extracted six aspects of this definition—the terms *undesirable, emotional, generalized, persistent, occurs in a minority of the population,* and *no origin in a gross neural lesion*—to evaluate work on experimental neurosis. Although the definition is hardly precise, it gives a basis for deciding whether the observed behavior in experimental neurosis can be considered comparable to human neurotic behavior, with necessary changes being made for species differences.

The classical work is reported by Pavlov (1927), Liddell (1956), Gantt (1944), and Masserman (1943). The references given contain summaries of some of the results.

In work in Pavlov's laboratory, neurotic reactions in dogs sometimes occurred when shock was used as a conditioned stimulus (CS) for food or when the dogs were required to make a progressively more difficult discrimination for food reinforcement. Some animals showed extreme general motor excitement; others became inhibited, drowsy, and refused food. It was observed that these pathological reactions became attached to particular stimuli. Dogs exposed to the waters of the famous Petrograd flood of 1924, for example, were retraumatized by a partial reproduction of the event. In general, in this work, all investigations were carried on in the usual typical conditioning situations, and generalization was not tested.

Liddell observed similar effects in sheep, dogs, pigs, and rabbits, using shock as a CS for a motor response or a difficult discrimination or extinction of a learned response for food. Some animals showed resistance to being attached to the experimental harness and restlessness during training after such experiences. Outside the training chamber, some heart-rate irregularities were observed, and decreased social behavior was observed in sheep returned to the flock. Some aggression toward the experimenters also occurred. Liddell followed some animals for several years after the first occurrence of disturbed behavior.

Gantt also presented some case histories of dogs whose behavior was followed for extended periods. Nick, the most famous, was studied for twelve years. The onset of neurotic behavior in Nick apparently followed training in a difficult discrimination for positive reinforcement. Nick showed restlessness, emotionality, and excitability in the experimental situation and avoidance or aggressiveness toward the experimenters outside. Other bizarre behaviors were noted, including sexual disturbances and unusual responses during conditioning trials. Attempts to eliminate these behaviors through rest periods and by feeding Nick in the experimental chamber were not successful, in that further work in conditioning invariably rearoused the original, or novel, bizarre behaviors.

Broadhurst concluded that none of these lines of investigation had shown that behavior had been produced experimentally that fulfilled all the conditions for neurosis given above. However, these studies provide anecdotal reports which give persuasive indications that persistent, generalized, and emotional behavior was obtained from several different training procedures. The other descriptive terms in the list previously given are not clearly relevant for breakdowns in behavior produced through experimental manipulation. The behavior frequently may be desirable, from at least the animal's point of view, and the special training procedures that produce the behavior may do so for a majority of animals subjected to them.

All the authors cited above presented theoretical interpretations of their work. The observations in Pavlov's laboratory contributed to the development of his theory of types of nervous systems. Liddell and Gantt developed specialized concepts, which have not had general acceptance in the mainstream of theorizing in learning.

Hebb (1947), Wolpe (1952), and Broadhurst (1961) used more familiar ideas, more closely tied to Hullian learning theory, to describe the data summarized above and other work. They posited that the phenomenon of experimental neurosis derives from the presence of anxiety (or "conditioned emotional responses," "fear," or "aversion," as this concept has been variously labeled) acquired as a response to stimuli present in the conditioning situation, following the principles of conditioning. That is, the neurotic symptoms observed are actually symptoms of fear conditioning, which mediates other, more overt behavior.

The use of the term "anxiety" ties the phenomena of experimental neurosis more closely to other experimental work in learning. However, an agreed-upon operational measure for anxiety has not been found. Both physiological and overt behavioral measures have been used, but they do not show the degree of correlation or agreement that would permit a well-defined conceptual dimension to emerge.

As with experimental neurosis, a wide variety of behaviors has been observed in studies of anxiety conditioning, and the specific behaviors that occur are related to specific environmental circumstances. Thus, in various situations, experimenters have observed most if not all the behaviors taken as signs of experimental neurosis, including general motor excitement, escape and avoidance of fear-associated stimuli, restlessness, disappearance of adaptive behavior, inability to perform previously learned discriminations, cardiac and respiratory disturbances, hyperirritability, eliminative disturbance, and unusual social behavior such as self-isolation or aggressiveness. All these behaviors, in humans, can represent signs of neurosis or anxiety. Thus, it appears reasonable to narrow the focus of research on experimental neurosis to behaviors that are found to result from situations productive of anxiety and to study the specific behaviors observed with more attention to the particular environmental circumstances that produce and sustain them. In fact, a trend toward analysis of specific behaviors appears to exist in current experimental work.

The establishment of fear reactions in animals has been studied extensively (Church, 1963; Solomon, 1964). A typical procedure is to follow a neutral stimulus with an aversive one, such as electric shock, and to observe the behavior that comes to be associated with the neutral stimulus under specific conditions. Use of shock is a simple way to induce anxiety, although, as Kessen and Mandler (1961) have noted, aversions can be acquired in the absence of pain, as was noted in the work with experimental neurosis. This view is also in agreement with clinical observations with humans.

Hebb's definition of neurosis, previously quoted, can be applied as well to specific fears or anxieties. Research with animals indicates that under well-controlled laboratory conditions, the observed responses to fear-producing situations are lawfully related to the associated environmental circumstances, among which are the stimuli associated with the aversive stimulation and the potential consequences of fear-mediated behaviors. Fears in animals and humans may be observed to fairly specific stimuli, such as snakes or heights, or to less definable situations, such as interpersonal threats. The investigation of such behaviors, carried out for both humans and animals, should show whether the functional processes involved are similar.

Although much work has been done on acquisition of fears in animals, research using humans is very limited. Watson and Rayner (1920) reported an early attempt to produce a fear reaction in a 9-month-old boy. They presented a white rat to the child just prior to a loud, frightening sound. The child acquired fear of the rat over a number of trials. Fear was expressed in crying and crawling away when the rat was presented, and in other behavior. Transfer was observed to a fur coat, a rabbit, a dog, and somewhat to cotton wool. Test of these reactions at the age of 1 year showed them to have survived the interval but apparently with decreased intensity. There were no data concerning possible exposure to similar stimuli in the interval.

Hebb's criteria for neurosis, which may be applied also to a conditioned fear reaction, are partly met in this study. The persistence of the reaction was tested only up to a few months. Some degree of generalization of the response was shown. The reaction is clearly undesirable (if not, perhaps, in the child's view) and had emotional components different from those of his pretraining reaction.

A number of studies have been done to condition anxietylike responses in humans other than children. Conditioning is usually assessed using physiological indicators, such as heart rate or GSR. Conditioned responses are readily obtained in standard conditioning situations, but in adults they do not obviously follow the same functional laws as they do in animals. Grings (1965) and Zeaman and Smith (1965) have reviewed some of this work. Factors that may be labeled *perceptual* and *cognitive* complicate the experimental situations. For example, conditioning appears highly discriminated, so that an acquired response is greatly attenuated or missing in situations unlike those in which conditioning occurred. Even in the laboratory setting, convincing instructions that the aversive stimulus has been discontinued, or the actual removal of shock electrodes, lead to immediate defusing of the conditioned stimulus as elicitor of a reaction. Also, conditioninglike responses can be created simply by instructing the subject that a given stimulus may be followed by shock, when no shock has been given. These facts obviously do not fit the conditioning models derived from animal learning. However, humans typically differ from experimental animals in that they come to the laboratory with an already learned repertoire of highly discriminated responses to the stimuli present there, including knowledge of the likely behavior of experimenters and the possibilities for delivery of aversive stimulation from laboratory apparatus, which thus do not have to be learned by direct experience in the situation. Thus, such data do not invalidate a learning model since they are not sufficiently elaborated, but they indicate that these models cannot be applied to human behavior in an a priori manner and that careful investigations of human-nonhuman differences are needed.

Perhaps the principal discrepancy between laboratory studies of conditioned fears in humans and the observations on fears that are seen in clinical practice is in the degree of generality of the behavior, that is, the variety of situations in which the fear may be observed. In laboratory studies subjects appear to discriminate rapidly between settings in which there is real danger (of shock or other unconditioned aversive stimulation) and very similar settings in which danger is absent. Although their reactions may be persistent under the former conditions, they disappear rapidly in the latter. This discrimination is not typical of human phobic reactions, which can be repeatedly evoked by stimuli that the victim recognizes as not realistically dangerous.

Some information about the development of more generalized phobialike aversive reactions in humans comes from research into therapeutic techniques. A major program to produce aversion to alcoholic beverages was conducted in the 1940s (Lemere & Voegtlin, 1950), during the course of which over 4,000 alcoholics were treated by aversive conditioning, with the smell and taste of alcohol as the conditioned stimulus and a powerful emetic, a mixture including emetine, as the unconditioned stimulus. Emetine produces nausea and vomiting a few minutes after administration, and preliminary signs of the reaction were such that exposure to the conditioned stimulus could be timed to precede the reaction. Precise timing was not possible but was apparently not necessary (Kamin, 1965). The principal data on the growth and generalization of aversion were the behavior of the alcoholics after treatment. Eighty-five percent of those treated were abstinent for at least 6 months.

No physiological or direct behavioral measures of the aversiveness of alcohol were taken, unfortunately, but verbal reports indicated that alcohol and sometimes other stimuli did in fact become aversive, so that thinking about drinking, seeing bottles of alcohol, etc., were repugnant. Thus a considerable degree of generalization of the conditioned fear, outside the laboratory, appears to have occurred in this work. However, it is uncertain that this generalization is of the sort observed in animal learning studies of responses to generalized stimuli, in view of the remarkable powers of discrimination between different settings that have been shown by human subjects in other studies, as discussed previously.

In a later study, Wallerstein (1957) repeated the Lemere and Voegtlin technique. After several days of conditioning he exposed fifty subjects to the smell and taste of alcohol in the conditioning chamber, with no drug administration. All cases apparently responded with either emesis or less severe signs of nausea. Again, no specific data were taken. Aversive stimulation as unpleasant as that used here is not generally usable with children or even normal adults, but pathological populations do offer research opportunities if therapeutic gain can be reasonably projected, although the well-controlled research that appears possible and desirable has not yet been done.

PATHOLOGICAL BEHAVIORS IN NONPSYCHOTIC CHILDREN

Although studies designed specifically to produce pathological behavior in humans are not numerous, many studies have attempted to demonstrate that it can be manipulated—either reduced or increased—by use of specific learning techniques. Such research is, of course, closely related to behavior-modification methods of psychotherapy, and most studies have had an intent to develop useful therapeutic methods. However, studies that attempted to control and measure the results of the procedures followed are of principal interest here. Useful research data concerning pathological behavior change, rather than therapeutic success, will be the criterion for selection.

Numerous studies have been made of the value of a simple conditioning technique for elimination of nocturnal enuresis. Mowrer and Mowrer (1938) analyzed this disturbance as a learning deficit and developed a simple device for treatment. A pad is placed under the child

in bed that will, when wet, activate an electric circuit to which a bell or buzzer or shock can be attached. The signal acts to terminate micturation and usually to waken the child. Treatment generally involves control by parents, under the direction of the therapist or experimenter. Lovibond (1964) and Jones (1960) reviewed studies testing variations of the device and provided complex analyses of the conditioning process involved, principally as involving classical conditioning and avoidance learning. The operations involved class the technique as punishment, when punishment is defined (e.g., by Azrin & Holz, 1966) as a procedure producing reduction of the future probability of a response as a result of stimulation contingent on the performance of the response.

Lovibond (1964) reviewed fifteen studies in which groups of enuretics were treated. Success rates in groups ran 33 to 100 percent for initial arrest of the behavior. Relapse rates ranged up to 45 percent under the various definitions given this term, but retreatment was generally successful at about the same rate as original treatment.

These studies did not use control groups or within-subject manipulations to investigate factors influencing the results of treatment. Werry and Cohrssen (1965) carried out a control-group study of hard-core cases from an enuresis clinic. Three groups were compared: twenty-seven subjects on a waiting list, twenty-one subjects given brief (six to eight sessions) therapy using suggestion and encouragement, and twenty-two subjects given conditioning treatment. The conditioning technique gave 50 percent improved and 30 percent cured, whereas the other two conditions left 70 percent of subjects unchanged. Conditioning was carried out entirely by parents, with only initial instructions from the therapist, so that the procedures actually followed were subject to inadequacies of implementation in the home to an extent greater than in most of the other studies that have been done. However, it is possible that individual differences in severity of the problem or presence of other pathological behaviors in the children gave a poorer prognosis for this sample of enuretics than for those in other studies that report higher cure rates. Werry and Cohrssen conjectured that hard-core enuretics were not common in previous studies, and the reports given of the kinds of subjects that have been treated leave room for uncertainty over this question.

A comparison among various treatment techniques, such as the one above, is helpful in evaluating the comparative therapeutic possibilities of the conditioning method but does not give much detailed insight into its operation since the groups compared differ on so many treatment variables—a flaw this study shares with other comparisons among diverse therapies.

The various demonstrations of elimination of enuresis using punishment support the view that enuresis represents a persistent failure to acquire or maintain acceptable operant control of the behavior. The data presently available appear to permit the conclusion that the use of mild punishment is highly effective, although the details of the operation of the technique are left obscure. For example, effectiveness of punishment with animals is known to depend on various environmental factors, including availability and adequacy of alternative behaviors. These may be relevant for treatment of enuretics.

Of greater importance, however, is the now fairly well-substantiated finding that development of new symptoms during treatment is uncommon. Successful treatment seems usually to be accompanied by an alleviation of other tensions in the client and the family. There is no published evidence at present to indicate that the danger of new maladaptive behaviors is at all serious. Thus these findings, while they do not contradict the common view that enuresis is symptomatic of some more profound character disorder, indicate that the suitability of direct treatment of the behavior need not depend on the solution of this question.

There are several studies of mild fearfulness in children. Various methods have been tried to eliminate fearful behavior toward specific situations. Some techniques that are available from animal studies, or are based on learning research, include:

1. Desensitization, in which the child is gradually exposed to the feared stimulus while in a state of relaxation or while eating, playing, or performing some other pleasurable or calming activity presumably antagonistic to anxiety (Lazarus & Abramovitz, 1962)

2. Vicarious desensitization, in which the child observes another person (model) fearlessly interacting with the feared object to an increasingly greater extent (Bandura, Grusec, & Menlove, 1967)

3. Gradual exposure with no attempt to produce behavior antagonistic to fear

4. Immediate prolonged unavoidable exposure to the feared object (flooding)

5. Operantly scheduled reward for gradual approach to the feared object or activity (Meyerson, Kerr, & Michael, 1967)

Two group studies will be considered first. Bandura, Grusec, and Menlove (1967) used a control-group design to investigate methods of eliminating fear of dogs in children whose behavior was typically not otherwise pathological. Four groups were compared. All children within a group met together for the treatment sessions. As a criterion measure, for each child actual approach to dogs was divided into fourteen steps and the groups were equated for average amount of approach on pretesting. Behavior change was measured by assessing each child's progress on the same fourteen steps after exposure to one of the several experimental conditions, in eight sessions.

In three of the four groups, subjects were

studied in a party atmosphere, set up for the occasion. In one of these groups and in the non-party group, a model was used who approached and played fearlessly with a dog kept in a small area near the group. Thus children observed the model, making gradual approaches to the dog over a period of eight sessions either in a party atmosphere (modeling-positive condition) or in a neutral setting (modeling-neutral). The degree to which subjects actually attended to the dog or model was not equated over these groups. In a second party group (exposure-positive), a dog was kept on a leash or in a pen nearby, but with no model. The last party group merely attended parties (positive context), with no dog or model present. Performance on posttest favored first the modeling-positive group and then the modeling-neutral. The other two did not differ significantly. That is, observing a model approach the dog appeared, on testing, to increase the extent of the children's own approach, but simply having a dog present during a party gave no advantage over no exposure.

An interpretation of this outcome is that vicarious desensitization operated in the first group (modeling-positive) more effectively than extinction alone or vicarious experience in a less relaxed context. Vicarious desensitization has no clear analogue in animal research, and the operations involved are best seen in research in imitation in children. The validity of the above interpretation depends on the extent to which other explanations can be eliminated. The degree of approach a child is willing to make to a dog is undoubtedly dependent on many factors other than fearfulness, and any of these might have been differentially manipulated in the different experimental conditions. Also, numerous differences among the experimental conditions could be conjectured, on the basis of the report given, that were not relevant to the variables of primary interest in the design.

Ritter (1968) used three groups of preadoles-cents to study techniques for eliminating fears of snakes. A twenty-nine-item test using actual graded approach to a snake was used to assess fear in both pre- and posttesting. Two 35-minute treatment sessions were used. One group (vicarious desensitization) observed the experimenter and a number of hired subjects pet a 4-foot snake in the far corner of the room in which the children sat. The models performed actions like those on the twenty-nine-item criterion test. The model's approach to the snake was not gradual, but the subjects were in a presumably neutral atmosphere, so that this group corresponds most closely to the modeling-neutral group in Bandura et al. rather than to a desensitization procedure, which should involve induction of some behavior incompatible with anxiety. In a second group (contact desensitization), the experimenter used physical contact between the experimenter and subjects, the bolder ones first, as a step to induce contact between the subjects and the snake. While the experimenter handled the snake, the subjects were urged to touch the experimenter. When subjects observed and touched the snake or watched others doing so, they received experimenter approval and support for further approaches. This group seems to be modeled on desensitization, using experimenter contact as a behavior incompatible with anxiety, but it also includes operant social rewards for approaches, some vicarious experiences, and instructions to approach the snake or experimenter. A third group, controls, was assessed only and was not contacted between test sessions. Results of posttesting, the day after treatment, showed that the contact-desensitization group made the greatest gains on the test. Eighty percent completed all steps. All differences between groups were significant. The control group showed very little change; the vicarious-desensitization group was intermediate. Fear ratings given for each completed step showed some change after the two sessions, but the decrease was not significantly greater for the experimental groups than for the controls, indicating that the changes in actual approach scores may have been influenced by factors other than fearfulness, such as change in the subject's desire to please the experimenter. However, the fear scale may not have been a reliable index of the presumed underlying state.

It is unfortunate that research such as the studies just reviewed have not analyzed in more detail the specific factors operating in these experimental situations. The problem lies partly in the use of the group-comparison experimental design. Different group conditions of therapy are not easily controlled so that two groups can be safely assumed to differ on only a single interesting variable (or small set of variables). The different experimental conditions studied vary along many dimensions, and some relevant variables, such as subject and experimenter relationship, will not be constant during the course of the sessions. Variables such as this last are also likely to be quite subtle and not easily measured.

Single experiments, of course, do not permit strong statements to be made about the generalizability to be expected for experimental conditions different from those actually observed. The procedures used above appear to be sufficiently straightforward to be replicated in important details, so that further, more analytical research is possible.

Meyerson, Kerr, and Michael (1967) report an unusual but straightforward method of eliminating fear of walking in a child with cerebral palsy. The boy, 7, would not walk unaided and may never have done so. Meyerson et al. offered rewards of tokens, exchangeable for toys, etc., for achievement of a series of approximations to the criterion behavior: unaided walking and falling. That is, at first, a token was given for scooting his chair across the room and pulling himself to a standing position at the experimenter's desk. More advanced steps followed. The boy played the game eagerly and demanded to be given new tasks for which he could earn tokens. Criterion behavior was achieved in four 20-minute sessions. The boy showed little of the emotionalism he had exhibited in previous training attempts.

The unusual feature of this approach is that a phobialike behavior was treated by an operant technique, with no attempt to deal with the emotional behavior presumably underlying the behavioral deficit. The use of the operant procedure permits frequent assessment of progress under the experimental conditions—a desirable feature not generally used in group-comparison research. Frequent measurement permits effects of different experimental conditions to be studied in the same child, although such manipulation was not done in this study.

As a result of studies such as those above, it has become a commonplace among practitioners of behavior-modification techniques that direct treatment of "symptoms" does not often result in development of serious new pathological behaviors. Cahoon (1968) discussed the question of symptomatic behavior from the behavioral viewpoint and gave several examples of situations in which behavioral treatment might produce new pathological behaviors. In a strict sense, for a behavior to be called a symptom, it should derive from some more basic pathological characteristic. Less strictly, any new pathological behavior that arises during treatment may be given the term. Some possibilities that might be expected on the basis of a behavioral model are:

1. If a behavior is a reaction to the presence or imminence of aversive stimulation and if, in a given instance, the behavior is prevented from occurring, then some other may arise to take its place, including avoidance, escape, aggression, and emotionality.

2. Treatment may add new behaviors to a client's repertoire directly. As an example, overaggressiveness may be learned by a client whose therapist attempts to train self-assertion if the client fails to master the more subtle modulations of assertive behavior. Such a behavior change could be called symptomatic only in the loose sense.

3. If a maladaptive behavior leading to reinforcement is eliminated, new (possibly maladaptive) learning may occur directed toward obtaining the reinforcement, or some previously acquired behavior may reappear. If the reinforcer is assumed to satisfy some need, then that need could be taken as a mediator for the new behavior, which would then be symptomatic in the strict sense.

4. A procedure designed to change the frequency of one response may result in changes in others also. Responses may be related in that similar cues or reinforcers maintain them or in that the occurrence of one blocks another, so that altering the frequency of one response may cause unexpected, undesirable changes elsewhere.

5. Since responses have consequences in the environment and expose the responder to new stimuli, changes in response patterns may lead to environmental alterations giving rise to new behavior. The reduction of patient and family tension following successful treatment of enuresis is an example.

Of the possibilities listed here, the development of new maladaptive behavior is probably most to be anticipated in treatment of behaviors such as fears, which are responses to aversive stimulation, or in treatment in which aversive stimulation is a part of the treatment procedure. However, learning models do not permit definitive predictions to be made about the frequency with which such substitute behavior will occur. Thus, if research reports do not often note such

symptoms, the finding does not present a paradox for behaviorism but simply marks an empirical phenomenon.

Buell, Stoddard, Harris, and Baer (1968) made careful measurements of a number of behaviors in a 3-year-old girl with an abnormally low rate of cooperative play and excessively babyish speech and behavior, in a nursey school. These and other behaviors were observed over several weeks, during which the girl's rate of play with playground equipment was being changed by use of social reinforcement and cuing. The intention of the study was to see whether the behavior change induced toward playground equipment would show effects in other areas of behavior. Play with equipment increased and declined markedly as reinforcement and cues were introduced for a time, then withdrawn for a few days, then introduced again, etc. None of the other behaviors showed changes corresponding to the experimentally produced changes in playground behavior, but several did show gradual shifts toward improvement over the course of the experiment. The data show no evidence that the induced changes in behavior had any undesirable consequences. However, the child's original problems were not seriously pathological.

Before presenting further studies of nonpsychotic children, it may be useful to preview one of the most important specific findings that has emerged from this research. This is that adult attention or withdrawal of attention, made contingent on a child's behavior, can have a powerful influence in many cases of pathological behavior. Most of the studies to follow have used attention as an independent variable. Both motor and emotional behaviors have been studied, and both "positive" and "punitive" attention have been used ("positive" and "punitive" express the purpose of the adults dispensing the attention, not the actual effect). One implication of these findings is that experimenters and therapists interacting with a patient are not best considered as "state" conditions in the patient's environment (e.g., as authoritarian in attitude or interpersonally attractive or warm and accepting) but that the classes of behaviors meant by these terms exert their influences on the child through moment-to-moment transactions and affect specific behaviors on which they may be made contingent.

Allen, Henke, Harris, Baer, and Reynolds (1967) studied a hyperactive but otherwise normal boy of 4 in a preschool class after casual observation before treatment had indicated no decrease in hyperactivity after 12 weeks in the school. The research procedure is readily adaptable to normal classroom teaching. It involves study of individual subjects rather than groups. The effects of different operations are tested sequentially, and the response to each is measured continually. The operations involve changes in teacher attention, with regard to its positive or negative quality and to the behaviors of the student on which it is made contingent.

The typical design, used here, requires collection of "base-rate" measures under specified conditions; then an experimental condition is introduced for a time, then varied, to check the effects of specific operations. The base-rate condition is usually that condition prevailing at the start of experimentation, but it may be any operationally describable condition.

In this study, careful observations were taken of hyperactive and task-relevant behaviors over several mornings, with no change from prior conditions. Then teacher attention (positive) was given contingent on continuous work on a single task for one minute, in an attempt to induce persistence at whatever task was undertaken. Attention was continued only so long as the boy continued with the school task. Task switching decreased by two-thirds in the first session and continued to decline over six sessions. Then the contingencies were reversed to check that positive attention contingent on performance

was the controlling variable. When task switching was reinforced, it doubled in the first day and increased over three sessions. Then attention was again made contingent on persistence, which quickly returned to the previously attained level and remained constant over 10 days. No data were provided for follow-up performance. This performance would be expected to depend on the conditions in effect after the end of the study, since the data indicate that task persistence was dependent on its social consequences.

Hart, Reynolds, Baer, Brawley, and Harris (1968) specifically studied both amount and distribution of attention in shaping cooperative play in a 5-year-old girl in a preschool class. An unusual amount of adult attention and approval given at random times, independent of the child's behavior, did not increase cooperative play with other children (the target behavior), but use of approval and attention contingent on such play was quite effective. The contingencies were altered several times to test that behavior depended on these variables, and the behavior showed quick adaptation to the changes, as in the previous study. The girl was not directly encouraged to engage in cooperative play; however, others were occasionally encouraged to interact with the subject. Thus effects of the combination of cues and instructions are confounded with contingent attention.

Disruptive classroom behaviors have been studied in several other reports. Careful data have been taken in several of these, e.g., Hall, Lund, and Jackson (1968), Thomas, Becker, and Armstrong (1968), Brown and Elliott (1965), and O'Leary and Becker (1967). The first three of these used teacher attention specifically to control and study disruptive behavior in classes of normal children. The children in the O'Leary and Becker study were described as emotionally disturbed. These studies indicate that positive teacher attention (praise, contact, smiles, etc.)

tends to produce increases in rates of the behaviors attended to, either studying or not studying. Ignoring these behaviors leads to a decrease in their rate.

The study of Thomas et al. shows careful division of attentive behaviors from the teacher into component acts and a similar division for disruptive behaviors from the children. Negative teacher attentions were of primary interest. Children were studied in their classroom. The teacher varied the amount and kind of attention given during regular class operation. The authors found that giving negative attentions contingent or unwanted behaviors, with very little positive attention, resulted in a great increase in these behaviors compared with the base-line condition, in which positive attentions for desired behavior predominated and little attention was given to undesired behavior. That is, when teacher attention was made contingent on disruptive acts, even negative attention increased, rather than decreased, their rate. This interesting finding, that disapproving comments do not always tend to suppress the behaviors they follow, was also noted by Browning (1967) in studying changes in rate of bragging behavior under various contingency conditions.

A possible explanation for the failure of contingent negative attention to suppress behavior may be found in the observations of Buehler, Patterson, and Furniss (1966) in an institution for delinquent girls. Ratings of ongoing behavior in the institution were taken for different categories of social reinforcement, including verbal and nonverbal interactions. Peer-peer and peer-staff interactions were both observed. Interaction categories were divided into positive and negative according to the judgment of the investigators. Results showed that peers reinforced each other positively for delinquent (institution-disapproved) behavior at rates far beyond that of the punishments administered by attendants for the same behaviors. Socially

conforming behavior was peer-reinforced negatively more often than positively. Adult and peer reinforcement systems thus acted, generally, in opposition. It may be that similar peer-reinforcement contingencies operate in classrooms of normal children in which the teacher provides a high rate of negative attention. O'Leary and Becker (1967) noted this possibility in working with a class of emotionally disturbed children, whose disruptive behavior they brought under control using token reinforcers for appropriate study behavior. Both individual children and the class as a whole were rewarded at intervals for gradually increasing periods of appropriate behavior.

In their study, Thomas et al. (1968) also commented on the possible influence of peer reinforcement, which they did not measure directly. The matter is important for interpretation of their data. In the absence of an understanding and investigation of peer reinforcement as a variable, the disapproving comments of the teacher appear to be positively reinforcing, as seems to be shown by the sensitivity of the criterion behaviors to changes in teacher disapproval. The validity of this interpretation can be defended only if there are no other variables that change in close correspondence with teacher attention. But in this study peer reinforcement may be such an auxiliary variable.

This problem is quite similar to that raised in connection with control-group research in psychotherapy, in which it was shown to be difficult to establish two conditions that differ only on known dimensions. The use of the single-subject design does not eliminate the difficulty. Replications under varied conditions are necessary to establish both the identity and the generality of those specific operations that produce observed effects.

Research using social reinforcement has not examined in detail the separate and combined effects of instructions, of contingent and noncontingent positive, neutral, or negative attention, and of the verbalizations and behaviors involved in this attention. Instructions appear to serve partly and perhaps primarily as cues as to what responses are to be reinforced. Research in use of instructions with adults indicates that the combination of contingent reinforcement with instructions should be more potent than either alone (Ayllon & Azrin, 1964). Exact specification of the nature of the attentive or instructional acts used is frequently difficult to determine from the published research reports. Detailed classifications of such behaviors, as attempted in the Thomas et al. and the Buehler et al. research, still need much investigation. Of course, considerable variability in the power of all these variables can be expected for different children and different circumstances.

However, research done so far, whatever its incompleteness, shows that a variety of behaviors can be successfully manipulated using social reinforcement. Other examples are Hart et al. (1964) on crying in preschoolers, Allen et al. (1964) on isolated playing and lack of peer interaction, Harris et al. (1964) on crawling in a regressive manner, and Johnston et al. (1966) on development of motor skills. None of these problems was severely pathological. No serious undesirable side effects were reported, although they were looked for. The principal variable appears to be contingent adult attention rather than specific instructions or total attention, although these effects were not separated for specific analysis.

More severe behavior problems have been studied using attention manipulation. Wolf, Birnbrauer, Williams, and Lawler (1965) used nonattending and candy rewards for undesired and desired behaviors (respectively) of a mentally retarded, brain-damaged girl in a token-economy classroom for retardates. The undesirable behaviors included frequent vomiting and such highly emotional behavior as tantrums and clothes tearing. These had previously been controlled by removing the girl from class—an unsatisfactory solution. For the experimental procedure the girl's undesirable behavior was ignored, insofar as possible, and candy was given for brief periods of appropriate behavior. The disturbed behavior disappeared over a 30-day period.

To test the effects of the contingencies, the original conditions were reestablished by providing teacher attention for early expressions of disturbance. The shift was intended to revive the emotional behaviors, but these did not recur. This result poses a problem for the interpretation of the manipulations of the study.

The failure to recapture the original behavior when the original contingencies were reintroduced casts doubt on the assumption that the experimental manipulation designated by the experimenters was actually responsible for the behavior change originally observed. Other factors that were not recognized may have operated in the setting. In work with humans in the classroom, the chances of interference from uncontrolled factors are much greater than in a controlled laboratory setting. Many of the cues and reinforcers available to the children are not well understood and cannot be easily held constant or assessed or described in this complex environment. Thus, the failure in this study to recapture the base-line behavior may indicate the irrelevance of the attention and candy in producing the effects observed; however, a plausible alternative is that the child found the token classroom itself reinforcing after the experimental contingencies had so changed her behavior as to give her the opportunity to learn to act effectively in the school environment. The new behaviors learned might then have produced sufficient reinforcement from the school so that the special social and tangible reinforcers were unnecessary. This possibility was mentioned but not further investigated in this study.

Gardner (1967) also used attention to control

severe emotional behavior, including tantrums, seizures, hair pulling, and head rolling, in a 10-year-old girl. This behavior was very disturbing to the parents, although the girl seemed relatively normal except during these outbursts. The experimenter instructed and supervised the parents, who apparently carried out the program he devised fairly rigorously. Attention was given for helping, happy behavior. Somatic complaints, the usual precursors of outbursts, were ignored. The overall level of positive attention was probably increased in this procedure. After a month, seizures and tantrums had disappeared and somatic complaints had been halved. After 26 weeks, parents were instructed to return to pretreatment conditions to test the effects of the attention manipulation. Complaints rose sharply, and a tantrum shortly occurred, so the treatment contingencies were reinstated, presumably permanently.

Some other studies using parents as the experimental agents have also been reported. Careful observations and data collection have been done in several. Examples are Hawkins et al. (1966) in treating an extremely brattish 4-year-old; O'Leary, O'Leary, and Becker (1967) in studying similar behavior in a seriously disturbed boy of 6; and Zeilberger, Sampen, and Sloane (1968); and Wahler et al. (1965). This last study was carried out in the laboratory. The others were done in the home. Positive attention, rewards, brief isolation, and verbal commands and instructions were all used in various combinations. These studies not only have reported successful control but give excellent guides for research techniques for further investigations, needed to separate variables in greater detail. All the children treated exhibited behaviors sufficiently extreme to qualify as seriously disturbed, if not psychotic. The elimination of the disturbed behaviors was not followed by new disturbances, insofar as the reports permit this question to be answered.

Results from studies such as those above, using single subjects or single-classroom designs, cannot be taken as conclusive evidence that the types of problems treated will generally be amenable to the manipulations that were found successful. The possibility exists that many or even most disturbed children with similar behaviors will not show great sensitivity to contingencies of adult attention or small tangible rewards. Research showing the power of these variables in a single individual does not elucidate the background factors that must exist before these variables can operate effectively. Such factors would derive from the child's history of adult interactions, which show great interchild variations. It seems likely, in single-subject research, that failures of experimental variables to control behavior will lead to early termination or modification of the research project more often than to publication of unsuccessful results, so that a count of published successes and failures is not representative of results that might be expected in wide applications.

However, given that the power of direct manipulation of the environment is demonstrated, adequate procedures for various existing circumstances should be obtainable through further research. Such research might concentrate on discovery of the variables in the child's environment or his performance repertoire that bear on the outcome to be expected from use of specific techniques. The results of such research would constitute a body of diagnostic procedures. In actual treatment the child's response to the treatment manipulations used gives such diagnostic information, but preliminary behavioral assessment is also feasible. If a chosen method does not have the intended effect or is producing unintended and undesired behavior changes, the use of immediate observation of the child's response makes possible detection of the discrepancy and selection of other treatment methods. It is on such direct observations of actual behavior changes, rather than on specialized and indirect assessment devices, that the behavior modifier will probably depend to determine what treatment is likely to produce the desired effects.

PSYCHOTIC BEHAVIOR

The most bizarre behavior patterns that can be observed in children are those usually diagnosed as schizophrenic or autistic. The diagnosis refers to interrelated patterns of behavior, whereas the studies to be reviewed here have been concerned with specific behaviors manifested by specific children. The emphasis on specific behaviors does not imply indifference to the child himself, however. It should be understood that many of the specific results reported are obtained from children in continuous treatment programs designed to bring about extensive changes in their behavior. It is perhaps some misunderstanding of this point that has led to criticism of operant work as leading to rigid, automatonlike behavior, as if the results obtained in a particular procedure were the limit that operant techniques could attain. In fact, there is rapid progress in development of training methods using operant techniques, and the potential usefulness of such training has not been reached.

Perhaps the most dramatic problem seen in seriously disturbed children is self-destructive behavior, including head banging, self-biting of hands or shoulders, and similar acts. Inability to control these behaviors makes most other forms of treatment impossible, since the child must be restrained for all but the brief periods when he can be given continous attention.

Lovaas, Freitag, Gold, and Kassorla (1965) report data on this problem from a 9-year-old schizophrenic girl. Self-destructiveness dated from her third year. She would bang her head and arms and pinch and slap herself. She had little appropriate verbal or social behavior.

Rocking and clapping to music, behaviors incompatible with self-punishment, were shaped using operant training. Reinforcement for these behaviors was withdrawn, introduced again, and then withdrawn again. This training in incompatible behavior produced a decrease in self-destructive acts, but when the incompatible behavior was not reinforced, self-destructive behavior gradually returned. Training in bar-pressing for candy showed a similar result when candy was discontinued. These data show the influence of environmental circumstances on self-destructive behaviors, which were greatly altered without use of restraints following rather simple procedures. A further investigation was then undertaken to discover whether social factors in the environment controlled self-destruction. It was found that when the experimenter completely ignored these acts, they decreased in frequency; but if they were followed by sympathetic comment, their rate increased. These results were found over numerous sessions in which these variables were repeatedly introduced and removed. Lovaas et al. interpreted these results as evidence that self-destructive behavior could be maintained by following its occurrences with social reinforcement, as was frequently seen to occur in the hospital setting. It was also noted that the child's behavior changed rapidly from session to session, following changes in the contingencies used, which indicated that the child was capable of observing the consequences of her self-destructive acts and using these consequences and other events as cues to increase or decrease their rate. That is, the behaviors were under fairly sensitive environmental control.

Lovaas later used electric shock to extinguish self-destructive behavior in two children (Bucher & Lovaas, 1968). Both had a history of at least five years of self-destructive behavior, which was severe at the time of treatment. They were kept in restraints during the day and would begin to injure themselves immediately upon being released. Extinction was tried first, with one subject. He was left without restraints, and no attention was given to his behavior, for 90-minute sessions. His rate dropped from 3,000 acts per hour in the first session to 15 in the eighth. Extinction appears thus to be successful but impractical, even for this boy, who was considered a "careful" hitter. A brief, potent electric shock was then introduced, contingent on occurrence of a self-destructive act. Punishment was then given twelve times over fifteen sessions, but not for every occurrence of the punishable act. The rate dropped to zero and stayed there over eight sessions.

Two further facts of interest were shown. First, the boy quickly formed a discrimination between the experimenter, who delivered shock, and other persons, who did not, and regulated self-destructive acts accordingly. This seems remarkable in a child whose ability to discriminate or even notice persons appeared very poor to a casual observer. If such discriminations were frequent in behavior-modification work, it should be expected than any child whose pathological behavior had been brought under control in a specific experimental setting would continue to manifest his usual behavior outside, where the reinforcers that had previously maintained it would continue to operate. Fortunately, this extreme discrimination is not always observed, for reasons that are not often clear. Also, in many cases, changes can be made in the contingencies experienced by the child outside the laboratory as well as inside by extending the experimental procedure to the wider environment. In the ward setting, staff personnel can be trained in proper methods of interaction with the self-destructive child, so that his behavior is not positively reinforced on the ward.

The second finding of interest in this study— in the work with the second child, a girl— concerns the relation between self-destructive behav-iors and crying and eye-avoidance of adults. Both behaviors were recorded through most sessions. It was found that all these behaviors rose and fell together. Since all were undesirable and no new undesirable consequences were seen, this phenomenon resulted in more widespread improvement in behavior than had been directly intended. Tate and Baroff (1966) also reported such behavior change following suppression of self-destructive behavior. They observed greater accessibility to adaptive interactions with adults: more smiling, talking, attending, etc.

The use of electric shock as punishment for undesired behavior in children is quite unusual. These studies show that self-destructive behavior may be modified quickly and lastingly by use of shock. For children who show a high rate of self-destructive acts or who may inflict serious damage on themselves, this technique can produce quick elimination and so seems uniquely effective in this respect. In the studies cited, no undesirable side effects of shock were seen, at least beyond the period of shock use, and in fact decrease in self-punitiveness seemed to open the way for new, more positive modes of interaction with the environment.

A very common behavior among psychotic children is repetitive gross motor activity, such as rocking and waving hands and arms in a stereotyped manner. Some children appear to engage in such behavior most of their waking hours. The behavior does not appear to be maintained by adult attention, although, like self-punitive behavior, it is accompanied by lack of responsiveness to the environment. Lovaas, Schaeffer, and Simmons (1965) report two cases (identical twins) treated using brief electric shock. When shock was made contingent on the onset of repetitive behavior, the behavior was suppressed from the first session. It did not recur in further sessions (in some of which shock was used for other purposes) for 10 months. This program was concurrent with two other uses of shock for these children, which will also be described. These uses involved study of methods for building social behavior, which was designed to make the children more responsive to social controls.

The twins were judged to have acquired no responsiveness to symbolic prohibitions from adults. The word "no" had no visible effects in pretesting. Also they did not look at or touch adults or respond to the request "Come here." To shape these behaviors, shock was delivered to the feet through a floor grid. Shock was made contingent on failure to respond to the verbal request "come here," which was accompanied at first by beckoning gestures and by a second experimenter shoving the child toward the first. Both subjects quickly acquired the response and soon came to display signs of pleasure in performing the avoidance response of running to, hugging, and kissing the experimenter. These behaviors continued during extinction (no-shock) sessions over ten months. It is reasonable to infer that the adults in this study had acquired a socially positive value to the subjects, under certain conditions, through their association with relief from shock. Shock, used in this manner, did not result in an increase in visible anxiety, maladaptive behavior, or withdrawal from adults.

Also, in the shock sessions, the word "no" was always paired with shock use, and this word was later demonstrated to have power to suppress an ongoing operant response (bar-pressing for candy), indicating that it had acquired anxiety-evoking properties, as was desired.

Some other effects were also tested after the preceding training had been completed. In a room quite different from the experimental room, raters unfamiliar with the program rated several aspects of each child's behavior in sessions in which the raters interacted "casually" with the children. They rated dependency on adults, responsiveness, affection seeking, pathological behaviors, anxiety, and others. There

were two conditions. In one, the child was given a brief noncontingent shock just prior to the interactions (as a "reminder" of the experimental sessions). In the other condition, shock was not given. Differences between the two conditions showed small increases in the direction of improvement for the sessions with shock use in all ratings but a "happiness-contentment" scale.

Another test of the power that persons had acquired as positive reinforcers used rate of lever-pressing as a measure. It had been previously found that the twins would press for candies, but this behavior extinguished when a 5-second view of an adult was presented through a window. After training using shock, as described above, in which the adult was associated with relief from shock, the twins' rate of lever-pressing for a view of the adult rose abruptly. However, the magnitude of the effect decreased over time, indicating that no permanent symbolic value of the experimenter's face had been transferred to the lever-pressing situation.

Risley (1968), in an extensive single-subject study, used shock to suppress inappropriate aggressive and climbing behavior in an autistic girl after several other techniques had not succeeded. Suppression was accompanied by increases in eye contact with the experimenter. No increase in undesirable behavior was seen. Shock did not suppress eating behavior or lead to observable anxiety, emotionality, or avoidance of the experimenter. Risley also found fast discriminations between shocked and unshocked conditions, in that the girl's behavior was virtually unchanged outside the experimental situation until shock was applied there also. The presence or absence of the experimenter was also quickly detected.

Food has also been used with autistic children to establish persons as symbolic reinforcers (Lovaas, Freitag, Kinder, Rubenstein, Schaeffer, & Simmons, 1966). At first the word "good" was given following a bit of food, but the word later showed no reinforcing effects. Then these authors tried to obtain this effect by making the cue more noticeable, since failure to respond to stimulation is common in autistics. To obtain food, two subjects were required to approach an adult when the adult performed a particular action: saying "good" or patting the child on the back. Thus the child could not fail to notice the cue if he learned to obtain reinforcement. Both subjects then learned a bar-press response to obtain the verbal cue, indicating that it had acquired reinforcing value. Cues maintained their effectiveness in the bar-press situation so long as they continued to be intermittently associated with food delivery.

Lovaas et al. considered this an analogue of common child-raising practices, in which parents and certain cues they emit continue to be positively reinforcing through their association with primary reinforcers, which parents occasionally deliver contingent on the cues and on certain responses from their children.

Study of early learning in normal children has shown the importance of the development of speech and imitative skills for the mastery of complex patterns of social and intellectual behavior. Neither of these skills is commonly available to schizophrenic children, who do not attend to, understand, or use speech to a practically useful extent. Once such a child has learned to use adult behavior as cues for his own, however, the adult may use this control to train further appropriate behaviors, including speech and imitation. Metz (1965), Lovaas, Berberich, Perloff, and Schaeffer (1966), Risley and Wolf (1967), and Lovaas, Freitas, Guilani, Nelson, and Whalen (1967) have presented data gathered from studying methods for training these behaviors. Speech imitation is already available in some of these children, who occasionally mimic what they hear. Direct reinforcement for repeating the experimenter's words was used by Risley and Wolf (1967). Initially they shaped

the desired vocalization by giving reinforcement for approximate copies, until more precise reproduction could be achieved. When reliable imitation of various words was obtained, an appropriate object or picture was paired with the experimenter's presentation of each word and the verbal component of the stimulus was gradually removed, so that the child was naming rather than imitating. The training process was found to be positively accelerated; that is, new verbal imitations and transfers to objects were learned at an increasing rate. Later, phrases to describe simple wants and situations were taught, so that the child began to acquire some verbal control and verbally expressed comprehension of his environment.

Risley and Wolf (1967) and Lovaas et al. (1966) both showed the importance of the contingent positive reinforcement in this training. Omission of reinforcement or of its contingent delivery had deleterious effects on the training that had already been achieved. The complexity of the training situation and the several stages through which the child must be moved make possible a large variety of different training techniques, whose relative effectiveness has only begun to be examined.

DISCUSSION AND SUMMARY

The preceding review permits two general conclusions about the value of learning models in research with behavior problems of children. The first is that these models have led to the development of quite effective techniques for controlling and reducing such behavior for a wide variety of problems. The data show clearly that pathological behavior can be effectively influenced through direct manipulation of the contingencies of the environment in which it occurs. There is no indication that direct treatment methods leave a serious residue of untouched emotional conflicts, unreconstructed personality inadequacies, or substituted symptomatic behavior.

Much of the research reported here has been collected only within the past few years, and for the most part the techniques that are now available for therapy were developed quite recently, so that application of these methods is not yet widespread. However, data on the treatment of enuresis using conditioning have been available since the 1930s; but in spite of a heavy preponderance of favorable reports, the technique has been little used. Thus, although research using learning models appears to have produced some valuable findings, it has not evoked a corresponding degree of application. It remains to be seen if the methods studied in more recent research will make their way into the repertoire of standard therapeutic techniques.

The second conclusion to be drawn from this review is that the designs used in research reported in these studies are useful methods of investigation of pathological behavior problems. The two designs discussed were the comparison-group design and the single-subject design. In a sense, this conclusion should precede the first one mentioned, since it is the careful use of these designs that makes possible the analysis of pathological behavior as presented here. These research methods are standard throughout psychological research, although they have not been frequently used in research in nonbehavioral therapies. (Client-centered therapy is the notable exception.) For example, the use of the single-subject design with controlled stimulation, frequent and careful observations of behavior, and programmed changes in treatment variables is almost unique to research using learning models. The typical clinical case report, even in a detailed presentation, is not representative of these designs since adequate measurement, control, and manipulation of variables have been rare in this literature.

Neither of these designs is without flaws. The group-comparison design is inefficient for the study of different experimental conditions in that it typically obtains only a small amount of data from each subject. In research in psychotherapy or in manipulation of pathological behavior, the published reports using this design are often too incomplete to permit replication, although this is partly a result of the types of therapy typically studied. Replication of a dynamically oriented therapy or a "no-treatment" condition is especially difficult because of the nonoperational nature of the treatment variables described in these conditions. Also, the different groups included are usually given treatment conditions that differ in variables other than those of interest to the experimenter, so that crucial group differences in treatment may be unsuspected and so unreported. Group comparisons appear to have been more frequently used to compare different schools of therapy rather than to test variables or techniques for manipulating pathological behavior, although there are some exceptions, including, in addition to those already discussed, Rachman (1965), Lomont and Edwards (1967), and Turner and Young (1966).

The single-subject design, on the other hand, is highly efficient in that considerable data are collected from each subject. Experimental variables are often fairly clearly defined in operational terms, so that replications can be done fairly exactly. But any single study or small set of studies leaves the breadth of applicability of the technique uncertain, since many background factors, which may be important for the observed effects, will be left unexplored by the manipulations that are actually used. Such factors could involve unnoticed variables that change concomitantly with the primary experimental manipulation or individual differences among persons, such as are of concern in traditional therapy. Group research is not free from this last difficulty, as can be seen by surveying the many groups of enuretics that have been treated. It is still possible to conjecture, as do Werry and Cohrssen (1965), that patients typical of those seen at enurectic clinics have not often been included in these groups, in spite of numerous statements in these studies to the contrary.

Thus neither of the two types of designs is able to give final and unchallengeable answers for the problems that confront behavior-modification research. However, the two designs complement each other in their uses. The single-subject design seems better as a tool for the functional analysis of effective variables, and the comparison-group design seems better to demonstrate the generality of particular techniques.

Neither of the two conclusions reached here has gained any great degree of acceptance among workers most directly concerned with the psychopathology of children. The research designs for the manipulation of behavior have been little used, and the resulting information has not led to extensive changes in current therapeutic practices. The behavior-modification approach continues to represent a minority view.

The principal reasons for this lack of general acceptance in spite of remarkable successes in investigation of behavioral manipulations may involve the disparity between the conceptual systems used in research in learning, on the one hand, and traditional dynamic viewpoints, on the other. This disparity makes it appear to supporters of dynamic models that learning research neglects certain crucial variables. The dynamic emphasis is on intrapsychic events, often to the neglect of environmental controls, whereas learning models emphasize these latter variables. Also, hypothesis verification in the study of traditional therapeutic methods is based not on research of the type that has been reviewed in this paper but on reasoning within the framework of a theoretical model, augmented by close observation of individuals or groups in treatment but without the degree of manipulation and control the single-subject and group designs require.

It appears that these methods of hypothesis formation and testing are widely considered to be sufficiently fruitful to have produced a basis for suspicion or rejection of the learning models and their data. Thus reported data from learning models are largely unpersuasive to advocates of the traditional views. Instead, there is distrust of the adequacy of the behavioral data being produced and of the genuine replicability or validity of the reported outcomes. In the absence of a competing body of research data, there is an exaggerated dependence on theory, authority, and personal experience.

Against this attitude, one can only repeat a frequently reiterated caution, that the data and treatment techniques available from learning research should be taken seriously and should be treated to close and adequate inspection on empirical grounds, as they deserve and as has been attempted here. The value of increasing our practical understanding of methods for changing pathological behavior is too great to be outweighed or retarded by theoretical preoccupations.

REFERENCES

Allen, K. E., Hart, B. M., Buell, J. S., Harris, F. R., & Wolf, M. M. Effects of social reinforcement on isolate behavior of a nursery school child. *Child Development,* 1964, **35,** 511–518.

Allen, K. E., Henke, L. B., Harris, F. R., Baer, D. M., & Reynolds, N. J. Control of hyperactivity by social reinforcement of attending behavior. *Journal of Educational Psychology,* 1967, **58,** 231–237.

Ayllon, T., & Azrin, N. H. Reinforcement and instructions with mental patients. *Journal of the Experimental Analysis of Behavior,* 1964, **7,** 327–331.

Azrin, N. H., & Holz, W. C. Punishment. In W. K. Honig (Ed.), *Operant behavior*. New York: Appleton Century Crofts, 1966.

Bandura, A., Grusec, J. E., & Menlove, F. L. Vicarious extinction of avoidance behavior. *Journal of Personality and Social Psychology,* 1967, **5,** 16–23.

Bijou, S. W. A functional analysis of retarded development. In N. R. Ellis (Ed.), *International review of mental retardation.* Vol. 1. New York: Academic, 1966.

Broadhurst, P. Abnormal animal behavior. In H. J. Eysenck (Ed.), *Handbook of abnormal psychology.* New York: Basic Books, 1961.

Brown, P., & Elliott, R. Control of aggression in nursery school children. *Journal of Experimental Child Psychology,* 1965, **2,** 102–107.

Browning, R. M. A same-subject design for simultaneous comparison of three reinforcement contingencies. *Behavior Research and Therapy,* 1967, **5,** 237–243.

Bucher, B., & Lovaas, O. I. Use of aversive stimulation in behavior modification. In M. R. Jones (Ed.), *Miami symposium on the prediction of behavior, 1967: Aversive stimulation.* Coral Gables, Fla.: University of Miami Press, 1968.

Buehler, R. E., Patterson, G. R., & Furniss, J. M. The reinforcement of behavior in institutional settings. *Behavior Research and Therapy,* 1966, **4,** 157–167.

Buell, J., Stoddard, P., Harris, F. R., & Baer, D. M. Collateral social development accompanying reinforcement of outdoor play in a preschool child. *Journal of Applied Behavior Analysis,* 1968, **1,** 167–174.

Cahoon, D. D. Symptom substitution and the

behavior therapies: A reappraisal. *Psychological Bulletin,* 1968, **69,** 149–156.

Church, R. M. The varied effects of punishment on behavior. *Psychological Review,* 1963, **70,** 369–402.

Dollard, J., & Miller, N. E. *Personality and psychotherapy.* New York: McGraw-Hill, 1950.

Ferster, C. B. Positive reinforcement and behavior deficits of autistic children. *Child Development,* 1961, **32,** 437–450.

Gantt, W. H. *Experimental basis for neurotic behavior: Origin and development of artificially produced disturbances of behavior in dogs.* New York: Hoeber-Harper, 1944.

Gardner, J. E. Behavior therapy treatment approach to a psychogenic seizure case. *Journal of Consulting Psychology,* 1967, **31,** 209–212.

Grings, W. W. Verbal-perceptual factors in the conditioning of autonomic responses. In W. F. Prokasy (Ed.), *Classical conditioning: A symposium.* New York: Appleton Century Crofts, 1965.

Hall, R. V., Lund, D., & Jackson, D. Effects of teacher attention on study behavior. *Journal of Applied Behavior Analysis,* 1968, **1,** 1–12.

Harris, R. R., Johnston, M. K., Kelley, C. S., & Wolf, M. M. Effects of positive social reinforcement on regressed crawling of a nursery school child. *Journal of Educational Psychology,* 1964, **55,** 35–41.

Hart, B. M., Allen, K. E., Buell, J. S., Harris, F. R., & Wolf, M. M. Effects of social reinforcement on operant crying. *Journal of Experimental Child Psychology,* 1964, **1,** 145–153.

Hart, B. M., Reynolds, N. J., Baer, I. M., Brawley, E. R., & Harris, F. R. Effects of contingent and non-contingent social reinforcement on the cooperative play of a preschool child. *Journal of Applied Behavior Analysis,* 1968, **1,** 73–78.

Hawkins, R. P., Peterson, R. F., Schweid, E., & Bijou, S. W. Behavior therapy in the home: Amelioration of problem parent-child relations with the parent in a therapeutic role. *Journal of Experimental Child Psychology,* 1966, **4,** 99–107.

Hebb, D. O. Spontaneous neurosis in chimpanzees: Theoretical relations with clinical and experimental phenomena. *Psychosomatic Medicine,* 1947, **9,** 3–16.

Johnston, M. K., Kelley, C. S., Harris, F. R., & Wolf, M. M. An application of reinforcement principles to development of motor skills of a young child. *Child Development,* 1966, **37,** 379–387.

Jones, H. G. The behavioral treatment of enuresis nocturna. In H. J. Eysenck (Ed.), *Behavior therapy and the neuroses.* New York: Pergamon, 1960.

Kamin, L. J. Temporal and intensity characteristics of the CS. In W. F. Prokasy (Ed.), *Classical conditioning: A symposium.* New York: Appleton Century Crofts, 1965.

Kessen, W., & Mandler, G. Anxiety, pain, and the inhibition of distress. *Psychological Review,* 1961, **68,** 396–404.

Lazarus, A. A., & Abramovitz, A. The use of "emotive imagery" in the treatment of children's phobias. *Journal of Mental Science,* 1962, **108,** 191–195.

Lemere, R., & Voegtlin, W. L. An evaluation of the aversion treatment of alcoholism. *Quarterly Journal of Studies on Alcohol,* 1950, **11,** 199–204.

Liddell, H. S. *Emotional hazards in animals and man.* Springfield, Ill.: Charles C Thomas, 1956.

Lomont, J. F., & Edwards, J. E. The role of relaxation in systematic desensitization. *Behavior Research and Therapy,* 1967, **5,** 11–26.

Lovaas, O. I., Berberich, J. P., Perloff, B. F., & Schaeffer, B. Acquisition of imitative speech in schizophrenic children. *Science,* 1966, **151,** 705–707.

Lovaas, O. I., Freitag, G., Gold, V. J., & Kassorla, I. C. Experimental studies in childhood schizophrenia: Analysis of self-destructive behavior. *Journal of Experimental Child Psychology,* 1965, **2,** 67–84.

Lovaas, O. I., Freitag, G., Kinder, M. I., Rubenstein, B. D., Schaeffer, B., & Simmons, J. Q. Establishment of social reinforcers in schizophrenic children using food. *Journal of Experimental Child Psychology,* 1966, **4,** 109–125.

Lovaas, O. I., Freitas, L., Guilani, B., Nelson, K., & Whalen, C. Building social and preschool behaviors in schizophrenic children through nonverbal imitation training. *Behavior Research and Therapy,* 1967, **5,** 171–181.

Lovaas, O. I., Schaeffer, B., & Simmons, J. Q. Experimental studies in childhood schizophrenia: Building social behavior in autistic children by use of electric shock. *Journal of Experimental Research in Personality,* 1965, **1,** 99–109.

Lovibond, S. H. *Conditioning and enuresis.* New York: Macmillan, 1964.

Masserman, J. H. *Behavior and neurosis: An experimental psychoanalytic approach to psychobiologic principles.* Chicago: University of Chicago Press, 1943.

Metz, J. R. Conditioning generalized imitation in autistic children. *Journal of Experimental Child Psychology,* 1965, **2,** 389–399.

Meyerson, L., Kerr, N., & Michael, J. L. Behavior modification in rehabilitation. In S. W. Bijou & D. M. Baer (Eds.), *Child development: Readings in experimental analysis.* New York: Appleton Century Crofts, 1967.

Mowrer, O. H., & Mowrer, W. M. Enuresis: A method for its study and treatment. *American Journal of Orthopsychiatry,* 1938, **8,** 436–459.

O'Leary, K. D., & Becker, W. C. Behavior modification of an adjustment class: A token reinforcement program. *Exceptional Children,* 1967, **33,** 637–642.

O'Leary, K. D., O'Leary, S., & Becker, W. C. Modification of a deviant sibling interaction pattern in the home. *Behavior Research and Therapy,* 1967, **5,** 113–120.

Pavlov, I. P. *Conditioned reflexes.* London: Oxford, 1927.

Rachman, S. Studies in desensitization. 1. The separate effects of relaxation and desensitization. *Behavior Research and Therapy,* 1965, **3,** 245–251.

Risley, T. R. The effects and side effects of punishing the autistic behaviors of a deviant child. *Journal of Applied Behavior Analysis,* 1968, **1,** 21–34.

Risley, T. R., & Wolf, M. M. Establishing functional speech in echolalic children. *Behavior Research and Therapy,* 1967, **5,** 73–88.

Ritter, B. The group desensitization of children's snake phobias using vicarious and contact desensitization procedures. *Behavior Research and Therapy,* 1968, **6,** 1–6.

Solomon, R. L. Punishment. *American Psychologist,* 1964, **19,** 239–253.

Tate, B. G., & Baroff, G. S. Aversive conditioning of self-injurious behavior in a psychotic boy. *Behavior Research and Therapy,* 1966, **4,** 281–287.

Thomas, D. R., Becker, W. C., & Armstong, M.

Production and elimination of disruptive classroom behavior by systematically varying teacher's behavior. *Journal of Applied Behavior Analysis,* 1968, **1,** 35–45.

Turner, R. K., & Young, G. C. CNS stimulant drugs and conditioning treatment of nocturnal enuresis: A long term followup study. *Behavior Research and Therapy,* 1966, **4,** 225–228.

Wahler, R. G., Winkel, G. H., Peterson, R. F., & Morrison, D. C. Mothers as behavior therapists for their own children. *Behavior Research and Therapy,* 1965, **3,** 113–124.

Wallerstein, R. S. *Hospital treatment of alcoholism.* New York: Basic Books, 1957.

Watson, J. B., & Rayner, R. Conditioned emotional reactions. *Journal of Experimental Psychology,* 1920, **3,** 1–4.

Werry, J. S., & Cohrssen, J. Enuresis—An etiologic and therapeutic study. *Journal of Pediatrics,* 1965, **67,** 423–431.

Wolf, M. M., Birnbrauer, J. S., Williams, T., & Lawler, J. A note on apparent extinction of the vomiting behavior of a retarded child. In L. P. Ullmann & L. J. Krasner (Eds.), *Case studies in behavior modification.* New York: Holt, 1965.

Wolpe, J. Experimental neuroses as learned behavior. *British Journal of Psychology,* 1952, **43,** 243–268.

Zeaman, D., & Smith, R. W. Review of some recent findings in human cardiac conditioning. In W. F. Prokasy (Ed.), *Classical conditioning: A symposium.* New York: Appleton Century Crofts, 1965.

Zeilberger, J., Sampen, S. E., & Sloane, H. N., Jr. Modification of a child's problem behaviors in the home with the mother as therapist. *Journal of Applied Behavior Analysis,* 1968, **1,** 47–53.

40 Psychoanalytic Theory and Related Approaches

Bernard F. Riess

Among the many defects for which psychoanalysis has been criticized since its inception, by far the most frequently mentioned is the low production of solid "research" by practitioners of this approach. In addition to the allegation of too little research, and sometimes given in the same sentence, is the reproach that psychoanalytic theories do not provide testable hypotheses. On another level, the analyst is blamed because he places his therapeutic relationship above the values of the "hard-nosed" researchers and will not tolerate experimental intrusions into his work.

In recent years these attacks from the laboratory people have been supported by a new argument, namely, that psychoanalysis is too long and too costly rather than too mystical. It seems easier to accept a short, nonmethodological, and nonconceptual mode of treatment than one longer and based, at least, on an underlying and explicit set of assumptions.

If the criticisms of psychoanalysis as a general approach to treatment are valid, they apply in even greater force to the specialty of child psychoanalysis. The amount of direct research in this area is minuscule if one uses conventional standards to measure the research methodology.

There are many reasons for the "deplorable" situation in both child and adult psychoanalysis. *Research* requires an attitude which in some respects is antagonistic to a fundamental assumption of all analytic therapy, namely, that the therapist maintain an interested, empathic, but nonjudgmental stance vis-à-vis his patient. The therapist-analyst is constantly *searching*, but his interests are not in *re*-searching with his patient, for he is convinced that no situation can be replicated on the same subject and that no two subjects can be adequately matched. Thus the sacred elements of "control" and "repeatability" seem to be beyond the realm of possibility. The distinction between "search" and "research" remains a formidable barrier to communication with the experimentalist. The research-motivated student must therefore fall back on analogic studies, investigations which present an "as if this were therapy" approach to people who act "as if they were patients" in the presence of the experimenter "as if he were the therapist."

Again, the analyst resists the intrusion of experimentally introduced variables into the treatment process because of concern for the relationship with the patient and for the goal of treatment, which is the increased efficiency of the patient. The distinction has been beautifully worded by Erikson (1940):

> But to learn the properties and the range of an instrument is one thing—to learn to use it unselfconsciously and firmly, another. It is good to be explicit for the sake of training; for the sake of therapy, it is necessary to act with intuitive regard for implied probabilities and possibilities. The scientific world wants to know why we are so sure to be on the right track; the patient only that we are sure.

Erikson's assertion, however, does not imply that experimental variables cannot be employed by the analyst. It has been repeatedly shown that experimental variations carefully introduced and explained to the patient do not disturb the relationship between the two participants but can be of help in sharpening the therapist's armamentarium.

On a much more fundamental level, we shall have to seek for the lack of really relevent analytic research in child psychopathology in the essence of psychoanalysis itself. The interest in childhood and adolescence, which started with Freud's case of *Phobia in a Five-year-old Boy,* or Little Hans, has been, for the most part, retrospective, and its goal postdictive. That is, the events of childhood were sought in order to clarify the current, ongoing neurosis and behavior disturbances of the *adult* patient. The literature of retrospection is tremendous, but little direct observation of children has been published by psychoanalysts. Gerald Pearson, in a recent volume on child psychoanalysis (1968), says:

> With adults the technique of psychoanalysis consists in the use by the patient of free association—which involves a slight regression away from secondary process thinking toward primary process thinking. Under the spell of this tentative regres-

sion, the derivatives of the unconscious begin to manifest themselves. The work of the analyst is directed largely toward removing the conscious and unconscious resistances to free association and the conscious and unconscious defenses against the underlying unconscious drives. The temporary and self-imposed regression toward primary process thinking is combated by the patient because it threatens the organization of the ego. Through his need to get well or to understand his unconscious, the normal and the psychoneurotic adult with the help of his analyst can resolutely defy this threat and eventually achieve the rewards of so doing.

Psychoanalysis, therefore, as a method of treatment, is directed to the psychoneuroses and to certain of the borderline conditions in which the ego is moderately developed.

When he [the student of psychoanalysis] studies the psychoanalysis of children and adolescents, he finds that the technical situation is very different. From the beginning development of the child, there is a constant attempt to replace primary process thinking by the use of the secondary process and each step in this struggle produces a dearly won victory. Piaget has shown that there is a difference—a gradual developmental process—in the type of thinking up to seven years of age, from seven to twelve, and from twelve on. Zilboorg has expressed the opinion that these three stages represent the gradual triumph of the secondary process over the primary process. As each step forward in the struggle between the two types of thinking represents the development of a new phase in ego development and in ego mastery, the child holds on dearly to the new powers of his ego and is very loath to give them up. The closer he is to his new acquisition, the more he dreads losing it. Children, therefore, will not use free association.

For all children, therefore, a technical substitute for free association has to be found, and this is found largely in undirected play and by the use of technical measures which are not parameters—to use Eissler's term for the modifications of psychoanalytic technique required in the treatment of many borderline and psychotic cases—but which furnish the essence of the technique of the psychoanalysis of children and adolescents.

This lengthy quotation is necessary because it points to several issues relevant to research. In the first place, it emphasizes the role of developmental psychology, the orderly sequence of stages, which is believed to characterize the evolution of adult behavior. All research in child psychoanalysis is based on the hypothesis that staged or phased change is the basis for the determination of normality and hence deviations from it. Second, the quotation puts ego operations in the forefront of inquiry. From this it follows that data essential for the child psychoanalyst can and must come from the field of child psychology, which has as its special bailiwick the study of the reality conceptions of the developing organism.

Erik Erikson, in 1940, in a report to the American Psychoanalytic Association, tried to differentiate between the psychotherapy and the psychoanalysis of children. He stated that the core of child psychoanalysis consists of:

> 1) The systematic investigation of:
>
>   a) unconscious, or as yet unverbalized, pathogenic associations between certain facts, fantasies and affects;
>
>   b) defense mechanisms developed or rigidified in the attempt to deal with these associations.
>
> 2) The systematic, selective communication to the child of the results of such investigation.
>
> 3) The systematic check of the therapeutic situation, which must continue, until there is evidence that the child's ego mastery has become more adequate for his age and he can be expected not only to weather his next maturational crisis, but also to utilize his potentialities to reasonable advantage. [Erikson, pp. 371–372]

Esman (1965) makes the same point in stating:

> Thus it is apparent that, whatever the modality of therapy in question and irrespective of theoretical divergences and fashions of technique, child therapy and psychoanalysis are unseparably linked in their development and their influence. Their foundations both rest, ultimately, on the rock of

developmental evaluation and accurate, flexible application of rational interventions into the pathological developmental process.

Research, therefore, with children as with adult patients in psychoanalysis falls into several somewhat overlapping fields. First, and pragmatically important, is the question of whether analysis works. This leads to the field of outcome research. The difficulties in this type of investigation have been dealt with, for adults, in many publications. Briefly stated, outcome studies do not satisfy research requirements because (1) they usually lack adequately standarized initial values, or base lines; (2) they lack agreed-upon and independent criteria of change; and (3) they omit comparisons with no-treatment or differently treated groups of comparable subjects. All these defects attributed to adult psychoanalysis inhere in research on the psychoanalytic treatment of children. In addition, there is an almost unsolvable problem, that of differentiation between changes, gains or loses, arising from normal maturation and those allegedly produced by therapy.

The second area is that of diagnostic studies of the child. For the therapist, this is not merely a labeling process but one which should help determine the course of therapy. The psychoanalyst, unlike the early Rogerian or client-centered therapist, is convinced that diagnosis is essential in the determination of the most effective mode of approach to the child's difficulties. Current research has pointedly emphasized the need to differentiate among emotional, perceptual, and brain-damage factors in order to select appropriate therapies.

It has also become increasingly apparent that diagnosis of the child patient must take into account the milieu in which he develops. Although the totality of research data counterindicates the validity of such general labels as *schizogenic family,* family diagnostic techniques throw much light on the source of symptoms—the identifications and the pattern of child-rearing against which to view the symptoms presented by the patient.

Most studies, however, have dealt with the third area, that of process research. This is a general term which covers such discrete phenomena as the interaction of child and therapist, the "transference and countertransference" effects, play as a projection of personality and psychopathology, and most frequently, identification as the mechanism by means of which the child differentiates or fails to differentiate himself from the objects and *personae* of his world.

Historically, process investigations in child psychoanalysis have originated in a desire to validate the findings from the recalled or reinterpreted data of the adult patient. Freud masterfully reconstructed the psychological life of the child from work with adults, and his followers have been concerned ever since with validating these observations. However, recently, cross-validating techniques have evolved in which the primary data are derived from the *in vivo* observations of the child in treatment.

Originally, the focus of these studies was on the factors relating to the occurrence of the symptom, its presence or absence as a function of therapy. Currently, Neubauer (1968, pp. 39–40) writes as follows:

> Just as the adult's health may be judged from his ability to continue functioning, so we may say that the child's health is to be judged by his ability to continue his development: Thus, when we assess a child, we will not deal with the conflict or the pathology only in relation to his psychic structure—superego, ego, id—or to his past history (the "genetic" approach) as it has led to his present adaptation, but will also view the clinical findings in terms of their relevance to the future outcome.

Thus the finger is put on the weak link in analytic child therapy, namely, the comparison of the stage of development reached by the patient with what is known of the "normal" child's developmental behavior. How old the problem is may be seen in a quotation from Hartmann (1964), dated 1950:

> It appears to me desirable to note clearly the difference between [these] two possibilities: (1) the case in which phase-specific symptoms are mainly determined by what happened in earlier stages; and (2) the case in which both the vulnerability in question and its main determinants are specific of the phase in which they occur. This may help us to distinguish more clearly the specific features of a given phase from its genetic determinants; it may help us to differentiate more clearly the element of genetic continuity from the element of phase specificity. It should also prevent us from describing what is actually a specific disposition of a later phase as characteristic of its genetic antecedents, as is widely done in some analytic writings; the interpretation of very early object relations in terms of specific features of the oedipal phase, or of early prohibiting functions of the ego in terms specific of the super-ego being cases in point. [Hartmann, chap. 6]

Another, and not unimportant, research area is that of determining criteria for the selection of child psychoanalytic patients. It is important in this context to recognize that psychoanalysts of all schools agree on certain differentials which isolate analysis from nonanalytic psychotherapy. Psychoanalysis directs its therapeutic armament at two aspects of personality. It tries to make the id drives and their derivatives conscious, so that the conscious part of the ego will be able to know and deal with them. The task here is for the ego to learn to control impulses and so to strengthen itself. Second, the superego controls must be affected, generally in the direction of releasing the ego to deal with reality without guilt. Hence cases best suited for analysis are those in which the ego is relatively strong and the superego demanding and rigid. From the standpoint of age, it therefore follows that children in the latency period are easier and more productive patients than at earlier or later ages. However, this does not preclude younger youths or adolescents from psychoanalytic treatment.

Given these considerations, research is called for on the utility of the analytic approach for cases in which the diagnosis is not clear. Pearson (1968) devotes a worthwhile chapter to this problem. He makes the important distinction, so often neglected, that what is true of needs at latency is not necessarily so for the prelatent, pubertal, or postpubertal youngster. For the prelatency case, the best-validated and most useful criteria for analytic handling are those given by Anna Freud (1946). In latency, the complications as to choice of psychoanalysis or psychotherapy arise where the case is not one of clearly classic neurosis. Pearson (1968) specifies the following groups as in need of classic psychoanalysis: (1) those who show inhibitions in ego functions or who show marked ego restrictions—withdrawal, depression, limited range of interests and behaviors are positive indices; (2) children who show time-specific psychosexual regression such as the return to thumb-sucking, bed-wetting, temper tantrums; (3) cases of cross-sexual role wishes or actions, i.e., the boy who consistently wants to be a girl or acts like one; (4) antisocial children whose behavior is caused by the need for punishment because of conscious or unconscious superego guilt; (5) conversion syndromists who have ties, stuttering, and other physical symptoms with regression; (6) those with specific perversions.

If the considerations presented in this long introduction have validity, they point to the conclusion that scientifically satisfactory research in the psychoanalysis of children is limited in quantity and quality. However, if one expands the chapter heading to include research which is of importance and of practical value to the practitioner in child psychoanalysis, then a large

reservoir of material becomes available. The data have been accumulated by researchers in child development, in social psychology, and in mental-health clinics. The balance of this chapter will therefore deal with a few studies in each of several areas of concern to child analysts rather than try to cover the whole of the tremendous output of the many disciplines investigating childhood pathology.

OUTCOME AND LONGITUDINAL STUDIES

It is only recently that attempts have been made to follow up cases of adults treated in orthodox psychoanalysis to assay posttreatment change. The same kind of investigation, limited to psychoanalytic treatment, has yet to be done for children. However, we have some important and revealing longitudinal studies of the relationships between youthful conditions and adult behavior. Most of the longitudinal studies have attempted merely to see what relationships, if any, exist between initial personality and that of the adult. Some studies have tried to determine what disturbances in adults are foreshadowed by what can be derived from a study of the child. Both kinds of investigations can lead to much valuable material for the psychoanalyst.

For the period of infancy, an article by Orlansky (1949) on the relationship of infancy to adult personality gives a very thorough survey of all the relevant research in the first half of this century. Orlansky finds that the balance of the evidence is in favor of the primary effect of the constitution and the specific culture of the infant in determining adult personality as contrasted to the then prevalent conception of the Freudian position. The author also finds that the data fit a Horneyian and Frommian framework better than a Freudian one. As we shall see, neither Sigmund nor Anna Freud denied the primacy of "constitutional" factors but rather saw these as basic to the effect of nurturance on the infant. Nor were the early psychoanalysts pessimistic about the modifiability of behavior after the early years of life. Hartmann et al. (1946) had this to say about modifiability: "The basic nature of the personality and the basic functional interrelationship of the system of the ego and super-ego are fixed to some extent by the age of six, but after this age the child does not stop growing and developing, and growth and development modify existing structure." Thus constitutional and environmental factors are admittedly relevant to the dynamics of personality. What then can be said about the relationship of childhood disorder to adult disorder? If certain types of pathology in childhood are predictive of adult disturbance, then we can apply the criteria for child availability to classical analysis to these types and so operate in a preventive role.

Eisenberg (1960) summarizes thusly:

> Although it is generally assumed that emotional illnesses in childhood are precursors of psychiatric maladjustments in later life, it is somewhat disconcerting to learn that clear, scientific evidence has, until recently, been quite limited.
>
> Long-term studies of children diagnosed as psychiatrically ill have been few until the past decade. There are indications that the likelihood of psychiatric disability in adult life for disturbed children depends on the type of childhood disorder, certain illnesses showing a grave outlook and others a high rate of remission.
>
> Morris and coworkers [1954] found that children diagnosed as schizoid (shy and withdrawn) in an outpatient clinic did surprisingly well when re-evaluated ten years later; this suggests that implicit cultural standards on the part of clinicians may have led to a confusion of normal introversion with morbid withdrawal. Studies of schizophrenic children at Bellevue indicate that only about one-quarter achieve adjustment. A follow-up of autistic children revealed an over-all recovery rate in the same range. In this group, as in other studies, 50 percent of the children with useful speech by the age of 5 achieved at least a marginal community adjustment as contrasted with a rate of less than five percent for the non-speaking children.

O'Neal (1958) and his co-workers have reported on a thirty-year follow-up of children formerly patients at a St. Louis child-guidance clinic. In comparison with a control group selected for good adjustment, the clinic patients showed significantly greater disturbance as adults. Here again, the types of childhood pathology varied in their predictions for adult disturbance. Children were classified as neurotic, delinquent, and nondelinquent with aggressive antisocial behavior. Of these three groups, the neurotics contributed least to adult pathology, the delinquents provided the most sociopathic adults, and the "nondelinquents" the greatest number of adult psychotics. Among the questions raised by these data are these: Did the therapy in the clinic contribute to the differential nature of the results? Since classical analysis rarely works with aggressive antisocial youngsters because of the deficiency in ego strength, what kinds of treatment should be given to the third group cited in the study? This is particularly important since the individuals studied by O'Neal and his collaborators had been seen in a child-guidance clinic where the psychoanalytic method as such was not used. However, the same type of approach employed by these workers can and should be tried in a frankly psychoanalytic setting.

For a more recent survey of longitudinal studies of normal child development, Kagan's article (1964) is valuable. He contrasts the findings of the major time-extended investigations of children with a view to determining what areas of normal behavior can be predicted from a knowledge of the earlier history of the child. These studies provide a base line against which the clinician can come to a decision as to whether a certain behavioral item is to be expected at the time of its appearance and thus can determine the existence of pathology.

One of the most ambitious follow-up projects is that of Ricks and collaborators. They are using the total past and present case load of the Judge Baker Child Guidance Clinic in Boston in order to see how many of the children seen and treated at the clinic show up in adult treatment facilities, what changes there are between initial and adult diagnoses, and what the various childhood diagnoses contribute to adult pathology. The full evaluation of Ricks' research must await its final publication. Computer processing of this mass of information has delayed the summation of his efforts.

In summary of this section, it is clear that longitudinal studies of the long-range effects of psychoanalytic therapy are wanting and badly needed. Research with nonanalytic procedures has indicated the existence of differential results for different presenting pictures. From a preventive mental-health point of view, early decision as to intervention depends first on what types of disturbance are susceptible to what kinds of approaches. All we know at present is that certain symptom combinations show persistent effects later on in life. Zax and associates (1968) have studied the relationship of diagnosed disturbance in first-graders to their status upon reexamination in seventh grade. Twenty-three originally labeled moderately to severely maladjusted and forty-three not so designated youngsters were compared in the seventh grade. School marks, teachers' judgments, and SRA achievement tests were all inferior, and significantly so, for the older group. Thus, as Zax points out, early identification of maladjustment is possible and potentially profitable. What kind of therapy might prevent or ameliorate the disturbance is unfortunately not dealt with by the authors.

CHILD REARING

It is obvious from the whole body of writings in child psychoanalysis that the traumata for abnormal development and the stimuli for healthy adaptation arise from within the bed of family upbringing of children. One of the best summaries of the multifaceted analytic theorizing about child rearing is the volume by Winnicott (1965). Research, on the other hand, has been the province of the nonanalysts. *Mental Health of Children,* published by the National Institute of Mental Health (1965), lists studies under its auspices which have researched the area. Many of the investigations mentioned have not yet reached the stage of publication, hence the absence of complete citation.

One group of investigators (Mussen, P. H.) has identified two parental child-rearing practices associated with certain attributes of preschool children. The first is the degree to which parents control the child's activities and promote parental standards. The second is the degree to which the parent displays warmth and involvement in caretaking functions. It was found that parents who displayed a high degree of both of these characteristics were more likely to produce assertive, self-confident children who could establish friendly relationships with their peers. Children whose parents exerted a moderate degree of control but displayed little involvement with them were lacking in self-confidence and socialized to a lesser degree with their peers. Parents who exerted little control over their children, but were essentially warm in their relations with them, had children who were impulsive and lacking in self-sufficiency, but sociable.

Another investigator (Rosen, B. C.) found that achievement motivation was most likely to be high among boys who had been exposed to training both in achievement and in independence. The data indicated that a boy needs more independence training from his father than from his mother. A strong, authoritarian father will often overwhelm and crush his son, destroying his achievement motive in the process.

The same investigator is currently testing these generalizations in Brazil, a society whose institutions are more authoritarian in structure than ours. Preliminary findings indicate that the achievement motivation of Brazilian boys is lower than American boys of roughly comparable social class. The investigator attributes this reduced achievement motivation to the authoritarian pattern of family life in Brazil.

Theories on the relationships between treatment in early childhood and later personality differences are being tested by a research team (Whiting, J. W.) against information systematically collected in six parts of the world where families have different ways of life and different theories and methods of training their children. As a result of the work to date, these investigators now believe that self-control is not the single, unitary trait they at first assumed, and that while direct, conscious, and planned training is important in its development, the indirect, unplanned, and unintended ways in which it is developed—or sometimes overdeveloped to a crippling degree—are also extremely important.

That child-rearing patterns do have long-term effects on the child's personality has been demonstrated in a 30-year study (Crandall, V. J.) supported in part by NIMH. This study found that behavior displayed during the age period 3 to 6 is a relatively good predictor of behavior during early adulthood. Such personality characteristics as passive withdrawal from stressful situations, dependency on family, the ease with which anger is aroused, and intellectual achievement were relatively constant from the early school years through adulthood.

The scientists who conducted this investigation also studied the role the mother plays in shaping personality characteristics. They selected four traits that mothers displayed in relation to their children and related these traits to the children's later behavior as adults. A protective, affectionate mother who was deeply involved in helping her child had boys who excelled in intellectual activity. Independent, self-reliant sons frequently had mothers who were rather restrictive and insisted on rigid standards and rules. But a carping and critical mother often suppressed achievement striving in her sons. A girl's reaction to such a mother was more frequently the opposite—she became an independent, intellectually striving adult. The mother who demanded accelerated achievement from her child produced both boys and girls who displayed a high level of achievement and success as adults. The investigators concluded that the mother's behavior not only exerts a dominant and permanent influence on personality but possibly on intelligence as well. [National Institute of Mental Health, 1965, pp. 12–17]

The literature on the relationship between personality and child-rearing practices of parents is tremendous and has been extensively dealt with in Hoffman and Hoffman (1964). No attempt will be made in this chapter to summarize the material since it will be treated in other parts of this volume.

MATERNAL DEPRIVATION

Psychoanalytic writers have always insisted on the traumatic effects of maternal deprivation on the child and on his later development. Studies have been numerous and of varying degrees of experimental exactitude. In one in which the author deals with the conceptual bases of maternal deprivation, the summary explicates this.

Beres and Obers (1950) were among the early analysts to pay attention to maternal deprivation. They make a strong case for the modifiability of the effects of early infantile experience. Early institutionalization was found to cause distortions in psychic structure, immature ego, deficient superego development. But by the age of adolescence, over 50 percent of their thirty-seven cases were making favorable overt adjustment: "They (the adolescents) were working well whether in work situations or at school . . . and presented no overt disturbances in their behavior or in their relationship within their families or among friends."

It is apparent that the data on maternal deprivation are based on research of varying degrees of methodological rigor. Most of the data consist of descriptive clinical findings arrived at fortuitously rather than through planned research, and frequently the findings are based on retrospective analyses which have been narrowly directed toward verification of clinical hunches. [Yarrow, 1961]

Yarrow distinguishes four types of maternal deprivation: institutionalization, separation from the mother or mother substitute, multiple mothering (as in the *kibbutzim*), and distortions in the quality of mothering, e.g., rejection, overprotection. In most instances these types occur in combination rather than separately. According to Yarrow, there are few research reports on distortions of mothering, so that her review deals only with the first three kinds.

Institutionalization studies suffer from several methodological difficulties, such as the lack of specific data on early conditions of maternal care and inadequate information on the personality characteristics of the subjects. Psychoanalytic theorizing about the potential damage arising from institutional living emphasizes the lack of opportunity for adult identification and impaired ego development. Yarrow finds additional hypotheses in constitutional differences, varying sensitivities at different developmental stages, and amount and quality of sensory input.

Maternal separation, although never studied under pure conditions, appears clearly to operate as a stressor factor. Resultant behavior has been characterized in analytic terminology as anaclitic depression, mourning, and repression of the mother image. The quality and kind of mothering prior to separation play an important role in the development of symptomatology. Yarrow also points to the importance of the findings that not all children separated from their mother show impairment.

Multiple mothering takes place when continuity of the mother figure is complicated by the existence of other women who perform some of the nurturing tasks. Few studies have been made of this situation, and not one provides a crucial test of the hypotheses of the importance of the diffusion of the mother image.

The best critical appraisal of the research on maternal deprivation and its possible impact on children is found in a monograph by Casler (1961). This author evaluates all prior studies on the basis of their methodological rigor and internal consistencies. He makes the point that "full understanding of what goes on during maternal deprivation requires an acquaintance with several lines of research seemingly far removed from the central problem. . . . There are three major avenues by which the problems involved in maternal deprivation may be approached: the institutional, the cultural and the animal."

In dealing with studies of institutionalized children, Casler finds most of the research to be nondemonstrative of the common analytic hypothesis that mother love as an affect is, by its absence, productive of pathology. Instead he points to the fact that "neither Sigmund Freud nor Anna Freud consistently felt that the attachment to the mother was basic or 'instinctive.' "On the contrary, they seemed to prefer an explanation of the mother-child tie in terms of secondary conditioning. Since the mother accompanies so many of the infant's satisfying experiences, her very presence will eventually serve as a goal and a reinforcement. Note, however, that this rapprochement between psychoanalysis and learning theory is denied by Spitz, who suggests another—and highly interesting—connection: "When the child is gradually and progressively *deprived* of bodily closeness and skin contact, he *replaces* them by forming emotional ties."

Thus Casler suggests that the importance misplaced onto maternal love should be transferred to secondary gains supplied by the mother. These include skin contact and other sensory and perceptual stimuli. Among the symptoms studied in the research cited by Casler are such entities as intellectual retardation (IQ studies), social isolation, physical ill health, regurgitation, psychotic reactions, rhythmic rocking, excessive crying, paucity of smiling, apathy, and impairment of speech development.

From all three of the approaches mentioned initially, i.e., institutional, cultural, and animal, Casler comes to the following conclusions:

1. Emotional, physical, and intellectual malfunctioning is known to occur with frequency among children in many institutions.

2. Some authors have alleged that this malfunctioning is attributable to the deprivation of maternal love.

3. It is more likely, however, that deprivation of maternal love can have ill effects only after specific affective responsiveness has been achieved by the child (usually at about the age of 6 months). Ill effects found in children maternally deprived before this age probably have some other cause.

4. Evidence is accumulating, on both the human and the animal level, that this "other cause" is perceptual deprivation—the absolute or relative absence of tactile, vestibular, and other forms of stimulation.

5. Those forms of social stimulation necessary for proper language development, etc., can be provided within an institutional setting.

6. Recent neuroanatomical findings, especially those concerning the reticular formation, help to explain why perceptual stimulation is so important for normal development.

IDENTIFICATION

Erik Erikson has made the concept of identification central to any understanding of the growth and maturation of personality. Studies of the process whereby an individual finds out who he or she is are many and confusing. At the core of identification, however, is the determination of whether one is a boy or a girl. Sexual self-awareness is not simply the perceptual act of recognizing the presence or absence of a penis. Sexual identity involves both this organic element and also the elaboration of sexually expected behaviors and attitudes. From many researchers, it has been found that parental expectations and disciplinary methods, and not merely the genital structure, are also determinative of masculine and feminine behavior. One of the pioneering investigations in this field has been conducted by Sears, Rau, and Alpert (1965). Their conclusions are as follows:

1. Children of both sexes initially adopt feminine-maternal ways of behaving. The mechanisms involved may include either a modeling process, the efficiency of which is based on the responsiveness of the mother, or direct tuition, either intentional and verbalizable or not.

2. The boy develops a cognitive map of the male role at some point in his first three or four years and begins to shape his own behavior toward that role. To the extent that he has male models available (e.g., the father), the boy will be efficient in this shaping. The male characteristics are superimposed on, and replace, the female characteristics adopted earlier. There is no evidence in our data, however, that the father's responsiveness to his son's dependency supplications is a significant determinant of the development of masculinity.

3. Masculinity and femininity both appear to be more influenced by parental attitudes toward the control of sex and aggression than by any aspect of the availability or the behavior of models. Masculinity is associated with freedom of expression, and with parental non-punitiveness, whereas femininity is associated with the opposite. This principle holds for children of both sexes.

Several aspects of the data concerning boys were congruent with Freud's theory of defensive identification, but we have been unable to form a behavioral theory of their process comparable to that for primary identification, nor do the data appear to call for one. Since masculinity of the various qualities of conscience we measured proved to be unrelated to one another, there seems to be no pressing need for a single process to account for such diverse forms of behavior.

In summary, children's personalities seem to possess "something like" the kind of patterning of female-maternal qualities that we hypothesized in our theory of primary identification, but by age four this patterning in boys has all but broken down under the requirement that males model themselves after males. The anaclitic quality of the initial socialization process remains evident in girls at this age, but does not in boys. Whether the growth of masculinity in boys is largely a product of the male role map or of some process such as defensive identification will best be determined by research with boys just older and just younger than our boys and for both sexes the needed clarification of the primary identification process will require examination of the conditions and consequences of attachment and imitation in the first two years of life. We must know more about the mechanism itself before we can go much beyond our present study of its consequences.

In another study, other aspects of the same problem were considered by Biller (1968) in reference to boys only. Three aspects of sex role were considered: orientation or the perception of evaluation of the masculinity or femininity of the self, preference or attitudinal set toward socially deprived representations of sex role and adoption, and how masculine and/or feminine members of the child's milieu view his behavior. The role and behavior of the father were selected as hypothetically important antecedents of the child's behavior. These variables included availability, paternal dominance or power, maternal encouragement, intellectual level, and the physique of the child.

One hundred eighty-six boys in a North Carolina city were the study children, with a mean age of 5 years, 5 months. Questionnaires to the parents and some projective techniques

administered to the children yielded the data for the study. The results include the following:

> Father's absence seemed to inhibit orientation primarily, preference to a lesser extent and adoption not at all. . . . Father's behavior in the home appeared very important.
> Perceived father power was significantly related to all three aspects of masculine development, but in terms of strength of relationship, the order was orientation, preference and adoption. . . . The results suggest that the father's behavior (including the father's interaction with the mother) is very important in the development of orientation but decreasingly so for preference and adoption. A high level of maternal encouragement seems the most significant factor for preference development. In contrast, in addition to father power, mental age and physique appear to influence adoption. As one goes from orientation to preference to adoption, familial variables seem to have less influence and other variables increasingly seem to need to be taken into account.

GROUP THERAPY

Despite the widespread popularity of group therapy, there have been few attempts to research it, particularly with children. Case reports and impressionistic articles on transference, resistance, etc., are abundant and unimpressive to the searcher or researcher. Furthermore, psychoanalytic group therapy with children is almost entirely unreported. A search of the references shows only one study with any research aspect.

A research approach validated by outside observations and testing is described by Speers and Lansing (1965) in an exciting project at the outpatient service of the North Carolina University School of Medicine. The authors call this study one of testing the "feasibility and effectiveness of group therapy in the treatment of young psychotic children and of the collateral group therapy of their parents." Five children and their parents constituted the first group to be exposed to this regime. The present volume describes and summarizes 4 years of treatment. During the last 2 years, six additional children had had experience with the original group. It is important to note that all the youngsters were referred to the clinic as psychotic and were there diagnosed in the clinic after a careful work-up.

The hypothesis underlying the treatment was that "autism in psychotic children is a defensive attitude used to preserve infantile omnipotence. Thus, when autistic, the child omnipotently controls the 'distance' in the symbiosis, preventing engulfment of self from mother." Group analytic therapy first reduced the autistic defense and thereby enhanced the resulting panic. When the ragelike panic behavior was controlled, aggression was more goal-directed and the group became a reality because it served to protect the individual from himself. Play activity accompanied control and protection and also provided a measure of change as structured activities came to be tolerated. The parents also became part of the study and demonstrated the validity of the symbiotic construct. Children were found to act out the mothers' unconscious fantasies. The double bind of the mother's urging on the child her own fantasies and the verbal prohibitions against this was seen and used. This study is an excellent text in the analytic handling of severe childhood pathology and is replete with hypotheses to be followed in setting up comparable treatment situations. For instance, one might try to establish the validity of the double bind said by Wolberg (1968) to be productive of borderline states. Treatment of parents and borderline children, together with analytic interpretation of the simultaneous dos and donts of the mother, could be studies with regard to its preventive aspects.

CHILD PSYCHOANALYSIS AND PIAGET

The importance of phased understanding of child psychopathology has been repeatedly stressed in this chapter. Several attempts have

been made by analysts to work out a more complete description of the time order of the changes in behavior than that given by Freud. Thus Anna Freud, Marie Mahler, and Erik Erikson have all presented systematic sequences of normal development. It is now, however, becoming increasingly clear that any picture of child growth must take into account the brilliant and complex observations of Piaget and his school:

Since it deals with observations and theory concerning a major aspect of child development, it is relevant also to child psychiatry. Its importance lies, in the first place, in the hypothesis of an orderly succession of increasingly complex developmental events in the cognitive sphere and, secondly, in the fact that these events can be qualitatively described. Furthermore the scheme provides a framework for a bridge between the intellectual and motivational-emotional aspects of development, which on the whole have been treated separately in the study of children. The sequence of developmental steps gives an indication of what kinds of thinking may be expected of children at various age ranges. For example, although the two-year-old shows some capacity for recall or past events in his actions in play, he has not the necessary verbal structures for understanding a promise; the young child may be expected to be egocentric and animistic and unable to coordinate successive events in time or two aspects of a spatial situation; before the age of about 11 years concreteness in thinking may be expected.

At the level of theoretical analysis, it is possible to apply the concepts of assimilation and accommodation to affective phenomena. Piaget discusses the role of wishes, interests and the dominance of the subjective viewpoint in false reasoning in the pre-operational period, and considers this to be the nature of the child's thinking at this time, when he can achieve only to the period after the development of operational thinking, to cover instances in which the influence of motivational-emotional factors lead to a distortion of reality, when the available operational schemata necessary for correct inferences are not applied because of interference from subjective interests. These instances, for example, in cases of rationalization, could also be described in terms of an assimilation of reality which is distorted because there is little accommodation: the facts of reality are distorted to fit into the subject's beliefs when the latter are not altered to accommodate the facts.

These concepts can equally be applied to adaptation or maladaptation to social situations, i.e., to inter-personal relations, an aspect which is mentioned only briefly by Piaget in terms of "affective schemata" or ways of reacting to people. Adaptation to a social situation involves a balance between assimilation of the facts and accommodation to them. If one of the two is predominant, the action is maladaptive. When an individual attempts to use an established pattern of action, which has been learned in previous actual situations, in a situation where it is inappropriate, this might be described as excessive assimilation at the expense of accommodation, in that new patterns of behavior demanded by the situation are not developed because the individual refuses to accommodate his existing patterns. On the other hand the individual who changes with every wind that blows might be described as excessively accommodating without absorbing his experiences. [Flavell, 1963, pp. 40–42]

Wolff (1960) includes in his monograph on Piaget the following remarks about Piaget's importance for the psychoanalytic understand of the child:

Piaget's system is by far the richest reporting of theory and data on intellectual development that is or ever has been available in the field of child psychology. It includes the first and so far the only really detailed stage-analytic theory of intellectual development in existence.

Piaget's analysis of the object concept . . . provide[s] a solid anchor—a set of concrete reference data—for long-held and familiar speculations about the phenomenology of infancy, e.g., that the infant cannot differentiate between self and world.

In moving up the ladder from the infancy period . . . Piaget has succeeded remarkably well in conveying a general picture of the cognitive experience, dispositions, achievements, and limitations of the pre-schooler. It is a picture at once integrated and unitary, vivid and easy to grasp and retain, and large-

ly accurate when held up to the yardsticks of experimental evidence and everyday observation. Painted into this picture are the pre-schooler's cognitive egocentrism, his susceptibility to centration effects, his inability to deal with transformations as opposed to states. . . . Read what Erikson has to say about the affective and interpersonal aspects of the preoperational period and see how Piaget's analysis both complements and significantly adds to Erikson's account of how a sense of the "whole child" emerges more clearly in a stereoscopic integration of the two.

DIAGNOSIS

Earlier in this survey, the point was made that diagnosis was dependent on the criteria used to evaluate "normal" development. Thus, if one uses a Piagetian schema, intellectual aberration is viewed against Piaget's data on base lines. Within a more directly psychoanalytic setting, Neubauer has set up, in his agency, a system of child classification based on development. Group 1 consists of children in the normal range of development. Group 2 has those with transitional developmental disorders. In group 3 are children with disorders which inhibit growth, and finally, in group 4 are the children who show accelerated growth after a period of inhibition. What this classificatory scheme means is best described in Neubauer's own words (1968):

A clinical assessment of children in a community nursery school has revealed that the majority of these children are suffering from various emotional conflicts and disorders, and are thus outside the "norm." The clinical data are based on interviews with mothers and teachers, psychological tests, observation in the nursery, and individual interviews with the children. If we assembled the clinical findings according to the present diagnostic categories, most of the children would be diagnosed as suffering from a primary behavior disorder or reactive disorders, preneurotic or neurotic symptomatology. There were the usual conflicts in connection with body functions, such as sleep disorders, training difficulties, enuresis, speech disorders, and so forth. Many of the children have shown phobic manifestations or excessive compulsive conflicts; they have expressed insistence on ritualistic behavior or over-orderliness or messiness; there have been social conflicts in the area of isolation, over-control, and the like. These problems are all too well known.

When they are assessed in reference to the developmental progression of the child, however, we find that about half the children outside the normal range fall into the category of transitional disorders—which means either that the pathology is short lived, or that conflicts that appear in one phase of development are carried over into the next succeeding phases. In this way, strong fixations are avoided and progression permitted to take place—but this is, we must remember, progression with pathology. The rest of the children fall within the categories of more serious fixations, neurotic internalized conflicts, atypical disorders, and so forth.

Such findings are at first alarming, until we think of them in the light of what we know about children—namely, that they seem to suffer from more difficulties and problems than do adults, and particularly very young children; that they may have monosymptomatic pathology, which must be assessed separately; and finally, that the infantile neurosis is, after all, a normal condition. Freud's early finding as to the regularity of the infantile neurosis was, at that time, related to his findings on the oedipal conflict. During the last decade, it has become clear that children go into that phase of development with already existing conflicts that arose in earlier phases. Thus, one may extend Freud's formulation by saying that infantile disorders, including the infantile neurosis, are normally to be expected.

The question arises whether children with transitional disorders can overcome them in subsequent stages of development, and whether those transitional disorders that have a tendency to move into the category of permanent interference with development need therapeutic attention. We have as yet insufficient knowledge to be able to answer that question, in part because we are not too good at prediction, and in part because we still lack the criteria that would enable us to determine whether, in an individual child's succeeding developmental phases, it

is still possible to work toward the reorganization of the dynamic forces that have contributed to his present conflict, or whether that conflict has become, in effect, static and unmodifiable.

The clinical importance of this issue is clear, for its resolution will play a part in our decision as to the need for therapy. Today, some children may be in treatment too early, while others may have come to it too late, for we do not yet know how to make a clear decision in the matter of timing. Preventive intervention, if it is to be successful, will depend on surer timing, among other things. Intensive research and careful longitudinal studies of treated and non-treated children are needed, in order to assist us in finding some of the answers. A restatement of what constitutes normal development will surely be a significant by-product of such studies.

Nagera (1966) also stresses developmental diagnosis, based on a threefold ordering of the data. He divides disorders into (1) developmental interferences in which factors or persons in the child's environment fail to take the status of the child's ego and coping ability into account, (2) developmental conflicts experienced in varying amounts by every child, and (3) neurotic conflicts specified in orthodox terms as arising from the vicissitudes of id, ego, and superego.

Regardless of the semantic problem presented by such disparate systems as Anna Freud's, Neubauer's, and Nagera's, what is significant is the almost complete absence of modern techniques for evaluating complex systems. With modern computer processing, some diagnostic factors should emerge. In a precursor to such research, Collins et al. (1961) factor-analyzed the data on summary sheets for all children, except epileptics, psychotics, and severe retardates, in a psychiatric clinic. The data showed very small factor loadings. In other words, the children were a heterogeneous group. What factors then emerged were different for each sex and age level. For the 8- to 10-year group, each sex showed three factors. The boys' factors were rebelliousness, rootlessness, and anxiety. For girls, the factors were rebelliousness—this time, however, inclusive of the items specific for the boys' factor of rootlessness—social and scholastic failure, and anxiety. So here again, one finds the need for specificity about both stage of development and sex role or sex status. What is unique about Collins' study is the use of both computer techniques and factorial analysis in establishing clusters of items which build a diagnostic picture.

PLAY THERAPY

Ginott (1964), writing in a collection of articles on psychotherapy with children, finds it possible to summarize research in play therapy in a contribution of four pages and twenty-six references. Of these, most refer to analog research with adults. Lebo (1964), in the same volume, does a little better in discovering studies worth reporting. However, as far as practical assessment goes, the studies reported by Lebo answer few questions in an unambivalent fashion. His summary presents the present research status of play therapy in a succinct manner: "The greatest weakness of nondirective play therapy lies in this impetuous overlooking of the real need for a foundation in research. The most pressing need is for the employment of controls in play therapy." This statement is, indeed, characteristic not only of play therapy but of the whole of child psychoanalysis.

BODY IMAGE AND SELF-AWARENESS

This is the latest newcomer in the research popularity contest and comes with truly respectable documentation and theoretical underpinnings. Many of the research findings can be adequately fitted into the Freudian ego construct, a concept which emphasized the relationship between mental image and bodily sensation. To Freud (1927), the ego is "first and foremost a body ego; it is not merely a surface entity but is itself

the projection of a surface. . . . The ego is ultimately derived from bodily sensations, chiefly from those springing from the surface of the body." Fenichel (1945) writes:

> In the development of reality the conception of one's own body plays a very special role. At first there is only the perception of tension, that is, of an "inside" something. Later, with the awareness that an object exists to quiet this tension, we have an "outside" something. One's own body becomes something apart from the rest of the world. . . . The sum of the mental representations of the body and its organs, the so-called body-image, constitutes the idea of I and is of basic importance for the further formation of the ego.

It is superfluous here to point to the extent of bodily image involvement in the various stages of psychosexual development described in the psychoanalytic literature. Adler (1930) enriched his theories of organ inferiority with body-image references. Reich (1949) finds relationships between personality conflicts, muscle tonus, and the self-armoring of the patient.

If there is a large body of theoretical and case-history material to suggest the importance of the body in pathology, the research evidence is also accumulating. Fisher and Cleveland (1958) have carefully collected the research data to that date and added to it their own studies of what Fisher has called "barrier scores" on the Rorschach in relation to children's development. The chapter on sex differences in barrier scores among children is particularly rewarding because it again emphasizes the differentiating role played by age in setting up differential body images in girls and boys. These Rorschach findings are seen as congruent with studies of castration fears and Oedipal transferences. The authors cite Friedman's (1952) monograph, in which he finds sex and age differences in the responses to a variety of projective story- and picture-completion materials. Since the publication of this book by Fisher and Cleveland, there have been replications of the research data with little that is new or startling to report. However, the value of body image both in diagnosis and in treatment seems established.

One new dimension of body image may be mentioned in connection with the analytic treatment of children. Kestenberg, an analyst and movement specialist, in a series of papers (1965a, 1965b, 1967) has applied dance notation techniques to the study of children's movements. The observations have then been related to Anna Freud's developmental schedule.

SUMMARY

This chapter is a mixed grab-bag of research studies and critiques of research. If one conclusion can be lifted out of the bag, it is that much of analytic treatment, diagnosis, and study of childhood pathology is in desperate need of research. The absence of such investigation is not a disproof of the value of child psychoanalysis but a reflection of priorities in the demand for the skilled analysts' time. Where careful studies, such as those of the body-imagery school, have been made, they are apt to verify and enrich the analytic armamentarium. There is a vast storehouse of empirical and intuitive stimulation in the annual volumes of *The Psychoanalytic Study of the Child*. What is needed is the allocation of time, energy, and financial reward to psychoanalysts who are working with children and who want to sharpen their tools on the grindstone of research.

REFERENCES

Beres, D., & Obers, S. J. The effects of extreme deprivation in infancy on psychic structure in adolescence. Vol. 5. *The psychoanalytic study of the child.* New York: International Universities Press, 1950. Pp. 121–140.

Biller, H. B. A multi-aspect investigation of masculine development in kindergarten age boys. *Genetic Psychology Monographs,* 1968, **78,** 89–138.

Casler, L. Maternal deprivation: A critical review of the literature. *Monographs of the Society for Research in Child Development,* 1961, **26**(2), 1–52.

Collins, L. F., Maxwell, A. E., & Cameron, K. A factor analysis of some child psychiatric clinic data. *Journal of Mental Science,* 1961, **108,** 274ff.

Eisenberg, L. Emotionally disturbed children and youth. In J. Margolin (Ed.), *Children and youth in the 1960's.* White House Conference on Children and Youth. Washington, D.C.: U.S. Government Printing Office, 1960.

Erikson, E. H. Studies in the interpretation of play: I. Clinical observation of play disruption in children. *Genetic Psychology Monographs,* 1940, **22,** 557–671.

Esman, A. Treatment of personality disorders in children. In B. B. Wolman (Ed.), *Handbook of clinical psychology.* New York: McGraw-Hill, 1965.

Fenichel, O. *The psychoanalytic theory of neuroses.* New York: Norton, 1945.

Fisher, S., & Cleveland, S. *Body image and personality.* Princeton, N.J.: Van Nostrand, 1958.

Flavell, J. H. *The developmental psychology of Jean Piaget.* Princeton, N. J.: Van Nostrand, 1963.

Freud, A. *The psychoanalytic treatment of children.* London: Imago, 1946.

Freud, A. Special experiences of young children, particularly in times of social disturbance. In K. Soddy (Ed.), *Mental health and infant development.* Vol. I. New York: Basic Books, 1956.

Freud, S. *The ego and the id.* London: Hogarth, 1927.

Friedman, S. M. An empirical study of the castration and oedipal complexes. *Genetic Psychology Monographs,* 1952, **42,** 61–130.

Ginott, H. G. Research in play therapy. In M. Haworth (Ed.), *Child psychotherapy.* New York: Basic Books, 1964.

Hartmann, H. Psychoanalysis and developmental psychology. Vol. 5. *The psychoanalytic study of the child.* New York: International Universities Press, 1950. Pp. 7–18.

Hartmann, H. *Essays in ego psychology.* New York: International Universities Press, 1964.

Hartmann, H., Kris, E., & Lowenheim, R. M. Comment on the formation of psychic structure. Vol. 2. *The psychoanalytic study of the child.* New York: International Universities Press, 1946. Pp. 11–38.

Hoffman, M. L., & Hoffman, L. W. *Review of child development research.* New York: Russell Sage Foundation, 1964.

Kagan, J. American longitudinal research in psychological development. *Child Development,* 1964, **35,** 1–32.

Kestenberg, J. S. The role of movement patterns in development. I. Rhythm of movement. *Psychoanalytic Quarterly,* 1965, **34,** 1–36. (a)

Kestenberg, J. S. The role of movement patterns in development. II. Flow of tension and effort. *Psychoanalytic Quarterly,* 1965, **34,** 517–563. (b)

Kestenberg, J. S. The role of movement patterns in development. III. The control of shape. *Psychoanalytic Quarterly,* 1967, **36,** 356–409.

Lebo, D. The present status of research on non-directive play therapy. In M. Haworth (Ed.), *Child psychotherapy.* New York: Basic Books, 1964.

Morris, D. P., et al. Follow-up studies of shy, withdrawn children. *American Journal of Orthopsychiatry,* 1954, **24,** 743ff.

Nagera, H. *Early childhood disturbances, the infantile neurosis and the adult disturbances.* New York: International Universities Press, 1966.

National Institute of Mental Health. Mental health of children. *Publications of Health Service Bulletin,* 1965, No. 1396, 12–17.

Neubauer, P. Some issues in child therapy: The developmental treatment approach. In B. F. Riess (Ed.), *New directions in mental health.* New York: Grune & Stratton, 1968.

O'Neal, P. Childhood patterns predictive of adult schizophrenia. *American Journal of Psychiatry,* 1958, **115,** 385ff.

Orlansky, H. Infant care and personality. *Psychological Bulletin,* 1949, **46,** 1–48.

Pearson, G. H. J. (Ed.) *A handbook of child psychoanalysis.* New York: Basic Books, 1968.

Sears, R. R., Rau, L., & Alpert, R. *Identification and child rearing.* Stanford, Calif.: Stanford University Press, 1965.

Settlage, C. F. Psychoanalytic theory in relation to the nosology of childhood psychic disorders. *Journal of the American Psychoanalytic Association,* 1964, **12,** 776–801.

Speers, R. W., & Lansing, C. *Group Therapy in childhood psychosis.* Chapel Hill: University of North Carolina Press, 1965.

Winnicott, D. W. *The maturational processes and the facilitating environment.* New York: International Universities Press, 1965.

Wolberg, A. Patterns of interaction in families of borderline patients. In B. F. Reiss (Ed.), *New directions in mental health.* New York: Grune & Stratton, 1968.

Wolff, P. H. The developmental psychologies of Jean Piaget and psychoanalysis. *Psychological Issues,* 1960, **2,**(1, Whole No. 5).

Yarrow, L. J. Maternal deprivation. Toward an empirical and conceptual re-evaluation. *Psychological Bulletin,* 1961, **58,** 459–490.

Zax, M., Cowen, E. L., & Rappaport, J. Follow-up study of children identified early as emotionally disturbed. *Journal of Consulting and Clinical Psychology,* 1968, **32,** 369–374.

41 | Contributions of Biological and Organic Viewpoints

L. W. Sontag

The relative importance of the roles of biological constitution and environmental impact as determinants of behavior of individuals has been a controversial subject since the study of human behavior began to take form. This nature-nurture controversy has involved a variety of disciplines and has been reported on by unlimited numbers of scientists. Freud called attention to the importance of "constitution" as a determinant of the social adjustment of people. Years later, many disciples of Freud apparently forgot the emphasis he had placed upon constitution as one of the factors in determining human behavior. In the mid-1920s, a number of child-development institutions were established in the United States emphasizing the need for the study of *individual differences* in human beings, biological and behavioral, and the interrelation of the two. In his book *Free and Unequal,* Roger Williams (1953) emphasized constitution as a determinant of behavior. John B. Watson, on the other hand, deprecated the role of biological differences in the social-psychological behavior patterns human beings develop. By this time, however, it is extremely difficult for anyone to deny that there are many aspects of biological

function and constitution which do play roles as determinants of human behavior. It is becoming almost equally true that many aspects of social environment are agents in modifying biological functions.

The statement that biological function plays a role in behavior from the cradle to the grave is not enough. Actually, it plays a role from conception to the grave.

Dr. René Dubos (1968), member and professor of the Rockefeller Institute and a noted biochemist, has commented that until quite recently the custom was to regard the fetal and neonatal states as relatively uninvolved in the external environment, except for such instances as teratogenesis, overt infection, or other obvious threat. Subtle variations in the biological environment, factors germane to the environment of the mother, are now known to profoundly affect the growth, the development, and even the personality of the child.

This chapter will present some of the known relationships between biology and behavior and some of the mechanisms involved, as well as a discussion of biological factors currently being actively explored as possible behavioral determinants.

BIOLOGY OF THE FETAL PERIOD

In a research paper published in a 1934 issue of the *American Journal of Diseases of Children* (Sontag & Wallace, 1934), it was pointed out that the then marked apathy toward the possible role of fetal environment as a determinant of postnatal health and behavior did not constitute rational thinking. Current at that time among many members of the medical profession was an almost implicit assumption that there was no fetal concomitant of the life experiences of the mother during gestation. The term *psychosomatic* had come into being, and it expressed a recognition of the fact that in human beings emotion could adversely affect body function—e.g., in peptic ulcer, hypertension, blood sugar level, hyperthyroidism—and that many aspects of biological function were modified by emotional states. However, physicians generally disregarded the possibility that physiological changes of psychic origin in the host mother could, through placental interchange of humoral constituents, modify the biology and perhaps the behavior of the fetus. There was, then, a general tendency to consider birth as the introduction of the period in which environment might be assumed to be influencing the growth, development, and behavior of the human organism. It was with this background that we became interested in attempting to assess some of the parameters of the environment of the fetus, an interest which had previously been shared by a few and which, subsequently, has come to be shared by many others.

FETAL RESPONSES TO EXTERNAL AND MATERNAL STIMULI

Peiper (1925) found evidence that during the tenth lunar month of intrauterine development, the fetus is capable not only of perceiving certain sounds but also of responding to these auditory stimuli by sudden and convulsive movements. We (Sontag & Wallace, 1935a, 1936) studied the human fetus not only in terms of a motor response (sudden extensory movements of the arms and legs and arching of the back) but also in terms of changes in heart rate. The heart-rate response, usually a sharp acceleration, occurred within five to ten seconds of the application of the stimulus. Since the interval between stimulus and response was less than that required for the production, circulation, and placental transfer of the maternal humoral product to produce such a fetal response, we concluded that what we were dealing with was the Moro, or startle, response which can be elicited in the newborn. Peiper had called attention to the severity of the fetal movement felt by some women while listening to concerts. Forbes and Forbes (1927) described the case of a woman who, while attending a concert, experienced the sensation of great fetal activity every time the audience applauded. These reports might be interpreted as describing the same Moro response (fetal kick) as was presumed to be the basis of the recorded activity and heart-rate responses in our experiments. Whether or not such was the case was not clearly established. It was not clear whether the observations of these mothers were a description of a fetal startle reaction to a loud sound or a maternal psychosomatic response which modified fetal behavior through a biological mechanism, namely, placental interchange. Neither Peiper nor the Forbeses mentioned fetal heart rate. Peiper's and Forbes' reports again suggested the possibility that everyday events in the lives of pregnant women may, through mind-body relationships as a psychobiological mechanism, modify immediately the behavior of the fetus.

To explore this area of the possible modifications of fetal behavior as a result of induced psychosomatic changes in the mother, we (Sontag et al., 1968) designed an experiment in which mothers would be exposed for a predetermined period to music which they themselves had selected. Following a 15-minute control period, they listened to this music for a second 15-minute period, during which time their heart rate and that of their fetus was recorded and later translated into beats per minute in sequential 15-second periods. Analysis of the data revealed that the period of music produced a significant heart-rate change in the fetus and a less dramatic one in the mother. However, change in fetal heart rate required two full minutes after the introduction of the music stimulus to achieve its maximum level, in contrast to the almost instantaneous response of the fetus to the direct application of sound to the maternal abdomen in earlier experiments.

In the direct sound application described earlier, there was a marked startle reflex in the way of vigorous activity. No change in fetal activity was noted in the music experiment. These two findings suggest that the behavioral change of infant heart-rate acceleration was a somatic result of a psychosomatic mechanism of the host mother.

Much more marked changes in fetal behavior have been observed (Sontag, 1966) to result from severe emotional reactions of pregnant women (Ferreira, 1960; Turner, 1956) during the late months of pregnancy. The emotions (and their effects on the fetus) which we have had the opportunity to observe have been anguish and fear. In a group of women suffering severe emotional traumas during the last 6 weeks of pregnancy, the fetal heart rate was significantly above that measured on several occasions before the traumatic incident. Also, unlike the nontraumatic emotional stimulus in the music experiment, in these situations of emotional trauma there was a great accentuation of physical movement of the fetus. An example of the type of traumatic situation involved in producing changes in fetal heart rate and activity was the death of one woman's husband in an automobile accident one month before her child was born. A second example

was that of a woman whose husband suffered a psychotic break about 6 weeks before the delivery date, threatened to kill her, and forced her to seek refuge to avoid attack. Again, these emotionally induced fetal stimuli represent psychosomatic changes in the mother, expressed through humoral mechanisms and placental transfer as a biologically induced behavioral change.

In such instances of traumatic emotional experience in late pregnancy, there were measurable differences in the newborn infants and in their behavior for a number of months. Instances of colic, intolerance of formula, excessive crying, and hyperactivity were observed. They were squirming, crying infants, often with excessively red skin, and usually poor sleepers. It is perhaps unnecessary to add that the impact of such a behavioral pattern is, in turn, not conducive to an ideally loving and accepting state of mind on the part of the new mother.

Many years ago, we (Sontag & Wallace, 1935b) were able to demonstrate that the mother's smoking of a cigarette increased the rate of the fetal heartbeat. Recently, Hellman et al. (1961), using very heavy smokers as subjects, deprived his subjects of cigarettes for a 24-hour period before his experiment. He was able to show that fetal cardiac acceleration occurred in half his subjects when the mother was offered a cigarette and before she actually lit it. This work has a fascinating implication regarding the possible role of everyday living experiences in mother-child psychosomatic relationships.

In recent years a number of investigators have used animals in an attempt to assess the effects of various modifications of fetal environment. Ader and Conklin (1963) have demonstrated that pregnant rats fondled for ten minutes a day during pregnancy produced offspring which at maturity were less "neurotic" than were the offspring of continually caged mothers. Ader has also compared the degree of "neuroticism," as measured in the offspring of rat mothers fondled for several minutes a day during pregnancy, with that of mothers to whom electric shock had been administered daily in a situation where shock avoidance was impossible. Neuroticism in the offspring at 65 days, measured by the open-field test and by frequency of defecation, was significantly higher in the offspring of the shocked animals. Lieberman (1963) has mimicked emotional stress in mice by the injection of hydrocortisone, epinephrine, and norepinephrine and has produced "neurotic" mice. W. R. Thompson (1957) has demonstrated that the production of a conflictual situation, a "neurosis," in pregnant rats resulted in offspring which, at adolescence, showed differences in index of neurotic behavior defined in terms of open-field performance and frequency of urination and defecation.

BIRTH TRAUMA AND CASUALTIES OF PREGNANCY

Epidemiology, as a research tool in the study of the causation of mental defect and, to some degree, of mental illness, is one tool which has yielded some indirect information on the relationship of prenatal environment to postnatal behavior. Ali A. Kawi and Benjamin Pasamanick (1959) studied the pregnancy records of 372 white male children in Baltimore, all having reading disorders, as compared with histories of a control group. They established statistically that histories of what they called *casualties of pregnancy,* i.e., hypertension disease, bleeding before the third trimester, placentaprevia, premature separation of the placenta, were more common in those children in which reading disorders had been observed than in the control groups. They found also that epilepsy, mental deficiency, and behavioral disorders were more frequent in those cases in which casualties of pregnancy had occurred.

In 66 percent of 102 retarded children, D. H. Stott (1957) found that there had been undue stress during pregnancy, stresses frequently of an emotional nature, as compared with 30 percent of 450 controls. A. N. Antonov (1947) reports that children born during the seige of Leningrad in 1942 were significantly smaller and that the morbidity in this population was greater. His conclusion that the markedly restricted maternal nutrition during this period produced a prematurity which was the sole cause of the small birth weight is questionable. Others have found such reduced birth weight during periods of war-induced malnutrition but have considered reduced fetal calories as the cause. It is indeed unfortunate that Antonov made no study of the developmental patterns of behavior of the children born during the seige of Leningrad. Another factor, the marked increase in activity which we have found during maternal emotional disturbances, would also be expected to produce a lessened birth weight. Pasamanick and Knobloch (1966) have found that mental defect is more likely to result from pregnancies in which birth occurs during the winter months. They have attributed this phenomenon to the higher summer temperatures during the early period of gestation of the winter-born babies.

Analysts have repeatedly referred to the psychic trauma of birth, a phenomenon impossible to confirm with any objectivity. Nandor Fodor (1949) described in detail the analysts' concept of this psychic trauma and its presumed relationship to later thoughts and emotions. While firm evidence of the psychic trauma of birth is obviously impossible to obtain, it is of interest to note that growth-arrest scars, identifiable as having been laid down at birth, can be seen in up to 10 percent of the x-rays of 1- and 3-month-old infants (Garn et al., 1968). The scars occur in the tarsal round bones and in the distal end of the tibia—both rapidly growing areas at birth. It has not been possible to identify a single variable in the birth history of those infants with bone scars. Severe precipitous labor does tend to be associated with them, however, as does protein and vitamin malnutrition. Protracted labor, long only because of intermittent labor contractions, apparently does not cause scars. The scars are the same as those occurring during childhood from a severe illness or surgery. Their presence in some infants, resulting from the birth process, suggests that an experience severe enough to produce growth arrest might also have some psychic concomitants.

RELATIONSHIP OF FETAL ACTIVITY TO PRESCHOOL BEHAVIOR

It would be ideal if there existed a continuum of the study of the behavior of a group of human beings beginning with the fetus through the last three months of gestation and continuing through the neonatal period, the preschool years, and the years to adulthood. Ideally, such a study would include measures of fetal heart-rate lability-stability, fetal activity, and the response of both these functions to direct fetal stress (sound stimulation) and to maternal fetal stress (fatigue, maternal emotion, maternal illness, etc.). It would include information on the birth process and detailed measures of motor behavior, physical-physiological development, the development of perception and language, the learning of social organization, etc. Such a study would include intelligence, social interaction, specific skills, and a constellation of personality characteristics. Unfortunately, such a longitudinal study of this magnitude has never been done—and probably never will be. In attempting to relate the characteristics of fetal behavior to the developing pattern of postnatal behavior, we must, therefore, use our own limited longitudinal study and those of others for such segments of data at such ages as are available. From our studies we have observed the level of fetal activity (movement of the arms and legs) during the last two months of gestation as being predictive of certain aspects of social behavior at 2½ years of age (Sontag, 1963). Infants who had shown the higher levels of fetal activity

showed greater anxiety about peer aggression, more social apprehension, more reluctance to leave home for preschool sessions, and more reluctance to go to school. These statistical correlations were found in both the male and female groups but were higher among the males. A negative correlation existed between peer aggression and quick fetal movement in the male child which was not demonstrated in the females. Those children who had been more active fetuses, while not inactive at nursery school age, expressed their mobility in unaggressive ways, avoiding conflict when possible. Such observations and correlations do not, unfortunately, carry with them ready explanations as to the mechanisms of the relationships. One might speculate on the possibility that during fetal life "emotional stimuli" consist of a series of physiological stimuli, resulting in part from the mother's emotional changes, and that these stimuli have, at birth, left some impact on the infant psyche or behavior pattern, an impact which is a significant factor in early-childhood response to environment. In our studies of adult personality at Fels, we have found that the amount of social apprehension of nursery school children is predictive of the social apprehension in the same individuals at 20 to 25 years of age (Kagan & Moss, 1962).

CARDIAC VARIABILITY AS A BIOLOGICAL FACTOR

The variation in beat-by-beat (R-R) intervals is a relatively constant characteristic of an individual and has been shown to be replicable over long periods of time (Lacey & Lacey, 1962). The degree of this beat-by-beat variability, under resting conditions, is referred to as *cardiac lability-stability,* a physiological characteristic which has been shown to have a number of personality or behavioral correlates. Lacey, Kagan, Lacey, and Moss (1963) have found that in young adults the level of dependency material in interviews was much higher in cardiac labiles than in stabiles. Cardiac labile males were more reluctant to depend on love objects, had more conflicts over dependency, and exhibited more intense strivings for achievement. They showed more anxiety over erotic activity and more compulsive behavior; they vacillated with decisions and were more introspective. We have no glib explanation for these personality correlates of cardiac instability or why boys with a fluctuating heart rate showed more conflict over dependency, more compulsive personalities, and other characteristics mentioned. At this stage of our understanding we must accept the fact that certain biological characteristics of young people are most likely to be accompanied by a given constellation of behavioral or personality characteristics. Such findings bring into focus the question of what part of the incorporation of life experiences is a matter of the experiences themselves and what part is due to gene-determined or prenatally acquired physiological processes. It is interesting that in a small group the lability-stability of fetal heart rate was predictive of lability-stability of the same subjects as young adults. If this finding is confirmed, the character of the fetal heart rhythm would be predictive of certain aspects of adult personality (Sontag, 1963).

AUTONOMIC RESPONSES TO STRESS IN YOUNG ADULTS

There are interesting individual differences in the patterns of autonomic nervous system functioning in a variety of stress situations, such as the cold pressor test, the performance of mental arithmetic problems, flashing bright lights, loud noises, and other situations which have been described by Lacey et al. (1963) and Lacey (1967). Further research has shown that the role of the heart may be more complex than previously thought and that the cardiac response to situations which require an individual to perform mental work is an acceleration of the heart rate (Obrist, 1963; Steele & Koons, 1968). In those situations in which it is necessary to observe the environment carefully for information, the cardiac response is one of deceleration below resting levels. Thus, the individual differences in the cardiac response have become an area of increased research interest.

Kagan and the Laceys have found that there are also personality correlates—in this instance, differences in cognitive style or ways of thinking and perceiving—between the strong reactors and the weak. The following are a few examples: In a variety of picture-test situations, the strong cardiac reactors, or those with high heart-rate response, were prone to perceive situations imaginatively or as having affect. For example, when these subjects were shown, through tachistoscopic procedure, a picture of a man sitting at a desk writing, Kagan and Moss noted that they would comment not only on the fact that the man was writing or that he was a man or that he was sitting but, in addition, on whether the man looked sad or happy or angry. Shown a picture of a child drawing at a blackboard, they would comment that the child was happy or sad or was about to draw an elephant or a bear or a flower, not simply that it was a child. The nature of the perception was quite different both in affect and in imagination from that of the low cardiac reactors, who, under similar situations, saw only the child or the blackboard.

There appear to be a greater projection of the subject's emotions into the picture in the case of the high reactors and little or no projection on the part of the low reactors. Furthermore, personality assessment of another group of subjects has suggested a high degree of emotional and behavioral control in all kinds of situations on the part of low reactors, whereas the high reactors are more likely to act out their emotions. In other words, people with unstable cardiac rates are also unstable in their social behavior.

The word *psychosomatics* usually implies the

effect of emotions on body function. It is most commonly used in discussing various illnesses and dysfunctions. Allergies, many skin lesions, hypertension, peptic ulcer, large bowel dysfunction, etc., have generally been credited with a greater or lesser emotional factor in terms of etiology. Emotions, mediated through the autonomic nervous system, may cause dysfunction and sometimes gross pathology of organs. Much has been written describing the personality structure and the psychodynamics which are presumably responsible for such organ function—in other words, about the emotions most likely to express themselves organically. Since the dimensions of personality primarily involved are formed during infancy and early childhood, one of the most important aspects of psychosomatics, particularly in infancy and childhood, is the child's interaction with his parental environment and modification of that environment.

Few people are very much concerned about the psychodynamics of infantile eczema. They might well, however, be concerned with the way in which infantile eczema has changed the image of the infant love object in the eyes of the mother from one of a rewarding and reassuring evidence of her own charm and femininity to that of an unattractive creature in whom she finds little pleasure or pride. The psychosomatics of childhood (Sontag, 1946) may involve very heavily the manner in which the infant's body form, behavior pattern, and health modify his parental environment, which, in turn, immediately begins its modification of the developing infant personality (Bell, 1968). In short, the term *psychosomatics of infancy* must be considered as both the psychosomatics and the somatopsychics of infants—the way in which the body form and function of the infant modify its parents' behavior toward him and, therefore, in turn modify his behavior and developing personality.

The first basic emotional need of infancy and childhood is parental love, the sustaining protective device by which the child is able to withstand the unknown terrors of a hostile world. Characteristic of the infantile dependent state of the child is (1) the relative singleness of source of the love which will gratify his needs; (2) that love and warmth must be almost constantly expressed; (3) that he cannot sustain himself for any appreciable length of time on the anticipation of expressions of love and that such deeds and actions as he undertakes to secure this expression must have their immediate reward; (4) that his capacity to like himself during the very early years is dependent heavily upon the early satisfaction of his dependent love needs and then upon an adequate resolution of these needs and the development of adequate *independence*. Simplified to the extreme, the development of an effective personality and an adequate social-emotional adjustment consists, to a large degree, in the resolution of this infantile dependent need, with its satisfaction in parent or parent-figure love, into adequate ego defenses and gratification of ego needs. Adult personality may be considered to be the constellation of defenses and devices which have been acquired in an attempt to resolve infantile dependent need and achieve emotional comfort and freedom of function. An adequate personality could also be defined as one in which the ego defenses and devices are (1) adequate to maintain a reasonable degree of freedom from anxiety, (2) adequate and of such a nature as to permit the individual to use effectively his basic abilities, and (3) not antisocial or destructive to other individuals or society.

THE INFANT'S MODIFICATION OF PARENTAL ENVIRONMENT

It is unfortunate that too much of the research on parent-child interaction has neglected the effect of the various aspects of the child and his behavior on the parent. There are, of course, innumerable assessments, reports, and clinical observations of the differences in attitude of mothers toward their various children (Lasko, 1952; Schaefer & Bayley, 1963), but there has been too little concern about the morphology, motor behavior, ability to learn, health, and other factors as determinants of parents' attitudes and behavior toward their children. Sears et al. (1957) emphasize that the parent-to-child relationship, rather than an interplay of relationship, is overdrawn, as do Hawkins et al. (1966). Bronchial asthma in children is an excellent and forceful example of this reverse relationship and is one which too often has been overlooked in the disciplines of pediatrics and psychiatry. Traditionally, the psychodynamics of asthma are described as an unresolved dependency on mother—a need to be sustained, loved, and cared for by mother—a fear of hostility toward mother and of withdrawal of mother love. This need to be taken care of by a mother or a mother figure and the fear of its frustration or disruption are usually considered to be the dominant psychodynamic factors in bronchial asthma. Whether such a "pat" conclusion is justified, however, may be open to question. To anyone who has been the subject of severe attacks of bronchial asthma, that illness is a frightening thing. The patient is deprived of the breath of life. He is fearful constantly that the next breath may be his last. Those observing such a severe attack of asthma are also acutely aware of the catastrophic nature of the threat to life which is posed by the attack. Certainly a mother watching such an asthmatic attack in a young child must be terribly frightened and must respond to the child's need for reassurance with anguish, tension, and extreme protectiveness. What other personality structure could an asthmatic have than that of a dependent child, fearful of the unavailability of mother's life-conserving care?

Another kind of infant who modifies parental feeling and behavior and, therefore, parental attitude and environment is the hyperkinetic child.

It has been my observation in the Fels longitudinal study of the development of children that many of the hyperactive, hyperkinetic, erratic-sleeping, "into everything" 7-year-olds were, except for their limitations of mobility and ways of expression of hyperkinesis, not much different at birth. They were red, squalling, crying, screaming, fighting characters who were somewhat less cuddly than a normal young octopus. Aggression seemed apparent from the beginning, expressed first in screaming, crying, and erratic sleeping and by the age of 18 months, expressed also in aggressive mobility. The statement one often hears, "He never lets me have a minute's peace," is a very meaningful one as an expression of the resentment that the mother of such a child feels toward him for what he has done to the tranquillity she had had in life.

Whether such hyperkinesis results from minimal brain damage at birth or whether it is simply an extreme along the continuum of physical passivity-activity differs, of course, from child to child, but the impact of such a pattern of behavior on the parental acceptance of the child, i.e., the ability of parents to relate warmly and constructively to the child, is much the same. Expressed or repressed hostility is inevitable. The child, by reason of his biology, has modified his environment and has thus inevitably modified many aspects of his developing personality and behavior.

The child with infantile eczema, a clubfoot, or an ugly birthmark or who is a spastic or a mental defective or who suffers from any deviation which makes him less attractive will probably have a less advantageous parental environment through his failure to conform to the ideal infant image which had been created in his mother's anticipation of his birth. Any physical disadvantage a child has which interferes either with his acceptance by his peer group or with his ability to compete effectively in it constitutes a biological determinant of his developing behavioral patterns. The process of learning to master problems, one of the most important devices people acquire in their striving to avoid anxiety, is influenced by such biological characteristics as strength, size, deformity, and intelligence.

MOTOR DEVELOPMENT

The rate of motor development of a child is an important somatic factor in the somatopsychic development of his personality and the constellation of his ego defenses and devices. The child with precocious motor development is more likely to acquire self-assurance from his physical success experiences—the approval and admiration of parents and his superiority in physical contest or competition with peers. In contrast, a sense of inadequacy and futility may be engendered in the child with retarded motor development. Such slow development is expressed dramatically in an early series (Sontag, 1962) of Stanford-Binet IQs from the age of 30 months to 4 years. The rise is often due to the decreasing importance of motor skills in favor of cognitive ones in sequential age levels of Binets, plus perhaps the lowered anxiety level as motor skills more nearly approach age expectancy. My assumption here is that, other things being equal, the ability to perform physically or mentally is a tension-reducing characteristic.

PHYSICAL AND INTELLECTUAL VIGOR: CONSTITUTION

Life from the conception of a child entails a continuous battery of greater or lesser environmental impacts and interactions. I have described a few such impacts during fetal life. After birth, such environmental impacts and interactions are, of course, in part observable. However, the differences in the reactions of individual children at any given chronological, developmental, or biological age to what is, as far as can be observed,

an identical stimulus are impressive (Mussen & Jones, 1962). One of the determinants of such differences is the vigor of mind and body of a particular child. A perceived environmental threat—as, for example, the attempted bullying of one 8-year-old by another—may be responded to either by fight or by flight. The reaction can be either phobic or counterphobic.

A girl reaching sexual maturity at age 10 in a class in which that stage of development averages 12 years will, of course, react very differently and will generate a very different pattern of behavior from her male peers than she would if such maturity appeared at 14 years (Stone & Baker, 1939). A boy who has excellent coordination or a height of 6 feet 3 inches or who is 60 pounds overweight will leave his impact on his peer and teacher environment and will respond to his environment very differently than if his motor skills, body size, or proportions were nearer the norms (Jones & Bayley, 1950).

Thomas et al. (1963) refer to this constitutional individuality as *behavioral individuality* and attempt to describe the behavioral individuality of each child in terms of intensity of reaction and styles of functioning. They do not attempt to assess the relative significance of genetic, familial, prenatal influences and early life experiences as etiological determinants of such behavioral individuality. Obviously, in such a characteristic as intelligence, a genetic factor has been demonstrated. In many other characteristics—as, for example, musical ability—a biological-genetical factor is almost certainly involved.

Ample evidence of constitutional difference as a basis for behavioral difference is available in studies of lower animals. A variety of behavioral characteristics in different strains of mice under well-controlled conditions have been studied by W. R. Thompson at McGill University. Level of exploratory behavior (perhaps representing freedom from anxiety, curiosity, or instinctive food seeking) has been well demonstrated. A series of publications by Scott and Fuller (1951) have described the various behavior characteristics of different breeds of dogs as well as the importance of critical periods for modifying behavior patterns in any breed of dogs. At Manhattan Agriculture College, Guhl has described genetically determined patterns of group behavior, dominance, and fighting in chickens of different strains.

ILLNESS AND MALNUTRITION

While every human being is born with his individually inherited potential vitality or energy level, that energy level may, of course, be subject to frequent modification through illness and, in some populations, malnutrition. Such modification of energy level and, therefore, of behavior is not limited to the period of childhood. The adult with a nutritional or thyroid deficiency reacts differently to an environmental impact than he would in a state of excellent health. However, in childhood the processes of growth and more limited homeostatic capability make for much more dynamic and dramatic changes in energy level in response to nutritional deficiencies or illness. Furthermore, childhood is the period of personality formation, the time when the individual is most rapidly expanding his social adaptation. For the first time he is meeting and competing with fellow humans of a comparable age and physique.

Rachitic bones and flabby muscles, with their limiting effects on a child's ability to compete in a nursery school situation, have a quite different significance when viewed thirty years later than would a few months of lowered vitality resulting from a nutritional deficiency or other cause. The state of a child's physical well-being, then, is a dynamic factor in the whole process of his social adjustment and emerging personality. The primary tubercular infection of infancy,

which often goes unrecognized, can, and often does, produce a period of poor weight gain, lessened endurance, and increased apathy. Environmental pressures elicit a different and usually less adequate and resistive response during such a period. More than any other segment of life, childhood is a period of fluctuating adequacy of the whole organism to resist and successfully adjust to an expanding parade of environmental encroachments. The health of the child has another psychosomatic implication in addition to modifying his resistance to environmental impact. Severe illness can change that environment and the position of the child in it. Illness causes withdrawal of the child from his normal social situation and from contact and competition with others of his own age. Again he spends his hours in a quiescent state, often flat in bed. He is waited upon, perhaps even fed, by a mother as anxious and solicitous as during his early infancy. Illness for him means a regression or retreat to infancy, to its limited family circle and extreme state of helplessness. Illness is, then, in some ways a "desirable" state, and he is most apt not to give up all its advantages readily. If the episode is prolonged, he may emerge with a lapse in toilet training, food fussiness, or other attention-getting devices as sequelae. His modified behavior patterns and the regression of his social behavior are products of his somatopsychic illness.

Extremes of malnutrition, such as kwashiorkor (*Nutrition Reviews,* 1965, 1966; Zamenhof et al., 1968) completely modify behavior by incapacitating the victim. Although there are no immediately conclusive studies of the possible permanent retardation of mental growth from such a protein-calorie deficiency, it is not unlikely that malnutrition plays a significant role. The behavioral aspects of another nutritional deficiency, pellagra, with its occasional delirium and acute mania, is a more dramatic example of the biology of behavior.

SELF-IMAGE OR SELF-CONCEPT

The image every individual has of himself is, of course, the product of a complex sequence of life experiences, first with parents, then with his peer group, and then with the world (Anastasi, 1962), but it may also have a significant biological component. I am sure that anyone who has served as a psychiatric consultant to high school or college boys has been approached many times by anxious males whose genitalia were small in comparison with those of their fellow students. Every trip to the shower room reconfirmed that fact, with a resultant heightening of anxiety level as to the adequacy of their masculinity to function sexually. Self-image in such an instance is quite definitely determined in part by the morphology. Anxiety about boy-girl relationships, feelings of inadequacy and depression may then, in such instances, have one etiological component in body form.

Self-concept is shaped in some instances by the race and ethnic origin of the individual in relationship to the particular culture or subculture in which he is living. The self-image or self-concept of the Japanese-American living in California 50 years ago was, of course, likely to be vastly different from what it would have been if he had stayed in Japan or what it would be had he currently been living in California.

In a recent request for dietary information, information which was paid for in advance, forty-three children failed to fill out the diet records, although some 75 percent responded. The forty-three who failed to respond averaged 10 percent overweight as compared with the rest of the research population. One must assume, then, that their body image of obesity made them ashamed to report what they had eaten that week. The drab, unattractive, unrelating child, with the self-image of unattractiveness and resourcelessness, often has as one component some aspect of physical unattractiveness—obesity, acne, or just plain homeliness. Such a statement, of course, does not deny the importance of the almost limitless numbers of life experiences which contribute to perception of self and relationship to the world.

BIOCHEMICAL FACTORS

A number of gene-determined metabolic defects, or inborn errors of metabolism, are known. These inherited defects of function have, in many instances, direct behavioral components. Others quite possibly have indirect components in that they are factors delineating constitution. Admittedly, these defects are not for most mental-emotional problems the causes of mental disease. They are only dramatic examples of metabolic constitutional characteristics which may play a role in delineating behavior patterns. They do suggest, perhaps, that many metabolic differences are not of the "all-or-none" variety and that differences which are not dramatic or whose dimensions are not completely known may play a role in the socioemotional adjustment of man. A few examples of such inborn errors of metabolism, of which there are many, are:

1. *Wilson's disease* is autosomal recessive in its inheritance and is characterized by an absence of the plasma copper protein, ceruloplasmin, which has enzymatic properties. Its absence produces no clinically detectable abnormality in early life. However, it results in an excessive accumulation of copper in the internal organs and in the eye, and it produces a liver cirrhosis. Patients with Wilson's disease suffer from severe emotional disturbances, both neurotic and psychotic in nature.

2. *Agammaglobulinemia* is a disease caused by a sex-linked recessive gene and results in an absence of gamma globulin, which is necessary for the formation of antibodies. Here again is a condition not detectable clinically at birth and actually not damaging unless the individual is

called upon to synthesize antibodies against invading organisms or toxin. When such an environmental threat appears, however, the importance of the metabolic defect is such as to make survival unlikely.

3. *Sickle-cell anemia* is a dominant genetic characteristic in which a part of the normal hemoglobin is displaced by a slightly different and ineffective variety. An individual may carry the dominant gene for sickle-cell anemia and have the aberrant hemoglobin in his cell without suffering clinical evidence of malfunction. If, however, he decides to live at a high altitude, the sickling of his red cells becomes rapidly apparent and the usual vascular pathology ensues, together with evidence of inadequate oxygen-carrying capacity. Here again is a constitutional factor which, when confronted with a threatening environment, may cause a crippling disease with behavioral modification not found in others living at high altitudes.

4. *Phenylpyruvic oligophrenia* is inherent as an autosomal recessive trait and consists of a deficiency of phenylalanine hydroxylase. The resulting disturbances in phenylalanine metabolism are expressed in mental defect, yet this constitutional factor can be circumvented by special dietary procedure at an early age.

5. *Galactosemia* is a disease resulting from another metabolic defect of protein synthesis and is characterized not only by physical but by mental defects.

The role of brain damage from anoxia as a frequent determinant of behavior is well recognized. Premature separation of the placenta, mechanical interference with cord circulation, and aspects of severity of labor are common causes at or near term. Severe Rh incompatibility, with much fetal blood destruction, may occur considerably prior to fetal maturity, as may toxemia of pregnancy. The classically described fetal hyperactivity which accompanies fetal an-

oxia is often seen in toxemia, as is "slugging" in the corneal vessels of the mother's eye. How much of the fetal anoxia is caused by such slugging and how much is the result of placental thrombosis is unknown. Cerebral hemorrhage as a source of brain damage during the birth process is, of course, a determinant of behavior, as is congenital deafness and blindness.

CHROMOSOMAL ABNORMALITY

The discovery within the last decade or so of aneuploidy, or errors in the chromosomal number, has added an important facet to the problem of the biological basis of behavior. Approximately 1 percent of the mentally retarded in English institutions are chromatin positive (Jacobs et al., 1965). A considerable proportion of these have an XYY sex-chromosome constitution. Aberrations of sex chromosomes are being discovered increasingly as the number of cytological examinations increase. XXYY, XXX, and XXY are frequently found, as are mosaics in which two different patterns of sex-chromosomal abnormalities are found in the same subject.

Although the behavioral patterns found occurring in chromosomal abnormalities are in many instances not yet clearly defined, some are. The so-called supermale, with an XYY sex-chromosome complex accounting for his forty-seven chromosomes in contrast to the more conventional forty-six, is described as tall, of low or normal mentality, and aggressive and is often incarcerated for criminal or delinquent behavior. This gonosomal aneuploidy has also been found to have a suspiciously high incidence in the taller portion of the population of mental hospitals (Casey et al., 1966; Price et al., 1966; Telfer et al., 1968).

Mongolism, or Down's syndrome, is a well-known example of an autosomal abnormality, a constitutional condition in which the forty-seventh chromosome is an autosomal rather than a sex chromosome. Mongolism has, of course, many biological features as well as its characteristic mental defect.

Turner's syndrome, Noonan's syndrome, Klinefelder's syndrome, trisomy D, trisomy E, and monosomy are all examples of aneuploidy which have some behavioral components. Discovery of new polysomal aberrations will, undoubtedly, lead to the discovery of further behavioral aberrations.

ENDOCRINOLOGICAL FACTORS

In a paper titled "Steroid Hormones and the Neuropsychology of Development," Valenstein (1968) has reviewed much of the literature on the effect of sex hormones on animal behavior and has contributed much data in this very important field of investigation. In the study of human behavior, for obvious reasons, no mass experimental attack on the problem of the role of sex hormones has been made, yet nature has provided opportunities for studying the effects of certain endocrine abnormalities. Of these, cretinism is probably the best known. The behavioral component, mental retardation or idiocy, is associated with differences in many physical characteristics. Graves' disease has both its biological components and its behavioral ones, primarily restlessness, anxiety, and loss of energy. Tumors of the pineal gland produce not only precocious sexual development but also precocious sexual behavior. The behavioral effect of insulin shock was so obvious when first observed that insulin shock became a therapeutic agent of major importance in the treatment of schizophrenia. While the literature on the relationship of adrenochromes to abnormal behavior is still confused, there is enough evidence to justify the conclusion that they do exert a marked influence. Money and Lewis (1966) report that children exhibiting the adrenogenital syndrome have not only a precocious growth rate but an advanced IQ.

Charles Stockard (1941) called attention to the associated endocrine and behavioral differences in various breeds of dogs. Leathem, in a personal communication, has reported that the castration of female mice at certain stages of development by the injection of androgens has resulted in these females killing the males introduced into their cages for breeding purposes.

Recently, many efforts have been made to "transfer learning" from one animal to another by injecting RNA extracted from the brain of a trained animal into a naïve one on the assumption that the protein changes resulting from learning would remain intact and be incorporated in the RNA molecules of the recipient (Babich et al., 1965). There is a great deal of controversy and conflict over results of such experiments. Halas et al. (1966) report a failure to replicate the transfer of learned response by RNA injections, although they do report that the RNA-injected rats were more responsive to stimuli.

The current widespread use of marijuana and LSD, together with the tremendous increase in the use of tranquilizers, antipsychotics, and antidepressants, has brought the field of psychopharmacology to increased levels of prominence. *Confessions of an English Opium Eater* (DeQuincey, 1853) and, later, Huxley's description of the psychedelic effects of peyote described mood changes and sometimes delusions and hallucinations from these drugs. However, it was not until many years after DeQuincey and Huxley wrote about these psychotogenic drugs that the use of LSD and marijuana became widespread in this country. LSD has been described by various of its users as expanding the walls of consciousness and perception and as enhancing creativity, sexual pleasure, and appreciation of art and music. Certainly it is capable of producing bizarre delusions and hallucinations. It has been accused of inducing schizophrenia episodes, but evidence of this effect has not been clearly demonstrated. The effects of mescaline and peyote are somewhat similar. Marijuana users describe an enhanced perception of beauty and empathy and depth toward others, increased appreciation for music and art, and enhanced ability to solve problems. Alcohol, of course, continues to alleviate anxiety and lower inhibitions and interpersonal barriers. In excessive amounts, it is destructive of performance and is eventually hypnotic and anesthetic.

In recent years psychopharmacology has profoundly changed the practice of psychiatry. Augmenting and to a considerable degree supplementing the barbiturates as tranquilizers are a bevy of compounds. One of the first of these was chlorpromazine, and today there is an extensive list, including such compounds as meprobamate and chlordeazepoxide, some of which, together with reserpine, are used to reduce or control the manifestation of psychotic states. A number of drugs are available for use as mood elevators in depression, such as M.A.O. inhibitors and dibengazepenes. Their effectiveness in severe depression leaves much to be desired. The amphetamines are often effective in alleviating mild, and particularly reactive, depressed moods. They are also used extensively to combat fatigue and sleepiness, particularly by the military and by students.

These newer drugs then join those of earlier periods—cocaine, heroin, opium, hashish, morphine, etc.—as modifiers of human behavior, performance, and mood. There are, needless to say, the "good guys" and the "bad guys" among the behavior and mood-changing drugs, a distinction made by the laws of the land; but in many instances, these drugs are classified differently by various segments of the population. There are among the scientists who are concerned either experimentally or intellectually with the effects of behavior and mood drugs many who envision a time when the educative process, social interaction, and performance in the arts, to mention a few, will each have its pharmacological supplement—a pill to help Johnny encompass his mathematics assignment more effectively, another to facilitate communication and empathy at the directors' meeting, and still another to contribute to the production of a masterpiece in literature, art, or music. Whether the emergence of psychopharmacological procedures leads to quite such an enhancement of the lives and products of the human race and whether the effect on individual responses of human beings is quite so predictable and dependable remains to be seen.

EFFECT OF DRUGS ON PERFORMANCE

Convulsion-producing drugs such as Metrazol and picrotoxin have been used in attempts to enhance the maze-learning ability of rats. At proper dosage, learning was improved by 40 percent. McGaugh (1966) believes that drugs which enhance learning ability do not all work in the same manner. Krech (1967) calls attention to the fact that while some enhance learning, perhaps through improvement in processes of memory, others may act upon attentiveness or increased versatility in mode of attack on problems. He emphasizes also that drugs affecting learning ability act differently on different strains and individuals, just as do most other drugs.

Theories that biochemical abnormalities, as well as the presumed impairment of cerebral circulation, constitute or contribute to the etiology of schizophrenia have been popular for many years (Kety, 1960, 1967). There is, however, no confirmed evidence that circulation, oxygenation of the brain cells, or carbohydrate metabolism are directly responsible for the schizophrenic syndrome. McGeer et al. (1957) have reported a high concentration of aromatic compounds in the urine of schizophrenics and believe they have discovered qualitative differences in their patterns of excretion. Georgi et al. (1956) have reported abnormal but unidentified amines and indoles in the urine of schizophrenics.

Hallucinogenic derivatives of epinephrine,

possibly with the production of the hallucinogenic derivatives adrenochrome or adrenolutin, have been suggested as etiological agents in schizophrenia. This theory is also controversial and, while subject to the investigations of a number of scientists, has not yielded concrete evidence of the causes or mechanisms (Osmond, 1955).

Ceruloplasmin, a copper-containing globulin, had its period of popularity when presumably abnormal levels of it, together with qualitatively different forms of it, were found in the blood (Hoffer, 1957; Hoffer et al., 1954). Findings in this area could not be proved to be related to the paranoid ideas, catatonic behavior, and hallucinations with which they were presumably associated (Heath et al., 1958; Leach et al., 1958; Markowitz et al., 1955).

Wooley and Shaw (1954) reported that LSD in low concentration blocked serotonin effects on smooth muscle. They inferred that *mental changes* induced by this substance were produced by a suppression of serotonin level in the *brain*. Administration of 5-hydroxytryptamine, a precursor of serotonin, elevated brain serotonin levels yet produced symptoms similar to those produced by LSD (Heath et al., 1957), a contradiction that could not be explained. The correlation between serotonin level and perception and behavior is not impressive.

Of the many studies whose objectives were an evaluation of the role of gene inheritance as a determinant of the probability of a schizophrenic illness, perhaps the most impressive are those of Franz Kallman (1946), who shows, particularly in his studies of identical twins reared apart, that the probability of one twin suffering from schizophrenia if such a condition existed in his schizophrenic monozygotic sibling reared apart is much greater than chance. Through what biochemical or enzymatic mechanism such inheritance occurs is, as yet, unknown.

The biology of the cell and vascular deterioration and its behavioral concomitants constitute a fitting subject in the discussion of the biology of behavior. Certainly, arteriosclerosis of the brain vessels can produce deteriorating memory and delusions as well as less well-defined behavioral or personality changes. What part changes in protein synthesis or enzymes may play in these behavioral changes is not yet clear. Nor is it always apparent what role the changes in self-image and body function incident to aging may play in a given instance. Certainly there is no one-to-one correlation between the degree of arteriosclerosis of cerebral vessels as determined at autopsy and the severity of behavior changes present prior to death. It is also true, however, that vascular replacement surgery of the large vessels supplying blood to the brain has often accomplished much in restoring a more normal behavior pattern and memory.

THE BIOLOGY OF LEARNING

Many intervention programs for advancing the intelligence and performance capabilities of socially disadvantaged children have been initiated, and some efforts have been made to evaluate their success. Deutsch has produced evidence to show that an expected decline in IQ in a disadvantaged preschool group can be prevented by intervention procedures. Stoddard (1945) and Wellman (1945) were perhaps the first to demonstrate that performance on mental tests could be dramatically improved in preschool children who had been subjected to an enriched environment. The advent of the Head Start program has provided a marked stimulus to the attempt to evaluate the effects of such intervention on mental performance. While not all the reports of the beneficial effects of such programs are convincing (perhaps because of inadequate methodology), there continues to pile up more evidence that what Stoddard and Wellman found in terms of improved performance in what was once considered a biologically predetermined ability is valid. More recently, attempts have been made using experimental animals to determine whether there are anatomical and/or biochemical changes which result from "enrichment" programs for young animals, biological changes which are concomitants of the behavioral changes.

Krech et al. (1966) have raised postweanling rats in an "enriching" environment for eighty days, an environment replete with other adolescents, lights, noise, running wheels, and learning tasks. At the end of this period, both experimental and control rats were sacrificed and the brains of the two groups were examined chemically and morphologically. The experimental rats showed a thicker cortex, more glial cells, and larger neuronal cell bodies. Blood vessels supplying the brain were larger, and chemically, more cholinesterase was found in the brains of the experimental animals.

Afterimage, a short-term memory, and long-term memory are apparently dependent upon somewhat different electrochemical phenomena. The long-term memory, in contrast to the short-term, probably depends on synthesis of new proteins and perhaps enzymes in the minutes following the processing of information intake. The short-term memory depends upon an electrochemical process not involving protein synthesis. Short-term memory can be interrupted by introduction of electrical current immediately after the learning experiment. If application of the current is delayed, presumably until after the synthesis of new proteins, memory of the learning experience will not be lost. Puromycin, an antibiotic, when injected into laboratory animals just before or just after the learning experience, does not interfere with short-term memory but does interfere with development of long-term memory (Davis et al., 1965), apparently through the inhibition of synthesis of new proteins.

SUMMARY

The biological basis of behavior, or half of the nature-nurture controversy, is now clearly recognized, although in innumerable areas what is nature and what is nurture has not yet been clearly identified. Nor is it clear what biological components of behavior can be modified by nurture.

Biological mechanisms are operative during the fetal period in determining both the behavior of the fetus and, in some instances, its postnatal behavior. Maternal emotions—anxiety, grief, anger, exhilaration—apparently are capable, through an autonomic endocrine humoral path, of influencing the activity and heart rate of the fetus. Occasionally fetal behavioral modifications persist for a considerable period after birth. There are also behavioral correlates at nursery school age of fetal activity levels during the eight and ninth months of fetal development. Lability of heart rate during fetal life is predictive of cardiac lability at 20 years of age, and there are personality and behavioral correlates at age 20 of cardiac lability-stability.

Animal experiments in recent years have demonstrated that procedures which modified the emotional states of pregnant rats resulted in offspring more emotionally stable and less neurotic than control groups or groups in which maternal neurosis was deliberately created. These animal data reinforce earlier findings on the effect of human maternal emotions.

There are behavioral differences in the form of cognitive style, or ways of thinking and perceiving, of individuals who react with strong autonomic response to stress situations as compared with those whose responses are weaker. Whether this physiological perceptual behavior is the product of the physiological process or a mere gene-determined relationship is unknown.

The manner in which the body of an infant or a child and his physical behavior modify the individual's parental and peer environment and, consequently, his self-image, his perception of the world, and his relationship to it are important. An infant or child creates, to an important degree, the environment which shapes his personality. Rate of motor development as well as physical and intellectual vigor are important factors in the fight-or-flight, phobic-counterphobic behavior pattern. Illness and malnutrition modify energy level, method of coping, and degree of dependent relationship. Illness modifies parental environment. Such specific nutritional deficiencies as are involved in pellagra often produce specific behavioral changes such as delirium and mania. Obesity is an important determinant of self-image and, therefore, of behavior.

Gene-determined biochemical differences, known as *inborn errors of metabolism,* are responsible for gross behavioral inadequacies and mental retardation. Brain damage from anoxia during the fetal period or during childhood modifies behavior.

Chromosomal abnormality appears to be the biological basis for a number of modifications of behavior such as are seen in mongolism, the supermale, and the superfemale. Steroid hormones have been demonstrated to produce a variety of behavioral changes in laboratory animals, and deficiencies in thyroid function modify patterns of behavior in both man and laboratory animals. Efforts in the field of molecular biology to modify the process of learning have produced no convincing results.

In psychopharmacology the evolution of tranquilizers, antipsychotics, and antidepressants for the care and treatment of psychiatric problems has been paralleled by a tremendous and widespread nonmedical use of marijuana and LSD, and recent experiments with drugs to enhance learning and memory suggest the probability of expanded use of drugs for modifying behavior and learning in children and aging populations. Various theories of biological and metabolic changes in the brain cells have been propounded in an attempt to explain the biology of schizophrenia. Work in this area ranges from a study of oxygenation and carbohydrate metabolism of the brain to the isolation of metabolites from blood and urine. Various derivative abnormalities of ceruloplasmin and serotonin have been suggested as possible etiological factors. There is a well-demonstrated genetic factor. Aging of the cell and vascular deterioration have behavioral components in the form of learning ability and memory changes. What was formerly considered a gene-determined characteristic in the form of intelligence has now been demonstrated to be modifiable by various environmental enrichment procedures, which, in turn, have been demonstrated to produce biological changes as well as behavioral ones.

REFERENCES

Ader, R., & Conklin, P. M. Handling of pregnant rats: Effects of emotionality on their offspring. *Science,* 1963, **142,** 411–412.

Anastasi, A. Heredity, environment and the question "how"? In J. Rosenblith & W. Allinsmith (Eds.), *The causes of behavior: Readings in child development and educational psychology.* Boston: Allyn & Bacon, 1962. Pp. 21–27.

Antonov, A. N. Children born during the seige of Leningrad during 1942. *Journal of Pediatrics,* 1947, **30,** 250-259.

Babich, F. R., Jacobson, A., Bubash, S., & Jacobson, A. Transfer of a response to naive rats by injection of ribonucleic acid extracted from trained rats. *Science,* 1965, **148,** 656–657.

Bell, R. Q. A reinterpretation of the direction of effects in studies of socialization. *Psychological Review,* 1968, **75,** 81-93.

Casey, M. D., Segall, L. J., Street, D. R. K., & Blank, C. E. Sex chromosome abnormalities in two state hospitals for patients requiring special security. *Nature,* 1966, **209,** 641.

Davis, R. E., Bright, P. J., & Agranoff, B. W. Effects of ECS and puromycin on memory in fish. *Journal of Comparative Physiology and Psychology,* 1965, **60,** 162–166.

DeQuincey, T. *Confessions of an English opium eater.* Boston: Ticknor and Fields, 1853.

Dubos, Rene. Neonatal deprivations can be permanent ones. *Journal of the American Medical Association,* 1968, **205**(10), 34–35.

Ferreira, A. J. The pregnant mother's emotional attitude and its reflection upon the newborn. *American Journal of Orthopsychiatry,* 1960, **30,** 553–561.

Forbes, H. S., & Forbes, H. B. Fetal sense reaction: Hearing. *Journal of Comparative Psychology,* 1927, **7,** 353–355.

Fodor, N. *The search for the beloved.* New York: Hermitage House, 1949.

Garn, S. M., Silverman, F. N., Hertzog, K. P., & Rohmann, C. G. Lines and bands of increased radiographic density and their implications to growth and development. *Medical Radiography and Photography,* 1968, **44,** 58–59.

Georgi, F., Honegger, C. C., Jordan, D., Riedner, H. P., & Rottenberg, M. Zur Physiologie und Pathophysiologie Körpereigener Amine. *Klinische Wochenschrift,* 1956, **34,** 799.

Halas, E. S., Bradfield, K., Sandlie, M. E., Theye, F., & Beardsley, J. Changes in rat behavior due to RNA injection. *Physiology and Behavior,* 1966, **1,** 281–283.

Hawkins, R. P., Peterson, R. F., Schweid, E., & Bijou, S. W. Behavior therapy in the home: Amelioration of problem parent-child relations with the parent in a therapeutic role. *Journal of Experimental Child Psychology,* 1966, **4,** 99–107.

Heath, R. G., Leach, B. E., Byers, L. W., Martens, S., & Feigley, C. A. Pharmacological and biological psychotherapy. *American Journal of Psychiatry,* 1958, **114,** 683.

Heath, R. G., Martens, S., Leach, B. E., Cohen, M., & Feigley, C. A. Behavioral changes in nonpsychotic volunteers following the administration of taraxein, the substance obtained from serum of schizophrenic patients. *American Journal of Psychiatry,* 1958, **114,** 917.

Heath, R. G., Martens, S., Leach, B. E., Cohen, M., & Angel, C. Effect on behavior in humans with the administration of taraxein. *American Journal of Psychiatry,* 1957, **114,** 14.

Hellman, L. M., Johnson, H. L., Tolles, W. E., & Jones, E. H. Some factors affecting the fetal heart rate. *American Journal of Obstetrics and Gynecology,* 1961, **82,** 1055–1063.

Hoffer, A. Epinephrine derivatives as potential schizophrenic factors. *Journal of Clinical and Experimental Psychopathology,* 1957, **18,** 27.

Hoffer, A., Osmond, H., & Smythies, J. Schizophrenia: A new approach. II. Result of a year's research. *Journal of Mental Science,* 1954, **100,** 29.

Jacobs, P. A., Brunton, M., & Melville, M. M. Aggressive behaviour, mental sub-normality and the XYY male. *Nature,* 1965, **208,** 1351.

Jones, M. C., & Bayley, N. Physical maturing among boys as related to behavior. *Journal of Educational Psychology,* 1950, **41,** 129–148.

Kagan, J., & Moss, H. *Birth to maturity.* New York: Wiley, 1962.

Kallman, F. J. The genetic theory of schizophrenia. An analysis of 691 twin index families. *American Journal of Psychiatry,* 1946, **103,** 309–322.

Kawi, A. A., & Pasamanick, B. Prenatal and paranatal factors in the development of childhood reading disorders. *Monographs of the So-*

ciety for Research in Child Development, 1959, **24,** 1–80.

Kety, S. S. Recent biochemical theories of schizophrenia. In D. D. Jackson (Ed.), *The etiology of schizophrenia.* New York: Basic Books, 1960.

Kety, S. S. Current biochemical approaches to schizophrenia. *New England Journal of Medicine,* 1967, **276,** 325–331.

Krech, D. The chemistry of learning. Paper presented at the National Seminars on Innovation sponsored by the U.S. Office of Education and the Charles F. Kettering Foundation, Honolulu, July, 1967.

Krech, D., Rosenzweig, M. R., & Bennett, E. L. Environmental impoverishment, social isolation and changes in brain chemistry and anatomy. *Physiology and Behavior,* 1966, **1,** 99–104.

Lacey, J. I. Somatic response patterning and stress: Some revisions of activation theory. In M. H. Appley & R. Trumbull (Eds.), *Psychological stress: Issues in research.* New York: Appleton Century Crofts, 1967.

Lacey, J. I., Kagan, J., Lacey, B. C., & Moss, H. The visceral level: Situational determinants and behavioral correlates of autonomic response patterns. In P. J. Knapp (Ed.), *Expression of the emotions in man.* New York: International Universities Press, 1963.

Lacey, J. I., & Lacey, B. C. The law of initial value in the longitudinal study of autonomic constitution: Reproducibility of autonomic responses and response patterns over a four-year interval. *Annals of the New York Academy of Sciences,* 1962, **98,** 1257–1290, 1322–1326.

Lasko, J. K. Parent-child relationships. *American Journal of Orthopsychiatry,* 1952, **22,** 300–304.

Leach, B. E., Cohen, M., Heath, R. G., & Mar-
tens, S. Studies of the role of ceruloplasmin and albumin in adrenaline metabolism. *AMA Archives of Neurology and Psychiatry,* 1958, **79,** 730.

Lieberman, M. Early development stress and later behavior. *Science,* 1963, **141,** 824–825.

Markowitz, H., Gubler, C. J., Mahoney, J. P., Cartwright, G. E., & Wintrobe, M. M. Studies on copper metabolism. XIV. Copper, ceruplasmin and oxidase activity in sera of normal human subjects, pregnant women and patients with infection, hepatolenticular degeneration and the nephrotic syndrome. *Journal of Clinical Investigation,* 1955, **34,** 1498.

McGaugh, J. L. Time-dependent processes in memory storage. *Science,* 1966, **153,** 1351–1358.

McGeer, E. G., Brown, W. T., & McGeer, P. L. Aromatic metabolism in schizophrenia. II. Bi-dimensional urinary chromatograms. *Journal of Nervous and Mental Disorders,* 1957, **125,** 176.

McGeer, P. L., McNair, F. E., McGeer, E. G., & Gibson, W. C. Aromatic metabolism in schizophrenia. I. Statistical evidence for aromaturia. *Journal of Nervous and Mental Disorders,* 1957, **125,** 166.

Money, J., & Lewis, V. IQ genetics and accelerated growth: Adrenogenital syndrome. *Bulletin of The Johns Hopkins Hospital,* 1966, **118,** 365–373.

Mussen, P. H., & Jones, Mary C. Self-conceptions, motivations and interpersonal attitudes of late- and early-maturing boys. In J. Rosenblith & W. Allinsmith (Eds.), *The causes of behavior: Readings in child development and educational psychology.* Boston: Allyn & Bacon, 1962. Pp. 43–51.

Nutrition Reviews. Early weaning, diet, and intelligence. 1965, **23,** 211–213.

Nutrition Reviews. Subsequent growth of children treated for malnutrition. 1966, **24,** 267–269.

Obrist, P. Cardiovascular differentiation of sensory stimuli. *Psychosomatic Medicine,* 1963, **25,** 450–459.

Osmond, H. Inspiration and method in schizophrenia research. *Diseases of the Nervous System,* 1955, **16,** 101.

Pasamanick, B., & Knobloch, H. Retrospective studies on the epidemiology of reproductive casualty: Old and new. *Merrill-Palmer Quarterly of Behavior and Development,* 1966, **12**(1), 20.

Peiper, A. Sinnesempfindugen des kindes vor seiner geburt. *Monatsschrift fuer Kinderheilkunde,* 1925, **29,** 236.

Price, W. H., Strong, J. A., Whatmore, P. B., & McClemont, W. F. Criminal patients with XYY sex-chromosome complement. *Lancet,* 1966, **1,** 565–567.

Schaefer, E., & Bayley, N. Maternal behavior, child behavior, and their intercorrelations from infancy through adolescence. *Monographs of the Society for Research in Child Development,* 1963, **28**(3, Whole No. 87).

Scott, J. P., & Fuller, J. L. Research on genetics and social behavior at the Roscoe B. Jackson Memorial Laboratory, 1946-1951. A progress report. *Journal of Heredity,* 1951, **42,** 191–197.

Sears, R. R., Maccoby, E. E., & Levin, H. *Patterns of child rearing.* Evanston, Ill.: Row, Peterson, 1957.

Sontag, L. W. Some psychosomatic aspects of childhood. *The Nervous Child,* 1946, **5**(4), 296–304.

Sontag, L. W. Dynamics of personality formation. *Journal of Personality,* 1951, **1,** 119–130.

Sontag, L. W. Psychosomatics and somatopsychics from birth to three years. *Modern Problems in Pediatrics,* 1962, **7,** 139–156.

Sontag, L. W. Prevision du comportement de l'enfant par le comportement foetal. *Médécine et Hygiene,* 1963, **21,** 659. (a)

Sontag, L. W. Somatopsychics of personality and body functions. *Vita Humana,* 1963, **6,** 1–10. (b)

Sontag, L. W. Implications of fetal behavior and environmental stress. *Annals of the New York Academy of Science,* 1966, **134,** 782–786.

Sontag, L. W., Steele, William G., & Lewis, Michael. The fetal and maternal cardiac response to environmental stress. *Human Development,* 1969, **12,** 1–9.

Sontag, L. W., & Wallace, R. F. Preliminary report of the Fels Fund: The study of fetal activity. *American Journal of Diseases of Children,* 1934, **48,** 1050–1057.

Sontag, L. W., & Wallace, R. F. The movement response of the human fetus to sound stimuli. *Child Development,* 1935, **6,** 253–258. (a)

Sontag, L. W., & Wallace, R. F. The effect of cigarette smoking during pregnancy upon fetal heart rate. *American Journal of Obstetrics and Gynecology,* 1935, **29,** 77–82. (b)

Sontag, L. W., & Wallace, R. F. Changes in the rate of the human fetal heart in response to vibratory stimuli. *American Journal of Diseases of Children,* 1936, **51,** 583–589.

Steele, W. G., & Koons, P. B., Jr. Cardiac response to mental arithmetic under quiet and white noise distraction. *Psychonomic Science,* 1968, **11,** 273–274.

Stockard, C. R. The genetic and endocrinic basis for differences in form and behavior as elucidated by studies of contrasted pure-line dog breeds and their hybrids. *American Anatomical Memoirs,* Oct., 1941, **19.**

Stoddard, G. D. *The meaning of intelligence.* New York: Macmillan, 1945.

Stone, C. P., & Baker, R. G. The attitudes and interests of premenarcheal and postmenarcheal girls. *Journal of Genetic Psychology,* 1939, **54,** 27–71.

Stott, D. H. Physical and mental handicaps following a disturbed pregnancy. *Lancet,* 1957, **1,** 1006–1012.

Telfer, A., Baker, D., Clark, G. R., & Richardson, C. E. Incidence of gross chromosomal errors among tall criminal American males. *Science,* 1968, **159,** 1249–1250.

Thomas, A., Chess, S., Birch, H. G., Hertzig, M. E., & Korn, S. *Behavior individuality in early childhood.* New York: New York University Press, 1963.

Thompson, W. R. Influence of prenatal maternal anxiety on emotionality in young rats. *Science,* 1957, **125,** 698–699.

Turner, E. K. The syndrome in the infant resulting from maternal emotional tension during pregnancy. *Medical Journal of Australia,* 1956, **1,** 221–222.

Valenstein, E. S. Steroid hormones and the neuropsychology of development. In R. Isaacson (Ed.), *Neuropsychology of development.* New York: Wiley, 1968.

Wellman, B. L. IQ changes of preschool and nonpreschool groups during the preschool years: A summary of the literature. *Journal of Psychology,* 1945, **20,** 347–368.

Williams, R. *Free and unequal.* Austin: University of Texas Press, 1953.

Wooley, D. W., & Shaw, E. A biological and pharmacological suggestion about certain mental disorders. *Science,* 1954, **119,** 587.

Zamenhof, S., van Marthens, E., & Margolis, F. L. DNA (cell number) and protein in neonatal brain: Alteration by maternal dietary protein restriction. *Science,* 1968, **160,** 322–323.

42 The Predictability of Adult Mental Health from Childhood Behavior

Lawrence Kohlberg, Jean LaCrosse, and David Ricks[1]

The research area surveyed by this chapter, the predictability of mental health over time, is probably the single most important area of study of clinical theory and practice with children. For the past two generations, clinical work with children has been dominated by the child-guidance-clinic approach based on psychoanalytic or neo-psychoanalytic theories of child psychopathology. These theories have assumed that nonorganic types of psychopathology are formed in childhood around attempts to defend against experiences of emotional conflict and stress and that these types of psychopathology become relatively crystallized in the elementary school years. In the absence of treatment, it is believed that the defensive styles, and the resultant warping or malformation of personality, will endure into

[1] This review of the literature was supported by NICHD grant HD 02460-01 and by a small grant, from the Joint Commission on Mental Health of Children to the first author. A complete set of abstracts of each of the studies reviewed and a more detailed summary of them all have been made by the second author and deposited with E.R.I.C. and with the Joint Commission.

adulthood and will be expressed as adult symptomatology, given adult experiences of conflict or stress. Furthermore, it is believed that these forms of psychopathology, and the conflicts underlying them, tend to become more crystallized or rigid with time, so that they are more amenable to therapeutic intervention at an earlier than a later age. All these assumptions of child-guidance work must be assessed against longitudinal research findings.

While stressing (1) the importance of early experience in determining adult psychopathology and (2) the continuity of childhood and adult maladjustive attitudes, psychoanalytic theory did not assume the *predictability* (as opposed to the continuity) of adult pathology from childhood symptomatology. According to Freud (1920, republished 1955, pp. 167–168):

So long as we trace development from its final outcome backwards, the chain of events appears continuous, and we feel we have gained an insight which is completely satisfactory or even exhaustive. But if we proceed the reverse way, if we start from the premises inferred from the analysis and try to follow

1217

these up to the final result, then we no longer get the impression of an inevitable sequence of events which could not have been otherwise determined. We notice at once that there might have been another result, and that we might have been just as well able to understand and explain the latter. . . . Hence the chain of causation can always be recognized with certainty if we follow the line of analysis (i.e., reconstruction), whereas to predict it . . . is impossible.

If Freud's pessimistic views as to the possibility of predicting adult psychopathology from childhood behavior and experiences are correct, it does not have great significance for the diagnosis and treatment of adults, but it has shattering implications for the diagnosis and treatment of children. Treatment of children may be justified on the grounds of relieving the immediate distress to the child and to his environment caused by his presenting symptoms. However, selective use of public resources for intensive treatment of some and not other children must also be justified on the grounds that (1) it can be predicted that the children selected for treatment are likely to grow up to be disturbed adults unless treated and (2) treatment will tend to prevent such adult or later disturbance. Much clinical attention and concern have centered on the issue of whether psychotherapy does any good in the sense of preventing or reducing later maladjustment and distress. As the research reviews of Levitt (1957, 1963) and Lewis (1965) indicate, there is little hard evidence that psychotherapy helps treated children as compared with untreated "control" children also referred to a clinic. The whole question of the effectiveness of treatment of children cannot adequately be discussed or researched, however, until the prior question of prediction is studied. The essential findings reviewed by Levitt are that two-thirds to three-quarters of treated children get better but so do the same proportion of control children, who are referred but do not receive treatment through choice or accident. The gross implication is that two-thirds to three-quarters of

children diagnosed as "needing treatment" do not require treatment since they will get better through natural processes of development, whether or not they are treated, or that two-thirds to three-quarters of children referred for treatment are misdiagnosed in the sense that a diagnosis might be considered a prediction that the child's disturbance will continue without treatment. Long-term effectiveness of treatment, then, cannot be subject to research evaluation until we can isolate for treatment a group of children whose problems are predictive of their later maladjustment and whom we can compare with a control group of children who we can also reliably predict will show an equal likelihood of later maladjustment.

From a practical point of view, then, conception of preventive mental-health intervention imposes strong demands for predictability, demands far stronger than those assumed either by intrapsychic personality theories or by the therapy of adults based on these theories. Our review of research will indicate that at the present time we cannot meet these requirements for prediction since we cannot reliably select out the small group of children with adjustment disturbances who will end in jails and mental hospitals unless treated from the larger group of children with disturbances or from obviously bad environments who will not. In the absence of such predictability, it seems impossible to socially justify the use of public funds to intensively treat a small proportion of the child population. The obvious practical alternative is to focus more heavily on *ecological, community mental-health,* and *psychoeducational* approaches. These approaches are oriented to creating an environment in which the cognitive skills, coping, and ego development of all children are facilitated, rather than to segregating children into special therapeutic environments radically different from that in which most of the child's coping efforts are directed. Community and psychoeducational approaches must, of course, focus more upon children with manifest problems than upon those without manifest problems and more upon children with severe problems than upon children with less severe problems. But these distinctions are fluid since diagnostic decisions about long-term placement in individual therapy or in segregated treatment groups are not required. It is assumed that children presenting problems are likely to continue to have problems for some time, whether the problems are situational or intrapsychic. This is not necessarily because the problems are fixed in the personality but is because behavior leading to task failure and social rejection tends to create further problems based on failure and rejection. Such problems are not only problems to the children who have them, but they cause trouble for the other children and adults around the problem child. The attitudes of the group constitute a major determinant of the attitudes of the individual but are themselves shaped by the attitudes of problem individuals. The community or psychoeducational approach, then, does not rest on a sharp distinction between problems in the child's environment and problems in the child's personality. The general conclusion is that mental-health services should be aimed at minimizing the amount of failure, rejection, and misery in children generally, and the problem child is a focus insofar as he overtly represents a large contribution to the sum total of failure, misbehavior, and unhappiness in the group.

Our review, then, will stress the gap which exists between our current ability to predict and the ability assumed by systems of mental-health intervention which sharply separate out a few children for intensive individual treatment. On the more positive side, however, the predictability literature can and does add substantially to our knowledge of the development of psychopathology even though it indicates poor prediction from a selection point of view. We have quoted Freud's statement that an accurate retrospective knowledge of the development of psychopathology

can be obtained and yet this knowledge does not imply the power of prediction in individual cases. It is obvious that if Freud's theory of the development of psychopathology were shown to be correct, it would be of extreme practical importance even if we were unable to predict or select particular children who would become adult problems. The research literature on prediction of later mental-health status is relevant to such a theoretical understanding of the development of pathology, and a finding may have theoretical importance without substantially adding to our power to predict or select for later outcome.

METHODOLOGICAL ISSUES: FOLLOW-UP AND FOLLOW-BACK DESIGNS

The distinctions just drawn immediately lead us into the most critical general issue of the design of life-history research. The issue is that of *follow-up* versus *follow-back* analysis.[2] Follow-up studies select types of children (or of traits) in childhood and follow them up to determine adult outcomes. Follow-back studies select types of adult adjustment outcome and analyze childhood school and clinical records to determine traits or symptoms associated with these outcomes. A study using this design is easier to do and is the customary first step in establishing an association between child and adult behavior. While follow-back studies may yield reliable knowledge as to *connections* between child and adult behavior, they ordinarily cannot provide knowledge usable for individual *prediction* of adult outcome from childhood behavior. Such prediction must take the form of *a statement of probability* that children with given characteristics will have an adult outcome of a given type. Before a characteristic

[2] We use the neologism *follow-back* rather than the usual term *retrospective*, which we take to mean the form of the follow-back design which uses childhood data based on the memory of the patient, his family, etc., that is the ordinary design of the clinical case study.

may be called a predictor of a given outcome, it must be shown that children with the characteristic are significantly more likely to develop the outcome than children without it, i.e., that the rate of children with the trait having the outcome is higher than the base rate for the outcome. As an example, Robins (1966) found that truancy constituted a predictor of alcoholism. Eleven percent of children who were truants as juveniles were diagnosed as alcoholic, whereas 8 percent of all her adults were alcoholic, the difference between 8 and 11 percent being statistically significant. This example also indicates that a characteristic can be a predictor in the statistical-significance sense and yet not be a useful predictor in any practical sense, since the difference between 8 and 11 percent rates of becoming alcoholic, by itself, is of no practical predictive value.

The question then arises as to how one does make a rational decision regarding the sorts of juvenile problems that index meaningfully high risks of later adjustment difficulties. Very arbitrarily, when it has been possible, we have selected for purposes of the present review evidence of a 50 percent or higher risk of later adjustment problems as a currently practical cutoff point for deciding which single variables are or are not predictive. Clearly, there is very ample room for disagreement with this unquestionably arbitrary decision, which represents a cutoff point between traits that are more predictive of illness and those more predictive of health.

Given the notion of probabilistic prediction, it is evident that neither follow-back nor retrospective studies can yield predictive probabilities. If an intuitive effort is made to use such studies for this purpose, it is likely to lead to serious error. As an example, Robins presents both follow-up and follow-back data on the relations of truancy and alcoholism. Follow-back analysis indicated that 75 percent of all alcoholics were truant as compared to 26 percent of psychi-

atrically healthy individuals. This suggests that truancy might be a useful predictor of alcoholism. As we have seen, follow-up figures indicate that this is not the case; only 11 percent of truants become alcoholics as compared to 8 percent of the remaining population. An understanding of continuity of (lower-class) adult alcoholism with childhood experience is aided by Robin's finding that an alcoholic dropout adaptation is very often preceded by a childhood dropout adaptation to school, but this understanding does not generate a useful probabilistic prediction of the adult fate of a school truant.

We have indicated that follow-back studies are almost useless for prognostic-prediction purposes but may be useful for a conceptual and causal understanding of a given outcome. Even here, however, great caution must be exercised in making causal inferences from follow-back studies. Mednick and McNeil (1968) catalog erroneous inferences that have been derived from concurrent and follow-back studies of schizophrenia which are not supported by follow-up longitudinal studies. *Concurrent* studies of the psychological functioning and family patterns of schizophrenics compared to control subjects lead to a variety of findings which are not supported by longitudinal studies. The effects of institutionalization upon the schizophrenic, and the effect of having a hospitalized family member upon the family, lead to a variety of effects which have been incorrectly viewed as antecedents or guides to the causal explanation of schizophrenics. A single dramatic example of the failure of concurrent data to be supported by follow-up study comes from work on the Minnesota Multiphasic Personality Inventory (MMPI) Schizophrenia Scale, based on items concurrently discriminating hospitalized schizophrenics from other patients and normals. High school scores on this scale turned out to be slightly negatively, not positively, predictive of schizophrenic outcome.

While *follow-back* studies are not liable to

many of the sources of bias of *concurrent* studies, they are liable to some forms of bias of their own. As an example, Albee et al. (1964) compared schizophrenics hospitalized in the Cleveland area with elementary school control classmates and found them to have been significantly lower in IQ than controls in the elementary school years. However, the study examined only schizophrenics hospitalized in the Cleveland area, i.e., nonmobile Ss. The control records of elementary school classes might have included children who later became schizophrenic, as many of these children had moved out of the area. Mobile individuals are known to be of higher IQ than nonmobile individuals, so that the IQ differences found by Albee et al. may have been due to low mobility, not to a predisposition to schizophrenia. Mednick and Schulsinger (1967) did not find any IQ differences when they used a follow-up design. While high-risk Ss (children of schizophrenic mothers) are slightly lower (4 points) in IQ than low-risk controls, high-risk Ss who become schizophrenic in adolescence are no lower in elementary school IQ than are Ss who do not break down.

If carefully controlled follow-back studies, such as that of Albee et al., are prone to systematic bias and errors, one can imagine the amount of error involved in clinical research based on the *concurrent* functioning and *retrospective* reports of adult patients. The typical clinician sees a patient for a period of months or years and constructs a picture of the patient's past and future unchecked against later data. It is the purpose of this chapter to summarize what evidence we have which aids in providing the clinician with such a longitudinal perspective. Its focus, then, will be upon the findings of follow-up studies, though we have also reviewed and tabulated follow-back studies. Our review first briefly considers theoretical strategies of prediction in the more extensively studied area of longitudinal analyses of normal development. Next we show some parallel

issues of theoretical strategy in the study of maladjustment by considering the relations between *developmental-adaptive* and *symptomatic* approaches to prediction. We then consider in detail first *cognitive* and then *affective* predictions of later adjustment. Then we consider *social-adaptational behaviors* which are composites of the cognitive, the affective, and the situational. Finally, we take up two contrasting cases of relatively successful prediction—delinquency and schizophrenia. Successful prediction for the first comes from the developmental-social situational model. Successful prediction for the second comes from a biological pathology model combining heredity, organic damage, and environmental stress rather than from either the developmental or psychogenic psychopathology models. We conclude by considering the practical implications of our current knowledge in the area of prediction.

THEORY AND FINDINGS ON THE PREDICTABILITY OF NORMAL PERSONALITY DIFFERENCES

In addition to the distinction of follow-up and follow-back analyses, a number of general conceptual distinctions in the study of personality continuity must be made in considering the research findings. These distinctions have been elaborated by Bloom (1964), by Emmerich (1966), by Ausubel and Sullivan (1970), by the writers (Kohlberg, 1969; Kohlberg & Zigler, 1967), and by Block and Haan (1971) in reviewing longitudinal findings on normal personality development. Continuity of personality development may be studied using the three following systems of assumptions:

1. The assumption of trait stability. In this approach, one examines the correlation between an adult behavior trait (or symptom) and a similar childhood behavior trait.

2. The assumption of continuity through invariant developmental sequences.

3. The assumption of stability of idiographic individuality, of the individual's distinctive or unique organization of his various traits.

A bald summary of the findings on normal personality using these three approaches may be derived from the surveys of Ausubel and Sullivan (1970), Emmerich (1966), Bloom (1964), and Kohlberg (1969). Trait stability is found primarily in the area of temperament; of genetically linked style of response to stimuli (activity-passivity, introversion-extroversion, etc.). All reviews are consistent with the conclusion of Escalona and Heider (1959):

> Our best predictive successes have occurred in regard to the formal aspects of behavior. With few exceptions, we have been better able to forecast *how* a child goes about moving, thinking, speaking, playing than what he is likely to do, think, speak or play.

An understanding of findings on stability, then, rests on distinguishing between traits of form and traits of (motivational) content. Second, it rests on distinguishing traits defined by adaptational and age-developmental dimensions from those which have no direct relation to development or whose developmental and adaptational significance varies at varying age periods. Temperamental traits are formal traits which do not define age trends. Temperamental differences are relatively situation-free; they are not clearly characterizable as adaptive-maladaptive (socially good or bad); they are manifested at all developmental levels, and development is not definable in terms of them (children do not become more or less introverted with age). In the case of traits of content, these other factors become involved and predictability becomes much poorer. This is typically the case in the motivational area. Traits such as aggression, selfishness, anxiety, and dependency show very low stability, and if they show

moderate (that is = .20 to .60) stability in one sex, they do not in the other. This poorer stability of motivational traits and needs is partly due to the fact that most such traits have one adaptive or developmental value at one age and a second at another. Physical aggression may not be maladaptive or immature in a middle-class boy aged 5, but it is in a middle-class boy aged 12. Physical aggression is maladaptive in a girl at any age. Nor surprisingly, then, aggression at 5 and at age 12 correlates poorly in boys and not at all in girls (Kagan & Moss, 1962; MacFarlane, Allen, & Honzik, 1954).

In addition to temperamental and motivational traits, there is a third type of trait, that which is defined by age-developmental trends and by adaptational significance. In traits of this sort, prediction is based not on the assumption that children stay the same but rather that children who are developmentally advanced at an early age will be developmentally advanced at a later age. These traits always have a cognitive component. They are the most stable or predictive traits yet found, being more predictive than temperamental traits. General intelligence, or IQ, is the best established of such traits. It has been repeatedly found that half of the reliable variation in adult IQ is predictable from IQ scores on school entrance at first grade; that is, r's are in the .60s, accounting for about half of the reliable variation when test-retest variation is subtracted from that variance (Bloom, 1964; Jensen, 1969). General intelligence is only one of a number of cognitive ability and style traits which show these characteristics. As an example, Witkin et al. (1967) have defined a cognitive-style dimension termed *global versus analytic* approach or *psychological differentiation* indicated in the perceptual realm by "field independence versus dependence." This, in turn, is measured by the ability to adjust a luminous rod to an upright position in a dark room without distorting the upright to correspond to a tilted luminous frame behind it. Correlation of field independence at age 24 with field independence at age 14 was .84 and with field independence at age 10 was .66 in a male sample (correlations were similar for females, who were not, however, studied past age 17). While part of this stability is probably due to IQ (with which the measure is correlated), field independence is clearly a stable variable. Other attention and cognitive-style variables which have developmental components appear to be equally promising from the point of view of trait stability (Kagan, 1970).

We have so far discussed predictions of relative maturity from a trait approach. Much serious work on the predictability of relative maturity over time has also been oriented to a stage-sequential model. Most theories of personality formation do not assume trait stability. They assume rather that personality undergoes radical transformations in development but that there is continuity in the individual's development through these transformations. In other words, they conceptualize personality development as an orderly sequence of change, with the individual's location at a later point in the sequence being related to his position at earlier points in the sequence.

In this view, early experience determines the choice of one or another path or sequence of development. It does not lead to the stamping in or fixation of traits carried from situation to situation throughout life. As stated by Anderson (1957), "The young organism is fluid, subsequent development can go in any one of many directions. But once a choice is made and direction is set, cumulative and irreversible changes take place."

While continuity in personality development may be defined in terms of a number of alternative sequences available to different individuals in different social settings, most developmental theories of personality have employed some notion of a single, universal sequence of personality stages (Erikson, 1950; Freud, 1938; Gesell, 1954; Piaget, 1928). Such stage theories view the child's social behavior as reflections of age-typical world views and coping mechanisms rather than as reflections of fixed character traits. As the child moves from stage to stage, developmental theorists expect his behavior to change radically but to be predictable in terms of knowledge of his prior location in the stage sequence and of the intervening experiences stimulating or retarding movement to the next stage. The implication for research is that satisfactory definition or measurement of age development requires definition of changes in the shape, pattern, or organization of responses, representing different psychological organizations at varying points in development. The stage doctrine hypothesizes that these qualitatively different types of organization are sequential and hence that the individual's developmental status is predictable or cumulative in the sense of continuity of position on an ordinal scale.

At present, the stage approach has been especially employed in three areas: cognitive development, ego development, and moral development. With regard to cognitive development, we have indicated that psychometric approaches to cognitive maturity clearly indicate stability from late preschool to adulthood in IQ, conceived as cumulative maturity (mental age) in "number of right answers." More recent approaches to intelligence based upon Piaget methods indicate that stage measures of maturity increase predictability even farther, at least over the short (three years) span structured. While psychometric and Piaget measures of cognitive maturity correlate with one another (= .60 to .70), factor analysis clearly separates psychometric and Piaget stage measures of cognition from one another (Kohlberg & De Vries, 1969). The Piaget stage measures are, in turn, predictable over time beyond expectations based on IQ, due to the fact that advance in an invariant sequence of stage favors further advance in the series (Kohn, 1969).

With regard to moral maturity, longitudinal

study indicates that children go through an invariant sequence of six stages of moral thought (Kohlberg, 1969). At one stage an individual child judges in terms of punishment and obedience; still later, in terms of maintenance of a social system of role expectations and authority; still later, in terms of moral principles. The moral ideology of the child, then, looks very different at various ages. Nevertheless, his position relative to other children, who are also changing, remains quite constant after age 13. The correlation between moral-maturity scores at age 16 (or age 13) and at age 25 is .78. At earlier ages (e.g., age 10), moral-maturity scores are much less predictive of adult status.

A number of writers have defined stages of ego development which include or parallel stages of moral development (Harvey, Hunt, & Schroeder, 1961; Vanden Daele, 1968; Loveinger, 1966). These stages are based on level of conceptualization of the self, the ego-ideal, of interpersonal relations, and of social values. Age-developmental trends in these stages are similar to those found for moral stages (Sullivan, McCullough, & Stager, 1970; Vanden Daele, 1968). While predictability over time has not yet been examined on these measures, the parallels with moral-stage measures suggest they will be relatively high. All three areas are correlated with one another; that is, measures of cognitive stage, of ego maturity, and of moral maturity range between .40 and .66 (Kohlberg, 1969; Sullivan & McCollough, 1970; Vanden Daele, 1968). Each area, however, may be distinguished from the other by factor analytic methods. There are reasons for thinking that the relations between the areas are such that cognitive development is a precondition to ego development and ego development a precondition to moral development. Cognitive development is more general than ego development, which represents cognitively based functioning in the domain of the social self. Ego development is more general than moral develop-

ment, which represents conceptual level of the social self in areas where there is a conflict of interests between persons. The precondition relation implies that the more specific (e.g., moral development) depends upon the more general (e.g., cognitive development), but not vice versa. Stated in other terms, one might expect that cognitively retarded children will be retarded in moral development (or ego development) but that cognitively advanced children need not be advanced in moral development (or ego development). In fact, the evidence suggests just this, that moral maturity is linearly related to IQ at the below-average IQ levels but that it is not correlated with IQ at the above-average levels. The same relation seems to hold with ego development. All high-moral children are relatively high on ego development, but not vice versa (Sullivan, McCullough, & Stager, 1970).

In summary, successful prediction in the cognitive, ego, and moral areas derives from the following conditions: (1) assessment in terms of an invariant sequence of developmental stages and (2) assessment in terms of a general level of optimal competence having cognitive components. These two conditions are linked in the sense that almost all culturally universal and regular age-developmental trends or sequences have heavy cognitive-competence components (Kohlberg, 1969). If the findings from the stage approach are combined with the findings from the intellectual-ability, cognitive-style, and coping-style studies discussed earlier, they provide a broad and relatively predictive description and measurement of ego development, including cognitive, moral, and self-conceptual components. Such descriptions constitute the best general tool for long-range prediction which normal child-development studies are at present able to provide the clinician.

We have so far discussed prediction from cognitive-hierarchical models of ego and moral development. Other fruitful stage models come from embryological models of ego and moral development, such as Erikson's (1950, 1964). Following Loveinger (1966), we may distinguish hierarchical from embryological models in that the former assume that each earlier mode of functioning (stage) is transformed into or integrated into the next stage of functioning whereas embryological modes define stages as distinctive age-developmental tasks. In this model, solution of one task facilitates solution of the next but the next task is faced regardless of the outcome of the earlier (in other words, a later stage organization is not a transformation of the earlier stage organization; it only builds upon it). Furthermore, the Erikson model defines stages as points of choice or bifurcation between individuals;[3] i.e., it spreads individuals along dimensions of individual difference, as well as defining them as more or less mature (Emmerich, 1966).

A third approach to personality prediction has been the idiographic or ipsitive one (Block & Haan, 1971; Rabson, 1969; Shirley, 1941). This approach is concerned with the relative salience of traits to one another in the individual, with their organization, and with the individual's style or manner of expressing these traits, rather than with the individual's rank on a trait compared with the rank of others. The studies cited offer evidence of some stability on idiographic personality organization, though it seems to vary widely from individual to individual (Block & Haan, 1971; Rabson, 1969). Part of the appeal of the approach is the fact that children have recognizably discernible individualities maintained from early childhood to adulthood (Shirley, 1941).

[3] When an indivudal child confronts a task (e.g., the crisis of autonomy shame), he does not simply pass from organizing the world as based on symbiosis to basing it upon the interactions of distinct wills, but he becomes differentiated from other children on various dimensions of autonomy, shame, etc. Emmerich (1966) is engaged in a program of research to map personality continuity from this more complex stage view, but we do not yet have much longitudinal evidence which bears upon it. Ultimately, however, it may build a richer base of prediction than the hierarchical approach.

Many of these unique characteristics are stylistic configurations, the behavioral analogues of the baby's fingerprint or facial configuration. The question about such manifestations of individuality is how they may be used to understand or predict later development and adaptation. The recognition of an adult's face in a group of pictures of babies casts no direct light on the predictability of adult physical growth and health from infant status. Theory and research using the idiographic approach are not yet advanced enough to cast light on these problems in the psychological domain.

We have so far discussed alternative models of prediction as if prediction were an end in itself. From a practical as well as a theoretical viewpoint, however, one of the ultimate payoffs of prediction studies is the definition of critical periods in development. The primary example of such an effort comes from Bloom's (1964) analysis of the longitudinal studies of the development of intelligence. Bloom has integrated data on longitudinal prediction with age-developmental growth data and with experimental intervention data to argue that the preschool period (ages 1 to 5) is a critical period for educational intervention in the stimulation of general intelligence. To a considerable extent, Bloom's rationale is the fundamental rationale of Head Start and other preschool programs for intellectual stimulation, especially of the disadvantaged. Bloom's argument stems from two primary findings:

1. Adult intelligence is predictable from IQ at first grade ($r = .60$ to $.70$), but it is not predictable from IQ type measures at age 1 to 2.
2. The preschool period (1 to 5) is a period of extremely rapid natural growth in general intelligence. Using various scaling rationales, Bloom estimates that about half of adult intellectual functioning has developed by age 6.

Bloom ties these findings together by the assumption that about half of the variance in adult

IQ is predictable from IQ at age 6 because about half of adult intelligence has developed during this period. Since adult IQ is not predictable from IQ at age 1, it is not an inborn or hereditary characteristic. Since adult IQ is predictable from IQ at age 6, however, intellectual development in this rapid period of intellectual growth (ages 1 to 5) is a relatively irreversible result of cognitive-environmental stimulation in this period. Later stimulation cannot offset deprivation in the preschool period, he believes, because if it could, adult status would not be so predictable from status at age 6. Cognitive stimulation, however, can to a considerable extent overcome potential deprivation in the earlier period up until this stabilization (or rapid increase of predictability) of IQ.

Essentially it is Bloom's assumption that a critical period is defined by rapid stabilization (increased predictability) with age, which is necessary to operationalize the argument for the early diagnosis and treatment of emotional disturbance in childhood which underlies child-guidance and preventive mental-health approaches. The usual theoretical assumption concerning neurosis, for instance, is that neuroses or stable defensive reactions to intrapsychic conflict crystallize or stabilize in the early school years. In Bloom's logic, this implies that neurotic types of emotional disturbance in adulthood are not well predicted by preschool functioning but are predictable from late-latency (ages 9 to 12) functioning. If this were the case, it would seem that this rapid period of increased predictability (from age 7 to age 11) would be the period of choice for preventive and therapeutic intervention.

While Bloom's logic is powerful, it has not held up well with regard to the area of intelligence as such. This is because the rapid increase of predictability of intelligence between age 1 and age 5 is in very large part to be explained as the appearance of a latent hereditary component in general intelligence and secondarily as the appearance of a latent cultural or home factor, which continues to shape intellectual development through childhood. The evidence supporting this conclusion is about as strong as any evidence in social science and has been thoroughly reviewed from this point of view by Jensen (1969) and by Kohlberg (1968). Essentially, baby tests fail to predict adult intelligence because they are not good tests of cognition or intelligence; they are tests of noncognitive sensory and motor maturation. Accordingly, they fail to pick up the hereditary component of intelligence, which the Stanford-Binet does pick up at age 5 to 6. As proof, the correlation of the IQs of foster children and adoptive children with the IQs of their real mothers (from whom they are completely separated) increases markedly in the preschool critical period (evidence reviewed in Kohlberg, 1968 and Jensen, 1969). Because of these facts, the optimistic notion that preschool education would markedly raise IQ in stable or long-range predictive ways has proved false (Jensen, 1969; Kohlberg, 1968).

While the application of Bloom's critical-period logic to intelligence has been a little disappointing, the logic is sound when not applied to a largely hereditary trait. An example of its application to a more environmentally determined trait comes from the Kohlberg (1969) work on morality. While IQ and other biological factors contribute something to moral maturity, there is little reason to believe that adult moral character is in any large part a direct hereditary-biological product. Adult moral character does not seem to be predictable until preadolescence (12 to 13), a very late time for a hereditary characteristic to be manifested (Kohlberg, 1969, Peck & Havighurst, 1960). As mentioned earlier, adult (age 25) moral maturity is predictable from maturity at age 13 ($r = .78$ to $.92$) but not from maturity at age 10 ($r = .20$ to $.24$). While this may be due to the inadequacy of our measures of moral character at age 10, it seems more likely that it is the result of the rapid moral growth at ages 9 to 12, in which most children move from "preconventional" to "conventional" morality. Following this rationale, Blatt and Kohlberg (1972) have developed public school programs of classroom moral discussion for this preadolescent period. These programs are based on (1) cognitive conflict through argument, and (2) exposure to the next stage of thinking above the child's own through cultivating arguments between adjacent stages. Preliminary results indicate that these programs move most children up one stage and that the advance is retained (compared with a control group) one year after the educational intervention.

The example is cited as a tentative but relatively clear case of intervention into ego development that clearly makes use of longitudinal prediction findings suggesting a critical period for intervention, in this case the period of preadolescence.

APPLICATION TO THE PREDICTION OF MENTAL-HEALTH DEVELOPMENTAL-ADAPTATIONAL AND SYMPTOMATIC APPROACHES

In mental-health research and practice, neither the "trait-stability" nor the "stage-developmental" model has been elaborated in pure form.

The trait-stability approach in pure form would imply the existence of symptomatic traits in children exactly corresponding to adult diagnostic traits or labels of psychopathology. While child psychiatric diagnosis does not make definite assumptions about the exact relationship of diagnosis to prognosis, many of the diagnostic categories of child psychiatry [as formulated by the Group for Advancement of Psychiatry (GAP) report, 1966] represent applications of adult psychiatric categories to children. Such categories as *psychoneurotic disorder, anxiety type, psychoneurotic disorder, phobic type, oppositional or passive-aggressive personality* are essen-

tially defined in a fashion similar to that employed in adult diagnosis. (Other diagnostic categories are peculiar to children, however; e.g., there is no adult analogue to a "learning block" diagnosis.) It is not clear in such writing as the GAP report that parallelism in diagnostic definition implies the assumption of trait stability of prognosis, e.g., that a diagnosis of "psychoneurotic disorder, phobic type" is a prognosis, if the subject is untreated, of an adult diagnosis as "psychoneurotic disorder, phobic type." If diagnosis is not prognosis, however, it is difficult to understand the rationale of applying adult diagnostic labels to children. There is certainly a simplified version of psychoanalytic theory which might lead to equating childhood and adult diagnostic categories. In this version an adult diagnostic category represents a pathological adaptation to a childhood emotional conflict, with the emotional conflict and the pathological adaptation or symptomatology both being fixed or frozen in childhood as a constellation continuing into adulthood and defining a diagnostic entity. Most clinicians, however, are oriented to more complex and less reductionistic notions of the relations between pathology and development, such as those formulated by Erikson (1950, 1964). In these more complex models, a childhood conflict is maintained as a theme in later development but its relationship to type of pathology, or indeed its healthy or unhealthy resolution is determined by developmental events up through adulthood.

Unfortunately, few longitudinal studies have yet been conducted which might shed direct light on either the fixed diagnosis (trait-stability) or the more developmental or stage-sequential models of psychopathology. Accordingly, our review of the literature will simply make a general distinction between a diluted form of the pure-trait-stability approach, which we shall call the *symptomatic approach*, and a diluted form of the stage-developmental approach, which we shall call the *developmental-adaptational* approach. The developmental-adaptational approach focuses upon prediction of later difficulty based upon relative level of development of traits of direct adaptational significance, such as intelligence, ego development, and moral development. It assumes that all children are changing on these traits but that relative arrest at an earlier time is likely to predict to relative arrest at a later time. The term *developmental-adaptational* is meant to stress the fact that almost all traits on which there are clear trends of age development are also traits generally recognized by the society to be "good" or "adaptive" regardless of clinical or psychological knowledge or viewpoint and that, conversely, almost all traits considered good by society show age-developmental trends.[4] The contrast between the two approaches may be suggested by comparing traits of "withdrawal" and "antisocial behavior." Withdrawal as a trait which does not increase with age and which is stable over time is largely a temperamental trait without strong adaptational value as judged by the culture. The symptomatic approach has sometimes read into this temperamental trait a mental-health significance by assuming that it is a weak form of an adult symptom which it will prognose. As an example, Wilkinson (1928) conducted a famous study comparing teachers' and clinicians' judgments of maladaptation in children and found that teachers viewed hyperaggressive behaviors as "sicker" than shyness whereas clinicians put much more emphasis on withdrawn behavior. Presumably teachers were responding to the bothersome here and now in behavior and

to the violation of rules, while the clinicians were prognosing long-range mental illness of the order of schizophrenia and neurotic withdrawal. As teachers have become increasingly exposed to mental-health concepts, their judgments of children's mental-health status have come closer to that of the clinicians (Schrupp & Gjerde, 1958; Stoeffer, 1952). The longtitudinal evidence unfortunately suggests that the clinicians should have been influenced by the teachers, rather than vice versa. In reality, the teacher's criterion of strong antisocial behavior does predict to adult maladjustment whereas shyness and withdrawal do not. As our review will indicate, shyness and withdrawal in elementary school children do not predict to schizophrenia or to other forms of adult maladaptation. In contrast, our review of childhood antisocial behavior indicates that it does predict to adult antisocial behavior as well as to other forms of adult maladjustment.

As a stable trait, withdrawal or shyness is temperamental, not developmental, since there are no regular age-developmental trends toward increased extroversion. In contrast, there are some gross age trends in decline of antisocial behavior, and there are also much more regular trends of moral character development which tend to underlie such age declines in antisocial behavior. While shyness is nondevelopmental and temperamental, then, antisocial behavior is to a considerable extent developmental. Second, shyness carries no direct environmental-adaptational consequences with it, whereas antisocial behavior elicits counteragression and punishment, promoting a vicious circle in child-environment interaction. For such reasons, then, a developmental-adaptational trait such as antisocial behavior or moral character seems to be more predictive than "symptomatic" traits such as withdrawal, which have temperamental components.

A more general comparison of the predictive value of the two approaches forms a focus of the

---

[4] One of the writers (Kohlberg, 1969) has discussed elsewhere the complex issue of whether age development is toward the socially defined good because age development is a process of socialization and education or whether basic, culturally universal norms or equilibria of adaptation determine both society's conception of the good and the process of age development. Whether due to socialization or natural development, the fact is that there are very few traits considered good or bad which are not heavily related in a positive direction to age development.

longitudinal research program of Kellam and Schiff (1967). These researchers have had teachers rate 2,000 ghetto children yearly on a four-point scale for six adaptive tasks (social contact, authority acceptance, maturation, cognitive authority acceptance, maturation, cognitive achievement, concentration, and global adaptation). These same children were independently rated by clinical psychologists in an unstructured situation on six symptomatic scales (flatness, depression, anxiety, hyperkinesis, bizarreness, and global mental health). There were moderate concurrent correlations between the clinicians' ratings of sickness and the teachers' ratings on social contact, maturation, and global adaptation. Over time in school, these correlations increased and their pattern changed. In later grades the relation between symptomatic and teacher adaptive ratings was heavily determined by the "hyperaggressive, immature, underachieving constellation" in contrast to the "withdrawn, immature constellation" picked up by the two sets of ratings earlier. Stated differently, the clinicians responded to an initial shy, fearful, withdrawn reaction to school entrances as "sick." As the children grew used to school, some of the withdrawn children became well adjusted while others became hyperaggressive and inattentive. Of even greater interest is Kellam and Schiff's finding that the teachers' adaptation ratings predicted to later symptomatic ratings better than the symptomatic ratings predicted to later adaptation ratings. Children rated maladaptive by teachers at the beginning of first grade had a good probability of being considered symptomatic at the end of first grade, though the reverse relation did not hold. These relations were not as strong over longer periods of time but showed the same patterns.

To summarize the findings of Kellam and Schiff, adaptational and symptomatic ratings were correlated but adaptational ratings were better predictors to later ratings, both adaptational and symptomatic, than were the symptomatic ratings.

The implications of the finding are the same as those made in our comparison of the predictive value of withdrawal and antisocial behavior. Adaptive ratings are predictive over time for the same reasons that intellectual maturity and moral maturity are predictive over time—because adaptive traits are cumulative and age-developmental whereas symptomatic traits are not and because positive adaptive traits are supported by the environment whereas the positive pole of symptomatic traits is not.

Kellam and Schiff's findings support some further generalizations. While most predictive studies rely on the correlation coefficient, it is seldom the case that the relative position of the child who is above some "milestone" level of adequacy or maturity on a trait predicts in the same sense as does the relative position of the child below that level. More specifically, the following generalizations frequently obtain:

1. In regard to developmental-adaptational traits, children who have attained an adequate level seldom lose a positive place on the trait while children at an immature or low level on the trait more frequently come up to an adequate level on it.[5] Kellam and Schiff found that for both adaptive and symptomatic ratings, one can predict better that well-adjusted children will

---

[5] One of the most dramatic long-range examples of this generalization comes from the Glueck (1966) study of delinquency. Almost none of their control group ever became delinquent or criminal, i.e., adolescent nondelinquency is a tendency never lost. In contrast, the delinquent group became increasingly nondelinquent with age in the period 17 to 29, so that only 29 percent were actively criminal at age 29. Thus adolescent nondelinquency is an almost perfect predictor of adult noncriminality but serious adolescent delinquency is only a moderate (29 percent) predictor of adult criminality. The same relation holds for predicting adolescent delinquency from elementary school family background. Using the Glueck prediction tables, Tait and Hodges (1962) correctly predicted "no later delinquency" in 95 percent of cases (referred for school misbehavior) but correctly predicted delinquency in only 36 percent of the cases.

stay well adjusted than that poorly adjusted children will stay poorly adjusted. We can diagnose the "healthy" better than the "ill." However, this finding is much more marked for adaptational than symptomatic tests. While children positive on adaptational traits are unlikely to become negative, children free of symptoms are more likely to become symptomatic. As discussed in the next section, all developmental-adaptational traits have cognitive ability components, and basic cognitive competences are irreversible, i.e., they are never lost. In contrast, most affective traits are related to current developmental and situational factors and are more or less reversible. Many emotional symptoms come and go according to the current situation of the child in relation to family, school, and peer group.

2. We have said that a positive level is more likely to be predictive than a negative level with regard to a developmental-adaptational trait. This finding, however, is with regard to predicting to the same trait later in time. If one wished

to predict to the concurrent relation of an adaptational trait to another emotional trait, a second generalization holds. This is that low status on the adaptational trait predicts to emotional disturbance but that high status on the trait is less likely to predict to being positive on the emotional trait. This is because the significance of developmental-adaptational traits for predicting to happiness or social-emotional status is often that of a necessary, not a sufficient, condition. This was noted earlier, when evidence was discussed suggesting that "stupid" children were retarded in ego and moral development while "bright" children need not be advanced. In regard to emotional tone and self-esteem, the "necessary but not sufficient condition" is even more basic. A retarded child is fairly likely to be disturbed; a bright child is less likely to be well adjusted. Brightness and success do not make a child happy, but it is hard to be happy without a certain minimal level of these attributes (a truism first amplified by Aristotle).[6]

---

[6] An example of the masking of the two generalizations just presented by use of the correlation coefficient comes from a longitudinal study by Havighurst et al. (1962) (and is more fully discussed in the next section). Two relatively good predictors to young adult adjustment (as globally rated) were sixth-grade IQ and tenth-grade adjustment scores on the California Psychological Inventory (CPI). The correlation between IQ and adult adjustment was .48, and between the CPI and adult adjustment, .58—roughly the same. The predictive powers of the two measures are very different, however, and reflect the two generalizations made. The CPI is a measure of adjustment predicting later adjustment. As such, it is a good predictor to later absence of maladjustment but is neither a good predictor to later good adjustment nor a good positive predictor of maladjustment. A moderate (upper three quartiles) score on the CPI is an indicator that a moderate level of adjustment will not be lost later, though a low score is not an indicator that a moderate level of adjustment will not be attained. If a child had a moderate score on CPI adjustment, he had less than a 1 percent chance of being in the bottom adult adjustment group (as compared with a 10 percent random probability). Expressed differently, almost all (77 percent) of the bottom adult adjustment group came from the bottom-quartile children on the CPI. How-

ever, most of the bottom-quartile children did not end up in the bottom adjustment group; i.e., being in the bottom quartile is not a good predictor of later poor adjustment. Furthermore, while a moderate score predicts absence of a later maladjustment, neither a moderate nor a good score predicts good later adjustment. The random probability of being in the top level of adjustment was 15 percent; the probability if the child was in the top quartile on the CPI was little better (23 percent).

In contrast to CPI adjustment, the IQ measure predicts on the necessary-but-not-sufficient rationale. A moderate score on IQ is not a good predictor of later absence of maladjustment, as is the CPI. Over 5 percent of the moderately intelligent (upper three quartiles) were in the bottom adjustment group (compared with a 10 percent random probability). Again, a high quartile score in IQ is not a good predictor of high adjustment (34 percent, compared with 15 percent randomly), but a low quartile score is a good predictor of *failure* to attain high adjustment (1 percent, compared with 15 percent). Both these findings reflect the necessary-but-not-sufficient rationale. Until longitudinal researchers break down correlation coefficients into such predictive contingencies, it will be difficult to either understand or make prac-

We have reported the preliminary findings of one major longitudinal study of problem behavior in an unselected group of (lower-class black) children, the Kellam and Schiff study. The other major longitudinal study of problem behavior between the ages of 2 and 14 (based on mothers' reports for a random sample of children representative of the city of Berkeley) is that of MacFarlane, Allen, and Honzik (1954). These authors classify problem behavior in terms of the age-developmental trends which they found. Reworking their classifications slightly, we arrive at the following groupings:

1. *Developmental-adaptational traits.* These are (*a*) problem behaviors which decline steadily with age throughout childhood or (*b*) behaviors such as lying which are "discovered" in preschool but decline throughout the school years. This group includes fears, overactivity, speech problems, destructiveness, lying, negativism, temper tantrums, enuresis, thumbsucking.

2. *Temperamental traits.* These are clusters of problems related to temperament and not regularly related to age. They include shyness, oversensitiveness, somberness, reserve, and to some extent irritability and jealousy.

3. *Phase-specific reactions to developmental crises.* These are clusters of problem behaviors which increased dramatically at two time points; the first time point is the "5-to-7" shift of school entrance, latency, or concrete operational thought, and the second is the "10-to-13" shift of puberty, junior high school entrance, or formal operational thought. These phase-specific traits include restless sleep, distrubing dreams, physical timidity, irritability, overdependence, and jealousy. (There was some overlap between these and the temperamental traits).

In terms of long-range predictability, the best steady predictors were the temperamental traits (as we would expect). The correlations between one of these traits at age 7 and the same trait at age 14 ranged from .40 to .60 and were relatively steady over the years. In terms of short-range prediction, the best predictors were the developmental-adaptational traits. Trait maturity at 1 year correlated relatively well with maturity the next year, but the longer the separation in time, the lower the correlation. A third type of prediction characterized the phase-specific reactions. Here the traits correlated well with themselves between the periods 5 to 7 and 10 to 13 but not as well in the intervening years. These phase-specific reactions determined or colored the overall prediction of problematic behavior over time, in terms of a measure of overall number of problem behaviors. Among boys, the number of problems at age 14 correlated -.07 with the number of problems at age 5, .73 with the number of problems at age 6, and .36 with the number of problems at age 8. Thus phase-specific reactions partly obscure long-range consistencies of temperament and development (as in the low correlation of -.07 between the ages 5 and 14) and partly lead to high correlations between ages of turbulence (6 and 13).

The MacFarlane study, then, like the Kellam and Schiff study, indicates that the imposition of fixed diagnostic categories of pathology onto symptomatic behavior is doomed to predictive and prognostic failure in the absence of a base in systematic observation of the regularities and perturbations of development.

With regard to temperament, the most comprehensive study of the relations of early temperamental traits to behavior disorders is that of Thomas, Chess, and Birch (1968) (though its follow-up data cover only the years from infancy to the early elementary school years). According to these authors:

> No single temperamental trait acted alone in influencing the course of the child's development. Rather, combinations of traits forming patterns and clusters tended to result in an indirect risk for developing behavior disorders. A given pattern of temperament did not, as such, result in a behaviorial

disturbance. Deviant as well as normal development was the result of the interaction between the child with given characteristics of temperament and significant features of the familial and extra-familial environment.

In other words, a temperamental trait could be a source of friction or difficulty with parents and school if handled in certain ways by these environmental agents but was not itself a direct prediction of a specific trait of disturbance. The disturbances studied by the authors were often of a transitory, developmental nature.[7] In any case, most temperamental and interpersonal traits are not clearly predictive of level of adult adjustment. While Kagan and Moss (1962) found low and occasionally moderate prediction of adult traits from similar childhood traits, they did not find measures of adult anxiety and conflict (based on interview and thematic perception measures) predicted by childhood traits.

The findings just discussed reinforce our earlier conclusions about the "developmental-adaptational" and the "emotional-symptomatic." The Kellam and Schiff data suggested that the symptomatic-emotional was more a consequence than a cause of developmental-adaptational difficulties. Ratings on the developmental-adaptational predicted to the later symptomatic, but the reverse was not the case. Thomas, Chess, and Birch (1968) come to a similar conclusion. According to these authors (p. 186):

> Common to Freudian, neo-Freudian and most learning theories is the assumption that anxiety and intrapsychic conflict is the basic chronic pathogenic force and the basic maneuver leading to symptom-formation is the reduction or avoidance of such anxiety and intrapsychic conflict. Our longitudinal data made it possible to determine the time relations be-

tween anxiety and symptom-formation, and our guidance procedures, focused on the direct elimination of symptoms, have given us the opportunity to determine the consequences of symptom removal. As has been demonstrated in the case histories, in the young child anxiety has not been evident as an initial factor preceding and determining symptom development. Where anxiety has arisen, it has been more a consequence than a cause, though it then affects the symptoms and the expression. Similarly the removal of symptoms had had positive consequences for the child's functioning and has not resulted in the appearance of overt anxiety or of new substitutive symptoms.

The findings of Thomas, Chess, and Birch were based largely on phenomena in children younger than the classic latency age for the crystallization of intrapsychic conflict. Our review will support their conclusion, however, in that emotional symptomatology is not nearly as reliable a predictor of adult maladjustment as are social character and cognitive adaptation.[8]

In summary, then:

1. Developmental-adaptational traits predict better over time both to themselves and to other traits than do symptomatic-affective traits.

2. Positive status on a developmental-adaptational trait is more predictive of later absence of maladjustment on the trait than is negative status on the trait predictive of later maladjustment on it.

3. The significance of low status on developmental-adaptational traits for predicting other mental-health traits is more clear-cut than is that of high status on the traits.

4. Much stably predictive symptomatic behavior is really temperamental and has little direct or long-range negative mental-health implications.

---

[7] It seems plausible to think that as the child moves to adulthood, he develops more latitude to select an environment compatible with his temperament. Thus a highly "withdrawn" or "introverted" child can be predicted to be not disturbed but to seek a relatively sheltered, stable, quiet, "undemanding" occupation and marital adjustment.

[8] Some qualification of this conclusion is required by findings on psychosis. Intense anxiety is a characteristic of a phase of reactive schizophrenia, and childhood anxiety is a predictor of it. However, our review of schizophrenia suggests that the predisposition to such anxiety and to schizophrenic defenses against it has heavy biological roots.

5. Much symptomatic behavior is specific to developmental phases or crises and may either predict only from one transition era (5 to 7) to another (10 to 13) or not predict at all.

COGNITIVE AND SCHOOL-ACHIEVEMENT PREDICTORS OF ADJUSTMENT

In contrasting developmental-adaptational and symptomatic approaches to the prediction of adult mental health, we assumed that developmental-adaptational traits had a cognitive structural base generating long-range predictiveness in a way that symptomatic-affective traits did not. Our survey of normal development indicated that predictability of a measure to the same measure in adulthood was maximum for measures of development with a heavy cognitive-ability base, including IQ, "differentiation," and moral-judgment maturity, all yielding ten-year predictions or correlations in the .70s and .80s. In part, this is because the development of cognitive traits is largely cumulative, sequential, and irreversible, whereas much of the development of affective traits and experiences is not clearly sequential or irreversible. To conscious experience, moods change, anxieties disappear, loves and hates fade, the emotion of yesterday is weak, and the emotion of today does not clearly build on the emotion of yesterday. The trauma theory of neurosis is dead; the evidence for irreversible effects of early-childhood trauma is extremely slight. Early-childhood maternal deprivation, parental mistreatment, separation, incest—all seem to have much slighter effects upon adult adjustment (unless supported by continuing deprivation and trauma throughout childhood) than anyone seemed to anticipate (Kadushin, 1967; Yarrow, 1964). (See the section "Prediction of Psychoses," below.)

According to cognitive-developmental theory (and parts of psychoanalytic theory), affective phenomena live on through memories or cog-nitive storage mechanisms, which are themselves transformed in cognitive and emotional development and through cognitive-style defensive operations screening such cognitions (Piaget, 1968). Accordingly, the enduring effects of emotional experience are not due to the fixation of traumatic experiences in memory but are rather due to sequences of emotional development which have cognitive-structural components. This, at least, is the assumption of the cognitive-developmental approach of Piaget, Werner, and others (Kohlberg, 1966, 1968, 1969). The approach assumes that emotional development and cognitive development are a single domain considered from two different perspectives (Kohlberg, 1969; Kohlberg & Zigler, 1967; Piaget, 1957). Not all emotional phenomena are indicators of emotional development. Emotional development refers to age-developmental trends in the differentiation and integration of affective responses and in the organization of the objects which elicit them. Emotional development, then, implies a structural or organizational component; it implies irreversible structural transformations in the organization of social-emotional responses. As so conceived, the structural development of emotion has basic dimensions in common with the structural development of cognition. These common dimensions may be very general, as in the general notion of differentiation used by Witkin et al. (1962) to order correlations between intellectual and emotional tasks. They may also be much more specific to given stages and tasks. As an example, Piaget has postulated the emergence of the property of reciprocity in the years 4 to 8, an emergence exhibited both in the child's logic (e.g., "I am my brother's brother" is an awareness of a logical relation of reciprocity) and in his social or moral judgments and action. In accordance with this hypothesis, it has been shown that the concept of moral reciprocity is highly correlated with Piaget's concrete operational cognitive tasks among children in this period (Kohlberg,

1970). As another example, the child's stabilization of a gender identity ("I am and will always
be a boy") is highly correlated with the phenomenon of concept stabilization, termed *conservation* by Piaget (Kohlberg, 1966). Because of
this parallelism of cognitive and affective development, the research literature indicates that wherever a reliable culturally general age-developmental trend in the emotional area has been
found, maturity on this trend is found to correlate with measures of cognitive maturity such
as the Stanford-Binet. These correlations are
found in such diverse areas as children's fears
(Jersild, 1943), humor and laughter (Levine, 1968),
sex-role identification (Kohlberg & Zigler, 1967),
moral development (Kohlberg, 1969, 1970), capacity to delay gratification (Mischel, 1963),
differentiated expression of affect (Ellinwood,
1969), and capacity for cooperative play (Parten
& Newhall, 1943).

The reasons why the cognitive-structural
components of emotional development are
largely disregarded by clinicians and child-care
workers are easy to understand. The cognitive
component of emotional development is largely
reflected in *capacity,* in maturity of *perception*
of the social-emotional situation, and the child's
performance or his overt response to his perception is not always at the maturity level of
his perception. Hence, examples of infantile
behavior in the bright child are easy to enumerate.
However, there is clear evidence that the long-
range trend is for behavior to move up to or conform to perceptions and that the occasional
dramatic failures of control of the child mature
in social perception are the colorful exception
rather than the long-range developmental rule,
at least in the moral domain (Kohlberg, 1969).

According to the parallelist or cognitive-
developmental view, it is not correct to phrase
these correlations as implying a single causal
direction in the relation of cognitive and emotional development. As a rough generalization,
however, it may be stated that general cognitive
development is more a cause than an effect of
emotional development. Cognitive development
is general; there is a strong general factor in
every test of intellectual maturity. Emotional
development is more specific to a given area;
there is less clearly such a thing as general emotional development. (To the extent that there
is, it is termed *ego-development,* a term implying
a cognitive-structural core.) Cognitive development is not only general, it is relatively autonomous; it is less sensitive to, or needful of, specific
forms of social experience. Furthermore, as
noted previously, there is a heavy hereditary
component of general intelligence. All these
considerations partially justify us in treating
cognitive maturity |a joint function of chrono-
logical age (CA) and IQ] as a causal antecedent
of emotional maturity and adjustment. As we
shall see, this assumption is justified by the fact
that IQ not only is concurrently correlated with
social maturity and adjustment measures but
predicts to them better than they predict to later
cognitive maturity.[9]

We have so far considered a developmental
rationale for intelligence as a mental-health
predictor: the rationale that a cognitively mature
child is more likely to be mature on age dimensions of emotional development. As is generally
the case for developmental-adaptational traits,
there is a second rationale for intelligence as a
mental-health predictor: the fact that it is socially

---

[9] There is, of course, a sense in which emotional retardation and conflict are the cause rather than the consequence of
intellectual retardation in schoolchildren. A child who becomes psychotic is likely to show a marked drop in IQ score.
In other cases, however, emotional conflict as a cause of
long-term poor intellectual functioning is better documented
in the areas of cognitive styles and school achievement than
it is in the area of general intelligence.

rewarded or leads to success.[10] Every measure of success or status in childhood is correlated with IQ, the most significant measures perhaps being school achievement and peer-group popularity or esteem. The correlations between IQ and the child's peer status, together with other mental-health correlates of IQ are summarized in Table 42-1 (in a format similar to that used in the remainder of this chapter).

Given the background of theory and data, we need not share Anderson's surprise when he says (1960, p. 91):

> We were surprised at the emergence of the intelligence factor in a variety of our instruments (family attitudes, responsibility, maturity and adjustment) in spite of our attempts to minimize intelligence in selecting our personality measures. Next we were surprised that for prediction over a long time, the intelligence quotient seems to carry a heavy predictive load in most of our measures of outcomes. It should be noted that in a number of studies, adjustment at both the child and adult level, whenever intelligence is included, emerges as a more significant factor than personality measures.

Some of the findings on intelligence as a predictor, to which Anderson's comments are relevant, are summarized in Table 42-2.

We may document the meaning of Anderson's comments by asking the question: What psychological test or instrument given to school-age (6 to 12) children will best predict their overall adult adjustment? Would that test be the Rorschach, the CPI, the MMPI, the various inventories of adjustment, the Manifest Anxiety

Scale, the Bower (1960) self-report screening tests? In terms of our current limited longitudinal knowledge, the answer to this question would have to be: No personality or adjustment test at all, but rather the IQ test.

One major study which points to this conclusion is that of Havighurst et al. (1962). This longitudinal study related sixth- and tenth-grade variables to young adult adjustment in 400 small-city adolescents. The measure of adjustment was a rating based on pooling interview and objective data, job success, educational progress, marital success, and personal competence and satisfaction. The best childhood correlates of this adjustment measure were (1) sixth-grade IQ, $r = .48$; (2) sixth-grade leadership ratings (pooled peer and teacher), $r = .52$; (3) tenth-grade CPI adjustment scores, $r = .58$; and (4) socioeconomic status of parents, $r = .48$. While the tenth-grade CPI correlated slightly better with young adult adjustment than did the IQ test, this would not have been true if the CPI (given at age 16) had been given at the earlier time period (age 12), when the IQ test was given. Another major study indicating the predictive value of IQ is the Anderson et al. (1959) study. This study investigated the young-adult (age 30) adjustment of children who had been in the Minnesota preschool system, using various subsamples and various measures (inventory, life data, and interview assessments) of adjustment. Across the various samples and measures of adult adjustment, the best and most consistent predictor among thirty-eight early-childhood (ages 2 to 5) measures was IQ. Correlations between early-childhood IQ and adult adjustment measures ranged from .30 to .36. (As in the Havighurst et al. study, the socioeconomic status and cultural richness of the parental home predicted almost as well and as consistently to adult adjustment as did IQ, predicting better than any of the child personality variables.) A third major study

---

[10] A third, somewhat distinct rationale for IQ as a mental-health predictor arises directly from the conception of intelligence or mental age as problem-solving ability. The research designs necessary to disentangle these three theoretically distinct roles of intelligence are discussed in Kohlberg and Zigler (1967) but have not been employed in the mental-health area. Accordingly, our review will not attempt to differentiate them in the present data.

TABLE 42-1   INTELLIGENCE IN RELATIONSHIP TO CONCURRENT ADJUSTMENT

Age or Grade	*Relationship*	*References*
2nd-6th grades	Positive relationship between level of intelligence and degree of peer acceptance; 10- to 15-point IQ difference typical between children at opposite extremes of peer-acceptance distribution.	Anderson (1960); Bonney (1943, 1955); Cassel & Martin (1964); Gronlund & Holmlund (1958); Havighurst et al. (1962); Sells et al. (1967)
6th grade	Positive relationship between teachers' ratings of adjustment and intelligence level.	Smith (1958); Terman & Oden (1959)
Mean CA = 11 yr	Gifted children scored better than normals on 7 "character tests" assessing, e.g., wholesomeness of preferences and attitudes, emotional stability.	Terman & Oden (1959)
6th grade	Positive relationship between favorable scores on Thorpe, Clarke, and Tieg Mental Health Analysis, Form A, and age-grade relationship.	Bedoian (1953)
9 yr	Low, negative relationship between Children's Manifest Anxiety Scale and verbal portion of Otis Quick-Scoring Mental-Ability Test.	Cowen et al. (1965); McCandless & Castaneda (1956)
	Mental retardation associated with emotional disturbance in most studies reviewed, though disturbance ranged from 10 to 50% of retardates in various studies.	Garfield (1963)
4th, 5th, 6th grades	Negative relationship between group-test IQ scores and identification as emotionally handicapped.	Bower (1960); Maxwell (1961); Stennett (1966)
6th grade	Delinquency and low IQ associated.	Anderson et al. (1959); Havighurst et al. (1962); McCord et al. (1959); Terman & Oden (1959)
15 yr	Delinquency and low IQ associated.	Anderson (1960); Anderson et al. (1959)
	Poor moral character, moral judgment, moral behavior associated with low IQ.	Peck & Havighurst (1960; Kohlberg (1969)
	Low ego maturity and low ego strength associated with low IQ.	Peck & Havighurst (1960); Kohlberg (1969)
	Maturity of sex-role attitudes associated with high IQ.	Kohlberg & Zigler (1967)
5–14 yr	Number of adjustment problems in an unselected sample negatively correlated with IQ ($r = .10$ to $.41$ at various ages).	MacFarlane et al. (1954)

TABLE 42-2   SCHOOL-AGE INTELLIGENCE AS A PREDICTOR OF ADULT ADJUSTMENT

Age or Grade	Relationship	References
Mean CA = 11 yr	In mid-40s, general adjustment of gifted individuals as good as or better than in unselected population. In late 20s and mid-40s, marital adjustments as good as or better than in unselected population.	Terman & Oden (1959) (L)*
Childhood	Lower rate of adequate personal-social adjustment for retardates than for "normal" controls.	Miller (1965) (L)
16 yr	For 36-year-old males, uncontrolled and fearful, withdrawn maladjustments moderately associated with relatively low IQ. For females, comparable IQ- adjustment relationships generally low and insignificant.	Anderson (1957): Bayley (1968) (L); Havighurst et al. (1962)
Mean CA = 11 yr	For gifted Ss, rates of alcoholism and homosexuality below rate for unselected population. Suicide rates essentially equivalent.	Terman & Oden (1959) (L)
Mean CA = 15 yr	For Ss with high risk for schizophrenia, no relationship between WISC Full Scale IQ and emergence of psychiatric illness during a 5-year follow-up. Picture-arrangement scores lower for Ss with "sick" outcome.	Mednick & Schulsinger (1967) (L)
2–5 yr	Direction of change in adjustment positively related to direction of IQ change.	Despert & Pierce (1946) (L)

*L indicates longitudinal or follow-up evidence for natural history of predictor.

leading to the same conclusions is Terman and Oden's (1959) adult follow-up of Terman's gifted children and their average-IQ controls. This study indicated that the gifted were more successful occupationally, maritally, and socially than the average group, were lower in morally deviant forms of psychopathology (e.g. alcoholism, homosexuality), and were equivalent in intrapsychic forms of psychopathology (psychosis and suicide).

A fourth major study is Miller's (1965) follow-up of the adult adjustment of noninstitutionalized mentally retarded children in comparison with an average control group from the same low-income urban area. Clear differences between the groups were found, though they were less than our stereotypes of retardation might anticipate. While almost all normals were self-supporting, two-thirds of the retarded were also. Retardates had somewhat more criminal offenses, divorces, etc.

In summary, it is correct to state that the childhood test best predicting adult adjustment is the IQ test, but this is more a testimony to the poorness of personality tests than it is to the predictive power of IQ tests. A crude quantitative estimate of the predictive power of IQ is the statement that 20 to 35 percent of the reliable variation in gross ratings or estimates of adjustment in a representative sample of adults can be predicted from elementary school IQ scores. Such a crude statement needs to be

qualified by the following interpretive generalizations:

1. It is difficult to separate out the effects
of parental socioeconomic status and child's IQ.
Some of the predictive power of IQ may be due
to the correlated status factor.

2. A statement in terms of correlation and
variance is somewhat misleading in light of the
fact that the relation of IQ to emotional maturity
and adjustment is that intelligence is a necessary,
not sufficient, condition to attain high maturity
or adjustment scores (as discussed in the previous
section). This implies:

   a. Bright (compared with average) children
   or average (compared with dull) children
   are almost as likely to show the crudest
   and most extreme forms of adult maladjustment, e.g., psychosis, suicide, and criminal behaviors (though there are statistically
   significant differences in the delinquent and
   criminal category). These categories of maladjustment have little relation to general ego
   or personality maturity or competence.

   b. Even for less extreme forms of maladjustment, moderate or high IQ is not a guarantee
   against later poor adjustment, in the sense in
   which a moderate level on an adjustment
   test was found to be (see the previous section). Low IQ, however, may be a guarantee
   against a prediction of later high adjustment. In other words, high IQ predicts
   better to extremely good adjustment than
   low IQ predicts to extremely poor adjustment, although high IQ is no guarantee
   of high adjustment, merely a necessary
   condition for it.

3. The relation of IQ to adjustment is not
fixed throughout the life cycle since the true correlation of emotional and intellectual traits is
more a matter of mental age than it is one of
IQ as such. Most childhood traits of social
maturity are better correlated with mental age

than with either IQ or CA. This implies:

   a. A bright child may reach a given level of
   ego or emotional maturity faster than the
   duller child, but at a later age there may
   be no difference between the two children
   on the emotional trait. Moral character
   continues to develop in many of the less
   bright children until the late twenties, so
   that they tend to catch up with the brighter
   children in this regard (Kohlberg, 1969).

   b. Maturity (mental age) brings problems
   as well as solves them. Because bright
   children face development tasks earlier,
   they sometimes look more disturbed than
   their same-age duller counterparts. Mac-
   Farlane et al. (1954) found that bright children aged 2 to 4 had slightly *more* problems
   than average children (at age 3, r between
   IQ and problems was $+.11$). Thereafter,
   bright children had fewer problems than
   the duller, increasingly so up until adolescence ($r = .41$). With adolescence, however (e.g., age 14), the advantage of the
   bright children (especially the boys) markedly dropped, presumably because they were
   again facing problems later faced by the
   duller boys.

We have discussed the predictive power of
IQ at length because IQ has been the only cognitive variable (other than school achievement
or performance) extensively studied in longitudinal studies of adjustment. We would seriously underestimate the value and power of
cognitive variables in predicting mental health,
however, if we assumed that they were covered
by the IQ score. As already noted, all systematic
developmental observations of ego development
or ego strength have a heavy cognitive base.
Most promising for mental-health prediction are:

1. Measures of Piaget cognitive-structural
   level
2. Measures of cognitive style and attention

3. Measures of ego or self-conceptual level
4. Measures of moral-judgment maturity

All these measures have been shown to be concurrent correlates of social maturity and to function independent of IQ. All have been shown to be stable or predictive of themselves over time (studies reviewed in Kohlberg, 1969, 1971). We can only recommend that future longitudinal studies of mental health and adjustment add some of these measures to the ubiquitous IQ measure.

Our discussion of cognitive predictors of adjustment has so far avoided the major cognitive focus of both laymen and clinicians in looking at childhood problems, namely, the problem of poor school achievement. Most research and practice in this area have been dominated by an assumption which might almost be labeled the *American education myth:* the assumption that objectively graded and measured school achievement is a basic or necessary ground for adult cognitive maturity or for adult adjustment or success. One of the writers has documented the many research considerations which should lead educational planners to question this assumption (Kohlberg, 1971). In the present section, we shall briefly review evidence which leads us to question this assumption as it is involved in clinical approaches to learning blocks.

It is difficult not to view the American educational myth as underlying many clinical analyses of poor school learning or achievement which view underachievement as reflecting either a brain dysfunction *(dyslexia)* or an emotional illness, disorder, or syndrome *(learning block).* When the transactions between schools and children are looked at in detail, it becomes more difficult to define failures in these transactions as the overt symptoms of a disease entity located in the child. An example of a somewhat uncritical approach of clinicians to the educational pro-

cess is the GAP report (1967) taxonomy, in which "learning failure" is included as one of a group of "developmental deviations in cognitive functions including developmental lags or other deviations in the capacity for symbolic or abstract thinking, among these the functions of reading, writing, and working arithmetic problems. Some children may exhibit the persistence of prelogical thought processes, some may be mildly retarded. Children who are significantly precocious or accelerated in their intellectual development can also be considered in this category."[11]

The basic defect of the GAP classification of learning failures is its confusion of school achievement with basic cognitive development. This confusion may be based on the finding that cognitive maturity or IQ scores correlate as well with an achievement test as does another achievement test (Bloom, 1964; Jensen, 1969). This finding indicates, however, the lack of generality and longitudinal stability of school achievement tests when the intelligence factor is removed, rather than that general and cognitive maturity is based on school learning. Basic general intelligence predicts later school achievement well, but school achievement does not predict later general intelligence well. Second-grade IQ predicts to high school reading achievement tests about as well as do second-grade achievement tests, but second-grade achievement tests do not predict to high school IQ nearly as well as second-grade IQ tests.

Put in other terms, one cannot equate "capacity for symbolic or abstract thinking" with "the functions of reading, writing, and working arith-

---

[11] Our discussion of research findings on the role of IQ contrasts strikingly with patterns of clinical thought which include brightness or intellectual acceleration among the "developmental deviations." That very bright children are sometimes bored and dissatisfied with school is certainly a fact but hardly a basis for labeling brightness a developmental deviation. It is perhaps more appropriate to locate the deviations in a school incapable of handling bright children than to label brightness itself as a deviation.

metic problems," and one cannot equate poor school achievement with basic lags in basic thought development, such as "the persistence of prelogical thought processes." Accordingly, one cannot call poor school learning a developmental deviation in the sense of a distortion of a basic natural developmental sequence due to some pathological force in the child or his environment.

Because school learning or achievement cannot be equated with basic cognitive development, it does not play the direct role in later social-emotional development and adaptation that cognitive development does. As a gross developmental-adaptational trait, school achievement correlates with most childhood measures of adjustment or absence of pathology and has a moderate predictive power to adult adjustment measures. This is indicated by Table 42-3, which shows a moderate association between low school achievement and almost every obvious form of adult maladjustment except suicide and neurosis. However, the more systematic studies listed in Table 42-3 indicated that the long-range predictive power of school grades or tests for later success or adjustment seems to be in almost no way due to the achievements or learnings themselves. It is rather due to other variables with which school achievement is correlated, including (1) IQ, (2) attention or steadiness, (3) acceptance of authority and inhibition of deviant, distractible, and rule-defying behavior, and (4) the status screening attendant on graduating from a (good) college. When some or all of these are controlled, school achievement does not turn out to be a predictor of later adjustment. Almost all the studies cited in Table 42-3 which partial out the factors cited find no remaining predictive power to the school-achievement variable.

The most obvious expected outcome of school achievement is job success. With IQ controlled,

TABLE 42-3   SCHOOL ACHIEVEMENT AND ADJUSTMENT OUTCOME

Age or Grade	Relationship	Research Design*	References
4th, 5th, 6th grades	Minimal indication of relationship between achievement and adjustment in 7th, 8th, and 9th grades which continue measurement. Does not include achievement measures.	L	Stennett (1966)
6th, 7th grades	Dropping out of school associated with low achievement. In turn, dropping out of school associated with delinquency, undesirable job, poor job adjustment.	L	Havighurst et al. (1962)
Childhood	Evidence conflicting regarding association of low achievement and delinquent or sociopathic (or psychopathic) outcomes.	R-I L L L L, R-I R-I	Friedlander (1945) Glueck & Glueck (1959) Havighurst et al. (1962) Powers & Witmer (1951) Robins (1966) Wittman (1948)

* L: Longitudinal evidence for natural history of predictor.
R-I: Ss group according to known outcome; predictive data gathered independently in juvenile period.

however, the only way in which school achievement furthers job success is through facilitating entrance into college. One source for this generalization comes from a large-scale study by Coombs and Cooley (1968) of the later (early twenties) job success of two groups: high school dropouts and high school graduates who did not go on to college. Both groups were equivalent in class background and in IQ. The male dropouts were doing slightly *better,* not worse, in terms of income and job status than the high school graduates (mainly due to their longer job experience). Another source for this generalization comes from studies of the prediction of later job achievement from high school and college grades. With intelligence and sheer college graduation controlled, there appears to be no relationship between high school or college grades and later success. In one such study, Little (1967) noted:

> . . .although differences in level of education (college–non-college) produced important differences in attained level of occupations, differences in high school performance had very little effect on the level of occupations attained in any of the groups. The median percentile rank in high school achievement of male graduates who were in occupations that had prestige scores below 70 was the same as the rank of all male high school graduates. Students who were high-achieving in high school who did not go to college failed to obtain occupations that were substantially better than the occupations of their lower ranking classmates. Even more remarkable is the fact that low-achieving students who attended college attained occupations equivalent to their much higher-ranking college classmates. The correlation coefficient between rank in high school graduating class and prestige score on a trained occupation was found to be .08.

In summary, then, graduating from college (and graduate school) predicts to occupational success but graduating from high school does not. While high school academic achievement aids college entrance because of current college

screening procedures, there is no convincing evidence that high school or college grades are themselves predictors of occupational achievement, particularly if intelligence is controlled.

Turning to general adult adjustment, one of the studies best controlling other factors is that of Robins (1966). This study followed up the adult adjustment of mainly lower-class white children referred to a child-guidance clinic. School achievement did not differentiate children later becoming psychotic or neurotic from those who were well as adults. Low achievement did predict to later alcoholism and criminal or sociopathic behavior. This, however, was due to the fact that children engaging in antisocial behavior and truancy also did poorly in school. When antisocial behavior (including school truancy) was controlled, there was no remaining power of school grades to predict to sociopathic or alcoholic adult disorders.[12]

In summary, school achievement, a developmental-adaptational trait, is a relatively good gross predictor of adult adjustment. Its predictive power markedly diminishes or disappears when socioeconomic status, IQ, distractibility, and restraint of impulse are controlled for. In light of these facts and of the American anxiety and preoccupation with school achievement, it is

[12] In a second major study, focused more upon school attendance, Robins (1967) makes the same point in more depth. The study involved two black groups, neither of whom had been referred to a clinic. Members of the first group either had been severe elementary truants (20 percent nonattendance), had been retarded a year in school, or both. Members of the second group (matched for IQ, father presence, and socioeconomic status) attended school regularly. The children who did not attend school regularly were more likely to be delinquents, to be homicidal or murdered, to be acting-out alcoholics, and to drop out of school. In other words, early school truancy was a good predictor of various forms of adult antisocial or rule-deviant behavior (but not of drug or alcoholic consumption or addiction as such). It should be noted that the predictive trait was not school learning or achievement; it was essentially the willingness (or home pressure) to attend or sit through school.

necessary to look with caution at clinical treatment of school underachievement as prognostic or diagnostic entities with a disease or syndrome flavor. In a more positive vein, the longitudinal findings do suggest that something like a critical period in the formation of abilities and attitudes (other than general intelligence) positive for school learning occurs in or is set or stabilized in the period of early elementary school (age 5 to 9). Bloom (1964) surveys longitudinal findings suggesting that adolescent or adult intelligence is to a considerable extent (about 50 percent of the variance) stabilized or predictable by first grade, whereas adolescent school achievement is predictable to the same extent only at age 9 (end of grade 3). It appears, then, that the factors which contribute to school achievement other than intelligence are to a considerable extent set in the first three grades. To some extent, these factors are sheer skill factors; e.g., if a child has more skills in first grade, he accumulates further skills in the second. In large part, however, this stabilization of school achievement is based on the stabilization of factors of interest in learning, attention, and sense of competence. The single best predictor of school achievement, after IQ is classroom attention as measured by various methods (Jackson, 1968). Classroom attention is, however, a more general aspect of an attentional capacity reflected in testing situations, in psychomotor tasks, and in social behavior (Grim, Kohlberg, & White, 1968).[13]

A second basic correlate of school achievement appears to be a sense of agency, an "internal locus of control" over one's destiny and the outcomes of one's efforts (Coleman et al., 1966). (Attention and internal locus of control are, in

[13] This capacity is related not only to the ability to profit from school learning but also to the ability to profit from psychoeducational and therapeutic experiences. The best predictor of improvement in day-school treatment for young disturbed children was a pretherapy rating of attention (Mayers, 1966).

turn, empirically related.) The point is that not only interest but ego-strength factors are related to school learning in the early school years. In this regard, attention is only one of a number of ego-strength factors associated with school learning, including sense of competence, achievement, motivation, delay of reward, and analytic cognitive style. Partly because underachievement is associated with defects in these ego-strength variables (as well with low IQ), underachievement is a statistical predictor to all the major forms of adult maladjustment. But it seems likely that early school failure is itself an environmental cause of later low status on some of these ego variables. In this sense, psychoeducational intervention to create more positive school attitudes and sets in the early school years might do much to reduce the disinterest in learning and the anxiety about failure characteristic of the child with a learning block. Such intervention, however, would be oriented toward the cultivation of positive attitudes toward learning, not toward bringing children up to a fixed, normal level of school achievement. Such intervention, also, would not be based on the notion that the educational environment is fixed and that the defective learning sets of the child are the expression of fixed intrapsychic problems generated outside the school environment.

EMOTIONAL PREDICTORS OF ADULT ADJUSTMENT

The fundamental assumptions of a field are indicated by its unquestioned labels. In child clinical thought, the label *emotionally disturbed* is used to refer to all nonorganic forms of childhood maladjustment. This section examines this assumption by asking whether childhood signs of "emotional disturbance" are predictors of adult maladjustment. It focuses, then, on the emotional as opposed to the cognitive and on the emotional as opposed to the behavioral (e.g., antisocial behavior, poor peer relations). Previously, we grouped traits of overt social behavior and of cognitive functioning together as *developmental-adaptive* and contrasted them with *symptomatic* traits of affective functioning. We concluded that developmental-adaptive traits were better long-range predictors than symptomatic traits. If true, this conclusion upsets the claims to expertise of the child clinical psychologist or psychiatrist, whose traditional diagnostic skills center on observation and interpretation of emotional responses in interviews, projective tests, and life situations.

In adults, the distinction between emotional disturbance and other forms of maladaptation is indicated by the label of *neurosis* as opposed to *psychosis* (where emotional disturbance is associated with cognitive or thought disorder) and by *neurosis* versus *character disorder and sociopathy* (involving criminal, antisocial, or unethical behaviors). Accordingly, the first way of posing the problem is to ask whether we can find childhood predictors of adult neurosis. The second way of posing the problem is to ask whether emotional behavior or symptoms in children (including a diagnosis as neurotic) predict adult maladjustment in ways in which cognitive status or overt social behavior does not.

Our answers to these questions are limited by two factors. The first limitation is that long-range follow-up studies of the predictive utility of the modern psychodiagnostic procedures have not been conducted. While post-World War II diagnosis in a child-guidance clinic involves integrating data from an intelligence test, projective tests, a psychiatric interview, and a family history, the follow-up studies of child clinic populations have relied upon prewar childhood diagnostic data on emotional functioning. The second limitation is that the number of well-designed follow-up studies concerned with adult neurosis (as compared with adult criminality or psychosis) is extremely small.

Within the limits of such data, the findings are largely negative. They may be summarized in the following (and overlapping) generalizations:

1. We have little practical ability to predict which children will be adult neurotics (as opposed to being well adults). The childhood behavior of adult neurotics is distinguishable from the behavior of children who become psychotics or criminals (or sociopaths) but not distinguishable from children who become normal.

2. Children who are referred to guidance clinics for emotional problems without concurrent cognitive and antisocial behavior problems are almost as likely to be well adults as is a random sample of the population.

3. While emotional symptoms often accompany cognitive defect and antisocial behavior in children who later become psychotic or sociopathic, systematic inclusion of these symptoms adds little to a prediction based on cognitive functioning or antisocial behavior itself.

A summary of the findings involved is presented as Table 42-4.

Probably the most careful and informative survey of the follow-up implications of emotional symptomatology comes from the study of Robins (1966). This study follows up 524 white children, mostly lower-class, seen in a child-guidance clinic in the 1920s and 1930s. The majority (73 percent) of these children were referred for antisocial behaviors (37 percent being referred by the juvenile court). The remaining 27 percent of the children were referred for (1) learning problems (10 percent), (2) temper tantrums (5 percent), and (3) other emotional symptoms (12 percent). Of this 27 percent referred for learning and emotional symptoms, 30 percent were well as adults as compared with 52 percent of a control group matched for social background. They were twice as likely to become alcoholic or schizophrenic as the controls but not more likely to become adult neurotics. They were also more likely to become hys-

TABLE 42-4 EMOTIONAL PROBLEMS AND ADJUSTMENT OUTCOME

Problem	Age or Grade at Assessment	Nonspecific Psychiatric Illness*	Psychosis*	Sociopathic Personality*	Alcoholism*	Hysteria*	Neurosis*	References
Manifest anxiety, fears	High school		R-II:PR† (M)					Bower et al. (1960)
	Childhood		R-I:p>50%† (M) (F, NS)					Gardner (1967)
Apprehensiveness	Childhood		R-I: p<50%	R-I:p<50%				Friedlander (1945)
Worry, ruminativeness	Childhood		L:p<50%, BR	L:NS	L:NS	L:NS	L:NS	Robins (1966)
Phobias	Childhood		R-I:p<50%† (M) (F, NS)					Gardner (1967)
School phobia	4–11 yrs.							Coolidge et al. (1964)
Apathy	Childhood		R-I: p>50%					Birren (1944)
	High school		R-II:PR† (M)					Bower et al. (1960)
Depression, unhappiness	Childhood		L:p<50%, BR	L:NS	L:NS	L:NS	L:NS	Robins (1966)
	High school		R-II:PR† (M)					Bower et al. (1960)
Sustained depression	Childhood		R-I:p>50%	R-I:p<50%				Friedlander (1945)
Suicidal ideas	Childhood	L:PR†						Robins (1966)
Emotional instability	Childhood		R-II:PRª					Pollin et al. (1966)
Easily upset emotional balance	Childhood		R-I:p>50%	R-I:p> 50%				Friedlander (1945)
Irritability	5–12 yrs.	L:NS	R-II:PRª					Pollack et al. (1966) Robins (1966)
Temper tantrums	Childhood	L:NS						Robins (1966)

*L: Longitudinal evidence for natural history of predictor.

R-I: Ss group according to known outcome; predictive data gathered independently in juvenile period.

R-II: Ss grouped according to known outcome; predictive data retrospectively recalled.

$p>50\%$: Predictor present in more than 50 percent of sample.

$p<50\%$: Predictor present in less than 50 percent of sample.

BR: Incidence of outcome significantly higher than base rate for outcome.

PR: Positive relationship.

NS: Not significant or no clear relationship apparent.

M: Males only.

F: Females only.

NR: No relationship.

†Adverse predictor or outcome significantly more prevalent than in comparison group(s).

[a] Adverse predictor or outcome more prevalent than in comparison group(s), but no statistical tests reported.

terics in a context in which *hysteric* was less a label for intrapsychic neurosis than a label for women with a history of sexual promiscuity, somatic symptoms and complaints, and inability to work to support themselves.

In contrast to a clear, positive association (discussed later) between number of antisocial problems and likelihood of adult adjustment problems, Robins (1966) found little relationship between number of physical and emotional problems and probability of a maladjusted outcome. Only at the extreme end of the scale, among children with nine or more such problems, was there a significant increase in the probability of adult maladjustment. When psychosomatic and emotional problems accompanied antisocial behavior, they did not alter the likelihood of later adjustment problems from that predicted on the basis of antisocial problems alone.

The other major longitudinal study of a group including referral for emotional symptoms is that of Morris et al. (1954), Michael (1956), and Michael (1957). They found that children referred for withdrawal and associated emotional symptomatology were no more likely to be either psychotic or otherwise maladjusted than was a random sample of the population.

When one turns from "reasons for referral" to notations of presence of emotional symptoms, one reaches a somewhat richer though still confusing picture. Working with the larger sample and more complete records provided by the Judge Baker Guidance Center, Ricks and Berry (1969) indicated somewhat more power of physical and emotional complaints to predict schizophrenia. Field's (1969) study checked for the presence or absence of neurotic symptoms in four groups of boys who had been classified by adult outcome as being either chronic schizophrenic, released schizophrenic, character disordered, or socially adjusted. Chronic schizophrenics revealed the greatest number of early neurotic symptoms, and the released schizophrenics next, followed

by socially adequate subjects and character disorders. People who were later chronic schizophrenics were especially high in frequency of early obsessional symptoms; symptoms of apathy and lack of initiative were most frequent in both chronic and released schizophrenics. Working with a partially overlapping set of cases, Gardner (1967) found obsessive compulsive traits in 30 percent of a set of boys who were later schizophrenic, as compared with 4 percent of boys who were later socially adjusted. She also found higher frequencies of general anxiety and of phobias in those boys who were later schizophrenic. Since none of these areas of concern differentiated between girls who were later schizophrenic and those who were not, they seem to have predictive power only for boys. In these same studies, Fleming and Ricks (1969) working with cases for whom five or more therapy-hour reports were available, found that reported feelings of anxiety, vulnerability, unreality of daily experience, and isolation and alienation from others distinguished youngsters who became schizophrenic from child-guidance-center cases who turned out well.

These results suggest mildly predictive relations of emotional symptomatology in childhood to later schizophrenia. For schizophrenia, there are, however, better predictors than emotional symptomatology (discussed in the section on schizophrenia) but consistent with these relations. As Table 42-4 suggests, outside of a possible predictive relation to schizophrenia, fears, nervousness, irritability, and temper do not predict to other forms of adult disorder.

The Robins (1966) study found no significant difference in childhood emotional symptomatology between clinic cases who became neurotic and those who were well as adults. With regard to girls who became hysterics, adolescent sexual misbehavior and associated running away and truancy were better childhood predictors than were emotional symptoms themselves (e.g., 80 percent of those diagnosed hysterics as adults had records of adolescent sexual misbehavior, as opposed to 25 percent of those growing up to be well). The same was true of alcoholism, better predicted by childhood acting-out behavior than by emotional symptoms as such.

With regard to adjustment in a representative or normal sample, the Livson and Peskin (1967) study indicates that negative emotional symptoms in childhood do not predict to adult adjustment, a finding consistent with those of MacFarlane et al. Some positive traits, however, are at some ages mildly related to adult status.

In summary, the development of evidence for predicting adult maladjustment on the basis of emotional symptoms independent of overt deviant behavior and poor intellectual functioning remains a task for the future. One might anticipate that a focus upon emotional development rather than upon emotional symptoms might be a more fruitful approach for prediction. The greatest focus in observation of emotional problems has been on intensity of dysphoric responses. The MacFarlane and the Livson and Peskin studies suggest that variations in intensity of emotional response are often determined by temperament and by the phase in solution of a developmental task at which the child is observed rather than by some underlying disposition to illness. As as example, fears of death, violence, and mutilation (and phobic displacements of these fears) are a developmentally normal phenomenon for boys in the 4- to 8-year-old period and are usually developmentally resolved then or subsequently. Predictive studies using *fear* or *phobias* as a category are likely to fasten on the intensity of these fears as a sign of pathology. In fact, there is no reason to believe that intensity of expression of a developmental concern is a predictor of failure to resolve the problem. Intensity is rather determined by a variety of developmental, temperamental, and situational factors regulating expression of the response. More

predictively useful observations are likely to focus on the child's awareness of, and mode of coping with, the developmental task in question. Anna Freud's research group is now attempting to develop such a system of longitudinal observation of the emotional side of ego development. It is to such developmental efforts, as well as to longitudinal studies relating longitudinal projective test and interview data to adult outcome, that clinicians must look to support their belief that they can prognose by observation of fantasy and emotional response.

PSYCHOSEXUAL PREDICTORS OF LATER ADJUSTMENT

Among the various childhood emotional attitudes and symptoms relevant to later adjustment, the most important for diagnostic theory are the psychosexual ones. The most theoretically unified and systematic theories and taxonomies of psychopathology are the psychoanalytic schemes based on libido theory (Fenichel, 1945). In essence, the psychoanalytic theory of psychopathology assumes the following:

1. Adult sexual perversions represent adult expressions of early childhood maturational stages of the sexual instinct.

2. Underneath every neurosis is a repressed perversion which the neurosis defends against (phallic-Oedipal for the hysteric, anal-sadistic for the obsessional, etc.).

3. Underneath every psychosis is an even earlier or more primitive perversion with narcissistic components (e.g., narcissistic homosexuality for the paranoid).

4. Underneath every character disorder is a repressed perversion "acted out" rather than "symptomatized," as in neurosis.

While the later thinking of Freud was increasingly concerned with the independent roles of anxiety, aggression, and ego development in determining mental illness and health, these fundamental assumptions of the libido theory of psychopathology have never been abandoned by psychoanalytic theory.

In contrast to the Freudian view, interpersonal, cognitive-developmental, and ego-developmental theories of psychosexuality (Ausubel, 1952; Kohlberg, 1966; Simon & Gagnon, 1969; Sullivan, 1953) do not assume strong childhood sexual drives but do assume that adolescent and adult sexual deviation and pathology reflect childhood distortions in ego development and in interpersonal attitudes. These childhood distortions are not specifically sexually or libidinally driven until early or late adolescence, but they are sexual in the sense that stressful interpersonal relations are imaged in a concrete or primitive cognitive symbolism of actions between bodies to be sought or avoided. As one example, American male slum and reformatory preadolescent and adolescent cultures overtly symbolize or define relations of aggressive domination and reciprocal passive subordination between males (as well as between males and females) in terms of sexual relations. This tendency is not peculiarly subcultural; it depends upon a universal body symbolism of interpersonal relationships which designates the weaker as feminine and vice versa. Combinations of stressful orientation toward dominance-subordination with uncertainties about sex identity then can generate preoccupation with, or identification with, homosexual patterns. As an example, Oversey (1950) reports that overt homosexual dreams of heterosexual men occur in a context of immediate situational concern about occupational problems requiring submissiveness.

With specific regard to overt deviant sexual behavior, an ego-developmental theory would postulate such behavior to be the complex result of (1) general weakness of ego control, such as is involved in deviant behavior in general; (2) a generally immature orientation toward emotional or love relations such that relational needs are defined in terms of isolated bodily acts between nonintimates; (3) a variety of anxieties or concerns about particular forms of interpersonal relationships; and (4) subcultural sexual norms and sexual opportunities. Both libidinal and ego development views hold that sexual deviance is not an isolated behavior, but the libidinal theory derives more general trends of character and pathology from sexual distortions or conflicts and the ego-developmental theory tends to derive sexual distortions from more general ego-developmental trends.

Unfortunately, there is little longitudinal research bearing clearly on these issues; the existing research is mainly retrospective rather than "follow-up" research. For example, major studies of male homosexuality have been based on the recall of childhood of self-acknowledged homosexuals (Chang & Block, 1960) in psychotherapy (Bieber et al., 1962) or in prisons (Gebhard, 1965; Holeman & Winokur, 1965). The character of self-acknowledged homosexuals in trouble (prison or psychotherapy) differs in all sorts of way from the character both of heterosexuals and of well-adjusted homosexuals who do not come to psychiatric attention. Furthermore, retrospection is even more suspect in this area than in others. As an example, self-acknowledged passive or "feminine" male homosexuals communicate in various ways that they do or did not identify with, or feel as close to, their fathers as they do with their mothers (Bieber et al., 1962; Chang & Block, 1960). It is hardly surprising to find that adult males who are identified with a feminine role feel closer to a female than a male parent, since a large research literature indicates that felt identification is largely determined by prior perceived similarity to the person identified with (Kohlberg, 1966). It is a long jump to conclude that low father identification or high mother identification causes male homosexuality. The available longitudinal evidence indicates no particular relation between father absence and male homosexuality or marked effeminacy, but it does indicate some relation between marked marital strife and later male homosexuality or markedly deviant effeminacy (McCord & Thurber, 1962).

Turning from parent identification to actual early effeminacy or homosexual behavior, a number of retrospective studies concur with the findings of Gebhard (1965) and Holeman and Winokur (1965) that a large proportion of self-acknowledged adult homosexuals of the passive or effeminate varieties had homosexual experiences or displayed effeminate behavior in the elementary years. However, it is also clear that many well adults retrospect similar behaviors and experience (Kinsey, 1948; Gebhard, 1965). If retrospective data are to be trusted, it seems likely that childhood difficulties in sexual identification or deviant childhood sexual experiences may be necessary but far from sufficient or predictive conditions for adult sexual deviation.

If one turns to actual follow-up studies, the picture is less clear-cut. Most longitudinal studies of normals indicate low stability of measures of sex-role identification, or masculinity-femininity of interests and attitudes (reviewed in Kohlberg, 1966). A rather high correlation of .63 was found by Kagan and Moss (1962) between boys' masculine interests in elementary school and those in adulthood. This seems to be somewhat inflated, however, because it is based on rating the gross motor activities more favored by the lower-class and less intelligent boys as masculine, so that much of the stability seems related to social class and intelligence. In any case, there is little or no correlation between standard measures of masculinity-femininity, or sex-role identification, and measures of either general adjustment or normal heterosexuality (evidence reviewed in Kohlberg, 1966).

In summary, longitudinal findings from the most studied area of sexual pathology, male homosexuality, provide little basis for predicting which school-age boys will become homosexual

and which will not and provide no clear support for common notions suggested by adult recall data that a strong positive relation to the father and a clear masculine identification are necessary to avoid a pattern of adult male homosexuality.

With regard to the more general prediction of adult sex deviance from sexually deviant childhood behavior, the major longitudinal data come from Robins (1966). Her general findings are that overtly deviant childhood sex behaviors do not predict to overtly deviant adult sex behavior. Instead, deviant childhood sexual behavior seems to mean much the same thing as nonsexually deviant or antisocial behavior from a predictive point of view. More specifically, Robins found that the 8 percent of the male clinic children referred for sex problems were no more likely to have sex problems as adults than were other groups showing the same behavior. Both this group of boys and the boys referred for theft had a 6 percent chance of ending up as adults who engaged in a sex crime. To the extent to which sexual problems or sexual perversions in boys were predictive of adult outcome, they were predictive of a criminal or sociopathic outcome, not an outcome of specifically sexual difficulty.

For girls, sexual behavior noted was primarily adolescent sexual intercourse or promiscuity. Two groups of adult women showed this behavior equally (75 percent) in their childhood records: the sociopaths and the hysterics. These women generally had similar childhood behavioral symptoms. The finding is interesting since it suggests the psychoanalytic view that sexual concerns lie behind the perceived body concerns and dysfunctions of hysterical women. In another context, however, taken with the male data, it merely suggests that childhood sexual acting out is one of many expressions of the poor controls of boys and girls who later become sociopaths or hysterics. In this context, Robins suggests that hysteria may be a feminine nonaggressive variation of the poor ego and moral control found in the sociopath, behavior found in women with poor marriage and employment histories who construct somatic and emotional excuses for their deviant social behavior (see also Sullivan, 1953).

In summary, there are little basic data on the role of childhood sexual attitudes and symptoms as prognostic of later sexual psychopathology. The limited evidence suggests that insofar as deviant childhood sexual behavior is predictive, it predicts in the same way as nonsexual deviant behavior: to deviant or irresponsible social behavior in adulthood. This finding seems most compatible with ego-developmental views of psychosexual development.

SOCIAL-BEHAVIOR PREDICTORS OF LATER ADJUSTMENT—ANTISOCIAL BEHAVIOR

We have so far considered assessments of psychological inner states, cognitive or affective, as predictors of later adjustment. We now turn to common-sense assessments of overt social conduct and functioning as predictors of later mental-health status. Three main subareas of research will be evaluated for their value in predicting eventual adjustment status: antisocial behavior, withdrawn forms of behavior, and finally, overall status and functioning in the peer group.

The *American College Dictionary* defines *antisocial* as "opposed to social order, or to the principles on which society is constituted." In classifying behavior as antisocial, ambiguity seems to center on what one regards as a violation of principles. One investigator may classify problem drinking as antisocial; another may not. The adaptational patterns deemed antisocial in the present discussion will encompass (1) aggressive or violent behavior involving violation of explicit or implicit rules regarding personal and property rights and (2) disobedience, which violates explicit or implicit rules intended

to maintain group cohesiveness and interpersonal trust.

The longitudinal research evidence suggests that antisocial behavior—particularly when some estimate of severity is taken into account—is the single most powerful predictor of later adjustment problems of any childhood behavior studied. (See Table 42-5.) More specifically, various forms and dimensions of juvenile antisocial behavior appear to be associated with psychiatric diagnoses of sociopathic personality, alcoholism, hysteria, and schizophrenia and with extent of adult criminal antisocial problems (above and beyond diagnostic categories). In contrast, presence of juvenile antisocial behavior seems to counterindicate later well—or neurotic—outcomes.

As we suggested previously, the predictive power of antisocial behavior is best understood in light of a broad age-developmental trend toward a decline in antisocial behavior. The predictive relation, then, is that all antisocial adults (and many other maladjusted adults) engaged in antisocial behavior as children but that many well adults also engaged in childhood antisocial behavior. Stated differently, we can predict that almost no children who are free of antisocial behavior will become antisocial adults, whereas only a moderate proportion of all children engaging in antisocial behavior will become antisocial adults.

The documentation of these statements comes from a number of sources. One of the most clear-cut is the Robins (1966) study. Robins found that "it is particularly striking that *no* child without frequent or serious anti-social behavior became a sociopathic adult." In contrast, "the percentage of children with frequent and serious episodes of anti-social behavior who became sociopathic personalities was 37%." Among the clinic children without frequent and serious episodes, only 5 percent became sociopathic personalities, and in the control lower-class children, only 2 percent became sociopathic

TABLE 42-5   RELATIONSHIP OF ANTISOCIAL BEHAVIOR TO ADJUSTMENT OUTCOME*

General Adjustment		Antisocial							References
		Presence of Nonspecific Antisocial Behavior							
Poor Adjustment	Psychiatric Illness	Psychoses (Mostly Schizophrenia)	Delinquency and/or Crime	Sociopathic Personality	Neuroses (Other Than Hysteria)	Hysteria	Alcoholism or Problem Drinking	Psychiatrically Healthy	
L:p > 50%[a]									Havighurst et al. (1962)
	L:p > 50%*	L:p < 50% R-I:p > 50%(M)	L:p > 50%[a] (M); p < 50%[a] (F)	L:p < 50%, BR** R-I:p > 50%	L:NR R-I:NR**(M)	L:p < 50% R-I:p > 50%(F)	L:p < 50% R-I:p > 50%(M)	L:NR R-I:p > 50%(M)	Robins (1966) Field (1969)
	L:p < 50%*								Levitt (1963)
		R-II[a]							Edwards & Langley (1936)
		L:p < 50%[a]							Michael et al. (1957)
									Pollack et al. (1966)
									Gardner (1967)
							R-I:PR** (M)		Jones (in press)
			L:p < 50%*						Michael (1956)
p > 50%[a] p < 50%		R-I:p < 50%		R-I:p > 50%					Roff (1961) Roff (1963a, b); 1967
									Friedlander (1945)

Target of Antisocial Behavior

R-I: peers**	R-I: Chld., Adlt., strngrs., adlt. acquaint., parents, auth. fig., org.**	R-I:No one**		R-I:Sibs**	R-I:No one**	Robins (1966)
Theft						
R-I:p < 50%[a] (M)						Frazee (1953)
R-I:p > 50%	L:p < 50%, BR** R-I:p > 50%	L:NS R-I:p < 50%	L:NS R-I:p < 50%(F)	L:p < 50%, BR** R-I:p > 50%(M)	R-I:p < 50%	Robins (1966)
Physical Aggression						
L:NS	L:p < 50%, BR**	L:NS	L:NS	L:NS		Robins (1966)
					R-II:PR[a]	Edwards & Langley (1936)
Running Away From Home						
L:NS R-I:p > 50%(M)	L:p < 50%, BR** R-I:p > 50%	L:NS R-I:p < 50% (M)	L:NS R-I:p > 50%(F)	L:p < 50%, BR** R-I:p > 50%(M)	R-I:p < 50%	Robins (1966) Frazee (1953) Nameche et al. (1964) Edwards & Langley (1936)
Truancy						
L:NS:R-I: p > 50% (M)	L:p < 50%, BR** p > 50%(M)	L:NS R-I:p < 50% (M)	L:NS	L:p < 50%, BR** RI:p > 50%(M)	R-I:p < 50%(M)	Robins (1966) Frazee (1953) Nameche et al. (1964) Glueck (1966)

* See Table 42-4 for key.

personalities.[14]   If we disregard diagnostic labels and look at criminal records, the relations are equally striking.   Two-thirds of the clinic children referred for antisocial difficulties had a record of adult "serious" (nontraffic) arrest. In contrast, less than one-quarter of the children referred for other reasons and less than one-quarter of the controls had adult arrest records.[15] Field (1969) has reported essentially equivalent findings as to relations between childhood antisocial behavior of children referred to a child-guidance clinic and later diagnosis as "character disorder" (grossly equivalant to *delinquent* or *sociopathic character* labels) or later adult arrests. Another basic study yielding similar clear-cut results is that of the Gluecks (1959).   Most of their delinquent group of 500 lower-class boys were so defined because of arrests for burglary, robbery, or larceny other than petty theft (86 percent) during the ages of 9 to 17.   In the next eight-year period (ages 17 to 25), 80 percent of these delinquents were arrested at least once and 34 percent were arrested at least once a year. In the next six-year period (ages 25 to 31), however, only 60 percent were arrested and only

19 percent were arrested at least once a year. In other words, the probability of a delinquent boy becoming a serious criminal in the 25-to-31 period was about 50 percent.   In contrast, only 10 percent of the control group from the same neighborhood were ever arrested as adults, and many of these arrests were not for severely antisocial behavior but rather for drunkenness, gambling, adultery, drug use, etc.

In summary, it is clear that relatively severe or frequent childhood antisocial behavior is a necessary but not sufficient condition for predicting adult antisocial behavior.   It is also clear that antisocial behavior declines with age, particularly in the period from age 25 to age 40. Age of first appearance of childhood antisocial behavior has not yet been shown to be predictive. In the Robins study, the majority of children who grew up to be sociopathic displayed clear antisocial behavior in the age period from 7 to 10. Severity of antisocial behavior was correlated with earliness of onset, so we do not know whether early onset independently predicts to adult antisocial difficulties.   No specific type of antisocial behavior was predictive of adult antisocial difficulties, though children engaging in "frequent and severe" antisocial behavior typically violated the law and engaged in theft in both the Field and Robins studies and the Glueck studies.[16]

---

[14] Robins defines a *sociopathic personality* as a "syndrome of gross repetitive failure to conform to social norms in many areas of life in the absence of thought disturbance suggestive of psychosis." Prognosis, based on life history and interview data, involved "failure to conform in at least five life areas (work, marriage, drugs, alcohol, arrests, belligerency, sexual behavior, vagrancy, pathological lying, etc." Neither Robins' nor any other longitudinal study yet provides any considered direct validation for the concept of a psychopathic or sociopathic personality conceived as a disease entity or as a character disorder established in very early childhood.   Stated differently, given two children engaged in repetitive antisocial behavior, there is currently no evidence that a psychiatric diagnosis as a psychopathic personality has any predictive value over and above the antisocial behavior itself. It is to be hoped that the Gluecks (1959) follow-up of delinquents into adulthood will investigate this issue.

[15] Arrest figures for women were lower than for men, but their relations to earlier antisocial behavior (also lower among girls) was the same.

[16] While this and other evidence are not clear-cut, they suggest that a most meaningful distinction between various forms of antisocial behavior is not psychological but legal. Nonlegal forms of antisocial behavior include disobedience, truancy, running away, pathological lying, some sexual problems, and aggressive behavior short of legal assault. The common legal forms in juveniles are various forms of theft, some sexual perversions, serious vandalism, and assault. Except for pathological lying, nonlegal forms of antisocial behavior were not specifically predictive to sociopathic or criminal outcome but were also common in other forms of maladjustment.   While 30 percent of children with forms of behavior leading to arrest became adult sociopaths, only 5 percent with other forms of antisocial behavior became sociopaths.

We have so far discussed antisocial behavior as predictive of criminal and sociopathic outcomes. It also seems to be predictive (though less so) to all other nonneurotic forms of adult maladjustment. Robins found that of the children referred for antisocial behavior, 84 percent were sick as adults, as compared with 70 percent of the children referred for other reasons and 52 percent of the controls. Antisocial children were more often sociopathic, alcoholic, or psychotic than either controls or children referred for other reasons, and they were less likely to be neurotic. In fact, nonantisocial symptoms added nothing to the prediction of adult adjustment status in these other categories. As an example, a child had only a 15 percent chance of being a well adult if he had six antisocial symptoms and only a 5 percent chance of being well if he had ten or more antisocial symptoms. The number of nonantisocial symptoms the child had added nothing to the prediction of adult sickness or health.

In general, the distinction between antisocial (sociopathic) and other maladjustment outcomes is predicted by higher frequency and seriousness of antisocial behavior in children who later are diagnosed as sociopathic but not by the absence of antisocial behavior in children ending with other disorders of a nonneurotic kind. In general, Robins' findings on the predictive value of antisocial behavior for noncriminal forms of adult maladjustment is confirmed by the studies of Field (1969) and Roff (1961, 1963, 1967).

We have so far discussed relatively serious forms of antisocial behavior. Sheer aggressiveness in schoolchildren is less clearly predictive of adult maladjustment. Havighurst et al. (1962) found a low negative ($r = -.24$) correlation between teacher- and peer-rated aggressive maladjustment at grade 6 and rated adult adjustment at age 20. Of the top 10 percent on ratings of aggressive maladjustment, almost none achieved an adult-adjustment rating that was better than average, though not all were at the bottom in adjustment.

In summary, then, childhood severe antisocial behavior is a necessary condition for the prediction of severe adult antisocial behavior, and milder forms of antisocial behavior are relatively good predictors of all forms of adult maladjustment. The predictive power of antisocial behavior does not appear to depend on specific types of antisocial behavior or upon particular kinds of aggressive, sexual, or other motives but seems to reflect the fact that distortions of ego development and distortions in the child's relation to his environment are necessary conditions for relatively frequent or severe forms of antisocial behavior.

SOCIAL BEHAVIOR—WITHDRAWAL AND OVERDEPENDENCY

Considerable research attention has been devoted to examining the mental-health outcomes of childhood withdrawal or restriction of social interaction. (See Table 42-6.) A wide variety of terms has been used in this connection, including *withdrawal, introversion, seclusiveness, shut-in-ness, daydreaming,* and *shyness.* The major findings concerning this variable were mentioned in previous sections, i.e., that withdrawal does not predict any effective way to later maladjustment. In the section on "Prediction of Psychoses," below, we shall document the finding that withdrawal in a child who is not overtly psychotic is not a useful predictor of later schizophrenia. These findings are summarized in Table 42-8 in that section. Table 42-8 indicates that follow-up studies report no relation of withdrawal to later psychosis. Mednick and Schulsinger (1969) find that children of schizophrenic mothers are more withdrawn than controls. Among these children of schizophrenic mothers, however, there is no relation between childhood withdrawal and later

TABLE 42-6   RELATIONSHIP OF WITHDRAWN BEHAVIOR TO ADJUSTMENT OUTCOME*

Age or Grade at Assessment	Withdrawn Behavior in Relationship to Outcome	Type of Investigation	References
General Adjustment			
Grammar school	"Improved adjustment" (8–10 years later): 100%(M)	L	Burns (1952)
6th, 7th, and 9th grades	Average or better adjustment (19–20 years old): 51%	L	Havighurst et al. (1962)
Childhood	Satisfactorily adjusted (16–27 years later): 65%, directly interviewed; 75%, followed through relatives	L	Morris et al. (1954)
Childhood	Psychiatric health vs. illness (30 years later): NS	L	Robins (1966)
6–22 yr	Improved adjustment (2–8 years later): 59%	L	Walcott (1932)
Psychosis			
Mean CA = 9 yrs.	Institutionalized for psychiatric illness: introverts, 0.6%; ambiverts 7.0%	L	Michael et al. (1957)
	Psychotic cases with history or withdrawn problems:		
School age	"Apathetic": 50%+	R-I	Birren (1944)
High school	"Pathologically shy": 9%[L] (M)	R-II	Bower et al. (1960)
Childhood	"Inaccessibility": PR "Daydreaming," "extreme quietness," "timidity": NR	R-II	Edwards & Langley (1936)
Childhood	"Social withdrawal": PR	R-II	Schofield & Balian (1959)
5–16 yr	"Shy, listless, lack of interest": 78%(M) "Excessive daydreaming": 65%(M) "Seclusiveness": 26%(M)	R-I R-I R-I	Frazee (1953)
Childhood	"Daydreaming": 94% "Preferred being alone": 50%	R-I	Friedlander (1945)
Childhood	"Extremely shy, backward, passive": 24%	R-II	Kasanin & Veo (1932)
5–12 yr	"Shy": PR	R-II	Pollack et al. (1966)
Childhood	Withdrawal: PR, postpuberty only	R-I	Veo (1931)

*See Table 42-4 for key.

psychosis. This finding is consistent with other follow-up studies, such as those of Morris, Michael, et al. In contrast, follow-back studies often do report a relationship. The discrepancies between follow-back and follow-up studies are probably largely due to the fact that high withdrawal in children is not a stable characteristic. Although introverted and passive social styles are relatively stable temperamental characteristics, judgments of high withdrawal are not (Havighurst et al., 1962; MacFarlane et al., 1952). Withdrawal problems are associated with specific developmental phases and crises, as was discussed previously. As a result, retrospective studies may find that schizophrenics were withdrawn sometime in their life prior to psychosis, but this does not indicate that a child's withdrawn behavior is predictive to later psychosis.

In fact, insofar as there is any relation of withdrawal to later psychosis, it would appear to be a form of withdrawal which is unstable, rather than a consistent personality style. Withdrawn, anxious adjustment problems in combination with acting-out behavior problems appeared to predict psychosis better than either did separately. Individuals with both sets of behavior problems had a higher rate of psychiatric hospitalization than did individuals with only inner or only outer juvenile difficulties (Michael et al., 1957).

The suggestion that prepsychotics may show both withdrawn and aggressive behavior indicates the necessity of the basic distinction in conceptualizing withdrawal suggested by Roff (1965). This is the distinction between seclusiveness, or active avoidance of social contact, and shyness or introversion, i.e., discomfort or passivity about initiating social interaction or seeking a social response. Active seclusiveness is a form of behavior which is as noticeable, as potentially embarrassing, and as self-assertive as is the dependent attention seeking which the shy child avoids. Thus there are a few hints that children who later become schizophrenic are sometimes seclusive, sometimes overdependent, and sometimes aggressive or antisocial but that few preschizophrenic children are shy or withdrawn in the usual sense. Related to the distinction between seclusiveness and withdrawal is the distinction by Field (1969) between withdrawal from the community (peers and school) and withdrawal from family members, which usually requires an active seclusiveness rather than an avoidance of social initiative.

Field (1969), using stringent criteria for withdrawal and distinguishing between withdrawal from community activities such as schools and gangs and the more encompassing withdrawal of removing oneself from family members, found that both chronic (56 percent) and released (50 percent) adult schizophrenics had been withdrawn from the community during adolescence but that only those who were later chronic (46 percent) frequently withdrew from the family as well. Comparable degrees of withdrawal in adolescent boys who were later character-disordered or socially adequate (untraceable through records of arrest or hospitalization) were from 10 to 16 percent, well below the preschizophrenic proportions.

In a related study using the same subjects, Berry and Ricks (1969) found a similar pattern in half of the boys in their sample who were later chronic. It should be noted, however, that the methodology of these studies was partly follow-back in that not all cases were followed up and there was no control group followed up.

In summary, a stable withdrawn, introverted, or shy personality or school adjustment is not predictive of psychosis. A sizable proportion of psychotics, however, seem to go through an adolescent phase of seclusiveness and detachment from their family which is not inconsistent with tendencies to dependency and aggression at other times or in other contexts.

Turning from psychosis to other adult outcomes; shy, withdrawn, and inhibited children are unlikely to have criminal or psychopathic outcomes and are no more likely to become neurotic than controls (Robins, 1966). The Michael, Morris et al. studies report similar results. These studies indicate that *introverted* or *internal-reactor individuals*[17] had found relatively sheltered styles of adult life, e.g., had jobs that were characterized by stability and security and had an unusually low divorce rate relative to general population. In general, their adjustment was rated as being as good as that of a random sample of the population.

If withdrawal is not a clear-cut predictor of adult-adjustment outcome, neither is its superficial opposite, overdependency or excessive demands for attention. Excessive demandingness and dependency upon the mother were the major characteristics of Levy's (1943) cases of *Maternal Overprotection*. The large majority of these children had adequate adult adjustments, both those treated and those not treated. Eleven percent were believed to have serious forms of psychopathology at adolescence and adulthood, not markedly different from a random population sample. Those who did have serious adult pathology were primarily antisocial or sociopathic. In other words, overdependency does not predict directly to adult neurotic behavior of an overdependent variety, nor is it generally predictive of adult adjustment. There is, however, some evidence that overdependency is slightly predictive of later psychosis in a lower-class setting. Robins (1966) found that 20 percent of clinic children showing overdependency became schizophrenic, as compared with 6 percent in the total clinic sample. As we have noted earlier, a polymor-

phous pattern of overseclusiveness, overdependency, and overaggressiveness seems to be somewhat characteristic of preschizophrenics, the common denominator perhaps being overt insensitivy to the reactions of others toward interpersonal deviance, whether of a demanding or a seclusive kind. In any case, the dependency of children who later became psychotic was not the primary problem for which they were referred to the clinic but was a side issue recorded in the notes (Robins, 1966).

In summary, the contrast between the predictiveness of antisocial behavior and that of behaviors on the withdrawal-overdependent role is marked. Antisocial behavior predicts well and predicts on the level of "like is to like." In contrast, withdrawal and overdependency predict poorly, and their possible predictive value is not based on a prediction of like to like. Some further perspective on this contrast between the antisocial and the withdrawn or dependent is presented in our next section, on global peer adjustment.

PEER RELATIONS AS PREDICTORS

In previous sections we noted that antisocial behavior was an excellent predictor of antisocial adult adjustment as well as of other difficulties. We also saw that additional social-behavior categories, such as the withdrawn, the overdependent, and the anxious, seemed to add little predictive power to the antisocial classification. We shall now survey evidence suggesting that peer acceptance and stable relations with peers does add additional power to predictions based on considering antisocial behavior alone. This evidence is summarized in Table 42-7.

In a certain sense, this evidence suggests that children are better diagnosticians than are adult clinicians, i.e., that their spontaneous evaluations of each other are more predictive than are the ratings of adults on mental-health behavior. An

---

[17] As defined by the investigators, *internal reactors* are those showing predominantly shy, withdrawn, anxious, or fearful behavior; those who are tending to develop neuroses; or those who are bothering themselves rather than others (Michael et al., 1957, p. 743).

example is the findings from a longitudinal study of children with high risk for schizophrenia (Mednick & Schulsinger, 1969). In this study, psychiatric ratings on adjustment were found to discriminate high-risk children with schizophrenic mothers from controls (in the direction of children with a schizoid temperament being rated as more poorly adjusted). Psychiatric ratings, however, failed to discriminate high-risk children who later became psychotic from those who did not. While psychiatric ratings did not predict psychotic breakdown, peer relations did.

Comparing two carefully matched groups of adolescents with a high risk for schizophrenia, the study found that about half of those who "broke down" into some psychiatric disorder during the first five years of study were more disturbing to classmates—a much higher proportion than those who were still functioning (see Table 42-7). This difference occurred in spite of rigorous matching for age, IQ, sex, social class, and childhood rearing conditions; without this matching, the differences could have been expected to be even greater. This is an example of data pointing to the need for clinical assessment to attend to peer relations with the same care and sensitivity which is now largely restricted to considering the child's relations to his family. Presumably the psychiatric ratings which failed to predict which children would become psychotic and which would not partly suffered from the lack of such organized sensitivity to peer relations.

It is not surprising to find that teachers as well as psychiatrists are insensitive or inaccurate in their perception of peer relations. Analysis of teachers' spontaneous comments in cumulative records indicated that males with apparently healthy outcomes, rather than with known schizophrenic outcomes, were the ones described significantly more often as lacking friends (Warnken & Siess, 1965). In contrast, more accurate evaluations of peer data by Roff and his colleagues (1969a, b) and by Mednick and Schulsinger indicate that children who later become schizophrenic do, in fact, have less adequate peer relations.

In considering the data on predictions from peer acceptance, we must first consider briefly the concurrent attributes of the child which influence peer acceptance-rejection. These may be divided into the following characteristics:

1. "Extraneous" status variables—e.g., socioeconomic status, race, physical attractiveness, physical growth, physical dress
2. Personality variables considered "good" or "well-adjusted" by clinicians
3. Personality variables usually overlooked by clinicians

Obviously, the last category of variables is the one most worth research attention, although it is the one least studied. With regard to the extraneous variables, research evidence documents their influence on peer assessment, though it also suggests that they are somewhat less important than one might anticipate. As an example, in elementary school ratings integrated by race and class, minority-group status and low socioeconomic status do not appear to play a large part in or do not determine sociometric rejection (Sells et al., 1967). Furthermore, extraneous variables are confounded with "relevant" variables (intelligence, restraint of antisocial behavior, etc.) which, to some extent, directly predict adjustment. It is well documented that in high school, family status heavily determines the prestige of various cliques, but this does not mean that failure to have some reciprocal relations with one's peers (of whatever status) is due to social-status variables.

The "good" personality variables related to peer acceptance may be divided into two groups: ego-strength or ego-development variables (all positively related to age development) and personality-adjustment variables (all uncorrelated with development). The evidence suggests that both sets of variables relate to peer acceptance

TABLE 42-7   PEER RELATIONSHIPS AND ADJUSTMENT OUTCOME*

Age or Grade at Assessment	Relationship	Research Design	References
General Adjustment			
Nursery school	Difficulties with other children negatively related to adjustment success in elementary school.	R-I	Van Alstyne & Hattwick (1939)
6th, 9th grades	Positive relationship between peer standing and high school success as indexed by academic rank, participation.	L L L L	Gronlund & Holmlund (1958) Havighurst et al. (1962) Sells et al. (1967) Ullman (1957)
6th, 7th, 9th grades	Positive relationship between combined peer-teacher ratings of "social leadership talent" and general adjustment at 19–20 years.	L	Havighurst et al. (1962)
Antisocial Behavior			
3d–6th grade	For upper SEC octiles, low peer status associated with delinquent outcome.[a] Lowest SEC octile: NR (M).	L L	Roff & Sells (1968) Sells et al. (1967)
Childhood	Degree of involvement in delinquent gang positively related to criminal outcome*: regular or irregular involvement, $p > 50\%$; no involvement, $p < 50\%$ (M).	L	McCord et al. (1959)
Childhood	Delinquency associated with having older companions: $p < 50\%$[a] (M).	L	Glueck (1966)
Childhood	Having "bad associates" related to outcome of sociopathic personalities: BR; $p > 50\%$.	L	Robins (1966)
Childhood	History of "bad associates" in group of known sociopathic personalities: $p > 50\%$[a] (M); BR.	L:R-I	Robins (1966)
Childhood	Young adult bad conduct related to history of poor peer relationships: $p > 50\%$* (M).	R-I	Roff (1961)

Neuroses			
Childhood	History of poor peer relationships: $p > 50\%$* (M).	R-I	Roff (1957, 1959)
Childhood	History of "bad associates": NR.	R-I	Robins (1966)
Homosexuality			
Childhood	History of poor peer relationships: $p > 50\%$* (M).	R-I	Roff (1966)
Schizoid Personality			
Childhood	History of poor peer relationships: $p > 50\%$* (M).	R-I	Roff (1965)
Chronic Brain Syndrome			
Childhood	Trouble with contemporaries associated with outcome of chronic brain syndrome: BR, $p < 50\%$.	L	Robins (1966)
Alcoholism			
Childhood	History of "bad associates": $p < 50\%$[a] (M).	R-I	Robins (1966)
Hysteria			
Childhood	History of "bad associates": $p > 50\%$ (F).	R-I	Robins (1966)
Well			
Childhood	History of "bad associates": $p < 50\%$.	R-I	Robins (1966)

*See Table 42-4 for key.

but that long-range correlates of peer acceptance may be more in the *ego-maturity* than the *social-adjustment* category. Relevant ego-maturity variables related to peer acceptance in elementary school (though not necessarily in preschool) are:

1. Intelligence
2. Control of antisocial behavior
3. Attention, or control of distractible or "foolish" behavior
4. Moral behavior and moral-judgment maturity
5. Capacity for cooperative interaction, a variable itself related to these other variables and to age (Parten & Newhall, 1943)

The evidence for the effect of intelligence on peer status was summarized in Table 42-1. The effect of antisocial behavior, almost self-evident, is amply documented (Northway, 1944; Sells et al., 1967; Smith, 1950). It is interesting, however, that the major negative influence on status in these studies comes from rule defiance rather than from aggressiveness in the more psychological sense. The relation of peer status to both moral-judgment maturity and moral behavior or character is well documented (Kohlberg, 1958, 1964, 1971). With IQ and social class controlled, sociometric integrates were found to be significantly more mature in moral judgment than were isolates. This effect was much stronger than the social-class effect. Gilliland (1965) found correlations in the .60s between high school peer ratings of moral character and tested maturity of moral judgment, a higher correlation than the correlation of .40 to .50 found between teacher ratings of moral character and tested maturity of moral judgment. These combined findings indicate that moral maturity is an important correlate of peer integration and suggest that moral maturity is better reflected in the positive judgments of peers than in the ratings of teachers.[18]

[18] Obviously, the relevance of moral or ego maturity to peer ratings depends on the general moral level of the group.

While moral and ego maturity are correlated with peer acceptance, we do not know the lines of causation involved in this relation. In part, social maturity causes peer integration; in part, peer integration stimulates ego and moral maturity by the provision of more experiences of role taking and by a greater sense of security, which positively influences development.

With regard to adjustment rather than development, there is also a clear relation between peer integration and adult ratings of adjustment and positive sociability; the well-liked, highly accepted child is described by his peers and is seen by observers as engaging in relatively comfortable, friendly, give-and-take interactions with other individuals and with groups (Bonney, 1955; Bonney & Powell, 1953; Gronlund & Anderson, 1957; Northway, 1944; Smith, 1950). Teachers apparently rate the high-peer-status child favorably (Bonney, 1955). Furthermore, he looks relatively healthy on tests intended to measure adjustment—although it should be noted that the validity of some of these tests and the age norms seem questionable (Bedoian, 1953; Bonney, 1955). Children who are problem-free, from a clinical point of view, tend to be well liked by their peers compared with children judged to be emotionally handicapped by school clinicians (Bower, 1960).

While schoolchildren orient positively to friendly, outgoing charm and communicativeness in their peers (as opposed to anxious withdrawal in their peers), there is evidence that it weighs less with them than it does with adults interested in mental health. We have noted frequently the overemphasis of clinicians on withdrawal as poor mental health. Children do not seem to have this bias, since withdrawal itself seems to be uncorrelated with low peer status ($r = .10$), whereas antisocial behavior (in varying combinations with anxiety) is correlated with low peer status (Glidewell, in preparation). One of the writers has had longitudinal experience in which he was initially surprised to find certain charming, apparently "well-adjusted" children labeled as *isolates* and certain inhibited, apparently poorly adjusted children labeled as *stars,* only to find over the years that the sociometric ratings were sounder than were his clinical impressions of sociability and adjustment. Adults do not make their sociometric evaluations of other adults on the same basis as that on which they evaluate children but are more impressed by long-term character. Preadolescent children seem to react also less to sociability than to character.

While extremes of sociometric status in repeated observations are useful predictors, momentary sociometric rank is not a particularly stable variable. Sells et al. (1967) correlated identical measures on the same individuals on a year-to-year basis over a four-year period. In general, despite changes within individuals, in peer-group composition, and in school structures, a consistent picture of moderate stability emerged, with positive peer-choice scores being somewhat more stable than negative peer-choice scores. For example, the range of one-year stability coefficients for several subsamples was .46 to .57 for positive peer-choice scores and .35 to .48 for negative peer-choice scores. Over greater lengths of time, there were reductions in stability, with the greatest reduction occurring at the transition from elementary to junior high school. When extremes of sociometric status (upper and lower 10 percent) are taken, the stability is considerably higher (Havighurst et al., 1962).

Our discussion of peer evaluations and relations indicates that they are influenced by extraneous status variables, by ego maturity, and by personality-adjustment factors. The longitudinal literature does not separate these variables. It does indicate that peer ratings add substantially to the prediction due to IQ and antisocial behavior, the two variables showing the greatest power in our review up to this point. The two most powerful sixth-grade predictors of adult adjustment in the Havighurst et al. study were IQ ($r = .48$) and pooled peer and adult ratings of social

leadership ($r = .52$). Again, peer ratings have the familiar pattern: rejected children may do better over time, while acceptance is a guarantee of absence of later poor adjustment.

Turning to more clinical analysis of outcome, the major work has been done by Roff and his colleagues (Roff, 1969a, b). Roff has identified adults who had child-guidance clinic records and defined their adult mental-health status in terms of military-service information. Culling through the files of those clinics that systematically obtained information from school, clinic, and community personnel regarding each case, an abstract for each subject regarding his childhood peer relationships was compiled. These abstracts were sorted by raters, independently of knowledge of outcome, into categories of *good, poor,* and *undecided* peer relationships. Regardless of the specific outcome, the consistent finding has been that between two-thirds and three-quarters of the individuals with psychiatric difficulties at (or during) the time of contact with the military have had histories of poor peer relationships. In contrast, the incidence of poor juvenile peer relationships in histories of men with child-guidance clinic histories but apparently adequately adjusted outcomes in military service runs about one-quarter.

Despite the paucity of detailed information, some picture of specific characteristics of juvenile peer relations distinctively associated with later specific kinds of adjustment difficulties may be constructed. Individuals destined for some sort of an antisocial adjustment outcome appear to have some peer ties, despite evidence suggesting that they are usually relatively low in peer status (Roff & Sells, 1968). The distinguishing characteristics appear to be the kind of friends the individual has and the sorts of people who are targets of his aggression. Longitudinal evidence (McCord et al., 1959; Robins, 1966) suggests that degree of involvement in a delinquent peer reference group—or the presence or absence of bad associates—is fairly distinctively associated with antisocial outcomes such as delinquency or sociopathic personality.

Robins' comparisons (1966) of the objects of antisocial behavior observed in the histories of different outcome groups suggest that sociopaths typically direct attacks against peers outside their immediate circle of friends. In contrast with the sociopath, the individual with an alcoholic outcome, though tending to have bad associates, apparently focuses his attacks not on children outside the family but rather on his sibs.

Qualitative characteristics of peer-relationship problems have most frequently been examined in relationship to a known psychotic (usually schizophrenic) outcome. Such evidence suggests that peer difficulties characterized by behaviors that would militate against ties with any peers may be relatively common. On the side of peer reactions to the individual, rejection, isolation, and scapegoating have been relatively frequent. In addition, aggression seems to be a common part of the picture (Roff, 1969a, b). In keeping with this picture are Robin's finding that the target of antisocial behavior most frequently used by the prepsychotic was a child with whom the individual was acquainted.

Roff (1969a, b) has suggested that when samples of child-guidance cases with various types of adult maladjustments are broken into those under 12 and those already into adolescence, as he has been able to do in some of his studies, the younger groups will show a good deal of undifferentiated active unpleasantness in social relationships while the older groups will show tendencies to "jell" into patterns closer to their adult syndromes. It is possible in many records to follow the transition from angry, rebellious, generally provocative behavior during the gradeschool years to more passive, apathetic, resigned behavior during high school.

Summary: Undifferentiated peer problems seem relatively promising as a nonspecific predictor of later adjustment difficulties. If the particular forms and temporal sequences of peer difficulties are examined, particular kinds of outcomes may be predictable. Confirmation of Roff's hypothesis that syndromes begin to "jell" in adolescence and more differentiated understanding of how particular peer relationships are associated with particular diagnostic outcomes will depend on the vast enterprise of naturalistic observation and longitudinal research.

THE PREDICTION OF PSYCHOSES

The core credibility of the mental-illness concept lies in the clinical observation of psychoses, especially schizophrenia. Delinquency, character disorders, neuroses, and learning failures can readily be interpreted as due to retardation in cognitive and social development or to social learning of maladaptive values and behavior. Since general processes of learning and development are equally applicable to all children, the differences between these disorders and normal personality patterns can be viewed as matters of degree only. However, it is extremely difficult to look at schizophrenic behavior in these terms. The core phenomena of adult schizophrenia—apathy, emotional withdrawal, and thought disorder—appear to be qualitatively different from normal behavior, from other forms of maladjustment, and from the earlier behavior of the patient himself. To the extent that there is a true discontinuity between normal and schizophrenic behavior or between preschizophrenic and schizophrenic behavior, schizophrenia, and to a lesser extent the other psychoses, would seem to fit the disease model of mental disorder.

The degree of discontinuity between premorbid personality and the characteristics observable during schizophrenia differs from patient to patient, so that investigators have been led to distinguish between "process schizophrenics" and "reactive" patients, who seem to develop the disorder in relation to a current stress after an ordinary childhood and adolescent history. Clinical theories of schizophrenia usually attempt to explain the apparent discontinuity between prepsychotic and psychotic behavior by positing an underlying schizophrenic disposition or schizophrenic process that becomes manifest during the overt psychosis. While the schizophrenic process is sometimes considered genetic or biochemical, it is assumed by psychoanalytic and neopsychoanalytic theories to be psychological or psychogenic. Both biogenic and psychogenic theories typically ascribe the onset of overt psychoses to environmentally related precipitating factors, but these are assumed to have greater weight in reactive disorders and less weight in process. The theories disagree, however, as to the biogenic or psychogenic origins of the predisposition to schizophrenia. The question is critical, not only for an understanding of schizophrenia but also for the whole application of mental-disease models to all forms of maladaptive behavior. If schizophrenia is understandable as a disease with a psychogenic origin, then it is feasible to extend the disease model to other psychogenic disorders. This has been the tradition of psychoanalytic psychiatry, which looks at all maladaptive behavior as symptomatic of underlying pathology, e.g., of fixation, of conflict, of defenses, and of character types built on these. If, however, schizophrenia has a biological base, then it may be warranted to consider it as a psychiatric disease and yet not extend the mental-illness concept beyond schizophrenia to the general province of maladaptive behavior. Current research gives considerable support to the latter view. Our review will suggest that the development of schizophrenia is built upon a biological predisposition to a disease state and in this regard is different from other forms of maladaptation. As a result, the findings on schizophrenia are not generalizable to the prediction of other forms of adult maladjustment.

The gross findings on childhood behavior patterns predictive of schizophrenia are summarized in Table 42-8. The findings indicate that schizophrenia is not an extension of (or well predicted by) the emotional withdrawal, anxiety, and poor intellectual functioning considered to be common characteristics of adult schizophrenia. Follow-back studies, particularly those focusing on adolescent records (Fleming & Ricks, 1969), indicate some association between these characteristics and adult psychosis, but follow-up studies typically fail to confirm these associations. In our discussion of follow-back versus follow-up research strategies, we gave some reasons for these discrepancies. Very often, they are due to failure to control the comparison groups on all relevant variables. Sometimes the control groups contain psychotics who were not followed up, or differences between the groups are due to irrelevant factors such as differential loss of patients and comparison subjects from the study samples. In other cases, the discrepancy is due to the fact that a genuine statistical association is not a predictor since one deals with two quite different regression lines in predicting back and predicting forward (Roff, 1969a, b). As an example, some studies indicate a larger proportion of schizophrenics as withdrawn under follow-back, as compared with controls. However, longitudinal study, at this point, indicates no predictive value to withdrawn behavior. Morris et al. (1954) examined the later adjustment of fifty-four children referred to a child-guidance clinic for shy, withdrawn, anxious, and fearful behavior, most of whom had been untreated. Available subjects were psychiatrically interviewed as adults; the remainder were followed up indirectly. Over two-thirds were satisfactorily adjusted, and only one shy child was psychotic—a rate equivalent to that in the general population. In fact, of all the children referred to the clinic, introverted or withdrawn children were least likely to become psychotic (0.6 percent) compared with extroverts (4 percent) and ambiverts (7 percent) (Michael et al., 1957). A less extensive longitudinal study by Burns (1952) yielded similar results.

TABLE 42-8 BIRTH, CHILDHOOD, AND ADOLESCENT CHARACTERISTICS RELATED TO PSYCHOTIC OUTCOME*

Age at Assessment	Variable	Design	References
Paranatal complications and deviant physiological functioning			
Birth	Low birth weight, compared with sibs.	R-I	Lane & Albee (1966)
	Low birth weight; more birth complications; neonatal asphyxia; weaker, shorter, compared with genetically identical twin.	R-I and R-II	Stabenau & Pollin (1969)
	Moderate to severe paranatal abnormality greater than 50%.	R-II	Pollack et al. (1966)
	Birth injuries or complications.	R-I	Mednick & Shulsinger (1969)
Early childhood	Index twin is fussier; more troublesome, fragile, and helpless; less active physically; less able to master motor tasks of development.	R-II	Stabenau & Pollin (1969)
Childhood	Slow motor development, poor coordination, unusual gait, hyperreactive reflexes, speech defects.	R-II	Ricks & Nameche (1966)
Adolescence	C1 syndrome found in half of later chronic male schizophrenics: hypoactivity, rigidity, abnormalities of speech output, abnormal gait, poor coordination, impaired attention span, tantrums, and disorganized destructive episodes.	R-I	Berry & Ricks (1969)
	C2 syndrome found in one-third of later chronic male schizophrenics: hyperactivity, incorrigibility, short attention span, overreaction to frustration, enuresis, tantrums.	R-I	
	Physically weak and unathletic.	R-I	Ricks & Nameche (1966)
	Conditioning responses characterized by fast latency, poor habituation, lack of extinction of conditioned emotional responses, and rapid recovery of g.s.r. responses after arousal.	L	Mednick & Shulsinger (1969)
Antisocial Behavior			
Childhood and adolescence	Presence and frequency of antisocial behavior predict to psychotic outcomes by both follow-up and follow-back studies.	R-I and L	Michael et al. (1957) Morris et al. (1956) Robins (1966) Roff (1961, 1963, 1967)
	Excellent school deportment records.	R-II	Schofield & Balian (1959)

1264

Age at Assessment	Variable	Design	References
	Deviant Emotional Functioning		
Adolescence	Signs of anxiety, phobias, obsessive-compulsive ruminations (males).	R-I R-I L	Gardner (1967) Field (1969) Friedlander (1945)
	Self-reported anxiety, feelings of vulnerability, feelings of unreality, sense of isolation and alienation.	R-I	Fleming & Ricks (1969)
	Intelligence		
2nd, 6th, 8th grades	In deprived urban population, schizophrenic outcome associated with low IQ relative to population means, classroom peers, and siblings.	R-I	Albee et al. (1964) Lane & Albee (1965)
K-9th grades	In suburban population, no relationship between schizophrenic outcome and IQ, except that IQ scores are lower than those of sibs.	R-I	Schaffner et al. (1967)
2nd–6th grades	No decline in IQ with onset of schizophrenia.	R-I	Albee et al. (1964)
High school	Schizophrenic outcome associated with low IQ.	R-I	Bower et al. (1960)
Young adult	Hebephrenic and simple schizophrenic outcomes associated with low IQ.	R-I	Mason (1956)
Adolescence	No relationship between IQ and breakdown in high-risk subjects.	L	Mednick & Shulsinger (1969)
	School Achievement		
Childhood and high school	School work more often difficult and good grades less easily achieved.	R-II	Schofield & Balian (1959)
5-12 yr	Low achievement.	R-I	Pollack et al. (1966)
High school	Low achievement, declining with age.	R-I	Bower et al. (1960)
School years	Relationship varies, depending on outcome of comparison group: 1. High achievement relative to psychopaths 2. Low achievement relative to apparently normal outcome 3. Comparable achievement relative to intellectually duller subjects with adequately adjusted or "constitutionally" psychotic outcomes.	R-I	Wittman (1948) Frazee (1953) Robins (1966) Birren (1944)

1265

TABLE 42-8 BIRTH, CHILDHOOD, AND ADOLESCENT CHARACTERISTICS RELATED TO PSYCHOTIC OUTCOME* *(Continued)*

Age at Assessment	Variable	Design	References
	Withdrawal		
Mean CA = 9 yr	Institutionalized for psychiatric illness: introverts, 0.6%[b]; ambiverts 7.0%[a]	L	Michael et al. (1957)
School age	"Apathetic": 50%[a]	R-I	Birren (1944)
	"Apathetic and lacking in initiative"	R-I	Field (1969)
High school	"Pathologically shy": 9%[L](M)	R-II	Bower et al. (1960)
	"Withdrawal in both home and community"	R-I	Field (1969)
	"Passive"	R-I	Field (1969)
Childhood	"Inaccessibility": PR[a]	R-II	Edwards & Langley (1936)
	"Daydreaming," "extreme quietness," "timidity": NR[b]		
	"Social withdrawal": PR[a]	R-II	Schofield & Balian (1959)
5–16 yr	"Shy, listless, lack of interest": 78%[a](M)	R-I	Frazee (1953)
	"Excessive daydreaming": 65%[a](M)		
	"Seclusiveness": 26%[a](M)		
Childhood	"Day dreaming": 94%[a]	R-I	Friedlander (1945)
	"Preferred being alone": 50%[a]		
	"Extremely shy, backward, passive": 24%[c]	R-II	Kasanin & Veo (1932)
5–12 yr	"Shy": PR[a]	R-II	Pollack et al. (1966)
Childhood	Withdrawal: Pr, postpuberty[c].	R-I	Veo (1931)
	Poor Peer Relations		
Childhood	Trouble with contemporaries: NS.	L	Robins (1966)
	Associated with relative difficulty in initiating social contacts.[a]	R-II	Pollin et al. (1966)
5–12 yr	Associated with difficulty relating to peers (few or no friends, scapegoating were most common problems).[a]	R-II	Pollack et al. (1966)
5–16 yr	Associated with lack of friends, being easily led ($p >$ 50%); no evidence of normal peer interaction or leadership skills[a] (M).	R-I	Frazee (1953)
Up to 12 yr	Associated with poor peer relationships: $p >$ 50%* (M)	R-I	Roff (1963a, b)

1266

TABLE 42-8   BIRTH, CHILDHOOD, AND ADOLESCENT CHARACTERISTICS RELATED TO PSYCHOTIC OUTCOME* *(Continued)*

Age at Assessment	Variable	Design	References
Adolescence	Lack of involvement in social life.	R-I	Ricks & Nameche (1966)
K–high	Lack of friends: NR*.	R-I	Warnken & Siess (1965)
High school	Associated with low degree of liking by others,* lack of participation in group activities,* little interest in opposite sex.*	R-II	Bower et al. (1960)

*See Table 42-4 for key.

While a significant portion of psychotics were withdrawn, the proportion of extremely withdrawn children who become psychotic is slight or nonpredictive. Since psychosis is a rare category and at least ordinary degrees of withdrawal a common one, the predictive power of withdrawal is nothing. The partial truth represented by the notion that withdrawal in childhood is a forerunner of schizophrenia seems to be that children who later become schizophrenic are more likely to have poor peer relations than are normals. Roff's follow-back studies (1961a, b; 1963a, b; 1967), however, do not suggest that the preschizophrenic poor peer relations are especially likely to be of a withdrawn nature. Rather, they are more likely to be due to antisocial behavior, transitory and nonreciprocal relations, etc. In this regard, the social difficulties of preschizophrenics do not appear very different from those of children who later become neurotic, delinquent, or sexually deviant (Roff, 1961a, b; 1963a, b; 1967).

The qualifications with regard to withdrawal as a predictor of schizophrenia apply to all the other behaviors summarized in Table 42-8. Furthermore, more qualitative or holistic diagnostic approaches seem little better for the prediction of schizophrenia. In the test interpretations of adolescent children tested at a child-study bureau who later became schizophrenic, Birren (1944)

found nothing which differentiated these children from a control group. (This test interpretation was based primarily on psychometric tests, however.) Mednick (Mednick & McNeil, 1968; Mednick & Schulsinger, 1967, 1969) found that psychiatric ratings and evaluations failed to predict which children of schizophrenic mothers would become schizophrenic and which would remain well; e.g., "an experienced psychiatrist found these two groups equivalent in level of adjustment."

We may conclude, then, that schizophrenia cannot at present be satisfactorily predicted on the basis of commonsense or psychiatric stereotypes of the preschizophrenic personality. As an example of the danger of these stereotypes, we may cite a not unusual case (personal communication, Norman Paul). A middle-class child manifesting disturbed behavior in first grade was placed in treatment with an experienced child psychoanalyst. The analyst recommended residential treatment because the child was preschizophrenic. The child was diagnosed and accepted for residential care by a progressive residential treatment center for children. At the last moment, the parents balked at institutionalizing the child and found a psychiatrist who disagreed with the diagnosis. Some years later, the child is making an adequate adjustment. One wonders whether institutionalization would not have been a self-fulfilling prophecy.

Although later schizophrenia is not satisfactorily predictable on behavior grounds, biological considerations allow a high rate of longitudinal prediction of schizophrenic breakdown. While frequently criticized, Kallman's (1946) evidence for genetic transmission of schizophrenia has received considerable research support. The criticism of these data has about the same status as the criticisms of the notion that IQ does not have a strong genetic base (criticism most recently refuted by Jensen, 1969). The broad import of Kallman's data in terms of heredity-environment issues is well discussed by Meehl (1954). The predictive value of the genetic factor is well enough documented by the Mednick and Schulsinger study. In this study, 200 "high-risk" children of schizophrenic mothers were followed into late adolescence along with a parallel control group matched in all respects except birth to a schizophrenic parent. Over 10 percent of the high-risk group had become psychotic by late adolescence, as compared with less than 1 percent of the control group. This difference cannot be attributed to the effects of mothering by a psychotic parent or to maternal separation for reasons discussed by Mednick and Schulsinger (1967). While the genetic factor gives some clue to prediction of schizophrenia, a much more powerful biological predictor has been found by the Mednick study. The study involves the comparison of "well-outcome" with "sick-outcome" groups among the high-risk children, the latter being the group which has become psychotic. Mednick (1969) finds that 70 percent of the sick-outcome group had perinatal birth injuries or complications, as compared with 15 percent of the well-outcome group (with many of this 15 percent still having a chance of becoming psychotic).

Furthermore, the factor of birth complications is found to relate closely to a schizophrenic pattern of galvanic skin response (g.s.r.) reactivity

which includes the following components:

1. Fast latency
2. Poor habituation
3. Lack of extinction of a conditioned emotional response
4. Rapid recovery of g.s.r. responses after stimulus arousal

The notions derived from the longitudinal research on schizophrenia seem consistent with a body of biologically oriented research on schizophrenia recently reviewed by Mirsky (1969). In particular, the chronic (process)/episodic (reactive) distinction noted in the studies of Ricks and his colleagues seems to be mirrored in the biological distinctions at the adult level. Mirsky (1969) suggests that there seem to be two major types of patient: the nuclear-chronic and the periodic-paranoial. According to Mirsky, the nuclear-chronic type of patient generally tend to give the impression of an individual with a badly made brain; in the second type of patient, brain damage is not so obvious.

> The case that is being made, therefore, is for two basically distinct types of brain pathology in schizophrenia: in the chronic-nuclear cases it is one of long standing that may be associated, in particular, with diffuse frontal lobe damage including destruction of tissue. . . . This is the group described as stuporous, blunted and withdrawn. In the episodic, paranoial group, on the other hand, the damage may preferentially be found in the septal hippocampal and temporal lobe areas, although frontal damage may occur as well. This latter population is more likely to be characterized as having personality difficulties and to be described as aggressive and assaultive or fragmented and bizarre.

Mirsky's review is summarized in Table 42-9.

While closely linked to birth injuries, this pattern independently predicts sick outcome. Mednick believes that it is a response to hippocampal damage, which in animals has been found linked to very fast and intense avoidance conditioning. The implication is that this provides a biological base for a pattern of schizophrenic withdrawal and thought disorder when the child is subjected to adolescent life experience arousing strong anxiety.

Regardless of our eventual understanding of the etiological basis of schizophrenia, the Mednick study demonstrates that a biological predisposition forms a powerful basis for its prediction, in comparison with the weakness of purely psychogenic approaches to prediction.

It is likely that environmental factors will be found to predict to later psychosis, once the biological factors are systematically considered.

With regard to prediction from the environment, Wolman, in a series of longitudinal and observational studies (1957, 1965, 1966, 1969), pointed to the possibility of predicting schizophrenia from early intrafamilial relations. In normal families the parental attitude is *vectorial;* the parents offer to the child affection and security, and the child-versus-parent attitude is *instrumental,* that is, the child expects to be loved and protected. In families that produce schizophrenics, the social roles are reversed. The parents demand love and affection from the child, and the child is forced to become the protector of his protector, that is, to develop a too early, morbid, hypervectorial attitude. These children continue to grow in the direction of schizophrenia; when the parental pressures are not too harsh, the children will develop obsessive neuroses, phobias, or latent schizophrenia, called by Wolman *hypervectorial disorders.* In extreme cases, the child will end up in a full-blown schizophrenia (*vectoriasis praecox*).

Apparently in addition to biological factors, gross estimates of level of ego development and of social competence predict to type and level of adaptation of schizophrenics in both premorbid, psychotic, and postpsychotic phases, as demonstrated by the Phillips and Zigler research program (e.g., Phillips & Zigler, 1961). These ego-develop-

mental factors are related to, but distinguishable from, the heuristically valuable "process-reactive" distinction.

Our review so far has discussed the prediction of postchildhood psychosis. When we turn to prediction of the outcome of childhood psychosis, some prevalent clinical stereotypes are also jolted. A recent study and literative review (Menolascino & Eaton, 1968) confirms Eisenberg's (1957) review suggesting that one-fourth to one-third of children diagnosed as overtly psychotic or schizophrenic attain an adequate adult adjustment with or without treatment, that another 40 percent attain a marginal adjustment level, and that a large number of the remaining 30 percent develop a clear organic symptomatology. In the Menolascino and Eaton (1968) study:

> 12 cases underwent change in formal diagnosis from childhood schizophrenia to chronic brain syndrome with psychosis as did one case of early infantile autism. Our follow-up study suggests that chronic brain syndrome with psychosis is more common than has generally been recognized. Most of these psychotic youngsters might have been diagnosed as early infantile autism, childhood schizophrenia or mental deficiency, depending upon the clinician's orientation.

One may conclude that a substantial proportion (at least 25 percent of childhood psychotics without organic symptoms are misdiagnosed or recover, while a large proportion of those who deteriorate have organic or biological factors involved. The common notion that childhood psychosis is the result of extreme and irreversible psychic trauma and deprivation in infancy has received little support from the longitudinal literature. This literature indicates that early parental deprivation and early trauma are extremely weak predictors in themselves of either psychosis or other "extreme" forms of disorder (literature review by Kadushin, 1967). While early maternal separation and trauma seem to play some role in interaction with other biological

TABLE 42-9 BASES OF SCHIZOPHRENIA (TENTATIVE NEUROPSYCHOLOGICAL SCHEMATIZATION OF THE SCHIZOPHRENIAS)

Diagnostic Label	Nuclear, chronic; process	Periodic, episodic, paranoial; reactive		Paranoid
Fundamental lesion or damage	*Hyperfunction of central mesodiencephalic core—structural (?) functional (?)*			
Additional cortical damage	Widespread loss in frontal systems	Frontal or temporal or both		Minimal or absent?
Onset	Early—childhood or adolescence	Late adolescence, early adulthood		
		May follow head trauma Life stress Late sequela of epilepsy		Life stress?
Development	Initial hyperfunction of ARAS; poor inhibitory control by cortex—leads to massive permanent overdamp to control sensory inflow	Defective, fragile but partial control of overstimulation		Tight, rigid control of overstimulation (usually adequate cortical mechanisms)
Symptoms	Blunting, withdrawn, catatonic, affectless, stupor	Periodic florid "productive" symptoms		Paranoid systems
		Disconnected, fragmented, delusional thought. Frontal (?)	Hostile, aggressive, assaultive, destructive. Temporal (?)	
EEG studies	Abnormally slow; poor response to stimuli may be "recovered" & fast normal	Normal background but fast; focally abnormal drug-activated foci		Normal background but fast
Evoked potential studies—recovery cycle and 2-tone correlation	Normal	Pathological during active symptom period		Normal
Behavior on attention-type tests	Poor	Variable; if good, falls with arousal		Good, but falls with arousal (?)
Response to phenothiazines	Poor	Good		Poor (?)

* Source: P. H. Mussen and M. R. Rosenzweig (Eds.), Annual Review of Psychology, *vol. 20, Palo Alto, Calif.: Annual Reviews, Inc., 1969.*

and developmental factors, they do not play the direct causal and predictive role in the genesis of severe disorders which has frequently been suggested.

CONCLUSIONS

Because the initiative for this review came from the Joint Commission on Mental Health of Children, we shall summarize its implications in terms of its policy implications for the child-clinical professions. For policy purposes, we need to stress more its negative than its positive implications because the negative conclusions are jolting for current views and practices.

In a thoughtful brief earlier research review, Lewis (1965) concludes: "The continuity hypothesis, that emotionally disturbed children will become mentally ill adults, has received only mild research support. The extent to which a childhood predisposition to mental illness influences appearance of problems in adult life is not entirely clear, but it is apparently not a determining (clearly predictive) factor." With two major exceptions, our own more extensive research review generates the same pessimistic conclusion, similar to Freud's conclusion quoted in the introduction. The first major exception to this conclusion is that at least some forms of schizophrenia in adulthood are predictable in terms of a biological disposition detectable in childhood and caused by a compound cf hereditary and perinatal brain-damage factors (the Mednick program's findings). The second major exception is that criminality and poor moral character (sociopathy and character disorders) are clearly predictable from a compound of family environment factors and from the occurrence of overt antisocial behavior in childhood. One form of prediction is biological; the other is in terms of environment and overt antisocial or immoral behavior. In neither case is intrapsychic

emotional disturbance a useful or basic aspect of the predictive picture, though emotional disturbance is involved in both schizophrenia and criminality. On emotional-disturbance grounds alone, however, prediction is currently impossible. Childhood emotional-disturbance symptoms are not now useful predictors. Neither is adult neurotic emotional disturbance currently predictable from childhood symptoms. Put bluntly, there is no research evidence yet available indicating that clinical analysis of the child's emotional status or dynamics leads to any more effective prognosis of adult mental health or illness than could be achieved by the man on the street who believes psychosis is hereditary and that criminality is the result of bad homes and neighborhoods in the common-sense meaning of that concept.

Clearly, the first implication of these negative findings is that further research is needed. If the child-clinical professions are ever to distinguish the children needing treatment from those who do not, it will depend upon further longitudinal research.

The few well-designed longitudinal studies in schizophrenia and in delinquency generate a remarkable power of prediction and lead to a greater optimism about prediction than do Freud's opinions on the topic. There have as yet been no well-designed follow-up studies of mental health outcomes other than schizophrenia and delinquency. It is likely that such studies would generate as powerful and as shattering findings as have the Mednick and Schulsinger study of schizophrenia and the Glueck study of delinquency.

Our review indicates that basic, sound follow-up design is an absolute necessity for predictive research. The single well-designed follow-up study of schizophrenia is the Mednick and Schulsinger study, and that study has contributed more basic positive knowledge on the prediction of schizophrenia than the two-score follow-back studies relying on clinic and school records and the hundreds of retrospective and concurrent studies. If the Glueck longitudinal study of delinquency is completed or fully analyzed, it is likely to generate similar results.

Basic child-clinical research *is* longitudinal research; the field of good clinical research is essentially equivalent to the field of well-designed longitudinal study. The distinction between basic clinical research and basic developmental research is that basic clinical research is concerned with individuality in children in relation to individuality in later outcomes. In John Dewey's (1930) words, "the field of individual psychology is the field of study of life careers." While basic dimensions of development may be at least provisionally charted by cross-sectional studies, individuality in development cannot. Basically, clinical psychology as a research discipline is the study of lives or of life careers.[19] Accordingly, longitudinal research must be the first order of business of the child-clinical community if it is to be established on a basis of research knowledge. We shall not review the promising and unpromising approaches and behavior areas for such research since we have done this in detail in earlier sections. From a practical point of view, however, what is most urgently needed is a longitudinal evaluation of the current standard methods and concepts of psychodiagnosis, involving the psychiatric interview, the family interview, and the projective tests. There is a fairly adequate body of data in the various core longitudinal studies (the Glueck study, and the Denver, Fels, and Berkeley studies), as well as in the files of clinics, to perform this task.

Turning to implications for diagnosis and treatment, a nihilistic implication of the con-

[19] The other basic focus of clinical study—experimental or therapeutic intervention into personality—also requires a longitudinal design.

clusions would be to say they do not justify expansion of mental-health services for school-age children. The rationale for expansion of childhood mental-health services rests on the assumption that such services will reduce or prevent mental illness in later life at less social cost and with less individual suffering than will a focus upon mental-health services for adults. This rationale, in turn, rests on two further assumptions. The first is that there is a continuity between mental health in childhood and mental health in adulthood. The second is that the environmental factors contributing to mental health or illness are more amenable to social intervention in childhood than later in life.

The evidence we have reviewed does not contradict either of these two assumptions in theory, but it contradicts the way they have been translated into child-guidance clinic practice. The notion that mental-health dispositions are largely formed in childhood assumes continuity in development, but it does not imply that this continuity is one of fixation or stabilization of mental-health traits in the childhood years. Theories of ego development assume that humans move through a series of stages and developmental tasks or crises and that retardation or conflict at one stage colors task solutions at later stages. They do not assume that the adult's traits or mental-health status are the same as those he showed in childhood. Diagnosis of childhood emotional disturbance does not itself assume that diagnosis is prognosis. If the major purpose of diagnosis is for the guidance of treatment, diagnosis does not assume that the withdrawn child is the schizophrenic adult, that the phobic child is the phobic adult, that the disturbed child is the mentally ill adult. However, if diagnosis is also viewed as a device for selecting some children for treatment (therapy or special classes) which is scarce and publicly supported, so that treatment should go to those most likely to have adult mental-health problems if untreated, our review indicates that current diagnosis is unsuccessful. In summary, while the provision of mental-health services to children does not assume that we can predict which children will have mental-health problems as adults, a heavy concentration of these services on a few children through procedures of diagnosis and treatment does rest on this unjustified assumption.

If heavy concentration of mental-health services on a few children cannot be justified, it is obvious that more of a community–mental-health or reeducation approach to mental-health services should be adopted. The basic characteristic of these approaches is that they are oriented to creating an environment in which the coping and ego development of all children are facilitated, rather than to segregating children into a special therapeutic environment radically different from that in which most of the child's coping efforts are directed. While children with problems should receive more attention than those without manifest problems and children with severe problems should receive more than those with less severe problems, these distinctions can be fluid since diagnostic decisions about long-term placement in segregated treatment groups are not required in community approaches.

Problem behavior in general may be classified into the following groups:

1. Troublesome behaviors which crystallize in a certain age period, i.e., which first appear at a certain age period and whose appearance is prognostic of long-term maintenance of the behavior without intervention.
2. Age-characteristic troublesome behaviors which may be expected to decline with further age development.
3. Situationally induced transitory behaviors
4. Troublesome behaviors which will persist and which reflect very early experiences or genetic determinants and which are therefore not curable.

Conventional treatment presupposes that we can separate out problems of class 1 to focus upon, but our review indicates that we cannot do this with present diagnostic methods. While it would be useful to distinguish among these types of problems where possible, even in a psychoeducational approach, the approach does not assume it is possible or necessary to do this. The approach assumes that children presenting problems are likely to continue to have problems for some time, whether the problems are situational or intrapsychic. This is not necessarily because the problems are fixed in the personality but because behavior leading to task failure and social rejection tends to create the further problems which failure and rejection cause. Furthermore, these problems not only are problems to the children who have them but cause problems for the other children and adults around the problem child.

In addition to making the assumption that we can prognose adult status, the diagnosis and treatment approach makes the assumption that childhood is an effective period for therapeutic intervention. This again involves a number of assumptions in addition to the assumption that mental-health dispositions are especially sensitive to environmental influence in the childhood years. The assumption that *treatment* of already diagnosed disturbance is especially effective in childhood is quite different from the assumption that disturbance may be most effectively *prevented* in childhood by interventive efforts. The treatment assumption seems especially questionable with regard to insight or psychoanalytically oriented modes of therapy. Classical insight therapy typically presupposes a quite high level of ego development, which is why it is generally held to be most effective with neurotics. Hence, while the critical-period notion suggests therapy at the earliest appearance of symptoms, the therapeutic requirement of ego maturity suggests a later period as optimal for therapy. In contrast to the diagnosis and treatment approach, the community mental-health approach does not assume that intrapsychic disturbances are necessarily most effectively treated in childhood. It does assume that certain developmental tasks may be best facilitated at certain ages, i.e., that creation of an optimal environment at given ages should have reference to such tasks and that special attention should be directed to those with difficulties in accomplishing these tasks at certain ages. Aid in accomplishing these tasks is psychoeducational; i.e., it involves various combinations of education, environmental manipulation, and therapy as usually conceived.

We have so far treated the findings on prognosis of mental-health status in purely negative terms. We have said that these findings do not generally support the assumptions of large-scale diagnosis and treatment approaches and that psychoeducational or community mental-health approaches do not require these assumptions. We shall now go on to consider some of the more positive findings on longitudinal stability and age development as they suggest a focus of psychoeducational mental-health efforts.

The nature of the psychoeducational approach toward mental health is essentially one in which the focus of mental-health interest is upon ego development and in which ego development is conceived to be integrally related to the child's cognitive and social learning and adaptation in the school and home environment. In other words, the improvement of the child's mental health in a school setting involves a cultivation of ego maturity as this related to school learning and the formation of social values and relationships to other children and to the teacher. Enhancement of school learning and of social relationships is viewed as both a result and a cause of enhancement of ego development. The findings we have reviewed support this position in suggesting that the best predictors of absence of adult mental illness and maladjustment are the *presence* of various forms of competence and ego maturity rather than the *absence* of problems and symptoms as such. The more prognostic negative traits of children are traits of ego weakness and of intellectual and social failure rather than symptoms as such.

Within the general psychoeducational or ego development approach just stressed, the findings suggest two critical-period foci of mental-health intervention. The first is a concern for cognitive orientation, interest, style, and attention in the years 6 to 9. The second is a special concern for peer relations (and relations to adults) in the years 9 to 12, when moral-character development appears to become crystallized. In both of these areas, there is a continuum between the efforts of a humane education to stimulate ego development and more therapeutic efforts to achieve the same end.

REFERENCES

Albee, G. W., Lane, E. A., & Reuter, J. M. Childhood intelligence of future schizophrenics and neighborhood peers. *Journal of Psychology,* 1964, **58,** 141–144.

Anderson, J. E. Relations of attitude to adjustment. *Education,* 1952, **73,** 210–218.

Anderson, J. E. Development. In D. Harris (Ed.), *The concept of development.* Minneapolis: University of Minnesota Press, 1957.

Anderson, J. E. The prediction of adjustment over time. In I. Iscoe & H. Stevenson (Eds.), *Personality development in children.* Austin: University of Texas Press, 1960.

Anderson, J. E., Harris, D. R., Werner, E., & Gallistel, E. *A study of children's adjustment over time.* Minneapolis: Institute of Child Development and Welfare, 1959.

Ausubel, D. *Ego development and the personality disorders.* New York: Grune & Stratton, 1952.

Ausubel, D., & Sullivan, E. *Theories and problems of child development.* 2nd ed. New York: Grune & Stratton, 1970.

Barthell, C., & Holmes, D. S. High school yearbooks: A nonreactive measure of social isolation in graduates who later became schizophrenic. *Journal of Abnormal Psychology,* 1968, **73**, 313–316.

Bayley, N. Behavioral correlates of mental growth: Birth to thirty-six years. *American Psychologist,* 1968, **23**, 1–17.

Bedoian, V. H. Mental health analyses of socially over-accepted, socially underaccepted, over-age and under-age pupils in the sixth grade. *Journal of Educational Psychology,* 1953, **44**, 336–371.

Bender, L., & Grugett, A. E., Jr. A follow-up report on children who had atypical sexual experience. *American Journal of Orthopsychiatry,* 1952, **22**, 825–837.

Berry, J., & Ricks, D. F. Family and symptom patterns that precede schizophrenia. In M. Roff & D. F. (Eds.), *Life history studies in psychopathology.* Minneapolis: University of Minnesota Press, 1969.

Bieber, I., et al. *Homosexuality.* New York: Basic Books, 1962.

Birren, J. E. Psychological examinations of children who later became psychotic. *Journal of Abnormal and Social Psychology,* 1944, **39**, 84–96.

Blatt, M., & Kohlberg, L. The effects of a classroom discussion program upon the moral levels of preadolescents. In Kohlberg and Turiel, 1972.

Block, J., & Haan, N. *Personality development from adolescence to adulthood.* New York: Appleton Century Crofts, 1971.

Bloom, B. S. *Stability and change in human characteristics.* New York: Wiley, 1964.

Bonney, M. E. The relative stability of social, intellectual, and academic status in grades II to IV, and the inter-relationships between these various forms of growth. *Journal of Educational Psychology,* 1943, **34**, 88–102.

Bonney, M. E. Social behavior differences between second grade children of high and low sociometric status. *Journal of Educational Research,* 1955, **48**, 481–495.

Bonney, M. E., & Nicholson, E. L. Comparative social adjustments of elementary school pupils with and without preschool training. *Child Development,* 1958, **29**, 125–133.

Bonney, M. E., & Powell, J. Differences in social behavior between sociometrically high and sociometrically low children. *Journal of Educational Research,* 1953, **46**, 481–495.

Bower, E. M. *Early identification of emotionally handicapped children in school.* Springfield, Ill.: Charles C Thomas, 1960.

Bower, E. M., & Lambert, N. M. In-school screening of children with emotional handicaps. In N. J. Long, W. C. Morse, & Ruth G. Newman (Eds.), *Conflict in the classroom.* Belmont, Calif.: Wadsworth, 1965. Pp. 128–134.

Bower, E. M., Shellhammer, T. A., & Daily, J. M. School characteristics of male adolescents who later become schizophrenic. *American Journal of Orthopsychiatry,* 1960, **30**, 712–729.

Bronner, A. Treatment and what happened afterward. *American Journal of Orthopsychiatry,* 1944, **14**, 28–33.

Burns, C. Pre-schizophrenic symptoms in pre-adolescents' withdrawal and sensitivity. *The Nervous Child,* 1952, **10,** 120–128.

Cassel, R. N., & Martin, G. Comparing peer status ratings of elementary pupils with their guidance data and learning efficiency indices. *Journal of Genetic Psychology,* 1964, **105,** 39–42.

Chang, J., & Block, J. A study of identification in male homosexuals. *Journal of Consulting and Clinical Psychology,* 1960, **24,** 307–310.

Coleman, J. S., et al. *Equality of educational opportunity.* Washington, D.C.: U.S. Government Printing Office, 1966.

Coolidge, J. C., Brodie, R. D., & Feeney, B. A ten-year follow-up study of sixty-six school-phobic children. *American Journal of Orthopsychiatry,* 1964, **34,** 675–684.

Coombs, J., & Cooley, W. Dropouts in high school and after. *American Journal of Educational Research,* 1968, **5,** 343–363.

Cowen, E. L., Zax, M., Klein, R., Izzo, L. D., & Trost, M. A. The relation of anxiety in school children to school record, achievement, and behavioral measures. *Child Development,* 1965, **36,** 685–695.

Davids, A. Intelligence in childhood schizophrenics, other emotionally disturbed children, and their mothers. *Journal of Consulting Psychology,* 1958, **22,** 159–163.

Despert, J. L., & Pierce, H. O. The relation of emotional adjustment to intellectual function. *Genetic Psychology Monographs,* 1946, **34,** 3–56.

Dewey, J. Experience and conduct. In C. Murchison (Ed.), *Psychologies of 1930.* Worcester, Mass.: Clark University Press, 1930.

Edwards, A. S., & Langley, L. D. Childhood manifestations and adult psychoses. *American Journal of Orthopsychiatry,* 1936, **6,** 103–109.

Eisenberg, L. The course of childhood schizophrenia. *Archives of Neurology,* 1957, **78,** 69–83.

Ellinwood, C. Structural development in the expression of emotion by children. Unpublished doctoral dissertation, University of Chicago, 1969.

Emmerich, W. Continuity and stability in early social development. II. Teacher ratings. *Child Development,* 1966, **37,** 17–27.

Erikson, E. *Childhood and society.* New York: Norton, 1950.

Erikson, E. *Insight and responsibility.* New York: Norton, 1964.

Escalona, S. K., & Heider, G. M. *Prediction and outcome.* New York: Basic Books, 1959.

Fenichel, O. *Psychoanalytic theory of the neuroses.* New York: Norton, 1945.

Field, H. Prediction of character disorder and psychotic outcome from childhood behavior. Unpublished thesis. New York: Teacher's College, Columbia University, 1969.

Fleming, P., & Ricks, D. F. Emotions of children before schizophrenia and character disorder. In M. Roff & D. F. Ricks (Eds.), *Life history studies in psychopathology.* Minneapolis: University of Minnesota Press, 1969.

Frazee, H. E. Children who later became schizophrenic. *Smith College Studies in Social Work,* 1953, **23,** 125–149.

Freeberg, N. E., & Payne, D. T. Parental influence on cognitive development in early childhood: A review. *Child Development,* 1967, **38,** 65–87.

Freud, S. *The basic writings of Sigmund Freud.* New York: Modern Library, 1938.

Freud, S. The psychogenesis of a case of homosexuality in a woman. (1920) Vol. 18. *The complete psychological works of Sigmund Freud.* London: Hogarth, 1955.

Friedlander, D. Personality development of twenty-seven children who later became psychotic. *Journal of Abnormal and Social Psychology,* 1945.

Gallagher, J. J., & Crowder, T. The adjustment of gifted children in the regular classroom. *Exceptional Children,* 1956, **23,** 306–312, 317–319.

Gardner, G. G. The relationship between childhood neurotic symptomatology and later schizophrenia in males and females. *Journal of Nervous and Mental Disorders,* 1967, **144,** 97–100.

Garfield, S. L. Abnormal behavior and mental deficiency. In N. R. Ellis (Ed.), *Handbook of mental deficiency.* New York: McGraw-Hill, 1963. Pp. 574–601.

Gebhard, P. H., Gagnon, J. H., Pomeroy, W. B., & Christenson, C.V. *Sex offenders: An analysis of types.* New York: Harper & Row, 1965.

Gesell, A. The ontogenesis of infant behavior. In L. Carmichael (Ed.), *Manual of child psychology.* New York: Wiley, 1954.

Gilliland. Correlations between high school peer ratings of moral character and tested moral judgment levels. Unpublished master's thesis. Provo, Utah: Brigham Young University, 1965.

Glidewell, J. C. The prevalence of maladjustment in elementary schools. Draft of report prepared for the National Commission on the Mental Health of Children, 1967.

Glueck, E. T. Distinguishing delinquents from pseudodelinquents. *Harvard Educational Review,* 1966, **36,** 119–130.

Glueck, S., & Glueck, E. *Predicting delinquency and crime.* Cambridge; Mass.: Harvard University Press, 1959.

Grim, P., Kohlberg, L., & White, S. Some relationships between conscience and attentional processes. *Journal of Personality and Social Psychology,* 1968, **8,** 239–252.

Gronlund, N. E., & Anderson, L. Personality characteristics of socially accepted, socially neglected, and socially rejected junior high school pupils. *Educational Administration and Supervision,* 1957, **43,** 329–339.

Gronlund, N. E., & Holmlund, W. S. The value of elementary school sociometric status scores for predicting pupil's adjustment in high school. *Educational Administration and Supervision,* 1958, **44,** 225–260.

Haan, N. Proposed model of ego functioning: Copying and defense mechanisms in relationship to IQ change. *Psychological Monographs,* 1963, **77** (8, Whole No. 571), 1–23.

Harvey, O. J., Hunt, D., & Schroeder, D. *Conceptual systems.* New York: Wiley, 1961.

Havighurst, R. J., Bowman, P. H., Liddle, G. P., Matthews, C. V., & Pierce, J. V. *Growing up in River City.* New York: Wiley, 1962.

Holeman, R. E., & Winokur, G. Effeminate homosexuality: A disease of childhood. *American Journal of Orthopsychiatry,* 1965, **35,** 48–56.

Jackson, D. D. (Ed.) *The etiology of schizophrenia.* New York: Basic Books, 1960.

Jackson, P. *Life in classrooms.* New York: Holt, 1968.

Jensen, A. R. How much can we boost I.Q. and scholastic achievement? *Harvard Educational Review,* 1969, **39** (1), 1–123.

Jersild, A. Children's fears. In R. Barker & H. Wright (Eds.), *Child Behavior and development.* New York: McGraw-Hill, 1943.

Jones, M. C. Personality correlates and antecedents of drinking patterns in adult males. *Journal of Consulting Psychology,* in press.

Kadushin, A. Reversibility of trauma: A follow-up study of children adopted when older. *Social Work,* 12 (4), October, 1967.

Kagan, J., & Moss, H. Personality and social development: Family and peer influences. *Review of Educational Research,* 1961, **31,** 463–474.

Kagan, J., & Moss H. *From birth to maturity.* New York: Wiley, 1962.

Kallman, F. Twin index studies in schizophrenia. *American Journal of Psychiatry,* 1946, **103,** 309.

Kasanin, J., & Veo, L. A study of the school adjustment of children who later in life became psychotic. *American Journal of Orthopsychiatry,* 1932, **2,** 212–230.

Kellam, S. G., & Schiff, S. K. Adaptation and mental illness in the first-grade classrooms of an urban community. *Psychiatric Research Report,* 1967, **21,** 79–91.

Kellam, S. G., & Schiff, S. K. The Woodlawn Mental Health Center: A community mental health center mode. *The Social Service Review,* 1966, **60,** 255–263.

Kennedy, W. A. School phobia: Rapid treatment of fifty cases. *Journal of Abnormal Psychology,* 1965, **70,** 285–289.

Kinsey, A. C., Pomeroy, W. B., & Martin, C.F. *Sexual behavior in the human male.* Philadelphia: Saunders, 1948.

Kohlberg, L. The development of modes of moral thinking and choice in the years ten to sixteen. Unpublished doctoral dissertation. University of Chicago, 1958.

Kohlberg, L. Development of moral character and ideology. In. M. L. Hoffman (Ed.), *Review of child development research.* Vol. 1. New York: Russell Sage Foundation, 1964.

Kohlberg, L. A cognitive-developmental analysis of children's sex-role concepts and attitudes.

In E. Maccoby (Ed.), *The development of sex differences.* Stanford, Calif.: Stanford University Press, 1966.

Kohlberg, L. Early education: A cognitive-developmental approach. *Child Development,* 1968.

Kohlberg, L. Stage and sequence: The cognitive-developmental approach to socialization. In D. Goslin (Ed.), *Handbook of socialization theory and research.* Chicago: Rand McNally, 1969.

Kohlberg, L. From is to ought: How to commit the naturalistic fallacy and get away with it. In T. Mischel (Ed.), *Cognitive development and epistemology.* New York: Academic, 1971.

Kohlberg, L., & De Vries, R. Relations between Piaget and psychometric assessments of intelligence. Paper presented at Conference on the Natural Curriculum, Urbana, Ill., 1969.

Kohlberg, L., & Turiel, E. Moralization, the cognitive-developmental approach. New York: Holt, 1972 (in press).

Kohlberg L., & Zigler, E. The impact of cognitive maturity on sex-role attitudes in the years four to eight. *Genetic Psychology Monographs,* 1967, **75,** 89–165.

Kohn, N. Performance of Negro children of varying social class background on Piagetian tasks. Unpublished doctoral dissertation. University of Chicago, 1969.

Lane, E. A., & Albee, G. W. Early childhood intellectual differences between schizophrenic adults and their siblings. *Journal of Abnormal and Social Psychology,* 1964, **68,** 193–195.

Lane, E. A., & Albee, G. W. Childhood intellectual differences between schizophrenic adults and their siblings. *American Journal of Orthopsychiatry,* 1965, **35,** 747–753.

Lane, E. A., & Albee, G. W. The comparative birth weights of adult schizophrenics and their siblings. *Journal of Psychology,* 1966, **64,** 227–231.

Lane, E. A., & Albee, G. W. Intellectual antecedents of schizophrenia. Paper presented at the Second Conference on Life History Research in Psychopathology, University of Minnesota, Minneapolis, April 18–19, 1968.

Levine, J. Humor. In *International encyclopedia of social sciences.* New York: Macmillan, 1968.

Levitt, E. E. The results of psychotherapy with children: An evaluation. *Journal of Consulting Psychology,* 1957, **21,** 189–196.

Levitt, E. E. Psychotherapy with children: A further evaluation. *Behaviour Research and Therapy Quarterly,* 1963, **1,** 45–51.

Levy, D. M. *Maternal overprotection.* New York: Columbia University Press, 1943.

Lewis, W. W. Continuity and intervention in emotional disturbance: A review. *Exceptional Children,* 1965.

Littell, W. M. The Wechsler Intelligence Scale for Children: Review of a decade of research. *Psychological Bulletin,* 1960, **57,** 132–164.

Little, J. K. The occupations of non-college youth. *American Journal of Educational Research,* 1967, **4,** 147–154.

Livson, N., & Peskin, H. The prediction of adult psychological health in a longitudinal study. *Journal of Abnormal and Social Psychology,* 1967, **72,** 509–518.

Loevinger, J. The meaning and measurement of ego development. *American Psychology,* 1966, 195–206.

MacFarlane, J., Allen, L., & Honzik, N. *A developmental study of behavior problems of normal children between 21 months and four years.* Berkeley: University of California Press, 1954.

Mason, C. F. Pre-illness intelligence of mental hospital patients. *Journal of Consulting Psychology,* 1956, **20,** 297–300.

Maxwell, A. E. Discrepancies between the pattern of abilities for normal and neurotic children. *Journal of Mental Science,* 1961, **107,** 300–307.

Mayers, F. Correlates of outcome in psychotherapy. Unpublished dissertation, University of Chicago, 1966.

McCandless, B. R., & Castaneda, A. Anxiety in children, school achievement, and intelligence. *Child Development,* 1956, **27,** 379–382.

McCord, W., McCord, J., & Zola, I. K. *Origins of crime: A new evaluation of the Cambridge-Somerville youth study.* New York: Columbia University Press, 1959.

McCord, J., & Thurber, E. Some effects of paternal absence on male children. *Journal of Abnormal and Social Psychology,* 1962, **64,** 361–369.

McHugh, A. F. WISC performance in neurotic and conduct disturbances. *Journal of Clinical Psychology,* 1963, **19,** 423–424.

Mednick, S. A. Prediction of breakdown in a high-risk group for schizophrenia. Paper presented at the Society for Research in Child Development meetings, Santa Monica, Calif., March 24, 1969.

Mednick, S. A., & McNeil, T. F. Current methodology in research on the etiology of schizophrenia. Serious difficulties which suggest the use of the high-risk group method. *Psychological Bulletin,* 1968.

Mednick, S. A., & Schulsinger, F. Some premorbid characteristics related to breakdown in children with schizophrenic mothers. Paper prepared for the Conference on Transmission of Schizophrenia, Dorado Beach, Puerto Rico, June 25–July 1, 1967. Sponsored by the Foundation's Fund for Research in Psychiatry.

Mednick, S. A., & Schulsinger, F. Factors related to breakdown in children at high risk for schizophrenia. In M. Roff & D. F. Ricks (Eds.) *Life history studies in psychopathology.* Minneapolis: University of Minnesota Press, 1969.

Meehl, P. E. *Clinical vs. statistical prediction: A theoretical analysis and a review of the evidence.* Minneapolis: University of Minnesota Press, 1954.

Menolascino, F., & Eaton, L. Psychosis of childhood: A five year follow-up of experiences in a mental retardation clinic. In S. Chess and A. Thomas (Eds.), *Annual progress in child psychiatry and child development, 1968.* New York: Brunner/Mazel, 1968.

Michael, C. M. Follow-up studies of introverted children. III. Relative incidence of criminal behavior. *Journal of Criminal Law and Criminology,* 1956, **47,** 414–422.

Michael, C. M., Morris, D. P., & Soroker, E. Follow-up studies of shy, withdrawn children. II. Relative incidence of schizophrenia. *American Journal of Orthopsychiatry,* 1957, **27,** 331–337.

Miller, E. L. Ability and social adjustment at midlife of persons earlier judged mentally deficient. *Genetic Psychology Monographs,* 1965, **72,** 139–198.

Mirsky, I. A. In P. H. Mussen and M. R. Rosenzweig (Eds.), *Annual review of psychology.* Palo Alto, Calif: Annual Reviews, Inc., 1969.

Mischel, W. Delay of gratification and deviant behavior. Paper read at meeting of the Society for Research in Child Development. Berkeley, Calif.: April, 1963.

Morgan, E., Sutton-Smith, B., & Rosenberg, B. G. Age changes in the relation between anxiety and achievement. *Child Development,* 1960, **31,** 515–519.

Morris, D. P., Soroker, E., & Burrus, G. Follow-up studies of shy, withdrawn children. I. Evaluation of later adjustment. *American Journal of Orthopsychiatry,* 1954, **24,** 743–754.

Morris, H. H., Jr., Escoll, P. J., & Wexler, R. Aggressive behavior disorders of childhood: A follow-up study. *American Journal of Psychiatry,* 1956, **112,** 991–997.

Mowrer, O. H. *The crisis of psychiatry and religion.* Princeton, N.J.: Van Nostrand, 1961.

Muma, J. R. Peer evaluation and academic performance. *The Personnel and Guidance Journal,* 1965, **44,** 405–409.

Nameche, G., Waring, M., & Ricks, D. Early indictators of outcome in schizophrenia. *Journal of Nervous Mental Disorders,* 1964, **139,** 232–240.

Northway, M. L. Outsiders: A study of the personality patterns of children least acceptable to their age-mates. *Sociometry,* 1944, **7,** 10–25.

Oversey, L. The homosexual conflict, an adaptational analysis. *Psychiatry,* 1950, **17,** 243–250.

Parten, M., & Newhall, N. Study of social development. In R. Barker & H. Wright (Eds.), *Child behavior and development.* New York: McGraw-Hill, 1943.

Peck, R. F., & Havighurst, R. J. *The psychology of character development.* New York: Wiley, 1960.

Pervin, L. A. Performance and satisfaction as a function of individual-environment fit. *Psychological Bulletin,* 1968, **69,** 56–68.

Phillips, L., & Zigler, E. Social competence and outcome in psychiatric disorder. *Journal of*

Abnormal and Social Psychology, 1961, **63,** 264–271.

Piaget, J. *The child's conception of the world.* New York: Harcourt, Brace, 1928.

Piaget, J. *Logic and psychology.* New York: Basic Books, 1957.

Piaget, J. On the development of memory and identity. In *Heinz Werner Lecture Series.* (1967) Vol. 2. Worcester, Mass.: Clark University Press, 1968.

Pollack, M., Woerner, M. G., Goodman, W., & Greenberg, I. W. Childhood development patterns of hospitalized adult schizophrenic and non-schizophrenic patients and their siblings. *American Journal of Orthopsychiatry,* 1966, **36,** 510–517.

Pollin, W., Stabenau, J. R., Mosher, L., & Jopin, J. Life history differences in identical twins discordant for schizophrenia. *American Journal of Orthopsychiatry,* 1966, **36,** 492–509.

Powers, E., & Witmer, H. An experiment in the prevention of delinquency: The Cambridge-Somerville youth study. New York: Columbia University Press, 1951.

Rabson, A. An ideographic approach to personality prediction. Unpublished paper read for the Society for Research in Child Development. Santa Monica, Calif., April, 1969.

Ricks, D. F., & Berry, J. C. Family and symptom patterns that precede schizophrenia. In M. Roff & D. F. Ricks (Eds.), *Life history studies in psychopathology.* Minneapolis: University of Minnesota Press, 1969.

Ricks, D. F., & Nameche, G. Symbiosis, sacrifice, and schizophrenia. *Mental Hygiene,* 1966, **50,** 541–551.

Robins, L. N. *Deviant children grown up: A sociological and psychiatric study of sociopathic personality.* Baltimore: Williams & Wilkins, 1966.

Robins, L. N. In praise of school records. Paper presented at First Conference on Life History Research in Psychopathology, Columbia University, New York, May 12, 1967.

Robins, L. N., & Murphy, G. E. Drug use in a normal population of young Negro men. *American Journal of Public Health,* 1967, **57,** 1580–1596.

Robins, L. N., Murphy, G. E., & Breckenridge, M. S. Drinking behavior in young urban Negro men. *Quarterly Journal of Studies in Alcohol,* in press.

Robins, L. N., & O'Neal, P. The adult prognosis for runaway children. *American Journal of Orthopsychiatry,* 1959, **29,** 752–761.

Roff, M. *Preservice personality problems and subsequent adjustment to military service: The prediction of psychoneurotic reactions.* School of Aviation Medicine, USAF, Report No. 57–136, November, 1957.

Roff, M. *Preservice personality problems and subsequent adjustment to military service: A replication of "The prediction of psychoneurotic reactions."* School of Aviation Medicine, USAF, Report No. 58–151, February, 1959.

Roff, M. Childhood social interactions and young adult bad conduct. *Journal of Abnormal and Social Psychology,* 1961, **63,** 333–337. (a)

Roff, M. *The service-related experience of a sample of juvenile delinquents.* U.S. Army Medical Research and Development Command and U.S. Public Health Service, Report No. 61-1, 1961. (b)

Roff, M. Childhood social interactions and young adult psychosis. *Journal of Clinical Psychology,* 1963, **19,** 152–157. (a)

Roff, M. *The service-related experience of a*

sample of juvenile delinquents. II. A replication on a larger sample in another state. U.S. Army Medical Research and Development Command and U.S. Public Health Service, Report No. 63-2, 1963. (b)

Roff, M. *Some developmental aspects of schizoid personality.* U.S. Army Medical Research and Development Command, Report No. 65-4, March, 1965.

Roff, M. *Some childhood and adolescent characteristics of adult homosexuals.* U.S. Army Medical Research and Development Command, Report No. 66-5, May, 1966.

Roff, M. *The service-related experience of a sample of juvenile delinquents. IV. Results with a second Minnesota sample.* U.S. Army Medical Research and Development Command and U.S. Public Health Service, Report No. 67-6, 1967.

Roff, M. Some life history factors in relation to various types of adult maladjustment. In M. Roff & D. F. Ricks (Eds.), *Life history studies in psychopathology.* Minneapolis: University of Minnesota Press, 1969. (a)

Roff, M. Some problems and strategies in life history research. In M. Roff & D. F. Ricks (Eds.), *Life history studies in psychopathology.* Minneapolis: University of Minnesota Press, 1969. (b)

Roff, M., & Sells, S. B. Juvenile delinquency in relation to peer acceptance-rejection and socioeconomic status. *Psychology in the Schools,* 1968, **5,** 3–18.

Rogers, C. R. The criteria used in a study of mental-health problems. *Educational Research Bulletin,* 1942, **21,** 28–40. (a)

Rogers, C. R. Mental health findings in three elementary schools. *Educational Research Bulletin,* 1942, **21,** 69–86. (b)

Rowley, V. N., & Stone, F. Beth. A further note on the relationship between WISC functioning and the CMAS. *Journal of Clinical Psychology,* 1963, **19,** 426.

Santostefano, S. G. A developmental study of the cognitive control "leveling-sharpening," *Merrill-Palmer Quarterly,* 1964, **10,** 343–360.

Santostefano, S. G., & Paley, E. Development of cognitive controls in children. *Child Development,* 1964, **35,** 939–949.

Schaffner, A., Albee, G.W., & Lane, E. A. Intellectual differences between suburban schizophrenics and their siblings. *Journal of Consulting Psychology,* 1967, **31,** 326–327.

Schiff, S. K., & Kellam, S. G. A community-wide mental health program of prevention and early treatment in first grade. *Psychiatric Research Report,* 1967, **21,** 92–102.

Schofield, W., & Balian, L. A comparative study of the personal histories of schizophrenic and nonpsychiatric patients. *Journal of Abnormal and Social Psychology,* 1959, **59,** 216–225.

Sells, S. B., & Roff, M. Peer acceptance-rejection and birth order. *Psychology in the Schools,* 1964, **1,** 156–162.

Sells, S. B., & Roff, M. Family influence as reflected in peer acceptance-rejection resemblance of siblings as compared with random sets of school children. *Psychology in the Schools,* 1965, **2,** 133–137.

Sells, S. B., Roff, M., Cox, S. H., & Mayer, M. *Peer acceptance-rejection and personality development.* Office of Education, final report of Project OE 5-0417, Contract OE 2-10-051, January, 1967.

Shellow, R., Schamp, J. R., Liebow, E., & Unger, E. Suburban runaways of the 1960's. *Child Development Monographs,* 1967, **32** (3).

Shirley, M. Impact of mother's personality on the young child. *Smith College Studies in Social Work,* 1941, **12,** 15–64.

Silverman, J. Scanning control mechanism and "cognitive filtering" in paranoid and non-paranoid schizophrenia. *Journal of Consulting Psychology,* 1964, **28,** 385–393.

Simon, W., & Gagnon, J. On psychosexual development. In D. Goslin (Ed.), *Handbook of socialization theory and research.* Chicago: Rand McNally, 1969.

Smith, G. H. Sociometric study of least-liked and best-liked children. *Elementary School Journal,* 1950, **51,** 77–85.

Smith, L. M. The concurrent validity of six personality and adjustment tests for children. *Psychology Monographs: General and Applied,* 1958, **72.**

Sobel, D. E. Children of schizophrenic patients: Preliminary observations on early development. *American Journal of Psychiatry,* 1961, **118,** 512–517.

Stabenau, J., & Pollin, R. Chapter in M. Roff and D. Ricks (Eds.), *Life history studies in psychopathology.* Minneapolis: University of Minneapolis Press, 1969.

Stennett, R. G. Emotional handicap in the elementary years: Phase or disease? *American Journal of Orthopsychiatry,* 1966, **36,** 444–449.

Stewart, R. S. Personality maladjustment and reading achievement. *American Journal of Orthopsychiatry,* 1950, **20,** 410–417.

Sullivan, E. V., McCullough, G., & Stager, M. A developmental study of the relationship between conceptual, ego and moral development. *Child Development,* 1970, **64.**

Sullivan, H. S. *An interpersonal theory of psychiatry.* New York: Norton, 1953.

Tait, C., & Hodges, E. *Delinquents, their families and the community.* Springfield, Ill.: Charles C Thomas, 1962.

Teigland, J. J., Winkler, R. C., Munger, P. F., & Kranzler, G. D. Some concomitants of underachievement at the elementary school level. *The Personnel and Guidance Journal,* 1966, **44,** 950–955.

Terman, L. M., & Oden, M. *The gifted group at mid-life: thirty-five years' follow-up of the superior child.* Vol. V. Stanford, Calif.: Stanford University Press, 1959.

Thomas, A., Chess, S., & Birch, H. *Temperament and behavior disorders in children.* New York: New York University Press, 1968.

Ullman, C. A. Teachers, peers and tests as predictors of adjustment. *Journal of Educational Psychology,* 1957, **48,** 257–267.

Van Alstyne, D., & Hattwick, L. A. A follow-up study of the behavior of nursery school children. *Child Development,* 1939, **10,** 43–70.

Vandenberg, S. G. Innate abilities: One or many? *Acta Genetica,* 1965, **14,** 41–47. (Cited in Mednick & Schulsinger, 1967, p. 13.)

Vanden Daele, L. A developmental study of the ego-ideal. *Genetic Psychology Monographs,* 1968, **78,** 191–256.

Veo, L. A personality study of six adolescents who later became psychotic. Unpublished dissertation. Smith College, 1930. (Also in *Smith College Studies in Social Work,* 1931, **1,** 317–363.)

Walcott, E. Daydreamers: A study of their adjustment in adolescence. *Smith College Studies in Social Work,* 1932, **2,** 283, 335.

Warnken, R. G., & Siess, T. F. The use of the cumulative record in the prediction of behavior. *The Personnel and Guidance Journal,* 1965, **44,** 231–237.

Wechsler, D. *The measurement and appraisal of adult intelligence.* Baltimore: Williams & Wilkins, 1958.

Wheway, Jane P. Intelligence and delinquency. *Durham Research Review,* 1958, **2,** 208–214.

White, B. L. An experimental approach to the effects of experience on early human behavior. In J. P. Hill (Ed.), *Minnesota symposia on child psychology.* Vol. I. Minneapolis: University of Minnesota Press, 1967. Pp. 201–226.

White, S. Some general outlines of the matrix of developmental changes between five and seven years. *Bulletin of the Orton Society,* 1970, **20,** 41–57.

Witkin, H. A., Dyk, R. B., Faterson, H. F., Goodenough, D. R., & Karp, S. A. *Psychological differentiation: Studies in development.* New York: Wiley, 1962.

Witkin, H. A., Goodenough, D. R., & Karp, S. A. Stability of cognitive style from childhood to young adulthood. *Journal of Personality and Social Psychology,* 1967, **7,** 291–300.

Wittman, M. P. Diagnostic and prognostic significance of the shut-in personality type as a pro-dromal factor in schizophrenia. *Journal of Clinical Psychology,* 1948, **4,** 211–214.

Wolf, M. G. Effects of emotional disturbance in childhood on intelligence. *American Journal of Orthopsychiatry,* 1965, **35,** 906–908.

Wolman, B. B. Explorations. *American Journal of Psychotherapy,* 1957, **11,** 560–588.

Wolman, B. B. Family dynamics and schizophrenia. *Journal of Health and Human Behavior,* 1965, **6,** 147–155.

Wolman, B. B. *Vectoriasis praecox or the group of schizophrenias.* Springfield, Ill.: Charles C Thomas, 1966.

Wolman, B. B. *Children without childhood: A study in childhood schizophrenia.* New York: Grune & Stratton, 1969.

Yarrow, L. J. Separation from parents during early childhood. In M. Hoffman and L. Hoffman (Eds.), *Review of child development research.* New York: Russell Sage Foundation, 1964.

Zander, A. F., & Van Egmond, E. E. Relationship of intelligence and social power to the interpersonal behavior of children. *Journal of Educational Psychology,* 1958, **49,** 257–268.

Zax, M., Cowen, E. L., Izzo, L. D., & Trost, M. A. Identifying emotional disturbance in the school setting. *American Journal of Orthopsychiatry,* 1964, **34,** 446–454.

part ix | The Clinical Professions

43 | The Clinical Child Psychologist

Alan O. Ross

HISTORY

In 1896 Lightner Witmer opened a psychological clinic at the University of Pennsylvania, and with it, clinical child psychology was born. The first case seen at that clinic was a boy who had inordinate difficulty learning how to spell. As Misiak and Sexton (1966) point out, this boy was the first formal clinic case in the history of American psychology. A few years later, in 1909, a clinic for exceptional children was started at Clark and another at the University of Minnesota under James B. Miner. J. E. Wallace Wallin opened a psychoeducational clinic at the University of Pittsburgh in 1912, reflecting the then current focus on learning difficulties. This early focus eventually gave way to a preoccupation with the internalized neurotic problems of children, only to be reawakened in the 1960s as a corollary of society's increasing concern with problems of educational achievement.

It will be noted that clinical psychology in its general and primarily adult-oriented form also traces its origins to Witmer's psychological clinic (see, for example, Sundberg & Tyler, 1962). These claims are easily reconciled if one recalls that in the early days students of clinical psychology were almost exclusively interested in children and questions of their development. It can thus be said that *clinical psychology* was originally synonymous with *clinical child psychology* and that it began to assume an adult orientation only as a result of the action demands of World War II. Indeed, as Sundberg and Tyler (1962) remark, up to the Second World War almost all clinics in which psychologists worked were designed to serve the needs of children.

As pointed out elsewhere (Ross, 1959), clinical child psychology represents the convergence of the developmental with the clinical point of view in psychology. The early pioneers of mental testing, who are generally considered the forerunners of clinical psychology, worked predominantly with children. Francis Galton, whom Watson (1953) names one of the earliest contributors to clinical psychology, is, in another history of psychology (Dennis, 1949), viewed as one of the important early contributors to child psychology. This merging of the developmental and the clinical points of view continues through such figures as G. Stanley Hall, Binet, Goddard, and Terman. All these men are claimed as ancestors by both clinical and child psychology, strongly suggesting that they are probably best viewed as early clinical child psychologists.

The first clinic designed to help disturbed children other than those with learning difficulties was organized by William Healy in 1909, and the first psychologist to join this "Juvenile Psychopathic Institute," now Chicago's Institute for Juvenile Research, was Grace M. Fernald. This clinic interested itself in the problems of young delinquents, and its function was at first primarily diagnostic. In 1913 Augusta F. Bronner joined the staff, and when she and Healy moved to Boston in 1917 to organize the Judge Baker Foundation (now the Judge Baker Guidance Center), their activities became more treatment-oriented.

Much of the work of these early pioneers involved mental testing and the development of instruments necessary to carry out this task. Finding out the intellectual strengths and weaknesses of a given child led naturally to attempts to help the child overcome his difficulties, and while these efforts consisted largely of advice, guidance, and remedial teaching, one can trace into these early days the clinical child psychologist's threefold function of testing, treatment, and research.

At about that point in the development of the field, the clinicians and the students of child psychology went divergent ways. With the establishment of child-welfare research stations—the one in Iowa opened in 1917—the interests of research-oriented child psychologists shifted to studies of maturation and physical development, the nature-nurture controversy spawned much and often inconclusive research, and longitudinal studies were launched which at times were other than productive. The clinicians, on the other hand, became more and more deeply engrossed in working in the clinics of the burgeoning child-guidance movement. By 1920 the team approach to the study and treatment of psychologically disturbed children had become crystallized, and the clinical psychologist on the child-guidance team began to immerse himself in testing, treatment, and training, with research conducted "when time permitted." Not only did the ever-increasing service demands in the clinics divert clinicians from their early interest in child psychology research, but the theoretical orientation of most child-guidance clinics became more and more Freudian, a stance that found little resonance among the scientists at the research centers.

For some 40 years child psychology and clinical child psychology had little to offer one another. There is thus some merit in the insistence of some that it is incorrect to say that clinical child psychology represents the clinical application of child psychology. These critics suggest that the specialty owes its existence not to child psychology but to the child-guidance movement, in whose clinics the clinical psychologist became a clinical child psychologist when he had to adapt his clinical skills to the problems of children. In a field where demand for trained professional personnel far outstrips the supply, individuals will come from various directions to try to meet the demand. Indeed, many present-day clinical child psychologists were trained as general clinical psychologists and acquired their skills for work with children in the setting of the child-guidance clinic. This does not alter the fact, however, that the earliest clinicians who worked with children had been trained as child psychologists, nor does it contradict the observation that, as we shall see, child psychology and clinical child psychology have once again come to interact and to contribute to one another.

From the point of view of the history of science, the role John B. Watson (might have) played in the development of clinical child psychology is of interest. The founder of American behaviorism turned to the study of normal infants in 1916 while working at the Phipps Clinic in Baltimore. In this context he and Raynor (Watson & Raynor, 1920) conducted the fear-conditioning study of the famous Albert, and this work eventually led to the equally famous case of Peter, whom Mary Cover Jones (1924) treated for various fears by the application of conditioning principles. The time was apparently not ripe for this approach to become incorporated in the work of clinics treating children, and with a few unassimilated exceptions, some forty years passed before psychologists treating children with psychological disorders returned to the application of conditioning principles (see Chapter 29 of this manual).

At any rate, consciousness, sensation, image, and feeling, the very concepts that Watson had cast out of American psychology, began to occupy the attention of clinical child psychologists more and more. As child-guidance clinics became increasingly psychoanalytic in their approach, the team member who was the specialist in mental testing came to be asked questions not only about intellectual development but also about such personality factors as conflicts, anxieties, fantasies, and defenses. The newly available Rorschach method and similar devices seemed to help in arriving at answers, and beginning in the 1930s, the psychologist's armamentarium came to include not only intelligence tests but also projective techniques.

Up to that time it had been curiosity in a subject matter, such as intellectual development, that had guided the activities of psychologists. It had led them to construct the needed instruments, designed for children and standardized on children. Now the activities of psychologists came to be determined not by their own curiosity but by questions asked by members of a different discipline. Instead of developing child-specific instruments, psychologists working with children simply took the tools others had fashioned for work with adults and began using them—unchanged—with children. The stimulus cards of the Rorschach are identical for adults and children, and until a modification of the Thematic Apperception Test became available for young children (Bellak & Bellak, 1949), psychologists used the same pictures, regardless of the age of the subject. This unimaginative approach of taking clinical psychology and applying it in work with children might be called *child clinical psychology;* it is not *clinical child psychology!*

An individual who conducts psychological testing, even when it includes diagnostic personality assessment, does not fit smoothly into the logistics of a child-guidance clinic. On the traditional team, the physician conducted the treatment of the child, the social worker did counseling with the mother, and the psychologist engaged in testing. But testing is done once, at the beginning of the clinic contact, when the decision about disposition of the case is to be made. As soon as a family entered treatment, thus tying up two-thirds of the team, the psychologist had nothing more to do with the case, and when all available treatment time was filled, he literally was idle. The notion of the trinitarian treatment team is thus a rather forced concept. Ideally, the psychologist should have used his unoccupied time by engaging in sorely needed research on clinic procedures and clinical problems. Yet, having become isolated from the mainstream of American academic psychology and operating in a frame of reference for which traditional research methods were ill-suited, psychologists working in child-guidance clinics contributed little if any meaningful research. As the demand for services kept increasing and the shortage of therapists became more and more critical, the "idle" psychologist found himself also doing treatment, an occupation that in many instances usurped even the time previously devoted to testing, which came to be relegated to students and junior staff. Some welcomed this state of affairs because they saw the psychologist doing something that seemed prestigious, socially constructive, and important; others deplored this trend and asked who was to do the essential research if the psychologist, who by training should be the logical team member for this task, engaged in an activity that might as readily be done by others.

Beginning about 1950, the history of clinical child psychology took a new turn. Psychologists engaged in clinical work with children had become indistinguishable from other clinical psychologists both by method and by training. There now began to emerge an identity and an insistence that work with children required special skills and specialized training. The designation *clinical child psychologist* came to be used here and there, and the publication of *The Practice of Clinical Child Psychology* (Ross, 1959) seemed to signal the reestablishment and renewed recognition of this old specialty. Within a few years, the Division of Clinical Psychology of the American Psychological Association (APA) sanctioned the formation of a Section on Clinical Child Psychology. Job descriptions began to use the term *clinical child psychologist,* universities developed courses with that designation, and— following the lead of the University of Minnesota—several doctoral programs in clinical child psychology became established.

A new generation of clinical child psychologists seemed to awaken to the fact that psychology is a source of principles and methods that can be applied in the clinical situation. The importance of developmental phenomena in the study and treatment of children with psychological disorders was once again recognized, and the contribution of psychology to the understanding of learning difficulties was rediscovered, thus renewing an interest that had led Witmer

to open his clinic. The tools of an adult-oriented clinical psychology and the constructs of psychoanalysis, though viewed as important, were no longer deemed sufficient as new and specialized techniques for the study of children were explored (e.g., Santostefano, 1962) and the theories of Heinz Werner, Jean Piaget, and B. F. Skinner began to be applied.

With increasing sophistication, clinical child psychologists were once again turning to research, many persuading their employing agencies that this endeavor is an important and necessary part of a psychologist's professional responsibility. It became more and more difficult to fill vacant positions unless it was explicitly specified that research was one of the incumbent's functions. Some of the larger and more forward-looking child-guidance clinics established full-time research positions to which they appointed clinical child psychologists, sometimes with the title of director of research. Soon clinical child psychologists began looking for publication outlets, and the Section on Clinical Child Psychology of the APA explored the feasibility of establishing a journal in that specialty. A survey revealed that this step was neither desirable nor necessary, particularly since, with its April, 1965, issue, the *Journal of Consulting and Clinical Psychology,* the APA publication in the area of clinical psychology, explicitly declared itself open to work from the child as well as the adult field.

It may be no coincidence that this trend in clinical child psychology paralleled the development of what has been called the *new child psychology.* After decades of observing, recording, and classifying what children do, a new generation of child psychologists has emerged who study how children do what they do. The field has passed through its botanizing stage and entered its experimental period. Sophisticated research methods are now being applied to questions of neonatal development, infant learning, child perception, conceptual styles, self-control, and social learning. Many of these issues bear directly on the problems encountered by the clinician, so that child psychology once again has something to contribute that can be applied in working with children who manifest psychological problems. The relevance of the experimental work to clinical issues may, at least in part, be due to the fact that many of the new generation of child psychologists had received clinical training as graduate students, so that their interests are cognate to those of the clinicians.

In a brief overview of the history of a field, it is hazardous to single out individual contributions because it is impossible not to be selective and thus omit many with equal or greater merit than those mentioned. Nonetheless, some representative work in the field of clinical child psychology cannot be omitted. It is not generally known, for example, that Carl Rogers was, at one time, director of the Rochester Guidance Center and that he wrote *The Clinical Treatment of the Problem Child* (1939) many years before his better-known publications appeared. Familiar are the names of some of the developers of intelligence tests, such as Grace Arthur (1943),[1] Grace Kent (1950), and Florence Goodenough (1926), and of tests of social competence, such as Edgar A. Doll (1953). Several clinical child psychologists worked to make the Rorschach method applicable to children; among these are Ames and her co-workers (1952), Florence Halpern (1953), and Nettie Ledwith (1959, 1960). Seymour Sarason (1953) brought a psychological orientation to the problem of mental deficiency, while Virginia Axline (1947), Haim Ginott (1961), and Clark Moustakas (1953, 1959) contributed to child therapy from the psychologist's point of view. Eugene Levitt (1957, 1963) concerned himself with the effectiveness of child psychotherapy, and E. K. Beller (1962)

[1] Dates refer to representative publications.

showed how clinical records can be constructively used in research. A total reorientation to helping emotionally disturbed children was pioneered by Nicholas Hobbs (1966), and Sidney Bijou (1965) was instrumental in bringing operant principles to bear on teaching the retarded. Recent years have seen psychologists increasingly bringing their research skills and research background to bear on clinical problems. Since intensive research training is the characteristic that most clearly differentiates the clinical child psychologist from other professionals in the clinical field, it is in applying research findings to practice that future contributions of clinical child psychologists are likely to be made.

PROFESSIONAL ORGANIZATION

When a distinct and explicit specialization in clinical child psychology was first delineated (Ross, 1959), it was necessary to point out that organizationally the clinical child psychologist was like a man without a country. The Division of Clinical Psychology of the APA was composed of members whose work and interests dealt primarily with adults, and the Division of Developmental Psychology was more representative of research than clinical interests. While the American Orthopsychiatric Association had originally admitted to membership only those who had clinical experience in child-guidance clinics, so that the clinical psychologists among the members were clinical child psychologists, this organization has since modified its membership criteria, so that at this point experience in clinical work with children is no longer a prerequisite.

In March, 1961, five psychologists who had been active on the Committee on Clinical Psychology of the American Association of Psychiatric Clinics for Children and who were attending the American Orthopsychiatric Association meetings in New York met at lunch to discuss professional issues facing clinical child psychologists.

Out of a shared concern regarding matters of training, practice, and organizational identity, they decided to form an interest group of clinical child psychologists who were members of the APA. A notice in several professional news media brought replies from fifty-one interested individuals, whereupon a meeting was scheduled for the following APA convention, which was held on August 31, 1961, and attended by forty-eight people.

Informal discussion during this meeting, chaired by Lovick Miller, revealed that the participants shared an interest in such questions as where, whether, and how clinical child psychology was taught, where they belonged within the organizational structure of the APA, and how they might communicate their interests to each other and to psychologists in general. To further their interests in these and related matters, the group voted to establish an organization, leaving the specific structure to be worked out by a steering committee headed by Alan O. Ross. Since another thirty-six individuals expressed interest in belonging to the group in the course of the same convention, the informal "charter" membership totaled eighty-four.

The steering committee took steps to organize an interest group and establish a newsletter, of which Allan Barclay was the first editor. When the Division of Clinical Psychology modified its bylaws in 1963 to permit the creation of sections within the division, the group became Section I, the Section on Clinical Child Psychology. Lovick Miller was elected first chairman of the section, which quickly grew in size and activity. By 1970 the membership totaled 773. Symposia dealing with topics of interest to clinical child psychologists are now a regular part of the annual meetings of the APA, and a number of active committees are working on substantive professional issues. For the historical record it might be noted that the following were the first five chairmen of the section: Lovick Miller, Theodore Leventhal, S.

Thomas Cummings, Sebastiano G. Santostefano, and Zanwil Sperber.

The section has been successful in giving clinical child psychologists an organizational home and a voice in the affairs of psychology. Its officers and members are increasingly contacted for advice on matters affecting clinical work with children, and through publications such as a directory of training resources and a monograph on psychological contributions to clinical work with children, the section supports the continuing growth of the profession.

TRAINING IN CLINICAL CHILD PSYCHOLOGY

There is no uniform preparation for the profession of clinical child psychology, and individuals enter it by various routes. Almost all graduate programs in clinical psychology now include some work with children, although in different degrees of emphasis. Some future clinical child psychologists train in one of these programs, take an internship in a setting serving a heterogeneous population, and then specialize in work with children by acquiring experience in an appropriate professional position. Many child-serving institutions give psychologists coming from this background intensive supervision during their first few years of work, thus ensuring their professional competence. Other individuals, trained in a general clinical psychology program, begin specializing in work with children by selecting for their internship an agency such as a child-guidance clinic, a children's hospital, a residential treatment school, or a similar specialized setting serving children. An increasing number of psychologists take explicit postdoctoral training in clinical child psychology, training that usually lasts two years and may come immediately after, or a few years following, the receipt of the Ph.D. degree. In a number of graduate programs, a student can combine preparation in clinical psychology with studies of child psychology, thus approximating the experience an integrated program in clinical child psychology would offer. Finally, there are a few graduate programs in clinical child psychology where a Ph.D. candidate can specifically prepare for a career in this field through a planned sequence of courses, seminars, practica, and internship. Whatever a particular individual psychologist's training, it will have included not only preparation for clinical practice but also intensive work in relevant research, including a research-based doctoral dissertation. Such graduate training follows what has come to be known as the *scientist-practitioner model.*

Among those responsible for the graduate training of clinical psychologists, opinions differ as to the desirability of predoctoral specialization. A survey of universities conducted in 1955 revealed an overwhelming rejection of predoctoral specialization in clinical child psychology. The respondents felt that such specialized training properly belongs in postdoctoral programs, although those offering such programs were then, and continue to be, few in number. In 1968 only five of the seventy-one doctoral programs in clinical psychology approved by the APA had made an explicit announcement that they were offering a doctorate in clinical child psychology (Ross & Blackwell, 1967). Only the Institute of Child Development at the University of Minnesota was listed as offering postdoctoral training in this specialty (*ibid.*), although there were twelve practicum agencies, able to accept a total of forty postdoctoral trainees into programs independent of university departments of psychology (Rie et al., 1967).

Because of a variety of critical issues facing clinical psychology, a conference on the professional preparation of clinical psychologists was held in Chicago in the summer of 1965. Among the fifty-eight voting members of this conference were four who had been invited specifically because of their identity as clinical child psychol-

ogists, and at least two others identified themselves with that specialty. Questions of specialty training came repeatedly under discussion during the five-day meeting, and many different opinions were expressed. The report of the conference (Hoch, Ross, & Winder, 1966) reflects the consensus that while some psychology departments might wish to offer specialized predoctoral programs, training in clinical child psychology is more appropriately placed in the postdoctoral years. In fact, the conference called for required postdoctoral training for anyone planning to teach or practice a specialty such as clinical child psychology. If this call is ever to be heeded, more postdoctoral traineeships will have to be created, and the conference took cognizance of this fact. The conference also strongly encouraged all programs in clinical psychology to increase their emphasis on developmental aspects of human behavior, having recognized that most such programs were inadequate in this important respect.

An essential and integral part of the doctoral training of clinical child psychologists is the internship, a year's experience in a clinical setting where the student can acquire practical skills, professional attitudes, and an understanding of clinical problems under close and intensive supervision. While not all clinical child psychologists obtain their internship in a setting serving children, for those who wish to do so the availability and quality of such settings are a critical question. A survey of practicum training resources conducted by the Section on Clinical Child Psychology and published in 1967 revealed that sixty-six agencies were offering a total of 185 traineeships to qualified applicants (Rie et al., 1967). These agencies ranged from clinics operated by university psychology departments, through mental hospitals with a children's service, to community child-guidance clinics. Thirty-five of these agencies had been approved for internship training by the APA, thus ensuring that they maintained certain minimal standards. In almost all settings, the trainee received supervised experience in assessment and treatment of children and parents, but the number of cases seen for these purposes varied greatly. Some settings operated on the assumption that the best form of training is extensive exposure to a great number of different children, so that some students were reported to have seen as many as 100 diagnostic cases. Others, believing that intensive work with a few carefully selected cases provides the best experience, gave the student as few as twelve such cases during a full-time one-year training period. Regardless of the size of the student's case load, the number of hours devoted to individual supervision of his work was uniformly high (eight to 10 hours per week), supervision being provided not only by senior psychologists but also by members of other disciplines on the staff of these agencies.

Anyone preparing to engage in clinical work with children must learn something about adults, and in that respect he shares a common core with students in general clinical psychology. In common with other psychologists, he must know statistics and research design, learning, perception, and personality, as well as physiological and social psychology. He must study individual testing, abnormal psychology, and various aspects and techniques of behavior modification. Beyond this basic core of clinical psychology, the clinical child psychology student must become immersed in developmental psychology from infancy through (at least) adolescence; he must know about mental retardation, speech disorders, and learning difficulties. He must understand the family and the school and be familiar with their impact on the child and how to modify that impact, where necessary. He must learn techniques for the observation of children. He must discover how to talk and relate to children, although the latter may well be a temperamental matter, better the subject of careful student selection than of teaching. Be that as it may, the plethora of things to

be mastered to become a clinical child psychologist undoubtedly calls for more than four years of training. The usual four-year predoctoral program in clinical psychology (which includes the one-year internship) simply does not allow enough time for the mastery of all the necessary material and skills. The Chicago conference was correct in calling for an expanded use of the postdoctoral years for specialty training, because proper preparation for clinical child psychology must span at least four predoctoral and two postdoctoral years.

There thus exists an urgent need for increased postdoctoral training programs. These must include not only supervised practice but also courses and seminars on content not covered in predoctoral training. The nonacademic centers where almost all postdoctoral training is taking place at the time of this writing may not possess the resources and structure for a systematic, integrated academic-practice program, and the university may well come to be viewed as a more suitable setting. If the recommendations of the Chicago conference have their desired impact, the coming years should see an increase in the number of university-based postdoctoral training programs in clinical child psychology.

TRENDS FOR THE FUTURE

Having come into its own in terms of a distinct identity only a few short years ago, clinical child psychology is a field in transition. Members of the profession are emerging from child-guidance clinics, where they had been submerged in the "team" for several decades. Some are establishing psychological centers where cases are treated by one of a variety of available methods and by one or more individuals, depending on the needs of the case and not on the demands of tradition. Others are found in residential treatment centers, where they are often in charge of programs. Some operate in specialized and regular schools, where they are returning to the psychoeducational emphasis of the early pioneers in the field (Sarason et al., 1966). There are clinical child psychologists working in pediatric settings and in institutions for the mentally retarded or the socially maladjusted delinquent. Some of the public school systems have come to look to the clinical child psychologist for consultation on problems of adaptation and effectiveness. In the major cities, clinical child psychologists enter individual or group practice. In some respects at the opposite pole, members of the profession are on university faculties, where they engage in practice, research, and teaching, often in close interaction with their colleagues in child psychology, with whom they once again find problems and interests in common.

No matter where they work, clinical child psychologists are increasing their research activity. If the trend continues, they will come to apply in their clinical work not only the findings of their own studies but also those of their colleagues in other areas of psychology, particularly child psychology. The scientist-professional model, reaffirmed at the Chicago conference (Hoch, Ross, & Winder, 1966), is critical for the future of clinical child psychology, and ultimately, the programmatic definition of clinical child psychology as the clinical application of child psychology should be fully implemented.

REFERENCES

Ames, L. B., Learned, J., Metraux, R. W., & Walker, R. N. *Child Rorschach responses: Developmental trends from two to ten years.* New York: Hoeber-Harper, 1952.

Arthur, G. *A point scale of performance tests. Vol. 1. Clinical manual.* (2nd ed.) New York: Commonwealth Fund, 1943.

Axline, V. M. *Play therapy.* Boston: Houghton Mifflin, 1947.

Bellak, L., & Bellak, S. S. *Manual of instruction for the Children's Apperception Test.* New York: C.P.S. Company, 1949.

Beller, E. K. *Clinical process.* New York: Free Press, 1962.

Bijou, S. W. Application of operant principles to the teaching of reading, writing, and arithmetic to retarded children. In *New frontiers in special education.* Washington, D.C.: National Education Association, 1965.

Dennis, W. Historical beginnings of child psychology. *Psychological Bulletin,* 1949, **46,** 224–235.

Doll, E. A. *The measurement of social competence: A manual for the Vineland Social Maturity Scale.* Minneapolis: Educational Test Bureau, 1953.

Ginott, H. G. *Group psychotherapy with children: The theory and practice of play-therapy.* New York: McGraw-Hill, 1961.

Goodenough, F. L. *Measurement of intelligence by drawings.* Tarrytown-on-Hudson: World, 1926.

Halpern, F. *A clinical approach to children's Rorschachs.* New York: Grune & Stratton, 1953.

Hobbs, N. Helping disturbed children: Psychological and ecological strategies. *American Psychologist,* 1966, **21,** 1105–1115.

Hoch, E. L., Ross, A. O., & Winder, C. L. (Eds.) *Professional preparation of clinical psychologists.* Washington, D.C.: American Psychological Association, 1966.

Jones, M. C. A laboratory study of fear: The case of Peter. *Journal of Genetic Psychology,* 1924, **31,** 308–315.

Kent, G. H. *Mental tests in clinics for children.* Princeton, N.J.: Van Nostrand, 1950.

Ledwith, N. H. *Rorschach responses of elementary school children.* Pittsburgh: University of Pittsburgh Press, 1959.

Ledwith, N. H. *A Rorschach study of child development.* Pittsburgh: University of Pittsburgh Press, 1960.

Levitt, E. E. The results of psychotherapy with children: An evaluation. *Journal of Consulting Psychology,* 1957, **21,** 189–196.

Levitt, E. E. Psychotherapy with children: A further evaluation. *Behaviour Research and Therapy,* 1963, **1,** 45–51.

Misiak, H., & Sexton, V. S. *History of psychology: An overview.* New York: Grune & Stratton, 1966.

Moustakas, C. E. *Children in play therapy.* New York: McGraw-Hill, 1953.

Moustakas, C. E. *Psychotherapy with children: The living relationship.* New York: Harper, 1959.

Rie, H. E., Bromberg, R. L., & Rynerson, M. N. *Directory of practicum training resources in clinical child psychology.* Columbus, Ohio: Section on Clinical Child Psychology, 1967.

Rogers, C. R. *The clinical treatment of the problem child.* Boston: Houghton Mifflin, 1939.

Ross, A. O. *The practice of clinical child psychology.* New York: Grune & Stratton, 1959.

Ross, S., & Blackwell, E. K. *Graduate study in psychology: 1968–69.* Washington: American Psychological Association, 1967.

Santostefano, S. Miniature situation tests as a way of interviewing children. *Merrill-Palmer Quarterly,* 1962, **8,** 261–269.

Sarason, S. B. *Psychological problems in mental deficiency.* (2nd ed.) New York: Harper, 1953.

Sarason, S. B., Levine, M., Goldenberg, I. I., Cherlin, D. L., & Bennett, E. M. *Psychology in community settings: Clinical, educational, vocational, social aspects.* New York: Wiley, 1966.

Sundberg, N. D., & Tyler, L. E. *Clinical psychology: An introduction to research and practice.* New York: Appleton Century Crofts, 1962.

Watson, J. B., & Raynor, R. Conditioned emotional reactions. *Journal of Experimental Psychology,* 1920, **3,** 1–14.

Watson, R. I. A brief history of clinical psychology. *Psychological Bulletin,* 1953, **50,** 321–346.

44 | The Child Psychologist

Stuart M. Finch

The child psychiatrist as we know him today is a relative newcomer to the medical as well as the mental-health scene. Although he may be said to have existed in unofficial form and barely discernible numbers since the nineteenth century, he came into his own only quite recently.

The training requirements for certification in child psychiatry, to be discussed in more detail later, are graduation from an accredited medical school with or without one year of approved internship, two years of training in adult psychiatry, and two years of training in child psychiatry—again in approved programs. Examinations are given first in adult and then in child psychiatry.

This is quite a change from the earlier period of child psychiatry. Actually, it is impossible to date the beginning of this specialty. Probably the most comprehensive historical review of the subject was published by Lawson Lowrey (1944). He divides the history into three periods—the first from 1846 to about 1909, the second from 1909 until 1919, and the third from then until the time of his writing. One certainly could add another period: from about the end of World War II until the present time.

HISTORICAL REVIEW

Although it is difficult to outline in specific detail the history of child psychiatry, a brief review may be useful.

According to Lowry and others, the period from about the middle of the last century until approximately 1909 saw developing interest by European psychiatrists in mentally retarded children, perhaps sparked by Itard's work in France. One of his pupils, Seguin, eventually moved to the United States and became the superintendent of a school for the mentally retarded in Massachusetts. This institution later was renamed the Walter Fernald State School. Fernald is given credit by Lowrey for major innovations in the care and treatment of the retarded in the United States. The original thinking, particularly in Europe, was that all retarded should be institutionalized lest they commit crimes. Fernald, who remained superintendent of the institution in Massachusetts for many years, pioneered such concepts as the categorizing of degrees of mental retardation, foster care, and special education.

It is interesting that the very roots of child psychiatry were in the care of the mentally retarded. Many years later, when child psychiatry became more accepted, it had moved away from this field and only recently has it made attempts to get back into the area of mental retardation.

It is probably fair to say, still following Lowrey, that most of the interest in psychiatry of children remained with the retarded until approximately 1909. There was a gradual expansion in the number of institutions caring for the retarded, and a slow improvement took place in the services to these children.

The year 1909 is important primarily because William Healy at that point began his work at the Juvenile Psychopathic Institute, which was at that time associated with the Chicago Juvenile Court. Healy's work heralded an era of attention to the juvenile delinquent. It was during the following ten-year period that some already established psychiatric institutes were beginning to devote increasing attention to the family and the child. The whole concept of the social worker was born. One of the pioneers in this field was Adolf Meyer, who enlisted the help of his wife for various social work types of involvement, including home visiting. We now begin to see the emergence of the orthopsychiatric team, with psychiatrist, psychologist, and social worker all addressing themselves to mental-health problems of youth. In 1917 Healy moved to Boston to head the Judge Baker Foundation.

During the years between 1909 and 1919, there were comparatively few clinics or other agencies in the country providing psychiatric service to youngsters. In the main, these efforts were concerned with the juvenile delinquent. Also during these years there were rapid growth and expansion in the fields of both psychiatric social work and psychology. There was a spread of the use of standardized intellectual testing. That which we now accept as training in child psychiatry in essence did not exist.

The third period, as described by Lowrey, from about 1909 until about 1944, saw a remarkable growth in the whole field of child guidance. The Commonwealth Fund was instrumental in the beginning of this, financing, under the auspices of the National Committee for Mental Hygiene, pilot child-guidance clinics scattered around the country. Additional such clinics were begun by various states and localities. A few inpatient services for the psychiatric care of children were established in the country.

The whole idea of the child-guidance clinic arose from the wishful concept that early detection and treatment of the emotional problems in children would in the long run practically eradicate subsequent problems in juvenile delinquency and adult emotional and mental troubles. There was great hope held for the preventive and therapeutic value of the child-guidance clinic in the beginning. However, as time went on, it became increasingly evident that the treatment of children was not as easy as had been hoped and, even more important, that the treatment of their parents did not always succeed. Furthermore, the numbers of children who needed such help far outweighed the available resources. Many of the families who needed this type of help most did not seek it.

With the rapid proliferation of child-guidance clinics throughout the country, it became impossible to have psychiatric direction in every one of them. The training of child psychiatrists was a sort of hit-or-miss activity, and relatively few individuals were being trained each year. The standards for the operation of such child-guidance clinics were diffuse and vague, and there was great variation in staffing from one clinic to another and from one state to another.

The period from approximately the end of the

Second World War until the present has seen many further developments in the area of child psychiatry. There has been not only an increase in the number of child-psychiatry facilities, both inpatient and outpatient, but a much greater standardization both of the operation of these clinics and institutions and of the training of the child psychiatrist himself.

It was in 1948 that the American Association of Psychiatric Clinics for Children was formed. The purposes of the AAPCC as outlined in their bylaws, are as follows:

A. To provide for the coordination of the activities of psychiatric clinics serving children in the United States, its territories and the Dominion of Canada.
B. To help maintain the highest possible standards of clinic practice.
C. To provide opportunities for the exchange of ideas, and for mutual help in the study and solution of clinic problems.
D. To promote the training of clinic personnel.
E. To cooperate with appropriate groups or organizations doing professional placement work in the clinic field.
F. To cooperate with appropriate organizations throughout the world whose purposes may, in whole or in part, coincide with those of the Association.
G. To carry on such other activities as may advance the field of child psychiatry.

The AAPCC sets qualifications for a clinic's membership in the organization. These have to do with the key personnel of the clinic, including the psychiatrist, chief psychologist, and chief psychiatric social worker. The general intent of this organization was and is to upgrade and standardize those clinics serving psychiatric needs of children. Certain of the clinics have been designated as training clinics and are authorized to grant certificates of AAPCC-approved training to child psychiatry fellows who have successfully completed two years of training.

The other sizable step forward in the standardization and improvement of child-psychiatry training was the establishment of child psychiatry as an official subspecialty in 1959. The details of this are explained later in this chapter.

CONTENT OF TRAINING

A child psychiatrist is the one member of the orthopsychiatric team who brings a background of medical training. This statement, while in no way diminishing the contributions and special talents of the other members of the expanding team, does have importance. Medicine has long had in our society the responsibility of treating illness and, whenever possible, preventing it. Physicians have traditionally been educated to take this responsibility and have been examined to determine their competence and then given the legal right to practice. While most state laws regarding the practice of medicine were written many years ago and are oriented toward organic illness, mental and emotional illness can and perhaps should be included. Certainly other mental-health professionals are competent to deal with many mental-health problems, but more often than not, they feel more comfortable with the consultation and backing of a physician, who may have to assume the final responsibility.

The child psychiatrist comes to his position after a rather long and arduous training period. His admission to medical school is usually preceded by four years of college. His medical school curriculum includes exposure to all areas of medicine and may be followed by at least one year of internship. If he follows the traditional path, he then takes two years of residency training in adult psychiatry and, next, two years of training in child psychiatry. After one year of subsequent practice, he may be accepted for the written examination for certification in adult psychiatry by the American Board of Psychiatry and Neurology, Inc. If he succeeds in this examination, he is then eligible for the oral examination, which again includes both psychiatry and neurology. If he is successful, he may then apply for examination in child psychiatry. This covers the various age groups from infancy through adolescence. It also tests the candidate's knowledge of literature, history, psychopharmacology, child psychology, community psychiatry, and other areas. Success in this examination makes the candidate a diplomate of the American Board of Psychiatry and Neurology, Inc., certified in psychiatry and child psychiatry.

As of this writing, there are approximately 600 certified child psychiatrists in the United States. Certainly this small number does not represent the total effort of psychiatrists in work with children or adolescents. A survey a few years ago revealed that approximately 2,700 of the members of the American Psychiatric Association were willing to consult about or even to treat children.

For the nonmedical reader a brief explanation of some of the complexities of medical licensure and practice in the United States seems appropriate at this point. Each state has a medical licensing board, which grants the privilege of practicing medicine to those physicians who successfully pass the examinations. Many states have a reciprocal agreement with other states. National board examinations are given throughout the country, and some states accept these in lieu of their own state board examinations. No child psychiatrist can practice without a valid license in his particular state.

Perhaps the most comprehensive treatise on the subject of career training in child psychiatry resulted from the 1963 conference held in Washington and cosponsored by the American Academy of Child Psychiatry and the American Psychiatric Association. The report on this conference was published by the American Psychiatric Association in 1964. In this book the initial question posed is why child psychiatry should be established as a subspecialty in psychiatry and thus require training above and beyond that of adult psychiatry. In answer, the authors point out a number of things which would seem worth quoting in regard to the special skills and abilities required of the child psychiatrist. These are:

A continual awareness of the importance of growth and maturation to a child's functioning and the constant relevance of developmental phase to the child's thinking, feeling and behaving. . . .

An awareness that there are multiple physical, intellectual, and emotional lines of development in the growing child, and that the development in these several areas may not proceed at equal rates. . . .

A knowledge of the physical and psychological aspects of normal and pathological development and of the interaction of the multiple forces in health and disease. . . .

A realization that while change is resisted by children, as it is by adults, and is often felt as a threat rather than something to be desired, there is an inherent biological and psychological striving for growth and development. . . .

A simultaneous appreciation of the child functioning as a discrete psychobiologic organism and as a unit interacting within a family, and, gradually, within an ever-expanding society. . . .

The capacity to collaborate with other medical and nonmedical professional disciplines — pediatricians and other physicians, psychiatric social workers, clinical psychologists, nurses, teachers, et al. — in the comprehensive diagnosis and treatment of children. . . .

Cognizance of the relative lack of a stabilized symptom picture in children. . . .

A recognition that diagnosis in child psychiatry includes not only a dynamic and genetic evaluation of the presenting symptoms and underlying pathology, but also an appraisal of the positive aspects of the personality or those assets or strengths used by the child currently and in the past in coping with both the usual everyday experiences and extraordinary events. . . .

A specialized kind of interviewing skill which includes an exceptional flexibility to communicate with children at various developmental levels, both verbally and nonverbally. . . .

An understanding that the goal of the child psychiatrist is not just the immediate relief of clinical symptoms, but, more fundamentally, the removal of roadblocks to the child's continued growth, enabling him to progress securely through succeeding developmental stages. The ultimate goal is prevention; this may be accomplished by various means, for example, parent education, early detection and treatment, and research.... [American Psychiatric Association, 1964]

THE TRAINING PROGRAM

Two years of special training in work with children and their families when added to the two years of adult psychiatric training might at first glance seem to be ample time. Yet when one outlines the various experiences which should be included in this period, two years becomes a relatively short time. While training programs vary considerably, we can list some of the important features provided in optimal training programs.

Diagnostic Experience

The child fellow should have an opportunity under the supervision to interview children of various ages, including adolescents and their parents. He should learn to formulate the dynamics of the child's illness as well as of the family problems and to plan an appropriate treatment approach. He needs an opportunity to work in collaboration with other members of the mental-health team, including social workers, psychologists, nurses, and teachers, in reaching decisions about psychopathology and how it should be managed. Each case should be carefully and thoroughly studied, and the number of cases, the ages of the children, and the types of psychopathology should be sufficiently varied so that the child fellow has a broad experience.

Specific training in the use of play materials is essential to this experience. A child is usually brought to a psychiatrist because some adult—the parents or perhaps the teacher—has felt that the child needed help. The child himself may be either totally unaware of his difficulties or at best only dimly so. Certainly he is not acquainted with the whole idea of psychiatric treatment and is confused about the strange physician he is forced to see. For example, the pediatrician must also examine children, but his goal is one of making the youngster comfortable and cooperative during the physical examination. The child psychiatrist has as his goal learning about the youngster's mental and emotional processes during the diagnostic evaluation. In younger children especially, a formal psychiatric interview would be totally useless. It is necessary for the trainee to learn to accept children on their own level and to allow them to express themselves in their own way. Since in younger children play is a form of expression, the child psychiatrist must learn to use and understand the child's play. He substitutes play materials for the stethoscope, the ophthalmoscope, or the syringe. He learns, for example, to sit on the floor with a small child and watch him build blocks until they topple. He may watch an 8-year-old girl set up a dollhouse scene depicting some of her own problems from home. He evaluates the reaction of the 9-year-old boy to the loss of a checker game. All these observations help him understand children better and will serve him well when he becomes involved in therapy of youngsters.

Exposure to Normal Children

The child fellow should have an opportunity to see normal youngsters of various ages. This is most often provided during his training in a school setting. He should be given the opportunity to observe regular classroom situations from nursery school through high school. If the child fellow is really to understand youngsters, it is necessary that he have sufficient exposure to children functioning in what we think of as normal situations. Certainly, when one thinks of a child psychiatrist evaluating the reactions of a 10-year-old sent to him for consultation, it is difficult to conceive that he could carry through this examination adequately if he did not have a thorough understanding of healthy 10-year-old behavior. So it is with any other age child who is brought to him for consultation.

Therapeutic Experience

During his training, the child psychiatrist should have an opportunity to treat children of various ages and with different emotional problems, and he should see them in inpatient as well as outpatient and perhaps day-care settings. He should engage in, under supervision, treatment of children, treatment of the entire family, short-term therapy, and more intensive therapy. He should become familiar with the use of drugs and other methods, as well as modes of collaboration. He may, for instance, take a child into treatment and work in collaboration with a social worker who is treating the parents. He might on his next case treat the parents and have someone else see the child. Still another possibility would be that he would see both child and parents, and perhaps the siblings as well. In general, the treatment experience should be gauged to give the fellow a basic knowledge of psychodynamics and how to apply this knowledge therapeutically.

Consultation

Many child-psychiatry training programs provide a graduated experience in consultation. They begin by having the trainee accompany a senior staff member to the agency to which the latter consults. After "sitting in" for a year, the fellow begins to consult on his own, with supervision as required. The principles of consultation are relatively simple, and if they are learned in one agency, they usually apply to other agencies with only minor modifications. For example, the consultant at a juvenile court, at a school, or in a community mental-health center does not function in different worlds. He is there primarily to add his own knowledge of child development and

psychopathology to the total scene. He can at times see one youngster and give ideas and suggestions perhaps to the teacher or the principal or even the parents. Most important, he can try to understand the duties and responsibilities of the agency and how he can best bring his own knowledge into this situation. He learns to recognize that he is not a schoolteacher, not an administrator, not even a juvenile judge, but that his special field of competence may be useful to these people. Such questions as "What do we do with the aggressive child?" and "How do we handle divorce problems with the youngsters?" are examples of the kind of problems he may help to solve. Many schools and agencies will initially expect to use him primarily as an evaluator of individual children, which is rarely the most economic use of his time (in contrast to his teaching functions as a disseminator of mental-health principles and management techniques). By his own melding into the agency functioning, by his understanding of the needs of children, and by his knowledge of the function of personality and its growth, he may assist others to do their work more effectively.

State Hospitals

Many child-psychiatry programs provide the trainee with exposure to state hospitals. The average child-psychiatry program cannot give such exposure to the vast problems encountered in the state hospital system. The trainee should learn what it means to send a youngster to a state mental hospital and what treatment he will receive, and it is only by spending time there that he will begin to learn this. Children and adolescents who are sent to state hospitals form a special and sizable group of youngsters. Every child fellow should be thoroughly acquainted with how his own state, as well as others, is prepared to handle this problem and what contributions he himself may make to these programs.

State Homes for the Retarded

Many child-psychiatry training programs provide some experience for their trainees in institutions for the mentally retarded. The average training facility does see some mentally retarded youngsters for evaluation and treatment. However, every child psychiatrist should have exposure to the institutional care of the more severely retarded. Those trainees with a special interest in this field should spend additional time in such institutions.

Pediatric Services

Most university-based child-psychiatry training programs maintain a close liaison with the department of pediatrics. Senior child psychiatrists supervise child fellows in answering consultations from both outpatient and inpatient pediatric services. In addition, there are usually combined staff meetings in which specific cases as well as general problems are discussed. This is a two-way street: the child psychiatrist has the opportunity to learn to deal with physically ill children, and he can assist the pediatrician to recognize the feeling component of his patients and to manage certain types of emotionally disturbed children.

Seminars and Conferences

An important ingredient of all training programs in child psychiatry is the seminar. These are usually several in number, and they cover a variety of topics, including literature, child development, childhood psychopathology, and principles of treatment. In addition, the program usually presents clinical conferences relating to specific problems of diagnosis and management. A continuous case conference, in which the group follows the treatment of a child and his family over a period of time, is also common.

THE CHILD PSYCHIATRIST IN VARIOUS SETTINGS

One can at best give only a partial list of the various settings in which child psychiatrists are working. It is most usual to find a child psychiatrist involved in more than one of these areas. It is also important to realize that the majority of child psychiatrists, having been trained also in adult psychiatry, do spend a certain amount of their time treating adults. There are probably a number of reasons for this, not the least of which is that working with disturbed children is quite taxing and is probably made easier if it is occasionally interspersed with work with adults.

Academic Setting

All the four-year medical schools in the United States have departments of psychiatry, but by no means all of them have sections of child psychiatry. Where such sections do exist, they vary greatly in size. One may have only one child psychiatrist on its staff, while another has a large service which includes inpatient, outpatient, and day care. The large, multidisciplinary staff of such an institution may even rival the adult side of the department in size. The academic child psychiatrist spends the majority of his time, of course, teaching and doing research. The service he performs is built around the research and teaching responsibilities which he has. Some child-psychiatry divisions have formal two-year child fellow training programs, while others do not. In the past few years it has become increasingly common to find child psychiatrists being named as chairmen of departments of psychiatry. There are only about two departments of child psychiatry in medical schools in the United States. The remainder are all sections within general departments.

Child-guidance Clinics

These clinics, first begun on a pilot basis in the 1920s, have multiplied remarkably in the ensuing years. There are now several hundred child-guidance clinics in many cities throughout the United States. These vary considerably in size and in personnel involved. While most child-guidance clinics may prefer to have as director a fully trained, board-certified child psychiatrist, there are not enough of these to go around. In any case, many are administered by other members of the mental-health team, such as social workers or psychologists. These usually have a child psychiatrist consultant, who may spend only a few hours a week at the clinic. This leads us into a rather fuzzy area which has not been totally clarified, namely, that of medical responsibility. If there is no psychiatrist or medical physician on the staff, then of course, the non-medical personnel must assume the responsibility for the patients. This necessitates a close working relationship with physicians in the community to ensure the fact that organic illness is not overlooked.

State Hospitals

A growing number of state hospitals in recent years have been adding children's units. Prior to that, youngsters either were not admitted to state hospitals or, unfortunately, were mixed in with adult patients. In such hospitals there usually was little in the way of a program for children, and the youngsters were continuously exposed to the psychopathology of the adult patients. They received little if any schooling.

The new concept of children's units in state hospitals is a wise one. Such units are often built on the state hospital grounds but as separate buildings. They include recreational-occupational therapy and school classrooms. Again, on a nationwide basis, it would appear that such units have been constructed more rapidly than the supply of child psychiatrists has increased to staff them. Some of them have remained closed because of this, while others have opened with an adult psychiatrist taking charge.

Various child psychiatrists have expressed differing feelings about the relationship of a children's unit in a state hospital to the parent hospital. Some advocate almost total autonomy of the children's unit, while others feel that more is to be gained by retaining at least some relationship with the parent hospital. One of the difficulties arises because the cost of hospitaliza-

tion of a child is greater than that of an adult, due to the additional services which must be provided. This means that a proportionately larger share of the overall budget must be given to the children's unit if it is to succeed. Many state hospital superintendents, especially if they are not interested in the care of children, resent this.

Private Practice

The majority of child psychiatrists do see at least some private patients, and a few are engaged in full-time private practice. The national distribution of child psychiatrists is uneven, as is the distribution of the rest of the medical profession, particularly in the specialties. The concentration is in large urban areas, especially in wealthy communities.

The child psychiatrist in private practice, at least the one who spends the majority of his time in this endeavor, is faced with many problems. In the first place, the demands for his service are usually great. He is asked to see far more patients than he can possibly take into treatment. If he is analytically trained, a great deal of his effort may go into treating a relatively few patients. He is also faced with the problem of effecting change in parents. Many child psychiatrists in private practice work out arrangements with social workers, psychologists, or others who will treat or guide parents while the physician is treating the child. In other situations the youngster may be the prime focus of treatment, with the child psychiatrist himself seeing the parents only on occasion. In work with older adolescents, it is sometimes less necessary to treat the parents of the patient.

It has long been recognized that the practice of diagnostic and therapeutic work with children is extremely demanding. This has resulted in many child psychiatrists either leaving the field or at least diminishing the amount of time devoted to it. Surveys by the American Psychiatric Association would indicate that many child psychiatrists who originally classified themselves as practicing predominantly in this area have subsequently classified themselves as doing some other type of practice. The unfortunate result has been a very slow gain in the number of child psychiatrists who label themselves as such.

The busy private practitioner of child psychiatry finds himself at a disadvantage in attempting to maintain adequate communication not only with the immediate family of the child but with the school and other agencies who may be involved.

Community Mental-health Agencies

Community psychiatry, one of the newest subspecialties, places a strong emphasis on prevention. It is quite natural that child psychiatrists should be drawn to this branch of psychiatry. Many of its concepts deal with the early recognition and prevention of mental and emotional disease, toward which child psychiatry has been oriented for many years. The nationwide movement in the direction of community psychiatry has led to the establishment of many preventive, emergency, and partial-care services in local areas.

Child psychiatrists have often been sought as directors of community mental-health clinics. While their training in working with adults, children, and families in some ways qualifies them to direct such an operation, unfortunately there are far too few child psychiatrists in this country to even begin to provide the necessary leadership for such agencies.

If the child psychiatrist finds himself as the director of a community mental-health clinic, he literally becomes a "jack-of-all-trades." He may, on the one hand, be trying to establish a suicide-prevention center while, on the other, be developing the necessary primary-prevention services as well as an educational program and other such activities. He is literally "on the front line."

There are many fields of knowledge which can contribute to community mental-health programs, such as community organization, community development, and mental-health education. Since these are specialties in themselves, no director can pretend to be expert in them all, and child-psychiatry training programs do not, on the whole, attempt to teach their content but try instead to familiarize residents with their function.

It is probably fair to say that community psychiatry has too often been offered as a panacea for mental health to the public and that, like so many of its predecessors, it will not eradicate all mental problems. The public often has unrealistic expectations from the community mental-health center and, when the center fails to meet these, may reduce its support. It is not only the professional future of the child psychiatrist which is in jeopardy in such a situation but also that of all his colleagues and co-workers. The public must be educated to realize the limitations as well as the potentials of community mental-health programs.

Pediatric Hospitals

A growing number of pediatric hospitals around the country have established divisions of child psychiatry. A majority of those who have not are currently searching for personnel to establish such units. The child psychiatrist in a pediatric hospital serves primarily as a consultant to the pediatricians and other physicians. His activities are generally divided into three broad areas. He provides consultation service to pediatricians who refer selected patients to him. He usually establishes seminars or case conferences to give the pediatricians a broader and better understanding of the principles of emotional development as well as the management of the less serious psychiatric problems in children and their families. He may also provide a small outpatient service unit with ongoing treatment cases being cared for.

Most large pediatric hospitals do not feel that their range of services is complete without child psychiatry. The psychologist and the psychiatric social worker are frequently a part of such an operation and at times must carry the entire burden because the institution is unable to find a child psychiatrist.

School Systems

Many child psychiatrists serve as consultants to school systems, most often on a part-time basis. Only a few of our largest school systems have a full-time child psychiatrist attached to the central staff. These child psychiatrists have commonly found that in the beginning the school system's expectation of his services differs from his own. The school system most often starts out hoping that he will evaluate and even treat seriously disturbed youngsters who have proved difficult to manage in school. The psychiatrist, on the other hand, hopes that his main function will be that of a true consultant, who meets with classroom teachers, school administrators, and special-services personnel periodically to discuss the problems that arise in the classroom as well as in the school system itself. Individual cases may, of course, be presented to him at times, but he hopes to use these as a vehicle for disseminating broader mental-health concepts to the teachers and administrators.

When the child psychiatrist deals directly with individual pupils, his total time is rapidly consumed by a relatively few youngsters, with little carry-over to the larger school population. The teachers and administrators learn little from him about mental-health principles and often continue to contribute unwittingly to the development of further problems. In summary, the child psychiatrist in this situation must gradually help the school personnel to realize where his most basic contribution may lie and that this may differ from their expectation.

THE CHILD PSYCHIATRIST AND THE CHILD ANALYST

Psychoanalysis, of course, originated in Freud's work with adults. It was only natural that as he and his co-workers delved more into the early childhood memories of their adult patients, their interest would be stimulated in seeking confirmation of some of these findings by direct observation of children. The most famous early attempt at this was outlined by Freud in 1909 in a paper entitled "Analysis of a Phobia in a Five-year-old Boy." This child was the son of a colleague of Freud's living in another town, with much of the "analysis" carried on by correspondence between Freud and the patient's father.

Some of the earliest professionals who became interested in applying the concepts of psychoanalysis to children were educators, and only somewhat later did psychiatrists follow suit. Hug-Hellmuth was one of the pioneers in this field. Two schools of child-analytic thought gradually developed in Europe, one headed by Anna Freud (Sigmund Freud's daughter, who is still living and productive) and the other headed by Melanie Klein in England.

In the United States there has been relatively little uniformity in the development of child analysis (particularly as it relates to child psychiatry). Training in adult analysis is a prerequisite for training in child analysis. All child-analytic training is done under the auspices of the various psychoanalytic institutes around the country. The programs differ in each of the institutes, although the American Psychoanalytic Association is making efforts to standardize them. In general, a curriculum is offered the potential child analyst which includes seminars in child development, child psychopathology, and diagnosis and treatment (as do child-psychiatry residency training programs). The candidate is expected to analyze under supervision several youngsters, usually two of latency age and one of adolescent age.

These child analysts have had training in formal child psychiatry. Some of the child-psychiatry training programs in this country are much more analytically oriented than others, and in these a far greater percentage of the candidate's time is spent in analytic work. The total number of graduating child analysts each year, however, is quite small. To complicate matters, it has been shown that after ten or fifteen years many of these individuals are no longer themselves seeing children in analysis but are supervising others.

THE CHILD PSYCHIATRIST AND THE ADOLESCENT

Many of the most basic concepts of child psychiatry stem from concern about the adolescent. William Healy, who began his work with delinquent adolescents, stimulated much of the early work in child psychiatry in the United States. As child-psychiatry training programs have developed, they have tended to include at least the midadolescent in their programs. Child psychiatrists feel that the teen-ager still faces many of the difficulties of his less emancipated younger sibling. He still goes to school, he is still a "minor," he is still a responsibility of his parents.

One need only take a closer look at teen-agers to realize that they are not a homogeneous group. One cannot compare a 13-year-old with a 19-year-old. The former is just coming into adolescence and just emerging from dependent childhood. The latter is verging on adult life, although he is denied many of its privileges. Paradoxically, he is asked to serve in the armed services but may not vote. He may well be in college and possess more intellectual knowledge than his parents, but in many states he cannot marry without their consent and cannot drink alcoholic beverages.

The adolescent group has been relatively neglected by medicine in general, as well as by psychiatry specifically. For example, the pediatrician typically tends to devote his primary efforts to infants and small children through grade school ages. The internist, on the other hand, spends the majority of his time dealing with adults. Even treating an adolescent in a general hospital has often been a difficult problem. He does not really belong on the pediatric ward, and he may not fit comfortably on the adult wards. The same situation has tended to be true in psychiatry. The child psychiatrist more often than not has spent the majority of his time dealing with preadolescent youngsters, whereas the general psychiatrist has confined himself for the most part to adult patients. While training in psychiatry of adolescence has been an integral part of most child-psychiatry training programs for many years, over the past few years society, as well as medicine and psychiatry, has increased its interest in the problems of the adolescent. This had led child psychiatrists to begin seeing greater numbers of young teen-agers. At the same time many adult psychiatrists have become interested in the older teen-ager, particularly the college student.

One result has been the formation of societies and councils for adolescent psychiatry around the country. These are composed of general and child psychiatrists who have special interests in the teen-age group and who have organized themselves in order to pursue this interest together. It would seem a strong probability, however, that adolescent psychiatry will never become an official subspecialty within the general field, as has child psychiatry.

Perhaps the most succinct statement about the psychiatry of adolescence was the following position statement published by the American Psychiatric Association:

> By 1967 about 50 percent of the total U.S. population will be under 25 years of age. Already, according to statistics of the National Institute of Mental Health, outpatient psychiatric clinics in the U.S. serve more persons in the 10 to 19 age group

than in any other decade of life. One-fourth of all clinic patients in 1963 were adolescents.

The recent increase in the inpatient adolescent population is especially striking: the number of patients aged 10 to 14 in state and county mental hospitals was 325 percent higher in 1963 than in 1950. (These statistics do not include the large number of adolescents in private psychiatric hospitals and in special schools, for whom statistics are not available.) If the present trend continues, NIMH predicts that during the next decade there will be an increase of about 90 percent in the rate young people are hospitalized in state and county mental hospitals.

From the biological standpoint adolescence can be considered to begin with the first physical evidence of sexual maturation and to end with the complete development of primary and secondary sexual characteristics. It encompasses the years from about ages 10 to 18 in girls and 12 to 20 in boys. Understanding this period, in which unique developmental tasks are accomplished, is important as part of the psychiatrist's total knowledge of personality development. There is a wide and varied spectrum of behavior disorders in this age group which bring both challenges and satisfactions in the areas of treatment, training, and research.

The American Psychiatric Association recommends that both the child psychiatrist and the general psychiatrist undergo training aimed at enhancing their effectiveness in dealing with the emotional problems of adolescents. The training of the child psychiatrist should include work with older adolescents. In turn the general psychiatrist, especially if he is interested in working with the older adolescents, should undergo training with the younger adolescent, thereby enhancing his knowledge of developmental processes and learning problems and of how to work with the family and schools. Opportunities for such training exist in many settings, including hospitals, clinics, courts, schools, and private practice.

In regard to inpatient care, the American Psychiatric Association recommends that every public mental hospital and every general hospital admitting patients to a psychiatric unit establish an inpatient adolescent service. This service, headed by an adequately trained and especially interested psychiatrist, assisted by ancillary staff, should control the treatment program of all adolescents in the hospital, whether or not there is a separate ward or building set aside for them. Treatment and rehabilitation programs in such inpatient programs should be geared to the special needs of adolescents.

The American Psychiatric Association also recommends an increase in the number of day treatment facilities, psychiatrically oriented boarding schools, and clinics serving adolescents. Expansion of such facilities would increase the opportunities for training and research with this age group.

The American Psychiatric Association recommends that the child psychiatrist and general psychiatrist work closely with members of related disciplines in dealing with adolescents and their families. Such multidisciplinary efforts should also be carried on in relation to research: only through multidisciplinary research, both applied and clinical, can we increase our understanding of the many and complex reasons for psychiatric disorders of adolescents and their families. In the long run results of such research will lead to more effective treatment methods.

A COMPOSITE PICTURE OF THE CHILD PSYCHIATRIST

The most basic difference between the child psychiatrist and other child mental-health personnel is, of course, his M.D. degree. In essence, he is first a physician and second a psychiatrist. There have been long and heated arguments about the wisdom of medical training for someone who is to spend his professional life dealing with mentally and emotionally disturbed people. There are some who believe that such training is unnecessary and even more who believe that the psychiatrist-physician soon forgets much of the medicine he has learned. There is still another school of thought which feels that medical school training, with its respect for organic illness and, even more important, its training for the assumption of responsibility for the care of the ill, is of great importance. At present, however, all psychiatrists are by law physicians licensed to practice medicine, with the traditional aura of "authority" accorded physicians.

They would seem also to have the additional advantage of greater acceptance by nonpsychiatric physicians. The psychiatrist's acceptance by the "brotherhood of medicine" is perhaps in question. The average psychiatrist calls upon other physicians to evaluate the medical problems of his patients. He is, however, in a position to be on the alert for organic problems. It also should be remembered that many of the current advances in psychiatry do deal with organic and biological knowledge, and the most effective psychiatrists stay reasonably abreast with these.

In addition to his basic medical background, the child psychiatrist is trained to understand the mental and emotional functioning of adults as well as children. His skills in interviewing, diagnostic evaluation, and therapy are based on several years of intensive training. While he may eventually decide upon one particular area of child psychiatry, he has been trained in many. He has evaluated normal children as well as disturbed ones. He has worked with parents as well as with children of all ages. He has frequently worked in close cooperation with other physicians, and his medical identity enhances his capacity to communicate with them.

The child psychiatrist has spent considerable time learning how to work effectively with the members of the other mental-health disciplines. Not only is he a member of the small original orthopsychiatric team of child psychiatrist, psychologist, and social worker, but his team function has expanded to include the special educator, the mental-health–public-health nurse, and many others.

Eventually he has chosen one or more areas in which he spends the majority of his time. He may choose these by age, preferring to work with preschool children or grade school children or even adolescents. He may have chosen to work with one or more types of difficulties, such as psychotic children or delinquent youngsters. He may have made his choice in terms of overall responsibility and thus devoted his efforts to community mental health, to state or federal government, to academic work, to consultation, or to any variety of these.

In terms of service need, there are far too few child psychiatrists in our country today. The reasons for this are manifold. In the first place, there is a general shortage of physicians. Even with the graduates of the eighteen to twenty new medical schools now being organized, the number of physicians serving our country will be less than optimum. Further, any medical student will have to choose from many specialties as well as general practice. Somewhere slightly below 10 percent of the medical school graduates will choose psychiatry as a specialty, and only a few of these will go on to become child psychiatrists. Certainly it would not appear that this number will grow remarkably in the foreseeable future, and therefore, our serious shortage will continue.

REFERENCES

American Psychiatric Association. Career training in child psychiatry. Report of the Conference on Training in Child Psychiatry, Washington, organized and conducted by the American Academy of Child Psychiatry and the American Psychiatric Association, Jan. 10–15, 1963. Washington: American Psychiatric Association, 1964.

American Psychiatric Association. Position statement on psychiatry of adolescence. *American Journal of Psychiatry,* 1967, **123,** 1031.

Freud, S. Analysis of a phobia in a five-year-old boy. (1909) In *Collected papers.* Vol. 3. New York: Basic Books, 1959. Pp. 149–289.

Lowry, L.G. Psychiatry for children: Brief history of developments. *American Journal of Psychiatry,* 1944, **101,** 375–388.

45 | The School Psychologist

Paul Eiserer

The relationship of the profession of school psychology to child psychopathology as considered in this volume is significant but not inclusive of the spectrum of roles (or functions) that have come to characterize school psychology in action. Another way to state it is that insofar as the kinds of pathology described in this volume are found in the schools, the school psychologist is profoundly concerned but this involvement constitutes but one part of his commitment to the entire school population. Some of the problems described are rarely, if ever, found in the schools; others are found with some frequency. Some maladjustments are identified in early stages of development, while others are in advanced stages.

As a practical matter, the schools are interested in the educability rather than in the pathology of children, and in the main the responsibility for treatment and care of the psychiatrically disabled lies outside the domain of the schools. Severe disorders which develop in the preschool years may never come to the attention of the schools and are dealt with through other mo-

dalities. Disorders which originate or become more serious during years of school attendence do indeed suggest an involvement of the schools and of the school psychologist as one member of the mental-health team. Since he is a significant member of this team, we are, of course, interested in the roles which he plays and in his competence to fulfill them. It is also important to note, however, something of his other roles so that a balanced picture of his broader contribution to the mission of the schools can be appreciated.

It will be the goal of this chapter to set forth the history, present status, and future prospects of school psychology so that the reader may better appreciate what can be expected of school psychology as it relates to the subject matter of this manual.

HISTORICAL DEVELOPMENT

The evolution of psychological services in schools is a twentieth-century phenomenon. Developments in psychology and education which

1310

shaped the origins and continuing growth of school psychology are discussed in some detail in a recent publication (Wallin & Ferguson, 1967). A reading of this chapter reminds us that diverse and complex forces contributed to the present status and problems of school psychology. The emergence of psychology both as a science and as a profession and the changing character of the school as a social institution provide the intricately fashioned fabric within which school psychology must be viewed. Just as a perspective on *past* growth yields knowledge of current status and problems, so is it certain that the *present-day* character of psychology and education must be comprehended for solving present problems and forecasting future trends.

Although its historical roots have been traced to the beginning of the twentieth century, school psychology has emerged as a viable entity within psychology's many mansions and as a visible profession in the school community only within the past decade. One writer locates the first use of the term *school psychology* in the literature in the early 1920s. The appearance of a dozen books about school psychology within the past decade attests to a new sense of professional identity among psychologists employed in public schools, who in earlier times functioned very much as lonely entrepreneurs in the vast reaches of the public schools.

Many of the functions currently performed by school psychologists have been performed somewhere by someone since the turn of the century. It is not the purpose here to document the growth of school psychology from early efforts to diagnose learning disability to the complex responsibilities of the behavior scientist-at-large occupying himself with myriad problems in the growth and development of children and youth. Concepts of the past are always relative, but from the standpoint of a hardheaded historian, the development of school psychology is best viewed as a current event. Such a perspective has definite advantages. It can view controversy about origins, anxiety about identity or functions, concern for professional definition, visibility or self-protection as somewhat premature or even pointless. It can say to would-be historians or to overly self-conscious professionalism—stop trying to write history, make it!

If one were to ask the ordinary citizen, "What is a school psychologist?" the most probable answer would be, "I imagine that he is a psychologist who works in the schools." Such a response would achieve wide consensus among laymen and professionals alike. If one followed with the question, "What does he do?" the consensus would disappear, for layman and professional alike. The fact is that psychologists employed in school systems perform such a variety of functions that particular knowledge rather than general description is necessary to answer the question in a specified place at a particular time.

It has not always been so. There was a time when "the school psychologist is a psychometrician" was an accurate job description rather than a derogatory stereotype. But that day has passed, and we are faced by the almost impossible task of writing about school psychology as a profession when it is more particularistic and less general than it has ever been.

A sense of the magnitude of growth in the number of psychologists for the schools is conveyed in a recent study (Magary & Meacham, 1963). A survey of state departments of education indicated that there were 520 school psychologists by 1950; by 1960 the number was 2,724, an increase of more than 500 percent. This rapid increase is attributed to "financial support from the state level; training programs in the colleges and universities; special certification requirements and the designation of school psychology as a specific profession; and increasing demand for services in rural as well as the urban areas." Five years later (1968), a pamphlet issued by the Division of School

Psychologists of the American Psychological Association stated that there are "approximately 5,000. . .school psychologists." The source of information is not given.

One measure of the availability of psychologists in the schools is the ratio of pupils to psychologists. In a study of urban school systems (Mullen, 1967), it was found that the ratio varied in 1966 from 1:2,000 to 1:24,300, with the median at 1:9,000. This was contrasted with 1950 figures of 1:2,200 to 1:68,000, with the median at 1:18,500. In more affluent suburban schools it is not uncommon to find ratios of 1:1,000 or even 1:500. Although present estimates seem to indicate that more favorable ratios have been achieved during the past decade, simple conclusions cannot be drawn from such data alone. Types of services rendered, level of performance, availability of supporting personnel such as social workers, psychiatrists, and remedial personnel, among other factors, must be appraised to provide meaningful interpretation. Field studies of the effectiveness of psychological services simply are not available. Yet the demands of the schools for more school psychologists are greater than ever.

Since the ways in which psychology, through basic research and practical application, can actually serve the schools through direct employment of psychologists are really in early stages of exploration, it is not possible to visualize what an optimum pupil-psychologist ratio might be.

FACTORS INFLUENCING SCHOOL PSYCHOLOGY ROLES

No social institution exists in a vacuum. Educational historians and sociologists have amply documented the societal forces which shape and condition the school as a social institution. Thus the aims and means which characterize schools originate in past and current events outside the schools. It follows that in complex ways the same influences impinge upon the roles enacted by persons within the schools, namely, teachers, administrators, supervisors, and special-services personnel, including psychologists. From this general proposition we may proceed to identify some of the factors which determine whether schools have psychological services at all and, if they do, the particular form of such services in a given situation.

For purposes of analysis, the assumed determinants are grouped under three major categories: community factors outside the schools, factors within the school as a social system, and factors associated with school psychology itself as a "profession."

Community Factors

In a broad sense, the community determines what it expects the schools to accomplish. If the goals are limited in scope, the types of skills required to achieve them are also likely to be limited. If the goals are comprehensive and complex, it will be expected that a larger variety of skills and specialized personnel will be required to attain them. Thus, if the purposes are defined in terms of the three R's, it will be expected generally that teachers alone should be competent to achieve them. If purposes are more comprehensive—for example, if they include emotional, social, and moral as well as intellectual dimensions—it is more likely to be recognized that such ambitious aims will require that teachers have available supporting specialized personnel to assist in their attainment.

To move from the general to the specific, it is still widely believed that the local community determines educational goals in a significant sense. Although some writers have described this belief as, in part at least, a pervasive myth, the belief is maintained because of such practices as electing school board officials and voting on school budgets. Since we have no national board of education, no national educational bureaucracy, and no national system of surveillance of schools and since we have, indeed, approximately 25,000 school districts, we may infer that we have something less than a monolithic system of education.

It appears probable that the extent to which individuals and groups believe that they exercise direct influence on schools is dependent upon the size of the community. In large systems, such as are found in urban centers, the existence and type of psychological services are more likely to be determined by the official educational bureaucracy and the municipal government than by individual parent or citizen or smaller pressure groups within the community.

In smaller communities, such as encircle our metropolitan areas, the situation is much different. Parents do indeed exert influence, albeit less than they think they do. In such communities parents and small groups, through voting procedures and informal intervention, have a voice in the availability and type of psychological service. In middle- and upper-class suburban communities the "mental-health" attitudes of the community are reflected in the amount and type of psychology found in the school. In these communities of affluence and high educational attainment, we find a generally positive attitude toward psychology as a discipline which can contribute significantly to the achievement of the educational mission. This is true whether the psychologist's role is seen as removing obstacles to college entrance or as achieving the well-rounded individual development of pupils. The distribution of psychological services is quite similar to that for medical, psychiatric, and other mental-health services. Thus we see a cluster of intercorrelated variables of social class, education, and wealth associated with psychology in the schools.

Wherever found, psychology in the school is likely to have its mission determined to a significant degree by the educational mission, which, in turn, reflects community aims and beliefs about how to achieve them. If the school is organized chiefly around intellectual purposes, the psychologist is expected to contribute to them; if the school is expected to intervene directly in emotional or social dysfunctions in pupils, the psychologist will be expected to be a significant participant.

This brief statement hardly does justice to the complex and interactive nature of community impingement upon schools; it is merely suggestive of the reality that schools and their practices cannot be understood by limiting our analysis to factors inside the schools or to the entrepreneurial aspirations of a professional group such as school psychologists.

Before leaving the larger community, one should take note of the impact of one special institution upon school psychology practice, namely, state government. The major influence to be noted here is the legislation affecting special education in the schools. In many states the aspirations of powerful groups of parents have been translated into legislative mandates requiring schools to classify and provide education for particular groups of atypical children such as the mentally retarded or the neurologically impaired. Such legislation either requires or creates a role for school psychology in the diagnosis, classification, placement, and education of atypical children. By providing matching funds to local districts, state governments have made psychological services more readily available in communities which previously would not initiate action in these areas. Thus a form of direct state intervention has created positions in schools and often paved the way for a wider display of psychological knowledge and skill than intended in the original legislation.

Factors within the School System

Factors within schools probably exert a more important influence upon *function* than upon *decisions* to employ psychologists in the first place. In a hierarchical system, the attitudes of persons occupying positions of power carry considerable weight throughout the system. The school superintendent and principals of schools would be expected to be in strategic position to influence the operational role of the school psychologist. How each of these leaders translates educational aims into operational roles will affect what a psychologist can or cannot do. Even within a single school system, one can observe differences among schools in relation to the beliefs and attitudes of particular administrators.

One principal who "runs a tight ship" may insist on close supervision of the psychologist's activities within his school, whereas another might give a "free hand" within broadly defined general guidelines. A principal who is insecure in his relationships with teachers or parents may be oversensitive about permitting a psychologist to function independently within his school. He may wish all referrals to be channeled through his office and may require continuous clearance of what the psychologist is doing. Another principal may trust the professional judgment of the psychologist to keep him informed of significant issues as they develop. Certainly these different attitudes will affect the work of the psychologist.

Since teachers are on the "firing line" with pupils, their attitudes are critical. If they are acceptant of the psychologist, are fully informed of his competence and style, and have experienced success in the past, they will make better use of his services and be comfortable in working with him. If they feel threatened by his presence, have had unfavorable past experiences with psychologists, or suspect that he may be involved in decisions that might negatively affect their personal status, they will avoid or be on guard against the type of involvement that produces good results for pupils.

The psychologist's role is related to the functions carried out by other special-services personnel. Guidance counselors, reading and speech specialists, psychiatric consultants, social workers, even the school nurse offer specialized assistance to achieve the overall mission of the school. All too often, jurisdictional disputes or power struggles arise among these personnel because of lack of explicit specifications of roles or because the persons occupying the roles seek to operate beyond the definitions. Since definitions are always abstractions, there is room for idiosyncratic interpretation and potential role conflict.

It is of the very nature of these specialties that they overlap in aspiration, training, and function, making it necessary to work out agreements in concrete situations. The conflict alluded to above need not be destructive; indeed, it may pose a creative opportunity to define roles in realistic and functional ways to serve the particular school, rather than by a priori standards.

The roles of superintendent, principal, and teacher have achieved such standardization that they may seem interchangeable from system to sysyem. In the main, this is a consequence of historical development. Among specialists, speech and reading personnel have fairly clear roles, and the adjectives suggest how they are circumscribed. However, psychologists and guidance personnel, especially as they project broad and amorphous concepts of their potential roles, face the necessity and creative opportunity to accommodate their roles, one to another, on a functional rather than predetermined basis. Some school psychologists seem overly distressed by the great variety of expectations of them and long for a more clearly delineated specification of role. Others see such possibility as premature if not inimical to professional functioning.

School Psychology as a Profession

Until recently, school psychologists have been single entrepreneurs, rarely organizing for collective action. Only in the past two decades has school psychology become identified as a legitimate specialty within psychology or education. Once the term pointed to a psychologist who happened to be employed in a school; now the term refers to a *subdiscipline,* or type of "applied psychology" within the schools.

School psychologists are more self-conscious about their identity than ever before. Concern for higher and more standardized certification requirements, accreditation of training programs, even ABPP diplomate status attest to this awareness. The development of national, state, and local associations of school psychologists is further evidence. Yet these developments have occurred within a period of maximum fluidity in role definition and of some anxiety about what the profession stands for. Indeed "school" psychology does not stand for a substantive area within psychology. At best, it defines where certain psychologists work. The same may be said for industrial or "military" psychology.

One view is that the psychologist who works within the schools draws upon the knowledge and skills available to him from substantive fields to make applications relevant to the problems to which psychologists can contribute solutions. Thus he draws upon clinical, educational, developmental, social, and measurement psychology to assist him in his endeavors. Or, to put it another way, he levies upon knowledge in learning, perception, motivation, group processes, measurement, diagnosis, behavior modification, and social change to deal with problems considered important to the educational mission.

If the above statement is valid, it has many implications for standards of training and certification. Above all, it has substantial relevance to the ways in which the psychologist himself defines his professional identity in the face of change and flexibility. The main point here is to highlight the freedom, with its attendant anxiety, available to the psychologist to play a creative role in serving the schools. Within the limits of his competence and the expectations existing within the social context of his position, he can experiment, in part at least, with new ways of using psychological knowledge and skills in the solution of educational problems. Although ambiguity means anxiety for some, it means opportunity for others. Psychologists, like most people, more clearly see the limitations upon their freedom than the opportunities which freedom presents. While there may be less freedom than idealists assume, there is also more freedom than realists contend. This is a way of saying that the chance for a school psychologist to define his professional role is usually greater than he imagines.

PREPARATION OF SCHOOL PSYCHOLOGISTS

A preconference survey conducted for the Thayer Conference of 1954 (Cutts, 1955) disclosed very limited opportunities for training in school psychology. Obviously, opportunities for preparation in psychology and education for employment in the schools had been available, but not on a systematic, formal basis. Of eighteen institutions providing fairly complete information for the survey, only five reported formal programs leading to the doctorate.

Ten years later another survey (Bardon, 1964) yielded a report that seventy-nine institutions were offering training programs. The development and expansion of training programs are in so fluid a state that statements of the number of programs must be viewed with caution. In the professional literature one finds estimates that vary between seventy-five and ninety programs. In any event, the figures suffice to support the view that training in this field has experienced the greatest current growth of any area of psychology. Of the seventy-nine institutions, forty-nine offered the doctorate and thirty granted a subdoctoral degree only. In an informal survey by the writer in 1965, it was found that nineteen programs were in effect prior to 1956. Between 1956 and 1960, twenty-three programs were established; during the years 1961 to 1965, thirty-one additional programs were started. Thus fifty-four, or 74 percent, of current programs were established within a ten-year period.

It is not surprising that a field in which training programs have developed so rapidly would be faced with myriad problems. Among these problems are levels of training, curricula, financial support, admission criteria, intrauniversity relationships. A brief discussion of each of these issues will illustrate the differing viewpoints which are inevitable in this phase of development. Since the Thayer Conference represented the first national appraisal of the functions, qualifications, and training of school psychologists, it now serves as a convenient landmark for viewing developments since 1954.

Levels of Training

The level of training appropriate for effective functioning in the schools has been, is now, and will continue to be a matter of some controversy. Although reliable figures are hard to come by, it is estimated that about 25 percent of school psychologists held the doctorate fifteen years ago, and in all probability the same pertains today. Although there has been a substantial increase in institutions offering doctoral-level training, their output has not been substantial. Furthermore, there has probably been a proportionate increase of subdoctorally trained psychologists entering the field.

Supply and demand operate as significant factors in maintaining the above situation. The demands of the schools for psychological services accompanied by attractive salaries and improved employment conditions appeal to many persons to whom the doctorate seems too far away or the requirements too demanding. Another damping effect is probably the ratio of 3:1 of women over men in the profession. Few fields of psychology offer as appealing an opportunity to combine professional and personal aspirations for women as school psychology. Of great importance also has been the lack of financial subsidy for doctoral study in this field. It will be considered in greater detail below.

Without going into details surrounding the issue of training levels, a consensus has been developing among psychologists, at least, that there is need and legitimacy for preparing psychologists in two-year and four-year (doctorate) programs if the demands of schools are to be met. This view reflects an upward thrust from the prevailing condition ten years ago, when a one-year (master's) program was the typical subdoctoral level of preparation. This upgrading is also evident in changes in state certification requirements.

A corollary problem has to do with coordinating level of preparation with the rising expectations of schools that psychologists assume greater and more complex responsibilities. In general, psychologists with greater preparation will gravitate toward positions of greater responsibility and remuneration. Under present circumstances it is essential to assume that psychologists with subdoctoral preparation are adequately trained to function in significant and meaningful ways in the schools. Certification procedures provide one way to ensure effective preparation in a two-level system that is both meaningful to participants and reasonably enforceable.

Programs of Study

Earlier in this essay the point was emphasized that many models of psychological service now exist and will continue to do so because of developments both in psychology and in education. It makes sense to argue that many models of training are also necessary. Analysis of presently formulated programs, particularly at the doctoral level, makes clear many similarities in requirements as well as the differences which distinguish one program from another. The Education and

Training Board of the APA was authorized in 1967 to proceed with the accreditation of training programs in school psychology. Success with such efforts of the APA in clinical and counseling psychology provided the background for the movement in this direction. It is notable that this step was taken even though no single state requires doctoral preparation as the only certification level for school psychologists. The accreditation program at present is limited to doctoral programs only.

There is little doubt that school psychologists collectively are assuming greater responsibility than ever before for defining programs of training, for ensuring quality, and for upgrading the competences to be made available to the schools generally.

Financial Support

One of the most serious deterrents to the production of highly qualified psychologists for the schools has been the meagerness of financial support for training. Despite traditional insistence on local autonomy and state responsibility for education, the only meaningful financial support for programs has come from the federal government. In 1964 only twelve universities reported that U.S. Public Health Service (National Institute of Mental Health) stipends were available, and seven reported stipends from the U.S. Office of Education. In the main, financial subsidy has been available only for doctoral study.

States have been particularly delinquent in meeting their responsibilities. Many states have responded to needs in special education by legislation, mandating that schools provide specialized services, without corresponding efforts to make the necessary personnel available. In view of competition with more heavily subsidized graduate study programs in psychology and other disciplines, it appears improbable that the supply of doctorally trained school psychologists will increase substantially in the immediate future.

Admission Criteria

An issue of considerable controversy in the past has been whether teaching experience should be a prerequisite for the school psychologist. Fifteen years ago participants in the Thayer Conference divided about equally, one-half in favor and the other half against. Participants, who themselves had backgrounds in education, favored the requirement; those with other backgrounds believed the requirement to be restrictive. Since 1954 teaching experience has been gradually relinquished as a prerequisite for admission, as well as in state certification codes. This change does not minimize the desirability of requiring that school psychologists have a thorough familiarity both with schools generally and with the classroom and teaching particularly. It does suggest that the desired competence can be acquired by other means, notably through fieldwork and internship experience. Although this assumption has not been tested systematically, informal evidence supports the view that this procedure has validity, especially for doctoral study.

Universities vary widely in the amount of previous preparation in psychology required for admission to programs of study—from none to undergraduate major. Since many programs require competence both in psychology and in education, graduate study can be geared to individual needs: for a student with substantial previous work in psychology, more work in education is feasible; for students with preparation in education, more graduate work in psychology can be provided.

Intrauniversity Relationships

Of the seventy-nine training programs reviewed in 1964, thirty-seven were located in departments of psychology, thirty were in departments or schools of education, and twelve were administered by joint committees composed of representatives from departments of psychology and education. Whether there are systematic differences in type or quality of curricula resulting from the location of responsibility for training has not been determined. The point is raised here because of persistent problems alleged to occur in academic versus professional areas in training programs in clinical and counseling psychology.

Substance of Training Programs

The content of training programs is a consequence of many factors: the particular requirements of state certification programs, the views of faculty responsible for programs in universities, and the indirect influences of schools as employers and of organizations of school psychologists. State certification programs probably exert strongest influence on programs aimed specifically at meeting state requirements on minimum levels. This influence is seen in course requirements rather than in level of functional competence achieved since the university alone determines quality of performance during training. In the degree that university programs exceed state requirements, the faculty of the institution exerts major influence over that part of the program which exceeds state stipulations.

Some states have instituted *program certification* with selected universities. This means that since the program is approved, the university gains flexibility in achieving program goals and the student can be certified upon completion of the program. This arrangement is especially advantageous for doctoral programs which include a longer period of preparation; such programs can be freer in experimentation with training designs.

Reference has previously been made to two levels of training for school psychologists: two-year and four-year (doctorate) programs. Although detailed comparisons of the content of training at different institutions have not been made, available material permits some useful comments.

The major differences between two- and four-year programs are that the latter usually include an academic one-year internship in a school system, intensive training in research culminating in the doctoral dissertation, and more extended practicum experience in diagnosis and remedial work. Undoubtedly there are also other outcomes from the longer period of training, such as greater theoretical sophistication in psychology and more skill in integrating the earlier components of training. It might be expected, then, that the doctorally trained person can, on job entry, perform a wider variety of roles in the schools and perform them at a higher level of expertness. It seems probable also that persons trained at this level will eventually assume greater supervisory and administrative responsibilities in special-service functions in the schools. Experience confirms these expectations.

Although there may be differences in some institutions, the first two years of the doctoral program and the two-year terminal program are quite similar in program content. Personality, measurement, development, learning, social, and educational psychology are common foundational courses to provide a broad-based understanding of psychological theory and of the methods of inquiry used by psychologists in studying a wide range of behavioral phenomena.

Skill attainment in the administration and interpretation of psychological and educational tests—individual and group—is expected. In practicum courses, these skills are put to work under close supervision to ensure a reasonable degree of independence in dealing with actual problems. Obviously, not all tests can be studied intensively, but a fair sampling is made on the assumption that the student will acquire a facility which will be transferable to other tests as he acquires further experience.

In addition, courses in remedial methods appropriate to the schools, statistics, behavior deviations, and special education are characteristic. Most programs require work in such educational areas as history, curriculum, administration, teaching methods, and guidance. For the student terminating his study at the end of two years, a shorter (than one year) form of internship is required.

As programs have evolved over the past decade, they have reflected more commonality than difference, although there remains much diversity in particular courses and program styles.

FUNCTIONS OF THE SCHOOL PSYCHOLOGIST

Other chapters in this book describe in great detail the diagnostic and treatment methods relevant to psychopathological phenomena in children. Hence, no attempt is made here to cover the same ground. Rather it is my purpose to consider within the context of the school the functions of the school psychologist in these areas in a way that will be complementary to the previous discussions since the school psychologist's role in dealing with pathological problems is but one facet of his total diagnostic and therapeutic activity. The contemporary school psychologist is concerned with problems and issues that go far beyond those considered in this manual.

The Diagnostic Function

No function of psychology in the schools is more honored by time or more widely practiced than diagnosis. Although the word literally means to "know between" and generally means "scientific discrimination of any kind," it evokes aversive associations for many educators and psychologists because of its traditional use in "diagnosing disease." Some writers prefer to use such terms as *assessment*, *evaluation*, or *appraisal*, even though they are not synonyms for *diagnosis*. Scientific discriminations are indeed what are sought when requests for diagnosis are made.

When a teacher refers a child because of academic difficulty or disturbance in the classroom, the psychologist assumes a diagnostic stance, that is, he first seeks to achieve a clear definition of the problem by differentiating the real problem from presumed, or "non," problems and then seeks to differentiate the probable factors contributing to the problem. The kinds of observations made, the tests used, and subsequent analyses of data obtained should illuminate the problem and lead to proposals for action. The issue is the relevance of his concepts and instruments to the problem, not whether he is clinically or educationally oriented.

The goal of diagnostic activity in the schools is to achieve a functional analysis of educational possibilities. Classification is considered useful only to enhance learning. Classification according to psychiatric criteria is not the aim unless there are demonstrable educational implications. Thus pupils of different diagnostic classifications according to psychiatric criteria may be placed together if educational requirements are similar and achievable under school conditions.

Frequently, the diagnostic efforts performed outside the school by persons with different intent may have to be supplemented in order to achieve the kind of analysis in which the tasks of the school may become evident. The point is not so much who is correct as that different purposes in making diagnoses can lead to different results.

It may be useful to refer briefly to some of the more common problems encountered by the school psychologist. Perhaps the most frequent type of problem detected by teachers reflects some learning difficulty of the child. This is understandable given the school's preoccupation with cognitive learning and the teacher's concern that each child demonstrate reasonable progress. Although learning difficulties may be the outer form of more profound inner disturbance, it is sufficient for referral purposes that teachers be attuned to the varied manifestations of learning problems. The first signs may be evident in the child's deviation from expected group norms or in decrements from his own past performance. The referral may lead to intellectual remediation or to a search for underlying emotional or organic factors.

Behavior disturbances in the classroom are another common cause for referral. Disruptions of the usual classroom procedures which are intense or persist over a period of time surely warrant further investigation. In selected instances classroom disturbances may merely reveal a teacher's inability to handle certain kinds of disciplinary problems. If so, work with her may soon resolve them. In most instances work with the child by the psychologist is called for.

Teachers have frequently been maligned for failure to detect the need of the child who is shy or overly conforming to classroom routines as a way of adapting to inner conflicts. The classic Wickman study of forty years ago formed the basis for much of this criticism. Subsequent studies have, however, shown teachers to be able to note signs of potential difficulty in a wide range of manifest behaviors, including those of outward placidity. This change is due in part to the more recent mental-health education of teachers, on both a preservice and an in-service basis.

Many pupils of normal social and emotional adjustment encounter learning difficulties at certain stages of their academic careers. Not all problems are personality problems in the narrow use of the term. Specific learning disabilities may prevent an otherwise normally functioning child from realizing his full learning potential. The learning potential of an entire class may be depressed because of poor teaching or inappropriate curricula. Conflict within the staff of a school may be reflected in classroom behavior. Such problems require diagnosis even though individual psychopathology is not at issue. Other concepts and certainly different diagnostic techniques are required to develop a basis for helpful intervention.

In addition, the school psychologist is asked to serve the entire pupil population by working toward optimum conditions for learning and personality development. Again, a diagnostic stance is called for to assess current status in the school population, the introduction of innovative practices, and their subsequent evaluation. Concepts and skills may be required from developmental and social psychology to grapple with these issues.

Of interest here is the growing variety of problems now being presented to the psychologist in the schools. Whereas in an earlier period most of the problems referred for diagnosis consisted of the difficulties of individual pupils as perceived in the classroom, the variety of other problems has greatly increased. A few of these problems are:

Problems in classroom management
Morale of staff in a school
Needs of teachers for better knowledge about child growth and development
Appropriateness of curricula for particular groups of children
Effectiveness of given programs of instruction and remediation
Citizen criticism of the school or of particular practices

This list does not exhaust the possibilities of problems in the schools which are increasingly being brought to the attention of the school psychologist. The issue here is not what kind of psychologist the school psychologist may be but whether he can bring appropriate knowledge and skill to bear upon the problem. It is suggested that all the problems listed above require diagnosis in the same sense that the problems of individual pupils do. The issue is the same: the problem(s) must be clearly delineated and relevant data collected for making scientific discriminations among contributing factors. Because clinical psychologists have not been prepared to deal with these kinds of problems, they have been perceived as outdated. To emphasize the point—clinical knowledge, concepts, and tests are not outmoded; it is just that many clinical psychologists are ill-equipped to cope with these problems. Clinical knowledge and skill might be relevant to an analysis of any of the problems stated above.

If interventions by the school in any significant way do not result from a diagnosis, it becomes pretty clear that other agencies and programs are needed for the child. The matter of exclusion from school is desirably a highly pragmatic affair, since a whole host of complex factors should be evaluated before concluding that schools are not capable of an important contribution.

Remedial Functions

The school psychologist's role in the remedial area may be viewed in several dimensions: direct participation, coordination, and consultation.

Direct participation refers to the psychologist's rendering of direct counseling or therapeutic services to clients through such modalities as individual or group counseling and play therapy. Although the issue of psychotherapy in the schools has been a bone of contention for some years, it is the author's view that it is a false issue. It is generally agreed that long-term, intensive counseling is inappropriate as a school function. But the application of psychodynamic or behaviorally oriented principles as intervention techniques can hardly be proscribed if psychology is to contribute to effective school learning and pupil development.

The real issues have to do with available time, qualifications of personnel, and decisions as to whether the school or some extraschool agency is the better locus of intervention. So long as intervention or remedial techniques are equated with "medical" treatment and it is misleading or illogical to do so, controversy will continue.

The issues are really, after satisfactory diagnostic evaluation is at hand, what should be done, who shall do it, and in what place. Confronting these issues on a pragmatic basis in a particular place should lead to better solutions than generalizations about functions or professional prerogatives.

At best, the school psychologist in most situations today will devote a rather small portion of his time in rendering direct remedial services to pupils. The greater portion of the school psychologist's time in the remedial role is allocated to the *coordinating function*. This includes a significant part in planning the strategies of intervention required in the individual case. Included may be referral processes outside the school, coordination of school personnel, curriculum adjustments, and ensuring intercommunication among those involved in the case. Where outside-the-school persons or agencies are involved, he may serve as the liaison person in the school. Evaluation of progress may fall to him. He may play a leading part in case conferences whenever they are convened throughout the process.

This function requires an overall perspective of the pupils' educational and personality needs as diagnosed, an intimate knowledge of therapeutic resources available, an ability to mobilize these resources at focal points of maximum impact, sensitivity in relating cooperating personnel one to another, and persistence in monitoring the component parts of the overall strategy.

The *consultative function* in therapeutics refers to the fact that the psychologist frequently seeks to achieve remedial results by working through other personnel. In discharging his role in this respect, he must know the talents and capabilities of others so that they can be maximally matched to pupil needs. He may perform supervisory functions, in that continuous review of techniques and process are integral aspects directing the intervention through others. His prescriptions must be tailored to the capacities and sensitivities of the proxy. He may have to lower his aspiration in one instance and raise it in another; realism and adaptability of strategy are essential.

Another view of consultation is feasible, of course. The direction of the planned change may be placed entirely in the hands of a teacher. In such an instance, the school psychologist stands ready to be called upon for assistance in thinking through alternatives, offering suggestions, evaluating consequences. The important point is that the responsibility lies elsewhere and the school psychologist constitutes an available source of support, information, and advice as needed.

Education

The educational goal of the school psychologist in relation to psychopathology includes informal and systematic efforts to inform and guide school personnel toward a better understanding of behavior deviations as manifest in school and of possibilities for identification, remediation, and prevention of such deviations.

Opportunities for informal education include consultation, case conferences, and perhaps the daily operation of special-services personnel as they assist teachers and administrators in the achievement of their instructional mission. Some of the most significant learning moments occur in the context of dealing with specific problems when the purpose is not only solution of the immediate problem but acquisition of insights of a more enduring and generalizable character. Such opportunities are not so much planned as seized upon as they occur within normal operations.

Systematic efforts to educate may take the form of courses, conferences, seminars, and institutes with relevant constituencies. Bulletins, reading lists, interpretive papers, and other written media may also be used. These efforts are distinguished from university courses by their ad hoc character, their immediacy of interest and relevance to "real" problems in the schools. The school psychologist directly and by bringing in specialists from outside the school can make an important contribution in updating knowledge and increasing skill whenever needed.

Research

Historically, research has not been a major function of school psychologists despite much rhetoric about its desirability. However, in very recent times and especially for those trained at the doctoral level, greater emphasis has been made that there should be an increasing allocation of the school psychologist's time and energy to research. Many writers view the schools as a vast ready-made "laboratory," within which a myriad of problems about growth and development can be most fruitfully studied. Some of the possibilities have been set forth in detail in a recent publication (Itkin, 1967).

In relation to the substance of this book, it seems apparent that many issues can best be examined within the framework of the schools: longitudinal studies of a wide range of phenomena, prediction studies, such as forecasting delinquency or dropout, interactions of intellectual function with emotional disturbance, efficacy of detection methods, remedial methods in a complex social system, and many others. Such studies can hardly be essayed by one individual, but cooperative teams involving school, university, and community personnel, competent and well financed, can begin to make inroads on previously intractable problems. Sophisticated research in the schools will not become a reality until more school psychologists with high-level research training become available and school personnel generally create a climate favorable to investigation and the discovery of new knowledge.

In addition to the discovery of fundamental and applied knowledge, a significant research endeavor lies in the application in the schools of knowledge obtained elsewhere. Knowledge obtained in university laboratories or in other community agencies and contexts can be tested in the schools through skillful leadership by the school psychologist. The so-called "lag" between discovery and application has been noted for a long time. While resistance to change, inertia, and lack of recognition of relevance are often adduced as reasons for the lag, it may well be that the most crucial problem lies in the fact that knowledge discovered in one context may have "untested" applicability to other situations. Furthermore, circumscribed studies with arbitrary controls may simply be irrelevant or trivial in contrast to the ongoing problems of a functioning social institution. Thus the schools as a context both for discovery and for field testing become indeed an untapped reservoir for learning more about the superior and maladaptive functioning of children and youth.

Prevention of Maladjustment in the Schools

One of the persistent themes in the literature about mental health and education during the past fifty years has been the belief that adult pathology can be prevented or at least substantially reduced in frequency or severity through mental-health programs, practices, and techniques in the schools. One of the volumes of the Joint Commission is devoted to this possibility (Allinsmith & Goethals, 1962). It can be said without fear of contradiction that there is no reliable evidence that these expectations have been realized. An avalanche of books and articles, many of them hortatory and rhetorical, attest to the lively interest of mental-health professionals, educators, and laymen in furthering these objectives. A great variety of programs in the schools have come and gone, most of them localized and fragmentary. Well intentioned

as many of these efforts were, they were bound to fail in part because of the incredible naïveté of the proponents. The messianic ardor of many of the advocates of "prevention of mental illness through education" lacked both a sound conceptual basis and a sound methodological basis for programming. One of the most perceptive observers and participants in the mental-health movement, George S. Stevenson (1944), illuminated these issues a quarter of a century ago, and his analysis remains completely relevant today.

Stevenson pointed out that prevention as a concept was global and undifferentiated, thus an inadequate conceptual basis for sound planning. His analysis of different kinds of "prevention" made clear that hopes for the elimination of mental illness were utopian in the light of existing knowledge of causation. His argument remains valid today. However, Stevenson was strongly in favor of procedures which have since come to be labeled *secondary* or *tertiary* prevention, and it is in these roles that the contemporary school psychologist can make a significant contribution.

All those measures which permit early identification of disorders, incipient or manifest, are in the proper direction. Enumeration and discussion of many of these measures have been set forth by Allinsmith and Goethals (1962).

The Promotion of Healthy Development

In viewing the problem of prevention through education, many recent writers have approached it from another standpoint. Instead of searching for "causes" of pathology, the argument runs along the following lines: What is known from behavioral science about the conditions and requirements for human development, for the acquisition of diversified competence, for enhancing the development of human potential that is relevant to the schools? To put the question in these terms is to bring educational and mental-health aims into intimate dialogue, for on this plane educational philosophy might well include "mental-health objectives." It may turn out to be the "sound mind in a sound body" axiom of ancient vintage.

The point to be stressed here is that we should put to work whatever knowledge we now have from all the sciences of man. This is a large order, but it deserves the best that we can do. The advantage of this framework is that it may lay divisive arguments to rest and focus on the task at hand. For example, the old question as to whether the schools should attend to cognitive or emotional development simply becomes irrelevant and trivial. As Sanford (1966) so brilliantly illustrates, educators must focus on human development in all of its dimensions.

If the foregoing view has substance, it suggests that the school psychologist might well move toward a role as a behavioral scientist-strategist in the schools. In this sense his client is the school system as well as the constituent groups and individuals. This does not place him in a superordinate role in the system, but it does suggest that in whatever capacity he functions, he must attend to systemwide phenomena as well as the functions of growing persons. It does not suggest that most of today's school psychologists can effectively perform this function, but it does argue that psychologists who function in schools in the future may be expected to function differently than in the past.

PROSPECTS

It has been stated previously that models of psychological practice and application are conditioned by many factors inside and outside of the schools. In a broad sense, developments within psychology as a science and profession determine the kinds of knowledge and skill which are potentially available for assisting educators to achieve the educational mission. It is easy to see historically how the development of knowledge about individual differences, with the associated growth of tests and measurements, made available valuable knowledge and tools for furthering educational purpose.

Not all developments within psychology, however, have so immediate and direct a relevance to education. It is not so readily apparent how advances in experimental methodology, characteristic of university laboratories, might be relevant. Yet studies of operant conditioning, to take a current example of great interest, have had profound impact on recent developments in programmed instruction and educational technology in its widest sense. At any one point in time, psychologists will differ widely in their judgments of those aspects of psychology which have greatest salience for education. It may well be that some current studies of brain functioning may eventually have more impact on schools than any presently more popular field such as tests, learning, or motivation. The task at any one time is to assess the priority of existing specialties for maximizing application to education.

The other broad facet to be considered relates to the way in which educational aims are defined. What schools seek to accomplish and the problems encountered in such a quest set the stage for assistance from the science and profession of psychology. The traditional view has been that the community sets educational purpose and psychology is called upon to help achieve it. If classification of pupils for learning is desired, certain areas of psychology seem best equipped to contribute toward that end. If the school includes mental-health objectives within its purpose, other specialties within psychology are summoned to assist. So it goes. As one views the history of education in this century, one gets a strong sense of the interplay of the two forces alluded to above. Since both psychology and education are constantly changing and will continue to do so, no model of psychological service to schools should be viewed as permanent.

The kinds of controversy found in the literature today about "clinical" versus "educational" models seem pointless when the issues are viewed in broad context. The conflict arises partly because models are contrived outside the schools and assumed to be readily grafted upon the schools. Models of "learning" have proved just as difficult to apply in classrooms as models of "therapy." Whether educational or clinical psychology, as presently defined, has more to contribute to education cannot be settled by a prior assumption or argument. The issue will be determined by demonstrated relevance to educational purpose, and this determination cannot be preempted by psychology alone.

This is not to say that psychologists will have no voice in setting educational goals as well as in providing means for their attainment. Psychology has much to offer, and the public, as well as individual psychologists, has often asked for more than psychology can deliver. Today psychology rides high in public esteem and is greatly tempted to offer unverified assertions and untested technologies to eager consumers.

One of the great values of psychological services in education is their responsiveness to needs in particular situations. This is attested both by historical development and by diversity of current functions. Magary (1967) has documented the many orientations and the special pleading of writers in the field. The accuracy of his delineation of the present state of affairs makes clear that functional and operational diversity as well as theoretical multidimensionality are the order of the day.

It becomes equally clear that the stance of school psychology vis-à-vis the psychopathology of children cannot be described in unequivocal terms. Although it seems evident that school psychologists can hardly ignore the existence of severe disturbances in school-age children, approaches to dealing with them will vary widely. In one instance the psychologist will employ the techniques described elsewhere in this volume to diagnose difficulties and institute remedial or referral services. While this practice is widespread it may change in several respects. Schools employing several psychologists may move toward specialization; that is, some well-trained clinical specialists may deal with problems of emotional majadjustment, while other psychologists may concentrate on educational or developmental issues of wider scope. On the other hand, the growth of community services such as the mental-health center may make it expedient for schools to purchase the required diagnostic services from outside the system while psychologists in the schools address themselves to other problems.

If school psychology is indeed a profession, it may evolve in the direction of the medical profession with respect to strategy in deployment of resources. Basically, a "general practitioner" will be the front-line professional, with referral to specialists to deal more intensively with particular problems. By present categories, for example, educational, clinical, developmental, and social psychologists may be available to deal with particular problems in greater depth than a generalist can do. In addition, the multi-level concept of psychological functions may suggest the evolution of "technician" levels, so that lower-level functions can be performed by less than professionally trained psychologists. Overall strategy and integration would be provided by top-level personnel.

To the writer, present contentions that the school psychologist should be a clinician or an educational learning specialist or a research specialist are misleading. Indeed, all the services implied by these terms are needed to achieve the school's mission. It seems unlikely on the basis of developments within both education and psychology that the generalist can embrace the scope and intensity of competence required. It is also restrictive to limit a specialist to particular services such as diagnosis, remediation, consultation, or research when all these emphases are needed in the schools. No institution in our culture demands so much or is entitled to so much. What is needed is not special pleading for one function or another but an overall strategy that will optimally serve the schools.

This view disputes much writing in the field which argues the merits of particular formulations aimed at defining a *school psychologist*. While each view has its own merits, each falls short of an inclusive conception as to how the now highly developed and differentiated science and profession of psychology can serve education, with its pluralistic and differentiated aims. This line of thought suggests that the "school" in *school psychologist* is out of date if the search is for a generic school psychologist. Teams of psychologists should be developed to serve schools which are organized in units large enough to support them. Thus both scope and specialization now characteristic of psychology can be achieved in the service of education.

REFERENCES

Allinsmith, W., & Goethals, G. W. *The role of the schools in mental health.* New York: Basic Books, 1962.

Bardon, J. I. Problems and issues in school psychology—1964. *Journal of School Psychology,* 1964, **3**(2), 1–42.

Cutts, N. E. (Ed.) *School psychologists at mid-century.* Washington: American Psychological Association, 1955.

Eiserer, P. E. *The school psychologist.* Washington: Center for Applied Research in Education, 1963.

Gottsegen, M. G., & Gottsegen, G. B. (Eds.) *Professional school psychology.* New York: Grune & Stratton, 1960 (Vol. 1), 1963 (Vol. 2).

Gray, S. W. *The psychologist in the schools.* New York: Holt, 1963.

Itkin, W. The school psychologist's role in research. In J. F. Magary (Ed.), *School psychological services.* Englewood Cliffs, N.J.: Prentice-Hall, 1967. Pp. 590–616.

Magary, J. F. (Ed.) *School psychological services.* Englewood Cliffs, N.J.: Prentice-Hall, 1967.

Magary, J. F., & Meacham, M. L. The growth of school psychology in the last decade. *Journal of School Pyschology,* 1963, **1,** 5–13.

Mullen, F. A. The role of the school psychologist in the urban school system. In J. F. Magary (Ed.) *School psychological services.* Englewood Cliffs, N.J.: Prentice-Hall, 1967. Pp. 30–67.

Reger, R. *School psychology.* Springfield, Ill.: Charles C Thomas, 1965.

Sanford, N. *Self and society.* New York: Atherton, 1966.

Stevenson, G. S. The prevention of personality disorders. In J. Mcv. Hunt (Ed.), *Personality and the behavior disorders.* Vol. 2. New York: Ronald, 1944. Pp. 1164–1191.

Valett, R. E. *The practice of school psychology.* New York: Wiley, 1963.

Wallin, J. E. W., & Ferguson, D.G. The development of school psychological services. In J. F. Magary (Ed.), *School psychological services.* Englewood Cliffs, N.J.: Prentice-Hall, 1967. Pp. 1–29.

White, M. A., & Harris, M. W. *The school psychologist.* New York: Harper, 1961.

46 | The Guidance Worker

Daisy K. Shaw

The term *guidance worker* covers a broad spectrum of occupations in the fields of education and the social sciences. Just as the term *health worker* may be applied to a variety of medical specialties, ranging from senior clinical professor to hospital attendant, the designation of *guidance worker* may include professionals representing a number of distinct though interrelated disciplines as well as auxiliary personnel and paraprofessionals.

In recent years, the need for coordination among the various services in the field of mental health and the growing support for an interdisciplinary approach have led to the development of the *pupil personnel* concept. The teamwork inherent in this concept has served to reduce overlapping in services to children and has also enhanced the contribution of each discipline involved.

While there is some variation in the composition of the pupil personnel team from one setting to another, the following titles are listed in *Certification Requirements for School Pupil Personnel Workers,* published in 1967 by the U.S. Department of Health, Education and Welfare:

A. School Counselors
B. School Psychologists, School Psychometrists, and School Psychological Examiners
C. School Social Workers, School Medical Personnel, and School Attendance Personnel

It is interesting to note that this bulletin is a retitling of the 1963 edition of *Guidance Workers Certification Requirements.* The explanation given in the Foreword by Nolan Estes, associate commissioner for elementary and secondary education, is: "Since guidance is considered in many areas today to be one of the pupil personnel services and the counselor, thus, one of the pupil personnel workers, the change in title appeared to be in accord with current thinking in the profession."

Most guidance workers function in the school setting, and there is a substantial body of opinion which holds that the teacher is the school's basic guidance worker since he has the closest and most continuing relationship with his pupils. There is general agreement, however, that the distinctive professional in the field of guidance is the *school counselor,* who works closely with other pupil personnel specialists in supplying supportive services to the teacher. School administrators, especially the principal, vice-principal, and dean, also exert a profound influence on the emotional and social climate of the school. "Paraprofessionals," who may also be identified as *school aides, auxiliary assistants, guidance aides, or family assistants,* have recently joined the educational scene. Even the school secretary and the custodian have roles to play in carrying out the school's guidance policies.

What is guidance? It has been defined as a point of view, a process, and a group of services. It has its philosophical roots in our fundamental concepts of democracy and equal opportunity and in our belief in the integrity and uniqueness of the individual. Guidance services exist primarily for the child, to aid him in the process of self-understanding and self-actualization. In this context, guidance is understood as an essential ingredient in the education of *all* children, pursuing objectives that are both preventive and therapeutic.

BRIEF HISTORY OF THE GUIDANCE MOVEMENT

Most authorities on the history of the guidance movement agree that formal counseling was introduced in 1908, when Frank Parsons established the first "vocational bureau" in Boston. His purpose was to assist young men in making vocational choices based upon their occupational aptitudes and interests. As the vocational guidance movement expanded, it came to be recognized as a continuing process, with counseling as its core. In 1913 the National Vocational Guidance Association was organized, with mem-

bers representing the fields of education, psychology, business, government, and social work.

Throughout its history, many disciplines have contributed their special theories to the field of guidance and counseling; at times this segmented approach has led to difficulties in defining the role of the counselor. In 1925 Arthur Payne, in his book *Organization of Vocational Guidance,* reported 103 definitions of vocational guidance, and in 1935 Harry Kitson, in *Occupations,* found the term *guidance* applied to a weird assortment of unrelated activities: counseling of individuals on any matter, group instruction, home visiting, trips to factories, probation work, teaching pupils how to study, chaperoning dances, club leadership, the giving of tests—whatever could not be easily classified was called *guidance.* He went on to add: "Everybody and anybody performs these services: principals, assistant principals, school psychologists, visiting teachers, deans, class advisers, homeroom teachers, teachers of subject-matter courses: all may claim to be doing guidance."

Since Alfred Binet published his first intelligence test, the field of psychometrics has been closely allied with that of counseling. In recent years both psychologists and counselors have adopted a holistic approach to personality, and while recognizing the importance of data secured through testing, most have acknowledged the limitations of test scores, particularly where socioeconomic, linguistic, and motivational factors tend to affect the results.

During the 1940s and 1950s great impetus was given to the guidance movement. The need for the screening, testing, and placement of military personnel during the war years, followed by the counseling of returning veterans, brought about a proliferation of guidance services. There was an expansion of counseling concepts not only in schools but also in business and industry, vocational rehabilitation centers, community agencies, pastoral settings, and other areas. The establishment of guidance institutes in colleges and universities under the National Defense Education Act of 1958 encouraged high-caliber professional leadership.

Professional organizations have grown in size and influence. The national voice of the counseling profession is the American Personnel and Guidance Association (APGA), formed in 1950 from a consolidation of the National Vocational Guidance Association and several other organizations. Its membership totals 27,222. Its official organ is the *Personnel and Guidance Journal,* a monthly publication. Among the subdivisions of the APGA are the American School Counselors' Association, which publishes the *School Counselor,* the National Vocational Guidance Association, which publishes the *Vocational Guidance Quarterly,* the American Rehabilitation Counseling Association, the Association for Counselor Education and Supervision, and the Association for Measurement and Evaluation in Guidance.

THE SCHOOL COUNSELOR—WHO IS HE? WHAT DOES HE DO?

Although there is a great deal of counseling activity outside the school setting (in government services, community clinics and agencies, business and industry, religious organizations, and others), our main focus of interest is the school counselor.

As of January 1, 1966, fifty-three states and outlying areas had specific guidance certification requirements for counselors on the secondary school level, and three on the elementary school level. Although state departments of education have the prerogative of setting standards for counselor training, there is considerable similarity in their requirements. In most cases, from 1 to 5 years of teaching experience is mandated (although there is a trend toward substitution of other types of experience for this requirement). In addition, formal course work is required, the most typical being 30 hours of specialized work at the graduate level. In some states a temporary certificate may be issued upon completion of 18 hours of course work.

Areas covered by course work generally include the following:

Understanding the individual
   principles and practices of guidance
Counseling techniques
Occupational and educational information
Tests and measurement
Organization of the guidance program
Group procedures
Practicum or supervised experience

There is a continuing trend toward upgrading requirements for counselor certification. C. Gilbert Wrenn (1962, pp. 167–168), representing the Commission on Guidance in American Schools, proposed a minimal two-year graduate program including the following:

1. One major core in psychology, including developmental and child psychology, personality growth and dynamics, and group psychology.
2. A second major core in the study of societal forces and culture changes involving the graduate areas of sociology, anthropology, economics and international relations.
3. An understanding of the basic educational philosophies and school curriculum patterns.
4. Provision for the essential applied or technique courses in counseling, measurement, educational and occupational information, to the extent of *not more* than one-fourth of the total graduate program.
5. Supervised experience in both individual counseling and planned group situations to the extent of *not less* than one-fourth of the total graduate program.

6. An elementary understanding of research methods and cautions, including an introduction to electronic computer programming and the outcomes to be expected from computer use.
7. Introduction to the problems of ethical relationships and legal responsibilities in counseling.

Clearly, there is increasing support for a thorough grounding in the behavioral sciences—psychology, sociology, anthropology—supplemented by advanced training in application of relevant techniques.

Basic to the counselor's ability to function in a helping relationship is his personality. Without denying the importance of methodology and scientific understanding, it is fairly obvious that desirable personal traits constitute an important variable in all counseling relationships. Many studies have been made of the "basic qualities" of an effective counselor. A policy statement issued by the APGA (1961, pp. 402–407) enumerates the following:

1) Belief in the worth inherent in each individual, in his capacity for change, and in his ability to develop under conditions that are favorable to him.
2) Commitment to human values
3) Alertness to the world
4) Open-mindedness
5) Talent to communicate

DELINEATION OF ROLE AND FUNCTION

One of the major concerns of professional associations in the field of counseling is the delineation of the role and function of the counselor. When should a person in need of help turn to a counselor, when to a social worker or psychologist? If we study the literature of each discipline in search of "functions," we find a striking commonality of goals. All the disciplines mentioned above seek to assist the individual in understanding himself and developing personal decision-making competencies, to help children who are experiencing adjustment problems through individual or group counseling, to help parents understand children's needs, and to provide consultation to teachers and other staff members which will imbue them with sound principles of mental health. Practitioners in all three disciplines are seeking closer involvement with the home and the community. Arbuckle (1967) finds such similarity among the three that he has proposed an "ecumenical movement" to create a new functional title, *school counseling psychologist.*

On the other hand, it is obvious that the differences among professional counselors in various work settings may be greater than among practitioners of separate disciplines in the same setting. Hoyt (1967) reports that categorical legislation supporting guidance for the gifted, the slow learner, the physically handicapped, the college-bound, the culturally disadvantaged, the economically depressed, the dropout, and many others has led to further differentiation.

Some educators view the counselor as a generalist, dedicated to furthering the optimum development of *all* the children. Others see him as the person who deals with crisis situations in the life of the child or his family. Is the counselor's function to be largely preventative and developmental or therapeutic and remedial or both? Studies of the responsibilities of school counselors have produced, not scores, but literally hundreds of duties which are considered to be within the purview of guidance. The counselor who is working with a small group of emotionally disturbed children may be performing quite differently from the college adviser in the secondary school or from the "career counselor." Yet all three are counselors who have experienced the same basic preparation for their work.

ELEMENTARY SCHOOL GUIDANCE

While much of secondary school guidance is service-oriented, guidance in the elementary schools is largely preventative and developmental. Guidance in the elementary schools was launched in the late 1940s and has experienced remarkable growth in the last few years as the benefits of early identification have become apparent. Further impetus has been given to elementary school guidance by the development of numerous preschool projects, particularly for the disadvantaged.

Certain basic concepts which underlie the development of an elementary school guidance program were outlined in a bulletin used by the New York City public schools (Board of Education of the City of New York, 1956):

1. Guidance includes personal and social as well as educational and vocational areas.
2. Guidance must be related to a functional curriculum to meet children's needs.
3. The guidance point of view must pervade the thinking of the personnel of the school in their attitude toward children, in their emphasis on growth and development and in the development of mental health concepts.
4. Sound guidance is based upon knowledge of children and an interest in learning about them.
5. Guidance is based on the recognition of the child as an individual.
6. Guidance takes into consideration the emotional needs of children, and as far as possible, implements these needs.
7. Guidance is inseparable from teaching.
8. No single technique of guidance is effective under all conditions.
9. Guidance is concerned with causes as well as symptoms.
10. Developmental problems are normal.

In many schools the elementary school counselor acts chiefly as a consultant, assisting the teacher in the identification of pupil strengths and weaknesses and planning with the teacher ways of developing the strengths and overcoming the weaknesses.

Although it has often been stated that elementary guidance should not be problem-centered, it is a fact of life that most counselors devote a substantial portion of their time to working with pupils who manifest learning and adjustment problems. Parental involvement requires that counselors be equipped to deal effectively with school-home and school-community relationships. At the same time, other pupil personnel workers may be involved and there may be need for coordination of services. This task often devolves upon the counselor, although in some schools an administrator is charged with the responsibility for coordination.

While standardization of function in elementary guidance is well-nigh impossible, there is general agreement on its objectives. It seeks to prevent personality maladjustment and to enhance learning ability. It is designed to prevent, through the cooperative efforts of teachers, parents, and pupil personnel workers, emotional disturbances from developing in young children, to assist children with learning difficulties when these are caused by emotional problems, to help teachers recognize the symptoms of emotional difficulties so that proper referrals can be made to appropriate community agencies, to interpret to parents facts about child development and the learning process, to provide occupational information to teachers and pupils, and to sensitize teachers to the developmental needs of pupils.

SECONDARY SCHOOL GUIDANCE

The role and functions of the secondary school counselor are based upon the needs of adolescents in an urban society. The guidance program is concerned with all the children: the normal, the gifted, the slow, the disadvantaged, the troubled. A statement on the role of the secondary school counselor, issued in August, 1966, by the American School Counselors' Association, a division of the APGA, includes the following:

A secondary school counselor is a professional educator with specialized graduate-level training in counseling and related guidance services whose major concern is for the normal, developmental needs and problems of all the pupils for whom he is responsible. . . .

Through the counseling relationship, he helps each pupil to understand himself in relation to the social and psychological world in which he lives, accept himself as he is, develop personal decision-making competencies, and resolve special problems.

He helps parents by acting as a consultant to them regarding the growth and development of their children. . . .

He serves as a consultant to members of the staff by sharing appropriate individual pupil data with them, helping them to identify pupils with special needs and problems, participating in the in-service training programs. . . .

He collects and disseminates to pupils and their parents information concerning school offerings, opportunities for further education, careers and career training opportunities.

In his working environment, he should be free from administrative and clerical assignments which would interfere with his responsibilities as a professional school counselor; should have physical facilities appropriate to his work; should have paid clerical assistance and equipment. . . . It is recommended that his pupil load should not exceed 250 to 300 pupils.

The above statement was based on an extensive study by many school counselors and, according to an introductory note, represents a description of what should be, rather than what is. Can the average school counselor realistically carry out this mandate on behalf of "each" pupil? Only if certain preconditions exist in the school setting: administrative understanding and support; collaborative interaction and joint planning with other staff members, including other pupil personnel workers; a viable case load; and a favorable working environment. There are many role determinants for the guidance counselor: the principal, the teachers, other members of the pupil personnel team, the pupils, the parents, the school, the community, the counselor himself. Since roles are interactive systems of behavior, no single influence can structure the counselor's role completely. Yet it is apparent that the counselor enjoys a lesser degree of professional autonomy in his work because he is usually more vulnerable than the psychologist or the social worker to outside influences.

The counselor's task is further complicated by the challenges of new programs developed in the war against poverty. Society's expectations of the counselor grow more awesome as the educational enterprise becomes more complex. The physician may consider that he has fulfilled his primary mission by healing the sick, the lawyer by giving legal aid, the businessman by managing a profitable enterprise. However, the counselor's responsibilities now extend far beyond his stated functions and include efforts to overcome the effects of poverty upon the disadvantaged, to raise aspirational levels and provide cultural enrichment through school and community resources; participation in programs of sex education; combating of drug addiction; promotion of integration; combating of racism; reduction of community tensions; mobilization of the community's resources in behalf of children; and engagement in a variety of activities to help bridge the generation gap.

GUIDANCE FOR THE HANDICAPPED

The American dream of equal educational opportunity for all applies to handicapped children as well—the physically handicapped, the mentally retarded, the emotionally disturbed. Early identification, proper grade or school placement, supportive counseling, and vocational guidance and follow-up are among the responsibilities of the guidance worker. Handicapped children require an environment of stimulation, motivation, and acceptance to an even greater degree than do their more normal classmates if they are to achieve self-fulfillment and make their maximum contribution to society.

Cruickshank (1956) points out that the counselor for the handicapped pupil in high school must be capable of honest diagnosis and prognosis and that he must have the patience, imagination, and depth of understanding to help a pupil utilize his capacities to the limit. He should help the pupil:

1. To know his strengths and weaknesses, his potentialities and limitations.
2. To learn about occupations through a variety of educational and career materials.
3. To make wise decisions in relating job demands and requirements to aspirations, goals and opportunities.
4. To understand some of the problems that will confront him in meeting people who are not sympathetic or honest in their dealings with handicapped individuals.
5. To acquire a philosophy that will provide motivation for sound living and for conscientious planning, with faith in himself and in society.

In describing the guidance needs of the handicapped, Ratchick and Koenig (1963, p. 38) state:

> The growth and development of these children is not only the concern of those who teach the handicapped. It is also a matter of importance to every citizen, every parent, every person who may come in contact with them.... Finally, it is a matter of conscience and professional pride to all who are involved in guidance, for no program that ignores these children can be considered true guidance.

COUNSELING OUTSIDE THE SCHOOL SETTING

With the proliferation of community action programs and the assumption of increased responsibility by social and welfare agencies for ameliorating the social and economic pathology of the slums, guidance workers are now employed in many areas outside the schools. Some of the services offered are highly professional; others are only marginally relevant to the counselor's training. Many jobs in government services, business and industry, and probation work with juvenile delinquents utilize other skills in addition to counseling. In many community agencies, counselors are part of a staff that includes psychiatrists, psychiatric social workers, psychologists, casework aides, health workers, and other types of personnel (Moser & Moser, 1963, p. 308).

The school guidance counselor works closely with agency personnel in securing skilled professional help for the troubled child and his family. Through sustained contacts, the agency assists the client in the ultimate solution of the problem. It gives the school a strong ally in the performance of a job which the school cannot do alone.

Since referrals are of such significance, they are made only after careful study by the school staff. The classroom teacher refers the case to the counselor, who in turn confers with other pupil personnel workers on the staff of the school. After several interviews with the pupil, consultation with the parents, and careful study of the records, the counselor will decide whether or not the services of a community agency are indicated. If the specialized services required by the pupil or his family cannot be obtained in the school, the counselor must then locate an agency whose services are available. At this point, the counselor usually discusses the case with the agency's intake worker. Then he prepares the child and parents for the referral. Most agencies prefer to have the parent make the initial appointment. However, in some cases, the counselor may make the appointment with the intake worker with the parent's consent.

Types of agencies which employ counselors as well as other pupil personnel specialists are described below.

Family service agencies. Family agencies focus their attention upon the entire family group, even if the problem is manifested by only one member. Withdrawn or aggressive behavior in school or in the community, inability to make or keep friends, and failure to achieve are but a few symptoms that may reflect home difficulties.

Mental hygiene clinics. Child-guidance clinics provide diagnostic and treatment services for a wide range of emotional problems, from school phobia to psychosis requiring institutional placement. The team approach is generally used, with social worker, psychologist, and psychiatrist meeting to discuss their findings and plan for treatment. Both psychotherapy and environmental modification are utilized. Usually the parents are also seen while the child is in treatment. Liaison with the school guidance counselor is extremely important for implementation of recommendations made by the clinical team.

Agencies for the handicapped. Vocational rehabilitation counselors are key members of the rehabilitation team. With increased public awareness of the needs of the handicapped has come a stress on the positive factors in the personality of the individual. Efforts are made to achieve maximum rehabilitation through a multidisciplinary approach. Educational and vocational guidance is coordinated with a program of medical rehabilitation.

Welfare and other social services. While welfare departments do not generally employ counselors as such, family caseworkers often perform guidance services which affect children, particularly those in the Aid to Dependent Children category. Frequently, inadequate home conditions and family disruption necessitate legal action by welfare officials.

Protective care agencies. "If a fellow needs a friend—Big Brothers holds out a hand" describes the type of service given by the Big Brothers (and Big Sisters) organizations. Qualified adult volunteers each take one boy under their wing. It is hoped that, in this way, the replacement of the missing father-son relationship will help overcome tendencies toward delinquency, truancy, and antisocial behavior.

Correctional agencies. Probation officers provide casework services for children up to 16 who are in need of court intervention. Both intake services and sustained contacts with clients after court hearings are carried out by personnel with varied levels of training in guidance and counseling.

Vocational counseling agencies. As occupational choice grows more complex, adolescents faced with the problem of career choice need the help of counselors specially trained in the appraisal of personal characteristics and knowledgeable in the field of occupational information. Theoretically, the school guidance counselor who knows the student well should be able to offer this type of service. In actual practice, however, the average counselor is so overwhelmed with a multiplicity of functions and an enormous caseload that vocational counseling rarely receives adequate attention. Many nonprofit agencies provide highly trained counselors and psychologists who work with each client to determine the best possible course of action open to him. Through interviews with both the pupil and his parents, the use of ability, aptitude, and interest tests, and study of the client's history, realistic plans are cooperatively developed. Frequently a case conference is held, including the school counselor, to pool the information gleaned from the tests and to help develop a plan for the client.

Settlement houses. Settlement houses have traditionally offered a wide range of services, including recreational facilities, educational programs, day camps, summer camps, visiting nurse service, and mental-hygiene services. Personnel vary in their background and training. Current emphasis is on heavy involvement with the community.

In recent years many voluntary agencies have enlarged the scope of their activities. The staff of one such agency, the Manhattan Society for Mental Health (1963), includes psychiatric and group social workers and research, education, and community relations consultants. An overview of the activities of this agency, as listed in Table 46-1, will indicate the breadth and variety of its services.

THE PARAPROFESSIONAL AND THE NONPROFESSIONAL IN GUIDANCE WORK

The last few years have witnessed the growth of the *new-careers movement* in education and social services. Pearl and Riessman (1965) have described this as an attempt to establish a new entry level to old careers and at the same time to enable an economically and educationally disadvantaged individual to make a meaningful contribution to society. Awareness of the communications gap between disadvantaged children and their parents on the one hand and middle-class teachers and counselors on the other led to the development of a new type of worker who could forge stronger links between the school and the community. New resources for the training and employment of the poor became available to school systems through the Office of Economic Opportunity, the Manpower Development Training Act, Title I of the Elementary and Secondary Education Act, the Nelson-Scheuer Amendment to the Poverty Act, and the Javits-Kennedy Act for Impacted Areas. Bowman and Klopf (1967, pp. 2–4) have described several innovations in these new programs for auxiliary personnel:

1. Emphasis on the right of all persons to essential human services.
2. A shift from the creation of entry level jobs leading nowhere to the concept of a career ladder, with training available at each step for those seeking upward mobility.
3. The involvement of low-income workers as participants in the process of problem-solving rather than as mere recipients of the wisdom of professionals.
4. A systematic approach to the program, including role development, training and institutionalization of auxiliary personnel as an integral part of public service.

Many benefits in addition to the possibility of increasing the scope and effectiveness of the professional are seen as accruing to both school and community from the employment of auxiliary personnel. Bowman and Klopf (1967, pp. 6–7) write:

The auxiliary who has actually lived in disadvantaged environments often speaks to the disadvantaged child or youth in a way that is neither strange nor threatening. He may help the new pupil to adjust to the unfamiliar world of the school without undue defensiveness; to fill the gaps, if any, in his preparation for learning; and to build upon his strengths, which may have more relevance to the new situation than the child himself realizes. This cultural bridge is seen as an asset, in and of itself, even if there were no need to provide jobs for the poor.

Moreover, the low-income auxiliary, having faced up to and overcome some of the difficulties and frustrations the children now face, may serve to motivate the child to further effort. His very presence in a role of some status in the school says to the child: "It can be done; it is worth trying to do; you, too, can succeed here." This has far more meaning than the story of a Ralph Bunche or a Felisa Rincon de Gautier to one who obviously lacks the exceptional ability of those great but remote persons.

Naturally, this message would be imparted more forcefully if the faculty, too, were mixed in terms of socio-economic background. As work-study programs become increasingly available, economic

TABLE 46-1   PROGRAM ACTIVITIES OF THE MANHATTAN SOCIETY FOR MENTAL HEALTH

Service or Activity	*Nature of Service*	*Groups or Persons Serviced*
Information and referral service	Information and consultation about use of resources; short-term counselling; referral to public voluntary and private agencies, institutions, and practitioners.	Patients, prospective patients, relatives, professional persons, and other interested parties
Job information service for psychiatrists	Seeks out information about job opportunities in public and voluntary agencies and institutions and brings it to the attention of psychiatrists with available time.	Community agencies and institutions and psychiatrists
Vocational rehabilitation unit	Work experience and training in clerical skills in a realistic office setting.	Psychiatric patients, referred by public and voluntary agencies and private psychiatrists, formerly or presently hospitalized or in current treatment
Mental-health education and film library	Supplies films, printed materials, special data, program consultation; organizes special programs.	Parents, teachers, guidance personnel, students, lay groups, etc.
Consultation services to agencies	Consultation about program development and problems.	Public and voluntary community agencies giving health and social services
Volunteer services	Screens and refers volunteers to Manhattan State Hospital and other mental-health services.	Mental-hospital staffs and patients served by their programs
Judson Health Center mental-health project	Consultation and evaluation of Judson Health Center's program of preventive services.	Judson Health Center professional staff
Research	Study of community mental-health resources and dissemination of findings; support of and participation in research work by other organizations.	Mental-health services to the community, under public or voluntary auspices
Community organization and legislative activities	Participation in the work of coordinating and planning groups; action to improve mental-health services; advice on legislation and public agency budgets; action to correct special problems.	Community mental-health agencies and the general public

integration may become more frequent in school faculties. Meantime, the low-income auxiliary sometimes provides incentive to poor pupils which would otherwise be lacking.

Further, the auxiliary from the child's own neighborhood may be able to interpret to the middle class professional some aspects of the behavior of a child who is non-responding in a school situation. The auxiliary may, in turn, interpret the goals of the school and the learning-teaching process to both parent and child. To reach the child for a few hours a day without reaching those who influence his mode of living may be of little avail. The parent who doesn't understand a school official sometimes finds a neighbor serving as a school auxiliary helpful.

Despite initial misgivings on the part of guidance counselors regarding the activities of non-professionals and the possible loss of confidentiality, the program has worked quite well in practice. Informal surveys of counseling staffs have reported generally favorable reactions. Ways in which guidance aides can extend the work of the counselor were outlined in a statement prepared by a group of counselors and supervisors for the New York City Bureau of Educational and Vocational Guidance in March, 1968. The following are excerpts from this statement:

I. The Principles and Purposes of the Para-Professional Worker in the Guidance Services of our schools (elementary, middle, and senior high)
   A. To involve the community in the guidance program of the school by providing the opportunities for trained, indigenous, interested adults to prepare for a career in the guidance programs of the public schools in New York City
   B. To meet the expanding guidance needs of our students by providing additional personnel entitled "Guidance Assistants"
   C. To provide work experience for interested people from the community which may in

time and with further training lead them to full professional status.

II. General Job Description
    To assist the Guidance Counselor in working with individuals and groups, with special emphasis on establishing closer ties with parents and other members of the community

III. The Functions of the Guidance Assistant are:
    A. To interview individual students re new admissions, remedial assistance, "incentives" (calling in students who are doing well and showing improvement), truancy, absence or cutting problems, assisting with the mechanical details of class programming, gathering data for the counselor involved with an exit interview
    B. To obtain information in the school for the Guidance Counselor with respect to school records, report cards, teacher evaluation of students, college transcripts, occupational and vocational information
    C. Act as office receptionist to screen the student and determine the nature of immediate or future appointment needs, answer the telephone, distribute applications for working papers, transportation, lunch, etc., and direct students and parents to proper offices and personnel
    D. Assist the Guidance Counselor with bi-lingual interviews and letters
    E. Fill out court reports, welfare forms and employment papers
    F. Visit homes and institutions for the purpose of obtaining relevant information which will be of benefit to the student
    G. Attend P.T.A. and Neighborhood Action meetings
    H. Assist in mass distribution of guidance material
    I. Perform basic clerical duties such as filing records, gathering data from records, pulling records, maintaining records and arranging appointments
    J. Assist the counselor in special testing situations
    K. Give tutorial help to students who exhibit

learning difficulties under the direction and with the consultation of the Guidance Counselor

L. Help interpret the goals of the educational process to parents and other members of the child's family and interested community groups

M. Interpret for the Guidance Counselor the existing attitudes of parents toward the school, the schools policies and students' progress

N. Participate in weekly group conferences with Social Worker, Psychologist, Guidance Counselors, teachers and other pupil personnel re progress of children

O. Participate in other guidance projects as they relate to the particular needs of the school or district in which they work

P. Help with and go on field trips with students in the area particularly related to guidance, i.e., articulation with other schools

Q. Give interim supportive help to a youngster in a crisis situation.

This program is, of course, in its formative stages. There are many who will not agree that the "guidance assistant" should play so active a role in interviewing students regarding such problems as absence and truancy, even though it is assumed that the assistant will work under the counselor's supervision. Others will ask: If all this can be done by the paraprofessional, what will be left for the counselor to do? One possible answer, not to be taken facetiously, is that the counselor may then have time for counseling.

TECHNIQUES OF GUIDANCE

Techniques employed by guidance workers are, in many cases, similar to those used by other pupil personnel workers. The difference is in the degree and depth of their use rather than in the choice of techniques.

Appraising Pupils through Tests and Measurements

Any sequential guidance service provides for the use and interpretation of a variety of tests—general ability, aptitude, achievement, interest, and personality. Projective tests are also used, but these should be administered and interpreted only by a qualified clinician.

Test results are useful in grouping pupils, identifying pupils who need special diagnostic study and remedial instruction, helping the pupil set educational and vocational goals, reporting progress to parents, and evaluating the instructional program (Mortensen & Schmuller, 1966, Chap. 7).

Serious question has arisen about the validity of traditional appraisal methods when tests designed for a middle-class population are administered to disadvantaged children, particularly to those of minority groups. Obviously, children whose verbal and sensory experiences have been inadequate should not be penalized by test results which merely reflect their impoverished environment. Since test scores are meaningful only in the light of an individual's personal history, guidance workers should exercise great caution in their use.

Collecting Information about the Individual

Closely related to the use of tests in the guidance program is the need for recording such data in a systematic manner. The purpose of maintaining a cumulative record and a guidance data record for each pupil is to help teachers, counselors, and other staff members gain a better understanding of each pupil's abilities, interests, aptitudes, disabilities, etc. (Humphreys, Traxler, & North, 1967, Chap. 6). Careful analysis of pupil data will assist the teacher and others to provide adaptation of the curriculum to meet the needs of the individual child and to guide each pupil educationally, personally, and vocationally. Accurate record keeping will also provide a basis for reporting to parents the progress and needs of their children.

Observation is an integral part of every other guidance technique. Directed observation may be recorded by the teacher or counselor in the form of anecdotal records. A true anecdotal record reports only incidents of behavior, without the personal interpretation of the observer. A cumulative record of this type will give the counselor an insight into a child's social and emotional development.

The Counseling Interview

The aim of counseling is to foster self-understanding and growth on the part of the counselee. The major procedure through which this is effected is the face-to-face counseling interview, in which we find a continuum from the simple interview for giving and getting information; to the advisement interview, which is more structured and involves some degree of interpretation; to the true counseling interview, which involves making of choices and resolution of problems; to psychotherapy, which aims to change behavior in a clinic setting and requires increased ego involvement on the part of both counselor and counselee (Mortensen & Schmuller, 1966, pp. 342–343). Counseling and psychotherapy are closely related, but while counseling is the primary tool of the counselor, psychotherapy requires professional training and skills in diagnosis and treatment which are within the province of the clinician. Leona Tyler (1953, p. 12) points out an important distinction between the two: "The aim of therapy is generally considered to be personality change of some sort. . . . Counseling [is used] to refer to a helping process the aim of which is not to change the person but to enable him to utilize the resources he now has for coping with life."

Over the years, the course of counseling has been influenced by many schools of thought.

All agree that, in his basic approach, the counselor must communicate a sense of caring for his counselee. The question arises: Should the counselor attempt to direct the interview toward goals which he (the counselor) has determined would be in the client's best interests, or should he serve as a sounding board, hopefully leading the client to solve his own problems? Countless volumes have been written on theories of counseling. We shall do no more than outline the major trends:

1. *Directive counseling.* This type of counseling or advice giving, in which the counselor studies all available data, reaches a conclusion (as, for example, that a student should change his course from academic to vocational), and then attempts to impose it upon the client, has been frowned upon by nearly all professionally trained counselors. Leaders in guidance and counseling agree that the counselee should be encouraged to assume as much responsibility as possible. Nevertheless, a great deal of counseling, particularly that given by untrained or partially trained teachers, advisers, and deans, is of this dogmatic variety.

2. *Client-centered counseling.* The leading exponent of the client-centered, or nondirective, school of counseling is Carl R. Rogers, whose book *Counseling and Psychotherapy,* published in 1942, has had tremendous influence on the counseling profession. In client-centered counseling, the counselor tries to create a permissive atmosphere that will encourage the client to speak freely about his problems in a series of interviews until he arrives at a conclusion or solution of his problems. The counselor reflects the client's feelings and frequently makes noncommittal comments such as "Tell me more about that," "Uh-uh," "So you feel . . . ." This type of counseling is very time-consuming, but its advocates claim for it significant therapeutic values (Humphreys, Traxler, & North, 1967, Chap. 7).

3. *Behavioral counseling.* Recently, a quiet revolution has been taking place in the field of counseling in response to the search for more effective ways of reaching our young people in need of help. Utilizing the findings of behavioral science and learning theory, a new school of thought has developed which sees client goals as specific rather than global. John D. Krumboltz, one of the leaders in this movement, proposes four approaches: (a) operant learning, (b) imitative learning, or the use of behavior models, (c) cognitive learning, and (d) emotional learning using classical conditioning (Krumboltz, 1966, chap. 1).

4. *Eclectic counseling.* Many counselors tend to take a middle position between various extremes. In the eclectic approach, the counselor utilizes the techniques which seem to him most appropriate to the needs and personality of the client.

There is a paucity of research findings on the comparative effectiveness of one method of counseling over another. Two points are clear: First, that the counselor generally uses the approach with which he personally feels most comfortable; and second, that client satisfaction is usually determined by the personal regard and warmth of the counselor.

Group Procedures

Group work has been advanced by some as a substitute for individual guidance when counselor-pupil ratios of 1 to 1,000, for example, make it impossible for the counselor to have a one-to-one relationship with each pupil. Others see unique values in group learning experiences as a supplement to individual counseling.

Leo Goldman (1962, pp. 518–522) pointed out meaningful differences in process and in group composition as bases for distinguishing group guidance, group counseling, and group therapy.

Group guidance is generally conducted in a classroom setting, with a teacher or counselor as the group leader. The primary purpose is to impart educational and vocational information. Many courses in group guidance also provide for discussion of personal and social problems.

Group counseling (sometimes referred to as *multiple counseling*) is generally limited to groups of not more than ten, led by a counselor. It emphasizes attitudes, opinions, and deeper feelings rather than cognitive elements. Usually all members of the group have a common problem; discussion is free and open, and interaction and mutual help among the members is encouraged. The objectives are similar to those of individual counseling: growth in self-direction and decision-making ability, self-evaluation, and behavioral change.

Group therapy is an intensive form of group counseling which should be used only by qualified psychologists and psychiatrists to help individuals with severe emotional and social problems.

Role of the Guidance Worker in Mental Health

As we have seen, "guidance" is a vast umbrella sheltering workers with varying degrees of education, training, and experience who perform varying functions in situations affected by a host of differential factors. The guidance worker has an important role to play in providing preventative, developmental, and remedial services in the school, the home, and the community. Counseling is an emerging profession, with its own body of theoretical knowledge, professional identity, and societal role. As Gilbert Wrenn (1962, p. 1) pointed out, guidance is an American phenomenon, based on our value system of equal opportunity and the concept of progress.

REFERENCES

American Personnel and Guidance Association. *A statement of policy: Standards for the prepa-*

ration of school counselors. Washington, D.C.: December, 1961. Pp. 402–407.

Arbuckle, D. S. Counselor, social worker, psychologist: Let's "ecumenicalize." *Personnel and Guidance Journal,* 1967, **45,** 532–538.

Board of Education of the City of New York. *Guidance of children in elementary schools.* New York: Board of Education, 1956.

Bowman, G. W., & Klopf, G. J. *New careers and roles in the American school.* New York: Bank Street College of Education, 1967. Pp. 2–4.

Cruickshank, W. D. *Psychology of exceptional children and youth.* Englewood Cliffs, N.J.: Prentice-Hall, 1956.

Goldman L. Group guidance: Content and process. *Personnel and Guidance Journal,* 1962, **40,** 518–522.

Hoyt, K. B. Attaining the promise of guidance for all. *Personnel and Guidance Journal,* 1967, **45,** 624–630.

Humphreys, J. A., Traxler, A. E., & North, R. D. *Guidance services.* Chicago: Science Research Associates, 1967. Chaps. 6, 7.

Krumboltz, J. D. *Revolution in counseling: Implications of behavioral science.* Boston: Houghton Mifflin, 1966.

Manhattan Society for Mental Health. *Working for mental health in the changing city: Five year report 1958–1962.* New York, 1963. Pp. 10–11.

Mortensen, D. G., & Schmuller, A. M. *Guidance in today's schools.* New York: Wiley, 1966. Chap. 7 and pp. 342–343.

Moser, L. E., & Moser, R. S. *Counseling and guidance: An exploration.* Englewood Cliffs, N.J.: Prentice-Hall, 1963. P. 308.

Pearl, A., & Riessman, F. *New careers for the poor: The nonprofessional in human services.* New York: Free Press, 1965.

Ratchick, I., & Koenig, F. G. *Guidance and the physically handicapped child.* Chicago: Science Research Associates, 1963. P. 38.

Tyler, L. *The work of the counselor.* New York: Appleton-Century-Crofts, 1953. P. 12.

Wrenn, C. G. *The counselor in a changing world.* Washington: American Personnel and Guidance Association, 1962. Pp. 1, 167–168.

Name Index

Subject Index